# WE BELIEVE

## Doctrines and Principles
### of
### The Church of Jesus Christ
### of Latter-day Saints

### by
### Rulon T. Burton

Cover Design by Greg Thurber
Cover material: Kivar Firenze

The selection and assembly of this material and the wording of the numbered doctrinal statements, including the List of Doctrines is the sole responsibility of Rulon T. Burton. This is not an official publication of The Church of Jesus Christ of Latter-day Saints and does not necessarily represent the official position or teachings of The Church of Jesus Christ of Latter-day Saints.

Library of Congress Control Number 200409259


ISBN 0-9748790-3-7
**Library Edition**

Printed in the United States of America
By Sterling Press of Salt Lake City, Utah


TABERNACLE BOOKS, INC., Publisher
**13267 So. Berry Lane, Draper , UT 84020**
**(801) 816-9810  Fax (801) 501-8348**
**www.tabernaclebooks.com**
**english@utah-inter.net**

# TABLE OF CONTENTS

# ACKNOWLEDGEMENTS

The public may not generally be interested in the acknowledgments that follow, but I have such feelings of gratitude for the assistance rendered me in bringing this book to its published form that I must express my thanks on this page. This is a big book, four times the size of ordinary books. It contains thousands of quotations and references. All this has demanded hundreds of hours of editing, involving many people.

Susan Roylance must be mentioned for her special typesetting and layout assistance. For what might have been a normal commercial venture, she went well beyond the second mile and contributed generously of her time, giving most valuable and appreciated suggestions. Thank you Susan.

Larry E. Dahle of Brigham Young University reviewed every doctrinal statement and gave beneficial suggestions for which I am truly grateful. John Welch, also of Brigham Young University, spent time with the manuscript, and in conference with me, making helpful suggestions with regard to the doctrinal statements. Both of these scholars contributed of their time without compensation.

Many other people contributed their time without pay to review all or portions of the book. Dortha Robinson needs special mention. She has read every word of the manuscript and some large blocks of it several times—which resulted in improvements to the manuscript. But she is not the only one. My friend William Partridge read the entire manuscript and gave worthwhile suggestions that were incorporated. Elizabeth B. Hodson, my sister, also read the entire manuscript. She also checked a block of references for me. Her suggestions have been implemented and her dedication appreciated. Heather R. Burton and her husband (my son) Justin O. Burton helped with scripture references and worked up the scripture index, all of which was time consuming and most helpful. Karen M. Burton reviewed all the doctrinal statements from a new convert's perspective. Her husband, Gideon O. Burton (another son) helped me with the introduction, with the sample pages, and with many hours of discussion. My daughter Charlotte B. Mortimer and her husband Jeffrey P. Mortimer participated in checking many references and in the analysis and review of much of the book. I would like also to mention Dale Putnam, who is now deceased, who gave me an idea that was of significant benefit in the way the quotations of prophets were styled. His wife, Billie, has read and edited portions of the book, and, along with the others mentioned in the paragraph, did so in love, without pay. Roger Andrus insisted the scripture index be created and included in the book.

Professional editors and readers were of great assistance, all of whom worked for less than their normal rate as a labor of love for a special book. These include Audrey Southcot, who read and marked the entire finished manuscript, and Debie Rossi, who also read and marked the entire manuscript. Camille West did a block of editing and, along with Debie Rossi, assisted me in a final review of all the doctrinal statements. Dale Longmore carefully read and edited a large segment of the book and his work is appreciated. Irene Peters and Laurel Ross edited smaller portions of the book. Without them, and all these other good people, this book could not have been published in the excellent quality in which it now comes to the public.

Greg Thurber is our graphic artist. I love his good spirit and talent. Jamie and Marcie Omer gave needed advice and assistance in evaluating the book jacket. The computer edition of *We Believe* has been made possible through the help of Gary Hansen. Jim Owen of Sterling Press has been marvelous to work with. I am indebted to Steve Schermerhorn, who did resourcing of people to assist me, and for volunteering his services to do the high resolution processing of the text at a reduced rate, because of the nature of the book. Darren Nelson energetically assisted with typesetting at a crucial time and refused compensation.

Finally, thanks to you, Jo, for being a loving and encouraging support and companion during almost ten years of researching and writing the book—while your husband was sequestered in his study. Not all wives would have been so lovingly patient.

—Rulon T. Burton, April 1994

# INTRODUCTION

## 1. How *We Believe* Came To Be

Over a period of many years, three unrelated incidents—when taken together—caused me to begin this book.

I was teaching a gospel doctrine class when a brother raised his hand and asked, "Would you please explain the doctrine of justification to us?" "What doctrine of justification?" I asked myself. I really didn't know whether the Church taught a doctrine by that name. In fact, I even wondered if this brother knew something I didn't know, but should.

After class I looked up "Justification" in the topical guide and I found a few references that seemed applicable (D&C 20:30; Romans 3:24; and Moses 6:60). But taken singly or together, these did not seem to help. By this time I had taken about an hour and Sunday dinner was waiting. I looked outside the Standard Works to find what general authorities might have said on the subject. The section on justification in *Mormon Doctrine* was very interesting to me, yet I could not find something similar said by other general authorities, and I was cautious about anything not repeated by other prophets. I looked in *Doctrines of Salvation,* in *The Teachings of Joseph Smith* and in Talmage's *Articles of Faith,* but only found a reference to Martin Luther's "justification by faith alone." More confused than enlightened, I joined the family for dinner and gave up the project.

How many teachers in the Church have had this same kind of frustrating experience! It would be most helpful, I began to think, if we had a reference book that grouped the words of modern and ancient prophets together so we could see how their united testimonies established each doctrine of the Church. *We Believe* began to formulate in my mind.

An earlier incident involved a meeting with Joseph Fielding Smith in his office in the late 1950s. At the time I was teaching the gospel to someone belonging to a fundamentalist group. There was a problem with a statement attributed to Brigham Young in the *Journal of Discourses.* During our visit with the Apostle he graciously resolved my investigator's concern, which happily led to this person eventually being baptized.

I have never forgotten the simple, satisfying answer Elder Smith gave to this quandary over doctrine. It is a mistake, he told us, to take one quotation of a prophet and isolate it from all other teachings dwelling on the same subject. He urged us to always consider what else has been said by authority on a given question and not to rely on one excerpt alone. In this case, no other prophet or general authority had said anything like the quotation that had disturbed my investigator. This counsel stayed with me and became my guideline for recognizing true doctrine. Later I would discover that Elder Smith was teaching us a principle that prophets have taught ever since Paul, a key doctrine *about* doctrine called the "Law of Witnesses" (see below).

The third incident occurred with my attending a stake conference. Speaking to an adult meeting, one of the general authorities of the Church admonished us to stay with the Church lesson manuals in our teaching. He said something that particularly caught my interest: "If you feel a need to supplement your lessons, use only those sources that are official publications of the Church." This made sense to me, much as Elder Smith's advice to rely only on repeated teachings of the prophets.[1]

However, the average Church member may have only a few of such official publications, and is likely missing some of the more central ones, such as the Conference Reports from years past.[2] Wouldn't it be useful, I thought, if there were a reference work to the doctrines of the Church that drew only upon official, authoritative sources and that presented as doctrines only what had been repeated by multiple prophets? And so I began a decade-long research on Church doctrine that has culminated in *We Believe.*

I think you will find *We Believe* of particular benefit whenever you may feel hazy about what you have heard taught in a class or over a pulpit. A few minutes in these pages can take you to a specific doctrine or principle that gives you some pretty good answers to your questions. Of course, this work can be a valuable aid for preparing talks, giving lessons in church and in family home evenings. It can help parents answer questions for their children. It can help members answer questions for non-member friends and investigators. It can be particularly helpful for new converts.

New converts have a testimony of only a few key doctrines of the gospel and are usually eager to learn more about the doctrines and principles of the Church, about what *we believe*. They will find much in this volume.

Constructing *We Believe* has given me a much deeper appreciation of the prophets. In this book you will find Moses is sometimes followed by George Q. Morris, Alma by President Joseph F. Smith, or Peter preceded by Matthew Cowley. I have found this intermingling of ancient prophets with modern prophets to be a testimony both of the inspired role of prophets and of the unity of the gospel.

*We Believe* has increased my desire to read the scriptures and to listen to the latter-day prophets, the chosen vessels of the Lord.

Often the wording of their messages is particularly beautiful and the phraseology marvelously polished: their messages are permeated with the spirit of the Holy Ghost! I leave you with an example of such prophetic clarity, the words of Joseph Fielding Smith that have been my guiding principle in this work:

> It is wrong to take one passage of scripture and isolate it from all other teachings dwelling on the same subject. We should bring together all that has been said by authority on the question. . . . Therefore we must find out what else has been said about salvation. *(Teachings of the Latter-Day Prophets, p. 615)*

## 2. Answers to Questions about *We Believe*

### Why We Believe?

This book is called *We Believe* for two reasons. First, I wished to emulate the doctrinal simplicity we find in the thirteen Articles of Faith. Thus, each doctrine of the Church has been summarized in a single sentence at the top of each entry (see "What are Doctrinal Statements?" below).

The words "we believe" could precede each of these statements. Second, only divinely-appointed prophets of the Church may establish officially what *we believe*. Accordingly, the doctrines and principles set forth in this book are based on the verbatim words of the *prophets* and not on personal opinion or in commentary.

### What are Doctrinal Statements?

Doctrinal Statements are single-sentence summaries of each doctrine or principle. Each is preceded by a number for ease of reference. These Doctrinal Statements—there are a total of 898—serve as headings that group together the words of the prophets that establish each doctrine. For example, the following Doctrinal Statement is found under the topic REVELATION: Law of Witnesses—

655. When the Lord wants the people to learn any essential truth, he will teach it to them over and over again through the witnesses of prophets.

Following this Doctrinal Statement are found the prophets' words that make up this particular doctrine.

These Doctrinal Statements are what make *We Believe* more important than a mere compilation of quotations. Typical compilations do little more than group quotations under general subjects. In contrast, the Doctrinal Statements of *We Believe* provide concise summaries that encapsulate specific principles and doctrines of the Church; these lead readers directly to the combined testimonies of several authorities on that same specific point.

For example, under the topic, "AMERICA," one finds Doctrinal Statement #23: "The American constitution is inspired of God," followed by quotations on the constitution's inspired nature by Joseph Smith, George Albert Smith, Ezra Taft Benson, J. Reuben Clark, Jr., and Mark E. Petersen.

### How is We Believe Organized?

A **List of Doctrines** precedes each general topic and consists of all the Doctrinal Statements that occur in the complete entries that follow. A complete entry consists of a Doctrinal Statement followed by those witnesses and testimonies of the prophets—in their original words—that establish it as doctrine. (See Sample Pages.)

This organization is meant to provide access to specific Church doctrines and is additionally intended to aid in the integrated understanding of doctrines as they relate to one another. This is accomplished structurally by grouping all Doctrinal Statements together at the beginning of each topic, along with relevant Doctrinal Statements from other topics. This listing allows readers to gain a sense of how all Church doctrines and principles coordinate with one another.

In the List of Doctrines for the topic **Prayer**, for example, there are several references to "Doctrines on **Prayer** Located in Other Topics." (This is true for each topic. There is provision for doctrines in the current topic that may be found in other topics, elsewhere.) In this particular case, these cross-references help us understand that we cannot isolate the principle of prayer from the principles of parenting, fasting, and testimony. Because the book is organized sequentially by Doctrinal Statement numbers, one may easily move from studying the prophets' words on prayer to studying their statements on these complementary subjects.

This kind of organization reflects the important need to coordinate our understanding of gospel principles with one another that Elder Neal A. Maxwell bore testimony to in a 1993 general conference of the Church:

> [T]he gospel's principles do require synchronization. When pulled apart from each other or isolated, men's interpretations and implementations of these doctrines may be wild. ¶ Love, if not checked by the seventh commandment, could become carnal. The fifth commandment's laudable emphasis upon honoring parents, unless checked by the first commandment, could result in unconditional loyalty to errant parents rather than to God. . . . ¶ Thus, the fulness of the gospel of Jesus Christ is greater than any of its parts. . . . CR1993Apr:97

By assessing statements on doctrine in light of corollary doctrines we avoid the subtle danger of taking a prophet's statement on Church principles out of the context of those coordinate doctrines which inform, limit or complement it.

### What is meant by "The Law of Witnesses?"
True doctrine is authenticated when many prophets repeat, or "witness" it. Paul, citing Moses, taught the Corinthians, "In the mouth of two or three witnesses shall every word be established" (2 Corinthians 13:1). God's authoritative teachings are always in accordance with this law of witnesses. Every gospel truth is given to us from God through the recorded witnesses of two or more prophets in written scriptures.

In a 1984 general conference address, a latter-day prophet, Elder Boyd K. Packer, provided his witness to the Law of Witnesses doctrine, calling it "a basic doctrine of the Church:"

> [I]nstruction vital to our salvation is not hidden in an obscure verse or phrase in the scriptures. To the contrary, essential truths are repeated over and over again. CR1984Oct:97

Each Doctrinal Statement in *We Believe* is supported according to the Law of Witnesses by quotations of the words of several prophets, derived from official Church sources.

### What "Authoritative Sources" are used?
The Authoritative Sources recognized in *We Believe* are the words of prophets as set forth in ancient and modern scripture (the Standard Works) and the continuing revelation to latter-day prophets.

The words of prophets that are binding scripture on the Saints and the world will always be *officially published by the Church*. One may find them in:

- **The Standard Works**
- **Conference reports**
- **Church-published books** and those writings of Apostles that are published by authority of the First Presidency of the Church or the Quorum of the Twelve.[3]
- **Church-published manuals** —priesthood and Relief Society manuals, institute and other lesson manuals. (See Gospel Principles, pp. 49, 51-52)

Accordingly, *We Believe* quotes only from official Church publications.[4] *We Believe* endeavors to follow closely the Lord's pattern for teaching his children on earth. Although general authorities and many others who are not Apostles or prophets, give profitable teachings, the Lord has chosen his prophets as his exclusive agents to teach authoritative doctrine.[5]

## Endnotes for Introduction

1.   The words of this general authority, like the counsel I received from Joseph Fielding Smith, have been corroborated by other prophets in the Church.  President J. Reuben Clark, speaking on behalf of the First Presidency to seminary, institute, and Church school teachers, repeated the need to stay with authoritative teachings of the Standard Works and the latter-day prophets:

> You are to teach this Gospel using as your sources and authorities the Standard Works of the Church, and the words of those whom God has called to lead His people in these last days.  You are not, whether high or low, to intrude into your work your own peculiar philosophy, no matter what its source or how pleasing or rational it seems to you to be. . . .
>
> You are not, whether high or low, to change the doctrines of the Church or to modify them, as they are declared by and in the Standard Works of the Church and by those whose authority it is to declare the mind and will of the Lord to the Church.  The Lord has declared he is "the same yesterday, today, and forever." *(Messages of the First Presidency, 6:55)*.  (See the topic, "TEACHING" in this book.)

2.   In the process of gathering together the many official publications of the Church I discovered just how many there are and how difficult they can be to obtain.  It took me three years, for example, to acquire a copy of the April 1946 conference report.

In addition to the Standard Works and conference reports, official church publications include *Articles of Faith, Discourses of Brigham Young, Gospel Principles, History of the Church* (7 volumes), *The House of the Lord, HYMNS, Jesus the Christ, Priesthood and Church Government, Teachings of the Latter-day Prophets, Teachings of the Prophet Joseph Smith, Church History and Modern Revelation;* the missionary discussions; and a host of various manuals for priesthood, Relief Society, seminary, institute and Church auxiliaries. (See Bibliography A.)

3.   "The Church of Jesus Christ of Latter-day Saints accepts four books as scripture: the Bible, the Book of Mormon, the Doctrine and Covenants, and the Pearl of Great Price. These books are called the Standard Works of the Church. . . . ¶ *In addition to these four books of scripture, the inspired words of our living prophets become scripture to us. Their words come to us through conferences, Church publications, and instructions to local priesthood leaders."* [Italics added] (Gospel Principles, pp. 49,51-52.)

Although the Church sponsors the Church magazines, the Ensign, New Era, and Friend, only the First Presidency Message in the Ensign carries authority as Church-published.  Conference talks are supplied to the Ensign in advance of their official corrected publication later in bound volumes called conference reports.

4.   "Secondary" sources are not referenced. *Journal of Discourses, Doctrines of Salvation, Mormon Doctrine, The Miracle of Forgiveness* and other valuable books have not been drawn upon because they are not *official,* not Church-published.  A "back door" exists by which passages from these books become legitimate doctrinal support.  It is when prophets cite them within an official context, such as a general conference address.

An exception to this policy of not referencing "secondary source" is some occasional referencing to the Messages of the First Presidency by James R. Clark, published by Bookcraft, Inc., 1965. (Cited as MOFP.)  Messages contained therein are quoted only if they have been previously published officially by the First Presidency or by the President of the Church. This source is quoted for ease of locating these previously published messages, which otherwise are very difficult for the general public to access.

5.   *We Believe* quotes only prophets (including Apostles and some latter-day Church patriarchs— since Apostles and Church patriarchs are ordained prophets).  Some biblical writers, however, are not known to be prophets.  Quotations from such writers are still included in this book since latter-day prophets have declared the witnesses of these writers to be the word of God. ("We believe the Bible to be the word of God as far as it is translated correctly. . . ." Joseph Smith, eighth Article of Faith.)  New Testament writers unknown to be prophets include Matthew, Mark, Luke, Acts (Luke),

and Jude. To distinguish these writers from known prophets, the name of the writer or book is preceded by the words **Recorded in**. For example, **Recorded in Luke.**

Old Testament books not known to be *entirely* written by prophets are quoted the same way. These include 1 and 2 Chronicles, Ecclesiastes, Esther, Job, Judges, 1 and 2 Kings, Psalms, Proverbs, Ruth, 1 and 2 Samuel, and The Song of Solomon. Passages from these books are generally cited with the words **Recorded in** preceding the name of the book.

The first five books of the Bible are reputed to have been written by Moses. However, some of the language in these books refers to Moses in the second person. This makes it awkward to cite such passages as having been written by Moses himself. For this reason some passages from these first five books of the Bible are also quoted with the words **Recorded in** preceding the name of the book, as follows: **Recorded in Genesis; Recorded in Exodus; Recorded in Leviticus; Recorded in Numbers;** and, **Recorded in Deuteronomy.**

# SAMPLE PAGES

## List of Doctrines
## JOY AND HAPPINESS

363. Happiness is the object and design of our existence.

364. True happiness and joy are not found in the frivolous or carnal pleasures of the world.

365. When we are actively engaged in a virtuous cause, we can experience true happiness.

366. Keeping the commandments of God fosters happiness.

367. Only by entering the Kingdom of God (the Celestial Kingdom) can we realize a fullness of joy.

*Doctrines on JOY AND HAPPINESS Located in Other Topics*

35. We cannot receive a fullness of joy in the Celestial Kingdom without the resurrection, in which the spirit and the body are inseparably reunited.

126. In the Spirit World, after death, there is a separation of spirits which lasts until the resurrection and final judgment; the wicked go into a state of outer darkness, and the righteous go into a state of happiness.

188 In the Garden of Eden, Adam and Eve were in a state of innocence, not understanding good and evil, and having neither joy nor misery.

293. Before God sent us to the earth, He prepared a "plan of salvation" for us.

302. A physical body is essential to obtaining a fullness of joy in the Celestial Kingdom of God.

740. Happiness comes from serving others.

750. It is more blessed to give than to receive; (there is more joy in serving than in being served).

760. We experience joy when we choose the good and reject the evil.

762. The person who persists in sin cannot have joy, for wickedness never was happiness.

874. The worldly wise, who will not humble themselves before God, will never enjoy eternal happiness.

# SAMPLE PAGES

When a Church President has spoken as an Apostle before becoming President, "Elder" is indicated. When he speaks after becoming the Church President, "President" is indicated.

Each doctrine of the Church is summarized in a single sentence and assigned a number for ease of reference—not for emphasis or priority.

References always indicate an official, Church-published source. (See List of Abbreviations under Bibliography A at the end of this book.)

in the light and frivolous pleasures of the world, or in matters pertaining strictly to the world, will be sadly disappointed, because it is said that a man whose heart is wedded to the things of the world is carnally minded, and we are told in the scriptures that to be carnally minded, or altogether worldly minded, is death, but to be spiritually minded is life eternal. There it is, and we should remember that as Latter-day Saints we must not give ourselves wholly and completely to worldly things, loving them above everything else. We have to deal with them, and we need them, too, but we must be spiritually minded if we will attain to a fulness of joy. CR1932Oct:10

**George Q. Cannon**

It is not given to men and women on the earth to be entirely satisfied, if they seek for satisfaction and happiness in worldly things. There is only one way in which perfect happiness can be obtained, and that is by having the Spirit of God. (Gospel Truth, 2:317-18) TLDP:319

A complete entry consists of a numbered Doctrinal Statement, followed by those witnesses and testimonies of the prophets—in their original words—that establish it as doctrine.

**Related Witnesses:**

**President David O. McKay**

Pleasure is not the purpose of man's existence. Joy is. (Church News; Gospel Ideals, p. 492) TLDP:318

One prophet citing another provides a second authoritative witness to the same truth.

365.    When we are actively engaged in a virtuous cause we can experience true happiness.

**Joseph Smith,**
*quoted by Elder Joseph Fielding Smith*

Happiness is the object and design of our existence; and will be the end thereof, if we pursue the path that leads to it; and this path is virtue, uprightness, faithfulness, holiness, and keeping all the commandments of God. (An essay recorded in the Journal History, Aug. 27, 1842) HC5:134-35; TPJS:255-56; DGSM:27

**Joseph Smith,**
*receiving the Word of the Lord*

Verily I say, men should be anxiously engaged in a good cause, and do many things of their own free will, and bring to pass much righteousness; 28. For the power is in them, wherein they are agents unto themselves. And inasmuch as men do good they shall in nowise lose their reward. (Revelation for the elders of the Church, Aug. 1, 1831; the Lord instructs the Saints to counsel with each other and with the Lord) D&C 58:27-28

Background statements clarify the contexts of prophetic witnesses and aid proper interpretation by indicating audience, date or period, location, purpose, or historical background.

**President Spencer W. Kimball**

The way for each person and each family to guard against the slings and arrows of the Adversary and

to prepare for the great day of the Lord, is to hold fast to the iron rod, to exercise greater faith, to repent of our sins and shortcomings, and to be anxiously engaged in the work of His kingdom on earth, which is the Church of Jesus Christ of Latter-day Saints. Herein lies the only true happiness for all our Father's children. CR1982Oct:4

**Rudger Clawson**

[Man] may get great happiness from what he does do in righteousness. . . . CR1932Oct:9

**President David O. MCkay**

Man's greatest happiness comes from losing himself for the good of others. CR1963Oct:8

**Elder David O. McKay**

Actions in harmony with divine law and the laws of nature will bring happiness and those in opposition to divine truth, misery. Man is responsible not only for every deed, but also for every idle word and thought. CR1950Apr:33

**Related Witnesses:**

**President David O. McKay**

The first condition of happiness is a clear conscience. No man who does wrong or who is unvirtuous will be happy. . . . (Church News; Gospel Ideals, p. 498) TLDP:320

**Elder Heber J. Grant**

Make a motto in life; always try to assist someone else to carry his burden. The true key to happiness in life is to labor for the happiness of others. (To students at University of Utah, 1901) (Gospel Standards, p. 161) TLDP:320

**George Q. Cannon**

Whence comes your enjoyment? Whence come the glorious feelings that you have when you feel the best? Do they come from the outside? Do external circumstances produce real happiness of the kind that I describe? Doubtless, they contribute to happiness; but the purest joy, the greatest happiness, that which is most heavenly proceeds from within. A man must carry the principles of happiness and the love of God in his own breast, or he will not be happy. ¶ It is not true enjoyment when it comes from any other source. Not without therefore, must we expect happiness and exaltation, but from within. Deity is within us, and its development brings happiness and joy inexpressible. (Gospel Truth, 1:99) TLDP:319

**Nephi, son of Lehi**

And it came to pass that we lived after the manner of happiness. (Nephi writes on plates shortly after the death of his father Lehi, 569-559 B.C.) 2Ne.5:27

**Marion G. Romney**

The key to happiness is to get the Spirit and keep it. CR1961Oct:61

"Related Witnesses" includes testimonies of prophets that do not establish a given doctrine alone, but provide important support to the complete doctrine.

# FOREWORD
## The Doctrinal Difference

*We Believe* makes it an easy matter to discern those beliefs that Mormons hold somewhat in common with other Christians—beliefs such as the divine nature of Jesus Christ; the reality of the resurrection and the Atonement; the need to exercise faith in Christ; service and charity to others; and the need to repent and change our lives.

At the same time, *We Believe* makes it possible to discern the specific doctrines and teachings that make The Church of Jesus Christ of Latter-day Saints distinct from other religions. These fall under four major categories of doctrine:

1. *Authority,*
2. *The Nature of God,*
3. *Revelation,* and
4. *Ordinances and Covenants.*

Mormon doctrine also addresses three primary questions about life:

5. *Where Do We Come From?*
6. *Why Are We Here?* and
7. *Where Are We Going?*

The topics in *We Believe* that deal with these seven doctrinal areas that distinguish Mormonism, or The Church of Jesus Christ of Latter-day Saints, are as follows:

### 1. Authority
- Priesthood Authority and Power
- Priesthood and Church Government
- Prophets, Seers and Revelators
- Sustaining Church Leaders

### 2. The Nature of God
- God

### 3. Revelation
- Revelation

### 4. Ordinances and Covenants
- Ordinances
- Baptism
- Covenants with God
- Sacrament of the Lord's Supper
- Temples

### 5. Where Do We Come From?
- Pre-Mortal Life

### 6. Why Are We Here? —*we are individual persons of infinite worth, having free agency!*
- Man: Mankind
- Mortal Life on Earth
- Agency
- Joy and Happiness

### 7. Where Are We Going?
- Death
- Degrees of Glory
- Hell

# List of Doctrines

## ADVERSITY

*Doctrines Located in This Topic*

1. Life on earth is a probationary state in which every individual who attains the age of accountability is tested.

2. Hardships and afflictions prepare us to enter the kingdom of heaven.

3. The Lord helps us bear tribulations.

4. We are given the particular tests and challenges we personally need for our eternal salvation—our exaltation.

5. Suffering can refine, purify, and perfect our nature.

6. We are to be patient in afflictions.

7. Those who live godly lives can expect criticism for their well doing.

8. Physical handicaps or disease are not necessarily the result of sin.

9. Some afflictions come upon us because of our own transgressions, that we might learn obedience by the things we suffer.

10. God does not suffer us to be tried or tested beyond that which we are able to bear.

*Doctrines on ADVERSITY Located in Other Topics*

17. Only by being exposed to evil can we recognize and embrace good; we taste the bitter fruits of life that we may learn to prize the good.

71. After we receive the more sure word of prophecy, that our calling and election is made sure, we may receive the Second Comforter, which carries the promise of eternal life.

184. Faith overcomes fear and doubt.

469. Those who successfully meet the trials of life on earth will inherit eternal life in the celestial kingdom of glory.

471. Mortality is a time for testing and trial, to prove whether we will keep the commandments of God.

508. The work of the Lord thrives under opposition and persecution.

509. We are to bear persecution with patience.

723. Answers to personal problems can come through scripture study.

# ADVERSITY

1. **Life on earth is a probationary state in which every individual who attains the age of accountability is tested.**

### Elder Joseph Fielding Smith

In the pre-existence we dwelt in the presence of God our Father. When the time arrived for us to be advanced in the scale of our existence and pass through this mundane probation, councils were held and the spirit children were instructed in matters pertaining to conditions in mortal life, and the reason for such an existence. In the former life we were spirits. In order that we should advance and eventually gain the goal of perfection, it was made known that we would receive tabernacles of flesh and bones and have to pass through mortality where we would be tried and proved to see if we, by trial, would prepare ourselves for exaltation. We were made to realize, in the presence of our glorious Father, who had a tangible body of flesh and bones which shone like the sun, that we were, as spirits, far inferior in our station to him. (Article in Church News, June 12, 1949) DGSM:14

### George Q. Morris

So these are real blessings. We come to the earth with all these conditions arranged as they are so that we have to struggle constantly against evil, struggle to preserve our lives, struggle for everything of true value—that is the thing for us to understand—this is the course of life that is most desirable, and for our good. We have no need to find fault with these conditions. The Lord has ordained them all for our welfare and happiness. CR1958Apr:39-40

### President Brigham Young,
### *quoted by John A. Widtsoe*

All intelligent beings who are crowned with crowns of glory, immortality, and eternal lives must pass through every ordeal appointed for intelligent beings to pass through, to gain their glory and exaltation. Every calamity that can come upon mortal beings will be suffered to come upon the few, to prepare them to enjoy the presence of the Lord. If we obtain the glory that Abraham obtained, we must do so by the same means that he did. If we are ever prepared to enjoy the society of Enoch, Noah, Melchizedek, Abraham, Isaac, and Jacob, or of their faithful children, and of the faithful Prophets and Apostles, we must pass through the same experience, and gain the knowledge, intelligence, and endowments that will prepare us to enter into the celestial kingdom of our Father and God. *(Sermon in Provo, Utah, Aug. 26, 1860, JD8:150)* DBY:345

### Recorded in Deuteronomy

And thou shalt remember all the way which the LORD thy God led thee these forty years in the wilderness, to humble thee, and to prove thee, to know what was in thine heart, whether thou wouldest keep his commandments, or no. (*Revelation to Moses for the children of Israel*) Deut.8:2

### Bruce R. McConkie

[T]his life never was intended to be easy. It is a probationary estate in which we are tested physically, mentally, morally, and spiritually. We are subject to disease and decay. We are attacked by cancer, leprosy, and contagious diseases. We suffer pain and sorrow and afflictions. Disasters strike; floods sweep away our homes; famines destroy our food; plagues and wars fill our graves with dead bodies and our broken homes with sorrow. ¶ We are called upon to choose between the revealed word of God and the soul-destroying postulates of the theoretical sciences. Temptations, the lusts of the flesh, evils of every sort—all these are part of the plan, and must be faced by every person privileged to undergo the experiences of mortality. ¶ The testing processes of mortality are for all men, saints and sinners alike. Sometimes the tests and trials of those who have received the gospel far exceed any imposed upon worldly people. Abraham was called upon to sacrifice his only son. Lehi and his family left their lands and wealth to live in a wilderness. Saints in all ages have been commanded to lay all that they have upon the altar, sometimes even their very lives. CR1976Oct:157-58

### Boyd K. Packer

We live in a day when the adversary stresses on every hand the philosophy of instant gratification. We seem to demand *instant* everything, including instant solutions to our problems. ¶ We are indoctrinated that somehow we should always be instantly emotionally comfortable. When that is not so, some become anxious—and all too frequently seek relief from counseling, from analysis, and even from medication. ¶ It was meant to be that life would be a challenge. To suffer some anxiety, some depression, some disappointment, even some failure is normal. ¶ Teach our members that if they have a good, miserable day once in a while, or several in a row, to stand steady and face them. Things will straighten out. ¶ There is great purpose in our struggle in life. (That All May Be Edified, p. 94) TLDP:8-9

### Elder Spencer W. Kimball

We knew before we were born that we were coming to earth for bodies and experience and that we would have joys and sorrows, ease and pain, comforts and hardships, health and sickness, successes and disappointments, and we knew also that after a period of life we would die. We accepted all these eventualities with a glad heart, eager to accept both the favorable and the unfavorable. We eagerly accepted the chance to come earthward even though it might be for only a day or a year. Perhaps we were not so much concerned whether we would die of disease, of accident, or of senility. We were willing to take life as it came and as we might organize and control it, and this without murmur, complaint, or unreasonable demands. (Faith Precedes the Miracle, p. 106) DGSM:28

**Related Witnesses:**

**Joseph Smith,**
*receiving the Word of the Lord*
[K]now thou, my son, that all these things shall give thee experience, and shall be for thy good. (*Revelation received in Liberty Jail, March 1839*) D&C 122:7

**Recorded in Luke**
Confirming the souls of the disciples, and exhorting them to continue in the faith, and that we must through much tribulation enter into the kingdom of God. (*Report on the ministry of Paul and Barnabas*) Acts 14:22

**Author's Note:** In this doctrinal statement, "Life on earth is a probationary state in which every individual is tested," the phrase, ". . . every individual is tested" must make room for the fact that there are infants and mentally deficient individuals who may not be tested in the same way as the rest of mankind.

---

2.  Hardships and afflictions prepare us to enter the kingdom of heaven.

**Elder Spencer W. Kimball**
Is there not wisdom in his [God's] giving us trials that we might rise above them, responsibilities that we might achieve, work to harden our muscles, sorrows to try our souls? Are we not exposed to temptations to test our strength, sickness that we might learn patience, death that we might be immortalized and glorified? (Faith Precedes the Miracle, p. 97) DGSM:28

**Joseph Smith,**
*receiving the Word of the Lord*
My son, peace be unto thy soul; thine adversity and thine afflictions shall be but a small moment; 8. And then, if thou endure it well, God shall exalt thee on high; thou shalt triumph over all thy foes. (*Revelation received while in Liberty Jail, March 20, 1839*) D&C 121:7-8

**Joseph Smith,**
*receiving the Word of the Lord*
And all they who suffer persecution for my name, and endure in faith, though they are called to lay down their lives for my sake yet shall they partake of all this glory. 36. Wherefore, fear not even unto death; for in this world your joy is not full, but in me your joy is full. (*Revelation Dec. 16, 1833*) D&C 101:35-36

**Joseph Smith,**
*receiving the Word of the Lord*
For verily I say unto you, blessed is he that keepeth my commandments, whether in life or in death; and he that is faithful in tribulation, the reward of the same is greater in the kingdom of heaven. 3. Ye cannot behold with your natural eyes, for the present time, the design of your God concerning those things which shall come hereafter, and the glory which shall follow after much tribulation. 4. For after much tribulation come the blessings. Wherefore the day cometh that ye shall be crowned with much glory; the hour is not yet, but is nigh at hand. (*Revelation to the elders of the Church, Aug. 1, 1831*) D&C 58:2-4

**Joseph Smith,**
*quoted by President John Taylor*
You will have all kinds of trials to pass through. And it is quite as necessary for you to be tried as it was for Abraham and other men of God, and (said he) God will feel after you, and He will take hold of you and wrench your very heart strings, and if you cannot stand it you will not be fit for an inheritance in the Celestial Kingdom of God. (*In Bowery, June 18, 1883, JD24:197*) TLDP:5

**Paul**
So that we ourselves glory in you in the churches of God for your patience and faith in all your persecutions and tribulations that ye endure: 5. Which is a manifest token of the righteous judgment of God, that ye may be counted worthy of the kingdom of God, for which ye also suffer: (*Letter to the Church at Thessalonica, comprising Jews and many pagan converts, A.D. 50*) 2Thess.1:4-5

**Melvin J. Ballard**
Why does the Lord permit us to suffer while in the body? Does that have any part in the divine plan? We never know joy until we have tasted sorrow. Things are only understood by their opposites. To appreciate good we must know what evil is. To have a siege of sickness makes one appreciate health. To live in a mortal body full of pain, of sorrow, decrepitude, and ultimately death, is all a preparation to make one understand what it means when the day shall come that death is swallowed up, that the grave

will be no longer a part of man's experiences, but that he is in an immortal body that knows no death, no disease and no decay, a body that is also perfect, without the handicaps that we have experienced in mortality. ¶ I have been convinced that every man or woman who has tasted the bitter sting of sickness and death, when loved ones have been snatched away, knows what hell means. I think there is no sorrow or torture that will ever come to those who are consigned to that punishment that will be any more intense than the pain and sorrow that tears human hearts when death takes loved ones away. So we all may know something of that sorrow and torture, and perhaps it is good that we should know it, when its opposite, freedom from pain and sickness and death, comes to us. (Sermons and Missionary Services of Melvin J. Ballard, p. 181) TLDP:6-7

### Marion G. Romney,
### also quoting Joseph Smith
Our mission, as a church, is to bring people to a knowledge of Christ and thus avoid all unnecessary suffering. We are aware, however, that should all men accept and live his teachings, adversity and affliction would still abound because, in the words of the Prophet Joseph Smith, "Men have to suffer that they may come upon Mount Zion and be exalted above the heavens." (HC5:556) ¶ This does not mean that we crave suffering. We avoid all we can. However, we now know, and we all knew when we elected to come into mortality, that we would here be proved in the crucible of adversity and affliction. CR1969Oct:57

### President Brigham Young
My people must be tried in all things, that they may be prepared to receive the glory that I have for them, even the glory of Zion; and he that will not bear chastisement is not worthy of my kingdom. (Revelation received Jan. 14, 1847) D&C 136:31

### Elder Ezra Taft Benson
While I do not believe in stepping out of the path of duty to pick up a cross I don't need, a man is a coward who refuses to pick up a cross that clearly lies within his path. No cross, no crown. No gall, no glory. No thorns, no throne. ACR(Taipei)1975:3

### Jacob, brother of Nephi,
### quoted by Nephi
But, behold, the righteous, the saints of the Holy One of Israel, they who have believed in the Holy One of Israel, they who have endured the crosses of the world, and despised the shame of it, they shall inherit the kingdom of God, which was prepared for them from the

foundation of the world, and their joy shall be full forever. (Jacob teaches the people of Nephi, 559-545 B.C.) 2Ne.9:18

### Elder Lorenzo Snow
It is necessary that we suffer in all things, that we may be qualified and worthy to rule, and govern all things, even as our Father in Heaven and His eldest son, Jesus. (Millennial Star 13:363, 1851) DGSM:28

### James
Blessed is the man that endureth temptation: for when he is tried, he shall receive the crown of life, which the Lord hath promised to them that love him. (Letter to his brethren in the Church) James 1:12

### Recorded in Luke
Confirming the souls of the disciples, and exhorting them to continue in the faith, and that we must through much tribulation enter into the kingdom of God. (Report of the ministry of Paul and Barnabas) Acts 14:22

### Jesus,
### recorded in Mark
And ye shall be hated of all men for my name's sake: but he that shall endure unto the end, the same shall be saved. (Jesus to his disciples) Mark 13:13

### Jesus,
### quoted by Mormon
And blessed are all ye who are persecuted for my name's sake, for theirs is the kingdom of heaven. 11. And blessed are ye when men shall revile you and persecute you, and shall say all manner of evil against you falsely, for my sake; 12. For ye shall have great joy and be exceedingly glad, for great shall be your reward in heaven; for so persecuted they the prophets who were before you. (The resurrected Jesus Christ to the Nephite people, A.D. 34) 3Ne.12:10-12

**Related Witnesses:**
### Elder Spencer W. Kimball
Being human, we would expel from our lives physical pain and mental anguish and assure ourselves of continual ease and comfort, but if we were to close the doors upon sorrow and distress, we might be excluding our greatest friends and benefactors. Suffering can make saints of people as they learn patience, long-suffering, and self-mastery. The sufferings of our Savior were part of his education. (Faith Precedes the Miracle, p. 98) DGSM:28

### Joseph Smith,
### receiving the Word of the Lord
If thou art called to pass through tribulation; if thou art in perils among false brethren; if thou art in perils among robbers; if thou art in perils by land or by sea; 6. If thou art accused with all

manner of false accusations; if thine enemies fall upon thee; if they tear thee from the society of thy father and mother and brethren and sisters; and if with a drawn sword thine enemies tear thee from the bosom of thy wife, and of thine offspring, and thine elder son, although but six years of age, shall cling to thy garments, and shall say, My father, my father, why can't you stay with us? O, my father, what are the men going to do with you? and if then he shall be thrust from thee by the sword, and thou be dragged to prison, and thine enemies prowl around thee like wolves for the blood of the lamb; 7. And if thou shouldst be cast into the pit, or into the hands of murderers, and the sentence of death passed upon thee; if thou be cast into the deep; if the billowing surge conspire against thee; if fierce winds become thine enemy; if the heavens gather blackness, and all the elements combine to hedge up the way; and above all, if the very jaws of hell shall gape open the mouth wide after thee, know thou, my son, that all these things shall give thee experience, and shall be for thy good. 8. The Son of Man hath descended below them all. Art thou greater than he? 9. Therefore, hold on thy way, and the priesthood shall remain with thee; for their bounds are set, they cannot pass. Thy days are known, and thy years shall not be numbered less; therefore, fear not what man can do, for God shall be with you forever and ever. (*Revelation received while in Liberty Jail, March 1839*) D&C 122:5-9

**Joseph Smith,**
*receiving the Word of the Lord*
[A]nd all things wherewith you have been afflicted shall work together for your good, and to my name's glory, saith the Lord. (*Revelation for the Saints in Missouri, Aug. 6, 1833*) D&C 98:3

**Elder David O. McKay**
There is no development of character without resistance; there is no growth of spirituality without overcoming. CR1945Oct:133

**Paul**
And not only so, but we glory in tribulations also: knowing that tribulation worketh patience; 4. And patience, experience; and experience, hope: 5. And hope maketh not ashamed; because the love of God is shed abroad in our hearts by the Holy Ghost which is given unto us. (*Letter to the Church in Rome, about A.D. 55*) Rom.5:3-5

**Elder Ezra Taft Benson**
We can meet every reversal that can possibly come with the help of the Lord. Every reversal can be turned to our benefit and blessing and can make us stronger, more courageous, more godlike. ACR(Manilla)1975:11

**Elder John Taylor**
I used to think, if I were the Lord, I would not suffer people to be tried as they are. But I have changed my mind on that subject. Now I think I would, if I were the Lord, because it purges out the meanness and corruption that stick around the Saints, like flies around molasses. (*Speech Aug. 9, 1857, JD5:115* ) DGSM:29

**Lehi,**
*quoted by his son Nephi*
Nevertheless, Jacob, my first-born in the wilderness, thou knowest the greatness of God; and he shall consecrate thine afflictions for thy gain. (*Lehi to his son, Jacob, between 588-570 B.C.*) 2Ne.2:2

**Peter**
Beloved, think it not strange concerning the fiery trial which is to try you, as though some strange thing happened unto you: 13. But rejoice, inasmuch as ye are partakers of Christ's sufferings; that, when his glory shall be revealed, ye may be glad also with exceeding joy. 14. If ye be reproached for the name of Christ, happy are ye; for the spirit of glory and of God resteth upon you: on their part he is evil spoken of, but on your part he is glorified. (*To the churches in modern Asia Minor, about A.D. 60*) 1Pet.4:12-14

3.  The Lord helps us bear tribulations.

**Recorded in Psalms**
Cast thy burden upon the LORD, and he shall sustain thee: he shall never suffer the righteous to be moved. Ps.55:22

**President Brigham Young,**
*quoted by John A. Widtsoe*
I know it is hard to receive chastisement, for no chastisement is joyous, but grievous at the time it is given; but if a person will receive chastisement and pray for the Holy Spirit to rest upon him, that he may have the Spirit of truth in his heart, and cleave to that which is pleasing to the Lord, the Lord will give him grace to bear the chastisement, and he will submit to and receive it, knowing that it is for his good. (*Sermon Oct. 6, 1855, JD3:47*) DBY:227

**Jesus,**
*recorded in Matthew*
Come unto me, all ye that labour and are heavy laden, and I will give you rest. 29. Take my yoke upon you, and learn of me; for I am meek and lowly in heart: and ye shall find rest unto your souls. 30. For my yoke is easy, and my burden is light. (*Addressing the multitude*) Matt.11:28-30

## Alma, the younger,
### quoted by Mormon

And now, O my son Helaman, behold, thou art in thy youth, and therefore, I beseech of thee that thou wilt hear my words and learn of me; for I do know that whosoever shall put their trust in God shall be supported in their trials, and their troubles, and their afflictions, and shall be lifted up at the last day. (*Alma instructs his son, Helaman, about 73 B.C.*) Alma 36:3

## Alma, the younger,
### quoted by Mormon

And now my son, Shiblon, I would that ye should remember, that as much as ye shall put your trust in God even so much ye shall be delivered out of your trials, and your troubles, and your afflictions, and ye shall be lifted up at the last day. (*Alma instructs his righteous son, Shiblon, about 73 B.C.*) Alma 38:5

### Elder Ezra Taft Benson

We all have our difficulties, our problems, our reversals. "Whom the Lord loveth He chasteneth." (Heb.12:6) It is in the depths that men and women learn the lessons that help to build strong men and women, not at the pinnacle of success. In the hour of a man's success is his greatest danger. It sometimes takes a reversal to make us appreciate our blessings and to develop us into strong, courageous characters. We can meet every reversal that can possibly come with the help of the Lord. Every reversal can be turned to our benefit and blessing and can make us stronger, more courageous, more godlike. ACR(Manilla)1975:11

### Joseph Smith

Verily I say unto you my friends, fear not, let your hearts be comforted; yea, rejoice evermore, and in everything give thanks; 2. Waiting patiently on the Lord, for your prayers have entered into the ears of the Lord of Sabaoth, and are recorded with this seal and testament—the Lord hath sworn and decreed that they shall be granted. 3. Therefore, he giveth this promise unto you, with an immutable covenant that they shall be fulfilled; and all things wherewith you have been afflicted shall work together for your good, and to my name's glory, saith the Lord. (*Revelation for the Saints in Missouri, Aug. 6, 1833*) D&C 98:1-3

## Joseph Smith,
### receiving the Word of the Lord

Be patient in afflictions, for thou shalt have many; but endure them, for, lo, I am with thee, even unto the end of thy days. (*Revelation to Joseph Smith and Oliver Cowdery, July 1830*) D&C 24:8

### Jacob, brother of Nephi

But behold, I, Jacob, would speak unto you that are pure in heart. Look unto God with firmness of mind, and pray unto him with exceeding faith, and he will console you in your afflictions, and he will plead your cause, and send down justice upon those who seek your destruction. (*Jacob's address to the Nephites, those who are pure in heart, 544-421 B.C.*) Jacob 3:1

### Elder John Taylor

I rejoice in afflictions, for they are necessary to humble and prove us, that we may comprehend ourselves, become acquainted with our weakness and infirmities; and I rejoice when I triumph over them, because God answers my prayers, therefore I feel to rejoice all the day long. (*Report of mission to Europe Aug. 22, 1852, JD1:17*) TLDP:5

**Related Witnesses:**
### Peter

Wherefore let them that suffer according to the will of God commit the keeping of their souls to him in well doing, as unto a faithful Creator. (*Letter to the churches in modern Asia Minor, about A.D. 60*) 1Pet.4:19

## Joseph Smith,
### receiving the Word of the Lord

My son, peace be unto thy soul; thine adversity and thine afflictions shall be but a small moment; 8. And then, if thou endure it well, God shall exalt thee on high; thou shalt triumph over all thy foes. 9. Thy friends do stand by thee, and they shall hail thee again with warm hearts and friendly hands. 10. Thou art not yet as Job; thy friends do not contend against thee, neither charge thee with transgression, as they did Job. (*The Lord to Joseph while he is in Liberty Jail, March 20, 1839*) D&C 121:7-10

## Jesus,
### quoted by John

These things I have spoken unto you, that in me ye might have peace. In the world ye shall have tribulation: but be of good cheer; I have overcome the world. (*Speaking to his apostles*) John 16:33

### Mormon

And it came to pass that the voice of the Lord came to them in their afflictions, saying: Lift up your heads and be of good comfort, for I know of the covenant which ye have made unto me; and I will covenant with my people and deliver them out of bondage. 14. And I will also ease the burdens which are put upon your shoulders, that even you cannot feel them upon your backs, even while you are in bondage; and this will I do that ye may stand as witnesses for me hereafter, and that ye may know of a surety that

I, the Lord God, do visit my people in their afflictions. 15. And now it came to pass that the burdens which were laid upon Alma and his brethren were made light; yea, the Lord did strengthen them that they could bear up their burdens with ease, and they did submit cheerfully and with patience to all the will of the Lord. (*Amulon puts taskmasters over Alma, the converted priest of King Noah, and his people; the Lord eventually delivers them from bondage, 145-121 B.C.*) Mosiah 24:13-15

---

4.   **We are given the particular tests and challenges we personally need for our eternal salvation— our exaltation.**

**Bruce R. McConkie**

[T]his life never was intended to be easy. . . . ¶ The testing processes of mortality are for all men, saints and sinners alike. Sometimes the tests and trials of those who have received the gospel far exceed any imposed upon worldly people. Abraham was called upon to sacrifice his only son. Lehi and his family left their lands and wealth to live in a wilderness. Saints in all ages have been commanded to lay all that they have upon the altar, sometimes even their very lives. ¶ As to the individual trials [or] problems that befall any of us, all we need say is that in the wisdom of Him who knows all things, and who does all things well, all of us are given the particular and specific tests that we need in our personal situations. CR1976Oct:157-58

**Boyd K. Packer**

Our lives are made up of thousands of everyday choices. Over the years these little choices will be bundled together and show clearly what we value. ¶ The crucial test of life, I repeat, does not center in the choice between fame and obscurity, nor between wealth and poverty. The greatest decision of life is between good and evil. ¶ We may foolishly bring unhappiness and trouble, even suffering, upon ourselves. These are not always to be regarded as penalties imposed by a displeased Creator. They are part of the lessons of life, part of the test. ¶ Some are tested by poor health, some by a body that is deformed or homely. Others are tested by handsome and healthy bodies; some by the passion of youth; others by the erosions of age. ¶ Some suffer disappointment in marriage, family problems; others live in poverty and obscurity. Some (perhaps this is the hardest test) find ease and luxury. ¶ All are part of the test, and there is more equality in this testing than sometimes

we suspect. ¶ It is possible to be both rich and famous and at the same time succeed spiritually. But the Lord warned of the difficulty of it when He talked of camels and needles (see Matt.19:24). CR1980Oct:29

**President Brigham Young**

There is not a single condition of life that is entirely unnecessary; there is not one hour's experience but what is beneficial to all those who make it their study, and aim to improve upon the experience they gain. What becomes a trial to one person is not noticed by another. (*Remarks in Tabernacle, May 25, 1862, JD9:292*) TLDP:5

**Joseph Smith,**
*quoted by President John Taylor*

You will have all kinds of trials to pass through. And it is quite as necessary for you to be tried as it was for Abraham and other men of God, and (said he) God will feel after you, and He will take hold of you and wrench your very heart strings, and if you cannot stand it you will not be fit for an inheritance in the Celestial Kingdom of God. (*In Bowery, June 18, 1883, JD24:197*) TLDP:5

**Elder Ezra Taft Benson**

We all have our difficulties, our problems, our reversals. "Whom the Lord loveth He chasteneth." (Heb.12:6) It is in the depths that men and women learn the lessons that help to build strong men and women, not at the pinnacle of success. In the hour of a man's success is his greatest danger. It sometimes takes a reversal to make us appreciate our blessings and to develop us into strong, courageous characters. We can meet every reversal that can possibly come with the help of the Lord. Every reversal can be turned to our benefit and blessing and can make us stronger, more courageous, more godlike. ACR(Manilla)1975:11

**Elder Heber J. Grant**

We sometimes meet people who say they would like to have witnessed the trials of the early Saints and taken a part in them, but I have no wish to nominate myself for a martyr. I tell you what I do desire: it is to be tested and tried only so far as is necessary to qualify me for the duties which have been imposed upon me, and to gain an exaltation in the presence of my Heavenly Father. CR1898Apr:15

**Related Witnesses:**

**President Brigham Young,**
*quoted by John A. Widtsoe*

When we look at the Latter-day Saints, we ask, is there any necessity of their being persecuted? Yes, if they are disobedient. Is there any necessity of chastening a son or a daughter? Yes, if they are disobedient. But suppose they are perfectly obedient to every requirement of their parents, is there any necessity of chastening them then? If there is, I do not understand the principle of it. I have not yet been able to see the necessity of chastening an obedient child, neither have I been able to see the necessity of chastisement from the Lord upon a people who are perfectly obedient. (*In old Tabernacle, Nov. 29, 1868, JD12:308*) DBY:350

**Orson Pratt**

Suppose we were created in the celestial world without a knowledge of that which we term pain, could we learn to sense it by seeing others suffer? No, no more than a person born in a dungeon and kept there until he reached the years of manhood, without the least gleam of light, could, while in that condition, be instructed about the principle of light. Why could he not be instructed? Because it is something he never has experienced. You tell him that light produces beautiful colors, such as red, blue, green, etc., what would he know about these colors? Nothing at all; his experience has not been called to grasp them; such a thing as a ray of light never penetrated his dungeon. But when he is permitted to experience the nature of light, when he sees the various colors, he then learns something which he never could reason out. So with regard to ourselves. We, in our first state of existence, never having seen misery among any of the immortal beings, and never experiencing it in our spiritual personages, how could we know anything about it? I do not think we could possibly comprehend the nature of it. We could not reason out the difference between happiness and misery. Why? For the want of experience. . . . We learn quite an experience here: we learn what it is to be miserable, we learn what it is to be unhappy, and we can now contrast misery with happiness; and we can say in our hearts, if I could only get rid of sickness, and pain, and sorrow, the effects of this death, how I could appreciate it! We often give expression to such feelings, when we are deeply afflicted. The Lord intends to free us, if we keep his commandments, after having suffered sufficiently long through this state of sickness and feebleness, this state of suffering and sorrow, which we have endured for so many years. . . . Yes, suppose the Lord were to appoint to you a kingdom; suppose he were to say to you, "Son, yonder are materials which you may organize by my power into a world; and you may place upon it your own offspring, as I did my offspring upon the world upon which you dwelt." What kind of person would you be if you had no

experience? What? Go and create a world, and then people that world with your own offspring, and not know the difference between good and evil, between sickness and health, between pain and happiness, having no knowledge of these by experience. I think that such a one would not be fit to be entrusted with a world that was to undergo and pass through the same ordeals that our creation is now experiencing. (*In 14th Ward, 1878, JD19:288-89*) TLDP:5-6

**Moses**

And thou shalt remember all the way which the LORD thy God led thee these forty years in the wilderness, to humble thee, and to prove thee, to know what was in thine heart, whether thou wouldest keep his commandments, or no. (*Revelation to Moses for the children of Israel*) Deut.8:2

---

5.   Suffering can refine, purify, and perfect our nature.

**James E. Faust**

From the refiner's fire of economic difficulty may come eternal blessings which can help save families and exalt their members by their being united and strengthened. CR1982Oct:131

**James E. Faust**

Some of the blessings available in overcoming economic adversity are: ¶ First, and perhaps most important, our faith and testimony can be strengthened. . . . ¶ Second, we may learn the need for humility. Our dependence upon the Lord becomes a means of developing teachableness, an important aspect of humility. ¶ Third, family members learn cooperation and love for each other by being forced to draw closer together to survive. ¶ Fourth, personal dignity and self-respect may be achieved. . . . ¶ Fifth, we can become stronger and more resilient. . . . ¶ Sixth, we learn patience. . . . ¶ Seventh, we rise to heights previously unobtainable by the use of talents and skills which might not have been developed otherwise. Economic necessity opens the way for profitable learning experiences. ¶ Eighth, we can learn to trust the Lord and thus overcome fear. CR1982Oct:129,131

**Howard W. Hunter**

What makes us imagine that we may be immune from the same experiences that refined the lives of former-day Saints? We must remember that the same forces of resistance which prevent our progress afford us also opportunities to overcome. God will have a tried people! CR1980Apr:36-37

### Elder Spencer W. Kimball

Being human we would expel from our lives sorrow, distress, physical pain and mental anguish and assure ourselves of continual ease and comfort, but if we closed the doors upon such, we might be evicting our greatest friends and benefactors. Suffering can make Saints of people as they learn patience, long suffering and self-mastery. The sufferings of our Savior were part of his education. (Brigham Young University Speeches of the Year, Dec. 6, 1955, p. 5) TLDP:7

### Elder Ezra Taft Benson

It is not on the pinnacle of success and ease where men and women grow most. It is often down in the valley of heartache and disappointment and reverses where men and women grow into strong characters. ACR(Stockholm)1974:70

### Elder Ezra Taft Benson

We all have our difficulties, our problems, our reversals. "Whom the Lord loveth He chasteneth." (Heb.12:6) It is in the depths that men and women learn the lessons that help to build strong men and women, not at the pinnacle of success. In the hour of a man's success is his greatest danger. It sometimes takes a reversal to make us appreciate our blessings and to develop us into strong, courageous characters. We can meet every reversal that can possibly come with the help of the Lord. Every reversal can be turned to our benefit and blessing and can make us stronger, more courageous, more godlike. ACR(Manilla)1975:11

### Elder John Taylor

I used to think, if I were the Lord, I would not suffer people to be tried as they are; but I have changed my mind on that subject. Now I think I would, if I were the Lord, because it purges out the meanness and corruption that stick around the Saints, like flies around molasses. *(Speech Aug. 9, 1857, JD5:115)* DGSM:29

### George Q. Cannon

The Lord our God is working with us; He is trying us, probably with trials of a new sort that he may approve of us in every respect. If we have set out to obtain Celestial glory, the precious and inestimable gift of eternal lives, there is no trial necessary for our purification and perfection as Saints of God that we will not have to meet, contend with and overcome. Such trials will come in various shapes, on the right hand and on the left, whether they be in having everything move on prosperously, or in adversity, hardship and the laying down of our lives for the truth, until the design is fully accomplished and the dross of our natures is purified and these earthly tabernacles are redeemed

from everything that is groveling and low and brought into entire subjection to the mind and will of God. *(In Tabernacle, Oct. 23, 1864, JD10:347)* TLDP:8

---

6.    We are to be patient in afflictions.

### Joseph Smith,
*receiving the Word of the Lord*

Be patient in afflictions, for thou shalt have many; but endure them, for, lo, I am with thee, even unto the end of thy days. (*Revelation to Joseph Smith and Oliver Cowdery, July 1830*) D&C 24:8

### Joseph Smith,
*receiving the Word of the Lord*

Be patient in afflictions, revile not against those that revile. Govern your house in meekness, and be steadfast. (*Revelation for Thomas B. Marsh, Sept. 30, 1830*) D&C 31:9

### Elder Spencer W. Kimball

Is there not wisdom in his [God's] giving us trials that we might rise above them, responsibilities that we might achieve, work to harden our muscles, sorrows to try our souls? Are we not exposed to temptations to test our strength, sickness that we might learn patience, death that we might be immortalized and glorified? (Faith Precedes the Miracle, p. 97) DGSM:28

### Elder Spencer W. Kimball

Suffering can make saints of people as they learn patience, long-suffering, and self-mastery. The sufferings of our Savior were part of his education. (Faith Precedes the Miracle, p. 98) DGSM:28

### King Benjamin,
*quoted by Mormon*

For the natural man is an enemy to God, and has been from the fall of Adam, and will be, forever and ever, unless he yields to the enticings of the Holy Spirit, and putteth off the natural man and becometh a saint through the atonement of Christ the Lord, and becometh as a child, submissive, meek, humble, patient, full of love, willing to submit to all things which the Lord seeth fit to inflict upon him, even as a child doth submit to his father. (*King Benjamin addresses his people, about 124 B.C.*) Mosiah 3:19

### Joseph Smith

Verily I say unto you my friends, fear not, let your hearts be comforted; yea, rejoice evermore, and in everything give thanks; 2. Waiting patiently on the Lord, for your prayers have entered into the ears of the Lord of Sabaoth, and are recorded with this seal and testament—the Lord hath sworn and decreed that they shall be granted. 3. Therefore, he giveth this promise unto you, with an immutable covenant that they shall be fulfilled; and all things wherewith you have been afflicted shall work together for your good, and to my name's glory, saith the Lord. (*Revelation received Aug. 6, 1833 in consequence of the persecution of the Saints in Missouri*) D&C 98:1-3

### James

Take, my brethren, the prophets, who have spoken in the name of the Lord, for an example of suffering affliction, and of patience. 11. Behold, we count them happy which endure. Ye have heard of the patience of Job, and have seen the end of the Lord; that the Lord is very pitiful, and of tender mercy. (*To his brethren in the Church*) James 5:10-11

### Peter

For what glory is it, if, when ye be buffeted for your faults, ye shall take it patiently? but if, when ye do well, and suffer for it, ye take it patiently, this is acceptable with God. 21. For even hereunto were ye called: because Christ also suffered for us, leaving us an example, that ye should follow his steps: 22. Who did no sin, neither was guile found in his mouth: 23. Who, when he was reviled, reviled not again; when he suffered, he threatened not; but committed himself to him that judgeth righteously:(*Peter writes to the churches in modern Asia Minor, about A.D. 60*) 1Pet.2:20-23

### Orson F. Whitney,
#### *quoted by Elder Spencer W. Kimball*

No pain that we suffer, no trial that we experience is wasted. It ministers to our education, to the development of such qualities as patience, faith, fortitude and humility. All that we suffer and all that we endure, especially when we endure it patiently, builds up our characters, purifies our hearts, expands our souls, and makes us more tender and charitable, more worthy to be called the children of God . . . and it is through sorrow and suffering, toil and tribulation, that we gain the education that we come here to acquire and which will make us more like our Father and Mother in heaven. (Faith Precedes the Miracle, p. 98) DGSM:28-29

---

7.  **Those who live godly lives can expect criticism for their well doing.**

### Peter

For what glory is it, if, when ye be buffeted for your faults, ye shall take it patiently? but if, when ye do well, and suffer for it, ye take it patiently, this is acceptable with God. (*Letter to the church-*

es in (modern) Asia Minor, about A.D. 60) 1Pet.2:20

### Peter

But and if ye suffer for righteousness' sake, happy are ye: and be not afraid of their terror, neither be troubled; 15. But sanctify the Lord God in your hearts: and be ready always to give an answer to every man that asketh you a reason of the hope that is in you with meekness and fear: 16. Having a good conscience; that, whereas they speak evil of you, as of evildoers, they may be ashamed that falsely accuse your good conversation in Christ. 17. For it is better, if the will of God be so, that ye suffer for well doing, than for evil doing. (*Peter to the churches in modern Asia Minor, about A.D. 60*) 1Pet.3:14-17

### President Spencer W. Kimball

Always remember that if this were not the Lord's work, the adversary would not pay any attention to us. If the Church were merely a church of men and women, teaching only the doctrines of men, we would encounter little or no criticism or resistance—but because this is the Church of Him whose name it bears, we must not be surprised when criticisms or difficulties arise. With faith and good works, the truth will prevail. This is His Work. There is none other like it. Let us, therefore, press forward, lengthening our stride and rejoicing in our blessings and opportunities. CR1981Apr:105-06

### Howard W. Hunter

What makes us imagine that we may be immune from the same experiences that refined the lives of former-day Saints? We must remember that the same forces of resistance which prevent our progress afford us also opportunities to overcome. God will have a tried people! CR1980Apr:36-37

### Paul

Persecutions, afflictions, which came unto me at Antioch, at Iconium, at Lystra; what persecutions I endured: but out of them all the Lord delivered me. 12. Yea, and all that will live godly in Christ Jesus shall suffer persecution. 13. But evil men and seducers shall wax worse and worse, deceiving, and being deceived. (*Letter to his assistant Timothy, about A.D. 64*) 2Tim.3:11-13

**Related Witnesses:**

### John

Marvel not, my brethren, if the world hate you. (*Letter to the churches in Asia*) 1Jn.3:13

### President Brigham Young,
#### *quoted by John A. Widtsoe*

The people of the Most High God must be tried. It is written that they will be tried in all things, even as Abraham was tried. (*In Bowery, June 28, 1857*) DBY:345

**Joseph Smith**

From apostates the faithful have received the severest persecutions. Judas was rebuked and immediately betrayed his Lord into the hands of His enemies, because Satan entered into him. There is a superior intelligence bestowed upon such as obeyed the Gospel with full purpose of heart, which, if sinned against, the apostate is left naked and destitute of the Spirit of God, and he is, in truth, nigh unto cursing, and his end is to be burned. When once that light which was in them is taken from them they become as much darkened as they were previously enlightened, and then, no marvel, if all their power should be enlisted against the truth, and they, Judas like, seek the destruction of those who were their greatest benefactors. What nearer friend on earth, or in heaven, had Judas than the Savior? (*Written message to the elders of the Church in Kirtland and elsewhere, Jan. 1834*) HC2:23

8. **Physical handicaps or disease are not necessarily the result of sin.**

**Joseph Smith**

Yet many of the righteous shall fall a prey to disease to pestilence and by reason of the weakness of the flesh and yet be saved in the Kingdom of God so that it is an unhallowed principle to say that such and such have transgressed because they have been preyed upon by disease or death for all flesh is subject to death and the Saviour has said—"Judge not lest ye be judged." (The Words of Joseph Smith, p. 15) TLDP:4

**Boyd K. Packer**

Some are tested by poor health, some by a body that is deformed or homely. Others are tested by handsome and healthy bodies; some by the passion of youth; others by the erosions of age. CR1980Oct:29

**Melvin J. Ballard**

Why does the Lord permit us to suffer while in the body? Does that have any part in the divine plan? We never know joy until we have tasted sorrow. Things are only understood by their opposites. To appreciate good we must know what evil is. To have a siege of sickness makes one appreciate health. To live in a mortal body full of pain, of sorrow, decrepitude, and ultimately death, is all a preparation to make one understand what it means when the day shall come that death is swallowed up, that the grave will be no longer a part of man's experiences, but that he is in an immortal body that knows

no death, no disease and no decay, a body that is also perfect, without the handicaps that we have experienced in mortality. ¶ I have been convinced that every man or woman who has tasted the bitter sting of sickness and death, when loved ones have been snatched away, knows what hell means. I think there is no sorrow or torture that will ever come to those who are consigned to that punishment that will be any more intense than the pain and sorrow that tears human hearts when death takes loved ones away. So we all may know something of that sorrow and torture, and perhaps it is good that we should know it, when its opposite, freedom from pain and sickness and death, comes to us. (Sermons and Missionary Services of Melvin J. Ballard, p. 181) TLDP:6-7

9. **Some afflictions come upon us because of our own transgressions, that we might learn obedience by the things we suffer.**

**Boyd K. Packer**

We may foolishly bring unhappiness and trouble, even suffering, upon ourselves. These are not always to be regarded as penalties imposed by a displeased Creator. They are part of the lessons of life, part of the test. CR1980Oct:29

**Joseph Smith,**
*receiving the Word of the Lord*

And my people must needs be chastened until they learn obedience, if it must needs be, by the things which they suffer. (*Revelation for Zion's Camp, June 22, 1834*) D&C 105:6

**Joseph Smith,**
*receiving the Word of the Lord*

Verily I say unto you, concerning your brethren who have been afflicted, and persecuted, and cast out from the land of their inheritance— 2. I, the Lord, have suffered the affliction to come upon them, wherewith they have been afflicted, in consequence of their transgressions; 3. Yet I will own them, and they shall be mine in that day when I shall come to make up my jewels. 4. Therefore, they must needs be chastened and tried, even as Abraham, who was commanded to offer up his only son. 5. For all those who will not endure chastening, but deny me, cannot be sanctified. 6. Behold, I say unto you, there were jarrings, and contentions, and envyings, and strifes, and lustful and covetous desires among them; therefore by these things they polluted their inheritances. 7. They were slow to hearken unto the voice of the Lord their God; therefore, the Lord their God is slow to hearken unto their prayers, to answer them in the day of their trouble. 8. In the day of their peace they esteemed lightly my counsel; but, in the day of their trouble, of necessity they feel after me. 9. Verily I say unto you, notwithstanding their sins, my bowels are filled with compassion towards them. I will not utterly cast them off; and in the day of wrath I will remember mercy. (*Revelation received Dec. 16, 1833*) D&C 101:1-9

**President Spencer W. Kimball**

There are many causes for human suffering—including war, disease, and poverty—and the suffering that proceeds from each of these is very real, but I would not be true to my trust if I did not say that the most persistent cause of human suffering, that suffering which causes the deepest pain, is sin—the violation of the commandments given to us by God. (*To Weber State College, Ogden, Utah, Nov. 4, 1977*) TLDP:4

**Recorded in Proverbs**

My son, despise not the chastening of the LORD; neither be weary of his correction: 12. For whom the LORD loveth he correcteth; even as a father the son in whom he delighteth. Prov.3:11-12

**President Joseph F. Smith**

Sometimes we are prone to charge God with causing our afflictions and our troubles; but if we could see as God sees, if we could understand as he understands, if we could trace the effects back to the cause, and that truly, by the spirit of correct understanding, we would unquestionably discover that our trouble, or suffering, or affliction is the result of our own indiscretion or lack of knowledge, or of wisdom. It was not the hand of God that put affliction and trouble upon us. . . . ¶ You will suffer the consequences of your own mistakes, of your own errors, though they bring sorrow, or sickness, or death! So I acknowledge the hand of the Lord in this free agency that he has given to the children of men; but I acknowledge the hand of man in the consequences of his own acts, following his disobedience to the law of God. I do not charge the weaknesses, the mistakes or errors, the crimes and wickedness of men, and the evils that exist in the world, to God the Father, for he is not a God of evil, of wickedness, of strife, of anger, of sorrow, of sickness, and of imperfection. ("A Message to the Soldier Boys of 'Mormondom'," IE1917Jul:822-23) TLDP:4

**President Brigham Young,**
*quoted by John A. Widtsoe*

When we look at the Latter-day Saints, we ask, is there any necessity of their being persecuted?

Yes, if they are disobedient. Is there any necessity of chastening a son or a daughter? Yes, if they are disobedient. But suppose they are perfectly obedient to every requirement of their parents, is there any necessity of chastening them then? If there is, I do not understand the principle of it. I have not yet been able to see the necessity of chastening an obedient child, neither have I been able to see the necessity of chastisement from the Lord upon a people who are perfectly obedient. Have this people been chastened? Yes they have. (*In old Tabernacle, Nov. 29, 1868, JD12:308*) DBY:350

**Related Witnesses:**

**James**

Let no man say when he is tempted, I am tempted of God: for God cannot be tempted with evil, neither tempteth he any man: (*James writes to his brethren in the Church*) James 1:13

**Joseph Smith,**
*receiving the Word of the Lord*

Therefore, fear not, little flock; do good; let earth and hell combine against you, for if ye are built upon my rock, they cannot prevail. (*Revelation to Joseph Smith and Oliver Cowdery, April 1829*) D&C 6:34

---

10. **God does not suffer us to be tried or tested beyond that which we are able to bear.**

**Paul**

There hath no temptation taken you but such as is common to man: but God is faithful, who will not suffer you to be tempted above that ye are able; but will with the temptation also make a way to escape, that ye may be able to bear it. (*To the Church at Corinth, Greece, about A.D. 55*) 1Cor.10:13

**Neal A. Maxwell**

The Lord knows our bearing capacity, both as to coping and to comprehending, and He will not give us more to bear than we can manage at the moment, though to us it may seem otherwise. (See D&C 50:40; 78:18.) Just as no temptation will come to us from which we cannot escape or which we cannot bear, we will not be given more trials than we can sustain. (See 1Cor.10:13.) CR1982Oct:97

**Alma, the younger,**
*quoted by Mormon*

But that ye would humble yourselves before the Lord, and call on his holy name, and watch and pray continually, that ye may not be tempted above that which ye can bear, and thus be led by the Holy Spirit, becoming humble, meek, submissive, patient, full of love and all long-suffering; (*Alma preaches repentance to his brethren in the gospel, about 82 B.C.*) Alma 13:28

### President Brigham Young,
*quoted by John A. Widtsoe*

I know it is hard to receive chastisement, for no chastisement is joyous, but grievous at the time it is given; but if a person will receive chastisement and pray for the Holy Spirit to rest upon him, that he may have the Spirit of truth in his heart, and cleave to that which is pleasing to the Lord, the Lord will give him grace to bear the chastisement, and he will submit to and receive it, knowing that it is for his good. (*In Bowery, Oct. 6, 1855*) DBY:227

**Related Witnesses:**

### Joseph Smith,
*receiving the Word of the Lord*

Behold, ye are little children and ye cannot bear all things now; ye must grow in grace and in the knowledge of the truth. (*Revelation for the elders of the Church, May 1831*) D&C 50:40

### Joseph Smith,
*receiving the Word of the Lord*

And ye cannot bear all things now; nevertheless, be of good cheer, for I will lead you along. The kingdom is yours and the blessings thereof are yours, and the riches of eternity are yours. (*Revelation, March 1832*) D&C 78:18

---

**HYMNS Written by Prophets Applicable to this Topic**

### Elder Joseph Fielding Smith
*Does the Journey Seem Long?*
HYMNS:127

Does the journey seem long,
The path rugged and steep?
Are there briars and thorns on the way?
Do sharp stones cut your feet
As you struggle to rise
To the heights thru the heat of the day?

Is your heart faint and sad,
Your soul weary within,
As you toil 'neath your burden of care?
Does the load heavy seem
You are forced now to lift?
Is there no one your burden to share?

Let your heart be not faint
Now the journey's begun;
There is One who still beckons to you.
So look upward in joy
And take hold of his hand;
He will lead you to heights that are new—

A land holy and pure,
Where all trouble doth end,
And your life shall be free from all sin,
Where no tears shall be shed,
For no sorrows remain.
Take his hand and with him enter in.

# List of Doctrines

## AGENCY

*Doctrines Located in This Topic*

11. We have the ability to discern between good and evil and the agency to choose between the two.

12. God will not force any person to do good, nor can a person be forced by Satan to do evil.

13. Before the earth was created, the spirits of all people were free to act for themselves.

14. We are each responsible for the choices we make through the exercise of our agency—and we must accept the immediate and eternal consequences of those decisions.

15. Good comes from God and evil comes from the devil.

16. We can discern between good and evil when we have the Spirit of God.

17. Only by being exposed to evil can we recognize and embrace good; we taste the bitter fruits of life that we may learn to prize the good.

18. Power to overcome Satan and his evil influence comes from God.

19. In their exercise of agency, those who choose good will be rewarded.

20. We have a dual nature: one, related to the earthly life; the other, akin to the divine; by following after the enticings of the Spirit we can overcome the inclinations of the flesh.

21. The Lord permits the righteous to be slain by the wicked that the wicked might exercise their agency and receive a just judgment at the last day.

*Doctrines on AGENCY*
*Located in Other Topics*

158. In the premortal existence the devil's plan was to destroy the agency of the spirit sons and daughters of God.

193. Adam voluntarily partook of the fruit of the tree of knowledge of good and evil with knowledge of the consequences.

386. Our final state after this life is determined by the choices we make (during this life and in the spirit world hereafter).

387. We receive our reward from him whom we choose to follow, whether we choose the Lord and the reward of exaltation, or the devil and the reward of damnation.

556. When the plan of salvation was presented in the premortal world, each person had the opportunity of accepting or rejecting it.

749. We are to be eagerly engaged in doing many things of our own free will (we are not to wait for specific commands or formal church callings to do good works).

# AGENCY

11. We have the ability to discern between good and evil and the agency to choose between the two.

**Alma, the younger,**
*quoted by Mormon*

Wherefore, he gave commandments unto men, they having first transgressed the first commandments as to things which were temporal, and becoming as Gods, knowing good from evil, placing themselves in a state to act, or being placed in a state to act according to their wills and pleasures, whether to do evil or to do good— (*Alma responds to the chief ruler, Antionah, regarding Adam and Eve's expulsion from the Garden of Eden, about 82 B.C.*) Alma 12:31

**Lehi,**
*quoted by his son Nephi*

And the Messiah cometh in the fulness of time, that he may redeem the children of men from the fall. And because that they are redeemed from the fall they have become free forever, knowing good from evil; to act for themselves and not to be acted upon, save it be by the punishment of the law at the great and last day, according to the commandments which God hath given. (*Lehi teaches his sons, between 588-570 B.C.*) 2Ne.2:26

**Samuel, the Lamanite,**
*quoted by Mormon*

And now remember, remember, my brethren, that whosoever perisheth, perisheth unto himself; and whosoever doeth iniquity, doeth it unto himself; for behold, ye are free; ye are permitted to act for yourselves; for behold, God hath given unto you a knowledge and he hath made you free. 31. He hath given unto you that ye might know good from evil, and he hath given unto you that ye might choose life or death; and ye can do good and be restored unto that which is good, or have that which is good restored unto you; or ye can do evil, and have that which is evil restored unto you. (*Preaching to the Nephites, about 6 B.C.*) Hel.14:30-31

**Charles W. Penrose**

For man in spirit form, in his spirit nature, is an independent entity. It is an organized being, a son of God or a daughter of God, as the case may be, and in the spirit birth he obtained not only an eternal organization, but power and intelligence by which he can determine and understand light from darkness, truth from error, and choose between that which is right and that which is wrong. In the Pearl of Great Price we read that God gave him that power. . . . ¶ Here [Moses 4:2-3] we read that that power of choice,

the gift, the ability to understand right from wrong, to understand light from darkness, was given to the spirit of man by the Lord and He gave to him that agency, power in himself to choose the good and refuse the evil, to choose the light or the darkness as he willed. CR1914Oct:40

---

12. God will not force any person to do good, nor can a person be forced by Satan to do evil.

**Charles W. Penrose**

Here [Moses 4:2-3] we read that that power of choice, the gift, the ability to understand right from wrong, to understand light from darkness, was given to the spirit of man by the Lord and He gave to him that agency, power in himself to choose the good and refuse the evil, to choose the light or the darkness as he willed. So because of that, man can be brought to judgment for the deeds that he performs, for he is not forced to do evil, neither is he forced to do right. The power of volition is in the spirit man and he brings it with him when he is born into the earthly sphere, and so we can do good or do evil as we elect, and therefore we will be brought to judgment and every man will be judged according to the deeds done while in the body; according to his works, so will his future be determined. CR1914Oct:40

**Elder Joseph F. Smith**

God has given to all men an agency and has granted to us the privilege to serve him or serve him not, to do that which is right or that which is wrong, and this privilege is given to all men irrespective of creed, color or condition. The wealthy have this agency, the poor have this agency, and no man is deprived by any power of God from exercising it in the fullest and in the freest manner. (*General conference, April 1883; JD24:175*) MPSG1989:127

**Joseph Smith,**
*translating the Book of Moses*

And I, the Lord God, commanded the man, saying: Of every tree of the garden thou mayest freely eat, 17. But of the tree of the knowledge of good and evil, thou shalt not eat of it, nevertheless, thou mayest choose for thyself, for it is given unto thee; but, remember that I forbid it, for in the day thou eatest thereof thou shalt surely die. (*The Lord reveals to Moses the placing of man in the Garden of Eden*) Moses 3:16-17

**Joseph Smith,**
*quoted by Elder Joseph Fielding Smith*

He [Joseph Smith] then observed that Satan

was generally blamed for the evils which we did, but if he was the cause of all our wickedness, men could not be condemned. The devil could not compel mankind to do evil; all was voluntary. Those who resisted the Spirit of God, would be liable to be led into temptation, and then the association of heaven would be withdrawn from those who refused to be made partakers of such great glory. God would not exert any compulsory means, and the devil could not; and such ideas as were entertained [on these subjects] by many were absurd. . . . (*Joseph's paraphrased discourse to the Saints, Nauvoo, Ill., May 1841, TPJS:187*) DGSM:31

**Related Witnesses:**

**James**

Submit yourselves therefore to God. Resist the devil and he will flee from you. 8. Draw nigh to God, and he will draw nigh to you. Cleanse your hands, ye sinners; and purify your hearts, ye double minded. (*Letter to his brethren in the Church*) James 4:7-8

---

13. Before the earth was created, the spirits of all people were free to act for themselves.

**Marion G. Romney**

In the Garden of Eden, God endowed Adam and all his posterity with that free agency which they had enjoyed in the spirit world. CR1976Apr:120

**Joseph Smith,**
*translating the Book of Moses*

Wherefore, because that Satan rebelled against me, and sought to destroy the agency of man, which I, the Lord God, had given him, and also, that I should give unto him mine own power; by the power of mine Only Begotten, I caused that he should be cast down; (*The Lord describes to Moses Satan's rebellion in the premortal world*) Moses 4:3

**President Wilford Woodruff**

With regard to the rights of the human family, I wish to say that God has given unto all of his children of this dispensation, as he gave unto all of the children of previous dispensations, individual agency. This agency has always been the heritage of man under the rule and government of God. He possessed it in the heaven of heavens before the world was, and the Lord maintained and defended it there against the aggression of Lucifer and those that took sides with him, to the overthrow of Lucifer and one-third part of the heavenly hosts. By virtue of this agency you and I and all mankind are made

responsible beings, responsible for the course we pursue, the lives we live, the deeds we do in the body. ("Discourse," Millennial Star, Oct. 1889, p. 642) DGSM:30

**Alma, the younger,**
*quoted by Mormon*

And this is the manner after which they were ordained—being called and prepared from the foundation of the world according to the foreknowledge of God, on account of their exceeding faith and good works; in the first place being left to choose good or evil; . . . (*Alma instructs the people how God calls and ordains men to preach, about 82 B.C.*) Alma 13:3

**Charles W. Penrose**

The power of volition is in the spirit man and he brings it with him when he is born into the earthly sphere, and so we can do good or do evil as we elect, and therefore we will be brought to judgment and every man will be judged according to the deeds done while in the body; according to his works, so will his future be determined. CR1914Oct:40

**Elder Joseph Fielding Smith**

The spirits of men were not equal. They may have had an equal start, and we know they were all innocent in the beginning; but the right of free agency which was given to them enabled some to outstrip others, and thus, through the eons of immortal existence, to become more intelligent, more faithful for they were free to act for themselves, to receive the truth or rebel against it. (Article in IE19:318-19) MPSG1985:78

---

14. We are each responsible for the choices we make through the exercise of our agency—and we must accept the immediate and eternal consequences of those decisions.

**Joseph Smith**

We believe that men will be punished for their own sins, and not for Adam's transgression. (*The second of the thirteen Articles of Faith; letter to John Wentworth, March 1, 1842*) AofF:2

**Joseph Smith,**
*quoted by Elder Joseph Fielding Smith*

He [Joseph Smith] then observed that Satan was generally blamed for the evils which we did, but if he was the cause of all our wickedness, men could not be condemned. The devil could not compel mankind to do evil; all was voluntary. Those who resisted the Spirit of God, would be liable to be led into temptation, and then the association of heaven would be withdrawn from those who refused to be made partakers of such great glory. God would not exert any compulsory means, and the devil could not; and such ideas as were entertained [on these subjects] by many were absurd. . . . (*Joseph's paraphrased discourse to the Saints, Nauvoo, Ill., May 1841*) TPJS:187;DGSM:31

### Joseph Smith,
#### *receiving the Word of the Lord*
And they who remain shall also be quickened; nevertheless, they shall return again to their own place, to enjoy that which they are willing to receive, because they were not willing to enjoy that which they might have received. 33. For what doth it profit a man if a gift is bestowed upon him, and he receive not the gift? Behold, he rejoices not in that which is given unto him, neither rejoices in him who is the giver of the gift. 34. And again, verily I say unto you, that which is governed by law is also preserved by law and perfected and sanctified by the same. 35. That which breaketh a law, and abideth not by law, but seeketh to become a law unto itself, and willeth to abide in sin, and altogether abideth in sin, cannot be sanctified by law, neither by mercy, justice, nor judgment. Therefore, they must remain filthy still. (*Revelation received Dec. 27/28, 1832*) D&C 88:32-35

### President Joseph F. Smith
We believe in the free agency of man, and therefore in his individual responsibility. (*Address from the First Presidency of the Church to the World, delivered to and accepted by vote of the Church in General Conference, Apr. 1907*) CR1907Apr(Appendix)4

### President Brigham Young,
#### *quoted by John A. Widtsoe*
The volition of the creature is free; this is a law of their existence and the Lord cannot violate his own law; were he to do that, he would cease to be God. He has placed life and death before his children, and it is for them to choose. If they choose life, they receive the blessing of life; if they choose death, they must abide the penalty. This is a law which has always existed from all eternity, and will continue to exist throughout all the eternities to come. Every intelligent being must have the power of choice, and God brings forth the results of the acts of his creatures to promote his Kingdom and subserve his purposes in the salvation and exaltation of his children. (*Sermon, Aug. 1866, JD11:272*) DBY:62; DGSM:31

### President Wilford Woodruff
With regard to the rights of the human family, I wish to say that God has given unto all of his children of this dispensation, as he gave unto all of the children of previous dispensations, individual agency. This agency has always been the heritage of man under the rule and government of God. He possessed it in the heaven of heavens before the world was, and the Lord maintained and defended it there against the aggression of Lucifer and those that took sides with him, to the overthrow of Lucifer and one-third part of the heavenly hosts. By virtue of this agency you and I and all mankind are made responsible beings, responsible for the course we pursue, the lives we live, the deeds we do in the body. (Millennial Star 51:642, 1889) DGSM:30

### Samuel, the Lamanite,
#### *quoted by Mormon*
And now remember, remember, my brethren, that whosoever perisheth, perisheth unto himself; and whosoever doeth iniquity, doeth it unto himself; for behold, ye are free; ye are permitted to act for yourselves; for behold, God hath given unto you a knowledge and he hath made you free. 31. He hath given unto you that ye might know good from evil, and he hath given unto you that ye might choose life or death; and ye can do good and be restored unto that which is good, or have that which is good restored unto you; or ye can do evil, and have that which is evil restored unto you. (*Samuel preaches to the Nephites, about 6 B.C.*) Hel.14:30-31

### Elder Joseph Fielding Smith
Each may act for himself. It was Satan's plan to destroy this agency and force men to do his will. There could be no satisfactory existence without this great gift. Men must have the privilege to choose even to the extent that they may rebel against the divine decrees. Of course salvation and exaltation must come through the free will without coercion and by individual merit in order that righteous rewards may be given and proper punishment be meted out to the transgressor. (Answers to Gospel Questions, 2:20) TLDP:10

---

15. **Good comes from God and evil comes from the devil.**

#### Mormon
Wherefore, all things which are good cometh of God; and that which is evil cometh of the devil; for the devil is an enemy unto God, and fighteth against him continually, and inviteth and enticeth to sin, and to do that which is evil continually. 13. But behold, that which is of God inviteth and enticeth to do good continually; wherefore, every thing which inviteth and enticeth to do good, and to love God, and to serve him, is inspired of God. (*Mormon preaches in the synagogue, prior to A.D. 384*) Moro.7:12-13

### Lehi,
#### quoted by his son Nephi

Wherefore, men are free according to the flesh; and all things are given them which are expedient unto man. And they are free to choose liberty and eternal life, through the great Mediator of all men, or to choose captivity and death, according to the captivity and power of the devil; for he seeketh that all men might be miserable like unto himself. 28. And now, my sons, I would that ye should look to the great Mediator, and hearken unto his great commandments; and be faithful unto his words, and choose eternal life, according to the will of his Holy Spirit; 29. And not choose eternal death, according to the will of the flesh and the evil which is therein, which giveth the spirit of the devil power to captivate, to bring you down to hell, that he may reign over you in his own kingdom. (*Lehi to his sons, between 588-570 B.C.*) 2Ne.2:27-29

#### Elder Wilford Woodruff

These two principles do exist, good and evil, God and the Devil. Whatever leads to good and to do good is of God. Whatever leads to evil and to do evil is of the Devil. God has labored from the creation of man to lead him to keep the celestial law, that he may inherit a celestial glory and partake of eternal life, the greatest of all the gifts of God to man; while the devil, with all the fallen angels, has labored from the creation to lead man astray, to lead him down to the perdition of ungodly men, that he may have dominion over him. (*Epistle to the Saints Abroad, Oct. 1886*) (Discourses of Wilford Woodruff, p. 239) TLDP:231

**Related Witnesses:**
#### President Joseph F. Smith

By every possible means he seeks to darken the minds of men and then offers them falsehood and deception in the guise of truth. Satan is a skillful imitator, and as genuine gospel truth is given the world in ever-increasing abundance, so he spreads the counterfeit coin of false doctrine. Beware of his spurious currency, it will purchase for you nothing but disappointment, misery and spiritual death. The "Father of Lies" he has been called, and such an adept has he become through the ages of practice in his nefarious work, that were it possible he would deceive the very elect. (Juvenile Instructor, Sept. 1902, p. 562) DCSM:23

#### Joseph Smith

And while we were yet in the Spirit, the Lord commanded us that we should write the vision; for we beheld Satan, that old serpent, even the devil, who rebelled against God, and sought to take the kingdom of our God and his Christ— 29. Wherefore, he maketh war with the saints of God, and encompasseth them round about. 30. And we saw a vision of the sufferings of those with whom he made war and overcame, for thus came the voice of the Lord unto us: (*Vision to Joseph Smith and Sidney Rigdon, Feb. 16, 1832*) D&C 76:28-30

---

16. **We can discern between good and evil when we have the Spirit of God.**

#### President Brigham Young

People are liable in many ways to be led astray by the power of the adversary, for they do not fully understand that it is a hard matter for them to always distinguish the things of God from the things of the devil. There is but one way by which they can know the difference, and that is by the light of the spirit of revelation, even the spirit of our Lord Jesus Christ. Without this we are all liable to be lead astray and forsake our brethren, forsake our covenants and the Church and kingdom of God on earth. . . . ¶ Consequently, it becomes us, as Saints, to cleave to the Lord with all our hearts and seek unto Him until we do enjoy the light of His Spirit, that we may discern between the righteous and the wicked, and understand the difference between false spirits and true. (*In Bowery, Oct. 6, 1855, JD3:43-44*) TLDP:232

#### Mormon

But behold, that which is of God inviteth and enticeth to do good continually; wherefore, every thing which inviteth and enticeth to do good, and to love God, and to serve him, is inspired of God. 14. Wherefore, take heed, my beloved brethren, that ye do not judge that which is evil to be of God, or that which is good and of God to be of the devil. 15. For behold, my brethren, it is given unto you to judge, that ye may know good from evil; and the way to judge is as plain, that ye may know with a perfect knowledge, as the daylight is from the dark night. 16. For behold, the Spirit of Christ is given to every man, that he may know good from evil; wherefore, I show unto you the way to judge; for every thing which inviteth to do good, and to persuade to believe in Christ, is sent forth by the power and gift of Christ; wherefore ye may know with a perfect knowledge it is of God. (*Mormon preaches in the synagogue, prior to A.D. 384*) Moro.7:13-16

**Related Witnesses:**
### Joseph Smith,
*translating the Book of Moses*
Blessed be the name of my God, for his Spirit hath not altogether withdrawn from me, or else where is thy glory, for it is darkness unto me? And I can judge between thee and God; for God said unto me: Worship God, for him only shalt thou serve. 16. Get thee hence, Satan; deceive me not; for God said unto me: Thou art after the similitude of mine Only Begotten. 17. And he also gave me commandments when he called unto me out of the burning bush, saying: Call upon God in the name of mine Only Begotten, and worship me. 18. And again Moses said: I will not cease to call upon God, I have other things to inquire of him: for his glory has been upon me, wherefore I can judge between him and thee. Depart hence, Satan. (*Revelation to Joseph Smith, 1830; Satan appears to Moses*) Moses 1:15-18

---

17.  Only by being exposed to evil can we recognize and embrace good; we taste the bitter fruits of life that we may learn to prize the good.

### Joseph Smith,
*receiving the Word of the Lord*
And it must needs be that the devil should tempt the children of men, or they could not be agents unto themselves; for if they never should have bitter they could not know the sweet— (*Revelation to Joseph, Sept. 1830*) D&C 29:39

### George Q. Morris
If we cannot be good, except as we resist and overcome evil, then evil must be present to be resisted. ¶ So this earth life is set up according to true principles, and these conditions that followed the transgression [of Adam] were not, in the usual sense, penalties that were inflicted upon us. All these . . . that seem to be sad inflictions of punishment, sorrow, and trouble are in the end not that. They are blessings. We have attained a knowledge of good and evil, the power to prize the sweet, to become agents unto ourselves, the power to obtain redemption and eternal life. These things had their origin in this transgression. The Lord has set the earth up so we have to labor if we are going to live, which preserves us from the curse of idleness and indolence; and though the Lord condemns us to death—mortal death—it is one of the greatest blessings that come to us here because it is the doorway to immortality, and we can never attain immortality without dying. ¶

So these are all real blessings. We come to the earth with all these conditions arranged as they are so that we have to struggle constantly against evil, struggle to preserve our lives, struggle for everything of true value—that is the thing for us to understand—this is the course of life that is most desirable, and for our good. We have no need to find fault with these conditions. The Lord has ordained them all for our welfare and happiness. CR1958Apr:39

### Joseph Smith,
*translating the Book of Moses*
And the Lord spake unto Adam, saying: Inasmuch as thy children are conceived in sin, even so when they begin to grow up, sin conceiveth in their hearts, and they taste the bitter, that they may know to prize the good. (*The record of Moses; Enoch recounts God speaking to Adam*) Moses 6:55

### President Brigham Young
Can the people comprehend that there is not, has not been, and never can by any method, scheme, or plan devised by any being in this world for intelligence to eternally exist and obtain an exaltation, without knowing the good and the evil—without tasting the bitter and the sweet? Can the people understand that it is actually necessary for opposite principles to be placed before them, or this state of being would be no probation, and we should have no opportunity for exercising the agency given us? Can they understand that we cannot obtain eternal life unless we actually know and comprehend by our experience the principle of good and the principle of evil, the light and the darkness, truth, virtue, and holiness, —also vice, wickedness, and corruption? (*In Tabernacle Sept. 1, 1859, JD7:237*) TLDP:232

### President Brigham Young
I will tell you a truth; it is God's truth; it is eternal truth: neither you nor I would ever be prepared to be crowned in the celestial kingdom of our Father and our God, without devils in this world. Do you know that the Saints never could be prepared to receive the glory that is in reserve for them, without devils to help them to get it? Men and women never could be prepared to be judged and condemned out of their own mouths, and to be set upon the left hand, or to have it said to them, "Go away into everlasting darkness", without the power both of God and the devil. We are obliged to know and understand them, one as well as the other, in order to prepare us for the day that is coming, and for our exaltation. Some of you may think that this is a curious principle, but it is true. Refer to the Book of Mormon, and you will find that Nephi and others taught that we actually need evil, in

order to make this a state of probation. We must know the evil in order to know the good. There must needs be an opposition in all things. All facts are demonstrated by their opposites, You will learn this in the Bible, the Book of Mormon, and in the revelations given through Joseph. We must know and understand the opposition that is in all things, in order to discern, choose, and receive that which we do know will exalt us to the presence of God. You cannot know the one without knowing the other. This is a true principle. *(In Bowery, June 28, 1857, JD4:373)* TLDP:129

**President John Taylor**

Why is it that good men should be tried? Why is it, in fact, that we should have a devil? Why did not the Lord kill him long ago? Because he could not do without him. He needed the devil and a great many of those who do his bidding just to keep men straight, that we may learn to place our dependence upon God, and trust in Him, and to observe his laws and keep his commandments. *(At Grantsville, Oct. 29, 1882, JD23:336)* TLDP:139

**Related Witnesses:**

**Joseph Smith,**
*translating the Book of Moses*

And in that day Adam blessed God and was filled, and began to prophesy concerning all the families of the earth, saying: Blessed be the name of God, for because of my transgression my eyes are opened, and in this life I shall have joy, and again in the flesh I shall see God. 11. And Eve, his wife, heard all these things and was glad, saying: Were it not for our transgression we never should have had seed, and never should have known good and evil, and the joy of our redemption, and the eternal life which God giveth unto all the obedient. *(The record of Moses; Adam realizes that through Adam and Eve's transgression they may receive joy, and he, therefore, blesses the name of God)* Moses 5:10-11

**John A. Widtsoe**

Free agency—the untrammeled will, the right to choose and act for oneself, to obey or disobey law—is a fundamental, unalterable, everlasting quality of man. Divinity stands aside for it. By its exercise, man progresses gloriously or retrogrades dishonorably. Before the earth was, pre-existent man accepted, without compulsion, the Father's plan of salvation. On earth, man, if worthy the name, tests and tries, sifts and refines, accepts or rejects, the offerings placed before him. Throughout eternity, he will use this inherent right. Thereby, and thereby only, will he find eternal joy. Without free agency there is no manhood; with it, man

becomes of the likeness of God. (Man and the Dragon, p. 161) TLDP:10

---

**18.　Power to overcome Satan and his evil influence comes from God.**

**Paul**

There hath no temptation taken you but such as is common to man: but God is faithful, who will not suffer you to be tempted above that ye are able; but will with the temptation also make a way to escape, that ye may be able to bear it. *(Paul writes to the Church at Corinth, Greece, about A.D. 55)* 1Cor.10:13

**Peter**

The Lord knoweth how to deliver the godly out of temptations, and to reserve the unjust unto the day of judgment to be punished: *(Peter writes to members of the Church, about A.D. 60 to 64)* 2Pet.2:9

**Joseph Smith,**
*receiving the Word of the Lord*

Behold, and hearken, O ye elders of my church, saith the Lord your God, even Jesus Christ, your advocate, who knoweth the weakness of man and how to succor them who are tempted. *(Revelation received Aug. 13, 1831)* D&C 62:1

**Related Witnesses:**

**Joseph Smith**

But, exerting all my powers to call upon God to deliver me out of the power of this enemy which had seized upon me, and at the very moment when I was ready to sink into despair and abandon myself to destruction—not to an imaginary ruin, but to the power of some actual being from the unseen world, who had such marvelous power as I had never before felt in any being—just at this moment of great alarm, I saw a pillar of light exactly over my head, above the brightness of the sun, which descended gradually until it fell upon me. 17. It no sooner appeared than I found myself delivered from the enemy which held me bound. When the light rested upon me I saw two Personages, whose brightness and glory defy all description, standing above me in the air. One of them spake unto me, calling me by name and said, pointing to the other—This is My Beloved Son. Hear Him! *(Joseph Smith delivered from the power of darkness by the visitation of the Father and the Son, Spring of 1820)* JS-H 1:16-17

**Jesus,**
*quoted by Mormon*

Behold, verily, verily, I say unto you, ye must watch and pray always lest ye enter into temptation; for Satan desireth to have you, that he may sift you as wheat. 19. Therefore ye must always pray unto the Father in my name; (*The resurrected Jesus commands the Nephite people to pray, A.D. 34*) 3Ne.18:18-19

---

**19. In their exercise of agency, those who choose good will be rewarded.**

### Jesus,
*recorded in Mark*

Then Peter began to say unto him, Lo, we have left all, and have followed thee. 29. And Jesus answered and said, Verily I say unto you, There is no man that hath left house, or brethren, or sisters, or father, or mother, or wife, or children, or lands, for my sake, and the gospel's, 30. But he shall receive an hundredfold now in this time, houses, and brethren, and sisters, and mothers, and children, and lands, with persecutions; and in the world to come eternal life. (*Jesus teaches Peter of the rewards to those who follow Christ*) Mark 10:28-30

### Joseph Smith,
*receiving the Word of the Lord*

Fear not to do good, my sons, for whatsoever ye sow, that shall ye also reap; therefore, if ye sow good ye shall also reap good for your reward. (*Revelation to Joseph Smith and Oliver Cowdery, April 1829*) D&C 6:33

### Joseph Smith,
*receiving the Word of the Lord*

For the power is in them, wherein they are agents unto themselves. And inasmuch as men do good they shall in nowise lose their reward. (*Revelation for the elders of the Church, Aug. 1, 1831*) D&C 58:28

### Joseph Smith,
*receiving the Word of the Lord*

But learn that he who doeth the works of righteousness shall receive his reward, even peace in this world and eternal life in the world to come. (*Revelation received Aug. 7, 1831*) D&C 59:23

### Recorded in Proverbs

The wicked worketh a deceitful work: but to him that soweth righteousness shall be a sure reward. Prov.11:18

### Elder Joseph Fielding Smith

Of course salvation and exaltation must come through the free will without coercion and by individual merit in order that righteous rewards may be given and proper punishment be meted out to the transgressor. (Answers to Gospel Questions, 2:20) TLDP:10

### Elder Joseph Fielding Smith

Without free agency we would amount to very

little, and the Lord granted unto us our agency, that we might act for ourselves—to choose the good, or to choose the evil if we desire—with the understanding that we would reap the reward of our labors in this life. ("The Essential Value of Genealogical Research," Utah Genealogical and Historical Magazine, Jan. 1918, p. 16) TLDP:11-12

### Elder Harold B. Lee

Salvation means the attainment of the eternal right to live in the presence of God the Father and the Son as a reward for a good life in mortality. (Lesson in the Junior M Man and Junior Gleaner Manual, 1950, see Stand Ye in Holy Places, p. 334) TLDP:154

### Bruce R. McConkie

Jesus . . . makes a pronouncement of wondrous import: If thou wilt enter into life, keep the commandments. This is the sum and substance of the whole matter. Salvation, eternal life, rewards in all their degrees and varieties—all come by obedience to the laws and ordinances of the gospel. Salvation must be won; it is not a free gift. "Let us hear the conclusion of the whole matter: Fear God, and keep his commandments: for this is the whole duty of man." (Eccl.12:13) But what of grace? Grace is the love, mercy, and condescension of God in making salvation available to men. "It is by grace that we are saved, after all we can do." (2Ne.25:23) Eternal life is freely available; salvation is free in that all may drink of the waters of life; all may come and partake; but none gains so high a reward as eternal life until he is tried and tested and found worthy, as were the ancients. . . . ¶ Eternal life can come to those only who put first in their lives the things of God's kingdom; who love the riches of eternity more than a handful of mortal pelf; who are willing to forsake all and follow Christ. Where a man's treasure is, there will his heart be also. (The Mortal Messiah, 3:302) TLDP:161

---

**20. We have a dual nature: one, related to the earthly life; the other, akin to the divine; by following after the enticings of the Spirit we can overcome the inclinations of the flesh.**

### Elder David O. McKay

Man has a dual nature; one, related to the earthly or animal life; the other, akin to the divine. Whether a man remains satisfied within what we designate the animal world, satisfied with what the animal world will give him, yielding without effort to the whim of his appetites and passions and slipping farther and farther into the realm of indulgence, or whether, through self-mastery, he rises toward intellectual, moral, and spiritual enjoyments depends upon the kind of choice he makes every day, nay, every hour of his life. . . . CR1949Apr:13; DGSM:21

### King Benjamin,
*quoted by Mormon*

For the natural man is an enemy to God, and has been from the fall of Adam, and will be, forever and ever, unless he yields to the enticings of the Holy Spirit, and putteth off the natural man and becometh a saint through the atonement of Christ the Lord, and becometh as a child, submissive, meek, humble, patient, full of love, willing to submit to all things which the Lord seeth fit to inflict upon him, even as a child doth submit to his father. (*King Benjamin addresses his people, about 124 B.C.*) Mosiah 3:19

### Lehi,
*quoted by his son Nephi*

Wherefore, men are free according to the flesh; and all things are given them which are expedient unto man. And they are free to choose liberty and eternal life, through the great Mediator of all men, or to choose captivity and death, according to the captivity and power of the devil; for he seeketh that all men might be miserable like unto himself. 28. And now, my sons, I would that ye should look to the great Mediator, and hearken unto his great commandments; and be faithful unto his words, and choose eternal life, according to the will of his Holy Spirit; 29. And not choose eternal death, according to the will of the flesh and the evil which is therein, which giveth the spirit of the devil power to captivate, to bring you down to hell, that he may reign over you in his own kingdom. (*Lehi to his sons, between 588-570 B.C.*) 2Ne.2:27-29

### President Brigham Young

God has placed in us a pure spirit; when this reigns predominant, without let or hindrance, and triumphs over the flesh and rules and governs and controls as the Lord controls the heavens and the earth, this I call the blessing of sanctification. Will sin be perfectly destroyed? No, it will not, for it is not so designed in the economy of Heaven. . . . ¶ Do not suppose that we shall ever in the flesh be free from temptations to sin. (*In Tabernacle, May 24, 1863, JD10:173*) TLDP:604

### President Spencer W. Kimball

[T]he highest achievement of spirituality comes as we conquer the flesh. We build character as we encourage people to care for their own needs. ¶ As givers [of welfare service] gain control of their desires and properly see other[s'] needs in light of their own wants, then the pow-

ers of the gospel are released in their lives. They learn that by living the great law of consecration they insure not only temporal salvation, but also spiritual sanctification. CR1977Oct:123

### Charles W. Penrose

For man in spirit form, in his spirit nature, is an independent entity. It is an organized being, a son of God or a daughter of God, as the case may be, and in the spirit birth he obtained not only an eternal organization, but power and intelligence by which he can determine and understand light from darkness, truth from error, and choose between that which is right and that which is wrong. In the Pearl of Great Price we read that God gave him that power. . . . ¶ Here [Moses 4:2-3] we read that that power of choice, the gift, the ability to understand right from wrong, to understand light from darkness, was given to the spirit of man by the Lord and He gave to him that agency, power in himself to choose the good and refuse the evil, to choose the light or the darkness as he willed. So because of that, man can be brought to judgment for the deeds that he performs, for he is not forced to do evil, neither is he forced to do right. The power of volition is in the spirit man and he brings it with him when he is born into the earthly sphere, and so we can do good or do evil as we elect, and therefore we will be brought to judgment and every man will be judged according to the deeds done while in the body; according to his works, so will his future be determined. CR1914Oct:40

### Related Witnesses:
### Elder David O. McKay

Man is a spiritual being, a soul, and at some period of his life everyone is possessed with an irresistible desire to know his relationship to the infinite. He realizes that he is not just a physical object that is to be tossed for a short time from bank to bank, only to be submerged finally in the everflowing stream of life. There is something within him which urges him to rise above himself, to control his environment, to master the body and all things physical and live in a higher and more beautiful world. CR1928Oct:37; DGSM:21

### Elder Joseph Fielding Smith

The Spirit of the Lord will not dwell in unclean tabernacles, and when the spirit is withdrawn, darkness supersedes the light, and apostasy will follow. This is one of the greatest evidences of the divinity of this latter-day work. In other organizations men may commit all manner of sin and still retain their membership, because they have no companionship with the Holy Ghost to lose; but in the Church when a man sins and continues without repentance, the Spirit is withdrawn, and when he is left to himself the adversary takes possession of his mind and he denies the faith. (Doctrines of Salvation, 3:309) TLDP:632

**Paul**

For, brethren, ye have been called unto liberty; only use not liberty for an occasion to the flesh, but by love serve one another. (*Paul's letter to the churches of Galatia in Asia Minor, about A.D. 55*) Gal.5:13

---

21. **The Lord permits the righteous to be slain by the wicked that the wicked might exercise their agency and receive a just judgment at the last day.**

**Mormon,**
*also quoting Alma, the younger*

And when Amulek saw the pains of the women and children who were consumed in the fire, he also was pained; and he said unto Alma: How can we witness this awful scene? Therefore let us stretch our hands, and exercise the power of God which is in us, and save them from the flames. 11. But Alma said unto him: The spirit constraineth me that I must not stretch forth mine hand; for behold the Lord receiveth them up unto himself, in glory; and he doth suffer that they may do this thing, or that the people may do this thing unto them, according to the hardness of their hearts, that the judgments which he shall exercise upon them in his wrath may be just; and the blood of the innocent shall stand as a witness against them, yea, and cry mightily against them at the last day. (*Alma speaks on the fate of those believers in the word of God who are burned, about 82 B.C.*) Alma 14:10-11

**Moroni, the Prophet General,**
*quoted by Mormon*

For the Lord suffereth the righteous to be slain that his justice and judgment may come upon the wicked; therefore ye need not suppose that the righteous are lost because they are slain; but behold, they do enter into the rest of the Lord their God. (*General Moroni complains of Pahoran of the government's neglect of the armies, about 62 B.C.*) Alma 60:13

**President Heber J. Grant,**
**J. Reuben Clark, Jr., David O. McKay**
(First Presidency)

"For the Lord suffereth the righteous to be slain that his justice and judgment may come upon the wicked; therefore ye need not suppose that the righteous are lost because they are slain; but behold, they do enter into the rest of the Lord their God." (Alma 60:7,12-13) ¶ In this terrible war

now waging, thousands of our righteous young men in all parts of the world and in many countries are subject to a call into the military service of their own countries. Some of these, so serving, have already been called back to their heavenly home; others will almost surely be called to follow. But "behold," as Moroni said, the righteous of them who serve and are slain "do enter into the rest of the Lord their God," and of them the Lord has said "those that die in me shall not taste of death, for it shall be sweet unto them." (D&C 42:46) Their salvation and exaltation in the world to come will be secure. That in their work of destruction they will be striking at their brethren will not be held against them. That sin, as Moroni of old said, is to the condemnation of those who "sit in their places of power in a state of thoughtless stupor," those rulers in the world who in a frenzy of hate and lust for unrighteous power and dominion over their fellow men, have put into motion eternal forces they do not comprehend and cannot control. God, in His own due time, will pass sentence upon them. ¶ "Vengeance is mine; I will repay, saith the Lord." (Rom.12:19) CR1942Apr:95-96

**Joseph Smith,**
*receiving the Word of the Lord*

Verily I say unto you, my friends, behold, I will give unto you a revelation and commandment, that you may know how to act in the discharge of your duties concerning the salvation and redemption of your brethren, who have been scattered on the land of Zion; 2. Being driven and smitten by the hands of mine enemies, on whom I will pour out my wrath without measure in mine own time. 3. For I have suffered them thus far, that they might fill up the measure of their iniquities, that their cup might be full; (*Revelation at Kirtland, Ohio, Feb. 24, 1834; why the Lord permitted persecution*) D&C 103:1-3

**Related Witnesses:**

**Joseph Smith,**
*receiving the Word of the Lord*

And even if they do unto you even as they have done unto me, blessed are ye, for you shall dwell with me in glory. (*Revelation to Joseph Smith and Oliver Cowdery, April 1829*) D&C 6:30

**Joseph Smith,**
*receiving the Word of the Lord*

And that you be firm in keeping the commandments wherewith I have commanded you; and if you do this, behold I grant unto you eternal life, even if you should be slain. (*Revelation received at the request of Martin Harris*) D&C 5:22

---

# List of Doctrines

## AMERICA

*Doctrines Located in This Topic*

22. The Lord prepared and preserved the American continent (the Western Hemi-
sphere) as a land choice
above all other lands.

23. The United States Constitution is inspired of God.

24. The American continent
(North and South America)
has been selected by the
Lord as a land of inheritance
for the descendants of
Joseph and all others whom
the Lord chooses to lead out
of other countries.

*Doctrines on AMERICA
Located in Other Topics*

638. The land of America was
prepared for the restoration
of all things in the latter
days.

730. At His second coming, the
Savior will appear first to
those in the New Jerusalem
in America, then to the
Jews in Jerusalem, and
finally to all the world.

897. Zion (the New Jerusalem)
will be established upon
the American continent.

# AMERICA

22. The Lord prepared and preserved the American continent (the Western Hemisphere) as a land choice above all other lands.

### Nephi, son of Lehi

And inasmuch as ye shall keep my commandments, ye shall prosper, and shall be led to a land of promise; yea, even a land which I have prepared for you; yea, a land which is choice above all other lands. (*The Lord speaks to Nephi in response to his prayer, 600-692 B.C.*) 1Ne.2:20

### J. Reuben Clark, Jr.

This has always been a mighty land in God's plan. It was in the valley of Adam-ondi-Ahman that Adam, prior to his death, called the great high priests together and there bestowed upon them his last blessing. The Lord appearing there, his posterity proclaimed Adam to be Michael, the Prince, the Archangel. (D&C107:53,54) It is to that same spot that Adam, as the Ancient of Days, shall come to visit his people (D&C116), when judgment shall be set and the books opened. (Dan.7:9 ff; Rev.20:4) ¶ It is here on this land that the New Jerusalem shall be built "unto the remnant of the seed of Joseph"—ourselves and those others, the literal descendants of Lehi. (Ether13:5 ff; 1Ne.14:1,2; 2Ne.14:18) And finally, it is here on this hemisphere that Zion shall be built. (tenth Article of Faith) It is this fact and purpose, the building of Zion on this hemisphere, which is Zion, which seem to be the dominant elements in all of God's dealings with them who possess this land, for Isaiah, speaking more than 2,500 years ago, declared that "out of Zion shall go forth the law, and the word of the Lord from Jerusalem." (Isa.2:3) ¶ Thus America's ultimate God-given destiny, planned by the Creator and testified by ancient and modern prophecy and revelation, is that out of her shall go forth the law. (*To M.I.A. Conference, June 9, 1940*) MOFP6:97

### Lehi,
*quoted by his son Nephi*

But, said he, notwithstanding our afflictions, we have obtained a land of promise, a land which is choice above all other lands; a land which the Lord God hath covenanted with me should be a land for the inheritance of my seed. Yea, the Lord hath covenanted this land unto me, and to my children forever, and also all those who should be led out of other countries by the hand of the Lord. (*Lehi to his sons, between 588-570 B.C.*) 2Ne.1:5

### Moroni, son of Mormon

And the Lord would not suffer that they should stop beyond the sea in the wilderness, but he would that they should come forth even unto the land of promise, which was choice above all other lands, which the Lord God had preserved for a righteous people. 8. And he had sworn in his wrath unto the brother of Jared, that whoso should possess this land of promise, from that time henceforth and forever, should serve him, the true and only God, or they should be swept off when the fulness of his wrath should come upon them. (*Moroni's abridgement of the record of the Jaredites covering the period of time of the Tower of Babel*) Ether 2:7-8

### Elder Ezra Taft Benson

Only in this land, under this God-inspired Constitution, under an environment of freedom, could it have been possible to have established the Church and kingdom of God and restored the gospel in its fulness. It is our responsibility, my brethren and sisters, to see that this freedom is maintained, so that the Church can flourish in the future. CR1954Oct:121

**Related Witnesses:**

### Moroni, son of Mormon

And when thou hast done this thou shalt go at the head of them down into the valley which is northward. And there will I meet thee, and I will go before thee into a land which is choice above all the lands of the earth. (*Moroni's abridgement of the record of the Jaredites covering the period of time of the Tower of Babel; the Lord responds to the prayer of the brother of Jared*) Ether 1:42

---

23. The United States Constitution is inspired of God.

### Joseph Smith,
*receiving the Word of the Lord*

And for this purpose have I established the Constitution of this land, by the hands of wise men whom I raised up unto this very purpose, and redeemed the land by the shedding of blood. (*Revelation at the time of great persecution in Missouri, Dec. 16, 1833, affirming the purpose of the Constitution was to protect the rights and agency of individuals—see 101:77-79*) D&C 101:80

### President George Albert Smith

[T]he Lord in his wisdom saw the necessity of giving us a nation in which we could thrive. In no other nation under heaven could the Church have been organized and gone forward as we have in this nation. The founding of the United States was not an accident. The giving to us of the Constitution of the United States was not an accident. Our Heavenly Father knew what would be needed, and so he paved the way to give us the Constitution. It came under the influence of prayer, and he guided those who framed that wonderful document. ¶ I hope that the membership of this Church will not be deceived into thinking that other plans, other forms of government, other systems of direction whatsoever, are desirable. I want to say to you without any hesitation that no form of government in the world can be compared favorably with the government God gave to us. This is his plan. CR1947Apr:163

**Elder Ezra Taft Benson**
Having declared America to be a land of liberty, God undertook to raise up a band of inspired and intelligent leaders who would write a constitution of liberty and establish the first free people in modern times. The hand of God in this undertaking is clearly indicated by the Lord himself in a revelation to the Prophet Joseph Smith in these words: ¶ ". . . I established the Constitution of this land, by the hands of wise men whom I raised up unto this very purpose. . . ." (D&C 101:80) ¶ . . . God declared that the United States Constitution was divinely inspired for the specific purpose of eliminating bondage and the violation of the rights and protection which belongs to "all flesh." (Ibid., 101:77-80) CR1961Oct:69-71

**Joseph Smith,**
*quoted by Elder Joseph Fielding Smith*
[T]he Constitution of the United States is a glorious standard; it is founded in the wisdom of God. It is a heavenly banner; it is to all those who are privileged with the sweets of liberty, like the cooling shades and refreshing waters of a great rock in a thirsty and weary land. It is like a great tree under whose branches men from every clime can be shielded from the burning rays of the sun. (*Epistle to the Church from Liberty Jail, March 25, 1839*) TPJS:147

**J. Reuben Clark, Jr.**
The Church unequivocally declares, nothing doubting, that God Himself set up the Constitution of the United States, and that He so declared, saying: "I established the Constitution of this land, by the hands of wise men whom I raised up unto this very purpose," and the Constitution shall "be maintained for the rights and protection of all flesh, according to just and holy principles." (D&C 101:80,77) ¶ The Church further declares that such laws must be framed "and held inviolate as will secure to each individual the free exercise of conscience, the right and control of property, and the protection of life." (D&C 134:2) ¶ The

Church has, for one hundred years, accepted as complying with the divine mandate, the form of government set up under the Constitution. (*To Citizens' Conference on Government Management, Estes Park, Colo., 1939*) MOFP6:67

**Mark E. Petersen**
As you read in the Doctrine and Covenants, he also gave us our form of government. The Constitution of the United States was revelation from God virtually. I do not say word for word, but I say that God raised up the men who wrote it, and inspired them in its writing so that this type of government—a free government—would be established here for one particular purpose. That was to provide the climate under which God would have such religious freedom, freedom of speech, freedom of the press, and all of the other freedoms, that this true Church could develop, later to send these things—the teachings of the gospel—out to all the world and especially to the house of Lehi. ("Our Divine Destiny," Brigham Young University Speeches of the Year, Feb. 20, 1968, p. 8) TLDP:21-22

**Related Witnesses:**

**Mark E. Petersen**
The United States is a different kind of nation from any other nation. The United States was God-given—raised up by the Almighty to provide the proper conditions under which the Church could be restored in this day and to provide the freedom as well as the armed might to permit us as missionaries to travel the world with the passports of a great country which would protect us wherever we went. ("Our Divine Destiny," Brigham Young University Speeches of the Year, Feb. 20, 1968, p. 3) TLDP:20

**Joseph Smith**
We believe that governments were instituted of God for the benefit of man; and that he holds men accountable for their acts in relation to them, both in making laws and administering them, for the good and safety of society. 2. We believe that no government can exist in peace, except such laws are framed and held inviolate as will secure to each individual the free exercise of conscience, the right and control of property, and the protection of life. (*Declaration of belief regarding governments and laws, Aug. 17, 1835*) D&C 134:1-2

---

24. The American continent (North and South America) has been selected by the Lord as a land of inheritance for the descendants of Joseph and all others whom the Lord chooses to lead out of other countries.

### J. Reuben Clark, Jr.

It is here on this land that the New Jerusalem shall be built "unto the remnant of the seed of Joseph"—ourselves and those others, the literal descendants of Lehi. (Ether13:5 ff; 1Ne. 14:1,2; 2Ne.10:18) And finally, it is here on this hemisphere that Zion shall be built. (tenth Article of Faith) It is this fact and purpose, the building of Zion on this hemisphere, which is Zion, which seem to be the dominant elements in all of God's dealings with them who possess this land, for Isaiah, speaking more than 2,500 years ago, declared that "out of Zion shall go forth the law, and the word of the Lord from Jerusalem." (Isa.2:3) (*To M.I.A. conference, June 9, 1940*) MOFP:6:97

### Lehi,
#### *quoted by his son Nephi*

But, said he, notwithstanding our afflictions, we have obtained a land of promise, a land which is choice above all other lands; a land which the Lord God hath covenanted with me should be a land for the inheritance of my seed. Yea, the Lord hath covenanted this land unto me, and to my children forever, and also all those who should be led out of other countries by the hand of the Lord. (*Lehi, descendent of Joseph, to his sons, between 588-570 B.C.*) 2Ne.1:5

### James E. Talmage

Unto Nephi, son of Lehi, was shown the future of his people, including the degeneracy of a branch thereof, afterward known as Lamanites and in modern times as American Indians. The coming of a man from among the Gentiles, across the deep waters, was revealed in such plainness as to positively identify that man with Columbus; and the coming of other Gentiles to this land, out of captivity, is equally explicit. . . . (1Ne.13:10-13) JTC:757

### Related Witnesses:
#### Nephi, son of Lehi

And I looked and beheld a man among the Gentiles, who was separated from the seed of my brethren by the many waters; and I beheld the Spirit of God, that it came down and wrought upon the man; and he went forth upon the many waters, even unto the seed of my brethren, who were in the promised land. 13. And it came to pass that I beheld the Spirit of God, that it wrought upon other Gentiles; and they went forth out of captivity, upon the many waters. 14. And it came to pass that I beheld many multitudes of the Gentiles upon the land of promise; (*An angel shows Nephi, descendent of Joseph, the discovery and colonizing of America, 600-592 B.C.*) 1Ne.13:12-14

### Nephi, son of Lehi

For it sufficeth me to say that we are descendants of Joseph. (*The writings of Nephi, 600-592 B.C.*) 1Ne.6:2

### Nephi, son of Lehi

And it came to pass that my father, Lehi, also found upon the plates of brass a genealogy of his fathers; wherefore he knew that he was a descendant of Joseph; yea, even that Joseph who was the son of Jacob, who was sold into Egypt, and who was preserved by the hand of the Lord, that he might preserve his father, Jacob, and all his household from perishing with famine. 15. And they were also led out of captivity and out of the land of Egypt, by that same God who had preserved them. 16. And thus my father, Lehi, did discover the genealogy of his fathers. And Laban also was a descendant of Joseph, wherefore he and his fathers had kept the records. (*The writings of Nephi, 600-592 B.C.*) 1Ne.5:14-16

### Elder Ezra Taft Benson

God revealed to his ancient American prophets that shortly after the discovery of America there would be peoples in Europe who would desire to escape the persecution and tyranny of the Old World and flee to America. (1Ne.13:13-16) CR1961Oct:69-71

# List of Doctrines

## APOSTASY

*Doctrines Located in This Topic*

*Doctrines on APOSTASY Located in Other Topics*

### (1) General Apostasy

25. A great apostasy from the Savior's church was foretold by prophets.

26. A universal apostasy took place in the early centuries of the Christian era, sometime after the death of Christ.

27. Present-day Christian churches have departed from the principles of the original Christian faith.

### (2) Personal Apostasy

28. Apostasy involves teaching or practicing false doctrine; having an apostate opinion, and either practicing or preaching it (after being corrected by one's bishop or higher authority) is apostasy.

29. A person who falls away after having been enlightened by the Spirit of God becomes more hardened— worse than if that person had never known the things of God.

506. Apostates are prone to persecute the Church.

– 28 –

# APOSTASY

## (1) General Apostasy
## (2) Personal Apostasy

### (1) General Apostasy

**25. A great apostasy from the Savior's church was foretold by prophets.**

**Hugh B. Brown**
Prophecy and history predict and record a great and universal apostasy which was to be followed by a restoration as predicted by John in Revelation. The fact of the great apostasy is attested by both sacred and secular writ, and history bears witness that it became universal. CR1964Oct:102

**James E. Talmage**
The foreknowledge of God made plain to Him even from the beginning this falling away from the truth; and, through inspiration the prophets of old uttered solemn warnings of the approaching dangers. AF:184

**James E. Talmage**
We affirm that the great apostasy was foretold by the Savior Himself while He lived as a Man among men, and by His inspired prophets both before and after the period of His earthly probation. (The Great Apostasy, p. 19) DGSM:59

**Mark E. Petersen**
Hard to believe though it is, the scriptures themselves foretold the sad division in Christianity, leading to the formation of the many denominations of today. They refer to it as a falling away, an apostasy from the original gospel. CR1969Oct:118

**Related Witnesses:**
**Amos**
Behold, the days come, saith the Lord GOD, that I will send a famine in the land, not a famine of bread, nor a thirst for water, but of hearing the words of the LORD: 12. And they shall wander from sea to sea, and from the north even to the east, they shall run to and fro to seek the word of the LORD, and shall not find it. (*Amos prophesies the downfall of Israel, about 770-750 B.C.*) Amos 8:11-12

**Isaiah**
The earth also is defiled under the inhabitants thereof; because they have transgressed the laws, changed the ordinance, broken the everlasting covenant. 6. Therefore hath the curse devoured the earth, and they that dwell therein are desolate: therefore the inhabitants of the earth are burned, and few men left. (*Isaiah prophesies, 740-659 B.C.*) Isa.24:5-6

**Jesus,**
*recorded in Matthew*
For there shall arise false Christs, and false prophets, and shall shew great signs and wonders; insomuch that, if it were possible, they shall deceive the very elect. (*Jesus to his disciples at the Mount of Olives*) Matt.24:24

**Jesus,**
*recorded in Matthew*
Another parable put he forth unto them, saying, The kingdom of heaven is likened unto a man which sowed good seed in his field: 25. But while men slept, his enemy came and sowed tares among the wheat, and went his way. 26. But when the blade was sprung up, and brought forth fruit, then appeared the tares also. 27. So the servants of the householder came and said unto him, Sir, didst not thou sow good seed in thy field? from whence then hath it tares? 28. He said unto them, An enemy hath done this. The servants said unto him, Wilt thou then that we go and gather them up? 29. But he said, Nay; lest while ye gather up the tares, ye root up also the wheat with them. 30. Let both grow together until the harvest: and in the time of harvest I will say to the reapers, Gather ye together first the tares, and bind them in bundles to burn them: but gather the wheat into my barn. (*Jesus teaches the people in parables*) Matt.13:24-30

**Joseph Smith,**
*receiving the Word of the Lord*
Verily, thus saith the Lord unto you my servants, concerning the parable of the wheat and of the tares: 2. Behold, verily I say, the field was the world, and the apostles were the sowers of the seed; 3. And after they have fallen asleep the great persecutor of the church, the apostate, the whore, even Babylon, that maketh all nations to drink of her cup, in whose hearts the enemy, even Satan, sitteth to reign—behold he soweth the tares; wherefore, the tares choke the wheat and drive the church into the wilderness. (*Revelation, Dec. 6, 1832; the Lord gives the meaning of the parable of the wheat and the tares*) D&C 86:1-3

**Peter**
But there were false prophets also among the people, even as there shall be false teachers among you, who privily shall bring in damnable heresies, even denying the Lord that bought them, and bring upon themselves swift destruction. 2. And many shall follow their pernicious ways; by reason of whom the way of truth shall be evil spoken of. 3. And through covetousness shall they with feigned words

make merchandise of you: whose judgment now of a long time lingereth not, and their damnation slumbereth not. (*Letter to members of the Church, about* A.D. *60 to 64*) 2Pet.2:1-3

**Paul**

For the time will come when they will not endure sound doctrine; but after their own lusts shall they heap to themselves teachers, having itching ears; 4. And they shall turn away their ears from the truth, and shall be turned unto fables. (*Paul writes to his assistant Timothy, about A.D. 64*) 2Tim.4:3-4

**Paul**

Now we beseech you, brethren, by the coming of our Lord Jesus Christ, and by our gathering together unto him, 2. That ye be not soon shaken in mind, or be troubled, neither by spirit, nor by word, nor by letter as from us, as that the day of Christ is at hand. 3. Let no man deceive you by any means: for that day shall not come, except there come a falling away first, and that man of sin be revealed, the son of perdition; 4. Who opposeth and exalteth himself above all that is called God, or that is worshipped; so that he as God sitteth in the temple of God, shewing himself that he is God. 5. Remember ye not, that, when I was yet with you, I told you these things? 6. And now ye know what withholdeth that he might be revealed in his time. 7. For the mystery of iniquity doth already work: only he who now letteth will let, until he be taken out of the way. 8. And then shall that Wicked be revealed, whom the Lord shall consume with the spirit of his mouth, and shall destroy with the brightness of his coming: 9. Even him, whose coming is after the working of Satan with all power and signs and lying wonders, 10. And with all deceivableness of unrighteousness in them that perish; because they received not the love of the truth, that they might be saved. 11. And for this cause God shall send them strong delusion, that they should believe a lie: 12. That they all might be damned who believed not the truth, but had pleasure in unrighteousness. (*Paul writes to the Church at Thessalonica, comprising Jews and many pagan converts,* A.D. *50*) 2Thess.2:1-12

**Paul,**
*recorded in Acts*

For I know this, that after my departing shall grievous wolves enter in among you, not sparing the flock. 30. Also of your own selves shall men arise, speaking perverse things, to draw away disciples after them. (*To the elders of the Church*) Acts 20:29-30

**26. A universal apostasy took place in the early centuries of the Christian era, sometime after the death of Christ.**

**James E. Talmage**

For over seventeen hundred years on the eastern hemisphere, and for more than fourteen centuries on the western, there appears to have been silence between the heavens and the earth. Of direct revelation from God to man during this long interval, we have no authentic record. As already shown, the period of apostolic ministry on the eastern continent probably terminated before the dawn of the second century of the Christian era. The passing of the apostles was followed by the rapid development of a universal apostasy as had been foreseen and predicted. ¶ In the accomplishment of this great falling away, external and internal causes cooperated. Among the disintegrating forces acting from without, the most effective was the persistent persecution to which the saints were subjected, incident to both Judaistic and pagan opposition. Vast numbers who had professed membership and many who had been officers in the ministry deserted the Church; while a few were stimulated to greater zeal under the scourge of persecution. The general effect of opposition from the outside—of external causes of decline in faith and works considered as a whole—was the defection of individuals, resulting in a widespread apostasy from the Church. But immeasurably more serious was the result of internal dissension, schism and disruption, whereby an absolute apostasy of the Church from the way and word of God was brought about. JTC:745; DGSM:59-60

**President Spencer W. Kimball**

This is not a continuous church, nor is it one that has been reformed or redeemed. It has been restored after it was lost. It was lost—the gospel with its powers and blessings—sometime after the Savior's crucifixion and the loss of his apostles. The laws were changed, the ordinances were changed, and the everlasting covenant was broken that the Lord Jesus Christ gave to his people in those days. There was a long period of centuries when the gospel was not available to people on this earth, because it had been changed. (*Paris France Area Conference, Aug. 1976*) DGSM:60

**Elder Spencer W. Kimball**

In the early centuries of the Christian era, the apostasy came not through persecution, but by relinquishment of faith caused by the superimposing of a man-made structure upon and over the divine program. Many men with no pretense nor claim to revelation, speaking without divine authority or revelation, depending only upon their own brilliant minds, but representing as they claim the congregations of the Christians and in long conference and erudite councils, sought the creation process to make a God which all could accept. ¶ The brilliant minds with their philosophies, knowing much abut the Christian traditions and the pagan philosophies, would combine all elements to please everybody. They replaced the simple ways and program of the Christ with spectacular rituals, colorful display, impressive pageantry, and limitless pomposity, and called it christianity. They had replaced the glorious, divine plan of exaltation of Christ with an elaborate, colorful, man-made system. They seemed to have little idea of totally dethroning the Christ, nor terminating the life of God, as in our own day, but they put together an incomprehensible God idea. (1966; Teachings of Spencer W. Kimball, p. 425) DGSM:60

**Related Witnesses:**
**President Brigham Young,**
*quoted by John A. Widtsoe*
[T]he Gospel of the kingdom that Jesus undertook to establish in his day and the Priesthood were taken from the earth. (*In new Tabernacle, Aug. 1872; JD15:126*) DGSM:62; DBY:107

**Elder Ezra Taft Benson**
Following the great apostasy from the principles and laws of Christ, the world became enslaved in a cloak of darkness. This long night of Christian apostasy placed an oppressive tyranny on the minds of men, which were shackled by chains of false priestly tradition. Truth had been turned to superstition, joy to despair, and worship into ritual. ACR(London)1976:49

**Joseph Smith**
My object in going to inquire of the Lord was to know which of all the sects was right, that I might know which to join. No sooner, therefore, did I get possession of myself, so as to be able to speak, than I asked the Personages who stood above me in the light, which of all the sects was right (for at this time it had never entered into my heart that all were wrong)—and which I should join. 19. I was answered that I must join none of them, for they were all wrong; and the Personage who addressed me said that all their creeds were an abomination in his sight; that those professors were all corrupt; that: "They draw near to me with their lips, but their hearts are far from me, they teach for doctrines the commandments of men, having a form of godliness, but they deny the power thereof." (*Vision of the Father and the Son; the Lord responds to*

*Joseph's desire to know which of all the sects was right, spring of 1820*) JS-H 1:18-19

**James E. Talmage**
The most important of the internal causes by which the apostasy of the Primitive Church was brought about may be thus summarized: (1) The corrupting of the simple doctrines of the gospel of Christ by admixture with so-called philosophic systems. (2) Unauthorized additions to the prescribed rites of the Church and the introduction of vital alterations in essential ordinances. (3) Unauthorized changes in Church organization and government. JTC:748-49; DGSM:60

**John**
And unto the angel of the church of the Laodiceans write; These things saith the Amen, the faithful and true witness, the beginning of the creation of God; 15. I know thy works, that thou art neither cold nor hot: I would thou wert cold or hot. 16. So then because thou art lukewarm, and neither cold nor hot, I will spue thee out of my mouth. (*John is instructed to write to the Church of Laodiceans*) Rev.3:14-16

---

**27.  Present-day Christian churches have departed from the principles of the original Christian faith.**

**Bruce R. McConkie**
Has no one read the promises made of old that the Lord Jesus cannot return "except there come a falling away first" (2Thess.2:1-12); that before that day, "darkness shall cover the earth, and gross darkness the people" (Isa.60:2; D&C 112:23-24); that the whole earth "is defiled under the inhabitants thereof; because they have transgressed the laws, changed the ordinance, broken the everlasting covenant" (Isa.24:5)? ¶ Does anyone really suppose that the sects of modern Christendom—with their silks and robes and rituals; with their notions of a salvation without works and by grace alone; with neither signs, nor miracles, nor apostles, nor prophets, nor revelation—does anyone really believe such a Christianity is the same as that of Jesus and Peter and Paul? (The Mortal Messiah, 3:436-37) TLDP:30

**Joseph Smith**
. . . I asked the Personages who stood above me in the light, which of all the sects was right (for at this time it had never entered into my heart that all were wrong)—and which I should join. 19. I was answered that I must join none of them, for they were all wrong; and the Personage who addressed me said that all their

creeds were an abomination in his sight; that those professors were all corrupt; that: "they draw near to me with their lips, but their hearts are far from me, they teach for doctrines the commandments of men, having a form of godliness, but they deny the power thereof." (*Vision to Joseph Smith of the Father and the Son, spring of 1820*) JS-H 1:18-19

### Parley P. Pratt

The modern world, called "Christian," claims to have perpetuated the system called "Christianity", while, at the same time, it declares, that the miraculous gifts of the Spirit have ceased. ¶ With as much propriety it might be contended, that the magnet had been perpetuated, but had lost its magnetic properties; that water was perpetuated with all its virtues, but had lost its power to quench thirst, or seek its own level; that fire was still fire, but had lost its heat. ¶ How, we inquire, can Christianity have been perpetuated, while its virtues, its legitimate powers, its distinguishing features, its very life and essence have ceased from among men? Or, of what use is it if it does exist? (Key to the Science of Theology, pp. 109-10) TLDP:29

### Elder John Taylor

There is no more similarity between christianity, as it now exists, with all its superstitions, corruptions, jargons, contentions, divisions, weakness, and imbecility, and this KINGDOM OF GOD, as spoken of in the Scriptures, than there is between light and darkness; and it would no more compare with things to come, than an orange would compare with the earth, or a taper with the glorious luminary of day. (The Government of God, p. 92) TLDP:29

### Elder Joseph Fielding Smith

The Lord has declared that unless we are one we are not his, and where his gospel has taken hold of the people there cannot be such bitterness of feeling, contention and bloodshed, as we find over the greater portion of the earth today. The present condition of the world is an incontrovertible evidence that the power and purity of the gospel is not to be found in their churches and that they are not in fellowship with the Lord. (Doctrines of Salvation, 3:36-37) TLDP:29-30

**Related Witnesses:**

### Joseph Smith

If the whole tree is corrupt, are not its branches corrupt? If the Catholic religion is a false religion, how can any true religion come out of it? If the Catholic church is bad, how can any good thing come out of it? The character of the old churches have always been slandered by all apostates since the world began. ¶ .... It is in the order of heavenly things that God should

always send a new dispensation into the world when men have apostatized from the truth and lost the priesthood; but when men come out and build upon other men's foundations, they do it on their own responsibility, without authority from God; and when the floods come and the winds blow, their foundations will be found to be sand, and their whole fabric will crumble to dust. (*Sermon in a meeting in the Grove, east of the Nauvoo Temple, June 16, 1844*) HC6:478-79

### Bruce R. McConkie

False creeds make false churches. There is no salvation in believing a lie. Every informed, inspired, and discerning person is revolted by the absurdities and scripture-defying pronouncements in the creeds of Christendom, whose chief function is to define and set forth the nature and kind of Being that God is. (The Mortal Messiah, 1:30) TLDP:35

### Joseph Smith

All men are liars who say they are of the true Church without the revelations of Jesus Christ and the Priesthood of Melchizedek, which is after the order of the Son of God. (*Sermon in a meeting in the Grove, east of the Nauvoo Temple, June 16, 1844*) HC6:478

### Jesus,
### *recorded in Matthew*

Ye hypocrites, well did Esaias prophesy of you, saying, 8. This people draweth nigh unto me with their mouth, and honoureth me with their lips; but their heart is far from me. 9. But in vain they do worship me, teaching for doctrines the commandments of men. (*Jesus answers the scribes and Pharisees who contend against him*) Matt.15:7-9

### Isaiah

Wherefore the Lord said, Forasmuch as this people draw near me with their mouth, and with their lips do honour me, but have removed their heart far from me, and their fear toward me is taught by the precept of men: 14. Therefore, behold, I will proceed to do a marvellous work among this people, even a marvellous work and a wonder: for the wisdom of their wise men shall perish, and the understanding of their prudent men shall be hid. (*Isaiah prophesies, about 700 B.C.*) Isa.29:13-14

### Paul

For the time will come when they will not endure sound doctrine; but after their own lusts shall they heap to themselves teachers, having itching ears; 4. And they shall turn away their ears from the truth, and shall be turned unto fables. (*Paul writes to his assistant Timothy, about A.D. 64*) 2Tim.4:3-4

### Paul

For I know this, that after my departing shall

grievous wolves enter in among you, not sparing the flock. 30. Also of your own selves shall men arise, speaking perverse things, to draw away disciples after them. (*To the elders of the Church*) Acts 20:29-30

**Peter**

But there were false prophets also among the people, even as there shall be false teachers among you, who privily shall bring in damnable heresies, even denying the Lord that bought them, and bring upon themselves swift destruction. 2. And many shall follow their pernicious ways; by reason of whom the way of truth shall be evil spoken of. 3. And through covetousness shall they with feigned words make merchandise of you: whose judgment now of a long time lingereth not, and their damnation slumbereth not. (*Letter to members of the Church, about 60 to A.D. 64*) 2Pet.2:1-3

---

### (2) Personal Apostasy

**Author's Note:** Dallin H. Oaks writes: "For purposes of church discipline, the Church currently defines apostasy as (1) repeatedly acting in clear, open, and deliberate public opposition to the Church or its leaders; (2) persisting in teaching as church doctrine information that is not church doctrine, after being corrected by one's bishop or higher authority; or (3) continuing to follow the teachings of apostate cults (such as those that advocate plural marriage) after being corrected by one's bishop or higher authority. Total inactivity in the Church or merely attending another church does not constitute apostasy." (The Lord's Way, p. 247)

28. **Apostasy involves teaching or practicing false doctrine; having an apostate opinion, and either practicing or preaching it (after being corrected by one's bishop or higher authority) is apostasy.**

**President Joseph F. Smith**

A man who does not believe in the atoning blood of Jesus Christ . . . who denies that truth and who persists in his unbelief is not worthy of membership in the Church. He may be considered harmless and of no great danger to others, particularly, as long as he keeps his mouth shut and does not advocate his pernicious doctrines, and be permitted to remain a member of the Church; but the moment you find him trying to poison the minds of somebody else—the innocent, the unsus-

pecting, the unwary—trying to sow the seeds of death and apostasy and unbelief and infidelity in the minds of innocent people, that moment it becomes the duty of the bishop of the ward where the man resides to take him up and try him. . . . Let him be cut off; let him go his way; but let it be understood that it is because of his unbelief, his unrepentance, his unwillingness to hearken to the law of God and to the right of the presidency in the Holy Priesthood of the Church. (*To Saints of Parowan Stake, Sept. 13, 1917*) MOFP5:83; IE1917Nov:7,11

**Elder Joseph Fielding Smith**

Every man that teaches holds a great responsibility, and he that teaches error and leads men from the path of truth is committing one of the greatest crimes that it is possible for man to commit. If he, through his teachings, is presenting false doctrine, and leading men astray from that which is eternal truth, away from the kingdom of God, he is taking upon himself a grave responsibility for which he will have to answer at the judgment seat of God. ¶ The Lord said in one of the early revelations before the organization of the Church that the worth of souls is great in the sight of God. Then he said if a man should labor all his days and convert but one soul, he should have great joy in the kingdom of our Father, and if he should convert many souls, then much greater would be that joy. Reversing the picture, he who blinds one soul, he who spreads error, he who destroys, through his teachings, divine truth, truth that would lead a man to the kingdom of God and to its fulness, how great shall be his condemnation and his punishment in eternity. For the destruction of a soul is the destruction of the greatest thing that has ever been created. . . . ¶ No matter what you teach, if it is not of God, it is darkness. And eventually, no matter how well it may be received, it must come to an end. (Take Heed to Yourselves! pp. 190-91) TLDP:668

**Nephi, son of Lehi**

Yea, and there shall be many which shall teach after this manner, false and vain and foolish doctrines, and shall be puffed up in their hearts, and shall seek deep to hide their counsels from the Lord; and their works shall be in the dark. 10. And the blood of the saints shall cry from the ground against them. 11. Yea, they have all gone out of the way; they have become corrupted. . . . 15. O the wise, and the learned, and the rich, that are puffed up in the pride of their hearts, and all those who preach false doctrines, and all those who commit whoredoms, and pervert the right way of the Lord, wo, wo, wo be unto them, saith the Lord God Almighty, for they shall be thrust down to hell! (*Nephi fore-tells of the last days and the coming forth of the Book of Mormon, 559-545 B.C.*) 2Ne.28:9-11,15

### J. Reuben Clark, Jr.

For any Latter-day Saint psychologist, chemist, physicist, geologist, archeologist, or any other scientist to explain away, or misinterpret, or evade or elude, or most of all, to repudiate or to deny, the great fundamental doctrines of the Church in which he professes to believe, is to give the lie to his intellect, to lose his self-respect, to bring sorrow to his friends, to break the hearts and bring shame to his parents, to besmirch the Church and its members, and to forfeit the respect and honor of those whom he has sought, by his course, to win as friends and helpers. ¶ I prayerfully hope there may not be any such among the teachers of the Church school system, but if there are any such, high or low, they must travel the same route as the teacher without the testimony. Shame and pre-text and evasion and hypocrisy have, and can have, no place in the Church school system, or in the character building and spiritual growth of our youth. ¶ Another thing which must be watched in our Church institutions is this: It must not be possible for men to keep positions of spiritual trust who, not being converted themselves, being really unbelievers, seek to turn aside the beliefs, education, and activities of our youth, and our aged also, from the ways they should follow, into other paths of educa-tion, beliefs, and activities, which (though leading where the unbeliever would go) do not bring us to the places where the Gospel would take us. That this works as a conscience-balm to the unbeliever who directs it is of no impor-tance. This is the grossest betrayal of trust. . . . (*Speaking in behalf of First Presidency [see letter of First Presidency, MOFP6:208-09] to seminary, institute, and Church school teach-ers at Aspen Grove*) (Entire speech published in Deseret News, Church Section, Aug. 13, 1938 and in IE1938Sep:520ff; copied in MOFP6:44-58. The speech was extracted for use as Lesson 18 of the Melchizedek Priest-hood Course of Study 1969-70, p. 129ff) MOFP6:53; TLDP:669-70

### Related Witnesses:

### Peter

But there were false prophets also among the people, even as there shall be false teachers among you, who privily shall bring in damnable heresies, even denying the Lord that bought them, and bring upon themselves swift destruction. (*Peter to members of the Church, about A.D. 60 to 64*) 2Pet.2:1-2

### Bruce R. McConkie

No man, before the judgment bar, will be excused for believing false doctrines or doing evil acts on the excuse that he followed a minis-ter, who he supposed taught true principles and gave good counsel, but who in fact declared false doctrine and wrought evil works. No mat-ter that, in showy piety, we bear grievous bur-dens in the name of religion (as all the Jews did), or win great theological conflicts (as the Rabbis and scribes were wont to do), or display a superabundance of supposed good works (as some modern religionists suppose they do); no matter what else we may do in a false hope of gaining salvation—all that will matter in the day of judgment will be whether we have kept, truly and faithfully, the commandments of God. Let false ministers be damned, if such is the judgment they deserve; the members of their congregations must nonetheless work out their salvation by conforming to true principles of religion. (The Mortal Messiah, 3:391) TLDP:322

---

29. A person who falls away after hav-ing been enlightened by the Spirit of God becomes more hardened—worse than if that person had never known the things of God.

### Mormon

And thus we can plainly discern, that after a people have been once enlightened by the Spirit of God, and have had great knowledge of things pertaining to righteousness, and then have fall-en away into sin and transgression, they become more hardened, and thus their state becomes worse than though they had never known these things. (*The Amalekites and Amulonites, after the order of the Nehors, slay the peaceful Anti-Nephi-Lehies, 90 to 77 B.C.*) Alma 24:30

### Joseph Smith

Strange as it may appear at first thought, yet it is no less strange than true, that notwithstand-ing all the professed determination to live godly, apostates after turning from the faith of Christ, unless they have speedily repented, have sooner or later fallen into the snares of the wicked one, and have been left destitute of the Spirit of God, to manifest their wickedness in the eyes of multitudes. From apostates the faithful have received the severest persecutions. Judas was rebuked and immediately betrayed his Lord into the hands of His enemies, because Satan entered into him. There is a superior intelligence bestowed upon such as obeyed the Gospel with full purpose of heart, which, if sinned against, the apostate is left naked and destitute of the Spirit of God, and he is, in truth, nigh unto cursing, and his end is to be burned. When once that light which was in them is taken from them they become as much darkened as they were previously enlightened, and then, no marvel, if all their power should be enlisted against the truth, and they, Judas like, seek the destruction of those who were their greatest benefactors. What nearer friend on earth, or in heaven, had Judas than the Savior? And his first object was to destroy Him. . . . From what source emanated the principle which has ever been manifested by apostates from the true Church to persecute with double diligence, and seek with double perseverance, to destroy those whom they once professed to love, with whom they once communed, and with whom they once covenanted to strive with every power in righteousness to obtain the rest of God? Perhaps our brethren will say the same that caused Satan to seek to overthrow the kingdom of God, because he himself was evil, and God's kingdom is holy. (*Written message to the elders of the Church in Kirtland and elsewhere, Jan. 1834*) HC2:23

### Elder Joseph Fielding Smith

When a man who was once enlightened loses the Spirit of truth, the darkness which takes its place is overwhelming. Alma gives us a good example of this in teaching Zeezrom. (Alma 12:9-11) CHMR2:125

### Elder Harold B. Lee

It seems a curious thing that in all dispensations, our worst enemies have been those within—who have betrayed the works of the Lord. There were the sons of Mosiah and the younger Alma before their miraculous conversions. It was so in the days of the Master, who said of his betrayer, Judas, "Have not I chosen you twelve, and one of you is a devil?" (John 6:70) Likewise did Joseph Smith have his betrayers. ¶ We may well expect to find our Judases among those professing membership, but, unfortunately for them, they are laboring under some kind of evil influences or have devious motives. CR1968Oct:61

### Related Witnesses:

#### Alma, the younger,
#### *quoted by Mormon*

And therefore, he that will harden his heart, the same receiveth the lesser portion of the word; and he that will not harden his heart, to him is given the greater portion of the word, until it is given unto him to know the mysteries of God

until he know them in full. 11. And they that will harden their hearts, to them is given the lesser portion of the word until they know nothing concerning his mysteries; and then they are taken captive by the devil, and led by his will down to destruction. Now this is what is meant by the chains of hell. (*Alma contends with the lawyer Zeezrom, about 82 B.C.*) Alma 12:10-11

# List of Doctrines

## ATONEMENT OF JESUS CHRIST

*Doctrines Located in This Topic*

### (1) Focusing on the Atonement

30. The Fall of Adam brought physical and spiritual death to all people and thus established the need for an atonement.

31. Adam and Eve were commanded to sacrifice animals in similitude of the future sacrifice that Christ would make to redeem all people from the Fall of Adam.

32. The sacrifice of animals (and burnt offerings) ended with the fulfillment of that portion of the law by Jesus Christ, culminating in His own sacrifice on the cross.

### (2) Salvation from Physical Death

33. The Atonement of Christ secures the universal and unconditional resurrection of the body for both the wicked and the righteous.

34. Without the atoning sacrifice of Jesus Christ there would be no resurrection of our bodies.

35. We cannot receive a fulness of joy in the celestial kingdom without the resurrection, in which our spirits and our bodies are inseparably reunited.

### (3) Salvation from Sin

36. Because we sin, we would all be forever banned from the presence of God were it not for the Atonement of Christ.

37. The Atonement of Christ makes it possible for us to return to the presence of the Lord.

38. Jesus Christ is the author of our salvation and there is no other name given whereby we can be saved.

39. The atoning Savior was Himself free from sin.

40. Christ died that we might live: the Atonement was an act of pure love on the part of Jesus Christ, the Son of God, who laid down His life for us all.

41. The Atonement of Jesus Christ began in Gethsemane prior to His crucifixion.

42. The Savior descended below all things; He bore the weight, the responsibility, and the burden of taking upon Himself the sins of all, that He might raise Himself and others above all things.

43. Christ suffered emotional and spiritual agony, He suffered in both body and spirit, beyond that which any mortal could endure, in offering Himself as a ransom for us all.

# ATONEMENT continued

44. Christ had the power to lay down His life and the power to take it up again, but no one could take His life from Him.

45. Were it not for the Atonement, mercy could not be extended to sinners who, though they might repent, would nevertheless be compelled to suffer the rigorous demands of justice.

46. The Atonement of Christ makes possible the forgiveness of sins for the repentant person.

47. Redemption from *spiritual* death through Christ's atonement is conditioned on obedience to the laws and ordinances of the gospel.

48. Unrepentant persons cannot receive the full benefit of the Atonement; they will be resurrected but they must suffer for their sins.

*Doctrines on the ATONEMENT*
*Located in Other Topics*

## (1) Focusing on the Atonement

264. Jesus Christ was chosen and foreordained to come to earth to perform the atoning sacrifice.

695. Jesus instituted the sacrament as the symbol of His atoning sacrifice.

## (2) Salvation from Physical Death

141. All people will be *saved* from death, but not all will receive the *salvation of exaltation* or *eternal life* in the celestial kingdom of God.

647. The resurrection is universal: every person will be saved from *physical* death regardless of whether he or she has done good or evil in this life.

## (3) Salvation from Sin

390. Through the Atonement of Christ, mercy is available to all.

695. Jesus instituted the sacrament as the symbol of His atoning sacrifice.

# ATONEMENT OF JESUS CHRIST

## (1) Focusing on the Atonement
## (2) Salvation from Physical Death
## (3) Salvation from Sin

**Author's Note:** The Bible Dictionary says that **atonement** "describes the setting 'at one' of those who have been estranged, and denotes the reconciliation of man to God. Sin is the cause of the estrangement, and therefore the purpose of atonement is to correct or overcome the consequences of sin. From the time of Adam to the death of Jesus Christ, true believers were instructed to offer animal sacrifices to the Lord. These sacrifices were symbolic of the forthcoming death of Jesus Christ, and were done by faith in Him (Moses 5:5-8)." (BD:617)

Hugh W. Nibley depicts **atonement** in this manner: "There is not a word among those translated as 'atonement' which does not plainly indicate the return to a former state or condition; one rejoins the family, returns to the Father, becomes united, reconciled, embracing and sitting down happily with others after a sad separation. We want to get back, but to do that we must resist the alternative, being taken into the community of the 'prince of this world' (John 12:31)." ("The Meaning of the Atonement," p. 26)

Bruce R. McConkie defines **atonement**: "To atone is to . . . pay the penalty. Thus the atonement of Christ is designed to ransom men from the effects of the fall of Adam in that both spiritual and temporal death are conquered; their lasting effect is nullified." (DGSM:23)

**Redemption** is tied into Atonement and is defined by Bruce R. McConkie thus: "Redemption is of two kinds: conditional and unconditional. *Conditional redemption* is synonymous with exaltation or eternal life. It comes by grace of God coupled with good works and includes redemption from the effects of both the temporal and spiritual fall. . . . *Unconditional redemption* is redemption from the effects of the temporal but not the spiritual fall. It consists in obtaining the free gift of immortality but being denied 'the eternal life which God giveth unto all the obedient.' (Moses 5:11) It comes by grace alone without works." (Mormon Doctrine, p. 623)

## (1) Focusing on the Atonement

30. The Fall of Adam brought physical and spiritual death to all people and thus established the need for an atonement.

### Jacob, brother of Nephi,
*quoted by Nephi*

For as death hath passed upon all men, to fulfil the merciful plan of the great Creator, there must needs be a power of resurrection, and the resurrection must needs come unto man by reason of the fall; and the fall came by reason of transgression; and because man became fallen they were cut off from the presence of the Lord. 7. Wherefore, it must needs be an infinite atonement—save it should be an infinite atonement this corruption could not put on incorruption. Wherefore, the first judgment which came upon man must needs have remained to an endless duration. And if so, this flesh must have laid down to rot and to crumble to its mother earth, to rise no more. 8. O the wisdom of God, his mercy and grace! For behold, if the flesh should rise no more our spirits must become subject to that angel who fell from before the presence of the Eternal God, and became the devil, to rise no more. 9. And our spirits must have become like unto him, and we become devils, angels to a devil, to be shut out from the presence of our God, and to remain with the father of lies, in misery, like unto himself; yea, to that being who beguiled our first parents, who transformeth himself nigh unto an angel of light, and stirreth up the children of men unto secret combinations of murder and all manner of secret works of darkness. 10. O how great the goodness of our God, who prepareth a way for our escape from the grasp of this awful monster; yea, that monster, death and hell, which I call the death of the body, and also the death of the spirit. 11. And because of the way of deliverance of our God, the Holy One of Israel, this death, of which I have spoken, which is the temporal, shall deliver up its dead; which death is the grave. 12. And this death of which I have spoken, which is the spiritual death, shall deliver up its dead; which spiritual death is hell; wherefore, death and hell must deliver up their dead, and hell must deliver up its captive spirits, and the grave must deliver up its captive bodies, and the bodies and the spirits of men will be restored one to the other; and it is by the power of the resurrection of the Holy One of Israel. 13. O how great the plan of our

God! For on the other hand, the paradise of God must deliver up the spirits of the righteous, and the grave deliver up the body of the righteous; and the spirit and the body is restored to itself again, and all men become incorruptible, and immortal, and they are living souls, having a perfect knowledge like unto us in the flesh, save it be that our knowledge shall be perfect. (*Jacob recounts to the people of Nephi the covenants of the Lord made to the house of Israel, 559-545 B.C.*) 2Ne.9:6-13

**J. Reuben Clark, Jr.**

Adam became mortal; spiritual death came to him; and mortal death came to him. This was the first great crisis in the history of mankind. Indeed, it may be said to have produced mankind. ¶ In order for him to get back to the place whence he began, it was necessary that there should be an atonement for this disobedience. ¶ Quite obviously, Adam could not retrace his steps; he could not un-eat. He was mortal. No matter how good any of his children might be, they, also mortal, had no more power than had he. So, to pay for the disobedience, it took a Being conceived by the Infinite, not subject to death as were Adam's posterity; someone to whom death was subject; someone born of woman but yet divine. He alone could make the sacrifice which would enable us to have our bodies and our spirits reunited in the due time of the Lord and then go back to the Father, thus reunited; and finally, body and spirit together, we might go on through all the eternities. CR1955Oct:23

**Alma, the younger,**
*quoted by Mormon*

But behold, it was appointed unto man to die—therefore, as they were cut off from the tree of life they should be cut off from the face of the earth—and man became lost forever, yea, they became fallen man. 7. And now, ye see by this that our first parents were cut off both temporally and spiritually from the presence of the Lord; and thus we see they became subjects to follow after their own will. 8. Now behold, it was not expedient that man should be reclaimed from this temporal death, for that would destroy the great plan of happiness. 9. Therefore, as the soul could never die, and the fall had brought upon all mankind a spiritual death as well as a temporal, that is, they were cut off from the presence of the Lord, it was expedient that mankind should be reclaimed from this spiritual death. 10. Therefore, as they had become carnal, sensual, and devilish, by nature, this probationary state became a state for them to prepare; it became a preparatory state. 11. And now remember, my son, if it were not for the plan of redemption, (laying it aside) as soon as they were dead their souls were miserable, being cut off from the presence of the Lord. 12. And now, there was no means to reclaim men from this fallen state, which man had brought upon himself because of his own disobedience; 13. Therefore, according to justice, the plan of redemption could not be brought about, only on conditions of repentance of men in this probationary state, yea, this preparatory state; for except it were for these conditions, mercy could not take effect except it should destroy the work of justice. Now the work of justice could not be destroyed; if so, God would cease to be God. 14. And thus we see that all mankind were fallen, and they were in the grasp of justice; yea, the justice of God, which consigned them forever to be cut off from his presence. 15. And now, the plan of mercy could not be brought about except an atonement should be made; therefore God himself atoneth for the sins of the world, to bring about the plan of mercy, to appease the demands of justice, that God might be a perfect, just God, and a merciful God also. (*Alma speaks to his son, Corianton, concerning the resurrection of the dead, about 73 B.C.*) Alma 42:6-15

**President Joseph Fielding Smith**

We believe that he [Christ] came into the world to ransom men from the temporal and spiritual death brought into the world through the fall of Adam, and we have in our hearts unbounded gratitude that through the shedding of his blood all men are raised in immortality, while those who believe and obey his laws are raised also unto eternal life. ("The First Prophet of the Last Dispensation," EN1971Aug:6) TLDP:37

**Elder Joseph Fielding Smith**

Justice made certain demands, and Adam could not pay the price, so mercy steps in. The Son of God says: "I will go down and pay the price. I will be the Redeemer and redeem men from Adam's transgression. I will take upon me the sins of the world and redeem or save every soul from his own sins who will repent." That is the only condition. The Savior does not save anybody from his individual sins only on condition of his repentance. So the effect of Adam's transgression was to place all of us in the pit with him. Then the Savior comes along, not subject to that pit, and lowers the ladder. He comes down into the pit and makes it possible for us to use the ladder to escape. . . . ¶ This was precisely the condition that Adam placed himself and his posterity in, when he partook of the forbidden fruit. All being together in the pit, none could gain the surface and relieve the others. The pit was banishment from the presence of the Lord and temporal death, the dissolution of the body. And all being subject to death, none could provide the means of escape. ¶ Therefore, in his infinite mercy, the Father heard the cries of his children and sent his Only Begotten Son, who was not subject to death nor to sin, to provide the means of escape. This he did through his infinite atonement and the everlasting gospel. (Doctrines of Salvation, 1:123) TLDP:48-49,50

### Anthon H. Lund

We learn in the revelations of the Lord that the fall extended to all, and that the grievous consequence of the fall was banishment from the presence of our Heavenly Father. The consequences of the fall were both temporal and spiritual. Jesus came; He made the sacrifice. He did it willingly. He was without blemish or fault. No sin was found in Him, and as such He was proper subject for the sacrifice. CR1912Apr:12

### President John Taylor

Was it known that man would fall? Yes. We are clearly told that it was understood that man should fall, and it was understood that the penalty of departing from the law would be death, death temporal. And there was a provision made for that. Man was not able to make that provision himself, and hence we are told that it needed the atonement of a God to accomplish this purpose; and the Son of God presented Himself to carry out that object. *(At Provo, Utah, Aug. 28, 1881, JD22:300)* TLDP:41

### President John Taylor

Death was "passed upon all men to fulfill the *merciful plan* of the great Creator;" and furthermore, that the resurrection came "by reason of the fall." For if man had not sinned, there would have been no death, and if Jesus had not atoned for the sin, there would have been no resurrection. Hence these things are spoken of as being according to the merciful plan of God. This corruption could not have put on incorruption, and this mortality could not have put on immortality; for, as we have elsewhere shown, man by reason of any thing that he himself could do or accomplish, could only exalt himself to the dignity and capability of man and therefore it needed the atonement of a God, before man, through the adoption, could be exalted to the Godhead. (The Mediation and Atonement, pp. 132-33) TLDP:39-40

---

31.    Adam and Eve were commanded to sacrifice animals in similitude of the future sacrifice that Christ would make to redeem all people from the Fall of Adam.

### Joseph Smith,
### *translating the Book of Moses*

And he gave unto them commandments, that they should worship the Lord their God, and should offer the firstlings of their flocks, for an offering unto the Lord. And Adam was obedient unto the commandments of the Lord. 6. And after many days an angel of the Lord appeared unto Adam, saying: Why dost thou offer sacrifices unto the Lord? And Adam said unto him: I know not, save the Lord commanded me. 7. And then the angel spake, saying: This thing is a similitude of the sacrifice of the Only Begotten of the Father, which is full of grace and truth. 8. Wherefore, thou shalt do all that thou doest in the name of the Son, and thou shalt repent and call upon God in the name of the Son forevermore. 9. And in that day the Holy Ghost fell upon Adam, which beareth record of the Father and the Son, saying: I am the Only Begotten of the Father from the beginning, henceforth and forever, that as thou hast fallen thou mayest be redeemed, and all mankind, even as many as will. (*Revelation to Moses concerning Adam and Eve after they were driven out of the Garden of Eden*) Moses 5:5-9

### Elder Joseph F. Smith

The Lord designed in the beginning to place before man the knowledge of good and evil, and gave him a commandment to cleave to good and abstain from evil. But if he should fail, he would give to him the law of sacrifice and provide a Savior for him, that he might be brought back again into the presence and favor of God and partake of eternal life with him. This was the plan of redemption chosen and instituted by the Almighty before man was placed on the earth. And when man did fall by transgressing the law which was given him, the Lord gave to him the law of sacrifice, and made it clear to his understanding, that it was for the purpose of reminding him of that great event that should transpire in the meridian of time, whereby he and all his posterity might be brought forth by the power of redemption and resurrection from the dead, and partake of eternal life with God in his kingdom. For this reason Adam and his posterity, from generation to generation, observed this law, and continually looked forward to a time when there should be provided for them a means of redemption from the fall and restoration from death to life, for death was the penalty of the law transgressed, which man was powerless to avert, that fiat of God being, "In the day that thou eatest thereof, thou shalt surely die," and this penalty was to follow upon all flesh, all being as helpless and dependent as he was in this matter. . . . ¶ In anticipation, therefore, of this great sacrifice which was to be offered for Adam and his seed, they offered sacrifices. . . . ¶ They would take the firstlings of their flocks, the best fruits of their fields, and those things which were emblematic of purity, innocence, and perfection, symbolical of him who was without sin, and as "a lamb slain from the foundation of the world," and offer sacrifices unto God in memory of him, and the matchless and wonderful deliverance to be wrought out for them by him. (Gospel Doctrine, pp. 202-03) TLDP:52

**Bruce R. McConkie**
For four thousand long years, from Adam to that bleak day when our Lord was lifted up by sinful men, all of his righteous followers sought remission of their sins through sacrifice. It was an ordinance of the Melchizedek Priesthood: it antedated the law of Moses by two and a half millenniums. . . . For our purposes now it suffices to know that there neither was nor could have been any ordinance or system devised that would have dramatized more perfectly the coming eternal sacrifice that was and is the heart and core of revealed religion. . . . ¶ After the final great sacrifice on the cross, the use for the similitude that looked forward to our Lord's death ceased. Blood sacrifices became a thing of the past. New symbolisms, found in the sacrament of the Lord's supper, were adopted so that the saints might look back with reverence and worship upon his atoning ordeal. (The Promised Messiah, pp. 379-80) TLDP:52

**Related Witnesses:**
**President John Taylor**
Jesus had to take away sin by the sacrifice of Himself, the just for the unjust, but, previous to this grand sacrifice, these animals had to have their blood shed as types, until the great antitype should offer up Himself once for all. (The Mediation and Atonement, pp. 149-50) TLDP:43

**Elder Joseph Fielding Smith**
All the sacrifices of old, from the days of Adam to the atonement of Jesus Christ by blood were in the similitude of and a reminder of the great sacrifice, and pointed forward to its fulfillment by Jesus upon the cross. (Answers to Gospel Questions, 1:188) TLDP:17

---

32. **The sacrifice of animals (and burnt offerings) ended with the fulfillment of that portion of the law by Jesus Christ, culminating in His own sacrifice on the cross.**

**Bruce R. McConkie**
After the final great sacrifice on the cross, the use for the similitude that looked forward to our Lord's death ceased. Blood sacrifices became a thing of the past. New symbolisms, found in the sacrament of the Lord's supper, were adopted so that the saints might look back with reverence and worship upon his atoning ordeal. (The Promised Messiah, pp. 380) TLDP:52

**President John Taylor**
Jesus had to take away sin by the sacrifice of Himself, the just for the unjust, but, previous to this grand sacrifice, these animals had to have their blood shed as types, until the great antitype should offer up Himself once for all. (The Mediation and Atonement, p. 150) TLDP:43

**Bruce R. McConkie**
He came as the living Paschal Lamb to put a divine seal upon all the sacrifices, all the trespass offerings, all the peace offerings ever offered by either Melchizedek or Aaronic authority since the world began. He came to fulfill the law that he himself had given to Moses, to bring redemption, to atone for the sins of the world. He came as the Lamb of God. He was appointed unto death, and all else incident to his mortal probation was truly incidental. (The Mortal Messiah, 1:140-41) TLDP:38

**Paul**
In burnt offerings and sacrifices for sin thou hast had no pleasure. 7. Then said I, Lo, I come (in the volume of the book it is written of me,) to do thy will, O God. 8. Above when he said, Sacrifice and offering and burnt offerings and offering for sin thou wouldest not, neither hadst pleasure therein; which are offered by the law; 9. Then said he, Lo, I come to do thy will, O God. He taketh away the first, that he may establish the second. 10. By the which will we are sanctified through the offering of the body of Jesus Christ once for all. 11. And every priest standeth daily ministering and offering oftentimes the same sacrifices, which can never take away sins: 12. But this man, after he had offered one sacrifice for sins for ever, sat down on the right hand of God; 13. From henceforth expecting till his enemies be made his footstool. 14. For by one offering he hath perfected for ever them that are sanctified. (*Letter to the Jewish members of the Church, about A.D. 60*) Heb.10:6-14

**Jesus,**
*quoted by Mormon*
And ye shall offer up unto me no more the shedding of blood; yea, your sacrifices and your burnt offerings shall be done away, for I will accept none of your sacrifices and your

burnt offerings. 20. And ye shall offer for a sacrifice unto me a broken heart and a contrite spirit. (*The voice of the resurrected Jesus Christ immediately before he visited the Nephites, A.D. 34*) 3Ne.9:19-20

---

## (2) Salvation from Physical Death

33. **The Atonement of Christ secures the universal and unconditional resurrection of the body for both the wicked and the righteous.**

### Elder Joseph F. Smith
Every creature that is born in the image of God will be resurrected from the dead. . . . But just as sure as we go down into the grave, through the transgression of our first parents, by whom death came into the world, so sure will we be resurrected from the dead by the power of Jesus Christ. It matters not whether we have done well or ill, whether we have been intelligent or ignorant, or whether we have been bondsmen or slaves or freemen, all men will be raised from the dead. (Millennial Star, March 1896, p. 162) DGSM:88

### Paul
For since by man came death, by man came also the resurrection of the dead. 22. For as in Adam all die, even so in Christ shall all be made alive. 23. But every man in his own order: Christ the firstfruits; afterward they that are Christ's at his coming. (*Letter to the Church at Corinth, Greece, about A.D. 55*) 1Cor.15:21-23

### James E. Talmage
But besides this universal application of the atonement, whereby all men are redeemed from the effects of Adam's transgression both with respect to the death of the body and inherited sin, there is application of the same great sacrifice as a means of propitiation for individual sins through the faith and good works of the sinner. This twofold effect of the atonement is implied in the article of our faith now under consideration. The first effect is to secure to all mankind alike, exemption from the penalty of the fall, thus providing a plan of *General Salvation*. The second effect is to open a way for *Individual Salvation* whereby mankind may secure remission of personal sins . . . conditioned on individual compliance with prescribed requirements—"obedience to the laws and ordinances of the Gospel." AF:78-79

### Amulek,
#### *quoted by Mormon*
Therefore the wicked remain as though there had been no redemption made, except it be the loosing of the bands of death; for behold, the day cometh that all shall rise from the dead and stand before God, and be judged according to their works. 42. Now, there is a death which is called a temporal death; and the death of Christ shall loose the bands of this temporal death, that all shall be raised from this temporal death. 43. The spirit and the body shall be reunited again in its perfect form; both limb and joint shall be restored to its proper frame, even as we now are at this time; and we shall be brought to stand before God, knowing even as we know now, and have a bright recollection of all our guilt. 44. Now, this restoration shall come to all, both old and young, both bond and free, both male and female, both the wicked and the righteous; and even there shall not so much as a hair of their heads be lost; but everything shall be restored to its perfect frame, as it is now, or in the body, and shall be brought and be arraigned before the bar of Christ the Son, and God the Father, and the Holy Spirit, which is one Eternal God, to be judged according to their works, whether they be good or whether they be evil. 45. Now, behold, I have spoken unto you concerning the death of the mortal body, and also concerning the resurrection of the mortal body. I say unto you that this mortal body is raised to an immortal body, that is from death, even from the first death unto life, that they can die no more; their spirits uniting with their bodies, never to be divided; thus the whole becoming spiritual and immortal, that they can no more see corruption. (*Amulek answers the lawyer Zeezrom, foretelling Christ's redemption of man and the final judgment, about 82 B.C.*) Alma 11:41-45

### Marion G. Romney
The atonement of the Master is the central point of world history. Without it, the whole purpose for the creation of the earth and our living upon it would fail. . . . ¶ [W]ithout it, no man or woman would ever be resurrected. . . . And so all the world, believers and nonbelievers, are indebted to the Redeemer for their certain resurrection, because the resurrection will be as wide as was the fall, which brought death to every man. CR1953Oct:34-35

### Moroni, son of Mormon
Behold he created Adam, and by Adam came the fall of man. And because of the fall of man came Jesus Christ, even the Father and the Son; and because of Jesus Christ came the redemption of man. 13. And because of the redemption of man, which came by Jesus Christ, they are brought back into the presence of the Lord; yea, this is wherein all men are redeemed, because

the death of Christ bringeth to pass the resurrection, which bringeth to pass a redemption from an endless sleep, from which sleep all men shall be awakened by the power of God when the trump shall sound; and they shall come forth, both small and great, and all shall stand before his bar, being redeemed and loosed from this eternal band of death, which death is a temporal death. (*Moroni addresses those who deny the revelations of God, A.D. 400-421*) Morm.9:12-13

### Elder Joseph Fielding Smith

So Jesus did for us something that we could not do for ourselves, through his infinite atonement. On the third day after the crucifixion he took up his body and gained the keys of the resurrection, and thus has power to open the graves for all men, but this he could not do until he had first passed through death himself and conquered. (Doctrines of Salvation, 1:128) DGSM:88

### Jacob, brother of Nephi,
### *quoted by Nephi*

And this death of which I have spoken, which is the spiritual death, shall deliver up its dead; which spiritual death is hell; wherefore, death and hell must deliver up their dead, and hell must deliver up its captive spirits, and the grave must deliver up its captive bodies, and the bodies and the spirits of men will be restored one to the other; and it is by the power of the resurrection of the Holy One of Israel. (*Jacob teaches the doctrine of the Atonement to the people of Nephi, 559-545 B.C.*) 2Ne.9:12

**Related Witnesses:**

### Paul

Why should it be thought a thing incredible with you, that God should raise the dead? (*Paul testifies before King Agrippa of the appearance of Jesus on the road to Damascus*) Acts 26:8

### Jesus,
### *recorded in Matthew*

And the graves were opened; and many bodies of the saints which slept arose, 53. And came out of the graves after his resurrection, and went into the holy city, and appeared unto many. (*Jesus is crucified and the first resurrection begins*) Matt.27:52-53

---

34.  Without the atoning sacrifice of Jesus Christ there would be no resurrection of our bodies.

### Jacob, brother of Nephi,
### *quoted by Nephi*

Wherefore, it must needs be an infinite atonement—save it should be an infinite atonement this corruption could not put on incorruption.

Wherefore, the first judgment which came upon man must needs have remained to an endless duration. And if so, this flesh must have laid down to rot and to crumble to its mother earth, to rise no more. (*Jacob teaches the doctrine of the Atonement to the people of Nephi, 559-545 B.C.*) 2Ne.9:7

### J. Reuben Clark, Jr.

He alone could make the sacrifice which would enable us to have our bodies and our spirits reunited in the due time of the Lord and then go back to the Father, thus reunited; and finally, body and spirit together, we might go on through all the eternities. CR1955Oct:23

### Melvin J. Ballard

Would he not be a wonderful friend? That is the kind of friend the world has in Jesus Christ. The mortgage of death was foreclosed, and death claimed its own. The grave received the body, and there it would stay forever and forever, were it not that Jesus Christ has interceded. He has settled with the holder of the mortgage. The price he paid was his life; in some way not yet perhaps fully comprehended and understood by us, he attained in that sacrifice a value of worth recognized, bartered for and exchanged and given to the holder of the mortgage and satisfied the claims upon these earth bodies. He has purchased us; he has redeemed us; he has bought us; and we belong to him. And now he proposed to give back these bodies glorified. (Sermons and Missionary Services of Melvin J. Ballard, pp. 169-70) TLDP:50

### Elder Joseph Fielding Smith

What a dreadful situation we would have been in without this infinite atonement! Our bodies returning to the dust there to remain forever; our spirits becoming subject to Satan, and we would have had no recourse. How grateful we should be for the mercies of our Eternal Father and his beloved Son that the way was opened for our escape. (Answers to Gospel Questions, 2:138) TLDP:50-51

### Bruce R. McConkie

If there were no atoning sacrifice our bodies would rot and decay and remain forever in the grave—temporal death would reign supreme. If there were no atoning sacrifice our spirits, in bondage to sin, would be cast out of the presence of God forever—spiritual death would reign supreme. If there were no atoning sacrifice, as the Book of Mormon says, all men would be subject to death, hell, the devil and endless torment forever. ACR(Nuku'alofa)1976:21

35. We cannot receive a fulness of joy in the celestial kingdom without the resurrection, in which our spirits and our bodies are inseparably reunited.

**Charles W. Penrose**

The Lord has shown to us that the elements are eternal and that it requires the eternal union of spirit and element to obtain a fulness of joy. For the spirit part of man and the earthly, or temporal part just now, shall be united together perpetually, eternally, the body and the spirit being made one again, only joined together after the power of an endless life, that without that union a fulness of joy cannot be obtained. CR1914Oct:35

**Joseph Smith**

For man is spirit. The elements are eternal, and spirit and element, inseparably connected, receive a fulness of joy; 34. And when separated, man cannot receive a fulness of joy. (*Revelation received at Kirtland, Ohio, May 6, 1833*) D&C 93:33-34

**Joseph Smith**

And the spirit and the body are the soul of man. 16. And the resurrection from the dead is the redemption of the soul. 17. And the redemption of the soul is through him that quickeneth all things, in whose bosom it is decreed that the poor and the meek of the earth shall inherit it. 18. Therefore, it must needs be sanctified from all unrighteousness, that it may be prepared for the celestial glory; 19. For after it hath filled the measure of its creation, it shall be crowned with glory, even with the presence of God the Father; 20. That bodies who are of the celestial kingdom may possess it forever and ever; for, for this intent was it made and created, and for this intent are they sanctified. (*Revelation received Dec. 27/28, 1832; the "olive leaf message of peace"*) D&C 88:15-20

**Melvin J. Ballard**

He has purchased us; he has redeemed us; he has bought us; and we belong to him. And now he proposed to give back these bodies glorified. To those who keep the full law he promises to give a celestial body, full of celestial power and glory and splendor; and to those who keep the terrestrial law, a body not so glorious, but still glorious and splendid; and telestial bodies to those who keep the telestial law; thus he extends to each this privilege. This is what the Lord Jesus Christ has done for man. (Sermons and Missionary Services of Melvin J. Ballard, pp. 169-70) TLDP:50

**Related Witnesses:**

**J. Reuben Clark, Jr.**

His real mission was to redeem man from the Fall of Adam by the atonement He made. We declare this is the greatest gift that ever came to man, for without it there would be no immortality of the soul, which is "the spirit and the body of man." ("I Am the Resurrection and the Life," IE1943Jan:63) TLDP:38

**President Joseph F. Smith**

For the dead had looked upon the long absence of their spirits from their bodies as a bondage. (*Vision regarding the Savior's visit to the spirits of the dead, Oct. 3, 1918*) D&C 138:50

**Joseph Smith,**
*receiving theWord of the Lord*

For as ye have looked upon the long absence of your spirits from your bodies to be a bondage, I will show unto you how the day of redemption shall come. . . . (*Revelation received March 7, 1831*) D&C 45:17

---

## (3) Salvation from Sin

36. Because we sin, we would all be forever banned from the presence of God were it not for the Atonement of Christ.

**Marion G. Romney**

All men have sinned. Each person is therefore unclean to the extent to which he has sinned, and because of that uncleanness is banished from the presence of the Lord so long as the effect of his own wrongdoing is upon him. ¶ Since we suffer this spiritual death as a result of our own transgressions, we cannot claim deliverance therefrom as a matter of justice. Neither has any man the power within himself alone to make restitution so complete that he can be wholly cleansed from the effect of his own wrongdoing. If men are to be freed from the results of their own transgressions and brought back into the presence of God, they must be the beneficiaries of some expedient beyond themselves which will free them from the effect of their own sins. For this purpose was the atonement of Jesus Christ conceived and executed. ¶ This was the world's supreme act of charity, performed by Jesus out of his great love for us. He not only thereby met the demands of the law of justice—which would have left us forever marred by the effects of our own transgressions—but made effective the law of mercy, through which all men may be cleansed from their own sins. CR1982Apr:9

### Bruce R. McConkie

If there were no atoning sacrifice, our spirits, in bondage to sin, would be cast out of the presence of God forever—spiritual death would reign supreme. If there were no atoning sacrifice, as the Book of Mormon says, all men would be subject to death, hell, the devil and endless torment forever. ACR(Nuku'alofa) 1976:21

### Anthon H. Lund

The sacrifice that was to be made for the human family could only be made by one who had not sinned Himself. It would have to be done by One who voluntarily offered to do this, in order that justice might be satisfied and mercy extended to the sinner. We learn in the revelations of the Lord that the fall extended to all, and that the grievous consequence of the fall was banishment from the presence of our Heavenly Father. The consequences of the fall were both temporal and spiritual. Jesus came; He made the sacrifice. He did it willingly. He was without blemish or fault. No sin was found in Him, and as such He was proper subject for the sacrifice. CR1912Apr:12

### Amulek,
*quoted by Mormon*

And now, behold, I will testify unto you of myself that these things are true. Behold, I say unto you, that I do know that Christ shall come among the children of men, to take upon him the transgressions of his people, and that he shall atone for the sins of the world; for the Lord God hath spoken it. 9. For it is expedient that an atonement should be made; for according to the great plan of the Eternal God there must be an atonement made, or else all mankind must unavoidably perish; yea, all are hardened; yea, all are fallen and are lost, and must perish except it be through the atonement which it is expedient should be made. 10. For it is expedient that there should be a great and last sacrifice; yea, not a sacrifice of man, neither of beast, neither of any manner of fowl; for it shall not be a human sacrifice; but it must be an infinite and eternal sacrifice. 11. Now there is not any man that can sacrifice his own blood which will atone for the sins of another. Now, if a man murdereth, behold will our law, which is just, take the life of his brother? I say unto you, Nay. 12. But the law requireth the life of him who hath murdered; therefore there can be nothing which is short of an infinite atonement which will suffice for the sins of the world. (*Amulek teaches the people about the atonement of Christ, 74 B.C.*) Alma 34:8-12

### Related Witnesses:
### Elder Joseph F. Smith

Men cannot forgive their own sins; they cannot cleanse themselves from the consequences of their sins. Men can stop sinning and can do right in the future, and so far their acts are acceptable before the Lord and worthy of consideration. But who shall repair the wrongs they have done to themselves and to others, which it seems impossible for them to repair themselves? By the atonement of Jesus Christ the sins of the repentant shall be washed away; though they be crimson they shall be made white as wool. CR1899Apr:41

### Paul

For all have sinned, and come short of the glory of God; (*Letter to the Church in Rome, about A.D. 55*) Rom.3:23

---

37. **The Atonement of Christ makes it possible for us to return to the presence of the Lord.**

### Joseph Smith,
*quoted by Elder Joseph Fielding Smith*

But that man was not able himself to erect a system, or plan with power sufficient to free him from a destruction which awaited him is evident from the fact that God, as before remarked, prepared a sacrifice in the gift of His own Son who should be sent in due time, to prepare a way, or open a door through which man might enter into the Lord's presence, whence he had been cast out for disobedience. (*In epistle to elders of the Church in Kirtland and elsewhere, Jan. 1834*) TPJS:58

### Samuel, the Lamanite,
*quoted by Mormon*

For behold, he surely must die that salvation may come; yea, it behooveth him and becometh expedient that he dieth, to bring to pass the resurrection of the dead, that thereby men may be brought into the presence of the Lord. 16. Yea, behold, this death bringeth to pass the resurrection, and redeemeth all mankind from the first death—that spiritual death; for all mankind, by the fall of Adam being cut off from the presence of the Lord, are considered as dead, both as to things temporal and to things spiritual. 17. But behold, the resurrection of Christ redeemeth mankind, yea, even all mankind, and bringeth them back into the presence of the Lord. 18. Yea, and it bringeth to pass the condition of repentance, that whosoever repenteth the same is not hewn down and cast into the fire; but whosoever repenteth not is hewn down and cast into the fire; and there cometh upon them again a spiritual death, yea, a second death, for they are cut off again as to things pertaining to righteousness. (*Samuel, the Lamanite, preaches to the Nephites that Christ, through his death and resurrection, redeems men from temporal and spiritual death, about 6 B.C.*) Hel.14:15-18

### Jacob, brother of Nephi,
### *quoted by Nephi*

And he cometh into the world that he may save all men if they will hearken unto his voice; for behold, he suffereth the pains of all men, yea, the pains of every living creature, both men, women, and children, who belong to the family of Adam. (*Jacob to the people of Nephi, 559-545 B.C.*) 2Ne.9:21

### Bruce R. McConkie

He came to bear their sins, to carry them as Azazel to a land apart. He came as the great and Eternal High Priest to rend the veil of the temple, that all men might enter the Holy of Holies and dwell forever in the Divine Presence. (The Mortal Messiah, 1:140-41) TLDP:38

### President Brigham Young,
### *quoted by John A. Widtsoe*

Can all the wisdom of the world devise means by which we can be redeemed, and return to the presence of our Father and Elder Brother, and dwell with holy angels and celestial beings? No, it is beyond the power and wisdom of the inhabitants of the earth that now live, or that ever did or ever will live, to prepare or create a sacrifice that will pay this divine debt. But God provided it, and his Son has paid it, and we, each and every one, can now receive the truth and be saved in the Kingdom of God. Is it clear and plain? It is to me, and if you have the Spirit of God, it is as plain to you as anything else in the world. (*In Ogden, Utah, July 10, 1870, JD14:71*) DBY:59

### Elder Joseph F. Smith

But who shall repair the wrongs they have done to themselves and to others, which it seems impossible for them to repair themselves? By the atonement of Jesus Christ the sins of the repentant shall be washed away; though they can be crimson they shall be made white as wool. This is the promise given to you. CR1899Oct:41

### Related Witnesses:
### Joseph Smith,
### *translating the Book of Moses*

For behold, this is my work and my glory—to bring to pass the immortality and eternal life of man. (*The Lord talks to Moses, face to face; revelation to Joseph Smith, 1830*) Moses 1:39

**38.** Jesus Christ is the author of our salvation and there is no other name given whereby we can be saved.

### Joseph Smith,
### *receiving the Word of the Lord*

Take upon you the name of Christ, and speak the truth in soberness. 22. And as many as repent and are baptized in my name, which is Jesus Christ, and endure to the end, the same shall be saved. 23. Behold, Jesus Christ is the name which is given of the Father, and there is none other name given whereby man can be saved; 24. Wherefore, all men must take upon them the name which is given of the Father, for in that name shall they be called at the last day; (*Revelation received June 1829*) D&C 18:21-24

### George F. Richards

We realize that there is no virtue for salvation and exaltation outside of the atoning blood of Jesus Christ, our Savior. There is no other name under heaven by which man may obtain salvation. The whole plan of salvation is founded upon revelation and Jesus Christ; rejecting these there is no foundation left upon which to build nor to stand. The ordinances of the Gospel have virtue in them by reason of the atoning blood of Jesus Christ, and without it there would be no virtue in them for salvation. CR1916Apr:53-54

### King Benjamin,
### *quoted by Mormon*

And moreover, I say unto you, that there shall be no other name given nor any other way nor means whereby salvation can come unto the children of men, only in and through the name of Christ, the Lord Omnipotent. (*King Benjamin makes known to the people the things told to him by an angel of God, about 124 B.C.*) Mosiah 3:17

### President Joseph Fielding Smith

We believe that salvation was, and is, and is to come in and through the atoning blood of Christ, the Lord Omnipotent, and that there is no other name given under heaven whereby men can become inheritors of eternal glory in the kingdoms which are ahead. ("The First Prophet of the Last Dispensation," EN1971Aug:6) TLDP:37

### Nephi, son of Lehi

And now, my brethren, I have spoken plainly that ye cannot err. And as the Lord God liveth that brought Israel up out of the land of Egypt, and gave unto Moses power that he should heal the nations after they had been bitten by the poisonous serpents, if they would cast their eyes unto the serpent which he did raise up before them, and also gave him power that he should smite the rock and the water should come forth; yea, behold I say unto you, that as these things are true, and as the Lord God liveth, there is none other name given under heaven save it be this Jesus Christ, of which I have spoken, whereby man can be saved. (*The writings of Nephi, 559-545 B.C.*) 2Ne.25:20

---

### 39. The atoning Savior was Himself free from sin.

#### Joseph Smith,
*receiving the Word of the Lord*
Listen to him who is the advocate with the Father, who is pleading your cause before him— 4. Saying: Father, behold the sufferings and death of him who did no sin, in whom thou wast well pleased; behold the blood of thy Son which was shed, the blood of him whom thou gavest that thyself might be glorified; (*Revelation, March 7, 1831; Christ will intercede with the Father*) D&C 45:3-4

#### Elder Joseph Fielding Smith
The whole plan of redemption is based on vicarious sacrifice. One without sin standing for the whole human family, all of whom were under the curse. It is most natural and just that he who commits the wrong should pay the penalty—atone for his wrongdoing. Therefore, when Adam was the transgressor of the law, justice demanded that he, and none else, should answer for the sin and pay the penalty with his life. ¶ But Adam, in breaking the law, himself became subject to the curse, and being under the curse could not atone for, or undo, what he had done. Neither could his children, for they also were under the curse, and it required one who was not subject to the curse to atone for that original sin. Moreover, since we were all under the curse, we were also powerless to atone for our individual sins. ¶ It, therefore, became necessary for the Father to send his Only Begotten Son, who was free from sin, to atone for our sins as well as for Adam's transgression, which justice demanded should be done. He accordingly offered himself a sacrifice for sins, and through his death upon the cross took upon himself both Adam's transgression and our individual sins, thereby redeeming us from the fall, and from our sins, on condition of repentance. (Doctrines of Salvation, 1:126) TLDP:41-42

#### John
And ye know that he was manifested to take away our sins; and in him is no sin. (*John writes to the churches in Asia*) 1Jn.3:5

#### Anthon H. Lund
This earth was prepared for us; this was the school we had to pass through; and the Lord, seeing what would take place, prepared the Lamb "slain from the foundation of the world" [Rev.13:8] to atone for men, and regain all that was lost in the Fall. Jesus accepted of this mission. The sacrifice that was to be made for the human family could only be made by one who had not sinned Himself. It would have to be done by One who voluntarily offered to do this, in order that justice might be satisfied and mercy extended to the sinner. We learn in the revelations of the Lord that the fall extended to all, and that the grievous consequence of the fall was banishment from the presence of our Heavenly Father. The consequences of the fall were both temporal and spiritual. Jesus came; He made the sacrifice. He did it willingly. He was without blemish or fault. No sin was found in Him, and as such He was proper subject for the sacrifice. CR1912Apr:12

#### Paul
Seeing then that we have a great high priest, that is passed into the heavens, Jesus the Son of God, let us hold fast our profession. 15. For we have not an high priest which cannot be touched with the feeling of our infirmities; but was in all points tempted like as we are, yet without sin. (*Paul writes to the Jewish members of the Church, about A.D. 60*) Heb.4:14-15

---

### 40. Christ died that we might live: the Atonement was an act of pure love on the part of Jesus Christ, the Son of God, who laid down His life for us all.

#### Hugh B. Brown
The transgression of Adam, together with all of its consequences, was foreseen and the expiation provided for before the foundations of the world were laid. In that primeval council, of which the scriptures speak, when "all the sons of God shouted for joy" (see Job 38:7), Christ offered himself as a ransom, He was not coerced or required to make this sacrifice. His free agency was in no way infringed or trammeled. It was a freewill, love-inspired offer, which could have been withdrawn at any time. It was optional until the very time of his crucifixion. . . . ¶ Why should Christ have volunteered to make this sacrifice? What was the motive that inspired and sustained him from the

time of that council in heaven until the moment of his agonized cry, "It is finished"? (John 19:30) The answer to this question is two-fold: first, his undeviating devotion to his Father's will. He said: ". . . My meat is to do the will of him that sent me, and to finish his work," (Ibid. 4:34) ¶ Second was his supernal and all-embracing love for mankind, who, without his mediation, would have remained in the total gloom of desiring without hope throughout eternity. CR1962Apr:108; TLDP:43

### Nephi, son of Lehi

He doeth not anything save it be for the benefit of the world; for he loveth the world, even that he layeth down his own life that he may draw all men unto him. Wherefore, he commandeth none that they shall not partake of his salvation. . . . For he doeth that which is good among the children of men; (*The writings of Nephi, 559-545 B.C.*) 2Ne.26:24,33

### Marion G. Romney

If men are to be freed from the results of their own transgressions and brought back into the presence of God, they must be the beneficiaries of some expedient beyond themselves which will free them from the effect of their own sins. For this purpose was the atonement of Jesus Christ conceived and executed. This was the world's supreme act of charity, performed by Jesus out of his great love for us. He not only thereby met the demands of the law of justice—which would have left us forever marred by the effects of our own transgressions—but made effective the law of mercy, through which all men may be cleansed from their own sins. CR1982Apr:9

### Elder Joseph Fielding Smith

One of the greatest sins, both in magnitude and extent—for it enters into the lives of every one of us without exception to some degree—is the sin of ingratitude. When we violate a commandment, no matter how small and insignificant we may think it to be, we show our ingratitude to our Redeemer. It is impossible for us to comprehend the extent of his suffering when he carried the burden of the sins of the whole world, a punishment so severe that we are informed that blood came from the pores of his body, and this was before he was taken to the cross. The punishment of physical pain coming from the nails driven in his hands and feet, was not the greatest of his suffering, excruciating as that surely was. The greater suffering was the spiritual and mental anguish coming from the load of our transgressions which he carried. If we understood the extent of that suffering and his suffering on the cross, surely none of us

would wilfully be guilty of sin. We would not give way to the temptations, the gratification of unholy appetites and desires and Satan could find no place in our hearts. As it is, whenever we sin, we show our ingratitude and disregard of the suffering of the Son of God by and through which we shall rise from the dead and live forever. If we really understood and could feel even to a small degree, the love and gracious willingness on the part of Jesus Christ to suffer for our sins we would be willing to repent of all our transgressions and serve him. (The Restoration of All Things, p. 199) TLDP:44-45

**Related Witnesses:**

### Jesus,
#### *quoted by John*

Greater love hath no man than this, that a man lay down his life for his friends. (*Jesus discourses on perfect love*) John 15:13

### Nephi, son of Lehi

And he said unto me: Knowest thou the condescension of God? 17. And I said unto him: I know that he loveth his children; nevertheless, I do not know the meaning of all things. 18. And he said unto me: Behold, the virgin whom thou seest is the mother of the Son of God, after the manner of the flesh. 19. And it came to pass that I beheld that she was carried away in the Spirit; and after she had been carried away in the Spirit for the space of a time the angel spake unto me, saying: Look! 20. And I looked and beheld the virgin again, bearing a child in her arms. 21. And the angel said unto me: Behold the Lamb of God, yea, even the Son of the Eternal Father! Knowest thou the meaning of the tree which thy father saw? 22. And I answered him, saying: Yea, it is the love of God, which sheddeth itself abroad in the hearts of the children of men; wherefore, it is the most desirable above all things. (*Nephi in a vision sees the mother of the Son of God and learns the condescension of God, 600-592 B.C.*) 1Ne.11:16-22

---

41.  **The Atonement of Jesus Christ began in Gethsemane prior to His crucifixion.**

#### Elder Joseph Fielding Smith

We get into the habit of thinking, I suppose, that his great suffering was when he was nailed to the cross by his hands and his feet and was left there to suffer until he died. As excruciating as that pain was, that was not the greatest suffering he had to undergo, for in some way which I cannot understand, but which I accept on faith, and which you must accept on faith, he carried on his back the burden of the sins of the whole world . . . was our Savior and Redeemer of a fallen world, and so great was his suffering before he ever went to the cross we are informed, that blood oozed from the pores of his body, and he prayed to his Father that the cup might pass if it were possible, but not being possible he was willing to drink. CR1947-Oct:147-48; MPSG1988:66

### James E. Talmage

Christ's agony in the garden is unfathomable by the finite mind, both as to intensity and cause. The thought that He suffered through fear of death is untenable. Death to Him was preliminary to resurrection and triumphal return to the Father from whom He had come, and to a state of glory even beyond what He had before possessed; and, moreover, it was within His power to lay down His life voluntarily. He struggled and groaned under a burden such as no other being who has lived on earth might even conceive as possible. It was not physical pain, nor mental anguish alone, that caused Him to suffer such torture as to produce an extrusion of blood from every pore; but a spiritual agony of soul such as only God was capable of experiencing. No other man, however great his powers of physical or mental endurance, could have suffered so; for his human organism would have succumbed, and syncope would have produced unconsciousness and welcome oblivion. In that hour of anguish Christ met and overcame all the horrors that Satan, "the prince of this world" could inflict. The frightful struggle incident to the temptations immediately following the Lord's baptism was surpassed and overshadowed by this supreme contest with the powers of evil. ¶ In some manner, actual and terribly real though to man incomprehensible, the Savior took upon Himself the burden of the sins of mankind from Adam to the end of the world. Modern revelation assists us to a partial understanding of the awful experience. In March 1830, the glorified Lord, Jesus Christ, thus spake: "For behold, I, God, have suffered these things for all, that they might not suffer if they would repent, but if they would not repent, they must suffer even as I, which suffering caused myself, even God, the greatest of all, to tremble because of pain, and to bleed at every pore, and to suffer both body and spirit: and would that I might not drink the bitter cup and shrink—Nevertheless, glory be to the Father, and I partook and finished my preparations unto the children of men." [D&C 19:16-19] ¶ From the terrible conflict in Gethsemane, Christ

emerged a victor. Though in the dark tribulation of that fearful hour He had pleaded that the bitter cup be removed from His lips, the request, however oft repeated, was always conditional; the accomplishment of the Father's will was never lost sight of as the object of the Son's supreme desire. The further tragedy of the night, and the cruel inflictions that awaited Him on the morrow, to culminate in the frightful tortures of the cross, could not exceed the bitter anguish through which He had successfully passed. JTC:613; DCSM:38

### Jesus,
### *recorded in Matthew*

Then cometh Jesus with them unto a place called Gethsemane, and saith unto the disciples, Sit ye here, while I go and pray yonder. 37. And he took with him Peter and the two sons of Zebedee, and began to be sorrowful and very heavy. 38. Then saith he unto them, My soul is exceeding sorrowful, even unto death: tarry ye here, and watch with me. 39. And he went a little further, and fell on his face, and prayed, saying, O my Father, if it be possible, let this cup pass from me: nevertheless not as I will, but as thou wilt. 40. And he cometh unto the disciples, and findeth them asleep, and saith unto Peter, What, could ye not watch with me one hour? 41. Watch and pray, that ye enter not into temptation: the spirit indeed is willing, but the flesh is weak. 42. He went away again the second time, and prayed, saying, O my Father, if this cup may not pass away from me, except I drink it, thy will be done. 43. And he came and found them asleep again: for their eyes were heavy. 44. And he left them, and went away again, and prayed the third time, saying the same words. 45. Then cometh he to his disciples, and saith unto them, Sleep on now, and take your rest: behold, the hour is at hand, and the Son of man is betrayed into the hands of sinners. 46. Rise, let us be going: behold, he is at hand that doth betray me. (*Jesus prays in Gethsemane*) Matt.26:36-46

### Jesus,
### *recorded in Luke*

And he came out, and went, as he was wont, to the mount of Olives; and his disciples also followed him. 40. And when he was at the place, he said unto them, Pray that ye enter not into temptation. 41. And he was withdrawn from them about a stone's cast, and kneeled down, and prayed, 42. Saying, Father, if thou be willing, remove this cup from me: nevertheless not my will, but thine, be done. 43. And there appeared an angel unto him from heaven, strengthening him. 44. And being in an agony he prayed more earnestly: and his sweat was as it were great drops of blood falling down to the ground. (*Jesus suffers in Gethsemane*) Luke 22:39-44

**Bruce R. McConkie**

To this we add, if we interpret the holy word aright, that all of the anguish, all of the sorrow, and all of the suffering of Gethesemane recurred during the final three hours on the cross, the hours when darkness covered the land. Truly there was no sorrow like unto his sorrow, and no anguish and pain like unto that which bore in with such intensity upon him. (The Millennial Messiah, 4:323 n.22) DGSM:25

**President John Taylor**

The suffering of the Son of God was not simply the suffering of personal death; for in assuming the position that He did in making an atonement for the sins of the world He bore the weight, the responsibility, and the burden of the sins of all men, which, to us, is incomprehensible. . . . ¶ Groaning beneath this concentrated load, this intense, incomprehensible pressure, this terrible exaction of Divine justice, from which feeble humanity shrank, and through the agony thus experienced sweating great drops of blood He was led to exclaim, "Father, if it be possible, let this cup pass from me." He had wrestled with the superincumbent load in the wilderness. He had struggled against the powers of darkness that had been let loose upon him there; placed below all things, His mind surcharged with aging and pain, lonely and apparently helpless and forsaken, in his agony the blood oozed from His pores. Thus rejected by His own, attacked by the powers of darkness, and seemingly forsaken by His God, on the cross He bowed beneath the accumulated loan, and cried out in anguish, "My God, my God, why hast thou forsaken me!" When death approached to relieve Him from His horrible position, a ray of hope appeared through the abyss of darkness with which He had been surrounded, and in a spasm of relief, seeing the bright future beyond, He said, "It is finished! Father, into thy hands I commend my spirit." (The Mediation and Atonement, pp. 150-51) TLDP:44

**Related Witnesses:**

**Joseph Smith,**

*receiving the Word of the Lord*

For behold, I, God, have suffered these things for all, that they might not suffer if they would repent; 17. But if they would not repent they must suffer even as I; 18. Which suffering caused myself, even God, the greatest of all, to tremble because of pain, and to bleed at every pore, and to suffer both body and spirit—and would that I might not drink

the bitter cup, and shrink— 19. Nevertheless, glory be to the Father, and I partook and finished my preparations unto the children of men. (*Christ announces himself in a revelation to Joseph, March 1830*) D&C 19:16-19

---

42. **The Savior descended below all things; He bore the weight, the responsibility, and the burden of taking upon Himself the sins of all, that He might raise Himself and others above all things.**

**President John Taylor**

In the economy of God pertaining to the salvation of the human family, we are told in the Scriptures that it was necessary that Christ should descend below all things, that He might be raised above all things; as stated above, He had to "become subject to man in the flesh." It was further necessary that He should descend below all things, in order that He might raise others above all things; for if He could not raise Himself and be exalted through those principles brought about by the atonement, He could not raise others; He could not do for others what He could not do for Himself, and hence it was necessary for Him to descend below all things, that by and through the same power that He obtained His exaltation, they also, through His atonement, expiation and intercession, might be raised to the same power with Him; and, as He was the Son of God, that they might also be the adopted sons of God. (The Mediation and Atonement, pp. 144-45) TLDP:40

**President John Taylor**

As a God, He [Christ] descended below all things, and made Himself subject to man in man's fallen condition; as a man, He grappled with all the circumstances incident to His sufferings in the world. Anointed, indeed, with the oil of gladness above His fellows, He struggled with and overcame the powers of men and devils, of earth and hell combined; and aided by this superior power of the Godhead, He vanquished death, hell and the grave, and arose triumphant as the Son of God, the very eternal Father, the Messiah, the Prince of peace, the Redeemer, the Savior of the world; having finished and completed the work pertaining to the atonement, which His Father had given Him to do as the Son of God and the Son of Man. As the Son of Man, He endured all that it was possible for flesh and blood to endure; as the Son of God He triumphed over all, and forever ascended to the right hand of God, to further carry out the designs of Jehovah pertaining to the world and to the human family. (The Mediation and Atonement, pp. 150-51) TLDP:44

**Joseph Smith,**
*receiving the Word of the Lord*

The Son of Man hath descended below them all. Art thou greater than he? (*Revelation received in Liberty Jail, March 1839*) D&C 122:8

**Joseph Smith**

He that ascended up on high, as also he descended below all things, in that he comprehended all things, that he might be in all and through all things, the light of truth; (*Revelation received Dec. 27/28, 1832; the Lord declares all things are controlled and governed by the light of Christ*) D&C 88:6

**Jacob, brother of Nephi,**
*quoted by Nephi*

And he cometh into the world that he may save all men if they will hearken unto his voice; for behold, he suffereth the pains of all men, yea, the pains of every living creature, both men, women, and children, who belong to the family of Adam. (*Jacob teaches the doctrine of the Atonement to the people of Nephi, 559-545 B.C.*) 2Ne.9:21

**Related Witnesses:**

**Joseph Smith,**
*receiving the Word of the Lord*

If thou art called to pass through tribulations; if thou art in perils among false brethren; if thou art in perils among robbers; if thou art in perils by land or by sea; 6. If thou art accused with all manner of false accusations; if thine enemies fall upon thee; if they tear thee from the society of thy father and mother and brethren and sister; and if with a drawn sword thine enemies tear thee from the bosom of thy wife, and of thine offspring, and thine elder son, although but six years of age, shall cling to thy garments, and shall say, My father, my father, why can't you stay with us? O, my father, what are the men going to do with you? and if then he shall be thrust from thee by the sword, and thou be dragged to prison, and thine enemies prowl around thee like wolves for the blood of the lamb; 7. And if thou shouldst be cast into the pit, or into the hands of murderers, and the sentence of death passed upon thee; if thou be cast into the deep; if the billowing surge conspire against thee; if fierce winds become thine enemy; if the heavens gather blackness, and all the elements combine to hedge up the way; and above all, if the very jaws of hell shall gape open the mouth wide after thee, know thou, my son, that all these things shall give thee experience, and shall be for thy good. 8. The Son of Man hath descended below them all. Art thou greater than he?

(*Epistle to the Church, Mar. 1839; the Lord comforts Joseph that his adversities are for his experience*) D&C 122:5-8);HC3:301

---

**43.** Christ suffered emotional and spiritual agony, He suffered in both body and spirit, beyond that which any mortal could endure, in offering Himself as a ransom for us all.

**James E. Talmage**

Christ's agony in the garden is unfathomable by the finite mind, both as to intensity and cause. The thought that He suffered through fear of death is untenable. Death to Him was preliminary to resurrection and triumphal return to the Father from whom He had come, and to a state of glory even beyond what He had before possessed; and, moreover, it was within His power to lay down His life voluntarily. He struggled and groaned under a burden such as no other being who has lived on earth might even conceive as possible. It was not physical pain, nor mental anguish alone, that caused Him to suffer such torture as to produce an extrusion of blood from every pore; but a spiritual agony of soul such as only God was capable of experiencing. No other man, however great his powers of physical or mental endurance, could have suffered so; for his human organism would have succumbed, and syncope would have produced unconsciousness and welcome oblivion. In that hour of anguish Christ met and overcame all the horrors that Satan, "the prince of this world" could inflict. JTC:613

**Joseph Smith,**
*receiving the Word of the Lord*

For behold, I, God, have suffered these things for all, that they might not suffer if they would repent; 17. But if they would not repent they must suffer even as I; 18. Which suffering caused myself, even God, the greatest of all, to tremble because of pain, and to bleed at every pore, and to suffer both body and spirit—and would that I might not drink the bitter cup, and shrink—. . . . 20. Wherefore, I command you again to repent, lest I humble you with my almighty power; and that you confess your sins, lest you suffer these punishments of which I have spoken, of which in the smallest, yea, even in the least degree you have tasted at the time I withdrew my Spirit. (*A commandment of God to Martin Harris received March 1830*) D&C 19:16-18,20

**Elder Joseph Fielding Smith**

It is impossible for us to comprehend the extent of his suffering when he carried the burden of the sins of the whole world, a punishment so severe that we are informed that blood came from the pores of his body, and this was before he was taken to the cross. The punishment of physical pain coming from the nails driven in his hands and feet, was not the greatest of his suffering, excruciating as that surely was. The greater suffering was the spiritual and mental anguish coming from the load of our transgressions which he carried. If we understood the extent of that suffering and his suffering on the cross, surely none of us would wilfully be guilty of sin. We would not give way to the temptations, the gratification of unholy appetites and desires and Satan could find no place in our hearts. (The Restoration of All Things, p. 199) TLDP:44-45

**Elder Joseph Fielding Smith**

We cannot comprehend the great suffering that the Lord had to take upon himself to bring to pass this redemption from death and from sin. . . . ¶ . . . [S]o great was his suffering before he ever went to the cross we are informed, that blood oozed from the pores of his body, and he prayed to his Father that the cup might pass if it were possible, but not being possible he was willing to drink. CR1947-Oct:147-48; MPSG88:68; DCSM:37-38

**King Benjamin,**
*quoted by Mormon*

And lo, he shall suffer temptations, and pain of body, hunger, thirst, and fatigue, even more than man can suffer, except it be unto death; for behold, blood cometh from every pore, so great shall be his anguish for the wickedness and the abominations of his people. (*King Benjamin addresses his people about 124 B.C.; the Lord Omnipotent shall minister among men in a tabernacle of clay*) Mosiah 3:7

**Marion G. Romney**

The suffering he undertook to endure, and which he did endure, equaled the combined suffering of all men. CR1969Oct:57

**Related Witnesses:**

**Jesus,**
*recorded in Luke*

And being in an agony he prayed more earnestly: and his sweat was as it were great drops of blood falling down to the ground. (*Jesus suffers in Gethsemane*) Luke 22:44

**Nephi, son of Lehi**

And all these things must surely come, saith the prophet Zenos. And the rocks of the earth must rend; and because of the groanings of the earth, many of the kings of the isles of the sea shall be wrought upon by the Spirit of God, to exclaim: The God of nature suffers. (*Nephi writes the prophecies of the prophet Zenos, between 588 and 570 B.C.*) 1Ne.19:12

**Jesus,**
*recorded in Matthew*

And about the ninth hour Jesus cried with a loud voice, saying, Eli, Eli, lama sabachthani? that is to say, My God, my God, why hast thou forsaken me? (*Jesus Christ is crucified*) Matt.27:46

---

**44. Christ had the power to lay down His life and the power to take it up again, but no one could take His life from Him.**

**Jesus,**
*quoted by John*

Therefore doth my Father love me, because I lay down my life, that I might take it again. 18. No man taketh it from me, but I lay it down of myself. I have power to lay it down, and I have power to take it again. This commandment have I received of my Father. (*John's record of the words of the Savior*) John 10:17-18

**Jesus,**
*quoted by John*

For as the Father hath life in himself; so hath he given to the Son to have life in himself; . . . (*Jesus answers the Jews who sought to kill him* ) John 5:26

**Marion G. Romney**

No one could have taken his life had he not been willing to give it. . . . It was, therefore, through acts of infinite love and mercy that he vicariously paid the debt of the broken law and satisfied the demands of justice. CR1982Apr:8-9; MPSG88:66

**J. Reuben Clark, Jr.**

So as I conceive it, we must stand adamant for the doctrine of the atonement of Jesus the Christ, for the divinity of his conception, for his sinless life, and for, shall I say, the divinity of his death, his voluntary surrender of life. He was not killed; he gave up his life. . . . ¶ It is our mission, perhaps the most fundamental purpose of our work, to bear constant testimony of Jesus the Christ. We must never permit to enter into our thoughts and certainly not into our teachings the idea that he was merely a great teacher, a great philosopher, the builder of a great system of ethics. It is our duty, day after day, year in and year out, always to declare that Jesus of Nazareth was the Christ who brought redemption to the world and to all the inhabitants thereof. CR1955Oct:23-24

**Lehi,**
*quoted by his son, Nephi*

Wherefore, how great the importance to make these things known unto the inhabitants of the earth, that they may know that there is no flesh that can dwell in the presence of God, save it be through the merits, and mercy, and grace of the Holy Messiah, who layeth down his life according to the flesh, and taketh it again by the power of the Spirit, that he may bring to pass the resurrection of the dead, being the first that should rise. (*Lehi teaches his son, Jacob, about the redemption of man from the fall of Adam, between 588-570 B.C.*) 2Ne.2:8

### Elder Joseph Fielding Smith

Jesus was the only person who ever came into this world who had power over death, and having that great power, by the shedding of his blood on the cross, he could redeem us and get the power of the resurrection. After he came forth from the tomb, he had all power to call every other person forth from the grave. And after he came forth, on the third day after his crucifixion he opened the graves of the righteous saints who had lived from the days of Adam to the time of his crucifixion. (Doctrines of Salvation, 2:269) DGSM:88

### Related Witnesses:

#### Paul

For our conversation is in heaven; from whence also we look for the Saviour, the Lord Jesus Christ: 21. Who shall change our vile body, that it may be fashioned like unto his glorious body, according to the working whereby he is able even to subdue all things unto himself. (*Letter from Rome to the Church at Philippi in Macedonia*) Philip.3:20-21

### James E. Talmage

Christ's agony in the garden is unfathomable by the finite mind, both as to intensity and cause. The thought that He suffered through fear of death is untenable. Death to Him was preliminary to resurrection and triumphal return to the Father from whom He had come, and to a state of glory even beyond what He had before possessed; and, moreover, it was within His power to lay down His life voluntarily. JTC:613

---

45.  Were it not for the Atonement, mercy could not be extended to sinners who, though they might repent, would nevertheless be compelled to suffer the rigorous demands of justice.

### Boyd K. Packer,
#### *also quoting Paul*

Each of us lives on a kind of spiritual credit. One day the account will be closed, a settlement demanded. However casually we may view it now, when that day comes and the foreclosure is imminent, we will look around in restless agony for someone, anyone, to help us. ¶ And, by eternal law, mercy cannot be extended save there be one who is both willing and able to assume our debt and pay the price and arrange the terms for our redemption. ¶ Unless there is a mediator, unless we have a friend, the full weight of justice untempered, unsympathetic, must, positively must fall on us. The full recompense for every transgression, however minor or however deep, will be exacted from us to the uttermost farthing. ¶ But know this: Truth, glorious truth, proclaims there is such a Mediator. ¶ "For there is one God, and one mediator between God and men, the man Christ Jesus." (1Tim.2:5) ¶ Through Him mercy can be fully extended to each of us without offending the eternal law of justice. ¶ This truth is the very root of Christian doctrine. You may know much about the gospel as it branches out from there, but if you only know the branches and those branches do not touch that root, if they have been cut free from that truth, there will be no life nor substance nor redemption in them. CR1977Apr:80

### Alma, the younger,
#### *quoted by Mormon*

Therefore, according to justice, the plan of redemption could not be brought about, only on conditions of repentance of men in this probationary state, yea, this preparatory state; for except it were for these conditions, mercy could not take effect except it should destroy the work of justice. Now the work of justice could not be destroyed; if so, God would cease to be God. 14. And thus we see that all mankind were fallen, and they were in the grasp of justice; yea, the justice of God, which consigned them forever to be cut off from his presence. 15. And now, the plan of mercy could not be brought about except an atonement should be made; therefore God himself atoneth for the sins of the world, to bring about the plan of mercy, to appease the demands of justice, that God might be a perfect, just God, and a merciful God also. . . . 22. But there is a law given, and a punishment affixed, and a repentance granted; which repentance mercy claimeth; otherwise, justice claimeth the creature and executeth the law, and the law inflicteth the punishment; if not so, the works of justice would be destroyed, and God would cease to be God. 23. But God ceaseth not to be God, and mercy claimeth the penitent, and mercy cometh because of the atonement; and the atonement bringeth to pass the resurrection of the dead; and the resurrection of the dead bringeth back men into the presence of God; and thus they are restored into his presence, to be judged according to their works, according to the law and justice. 24. For behold, justice exerciseth all his demands, and also mercy claimeth all which is her own; and thus, none but the truly penitent are saved. 25. What, do ye suppose that mercy can rob justice? I say unto you, Nay; not one whit. If so, God would cease to be God. (*Alma speaks to his son Corianton, concerning the resurrection of the dead, about 73 B.C.*) Alma 42:13-15,22-25

### Amulek,
*quoted by Mormon*

And behold, this is the whole meaning of the law, every whit pointing to that great and last sacrifice; and that great and last sacrifice will be the Son of God, yea, infinite and eternal. 15. And thus he shall bring salvation to all those who shall believe on his name; this being the intent of this last sacrifice, to bring about the bowels of mercy, which overpowereth justice, and bringeth about means unto men that they may have faith unto repentance. 16. And thus mercy can satisfy the demands of justice, and encircles them in the arms of safety, while he that exercises no faith unto repentance is exposed to the whole law of the demands of justice; therefore only unto him that has faith unto repentance is brought about the great and eternal plan of redemption. (*Amulek teaches the people about the atonement of Christ, 74 B.C.*) Alma 34:14-16

### Abinadi,
*quoted by Mormon*

Yea, even so he shall be led, crucified, and slain, the flesh becoming subject even unto death, the will of the Son being swallowed up in the will of the Father. 8. And thus God breaketh the bands of death, having gained the victory over death; giving the Son power to make intercession for the children of men— 9. Having ascended into heaven, having the bowels of mercy; being filled with compassion towards the children of men; standing betwixt them and justice; having broken the bands of death, taken upon himself their iniquity and their transgressions, having redeemed them, and satisfied the demands of justice. (*Abinadi preaches to King Noah and his people of the intercession of Christ, about 148 B.C.*) Mosiah 15:7-9

**Related Witnesses:**
### Mormon

Wherefore, my beloved brethren, have miracles ceased because Christ hath ascended into heaven, and hath sat down on the right hand of God, to claim of the Father his rights of mercy which he hath upon the children of men? 28. For he hath answered the ends of the law, and he claimeth all those who have faith in him; and they who have faith in him will cleave unto every good thing; wherefore he advocateth the cause of the children of men; and he dwelleth eternally in the heavens. (*Mormon preaches in the synagogue, prior to A.D. 384*) Moro.7:27-28

46. **The Atonement of Christ makes possible the forgiveness of sins for the repentant person.**

### Joseph Smith,
*receiving the Word of the Lord*

For behold, I, God, have suffered these things for all, that they might not suffer if they would repent; (*A commandment of God for Martin Harris received by revelation, March 1830*) D&C 19:16

### Elder Spencer W. Kimball

Every normal individual is responsible for the sins he commits, and would be similarly liable to the punishment attached to those broken laws. However, Christ's death on the cross offers us exemption from the eternal punishment for most sins. He took upon himself the punishment for the sins of the world, with the understanding that those who repent and come unto him will be forgiven of their sins and freed from the punishment. (The Miracle of Forgiveness, p. 133) MPSG88:67

### Lehi,
*quoted by his son Nephi*

Wherefore, redemption cometh in and through the Holy Messiah; for he is full of grace and truth. 7. Behold, he offereth himself a sacrifice for sin, to answer the ends of the law, unto all those who have a broken heart and a contrite spirit; and unto none else can the ends of the law be answered. (*Lehi teaches his son, Jacob, about the redemption of man from the fall of Adam, between 588-570 B.C.*) 2Ne.2:6-7

### King Benjamin,
*quoted by Mormon*

For behold, and also his blood atoneth for the sins of those who have fallen by the transgression of Adam, who have died not knowing the will of God concerning them, or who have ignorantly sinned. 12. But wo, wo unto him who knoweth that he rebelleth against God! For salvation cometh to none such except it be through repentance and faith on the Lord Jesus Christ. (*King Benjamin to his people, about 124 B.C.*) Mosiah 3:11-12

### James E. Talmage

But besides this universal application of the

atonement, whereby all men are redeemed from the effects of Adam's transgression both with respect to the death of the body and inherited sin, there is application of the same great sacrifice as a means of propitiation for individual sins through the faith and good works of the sinner. This twofold effect of the atonement is implied in the article of our faith now under consideration. [article 3] The first effect is to secure to all mankind alike, exemption from the penalty of the fall, thus providing a plan of *General Salvation*. The second effect is to open a way for *Individual Salvation* whereby mankind may secure remission of personal sins . . . conditioned on individual compliance with prescribed requirements—"obedience to the laws and ordinances of the Gospel." AF:78-79

---

**47. Redemption from *spiritual* death through Christ's atonement is conditioned on obedience to the laws and ordinances of the gospel.**

**Joseph Smith**

We believe that through the Atonement of Christ, all mankind may be saved, by obedience to the laws and ordinances of the Gospel. (*The third of the thirteen Articles of Faith; letter to John Wentworth, March 1, 1842*) AofF:3

**President Joseph F. Smith**

[T]hrough his atonement, and by obedience to the principles of the gospel, mankind might be saved. (*Vision to President Smith regarding the Savior's visit to the spirits of the dead, Oct. 3, 1918*) D&C 138:4

**James E. Talmage**

The first effect [of the atonement] is to secure to all mankind alike, exemption from the penalty of the fall, thus providing a plan of *General Salvation*. The second effect is to open a way for *Individual Salvation* whereby mankind may secure remission of personal sins . . . conditioned on individual compliance with prescribed requirements—"obedience to the laws and ordinances of the Gospel." AF:78-79

**Paul**

And being made perfect, he became the author of eternal salvation unto all them that obey him; (*Paul writes to the Jewish members of the Church, about A.D. 60*) Heb.5:9

**Marion G. Romney**

There is another phase of the atonement which makes me love the Savior even more, and fills my soul with gratitude beyond expression. . . . In addition to atoning for Adam's transgression, thereby bringing about the resurrection, the

Savior by his suffering paid the debt for my personal sins. He paid the debt for your personal sins and for the personal sins of every living soul that ever dwelt upon the earth. But this he did conditionally. ¶ The benefits of this suffering for our individual transgressions will not come to us unconditionally in the same sense that the resurrection will come, regardless of what we do. If we partake of the blessings of the atonement as far as our individual transgressions are concerned, we must obey the law. CR1953Oct:35; MGSP:10

**Jacob, brother of Nephi,**
*quoted by Nephi*

And he cometh into the world that he may save all men if they will hearken unto his voice; for behold, he suffereth the pains of all men, yea, the pains of every living creature, both men, women, and children, who belong to the family of Adam. (*Jacob teaches the doctrine of the Atonement to the people of Nephi, 559-545 B.C.*) 2Ne.9:21

**Amulek,**
*quoted by Mormon*

And he shall come into the world to redeem his people; and he shall take upon him the transgressions of those who believe on his name; and these are they that shall have eternal life, and salvation cometh to none else. 41. Therefore the wicked remain as though there had been no redemption made, except it be the loosing of the bands of death; for behold, the day cometh that all shall rise from the dead and stand before God, and be judged according to their works. (*Amulek answers the lawyer Zeezrom, foretelling Christ's redemption of man and the final judgment, about 82 B.C.*) Alma 11:40-41

**Related Witnesses:**

**King Benjamin,**
*quoted by Mormon*

For behold, and also his blood atoneth for the sins of those who have fallen by the transgression of Adam, who have died not knowing the will of God concerning them, or who have ignorantly sinned. 12. But wo, wo unto him who knoweth not that he rebelleth against God! For salvation cometh to none such except it be through repentance and faith on the Lord Jesus Christ. (*King Benjamin to his people, about 124 B.C.*) Mosiah 3:11-12

**Jesus,**
*quoted by John*

Jesus said unto her, I am the resurrection, and the life: he that believeth in me, though he were dead, yet shall he live: 26. And whosoever liveth and believeth in me shall never die. Believest thou this? (*Jesus responds to Martha prior to raising her brother Lazarus from the dead)* John 11:25-26

**Joseph Smith,**
*receiving the Word of the Lord*

Wherefore, it came to pass that the devil tempted Adam, and he partook of the forbidden fruit and transgressed the commandment, wherein he became subject to the will of the devil, because he yielded unto temptation. 41. Wherefore, I, the Lord God, caused that he should be cast out from the Garden of Eden, from my presence, because of his transgression, wherein he became spiritually dead, which is the first death, even that same death which is the last death, which is spiritual, which shall be pronounced upon the wicked when I shall say: Depart, ye cursed. 42. But, behold, I say unto you that I, the Lord God, gave unto Adam and unto his seed, that they should not die as to the temporal death, until I, the Lord God, should send forth angels to declare unto them repentance and redemption, through faith on the name of mine Only Begotten Son. 43. And thus did I, the Lord God, appoint unto man the days of his probation—that by his natural death he might be raised in immortality unto eternal life, even as many as would believe; *(Revelation in presence of six elders, Sept. 1830)* D&C 29:40-43

**Joseph Smith,**
*quoted by Elder Joseph Fielding Smith*

I . . . spoke to the people, showing them that to get salvation we must not only do some things, but everything which God has commanded. Men may preach and practice everything except those things which God commands us to do, and will be damned at last. We may tithe mint and rue, and all manner of herbs, and still not obey and teach others to obey God in just what He tells us to do. It mattereth not whether the principle is popular or unpopular, I will always maintain a true principle, even if I stand alone in it. *(In Nauvoo, Ill., Feb. 21, 1844)* TPJS:332; DGSM:48

**Jacob, brother of Nephi,**
*quoted by Nephi*

Therefore, cheer up your hearts, and remember that ye are free to act for yourselves—to choose the way of everlasting death or the way of eternal life. 24. Wherefore, my beloved brethren, reconcile yourselves to the will of God, and not to the will of the devil and the flesh; and remember, after ye are reconciled unto God, that it is only in and through the grace of God that ye are saved. 25. Wherefore, may God raise you from death by the power of the resurrection, and also from everlasting death by the power of the atonement, that ye may be received into the eternal kingdom of God, that ye may praise him through grace divine. Amen. *(Jacob to the people of Nephi, 559-545 B.C.)* 2Ne.10:23-25

**Joseph Smith,**
*translating the Book of Moses*

For behold, this is my work and my glory—to bring to pass the immortality and eternal life of man. *(The Lord talks to Moses face to face)* Moses 1:39

**Job**

For I know that my redeemer liveth, and that he shall stand at the latter day upon the earth: 26. And though after my skin worms destroy this body, yet in my flesh shall I see God: 27. Whom I shall see for myself, and mine eyes shall behold, and not another; though my reins be consumed within me. *(Job prophecies of his own resurrection and exaltation)* Job 19:25-27

---

48. **Unrepentant persons cannot receive the full benefit of the Atonement; they will be resurrected but they must suffer for their sins.**

**Amulek,**
*quoted by Mormon*

And I say unto you again that he cannot save them in their sins; for I cannot deny his word, and he hath said that no unclean thing can inherit the kingdom of heaven; therefore, how can ye be saved, except ye inherit the kingdom of heaven? Therefore, ye cannot be saved in your sins. . . . 41. Therefore the wicked remain as though there had been no redemption made, except it be the loosing of the bands of death; for behold, the day cometh that all shall rise from the dead and stand before God, and be judged according to their works. *(Amulek contends with the lawyer Zeezrom, about 82 B.C.)* Alma 11:37,41

**Elder Joseph Fielding Smith**

He [the Only Begotten Son] accordingly offered himself a sacrifice for sins, and through his death upon the cross took upon himself both Adam's transgression and our individual sins, thereby redeeming us from the fall, and from our sins, on condition of repentance. (Doctrines of Salvation, 1:126) TLDP:41-42

**James E. Talmage**

The effect of Christ's Atonement upon the race is twofold: ¶ 1. The eventual resurrection of all men, whether righteous or wicked. This constitutes Redemption from the Fall, and, since the Fall came through individual transgression, in all justice relief therefrom must be made universal and unconditional. Thus we read:

"Therefore as by the offence of one judgment came upon all men to condemnation: even so by the righteousness of one the free gift came upon all men unto justification of life" (Romans 5:18). ¶ 2. The providing of a means whereby reparation may be made and forgiveness be obtained for individual sin. This constitutes Salvation and is made available to all through Obedience to the laws and ordinances of the Gospel. ¶ Between redemption from the power of death and salvation in the Kingdom of Heaven there is a vital difference. Man alone cannot save himself: Christ alone cannot save him. The plan of salvation is co-operative. The Atonement effected by the Lord Jesus Christ has opened the way; it is left to every man to enter therein and be saved or to turn aside and forfeit salvation. God will force no man either into heaven or into hell. ("The Co-operative Plan of Salvation," IE1917Jun:705) TLDP:37

**Related Witnesses:**

### King Benjamin,
*quoted by Mormon*

For the natural man is an enemy to God, and has been from the fall of Adam, and will be, forever and ever, unless he yields to the enticings of the Holy Spirit, and putteth off the natural man and becometh a saint through the atonement of Christ the Lord, and becometh as a child, submissive, meek, humble, patient, full of love, willing to submit to all things which the Lord seeth fit to inflict upon him, even as a child doth submit to his father. (*King Benjamin addresses his people, about 124 B.C.*) Mosiah 3:19

### Elder Joseph F. Smith

When we commit sin, it is necessary that we repent of it and make restitution as far as lies our power. When we cannot make restitution for the wrong we have done, then we must apply for the grace and mercy of God to cleanse us from the iniquity. ¶ Men cannot forgive their own sins, they cannot cleanse themselves from the consequences of their sins. Men can stop sinning and can do right in the future, and so far their acts are acceptable before the Lord and worthy of consideration. But who shall repair the wrongs they have done to themselves and to others, which it seems impossible for them to repair themselves? By the atonement of Jesus Christ the sins of the repentant shall be washed away; though they can be crimson they shall be made white as wool. This is the promise given to you. We who have not paid our tithing in the past, and are therefore under obligations to the Lord, which we are not in position to discharge,

the Lord requires that no longer at our hands, but will forgive us for the past if we will observe this law honestly in the future. That is generous and kind, and I feel grateful for it. CR1899Oct:41

### Joseph Smith,
*receiving the Word of the Lord*

Therefore I command you to repent—repent, lest I smite you by the rod of my mouth, and by my wrath, and by my anger, and your sufferings be sore—how sore you know not, how exquisite you know not, yea, how hard to bear you know not. 16. For behold, I, God, have suffered these things for all, that they might not suffer if they would repent; 17. But if they would not repent they must suffer even as I; 18. Which suffering caused myself, even God, the greatest of all, to tremble because of pain, and to bleed at every pore, and to suffer both body and spirit—and would that I might not drink the bitter cup, and shrink— 19. Nevertheless, glory be to the Father, and I partook and finished my preparations unto the children of men. 20. Wherefore, I command you again to repent, lest I humble you with my almighty power; and that you confess your sins, lest you suffer these punishments of which I have spoken, of which in the smallest, yea, even in the least degree you have tasted at the time I withdrew my Spirit. (*A commandment of God for Martin Harris given by revelation March 1830*) D&C 19:15-20

---

**HYMNS Written by Prophets
Applicable to this Topic**

### Gordon B. Hinckley
*My Redeemer Lives*
HYMNS:135

I know that my Redeemer lives,
Triumphant Savior, Son of God,
Victorious over pain and death,
My King, my Leader, and my Lord.

He lives, my one sure rock of faith,
The one bright hope of men on earth,
The beacon to a better way,
The light beyond the veil of death.

Oh, give me thy sweet Spirit still,
The peace that comes alone from thee,
The faith to walk the lonely road
That leads to thine eternity.

### Bruce R. McConkie
*I Believe in Christ*
HYMNS:134

I believe in Christ; he is my King!
With all my heart to him I'll sing;
I'll raise my voice in praise and joy,
In grand amens my tongue employ.
I believe in Christ; he is God's Son.
On earth to dwell his soul did come.
He healed the sick; the dead he raised.
Good works were his; his name be praised.

I believe in Christ; oh, blessed name!
As Mary's Son he came to reign
'Mid mortal men, his earthly kin,
To save them from the woes of sin.
I believe in Christ, who marked the path,
Who did gain all his Father hath,
Who said to men: "Come, follow me,
That ye, my friends, with God may be."

I believe in Christ—my Lord, my God!
My feet he plants on gospel sod.
I'll worship him with all my might;
He is the source of truth and light.
I believe in Christ; he ransoms me.
From Satan's grasp he sets me free,
And I shall live with joy and love
In his eternal courts above.

I believe in Christ; he stands supreme!
From him I'll gain my fondest dream;
And while I strive through grief and pain,
His voice is heard: "Ye shall obtain."
I believe in Christ; so come what may,
With him I'll stand in that great day
When on this earth he comes again
To rule among the sons of men.

### John A. Widtsoe
*How Long, O Lord Most Holy*
HYMNS:126

How long, O Lord most holy and true,
Shall shadowed hope our joy delay?
Our hearts confess, our souls believe
Thy truth, thy truth, thy light,
    thy will, thy way!

Thy truth has made our prison bright;
Thy light has dimmed the dying past.
We bend beneath thy loving will
And seek thy onward, onward path at last.

Eternal Father, gentle Judge!
Speed on the day, redemption's hour.
Set up thy kingdom; from thy house
Unlock for us, for us the prison tow'r.

From grim confusion's awful depth
The wail of hosts, faith's urgent plea:
Release our anguished, weary souls;
Swing wide, swing wide the gates,
    and set us free!

### Elder Joseph Fielding Smith
*Does the Journey Seem Long?*
HYMNS:127

Does the journey seem long,
The path rugged and steep?
Are there briars and thorns on the way?
Do sharp stones cut your feet
As you struggle to rise
To the heights thru the heat of the day?

Is your heart faint and sad,
Your soul weary within,
As you toil 'neath your burden of care?
Does the load heavy seem
You are forced now to lift?
Is there no one your burden to share?

Let your heart be not faint
Now the journey's begun;
There is One who still beckons to you.
So look upward in joy
And take hold of his hand;
He will lead you to heights that are new—

A land holy and pure,
Where all trouble doth end,
And your life shall be free from all sin,
Where no tears shall be shed,
For no sorrows remain.
Take his hand and with him enter in.

# List of Doctrines

## BAPTISM

*Doctrines Located in This Topic*

49. Baptism is required for all persons (who are capable of repentance) for entrance into the kingdom of God.

50. Baptism is necessary before a person can receive the gift of the Holy Ghost.

51. Baptism is required of children only when they arrive at the age of accountability—when they are capable of repentance.

52. Only those who have truly repented may be baptized.

53. Baptism is an ordinance of the gospel entered into with a covenant.

54. The covenant of baptism is a solemn promise that we are willing to take upon us the name of Jesus Christ and keep His commandments, with a determination to serve Him to the end.

55. The specific form and words of the baptismal ordinance have been prescribed by revelation from the Lord.

56. The person being baptized shall be immersed in water.

57. Baptism by immersion in water symbolizes the death, burial, and resurrection of Christ.

58. Baptism is a new birth; it is symbolic of our new life in the kingdom of God.

59. Baptism in connection with the gift of the Holy Ghost is a cleanser and a purifier.

60. Baptism was practiced in the former ages of the world, beginning with Adam.

*Doctrines on BAPTISM Located in Other Topics*

73. Little children have no need of repentance or baptism.

110. Baptism is an everlasting covenant between God and a new member of His Church.

132. We are to perform vicarious baptisms for the dead.

137. To merit the gift of eternal life in the celestial kingdom, we must be baptized and receive the gift of the Holy Ghost, render obedience to the laws and ordinances of the gospel, and endure to the end.

213. Parents are commanded to teach their children by the time they are eight years old to understand the doctrines of faith, repentance, and baptism.

296. The first principles and ordinances of the gospel are faith in the Lord Jesus Christ, repentance, baptism by immersion, and the laying on of hands for the gift of the Holy Ghost.

316. The gift of the Holy Ghost is bestowed on those who have repented of their sins and have been properly baptized.

# BAPTISM

49. Baptism is required for all persons (who are capable of repentance) for entrance into the kingdom of God.

### Jesus,
#### *quoted by John*

Jesus answered and said unto him, Verily, verily, I say unto thee, Except a man be born again, he cannot see the kingdom of God. 4. Nicodemus saith unto him, How can a man be born when he is old? can he enter the second time into his mother's womb, and be born? 5. Jesus answered, Verily, verily, I say unto thee, Except a man be born of water and of the Spirit, he cannot enter into the kingdom of God. (*Jesus tells Nicodemus men must be born again*) John 3:3-5

### Joseph Smith,
#### *quoted by Elder Joseph Fielding Smith*

Except a man be born again he cannot see the kingdom of God. Nicodemus saith unto him, How can a man be born when he is old? can he enter the second time into his mother's womb, and be born? — Jesus answered, Verily, verily, I say unto thee, Except a man be born of water, and of the Spirit, he cannot enter into the kingdom of God. This strong and positive answer of Jesus, as to water baptism, settles the question: If God is the same yesterday, today, and forever: it is no wonder he is so positive in the great declaration: He that believes and is baptized shall be saved, and he that believes not shall be damned! There was no other name given under heaven, nor no other ordinance admitted, whereby men could be saved: No wonder the Apostle said, being "buried with him in baptism," ye shall rise from the dead! No wonder Paul had to arise and be baptized and wash away his sins: No wonder the angel told good old Cornelius that he must send for Peter to learn how to be saved: Peter could baptize, and angels could not, so long as there were legal officers in the flesh holding the keys of the kingdom, or the authority of the priesthood. (*Editorial in Times and Seasons, Sept. 1, 1842*) TPJS:264-65

### Joseph Smith,
#### *receiving the Word of the Lord*

Verily, verily, I say unto you, they who believe not on your words, and are not baptized in water in my name, for the remission of their sins, that they may receive the Holy Ghost, shall be damned, and shall not come into my Father's kingdom where my Father and I am. (*Revelation on priesthood received with six elders, Sept. 22/23, 1832*) D&C 84:74

### Joseph Smith,
#### *quoted by Elder Joseph Fielding Smith*

Baptism is a sign to God, to angels, and to heaven that we do the will of God, and there is no other way beneath the heavens whereby God hath ordained for man to come to Him to be saved, and enter into the Kingdom of God, except faith in Jesus Christ, repentance, and baptism for the remission of sins, and any other course is in vain; then you have the promise of the gift of the Holy Ghost. (*In Grove near Nauvoo Temple, March 20, 1842*) DGSM:43; TPJS:198

### Jacob, brother of Nephi,
#### *quoted by Nephi*

And he commandeth all men that they must repent, and be baptized in his name, having perfect faith in the Holy One of Israel, or they cannot be saved in the kingdom of God. 24. And if they will not repent and believe in his name, and be baptized in his name, and endure to the end, they must be damned; for the Lord God, the Holy One of Israel, has spoken it. (*Jacob teaches the Nephites in the temple, 559-545 B.C.*) 2Ne.9:23-24

### Elder Wilford Woodruff

No man can enter into the kingdom of God except he is born of the water and of the Spirit. Men may be judged and their bodies lie in the grave until the last resurrection, to come forth and receive of the telestial glory, but no man will receive of the celestial glory except it be through the ordinances of the House of God. (*In Tabernacle, June 30, 1878, JD19:361*) TLDP:53

### Related Witnesses:
### Joseph Smith

The person who is called of God and has authority from Jesus Christ to baptize, shall go down into the water with the person who has presented himself or herself for baptism, and shall say, calling him or her by name: Having been commissioned of Jesus Christ, I baptize you in the name of the Father, and of the Son, and of the Holy Ghost. Amen. 74. Then shall he immerse him or her in the water, and come forth again out of the water. (*Revelation on Church Organization and Government, April 1830*) D&C 20:73-74

### Joseph Smith,
#### *receiving the Word of the Lord*

And they are they who are ordained of me to baptize in my name, according to that which is written; (*Revelation received June 1829*) D&C 18:29

### John the Baptist,
*quoted by Joseph Smith*

Upon you my fellow servants, in the name of Messiah I confer the Priesthood of Aaron, which holds the keys of the ministering of angels, and of the gospel of repentance, and of baptism by immersion for the remission of sins; and this shall never be taken again from the earth, until the sons of Levi do offer again an offering unto the Lord in righteousness. (*The ordination of Joseph Smith and Oliver Cowdery to the Aaronic Priesthood by the hands of John the Baptist, May 15, 1829*) D&C 13:1

### Joseph Smith,
*receiving the Word of the Lord*

Behold, I say unto you that all old covenants have I caused to be done away in this thing; and this is a new and an everlasting covenant, even that which was from the beginning. 2. Wherefore, although a man should be baptized an hundred times it availeth him nothing, for you cannot enter in at the strait gate by the law of Moses, neither by your dead works. 3. For it is because of your dead works that I have caused this last covenant and this church to be built up unto me, even as in days of old. 4. Wherefore, enter ye in at the gate, as I have commanded, and seek not to counsel your God. Amen. (*Revelation received April 1830, given in consequence of persons desiring to join the Church without rebaptism*) D&C 22:1-4

**Author's Note:** The witnesses of the foregoing prophets were directed toward adult audiences. Latter-day revelation makes it clear that baptism is required for all persons who are *capable* of repentance, hence, excluding little children and probably the mentally incompetent. (D&C 20:71, and Moro.8:10)

---

50. Baptism is necessary before a person can receive the gift of the Holy Ghost.

### Peter

Now when they heard this, they were pricked in their heart, and said unto Peter and to the rest of the apostles, Men and brethren, what shall we do? 38. Then Peter said unto them, Repent, and be baptized every one of you in the name of Jesus Christ for the remission of sins, and ye shall receive the gift of the Holy Ghost. (*Peter addresses the people on the day of Pentecost when about 3,000 people were baptized*) Acts 2:37-38

### Joseph Smith

We believe that the first principles and ordinances of the Gospel are: first, Faith in the Lord Jesus Christ; second, Repentance; third, Baptism by immersion for the remission of sins; fourth, Laying on of hands for the gift of the Holy Ghost. (*The fourth of the thirteen Articles of Faith; letter to John Wentworth, March 1, 1842*) AofF:4

### Joseph Smith,
*quoted by Elder Joseph Fielding Smith*

Cornelius received the Holy Ghost before he was baptized, which was the convincing power of God unto him of the truth of the Gospel, but he could not receive the gift of the Holy Ghost until after he was baptized. Had he not taken this sign or ordinance upon him, the Holy Ghost, which convinced him of the truth of God, would have left him. (*In Grove by Nauvoo Temple*) TPJS:199; DGSM:44

### Joseph Smith,
*translating the Book of Moses*

And he also said unto him: If thou wilt turn unto me, and hearken unto my voice, and believe, and repent of all thy transgressions, and be baptized, even in water, in the name of mine Only Begotten Son, who is full of grace and truth, which is Jesus Christ, the only name which shall be given under heaven, whereby salvation shall come unto the children of men, ye shall receive the gift of the Holy Ghost, asking all things in his name, and whatsoever ye shall ask, it shall be given you. (*The record of Moses: Enoch recounts God speaking to Adam*) Moses 6:52

### Joseph Smith,
*receiving the Word of the Lord*

But now I give unto thee a commandment, that thou shalt baptize by water, and they shall receive the Holy Ghost by the laying on of the hands, even as the apostles of old. (*Revelation to Joseph Smith and Sidney Rigdon, Dec. 1830*) D&C 35:6

### Joseph Smith

Yea, repent and be baptized, every one of you, for a remission of your sins; yea, be baptized even by water, and then cometh the baptism of fire and of the Holy Ghost. (*Revelation for Ezra Thayre and Northrop Sweet, Oct. 1830*) D&C 33:11

### Joseph Smith

Believe on the name of the Lord Jesus, who was on the earth, and is to come, the beginning and the end; 13. Repent and be baptized in the name of Jesus Christ, according to the holy commandment, for the remission of sins; 14. And whoso doeth this shall receive the gift of the Holy Ghost, by the laying on of the hands of the elders of the church. (*Revelation, March 1831*) D&C 49:12-14

### Nephi, son of Lehi

And also, the voice of the Son came unto me, saying: He that is baptized in my name, to him will the Father give the Holy Ghost, like unto me; wherefore, follow me, and do the things which ye have seen me do. 13. Wherefore, my beloved brethren, I know that if ye shall follow the Son, with full purpose of heart, acting no hypocrisy and no deception before God, but with real intent, repenting of your sins, witnessing unto the Father that ye are willing to take upon you the name of Christ, by baptism—yea, by following your Lord and your Savior down into the water, according to his word, behold, then shall ye receive the Holy Ghost; yea, then cometh the baptism of fire and of the Holy Ghost; and then can ye speak with the tongue of angels, and shout praises unto the Holy One of Israel. (*Nephi tells why Christ was baptized, between 559-545 B.C.*) 2Ne.31:12-13

**Related Witnesses:**

### Nephi, son of Lehi

Wherefore, do the things which I have told you I have seen that your Lord and your Redeemer should do; for, for this cause have they been shown unto me, that ye might know the gate by which ye should enter. For the gate by which ye should enter is repentance and baptism by water; and then cometh a remission of your sins by fire and by the Holy Ghost. (*Nephi's writings, between 559-545 B.C.*) 2Ne.31:17

---

51. **Baptism is required of children only when they arrive at the age of accountability—when they are capable of repentance.**

### Orson F. Whitney

Little children, too young to have sinned, and therefore incapable of repentance, are exempt from baptism, and it is a sin to baptize them, involving as it does the vain use of a sacred ordinance. [See Moro.8:8-10,19,22.] Redeemed by the blood of Christ from the foundation of the world, their innocence and purity are typical of the saved condition of men and women, who must become like them before entering the Kingdom of Heaven. [See D&C 29:46-47, 74:6.] As children advance in years, however, they become accountable, and must yield obedience to the requirements of the Gospel. [See Moses 6:55.] Eight years is the recognized age of accountability in the Church of Christ. [See D&C 68:25-27.] (Saturday Night Thoughts, p. 248) TLDP:60

### Joseph Smith

And you must preach unto the world, saying:

You must repent and be baptized, in the name of Jesus Christ; 42. For all men must repent and be baptized, and not only men, but women, and children who have arrived at the years of accountability. (*Revelation received June 1829*) D&C 18:41-42

### Joseph Smith

And again, inasmuch as parents have children in Zion, or in any of her stakes which are organized, that teach them not to understand the doctrine of repentance, faith in Christ the Son of the living God, and of baptism and the gift of the Holy Ghost by the laying on of the hands, when eight years old, the sin be upon the heads of the parents. 26. For this shall be a law unto the inhabitants of Zion, or in any of her stakes which are organized. 27. And their children shall be baptized for the remission of their sins when eight years old, and receive the laying on of the hands. (*Revelation, Nov. 1831*) D&C 68:25-27

### Mormon

Listen to the words of Christ, your Redeemer, your Lord and your God. Behold, I came into the world not to call the righteous but sinners to repentance; the whole need no physician, but they that are sick; wherefore, little children are whole, for they are not capable of committing sin; wherefore the curse of Adam is taken from them in me, that it hath no power over them; and the law of circumcision is done away in me. 9. And after this manner did the Holy Ghost manifest the word of God unto me; wherefore, my beloved son, I know that it is solemn mockery before God, that ye should baptize little children. 10. Behold I say unto you that this thing shall ye teach—repentance and baptism unto those who are accountable and capable of committing sin; yea, teach parents that they must repent and be baptized, and humble themselves as their little children, and they shall all be saved with their little children. 11. And their little children need no repentance, neither baptism. Behold, baptism is unto repentance to the fulfilling the commandments unto the remission of sins. (*Mormon writes to his son Moroni, prior to A.D. 384*) Moro.8:8-11

### Elder Wilford Woodruff

With regard to redemption, Paul said: All children of Adam are redeemed from the fall by the atoning blood of Jesus, and all infants are redeemed as well as other people. There is no infant or child that has died before arriving at the years of accountability, but what is redeemed, and is therefore entirely beyond the tormented of hell, to use a sectarian term. And any doctrine, such as the sprinkling of infants, or any religious rite for little children, is of no effect whatever, neither in this world nor in the world to come. It

is a man-made doctrine, and therefore not ordained of God; and I will defy any man to find in
any of the records of divine truth any ordinance
instituted for the salvation of little innocent children; it would be unnecessary on the face of it,
and the only thing that can be found is where
Jesus took the little ones in his arms and blessed
them, which is and would be perfectly right to do
according to the order of God. But the sprinkling
of infants or the doctrine that infants go to hell
under any circumstances, is a doctrine ordained
of man and not of God, and is therefore of no
avail and entirely wrong and displeasing in the
sight of God. So much about the infants. I will
say again they are redeemed by the blood of
Jesus Christ, and when they die, whether of
Christian, Pagan or Jewish parentage, their spirits are taken home to God who gave them, and
never go to suffer torments of any kind. (*In
Tabernacle, May 14, 1882, JD23:126*) TLDP:60
**Related Witnesses:**

### Joseph Smith

No one can be received into the church of
Christ unless he has arrived unto the years of
accountability before God, and is capable of
repentance. (*Revelation on Church Organization and Government, April 1830; laws governing repentance, justification, sanctification, and
baptism are set forth*) D&C 20:71

---

## 52. Only those who have truly re-
pented may be baptized.

### Joseph Smith

And again, by way of commandment to the
church concerning the manner of baptism—All
those who humble themselves before God, and
desire to be baptized, and come forth with broken hearts and contrite spirits, and witness
before the church that they have truly repented
of all their sins, and are willing to take upon
them the name of Jesus Christ, having a determination to serve him to the end, and truly
manifest by their works that they have received
of the Spirit of Christ unto the remission of
their sins, shall be received by baptism into his
church. (*Revelation on Church Organization
and Government, April 1830*) D&C 20:37

### Moroni, son of Mormon

And now I speak concerning baptism. Behold,
elders, priests, and teachers were baptized; and
they were not baptized save they brought forth
fruit meet that they were worthy of it. 2. Neither
did they receive any unto baptism save they
came forth with a broken heart and a contrite
spirit, and witnessed unto the church that they

truly repented of all their sins. 3. And none were
received unto baptism save they took upon them
the name of Christ, having a determination to
serve him to the end. (*Moroni writes a few last
things in his record*) Moro.6:1-3

### Mormon

And the first fruits of repentance is baptism; and
baptism cometh by faith unto the fulfilling the
commandments; and the fulfilling the commandments bringeth remission of sins; . . . (*Mormon
writes to his son Moroni, prior to A.D. 384*)
Moro.8:25

### Joseph Smith

No one can be received into the church of
Christ unless he has arrived unto the years of
accountability before God, and is capable of
repentance. (*Revelation on Church Organization and Government, April 1830; laws governing repentance, justification, sanctification, and
baptism are set forth*) D&C 20:71

### President Joseph F. Smith

No person can be properly baptized unless he has
faith in the Lord Jesus Christ, and has repented of
his sins, with a repentance that need not be repented of. ("Baptism," IE1911Jan:266) TLDP:55

### Francis M. Lyman

I must be contrite in spirit and my heart broken
and tender, for the Lord has prescribed that all
those who humble themselves before God and
desire to be baptized should come forth with
broken hearts and contrite spirits, and witness
before the Church that they have truly repented
of their sins and are willing to take upon them
the name of Jesus Christ, having a determination to serve Him to the end. CR1897Oct:16

---

## 53. Baptism is an ordinance of the
gospel entered into with a covenant.

### Elder Joseph Fielding Smith

Every person baptized into this Church has made
a covenant with the Lord to keep his commandments. (Doctrines of Salvation, 2:238) DGSM:43

### Elder Joseph Fielding Smith

Every baptized person who has fully repented,
who comes into the Church with a broken heart
and a contrite spirit, has made a covenant to continue with that broken heart, with that contrite
spirit, which means a repentant spirit. He makes
a covenant that he will do that. CR1941Oct:93

### John A. Widtsoe

This understanding of the promise to Abraham
places a heavy responsibility upon all who
accept the gospel. As children of Abraham, they
are under obligation to do the works of Abraham. The waters of baptism carry with them the

promise on the part of the candidate that he will conform his life to the gospel of Jesus Christ, which, of course, was the gospel given, accepted, and practiced by Father Abraham. (Evidences and Reconciliations, p. 400) DGSM:58

### James E. Talmage

The Special Purpose of Baptism is to afford admission to the Church of Christ with remission of sins. What need of more words to prove the worth of this divinely appointed ordinance? What gift could be offered the human race greater than a sure means of obtaining forgiveness for transgression? Justice forbids the granting of universal and unconditional pardon for sins committed except through obedience to ordained law; but means simple and effective are provided whereby the penitent sinner may enter into a covenant with God, sealing that covenant with the sign that commands recognition in heaven, that he will submit himself to the laws of God; thus he places himself within the reach of Mercy, under whose protecting influence he may win eternal life. AF:111

### Bruce R. McConkie

In the waters of baptism, we make a covenant with the Lord. We adopt, as individuals, all the terms and conditions of the new and everlasting covenant. This plan of salvation which was ordained in the councils of eternity, which is the gospel of Christ, is an everlasting, eternal covenant. Now a covenant is a contract. In the case of the gospel, it's a contract between God in heaven and man on earth. The gospel is a new and everlasting covenant. It is new to us, to the people in the world, because it's been revealed anew. But it's everlasting in the sense that it goes on eternally. Its laws are infinite; they apply everywhere to all people in all ages and on all worlds. Well, when we believe the truth, then we are baptized. And the ordinance of baptism is a procedure and the way that God has ordained for us to accept the terms and conditions of the plan of salvation. ¶ If you will read in the eighteenth chapter of Mosiah the account that took place at the waters of Mormon, you'll read what members of the Church do when they come in by baptism. They covenant to do certain things; for instance, one of the list of covenants there listed, recited is this: I covenant to stand as a witness of Christ, at all times, and in all places, and under all circumstances that I may be in even until death. That's one of the covenants we make. Now the overall covenant that we make is to keep the commandments. And the Lord, on his part, covenants with us that if we do what we there and then agree, he will pour out his Spirit upon

us more abundantly, and he will give us eternal life in his kingdom. In other words, we in effect sign the everlasting covenant by the ordinance of baptism, and we make its terms and conditions binding upon us, and this is what makes us different from the generality of mankind. We receive the gift of the Holy Ghost, which is the right to the constant companionship of that member of the Godhead. And if we are guided thereby, then the sanctifying, cleansing, purifying, perfecting processes begin to operate in our lives, and in literal reality we become the saints of God, a peculiar and distinct people. That's what happens to us at least, if we keep our covenants—the covenants made in the waters of baptism. ACR(Brisbane)1976:15

### Related Witnesses:

#### Alma, the elder,
#### *quoted by Mormon*

Behold, here are the waters of Mormon (for thus were they called) and now, as ye are desirous to come into the fold of God, and to be called his people, and are willing to bear one another's burdens, that they may be light; 9. Yea, and are willing to mourn with those that mourn; yea, and comfort those that stand in need of comfort, and to stand as witnesses of God at all times and in all things, and in all places that ye may be in, even until death, that ye may be redeemed of God, and be numbered with those of the first resurrection, that ye may have eternal life— 10. Now I say unto you, if this be the desire of your hearts, what have you against being baptized in the name of the Lord, as a witness before him that ye have entered into a covenant with him, that ye will serve him and keep his commandments, that he may pour out his Spirit more abundantly upon you? (*Mormon records Alma organizing the Church of Christ, about 148 B.C.*) Mosiah 18:8-10

---

54. The covenant of baptism is a solemn promise that we are willing to take upon us the name of Jesus Christ and keep His commandments, with a determination to serve Him to the end.

### Joseph Smith

And again, by way of commandment to the church concerning the manner of baptism—All those who humble themselves before God, and desire to be baptized, and come forth with broken hearts and contrite spirits, and witness before the church that they have truly repented of all their sins, and are willing to take upon them the name of Jesus Christ, having a determination to serve him to the end, and truly manifest by their works that they have received of the Spirit of Christ unto the remission of their sins, shall be received by baptism into his church. (*Revelation on Church Organization and Government, April 1830*) D&C 20:37

### Elder Joseph Fielding Smith

Every person baptized into this Church has made a covenant with the Lord to keep his commandments. We are to serve the Lord with all the heart, and all the mind, and all the strength that we have, and that too in the name of Jesus Christ. Everything that we do should be done in the name of Jesus Christ. ¶ In the waters of baptism, we covenanted that we would keep these commandments; that we would serve the Lord; that we would keep this first and greatest of all commandments, and love the Lord our God; that we would keep the next great commandment, we would love our neighbor as ourselves; and with all the might that we have, with all the strength, with all our hearts, we would prove to him that we would "live by every word that proceedeth forth from the mouth of God;" that we would be obedient and humble, diligent in his service, willing to obey, to hearken to the counsels of those who preside over us and do all things with an eye single to the glory of God. (Doctrines of Salvation, 2:238) DGSM:43

### King Benjamin,
### *quoted by Mormon*

And now, because of the covenant which ye have made ye shall be called the children of Christ, his sons, and his daughters; for behold, this day he hath spiritually begotten you; for ye say that your hearts are changed through faith on his name; therefore, ye are born of him and have become his sons and his daughters. 8. And under this head ye are made free, and there is no other head whereby ye can be made free. There is no other name given whereby salvation cometh; therefore, I would that ye should take upon you the name of Christ, all you that have entered into the covenant with God that ye should be obedient unto the end of your lives. 9. And it shall come to pass that whosoever doeth this shall be found at the right hand of God, for he shall know the name by which he is called; for he shall be called by the name of Christ. (*King Benjamin addresses the people after they entered into a covenant with God to keep all his commandments, about 124 B.C.*) Mosiah 5:7-9

### Nephi, son of Lehi

Wherefore, my beloved brethren, I know that if ye shall follow the Son, with full purpose of heart, acting no hypocrisy and no deception before God, but with real intent, repenting of your sins, witnessing unto the Father that ye are willing to take upon you the name of Christ, by baptism—yea, by following your Lord and your Savior down into the water, according to his word, behold, then shall ye receive the Holy Ghost; yea, then cometh the baptism of fire and of the Holy Ghost; and then can ye speak with the tongue of angels, and shout praises unto the Holy One of Israel. (*Nephi tells why Christ was baptized, between 559-545 B.C.*) 2Ne.31:13

### President Joseph F. Smith

Before performing a baptism, it should be known to those who officiate, and, in fact, to the Church, that the candidate for baptism is willing to conform to all these things. Further, that he is willing to take upon himself the name of Jesus Christ; to speak the truth in soberness; that he has determined to serve God to the end, and that he is willing to manifest by his works that he has received of the Spirit of Christ unto the remission of his sins. ("Baptism," IE1911-Jan:266) TLDP:57

### Related Witnesses:
### Joseph Smith

And as many as repent and are baptized in my name, which is Jesus Christ, and endure to the end, the same shall be saved. 23. Behold, Jesus Christ is the name which is given of the Father, and there is none other name given whereby man can be saved; 24. Wherefore, all men must take upon them the name which is given of the Father, for in that name shall they be called at the last day; 25. Wherefore, if they know not the name by which they are called, they cannot have place in the kingdom of my Father. (*Revelation received June 1829*) D&C 18:22-25

### Alma, the elder,
### *quoted by Mormon*

Now I say unto you, if this be the desire of your hearts, what have you against being baptized in the name of the Lord, as a witness before him that ye have entered into a covenant with him, that ye will serve him and keep his commandments, that he may pour out his Spirit more abundantly upon you? (*Alma organizes the Church of Christ, about 148 B.C.*) Mosiah 18:10

---

55. The specific form and words of the baptismal ordinance have been prescribed by revelation from the Lord.

### Joseph Smith

Baptism is to be administered in the following manner unto all those who repent— 73. The person who is called of God and has authority from Jesus Christ to baptize, shall go down into the water with the person who has presented himself or herself for baptism, and shall say, calling him or her by name: Having been commissioned of Jesus Christ, I baptize you in the name of the Father, and of the Son, and of the Holy Ghost. Amen. 74. Then shall he immerse him or her in the water, and come forth again out of the water. (*Revelation on Church Organization and Government, April 1830*) D&C 20:72-74

### Jesus,
#### quoted by Mormon

And it came to pass that he spake unto Nephi (for Nephi was among the multitude) and he commanded him that he should come forth. 19. And Nephi arose and went forth, and bowed himself before the Lord and did kiss his feet. 20. And the Lord commanded him that he should arise. And he arose and stood before him. 21. And the Lord said unto him: I give unto you power that ye shall baptize this people when I am again ascended into heaven. 22. And again the Lord called others, and said unto them likewise; and he gave unto them power to baptize. And he said unto them: On this wise shall ye baptize; and there shall be no disputations among you. 23. Verily I say unto you, that whoso repenteth of his sins through your words and desireth to be baptized in my name, on this wise shall ye baptize them—Behold, ye shall go down and stand in the water, and in my name shall ye baptize them. 24. And now behold, these are the words which ye shall say, calling them by name, saying: 25. Having authority given me of Jesus Christ, I baptize you in the name of the Father, and of the Son, and of the Holy Ghost. Amen. 26. And then shall ye immerse them in the water, and come forth again out of the water. 27. And after this manner shall ye baptize in my name; for behold, verily I say unto you, that the Father, and the Son, and the Holy Ghost are one; and I am in the Father, and the Father in me, and the Father and I are one. 28. And according as I have commanded you thus shall ye baptize. And there shall be no disputations among you, as there have hitherto been; neither shall there be disputations among you concerning the points of my doctrine, as there have hitherto been. (*The resurrected Jesus Christ addresses his Nephite disciples, A.D. 34*) 3Ne.11:18-28

### Joseph Smith,
#### receiving the Word of the Lord

And they are they who are ordained of me to baptize in my name, according to that which is written; 30. And you have that which is written before you; wherefore, you must perform it

according to the words which are written. (*Revelation received June 1829*) D&C 18:29-30

### Elder Joseph F. Smith

Baptism without divine authority is not valid. It is a symbol of the burial and resurrection of Jesus Christ, and must be done in the likeness thereof, by one commissioned of God, in the manner prescribed, otherwise it is illegal and will not be accepted by Him, nor will it effect a remission of sins. . . . (*In Tabernacle, Sept. 30, 1877, JD19:190*) TLDP:54-55

---

## 56. The person being baptized shall be immersed in water.

### Joseph Smith

Baptism is to be administered in the following manner unto all those who repent— 73. The person who is called of God and has authority from Jesus Christ to baptize, shall go down into the water with the person who has presented himself or herself for baptism, and shall say, calling him or her by name: Having been commissioned of Jesus Christ, I baptize you in the name of the Father, and of the Son, and of the Holy Ghost. Amen. 74. Then shall he immerse him or her in the water, and come forth again out of the water. (*Revelation on Church Organization and Government, April 1830*) D&C 20:72-74

### Jesus,
#### quoted by Mormon

Verily I say unto you, that whoso repenteth of his sins through your words and desireth to be baptized in my name, on this wise shall ye baptize them—Behold, ye shall go down and stand in the water, and in my name shall ye baptize them. 24. And now behold, these are the words which ye shall say, calling them by name, saying: 25. Having authority given me of Jesus Christ, I baptize you in the name of the Father, and of the Son, and of the Holy Ghost. Amen. 26. And then shall ye immerse them in the water, and come forth again out of the water. 27. And after this manner shall ye baptize in my name. . . . (*The resurrected Jesus Christ addresses his Nephite disciples, A.D. 34*) 3Ne.11:23-27

### Joseph Smith

We believe that the first principles and ordinances of the Gospel are: first, Faith in the Lord Jesus Christ; second, Repentance; third, Baptism by immersion for the remission of sins; fourth, Laying on of hands for the gift of the Holy Ghost. (*The fourth of the thirteen Articles of Faith; letter to John Wentworth, March 1, 1842*) AofF:4

### Elder Joseph F. Smith

Baptism means immersion in water, and is to be administered by one having authority, in the name of the Father, and of the Son, and of the Holy Ghost. Baptism without divine authority is not valid. It is a symbol of the burial and resurrection of Jesus Christ, and must be done in the likeness thereof, by one commissioned of God, in the manner prescribed, otherwise it is illegal and will not be accepted by him, nor will it effect a remission of sins, the object for which it is designed, but whosoever hath faith, truly repents and is "buried with Christ in baptism," by one having divine authority, shall receive a remission of sins, and is entitled to the gift of the Holy Ghost by the laying on of hands. (*In new Tabernacle, Sept. 1877, JD19:190*) DGSM:43

### Elder Joseph Fielding Smith

The evidence is perfectly clear in the New Testament, and this is confirmed in the teachings and writings of the first centuries, that there was but one mode of baptism practiced in the primitive Church of Jesus Christ, and taught by the early disciples. This mode was burial in water and definitely for the remission of sins. I feel that I can say without successful contradiction that there is not a syllable in the entire New Testament that can, by any sense of reason, be interpreted in defense of sprinkling or pouring water on the head of the person as baptism. It is needless for me to go into a lengthy discussion of the meaning of the word Baptize because it is universally conceded that the word in the Greek means to plunge or immerse, and that is the meaning the Savior and his apostles gave to the word if we are to judge them by their actions. (The Restoration of All Things, pp. 206-07) TLDP:54

### James E. Talmage

The Latter-day Saints hold that the scriptures are devoid of ambiguity regarding the acceptable mode of baptism; and they boldly declare their belief that bodily immersion by a duly commissioned servant or representative of the Savior is the only true form. . . . ¶ Scriptural authority, the revealed word of God through the mouths of ancient and latter-day prophets, prescribes immersion as the true form of baptism. AF:124

**Related Witnesses:**

### Joseph Smith,
*quoted by Elder Joseph Fielding Smith*

[T]he word baptize is derived from the Greek verb "baptiso," and means to immerse or overwhelm. . . . (Editorial in Times and Seasons, Sept. 1842) DGSM:43; TPJS:262

---

**57. Baptism by immersion in water symbolizes the death, burial, and resurrection of Christ.**

### Joseph Smith

Herein is glory and honor, and immortality and eternal life—The ordinance of baptism by water, to be immersed therein in order to answer to the likeness of the dead, that one principle might accord with the other; to be immersed in the water and come forth out of the water is in the likeness of the resurrection of the dead in coming forth out of their graves; hence, this ordinance was instituted to form a relationship with the ordinance of baptism for the dead, being in likeness of the dead. 13. Consequently, the baptismal font was instituted as a similitude of the grave, and was commanded to be in a place underneath where the living are wont to assemble, to show forth the living and the dead, and that all things may have their likeness, and that they may accord one with another—that which is earthly conforming to that which is heavenly, as Paul hath declared, 1 Corinthians 15:46, 47, and 48. . . . (*Joseph writes to the Church giving further directions on baptism for the dead, Sept. 6, 1842*) D&C 128:12-13

### Elder Joseph F. Smith

Baptism means immersion in water, and is to be administered by one having authority, in the name of the Father, and of the Son, and of the Holy Ghost. Baptism without divine authority is not valid. It is a symbol of the burial and resurrection of Jesus Christ, and must be done in the likeness thereof, by one commissioned of God, in the manner prescribed, otherwise it is illegal and will not be accepted by him, nor will it effect a remission of sins, the object for which it is designed. . . . (*In new Tabernacle, Sept. 1877, JD19:190*) DGSM:43

### Paul

Know ye not, that so many of us as were baptized into Jesus Christ were baptized into his death? 4. Therefore we are buried with him by baptism into death: that like as Christ was raised up from the dead by the glory of the Father, even so we also should walk in newness of life. 5. For if we have been planted together in the likeness of his death, we shall be also in the likeness of his resurrection: (*Paul writes to the Church in Rome regarding baptism, about A.D. 55*) Rom.6:3-5

### Bruce R. McConkie

It is common among us to say that baptisms are performed in similitude of the death, burial and resurrection of Christ, and that they should therefore be performed by immersion. This is true, but it is an oversimplification and tells only part of the story. Baptism is a new birth; it is symbolical of our new life in the kingdom of God, which new birth is a living reality because of the shedding of the blood of Christ, or in other words because of his death, burial and resurrection. The new birth grows out of the atonement wrought by our Lord; the newness of life comes to the repentant sinner because he has bowed to the will of the Lord; and has been immersed in water by a legal administrator. (The Promised Messiah, pp. 389-90) TLDP:59

---

58. Baptism is a new birth; it is symbolic of our new life in the kingdom of God.

### President David O. McKay

Membership is obtained by baptism, which is at once a burial and a birth—a burial of the old person, with all his frailties, faults, and sins, if any, and a coming forth to walk in a newness of life. Backbiting, faultfinding, slander, profanity, uncontrolled temper, avarice, jealousy, hatred, intemperance, fornication, lying, cheating, are all buried. That is part of what baptism by immersion signifies. "Except a man be born again, he cannot see the kingdom God," (John 3:3) said Jesus to Nicodemus. He comes forth to walk in a newness of life, signifying that in the new life ahead there will be an effort to maintain honesty, loyalty, chastity benevolence, and of doing good to men. CR1958Oct:90

### Bruce R. McConkie

It is common among us to say that baptisms are performed in similitude of the death, burial and resurrection of Christ, and that they should therefore be performed by immersion. This is true, but it is an oversimplification and tells only part of the story. Baptism is a new birth; it is symbolical of our new life in the kingdom of God, which new birth is a living reality because of the shedding of the blood of Christ, or in other words because of his death, burial and resurrection. The new birth grows out of the atonement wrought by our Lord; the newness of life comes to the repentant sinner because he has bowed to the will of the Lord; and has been immersed in water by a legal administrator. (The Promised Messiah, pp. 389-90) TLDP:59

### Paul

Know ye not, that so many of us as were baptized into Jesus Christ were baptized into his death? 4. Therefore we are buried with him by baptism into death: that like as Christ was raised up from the dead by the glory of the Father, even so we also should walk in newness of life. 5. For if we have been planted together in the likeness of his death, we shall be also in the likeness of his resurrection: (Paul writes to the Church in Rome regarding baptism, about A.D. 55) Rom.6:3-5

### Elder Harold B. Lee

The Master's admonition to Nicodemus, who came confessing Jesus as a teacher come of God, and undoubtedly seeking to know, like so many others who are true seekers after truth, just what he must do to be saved. He was told that he must be born again if he would see the kingdom of God. This statement the Master clarified when he explained, "Except a man be born of water and of the Spirit, he cannot enter into the kingdom of God" (John 3:5). . . . ¶ This new birth, then, was to be accomplished through the medium of baptism by immersion and by the laying on of hands for the conferring of the Holy Ghost, as the disciples, thereafter as they went out among the people, administered these sacred ordinances. CR1961Apr:32

### Elder Harold B. Lee

When you think about it there is so much promised in the gospel for so little required on our part; for example, the ordinance of baptism is given us for the remission of sins, for entrance into the kingdom—a new birth. . . . CR1956Apr:110

### Henry D. Moyle

Let us stop and think for a moment what a young missionary has to accomplish before he leads the convert down into the waters of baptism. He must first teach him the Word of Wisdom, and that means teach him in practically all cases to give up practices which have been lifelong and confirmed and live virtually a new life and to have the investigator commit himself to the keeping of this commandment of the Lord from the time of his baptism until the Lord calls him home. CR1961Oct:44

---

59. Baptism in connection with the gift of the Holy Ghost is a cleanser and a purifier.

### Marion G. Romney

In final preparation for Church membership, and as evidence of our willingness to take upon us the name of Christ and of our commandments, we were baptized by immersion for the remission of sin. . . . Thus prepared we were confirmed members of the Church and given the gift of the Holy Ghost. Through these principles and ordinances we were cleansed and purified. Having thus washed our garments in the blood of Christ, we entered through the straight gate and stood redeemed on the narrow way which leads to life eternal. It should have then been, and it should now be, the controlling desire of every Church member, and it is the desire of every member who is on the way to eternal life always to retain this redeemed status. CR1956Oct:17

### Bruce R. McConkie

In other words, we in effect sign the everlasting covenant by the ordinance of baptism, and we make its term and conditions binding upon us, and this is what makes us different from the generality of mankind. We receive the gift of the Holy Ghost, which is the right to the constant companionship of that member of the Godhead. And if we are guided thereby, then the sanctifying, cleansing, purifying, perfecting processes begin to operate in our lives, and in literal reality we become the saints of God, a peculiar and distinct people. That's what happens to us at least, if we keep our covenants— the covenants made in the waters of baptism. ACR(Brisbane)1976:15

### Jesus,
#### quoted by Mormon

Now this is the commandment: Repent, all ye ends of the earth, and come unto me and be baptized in my name, that ye may be sanctified by the reception of the Holy Ghost, that ye may stand spotless before me at the last day. (*The resurrected Jesus calls on the Nephites to repent in contemplation of the final judgment, A.D. 34*) 3Ne.27:20

### Related Witnesses:
#### Alma, the younger,
#### quoted by Mormon

Now they, after being sanctified by the Holy Ghost, having their garments made white, being pure and spotless before God, could not look upon sin save it were with abhorrence; and there were many, exceedingly great many, who were made pure and entered into the rest of the Lord their God. (*Alma instructs the people that high priests were ordained because of righteousness, about 82 B.C.*) Alma 13:12

### Peter

Elect according to the foreknowledge of God the Father, through sanctification of the Spirit, unto obedience and sprinkling of the blood of Jesus Christ: Grace unto you, and peace, be multiplied. (*Peter writes to the churches in modern Asia Minor, about A.D. 60*) 1Pet.1:2

### Joseph Smith,
#### quoted by Elder Joseph Fielding Smith

[T]he effect of the Holy Ghost upon a Gentile is to purge out the old blood, and make him actually of the seed of Abraham. That man that has none of the blood of Abraham (naturally) must have a new creation by the Holy Ghost. In such a case, there may be more of a powerful effect upon the body, and visible to the eye, than upon an Israelite, while the Israelite at first might be far before the Gentile in pure intelligence. (*The Prophet instructs the Twelve in Nauvoo, June 27, 1839*) TPJS:150; HC3:380

### Parley P. Pratt

[The Holy Ghost] quickens all the intellectual faculties, increases, enlarges, expands, and purifies all the natural passions and affections, and adapts them, by the gift of wisdom, to their lawful use. (Key to the Science of Theology, pp. 61-62) DGSM:45

### Orson Pratt

If the Father possesses infinite wisdom and knowledge, why, some may ask, can he not get along with his work without the assistance of the Son and Holy Spirit? We answer, the Son is necessary to reconcile fallen man to the Father; the Holy Spirit is necessary to sanctify and purify the affections of men, and also to dwell in them as a teacher of truth. (Masterful Discourses and Writings of Orson Pratt, pp. 313-14) TLDP:230

---

### 60. Baptism was practiced in the former ages of the world, beginning with Adam.

### James E. Talmage

The Establishment of Baptism dates from the time of the earliest history of the race. When the Lord manifested Himself to Adam after the expulsion from the Garden of Eden, He promised the patriarch of the race: "If thou wilt turn unto me, and hearken unto my voice, and believe, and repent of all thy transgressions, and be baptized, even in water, in the name of mine Only Begotten Son, who is full of grace and truth, which is Jesus Christ, the only name which shall be given under heaven, whereby salvation shall come unto the children of men, ye shall receive the gift of the Holy Ghost, asking all things in his name, and whatsoever ye shall ask, it shall be given you. And it came to pass, when the Lord had spoken with Adam, our father, that Adam cried unto the Lord, and he was caught away by the Spirit of the Lord, and was carried down into the water, and was laid under the water, and was brought forth out of the water. And thus he was baptized, and the Spirit of God descended upon him, and thus he was born of the Spirit, and became quickened in the inner man." Enoch preached the doctrine of repentance and baptism, and baptized the penitent believers; and as many as accepted these teachings and submitted to the requirements of the Gospel became Sanctified in the sight of God. AF:110-11

### Bruce R. McConkie

Every baptism—properly performed by a legal administrator!—from Adam to Christ was itself a Messianic prophecy. It bore record of Christ, who was to come, and was so understood by the saints of old. . . . ¶ Baptism began with Adam. . . . He was then taught that "by the blood ye are sanctified," meaning that the cleansing power of baptism rests upon and grows out of the atoning sacrifice of the Only Begotten. (Moses 6:59-68) That is to say, without the atonement and without the shedding of the blood of God's Son, neither baptism nor any ordinance would have any efficacy, virtue, or force in and after the resurrection of the dead. (The Promised Messiah, pp. 386-87) TLDP:57

### Joseph Smith,
*quoted by Elder Joseph Fielding Smith*

In the former ages of the world, before the Savior came in the flesh, "the saints" were baptized in the name of Jesus Christ to come, because there never was any other name whereby men could be saved; and after he came in the flesh and was crucified, risen from the dead and ascended into heaven, that they might be buried in baptism like him, and be raised in glory like him, that as there was but one Lord, one faith, one baptism, and one God and father of us all, even so there was but one door to the mansions of bliss. Amen. (Times and Seasons, Sept. 1842) DGSM:43; TPJS:266

**Related Witnesses:**

### Joseph Smith,
*translating the Book of Moses*

And it came to pass, when the Lord had spoken with Adam, our father, that Adam cried unto the Lord, and he was caught away by the Spirit of the Lord, and was carried down into the water, and was laid under the water, and was brought forth out of the water. 65. And thus he was baptized, and the Spirit of God descended upon him, and thus he was born of the Spirit, and became quickened in the inner man. (*The record of Moses: Enoch testifies to the people; he tells of Adam's baptism*) Moses 6:64-65

### Enoch,
*quoted by Joseph Smith,*
*translating the Book of Moses*

And he gave unto me a commandment that I should baptize in the name of the Father, and of the Son, which is full of grace and truth, and of the Holy Ghost, which beareth record of the Father and the Son. (*The record of Moses: Enoch is commanded to baptize*) Moses 7:11

### Joseph Smith,
*translating the Book of Moses*

And it came to pass that Noah continued his preaching unto the people, saying: Hearken, and give heed to my words; 24. Believe and repent of your sins and be baptized in the name of Jesus Christ, the Son of God, even as our fathers, and ye shall receive the Holy Ghost, that ye may have all things made manifest; and if ye do not this, the floods will come in upon you; nevertheless they hearkened not. (*The record of Moses: Noah preaches repentance and baptism*) Moses 8:23-24

### Joseph Smith

Therefore, he took Moses out of their midst, and the Holy Priesthood also; 26. And the lesser priesthood continued, which priesthood holdeth the key of the ministering of angels and the preparatory gospel; 27. Which gospel is the gospel of repentance and of baptism, and the remission of sins, and the law of carnal commandments, which the Lord in his wrath caused to continue with the house of Aaron among the children of Israel until John, whom God raised up, being filled with the Holy Ghost from his mother's womb. (*Baptism administered by lessor priesthood among the children of Israel*) D&C 84:25-27

### Elder Harold B. Lee

Baptism of water and of the Spirit by those having authority are the necessary ordinances for this cleansing, for as the Lord told Adam, ". . . by the water ye keep the commandment, by the Spirit are ye justified, and by the blood are ye sanctified." (Moses 6:60) CR1961Apr:33

---

**HYMNS Written by Prophets**
**Applicable to this Topic**

### Parley P. Pratt
*Father in Heaven, We Do Believe*
HYMNS:180

Father in Heav'n, we do believe
The promise thou hast made;
Thy word with meekness we receive,
Just as thy Saints have said.

We now repent of all our sin
And come with broken heart,
And to thy covenant enter in
And choose the better part.

O Lord, accept us while we pray,
And all our sins forgive;
New life impart to us this day,
And bid the sinners live.

Humbly we take the sacrament
In Jesus' blessed name;
Let us receive thru covenant
The Spirit's heav'nly flame.

We will be buried in the stream
In Jesus' blessed name,
And rise, while light shall on us beam
The Spirit's heav'nly flame.

Baptize us with the Holy Ghost
And seal us as thine own,
That we may join the ransomed host
And with the Saints be one.

# List of Doctrines

## BIBLE

*Doctrines Located in This Topic*

*Doctrines on BIBLE*
*Located in Other Topics*

61. The Bible is the word of God as far as it is translated correctly.

62. In the compilation and translation of the Bible many plain and precious truths were omitted.

69. The Book of Mormon sustains the Bible and is in harmony with it.

655. When the Lord wants the people to learn any essential truth, He will teach it to them over and over again through the witnesses of prophets.

658. True doctrine is in harmony with the recorded revealed word of God in all scriptures (i.e., the Standard Works).

(See topic SCRIPTURE.)

# BIBLE

**61. The Bible is the word of God as far as it is translated correctly.**

**Joseph Smith**

We believe the Bible to be the word of God as far as it is translated correctly; we also believe the Book of Mormon to be the word of God. (*The eighth of the thirteen Articles of Faith; letter to John Wentworth, March 1, 1842*) AofF:8

**James E. Talmage**

The Church of Jesus Christ of Latter-day Saints accepts the Holy Bible as the foremost of her standard works, first among the books which have been proclaimed as her written guides in faith and doctrine. In the respect and sanctity with which the Latter-day Saints regard the Bible they are of like profession with Christian denominations in general, but differ from them in the additional acknowledgment of certain other scriptures as authentic and holy, which others are in harmony with the Bible, and serve to support and emphasize its facts and doctrines. ¶ The historical and other data upon which is based the current Christian faith as to the genuineness of the Biblical record are accepted as unreservedly by the Latter-day Saints as by the members of any sect; and in literalness of interpretation this Church probably excels. ¶ Nevertheless, the Church announces a reservation in the case of erroneous translation, which may occur as a result of human incapacity; and even in this measure of caution we are not alone, for Biblical scholars generally admit the presence of errors of the kind—both of translation and of transcription of the text. The Latter-day Saints believe the original records to be the word of God unto man, and, as far as these records have been translated correctly, the translations are regarded as equally authentic. The English Bible professes to be a translation made through the wisdom of man; in its preparation the most scholarly men have been enlisted, yet not a version has been published in which errors are not admitted. However, an impartial investigator has cause to wonder more at the paucity of errors than that mistakes are to be found at all. ¶ There will be, there can be, no absolutely reliable translation of these or other scriptures unless it be effected through the gift of translation, as one of the endowments of the Holy Ghost. The translator must have the spirit of the prophet if he would render in another tongue the prophet's words; and human wisdom alone leads not to that possession. Let the Bible then be read reverently and with prayerful care, the reader ever seeking the light of the Spirit that he may discern between truth and the errors of men. AF:214-15

**Related Witnesses:**

**Joseph Smith,**
*quoted by Elder Joseph Fielding Smith*

Upon my return from Amherst Conference, I resumed the translation of the Scriptures. From sundry revelations which had been received, it was apparent that many important points touching the salvation of men, had been taken from the Bible, or lost before it was compiled. (*Joseph's journal entry, Feb. 16, 1832*) TPJS:9-11

**Joseph Smith**

[Moroni] commenced quoting the prophecies of the Old Testament. He first quoted part of the third chapter of Malachi; and he quoted also the fourth or last chapter of the same prophecy, though with a little variation from the way it reads in our Bibles. . . . 40. In addition to these, he quoted the eleventh chapter of Isaiah. . . . He quoted also the third chapter of Acts, twenty-second and twenty-third verses, precisely as they stand in our New Testament. . . . 41. He also quoted the second chapter of Joel from the twenty-eighth verse to the last. . . . He quoted many other passages of scripture, and offered many explanations which cannot be mentioned here. (*The angel Moroni instructs Joseph, Sept. 21, 1823*) JS-H 1:36,40-41

**President Brigham Young,**
*quoted by John A. Widtsoe*

Take the Bible just as it reads; and if it be translated incorrectly and there is a scholar on the earth who professes to be a Christian, and he can translate it any better than King James's translators did it, he is under obligation to do so. If I understood Greek and Hebrew as some may profess to do, and I knew the Bible was not correctly translated, I should feel myself bound by the law of justice to the inhabitants of the earth to translate that which is incorrect and give it just as it was spoken anciently. Is that proper? Yes, I would be under obligation to do it. But I think it is translated just as correctly as the scholars could get it, although it is not correct in a great many instances. But it is no matter about that. Read it and observe it and it will not hurt any person in the world. (*In new Tabernacle, Aug. 27, 1871, JD14:226*) DBY:124

**Author's Note:** With regard to the phrase in D-61, "as far as it is translated correctly," Robert Matthews writes: "Here the word *translated* appears to be used in a broader sense to mean *transmitted,* which would include not only translation of languages but also copying, editing, deleting from, and adding to documents. The Bible has undergone a much more serious change than merely translation from one language to another." (A Bible! A Bible!, p. 72) ¶ Joseph Smith approached God in the First Vision by reason of having read from the Bible a passage from James 1:5; God responded in vision and did not refute but rather appeared in confirmation of Joseph's faith in the Bible. ". . . I came to the conclusion that I must either remain in darkness and confusion, or else do as James directs, that is, 'ask of God.'" (JS-H 1:13)

---

## 62. In the compilation and translation of the Bible many plain and precious truths were omitted.

### President Brigham Young,
*quoted by John A. Widtsoe*

The Bible is true. It may not all have been translated aright, and many precious things may have been rejected in the compilation and translation of the Bible; but we understand, from the writings of one of the Apostles, that if all the sayings and doings of the Savior had been written, the world could not contain them. I will say that the world could not understand them. They do not understand what we have on record, nor the character of the Savior, as delineated in the Scriptures; and yet it is one of the simplest things in the world, and the Bible, when it is understood, is one of the simplest books in the world, for, as far as it is translated correctly, it is nothing but truth, and in truth there is no mystery save to the ignorant. The revelations of the Lord to his creatures are adapted to the lowest capacity, and they bring life and salvation to all who are willing to receive them. (*In Tabernacle, May 12, 1871, JD14:135*) DBY:124

### Joseph Smith,
*quoted by Elder Joseph Fielding Smith*

Upon my return from Amherst conference, I resumed the translation of the Scriptures. From sundry revelations which had been received, it was apparent that many important points touching the salvation of man, had been taken from the Bible, or lost before it was compiled. (*Joseph's journal entry, Feb. 16, 1832*) TPJS:9-11; HC1:245

### Joseph Smith

I believe the Bible as it reads when it came from the pen of the original writers. Ignorant translators, careless transcribers, or designing and corrupt priests have committed many errors. (*At the Stand, east of the Nauvoo Temple, Oct. 15, 1843*) HC6:57

### Nephi, son of Lehi

And it came to pass that I, Nephi, beheld that they did prosper in the land; and I beheld a book, and it was carried forth among them. 21. And the angel said unto me: Knowest thou the meaning of the book? 22. And I said unto him: I know not. 23. And he said: Behold it proceedeth out of the mouth of a Jew. And I, Nephi, beheld it; and he said unto me: The book that thou beholdest is a record of the Jews, which contains the covenants of the Lord, which he hath made unto the house of Israel; and it also containeth many of the prophecies of the holy prophets; and it is a record like unto the engravings which are upon the plates of brass, save there are not so many; nevertheless, they contain the covenants of the Lord, which he hath made unto the house of Israel; wherefore, they are of great worth unto the Gentiles. 24. And the angel of the Lord said unto me: Thou hast beheld that the book proceeded forth from the mouth of a Jew; and when it proceeded forth from the mouth of a Jew it contained the fulness of the gospel of the Lord, of whom the twelve apostles bear record; and they bear record according to the truth which is in the Lamb of God. . . . 28. Wherefore, thou seest that after the book hath gone forth through the hands of the great and abominable church, that there are many plain and precious things taken away from the book, which is the book of the Lamb of God. 29. And after these plain and precious things were taken away it goeth forth unto all the nations of the Gentiles; and after it goeth forth unto all the nations of the Gentiles, yea, even across the many waters which thou hast seen with the Gentiles which have gone forth out of captivity, thou seest—because of the many plain and precious things which have been taken out of the book, which were plain unto the understanding of the children of men, according to the plainness which is in the Lamb of God—because of these things which are taken away out of the gospel of the Lamb, an exceedingly great many do stumble, yea, insomuch that Satan hath great power over them. . . . 40. And the angel spake unto me, saying: These last records, which thou hast seen among the Gentiles, shall establish the truth of the first, which are of the twelve apostles of the Lamb, and shall make known the plain and precious things which have been taken away from them; and shall make known to all kindreds, tongues, and people, that the Lamb of God is the Son of the Eternal Father, and the Savior of the world; and that all men must come unto him, or they cannot be saved. (*An angel shows Nephi the Bible and informs him of changes made in it, 600-592 B.C.*) 1Ne.13:20-24,28-29,40

# List of Doctrines

## BOOK OF MORMON

*Doctrines Located in This Topic*

63. The Book of Mormon is the word of God.

64. The Book of Mormon contains the fulness of the gospel of Jesus Christ.

65. Joseph Smith translated the Book of Mormon by the power of God.

66. The Lord caused the ancient Book of Mormon plates to be delivered to Joseph Smith.

67. The purpose of the Book of Mormon is to persuade all people to believe that Jesus is the Christ, the Eternal God.

68. A person may learn that the Book of Mormon is true by reading it and by asking of God, who will manifest the truth of it by the power of the Holy Ghost.

69. The Book of Mormon sustains the Bible and is in harmony with it.

*Doctrines on BOOK OF MORMON Located in Other Topics*

644. The Lord gave Joseph Smith the gift to translate the Book of Mormon plates, that this generation would have the word of the Lord.

(See topic SCRIPTURE.)

# BOOK OF MORMON

### 63. The Book of Mormon is the word of God.

#### Joseph Smith

We believe the Bible to be the word of God as far as it is translated correctly; we also believe the Book of Mormon to be the word of God. (*The eighth of the thirteen Articles of Faith; letter to John Wentworth, March 1, 1842*) AofF:8

#### Marion G. Romney

The first reason for reading the Book of Mormon which I want to mention is that it is approved by the highest authority in the universe, the Lord himself. . . . ¶ After the Prophet Joseph Smith had translated that part of the record which he had been told to translate, the Lord said: ". . . and as your Lord and your God liveth it is true," . . . (D&C 17:6) CR1949Apr:37

#### Joseph Smith

Sunday, 28.—I spent the day in the council with the Twelve Apostles at the house of President Young, conversing with them upon a variety of subjects. Brother Joseph Fielding was present, having been absent four years on a mission to England. I told the brethren that the Book of Mormon was the most correct of any book on earth, and the keystone of our religion, and a man would get nearer to God by abiding by its precepts, than by any other book. (*Nov. 28, 1841, Joseph counsels with the Twelve in Nauvoo, Ill.*) HC4:461

#### Elder Heber J. Grant

I rejoice in the wonderful spirit of the Book of Mormon. I believe that it is one of the greatest missionaries in the hands of the Elder that it is possible for him to have. I believe that no man can open that book and read it with a prayerful heart, and ask God, in the name of Jesus Christ, for a testimony regarding its divinity, but what the Lord will manifest unto him by His Spirit the truth of the book. Now that is the promise made in the book itself and God has performed it; He has done it in thousands of cases. There is a mark of divinity in this book; and I maintain that no man can read, for instance the 36th chapter, the commandments of Alma to his son Helaman without receiving an impression of this kind. CR1908Apr:57

#### Joseph Smith,
*receiving the Word of the Lord*

I tell thee these things as a witness unto thee—that the words or the work which thou hast been writing are true. (*Revelation to Joseph and Oliver Cowdery regarding the Book of Mormon, April 1829*) D&C 6:17

#### Joseph Smith,
*receiving the Word of the Lord*

Behold, I have manifested unto you, by my Spirit in many instances, that the things which you have written are true; wherefore you know that they are true. 3. And if you know that they are true, behold, I give unto you a commandment, that you rely upon the things which are written; 4. For in them are all things written concerning the foundation of my church, my gospel, and my rock. (*Revelation directed to Oliver Cowdery regarding his writing the words of the Book of Mormon as Joseph translated them, received June 1829*) D&C 18:2-4

**Related Witnesses:**
#### Moroni, son of Mormon

And when ye shall receive these things, I would exhort you that ye would ask God, the Eternal Father, in the name of Christ, if these things are not true; and if ye shall ask with a sincere heart, with real intent, having faith in Christ, he will manifest the truth of it unto you, by the power of the Holy Ghost. 5. And by the power of the Holy Ghost ye may know the truth of all things. (*The final writings of Moroni in the Book of Mormon, about A.D. 421*) Moro.10:4-5

#### Nephi, son of Lehi

And now, my beloved brethren, and also Jew, and all ye ends of the earth, hearken unto these words and believe in Christ; and if ye believe not in these words believe in Christ. And if ye shall believe in Christ ye will believe in these words, for they are the words of Christ, and he hath given them unto me; and they teach all men that they should do good. 11. And if they are not the words of Christ, judge ye—for Christ will show unto you, with power and great glory, that they are his words, at the last day; and you and I shall stand face to face before his bar; and ye shall know that I have . been commanded of him to write these things, notwithstanding my weakness. 12. And I pray the Father in the name of Christ that many of us, if not all, may be saved in his kingdom at that great and last day. (*Nephi writes, between 559-545 B.C.*) 2Ne.33:10-12

#### Jesus,
*quoted by Mormon*

For in that day, for my sake shall the Father work a work, which shall be a great and a marvelous work among them; and there shall be among them those who will not believe it, although a man shall declare it unto them. 10. But behold, the life of my servant shall be in my hand; therefore they shall not hurt him, although he shall be marred because of them.

not true; and if ye shall ask with a sincere heart, with real intent, having faith in Christ, he will manifest the truth of it unto you, by the power of the Holy Ghost. 5. And by the power of the Holy Ghost ye may know the truth of all things. (*Moroni's final writings, about* A.D. *421*) Moro.10:4-5

### N. Eldon Tanner

I invite and encourage each and every one of you to investigate and to read the Book of Mormon, to test and enjoy the promise contained therein, which is: "And when ye shall receive these things, I would exhort you that ye would ask God, the Eternal Father, in the name of Christ, if these things are not true; and if ye shall ask with a sincere heart, with real intent, having faith in Christ, he will manifest the truth of it unto you, by the power of the Holy Ghost. ¶ And by the power of the Holy Ghost ye may know the truth of all things." (Moro.10:4-5) ¶ This promise, and my testimony, I leave with you in the name of Jesus Christ. Amen. CR1972Apr:59

### Marion G. Romney

The Holy Ghost not only bears witness to the divinity of the Father and the Son; he also bears witness to the truth, particularly gospel truths. ¶ ". . . .[W]hen you shall read these things [speaking of the gospel truths contained in the Book of Mormon], . . . I would exhort you," wrote Moroni, "that ye would ask God, the Eternal Father, in the name of Christ, if these things are not true; and if ye shall ask with a sincere heart, with real intent, having faith in Christ, he will manifest the truth of it unto you, by the power of the Holy Ghost." ¶ And then he adds this great promise: ¶ "And by the power of the Holy Ghost ye may know the truth of all things." (Moro.10:4-5) ¶ Hundreds and thousands of people have accepted and acted upon this challenge and thereafter borne witness, by the power of the Holy Ghost, to its truth. CR1974Apr:132

### Elder Ezra Taft Benson

Now God expects us to use the Book of Mormon in several ways. We are to read it ourselves—carefully, prayerfully—and ponder as we read, as to whether this book is the work of God or of an unlearned youth. And then when we are finished reading the things in the book, Moroni exhorts us to put them to the test in these words: ¶ "And when ye shall receive these things, I would exhort you that ye would ask God, the Eternal Father, in the name of Christ, if these things are not true; and if ye shall ask with a sincere heart, with real intent, having faith in Christ, he will manifest the truth of it unto you, by the power of the Holy

Ghost." (Moro.10:4) I have done as Moroni exhorts, and I can testify to you that this book is from God and so is verily true. CR1975Apr:95

**Related Witnesses:**

### LeGrand Richards

How could any sane person, a lover of truth, read that testimony and then not want to know whether that book is true, and then read the promise in the latter part of it, that if any man would read it and ask God the Eternal Father, in the name of Jesus Christ, having faith that the Lord would manifest the truth of it unto him by the power of the Holy Ghost. (See Moro.10:4-5.) CR1976Oct:94

---

### 69. The Book of Mormon sustains the Bible and is in harmony with it.

### Anthony W. Ivins

This book [Book of Mormon] is the strongest corroborative evidence to the divinity of the things contained in the Bible, that there is in the world. It is the strongest evidence of the divinity of the mission of the Redeemer of the world, that can be found, the Bible alone excepted. . . . Not one line in it, not one doctrine which it teaches, not one truth which it sets forth, has been found to be out of harmony with the word of the Lord, as contained in the Bible, and as it has come to us through his inspired servants—a thing which can be said of no other book in the world. CR1921Apr:20-21

### Nephi, son of Lehi

And the angel spake unto me, saying: These last records, which thou hast seen among the Gentiles, shall establish the truth of the first, which are of the twelve apostles of the Lamb, and shall make known the plain and precious things which have been taken away from them; and shall make known to all kindreds, tongues, and people, that the Lamb of God is the Son of the Eternal Father, and the Savior of the world; and that all men must come unto him, or they cannot be saved. (*An angel reveals the Lord's mercy toward the Gentiles, 600-592* B.C.) 1Ne.13:40

### President Heber J. Grant

The Book of Mormon is in absolute harmony from start to finish with other sacred scriptures. There is not a doctrine taught in it that does not harmonize with the teachings of Jesus Christ. . . . It is in every way a true witness for God, and it sustains the Bible and is in harmony with the Bible. CR1929Apr:128-29

### President Heber J. Grant

The Book of Mormon does not in any degree

conflict with or take the place of the Holy Bible, but is the strongest corroborative evidence in existence of the divine origin of that sacred record. CR1930Apr:10

### President Heber J. Grant

All my life I have been finding additional evidences that the Bible is the Book of books, and that the Book of Mormon is the greatest witness for the truth of the Bible that has ever been published. (*"The President Speaks: Excerpts from the Utterances of Heber J. Grant," IE1936Nov:660*) TLDP:612

### Joseph Smith

And gave him power from on high, by the means which were before prepared, to translate the Book of Mormon; 9. Which contains a record of a fallen people, and the fulness of the gospel of Jesus Christ to the Gentiles and to the Jews also; 10. Which was given by inspiration, and is confirmed to others by the ministering of angels, and is declared unto the world by them— 11. Proving to the world that the holy scriptures are true, and that God does inspire men and call them to his holy work in this age and generation, as well as in generations of old; 12. Thereby showing that he is the same God yesterday, today, and forever. Amen. (*Revelation on Church Organization and Government, April 1830; the Book of Mormon proves the divinity of the latter-day work*) D&C 20:8-12

### Joseph, son of Jacob (Israel),
### quoted by Lehi,
### who is quoted by his son Nephi

But a seer will I raise up out of the fruit of thy loins; and unto him will I give power to bring forth my word unto the seed of thy loins—and not to the bringing forth my word only, saith the Lord, but to the convincing them of my word, which shall have already gone forth among them. 12. Wherefore, the fruit of thy loins shall write; and the fruit of the loins of Judah shall write; and that which shall be written by the fruit of thy loins, and also that which shall be written by the fruit of the loins of Judah, shall grow together, unto the confounding of false doctrines and laying down of contentions, and establishing peace among the fruit of thy loins, and bringing them to the knowledge of their fathers in the latter days, and also to the knowledge of my covenants, saith the Lord. (*Lehi quotes Joseph in Egypt who tells of the word of the Lord that came to him*) 2Ne.3:11-12

### James E. Talmage,
### also quoting Ezekiel

Ezekiel saw in vision the coming together of the stick of Judah, and the stick of Joseph, signifying the Bible and the Book of Mormon. The passage last referred to reads, in the words of Ezekiel: "The word of the Lord came again unto me, saying, Moreover, thou son of man, take thee one stick, and write upon it, For Judah, and for the children of Israel his companions: then take another stick, and write upon it, For Joseph, the stick of Ephraim, and for all the house of Israel his companions: And join them one to another into one stick; and they shall become one in thine hand." ¶ When we call to mind the ancient custom in the making of books—that of writing on long strips of parchment and rolling the same on rods or sticks, the use of the word "stick" as equivalent to "book" in the passage becomes apparent. At the time of this utterance, the Israelites had divided into two nations known as the kingdom of Judah and that of Israel, or Ephraim. Plainly the separate records of Judah and Joseph are here referred to. Now, as we have seen, the Nephite nation comprised the descendants of Lehi who belonged to the tribe of Manasseh, of Ishmael who was an Ephraimite, and of Zoram whose tribal relation is not definitely stated. The Nephites were then of the tribes of Joseph; and their record or "stick" is as truly represented by the Book of Mormon as is the "stick" of Judah by the Bible. ¶ That the bringing forth of the record of Joseph or Ephraim was to be accomplished through the direct power of God is evident from the Lord's exposition of the vision of Ezekiel, wherein He says: "Behold, I will take the stick of Joseph . . . and will put them with him, even with the stick of Judah." AF:249-50

### Ezekiel

The word of the LORD came again unto me, saying, 16. Moreover, thou son of man, take thee one stick, and write upon it, For Judah, and for the children of Israel his companions: then take another stick, and write upon it, For Joseph, the stick of Ephraim, and for all the house of Israel his companions: 17. And join them one to another into one stick; and they shall become one in thine hand. 18. And when the children of thy people shall speak unto thee, saying, Wilt thou not shew us what thou meanest by these? 19. Say unto them, Thus saith the Lord GOD; Behold, I will take the stick of Joseph, which is in the hand of Ephraim, and the tribes of Israel his fellows, and will put them with him, even with the stick of Judah, and make them one stick, and they shall be one in mine hand. (*Revelation to the prophet Ezekiel*) Ezek.37:15-19

### Joseph Smith

We believe the Bible to be the word of God as

far as it is translated correctly; we also believe the Book of Mormon to be the word of God. (*The eighth of the thirteen Articles of Faith; letter to John Wentworth, March 1, 1842*) AofF:8

**President Brigham Young**

No man can say that this book (laying his hand on the Bible) is true, is the word of the Lord, is the way, is the guide-board in the path, and a charter by which we may learn the will of God; and at the same time say that the Book of Mormon is untrue; if he has had the privilege of reading it, or of hearing it read, and learning its doctrines. There is not that person on the face of the earth who has had the privilege of learning the Gospel of Jesus Christ from these two books, that can say that one is true, and the other is false. No Latter-day Saint, no man or woman, can say the Book of Mormon is true, and at the same time say that the Bible is untrue. If one be true, both are; and if one be false, both are false. (*In Tabernacle, July 11, 1852, JD1:38*) TLDP:611

**Related Witnesses:**

**Joseph Smith**

And the Book of Mormon and the holy scriptures are given of me for your instruction; and the power of my Spirit quickeneth all things. (*Revelation for Ezra Thayre and Northrop Sweet, Oct. 1830*) D&C 33:16

**Joseph Smith**

And again, the elders, priests and teachers of this church shall teach the principles of my gospel, which are in the Bible and the Book of Mormon, in the which is the fulness of the gospel. (*Revelation "embracing the law of the Church," Feb. 9, 1831*) D&C 42:12

**Nephi, son of Lehi**

And because my words shall hiss forth—many of the Gentiles shall say: A Bible! A Bible! We have got a Bible, and there cannot be any more Bible. 4. But thus saith the Lord God: O fools, they shall have a Bible; and it shall proceed forth from the Jews, mine ancient covenant people. And what thank they the Jews for the Bible which they receive from them? Yea, what do the Gentiles mean? Do they remember the travails, and the labors, and the pains of the Jews, and their diligence unto me, in bringing forth salvation unto the Gentiles? . . . 10. Wherefore, because that ye have a Bible ye need not suppose that it contains all my words; neither need ye suppose that I have not caused more to be written. 11. For I command all men, both in the east and in the west, and in the north, and in the south, and in the islands of the sea, that they shall write the words which I speak unto them; for out of the books which shall be written I will

judge the world, every man according to their works, according to that which is written. (*The Lord speaks to Nephi about the latter-day Gentiles, 559-545 B.C.*) 2Ne.29:3-4,10-11

**HYMNS Written by Prophets Applicable to this Topic**

**Parley P. Pratt**
*An Angel from on High*
HYMNS:13

An angel from on high
The long, long silence broke;
Descending from the sky,
These gracious words he spoke:
Lo! in Cumorah's lonely hill
A sacred record lies concealed.
Lo! in Cumorah's lonely hill
A sacred record lies concealed.

Sealed by Moroni's hand,
It has for ages lain
To wait the Lord's command,
From dust to speak again.
It shall again to light come forth
To usher in Christ's reign on earth.
It shall again to light come forth
To usher in Christ's reign on earth.

It speaks of Joseph's seed
And makes the remnant known
Of nations long since dead,
Who once had dwelt alone.
The fulness of the gospel, too,
Its pages will reveal to view.
The fulness of the gospel, too,
Its pages will reveal to view.

The time is now fulfilled,
The long-expected day;
Let earth obedience yield
And darkness flee away.
Remove the seals; be wide unfurled
Its light and glory to the world.
Remove the seals; be wide unfurled
Its light and glory to the world.

Lo! Israel filled with joy
Shall now be gathered home,
Their wealth and means employ
To build Jerusalem,
While Zion shall arise and shine
And fill the earth with truth divine,
While Zion shall arise and shine
And fill the earth with truth divine.

# List of Doctrines

## CALLING AND ELECTION

*Doctrines Located in This Topic*

70. Church members are to strive to make their calling and election sure.

71. After we receive the more sure word of prophecy, that our calling and election is made sure, we may receive the Second Comforter, which carries the promise of eternal life.

# CALLING AND ELECTION

**70. Church members are to strive to make their calling and election sure.**

**Marion G. Romney,**
*also quoting Joseph Smith and Peter*

The theme I have in mind to discuss is "Making One's Calling and Election Sure." To do this one must receive a divine witness that he will inherit eternal life. . . . ¶ The fullness of eternal life is not attainable in mortality, but the peace which is its harbinger and which comes as a result of making one's calling and election sure is attainable in this life. The Lord has promised that ". . . he who doeth the works of righteousness shall receive his reward, even peace in this world, and eternal life in the world to come" (D&C 59:23). . . . ¶ Now I come directly to my theme: ¶ I take my text from Second Peter, and as he did, I direct my remarks ". . . to them that have obtained like precious faith with us. . . ." (2Pet. 1:1) ¶ Peter, having put the Saints in remembrance of gospel fundamentals, admonished them to ". . . give diligence to make your calling and election sure: for if ye do these things, ye shall never fall." (Ibid.1:10) ¶ By making their calling and election sure, the Saints were to gain entrance ". . . into the everlasting kingdom of our Lord and Savior Jesus Christ." To this fact Peter bore powerful witness. He reviewed his experience on the Mount of Transfiguration with James and John, where he says they heard the voice of ". . . God the Father . . ." declare of Jesus, "This is my beloved Son, in whom I am well pleased." Then by way of instruction that such an experience did not of itself make one's calling and election sure, he added, "We have also a more sure word of prophecy; . . ." (Ibid.1:11, 17, 19) ¶ Speaking on Sunday the 14th of May, 1843, the Prophet Joseph Smith took this statement of Peter for his text. From the Prophet's sermon I quote: ¶ "Notwithstanding the apostle exhorts them to add to their faith, virtue, knowledge, temperance, etc., yet he exhorts them to make their calling and election sure. And though they had heard an audible voice from heaven bearing testimony that Jesus was the Son of God, yet he says we have a more sure word of prophecy. . . . Now wherein could they have a more sure word of prophecy than to hear the voice of God, This is my beloved son, etc.," Answering his own questions, the Prophet continued, "Though they might hear the voice of God and know that Jesus was the Son of God, this would be no evidence that their election and calling was made sure, that they had part with Christ, and were joint heirs with Him. They then would want that more

sure word of prophecy, that they were sealed in the heavens and had the promise of eternal life in the kingdom of God. Then, having this promise sealed unto them, it was an anchor to the soul, sure and steadfast. Though the thunders might roll and lightnings flash, and earthquakes bellow, and war gather thick around, yet this hope and knowledge would support the soul in every hour of trial, trouble and tribulation." ¶ Then speaking directly to his listeners, the Prophet continued: ¶ ". . . I would exhort you to go on and continue to call upon God until you make your calling and election sure for yourselves, by obtaining this more sure word of prophecy. . . ." (HC5:388-389) CR1965Oct:20-21; DGSM:52

**Marion G. Romney**

This gift of eternal life in the world to come may not, of course, be fully realized during earth life. An assurance that it will be obtained in the world to come may, however, be had in this world. As a matter of fact, the blessings of the celestial kingdom are promised only to those who have such an assurance. According to the vision, a successful candidate for these blessings must qualify on three counts. First, he must have "received the testimony of Jesus, and believed on his name" and have been "baptized after the manner of his burial"; second, he must have received "the Holy Spirit by the laying on of the hands of him who is ordained and sealed unto this power"; and third, he must be "sealed by the Holy Spirit of promise." (D&C 76:51-53) ¶ The Prophet Joseph taught that one so sealed would have within himself an assurance born of the Spirit that he would obtain eternal life in the world to come. He urgently and repeatedly admonished the Saints of his day to obtain such an assurance by making their calling and election sure. It is this assurance within a person that brings to him that peace in this world which will sustain him in every tribulation. (Learning for the Eternities, p. 95) TLDP:153

**Marion G. Romney,**
*also quoting Joseph Smith*

"It is one thing to be on the mount and hear the excellent voice, etc., and another to hear the voice declare to you, You have a part and lot in that kingdom." (HC5:403) ¶ That passage from the Prophet's writings has been on my mind a great deal. He gave it at the end of a long sermon, in which he has been urging the people of his day to make their calling and their election sure. He himself had made his calling and election sure. ¶ The Lord said to the Prophet Joseph Smith on one occasion, ¶ "For I am the Lord thy God, and will be with thee even unto the end of the world, and through all eternity; for verily I seal upon you your exaltation, and prepare a throne for you in the kingdom of my Father, with Abraham your Father." (D&C 132:49) ¶ And then the Lord specifies in the next sentence the conditions that brought that great blessing to the Prophet Joseph. ¶ "Behold, I have seen your sacrifices, and will forgive all your sins; I have seen your sacrifices in obedience to that which I have told you." (D&C 132:50) ¶ He gave that same witness to Heber C. Kimball. I suppose that a man who had that witness would be enjoying the more sure word of prophecy, which the Prophet defines as ¶ ". . . a man's knowing that he is sealed up unto eternal life, by revelation and the spirit of prophecy, through the power of the Holy Priesthood." (D&C 131:5) CR1954Apr:132

**Joseph Smith**

Though they might hear the voice of God and know that Jesus was the Son of God, this would be no evidence that their election and calling was made sure, that they had part with Christ, and were joint heirs with Him. They then would want that more sure word of prophecy, that they were sealed in the heavens and had the promise of eternal life in the kingdom of God. . . . ¶ . . . . Then I would exhort you to go on and continue to call upon God until you make your calling and election sure for yourselves, by obtaining this more sure word of prophecy, and wait patiently for the promise until you obtain it. (*Sermon on Sunday, May 14, 1843*) HC5:388-89

**Joseph Smith**

Contend earnestly for the like precious faith with the Apostle Peter, "and add to your faith virtue," knowledge, temperance, patience, godliness, brotherly kindness, charity; "for if these things be in you, and abound, they make you that ye shall neither be barren nor unfruitful in the knowledge of our Lord Jesus Christ." Another point, after having all these qualifications, he lays this injunction upon the people "to make your calling and election sure." He is emphatic upon this subject—after adding all this virtue, knowledge, &c., "Make your calling and election sure." What is the secret—the starting point? "According as His divine power hath given unto us all things that pertain unto life and godliness." How did he obtain all things? Through the knowledge of Him who hath called him. There could not anything be given, pertaining to life and godliness, without knowledge. . . . ¶ Salvation is for a man to be saved from all his enemies; for until a man can triumph over death, he is not saved. A knowledge of the priesthood alone will do this. . . . ¶

We have no claim in our eternal compact, in relation to eternal things, unless our actions and contracts and all things tend to this end. But after all this, you have got to make your calling and election sure. If this injunction would lie largely on those to whom it was spoken, how much more those of the present generation! ¶ 1st key: Knowledge is the power of salvation. 2nd key: Make your calling and election sure. 3rd key: It is one thing to be on the mount and hear the excellent voice. &c., &c., and another to hear the voice declare to you, You have a part and lot in that kingdom. (*Discourse Sunday, May 21, 1842 in Kirtland Temple*) HC5:402-3

**Peter**

Wherefore the rather, brethren, give diligence to make your calling and election sure: for if ye do these things, ye shall never fall: 11. For so an entrance shall be ministered unto you abundantly into the everlasting kingdom of our Lord and Saviour Jesus Christ. 12. Wherefore I will not be negligent to put you always in remembrance of these things, though ye know them, and be established in the present truth. (*Peter writes to members of the Church, about* A.D. *60 to 64*) 2Pet.1:10-12

**Related Witnesses:**

**Joseph Smith**

The more sure word of prophecy means a man's knowing that he is sealed up unto eternal life, by revelation and the spirit of prophecy, through the power of the Holy Priesthood. (*Revelation, May 17, 1843*) D&C 131:5

**Joseph Smith**

This principle ought (in its proper place) to be taught, for God hath not revealed anything to Joseph, but what he will make known to the Twelve, and even the least saint may know all things as fast as he is able to bear them, for the day must come when no man need say to his neighbor, know ye the Lord; for all shall know him (who remain) from the least to the greatest. How is this to be done? It is to be done by this sealing power, and the other Comforter spoken of, which will be manifest by revelation. (*Instructions to the brethren at a conference of the Twelve, June 27, 1839 in Commerce, Ill.*) HC3:380

**Joseph Smith,**
*receiving the Word of the Lord*

Wherefore, I now send upon you another Comforter, even upon you my friends, that it may abide in your hearts, even the Holy Spirit of promise; which other Comforter is the same that I promised unto my disciples, as is recorded in the testimony of John. 4. This Comforter is the promise which I give unto you of eternal life, even the glory of the celestial kingdom; (*Revelation Dec. 27/28, 1832; the "olive leaf message of peace"*) D&C 88:3-4

### Peter

For we have not followed cunningly devised fables, when we made known unto you the power and coming of our Lord Jesus Christ, but were eyewitnesses of his majesty. 17. For he received from God the Father honour and glory, when there came such a voice to him from the excellent glory, This is my beloved Son, in whom I am well pleased. 18. And this voice which came from heaven we heard, when we were with him in the holy mount. 19. *We have also a more sure word of prophecy;* [italics added] whereunto ye do well that ye take heed, as unto a light that shineth in a dark place, until the day dawn, and the day star arise in your hearts: 20. Knowing this first, that no prophecy of the scripture is of any private interpretation. (*Peter writes to members of the Church, about A.D. 60 to 64*) 2Pet.1:16-20

### Melvin J. Ballard

And what does it mean to keep your second estate? It means to subscribe to all of the laws of the gospel of the Son of God. That is what it means to keep your second estate, to make your calling and election sure. And they who keep their second estate shall have glory added upon their heads forever and forever. (Sermons and Missionary Services of Melvin R. Ballard, p. 224) TLDP:64

**Author's Note:** Perhaps we should be a little more occupied with doing works of righteousness than with simply striving for the Lord's blessing on ourselves. According to Joseph Smith, as cited above, "We have no claim in our eternal compact, in relation to eternal things, unless our actions and contracts and all things tend to this end." In Mosiah 26th chapter, the Lord assured Alma of eternal life in response to Alma's prayer—a prayer *not for himself* but a prayer that he be given wisdom to judge righteously certain misled Church members. ¶ Though a person might have his calling and election made sure *there remains a possibility that he may fall from grace.* "But there is a possibility that man may fall from grace and depart from the living God; Therefore let the church take heed and pray always, lest they fall into temptation; Yea, and even let those who are sanctified take heed also." (D&C 20:32-34) ¶ *But it appears that according to the Prophet Joseph Smith, to fall from grace thereafter would be a permanent fall!* "The doctrine that the Presbyterians and Methodists have quarreled so

much about—once in grace, always in grace, or falling away from grace, I will say a word about. They are both wrong. Truth takes a road between them both, for while the Presbyterian says 'once in grace, you cannot fall;' the Methodist says: 'You can have grace today, fall from it tomorrow, next day have grace again; and so follow on, changing continually.' But the doctrine of the Scriptures and the spirit of Elijah would show them both false, and take a road between them both; for, according to the Scripture, if men have received the good word of God, and tasted of the powers of the world to come, if they shall fall away, it is impossible to renew them again, seeing they have crucified the Son of God afresh, and put Him to an open shame; so there is a possibility of falling away; you could not be renewed again, and the power of Elijah cannot seal against this sin, for this is a reserve made in the seals and power of the Priesthood." ¶ Bruce R. McConkie writes, "[T]he added blessing of having one's calling and election made sure is itself an encouragement to avoid sin and a hedge against its further commission. By that long course of obedience and trial which enabled them to gain so great a blessing the sanctified saints have charted a course and developed a pattern of living which avoids sin and encourages righteousness. . . . But suppose such persons become disaffected and the spirit of repentance leaves them—which is a seldom and almost unheard of eventuality—still, what then? The answer is—and the revelations and teachings of the Prophet Joseph Smith so recite!—they must pay the penalty of their own sins, for the blood of Christ will not cleanse them. Or if they commit murder or adultery, they lose their promised inheritance because these sins are exempt from the sealing promises. Or if they commit the unpardonable sin, they become sons of perdition." (Doctrinal New Testament Commentary, 3:343)

---

71. After we receive the more sure word of prophecy, that our calling and election is made sure, we may receive the Second Comforter, which carries the promise of eternal life.

### Joseph Smith

There are two Comforters spoken of. One is the Holy Ghost, the same as given on the day of Pentecost, and that all Saints receive after faith, repentance, and baptism. . . . ¶ The other Comforter spoken of is a subject of great interest, and perhaps understood by few of this generation. After a person has faith in Christ, repents of his sins, and is baptized for the remission of his sins and receives the Holy Ghost, (by the laying on of hands), which is the first Comforter, then let him continue to humble himself before God, hungering and thirsting after righteousness, and living by every word of God, and the Lord will soon say unto him, Son, thou shalt be exalted. When the Lord has thoroughly proved him, and finds that the man is determined to serve him at all hazards, then the man will find his calling and his election made sure, then it will be his privilege to receive the other Comforter, which the Lord hath promised the saints, as is recorded in the testimony of St. John, in the 14th chapter, from the 12th to the 27th verses. . . . (*Instruction at a conference of the Twelve, June 27, 1839*) HC3:380-81; TPJS:150; DGSM:52

### Bruce R. McConkie,
*also quoting Jeremiah and Joseph Smith*

Having in mind these concepts about the Second Comforter, and knowing that all those who so obtain have their callings and elections made sure, let us catch the vision, if we can, of one of the great prophetic utterances of Jeremiah. "Behold, the days come, saith the Lord . . . that I will make a new covenant with the house of Israel, and with the house of Judah." Hear it and mark it well: it will be a new covenant, a new and an everlasting covenant: it will be the fulness of the everlasting gospel, not in name only, but in fact and in deed, in active operation in the lives of men. . . . ¶ "But this shall be the covenant that I will make with the house of Israel; after those days, saith the Lord. I will put my law in their inward parts, and write it in their hearts; and will be their God, and they shall be my people." There will be a day when latter-day Israel will serve the Lord with all their hearts and make themselves worthy of the fulness of his glory. "And they shall teach no more every man his neighbour, and every man his brother, saying, Know the Lord: for they shall all know me, from the least of them unto the greatest of them, saith the Lord: for I will forgive their iniquity, and I will remember their sin no more." (Jer.31:31-34) . . . . ¶ . . . . The Prophet [Joseph Smith] speaks of making one's calling and election sure and of the sealing power whereby "we may be sealed up unto the day of redemption." Then he says: "This principle ought (in its proper place) to be taught, for God hath not revealed anything to Joseph, but what He will make known unto the Twelve, and even the least Saint may know all things as fast as he is able to bear them, for the day must come when no man need say to

his neighbor, Know ye the Lord: for all shall know Him (who remain) from the least to the greatest." (The Millennial Messiah, pp. 681-82) TLDP:403-04

### Related Witnesses:
#### Peter

Wherefore the rather, brethren, give diligence to make your calling and election sure: for if ye do these things, ye shall never fall: 11. For so an entrance shall be ministered unto you abundantly into the everlasting kingdom of our Lord and Saviour Jesus Christ. 12. Wherefore I will not be negligent to put you always in remembrance of these things, though ye know them, and be established in the present truth. (*Peter writes to members of the Church, about A.D. 60–64*) 2Pet.1:10-12

#### Marion G. Romney

The fullness of eternal life is not attainable in mortality, but the peace which is its harbinger and which comes as a result of making one's calling and election sure is attainable in this life. The Lord has promised that ". . . he who doeth the works of righteousness shall receive his reward, even peace in this world, and eternal life in the world to come." (D&C 59:23) CR1965Oct:20

#### Joseph Smith,
*receiving the Word of the Lord*

Verily, thus saith the Lord unto you who have assembled yourselves together to receive his will concerning you: 2. Behold, this is pleasing unto your Lord, and the angels rejoice over you; the alms of your prayers have come up into the ears of the Lord of Sabaoth, and are recorded in the book of the names of the sanctified, even them of the celestial world. 3. Wherefore, I now send upon you another Comforter, even upon you my friends, that it may abide in your hearts, even the Holy Spirit of promise; which other Comforter is the same that I promised unto my disciples, as is recorded in the testimony of John. 4. This Comforter is the promise which I give unto you of eternal life, even the glory of the celestial kingdom; (*Revelation, Dec. 27/28, 1832*) D&C 88:1-4

#### John

I will not leave you comfortless: I will come to you. . . . 21. He that hath my commandments, and keepeth them, he it is that loveth me: and he that loveth me shall be loved of my Father, and I will love him, and will manifest myself to him. . . . 23. Jesus answered and said unto him, If a man love me, he will keep my words: and my Father will love him, and we will come unto him, and make our abode with him. (*Jesus, on the occasion of the Last Supper with the Twelve, promises the Second Comforter*) John 14:18,21,23

**Elder Joseph Fielding Smith**

Those who press forward in righteousness, living by every word of revealed truth, have power to make their calling and election sure. They receive the more sure word of prophecy and know by revelation and the authority of the priesthood that they are sealed up unto eternal life. They are sealed against all manner of sin and blasphemy against the Holy Ghost and the shedding of innocent blood. (Doctrines of Salvation, 2:46) TLDP:64

**President Joseph F. Smith**

Whoever will keep the commandments of God, no matter whether it be you or any other people, they will rise and not fall, they will lead and not follow, they will go upward and not downward; God will exalt them and magnify them before the nations of the earth, and he will set the seal of his approval upon them, will name them as his own. ("A Sermon on Purity," Improvement Era, May 1903, p. 506) TLDP:436

**Joseph Smith,**
*receiving the Word of the Lord*

For whoso is faithful unto the obtaining these two priesthoods of which I have spoken, and the magnifying their calling, are sanctified by the Spirit unto the renewing of their bodies. 34. They become the sons of Moses and of Aaron and the seed of Abraham, and the church and kingdom, and the elect of God. 35. And also all they who receive this priesthood receive me, saith the Lord; 36. For he that receiveth my servants receiveth me; 37. And he that receiveth me receiveth my Father; 38. And he that receiveth my Father receiveth my Father's kingdom; therefore all that my Father hath shall be given unto him. (*Revelation on priesthood, Sept. 22/23, 1832*) D&C 84:33-38

**President Brigham Young,**
*quoted by John A. Widtsoe*

If you will follow the doctrines, and be guided by the precepts of that book [the Bible], it will direct you where you may see as you are seen, where you may converse with Jesus Christ, have the visitation of angels, have dreams, visions, and revelations, and understand and know God for yourselves." (*Discourse in July 1853, JD1:243*) DBY:126

# List of Doctrines

## CHILDREN

*Doctrines Located in This Topic*

72. Children are innocent and are not under penalty of sin when born into mortality.

73. Little children have no need of repentance or baptism.

74. Little children who die before they reach the age of accountability are saved in the celestial kingdom.

75. Little children (babies) are to be blessed before the Church.

76. Children should respect and honor their parents.

77. We are to learn in our youth to keep the commandments of God.

*Doctrines on CHILDREN Located in Other Topics*

51. Baptism is required of children only when they arrive at the age of accountability—when they are capable of repentance.

565. Every spirit born on earth is innocent.

862. Parents are to support their minor children.

(See topic FAMILY AND PARENTHOOD.)

# CHILDREN

**72. Children are innocent and are not under penalty of sin when born into mortality.**

### Elder Joseph Fielding Smith

It is a false doctrine which prevails in the world that children have to be cleansed from original sin. The posterity of Adam in no way whatever is subject to original sin. Even should parents be guilty, that does not place any sin on the soul of the child. Little children are not under the cloud of sin. MPSG1972-73:124

### Joseph Smith

Every spirit of man was innocent in the beginning; and God having redeemed man from the fall, men became again, in their infant state, innocent before God. (*Revelation at Kirtland, Ohio, May 6, 1833*) D&C 93:38

### Delbert L. Stapley

We learn from this revelation [D&C 93:38] that in the beginning of mortal life all mankind is innocent before God and, therefore, is like the beginning river of water, pure and undefiled. As the polluted tributaries of water enter the main stream, our lives too become polluted when we allow tributaries of evil and wickedness to enter. It is these tributaries of evil we must be concerned about and fortify ourselves against. Wickedness never was happiness, but to the contrary, it is depressing; it destroys conscience and ultimately the spiritual life of the constant, erring individual. CR1971Oct:105

### Mormon

Listen to the words of Christ, your Redeemer, your Lord and your God. Behold, I came into the world not to call the righteous but sinners to repentance; the whole need no physician, but they that are sick; wherefore, little children are whole, for they are not capable of committing sin; wherefore the curse of Adam is taken from them in me, that it hath no power over them; and the law of circumcision is done away in me. 9. And after this manner did the Holy Ghost manifest the word of God unto me; wherefore, my beloved son, I know that it is solemn mockery before God, that ye should baptize little children. 10. Behold I say unto you that this thing shall ye teach—repentance and baptism unto those who are accountable and capable of committing sin; yea, teach parents that they must repent and be baptized, and humble themselves as their little children, and they shall all be saved with their little children. 11. And their little children need no repentance, neither baptism. Behold, baptism is unto repentance to the fulfilling the commandments unto the remission of sins. 12. But little children are alive in Christ, even from the foundation of the world; if not so, God is a partial God, and also a changeable God, and a respecter to persons; for how many little children have died without baptism! 13. Wherefore, if little children could not be saved without baptism, these must have gone to an endless hell. 14. Behold I say unto you, that he that supposeth that little children need baptism is in the gall of bitterness and in the bonds of iniquity; for he hath neither faith, hope, nor charity; wherefore, should he be cut off while in the thought, he must go down to hell. 15. For awful is the wickedness to suppose that God saveth one child because of baptism, and the other must perish because he hath no baptism. (*Mormon writes to his son Moroni, prior to A.D. 384*) Moro.8:8-15

### King Benjamin, *quoted by Mormon*

And even if it were possible that little children could sin they could not be saved; but I say unto you they are blessed; for behold, as in Adam, or by nature, they fall, even so the blood of Christ atoneth for their sins. 17. And moreover, I say unto you, that there shall be no other name given nor any other way nor means whereby salvation can come unto the children of men, only in and through the name of Christ, the Lord Omnipotent. 18. For behold he judgeth, and his judgment is just; and the infant perisheth not that dieth in his infancy; but men drink damnation to their own souls except they humble themselves and become as little children, and believe that salvation was, and is, and is to come, in and through the atoning blood of Christ, the Lord Omnipotent. (*King Benjamin makes known to the people the things told to him by an angel of God, about 124 B.C.*) Mosiah 3:18

### Related Witnesses:
### Joseph Smith

We believe that men will be punished for their own sins, and not for Adam's transgression. (*The second of the thirteen Articles of Faith; letter to John Wentworth, March 1, 1842*) AofF:2

### Elder Joseph Fielding Smith

No matter what David said [Ps.51:5] "Behold, I was shapen in iniquity; and in sin did my mother conceive me," he was not born in sin. In the midst of his sorrow because he violated the moral law, he may have felt his sin keenly and in this manner expressed himself, but this did not make the statement true that his parents were guilty of sin and that he partook of it in his birth. Let it be remembered that David was speaking only for and of himself, and that his words cannot in justice be universally applied. MPSG1972-73:123

---

### 73. Little children have no need of repentance or baptism.

**James E. Talmage**
The Church of Jesus Christ of Latter-day Saints teaches as a doctrine founded on reason, justice, and scripture, that all children are innocent in the sight of God, and that, until they reach an age of personal responsibility, baptism is neither requisite nor proper in their behalf; that, in short, they are saved through the atonement of Christ. AF:79

**Joseph Smith**
"Do you believe in the baptism of infants?" asks the Presbyterian. No. "Why?" Because it is nowhere written in the Bible. Circumcision is not baptism, neither was baptism instituted in the place of circumcision. Baptism is for remission of sins. Children have no sins. Jesus blessed them and said, "Do what you have seen me do." Children are all made alive in Christ, and those of riper years through faith and repentance. (*To the Saints in the Grove, Nauvoo, Ill., July 1843*) HC5:499

**Mormon**
Listen to the words of Christ, your Redeemer, your Lord and your God. Behold, I came into the world not to call the righteous but sinners to repentance; the whole need no physician, but they that are sick; wherefore, little children are whole, for they are not capable of committing sin; wherefore the curse of Adam is taken from them in me, that it hath no power over them; and the law of circumcision is done away in me. 9. And after this manner did the Holy Ghost manifest the word of God unto me; wherefore, my beloved son, I know that it is solemn mockery before God, that ye should baptize little children. 10. Behold I say unto you that this thing shall ye teach—repentance and baptism unto those who are accountable and capable of committing sin; yea, teach parents that they must repent and be baptized, and humble themselves as their little children, and they shall all be saved with their little children. 11. And their little children need no repentance, neither baptism. Behold, baptism is unto repentance to the fulfilling the commandments unto the remission of sins. 12. But little children are alive in Christ, even from the foundation of the world; if not so, God is a partial God, and also a changeable God, and a respecter to persons; for how many little children have died without baptism! 13. Wherefore, if little children could not be saved without baptism, these must have gone to an endless hell. 14. Behold I say unto you, that he that supposeth that little children need baptism is in the gall of bitterness and in the bonds of iniquity, for he hath neither faith, hope, nor charity; wherefore, should he be cut off while in the thought, he must go down to hell. 15. For awful is the wickedness to suppose that God saveth one child because of baptism, and the other must perish because he hath no baptism. (*Mormon writes to his son Moroni, prior to A.D. 384*) Moro.8:8-15

**Joseph Smith**
For all men must repent and be baptized, and not only men, but women, and children who have arrived at the years of accountability. (*Revelation received June 1829*) D&C 18:42

**Related Witnesses:**
**Jesus,**
*recorded in Matthew*
Then were there brought unto him little children, that he should put his hands on them, and pray: and the disciples rebuked them. 14. But Jesus said, Suffer little children, and forbid them not, to come unto me: for of such is the kingdom of heaven. (*Jesus ministers to the multitude*) Matt.19:13-14

**Jesus,**
*quoted by Mormon*
And when he had said these words, he wept, and the multitude bare record of it, and he took their little children, one by one, and blessed them, and prayed unto the Father for them. 22. And when he had done this he wept again; 23. And he spake unto the multitude, and said unto them: Behold your little ones. 24. And as they looked to behold they cast their eyes towards heaven, and they saw the heavens open, and they saw angels descending out of heaven as it were in the midst of fire; and they came down and encircled those little ones about, and they were encircled about with fire; and the angels did minister unto them. (*The resurrected Jesus instructs the Nephite people, A.D. 34*) 3Ne.17:21-24

**Joseph Smith**
No one can be received into the church of Christ unless he has arrived unto the years of accountability before God, and is capable of repentance. (*Revelation on Church Organization and Government, April 1830*) D&C 20:71

### Joseph Smith,
#### *receiving the Word of the Lord*

But behold, I say unto you, that little children are redeemed from the foundation of the world through mine Only Begotten; 47. Wherefore, they cannot sin, for power is not given unto Satan to tempt little children, until they begin to become accountable before me; (*Revelation received in presence of six elders, Sept. 1830*) D&C 29:46-47

### Elder Joseph Fielding Smith

Since all mankind come into the world innocent so far as this mortal life is concerned, and there is no sin laid to their charge, should they die in their childhood before they are accountable for their deeds, it would be manifestly unjust to condemn them. . . . It is not the fault of little children who die that their parents do not come into the Church and refuse to accept the gospel. Through the mercy and justice of our Eternal Father, every soul is entitled to hear the gospel. If they do not have the privilege in this mortal life, then they will have it in the spirit world, where it is preached to the dead and even the dead will be judged according to their works. MPSG1972-73:120

---

74. Little children who die before they reach the age of accountability are saved in the celestial kingdom.

### Joseph Smith

And I also beheld that all children who die before they arrive at the years of accountability are saved in the celestial kingdom of heaven. (*Vision received in Kirtland Temple, Jan. 21, 1836*) D&C 137:10

### Joseph Smith

All who have died without a knowledge of this Gospel, who would have received it if they had been permitted to tarry, shall be heirs of the celestial kingdom of God; also all that shall die henceforth without a knowledge of it, who would have received it with all their hearts, shall be heirs of that kingdom, for I, the Lord, will judge all men according to their works, according to the desire of their hearts. ¶ And I also beheld that all children who die before they arrive at the years of accountability, are saved in the celestial kingdom of heaven. (*The Prophet instructs the Twelve in Nauvoo, Ill., June 27, 1839*) HC2:380-81

### Elder Joseph Fielding Smith,
#### *also quoting Joseph Smith*

Little children who die before the age of accountability are saved in the celestial kingdom. The Prophet Joseph Smith received this knowledge by vision in the Kirtland Temple, January 21, 1836. On that occasion it was shown that ". . . all children who die before they arrive at the years of accountability are saved in the celestial kingdom of heaven." [HC2:381] MPSG1972-73:120-21

### President Joseph F. Smith,
#### *quoted by Elder Joseph Fielding Smith*

But, with little children who are taken away in infancy and innocence before they have reached the years of accountability, and are not capable of committing sin, the gospel reveals to us the fact that they are redeemed, and Satan has no power over them. Neither has death any power over them. They are redeemed by the blood of Christ, and they are saved just as surely as death has come into the world through the fall of our first parents. MPSG1972-73:121

### Abinadi,
#### *quoted by Mormon*

And little children also have eternal life. (*Abinadi preaches to King Noah and his people of the intercession of Christ, about 148 B.C.*) Mosiah 15:25

### Mormon

Listen to the words of Christ, your Redeemer, your Lord and your God. Behold, I came into the world not to call the righteous but sinners to repentance; the whole need no physician, but they that are sick; wherefore, little children are whole, for they are not capable of committing sin; wherefore the curse of Adam is taken from them in me, that it hath no power over them; and the law of circumcision is done away in me. . . . 10. Behold I say unto you that this thing shall ye teach—repentance and baptism unto those who are accountable and capable of committing sin; yea, teach parents that they must repent and be baptized, and humble themselves as their little children, and they shall all be saved with their little children. 11. And their little children need no repentance, neither baptism. Behold, baptism is unto repentance to the fulfilling the commandments unto the remission of sins. (*Mormon writes to his son Moroni, prior to A.D. 384*) Moro.8:8,10-11

### Joseph Smith,
#### *receiving the Word of the Lord*

But behold, I say unto you, that little children are redeemed from the foundation of the world through mine Only Begotten; 47. Wherefore, they cannot sin, for power is not given unto Satan to tempt little children, until they begin to become accountable before me; 48. For it is given unto them even as I will, according to mine own pleasure, that great things may be required at the hand of their fathers. 49. And, again, I say unto you, that whoso having knowledge, have I not commanded to repent? 50. And he that hath no understanding, it remaineth in me to do according as it is written. And now I declare no more unto you at this time. Amen. (*Revelation from the Lord received in presence of six elders, Sept. 1830*) D&C 29:46-50

### James E. Talmage

The Church of Jesus Christ of Latter-day Saints teaches as a doctrine founded on reason, justice, and scripture, that all children are innocent in the sight of God, and that, until they reach an age of personal responsibility, baptism is neither requisite nor proper in their behalf; that, in short, they are saved through the atonement of Christ. AF:79

---

75. Little children (babies) are to be blessed before the Church.

### Joseph Smith

Every member of the church of Christ having children is to bring them unto the elders before the church, who are to lay their hands upon them in the name of Jesus Christ, and bless them in his name. (*Revelation on Church Organization and Government, April 1830*) D&C 20:70

### President John Taylor,
*in behalf of the Quorum of the Twelve,*
*also quoting Joseph Smith*

We have nothing to say against a father blessing his children, the genius of the Priesthood being primarily patriarchal, with God himself the great Father of us all at the head. Indeed we claim that every man holding the Melchizedek Priesthood is a patriarch in his own home, with the right to bless all his children and grandchildren, even all the fruits of his loins. Nor do we object to the father taking his babe on the eighth day and giving it a father's blessing. But we do not think that this privilege whether exercised or unimproved, should interfere with our obedience to that law of the Lord wherein it is stated [D&C 20:70] "Every member of the Church of Christ having children, is to bring them unto the Elders before the Church, who are to lay their hands upon them in the name of Jesus Christ and bless them in his name." Outside of the all important fact that this is a direct command of Jehovah, and as such should be studiously complied with without hesitancy or objection, we think quite a number of excellent reasons can be adduced to prove that this

command is attended with beneficial results to babe and to parents, who by bringing their child before the Church manifest their faith in the sight of their brethren and sisters, in God's word and in his promises, as well as their thankfulness to him for increasing their posterity and for the safe delivery of his handmaiden. The child is also benefited by the united faith and responsive prayers of the assembled Saints. . . . (*Published Message of acting First Presidency, i.e. John Taylor and the Quorum of the Twelve*) (In Millennial Star, April 1878, No. 15, p. 235; and in Deseret News) MOFP2:311-12; DCSM:43 (in part)

### President Wilford Woodruff,
### George Q. Cannon and Joseph F. Smith
(First Presidency)

Hereafter, therefore, we desire the Latter-day Saints, under the direction of the Presidents of Stakes and the Bishops, to meet in their several places of worship on the afternoon of the first Sunday in each month, whenever it can be done conveniently, and devote the meeting to the administration of the Sacrament, to the bearing of testimony by the members of the Church, to the blessing of children and the confirming of members in the Church, and to such other services as have usually been attended to at such meetings. (Published Message of the First Presidency in Deseret Evening News, Nov. 7, 1896) MOFP3:282

**Related Witnesses:**

### Joseph Smith

Children have no sins. Jesus blessed them and said, "Do what you have seen me do." (*To Saints in the Grove, Nauvoo, Ill., July, 1843*) HC5:499

### Jesus,
*quoted by Mormon*

And when he had said these words, he wept, and the multitude bare record of it, and he took their little children, one by one, and blessed them, and prayed unto the Father for them. 22. And when he had done this he wept again; 23. And he spake unto the multitude, and said unto them: Behold your little ones. 24. And as they looked to behold they cast their eyes towards heaven, and they saw the heavens open, and they saw angels descending out of heaven as it were in the midst of fire; and they came down and encircled those little ones about, and they were encircled about with fire; and the angels did minister unto them. (*The resurrected Jesus instructs the Nephite people, A.D. 34*) 3Ne.17:21-24

**Author's Note:** The following instructions appear in the 1991 Supplement to the 1989 General Handbook of Instructions published by the Church: "Every member of the church of Christ having children is to bring them unto the elders before the church, who are to lay their hands upon them in the name of Jesus Christ, and bless them in his name" (D&C 20:70). In conformity with this revelation, only those who hold the Melchizedek Priesthood should participate in the ordinance of naming and blessing children. This instruction supersedes previous instructions. . . ."

---

## 76. Children should respect and honor their parents.

### Moses
Honour thy father and thy mother: that thy days may be long upon the land which the LORD thy God giveth thee. (*The Lord reveals the fifth of the Ten Commandments to Moses*) Ex.20:12

### President Joseph F. Smith
Young men should be scrupulously careful to impress upon their minds the necessity of consulting with father and mother in all that pertains to their actions in life. Respect and veneration for parents should be inculcated into the hearts of the young people of the Church—father and mother to be respected, their wishes to be regarded—and in the heart of every child should be implanted this thought of esteem and consideration for parents which characterized the families of the ancient patriarchs. ¶ God is at the head of the human race; we look up to him as the Father of all. We cannot please him more than regarding and respecting and honoring our fathers and our mothers who are the means of our existence here upon the earth. (IE1902Feb:307) DGSM:82

### Paul
Children, obey your parents in the Lord: for this is right. 2. Honour thy father and mother; (which is the first commandment with promise;) 3. That it may be well with thee, and thou mayest live long on the earth. 4. And, ye fathers, provoke not your children to wrath: but bring them up in the nurture and admonition of the Lord. (*Paul's letter to the Saints at Ephesus in Asia Minor, about A.D. 62*) Eph.6:1-4

### N. Eldon Tanner
We have the old commandment, "Honor thy father and thy mother that thy days may be long upon the land which the Lord thy God giveth thee." Children should be taught and trained to honor their father and their mother. Their parents gave them life and cared for them when they could not care for themselves.

Every child of every age should love and honor his parents. CR1963Apr:136; DGSM:82

### Jesus,
#### *recorded in Matthew*
For God commanded, saying, Honour thy father and mother: and, He that curseth father or mother, let him die the death. 5. But ye say, Whosoever shall say to his father or his mother, It is a gift, by whatsoever thou mightest be profited by me; 6. And honour not his father or his mother, he shall be free. Thus have ye made the commandment of God of none effect by your tradition. (*Jesus answers the scribes and Pharisees who contend against him*) Matt.15:4-6

### Nephi, son of Lehi
And now, they said: We know of a surety that the Lord is with thee, for we know that it is the power of the Lord that has shaken us. And they fell down before me, and were about to worship me, but I would not suffer them, saying: I am thy brother, yea, even thy younger brother; wherefore, worship the Lord thy God, and honor thy father and thy mother, that thy days may be long in the land which the Lord thy God shall give thee. (*Nephi answers his rebellious brothers, about 591 B.C.*) 1Ne.17:55

### President Spencer W. Kimball
It is not enough to honor our parents in some narrow way. If we truly honor them, we will seek to emulate their best characteristics and to fulfill their highest aspirations for us. No gift purchased from a store can begin to match in value to parents some simple, sincere words of appreciation. Nothing we could give them would be more prized than righteous living for each youngster. Even where parents have not great strength of testimony, they will take pride in the strength and conviction of their children, if the relationship between them is a tolerant, loving, supporting one. (The Teachings of Spencer W. Kimball, p. 348) TLDP:76-77

### Related Witnesses:
#### Recorded in Exodus
And he that smiteth his father, or his mother, shall be surely put to death. . . . And he that curseth his father, or his mother, shall surely be put to death. (*The Lord reveals his laws*) Ex.21:15,17

#### Recorded in Proverbs
My son, keep thy father's commandment, and forsake not the law of thy mother: 21. Bind them continually upon thine heart, and tie them about thy neck. 22. When thou goest, it shall lead thee; when thou sleepest, it shall keep thee; and when thou awakest, it shall talk with thee. Prov.6:20-22

**Author's Note:** A dictionary definition of *to honor*: "To regard with honor or respect. To treat with courtesy." (Funk & Wagnalls, p. 643)

---

## 77. We are to learn in our youth to keep the commandments of God.

### Alma, the younger,
### *quoted by Mormon*

O, remember, my son, and learn wisdom in thy youth; yea, learn in thy youth to keep the commandments of God. 36. Yea, and cry unto God for all thy support; yea, let all thy doings be unto the Lord, and whithersoever thou goest let it be in the Lord; yea, let all thy thoughts be directed unto the Lord; yea, let the affections of thy heart be placed upon the Lord forever. 37. Counsel with the Lord in all thy doings, and he will direct thee for good; yea, when thou liest down at night lie down unto the Lord, that he may watch over you in your sleep; and when thou risest in the morning let thy heart be full of thanks unto God; and if ye do these things, ye shall be lifted up at the last day. (*Alma instructs his son, Helaman, about 73 B.C.*) Alma 37:35-37

### President Spencer W. Kimball

If we truly honor [our parents], we will seek to emulate their best characteristics and to fulfill their highest aspirations for us. . . . Nothing we could give them would be more prized than righteous living for each youngster. (The Teachings of Spencer W. Kimball, p. 348) TLDP:76-77

### Paul

Let no man despise thy youth; but be thou an example of the believers, in word, in conversation, in charity, in spirit, in faith, in purity. (*Paul writes to his assistant Timothy, about A.D. 64*) 1Tim.4:12

### Marion G. Romney,
### *also quoting Joseph Smith*

I plead with you young Aaronic Priesthood bearers—and all of us—to determine now, in your youth, to put your trust in the Lord, and by obeying his commandments earn the right to receive specific blessings he has promised for specific types of living—those given in the Word of Wisdom, for example, when he said that "all saints who remember to keep and do these sayings, walking in obedience to the commandments, shall receive health in their navel and marrow to their bones; . . ." CR1979Apr:57

### Paul

Flee also youthful lusts: but follow righteousness, faith, charity, peace, with them that call on the Lord out of a pure heart. 23. But foolish and unlearned questions avoid, knowing that they do gender strifes. (*Paul writes to his assistant Timothy, about A.D. 64*) 2Tim.2:22-23

**Related Witnesses:**

### Recorded in Luke

And the child grew, and waxed strong in spirit, filled with wisdom: and the grace of God was upon him. . . . And Jesus increased in wisdom and stature, and in favour with God and man. (*Luke writes concerning Jesus as a youth*) Luke 2:40,52

# List of Doctrines

## CHURCH DISCIPLINE

*Doctrines Located in This Topic*

78. Church discipline is administered to save the souls of transgressors.

79. Church discipline is administered to safeguard the purity, integrity, and good name of the Church.

80. Church discipline is ecclesiastical only and can only affect a member's standing in the Church.

*Doctrines on CHURCH DISCIPLINE Located in Other Topics*

226. The Church receives back into fellowship those transgressors who repent.

# CHURCH DISCIPLINE

**Author's Note:** The following statement appears in the "General Handbook of Instructions," page 10-11, published by The Church of Jesus Christ of Latter-day Saints, March 1989:¶ "The purposes of Church discipline are to (1) save the souls of transgressors; (2) protect the innocent; and (3) safeguard the purity, integrity, and good name of the Church. Church discipline includes giving cautions in private interviews, imposing restrictions in probations, and withdrawing fellowship or membership." Informal discipline is administered by a bishop or stake president without participation of counselors or a disciplinary council. Formal discipline is administered in a *disciplinary council, formerly called a church "court."* [Emphasis and italics added for clarification to reflect the current change in nomenclature.]

## 78. Church discipline is administered to save the souls of transgressors.

### N. Eldon Tanner

It is abundantly clear that the cases which are to be handled by the Church include, but are not limited to, fornication, adultery, homosexual acts, abortion, or other infractions of the moral code; intemperance; criminal acts involving moral turpitude such as burglary, dishonesty, theft, or murder; apostasy; open opposition to and deliberate disobedience to the rules and regulations of the Church; cruelty to spouse or children; advocating or practicing so-called plural marriage; or any unchristianlike conduct in violation of the law and order of the Church. ¶ Brethren, we must realize the seriousness and importance of this subject. It is so important that you deal with these cases, that you know when there is iniquity and when you find it that you be kind enough to show an interest in the transgressor and bring him to repentance. As you do this the Lord will bless you, strengthen you, and direct you in carrying out the work to which you have been assigned. ¶ It is important, however, that when it is necessary to disfellowship or excommunicate a person you show great love and concern and put forth every effort to help him clear up his life and return to full fellowship in the Church. ACR(Sao Paulo)1975:49

### Elder Harold B. Lee

The more we give to a person in the Church, the more the Lord expects of him. We wouldn't baptize an individual unless we are assured that that individual has repented of his sins. We wouldn't think of conferring the Holy Ghost upon him unless we felt that he was prepared to receive it. We wouldn't give to him the holy priesthood, which would only be a burden he is not prepared to carry, unless he was worthy of it. And so it is when one has sinned so seriously that to hold further membership or to hold the holy priesthood would be as a stumbling block and burden rather than a blessing. In the wisdom of the Lord, these privileges are taken from him that he might be ground as "clay in the hands of the potter," again tried and tested, until he is again worthy to receive these holy blessings. (*Address to Brigham Young University student body, 1956*) (Stand Ye in Holy Places, p. 119) TLDP:79

### Elder Harold B. Lee

I was in a stake conference recently where one of the bishops frankly stated that he had determined that he would never excommunicate any person no matter what the sin. I told him that if this was his true feeling, then he was in the wrong position—as a common judge in Israel. . . . When we let members lead a double and destructive life, instead of doing them a favor as we suppose, we damage them, sometimes, irreparably. We must let the light of gospel standards shine fully, and not try to deflect the penetrating rays of its standards. The gospel is to save men, not to condemn them, but to save it is sometimes necessary to confront and to discipline as the Lord has directed us. When individuals are on the wrong path, our task is to redirect them lovingly, and not to watch idly from our vantage point on the straight and narrow path. (*Address given at Regional Representatives' seminar, Oct. 1/2, 1969*) TLDP:81

### John A. Widtsoe

It should always be remembered that the Church exists to save, not to condemn men. . . . ¶ Should it be necessary to call a person to a church trial, those composing the council must use every endeavor to bring about reconciliation or confession in humility. Excommunication should be the last resort. ¶ All should be eager to keep those who are in the Church in full fellowship with the community of Saints. PCG:215

### John A. Widtsoe

Members who have been disfellowshipped or excommunicated should not be avoided or persecuted by the membership of the Church. On the contrary, they should be dealt with kindly and prayerfully, in the hope that they may turn from their mistakes, and receive again the full privileges of Church membership. Every effort should be made to show love to such persons, so that they may be encouraged to live so as to merit, again, the full privileges of the Church. PCG:213

### James E. Talmage

The essential purpose of the Gospel of Jesus Christ is to save mankind from sin, and to enable the sinner to retrieve his character through contrite repentance and by further compliance with the laws and ordinances based on the Atonement wrought by the Savior of the race. ("Judiciary System of The Church of Jesus Christ of Latter-day Saints," IE1919-Apr:498-99) TLDP:78

**Related Witnesses:**

### Joseph Smith,
### *receiving the Word of the Lord*

For I the Lord cannot look upon sin with the least degree of allowance; 32. Nevertheless, he that repents and does the commandments of the Lord shall be forgiven; 33. And he that repents not, from him shall be taken even the light which he has received; for my Spirit shall not always strive with man, saith the Lord of Hosts. (*Revelation received during conference of elders of the Church, Nov. 1, 1831*) D&C 1:31-33

### Elder Joseph Fielding Smith

In other organizations men may commit all manner of sin and still retain their membership, because they have no companionship with the Holy Ghost to lose: but in the Church when a man sins and continues without repentance, the Spirit is withdrawn, and when he is left to himself the adversary takes possession of his mind and he denies the faith. (Doctrines of Salvation, 3:309) TLDP:632

---

79. **Church discipline is administered to safeguard the purity, integrity, and good name of the Church.**

### President John Taylor

What are bishops' courts [now "disciplinary councils"] and high councils for? That when men transgress the laws of God, they shall be tried according to the laws of the Church, and if found guilty, and are worthy of such action, they shall be cast out; that the pure and the righteous may be sustained, and the wicked and corrupt, the ungodly and impure, be dealt with according to the laws of God. This is necessary in order to maintain purity throughout the Church, and to cast off iniquity therefrom. (*At Manti, Utah, May 19, 1883, JD24:171*) TLDP:77

### President Joseph F. Smith

[If a person starts] sowing the seeds of dissension and of disobedience and rebellion in the hearts of others, he becomes a dangerous person, poisoning the minds of the innocent, misleading those who are unwary, stirring up dissension and discontent in the hearts of those who ought to be in harmony with the bishop and with the ward, and thereby sowing the seeds of disunion, disorganization and disintegration. Such a man becomes dangerous, although he may be moral and virtuous, and a strictly temperate man, so far as his life is concerned. At the same time he is persisting in a wrong course. He is persisting in that which is in opposition to the Priesthood and to the organizations of the Church. ¶ Therefore he is in opposition to divine authority; he is sowing the seeds of dissension in the hearts of others; and if he carries that to the extreme, like the murderer or the adulterer, or like the thief and the robber, *he may be dealt with for his fellowship in the Church and for his membership, and be cut off from the Church, just for his rebellion* [italics added]. . . . ¶ If we were to resort to rebellion and unbelief and all kinds of iniquity, *if those conditions existed in our wards, do you think it could said of us that the Church of Jesus Christ of Latter-day Saints is the Church of Christ, and that the gospel we teach will purify men and bring them to a knowledge of the truth of the standard of the Lord Jesus Christ, which is the perfect standard?* [Italics added] No; it could not be said; it would not be said; and it would be a dishonor to the Lord, a disgrace to the bishop and his counselors, a disgrace to that stake of Zion, to the high council and the presidency of that stake. It would be understood that men professing to be members of the Church were guilty of works of abomination and rebellion in the midst of the House of Israel. *It would be a disgrace to the presiding authorities to permit it.* [Italics added] (*From an address on "Principles of Government in the Church" delivered Sept. 1917*) (Published by the First Presidency in the Improvement Era, IE1917Nov:3-11) MOFP5:84,87

### President John Taylor

When it has been found necessary *for the well being of the Church of Christ* [italics added] to withdraw fellowship from any of its members, on account of their misdoings or apostasy, and such members have been duly tried by the Bishop and his counselors and the case decided upon, and no appeal taken, then such action should be made public by announcement at a meeting of the Saints in the ward in which the offending parties reside. This public announcement will in the great majority of cases satisfy the demands of justice and the law of the

Lord. (Published in Deseret News, April 17, 1878; See MOFP2:313) TLDP:80-81
**Related Witnesses:**
### Anthony W. Ivins
[T]he civil law is given for the protection and control of our temporal affairs, while the Priesthood is conferred upon us for the control and development of the Church. . . . ("Right Relationship between the Church and the State," IE1923Jun:685) TLDP:77-78

80. Church discipline is ecclesiastical only and can only affect a member's standing in the Church.

### President Joseph F. Smith,
### John R. Winder, Anthon H. Lund
(First Presidency)
The courts [now, "disciplinary councils"] of the Church are entirely ecclesiastical. They adjudicate between Church members in matters of dispute and in the promotion of Church discipline. Litigation among them is deprecated, and it is deemed wrong for brother to go to law against brother. But no penalty is enforced other than disfellowshipment, or excommunication, as the extreme punishment. The courts of law are recognized in their secular capacity and their decisions are honored and observed. (Published by First Presidency in Deseret News, Christmas, 1903) MOFP4:82
### Joseph Smith,
*receiving the Word of the Lord*
And again, every person who belongeth to this church of Christ, shall observe to keep all the commandments and covenants of the church. 79. And it shall come to pass, that if any persons among you shall kill they shall be delivered up and dealt with according to the laws of the land; for remember that he hath no forgiveness; and it shall be proved according to the laws of the land. 80. And if any man or woman shall commit adultery, he or she shall be tried before two elders of the church, or more, and every word shall be established against him or her by two witnesses of the church, and not of the enemy; but if there are more than two witnesses it is better. 81. But he or she shall be condemned by the mouth of two witnesses; and the elders shall lay the case before the church, and the church shall lift up their hands against him or her, that they may be dealt with according to the law of God. 82. And if it can be, it is necessary that the bishop be present also. 83. And thus ye shall do in all cases which shall come before you. 84. And if a man or woman shall rob, he or she shall be

delivered up unto the law of the land. 85. And if he or she shall steal, he or she shall be delivered up unto the law of the land. 86. And if he or she shall lie, he or she shall be delivered up unto the law of the land. 87. And if he or she do any manner of iniquity, he or she shall be delivered up unto the law, even that of God. (*Revelation "embracing the law of the Church" Feb. 9, 1831*) D&C 42:78-87
### Joseph Smith
We do not believe it just to mingle religious influence with civil government, whereby one religious society is fostered and another proscribed in its spiritual privileges, and the individual rights of its members, as citizens, denied. 10. We believe that all religious societies have a right to deal with their members for disorderly conduct, according to the rules and regulations of such societies; provided that such dealings be for fellowship and good standing; but we do not believe that any religious society has authority to try men on the right of property or life, to take from them this world's goods, or to put them in jeopardy of either life or limb, or to inflict any physical punishment upon them. They can only excommunicate them from their society, and withdraw from them their fellowship. 11. We believe that men should appeal to the civil law for redress of all wrongs and grievances, where personal abuse is inflicted or the right of property or character infringed, where such laws exist as will protect the same; . . . (*Declaration of belief regarding governments and laws, Aug. 17, 1835*) D&C 134:9-11
### James E. Talmage,
*also quoting Joseph Smith*
That the courts of the Church [now "disciplinary councils"] in no sense assume to oppose or supersede the secular law is shown in a revelation given as early as 1831, wherein it is expressly required that if members of the Church commit crime, if they kill, or rob, or lie, they "shall be delivered up unto the law of the land." (See D&C 42.) ("Judiciary System of The Church of Jesus Christ of Latter-day Saints," IE1919Apr:498-99) TLDP:78
### President Joseph F. Smith
[T]he bishoprics, and the presidents of stakes, have . . . jurisdiction over the membership or the standing of men and women in their wards and in their stakes. CR1913Apr:5
### Anthony W. Ivins
It is true that a system of Church courts [now "disciplinary councils"] has been given, and judges provided whose duty it is to watch over the Church, to hear cases where differences may exist between Church members, and to

take cognizance of cases where the rules governing the conduct of members, whose acts may be un-Christian, immoral, or opposed to justice and righteousness, are concerned. ¶ This system begins with the teachers, who are expected to be familiar with the lives and conduct of the members of their wards, and who seek to induce, by persuasion and love, those who may have departed from the way of the Lord, to return to it. Where members refuse, or neglect to be governed by the council of the teachers, their case may be taken to the bishopric, and if they fail to reach a satisfactory adjustment may be carried to the high council, and from there appealed to the First Presidency. ¶ These Church courts [now "disciplinary councils"], while corresponding closely to our civil courts, differ entirely from the latter in this respect. Whether it be the decision of a bishop's court, a high council or the First Presidency, no effort is made to enforce the decree contrary to the will of the accused. Disinterested men hear the case, there are no lawyers to interpret, or misinterpret the law, the accused has the right to appear and speak in his own behalf, and to introduce evidence, after which the decision is rendered. If the accused refuses to submit to the findings of the court [disciplinary council], the only penalty attached is the withdrawal of the hand of fellowship, or excommunication from the Church, after which he is permitted to go his way in peace to dwell in his soul. ¶ The purpose of this review, brief and very imperfect as it is, is to call your attention to the fact that the civil law is given for the protection and control of our temporal affairs, while the Priesthood is conferred upon us for the control and development of the Church: that the former differs from the latter in that one is compulsory, the other entirely voluntary. To the civil law all men must submit, regardless of race, creed or condition, while to the priesthood man may submit or not, as he may choose.("Right Relationship between the Church and the State," IE1923Jun:685) TLDP:77-78

### President Wilford Woodruff,
### George Q. Cannon, Joseph F. Smith
(First Presidency)
### The Council of the Twelve Apostles

We declare that no Bishop's or other court [now "disciplinary council"] in this Church claims or exercises the right to supersede, annul or modify a judgment of any civil court. Such courts [disciplinary councils], while established to regulate Christian conduct, are purely ecclesiastical, and their punitive powers go no further than the suspension or excommunication of members from Church fellowship. (*Official Declaration, Dec. 12, 1889*) MOFP3:185

### Related Witnesses:
#### John A. Widtsoe

There are really only three kinds of offenses of which the Church takes cognizance. First and most serous is the breaking of the moral law in any of its divisions. Second, deliberate disobedience to the regulations of the Church, which renders a person liable to such punishment as the Church can properly mete out to its members. Third, the incorrect interpretation of doctrine, coupled with an unwillingness to accept the correct view after proper explanations of the doctrine have been made. The first two types of violation are of conduct, the third of belief. All imply non-conformity to the practices of the Church or non-acceptance of its teachings. PCG:214

# List of Doctrines

## CHURCH OF JESUS CHRIST

*Doctrines Located in This Topic*

81. The Church of Jesus Christ of Latter-day Saints is the only true and living church upon the face of the whole earth.

82. The restored church of Jesus Christ was organized on April 6, 1830, by divine revelation that specified this precise date.

83. All people are to come unto Christ by belonging to His church.

84. The Church of Jesus Christ of Latter-day Saints is a Christian church, built on and centered in Christ.

85. The precise name of the Lord's church in the last days was given by revelation, namely: The Church of Jesus Christ of Latter-day Saints.

86. One of the (threefold) missions of the Church is to perfect the Saints.

87. One of the (threefold) missions of the Church is to proclaim the gospel to the world.

88. One of the (threefold) missions of the Church is to perform vicarious ordinances for the redemption of the dead.

89. The Church of Jesus Christ of Latter-day Saints is founded on the revelations of God.

90. The latter-day church of Christ has the same organization that Jesus Himself established while He was on the earth.

91. Where two or three disciples of the Lord are gathered together in His name, His spirit will be with them.

*Doctrines on CHURCH OF JESUS CHRIST Located in Other Topics*

594. The Church of Jesus Christ of Latter-day Saints is directed and governed by revelation from God through priesthood authorities.

643. The Church of Jesus Christ of Latter-day Saints was organized in these latter days by divine authority.

667. Revelation to individuals and to the Church comes line upon line, precept upon precept.

# CHURCH OF JESUS CHRIST

**81.** The Church of Jesus Christ of Latter-day Saints is the only true and living church upon the face of the whole earth.

**Joseph Smith,**
*receiving the Word of the Lord*
And also those to whom these commandments were given, might have power to lay the foundation of this church, and to bring it forth out of obscurity and out of darkness, the only true and living church upon the face of the whole earth, with which I, the Lord, am well pleased, speaking unto the church collectively and not individually— (*Revelation received during conference of elders of the Church, Nov. 1, 1831*) D&C 1:30

**James E. Talmage**
The Church of Jesus Christ stands, in a particular sense, alone. Not even a hostile commentator or an unfavorable critic has ever yet ventured to put forth the assertion that this Church has any relationship of origin and development with any other church or denomination on the face of the earth. We are not regarded as an offshoot of any mother church. Churches generally treat us for what we are, a body of religionists standing alone in the world. . . . ¶ We have been severely criticized because of the declaration that the sects and denominations of that day were wrong. [JS-H 1:19] Remember, please, the declaration was not of Joseph. He had not before known that to be the case. Those words were the words of One greater than he, greater than you, greater than all of us here assembled, the words of the Son of God. . . . ¶ This Church, therefore, from its beginning, has been unique, for the organization of the Church was forecasted in this declaration that at the time of Joseph Smith's first vision there was no Church of Jesus Christ upon the earth. . . . CR1920Apr:100,02-03

**President Joseph F. Smith**
The Church of Jesus Christ of Latter-day Saints is no partisan Church. It is not a sect. It is THE CHURCH OF JESUS CHRIST OF LATTER-DAY SAINTS. It is the only one today existing in the world that can and does legitimately bear the name of Jesus Christ and his divine authority. I make this declaration in all simplicity and honesty before you and before all the world, bitter as the truth may seem to those who are opposed and who have no reason for that opposition. It is nevertheless true and will remain true until he who has a right to rule among the nations of the earth and among the

individual children of God throughout the world shall come and take the reins of government and receive the bride that shall be prepared for the coming of the Bridegroom. (Gospel Doctrine, p. 412) TLDP:84

**John A. Widtsoe**
The Church of Christ possesses real authority, derived from God, and in its work represents God. Such a Church, alone, can appeal to the human understanding. A Church without authority is limp and helpless. Authority is the final test of a true Church. Does it attempt to officiate for God? Does its Priesthood possess authority? From the beginning, the Church of God has been given direct, divine authority so that its work might not be questioned. The angel walked with Adam, the Lord spoke to Abraham, Jesus in person came on earth, the Father and the Son came to Joseph Smith—in all ages, when the Church has been fully established, the Priesthood has been conferred by authoritative beings. The authority of the Church is real and genuine and possesses power. By its power it shall be known. (A Rational Theology, pp. 116-17) TLDP:83

**Related Witnesses:**
**Joseph Smith**
My object in going to inquire of the Lord was to know which of all the sects was right, that I might know which to join. No sooner, therefore, did I get possession of myself, so as to be able to speak, than I asked the Personages who stood above me in the light, which of all the sects was right (for at this time it had never entered into my heart that all were wrong)—and which I should join. 19. I was answered that I must join none of them, for they were all wrong; and the Personage who addressed me said that all their creeds were an abomination in his sight; that those professors were all corrupt; that: "They draw near to me with their lips, but their hearts are far from me, they teach for doctrines the commandments of men, having a form of godliness, but they deny the power thereof." (*Vision of the Father and the Son, spring of 1820*) JS-H 1:18-19

---

**82.** The restored church of Jesus Christ was organized on April 6, 1830, by divine revelation that specified this precise date.

**Joseph Smith**
In this manner did the Lord continue to give us instructions from time to time, concerning the

duties which now devolved upon us; and among many other things of the kind, we obtained of Him the following, by the spirit of prophecy and revelation; which not only gave us much information, but also pointed out to us the precise day upon which, according to His will and commandment, we should proceed to organize His Church once more here upon the earth: . . . (*Journal entry regarding the receipt of the revelation contained in Section 20 of the Doctrine and Covenants, April 1830, which revelation states April 6, 1830 to be the date the Church should be organized*) HC1:64; DCSM:39-40

### Joseph Smith

The rise of the Church of Christ in these last days, being one thousand eight hundred and thirty years since the coming of our Lord and Savior Jesus Christ in the flesh, it being regularly organized and established agreeable to the laws of our country, by the will and commandments of God, in the fourth month, and on the sixth day of the month which is called April—2. Which commandments were given to Joseph Smith, Jun., who was called of God, and ordained an apostle of Jesus Christ, to be the first elder of this church; 3. And to Oliver Cowdery, who was also called of God, an apostle of Jesus Christ, to be the second elder of this church, and ordained under his hand; 4. And this according to the grace of our Lord and Savior Jesus Christ, to whom be all glory, both now and forever. Amen. (*Revelation on Church Organization and Government, April 1830*) D&C 20:1-4

### President Harold B. Lee

April 6, 1973, is a particularly significant date because it commemorates not only the anniversary of the organization of The Church of Jesus Christ of Latter-day Saints in this dispensation, but also the anniversary of the birth of the Savior, our Lord and Master, Jesus Christ. CR1973Apr:4; DCSM:40

### James E. Talmage

The time of the Messiah's birth is a subject upon which specialists in theology and history, and those who are designated in literature "the learned," fail to agree. . . . ¶ Without attempting to analyze the mass of calculation data relating to this subject, we accept the Dionysian basis as correct with respect to the year, which is to say that we believe Christ to have been born in the year known to us as 1 B.C., and, as shall be shown, in an early month of that year. In support of this belief we cite the inspired record known as the "Revelation on Church Government, given through Joseph the Prophet, in April, 1830," which opens with these words: "The rise

of the Church of Christ in these last days, being one thousand eight hundred and thirty years since the coming of our Lord and Saviour Jesus Christ in the flesh. . . ." ¶ As to the season of the year in which Christ was born, there is among the learned as great a diversity of opinion as that relating to the year itself. It is claimed by many Biblical scholars that December 25th, the day celebrated in Christendom as Christmas, cannot be the correct date. We believe April 6th to be the birthday of Jesus Christ as indicated in a revelation of the present dispensation already cited in which that day is made without qualification the completion of the one thousand eight hundred and thirtieth year since the coming of the Lord in the flesh. This acceptance is admittedly based on faith in modern revelation, and in no wise is set forth as the result of chronological research or analysis. We believe that Jesus Christ was born in Bethlehem of Judea, April 6, 1 B.C. JTC:102-04

### Joseph Smith

The day was spent in a very agreeable manner, in giving and receiving knowledge which appertained to this last kingdom—it being just 1800 years since the Savior laid down His life that men might have everlasting life, and only three years since the Church had come out of the wilderness, preparatory for the last dispensation. (*Journal entry of April 6, 1833*) HC1:337; DCSM:40

### Joseph Smith,
#### *receiving the Word of the Lord*

Behold, there shall be a record kept among you; and in it thou shalt be called a seer, a translator, a prophet, an apostle of Jesus Christ, an elder of the church through the will of God the Father, and the grace of your Lord Jesus Christ, 2. Being inspired of the Holy Ghost to lay the foundation thereof, and to build it up unto the most holy faith. 3. Which church was organized and established in the year of your Lord eighteen hundred and thirty, in the fourth month, and on the sixth day of the month which is called April. (*Revelation given at the organization of the Church, April 6, 1830; Joseph Smith is called by the Lord to be a seer, translator, prophet, Apostle and elder of the Church*) D&C 21:1-3

### Elder Joseph Fielding Smith

This Church is not a new Church. Many people think it is. It did not have its beginning on the 6th day of April, 1830. It was organized in the days of Adam, and it has been on the earth every time the Lord has had servants who would do his will. (Take Heed to Yourselves!, p. 228) TLDP:85

### James E. Talmage

In the first section of the Doctrine and Covenants . . . after reciting his purposes and plans and the partial realization of such in the bringing forth of this Gospel in this age, he [the Lord] speaks of those who were charged with authority in that day to administer the affairs of the Church, those to whom these commandments were given, and explains that the commandments were given that his servants might have power to lay the foundation of this Church and to bring it forth out of obscurity and out of darkness. CR1928Oct:118

---

### 83. All people are to come unto Christ by belonging to His church.

#### N. Eldon Tanner

Some people ask the reason for an organized church. They feel they can work out their salvation alone, and that there is no need to attend church meetings or fill other requirements as long as they are honest and honorable and do good to their fellowmen. But the Lord has given us instructions that we should belong to a church; and this, his church, has the same organization that Jesus Christ himself established while he was on the earth. We have many explicit declarations from the Lord that make this clear, and also that we need to encourage and help one another. . . . ¶ To accomplish God's purposes and to prove ourselves, it is necessary that we work within his church and under the direction of his authorized servants. We need the strength that comes from association with others who are seeking the same goals. CR1977Apr:64-65

#### Joseph Smith,
#### *receiving the Word of the Lord*

And for this cause have I said: If this generation harden not their hearts, I will establish my church among them. 54. Now I do not say this to destroy my church, but I say this to build up my church; 55. Therefore, whosoever belongeth to my church need not fear, for such shall inherit the kingdom of heaven. 56. But it is they who do not fear me, neither keep my commandments but build up churches unto themselves to get gain, yea, and all those that do wickedly and build up the kingdom of the devil—yea, verily, verily, I say unto you, that it is they that I will disturb, and cause to tremble and shake to the center. . . . 69. And now, behold, whosoever is of my church, and endureth of my church to the end, him will I establish upon my rock, and the gates of hell shall not prevail against them.

*(Revelation received at Harmony, Penn., summer 1828)* D&C 10:53-56,69

#### Mormon

Blessed art thou, Alma, and blessed are they who were baptized in the waters of Mormon. . . . 16. And blessed are they because of their exceeding faith in the words alone which thou hast spoken unto them. 17. And blessed art thou because thou hast established a church among this people; and they shall be established, and they shall be my people. 18. Yea, blessed is this people who are willing to bear my name; for in my name shall they be called; and they are mine. . . . 21. And he that will hear my voice shall be my sheep; and him shall ye receive into the church, and him will I also receive. 22. For behold, this is my church; whosoever is baptized shall be baptized unto repentance. And whomsoever ye receive shall believe in my name; and him will I freely forgive. . . . 28. Therefore I say unto you, that he that will not hear my voice, the same shall ye not receive into my church, for him I will not receive at the last day. *(The voice of the Lord to Alma)* Mosiah 26:15-18,21-22,28

#### Recorded in Acts,
#### *which also quotes Peter*

Now when they heard this, they were pricked in their heart, and said unto Peter and to the rest of the apostles, Men and brethren, what shall we do? 38. Then Peter said unto them, Repent, and be baptized every one of you in the name of Jesus Christ for the remission of sins, and ye shall receive the gift of the Holy Ghost. 39. For the promise is unto you, and to your children, and to all that are afar off, even as many as the Lord our God shall call. 40. And with many other words did he testify and exhort, saying, Save yourselves from this untoward generation. 41. Then they that gladly received his word were baptized: and the same day there were added unto them about three thousand souls. 42. And they continued stedfastly in the apostles' doctrine and fellowship, and in breaking of bread, and in prayers. 43. And fear came upon every soul: and many wonders and signs were done by the apostles. 44. And all that believed were together, and had all things common; 45. And sold their possessions and goods, and parted them to all men, as every man had need. 46. And they, continuing daily with one accord in the temple, and breaking bread from house to house, did eat their meat with gladness and singleness of heart, 47. Praising God, and having favour with all the people. And the Lord added to the church daily such as should be saved. *(Peter addresses the people on the day of Pentecost when about 3,000 people were baptized*) Acts 2:37-47

### Mormon

Yea, verily I say unto you, if ye will come unto me ye shall have eternal life. Behold, mine arm of mercy is extended towards you, and whosoever will come, him will I receive; and blessed are those who come unto me. . . . 17. And as many as have received me, to them have I given to become the sons of God; and even so will I to as many as shall believe on my name, for behold, by me redemption cometh, and in me is the law of Moses fulfilled. . . . 20. And ye shall offer for a sacrifice unto me a broken heart and a contrite spirit. And whoso cometh unto me with a broken heart and a contrite spirit, him will I baptize with fire and with the Holy Ghost, even as the Lamanites, because of their faith in me at the time of their conversion, were baptized with fire and with the Holy Ghost, and they knew it not. 21. Behold, I have come unto the world to bring redemption unto the world, to save the world from sin. 22. Therefore, whoso repenteth and cometh unto me as a little child, him will I receive, for of such is the kingdom of God. Behold, for such I have laid down my life, and have taken it up again; therefore repent, and come unto me ye ends of the earth, and be saved. (*The voice of the resurrected Jesus Christ to the Nephites immediately before he visited them, A.D. 34*) 3Ne.9:14,17,20-22

### Related Witnesses:

### Mormon

And after this manner he did baptize every one that went forth to the place of Mormon; and they were in number about two hundred and four souls; yea, and they were baptized in the waters of Mormon, and were filled with the grace of God. 17. And they were called the church of God, or the church of Christ, from that time forward. And it came to pass that whosoever was baptized by the power and authority of God was added to his church. (*Mormon records Alma organizing the Church of Christ, about 148 B.C.*) Mosiah 18:16-17

### Mormon

And it came to pass that in this same year there was exceedingly great prosperity in the church, insomuch that there were thousands who did join themselves unto the church and were baptized unto repentance. 25. And so great was the prosperity of the church, and so many the blessings which were poured out upon the people, that even the high priests and the teachers were themselves astonished beyond measure. 26. And it came to pass that the work of the Lord did prosper unto the baptizing and uniting to the church of God, many souls, yea, even tens of thousands. 27. Thus we may see that the Lord is merciful unto all who will, in the sincerity of their hearts, call upon his holy name. 28. Yea, thus we see that the gate of heaven is open unto all, even to those who will believe on the name of Jesus Christ, who is the Son of God. (*Tens of thousands join the Church of God, about 43 B.C.*) Hel.3:24-28

### Moroni, son of Mormon

And after they had been received unto baptism, and were wrought upon and cleansed by the power of the Holy Ghost, they were numbered among the people of the church of Christ; . . . (*Moroni writes for the benefit of the Lamanites, A.D. 400-421*) Moro.6:4

### President Joseph F. Smith

Our religion is founded on the revelations of God. The Gospel we proclaim is the Gospel of Christ, restored to earth in this the dispensation of the fulness of times. The high claim of the Church is declared in its title—THE CHURCH OF JESUS CHRIST OF LATTER-DAY SAINTS. Established by divine direction, its name was prescribed by Him whose Church it is—Jesus the Christ. (*Address from the First Presidency of the Church to the world, delivered to and accepted by vote of the Church in general conference, April 1907*) CR1907-Apr(Appendix)3-4

---

## 84. The Church of Jesus Christ of Latter-day Saints is a Christian church, built on and centered in Christ.

### President Joseph F. Smith

Our religion is founded on the revelations of God. The Gospel we proclaim is the Gospel of Christ, restored to earth in this the dispensation of the fulness of times. The high claim of the Church is declared in its title—THE CHURCH OF JESUS CHRIST OF LATTER-DAY SAINTS. Established by divine direction, its name was prescribed by Him whose Church it is—Jesus the Christ. ¶ The religion of this people is pure Christianity. Its creed is expressive of the duties of practical life. Its theology is based on the doctrines of the Redeemer. ¶ If it be true Christianity to accept Jesus Christ in person and in mission as divine; to revere Him as the Son of God, the crucified and risen Lord, through whom alone can mankind attain salvation; to accept His teachings as a guide, to adopt as a standard and observe as a law the ethical code He promulgated; to comply with the requirements prescribed by Him as essential to membership in His Church, namely, faith, repentance, baptism by immersion for the remission of sins, and the laying on of hands for the gift of the Holy Ghost,—if this be Christianity, then are we Christians, and the Church of Jesus Christ of Latter-day Saints is a Christian church. (*Address from the First Presidency of the Church to the world, delivered to and accepted by vote of the Church in general conference, April 1907*) CR1907-Apr(Appendix)3-4

### Elder Wilford Woodruff

The full set time is come for the Lord to set His hand to accomplish these mighty events; and as He has done in other ages, so has He done now—He has raised up a Prophet, and is revealing unto him His secrets. Through that Prophet He has brought to light the fullness of the everlasting Gospel to the present generation, and is again once more for the last time establishing His Church upon the foundation of the ancient Apostles and Prophets, which is revelation, Jesus Christ being the chief corner stone. (*Remarks at a conference of the Twelve, Boylston Hall, Boston, Mass., Sept. 10, 1843*) HC6:24

### Jesus,
#### quoted by Mormon

And they said unto him: Lord, we will that thou wouldst tell us the name whereby we shall call this church; for there are disputations among the people concerning this matter. . . . 5. Have they not read the scriptures, which say ye must take upon you the name of Christ, which is my name? For by this name shall ye be called at the last day; 6. And whoso taketh upon him my name, and endureth to the end, the same shall be saved at the last day. 7. Therefore, whatsoever ye shall do, ye shall do it in my name; therefore ye shall call the church in my name; and ye shall call upon the Father in my name that he will bless the church for my sake. 8. And how be it my church save it be called in my name? For if a church be called in Moses' name then it be Moses' church; or if it be called in the name of a man then it be the church of a man; but if it be called in my name then it is my church, if it so be that they are built upon my gospel. 9. Verily I say unto you, that ye are built upon my gospel; therefore ye shall call whatsoever things ye do call, in my name; therefore if ye call upon the Father, for the church, if it be in my name the Father will hear you; 10. And if it so be that the church is built upon my gospel then will the Father show forth his own works

in it. (*The resurrected Jesus instructs his twelve Nephite disciples, A.D. 34*) 3Ne.27:3,5-10

### James E. Talmage,
#### also quoting Joseph Smith

"For thus shall my Church be called in the last days, even the Church of Jesus Christ of Latter-day Saints" (D&C 115:3-4). ¶ The name thus conferred is a self-explanatory and exclusive title of distinction and authority. It is an epitome of the cardinal truths and of the philosophical basis of the system commonly called "Mormonism." Every prayer that is offered, every ordinance administered, every doctrine proclaimed by the Church, is voiced in the name of Him whose Church it is. (The Vitality of Mormonism, pp.40-41) TLDP:86

### Related Witnesses:
#### Paul

Now therefore ye are no more strangers and foreigners, but fellowcitizens with the saints, and of the household of God; 20. And are built upon the foundation of the apostles and prophets, Jesus Christ himself being the chief corner stone; (*Paul writes to the Saints at Ephesus in Asia Minor, about A.D. 62*) Eph.2:19-20

### Jesus,
#### recorded in Luke

And he beheld them, and said, What is this then that is written, The stone which the builders rejected, the same is become the head of the corner? (*Jesus speaks to the chief priests who oppose him*) Luke 20:17 (see vs 8-17)

### Peter

Unto you therefore which believe he is precious: but unto them which be disobedient, the stone which the builders disallowed, the same is made the head of the corner, (*Letter to the churches in modern Asia Minor, about A.D. 60*) 1Pet.2:7

### Paul,
#### quoted by Joseph Smith,
#### translating 1 Timothy

But if I tarry long, that thou mayest know how thou oughtest to behave thyself in the house of God, which is the church of the living God. 16. The pillar and ground of the truth is, (and without controversy, great is the mystery of godliness,) God was manifest in the flesh, justified in the Spirit, seen of angels, preached unto the Gentiles, believed on in the world, received up into glory. (*Letter to Paul's assistant Timothy, about A.D. 64*) JST(1Tim.3:15-16 in appendix)

### Paul

For this is good and acceptable in the sight of God our Saviour; 4. Who will have all men to be saved, and to come unto the knowledge of the truth. 5. For there is one God, and one mediator between God and men, the man Christ Jesus; 6. Who gave himself a ransom for all, to be testified in due time. (*Letter to Paul's assistant Timothy, about A.D. 64*) 1Tim.2:3-6

---

**85. The precise name of the Lord's church in the last days was given by revelation, namely: The Church of Jesus Christ of Latter-day Saints.**

### Joseph Smith,
*receiving the Word of the Lord*
And also unto my faithful servants who are of the high council of my church in Zion, for thus it shall be called, and unto all the elders and people of my Church of Jesus Christ of Latter-day Saints, scattered abroad in all the world; 4. For thus shall my church be called in the last days, even The Church of Jesus Christ of Latter-day Saints. (*Revelation addressed to the presiding officers of the Church*) D&C 115:3-4
**President Joseph F. Smith**
Our religion is founded on the revelations of God. The Gospel we proclaim is the Gospel of Christ, restored to earth in this the dispensation of the fulness of times. The high claim of the Church is declared in its title—THE CHURCH OF JESUS CHRIST OF LATTER-DAY SAINTS. Established by divine direction, its name was prescribed by Him whose Church it is—Jesus the Christ. (*Address from the First Presidency of the Church to the world, delivered to and accepted by vote of the Church in general conference, April 1907*) CR1907Apr(Appendix)3-4
### James E. Talmage,
*also quoting Joseph Smith*
"For thus shall my Church be called in the last days, even the Church of Jesus Christ of Latter-day Saints" (D&C 115:3-4). ¶ The name thus conferred is a self-explanatory and exclusive title of distinction and authority. It is an epitome of the cardinal truths and of the philosophical basis of the system commonly called "Mormonism." Every prayer that is offered, every ordinance administered, every doctrine proclaimed by the Church, is voiced in the name of Him whose Church it is. (The Vitality of Mormonism, pp.40-41) TLDP:86
**Related Witnesses:**
### Jesus,
*quoted by Mormon*
And they said unto him: Lord, we will that thou wouldst tell us the name whereby we shall call this church; for there are disputations among the

people concerning this matter. . . . 5. Have they not read the scriptures, which say ye must take upon you the name of Christ, which is my name? For by this name shall ye be called at the last day; 6. And whoso taketh upon him my name, and endureth to the end, the same shall be saved at the last day. 7. Therefore, whatsoever ye shall do, ye shall do it in my name; therefore ye shall call the church in my name; and ye shall call upon the Father in my name that he will bless the church for my sake. 8. And how be it my church save it be called in my name? For if a church be called in Moses' name then it be Moses' church; or if it be called in the name of a man then it be the church of a man; but if it be called in my name then it is my church, if it so be that they are built upon my gospel. 3Ne.27:3,5-8

---

**86. One of the (threefold) missions of the Church is to perfect the Saints.**

### President Spencer W. Kimball
My brothers and sisters, as the Brethren of the First Presidency and the twelve have meditated upon and prayed about the great latter-day work the Lord has given us to do, we are impressed that the mission of the Church is threefold: ¶ To proclaim the gospel of the Lord Jesus Christ to every nation, kindred, tongue, and people; ¶ To perfect the Saints by preparing them to receive the ordinances of the gospel and by instruction and discipline to gain exaltation; ¶ To redeem the dead by performing vicarious ordinances of the gospel for those who have lived on the earth. ¶ All three are part of one work—to assist our Father in Heaven and His Son, Jesus Christ, in Their grand and glorious mission "to bring to pass the immortality and eternal life of man." (Moses 1:39) CR1981Apr:3
### J. Reuben Clark, Jr.
The mission of the Church is first, to teach, encourage, assist, and protect the individual member in his striving to live the perfect life, temporally and spiritually, as laid down in the Gospel,—"Be ye perfect, even as your Father which is in Heaven is perfect," said the Master; secondly, the Church is to maintain, teach, encourage, and protect, temporally and spiritually, the membership as a group in its living of the Gospel; thirdly, the Church is militantly to proclaim the truth, calling upon all men to repent, and to live in obedience to the Gospel, "for every knee must bow and every tongue confess." (*Speaking in behalf of First Presidency [see letter of First Presidency, MOFP6:208-09] to seminary, institute, and*

*Church school teachers at Aspen Grove, Utah)* (Entire speech published in Deseret News, Church Section, Aug. 13, 1938 and in IE1938-Sep:520ff; copied in MOFP6:44-58. The speech was extracted for use as Lesson 18 of the Melchizedek Priesthood Course of Study 1969-70, p. 129ff) MOFP6:45; TLDP:871

### Paul

And he gave some, apostles; and some, prophets; and some, evangelists; and some, pastors and teachers; 12. For the perfecting of the saints, for the work of the ministry, for the edifying of the body of Christ: 13. Till we all come in the unity of the faith, and of the knowledge of the Son of God, unto a perfect man, unto the measure of the stature of the fulness of Christ: 14. That we henceforth be no more children, tossed to and fro, and carried about with every wind of doctrine, by the sleight of men, and cunning craftiness, whereby they lie in wait to deceive; *(Paul writes to the Saints at Ephesus in Asia Minor, about A.D. 62)* Eph.4:11-14

### Moroni, son of Mormon

And after they had been received unto baptism, and were wrought upon and cleansed by the power of the Holy Ghost, they were numbered among the people of the church of Christ; and their names were taken, that they might be remembered and nourished by the good word of God, to keep them in the right way, to keep them continually watchful unto prayer, relying alone upon the merits of Christ, who was the author and the finisher of their faith. 5. And the church did meet together oft, to fast and to pray, and to speak one with another concerning the welfare of their souls. 6. And they did meet together oft to partake of bread and wine, in remembrance of the Lord Jesus. 7. And they were strict to observe that there should be no iniquity among them; and whoso was found to commit iniquity, and three witnesses of the church did condemn them before the elders, and if they repented not, and confessed not, their names were blotted out, and they were not numbered among the people of Christ. 8. But as oft as they repented and sought forgiveness, with real intent, they were forgiven. 9. And their meetings were conducted by the church after the manner of the workings of the Spirit, and by the power of the Holy Ghost; for as the power of the Holy Ghost led them whether to preach, or to exhort, or to pray, or to supplicate, or to sing, even so it was done. *(Instructions recorded in the last record of Moroni, about A.D. 400-421)* Moro.6:4-9

### Peter

Feed the flock of God which is among you, taking the oversight thereof, not by constraint, but willingly; not for filthy lucre, but of a ready mind; *(Letter to the churches in modern Asia Minor, about A.D. 60)* 1Pet.5:2

### President Joseph F. Smith

We proclaim the objects of this organization to be, the preaching of the Gospel in all the world, the gathering of scattered Israel, and the preparation of a people for the coming of the Lord. *(Address from the First Presidency of the Church to the world, delivered to and accepted by vote of the Church in general conference, April 1907)* CR1907Apr(Appendix)4

### Elder David O. McKay

The mission of the Latter-day Saints may be considered in two great aspects; one, the proclamation to the world of the restoration of the gospel of Jesus Christ—the declaration to all mankind that God the Father and his Son Jesus Christ appeared in this dispensation to the Prophet Joseph Smith. That in itself is a wonderful message. ¶ The other great purpose of the Church is to translate truth into a better social order, or in other words, to make our religion effective in the individual lives of men, and in improving social conditions. CR1927Oct:11

### Related Witnesses:

### Mormon

For it came to pass that they did deceive many with their flattering words, who were in the church, and did cause them to commit many sins; therefore it became expedient that those who committed sin, that were in the church, should be admonished by the church. 7. And it came to pass that they were brought before the priests, and delivered up unto the priests by the teachers; and the priests brought them before Alma, who was the high priest. . . . 9. And it came to pass that Alma did not know concerning them; but there were many witnesses against them; yea, the people stood and testified of their iniquity in abundance. . . . 13. And now the spirit of Alma was again troubled; and he went and inquired of the Lord what he should do concerning this matter, for he feared that he should do wrong in the sight of God. 14. And it came to pass that after he had poured out his whole soul to God, the voice of the Lord came to him, saying: . . . 19. And because thou hast inquired of me concerning the transgressor, thou art blessed. . . . 21. And he that will hear my voice shall be my sheep; and him shall ye receive into the church, and him will I also receive. 22. For behold, this is my church; whosoever is baptized shall be baptized unto repentance. And whomsoever ye receive shall believe in my name; and him will I freely forgive. *(Mormon records that members of the Church are led into sin; the voice of the Lord to Alma)* Mosiah 26:6-7,9,13-14,19,21-22

### Jesus,
### *recorded in Luke*

But I have prayed for thee, that thy faith fail not: and when thou art converted, strengthen thy brethren. (*Jesus talks to Peter, prior to departing for Gethsemane*) Luke 22:32

### Peter

As every man hath received the gift, even so minister the same one to another, as good stewards of the manifold grace of God. (*Letter to the churches in modern Asia Minor, about A.D. 60*) 1Pet.4:10

### Joseph Smith,
### *receiving the Word of the Lord*

Wherefore, be faithful; stand in the office which I have appointed unto you; succor the weak, lift up the hands which hang down, and strengthen the feeble knees. (*Revelation for his newly called counselor in the First Presidency, Frederick G. Williams, March 1832*) D&C 81:5

### Paul,
### *recorded in Acts*

Take heed therefore unto yourselves, and to all the flock, over the which the Holy Ghost hath made you overseers, to feed the church of God, which he hath purchased with his own blood. . . . 35. I have shewed you all things, how that so labouring ye ought to support the weak, and to remember the words of the Lord Jesus, how he said, It is more blessed to give than to receive. (*Paul counsels the elders of the Church from Ephesus*) Acts 20:28,35

---

87. One of the (threefold) missions of the Church is to proclaim the gospel to the world.

### President Joseph F. Smith

We proclaim the objects of this organization to be, the preaching of the Gospel in all the world, the gathering of scattered Israel, and the preparation of a people for the coming of the Lord. (*Address from the First Presidency of the Church to the world, delivered to and accepted by vote of the Church in general conference, April 1907*) CR1907Apr(Appendix)4

### President Spencer W. Kimball

My brothers and sisters, as the Brethren of the First Presidency and the twelve have meditated upon and prayed about the great latter-day work the Lord has given us to do, we are impressed that the mission of the Church is threefold: ¶ To proclaim the gospel of the Lord Jesus Christ to

every nation, kindred, tongue, and people; ¶ To perfect the Saints by preparing them to receive the ordinances of the gospel and by instruction and discipline to gain exaltation; ¶ To redeem the dead by performing vicarious ordinances of the gospel for those who have lived on the earth. ¶ All three are part of one work—to assist our Father in Heaven and His Son, Jesus Christ, in Their grand and glorious mission "to bring to pass the immortality and eternal life of man." (Moses 1:39) CR1981Apr:3

### Elder David O. McKay

The mission of the Latter-day Saints may be considered in two great aspects; one, the proclamation to the world of the restoration of the gospel of Jesus Christ—the declaration to all mankind that God the Father and his Son Jesus Christ appeared in this dispensation to the Prophet Joseph Smith. That in itself is a wonderful message. ¶ The other great purpose of the Church is to translate truth into a better social order, or in other words, to make our religion effective in the individual lives of men, and in improving social conditions. CR1927Oct:11

### John A. Widtsoe

The plan of eternal progress involves every living soul who comes upon earth. To the Church is committed the huge task of keeping alive this plan and of carrying it to all the nations. The Church, then, is a great missionary organization. PCG:181

**Related Witnesses:**

### Joseph Smith,
### *receiving the Word of the Lord*

Behold, I sent you out to testify and warn the people, and it becometh every man who hath been warned to warn his neighbor. (*Revelation Dec. 27/28, 1832*) D&C 88:81

### Joseph Smith,
### *receiving the Word of the Lord*

Remember the worth of souls is great in the sight of God; 11. For, behold, the Lord your Redeemer suffered death in the flesh; wherefore he suffered the pain of all men, that all men might repent and come unto him. 12. And he hath risen again from the dead, that he might bring all men unto him, on conditions of repentance. 13. And how great is his joy in the soul that repenteth! 14. Wherefore, you are called to cry repentance unto this people. 15. And if it so be that you should labor all your days in crying repentance unto this people, and bring, save it be one soul unto me, how great shall be your joy with him in the kingdom of my Father! 16. And now, if your joy will be great with one soul that you have brought unto me into the kingdom of my Father, how great will be your joy if you should bring many souls unto me! (*Revelation received June 1829*) D&C 18:10-16

**Joseph Smith**

Now behold, a marvelous work is about to come forth among the children of men. 2. Therefore, O ye that embark in the service of God, see that ye serve him with all your heart, might, mind and strength, that ye may stand blameless before God at the last day. 3. Therefore, if ye have desires to serve God ye are called to the work; 4. For behold the field is white already to harvest; and lo, he that thrusteth in his sickle with his might, the same layeth up in store that he perisheth not, but bringeth salvation to his soul; 5. And faith, hope, charity and love, with an eye single to the glory of God, qualify him for the work. (*Revelation for Joseph Smith, Sr., Feb. 1829*) D&C 4:1-5

**Jesus,**
*recorded in Mark*

And he said unto them, Go ye into all the world, and preach the gospel to every creature. (*Jesus organizes his disciples*) Mark 16:15

**Paul**

For though I preach the gospel, I have nothing to glory of: for necessity is laid upon me; yea, woe is unto me, if I preach not the gospel! (*Letter to the Church at Corinth, Greece, about A.D. 55*) 1Cor.9:16

**Mormon**

Now they were desirous that salvation should be declared to every creature, for they could not bear that any human soul should perish; yea, even the very thoughts that any soul should endure endless torment did cause them to quake and tremble. (*The sons of Mosiah choose to go preach to the Lamanites, about 92 B.C.*) Mosiah 28:3

---

88. One of the (threefold) missions of the Church is to perform vicarious ordinances for the redemption of the dead.

**Elder Ezra Taft Benson,**
*also quoting Joseph Smith,*
*who is quoting Paul*

Our members need to be taught that it is not sufficient for a husband and wife to be sealed in the temple to guarantee their exaltation—they must also be eternally linked with their progenitors and see that the work is done for those ancestors. "They without us," said the Apostle Paul, "cannot be made perfect—neither can we without our dead be made perfect" (D&C 128:15). Our members should therefore understand that they have an individual responsibility to see that they are linked to their progenitors. (*To Regional Representatives, April 3, 1981*) DGSM:86

**Joseph Smith**

In the days of Noah, God destroyed the world by a flood, and He has promised to destroy it by fire in the last days: but before it should take place, Elijah should first come and turn the hearts of the fathers to the children, &c. ¶ Now comes the point. What is this office and work of Elijah? It is one of the greatest and most important subjects that God has revealed. He should send Elijah to seal the children to the fathers, and the fathers to the children. ¶ Now was this merely confined to the living, to settle difficulties with families on earth? By no means. It was a far greater work. Elijah! what would you do if you were here? Would you confine your work to the living alone? No; I would refer you to the Scriptures, where the subject is manifest: that is, without us, they could not be made perfect, nor we without them; the fathers without the children, nor the children without the fathers. ¶ I wish you to understand this subject, for it is important; and if you will receive it, this is the spirit of Elijah, that we redeem our dead, and connect ourselves with our fathers which are in heaven, and seal up our dead to come forth in the first resurrection; and here we want the power of Elijah to seal those who dwell on earth to those who dwell in heaven. This is the power of Elijah and the keys of the kingdom of Jehovah. (*At the Stand in a meeting at Nauvoo, Ill., March 10, 1844*) HC6:251-52

**Joseph Smith,**
*quoted by Elder Joseph Fielding Smith*

[F]or every man who wishes to save his father, mother, brothers, sisters and friends, must go through all the ordinances for each one of them separately, the same as for himself, from baptism to ordination, washing and anointings, and receive all the keys and powers of the Priesthood, the same as for himself. (*General conference of the Church, April 8, 1844*) HC6:319; TPJS:363

**President Spencer W. Kimball**

My brothers and sisters, as the Brethren of the First Presidency and the twelve have meditated upon and prayed about the great latter-day work the Lord has given us to do, we are impressed that the mission of the Church is threefold: ¶ To proclaim the gospel of the Lord Jesus Christ to every nation, kindred, tongue, and people; ¶ To perfect the Saints by preparing them to receive the ordinances of the gospel and by instruction and discipline to gain exaltation; ¶ To redeem the dead by performing vicarious ordinances of the gospel for those who have lived on the earth. ¶ All three are part of one work—to assist our Father in Heaven and His Son, Jesus

Christ, in Their grand and glorious mission "to bring to pass the immortality and eternal life of man." (Moses 1:39) CR1981Apr:3

**Rudger Clawson**

And so we have two great churches, one in heaven, the other upon the earth. They are moving along parallel lines, and the temple of God, it appears to me, is the connecting link that connects the heavens with the earth, because it is through the temple that we will be able to reach our dead and not otherwise. To pray for the dead may not be of any real assistance to them. To actually help them we must do a work for them. CR1933Apr:77-78; DGSM:85

**John A. Widtsoe**

In our pre-existent state, in the day of the great council, we made a certain agreement with the Almighty. The Lord proposed a plan, conceived by him. We accepted it. Since the plan is intended for all men, we become parties to the salvation of every person under the plan. We agreed, right then and there, to be not only saviors for ourselves, but measurably saviors for the whole human family. We went into partnership with the Lord. The working out of the plan became then not merely the Father's work, and the Savior's work, but also our work. The least of us, the humblest, is in partnership with the Almighty in achieving the purpose of the eternal plan of salvation. (In Utah Genealogical and Historical Magazine, Oct. 1934) MPSG1967:87; DCSM:8

**Related Witnesses:**

**Joseph Smith,**
*quoted by Elder Joseph Fielding Smith*

In regard to the law of the priesthood, there should be a place where all nations shall come up from time to time to receive their endowments; and the Lord has said this shall be the place for the baptisms for the dead. Every man that has been baptized and belongs to the kingdom has a right to be baptized for those who have gone before; and as soon as the law of the Gospel is obeyed here by their friends who act as proxy for them, the Lord has administrators there to set them free. A man may act as proxy for his own relatives; the ordinances of the Gospel which were laid out before the foundations of the world have thus been fulfilled by them, and we may be baptized for those whom we have much friendship for; but it must first be revealed to the man of God, lest we should run too far. (*Address at the Stand in Nauvoo, Ill., May 12, 1844*) HC6:365-66; TPJS:367

**N. Eldon Tanner**

We know by the scriptures that the gospel is preached to the dead and the dead are to be judged according to men in the flesh and live according to God in the spirit. Thus baptism is necessary for those who, during their lifetime, had not opportunity for this ordinance of baptism by immersion for the remission of sin. CR1979Mar-Apr:20; DGSM:86

**Joseph Smith,**
*receiving the Word of the Lord*

For there is not a place found on earth that he may come to and restore again that which was lost unto you, or which he hath taken away, even the fulness of the priesthood. 29. For a baptismal font there is not upon the earth, that they, my saints, may be baptized for those who are dead— 30. For this ordinance belongeth to my house, and cannot be acceptable to me, only in the days of your poverty, wherein ye are not able to build a house unto me. 31. But I command you, all ye my saints, to build a house unto me; and I grant unto you a sufficient time to build a house unto me; and during this time your baptisms shall be acceptable unto me. 32. But behold, at the end of this appointment your baptisms for your dead shall not be acceptable unto me; and if you do not these things at the end of the appointment ye shall be rejected as a church, with your dead, saith the Lord your God. (*Revelation to Joseph Smith, Jan. 19, 1841*) D&C 124:28-32

**Joseph Smith**

And now, my dearly beloved brethren and sisters, let me assure you that these are principles in relation to the dead and the living that cannot be lightly passed over, as pertaining to our salvation. For their salvation is necessary and essential to our salvation, as Paul says concerning the fathers—that they without us cannot be made perfect—neither can we without our dead be made perfect. . . . 18. I might have rendered a plainer translation to this, but it is sufficiently plain to suit my purpose as it stands. It is sufficient to know, in this case, that the earth will be smitten with a curse unless there is a welding link of some kind or other between the fathers and the children, upon some subject or other— and behold what is that subject? It is the baptism for the dead. For we without them cannot be made perfect; neither can they without us be made perfect. Neither can they nor we be made perfect without those who have died in the gospel also; for it is necessary in the ushering in of the dispensation of the fulness of times, which dispensation is now beginning to usher in, that a whole and complete and perfect union, and welding together of dispensations, and keys, and powers, and glories should take place, and be revealed from the days of Adam even to the present time. (*Joseph writes to the Church giving further directions on baptism for the dead, Sept. 6, 1842*) D&C 128:15,18

**President Joseph F. Smith**

Thus was the gospel preached to those who had died in their sins, without a knowledge of the truth, or in transgression, having rejected the prophets. 33. These were taught faith in God, repentance from sin, vicarious baptism for the remission of sins, the gift of the Holy Ghost by the laying on of hands. (*Vision regarding the Savior's visit to the spirits of the dead, Oct. 3, 1918*) D&C 138:32-33

---

**89. The Church of Jesus Christ of Latter-day Saints is founded on the revelations of God.**

**President Joseph F. Smith**

Our religion is founded on the revelations of God. The Gospel we proclaim is the Gospel of Christ, restored to earth in this the dispensation of the fulness of times. The high claim of the Church is declared in its title—THE CHURCH OF JESUS CHRIST OF LATTER-DAY SAINTS. Established by divine direction, its name was prescribed by Him whose Church it is—Jesus the Christ. (*Address from the First Presidency of the Church to the world, delivered to and accepted by vote of the Church in general conference, April 1907*) CR1907Apr(Appendix)3

**Elder Wilford Woodruff**

The full set time is come for the Lord to set His hand to accomplish these mighty events; and as He has done in other ages, so has He done now—He has raised up a Prophet, and is revealing unto him His secrets. Through that Prophet He has brought to light the fullness of the everlasting Gospel to the present generation, and is again once more for the last time establishing His Church upon the foundation of the ancient Apostles and Prophets, which is revelation, Jesus Christ being the chief corner stone. (*Remarks at a conference of the Twelve, Boylston Hall, Boston, Mass., Sept. 10, 1843*) HC6:24

**Elder Harold B. Lee,**
*also quoting Parley P. Pratt*

We sometimes hear people who talk about the Church as a democracy. Well, it isn't any such thing. Democracy means a government where the sole authority is vested in the people—the right to nominate, the right to release, to change. The Church is not a democracy. It is more like a kingdom than a democracy—and yet it is not wholly like a kingdom, except that we accept the Lord as the king, who has under His direction an earthly head who operates and becomes His mouthpiece. It is an organization that is defined more accurately as a *theocracy*, which means that it is something like a kingdom as the world would define it, and yet something like a democracy. . . . ¶ Let me read you something by Parley P. Pratt that appeared in the *Millennial Star* in 1845. It was called a "Proclamation." ¶ "The legislative, judicial, and executive power is vested in Him (the Lord). He reveals the laws, and he elects, chooses, or appoints the officers; and holds the right to reprove, to correct, or even to remove them at pleasure. Hence the necessity of a constant intercourse by direct revelation between Him and His Church. As a precedent for the foregoing facts, we refer to the examples of all ages as recorded in the Scriptures. ¶ "This order of government began in Eden—God appointed Adam to govern the earth and gave him laws. ¶ "It was perpetuated in a regular succession from Adam to Noah to Melchizedek, Abraham, Isaac, Jacob, Joseph, Moses, Samuel, the prophets, John, Jesus and his apostles. All, and each of which were chosen by the Lord, and not by the people." (Millennial Star, 5:150, [March 1843]) (Stand Ye in Holy Places, pp. 150-51) TLDP:83

**Elder Wilford Woodruff**

The Lord never had—and never will have to the end of time—a Church on earth without Prophets, Apostles, and inspired men. Whenever the Lord had a people on the earth that He acknowledged as such, that people were led by revelation. No man can find anything contrary to this. When the gospel was given to the Jews, all the gifts and graces and powers thereof, accompanied it. It was accompanied by the Eternal Priesthood—which is after the order of the Son of God, without which no man can administer in the ordinances of life and salvation. (*In Tabernacle, July 20, 1883, JD24:240*) TLDP:86

**Charles W. Penrose**

[W]e take the word of the Lord, and don't let us forget that it is the word of the Lord that has come to us, and this Church is founded upon it. Christ prayed to the Father concerning His disciples, "Father sanctify them through thy truth: thy word is truth." The word of the Lord . . . is truth and can be relied upon, and we can take our stand upon it and bring everything to it, and that should be with us the standard. CR1918Apr:21

**Related Witnesses:**

**Joseph Smith,**
*receiving the Word of the Lord*

For verily I say unto you that I am Alpha and

Omega, the beginning and the end, the light and the life of the world—a light that shineth in darkness and the darkness comprehendeth it not. 8. I came unto mine own, and mine own received me not; but unto as many as received me gave I power to do many miracles, and to become the sons of God; and even unto them that believed on my name gave I power to obtain eternal life. (*Revelation received March 7, 1831*) D&C 45:7-8

---

90. The latter-day church of Christ has the same organization that Jesus Himself established while He was on the earth.

### N. Eldon Tanner

Some people ask the reason for an organized church. They feel they can work out their salvation alone, and that there is no need to attend church meetings or fill other requirements as long as they are honest and honorable and do good to their fellowmen. But the Lord has given us instructions that we should belong to a church; and this, his church, has the same organization that Jesus Christ himself established while he was on the earth. We have many explicit declarations from the Lord that make this clear. . . . CR1977Apr:64

### Joseph Smith

We believe in the same organization that existed in the Primitive Church, namely, apostles, prophets, pastors, teachers, evangelists, and so forth. (*The sixth of the thirteen Articles of Faith; letter to John Wentworth of the Chicago Democrat, March 1, 1842*) AofF:6

### Elder Wilford Woodruff

The full set time is come for the Lord to set His hand to accomplish these mighty events; and as He has done in other ages, so has He done now—He has raised up a Prophet, and is revealing unto him His secrets. Through that Prophet He has brought to light the fullness of the everlasting Gospel to the present generation, and is again once more for the last time establishing His Church upon the foundation of the ancient Apostles and Prophets, which is revelation, Jesus Christ being the chief corner stone. (*Remarks at a conference of the Twelve, Boylston Hall, Boston, Mass., Sept. 10, 1843*) HC6:24

**Related Witnesses:**

### Paul

Now therefore ye are no more strangers and foreigners, but fellowcitizens with the saints, and of the household of God; 20. And are built

upon the foundation of the apostles and prophets, Jesus Christ himself being the chief corner stone; (*Paul writes to the Saints at Ephesus in Asia Minor, about A.D. 62*) Eph.2:19-20

### Elder John Taylor

[The kingdom of God] has its First Presidency, its Prophets and Apostles, its Seventies and High Priests, its Bishops, Teachers, and Deacons, and every appendage that is necessary to completeness, and to promote the happiness and welfare of government on this earth and in the heavens. Or, in other words, this organization is a pattern of things in the heavens and is the mediums or channels through which the blessings of God flow to his people on the earth, and through which intelligence is communicated concerning all subjects with which the Saints are concerned, whether they relate to this world or to the world which is to come. (*In Tabernacle, Oct. 7, 1859, JD7:323*) TLDP:85-86

### Paul

And he gave some, apostles; and some, prophets; and some, evangelists; and some, pastors and teachers; 12. For the perfecting of the saints, for the work of the ministry, for the edifying of the body of Christ: 13. Till we all come in the unity of the faith, and of the knowledge of the Son of God, unto a perfect man, unto the measure of the stature of the fulness of Christ: 14. That we henceforth be no more children, tossed to and fro, and carried about with every wind of doctrine, by the sleight of men, and cunning craftiness, whereby they lie in wait to deceive; (*Paul writes to the Saints at Ephesus in Asia Minor, about A.D. 62*) Eph.4:11-14

### Recorded in Luke

And when they had ordained them elders in every church, and had prayed with fasting, they commended them to the Lord, on whom they believed. (*Luke's report of the ministry of Paul and Barnabas*) Acts 14:23

### Joseph Smith

And again, the offices of elder and bishop are necessary appendages belonging unto the high priesthood. 30. And again, the offices of teacher and deacon are necessary appendages belonging to the lesser priesthood, which priesthood was confirmed upon Aaron and his sons. (*Revelation on priesthood received with six elders, Sept. 22/23, 1832*) D&C 84:29-30

### Jesus, *recorded in Luke*

Therefore also said the wisdom of God, I will send them prophets and apostles, and some of them they shall slay and persecute: 50. That the blood of all the prophets, which was shed from the foundation of the world, may be required of this generation;   *(Jesus reproaches the lawyers)* Luke 11:49-50

### J. Reuben Clark, Jr.

The Church is the organized Priesthood of God, the Priesthood can exist without the Church, but the Church cannot exist without the Priesthood. *(Speaking in behalf of First Presidency [see letter of First Presidency, MOFP6:208-09] to seminary, institute, and church school teachers at Aspen Grove)* (Entire speech published in Deseret News, Church Section, Aug. 13, 1938 and in IE1938Sep:520ff; copied in MOFP6:44-58. The speech was extracted for use as Lesson 18 of the Melchizedek Priesthood Course of Study 1969-70, p. 129ff) MOFP6:45; TLDP:87

**Author's Note:**The restored church was organized as described in the head note to a revelation given to Joseph Smith, the Prophet, at Fayette, New York, April 6, 1830. "This revelation was given at the organization of the Church, on the date named, in the home of Peter Whitmer, Sen. Six men, who had previously been baptized, participated. By unanimous vote these persons expressed their desire and determination to organize, according to the commandment of God; see Section 20. They also voted to accept and sustain Joseph Smith, Jun., and Oliver Cowdery as the presiding officers of the Church. With the laying on of hands, Joseph then ordained Oliver an elder of the Church; and Oliver similarly ordained Joseph. After administration of the sacrament, Joseph and Oliver laid hands upon the participants individually, for the bestowal of the Holy Ghost and for the confirmation of each as a member of the Church." (See heading to D&C 21.) (HC1:74-79)

---

91. Where two or three disciples of the Lord are gathered together in His name, His spirit will be with them.

### Joseph Smith,
### *receiving the Word of the Lord*

Verily, verily, I say unto you, as I said unto my disciples, where two or three are gathered together in my name, as touching one thing, behold, there will I be in the midst of them—even so am I in the midst of you. *(Revelation to Joseph Smith and Oliver Cowdery, April 1829)* D&C 6:32

### Jesus,
### *recorded in Matthew*

Again I say unto you, That if two of you shall agree on earth as touching any thing that they shall ask, it shall be done for them of my Father which is in heaven. 20. For where two or three are gathered together in my name, there am I in the midst of them. *(Jesus teaches his disciples)* Matt.18:19-20

### John A. Widtsoe

At times it has seemed to me that the spirit that has moved upon those who have spoken and listened in the small gatherings in the mission field has been even stronger and more powerful than we feel here at home. It often happens that, when far away from home, far from the sheltered protection of the temple, the tabernacle, and stakes of Zion, we draw more heavily upon the spiritual forces about us. CR1934Apr:113

**Related Witnesses:**

### Joseph Smith,
### *receiving the Word of the Lord*

And, as it is written—Whatsoever ye shall ask in faith, being united in prayer according to my command, ye shall receive. *(Revelation received Sept. 1830)* D&C 29:6

### Joseph Smith

A revelation of Jesus Christ unto his servant Joseph Smith, Jun., and six elders, as they united their hearts and lifted their voices on high. *(Revelation on priesthood received with six elders, Sept. 22/23, 1832)* D&C 84:1

# List of Doctrines

## CONSECRATION AND SACRIFICE

*Doctrines Located in This Topic*

### (1) The Law of Consecration

92. Members of the Church are to live the law of consecration when called upon to do so: they are to be ready at all times to consecrate their time, talents, money, and property to the building up of the kingdom of God on earth.

93. Disciples of Christ should be more concerned with building up the kingdom of God than with acquiring the things of this world.

94. Persons who have acquired more possessions than they can manage and use properly are to freely impart the surplus to the needy.

95. Those who refuse to share what they have will not gain exaltation.

### (2) The Law of Sacrifice

96. Members of the Church are to live the law of sacrifice: to be willing to make whatever sacrifices the Lord requires for the sake of the gospel.

*Doctrines on CONSECRATION AND SACRIFICE Located in Other Topics*

828. The law of tithing was instituted because the people could not abide the greater law of consecration.

851. The devil tempts us to covet riches and the material things of the earth.

855. We are to impart of our substance for the benefit of those less fortunate.

869. We are to be very generous in the giving of fast offerings.

# CONSECRATION AND SACRIFICE

**(1) The Law of Consecration**
**(2) The Law of Sacrifice**

## (1) The Law of Consecration

92. Members of the Church are to live the law of consecration when called upon to do so: they are to be ready at all times to consecrate their time, talents, money, and property to the building up of the kingdom of God on earth.

**Bruce R. McConkie,**
*also quoting Joseph Smith*
. . . I shall now set forth some of the principles of sacrifice and consecration to which the true saints must conform if they are ever to go where God and Christ are and have an inheritance with the faithful saints of ages past. ¶ . . . . The law of sacrifice is a celestial law; so also is the law of consecration. . . . ¶ Sacrifice and consecration are inseparably intertwined. The law of consecration is that we consecrate our time, our talents, and our money and property to the cause of the Church; such are to be available to the extent they are needed to further the Lord's interests on earth. . . . ¶ We are not always called upon to live the whole law of consecration and give of all our time, talents, and means to the building up of the Lord's earthly kingdom. Few of us are called upon to sacrifice much of what we possess, and at the moment there is only an occasional martyr in the cause of revealed religion. ¶ But what the scriptural account means is that to gain celestial salvation we must be able to live these laws to the full if we are called upon to do so. Implicit in this is the reality that we must in fact live them to the extent we are called upon so to do. . . . ¶ Now I think it is perfectly clear that the Lord expects far more of us than we sometimes render in response. We are not as other men. We are the saints of God and have the revelations of heaven. Where much is given much is expected. We are to put first in our lives the things of his kingdom. . . . ¶ We have made . . . solemn, sacred, holy covenants, pledging ourselves before gods and angels. ¶ We are under covenant to live the law of obedience.¶ We are under covenant to live the law of sacrifice. ¶ We are under covenant to live the law of consecration. . . . ¶ It is our privilege to consecrate our time, talents, and means to build up his kingdom. We are called upon to sacrifice, in one degree or another, for the furtherance of his work. Obedience is essential to salvation; so,

also, is service; and so, also, are consecration and sacrifice. CR1975Apr:74-76

**Marion G. Romney,**
*also quoting J. Reuben Clark, Jr.*
The basic principle and the justification for the law of consecration "is that everything we have belongs to the Lord; therefore, the Lord may call upon us for any and all of the property which we have, because it belongs to Him." [See D&C 104:14-17, 54-57.] (J. Reuben Clark, Jr., in Conference Report, Oct. 1942, p. 55) (*First Presidency Message, Feb. 1979; EN1979Feb:3*) DCSM:422

**George Q. Cannon**
Those who have faith and who rise to the comprehension of the dignity and exaltation that God intends to bestow upon us will not hesitate to give everything they have to the Lord, but it requires faith. The Lord might require us to lay down our lives. That would require faith, would it not? Yes. But what is the promise? That we shall have eternal life and be exalted in His presence. Therefore, those who wish to attain to this exaltation must cherish sublimity of feeling, sublimity of self-sacrifice. They must not only be willing to pay their tithing but be willing to give everything they have on the earth—wives and children and everything else. (Gospel Truth, 1:112-13) TLDP:100

**President Brigham Young**
You think that your business needs your continual and undivided attention, that you must attend to this, or to that, before you can dedicate yourselves and families to the Lord. There may perhaps be some few here this morning who feel they ought to be plowing, fencing, building, or attending to some minor affair, and cannot possibly spend time to remain at the Conference. If you will hearken to the counsel of your humble servant, you will say to the fields, the flocks, and the herds, to the gold and the silver, to the goods and chattels, to the tenements and the possessions, and to all the world—Stand aside, get away from my thoughts, for I am going up to worship the Lord. Let it all go by the board, brethren, and who cares? I do not. Your oxen and horses will not live for ever, they will die occasionally; and sometimes we are deprived by death of our children and other members of our families. I say, let the dead bury the dead, let the corn and the wheat, and all other things take care of themselves, but let us dedicate ourselves, our families, our substance, our times, our talents, and everything we have upon the face of this world, with all that will hereafter be entrusted to us, to the Lord our God; let the whole be devoted to the building up of His kingdom upon the earth, and

whether you are called here or there, it makes no matter; but . . . let every heart be humble, watchful, and prayerful, dedicating themselves unto the Lord. *(Delivered at opening of new Tabernacle, April 6, 1852, JD1:200)* TLDP:99-100

**President Spencer W. Kimball**

Consecration is the giving of one's time, talents, and means to care for those in need—whether spiritually or temporally—and in building the Lord's kingdom. In Welfare Services, members consecrate as they labor on production projects, donate materials to Deseret Industries, share their professional talents, give a generous fast offering, and respond to ward and quorum service projects. They consecrate their time in their home or visiting teaching. We consecrate when we give of ourselves. CR1977Oct:124

**Related Witnesses:**

**Marion G. Romney**

In light of the fact that we are not now required to live the law of consecration and the further fact that we have the welfare program which, as President Clark said, if put "thoroughly into operation . . . we shall not be . . . far from carrying out the great fundamentals of the United Order," I suppose the best way to live the principles of the law of consecration is to abide by the principles and practices of the welfare program. ¶ These principles and practices include avoiding idleness and greed, contributing liberal fast offerings and other welfare donations, paying a full tithing, and complying with the purpose for which the First Presidency organized the program [set forth by J. Reuben Clark in CR1936Oct:111]. *(First Presidency Message, Feb.1979)* EN1979Feb:4

**President Joseph F. Smith**

Zion can only be built up by the law that God revealed for that purpose, which is the law of consecration—not the law of tithing. The law of tithing was instituted because the people could not abide the greater law. If we could live up to the law of consecration, then there would be no necessity for the law of tithing, because it would be swallowed up in the greater law. The law of consecration requires all; the law of tithing only requires one-tenth of your increase annually. (Millennial Star, June 1984, p. 386) TLDP:106

**Joseph Smith,**
*receiving the Word of the Lord*

I, the Lord, stretched out the heavens, and built the earth, my very handiwork; and all things therein are mine. 15. And it is my purpose to provide for my saints, for all things are mine. 16. But it must needs be done in mine own way; and behold this is the way that I, the Lord, have decreed to provide for my saints, that the poor shall be exalted, in that the rich are made low.

17. For the earth is full, and there is enough and to spare; yea, I prepared all things, and have given unto the children of men to be agents unto themselves. 18. Therefore, if any man shall take of the abundance which I have made, and impart not his portion, according to the law of my gospel, unto the poor and the needy, he shall, with the wicked, lift up his eyes in hell, being in torment. *(Revelation concerning the United Order, April 23, 1834)* D&C 104:14-18

**Joseph Smith,**
*receiving the Word of the Lord*

And behold, thou wilt remember the poor, and consecrate of thy properties for their support that which thou hast to impart unto them, with a covenant and a deed which cannot be broken. 31. And inasmuch as ye impart of your substance unto the poor, ye will do it unto me; and they shall be laid before the bishop of my church and his counselors, two of the elders, or high priests, such as he shall appoint or has appointed and set apart for that purpose. 32. And it shall come to pass, that after they are laid before the bishop of my church, and after that he has received these testimonies concerning the consecration of the properties of my church, that they cannot be taken from the church, agreeable to my commandments, every man shall be made accountable unto me, a steward over his own property, or that which he has received by consecration, as much as is sufficient for himself and family. 33. And again, if there shall be properties in the hands of the church, or any individuals of it, more than is necessary for their support after this first consecration, which is a residue to be consecrated unto the bishop, it shall be kept to administer to those who have not, from time to time, that every man who has need may be amply supplied and receive according to his wants. 34. Therefore, the residue shall be kept in my storehouse, to administer to the poor and the needy, as shall be appointed by the high council of the church, and the bishop and his council; 35. And for the purpose of purchasing lands for the public benefit of the church, and building houses of worship, and building up of the New Jerusalem which is hereafter to be revealed— *(Laws governing the consecration of properties are set forth)* D&C 42:30-35

**J. Reuben Clark, Jr.**

The basic principle of all the revelations on the United Order is that everything we have belongs to the Lord; therefore, the Lord may call upon us for any and all of the property which we have, because it belongs to him. This, I repeat, is the basic principle. (D&C 104:14-17,54-57) CR1942Oct:55

**93.** Disciples of Christ should be more concerned with building up the kingdom of God than with acquiring the things of this world.

### Jesus,
#### quoted by Mormon

Lay not up for yourselves treasures upon earth, where moth and rust doth corrupt, and thieves break through and steal; 20. But lay up for yourselves treasures in heaven, where neither moth nor rust doth corrupt, and where thieves do not break through nor steal. 21. For where your treasure is, there will your heart be also. *(Jesus addresses the Nephite multitude on the American continent, after his crucifixion, A.D. 34)* 3Ne.13:19-21

### Jesus,
#### quoted by Joseph Smith,
#### translating Matthew

Wherefore, seek not the things of this world but seek ye first to build up the kingdom of God, and to establish his righteousness, and all these things shall be added unto you. *(Jesus teaches his disciples)* JST(Matt.6:33 fn. a.)

#### President John Taylor

I will promise the Latter-day Saints that if they will go into these things allowing God to dictate in the interests if Israel and the building up of his Zion on the earth, and take themselves and their individual interests out of the question, feeling they are acting for him and his kingdom, they will become the wealthiest of all people, and God will bless them and pour out wealth and intelligence and all the blessings that earth can afford. *(At Kaysville, March 2, 1879, JD20:164)* TLDP:105

#### President Brigham Young

Let it all go by the board, brethren, and who cares? I do not. Your oxen and horses will not live for ever, they will die occasionally; and sometimes we are deprived by death of our children and other members of our families. I say, let the dead bury the dead, let the corn and the wheat, and all other things take care of themselves, but let us dedicate ourselves, our families, our substance, our times, our talents, and everything we have upon the face of this world, with all that will hereafter be entrusted to us, to the Lord our God; let the whole be devoted to the building up of His kingdom upon the earth, and whether you are called here or there, it makes no matter; but . . . let every heart be humble, watchful, and prayerful, dedicating themselves unto the Lord. *(Delivered at opening of new Tabernacle, April 6, 1852, JD1:200)* TLDP:99-100

### Joseph Smith

Seek not for riches but for wisdom, and behold the mysteries of God shall be unfolded unto you, and then shall you be made rich. Behold, he that hath eternal life is rich. *(Revelation for Oliver Cowdery, April 1829)* D&C 6:7

### Jesus,
#### quoted by Mormon

Therefore take no thought, saying, What shall we eat? or, What shall we drink? or, Wherewithal shall we be clothed? 32. For your heavenly Father knoweth that ye have need of all these things. 33. But seek ye first the kingdom of God and his righteousness, and all these things shall be added unto you. *(Jesus teaches the twelve disciples)* 3Ne.13:31-33

### Jesus,
#### recorded in Matthew

Therefore I say unto you, Take no thought for your life, what ye shall eat, or what ye shall drink; nor yet for your body, what ye shall put on. Is not the life more than meat, and the body than raiment? 26. Behold the fowls of the air: for they sow not, neither do they reap, nor gather into barns; yet your heavenly Father feedeth them. Are ye not much better than they? 27. Which of you by taking thought can add one cubit unto his stature? 28. And why take ye thought for raiment? Consider the lilies of the field, how they grow; they toil not, neither do they spin: 29. And yet I say unto you, That even Solomon in all his glory was not arrayed like one of these. 30. Wherefore, if God so clothe the grass of the field, which to day is, and to morrow is cast into the oven, shall he not much more clothe you, O ye of little faith? 31. Therefore take no thought, saying, What shall we eat? or, What shall we drink? or, Wherewithal shall we be clothed? 32. (For after all these things do the Gentiles seek:) for your heavenly Father knoweth that ye have need of all these things. 33. But seek ye first the kingdom of God, and his righteousness; and all these things shall be added unto you. *(Jesus teaches his disciples)* Matt.6:25-33

**Related Witnesses:**

### Orson F. Whitney

What more eloquent preaching of the Gospel has there ever been, in this or any previous age, than the great gathering movement which has been going on since Joseph Smith lifted up the standard of the restored Gospel in this dispensation? There is no more eloquent preaching than when men and women will forsake their native land, their homes, their parents, their children, their material possessions—every earthly thing, and cross the stormy ocean, the heated plains, the frosty mountains, many of them laying down their lives, to be buried in lonely graves by the wayside; pulling hand carts, wading rivers, crossing deserts, climbing mountains, and settling in a barren waste—all for what? Was it for gold and silver, houses and lands, flocks and herds, and the betterment of their temporal condition? Was it for the honors of men and the applause of the world that they did these things? No, it was because they loved God and wanted to build up His kingdom. CR1915Apr:101

94. **Persons who have acquired more possessions than they can manage and use properly are to freely impart the surplus to the needy.**

### Marion G. Romney

While we await the redemption of Zion and the earth and the establishment of the United Order, we as bearers of the priesthood should live strictly by the principles of the United Order insofar as they are embodied in present church practices, such as fast offering, tithing, and the welfare activities. Through these practices we could as individuals, if we were of a mind to do so, implement in our own lives all the basic principles of the United Order. ¶ As you will recall, the principles underlying the United Order are consecration and stewardship and then the contribution of surpluses into the bishop's storehouse. . . . ¶ What prohibits us from giving as much in fast offerings as we would have given in surpluses under the United Order? Nothing but our own limitations. CR1966Apr:100

### Elder Joseph F. Smith,
*also quoting Joseph Smith*

Everyone should be increasing, improving, and advancing in some way, and accomplishing something for his or her good and for the good of the whole. ¶ Then again, it is written that "it is not given that one man should possess that which is above another." [D&C 49:20] Of course, there is some allowance to be made for this expression. A man who has ability superior to another man, and who is able to manage and control larger affairs than another, may possess far more than another who is not able to control and manage as much as he. But if they each had what they were capable of managing and of using wisely and prudently, they would each have alike. . . . I never expect to see the day when we shall come to the iron bedstead plan—that if a man be too long for the bedstead he will have to be shortened to fit it; or if it be too short, he will have to be stretched out. I expect

to see every man a steward over his inheritance, and I expect to see every man manage his inheritance according to the light and wisdom that he possesses and in accordance with his capacity for managing. If his capacity is greater than another's he will have more than another, because he cannot be curtailed in his liberties or rights to do good and to magnify, to enlarge, to increase, to be greater and better, because there is another that cannot be as great or good as he. What is meant then by this passage which says that it is not given that one man should possess that which is above another? I take it that in part at least it means this: It is not right for one man, because of superior advantages that he may possess in a social or financial way, or in any other way, to take advantage of others and to deprive them of that which naturally and rightfully belongs to them. I understand, too, that it is not right for men to combine together in order to oppress their fellow beings and to take advantage of them. . . . Furthermore, the Lord requires that when men have abundance they shall be humble, as economical and as prudent in the management of their abundance as the man who possesses much less is expected to be prudent and economical in the management of that which is given to him. . . . ¶ . . . . Some man possesses here [citing certain homesteads] more than he is capable of controlling, more than he can wisely handle, and he is simply half-doing or quarter-doing that which should be done, and in a sense he is depriving others of privileges that they should enjoy. . . . Here is an exemplification of the word of the Lord that it is not given that one man should possess that which is above another. This man has more than he can attend to. That 1,800 acres of land more or less ought to be divided up. . . . Why should the wealthy, because they are wealthy, monopolize the land, when they themselves cannot cultivate it as it ought to be? It is a wrong principle, and I think advice and counsel might properly be given to some of these rich men that have large tracts of land here in this valley in which we live or elsewhere which they cannot use wisely or profitably, to persuade them to divide it up with their children or with somebody else's children. . . . CR1898Oct:23-24

### Paul

For I mean not that other men be eased, and ye burdened: 14. But by an equality, that now at this time your abundance may be a supply for their want, that their abundance also may be a supply for your want: that there may be equality: 15. As it is written, He that had gathered much had nothing over; and he that had gathered little had no lack. (*Letter to the Church at Corinth, Greece, about* A.D. *55*) 2Cor.8:13-15

**Related Witnesses:**

**J. Reuben Clark, Jr.**

The basic principle of all the revelations on the United Order is that everything we have belongs to the Lord; therefore, the Lord may call upon us for any and all of the property which we have, because it belongs to him. This, I repeat, is the basic principle (D&C 104: 14-17, 54-57). . . . ¶ . . . . Now, that part of a man's property which was not turned back to him [in the operation of the United Order], if he had more than was needed under this rule of "equality" already stated, became the common property of the Church, and that common property was used for the support of the poor of the Church. It is spoken of in the revelations as the "residue" of property. (D&C 42:34-36). . . . ¶ . . . . I repeat that whatever a steward realized from the portion allotted to him over and above that which was necessary in order to keep his family under the standard provided, as already stated above, was turned over by the steward to the bishop, and this amount of surplus, plus the residues to which I have already referred, went into the bishop's storehouse (D&C 51:13, and citations above), and the materials of the storehouse were to be used in creating portions, as above indicated, for caring for the poor (D&C 78:3), the widows and orphans (D&C 83:6), and for the elders of the Church engaged in the ministry, who were to pay for what they received if they could, but if not, their faithful labors should answer their debt to the bishop. (D&C 72:11ff) CR1942Oct:55-56

**Mormon**

And now, because of the steadiness of the church they began to be exceedingly rich, having abundance of all things whatsoever they stood in need—an abundance of flocks and herds, and fatlings of every kind, and also abundance of grain, and of gold, and of silver, and of precious things, and abundance of silk and fine-twined linen, and all manner of good homely cloth. 30. And thus, in their prosperous circumstances, they did not send away any who were naked, or that were hungry, or that were athirst, or that were sick, or that had not been nourished; and they did not set their hearts upon riches; therefore they were liberal to all, both old and young, both bond and free, both male and female, whether out of the church or in the church, having no respect to persons as to those who stood in need. 31. And thus they did prosper and become far more wealthy than those who did not belong to their church. (*Those who*

*were strong in the faith considered themselves equals, the priests supported themselves and the people cared for the poor, 91* B.C.) Alma 1:29-31

**Jacob, brother of Nephi**

And the hand of providence hath smiled upon you most pleasingly, that you have obtained many riches; and because some of you have obtained more abundantly than that of your brethren ye are lifted up in the pride of your hearts, and wear stiff necks and high heads because of the costliness of your apparel, and persecute your brethren because ye suppose that ye are better than they. 14. And now, my brethren, do ye suppose that God justifieth you in this thing? Behold, I say unto you, Nay. But he condemneth you, and if ye persist in these things his judgments must speedily come unto you. (*Jacob denounces the love of riches, addressing the Nephites 544-421* B.C.) Jacob 2:13-14

**Recorded in Leviticus**

And if thy brother be waxen poor, and fallen in decay with thee; then thou shalt relieve him: yea, though he be a stranger, or a sojourner; that he may live with thee. 36. Take thou no usury of him, or increase: but fear thy God; that thy brother may live with thee. 37. Thou shalt not give him thy money upon usury, nor lend him thy victuals for increase. 38. I am the LORD your God, which brought you forth out of the land of Egypt, to give you the land of Canaan, and to be your God. (*Each seventh year to be kept as a sabbath year—each fiftieth year to be one of jubilee, in which liberty is proclaimed throughout the land*) Lev.25:35-38

---

**95. Those who refuse to share what they have will not gain exaltation.**

**George Q. Cannon**

Those who have faith and who rise to the comprehension of the dignity and exaltation that God intends to bestow upon us will not hesitate to give everything they have to the Lord, but it requires faith. . . . Therefore, those who wish to attain to this exaltation must cherish sublimity of feeling, sublimity of self-sacrifice. They must not only be willing to pay their tithing but be willing to give everything they have on the earth—wives and children and everything else. . . . But if I am not willing to do this, I cannot hope to attain to that exaltation and receive that fullness which the Lord has promised unto us, if we are faithful. . . . (Gospel Truth, 1:112-13) TLDP:100

**Joseph Smith,**
*receiving the Word of the Lord*

Wo unto you rich men, that will not give your

substance to the poor, for your riches will canker your soul; and this shall be your lamentation in the day of visitation, and of judgment, and of indignation: The harvest is past, the summer is ended, and my soul is not saved! 17. Wo unto you poor men, whose hearts are not broken, whose spirits are not contrite, and whose bellies are not satisfied, and whose hands are not stayed from laying hold upon other men's goods, whose eyes are full of greediness, and who will not labor with your own hands! 18. But blessed are the poor who are pure in heart, whose hearts are broken, and whose spirits are contrite, for they shall see the kingdom of God coming in power and great glory unto their deliverance; for the fatness of the earth shall be theirs. (*Revelation received at Kirtland, Ohio, June 1831*) D&C 56:16-18

**Joseph Smith,**
*receiving the Word of the Lord*

I, the Lord, stretched out the heavens, and built the earth, my very handiwork; and all things therein are mine. 15. And it is my purpose to provide for my saints, for all things are mine. 16. But it must needs be done in mine own way; and behold this is the way that I, the Lord, have decreed to provide for my saints, that the poor shall be exalted, in that the rich are made low. 17. For the earth is full, and there is enough and to spare; yea, I prepared all things, and have given unto the children of men to be agents unto themselves. 18. Therefore, if any man shall take of the abundance which I have made, and impart not his portion, according to the law of my gospel, unto the poor and the needy, he shall, with the wicked, lift up his eyes in hell, being in torment. (*Revelation concerning the United Order, April 23, 1834*) D&C 104:14-18

**Related Witnesses:**

**Mormon**

And thus, in their prosperous circumstances, they did not send away any who were naked, or that were hungry, or that were athirst, or that were sick, or that had not been nourished; and they did not set their hearts upon riches; therefore they were liberal to all, both old and young, both bond and free, both male and female, whether out of the church or in the church, having no respect to persons as to those who stood in need. (*Those who were strong in the faith considered themselves equals, the priests supported themselves and the people cared for the poor, 91 B.C.*) Alma 1:30

**Elder Joseph F. Smith**

The moment a community begin to be wrapt up in themselves, become selfish, become

engrossed in the temporalities of life, and put their faith in riches, that moment the power of God begins to withdraw from them, and if they repent not the Holy Spirit will depart from them entirely, and they will be left to themselves. That which was given them will be taken away, they will lose that which they had, for they will not be worthy of it. God is just, as well as merciful, and we need not expect favors at the hand of the Almighty except as we merit them, at least in the honest desires of our hearts; and the desire and intent will not always avail unless our acts correspond. (*In general conference, April 8, 1883*) (Gospel Doctrine, p. 51) TLDP:440

**Jesus,**
*recorded in Mark*

If any man have ears to hear, let him hear. 24. And he said unto them, Take heed what ye hear: with what measure ye mete, it shall be measured to you: and unto you that hear shall more be given. 25. For he that hath, to him shall be given: and he that hath not, from him shall be taken even that which he hath. (*Jesus explains the parable of the sower to the Twelve*) Mark 4:23-25

---

### (2) The Law of Sacrifice

96. Members of the Church are to live the law of sacrifice: to be willing to make whatever sacrifices the Lord requires for the sake of the gospel.

**Joseph Smith**

Let us here observe, that a religion that does not require the sacrifice of all things never has power sufficient to produce the faith necessary unto life and salvation; for, from the first existence of man, the faith necessary unto the enjoyment of life and salvation never could be obtained without the sacrifice of all earthly things. It was through this sacrifice, and this only, that God has ordained that men should enjoy eternal life; and it is through the medium of the sacrifice of all earthly things that men do actually know that they are doing the things that are well pleasing in the sight of God. When a man has offered in sacrifice all that he has for the truth's sake, not even withholding his life, and believing before God that he has been called to make this sacrifice because he seeks to do his will, he does know, most assuredly, that God does and will accept his sacrifice and offering, and that he has not, nor will not seek his face in vain. (*Lectures on Faith delivered to the School of the Prophets, 1834-35*) LOF6:7

### Bruce R. McConkie,
*also quoting Joseph Smith*

. . . I shall now set forth some of the principles of sacrifice and consecration to which the true saints must conform if they are ever to go where God and Christ are and have an inheritance with the faithful saints of ages past. ¶ . . . . The law of sacrifice is a celestial law; so also is the law of consecration. . . . ¶ Sacrifice and consecration are inseparably intertwined. The law of consecration is that we consecrate our time, our talents, and our money and property to the cause of the Church; such are to be available to the extent they are needed to further the Lord's interests on earth. ¶ The law of sacrifice is that we are willing to sacrifice all that we have for the truth's sake—our character and reputation; our honor and applause; our good name among men; our houses, lands, and families; all things, even our very lives if need be. ¶ Joseph Smith said, "A religion that does not require the sacrifice of all things never has power sufficient to produce the faith necessary [to lead] unto life and salvation" (Lectures on Faith, p. 58). ¶ We are not always called upon to live the whole law of consecration and give of all our time, talents, and means to the building up of the Lord's earthly kingdom. Few of us are called upon to sacrifice much of what we possess, and at the moment there is only an occasional martyr in the cause of revealed religion. ¶ But what the scriptural account means is that to gain celestial salvation we must be able to live these laws to the full if we are called upon to do so. Implicit in this is the reality that we must in fact live them to the extent we are called upon so to do. . . . ¶ Now I think it is perfectly clear that the Lord expects far more of us than we sometimes render in response. We are not as other men. We are the saints of God and have the revelations of heaven. Where much is given much is expected. We are to put first in our lives the things of his kingdom. . . . ¶ We have made . . . solemn, sacred, holy covenants, pledging ourselves before gods and angels. ¶ We are under covenant to live the law of obedience. ¶ We are under covenant to live the law of sacrifice. ¶ We are under covenant to live the law of consecration. . . . ¶ It is our privilege to consecrate our time, talents, and means to build up his kingdom. We are called upon to sacrifice, in one degree or another, for the furtherance of his work. Obedience is essential to salvation; so, also, is service; and so, also, are consecration and sacrifice. CR1975Apr:74-76

### George Q. Cannon

If we cannot sacrifice everything there is upon the face of the earth, that men hold dear to them, then we are unworthy of that great salva-tion that God has promised unto the faithful. The man that cannot bring every appetite into subjection to the mind and will of God, that cannot forego everything of this kind, and that is not willing to sacrifice houses and lands, and father and mother, wives and children and everything that men hold dear to them, is unworthy of that great salvation that God has in store for His faithful children. . . . ¶ If we value this salvation as we should, there is nothing that will stand between us and it. . . . We must love the Gospel of the Lord Jesus Christ, and the cause that He established, better than we do our wives and children, better than we do our own lives. There is nothing upon the face of the earth that we should love as we do the Gospel. God requires this of us. *(In Assembly Hall, Nov. 20, 1881, JD23:100)* TLDP:589-90

### Jesus,
*recorded in Matthew*

And every one that hath forsaken houses, or brethren, or sisters, or father, or mother, or wife, or children, or lands, for my name's sake, shall receive an hundredfold, and shall inherit ever-lasting life. (*Jesus teaches of the difficulty for a rich man to enter into the kingdom of God*) Matt.19:29

### Joseph Smith,
*receiving the Word of the Lord*

And all they who suffer persecution for my name, and endure in faith, though they are called to lay down their lives for my sake yet shall they partake of all this glory. 36. Wherefore, fear not even unto death; for in this world your joy is not full, but in me your joy is full. 37. Therefore, care not for the body, neither the life of the body; but care for the soul, and for the life of the soul. 38. And seek the face of the Lord always, that in patience ye may possess your souls, and ye shall have eternal life. 39. When men are called unto mine everlasting gospel, and covenant with an everlasting covenant, they are accounted as the salt of the earth and the savor of men; 40. They are called to be the savor of men; therefore, if that salt of the earth lose its savor, behold, it is thenceforth good for nothing only to be cast out and trod-den under the feet of men. (*Revelation Dec. 16, 1833; the Saints are chastened and afflicted because of transgressions*) D&C 101:35-40

### John A. Widtsoe

The Savior gave of himself, gave His very life that we might live. To sacrifice that others might be blessed was His word, His work, His life. Sacrifice is the evidence of true love. Without sacrifice love is not manifest. Without sacrifice there is no real love, or kindness. . . .

We love no one unless we sacrifice for him. We can measure the degree of love that we possess for any man or cause, by the sacrifice we make for him or it. . . . Sacrifice lifts us toward the likeness of God, the likeness of our Elder Brother Jesus Christ. CR1943Apr:38

**Related Witnesses:**

**Melvin J. Ballard**

What did it mean to have in the world, during his ministry, for three brief years the Lord Jesus Christ—not the Father, just the Son? It was the most wonderful privilege the world has ever had. What would you give tonight for the privilege of standing in the presence of the Son for five minutes? You would give all your earthly possessions for that privilege. Then can you comprehend the full meaning and significance of the statement that those who gain celestial glory will have the privilege of dwelling in the presence of the Father and the Son forever and ever? That in itself, will be reward enough for the struggle to obtain the prize. Yea, it is beyond price and earthly possessions. Even the giving of life itself would be a trifle for the privilege to dwell forever and ever in the presence of the Father and the Son. (Sermons and Missionary Services of Melvin J. Ballard, pp. 242-43) TLDP:591

**Joseph Smith,**
*receiving the Word of the Lord*

And whoso layeth down his life in my cause, for my name's sake, shall find it again, even life eternal. 14. Therefore, be not afraid of your enemies, for I have decreed in my heart, saith the Lord, that I will prove you in all things, whether you will abide in my covenant, even unto death, that you may be found worthy. 15. For if ye will not abide in my covenant ye are not worthy of me. (*Revelation received Aug. 6, 1833 in consequence of persecution of Saints in Missouri*) D&C 98:13-15

**John A. Widtsoe**

The question as to individual responsibility for the welfare of the Church was asked in the early days of members of the Church. Several of the men who labored with the Prophet Joseph Smith came to him in those early days and said: "What shall we do?" They might have said: "What shall we do to be saved?" The Lord in every instance gave an answer. We have a series of short revelations in the Doctrine and Covenants, which are the answers to that question. I find in every one a significant statement, worded almost identically in all of these revelations, to Hyrum Smith, David Whitmer, Oliver Cowdery, and others of less fame in the Church: "Keep my commandments, and seek to bring forth and establish the cause of Zion." That is our business, the business

of the Latter-day Saints. ¶ From one point of view, it is selfish enough, perhaps, to keep the commandments that I may be blessed, but it is something even greater to keep the commandments that Zion may be established. As the foundation of his great cause, the Lord gave the law of sacrifice. Unless we give of ourselves we cannot build Zion, or anything else worthy of the great cause that the Lord has given us. The law of sacrifice, from the day of Adam to the present day, in one form or another, is the basic principle of life among the communities of Saints. ¶ So we need, in this Church and Kingdom, for our own and the world's welfare, a group of men and women in their individual lives who shall be as a light to the nations, and rally standards for the world to follow. Such a people must be different from the world as it now is. There is no opportunity for Latter-day Saints to say we shall be as the world is, unless the world has the same aim that we have. We are here to build Zion to Almighty God, for the blessing of all the world. In that aim we are unique and different from all other peoples. We must respect that obligation, and not be afraid of it. We cannot walk as other men, or talk as other men, or do as other men, for we have a different destiny, obligation, and responsibility placed upon us, and we must fit ourselves for that great destiny and obligation. CR1940Apr:36

**Peter**

To whom coming, as unto a living stone, disallowed indeed of men, but chosen of God, and precious, 5. Ye also, as lively stones, are built up a spiritual house, an holy priesthood, to offer up spiritual sacrifices, acceptable to God by Jesus Christ. 6. Wherefore also it is contained in the scripture, Behold, I lay in Sion a chief corner stone, elect, precious: and he that believeth on him shall not be confounded. . . . 9. But ye are a chosen generation, a royal priesthood, an holy nation, a peculiar people; that ye should shew forth the praises of him who hath called you out of darkness into his marvellous light: (*Peter writes to the churches in modern Asia Minor, about* A.D. 60) 1Pet.2:4-6,9

**Joseph Smith,**
*receiving the Word of the Lord*

Verily I say unto you, all among them who know their hearts are honest, and are broken, and their spirits contrite, and are willing to observe their covenants by sacrifice—yea, every sacrifice which I, the Lord, shall command— they are accepted of me. . . . (*Revelation dealing with the affairs of the persecuted Saints in Missouri, Aug. 2, 1833*) D&C 97:8

**Moses**

And he said, Take now thy son, thine only son

Isaac, whom thou lovest, and get thee into the land of Moriah; and offer him there for a burnt offering upon one of the mountains which I will tell thee of. . . . 10. And Abraham stretched forth his hand, and took the knife to slay his son. 11. And the angel of the LORD called unto him out of heaven, and said, Abraham, Abraham: and he said, Here am I. 12. And he said, Lay not thine hand upon the lad, neither do thou any thing unto him: for now I know that thou fearest God, seeing thou hast not withheld thy son, thine only son from me. (*Abraham shows great obedience to the Lord by his willingness to sacrifice Isaac*) Gen.22:2,10-12

### Daniel H. Wells

We talk a great deal about sacrifices, when strictly there is no such thing; it is a misnomer—it is a wrong view of the subject, for what we do in the kingdom of God is the best investment we can possibly make. It pays the best, which ever way we may look at it, it is the principle of all others to be appreciated—and is the best investment we can make of all that pertains to us in this life. (*In Tabernacle, March 1, 1857, JD4:253*) TLDP:590-91

### President Brigham Young

The Lord has led the people through scenes of sorrow and affliction; but what have we passed through here during the two last years? Nothing, comparatively speaking. I can say that I do not consider that I have ever suffered anything for this kingdom—nothing in the least. I have never sacrificed anything, without it be the evil propensities that are sown in our nature, springing from the seed that was sown at the fall. May that be termed a sacrifice? I will not call it so. What do we possess on this earth? Do we even own our bodies? Had we the power to produce them? Is the intelligence in these bodies our own? Did we organize and implant it? No human being has had power to organize his own existence. Then there is a greater than we. Are we our own in our bodies? Are we our own in our spirits? We are not our own. We belong to our progenitors—to our Father and our God. ¶ We say that we have lost an ox, a cow, or a horse; or, "I left my farm, my house, and have sacrificed a great deal for this work." This is a mistake. You had nothing to lose. Not one particle of all that comprises this vast creation of God is our own. Everything we have has been bestowed upon us for our action, to see what we would do with it—whether we would use it for eternal life and exaltation or for eternal death and degradation, until we cease operating in this existence. We have nothing to sacrifice; then let us not talk about sacrificing. (*In Tabernacle, June 3, 1860, JD8:66-67*) TLDP:590

### Joseph Smith,
*translating the Book of Moses*

And he gave unto them commandments, that they should worship the Lord their God, and should offer the firstlings of their flocks, for an offering unto the Lord. And Adam was obedient unto the commandments of the Lord. 6. And after many days an angel of the Lord appeared unto Adam, saying: Why dost thou offer sacrifices unto the Lord? And Adam said unto him: I know not, save the Lord commanded me. 7. And then the angel spake, saying: This thing is a similitude of the sacrifice of the Only Begotten of the Father, which is full of grace and truth. 8. Wherefore, thou shalt do all that thou doest in the name of the Son, and thou shalt repent and call upon God in the name of the Son forevermore. (*The record of Moses: concerning Adam and Eve after they were driven out of the Garden of Eden*) Moses 5:5-8

### Elder Joseph Fielding Smith

[I]n the early days of the Church, the brethren came to the Prophet Joseph Smith asking what the Lord would have them do. The answer given to them was "to bring forth the cause of Zion." That is our work, to establish Zion, to build up the kingdom of God, to preach the gospel to every creature in the world, that not one soul may be overlooked where there is the possibility for us to present unto him the truth. CR1951Apr:152-53

### Joseph Smith,
*quoted by Elder Joseph Fielding Smith*

When we consecrate our property to the Lord it is to administer to the wants of the poor and needy, for this is the law of God; it is not for the benefit of the rich, those who have no need; and when a man consecrates or dedicates his wife and children, he does not give them to his brother, or to his neighbor, for there is no such law. . . . Now for a man to consecrate his property, wife and children, to the Lord, is nothing more nor less than to feed the hungry, clothe the naked, visit the widow and fatherless, the sick and afflicted, and do all he can to administer to their relief in their afflictions, and for him and his house to serve the Lord. In order to do this, he and all his house must be virtuous, and must shun the very appearance of evil. (*In letter to the Church from Liberty Jail, Dec. 16, 1838*) TPJS:127

### Paul

By faith Abraham, when he was tried, offered up Isaac: and he that had received the promises offered up his only begotten son, (*Letter to the Jewish members of the Church on faith, about A.D. 60*) Heb.11:17

# List of Doctrines

## CONVERSION: Spiritual Rebirth

*Doctrines Located in This Topic*

97. A person who *accepts* divine truth must obtain it by the Spirit of God from someone who *teaches* by that same Spirit.

98. A person must be "born again" (must experience a spiritual rebirth) in order to receive eternal salvation in the celestial kingdom of God.

99. To be converted is to have a change of heart—a heart that has been penetrated by the Spirit of the Lord.

100. People are not truly converted by miracles.

101. We must keep all the commandments and endure to the end in order to receive the gift of eternal life in the celestial kingdom of God.

# CONVERSION: Spiritual Rebirth

97. A person who *accepts* divine truth must obtain it by the Spirit of God from someone who *teaches* by that same Spirit.

### Joseph Smith

And again, he that receiveth the word of truth, doth he receive it by the Spirit of truth or some other way? 20. If it be some other way it is not of God. 21. Therefore, why is it that ye cannot understand and know, that he that receiveth the word by the Spirit of truth receiveth it as it is preached by the Spirit of truth? 22. Wherefore, he that preacheth and he that receiveth, understand one another, and both are edified and rejoice together. (*Revelation for the elders of the Church, May 1831*) D&C 50:19-22

### President Brigham Young, quoted by John A. Widtsoe

The preacher needs the power of the Holy Ghost to deal out to each heart a word in due season, and the hearers need the Holy Ghost to bring forth the fruits of the preached word of God to his glory. (*In Bowery, Sept. 16, 1860, JD8:167*) DBY:333

### Elder Joseph Fielding Smith

People are converted by their hearts being penetrated by the Spirit of the Lord when they humbly hearken to the testimonies of the Lord's servants. CHMR1:40; DCSM:13

### Mormon

And now, as the preaching of the word had a great tendency to lead the people to do that which was just—yea, it had had more powerful effect upon the minds of the people than the sword, or anything else, which had happened unto them—therefore Alma thought it was expedient that they should try the virtue of the word of God. (*Alma heads a mission to reclaim the apostate Zoramites, about 74 B.C.*) Alma 31:5

**Related Witnesses:**

### Elder Joseph Fielding Smith, also quoting Isaiah

This revelation [D&C 5:7-10] declared that this generation shall have the word of the Lord through Joseph Smith. There may be some who think that this is unreasonable, and the Lord should use some miraculous means to convert the world. Frequently when strangers . . . hear the story of the coming forth of the Book of Mormon, they ask if the plates are in some museum where they may be seen. Some of them with some scientific training, express themselves to the effect that if the scholars could see and examine the plates and learn to

read them, they would then bear witness to the truth of the Book of Mormon and the veracity of Joseph Smith, and the whole world would then be converted. When they are informed that the angel took the plates back again, they turn away in their skepticism, shaking their heads. But the Lord has said: "For my thoughts are not your thoughts, neither are your ways my ways, saith the Lord. For as the heavens are higher than the earth, so are my ways higher than your ways, and my thoughts than your thoughts." (Isa.55:8-9) We have learned that people are not converted by miracles or by examining records. If the Lord had placed the [Book of Mormon] plates where the scholars could examine them, they would have scoffed at them just as much as they do today. People are converted by their hearts being penetrated by the Spirit of the Lord when they humbly hearken to the testimonies of the Lord's servants. The Jews witnessed the miracles of our Lord, but this did not prevent them from crying out against him and having him crucified. CHMR1:39-40; DCSM:13

### Marion G. Romney

Conversion is effected by divine forgiveness, which remits sins. The sequence is something like this. An honest seeker hears the message. He asks the Lord in prayer if it is true. The Holy Spirit gives him a witness. This is a testimony. If one's testimony is strong enough he repents and obeys the commandments. By such obedience he receives divine forgiveness which remits sin. Thus he is converted to a newness of life. His spirit is healed. CR1963Oct:24

### John A. Widtsoe

[Y]ou know there is a great symbolism in irrigation. As a lifelong student of the subject I have always been impressed by the fact that the dry desert soil contains nearly all the elements of fertility. All that it needs is the enlivening power of a stream of water to flow over that soil. Suddenly the land begins to yield, and it becomes powerful. Is it not so in our spiritual lives, I wonder? Men according to our theology are children of God, not created under the old idea, but being literally children of Almighty God, contain all the elements under the law of eternal progression that will lead them into the likeness of their Father in heaven. When this being, this divine being, because in one sense we are all divine, is touched by the power of the Holy Ghost, the Holy Spirit, the power that flows from God, suddenly a man blossoms into a new life, new possibilities arise, new powers develop. As I have lived in the Church of Jesus

Christ of Latter-day Saints as a member since my very early boyhood, I have come to understand that perhaps the greatest miracle in the gospel of the Lord Jesus Christ is the transformation that comes to a man or a woman who in faith accepts the truth of the gospel, and who then lives it in his or her life. That transformation is marvelous. I have seen it in the mission field, where I first heard the gospel. I have seen it here at home. I see it every day. Every person has a measure of God's Spirit given to him. We are all in God's presence through his Holy Spirit. As new and greater truths come, as the understanding of them develops within us if we accept and live them, we are transformed from ordinary men into new powers and possibilities. ¶ The weavers of the midlands in England, the coal miners of Wales, the fishermen in Norway, the trudging farmers of Denmark, very common ordinary people, who accept the gospel from the lips of some humble Mormon missionary become so changed by those enlightening truths of the gospel that they are not the same people any longer. They have been fertilized, so to speak, by the Spirit of God that flows from eternal truth just as in irrigation the barren, dry, soil is fertilized by diverting the stream of water from the irrigation ditch onto the thirsty land. CR1952Apr:33-34

**Isaiah**

For my thoughts are not your thoughts, neither are your ways my ways, saith the LORD. 9. For as the heavens are higher than the earth, so are my ways higher than your ways, and my thoughts than your thoughts. (*Isaiah teaches: Seek the Lord while he is near, 740-659 B.C.*) Isa.55:8-9

**Orson F. Whitney**

It is all-important that we should possess that Spirit, whether we preach or sing or pray. Prayers unprompted by it do not ascend to Heaven; sermons uninspired by it fail to touch the heart of the hearer; and the songs that are sung in our worshiping assemblies, if not in tune with it, are but discords in the ear of Deity. CR1931Apr:61

---

**98. A person must be "born again" (must experience a spiritual rebirth) in order to receive eternal salvation in the celestial kingdom of God.**

**Joseph Smith,**
*quoted by Elder Joseph Fielding Smith*

[T]he Son of God came into the world to redeem it from the fall. But except a man be born again, he cannot see the kingdom of God.

This eternal truth settles the question of all men's religion. A man may be saved, after the judgment, in the terrestrial kingdom, or in the telestial kingdom, but he can never see the celestial kingdom of God, without being born of water and the Spirit. (In Evening and Morning Star, Aug. 1832) DGSM:49; TPJS:12

**Elder Harold B. Lee**

A man must be "born again" if he would reach perfection, in order to see or enter into the kingdom of God. . . . ¶ You cannot have a Christlike life, as the test would have it, without being born again. One would never be happy in the presence of the Holy One of Israel without this cleansing and purifying. (Stand Ye in Holy Places, pp. 210, 213) TLDP:654

**Jesus,**
*recorded by John*

Jesus answered and said unto him, Verily, verily, I say unto thee, Except a man be born again, he cannot see the kingdom of God. 4. Nicodemus saith unto him, How can a man be born when he is old? can he enter the second time into his mother's womb, and be born? 5. Jesus answered, Verily, verily, I say unto thee, Except a man be born of water and of the Spirit, he cannot enter into the kingdom of God. 6. That which is born of the flesh is flesh; and that which is born of the Spirit is spirit. 7. Marvel not that I said unto thee, Ye must be born again. 8. The wind bloweth where it listeth, and thou hearest the sound thereof, but canst not tell whence it cometh, and whither it goeth: so is every one that is born of the Spirit. (*Jesus tells Nicodemus men must be born again*) John 3:3-8

**George Q. Cannon**

We need to be born again, and have new hearts put in us. There is too much of the old leaven about us. We are not born again as we should be. Do you not believe that we ought to be born again? Do you not believe that we should become new creatures in Christ Jesus, under the influence of the Gospel? All will say, yes, who understand the Gospel. You must be born again. You must have new desires, new hearts, so to speak, in you. But what do we see? We see men following the ways of the world just as much as though they made no pretensions to being Latter-day Saints. Hundreds of people who are called Latter-day Saints you could not distinguish from the world. They have the same desires, the same feelings, the same aspirations, the same passions as the rest of the world. Is this how God wants us to be? No; He wants us to have new hearts, new desires. He wants us to be a changed people when we embrace His Gospel, and to be animated by entirely new motives, and have a faith that will lay hold of the promises of God. CR1899Oct:50

**Alma, the younger,**
*quoted by Mormon*

Now I say unto you that ye must repent, and be born again; for the Spirit saith if ye are not born again ye cannot inherit the kingdom of heaven; therefore come and be baptized unto repentance, that ye may be washed from your sins, that ye may have faith on the Lamb of God, who taketh away the sins of the world, who is mighty to save and to cleanse from all unrighteousness. (*Alma preaches to the people in Gideon, about 83 B.C.*) Alma 7:14

**Mark E. Petersen**

We receive confirmation by the laying on of hands and are given the gift of the Holy Ghost. But we must remember that in that ordinance we also receive a newness of life. If we are sincere, we are literally born again. In a very real sense we become different and better persons. We receive a new heart. We put away the man of sin, as Paul describes it, and take upon ourselves the name and the image of Christ. (See Col.3:9-10.) ¶ We need that rebirth so that others may believe through us that indeed Jesus was sent from heaven by his father, that he is the Savior, and that we are his servants, authorized to lead them in the way of truth. That is the beginning of their salvation and an extension of ours. ¶ We must constantly preserve the effect of his rebirth in our own lives. We seek rebirth for others through our ministry, but we cannot give something we ourselves do not possess. If our house is not properly structured, we can hardly be effective architects and builders in the lives of others. ("The Image of a Church Leader," EN1980Aug:5) TLDP:657

**Alma, the younger,**
*quoted by Mormon*

For, said he, I have repented of my sins, and have been redeemed of the Lord; behold I am born of the Spirit. 25. And the Lord said unto me: Marvel not that all mankind, yea, men and women, all nations, kindreds, tongues and people, must be born again; yea, born of God, changed from their carnal and fallen state, to a state of righteousness, being redeemed of God, becoming his sons and daughters; 26. And thus they become new creatures; and unless they do this, they can in nowise inherit the kingdom of God. 27. I say unto you, unless this be the case, they must be cast off; and this I know, because I was like to be cast off. 28. Nevertheless, after wading through much tribulations, repenting nigh unto death, the Lord in mercy hath seen fit to snatch me out of an everlasting burning, and I am born of God. 29. My

soul hath been redeemed from the gall of bitterness and bonds of iniquity. I was in the darkest abyss; but now I behold the marvelous light of God. My soul was racked with eternal torment; but I am snatched, and my soul is pained no more. (*Alma recovers and is able to speak to the Nephite people after an angel appeared to him and he was physically helpless for three days, 100-92 B.C.*) Mosiah 27:24-29

**Related Witnesses:**

**Mormon,**
*also quoting King Benjamin*

And they all cried with one voice, saying: Yea, we believe all the words which thou hast spoken unto us; and also, we know of their surety and truth, because of the Spirit of the Lord Omnipotent, which has wrought a mighty change in us, or in our hearts, that we have no more disposition to do evil, but to do good continually. 5. And we are willing to enter into a covenant with our God to do his will, and to be obedient to his commandments in all things that he shall command us, all the remainder of our days, that we may not bring upon ourselves a never-ending torment, as has been spoken by the angel, that we may not drink out of the cup of the wrath of God. 6. And now, these are the words which king Benjamin desired of them; and therefore he said unto them: Ye have spoken the words that I desired; and the covenant which ye have made is a righteous covenant. 7. And now, because of the covenant which ye have made ye shall be called the children of Christ, his sons, and his daughters; for behold, this day he hath spiritually begotten you; for ye say that your hearts are changed through faith on his name; therefore, ye are born of him and have become his sons and daughters. (*King Benjamin receives the response of the people to his address and continues his address, about 124 B.C.*) Mosiah 5:2,5-7

**Matthew Cowley**

Of those who sought the kingdom of God, Christ required complete conversion, or the second birth as explained by him to Nicodemus: "The kingdom of God is within you;" therefore, conversion must needs come from within. And by conversion the kingdom of God within man impels him to reach out for the guidance and tuition of the organized kingdom of God with which he will seek affiliation. ¶ If the kingdom within man does not impel him to an earnest quest for the established kingdom among men, then the kingdom within has not attained unto its fullest expression. "Seek, and ye shall find," said the Master. (Matthew Cowley Speaks, p. 41) TLDP:654

**99. To be converted is to have a change of heart—a heart that has been penetrated by the Spirit of the Lord.**

### Elder Harold B. Lee

To become converted, according to the scriptures, meant having a change of heart and the moral character of a person turned from the controlled power of sin into a righteous life. It meant to "wait patiently on the Lord" until one's prayers can be answered. . . . ¶ Conversion must mean more than just being a "card carrying" member of the Church with a tithing receipt, a membership card, a temple recommend, etc. It means to overcome the tendencies to criticize and to strive continually to improve inward weaknesses and not merely the outward appearances. CR1971Apr:92

### Elder Joseph Fielding Smith

People are converted by their hearts being penetrated by the Spirit of the Lord when they humbly hearken to the testimonies of the Lord's servants. CHMR1:39-40; DCSM:13

### Marion G. Romney

While conversion may be accomplished in stages, one is not really converted in the full sense of the term unless and until he is at heart a new person. *Born again* is the scriptural term. ¶ In one who is wholly converted, desire for things inimical to the gospel of Jesus Christ has actually died, and substituted therefore is a love of God with a fixed and controlling determination to keep his commandments. (Look to God and Live, p. 109) TLDP:655

### Marion G. Romney

Now since eternal life is the greatest of all the gifts of God, and obtaining it is conditioned upon being converted and healed, it is vital that we who are seeking eternal life understand what it means to be converted and healed. Converted means to turn from one belief or course of action to another. Conversion is a spiritual and moral change. *Converted* implies not merely mental acceptance of Jesus and his teachings but also a motivating faith in him and his gospel. A faith which works a transformation, an actual change in one's understanding of life's meaning and in his allegiance to God in interest, in thought, and in conduct. In one who is really wholly converted, desire for things contrary to the gospel of Jesus Christ has actually died. And substituted therefore is a love of God, with a fixed and controlling determination to keep his commandments. ¶ Paul said that such an one would walk in newness of life. (See Romans 6:4.) Peter taught that by walking in this newness of life and developing within himself faith, virtue, knowledge, temperance, patience, godliness, brotherly kindness, and charity, one becomes a partaker of the divine nature. (See 2 Pet.1:4-7.) That is to say, he becomes like God. ACR(Munich)1977:8

**Related Witnesses:**

### Mormon

And it came to pass that while they were thus conversing one with another, they heard a voice as if it came out of heaven; and they cast their eyes round about, for they understood not the voice which they heard; and it was not a harsh voice, neither was it a loud voice; nevertheless, and notwithstanding it being a small voice it did pierce them that did hear to the center, insomuch that there was no part of their frame that it did not cause to quake; yea, it did pierce them to the very soul, and did cause their hearts to burn. (*God the Father testifies of his Beloved Son, A.D. 34*) 3Ne.11:3

---

**100. People are not truly converted by miracles.**

### James E. Talmage

Men have been led to the light through manifestations of the miraculous; but events in the lives of these show that they are either such as would have found a knowledge of the truth in some other way, or they are but superficially affected, and as soon as the novelty of the new sensation has exhausted itself they wander again into the darkness from which they had for the time emerged. Miracles are not primarily intended, surely they are not needed, to prove the power of God; the simpler occurrences, the more ordinary works of creation do that. But unto the heart already softened and purified by the testimony of the truth, to the mind enlightened through the Spirit's power and conscious of obedient service in the requirements of the Gospel, the voice of miracles comes with cheering tidings, with fresh and more abundant evidences of the magnanimity of an all-merciful God. AF:199

### Joseph Smith,
*receiving the Word of the Lord*

Behold, if they will not believe my words, they would not believe you, my servant Joseph, if it were possible that you should show them all these things which I have committed unto you. 8. Oh, this unbelieving and stiffnecked generation—mine anger is kindled against them. 9. Behold, verily I say unto you, I have reserved those things which I have entrusted unto you, my servant Joseph, for a wise purpose in me, and it shall be made known unto future generations; 10. But this generation shall have my word through you; (*Revelation received at the request of Martin Harris, March 1829*) D&C 5:7-10

### Elder Joseph Fielding Smith,
#### *also quoting Isaiah*

This revelation [D&C 5:7-10] declared that this generation shall have the word of the Lord through Joseph Smith. There may be some who think that this is unreasonable, and the Lord should use some miraculous means to convert the world. Frequently when strangers . . . hear the story of the coming forth of the Book of Mormon, they ask if the plates are in some museum where they may be seen. Some of them with some scientific training, express themselves to the effect that if the scholars could see and examine the plates and learn to read them, they would then bear witness to the truth of the Book of Mormon and the veracity of Joseph Smith, and the whole world would then be converted. When they are informed that the angel took the plates back again, they turn away in their skepticism, shaking their heads. But the Lord has said: "For my thoughts are not your thoughts, neither are your ways my ways, saith the Lord. For as the heavens are higher than the earth, so are my ways higher than your ways, and my thoughts than your thoughts." (Isa.55:8-9) We have learned that people are not converted by miracles or by examining records. If the Lord had placed the [Book of Mormon] plates where the scholars could examine them, they would have scoffed at them just as much as they do today. People are converted by their hearts being penetrated by the Spirit of the Lord when they humbly hearken to the testimonies of the Lord's servants. The Jews witnessed the miracles of our Lord, but this did not prevent them from crying out against him and having him crucified. CHMR1:39-40; DCSM:13

### Jesus,
#### *recorded in Luke*

And he said unto him, If they hear not Moses and the prophets, neither will they be persuaded, though one rose from the dead. (*Jesus gives the parable of the rich man and Lazarus; the rich man requests that Lazarus be sent from heaven to warn his brothers.*) Luke 16:31

### President Brigham Young,
#### *quoted by John A. Widtsoe*

Miracles, or these extraordinary manifestations of the power of God, are not for the unbeliever; they are to console the Saints, and to strengthen and confirm the faith of those who love, fear, and serve God, and not for outsiders. (*In Bowery, June 30, 1867, JD12:97*) DBY:341

### Related Witnesses:
### James E. Talmage

[W]e are not justified in regarding the evidence of miracles as proof of authority from heaven; on the other hand, the scriptures aver that spiritual powers of the baser sort have wrought miracles, and will continue so to do, to the deceiving of many who lack discernment. If miracles be accepted as infallible evidence of godly power, the magicians of Egypt, through the wonders which they accomplished in opposition to the ordained plan for Israel's deliverance, have as good a claim to our respect as has Moses. John the Revelator saw in vision a wicked power working miracles, and thereby deceiving many, doing great wonders, even bringing fire from heaven. Again, he saw unclean spirits, whom he knew to be "the spirits of devils, working miracles.". . . ¶ Satan has shown himself to be an accomplished strategist and a skillful imitator; the most deplorable of his victories are due to his simulation of good, whereby the undiscerning have been led captive. Let no one be deluded with the thought that any act, the immediate result of which appears to be benign, is necessarily productive of permanent good. It may serve the dark purposes of Satan to play upon the human sense of goodness, even to the extent of healing the body and apparently of thwarting death. ¶ The restoration of the Priesthood to earth in this age of the world was followed by a phenomenal growth of the vagaries of spiritualism, whereby many were led to put their trust in Satan's counterfeit of God's eternal power. The development of the healing gift in the Church today is imitated in a degree comparable to that with which the magicians simulated the miracles of Moses, by the varied faith cures and their numerous modifications. For those to whom miraculous signs are all-sufficient, the imitation will answer as well as would the real; but the soul who regards the miracle in its true nature as but one element of the system of Christ, possessing value as a positive criterion only as it is associated with the numerous other characteristics of the Church, will not be deceived. AF:209,211

---

101. We must keep all the commandments and endure to the end in order to receive the gift of eternal life in the celestial kingdom of God.

## Joseph Smith,
### *receiving the Word of the Lord*

And, if you keep my commandments and endure to the end you shall have eternal life, which gift is the greatest of all the gifts of God. (*Revelation for David Whitmer, June 1829*) D&C 14:7

## Joseph Smith

If thou wilt do good, yea, and hold out faithful to the end, thou shalt be saved in the kingdom of God, which is the greatest of all the gifts of God; for there is no gift greater than the gift of salvation. (*Revelation for Oliver Cowdery, April 1829*) D&C 6:13

## Elder Joseph Fielding Smith

Baptism is not merely a door into the kingdom, which entitles us to enter, bringing with us a trail of sins unrepented of. It is not that at all. We must not enter that door until our hearts are humble, our spirits contrite, and we give the assurance that we will serve the Lord in faithfulness and righteousness to the end. CR1941Oct:93-94

## King Benjamin,
### *quoted by Mormon*

And again I say unto you as I have said before, that as ye have come to the knowledge of the glory of God, or if ye have known of his goodness and have tasted of his love, and have received a remission of your sins, which causeth such exceedingly great joy in your souls, even so I would that ye should remember, and always retain in remembrance, the greatness of God, and your own nothingness, and his goodness and long-suffering towards you, unworthy creatures, and humble yourselves even in the depths of humility, calling on the name of the Lord daily, and standing steadfastly in the faith of that which is to come, which was spoken by the mouth of the angel. 12. And behold, I say unto you that if ye do this ye shall always rejoice, and be filled with the love of God, and always retain a remission of your sins; and ye shall grow in the knowledge of the glory of him that created you, or in the knowledge of that which is just and true. (*King Benjamin to his people, about 124 B.C.*) Mosiah 4:11-12

## Related Witnesses:
### Alma, the younger,
### *quoted by Mormon*

And now behold, I ask of you, my brethren of the church, have ye spiritually been born of God? Have ye received his image in your countenances? Have ye experienced this mighty change in your hearts? 15. Do ye exercise faith in the redemption of him who created you? Do you look forward with an eye of faith, and view this mortal body raised in immortality, and this corruption raised in incorruption, to stand before God to be judged according to the deeds which have been done in the mortal body? 16. I say unto you, can you imagine to yourselves that ye hear the voice of the Lord, saying unto you, in that day: Come unto me ye blessed, for behold, your works have been the works of righteousness upon the face of the earth? 17. Or do ye imagine to yourselves that ye can lie unto the Lord in that day, and say— Lord, our works have been righteous works upon the face of the earth—and that he will save you? 18. Or otherwise, can ye imagine yourselves brought before the tribunal of God with your souls filled with guilt and remorse, having a remembrance of all your guilt, yea, a perfect remembrance of all your wickedness, yea, a remembrance that ye have set at defiance the commandments of God? 19. I say unto you, can ye look up to God at that day with a pure heart and clean hands? I say unto you, can you look up, having the image of God engraven upon your countenances? 20. I say unto you, can ye think of being saved when you have yielded yourselves to become subjects to the devil? 21. I say unto you, ye will know at that day that ye cannot be saved; for there can no man be saved except his garments are washed white; yea, his garments must be purified until they are cleansed from all stain, through the blood of him of whom it has been spoken by our fathers, who should come to redeem his people from their sins. 22. And now I ask of you, my brethren, how will any of you feel, if ye shall stand before the bar of God, having your garments stained with blood and all manner of filthiness? Behold, what will these things testify against you? 23. Behold will they not testify that ye are murderers, yea, and also that ye are guilty of all manner of wickedness? 24. Behold, my brethren, do ye suppose that such an one can have a place to sit down in the kingdom of God, with Abraham, with Isaac, and with Jacob, and also all the holy prophets, whose garments are cleansed and are spotless, pure and white? 25. I say unto you, Nay; except ye make our Creator a liar from the beginning, or suppose that he is a liar from the beginning, ye cannot suppose that such can have place in the kingdom of heaven; but they shall be cast out for they are the children of the kingdom of the devil. 26. And now behold, I say unto you, my brethren, if ye have experienced a change of heart, and if ye have felt to sing the song of redeeming love, I would ask, can ye feel so now? 27. Have ye walked, keeping yourselves blameless before God? Could ye say, if ye were called to die at this time, within yourselves, that ye have been sufficiently humble? That your garments have been cleansed and made white through the blood of Christ, who will come to redeem his people from their sins? 28. Behold, are ye stripped of pride? I say unto you, if ye are not ye are not prepared to meet God. Behold ye must prepare quickly; for the kingdom of heaven is soon at hand, and such an one hath not eternal life. 29. Behold, I say, is there one among you who is not stripped of envy? I say unto you that such an one is not prepared; and I would that he should prepare quickly, for the hour is close at hand, and he knoweth not when the time shall come; for such an one is not found guiltless. 30. And again I say unto you, is there one among you that doth make a mock of his brother, or that heapeth upon him persecutions? 31. Wo unto such an one, for he is not prepared, and the time is at hand that he must repent or he cannot be saved! (*Alma preaches to the Church about spiritual rebirth, 83 B.C.*) Alma 5:14-31

# List of Doctrines

## COVENANT PEOPLE

*Doctrines Located in This Topic*

102. The Lord covenanted with Abraham that through his descendants all the families of the earth would be blessed with the gospel.

103. The descendants of Israel are the covenant people through the chosen lineage of Abraham, Isaac, and Jacob.

104. In the premortal existence, because of their faithfulness, the people of Israel were foreordained to become a chosen nation on earth.

105. Many of the valiant and noble spirits in the premortal world were chosen and foreordained to be born into the family of Jacob (Israel).

106. Each individual's placement among the tribes, families, and nations of this world was determined by the kind of life he or she lived in the premortal state.

107. All who receive the gospel are designated of Abraham's seed; hence, the blessings of Abraham are for everyone who embraces the gospel.

# COVENANT PEOPLE

102. The Lord covenanted with Abraham that through his descendants all the families of the earth would be blessed with the gospel.

### John A. Widtsoe
This covenant with Abraham was also a call to leadership. Therefore, it has been interpreted to mean that Abraham and his descendants were chosen to conserve in purity and to advance on earth the eternal plan for human salvation. Consequently, the seed of Abraham are often spoken of as the chosen or covenant people. (*IE1945Jun:349*) DGSM:57

### Elder Joseph Fielding Smith
When the Lord called Abraham out of Ur, the land of his fathers, he made certain covenants with him because of his faithfulness. One promise was that through him and his seed after him all nations of the earth should be blessed. This blessing is accomplished in several ways. 1. Through Jesus Christ who came through the lineage of Abraham; 2. Through the priesthood which was conferred upon Abraham and his descendants; 3. Through the scattering of Israel among all nations by which the blood of Israel was sprinkled among the nations, and thus the nations partake of the leaven of righteousness, on condition of their repentance, and are entitled to the promises made to the children of Abraham; and 4. In the fact that the Lord covenanted with Abraham that after his time all who embraced the gospel should be called by his name, or, should be numbered among his seed, and should receive the Holy Ghost. (Doctrines of Salvation, 3:246) DGSM:57

### Abraham,
*quoted by Joseph Smith*
And I will make of thee a great nation, and I will bless thee above measure, and make thy name great among all nations, and thou shalt be a blessing unto thy seed after thee, that in their hands they shall bear this ministry and Priesthood unto all nations; 10. And I will bless them through thy name; for as many as receive this Gospel shall be called after thy name, and shall be accounted thy seed, and shall rise up and bless thee, as their father; 11. And I will bless them that bless thee, and curse them that curse thee; and in thee (that is, in thy Priesthood) and in thy seed (that is, thy Priesthood), for I give unto thee a promise that this right shall continue in thee, and in thy seed after thee (that is to say, the literal seed, or the seed of the body) shall all the families of the earth be bless-

ed, even with the blessings of the Gospel, which are the blessings of salvation, even of life eternal. (*Jehovah appears to Abraham in response to prayer*) Abr.2:9-11

### Parley P. Pratt
In the lineage of Abraham, Isaac, and Jacob, according to the flesh, was held the right of heirship to the keys of Priesthood for the blessings and for the salvation of all nations. From this lineage sprang the Prophets, John the Baptist, Jesus, and the Apostles; and from this lineage sprang the great prophet and restorer in modern times, and the Apostles who hold the keys under his hand. It is true, that Melchizedek and the fathers before him held the same Priesthood, and that Abraham was ordained and blessed under his hand, but this was an older branch of the chosen seed. I am speaking more fully of those who have lived since the older branches have passed away, and since the transfer of the keys to Abraham and his seed. No Ishmaelite, no Edomite, no Gentile, has since then been privileged to hold the presiding keys of Priesthood, or of the ministry of salvation. In this peculiar lineage, and in no other, should all the nations be blessed. From the days of Abraham until now, if the people of any country, age or nation have been blessed with the blessings peculiar to the everlasting covenant of the Gospel, its sealing powers, Priesthood, and ordinances, it has been through the ministry of the lineage, and the keys of Priesthood held by the lawful heirs according to the flesh. (*In Tabernacle, general conference, April 10, 1853, JD1:261*) TLDP:113

### Joseph Smith,
*receiving the Word of the Lord*
Abraham received promises concerning his seed, and of the fruit of his loins—from whose loins ye are, namely, my servant Joseph—which were to continue so long as they were in the world; and as touching Abraham and his seed, out of the world they should continue; both in the world and out of the world should they continue as innumerable as the stars; or, if ye were to count the sand upon the seashore ye could not number them. 31. This promise is yours also, because ye are of Abraham, and the promise was made unto Abraham; and by this law is the continuation of the works of my Father, wherein he glorifieth himself. (*The Lord reveals to Joseph the new and everlasting covenant, July 12, 1843 [1831]*) D&C 132:30-31

**Related Witnesses:**
### Moses
And when Abram was ninety years old and nine,

the LORD appeared to Abram, and said unto him, I am the Almighty God; walk before me, and be thou perfect. 2. And I will make my covenant between me and thee, and will multiply thee exceedingly. 3. And Abram fell on his face: and God talked with him, saying, 4. As for me, behold, my covenant is with thee, and thou shalt be a father of many nations. 5. Neither shall thy name any more be called Abram, but thy name shall be Abraham; for a father of many nations have I made thee. 6. And I will make thee exceeding fruitful, and I will make nations of thee, and kings shall come out of thee. 7. And I will establish my covenant between me and thee and thy seed after thee in their generations for an everlasting covenant, to be a God unto thee, and to thy seed after thee. (*The Lord appears to Abram, changes his name to Abraham and covenants with him*) Gen.17:1-7

### Moses

That in blessing I will bless thee, and in multiplying I will multiply thy seed as the stars of the heaven, and as the sand which is upon the sea shore; and thy seed shall possess the gate of his enemies; 18. And in thy seed shall all the nations of the earth be blessed; because thou hast obeyed my voice. (*The Lord blesses Abraham because he was willing to obey and sacrifice Isaac*) Gen.22:17-18

### Moses

And I will make of thee a great nation, and I will bless thee, and make thy name great; and thou shalt be a blessing: 3. And I will bless them that bless thee, and curse him that curseth thee: and in thee shall all families of the earth be blessed. (*The Lord instructs Abram [Abraham]*) Gen.12:2-3

---

103. The descendants of Israel are the covenant people through the chosen lineage of Abraham, Isaac, and Jacob.

### Parley P. Pratt

In the lineage of Abraham, Isaac, and Jacob, according to the flesh, was held the right of heirship to the keys of Priesthood for the blessings and for the salvation of all nations. From this lineage sprang the Prophets, John the Baptist, Jesus, and the Apostles; and from this lineage sprang the great prophet and restorer in modern times, and the Apostles who hold the keys under his hand. It is true, that Melchizedek and the fathers before him held the same Priesthood, and that Abraham was ordained and blessed under his hand, but this was an older branch of the cho-

sen seed. I am speaking more fully of those who have lived since the older branches have passed away, and since the transfer of the keys to Abraham and his seed. . . . In this peculiar lineage, and in no other, should all the nations be blessed. From the days of Abraham until now, if the people of any country, age or nation have been blessed with the blessings peculiar to the everlasting covenant of the Gospel, its sealing powers, Priesthood, and ordinances, it has been through the ministry of the lineage, and the keys of Priesthood held by the lawful heirs according to the flesh. (*In Tabernacle, general conference, April 10, 1853, JD1:261*) TLDP:113

### Parley P. Pratt

Knowing of the covenants and promises made to the fathers, as I now know them, and the rights of heirship to the Priesthood, as manifested in the election of God, I would never receive any man as an Apostle or a Priest, holding the keys of restoration, to bless the nations, while he claimed to be of any other lineage than Israel. ¶ The word of the Lord, through our Prophet and founder, to the chosen instruments of the modern Priesthood, was this—"Ye are lawful heirs according to the flesh, and your lives have been his with Christ in God." That is to say, they have been held in reserve during the reign of Mystic Babel, to be born in due time, as successors to the Apostles and Prophets of old, being their children, of the same royal line. They have come forth, at length, as heirs to the keys of power, knowledge, glory and blessings, to minister to all the nations of the Gentiles, and afterwards to restore the tribes of Israel. They are of the royal blood of Abraham, Isaac, and Jacob, and have a right to claim the ordination and endowments of the Priesthood, inasmuch as they repent, and obey the Lord God of their fathers. ¶ Those who are not of this lineage, whether they are Gentiles, Edomites, or Ishmaelites, or whatever nation, have a right to remission of sins and the Gift of the Holy Spirit, through their ministry, on conditions of faith, repentance, and baptism, in the name of Jesus Christ. Through this Gospel they are adopted into the same family, and are counted for the seed of Abraham. . . . (*In Tabernacle, general conference, April 10, 1853, JD1:262-63*) TLDP:109-10

### Elder Joseph Fielding Smith

[T]he choosing of a special race, and the conferring upon it of peculiar covenants and obligations, which other nations would not keep, had the effect of segregating this race from other races. If no special covenant or peculiar practice had been given to Israel, with the strict commandment not to mix with other peoples, Israel would have disappeared as a nation in the course of a very few years. Even as it was it took years of training and constant guidance on the part of divinely appointed prophets to impress upon the people the sacredness of their special call. Moreover, they had to suffer for the transgression of the law and the breaking of covenants, be whipped and suffer bondage before they could learn their lesson. (The Way to Perfection, pp. 129-30) DGSM:58

**Moses**

And God appeared unto Jacob again, when he came out of Padan-aram, and blessed him. 10. And God said unto him, Thy name is Jacob: thy name shall not be called any more Jacob, but Israel shall be thy name: and he called his name Israel. 11. And God said unto him, I am God Almighty: be fruitful and multiply; a nation and a company of nations shall be of thee, and kings shall come out of thy loins; (*God blesses Jacob and changes his name to Israel*) Gen.35:9-11

**Elder Joseph Fielding Smith**

Every person who embraces the Gospel becomes of the house of Israel. In other words, they become members of the chosen lineage, or Abraham's children through Isaac and Jacob unto whom the promises were made. The great majority of those who become members of the Church are literal descendants of Abraham through Ephraim, son of Joseph. Those who are not literal descendants of Abraham and Israel must become such, and when they are baptized and confirmed they are grafted into the tree and are entitled to all the rights and privileges as heirs. (*"How One May Become of the House of Israel," IE1923Oct:1149*) TLDP:112-13

**Elder Joseph Fielding Smith**

Nor is this covenant confined to mortal life. It extends beyond the grave and into the celestial kingdom. The children of Abraham, if they will keep the covenant as they receive it in the house of the Lord, shall, as Abraham their father, continue on through all eternity to increase, and there shall be no end to their posterity. In this way the blessings of Abraham, Isaac, and Jacob are extended to them, and they become partakers to the fullest extent. For there is to be a continuation of the "seeds forever" among those who receive exaltation in the kingdom of God. This is the promise and there shall come through Abraham kings and priests and rulers, not only on this earth but in the heavens, and so shall it be worlds without end. (The Way to Perfection, p. 96) TLDP:113

**Orson Hyde**

O Thou, Who didst covenant with Abraham, Thy friend, and who didst renew that covenant with Isaac, and confirm the same with Jacob with an oath, that Thou wouldst not only give them this land for an everlasting inheritance, but that Thou wouldst also remember their seed forever. Abraham, Isaac, and Jacob have long since closed their eyes in death, and made the grave their mansion. Their children are scattered and dispersed abroad among the nations of the Gentiles like sheep that have no shepherd, and are still looking forward for the fulfillment of those promises which Thou didst make concerning them; and even this land, which once poured forth nature's richest bounty, and flowed, as it were, with milk and honey, has, to a certain extent, been smitten with barrenness and sterility since it drank from murderous hands the blood of Him who never sinned. (*Prayer uttered on the Mount of Olives*) HC4:456-57

**Related Witnesses:**

**Isaac,**
*quoted by Moses*

And God Almighty bless thee, and make thee fruitful, and multiply thee, that thou mayest be a multitude of people; 4. And give thee the blessing of Abraham, to thee, and to thy seed with thee; that thou mayest inherit the land wherein thou art a stranger, which God gave unto Abraham. (*Isaac blesses Jacob*) Gen.28:3-4

**President Harold B. Lee**

Those born to the lineage of Jacob, who was later to be called Israel, and his posterity, who were known as the children of Israel, were born into the most illustrious lineage of any of those who came upon the earth as mortal beings. CR1973Oct:7

**Recorded in Exodus**

And Moses went up unto God, and the LORD called unto him out of the mountain, saying, Thus shalt thou say to the house of Jacob, and tell the children of Israel; 4. Ye have seen what I did unto the Egyptians, and how I bare you on eagles' wings, and brought you unto myself. 5. Now therefore, if ye will obey my voice indeed, and keep my covenant, then ye shall be a peculiar treasure unto me above all people: for all the earth is mine: 6. And ye shall be unto me a kingdom of priests, and an holy nation. These are the words which thou shalt speak unto the children of Israel. (*The Lord covenants to make Israel a peculiar treasure, a kingdom of priests, and an holy nation*) Ex.19:3-6

104. In the premortal existence, because of their faithfulness, the people of Israel were foreordained to become a chosen nation on earth.

### Bruce R. McConkie

Israel is an eternal people. Members of that chosen race first gained their inheritance with the faithful in the pre-mortal life. Israel was a distinct people in the pre-existence. Many of the valiant and noble spirits in that first estate were chosen, elected, and foreordained to be born into the family of Jacob, so as to be natural heirs of all of the blessings of the gospel. (Doctrinal New Testament Commentary, 2:284) DGSM:56

### Bruce R. McConkie

Abraham's mortal seed, because of long ages of preparation and devotion, while they yet dwelt as spirits in the presence of their Eternal Father earned the "right" to the gospel and the priesthood and an eventual inheritance of eternal life (Abr.2:10-12). That is, they were foreordained to be the children of the father of the faithful and to work the works of righteousness as did faithful Abraham. Though the gospel is for all men, in due course . . . yet some are entitled to receive it before it is presented to others. The Lord sends forth his word on a priority basis. It goes to all men eventually, but some are entitled to hear the voice before others. (The Promised Messiah, p. 507) DGSM:57

### Elder Joseph Fielding Smith

The numbers of the children of Israel were known and the bounds of their habitation fixed, in the days of old when the Lord divided to the nations their inheritance. We conclude, therefore, that there must have been a division of the spirits of men in the spiritual world, and those who were appointed to be the children of Israel were separated and prepared for a special inheritance. (Doctrines of Salvation, 1:59) TLDP:202-03

### Elder Joseph Fielding Smith

Through this covenant people the Lord reserved the right to send into the world a chosen lineage of faithful spirits who were entitled to special favors based on pre-mortal obedience. (The Way to Perfection, pp. 129-30) DGSM:58

### President Harold B. Lee

Those born to the lineage of Jacob, who was later to be called Israel, and his posterity, who were known as the children of Israel, were born into the most illustrious lineage of any of those who came upon the earth as mortal beings. ¶ All these rewards were seemingly promised, or foreordained, before the world was. Surely these matters must have been determined by the kind of lives we had lived in that premortal spirit world. Some may question these assumptions, but at the same time they will accept without any question the belief that each one of us will be judged when we leave this earth according to his or her deeds during our lives here in mortality.

Isn't it just as reasonable to believe that what we have received here in this earth [life] was given to each of us according to the merits of our conduct before we came here? CR1973Oct:7-8

### Recorded in Deuteronomy

Remember the days of old, consider the years of many generations: ask thy father, and he will shew thee; thy elders, and they will tell thee. 8. When the most High divided to the nations their inheritance, when he separated the sons of Adam, he set the bounds of the people according to the number of the children of Israel. 9. For the LORD's portion is his people; Jacob is the lot of his inheritance. (*Israel was known in the pre-mortal world*) Deut.32:7-9

---

105. **Many of the valiant and noble spirits in the premortal world were chosen and foreordained to be born into the family of Jacob (Israel).**

### Bruce R. McConkie

Israel was a distinct people in the pre-existence. Many of the valiant and noble spirits in that first estate were chosen, elected, and foreordained to be born into the family of Jacob, so as to be natural heirs of all of the blessings of the gospel. (Doctrinal New Testament Commentary, 2:274) MPSG1987:41

### President Harold B. Lee

Those born to the lineage of Jacob, who was later to be called Israel, and his posterity, who were known as the children of Israel, were born into the most illustrious lineage of any of those who came upon the earth as mortal beings. ¶ All these rewards were seemingly promised, or foreordained, before the world was. Surely these matters must have been determined by the kind of lives we had lived in that premortal spirit world. . . . Isn't it just as reasonable to believe that what we have received here in this earth [life] was given to each of us according to the merits of our conduct before we came here? CR1973Oct:7-8

### Elder Joseph Fielding Smith

The numbers of the children of Israel were known and the bounds of their habitation fixed, in the days of old when the Lord divided to the nations their inheritance. We conclude, therefore, that there must have been a division of the spirits of men in the spiritual world, and those who were appointed to be the children of Israel were separated and prepared for a special inheritance. (Doctrines of Salvation, *1:59*) TLDP:202-03

**Related Witnesses:**

### George Q. Cannon

Hence, as it is a great advantage to be born in

the covenant, it is but reasonable to suppose that noble spirits will seek the opportunity to come into families where they will have all the blessings and promises which pertain to the covenant. The Latter-day Saints will undoubtedly become a great people, for God has made promises to them, and this will be one of the means by which their greatness will be developed. (Gospel Truth, 2:87) TLDP:114

---

106. **Each individual's placement among the tribes, families, and nations of this world was determined by the kind of life he or she lived in the premortal state.**

**President Harold B. Lee**
You are now born into a family to which you have come, into the nations through which you have come, as a reward for the kind of lives you lived before you came here and at a time in the world's history, as the Apostle Paul taught the men of Athens and as the Lord revealed to Moses, determined by the faithfulness of each of those who lived before this world was created. CR1973Oct:7

**George Q. Cannon,**
*also quoting Joseph Smith*
It was arranged before we came here how we should come and through what lineage we should come. . . . As the Lord has taught us . . . our Priesthood has been hid with God. He says: ¶ "Therefore, thus saith the Lord unto you, with whom the priesthood hath continued through the lineage of your fathers— ¶ For Ye are lawful heirs, according to the flesh, and have been hid from the world with Christ in God— ¶ Therefore your life and the priesthood have remained, and must needs remain through you and your lineage until the restoration of all things spoken by the mouths of all the holy prophets since the world began." [D&C 86:8-10] ¶ I am convinced that it was predestined [predetermined] before I was born that I should come through my father as I am that I stand here. (Gospel Truth, 2:89) TLDP:114

**President David O. McKay**
From this revelation [Abraham 3:23], we may infer two things: first, that there were among those spirits [in the premortal life] different degrees of intelligence, varying grades of achievement, retarded and advanced spiritual attainment; second, that there were no national distinctions among those spirits such as Americans, Europeans, Asiatics, Australians, etc. Such "bounds of habitation" would have to be

"determined" when the spirits entered their earthly existence or second estate. . . . ¶ . . . . Our place in this world would then be determined by our own advancement or condition in the pre-mortal state, just as our place in our future existence will be determined by what we do here in mortality. ¶ When, therefore, the Creator said to Abraham, and to others of his attainment, "You I will make my rulers," there could exist no feeling of envy or jealousy among the million other spirits, for those who were "good and great" were but receiving their just reward. (Home Memories of President David O. McKay, pp. 228-30) DGSM:14

**Elder Harold B. Lee,**
*also quoting John*
There is no truth more plainly taught in the Gospel than that our condition in the next world will depend upon the kind of lives we live here. "All that are in the graves shall hear his voice, and shall come forth; they that have done evil, unto the resurrection of damnation" (John 5:28-29). Is it not just as reasonable to suppose that the conditions in which we now live have been determined by the kind of lives we lived in the pre-existent world of spirits? That the apostles understood this principle is indicated by their question to the Master when the man who was blind from his birth was healed of his blindness. "Master, who did sin, this man or his parents that he was born blind?" (John 9:2) Now perhaps you will have a partial answer to some of your questions as to why, if God is a just Father, that some of his children are born of an enlightened race and in a time when the Gospel is upon the earth, while others are born of a heathen parentage in a benighted, backward country. . . . ¶ The privilege of obtaining a mortal body on this earth is seemingly so priceless that those in the spirit world, even though unfaithful or not valiant, were undoubtedly permitted to take mortal bodies although under penalty of racial or physical or nationalistic limitations. Between the extremes of the "noble and the great" spirits, whom God would make his rulers, and the disobedient and the rebellious who were cast out with Satan, there were obviously many spirits with varying degrees of faithfulness. May we not assume from these teachings that the progress and development we made as spirits have brought privileges and blessings here according to our faithfulness in the spirit world? (Decisions for Successful Living, pp. 164-65) TLDP:497

**President Heber J. Grant**
We have been placed upon this earth because of our faithfulness in having kept our first estate.

The labors that we performed in the sphere that we left before we came here have had a certain effect upon our lives here, and to a certain extent they govern and control the lives that we lead here, just the same as the labors that we do here will control and govern our lives when we pass from this stage of existence. ("Reward of Conscience," IE1943Feb:75) TLDP:496

**Paul**

God that made the world and all things therein, seeing that he is Lord of heaven and earth, dwelleth not in temples made with hands; 25. Neither is worshipped with men's hands, as though he needed any thing, seeing he giveth to all life, and breath, and all things; 26. And hath made of one blood all nations of men for to dwell on all the face of the earth, and hath determined the times before appointed, and the bounds of their habitation; (Paul preaches on Mars' Hill about the Unknown God) Acts 17:24-26

**Related Witnesses:**

**Elder Joseph Fielding Smith**

Every man had his agency there [in the pre-mortal life], and men receive rewards here based upon their actions there, just as they will receive rewards hereafter for deeds done in the body. (Doctrines of Salvation, 1:66) TLDP:497

**Bruce R. McConkie**

Israel is an eternal people. Members of that chosen race first gained their inheritance with the faithful in the pre-mortal life. Israel was a distinct people in the pre-existence. Many of the valiant and noble spirits in that first estate were chosen, elected, and foreordained to be born into the family of Jacob, so as to be natural heirs of all of the blessings of the gospel. (Doctrinal New Testament Commentary, 2:284) MPSG1987:41

**Author's Note:** As to going so far as to say we all chose our parents in the premortal world, Joseph Fielding Smith once wrote that the scriptures do not bear this out. Accordingly, neither have I been able to find prophetic witnesses to this effect. Hence it may not be true. In any event, such appears not to be a doctrine of the Church. Elder Smith wrote: "We have no scriptural justification . . . for the belief that we had the privilege of choosing our parents and our life companions in the spirit world. This belief has been advocated by some, and it is possible that in some instances it is true. . . . Most likely we came where those in authority decided to send us. Our agency may not have been exercised to the extent of making choice of parents and posterity." (The Way to Perfection, pp. 44-45)

**107. All who receive the gospel are designated of Abraham's seed; hence, the blessings of Abraham are for everyone who embraces the gospel.**

**Abraham,**
*quoted by Joseph Smith*

[F]or as many as receive this Gospel shall be called after thy name, and shall be accounted thy seed, and shall rise up and bless thee, as their father; (*Jehovah appears to Abraham in response to prayer*) Abr.2:10

**John A. Widtsoe**

The oft-asked question, "Who are the children of Abraham?" is well answered in light of the revealed gospel. ¶ All who accept God's plan for his children on earth and who live it are the children of Abraham. Those who reject the gospel, whether children in the flesh, or others, forfeit the promises made to Abraham and are not children of Abraham. (Evidences and Reconciliations, p. 400) DGSM:58

**Elder Joseph Fielding Smith**

Is it necessary that we be of the house of Israel in order to accept the gospel and all the blessings pertaining to it? If so, how do we become of the house of Israel, by adoption or by direct lineage? ¶ Every person who embraces the gospel becomes of the house of Israel. In other words, they become members of the chosen lineage, or Abraham's children through Isaac and Jacob unto whom the promises were made. The great majority of those who become members of the Church are literal descendants of Abraham through Ephraim, son of Joseph. Those who are not literal descendants of Abraham and Israel must become such, and when they are baptized and confirmed they are grafted into the tree and are entitled to all the rights and privileges as heirs. (Doctrines of Salvation, 3:245-46) DGSM:58

**Paul**

Even as Abraham believed God, and it was accounted to him for righteousness. 7. Know ye therefore that they which are of faith, the same are the children of Abraham. 8. And the scripture, foreseeing that God would justify the heathen through faith, preached before the gospel unto Abraham, saying, In thee shall all nations be blessed. 9. So then they which be of faith are blessed with faithful Abraham. . . . 13. Christ hath redeemed us from the curse of the law, being made a curse for us: for it is written, Cursed is every one that hangeth on a tree: 14. That the blessing of Abraham might come on the Gentiles through Jesus Christ; that we might receive the promise of the Spirit through faith. . . . 16. Now to Abraham and his seed were the promises made. He saith not, And to seeds, as of many; but as of one, And to thy seed, which is Christ. . . . 29. And if ye be Christ's, then are ye Abraham's seed, and heirs according to the promise. (*Paul writes to the churches of Galatia in Asia Minor, about A.D. 55*) Gal.3:6-9,13-14,16,29

**Elder Joseph Fielding Smith,**
*also quoting Jesus and Joseph Smith*

No person can receive the Gospel without becoming of the seed of Abraham. If they are not of his blood by descent they become so by adoption. This is the meaning of the words of the Savior to the Jews: "And I say unto you, That many shall come from the east and west and shall sit down with Abraham, and Isaac, and Jacob, in the kingdom of heaven. But the children of the kingdom shall be cast out into outer darkness; there shall be weeping and gnashing of teeth." Moreover, the Lord revealed to Joseph Smith that all who receive the two Priesthoods become sons of Moses and of Aaron, and "the seed of Abraham, and the church and kingdom, and the elect of God." This is done by virtue of the covenant made with Abraham, which was renewed with Jacob and the tribes of Israel. (The Way to Perfection, pp. 89-90) TLDP:113

**Joseph Smith**

For whoso is faithful unto the obtaining these two priesthoods of which I have spoken, and the magnifying their calling, are sanctified by the Spirit unto the renewing of their bodies. 34. They become the sons of Moses and of Aaron and the seed of Abraham, and the church and kingdom, and the elect of God. (*Revelation on priesthood with six elders, Sept. 22/23, 1832*) D&C 84:33-34

**Parley P. Pratt**

By obeying the Gospel, or by adoption through the Gospel, we are all joint heirs with Abraham, and with his seed, and we shall by continuance in well doing, all be blessed in Abraham and his seed, no matter whether we are descended from Melchizedek, from Edom, from Ishmael, or whether we be Jews or Gentiles. On the principles of Gospel adoption, the blessing is broad enough to gather all good, penitent, obedient people under its wings and to extend to all nations the principles of salvation. We would therefore more cordially invite all nations to join themselves to this favored lineage, and come with all humility and penitence to its royal Priesthood, if they wish to be instructed and blessed, for to be blessed in this peculiar sense in any other way, or by any other institutions or government, they cannot, while the promises and covenants of God hold good to the elect seed. (*In Tabernacle, general conference, April 10, 1853, JD1:262-63*) TLDP:109-10

**Related Witnesses:**

**Jesus,**
*quoted by John*

If ye were Abraham's children, ye would do the works of Abraham. (*Jesus tells the Jews that simply being of the seed of Abraham is not enough*) John 8:39

**Joseph Smith,**
*quoted by Elder Joseph Fielding Smith*

This first Comforter or Holy Ghost has no other effect than pure intelligence. It is more powerful in expanding the mind, enlightening the understanding, and storing the intellect with present knowledge, of a man who is of the literal seed of Abraham, than one that is a Gentile, though it may not have half as much visible effect upon the body; for as the Holy Ghost falls upon one of the literal seed of Abraham, it is calm and serene; and his whole soul and body are only exercised by the pure spirit of intelligence; while the effect of the Holy Ghost upon a Gentile, is to purge out the old blood, and make him actually of the seed of Abraham. That man that has none of the blood of Abraham (naturally) must have a new creation by the Holy Ghost. In such a case, there may be more of a powerful effect upon the body, and visible to the eye, than upon an Israelite, while the Israelite at first might be far before the Gentile in pure intelligence. (*Joseph Smith instructs the brethren at a conference of the Twelve, June 1839*) TPJS:149-50; DGSM:57-58

**HYMNS Written by Prophets
Applicable to this Topic**

**Parley P. Pratt**
*The Morning Breaks*, Verses 3,4,5
HYMNS:1

The Gentile fulness now comes in,
And Israel's blessings are at hand.
Lo, Judah's remnant, cleansed from sin,
Lo, Judah's remnant, cleansed from sin,
Shall in their promised Canaan stand.

Jehovah speaks! Let earth give ear,
And Gentile nations turn and live,
His mighty arm is making bare,
His mighty arm is making bare
His cov'nant people to receive.

Angels from heav'n and truth from earth
Have met, and both have record borne;
Thus Zion's light is bursting forth,
Thus Zion's light is bursting forth
To bring her ransomed children home.

# List of Doctrines

## COVENANTS WITH GOD

*Doctrines Located in This Topic*

108. God's people are a covenant-making people.

109. The fulness of the gospel of Jesus Christ is the new and everlasting covenant between God and members of His Church.

110. Baptism is an everlasting covenant between God and a new member of His Church.

111. The oath and covenant of the priesthood is an everlasting covenant between God and each man who receives the Melchizedek Priesthood ordination.

112. The sealing ordinance of marriage is an everlasting covenant between God and those who are sealed.

113. We are to keep the sacred covenants we have made with God if we are to merit entrance into the celestial kingdom.

*Doctrines on COVENANTS WITH GOD Located in Other Topics*

53. Baptism is an ordinance of the gospel entered into with a covenant.

54. The covenant of baptism is a solemn promise that we are willing to take upon us the name of Jesus Christ and keep His commandments, with a determination to serve Him to the end.

92. Members of the Church are to live the law of consecration when called upon to do so: they are to be ready at all times to consecrate their time, talents, money, and property to the building up of the kingdom of God on earth.

96. Members of the Church are to live the law of sacrifice: to be willing to make whatever sacrifices the Lord requires for the sake of the gospel.

142. To receive exaltation (the highest degree in the celestial kingdom) a person must be married in the new and everlasting covenant.

414. A man receives the oath and covenant of the priesthood with a *covenant* of obedience.

415. A man receives the oath and covenant of the priesthood with a *covenant* of service to do the work assigned.

688. The Sabbath day is set apart for partaking of the sacrament (for renewing sacred covenants).

697. In partaking of the sacrament we renew solemn covenants with the Lord.

# COVENANTS WITH GOD

**108. God's people are a covenant-making people.**

### Marion G. Romney

Traditionally, God's people have been known as a covenant people. The gospel itself is the new and everlasting covenant. The posterity of Abraham through Isaac and Jacob is the covenant race. We come into the Church by covenant, which we enter into when we go into the waters of baptism. The new and everlasting covenant of celestial marriage is the gate to exaltation in the celestial kingdom. Men receive the Melchizedek Priesthood by an oath and covenant. CR1962Apr:17

### John A. Widtsoe

Everyone who receives an ordinance must make a covenant, else the ordinance is not fully satisfactory. He who is baptized covenants to keep the law of the Church; he who is administered to for sickness, and the administrators, covenant to use their faith to secure the desired healings; he who receives the temple endowment covenants to use in his life that which he has been taught; he who is ordained to the priesthood agrees to honor it, and so on with every ordinance. ¶ That places covenants high, as they should be. Knowledge of itself has little saving power. Only as it is used does knowledge become of value. The man who learns and promises to use that knowledge is of value to society. ("What Is the Need of Ordinances?" IE1948Feb:97) TLDP:117-18

### President Brigham Young

All Latter-day Saints enter the new and everlasting covenant when they enter this Church. They covenant to cease sustaining, upholding and cherishing the kingdom of the devil and the kingdoms of this world. They enter into the new and everlasting covenant to sustain the Kingdom of God and no other kingdom. They take a vow of the most solemn kind, before the heavens and earth, and that, too, upon the validity of their own salvation, that they will sustain truth and righteousness instead of wickedness and falsehood, and build up the Kingdom of God, instead of the kingdoms of this world. (At Bountiful, Utah, May 17, 1868, JD12:230) TLDP:118

### Related Witnesses:

### Marion G. Romney

A covenant is an agreement between two or more parties. An oath is a sworn attestation to the inviolability of the promises in the agreement. In the covenant of the priesthood the parties are the Father and the receiver of the priest-hood. Each party to the covenant undertakes certain obligations. The receiver undertakes to magnify his calling in the priesthood. The Father, by oath and covenant, promises the receiver that if he does so magnify his priesthood he will be sanctified by the Spirit unto the renewing of his body; (see D&C 84:33) that he will become a member of ". . . the church and kingdom, and the elect of God," (Ibid., 84:34) and receive the ". . . Father's kingdom; therefore," said the Savior, "all that my Father hath shall be given unto him." (Ibid., 84:38) CR1962Apr:17

### Joseph Smith

All covenants, contracts, bonds, obligations, oaths, vows, performances, connections, associations, or expectations, that are not made and entered into and sealed by the Holy Spirit of promise, of him who is anointed, both as well for time and for all eternity . . . are of no efficacy, virtue, or force in and after the resurrection from the dead; for all contracts that are not made unto this end have an end when men are dead. (Revelation relating to the new and everlasting covenant, July 12, 1843, [1831]) D&C 132:7

### Delbert L. Stapley

The Holy Priesthood is accepted by an oath and covenant and is binding upon those who receive it. They obligate themselves to keep faithfully all the commandments of God and to magnify their callings by honoring and exercising the priesthood in righteousness for the benefit and blessing of mankind. CR1959Apr:109

**Author's Note:** Ordinances are covenants, writes Joseph Fielding Smith: "Each ordinance and requirement given to man for the purpose of bringing to pass his salvation and exaltation is a covenant. Baptism for the remission of sins is a covenant. . . . ¶ "Keeping the Sabbath day holy is a covenant. . . . All of the Ten Commandments are everlasting covenants. The law of tithing is a form of an everlasting covenant . . . although some day we shall be given a higher form of this law known as consecration. ¶ "Marriage is an everlasting covenant, but not as some believe, the new and everlasting covenant." (Church News, May 6, 1939; Doctrines of Salvation, 1:152-53)

**109. The fulness of the gospel of Jesus Christ is the new and everlasting covenant between God and members of His Church.**

### Elder Joseph Fielding Smith

The new and everlasting covenant is the fulness of the gospel. It is composed of "All covenants, contracts, bonds, obligations, oaths, vows, performances, connections, associations, or expectations" that are sealed upon members of the Church by the Holy Spirit of promise, or the Holy Ghost, by the authority of the President of the Church who holds the keys. The President of the Church holds the keys of the Melchizedek Priesthood. He delegates authority to others and authorizes them to perform the sacred ordinances of the priesthood. ¶ Marriage for eternity is a new and everlasting covenant. Baptism is also a new and everlasting covenant, and likewise ordination to the priesthood, and every other covenant is everlasting and a part of the new and everlasting covenant which embraces all things. (Answers to Gospel Questions, 1:65) DCSM:46

### Elder Joseph Fielding Smith

What is the new and everlasting covenant? I regret to say that there are some members of the Church who are misled and misinformed in regard to what the new and everlasting covenant really is. *The new and everlasting covenant is the sum total of all gospel covenants and obligations.* (Doctrines of Salvation, 1:156) TLDP:118

### Marion G. Romney

Traditionally, God's people have been known as a covenant people. The gospel itself is the new and everlasting covenant. The posterity of Abraham through Isaac and Jacob is the covenant race. We come into the Church by covenant, which we enter into when we go into the waters of baptism. The new and everlasting covenant of celestial marriage is the gate to exaltation in the celestial kingdom. Men receive the Melchizedek Priesthood by an oath and covenant. CR1962Apr:17

### Joseph Smith,
*receiving the Word of the Lord*

Verily I say unto you, blessed are you for receiving mine everlasting covenant, even the fulness of my gospel, sent forth unto the children of men, that they might have life and be made partakers of the glories which are to be revealed in the last days, as it was written by the prophets and apostles in days of old. (*Revelation for several elders in the Church, Oct. 25, 1831*) D&C 66:2

**Related Witnesses:**

### Joseph Smith,
*receiving the Word of the Lord*

And as pertaining to the new and everlasting covenant, it was instituted for the fulness of my glory; and he that receiveth a fulness thereof must and shall abide the law, or he shall be damned, saith the Lord God. 7. And verily I say unto you, that the conditions of this law are these: All covenants, contracts, bonds, obligations, oaths, vows, performances, connections, associations, or expectations, that are not made and entered into and sealed by the Holy Spirit of promise, of him who is anointed, both as well for time and for all eternity, and that too most holy, by revelation and commandment through the medium of mine anointed, whom I have appointed on the earth to hold this power (and I have appointed unto my servant Joseph to hold this power in the last days, and there is never but one on the earth at a time on whom this power and the keys of this priesthood are conferred), are of no efficacy, virtue, or force in and after the resurrection from the dead; for all contracts that are not made unto this end have an end when men are dead. (*Revelation relating to the new and everlasting covenant, July 12, 1843, [1831]*) D&C 132:6-7

### President Brigham Young

All Latter-day Saints enter the new and everlasting covenant when they enter this Church. They covenant to cease sustaining, upholding and cherishing the kingdom of the devil and the kingdoms of this world. They enter into the new and everlasting covenant to sustain the Kingdom of God and no other kingdom. They take a vow of the most solemn kind, before the heavens and earth, and that, too, upon the validity of their own salvation, that they will sustain truth and righteousness instead of wickedness and falsehood, and build up the Kingdom of God, instead of the kingdoms of this world. (*At Bountiful, Utah, May 17, 1868, JD12:230*) TLDP:118

### Elder Wilford Woodruff

It was with no ordinary feelings that we took our departure from the Saints in Herefordshire on this occasion; for, less than four months since, I proclaimed the fullness of the Gospel in this region for the first time; but now, we were leaving between five and six hundred Saints, who were rejoicing in the new and everlasting covenant, and hundreds of others who were wishing to hear and obey. (Letter to Millennial Star, July 9, 1840) HC4:153

### Joseph Smith

Shall I, who have heard the voice of God, and communed with angels, and spake as moved by the Holy Ghost for the renewal of the everlasting covenant, and for the gathering of Israel in the last days,—shall I worm myself into a political hypocrite? Shall I, who hold the keys of the last kingdom, in which is the dispensation of the fullness of all things spoken by the mouths of all the holy Prophets since the world began, under the sealing power of the Melchizedek Priesthood,—shall I stoop from the sublime authority of Almighty God, to be handled as a monkey's cat's-paw, and pettify myself into a clown to act the farce of political demagoguery? (*Letter to James A. Bennett, Nauvoo, Ill., Nov. 13, 1843*) HC6:78

### Orson Hyde

My humble advice to all such is, that they repent and cast far from them these wicked traditions, and be baptized into the new and everlasting covenant, lest the Lord speak to them in His wrath, and vex them in His sore displeasure. (*Letter from Trieste concerning his journey to Jerusalem, Jan. 1842*) HC4:497

### Joseph Smith,
### *receiving the Word of the Lord*

And even so I have sent mine everlasting covenant into the world, to be a light to the world, and to be a standard for my people, and for the Gentiles to seek to it, and to be a messenger before my face to prepare the way before me. (*Revelation March 7, 1831*) D&C 45:9

### Isaiah

The earth also is defiled under the inhabitants thereof; because they have transgressed the laws, changed the ordinance, broken the everlasting covenant. (*Isaiah prophesies, 740-659 B.C.*) Isa.24:5

### Jeremiah

Behold, the days come, saith the LORD, that I will make a new covenant with the house of Israel, and with the house of Judah: 32. Not according to the covenant that I made with their fathers in the day that I took them by the hand to bring them out of the land of Egypt; which my covenant they brake, although I was an husband unto them, saith the LORD: 33. But this shall be the covenant that I will make with the house of Israel; After those days, saith the LORD, I will put my law in their inward parts, and write it in their hearts; and will be their God, and they shall be my people. 34. And they shall teach no more every man his neighbour, and every man his brother, saying, Know the LORD: for they shall all know me, from the least of them unto the greatest of them, saith the LORD; for I will forgive their iniquity, and I will remember their sin no more. (*He speaks of the last days*) Jer.31:31-34

---

110. Baptism is an everlasting covenant between God and a new member of His Church.

### Elder Joseph Fielding Smith

Baptism is also a new and everlasting covenant, and likewise ordination to the priesthood, and every other covenant is everlasting and a part of the new and everlasting covenant which embraces all things. (Answers to Gospel Questions, 1:65) DCSM:46

### Bruce R. McConkie

In the waters of baptism, we make a covenant with the Lord. We adopt, as individuals, all the terms and conditions of the new and everlasting covenant. This plan of salvation which was ordained in the counsels of eternity, which is the gospel of Christ, is an everlasting, eternal covenant. . . . In other words, we in effect sign the everlasting covenant by the ordinance of baptism, and we make its term and conditions binding upon us. . . . ACR(Brisbane)1976:15

### Joseph Smith,
### *receiving the Word of the Lord*

Behold, I say unto you that all old covenants have I caused to be done away in this thing; and this is a new and an everlasting covenant, even that which was from the beginning. 2. Wherefore, although a man should be baptized an hundred times it availeth him nothing, for you cannot enter in at the strait gate by the law of Moses, neither by your dead works. 3. For it is because of your dead works that I have caused this last covenant and this church to be built up unto me, even as in days of old. 4. Wherefore, enter ye in at the gate, as I have commanded, and seek not to counsel your God. Amen. (*Revelation received April 1830, given in consequence of persons desiring to join the Church without rebaptism*) D&C 22:1-4

### Marion G. Romney

We come into the Church by covenant, which we enter into when we go into the waters of baptism. The new and everlasting covenant of celestial marriage is the gate to exaltation in the celestial kingdom. Men receive the Melchizedek Priesthood by an oath and covenant. CR1962Apr:17

### Delbert L. Stapley

When baptized by an authorized servant of God, we covenant to do God's will and to obey his commandments. CR1965Oct:14

---

111. The oath and covenant of the priesthood is an everlasting covenant between God and each man who receives the Melchizedek Priesthood ordination.

**Joseph Smith,**
*receiving the Word of the Lord*

Therefore, all those who receive the priesthood, receive this oath and covenant of my Father, which he cannot break, neither can it be moved. (*Revelation on priesthood with six elders, Sept. 22/23, 1832*) D&C 84:40

**Delbert L. Stapley**

The Holy Priesthood is accepted by an oath and covenant and is binding upon those who receive it. They obligate themselves to keep faithfully all the commandments of God and to magnify their callings by honoring and exercising the priesthood in righteousness for the benefit and blessing of mankind. CR1959Apr:109

**Delbert L. Stapley**

The Father has promised his sons who receive the Holy Priesthood and faithfully abide by the conditions of its oath and covenant that they are to share in all that which the Father hath. The Father possesses kingdoms, thrones, principalities, powers, dominions, and exaltations. These the faithful will receive of him as heirs of God and joint-heirs with Jesus Christ. CR1961Apr:67

**Marion G. Romney,**
*also quoting Joseph Smith*

Traditionally, God's people have been known as a covenant people. . . . Men receive the Melchizedek Priesthood by an oath and covenant. ¶ . . . . In the covenant of the priesthood the parties are the Father and the receiver of the priesthood. Each party to the covenant undertakes certain obligations. The receiver undertakes to magnify his calling in the priesthood. The Father, by oath and covenant, promises the receiver that if he does so magnify his priesthood he will be sanctified by the Spirit unto the renewing of his body; (see D&C 84:33) that he will become a member of ". . . the church and kingdom, and the elect of God," (*Ibid.*, 84:34) and receive the ". . . Father's kingdom; therefore," said the Savior, "all that my Father hath shall be given unto him." (*Ibid.*, 84:38) CR1962Apr:17

**Elder Joseph Fielding Smith**

Baptism is also a new and everlasting covenant, and likewise ordination to the priesthood, and every other covenant is everlasting and a part of the new and everlasting covenant which embraces all things. (Answers to Gospel Questions, 1:65) DCSM:46

**Elder Joseph Fielding Smith**

Every man who is ordained to an office in the Melchizedek Priesthood should realize fully just what that ordination means. He receives the Priesthood with an oath and covenant that he will magnify his calling and be faithful therein. This oath and covenant when received in the fullness will entitle a man to become a member of the Church of the Firstborn, and the elect of God. He receives the fullness of the Father's kingdom and is entitled, if faithful to the end, "to all that the Father hath." This oath and covenant cannot be treated lightly, and if broken and altogether turned from, the man thus guilty has no forgiveness, that is to say, he will not again have these privileges granted to him which bring exaltation, or "all that the Father hath." He will stand aside without these blessings, but does not become a son of perdition because of this serious offense. The oath and covenant belonging to the Priesthood, pertains to the Melchizedek Priesthood and not to the Aaronic, although it is also a serious matter to turn away or violate that blessing. CHMR1:339

**Bruce R. McConkie**

The covenant which a man makes when he receives an office in the Melchizedek Priesthood is threefold: ¶ 1. That he will receive and make a part of his life and being the Holy Priesthood and that he will honor it as the holy power and authority which it is; ¶ 2. That he will magnify his calling in the priesthood; that is, that he will minister in the duties of the office, that he will do the work assigned; and ¶ 3. That he will live by every word that proceedeth forth from the mouth of God; that is to say, he will keep the commandments and work righteousness. ¶ The covenant which God makes is that he on his part will give the faithful all that his Father hath. In other words, he will give eternal life to those who keep their priesthood covenants. ¶ Now we have mentioned both an oath and a covenant where the Melchizedek Priesthood is concerned. The oath is the solemn promise of the Lord that all those who keep the priesthood covenant shall gain exaltation. That is to say, the Lord swears with an oath that his adopted and obedient sons shall be high priests forever after the order of Melchizedek (see D&C 76:57); they shall be joint heirs with his natural Son, who is Christ our Lord. ACR(Lima)1977:18

**Related Witnesses:**

**Elder Joseph F. Smith**

This makes [D&C 84:33-41] a very serious matter of receiving this covenant and this Priesthood; for those who receive it must, like God himself, abide in it, and must not fail, and must not be moved out of the way; for those who receive this oath and covenant and turn away from it, and cease to do righteously and to honor this covenant, and will to abide in sin, and repent not, there is no forgiveness for them either in this life or in the world to come. CR1898Apr:65

**Elder Harold B. Lee**

And with reference to the priesthood, when the Lord discusses in the 84th section the oath and covenant, exactly the same principle is implied. By the laying on of hands we get the promise of power and authority, but it will not be ours—worlds without end—unless we keep our part of the covenant. (Stand Ye in Holy Places, pp. 51-52) TLDP:333

**Elder Spencer W. Kimball**

One breaks the priesthood covenant by transgressing commandments—but also by leaving undone his duties. Accordingly, to break this covenant one needs only to do nothing. (The Teachings of Spencer W. Kimball, p. 497) TLDP:501

---

**112. The sealing ordinance of marriage is an everlasting covenant between God and those who are sealed.**

**Elder Joseph Fielding Smith**

Marriage for eternity is a new and everlasting covenant. (Answers to Gospel Questions, 1:65) DCSM:46

**Marion G. Romney**

The new and everlasting covenant of celestial marriage is the gate to exaltation in the celestial kingdom. . . . ¶ A covenant is an agreement between two or more parties. An oath is a sworn attestation to the inviolability of the promises in the agreement. CR1962Apr:17

**Joseph Smith**

In the celestial glory there are three heavens or degrees; 2. And in order to obtain the highest, a man must enter into this order of the priesthood [meaning the new and everlasting covenant of marriage]; (*Instructions given by the Prophet, May 16 and 17, 1843*) D&C 131:1-2

**Joseph Smith**

Except a man and his wife enter into an everlasting covenant and be married for eternity, while in this probation, by the power and authority of the Holy Priesthood, they will cease to increase when they die; that is, they will not have any children after the resurrection. But those who are married by the power and authority of the priesthood in this life, and continue without committing the sin against the Holy Ghost, will continue to increase and have children in the celestial glory. (*Instructions given Brother and Sister Benjamin Johnson, in presence of several elders, Ramus, Ill., May 16, 1843*) HC5:391

**President Harold B. Lee**

For remember, brethren, that only those who enter into the new and everlasting covenant of marriage in the temple for time and eternity, only those will have the exaltation in the celestial kingdom. That is what the Lord tells us. CR1973Oct:120

**President John Taylor
& George Q. Cannon**

(First Presidency)

The Lord has revealed to us by His special revelations, as clearly and positively as He ever did to any of the ancient Prophets, certain principles associated with the eternity of the marriage covenant, has given definite commands pertaining thereto, and made them obligatory upon us to carry out. He has made manifest to us those great and eternal principles which bind woman to man and man to woman, children to parents and parents to children, and has called upon us in the most emphatic and pointed manner to obey them. These glorious principles involve our dearest interests and associations in time and throughout the eternities that are to come. We are told that this is His everlasting covenant, and that it has existed from eternity; and, furthermore, that all covenants that relate only to time shall be dissolved at death and be no longer binding upon the human family. He has, moreover, told us that if we do not obey those principles we shall be damned. Believing these principles to be of God and from God, we have entered into eternal covenants with our wives under the most solemn promises and in the most sacred manner. (*General conference, April 4, 1885*) MOFP3:9-10

**James E. Talmage**

Marriage covenants authorized and sealed by that God-given power, endure, if the parties thereto are true to their troth, not through mortal life alone, but through time and all eternity. Thus the worthy husband and wife who have been sealed under the everlasting covenant shall come forth in the day of the resurrection to receive their heritage of glory, immortality, and eternal lives. (Young Women's Journal, Oct. 1914, p. 604) DGSM:77

**Delbert L. Stapley**

In connection with all ordinances pertaining to the temples of our God, men and women accept covenants and obligations which relate to the endowment and to the eternity of the marriage and family relationship. CR1965Oct:14

**Related Witnesses:**

**Joseph Smith,**
*receiving the Word of the Lord*

Verily, thus saith the Lord unto you my servant

Joseph, that inasmuch as you have inquired of my hand to know and understand wherein I, the Lord, justified my servants Abraham, Isaac, and Jacob, as also Moses, David and Solomon, my servants, as touching the principle and doctrine of their having many wives and concubines— 2. Behold, and lo, I am the Lord thy God, and will answer thee as touching this matter. 3. Therefore, prepare thy heart to receive and obey the instructions which I am about to give unto you; for all those who have this law revealed unto them must obey the same. 4. For behold, I reveal unto you a new and an everlasting covenant; and if ye abide not that covenant, then are ye damned; for no one can reject this covenant and be permitted to enter into my glory. 5. For all who will have a blessing at my hands shall abide the law which was appointed for that blessing, and the conditions thereof, as were instituted from before the foundation of the world. *(Revelation received 1831, recorded at Nauvoo, Ill., July 12, 1843, relating to the new and everlasting covenant, including the eternal nature of the marriage covenant, as also plurality of wives)* D&C 132:1-5

**Author's Note:** Marriage is not the only new and everlasting covenant: "Each ordinance and requirement given to man for the purpose of bringing to pass his salvation and exaltation is a covenant. Baptism for the remission of sins is a covenant.... ¶ Keeping the Sabbath day holy is a covenant. . . . All of the Ten Commandments are everlasting covenants. The law of tithing is a form of an everlasting covenant . . . although some day we shall be given a higher form of this law known as consecration. ¶ Marriage is an everlasting covenant, but not as some believe, the new and everlasting covenant. The law of marriage to the Church, like the covenant of baptism, is new because it is not the marriage of the world, but for time and for all eternity." *(Doctrines of Salvation, 1:153)* ¶ Elder Joseph Fielding Smith also wrote that the new and everlasting covenant is all of the covenants: "What is the new and everlasting covenant? I regret to say that there are some members of the Church who are misled and misinformed in regard to what the new and everlasting covenant really is. The new and everlasting covenant is the sum total of all gospel covenants and obligations. . . ." (Doctrines of Salvation, 1:156)

113. We are to keep the sacred covenants we have made with God if we are to merit entrance into the celestial kingdom.

**Elder Joseph Fielding Smith**
The fate of the covenant breaker was most severe. "And the soul that sins against this covenant, and hardeneth his heart against it, shall be dealt with according to the laws of my church, and shall be delivered over to the buffetings of Satan until the day of redemption." The breaking of any covenant that our Father in heaven makes with us, is a dreadful thing. We make a covenant in the waters of baptism. Many have broken it, and hence lose the promised blessings. All through our lives we are called to enter into covenants and many members of the Church seemingly fail to realize the seriousness of a violation or to understand that punishment must inevitably follow. Solemn covenants are taken by members of the Church in the Temples. These covenants are to prepare us for an exaltation. Yet there are many who receive them who utterly fail to heed them, but presumably, they think the Lord has a short memory, or that he is so extremely merciful that he will break his promises and the punishment mentioned for the violation will not be inflicted. In this manner many deceive themselves. CHMR1:322-23

**Delbert L. Stapley**
Perhaps we should define the meaning and significance of a covenant. In a spiritual application a covenant is a solemn, binding compact between God and man whereby man agrees to keep God's commandments and serve him in righteousness and in truth unto the end. The gospel covenants and obligations bind Church members to obedience to laws and principles given of God which lead to happiness, love, and eternal joy. A covenant then is an agreement which includes obligations and is given as a principle with promise of blessings for obedience. . . . ¶ Perhaps in Church assemblies today we do not stress sufficiently the importance of gospel covenants and the Saints' obligation to them. It is our duty to learn and understand the sacred and binding nature of the covenants we accept at baptism and the covenants and obligations associated with all other ordinances of the gospel found along that narrow path which leads to life eternal. CR1959Apr:107-08

**Joseph Smith,**
*receiving the Word of the Lord*
For if ye will not abide in my covenant ye are not worthy of me. *(Revelation received Aug. 6, 1833, in consequence of the persecution of the Saints)* D&C 98:15

**Joseph Smith,**
*receiving the Word of the Lord*
I, the Lord, am bound when ye do what I say;

but when ye do not what I say, ye have no promise. D&C 82:10

### Joseph Smith,
*receiving the Word of the Lord*

The blasphemy against the Holy Ghost, which shall not be forgiven in the world nor out of the world, is in that ye commit murder wherein ye shed innocent blood, and assent unto my death, after ye have received my new and everlasting covenant, saith the Lord God; and he that abideth not this law can in nowise enter into my glory, but shall be damned, saith the Lord. (*Revelation relating to the new and everlasting covenant, July 12, 1843 [1831]; law given relative to blasphemy against the Holy Ghost*) D&C 132:27

### Related Witnesses:
### John A. Widtsoe

Everyone who receives an ordinance must make a covenant, else the ordinance is not fully satisfactory. He who is baptized covenants to keep the law of the Church; he who is administered to for sickness, and the administrators, covenant to use their faith to secure the desired healings; he who receives the temple endowment covenants to use in his life that which he has been taught; he who is ordained to the priesthood agrees to honor it, and so on with every ordinance. ¶ That places covenants high, as they should be. Knowledge of itself has little saving power. Only as it is used does knowledge become of value. The man who learns and promises to use that knowledge is of value to society. ("What Is the Need of Ordinances?" IE1948Feb:97) TLDP:117-18

### Recorded in Ecclesiastes

When thou vowest a vow unto God, defer not to pay it; for he hath no pleasure in fools: pay that which thou hast vowed. 5. Better is it that thou shouldest not vow, than that thou shouldest vow and not pay. (*Reflections of a son of David the king*) Eccl.5:4-5

---

### HYMNS Written by Prophets
### Applicable to this Topic

### Parley P. Pratt
*Father in Heaven, We Do Believe*
HYMNS:180

Father in Heav'n, we do believe
The promise thou hast made;
Thy word with meekness we receive,
Just as thy Saints have said.

We now repent of all our sin
And come with broken heart,
And to thy covenant enter in
And choose the better part.

O Lord, accept us while we pray,
And all our sins forgive;
New life impart to us this day,
And bid the sinners live.

Humbly we take the sacrament
In Jesus' blessed name;
Let us receive thru covenant
The Spirit's heav'nly flame.

We will be buried in the stream
In Jesus' blessed name,
And rise, while light shall on us beam
The Spirit's heav'nly flame.

Baptize us with the Holy Ghost
And seal us as thine own,
That we may join the ransomed host
And with the Saints be one.

# List of Doctrines

## CREATION

*Doctrines Located in This Topic*

114. Through His son Jesus Christ, God the Father created the earth and all things in the heavens and in the earth.

115. Adam, known as Michael, assisted Jesus Christ in the creation of the earth.

116. The elements are eternal; they were not created from nothing.

117. Mankind and all forms of life were created spiritually before they were created physically on the earth.

118. God created mankind in His own image and likeness.

119. The heavens, the earth, and all things upon the earth were created in six creative periods.

120. All plants and animals upon the earth were created for the benefit of human beings.

121. God the Father created other worlds through His son Jesus Christ.

**Author's Note:** A dictionary definition of *To Create:* "To originate or cause; to bring into being; to cause to exist; to make or form, by investing with new character;" (The New Webster Encyclopedic Dictionary of the English Language p. 201)

Bruce R. McConkie defines it as follows: "To create is to organize. It is an utterly false and uninspired notion to believe that the world or any other thing was created out of nothing, or that any created thing can be destroyed in the sense of annihilation. 'The elements are eternal' (D&C 93:33)." (Mormon Doctrine, p. 169)

Joseph Smith had this to say about the word "create," which he uttered just a few months before his death: "Now, the word create came from the baurau which does not mean to create out of nothing; it means to organize; the same as a man would organize materials and build a ship. Hence, we infer that God had materials to organize the world out of chaos—chaotic matter, which is element, and in which dwells all the glory. Element had an existence from the time He had. The pure principles of element are principles which can never be destroyed; they may be organized and re-organized, but not destroyed. They had no beginning, and can have no end." (TPJS:350-52; DGSM:16)

**114. Through His son Jesus Christ, God the Father created the earth and all things in the heavens and in the earth.**

**Elder Joseph Fielding Smith**

It was Jesus, our Redeemer, who, under the direction of his father, came down and organized matter and made this planet. . . . (Doctrines of Salvation, 1:74-75) DGSM:16

**Paul**

And to make all men see what is the fellowship of the mystery, which from the beginning of the world hath been hid in God, who created all things by Jesus Christ: (*Paul writes to the Saints at Ephesus in Asia Minor, about* A.D. 62) Eph.3:9

**Paul**

God, who at sundry times and in divers manners spake in time past unto the fathers by the prophets, 2. Hath in these last days spoken unto us by his Son, whom he hath appointed heir of all things, by whom also he made the worlds; 3. Who being the brightness of his glory, and the express image of his person, and upholding all things by the word of his power, when he had by himself purged our sins, sat down on the right hand of the Majesty on high; (*Paul writes to the Jewish members of the Church, about* A.D. 60) Heb.1:1-3

**Joseph Smith,**
*translating the Book of Moses*

And behold, the glory of the Lord was upon Moses, so that Moses stood in the presence of God, and talked with him face to face. And the Lord God said unto Moses: For mine own purpose have I made these things. Here is wisdom and it remaineth in me. 32. And by the word of my power, have I created them, which is mine Only Begotten Son, who is full of grace and truth. 33. And worlds without number have I created; and I also created them for mine own purpose; and by the Son I created them, which is mine Only Begotten. (*The Lord talks to Moses, face to face; revelation received in 1830*) Moses 1:31-33

**Mark E. Petersen**

So the scriptures teach that everything came into existence through Jesus Christ and it came about with full advance planning and purpose. The purpose was that this was a first step in our becoming like God. . . . ¶ May I make this crystal clear: Jesus Christ, our Redeemer and Savior, created all things under the direction of his Father, including life, and he did so according to a preconceived plan. He was the Creator of heaven and earth. This is the position we Latter-day Saints must take with respect to Jesus Christ. If we truly believe in him, we must believe his doctrine, and this is the doctrine of Christ. Are we willing to believe it? Are we willing to be Christians within the framework of this definition? I testify to you humbly as a servant of Christ—but also as one of his special witnesses—that these things are true. ("Christ the Creator," Brigham Young University Speeches of the Year, 1977, p. 197) TLDP:120

**John A. Widtsoe**

The creation of the earth, the details of which are not known, must have been marvelously and intensely appealing in its interest to the intelligent beings who, because of their exalted knowledge, had the necessary power over the elements and forces of the universe to accomplish the forming of an earth. Three great intelligent Beings were in supreme authority in the building of the earth; namely, God, the Father, his Son Jehovah, who became the Christ, and Michael, who became the first man, Adam. These three Beings were naturally the ones concerned in the making of an earth for the sojourn of the spirits, for it was through the agency of God, the Father, that the spirit beings were started on the road of eternal progression; it was about the mission of Jehovah, the Son of God, that the differences of opinion raged in the Great Council, and finally, it was Adam, or Michael, who was appointed to be the one to come upon the earth, and there to subject himself to death, so that the procreation of spirits in earthly tabernacles might be begun. (A Rational Theology, pp. 49-51) TLDP:120

**Bruce R. McConkie**
We know that Jehovah-Christ, assisted by "many of the noble and great ones" (Abr.3:22), of whom Michael is but the illustration, did in fact create the earth and all forms of plant and animal life on the face thereof. But when it came to placing man on earth, there was a change in Creators, that is, the Father himself became personally involved. All Things were created by the Son, using the power delegated by the Father, except man. In the spirit and again in the flesh, man was created by the father. There was no delegation of authority where the crowning creature of creation was concerned. (The Promised Messiah, p. 62) DGSM:18

**Related Witnesses:**

**John**
In the beginning was the Word, and the Word was with God, and the Word was God. 2. The same was in the beginning with God. 3. All things were made by him; and without him was not any thing made that was made. 4. In him was life; and the life was the light of men. 5. And the light shineth in darkness; and the darkness comprehended it not. . . . 14. And the Word was made flesh, and dwelt among us, (and we beheld his glory, the glory as of the only begotten of the Father,) full of grace and truth. (*The record of the Apostle John, testifying of the Savior*) John 1:1-5,14

**Abraham,**
*quoted by Joseph Smith*
Now the Lord had shown unto me, Abraham, the intelligences that were organized before the world was; and among all these there were many of the noble and great ones; . . . 24. And there stood one among them that was like unto God, and he said unto those who were with him: We will go down, for there is space there, and we will take of these materials, and we will make an earth whereon these may dwell; (*Abraham learns of pre-earth life and foreordination*) Abr.3:22,24

**115. Adam, known as Michael, assisted Jesus Christ in the creation of the earth.**

**John A. Widtsoe**
Three great intelligent Beings were in supreme authority in the building of the earth; namely, God, the Father, his Son Jehovah, who became the Christ, and Michael, who became the first man, Adam. These three Beings were naturally the ones concerned in the making of an earth for the sojourn of the spirits, for it was through the agency of God, the Father, that the spirit beings were started on the road of eternal progression; it was about the mission of Jehovah, the Son of God, that the differences of opinion raged in the Great Council, and finally, it was Adam, or Michael, who was appointed to be the one to come upon the earth, and there to subject himself to death, so that the procreation of spirits in earthly tabernacles might be begun. (A Rational Theology, pp. 49-51) TLDP:120

**Bruce R. McConkie**
We know that Jehovah-Christ, assisted by "many of the noble and great ones" (Abr.3:22), of whom Michael is but the illustration, did in fact create the earth and all forms of plant and animal life on the face thereof. (The Promised Messiah, p. 62) DGSM:18

**Elder Joseph Fielding Smith**
It was Jesus, our Redeemer, who, under the direction of his father, came down and organized matter and made this planet. . . . ¶ It is true that Adam helped to form this earth. He labored with our Savior Jesus Christ. I have a strong view or conviction that there were others also who assisted them. Perhaps Noah and Enoch; and why not Joseph Smith, and those who were appointed to be rulers before the earth was formed? (Doctrines of Salvation, 1:74-75) DGSM:16

**Related Witnesses:**

**President Brigham Young,**
*quoted by John A. Widtsoe*
When Father Adam came to assist in organizing the earth out of the crude material that was found, an earth was made upon which the children of men could live. After the earth was prepared Father Adam came and stayed here. . . . (*At Paris, Idaho, Aug. 31, 1873, JD16:167*) DBY:102

---

**116. The elements are eternal; they were not created from nothing.**

**Joseph Smith,**
*quoted by Elder Joseph Fielding Smith*
You ask the learned doctors why they say the

world was made out of nothing, and they will answer, "Doesn't the Bible say He created the world?" And they infer, from the word create, that it must have been made out of nothing. Now, the word create came from the word baurau, which does not mean to create out of nothing; it means to organize; the same as a man would organize materials and build a ship. Hence we infer that God had materials to organize the world out of chaos—chaotic matter, which is element, and in which dwells all the glory. Element had an existence from the time He had. The pure principles of element are principles which can never be destroyed; they may be organized and reorganized, but not destroyed. They had no beginning and can have no end. (*To the Church in general conference— to a congregation of 20,000—, "King Follett Sermon", April 7, 1844*) (See HC6:302-17, also see The Words of Joseph Smith, pp. 340-62) HC6:308-09; TPJS:354

**President Joseph F. Smith**
**Anthon H. Lund, Charles W. Penrose**
(First Presidency)
**The Council of the Twelve Apostles**
The scriptures plainly and repeatedly affirm that God is the Creator of the earth and the heavens and all things that in them are. In the sense so expressed the Creator is an Organizer. God created the earth as an organized sphere; but He certainly did not create, in the sense of bringing into primal existence, the ultimate elements of the materials of which the earth consists, for "the elements are eternal" (D&C 93:33). ¶ So also life is eternal, and not created; but life, or the vital force, may be infused into organized matter, though the details of the process have not been revealed unto man. (In pamphlet, "The Father and The Son; A Doctrinal Exposition by The First Presidency and The Twelve," published by the Church June 30, 1916. Reprinted in AF:420-26. See MOFP:5:23-34) AF:420

**John A. Widtsoe**
Matter in its essence is eternal, that is, everlasting. Whether the various known forms of matter may be converted one into the other is not definitely known, though it seems probable. Any such conversion would, however, leave the total quantity of matter or its equivalent unchanged. God, the supreme Power, cannot conceivably originate matter; he can only organize matter. Neither can he destroy matter; he can only disorganize it. God is the Master, who, because of his great knowledge, knows how to use the elements, already existing, for the building of whatever he may have in mind.

The doctrine that God made the earth or man from nothing becomes, therefore, an absurdity. The doctrine of the indestructibility of the essential elements of the universe makes possible much theological reasoning that would otherwise be impossible. (A Rational Theology, pp. 11-12) TLDP:121-22
**Related Witnesses:**
**Joseph Smith**
For man is spirit. The elements are eternal, and spirit and element, inseparably connected, receive a fulness of joy; (*Revelation received at Kirtland, Ohio, May 6, 1833*) D&C 93:33

---

117. Mankind and all forms of life were created spiritually before they were created physically on the earth.

**Elder Joseph Fielding Smith**
There is no account of the creation of man or other forms of life when they were created as spirits. There is just the simple statement that they were so created before the physical creation. The statements in Moses 3:5 and Genesis 2:5 are interpolations thrown into the account of the physical creation, explaining that all things were first created in the spirit existence in heaven before they were placed upon this earth. ¶ We were all created untold ages before we were placed on this earth. We discover from Abraham 3:22-28, that it was before the earth was formed that the plan of salvation was presented to the spirits, or "intelligences." This being true, then man, animals and plants were not created in the spirit at the time of the creation of the earth, but long before. (Doctrines of Salvation, 1:75-76) TLDP:120-21
**Joseph Smith,**
*translating the Book of Moses*
And every plant of the field before it was in the earth, and every herb of the field before it grew. For I, the Lord God, created all things, of which I have spoken, spiritually, before they were naturally upon the face of the earth. For I, the Lord God, had not caused it to rain upon the face of the earth. And I, the Lord God, had created all the children of men; and not yet a man to till the ground; for in heaven created I them; and there was not yet flesh upon the earth, neither in the water, neither in the air; . . . 7. And I, the Lord God, formed man from the dust of the ground, and breathed into his nostrils the breath of life; and man became a living soul, the first flesh upon the earth, the first man also; nevertheless, all things were before created; but

spiritually were they created and made according to my word. (*The Lord reveals to Moses the creation of the earth and of man*) Moses 3:5,7

**Mark E. Petersen**

Our religion tells us that God is our Father, and that we lived with him before we were born on this earth. It tells us further that every creature, microscopic and otherwise, was made by him before it lived here on the earth, and also that each one was made as a spirit before it was made in the flesh here in mortality. There were two creations, one in which God made all things in the spirit. That is, he made the real life, the real being, as a spirit, in the first creation. And then, in the second creation, he provided these mortal tabernacles in which he placed these spirits that he had created in the preexistence. ("We Believe in God, The Eternal Father," Brigham Young University Speeches of the Year, 1973, p. 247) TLDP:121

**President Joseph F. Smith,**
**John R. Winder, Anthon H. Lund**

(First Presidency)

By His almighty power He [God] organized the earth, and all that it contains, from spirit and element, which exist co-eternally with Himself. He formed every plant that grows, and every animal that breathes, each after its own kind, spiritually and temporally. . . . He made the tadpole and the ape, the lion and the elephant, but He did not make them in His own image, nor endow them with Godlike reason and intelligence. Nevertheless, the whole animal creation will be perfected and perpetuated in the Hereafter, each class in its 'distinct order or sphere,' and will enjoy 'eternal felicity.' That fact has been made plain in this dispensation (D&C 77:3). (Christmas greetings, Dec. 18, 1909) MOFP4:206

**Related Witnesses:**

**Bruce R. McConkie**

Man and all forms of life existed as spirit beings and entities before the foundations of this earth were laid. There were spirit men and spirit beasts, spirit fowls and spirit fishes, spirit plants and spirit trees. Every creeping thing, every herb and shrub, every amoeba and tadpole, every elephant and dinosaur—all things— existed as spirits, as spirit beings before they were placed naturally upon the earth. (The Millennial Messiah, pp. 642-43) DGSM:16

**Moses**

These are the generations of the heavens and of the earth when they were created, in the day that the LORD God made the earth and the heavens, 5. And every plant of the field before it was in the earth, and every herb of the field

before it grew: for the LORD God had not caused it to rain upon the earth, and there was not a man to till the ground. (*Revelation to Moses with respect to the Creation*) Gen.2:4-5

---

### 118. God created mankind in His own image and likeness.

**Moses**

And God said, Let us make man in our image, after our likeness: and let them have dominion over the fish of the sea, and over the fowl of the air, and over the cattle, and over all the earth, and over every creeping thing that creepeth upon the earth. 27. So God created man in his own image, in the image of God created he him; male and female created he them. (*Revelation to Moses with respect to the Creation*) Gen.1:26-27

**Mark E. Petersen**

The sectarian people have a hard time understanding the idea that man is made in the image of God and that God looks like a human being. But I ask you, he having made all these rules, he having created all things and now reproducing us after his own kind, how could we be other than the exact image and likeness of God? It had to be that way, because we're the offspring of God. And since we are the offspring of God, and since the law is that everything should reproduce after its own kind, and inasmuch as God would not break his own laws, he reproduced after his own kind and thus man looks like God and man is in the image and likeness of God. ("We Believe in God, the Eternal Father," Brigham Young University Speeches of the Year, 1973, p. 249) TLDP:122

**Moses**

This is the book of the generations of Adam. In the day that God created man, in the likeness of God made he him; 2. Male and female created he them; and blessed them, and called their name Adam, in the day when they were created. (*Revelation to Moses*) Gen.5:1-2

**Jesus,**
*quoted by Moroni, son of Mormon*

And never have I showed myself unto man whom I have created, for never has man believed in me as thou hast. Seest thou that ye are created after mine own image? Yea, even all men were created in the beginning after mine own image. 16. Behold, this body, which ye now behold, is the body of my spirit; and man have I created after the body of my spirit; and even as I appear unto thee to be in the spirit will I appear unto my people in the flesh. (*Christ* shows his spirit body to the brother of Jared, at the time of the Tower of Babel) Ether 3:15-16

**Abraham,**
*quoted by Joseph Smith*

And the Gods took counsel among themselves and said: Let us go down and form man in our image, after our likeness; and we will give them dominion over the fish of the sea, and over the fowl of the air, and over the cattle, and over all the earth, and over every creeping thing that creepeth upon the earth. 27. So the Gods went down to organize man in their own image, in the image of the Gods to form they him, male and female to form they them. (*Abraham learns about the creation of the earth*) Abr.4:26-27

**Joseph Smith,**
*translating the Book of Moses*

And I, God, said unto mine Only Begotten, which was with me from the beginning: Let us make man in our image, after our likeness; and it was so. And I, God, said: Let them have dominion over the fishes of the sea, and over the fowl of the air, and over the cattle, and over all the earth, and over every creeping thing that creepeth upon the earth. 27. And I, God, created man in mine own image, in the image of mine Only Begotten created I him; male and female created I them. (*The record of Moses: God makes man and gives him dominion over all things*) Moses 2:26-27

**Ammon, son of Mosiah,**
*quoted by Mormon*

Ammon said unto him: I am a man; and man in the beginning was created after the image of God, and I am called by his Holy Spirit to teach these things unto this people, that they may be brought to a knowledge of that which is just and true; (*Ammon responds to King Lamoni, about 90 B.C.*) Alma 18:34

**President Joseph F. Smith,**
**John R. Winder, Anthon H. Lund**
(First Presidency)

Man is the child of God, formed in the divine image and endowed with divine attributes, and even as the infant son of an earthly father and mother is capable in due time of becoming a man, so the undeveloped offspring of celestial parentage is capable, by experience through ages and aeons, of evolving into a God. (In The Origin of Man, official statement, Nov. 1909) MOFP4:206

**Marion G. Romney**

The truth I desire to emphasize today is that we mortals are in very deed the literal offspring of God. If men understood, believed, and accepted this truth and lived by it, our sick and dying society would be reformed and redeemed, and men would have peace here and now and eternal joy

in the hereafter. ¶ Members of The Church of Jesus Christ of Latter-day Saints accept this concept as a basic doctrine of their theology. The lives of those who have given it thought enough to realize its implications are controlled by it; it gives meaning and direction to all their thoughts and deeds. This is so because they know that it is the universal law of nature in the plant, animal, and human worlds for reproducing offspring to reach in final maturity the likeness of their parents. ¶ They reason that the same law is in force with respect to the offspring of God. Their objective is, therefore, to someday be like their heavenly parents. CR1973Apr:133

**Related Witnesses:**
**Paul**

Forasmuch then as we are the offspring of God, we ought not to think that the Godhead is like unto gold, or silver, or stone, graven by art and man's device. (*Paul preaches on Mars' Hill about the Unknown God*) Acts 17:29

---

**119. The heavens, the earth, and all things upon the earth were created in six creative periods.**

**John A. Widtsoe**

In the making of the earth, as in all other matters pertaining to the destiny of man, the work was done in complete and orderly harmony with the existing laws of the universe. The Mosaic six days represent successive stages in the building of the earth, each measured by ages of time. The forces of nature set steadily, though often slowly in the accomplishment of great works. (A Rational Theology, pp. 49-51) TLDP:119-120

**Abraham,**
*quoted by Joseph Smith*

4:1. And then the Lord said: Let us go down. And they went down at the beginning, and they, that is the Gods, organized and formed the heavens and the earth. . . . 4:31. . . . [A]nd they numbered the sixth time. . . . 5:1. And thus we will finish the heavens and the earth, and all the hosts of them. 5:2. And the Gods said among themselves: On the seventh time we will end our work, which we have counseled; and we will rest on the seventh time from all our work which we have counseled. (*Abraham learns about the creation of the earth*) Abr.4:1,31; Abr.5:1-2

**Recorded in Exodus**

For in six days the Lord made heaven and earth, the sea, and all that in them is, and rested the seventh day: wherefore the Lord blessed the sabbath day, and hallowed it. (*The Lord reveals the fourth of the Ten Commandments to Moses*) Ex.20:11

**Moses**

1:1. In the beginning God created the heaven and the earth. . . . 1:31. And God saw every thing that he had made, and, behold, it was very good. And the evening and the morning were the sixth day. . . . 2:1. Thus the heavens and the earth were finished, and all the host of them. 2:2. And on the seventh day God ended his work which he had made; and he rested on the seventh day from all his work which he had made. (*Revelation to Moses with respect to the Creation*) Gen.1:1,31; Gen.2:1-2

**Joseph Smith,**
*translating the Book of Moses*

2:1. [I]n the beginning I created the heaven, and the earth upon which thou standest. . . . 2:31. And I, God, saw everything that I had made, and, behold, all things which I had made were very good; and the evening and the morning were the sixth day. . . . 3:1. Thus the heaven and the earth were finished, and all the host of them. 3:2. And on the seventh day I, God, ended my work, and all things which I had made; and I rested on the seventh day from all my work, and all things which I had made were finished, and I, God, saw that they were good; (*The Lord explains the Creation to Moses; revelation received in 1830*) Moses 2:1,31; Moses 3:1-2

**Bruce R. McConkie**

But first, what is a day? It is a specified time period; it is an age, an eon, a division of eternity; it is the time between two identifiable events. And each day, of whatever length, has the duration needed for its purposes. One measuring rod is the time required for a celestial body to turn once on its axis. . . . ¶ There is no revealed recitation specifying that each of the "six days" involved in the creation was of the same duration. . . . (Common Consent, p. 11) DGSM:17

---

**120. All plants and animals upon the earth were created for the benefit of human beings.**

**Joseph Smith**

Verily I say, that inasmuch as ye do this, the fulness of the earth is yours, the beasts of the field and the fowls of the air, and that which climbeth upon the trees and walketh upon the earth; 17. Yea, and the herb, and the good things which come of the earth, whether for food or for raiment, or for houses, or for barns, or for orchards, or for gardens, or for vineyards; 18. Yea, all things which come of the earth, in the season thereof, are made for the benefit and the use of man, both to please the

eye and to gladden the heart; 19. Yea, for food and for raiment, for taste and for smell, to strengthen the body and to enliven the soul. 20. And it pleaseth God that he hath given all these things unto man; for unto this end were they made to be used, with judgment, not to excess, neither by extortion. (*Revelation received Aug. 7, 1831*) D&C 59:16-20

**Moses**

And God said, Behold, I have given you every herb bearing seed, which is upon the face of all the earth, and every tree, in the which is the fruit of a tree yielding seed; to you it shall be for meat. (*Revelation to Moses with respect to the Creation*) Gen.1:29

**Joseph Smith,**
*translating the Book of Moses*

And I, God, said unto man: Behold, I have given you every herb bearing seed, which is upon the face of all the earth, and every tree in the which shall be the fruit of a tree yielding seed; to you it shall be for meat. (*The record of Moses: God makes man and gives him dominion over all*) Moses 2:29

**Abraham,**
*quoted by Joseph Smith*

And the Gods said: Behold, we will give them every herb bearing seed that shall come upon the face of all the earth, and every tree which shall have fruit upon it; yea, the fruit of the tree yielding seed to them we will give it; it shall be for their meat. (*Abraham learns about the creation of the earth*) Abr.4:29

---

**121. God the Father created other worlds through His son Jesus Christ.**

**Joseph Smith,**
*translating the Book of Moses*

And by the word of my power, have I created them, which is mine Only Begotten Son, who is full of grace and truth. 33. And worlds without number have I created; and I also created them for mine own purpose; and by the Son I created them, which is mine Only Begotten. (*The Lord talks to Moses, face to face, revelation received in 1830*) Moses 1:32-33

**Joseph Smith**

And now, after the many testimonies which have been given of him, this is the testimony, last of all, which we give of him: That he lives! 23. For we saw him, even on the right hand of God; and we heard the voice bearing record that he is the Only Begotten of the Father— 24. That by him, and through him, and of him, the worlds are and were created, and the inhabitants thereof are begotten sons and daughters unto God. *(Vision to Joseph Smith and Sidney Rigdon, Feb. 16, 1832)* D&C 76:22-24

**Paul**

God, who at sundry times and in divers manners spake in time past unto the fathers by the prophets, 2. Hath in these last days spoken unto us by his Son, whom he hath appointed heir of all things, by whom also he made the worlds; *(Paul writes to the Jewish members of the Church, about A.D. 60)* Heb.1:1-2

**J. Reuben Clark, Jr.,
also quoting Joseph Smith**

The Son apparently had been organizing worlds before, interpreting the passage in the Book of Moses, where the Father said to Moses: "Worlds without number had He created; by His only Begotten Son had He made them." CR1949Oct:192-93

**Bruce R. McConkie**

After the Firstborn of the Father, while yet a spirit being, had gained power and intelligence that made him like unto God; after he had become, under the Father, the Creator of worlds without number; after he had reigned on the throne of eternal power as the Lord Omnipotent—after all this he yet had to gain a mortal and then an immortal body. ¶ After the Son of God "made flesh" his "tabernacle," and while he "dwelt among the sons of men" after he left his preexistent glory as we all do at birth; after he was born of Mary in Bethlehem of Judea—after all this he was called upon to work out his own salvation. ("Our Relationship with the Lord," Brigham Young University Speeches of the Year, 1981-82, p. 99) TLDP:747

**Elder Joseph Fielding Smith**

We know that our Heavenly Father is a glorified, exalted personage who has all power, all might, and all dominion, and that he knows all things. We testify that he, through his Only Begotten Son, is the Creator of this earth and of worlds without number, all of which are peopled by his spirit children. CR1971Apr:4-5

**Related Witnesses:**

**John,
quoted by Joseph Smith**

The worlds were made by him; men were made by him; all things were made by him, and through him, and of him. *(Revelation received at Kirtland, Ohio, May 6, 1833; John bore record of Jesus Christ)* D&C 93:10

**Bruce R. McConkie**

Further, the gospel is in operation in all the worlds created by the Father and the Son. Their work and their glory, in all the infinite creations that their hands have made, is to bring to pass immortality and eternal life for the children of the Father. Through the atonement of Christ, the inhabitants of all these worlds have power to become his sons and daughters, to become joint-heirs with him of all the glory of his Father's kingdom, to be adopted into the family of the Father, which is to say that the inhabitants of all worlds "are [thus] begotten sons and daughters unto God." (D&C 76:24) (The Promised Messiah, p. 286) TLDP:238

**President John Taylor**

It would appear that the translated residents of Enoch's city are under the direction of Jesus, who is the Creator of worlds: and that He, holding the keys of the government of other worlds, could, in His administrations to them, select the translated people of Enoch's Zion, if He thought proper, to perform a mission to these various planets, and as death had not passed upon them, they could be prepared by Him and made use of through the medium of the Holy Priesthood to act as ambassadors, teachers, or messengers to those worlds over which Jesus holds the authority. . . . ¶ Each kingdom, or planet, and the inhabitants thereof, were blessed with the visits and presence of their Creator, in their several times and seasons. (The Mediation and Atonement, pp. 76-77) TLDP:699

**Marion G. Romney**

Except for his mortal ministry accomplished on this earth, his service and relationship to other worlds and their inhabitants are the same as his service and relationship to this earth and its inhabitants. ("Jesus Christ: Lord of the Universe," IE1968Nov:46) TLDP:47

**Elder John Taylor**

Truly Jesus Christ created the worlds, and is Lord of Lords, and, as the Psalmist said, "judgeth among the Gods." (Psalm 82:1) Then Moses might have said with propriety, he is the "living God", and Christ, speaking of the flesh could say: I am the son of man; and Peter, enlightened by the Holy Ghost: Thou art the son of the living God—meaning our Father in Heaven, who is the Father of all spirits, and who, with Jesus Christ, his first begotten Son, and the Holy Ghost, are one in power, one in dominion, and one in glory, constituting the first presidency of this system, and this eternity. But they are as much three distinct persons as the sun, moon, and earth are three different bodies. (Times and Seasons, Feb. 15, 1845, The Gospel Kingdom, pp. 28-29) TLDP:230

# List of Doctrines

## DEATH

# DEATH continued

*Doctrines on DEATH*
*Located in Other Topics*

88.  One of the (threefold) missions of the Church is to perform vicarious ordinances for the redemption of the dead.

126.  In the spirit world, after death, there is a separation of spirits that lasts until the resurrection and final judgment; the wicked go into a state of outer darkness, and the righteous go into a state of happiness.

141.  All people will be *saved* from death, but not all will receive the *salvation of exaltation* or *eternal life* in the celestial kingdom of God.

194.  Because of the Fall of Adam all people became subject to physical, temporal death.

451.  In the Millennium there will be no more weeping, no sorrow or pain, and no fear of death.

453.  The great work of the Millennium shall be temple work for the redemption of the dead.

647.  The resurrection is universal: every person will be saved from *physical* death regardless of whether he or she has done good or evil in this life.

829.  Some mortals have been translated; in this state their bodies are changed so that they are not subject to disease, sorrow, or death.

830.  Translated beings eventually undergo a change equivalent to death.

(See topics ADVERSITY, ATONEMENT OF JESUS CHRIST: Salvation from Physical Death, and RESURRECTION.)

# DEATH

**(1) Death, Generally**
**(2) Postmortal Spirit World**
**(3) Work for the Dead**

### (1) Death, Generally

122. Death is a necessary part of God's plan for the salvation of all people.

#### Elder Joseph Fielding Smith
We came into this world to die. That was understood before we came here. It is part of the plan, all discussed and arranged long before men were placed upon the earth. When Adam was sent into this world, it was with the understanding that he would violate a law, transgress a law, in order to bring to pass this mortal condition which we find ourselves in today. (Doctrines of Salvation, 1:66) DGSM:21

#### Bruce R. McConkie
Our scriptures say: "Death hath passed upon all men, to fulfil the merciful plan of the great Creator." (2 Ne. 9:6) Where the true Saints are concerned there is no sorrow in death except that which attends a temporary separation from loved ones. Birth and death are both essential steps in the unfolding drama of eternity. ¶ We shouted for joy at the privilege of becoming mortal because without the tests of mortality there could be no eternal life. We now sing praises to the great Redeemer for the privilege of passing from this life because without death and the resurrection we could not be raised in immortal glory and gain eternal life. . . . ¶ Now, we do not seek death, though it is part of the merciful plan of the great Creator. Rather, we rejoice in life, and desire to live as long as we can be of service to our fellowmen. Faithful saints are a leaven of righteousness in a wicked world. ¶ But sometimes the Lord's people are hounded and persecuted. Sometimes He deliberately lets His faithful saints linger and suffer, in both body and spirit, to prove them in all things, and to see if they will abide in His covenant, even unto death, that they may be found worthy of eternal life. If such be the lot of any of us, so be it. CR1976Oct:158-59

#### Alma, the younger, *quoted by Mormon*
And now behold, if it were possible that our first parents could have gone forth and partaken of the tree of life they would have been forever miserable, having no preparatory state; and thus the plan of redemption would have been frus-trated, and the word of God would have been void, taking none effect. 27. But behold, it was not so; but it was appointed unto men that they must die; and after death, they must come to judgment, even that same judgment of which we have spoken, which is the end. (*Alma responds to the chief ruler, Antionah, regarding Adam and Eve's expulsion from the Garden of Eden, about 82 B.C.*) Alma 12:26-27

#### Alma, the younger, *quoted by Mormon*
But behold, it was appointed unto man to die— therefore, as they were cut off from the tree of life they should be cut off from the face of the earth—and man became lost forever, yea, they became fallen man. 7. And now, ye see by this that our first parents were cut off both temporally and spiritually from the presence of the Lord; and thus we see they became subjects to follow after their own will. 8. Now behold, it was not expedient that man should be reclaimed from this temporal death, for that would destroy the great plan of happiness. (*Alma speaks to his son Corianton, about 73 B.C.; mortality is a probationary time to enable man to repent and serve God*) Alma 42:6-8

#### Jacob, brother of Nephi
For as death hath passed upon all men, to fulfil the merciful plan of the great Creator, there must needs be a power of resurrection, and the resurrection must needs come unto man by reason of the fall; and the fall came by reason of transgression; and because man became fallen they were cut off from the presence of the Lord. (*Jacob recounts to the people of Nephi the covenants of the Lord made to the house of Israel, 559-545 B.C.*) 2Ne.9:6

**Related Witnesses:**

#### Joseph Smith, *receiving the Word of the Lord*
Wherefore, fear not even unto death; for in this world your joy is not full, but in me your joy is full. (*Revelation received Dec. 16, 1833*) D&C 101:36

---

123. There is no tragedy in death.

#### Elder Spencer W. Kimball
If we say that early death is a calamity, disaster or a tragedy, would it not be saying that mortality is preferable to earlier entrance into the spirit world and to eventual salvation and exaltation? If mortality be the perfect state, then death would be a frustration but the Gospel teaches us there is not tragedy in death, but only in sin.

*(Speech at Brigham Young University, Dec. 1955)* DGSM:84

**Elder Joseph F. Smith**

All fear of this death has been removed from the Latter-day Saints. They have no dread of the temporal death, because they know that as death came upon them by the transgression of Adam, so by the righteousness of Jesus Christ shall life come unto them, and though they die, they shall live again. Possessing this knowledge, they have joy even in death, for they know that they shall rise again and shall met again beyond the grave. They know that the spirit dies not at all; that it passes through no change, except the change from imprisonment in this mortal clay to freedom and to the sphere in which it acted before it came to this earth. CR1899Oct:70-71

**Jesus,**
*recorded in Matthew*

And fear not them which kill the body, but are not able to kill the soul: but rather fear him which is able to destroy both soul and body in hell. *(Jesus instructs the Twelve Apostles; they shall expect persecution)* Matt.10:28

**Joseph Smith,**
*receiving the Word of the Lord*

And it shall come to pass that those that die in me shall not taste of death, for it shall be sweet unto them; . . . *(Revelation received Feb. 9, 1831; administration to the sick)* D&C 42:46

**Mormon**

And they did look upon shedding the blood of their brethren with the greatest abhorrence; and they never could be prevailed upon to take up arms against their brethren; and they never did look upon death with any degree of terror, for their hope and views of Christ and the resurrection; therefore, death was swallowed up to them by the victory of Christ over it. *(Upright, zealous members of the Church choose death at the hands of their enemies rather than taking the sword against them)* Alma 27:28

**President Brigham Young**

We shall turn round and look upon it [the valley of death] and think, when we have crossed it, why this is the greatest advantage of my whole existence, for I have passed from a state of sorrow, grief, mourning, woe, misery, pain, anguish and disappointment into a state of existence, where I can enjoy life to the fullest extent as far as that can be done without a body. My spirit is set free, I thirst no more, I want to sleep no more, I hunger no more, I tire no more, I run, I walk, I labor, I go, I come, I do this, I do that, whatever is required of me, nothing like pain or weariness, I am full of life, full of vigor,

and I enjoy the presence of my heavenly Father. *(Funeral sermon 14th Ward, July 1874, JD17:142)* DGSM:83

---

**124. At death our physical bodies die, while our spirits continue to live.**

**Recorded in Ecclesiastes**

Then shall the dust return to the earth as it was: and the spirit shall return unto God who gave it. *(Reflections of a son of David the king)* Eccl.12:7

**Marion G. Romney**

Our probation here on earth will, of course, be terminated by death, death being the dissolution of the soul—the separation of the body and the spirit. CR1976Apr:119

**Alma, the younger,**
*quoted by Mormon*

And we see that death comes upon mankind, yea, the death which has been spoken of by Amulek, which is the temporal death; nevertheless there was a space granted unto man in which he might repent; therefore this life became a probationary state; a time to prepare to meet God; a time to prepare for that endless state which has been spoken of by us, which is after the resurrection of the dead. . . . 27. But behold, it was not so; but it was appointed unto men that they must die; and after death, they must come to judgment, even that same judgment of which we have spoken, which is the end. *(Alma responds to the chief ruler, Antionah, regarding Adam and Eve's expulsion from the Garden of Eden, about 82 B.C.)* Alma 12:24,27

**Alma, the younger,**
*quoted by Mormon*

Now, concerning the state of the soul between death and the resurrection—Behold, it has been made known unto me by an angel, that the spirits of all men, as soon as they are departed from this mortal body, yea, the spirits of all men, whether they be good or evil, are taken home to that God who gave them life. . . . *(Alma speaks to his son Corianton, concerning the resurrection of the dead, about 73 B.C.)* Alma 40:11

**President Joseph F. Smith**

The spirits of all men, as soon as they depart from this mortal body, whether they are good or evil, we are told in the Book of Mormon, are taken home to that God who gave them life, where there is a separation, a partial judgment, and the spirits of those who are righteous are received into a state of happiness which is called paradise, a state of rest, a state of peace, where they expand in wisdom, where they have respite from all their troubles, and where care and sorrow do not annoy. The wicked, on the contrary, have no part nor portion in the Spirit of the Lord, and they are cast into outer darkness, being led captive, because of their own iniquity, by the evil one. And in this space between death and the resurrection of the body, the two classes of souls remain, in happiness or in misery, until the time which is appointed of God that the dead shall come forth and be reunited both spirit and body, and be brought to stand before God and be judged according to their works. This is the final judgment. (Gospel Doctrine, p. 448) DGSM:84

**Related Witnesses:**

### Recorded in Matthew

And the graves were opened; and many bodies of the saints which slept arose, 53. And came out of the graves after his resurrection, and went into the holy city, and appeared unto many. (*Jesus is crucified and the first resurrection begins*) Matt.27:52-53

### Paul

For we brought nothing into this world, and it is certain we can carry nothing out. (*Paul writes to his assistant Timothy, about A.D. 64* ) 1Tim.6:7

### James

For as the body without the spirit is dead, so faith without works is dead also. (*James writes to his brethren in the Church*) James 2:26

---

### 125. Spiritual death is separation from the presence of God.

#### Elder Joseph Fielding Smith

Adam transgressed and the penalty was death. It came in two-fold form—first, spiritual and secondly, temporal or mortal. The first was banishment from the presence of the Lord, the second the dissolution of the body. The redemption from the spiritual death is brought about through repentance and obedience to the gospel. The redemption from the mortal death is through the resurrection from the grave. (The Restoration of All Things, p. 22) TLDP:186

#### Alma, the younger,
*quoted by Mormon*

Therefore, as the soul could never die, and the fall had brought upon all mankind a spiritual death as well as a temporal, that is, they were cut off from the presence of the Lord, it was expedient that mankind should be reclaimed from this spiritual death. (*Alma speaks to his son Corianton concerning the resurrection of the dead, about 73 B.C.*) Alma 42:9

#### Joseph Smith,
*receiving the Word of the Lord*

Wherefore, it came to pass that the devil tempted Adam, and he partook of the forbidden fruit and transgressed the commandment, wherein he became subject to the will of the devil, because he yielded unto temptation. 41. Wherefore, I, the Lord God, caused that he should be cast out from the Garden of Eden, from my presence, because of his transgression, wherein he became spiritually dead, which is the first death, even that same death which is the last death, which is spiritual, which shall be pronounced upon the wicked when I shall say: Depart, ye cursed. (*Revelation received in presence of six elders, Sept. 1830*) D&C 29:40-41

#### James E. Talmage

The Immediate Result of the Fall was the substitution of mortality, with all its attendant frailties, for the vigor of the primeval deathless state. Adam felt directly the effects of transgression in finding a barren and dreary earth, with a relatively sterile soil, instead of the beauty and fruitfulness of Eden. In place of pleasing and useful plants, thorns and thistles sprang up; and the man had to labor arduously, under the conditions of physical fatigue and suffering, to cultivate the soil that he might obtain necessary food. Upon Eve fell the penalty of bodily infirmity; pains and sorrows, which since have been regarded as the natural lot of womankind, came upon her, and she was made subject to her husband's authority. Having lost their sense of former innocence they became ashamed of their nakedness, and the Lord made for them garments of skins. Upon both the man and the woman was visited the penalty of spiritual death; for in that very day they were banished from Eden and cast out from the presence of the Lord. AF:61

**Related Witnesses:**

#### Jacob, brother of Nephi

For as death hath passed upon all men, to fulfil the merciful plan of the great Creator, there must needs be a power of resurrection, and the resurrection must needs come unto man by reason of the fall; and the fall came by reason of transgression; and because man became fallen they were cut off from the presence of the Lord. 7. Wherefore, it must needs be an infinite atonement—save it should be an infinite atonement this corruption could not put on incorruption. Wherefore, the first judgment which came upon man must needs have remained to an endless duration. And if so, this flesh must have laid down to rot and to crumble to its mother earth, to rise no more. 8. O the wisdom of God, his mercy and grace! For behold, if the flesh should rise no more our spirits must become subject to that angel who fell from before the presence of the Eternal God, and became the devil, to rise no more. 9. And our spirits must have become like unto him, and we become devils, angels to a devil, to be shut out from the presence of our God, and to remain with the father of lies, in misery, like unto himself; yea, to that being who beguiled our first parents, who transformeth himself nigh unto an angel of light, and stirreth up the children of men unto secret combinations of murder and all manner of secret works of darkness. 10. O how great the goodness of our God, who prepareth a way for our escape from the grasp of this awful monster; yea, that monster, death and hell, which I call the death of the body, and also the death of the spirit. (*Jacob teaches the doctrine of the atonement to the people of Nephi, 559-545 B.C.*) 2Ne.9:6-10

## (2) The Postmortal Spirit World

126. In the spirit world, after death, there is a separation of spirits that lasts until the resurrection and final judgment; the wicked go into a state of outer darkness, and the righteous go into a state of happiness.

### President Joseph F. Smith

The spirits of all men, as soon as they depart from this mortal body, whether they are good or evil, we are told in the Book of Mormon, are taken home to that God who gave them life, where there is a separation, a partial judgment, and the spirits of those who are righteous are received into a state of happiness which is called paradise, a state of rest, a state of peace, where they expand in wisdom, where they have respite from all their troubles, and where care and sorrow do not annoy. The wicked, on the contrary, have no part or portion in the Spirit of the Lord, and they are cast into outer darkness, being led captive, because of their own iniquity, by the evil one. And in this space between death and the resurrection of the body, the two classes of souls remain, in happiness or in misery, until the time which is appointed of God that the dead shall come forth and be reunited both spirit and body, and be brought to stand before God, and be judged according to their works. (Gospel Doctrine, p. 448) DGSM:84; TLDP:637-38

### Alma, the younger, *quoted by Mormon*

And then shall it come to pass, that the spirits of those who are righteous are received into a state of happiness, which is called paradise, a state of rest, a state of peace, where they shall rest from all their troubles and from all care, and sorrow. . . . 14. Now this is the state of the souls of the wicked, yea, in darkness, and a state of awful, fearful looking for the fiery indignation of the wrath of God upon them; thus they remain in this state, as well as the righteous in paradise, until the time of their resurrection. (*Alma speaks to his son Corianton, concerning the resurrection of the dead, about 73 B.C.*) Alma 40:12,14

### James E. Talmage, *also quoting Alma, the younger*

Paradise . . . is not Heaven, if by the latter term we understand the abode of the Eternal Father and His celestialized children. Paradise is a place where dwell righteous and repentant spirits between bodily death and resurrection. Another division of the spirit world is reserved for those disembodied beings who have lived lives of wickedness and who remain impenitent even after death. Alma, a Nephite prophet, thus spake of the conditions prevailing among the departed: ¶ "Now concerning the state of the soul between death and the resurrection. Behold, it has been made known unto me, by an angel, that the spirits of all men, as soon as they are departed from this mortal body; yea, the spirits of all men, whether they be good or evil, are taken home to that God who gave them life. And then shall it come to pass that the spirits of those who are righteous, are received into a state of happiness, which is called paradise; a state of rest; a state of peace, where they shall rest from all their troubles and from all care, and sorrow, &c. And then shall it come to pass, that the spirits of the wicked, yea, who are evil . . . these shall be cast out into outer darkness; there shall be weeping, and wailing, and gnashing of teeth; and this because of their own iniquity; being led captive by the will of the devil. Now this is the state of the souls of the wicked: yea, in darkness, and a state of awful, fearful, looking for the fiery indignation of the wrath of God upon them; thus they remain in this state, as well as the righteous in paradise, until the time of their resurrection." [Alma 40:11-14] JTC:671-72

### President Joseph F. Smith

And there were gathered together in one place an innumerable company of the spirits of the just, who had been faithful in the testimony of Jesus while they lived in mortality; . . . 18. While this vast multitude waited and conversed, rejoicing in the hour of their deliverance from the chains of death, the Son of God appeared, declaring liberty to the captives who had been faithful; 19. And there he preached to them the everlasting gospel, the doctrine of the resurrection and the redemption of mankind from the fall, and from individual sins on conditions of repentance. 20. But unto the wicked he did not go, and among the ungodly and the unrepentant who had defiled themselves while in the flesh, his voice was not raised; 21. Neither did the rebellious who rejected the testimonies and the warnings of the ancient prophets behold his presence, nor look upon his face. 22. Where these were, darkness reigned, but among the righteous there was peace; . . . (*Vision regarding the Savior's visit to the spirits of the dead, Oct. 3, 1918*) D&C 138:12,18-22

### James E. Talmage

While as a practice it would be critically unfair to deduce doctrinal principles from parabolic incidents [See Lazarus and the Rich man in Luke 16:19-31.], we cannot admit that Christ would teach falsely even in parable; and therefore we accept as true the portrayal of conditions in the world of the disembodied. That righteous and unrighteous dwell apart during the interval between death and resurrection is clear. Paradise, or as the Jews like to designate that blessed abode, "Abraham's bosom," is not the place of final glory, any more than the hell to which the rich man's spirit was consigned is the final habitation of the condemned. To that preliminary or intermediate state, however, men's works do follow them; and the dead shall surely find that their abode is that for which they have qualified themselves while in the flesh. JTC:468

**Related Witnesses:**

### George Q. Cannon

I have thought sometimes that some of our people are inclined to think there is no hell and that nobody is going to hell. I tell you there will be a large number of people go to hell; they will suffer torment and will go where there is weeping and wailing and gnashing of teeth; they will be in outer darkness and suffer far beyond anything we can conceive of. Latter-day Saints especially who commit sin, if they die in their sin, will go to hell, and they will suffer torment there until the day of redemption. But think of the length of time during which they will be in this torment! (Gospel Truth, 1:85) TLDP:639

### Joseph Smith

Hades, the Greek, or Shaole, the Hebrew: these two significations mean a world of spirits. Hades, Shaole, paradise, spirits in prison, are all

one: it is a world of spirits. ¶ The righteous and the wicked all go to the same world of spirits until the resurrection. . . . ¶ The great misery of departed spirits in the world of spirits, where they go after death, is to know that they come short of the glory that others enjoy and that they might have enjoyed themselves, and they are their own accusers. (*At the Stand in Nauvoo, Ill., June 11, 1843*) HC5:425

### James E. Talmage

The scriptures prove, that at the time of man's final judgment he will stand before the bar of God, clothed in his resurrected body, and this, irrespective of his condition of purity or guilt. While awaiting the time of their coming forth, disembodied spirits exist in an intermediate state, of happiness and rest or of suffering and suspense, according to their works in mortality. AF:466

### James E. Talmage

As rewards for righteous deeds are proportionate to deserving acts, so the punishment prescribed for sin is made adequate to the offense. But, be it remembered, both rewards and punishments are natural consequences. Punishment is inflicted upon the sinner for disciplinary and reformatory purposes and in accordance with justice. There is nothing of vindictiveness or of desire to cause suffering manifest in the divine nature; on the contrary, our Father is cognizant of every pang, and permits such to afflict for beneficent purposes only. God's mercy is declared in the retributive pains that He allows, as in the blessings of peace that issue from Him. It is scarcely profitable to speculate as to the exact nature of the spiritual suffering imposed as punishment for sin. Comparison with physical pain, such as the tortures of fire in a sulphurous lake, serve to show that the human mind is incapable of comprehending the extent of these penalties. The sufferings entailed by the fate of condemnation are more to be feared than are any possible inflictions of physical torture; the mind, the spirit, the whole soul is doomed to suffer, and the torment is known by none in the flesh. AF:53-54

### President Joseph F. Smith

I beheld that the faithful elders of this dispensation, when they depart from mortal life, continue their labors in the preaching of the gospel of repentance and redemption, through the sacrifice of the Only Begotten Son of God, among those who are in darkness and under the bondage of sin in the great world of the spirits of the dead. (*Vision to President Joseph F. Smith regarding the Savior's visit to the spirits of the dead, Oct. 3, 1918*) D&C 138:57

**Author's Note:** For the present, we do not know what level of righteousness is required to merit "paradise," a state of happiness, and what level of wickedness consigns a person to state of "outer darkness." Nor are we taught the exact dividing line between the righteous and the wicked in the spirit world. Clearly all righteous people are not equally righteous, and all wicked people are not equally wicked. Perhaps it is enough for us to know that we should be as righteous as we know how.

---

127. In the postmortal spirit world the spirits of the righteous enter a condition of peace and rest, called paradise, until their resurrection.

**Alma, the younger,**
*quoted by Mormon*
And then shall it come to pass, that the spirits of those who are righteous are received into a state of happiness, which is called paradise, a state of rest, a state of peace, where they shall rest from all their troubles and from all care, and sorrow. . . . 14. . . . until the time of their resurrection. (*Alma speaks to his son Corianton, concerning the resurrection of the dead, about 73 B.C.*) Alma 40:12,14

**Bruce R. McConkie**
Paradise—the abode of righteous spirits, as they await the day of their resurrection; paradise—a place of peace and rest where the sorrows and trials of [t]his life have been shuffled off, and where the saints continue to prepare for a celestial heaven; paradise—not the Lord's eternal kingdom, but a way station along the course leading to eternal life, a place where the final preparation is made for that fulness of joy which comes only when body and spirit are inseparably connected in immortal glory! (The Millennial Messiah, 4:222) DGSM:84

**Jacob, brother of Nephi,**
*quoted by Nephi*
O how great the plan of our God! For on the other hand, the paradise of God must deliver up the spirits of the righteous, and the grave deliver up the body of the righteous; and the spirit and the body is restored to itself again, and all men become incorruptible, and immortal, and they are living souls, having a perfect knowledge like unto us in the flesh, save it be that our knowledge shall be perfect. (*Jacob teaches the doctrine of the Atonement to the people of Nephi, 559-545 B.C.*) 2Ne.9:13

**Moroni, son of Mormon**
And now I bid unto all, farewell. I soon go to rest in the paradise of God, until my spirit and body shall again reunite, and I am brought forth triumphant through the air, to meet you before the pleasing bar of the great Jehovah, the Eternal Judge of both quick and dead. Amen. (*Moroni's final writings, about A.D. 421*) Moro.10:34

**President Joseph F. Smith**
The spirits of all men, as soon as they depart from this mortal body, whether they are good or evil, we are told in the Book of Mormon, are taken home to that God who gave them life, where there is a separation, a partial judgment, and the spirits of those who are righteous are received into a state of happiness which is called paradise, a state of rest, a state of peace, where they expand in wisdom, where they have respite from all their troubles, and where care and sorrow do not annoy. (Gospel Doctrine, p. 448) DGSM:84; TLDP:637-38

**Related Witnesses:**
**President Brigham Young**
The brightness and glory of the next apartment is inexpressible. It is not encumbered with this clog of dirt we are carrying around here so that when we advance in years we have to be stubbing along and to be careful lest we fall down. . . . ¶ Here, we are continually troubled with ills and ailments of various kinds . . . but in the spirit world we are free from all this and enjoy life, glory, and intelligence . . . and we shall enjoy the society of the just and the pure who are in the spirit world until the resurrection. (*At funeral services of Aurelia Spencer, 13th Ward, Sept. 16, 1871, JD14:231*) TLDP:638

**Mormon**
And it came to pass that the seventy and first year passed away, and also the seventy and second year, yea, and in fine, till the seventy and ninth year had passed away; yea, even an hundred years had passed away, and the disciples of Jesus, whom he had chosen, had all gone to the paradise of God, save it were the three who should tarry; and there were other disciples ordained in their stead; and also many of that generation had passed away. (*Mormon abridges the account of Nephi, son of Nephi, one of the disciples of Christ, A.D. 36-60*) 4Ne.1:14

---

### (3) Work for the Dead

128. All who have died without the opportunity to hear and to receive the gospel shall be given that opportunity in the spirit world.

### Elder Joseph Fielding Smith

In the justice of the Father, he is going to give to every man the privilege of hearing the gospel. Not one soul shall be overlooked or forgotten. This being true, what about the countless thousands who have died and never heard of Christ, never had an opportunity of repentance and remission of their sins, never met an elder of the Church holding the authority? Some of our good Christian neighbors will tell you they are lost forever, that they cannot believe in the grave, for there is no hope beyond. ¶ Would that be fair? Would it be just? No! the Lord is going to give to every man the opportunity to hear and to receive eternal life, or a place in his kingdom. We are very fortunate because we have had that privilege here and have passed from death into life. (Doctrines of Salvation, 2:132) DGSM:84

### Peter

For for this cause was the gospel preached also to them that are dead, that they might be judged according to men in the flesh, but live according to God in the spirit. (*Peter writes to the churches in modern Asia Minor, about A.D. 60*) 1Pet.4:6

### President Joseph F. Smith

But behold, from among the righteous, he organized his forces and appointed messengers, clothed with power and authority, and commissioned them to go forth and carry the light of the gospel to them that were in darkness, even to all the spirits of men; and thus was the gospel preached to the dead. 31. And the chosen messengers went forth to declare the acceptable day of the Lord and proclaim liberty to the captives who were bound, even unto all who would repent of their sins and receive the gospel. 32. Thus was the gospel preached to those who had died in their sins, without a knowledge of the truth, or in transgression, having rejected the prophets. 33. These were taught faith in God, repentance from sin, vicarious baptism for the remission of sins, the gift of the Holy Ghost by the laying on of hands. 34. And all other principles of the gospel that were necessary for them to know in order to qualify themselves that they might be judged according to men in the flesh, but live according to God in the spirit. . . . 57. I beheld that the faithful elders of this dispensation, when they depart from mortal life, continue their labors in the preaching of the gospel of repentance and redemption, through the sacrifice of the Only Begotten Son of God, among those who are in darkness and under the bondage of sin in the great world of the spirits of the dead. (*Vision regarding the Savior's visit to the spirits of the dead, Oct. 3, 1918*) D&C 138:30-34,57

### Joseph Smith,
#### quoted by Elder Joseph Fielding Smith

I have a declaration to make as to the provisions which God hath made to suit the conditions of man—made for before the foundation of the world. What has Jesus said? All sin, and all blasphemies, and every transgression, except one, that man can be guilty of, may be forgiven; and there is a salvation for all men, either in this world or the world to come, who have not committed the unpardonable sin, there being a provision either in this world or the world of spirits. Hence God hath made a provision that every spirit in the eternal world can be ferreted out and saved unless he has committed that unpardonable sin which cannot be remitted to him either in this world or the world of spirits. God has wrought out a salvation for all men, unless they have committed a certain sin; and every man who has a friend in the eternal world can save him, unless he has committed the unpardonable sin. And so you can see how far you can be a savior. (*To the Church in general conference—a congregation of 20,000, "King Follett Sermon", April 7, 1844*) (See HC6:302-17, also see The Words of Joseph Smith, pp. 340-62.) TPJS:356-57

### President Lorenzo Snow

I believe . . . that when the Gospel is preached to the spirits in prison, the success attending that preaching will be far greater than that attending the preaching of our Elders in this life. I believe there will be very few indeed of those spirits who will not gladly receive the Gospel when it is carried to them. The circumstances there will be a thousand times more favorable. (Millennial Star, Jan. 22, 1894, p. 49) TLDP:639

### Related Witnesses:
#### James E. Talmage

The Latter-day Saints believe and teach that repentance will be possible, and indeed required of the yet unrepentant, even after death; and they affirm that this doctrine is supported by scripture both ancient and modern. HL:67-68

### Charles W. Penrose

There are hundreds of thousands who have heard the Gospel in the flesh and through fear or folly have not embraced it, having been afraid to come forward and join themselves with this unpopular people, when they pass away from this stage of being into the spirit world will be prepared to receive it when it is being preached among the spirits that are there. CR1906Apr:86

129. **Prophets and other priesthood holders who have departed this earth will be occupied in teaching the gospel to the dead in the spirit world.**

### President Brigham Young

If the Elders of Israel in these latter times go and preach to the spirits in prison, they associate with them, precisely as our Elders associate with the wicked in the flesh, when they go to preach to them. *(In Tabernacle, Dec. 3, 1854, JD2:137)* TLDP:639

### Elder Joseph Fielding Smith

The Lord has so arranged his plan of redemption that all who have died without this opportunity shall be given it in the spirit world. There the elders of the Church who have died are proclaiming the gospel to the dead. All those who did not have an opportunity here to receive it, who there repent and receive the gospel, shall be heirs of the celestial kingdom of God. (Doctrines of Salvation, 2:132) DGSM:84

### Charles W. Penrose

There are hundreds of thousands who have heard the Gospel in the flesh and through fear or folly have not embraced it, having been afraid to come forward and join themselves with this unpopular people, when they pass away from this stage of being into the spirit world will be prepared to receive it when it is being preached among the spirits that are there. For the work that Christ did after He departed from the flesh and went and preached to the spirits in prison who were disobedient in the days of Noah, will have to be repeated now by the servants of God who have gone beyond the veil, and it will be continued by those who shall follow after. While the Saints upon the earth are ministering in the temples that have been reared, and performing the necessary ordinances that pertain to the flesh which cannot be attended to by people in the spirit land, the prophets of the living God, who sealed their testimony with their blood, and their faithful brethren who have followed after them, are now laboring among the people behind the veil that they may be prepared to receive the blessings that shall come to them through the labors of the Saints in the flesh. . . . The powers of the Holy Priesthood which God has revealed are inseparably connected, he has told us, with the powers that are behind the veil. They are working together in harmony, and the time will come and it is not far distant, when the veil will be taken away which separates us from our brethren who have gone before, and

we will work with them, and they with us. We will be in perfect harmony; and the Priesthood behind the veil will reveal to the Priesthood in the flesh in the holy Temples of God where these conversations will take place, the names of those for whom we must officiate which we cannot obtain by the means now at our command. This is the Lord's work, and it is not only going on here in the flesh, but it is going on in the world behind the veil among the spirits that have departed. Every man who has been called to hold the Priesthood should endeavor to qualify himself for the work that lies before him, both that which he will be called to do while he dwells in the body, and that which he will have to perform when he goes out of the body; for it is a fact that when we go away from here we will take with us that which we have spiritual. That intelligence which we gain, that knowledge of principle, that fellowship we have with the heavens, that Holy Priesthood which we bear, that divine spirit by which we have been inspired, and all the powers that we have gained in being exercised in the duties of the Holy Priesthood, will be strength and power and might to us when we depart from the body and are delivered from the weakness of mortality, and called to labor in the world of spirits. The same authority, the same power, the same intelligence, the same experiences that we have had here we will have there. . . . Therefore every man holding the Priesthood should endeavor to qualify himself for the work of the ministry, in time and in eternity, so that we may labor under the direction of the Captain of our salvation until redemption shall come to all the race, and "every knee shall bow and every tongue confess that Jesus is the Christ to the glory of God the Father." CR1906Apr:86-87

### Peter

For Christ also hath once suffered for sins, the just for the unjust, that he might bring us to God, being put to death in the flesh, but quickened by the Spirit: 19. By which also he went and preached unto the spirits in prison; 20. Which sometime were disobedient, when once the longsuffering of God waited in the days of Noah, while the ark was a preparing, wherein few, that is, eight souls were saved by water. *(Peter writes to the churches in modern Asia Minor, about A.D. 60)* 1Pet.3:18-20

### President Brigham Young

Jesus was the first man that ever went to preach to the spirits in prison, holding the keys of the Gospel of salvation to them. Those keys were delivered to him in the day and hour that he went into the spirit world, and with them he opened the door of salvation to the spirits in prison. *(In Tabernacle, March 15, 1857, JD4:285)* TLDP:639

### President Joseph F. Smith

I have always believed, and still do believe with all my soul, that such men as Peter and James and the twelve disciples chosen by the Savior in his time, have been engaged all the centuries that have passed since their martyrdom for the testimony of Jesus Christ, in proclaiming liberty to the captives in the spirit world and in opening their prison doors . . . . Their special calling and anointing of the Lord himself was to save the world, to proclaim liberty to the captives, and the opening of the prison doors to those who were bound in chains of darkness, superstition, and ignorance. I believe that the disciples who have passed away in this dispensation—Joseph, the Prophet, and his brother Hyrum, and Brigham, and Heber, and Willard, and Daniel and John, and Wilford and all the rest of the prophets who have lived in this dispensation, and who have been intimately associated with the work of redemption and the other ordinances of the gospel of the Son of God in this world, are preaching that same gospel that they lived and preached here, to those who are in darkness in the spirit world and who had not the knowledge before they went. The gospel must be preached to them. We are not perfect without them—they cannot be perfect without us. (Young Women's Journal, 1911, Gospel Doctrine, pp. 460-61) TLDP:640

### President Joseph F. Smith

As I pondered over these things which are written, the eyes of my understanding were opened, and the Spirit of the Lord rested upon me, and I saw the hosts of the dead, both small and great. 12. And there were gathered together in one place an innumerable company of the spirits of the just, who had been faithful in the testimony of Jesus while they lived in mortality. . . . 16. They were assembled awaiting the advent of the Son of God into the spirit world, to declare their redemption from the bands of death. . . . 18. While this vast multitude waited and conversed, rejoicing in the hour of their deliverance from the chains of death, the Son of God appeared, declaring liberty to the captives who had been faithful; 19. And there he preached to them the everlasting gospel, the doctrine of the resurrection and the redemption of mankind from the fall, and from individual sins on conditions of repentance. 20. But unto the wicked he did not go, and among the ungodly and the unrepentant who had defiled themselves while in the flesh, his voice was not raised; 21. Neither did the rebellious who rejected the testimonies and the warnings of the ancient prophets behold his presence, nor look upon his face. 22. Where these were, darkness reigned, but among the righteous there was peace; . . . 25. I marveled, for I understood that the Savior spent about three years in his ministry among the Jews and those of the house of Israel, endeavoring to teach them the everlasting gospel and call them unto repentance; 26. And yet, notwithstanding his mighty works, and miracles, and proclamation of the truth, in great power and authority, there were but few who hearkened to his voice, and rejoiced in his presence, and received salvation at his hands. 27. But his ministry among those who were dead was limited to the brief time intervening between the crucifixion and his resurrection; 28. And I wondered at the words of Peter—wherein he said that the Son of God preached unto the spirits in prison, who sometime were disobedient, when once the long-suffering of God waited in the days of Noah—and how it was possible for him to preach to those spirits and perform the necessary labor among them in so short a time. 29. And as I wondered, my eyes were opened, and my understanding quickened, and I perceived that the Lord went not in person among the wicked and the disobedient who had rejected the truth, to teach them; 30. But behold, from among the righteous, he organized his forces and appointed messengers, clothed with power and authority, and commissioned them to go forth and carry the light of the gospel to them that were in darkness, even to all the spirits of men; and thus was the gospel preached to the dead. 31. And the chosen messengers went forth to declare the acceptable day of the Lord and proclaim liberty to the captives who were bound, even unto all who would repent of their sins and receive the gospel. 32. Thus was the gospel preached to those who had died in their sins, without a knowledge of the truth, or in transgression, having rejected the prophets. 33. These were taught faith in God, repentance from sin, vicarious baptism for the remission of sins, the gift of the Holy Ghost by the laying on of hands. 34. And all other principles of the gospel that were necessary for them to know in order to qualify themselves that they might be judged according to men in the flesh, but live according to God in the spirit. . . . 36. Thus was it made known that our Redeemer spent his time during his sojourn in the world of spirits, instructing and preparing the faithful spirits of the prophets who had testified of him in the flesh. 37. That they might carry the message of redemption unto all the dead, unto whom he could not go personally, because of their rebellion and transgression, that they through the ministration of his servants might also hear his words. (*Vision regarding the Savior's visit to the spirits of the dead, Oct. 3, 1918*) D&C 138:11-12,16,18-22,25-34,36-37

### Joseph Smith

And also they who are the spirits of men kept in prison, whom the Son visited, and preached the gospel unto them, that they might be judged according to men in the flesh; . . . (*Vision to Joseph Smith and Sidney Rigdon, Feb. 16, 1832*) D&C 76:73

**Related Witnesses:**

### President Wilford Woodruff

If the veil could be taken from our eyes and we could see into the spirit world, we would see that Joseph Smith, Brigham Young and John Taylor had gathered together every spirit that ever dwelt in the flesh in this Church since its organization. We would also see the faithful apostles and elders of the Nephites who dwelt in the flesh in the days of Jesus Christ. In that assembly we would also see Isaiah and every prophet and apostle that ever prophesied of the great work of God. In the midst of those spirits we would see the Son of God, the Savior, who presides and guides and controls the preparing for the kingdom of God on the earth and in heaven. . . . The Son of God stands in the midst of that body of celestial spirits, and teaches them their duties concerning the day in which we live, and instructs them what they must do to prepare and qualify themselves to go with him to the earth when he comes to judge every man according to the deeds done in the body. (The Vision, or The Degrees of Glory, p. 96) TLDP:638

### President Brigham Young,
*quoted by John A. Widtsoe*

Father Smith and Carlos and Brother Partridge, yes, and every other good Saint, are just as busy in the spirit world as you and I are here. . . . What are they doing there? They are preaching, preaching all the time. . . . (*In Bowery, June 22, 1856, JD3:370*) DBY:378

**Author's Note:** Since sisters as well as priesthood holders are engaged in this work on earth, it is logical that they likewise will be so engaged in the spirit world. Joseph Fielding Smith wrote: "Neither will the work in the spirit world be carried on exclusively by the men holding the Priesthood. The sisters who have made covenant with the Lord and who have received blessings and power in the temples will also have much to do in that work. This was made very clear by President [Joseph F.] Smith at the funeral of Sister Mary A. Freeze, when he said: 'Now, among all these millions of spirits that have lived on the earth and have passed away, from generation to generation, since the beginning of the world, without the knowledge of the Gospel—among them you may count that at least one-half are women. Who is going to preach the Gospel to the women? Who is going to carry the testimony of Jesus Christ to the hearts of the women who have passed away without a knowledge of the Gospel? Well, to my mind, it is a simple thing. These good sisters who have been set apart, ordained to the work, called to it, authorized by the authority of the Holy Priesthood to minister for their sex, in the House of God for the living and for the dead, will be fully authorized and empowered to preach the Gospel and minister to the women while the elders and prophets are preaching it to the men. The things we experience here are typical of the things of God, and the life beyond us'." — Gospel Doctrine pp. 581-82. (The Way To Perfection, p. 320)

---

130. **All who die without knowledge of the gospel, who would have received it with all their hearts while on earth, will inherit the celestial kingdom.**

### Bruce R. McConkie

The doctrine of salvation for the dead is that all who die without a knowledge of the gospel, without a knowledge of Christ and his atoning sacrifice, without having the opportunity to believe and obey in this life and thereby qualify for celestial salvation—the doctrine of salvation for the dead is that all such, if they would have received the gospel with all of their hearts, had it been available to them, such shall hear and believe and obey in the spirit world and thereby become heirs of the celestial kingdom of heaven. Gospel ordinances—baptisms, endowments, marriages, sealing—will be performed for them vicariously by those yet in mortality. (The Promised Messiah, pp. 240-41) TLDP:596-97

### Joseph Smith

I saw Father Adam and Abraham; and my father and my mother; my brother Alvin, that has long since slept; 6. And marveled how it was that he had obtained an inheritance in that kingdom, seeing that he had departed this life before the

Lord had set his hand to gather Israel the second time, and had not been baptized for the remission of sins. 7. Thus came the voice of the Lord unto me, saying: All who have died without a knowledge of this gospel, who would have received it if they had been permitted to tarry, shall be heirs of the celestial kingdom of God; 8. Also all that shall die henceforth without a knowledge of it, who would have received it with all their hearts, shall be heirs of that kingdom. 9. For I, the Lord, will judge all men according to their works, according to the desire of their hearts. (*Vision received in Kirtland Temple; Joseph sees his brother Alvin in the celestial kingdom, Jan. 21, 1836*) D&C 137:5-9

**Elder Joseph Fielding Smith**
All who hear and believe, repenting and receiving the gospel in its fulness, whether living or dead, are heirs of salvation in the celestial kingdom of God. (Doctrines of Salvation, 2:133) DGSM:85

**Elder Joseph Fielding Smith**
Those who keep the full law and obey all the commandments of God are heirs of full salvation in the celestial kingdom, the glory of which the sun is spoken of as being typical. These overcome all things and receive a fulness of the blessings, power, and glory of the Father. All who have died without a knowledge of the gospel, or the opportunity to receive it, who would have accepted it had the opportunity been presented to them while living, are also heirs of this kingdom. (Doctrines of Salvation, 2:21) TLDP:129

**Related Witnesses:**
**President John Taylor**
He [Christ] has told us . . . to build Temples. What for? To administer in them. Who for? For the dead who have died without a knowledge of the Gospel, that they might participate with us in the blessings which they had not the privilege of enjoying on the earth. . . . We are making preparations for saving the dead, according to the word of God. (*At quarterly conference of Salt Lake Stake, Jan. 6, 1879, JD20:118*) TLDP:675

**President Joseph F. Smith**
Thus was the gospel preached to those who had died in their sins, without a knowledge of the truth, or in transgression, having rejected the prophets. 33. These were taught faith in God, repentance from sin, vicarious baptism for the remission of sins, the gift of the Holy Ghost by the laying on of hands. 34. And all other principles of the gospel that were necessary for them to know in order to qualify themselves that they might be judged according to men in

the flesh, but live according to God in the spirit. (*Vision regarding the Savior's visit to the spirits of the dead, Oct. 3, 1918*) D&C 138:32-34

---

**131. The prophet Elijah restored to Joseph Smith the sealing power— power to seal together those who dwell on earth, and to seal those on earth to those who dwell in heaven.**

**Elder Joseph Fielding Smith**
The keys that Elijah held were the keys of the everlasting priesthood, the keys of the sealing power, which the Lord gave unto him. And that is what he . . . gave to the Prophet Joseph Smith; and that included a ministry of sealing for the living as well as the dead and it is not confined to the living and it is not confined to the dead, but includes them both. . . . ¶ Elijah's mission was the sealing power. He held the keys by which the parents could be sealed together and children sealed to parents. He bestowed these keys upon the Prophet Joseph Smith. And that applies to the dead as well as the living since the coming of the Lord Jesus Christ. ¶ But what was the nature of his mission to the earth in these latter days? It was to restore power and authority which once was given to men on the earth and which is essential to the complete salvation and exaltation of man in the kingdom of God. In other words, Elijah came to restore to the earth, by conferring on mortal prophets duly commissioned of the Lord, the fulness of the power of priesthood. This priesthood holds the keys of binding and sealing on earth and in heaven of all the ordinances and principles pertaining to the salvation of man, that they may thus become valid in the celestial kingdom of God. (Doctrines of Salvation, 2:111-12,17) DCSM:7

**Elder Joseph Fielding Smith**
According to that which has been revealed through the restoration of the sealing power of Elijah, the crowning blessing in the restoration of his keys, is the authority to seal both on earth and in heaven, husbands and wives and children to parents. Malachi said that if this authority was not restored the Lord would "come and smite the earth with a curse." Elijah, when he delivered his authority, said that the great and dreadful day of the Lord was near, even at the doors. (The Restoration of All Things, pp. 252-53) TLDP:190-91

**Joseph Smith**
What is this office and work of Elijah? It is one

of the greatest and most important subjects that God has revealed. He should send Elijah to seal the children to the fathers, and the fathers to the children. ¶ Now was this merely confined to the living, to settle difficulties with families on earth? By no means. It was a far greater work. Elijah! what would you do if you were here? Would you confine your work to the living alone? No; I would refer you to the Scriptures, where the subject is manifest: that is, without us, they could not be made perfect, nor we without them; the fathers without the children, nor the children without the fathers. . . . ¶ The doctrine or sealing power of Elijah is as follows:—If you have power to seal on earth and in heaven, then we should be wise. The first thing you do, go and seal on earth your sons and daughters unto yourself, and yourself unto your fathers in eternal glory. *(Sunday sermon on Elijah and Elias, March 10, 1844)* HC6:251-52,54

**Related Witnesses:**

**Elder Joseph Fielding Smith**

I am sure you agree with me that he has already appeared, for we have it so recorded by the testimony of witnesses. [See section 110.] It was on the third day of April, 1836, when he came to the Kirtland Temple, to Joseph Smith and Oliver Cowdery, and conferred upon them the keys of his priesthood and told them that he came in fulfillment of the prophecy of Malachi, to turn the hearts of the fathers to the children and the children to their fathers, lest the whole earth be smitten with a curse. CR1948Apr:132

**LeGrand Richards**

Just think of the consequences if the hearts of the fathers are not turned to their children and the hearts of the children turned to the fathers, and no one in this world outside of this Church can tell you the true meaning of those words, nor would we be able to do so except for the fact that Elijah did come and appeared to the Prophet Joseph Smith and Oliver Cowdery in the Kirtland Temple, and he revealed these great truths to them. That accounts for our building these holy temples all over the world, so that with the power of the priesthood of God that has been restored in our day, men and women can be sealed together for time and for all eternity and know that their children shall be born under the new and everlasting covenant and shall be theirs throughout the countless ages of eternity. CR1962Oct:109

**Joseph Smith**

After this vision had closed, another great and glorious vision burst upon us; for Elijah the prophet, who was taken to heaven without tasting death, stood before us, and said: 14.

Behold, the time has fully come, which was spoken of by the mouth of Malachi—testifying that he [Elijah] should be sent, before the great and dreadful day of the Lord come— 15. To turn the hearts of the fathers to the children, and the children to the fathers, lest the whole earth be smitten with a curse— 16. Therefore, the keys of this dispensation are committed into your hands; and by this ye may know that the great and dreadful day of the Lord is near, even at the doors. *(Visions manifested to Joseph Smith and Oliver Cowdery in the Kirtland Temple, April 3, 1836)* D&C 110:13-16

**Mark E. Petersen**

Adam brought the keys of the First Presidency. Joseph Smith received the keys of the First Presidency from Adam, who came back and visited him. Joseph Smith received the power of the gathering of Israel through Moses, who came back to see him. Elijah brought back the powers that we use in connection with our temple work. ACR(Mexico City)1972:61

**Boyd K. Packer**

I have found that many members of the Church have a very limited view of what the sealing power is. Since it is used most frequently in connection with temple marriages, the word seal has come to mean, in the minds of many Church members, simply that—sealing two people in the eternal marriage bond. It is also used to designate the ordinance by which children who have not been born in the covenant are "sealed" to their parents. Other members of the Church have the idea that the sealing authority that Elijah brought had to do solely with baptism for the dead. ¶ The authority is much more inclusive than that. The keys of the sealing power are synonymous with the keys of the everlasting priesthood. . . . ¶ Peter was to hold the sealing power, that authority which carries the power to bind or seal on earth or to loose on earth and it would be so in the heavens. Those keys belong to the President of the Church—to the prophet, seer, and revelator. That sacred sealing power is with the Church now. Nothing is regarded with more sacred contemplation by those who know the significance of this authority. Nothing is more closely held. There are relatively few men who hold this sealing power upon the earth at any given time—in each temple are brethren who have been given the sealing power. No one can get it except from the prophet, seer, and revelator and President of The Church of Jesus Christ of Latter-day Saints. It is more closely held than any other authority. I am an Apostle and in company with fourteen other men now living hold all of the keys. I have the sealing power. It was given to me at the time of my ordination, as is true of all the Brethren who hold membership in the First Presidency and the Quorum of the Twelve. I can seal and I can loose according to the directions given by the President of the Church. But I cannot give this authority to another. If another is to have it, he must get it from that one man on the earth who has the right to exercise all the keys of the priesthood. We know from the revelations that there will be but one at a time on the earth who has this right. (The Holy Temple, pp. 84-85) TLDP:619

**Joseph Smith**

I wish you to understand this subject, for it is important; and if you will receive it, this is the spirit of Elijah, that we redeem our dead, and connect ourselves with our fathers which are in heaven, and seal up our dead to come forth in the first resurrection; and here we want the power of Elijah to seal those who dwell on earth to those who dwell in heaven. This is the power of Elijah and the keys of the kingdom of Jehovah. (*Sermon, March 10, 1844*) HC6:252; DGSM:86

**Author's Note:** The importance of this mission of Elijah can be seen by its early mention to the boy Joseph by the angel Moroni in 1823: "And again, he quoted the fifth verse thus: Behold, I will reveal unto you the Priesthood, by the hand of Elijah the prophet, before the coming of the great and dreadful day of the Lord. 39. He also quoted the next verse differently: And he shall plant in the hearts of the children the promises made to the fathers, and the hearts of the children shall turn to their fathers. If it were not so, the whole earth would be utterly wasted at his coming." (JS-H 1:38-39) ¶ And, Malachi foretold the event some four hundred years before the birth of Christ: "Behold, I will send you Elijah the prophet before the coming of the great and dreadful day of the LORD: 6. And he shall turn the heart of the fathers to the children, and the heart of the children to their fathers, lest I come and smite the earth with a curse." (Mal.4:5-6)

---

### 132. We are to perform vicarious baptisms for the dead.

**Joseph Smith**

It is not only necessary that you should be baptized for your dead, but you will have to go through all the ordinances for them, the same as you have gone through to save yourselves. (*To*

*the Church in Nauvoo, Ill., May 12, 1844*) HC6:365; DGSM:86

**Joseph Smith**

. . . I now resume the subject of the baptism for the dead, as that subject seems to occupy my mind, and press itself upon my feelings the strongest, since I have been pursued by my enemies. . . . 5. You may think this order of things to be very particular; but let me tell you that it is only to answer the will of God, by conforming to the ordinance and preparation that the Lord ordained and prepared before the foundation of the world, for the salvation of the dead who should die without a knowledge of the gospel. (*Joseph writes to the Church giving further directions on baptism for the dead, Sept. 6, 1842*) D&C 128:1,5

**Elder Heber J. Grant**

The Latter-day Saints [believe] in baptism for the dead, in salvation for those who [have] died without a knowledge of the Gospel—that all human beings should have the privilege of receiving or rejecting the Gospel. ("Sunday Services," Deseret Weekly, April 23, 1892, p. 593) TLDP:61

**Boyd K. Packer**

We have been authorized to perform baptisms vicariously so that when they [the dead] hear the gospel preached and desire to accept it, that essential ordinance will have been performed. They need not ask for any exemption from that essential ordinance. Indeed, the Lord Himself was not exempted from it. CR1975Oct:147

**N. Eldon Tanner**

We know by the scriptures that the gospel is preached to the dead and the dead are to be judged according to men in the flesh and live according to God in the spirit. Thus baptism is necessary for those who, during their lifetime, had no opportunity for this ordinance of baptism by immersion for the remission of sin. CR1979Apr:20

**Paul**

Else what shall they do which are baptized for the dead, if the dead rise not at all? why are they then baptized for the dead? (*Paul writes to the Church at Corinth, Greece, about A.D. 55*) 1Cor.15:29

**Elder Wilford Woodruff,**
*also quoting Paul*

They will not baptize anybody in the spirit world; there is no baptism there; there is no marrying or giving in marriage there; all these ordinances have to be performed on the earth. Paul says, in referring to this subject—"Why are ye baptized for the dead? If the dead rise not why then are ye baptized for the dead?" The

Lord holds us responsible for going to and building Temples, that we may attend therein to the ordinances necessary for the salvation of the dead. *(In new Tabernacle, Sept. 12, 1875, JD18:114)* TLDP:61

**President Wilford Woodruff**

We have a great work before us in the redemption of our dead. . . . Those persons may receive their testimony, but they cannot be baptized in the spirit world, for somebody on the earth must perform this ordinance for them in the flesh before they can receive part in the first resurrection, and be worthy of eternal life. It takes as much to save a dead man as a living one. . . . Have we any time to spend in trying to get rich and in neglecting our dead? I tell you no. *(At Bountiful, Utah, June 26, 1881, JD22:234)* TLDP:61

**President Joseph F. Smith**

Thus was the gospel preached to those who had died in their sins, without a knowledge of the truth, or in transgression, having rejected the prophets. 33. These were taught faith in God, repentance from sin, vicarious baptism for the remission of sins, the gift of the Holy Ghost by the laying on of hands. *(Vision regarding the Savior's visit to the spirits of the dead, Oct. 3, 1918)* D&C 138:32-33

---

133. The Saints in the latter days cannot be made perfect without doing the ordinance work for their dead, nor can the dead be made perfect without this work being done for them.

**James E. Talmage**

One of the fundamental principles underlying the doctrine of salvation for the dead, is that of the mutual dependance of the fathers and the children. Family lineage and the sequence of generations in each particular line of descent are facts, and cannot be changed by earth; on the other hand it is evident from the olden scriptures . . . attested by the equally sure word of modern revelation, that the family relationships of earth are recognized in the spirit world. Neither the children nor the fathers, neither progenitors nor descendants, can alone attain perfection; and the requisite co-operation is effected through baptism and related ordinances, administered to the living in behalf of the dead. ¶ In this way and through this work are the hearts of the fathers and those of the children turned toward each other. As the living children learn that without their ancestors

they cannot attain a perfect status in the eternal world, their own faith will be strengthened and they will be willing to labor for the redemption and salvation of their dead. And the dead, learning through the preaching of the Gospel in their world, that they are dependent upon their descendants as vicarious saviors, will turn with loving faith and prayerful effort toward their children yet living. HL:83-84

**Joseph Smith**

And now, my dearly beloved brethren and sisters, let me assure you that these are principles in relation to the dead and the living that cannot be lightly passed over, as pertaining to our salvation. For their salvation is necessary and essential to our salvation, as Paul says concerning the fathers—that they without us cannot be made perfect—neither can we without our dead be made perfect. 18. I might have rendered a plainer translation to this, but it is sufficiently plain to suit my purpose as it stands. It is sufficient to know, in this case, that the earth will be smitten with a curse unless there is a welding link of some kind or other between the fathers and the children, upon some subject or other—and behold what is that subject? It is the baptism for the dead. For we without them cannot be made perfect; neither can they without us be made perfect. Neither can they nor we be made perfect without those who have died in the gospel also; for it is necessary in the ushering in of the dispensation of the fulness of times, which dispensation is now beginning to usher in, that a whole and complete and perfect union, and welding together of dispensations, and keys, and powers, and glories should take place, and be revealed from the days of Adam even to the present time. And not only this, but those things which never have been revealed from the foundation of the world, but have been kept hid from the wise and prudent, shall be revealed unto babes and sucklings in this, the dispensation of the fulness of times. *(Joseph writes to the Church giving further directions on baptism for the dead, Sept. 6, 1842)* D&C 128:15,18

**President Brigham Young**

We have a work to do just as important in its sphere as the Savior's work was in its sphere. Our fathers cannot be made perfect without us; we cannot be made perfect without them. They have done their work. . . . We are now called upon to do ours; which is to be the greatest work man ever performed on the earth. Millions of our fellow creatures who have lived upon the earth and died without a knowledge of the Gospel must be officiated for in order that they may inherit eternal life (that is, all that would have received the Gospel). And we are called upon to enter into this work. *(At Logan, Utah, Aug. 15, 1876, JD18:213)* TLDP:592-93

### Elder Ezra Taft Benson,
### *also quoting Paul*

Our members need to be taught that it is not sufficient for a husband and wife to be sealed in the temple to guarantee their exaltation—they must also be eternally linked with their progenitors and see that the work is done for those ancestors. "They without us," said the Apostle Paul, "cannot be made perfect—neither can we without our dead be made perfect" (D&C 128:15). Our members should therefore understand that they have an individual responsibility to see that they are linked to their progenitors. *(To regional representatives, April 3, 1981)* DGSM:86

### Joseph Smith

In the days of Noah, God destroyed the world by a flood, and He has promised to destroy it by fire in the last days: but before it should take place, Elijah should first come and turn the hearts of the fathers to the children, &c. ¶ Now comes the point. What is this office and work of Elijah? It is one of the greatest and most important subjects that God has revealed. He should send Elijah to seal the children to the fathers, and the fathers to the children. ¶ Now was this merely confined to the living, to settle difficulties with families on earth? By no means. It was a far greater work. Elijah! what would you do if you were here? Would you confine your work to the living alone? No; I would refer you to the Scriptures, where the subject is manifest: that is, without us, they could not be made perfect, nor we without them; the fathers without the children, nor the children without the fathers. ¶ I wish you to understand this subject, for it is important; and if you will receive it, this is the spirit of Elijah, that we redeem our dead, and connect ourselves with our fathers which are in heaven, and seal up our dead to come forth in the first resurrection; and here we want the power of Elijah to seal those who dwell on earth to those who dwell in heaven. This is the power of Elijah and the keys of the kingdom of Jehovah. *(Sermon at the Stand, Nauvoo, Ill., Mar. 10, 1844)* HC6:251-52

### John A. Widtsoe

In our preexistent state, in the day of the great council, we made a certain agreement with the Almighty. The Lord proposed a plan, conceived by him. We accepted it. Since the plan is intended for all men, we become parties to the salvation of every person under that plan. We agreed, right then and there, to be not only saviours for ourselves but measurably, saviours for the whole human family. We went into a partnership with the Lord. The working out of the plan became then not merely the Father's work, and the Saviour's work, but also our work. The least of us, the humblest, is in partnership with the Almighty in achieving the purpose of the eternal plan of salvation. (Utah Genealogical and Historical Magazine, Oct. 1934) DCSM:8; MPSG1967:87

### Related Witnesses:
### Paul

God having provided some better thing for us, that they without us should not be made perfect. *(Paul writes to the Jewish members of the Church on faith, about A.D. 60)* Heb.11:40

### Elder Joseph Fielding Smith

There is a feeling existing among some members of the Church that because the Prophet declared that we without our dead cannot be made perfect, the work in the temples will have to be performed for all the dead. This is an error. What is intended by this remark is that we cannot be made perfect without our dead who are worthy and entitled to salvation. There will be a great host of the dead who will not be entitled to the ordinances of exaltation and who will not be made perfect. Perfection is in the celestial kingdom only, and those who enter the other kingdoms and who are restricted will be as countless as the stars of heaven. Few, there will be, who will be saved. (Matt.7:13-14) CHMR2:329-30

### Joseph Smith

It is not only necessary that you should be baptized for your dead, but you will have to go through all the ordinances for them, the same as you have gone through to save yourselves. *(To the Church in Nauvoo, Ill., May 12, 1844)* HC6:365; DGSM:86

### Elder Wilford Woodruff

No man can enter into the kingdom of God except he is born of the water and of the Spirit. Men may be judged and their bodies lie in the grave until the last resurrection, to come forth and receive of the telestial glory, but no man will receive of the celestial glory except it be through the ordinances of the House of God. *(In Tabernacle, June 30, 1878, JD19:361)* TLDP:53

### Elder Wilford Woodruff,
### *also quoting Paul*

They will not baptize anybody in the spirit world; there is no baptism there; there is no marrying or giving in marriage there; all these ordinances have to be performed on the earth. Paul says, in referring to this subject—"Why are ye baptized for the dead? If the dead rise not why then are ye baptized for the dead?" The Lord holds us responsible for going to and building Temples, that we may attend therein to the ordinances necessary for the salvation of the dead. *(In new Tabernacle, Sept. 12, 1875, JD18:114)* TLDP:61

### Elder Joseph Fielding Smith

Why is this such a grave responsibility? For two reasons. First, because we cannot enter into the perfect life without our worthy dead who have not been blessed as we have with the Gospel. Second, because they who have lived worthy lives, but in darkness, because the Gospel did not come to them in life, are also heirs of salvation. (The Way to Perfection, p. 153) TLDP:592

---

134. The hearts of the children shall be turned to their ancestors in such a manner that the children will desire to seek the records of their dead ancestors and perform the necessary ordinances for them.

### Elder Joseph Fielding Smith

The fathers are our dead ancestors who died without the privilege of receiving the gospel, but who received the promise that the time would come when that privilege would be granted them. The children are those now living who are preparing genealogical data and who are performing the vicarious ordinances in the temples. ¶ The turning of the hearts of the children to the fathers is placing or planting in the hearts of the children that feeling and desire which will inspire them to search out the records of the dead. Moreover the planting of the desire and inspiration in their hearts is necessary. This they must have in order that they might go into the house of the Lord and perform the necessary labor for their fathers, who died without a knowledge of the gospel, or without the privilege of receiving the fulness of the gospel. (Doctrines of Salvation, 2:127-28) DCSM:7-8

### Melvin J. Ballard

The dead know where their records are, so you are to search until you have gone as far as you can. But, of course, there are hosts of men and women in the Spirit World whose records don't exist anywhere on the earth, but whose record is in the Spirit World. ¶ When you have done all you can and have reached the limit, what

will happen? As always in the past, man's extremity is God's opportunity: The Lord never helps us while we can help ourselves. This is our day. We don't expect Him to do miraculous things that we can do ourselves. When we have done our utmost, then will come God's opportunity. Don't think for a moment that the temples will close. They will go on all through the Millennium. Great hosts of the dead in the Spirit World are waiting for this work. Should it not stir us to do everything to relieve them of their distress? It surely should. When we have done our utmost, then will come the day when the authorities that preside on the other side will come and make known all who have received the Gospel in the Spirit World, and everyone entitled to have their work done. That is the simplest thing in the world. When the Lord is ready, it will be very simple and very easy. We can speed that day by doing now the work that we can do. ("The Inspiration of Temple Work," Utah Genealogical and Historical Magazine, Oct. 1932, pp 148-49) TLDP:602

### George F. Richards

We have our dead also to seek after, those of our immediate ancestors, our blood kindred, many of whom were noble men and women who lived their lives here in mortality, according to the best light and knowledge they had, but were deprived of the privileges which we enjoy of the Gospel and its saving ordinances. We have the responsibility of finding these out by genealogical research, obtaining information which is necessary to identify them upon the records of the Church and of the Temple, and then after receiving these saving ordinances ourselves, to act vicariously for the dead in receiving those ordinances. . . . ¶ The Lord has said through the Prophet Joseph that there is no greater responsibility that he has laid upon us than that of looking after our kindred dead. ¶ This missionary work for the living and the dead is the highest service in which man can be employed, and, I think I might say, that can employ the attention of the Gods, for all that we know of their works that have been revealed unto us are looking to this worthy end the saving of the souls of men. CR1939Oct:109-10

### Joseph Smith

The Bible says, "I will send you Elijah the Prophet before the coming of the great and dreadful day of the Lord; and he shall turn the hearts of the fathers to the children, and the hearts of the children to the fathers, lest I come and smite the earth with a curse." Now, the word turn here should be translated bind, or seal. But what is the object of this important mission? or how is it to be fulfilled? . . . By building their temples, erecting their baptismal fonts, and going forth and receiving all the ordinances, baptisms, confirmations, washings, anointings, ordinations and sealing powers upon their heads, in behalf of all their progenitors who are dead, and redeem them that they may come forth in the first resurrection and be exalted to thrones of glory with them; and herein is the chain that binds the hearts of the fathers to the children, and the children to the fathers, which fulfills the mission of Elijah. (*Discourse on the sealing power in the Priesthood, at southeast corner of Nauvoo Temple, Jan. 21, 1844*) HC6:183-84

**Related Witnesses:**

### Matthew Cowley

It is a matter of historical record that God was to send Elijah the prophet before the coming of the great and dreadful day of the Lord to turn the hearts of the children to the fathers and the hearts of the fathers to the children, lest the earth be smitten with a curse. It is a matter of historical fact that in this dispensation Elijah has returned to the earth, for the hearts of the children have been turned to their parents and those of the parents to the children. CR1950Oct:25

### Joseph Smith

He also quoted the next verse differently: "And he shall plant in the hearts of the children the promises made to the fathers, and the hearts of the children shall turn to their fathers. If it were not so the whole earth would be utterly wasted at his coming." (*Joseph relates the angel Moroni's visit to him, Sept. 21, 1823*) JS-H 1:39

### Malachi

Behold, I will send you Elijah the prophet before the coming of the great and dreadful day of the LORD: 6. And he shall turn the heart of the fathers to the children, and the heart of the children to their fathers, lest I come and smite the earth with a curse. (*The prophet Malachi to the people, about 430 B.C.*) Mal.4:5-6

### Jesus,
### *quoting Malachi,*
### *quoted by Mormon*

Behold, I will send you Elijah the prophet before the coming of the great and dreadful day of the Lord; 6. And he shall turn the heart of the fathers to the children, and the heart of the children to their fathers, lest I come and smite the earth with a curse. (*The resurrected Jesus Christ teaches the Nephite people, A.D. 34*) 3Ne.25:5-6

### Joseph Smith

Behold, I will reveal unto you the Priesthood, by the hand of Elijah the prophet, before the coming of the great and dreadful day of the Lord. 2. And he shall plant in the hearts of the children the promises made to the fathers, and the hearts of the children shall turn to their fathers. 3. If it were not so, the whole earth would be utterly wasted at his coming. (*Extract from words of the angel Moroni to Joseph Smith, Sept. 21, 1823*) D&C 2:1-3

### Joseph Smith

After this vision had closed, another great and glorious vision burst upon us; for Elijah the prophet, who was taken to heaven without tasting death, stood before us, and said: 14. Behold, the time has fully come, which was spoken of by the mouth of Malachi—testifying that he [Elijah] should be sent, before the great and dreadful day of the Lord come— 15. To turn the hearts of the fathers to the children, and the children to the fathers, lest the whole earth be smitten with a curse— 16. Therefore, the keys of this dispensation are committed into your hands; and by this ye may know that the great and dreadful day of the Lord is near, even at the doors. (*Visions manifested to Joseph Smith and Oliver Cowdery in the Kirtland Temple, April 3, 1836*) D&C 110:13-16

# List of Doctrines

## DEGREES OF GLORY

*Doctrines Located in This Topic*

### (1) The Celestial Kingdom

135. Eternal life means life in the celestial kingdom of God.

136. The aim of the gospel and the Church is to bring all people into the celestial kingdom of God (not into the terrestrial or telestial kingdoms).

137. To merit the gift of eternal life in the celestial kingdom, we must be baptized and receive the gift of the Holy Ghost, render obedience to the laws and ordinances of the gospel, and endure to the end.

138. If those who did not have opportunity to accept the gospel in mortality accept it in the spirit world, they may inherit the celestial kingdom.

139. In the celestial kingdom there are three heavens or degrees.

140. Salvation in its truest sense means exaltation in the highest degree of the celestial kingdom.

141. All people will be *saved* from death, but not all will receive the *salvation of exaltation* or *eternal life* in the celestial kingdom of God.

142. To receive exaltation (the highest degree in the celestial kingdom) a person must be married in the new and everlasting covenant.

143. Those who inherit the highest degree of the celestial kingdom will have eternal increase, becoming parents of spirit offspring.

144. Those who inherit exaltation in the celestial kingdom will thereafter become gods.

145. The celestial kingdom was prepared, before the world began, to receive the faithful.

### (2) The Terrestrial Kingdom

146. The terrestrial kingdom exceeds the telestial kingdom in glory, in power, in might, and in dominion.

147. Honorable people of the earth who refused the gospel in mortality, but in the spirit world repented and accepted it, will inherit the terrestrial kingdom.

148. Those who accepted the gospel in mortality but were not valiant, may not inherit the celestial kingdom.

149. The torment of those who are damned is the knowledge that if they had kept the commandments they might have achieved a greater glory.

### (3) The Telestial Kingdom

150. The glory and grandeur of the telestial kingdom surpasses all human understanding.

151. Those who will inherit the telestial kingdom will be the wicked people of the earth, such as adulterers and deliberate liars.

152. Those who are to inhabit the telestial kingdom are first cast down to hell in the spirit world before they are redeemed from the devil in the last resurrection.

153. The inhabitants of the telestial kingdom will be as innumerable as the stars.

154. The telestial kingdom is comprised of several subdivisions.

*Doctrines on DEGREES OF GLORY Located in Other Topics*

74. Little children who die before they reach the age of accountability are saved in the celestial kingdom.

101. We must keep all the commandments and endure to the end in order to receive the gift of eternal life in the celestial kingdom of God.

171. The earth will be sanctified and will become the celestial kingdom, which the righteous shall inherit.

208. Married persons who achieve exaltation (in the highest degree of the celestial kingdom) will enjoy eternal increase, having children in the celestial kingdom.

302. A physical body is essential to obtaining a fulness of joy in the celestial kingdom of God.

367. Only by entering the kingdom of God (the celestial kingdom) can we realize a fulness of joy.

383. Every person in the final judgment will be saved in a kingdom of glory (except the sons of perdition, who are cast into outer darkness).

384. There are three principle kingdoms, or degrees of glory, to which we are assigned after mortality.

385. At the final judgment we will be assigned to that degree of glory that we are willing to receive and able to abide.

427. Without charity (the pure love of Christ), we cannot enter into the celestial kingdom.

436. The temple marriage sealing ordinance is essential for exaltation in the celestial kingdom (it is a prerequisite to exaltation in the highest degree of the celestial kingdom).

## DEGREES OF GLORY continued

492. We must receive all the essential ordinances of the gospel if we are to gain exaltation in the celestial kingdom of God.

761. Because no unclean thing can inherit the celestial kingdom, we cannot enter that kingdom unless we have repented of our sins.

# DEGREES OF GLORY

**(1) The Celestial Kingdom**
**(2) The Terrestrial Kingdom**
**(3) The Telestial Kingdom**

## (1) The Celestial Kingdom

135. Eternal life means life in the celestial kingdom of God.

### Bruce R. McConkie
Eternal life is life in the highest heaven of the celestial world; it is exaltation; it is the name of the kind of life God lives. It consists of a continuation of the family unit in eternity. ("The Salvation of Little Children," EN1977Apr:5) TLDP:604

### Joseph Smith,
*receiving the Word of the Lord*
This Comforter is the promise which I give unto you of eternal life, even the glory of the celestial kingdom; (*Revelation received Dec. 27/28, 1832*) D&C 88:4

### Joseph Smith,
*receiving the Word of the Lord*
Therefore, I must gather together my people, according to the parable of the wheat and the tares, that the wheat may be secured in the garners to possess eternal life, and be crowned with celestial glory, when I shall come in the kingdom of my Father to reward every man according as his work shall be; (*Revelation received Dec. 16, 1833*) D&C 101:65

### Orson F. Whitney
God's greatest gift is eternal life, but that pertains to Eternity. The greatest blessing that our Heavenly Father can bestow upon us in time, or while we are here, is the power to lay hold upon eternal life. The everlasting Gospel, through obedience to its every requirement, and the gift of the Holy Ghost, gives this power. It not only saves—it exalts men to where God and Christ dwell in the fulness of celestial glory. CR1929Oct:30

**Related Witnesses:**
### Joseph Smith
Here, then, is eternal life—to know the only wise and true God; and you have got to learn how to be gods yourselves, and to be kings and priests to God, the same as all gods have done before you, namely, by going from one small degree to another, and from a small capacity to a great one; from grace to grace, from exaltation to exaltation, until you attain to the resurrection of the dead, and are able to dwell in everlasting burnings, and to sit in glory, as do those who sit enthroned in everlasting power.(*To the Church in General Conference—a congregation of 20,000—, "King Follett Sermon", April 7, 1844*) (See HC6:302-317, also see The Words of Joseph Smith, pp. 340-62.) HC6:306

### Marion G. Romney
Eternal life is the quality of life which God himself enjoys. The gospel plan, authored by the Father and put into operation by the atonement of Jesus Christ, brings eternal life within the reach of every man. The Lord gave this assurance when he said, ". . . if you keep my commandments and endure to the end you shall have eternal life, . . . " CR1965Oct:20

### Joseph Smith,
*translating the Book of Moses*
For behold, this is my work and my glory—to bring to pass the immortality and eternal life of man. (*The Lord talks to Moses face to face*) Moses 1:39

---

136. The aim of the gospel and the Church is to bring all people into the celestial kingdom of God (not into the terrestrial or telestial kingdoms).

### Elder George Albert Smith
The gospel has been restored in these latter days to prepare men for the celestial kingdom. This gospel has not been given to qualify men for any other kingdom, but has been given to us to prepare us that we may dwell upon this earth when it has been celestialized, when our Redeemer will dwell here and he will be our lawgiver and our king. CR1926Oct:102-03

### John A. Widtsoe
Now the concern of the Church is to bring all men into the celestial kingdom. It has no interest in the other, lower kingdoms. Every doctrine, principle, and item of organization within the Church pertains to the celestial glory. The manner of entrance into this the highest kingdom, is therefore made clear. Any person who wishes to enter it must have faith and repent from his sins. Then he must be baptized, and receive the gift of the Holy Ghost by one who has divine authority to perform such ordinances. There are principles and ordinances which in their entirety belong peculiarly to the higher kingdom. ¶ After having laid the foundation for his claim to celestial membership and association, he must, to receive all available blessings of this kingdom, comply with the

many requirements of life within the Church. He belongs to "those who are valiant and inspired with the true independence of heaven, who will go forth boldly in the service of their God leaving others to do as they please, determined to do right, though all mankind should take the opposite course." All this having been done, he is qualified to enter the celestial kingdom. Indeed, he is then, even on earth, in the celestial kingdom of God. (Evidences and Reconciliations, pp. 200-01) TLDP:163-64

### George Q. Cannon

I think it is of great importance to us as a people to know what we shall do. Are we content to aim for telestial glory? I never heard a prayer offered, especially in the family circle, in which the family does not beseech God to give them celestial glory. Telestial glory is not in their thoughts. Terrestrial glory may be all right for honorable Gentiles, who have not faith enough to believe the Gospel and who do right according to the best knowledge they have; but celestial glory is our aim. . . . ¶ . . . . All that I am on this earth for is to get celestial glory. CR1900Apr:55-56

### Orson F. Whitney

God's greatest gift is eternal life, but that pertains to Eternity. The greatest blessing that our Heavenly Father can bestow upon us in time, or while we are here, is the power to lay hold upon eternal life. The everlasting Gospel, through obedience to its every requirement, and the gift of the Holy Ghost, gives this power. It not only saves—it exalts men to where God and Christ dwell in the fulness of celestial glory. CR1929Oct:30

### Orson F. Whitney

The gospel of Christ is more than "the power of God unto salvation;" it is the power of God unto exaltation, and was instituted as such before this earth rolled into existence, before Adam fell, and consequently before man had need of redemption and salvation. It is the way of eternal progress, the path to perfection. . . . CR1920Apr:122

### Related Witnesses:
### Joseph Smith,
### translating the Book of Moses

For behold, this is my work and my glory—to bring to pass the immortality and eternal life of man. (The Lord talks to Moses face to face) Moses 1:39

### Elder Wilford Woodruff

I always have said and believed, and I believe today, that it will pay you and me and all the sons and daughters of Adam to abide the celestial law, for celestial glory is worth all we pos-

sess; if it calls for every dollar we own and our lives into the bargain, if we obtain an entrance into the celestial kingdom of God it will amply repay us. The Latter-day Saints have started out for celestial glory, and if we can only manage to be faithful enough to obtain an inheritance in the kingdom, where God and Christ dwell, we shall rejoice through the endless ages of eternity. (General conference, Oct. 9, 1874, JD17:250) TLDP:128-29

### Marion G. Romney

This gift of eternal life in the world to come may not, of course, be fully realized during earth life. An assurance that it will be obtained in the world to come may, however, be had in this world. As a matter of fact, the blessings of the celestial kingdom are promised only to those who have such an assurance. According to the vision, a successful candidate for these blessings must qualify on three counts. First, he must have "received the testimony of Jesus, and believed on his name" and have been "baptized after the manner of his burial;" second, he must have received "the Holy Spirit by the laying on of the hands of him who is ordained and sealed unto this power;" and third, he must be "sealed by the Holy Spirit of promise." (D&C 76:51-53) (Learning for the Eternities, p. 95) TLDP:66

---

137. To merit the gift of eternal life in the celestial kingdom, we must be baptized and receive the gift of the Holy Ghost, render obedience to the laws and ordinances of the gospel, and endure to the end.

### Nephi, son of Lehi

For the gate by which ye should enter is repentance and baptism by water; and then cometh a remission of your sins by fire and by the Holy Ghost. 18. And then are ye in this strait and narrow path which leads to eternal life; yea, ye have entered in by the gate; ye have done according to the commandments of the Father and the Son; and ye have received the Holy Ghost, which witnesses of the Father and the Son, unto the fulfilling of the promise which he hath made, that if ye entered in by the way ye should receive. 19. And now, my beloved brethren, after ye have gotten into this strait and narrow path, I would ask if all is done? Behold, I say unto you, Nay; for ye have not come thus far save it were by the word of Christ with unshaken faith in him, relying wholly upon the merits of him who is mighty to save. 20. Wherefore, ye must press forward with a steadfastness in Christ, having a perfect brightness of hope, and a love of God and of all men. Wherefore, if ye shall press forward, feasting upon the word of Christ, and endure to the end, behold, thus saith the Father: Ye shall have eternal life. (*Nephi's writings, between 559-545 B.C.*) 2Ne.31:17-20

**Joseph Smith**

And again we bear record—for we saw and heard, and this is the testimony of the gospel of Christ concerning them who shall come forth in the resurrection of the just— 51. They are they who received the testimony of Jesus, and believed on his name and were baptized after the manner of his burial, being buried in the water in his name, and this according to the commandment which he has given— 52. That by keeping the commandments they might be washed and cleansed from all their sins, and receive the Holy Spirit by the laying on of the hands of him who is ordained and sealed unto this power; 53. And who overcome by faith, and are sealed by the Holy Spirit of promise, which the Father sheds forth upon all those who are just and true. . . . 62. These shall dwell in the presence of God and his Christ forever and ever. . . . 70. These are they whose bodies are celestial, whose glory is that of the sun, even the glory of God, the highest of all, whose glory the sun of the firmament is written of as being typical. (*Vision to Joseph Smith and Sidney Rigdon, Feb. 16, 1832*) D&C 76:50-53,62,70

**John A. Widtsoe**

The manner of entrance into this the highest kingdom, is therefore made clear. Any person who wishes to enter it must have faith and repent from his sins. Then he must be baptized, and receive the gift of the Holy Ghost by one who has divine authority to perform such ordinances. There are principles and ordinances which in their entirety belong peculiarly to the higher kingdom. ¶ After having laid the foundation for his claim to celestial membership and association, he must, to receive all available blessings of this kingdom, comply with the many requirements of life within the Church. He belongs to "those who are valiant and inspired with the true independence of heaven, who will go forth boldly in the service of their God leaving others to do as they please, determined to do right, though all mankind should take the opposite course." All this having been done, he is qualified to enter the celestial kingdom. Indeed, he is then, even on earth, in the celestial kingdom of God. . . . (*Evidences and Reconciliations, pp. 200-01*) TLDP:163-64

**Related Witnesses:**

**President Joseph F. Smith**

We believe that salvation is for no select few, but that all men may be saved through obedience to the laws and ordinances of the Gospel. (*Address from the First Presidency of the Church to the world, accepted by vote of the Church in general conference*) CR1907Apr(Appendix)4

**Joseph Smith**

A man may be saved, after the judgment, in the terrestrial kingdom or in the telestial kingdom but he can never see the celestial kingdom of God without being born of the water and the Spirit. He may receive a glory like unto the moon [i.e., of which the light of the moon is typical], or a star [i.e., of which the light of the stars is typical], but he can never come unto Mount Zion and unto the city of the living God, the heavenly Jerusalem, and to an innumerable company of angels; to the general assembly and Church of the Firstborn, which are written in heaven and to God the judge of all, and to the spirits of just men made perfect, and to Jesus the Mediator of the new covenant, unless he becomes as a little child, and is taught by the Spirit of God. (*Article in the Star, Aug. 1832*) HC1:283

**Joseph Smith**

We believe that through the Atonement of Christ, all mankind may be saved, by obedience to the laws and ordinances of the Gospel. (*The third of the thirteen Articles of Faith; letter to John Wentworth, March 1, 1842*) AofF:3

**Elder Joseph Fielding Smith**

Not all shall obtain the blessing of eternal life who partake of the blessing of immortality. The scriptures point out very clearly a difference. Immortality is the gift of God, through Jesus Christ, to all men; by which they come forth in the resurrection to die no more, whether they have obeyed him or rebelled against him. This great gift is theirs; even the wicked receive it through the grace of Jesus Christ, and shall have the privilege of living forever, but they will have to pay the price of their sins in torment with the devil before they are redeemed. ¶ Eternal life is a special blessing granted to a certain class because of their obedience to the commands of God. It is the greatest of all the gifts of God. (D&C 14:7) Those who receive it "are rich," for they obtain the riches of eternity, but it is only by traveling through the strait gate and path. (The Way to Perfection, pp. 328-29) TLDP:155-56

**Bruce R. McConkie**

Thus all men—except the sons of perdition who are cast out into an eternal hell—are saved, in that they become immortal and go to a telestial or terrestrial inheritance, but only those who believe and obey become inheritors of that celestial rest which the whole body of revealed writ speaks of as salvation. ¶ Eternal life is the name of the kind of life which God lives and is therefore "the greatest of all the gifts of God" (D&C 14:7); and because those who gain it become like God, they are one with him. (The Promised Messiah, p. 130) TLDP:154-55

---

138. **If those who did not have opportunity to accept the gospel in mortality accept it in the spirit world, they may inherit the celestial kingdom.**

### Elder Joseph Fielding Smith
All who have not had the privilege of repentance and acceptance of the plan of salvation in this life will have that opportunity in the world of spirits. ¶ Those who repent there and believe when the message is declared to them are heirs of salvation and exaltation. The ordinances which pertain to the mortal life will be performed for them in the temples. (Doctrines of Salvation, 2:134-35) TLDP:596

### Bruce R. McConkie
There is no such thing as a second chance to gain salvation. This life is the time and day of our probation. After this day of life, which is given us to prepare for eternity, then cometh the night of darkness where there can be no labor performed. ¶ For those who do not have an opportunity in this life, the first chance to gain salvation will come in the spirit world. If those who hear the word for the first time in the realms ahead are the kind of people who would have accepted the gospel here, had the opportunity been afforded them, they will accept it there. Salvation for the dead is for those whose first chance to gain salvation is in the spirit world. ¶ . . . . Those who reject the gospel in this life and then receive it in the spirit world go not to the celestial, but to the terrestrial kingdom. ("The Seven Deadly Heresies," Brigham Young University Speeches of the Year, 1980) DCSM:165

### Joseph Smith,
*receiving the Word of the Lord*
All who have died without a knowledge of this gospel, who would have received it if they had been permitted to tarry, shall be heirs of the celestial kingdom of God; 8. Also all that shall die henceforth without a knowledge of it, who would have received it with all their hearts, shall be heirs of that kingdom. 9. For I, the Lord, will judge all men according to their

works, according to the desire of their hearts. (*Vision to Joseph Smith in Kirtland Temple; Joseph sees his brother Alvin in the celestial kingdom, Jan. 21, 1836*) D&C 137:7-9

### Melvin J. Ballard
Now, I wish to say to you that those who died without law, meaning the pagan nations, for lack of faithfulness, for lack of devotion, in the former life, are obtaining all that they are entitled to. I don't mean to say that all of them will be barred from entrance into the highest glory. Any one of them who repents and complies with the conditions might also obtain celestial glory, but the great bulk of them will only obtain terrestrial glory. (Sermons of Melvin J. Ballard, p. 251) DCSM:164

### President Brigham Young
Millions of our fellow creatures who have lived upon the earth and died without a knowledge of the Gospel must be officiated for in order that they may inherit eternal life (that is, all that would have received the Gospel). And we are called upon to enter into this work. (*At Logan, Utah, Aug. 15, 1876, JD18:213*) TLDP:592-93

**Related Witnesses:**
### President Joseph F. Smith
Thus was the gospel preached to those who had died in their sins, without a knowledge of the truth, or in transgression, having rejected the prophets. 33. These were taught faith in God, repentance from sin, vicarious baptism for the remission of sins, the gift of the Holy Ghost by the laying on of hands. 34. And all other principles of the gospel that were necessary for them to know in order to qualify themselves that they might be judged according to men in the flesh, but live according to God in the spirit. 35. And so it was made known among the dead, both small and great, the unrighteous as well as the faithful, that redemption had been wrought through the sacrifice of the Son of God upon the cross. (*Vision of the Savior's visit to the spirits of the dead, Oct. 3, 1918*) D&C 138:32-35

---

139. **In the celestial kingdom there are three heavens or degrees.**

### Joseph Smith
In the celestial glory there are three heavens or degrees; . . . (*Instructions given by the Prophet, May 16/17, 1843*) D&C 131:1

### President Spencer W. Kimball,
*also quoting Joseph Smith*
No one who rejects the covenant of celestial marriage can reach exaltation in the eternal kingdom of God. ¶ "In the celestial glory there

are three heavens or degrees; ¶ And in order to obtain the highest, a man must enter into this order of the priesthood [meaning the new and everlasting covenant of marriage]; . . ." ¶ The Lord says further in the 132nd section of the Doctrine and Covenants: ¶ No one can reject this covenant and be permitted to enter into my glory. (D&C 132:4) ¶ No one! It matters not how righteous they may have been, how intelligent or how well trained they are. No one will enter this highest glory unless he enters into the covenant, and this means the new and everlasting covenant of marriage. ("The Importance of Celestial Marriage," EN1979Oct:5-6) DCSM:325-26

### John A. Widtsoe

Naturally, those who enter the celestial kingdom are of various attainments. There is not absolute uniformity anywhere among the children of God. Their innate capacities and their use of the law of free agency make them different, often widely so. Therefore, the members of the highest kingdom are also grouped, according to the Prophet Joseph Smith, into three "degrees." [See D&C 131:1.] (Evidences and Reconciliations, pp. 200-01) TLDP:163-64

### Related Witnesses:

#### Bruce R. McConkie

Eternal life is life in the highest heaven of the celestial world; it is exaltation; it is the name of the kind of life God lives. It consists of a continuation of the family unit in eternity. ("The Salvation of Little Children," EN1977Apr:5) TLDP:604

---

## 140. Salvation in its truest sense means exaltation in the highest degree of the celestial kingdom.

### Bruce R. McConkie,
#### *also quoting Joseph Smith*

Salvation means eternal life; the two terms are synonymous; they mean exactly the same thing. Joseph Smith said, "Salvation consists in the glory, authority, majesty, power and dominion which Jehovah possesses and in nothing else." (Lectures on Faith, pp. 63-67) We have come to speak of this salvation as exaltation—which it is—but all of the scriptures in all of the standard works call it salvation. I know of only three passages in all our scriptures which use salvation to mean something other and less than exaltation. ("The Salvation of Little Children," EN1977Apr:5) TLDP:154-55

### Joseph Smith

[F]or salvation consists in the glory, authority, majesty, power and dominion which Jehovah possesses and in nothing else; and no being can possess it but himself or one like him. (*Lectures on Faith delivered to the School of the Prophets, 1834-35*) LOF7:9

### President Brigham Young

What is life and salvation? It is to take that course wherein we can abide forever and ever, and be exalted to thrones, kingdoms, governments, dominions, and have full power to control the elements, according to our pleasure to all eternity. (*Special conference, Aug. 14, 1853, JD1:275*) TLDP:154

### Bruce R. McConkie

Eternal life: what is it and when shall its glories and blessing rest upon the saints? It is full salvation; it is an inheritance in the highest heaven; it is exaltation. It is to sit down with Abraham, Isaac, and Jacob in the kingdom of God, to go no more out. (The Mortal Messiah, 3:50-51) TLDP:154

### Bruce R. McConkie,
#### *also quoting Joseph Smith*

Eternal life is the name of the kind of life which God lives and is therefore "the greatest of all the gifts of God" (D&C 14:7); and because those who gain it become like God, they are one with him. ¶ Exaltation consists of an inheritance in the highest heaven of the celestial world, where alone the family unit continues and where each recipient gains for himself an eternal family unit, patterned after the family of God our Heavenly Father, so that every exalted person lives the kind of life which God lives and is therefore one with him. ¶ Salvation consists in gaining—and this is Joseph Smith's language—"the glory, authority, majesty, power and dominion which Jehovah possesses and in nothing else; and no being can possess it but himself or one like him" (Lectures on Faith, cited in Mormon Doctrine, 2nd ed., p. 258), and since he is one with his Father, so also are all saved beings. Truly, "There is no gift greater than the gift of salvation." (D&C 6:13) ¶ Thus, to be saved, to gain exaltation, to inherit eternal life, all means to be one with God, to live as he lives, to think as he thinks, to act as he acts, to possess the same glory, the same power, the same might and dominion that he possesses. (The Promised Messiah, p. 130) TLDP:154-55

### Bruce R. McConkie

Thus all men—except the sons of perdition who are cast out into an eternal hell—are saved, in that they become immortal and go to a telestial or terrestrial inheritance, but only those who believe and obey become inheritors of that celestial rest which the whole body of revealed writ speaks of as salvation. (The Promised Messiah, p. 130) TLDP:154-55

### Elder Harold B. Lee

Salvation means the attainment of the eternal right to live in the presence of God the Father and the Son as a reward for a good life in mortality. (Stand Ye in Holy Places, p. 334) TLDP:154

### Elder Heber J. Grant

God tells us in the Doctrine and Covenants there is no gift greater than the gift of salvation. We as Latter-day Saints have all started out for the gift of salvation, and we should so order our lives that when we have finished our work we shall be worthy to go back into the presence of our Father, and be worthy not only to receive an exaltation ourselves, but also to receive our wives and our children that have been sealed unto us that we shall possess them. No amount of testimony, no amount of knowledge, even knowledge that this is God's work will ever save a man . . . but the keeping of the commandments of God will entitle him to that blessing. CR1900Oct:59

### Orson F. Whitney

The gospel of Christ is more than "the power of God unto salvation;" it is the power of God unto exaltation, and was instituted as such before this earth rolled into existence, before Adam fell, and consequently before man had need of redemption and salvation. It is the way of eternal progress, the path to perfection. . . . CR1920Apr:122

**Related Witnesses:**

### Mark E. Petersen

The meaning of complete salvation is that we become like the Savior in word and thought and deed. We can measure our progress toward salvation merely by determining how Christlike we are. If we are not becoming more like Him in our everyday living, we are not advancing toward salvation as we should. ¶ Becoming Christlike is a matter of daily spiritual growth. As a flower develops from a seed, as a mature adult develops from a tiny child, so we can grow spiritually day by day, eventually into Christlike personalities. CR1982Oct:20

---

**141. All people will be *saved* from death, but not all will receive the *salvation of exaltation* or *eternal life* in the celestial kingdom of God.**

### Bruce R. McConkie

Thus all men—except the sons of perdition who are cast out into an eternal hell—are saved, in that they become immortal and go to a telestial or terrestrial inheritance, but only those who believe and obey become inheritors of that celestial rest which the whole body of revealed writ speaks of as salvation. ¶ Eternal life is the name of the kind of life which God lives and is therefore "the greatest of all the gifts of God" (D&C 14:7); and because those who gain it become like God, they are one with him. (The Promised Messiah, p. 130) TLDP:154-55

### Bruce R. McConkie

By one degree of obedience or another, all men, in this life, develop either celestial, terrestrial, or telestial bodies (or in the case of those destined to be sons of perdition, bodies of a baser sort). In the resurrection all men receive back again "the same body which was a natural body," whether it be celestial, terrestrial, or what have you. That body is then quickened by the glory attending its particular type, and the person receiving the body then goes automatically, as it were, to the kingdom of glory where that degree of glory is found. (D&C 76; 88:16-33; 1Cor.15:35-38) (The Mortal Messiah, 2:80-81) TLDP:566

### Elder John Taylor

As eternal beings we all have to stand before him to be judged; and he has provided different degrees of glory—the celestial, the terrestrial, and the telestial glories—which are provided according to certain unchangeable laws which cannot be controverted. . . . For those who are willing to yield to obedience to his commands at all times and carry out his purposes upon the earth, and who are willing to abide a celestial law, he has prepared for them a celestial glory, that they may be with him for ever and ever. And what about the others? They are not prepared to go there any more than lead is prepared to stand the same test as gold or silver; and there they cannot go. And there is a great gulf between them. But he [God] will do with them just as well as he can. A great many of these people in the world, thousands and hundreds of millions of them, will be a great deal better off through the interposition of the Almighty that they have any idea of. But they cannot enter into the celestial kingdom of God; where God and Christ are they cannot come. *(At quarterly conference of Salt Lake Stake, Jan. 6, 1879, JD20:118)* TLDP:325

### Melvin J. Ballard

He has purchased us; he has redeemed us; he has bought us; and we belong to him. And now he proposed to give back these bodies glorified. To those who keep the full law he promises to give a celestial body, full of celestial power and glory and splendor; and to those who keep the terrestrial law, a body not so glorious, but still glorious and splendid; and telestial bodies to those who keep the telestial law; thus he extends to each this privilege. This is what the Lord Jesus Christ has done for man. (Sermons and Missionary Services of Melvin J. Ballard, pp. 169-70) TLDP:50

**Joseph Smith**
And the spirit and the body are the soul of man. 16. And the resurrection from the dead is the redemption of the soul. 17. And the redemption of the soul is through him that quickeneth all things, in whose bosom it is decreed that the poor and the meek of the earth shall inherit it. 18. Therefore, it must needs be sanctified from all unrighteousness, that it may be prepared for the celestial glory; 19. For after it hath filled the measure of its creation, it shall be crowned with glory, even with the presence of God the Father; 20. That bodies who are of the celestial kingdom may possess it forever and ever; for, for this intent was it made and created, and for this intent are they sanctified. 21. And they who are not sanctified through the law which I have given unto you, even the law of Christ, must inherit another kingdom, even that of a terrestrial kingdom, or that of a telestial kingdom. 22. For he who is not able to abide the law of a celestial kingdom cannot abide a celestial glory. (*Revelation received Dec. 27/28, 1832; the "olive leaf message of peace"*) D&C 88:15-22

**Related Witnesses:**
**Joseph Smith**
A man may be saved, after the judgment, in the terrestrial kingdom or in the telestial kingdom but he can never see the celestial kingdom of God without being born of the water and the Spirit. He may receive a glory like unto the moon [i.e., of which the light of the moon is typical], or a star [i.e., of which the light of the stars is typical], but he can never come unto Mount Zion and unto the city of the living God, the heavenly Jerusalem, and to an innumerable company of angels; to the general assembly and Church of the Firstborn, which are written in heaven and to God the judge of all, and to the spirits of just men made perfect, and to Jesus the Mediator of the new covenant, unless he becomes as a little child, and is taught by the Spirit of God. (Article in the Star, Aug. 1832) HC1:283

**Melvin J. Ballard**
Now, I wish to say to you that those who died without law, meaning the pagan nations, for lack of faithfulness, for lack of devotion, in the former life, are obtaining all that they are entitled to. I don't mean to say that all of them will be barred from entrance into the highest glory.

Any one of them who repents and complies with the conditions might also obtain celestial glory, but the great bulk of them will only obtain terrestrial glory. (Sermons of Melvin J. Ballard, p. 251) DCSM:164

---

142. **To receive exaltation (the highest degree in the celestial kingdom) a person must be married in the new and everlasting covenant.**

**Joseph Smith**
In the celestial glory there are three heavens or degrees; 2. And in order to obtain the highest, a man must enter into this order of the priesthood [meaning the new and everlasting covenant of marriage]; 3. And if he does not, he cannot obtain it. 4. He may enter into the other, but that is the end of his kingdom; he cannot have an increase. (*Instructions given by the Prophet, May 16/17, 1843*) D&C 131:1-4

**President Spencer W. Kimball,**
*also quoting Joseph Smith*
One young man said that he expected to reach exaltation in the celestial kingdom as one of the Lord's messengers, without having to marry. He does not understand. No one who rejects the covenant of celestial marriage can reach exaltation in the eternal kingdom of God. ¶ "In the celestial glory there are three heavens or degrees; ¶ And in order to obtain the highest, a man must enter into this order of the priesthood [meaning the new and everlasting covenant of marriage]; ¶ And if he does not, he cannot obtain it. ¶ He may enter into the other, but that is the end of his kingdom; he cannot have an increase." (D&C 131:1-4) ¶ He cannot have an increase! He cannot have exaltation! ¶ The Lord says further in the 132nd section of the Doctrine and Covenants: ¶ No one can reject this covenant and be permitted to enter into my glory. (D&C 132:4) ¶ No one! It matters not how righteous they may have been, how intelligent or how well trained they are. No one will enter this highest glory unless he enters into the covenant, and this means the new and everlasting covenant of marriage. ("The Importance of Celestial Marriage," EN1979Oct:5-6) DCSM:325-26

**John A. Widtsoe**
Naturally, those who enter the celestial kingdom are of various attainments. There is not absolute uniformity anywhere among the children of God. Their innate capacities and their use of the law of free agency make them different, often widely so. Therefore, the members of the highest kingdom are also grouped,

according to the Prophet Joseph Smith into three "degrees." [See D&C 131:1.] ¶ To enter the highest of these degrees in the celestial kingdom is to be exalted in the kingdom of God. Such exaltation comes to those who receive the higher ordinances of the Church, such as the temple endowment, and afterwards are sealed in marriage for time and eternity, whether on earth or in the hereafter. Those who are so sealed continue the family relationship eternally. Spiritual children are begotten by them. They carry on the work of salvation for the hosts of waiting spirits. They who are so exalted become even as the gods. They will be "from everlasting to everlasting, because they continue; . . ." [See D&C 132:20.] (Evidences and Reconciliations, pp. 200-01) TLDP:163-64

### Elder Spencer W. Kimball,
*also quoting President Brigham Young*
If one is going to be in God's kingdom of exaltation, where God dwells in all his glory, one will be there as a husband or a wife and not otherwise. Regardless of his virtues, the single person, or the one married for this life only, cannot be exalted. All normal people should marry and rear families. To quote Brigham Young: "No man can be perfect without the woman, so no woman can be perfect without a man. . . . I tell you the truth as it is in the bosom of eternity. If he wishes to be saved, he cannot be saved without a woman by his side." (Miracle of Forgiveness, p. 245) TLDP:380

### Elder Joseph F. Smith
When we become like him you will find that we will be presented before him in the form in which we were created, male and female. The woman will not go there alone, and the man will not go there alone, and claim exaltation. They may attain a degree of salvation alone, but when they are exalted they will be exalted according to the law of the celestial kingdom. They cannot be exalted in any other way, neither the living nor the dead. It is well for us to learn something about why we build temples, and why we administer in them for the dead as well as for the living. We do this that we may become like unto him, and dwell with him eternally; that we may become sons of God, heirs of God and joint heirs with Jesus Christ. (*Sermon in 1898*) (Gospel Doctrine, p. 276) TLDP:162-63

**Related Witnesses:**
### Joseph Smith,
*quoted by Elder Joseph Fielding Smith*
Except a man and his wife enter into an everlasting covenant and be married for eternity, while in this probation, by the power and

authority of the Holy Priesthood, they will cease to increase when they die; that is, they will not have any children after the resurrection. But those who are married by the power and authority of the priesthood in this life, and continue without committing the sin against the Holy Ghost, will continue to increase and have children in the celestial glory. (*Instructions given Brother and Sister Benjamin Johnson, in presence of several brethren, Ramus, Ill., May 16, 1843*) TPJS:300-01

### Joseph Smith,
*receiving the Word of the Lord*
For behold, I reveal unto you a new and an everlasting covenant; and if ye abide not that covenant, then are ye damned; for no one can reject this covenant and be permitted to enter into my glory. 5. For all who will have a blessing at my hands shall abide the law which was appointed for that blessing, and the conditions thereof, as were instituted from before the foundation of the world. 6. And as pertaining to the new and everlasting covenant, it was instituted for the fulness of my glory; and he that receiveth a fulness thereof must and shall abide the law, or he shall be damned, saith the Lord God. (*Revelation relating to the new and everlasting covenant, including the eternal nature of the marriage covenant, July 12, 1843, [1831]*) D&C 132:4-6

### Elder Joseph Fielding Smith,
*also quoting Joseph Smith*
Those who gain exaltation in the celestial kingdom are those who are members of the Church of the Firstborn; in other words, those who keep all the commandments of the Lord. . . . ¶ The higher ordinances in the temple of God pertain to exaltation in the celestial kingdom. . . . In order to receive this blessing, one must keep the full law, must abide the law by which that kingdom is governed; for, "he who is not able to abide the law of a celestial kingdom cannot abide a celestial glory." (Doctrines of Salvation, 2:41-42) DGSM:91

---

**143. Those who inherit the highest degree of the celestial kingdom will have eternal increase, becoming parents of spirit offspring.**

### John A. Widtsoe
To enter the highest of these degrees in the celestial kingdom is to be exalted in the kingdom of God. Such exaltation comes to those who receive the higher ordinances of the Church, such as the temple endowment, and

afterwards are sealed in marriage for time and eternity, whether on earth or in the hereafter. Those who are so sealed continue the family relationship eternally. Spiritual children are begotten by them. They carry on the work of salvation for the hosts of waiting spirits. They who are so exalted become even as the gods. They will be "from everlasting to everlasting, because they continue; . . ." [D&C 132:20] (Evidences and Reconciliations, pp. 200-01) TLDP:163-64

**President Joseph F. Smith,**
**Anthon H. Lund, Charles W. Penrose**
(First Presidency)
**The Council of the Twelve Apostles**

So far as the stages of eternal progression and attainment have been made known through divine revelation, we are to understand that only resurrected and glorified beings can become parents of spirit offspring. Only such exalted souls have reached maturity in the appointed course of eternal life; and the spirits born to them in the eternal worlds will pass in due sequence through the several stages or estates by which the glorified parents have attained exaltation. ("The Father and the Son," IE1916Aug:942) TLDP:160

**Hugh B. Brown,**
*also quoting Jesus,*
*and President Lorenzo Snow*

One of the first commandments given to Adam and Eve was to multiply and replenish the earth and subdue it. This injunction has never been revoked. When the father and mother and children are sealed together by the same divine authority as was given to Peter, celestial marriage commences an eternal family. Christ said to Peter: "And I will give unto thee the keys of the kingdom of heaven: and whatsoever thou shalt bind on earth shall be bound in heaven; and whatsoever thou shalt loose on earth shall be loosed in heaven." (Matt 16:19) All who are faithful to the teachings of the gospel will continue as a family into the highest degree of the celestial kingdom and will be crowned with immortality, eternal life, and eternal increase. . . . ¶ . . . . President Lorenzo Snow gave an intimation of what eternal marriage meant: "A man and a woman in the other life, having celestial bodies, free from sickness and disease, glorified and beautified beyond description, standing in the midst of their posterity, governing and controlling them, administering life, exaltation and glory, world without end." CR1966Oct:103-04

**President Brigham Young**

The Lord has blessed us with the ability to enjoy an eternal life with the Gods, and this is pronounced the greatest gift of God. The gift of eternal life, without a posterity, to become an angel, is one of the greatest gifts that can be bestowed; yet the Lord has bestowed on us the privilege of becoming fathers of lives. What is a father of lives, as mentioned in the Scriptures? A man who has a posterity to an eternal continuance. That is the blessing Abraham received, and it perfectly satisfied his soul. He obtained the promise that he should be the father of lives. *(In Tabernacle, May 20, 1860, JD8:63)* TLDP:159

**Delbert L. Stapley,**
*also quoting Joseph Smith*

How sublime, comprehensive, significant, and important the endowment becomes when we understand it. When one has been endowed according to the order of temple rights and ordinances, then he or she is prepared for eternal sealing of husband to wife, wife to husband, and children to both, by men authorized and possessing the keys of this sealing power. Families thus united may go on to perfection, exaltation, and eternal happiness together. ¶ We learn this from the writings of the Prophet Joseph Smith, found in both the 131st and 132nd sections of the Doctrine and Covenants. The Lord, speaking to the Prophet, said, ¶ "In the celestial glory there are three heavens, or degrees; ¶ And in order to obtain the highest a man must enter into this order of the priesthood, [meaning the new and the everlasting covenant of marriage]; ¶ And if he does not he cannot obtain it. ¶ He may enter into the others, but that is the end of his kingdom; he cannot have an increase." (D&C 131:1-4) ¶ Those who do not enter this order of the priesthood, that is, the eternal covenant of marriage, become angels of God in a separate and single state forever and ever, and thus are without increase of posterity in the eternal world; therefore without posterity they have no need of a kingdom. CR1955Apr:67

**Joseph Smith,**
*quoted by Elder Joseph Fielding Smith*

Except a man and his wife enter into an everlasting covenant and be married for eternity, while in this probation, by the power and authority of the Holy Priesthood, they will cease to increase when they die; that is, they will not have any children after the resurrection. But those who are married by the power and authority of the priesthood in this life, and continue without committing the sin against the Holy Ghost, will continue to increase and have children in the celestial glory. *(Instructions given Brother and Sister Benjamin Johnson in presence of several brethren, Ramus, Ill., May 16, 1843)* TPJS:300-01

### Delbert L. Stapley

As sons and daughters of God, we are required to purify and perfect ourselves in righteousness, otherwise, we cannot be with him nor enjoy eternal lives and glory in his kingdom. To become like God we must possess the powers of Godhood. For such preparation there are important covenants, obligations, and ordinances for mankind to receive beyond the requirement of baptism and the laying on of hands for the reception of the Holy Ghost. Every person is to receive his or her endowments in the house of the Lord which permit them, if faithful and true, to pass by the angels who stand as sentinels guarding the way to eternal glory in the mansions of God. The everlasting covenant of marriage ordained of God for man and woman, also is to be entered into and the marriage contract sealed eternally by the authority of the Holy Priesthood of God. Otherwise, the highest degree of the celestial kingdom cannot be attained nor Godhood acquired, which exalted condition assures continuation of the lives forever. CR1961Apr:66

**Related Witnesses:**

### President Brigham Young

We understand that we are to be made kings and Priests unto God; now if I be made the king and lawgiver to my family, and if I have many sons, I shall become the father of many fathers, for they will have sons, and their sons will have sons, and so on, from generation to generation, and, in this way, I may become the father of many fathers, or the king of many kings. This will constitute every man a prince, king, lord, or whatever the Father sees fit to confer upon us. ¶ In this way we can become King of kings, and Lord of lords, or, Father of fathers, or Prince of princes, and this is the only course, for another man is not going to raise up a kingdom for you. *(In Bowery, Provo, Utah, July 14, 1855, JD3:265-66)* TLDP:159

### George Q. Cannon

If I have children; if I have a wife, I shall have them in eternity. I shall preside over that family no matter how small it may be, or how large it may extend. They will be my kingdom; for this is the promise of God. What is there that is more delightful in the contemplation of the future than this thought, that those with whom we are associated here, with whom our lives and happiness is entwined, who give unto us the greatest pleasure, because of the love we have for them and they have for us; that that union shall be perpetuated throughout eternity, and that there shall be an increase of that love and of that union and an increase also of that power, because the power of procreation is promised—the greatest power that man possesses on earth. That is promised unto those who are faithful. . . . Therefore, it can be said of us as it was said of our Lord and Savior, "to the increase of His kingdom there shall be no end." Why? Because of this principle that I spoke of—the principle of procreation. By it, and through that principle the worlds are peopled. The planetary orbs which stud our heavens so gloriously are peopled by that principle—the principle of procreation. God possesses it, and we as His children inherit the power. If we do what is right He promises to bestow it upon us. CR1899Apr:20

---

**144. Those who inherit exaltation in the celestial kingdom will thereafter become gods.**

### Elder Wilford Woodruff

There are a few individuals in this dispensation who will inherit celestial glory, and a few in other dispensations; but before they receive their exaltation they will have to pass through and submit to whatever dispensation God may decree. But for all this they will receive their reward—they will become Gods, they will inherit thrones, kingdoms, principalities and powers through the endless ages of eternity, and to their increase there will be no end, and the heart of man has never conceived of the glory that is in store for the sons and daughters of God who keep the celestial law. *(Funeral services of two young children, Wanship, Utah, JD18:39)* TLDP:130

### Joseph Smith

And who overcome by faith, and are sealed by the Holy Spirit of promise, which the Father sheds forth upon all those who are just and true. 54. They are they who are the church of the Firstborn. 55. They are they into whose hands the Father has given all things— 56. They are they who are priests and kings, who have received of his fulness, and of his glory; 57. And are priests of the Most High, after the order of Melchizedek, which was after the order of Enoch, which was after the order of the Only Begotten Son. 58. Wherefore, as it is written, they are gods, even the sons of God— 62. These shall dwell in the presence of God and his Christ forever and ever. 70 These are they whose bodies are celestial, whose glory is that of the sun, even the glory of God, the highest of all, whose glory the sun of the firmament is written of as being typical. *(Vision to Joseph Smith and Sidney Rigdon, Feb. 16, 1832)* D&C 76:53-58,62,70

**John A. Widtsoe**

To enter the highest of these degrees in the celestial kingdom is to be exalted in the kingdom of God. Such exaltation comes to those who receive the higher ordinances of the Church, such as the temple endowment, and afterwards are sealed in marriage for time and eternity, whether on earth or in the hereafter. Those who are so sealed continue the family relationship eternally. Spiritual children are begotten by them. They carry on the work of salvation for the hosts of waiting spirits. They who are so exalted become even as the gods. They will be "from everlasting to everlasting, because they continue; . . ." [See D&C 132:20.] (Evidences and Reconciliations, pp. 200-01) TLDP:163-64

**Joseph Smith,**
*quoted by Elder Joseph Fielding Smith*

How consoling to the mourners when they are called to part with a husband, wife, father, mother, child, or dear relative, to know that, although the earthly tabernacle is laid down and dissolved, they shall rise again to dwell in everlasting burnings in immortal glory, not to sorrow, suffer, or die any more; but they shall be heirs of God and joint heirs with Jesus Christ. What is it? To inherit the same power, the same glory and the same exaltation, until you arrive at the station of a God, and ascend the throne of eternal power, the same as those who have gone before. What did Jesus do? Why; I do the things I saw my Father do when worlds came rolling into existence. My Father worked out his kingdom with fear and trembling, and I must do the same; and when I get my kingdom, I shall present it to my Father, so that he may obtain kingdom upon kingdom, and it will exalt him in glory. He will then take a higher exaltation, and I will take his place, and thereby become exalted myself. So that Jesus treads in the tracks of his Father, and inherits what God did before; and God is thus glorified and exalted in the salvation and exaltation of all his children. It is plain beyond disputation, and you thus learn some of the first principles of the Gospel, about which so much hath been said. (*To the Church in general conference—a congregation of 20,000—"King Follett Sermon", April 7, 1844*) (See HC6:302-317, also see The Words of Joseph Smith, pp. 340-62.) TPJS:347-48

**Related Witnesses:**

**Joseph Smith**

Here, then, is eternal life—to know the only wise and true God; and you have got to learn how to be gods yourselves, and to be kings and priests to God, the same as all gods have done

before you, namely, by going from one small degree to another, and from a small capacity to a great one; from grace to grace, from exaltation to exaltation, until you attain to the resurrection of the dead, and are able to dwell in everlasting burnings, and to sit in glory, as do those who sit enthroned in everlasting power. (*To the Church in general conference—a congregation of 20,000—"King Follett Sermon", April 7, 1844*)(Full Sermon: HC6:302-317, also see WJS:340-62) HC6:306

**Joseph Smith,**
*receiving the Word of the Lord*

And again, verily I say unto you, if a man marry a wife by my word, which is my law, and by the new and everlasting covenant, and it is sealed unto them by the Holy Spirit of promise, by him who is anointed, unto whom I have appointed this power and the keys of this priesthood; and it shall be said unto them—Ye shall come forth in the first resurrection; and if it be after the first resurrection, in the next resurrection; and shall inherit thrones, kingdoms, principalities, and powers, dominions, all heights and depths—then shall it be written in the Lamb's Book of Life, that he shall commit no murder whereby to shed innocent blood, and if ye abide in my covenant, and commit no murder whereby to shed innocent blood, it shall be done unto them in all things whatsoever my servant hath put upon them, in time, and through all eternity; and shall be of full force when they are out of the world; and they shall pass by the angels, and the gods, which are set there, to their exaltation and glory in all things, as hath been sealed upon their heads, which glory shall be a fulness and a continuation of the seeds forever and ever. 20. Then shall they be gods, because they have no end; therefore shall they be from everlasting to everlasting, because they continue; then shall they be above all, because all things are subject unto them. Then shall they be gods, because they have all power, and the angels are subject unto them. (*Revelation relating to the new and everlasting covenant, including the eternal nature of the marriage covenant, July 12, 1843 [1831]*) D&C 132:19-20

**President Spencer W. Kimball**

Now, the sealing for eternity gives to you eternal leadership. The man will have the authority of the priesthood, and if he keeps his life in order he will become a god. . . . The Lord created this earth for us and made it a beautiful place to live. He promised us that if we would live the right way we could come back to him and be like him. ACR(Sao Paulo)1975:43

### President Spencer W. Kimball

Man can transform himself and he must. Man has in himself the seeds of godhood, which can germinate and grow and develop. As the acorn becomes the oak, the mortal man becomes a god. It is within his power to lift himself by his very bootstraps from the plane on which he finds himself to the plane on which he should be. It may be a long, hard lift with many obstacles, but it is a real possibility. (*Sermon at Brigham Young University, Sept. 1974*) (Teachings of Spencer W. Kimball, p. 28) DGSM:52

### Elder Joseph F. Smith

It is well for us to learn something about why we build temples, and why we administer in them for the dead as well as for the living. We do this that we may become like unto him, and dwell with him eternally; that we may become sons of God, heirs of God and joint heirs with Jesus Christ. (*Sermon, June 12, 1898*) (Gospel Doctrine, p. 276) TLDP:162-63

---

145. The celestial kingdom was prepared, before the world began, to receive the faithful.

### Jesus,
### *recorded in Matthew*

Then shall the King say unto them on his right hand, Come, ye blessed of my Father, inherit the kingdom prepared for you from the foundation of the world: . . . (*Jesus gives the parable of the sheep and the goats; the sheep are placed on his right hand at the Lord's Second Coming*) Matt.25:34

### Jacob, brother of Nephi,
### *quoted by Nephi*

But, behold, the righteous, the saints of the Holy One of Israel, they who have believed in the Holy One of Israel, they who have endured the crosses of the world, and despised the shame of it, they shall inherit the kingdom of God, which was prepared for them from the foundation of the world, and their joy shall be full forever. (*Jacob teaches the people of Nephi, 559-545 B.C.*) 2 Ne.9:18

### Paul

In hope of eternal life, which God, that cannot lie, promised before the world began; (*Letter to his companion Titus, about A.D. 64*) Titus 1:2

**Related Witnesses:**

### Joseph Smith

The heavens were opened upon us, and I beheld the celestial kingdom of God, and the glory thereof, whether in the body or out I cannot tell. 2. I saw the transcendent beauty of the gate through which the heirs of that kingdom will enter, which was like unto circling flames of fire; 3. Also the blazing throne of God, whereon was seated the Father and the Son. (*Vision to Joseph Smith in Kirtland Temple, Jan. 21, 1836*) D&C 137:1-3

### Orson F. Whitney

The gospel of Christ is more than "the power of God unto salvation;" it is the power of God unto exaltation, and was instituted as such before this earth rolled into existence, before Adam fell, and consequently before man had need of redemption and salvation. It is the way of eternal progress, the path to perfection. . . . CR1920Apr:122

---

## (2) The Terrestrial Kingdom

146. The terrestrial kingdom exceeds the telestial kingdom in glory, in power, in might, and in dominion.

### Joseph Smith

And again, we saw the glory of the telestial, which glory is that of the lesser, even as the glory of the stars differs from that of the glory of the moon in the firmament. 91. And thus we saw the glory of the terrestrial which excels in all things the glory of the telestial, even in glory, and in power, and in might, and in dominion. (*Vision to Joseph Smith and Sidney Rigdon, Feb. 16, 1832*) D&C 76:81,91

### President Brigham Young

The glory of the telestial world no man knows, except he partakes of it; and yet, in that world they differ in glory as the stars in the firmament differ one from the other. The terrestrial glory is greater still, and the celestial is the greatest of all; that is the glory of God the Father, where our Lord Jesus Christ reigns. (*In Tabernacle, Aug. 15, 1852, JD6:293*) TLDP:128

### Elder Wilford Woodruff

No man will receive a celestial glory unless he abides a celestial law; no man will receive a terrestrial glory unless he abides a terrestrial law, and no man will receive a telestial glory unless he abides a telestial law. There is a great difference between the light of the sun at noonday and the glimmer of the stars at night, but that difference is no greater than the difference of the glory in the several portions of the kingdom of God. (*General conference, Oct. 9, 1874, JD17:250*) TLDP:357

### Melvin J. Ballard

When you see men and women in the resurrection, we shall see them in very bloom of their glorious manhood and womanhood, and he has promised all who would keep his command-ments and obey the gospel of the Lord Jesus Christ, the restoration of their houses, glorified, immortalized, celestialized, fitted to dwell in the presence of God. ¶ To those who cannot subscribe to those terms, and yet obey others, the lesser law, Jesus has promised a terrestrial body, not so glorious, and yet immortal and eternal, and still to those who cannot do so much, but only obey in part, a telestial body suited to the kingdom in which they dwell. Thus we fix our status in that resurrection, though the resurrection is a fact without our action. Our action makes it either glorious—the resurrection of the just; or the resurrection of the unjust. (Sermons and Missionary Services of Melvin J. Ballard, p. 186) TLDP:565-66

### Melvin J. Ballard

To those who keep the full law he promises to give a celestial body, full of celestial power and glory and splendor; and to those who keep the terrestrial law, a body not so glorious, but still glorious and splendid; and telestial bodies to those who keep the telestial law; thus he extends to each this privilege. This is what the Lord Jesus Christ has done for man. (Sermons and Missionary Services of Melvin J. Ballard, pp. 169-70) TLDP:50

**Related Witnesses:**

### Bruce R. McConkie

By one degree of obedience or another, all men, in this life, develop either celestial, terrestrial, or telestial bodies (or in the case of those des-tined to be sons of perdition, bodies of a baser sort). In the resurrection all men receive back again "the same body which was a natural body," whether it be celestial, terrestrial, or what have you. That body is then quickened by the glory attending its particular type, and the person receiving the body then goes automatically, as it were, to the kingdom of glory where that degree of glory is found. (D&C 76; 88:16-33; 1Cor.15:35-38) (Doctrinal New Testament Commentary, 1:196) TLDP:566

### James E. Talmage

The three kingdoms of widely differing glories are organized on an orderly plan of gradation. We have seen that the telestial kingdom com-prises several subdivisions; this also is the case, we are told, with the celestial; and, by analogy, we conclude that a similar condition prevails in the terrestrial. Thus the innumerable degrees of merit amongst mankind are provided for in an infinity of graded glories. The celestial kingdom is supremely honored by the personal ministra-tions of the Father and the Son. The terrestrial kingdom will be administered through the higher,

without a fulness of glory. The telestial is gov-erned through the ministrations of the terrestrial, by "angels who are appointed to minister for them." ¶ Exaltation in the kingdom of God implies attainment to the graded orders of the Holy Priesthood, and with these the ceremonies of the endowment are directly associated. HL:83

### Elder Joseph Fielding Smith

This earth will become a celestial kingdom when it is sanctified. Those who enter the ter-restrial kingdom will have to go to some other sphere which will be prepared for them. Those who enter the telestial kingdom, likewise will have to go to some earth which is prepared for them, and there will be another place which is hell where the devil and those who are pun-ished to go with him will dwell. (Answers to Gospel Questions, 2:208-10) TLDP:127

---

**147. Honorable people of the earth who refused the gospel in mortal-ity, but in the spirit world re-pented and accepted it, will inher-it the terrestrial kingdom.**

### Elder Joseph Fielding Smith

Into the terrestrial kingdom will go all those who are honorable and who have lived clean virtuous lives, but who would not receive the Gospel, but in the spirit world repented and accepted it as far as it can be given unto them. Many of these have been blinded by tradition and the love of the world, and have not been able to see the beauties of the Gospel. CHMR1:287-88; DGSM:92

### James E. Talmage

The Terrestrial Glory—We read of others who receive glory of a secondary order, differing from the highest as "the moon differs from the sun in the firmament." These are they who, though honorable, failed to comply with the requirements for exaltation, were blinded by the craftiness of men and unable to receive and obey the higher laws of God. They proved "not valiant in the testimony of Jesus," and therefore are not entitled to the fulness of glory. AF:83

### George Q. Cannon

Terrestrial glory may be all right for honorable Gentiles, who have not faith enough to believe the Gospel and who do right according to the best knowledge they have; but celestial glory is our aim. . . . ¶ . . . . All that I am on this earth for is to get celestial glory. CR1900Apr:55-56

**Related Witnesses:**

### Joseph Smith

And again, we saw the terrestrial world, and

behold and lo, these are they who are of the ter-restrial, whose glory differs from that of the church of the Firstborn who have received the fulness of the Father, even as that of the moon differs from the sun in the firmament. 72. Be-hold, these are they who died without law; 73. And also they who are the spirits of men kept in prison, whom the Son visited, and preached the gospel unto them, that they might be judged ac-cording to men in the flesh; 74. Who received not the testimony of Jesus in the flesh, but afterwards received it. 75. These are they who are honorable men of the earth, who were blinded by the craftiness of men. 76. These are they who receive of his glory, but not of his full-ness. 77. These are they who receive of the presence of the Son, but not of the fulness of the Father. 78. Wherefore, they are bodies ter-restrial, and not bodies celestial, and differ in glory as the moon differs from the sun. 79. These are they who are not valiant in the testi-mony of Jesus; wherefore, they obtain not the crown over the kingdom of our God. (*Vision to Joseph Smith and Sidney Rigdon, Feb. 16, 1832*) D&C 76:71-79

### President Brigham Young,
*quoted by John A. Widtsoe*

Some might suppose that it would be a great blessing to be taken and carried directly into heaven and there set down, but in reality that would be no blessing to such persons; they could not reap a full reward, could not enjoy the glory of the kingdom, and could not com-prehend and abide the light thereof, but it would be to them a hell intolerable and I sup-pose would consume them much quicker than would hell fire. It would be no blessing to you to be carried into the celestial kingdom, and obliged to stay therein, unless you were pre-pared to dwell there. (*In Tabernacle, March 1856, JD3:221*) DBY:95; DGSM:92

---

### 148. Those who accepted the gospel in mortality but were not valiant, may not inherit the celestial king-dom.

### Joseph Smith

And again, we saw the terrestrial world, and behold and lo, these are they who are of the ter-restrial, whose glory differs from that of the church of the Firstborn who have received the fulness of the Father, even as that of the moon differs from the sun in the firmament. . . . 79. These are they who are not valiant in the testi-mony of Jesus; wherefore, they obtain not the

crown over the kingdom of our God. (*Vision to Joseph Smith and Sidney Rigdon, Feb. 16, 1832*) D&C 76:71,79

### President Brigham Young

Those men, or those women, who [allow them-selves to be] led entirely by another person, sus-pending their own understanding, and pinning their faith upon another's sleeve, will never be capable of entering into the celestial glory, to be crowned as they anticipate; they will never be capable of becoming Gods. They cannot rule themselves, to say nothing of ruling others, but they must be dictated to every trifle, like a child. . . . They never can hold scepters of glory, majesty, and power in the celestial kingdom. Who will? Those who are valiant and inspired with the true independence of heaven, who will go forth boldly to do as they please, determined to do right, though all mankind besides should take the opposite course. (*In Tabernacle, Feb. 20, 1853, JD1:312*) TLDP:127

### Elder Joseph Fielding Smith

The terrestrial kingdom. Into this kingdom will go all those who have lived clean lives, but were not willing to receive the gospel; also those who have lived clean lives but who, notwithstanding their membership in the Church, were not valiant, and those who refused to receive the gospel when they lived on the earth, but in the spirit world accepted the testimony of Jesus. All who enter this kingdom must be of that class who have been morally clean. (Answers to Gospel Questions, 2:208-10) TLDP:127

### Related Witnesses:

### Bruce R. McConkie

To be valiant in the testimony of Jesus is to bri-dle our passions, control our appetites, and rise above carnal and evil things. It is to overcome the world as did he who is our prototype and who himself was the most valiant of all our Father's children. It is to be morally clean, to pay our tithes and offerings, to honor the Sabbath day, to pray with full purpose of heart, to lay our all upon the altar if called upon to do so. ¶ To be valiant in the testimony of Jesus is to take the Lord's side on every issue. It is to vote as he would vote. It is to think what he thinks, to believe what he believes, to say what he would say and do what he would do in the same situation. It is to have the mind of Christ and be one with him as he is one with his Father. CR1974Oct:46

### Elder George Albert Smith

We [Latter-day Saints] will not be judged as our brothers and sisters of the world are judged; but according to the greater opportunities placed in our keeping. We will be among those who have received the word of the Lord, who have heard His sayings, and if we do them it will be to us eternal life, but if we fail condemnation will result. CR1906Oct:47

**Author's Note:** According to Elder Ezra Taft Benson: "Concerning those who will receive the terrestrial, or lesser, kingdom, the Lord said, 'These are they who are not valiant in the testimony of Jesus; wherefore, they obtain not the crown over the kingdom of our God.' (D&C 76:79) Not to be valiant in one's testimony is a tragedy of eternal consequence. These are members who know this latter-day work is true, but who fail to endure to the end. Some may even hold temple recommends, but do not magnify their callings in the Church. Without valor, they do not take an affirmative stand *for* the kingdom of God. Some seek the praise, adulation, and honors of men; others attempt to conceal their sins; and a few criticize those who preside over them. . . . ¶ President Joseph F. Smith said, 'There are at least three dangers that threaten the Church from within, . . . they are flattery of prominent men in the world, false educational ideas, and sexual impurity'." (Teachings of Ezra Taft Benson, pp. 392-93)

149. **The torment of those who are damned is the knowledge that if they had kept the commandments they might have achieved a greater glory.**

**Elder Joseph Fielding Smith**
This earth will become a celestial kingdom when it is sanctified. Those who enter the terrestrial kingdom will have to go to some other sphere which will be prepared for them. Those who enter the telestial kingdom, likewise will have to go to some earth which is prepared for them, and there will be another place which is hell where the devil and those who are punished to go with him will dwell. Of course, those who enter the telestial kingdom, and those who enter the terrestrial kingdom will have the eternal punishment which will come to them in knowing that they might, if they had kept the commandments of the Lord, have returned to his presence as his sons and his daughters. This will be a torment to them, and in that sense it will be hell. (Answers to Gospel Questions, 2:208-10) TLDP:127

**John A. Widtsoe**
Those who dwell in the lower [glory] may look wistfully to the higher as we do here. The hell

on the other side will be felt in some such way. (Message of the Doctrine and Covenants, p.167) DCSM:166

**Joseph Smith**
A man is his own tormentor and his own condemner. Hence the saying, They shall go into the lake that burns with fire and brimstone. The torment of disappointment in the mind of man is as exquisite as a lake burning with fire and brimstone. I say, so is the torment of man. (*To the Church in general conference—a congregation of 20,000—"King Follett Sermon", April 7, 1844*) (See HC6:302-317, also see The Words of Joseph Smith, pp. 340-62.) HC6:314

## (3) The Telestial Kingdom

150. **The glory and grandeur of the telestial kingdom surpasses all human understanding.**

**Joseph Smith**
And again, we saw the glory of the telestial, which glory is that of the lesser, even as the glory of the stars differs from that of the glory of the moon in the firmament. . . . 89. And thus we saw, in the heavenly vision, the glory of the telestial, which surpasses all understanding;(*Vision to Joseph Smith and Sidney Rigdon, Feb. 16, 1832*) D&C 76:81,89

**Joseph Smith**
And thus I beheld, in the vision of heav'n, ¶ The telestial glory, dominion and bliss, ¶ Surpassing the great understanding of men, — ¶ Unknown, save reveal'd, in a world vain as this. (*Verse 64 of a 78 verse poem: "The Answer to W. W. Phelps, Esq., A Vision"*) (Published by Joseph Smith in Nauvoo, Ill., Feb. 1, 1843 in the Times and Seasons) MOFP1:166

**John A. Widtsoe**
The book [Doctrine and Covenants] explains clearly that the lowest glory to which man is assigned is so glorious as to be beyond the understanding of man. It is a doctrine fundamental in Mormonism that the meanest sinner, in the final judgment, will receive a glory which is beyond human understanding, which is so great that we are unable to describe it adequately. Those who do well will receive an even more glorious place. . . . ¶ The Gospel is a gospel of tremendous love. Love is at the bottom of it. The meanest child is loved so dearly that his reward will be beyond the understanding of mortal man. (Message of the Doctrine and Covenants, p.167) DCSM:166

**James E. Talmage**

Even the telestial glory "surpasses all understanding; And no man knows it except him to whom God has revealed it." AF:84

---

151. **Those who will inherit the telestial kingdom will be the wicked people of the earth, such as adulterers and deliberate liars.**

**Elder Joseph Fielding Smith,**
*also quoting Joseph Smith*

The telestial kingdom. Into this kingdom will go all of those who have been unclean in their lives. See verses 98 to 112, in Section 76 [of the Doctrine and Covenants]. These people who enter there will be the unclean; the liars, sorcerers, adulterers, and those who have broken their covenants. Of these the Lord says: ¶ "These are they who are cast down to hell and suffer the wrath of Almighty God, until the fulness of times, when Christ shall have subdued all enemies under his feet, and shall have perfected his work;" [D&C 76:106] ¶ Yet these, after they have been punished for their sins and having been turned over to the torments of Satan, shall eventually, come forth, after the millennium, to receive the telestial kingdom. (Answers to Gospel Questions, 2:208-10) TLDP:127

**Joseph Smith**

And again, we saw the glory of the telestial, which glory is that of the lesser, even as the glory of the stars differs from that of the glory of the moon in the firmament. . . . 99. For these are they who are of Paul, and of Apollos, and of Cephas. 100. These are they who say they are some of one and some of another—some of Christ and some of John, and some of Moses, and of Elias, and some of Esaias, and some of Isaiah, and some of Enoch; 101. But received not the gospel, neither the testimony of Jesus, neither the prophets, neither the everlasting covenant. . . . 103. These are they who are liars, and sorcerers, and adulterers, and whoremongers, and whosoever loves and makes a lie. (*Vision to Joseph Smith and Sidney Rigdon, Feb. 16, 1832*) D&C 76:81,99-101,103

**James E. Talmage,**
*also quoting Joseph Smith*

The Telestial Glory —The revelation continues: "And again, we saw the glory of the telestial, which glory is that of the lesser, even as the glory of the stars differs from that of the glory of the moon in the firmament. These are they who received not the gospel of Christ, neither the testimony of Jesus. These are they who deny not

the Holy Spirit. These are they who are thrust down to hell. These are they who shall not be redeemed from the devil until the last resurrection, until the Lord, even Christ the Lamb, shall have finished his work." We learn further that the inhabitants of this kingdom are to be graded among themselves, comprising as they do the unenlightened among the varied opposing sects and divisions of men, and sinners of many types, whose offenses are not those of utter perdition: "For as one star differs from another star in glory, even so differs one from another in glory in the telestial world; For these are they who are of Paul, and of Apollos, and of Cephas. These are they who say they are some of one and some of another —some of Christ, and some of John, and some of Moses, and some of Elias, and some of Esaias, and some of Isaiah, and some of Enoch; But received not the gospel, neither the testimony of Jesus, neither the prophets, neither the everlasting covenant." Evidently a considerable part of the human family will fail of all glory beyond that of the telestial kingdom, for we are told: "But behold, and lo, we saw the glory and the inhabitants of the telestial world, that they were as innumerable as the stars in the firmament of heaven, or as the sand upon the seashore." They are thus not wholly rejected; their every merit will be respected. "For they shall be judged according to their works, and every man shall receive according to his own works, his own dominion, in the mansions which are prepared; And they shall be servants of the Most High, but where God and Christ dwell they cannot come, worlds without end." AF:369-70

**President Heber J. Grant,**
**J. Reuben Clark, Jr., David O. McKay,**
(First Presidency)
*also quoting Joseph Smith*

In the great revelation on the three heavenly glories, the Lord said, speaking of those who will inherit the lowest of these, or the telestial glory: ¶ "These are they who are liars, and sorcerers, and adulterers, and whoremongers, and whosoever loves and makes a lie." — (D&C 76:103) ¶ The doctrine of this Church is that sexual sin— the illicit sexual relations of men and women— stands, in its enormity, next to murder. ¶ The Lord has drawn no essential distinctions between fornication, adultery, and harlotry or prostitution. Each has fallen under His solemn and awful condemnation. ¶ . . . . By virtue of the authority in us vested as the First Presidency of the Church, we warn our people who are offending, of the degradation, the wickedness, the punishment that attend upon unchastity. . . . CR1942Oct:11

**152. Those who are to inhabit the telestial kingdom are first cast down to hell in the spirit world before they are redeemed from the devil in the last resurrection.**

### Elder Joseph Fielding Smith

Those who enter into the telestial kingdom . . . are the ungodly, the filthy who suffer the wrath of God on earth, who are thrust down to hell where they will be required to pay the uttermost farthing before their redemption comes. These are they who receive not the gospel of Christ and consequently could not deny the Holy Spirit while living on the earth. ¶ They have no part in the first resurrection and are not redeemed from the devil and his angels until the last resurrection, because of their wicked lives and their evil deeds. Nevertheless, even these are heirs of salvation, but before they are redeemed and enter the kingdom, they must repent of their sins, and receive the gospel, and bow the knee, and acknowledge that Jesus is the Christ, the Redeemer of the world. (Doctrines of Salvation, 2:22) DGSM:93

### James E. Talmage

Even to hell there is an exit as well as an entrance; and when sentence has been served, commuted perhaps by repentance and its attendant works, the prison doors shall open and the penitent captive be afforded opportunity to comply with the law, which he aforetime violated. . . . ¶ The inhabitants of the telestial world—the lowest of the kingdoms of glory prepared for resurrected souls, shall include those "who are thrust down to hell" and "who shall not be redeemed from the devil until the last resurrection." (D&C 76:82-85) And though these may be delivered from hell and attain to a measure of glory with possibilities of progression, yet their lot shall be that of "servants of the Most High, but where God and Christ dwell they cannot come, worlds without end." (v.112) ¶ Deliverance from hell is not admittance to heaven. (The Vitality of Mormonism, pp. 255-56) DGSM:93

### Elder Joseph Fielding Smith,
*also quoting Joseph Smith*

All liars, and sorcerers, and adulterers and all who love and make a lie, shall not receive the resurrection at this time, but for a thousand years shall be thrust down into hell where they shall suffer the wrath of God until they pay the price of their sinning, if it is possible, by the things which they shall suffer. [See Church News, April 23, 1932, p. 6.] ¶ These are the "Spirits of men who are to be judged and are found under condemnation; And these are the rest of the dead; and they live not again until the thousand years are ended, neither again, until the end of the earth" [See D&C 88:100-01.]. . . . ¶ These are the hosts of the telestial world who are commanded to "suffer the wrath of God on earth"; and who are "cast down to hell and suffer the wrath of Almighty God, until the fulness of times, when Christ shall have subdued all enemies under his feet, and shall have perfected his work" [Era, vol 45, p 781; D&C 76:104-06]. . . . ¶ This suffering will be a means of cleansing, or purifying, and through it the wicked shall be brought to a condition whereby they may, through the redemption of Jesus Christ, obtain immortality. Their spirits and bodies shall be again united, and they shall dwell in the telestial kingdom. But this resurrection will not come until the end of the world. (Doctrines of Salvation, 2:295-98) TLDP:564-65

### Joseph Smith

And again, we saw the glory of the telestial, which glory is that of the lesser, even as the glory of the stars differs from that of the glory of the moon in the firmament. . . . 84. These are they who are thrust down to hell. 85. These are they who shall not be redeemed from the devil until the last resurrection, until the Lord, even Christ the Lamb, shall have finished his work. . . . 104. These are they who suffer the wrath of God on earth. 105. These are they who suffer the vengeance of eternal fire. 106. These are they who are cast down to hell and suffer the wrath of Almighty God, until the fulness of times, when Christ shall have subdued all enemies under his feet, and shall have perfected his work;(*Vision to Joseph Smith and Sidney Rigdon, Feb. 16, 1832*) D&C 76:81,84-85,104-06

### Related Witnesses:
#### President Brigham Young

Jesus will bring forth, by his own redemption, every son and daughter of Adam, except the sons of perdition. . . . Others will suffer the wrath of God—will suffer all the Lord can demand at their hands, or justice can require of them; and when they have suffered the wrath of God till the utmost farthing is paid, they will be brought out of prison. *(In Bowery, Aug. 26, 1860, JD8:154)* TLDP:330

#### Parley P. Pratt

The spirit world is not the heaven where Jesus Christ, his Father, and other beings dwell, who have, by resurrection or translation, ascended to eternal mansions, and been crowned and seated on thrones of power; but it is an intermediate state, a probation, a place of preparation, improvement, instruction, or education, where spirits are chastened and improved, and where, if found worthy, they may be taught a knowledge of the Gospel. In short, it is a place where the Gospel is preached, and where faith, repentance, hope and charity may be exercised; a place of waiting for the resurrection or redemption of the body; while, to those who deserve it, it is a place of punishment, a purgatory or hell, where spirits are buffeted till the day of redemption. (Key to the Science of Theology, pp. 132-33) TLDP:637

**President Joseph F. Smith**

God will not condemn any man to utter destruction, neither shall any man be thrust down to hell irredeemably, until he has been brought to the possession of the greater light that comes through repentance and obedience to the laws and commandments of God; but if, after he has received light and knowledge, he shall sin against the light and will not repent, then, indeed, he becomes a lost soul, a son of perdition. ("I Know That My Redeemer Lives," IE1908Mar:381) TLDP:634

**George Q. Cannon**

I have thought sometimes that some of our people are inclined to think there is no hell and that nobody is going to hell. I tell you there will be a large number of people go to hell; they will suffer torment and will go where there is weeping and wailing and gnashing of teeth; they will be in outer darkness and suffer far beyond anything we can conceive of. Latter-day Saints especially who commit sin, if they die in their sin, will go to hell, and they will suffer torment there until the day of redemption. But think of the length of time during which they will be in this torment! (Gospel Truth, 1:85) TLDP:639

**Bruce R. McConkie**

Messianic prophecies . . . describe in a most graphic way how the Lord saves men from the direful fate that would be theirs if he had not atoned for their sins. It is known as freeing the hosts of men from prison—from the prison of death, of hell, of the devil, and of endless torment. And how apt and pointed the illustration is, for the prisons of ancient times were hell holes of death, disease, and despair. They were dungeons of filth, corruption, and creeping denizens. Sheol itself was known as the pit, the dungeon of despair, the nether realms of torment, the Hades of hell. To be in prison was worse than a living hell, and to be freed therefrom was to arise from death to life. It is no wonder that the prophetic mind seized upon this illustration to teach what the Redeemer would do to ransom men from the fate that would be

theirs if there were no atonement. (The Promised Messiah, pp. 238-39) TLDP:51

---

**153. The inhabitants of the telestial kingdom will be as innumerable as the stars.**

**Joseph Smith**

And again, we saw the glory of the telestial, which glory is that of the lesser, even as the glory of the stars differs from that of the glory of the moon in the firmament. . . . 109. But behold, and lo, we saw the glory and the inhabitants of the telestial world, that they were as innumerable as the stars in the firmament of heaven, or as the sand upon the seashore; (*Vision to Joseph Smith and Sidney Rigdon, Feb. 16, 1832*) D&C 76:81,109

**Elder Joseph Fielding Smith**

Those who enter into the telestial kingdom, where their glories differ as do the stars of heaven in their magnitude, and who are innumerable as the sands of the seashore, are the ungodly, the filthy who suffer the wrath of God on the earth. . . . (Doctrines of Salvation, 2:22) DGSM:93

**James E. Talmage,**
*also quoting Joseph Smith*

Evidently a considerable part of the human family will fail of all glory beyond that of the telestial kingdom, for we are told: "But behold, and lo, we saw the glory and the inhabitants of the telestial world, that they were as innumerable as the stars in the firmament of heaven, or as the sand upon the seashore." [D&C 76:81] They are thus not wholly rejected; their every merit will be respected. "For they shall be judged according to their works, and every man shall receive according to his own works, his own dominion, in the mansions which are prepared; And they shall be servants of the Most High, but where God and Christ dwell they cannot come, worlds without end." [D&C 76:112] AF:370

**Related Witnesses:**

**President John Taylor**

As eternal beings we all have to stand before him to be judged; and he has provided different degrees of glory—the celestial, the terrestrial, and the telestial glories—which are provided according to certain unchangeable laws which cannot be controverted. What will he do with them? For those who are ready to listen to him and be brought under the influence of the Spirit of God and be led by the principles of revelation and the light of heaven, and who are willing to yield to obedience to his commands at all times and carry out his purposes upon the earth, and who are willing to abide a celestial law, he has prepared for them a celestial glory, that they may be with him for ever and ever. And what about the others? They are not prepared to go there any more than lead is prepared to stand the same test as gold or silver; and there they cannot go. And there is a great gulf between them. But he [God] will do with them just as well as he can. A great many of these people in the world, thousands and hundreds of millions of them, will be a great deal better off through the interposition of the Almighty that they have any idea of. But they cannot enter into the celestial kingdom of God; where God and Christ are they cannot come. *(Quarterly conference, Salt Lake Stake, in Salt Lake Theater, Jan. 6, 1879, JD20:116)* TLDP:325

differ one from the other. The terrestrial glory is greater still, and the celestial is the greatest of all; that is the glory of God the Father, where our Lord Jesus Christ reigns. *(In Tabernacle, Aug. 15, 1852, JD6:293)* TLDP:128

## 154. The telestial kingdom is comprised of several subdivisions.

### Joseph Smith
And again, we saw the glory of the telestial, which glory is that of the lesser, even as the glory of the stars differs from that of the glory of the moon in the firmament. . . . 98. And the glory of the telestial is one, even as the glory of the stars is one; for as one star differs from another star in glory, even so differs one from another in glory in the telestial world; . . . *(Vision to Joseph Smith and Sidney Rigdon, Feb. 16, 1832)* D&C 76:81,98

### Elder Joseph Fielding Smith
Those who enter into the telestial kingdom, where their glories differ as do the stars of heaven in their magnitude, and who are innumerable as the sands of the seashore, are the ungodly, the filthy who suffer the wrath of God on earth. . . . (Doctrines of Salvation, 2:296) DGSM:93

### James E. Talmage
The three kingdoms of widely differing glories are organized on an orderly plan of gradation. We have seen that the telestial kingdom comprises several subdivisions; this also is the case, we are told, with the celestial; and, by analogy, we conclude that a similar condition prevails in the terrestrial. Thus the innumerable degrees of merit amongst mankind are provided for in an infinity of graded glories. HL:83

### President Brigham Young
The glory of the telestial world no man knows, except he partakes of it; and yet, in that world they differ in glory as the stars in the firmament

# List of Doctrines

## DEVIL

*Doctrines Located in This Topic*

155. There is a spirit personage known as the devil.

156. In the premortal existence the devil was an angel of God in a position of authority with God.

157. In the premortal existence the devil was ambitious and sought to exalt himself to the glory and honor of God.

158. In the premortal existence the devil's plan was to destroy the agency of the spirit sons and daughters of God.

159. The devil and his followers failed to keep their First Estate (in the premortal life); hence, they were denied the privilege of being born into the world and receiving mortal bodies.

160. There is a place prepared for the devil and his followers called hell.

161. The devil seeks to destroy our souls.

162. The devil has power that in certain circumstances can be exerted upon our physical bodies.

163. The devil is the author of all sin, the source of all evil on earth.

164. The devil attempts to deceive us by appearing at times as an angel of light.

165. The devil is the father of all lies.

166. The devil attempts to beguile us so that he may drag our souls down to hell.

167. The devil authors false doctrines.

168. The priesthood of God has power over the devil.

169. The devil will be bound when he is no longer needed.

170. Satan tempts us to worship him instead of God.

*Doctrines on DEVIL*
*Located in Other Topics*

18. Power to overcome Satan and his evil influence comes from God.

197. The Fall of Adam subjected all people to the enticings of Satan.

261. God has power over the devil.

445. In the Millennium, Satan will be bound and unable to tempt any person.

446. The devil will be loosed for a short time after the Millennium and wickedness will again abound upon the earth.

# DEVIL continued

447. After the Millennium, a final war between the devil with his hosts and the hosts of heaven will result in the expulsion of the devil from the earth forever.

507. Satan influences people to persecute the Saints.

534. We are to pray that we can conquer Satan.

566. The devil rebelled against God in the premortal world, sought to take control of the kingdom of God, and there was war in heaven.

567. As a result of the war in the premortal world, the devil and a third part of the hosts of heaven were thrust out.

579. The Lord gives His authorized servants power over devils.

616. Righteousness binds the devil; we are to take upon us the armor of righteousness as a protection against the evil one.

791. Satan is called Perdition.

792. Those in mortality who sink to the level of perdition (and the premortal hosts of heaven who followed Satan) are sons of perdition.

# DEVIL

**Author's Note:** The devil is referred to in scripture by the following names:

**Adversary**, 1Ne.15:24, D&C 82:5, 1Pet.5:8;
**Beelzebub**, Matt.12:24;
**Belial**, 2Cor.6:15; 1Sam.2:12;
**Dragon**, Rev.12:7-9;
**Destroyer**, 1Cor.10:10, D&C 61:19;
**Father of all lies**, Moses 4:4, Ether 8:25, 2Ne.2:18;
**Lucifer**, (meaning, torchbearer, see CHMR1:281)
    D&C 76:25-26, Isa.14:12-15;
**Perdition**, D&C 76:26;
**Prince of Devils**, Matt.9:34; Mark 3:22;
**Prince of the power of the air**, Eph.2:2
**Satan**, Moses 4:4, D&C 76:28, Rev.12:9;
**Son of the Morning**, D&C 76:25-27, Isa.14:12-15;
**Tempter**, Matt.4:1-3;
**That old serpent**, D&C 76:28, D&C 88:110, 2Ne.2:18.

## 155. There is a spirit personage known as the devil.

### James E. Talmage

We have had occasion to refer frequently to the author of evil among men. This is Satan, the adversary or opponent of the Lord, the chief of evil spirits, called also the Devil, Beelzebub, or the Prince of Devils, Perdition, and Belial. The figurative appellations dragon and serpent are applied to Satan when reference is made to his fall. We learn from the revealed word that Satan was once an angel of light, then known as Lucifer, a Son of the Morning; but his selfish ambition led him to aspire to the glory and power of the Father. . . . AF:56-57

### Joseph Smith,
*translating the Book of Moses*

Wherefore, because that Satan rebelled against me, and sought to destroy the agency of man, which I, the Lord God, had given him, and also, that I should give unto him mine own power; by the power of mine Only Begotten, I caused that he should be cast down; 4. And he became Satan, yea, even the devil, the father of all lies, to deceive and to blind men, and to lead them captive at his will, even as many as would not hearken unto my voice. *(Revelation received 1830, Moses describes the fall of Satan)* Moses 4:3-4

### President Brigham Young,
*quoted by John A. Widtsoe*

There was a devil in heaven, and he strove to possess the birthright of the Savior. He was a liar from the beginning, and loves those who love and make lies, as do his imps and followers here on the earth. *(In Tabernacle, June 3, 1860, JD8:279)* DBY:68

### Joseph Smith

And this we saw also, and bear record, that an angel of God who was in authority in the presence of God, who rebelled against the Only Begotten Son whom the Father loved and who was in the bosom of the Father, was thrust down from the presence of God and the Son, 26. And was called Perdition, for the heavens wept over him—he was Lucifer, a son of the morning. 27. And we beheld, and lo, he is fallen! is fallen, even a son of the morning! 28. And while we were yet in the Spirit, the Lord commanded us that we should write the vision; for we beheld Satan, that old serpent, even the devil, who rebelled against God, and sought to take the kingdom of our God and his Christ— *(Vision to Joseph and Sidney Rigdon, Feb. 16, 1832)* D&C 76:25-28

### John

And there was war in heaven: Michael and his angels fought against the dragon; and the dragon fought and his angels. 8. And prevailed not; neither was their place found any more in heaven. 9. And the great dragon was cast out, that old serpent, called the Devil, and Satan, which deceiveth the whole world: he was cast out into the earth, and his angels were cast out with him. *(John sees the War in Heaven)* Rev.12:7-9

### Moroni, son of Mormon

For it cometh to pass that whoso buildeth it up seeketh to overthrow the freedom of all lands, nations, and countries; and it bringeth to pass the destruction of all people, for it is built up by the devil, who is the father of all lies; even that same liar who beguiled our first parents, yea, even that same liar who hath caused man to commit murder from the beginning; who hath hardened the hearts of men that they have murdered the prophets, and stoned them, and cast them out from the beginning. (*Moroni writes for the benefit of the Gentiles, about* A.D. *419-420*) Ether 8:25

## 156. In the premortal existence the devil was an angel of God in a position of authority with God.

### Joseph Smith
And this we saw also, and bear record, that an angel of God who was in authority in the presence of God, who rebelled against the Only Begotten Son whom the Father loved and who was in the bosom of the Father, was thrust down from the presence of God and the Son, 26. And was called Perdition, for the heavens wept over him—he was Lucifer, a son of the morning. 27. And we beheld, and lo, he is fallen! is fallen, even a son of morning! 28. And while we were yet in the Spirit, the Lord commanded us that we should write the vision; for we beheld Satan, that old serpent, even the devil, who rebelled against God, and sought to take the kingdom of our God and his Christ— (*Vision to Joseph Smith and Sidney Rigdon, Feb. 16, 1832*) D&C 76:25-28

### Elder Joseph Fielding Smith
Just what authority Lucifer held before his rebellion we do not know, but he was an angel of light, his name, Lucifer, meaning torchbearer. Agency was given unto the spirits of men, and they had their talents and individual traits of character there as they do here. It was due to this fact that Lucifer, who was proud and ambitious, rebelled against the Father when his plan for the salvation of fallen man was rejected. (See Moses 4:1-4 and Abr:3:27-28.) CHMR1:281

**Related Witnesses:**

### Lehi,
#### quoted by his son Nephi
And I, Lehi, according to the things which I have read, must needs suppose that an angel of God, according to that which is written, had fallen from heaven; wherefore, he became a devil, having sought that which was evil before God. (*Lehi teaches his sons, between 588-570 B.C.*) 2Ne.2:17

### James E. Talmage
Satan . . . is the foremost of the angels who were thrust down, and the instigator of the ruin of those who fall in this life; AF:57

## 157. In the premortal existence the devil was ambitious and sought to exalt himself to the glory and honor of God.

### James E. Talmage
We have had occasion to refer frequently to the author of evil among men. This is Satan, the adversary or opponent of the Lord, the chief of evil spirits, called also the Devil, Beelzebub, or the Prince of Devils, Perdition, and Belial. The figurative appellations dragon and serpent are applied to Satan when reference is made to his fall. We learn from the revealed word that Satan was once an angel of light, then known as Lucifer, a Son of the Morning; but his selfish ambition led him to aspire to the glory and power of the Father. . . . AF:56-57

### Isaiah
How art thou fallen from heaven, O Lucifer, son of the morning! how art thou cut down to the ground, which didst weaken the nations! 13. For thou hast said in thine heart, I will ascend into heaven, I will exalt my throne above the stars of God: I will sit also upon the mount of the congregation, in the sides of the north: 14. I will ascend above the heights of the clouds; I will be like the most High. (*Lucifer is cast out of heaven for rebellion*) Isa.14:12-14

### J. Reuben Clark, Jr.
I do not know whether Satan was offering a new plan or whether he had offered it before, but it sounded as if he thought it was a new plan. Satan offered the Father to take over all the spirits in the great council and save them all. Nobody was going to be lost, and all he asked of the Father was that the Father abdicate. He did not use that word. Maybe it is not used up in heaven, but we know what it means down here. The Father was to turn all of his power over to Satan, was to disappear, get out of the picture. ¶ The Son apparently had been organizing worlds before, interpreting the passage in the Book of Moses, where the Father said to Moses: "Worlds without number had He created; by His only Begotten Son had He made them." ¶ What Satan wanted, quite evidently, was the full possession, ownership, of this creation of spirits that is involved in the peopling of this earth; so he tried to get them by gift, and that being denied, he is following along and trying to get us through the commission of sin. If we sin sufficiently we become his subjects. ¶ As I read the scriptures, Satan's plan required one of two things: Either the compulsion of the mind, the spirit, the intelligence of man, or else saving men in sin. I

question whether the intelligence of man can be compelled. Certainly men cannot be saved in sin, because the laws of salvation and exaltation are founded in righteousness, not in sin. CR1949Oct:192-93

**Joseph Smith,**
*translating the Book of Moses*
Wherefore, because that Satan rebelled against me, and sought to destroy the agency of man, which I, the Lord God, had given him, and also, that I should give unto him mine own power; by the power of mine Only Begotten, I caused that he should be cast down; (*The record of Moses: the Lord describes Satan's rebellion in the premortal world*) Moses 4:3

**Joseph Smith,**
*receiving the Word of the Lord*
And it came to pass that Adam, being tempted of the devil—for, behold, the devil was before Adam, for he rebelled against me, saying, Give me thine honor, which is my power: and also a third part of the hosts of heaven turned he away from me because of their agency; (*Revelation received Sept. 1830*) D&C 29:36

---

**158. In the premortal existence the devil's plan was to destroy the agency of the spirit sons and daughters of God.**

**Elder Joseph Fielding Smith**
The Lord gave to man his free agency in the pre-existence. This great gift of agency, that is the privilege given to man to make his own choice, has never been revoked, and it never will be. It is an eternal principle giving freedom of thought and action to every soul. No person, by any decree of the Father, has ever been compelled to do good; no person has ever been forced to do good; no person has ever been forced to do evil. Each may act for himself. It was Satan's plan to destroy this agency and force men to do his will. There could be no satisfactory existence without this great gift. Men must have the privilege to choose even to the extent that they may rebel against the divine decrees. Of course salvation and exaltation must come through the free will without coercion and by individual merit in order that righteous rewards may be given and proper punishment be meted out to the transgressor. (Answers to Gospel Questions, 2:20) TLDP:10

**Joseph Smith,**
*translating the Book of Moses*
Wherefore, because that Satan rebelled against me, and sought to destroy the agency of man,

which I, the Lord God, had given him, and also, that I should give unto him mine own power; by the power of mine Only Begotten, I caused that he should be cast down; 4. And he became Satan, yea, even the devil, the father of all lies, to deceive and to blind men, and to lead them captive at his will, even as many as would not hearken unto my voice. (*Revelation received 1830, Moses describes the fall of Satan*) Moses 4:3-4

**James E. Talmage**
We learn from the revealed word that Satan was once an angel of light, then known as Lucifer, a Son of the Morning; but his selfish ambition led him to aspire to the glory and power of the Father, to secure which he made the pernicious proposition to redeem the human family by compulsion; and, failing in this purpose, he headed an open rebellion against the Father and the Son, drawing a third of the hosts of heaven into his impious league. These rebellious spirits were expelled from heaven, and have since followed the impulses of their wicked natures by seeking to lead human souls into their own condition of darkness. They are the devil and his angels. The right of free agency, maintained and vindicated by the war in heaven, prevents the possibility of compulsion being employed in this fiendish work of degradation; but the powers of these malignant spirits to tempt and persuade are used to the utmost. Satan tempted Eve to transgress the law of God; it was he who imparted the secret of murder for gain to the fratricide, Cain. ¶ Satan exerts a mastery over the spirits that have been corrupted by his practices; he is the foremost of the angels who were thrust down, and the instigator of the ruin of those who fall in this life; he seeks to molest and hinder mankind in good efforts, by tempting to sin; or it may be by imposing sickness, or possibly death. Yet in all these malignant doings, he can go no farther than the transgressions of the victim may enable him, or the wisdom of God may permit; and at any time he may be checked by the superior power. . . . AF:56-57

**J. Reuben Clark, Jr.**
Satan offered the Father to take over all the spirits in the great council and save them all. Nobody was going to be lost, and all he asked of the Father was that the Father abdicate. He did not use that word. Maybe it is not used up in heaven, but we know what it means down here. The Father was to turn all of his power over to Satan, was to disappear, get out of the picture. . . . ¶ . . . . What Satan wanted, quite evidently, was the full possession, ownership, of this creation of spirits that is involved in the peopling of this earth; so he tried to get them by

gift, and that being denied, he is following along and trying to get us through the commission of sin. If we sin sufficiently we become his subjects. ¶ As I read the scriptures, Satan's plan required one of two things; Either the compulsion of the mind, the spirit, the intelligence of man, or else saving men in sin. I question whether the intelligence of man can be compelled. Certainly men cannot be saved in sin, because the laws of salvation and exaltation are founded in righteousness, not in sin. CR1949Oct:193

159. **The devil and his followers failed to keep their First Estate (in the premortal life); hence, they were denied the privilege of being born into the world and receiving mortal bodies.**

### Elder Joseph Fielding Smith
The punishment of Satan and the third of the host of heaven who followed him, was that they were denied the privilege of being born into this world and receiving mortal bodies. They did not keep their first estate and were denied the opportunity of eternal progression. The Lord cast them out into the earth, where they became the tempters of mankind—the devil and his angels. (Doctrines of Salvation, 1:65) DGSM:15

### Joseph Smith
The spirits in the eternal world are like the spirits in this world. When those have come into this world and received tabernacles, then died and again have risen and received glorified bodies, they will have an ascendancy over the spirits who have received no bodies, or kept not their first estate, like the devil. The punishment of the devil was that he should not have a habitation like men. The devil's retaliation is, he comes into this world, binds up men's bodies, and occupies them himself. When the authorities come along, they eject him from a stolen habitation. (*In the Nauvoo Temple, from a discourse on the first chapter of Second Peter, May 21, 1843*) HC5:403

### Abraham,
### *quoted by Joseph Smith*
Now the Lord had shown unto me, Abraham, the intelligences that were organized before the world was; and among all these there were many of the noble and great ones; 23. And God saw these souls that they were good, and he stood in the midst of them, and he said: These I will make my rulers; for he stood among those

that were spirits, and he saw that they were good; and he said unto me: Abraham, thou art one of them; thou wast chosen before thou wast born. 24. And there stood one among them that was like unto God, and he said unto those who were with him: We will go down, for there is space there, and we will take of these materials, and we will make an earth whereon these may dwell; 25. And we will prove them herewith, to see if they will do all things whatsoever the Lord their God shall command them; 26. And they who keep their first estate shall be added upon; and they who keep not their first estate shall not have glory in the same kingdom with those who keep their first estate; and they who keep their second estate shall have glory added upon their heads for ever and ever. 27. And the Lord said: Whom shall I send? And one answered like unto the Son of Man: Here am I, send me. And another answered and said: Here am I, send me. And the Lord said: I will send the first. 28. And the second was angry, and kept not his first estate; and, at that day, many followed after him. (*Abraham learns about the creation of the earth and the second estate of man*) Abr.3:22-28

**Related Witnesses:**
### Bruce R. McConkie
We do know their [the evil spirits] curse is to be denied tabernacles, and we surmise that the desire for such tenancy is so great that they, when permitted, even enter the bodies of beasts. [Matt.8:31-32] (The Mortal Messiah, 2:282) TLDP:645

### President Brigham Young,
### *quoted by John A. Widtsoe*
The spirits of devils have been deprived of bodies, and that constitutes their curse, that is to say, speaking after the manner of men, you shall be wanderers on the earth, you have got to live out of doors all the time you live. ¶ That is the situation of the spirits that were sent to the earth, when the revolt took place in heaven, when Lucifer, the Son of the Morning, was cast out. Where did he go? He came here, and one-third part of the spirits in heaven came with him. (*In Bowery, June 22, 1856, JD3:368-69*) DBY:68

### Joseph F. Merrill
According to our teachings, Satan and an army of supporters were cast down to earth from the premortal spirit world. They are spirit brothers of ours, and are real persons having spirit bodies. CR1941Apr:49

### Peter
For . . . God spared not the angels that sinned, but cast them down to hell, and delivered them

into chains of darkness, to be reserved unto judgment; (*In letter to members of the Church, about A.D. 60 to 64*) 2Pet.2:4

## 160. There is a place prepared for the devil and his followers called hell.

**Joseph Smith,**
*receiving the Word of the Lord*
And it came to pass that Adam, being tempted of the devil—for, behold, the devil was before Adam, for he rebelled against me, saying, Give me thine honor, which is my power; and also a third part of the hosts of heaven turned he away from me because of their agency; 37. And they were thrust down, and thus came the devil and his angels; 38. And, behold, there is a place prepared for them from the beginning, which place is hell. (*Revelation received Sept. 1830*) D&C 29:36-38

**Bruce R. McConkie**
[T]he devils know their eventual destiny is to be cast out into the eternal hell from whence there is no return. . . . (Doctrinal New Testament Commentary, 1:311) TLDP:645-46

**Jacob, brother of Nephi,**
*quoted by Nephi*
And assuredly, as the Lord liveth, for the Lord God hath spoken it, and it is his eternal word, which cannot pass away, that they who are righteous shall be righteous still, and they who are filthy shall be filthy still; wherefore, they who are filthy are the devil and his angels; and they shall go away into everlasting fire, prepared for them; and their torment is as a lake of fire and brimstone, whose flame ascendeth up forever and ever and has no end. (*Jacob teaches the people of Nephi, 559-545 B.C.*) 2Ne.9:16

**Jesus,**
*recorded in Matthew*
Then shall he say also unto them on the left hand, Depart from me, ye cursed, into everlasting fire, prepared for the devil and his angels: (*Jesus gives the parable of the sheep and the goats; the sheep are placed on his right hand at the Lord's Second Coming*) Matt.25:41

**Nephi, son of Lehi**
But behold, I say unto you, the kingdom of God is not filthy, and there cannot any unclean thing enter into the kingdom of God; wherefore there must needs be a place of filthiness prepared for that which is filthy. 35. And there is a place prepared, yea, even that awful hell of which I have spoken, and the devil is the preparator of it; wherefore the final state of the souls of men is to dwell in the kingdom of

God, or to be cast out because of that justice of which I have spoken. (*Nephi interprets his father Lehi's dream to his brothers, between 600-592 B.C.*) 1Ne.15:34-35

## 161. The devil seeks to destroy our souls.

**Joseph Smith**
Satan stirreth them up, that he may lead their souls to destruction. . . . 27. And thus he goeth up and down, to and fro in the earth, seeking to destroy the souls of men. (*Revelation in respect to the lost 116 manuscript pages, 1828*) D&C 10:22,27

**President Heber J. Grant,**
**J. Reuben Clark, Jr., David O McKay**
(First Presidency)
Satan is making war against all the wisdom that has come to men through their ages of experience. He is seeking to overturn and destroy the very foundations upon which society, government and religion rest. He aims to have man adopt theories and practices which he induced their forefathers, over the ages, to adopt and try, only to be discarded by them when found unsound, impractical, and ruinous. He plans to destroy liberty and freedom—economic, political, and religious, and to set up in place thereof the greatest, most widespread, and the most complete tyranny that has ever oppressed men. He is working under such perfect disguise that many do not recognize either him or his methods. There is no crime he would not commit, no debauchery he would not set up, no plague he would not send, no heart he would not break, no life he would not take, no soul he would not destroy. He comes as a thief in the night, he is a wolf in sheep's clothing. Without their knowing it, the people are being urged down paths that lead only to destruction. Satan never before had so firm a grip on this generation as he has now. (*"The Message of the First Presidency to the Church"*) IE1942Nov:761

**Peter**
Be sober, be vigilant; because your adversary the devil, as a roaring lion, walketh about, seeking whom he may devour: (*Peter to the churches in modern Asia Minor, about A.D. 60*) 1Pet.5:8

**President Spencer W. Kimball**
[T]he evil one knows where to attack. He is going to attack the home. He is going to try to destroy the family. That is what he wants to do. And you will see that all these workings of Satan . . . have a final result of destroying the family, the parents, the loved ones. That is what

this Satan would like to do. Let us make up our minds he will not do it in our families. CR1975Oct:165

### Nephi, son of Lehi

For the kingdom of the devil must shake, and they which belong to it must needs be stirred up unto repentance, or the devil will grasp them with his everlasting chains, and they be stirred up to anger, and perish; 20. For behold, at that day shall he rage in the hearts of the children of men, and stir them up to anger against that which is good. 21. And others will he pacify, and lull them away into carnal security, that they will say: All is well in Zion; yea, Zion prospereth, all is well—and thus the devil cheateth their souls, and leadeth them away carefully down to hell. (*Nephi foretells of the last days, 559-545 B.C.*) 2Ne.28:19-21

### Joseph F. Merrill

According to our teachings, Satan and an army of supporters were cast down to earth from the premortal spirit world. They are spirit brothers of ours, and are real persons having spirit bodies. As surely as we live they live also. They are trying to handicap and thwart the work of the Lord. Wherever the Saints are found there the devil is also. If Satan can overcome the Saints, he will have all the world subject to him. He is a deceiver, the father of lies, the source of evil, the enemy of all righteousness. ¶ He has great power in the earth. He has deceived and is deceiving, some people who have been and may now be members of the Church, but members in grave danger. One of his schemes is to give them a type of revelation, inducing them to believe that these come from heaven instead of from the devil. It is these people that are in urgent need of a warning. CR1941Apr:49

### Lehi,
#### *quoted by his son Nephi*

And now, my sons, I would that ye should look to the great Mediator, and hearken unto his great commandments; and be faithful unto his words, and choose eternal life, according to the will of his Holy Spirit; 29. And not choose eternal death, according to the will of the flesh and the evil which is therein, which giveth the spirit of the devil power to captivate, to bring you down to hell, that he may reign over you in his own kingdom. (*Lehi to his sons, between 588-570 B.C.*) 2Ne.2:28-29

### Bruce R. McConkie

Lucifer leads the armies of hell against all men, and more especially against those who are instrumental in furthering the Lord's work. (The Mortal Messiah, 2:282) TLDP:645

### Related Witnesses:
#### Amulek,
#### *quoted by Mormon*

But Amulek stretched forth his hand, and cried the mightier unto them, saying: O ye wicked and perverse generation, why hath Satan got such great hold upon your hearts? Why will ye yield yourselves unto him that he may have power over you, to blind your eyes, that ye will not understand the words which are spoken, according to their truth? (*Amulek answers the lawyers and the people in Ammonihah, about 82 B.C.*) Alma 10:25

### Mormon

And thus we see the end of him who perverteth the ways of the Lord; and thus we see that the devil will not support his children at the last day, but doth speedily drag them down to hell. (*Korihor, a disciple of the devil, is killed by his people, about 74 B.C.*) Alma 30:60

---

### 162. The devil has power that in certain circumstances can be exerted upon our physical bodies.

### Bruce R. McConkie

Why did the demons desire to enter the bodies of the swine? or, for that matter, how came they to take up tenancy in the body of the man? We cannot tell and do not know how it is that evil spirits—few or many—gain entrance into the bodies of mortal men. We do know that all things are governed by law, and that Satan is precluded from taking possession of the bodies of the prophets and other righteous people. Were it not so, the work of God would be thwarted—always and in all instances—for Lucifer leads the armies of hell against all men, and more especially against those who are instrumental in furthering the Lord's work. ¶ There must be circumstances of depression and sin and physical weakness that within the restrictions of divine control, permit evil spirits to enter human bodies. We do know their curse is to be denied tabernacles, and we surmise that the desire for such tenancy is so great that they, when permitted, even enter the bodies of beasts. (The Mortal Messiah, 2:282) TLDP:645

### President Brigham Young

You are aware that many think that the devil has rule and power over both body and spirit. Now, I want to tell you that he does not hold any power over man, only so far as the body overcomes the spirit that is in a man, through yielding to the spirit of evil. The spirit that the Lord puts into a tabernacle of flesh, is under the dictation of the Lord Almighty; but the spirit and body are united in order that the spirit may have a tabernacle, and be exalted; and the spirit is influenced by the body, and the body by the spirit. ¶ In the first place the spirit is pure, and under the special control and influence of the Lord, but the body is of the earth, and is subject to the power of the devil, and is under the mighty influence of that fallen nature that is of the earth. If the spirit yields to the body, the devil then has power to overcome both the body and spirit of that man, and he loses both. *(In Tabernacle, April 6, 1855, JD2:255-56)* TLDP:135

### Joseph Smith

The spirits in the eternal world are like the spirits in this world. When those have come into this world and received tabernacles, then died and again have risen and received glorified bodies, they will have an ascendancy over the spirits who have received no bodies, or kept not their first estate, like the devil. The punishment of the devil was that he should not have a habitation like men. The devil's retaliation is, he comes into this world, binds up men's bodies, and occupies them himself. When the authorities come along, they eject him from a stolen habitation. *(In the Nauvoo Temple, from a discourse on the first chapter of Second Peter, May 21, 1843)* HC5:403

### Related Witnesses:

#### Recorded in Luke

[T]he devil threw him down, and tare him. *(Jesus heals a child from an unclean spirit)* Luke 9:42

#### Recorded in Luke

And in the synagogue there was a man, which had a spirit of an unclean devil, and cried out with a loud voice, 34. Saying, Let us alone; what have we to do with thee, thou Jesus of Nazareth? art thou come to destroy us? I know thee who thou art; the Holy One of God. 35. And Jesus rebuked him, saying, Hold thy peace, and come out of him. And when the devil had thrown him in the midst, he came out of him, and hurt him not. 36. And they were all amazed, and spake among themselves, saying, What a word is this! for with authority and power he commandeth the unclean spirits, and they come out. *(Jesus casts out a devil)* Luke 4:33-36

#### Recorded in Matthew

And when he was come to the other side into the country of the Gergesenes, there met him two possessed with devils, coming out of the tombs, exceeding fierce, so that no man might pass by that way. 29. And, behold, they cried out, saying, What have we to do with thee, Jesus, thou Son of God? art thou come hither to torment us before the time? 30. And there was a good way off from them an herd of many swine feeding. 31. So the devils besought him, saying, If thou cast us out, suffer us to go away into the herd of swine. 32. And he said unto them, Go. And when they were come out, they went into the herd of swine: and, behold, the whole herd of swine ran violently down a steep place into the sea, and perished in the waters. 33. And they that kept them fled, and went their ways into the city, and told every thing, and what was befallen to the possessed of the devils. *(Jesus casts out devils)* Matt.8:28-33

### Joseph Smith

I was seized upon by some power which entirely overcame me, and had such an astonishing influence over me as to bind my tongue so that I could not speak. Thick darkness gathered around me, and it seemed to me for a time as if I were doomed to sudden destruction. *(Vision to Joseph of the Father and the Son, spring of 1820)* JS-H 1:15

### Elder Joseph Fielding Smith

It may seem strange to us, but it is the fact that Satan exercises dominion and has some control over the elements. This he does by powers which he knows, but which are hidden from weak mortal men. We read in the book of Job that when the sons and daughters were celebrating in the eldest brother's house, there came a great wind and it smote the four corners of the house, killing them all. Again there came down fire and burned Job's sheep. This was the work of the adversary. Paul speaks of Satan as the "prince of the power of the air." (Eph. 2:2) CHMR2:225

---

### 163. The devil is the author of all sin, the source of all evil on earth.

#### Mormon

And behold, it is he who is the author of all sin. And behold, he doth carry on his works of darkness and secret murder, and doth hand down their plots, and their oaths, and their covenants, and their plans of awful wickedness, from generation to generation according as he can get hold upon the hearts of the children of men. *(Mormon abridges the records of Helaman, 24 B.C.; the Gadianton Robbers' secret oaths and covenants came from Satan who is responsible for sin from the beginning of time)* Hel.6:30

### James E. Talmage

We have had occasion to refer frequently to the author of evil among men. This is Satan, the adversary or opponent of the Lord, the chief of evil spirits, called also the Devil, Beelzebub, or the Prince of Devils, Perdition, and Belial. The figurative appellations dragon and serpent are applied to Satan when reference is made to his fall. AF:56

### Mormon

Wherefore, all things which are good cometh of God; and that which is evil cometh of the devil; for the devil is an enemy unto God, and fighteth against him continually, and inviteth and enticeth to sin, and to do that which is evil continually. 13. But behold, that which is of God inviteth and enticeth to do good continually; wherefore, every thing which inviteth and enticeth to do good, and to love God, and to serve him, is inspired of God. . . . 17. But whatsoever thing persuadeth men to do evil, and believe not in Christ, and deny him, and serve not God, then ye may know with a perfect knowledge it is of the devil; for after this manner doth the devil work, for he persuadeth no man to do good, no, not one; neither do his angels; neither do they who subject themselves unto him. (*Mormon preaches in the synagogue, prior to* A.D. *384*) Moro.7:12-13,17

### Joseph Smith

Verily, verily, I say unto you, that Satan has great hold upon their hearts; he stirreth them up to iniquity against that which is good; 21. And their hearts are corrupt, and full of wickedness and abominations; and they love darkness rather than light, because their deeds are evil; therefore they will not ask of me. 22. Satan stirreth them up, that he may lead their souls to destruction. 23. And thus he has laid a cunning plan, thinking to destroy the work of God; but I will require this at their hands, and it shall turn to their shame and condemnation in the day of judgment. 24. Yea, he stirreth up their hearts to anger against this work. 25. Yea, he saith unto them: Deceive and lie in wait to catch, that ye may destroy; behold, this is no harm. And thus he flattereth them, and telleth them that it is no sin to lie that they may catch a man in a lie, that they may destroy him. 26. And thus he flattereth them, and leadeth them along until he draggeth their souls down to hell; and thus he causeth them to catch themselves in their own snare. 27. And thus he goeth up and down, to and fro in the earth, seeking to destroy the souls of men. (*Revelation in respect to the lost 116 manuscript pages, 1828*) D&C 10:20-27

### Abinadi,
### *quoted by Mormon*

For they are carnal and devilish, and the devil has power over them; yea, even that old serpent that did beguile our first parents, which was the cause of their fall; which was the cause of all mankind becoming carnal, sensual, devilish, knowing evil from good, subjecting themselves to the devil. (*Abinadi preaches to King Noah and his people, about 148* B.C.) Mosiah 16:3

**Related Witnesses:**

### Elder Joseph Fielding Smith

The devil is the author of false religions. He is perfectly willing that men should worship something and in some manner. He makes them think they are worshipping Jesus Christ and his Father but sees to it that many false doctrines contrary to the plan of salvation are introduced among men. He is the author of confusion and laughs at the divided condition existing among the religious denominations. (Man: His Origin and Destiny, pp. 292-93) TLDP:138

### Joseph Smith

And it must needs be that the devil should tempt the children of men, or they could not be agents unto themselves; for if they never should have bitter they could not know the sweet— (*Revelation received Sept. 1830*) D&C 29:39

### James E. Talmage

He is the author of sophistry and degrading skepticism, and of the whole foul mass of the philosophy and science "falsely so called," by which mankind are led to doubt the word of God, to becloud the Scriptures with vain imaginings and private interpretations, and to narcotize the mind with the poison of human invention as a substitute for revealed truth. (The Vitality of Mormonism, p. 347) TLDP:138-39

### Joseph Smith,
### *translating the Book of Moses*

And there came generation upon generation; and Enoch was high and lifted up, even in the bosom of the Father, and of the Son of Man; and behold, the power of Satan was upon all the face of the earth. 25. And he saw angels descending out of heaven; and he heard a loud voice saying: Wo, wo be unto the inhabitants of the earth. 26. And he beheld Satan; and he had a great chain in his hand, and it veiled the whole face of the earth with darkness; and he looked up and laughed, and his angels rejoiced. (*Revelation to Moses regarding Enoch's view of earth*) Moses 7:24-26

### Mormon

And many more things did the people imagine up in their hearts, which were foolish and vain; and they were much disturbed, for Satan did stir them up to do iniquity continually; yea, he did go about spreading rumors and contentions upon all the face of the land, that he might harden the hearts of the people against that which was good and against that which should come. (*The unbelievers say it is not reasonable to believe in Christ and his coming in Jerusalem, about 1 B.C.*) Hel.16:22

---

## 164. The devil attempts to deceive us by appearing at times as an angel of light.

### Elder John Taylor

It is not every revelation that is of God, for Satan has the power to transform himself into an angel of light; he can give visions and revelations as well as spiritual manifestations and table-rappings. (Millennial Star, March 1857, p. 197) TLDP:134

### Jacob, brother of Nephi,
### *quoted by Nephi*

And our spirits must have become like unto him, and we become devils, angels to a devil, to be shut out from the presence of our God, and to remain with the father of lies, in misery, like unto himself; yea, to that being who beguiled our first parents, who transformeth himself nigh unto an angel of light, and stirreth up the children of men unto secret combinations of murder and all manner of secret works of darkness. (*To the people of Nephi, 559-545 B.C.*) 2Ne.9:9

### Paul

For such are false apostles, deceitful workers, transforming themselves into the apostles of Christ. 14. And no marvel; for Satan himself is transformed into an angel of light. 15. Therefore it is no great thing if his ministers also be transformed as the ministers of righteousness; whose end shall be according to their works. (*Paul's letter to the Church at Corinth in Greece, about A.D. 55*) 2Cor.11:13-15

**Related Witnesses:**

### Joseph Smith

If it be the devil as an angel of light, when you ask him to shake hands he will offer you his hand, and you will not feel anything; you may therefore detect him. (*Instructions given at Nauvoo, Ill., Feb. 9, 1843; keys given whereby messengers from beyond the veil may be identified*) D&C 129:8

### Mormon

And Korihor put forth his hand and wrote, saying: I know that I am dumb, for I cannot speak; and I know that nothing save it were the power of God could bring this upon me; yea, and I always knew that there was a God. 53. But

behold, the devil hath deceived me; for he appeared unto me in the form of an angel, and said unto me: Go and reclaim this people, for they have all gone astray after an unknown God. And he said unto me: There is no God; yea, and he taught me that which I should say. And I have taught his words; and I taught them because they were pleasing unto the carnal mind; and I taught them, even until I had much success, insomuch that I verily believed that they were true; and for this cause I withstood the truth, even until I have brought this great curse upon me. (*Korihor, a disciple of the devil, confesses, about 74 B.C.*) Alma 30:52-53

### Joseph Smith

And again, what do we hear? Glad tidings from Cumorah! Moroni, an angel from heaven, declaring the fulfillment of the prophets—the book to be revealed. A voice of the Lord in the wilderness of Fayette, Seneca county, declaring the three witnesses to bear record of the book! The voice of Michael on the banks of the Susquehanna, detecting the devil when he appeared as an angel of light! The voice of Peter, James, and John in the wilderness between Harmony, Susquehanna county, and Colesville, Broome county, on the Susquehanna river, declaring themselves as possessing the keys of the kingdom, and of the dispensation of the fulness of times! (*Epistle to the Church, Sept. 6, 1842, at Nauvoo, Ill.; all of the keys, powers, and authorities have been restored*) D&C 128:20

### Anthony W. Ivins

Knowing that his dominion over the people of the earth is to be broken, and that certain defeat awaits him, he [Lucifer] arrays himself in the livery of Christ, and masquerading as his representative, in the words of Shakespeare, wins the hearts of men by honest trifles which are true, while he betrays them, and leads them away to deepest consequences. CR1934Apr:98

### Joseph Smith,
### *translating the Book of Moses*

And it came to pass that when Moses had said these words, behold, Satan came tempting him, saying: Moses, son of man, worship me. 13. And it came to pass that Moses looked upon Satan and said: Who art thou? For behold, I am a son of God, in the similitude of his Only Begotten; and where is thy glory, that I should worship thee? 14. For behold, I could not look upon God, except his glory should come upon me, and I were transfigured before him. But I can look upon thee in the natural man. Is it not so, surely? (*The record of Moses: Satan appears to Moses*) Moses 1:12-14 (See verses 12-23.)

## 165. The devil is the father of all lies.

### Joseph F. Merrill

According to our teachings, Satan and an army of supporters were cast down to earth from the premortal spirit world. They are spirit brothers of ours, and are real persons having spirit bodies. As surely as we live they live also. They are trying to handicap and thwart the work of the Lord. Wherever the Saints are found there the devil is also. If Satan can overcome the Saints, he will have all the world subject to him. He is a deceiver, the father of lies, the source of evil, the enemy of all righteousness. CR1941Apr:49

### Moroni, son of Mormon

Wherefore, the Lord commandeth you, when ye shall see these things come among you that ye shall awake to a sense of your awful situation, because of this secret combination which shall be among you; or wo be unto it, because of the blood of them who have been slain; for they cry from the dust for vengeance upon it, and also upon those who built it up. 25. . . . for it is built up by the devil, who is the father of all lies; even that same liar who beguiled our first parents, yea, even that same liar who hath caused man to commit murder from the beginning; who hath hardened the hearts of men that they have murdered the prophets, and stoned them, and cast them out from the beginning. (*Moroni writes for the benefit of the Gentiles, about A.D. 419-420*) Ether 8:24-25

### President Joseph F. Smith

Let it not be forgotten that the evil one has great power in the earth, and that by every possible means he seeks to darken the minds of men, and then offers them falsehood and deception in the guise of truth. Satan is a skilful imitator, and as genuine gospel truth is given the world in ever-increasing abundance, so he spreads the counterfeit coin of false doctrine. Beware of his spurious currency, it will purchase for you nothing but disappointment, misery and spiritual death. The "father of lies" he has been called, and such an adept has he become, through the ages of practice in his nefarious work, that were it possible he would deceive the very elect. (Gospel Doctrine, p. 376) TLDP:137

### Joseph Smith,
### *translating the Book of Moses*

And he became Satan, yea, even the devil, the father of all lies, to deceive and to blind men, and to lead them captive at his will, even as many as would not hearken unto my voice. (*Revelation received in 1830; Moses describes the fall of Satan*) Moses 4:4

### Lehi,
### *quoted by his son Nephi*

And because he had fallen from heaven, and had become miserable forever, he sought also the misery of all mankind. Wherefore, he said unto Eve, yea, even that old serpent, who is the devil, who is the father of all lies, wherefore he said: Partake of the forbidden fruit, and ye shall not die, but ye shall be as God, knowing good and evil. 19. And after Adam and Eve had partaken of the forbidden fruit they were driven out of the garden of Eden, to till the earth. (*Lehi explains the fall of Adam to his sons, 588-570 B.C.*) 2Ne.2:18-19

### Related Witnesses:
### Recorded in Luke

But a certain man named Ananias, with Sapphira his wife, sold a possession, 2. And kept back part of the price, his wife also being privy to it, and brought a certain part, and laid it at the apostles' feet. 3. But Peter said, Ananias, why hath Satan filled thine heart to lie to the Holy Ghost, and to keep back part of the price of the land? (*Early Saints practice a united order*) Acts 5:1-3

### President Brigham Young,
### *quoted by John A. Widtsoe*

There was a devil in heaven, and he strove to possess the birthright of the Savior. He was a liar from the beginning, and loves those who love and make lies, as do his imps and followers here on the earth. (*In the Tabernacle, June 3, 1860, JD8:279*) DBY:68

---

## 166. The devil attempts to beguile us so that he may drag our souls down to hell.

### President Brigham Young,
### *quoted by John A. Widtsoe*

The adversary presents his principles and arguments in the most approved style, and in the most winning tone, attended with the graceful attitudes; and he is very careful to ingratiate himself into the favor of the powerful and influential of mankind, uniting himself with popular parties, floating into offices of trust and emolument by pandering to popular feeling, though it should seriously wrong and oppress the innocent. (*In Tabernacle, June 3, 1866, JD11:238*) DBY:69

### Nephi, son of Lehi

For the kingdom of the devil must shake, and they which belong to it must needs be stirred up unto repentance, or the devil will grasp them with his everlasting chains, and they be stirred up to anger, and perish; 20. For behold, at that day shall he rage in the hearts of the children of men, and stir them up to anger against that which is good. 21. And others will he pacify, and lull them away into carnal security, that they will say: All is well in Zion; yea, Zion prospereth, all is well—and thus the devil cheateth their souls, and leadeth them away carefully down to hell. 22. And behold, others he flattereth away, and telleth them there is no hell; and he saith unto them: I am no devil, for there is none—and thus he whispereth in their ears, until he grasps them with his awful chains, from whence there is no deliverance. (*Nephi foretells the last days, 559-545 B.C.*) 2Ne.28:19-22

**Joseph Smith,**
*receiving the Word of the Lord*
Yea, he saith unto them: Deceive and lie in wait to catch, that ye may destroy; behold, this is no harm. And thus he flattereth them, and telleth them that it is no sin to lie that they may catch a man in a lie, that they may destroy him. 26. And thus he flattereth them, and leadeth them along until he draggeth their souls down to hell; and thus he causeth them to catch themselves in their own snare. 27. And thus he goeth up and down, to and fro in the earth, seeking to destroy the souls of men. 28. Verily, verily, I say unto you, wo be unto him that lieth to deceive because he supposeth that another lieth to deceive, for such are not exempt from the justice of God. 29. Now, behold, they have altered these words, because Satan saith unto them: He hath deceived you—and thus he flattereth them away to do iniquity, to get thee to tempt the Lord thy God. (*Revelation in respect to lost 116 manuscript pages, 1828*) D&C 10:25-29

**Marvin J. Ashton**
Satan and his forces were never more strongly arrayed than today. He is cunning. He is successful. One of the most subtle and effective tools he is using among us today is the convincing of some that they have arrived, they have reached their destination, they have earned a rest, they aren't needed anymore, they are out of danger, they are beyond temptation, and they can take pride in their accomplishments. CR1972Apr:61

**Related Witnesses:**
**Jacob, brother of Nephi**
And he was learned, that he had a perfect knowledge of the language of the people; wherefore, he could use much flattery, and much power of speech, according to the power of the devil. (*Jacob refutes the wicked man Sherem, 544-421 B.C.*) Jacob 7:4

## 167. The devil authors false doctrines.

**President Joseph F. Smith**
Let it not be forgotten that the evil one has great power in the earth, and that by every possible means he seeks to darken the minds of men, and then offers them falsehood and deception in the guise of truth. Satan is a skilful imitator, and as genuine gospel truth is given the world in ever-increasing abundance, so he spreads the counterfeit coin of false doctrine. Beware of his spurious currency, it will purchase for you nothing but disappointment, misery and spiritual death. The "father of lies" he has been called, and such an adept has he become, through the ages of practice in his nefarious work, that were it possible he would deceive the very elect. (Gospel Doctrine, p. 376) TLDP:137

**Elder Joseph Fielding Smith,**
*also quoting Joseph Smith*
He will lay temptations in the path of every individual to cause them to commit sin. He has taught the world false doctrines under the guise of truth and many have followed him. He appeared to Moses saying: ¶ ". . . Moses, son of man, worship me. ¶ "And it came to pass that Moses looked upon Satan and said : Who art thou? For behold, I am a son of God, in the similitude of His Only Begotten and where is thy glory, that I should worship thee?" [Moses 1:12-13] ¶ We should be on guard always to resist Satan's advances. He will appear to us in a person of a friend or a relative in whom we have confidence. He has power to place thoughts in our minds and to whisper to us in unspoken impressions to entice us to satisfy our appetites or desires and in various other ways he plays upon our weaknesses and desires. (Answers to Gospel Questions, 3:81) TLDP:137

**Elder Joseph Fielding Smith**
The devil is the author of false religions. He is perfectly willing that men should worship something and in some manner. He makes them think they are worshipping Jesus Christ and his Father but sees to it that many false doctrines contrary to the plan of salvation are introduced among men. He is the author of confusion and laughs at the divided condition existing among the religious denominations. He it was who brought to pass the great apostasy from the religion and Church of Jesus Christ in former days. Satan is exercising great power and has led the great majority of mankind away from the commandments of God, even while he makes them think that they are serving him. In these latter days he is extremely busy and dominates the thinking and the philosophies of the world and

has led many people into "strong delusion, that they should believe a lie." (Man: His Origin and Destiny, pp. 292-93) TLDP:138

**James E. Talmage**

A liar and a murderer from the beginning! He it was who beguiled the mother of the race, and that by the most dangerous of all falsehoods, the half-truth, in the use of which he is a past master. . . . ¶ Primordially he and his angels were "cast out into the earth," and here they have since been, going up and down in the world, seeking whom they may deceive. ¶ He is the author of sophistry and degrading skepticism, and of the whole foul mass of the philosophy and science "falsely so called," by which mankind are led to doubt the word of God, to becloud the Scriptures with vain imaginings and private interpretations, and to narcotize the mind with the poison of human invention as a substitute for revealed truth. ¶ He is an adept at compounding mixtures of truth and falsehood, with just enough of the one to inspire a dangerous confidence, and of the other a toxic portion. ¶ Beware of his prescriptions, his tonics and medicaments. Remember that water may be crystal clear, and yet hold in solution the deadliest of poisons. ¶ He it is who has deceived peoples, tribes and races, into servile submission to self-constituted rulers, and made of the masses slaves of autocrats, rather than to assert and maintain their rights as free men, whatever the effort and sacrifice be. (The Vitality of Mormonism, p. 347) TLDP:138

---

**168. The priesthood of God has power over the devil.**

**Elder Spencer W. Kimball**

Not even Lucifer, the Star of the Morning, the arch-enemy of mankind can withstand the power of the priesthood of God. CR1964Apr:96

**Heber C. Kimball**

I have no fears of anything myself; I do not fear all the devils in hell nor on the earth. I have seen the time, whether in the body or out of it, I do not know, but I saw legions of devils; they came by thousands and tens of thousands, and thousands of men will, no doubt, give way before them and yield the field; but when they came against me and my brethren, we having the priesthood had power to withstand them all, for we were of God. You have heard President Young preach that a man, with the power of God upon him, all the devils in hell could not do anything with him; but if a man enters into the spirit world in his sins, the devil will have power over

him to lead him captive at his will. ("Remarks," Deseret News, Aug. 20, 1862, p. 58) TLDP:139

**Elder Joseph F. Smith**

The hatred of the wicked always has and always will follow the Priesthood and the Saints. The devil will not lose sight of the power of God vested in man—the Holy Priesthood. He fears it, he hates it, and will never cease to stir up the hearts of the debased and corrupt in anger and malice towards those who hold this power, and to persecute the Saints, until he is bound. (At St. George, Utah, April 2, 1877, JD19:24) TLDP:139

**Related Witnesses:**

**Joseph Smith,**
*translating the Book of Moses*

And it came to pass that Moses looked upon Satan and said: Who art thou? For behold, I am a son of God, in the similitude of his Only Begotten; and where is thy glory, that I should worship thee? 14. For behold, I could not look upon God, except his glory should come upon me, and I were transfigured before him. But I can look upon thee in the natural man. Is it not so, surely? 15. Blessed be the name of my God, for his Spirit hath not altogether withdrawn from me, or else where is thy glory, for it is darkness unto me? And I can judge between thee and God; for God said unto me: Worship God, for him only shalt thou serve. 16. Get thee hence, Satan; deceive me not; for God said unto me: Thou art after the similitude of mine Only Begotten. 17. And he also gave me commandments when he called unto me out of the burning bush, saying: Call upon God in the name of mine Only Begotten, and worship me. 18. And again Moses said: I will not cease to call upon God, I have other things to inquire of him: for his glory has been upon me, wherefore I can judge between thee and him. Depart hence, Satan. 19. And now, when Moses had said these words, Satan cried with a loud voice, and ranted upon the earth, and commanded, saying: I am the Only Begotten, worship me. 20. And it came to pass that Moses began to fear exceedingly; and as he began to fear, he saw the bitterness of hell. Nevertheless, calling upon God, he received strength, and he commanded, saying: Depart from me, Satan, for this one God only will I worship, which is the God of glory. 21. And now Satan began to tremble, and the earth shook; and Moses received strength, and called upon God, saying: In the name of the Only Begotten, depart hence, Satan. 22. And it came to pass that Satan cried with a loud voice, with weeping, and wailing, and gnashing of teeth; and he departed hence, even from the presence of Moses, that he beheld him not. (*Satan appears to Moses*) Moses 1:13-22

---

### 169. The devil will be bound when he is no longer needed.

#### Elder John Taylor

Who is Satan? A being powerful, energetic, deceptive, insinuating; and yet necessary to develop the evil, as there are bitters, to make us appreciate the sweet; darkness, to make us appreciate the light; evil and sorrows, that we may appreciate the good; error that we may by enabled to appreciate truth; misery, in order that we may appreciate happiness. . . . ¶ But again, who is Satan? He is a being of God's own make, under his control, subject to his will, cast out of heaven for rebellion; and when his services can be dispensed with, an angel will cast him into the bottomless pit. Can he fight against and overcome God? verily, No! Can he alter the designs of God? verily, No! Satan may rage, but the Lord can confine him within proper limits. He may instigate rebellion against God, but the Lord can bind him in chains. (The Government of God, pp. 80-81) TLDP:141

#### George Q. Cannon

We talk about Satan being bound. Satan will be bound by the power of God; but he will be bound also by the determination of the people of God not to listen to him, not to be governed by him. The Lord will not bind him and take his power from the earth while there are men and women willing to be governed by him. That is contrary to the plan of salvation. To deprive men of their agency is contrary to the purposes of our God. There was a time on this continent, of which we have an account, when the people were so righteous that Satan did not have power among them. Nearly four generations passed away in righteousness. They lived in purity, and died without sin. That was through their refusal to yield to Satan. It is not recorded that Satan had no power in other parts of the earth during that period. According to all history that we have in our possession, Satan had the same power over men who were willing to listen to him. But in this land he did not have power, and he was literally bound. I believe that this will be the case in the millennium. CR1897Oct:65

#### Elder Joseph F. Smith

The hatred of the wicked always has and always will follow the Priesthood and the Saints. The devil will not lose sight of the power of God vested in man—the Holy Priesthood. He fears it, he hates it, and will never

cease to stir up the hearts of the debased and corrupt in anger and malice towards those who hold this power, and to persecute the Saints, until he is bound. (*At St. George, Utah, April 2, 1877, JD19:24*) TLDP:139

**Related Witnesses:**
#### Delbert L. Stapley

The only way Satan can be bound is for people to forsake his temptations and enticements to do evil, and to talk uprightly and circumspectly before the Lord. (See 1Tim.6:5-7.) CR1971-Oct:101

---

### 170. Satan tempts us to worship him instead of God.

#### President Brigham Young, *quoted by John A. Widtsoe*

Who owns this earth? Does the Devil? No, he does not, he pretended to own it when the Savior was here, and promised it all to him if he would fall down and worship him; but he did not own a foot of land, he only had possession of it. He was an intruder, and is still; this earth belongs to him that framed and organized it, and it is expressly for his glory and the possession of those who love and serve him and keep his commandments; but the enemy has possession of it. (*In new Tabernacle, April 28, 1872, JD15:5*) DBY:68

#### Joseph Smith, *translating the Book of Moses*

Behold Satan hath come among the children of men, and tempteth them to worship him; and men have become carnal, sensual, and devilish, and are shut out from the presence of God. (*The record of Moses; Enoch preaches to the people*) Moses 6:49

#### Joseph Smith, *translating the Book of Moses*

And it came to pass that when Moses had said these words, behold, Satan came tempting him, saying: Moses, son of man, worship me. . . . 19. And now, when Moses had said these words, Satan cried with a loud voice, and ranted upon the earth, and commanded, saying: I am the Only Begotten, worship me. 20. And it came to pass that Moses began to fear exceedingly; and as he began to fear, he saw the bitterness of hell. Nevertheless, calling upon God, he received strength, and he commanded, saying: Depart from me, Satan, for this one God only will I worship, which is the God of glory. 21. And now Satan began to tremble, and the earth shook; and Moses received strength, and called upon God, saying: In the name of the Only Begotten, depart hence, Satan. 22. And it came to pass that Satan cried with a loud voice, with weeping, and wailing, and gnashing of teeth; and he departed hence, even from the presence of Moses, that he beheld him not. (*Revelation to Joseph Smith, 1830; Satan appears to Moses*) Moses 1:12,19-22

**James E. Talmage**

The effrontery of his offer was of itself diabolical. Christ, the Creator of heaven and earth, tabernacled as He then was in mortal flesh, may not have remembered His preexistent state, nor the part He had taken in the great council of the Gods; while Satan, an unembodied spirit—he the disinherited, the rebellious and rejected son—seeking to tempt the Being through whom the world was created by promising Him part of what was wholly His, still may have had, as indeed he may yet have, a remembrance of those primeval scenes. In that distant past, antedating the creation of the earth, Satan, then Lucifer, a son of the morning, had been rejected; and the Firstborn Son had been chosen. Now that the Chosen One was subject to the trials incident to mortality, Satan thought to thwart the divine purpose by making the Son of God subject to himself. He who had been vanquished by Michael and his hosts and cast down as a defeated rebel, asked the embodied Jehovah to worship him. "Then saith Jesus unto him, Get thee hence, Satan: for it is written, Thou shalt worship the Lord thy God, and him only shalt thou serve. Then the devil leaveth him, and behold, angels came and ministered unto him." JTC:132-33

**Jesus,**
*recorded in Luke*

And Jesus being full of the Holy Ghost returned from Jordan, and was led by the Spirit into the wilderness, 2. Being forty days tempted of the devil. And in those days he did eat nothing: and when they were ended, he afterward hungered. 3. And the devil said unto him, If thou be the Son of God, command this stone that it be made bread. 4. And Jesus answered him, saying, It is written, That man shall not live by bread alone, but by every word of God. 5. And the devil, taking him up into an high mountain, shewed unto him all the kingdoms of the world in a moment of time. 6. And the devil said unto him, All this power will I give thee, and the glory of them: for that is delivered unto me; and to whomsoever I will I give it. 7. If thou therefore wilt worship me, all shall be thine. 8. And Jesus answered and said unto him, Get thee behind me, Satan: for it is written, Thou shalt worship the Lord thy God, and him only shalt

thou serve. 9. And he brought him to Jerusalem and set him on a pinnacle of the temple, and said unto him, If thou be the Son of God, cast thyself down from hence: 10. For it is written, He shall give his angels charge over thee, to keep thee: 11. And in their hands they shall bear thee up, lest at any time thou dash thy foot against a stone. 12. And Jesus answering said unto him, It is said, Thou shalt not tempt the Lord thy God. 13. And when the devil had ended all the temptation, he departed from him for a season. (*Jesus fasts 40 days and is tempted of the devil*) Luke 4:1-13

**Related Witnesses:**

**Bruce R. McConkie**

False worship brings damnation. (The Millennial Messiah, p. 435) TLDP:751

# List of Doctrines

## EARTH

# EARTH

171. The earth will be sanctified and will become the celestial kingdom, which the righteous shall inherit.

**Elder Joseph Fielding Smith**

In that great change, or resurrection, which shall come to this earth, it shall be sanctified, celestialized and made a fit abode even for God the Father, who shall grace it with his presence. (D&C 88:19) Then shall the righteous, those who have become sanctified through the law of God, possess it for ever as their abode. This earth is destined to become the everlasting residence of its inhabitants who gain the glory of the celestial kingdom. It shall become in that day like the throne of God and shall shine forth with all the splendor and brightness of celestial glory in its eternal, sanctified and glorious state. (The Way to Perfection, p. 351) DGSM:105

**Elder Joseph Fielding Smith**

It is not the fault of the earth that wickedness prevails upon her face, for she has been true to the law which she received and that law is the celestial law. Therefore the Lord says that the earth shall be sanctified from all unrighteousness, that bodies who are of the celestial kingdom may possess it forever and ever; for, for this intent was it made and created, and for this intent are they—the celestial beings—sanctified. It is very strange that members of the Church should fail to understand the plain meaning of this revelation. The Lord did not say this earth shall be one-third celestial, and one-third terrestrial, and one-third telestial, but that the earth was made and created to become a celestial body upon whose face the meek and the poor, who have received their part in the celestial kingdom, shall find their eternal abode. God himself shall make his abode upon it. Moreover, the revelation is very clear in the statement that all who cannot abide the celestial law, or the law of the Gospel, must abide another kingdom. They will have to be transplanted to some other sphere which, without doubt, has been given the law of a terrestrial kingdom, or of a telestial kingdom, in anticipation of a place where bodies who are of the terrestrial spirit or telestial spirit may find their eternal abode. CHMR1:367

**Joseph Smith,**
*receiving the Word of the Lord*

[I]t is decreed that the poor and the meek of the earth shall inherit it. 18. Therefore, it must needs be sanctified from all unrighteousness, that it may be prepared for the celestial glory;

19. For after it hath filled the measure of its creation, it shall be crowned with glory, even with the presence of God the Father; 20. That bodies who are of the celestial kingdom may possess it forever and ever; for, for this intent was it made and created, and for this intent are they sanctified. . . . 25. And again, verily I say unto you, the earth abideth the law of a celestial kingdom, for it filleth the measure of its creation, and transgresseth not the law— 26. Wherefore, it shall be sanctified; yea, notwithstanding it shall die, it shall be quickened again, and shall abide the power by which it is quickened, and the righteous shall inherit it. (*Revelation received Dec. 27/28, 1832*) D&C 88:17-20,25-26

**President George Albert Smith**

If we live for it, our Heavenly Father will give to us eternal life in the celestial kingdom—and that celestial kingdom will be this earth which we dwell upon, when it is cleansed and purified and when it becomes the kingdom that will be presided over by Jesus Christ our Lord. (Published by the Church in Deseret News, Church Section, May 26, 1945)

**Joseph Smith**

The place where God resides is a great Urim and Thummim. 9. This earth, in its sanctified and immortal state, will be made like unto crystal and will be a Urim and Thummim to the inhabitants who dwell thereon, whereby all things pertaining to an inferior kingdom, or all kingdoms of a lower order, will be manifest to those who dwell on it; and this earth will be Christ's. 10. Then the white stone mentioned in Revelation 2:17, will become a Urim and Thummim to each individual who receives one, whereby things pertaining to a higher order of kingdoms will be made known; 11. And a white stone is given to each of those who come into the celestial kingdom, whereon is a new name written, which no man knoweth save he that receiveth it. The new name is the key word. (*Revelation, April 2, 1830*) D&C 130:8-11

**Orson Pratt**

After the thousand years here referred to [Rev. 20:5], this earth will die; it will pass through a change similar to that of our bodies; it will pass away, as an organized world, but not a particle, however, will be destroyed or annihilated; it will all exist, and when it is resurrected again, it will be a new earth. Then those immortal beings who come up out of their graves, at the beginning of the thousand years, will again descend from heaven upon the new earth; and the earth will be eternal; and the beings that inhabit it will be eternal. And the earth will at that time have no more need of the light of a luminary like our sun, or any artificial light, for it will be a globe of light; for when God makes this earth immortal, he will make it glorious like the inhabitants that will be permitted to live upon it. They will become immortal, and be crowned with crowns of glory, and light will radiate from their personages and countenances; so will the earth radiate its light, and shine forth in celestial splendor. *(Fourteenth Ward, 1878, JD19:290)* TLDP:148

**Charles W. Penrose**

Thus the inhabitants of Earth with the few exceptions that are beyond the power of redemption will eventually be saved. And the globe on which they passed their probation, having kept the law of its being, will come into remembrance before its Maker. It will die like its products. But it will be quickened again and resurrected in the celestial glory. It has been born of the water, it will also be born of the Spirit. Purified by fire from all the corruptions that once defiled it, developed into its perfections as one of the family of worlds fitted for the Creator's presence, all its latent light awakened into scintillating action, it will move up into its place among the orbs governed by celestial time, and shining "like a sea of glass mingled with fire," every tint and color of the heavenly bow radiating from its surface, the ransomed of the Lord will dwell upon it; the highest beings of the ancient orbs will visit it; the garden of God will again adorn it; the heavenly government will prevail in every part; Jesus will reign as its King; the river of life will flow out from the regal throne; the tree of life, whose leaves were for the healing of the nations, will flourish upon the banks of the heavenly stream, and its golden fruit will be free for the white-robed throng, that they may eat and live forever. This perfected Earth and its saved inhabitants will then be presented to the Eternal Father as the finished work of Christ, and all things will be subject unto the Great Patriarch, Architect, Creator, Ruler, the Almighty, to whom be obedience and reverence and praise in all the countless worlds that shine as jewels in His universal crown! ("Leaves from the Tree of Life," Contributor, Sept. 1881, pp. 364-65) TLDP:145

**Charles W. Penrose,**
*also quoting Joseph Smith*

As there is much misunderstanding in regard to the origin of the earth, so there is concerning its destiny. It is stated in scripture that "the earth and the works therein shall be burned up." The conclusion is leaped at from that remark that the earth is then to be destroyed and be no more. But those who entertain that notion neglect to read that which follows, i.e., "Nevertheless, we according to his promise look for new heavens and a new earth wherein dwelleth righteousness." (2Pet.3:10-13) The lesson learned from these verses is that this globe is to be purified by fire and the "elements to melt with fervent heat," but not to be annihilated. As it was once, in "the flood," cleansed by the baptism of water, so it is to be regenerated by the baptism of fire and the Holy Ghost, and made a fit habitation for "righteousness" and the righteous, that God may dwell among men and stand upon his "footstool" and commune with man as he did before sin entered the world, and "death by sin." This globe will thus be restored to its primeval beauty and purity when God looked upon it and saw that everything therein was "very good." (See Rev., chap. 21 and 22.) ¶ The destiny of this globe is to be fitted as a habitation for the righteous and "meek" of the earth, who will inherit it in their resurrected state. The Lord has revealed that "the earth abideth the law of its creation," and when it has fully filled the measure thereof, "it shall be crowned with glory; even with the presence of the Father;" that "although it shall die, it shall be quickened again" and shall be inhabited by beings clothed with the celestial glory: that "for this intent was it made and created." (See D&C 88:17-26.) ("The Age and Destiny of the Earth," IE1909May:508-09) TLDP:147

**James E. Talmage**

According to the scriptures the earth has to undergo a change analogous to death, and is to be regenerated in a way comparable to a resurrection. References to the elements melting with heat, and to the earth being consumed and passing away, such as occur in many scriptures already cited, are suggestive of death; and the new earth, really the renewed or regenerated planet, may be likened to a resurrected organism. The change has been called a transfiguration. Every created thing that fills the measure of its creation is to advance in the scale of progression, be it an atom or a world, an animalcule, or man—the direct and literal offspring of Deity. In speaking of the degrees of glory provided for His creations, and of the laws of regeneration and sanctification, the Lord, in a revelation dated 1832, speaks plainly of the approaching death and subsequent quickening of the earth: "And again, verily I say unto you, the earth abideth the law of a celestial kingdom, for it filleth the measure of its creation, and transgresseth not the law—Wherefore, it shall be sanctified; yea, notwithstanding it shall die, it shall be quickened again, and shall abide the power by which it is quickened, and the righteous shall inherit it." AF:341-42

**Related Witnesses:**

**Elder George Albert Smith**

God has said if we will honor Him, and keep His commandments—if we will observe His laws He will fight our battles and destroy the wicked, and when the time comes He will come down in heaven—not from heaven—but He will bring heaven with Him—and this earth upon which we dwell, will be the celestial kingdom. CR1942Oct:49; DGSM:105

**Joseph Smith,**
*receiving the Word of the Lord*

And again, verily, verily, I say unto you that when the thousand years are ended, and men again begin to deny their God, then will I spare the earth but for a little season; 23. And the end shall come, and the heaven and the earth shall be consumed and pass away, and there shall be a new heaven and a new earth. 24. For all old things shall pass away, and all things shall become new, even the heaven and the earth, and all the fulness thereof, both men and beasts, the fowls of the air, and the fishes of the sea; 25. And not one hair, neither mote, shall be lost, for it is the workmanship of mine hand. (*Revelation in presence of six elders, Sept. 1830*) D&C 29:22-25

**Orson Pratt**

Righteousness will abide upon its face, during a thousand years, and the Saviour will bless it with his personal presence: after which the end soon comes, and the earth itself will die, and its elements be dissolved through the agency of a fire. . . . But all mankind are made alive from the first death through the resurrection, so the earth will again be renewed, its elements will again be collected, they will be recombined and reorganized as when it first issued from the womb of chaos. (*Discourse by "Professor Orson Pratt," JD1:331*) TLDP:147

**Elder Joseph Fielding Smith**

From these and other revelations, we are taught that this earth upon which we dwell, is passing through the same experiences and destiny that countless other earths have passed through; that is, to endure for a period of time in a temporal, or mortal state, as a habitation for mortal beings who are being schooled in the mortal probation. When that period of temporality is ended, then like its inhabitants it shall die, pass through the resurrection and be raised to an immortal, unchangeable condition, as the eternal abode

for such inhabitants as the Lord in his wisdom will place upon it. When Adam fell, he brought death into the world, and that death was passed on to every living creature, even the earth, itself, partook of the fall. When it has filled the measure of its temporal existence, it will die and be consumed by fire, but that is not to be the end of this earth. Neither is this mortal death to be something which is to occur millions of years hence or even thousands of years in the future. The earth is now growing old. Soon it is to be changed and brought back very largely to the condition in which it was found before man transgressed in the Garden of Eden and brought upon himself and the earth the temporal change. In this changed condition, which is shortly to take place, the earth will endure for one thousand years as a terrestrial sphere in purity and sanctification. The Savior will come to reign and take his rightful place. All kingdoms and governments will come to an end, and be superseded by Christ's government. There will be no more war, but peace and righteousness, for the knowledge of the Lord shall cover the earth as the waters do the sea. (The Restoration of All Things, pp. 291-92) TLDP:147-48

**John**

And I saw a new heaven and a new earth: for the first heaven and the first earth were passed away; and there was no more sea. . . . 3. And I heard a great voice out of heaven saying, Behold, the tabernacle of God is with men, and he will dwell with them, and they shall be his people, and God himself shall be with them, and be their God. 4. And God shall wipe away all tears from their eyes; and there shall be no more death, neither sorrow, nor crying, neither shall there be any more pain: for the former things are passed away. (*The Apostle John sees the earth in its millennial status*) Rev.21:1,3-4

**President Brigham Young,**
*quoted by John A. Widtsoe*

The earth will abide its creation, and will be counted worthy of receiving the blessings designed for it, and will ultimately roll back into the presence of God who formed it and established its mineral, vegetable, and animal kingdoms. These will all be retained upon the earth, come forth in the resurrection, and abide for ever and for ever. (*In Tabernacle, March 1860, JD8:8*) DBY:101-02; DGSM:105

**Moroni, son of Mormon**

And there shall be a new heaven and a new earth; and they shall be like unto the old save the old have passed away, and all things have become new. (*Moroni's abridgement of the*

*writings of Ether, who wrote, about 550 B.C.)*
Ether 13:9

**Joseph Smith**

I remarked to my family and friends present, that when the earth was sanctified and became like a sea of glass, it would be one great urim and thummim, and the Saints could look in it and see as they are seen. (*Remarks at dinner, Feb. 1843*) HC5:279; DGSM:105

**Joseph Smith**

Q. What is the sea of glass spoken of by John, 4th chapter, and 6th verse of the Revelation? A. It is the earth, in its sanctified, immortal, and eternal state. (*Revelation to Joseph Smith in connection with his translating of the scriptures, March 1832*) D&C 77:1

**Joseph Smith**

And he that liveth in righteousness shall be changed in the twinkling of an eye, and the earth shall pass away so as by fire. (*Revelation: message for the nations of the earth, Feb. 1831*) D&C 43:32

**Isaiah**

Lift up your eyes to the heavens, and look upon the earth beneath: for the heavens shall vanish away like smoke, and the earth shall wax old like a garment, and they that dwell therein shall die in like manner: but my salvation shall be for ever, and my righteousness shall not be abolished. (*Isaiah prophesies of the last days*) Isa.51:6

**Isaiah**

For, behold, I create new heavens and a new earth: and the former shall not be remembered, nor come into mind. (*Isaiah prophesies the rejoicing and triumph of the Lord's people during the millennium*) Isa.65:17

**Isaiah**

For as the new heavens and the new earth, which I will make, shall remain before me, saith the LORD, so shall your seed and your name remain. (*Isaiah prophesies the rejoicing and triumph of the Lord's people during the millennium*) Isa.66:22

**Recorded in Psalms**

Of old hast thou laid the foundation of the earth: and the heavens are the work of thy hands. 26. They shall perish, but thou shalt endure: yea, all of them shall wax old like a garment; as a vesture shalt thou change them, and they shall be changed: Ps.102:25-26

**HYMNS Written by Prophets
Applicable to this Topic**

**Parley P. Pratt**
*Come, O Thou King of Kings,* 2nd verse
HYMNS:59

Come, make an end to sin
And cleanse the earth by fire,
And righteousness bring in,
That Saints may tune the lyre
With songs of joy, a happier strain,
To welcome in thy peaceful reign.

# List of Doctrines

## FAITH AND BELIEF IN CHRIST

*Doctrines Located in This Topic*

172. Faith in the Lord Jesus Christ is the first principle of the gospel.

173. Faith is the principle of righteous action; it will cause a person to do good works, whereas passive belief will not.

174. To obtain eternal life in the celestial kingdom, a person must have faith in Christ, keep the commandments, and endure to the end.

175. Only faith that is followed by repentance is faith that saves.

176. To obtain exaltation a person must have knowledge that God exists and have a correct idea of His character and attributes.

177. To obtain exaltation a person must have knowledge that the course of life that he or she is pursuing is according to the will of God.

178. Faith is a principle of power that enables us to work miracles.

179. The elder who has sufficient faith in Christ may heal the sick.

180. The person who has faith to be healed may be healed.

181. Christ can do all things for those who exercise sufficient faith in Him.

182. Faith in Christ does not come from signs; signs follow those who believe.

183. Those who believe the testimony of the prophets will receive the manifestations of the Holy Ghost.

184. Faith overcomes fear and doubt.

185. A desire to believe can begin the establishment of faith in Christ.

186. Faith in Christ is increased by obedience to the word of God.

187. By the exercise of faith in Christ, knowledge of divine truths can be received through the power of the Holy Ghost.

*Doctrines on FAITH AND BELIEF IN CHRIST Located in Other Topics*

241. Some are given the gift of faith to heal the sick.

242. Some are given the gift of faith to be healed.

245. Some are given the gift of faith.

# FAITH AND BELIEF IN CHRIST continued

295. Those who receive Christ and believe on His name are given power to become (spiritually reborn) sons and daughters of God.

296. The first principles and ordinances of the gospel are faith in the Lord Jesus Christ, repentance, baptism by immersion, and the laying on of hands for the gift of the Holy Ghost.

310. By faith we are saved by the grace of God, not by works alone without true faith.

516. The Lord answers the prayers of His servants according to the degree of their faith (and His holy purposes).

526. The Spirit of God is received through the prayer of faith.

# FAITH AND BELIEF IN CHRIST

172. Faith in the Lord Jesus Christ is the first principle of the gospel.

**Elder Joseph Fielding Smith**

The first principle of the gospel is faith in the Lord Jesus Christ; and of course we are not going to have faith in the Lord Jesus Christ without having faith in his Father. Then if we have faith in God the Father and the Son and are guided, as we ought to be, by the Holy Ghost, we will have faith in servants of the Lord through whom he has spoken. (Doctrines of Salvation, 2:303) DGSM:35

**Joseph Smith**

We believe that the first principles and ordinances of the Gospel are: first, Faith in the Lord Jesus Christ; second, Repentance; third, Baptism by immersion for the remission of sins; fourth, Laying on of hands for the gift of the Holy Ghost. (*The fourth of the thirteen Articles of Faith; letter to John Wentworth, March 1, 1842*) AofF:4

**James E. Talmage**

Although faith is called the first principle of the Gospel of Christ, though it be in fact the foundation of religious life, yet even faith is preceded by sincerity of disposition and humility of soul, whereby the word of God may make an impression upon the heart. No compulsion is used in bringing men to a knowledge of God; yet, as fast as we open our hearts to the influences of righteousness, the faith that leads to life eternal will be given us of our Father. AF:97

**Related Witnesses:**

**Joseph Smith**

As faith, then, is the principle by which the heavenly hosts perform their works, and by which they enjoy all their felicity, we might expect to find it set forth in a revelation from God as the principle upon which his creatures here below must act in order to obtain the felicities enjoyed by the saints in the eternal world; and that, when God would undertake to raise up men for the enjoyment of himself, he would teach them the necessity of living by faith, and the impossibility there was of their enjoying the blessedness of eternity without it. . . . (*Lectures on Faith delivered to the School of the Prophets, 1834-35*) LOF7:6

**Joseph Smith**

In him [God] the principle of faith dwells independently, and he is the object in whom the faith of all other rational and accountable beings centers for life and salvation. (*Lectures on Faith delivered to School of Prophets, 1834-35*) LOF2:2

**Jacob, brother of Nephi,**
*quoted by Nephi*

And he commandeth all men that they must repent, and be baptized in his name, having perfect faith in the Holy One of Israel, or they cannot be saved in the kingdom of God. (*Jacob teaches the people of Nephi, 559-545 B.C.*) 2Ne.9:23

**Stephen L. Richards**

Why is it so difficult to accept things on faith? I think I can suggest an answer. It is because we are so conceited. Men of the world are in the world only because they adopt the philosophy of the world, which is the philosophy of self-sufficiency. It is not a humble philosophy—it is highly egotistical. It makes men themselves the arbiters of all things. They look to no higher source than themselves for the solution of all questions. ¶ . . . I think that altogether too often we permit thinking complexes and sophisticated reasoning to warp our intuitive judgment and entrammel the spontaneous feelings and emotions of our souls. So, when I prescribe that acceptance of Christ as a condition of orthodoxy, I mean acceptance without reservation—a whole-souled intelligent, joyous acceptance of him that proclaims him Lord, Savior, Redeemer and Mediator with the Father and lays claim on his mercy, his grace and his love for all the finer things we know in life. What hope—what peace and satisfaction such a full acceptance of the Christ brings to the heart of man, only those who have received a testimony of Jesus will ever know. CR1935Apr:30-31

**Nephi, son of Lehi**

And now, my beloved brethren, after ye have gotten into this strait and narrow path, I would ask if all is done? Behold, I say unto you, Nay; for ye have not come thus far save it were by the word of Christ with unshaken faith in him, relying wholly upon the merits of him who is mighty to save. (*Nephi writes, between 559-545 B.C.*) 2Ne.31:19

**Paul**

But without faith it is impossible to please him: for he that cometh to God must believe that he is, and that he is a rewarder of them that diligently seek him. (*Paul writes to the Jewish members of the Church on faith, about A.D. 60*) Heb.11:6

**Moroni, son of Mormon**

For if there be no faith among the children of men God can do no miracle among them; wherefore, he showed not himself until after their faith. (*Moroni recounts the wonders and marvels done by faith, about A.D. 419-420*) Ether 12:12

### Moroni, son of Mormon

For thus didst thou manifest thyself unto thy disciples; for after they had faith, and did speak in thy name, thou didst show thyself unto them in great power. (*Moroni sees Jesus face to face and responds, about* A.D. *419*) Ether 12:31

---

173. Faith is the principle of righteous action; it will cause a person to do good works, whereas passive belief will not.

### James E. Talmage

The terms faith and belief are sometimes regarded as synonyms; nevertheless each of them has a specific meaning in our language, although in earlier usage there was little distinction between them, and therefore the words are used interchangeably in many scriptural passages. Belief, in one of its accepted senses, may consist in a merely intellectual assent, while faith implies such confidence and conviction as will impel to action. Dictionary authority justifies us in drawing a distinction between the two, according to present usage in English; and this authority defines belief as a mental assent to the truth or actuality of anything, excluding, however, the moral element of responsibility through such assent, which responsibility is included by faith. Belief is in a sense passive, an agreement or acceptance only; faith is active and positive, embracing such reliance and confidence as will lead to works. Faith in Christ comprises belief in Him, combined with trust in Him. One cannot have faith without belief; yet he may believe and still lack faith. Faith is vivified, vitalized, living belief. AF:87-88

### Joseph Smith

If men were duly to consider themselves, and turn their thoughts and reflections to the operations of their own minds, they would readily discover that it is faith, and faith only, which is the moving cause of all action in them; that without it both mind and body would be in a state of inactivity, and all their exertions would cease, both physical and mental. ¶ 11. . . . Would you exert yourselves to obtain wisdom and intelligence, unless you did believe that you could obtain them? Would you have ever sown, if you had not believed that you would reap? . . . In a word, is there anything that you would have done either physical or mental, if you had not previously believed? Are not all your exertions of every kind, dependent on your faith? Or, may we not ask, what have you, or what do you possess, which you have not obtained by reason of your faith? Your food, your raiment, your lodgings, are they not all by reason of your faith? Reflect, and ask yourselves if these things are not so. Turn your thoughts on your own minds, and see if faith is not the moving cause of all action in yourselves; and, if the moving cause in you, is it not in all other intelligent beings? (*Lectures on Faith delivered to the School of the Prophets, 1834-35*) LOF1:10-11

### James

What doth it profit, my brethren, though a man say he hath faith, and have not works? can faith save him? 15. If a brother or sister be naked, and destitute of daily food, 16. And one of you say unto them, Depart in peace, be ye warmed and filled; notwithstanding ye give them not those things which are needful to the body; what doth it profit? 17. Even so faith, if it hath not works, is dead, being alone. 18. Yea, a man may say, Thou hast faith, and I have works: shew me thy faith without thy works, and I will shew thee my faith by my works. 19. Thou believest that there is one God; thou doest well: the devils also believe, and tremble. 20. But wilt thou know, O vain man, that faith without works is dead? 21. Was not Abraham our father justified by works, when he had offered Isaac his son upon the altar? 22. Seest thou how faith wrought with his works, and by works was faith made perfect? 23. And the scripture was fulfilled which saith, Abraham believed God, and it was imputed unto him for righteousness: and he was called the Friend of God. 24. Ye see then how that by works a man is justified, and not by faith only. 25. Likewise also was not Rahab the harlot justified by works, when she had received the messengers, and had sent them out another way? 26. For as the body without the spirit is dead, so faith without works is dead also. (*Letter to his brethren in the Church*) James 2:14-26

### John A. Widtsoe

The problem of faith as of every gift of the Lord, is twofold: to secure it, and to use it. We speak easily of faith, but altogether too often fail to use it. We recall that it is knowledge, high knowledge, but forget that it is also power, mighty power, and therefore fail to use the greatest force placed within our reach in every issue of life. It has been said: "Without faith it is impossible to please God;" and it may have been added that without the use of faith it is impossible to win the full happiness in life that the Lord has destined for his children. ¶ Latter-day Saints, trained in these truths, possessing a religion resting upon faith, should eagerly use their knowledge for their own and others' good. They should remember that faith may deliver us from evil and secure for us the good that we need. (Man and the Dragon, p. 142,) TLDP:181

**President Brigham Young**

I know nothing about faith in the Lord, without works corresponding therewith; they must go together, for without works you cannot prove that faith exists. We might cry out, until the day of our death, that we love the Savior, but if we neglected to observe his sayings he would not believe us. (At Nephi, Utah, April 18, 1874, JD17:40) TLDP:180

**Joseph Smith**

Yea, signs come by faith, unto mighty works, for without faith no man pleaseth God; and with whom God is angry he is not well pleased; wherefore, unto such he showeth no signs, only in wrath unto their condemnation. (Revelation Aug. 1831) D&C 63:11

**Related Witnesses:**

**James E. Talmage**

I do not realize that we need to speak of faith and works as distinct from each other. There is no true faith without works. It is only belief if the works be left out. And in that sense, the sense in which Paul, the scholar, the student of language, the master of philosophy of his day, used the term, he meant by the use of the term faith, faith as God understands it, faith as it has been declared in the divine word, which means work, effort, sacrifice, service. ("Prove thy Faith by Thy Works," IE1914Aug:943) TLDP:181

**Joseph Smith**

As we have seen in our former lectures . . . faith was the principle of action and of power in all intelligent beings, both in heaven and on earth. . . . (Lectures on Faith delivered to the School of the Prophets, 1834-35) LOF7:2

**Alma, the younger,**
*quoted by Mormon*

And see that ye have faith, hope, and charity, and then ye will always abound in good works. . . . 27. And now, may the peace of God rest upon you, and upon your houses and lands, and upon your flocks and herds, and all that you possess, your women and your children, according to your faith and good works, from this time forth and forever. And thus I have spoken. Amen. (Alma preaches to the people in Gideon, about 83 B.C.) Alma 7:24,27

**Ammon, son of Mosiah,**
*quoted by Mormon*

Yea, he that repenteth and exerciseth faith, and bringeth forth good works, and prayeth continually without ceasing—unto such it is given to know the mysteries of God; yea, unto such it shall be given to reveal things which never have been revealed; yea, and it shall be given unto such to bring thousands of souls to repentance, even as it has been given unto us to bring these our brethren to repentance. (Ammon addresses his brethren, 90-77 B.C.) Alma 26:22

**Jesus,**
*recorded in Luke*

Bring forth therefore fruits worthy of repentance, and begin not to say within yourselves, We have Abraham to our father: for I say unto you, That God is able of these stones to raise up children unto Abraham. (John the Baptist preaches the baptism of repentance) Luke 3:8

**Jesus,**
*recorded in Luke*

And why call ye me, Lord, Lord, and do not the things which I say? (Jesus teaches his disciples obedience) Luke 6:46

**Author's Note:** About the need for *action*: "Emphasis on the outward deed prevents us from substituting mere good wishes for actual performance. It reminds us that we are not pure spirits but embodied spirits, and that we must teach our bodies as well as our hearts to be kind, our lips as well as our thoughts to be clean." (Lectures on Faith in Historical Perspective, p. 174, Dennis F. Rasmussen)

---

**174. To obtain eternal life in the celestial kingdom, a person must have faith in Christ, keep the commandments, and endure to the end.**

**Joseph Smith**

That as many as would believe and be baptized in his holy name, and endure in faith to the end, should be saved— . . . 29. And we know that all men must repent and believe on the name of Jesus Christ, and worship the Father in his name, and endure in faith on his name to the end, or they cannot be saved in the kingdom of God. (Revelation on Church Organization and Government, April 1830) D&C 20:25,29

**Elder Joseph Fielding Smith**

Unless a man will adhere to the doctrine and walk in faith, accepting the truth and observing the commandments as they have been given, it will be impossible for him to receive eternal life, no matter how much he may confess with his lips that Jesus is the Christ, or believe that his Father sent him into the world for the redemption of man. So James is right when he says the devils "believe and tremble," but they do not repent. So it is necessary, not merely that we believe, but that we repent, and in faith perform good works until the end; and then shall we receive the reward of the faithful and a place in the celestial kingdom of God. (Doctrines of Salvation, 2:311) DGSM:36

**Nephi, son of Lehi**

And now, my beloved brethren, after ye have gotten into this strait and narrow path, I would ask if all is done? Behold, I say unto you, Nay; for ye have not come thus far save it were by the word of Christ with unshaken faith in him, relying wholly upon the merits of him who is mighty to save. 20. Wherefore, ye must press forward with a steadfastness in Christ, having a perfect brightness of hope, and a love of God and of all men. Wherefore, if ye shall press forward, feasting upon the word of Christ, and endure to the end, behold, thus saith the Father: Ye shall have eternal life. 21. And now, behold, my beloved brethren, this is the way; and there is none other way nor name given under heaven whereby man can be saved in the kingdom of God. And now, behold, this is the doctrine of Christ, and the only and true doctrine of the Father, and of the Son, and of the Holy Ghost, which is one God, without end. Amen. (*Nephi writes, between 559-545 B.C.*) 2Ne.31:19-21

**Related Witnesses:**

**Joseph Smith**

And who overcome by faith, and are sealed by the Holy Spirit of promise, which the Father sheds forth upon all those who are just and true. . . . 60. And they shall overcome all things. . . . 62. These shall dwell in the presence of God and his Christ forever and ever. . . . 70. These are they whose bodies are celestial, whose glory is that of the sun, even the glory of God, the highest of all, whose glory the sun of the firmament is written of as being typical. (*Vision to Joseph Smith and Sidney Rigdon, Feb. 16, 1832*) D&C 76:53,60,62,70

**President Brigham Young**

I know nothing about faith in the Lord, without works corresponding therewith; they must go together, for without works you cannot prove that faith exists. We might cry out, until the day of our death, that we love the Savior, but if we neglected to observe his sayings he would not believe us. (*At Nephi, Utah, April 18, 1874, JD17:40*) TLDP:180

**President Heber J. Grant**

Of what good are our faith, our repentance, our baptism, and all the sacred ordinances of the gospel by which we have been made ready to receive the blessings of the Lord, if we fail, on our part, to keep the commandments? All that we expect, or all that we are promised, is predicated on our own actions, and if we fail to act, or to do the work which God has required of us, we are little better than those who have not received the principles and ordinances of the gospel. We have only started, and when we rest there, we are not following our faith by our works, and are under condemnation: our salvation is not attained. (Gospel Standards, p. 6) TLDP:180-81

**Joseph Smith,**
*receiving the Word of the Lord*

And all they who suffer persecution for my name, and endure in faith, though they are called to lay down their lives for my sake yet shall they partake of all this glory. (*Revelation at the time of great persecution in Missouri, Dec. 16, 1833*) D&C 101:35

**James E. Talmage**

Faith Essential to Salvation—Inasmuch as salvation is attainable only through the mediation and atonement of Christ, and since this is made applicable to individual sin in the measure of obedience to the laws of righteousness, faith in Jesus Christ is indispensable to salvation. But no one can effectively believe in Jesus Christ and at the same time doubt the existence of either the Father or the Holy Ghost; therefore faith in the entire Godhead is essential to salvation. Paul declares that without faith it is impossible to please God, "for he that cometh to God must believe that he is, and that he is a rewarder of them that diligently seek him." The scriptures abound in assurances of salvation to those who exercise faith in God, and obey the requirements which that faith makes plain. . . . AF:96

---

**175. Only faith that is followed by repentance is faith that saves.**

**Orson Pratt,**
*also quoting Paul*

The first effect of true faith is a sincere, true, and thorough repentance of all sins. . . . ¶ . . . . What does Paul mean when he says, "Therefore being justified by faith, we have peace with God, through our Lord Jesus Christ?" He means that faith is the starting point—the foundation and cause of our repentance and baptism which bring remission or justification; and being the cause which leads to those results, it is not improper to impute justification to faith. . . . All will admit that to believe with the heart leads to and includes repentance. ("True Faith," in Lectures on Faith, pp. 76-77) TLDP:178

## Joseph Smith,
### *receiving the Word of the Lord*

But, behold, I say unto you that I, the Lord God, gave unto Adam and unto his seed, that they should not die as to the temporal death, until I, the Lord God, should send forth angels to declare unto them repentance and redemption, through faith on the name of mine Only Begotten Son. 43. And thus did I, the Lord God, appoint unto man the days of his probation—that by his natural death he might be raised in immortality unto eternal life, even as many as would believe; 44. And they that believe not unto eternal damnation; for they cannot be redeemed from their spiritual fall, because they repent not; (*Revelation in presence of six elders, Sept. 1830*) D&C 29:42-44

### Joseph Smith

And that the Lamanites might come to the knowledge of their fathers, and that they might know the promises of the Lord, and that they may believe the gospel and rely upon the merits of Jesus Christ, and be glorified through faith in his name, and that through their repentance they might be saved. Amen. (*Revelation regarding the lost manuscript pages and the purpose of the Book of Mormon plates, July 1828*) D&C 3:20

### Jacob, brother of Nephi,
#### *quoted by Nephi*

And if they will not repent and believe in his name, and be baptized in his name, and endure to the end, they must be damned; for the Lord God, the Holy One of Israel, has spoken it. (*Jacob teaches the people of Nephi, 559-545 B.C.*) 2Ne.9:24

### Amulek,
#### *quoted by Mormon*

And thus he shall bring salvation to all those who shall believe on his name; this being the intent of this last sacrifice, to bring about the bowels of mercy, which overpowereth justice, and bringeth about means unto men that they may have faith unto repentance. 16. And thus mercy can satisfy the demands of justice, and encircles them in the arms of safety, while he that exercises no faith unto repentance is exposed to the whole law of the demands of justice; therefore only unto him that has faith unto repentance is brought about the great and eternal plan of redemption. 17. Therefore may God grant unto you, my brethren, that ye may begin to exercise your faith unto repentance, that ye begin to call upon his holy name, that he would have mercy upon you; (*Amulek teaches the people about the atonement of Christ, 74 B.C.*) Alma 34:15-17

### Related Witnesses:
#### Mormon

And it came to pass that many of the Lamanites did come down into the land of Zarahemla, and did declare unto the people of the Nephites the manner of their conversion, and did exhort them to faith and repentance. (*Righteous Lamanites preach to the wicked Nephites, about 30 B.C.*) Hel.6:4

### Samuel, the Lamanite,
#### *quoted by Mormon*

And behold, ye do know of yourselves, for ye have witnessed it, that as many of them as are brought to the knowledge of the truth, and to know of the wicked and abominable traditions of their fathers, and are led to believe the holy scriptures, yea, the prophecies of the holy prophets, which are written, which leadeth them to faith on the Lord, and unto repentance, which faith and repentance bringeth a change of heart unto them— 8. Therefore, as many as have come to this, ye know of yourselves are firm and steadfast in the faith, and in the thing wherewith they have been made free. (*To the Nephites, about 6 B.C.*) Hel.15:7-8

---

## 176. To obtain exaltation a person must have knowledge that God exists and have a correct idea of His character and attributes.

### Joseph Smith,
#### *also quoting Paul*

[F]or faith could not center in a Being of whose existence we have no idea, because the idea of his existence in the first instance is essential to the exercise of faith in him. Romans 10:14: "How then shall they call on him in whom they have not believed? and how shall they believe in him of whom they have not heard? and how shall they hear without a preacher (or one sent to tell them)? So, then faith comes by hearing the word of God." (New Translation) ¶ 2. Let us here observe, that three things are necessary in order that any rational and intelligent being may exercise faith in God unto life and salvation. ¶ 3. First, the idea that he actually exists. ¶ 4. Secondly, a correct idea of his character, perfections, and attributes. ¶ 5. Thirdly, an actual knowledge that the course of life which he is pursuing is according to his will. For without an acquaintance with these three important facts, the faith of every rational being must be imperfect and unproductive; but with this understanding it can become perfect and fruitful, abounding in righteousness, unto the praise and glory of God the Father, and the Lord Jesus Christ. (*Lectures on Faith delivered to the School of the Prophets, 1834-35*) LOF3:2-5

### Jesus,
#### *quoted by John*

And this is life eternal, that they might know thee the only true God, and Jesus Christ, whom thou hast sent. (*Jesus offers the great intercessory prayer for his Apostles*) John 17:3

### Joseph Smith,
#### *receiving the Word of the Lord*

This is eternal lives—to know the only wise and true God, and Jesus Christ, whom he hath sent. I am he. Receive ye, therefore, my law. (*Revelation relating to the new and everlasting covenant, including the eternal nature of the marriage covenant, July 12, 1843, [1831]*) D&C 132:24

### Elder Spencer W. Kimball,
#### *also quoting Jesus and Joseph Smith*

As members of The Church of Jesus Christ of Latter-day Saints, we declare in all solemnity the reality of God the Eternal Father and his Son Jesus Christ, as like as any father and son, yet distinct individuals. On more than one occasion the Christ has made known that a knowledge and acquaintance with God is basic to exaltation. ¶ "This is eternal lives—to know the only wise and true God, and Jesus Christ, whom he hath sent. I am he." And then his command: "Receive ye therefore, my law." (D&C 132:24) CR1964Apr:93

### George Q. Morris,
#### *also quoting Jesus*

What is eternal life? What is immortality? What is exaltation and salvation? The Lord says: "And this is life eternal, that they might know thee the only true God, and Jesus Christ, whom thou hast sent." (John 17:3) CR1959Oct:47

**Related Witnesses:**

### Paul

How then shall they call on him in whom they have not believed? and how shall they believe in him of whom they have not heard? and how shall they hear without a preacher? (*Letter to the Church in Rome, about A.D. 55; faith comes by hearing the gospel taught by legal administrators sent of God*) Rom.10:14

### Henry D. Moyle

I know with all my heart that God lives and that Jesus is the Christ, and I want for nothing but to dedicate my life, my energy, to proclaiming this testimony to the world, to let my fellow men know that there can be no joy in life, and certainly no salvation hereafter, unless we understand the laws of God, given to us for our happiness and our salvation, and in turn lend obedience to them. CR1951Oct:12

### Elder Spencer W. Kimball,
#### *also quoting Joseph Smith*

The ultimate and greatest of all knowledge, then, is to know God and his program for our exaltation. We may know him by sight, by sound, by feeling. While relatively few ever do really know him, everyone may know him, not only prophets—ancient and modern—but, as he said: ¶ ". . . every soul who forsaketh his sins and cometh unto me, and calleth on my name, and obeyeth my voice, and keepeth my commandments, shall see my face and know that I am." (D&C 93:1) CR1968Oct:130

---

177. To obtain exaltation a person must have knowledge that the course of life that he or she is pursuing is according to the will of God.

### Joseph Smith

Let us here observe, that three things are necessary in order that any rational and intelligent being may exercise faith in God unto life and salvation. ¶ 3. First, the idea that he actually exists. ¶ 4. Secondly, a correct idea of his character, perfections, and attributes. ¶ 5. Thirdly, an actual knowledge that the course of life which he is pursuing is according to his will. For without an acquaintance with these three important facts, the faith of every rational being must be imperfect and unproductive; but with this understanding it can become perfect and fruitful, abounding in righteousness, unto the praise and glory of God the Father, and the Lord Jesus Christ. (*Lectures on Faith delivered to the School of the Prophets, 1834-35*) LOF3:2-5

### Joseph Smith

An actual knowledge to any person, that the course of life which he pursues is according to the will of God, is essentially necessary to enable him to have that confidence in God, without which no person can obtain eternal life. It was this that enabled the ancient saints to endure all their afflictions and persecutions, and to take joyfully the spoiling of their goods, knowing (not believing merely) that they had a more enduring substance. (Heb.10:34) ¶ 3. Having the assurance that they were pursuing a course which was agreeable to the will of God, they were enabled to take, not only the spoiling of their goods, and the wasting of their substance, joyfully, but also to suffer death in its most horrid forms; knowing (not merely believing) that when this earthly house of their tabernacle was dissolved, they had a building of

God, a house not made with hands, eternal in the heavens. (2Cor.5:1) ¶ 4. Such was, and always will be, the situation of the saints of God, that unless they have an actual knowledge that the course they are pursuing is according to the will of God they will grow weary in their minds, and faint; for such has been, and always will be, the opposition in the hearts of unbelievers and those that know not God against the pure and unadulterated religion of heaven (the only thing which insures eternal life), that they will persecute to the uttermost all that worship God according to his revelations, receive the truth in the love of it, and submit themselves to be guided and directed by his will; and drive them to such extremities that nothing short of an actual knowledge of their being the favorites of heaven, and of their having embraced the order of things which God has established for the redemption of man, will enable them to exercise that confidence in him, necessary for them to overcome the world, and obtain that crown of glory which is laid up for them that fear God. (*Lectures on Faith delivered to the School of the Prophets, 1834-35*) LOF6:2-4

### Bruce R. McConkie

All the faithful Saints, all of those who have endured to the end, depart this life with the absolute guarantee of eternal life. ¶ There is no equivocation, no doubt, no uncertainty in our minds. Those who have been true and faithful in this life will not fall by the wayside in the life to come. If they keep their covenants here and now and depart this life firm and true in the testimony of our blessed Lord, they shall come forth with an inheritance of eternal life. ¶ We do not mean to say that those who die in the Lord, and who are true and faithful in this life, must be perfect in all things when they go into the next sphere of existence. There was only one perfect man—the Lord Jesus whose Father was God. ¶ There have been many righteous souls who have attained relative degrees of perfection, and there have been great hosts of faithful people who have kept the faith, and lived the law, and departed this life with the full assurance of an eventual inheritance of eternal life. . . . ¶ But what we are saying is that when the saints of God chart a course of righteousness, when they gain sure testimonies of the truth and divinity of the Lord's work, when they keep the commandments, when they overcome the world, when they put first in their lives the things of God's kingdom; when they do all these things, and then depart this life— though they have not yet become perfect—they shall nonetheless gain eternal life in our

Father's kingdom; and eventually they shall be perfect as God their Father and Christ His Son are perfect. CR1976Oct:158-59

### James E. Talmage

A condition essential to the exercise of a living, growing, sustaining faith in Deity is the consciousness on man's part that he is at least endeavoring to live in accordance with the laws of God as he has learned them. A knowledge that he is wilfully and wantonly sinning against the truth will deprive him of sincerity in prayer and faith and estrange him from his Father. He must feel that the trend of his life's course is acceptable, that with due allowance for mortal weakness and human frailty he is in some measure approved of the Lord; otherwise he is restrained from supplicating the throne of grace with confidence. The consciousness of earnest effort toward godly conduct is a power of itself, strengthening its possessor in sacrifice and under persecution, and sustaining him in all good works. AF:95-96

### Related Witnesses:

#### Stephen L. Richards

In this new teaching of God's plans for his children [the gospel investigator] is given matchless incentive for the development of noble character and high service to his fellow man. He is taught that the revelations set forth with certainty the stations to which men of ambition and ideals may aspire; that there are preferential conditions and places in the hereafter as in this life; and that the reward to the truly faithful will be placement in the highest degree of glory in the presence of the Father and the Son, there to dwell forever in an eternity of progression in knowledge, power, and goodness. ¶ Now, after these teachings and their assimilation by the investigator he is prepared for the call to repentance. He is prepared to review and appraise his life in light of the knowledge he has received. Perhaps never before in his experience has he thought seriously of the need for repentance. Now he knows that all men are called to repentance, not once only, but all during the course of their lives, that as they gain knowledge of the principles and laws of the perfect life, they have need to turn away from frailty, weakness, and imperfection. ¶ He becomes more keenly conscious of the commandments the Lord has given, of their transcendent importance not only to himself, but to the great society of men everywhere. He begins to realize the real significance of God's kingdom in the earth, and in the hearts of men. When he understands the paternity of man, his appreciation of the fraternity and brotherhood of man is enhanced. ¶ And so there arises within the heart of the investigator so led and instructed in the principles of truth a desire—a fervent, burning desire—to avail himself of the high privileges extended to him to ally himself with the kingdom of our Lord. He wishes for the kind of conviction and testimony he has heard and experienced from the missionary. ¶ He sees the happiness, the contentment, and the satisfaction which flow from such testimony. He has been taught, and he now knows that this great happiness may come to him only through humble prayer and study, so he acquires the philosophy of humility. He no longer regards himself as self-sufficient. He depends on the Lord, and his faith assures him his trust will be rewarded. CR1954Oct:95

**Paul**

For I am now ready to be offered, and the time of my departure is at hand. 7. I have fought a good fight, I have finished my course, I have kept the faith: 8. Henceforth there is laid up for me a crown of righteousness, which the Lord, the righteous judge, shall give me at that day: and not to me only, but unto all them also that love his appearing. (*Letter to his assistant Timothy, about A.D. 64*) 2Tim.4:6-8

**Mormon**

And it came to pass as he was thus pondering—being much cast down because of the wickedness of the people of the Nephites, their secret works of darkness, and their murderings, and their plunderings, and all manner of iniquities—and it came to pass as he was thus pondering in his heart, behold, a voice came unto him saying: 4. Blessed art thou, Nephi, for those things which thou hast done; for I have beheld how thou hast with unwearyingness declared the word, which I have given unto thee, unto this people. And thou hast not feared them, and hast not sought thine own life, but hast sought my will, and to keep my commandments. 5. And now, because thou hast done this with such unwearyingness, behold, I will bless thee forever; and I will make thee mighty in word and in deed, in faith and in works; yea, even that all things shall be done unto thee according to thy word, for thou shalt not ask that which is contrary to my will. (*Nephi, son of Helaman, ponders as he returns to his house, between 23 and 20 B.C.*) Hel.10:3-5

**Richard L. Evans**

And you who are tried and tempted by appetites, by evil in its subtle shapes; you who have been careless in your conduct, who have lived the kind of lives that fall short of what you know you should have lived—and are contending with conscience and are torn inside

yourselves: You also are not alone in life, for the Lord God who gave you life has also given the glorious principle of repentance, which, upon sincere turning away from false ways, can restore again the blessed peace that comes with quiet conscience. (Richard L. Evans: The Man and the Message, p. 139) TLDP:553-54

## 178. Faith is a principle of power that enables us to work miracles.

**J. Reuben Clark, Jr.**

As I think about faith, this principle of power, I am obliged to believe that it is an intelligent force. Of what kind, I do not know. But it is superior to and overrules all other forces of which we know. . . . ¶ You brethren, we brethren, have had this great power given unto us, this power of faith. What are we doing about it? Can you, can we, do the mighty things that the Savior did? Yes. They have been done by the members of the Church who had the faith and the righteousness so to do. Think of what is within your power if you but live the Gospel, if you but live so that you may invoke the power which is within you. CR1960Apr:21; DCSM:19

**Orson F. Whitney**

The turning of water into wine, the miraculous feeding of the multitude, the walking upon the waves, the healing of the sick, the raising of the dead, and other wonderful works wrought by the Savior, the apostles, and the ancient prophets—what were they but manifestations of an all-powerful faith, to possess which is to have the power to remove mountains—without picks and shovels. . . . Such a faith is not mere credulity: it is a divine energy, operating upon the natural laws and by natural processes—natural, though unknown to "the natural man," and termed by him supernatural. ¶ Faith is the beating heart of the universe—the incentive, the impulse, to all action, the mainspring of all achievement. Nothing was ever accomplished, small or great, commonplace or miraculous, that was not backed up by confidence in some power, human or superhuman, that impelled and pushed forward the enterprise. (Gospel Themes, p. 33) TLDP:180

**Mormon**

Whatsoever thing ye shall ask the Father in my name, which is good, in faith believing that ye shall receive, behold, it shall be done unto you. . . . 33. And Christ hath said: If ye will have faith in me ye shall have power to do whatsoever thing is expedient in me. . . . 35. . . . [H]as the day of miracles ceased? 36. Or have angels ceased to appear unto the children of men? Or has he withheld the power of the Holy Ghost from them? Or will he, so long as time shall last, or the earth shall stand, or there shall be one man upon the face thereof to be saved? 37. Behold I say unto you, Nay; for it is by faith that miracles are wrought; and it is by faith that angels appear and minister unto men; wherefore, if these things have ceased wo be unto the children of men, for it is because of unbelief, and all is vain. (*Mormon preaches in the synagogue, prior to A.D. 384*) Moro.7:26,33,35-37

### Joseph Smith,
### *also quoting Paul*

But faith is not only the principle of action, but [it is the principle] of power also, in all intelligent beings, whether in heaven or on earth. Thus says the author of the epistle to the Hebrews, (11:3) 14. "Through faith we understand that the worlds were framed by the word of God; so that things which are seen were not made of things which do appear." 15. By this we understand that the principle of power which existed in the bosom of God, by which the worlds were framed, was faith; and that it is by reason of this principle of power existing in the Deity, that all created things exist; so that all things in heaven, on earth, or under the earth exist by reason of faith as it existed in Him. 16. Had it not been for the principle of faith the worlds would never have been framed neither would man have been formed of the dust. It is the principle by which Jehovah works, and through which he exercises power over all temporal as well as eternal things. Take this principle or attribute—for it is an attribute—from the Deity, and he would cease to exist. 17. Who cannot see, that if God framed the worlds by faith, that it is by faith that he exercises power over them, and that faith is the principle of power? And if the principle of power, it must be so in man as well as in the Deity? This is the testimony of all the sacred writers, and the lesson which they have been endeavouring to teach to man. . . . ¶ 22. It was by faith that the worlds were framed. God spake, chaos heard, and worlds came into order by reason of the faith there was in HIM. So with man also; he spake by faith in the name of God, and the sun stood still, the moon obeyed, mountains removed, prisons fell, lions' mouths were closed, the human heart lost its enmity, fire its violence, armies their power, the sword its terror, and death its dominion; and all this by reason of the faith which was in him. (*Lectures on Faith delivered to the School of the Prophets, 1834-35*) LOF1:13-17,22

### Related Witnesses:
### John A. Widtsoe

Faith is power. A rational faith is based upon the use of human intelligence and prayer to God. The man of faith touches divinity, the source of power, the force of forces, and becomes as it were a transmitter, or conductor, of the boundless influence of God. As the electric current travels along copper wire, so does divine power reach man through faith. Faith enables man to endure and to accomplish. This is "the substance of things hoped for." (Man and the Dragon, pp. 140-41) TLDP:180

### Jesus,
### *recorded in Matthew*

If ye have faith as a grain of mustard seed, ye shall say unto this mountain, Remove hence to yonder place; and it shall remove; and nothing shall be impossible unto you. (*Jesus heals a lunatic boy and teaches his disciples the principle of faith*) Matt.17:20

### Joseph Smith

Faith comes by hearing the word of God. If a man has not faith enough to do one thing, he may have faith to do another: if he cannot remove a mountain, he may heal the sick. Where faith is there will be some of the fruits: all gifts and power which were sent from heaven, were poured out on the heads of those who had faith. (*Joseph remarks to the Saints newly arrived from England, April 1843*) HC5:355

### Paul

And what shall I more say? for the time would fail me to tell of Gedeon, and of Barak, and of Samson, and of Jephthae; of David also, and Samuel, and of the prophets: 33. Who through faith subdued kingdoms, wrought righteousness, obtained promises, stopped the mouths of lions, 34. Quenched the violence of fire, escaped the edge of the sword, out of weakness were made strong, waxed valiant in fight, turned to flight the armies of the aliens. 35. Women received their dead raised to life again: and others were tortured, not accepting deliverance; that they might obtain a better resurrection: (*Paul writes on faith to the Jewish members of the Church, about A.D. 60*) Heb.11:32-35

### Alma, the younger,
### *quoted by Mormon*

And Alma cried, saying: How long shall we suffer these great afflictions, O Lord? O Lord, give us strength according to our faith which is in Christ, even unto deliverance. And they broke the cords with which they were bound; and when the people saw this, they began to flee, for the fear of destruction had come upon them. 27. And it came to pass that so great was their fear that they fell to the earth, and did not obtain the outer door of the prison; and the earth shook mightily, and the walls of the prison were rent in twain, so that they fell to the earth; and the chief judge, and the lawyers, and priests, and teachers, who smote upon Alma and Amulek, were slain by the fall thereof. 28. And Alma and Amulek came forth out of the prison, and they were not hurt; for the Lord had granted unto them power, according to their faith which was in Christ. And they straightway came forth out of the prison; and they were loosed from their bands; and the prison had fallen to the earth, and every soul within the walls thereof, save it were Alma and Amulek, was slain; and they straightway came forth into the city. (*Alma and Amulek are delivered from prison, about 81 B.C.*) Alma 14:26-28

### Moroni, son of Mormon

Behold, it was the faith of Alma and Amulek that caused the prison to tumble to the earth. . . . 17. And it was by faith that the three disciples obtained a promise that they should not taste of death; and they obtained not the promise until after their faith. 18. And neither at any time hath any wrought miracles until after their faith; wherefore they first believed in the Son of God. . . . 30. For the brother of Jared said unto the mountain Zerin, Remove—and it was removed. And if he had not had faith it would not have moved; wherefore thou workest after men have faith. (*Moroni recounts the wonders and marvels done by faith, about A.D. 419-420*) Ether 12:13,17-18,30

### Recorded in Exodus

And Moses said unto the people, Fear ye not, stand still, and see the salvation of the LORD, which he will shew to you to day: for the Egyptians whom ye have seen to day, ye shall see them again no more for ever. 14. The LORD shall fight for you, and ye shall hold your peace. 15. And the LORD said unto Moses, Wherefore criest thou unto me? speak unto the children of Israel, that they go forward: 16. But lift thou up thy rod, and stretch out thine hand over the sea, and divide it: and the children of Israel shall go on dry ground through the midst of the sea. (*Moses speaks to the Israelites and parts the Red Sea*) Ex.14:13-16

---

## 179. The elder who has sufficient faith in Christ may heal the sick.

### Joseph Smith,
*receiving the Word of the Lord*

And whoso shall ask it in my name in faith, they shall cast out devils; they shall heal the sick; they shall cause the blind to receive their sight, and the deaf to hear, and the dumb to speak, and the lame to walk. (*Revelation to Joseph Smith and Sidney Rigdon, Dec. 1830*) D&C 35:9

### James

Is any sick among you? let him call for the elders of the church; and let them pray over him, anointing him with oil in the name of the Lord: 15. And the prayer of faith shall save the sick, and the Lord shall raise him up; and if he have committed sins, they shall be forgiven him. (*Letter to his brethren in the Church*) James 5:14-15

### James E. Talmage

Though the authority to administer to the sick belongs to the elders of the Church in general, some possess this power in an unusual degree, having received it as an especial endowment of the Spirit. Another gift, allied to this, is that of having faith to be healed, which is manifested in varying degrees. Not always are the administrations of the elders followed by immediate healings; the afflicted may be permitted to suffer in body, perhaps for the accomplishment of good purposes, and in the time appointed all must experience bodily death. But let the counsels of God be observed in administering to the afflicted; then if they recover, they live unto the Lord; and the assuring promise is added that those who die under such conditions die unto the Lord. AF:205

### Related Witnesses:

#### President Joseph Fielding Smith

We are ambassadors of the Lord Jesus Christ. Our commission is to represent him. We are directed to preach his gospel, to perform the ordinances of salvation, to bless mankind, to heal the sick and perhaps perform miracles, to do what he would do if he were personally present—and all this because we hold the holy priesthood. CR1971Apr:47

#### President Brigham Young,
*quoted by John A. Widtsoe*

When I lay hands on the sick, I expect the healing power and influence of God to pass through me to the patient, and the disease to give away. I do not say that I heal everybody I lay hands on; but many have been healed under my administration. Jesus said, on one occasion, "Who has touched me?" A woman had crept up behind him in the crowd, and touched the hem of his garment, and he knew it, because virtue had gone from him. Do you see the reason and propriety of laying hands on each other? When we are prepared, when we are holy vessels before the Lord, a stream of power from the

Almighty can pass through the tabernacle of the administrator to the system of the patient, and the sick are made whole; the headache, fever or other disease has to give away. My brethren and sisters, there is virtue in us if we will do right; if we live our religion we are the temples of God wherein he will dwell; if we defile ourselves, these temples God will destroy. (*In Ogden Tabernacle, July 10, 1870, JD14:72*) DBY:162

**Joseph Smith,**
*quoted by Elder Joseph Fielding Smith*
Because faith is wanting, the fruits are. No man since the world was had faith without having something along with it. The ancients quenched the violence of fire, escaped the edge of the sword, women received their dead, etc. By faith the worlds were made. A man who has none of the gifts has no faith; and he deceives himself, if he supposes he has. Faith has been wanting, not only among the heathen, but in professed Christendom also, so that tongues, healings, prophecy, and prophets and apostles, and all the gifts and blessings have been wanting. (*Journal entry Jan. 2, 1843*) TPJS:270; DGSM:36

---

**180. The person who has faith to be healed may be healed.**

**Joseph Smith,**
*receiving the Word of the Lord*
And again, it shall come to pass that he that hath faith in me to be healed, and is not appointed unto death, shall be healed. 49. He who hath faith to see shall see. 50. He who hath faith to hear shall hear. 51. The lame who hath faith to leap shall leap. (*Revelation "embracing the law of the Church," Feb. 9, 1831; administration to the sick*) D&C 42:48-51

**James E. Talmage**
Another gift . . . is that of having faith to be healed, which is manifested in varying degrees. Not always are the administrations of the elders followed by immediate healings; the afflicted may be permitted to suffer in body, perhaps for the accomplishment of good purposes, and in the time appointed all must experience bodily death. AF:205

**Joseph Smith**
The sick will be healed, the lame made to walk, the deaf to hear, and the blind to see, through your instrumentality. But let me tell you, that you will not have power, after the endowment to heal those that have not faith, nor to benefit them, for you might as well expect to benefit a

devil in hell as such as are possessed of his spirit, and are willing to keep it; for they are habitations for devils, and only fit for his society. (*Remarks made in meeting with the Council of the Twelve, Nov. 12, 1835*) HC2:309
**Related Witnesses:**
**Elder Harold B. Lee,**
*also quoting President Brigham Young*
If you want the blessing, don't just kneel down and pray about it. Prepare yourselves in every conceivable way you can in order to make yourselves worthy to receive the blessing you seek. ¶ Brigham Young illustrated this when he said: "You may go to some people here, and ask what ails them, and they answer, 'I don't know but we feel a dreadful distress in the stomach and in the back; we feel all out of order, and we wish you to lay hands on us.'" ¶ He said to these people, "Have you used any remedies?"—meaning herbs or whatever the pioneers had. "No," they said, "we wish the Elders to lay hands upon us, and we have faith that we shall be healed." President Young said: ¶ "That is very inconsistent according to my faith. If we are sick, and ask the Lord to heal us, and to do all for us that is necessary to be done, according to my understanding of the Gospel of salvation, I might as well ask the Lord to cause my wheat and corn to grow without my plowing the ground and casting in the seed. It appears consistent to me to apply every remedy that comes within the range of my knowledge, and then ask my Father in heaven, in the name of Jesus Christ, to sanctify that application to the healing of my body. . . . ¶ But supposing we were traveling in the mountains, and all we had or could get, in the shape of nourishment, was a little venison, and one or two were taken sick, without anything in the world in the shape of healing medicine within our reach, what should we do? According to my faith, ask the Lord Almighty to send an angel to heal the sick. This is our privilege. . . ." (Discourses of Brigham Young, p. 163) ¶ When we are situated that we cannot get anything to help ourselves, then we may call upon the Lord and His servants who can do all. But it is our duty to do what we can within our own power. (*In MIA June conference, June 1966*) (Stand Ye in Holy Places, pp. 244-45) TLDP:181-82
**Alma, the younger,**
*quoted by Mormon*
And it came to pass that Alma said unto him, taking him by the hand: Believest thou in the power of Christ unto salvation? 7. And he answered and said: Yea, I believe all the words that thou hast taught. 8. And Alma said: If thou

believest in the redemption of Christ thou canst be healed. 9. And he said: Yea, I believe according to thy words. 10. And then Alma cried unto the Lord, saying: O Lord our God, have mercy on this man, and heal him according to his faith which is in Christ. 11. And when Alma had said these words, Zeezrom leaped upon his feet, and began to walk; and this was done to the great astonishment of all the people; and the knowledge of this went forth throughout all the land of Sidom. (*Alma heals Zeezrom, who joins the Church, about A.D. 81*) Alma 15:6-11

### Jesus,
### recorded in Matthew

Then Jesus answered and said unto her, O woman, great is thy faith: be it unto thee even as thou wilt. And her daughter was made whole from that very hour. (*Jesus heals the daughter of a gentile woman*) Matt.15:28

### Bruce R. McConkie

O Father, there are those among us who are sick and afflicted, who suffer from disease, and who are not appointed unto death. O thou Great Physician, pour out thy healing power upon thy Saints. ¶ O Lord, increase our faith, and let the sick be healed and the dead raised even in greater numbers than at present. ¶ But above this, O thou God of healing, wilt thou cause him who came with healing in his wings also to heal us spiritually. CR1984Apr:46

### President Heber J. Grant,
### J. Reuben Clark, Jr., David O. McKay
(First Presidency)

We pray the Lord to heal all those who are stricken with disease and not appointed unto death. May He soften the pain of the wounded and bring to them health and strength. (*Dec. 1939; this message, drafted by President J. Reuben Clark, Jr., was an invocation and prayer for a war-torn world, IE1940Jan:9*) MOFP6:94

---

### 181. Christ can do all things for those who exercise sufficient faith in Him.

#### Nephi, son of Lehi

Yea, and how is it that ye have forgotten that the Lord is able to do all things according to his will, for the children of men, if it so be that they exercise faith in him? Wherefore, let us be faithful to him. (*Nephi exhorts his brethren who thereafter bind him with cords, about 600 to 592 B.C.*) 1Ne.7:12

#### Mormon

Whatsoever thing ye shall ask the Father in my name, which is good, in faith believing that ye shall receive, behold, it shall be done unto you. (*The Lord through Mormon, who preaches in the synagogue, prior to A.D. 384*) Moro.7:26

#### Joseph Smith

[T]hrough the whole history of the scheme of life and salvation, it is a matter of faith: every man received according to his faith—according as his faith was, so were his blessings and privileges; and nothing was withheld from him when his faith was sufficient to receive it. He could stop the mouths of lions, quench the violence of fire, escape the edge of the sword, wax valiant in fight, and put to flight the armies of the aliens; women could, by their faith, receive their dead children to life again; in a word, there was nothing impossible with them who had faith. All things were in subjection to the Former-day Saints, according as their faith was. By their faith they could obtain heavenly visions, the ministering of angels, have knowledge of the spirits of just men made perfect, of the general assembly and church of the firstborn, whose names are written in heaven, of God the judge of all, of Jesus the Mediator of the new covenant, and become familiar with the third heavens, see and hear things which were not only unutterable, but were unlawful to utter. (*Lectures on Faith delivered to the School of the Prophets, 1834-35*) LOF7:17

#### Paul

By faith Noah, being warned of God of things not seen as yet, moved with fear, prepared an ark to the saving of his house; by the which he condemned the world, and became heir of the righteousness which is by faith. 8. By faith Abraham, when he was called to go out into a place which he should after receive for an inheritance, obeyed; and he went out, not knowing whither he went. 9. By faith he sojourned in the land of promise, as in a strange country, dwelling in tabernacles with Isaac and Jacob, the heirs with him of the same promise: 10. For he looked for a city which hath foundations, whose builder and maker is God. 11. Through faith also Sara herself received strength to conceive seed, and was delivered of a child when she was past age, because she judged him faithful who had promised. 12. Therefore sprang there even of one, and him as good as dead, so many as the stars of the sky in multitude, and as the sand which is by the sea shore innumerable. 13. These all died in faith, not having received the promises, but having seen them afar off, and were persuaded of them, and embraced them, and confessed that they were strangers and pilgrims on the earth. 14. For they that say such things declare plainly that they seek a country. 15. And truly, if they had been mindful of that country from whence they came out, they might have had opportunity to have returned. 16. But now they desire a better country, that is, an heavenly: wherefore God is not ashamed to be called their God: for he hath prepared for them a city. 17. By faith Abraham, when he was tried, offered up Isaac: and he that had received the promises offered up his only begotten son, 18. Of whom it was said, That in Isaac shall thy seed be called: 19. Accounting that God was able to raise him up, even from the dead; from whence also he received him in a figure. 20. By faith Isaac blessed Jacob and Esau concerning things to come. 21. By faith Jacob, when he was a dying, blessed both the sons of Joseph; and worshipped, leaning upon the top of his staff. 22. By faith Joseph, when he died, made mention of the departing of the children of Israel; and gave commandment concerning his bones. 23. By faith Moses, when he was born, was hid three months of his parents, because they saw he was a proper child; and they were not afraid of the king's commandment. 24. By faith Moses, when he was come to years, refused to be called the son of Pharaoh's daughter; 25. Choosing rather to suffer affliction with the people of God, than to enjoy the pleasures of sin for a season; 26. Esteeming the reproach of Christ greater riches than the treasures in Egypt: for he had respect unto the recompence of the reward. 27. By faith he forsook Egypt, not fearing the wrath of the king: for he endured, as seeing him who is invisible. 28. Through faith he kept the passover, and the sprinkling of blood, lest he that destroyed the firstborn should touch them. 29. By faith they passed through the Red sea as by dry land: which the Egyptians assaying to do were drowned. 30. By faith the walls of Jericho fell down, after they were compassed about seven days. 31. By faith the harlot Rahab perished not with them that believed not, when she had received the spies with peace. (*Paul writes to the Jewish members of the Church on faith, about* A.D. *60*) Heb.11:7-31

---

## 182. Faith in Christ does not come from signs; signs follow those who believe.

### Joseph Smith,
#### receiving the Word of the Lord
And he that seeketh signs shall see signs, but not unto salvation. 8. Verily, I say unto you,

there are those among you who seek signs, and there have been such even from the beginning; 9. But, behold, faith cometh not by signs, but signs follow those that believe. 10. Yea, signs come by faith, not by the will of men, nor as they please, but by the will of God. 11. Yea, signs come by faith, unto mighty works, for without faith no man pleaseth God; and with whom God is angry he is not well pleased; wherefore, unto such he showeth no signs, only in wrath unto their condemnation. 12. Wherefore, I, the Lord, am not pleased with those among you who have sought after signs and wonders for faith, and not for the good of men unto my glory. (*Revelation received Aug. 1831*) D&C 63:7-12

### Elder Spencer W. Kimball
Signs will *follow* them that believe. He makes no promise that signs will create belief nor save nor exalt. Signs are the product of faith. They are born in the soil of unwavering sureness. They will be prevalent in the Church in about the same degree to which the people have true faith. (Instructor, Dec. 1959, The Teachings of Spencer W. Kimball, p. 500) TLDP:648

### Bruce R. McConkie
Miracles are part of the gospel. Signs follow those that believe. Where the doctrines of salvation are taught in purity and perfection, where there are believing souls who accept these truths and make them a part of their lives, and where devout souls accept Jesus as their Lord and serve him to the best of their ability, there will always be miracles. Such ever attend the preaching of the gospel to receptive and conforming people. Miracles stand as a sign and a witness of the truth and divinity of the Lord's work. Where there are no signs and miracles, none of these desired blessings will be found. (The Mortal Messiah, 2:10) TLDP:648

### Moroni, son of Mormon
And these signs shall follow them that believe—in my name shall they cast out devils; they shall speak with new tongues; they shall take up serpents; and if they drink any deadly thing it shall not hurt them; they shall lay hands on the sick and they shall recover; (*Moroni addresses those who deny the revelations of God,* A.D. *400-421*) Morm.9:24

### Related Witnesses:
#### Joseph Smith,
#### receiving the Word of the Lord
Behold, if they will not believe my words, they would not believe you, my servant Joseph, if it were possible that you should show them all these things [the plates] which I have committed unto you. . . . 10. But this generation shall

have my word through you; 11. And in addition to your testimony, the testimony of three of my servants, whom I shall call and ordain, unto whom I will show these things, and they shall go forth with my words that are given through you. (*Revelation received March 1829*) D&C 5:7,10-11

### Jesus,
#### *recorded in Luke*
Abraham saith unto him, They have Moses and the prophets; let them hear them. 30. And he said, Nay, father Abraham: but if one went unto them from the dead, they will repent. 31. And he said unto him, If they hear not Moses and the prophets, neither will they be persuaded, though one rose from the dead. (*Jesus gives the parable of the rich man and Lazarus*) Luke 16:29-31

### Howard W. Hunter
Thomas had said, "To see is to believe," but Christ answered: "To believe is to see." ¶ Faith has always been a necessary condition of a righteous life. . . . ¶ . . . . Faith gives a feeling of confidence in that which is not visible or susceptible of positive proof. CR1962Oct:23

### Mormon
And now Korihor said unto Alma: If thou wilt show me a sign, that I may be convinced that there is a God, yea, show unto me that he hath power, and then will I be convinced of the truth of thy words. 44. But Alma said unto him: Thou hast had signs enough; will ye tempt your God? Will ye say, Show unto me a sign, when ye have the testimony of all these thy brethren, and also all the holy prophets? The scriptures are laid before thee, yea, and all things denote there is a God; yea, even the earth, and all things that are upon the face of it, yea, and its motion, yea, and also all the planets which move in their regular form do witness that there is a Supreme Creator. (*Korihor demands of Alma a sign that there is a God*) Alma 30:43-44

---

183. Those who believe the testimony of the prophets will receive the manifestations of the Holy Ghost.

### Moroni, son of Mormon
And when ye shall receive these things, I would exhort you that ye would ask God, the Eternal Father, in the name of Christ, if these things are not true; and if ye shall ask with a sincere heart, with real intent, having faith in Christ, he will manifest the truth of it unto you, by the power of the Holy Ghost. (*The final writings of Moroni, about A.D. 421*) Moro.10:4

### Joseph Smith,
#### *receiving the Word of the Lord*
And the testimony of three witnesses will I send forth of my word. 16. And behold, whosoever believeth on my words, them will I visit with the manifestation of my Spirit; and they shall be born of me, even of water and of the Spirit— (*Revelation received March 1829*) D&C 5:15-16

### Moroni, son of Mormon
But he that believeth these things which I [Christ] have spoken, him will I visit with the manifestations of my Spirit, and he shall know and bear record. For because of my Spirit he shall know that these things are true; for it persuadeth men to do good. (*The word of the Lord given to Moroni by revelation A.D. 384-421*) Ether 4:11

### Elder George Albert Smith
It has been by faith that the men who have stood at the head of this work have been inspired, from time to time, to give the instruction that we have needed. It is by faith that we are edified on occasions like this, by those who minister in the name of the Lord, and the Comforter quickens their understanding, bringing things past to their remembrance and showing them things to come; thus evidencing the spirit of revelation. CR1913Oct:103

**Related Witnesses:**
### Mormon
And we, ourselves, also, through the infinite goodness of God, and the manifestations of his Spirit, have great views of that which is to come; and were it expedient, we could prophesy of all things. (*Response of the people to King Benjamin's address, about 124 B.C.*) Mosiah 5:3

### Joseph Smith
FAITH comes by hearing the word of God, through the testimony of the servants of God; that testimony is always attended by the Spirit of prophecy and revelation. (*The Prophet instructs the Twelve in Commerce, Ill., June 27, 1839*) HC3:379

### Joseph Smith,
#### *receiving the Word of the Lord*
Oliver Cowdery, verily, verily, I say unto you, that assuredly as the Lord liveth, who is your God and your Redeemer, even so surely shall you receive a knowledge of whatsoever things you shall ask in faith, with an honest heart, believing that you shall receive a knowledge concerning the engravings of old records, which are ancient, which contain those parts of my scripture of which has been spoken by the manifestation of my Spirit. (*Revelation for Oliver Cowdery, April 1829*) D&C 8:1

### Jacob, brother of Nephi

Behold, my brethren, he that prophesieth, let him prophesy to the understanding of men; for the Spirit speaketh the truth and lieth not. Wherefore, it speaketh of things as they really are, and of things as they really will be. . . . (*Jacob makes his record on plates of metal, 544-421 B.C.*) Jacob 4:13

### Alma, the younger,
*quoted by Mormon*

And now my beloved brethren, do you believe these things? Behold, I say unto you, yea, I know that ye believe them; and the way that I know that ye believe them is by the manifestation of the Spirit which is in me. . . . (*Alma preaches to the people in Gideon, about 83 B.C.*) Alma 7:17

### Moroni, son of Mormon

And again, I exhort you, my brethren, that ye deny not the gifts of God, for they are many; and they come from the same God. And there are different ways that these gifts are administered; but it is the same God who worketh all in all; and they are given by the manifestations of the Spirit of God unto men, to profit them. . . . 30. And again I would exhort you that ye would come unto Christ, and lay hold upon every good gift, and touch not the evil gift, nor the unclean thing. (*The final writings of Moroni, son of Mormon, about A.D. 421*) Moro.10:8,30 (see 8-18)

---

## 184. Faith overcomes fear and doubt.

### President Joseph F. Smith

The ancient prophets speak of "entering into God's rest;" what does it mean? To my mind, it means entering into the knowledge and love of God, having faith in his purpose and in his plan, to such an extent that we know we are right, and that we are not hunting for something else, we are not disturbed by every wind of doctrine, or by the cunning and craftiness of men who lie in wait to deceive. We know of the doctrine, that it is of God, and we do not ask any questions of anybody about it; they are welcome to their opinions, to their ideas and to their vagaries. The man who has reached that degree of faith in God that all doubt and fear have been cast from him, he has entered into "God's rest," and he need not fear the vagaries of men, nor their cunning and craftiness, by which they seek to deceive and mislead him from the truth. I pray that we may all enter into God's rest—rest from doubt, from fear, from apprehension of danger, rest from the religious turmoil of the world; from the cry that is going forth, here and

there—lo, here is Christ; lo, there is Christ; lo, he is in the desert, come ye out to meet him. The man who has found God's rest will not be disturbed by these vagaries of men. CR1909Oct:8

### Jesus,
*recorded in Mark*

For verily I say unto you, That whosoever shall say unto this mountain, Be thou removed, and be thou cast into the sea; and shall not doubt in his heart, but shall believe that those things which he saith shall come to pass; he shall have whatsoever he saith. (*Jesus address Peter and other disciples*) Mark 11:23

### Joseph Smith,
*receiving the Word of the Lord*

Look unto me in every thought; doubt not, fear not. 37. Behold the wounds which pierced my side, and also the prints of the nails in my hands and feet; be faithful, keep my commandments, and ye shall inherit the kingdom of heaven. Amen. (*Revelation to Joseph and to Oliver Cowdery, April 1829*) D&C 6:36-37

### Elder Harold B. Lee,
*also quoting Joseph Smith*

[F]aith, not doubt, is the beginning of all learning, whether in science or religion. It is faith in the wisdom of ages past that leads to further study, experimentation and new discovery. It is faith that seeks for spiritual knowledge and power by studying out in your own mind the matter in question, by applying all possible human wisdom to the solution of your problem and then asking God if your conclusion is right. If it is right, your bosom shall burn within you and you shall "feel" that it is right, but if your conclusion is not right, you shall have a stupor of thought that shall cause you to forget the thing that is wrong. (D&C 9:8-9) (Decisions for Successful Living, p. 194) TLDP:179

### Related Witnesses:
### Helaman, son of Alma, the younger,
*quoted by Mormon*

56:47 Now they never had fought, yet they did not fear death; and they did think more upon the liberty of their fathers than they did upon their lives; yea, they had been taught by their mothers, that if they did not doubt, God would deliver them. . . . 57:26. And now, their preservation was astonishing to our whole army, yea, that they should be spared while there was a thousand of our brethren who were slain. And we do justly ascribe it to the miraculous power of God, because of their exceeding faith in that which they had been taught to believe—that there was a just God, and whosoever did not doubt, that they should be preserved by his marvelous power. (*Helaman's two thousand stripling sons fight with miraculous power and none of them are slain, 62 B.C.)* Alma 56:47; 57:26

### Jesus,
#### recorded in Matthew

But when he saw the wind boisterous, he was afraid; and beginning to sink, he cried, saying, Lord, save me. 31. And immediately Jesus stretched forth his hand, and caught him, and said unto him, O thou of little faith, wherefore didst thou doubt? *(Peter walks on the sea with Jesus)* Matt.14:30-31

### Recorded in Exodus

And Moses said unto the people, Fear ye not, stand still, and see the salvation of the LORD, which he will shew to you to day: for the Egyptians whom ye have seen to day, ye shall see them again no more for ever. 14. The LORD shall fight for you, and ye shall hold your peace. 15. And the LORD said unto Moses, Wherefore criest thou unto me? speak unto the children of Israel, that they go forward: 16. But lift thou up thy rod, and stretch out thine hand over the sea, and divide it: and the children of Israel shall go on dry ground through the midst of the sea. *(Moses parts the Red Sea)* Ex.14:13-16

---

185. A desire to believe can begin the establishment of faith in Christ.

#### Alma, the younger,
##### quoted by Mormon

But behold, if ye will awake and arouse your faculties, even to an experiment upon my words, and exercise a particle of faith, yea, even if ye can no more than desire to believe, let this desire work in you, even until ye believe in a manner that ye can give place for a portion of my words. 28. Now, we will compare the word unto a seed. Now, if ye give place, that a seed may be planted in your heart, behold, if it be a true seed, or a good seed, if ye do not cast it out by your unbelief, that ye will resist the Spirit of the Lord, behold, it will begin to swell within your breasts; and when you feel these swelling motions, ye will begin to say within yourselves—It must needs be that this is a good seed, or that the word is good, for it beginneth to enlarge my soul; yea, it beginneth to enlighten my understanding, yea, it beginneth to be delicious to me. *(Alma teaches the poor, compares the word of God to a seed, about 74 B.C.)* Alma 32:27-28

#### John A. Widtsoe

Whoever in absolute desire to know the truth places himself in harmony with divine forces and approaches God in humble prayer, with full surrender of inherited or acquired prejudices, will learn to his complete satisfaction that there is a God in heaven, whose loving will is operative on earth. Just as the turning of the dial of the radio enables us to hear the messages of distant broadcasting stations, so we may tune ourselves in prayer for truth to hear the messages that come from heavenly places. Man is more than a machine; he can so purify himself, establish earnest desire, and forget his selfish needs, as to receive through prayer the final assurance of the existence of the Lord of Heaven and Earth. This method or test is within the reach of all, humble or great, rich or poor. Happy is the man who thus enters into the abundant knowledge of divine things. ("The Articles of Faith," IE1935May:288) TLDP:224

#### John A. Widtsoe

These . . . are the steps on the way to truth: Desire, prayer, study, and practice. They form the eternal price which must be paid for truth. ¶ This way must be found by each person for himself. Another cannot desire, pray, study, or practice in our stead and for us. Truth must be won individually. ¶ The way to truth is the way to a testimony of the truth of the restored gospel of Jesus Christ. Try it! It never fails those who travel it sincerely. Those who live most, live by truth. (Evidences and Reconciliations, 3:84-85) TLDP:705

#### Elder Harold B. Lee

With these truths made clear, then—first, that a testimony follows the exercise of faith, and second, that revelation by the power of the Holy Ghost is required for one to receive a testimony—the next question of our truth-seeking friend would naturally be, "Just how does one prepare himself to receive that divine witness called testimony?". . . ¶ As one reads this whole text [Alma 32], he finds clearly prescribed the way by which all may receive a testimony or "knowledge by revelation" as defined above: first, desire; second, belief; third, faith; forth, knowledge or testimony. . . . ¶ But now we must understand one thing more: Faith necessary to knowledge comes by "hearing the word of God," as Paul said. (Stand Ye in Holy Places, pp. 194-95) TLDP:686

#### James E. Talmage

Remove man's faith in the possibility of any desired success, and you rob him of the incentive to strive. He would not stretch forth his hand to seize did he not believe in the possibility of securing that for which he reaches. This principle becomes therefore the impelling force by which men struggle for excellence, ofttimes enduring vicissitudes and suffering that they may achieve their purposes. Faith is the secret of ambition, the soul of heroism, the motive power of effort. AF:93

**Related Witnesses:**

**James E. Talmage**

Although faith is called the first principle of the Gospel of Christ, though it be in fact the foundation of religious life, yet even faith is preceded by sincerity of disposition and humility of soul, whereby the word of God may make an impression upon the heart. No compulsion is used in bringing men to a knowledge of God; yet, as fast as we open our hearts to the influences of righteousness, the faith that leads to life eternal will be given us of our Father. AF:97

---

186. Faith in Christ is increased by obedience to the word of God.

**Jesus,**
*quoted by John*

If any man will do his will, he shall know of the doctrine, whether it be of God, or whether I speak of myself. (*Jesus teaches in the temple*) John 7:17

**Elder Joseph Fielding Smith**

If we want to have a living, abiding faith, we must be active in the performance of every duty as members of this Church. (Doctrines of Salvation, 2:311) DGSM:36

**Elder Harold B. Lee**

All the principles and ordinances of the gospel are in a sense but invitations to learning the gospel by the practice of its teachings. No person knows the principle of tithing until he pays tithing. No one knows the principle of the Word of Wisdom until he keeps the Word of Wisdom. Children, or grownups for that matter, are not converted to tithing, the Word of Wisdom, keeping the Sabbath day holy, or prayer by hearing someone talk about these principles. We learn the gospel by living it. (Stand Ye in Holy Places, p. 215) TLDP:439

**John A. Widtsoe**

There is only one way . . . to obtain and possess this mighty spirit . . . which guides the Church today and enlightens every soul, and that is by obeying strictly, with all our might, as far as we poor mortal beings are able, the laws of the Gospel. If we obey, if we practice in our lives the truths given us, then as certainly as we do that, the enlivening spirit of light, of revelation, of understanding will come to us, comprehension will enter our minds and hearts and we shall know the true joy of being Latter-day Saints. CR1934Oct:11

**John A. Widtsoe**

I was brought up in scientific laboratories, where I was taught to test things, never to be satisfied unless a thing was tested. We have the right to test the Gospel of the Lord Jesus Christ. By testing it I mean living it, trying it out. Do you question the Word of Wisdom? Try it. Do you question the law of tithing? Practice it. Do you doubt the virtue of attending meetings? Attend them. Only then shall we be able to speak of these things intelligently and in such a way as to be respected by those who listen to us. Those who live the Gospel of Jesus Christ gain this higher knowledge, this greater testimony, this ultimate assurance that leads to truth. It is the way to truth. CR1938Oct:129

**James E. Talmage**

A condition essential to the exercise of a living, growing, sustaining faith in Deity is the consciousness on man's part that he is at least endeavoring to live in accordance with the laws of God as he has learned them. A knowledge that he is wilfully and wantonly sinning against the truth will deprive him of sincerity in prayer and faith and estrange him from his Father. He must feel that the trend of his life's course is acceptable, that with due allowance for mortal weakness and human frailty he is in some measure approved of the Lord; otherwise he is restrained from supplicating the throne of grace with confidence. The consciousness of earnest effort toward godly conduct is a power of itself, strengthening its possessor in sacrifice and under persecution, and sustaining him in all good works. It was this knowledge of assured communion with God that enabled the saints of olden time to endure as they did, though their sufferings were extreme. Of them we read that some "were tortured, not accepting deliverance; that they might obtain a better resurrection: And others had trial of cruel mockings and scourgings, yea, moreover of bonds and imprisonment: They were stoned, they were sawn asunder, were tempted, were slain with the sword: they wandered about in sheepskins and goatskins; being destitute, afflicted, tormented; (Of whom the world was not worthy:) they wandered in deserts, and in mountains, and in dens and caves of the earth." As in former days so in the present, the saints have been sustained through all their sufferings by the sure knowledge of divine approval; and the faith of righteous men has ever grown through a consciousness of their sincere and devoted endeavor. AF:95-96

**Elder Joseph Fielding Smith**

A testimony of the gospel is a convincing

knowledge given by revelation to the individual who humbly seeks the truth. Its convincing power is so great that there can be no doubt left in the mind when the Spirit has spoken. It is the only way that a person can truly know that Jesus is the Christ and that his gospel is true. There are millions of people on the earth who believe that Jesus lived and died and that his work was for the salvation of souls; but unless they have complied with his commandments and have accepted his truth as it has been restored, they do not know and cannot know the full significance of his mission and its benefits to mankind. Only through humble repentance and submission to the plan of salvation can this be made known. The way is open to all if they will receive his truth and accept his ordinances and abide faithfully in them. (Answers to Gospel Questions, 3:31) TLDP:685

---

187. By the exercise of faith in Christ, knowledge of divine truths can be received through the power of the Holy Ghost.

### Moroni, son of Mormon
And when ye shall receive these things, I would exhort you that ye would ask God, the Eternal Father, in the name of Christ, if these things are not true; and if ye shall ask with a sincere heart, with real intent, having faith in Christ, he will manifest the truth of it unto you, by the power of the Holy Ghost. 5. And by the power of the Holy Ghost ye may know the truth of all things. (*The final writings of Moroni, about* A.D. *421*) Moro.10:4-5

### Moroni, son of Mormon
And now, I, Moroni, would speak somewhat concerning these things; I would show unto the world that faith is things which are hoped for and not seen; wherefore, dispute not because ye see not, for ye receive no witness until after the trial of your faith. 7. For it was by faith that Christ showed himself unto our fathers, after he had risen from the dead; and he showed not himself unto them until after they had faith in him; wherefore, it must needs be that some had faith in him, for he showed himself not unto the world. 8. But because of the faith of men he has shown himself unto the world, and glorified the name of the Father, and prepared a way that thereby others might be partakers of the heavenly gift, that they might hope for those things which they have not seen. (*Moroni recounts the wonders and marvels done by faith, about* A.D. *419-420*) Ether 12:6-8

### Elder Harold B. Lee
With these truths made clear, then—first, that a testimony follows the exercise of faith, and second, that revelation by the power of the Holy Ghost is required for one to receive a testimony—the next question of our truth-seeking friend would naturally be, "Just how does one prepare himself to receive that divine witness called testimony? . . . ¶ As one reads this whole text [Alma 32], he finds clearly prescribed the way by which all may receive a testimony or "knowledge by revelation" as defined above: first, desire; second, belief; third, faith; forth, knowledge or testimony. . . . ¶ But now we must understand one thing more: Faith necessary to knowledge comes by "hearing the word of God," as Paul said. (Stand Ye in Holy Places, pp. 194-95) TLDP:686

**Related Witnesses:**
### Joseph Smith
And the Spirit shall be given unto you by the prayer of faith; (*Revelation "embracing the law of the Church," Feb. 9, 1831*) D&C 42:14
### Elder Harold B. Lee
[N]either the Prophet Joseph Smith, nor any who have followed since, have ever received a personal visitation from the Master, nor have they ever received a special witness of his life and mission, except they have had a supreme faith. Until that faith had been tried and tested, only then did they receive the witness. CR1952Apr:127

---

**HYMNS Written by Prophets
Applicable to this Topic**

### Bruce R. McConkie
*I Believe in Christ*
HYMNS:134

I believe in Christ; he is my King!
With all my heart to him I'll sing;
I'll raise my voice in praise and joy,
In grand amens my tongue employ.
I believe in Christ; he is God's Son.
On earth to dwell his soul did come.
He healed the sick; the dead he raised.
Good works were his; his name be praised.

I believe in Christ; oh, blessed name!
As Mary's Son he came to reign
'Mid mortal men, his earthly kin,
To save them from the woes of sin.
I believe in Christ, who marked the path,
Who did gain all his Father hath,
Who said to men: "Come, follow me,
That ye, my friends, with God may be."

I believe in Christ—my Lord, my God!
My feet he plants on gospel sod.
I'll worship him with all my might;
He is the source of truth and light.
I believe in Christ; he ransoms me.
From Satan's grasp he sets me free,
And I shall live with joy and love
In his eternal courts above.

I believe in Christ; he stands supreme!
From him I'll gain my fondest dream;
And while I strive through grief and pain,
His voice is heard: "Ye shall obtain."
I believe in Christ; so come what may,
With him I'll stand in that great day
When on this earth he comes again
To rule among the sons of men.

### Elder Joseph Fielding Smith
*Does the Journey Seem Long?*
HYMNS:127

Does the journey seem long,
The path rugged and steep?
Are there briars and thorns on the way?
Do sharp stones cut your feet
As you struggle to rise
To the heights thru the heat of the day?

Is your heart faint and sad,
Your soul weary within,
As you toil 'neath your burden of care?
Does the load heavy seem
You are forced now to lift?
Is there no one your burden to share?

Let your heart be not faint
Now the journey's begun;
There is One who still beckons to you.
So look upward in joy
And take hold of his hand;
He will lead you to heights that are new—

A land holy and pure,
Where all trouble doth end,
And your life shall be free from all sin,
Where no tears shall be shed,
For no sorrows remain.
Take his hand and with him enter in.

### Parley P. Pratt
*Father in Heaven, We Do Believe*
HYMNS:180

Father in Heav'n, we do believe
The promise thou hast made;
Thy word with meekness we receive,
Just as thy Saints have said.

We now repent of all our sin
And come with broken heart,
And to thy covenant enter in
And choose the better part.

O Lord, accept us while we pray,
And all our sins forgive;
New life impart to us this day,
And bid the sinners live.

Humbly we take the sacrament
In Jesus' blessed name;
Let us receive thru covenant
The Spirit's heav'nly flame.

We will be buried in the stream
In Jesus' blessed name,
And rise, while light shall on us beam
The Spirit's heav'nly flame.

Baptize us with the Holy Ghost
And seal us as thine own,
That we may join the ransomed host
And with the Saints be one.

# List of Doctrines

## FALL OF ADAM

*Doctrines Located in This Topic*

188. In the Garden of Eden, Adam and Eve were in a state of innocence, not understanding good and evil, and having neither joy nor misery.

189. Before the Fall, Adam was not subject to death.

190. While in the Garden of Eden, Adam and Eve enjoyed the presence of God.

191. The Fall of Adam brought upon him spiritual death, the condition of being cut off from the presence of God.

192. The devil beguiled Eve to partake of the forbidden fruit.

193. Adam voluntarily partook of the fruit of the tree of knowledge of good and evil with knowledge of the consequences.

194. Because of the Fall of Adam all people became subject to physical, temporal death.

195. After the Fall, Adam and Eve were granted a probationary time to repent and serve God.

196. As a result of the Fall, Adam and Eve experienced pain and sorrow, which are part of mortality.

197. The Fall of Adam subjected all people to the enticings of Satan.

198. The body of flesh subjects us to enticements toward physical gratification.

199. The Fall of Adam was a necessary element in God's plan of salvation for His children.

200. The Fall of Adam and Eve made it possible for them to have children.

201. It was the design of the Lord that Adam and Eve (and all people born thereafter) should support themselves by their own labors.

*Doctrines on FALL OF ADAM
Located in Other Topics*

30. The Fall of Adam brought physical and spiritual death to all people and thus established the need for an atonement.

31. Adam and Eve were commanded to sacrifice animals in similitude of the future sacrifice that Christ would make to redeem all people from the Fall of Adam.

796. Because of the Fall of Adam all people were cut off from the presence of the Lord and are considered spiritually dead.

# FALL OF ADAM

188. In the Garden of Eden, Adam and Eve were in a state of innocence, not understanding good and evil, and having neither joy nor misery.

### Elder Joseph Fielding Smith

He [Adam] had knowledge, of course. He could speak. He could converse. There were many things he could be taught and was taught; but under the conditions in which he was living at that time it was impossible for him to visualize or understand the power of good and evil. He did not know what pain was. He did not know what sorrow was; and a thousand other things that have come to us in this life that Adam did not know in the Garden of Eden and could not understand and would not have known had he remained there. (Doctrines of Salvation, 1:107-8) DGSM:20

### Lehi,
#### quoted by his son Nephi

And they would have had no children; wherefore they would have remained in a state of innocence, having no joy, for they knew no misery; doing no good, for they knew no sin. (*Lehi teaches his sons that had Adam and Eve not transgressed God's plan of salvation would have been thwarted, between 588-570 B.C.*) 2Ne.2:23

### Joseph Smith,
#### translating the Book of Moses

And Eve, his wife, heard all these things and was glad, saying: Were it not for our transgression we never should have had seed, and never should have known good and evil, and the joy of our redemption, and the eternal life which God giveth unto all the obedient. (*The record of Moses: Adam realizes that through Adam and Eve's transgression they may receive joy and he therefore blesses the name of God*) Moses 5:11

**Related Witnesses:**

### President John Taylor

Thus we find: Firstly. That Adam and Eve both considered that they had gained, instead of suffered loss, through their disobedience to that law; for they made the statement, that if it had not been for their transgression they never would "have known good and evil." And again, they would have been incapable of increase; and without that increase the designs of God in relation to the formation of the earth and man could not have been accomplished; for one great object of the creation of the world was the propagation of the human species, that bodies might be prepared for those spirits who already existed, and who, when they saw the earth formed, shouted for joy. (The Mediation

and Atonement, pp. 130, 187) TLDP:182-83

### James E. Talmage

The Immediate Result of the Fall was the substitution of mortality, with all its attendant frailties, for the vigor of the primeval deathless state. . . . Having lost their sense of former innocence they became ashamed of their nakedness, and the Lord made for them garments of skins. Upon both the man and the woman was visited the penalty of spiritual death; for in that very day they were banished from Eden and cast out from the presence of the Lord. AF:61

---

189. Before the Fall, Adam was not subject to death.

### Lehi,
#### quoted by his son Nephi

And now, behold, if Adam had not transgressed he would not have fallen, but he would have remained in the garden of Eden. And all things which were created must have remained in the same state in which they were after they were created; and they must have remained forever, and had no end. (*Lehi explains the Fall of Adam, 588-570 B.C.*) 2Ne.2:22

### Elder Joseph Fielding Smith

Adam had a spiritual body until mortality came upon him through the violation of the law under which he was living, but he also had a physical body of flesh and bones. ¶ Now what is a spiritual body? It is one that is quickened by spirit not blood. . . . ¶ [W]hen Adam was in the Garden of Eden, he was not subject to death. There was no blood in his body and he could have remained there forever. This is true of all the other creations. (Doctrines of Salvation, 1:76-77) DGSM:19

### Elder Joseph Fielding Smith

When Adam came into this world, he was not subject to death. He was immortal. He could have lived forever. Had he remained in the Garden of Eden and not transgressed the law that had been given to him, he and Eve would have been there yet. (Doctrines of Salvation, 1:91) DGSM:21

### James E. Talmage

The Immediate Result of the Fall was the substitution of mortality, with all its attendant frailties, for the vigor of the primeval deathless state. AF:61

**Related Witnesses:**

### John A. Widtsoe

To subject an eternal being to the dominion of "earth-element"—that is, to forgetfulness, the many vicissitudes of earth, and eventual death—appeared to be a descent in power and station. The first man, to bring himself under such dominion and domination would have to break, or set aside, an established law; but unless this were done, the plan could not be inaugurated. Man, made to walk upright, must bend his back through the tunnel through the mountain which leads to a beautiful valley. Adam and Eve accepted the call to initiate the plan, and subjected themselves to earth conditions. That was the so-called fall of Adam, an act necessary for the winning of bodies of earth-element by man, and for the fulfilment of divine law. (Moses, 4:7-13; 5:10-11). . . . ¶ Here then, would be the condition of man after he had acquired an "earthly body" and then was separated from it by the process called death: He was rich in earth experience but without the earth-body to be used by him as an eternal tool to help him win his place among the realities of the universe. The "fall of Adam" had made possible the earth experience. (Evidences and Reconciliations, pp. 73-74) TLDP:184-85

---

**190. While in the Garden of Eden, Adam and Eve enjoyed the presence of God.**

**James E. Talmage**
The Scriptures inform us that, prior to his transgression in Eden, Adam held direct and personal communion with God; and that one of the immediate consequences of his fall, which was brought about through disobedience, was his forfeiture of that exalted association. He was shut out from the presence of God, and though he heard the Divine Voice he no longer was permitted to behold the Presence of the Lord. This banishment was to the man spiritual death; and its infliction brought into effect the predicted penalty, that in the day of his sin he would surely die. [Moses 3:17] (The Vitality of Mormonism, pp. 51-52) TLDP:186

**Elder Joseph Fielding Smith**
We find, then, Adam's status before the fall was: ¶ 1. He was not subject to death. ¶ 2. He was in the presence of God. He saw him just as you see your fathers: was in his presence, and learned his language. . . . ¶ 3. He had no posterity. ¶ 4. He was without knowledge of good and evil. (Doctrines of Salvation, 1:107-08) TLDP:185-86

**Elder Joseph F. Smith**
When Adam . . . partook of the forbidden fruit . . .

he was banished from the presence of God, and was thrust out into outer spiritual darkness. This was the first death. Yet living, he was dead—dead to God, dead to light and truth, dead spiritually; cast out from the presence of God. CR1899Oct:72; DGSM:20

**President Brigham Young,**
*quoted by John A. Widtsoe*
Adam was as conversant with his Father who placed him upon this earth as we are conversant with our earthly parents. The Father frequently came to visit his son Adam, and talked and walked with him. . . . (*In Tabernacle, Jan. 12, 1862, JD9:148*) DBY:104

**Related Witnesses:**
**Elder Joseph Fielding Smith**
Adam and Eve were chosen to come here as the primal parents of humanity. And they were placed in the Garden of Eden where there was no death and we read in the scriptures that they could have lived in that Garden forever, but not under the most favorable circumstances. For there, although they were in the presence of God, they were deprived of certain knowledge and understanding in a condition where they could not understand clearly things that were necessary for them to know. (*Speech to students at Brigham Young University, 1955*) DGSM:20

**Joseph Smith,**
*quoted by Elder Joseph Fielding Smith*
Adam received commandments and instructions from God; this was the order from the beginning. (*Remarks on priesthood at Church conference, Oct. 5, 1840*) TPJS:168

**Joseph Smith,**
*translating the Book of Moses*
And they heard the voice of the Lord God, as they were walking in the garden, in the cool of the day; and Adam and his wife went to hide themselves from the presence of the Lord God amongst the trees of the garden. (*Revelation received by Joseph in 1830, Moses describes the transgression of Adam and Eve*) Moses 4:14

**Moses**
And they heard the voice of the LORD God walking in the garden in the cool of the day: and Adam and his wife hid themselves from the presence of the LORD God amongst the trees of the garden. (*Moses describes the transgression of Adam and Eve*) Gen.3:8

---

**191. The Fall of Adam brought upon him spiritual death, the condition of being cut off from the presence of God.**

## Alma, the younger,
### *quoted by Mormon*

But behold, it was appointed unto man to die—therefore, as they were cut off from the tree of life they should be cut off from the face of the earth—and man became lost forever, yea, they became fallen man. 7. And now, ye see by this that our first parents were cut off both temporally and spiritually from the presence of the Lord; and thus we see they became subjects to follow after their own will. . . . 9. Therefore, as the soul could never die, and the fall had brought upon all mankind a spiritual death as well as a temporal, that is, they were cut off from the presence of the Lord, it was expedient that mankind should be reclaimed from this spiritual death. (*Alma speaks to his son Corianton; mortality is a probationary time to enable man to repent and serve God; about 73 B.C.*) Alma 42:6-7,9

### Elder Joseph F. Smith

When Adam, our first parent, partook of the forbidden fruit, transgressed the law of God, and became subject unto Satan, he was banished from the presence of God, and was thrust out into outer spiritual darkness. This was the first death. Yet living, he was dead—dead to God dead to light and truth, dead spiritually; cast out from the presence of God; communication between the Father and the Son was cut off. He was as absolutely thrust out from the presence of God as was Satan and the hosts that followed him. That was a spiritual death. But the Lord said that he would not suffer Adam nor his posterity to come to the temporal death until they should have the means by which they might be redeemed from the first death, which is spiritual. CR1899Oct:72; DGSM:20-21

### Joseph Smith,
#### *receiving the Word of the Lord*

Wherefore, it came to pass that the devil tempted Adam, and he partook of the forbidden fruit and transgressed the commandment, wherein he became subject to the will of the devil, because he yielded unto temptation. 41. Wherefore, I, the Lord God, caused that he should be cast out from the Garden of Eden, from my presence, because of his transgression, wherein he became spiritually dead, which is the first death, even that same death which is the last death, which is spiritual, which shall be pronounced upon the wicked when I shall say: Depart, ye cursed. (*Revelation received Sept. 1830; the Fall and Atonement bring salvation*) D&C 29:40-41

### James E. Talmage

The Immediate Result of the Fall was the substitution of mortality, with all its attendant frailties, for the vigor of the primeval deathless state. . . . Upon both the man and the woman was visited the penalty of spiritual death; for in that very day they were banished from Eden and cast out from the presence of the Lord. AF:61

### Joseph Smith,
#### *translating the Book of Moses*

And Adam and Eve, his wife, called upon the name of the Lord, and they heard the voice of the Lord from the way toward the Garden of Eden, speaking unto them, and they saw him not; for they were shut out from his presence. (*The record of Moses: Concerning Adam and Eve after they were driven out of the Garden of Eden*) Moses 5:4

**Related Witnesses:**

### Joseph Smith,
#### *translating the Book of Moses*

Behold Satan hath come among the children of men, and tempteth them to worship him; and men have become carnal, sensual, and devilish, and are shut out from the presence of God. (*The record of Moses: Enoch testifies to the people*) Moses 6:49

---

## 192. The devil beguiled Eve to partake of the forbidden fruit.

### James E. Talmage

Satan presented himself before Eve in the garden, and, speaking by the mouth of the serpent, questioned her about the commandments that God had given respecting the tree of knowledge of good and evil. Eve answered that they were forbidden even to touch the fruit of that tree, under penalty of death. Satan then sought to beguile the woman, contradicting the Lord's statement and declaring that death would not follow a violation of the divine injunction; but that, on the other hand, by doing that which the Lord had forbidden she and her husband would become like unto the gods, knowing good and evil for themselves. The woman was captivated by these representations; and, being eager to possess the advantages pictured by Satan, she disobeyed the command of the Lord, and partook of the fruit forbidden. She feared no evil, for she knew it not. Then, telling Adam what she had done, she urged him to eat of the fruit also. AF:58-59

### Joseph Smith,
#### *translating the Book of Moses*

And now the serpent was more subtle than any beast of the field which I, the Lord God, had made. 6. And Satan put it into the heart of the serpent, (for he had drawn away many after him,) and he sought also to beguile Eve, for he knew not the mind of God, wherefore he sought to destroy the world. 7. And he said unto the woman: Yea, hath God said—Ye shall not eat of every tree of the garden? (And he spake by the mouth of the serpent.) 8. And the woman said unto the serpent: We may eat of the fruit of the trees of the garden; 9. But of the fruit of the tree which thou beholdest in the midst of the garden, God hath said—Ye shall not eat of it, neither shall ye touch it, lest ye die. 10. And the serpent said unto the woman: Ye shall not surely die; 11. For God doth know that in the day ye eat thereof, then your eyes shall be opened, and ye shall be as gods, knowing good and evil. 12. And when the woman saw that the tree was good for food, and that it became pleasant to the eyes, and a tree to be desired to make her wise, she took of the fruit thereof, and did eat, and also gave unto her husband with her, and he did eat. (*Moses learns that Lucifer deceives Eve and she and Adam partake of the forbidden fruit*) Moses 4:5-12

### Moses

Now the serpent was more subtil than any beast of the field which the LORD God had made. And he said unto the woman, Yea, hath God said, Ye shall not eat of every tree of the garden? 2. And the woman said unto the serpent, We may eat of the fruit of the trees of the garden: 3. But of the fruit of the tree which is in the midst of the garden, God hath said, Ye shall not eat of it, neither shall ye touch it, lest ye die. 4. And the serpent said unto the woman, Ye shall not surely die: 5. For God doth know that in the day ye eat thereof, then your eyes shall be opened, and ye shall be as gods, knowing good and evil. 6. And when the woman saw that the tree was good for food, and that it was pleasant to the eyes, and a tree to be desired to make one wise, she took of the fruit thereof, and did eat, and gave also unto her husband with her; and he did eat. (*Lucifer deceives Eve and she and Adam partake of the forbidden fruit*) Gen.3:1-6

**Related Witnesses:**

### Lehi,
#### *quoted by his son Nephi*

And because he had fallen from heaven, and had become miserable forever, he sought also the misery of all mankind. Wherefore, he said unto Eve, yea, even that old serpent, who is the devil, who is the father of all lies, wherefore he said: Partake of the forbidden fruit, and ye shall not die, but ye shall be as God, knowing good and evil. (*Lehi teaches his sons, between 588-570 B.C.*) 2Ne.2:18

### James E. Talmage

Eve was fulfilling the foreseen purposes of God by the part she took in the great drama of the fall; yet she did not partake of the forbidden fruit with that object in view, but with intent to act contrary to the divine command, being deceived by the sophistries of Satan. . . . AF:63

### Abinadi,
#### *quoted by Mormon*

[Y]ea, even that old serpent that did beguile our first parents, which was the cause of their fall; which was the cause of all mankind becoming carnal, sensual, devilish, knowing evil from good, subjecting themselves to the devil. (*Abinadi preaches to King Noah and his people, about 148 B.C.*) Mosiah 16:3

### Joseph Smith

Wherefore, it came to pass that the devil tempted Adam, and he partook of the forbidden fruit and transgressed the commandment, wherein he became subject to the will of the devil, because he yielded unto temptation. (*Revelation received Sept. 1830*) D&C 29:40

---

193. Adam voluntarily partook of the fruit of the tree of knowledge of good and evil with knowledge of the consequences.

### Marion G. Romney

Adam voluntarily, and with full knowledge of the consequences, partook of the fruit of the tree of knowledge of good and evil, that men might be. . . . For his service we owe Adam an immeasurable debt of gratitude. (*Address to seminary and institute personnel, July 13, 1966*) DGSM:20

### James E. Talmage

Eve was fulfilling the foreseen purposes of God by the part she took in the great drama of the fall; yet she did not partake of the forbidden fruit with that object in view, but with intent to act contrary to the divine command, being deceived by the sophistries of Satan. . . . Adam's part in the great event was essentially different from that of his wife; he was not deceived; on the contrary he deliberately decided to do as Eve desired, that he might carry out the purposes of his Maker with respect to the race of men, whose first patriarch he was ordained to be. AF:63

### Elder Joseph Fielding Smith

Just why the Lord would say to Adam that he forbade him to partake of the tree is not made clear in the Bible account, but in the original as it comes to us in the Book of Moses it is made definitely clear. It is that the Lord said to Adam that if he wished to remain as he was in the garden, then he was not to eat the fruit, but if he desired to eat it and partake of death he was at liberty to do so. So really it was not in the true sense a transgression of a divine commandment. Adam made the wise decision, in fact the only decision that he could make. (Answers to Gospel Questions, 4:81) MGSP:9

**Related Witnesses:**

### Elder Joseph Fielding Smith

Adam and Eve were chosen to come here as the primal parents of humanity. And they were placed in the Garden of Eden where there was no death and we read in the scriptures that they could have lived in that Garden forever, but not under the most favorable circumstances. For there, although they were in the presence of God, they were deprived of certain knowledge and understanding in a condition where they could not understand clearly things that were necessary for them to know. Therefore, it became essential to their salvation and to ours that their nature should be changed. The only way it could be changed was by the violation of the law under which they were at that time. Mortality could not come without violation of that law and mortality was essential, a step towards our exaltation. Therefore, Adam partook of the forbidden fruit, forbidden in a rather peculiar manner for it is the only place in all the history where we read that the Lord forbade something and yet said, "Nevertheless thou mayest choose for thyself." He never said that of any sin. I do not look upon Adam's fall as a sin, although it was a transgression of the law. The temporal law. And he became subject to death. The partaking of that fruit created blood in his body and that blood became the life-giving influence of mortality. (Speech to students at Brigham Young University, 1955) DGSM:20

### Moses

And when the woman saw that the tree was good for food, and that it was pleasant to the eyes, and a tree to be desired to make one wise, she took of the fruit thereof, and did eat, and gave also unto her husband with her; and he did eat. (Lucifer deceives Eve and she and Adam partake of the forbidden fruit) Gen.3:6

### John A. Widtsoe

It is a thrilling thought that Adam and Eve were not coerced to begin God's work on earth. They chose to do so, by the exercise of their free agency. It is the lesson for all their children: Seek the truth, choose wisely, and carry the responsibility for our acts. (Evidences and Reconciliations, pp. 192-95) TLDP:189

## 194. Because of the Fall of Adam all people became subject to physical, temporal death.

### Alma, the younger, quoted by Mormon

Now Alma said unto him: This is the thing which I was about to explain, now we see that Adam did fall by the partaking of the forbidden fruit, according to the word of God; and thus we see, that by his fall, all mankind became a lost and fallen people. 23. And now behold, I say unto you that if it had been possible for Adam to have partaken of the fruit of the tree of life at that time, there would have been no death, and the word would have been void, making God a liar, for he said: If thou eat thou shalt surely die. 24. And we see that death comes upon mankind, yea, the death which has been spoken of by Amulek, which is the temporal death; nevertheless there was a space granted unto man in which he might repent; therefore this life became a probationary state; a time to prepare to meet God; a time to prepare for that endless state which has been spoken of by us, which is after the resurrection of the dead. (Alma responds to the chief ruler, Antionah, regarding Adam and Eve's expulsion from the Garden of Eden, about 82 B.C.) Alma 12:22-24

### Paul

For since by man came death, by man came also the resurrection of the dead. 22. For as in Adam all die, even so in Christ shall all be made alive. (Paul writes to the Church at Corinth, Greece, about A.D. 55) 1Cor.15:21-22

### Joseph Smith, translating the Book of Moses

And he said unto them: Because that Adam fell, we are; and by his fall came death; and we are made partakers of misery and woe. (Joseph Smith receives the revelation given Moses; Enoch testifies to the people) Moses 6:48

### James E. Talmage

The Immediate Result of the Fall was the substitution of mortality, with all its attendant frailties, for the vigor of the primeval deathless state. AF:61

### Elder Joseph Fielding Smith

When Adam came into this world, he was not subject to death. He was immortal. He could have lived forever. Had he remained in the Garden of Eden and not transgressed the law that had been given to him, he and Eve would have been there yet. (Doctrines of Salvation, 1:91) DGSM:21

### Orson F. Whitney

The death that came into the world by the fall

of Adam and Eve was death in very deed; it meant eternal banishment from the Divine Presence, the absolute death of spirit and body. . . . ("Significance of the Fall," IE1916Mar:402-03) TLDP:183

## 195. After the Fall, Adam and Eve were granted a probationary time to repent and serve God.

### Alma, the younger,
*quoted by Mormon*

Now behold, my son, I will explain this thing unto thee. For behold, after the Lord God sent our first parents forth from the garden of Eden, to till the ground, from whence they were taken—yea, he drew out the man, and he placed at the east end of the garden of Eden, cherubim, and a flaming sword which turned every way, to keep the tree of life— 3. Now, we see that the man had become as God, knowing good and evil; and lest he should put forth his hand, and take also of the tree of life, and eat and live forever, the Lord God placed cherubim and the flaming sword, that he should not partake of the fruit— 4. And thus we see, that there was a time granted unto man to repent, yea, a probationary time, a time to repent and serve God. 5. For behold, if Adam had put forth his hand immediately, and partaken of the tree of life, he would have lived forever, according to the word of God, having no space for repentance; yea, and also the word of God would have been void, and the great plan of salvation would have been frustrated. (*Alma speaks to his son Corianton; mortality is a probationary time to enable man to repent and serve God; about 73 B.C.*) Alma 42:2-5

### Bruce R. McConkie

Such is the divine will. Fall thou must, O mighty Michael. Fall? Yes, plunge down from thy immortal state of peace, perfection, and glory to a lower existence; leave the presence of thy God in the garden and enter the lone and dreary world; step forth from the garden to the wilderness; leave the flowers and fruits that grow spontaneously and begin the battle with thorns, thistles, briars, and noxious weeds; subject thyself to famine and pestilence; suffer with disease; know pain and sorrow; face death on every hand—but with it all bear children; provide bodies for all those who served with thee when thou led the hosts of heaven in casting out Lucifer, our common enemy. ¶ Yes, Adam, fall; fall for thine own good; fall for the good of all mankind; fall that man may be;

bring death into the world; do that which will cause an atonement to be made, with all the infinite and eternal blessings which flow therefrom. ¶ And so Adam fell as fall he must. But he fell by breaking a lesser law—so that he too, having thereby transgressed, would become subject to sin and need a Redeemer and be privileged to work out his own salvation, even as would be the case with all those upon whom the effects of his fall would come. (The Promised Messiah, pp. 220-21) TLDP:185

### James E. Talmage,
*also quoting Alma, the younger*

Alma, the Nephite prophet, comprehended the result that would have followed had Adam and his wife eaten of the tree of life; he thus explained the matter: "Now, we see that the man had become as God, knowing good and evil; and lest he should put forth his hand, and take also of the tree of life, and eat and live forever, the Lord God placed cherubim and the flaming sword, that he should not partake of the fruit—And thus we see, that there was a time granted unto man to repent, yea, a probationary time, a time to repent and serve God. For behold, if Adam had put forth his hand immediately, and partaken of the tree of life, he would have lived forever, according to the word of God, having no space for repentance; yea, and also the word of God would have been void, and the great plan of salvation would have been frustrated." [See Alma 42:2-5.] AF:60-61

### Alma, the younger,
*quoted by Mormon*

Therefore, as the soul could never die, and the fall had brought upon all mankind a spiritual death as well as a temporal, that is, they were cut off from the presence of the Lord, it was expedient that mankind should be reclaimed from this spiritual death. 10. Therefore, as they had become carnal, sensual, and devilish, by nature, this probationary state became a state for them to prepare; it became a preparatory state. (*Alma speaks to his son Corianton concerning the resurrection of the dead, about 73 B.C.*) Alma 42:9-10

### Alma, the younger,
*quoted by Mormon*

Now Alma said unto him: This is the thing which I was about to explain, now we see that Adam did fall by the partaking of the forbidden fruit, according to the word of God; and thus we see, that by his fall, all mankind became a lost and fallen people. . . . 24. . . . nevertheless there was a space granted unto man in which he might repent; therefore this life became a probationary state; a time to prepare to meet God;

a time to prepare for that endless state which has been spoken of by us, which is after the resurrection of the dead. . . . 26. And now behold, if it were possible that our first parents could have gone forth and partaken of the tree of life they would have been forever miserable, having no preparatory state; and thus the plan of redemption would have been frustrated, and the word of God would have been void, taking none effect. (*Alma responds to the chief ruler, Antionah, regarding Adam and Eve's expulsion from the Garden of Eden, about 82 B.C.*) Alma 12:22,24,26

**Related Witnesses:**

**James E. Talmage**

The Fall came not by Chance — It would be unreasonable to suppose that the transgression of Eve and Adam came as a surprise to the Creator. By His infinite foreknowledge, God knew what would be the result of Satan's temptation to Eve, and what Adam would do under the resulting conditions. Further, it is evident that the fall was foreseen to be a means whereby man could be brought into direct experience with both good and evil, so that of his own agency he might elect the one or the other, and thus be prepared by the experiences of a mortal probation for the exaltation provided in the beneficent plan of his creation: "For behold, this is my work and my glory—to bring to pass the immortality and eternal life of man" spake the Lord unto Moses. It was the purpose of God to place within the reach of the spirits begotten by Him in the heavens the means of individual effort, and the opportunity of winning not merely redemption from death but also salvation and even exaltation, with the powers of eternal progression and increase. Hence it was necessary that the spiritual offspring of God should leave the scenes of their primeval childhood and enter the school of mortal experience, meeting, contending with, and overcoming evil, according to their several degrees of faith and strength. Adam and Eve could never have been the parents of a mortal posterity had they not themselves become mortal; mortality was an essential element in the divine plan respecting the earth and its appointed inhabitants; and, as a means of introducing mortality, the Lord placed before the progenitors of the race a law, knowing what would follow. AF:62-63

**James E. Talmage**

This course of instruction [the Temple Endowment] includes a recital of the most prominent events of the creative period, the condition of our first parents in the Garden of Eden, their disobedience and consequent expulsion from that blissful abode, their condition in the lone and dreary world when doomed to live by labor and sweat, the plan of redemption by which the great transgression may be atoned . . . the absolute and indispensable condition of personal purity and devotion to the right in present life, and a strict compliance with Gospel requirements. HL:99-100

**Bruce R. McConkie**

The revealed accounts of the Creation are designed to accomplish two great purposes. Their *general purpose* is to enable us to understand the nature of our mortal probation, a probation in which all men are being tried and tested "to see if they will do all things whatsoever the Lord their God shall command them." (Abr. 3:25.) Their *specific purpose* is to enable us to understand the atoning sacrifice of the Lord Jesus Christ, which infinite and eternal Atonement is the very foundation upon which revealed religion rests. ("Christ and the Creation," EN1982Jun:13) TLDP:124

**Bruce R. McConkie**

One of the sweet and gracious doctrines of the gospel, a doctrine that brings comfort and serenity to the saints, is that those who are true and faithful in all things enter into the rest of the Lord their God. ¶ Mortality is the state in which men are tried and tested; in which they are subject to temptation, disease, sorrow, and death; in which there is violent opposition to every true principle; in which the generality of mankind is wafted hither and yon by every wind of doctrine; in which Satan has great hold upon the hearts of most of mankind. It is not a state of peace and rest; in it there is work and turmoil and dissension. It is a probationary estate where choices must be made, where all men, the saints included, are being tried and tested, to see if they choose liberty and eternal life through the atonement of Christ the Lord, or whether they will walk in subjection to the angel who fell from before the presence of the Eternal God and become the devil to rise no more. (The Promised Messiah, pp. 317-19) TLDP:472-73

---

**196. As a result of the Fall, Adam and Eve experienced pain and sorrow, which are part of mortality.**

**James E. Talmage**

The Immediate Result of the Fall was the substitution of mortality, with all its attendant frailties, for the vigor of the primeval deathless state. Adam felt directly the effects of transgression in finding a barren and dreary earth, with a relatively sterile soil, instead of the beauty and fruitfulness of Eden. In place of pleasing and useful plants, thorns and thistles sprang up; and the man had to labor arduously, under the conditions of physical fatigue and suffering, to cultivate the soil that he might obtain necessary food. Upon Eve fell the penalty of bodily infirmity; pains and sorrows, which since have been regarded as the natural lot of womankind, came upon her, and she was made subject to her husband's authority. AF:61

**Moses**

Unto the woman he said, I will greatly multiply thy sorrow and thy conception; in sorrow thou shalt bring forth children; and thy desire shall be to thy husband, and he shall rule over thee. (*The Lord teaches Adam and Eve the conditions of mortality*) Gen.3:16

**Joseph Smith,**
*translating the Book of Moses*

And he said unto them: Because that Adam fell, we are; and by his fall came death; and we are made partakers of misery and woe. (*The record of Moses; Enoch testifies to the people*) Moses 6:48

**Bruce R. McConkie**

Fall thou must, O mighty Michael. Fall? Yes, plunge down from thy immortal state of peace, perfection, and glory to a lower existence; leave the presence of thy God in the garden and enter the lone and dreary world; step forth from the garden to the wilderness; leave the flowers and fruits that grow spontaneously and begin the battle with thorns, thistles, briars, and noxious weeds; subject thyself to famine and pestilence; suffer with disease; know pain and sorrow; face death on every hand—but with it all bear children; provide bodies for all those who served with thee when thou led the hosts of heaven in casting out Lucifer, our common enemy. (The Promised Messiah, pp. 220-21) TLDP:185

**Orson F. Whitney**

In order that God's spirit children might have the opportunity to take bodies and undergo experiences on this earth, two heavenly beings came down in advance and became mortal for our sake. This is the true significance of the fall of Adam and Eve. It was not a mere yielding to temptation—they came on a mission, to pioneer this earthly wilderness, and open the way so that a world of waiting spirits might become souls, and make a stride forward in the great march of eternal progression. By the experience we gain here—the best of which comes from sorrow and tribulation—and by obedience to divine requirements, we accomplish successfully our earthly pilgrim-

age. We knew this in the life before, and rejoiced over it: "The morning stars sang together, and all the Sons of God shouted for joy" at the prospect—not of pain and death, but of eternal life and endless glory beyond! ("Significance of the Fall," IE1916Mar:402-03) TLDP:183

## 197. The Fall of Adam subjected all people to the enticings of Satan.

**Joseph Smith**

And it must needs be that the devil should tempt the children of men, or they could not be agents unto themselves; for if they never should have bitter they could not know the sweet— 40. Wherefore, it came to pass that the devil tempted Adam, and he partook of the forbidden fruit and transgressed the commandment, wherein he became subject to the will of the devil, because he yielded unto temptation. (*Revelation received Sept. 1830; the Fall and the Atonement bring salvation*) D&C 29:39-40

**Joseph Smith,**
*translating the Book of Moses*

And he said unto them: Because that Adam fell, we are; and by his fall came death; and we are made partakers of misery and woe. 49. Behold Satan hath come among the children of men, and tempteth them to worship him; and men have become carnal, sensual, and devilish, and are shut out from the presence of God. (*The record of Moses: Enoch testifies to the people*) Moses 6:48-49

**Abinadi,**
*quoted by Mormon*

For they are carnal and devilish, and the devil has power over them; yea, even that old serpent that did beguile our first parents, which was the cause of their fall; which was the cause of all mankind becoming carnal, sensual, devilish, knowing evil from good, subjecting themselves to the devil. 4. Thus all mankind were lost; and behold, they would have been endlessly lost were it not that God redeemed his people from their lost and fallen state. 5. But remember that he that persists in his own carnal nature, and goes on in the ways of sin and rebellion against God, remaineth in his fallen state and the devil hath all power over him. Therefore, he is as though there was no redemption made, being an enemy to God; and also is the devil an enemy to God. (*Abinadi preaches to King Noah and his people, about 148 B.C.*) Mosiah 16:3-5

**Marion G. Romney**

From the days of Adam until today, Satan has

fought against Christ for the souls of men. Every person who has reached the age of accountability, except Jesus, has yielded in some degree to sin, some more and some less, but all save Jesus only have yielded sufficiently to be barred from the presence of God. This means that every person must be cleansed through the atonement of Jesus Christ in order to reenter the society of God. ("Jesus—Savior and Redeemer," Brigham Young University Speeches of the Year, 1978, p. 11) TLDP:633

**Related Witnesses:**

**President Brigham Young**
If we are faithful to our religion, when we go into the spirit world, the fallen spirits—Lucifer and the third part of the heavenly hosts that came with him, and the spirits of wicked men who have dwelt upon this earth, the whole of them combined will have no influence over our spirits. Is that not an advantage? Yes. All the rest of the children of men are more or less subject to them, and they are subject to them as they were while here in the flesh. *(In Tabernacle, Sept. 1, 1859, JD7:240)* TLDP:638

**Joseph Smith**
But by the transgression of these holy laws man became sensual and devilish, and became fallen man. *(Revelation on Church Organization and Government, April 1830)* D&C 20:20

**Moroni, son of Mormon**
O Lord, thou hast said that we must be encompassed about by the floods. Now behold, O Lord, and do not be angry with thy servant because of his weakness before thee; for we know that thou art holy and dwellest in the heavens, and that we are unworthy before thee; because of the fall our natures have become evil continually; nevertheless, O Lord, thou hast given us a commandment that we must call upon thee, that from thee we may receive according to our desires. *(The brother of Jared prays to the Lord beginning his petition requesting the Lord to touch the 16 stones that they may shine in darkness, about the time of the Tower of Babel)* Ether 3:2

**George Q. Morris**
This being "conceived in sin" [Moses 6:55], as I understand it, is only that they are in the midst of sin. They come into the world where sin is prevalent, and it will enter into their hearts, but it will lead them "to taste the bitter, that they may know to prize the good." CR1958Apr:38; DGSM:21

**President Brigham Young**
You are aware that many think that the devil has rule and power over both body and spirit. Now, I want to tell you that he does not hold any

power over man, only so far as the body overcomes the spirit that is in a man, through yielding to the spirit of evil. The spirit that the Lord puts into a tabernacle of flesh, is under the dictation of the Lord Almighty; but the spirit and body are united in order that the spirit may have a tabernacle, and be exalted; and the spirit is influenced by the body, and the body by the spirit. ¶ In the first place the spirit is pure, and under the special control and influence of the Lord, but the body is of the earth, and is subject to the power of the devil, and is under the mighty influence of that fallen nature that is of the earth. If the spirit yields to the body, the devil then has power to overcome both the body and spirit of that man, and he loses both. *(In Tabernacle, April 6, 1855, JD2:255-56)* TLDP:135

---

### 198. The body of flesh subjects us to enticements toward physical gratification.

**Paul**
For they that are after the flesh do mind the things of the flesh; but they that are after the Spirit the things of the Spirit. 6. For to be carnally minded is death; but to be spiritually minded is life and peace. 7. Because the carnal mind is enmity against God: for it is not subject to the law of God, neither indeed can be. 8. So then they that are in the flesh cannot please God. *(Paul writes to the Church in Rome, about A.D. 55)* Rom.8:5-8

**Lehi,**
*quoted by his son Nephi*
And not choose eternal death, according to the will of the flesh and the evil which is therein, which giveth the spirit of the devil power to captivate, to bring you down to hell, that he may reign over you in his own kingdom. *(Lehi exhorts his sons to choose eternal life, between 588-570 B.C.)* 2Ne.2:29

**President Spencer W. Kimball**
The "natural man" is the "earthy man" who has allowed rude animal passions to overshadow his spiritual inclinations. CR1974Oct:161; DGSM:21

**President Brigham Young**
In the first place the spirit is pure, and under the special control and influence of the Lord, but the body is of the earth, and is subject to the power of the devil, and is under the mighty influence of that fallen nature that is of the earth. If the spirit yields to the body, the devil then has power to overcome both the body and spirit of that man, and he loses both.

*(In Tabernacle, Apr. 6, 1855, JD2:255-56)*
TLDP:135
**Related Witnesses:**
### Alma, the younger,
*quoted by Mormon*
Therefore, as the soul could never die, and the fall had brought upon all mankind a spiritual death as well as a temporal, that is, they were cut off from the presence of the Lord, it was expedient that mankind should be reclaimed from this spiritual death. 10. Therefore, as they had become carnal, sensual, and devilish, by nature, this probationary state became a state for them to prepare; it became a preparatory state. *(Alma speaks to his son Corianton concerning the resurrection of the dead, about 73 B.C.)* Alma 42:9-10
### Joseph Smith,
*translating the Book of Moses*
And Adam and Eve blessed the name of God, and they made all things known unto their sons and their daughters. 13. And Satan came among them, saying: I am also a son of God; and he commanded them, saying: Believe it not; and they believed it not, and they loved Satan more than God. And men began from that time forth to be carnal, sensual, and devilish. *(The record of Moses: Adam realizes that through Adam and Eve's transgression they may receive joy and eternal life, and he therefore blesses the name of God)* Moses 5:12-13
### Joseph Smith,
*translating the Book of Moses*
And he said unto them: Because that Adam fell, we are; and by his fall came death; and we are made partakers of misery and woe. 49. Behold Satan hath come among the children of men, and tempteth them to worship him; and men have become carnal, sensual, and devilish, and are shut out from the presence of God. *(The record of Moses: Enoch testifies to the people)* Moses 6:48-49
### Alma, the younger,
*quoted by Mormon*
And now, my son, all men that are in a state of nature, or I would say, in a carnal state, are in the gall of bitterness and in the bonds of iniquity; they are without God in the world, and they have gone contrary to the nature of God; therefore, they are in a state contrary to the nature of happiness. *(Alma speaks to his son Corianton concerning the resurrection of the dead, about 73 B.C.)* Alma 41:11
### Elder Joseph Fielding Smith
If we understood the extent of that suffering and his suffering on the cross, surely none of us would wilfully be guilty of sin. We would not

give way to the temptations, the gratification of unholy appetites and desires and Satan could find no place in our hearts. As it is, whenever we sin, we show our ingratitude and disregard of the suffering of the Son of God by and through which we shall rise from the dead and live forever. (The Restoration of All Things, p. 199) TLDP:44-45
### President Heber J. Grant,
### J. Reuben Clark, Jr., David O. McKay,
(First Presidency)
The doctrine of this Church is that sexual sin— the illicit sexual relations of men and women— stands, in its enormity, next to murder. ¶ The Lord has drawn no essential distinctions between fornication, adultery, and harlotry or prostitution. Each has fallen under His solemn and awful condemnation. ¶ You youths of Zion, you cannot associate in non-marital, illicit sexual relationships, which is fornication, and escape the punishments and the judgements which the Lord has declared against this sin. The day of reckoning will come just as certainly as night follows day. They who would palliate this crime and say that such indulgence is but a sinless gratification of a normal desire, like appeasing hunger and thirst, speak filthiness with their lips. Their counsel leads to destruction; their wisdom comes from the Father of Lies. CR1942Oct:11
### James E. Faust
Many years of listening to the tribulations of man have persuaded me that the satisfaction of all desires is completely counterproductive to happiness. Instant and unrestrained gratification is the shortest and most direct route to unhappiness. (Brigham Young University Speeches of the Year, 1974, p. 319) TLDP:319
### J. Reuben Clark, Jr.
There is some belief, too much I fear, that sex desire is planted in us solely for the pleasures of full gratification; that the begetting of children is only an unfortunate incident. The direct opposite is the fact. Sex desire was planted in us in order to be sure that bodies would be begotten to house the spirits; the pleasures of gratification of the desire is an incident, not the primary purpose of the desire. . . . ¶ As to sex in marriage, the necessary treatise on that for Latter-day Saints can be written in two sentences: Remember the prime purpose of sex desire is to beget children. Sex gratification must be had at that hazard. You husbands: be kind and considerate of your wives. They are not your property; they are not mere conveniences; they are your partners for time and eternity. CR1949Oct:194-95

### King Benjamin,
#### *quoted by Mormon*

For the natural man is an enemy to God, and has been from the fall of Adam, and will be, forever and ever, unless he yields to the enticings of the Holy Spirit, and putteth off the natural man and becometh a saint through the atonement of Christ the Lord, and becometh as a child, submissive, meek, humble, patient, full of love, willing to submit to all things which the Lord seeth fit to inflict upon him, even as a child doth submit to his father. *(King Benjamin relates the words of an angel spoken to him)* Mosiah 3:19

---

199. The Fall of Adam was a necessary element in God's plan of salvation for His children.

### President Brigham Young,
#### *quoted by John A. Widtsoe*

Did they [Adam and Eve] come out in direct opposition to God and to his government? No. But they transgressed a command of the Lord, and through that transgression sin came into the world. The Lord knew they would do this, and he had designed that they should. *(Instructions during visit to Davis and Weber counties, June 10-13, 1864, JD10:312)* DBY:103; DGSM:21

### Lehi,
#### *quoted by his son Nephi*

And now, behold, if Adam had not transgressed he would not have fallen, but he would have remained in the garden of Eden. And all things which were created must have remained in the same state in which they were after they were created; and they must have remained forever, and had no end. 23. And they would have had no children; wherefore they would have remained in a state of innocence, having no joy, for they knew no misery; doing no good, for they knew no sin. 24. But behold, all things have been done in the wisdom of him who knoweth all things. 25. Adam fell that men might be; and men are, that they might have joy. 26. And the Messiah cometh in the fulness of time, that he may redeem the children of men from the fall. And because that they are redeemed from the fall they have become free forever, knowing good from evil; to act for themselves and not to be acted upon, save it be by the punishment of the law at the great and last day, according to the commandments which God hath given. 27. Wherefore, men are free according to the flesh; and all things are given them which are expedient unto man. And they

are free to choose liberty and eternal life, through the great Mediator of all men, or to choose captivity and death, according to the captivity and power of the devil; for he seeketh that all men might be miserable like unto himself. *(The writings of Nephi, 559-545 B.C.)* 2Ne.2:22-27

### Joseph Smith,
#### *translating the Book of Moses*

And in that day Adam blessed God and was filled, and began to prophesy concerning all the families of the earth, saying: Blessed be the name of God, for because of my transgression my eyes are opened, and in this life I shall have joy, and again in the flesh I shall see God. 11. And Eve, his wife, heard all these things and was glad, saying: Were it not for our transgression we never should have had seed, and never should have known good and evil, and the joy of our redemption, and the eternal life which God giveth unto all the obedient. *(The record of Moses: Adam realizes that through Adam and Eve's transgression they may receive joy and eternal life, and he therefore blesses the name of God)* Moses 5:10-11

### Elder Joseph Fielding Smith

In order for mankind to obtain salvation and exaltation it is necessary for them to obtain bodies in this world, and pass through the experiences and schooling that are found only in mortality. . . . ¶ The fall of man came as a blessing in disguise, and was the means of furthering the purposes of the Lord in the progress of man, rather than a means of hindering them. (Doctrines of Salvation, 1:113-14) DGSM:21

### John A. Widtsoe

Clearly, the processes involved in the operation of the plan are beyond the full comprehension of man. Yet enough has been revealed to make the essentials of man's entrance upon earth, and progress in the hereafter, understandable to the human mind. ¶ To subject an eternal being to the dominion of "earth-element"—that is, to forgetfulness, the many vicissitudes of earth, and eventual death—appeared to be a descent in power and station. The first man, to bring himself under such dominion and domination would have to break, or set aside, an established law; but unless this were done, the plan could not be inaugurated. Man, made to walk upright, must bend his back through the tunnel through the mountain which leads to a beautiful valley. Adam and Eve accepted the call to initiate the plan, and subjected themselves to earth conditions. That was the so-called fall of Adam, an act necessary for the winning of bodies of earth-element by man, and for the fulfilment of divine law. (Pearl of Great Price, Moses, 4:7-13; 5:10, 11) Just how this "fall" was accomplished is not known, and probably cannot be understood by the mortal mind. One thing must be kept in mind: The fall was not a sin in the usually accepted sense of that word. It was a necessary act in a series of acts by which ultimately all men will win an eternal possession of their earth-bodies. In the gospel sense, the fall of Adam brought life, not death, into man's eternal existence. ¶ Here then, would be the condition of man after he had acquired an "earthly body" and then was separated from it by the process called death: He was rich in earth experience but without the earth-body to be used by him as an eternal tool to help him win his place among the realities of the universe. The "fall of Adam" had made possible the earth experience. (Evidences and Reconciliations, pp. 73-74) TLDP:184-85

**Lehi,**
*quoted by his son Nephi*
Adam fell that men might be; and men are, that they might have joy. *(Lehi teaches his sons, between 588-570 B.C.)* 2Ne.2:25

---

**200. The Fall of Adam and Eve made it possible for them to have children.**

**Lehi,**
*quoted by his son, Nephi*
And now, behold, if Adam had not transgressed he would not have fallen, but he would have remained in the garden of Eden. And all things which were created must have remained in the same state in which they were after they were created; and they must have remained forever, and had no end. 23. And they would have had no children; wherefore they would have remained in a state of innocence, having no joy, for they knew no misery; doing no good, for they knew no sin. 24. But behold, all things have been done in the wisdom of him who knoweth all things. *(Lehi teaches his sons that had Adam and Eve not transgressed, God's plan of salvation would have been thwarted, between 588-570 B.C.)* 2Ne.2:22-24

**Orson F. Whitney**
In order that God's spirit children might have the opportunity to take bodies and undergo experiences on this earth, two heavenly beings came down in advance and became mortal for our sake. This is the true significance of the fall of Adam and Eve. It was not a mere yielding to temptation—they came

on a mission, to pioneer this earthly wilderness, and open the way so that a world of waiting spirits might become souls, and make a stride forward in the great march of eternal progression. ("Significance of the Fall," IE1916Mar:402-03) TLDP:183

**Bruce R. McConkie**
Be fruitful! Multiply! Have children! The whole plan of salvation, including both immortality and eternal life for all the spirit hosts of heaven, hung on their compliance with this command. If they obeyed, the Lord's purposes would prevail. ¶ If they disobeyed, they would remain childless and innocent in their paradisiacal Eden, and the spirit hosts would remain in their celestial heaven—denied the experiences of mortality, denied a resurrection, denied a hope of eternal life, denied the privilege to advance and progress and become like their Eternal Father. That is to say, the whole plan of salvation would have been frustrated, and the purposes of God in begetting spirit children and in creating this earth as their habitat would have come to naught. ¶ "Be fruitful, and multiply." Provide bodies for my spirit progeny. Thus saith thy God. Eternity hangs in the balance. The plans of Deity are at the crossroads. There is only one course to follow: the course of conformity and obedience. Adam, who is Michael—the spirit next in intelligence, power, dominion, and righteousness to the great Jehovah himself—Adam, our father, and Eve, our mother, must obey. They must fall. They must become mortal. Death must enter the world. There is no other way. They must fall that man may be. (The Promised Messiah, pp. 220-21) TLDP:185

**Lehi,**
*quoted by his son Nephi*
Adam fell that men might be; and men are, that they might have joy. *(Lehi teaches his sons, between 588-570 B.C.)* 2Ne.2:25

**Joseph Smith,**
*translating the Book of Moses*
And Adam knew his wife, and she bare unto him sons and daughters, and they began to multiply and to replenish the earth. 3. And from that time forth, the sons and daughters of Adam began to divide two and two in the land, and to till the land, and to tend flocks, and they also begat sons and daughters. . . . 11. And Eve, his wife, heard all these things and was glad, saying: Were it not for our transgression we never should have had seed, and never should have known good and evil, and the joy of our redemption, and the eternal life which God giveth unto all the obedient. *(Revelation to Moses given to Joseph concerning*

*Adam and Eve after they were driven out of the Garden of Eden; Adam realizes that through Adam and Eve's transgression they may receive joy and he therefore blesses the name of God)* Moses 5:2-3,11
**Related Witnesses:**
### Moses
Unto the woman he said, I will greatly multiply thy sorrow and thy conception; in sorrow thou shalt bring forth children; and thy desire shall be to thy husband, and he shall rule over thee. *(The Lord teaches Adam and Eve the conditions of mortality)* Gen.3:16

---

**201. It was the design of the Lord that Adam and Eve (and all people born thereafter) should support themselves by their own labors.**

### George Q. Morris
The Lord has set the earth up so we have to labor if we are going to live, which preserves us from the curse of idleness and indolence; . . . ¶ So these are all real blessings. We come to the earth with all these conditions arranged as they are so that we have to struggle constantly against evil, struggle to preserve our lives, struggle for everything of true value—that is the course of life that is most desirable, and for our good. We have no need to find fault with these conditions. The Lord has ordained them all for our welfare and happiness. CR19-58Apr:39; DGSM:21

### Moses
[C]ursed is the ground for thy sake; in sorrow shalt thou eat of it all the days of thy life; 18. Thorns also and thistles shall it bring forth to thee; and thou shalt eat the herb of the field; 19. In the sweat of thy face shalt thou eat bread, till thou return unto the ground; for out of it wast thou taken: for dust thou art, and unto dust shalt thou return. *(The Lord teaches Adam and Eve the conditions of mortality)* Gen.3:17-19

### J. Reuben Clark, Jr.
From the foundation of the Church until now, idleness has been condemned as unworthy of Church members, as destructive of character, as violative of the true Christian life, as contrary to the command given to Adam as the law of this world "In the sweat of thy brow, thou shalt eat bread." The Lord has repeatedly spoken about it in our time. CR1940Oct:12-13

### Mark E. Petersen
That we should work for what we get is a divine principle. When the Lord placed Adam, the first man in the earth, he commanded him to work for his living, to earn his bread by the sweat of his brow. On Mount Sinai the Lord commanded men to labor. Philosophies which tend to cheapen the doctrine that men should work for their sustenance detract from the stability of the nation. They also have a moral effect upon the individual, robbing him of his self-respect, and undermining his character. CR1947Oct:109

### Joseph Smith,
*translating the Book of Moses*
[C]ursed shall be the ground for thy sake; in sorrow shalt thou eat of it all the days of thy life. 24. Thorns also, and thistles shall it bring forth to thee, and thou shalt eat the herb of the field. 25. By the sweat of thy face shalt thou eat bread, until thou shalt return unto the ground—for thou shalt surely die—for out of it wast thou taken: for dust thou wast, and unto dust shalt thou return. *(The record of Moses: the Lord teaches Adam and Eve the conditions of mortality)* Moses 4:23-25
**Related Witnesses:**
### Joseph Smith,
*translating the Book of Moses*
And it came to pass that after I, the Lord God, had driven them out, that Adam began to till the earth, and to have dominion over all the beasts of the field, and to eat his bread by the sweat of his brow, as I the Lord had commanded him. And Eve, also, his wife, did labor with him. *(The record of Moses: concerning Adam and Eve after they were driven out of the Garden of Eden)* Moses 5:1

### James E. Talmage
The Immediate Result of the Fall was the substitution of mortality, with all its attendant frailties, for the vigor of the primeval deathless state. Adam felt directly the effects of transgression in finding a barren and dreary earth, with a relatively sterile soil, instead of the beauty and fruitfulness of Eden. In place of pleasing and useful plants, thorns and thistles sprang up; and the man had to labor arduously, under the conditions of physical fatigue and suffering, to cultivate the soil that he might obtain necessary food. AF:61

---

# List of Doctrines

## FAMILY AND PARENTHOOD

### The Eternal Family

*Doctrines Located in This Topic*

202. The family is the most important of all institutions.

203. The Lord ordained the family unit to last into eternity.

204. The Lord commanded married couples to bring children into the world.

205. The power of procreation is a divine gift to be exercised only between husband and wife in the marriage relationship.

206. Husbands and wives normally should not curtail the birth of children; yet husbands must be considerate of their wives who have a great responsibility not only for bearing children but for caring for them through childhood (married couples should seek inspiration from the Lord in this regard).

207. Abortion is a sinful, evil practice and Church members are not to submit to or perform an abortion— except in specific rare instances.

208. Married persons who achieve exaltation (in the highest degree of the celestial kingdom) will enjoy eternal increase, having children in the celestial kingdom.

209. Fathers are the presiding authority in the home and have the responsibility for the direction and regulation of the home.

210. Husbands and wives are equal partners in the marriage and family relationship (even though the man in the righteous exercise of the priesthood presides in the home).

211. Parents are to provide and care for their children.

212. Parents are to teach their children to honor and respect their parents.

213. Parents are commanded to teach their children by the time they are eight years old to understand the doctrines of faith, repentance, and baptism.

214. Parents are commanded to teach the gospel to their children.

215. Parents are to teach their children to pray.

216. Parents are commanded to correct and discipline their children (in the spirit of love).

*Doctrines on FAMILY AND PARENTHOOD Located in Other Topics*

143. Those who inherit the highest degree of the celestial kingdom will have eternal increase, becoming parents of spirit offspring.

# FAMILY AND PARENTHOOD continued

722. Parents are to teach their children to study the scriptures.

862. Parents are to support their minor children.

863. Adult children have the responsibility to support their parents when they are in need.

864. If Church members are unable to sustain themselves, they are to call upon their own families, and then upon the Church, in that order.

# FAMILY AND PARENTHOOD

## The Eternal Family

**202. The family is the most important of all institutions.**

### Boyd K. Packer

I invoke the blessings of the Lord upon you, all of you here, with reference to your home and your families. It is the choicest of all life's experiences. I urge you to put it first. The center core of the Church is not the stake house; it is not the chapel; that is not the center of Mormonism. And, strangely enough, the most sacred place on earth may not be the temple, necessarily. The chapel, the stake house, and the temple are sacred as they contribute to the building of the most sacred institution in the Church—the home—and to the blessing of the most sacred relationships in the Church, the family. (*At Brigham Young University, 1963*) DGSM:79

### David B. Haight

The family is the basic unit of the Church. The Church exists mainly to help families return to live in the presence of God. ACR(Nuku'alofa) 1976:38

### President Joseph Fielding Smith

The family is the most important organization in time or in eternity. Our purpose in life is to create for ourselves eternal family units. There is nothing that will ever come into your family life that is as important as the sealing blessings of the temple and then keeping the covenants made in connection with this order of celestial marriage. CR1972Apr:13

### Elder Spencer W. Kimball

The family is the great plan of life as conceived and organized by our Father in heaven. CR1973Apr:151; DGSM:78

**Related Witnesses:**

### President Joseph F. Smith

The typical "Mormon" home is the temple of the family, in which the members of the household gather morning and evening, for prayer and praise to God, offered in the name of Jesus Christ, and often accompanied by the reading of scripture and the singing of spiritual songs. Here are taught and gently enforced, the moral precepts and religious truths, which, taken together, make up that righteousness which exalteth a nation, and ward off that sin which is a reproach to any people. . . . Here are our sons and daughters, submit them to any test of comparison you will: regard for truth, veneration for age, reverence for God, love of man, loyalty to country, respect for law, refinement of man-

ners, and, lastly . . . purity of mind and chastity of conduct. (*Address from the First Presidency of the Church to the world, delivered to and accepted by vote of the Church in general conference, April 1907*) CR1907Apr(Appendix)7

### President Harold B. Lee

Now, you husbands, remember that the most important of the Lord's work that you will ever do will be the work you do within the walls of your own home. Home teaching, bishopric's work, and other church duties are all important, but the most important work is within the walls of your home. (*October general conference, 1973*) DGSM:79

### Elder David O. McKay

Latter-day Saints, the responsibility of saving this sacred institution devolves largely upon you, for you know that the family ties are eternal. They should be eternal. There is nothing temporary in the home of the Latter-day Saint. There is no element of transitoriness in the family relationship of the Latter-day Saint home. That all such ties are eternal should be maintained. To the Latter-day Saint the home is truly the cell-unit of society: and parenthood is next to Godhood. CR1919Jun:77

### President Spencer W. Kimball

We have no choice . . . but to continue to hold up the ideal of the Latter-day Saint family. The fact that some do not now have the privilege of living in such a family is not reason enough to stop talking about it. We do discuss family life with sensitivity, however, realizing that many . . . do not presently have the privilege of belonging or contributing to such a family. But we cannot set aside this standard because so many other things depend upon it. (*Sermon, women's fireside, 1978*) DGSM:79

### Bruce R. McConkie

But we do know that our Eternal Father . . . lives in the family unit. We do know that we are his children, created in his image, endowed with power and ability to become like him. CR1974Apr:103

---

**203. The Lord ordained the family unit to last into eternity.**

### President Spencer W. Kimball

The greatest joys of true married life can be continued. The most beautiful relationships of parents and children can be made permanent. The holy association of families can be never-ending if husband and wife have been sealed in the holy bond of eternal matrimony. . . . ¶ . . . . In these temples, by duly constituted authority, are men who can seal husbands and wives and their children for all eternity. (The Teachings of Spencer W. Kimball, p. 291) DGSM:75

**President Joseph F. Smith**

Who are there besides the Latter-day Saints who contemplate the thought that beyond the grave we will continue in the family organization? the father, the mother, the children recognizing each other in the relations which they owe to each other and in which they stand to each other? this family organization being a unit in the great and perfect organization of God's work, and all destined to continue throughout time and eternity? ¶ We are living for eternity and not merely for the moment. Death does not part us from one another, if we have entered into sacred relationships with each other by virtue of the authority that God has revealed to the children of men. Our relationships are formed for eternity. (1917, Gospel Doctrine, p. 277) TLDP:190

**Elder George Albert Smith**

Children are the offspring of God, their spirits were begotten in the holy heavens of our Father, and they are given to us for our blessing. We, as stewards, are permitted to receive them in their infancy, to educate and prepare them, not alone that they may become great in this world and bring honor to us here, but, by observing the laws of God, that they might live again with us in the presence of our Father throughout the endless ages of eternity. CR1907Oct:36

**Related Witnesses:**

**Joseph Smith**

And now, my dearly beloved brethren and sisters, let me assure you that these are principles in relation to the dead and the living that cannot be lightly passed over, as pertaining to our salvation. For their salvation is necessary and essential to our salvation, as Paul says concerning the fathers—that they without us cannot be made perfect—neither can we without our dead be made perfect. . . . 18. I might have rendered a plainer translation to this, but it is sufficiently plain to suit my purpose as it stands. It is sufficient to know, in this case, that the earth will be smitten with a curse unless there is a welding link of some kind or other between the fathers and the children, upon some subject or other— and behold what is that subject? It is the baptism for the dead. For we without them cannot be made perfect; neither can they without us be made perfect. Neither can they nor we be made perfect without those who have died in the

gospel also; for it is necessary in the ushering in of the dispensation of the fulness of times, which dispensation is now beginning to usher in, that a whole and complete and perfect union, and welding together of dispensations, and keys, and powers, and glories should take place, and be revealed from the days of Adam even to the present time. . . . (*Joseph writes to the Church giving further directions on baptism for the dead, Sept. 6, 1842*) D&C 128:15,18

**Joseph Smith**

And that same sociality which exists among us here will exist among us there, only it will be coupled with eternal glory, which glory we do not now enjoy. (*Revelation April 2, 1830*) D&C 130:2

**Joseph Smith**

He also quoted the next verse differently: "And he shall plant in the hearts of the children the promises made to the fathers, and the hearts of the children shall turn to their fathers. If it were not so the whole earth would be utterly wasted at his coming." (*Joseph relates the angel Moroni's visit to him, Sept. 21, 1823*) JS-H 1:39

**Joseph Smith**

The Bible says, "I will send you Elijah the Prophet before the coming of the great and dreadful day of the Lord; and he shall turn the hearts [sic] of the fathers to the children, and the hearts [sic] of the children to the fathers, lest I come and smite the earth with a curse." Now, the word turn here should be translated *bind*, or seal. But what is the object of this important mission? or how is it to be fulfilled? . . . By building their temples, erecting their baptismal fonts, and going forth and receiving all the ordinances, baptisms, confirmations, washings, anointings, ordinations and sealing powers upon their heads, in behalf of all their progenitors who are dead, and redeem them that they may come forth in the first resurrection and be exalted to thrones of glory with them; and herein is the chain that binds the hearts of the fathers to the children, and the children to the fathers, which fulfills the mission of Elijah. (*Discourse at southeast corner of Nauvoo Temple, delivered to several thousand people, Jan. 21, 1844*) HC6:183-84

**Malachi**

Behold, I will send you Elijah the prophet before the coming of the great and dreadful day of the LORD: 6. And he shall turn the heart of the fathers to the children, and the heart of the children to their fathers, lest I come and smite the earth with a curse. (*The prophet Malachi to the people, about 430 B.C.*) Mal.4:5-6

**204.** The Lord commanded married couples to bring children into the world.

### President Heber J. Grant
### J. Reuben Clark, David O. McKay
*(First Presidency)*

The Lord has told us that it is the duty of every husband and wife to obey the command given to Adam to multiply and replenish the earth, so that the legions of choice spirits waiting for their tabernacles of flesh may come here and move forward under God's great design to become perfect souls, for without these fleshly tabernacles they cannot progress to their God-planned destiny. Thus, every husband and wife should become a father and a mother in Israel to children born under the holy, eternal covenant. CR1942Oct:12

### President Spencer W. Kimball

The Lord has spoken out very strongly in this matter, constantly and continuously. He said, as one of his important commandments, "Multiply and replenish the earth." (Genesis 1:28) That wasn't just a hoping so; it wasn't just something that would be kind of nice to do. The Lord said, "Go forward now, husband and the wife; love each other." They will have their children, and then they will work together for the children to see that they grow up in righteousness. *(Melbourne Australia Area Conference, 1976)* DGSM:79

### Elder George Albert Smith

How will those feel who fail to obey that first great command [multiply, and replenish the earth] when they stand in the presence of the creator, who says to them, as He said to those in olden times, "Suffer little children to come unto me, and forbid them not, for of such is the kingdom of heaven." How can they comply with that invitation if they have no children to take to the Father? They must remain childless throughout eternity. They have been blind to their rights and privileges. It is only by a proper understanding of the laws of God, and by compliance with the Gospel of Jesus Christ, only by doing what the Lord has said we should do, that we will enjoy the fulness of happiness that our Father in heaven has promised those who are faithful. I do not feel to censure, but with all my heart I pity the man and woman who grace their home with the lesser animals of God's creation, and keep away from their firesides those angels from His presence who might be theirs through time and through all eternity. I realize there are some men and women who are grieved because they are not

fathers and mothers, they are not blessed of the Lord in that particular, they have no children of their own, and by no fault of their own. I believe the Lord will provide in such cases. If they will do their duty in keeping the other commandments, their reproach will be taken away. I raise my voice among the sons and daughters of Zion, and warn you that if you dry up the springs of life and abuse the power that God has blessed you with, there will come a time of chastening to you, that all the tears you may shed will never remove. Remember the first great commandment [Gen.1:28]; fulfill that obligation. CR1907Oct:38

**Related Witnesses:**

### Moses

So God created man in his own image, in the image of God created he him; male and female created he them. 28. And God blessed them, and God said unto them, Be fruitful, and multiply, and replenish the earth, and subdue it: and have dominion over the fish of the sea, and over the fowl of the air, and over every living thing that moveth upon the earth. *(Revelation to Moses regarding the creation of man)* Gen.1:27-28

### Joseph Smith,
*translating the Book of Moses*

And I, God, blessed them, and said unto them: Be fruitful, and multiply, and replenish the earth, and subdue it, and have dominion over the fish of the sea, and over the fowl of the air, and over every living thing that moveth upon the earth. *(The record of Moses: God makes man and gives him dominion over all things)* Moses 2:28

### Joseph Smith,
*quoted by President Spencer W. Kimball*

And I God, blessed them (Man here is always in the plural. It was plural from the beginning.) and said unto them: Be fruitful, and multiply, and have dominion over [it]. (Moses 2:27-28) ("The Blessings and Responsibilities of Womanhood," EN1976Mar:71) DGSM:18

### Moses

And God blessed Noah and his sons, and said unto them, Be fruitful, and multiply, and replenish the earth. *(After the Flood, the Lord gives commandments to Noah and his sons)* Gen.9:1

### Elder Ezra Taft Benson

The establishment of a home is not only a privilege, but marriage and the bearing, rearing, and proper training of children is a duty of the highest order. CR1947Oct:23

### Joseph Smith

Wherefore, it is lawful that he should have one wife, and they twain shall be one flesh, and all this that the earth might answer the end of its creation; 17. And that it might be filled with the measure of man, according to his creation before the world was made. (*Revelation refuting the Shaker doctrine of celibacy, March 1831*) D&C 49:16-17

**President Brigham Young,**
*quoted by John A. Widtsoe*

The whole object of the creation of this world is to exalt the intelligences that are placed upon it, that they may live, endure, and increase for ever and ever. (*In the Tabernacle, Oct. 9, 1859, JD7:290*) DBY:57; DGSM:18

**Author's Note:** In Genesis 1:28 the Lord commanded Adam and Eve to multiply in the status of man and wife. The following scripture bears that out: "And the rib, which the LORD God had taken from man, made he a woman, and brought her unto the man. And Adam said, This is now bone of my bones, and flesh of my flesh: she shall be called Woman, because she was taken out of Man. Therefore shall a man leave his father and his mother, and shall cleave unto his wife: and they shall be one flesh. And they were both naked, the man and his wife, and were not ashamed." (Gen.2:22-25) ¶ That God intended that man and women bear children only as husband and wife and not outside of wedlock, note the following scriptures: "Marriage is honourable in all, and the bed undefiled: but whoremongers and adulterers God will judge." (Heb.13:4) "And again, verily I say unto you, that whoso forbiddeth to marry is not ordained of God, for marriage is ordained of God unto man." (D&C 49:15) See Topic MARRIAGE: Husband and Wife.

---

205. The power of procreation is a divine gift to be exercised only between husband and wife in the marriage relationship.

**Boyd K. Packer**

There was provided in our bodies—and this is sacred—a power of creation, a light, so to speak, that has the power to kindle other lights. This gift was to be used only within the sacred bonds of marriage. Through the exercise of this power of creation, a mortal body may be conceived, a spirit enter into it, and a new soul born into this life. ¶ This power is good. It can create and sustain family life, and it is in family life that we find the fountains of happiness. It is given to virtually every individual who is born into mortality. . . . ¶ It was necessary that

this power of creation have at least two dimensions: one, it must be strong; and two, it must be more or less constant. ¶ This power must be strong, for most men by nature seek adventure. Except for the compelling persuasion of these feelings, men would be reluctant to accept the responsibility of sustaining a home and a family. This power must be constant, too, for it becomes a binding tie in family life. CR1972 Apr:136-37

**Hugh B. Brown**

Latter-day Saints therefore believe that God is actually the third partner in this relationship and that bringing children into the world within the divinely sanctioned institution of marriage is part of his plan to bring to pass the immortality and eternal life of man. ("The LDS Concept of Marriage," IE1962Aug:574) TLDP:524-25

**Paul**

Marriage is honourable in all, and the bed undefiled: but whoremongers and adulterers God will judge. (*Letter to the Jewish members of the Church, about A.D. 60*) Heb.13:4

**Joseph Smith**

Wherefore, it is lawful that he should have one wife, and they twain shall be one flesh, and all this that the earth might answer the end of its creation; 17. And that it might be filled with the measure of man, according to his creation before the world was made. (*Revelation refuting the Shaker doctrine of celibacy, March 1831*) D&C 49:16-17

**Related Witnesses:**

**Elder Spencer W. Kimball**

The Lord organized the whole program in the beginning with a father who procreates, provides, and loves and directs, and a mother who conceives and bears and nurtures and feeds and trains. The Lord could have ordained it otherwise but chose to have a unit with responsibility and purposeful associations where children train and discipline each other and come to love, honor, and appreciate each other. The family is the great plan of life as conceived and organized by our Father in heaven. CR1973Apr:151; DGSM:78

**Moses**

And the LORD God said, It is not good that the man should be alone; I will make him an help meet for him. . . . ¶ 22. And the rib, which the LORD God had taken from man, made he a woman, and brought her unto the man. 23. And Adam said, This is now bone of my bones, and flesh of my flesh: she shall be called Woman, because she was taken out of Man. 24. Therefore shall a man leave his father and his mother, and shall cleave unto his wife: and they shall be one flesh. 25. And they were both naked, the man and his wife, and were not ashamed. (*The Lord places Adam in the Garden of Eden*) Gen.2:18,22-25

**President Brigham Young,**
*quoted by President Spencer W. Kimball*

Let me here say a word to console the feelings and hearts of all who belong to this Church. Many of the sisters grieve because they are not blessed with offspring. You will see the time when you will have millions of children around you. If you are faithful to your covenants, you will be mothers of nations. You will become Eves to earths like this, and when you have assisted in peopling one earth, there are millions of others still in the course of creation. And when they have endured a thousand million times longer than this earth, it is only as it were at the beginning of your creation. Be faithful and if you are not blessed with children in this time, you will be hereafter. (*An 1860 statement, quoted at fireside address in 1977*) DGSM:79

---

206. **Husbands and wives normally should not curtail the birth of children; yet husbands must be considerate of their wives who have a great responsibility not only for bearing children but for caring for them through childhood (married couples should seek inspiration from the Lord in this regard).**

**President David O. McKay,**
**Hugh B. Brown, N. Eldon Tanner**
(First Presidency)

We seriously regret that there should exist a sentiment or feeling among any members of the Church to curtail the birth of their children. We have been commanded to multiply and replenish the earth that we may have joy and rejoicing in our posterity. ¶ Where husband and wife enjoy health and vigor and are free from impurities that would be entailed upon their posterity, it is contrary to the teachings of the Church artificially to curtail or prevent the birth of children. We believe that those who practice birth control will reap disappointment by and by. ¶ However, we feel that men must be considerate of their wives who bear the greater responsibility not only of bearing children, but of caring for them through childhood. To this end the mother's health and strength should be conserved and the husband's consideration for his wife is

his first duty, and self-control a dominant factor in all their relationships. (*Letter to bishops, stake presidents, and mission presidents, April 14, 1969*) TLDP:529

**Hugh B. Brown,**
*quoted by Mark E. Petersen*

The Church has always advised against birth control and that is the only position the Church can take in view of our beliefs with respect to the eternity of the marriage covenant and the purpose of this divine relationship. There are, of course, circumstances under which people are justified in regulating the size of their families. ¶ Where the health of the mother is concerned, and where the welfare of other children would be adversely affected, parents sometimes, under the advice of their physicians, deem it wisdom to take precautionary measures. . . . ¶ The Church cannot give a blanket or over-all answer to the question which would be applicable to all situations. Seeking divine guidance and searching your own souls is recommended, but in a long lifetime of counseling on these matters, the General Authorities of the Church are united in recommending generally against birth control. (The Way of the Master, pp. 114-15) TLDP:529-30

**Elder Joseph Fielding Smith**

Is it proper and right in the sight of God for parents intentionally to prevent, by any means whatever, the spirits, the sons and daughters of our Heavenly Father, from obtaining earthly tabernacles? I have, of course, only reference to parents lawfully married, and specifically to Latter-day Saints. ¶ In a general way, and as a rule, the answer to this question is an emphatic negative. I do not hesitate to say that prevention is wrong. It brings in its train a host of social evils. It destroys the morals of a community and nation. It creates hatred and selfishness in the hearts of men and women, and perverts their natural qualities of love and service, changing them to hate and aversion. It causes death, decay, and degeneration instead of life, growth, and advancement. And finally, it disregards or annuls the great commandment of God to man, "Multiply and replenish the earth." ¶ I am now speaking of the normally healthy man and woman. But, that there are weak and sickly people who in wisdom, discretion and common sense *should be counted as exceptions, only strengthens the general rule.* [Italics added] ("A Vital Question," IE1908Oct:959-60) TLDP:529

**Related Witnesses:**
**J. Reuben Clark, Jr.**

As to sex in marriage, the necessary treatise on that for Latter-day Saints can be written in two sentences: Remember the prime purpose of sex desire is to beget children. Sex gratification must be had at that hazard. You husbands: be kind and considerate of your wives. They are not your property; they are not mere conveniences; they are your partners for time and eternity. CR1949Oct:194-95

**President David O. McKay**

The increasing tendency to look upon family life as a burden, and the ever-spreading practice of birth control, are ominous threats to the perpetuation of the United States. In the light of what the restored gospel teaches us regarding pre-existence, the eternal nature of the marriage covenant, and of family relationship, no healthy wife in the Church should shun the responsibilities of normal motherhood. (Treasures of Life, p. 57) TLDP:528

**President Harold B. Lee**

[W]e declare it is a grievous sin before God to adopt restrictive measures in disobedience to God's divine command from the beginning of time to "multiply and replenish the earth." Surely those who project such measures to prevent life or to destroy life before or after birth will reap the whirlwind of God's retribution, for God will not be mocked. CR1972Oct:63

**Elder Spencer W. Kimball**

Sterilization and tying of tubes and such are sins, and except under special circumstances it cannot be approved. (The Teachings of Spencer W. Kimball, p. 331) TLDP:529

**President Spencer W. Kimball**

As we look about us, we see many forces at work bent on the destruction of the family. . . . [A]bortion . . . bids well to become a national scandal and is a very grave sin. Another erosion of the family is unwarranted and selfish birth control. CR1979Oct:6

**George Q. Cannon**

We have heard that many of the diabolical practices of the world have been introduced . . . among some who profess to be Latter-day Saints, to prevent the bearing of children. No sin, unless it be that of murder, will meet with a greater condemnation from God than this evil of tampering with the fountains of life. Such sins will destroy the strength of any people that practices them, and the nation whose people yield to such vices is in great danger of destruction. No Saint can practice or encourage such corruption without incurring the displeasure of an offended God. (Juvenile Instructor, July 15, 1895, p. 451) TLDP:527

**Elder Joseph F. Smith**

Those who have taken upon themselves the responsibility of wedded life should see to it that they do not abuse the course of nature; that they do not destroy the principle of life within them, nor violate any of the commandments of God. The command which he gave in the beginning to multiply and replenish the earth is still in force upon the children of men. Possibly no greater sin could be committed by the people who have embraced this gospel than to prevent or to destroy life in the manner indicated. We are born into the world that we may have life, and we live that we may have a fulness of joy, and if we will obtain a fulness of joy, we must obey the law of our creation and the law by which we may obtain the consummation of our righteous hopes and desires—life eternal. CR1900Apr:40

**Author's Note:** The 1989 General Handbook of Instructions states at page 11-4: "Husbands must be considerate of their wives, who have a great responsibility not only for bearing children but also for caring for them through childhood. Husbands should help their wives conserve their health and strength. Married couples should seek inspiration from the Lord in meeting their marital challenges and rearing their children according to the teachings of the gospel."

---

207. **Abortion is a sinful, evil practice and Church members are not to submit to or perform an abortion— except in specific rare instances.**

**President Spencer W. Kimball,
N. Eldon Tanner, Marion G. Romney**
(First Presidency)
*also quoting Joseph Smith,*
*also quoting a previous First Presidency:*
*President David O. McKay,*
*Stephen L. Richards, J. Reuben Clark, Jr.*
*(First Presidency)*

In view of a recent decision of the United States Supreme Court, we feel it necessary to restate the position of the Church on abortion in order that there will be no misunderstanding of our attitude. ¶ The Church opposes abortion and counsels its members not to submit to or perform an abortion except in the rare cases where, in the opinion of competent medical counsel, the life or good health of the mother is seriously endangered or where the pregnancy was caused by rape and produces serious emotional trauma in the mother. Even then it should be done only after counseling with the local presiding priesthood authority and after receiving divine confirmation through prayer. ¶ Abortion must be considered one of the most revolting and sinful practices in this day, when we are witnessing the frightening evidence of permissiveness leading to sexual immorality. ¶ Members of the Church guilty of being parties to the sin of abortion must be subjected to the disciplinary action of the councils of the Church as circumstances warrant. In dealing with this serious matter, it would be well to keep in mind the word of the Lord stated in the 59th Section of the Doctrine and Covenants, verse 6. "Thou shalt not steal; neither commit adultery, nor kill, nor do anything like unto it." ¶ As to the amenability of the sin of abortion to the laws of repentance and forgiveness, we quote the following statement made by President David O. McKay and his counselors, Stephen L. Richards and J. Reuben Clark Jr., which continues to represent the attitude and position of the Church: ¶ "As the matter stands today, no definite statement has been made by the Lord one way or another regarding the crime of abortion, so far as is known, he has not listed it alongside the crime of the unpardonable sin and shedding of innocent human blood. That he has not done so would suggest that it is not in that class of crime and therefore that it will be amenable to the laws of repentance and forgiveness." ¶ This quoted statement, however, should not, in any sense, be construed to minimize the seriousness of this revolting sin. (Priesthood Bulletin, Feb. 1973, pp. 1-2) TLDP:530

**President Spencer W. Kimball**

Abortion, the taking of life, is one of the most grievous sins. We have repeatedly affirmed the position of the Church in unalterably opposing all abortions, except in two rare instances: When conception is the result of forcible rape and when competent medical counsel indicates that a mother's health would otherwise be seriously jeopardized. CR1976Oct:6

**Boyd K. Packer,**
*also quoting Joseph Smith*

In or out of marriage, abortion is not an individual choice. At a minimum, three lives are involved. ¶ The scriptures tell us, "Thou shalt not . . . kill, nor do *anything* like unto it" (D&C 59:6; italics added). ¶ Except where the wicked crime of incest or rape was involved, or where competent medical authorities certify that the life of the mother is in jeopardy, or that a severely defective fetus cannot survive birth, abortion is clearly a "thou shalt not." Even in these very exceptional cases, much sober

prayer is required to make the right choice. CR1990Oct:108

**Related Witnesses:**

**Russell M. Nelson,**
*also quoting a First Presidency:*
**John Taylor, George Q. Cannon**

Another contention raised is that a woman is free to choose what she does with her own body. To a certain extent this is true for all of us. We are free to think. We are free to plan. And then we are free to do. But once an action has been taken, we are never free from its consequences. . . . ¶ The woman's choice for her own body does not validate choice for the body of another. . . . The consequence of terminating the fetus therein involves the body and very life of another. These two individuals have separate brains, separate hearts, and separate circulatory systems. To pretend there is no child and no life there is to deny reality. ¶ . . . . Abortion sheds that innocent blood. ¶ . . . . Now, as a servant of the Lord, I dutifully warn those who advocate and practice abortion that they incur the wrath of Almighty God, who declared, "If men . . . hurt a woman with child, so that her fruit depart from her, . . . he shall be surely punished," (Exodus 21:22). ¶ . . . . The Church of Jesus Christ of Latter-day Saints has consistently opposed the practice of abortion. One hundred years ago the First Presidency wrote: "And we again take this opportunity of warning the Latter-day Saints against those . . . practices of foeticide and infanticide." [MOFP3:11] CR1985Apr:14-16

**Elder Ezra Taft Benson**

Let me warn the sisters, in all seriousness, that you who submit yourselves to an abortion or to an operation that precludes you from safely having additional healthy children are jeopardizing your exaltation and your future membership in the kingdom of God. ACR(Manilla)1975:9

**Elder Joseph F. Smith**

Possibly no greater sin could be committed by the people who have embraced this gospel than to prevent or to destroy life. . . . CR1900Apr:40

**President Harold B. Lee**

We declare it is a grievous sin before God to adopt restrictive measures in disobedience to God's divine command from the beginning of time to "multiply and replenish the earth." Surely those who project such measures to prevent life or to destroy life before or after birth will reap the whirlwind of God's retribution, for God will not be mocked. CR1972Oct:63

**208.** Married persons who achieve exaltation (in the highest degree of the celestial kingdom) will enjoy eternal increase, having children in the celestial kingdom.

### John A. Widtsoe

To enter the highest of these degrees in the celestial kingdom is to be exalted in the kingdom of God. Such exaltation comes to those who receive the higher ordinances of the Church, such as the temple endowment, and afterwards are sealed in marriage for time and eternity, whether on earth or in the hereafter. Those who are so sealed continue the family relationship eternally. Spiritual children are begotten by them. They carry on the work of salvation for the hosts of waiting spirits. They who are so exalted become even as the gods. They will be "from everlasting to everlasting, because they continue." [D&C 132:20] (Evidences and Reconciliations, pp. 200-01) TLDP:163-64

### Marion G. Romney

The plan provides that couples so married shall in eternity persist as husbands and wives and there progress until they eventually reach perfection and themselves become parents of spirit children. ("Scriptures as They Relate to Family Stability," EN1972Feb:58) TLDP:386

### Elder Lorenzo Snow

When two Latter-day Saints are united together in marriage, promises are made to them concerning their offspring that reach from eternity to eternity. They are promised that they shall have the power and the right to govern and control and administer salvation and exaltation and glory to their offspring, worlds without end. And what offspring they do not have here, undoubtedly there will be opportunities to have them hereafter. What else could man wish? A man and a woman in the other life, having celestial bodies, free from sickness and disease, glorified and beautified beyond description, standing in the midst of their posterity, governing and controlling them, administering life, exaltation and glory worlds without end! (At the Salt Lake Stake conference, Salt Lake City, Saturday, March 13, 1897) (Deseret Evening News, March 27, 1897, p. 9) TLDP:385

### James E. Talmage

Marriage covenants authorized and sealed by that God-given power, endure, if the parties thereto are true to their troth, not through mortal life alone, but through time and all eternity. Thus the worthy husband and wife who have been sealed under the everlasting covenant shall come forth in the day of the resurrection to receive their heritage of glory, immortality, and eternal lives. ¶ It is the blessed privilege of resurrected beings who attain an exaltation in the celestial kingdom to enjoy the glory of endless increase, to become the parents of generations of spirit-offspring, and to direct their development through probationary stages analogous to those through which they themselves have passed. ¶ Eternal are the purposes of God; never-ending progression is provided for His children, worlds without end. (Young Women's Journal, Oct. 1914, p. 604) DGSM:77

### Joseph Smith,
### *quoted by Elder Joseph Fielding Smith*

Except a man and his wife enter into an everlasting covenant and be married for eternity, while in this probation, by the power and authority of the Holy Priesthood, they will cease to increase when they die; that is, they will not have any children after the resurrection. But those who are married by the power and authority of the priesthood in this life, and continue without committing the sin against the Holy Ghost, will continue to increase and have children in the celestial glory. (*Instructions on the priesthood to Brother and Sister Benjamin F. Johnson at Ramus, Ill., May 1843*) HC5:391; TPJS:300-01; DGSM:77

### Joseph Smith

In the celestial glory there are three heavens or degrees; 2. And in order to obtain the highest, a man must enter into this order of the priesthood meaning the new and everlasting covenant of marriage; 3. And if he does not, he cannot obtain it. 4. He may enter into the other, but that is the end of his kingdom; he cannot have an increase. (*Instructions May 16 and 17, 1843*) D&C 131:1-4

### Joseph Smith,
### *receiving the Word of the Lord*

And again, verily I say unto you, if a man marry a wife by my word, which is my law, and by the new and everlasting covenant, and it is sealed unto them by the Holy Spirit of promise, by him who is anointed, unto whom I have appointed this power and the keys of this priesthood; and it shall be said unto them—Ye shall come forth in the first resurrection; and if it be after the first resurrection, in the next resurrection; and shall inherit thrones, kingdoms, principalities, and powers, dominions, all heights and depths— then shall it be written in the Lamb's Book of Life, that he shall commit no murder whereby to shed innocent blood, and if ye abide in my covenant, and commit no murder whereby to shed innocent blood, it shall be done unto them in all things whatsoever my servant hath put upon them, in time, and through all eternity; and shall be of full force when they are out of the world; and they shall pass by the angels, and the gods, which are set there, to their exaltation and glory in all things, as hath been sealed upon their heads, which glory shall be a fulness and a continuation of the seeds forever and ever. 20. Then shall they be gods, because they have no end; therefore shall they be from everlasting to everlasting, because they continue; then shall they be above all, because all things are subject unto them. Then shall they be gods, because they have all power, and the angels are subject unto them. (*Revelation relating to the new and everlasting covenant, including the eternal nature of the marriage covenant, July 12, 1843, [1831]*) D&C 132:19-20

**Elder Joseph Fielding Smith**
The doctrine of the eternity of the marriage covenant and the "continuation of the seeds forever and ever," is one of the most glorious principles of the Gospel. It is, in fact, the crowning principle which brings the fullness of exaltation to men and women who are willing to accept this eternal, holy and sacred ordinance. It is only in the celestial kingdom that the privilege of marriage and eternal increase will be found. Even in that kingdom there will be servants who are denied this privilege and glory. (D&C Sections 131 and 132:16-17) All who refuse to accept this principle and live in accordance with this covenant cannot be enlarged, but must remain separately and singly through all eternity. They cannot become sons and daughters of God. CHMR2:357-58

**Bruce R. McConkie**
In [the Millennial] day family units will be perfected according to the plans made in the heavens before the peopling of the earth. Celestial marriage in its highest and most glorious form will bind men and women together in eternal unions, and the resultant families will truly continue forever. (The Millennial Messiah, p. 655) TLDP:395-96

**Related Witnesses:**
### George Q. Cannon
And this is the blessing that God has promised to every faithful man and woman—that to the increase of their seed there shall be no end. This will constitute the great glory of eternity—the man presiding over his family and being lord over them. Thus it is that Jesus is called Lord of lords. He is Lord of lords because His brethren will exercise this power and authority over their posterity. (Gospel Truth, 1:117) TLDP:385

**Elder Joseph Fielding Smith**
The gift promised those who receive this covenant

of marriage and remain faithful to the end, that they shall "have no end," [D&C 132:20] means that they shall have the power of eternal increase. (The Way to Perfection, p. 24) DGSM:77

**President Brigham Young,**
*quoted by President Spencer W. Kimball*
Let me here say a word to console the feelings and hearts of all who belong to this Church. Many of the sisters grieve because they are not blessed with offspring. You will see the time when you will have millions of children around you. If you are faithful to your covenants, you will be mothers of nations. You will become Eves to earths like this, and when you have assisted in peopling one earth, there are millions of others still in the course of creation. And when they have endured a thousand million times longer than this earth, it is only as it were at the beginning of your creation. Be faithful and if you are not blessed with children in this time, you will be hereafter. (*An 1860 statement, quoted at fireside address in 1977*) DGSM:79

**President Brigham Young**
Those who are faithful will continue to increase, and this is the great blessing the Lord has given to, or placed within the reach of, the children of man, even to be capable of receiving eternal lives. ¶ To have such a promise so sealed upon our heads, which no power on earth, in heaven, or beneath the earth can take from us, to be sealed up to the day of redemption and have the promise of eternal lives, is the greatest gift of all. (*In Tabernacle, June 3, 1855, JD2:301*) TLDP:384-85

**Bruce R. McConkie**
Eternal life is life in the highest heaven of the celestial world; it is exaltation; it is the name of the kind of life God lives. It consists of a continuation of the family unit in eternity. ("The Salvation of Little Children," EN1977 Apr:5) TLDP:604

**Parley P. Pratt**
All persons who attain to the resurrection, and to salvation, without these eternal ordinances, or sealing covenants, will remain in a *single state*, in their saved condition, without the joys of eternal union with the other sex, and consequently without a crown, without a kingdom, without the power to increase. ¶ Hence, they are angels, and are not gods; and are ministering spirits, or servants, in the employ and under the direction of the Royal Family of heaven—the princes, kings and priests of eternity. (Key to the Science of Theology, pp. 169-70) TLDP:379

**Melvin J. Ballard**
What do we mean by endless or eternal increase? We mean that through the righteousness and

faithfulness of men and women who keep the commandments of God they will come forth with celestial bodies, fitted and prepared to enter into their great, high and eternal glory in the celestial kingdom of God; and unto them, through their preparation, there will come children, who will be spirit children. I don't think that is very difficult to comprehend and understand. The nature of the offspring is determined by the nature of the substance that flows in the veins of the being. When blood flows in the veins of the being, the offspring will be what blood produces, which is tangible flesh and blood, but when that which flows in the veins is spirit matter, a substance which is more refined and pure and glorious than blood, the offspring of such beings will be spirit children. By that I mean they will be in the image of the parents. They will have a spirit body and have a spark of the eternal or divine that always did exist in them. ¶ Unto such parentage will this glorified privilege come, for it is written in our scriptures that "the glory of God is to bring to pass the immortality and eternal life of man." So, it will be the glory of men and women that will make their glory like unto his. When the power of endless increase shall come to them, and their offspring, growing and multiplying through ages that shall come, they will be in due time, as we have been, provided with an earth like this, wherein they too may obtain earthly bodies and pass through all the experiences through which we have passed, and then we shall hold our relationship to them, the fulness and completeness of which has not been revealed to us, but we shall stand in our relationship to them as God, our Eternal Father, does to us, and thereby is this the most glorious and wonderful privilege that ever will come to any of the sons and daughters of God. (Sermons and Missionary Services of Melvin J. Ballard, pp. 239-40) TLDP:386

---

**209. Fathers are the presiding authority in the home and have the responsibility for the direction and regulation of the home.**

### President Joseph F. Smith

In the home the presiding authority is always vested in the father, and in all home affairs and family matters there is no other authority paramount. . . . The father presides at the table, at prayer, and gives general directions relating to his family life to whoever may be present. Wives and children should be taught to feel that the patriarchal order in the kingdom of God has been established for a wise and beneficent purpose, and should sustain the head of the household and encourage him in the discharge of his duties, and do all in their power to aid him in the exercise of the rights and privileges which God has bestowed upon the head of the home. This patriarchal order has its divine spirit and purpose, and those who disregard it under one pretext or another are out of harmony with the spirit of God's laws as they are ordained for recognition in the home. It is not merely a question of who is perhaps the best qualified. Neither is it wholly a question of who is living the most worthy life. It is a question largely of law and order, and its importance is seen often from the fact that the authority remains and is respected long after a man is really unworthy to exercise it. ¶ This authority carries with it a responsibility and a grave one, as well as its rights and privileges, and men can not be too exemplary in their lives, nor fit themselves too carefully to live in harmony with this important and God-ordained rule of conduct in the family organization. Upon this authority certain promises and blessings are predicated, and those who observe and respect this authority have certain claims on divine favor which they cannot have except they respect and observe the laws that God has established for the regulation and authority of the home. (1902, Gospel Doctrine, pp. 287-88) TLDP:505

### President Spencer W. Kimball

The Father is the head of every home, and even though the mother may be just as brilliant or more so, the father has been set apart by the Lord to look after his family. (The Teachings of Spencer W. Kimball, p. 344) TLDP:196

### Elder Ezra Taft Benson

Fathers, you cannot delegate your duty as the head of the home. Mothers, train up your children in righteousness; do not attempt to save the world and let your own family fall apart. An evening at home once a week is good protection against the breakdown of the family. ¶ The home is the rock foundation, the cornerstone of civilizations. This nation and others will never rise above their homes. The church, the schools, and even nations stand helpless before weakened and degraded homes. ACR(Taipei) 1975:3

**Related Witnesses:**

### President Brigham Young, *quoted by John A. Widtsoe*

Say your prayers always before going to work. Never forget that. . . . A father—the head of the family—should never miss calling his family together and dedicating himself and them to the Lord of Hosts, asking the guidance and direction of his Holy Spirit to lead them through the day—that very day. Lead us this day, guide us this day, preserve us this day, save us from sinning against thee or any being in heaven or on earth this day! If we do this every day, the last day we live we will be prepared to enjoy a higher glory. (*In new Tabernacle, Aug. 9, 1868, JD12:261)* DBY:44

### President Harold B. Lee

The greatest of the Lord's work you brethren will ever do as fathers will be within the walls of your own home. CR1973Apr:130; MPSG1976-77:221

### Paul

And, ye fathers, provoke not your children to wrath: but bring them up in the nurture and admonition of the Lord. (*Paul's letter to the Saints at Ephesus in Asia Minor, about A.D. 62)* Eph.6:4

---

210. Husbands and wives are equal partners in the marriage and family relationship (even though the man in the righteous exercise of the priesthood presides in the home).

### Marion G. Romney

With the Lord, the man is not without the woman, nor is the woman without the man. ¶ Husbands and wives should never forget these basic truths. They should remember their relationship and the purpose of it. ¶ They should be one in harmony, respect, and mutual consideration. Neither should plan or follow an independent course of action. They should consult, pray, and decide together. ¶ In the management of their homes and families, husbands and wives should counsel with each other in kindness, love, patience, and understanding . . . . ¶ Remember that neither the wife nor the husband is the slave of the other. Husbands and wives are equal partners, particularly Latter-day Saint husbands and wives. They should so consider themselves and so treat each other in this life, and then they will do so throughout eternity. . . . ¶ The woman is not inferior to the man. It is true, of course, that the man holds the priesthood and in the righteous exercise thereof presides in the home. This he is to do, however, in the spirit with which Christ presides over His church. ("In the Image of God," EN1978Mar:2,4) TLDP:388-89

### Joseph F. Merrill

A Latter-day Saint marriage is a union of two equal partners, obligated to build a home where mutual love, respect, trust, fidelity, tolerance,

patience, and kindness are some of the essential operating factors. And in the home where these prevail the ugly specter of divorce will never enter. CR1946Apr:29

### President Spencer W. Kimball

[O]ur partnerships with our eternal companions, our wives, must be full partnerships. . . . ¶ Our sisters do not wish to be indulged or to be treated condescendingly; they desire to be respected and revered as our sisters and our equals. . . . We will be judged, as the Savior said on several occasions, by whether or not we love one another and treat one another accordingly and by whether or not we are of one heart and one mind. We cannot be the Lord's if we are not one! CR1979Oct:71-72

### President Spencer W. Kimball

Brethren, love your wives. Be kind to your wives. They are not your chattels. They do not belong to you for your service. They are your partners. Love them; really love them, and stay close to them, and consider with them the family problems. And the Lord will bring down upon you blessings you have been unable to even imagine at this time. ACR(Stockholm)1974:104

### Elder Ezra Taft Benson

In the beginning, God placed a woman in a companion role with the priesthood. The Gods counseled and said that "it was not good that the man should be alone; wherefore, I will make a help meet for him." (Moses 3:18) Why was it not good for man to be alone? If it were only man's loneliness with which God was concerned, he might have provided other companionship. But he provided woman, for she was to be man's helpmeet. She was to act in partnership with him. ¶ In this pronouncement that it was not good for man to be alone, God declared a fundamental truth. The Lord gave woman a different personality and temperament than man. By nature woman is charitable and benevolent, man is striving and competitive. Man is at his best when complemented by a good woman's natural influence. She tempers the home and marriage relationship with her compassionate and loving influence. ¶ Yes, it is not good for man to be alone because a righteous woman complements what may be lacking in a man's natural personality and disposition. Nowhere is this complementary association more ideally portrayed than in the eternal marriage of our first parents, Adam and Eve. (Woman, p. 69) TLDP:736

### J. Reuben Clark, Jr.

As to sex in marriage, the necessary treatise on that for Latter-day Saints can be written in two sentences: Remember the prime purpose of sex desire is to beget children. Sex gratification must be had at that hazard. You husbands: be kind and considerate of your wives. They are not your property; they are not mere conveniences; they are your partners for time and eternity. CR1949Oct:194-95

## 211. Parents are to provide and care for their children.

**Paul**
But if any provide not for his own, and specially for those of his own house, he hath denied the faith, and is worse than an infidel. (*Paul writes to his assistant Timothy, about A.D. 64*) 1Tim.5:8

**King Benjamin,**
*quoted by Mormon*
And ye will not suffer your children that they go hungry, or naked. . . . (*King Benjamin concludes his discourse, about 124 B.C.*) Mosiah 4:14

**Joseph Smith**
All children have claim upon their parents for their maintenance until they are of age. (*Revelation received April 30, 1832*) D&C 83:4

**President Spencer W. Kimball**
Our Heavenly Father placed the responsibility upon parents to see that their children are well fed, well groomed and clothed, well trained, and well taught. Most parents protect their children with shelter—they tend and care for their diseases, provide clothes for their safety and their comfort, and supply food for their health and growth. But what do they do for their souls? (EN1978Apr:2) DGSM:81

**Related Witnesses:**
**Joseph Smith,**
*receiving the Word of the Lord*
And again, verily I say unto you, that every man who is obliged to provide for his own family, let him provide, and he shall in nowise lose his crown. . . . (*Revelation through Joseph Smith at a Church conference, Jan. 25, 1832*) D&C 75:28

## 212. Parents are to teach their children to honor and respect their parents.

**N. Eldon Tanner,**
*also quoting Moses*
We have the old commandment, "Honor thy father and thy mother that thy days may be long upon the land which the Lord thy God giveth thee." Children should be taught and trained to honor their father and their mother. Their parents gave them life and cared for them when

they could not care for themselves. Every child of every age should love and honor his parents. CR1963Apr:136

**Paul**
But if any widow have children or nephews, let them learn first to shew piety at home, and to requite their parents: for that is good and acceptable before God. (*Paul writes to his assistant Timothy, about A.D. 64*) 1Tim.5:4

**President Joseph F. Smith**
Young men should be scrupulously careful to impress upon their minds the necessity of consulting with father and mother in all that pertains to their actions in life. Respect and veneration for parents should be inculcated into the hearts of the young people of the Church—father and mother to be respected, their wishes to be regarded—and in the heart of every child should be implanted this thought of esteem and consideration for parents which characterized the families of the ancient patriarchs. ¶ God is at the head of the human race; we look up to him as the Father of all. We cannot please him more than regarding and respecting and honoring our fathers and our mothers who are the means of our existence here upon the earth. (IE1902Feb:307; Gospel Doctrine, p. 162) DGSM:82

**Related Witnesses:**
**President Heber J. Grant,**
**J. Reuben Clark, Jr., David O. McKay**
(First Presidency)
*also quoting Moses*
[T]housands of years ago, the Lord said to His Chosen People, "Honor thy father and thy mother that thy days may be long in the land which the Lord thy God giveth thee." The Lord asks you now to keep this commandment. (*Letter to Primary children*) TLDP:76; MOFP6:134-35

**President Spencer W. Kimball**
It is not enough to honor our parents in some narrow way. If we truly honor them, we will seek to emulate their best characteristics and to fulfill their highest aspirations for us. No gift purchased from a store can begin to match in value to parents some simple, sincere words of appreciation. Nothing we could give them would be more prized than righteous living for each youngster. Even where parents have not great strength of testimony, they will take pride in the strength and conviction of their children, if the relationship between them is a tolerant, loving, supporting one. (*Dedication of Independence Missouri Stake Center, Sept. 1978*) (The Teachings of Spencer W. Kimball, p. 348) TLDP:76-77

**Related Witnesses:**
**Recorded in Luke**

And he went down with them, and came to Nazareth, and was subject unto them: but his mother kept all these sayings in her heart. (*Luke writes concerning Jesus as a youth*) Luke 2:51

**Paul**

Children, obey your parents in the Lord: for this is right. 2. Honour thy father and mother; (which is the first commandment with promise;) (*Paul's letter to the Saints at Ephesus in Asia Minor, about A.D. 62*) Eph.6:1-2

**Recorded in Proverbs**

My son, keep thy father's commandment, and forsake not the law of thy mother: 21. Bind them continually upon thine heart, and tie them about thy neck. 22. When thou goest, it shall lead thee; when thou sleepest, it shall keep thee; and when thou awakest, it shall talk with thee. Prov.6:20-22

**Moses**

Honour thy father and thy mother: that thy days may be long upon the land which the LORD thy God giveth thee. (*The Lord reveals the fifth of the Ten Commandments to Moses*) Ex.20:12

**Paul**

Children, obey your parents in all things: for this is well pleasing unto the Lord. (*Paul writes from prison to the Church in Colossae, Asia Minor, about A.D. 60*) Col.3:20

---

**213. Parents are commanded to teach their children by the time they are eight years old to understand the doctrines of faith, repentance, and baptism.**

**Joseph Smith**

And again, inasmuch as parents have children in Zion, or in any of her stakes which are organized, that teach them not to understand the doctrine of repentance, faith in Christ the Son of the living God, and of baptism and the gift of the Holy Ghost by the laying on of the hands, when eight years old, the sin be upon the heads of the parents. 26. For this shall be a law unto the inhabitants of Zion, or in any of her stakes which are organized. 27. And their children shall be baptized for the remission of their sins when eight years old, and receive the laying on of the hands. 28. And they shall also teach their children to pray, and to walk uprightly before the Lord. (*Revelation at the request of several elders, Nov. 1831*) D&C 68:25-28

**Elder Joseph Fielding Smith**

Every soul is precious in the sight of God. We are all his children and he desires our salvation. Free agency is given to each individual, but still the Lord has placed the responsibility upon all parents in the Church to teach their children in light and truth. He has placed the obligation upon all parents that they must teach the first principles of the Gospel to their children, teach them to pray, and see that they are baptized when they are eight years of age. Parents cannot shirk or neglect this great responsibility without incurring the displeasure of a righteous God. He has not relinquished his claim upon his children when they are born into this world and therefore commands parents to teach their offspring so that they may be brought up in the truth of the everlasting Gospel. For parents to fail to do this places them in condemnation and the sin of such neglect will have to be answered with punishment on their own heads. This is the law unto Zion and all of her stakes. CHMR1:260

**Elder Spencer W. Kimball**

It is the responsibility of the parents to teach their children. The Sunday School, the Primary, the MIA and other organizations of the Church play a secondary role. . . . ¶ The Lord . . . gave us this law: when the child is eight years of age, he should have been trained—not that he should *begin* to be trained, as many of our parents surmise. (*Remarks to stake Junior Sunday School coordinators, April 1959*) (Teachings of Spencer W. Kimball, p. 332) TLDP:454

**Related Witnesses:**
**President Joseph F. Smith**

It is the duty of parents to teach their children the principles of the gospel, and to be sober-minded and industrious in their youth. They should be impressed from the cradle to the time they leave the parental roof to make homes and assume the duties of life for themselves, that there is a seed time and harvest, and as a man sows, so shall he reap. The sowing of bad habits in youth will bring forth nothing better than vice, and the sowing of the seeds of indolence will result invariably in poverty and lack of stability in old age. Evil begets evil, and good will bring forth good. ("Responsibilities of Life," Juvenile Instructor, Jan. 1917, p. 19) TLDP:453

---

**214. Parents are commanded to teach the gospel to their children.**

**Elder George Albert Smith**

In our homes, brethren and sisters, it is our privilege, nay, it is our duty, to call our families together to be taught the truths of the Holy Scriptures. In every home, children should be encouraged to read the word of the Lord, as it has been revealed to us in all dispensations. We should read the Bible, the Book of Mormon, the Doctrine and Covenants, and the Pearl of Great Price; not only read it in our homes, but explain it to our children, that they may understand the hand dealings of God with the peoples of the earth. Let us see if we cannot do more of this in the future than we have done in the past. Let each one in this congregation today ask himself: "Have I done my duty in my home in reading and in teaching the Gospel, as it has been revealed through the prophets of the Lord?" If we have not, let us repent of our neglect and draw our families around us and teach them the truth. CR1914Apr:12; DGSM:81

### Joseph Smith,
*receiving the Word of the Lord*
But I have commanded you to bring up your children in light and truth. 41. But verily I say unto you, my servant Frederick G. Williams, you have continued under this condemnation; 42. You have not taught your children light and truth, according to the commandments; and that wicked one hath power, as yet, over you, and this is the cause of your affliction. (*Leading brethren in the Church are commanded to set their houses in order; Kirtland, Ohio, May 6, 1833*) D&C 93:40-42

### Joseph Smith,
*translating the Book of Moses*
Wherefore teach it unto your children, that all men, everywhere, must repent, or they can in nowise inherit the kingdom of God, for no unclean thing can dwell there, or dwell in his presence; for, in the language of Adam, Man of Holiness is his name, and the name of his Only Begotten is the Son of Man, even Jesus Christ, a righteous Judge, who shall come in the meridian of time. 58. Therefore I give unto you a commandment, to teach these things freely unto your children, saying: 59. That by reason of transgression cometh the fall, which fall bringeth death, and inasmuch as ye were born into the world by water, and blood, and the spirit, which I have made, and so became of dust a living soul, even so ye must be born again into the kingdom of heaven, of water, and of the Spirit, and be cleansed by blood, even the blood of mine Only Begotten; that ye might be sanctified from all sin, and enjoy the words of eternal life in this world, and eternal life in the world to come, even immortal glory; 60. For by the water ye keep the commandment; by the Spirit ye are justified, and by the blood ye are sanctified; (*The record of Moses: Enoch recounts God speaking to Adam*) Moses 6:57-60

### Recorded in Deuteronomy
And these words, which I command thee this day, shall be in thine heart: 7. And thou shalt teach them diligently unto thy children, and shalt talk of them when thou sittest in thine house, and when thou walkest by the way, and when thou liest down, and when thou risest up. (*The people of Israel are commanded to teach their children*) Deut.6:6-7

### Recorded in Deuteronomy
Therefore shall ye lay up these my words in your heart and in your soul, and bind them for a sign upon your hand, that they may be as frontlets between your eyes. 19. And ye shall teach them your children, speaking of them when thou sittest in thine house, and when thou walkest by the way, when thou liest down, and when thou risest up. (*The people of Israel are taught that they must obey God's laws, and teach their children*) Deut.11:18-19

### King Benjamin,
*quoted by Mormon*
And ye will not suffer your children that they go hungry, or naked; neither will ye suffer that they transgress the laws of God, and fight and quarrel one with another, and serve the devil, who is the master of sin, or who is the evil spirit which hath been spoken of by our fathers, he being an enemy to all righteousness. 15. But ye will teach them to walk in the ways of truth and soberness; ye will teach them to love one another, and to serve one another. (*King Benjamin concludes his discourse, about 124 B.C.*) Mosiah 4:14-15

**Related Witnesses:**
### Elder Ezra Taft Benson
Parents are directly responsible for the righteous rearing of their children, and this responsibility cannot be safely delegated to relatives, friends, neighbors, the school, the church, or the state. CR1970Oct:21

### Recorded in Proverbs
Train up a child in the way he should go: and when he is old, he will not depart from it. Prov.22:6

---

## 215. Parents are to teach their children to pray.

### Joseph Smith
And they shall also teach their children to pray, and to walk uprightly before the Lord. (*Revelation Nov. 1831*) D&C 68:28

### Elder Spencer W. Kimball
Teach them to pray the Church way. Have them say their own individual prayers, of course, and use whatever influence they might have in their

own homes to get family prayer started every night and morning and so plan their own family lives after their marriage. (*Remarks to seminary and institute teachers at Brigham Young University, June 1962*) (Teachings of Spencer W. Kimball, p. 117) TLDP:491

**Elder Joseph Fielding Smith**

Of course there should be prayer and faith and love and obedience to God in the home. It is the duty of parents to teach their children these saving principles of the gospel of Jesus Christ. . . . [Y]ou must begin by teaching at the cradleside. You are to teach by example as well as precept. CR1948Oct:153

**President Heber J. Grant**

I am convinced that one of the greatest things that can come into any home to cause the boys and girls in that home to grow up in a love of God, and in a love of the gospel of Jesus Christ, is to have family prayer, not for the father of the family alone to pray, but for the mother and for the children to do so also, that they may partake of the spirit of prayer, and be in harmony, be in tune, to have the radio, so to speak, in communication with the Spirit of the Lord. I believe that there are very few that go astray, that very few lose their faith, who have once had a knowledge of the gospel, and who never neglect their prayers in their families, and their secret supplications to God. CR1923Oct:7-8

**President Spencer W. Kimball**

The home should be a place where reliance on the Lord is a matter of common experience, not reserved for special occasions. One way of establishing that is by regular, earnest prayer. It is not enough just to pray. It is essential that we really speak to the Lord, having faith that he will reveal to us as parents what we need to know and do for the welfare of our families. It has been said of some men that when they prayed, a child was likely to open his eyes to see if the Lord were really there, so personal and direct was the petition. CR1974Oct:161-62

**Related Witnesses:**

**President Brigham Young**

Mothers should teach their little ones to pray as soon as they are able to talk. ("General Epistle," Millennial Star, March 15, 1848, p. 85) TLDP:452

**Jesus,**
*quoted by Mormon*

Pray in your families unto the Father, always in my name, that your wives and your children may be blessed. (*The resurrected Jesus commands the Nephite people to pray, A.D. 34*) 3Ne.18:21

**216. Parents are commanded to correct and discipline their children (in the spirit of love).**

**President Spencer W. Kimball**

Discipline is probably one of the most important elements in which a mother and father can lead and guide and direct their children. It certainly would be well for parents to understand the rule given to the priesthood in section 121. Setting limits to what a child can do means to that child that you love him and respect him. If you permit the child to do all the things he would like to do without any limits, that means to him that you do not care much about him. (*Sydney Australia Area Conference, Feb. 1976*) DGSM:81-82

**President Joseph F. Smith**

The necessity, then, of organizing the patriarchal order and authority of the home rests upon principle as well as upon the person who holds that authority, and among the Latter-day Saints family discipline, founded upon the law of the patriarchs, should be carefully cultivated, and fathers will then be able to remove many of the difficulties that now weaken their position in the home, through unworthy children. (March 1902, Gospel Doctrine, pp. 288) TLDP:505

**James E. Faust**

May I suggest . . . ways to enrich family life: ¶ 1. Hold family prayer night and morning. . . . ¶ 2. Study the scriptures. All of us need the strength that comes from daily reading of the scriptures. . . . ¶ 3. Teach children to work. . . . ¶ 4. Teach discipline and obedience. . . . ¶ 5. Place a high priority on loyalty to each other. . . . ¶ 6. Teach principles of self-worth and self-reliance. One of the main problems in families today is that we spend less and less time together. Some spend an extraordinary amount of time, when they are together, in front of the television, which robs them of personal time for reinforcing feelings of self-worth. Time together is precious time—time needed to talk, to listen, to encourage, and to show how to do things. . . . ¶ 7. Develop family traditions. Some of the great strengths of families can be found in their own traditions. . . . ¶ 8. Do everything in the spirit of love. . . . ¶ . . . . As direction is given in the Church and in our homes, there should be no spirit of dictatorship and no unrighteous dominion. CR1983Apr:57-60

**King Benjamin,**
*quoted by Mormon*

And ye will not suffer your children that they go hungry, or naked; neither will ye suffer that they transgress the laws of God, and fight and quarrel one with another, and serve the devil, who is the master of sin, or who is the evil spirit which hath been spoken of by our fathers, he being an enemy to all righteousness. 15. But ye will teach them to walk in the ways of truth and soberness; ye will teach them to love one another, and to serve one another. (*King Benjamin addresses his people, about 124 B.C.*) Mosiah 4:14-15

**Related Witnesses:**
**Recorded in Proverbs**
Train up a child in the way he should go: and when he is old, he will not depart from it. Prov.22:6

**Recorded in Proverbs**
Chasten thy son while there is hope, and let not thy soul spare for his crying. Prov.19:18

**Paul**
And, ye fathers, provoke not your children to wrath: but bring them up in the nurture and admonition of the Lord. (*Letter to the Saints at Ephesus in Asia Minor, about A.D. 62*) Eph.6:4

**Recorded in 1 Samuel**
In that day I will perform against Eli all things which I have spoken concerning his house: when I begin, I will also make an end. 13. For I have told him that I will judge his house for ever for the iniquity which he knoweth; because his sons made themselves vile, and he restrained them not. (*The Lord speaks to the child Samuel*) 1Sam.3:12-13

**Joseph Smith**
Reproving betimes with sharpness, when moved upon by the Holy Ghost; and then showing forth afterwards an increase of love toward him whom thou hast reproved, lest he esteem thee to be his enemy; (*Revelation received in Liberty Jail, March 20, 1839; the priesthood should be used only in righteousness*) D&C 121:43

**Recorded in Proverbs**
My son, despise not the chastening of the LORD; neither be weary of his correction: 12. For whom the LORD loveth he correcteth; even as a father the son in whom he delighteth. Prov.3:11-12

**Recorded in Deuteronomy**
Thou shalt also consider in thine heart, that, as a man chasteneth his son, so the LORD thy God chasteneth thee. (*The Lord reminds Israel of their forty year test in the wilderness*) Deut.8:5

**Paul**
Now no chastening for the present seemeth to be joyous, but grievous: nevertheless afterward it yieldeth the peaceable fruit of righteousness

unto them which are exercised thereby. (*Letter to the Jewish members of the Church, about A.D. 60*) Heb.12:11

**Recorded in Proverbs**
Correct thy son, and he shall give thee rest; yea, he shall give delight unto thy soul. Prov.29:17

---

**HYMNS Written by Prophets**
**Applicable to this Topic**

**Orson F. Whitney**
*The Wintry Day, Descending to Its Close*
HYMNS:37

The wintry day, descending to its close,
Invites all wearied nature to repose,
And shades of night are falling dense and fast,
Like sable curtains closing o'er the past.
Pale through the gloom the newly fallen snow
Wraps in a shroud the silent earth below
As tho 'twere mercy's hand had spread the pall,
A symbol of forgiveness unto all.

I cannot go to rest, but linger still
In meditation at my window sill,
While, like the twinkling stars in heaven's dome,
Come one by one sweet memories of home.
And wouldst thou ask me where my fancy roves
To reproduce the happy scenes it loves,
Where hope and memory together dwell
And paint the pictured beauties that I tell?

Away beyond the prairies of the West,
Where exiled Saints in solitude were blest,
Where industry the seal of wealth has set
Amid the peaceful vales of Deseret,
Unheeding still the fiercest blasts that blow,
With tops encrusted by eternal snow,
The tow'ring peaks that shield the tender sod
Stand, types of freedom reared by nature's God.

The wilderness, that naught before would yield,
Is now become a fertile, fruitful field.
Where roamed at will the fearless Indian band,
The templed cities of the Saints now stand.
And sweet religion in its purity
Invites all men to its security.
There is my home, the spot I love so well,
Whose worth and beauty pen nor tongue can tell.

# List of Doctrines

## FASTING

# FASTING

**217. Church members are to fast for two consecutive meals on fast day (usually the first Sunday of each month).**

### President Heber J. Grant

When fasting, members of the Church are advised to abstain from two meals each Fast Day and to contribute as a donation the amount saved thereby for the support of the worthy poor. . . . (*Published statement from the First Presidency of the Church, March 26, 1932*) MOFP5:307

### President Heber J. Grant

Each member is asked to fast for two meals on the first Sunday in each month, and to give as a wholly voluntary contribution, the equivalent of these meals, which is used for the support of the poor. (*Published statement from the First Presidency of the Church, June 20, 1939*) MOFP6:72

### Delbert L. Stapley

Most Latter-day Saints, I think, understand the doing without two meals in connection with the monthly fast and giving the cash equivalent to the bishop as fast offerings, but I am wondering along with our fasting do we gather our families together and pray with them that they may enjoy the blessings of the Lord? CR1951Oct:123

### Mark E. Petersen

I believe that in many ways, here and now in mortality, we can begin to perfect ourselves. A certain degree of perfection is attainable in this life. I believe that we can be one hundred percent perfect, for instance, in abstaining from the use of tea and coffee. We can be one hundred percent perfect in abstaining from liquor and tobacco. We can be one hundred percent perfect in paying a full and honest tithing. We can be one hundred percent perfect in abstaining from eating two meals on fast day and giving to the bishop as fast offering the value of those two meals from which we abstain. CR1950Apr:153

### President David O. McKay

The regularly constituted fast consists of abstinence from food once each month, that is, it means missing two meals on the first Sunday of each month. The value of those two meals given as voluntary donation for the relief of those who are hungry or otherwise in distress constitutes the fast offering. Think what the sincere observance of this rule would mean spiritually if every man, woman, and child were to observe the fast and contribute the resultant offering, with the sincere desire of blessing the

less fortunate brother or sister or sorrowing child! ¶ It is God's way. You say people don't like charity? Why, it should not be administered as charity; but as a co-operative plan of mutual service adopted for the benefit of all. ("On Fasting," IE1963Mar:156-57) TLDP:198

**Related Witnesses:**
### President Heber J. Grant

Let me promise you here today that if the Latter-day Saints will honestly and conscientiously from this day forth, as a people, keep the monthly fast and pay into the hands of their bishops the actual amount that they would have spent for food for the two meals from which they have refrained; and if in addition to that they will pay their honest tithing, it will solve all of the problems in connection with taking care of the Latter-day Saints. We would have all the money necessary to take care of all the idle and all the poor. ¶ Every living soul among the Latter-day Saints that fasts two meals once a month will be benefited spiritually and be built up in the faith of the gospel of the Lord Jesus Christ—benefited spiritually in a wonderful way—and sufficient means will be in the hands of the bishops to take care of all the poor. (Church News, 1932, Gospel Standards, p. 123) TLDP:199

### Melvin J. Ballard

Our difficulty is that we have not all used the Lord's plan as we should. What ought that contribution, our fast offerings, be, to be the equivalent of two meals? I would like to suggest that there isn't anything that this present generation needs so much as the power of self-control; appetite is stronger than will. Men's passions dominate their lives. If there is one thing that we need to recover, it is the power of self-control over the physical body; to deny it good food . . . for two meals, [is to obtain] a mastery over self; and the greatest battle any of us shall ever fight is with self. (Sermons and Missionary Services of Melvin J. Ballard, p. 157) TLDP:199

---

**218. Fasting produces spiritual strength.**

### President David O. McKay

All the principles related to fasting seem to point to the fact that it produces (1) physical benefits; (2) intellectual activity; and (3) spiritual strength, which is the greatest of all benefits. This fine spiritual strength is derived by the subjection of the physical appetite to the will of the individual. . . . ¶ If there were no other virtue in fasting but gaining strength of character, that alone would be sufficient justification for its universal acceptance. ("On Fasting," IE1963Mar:156) TLDP:199

**Elder Ezra Taft Benson**

Periodic fasting can help clear up the mind and strengthen the body and the spirit. . . . To make a fast most fruitful, it should be coupled with prayer and meditation; physical work should be held to a minimum, and it's a blessing if one can ponder on the scriptures and the reason for the fast. CR1974Oct:92

**President Heber J. Grant**

Every living soul among the Latter-day Saints that fasts two meals once a month will be benefited spiritually and be built up in the faith of the gospel of the Lord Jesus Christ—benefited spiritually in a wonderful way—and sufficient means will be in the hands of the bishops to take care of all the poor. (June 1932, Gospel Standards, p. 123) TLDP:199

**President Heber J. Grant**

When fasting, members of the Church are advised to abstain from two meals each Fast Day . . . also by prayer in connection with fasting to develop spiritual power. No direct instruction is given in the Doctrine and Covenants regarding abstaining from water while fasting. In the Bible there are three references in connection with fasting and abstaining from water. These are: Exodus 34:28 and Deuteronomy 9:9-18, where it states that Moses "did neither eat bread nor drink water"; and Esther 4:16, where Esther asked the Jews to fast for her and to "neither eat nor drink." ¶ The spirit of fasting is the main thing to encourage. Too much stress should not be laid on technical details, but the self denial of food, striving for spiritual strength and donating for the benefit of the poor should constantly be in mind. (*Published statement from the First Presidency of the Church, March 26, 1932*) MOFP5:307-08

**Bruce R. McConkie**

In all ages the Lord has called upon his people to fast and pray and seek him with all their strength and power. Fasting—the abstaining from food and drink for a designated period—gives a man a sense of his utter dependence upon the Lord so that he is in a better frame of mind to get in tune with the Spirit. Moses and Jesus both fasted for forty days as they sought that oneness with the Father out of which great spiritual strength comes. (The Mortal Messiah, 2:152) TLDP:200

**Elder Spencer W. Kimball**

The law of the fast is another test [compared with the Word of Wisdom]. If we merely go without food to supply welfare funds it is much of the letter, but in real fasting, for spiritual blessings, come self-mastery and increased spirituality. CR1951Oct:87

**President Joseph F. Smith**

It is evident that the acceptable fast is that which carries with it the true spirit of love for God and man; and that the aim in fasting is to secure perfect purity of heart and simplicity of intention—a fasting unto God in the fullest and deepest sense—for such a fast would be a cure for every practical and intellectual error; vanity would disappear, love for our fellows would take its place, and we would gladly assist the poor and the needy. ("Observance of Fast Day," IE1902Dec:147) TLDP:199

**President Joseph F. Smith**

[Observing the law of the fast] would call attention to the sin of overeating, place the body in subjection to the spirit, and so promote communion with the Holy Ghost, and insure a spiritual strength and power which the people of the nation so greatly need. (Gospel Doctrine, pp. 237-38) MPSG1986:115

**Delbert L. Stapley**

It seems to me [fasting and prayer] is a source of strength, a source of power, a source of blessing that perhaps as a people we are not using enough; that it does have tremendous spiritual value to those who observe the law, and who apply it faithfully. . . . ¶ The Saints by fasting and praying can sanctify the soul and elevate the spirit to Christlike perfection, and thus the body would be brought into subjection to the spirit, promote communion with the Holy Ghost, and insure spiritual strength and power to the individual. ¶ By observing fasting and prayer in its true spirit, the Latter-day Saints cannot be overpowered by Satan tempting them to evil. CR1951Oct:122-23

**Related Witnesses:**

**Mormon**

. . . Alma did rejoice exceedingly to see his brethren; and what added more to his joy, they were still his brethren in the Lord; yea, and they had waxed strong in the knowledge of the truth; for they were men of a sound understanding and they had searched the scriptures diligently, that they might know the word of God. 3. But this is not all; they had given themselves to much prayer, and fasting; therefore they had the spirit of prophecy, and the spirit of revelation, and when they taught, they taught with power and authority of God. (*Mormon recounts the activities of the spiritually devoted sons of Mosiah*) Alma 17:2-3

### Alma, the younger,
#### quoted by Mormon

. . . Behold, I have fasted and prayed many days that I might know these things of myself. And now I do know of myself that they are true; for the Lord God hath made them manifest unto me by his Holy Spirit; and this is the spirit of revelation which is in me. (*Alma testifies to the people of the truth of his teachings, about 83 B.C.*) Alma 5:46

### Melvin J. Ballard

Our difficulty is that we have not all used the Lord's plan as we should. What ought that contribution, our fast offerings, be, to be the equivalent of two meals? I would like to suggest that there isn't anything that this present generation needs so much as the power of self-control; appetite is stronger than will. Men's passions dominate their lives. If there is one thing that we need to recover, it is the power of self-control over the physical body; to deny it good food that would not be injurious, for two meals, has obtained a mastery over self; and the greatest battle any of us shall ever fight is with self. ¶ I am charged to take possession of this house, this mortal tabernacle, and it is to be my servant. I am not to abuse it but keep it vigorous, clean, healthy, and strong. This exercise of controlling it once a month, that it must fast, is a healthy exercise of spiritual control over the material. If I can do this with regard to food, when this body craves something that is positively hurtful, then I have obtained power to say: "You cannot have it." Thus spiritual control over the body, in all its activities, may be secured, beginning with control over the appetite. (Sermons and Missionary Services of Melvin J. Ballard, p. 157) TLDP:199

### Recorded in Psalms

I humbled my soul with fasting; and my prayer returned into mine own bosom. Ps.35:13

### Elder Spencer W. Kimball

Failing to fast is a sin. In the 58th chapter of Isaiah, rich promises are made by the Lord to those who fast and assist the needy. . . . Inspiration and spiritual guidance will come with righteousness and closeness to our Heavenly Father. To omit to do this righteous act of fasting would deprive us of these blessings. (The Miracle of Forgiveness, p. 98) DGSM:34

---

219. Monthly fasting should be coupled with a desire to bless our fellow beings.

### President David O. McKay

The regularly constituted fast consists of abstinence from food once each month, that is, it means missing two meals on the first Sunday of each month. The value of those two meals given as voluntary donation for the relief of those who are hungry or otherwise in distress constitutes the fast offering. Think what the sincere observance of this rule would mean spiritually if every man, woman, and child were to observe the fast and contribute the resultant offering, with the sincere desire of blessing the less fortunate brother or sister or sorrowing child! ("On Fasting," IE1963Mar:156-57) TLDP:198

### President Joseph F. Smith

It is evident that the acceptable fast is that which carries with it the true spirit of love for God and man; and that the aim in fasting is to secure perfect purity of heart and simplicity of intention—a fasting unto God in the fullest and deepest sense—for such a fast would be a cure for every practical and intellectual error; vanity would disappear, love for our fellows would take its place, and we would gladly assist the poor and the needy. ("Observance of Fast Day," IE1902Dec:147) TLDP:199

### President Spencer W. Kimball

We must ever remind ourselves and all members of the Church to keep the law of the fast. We often have our individual reasons for fasting. But I hope members won't hesitate to fast to help us lengthen our stride in our missionary effort, to open the way for the gospel to go to the nations where it is not now permitted. It's good for us to fast as well as to pray over specific things and over specific objectives. CR1976Apr:172

### Elder David O. McKay

Consider for a moment this principle of fasting. It is as old as the human race and undoubtedly when first practiced was related to health. It is generally conceded that most people usually consume more food than the body requires. Overeating clogs the system with deleterious waste products. When such a condition exists a short fast is useful as a means of restoring the body to its normal active state. . . . ¶ Associated with this practice in the Church of Jesus Christ of Latter-day Saints is the giving of a fast offering, the underlying purpose and far-reaching benefits of which make the monthly observance of fast day one of the most significant features of this latter-day work. Besides the benefits already mentioned there are: First, all the spiritual uplift that comes from a Christ-like desire to serve one's fellowmen; and Second, an economic means which when carried out by a perfect and active organization will supply the needs of every worthy poor person within the confines of the organized branches of the Church. CR1932Apr:64-65

### Delbert L. Stapley
It also seems to me that fasting and prayer can be employed to bless others, and if we would faithfully observe the law, the blessings of our Heavenly Father would collectively be given to the people of the Church. CR1951Oct:122-23

---

### 220. One purpose of the monthly fast is to benefit the poor.

#### President Spencer W. Kimball
Each member should contribute a generous fast offering for the care of the poor and the needy. This offering should at least be the value of the two meals not eaten while fasting. ¶ "Sometimes we have been a bit penurious and figured that we had for breakfast one egg and that cost so many cents and then we give that to the Lord. I think that when we are affluent, as many of us are, that we ought to be very, very generous. . . . ¶ "I think we should . . . give, instead of the amount saved by our two meals of fasting, perhaps much, much more—ten times more when we are in a position to do it. [CR1974Apr:184]" *(President Kimball quotes his prior address)* CR1977Oct:126

#### President Joseph F. Smith
Fast day being on the Sabbath, it follows, of course, that all labor is to be abstained from. In addition, the leading and principle object of the institution of the fast among the Latter-day Saints, was that the poor might be provided with food and other necessities. It is, therefore, incumbent upon every Latter-day Saint to give to his bishop, on fast day, the food that he or his family would consume for the day, that it may be given to the poor for their benefit and blessing; or, in lieu of the food that its equivalent amount, or if the person is wealthy a liberal donation, in money be so reserved and dedicated to the poor. . . . ("Observance of Fast Day," IE1902Dec:148-49) TLDP:198

#### President David O. McKay
The regularly constituted fast consists of abstinence from food once each month, that is, it means missing two meals on the first Sunday of each month. The value of those two meals given as voluntary donation for the relief of those who are hungry or otherwise in distress constitutes the fast offering. Think what the sincere observance of this rule would mean spiritually if every man, woman, and child were to observe the fast and contribute the resultant offering, with the sincere desire of blessing the less fortunate brother or sister or sorrowing child! ¶ It is God's way. You say people don't like charity? Why, it should not be administered as charity; but as a co-operative plan of mutual service adopted for the benefit of all. ("On Fasting," IE1963Mar:156-57) TLDP:198

#### Elder David O. McKay
Associated with this practice in the Church of Jesus Christ of Latter-day Saints is the giving of a fast offering, the underlying purpose and far-reaching benefits of which make the monthly observance of fast day one of the most significant features of this latter-day work. Besides the benefits already mentioned there are: First, all the spiritual uplift that comes from a Christ-like desire to serve one's fellowmen; and Second, an economic means which when carried out by a perfect and active organization will supply the needs of every worthy poor person within the confines of the organized branches of the Church. CR1932Apr:65

#### Related Witnesses:
##### Marion G. Romney
Don't give just for the benefit of the poor, but give for your own welfare. Give enough so that you can give yourself into the kingdom of God through consecrating of your means and your time. Pay an honest tithing and a generous fast offering if you want the blessings of heaven. I promise every one of you who will do it that you will increase your own prosperity, both spiritually and temporally. The Lord will reward you according to your deeds. ("The Blessings of the Fast," EN1982Jul:4) TLDP:200

---

### 221. We are to fast using wisdom and discretion.

#### President Joseph F. Smith
The Lord instituted the fast on a reasonable and intelligent basis, and none of his works are vain or unwise. His law is perfect in this as in other things. Hence, those who can, are required to comply thereto; it is a duty from which they cannot escape; but let it be remembered that the observance of the fast day by abstaining twenty-four hours from food or drink is not an absolute rule, it is no iron-clad law to us, but is left with the people as a matter of conscience, to exercise wisdom and discretion. Many are subject in weakness, others are delicate in health, and others have nursing babes; of such it

should not be required to fast. Neither should parents compel their little children to fast. I have known children to cry for something to eat on fast day. In such cases, going without food will do them no good. Instead, they dread the day to come, and in place of hailing it, dislike it; while the compulsion engenders a spirit of rebellion in them, rather than a love for the Lord and their fellows. Better to teach them the principle, and let them observe it when they are old enough to choose intelligently, than to so compel them. ¶ But those should fast who can, and all classes among us should be taught to save the meals which they would eat, or their equivalent, for the poor. ("Observance of Fast Day," IE1902Dec:148-49) TLDP:198

### President Joseph F. Smith
I say to my brethren, when they are fasting, and praying for the sick, and for those that need faith and prayer, do not go beyond what is wise and prudent in fasting and prayer. The Lord can hear a simple prayer, offered in faith, in half a dozen words, and he will recognize fasting that may not continue more than twenty-four hours, just as readily and as effectually as He will answer a prayer of a thousand words and fasting for a month. CR1912Oct:122-34

### John A. Widtsoe
The Church urges all to observe the monthly fasts, and advises that fasts at other times be engaged in wisely, with due respect to the conditions and needs of the body. PCG:377

### Elder Ezra Taft Benson
Periodic fasting can help clear up the mind and strengthen the body and the spirit. The usual fast, the one we are asked to participate in for fast Sunday, is for 24 hours without food or drink. Some people feeling the need, have gone on longer fasts of abstaining from food but have taken the needed liquids. Wisdom should be used, and the fast should be broken with light eating. To make a fast most fruitful, it should be coupled with prayer and meditation; physical work should be held to a minimum, and it's a blessing if one can ponder on the scriptures and the reason for the fast. CR1974Oct:92

---

### 222. Fasting is to be coupled with prayer and meditation.

### Elder Ezra Taft Benson
To make a fast most fruitful, it should be coupled with prayer and meditation; physical work should be held to a minimum, and it's a bless-

ing if one can ponder on the scriptures and the reason for the fast. CR1974Oct:92

### John A. Widtsoe
The monthly fast should always be accompanied with prayer. It is well to call the household together on the day of fasting, to thank the Lord for blessings received and to supplicate by the members of the family. Individuals frequently undertake fasts when in special need of heavenly help. The Church urges all to observe the monthly fasts, and advises that fasts at other times be engaged in wisely, with due respect to the conditions and needs of the body. PCG:377

### Elder Joseph Fielding Smith
Fasting we may well assume is a religious custom that has come down from the beginning of time, and [is] always associated with prayer. (Answers to Gospel Questions, 1:88) TLDP:197

### President Joseph F. Smith
I say to my brethren, when they are fasting, and praying for the sick, and for those that need faith and prayer, do not go beyond what is wise and prudent in fasting and prayer. The Lord can hear a simple prayer, offered in faith, in half a dozen words, and he will recognize fasting that may not continue more than twenty-four hours, just as readily and as effectually as He will answer a prayer of a thousand words and fasting for a month. CR1912Oct:133-34

### Delbert L. Stapley
The Saints by fasting and praying can sanctify the soul and elevate the spirit to Christlike perfection, and thus the body would be brought into subjection to the spirit, promote communion with the Holy Ghost, and insure spiritual strength and power to the individual. ¶ By observing fasting and prayer in its true spirit, the Latter-day Saints cannot be overpowered by Satan tempting them to evil. CR1951Oct:122-23

### Related Witnesses:
### Mormon
Nevertheless the children of God were commanded that they should gather themselves together oft, and join in fasting and mighty prayer in behalf of the welfare of the souls of those who knew not God. (Alma sets the Church in Zarahemla in order, about 83 B.C.) Alma 6:6

### Isaiah
Is not this the fast that I have chosen? to loose the bands of wickedness, to undo the heavy burdens, and to let the oppressed go free, and that ye break every yoke? 7. Is it not to deal thy bread to the hungry, and that thou bring the poor that are cast out to thy house? when thou seest

the naked, that thou cover him; and that thou hide not thyself from thine own flesh? 8. Then shall thy light break forth as the morning, and thine health shall spring forth speedily: and thy righteousness shall go before thee; the glory of the LORD shall be thy rereward. 9. Then shalt thou call, and the LORD shall answer. . . . (*The Lord commands Isaiah to teach the people in fasting to serve the needy, thereby to be able to pray to the Lord and receive answers*) Isa.58:6-9

### Alma, the younger,
### *quoted by Mormon*

Behold, I say unto you they are made known unto me by the Holy Spirit of God. Behold, I have fasted and prayed many days that I might know these things of myself. And now I do know of myself that they are true; for the Lord God hath made them manifest unto me by his Holy Spirit; and this is the spirit of revelation which is in me. (*Alma testifies to the people of the truth of his teachings, about 83 B.C.*) Alma 5:46

### Mormon

But this is not all; they had given themselves to much prayer, and fasting; therefore they had the spirit of prophecy, and the spirit of revelation, and when they taught, they taught with power and authority of God. (*Mormon recounts the activities of the spiritually devoted sons of Mosiah*) Alma 17:3

### Mormon

And he caused that the priests should assemble themselves together; and they began to fast, and to pray to the Lord their God that he would open the mouth of Alma, that he might speak, and also that his limbs might receive their strength—that the eyes of the people might be opened to see and know of the goodness and glory of God. 23. And it came to pass after they had fasted and prayed for the space of two days and two nights, the limbs of Alma received their strength, and he stood up and began to speak unto them, bidding them to be of good comfort: (*After an angel appeared to Alma, the younger, he became dumb and physically help-less, 100-92 B.C.*) Mosiah 27:22-23

# List of Doctrines

## FORGIVENESS

*Doctrines Located in This Topic*

223. We are to forgive each other without condition, limitation, or exception.

224. When offended, we are to forgive the offending person and seek reconciliation.

225. God forgives those who forgive others.

226. The Church receives back into fellowship those transgressors who repent.

*Doctrines on FORGIVENESS Located in Other Topics*

46. The Atonement of Christ makes possible the forgiveness of sins for the repentant person.

523. We are to pray for forgiveness of our sins.

635. There can be complete divine forgiveness of sin.

780. The adulterer who repents can be forgiven.

# FORGIVENESS

**223. We are to forgive each other without condition, limitation, or exception.**

**N. Eldon Tanner,**
*also quoting Joseph Smith*
The Lord has said, "I, the Lord will forgive whom I will forgive, but of you it is required to forgive all men." (D&C 64:10) We are further admonished to forgive many times, even seventy times seven. We should stop and ask ourselves if we are prepared to ask the Lord to forgive us of our sins and trespasses only as we forgive our friends and neighbors. How wonderful it would be if we would all forgive and love our neighbors. Then it would be much easier for us to call upon the Lord to forgive us of any of our wrongdoings, and as we repent and bring forth fruits meet for repentance, we can expect God's forgiveness and mercy to be extended in our behalf. CR1974Apr:76

**Joseph Smith**
One of the most pleasing scenes that can transpire on earth, is, when a sin has been committed by one person against another, to forgive that sin: and then, according to the sublime and perfect pattern of the Savior, pray to our Father in heaven, to forgive also. ("A Friendly Hint to Missouri," Times and Seasons, March 15, 1844, p. 473) TLDP:206

**Elder Harold B. Lee**
I bear you my humble testimony, as one of the humblest among you: I know that there are powers that can draw close to one who fills his heart with . . . love. . . . I came to a night, some years ago, when on my bed, I realized that before I could be worthy of the high place to which I had been called, I must love and forgive every soul that walked the earth, and in that time I came to know and I received a peace and a direction, and a comfort, and an inspiration, that told me things to come and gave me impressions that I knew were from a divine source. CR1946Oct:146

**Jesus,**
*recorded in Matthew*
Then came Peter to him, and said, Lord, how oft shall my brother sin against me, and I forgive him? till seven times? 22. Jesus saith unto him, I say not unto thee, Until seven times: but, Until seventy times seven. (*Jesus teaches his disciples the principle of forgiveness*) Matt.18:21-22

**Elder Spencer W. Kimball**
Until seventy times seven! That seems very difficult indeed for us mortals, and yet there are still harder things to do. When they have repented and come on their knees to ask

forgiveness, most of us can forgive, but the Lord has required that we shall even forgive them if they do not repent nor ask forgiveness of us. CR1949Oct:129

**Elder Spencer W. Kimball**
Remember we must forgive even if our offender did not repent and ask forgiveness. Stephen yet in his young life mastered this principle. His accusers, unable to find anything against him other than fancied blasphemy, stoned him to death. Not waiting for them to repent, Stephen displayed his saintliness by using his last breath to forgive them saying: "Lord, lay not this sin to their charge." (Acts 7:60) They had taken his very life, and yet he forgave them. . . . The Lord Jesus also gave to us the lesson. Before they asked forgiveness, before they repented, while they were still in their murderous passion, he found it in his heart to forgive them and to ask his Father to ". . . forgive them; for they know not what they do." He did not wait till his crucifiers . . . should have a change of heart, but forgave them while they were yet covered with his life's blood. CR1949Oct:132

**Elder David O. McKay,**
*also quoting Jesus*
If we would have peace as individuals, we must supplant enmity with forbearance, which means to refrain or abstain from finding fault or from condemning others. . . . We shall have power to do this if we really cherish in our hearts the ideals of Christ, who said: "Therefore if thou bring thy gift to the altar, and there rememberest that thy brother hath ought against thee; Leave there thy gift before the altar, and go thy way; first be reconciled to thy brother, and then come and offer thy gift." (Matt.5:23-24) ¶ Note the Savior did not say if you have ought against him, but if you find that another has ought against you. CR1938Oct:133

**President Brigham Young,**
*quoted by John A. Widtsoe*
Do not throw away a man or a woman, old or young. If they commit an evil today, and another tomorrow, but wish to be Saints and to be forgiven, do you forgive them, not only seven times, but seventy times seven in a day, if their hearts are fully set to do right. Let us make it a point to pass over their weaknesses and say, "God bless you in trying to be better in time to come, and act as wise stewards in the Kingdom of God." (*In Tabernacle, March 17, 1871, JD8:368*) DBY:277

**Elder Lorenzo Snow**
There is a divinity within ourselves that is immortal and never dies. Thousands and thousands of

years hence we will be ourselves, and nobody else. . . . We are as children growing and increasing in knowledge and wisdom. Some of the . . . great prophets advanced themselves to that degree of knowledge, and develop[ed] their immortal possibilities to an extent that is perfectly astonishing. And you and I will have to advance in this line until we control those things that the world cannot possibly do. ¶ . . . . The Lord requires that men should forgive one another, even seventy times seven. And even if the party does not ask forgiveness, we are to forgive for a certain number of times. He that forgives not his brother, we are told, there remaineth in him the greater sin—that is, he is a greater sinner than the person that offended him. CR1898Apr:63

**President Joseph F. Smith**

It is extremely hurtful for any man holding the Priesthood, and enjoying the gift of the Holy Ghost, to harbor a spirit of envy, or malice, or retaliation, or intolerance toward or against his fellowmen. We ought to say in our hearts, let God judge between me and thee, but as for me, I will forgive. I want to say to you that Latter-day Saints who harbor a feeling of unforgiveness in their souls are more guilty and more censurable than the one who has sinned against them. CR1902Oct:86-7; DGSM:40

**Related Witnesses:**

**Orson F. Whitney**

We are required to forgive all men, for our own sakes, since hatred retards spiritual growth. (Gospel Themes, p. 144) TLDP:206

**Joseph Smith,**
*receiving the Word of the Lord*

[V]erily I say unto you, I, the Lord, forgive sins unto those who confess their sins before me and ask forgiveness, who have not sinned unto death. 8. My disciples, in days of old, sought occasion against one another and forgave not one another in their hearts; and for this evil they were afflicted and sorely chastened. 9. Wherefore, I say unto you, that ye ought to forgive one another; for he that forgiveth not his brother his trespasses standeth condemned before the Lord; for there remaineth in him the greater sin. 10. I, the Lord, will forgive whom I will forgive, but of you it is required to forgive all men. (*Revelation for the elders of the Church at Kirtland, Ohio, Sept. 11, 1831*) D&C 64:7-10

**Author's Note:** There are two separate recorded statements, that on the surface *appear* contrary to this Doctrinal Statement (D-223). These are isolated statements that I have not found repeated elsewhere (which means they do not

appear to comply with the Law of Witnesses). However, when understood in the *context* of each statement, neither appears to be contrary to this important doctrine that requires us *as individuals* to render unconditional forgiveness. ¶ The first is from President Heber J. Grant: In a General Conference speech President Heber J. Grant made a statement that, unless understood in context of the audience he was addressing, could *appear* contrary to this restated doctrine. President Grant was speaking to a restricted audience composed of *general authorities* of the Church and other *presiding priesthood holders*. The general public was not invited to the conference session due to the war emergency. He said, "There is nothing in the world that is more splendid than to have in our hearts a desire to forgive the sinner if he only repents. But I want to say, do not forgive the sinner if he does not repent. 'By this ye may know if a man repenteth of his sins—behold he will confess them and forsake them.' It is up to the Lord, however, and unless they confess their sins we [the Church] are not obliged to forgive, but when they really and truly repent, it is one of the obligations that rest upon us [the Church] to forgive those who have sinned." (CR1944-Apr:11) ¶ This statement, then, can easily be seen as not being contrary with this Doctrinal Restatement because President Grant is saying, in effect, do not offer the *Church's* forgiveness (i.e. fellowship) to a man unless he truly repents. As *individuals* we are to still required to forgive without condition, limitation or exception. ¶ The second statement appears in the Doctrine and Covenants and is on the subject of war. The Lord, through Joseph Smith, tells us *as a people* what to do when an enemy attacks us—it does *not* address how we as individuals should feel toward our enemies: "[I]f after thine enemy has come upon thee the first time, he repent and come unto thee praying thy forgiveness, thou shalt forgive him, and shalt hold it no more as a testimony against thine enemy—." This we should do up to the fourth time. "But if he trespass against thee the fourth time thou shalt not forgive him, but shalt bring these testimonies before the Lord." A people oppressed by an enemy nation must forgive the enemy when it repents. But when the enemy fights and repents repeatedly, then, on the fourth time, the people must no longer trust the "repentance" of the enemy and are thereafter to leave the matter in the hands of the Lord. ¶ Even thereafter, if the enemy repents and additionally makes restitution, the people are to forgive the enemy. Notwithstanding that, the

Lord is telling us as a people at what point we should cease to trust the aggressor, that there is a time when we must cease to grant the enemy Christian forgiveness—as a matter of preservation and defense. He yet emphasizes in the end this important principle of forgiveness that he wants us to learn. (See D&C 98:39-45.)

## 224. When offended, we are to forgive the offending person and seek reconciliation.

**Joseph Smith**

And if thy brother or sister offend thee, thou shalt take him or her between him or her and thee alone; and if he or she confess thou shalt be reconciled. (*Revelation "embracing the law of the Church," Feb. 9, 1831*) D&C 42:88

**Joseph Smith,**
*quoted by Elder Joseph Fielding Smith*

Ever keep in exercise the principles of mercy, and be ready to forgive our brother on the first intimations of repentance, and asking forgiveness; and should we even forgive our brother, or even our enemy, before he repent or ask forgiveness, our heavenly Father would be equally as merciful unto us. (*Joseph instructs the Apostles and seventies who are about to depart on their missions to Great Britain, July 2, 1839*) TPJS:155

**Elder Spencer W. Kimball**

It frequently happens that offenses are committed when the offender is not aware of it. Something he has said or done is misconstrued or misunderstood. The offended one treasures in his heart the offense, adding to it such other things as might give fuel to the fire and justify his conclusions. Perhaps this is one of the reasons why the Lord requires that the offended one should make the overtures toward peace. [Citing D&C 42:88.]. . . . ¶ Do we follow that command or do we sulk in our bitterness waiting for our offender to learn of it and to kneel to us in remorse? CR1949Oct:132

**Elder Spencer W. Kimball,**
*also quoting President Joseph F. Smith*

A common error is the idea that the offender must apologize and humble himself to the dust before forgiveness is required. Certainly, the one who does the injury should totally make his adjustment, but as for the offended one, he must forgive the offender regardless of the attitude of the other. Sometimes men get satisfactions from seeing the other party on his knees and grovelling in the dust, but that is not the gospel way. . . . ¶ In this regard the admonition of President Joseph F. Smith in 1902 is as applicable now as then: ¶ "We hope and pray that you will . . . forgive one another and never from this time forth . . . bear malice toward another fellow creature. ¶ ". . . . It is extremely hurtful for any man holding the gift of the Holy Ghost to harbor a spirit of envy, or malice, or retaliations, or intolerance toward or against his fellow man. We ought to say in our hearts, 'Let God judge between me and thee, but as for me, I will forgive.' I want to say to you that Latter-day Saints who harbor a feeling of unforgiveness in their souls are more censurable than the one who has sinned against them. Go home and dismiss envy and hatred from your hearts; dismiss the feeling of unforgiveness; and cultivate in your souls that spirit of Christ which cried out upon the cross, 'Father, forgive them; for they know not what they do.' This is the spirit that Latter-day Saints ought to possess all the day long." ¶ Yes, to be in the right we must forgive, and we must do so *without regard to whether or not our antagonist repents*, or how sincere is his transformation, or whether or not he asks our forgiveness. . . . ¶ Sometimes the spirit of forgiveness is carried to the loftiest height—to rendering assistance to the offender. Not to be revengeful, not to seek what outraged justice might demand, to leave the offender in God's hands—this is admirable. But to return good for evil, this is the sublime expression of Christian love. ¶ In this regard we have the stimulating example of President George Albert Smith. It was reported to him that someone had stolen from his buggy the buggy robe. Instead of being angry, he responded: "I wish we knew who it was, so that we could give him the blanket also, for he must have been cold; and some food also, for he must have been hungry." (The Miracle of Forgiveness, pp. 282-84) TLDP:206-07

**Jesus,**
*quoted by Mormon*

[I]f ye shall come unto me, or shall desire to come unto me, and rememberest that thy brother hath aught against thee— 24. Go thy way unto thy brother, and first be reconciled to thy brother, and then come unto me with full purpose of heart, and I will receive you. (*The resurrected Jesus Christ teaches the Nephite people, A.D. 34*) 3Ne.12:23-24

**Jesus,**
*recorded in Matthew*

Therefore if thou bring thy gift to the altar, and there rememberest that thy brother hath ought against thee; 24. Leave there thy gift before the altar, and go thy way; first be reconciled to thy brother, and then come and offer thy gift.

*(Jesus teaches the multitude, about A.D. 30)*
Matt.5:23-24

### Elder David O. McKay,
*also quoting Jesus*

If we would have peace as individuals, we must supplant enmity with forbearance, which means to refrain or abstain from finding fault or from condemning others. . . . We shall have power to do this if we really cherish in our hearts the ideals of Christ, who said: "Therefore if thou bring thy gift to the altar, and there rememberest that thy brother hath ought against thee; Leave there thy gift before the altar, and go thy way; first be reconciled to thy brother, and then come and offer thy gift." (Matt.5:23-24) ¶ Note the Savior did not say if you have ought against him, but if you find that another has ought against you. CR1938Oct:133

### 225. God forgives those who forgive others.

### Jesus,
*recorded in Matthew*

For if ye forgive men their trespasses, your heavenly Father will also forgive you: 15. But if ye forgive not men their trespasses, neither will your Father forgive your trespasses. *(Jesus teaches the disciples the Lord's Prayer)* Matt.6:14-15

### James E. Talmage

The first step toward the blessed state of forgiveness consists in the sinner confessing his sins; the second, in his forgiving others who have sinned against him; and the third in his showing his acceptance of Christ's atoning sacrifice by complying with the divine requirements. AF:99

### Joseph Smith

The nearer we get to our heavenly Father, the more we are disposed to look with compassion on perishing souls; we feel that we want to take them upon our shoulders, and cast their sins behind our backs. . . . If you would have God have mercy on you, have mercy on one another. *(In Relief Society meeting, at the Grove, Nauvoo, Ill., June 9, 1842)* HC5:24

### Joseph Smith,
*receiving the Word of the Lord*

My disciples, in days of old, sought occasion against one another and forgave not one another in their hearts; and for this evil they were afflicted and sorely chastened. 9. Wherefore, I say unto you, that ye ought to forgive one another; for he that forgiveth not his brother his trespasses standeth condemned before the Lord;

for there remaineth in him the greater sin. *(Revelation for the elders of the Church at Kirtland, Ohio, Sept. 11, 1831)* D&C 64:8-9

### Mormon

And ye shall also forgive one another your trespasses; for verily I say unto you, he that forgiveth not his neighbor's trespasses when he says that he repents, the same hath brought himself under condemnation. *(The voice of the Lord comes to Alma)* Mosiah 26:31

**Related Witnesses:**

### President Joseph F. Smith

I want to say to you that Latter-day Saints who harbor a feeling of unforgiveness in their souls are more guilty and more censurable than the one who has sinned against them. CR1902Oct:86-7; DGSM:40

### 226. The Church receives back into fellowship those transgressors who repent.

### Mormon

And whosoever repented of their sins and did confess them, them he did number among the people of the church; 36. And those that would not confess their sins and repent of their iniquity, the same were not numbered among the people of the church, and their names were blotted out. *(Alma judges those taken in iniquity according to the word of the Lord received by him, about 120-100 B.C.)* Mosiah 26:35-36

### J. Reuben Clark, Jr.,
*also quoting Joseph Smith*

I would like to point out that to me there is a great difference between confession and admission, after transgression is proved. I doubt much the efficacy of an admission as a confession. ¶ In ancient days, men made sacrifice that they might be forgiven. Today we are told that we must bring to the Lord for our forgiveness a humble heart and a contrite spirit. As to forgiveness, the Lord has said, "I, the Lord, will forgive whom I will forgive, but of you it is required to forgive all men," (D&C 64:10) which means, as I understand it, that where there is repentance, we shall forgive and receive into fellowship the repentant transgressor, leaving to God the final disposition of the sin. CR1950Apr:166-67

### Marion G. Romney

Finally, where one's transgressions are of such a nature as would, unrepented of, put in jeopardy his right to membership or fellowship in the Church of Jesus Christ, full and effective confession would, in my judgment, require confession by the repentant sinner to his bishop or other proper presiding Church officer—not that the Church officer could forgive the sin (this power rests in the Lord himself and those only to whom he specifically delegates it) but rather that the Church, acting through its duly appointed officers, might with full knowledge of the facts take such action with respect to Church discipline as the circumstances merit. CR1955Oct:125

### President Heber J. Grant

There is nothing in the world that is more splendid than to have in our hearts a desire to forgive the sinner if he only repents. But I want to say, do not forgive the sinner if he does not repent. "By this ye may know if a man repenteth of his sins—behold he will confess them and forsake them." It is up to the Lord, however, and unless they confess their sins we are not obliged to forgive, but when they really and truly repent, it is one of the obligations that rest upon us to forgive those who have sinned. (*Instructing a selected body of priesthood officers of the Church in their ecclesiastical capacities*) CR1944Apr:10

### Joseph Smith,
### *receiving the Word of the Lord*

For I the Lord cannot look upon sin with the least degree of allowance; 32. Nevertheless, he that repents and does the commandments of the Lord shall be forgiven; (*Revelation received during conference of elders of the Church, Nov. 1, 1831*) D&C 1:31-32

### President Spencer W. Kimball

I want to repeat to be sure that I am well understood. The Lord said, "Wherefore all manner of sins should be forgiven unto men, except the sinning against the Holy Ghost and the committing of murder." (See Matthew 12:31.) None of us will commit sin against the Holy Ghost (generally we do not know enough), and few of us will ever be involved in a murder. Therefore, the sins of mankind can be forgiven. But not by ignoring them; one must go to the proper ecclesiastical officials and clear his problems. The Lord offered a concluding thought, "Be ye clean that bear the vessels of the Lord." (D&C 38:42) All of us bear the vessels of the Lord, so that command is to every man, woman, youth, and child. ACR(Amsterdam)1976:4

### Bruce R. McConkie

We must remind ourselves of how the law of forgiveness operates, for the Lord, who himself ordained the laws, is also himself bound to uphold and sustain and conform to them. The Lord forgives sins, but he does it in harmony with the laws he ordained before the world was. ¶ All men sin and fall short of the glory of God;

all need repentance; all need forgiveness; and all can become free from sin by obedience to the laws and ordinances that comprise the cleansing process. For those who have not accepted the gospel . . . the course of forgiveness is to believe in the Lord Jesus Christ, to repent, to be baptized by immersion for the remission of sins, and to receive the gift of the Holy Ghost by the laying on of hands. The Holy Ghost is a sanctifier, and those who receive the baptism of fire have sin and evil burned out of their souls as though by fire. ¶ For those whose sins have thus been remitted and who sin after baptism—as all baptized souls do—the path to forgiveness consists of repenting and renewing the covenant made in the waters of baptism. Godly sorrow for sin, complete abandonment of the wrongful acts, confession to the Lord and to the church officers where need be, restitution if such is possible, and renewed obedience—these are all part of the cleansing process for those who, after baptism, fall from the strait and narrow path leading to eternal life. By doing these things and by then partaking worthily of the sacrament, so that the Spirit of the Lord will come again into the lives of the penitent persons, members of the kingdom gain forgiveness of sins. (The Mortal Messiah, 2:50-51) TLDP:205

### Elder Spencer W. Kimball

Our loving Father has given us the blessed principle of repentance as the gateway to forgiveness. All sins but those excepted by the Lord—basically, the sin against the Holy Ghost, and murder—will be forgiven to those who totally, consistently, and continuously repent in a genuine and comprehensive transformation of life. There is forgiveness for even the sinner who commits serious transgressions, for the Church will forgive and the Lord will forgive such things when repentance has reached fruition. ¶ Repentance and forgiveness are part of the glorious climb toward godhood. In God's plan, man must voluntarily make this climb, for the element of free agency is basic. Man chooses for himself, but he cannot control the penalties. They are immutable. Little children and mental incompetents are not held responsible, but all others will receive either blessings, advancements, and rewards, or penalties and deprivation, according to their reaction to God's plan when it is presented to them and to their faithfulness to that plan. The Lord wisely provided for this situation and made it possible that there might be good and evil, comfort and pain. The alternatives give us a choice and thereby growth and development. (The Miracle of Forgiveness, p. 14) TLDP:203

**Related Witnesses:**
**Joseph Smith,**
*receiving the Word of the Lord*

[V]erily I say unto you, I, the Lord, forgive sins unto those who confess their sins before me and ask forgiveness, who have not sinned unto death. (*Revelation for the elders of the Church at Kirtland, Ohio, Sept. 11, 1831*) D&C 64:7

**Joseph Smith**

Nevertheless, he that repents and does the commandments of the Lord shall be forgiven; (*Revelation received during conference of elders of the Church, Nov. 1, 1831*) D&C 1:32

---

**HYMNS Written by Prophets**
**Applicable to this Topic**

**Orson F. Whitney**
*The Wintry Day, Descending to Its Close*
HYMNS:37

The wintry day, descending to its close,
Invites all wearied nature to repose,
And shades of night are falling dense and fast,
Like sable curtains closing o'er the past.
Pale through the gloom the newly fallen snow
Wraps in a shroud the silent earth below
As tho 'twere mercy's hand had spread the pall,
A symbol of forgiveness unto all.

I cannot go to rest, but linger still
In meditation at my window sill,
While, like the twinkling stars in heaven's dome,
Come one by one sweet memories of home.
And wouldst thou ask me where my fancy roves
To reproduce the happy scenes it loves,
Where hope and memory together dwell
And paint the pictured beauties that I tell?

Away beyond the prairies of the West,
Where exiled Saints in solitude were blest,
Where industry the seal of wealth has set
Amid the peaceful vales of Deseret,
Unheeding still the fiercest blasts that blow,
With tops encrusted by eternal snow,
The tow'ring peaks that shield the tender sod
Stand, types of freedom reared by nature's God.

The wilderness, that naught before would yield,
Is now become a fertile, fruitful field.
Where roamed at will the fearless Indian band,
The templed cities of the Saints now stand.
And sweet religion in its purity
Invites all men to its security.
There is my home, the spot I love so well,
Whose worth and beauty pen nor tongue can tell.

**Parley P. Pratt**
*Father in Heaven, We Do Believe*
HYMNS:180

Father in Heav'n, we do believe
The promise thou hast made;
Thy word with meekness we receive,
Just as thy Saints have said.

We now repent of all our sin
And come with broken heart,
And to thy covenant enter in
And choose the better part.

O Lord, accept us while we pray,
And all our sins forgive;
New life impart to us this day,
And bid the sinners live.

Humbly we take the sacrament
In Jesus' blessed name;
Let us receive thru covenant
The Spirit's heav'nly flame.

We will be buried in the stream
In Jesus' blessed name,
And rise, while light shall on us beam
The Spirit's heav'nly flame.

Baptize us with the Holy Ghost
And seal us as thine own,
That we may join the ransomed host
And with the Saints be one.

**John A. Widtsoe**
*How Long, O Lord Most Holy and True*
HYMNS:126

How long, O Lord most holy and true,
Shall shadowed hope our joy delay?
Our hearts confess, our souls believe
Thy truth, thy truth, thy light,
thy will, thy way!

Thy truth has made our prison bright;
Thy light has dimmed the dying past.
We bend beneath thy loving will
And seek thy onward, onward path at last.

Eternal Father, gentle Judge!
Speed on the day, redemption's hour.
Set up thy kingdom; from thy house
Unlock for us, for us the prison tow'r.

From grim confusion's awful depth
The wail of hosts, faith's urgent plea:
Release our anguished, weary souls;
Swing wide, swing wide the gates, and set us free!

# List of Doctrines

## GATHERING

### The Scattering and Gathering of Israel

*Doctrines Located in This Topic*

227. It was foretold by prophecy that the people of Israel would be scattered among the nations of the earth because of their wickedness.

228. The Lord decreed that the Jews would be scattered among the nations of the world.

229. It was foretold by prophets that the gathering and redemption of Israel would take place in the latter days.

230. Moses delivered the keys of the gathering of Israel to Joseph Smith.

231. The Lord will gather Israel from the four corners of the earth: He will gather up His scattered peoples from all lands and nations.

232. The ten tribes will be gathered in from the "land of the north."

233. In the last days many Jews will return to Jerusalem still not believing in Jesus Christ.

234. Only when the Jews believe in Christ will the Lord fully and finally gather them to Jerusalem.

235. The object of gathering the people of God in any age is for their salvation, that they might obtain the ordinances administered in holy temples.

*Doctrines on GATHERING: The Scattering and Gathering of Israel Located in Other Topics*

894. Zion is wherever the organization of the Church of God is—where the pure in heart are gathered.

# GATHERING

## The Scattering and Gathering of Israel

227. It was foretold by prophecy that the people of Israel would be scattered among the nations of the earth because of their wickedness.

### James E. Talmage

It has been said, that "if a complete history of the house of Israel were written, it would be the history of histories, the key of the world's history for the past twenty centuries." Justification for this sweeping statement is found in the fact that the Israelites have been so completely dispersed among the nations as to give to this scattered people a place of importance as a factor in the rise and development of almost every large division of the human family. This work of dispersion was brought about by many stages, and extended through millenniums. It was foreseen by the early prophets; and the spiritual leaders of every generation prior to and immediately following the Messianic era predicted the scattering of the people, as an ordained result of their increasing wickedness. . . . AF:286

### Nephi, son of Lehi

Yea, even my father spake much concerning the Gentiles, and also concerning the house of Israel, that they should be compared like unto an olive-tree, whose branches should be broken off and should be scattered upon all the face of the earth. 13. Wherefore, he said it must needs be that we should be led with one accord into the land of promise, unto the fulfilling of the word of the Lord, that we should be scattered upon all the face of the earth. (*Nephi's writings, 600-592 B.C.*) 1Ne.10:12-13

### Elder Joseph Fielding Smith

In the Book of Jacob, chapter five, in the Book of Mormon, we have one of the most remarkable parables ever written. It is a parable of the scattering of Israel. The Lord revealed to Jacob that he would scatter Israel, and in this figure, Israel is a tame olive tree. It is an olive tree that begins to decay. The branches that are dying are cut off. But the gardener takes certain of those branches off that tree that seem to be decaying and plants them in all parts of the Lord's vineyard. . . . ¶ He planted them all over his vineyard, which is the world. . . . ¶ The interpretation of this parable is a story of the scattering of Israel and the mixing of the blood of Israel with the wild olive trees, or Gentile peoples, in all parts of the world. Therefore we find in China, Japan, India, and in all other countries that are inhabited by the Gentiles that the blood of Israel was scattered, or "grafted," among them. MPSG1972-73:280-81

### Related Witnesses:

#### Isaiah

Thus saith the LORD, Where is the bill of your mother's divorcement, whom I have put away? or which of my creditors is it to whom I have sold you? Behold, for your iniquities have ye sold yourselves, and for your transgressions is your mother put away. (*Isaiah speaks Messianically, [the Messiah speaks]*) Isa.50:1

#### Recorded in Leviticus

And I will scatter you among the heathen, and will draw out a sword after you: and your land shall be desolate, and your cities waste. (*Revelation to Moses for the children of Israel*) Lev.26:33

#### Recorded in Deuteronomy

The LORD shall cause thee to be smitten before thine enemies: thou shalt go out one way against them, and flee seven ways before them: and shalt be removed into all the kingdoms of the earth. . . . 37. And thou shalt become an astonishment, a proverb, and a byword, among all nations whither the LORD shall lead thee. . . . 64. And the LORD shall scatter thee among all people, from the one end of the earth even unto the other; and there thou shalt serve other gods, which neither thou nor thy fathers have known, even wood and stone. (*Israel, if disobedient, shall be cursed*) Deut.28:25,37,64

#### Nephi, son of Lehi

Wherefore, the things of which I have read are things pertaining to things both temporal and spiritual; for it appears that the house of Israel, sooner or later, will be scattered upon all the face of the earth, and also among all nations. 4. And behold, there are many who are already lost from the knowledge of those who are at Jerusalem. Yea, the more part of all the tribes have been led away; and they are scattered to and fro upon the isles of the sea; and whither they are none of us knoweth, save that we know that they have been led away. (*Nephi interprets the things he has read from the plates of brass, about 588-570 B.C.*) 1Ne.22:3-4

#### Bruce R. McConkie

Israel was scattered because she apostatized; because she broke the Ten Commandments; because she rejected the prophets and seers and turned to wizards that peep and mutter; because she forsook the covenant; because she gave heed to false ministers and joined false churches;

because she ceased to be a peculiar people and a kingdom of priests. When she became as the world, the Lord left her to suffer and live and be as the world then was. (The Millennial Messiah, p. 186) DGSM:65

### James E. Talmage

All the Jews in Palestine at the time of Christ's birth constituted but a small remnant of the great Davidic nation. The Ten Tribes, distinctively the aforetime kingdom of Israel, had then long been lost to history, and the people of Judah had been widely scattered among the nations. JTC:61

---

228. The Lord decreed that the Jews would be scattered among the nations of the world.

### Nephi, son of Lehi

And behold it shall come to pass that after the Messiah hath risen from the dead, and hath manifested himself unto his people, unto as many as will believe on his name, behold, Jerusalem shall be destroyed again; for wo unto them that fight against God and the people of his church. 15. Wherefore, the Jews shall be scattered among all nations; yea, and also Babylon shall be destroyed; wherefore, the Jews shall be scattered by other nations. (*Nephi explains Isaiah's prophecies, about 559-554 B.C.*) 2Ne.25:14-15

### Jesus,
### *recorded in Luke*

And they shall fall by the edge of the sword, and shall be led away captive into all nations: and Jerusalem shall be trodden down of the Gentiles, until the times of the Gentiles be fulfilled. (*Jesus tells of the signs that shall precede his Second Coming*) Luke 21:24

### Joseph Smith,
### *receiving the Word of the Lord*

And now ye behold this temple which is in Jerusalem, which ye call the house of God, and your enemies say that this house shall never fall. 19. But, verily I say unto you, that desolation shall come upon this generation as a thief in the night, and this people shall be destroyed and scattered among all nations. 20. And this temple which ye now see shall be thrown down that there shall not be left one stone upon another. 21. And it shall come to pass, that this generation of Jews shall not pass away until every desolation which I have told you concerning them shall come to pass. . . . 24. And this I have told you concerning Jerusalem; and when that day shall come, shall a remnant

be scattered among all nations; (*Christ reveals signs of his coming as given on the Mount of Olives*) D&C 45:18-21,24

**Related Witnesses:**
### Elder Brigham Young
### and Willard Richards

[F]or there is none other name under heaven given among men whereby we must be saved, but the name of Jesus Christ of Nazareth (Acts 4:10, 12); but of this the Jews were ignorant, although they themselves crucified Him; and they have been going about wandering among all the nations of the earth ever since, for the space of eighteen hundred years, trying to establish their own righteousness, which is of the law of Moses, which law can never make the comers thereto perfect (Heb.10:1); (*From "Election and Reprobation," in Millennial Star, about which Joseph Smith wrote, "It is one of the sweetest pieces that has been written in the last days"*) HC4:265

---

229. It was foretold by prophets that the gathering and redemption of Israel would take place in the latter days.

### Joseph Smith

It is also the concurrent testimony of all the Prophets, that this gathering together of all the Saints, must take place before the Lord comes to "take vengeance upon the ungodly," and "to be glorified and admired by all those who obey the Gospel." The fiftieth Psalm, from the first to the fifth verse inclusive, describes the glory and majesty of that event. (*"A Proclamation of the First Presidency of the Church to the Saints Scattered Abroad. . . ;" the Prophet encourages the Saints to gather to Nauvoo, Ill., Jan.15, 1841*) HC4:272

### James E. Talmage

Comparison with other prophecies relating to the gathering will conclusively prove that the great event was predicted to take place in the latter times, preparatory to the second coming of Christ. AF:250

**Related Witnesses:**
### Recorded in Psalms

The mighty God, even the LORD, hath spoken, and called the earth from the rising of the sun unto the going down thereof. 2. Out of Zion, the perfection of beauty, God hath shined. 3. Our God shall come, and shall not keep silence: a fire shall devour before him, and it shall be very tempestuous round about him. 4. He shall call to the heavens from above, and to the earth, that he may judge his people. 5. Gather my saints together unto me; those that have made a covenant with me by sacrifice. Ps.50:1-5

### Bruce R. McConkie

[E]ven the apostles sought yet to learn of the fulfillment of the prophetic word concerning Israel the chosen. "When they therefore were come together, . . . they asked of him, saying, Lord, wilt thou at this time restore again the kingdom to Israel?" ¶ . . . . The kingdom was not to be restored to Israel in their day. . . . The promised day of restoration, the day of Israel's triumph and glory, the day of millennial glory—all this lay ahead. It was scheduled for the last days. (The Millennial Messiah, 309-10) DGSM:66

### Moses

And the LORD shall scatter you among the nations, and ye shall be left few in number among the heathen, whither the LORD shall lead you. 28. And there ye shall serve gods, the work of men's hands, wood and stone, which neither see, nor hear, nor eat, nor smell. 29. But if from thence thou shalt seek the LORD thy God, thou shalt find him, if thou seek him with all thy heart and with all thy soul. 30. When thou art in tribulation, and all these things are come upon thee, even in the latter days, if thou turn to the LORD thy God, and shalt be obedient unto his voice; 31. (For the LORD thy God is a merciful God;) he will not forsake thee, neither destroy thee, nor forget the covenant of thy fathers which he sware unto them. (*Moses records that Israel shall be scattered among all the nations when they worship other gods*) Deut.4:27-31

---

### 230. Moses delivered the keys of the gathering of Israel to Joseph Smith.

### Joseph Smith

After this vision closed, the heavens were again opened unto us; and Moses appeared before us, and committed unto us the keys of the gathering of Israel from the four parts of the earth, and the leading of the ten tribes from the land of the north. (*Visions manifested to Joseph Smith and Oliver Cowdery in the Kirtland Temple, April 3, 1836*) D&C 110:11

### Elder Joseph Fielding Smith

Moses held the keys of the gathering of Israel. He received the first commission to gather them and lead them out of Egypt and plant them in their promised land. When Moses appeared on the mount with Elias, he conferred the keys of

this authority to lead Israel on Peter, James and John for the dispensation of the meridian of time. On the third day of April, 1836, this same Moses came to Joseph Smith and Oliver Cowdery in the Kirtland Temple and conferred upon them "the keys of the gathering of Israel from the four parts of the earth, and the leading of the ten tribes from the land of the north." In this way the authority for the gathering was restored. (The Restoration of All Things, p. 142) TLDP:211

### James E. Talmage

From the early days of Joseph Smith's ministry he taught the doctrine of the gathering as imposing a present duty upon the Church; and this phase of Latter-day Saint labor is one of its most characteristic features. Joseph Smith and Oliver Cowdery affirm that the commission for prosecuting this work was committed to the Church through them by Moses, who held authority as Israel's leader in the dispensation known specifically as the Mosaic. AF:17

### Related Witnesses:

### Joseph Smith

Behold, thus saith the Lord, it is a descendant of Jesse, as well as of Joseph, unto whom rightly belongs the priesthood, and the keys of the kingdom, for an ensign, and for the gathering of my people in the last days. (*Joseph answers certain questions on the writings of Isaiah, March 1838*) D&C 113:6

### President John Taylor

Why is it that you are here today? and what brought you here? Because the keys of the gathering of Israel from the four quarters of the earth have been committed to Joseph Smith, and he has conferred those keys upon others that the gathering of Israel may be accomplished, and in due time the same thing will be performed to the tribes in the land of the north. It is on this account, and through the unlocking of this principle, and through those means, that you are brought together as you are today. (*At dedication of Logan Temple, May 1884; JD25:179*) DGSM:66

---

### 231. The Lord will gather Israel from the four corners of the earth: He will gather up His scattered peoples from all lands and nations.

### Jacob, brother of Nephi

But behold, thus saith the Lord God: When the day cometh that they shall believe in me, that I am Christ, then have I covenanted with their fathers that they shall be restored in the flesh, upon the earth, unto the lands of their inheritance. 8. And it shall come to pass that they shall be gathered in from their long dispersion, from the isles of the sea, and from the four parts of the earth; and the nations of the Gentiles shall be great in the eyes of me, saith God, in carrying them forth to the lands of their inheritance. *(Jacob recites the words of the Lord to the people of Nephi, 559-545 B.C.)* 2Ne.10:7-8

### Moses

That then the LORD thy God will turn thy captivity, and have compassion upon thee, and will return and gather thee from all the nations, whither the LORD thy God hath scattered thee. *(Moses foretells the gathering of Israel)* Deut.30:3

### James E. Talmage

It is evident that the plan of gathering comprises: ¶ 1. Assembling in the land of Zion of the people of Israel from the nations of the earth. ¶ 2. Return of the Jews to Jerusalem. ¶ 3. Restoration of the Lost Tribes. ¶ The sequence of these events as here presented is that of convenience and has no significance as to the order in which the several gatherings are to be accomplished. AF:305

### Elder Joseph Fielding Smith

If all things are to be restored in the dispensation of the fulness of times, as Peter and Paul predicted, then there must come as part of that great restoration the gathering of Israel. It is well known that the prophets predicted the scattering of Israel into all parts of the earth, long before that dispersion commenced. This fact is one of the evidences of the divine origin of the prophecies in the Bible, since the scattering was literally fulfilled. ¶ The promise of the return of Israel was just as emphatically proclaimed and must be fulfilled just as surely as the dispersion. (The Restoration of All Things, p. 138) TLDP:208

### Nephi, son of Lehi

And he gathereth his children from the four quarters of the earth; and he numbereth his sheep, and they know him; and there shall be one fold and one shepherd; and he shall feed his sheep, and in him they shall find pasture. *(Nephi explains the prophecies written on the plates of brass, 588-570 B.C.)* 1Ne.22:25

### Joseph Smith

We believe in the literal gathering of Israel and in the restoration of the Ten Tribes; that Zion (the New Jerusalem) will be built upon the American continent; that Christ will reign personally upon the earth; and, that the earth will be renewed and receive its paradisiacal glory. *(The tenth of the thirteen Articles of Faith; letter to John Wentworth, March 1, 1842)* AofF:10

### Nephi, son of Lehi

And after our seed is scattered the Lord God will proceed to do a marvelous work among the Gentiles, which shall be of great worth unto our seed; wherefore, it is likened unto their being nourished by the Gentiles and being carried in their arms and upon their shoulders. 9. And it shall also be of worth unto the Gentiles; and not only unto the Gentiles but unto all the house of Israel, unto the making known of the covenants of the Father of heaven unto Abraham, saying: In thy seed shall all the kindreds of the earth be blessed. 10. And I would, my brethren, that ye should know that all the kindreds of the earth cannot be blessed unless he shall make bare his arm in the eyes of the nations. 11. Wherefore, the Lord God will proceed to make bare his arm in the eyes of all the nations, in bringing about his covenants and his gospel unto those who are of the house of Israel. 12. Wherefore, he will bring them again out of captivity, and they shall be gathered together to the lands of their inheritance; and they shall be brought out of obscurity and out of darkness; and they shall know that the Lord is their Savior and their Redeemer, the Mighty One of Israel. *(Nephi explains the prophecies written on the plates of brass, 588-570 B.C.)* 1Ne.22:8-12

### Isaiah

Fear not: for I am with thee: I will bring thy seed from the east, and gather thee from the west; 6. I will say to the north, Give up; and to the south, Keep not back: bring my sons from far, and my daughters from the ends of the earth; *(The Lord speaks to Israel)* Isa.43:5-6

### Isaiah

And it shall come to pass in that day, that the Lord shall set his hand again the second time to recover the remnant of his people, which shall be left, from Assyria, and from Egypt, and from Pathros, and from Cush, and from Elam, and from Shinar, and from Hamath, and from the islands of the sea. 12. And he shall set up an ensign for the nations, and shall assemble the outcasts of Israel, and gather together the dispersed of Judah from the four corners of the earth. *(Isaiah prophesies, 740-659 B.C.)* Isa.11:11-12

### Ezekiel

For thus saith the Lord GOD; Behold, I, even I, will both search my sheep, and seek them out. 12. As a shepherd seeketh out his flock in the day that he is among his sheep that are scattered; so will I seek out my sheep, and will deliver them out of all places where they have been scattered in the cloudy and dark day. 13. And I will bring them out from the people, and gather them from the countries, and will bring them to their own land, and feed them upon the mountains of Israel by the rivers, and in all the inhabited places of the country. 14. I will feed them in a good pasture, and upon the high mountains of Israel shall their fold be: there shall they lie in a good fold, and in a fat pasture shall they feed upon the mountains of Israel. 15. I will feed my flock, and I will cause them to lie down, saith the Lord GOD. 16. I will seek that which was lost, and bring again that which was driven away, and will bind up that which was broken, and will strengthen that which was sick: but I will destroy the fat and the strong; I will feed them with judgment. (*In the last days the Lord will gather the lost sheep of Israel*) Ezek.34:11-16

### President Brigham Young,
### Heber C. Kimball, Willard Richards
(First Presidency)

The Lord Jesus Christ . . . ere long, will set his feet again on Mount Olivet, and make himself manifest unto Israel, according to the predictions of the ancient prophets; for Israel must be gathered from all nations, and be again established in the land of their inheritance, and behold the wounds in the hands and side of Him whom they have pierced, and acknowledge Him as their Saviour, their Redeemer, the Holy One of Israel. The gathering of Israel has already commenced; Judea is receiving its ancient inhabitants, and the Holy City is re-building; which is one prominent sign of the near approach of the Messiah. ¶ . . . . The unparalleled spread of the Gospel, in so short a space of time [twenty-one years at this writing], and the rapid gathering of the saints, is another token of Messiah's near approach. (*First Presidency of the Church "Fifth General Epistle" to the Saints, April 7, 1851*) MOFP2:63-64

### James E. Talmage
I read that in the last days one of the conditions preceding the return of the Christ to earth shall be the gathering of the Jews at their ancient capital, and in the land round about; and that another sign shall be the gathering of the people who have been scattered among the nations. . . . CR1916Oct:76

### Elder Joseph Fielding Smith
The Lord has caused Israel to mix with the nations and bring the Gentiles within the blessings of the seed of Abraham. We are preaching the gospel now in all parts of the world, and for what purpose? To gather out from the Gentile nations the lost sheep of the house of Israel. It is by this scattering that the Gentile nations have been blessed, and if they will truly repent they are entitled to all the blessings promised to Israel, "which are the blessings of salvation,

even of life eternal." (Answers to Gospel Questions, 2:57) TLDP:210

**Related Witnesses:**
### Joseph Smith
And there shall be gathered unto it out of every nation under heaven; and it shall be the only people that shall not be at war one with another. . . . 71. And it shall come to pass that the righteous shall be gathered out from among all nations, and shall come to Zion, singing with songs of everlasting joy. (*Revelation received March 7, 1831*) D&C 45:69,71

### Joseph Smith
Yea, let the cry go forth among all people: Awake and arise and go forth to meet the Bridegroom; behold and lo, the Bridegroom cometh; go ye out to meet him. Prepare yourselves for the great day of the Lord. 11. Watch, therefore, for ye know neither the day nor the hour. 12. Let them, therefore, who are among the Gentiles flee unto Zion. 13. And let them who be of Judah flee unto Jerusalem, unto the mountains of the Lord's house. 14. Go ye out from among the nations, even from Babylon, from the midst of wickedness, which is spiritual Babylon. 15. But verily, thus saith the Lord, let not your flight be in haste, but let all things be prepared before you; and he that goeth, let him not look back lest sudden destruction shall come upon him. (*All are commanded to flee from Babylon, come to Zion, and prepare for the great day of the Lord*) D&C 133:10-15

### Jeremiah
For, lo, the days come, saith the LORD, that I will bring again the captivity of my people Israel and Judah, saith the LORD: and I will cause them to return to the land that I gave to their fathers, and they shall possess it. (*He speaks of the last days*) Jer.30:3

### Recorded in Psalms
O give thanks unto the LORD, for he is good: for his mercy endureth for ever. 2. Let the redeemed of the LORD say so, whom he hath redeemed from the hand of the enemy; 3. And gathered them out of the lands, from the east, and from the west, from the north, and from the south. Ps.107:1-3

---

## 232. The ten tribes will be gathered in from the "land of the north."

### President Brigham Young,
*quoted by John A. Widtsoe*

By and by the Jews will be gathered to the land of their fathers, and the ten tribes, who wandered into the north, will be gathered home. (*In*

*Tabernacle, April 14, 1867; general instructions to missionaries, JD12:38)* DBY:121

**President John Taylor**

Why is it that you are here today? and what brought you here? Because the keys of the gathering of Israel from the four quarters of the earth have been committed to Joseph Smith, and he has conferred those keys upon others that the gathering of Israel may be accomplished, and in due time the same thing will be performed to the tribes in the land of the north. (*At dedication of Logan Temple, May 1884, JD25:179)* DGSM:66

**Joseph Smith**

After this vision closed, the heavens were again opened unto us; and Moses appeared before us, and committed unto us the keys of the gathering of Israel from the four parts of the earth, and the leading of the ten tribes from the land of the north. (*Visions manifested to Joseph Smith and Oliver Cowdery in the Kirtland Temple, April 3, 1836)* D&C 110:11

**Joseph Smith**

And they who are in the north countries shall come in remembrance before the Lord; and their prophets shall hear his voice, and shall no longer stay themselves; and they shall smite the rocks, and the ice shall flow down at their presence. 27. And an highway shall be cast up in the midst of the great deep. . . . (*At the Second Coming the lost tribes of Israel shall return)* D&C 133:26-27

**Jeremiah**

In those days the house of Judah shall walk with the house of Israel, and they shall come together out of the land of the north to the land that I have given for an inheritance unto your fathers. (*Revelation to Jeremiah, about 628 B.C.)* Jer.3:18

**Moroni, son of Mormon**

And then also cometh the Jerusalem of old; and the inhabitants thereof, blessed are they, for they have been washed in the blood of the Lamb; and they are they who were scattered and gathered in from the four quarters of the earth, and from the north countries, and are partakers of the fulfilling of the covenant which God made with their father, Abraham. (*Moroni's abridgement of the writings of Ether, who wrote, about 550 B.C.)* Ether 13:11

**Related Witnesses:**

**Joseph Smith**

We believe in the literal gathering of Israel and in the restoration of the Ten Tribes; that Zion (the New Jerusalem) will be built upon the American continent; that Christ will reign personally upon the earth; and, that the earth will be renewed and receive its paradisiacal glory. (*The tenth of the thirteen Articles of Faith; letter to John Wentworth, March 1, 1842)* AofF:10

**Jesus,**
***quoted by Mormon***

And verily, verily, I say unto you that I have other sheep which are not of this land, neither of the land of Jerusalem, neither in any parts of that land round about whither I have been to minister. 2. For they of whom I speak are they who have not as yet heard my voice; neither have I at any time manifested myself unto them. 3. But I have received a commandment of the Father that I shall go unto them, and that they shall hear my voice, and shall be numbered among my sheep, that there may be one fold and one shepherd; therefore I go to show myself unto them. (*Jesus will visit others of the lost sheep of Israel)* 3Ne.16:1-3

**Jesus,**
***quoted by Mormon***

But now I go unto the Father, and also to show myself unto the lost tribes of Israel, for they are not lost unto the Father, for he knoweth whither he hath taken them. (*After Jesus tells the people to ponder his words, he tells them he will visit the lost tribes of Israel)* 3Ne.17:4

**Nephi, son of Lehi**

And it shall come to pass that the Jews shall have the words of the Nephites, and the Nephites shall have the words of the Jews; and the Nephites and the Jews shall have the words of the lost tribes of Israel; and the lost tribes of Israel shall have the words of the Nephites and the Jews. 14. And it shall come to pass that my people, which are of the house of Israel, shall be gathered home unto the lands of their possessions; and my word also shall be gathered in one. And I will show unto them that fight against my word and against my people, who are of the house of Israel, that I am God, and that I covenanted with Abraham that I would remember his seed forever. (*The Lord will remember the seed of Abraham forever)* 2Ne.29:13-14

---

**233. In the last days many Jews will return to Jerusalem still not believing in Jesus Christ.**

**Elder Wilford Woodruff**

The Jews have got to gather to their own land in unbelief. They will go and rebuild Jerusalem and their temple. They will take their gold and silver from the nations and will gather to the Holy Land, and when they have done this and rebuilt their city, the Gentiles . . . will go up against Jerusalem to battle and to take a spoil and a prey; and then when they have taken one-half of Jerusalem captive and distressed the Jews for the last time on the earth, their Great Deliverer, Shiloh, will come. They do not believe in Jesus of Nazareth now, nor ever will until he comes and sets his foot on Mount Olivet and it cleaves in twain, one part going towards the East and the other towards the West. Then, when they behold the wounds in his hands and in his feet, they will say, "Where did you get them?" and he will reply "I am Jesus of Nazareth, King of the Jews, your Shiloh, him whom you crucified." Then, for the first time will the eyes of Judah be opened. They will remain in unbelief until that day. This is one of the events that will transpire in the latter day. *(In 13th Ward, Jan. 12, 1873, JD15:277-78)* TLDP:349

**Elder Joseph Fielding Smith**
We are drawing near the great day for the appearing of our Lord in the clouds of glory to take his place as King of kings. Before that day can come, there must be a restoration of a remnant of Jews to Palestine, and a remnant of Israel to Zion. Israel has been gathering to Zion for one hundred years and more. The Jews are only commencing to gather. They will return to Jerusalem only partially believing in Jesus Christ, but not accepting him as their Redeemer. (The Restoration of All Things, p. 154) TLDP:208

**Related Witnesses:**

**James E. Talmage**
I read that in the last days one of the conditions preceding the return of the Christ to earth shall be the gathering of the Jews at their ancient capital, and in the land round about; and that another sign shall be the gathering of the people who have been scattered among the nations. . . . CR1916Oct:76

**George Q. Morris**
[Another item of the signs of the final preparatory work] is God's promise that he would gather Jews to Jerusalem, and I think perhaps we may well now *not* [italics added] continue saying the Jews are going to gather in Jerusalem. I think now we may well say they *have gathered.* The ultimate returns will come later as they develop this land and are joined by others. ¶ In a writing issued recently this statement was made: "About two million Jews have returned to restore land which has lain desolate for centuries. In little more than ten years fetid swamps have been transformed into fertile valleys. Orchards now blossom on stony hillsides.

Farms have sprouted the desert, and towns and cities have been built on the site of ancient settlements." (Know the World: Israel, "Around the World Program," by Peggy Mann) ¶ It goes on to explain . . . that this movement started about 1880 when pogroms against the Jews drove them from Europe, and they began to trickle into Palestine. . . . ¶ In 1948, with a population of 600,000, the Declaration of Independence was issued, and the State of Israel was established. An army of 35,000 Jews was opposed by an army of nearly 80,000 Arabs. In about nine months peace was declared, and they set up their government. They planted more than 53 million trees. Martyr's Forest has six million trees, one for each Jewish life lost in Nazi Europe. ¶ This statement by a writer is very interesting: ¶ "Strangely enough when the State of Israel was reborn in 1948, it was a nation of 600,000, the same number which the Bible reports that Moses led out of bondage in Egypt. It now numbers some two million, the same number which it is said populated the ancient Kingdom of Solomon, when Israel was in all its glory. (Idem)" ¶ That is why we may now say that the Jews have returned to Palestine. On a land one-tenth the size of Utah they have nearly a half million more people than we have in our whole Church. [In 1960] They have about 258 people for each square mile in Palestine, which is a dense population. We have about ten a square mile in Utah. [In 1960] CR1960Apr:101

**President Brigham Young,**
*quoted by John A. Widtsoe*
When the Savior visits Jerusalem, and the Jews look upon him, and see the wounds in his hands and in his side and in his feet, they will then know that they have persecuted and put to death the true Messiah, and then they will acknowledge him, *but not till then.* [Italics added] They have confounded his first and second coming, expecting his first coming to be as a mighty prince instead of as a servant. They will go back by and by to Jerusalem and own their Lord and Master. We have no feelings against them. *(In Tabernacle, Dec. 23, 1866, JD11:279)* DBY:122

**President Brigham Young,**
*quoted by John A. Widtsoe*
Jerusalem is not to be redeemed by the soft, still voice of the preacher of the Gospel of peace. Why? Because they were once the blessed of the Lord, the chosen of the Lord, the promised seed. They were the people from among whom should spring the Messiah; and salvation could be found only through that people. The Messiah

came through them, and they killed him; and they will be the last of all the seed of Abraham to have the privilege of receiving the New and Everlasting Covenant. You may hand out to them gold, you may feed and clothe them, but it is impossible to convert the Jews, until the Lord God Almighty does it. (*In Tabernacle, Dec. 3, 1854, JD2:142)* DBY:121

**Joseph Smith,**
*receiving the Word of the Lord*
And this I have told you concerning Jerusalem; and when that day shall come, shall a remnant be scattered among all nations; 25. But they shall be gathered again; but they shall remain until the times of the Gentiles be fulfilled. (*Revelation received March 7, 1831; signs and wonders to attend the Second Coming*) D&C 45:24-25

---

**234. Only when the Jews believe in Christ will the Lord fully and finally gather them to Jerusalem.**

**Jacob, brother of Nephi,**
*quoted by Nephi*
But behold, thus saith the Lord God: When the day cometh that they shall believe in me, that I am Christ, then have I covenanted with their fathers that they shall be restored in the flesh, upon the earth, unto the lands of their inheritance. 8. And it shall come to pass that they shall be gathered in from their long dispersion, from the isles of the sea, and from the four parts of the earth; and the nations of the Gentiles shall be great in the eyes of me, saith God, in carrying them forth to the lands of their inheritance. (*Jacob recites the words of the Lord to the people of Nephi, 559-545 B.C.*) 2Ne.10:7-8

**James E. Talmage**
It is evident from these and many other scriptures that the time of the full recovery or redemption of the Jews is to be determined by their acceptance of Christ as their Lord. When that time comes, they are to be gathered to the land of their fathers; and in the work of gathering, the Gentiles are destined to take a great and honorable part, as witness the further words of Nephi: "But behold, thus saith the Lord God: When the day cometh that they shall believe in me, that I am Christ, then have I covenanted with their fathers that they shall be restored in the flesh, upon the earth, unto the lands of their inheritance. And it shall come to pass that they shall be gathered in from their long dispersion, from the isles of the sea, and from the four parts of the earth; and the nations of the Gentiles

shall be great in the eyes of me, saith God, carrying them forth to the land of their inheritance. Yea, the kings of the Gentiles shall be nursing fathers unto them, and their queens shall become nursing mothers; wherefore, the promises of the Lord are great unto the Gentiles, for he hath spoken it, and who can dispute?" AF:303

**President Brigham Young,**
*quoted by John A. Widtsoe*
When the Savior visits Jerusalem, and the Jews look upon him, and see the wounds in his hands and in his side and in his feet, they will then know that they have persecuted and put to death the true Messiah, and then they will acknowledge him, but not till then. They have confounded his first and second coming, expecting his first coming to be as a mighty prince instead of as a servant. They will go back by and by to Jerusalem and own their Lord and Master. (*In Tabernacle, Dec. 23, 1866, JD11:279*) DBY:122

**Related Witnesses:**

**Isaiah,**
*quoted by Nephi, son of Lehi*
And he shall set up an ensign for the nations, and shall assemble the outcasts of Israel, and gather together the dispersed of Judah from the four corners of the earth. (*Nephi records the words of Isaiah from the brass plates, 559-545 B.C.*) 2Ne.21:12

**Nephi, son of Lehi**
Wherefore, he will bring them again out of captivity, and they shall be gathered together to the lands of their inheritance; and they shall be brought out of obscurity and out of darkness; and they shall know that the Lord is their Savior and their Redeemer, the Mighty One of Israel. (*Nephi expounds on the prophecies regarding the scattering and gathering of Israel written on the plates of brass, 588-570 B.C.*) 1Ne.22:12

**Bruce R. McConkie**
Now I call your attention to the facts, set forth in these scriptures, that the gathering of Israel consists of joining the true Church, of coming to a knowledge of the true God and of his saving truths, and of worshiping him in the congregations of the Saints in all nations and among all peoples. ACR(Mexico City)1972:45

---

**235. The object of gathering the people of God in any age is for their salvation, that they might obtain the ordinances administered in holy temples.**

**Joseph Smith**

What was the object of gathering the Jews, or the people of God in any age of the world?. . . ¶ The main object was to build unto the Lord a house whereby He could reveal unto His people the ordinances of His house and the glories of His kingdom, and teach the people the way of salvation; for there are certain ordinances and principles that, when they are taught and practiced, must be done in a place or house built for that purpose. ¶ It was the design of the councils of heaven before the world was, that the principles and laws of the priesthood should be predicated upon the gathering of the people in every age of the world. Jesus did everything to gather the people, and they would not be gathered, and He therefore poured out curses upon them. Ordinances instituted in the heavens before the foundation of the world, in the priesthood, for the salvation of men, are not to be altered or changed. All must be saved on the same principles. ¶ It is for the same purpose that God gathers together His people in the last days, to build unto the Lord a house to prepare them for the ordinances and endowments, washings and anointings, etc. . . . ¶ Why gather the people together in this place? For the same purpose that Jesus wanted to gather the Jews—to receive the ordinances, the blessings, and glories that God has in store for His Saints. (*At the Stand in Nauvoo, Ill., June 11, 1843*) HC5:423-424,427

**President Brigham Young,**
*quoted by John A. Widtsoe*

We have been gathered to the valleys of these mountains for the express purpose of purifying ourselves, that we may become polished stones in the temple of God. We are here for the purpose of establishing the Kingdom of God on the earth. To be prepared for this work it has been necessary to gather us out from the nations and countries of the world, for if we had remained in those lands we could not have received the ordinances of the holy Priesthood of the Son of God, which are necessary for the perfection of the Saints preparatory to his coming. (*In old Tabernacle, Feb. 16, 1868, JD12:161*) DBY:121

**George Albert Smith (1817-1875)**

What is the gathering for? Why was it that the Savior wished the children of Israel to gather together? It was that they might become united and provide a place wherein he could reveal unto them keys which have been hid from before the foundation of the world; that he could unfold unto them the laws of exaltation, and

make them a kingdom of Priests, even the whole people, and exalt them to thrones and dominions in the celestial world. (*In Tabernacle, March 18, 1855, JD2:214*) TLDP:209

**Related Witnesses:**

**Melvin J. Ballard**

When the day comes that the Gentile nations shall close their doors, and their time is ended so far as preaching the gospel is concerned, then cometh the day when the promise of the Lord made to the house of Israel—all branches of the house shall be remembered—and he shall fulfill his promises. I declare unto you that the day of the dawning of the redemption of all branches of the house of Israel is at hand. The Lord has brought the Latter-day Saints up into these mountains to put them in training to prepare them to perform a great service, even as he took Joseph away from his brethren, and separated him from them and took him into the land of Egypt to make him a Savior for all of the house of Israel. In a like manner he has separated and brought out from the nations of the world Joseph's descendants to make them in the last days a Savior to all the branches of the house of Israel. (Sermons and Missionary Services of Melvin J. Ballard, p. 145) TLDP:209

**President Spencer W. Kimball**

Now, the gathering of Israel consists of joining the true church and their coming to a knowledge of the true God. . . . Any person, therefore, who has accepted the restored gospel, and who now seeks to worship the Lord in his own tongue and with the Saints in the nations where he lives, has complied with the law of the gathering of Israel and is heir to all of the blessings promised the Saints in these last days. (*Honolulu Area Conference, June 1978*) (The Teachings of Spencer W. Kimball, p. 439) TLDP:212

**Elder Joseph Fielding Smith**

The Lord has caused Israel to mix with the nations and bring the Gentiles within the blessings of the seed of Abraham. We are preaching the gospel now in all parts of the world, and for what purpose? To gather out from the Gentile nations the lost sheep of the house of Israel. It is by this scattering that the Gentile nations have been blessed, and if they will truly repent they are entitled to all the blessings promised to Israel, "which are the blessings of salvation, even of life eternal." (Answers to Gospel Questions, 2:57) TLDP:210

## HYMNS Written by Prophets
## Applicable to this Topic

### Parley P. Pratt
*An Angel from on High,* 5th verse
HYMNS:13

Lo! Israel filled with joy
Shall now be gathered home,
Their wealth and means employ
To build Jerusalem,
While Zion shall arise and shine
And fill the earth with truth divine,
While Zion shall arise and shine
And fill the earth with truth divine.

### Parley P. Pratt
*Come, O Thou King of Kings*
HYMNS:59

Come, O thou King of Kings!
We've waited long for thee,
With healing in thy wings
To set thy people free.
Come, thou desire of nations, come;
Let Israel now be gathered home.

Come, make an end to sin
And cleanse the earth by fire,
And righteousness bring in,
That Saints may tune the lyre
With songs of joy, a happier strain,
To welcome in thy peaceful reign.

Hosannas now shall sound
From all the ransomed throng,
And glory echo round
A new triumphal song;
The wide expanse of heaven fill
With anthems sweet from Zion's hill.

Hail! Prince of life and peace!
Thrice welcome to thy throne!
While all the chosen race
Their Lord and Savior own,
The heathen nations bow the knee,
And ev'ry tongue sounds praise to thee.

### Parley P. Pratt
*The Morning Breaks,* verses 3,4)
HYMNS:1

The Gentile fulness now comes in,
And Israel's blessings are at hand.
Lo, Judah's remnant, cleansed from sin,
Lo, Judah's remnant, cleansed from sin,
Shall in their promised Canaan stand.

Jehovah speaks! Let earth give ear,
And Gentile nations turn and live.
His mighty arm is making bare,
His mighty arm is making bare
His cov'nant people to receive.

### John Taylor
*Go, Ye Messengers of Heaven*
HYMNS:327

Go, ye messengers of heaven,
Chosen by divine command;
Go and publish free salvation
To a dark, benighted land.

Go to island, vale, and mountain;
There fulfill the great command;
Gather out the sons of Jacob
To possess the promised land.

When your thousands all are gathered,
And their prayers for you ascend,
And the Lord has crowned with blessings
All the labors of your hand,

Then the song of joy and transport
Will from ev'ry land resound;
Then the nations long in darkness
By the Savior will be crowned.

# List of Doctrines

## GIFTS OF THE SPIRIT

### Spiritual Gifts and Talents

*Doctrines Located in This Topic*

236. Spiritual gifts are distributed among the members of the Church.

237. Some are given the gift of speaking in tongues; others are given the interpretation of tongues.

238. Some are given the gift of prophecy and revelation.

239. The testimony of Jesus is the spirit of prophecy.

240. Some are given the gift of visions.

241. Some are given the gift of faith to heal the sick.

242. Some are given the gift of faith to be healed.

243. Some are given the gift of casting out devils.

244. Some are given the gift of working miracles.

245. Some are given the gift of faith.

246. Those appointed by the Lord to watch over the Church are entitled to the discernment of all the gifts of the Spirit.

247. A gift from God may be taken away when a person fails to heed the counsel of God; the light received shall be taken from the person who does not repent.

*Doctrines on GIFTS OF THE SPIRIT Located in Other Topics*

92. Members of the Church are to live the law of consecration when called upon to do so: they are to be ready at all times to consecrate their time, talents, money, and property to the building up of the kingdom of God on earth.

559. As spirit children of God in the premortal world we were not all alike; each of us had different talents and dispositions.

644. The Lord gave Joseph Smith the gift to translate the Book of Mormon plates, that this generation would have the word of the Lord.

# GIFTS OF THE SPIRIT

## Spiritual Gifts and Talents

**236. Spiritual gifts are distributed among the members of the Church.**

### Elder Joseph Fielding Smith

That the Saints might not be deceived, the Lord pointed out to them the proper gifts of the Spirit (D&C:46) which are distributed among the members as the Lord sees good to bestow. Yet more than one gift may be received by any person who diligently seeks for these things. All members of the Church should seek for the gift of prophecy, for their own guidance, which is the spirit by which the word of the Lord is understood and his purpose made known. (See 1 Cor. 14:1) Men who are called to positions of responsibility in the government of the Church are entitled to have many gifts, and the President all of them, "lest there shall be any among you professing and yet be not of God." CHMR1:201

### Joseph Smith,
*receiving the Word of the Lord*

[S]eek ye earnestly the best gifts, always remembering for what they are given; 9. For verily I say unto you, they are given for the benefit of those who love me and keep all my commandments, and him that seeketh so to do; that all may be benefited that seek or that ask of me, that ask and not for a sign that they may consume it upon their lusts. 10. And again, verily I say unto you, I would that ye should always remember, and always retain in your minds what those gifts are, that are given unto the church. 11. For all have not every gift given unto them; for there are many gifts, and to every man is given a gift by the Spirit of God. 12. To some is given one, and to some is given another, that all may be profited thereby. 13. To some it is given by the Holy Ghost to know that Jesus Christ is the Son of God, and that he was crucified for the sins of the world. 14. To others it is given to believe on their words, that they also might have eternal life if they continue faithful. 15. And again, to some it is given by the Holy Ghost to know the differences of administration, as it will be pleasing unto the same Lord, according as the Lord will, suiting his mercies according to the conditions of the children of men. 16. And again, it is given by the Holy Ghost to some to know the diversities of operations, whether they be of God, that the manifestations of the Spirit may be given to every man to profit withal. 17. And again, verily I say unto

you, to some is given, by the Spirit of God, the word of wisdom. 18. To another is given the word of knowledge, that all may be taught to be wise and to have knowledge. 19. And again, to some it is given to have faith to be healed; 20. And to others it is given to have faith to heal. 21. And again, to some is given the working of miracles; 22. And to others it is given to prophesy; 23. And to others the discerning of spirits. 24. And again, it is given to some to speak with tongues; 25. And to another is given the interpretation of tongues. 26. And all these gifts come from God, for the benefit of the children of God. (*Revelation relative to the gifts of the Spirit, March 8, 1831*) D&C 46:8-26

### Paul

Now concerning spiritual gifts, brethren, I would not have you ignorant. 2. Ye know that ye were Gentiles, carried away unto these dumb idols, even as ye were led. 3. Wherefore I give you to understand, that no man speaking by the Spirit of God calleth Jesus accursed: and that no man can say that Jesus is the Lord, but by the Holy Ghost. 4. Now there are diversities of gifts, but the same Spirit. 5. And there are differences of administrations, but the same Lord. 6. And there are diversities of operations, but it is the same God which worketh all in all. 7. But the manifestation of the Spirit is given to every man to profit withal. 8. For to one is given by the Spirit the word of wisdom; to another the word of knowledge by the same Spirit; 9. To another faith by the same Spirit; to another the gifts of healing by the same Spirit; 10. To another the working of miracles; to another prophecy; to another discerning of spirits; to another divers kinds of tongues; to another the interpretation of tongues: 11. But all these worketh that one and the selfsame Spirit, dividing to every man severally as he will. (*Paul writes to the Church at Corinth, Greece, about A.D. 55*) 1Cor.12:1-11

### Moroni, son of Mormon

For behold, to one is given by the Spirit of God, that he may teach the word of wisdom; 10. And to another, that he may teach the word of knowledge by the same Spirit; 11. And to another, exceedingly great faith; and to another, the gifts of healing by the same Spirit; 12. And again, to another, that he may work mighty miracles; 13. And again, to another, that he may prophesy concerning all things; 14. And again, to another, the beholding of angels and ministering spirits; 15. And again, to another, all kinds of tongues; 16. And again, to another, the interpretation of languages and of divers kinds of tongues. 17. And all these gifts come by the Spirit of Christ; and they come unto every man severally, according as he will. (*Moroni's final writings, about A.D. 421*) Moro.10:9-17

### Marion G. Romney,
*also quoting Moroni*

Among the gifts of the spirit manifest in the Apostolic Church, Paul lists wisdom, knowledge, faith, healing, working of miracles, prophesy, discerning of spirits, diverse kinds of tongues, and the interpretation of tongues. The New Testament records numerous examples of the manifestation of these gifts. ¶ Among the Jaredites and Nephites, the manifestations of these gifts were likewise prevalent. Mormon testified that they would not cease except for unbelief, ". . . so long as time shall last, or the earth shall stand, or there shall be one man upon the face thereof to be saved." (Moroni 7:36) CR1956Apr:69

**Related Witnesses:**

### Joseph Smith,
*receiving the Word of the Lord*

If thou shalt ask, thou shalt receive revelation upon revelation, knowledge upon knowledge, that thou mayest know the mysteries and peaceable things—that which bringeth joy, that which bringeth life eternal. (*Revelation "embracing the law of the Church," Feb. 9, 1831*) D&C 42:61

### Joseph Smith,
*quoted by Elder Joseph Fielding Smith*

. . . Paul says, "To one is given the gift of tongues, to another the gift of prophecy, and to another the gift of healing;" and again: "Do all prophesy? do all speak with tongues? do all interpret?" evidently showing that all did not possess these several gifts; but that one received one gift, and another received another gift—all did not prophesy, all did not speak in tongues, all did not work miracles; but all did receive the gift of the Holy Ghost; sometimes they spake in tongues and prophesied in the Apostles' days, and sometimes they did not. The same is the case with us also in our administrations, while more frequently there is no manifestation at all, that is visible to the surrounding multitude. . . . (Editorial in Times and Seasons, June 15, 1842) TPJS:243-44; DGSM:45

### Joseph Smith

Because faith is wanting, the fruits are. No man since the world was had faith without having something along with it. The ancients quenched the violence of fire, escaped the edge of the sword, women received their dead, &c. By faith the worlds were made. A man who has none of the gifts has no faith; and he deceives himself, if he supposes he has. Faith

has been wanting, not only among the heathen, but in professed Christendom also, so that tongues, healings, prophecy, and prophets and apostles, and all the gifts and blessings have been wanting. (*Journal entry of the Prophet, Jan. 2, 1843*) HC5:218

### Joseph Smith

We believe in the gift of tongues, prophecy, revelation, visions, healing, interpretation of tongues, and so forth. (*The seventh of the thirteen Articles of Faith; letter to John Wentworth, March 1, 1842*) AofF:7

### Jesus,
*recorded in Mark*

And these signs shall follow them that believe; In my name shall they cast out devils; they shall speak with new tongues; 18. They shall take up serpents; and if they drink any deadly thing, it shall not hurt them; they shall lay hands on the sick, and they shall recover. (*The risen Jesus Christ to the eleven Apostles*) Mark 16:17-18

---

**237. Some are given the gift of speaking in tongues; others are given the interpretation of tongues.**

### Joseph Smith

And again, it is given to some to speak with tongues; 25. And to another is given the interpretation of tongues. 26. And all these gifts come from God, for the benefit of the children of God. (*Revelation relative to governing and conducting meetings, March 8, 1831*) D&C 46:24-26

### Paul

But the manifestation of the Spirit is given to every man to profit withal. 8. For to one is given by the Spirit the word of wisdom; . . . 10. . . . [T]o another divers kinds of tongues; to another the interpretation of tongues: (*Paul writes to the Church at Corinth, Greece, about A.D. 55*) 1Cor.12:7-8,10

### Elder Heber J. Grant

I know that there are no gifts, no graces, no authority, which were possessed in the days of the Savior by his apostles which are not possessed today by the people of God. I know that the gift of tongues and the interpretation thereof exist in this Church of Christ. CR1917Oct:14

### Elder Joseph F. Smith

There is perhaps no gift of the spirit of God more easily imitated by the devil than the gift of tongues. . . . ¶ I believe in the gifts of the Holy Spirit unto men, but I do not want the gifts of tongues, except when I need it. . . . ¶ So far as I am concerned, if the Lord will give me ability to teach the people in my native tongue, or in their own language to the understanding of those that hear me, that will be sufficient gift of tongues to me. Yet if the Lord gives you the gift of tongues, do not despise it, do not reject it. For if it comes from the Spirit of God, it will come to those who are worthy to receive it, and it is all right. CR1900Apr:41

**Related Witnesses:**

**Joseph Smith**

Be not so curious about tongues, do not speak in tongues except there be an interpreter present; the ultimate design of tongues is to speak to foreigners, and if persons are very anxious to display their intelligence, let them speak to such in their own tongues. The gifts of God are all useful in their place, but when they are applied to that which God does not intend, they prove an injury, a snare and a curse instead of a blessing. *(The risen Jesus Christ to the eleven Apostles)* HC5:31

**Jesus,**
*recorded in Mark*

And these signs shall follow them that believe; In my name shall they cast out devils; they shall speak with new tongues; *(The risen Jesus Christ to the eleven Apostles)* Mark 16:17

**Moroni, son of Mormon**

And these signs shall follow them that believe—in my name shall they cast out devils; they shall speak with new tongues; they shall take up serpents; and if they drink any deadly thing it shall not hurt them; they shall lay hands on the sick and they shall recover; *(Moroni calls upon those who do not believe in Christ to repent, A.D. 400-421)* Morm.9:24

**Joseph Smith**

We believe in the gift of tongues, prophecy, revelation, visions, healing, interpretation of tongues, and so forth. *(The seventh of the thirteen Articles of Faith; letter to John Wentworth, March 1, 1842)* AofF:7

---

**238.** Some are given the gift of prophecy and revelation.

**Joseph Smith**

And to others it is given to prophesy; *(Revelation relative to the gifts of the Spirit, March 8, 1831)* D&C 46:22

**Joseph Smith,**
*receiving the Word of the Lord*

If thou shalt ask, thou shalt receive revelation upon revelation, knowledge upon knowledge, that thou mayest know the mysteries and peaceable things—that which bringeth joy, that which bringeth life eternal. *(Revelation "embracing the law of the Church," Feb. 9, 1831)* D&C 42:61

**Paul**

But the manifestation of the Spirit is given to every man to profit withal. 8. For to one is given by the Spirit the word of wisdom; . . . 10. . . . [T]o another prophecy; *(Paul writes to the Church at Corinth, Greece, about A.D. 55)* 1Cor.12:7-8,10

**Joseph Smith**

We believe in the gift of tongues, prophecy, revelation, visions, healing, interpretation of tongues, and so forth. *(The seventh of the thirteen Articles of Faith; letter to John Wentworth, March 1, 1842)* AofF:7

**Joseph Smith**

Deny not the spirit of revelation, nor the spirit of prophecy, for wo unto him that denieth these things; *(Revelation for Hyrum Smith, May 1829)* D&C 11:25

**Related Witnesses:**

**Paul**

Now, brethren, if I come unto you speaking with tongues, what shall I profit you, except I shall speak to you either by revelation, or by knowledge, or by prophesying, or by doctrine? *(Paul writes to the Church at Corinth, Greece, about A.D. 55)* 1Cor.14:6

**Jacob, brother of Nephi**

Behold, great and marvelous are the works of the Lord. How unsearchable are the depths of the mysteries of him; and it is impossible that man should find out all his ways. And no man knoweth of his ways save it be revealed unto him; wherefore, brethren, despise not the revelations of God. *(Jacob makes his record on plates of metal, 544-421 B.C.)* Jacob 4:8

**Mormon**

But this is not all; they had given themselves to much prayer, and fasting; therefore they had the spirit of prophecy, and the spirit of revelation, and when they taught, they taught with power and authority of God. *(Mormon recounts the activities of the spiritually devoted sons of Mosiah)* Alma 17:3

**Elder Joseph Fielding Smith**

All members of the Church should seek for the gift of prophecy, for their own guidance, which is the spirit by which the word of the Lord is understood and his purpose made known. (See 1Cor.14:1.) CHMR1:201

**Bruce R. McConkie**

Most persons with the spirit of testimony, of inspiration, and of prophecy are prophets to themselves only, or to their families. Some are called to preside over and give inspired guidance to one organization or another. (The Promised Messiah, pp. 24-25) TLDP:606

**239. The testimony of Jesus is the spirit of prophecy.**

**John**

The testimony of Jesus is the spirit of prophecy. (*An angel teaches John about the testimony of Jesus*) Rev.19:10

**Bruce R. McConkie**

The testimony of Jesus is the spirit of prophecy; both testimony and prophecy come by the power of the Holy Ghost; and any person who receives the revelation that Jesus is the Lord is a prophet and can, as occasion requires and when guided by the Spirit, "prophesy of all things." (The Promised Messiah, p. 23) TLDP:539-40

**Joseph Smith**

If any person should ask me if I were a prophet, I should not deny it, as that would give me the lie; for, according to John, the testimony of Jesus is the spirit of prophecy; therefore if I profess to be a witness or teacher, and have not the spirit of prophecy, which is the testimony of Jesus, I must be a false witness; but if I be a true teacher and witness, I must possess the spirit of prophecy, and that constitutes a prophet; and any man who says he is a teacher or preacher of righteousness, and denies the spirit of prophecy, is a liar, and the truth is not in him; and by this key false teachers and impostors may be detected. (*Joseph explains the nature of a prophet to several prominent Gentiles in Nauvoo, Ill., Jan. 1, 1843*) HC5:215-16

**Elder Wilford Woodruff**

He [Brigham Young] is a prophet. I am a prophet, you are, and anybody is a prophet who has the testimony of Jesus Christ, for that is the spirit of prophecy. The Elders of Israel are prophets. A prophet is not so great as an Apostle. Christ has set in his Church, first, Apostles; they hold the keys of the kingdom of God. (*In Tabernacle, Dec. 12, 1869, JD13:165*) TLDP:684

**240. Some are given the gift of visions.**

**Elder Heber J. Grant**

Holy men and holy women have had heavenly visions, by the hundred and by the thousands, yea, by the tens of thousands since this Gospel was restored to the earth in our day. CR1912Oct:92

**President Brigham Young**

God never bestows upon His people, or upon an individual, superior blessings without a severe trial to prove them, to prove that individual, or that people, to see whether they will keep their covenants with Him, and keep in remembrance what He has shown them. Then the greater the vision, the greater the display of the power of the enemy. . . . ¶ So when individuals are blessed with visions, revelations, and great manifestations, look out, then the devil is nigh you, and you will be tempted in proportion to the vision, revelation, or manifestation you have received. (*In Tabernacle, Feb. 17, 1856, JD3:205-06*) TLDP:647-48

**Joel**

And it shall come to pass afterward, that I will pour out my spirit upon all flesh; and your sons and your daughters shall prophesy, your old men shall dream dreams, your young men shall see visions: (*Joel, a prophet of Judah, prophesies*) Joel 2:28

**Related Witnesses:**

**Joseph Smith**

We believe in the gift of tongues, prophecy, revelation, visions, healing, interpretation of tongues, and so forth. (*The seventh of the thirteen Articles of Faith; letter to John Wentworth, March 1, 1842*) AofF:7

**Joseph Smith**

We may look for angels and receive their ministration, but we are to try the spirits and prove them, for it is often the case that men make a mistake in regard to these things. God has so ordained that when he has communicated, no vision is to be taken but what you see by the seeing of the eye, or what you hear by the hearing of the ear. When you see a vision, pray for the interpretation; if you get not this, shut it up; there must be certainty in this matter. (*The Prophet instructs the Twelve on priesthood, in the vicinity of Commerce, Ill., July 2, 1839*) HC3:391-92

**Moses**

And God spake unto Israel in the visions of the night, and said, Jacob, Jacob. And he said, Here am I. (*The Lord sends Jacob and his family to Egypt; speaks to Jacob in vision*) Gen.46:2

**Ezekiel**

Now it came to pass in the thirtieth year, in the fourth month, in the fifth day of the month, as I was among the captives by the river of Chebar, that the heavens were opened, and I saw visions of God. (*Ezekiel the prophet receives a vision from God*) Ezek.1:1

**Daniel**

I saw in the night visions, and, behold, one like the Son of man came with the clouds of heaven, and came to the Ancient of days, and they brought him near before him. (*Daniel dreams visions and records them*) Dan.7:13

**Recorded in Acts**

Then spake the Lord to Paul in the night by a vision, Be not afraid, but speak, and hold not thy peace: (*Paul takes the gospel to the Gentiles and is instructed by the Lord*) Acts 18:9

**Nephi, son of Lehi**

And now I, Nephi, do not make a full account of the things which my father hath written, for he hath written many things which he saw in visions and in dreams; and he also hath written many things which he prophesied and spake unto his children, of which I shall not make a full account. (*Nephi begins the record of his people, about 600 B.C.*) 1Ne.1:16

**Nephi, son of Lehi**

Behold, he hath heard my cry by day, and he hath given me knowledge by visions in the nighttime. (*Nephi writes on plates shortly after the death of his father, Lehi, 588-570 B.C.*) 2Ne.4:23

**Joseph Smith**

Some few days after I had this vision, I happened to be in company with one of the Methodist preachers, who was very active in the before mentioned religious excitement; and, conversing with him on the subject of religion, I took occasion to give him an account of the vision which I had had. I was greatly surprised at his behavior; he treated my communication not only lightly, but with great contempt, saying it was all of the devil, that there were no such things as visions or revelations in these days; that all such things had ceased with the apostles, and that there would never be any more of them. (*Joseph testifies of the reality of the First Vision*) JS-H 1:21

---

**241. Some are given the gift of faith to heal the sick.**

**James E. Talmage**

Though the authority to administer to the sick belongs to the elders of the Church in general, some possess this power in an unusual degree, having received it as an especial endowment of the Spirit. Another gift, allied to this, is that of having faith to be healed, which is manifested in varying degrees. Not always are the administrations of the elders followed by immediate healings; the afflicted may be permitted to suffer in body, perhaps for the accomplishment of good purposes, and in the time appointed all must experience bodily death. But let the counsels of God be observed in administering to the afflicted; then if they recover, they live unto the Lord; and the assuring promise is added that those who die under such conditions die unto the Lord. AF:205

**Joseph Smith**

And again, to some it is given to have faith to

be healed; 20. And to others it is given to have faith to heal. (*Revelation relative to governing and conducting meetings, March 8, 1831*) D&C 46:19-20

**Related Witnesses:**

**Paul**

To another faith by the same Spirit; to another the gifts of healing by the same Spirit; (*Paul writes to the Church at Corinth, Greece, about A.D. 55*) 1Cor.12:9

**Joseph Smith**

We believe in the gift of tongues, prophecy, revelation, visions, healing, interpretation of tongues, and so forth. (*The seventh of the thirteen Articles of Faith; letter to John Wentworth, March 1, 1842*) AofF:7

**Moroni, son of Mormon**

And these signs shall follow them that believe—in my name shall they cast out devils; they shall speak with new tongues; they shall take up serpents; and if they drink any deadly thing it shall not hurt them; they shall lay hands on the sick and they shall recover; (*Moroni calls upon those who do not believe in Christ to repent, A.D. 400-421*) Morm.9:24

**Recorded in Mark**

And he ordained twelve, that they should be with him, and that he might send them forth to preach, 15. And to have power to heal sicknesses, and to cast out devils: (*Jesus chooses and ordains the Twelve Apostles*) Mark 3:14-15

**Jesus,**
**recorded in Matthew**

Heal the sick, cleanse the lepers, raise the dead, cast out devils: freely ye have received, freely give. (*Jesus instructs, empowers, and sends the Twelve Apostles forth to preach, to minister, and to heal the sick*) Matt.10:8

**Recorded in Mark**

And they cast out many devils, and anointed with oil many that were sick, and healed them. (*The Twelve Apostles are sent to preach repentance*) Mark 6:13

**President Brigham Young,**
**quoted by John A. Widtsoe**

When I lay hands on the sick, I expect the healing power and influence of God to pass through me to the patient, and the disease to give away. I do not say that I heal everybody I lay hands on; but many have been healed under my administration. Jesus said, on one occasion. "Who has touched me?" A woman had crept up behind him in the crowd, and touched the hem of his garment, and he knew it, because virtue had gone from him. Do you see the reason and propriety of laying hands on each other? When we are prepared, when we are holy vessels before the Lord, a stream of power from the Almighty can pass through the tabernacle of the administrator to the system of the patient, and the sick are made whole; the headache, fever or other disease has to give away. My brethren and sisters, there is virtue in us if we will do right; if we live our religion we are the temples of God wherein he will dwell; if we defile ourselves, these temples God will destroy. (*In Ogden Utah Tabernacle, July 10, 1870, JD14:72*) DBY:162

---

### 242. Some are given the gift of faith to be healed.

#### Joseph Smith,
*receiving the Word of the Lord*
And whosoever among you are sick, and have not faith to be healed, but believe, shall be nourished with all tenderness, with herbs and mild food, and that not by the hand of an enemy. . . . 48. And again, it shall come to pass that he that hath faith in me to be healed, and is not appointed unto death, shall be healed. 49. He who hath faith to see shall see. 50. He who hath faith to hear shall hear. 51. The lame who hath faith to leap shall leap. 52. And they who have not faith to do these things, but believe in me, have power to become my sons; and inasmuch as they break not my laws thou shalt bear their infirmities. (*Revelation "embracing the law of the Church," Feb. 9, 1831; administration to the sick*) D&C 42:43,48-52

#### Joseph Smith
And again, to some it is given to have faith to be healed; 20. And to others it is given to have faith to heal. (*Revelation relative to governing and conducting meetings, March 8, 1831*) D&C 46:19-20

#### Joseph Smith
The sick will be healed, the lame made to walk, the deaf to hear, and the blind to see, through your instrumentality. But let me tell you, that you will not have power, after the endowment to heal those that have not faith, nor to benefit them, for you might as well expect to benefit a devil in hell as such as are possessed of his spirit, and are willing to keep it; for they are habitations for devils, and only fit for his society. (*Remarks made in meeting with the Council of the Twelve, Nov. 12, 1835*) HC2:309

#### James E. Talmage
Another gift . . . is that of having faith to be healed, which is manifested in varying degrees. Not always are the administrations of the elders followed by immediate healings; the afflicted

may be permitted to suffer in body, perhaps for the accomplishment of good purposes, and in the time appointed all must experience bodily death. But let the counsels of God be observed in administering to the afflicted; then if they recover, they live unto the Lord; and the assuring promise is added that those who die under such conditions die unto the Lord. AF:205

#### Heber C. Kimball
It would be singular to have a priesthood that would not enable me to bless myself. I have laid hands upon myself when I could not get access to other Elders, and I have been healed just as soon as if anybody else had done it. (Deseret News Weekly, Aug. 20, 1862, p. 58) TLDP:651-52

#### Bruce R. McConkie
Every miracle is unique; no two are alike. Two blind men have their eyes opened by divine power, and each wondrous deed is as different from the other as are the two recipients of the heaven-sent goodness. Those few of Jesus' miracles which are recorded in any sort of detail were selected from the many by the spirit of inspiration; such accounts preserve for us patterns and types of miraculous acts, with a view to encouraging us—whatever our disabled or diseased condition may be—to ourselves rely on Him by whose power miracles are wrought, and to seek to gain an outpouring of his goodness and grace in our own lives. ¶ Further, all healings do not happen instantaneously; the prophetic fingers do not always snap and cause a prostrate sufferer to leap from his pallet as though by magic. A sightless one may be sent to wash the spittle and clay from his eyes in the pool of Siloam, a leper may be required to immerse seven times in Jordan; a suffering soul may be tested to the full before hearing the blessed words: "Be it unto thee according to thy faith." It is no less a miracle when shattered bones weld themselves together gradually than when they reform in an instant. A withered arm that attains its proper and perfect frame through a growth process may be an exhibition of as great a miracle as one that bursts suddenly into being. (The Mortal Messiah, 3:28) TLDP:652

**Related Witnesses:**
#### Recorded in Acts
And there sat a certain man at Lystra, impotent in his feet, being a cripple from his mother's womb, who never had walked: 9. The same heard Paul speak: who stedfastly beholding him, and perceiving that he had faith to be healed, 10. Said with a loud voice, Stand upright on thy feet. And he leaped and walked. (*Paul heals a cripple*) Acts 14:8-10

**Author's Note:** The very phenomenon of a priesthood blessing recipient feeling the great love of God and the marvelous power of His priesthood as it is transmitted through the administrating elders surrounding and lovingly placing hands on the head of the individual being blessed, brings peace and joy and contributes much to the healing process. "It is not the gift but the hand of the giver that is everything," writes Hugh Nibley. "It is the awareness in receiving the gift that it comes from the infinite and inexhaustible love [of God]" that counts. "Many a person afflicted with a sore but temporary illness," he writes, "upon being healed by the ministrations of the priesthood, has shouted for joy. But if he was bound to get well anyway, where is the thrill of it? Again, it is not the gift but the hand of the giver that is everything." (Approaching Zion, p. 147, by Hugh Nibley)

---

243. **Some are given the gift of casting out devils.**

### Jesus,
*recorded in Mark*

And these signs shall follow them that believe; In my name shall they cast out devils; they shall speak with new tongues; 18. They shall take up serpents; and if they drink any deadly thing, it shall not hurt them; they shall lay hands on the sick, and they shall recover. (*The risen Jesus Christ to the eleven Apostles*) Mark 16:17-18

### Moroni, son of Mormon

And these signs shall follow them that believe—in my name shall they cast out devils; they shall speak with new tongues; they shall take up serpents; and if they drink any deadly thing it shall not hurt them; they shall lay hands on the sick and they shall recover; (*Moroni calls upon those who do not believe in Christ to repent, A.D. 400-421*) Morm.9:24

### Joseph Smith,
*receiving the Word of the Lord*

And whoso shall ask it in my name in faith, they shall cast out devils; they shall heal the sick; they shall cause the blind to receive their sight, and the deaf to hear, and the dumb to speak, and the lame to walk. (*Revelation to Joseph and to Sidney Rigdon, Dec. 1830*) D&C 35:9

**Related Witnesses:**
### Jesus,
*recorded in Matthew*

Heal the sick, cleanse the lepers, raise the dead, cast out devils: freely ye have received, freely give. (*Jesus instructs, empowers, and sends the Twelve Apostles forth to preach, minister, and heal the sick*) Matt.10:8

### Recorded in Mark

And he ordained twelve, that they should be with him, and that he might send them forth to preach, 15. And to have power to heal sicknesses, and to cast out devils: (*Jesus instructs, empowers, and sends the Twelve Apostles forth to preach, minister, and heal the sick*) Mark 3:14-15

### Recorded in Mark

And they cast out many devils, and anointed with oil many that were sick, and healed them. (*The Twelve Apostles are sent to preach repentance*) Mark 6:13

### Mormon

And in the name of Jesus did he cast out devils and unclean spirits; and even his brother did he raise from the dead, after he had been stoned and suffered death by the people. 20. And the people saw it, and did witness of it, and were angry with him because of his power; and he did also do many more miracles, in the sight of the people, in the name of Jesus. (*Mormon records how Nephi preached repentance and faith in Christ, A.D. 31-32*) 3Ne.7:19-20

### Heber C. Kimball

I have no fears of anything myself; I do not fear all the devils in hell nor on the earth. I have seen the time, whether in the body or out of it, I do not know, but I saw legions of devils; they came by thousands and tens of thousands, and thousands of men will, no doubt, give way before them and yield the field; but when they came against me and my brethren, we having the priesthood had power to withstand them all, for we were of God. You have heard President Young preach that a man, with the power of God upon him, all the devils in hell could not do anything with him; but if a man enters into the spirit world in his sins, the devil will have power over him to lead him captive at his will. (Deseret News Weekly, Aug. 20, 1862, p. 58) TLDP:139

### Nephi, son of Lehi

And he spake unto me again, saying: Look! And I looked, and I beheld the Lamb of God going forth among the children of men. And I beheld multitudes of people who were sick, and who were afflicted with all manner of diseases, and with devils and unclean spirits; and the angel spake and showed all these things unto me. And they were healed by the power of the Lamb of God; and the devils and the unclean spirits were cast out. (*In a vision an angel shows Nephi the Lamb of God going among the people healing the sick*) 1Ne.11:31

### Elder John Taylor

The priesthood is placed in the church for this purpose, to dig, to plant, to nourish, to teach correct principles, and to develop the order of the kingdom of God, to fight the devils, and maintain and support the authorities of the church of Christ upon the earth. (*In Tabernacle, April 6, 1861*) (The Gospel Kingdom, p. 129) TLDP:336

## 244. Some are given the gift of working miracles.

**Joseph Smith**

And again, to some is given the working of miracles; (*Revelation relative to the gifts of the Spirit, March 8, 1831*) D&C 46:21

**Paul**

To another the working of miracles. . . . (*Paul writes to the Church at Corinth, Greece, about A.D. 55*) 1Cor.12:10

**Marion G. Romney**

[O]ne who has never received the gift of the Holy Ghost cannot possibly work miracles by his power. . . . ¶ Now, righteous men, bearing the holy priesthood of the living God and endowed with the gift of the Holy Ghost, who are magnifying their callings—and such are the only men upon the earth with the right to receive and exercise the gifts of the spirit—will do so circumspectly and in all humility. They will not spectacularly advertise their divine power nor boast about it. Neither will they display it for money. Of this you may be sure. CR1956Apr:72

**President Brigham Young,**
*quoted by John A. Widtsoe*

Miracles, or these extraordinary manifestations of the power of God, are not for the unbeliever; they are to console the Saints, and to strengthen and confirm the faith of those who love, fear, and serve God, and not for outsiders. (*In Bowery, June 30, 1867, JD12:97*) DBY:341

**Related Witnesses:**

**Mormon**

And in the name of Jesus did he cast out devils and unclean spirits; and even his brother did he raise from the dead, after he had been stoned and suffered death by the people. 20. And the people saw it, and did witness of it, and were angry with him because of his power; and he did also do many more miracles, in the sight of the people, in the name of Jesus. (*Nephi preaches repentance and faith in Christ, A.D. 31-32*) 3Ne.7:19-20

**Bruce R. McConkie,**
*also quoting Jesus*

If there is one thing that always attends and identifies those who believe in Christ it is this: they work miracles. Signs and gifts always attend their ministry. However much it may run counter to the course of Christendom, however severe the indictment may seem, speaking of the gifts of the Spirit, the word of the Lord is: "These signs shall follow them that believe." (Mark 16:17) "And if it so be that the church is built upon my gospel then will the Father show forth his own works in it." (3Ne.27:10) ¶ Anyone who believes what the apostles believed will receive the same gifts they enjoyed, will perform the same miracles, and will do the same works. "He that believeth on me, the works that I do shall he do also." (John 14:12) (The Promised Messiah, p. 298) TLDP:648-49

**Elder Joseph Fielding Smith**

A miracle is not, as many believe, the setting aside or overruling natural laws. Every miracle performed in Biblical days or now, is done on natural principles and in obedience to natural law. The healing of the sick, the raising of the dead, giving eyesight to the blind, whatever it may be that is done by the power of God, is in accordance with natural law. Because we do not understand how it is done, does not argue for the impossibility of it. Our Father in heaven knows many laws that are hidden from us. (Man: His Origin and Destiny, p. 484) TLDP:649

**Joseph Smith,**
*receiving the Word of the Lord*

Require not miracles, except I shall command you, except casting out devils, healing the sick, and against poisonous serpents, and against deadly poisons; (*Revelation, July 1830*) D&C 24:13

## 245. Some are given the gift of faith.

**Paul**

To another faith by the same Spirit. . . . (*Paul writes to the Church at Corinth, Greece, about A.D. 55*) 1Cor.12:9

**President Brigham Young,**
*quoted by John A. Widtsoe*

When you believe the principles of the Gospel and attain unto faith, which is a gift of God, he adds more faith, adding faith to faith. He bestows faith upon his creatures as a gift; but his creatures inherently possess the privilege of believing the Gospel to be true or false. (*In Tabernacle, March 5, 1860, JD8:17*) DBY:154

**John A. Widtsoe**

The gifts of faith are two: knowledge and power. These are to each other as the palm and fingers of a hand, or the charge and the gun to the speeding bullet. Where one is there is the other. These gifts were in the mind of the Apostle Paul when he defined faith as "the substance of things hoped for, the evidence of things not seen." From these chief gifts are derived many lesser ones, such as hope and courage, trust and contentment. Faith, once developed, contributes to the solution of every problem of life. (Man and the Dragon, p. 139) TLDP:178

**Related Witnesses:**

**Moroni, son of Mormon**

And he knoweth their faith, for in his name could they remove mountains; and in his name could they cause the earth to shake; and by the power of his word did they cause prisons to tumble to the earth; yea, even the fiery furnace could not harm them, neither wild beasts nor poisonous serpents, because of the power of his word. (*Moroni writes of the saints who preceded him; about* A.D. *419-420*) Morm.8:24

---

246. **Those appointed by the Lord to watch over the Church are entitled to the discernment of all the gifts of the Spirit.**

**Stephen L. Richards**

The gift of discernment is essential to the leadership of the Church. I never ordain a bishop or set apart a president of a stake without invoking upon him this divine blessing, that he may read the lives and hearts of his people and call forth the best within them. The gift and power of discernment in this world of contention between the forces of good and the power of evil is essential equipment for every son and daughter of God. There could be no such mass dissensions as endanger the security of the world, if its populations possessed this great gift in larger degree. . . . ¶ Every member in the restored Church of Christ could have this gift if he willed to do so. He could not be deceived with the sophistries of the world. He could not be led astray by pseudo-prophets and subversive cults. Even the inexperienced would recognize false teachings, in a measure at least. With this gift they would be able to detect something of the disloyal, rebellious, and sinister influences which not infrequently prompt those who seemingly take pride in the destruction of youthful faith and loyalties. Discerning parents will do well to guard their children against such influences and such personalities and teachings before irreparable damage is done. The true gift of discernment is often premonitory. A sense of danger should be heeded to be of value. We give thanks for a set of providential circumstances which avert an accident. We ought to be grateful every day of our lives for this

sense which keeps alive a conscience which constantly alerts us to the dangers inherent in wrongdoers and sin. CR1950Apr:163

**Joseph Smith**

And unto the bishop of the church, and unto such as God shall appoint and ordain to watch over the church and to be elders unto the church, are to have it given unto them to discern all those gifts lest there shall be any among you professing and yet be not of God. 28. And it shall come to pass that he that asketh in Spirit shall receive in Spirit; 29. That unto some it may be given to have all those gifts, that there may be a head, in order that every member may be profited thereby. (*Revelation relative to governing and conducting meetings, March 8, 1831*) D&C 46:27-29

**Abraham O. Woodruff**

The Saints should be guided by the Spirit of God, and subject to those who preside in the meetings. If the Bishop, who is a common judge in Israel, tells a person to restrain this gift, or any other gift, it is the duty of that person to do it. The Bishop has a right to the gift of discernment, whereby he may tell whether these spirits are of God or not, and if they are not they should not have place in the congregations of the Saints. No man or woman has a right to find fault with the Bishop for restraining him or her in any of these matters. The Bishop is the responsible party; and it is his privilege to say what shall be done under his presidency. CR1901Apr:12; DGSM:45

**Elder Joseph Fielding Smith**

Men who are called to positions of responsibility in the government of the Church are entitled to have many gifts, and the President all of them, "lest there shall be any among you professing and yet be not of God." CHMR1:201

**Joseph Smith**

And again, the duty of the President of the office of the High Priesthood is to preside over the whole church, and to be like unto Moses— 92. Behold, here is wisdom; yea, to be a seer, a revelator, a translator, and a prophet, having all the gifts of God which he bestows upon the head of the church. (*Revelation on priesthood received in council with the Twelve, March 28, 1835*) D&C 107:91-92

---

247. **A gift from God may be taken away when a person fails to heed the counsel of God; the light received shall be taken from the person who does not repent.**

### Elder Joseph F. Smith

[T]he moment a community [of Latter-day Saint people] begin to be wrapt up in themselves, become selfish, become engrossed in the temporalities of life, and put their faith in riches, that moment the power of God begins to withdraw from them, and if they repent not the Holy Spirit will depart from them entirely, and they will be left to themselves. That which was given them will be taken away, they will lose that which they had, for they will not be worthy of it. God is just, as well as merciful, and we need not expect favors at the hand of the Almighty except as we merit them, at least in the honest desires of our hearts; and the desire and intent will not always avail unless our acts correspond. (*General conference, April 8, 1883*) (Gospel Doctrine, p. 51) TLDP:440

### Joseph Smith,
*receiving the Word of the Lord*

And he that repents not, from him shall be taken even the light which he has received; for my spirit shall not always strive with man, saith the Lord of Hosts. (*Revelation received during conference of elders of the Church, Nov. 1, 1831*) D&C 1:33

### Joseph Smith

[W]hen we undertake to cover our sins, or to gratify our pride, our vain ambition, or to exercise control or dominion or compulsion upon the souls of the children of men, in any degree of unrighteousness, behold, the heavens withdraw themselves; the Spirit of the Lord is grieved; and when it is withdrawn, Amen to the priesthood or the authority of that man. (*Revelation received in Liberty Jail, March 20, 1839: why many are called and few chosen*) D&C 121:37

### Joseph Smith,
*receiving the Word of the Lord*

But with some I am not well pleased, for they will not open their mouths, but they hide the talent which I have given unto them, because of the fear of man. Wo unto such, for mine anger is kindled against them. 3. And it shall come to pass, if they are not more faithful unto me, it shall be taken away, even that which they have. (*Revelation for certain elders of the Church, Aug. 8, 1831*) D&C 60:2-3

### Elder Joseph Fielding Smith

The Spirit of the Lord will not dwell in unclean tabernacles, and when the spirit is withdrawn, darkness supersedes the light, and apostasy will follow. This is one of the greatest evidences of the divinity of this latter-day work. In other organizations men may commit all manner of sin and still retain their membership, because they have no companionship with the Holy Ghost to lose: but in the Church when a man sins and continues

without repentance, the Spirit is withdrawn, and when he is left to himself the adversary takes possession of his mind and he denies the faith. (Doctrines of Salvation, 3:309) TLDP:632

### Elder John Taylor

[W]here there is not a feeling of obedience, the Spirit of God will be withdrawn; people cannot retain it and be in rebellion against the authorities and counsels of the church and kingdom of God. (*In Bowery, Sept. 20, 1857, JD5:265*) TLDP:433

### Marion G. Romney

One who has never received the gift of the Holy Ghost cannot possibly work miracles by his power. . . . ¶ Now, righteous men, bearing the holy priesthood of the living God and endowed with the gift of the Holy Ghost, who are magnifying their callings—and such are the only men upon the earth with the right to receive and exercise the gifts of the spirit—will do so circumspectly and in all humility. They will not spectacularly advertise their divine power nor boast about it. Neither will they display it for money. Of this you may be sure. CR1956Apr:72

**Related Witnesses:**

### President Brigham Young

God never bestows upon His people, or upon an individual, superior blessings without a severe trial to prove them, to prove that individual, or that people, to see whether they will keep their covenants with Him, and keep in remembrance what He has shown them. Then the greater the vision, the greater the display of the power of the enemy. . . . ¶ So when individuals are blessed with visions, revelations, and great manifestations, look out, then the devil is nigh you, and you will be tempted in proportion to the vision, revelation, or manifestation you have received. (*In Tabernacle, Feb. 17, 1856, JD3:205-06*) TLDP:647-48

### Joseph Smith,
*receiving the Word of the Lord*

Behold, thou art Joseph, and thou wast chosen to do the work of the Lord, but because of transgression, if thou art not aware thou wilt fall. 10. But remember, God is merciful; therefore, repent of that which thou hast done which is contrary to the commandment which I gave you, and thou art still chosen, and art again called to the work; 11. Except thou do this, thou shalt be delivered up and become as other men and have no more gift. . . . 14. And this is the reason that thou hast lost thy privileges for a season— 15. For thou hast suffered the counsel of thy director to be trampled upon from the beginning. (*Revelation regarding the lost manuscript pages, July 1828*) D&C 3:9-11,14-15

# List of Doctrines

## GOD

*Doctrines Located in This Topic*

### (1) Attributes of Both Father and Son

248. God is a (glorified, exalted) personage in form like us; He has a body of flesh and bones as tangible as ours.

249. God is a just god; He is true and righteous in all things.

250. God is no respecter of persons (He has no favorites except upon grounds of their degree of righteousness).

251. God is merciful.

252. The Lord is a god of truth and cannot lie.

253. The works, designs, and purposes of God cannot be defeated by any person, but must come to pass.

254. All things on the earth and above the earth denote there is a God.

255. Prophets bear witness of God's existence.

256. God is omniscient: He knows all things.

257. God is omnipotent: He has all power, might, and authority.

258. God is omnipresent: through the medium of the Spirit, God is in direct communication with all things at all times.

259. God is the same yesterday, today, and forever; there is no variableness in Him.

260. God loves His children.

261. God has power over the devil.

### (2) Christ the Son

262. Before the earth was created Jesus Christ was with God the Father in a premortal life.

263. Jesus Christ is the firstborn spirit son of God.

264. Jesus Christ was chosen and foreordained to come to earth to perform the atoning sacrifice.

265. Christ was born on earth April 6 (not December 25).

266. Jesus Christ is the only Begotten Son of God in the flesh (in mortality).

267. Christ's spirit body, before His birth on earth, was the same in appearance as His earthly body.

# GOD continued

268. Through the process of death and resurrection, Jesus Christ's spirit was reunited with his body.

269. Christ had power to lay down His life and to take it up again.

270. The resurrected Jesus Christ is a glorified personage in form like man; He has a body of flesh and bones as tangible as man's.

271. The resurrected Jesus Christ possesses a fulness of the glory of the Father.

272. The mission of the Savior is to offer all the human race the sublime privilege of regaining the presence of the Father and of entering into His rest (in the celestial kingdom).

273. Jesus Christ is the mediator between God and all mankind; He is our advocate with the Father.

274. Jesus Christ is Jehovah, the God of the Old Testament.

275. Jesus Christ presides as the God of this world (under the Father).

276. Jesus Christ is the life and light of the world.

277. Only through Christ can we be saved.

278. Jesus Christ is the judge of all.

279. The Son, Jesus Christ, carries out the Father's will.

280. Jesus Christ, the Savior and Son of God, is sometimes referred to as the Father; He is father of the spiritually reborn.

### (3) The Father

281. God the Father is the supreme member of the Godhead.

282. God the Father carries the title of Elohim.

283. God the Father is the literal father of the spirits of all people.

284. God the Father is the spiritual and the physical parent of Jesus Christ.

285. When God the Father appears to mortals it is principally for the purpose of bearing record of the Son.

286. God the Father is to be the object of our worship.

287. God, the Eternal Father, is an exalted man.

## GOD continued

### (4) The Godhead

288. There is a Godhead consisting of God the Eternal Father, His son Jesus Christ, and the Holy Ghost.

289. Each member of the Godhead is physically separate and distinct from the other two.

290. The three members of the Godhead (God the Father, His son Jesus Christ, and the Holy Ghost) are united in purpose.

291. There is but one God, or Godhead, to whom the inhabitants of the earth are subject.

### Doctrines on GOD
### Located in Other Topics

114. Through His son Jesus Christ, God the Father created the earth and all things in the heavens and in earth.

121. God the Father created other worlds through His son Jesus Christ.

176. To obtain exaltation a person must have knowledge that God exists and have a correct idea of His character and attributes.

325. The Holy Ghost is one of three members of the Godhead.

# GOD

(1)  **Attributes of Both Father and Son**
(2)  **Christ the Son (Jehovah, Jesus Christ—
     Creator, Savior, Judge, "Father")**
(3)  **The Father**
(4)  **The Godhead**

## (1) Attributes of Both Father and Son

248.  God is a (glorified, exalted)
      personage in form like us; He has
      a body of flesh and bones as
      tangible as ours.

### Hugh B. Brown

The Church teaches that when God created man
in his own image, he did not divest himself of
that image. He is still in human form and is possessed of sanctified and perfected human qualities, which we all admire. All through the holy
scriptures, the Father and the Son are seen to be
separate and distinct personages. We affirm the
doctrine of the ancient scripture and of the
prophets that asserts that man was created in the
image of God and that God possessed such
human qualities as consciousness, will, love,
mercy, justice. In other words he is an exalted,
perfected, and glorified Being. CR1969Apr:51

### President Joseph F. Smith
### John R. Winder, Anthon H. Lund
(First Presidency)

God Himself is an exalted man, perfected,
enthroned, and supreme. By His almighty
power He organized the earth, and all that it
contains, from spirit and element, which exist
co-eternally with Himself. ("The Origin of
Man," IE1909Nov:81) TLDP:221

### James E. Talmage

[W]e know that both the Father and the Son are
in form and stature perfect men; each of them
possesses a tangible body, infinitely pure and
perfect and attended by transcendent glory, nevertheless a body of flesh and bones. AF:38

### President Brigham Young

Our Father in heaven is a personage of tabernacle, just as much as I am who stand before
you to-day, and he has all the parts and passions
of a perfect man, and his body is composed of
flesh and bones, but not of blood. *(To Sunday
School children in Tabernacle, July 24, 1877,
JD19:64)* TLDP:221

### Joseph Smith

The Father has a body of flesh and bones as
tangible as man's; the Son also; but the Holy
Ghost has not a body of flesh and bones, but is

a personage of Spirit. Were it not so, the Holy
Ghost could not dwell in us. . . . *(Revelation
received April 2, 1830)* D&C 130:22

### Stephen L. Richards

When Joseph came out of the grove, he had no
need to argue for a theory—he knew the facts.
God is in form like a man. He has a voice. He
speaks. He is considerate and kind. His Son is
a like but distinct person. He is obedient to the
Father and the mediator between God and man.
The presumption of God as a mere essence or
principle of power and force in the universe
was for all time exploded. The testimony is
direct and positive and irrefutable. Many have
not believed, but no one has ever had the
knowledge to disprove it. (Where is Wisdom?,
p. 31) TLDP:221-22

### Elder Joseph Fielding Smith

*Question*: "If God has a body of flesh and bones
plus spirit, how is it that his children were spirits, in the pre-existence?" *Answer*: According to
the gospel as revealed, we came here purposely
to obtain tabernacles of flesh and bones, and if
faithful to return to our Father to partake of his
fulness. This question the Lord has not fully explained, but there are sufficient reasons why we
should believe that he does have a tabernacle of
flesh and bones. MPSG1972-73:17

### President Joseph F. Smith

Jesus is the express image and likeness of His
Father; therefore, as Jesus is a personage of
flesh and bones, having a body as tangible as
that of man, bearing in it the wounds of the
nails and of the spear, so is the body of the
Father just as tangible; it is just as real as that of
the Son. (Millennial Star, Nov. 1, 1906, p. 690)
TLDP:221

### Abraham,
*quoted by Joseph Smith*

And the Gods took counsel among themselves
and said: Let us go down and form man in our
image, after our likeness. . . . 27. So the Gods
went down to organize man in their own image,
in the image of the Gods to form they him,
male and female to form they them. *(The Gods
plan the creation of the earth)* Abr.4:26-27

### Joseph Smith,
*translating the Book of Moses*

And I, God, said unto mine Only Begotten,
which was with me from the beginning: Let us
make man in our image, after our likeness; and it
was so. . . . 27. And I, God, created man in mine
own image, in the image of mine Only Begotten
created I him; male and female created I them.
*(The record of Moses: God makes man and gives
him dominion over all else)* Moses 2:26-27

### Moses

So God created man in his own image, in the image of God created he him; male and female created he them. (*Revelation to Moses with respect to the Creation*) Gen.1:27

### Jesus,
#### quoted by Moroni

And never have I showed myself unto man whom I have created, for never has man believed in me as thou hast. Seest thou that ye are created after mine own image? Yea, even all men were created in the beginning after mine own image. 16. Behold, this body, which ye now behold, is the body of my spirit; and man have I created after the body of my spirit; and even as I appear unto thee to be in the spirit will I appear unto my people in the flesh. (*Christ, before he is born into the world, shows himself to be in the image of man*) Ether 3:15-16

### Related Witnesses:
#### Joseph Smith

John 14:23—The appearing of the Father and the Son, in that verse, is a personal appearance; and the idea that the Father and the Son dwell in a man's heart is an old sectarian notion, and is false. (*Revelation, April 2, 1830*) D&C 130:3

#### Elder Lorenzo Snow

Through a continual course of progression, our heavenly Father has received exaltation and glory, and he points us out the same path; and inasmuch as he is clothed with power, authority, and glory, he says, "Walk ye up and come in possession of the same glory and happiness that I possess." (*In Tabernacle, Oct. 1857*) DGSM:92

### Mormon

And because he said unto them that Christ was the God, the Father of all things, and said that he should take upon him the image of man, and it should be the image after which man was created in the beginning; or in other words, he said that man was created after the image of God, and that God should come down among the children of men, and take upon him flesh and blood, and go forth upon the face of the earth— (*King Limhi recounts the history of his people to Ammon and the throng assembled; he says a prophet [Abinadi] was slain because he testified that Christ is the God and Father of all things*) Mosiah 7:27

### Ammon, son of Mosiah,
#### quoted by Mormon

Ammon said unto him: I am a man; and man in the beginning was created after the image of God. . . . (*Ammon responds to King Lamoni, about 90 B.C.*) Alma 18:34

### 249. God is a just god; He is true and righteous in all things.

#### Charles W. Penrose

[God] is not a mere force of etherial immateriality, but is the embodiment in His personality of light, truth, virtue, justice, mercy, energy and all the eternal verities. CR1916Apr:23

#### Joseph Smith

It is also necessary, in order to exercise faith in God unto life and salvation, that men should have the idea of the existence of the attribute justice in him; for without the idea of the existence of the attribute justice in the Deity, men could not have confidence sufficient to place themselves under his guidance and direction; for they would be filled with fear and doubt lest the judge of all the earth would not do right, and thus fear or doubt, existing in the mind, would preclude the possibility of the exercise of faith in him for life and salvation. But when the idea of the existence of the attribute justice in the Deity is fairly in the mind, it leaves no room for doubt to get into the heart, and the mind is enabled to cast itself upon the Almighty without fear and without doubt, and with the most unshaken confidence, believing that the Judge of all the earth will do right. ¶ 17. Let the mind once reflect sincerely and candidly upon the ideas of the existence of the . . . attributes in the Deity, and it will be seen that, as far as his attributes are concerned, there is a sure foundation laid for the exercise of faith in him for life and salvation. . . . Seeing, also, that justice is an attribute of the Deity, he will deal with them upon the principles of righteousness and equity, and a just reward will be granted unto them for all their afflictions and sufferings for the truth's sake. (*Lectures on Faith delivered to the School of the Prophets, 1834-35*) LOF4:13,17

#### Joseph Smith

O Lord God Almighty, hear us in these our petitions, and answer us from heaven, thy holy habitation, where thou sittest enthroned, with glory, honor, power, majesty, might, dominion, truth, justice, judgment, mercy, and an infinity of fulness, from everlasting to everlasting. (*Prayer given by revelation to be offered at dedication of Kirtland Temple, March 27, 1836*) D&C 109:77

#### Hugh B. Brown

We know Him to be a living being with every essential property and attribute of personality—that He thinks, wills, feels, and has purposes—that He is a moral being who requires righteousness and justice—but that in His love He is compassionate, merciful, and long suffering. (The Abundant Life, p. 21) TLDP:217

**John**

And they sing the song of Moses the servant of God, and the song of the Lamb, saying, Great and marvellous are thy works, Lord God Almighty; just and true are thy ways, thou King of saints. (*John sees in vision exalted Saints praising God in celestial glory*) Rev.15:3

**Related Witnesses:**

**Recorded in Psalms**

Justice and judgment are the habitation of thy throne: mercy and truth shall go before thy face. Ps.89:14

**Moroni, son of Mormon**

And he answered: Yea, Lord, I know that thou speakest the truth, for thou art a God of truth, and canst not lie. (*The Lord shows himself to the brother of Jared, about the time of the Tower of Babel*) Ether 3:12

---

**250. God is no respecter of persons (He has no favorites except upon grounds of their degree of righteousness).**

**Elder Joseph Fielding Smith**

[Respecter of persons] does not mean that the Lord does not respect those who obey him in all things more than he does the ungodly. Without question the Lord does respect those who love him and keep his commandments more than he does those who rebel against him. The proper interpretation of this passage is that the Lord is not partial and grants to each man, if he will repent, the same privileges and opportunities of salvation and exaltation. He is just to every man, both the righteous and the wicked. He will receive any soul who will turn from iniquity to righteousness, and will love him with a just love and bless him with all that the Father has to give; but let it not be thought that he will grant the same blessings to those who will not obey him and keep his law. If the Lord did bless the rebellious as he does the righteous, without their repentance, then he would be a respecter of persons. CHMR1:255; DCSM:6

**Rudger Clawson**

So, my brethren and sisters, if there are to be distinctions among us, they must not be based on our financial condition, but rather upon the principle of righteousness. One man is better than another if he is more righteous than the other. One man is more acceptable to the lord than another if he lives nearer to the Lord than the other. CR1899Apr:4

**Elder Joseph F. Smith**

God is not a respecter of persons. The rich man may enter into the kingdom of heaven as freely as the poor, if he will bring his heart and affections into subjection to the law of God and to the principle of truth; if he will place his affections upon God, his heart upon the truth, and his soul upon the accomplishment of God's purposes, and not fix his affections and his hopes upon the things of the world. (*General conference, Oct. 1875*) (*Gospel Doctrine*, pp. 260-61) TLDP:714

**Peter**

Then Peter opened his mouth, and said, Of a truth I perceive that God is no respecter of persons: 35. But in every nation he that feareth him, and worketh righteousness, is accepted with him. (*Peter in a vision is commanded to take the gospel to the Gentiles*) Acts 10:34-35

**Joseph Smith**

[W]e learn the following things respecting the character of God: . . . ¶ 17. . . . [T]hat he is no respecter of persons: but in every nation he that fears God and works righteousness is accepted of him. . . . ¶ 23. But it is also necessary that men should have an idea that he is no respecter of persons, for with the idea of all the other excellencies in his character, and this one wanting, men could not exercise faith in him; because if he were a respecter of persons, they could not tell what their privileges were, nor how far they were authorized to exercise faith in him, or whether they were authorized to do it at all, but all must be confusion; but no sooner are the minds of men made acquainted with the truth on this point, that he is no respecter of persons, than they see that they have authority by faith to lay hold on eternal life, the richest boon of heaven, because God is no respecter of persons, and that every man in every nation has an equal privilege. (*Lectures on Faith delivered to the School of the Prophets, 1834-35*) LOF:3:12,17,23

**Joseph Smith,**
*receiving the Word of the Lord*

And again, verily I say unto you, O inhabitants of the earth: I the Lord am willing to make these things known unto all flesh; 35. For I am no respecter of persons, (*Revelation received during conference of elders of the Church, Nov. 1, 1831*) D&C 1:34-35

**Joseph Smith,**
*receiving the Word of the Lord*

And for your salvation I give unto you a commandment, for I have heard your prayers, and the poor have complained before me, and the rich have I made, and all flesh is mine, and I am no respecter of persons. (*Revelation of commandments to Saints in conference, Jan. 2, 1831*) D&C 38:16

### Mormon

But little children are alive in Christ, even from the foundation of the world; if not so, God is a partial God, and also a changeable God, and a respecter to persons; for how many little children have died without baptism! (*Mormon writes to his son Moroni, prior to* A.D. *384*) Moro.8:12

### Rudger Clawson

Hence these glorious temples which have been erected in our midst, that ordinances may be performed therein for the living and the dead. In this we see again that God is no respecter of persons, and that He is feeling after the dead as well as after the living. We cannot be made perfect without our fathers and mothers and our ancestors, and they cannot be made perfect without us. CR1904Oct:37

### Bruce R. McConkie

Either God treats all men the same or he is not God. If he respects persons and shows partiality, he does not possess those attributes of perfection which make him the exalted being that he is. (The Promised Messiah, p. 286) TLDP:221

**Related Witnesses:**

### Nephi, son of Lehi

Behold, the Lord esteemeth all flesh in one; he that is righteous is favored of God. (*Nephi answers his rebellious brothers, about 591 B.C.*) 1Ne.17:35

### James E. Talmage

Now when we say that the Lord is not pleased with those churches, we do not mean that he is not pleased with the members thereof. We hold that God is no respecter of persons, but, on the contrary, that he will acknowledge good in any soul, no matter whether that person belongs to a church or not. But the Lord is not pleased with those churches that have been constructed by men and then labeled with his name. CR1928Oct:120

---

## 251. God is merciful.

### Nehemiah

[B]ut thou art a God ready to pardon, gracious and merciful, slow to anger, and of great kindness, and forsookest them not. (*Levites bless and praise the Lord*) Neh.9:17

### Ammon, son of Mosiah,
#### quoted by Mormon

Now my brethren, we see that God is mindful of every people, whatsoever land they may be in; yea, he numbereth his people, and his bowels of mercy are over all the earth. Now this is my joy, and my great thanksgiving; yea, and I will give thanks unto my God forever. Amen. (*Ammon extols the mercy of God who has not forgotten this branch of the tree of Israel, 90-77 B.C.*) Alma 26:37

### Joseph Smith

And again, it is equally important that men should have the idea of the existence of the attribute mercy in the Deity, in order to exercise faith in him for life and salvation; for without the idea of the existence of this attribute in the Deity, the spirits of the saints would faint in the midst of the tribulations, afflictions, and persecutions which they have to endure for righteousness' sake. But when the idea of the existence of this attribute is once established in the mind it gives life and energy to the spirits of the saints, believing that the mercy of God will be poured out upon them in the midst of their afflictions, and that he will compensate them in their sufferings, and that the mercy of God will lay hold of them and secure them in the arms of his love, so that they will receive a full reward for all their sufferings. ¶ 17. Let the mind once reflect sincerely and candidly upon the ideas of the existence of the . . . attributes in the Deity, and it will be seen that, as far as his attributes are concerned, there is a sure foundation laid for the exercise of faith in him for life and salvation. . . . And as mercy is also an attribute of the Deity, his saints can have confidence that it will be exercised towards them, and through the exercise of that attribute towards them comfort and consolation will be administered unto them abundantly, amid all their afflictions and tribulations. (*Lectures on Faith delivered to the School of the Prophets, 1834-35*) LOF4:15,17

### Recorded in Exodus

And the LORD passed by before him, and proclaimed, The LORD, The LORD God, merciful and gracious, longsuffering, and abundant in goodness and truth, 7. Keeping mercy for thousands, forgiving iniquity and transgression and sin. . . . (*The Lord appears to Moses on Mount Sinai*) Ex.34:6-7

### Paul

But God, who is rich in mercy, for his great love wherewith he loved us, 5. Even when we were dead in sins, hath quickened us together with Christ, (by grace ye are saved;) (*Letter to the Saints at Ephesus in Asia Minor, about A.D. 62*) Eph.2:4-5

### Joseph Smith

Glory, and honor, and power, and might, Be ascribed to our God; for he is full of mercy, Justice, grace and truth, and peace, Forever and ever, Amen. (*Revelation on priesthood received with six elders, Sept. 22/23, 1832*) D&C 84:102

### Recorded in Psalms

O give thanks unto the God of gods: for his mercy endureth for ever. 3. O give thanks to the Lord of lords: for his mercy endureth for ever. 4. To him who alone doeth great wonders: for his mercy endureth for ever. 5. To him that by wisdom made the heavens: for his mercy endureth for ever. 6. To him that stretched out the earth above the waters: for his mercy endureth for ever. 7. To him that made great lights: for his mercy endureth for ever: 8. The sun to rule by day: for his mercy endureth for ever: 9. The moon and stars to rule by night: for his mercy endureth for ever. 10. To him that smote Egypt in their firstborn: for his mercy endureth for ever: 11. And brought out Israel from among them: for his mercy endureth for ever: 12. With a strong hand, and with a stretched out arm: for his mercy endureth for ever. 13. To him which divided the Red sea into parts: for his mercy endureth for ever: 14. And made Israel to pass through the midst of it: for his mercy endureth for ever: 15. But overthrew Pharaoh and his host in the Red sea: for his mercy endureth for ever. 16. To him which led his people through the wilderness: for his mercy endureth for ever. 17. To him which smote great kings: for his mercy endureth for ever: 18. And slew famous kings: for his mercy endureth for ever: 19. Sihon king of the Amorites: for his mercy endureth for ever: 20. And Og the king of Bashan: for his mercy endureth for ever: 21. And gave their land for an heritage: for his mercy endureth for ever: 22. Even an heritage unto Israel his servant: for his mercy endureth for ever. 23. Who remembered us in our low estate: for his mercy endureth for ever: 24. And hath redeemed us from our enemies: for his mercy endureth for ever. 25. Who giveth food to all flesh: for his mercy endureth for ever. 26. O give thanks unto the God of heaven: for his mercy endureth for ever. Ps.136:2-26

**Related Witnesses:**

### Alma, the younger,
*quoted by Mormon*

O my son, I desire that ye should deny the justice of God no more. Do not endeavor to excuse yourself in the least point because of your sins, by denying the justice of God; but do you let the justice of God, and his mercy, and his long-suffering have full sway in your heart; and let it bring you down to the dust in humility. 31. And now, O my son, ye are called of God to preach the word unto this people. And now, my son, go thy way, declare the word with truth and soberness, that thou mayest bring souls unto repentance, that the great plan of mercy may have claim upon them. And may God grant unto you even according to my words. Amen. (*Alma speaks to his son Corianton concerning the resurrection of the dead, about 73 B.C.*) Alma 42:30-31

## 252. The Lord is a god of truth and cannot lie.

### Moroni, son of Mormon

And he answered: Yea, Lord, I know that thou speakest the truth, for thou art a God of truth, and canst not lie. (*The Lord shows himself to the brother of Jared, about the time of the Tower of Babel*) Ether 3:12

### Joseph Smith

He is a God of truth and cannot lie. . . . ¶ 22. And again, the idea that he is a God of truth and cannot lie, is equally as necessary to the exercise of faith in him as the idea of his unchangeableness. For without the idea that he was a God of truth and could not lie, the confidence necessary to be placed in his word in order to the exercise of faith in him could not exist. But having the idea that he is not man, that he cannot lie, it gives power to the minds of men to exercise faith in him. (*Lectures on Faith delivered to the School of the Prophets, 1834-35*) LOF3:16,22

### Joseph Smith

And lastly, but not less important to the exercise of faith in God, is the idea of the existence of the attribute truth in him; for without the idea of the existence of this attribute the mind of man could have nothing upon which it could rest with certainty—all would be confusion and doubt. But with the idea of the existence of this attribute in the Deity in the mind, all the teachings, instructions, promises, and blessings, become realities, and the mind is enabled to lay hold of them with certainty and confidence, believing that these things, and all that the Lord has said, shall be fulfilled in their time; and that all the cursings, denunciations, and judgments, pronounced upon the heads of unrighteous, will also be executed in the due time of the Lord: and, by reason of the truth and veracity of him, the mind beholds its deliverance and salvation as being certain. (*Lectures on Faith delivered to the School of the Prophets, 1834-35*) LOF4:16

### Joseph Smith

For God doth not walk in crooked paths, neither doth he turn to the right hand nor to the left, neither doth he vary from that which he hath said, therefore his paths are straight, and his course is one eternal round. (*Revelation regarding the lost manuscript pages, July 1828*) D&C 3:2

### Joseph Smith,
*receiving the Word of the Lord*
. . . I, the Lord, promise the faithful and cannot lie. (*Revelation through Joseph Smith, Aug. 13, 1831*) D&C 62:6

### Alma, the younger,
*quoted by Mormon*
I perceive that it has been made known unto you, by the testimony of his word, that he cannot walk in crooked paths; neither doth he vary from that which he hath said; neither hath he a shadow of turning from the right to the left, or from that which is right to that which is wrong; therefore, his course is one eternal round. (*Alma preaches to the people in Gideon, about 83 B.C.*) Alma 7:20

### Enos,
*quoted by Mormon*
And there came a voice unto me, saying: Enos, thy sins are forgiven thee, and thou shalt be blessed. 6. And I, Enos, knew that God could not lie; wherefore, my guilt was swept away. 7. And I said: Lord, how is it done? 8. And he said unto me: Because of thy faith in Christ, whom thou hast never before heard nor seen. (*Enos prays mightily and gains a remission of sins, 544-421 B.C.*) Enos 1:5-8

### Balaam
God is not a man, that he should lie; neither the son of man, that he should repent: hath he said, and shall he not do it? or hath he spoken, and shall he not make it good? (*The prophet Balaam replies to Balak, telling him what the Lord has spoken*) Num.23:19

### Paul
In hope of eternal life, which God, that cannot lie, promised before the world began; (*Letter to his companion Titus, about A.D. 64*) Titus 1:2

### Paul
Wherein God, willing more abundantly to shew unto the heirs of promise the immutability of his counsel, confirmed it by an oath: 18. That by two immutable things, in which it was impossible for God to lie, we might have a strong consolation, who have fled for refuge to lay hold upon the hope set before us: 19. Which hope we have as an anchor of the soul, both sure and stedfast, and which entereth into that within the veil; (*Letter to the Jewish members of the Church, about A.D. 60*) Heb.6:17-19

---

253. **The works, designs, and purposes of God cannot be defeated by any person, but must come to pass.**

### Joseph Smith
The works, and the designs, and the purposes of God cannot be frustrated, neither can they come to naught. 2. For God doth not walk in crooked paths, neither doth he turn to the right hand nor to the left, neither doth he vary from that which he hath said, therefore his paths are straight, and his course is one eternal round. (*Revelation regarding the lost manuscript pages, July 1828*) D&C 3:1-2

### Joseph Smith,
*receiving the Word of the Lord*
What I the Lord have spoken, I have spoken, and I excuse not myself; and though the heavens and the earth pass away, my word shall not pass away, but shall all be fulfilled, whether by mine own voice or by the voice of my servants, it is the same. (*Revelation received during conference of elders of the Church, Nov. 1, 1831*) D&C 1:38

### Abraham O. Woodruff
No weapon that has ever been formed against Zion has prospered. The efforts of the evil one to destroy the work of the Lord have only tended to spread it abroad. The persecutions which have been heaped upon this people have been the means of cementing us together, drawing us more closely to God, and making us more united and powerful. It is the heritage of the saints of God to be misrepresented and persecuted by the insincere and the wicked; but their efforts have never blocked the progress of the work of our Eternal Father. On the contrary, the labors of our most bitter enemies have been among the main factors in spreading the work abroad. The Lord has turned the wrath of the wicked to his own glory. Had it not been for the persecution of the Latter-day Saints, the mustard seed would not have been cast abroad; but in the attempt to destroy the mustard stalk, to which the Savior compared the Gospel, they have scattered the seed, and it has taken root wherever it has fallen. . . . I thank God that it is not his purposes which have failed, but the purposes of man. This should be an encouragement to every Latter-day Saint and a strong testimony that this is the work of God. It ought to be a testimony also to those who have sought to bring to naught the purposes of God. CR1901Oct:11-12

### Elder Joseph Fielding Smith
In his infinite wisdom, our Father has provided for every problem or difficulty that may arise to stop or hinder the progress of his work. No power on earth or in hell can overthrow or defeat that which God has decreed. Every plan of the Adversary will fail, for the Lord knows the secret thoughts of men, and sees the future

with a vision clear and perfect, even as though it were in the past. Jacob, son of Lehi, in his rejoicing declared: "O how great the holiness of our God! For he knoweth all things, and there is not anything save he knows it." (2Ne.9:20) He knew that Satan would try to frustrate the coming forth of the Book of Mormon by the stealing and changing of the manuscript, and provided for it hundreds of years before the birth of Jesus Christ. CHMR1:26; DCSM:10

**Related Witnesses:**

### Daniel
And there was given him dominion, and glory, and a kingdom, that all people, nations, and languages, should serve him: his dominion is an everlasting dominion, which shall not pass away, and his kingdom that which shall not be destroyed. (*Daniel dreams visions and records them*) Dan.7:14

### Jesus,
#### recorded in Matthew
Heaven and earth shall pass away, but my words shall not pass away. (*Signs of the Second Coming are spoken of by the Savior*) Matt.24:35

### Jesus,
#### quoted by Joseph Smith, translating Matthew
Although, the days will come, that heaven and earth shall pass away; yet my words shall not pass away, but all shall be fulfilled. (*Signs of the Second Coming are spoken of by the Savior*) JS-M 1:35

---

### 254. All things on the earth and above the earth denote there is a God.

#### Mormon
But Alma said unto him: Thou hast had signs enough; will ye tempt your God? Will ye say, Show unto me a sign, when ye have the testimony of all these thy brethren, and also all the holy prophets? The scriptures are laid before thee, yea, and all things denote there is a God; yea, even the earth, and all things that are upon the face of it, yea, and its motion, yea, and also all the planets which move in their regular form do witness that there is a Supreme Creator. (*Korihor demands of Alma a sign that there is a god*) Alma 30:44

#### Joseph Smith, translating the Book of Moses
And behold, all things have their likeness, and all things are created and made to bear record of me, both things which are temporal, and things which are spiritual; things which are in the heavens above, and things which are on the

earth, and things which are in the earth, and things which are under the earth, both above and beneath: all things bear record of me. (*The record of Moses: Enoch recounts God speaking to Adam*) Moses 6:63

#### Joseph Smith
We are sensible that, after a revelation of Jesus Christ, the works of creation, throughout their vast forms and varieties, clearly exhibit his eternal power and Godhead. (*Lectures on Faith delivered to the School of the Prophets, 1834-35*) LOF2:4

#### Joseph Smith
Behold, all these are kingdoms, and any man who hath seen any or the least of these hath seen God moving in his majesty and power. (*Revelation received Dec. 27/28, 1832; the "olive leaf message of peace"*) D&C 88:47

#### Joseph Smith
[T]he heavens declare the glory of a God, and the firmament showeth His handiwork; and a moment's reflection is sufficient to teach every man of common intelligence, that all these are not the mere productions of chance, nor could they be supported by any power less than an Almighty hand. . . . (*Epistle to the elders of the Church, Jan. 1834*) TPJS:56; DGSM:7

**Related Witnesses:**

#### Paul
For the invisible things of him from the creation of the world are clearly seen, being understood by the things that are made, even his eternal power and Godhead; (*Letter to the Church in Rome, about A.D. 55*) Rom.1:20

#### Nephi, son of Helaman
And now, seeing ye know these things and cannot deny them except ye shall lie, therefore in this ye have sinned, for ye have rejected all these things, notwithstanding so many evidences which ye have received; yea, even ye have received all things, both things in heaven, and all things which are in the earth, as a witness that they are true. (*Nephi speaks to the wicked Nephites*) Hel.8:24

#### John A. Widtsoe
Every process of nature is orderly. Chance, disorder, chaos are ruled out of the physical universe. If every condition involved in a system is precisely the same, the result, anywhere, everywhere, today or at any other time, will be the same. The sun does not rise in the east today and in the west tomorrow. That means that the phenomena of nature are products of law. The infinitely large or the infinitely small move in obedience to law. In man's earnest search for truth, no exception to this process has been found. . . . (Evidences and Reconciliations, pp. 19-21) DGSM:7

## 255. Prophets bear witness of God's existence.

### John A. Widtsoe

As a supplementary evidence is the further historical fact that a number of men have declared that they have seen God, and even spoken with Him, or that they have received messages from Him for themselves and others. The historicity of their claims is in most cases well established. That which was done, for example, by Paul the Apostle and Joseph Smith the Prophet after their heavenly experiences helps confirm the truth of their claims. (Evidences and Reconciliations, pp. 19-21) DGSM:7

### Joseph Smith

And while we meditated upon these things, the Lord touched the eyes of our understandings and they were opened, and the glory of the Lord shone round about. 20. And we beheld the glory of the Son, on the right hand of the Father, and received of his fulness; 21. And saw the holy angels, and them who are sanctified before his throne, worshiping God, and the Lamb, who worship him forever and ever. 22. And now, after the many testimonies which have been given of him, this is the testimony, last of all, which we give of him: That he lives! 23. For we saw him, even on the right hand of God; and we heard the voice bearing record that he is the Only Begotten of the Father— 24. That by him, and through him, and of him, the worlds are and were created, and the inhabitants thereof are begotten sons and daughters unto God. (*Vision to Joseph Smith and Sidney Rigdon, Feb. 16, 1832*) D&C 76:19-24

### Nephi, son of Lehi

Yea, I make a record in the language of my father, which consists of the learning of the Jews and the language of the Egyptians. 3. And I know that the record which I make is true; and I make it with mine own hand; and I make it according to my knowledge. . . . 7. And it came to pass that he returned to his own house at Jerusalem; and he cast himself upon his bed, being overcome with the Spirit and the things which he had seen. 8. And being thus overcome with the Spirit, he was carried away in a vision, even that he saw the heavens open, and he thought he saw God sitting upon his throne, surrounded with numberless concourses of angels in the attitude of singing and praising their God. 9. And it came to pass that he saw One descending out of the midst of heaven, and he beheld that his luster was above that of the sun at noon-day. 10. And he also saw twelve others following him, and their brightness did exceed that of the stars in the firmament. 11. And they came down and went forth upon the face of the earth; and the first came and stood before my father, and gave unto him a book, and bade him that he should read. (*Nephi tells of the vision of his father Lehi, about 600 B.C.*) 1Ne.1:2-3,7-11

### Stephen,
### recorded in Acts

But he, being full of the Holy Ghost, looked up stedfastly into heaven, and saw the glory of God, and Jesus standing on the right hand of God, 56. And said, Behold, I see the heavens opened, and the Son of man standing on the right hand of God. (*Stephen is stoned and receives a vision of the Father and the Son*) Acts 7:55-56

### Recorded in Luke

And Saul, yet breathing out threatenings and slaughter against the disciples of the Lord, went unto the high priest, 2. And desired of him letters to Damascus to the synagogues, that if he found any of this way, whether they were men or women, he might bring them bound unto Jerusalem. 3. And as he journeyed, he came near Damascus: and suddenly there shined round about him a light from heaven: 4. And he fell to the earth, and heard a voice saying unto him, Saul, Saul, why persecutest thou me? 5. And he said, Who art thou, Lord? And the Lord said, I am Jesus whom thou persecutest: it is hard for thee to kick against the pricks. 6. And he trembling and astonished said, Lord, what wilt thou have me to do? And the Lord said unto him, Arise, and go into the city, and it shall be told thee what thou must do. (*Jesus appears to Saul*) Acts 9:1-6

### Joseph Smith

So it was with me. I had actually seen a light, and in the midst of that light I saw two Personages, and they did in reality speak to me; and though I was hated and persecuted for saying that I had seen a vision, yet it was true; and while they were persecuting me, reviling me, and speaking all manner of evil against me falsely for so saying, I was led to say in my heart: Why persecute me for telling the truth? I have actually seen a vision; and who am I that I can withstand God, or why does the world think to make me deny what I have actually seen? for I had seen a vision; I knew it, and I knew that God knew it, and I could not deny it, neither dared I do it; at least I knew that by so doing I would offend God, and come under condemnation. (*Joseph testifies of the reality of the First Vision*) JS-H 1:25

## 256. God is omniscient: He knows all things.

### Nephi, son of Lehi

But the Lord knoweth all things from the beginning; wherefore, he prepareth a way to accomplish all his works among the children of men; for behold, he hath all power unto the fulfilling of all his words. And thus it is. Amen. (*Nephi discloses the Lord's command to him to make two sets of plates for a wise purpose unknown to Nephi, 600-592 B.C.*) 1Ne.9:6

### Marion G. Romney

As a member of the Godhead, and being one with the Father and the Son, the Holy Ghost is, as are the Father and the Son, omniscient. He comprehends all truth having a knowledge of [all] things. (D&C 93:24) ("The Holy Ghost," EN1974May:90) MGSP:7

### Joseph Smith

[W]ithout the knowledge of all things, God would not be able to save any portion of his creatures; for it is by reason of the knowledge which he has of all things, from the beginning to the end, that enables him to give that understanding to his creatures by which they are made partakers of eternal life; and if it were not for the idea existing in the minds of men that God had all knowledge it would be impossible for them to exercise faith in him. ¶ 17. Let the mind once reflect sincerely and candidly upon the ideas of the existence of the . . . attributes in the Deity, and it will be seen that, as far as his attributes are concerned, there is a sure foundation laid for the exercise of faith in him for life and salvation. For inasmuch as God possesses the attribute knowledge, he can make all things known to his saints necessary for their salvation; (*Lectures on Faith delivered to the School of the Prophets, 1834-35*) LOF4:11,17

### James E. Talmage

God is Omniscient—By Him matter has been organized and energy directed. He is therefore the Creator of all things that are created; and "Known unto God are all his works from the beginning of the world." His power and His wisdom are alike incomprehensible to man, for they are infinite. Being Himself eternal and perfect, His knowledge cannot be otherwise than infinite. To comprehend Himself, an infinite Being, He must possess an infinite mind. Through the agency of angels and ministering servants He is in continuous communication with all parts of creation, and may personally visit as He may determine. AF:39-40

### Lehi,
#### quoted by his son Nephi

But behold, all things have been done in the wisdom of him who knoweth all things. (*Lehi explains the fall of Adam, 588-570 B.C.*) 2Ne.2:24

### Joseph Smith

. . . God is the only supreme governor and independent being in whom all fullness and perfection dwell; who is omnipotent, omnipresent and omniscient; without beginning of days or end of life; and that in him every good gift and every good principle dwell; and that he is the Father of lights; in him the principle of faith dwells independently, and he is the object in whom the faith of all other rational and accountable beings center for life and salvation. (*Lectures on Faith delivered to the School of the Prophets, 1834-35*) LOF2:2; DGSM:8

**Related Witnesses:**

### King Benjamin,
#### quoted by Mormon

Believe in God; believe that he is, and that he created all things, both in heaven and in earth; believe that he has all wisdom, and all power, both in heaven and in earth; believe that man doth not comprehend all the things which the Lord can comprehend. (*King Benjamin addresses his people, about 124 B.C.*) Mosiah 4:9

---

## 257. God is omnipotent: He has all power, might, and authority.

### James E. Talmage

God is Omnipotent—He is properly called the Almighty. Man can discern proofs of the divine omnipotence on every side, in the forces that control the elements of earth and guide the orbs of heaven in their prescribed courses. Whatever His wisdom indicates as necessary to be done God can and will do. The means through which He operates may not be of infinite capacity in themselves, but they are directed by an infinite power. A rational conception of His omnipotence is power to do all that He may will to do. AF:40

### Joseph Smith

God is the only supreme governor and independent being in whom all fullness and perfection dwell; who is omnipotent, omnipresent and omniscient; without beginning of days or end of life; and that in him every good gift and every good principle dwell; and that he is the Father of lights; in him the principle of faith dwells independently, and he is the object in whom the faith of all other rational and accountable beings center for life and salvation. (*Lectures on Faith delivered to the School of the Prophets, 1834-35*) LOF2:2; DGSM:8

### Joseph Smith

Let the mind once reflect sincerely and candidly upon the ideas of the existence of the . . . attributes in the Deity, and it will be seen that, as far as his attributes are concerned, there is a sure foundation laid for the exercise of faith in him for life and salvation. . . . As he possesses the attribute power, he is able thereby to deliver them from the power of all enemies; (*Lectures on Faith delivered to the School of the Prophets, 1834-35*) LOF4:17

### Nephi, son of Lehi

But the Lord knoweth all things from the beginning; wherefore, he prepareth a way to accomplish all his works among the children of men; for behold, he hath all power unto the fulfilling of all his words. And thus it is. Amen. (*Nephi discloses the Lord's command to him to make two sets of plates for a wise purpose unknown to Nephi, 600-592 B.C.*) 1Ne.9:6

### King Benjamin,
### *quoted by Mormon*

Believe in God; believe that he is, and that he created all things, both in heaven and in earth; believe that he has all wisdom, and all power, both in heaven and in earth; believe that man doth not comprehend all the things which the Lord can comprehend. (*King Benjamin addresses his people, about 124 B.C.*) Mosiah 4:9

### King Benjamin,
### *quoted by Mormon*

For behold, the time cometh, and is not far distant, that with power, the Lord Omnipotent who reigneth, who was, and is from all eternity to all eternity, shall come down from heaven among the children of men, and shall dwell in a tabernacle of clay, and shall go forth amongst men, working mighty miracles, such as healing the sick, raising the dead, causing the lame to walk, the blind to receive their sight, and the deaf to hear, and curing all manner of diseases. (*The Lord speaks to King Benjamin*) Mosiah 3:5

### John

And I heard as it were the voice of a great multitude, and as the voice of many waters, and as the voice of mighty thunderings, saying, Alleluia: for the Lord God omnipotent reigneth. (*A vision of John the Revelator*) Rev.19:6

**Related Witnesses:**

### James E. Talmage

Let it not be assumed, however, that the fact of God's foreknowledge as to what *would* be under any given conditions, is a determining cause that such *must* be. Omnipotent though He be, He permits much that is contrary to His will. We cannot believe that vice and crime, injustice, intolerance, and unrighteous domina-tion of the weak by the strong, the oppression of the poor by the rich, exist by the will and determination of God. It is not His design or wish that even one soul be lost; on the contrary it was and is His work and glory "to bring to pass the immortality and eternal life of man." So also, it is not God's purpose to interfere with, far less to annul, the free agency of His children, even though those children prostitute their Divine birthright of freedom to the accomplishment of evil, and the condemnation of their souls. ("The Philosophical Basis of 'Mormonism'," IE1915Sep951) TLDP:218

**Author's Note:** God is omnipotent, yet He works within established parameters. The Church of Jesus Christ of Latter-day Saints, in contrast to the views of many in Catholicism or Protestantism, does not believe in an utterly transcendent Being—a God who recognizes no limitations.

---

**258. God is omnipresent: through the medium of the Spirit, God is in direct communication with all things at all times.**

### James E. Talmage

There is no part of creation, however remote, into which God cannot penetrate; through the medium of the Spirit the Godhead is in direct communication with all things at all times. It has been said, therefore, that God is everywhere present; but this does not mean that the actual person of any one member of the Godhead can be physically present in more than one place at one time. The senses of each of the Trinity are of infinite power; His mind is of unlimited capacity; His powers of transferring Himself from place to place are infinite; plainly, however, His person cannot be in more than one place at any one time. Admitting the personality of God, we are compelled to accept the fact of His materiality; indeed, an "immaterial being," under which meaningless name some have sought to designate the condition of God, cannot exist, for the very expression is a contradiction in terms. If God possesses a form, that form is of necessity of definite proportions and therefore of limited extension in space. It is impossible for Him to occupy at one time more than one space of such limits; and it is not surprising, therefore, to learn from the scriptures that He moves from place to place. AF:38-39

### President Brigham Young,
### *quoted by John A. Widtsoe*

[H]e knoweth every thought and intent of the

hearts of all living, for he is everywhere present by the power of his Spirit—his minister, the Holy Ghost. He is the Father of all, is above all, through all, and in you all; he knoweth all things pertaining to this earth, and he knows all things pertaining to millions of earths like this. (*In Tabernacle, Jan. 8, 1865, JD11:41*) DBY:19

### Elder Joseph Fielding Smith,
#### also quoting President Joseph F. Smith

President Joseph F. Smith has expressed it thus: "The Holy Ghost as a personage of Spirit can no more be omnipresent in person than can the Father or the Son, but by his intelligence, his knowledge, his power and influence over and through the laws of nature, he is and can be omnipresent throughout all the works of God." Thus when it becomes necessary to speak to us, he is able to do so by acting through the other Spirit, that is, through the Light of Christ. (Doctrines of Salvation, 1:40) TLDP:272

### Charles W. Penrose

The Father has a body of flesh and bones, the Son also, but the Holy Ghost is a "personage of Spirit" (D&C:130). In their personality neither of them can be in more than one place at one time, no matter how speedily or by what means he can move through illimitable space. But universally diffused throughout the immensity of space is an everywhere-present holy spirit that is not a personage, and by that essence God can be and is omnipresent and omniscient at will. . . . ¶ It pervades all worlds and "proceedeth from the presence of God throughout the immensity of space," being in all things, giving light to all things, and the law and power of God by which all things are governed, and by which "He comprehendeth all things, and all things are before Him and all things are round about Him, and He is above all things, and through all things, and in all things, and all things are by Him, and of Him, even God forever and ever." (John 1:1-9; Job 32:8; 1Cor.12:4-11; D&C:88:7-13, 41; and 93:29) Thus God can receive our prayers, know our thoughts, understand our desires and minister to our necessities. He has also at His command angels, and other divine intelligences, who operate in different spheres and worlds and constellations, who are endowed with power and authority to speak and act for Him in the grand order of His spiritual kingdom, according to eternal principles and the developments and needs of His creatures and creations. ("Whom Do the Latter-day Saints Worship?" IE1914Jun:706,709) TLDP:362-63

### Joseph Smith

God is the only supreme governor and independent being in whom all fullness and perfection dwell; who is omnipotent, omnipresent and omniscient; without beginning of days or end of life; and that in him every good gift and every good principle dwell; and that he is the Father of lights; in him the principle of faith dwells independently, and he is the object in whom the faith of all other rational and accountable beings center for life and salvation. (*Lectures on Faith delivered to the School of the Prophets, 1834-35*) LOF2:2; DGSM:8

### Related Witnesses:
#### Ammon, son of Mosiah,
##### quoted by Mormon

Now my brethren, we see that God is mindful of every people, whatsoever land they may be in; yea, he numbereth his people, and his bowels of mercy are over all the earth. Now this is my joy, and my great thanksgiving; yea, and I will give thanks unto my God forever. Amen. (*Ammon extols the mercy of God who has not forgotten this branch of the tree of Israel, 90-77 B.C.*) Alma 26:37

---

## 259. God is the same yesterday, today, and forever; there is no variableness in Him.

### Moroni, son of Mormon

For do we not read that God is the same yesterday, today, and forever, and in him there is no variableness neither shadow of changing? (*Moroni addresses those who deny the revelations of God, A.D. 400-421*) Morm.9:9

### Moroni, son of Mormon

And I would exhort you, my beloved brethren, that ye remember that he is the same yesterday, today, and forever, and that all these gifts of which I have spoken, which are spiritual, never will be done away, even as long as the world shall stand, only according to the unbelief of the children of men. (*The final writings of Moroni, about A.D. 421*) Moro.10:19

### Nephi, son of Lehi

For he is the same yesterday, to-day, and forever; and the way is prepared for all men from the foundation of the world, if it so be that they repent and come unto him. (*Nephi's writings, 600-592 B.C.*) 1Ne.10:18

### Lehi,
#### quoted by his son Nephi

And thou hast beheld in thy youth his glory; wherefore, thou art blessed even as they unto whom he shall minister in the flesh; for the Spirit is the same, yesterday, today, and forever. And the way is prepared from the fall of man, and salvation is free. *(Lehi to his son, Jacob, between 588-570 B.C.)* 2Ne.2:4

**Nephi, son of Lehi**

For behold, I am God; and I am a God of miracles; and I will show unto the world that I am the same yesterday, today, and forever; and I work not among the children of men save it be according to their faith. *(Nephi has been foretelling the coming forth of the Book of Mormon, now writes the words of the Lord, about 559-545 B.C.)* 2Ne.27:23

**Nephi, son of Lehi**

And I do this that I may prove unto many that I am the same yesterday, today, and forever; and that I speak forth my words according to mine own pleasure. And because that I have spoken one word ye need not suppose that I cannot speak another; for my work is not yet finished; neither shall it be until the end of man, neither from that time henceforth and forever. *(Nephi writes the word of the Lord regarding the witnesses of the Bible and Book of Mormon)* 2Ne.29:9

**Joseph Smith**

Thereby showing that he is the same God yesterday, today, and forever. Amen. . . . 17. By these things we know that there is a God in heaven, who is infinite and eternal, from everlasting to everlasting the same unchangeable God, the framer of heaven and earth, and all things which are in them; *(Revelation April 1830; the Book of Mormon proves the divinity of the latter-day work)* D&C 20:12,17

**Joseph Smith**

[W]e learn the following things respecting the character of God: ¶ 13. First, that he was God before the world was created, and the same God that he was after it was created. . . . ¶ 15. . . . that he changes not, neither is there variableness with him; but that he is the same from everlasting to everlasting, being the same yesterday, to-day, and for ever; and that his course is one eternal round, without variation. *(Lectures on Faith delivered to the School of the Prophets, 1834-35)* LOF3:12,13,15

**James**

Every good gift and every perfect gift is from above, and cometh down from the Father of lights, with whom is no variableness, neither shadow of turning. *(Letter to his brethren in the Church)* James 1:17

**Paul**

Jesus Christ the same yesterday, and to day, and for ever. *(Letter to the Jewish members of the Church, about A.D. 60)* Heb.13:8

**Bruce R. McConkie,**
*also quoting James, Paul and Moroni*

The everlasting gospel was with God in the beginning; it was taught in the councils of eternity before the foundations of this world were laid; we have it now; and it will continue forever, being enjoyed in its eternal fulness in those realms of light and joy where celestial beings abide. . . . ¶ Anyone who, with James, knows that the Almighty is a being "with whom is no variableness, neither shadow of turning" (James 1:17) thereby knows also that the gospel is everlasting and that all men are saved by conforming to the same eternal standards. ¶ Anyone who, with Paul, believes the statement "Jesus Christ the same yesterday, and to day, and for ever" (Heb.13:8), knows that Adam and Abraham, Moses and Elijah were saved by faith in the same person in whom the New Testament saints believed. ¶ Anyone who, with Moroni, knows, "That God is the same yesterday, and forever, and in him there is no variableness neither shadow of changing" (Morm.9:9), also knows, automatically and instinctively, that Adam had the gospel of Jesus Christ in the same literal sense that the same plan of salvation was enjoyed by Paul. (The Promised Messiah, pp. 285-87) TLDP:235-36

---

**260. God loves His children.**

**President Brigham Young**

[Our Father in Heaven] has eyes to see, and his eyes are upon all the works of his hands; he has ears, which are open to hear the prayers of little children, and he loves you, and knows you, for you are all his offspring; and his knowledge of you is so minute that, to use the language of the ancients, not a hair of your head falls to the ground unnoticed. This is the kind of God we worship. *(To Sunday School children in Tabernacle, July 24, 1877; JD19:64)* TLDP:220

**Boyd K. Packer**

Through this loving one more than you love yourself, you become truly Christian. Then you know, as few others know, what the word *Father* means when it is spoken of in the scriptures. You may then feel something of the love and concern that he has for us. ¶ It should have great meaning that of all the titles of respect and honor and admiration that could be given him, God himself, he who is the highest of all, chose to be addressed simply as Father. CR1972Apr:139

**John A. Widtsoe**

God, the Father, the supreme God, knows the equivalent of every phase of the Great Plan, which we are working out. He has had our experiences or their equivalents, and understands therefore the difficulties of our journey. His love for us is an understanding love. Our earth troubles we may lay fully before him, knowing that he understands how human hearts are touched by the tribulations and the joys of life. (A Rational Theology, p. 67) TLDP:220

### John

Herein is love, not that we loved God, but that he loved us, and sent his Son to be the propitiation for our sins. 11. Beloved, if God so loved us, we ought also to love one another. . . . 16. And we have known and believed the love that God hath to us. God is love; and he that dwelleth in love dwelleth in God, and God in him. (*John writes to the churches in Asia*) 1Jn.4:10-11,16

### Paul

That Christ may dwell in your hearts by faith; that ye, being rooted and grounded in love, 18. May be able to comprehend with all saints what is the breadth, and length, and depth, and height; 19. And to know the love of Christ, which passeth knowledge, that ye might be filled with all the fulness of God. (*Paul writes to the Saints at Ephesus in Asia Minor, about A.D. 62*) Eph.3:17-19

### President Heber J. Grant
### J. Reuben Clark, Jr., David O. McKay
(First Presidency)

We bear witness that God loves and cherishes His children who live righteously, even as He loved His Only Begotten Son, whom He suffered to endure the agony of death on the cross that we might be blessed by a resurrection from the dead and pass on to glory and eternal progression in His Service and Kingdom. ¶ We further testify that the Father who lets no sparrow fall to the ground unnoticed, guards and protects those who live righteously in Him. (Principles of the Gospel, 1943 edition, pp. i-iii); (*Message to armed forces personnel during World War II to encourage righteous living; emphasis on the love of God toward those who live righteously, for in the righteous God has special pleasure—yet, we know that God loves all of his children, including those who err*) MOFP6:192

### Jesus,
#### quoted by John

Greater love hath no man than this, that a man lay down his life for his friends. 14. Ye are my friends, if ye do whatsoever I command you. 15. Henceforth I call you not servants; for the servant knoweth not what his lord doeth: but I have called you friends; for all things that I have heard of my Father I have made known unto you. (*Jesus discourses on perfect love*) John 15:13-15

### Nephi, son of Lehi

And he said unto me: Knowest thou the conde-scension of God? 17. And I said unto him: I know that he loveth his children; nevertheless, I do not know the meaning of all things. 18. And he said unto me: Behold, the virgin whom thou seest is the mother of the Son of God, after the manner of the flesh. 19. And it came to pass that I beheld that she was carried away in the Spirit; and after she had been carried away in the Spirit for the space of a time the angel spake unto me, saying: Look! 20. And I looked and beheld the virgin again, bearing a child in her arms. 21. And the angel said unto me: Behold the Lamb of God, yea, even the Son of the Eternal Father! Knowest thou the meaning of the tree which thy father saw? 22. And I answered him, saying: Yea, it is the love of God, which sheddeth itself abroad in the hearts of the children of men; wherefore, it is the most desirable above all things. (*Nephi sees in vision the mother of the Son of God*) 1Ne.11:16-22

**Related Witnesses:**

### Joseph Smith

Be faithful and diligent in keeping the commandments of God, and I will encircle thee in the arms of my love. (*Revelation to Joseph Smith and Oliver Cowdery, April 1829*) D&C 6:20

### Lehi,
#### quoted by his son Nephi

But behold, the Lord hath redeemed my soul from hell; I have beheld his glory, and I am encircled about eternally in the arms of his love. (*Lehi exhorts his sons to put on the armor of God, 588-570 B.C.*) 2Ne.1:15

### Joseph Smith,
#### receiving the Word of the Lord

Verily, I say unto my servant Joseph Smith, Jun., or in other words, I will call you friends, for you are my friends, and ye shall have an inheritance with me— (*Revelation received at Kirtland, Ohio, May 6, 1833*) D&C 93:45

### Elder Spencer W. Kimball

Neither the Father Elohim nor the Son Jehovah would alienate himself from the children of men. It is they, the men, who cut themselves off if there be estrangement. Both the Father and the Son would gladly commune and associate with men. CR1964Apr:93

### Joseph Smith,
#### receiving the Word of the Lord

And again I say unto you, my friends, for from henceforth I shall call you friends, it is expedient that I give unto you this commandment, that ye become even as my friends in days when I was with them, traveling to preach the gospel in my power; (*Revelation on priesthood, Sept. 22/23, 1832*) D&C 84:77

## 261. God has power over the devil.

**Joseph Smith,**
*receiving the Word of the Lord*

Retaining all power, even to the destroying of Satan and his works at the end of the world, and the last great day of judgment, which I shall pass upon the inhabitants thereof, judging every man according to his works and the deeds which he hath done. (*Christ announces himself and gives a commandment of God for Martin Harris, March 1830*) D&C 19:3

**James E. Talmage**

Satan exerts a mastery over the spirits that have been corrupted by his practices; he is the foremost of the angels who were thrust down, and the instigator of the ruin of those who fall in this life; he seeks to molest and hinder mankind in good efforts, by tempting to sin; or it may be by imposing sickness, or possibly death. Yet in all these malignant doings, he can go no farther than the transgressions of the victim may enable him, or the wisdom of God may permit; and at any time he may be checked by the superior power. Indeed, even the operations of his utmost malice may be turned to the accomplishment of divine purposes. The scriptures prove to us that the days of Satan's power are numbered; his doom has been pronounced, and in the Lord's own time he will be completely overcome. He is to be bound during the millennial reign, and after that thousand years of peace he will be loosed for a little season, then his defeat will be made complete, and his power over the children of God will be destroyed. AF:57

**Elder Spencer W. Kimball**

Not even Lucifer, the Star of the Morning, the arch-enemy of mankind can withstand the power of the priesthood of God. CR1964Apr:96

**George Q. Cannon**

We talk about Satan being bound. Satan will be bound by the power of God; but he will be bound also by the determination of the people of God not to listen to him, not to be governed by him. The Lord will not bind him and take his power from the earth while there are men and women willing to be governed by him. That is contrary to the plan of salvation. To deprive men of their agency is contrary to the purposes of our God. There was a time on this continent, of which we have an account, when the people were so righteous that Satan did not have power among them. Nearly four generations passed away in righteousness. They lived in purity, and died without sin. That was through their refusal to yield to Satan. It is not recorded that Satan had no power in other parts of the earth during

that period. According to all history that we have in our possession, Satan had the same power over men who were willing to listen to him. But in this land he did not have power, and he was literally bound. I believe that this will be the case in the millennium. CR1897Oct:65

## (2) Christ the Son

### Jehovah, Jesus Christ—Creator, Savior, Judge, "Father"

## 262. Before the earth was created Jesus Christ was with God the Father in a premortal life.

**J. Reuben Clark, Jr.**

[The] Holy Writ plainly taught, and . . . Jesus himself declared, that he had an antemortal existence with the Father, that he lived with the Father in eternity from the very "beginning," during untold periods before he came to earth to take on a mortal body. (On the Way to Immortality and Eternal Life, p. 27) MPSG1968-69:12

**James E. Talmage**

No one who accepts Jesus Christ as the Son of God can consistently deny His antemortal existence, or question His position as one of the Godhead before He came to earth as Mary's Son. The common interpretation given to the opening words of John's Gospel sustains the view of Christ's primeval Godship: "In the beginning was the Word, and the Word was with God, and the Word was God." We read further, "And the Word was made flesh, and dwelt among us." The affirmations of the Redeemer support this truth. When His disciples dissented concerning His doctrine of Himself, He said: "What and if ye shall see the Son of Man ascend up where he was before?" On another occasion He spoke in this wise: "I came forth from the Father, and am come into the world: again, I leave the world, and go to the Father." And His disciples, pleased with this plain declaration confirming the belief which, perchance, they already entertained at heart, rejoined, "Lo, now speakest thou plainly, and speakest no proverb . . . by this we believe that thou camest forth from God." To certain wicked Jews who boasted of their descent from Abraham, and sought to hide their sins under the protecting mantle of the great patriarch's name, the Savior declared: "Verily, verily, I say unto you, Before Abraham was, I am." In solemn prayer the Son implored, "And now, O Father, glorify thou me with thine own self with the glory which I had with thee before the world was." Yet Christ was born a child among mortals; and it is consistent to infer that if His earthly birth was the union of a preexistent or antemortal spirit with a mortal body such also is the birth of every member of the human family. AF:174-75

### Joseph Smith,
*receiving the Word of the Lord*

And now, verily I say unto you, I was in the beginning with the Father, and am the Firstborn; . . . (*The Lord speaks by revelation at Kirtland, Ohio, May 6, 1833*) D&C 93:21

### James E. Talmage

Evidence is abundant that Jesus Christ was chosen and ordained to be the Redeemer of the world, even in the beginning. We read of His foremost position amongst the sons of God in offering Himself as a sacrifice to carry into effect the will of the Father. He it was, "Who verily was foreordained before the foundation of the world." AF:172

### John,
*quoted by Joseph Smith, translating John*

In the beginning was the gospel preached through the Son. And the gospel was the word, and the word was the Son, and the Son was with God and the Son was of God. . . . (*The record of the Apostle John, testifying of the Savior*) JST John 1:1

### Jesus,
*quoted by John*

For I came down from heaven, not to do mine own will, but the will of him that sent me. . . . 62. What and if ye shall see the Son of man ascend up where he was before? (*Jesus teaches the people after feeding the 5,000*) John 6:38,62

### Jesus,
*quoted by John*

I came forth from the Father, and am come into the world: again, I leave the world, and go to the Father. (*Jesus teaches his disciples*) John 16:28

### Jesus,
*quoted by John*

And now, O Father, glorify thou me with thine own self with the glory which I had with thee before the world was. (*Jesus offers the great intercessory prayer for his Apostles*) John 17:5

### Joseph Smith,
*also quoting John*

And John saw and bore record of the fulness of my glory, and the fulness of John's record is hereafter to be revealed. 7. And he bore record, saying: I saw his glory, that he was in the beginning, before the world was; 8. Therefore, in the beginning the Word was, for he was the Word, even the messenger of salvation— 9. The light and the Redeemer of the world; the Spirit of

truth, who came into the world, because the world was made by him, and in him was the life of men and the light of men. 10. The worlds were made by him; men were made by him; all things were made by him, and through him, and of him. 11. And I, John, bear record that I beheld his glory, as the glory of the Only Begotten of the Father, full of grace and truth, even the Spirit of truth, which came and dwelt in the flesh, and dwelt among us. (*The Lord reveals that John bore record of his glory; Kirtland, Ohio, May 6, 1833*) D&C 93:6-11

### Peter

Who verily was foreordained before the foundation of the world, but was manifest in these last times for you, (*Letter to the churches in modern Asia Minor, about A.D. 60*) 1Pet.1:20

**Related Witnesses:**

### President Joseph F. Smith

Among the spirit children of Elohim, the firstborn was and is Jehovah or Jesus Christ, to whom all others are juniors. (Gospel Doctrine, p. 70) MPSG1987:39

### Joseph Smith,
*quoted by Joseph Fielding Smith*

At the first organization in heaven we were all present, and saw the Savior chosen and appointed and the plan of salvation made, and we sanctioned it. (*Jan. 1841 at organization of a school of instruction*)(Words of Joseph Smith, p. 61) TPJS:181; MPSG1987:39

### Jesus,
*quoted by John*

Jesus said unto them, Verily, verily, I say unto you, Before Abraham was, I am. (*Jesus answers the disputing Jews*) John 8:58

### Abraham,
*quoted by Joseph Smith*

And there stood one among them that was like unto God, and he said unto those who were with him: We will go down, for there is space there, and we will take of these materials, and we will make an earth whereon these may dwell; (*Abraham learns of pre-earth life and foreordination*) Abr.3:24

---

## 263. Jesus Christ is the firstborn spirit son of God.

### President Joseph F. Smith

Among the spirit children or Elohim, the firstborn was and is Jehovah, or Jesus Christ, to whom all others are juniors. (Gospel Doctrine, p. 70) DGSM:9

### President Heber J. Grant

We believe absolutely that Jesus Christ is the

Son of God, begotten of God, the first-born in the spirit and the only begotten in the flesh; that He is the Son of God just as much as you and I are the sons of our fathers. (Millennial Star, Jan. 1922, p. 2) DGSM:9

### President John Taylor

He, in the nearness of His relationship to the Father, seems to occupy a position that no other person occupies. He is spoken of as His well beloved Son, as the Only Begotten of the Father—does not this mean the only begotten after the flesh? If He was the first born and obedient to the laws of His Father, did He not inherit the position by right to be the representative of God, the Savior and Redeemer of the world? And was it not His peculiar right and privilege as the firstborn, the legitimate heir of God, the Eternal Father, to step forth, accomplish and carry out the designs of His Heavenly Father pertaining to the redemption, salvation and exaltation of man? And being Himself without sin (which no other mortal was), He took the position of Savior and Redeemer, which by right belonged to Him as the first born. And does it not seem that in having a body specially prepared, and being the offspring of God, both in body and spirit, He stood pre-eminently in the position of the Son of God, or in the place of God, and was God, and was thus the fit and only personage capable of making an infinite atonement? (The Mediation and Atonement, pp. 135-37) TLDP:299

### President Joseph F. Smith,
### Anthon H. Lund, Charles W. Penrose
### (First Presidency)

There is no impropriety, therefore, in speaking of Jesus Christ as the Elder Brother of the rest of human kind. That He is by spiritual birth Brother to the rest of us is indicated in Hebrews: "Wherefore in all things it behoved him to be made like unto his brethren, that he might be a merciful and faithful high priest in things pertaining to God, to make reconciliation for the sins of the people." (Heb.2:17) Let it not be forgotten, however, that He is essentially greater than any and all others, by reason (1) of His seniority as the oldest, or firstborn; (2) of His unique status in the flesh as the offspring of a mortal mother and of an immortal, or resurrected and glorified, Father; (3) of His selection and foreordination as the one and only Redeemer and Savior of the race; and (4) of His transcendent sinlessness. MOFP5:34

### Paul

Who hath delivered us from the power of darkness, and hath translated us into the kingdom of his dear Son: 14. In whom we have redemption through his blood, even the forgiveness of sins:

15. Who is the image of the invisible God, the firstborn of every creature: (Letter from prison to the Church in Colossae, Asia Minor, about A.D. 60) Col.1:13-15

**Related Witnesses:**

### Joseph Smith,
### receiving the Word of the Lord

And now, verily I say unto you, I was in the beginning with the Father, and am the Firstborn; (The Lord speaks by revelation at Kirtland, Ohio, May 6, 1833) D&C 93:21

---

### 264. Jesus Christ was chosen and fore-ordained to come to earth to perform the atoning sacrifice.

### James E. Talmage

Evidence is abundant that Jesus Christ was chosen and ordained to be the Redeemer of the world, even in the beginning. We read of His foremost position amongst the sons of God in offering Himself as a sacrifice to carry into effect the will of the Father. He it was, "Who verily was foreordained before the foundation of the world." AF:172

### Peter

But with the precious blood of Christ, as of a lamb without blemish and without spot: 20. Who verily was foreordained before the foundation of the world, but was manifest in these last times for you, (Peter writes to the churches in modern Asia Minor about redemption by blood of Christ, about A.D. 60) 1Pet.1:19-20

### Elder Joseph F. Smith

The only begotten Son of God in this world came in it primarily to die. He is spoken of in the scriptures as the "Lamb slain from the foundation of the world." The meaning of this is that he was chosen to his mission as Redeemer of a fallen world, even before the foundations of the earth were laid. (The Restoration of All Things, pp. 283-84) TLDP:309

### Moroni, son of Mormon

Behold, I am he who was prepared from the foundation of the world to redeem my people. Behold, I am Jesus Christ. I am the Father and the Son. In me shall all mankind have life, and that eternally, even they who shall believe on my name; and they shall become my sons and my daughters. (Christ speaks as he shows his spirit body to the brother of Jared, at the time of the Tower of Babel) Ether 3:14

**Related Witnesses:**

### Joseph Smith,
### quoted by Joseph Fielding Smith

At the first organization in heaven we were all

present, and saw the Savior chosen and appointed and the plan of salvation made, and we sanctioned it. (*Jan. 1841 at organization of a school of instruction*) (Words of Joseph Smith, p. 61) TPJS:181; MPSG1987:39

### John

And all that dwell upon the earth shall worship him, whose names are not written in the book of life of the Lamb slain from the foundation of the world. (*The Apostle John sees the devil gain power over the nations*) Rev.13:8

### Joseph Smith,
### *translating the Book of Moses*

And behold, Enoch saw the day of the coming of the Son of Man, even in the flesh; and his soul rejoiced, saying: The Righteous is lifted up, and the Lamb is slain from the foundation of the world; and through faith I am in the bosom of the Father, and behold, Zion is with me. (*The record of Moses: Enoch foresees the coming of the Son of Man*) Moses 7:47

---

## 265. Christ was born on earth April 6 (not December 25).

### President Harold B. Lee

April 6, 1973, is a particularly significant date because it commemorates not only the anniversary of the organization of The Church of Jesus Christ of Latter-day Saints in this dispensation, but also the anniversary of the birth of the Savior, our Lord and Master, Jesus Christ. CR1973Apr:4; DCSM:40

### President Spencer W. Kimball

The name of Jesus Christ and what it represents has been plowed deep into the history of the world, never to be uprooted. Christ was born on the sixth of April. Being one of the sons of God and His only Begotten, his birth is of supreme importance. CR1975Apr:3-4

### Joseph Smith

The rise of the Church of Christ in these last days, being one thousand eight hundred and thirty years since the coming of our Lord and Savior Jesus Christ in the flesh. . . . (*Revelation on Church Organization and Government April 1830*) D&C 20:1

### Joseph Smith

The day [April 6, 1833] was spent in a very agreeable manner, in giving and receiving knowledge which appertained to this last kingdom—it being just 1800 years since the Savior laid down His life that men might have everlasting life, and only three years since the Church had come out of the wilderness, preparatory for the last dispensation. (*Journal entry of the Prophet, April 6, 1833*) HC1:337; DCSM:40

---

## 266. Jesus Christ is the only Begotten Son of God in the flesh (in mortality).

### President Heber J. Grant

We believe absolutely that Jesus Christ is the Son of God, begotten of God, the first-born in the spirit and the only begotten in the flesh; that He is the Son of God just as much as you and I are the sons of our fathers. (Millennial Star, Jan. 1922, p. 2) DGSM:9

### Melvin J. Ballard

One of the great questions that I have referred to that the world is concerned about, and is in confusion over, is as to whether or not his was a virgin birth, a birth wherein divine power interceded. Joseph Smith made it perfectly clear that Jesus Christ told the absolute truth, as did those who testify concerning him, the Apostles of the Lord Jesus Christ, wherein he is declared to be the very Son of God. And if God the Eternal Father is not the real Father of Jesus Christ, then are we in confusion; then is he not in reality the Son of God. But we declare that he *is* the Only Begotten of the Father in the flesh. ¶ Mary told the story most beautifully when she said that an angel of the Lord came to her and told her that she had found favor in the sight of God, and had come to be worthy of the fulfilment of the promises heretofore made, to become the virgin mother of the Redeemer of the world. She afterwards, referring to the event, said: "God hath done wonderful things unto me." "And the Holy Ghost came upon her," is the story. "and she came into the presence of the highest." No man or woman can live in mortality and survive the presence of the Highest except by the sustaining power of the Holy Ghost. So it came upon her to prepare her for admittance into the divine presence, and the power of the Highest, who is the Father, was present, and overshadowed her, and the holy Child that was born of her was called the Son of God. ¶ Men who deny this, or who think that it degrades our Father, have no true conception of the sacredness of the most marvelous power with which God has endowed mortal men—the power of creation. Even though that power may be abused and may become a mere harp of pleasure to the wicked, nevertheless it is the most sacred and holy and divine function with which God has endowed man. Made holy, it is retained by the Father of us all, and in his exercise of that great and marvelous creative power and function, he did not debase himself, degrade himself, nor debauch his daughter. Thus Christ became the literal Son of a divine Father, and no one else was worthy to be his father. (Sermons and Missionary Services of Melvin J. Ballard, pp. 166-67) TLDP:301

### President John Taylor
He, in the nearness of His relationship to the Father, seems to occupy a position that no other person occupies. He is spoken of as His well beloved Son, as the Only Begotten of the Father—does not this mean the only begotten after the flesh? (The Mediation and Atonement, p. 136) TLDP:299

### Joseph Smith
Jesus Christ is the heir of this Kingdom—the only begotten of the Father according to the flesh, and holds the keys over all this world. (*Address at the Stand in Nauvoo, Ill., Aug. 27, 1843*) HC5:556; MGSP:5

### Elder Joseph Fielding Smith
Our Father in heaven is the Father of Jesus Christ, both in the spirit and in the flesh. Our Savior is the Firstborn in the spirit, the Only Begotten in the flesh. ¶ I believe firmly that Jesus Christ is the Only Begotten Son of God in the flesh. He taught this doctrine to his disciples. He did not teach them that he was the Son of the Holy Ghost, but the Son of the Father. Truly, all things are done by the *power* of the Holy Ghost. It was through this power that Jesus was brought into this world, but not as the Son of the Holy Ghost, but the Son of God. . . . ¶ Christ was born a babe at Bethlehem. That is where he got his body, and the only physical body, or body of flesh and bones, that he ever had or ever will have. (Doctrines of Salvation, 1:18) TLDP:301

### Related Witnesses:
### John,
#### quoted by Joseph Smith, translating John
In the beginning was the gospel preached through the Son. And the gospel was the word, and the word was the Son, and the Son was with God and the Son was of God. . . . 13. He was born, not of blood, nor of the will of the flesh, nor of the will of man, but of God. 14. And the same word was made flesh, and dwelt among us, and we beheld his glory, the glory as of the Only Begotten of the Father, full of grace and truth. (*The record of the Apostle John, testifying of the Savior*) JST John 1:1,13-14

### James E. Talmage
That Child to be born of Mary was begotten of Elohim, the Eternal Father, not in violation of natural law but in accordance with a higher

manifestation thereof; and, the offspring from that association of supreme sanctity, celestial Sireship, and pure though mortal maternity, was of right to be called the 'Son of the Highest.' JTC:81; DGSM:9

### Recorded in Luke
And Joseph also went up from Galilee, out of the city of Nazareth, into Judaea, unto the city of David, which is called Bethlehem; (because he was of the house and lineage of David:) 5. To be taxed with Mary his espoused wife, being great with child. 6. And so it was, that, while they were there, the days were accomplished that she should be delivered. 7. And she brought forth her firstborn son, and wrapped him in swaddling clothes, and laid him in a manger; because there was no room for them in the inn. 8. And there were in the same country shepherds abiding in the field, keeping watch over their flock by night. 9. And, lo, the angel of the Lord came upon them, and the glory of the Lord shone round about them: and they were sore afraid. 10. And the angel said unto them, Fear not: for, behold, I bring you good tidings of great joy, which shall be to all people. 11. For unto you is born this day in the city of David a Saviour, which is Christ the Lord. 12. And this shall be a sign unto you; Ye shall find the babe wrapped in swaddling clothes, lying in a manger. 13. And suddenly there was with the angel a multitude of the heavenly host praising God, and saying, 14. Glory to God in the highest, and on earth peace, good will toward men. (*Luke records the birth of Jesus Christ, the Savior*) Luke 2:4-14

---

## 267. Christ's spirit body, before His birth on earth, was the same in appearance as His earthly body.

### Moroni, son of Mormon
And never have I showed myself unto man whom I have created, for never has man believed in me as thou hast. Seest thou that ye are created after mine own image? Yea, even all men were created in the beginning after mine own image. 16. Behold, this body, which ye now behold, is the body of my spirit; and man have I created after the body of my spirit; and even as I appear unto thee to be in the spirit will I appear unto my people in the flesh. (*Christ shows his spirit body to the brother of Jared, at the time of the Tower of Babel*) Ether 3:15-16

### President Joseph F. Smith,
### Anthon H. Lund, Charles W. Penrose
#### (First Presidency)
Jesus Christ is the Son of Elohim both as spiritu-

al and bodily offspring; that is to say, Elohim is literally the Father of the spirit of Jesus Christ and also of the body in which Jesus Christ performed His mission in the flesh, and which body died on the cross and was afterward taken up by the process of resurrection, and is now the immortalized tabernacle of the eternal spirit of our Lord and Savior. ("The Father and The Son; A Doctrinal Exposition by The First Presidency and The Twelve," pamphlet published by the Church, June 30, 1916. Reprinted in AF:420-426. See MOFP5:23-34) MOFP5:27

**Marion G. Romney**

Now who is Jesus Christ, and how could he bring about the resurrection when no other man nor all men put together could do so? The Scriptures respond to these questions. They make it clear that the spirit person Jesus Christ—as are the spirits of all men—is the Son of God, our Eternal Father. In this respect he is like all other men. He differs from all other men, however, by reason of the fact that men's bodies are begotten of mortal men and are, therefore, subject to death, being descendants and inheritors from Adam, while Christ's physical body was begotten of God, our Heavenly Father—an immortal being not subject to death. Christ, therefore, inherited from his Father the faculty to live on indefinitely. CR1975Apr:123-24

**Related Witnesses:**

**Orson Pratt**

The true God exists both in time and in space, and has as much relation to them as man or any other being. He has extension, and form, and dimensions, as well as man. He occupies space; has a body, parts, and passions; can go from place to place—can eat, drink, and talk, as well as man. Man resembles him in the features and form of his body, and he does not differ materially in size. When he has been seen among men, he has been pronounced, even by the wicked, as one of their own species. So much did he look like man, that some supposed him to be the carpenter's son. Like man, he had a Father; and he was *"the express image of the person of the Father."* The two persons were as much alike in form, in size, and in every other respect as fathers and sons are of the human race; indeed, the human race are *"his offspring,"* made in his likeness and image . . . after the image of his person. (The Kingdom of God, p. 4) TLDP:308

**President Joseph F. Smith,**
**Anthon H. Lund, Charles W. Penrose**
(First Presidency)
Jesus Christ is the Son of Elohim both as spiritual and bodily offspring; that is to say, Elohim is literally the Father of the spirit of Jesus Christ and also of the body in which Jesus Christ performed His mission in the flesh, and which body died on the cross and was afterward taken up by the process of resurrection, and is now the immortalized tabernacle of the eternal spirit of our Lord and Savior. ("The Father and The Son; A Doctrinal Exposition by The First Presidency and The Twelve," pamphlet published by the Church, June 30, 1916. Reprinted in AF:420-426. See MOFP5:23-34) MOFP5:27

**President Heber J. Grant**

We believe that Christ, divinely begotten, was born of woman, that He lived a mortal life, that He was crucified upon the cross, that He died, His spirit leaving His body, and was buried, and was on the third day resurrected, His spirit and body re-uniting. We believe this is the exact pattern we shall all follow. We believe that all men will be resurrected, that "men will be punished for their own sins, and not for Adam's transgression." MOFP6:33

**Bruce R. McConkie,**
*also quoting Joseph Smith*

"From eternity to eternity he is the same." (D&C 76:4) So it is written of that Lord who is both Jehovah and Jesus. And so it is. As the *Unembodied One*, while he dwelt in preexistence as the Firstborn spirit Son of the Eternal Elohim; as the *Embodied One*, while he dwelt among us, with his spirit shackled in a tabernacle of clay, a tabernacle created in the womb of Mary whose Son he was; as the *Disembodied One*, while he ministered for a moment among the spirits of the righteous dead; and finally as the *Reembodied One*, which he became when he rose from the dead, clothed with glory, immortality, and eternal life—in all of these states he was and is the same. (The Promised Messiah, pp. 197-98) TLDP:308

**President Spencer W. Kimball**

In order for Adam to regain his original state (to be in the presence of God), an atonement for this disobedience was necessary. In God's divine plan, provision was made for a redeemer to break the bonds of death and, through the resurrection, make possible the reunion of the spirits and bodies of all persons who had dwelt on earth. ¶ Jesus of Nazareth was the one who, before the world was created, was chosen to

---

268. Through the process of death and resurrection, Jesus Christ's spirit was reunited with his body.

come to earth to perform this service, to conquer mortal death. This voluntary action would atone for the fall of Adam and Eve and permit the spirit of man to recover his body, thereby reuniting body and spirit. ¶ Jesus Christ has influenced humanity more than anyone else who ever lived. CR1978Apr:7-8

**Elder Joseph Fielding Smith**
So Jesus did for us something that we could not do for ourselves, through his infinite atonement. On the third day after the crucifixion he took up his body and gained the keys of the resurrection, and thus has power to open the graves for all men, but this he could not do until he had first passed through death himself and conquered. (Doctrines of Salvation, 1:128) DGSM:87

**Related Witnesses:**

**Jesus,**
*recorded in Luke*
And as they thus spake, Jesus himself stood in the midst of them, and saith unto them, Peace be unto you. 37. But they were terrified and affrighted, and supposed that they had seen a spirit. 38. And he said unto them, Why are ye troubled? and why do thoughts arise in your hearts? 39. Behold my hands and my feet, that it is I myself: handle me, and see; for a spirit hath not flesh and bones, as ye see me have. (*The risen Christ appears to the Apostles and others*) Luke 24:36-39

**Mark E. Petersen**
Next we affirm the Jesus Christ of Nazareth is indeed the Christ—he who was born in Bethlehem on the first Christmas; he who answered the questions of the doctors in the temple when but twelve years old; he who was baptized of John; he who walked the plains of Palestine preaching his gospel, healing many who were sick, and raising some of the dead; he who was persecuted by the religious cults of the day, was condemned to the cross, but who conquered death and the grave in a glorious resurrection on the third day afterward. ¶ He *is* the Savior of mankind! He *is* the Redeemer of all flesh! He *did* arise from the grave. He *is* risen, as the angel said, in physical, corporeal reality. And he lives today! Our modern prophets have seen him face to face and have talked with him. We know that he lives and by his resurrection he will also give to each of us a victory over death, for we too shall be resurrected— physically and literally. We too shall live again. CR1980Apr:93-94

**John**
But Thomas, one of the twelve, called Didymus, was not with them when Jesus came.

25. The other disciples therefore said unto him, We have seen the Lord. But he said unto them, Except I shall see in his hands the print of the nails, and put my finger into the print of the nails, and thrust my hand into his side, I will not believe. 26. And after eight days again his disciples were within, and Thomas with them: then came Jesus, the doors being shut, and stood in the midst, and said, Peace be unto you. 27. Then saith he to Thomas, reach hither thy finger, and behold my hands; and reach hither thy hand, and thrust it into my side: and be not faithless, but believing. 28. And Thomas answered and said unto him, My Lord and my God. 29. Jesus saith unto him, Thomas, because thou hast seen me, thou hast believed: blessed are they that have not seen, and yet have believed. (*The risen Jesus appears to his assembled disciples*) John 20:24-29

**Jesus,**
*quoted by Mormon*
Arise and come forth unto me, that ye may thrust your hands into my side, and also that ye may feel the prints of the nails in my hands and in my feet, that ye may know that I am the God of Israel, and the God of the whole earth, and have been slain for the sins of the world. 15. And it came to pass that the multitude went forth, and thrust their hands into his side, and did feel the prints of the nails in his hands and in his feet; and this they did do, going forth one by one until they had all gone forth, and did see with their eyes and did feel with their hands, and did know of a surety and did bear record, that it was he, of whom it was written by the prophets, that should come. 16. And when they had all gone forth and had witnessed for themselves, they did cry out with one accord, saying: 17. Hosanna! Blessed be the name of the Most High God! And they did fall down at the feet of Jesus, and did worship him. (*The risen Jesus Christ appears to the Nephite people on the American continent soon after his ascension into heaven following the Crucifixion, A.D. 34*) 3Ne.11:14-17

---

**269. Christ had power to lay down His life and to take it up again.**

**President John Taylor**
One thing, as we read, is that the Father gave [Christ] power to have life in Himself; "For as the Father hath life in himself, so hath he given to the Son to have life in himself;" and further, He had power, when all mankind had lost their life, to restore life to them again; and hence He is the Resurrection and the Life, which power no other

man possesses. ¶ Another distinction is, that having this life in Himself, He had power, as He said, to lay down His life and to take it up again, which power was also given Him by the Father. This is also a power which no other being associated with this earth possesses. (The Mediation and Atonement, pp. 135-37) TLDP:299

**President John Taylor**
The Son hath life inherent in Himself, even as the Father hath life in Himself, He having received this power from the Father. Also, that He had power in Himself, as elsewhere stated, to lay down this body, and also to take it up again; and in this respect He differed from others. While man dies and lays down his body, he has not power under any circumstance to raise it again, only through the power of Jesus and His intercession and atonement; for the Redeemer has proclaimed Himself to be the Resurrection and the Life; and it is by this resurrective power which He possesses, as the gift of God through obedience to the will of the Father, that the dead shall hear the voice of God and shall live. Hence He not only becomes the first fruits of those that slept, having conquered death Himself and triumphed over it, but He also becomes the means of the resurrection of all men from the dead. (The Mediation and Atonement, pp. 146-47) TLDP:312

**Joseph Smith**
Jesus said that the Father wrought precisely in the same way as His Father had done before Him. As the Father had done before. He laid down His life, and took it up the same as His Father had done before. He did as He was sent, to lay down His life and take it up again; and then was committed unto Him the keys, &c. *(Sermon at the Stand in Nauvoo, Ill., June 16, 1844)* HC6:477

**Bruce R. McConkie**
Jesus only of all mankind—Jesus, the Son of the living God; Jesus, the Son of the mortal Virgin—this One Man of all men had power to live or to die; and having chosen to die, he had power to live again in glorious immortality, never again to see death. All this is according to the commandment of the Father. (The Mortal Messiah, 3:216-17) TLDP:313

**Elder Joseph F. Smith**
Jesus, the Only Begotten of the Father . . . had power to lay down His life and take it up again, and if we keep inviolate the covenants of the Gospel, remaining faithful and true to the end, we too, in his name and through his redeeming blood, will have power in due time to resurrect these our bodies after they shall have been committed to the earth. *(General conference, April 1876, JD18:277)* TLDP:560

**Elder Joseph Fielding Smith**
Christ is the "resurrection and the life" and the first fruits of them that slept. Therefore, none could pass from mortality to immortality until our Savior completed his work for the redemption of man and had gained the keys of the resurrection, being the *first* to rise, having "life in himself" and the power to lay down his life and take it up again, thus freeing all men from the bondage which the fall had placed upon them. (Doctrines of Salvation, 2:300-01) TLDP:700

---

270. The resurrected Jesus Christ is a glorified personage in form like man; He has a body of flesh and bones as tangible as man's.

**James E. Talmage**
[W]e know that both the Father and the Son are in form and stature perfect men; each of them possesses a tangible body, infinitely pure and perfect and attended by transcendent glory, nevertheless a body of flesh and bones. AF:38

**President Joseph F. Smith**
Jesus is the express image and likeness of His Father; therefore, as Jesus is a personage of flesh and bones, having a body as tangible as that of man, bearing in it the wounds of the nails and of the spear, so is the body of the Father just as tangible; it is just as real as that of the Son. (Millennial Star, Nov. 1, 1906, p. 690) TLDP:221

**President Joseph F. Smith**
The thing I want to impress upon you is that God is real, a creature of flesh and bones the same as you and I. Christ is the same but the Holy Ghost is a creature of spirit. ("Mutual Conference Is Well Attended," The Journal, Logan, Utah, March 14, 1911, p. 4) TLDP:228

**Elder Joseph Fielding Smith**
The Holy Ghost is the third member of the Godhead. He is a Spirit, in the form of a man. The Father and the Son are personages of tabernacle; they have bodies of flesh and bones. (Doctrines of Salvation, 1:38) TLDP:272

**Charles W. Penrose**
The Father has a body of flesh and bones, the Son also, but the Holy Ghost is a "personage of Spirit" (D&C:130). ("Whom Do the Latter-day Saints Worship?", IE1914Jun:706, 709) TLDP:362

**Related Witnesses:**
**Joseph Smith**
The Father has a body of flesh and bones as tangible as man's. The Son also; *(Revelation received April 2, 1830)* D&C 130:22

### Joseph Smith

For instance, Jesus said: Handle me and see, for a spirit hath not flesh and bones, as ye see me have. (*Instructions given at Nauvoo, Ill., Feb. 9, 1843; keys given whereby messengers from beyond the veil may be identified*) D&C 129:2

### Jesus,
#### recorded in Luke

And as they thus spake, Jesus himself stood in the midst of them, and saith unto them, Peace be unto you. 37. But they were terrified and affrighted, and supposed that they had seen a spirit. 38. And he said unto them, Why are ye troubled? and why do thoughts arise in your hearts? 39. Behold my hands and my feet, that it is I myself: handle me, and see; for a spirit hath not flesh and bones, as ye see me have. (*The risen Christ appears to the Apostles and others*) Luke 24:36-39

### Jesus,
#### quoted by Mormon

And it came to pass that when Jesus had spoken these words the whole multitude fell to the earth; for they remembered that it had been prophesied among them that Christ should show himself unto them after his ascension into heaven. 13. And it came to pass that the Lord spake unto them saying: 14. Arise and come forth unto me, that ye may thrust your hands into my side, and also that ye may feel the prints of the nails in my hands and in my feet, that ye may know that I am the God of Israel, and the God of the whole earth, and have been slain for the sins of the world. 15. And it came to pass that the multitude went forth, and thrust their hands into his side, and did feel the prints of the nails in his hands and in his feet; and this they did do, going forth one by one until they had all gone forth, and did see with their eyes and did feel with their hands, and did know of a surety and did bear record, that it was he, of whom it was written by the prophets, that should come. (*The risen Jesus Christ appears to the Nephite people on the American continent soon after his ascension into heaven following the Crucifixion, A.D. 34*) 3Ne.11:12-15

### Joseph Smith

It no sooner appeared than I found myself delivered from the enemy which held me bound. When the light rested upon me I saw two Personages, whose brightness and glory defy all description, standing above me in the air. One of them spake unto me, calling me by name and said, pointing to the other—This is My Beloved Son. Hear Him! (*Vision of the Father and the Son, spring of 1820*) JS-H 1:17

271. The resurrected Jesus Christ possesses a fulness of the glory of the Father.

### Elder Joseph Fielding Smith

The Savior did not have a fulness at first, but after he received his body and the resurrection all power was given unto him both in heaven and in earth. Although he was a God, even the Son of God, with power and authority to create this earth and other earths, yet there were some things lacking which he did not receive until after his resurrection. In other words he had not received the fulness until he got a resurrected body. (Doctrines of Salvation, 1:33) DGSM:9-10

### Elder Joseph Fielding Smith

Christ is also our Father because his father has given him of his fulness; that is, he has received a fulness of the glory of the Father. . . . ¶ The Father has honored Christ by placing his name upon him, so that he can minister in and through that name as though he were the Father; and thus, so far as power and authority are concerned, his words and acts become and are those of the Father. (Doctrines of Salvation, 1:29-30) TLDP:302-03

### Paul

1:19. For it pleased the Father that in him should all fulness dwell; . . . 2:9. For in him dwelleth all the fulness of the Godhead bodily. (*Paul writes from prison to the Church in Colossae, Asia Minor, about A.D. 60*) Col.1:19; 2:9

### John,
#### quoted by Joseph Smith

And I, John, saw that he received not of the fulness at the first, but received grace for grace; 13. And he received not of the fulness at first, but continued from grace to grace, until he received a fulness; 14. And thus he was called the Son of God, because he received not of the fulness at the first. 15. And I, John, bear record, and lo, the heavens were opened, and the Holy Ghost descended upon him in the form of a dove, and sat upon him, and there came a voice out of heaven saying: This is my beloved Son. 16. And I, John, bear record that he received a fulness of the glory of the Father; 17. And he received all power, both in heaven and on earth, and the glory of the Father was with him, for he dwelt in him. (*The Lord reveals that John bore record of his glory; Kirtland, Ohio, May 6, 1833*) D&C 93:12-17

### Joseph Smith,
#### receiving the Word of the Lord

The Father because he gave me of his fulness, and the Son because I was in the world and made flesh my tabernacle, and dwelt among the sons of men. (*The Lord speaks by revelation through Joseph Smith at Kirtland, Ohio, May 6, 1833*) D&C 93:4

**President John Taylor**

He is the Elect, the Chosen, and one of the Presidency in the heavens, and in Him dwells all the fulness of the Godhead bodily, which could not be said of us in any of these particulars. (The Mediation and Atonement, pp. 135-37) TLDP:299

**James E. Talmage**
*also quoting John,*
*as he is quoted by Joseph Smith*

Testimony of John the Apostle Concerning Christ's Development in Knowledge and Grace.—In a modern revelation, Jesus the Christ has confirmed the record of John the apostle, which record appears but in part in our compilation of ancient scriptures. John thus attests the actuality of natural development in the growth of Jesus from childhood to maturity: "And I, John, saw that he received not of the fulness at the first, but received grace for grace; And he received not of the fulness at first, but continued from grace to grace, until he received a fulness; And thus he was called the Son of God, because he received not of the fulness at the first" (D&C 93:12-14). Notwithstanding this graded course of growth and development after His birth in the flesh, Jesus Christ had been associated with the Father from the beginning, as is set forth in the revelation cited. We read therein: "And he [John] bore record, saying, I saw his glory that he was in the beginning before the world was; therefore in the beginning the Word was, for he was the Word, even the messenger of salvation, the light and the Redeemer of the world; the Spirit of truth, who came into the world, because the world was made by him, and in him was the life of men and the light of men. The worlds were made by him: men were made by him: all things were made by him, and through him, and of him. And I, John, bear record that I beheld his glory, as the glory of the Only Begotten of the Father, full of grace and truth, even the Spirit of truth, which came and dwelt in the flesh, and dwelt among us" (verses 7-11). JTC:119

---

272. **The mission of the Savior is to offer all the human race the sublime privilege of regaining the presence of the Father and of entering into His rest (in the celestial kingdom).**

**John A. Widtsoe**

The mission of the Savior and of His Church is to offer to all the human race the sublime privilege of regaining the presence of the Father and of entering into His rest. PCG:31

**President Brigham Young**

The errand of Jesus to earth was to bring his brethren and sisters back into the presence of the Father; he has done his part of the work, and it remains for us to do ours. There is not one thing that the Lord could do for the salvation of the human family that He has neglected to do; and it remains for the children of men to receive the truth or reject it; all that can be accomplished for their salvation, independent of them, has been accomplished in and by the Savior. . . . "Jesus paid the debt; he atoned for the original sin; he came and suffered and died on the cross." (*In new Tabernacle, July 18, 1869, JD13:59*) TLDP:309

**President Brigham Young,**
*quoted by John A. Widtsoe*

Can all the wisdom of the world devise means by which we can be redeemed, and return to the presence of our Father and Elder Brother, and dwell with holy angels and celestial beings? No, it is beyond the power and wisdom of the inhabitants of the earth that now live, or that ever did or ever will live, to prepare or create a sacrifice that will pay this divine debt. But God provided it, and his Son has paid it, and we, each and every one, can now receive the truth and be saved in the Kingdom of God. Is it clear and plain? It is to me, and if you have the Spirit of God, it is as plain to you as anything else in the world. (*In Ogden, Utah, Tabernacle, July 10, 1870, JD14:72*) DBY:59

**Jesus,**
*quoted by John*

Let not your heart be troubled: ye believe in God, believe also in me. 2. In my Father's house are many mansions: if it were not so, I would have told you. I go to prepare a place for you. 3. And if I go and prepare a place for you, I will come again, and receive you unto myself; that where I am, there ye may be also. 4. And whither I go ye know, and the way ye know. (*Jesus speaks to the Twelve of his many mansions*) John 14:1-4

**Related Witnesses:**

**Joseph Smith,**
*translating the Book of Moses*

For behold, this is my work and my glory—to bring to pass the immortality and eternal life of man. (*The Lord talks to Moses, face to face*) Moses 1:39

**President Spencer W. Kimball**

All three [missions of the Church] are part of

one work—to assist our Father in Heaven and His Son, Jesus Christ, in Their grand and glorious mission "to bring to pass the immortality and eternal life of man." (Moses 1:39) CR1981Apr:3

### John

But as many as received him, to them gave he power to become the sons of God, even to them that believe on his name: (*The record of the Apostle John, testifying of the Savior*) John 1:12

### Paul

[T]hat Christ Jesus came into the world to save sinners; of whom I am chief. (*Paul writes to his assistant Timothy, about A.D. 64*) 1Tim.1:15

### Joseph Smith

And this is the gospel, the glad tidings, which the voice out of the heavens bore record unto us— 41. That he came into the world, even Jesus, to be crucified for the world, and to bear the sins of the world, and to sanctify the world, and to cleanse it from all unrighteousness; 42. That through him all might be saved whom the Father had put into his power and made by him; (*Vision to Joseph Smith and Sidney Rigdon, Feb. 16, 1832*) D&C 76:40-42

### Jacob, brother of Nephi,
*quoted by Nephi*

And he cometh into the world that he may save all men if they will hearken unto his voice; for behold, he suffereth the pains of all men, yea, the pains of every living creature, both men, women, and children, who belong to the family of Adam. (*Jacob to the people of Nephi, 559-545 B.C.*) 2Ne.9:21

### Elder Joseph Fielding Smith

The only begotten Son of God in this world came in it primarily to die. He is spoken of in the scriptures as the "Lamb slain from the foundation of the world." The meaning of this is that he was chosen to his mission as Redeemer of a fallen world, even before the foundations of the earth were laid. His great mission is twofold. First, to redeem all men from death irrespective of their obedience or disobedience, their willingness to keep his commandments, or their rejection of those commandments, and this is done because since Adam, all men have been innocent of the cause of death in the world. Therefore they are redeemed from its consequences irrespective of their belief or lack of belief in the Son of God. Secondly, he came into the world to save all men from the consequences of their own sins if they are willing to repent. (The Restoration of All Things, pp. 283-84) TLDP:309

### J. Reuben Clark, Jr.

. . . His real mission was to redeem man from the Fall of Adam by the atonement He made.

We declare this is the greatest gift that ever came to man, for without it there would be no immortality of the soul, which is "the spirit and the body of man." ("I Am the Resurrection and the Life," IE1943Jan:63) TLDP:38

---

## 273. Jesus Christ is the mediator between God and all mankind; He is our advocate with the Father.

### Joseph Smith

Listen to him who is the advocate with the Father, who is pleading your cause before him— 4. Saying: Father, behold the sufferings and death of him who did no sin, in whom thou wast well pleased; behold the blood of thy Son which was shed, the blood of him whom thou gavest that thyself might be glorified; 5. Wherefore, Father, spare these my brethren that believe on my name, that they may come unto me and have everlasting life. (*Revelation March 7, 1831; Christ will intercede with the Father, with these words*) D&C 45:3-5

### Paul

For there is one God, and one mediator between God and men, the man Christ Jesus; 6. Who gave himself a ransom for all, to be testified in due time. (*Paul writes to his assistant Timothy, about A.D. 64*) 1Tim.2:5-6

### Elder Joseph Fielding Smith

When Adam was in the Garden of Eden, he was in the presence of God our Eternal Father. After his fall, he was driven out of the presence of the Father, who withdrew from Adam, and when children were born to Adam they, too, were shut out of the presence of the father. Then, according to the scriptures, Jesus Christ became the Advocate for Adam and his children, and also their Mediator standing between mankind and the Eternal Father, pleading our cause. From that time forth it was Jesus Christ who directed his servants on the earth and gave revelation and guidance to the prophets. (Answers to Gospel Questions, 3:5) TLDP:305

### Elder Joseph Fielding Smith

[T]he Father withdrew from having personal contact with his children and Jesus Christ as the advocate and mediator between God the Father and mankind comes upon the scene. (Man, His Origin and Destiny, p. 312) TLDP:305

### Bruce R. McConkie

He came into the world to ransom men from the temporal and spiritual death brought upon them by the fall of Adam. He came to satisfy the demands of divine justice and to bring mercy to the penitent. He came as a Mediator, as an

Intercessor, to plead the cause of all those who believe in him. CR1977Apr:16-17

### Boyd K. Packer,
*also quoting Paul*

[B]y eternal law, mercy cannot be extended save there be one who is both willing and able to assume our debt and pay the price and arrange the terms for our redemption. ¶ Unless there is a mediator, unless we have a friend, the full weight of justice untempered, unsympathetic, must, positively must fall on us. The full recompense for every transgression, however minor or however deep, will be exacted from us to the uttermost farthing. ¶ But know this: Truth, glorious truth, proclaims there is such a Mediator. ¶ "For there is one God, and one mediator between God and men, the man Christ Jesus." (1Tim.2:5) CR1977Apr:80

### Related Witnesses:
#### Mormon

For he hath answered the ends of the law, and he claimeth all those who have faith in him; and they who have faith in him will cleave unto every good thing; wherefore he advocateth the cause of the children of men; and he dwelleth eternally in the heavens. (*Mormon preaches about Christ in the synagogue, prior to A.D. 384*) Moro.7:28

#### John

My little children, these things write I unto you, that ye sin not. And if any man sin [JST(1Jn.1 fn. a "and repent"], we have an advocate with the Father, Jesus Christ the righteous: (*John writes to the churches in Asia*) 1Jn.2:1

#### Joseph Smith

The veil was taken from our minds, and the eyes of our understanding were opened. 2. We saw the Lord standing upon the breastwork of the pulpit, before us; and under his feet was a paved work of pure gold, in color like amber. 3. His eyes were as a flame of fire; the hair of his head was white like the pure snow; his countenance shone above the brightness of the sun; and his voice was as the sound of the rushing of great waters, even the voice of Jehovah, saying: 4. I am the first and the last; I am he who liveth, I am he who was slain; I am your advocate with the Father. (*Visions manifested to Joseph Smith and to Oliver Cowdery in the Kirtland Temple, April 3, 1836*) D&C 110:1-4

---

### 274. Jesus Christ is Jehovah, the God of the Old Testament.

### James E. Talmage

Jesus of Nazareth, who in solemn testimony to the Jews declared Himself the I Am or Jehovah, who was God before Abraham lived on earth, was the same Being who is repeatedly proclaimed as the God who made covenant with Abraham, Isaac, and Jacob; the God who led Israel from the bondage of Egypt to the freedom of the promised land, the one and only God known by direct and personal revelation to the Hebrew prophets in general. ¶ The identity of Jesus Christ with the Jehovah of the Israelites was well understood by the Nephite prophets, and the truth of their teachings was confirmed by the risen Lord who manifested Himself unto them shortly after His ascension from the midst of the apostles at Jerusalem. JTC:38

### James E. Talmage

Jesus Christ was and is Jehovah, the God of Adam and of Noah, the God of Abraham, Isaac, and Jacob, the God of Israel, the God at whose instance the prophets of the ages have spoken, the God of all nations, and He who shall yet reign on earth as King of kings and Lord of lords. JTC:4

### Bruce R. McConkie

Names applied to our Lord are numerous. Each has a differing shade of meaning and teaches some special thing relative to him and his work. But each refers to the same individual. Old Testament prophets refer to him as the Savior, Redeemer, Deliverer, Messiah, God of Israel, Jehovah, and so forth, all being names that identify the Only Begotten of the Father. (The Promised Messiah, p. 306) TLDP:300

### Elder Joseph Fielding Smith

All revelation since the fall has come through Jesus Christ, who is the Jehovah of the Old Testament. In all of the scriptures, where God is mentioned and where he has appeared, it was Jehovah who talked with Abraham, with Noah, Enoch, Moses and all the prophets. He is the God of Israel, the Holy One of Israel; the one who led that nation out of Egyptian bondage, and who gave and fulfilled the law of Moses. The Father has never dealt with man directly and personally since the fall, and he has never appeared except to introduce and bear record of the Son. (Doctrines of Salvation, 1:27) DGSM:4

### President Joseph F. Smith,
### Anthon H. Lund, Charles W. Penrose
(First Presidency)
*also quoting Jesus*
*as He is quoted by John*

In all His dealings with the human family Jesus the Son has represented and yet represents Elohim His father in power and authority. This is true of Christ in His preexistent, antemortal, or unembodied state, in which He was know as Jehovah; also during His embodiment in the flesh; and during His labors as a disembodied spirit in the realm of the dead; and since that period in His resurrected state. To the Jews He said: "I and my Father are one" (John 10:30; see also 17:11, 22); yet He declared "My Father is greater than I" (John 14:28); and further, "I am come in my Father's name" (John 5:43; see also 10:25). The same truth was declared by Christ Himself to the Nephites (see 3 Nephi 20:35 and 28:10), and has been reaffirmed by revelation in the present dispensation (D&C: 50:43). Thus the Father placed His name upon the Son; and Jesus Christ spoke and ministered in and through the Father's name; and so far as power, authority and Godship are concerned His words and acts were and are those of the father. ("The Father and The Son; A Doctrinal Exposition by The First Presidency and The Twelve," published by the Church in a pamphlet, June 30, 1916. Reprinted in AF:420-426. See MOFP:5:23-34) MOFP5:31-32

### Joseph Smith

The veil was taken from our minds, and the eyes of our understanding were opened. 2. We saw the Lord standing upon the breastwork of the pulpit, before us; and under his feet was a paved work of pure gold, in color like amber. 3. His eyes were as a flame of fire; the hair of his head was white like the pure snow; his countenance shone above the brightness of the sun; and his voice was as the sound of the rushing of great waters, even the voice of Jehovah, saying: 4. I am the first and the last; I am he who liveth, I am he who was slain; I am your advocate with the Father. (*Visions manifested to Joseph Smith and Oliver Cowdery in the Kirtland Temple, April 3, 1836*) D&C 110:1-4

### Abraham,
#### quoted by Joseph Smith

For I am the Lord thy God; I dwell in heaven; the earth is my footstool; I stretch my hand over the sea, and it obeys my voice; I cause the wind and the fire to be my chariot; I say to the mountains—Depart hence—and behold, they are taken away by a whirlwind, in an instant, suddenly. 8. My name is Jehovah, and I know the end from the beginning; therefore my hand shall be over thee. (*Jehovah appears to Abraham in response to prayer*) Abr.2:7-8

### James E. Talmage

Jesus, when once assailed with question and criticism from certain Jews who regarded their Abrahamic lineage as an assurance of divine preferment, met their abusive words with the declaration: "Verily, verily, I say unto you, Before Abraham was, I am." The true significance of this saying would be more plainly

expressed were the sentence punctuated and pointed as follows: "Verily, verily, I say unto you, Before Abraham, was I AM"; which means the same as had He said—Before Abraham, was I, Jehovah. JTC:37; MPSG1987:40

### Related Witnesses:
#### Jesus,
##### quoted by John

Art thou greater than our father Abraham, which is dead? and the prophets are dead: whom makest thou thyself? 54. Jesus answered, If I honour myself, my honour is nothing: it is my Father that honoureth me; of whom ye say, that he is your God: 55. Yet ye have not known him; but I know him: and if I should say, I know him not, I shall be a liar like unto you: but I know him, and keep his saying. 56. Your father Abraham rejoiced to see my day: and he saw it, and was glad. 57. Then said the Jews unto him, Thou art not yet fifty years old, and hast thou seen Abraham? 58. Jesus said unto them, Verily, verily, I say unto you, Before Abraham was, I am. 59. Then took they up stones to cast at him: but Jesus hid himself, and went out of the temple, going through the midst of them, and so passed by. (*Jesus answers the disputing Jews*) John 8:53-59

### Joseph Smith,
#### receiving the Word of the Lord

Thus saith the Lord your God, even Jesus Christ, the Great I AM, Alpha and Omega, the beginning and the end, the same which looked upon the wide expanse of eternity, and all the seraphic hosts of heaven, before the world was made; 2. The same which knoweth all things, for all things are present before mine eyes; 3. I am the same which spake, and the world was made, and all things came by me. (*Christ speaks to the Prophet giving revelation of commandments to Saints in conference, Jan. 2, 1831*) D&C 38:1-3

### Jesus,
#### quoted by Mormon

And it came to pass that the Lord spake unto them saying: 14. Arise and come forth unto me, that ye may thrust your hands into my side, and also that ye may feel the prints of the nails in my hands and in my feet, that ye may know that I am the God of Israel, and the God of the whole earth, and have been slain for the sins of the world. (*The risen Jesus Christ appears to the Nephite people on the American continent soon after his ascension into heaven following the crucifixion, A.D. 34*) 3Ne.11:13-14

### Jesus,
#### quoted by Mormon

Behold, I am he that gave the law, and I am he who covenanted with my people Israel; therefore, the law in me is fulfilled, for I have come to fulfil the law; therefore it hath an end. *(The resurrected Jesus teaches the Nephites, A.D. 34)* 3Ne.15:5

### Nephi, son of Lehi

And the God of our fathers, who were led out of Egypt, out of bondage, and also were preserved in the wilderness by him, yea, the God of Abraham, and of Isaac, and the God of Jacob, yieldeth himself, according to the words of the angel, as a man, into the hands of wicked men, to be lifted up, according to the words of Zenock, and to be crucified, according to the words of Neum, and to be buried in a sepulchre, according to the words of Zenos, which he spake concerning the three days of darkness, which should be a sign given of his death unto those who should inhabit the isles of the sea, more especially given unto those who are of the house of Israel. *(Nephi's writings, between 588 and 570 B.C.)* 1Ne.19:10

### Joseph Smith,
### *translating the book of Exodus*

. . . I am the Lord God Almighty; the Lord JEHOVAH. And was not my name known unto them? *(The Lord identifies himself to Moses as Jehovah)* JST(Ex.6:3 fn. c)

### Isaiah

Behold, God is my salvation; I will trust, and not be afraid: for the LORD JEHOVAH is my strength and my song; he also is become my salvation. *(Isaiah anticipates the millennial day)* Isa.12:2

### Recorded in Exodus

. . . God called unto him out of the midst of the bush, and said, Moses, Moses. And he said, Here am I. 5. And he said, Draw not nigh hither: put off thy shoes from off thy feet, for the place whereon thou standest is holy ground. 6. Moreover he said, I am the God of thy father, the God of Abraham, the God of Isaac, and the God of Jacob. And Moses hid his face; for he was afraid to look upon God. . . . 15. And God said moreover unto Moses, Thus shalt thou say unto the children of Israel, The LORD God of your fathers, the God of Abraham, the God of Isaac, and the God of Jacob, hath sent me unto you: this is my name for ever, and this is my memorial unto all generations. 16. Go, and gather the elders of Israel together, and say unto them, The LORD God of your fathers, the God of Abraham, of Isaac, and of Jacob, appeared unto me, saying, I have surely visited you, and seen that which is done to you in Egypt: *(Jehovah/Christ appears to Moses in the burning bush)* Ex.3:4-6,15-16

## 275. Jesus Christ presides as the God of this world (under the Father).

### President Spencer W. Kimball

Jesus Christ is the God of this world. He has made it very plain in his many self-introductions. CR1977Oct:112

### Hugh B. Brown

The vital and dynamic message of Mormonism is that there is a personal God in the heavens. He is omnipotent, omniscient, and omnipresent. He has not abated his power—he has not surrendered his sovereignty; he has not diluted his love; he changes not; and his plans never fail. We bear witness that his chief executive officer in the creation and direction of the affairs of this and other worlds is Jesus Christ the Lord, the Redeemer of the World, the Son of the Father. CR1962Oct:43

### Elder Ezra Taft Benson

Nearly two thousand years ago a perfect man walked the earth: Jesus the Christ. He was the son of a heavenly father and an earthly mother. He is the God of this world, under the Father. He taught men truth, that they might be free. His example and precepts provide the great standard, the only sure way, for all mankind. He became the first and only one who had the power to reunite his body with his spirit after death. By his power all men who have died shall be resurrected. Before him one day we all must stand to be judged by his laws. He lives today and in the not too distant future shall return, in triumph to subdue his enemies, to reward men according to their deeds, and to assume his rightful role to rule and reign in righteousness over the entire earth. CR1967Apr:58-59

### Elder Ezra Taft Benson

Yes, this same Jesus has already come to earth in our day. The Resurrected Christ—glorified, exalted, the God of this world under the Father—appeared to the boy Joseph Smith in 1820. This same Jesus who was the God of Abraham, Isaac, and Jacob, the God of Moses, the Creator of this earth, has come in our day. CR1964Apr:122

### Jesus,
### *quoted by Mormon*

And behold, I am the light and the life of the world; and I have drunk out of that bitter cup which the Father hath given me, and have glorified the Father in taking upon me the sins of the world, in the which I have suffered the will of the Father in all things from the beginning. 12. And it came to pass that when Jesus had spoken these words the whole multitude fell to the earth; for they remembered that it had been prophesied among them that Christ should show himself unto them after his ascension into heaven. 13. And it came to pass that the Lord spake unto them saying: 14. Arise and come forth unto me, that ye may thrust your hands into my side, and also that ye may feel the prints of the nails in my hands and in my feet, that ye may know that I am the God of Israel, and the God of the whole earth, and have been slain for the sins of the world. (*The risen Jesus Christ appears to the Nephite people on the American continent soon after his ascension into heaven following the Crucifixion, A.D. 34*) 3Ne.11:11-14

### James E. Talmage

We are to study Him as the Creator of the world, as the Word of Power, through whom the purposes of the Eternal Father were realized in the preparation of the earth for the abode of His myriad spirit children during the appointed period of their mortal probation. Jesus Christ was and is Jehovah, the God of Adam and of Noah, the God of Abraham, Isaac, and Jacob, the God of Israel, the God at whose instance the prophets of the ages have spoken, the God of all nations, and He who shall yet reign on earth as King of kings and Lord of lords. JTC:4

**Related Witnesses:**

### Elder Harold B. Lee

I bear you my witness, as the Spirit has before, and does now bear witness to my soul, that there has been entrusted to this, the true Church of Jesus Christ in these latter days, the true doctrines of salvation by which mankind may be redeemed, through the atonement of our Lord and Master, the Savior of the world. The Lord Jesus Christ does live and presides from his holy dwelling place, over this, his kingdom of God on this earth, through him who has been sustained this day as your President, a prophet, seer, and revelator. CR1970Apr:126

### President Joseph F. Smith

I declare to you that they are not one person, but that they are two persons, two bodies, separate and apart, and as distinct as are any father and son within the sound of my voice. Yet, Jesus is the Father of this world, because it was by him that the world was made. *(March 16, 1902)* (Gospel Doctrine, p. 68) TLDP:306

### Samuel, the Lamanite,
#### *quoted by Mormon*

And also that ye might know of the coming of Jesus Christ, the Son of God, the Father of heaven and of earth, the Creator of all things from the beginning; and that ye might know of the signs of his coming, to the intent that ye

might believe on his name. (*Samuel preaches to the Nephites that Christ, through his death and resurrection, redeems men from temporal and spiritual death, about 6 B.C.*) Hel.14:12

### Bruce R. McConkie

Christ-Messiah is God! ¶ Such is the plain and pure pronouncement of all the prophets of all the ages. In our desire to avoid the false and absurd conclusions contained in the creeds of Christendom, we are wont to shy away from this pure and unadorned verity; we go to great lengths to use language that shows there is both a Father and a Son, that they are separate Persons and are not somehow mystically intertwined as an essence or spirit that is everywhere present. Such an approach is perhaps essential in reasoning with the Gentiles of sectarianism; it helps to overthrow the fallacies formulated in their creeds. ¶ But having so done, if we are to envision our Lord's true status and glory, we must come back to the pronouncement of pronouncements, the doctrine of doctrines, the message of messages, which is that Christ is God. And if it were not so, he could not save us. Let all men, both in heaven and on earth, hear the proclamation and rejoice in its eternal verity; "The Lord is God, and beside him there is no Savior." (D&C 76:1) (The Promised Messiah, p. 98) TLDP:302

### President John Taylor

If He was the first born and obedient to the laws of His Father, did He not inherit the position by right to be the representative of God, the Savior and Redeemer of the world? And was it not His peculiar right and privilege as the firstborn, the legitimate heir of God, the Eternal Father, to step forth, accomplish and carry out the designs of His Heavenly Father pertaining to the redemption, salvation and exaltation of man? And being Himself without sin (which no other mortal was), He took the position of Savior and Redeemer, which by right belonged to Him as the first born. And does it not seem that in having a body specially prepared, and being the offspring of God, both in body and spirit, He stood preeminently in the position of the Son of God, or in the place of God, and was God, and was thus the fit and only personage capable of making an infinite atonement? (The Mediation and Atonement, pp. 135-37) TLDP:299

### Joseph Smith,
#### *receiving the Word of the Lord*

Hearken and listen to the voice of him who is from all eternity to all eternity, the Great I AM, even Jesus Christ— 2. The light and the life of the world; a light which shineth in darkness and the darkness comprehendeth it not; 3. The same which came in the meridian of time unto mine own, and mine own received me not; 4. But to as many as received me, gave I power to become my sons; and even so will I give unto as many as will receive me, power to become my sons. (*Revelation received Jan. 5, 1831*) D&C 39:1-4

**Author's Note:** Although Christ is God of this world, the devil would arrogantly claim, "I am the god of this world!" Satan has at times been called "the god of the world," referring to his role as ruler of darkness of the world. (See Eph.6:12.) Satan is not, of course, the *true* God of the world, except in the context that "worldly" people follow him and allow Satan to rule over them. ¶ Paul talked about "the god of this world" who "hath blinded the minds of them which believe not" (2Cor.4:4). Elder Harold B. Lee said that the coming of Christ as the Son of God "seemed to have intensified the hatred of the forces of evil. So powerful was Satan that the Master, you recall, spoke of him as the prince of this world. Said he, '. . . the prince of this world cometh, and hath nothing in me'." (John 14:30) (CR1965Oct:128)

---

276. Jesus Christ is the life and light of the world.

**Bruce R. McConkie**

Our understanding of the Light of Christ is limited. Finite powers and capacities cannot comprehend that which is infinite. But we do know certain basic principles, among which are these: ¶ 1. That it is the light which proceeds forth from the presence and person of Deity to fill immensity, and that it is therefore everywhere present; ¶ 2. That it is the agency of God's power, the law by which all things are governed. ¶ 3. That it is the divine power which gives life to all things and that if it were completely withdrawn life would cease; ¶ 4. That it enlightens the mind and quickens the understanding of every person born into the world (all have a conscience!); ¶ 5. That it strives with all men (the Holy Ghost testifies but does not strive) unless and until they rebel against light and truth, at which time the striving ceases, and in that sense the Spirit is withdrawn; ¶ 6. That those who hearken to its voice come unto Christ, receive his gospel, are baptized, and gain the gift of the Holy Ghost. (Moro.7:12-18; D&C 84:43-53; 88:7-13) (The Promised Messiah, pp. 208-09) DGSM:44

**Joseph Smith**

And now, remember the words of him who is

the life and light of the world, your Redeemer, your Lord and your God. Amen. (*Revelation received summer 1828*) D&C 10:70

**Joseph Smith**

He that ascended up on high, as also he descended below all things, in that he comprehended all things, that he might be in all and through all things, the light of truth; 7. Which truth shineth. This is the light of Christ. As also he is in the sun, and the light of the sun, and the power thereof by which it was made. 8. As also he is in the moon, and is the light of the moon, and the power thereof by which it was made; 9. As also the light of the stars, and the power thereof by which they were made; 10. And the earth also, and the power thereof, even the earth upon which you stand. 11. And the light which shineth, which giveth you light, is through him who enlighteneth your eyes, which is the same light that quickeneth your understandings; 12. Which light proceedeth forth from the presence of God to fill the immensity of space— 13. The light which is in all things, which giveth life to all things, which is the law by which all things are governed, even the power of God who sitteth upon his throne, who is in the bosom of eternity, who is in the midst of all things. (*Revelation Dec. 27/28, 1832*) D&C 88:6-13

**Jesus,**
*quoted by Mormon*

I am the light and the life of the world. I am Alpha and Omega, the beginning and the end. (*The voice of the resurrected Jesus Christ to the Nephites immediately before he visited them,* A.D. 34) 3Ne.9:18

**John**

That was the true Light, which lighteth every man that cometh into the world. (*The record of the Apostle John, testifying of the Savior*) John 1:9

**John,**
*quoted by Joseph Smith,*
*translating John*

In him was the gospel, and the gospel was the life, and the life was the light of men; 5. And the light shineth in the world, and the world perceiveth it not. 6. There was a man sent from God, whose name was John. 7. The same came into the world for a witness, to bear witness of the light, to bear record of the gospel through the Son, unto all, that through him men might believe. 8. He was not that light, but came to bear witness of that light, 9. Which was the true light, which lighteth every man who cometh into the world; JST(John 1:4-9 in Appendix)

**Joseph Smith**

For the word of the Lord is truth, and whatsoever

is truth is light, and whatsoever is light is Spirit, even the Spirit of Jesus Christ. 46. And the Spirit giveth light to every man that cometh into the world; and the Spirit enlighteneth every man through the world, that hearkeneth to the voice of the Spirit. (*Revelation received Sept. 22/23, 1832; the Spirit of Christ enlightens men*) D&C 84:45-46

### Joseph Smith,
*receiving the Word of the Lord*

And that I am the true light that lighteth every man that cometh into the world; . . . 9. The light and the Redeemer of the world; the Spirit of truth, who came into the world, because the world was made by him, and in him was the life of men and the light of men. (*The Lord speaks by revelation at Kirtland, Ohio, May 6, 1833*) D&C 93:2,9

### Jesus,
*quoted by John*

Then spake Jesus again unto them, saying, I am the light of the world: he that followeth me shall not walk in darkness, but shall have the light of life. (*Jesus teaches the people in the temple*) John 8:12

**Related Witnesses:**

### Jesus,
*quoted by John*

Jesus saith unto him, I am the way, the truth, and the life: no man cometh unto the Father, but by me. (*Jesus answers Thomas, who asks, "How can we know the way?"*) John 14:6

---

### 277. Only through Christ can we be saved.

### Jesus,
*quoted by John*

Jesus saith unto him, I am the way, the truth, and the life: no man cometh unto the Father, but by me. (*Jesus answers Thomas, who asks, "How can we know the way?"*) John 14:6

### James E. Talmage

I am thankful that the Church to which I belong preaches Christ and Him crucified, and resurrected, . . . the Christ that was the offspring in the flesh, as well as in the spirit, of the very Eternal Father, the Christ who is the Savior and Redeemer of mankind, beside whom there is none, beside whose name there is no name under heaven, whereby mankind may be saved. CR1916Apr:131

### George F. Richards

[We Latter-day Saints] . . . realize that there is no virtue for salvation and exaltation outside of the atoning blood of Jesus Christ, our Savior. There is no other name under heaven by which

man may obtain salvation. CR1916Apr:53

### Peter

Neither is there salvation in any other: for there is none other name under heaven given among men, whereby we must be saved. (*Peter and John are arrested and brought before the Jewish council; Peter answers the question, "By what power, or by what name, have ye done this?" by replying "by the name of Jesus Christ"*) Acts 4:12

### Bruce R. McConkie

He came to bring hope, to bring joy, to bring peace, to bring salvation; and his is the only name given under heaven whereby salvation comes. ¶ Our Lord—the Lord Jehovah, the Lord Jesus—is our hope and our salvation. He it is that hath brought life and immortality to light through the gospel. He has redeemed us from death, hell, the devil, and endless torment. CR1977Apr:17

### King Benjamin,
*quoted by Mormon*

And moreover, I say unto you, that there shall be no other name given nor any other way nor means whereby salvation can come unto the children of men, only in and through the name of Christ, the Lord Omnipotent. (*King Benjamin addresses his people, about 124 B.C.; the Lord Omnipotent shall minister among men in a tabernacle of clay*) Mosiah 3:17

### King Benjamin,
*quoted by Mormon*

And under this head ye are made free, and there is no other head whereby ye can be made free. There is no other name given whereby salvation cometh; therefore, I would that ye should take upon you the name of Christ, all you that have entered into the covenant with God that ye should be obedient unto the end of your lives. (*King Benjamin addresses the people after they entered into a covenant with God to keep all his commandments, about 124 B.C.*) Mosiah 5:8

### Jacob, brother of Nephi,
*quoted by Nephi*

[T]he keeper of the gate is the Holy One of Israel; and he employeth no servant there; and there is none other way save it be by the gate; for he cannot be deceived, for the Lord God is his name. (*Jacob teaches the people of Nephi, 559-545 B.C.*) 2Ne.9:41

**Related Witnesses:**

### Jesus,
*quoted by John*

Then said Jesus unto them again, Verily, verily, I say unto you, I am the door of the sheep. . . . 9. I am the door: by me if any man enter in, he shall be saved, and shall go in and out, and find pasture. (*Jesus teaches the people*) John 10:7,9

## 278. Jesus Christ is the judge of all.

### Jesus,
### *quoted by John*

For the Father judgeth no man, but hath committed all judgment unto the Son: . . . 27. And hath given him authority to execute judgment also, because he is the Son of man. . . . 30. I can of mine own self do nothing: as I hear, I judge: and my judgment is just; because I seek not mine own will, but the will of the Father which hath sent me. (*Jesus addresses the Jews*) John 5:22,27,30

### George Q. Cannon

The Lord says that He is coming "to recompense unto every man according to his work, and measure to every man according to the measure he has measured to his fellow man." This is in keeping with the words of Jesus: [Luke 6:37-38 is quoted]. (Gospel Truth, 1:92) TLDP:321

### President John Taylor

When we reflect upon the statement of creatures being judged without law, the question arises as to who are to be their judges. We may here state that Christ is called the judge of the quick and the dead, the judge of all the earth. (The Mediation and Atonement, pp. 155-57) TLDP:324

### President Joseph F. Smith

[C]alamities will befall the nations as signs of the coming of Christ to judgment. (Gospel Doctrine, p. 55) TLDP:327

### Recorded in Psalms

But the LORD shall endure for ever: he hath prepared his throne for judgment. 8. And he shall judge the world in righteousness, he shall minister judgment to the people in uprightness. Ps.9:7-8

### Paul

Henceforth there is laid up for me a crown of righteousness, which the Lord, the righteous judge, shall give me at that day: and not to me only, but unto all them also that love his appearing. (*Paul writes to his assistant Timothy, about A.D. 64*) 2Tim.4:8

### Peter

Him God raised up the third day, and shewed him openly; 41. Not to all the people, but unto witnesses chosen before of God, even to us, who did eat and drink with him after he rose from the dead. 42. And he commanded us to preach unto the people, and to testify that it is he which was ordained of God to be the Judge of quick and dead. (*Peter preaches about Christ*) Acts 10:40-42

### Related Witnesses:
### Elder John Taylor

It is written that Jesus will judge not after the sight of the eye, or after the hearing of the ear, but with righteousness shall he judge the poor, and reprove with equity the meek of the earth. (*In Tabernacle, Feb. 5, 1865, JD11:79*) TLDP:324

## 279. The Son, Jesus Christ, carries out the Father's will.

### President Brigham Young,
### *quoted by John A. Widtsoe*

He did nothing of himself. He wrought miracles and performed a good work on the earth; but of himself he did nothing. He said, "As I have seen my Father do, so do I. I came not to do my will, but the will of him that sent me." We must come to the conclusion that the Son of God did not suggest, dictate, act, or produce any manifestation of his power, of his glory, or of his errand upon the earth, only as it came from the mind and will of his Father. (*In Tabernacle, Nov. 29, 1857, JD6:96*) DBY:26

### Jesus,
### *quoted by John*

Jesus saith unto them, My meat is to do the will of him that sent me, and to finish his work. (*The disciples of Christ encourage him to eat*) John 4:34

### Jesus,
### *quoted by John*

Then answered Jesus and said unto them, Verily, verily, I say unto you, The Son can do nothing of himself, but what he seeth the Father do: for what things soever he doeth, these also doeth the Son likewise. . . . 30. I can of mine own self do nothing: as I hear, I judge: and my judgment is just; because I seek not mine own will, but the will of the Father which hath sent me. (*Jesus addresses the Jews*) John 5:19,30

### President Joseph F. Smith
### Anthon H. Lund, Charles W. Penrose
### (First Presidency)
### The Council of the Twelve

Thus the Father placed His name upon the Son; and Jesus Christ spoke and ministered in and through the Father's name; and so far as power, authority and Godship are concerned His words and acts were and are those of the Father. ("The Father and The Son; A Doctrinal Exposition by The First Presidency and The Twelve," published by the Church in a pamphlet, June 30, 1916. Reprinted in AF:420-426. See MOFP:5:23-34) AF:425

### President John Taylor

If He was the first born and obedient to the laws of His Father, did He not inherit the position by right to be the representative of God, the Savior and Redeemer of the world? And was it not His peculiar right and privilege as the firstborn, the legitimate heir of God, the Eternal Father, to step forth, accomplish and carry out the designs of His Heavenly Father pertaining to the redemption, salvation and exaltation of man? (The Mediation and Atonement, pp. 135-37) TLDP:299

**Related Witnesses:**

### Jesus,
#### recorded in Matthew

And he went a little further, and fell on his face, and prayed, saying, O my Father, if it be possible, let this cup pass from me: nevertheless not as I will, but as thou wilt. . . . 42. He went away again the second time, and prayed, saying, O my Father, if this cup may not pass away from me, except I drink it, thy will be done. (*Jesus suffers in Gethsemane*) Matt.26:39,42

### Jesus,
#### quoted by Mormon

And behold, I am the light and the life of the world; and I have drunk out of that bitter cup which the Father hath given me, and have glorified the Father in taking upon me the sins of the world, in the which I have suffered the will of the Father in all things from the beginning. (*The risen Jesus Christ appears to the Nephite people on the American continent soon after his ascension into heaven following the Crucifixion, A.D. 34*) 3Ne.11:11

### Joseph Smith,
#### quoted by Joseph Fielding Smith

He [our Lord] never transgressed or broke a commandment or law of heaven—no deceit was in His mouth, neither was guile found in His heart. (*Epistle to the elders of the Church generally, Jan. 1834*) TPJS:67; DGSM:10

---

**280. Jesus Christ, the Savior and Son of God, is sometimes referred to as the Father; He is father of the spiritually reborn.**

#### Bruce R. McConkie

Few doctrines are better known by members of the true Church than the doctrine of preexistence. We are well aware that all men are the children of God, the offspring of the Father, his sons and his daughters. We know that we were all born in his courts as spirit beings, long before the foundations of this earth were laid, and that the Lord Jehovah is in fact the Firstborn Son. What is not so well known is that nearly all the passages of scripture, both ancient and modern, which speak of God as our father and of men on earth being the sons of

God, have no reference to our birth in preexistence as the children of Elohim, but teach rather that Jehovah is our Father and we are his children. ¶ In setting forth that all men must be born again to gain salvation, we have seen that this means they must be "born of God, changed from their carnal and fallen state, to a state of righteousness, being redeemed of God, becoming his sons and daughters;" (Mosiah 27:25). Whose sons and whose daughters do we become when we are born again? Who is our new Father? The answer is Christ is our Father; we become his children by adoption; he makes us members of his family. Nowhere is this set forth better than in the words of King Benjamin to his Nephite subjects. (The Promised Messiah, pp. 351-52) TLDP:303

### King Benjamin,
#### quoted by Mormon

And now, because of the covenant which ye have made ye shall be called the children of Christ, his sons, and his daughters; for behold, this day he hath spiritually begotten you; for ye say that your hearts are changed through faith on his name; therefore, ye are born of him and have become his sons and his daughters. (*King Benjamin addresses the people after they entered into a covenant with God to keep all his commandments, about 124 B.C.*) Mosiah 5:7

#### Bruce R. McConkie

In 1916, the duly constituted heads of the earthly Church, who have the ultimate responsibility, under Deity, to interpret and promulgate the mind and will of the Lord to mortals, issued a document entitled *The Father and The Son: A Doctrinal Exposition by The First Presidency and The Twelve.* Therein are set forth, among other things, three distinct senses in which Christ is also known as the Father. These are: ¶ 1. He is the Father as Creator, the Father of the heavens and the earth. ¶ 2. He is the Father of those who abide in his gospel, the Father of all those who take upon themselves his name and are adopted into his family. ¶ 3. He is the Father by divine investiture of authority, meaning that the Father-Elohim has placed his name upon the Son, has given him his own power and authority, and has authorized him to speak in the first person as though he were the original or primal Father. (The Promised Messiah, p. 63) TLDP:300

### President Joseph F. Smith
### Anthon H. Lund, Charles W. Penrose
#### (First Presidency)
#### The Council of the Twelve

Jesus Christ the "Father" of Those Who Abide in His Gospel— A third sense in which Jesus Christ is regarded as the "Father" has reference to the relationship between Him and those who accept His Gospel and thereby become heirs of eternal life. . . . ¶ Salvation is attainable only through compliance with the laws and ordinances of the Gospel; and those who are thus saved become sons and daughters unto God in a distinctive sense. In a revelation given through Joseph the Prophet to Emma Smith the Lord Jesus addressed the woman as "My daughter," and said: "for verily I say unto you, all those who receive my gospel are sons and daughters in my kingdom" (D&C 25:1). In many instances the Lord has addressed men as His sons (e.g. D&C 9:1; 34:3; 121:7). ¶ That by obedience to the Gospel men may become sons of God, both as sons of Jesus Christ, and, through Him, as sons of His Father, is set forth in many revelations given in the current dispensation. ("The Father and The Son; A Doctrinal Exposition by The First Presidency and The Twelve," pamphlet published by the Church, June 30, 1916. Reprinted in AF:420-426. See MOFP5:23-34) MOFP5:27-29

**Elder Joseph Fielding Smith,**
*also quoting King Benjamin*

The Savior becomes our Father, in the sense in which this term is used in the scriptures, because he offers us life, eternal life, through atonement which he made for us. In the wonderful instruction given by King Benjamin we find this: "And now, because of the covenant which ye have made ye shall be called the children of Christ, his sons, and his daughters; for behold, this day he hath spiritually begotten you; for ye say that your hearts are changed through faith on his name; therefore, ye are born of him and have become his sons and daughters." ¶ So we become the children, sons and daughters of Jesus Christ, through our covenants of obedience to him. Because of his divine authority and sacrifice on the cross, we become spiritually begotten sons and daughters, and he is our Father. ¶ Christ is also our Father because his Father has given him of his fulness; that is, he has received a fulness of the glory of the Father. This is taught in Doctrine and Covenants 93:1-5, 16-17, and also by Abinadi in the 15th chapter of Mosiah. Abinadi's statement that he is "the Father, because he was conceived by the power of God," harmonizes with the Lord's own words in Section 93 that he is the Father because he has received of the fulness of the Father. Christ says he is the Son because, "I was in the world and made flesh my tabernacle, and dwelt among sons of men." Abinadi expresses this truth by saying he is "the Son because of the flesh." ¶ The Father has

honored Christ by placing his name upon him, so that he can minister in and through that name as though he were the Father; and thus, so far as power and authority are concerned, his words and acts become and are those of the Father. (Doctrines of Salvation, 1:29-30) TLDP:302-03

**Samuel, the Lamanite,**
*quoted by Mormon*

And also that ye might know of the coming of Jesus Christ, the Son of God, the Father of heaven and of earth, the Creator of all things from the beginning; and that ye might know of the signs of his coming, to the intent that ye might believe on his name. (*Samuel preaches to the Nephites that Christ, through his death and resurrection, redeems men from temporal and spiritual death, about 6 B.C.*) Hel.14:12

**Isaiah**

For unto us a child is born, unto us a son is given: and the government shall be upon his shoulder: and his name shall be called Wonderful, Counseller, The mighty God, The everlasting Father, The Prince of Peace. (*Isaiah predicts the birth of the Messiah*) Isa.9:6

**Related Witnesses:**

**Moroni, son of Mormon**

Behold, I am he who was prepared from the foundation of the world to redeem my people. Behold, I am Jesus Christ. I am the Father and the Son. In me shall all mankind have life, and that eternally, even they who shall believe on my name; and they shall become my sons and my daughters. (*The Lord shows himself to the brother of Jared, about the time of the Tower of Babel*) Ether 3:14

**Joseph Smith,**
*receiving the Word of the Lord*

Hearken unto the voice of the Lord your God, while I speak unto you, Emma Smith, my daughter; for verily I say unto you, all those who receive my gospel are sons and daughters in my kingdom. (*Revelation for Emma Smith, July 1830*) D&C 25:1

**Joseph Smith,**
*receiving the Word of the Lord*

Behold, I am Jesus Christ, the Son of God. I am the life and the light of the world. 29. I am the same who came unto mine own and mine own received me not; 30. But verily, verily, I say unto you, that as many as receive me, to them will I give power to become the sons of God, even to them that believe on my name. Amen. (*The Lord speaks in a revelation for Hyrum Smith, May 1829*) D&C 11:28-30

**Abinadi,**
*quoted by Mormon*

And now I say unto you, who shall declare his

generation? Behold, I say unto you, that when his soul has been made an offering for sin he shall see his seed. And now what say ye? And who shall be his seed? 11. Behold I say unto you, that whosoever has heard the words of the prophets, yea, all the holy prophets who have prophesied concerning the coming of the Lord—I say unto you, that all those who have hearkened unto their words, and believed that the Lord would redeem his people, and have looked forward to that day for a remission of their sins, I say unto you, that these are his seed, or they are heirs of the kingdom of God. 12. For these are they whose sins he has borne; these are they for whom he has died, to redeem them from their transgressions. And now, are they not his seed? 13. Yea, and are not the prophets, every one that has opened his mouth to prophesy, that has not fallen into transgression, I mean all the holy prophets ever since the world began? I say unto you that they are his seed. (*Abinadi preaches to King Noah and his people of the intercession of Christ, about 148 B.C.*) Mosiah 15:10-13

**Author's Note:** For a detailed discussion of four meanings of the term "Father," when applied to Deity in sacred writ, see pamphlet, "The Father and The Son; A Doctrinal Exposition by The First Presidency and The Twelve," published by the Church June 30, 1916. Reprinted in AF:420-426. (See MOFP5:23-34)

### (3) The Father

**Author's Note:** With one exception, this segment includes only those doctrines which deal with attributes of the Father that are not mutual with the Son. The exception is doctrine number 287: "God, the eternal Father, is an exalted man." We know that Christ, too, is now an exalted man.

### 281. God the Father is the supreme member of the Godhead.

#### John A. Widtsoe
God, the Father, the supreme God, knows the equivalent of every phase of the Great Plan, which we are working out. He has had our experiences or their equivalents, and understands therefore the difficulties of our journey. His love for us is an understanding love. Our earth troubles we may lay fully before him, knowing that he understands how human hearts

are touched by the tribulations and the joys of life. (A Rational Theology, p. 67) TLDP:220

#### Joseph Smith,
*quoted by Elder Joseph Fielding Smith*
Everlasting covenant was made between three personages before the organization of this earth, and relates to their dispensation of things to men on the earth; these personages, according to Abraham's record, are called God the first, the Creator; God the second, the Redeemer; and God the third, the witness or Testator. (*May 16, 1841*) TPJS:190; DGSM:8

#### President Brigham Young,
*quoted by John A. Widtsoe*
He is our Heavenly Father; he is also our God, and the Maker and upholder of all things in heaven and on earth. He sends forth his counsels and extends his providences to all living. He is the Supreme Controller of the universe. . . . [T]he hairs of our heads are numbered by him, and not a sparrow falleth to the ground without our Father; and he knoweth every thought and intent of the hearts of all living, for he is everywhere present by the power of his Spirit—his minister, the Holy Ghost. He is the Father of all, is above all, through all, and in you all; he knoweth all things pertaining to this earth, and he knows all things pertaining to millions of earths like this. (*In Tabernacle, Jan. 8, 1865, JD11:41*) DBY:19

#### Joseph Smith
. . . God is the only supreme governor and independent being in whom all fullness and perfection dwell; who is omnipotent, omnipresent and omniscient; without beginning of days or end of life; and that in him every good gift and every good principle dwell; and that he is the Father of lights; in him the principle of faith dwells independently, and he is the object in whom the faith of all other rational and accountable beings center for life and salvation. (*Lectures on Faith delivered to the School of the Prophets, 1834-35*) LOF2:2; DGSM:8

#### President Joseph F. Smith
#### Anthon H. Lund, Charles W. Penrose
(First Presidency)
#### The Council of the Twelve
In all His dealings with the human family Jesus the Son has represented and yet represents Elohim His Father in power and authority. This is true of Christ in His preexistent, antemortal, or unembodied state, in the which He was known as Jehovah; also during His embodiment in the flesh; and during His labors as a disembodied spirit in the realm of the dead; and since that period in His resurrected state. To the Jews He said: "I and My Father are one" (John

10:30; see also 17:11, 22) yet He declared "My Father is greater than I" (John 14:28); and further, "I am come in my Father's name" (John 5:43; see also 10:25). The same truth was declared by Christ Himself to the Nephites (see 3 Nephi 20:35 and 28:10), and has been reaffirmed by revelation in the present dispensation (D&C 50:43). Thus the Father placed His name upon the Son, and Jesus Christ spoke and ministered in and through the Father's name; and so far as power, authority, and Godship are concerned His words and acts were and are those of the Father. ("The Father and The Son; A Doctrinal Exposition by The First Presidency and The Twelve," published by the Church in a pamphlet, June 30, 1916. Reprinted in AF:420-426. See MOFP:5:23-34) MOFP5:31-32

**Elder Joseph Fielding Smith**

The presiding authority in the Universe is, God the Father, his Son Jesus Christ, and the Holy Ghost. . . . (Man, His Origin and Destiny, pp. 50-53) TLDP:243

**Jesus,**
*quoted by John*

My Father, which gave them me, is greater than all; and no man is able to pluck them out of my Father's hand. (*Jesus speaks of his sheep to whom he gives eternal life*) John 10:29

**Related Witnesses:**

**Jesus,**
*quoted by John*

But the Comforter, which is the Holy Ghost, whom the Father will send in my name, he shall teach you all things, and bring all things to your remembrance, whatsoever I have said unto you. . . . 28. Ye have heard how I said unto you, I go away, and come again unto you. If ye loved me, ye would rejoice, because I said, I go unto the Father: for my Father is greater than I. . . . 31. But that the world may know that I love the Father; and as the Father gave me commandment, even so I do. Arise, let us go hence. (*Jesus comforts the Twelve in anticipation of his crucifixion*) John 14:26,28,31

**Bruce R. McConkie**

We follow the Son as he follows his Father. We labor and strive to be like the Son as he is like the Father, and the Father and Son and Holy Ghost are one. For these holy Beings we have unbounded love, reverence, and worship. (The Promised Messiah, p. 13) TLDP:228

**Nephi, son of Lehi**

Know ye not that he was holy? But notwithstanding he being holy, he showeth unto the children of men that, according to the flesh he humbleth himself before the Father, and witnesseth unto the Father that he would be obedient unto him in keeping his commandments. . . . 12. And also, the voice of the Son came unto me, saying: He that is baptized in my name, to him will the Father give the Holy Ghost, like unto me; wherefore, follow me, and do the things which ye have seen me do. (*Nephi tells why Christ was baptized, between 559-545 B.C.*) 2Ne.31:7,12

---

## 282. God the Father carries the title of Elohim.

**President Joseph F. Smith**
**Anthon H. Lund, Charles W. Penrose**
(First Presidency)
**The Council of the Twelve**

. . . God the Eternal Father, whom we designate by the exalted name-title "Elohim," is the literal Parent of our Lord and Savior Jesus Christ, and of the spirits of the human race. Elohim is the Father in every sense in which Jesus Christ is so designated, and distinctively He is the Father of spirits. Thus we read in the Epistle to the Hebrews: "Furthermore we have had fathers of our flesh which corrected us, and we gave them reverence: shall we not much rather be in subjection unto the Father of spirits, and live?" (Heb.12:9). In view of this fact we are taught by Jesus Christ to pray: "Our Father which art in heaven, Hallowed be thy name" . . . ¶ . . . . Jesus Christ is the Son of Elohim both as spiritual and bodily offspring; that is to say, Elohim is literally the Father of the spirit of Jesus Christ and also of the body in which Jesus Christ performed His mission in the flesh, and which body died on the cross and was afterward taken up by the process of resurrection, and is now the immortalized tabernacle of the eternal spirit of our Lord and Savior. ("The Father and The Son; A Doctrinal Exposition by The First Presidency and The Twelve," pamphlet published by the Church June 30, 1916. Reprinted in AF:420-426. See MOFP5:23-34) AF:421

**President Brigham Young,**
*quoted by John A. Widtsoe*

I want to tell you, each and every one of you, that you are well acquainted with God our Heavenly Father, or the great Elohim. You are all well acquainted with him, for there is not a soul of you but what has lived in his house and dwelt with him year after year; and yet you are seeking to become acquainted with him, when the fact is, you have merely forgotten what you did know. (*In Tabernacle, Feb. 1857, JD4:216*) DBY:50

**James E. Talmage**
That Child to be born of Mary was begotten of Elohim, the Eternal Father, not in violation of natural law but in accordance with a higher manifestation thereof; JTC:81; DGSM:9
**President Joseph F. Smith**
**Anthon H. Lund, Charles W. Penrose**
(First Presidency)
**The Council of the Twelve**
[I]n all His dealings with the human family Jesus the Son has represented and yet represents Elohim His Father in power and authority. MOFP5:31-32
**President Joseph F. Smith**
**Anthon H. Lund, Charles W. Penrose**
(First Presidency)
**The Council of the Twelve**
Jesus Christ is the Son of Elohim both as spiritual and bodily offspring; that is to say, Elohim is literally the Father of the spirit of Jesus Christ and also of the body in which Jesus Christ performed His mission in the flesh, and which body died on the cross and was afterward taken up by the process of resurrection, and is now the immortalized tabernacle of the eternal spirit of our Lord and Savior. ("The Father and The Son; A Doctrinal Exposition by The First Presidency and The Twelve," pamphlet published by the Church June 30, 1916. Reprinted in AF:420-426. See MOFP5:23-34; "The Father and the Son," IE1916Aug:935) MOFP5:27; TLDP:230
**Elder Joseph F. Smith**
Among the spirit children of Elohim, the first-born was and is Jehovah or Jesus Christ, to whom all others are juniors. (Gospel Doctrine, p. 70) MPSG1987:39
**Elder Spencer W. Kimball**
Neither the Father Elohim nor the Son Jehovah would alienate himself from the children of men. It is they, the men, who cut themselves off if there be estrangement. Both the Father and the Son would gladly commune and associate with men. CR1964Apr:93

---

**283. God the Father is the literal father of the spirits of all people.**

**President Joseph F. Smith**
**Anthon H. Lund, Charles W. Penrose**
(First Presidency)
**The Council of the Twelve**
. . . God the Eternal Father, whom we designate by the exalted name-title "Elohim," is the literal Parent of our Lord and Savior Jesus Christ, and of the spirits of the human race. ("The Father and The Son; A Doctrinal Exposition by The First Presidency and The Twelve," pamphlet published by the Church June 30, 1916. Reprinted in AF:420-426. See MOFP:5:23-34) AF:421
**President Brigham Young,**
*quoted by John A. Widtsoe*
There is not a person here today but what is a son or a daughter of that Being [God our heavenly Father, Elohim]. In the spirit world their spirits were first begotten and brought forth, and they lived there with their parents for ages before they came here. (*In Tabernacle, Feb. 8, 1857, JD4:216*) DBY:50; DGSM:7
**President Brigham Young**
Man is the offspring of God. . . . We are as much the children of this great Being as we are the children of our mortal progenitors. We are flesh of his flesh, bone of his bone, and the same fluid that circulates in our bodies, called blood, once circulated in his veins as it does in ours. As the seeds of grains, vegetables and fruits produce their kind, so man is in the image of God. (*In Tabernacle, Feb. 23, 1862, JD9:283*) TLDP:212
**Paul**
Furthermore we have had fathers of our flesh which corrected us, and we gave them reverence: shall we not much rather be in subjection unto the Father of spirits, and live? (*Paul writes to the Jewish members of the Church on faith, about A.D. 60*) Heb.12:9
**President George Albert Smith**
There are thousands of members of this Church who know—it is not a question of imagination at all—they know that God lives and that Jesus is the Christ and that we are the children of God. He is the Father of our spirits. We have not come from some lower form of life, but God is the Father of our spirits, and we belong to the royal family, because he is our Father. CR1946Apr:125
**Paul**
For in him we live, and move, and have our being; as certain also of your own poets have said, For we are also his offspring. 29. Forasmuch then as we are the offspring of God, we ought not to think that the Godhead is like unto gold, or silver, or stone, graven by art and man's device. (*Paul preaches on Mars' Hill about the Unknown God*) Acts 17:28-29
**Recorded in Numbers**
And they fell upon their faces, and said, O God, the God of the spirits of all flesh, shall one man sin, and wilt thou be wroth with all the congregation? (*The congregation appeals to God not to punish them for the rebels' sake*) Num.16:22

**Jesus,**
*quoted by John*

Jesus saith unto her, Touch me not; for I am not yet ascended to my Father: but go to my brethren, and say unto them, I ascend unto my Father, and your Father; and to my God, and your God. (*The risen Christ appears to Mary Magdalene*) John 20:17

**Charles W. Penrose**

[T]he great Eternal God is our Father and we are begotten of Him or UNTO Him and to Him we owe allegiance, to Him we owe obedience, because He is our Father and our God and our King. We should obey Him because of His parentage to us; we should obey Him because we are His children and He has the right to our obedience, and being so high and exalted and lifted up, He understands us better than we understand ourselves and He has our destiny in His hands and He has power over life and over death and we should be obedient to Him because of our relationship to Him. CR1916Apr:16

**Paul**

The Spirit itself beareth witness with our spirit, that we are the children of God: 17. And if children, then heirs; heirs of God, and joint-heirs with Christ; if so be that we suffer with him, that we may be also glorified together. (*Letter to the Church in Rome, about A.D. 55*) Rom.8:16-17

**Joseph Smith,**
*quoted by Elder Joseph Fielding Smith*

God himself was once as we are now, and is an exalted man. . . . If the veil were rent today, . . . if you were to see him today, you would see him like a man in form—like yourselves in all the person, image, and very form as a man. . . . ¶ . . . . It is the first principle of the Gospel to know for a certainty the Character of God, and to know that we may converse with him as one man converses with another, and that he was once a man like us; yea, that God himself, the Father of us all, dwelt on an earth, the same as Jesus Christ himself did; and I will show it from the Bible. (*To the Church in general conference—to a congregation of 20,000—, "King Follett Sermon" April 7, 1844*) (See HC6:302-317, also see The Words of Joseph Smith, pp. 340-62.) TPJS:345-46; DGSM:7-8

**James E. Talmage**

The Father of our spirits has a full knowledge of the nature and disposition of each of His children, a knowledge gained by observation and experience in the long ages of our primeval childhood, when we existed as unembodied spirits, endowed with individuality and agency—a knowledge compared with which that gained by earthly parents through experience with their children in the flesh is infinitesimally small. (The Vitality of Mormonism, p. 320) TLDP:218

---

**284. God the Father is the spiritual and the physical parent of Jesus Christ.**

**Melvin J. Ballard**

One of the great questions that I have referred to that the world is concerned about, and is in confusion over, is as to whether or not his was a virgin birth, a birth wherein divine power interceded. Joseph Smith made it perfectly clear that Jesus Christ told the absolute truth, as did those who testify concerning him, the Apostles of the Lord Jesus Christ, wherein he is declared to be the very Son of God. And if God the Eternal Father is not the real Father of Jesus Christ, then are we in confusion; then is he not in reality the Son of God. But we declare that he *is* the Only Begotten of the Father in the flesh. ¶ Mary told the story most beautifully when she said that an angel of the Lord came to her and told her that she had found favor in the sight of God, and had come to be worthy of the fulfilment of the promises heretofore made, to become the virgin mother of the Redeemer of the world. She afterwards, referring to the event, said: "God hath done wonderful things unto me." "And the Holy Ghost came upon her," is the story, "and she came into the presence of the highest." No man or woman can live in mortality and survive the presence of the Highest except by the sustaining power of the Holy Ghost. So it came upon her to prepare her for admittance into the divine presence, and the power of the Highest, who is the Father, was present, and overshadowed her, and the holy Child that was born of her was called the Son of God. ¶ Men who deny this, or who think that it degrades our Father, have no true conception of the sacredness of the most marvelous power with which God has endowed mortal men—the power of creation. Even though that power may be abused and may become a mere harp of pleasure to the wicked, nevertheless it is the most sacred and holy and divine function with which God has endowed man. Made holy, it is retained by the Father of us all, and in his exercise of that great and marvelous creative power and function, he did not debase himself, degrade himself, nor debauch his daughter. Thus Christ became the literal Son of a divine

Father, and no one else was worthy to be his father. (Sermons and Missionary Services of Melvin J. Ballard, pp. 166-67) TLDP:301

### President Joseph F. Smith
### Anthon H. Lund, Charles W. Penrose
#### (First Presidency)
### The Council of the Twelve

Jesus Christ is the Son of Elohim both as spiritual and bodily offspring; that is to say, Elohim is literally the Father of the spirit of Jesus Christ and also of the body in which Jesus Christ performed His mission in the flesh, and which body died on the cross and was afterward taken up by the process of resurrection, and is now the immortalized tabernacle of the eternal spirit of our Lord and Savior. ("The Father and The Son; A Doctrinal Exposition by The First Presidency and The Twelve," published by the Church in a pamphlet, June 30, 1916. Reprinted in AF:420-426. See MOFP5:23-34) MOFP5:27

### President Heber J. Grant

We believe absolutely that Jesus Christ is the Son of God, begotten of God, the first-born in the spirit and the only begotten in the flesh; that He is the Son of God just as much as you and I are the sons of our fathers. ("Analysis of the Articles of Faith," Millennial Star, Jan. 5, 1922, p. 2) TLDP:301

### Marion G. Romney

Now who is Jesus Christ, and how could he bring about the resurrection when no other man nor all men put together could do so? The Scriptures respond to these questions. They make it clear that the spirit person Jesus Christ—as are the spirits of all men—is the Son of God, our Eternal Father. In this respect he is like all other men. He differs from all other men, however, by reason of the fact that men's bodies are begotten of mortal men and are, therefore, subject to death, being descendants and inheritors from Adam, while Christ's physical body was begotten of God, our Heavenly Father—an immortal being not subject to death. Christ, therefore, inherited from his Father the faculty to live on indefinitely. CR1975Apr:123-24

---

**285. When God the Father appears to mortals it is principally for the purpose of bearing record of the Son.**

### Elder Joseph Fielding Smith

All revelation since the fall has come through Jesus Christ, who is the Jehovah of the Old Testament. In all of the scriptures, where God is mentioned and where he has appeared, it was Jehovah who talked with Abraham, with Noah, Enoch, Moses and all the prophets. He is the God of Israel, the Holy One of Israel; the one who led that nation out of Egyptian bondage, and who gave and fulfilled the law of Moses. The Father has never dealt with man directly and personally since the fall, and he has never appeared except to introduce and bear record of the Son. (Doctrines of Salvation, 1:27) DGSM:4

### James E. Talmage

A general consideration of scriptural evidence leads to the conclusion that God the Eternal Father has manifested Himself to earthly prophets or revelators on very few occasions, and then principally to attest the divine authority of His Son, Jesus Christ. . . . [T]he Son was the active executive in the work of creation; throughout the creative scenes the Father appears mostly in a directing or consulting capacity. Unto Adam, Enoch, Noah, Abraham and Moses the Father revealed Himself, attesting the Godship of the Christ, and the fact that the Son was the chosen Savior of mankind. On the occasion of the baptism of Jesus, the Father's voice was heard, saying, "This is my beloved Son, in whom I am well pleased"; and at the transfiguration a similar testimony was given by the Father. On an occasion yet later, while Jesus prayed in anguish of soul, submitting Himself that the Father's purposes be fulfilled and the Father's name glorified, "Then came there a voice from heaven, saying, I have both glorified it, and will glorify it again." The resurrected and glorified Christ was announced by the Father to the Nephites on the western hemisphere, in these words: "Behold my beloved Son, in whom I am well pleased, in whom I have glorified my name: hear ye him." From the time of the occurrence last noted, the voice of the Father was not heard again among men, so far as the scriptures aver, until the spring of 1820, when both the Father and the Son ministered unto the prophet Joseph Smith, the Father saying, "This is my beloved Son, hear him!" These are the instances of record in which the Eternal Father has been manifest in personal utterance or other revelation to man apart from the Son. God the Creator, the Jehovah of Israel, the Savior and Redeemer of all nations, kindreds and tongues, are the same, and He is Jesus the Christ. JTC:39-40

### John,
#### *quoted by Joseph Smith,*
#### *translating John*

And no man hath seen God at any time, except he hath borne record of the Son; for except it is through him no man can be saved. (Revised Version) *(The record of the Apostle John)* JST(John 1:18 in Appendix)

**Related Witnesses:**

**Jesus,**
*quoted by Mormon*

Behold my Beloved Son, in whom I am well pleased, in whom I have glorified my name— hear ye him. *(God the Father testifies of his Beloved Son, A.D. 34)* 3Ne.11:7

**Joseph Smith**

It no sooner appeared than I found myself delivered from the enemy which held me bound. When the light rested upon me I saw two Personages, whose brightness and glory defy all description, standing above me in the air. One of them spake unto me, calling me by name and said, pointing to the other—This is My Beloved Son. Hear Him! *(Visitation of the Father and the Son, spring of 1820)* JS-H 1:17

**Joseph Smith**

For we saw him, even on the right hand of God; and we heard the voice bearing record that he is the Only Begotten of the Father— *(Vision to Joseph Smith and Sidney Rigdon, Feb. 16, 1832)* D&C 76:23

**Stephen,**
*recorded in Acts*

But he, being full of the Holy Ghost, looked up stedfastly into heaven, and saw the glory of God, and Jesus standing on the right hand of God, 56. And said, Behold, I see the heavens opened, and the Son of man standing on the right hand of God. *(Stephen is stoned and receives a vision of the Father and the Son)* Acts 7:55-56

**John,**
*quoted by Joseph Smith*

And I, John, bear record, and lo, the heavens were opened, and the Holy Ghost descended upon him in the form of a dove, and sat upon him, and there came a voice out of heaven saying: This is my beloved Son. *(The Lord reveals that John bore record of his glory, Kirtland, Ohio, May 6, 1833)* D&C 93:15

**Jesus,**
*quoted by Mormon*

And this is my doctrine, and it is the doctrine which the Father hath given unto me; and I bear record of the Father, and the Father beareth record of me, and the Holy Ghost beareth record of the Father and me; and I bear record that the Father commandeth all men, everywhere, to repent and believe in me. *(The resurrected Jesus Christ addresses his Nephite disciples, A.D. 34)* 3Ne.11:32

**Joseph F. Merrill**

Yes, God does live. The Father, Son, and Holy Ghost are three separate personal beings, alike in form, in whose image man is made. In order that these basic fundamental truths, lost to the world through centuries of erroneous teachings, might again be available to people of our day, a new revelation was necessary, and this was given to the fourteen-year-old Joseph Smith in the form of the most glorious vision ever given to mortal man, so far as the records indicate—a vision in which Father and Son appeared simultaneously. . . . CR1948Oct:59

**Author's Note:** Joseph Fielding Smith: There are too many passages [in the Bible] which declare very definitely that God did appear, "face to face," with his ancient servants. Therefore, passages which declare that no man has seen him, must be in error. The prophet Joseph Smith has given us a correction of John 1:18 as follows: "And no man hath seen God at any time, except he hath borne record of the Son; for except it is through him no man hath seen God at any time, except he hath borne record of the Son; for except it is through him no man can be saved." [JST(John 1:19 in Appendix)] (MPSG-72-73:16)

---

**286. God the Father is to be the object of our worship.**

**Bruce R. McConkie**

We do not worship the Son, and we do not worship the Holy Ghost. I know perfectly well what the scriptures say about worshiping Christ and Jehovah, but they are speaking in an entirely different sense—the sense of standing in awe and being reverentially grateful to him who has redeemed us. Worship in the true and saving sense is reserved for God the first, the Creator. ¶ Our revelations say that the Father "is infinite and eternal," that he created "man, male and female." ¶ And gave unto them commandments that they should love and serve him, the only living and true God, and that he should be the only being whom they should worship. (D&C 20:17-19] ¶ Jesus said: True worshippers shall [note that this is mandatory] worship the Father in spirit and in truth; for the Father seeketh such to worship him. ¶ For unto such hath God promised his Spirit. And they who worship him, must worship in spirit and in truth. [JST John 4:25-26] ¶ There is no other way, no other approved system of worship. ("Our Relationship with the Lord," in Brigham Young University Speeches of the Year, 1981-82, p. 98) TLDP:746-47

**President Joseph F. Smith**

We . . . accept without any question the doctrines we have been taught by the Prophet Joseph Smith and by the Son of God himself, that we pray to God, the Eternal Father, in the name of his only begotten Son, to whom also our father Adam and his posterity have prayed from the beginning. CR1916Oct:6

**Joseph Smith,**
*receiving the Word of the Lord*
And you shall fall down and worship the Father in my name. (*Revelation received June 1829*) D&C 18:40

**Jesus,**
*recorded in Luke*
And Jesus answered and said unto him, Get thee behind me, Satan: for it is written, Thou shalt worship the Lord thy God, and him only shalt thou serve. (*Jesus fasts 40 days and is tempted of the devil*) Luke 4:8

**Jesus,**
*recorded in Mark*
And thou shalt love the Lord thy God with all thy heart, and with all thy soul, and with all thy mind, and with all thy strength: this is the first commandment. (*A scribe asks Jesus in sincerity: "Which is the first commandment of all?"*) Mark 12:30

---

### 287. God, the Eternal Father, is an exalted man.

**Joseph Smith**
God himself was once as we are now, and is an exalted man, and sits enthroned in yonder heavens! That is the great secret. If the veil were rent today, and the great God who holds this world in its orbit, and who upholds all worlds and all things by His power, was to make himself visible,—I say, if you were to see him today, you would see him like a man in form—like yourselves in all the person, image, and very form as a man; for Adam was created in the very fashion, image and likeness of God, and received instruction from, and walked, talked and conversed with Him, as one man talks and communes with another. . . . It is the first principle of the gospel to know for a certainty the character of God, and to know that we may converse with Him as one man converses with another, and that He was once a man like us; yea, that God himself, the Father of us all, dwelt on an earth, the same as Jesus Christ Himself did. (*To the Church in general conference—to a congregation of 20,000, "King Follett Sermon" April 7, 1844*) (See HC6:302-317, also see The Words of Joseph Smith, pp. 340-62.) HC6:305

**President Joseph F. Smith**
**John R. Winder, Anthon H. Lund**
(First Presidency)
God Himself is an exalted man, perfected, enthroned, and supreme. By His almighty power He organized the earth, and all that it contains, from spirit and element, which exist co-eternally with Himself. ("The Origin of Man," IE1909Nov:81) TLDP:221

**Charles W. Penrose**
Christ was the Son of God, of God the Father; the Father of His Spirit was the Father of His body. He was an exalted man who had passed through all things that Jesus Christ, His Beloved Son, afterwards passed through. It was a repetition of the things that had been done from remote, eternal ages, the great plan of salvation for all the people of all the worlds that God has created. CR1916Apr:23

**Elder Joseph Fielding Smith**
God, our Eternal Father, is an immortal exalted Man, with a body of flesh and bones and eternal spirit, inseparably connected that cannot be divided and cannot die. (Man, His Origin and Destiny, pp. 50-53) TLDP:243

**James E. Talmage**
The Church proclaims the eternal truth: "As man is, God once was; as God is, man may be." With such a future, well may man open his heart to the stream of revelation, past, present, and to come. . . . AF:390

**Elder Lorenzo Snow**
As man now is, God once was. . . . ¶ We are the offspring of God, begotten by Him in the spirit world, where we partook of His nature as children here partake of the likeness of their parents. Our trials and sufferings give us experience, and establish within us principles of godliness. (*At Brigham City Tabernacle, prior to being sentenced by Judge Powers in the First District Court, Jan. 10, 1886, JD26:368*) TLDP:157

**Elder Lorenzo Snow**
Through a continual course of progression, our heavenly Father has received exaltation and glory, and he points us out the same path; and inasmuch as he is clothed with power, authority, and glory, he says, "Walk ye up and come in possession of the same glory and happiness that I possess." (*In Tabernacle, Oct. 1857*) DGSM:92

**Hugh B. Brown**
The Church teaches that when God created man in his own image, he did not divest himself of that image. He is still in human form and is possessed of sanctified and perfected human qualities, which we all admire. All through the

holy scriptures, the Father and the Son are seen to be separate and distinct personages. We affirm the doctrine of the ancient scripture and of the prophets that asserts that man was created in the image of God and that God possessed such human qualities as consciousness, will, love, mercy, justice. In other words he is an exalted, perfected, and glorified Being. CR1969Apr:51

### President Brigham Young

Our Father in heaven is a personage of tabernacle, just as much as I am who stand before you to-day, and he has all the parts and passions of a perfect man, and his body is composed of flesh and bones, but not of blood. *(To Sunday School children, in Tabernacle, July 24, 1877, JD19:64)* TLDP:221

### Orson Hyde

Remember that God, our heavenly Father, was perhaps once a child, and mortal like we ourselves, and rose step by step in the scale of progress, in the school of advancement; has moved forward and overcome, until He has arrived at the point where He now is. *(General conference, Oct. 6, 1853, JD1:123)* TLDP:221

### James E. Talmage

'Mormonism' claims that all nature, both on earth and in heaven, operates on a plan of advancement; that the very Eternal Father is a progressive Being; that his perfection, while so complete as to be incomprehensible by man, possesses this essential quality of true perfection—the capacity of eternal increase. AF:474

**Related Witnesses:**

### Joseph Smith

Where shall we find a prototype into whose likeness we may be assimilated, in order that we may be made partakers of life and salvation? or, in other words, where shall we find a saved being? for if we can find a saved being, we may ascertain without much difficulty what all others must be in order to saved. We think that it will not be a matter of dispute, that two beings who are unlike each other cannot both be saved; for whatever constitutes the salvation of one will constitute the salvation of every creature which will be saved; and if we find one saved being in all existence, we may see what all others must be, or else not be saved. We ask, then, where is the prototype? or where is the saved being? We conclude, as to the answer of this question, there will be no dispute among those who believe the Bible, that it is Christ: all will agree in this, that he is the prototype or standard of salvation; or, in other words, that he is a saved being. And if we should continue our interrogation, and ask how it is that he is

saved? the answer would be—because he is a just and holy being; and if he were anything different from what he is, he would not be saved; for his salvation depends on his being precisely what he is and nothing else; for if it were possible for him to change, in the least degree, so sure he would fail of salvation and lose all his dominion, power, authority and glory, which constitute salvation; for salvation consists in the glory, authority, majesty, power and dominion which Jehovah possesses and in nothing else; and no being can possess it but himself or one like him. *(Lectures on Faith delivered to the School of the Prophets, 1834-35)* LOF:7:9

---

## (4) The Godhead

**288. There is a Godhead consisting of God the Eternal Father, His son Jesus Christ, and the Holy Ghost.**

### President Joseph F. Smith

We believe in the Godhead, comprising the three individual personages, Father, Son, and Holy Ghost. *(Address from the First Presidency of the Church to the world, delivered to and accepted by vote of the Church in general conference, April 1907)* CR1907Apr(Appendix)4

### Mark E. Petersen

Those who say that there was no evidence of the Trinity in the Godhead in Old Testament times simply do not have all the facts. The Father, Son, and Holy Ghost have labored with and for this earth from its beginning and will do so until the end. (Isaiah for Today, p. 125) TLDP:227-28

### Joseph Smith

And he being the Only Begotten of the Father, full of grace and truth, and having overcome, received a fullness of the glory of the Father, possessing the same mind with the Father, which mind is the Holy Spirit, that bears record of the Father and the Son, and these three are one; or, in other words, these three constitute the great, matchless, governing and supreme power over all things; by whom all things were created and made that were created and made, and these three constitute the Godhead, and are one; the Father and the Son possessing the same mind, the same wisdom, glory, power, and fullness—filling all in all; the Son being filled with the fullness of the mind, glory, and power; or, in other words, the spirit, glory, and power, of the Father, possessing all knowledge and glory, and the same kingdom, sitting at the right hand of power, in the express image and likeness of the Father, mediator for man, being filled with the fullness of the mind of the Father; or, in other words, the Spirit of the Father, which Spirit is shed forth upon all who believe on his name and keep his commandments. (*Lectures on Faith delivered to the School of the Prophets, 1834-35*) LOF5:2

### Elder Joseph Fielding Smith

This reference [D&C 20:27-29], then, to the three as one God, must be interpreted to mean that they constitute one Godhead or Supreme Council, composed of three separate Personages, the Father, the Son, and the Holy Ghost. MPSG72-73:10

### Joseph Smith

We believe in God, the Eternal Father, and in His Son, Jesus Christ, and in the Holy Ghost. (*The first of the thirteen Articles of Faith; letter to John Wentworth, March 1, 1842*) AofF:1

### Joseph Smith

Which Father, Son, and Holy Ghost are one God, infinite and eternal, without end. Amen. (*Revelation on Church Organization and Government, April 1830*) D&C 20:28

### John

For there are three that bear record in heaven, the Father, the Word, and the Holy Ghost: and these three are one. (*John writes to the churches in Asia*) 1Jn.5:7

### Amulek,
#### quoted by Mormon

[E]very thing shall be restored to its perfect frame, as it is now, or in the body, and shall be brought and be arraigned before the bar of Christ the Son, and God the Father, and the Holy Spirit, which is one Eternal God, to be judged according to their works, whether they be good or whether they be evil. (*Amulek, foretelling Christ's redemption of man and the final judgment, answers the lawyer Zeezrom, about 82 B.C.*) Alma 11:44

### Joseph Smith,
#### quoted by Elder Joseph Fielding Smith

Everlasting covenant was made between three personages before the organization of this earth, and relates to their dispensation of things to men on the earth; these personages, according to Abraham's record, are called God the first, the Creator; God the second, the Redeemer; and God the third, the witness or Testator. (*May 16, 1841*) TPJS:190; DGSM:8

### Elder Joseph Fielding Smith

It is perfectly true, as recorded in the Pearl of Great Price and in the Bible, that to us there is but one God. Correctly interpreted God in this sense means Godhead, for it is composed of

Father, Son, and Holy Spirit. This Godhead presides over us, and to us, the inhabitants of this world, they constitute the only God, or Godhead. There is none other besides them. To them we are amenable, and subject to their authority, and there is no other Godhead unto whom we are subject. However, as the Prophet has shown, there can be, and are, other Gods. (Answers to Gospel Questions, 2:142) DCSM:41

### Related Witnesses:
#### Recorded in Matthew

And Jesus, when he was baptized, went up straightway out of the water: and, lo, the heavens were opened unto him, and he saw the Spirit of God descending like a dove, and lighting upon him: 17. And lo a voice from heaven, saying, This is my beloved Son, in whom I am well pleased. (*Jesus is baptized by John to fulfill all righteousness*) Matt.3:16-17

### Jesus,
#### quoted by Mormon

And now behold, these are the words which ye shall say, calling them by their name, saying: 25. Having authority given me of Jesus Christ, I baptize you in the name of the Father, and of the Son, and of the Holy Ghost. Amen. (*The resurrected Jesus Christ sets forth the mode and manner of baptism to his disciples, A.D. 34*) 3Ne.11:24-25

---

**289. Each member of the Godhead is physically separate and distinct from the other two.**

### Elder Joseph Fielding Smith

This reference [D&C 20:27-29], then, to the three as one God, must be interpreted to mean that they constitute one Godhead or Supreme Council, composed of three separate Personages, the Father, the Son, and the Holy Ghost. MPSG1972-73:10

### Elder Joseph Fielding Smith

I make bold to say that there is not within the lids of the Bible one single passage which can properly be construed to uphold the popular but erroneous doctrine that the Father and the Son and the Holy Ghost are in substance one, a spirit, or essence, and without body or parts or passions, incomprehensible and invisible. To the contrary, I maintain that throughout the scriptures there is ample evidence in numerous passages, teaching that the Eternal Father and his Son Jesus Christ and the Holy Ghost are separate entities, perfectly distinct and in person independent from each other. This is the doctrine clearly stated by our Savior. It is their epistles to the ancient saints. Any doctrine to the contrary contradicts what is plainly written and is a misinterpretation of these teachings. (The Restoration of All Things, pp. 51-52) TLDP:228

**Joseph Smith**

There is much said about God and the Godhead. The scriptures say there are Gods many and Lords many, but to us there is but one living and true God, and the heaven of heavens could not contain him; for he took the liberty to go into other heavens. The teachers of the day say that thy Father is God, the Son is God, and the Holy Ghost is God, and they are all in one body and one God. Jesus prayed that those that the Father had given him out of the world might be made one in them, as they were one; [one in spirit, in mind, in purpose]. If I were to testify that the Christian world were wrong on this point, my testimony would be true. Peter and Stephen testify that they saw the Son of Man standing on the right hand of God. Any person that had seen the heavens opened knows that there are three personages in the heavens who hold the keys of power, and one presides over all. (At the Stand, Nauvoo, Ill., June 11, 1843) HC5:426

**Bruce R. McConkie**

We learn these truths relative to the Gods we worship: ¶ 1. They are three in number, three separate persons: the first is the Father, the second, the Son; and the third, the Holy Ghost. They are three individuals who meet together, counsel in concert, and as occasion requires travel separately through all immensity. They are three holy men, two having bodies of flesh and bones, the third being a personage of spirit. ¶ 2. They are one and dwell in each other, meaning: They have the same mind one with another; they think the same thoughts, speak the same words, and perform the same acts—so much so that any thought, word, or act of one is the thought of the other. ¶ 3. They possess the same character, enjoy the same perfections, and manifest the same attributes, each one possessing all of these in their eternal and godly fulness. ¶ 4. Their unity in all things, their perfect oneness in mind, power, and perfections, marks the course and charts the way for faithful mortals, whose chief goal in life is to unite together and become one with them, thereby gaining eternal life for themselves. ¶ 5. Our Lord is the manifestation of the Father, meaning: God is in Christ revealing himself to men so that those who believe in the Son believe also in the Father, and into such the Father gives the Holy Ghost, and they being thus purified in Christ are fit to dwell with him and his Father forever. (The Promised Messiah, p. 120) TLDP:228-29

**Orson Pratt**

The Godhead may be further illustrated by a council, consisting of three men—all possessing equal wisdom, knowledge, and truth—together with equal qualifications in every other respect. Each person would be a separate distinct person or substance from the other two, and yet the three would form but one council. (Masterful Discourses and Writings of Orson Pratt, p. 313) TLDP:229

**Related Witnesses:**

**Joseph Smith**

It no sooner appeared than I found myself delivered from the enemy which held me bound. When the light rested upon me I saw two Personages, whose brightness and glory defy all description, standing above me in the air. One of them spake unto me, calling me by name and said, pointing to the other—This is My Beloved Son. Hear Him! (Vision of the Father and the Son, spring of 1820) JS-H 1:17

**Joseph Smith**

And now, after the many testimonies which have been given of him, this is the testimony, last of all, which we give of him: That he lives! 23. For we saw him, even on the right hand of God; and we heard the voice bearing record that he is the Only Begotten of the Father— 24. That by him, and through him, and of him, the worlds are and were created, and the inhabitants thereof are begotten sons and daughters unto God. (Vision to Joseph Smith and Sidney Rigdon, Feb. 16, 1832) D&C 76:22-24

**Jesus,**
*quoted by John*

Jesus saith unto her, Touch me not; for I am not yet ascended to my Father: but go to my brethren, and say unto them, I ascend unto my Father, and your Father; and to my God, and your God. (The risen Christ appears to Mary Magdalene) John 20:17

**Joseph Smith**

The Father has a body of flesh and bones as tangible as man's; the Son also; but the Holy Ghost has not a body of flesh and bones, but is a personage of Spirit. Were it not so, the Holy Ghost could not dwell in us. (Revelation, April 2, 1830) D&C 130:22

**Jesus,**
*recorded by John*

And this is life eternal, that they might know thee the only true God, and Jesus Christ, whom thou hast sent. (Jesus offers the great intercessory prayer for his Apostles) John 17:3

**Recorded in Matthew**

And Jesus, when he was baptized, went up straightway out of the water: and, lo, the heavens were opened unto him, and he saw the Spirit of God descending like a dove, and lighting upon him: 17. And lo a voice from heaven, saying, This is my beloved Son, in whom I am well pleased. (*Jesus is baptized by John to fulfill all righteousness*) Matt.3:16-17

### Joseph Smith

The heavens were opened upon us, and I beheld the celestial kingdom of God, and the glory thereof, whether in the body or out I cannot tell. 2. I saw the transcendent beauty of the gate through which the heirs of that kingdom will enter, which was like unto circling flames of fire; 3. Also the blazing throne of God, whereon was seated the Father and the Son. (*Vision to Joseph Smith in Kirtland Temple, Jan. 21, 1836*) D&C 137:1-3

### Mormon

Behold my Beloved Son, in whom I am well pleased, in whom I have glorified my name— hear ye him. (*God the Father testifies of his Beloved Son, A.D. 34*) 3Ne.11:7

### Peter

Therefore being by the right hand of God exalted, and having received of the Father the promise of the Holy Ghost, he hath shed forth this, which ye now see and hear. 34. For David is not ascended into the heavens: but he saith himself, The Lord said unto my Lord, Sit thou on my right hand. . . . 36. . . . God hath made that same Jesus, whom ye have crucified, both Lord and Christ. (*Peter addresses the people on the day of Pentecost when about 3,000 people were baptized*) Acts 2:33-34,36

### Stephen, *recorded in Acts*

But he, being full of the Holy Ghost, looked up stedfastly into heaven, and saw the glory of God, and Jesus standing on the right hand of God, 56. And said, Behold, I see the heavens opened, and the Son of man standing on the right hand of God. (*Stephen is stoned and receives a vision of the Father and the Son*) Acts 7:55-56

### 290. The three members of the Godhead (God the Father, His son Jesus Christ, and the Holy Ghost) are united in purpose.

### James E. Talmage

This unity is a type of completeness; the mind of any one member of the Trinity is the mind of the others; seeing as each of them does with the eye of perfection, they see and understand alike. Under any given conditions each would

act in the same way, guided by the same principles of unerring justice and equity. The oneness of the Godhead, to which the scriptures so abundantly testify, implies no mystical union of substance, nor any unnatural and therefore impossible blending of personality. Father, Son, and Holy Ghost are as distinct in their persons and individualities as are any three personages in mortality. Yet their unity of purpose and operation is such as to make their edicts one, and their will the will of God. AF:37

### Joseph Smith

Which Father, Son, and Holy Ghost are one God, infinite and eternal, without end. Amen. (*Revelation received April 1830; the Holy Ghost bears record of the Father and the Son*) D&C 20:28

### Elder Joseph Fielding Smith

There is a oneness in the godhead as well as a distinctness of personality. This oneness is emphasized in the sayings and writings of prophets and apostles in order to guard against the erroneous idea that these three may be distinct and independent deities and rivals for our worship. (IE1901Jan:228) DGSM:8

### Orson Pratt

The Godhead may be further illustrated by a council, consisting of three men—all possessing equal wisdom, knowledge, and truth—together with equal qualifications in every other respect. Each person would be a separate distinct person or substance from the other two, and yet the three would form but one council. Each alone possesses, by supposition, the same wisdom and truth that the three united or the one council possesses. The union of the three men in one council would not increase the knowledge or wisdom of either. Each man would be one part of the council when reference is made to his person; but the wisdom and truth of man would be the whole wisdom and truth of the council, and not a part. (Masterful Discourses and Writings of Orson Pratt, p. 313) TLDP:229

### Bruce R. McConkie

We learn these truths relative to the Gods we worship: ¶ 1. They are three in number, three separate persons: the first is the Father, the second, the Son; and the third, the Holy Ghost. They are three individuals who meet together, counsel in concert, and as occasion requires travel separately through all immensity. They are three holy men, two having bodies of flesh and bones, the third being a personage of spirit. ¶ 2. They are one and dwell in each other, meaning: They have the same mind one with another; they think the same thoughts, speak the same words, and perform the same acts—so much so that any thought, word, or act of one is the thought of the other. ¶ 3. They possess the same character, enjoy the same perfections, and manifest the same attributes, each one possessing all of these in their eternal and godly fulness. ¶ 4. Their unity in all things, their perfect oneness in mind, power, and perfections, marks the course and charts the way for faithful mortals, whose chief goal in life is to unite together and become one with them, thereby gaining eternal life for themselves. (The Promised Messiah, p. 120) TLDP:228-29

**Related Witnesses:**

### Marion G. Romney
As a member of the Godhead, and being one with the Father and the Son, the Holy Ghost is, as are the Father and the Son, omniscient. He comprehends all truth having a knowledge of [all] things. (D&C 93:24) ("The Holy Ghost," EN1974May:90) MGSP:7

### John
For there are three that bear record in heaven, the Father, the Word, and the Holy Ghost: and these three are one. (*John writes to the churches in Asia*) 1Jn.5:7

### Amulek,
*quoted by Mormon*
Now, this restoration shall come to all, both old and young, both bond and free, both male and female, both the wicked and the righteous; and even there shall not so much as a hair of their heads be lost; but every thing shall be restored to its perfect frame, as it is now, or in the body, and shall be brought and be arraigned before the bar of Christ the Son, and God the Father, and the Holy Spirit, which is one Eternal God, to be judged according to their works, whether they be good or whether they be evil. (*Amulek, foretelling Christ's redemption of man and the final judgment, answers the lawyer Zeezrom, about 82 B.C.*) Alma 11:44

### Nephi, son of Lehi
And now, behold, my beloved brethren, this is the way; and there is none other way nor name given under heaven whereby man can be saved in the kingdom of God. And now, behold, this is the doctrine of Christ, and the only and true doctrine of the Father, and of the Son, and of the Holy Ghost, which is one God, without end. Amen. (*Nephi's writings, between 559-545 B.C.*) 2Ne.31:21

### Jesus,
*quoted by Mormon*
And after this manner shall ye baptize in my name; for behold, verily I say unto you, that the Father, and the Son, and the Holy Ghost are one; and I am in the Father, and the Father in

me, and the Father and I are one. (*The resurrected Jesus Christ addresses his Nephite disciples, A.D. 34*) 3Ne.11:27

---

**291. There is but one God, or Godhead, to whom the inhabitants of the earth are subject.**

### Elder Joseph Fielding Smith
It is perfectly true, as recorded in the Pearl of Great Price and in the Bible, that to us there is but one God. Correctly interpreted God in this sense means Godhead, for it is composed of Father, Son, and Holy Spirit. This Godhead presides over us, and to us, the inhabitants of this world, they constitute the only God, or Godhead. There is none other besides them. To them we are amenable, and subject to their authority, and there is no other Godhead unto whom we are subject. However, as the Prophet has shown, there can be, and are, other Gods. (Answers to Gospel Questions, 2:142) DCSM:41

### Bruce R. McConkie
Our Godhead consists of the Father, Son and Holy Ghost. They are supreme over all, and though they administer their kingdoms through a hierarchy of appointed angels who also are exalted, one of whom is Adam or Michael, in the ultimate sense these members of the Eternal Godhead are the only Gods with whom we have to do. We worship the Father, in the name of the Son, by the power of the Holy Ghost. We follow the Son as he follows his Father. We labor and strive to be like the Son as he is like the Father, and the Father and Son and Holy Ghost are one. For these holy Beings we have unbounded love, reverence, and worship. (The Promised Messiah, p. 13) TLDP:228

### Joseph Smith
Which Father, Son, and Holy Ghost are one God, infinite and eternal, without end. Amen. (*Revelation on Church Organization and Government, April 1830*) D&C 20:28

### Joseph Smith
We believe in God, the Eternal Father, and in His Son, Jesus Christ, and in the Holy Ghost. (*The first of the thirteen Articles of Faith; Letter to John Wentworth, March 1, 1842*) AofF:1

**Related Witnesses:**

### Paul
For though there be that are called gods, whether in heaven or in earth, (as there be gods many, and lords many,) 6. But to us there is but one God, the Father, of whom are all things, and we

in him; and one Lord Jesus Christ, by whom are
all things, and we by him. (*Letter to the church
at Corinth, Greece, about A.D. 55)* 1Cor.8:5-6

**Amulek,**
*quoted by Mormon*

[E]very thing shall be restored to its perfect
frame, as it is now, or in the body, and shall be
brought and be arraigned before the bar of
Christ the Son, and God the Father, and the
Holy Spirit, which is one Eternal God, to be
judged according to their works, whether they
be good or whether they be evil. (*Amulek
answers the lawyer Zeezrom foretelling Christ's
redemption of man and the final judgment,
about 82 B.C.)* Alma 11:44

**John**

For there are three that bear record in heaven,
the Father, the Word, and the Holy Ghost: and
these three are one. (*John writes to the churches
in Asia)* 1Jn.5:7

---

**HYMNS Written by Prophets
Applicable to this Topic**

**Parley P. Pratt**
*Jesus, Once of Humble Birth*
HYMNS:196

Jesus, once of humble birth,
Now in glory comes to earth.
Once he suffered grief and pain;
Now he comes on earth to reign.
Now he comes on earth to reign.

Once a meek and lowly Lamb,
Now the Lord, the great I Am.
Once upon the cross he bowed;
Now his chariot is the cloud.
Now his chariot is the cloud.

Once he groaned in blood and tears;
Now in glory he appears.
Once rejected by his own,
Now their King he shall be known.
Now their king he shall be known.

Once forsaken, left alone,
Now exalted to a throne.
Once all things he meekly bore,
But he now will bear no more.
But he now will bear no more.

# List of Doctrines

## GOSPEL OF JESUS CHRIST
### The Plan of Salvation

*Doctrines Located in This Topic*

292. The work of God is to bring about immortality and eternal life for us, His children (to reunite our bodies and spirits and give us the fulness of His glory in the celestial kingdom).

293. Before God sent us to the earth He prepared a plan of salvation for us.

294. The gospel is the plan of salvation.

295. Those who receive Christ and believe on His name are given power to become (spiritually reborn) sons and daughters of God.

296. The first principles and ordinances of the gospel are faith in the Lord Jesus Christ, repentance, baptism by immersion, and the laying on of hands for the gift of the Holy Ghost.

297. The principles of the gospel are unchanging, eternal truths.

298. The blessings of salvation and exaltation are available to all, not to a select few.

299. The gospel is universally applicable to all people everywhere; it will bring to each person exactly what is necessary for salvation.

300. The gospel was preached from the beginning, starting with Adam.

301. Every person will at some time have opportunity to hear the gospel, whether on earth or in the spirit world.

302. A physical body is essential to obtaining a fulness of joy in the celestial kingdom of God.

*Doctrines on GOSPEL OF JESUS CHRIST Located in Other Topics*

64. The Book of Mormon contains the fulness of the gospel of Jesus Christ.

87. One of the (threefold) missions of the Church is to proclaim the gospel to the world.

96. Members of the Church are to live the law of sacrifice: to be willing to make whatever sacrifices the Lord requires for the sake of the gospel.

102. The Lord covenanted with Abraham that through his descendants all the families of the earth would be blessed with the gospel.

109. The fulness of the gospel of Jesus Christ is the new and everlasting covenant between God and members of His Church.

# GOSPEL OF JESUS CHRIST continued

136. The aim of the gospel and the Church is to bring all people into the celestial kingdom of God (not in the terrestrial or telestial kingdoms).

404. In the last days the fulness of the gospel is to be given first to the Gentiles (non-Jews) and thereafter to the Jews.

462. The preaching of the gospel has a more powerful effect on the minds of people who hear it, to lead them to do right, than anything else.

492. We must receive all the essential ordinances of the gospel if we are to gain exaltation in the celestial kingdom of God.

556. When the plan of salvation was presented in the premortal world, each person had the opportunity of accepting or rejecting it.

641. The restored gospel will remain on earth until the end of time, never to be taken away again.

642. The restoration of the gospel in the latter days is the "marvelous work and a wonder" of the Lord.

844. It is impossible for a person to be saved in ignorance of the saving principles of the gospel.

# GOSPEL OF JESUS CHRIST
## The Plan of Salvation

292. The work of God is to bring about immortality and eternal life for us, His children (to reunite our bodies and spirits and give us the fulness of His glory in the celestial kingdom).

### Joseph Smith,
*translating the Book of Moses*

For behold, this is my work and my glory—to bring to pass the immortality and eternal life of man. (*God talks to Moses face to face*) Moses 1:39

### Bruce R. McConkie

Further, the gospel is in operation in all the worlds created by the Father and the Son. Their work and their glory, in all the infinite creations that their hands have made, is to bring to pass immortality and eternal life for the children of the Father. Through the atonement of Christ, the inhabitants of all these worlds have power to become his sons and daughters, to become joint-heirs with him of all the glory of his Father's kingdom, to be adopted into the family of the Father, which is to say that the inhabitants of all worlds "are [thus] begotten sons and daughters unto God." (D&C 76:24) (The Promised Messiah, p. 286) TLDP:238

### Bruce R. McConkie

The gospel is the plan of salvation—the eternal plan of the Eternal Father. It is the laws and truths and powers by conformity to which the spirit children of the Father (Christ included) can advance and progress and become like him. It includes the creation and peopling of the earth, the testing processes of mortality, and death, the resurrection, and eternal judgment. It is founded and grounded upon the atoning sacrifice of Christ and is operative because he laid down his life for all men. . . . ¶ It is the gospel of God; the plan originated with the Father; it is his gospel. It concerns Jesus Christ our Lord because he was chosen to come into this world as the Son of God, to work out the infinite and eternal atonement, and to put into full force all of the terms and conditions of the Father's plan. The Son does the will of the Father; the Son did not devise a plan and suggest it to the Father; the Son obeyed and conformed and adopted. He espoused and championed the cause of his Father. (The Mortal Messiah, 4:380-81) TLDP:40

### Related Witnesses:
#### Marion G. Romney

. . . God has revealed the fact that it is his work

and glory to bring to pass their [his spiritual offspring] eternal life (Moses 1:39), which is the life God lives. CR1973Apr:133

### President Joseph F. Smith

It is the plan of life that the Almighty has restored to man in the latter days for the salvation of the souls of men, not only in the world to come, but in our present life, for the Lord has instituted his work that his people may enjoy the blessings of this life to the utmost; that they should be saved in this present life, as well as in the life to come, that they should lay the foundation here for immunity from sin and all its effects and consequences, that they may obtain an inheritance in the kingdom of God beyond this vale of tears. The gospel of Jesus Christ is the power of God unto salvation, and it is absolutely necessary for every man and woman in the Church of Christ to work righteousness, to observe the laws of God, and keep the commandments that he has given, in order that they may avail themselves of the power of God unto salvation in this life. CR1907Oct:2

### Elder George Albert Smith

What is this gospel to which we refer? It is the only power of God unto salvation, it is the only plan that will enable man to go back into the presence of his Maker and enjoy the celestial kingdom. It is the only plan that will bring peace and happiness to all the children of men, of every race and creed. CR1928Oct:93

### President Joseph F. Smith

We believe in the pre-existence of man as a spirit, and in the future state of individual existence, in which every soul shall find its place, as determined by justice and mercy, with opportunities of endless progression, in varied conditions of eternity. (*Address from the First Presidency of the Church to the world, delivered to and accepted by vote of the Church in general conference, April 1907*) CR1907Apr(Appendix)4

**Author's Note:** The expressions "immortality" and "eternal life," as set forth in this section (D-292), have been defined as follows: ¶ By George F. Richards: "The word immortal means not mortal; that is, not subject to the power of death. I would define immortality as being that state to which we attain in the progress of life when we have passed through death and the resurrection, the spirit and body being reunited and inseparably connected, constituting the soul of man prepared to receive a fulness of the glory of

God. Immortality is a means to an end, the end being the accomplishment of man's eternal salvation and glory. In support of this statement I call attention to the word of the Lord to the Prophet Joseph, as recorded in the Doctrine and Covenants, Sec. 93, verses 33 and 34, as follows: 'For man is spirit. The elements are eternal, and spirit and element, inseparably connected, receive a fulness of joy; And when separated, man cannot receive a fulness of joy.' Hence the importance of bringing about the immortality of man. ¶ The eternal life referred to means something more than that man shall not cease to live. I read the word of the Lord from the Doctrine and Covenants, Sec. 14, verse 7, as follows: 'And, if you keep my commandments and endure to the end you shall have eternal life, which gift is the greatest of all the gifts of God.' The revelations of the Lord indicate to us the height, depth and grandeur of the glory of God to which the righteous may attain. Eternal life, as here used, being the greatest gift of God, must include a fulness of glory of God, in his celestial kingdom. [Sec.76:54-60;132:20-24.] ¶ The Lord uses the expressions 'eternal life' and 'salvation' synonymously (see D&C 6:13) 'If thou wilt do good, yea, and hold out faithful to the end, thou shalt be saved in the kingdom of God, which is the greatest of all the gifts of God; for there is no gift greater than the gift of salvation.'" CR1916Apr:52 ¶ By Bruce R. McConkie: "Accordingly, eternal life is not a name that has reference only to the unending duration of a future life; immortality is to live forever in the resurrected state, and by the grace of God all men will gain this unending continuance of life. But only those who obey the fulness of the gospel law will inherit eternal life." (MPSG1967-68:6)

---

**293. Before God sent us to the earth, He prepared a plan of salvation for us.**

**Joseph Smith,**
*quoted by Elder Joseph Fielding Smith*
Spirits are eternal. At the first organization in heaven we were all present, and saw the Savior chosen and appointed and the plan of salvation made, and we sanctioned it. (*At the organization of a school of instruction, Jan. 1841*) (See Words of Joseph Smith, p. 60) TPJS:181; MPSG1987:39; DGSM:21
**Bruce R. McConkie**
We are his offspring. We were spirit children: he was glorified and exalted in the life that

went before. We could tell the difference between our spirit bodies and the glorified and exalted body which he possessed. He taught us eternal truths: there came into our hearts the great desire to progress and advance and become like him so that we could have glorified and exalted bodies and so that we could live in the family unit as he lived in the family unit. And as a consequence, he ordained and established what is called a plan of salvation. The Prophet Joseph Smith said, "God, himself, finding he was in the midst of spirits and glory," ordained laws whereby they progress and become like him. ACR(Brisbane)1976:14
**Elder Joseph F. Smith**
Our spirits . . . were in the councils of the heavens before the foundations of the earth were laid. We were there. We sang together with the heavenly hosts for joy when the foundations of the earth were laid, and when the plan of our existence upon this earth and redemption were mapped out. We were there; we were interested, and we took a part in this great preparation. . . . We were vitally concerned in the carrying out of these great plans and purposes, we understood them, and it was for our sakes they were decreed, and are to be consummated. (Deseret Weekly News, 1884, p. 130) MPSG1985:78-79
**John A. Widtsoe**
In our pre-existent state, in the day of the great council, we made a certain agreement with the Almighty. The Lord proposed a plan, conceived by him. We accepted it. Since the plan is intended for all men, we become parties to the salvation of every person under the plan. We agreed, right then and there, to be not only saviors for ourselves, but measurably saviors for the whole human family. We went into partnership with the Lord. The working out of the plan became then not merely the Father's work, and the Savior's work, but also our work. The least of us, the humblest, is in partnership with the Almighty in achieving the purpose of the eternal plan of salvation. . . . (Utah Genealogical and Historical Magazine, Oct. 1934) MPSG1967:87
**Related Witnesses:**
**Abraham,**
*quoted by Joseph Smith*
And there stood one among them that was like unto God, and he said unto those who were with him: We will go down, for there is space there, and we will take of these materials, and we will make an earth whereon these may dwell; 25. And we will prove them herewith, to see if they will do all things whatsoever the Lord their God shall command them; 26. And

they who keep their first estate shall be added upon; and they who keep not their first estate shall not have glory in the same kingdom with those who keep their first estate; and they who keep their second estate shall have glory added upon their heads for ever and ever. *(Abraham learns of pre-earth life and foreordination)* Abr.3:24-26

**Elder Joseph Fielding Smith**

At one time we were in the presence of our Eternal Father. . . . We knew what kind of a being he is. . . . And we wanted to be like him. And because we wanted to be like him, we are here. We could not be like him and stay in his presence, because we did not have glorious bodies of flesh and bones. We were just spirits, and the spirit does not have flesh and bones. But we saw him in his glory and it was made known to us that by keeping his commandments and observing every covenant that would be given to us on earth, we could come back again into his presence, receiving our bodies in the resurrection from the dead—our spirits and bodies being united again, inseparably, never again to be divided. ¶ If we will just be true and faithful to every covenant, to every principle of truth that he has given us, then after the resurrection we would come back into his presence and we would be just like he is. We would have the same kind of bodies—bodies that would shine like the sun. (Take Heed to Yourselves, p. 345) DGSM:28

**Elder Lorenzo Snow**

There is nothing the Latter-day Saints can imagine that would afford them happiness that God has not unfolded to us. He has prepared everything for the Latter-day Saints that they could possibly wish or imagine in order to effect their complete happiness throughout the vast eternities. (The Teachings of Lorenzo Snow, p. 63, [1897]) DGSM:28

**Marion G. Romney**

Abraham's account of the great pre-earth heavenly council identifies both God and Satan as participators in that council (read Abr.3). ¶ Marvelous and important is the knowledge revealed in that account—knowledge of things as they were in the distant past, concerning God the Father and his spirit children, and concerning his plans for the creation of this earth. It refers to the gospel plan and identifies Christ and Satan. CR1971Apr:22-23

**Joseph Smith,**
*translating the Book of Moses*

For behold, this is my work and my glory—to bring to pass the immortality and eternal life of man. *(God talks to Moses face to face)* Moses 1:39

**President Joseph F. Smith**

We believe in the pre-existence of man as a spirit, and in the future state of individual existence, in which every soul shall find its place, as determined by justice and mercy, with opportunities of endless progression, in varied conditions of eternity. *(Address from the First Presidency of the Church to the world, delivered to and accepted by vote of the Church in general conference, April 1907)* CR1907Apr(Appendix)4

---

**294. The gospel is the plan of salvation.**

**Bruce R. McConkie**

The gospel is the plan of salvation, the plan ordained and established by the Father to enable his spirit children to advance and progress and become like him. . . . ¶ The gospel "is the plan of salvation unto all men, through the blood of (God's) Only Begotten." (The Mortal Messiah, 2:8-9) TLDP:234

**Bruce R. McConkie**

The Church administers the gospel and offers salvation to all who will believe in Christ and live his laws. ¶ What is the fulness of the everlasting gospel? ¶ It is the plan of salvation—the Father's eternal plan to save his children. ¶ It is the begetting of spirit children, the teachings and testings of our premortal existence, the creation of worlds without number, and (for us) our inheritance here on planet earth. ¶ It is the fall of Adam, with its temporal and spiritual death, and the ransoming power of the Son of God, who abolished death and brought life and immortality to light through his laws. ¶ It is all of the laws, rites, and ordinances; all of the truths, powers, and performances; all of the keys, priesthoods, and privileges which bring to pass the immortality and eternal life of man. ¶ It is the atonement of Christ, the redemption of man, the opening of the graves, the wonder and glory of eternal life. ¶ It is faith, repentance, and baptism; it is the gifts of the Spirit, the revelations of heaven, and the unspeakable gift of the Holy Ghost. ¶ It is eternal marriage and eternal lives and eternal exaltation. It is to be one with the Father and the Son and to reign with them forever on their throne. ¶ It is the tests and trials of this mortal probation; it is sorrow and pain and death; it is overcoming the world and pursuing a godly course in spite of earth and hell; it is keeping the commandments and serving our fellowmen. ¶ And, finally , it is to sit down with Abraham, Isaac, and Jacob, and all the holy prophets, in the kingdom of God to go no more out. ("This Final Glorious Gospel Dispensation," EN1980Apr:21) TLDP:233-34

**Paul**

For I am not ashamed of the gospel of Christ: for it is the power of God unto salvation to every one that believeth; (*Letter to the Church in Rome, about A.D. 55*) Rom.1:16

**George F. Richards,**
*also quoting Paul*

We read in the Scriptures a definition of the Gospel given by the Apostle Paul to the Romans wherein he says, "I am not ashamed of the Gospel of Christ: for it is the power of God unto salvation." To enlarge a little upon that definition, we might say that the Gospel is the plan of the Gods in the councils of heaven before the world was, for the existence of this earth upon which we live and of man upon the earth, for the fall of man, for the redemption of man, and his exaltation through the atoning of Jesus Christ and obedience unto the laws and ordinances of the Gospel, and for the glorification of the earth. This plan involves also the acceptance of certain principles, the keeping of the commandments of the Lord, obeying his laws, rendering service to the Church, service to the Lord, service to fellow men, public service and private service, financial aid and spiritual blessing, and whatever else can be done for the blessing of mankind. CR1934Oct:72

**Orson F. Whitney**

The gospel is the plan of eternal progression, and perfection is its goal. CR1920Oct:36

**Elder Harold B. Lee**

The gospel is not merely a code of ethics or a social program, although "living upon the earth involves a plan of living together in order to cast out greed and avarice, selfishness, vice and wickedness, self-seeking for earthly power and dominion." The gospel is the plan of our Heavenly Father to guide mankind in their associations together in mortality to the end that eventually they shall be saved and exalted in the world to come. The gospel is divine truth, "it is all truth existent from eternity to eternity." The laws contained in the gospel are God's laws. They are not to be changed or modified to suit the whims of individuals and are designed to develop our inward souls through proper observance of and respect therefor. Any conduct on the part of an individual that does not advance him toward the goal of eternal life is not only wasted energy but actually becomes the basis of sin. (Decisions for Successful Living, p. 8) TLDP:233

**Marion G. Romney**

What do you think of when you think of the gospel of Jesus Christ? In my mind I have defined the gospel of Jesus Christ as the program which is established by the Lord by which he can bring his spirit children now in mortality back into his presence. ACR(Seoul)1975:2

**Related Witnesses:**

**Joseph Smith**

And this is the gospel, the glad tidings, which the voice out of the heavens bore record unto us— 41. That he came into the world, even Jesus, to be crucified for the world, and to bear the sins of the world, and to sanctify the world, and to cleanse it from all unrighteousness; 42. That through him all might be saved whom the Father had put into his power and made by him; (*Vision to Joseph Smith and Sidney Rigdon, Feb. 16, 1832*) D&C 76:40-42

---

295. **Those who receive Christ and believe on His name are given power to become (spiritually reborn) sons and daughters of God.**

**Moroni, son of Mormon**

Behold, I am Jesus Christ. I am the Father and the Son. In me shall all mankind have life, and that eternally, even they who shall believe on my name; and they shall become my sons and my daughters. (*Christ shows his spirit body to the brother of Jared, at the time of the Tower of Babel*) Ether 3:14

**Elder Harold B. Lee**

The Lord has given a plan, a three-fold plan, by which this unity might be fully realized. Unity centers in heaven, even as the Master prayed, "Father, that we might be one." The Saints might become one with the Father and the Son, spiritually begotten by baptism and through the Holy Ghost even unto the renewing of their bodies as the Lord tells us, and thus " . . . become the sons of Moses and Aaron . . . the church and kingdom, and the elect of God. . . ." (D&C 84:34) CR1950Apr:99

**Joseph Smith,**
*receiving the Word of the Lord*

I am Jesus Christ, the Son of God, who was crucified for the sins of the world, even as many as will believe on my name, that they may become the sons of God, even one in me as I am one in the Father, as the Father is one in me, that we may be one. (*Revelation to Joseph Smith and Sidney Rigdon, Dec. 1830*) D&C 35:2

**Joseph Smith,**
*receiving the Word of the Lord*

Behold, I am Jesus Christ, the Son of God. I
am the life and the light of the world. 29. I am
the same who came unto mine own and mine
own received me not; 30. But verily, verily, I
say unto you, that as many as receive me, to
them will I give power to become the sons of
God, even to them that believe on my name.
Amen. (*Revelation for Hyrum Smith, May
1829*) D&C 11:28-30

**Joseph Smith,**
*receiving the Word of the Lord*

But to as many as received me, gave I power to
become my sons; and even so will I give unto
as many as will receive me, power to become
my sons. (*Revelation received Jan. 5, 1831*)
D&C 39:4

**John**

But as many as received him, to them gave he
power to become the sons of God, even to them
that believe on his name: (*John writes of the
mission of Jesus Christ*) John 1:12

**Moroni, son of Mormon**

And after that he came men also were saved by
faith in his name; and by faith, they become the
sons of God. . . . (*Moroni records a sermon of
his father Mormon, given prior to A.D. 384*)
Moro.7:26

**Moroni, son of Mormon**

Wherefore, my beloved brethren, pray unto the
Father with all the energy of heart, that ye may
be filled with this love, which he hath bestowed
upon all who are true followers of his Son,
Jesus Christ; that ye may become the sons of
God; that when he shall appear we shall be like
him, for we shall see him as he is; that we may
have this hope; that we may be purified even as
he is pure. Amen. (*Mormon preaches in the
synagogue, prior to A.D. 384*) Moro.7:48

**President John Taylor**

It was further necessary that He [Christ] should
descend below all things, in order that He might
raise others above all things; for if He could not
raise Himself and be exalted through those
principles brought about by the atonement, He
could not raise others; He could not do for others what He could not do for Himself, and
hence it was necessary for Him to descend
below all things, that by and through the same
power that He obtained His exaltation, they
also, through His atonement, expiation and
intercession, might be raised to the same power
with Him; and, as He was the Son of God, that
they might also be the adopted sons of God.
(The Mediation and Atonement, pp. 144-45)
TLDP:40

**Related Witnesses:**
**Bruce R. McConkie**

Through the atonement of Christ, the inhabitants of all these worlds have power to become
his sons and daughters, to become joint-heirs
with him of all the glory of his Father's kingdom, to be adopted into the family of the
Father, which is to say that the inhabitants of all
worlds "are [thus] begotten sons and daughters
unto God." (D&C 76:24) (The Promised
Messiah, p. 286) TLDP:238

**Bruce R. McConkie**

Now we have mentioned both an oath and a
covenant where the Melchizedek Priesthood is
concerned. The oath is the solemn promise of
the Lord that all those who keep the priesthood covenant shall gain exaltation. That is to
say, the Lord swears with an oath that his
adopted and obedient sons shall be high
priests forever after the order of Melchizedek
(see D&C 76:57); they shall be joint heirs with
his natural Son, who is Christ our Lord.
ACR(Lima)1977:18

**Bruce R. McConkie**

In 1916, the duly constituted heads of the earthly Church, who have the ultimate responsibility,
under Deity, to interpret and promulgate the
mind and will of the Lord to mortals, issued a
document entitled *The Father and The Son: A
Doctrinal Exposition by The First Presidency
and The Twelve*. Therein are set forth, among
other things, . . . [these] distinct senses in which
Christ is also known as the Father. These are: ¶
1. He is the Father as Creator, the Father of the
heavens and the earth. ¶ 2. He is the Father of
those who abide in his gospel, the Father of all
those who take upon themselves his name and
are adopted into his family. (The Promised
Messiah, p. 63) TLDP:300

**Joseph Smith**

For whoso is faithful unto the obtaining these
two priesthoods of which I have spoken, and
the magnifying their calling, are sanctified by
the Spirit unto the renewing of their bodies. 34.
They become the sons of Moses and of Aaron
and the seed of Abraham, and the church and
kingdom, and the elect of God. (*Revelation on
priesthood received with six elders, Sept. 22/23,
1832*) D&C 84:33-34

---

296. The first principles and ordinances of the gospel are faith in
the Lord Jesus Christ, repentance, baptism by immersion, and
the laying on of hands for the gift
of the Holy Ghost.

**Joseph Smith**

We believe that the first principles and ordinances of the Gospel are: first, Faith in the Lord Jesus Christ; second, Repentance; third, Baptism by immersion for the remission of sins; fourth, Laying on of hands for the gift of the Holy Ghost. (*The fourth of the thirteen Articles of Faith; letter to John Wentworth, March 1, 1842*) AofF:4

**Elder Joseph Fielding Smith**

The first, or foundation principles, which must be received and obeyed are these: ¶ a. Faith in God and in the Atonement of Jesus Christ. ¶ b. Repentance from all sin. ¶ c. Baptism, by one having authority, in water by immersion for the remission of sin. ¶ d. Laying on of hands by one holding authority, for the gift of the Holy Ghost. ¶ e. A contrite spirit and a humble heart. ¶ f. Obedience to every other ordinance and principle of the Gospel, appertaining to the blessing of eternal life, and faithfulness to the end. (Man, His Origin and Destiny, pp. 50-53) TLDP:243-44

**President John Taylor**

Our mission has principally been to preach the first principles of the gospel, calling upon men everywhere to believe in the Lord God of heaven, he that created the heavens and the earth, the seas, and the fountains of waters; to believe in his Son, Jesus Christ, repenting of their sins, to be baptized for the remission of the same; and then we have promised them the Holy Ghost. In doing this the Lord has stood by us, sustaining those principles that we have advanced; and when we have ministered unto men the ordinances of the gospel they have received for themselves the witness of the Spirit, even the Holy Ghost, making known to them for a surety that the principles that they had received were from God. (*At Ephraim, Utah, Aug. 20, 1882, JD23:235-36*) TLDP:419

**Bruce R. McConkie**

The gospel "is the plan of salvation unto all men, through the blood of (God's) Only Begotten." It recognizes that "all men, everywhere, must repent, or they can in nowise inherit the kingdom of God, for no unclean thing can dwell there, or dwell in his presence." (Moses 6:57-62) It consists of hearkening unto the voice of God and believing in his Only Begotten; of forsaking the world and repenting of one's sins; of being baptized in water for the remission of sins; of receiving the gift of the Holy Ghost, so that the newly born saint may be sanctified and become pure and spotless; and of then enduring to the end and working the works of righteousness all one's days. "And

this is my gospel—repentance and baptism by water, and then cometh the baptism of fire and the Holy Ghost, even the Comforter, which showeth all things, and teacheth the peaceable things of the kingdom." (D&C 39:6) (The Mortal Messiah, 2:8-9) TLDP:234

**Related Witnesses:**

**President Joseph F. Smith**

In the theological sense, the gospel means more than just the tidings of good news, with accompanying joy to the souls of men, for it embraces every principle of eternal truth. There is no fundamental principle, or truth, anywhere in the universe, that is not embraced in the gospel of Jesus Christ, and it is not confined to the simple first principles, such as faith in God, repentance from sin, baptism for the remission of sins, and the laying on of hands for the gift of the Holy Ghost, although these are absolutely essential to salvation and exaltation in the kingdom of God. ¶ The laws known to man as the "laws of nature," through which the earth and all things on it are governed, as well as the laws which prevail throughout the entire universe, through which heavenly bodies are controlled and to which they are obedient in all things, are all circumscribed and included in the gospel. Every natural law or scientific principle that man has truly discovered, but which was always known to God, is a part of the gospel truth. There never was and never will be any conflict between truth revealed by the Lord to his servants, the prophets, and truth revealed by him to the scientist, who makes his discoveries through his research and study. (Gospel Doctrine, pp. 85-86) TLDP:238

**Joseph Smith,**
*receiving the Word of the Lord*

And this is my gospel—repentance and baptism by water, and then cometh the baptism of fire and the Holy Ghost, even the Comforter, which showeth all things, and teacheth the peaceable things of the kingdom. (*Revelation received Jan. 5, 1831*) D&C 39:6

**Joseph Smith,**
*translating the Book of Moses*

And he also said unto him: If thou wilt turn unto me, and hearken unto my voice, and believe, and repent of all thy transgressions, and be baptized, even in water, in the name of mine Only Begotten Son, who is full of grace and truth, which is Jesus Christ, the only name which shall be given under heaven whereby salvation shall come unto the children of men, ye shall receive the gift of the Holy Ghost, asking all things in his name, and whatsoever ye shall ask, it shall be given you. (*The record of*

*Moses: Enoch recounts God speaking to Adam)*
Moses 6:52

**Author's Note:** Earlier editions of the Articles of Faith tied the fourth article with the third: "3. We believe that, through the atonement of Christ, all mankind may be saved, by obedience to the laws and ordinances of the Gospel. 4. We believe that these ordinances are: [etc.]" (See Ready References, published by The Deseret News Co. 1887, printed in "An 1877 Mormon Catechism for Children Together with Ready Reference," republished by Jerry Burnett and Charles Pope, Mormon Heritage Publishers, Salt Lake City, Utah 1976)

---

### 297. The principles of the gospel are unchanging, eternal truths.

**President Heber J. Grant,**
**J. Reuben Clark, Jr., David O. McKay**
(First Presidency)

The principles of the gospel are all-embracing—they are everlasting, unchangeable, ultimate truth. They will fit every situation, every problem, every contingency that may arise in the life of man. There are no local problems, no peculiar situations, in ward or stake, that may not be solved under these principles. It will not do for any Church officer or member to work out for himself a different course from that prescribed. This will lead to disorder, and the Lord's house is a house of order. When new light is needed, or further instructions, the Lord will make them known through His appointed representative. What we should seek is wisdom to apply the old and true principles to new situations. Let us not suppose that man has recently changed in his essential qualities or habits, for this is not true; all that has happened today is that some basic passions which, through the generations, mankind had brought under control, have now broken loose in something of their primeval strength. They are not new passions. We possess the principles which brought them under subjection once; these principles were given to man in the very beginning for this exact purpose; we must now apply them again to conquer these same old foes of righteousness. This is not a new world; it is an old and sinful world again returned, and now once more to be reconquered and rejuvenated. CR1942Oct:14

**President John Taylor**

There is not a principle associated with the Gospel of the Son of God but what is eternal in its nature and consequences, and we cannot with impunity trample upon any principle that is correct without having to suffer the penalty thereof before God and the holy angels, and in many instances before men. The principles of the Gospel being eternal, they were framed and originated with the Almighty in eternity before the world was, according to certain eternal laws, and hence the Gospel is called the everlasting Gospel. *(At American Fork, Utah, Nov. 28, 1879, JD21:112)* TLDP:234

**Elder John Taylor**

We are not connected with a something that will exist only for a few years, some of the peculiar ideas and dogmas of men, some nice theory of their forming; the principles that we believe in reach back into eternity, they originated with the Gods in the eternal worlds, and they reach forward to the eternities that are to come. We feel that we are operating with God in connection with those who were, with those who are, and with those who are to come. *(General conference, Oct. 7, 1874, JD17:206)* TLDP:234

**John A. Widtsoe**

The Gospel itself, the so-called plan of salvation, or Great Plan, in obedience to which men guide their earth-lives, is eternal. It is not a temporary or transient thing, made primarily for the handful of men and women on earth, but it is an eternal plan based upon the everlasting relationships of the elements of the universe—a plan which, in some form, is adapted everywhere and forever to the advancement of personal beings. This must be so, for as it leads always to the same definite end, in accordance with the law of cause and effect, it must have a universal meaning. . . . ¶ The Gospel may be said to be The Philosophy of Eternalism. The Gospel is immersed in the ocean of eternity. (A Rational Theology, p. 15) TLDP:235

**Elder Harold B. Lee**

The gospel is divine truth, "it is all truth existent from eternity to eternity." The laws contained in the gospel are God's laws. They are not to be changed or modified to suit the whims of individuals and are designed to develop our inward souls through proper observance of and respect therefor. (Decisions for Successful Living, p. 8) TLDP:233

**Elder Wilford Woodruff**

No man ever did or ever will obtain salvation only through the ordinances of the Gospel and through the name of Jesus. There can be no change in the Gospel; all men that are saved from Adam to infinitum are saved by the one system of salvation. The Lord may give many laws and commandments to suit the varied circumstances and conditions of his children throughout the world, such as giving a law of carnal commandments to Israel, but the laws and principles of the Gospel do not change. *(In Bowery, June 12, 1863, JD10:217)* TLDP:234-35

### Elder Joseph Fielding Smith

I think the idea prevails throughout the so-called "Christian" world that the plan that was given from the days of Adam until the days of Jesus Christ was a different plan—something other than what our Savior gave—and that the gospel of Jesus Christ as introduced by him is another system entirely from that which was in force or required of mankind before the coming of our Lord in his ministry. But that is not true. The decrees of the Almighty are unchangeable so far as the laws pertaining to the kingdom of God are concerned. They always were what they are today. We have not changed them. They are not different from what people had to subscribe to from the days of Adam on down. (Seek Ye Earnestly, pp.407-08) TLDP:235

**Related Witnesses:**

### Elder George Albert Smith

What is this gospel to which we refer? It is the only power of God unto salvation, it is the only plan that will enable man to go back into the presence of his Maker and enjoy the celestial kingdom. It is the only plan that will bring peace and happiness to all the children of men, of every race and creed. CR1928Oct:93

### Peter

Be it known unto you all, and to all the people of Israel, that by the name of Jesus Christ of Nazareth, whom ye crucified, whom God raised from the dead, even by him doth this man stand here before you whole 11. This is the stone which was set at nought of you builders, which is become the head of the corner. 12. Neither is there salvation in any other: for there is none other name under heaven given among men, whereby we must be saved. *(Under arrest, Peter testifies before the Jewish rulers, elders and scribes)* Acts 4:10-12

### Paul

Beware lest any man spoil you through philosophy and vain deceit, after the tradition of men, after the rudiments of the world, and not after Christ. *(Letter from prison to the Church in Colossae, Asia Minor, about A.D. 60)* Col.2:8

### Paul

One Lord, one faith, one baptism, *(Letter to the Saints at Ephesus in Asia Minor declaring one Lord, one faith, one baptism, about A.D. 62)* Eph.4:5

## 298. The blessings of salvation and exaltation are available to all, not to a select few.

### John A. Widtsoe

Man's earth-career is designed to enable him to acquire more power, more development, and therefore more joy. In the nature of existence, it is impossible for an intelligent being to attain the highest degree of joy unless other like beings move along with him. The Great Plan will succeed only if all, or at least a majority of those who accepted it are saved. The Church, a part of the Great Plan, must have as its main purpose the saving of all human beings. All must be saved! The work of the Church cannot be completed until all have at least heard the truth and have been given the chance to accept it. There can be no talk of a few souls before the throne of God, with the many in hell. The great mission of the Church must always be to bring all men into a knowledge and acceptance of the truth. This is the cementing purpose of the Church. (A Rational Theology, p. 122) TLDP:411

### Peter

Then Peter opened his mouth, and said, Of a truth I perceive that God is no respecter of persons: 35. But in every nation he that feareth him, and worketh righteousness, is accepted with him. *(Peter in a vision is commanded to take the gospel to the Gentiles)* Acts 10:34-35

### President Joseph F. Smith

We believe that salvation is for no select few, but that all men may be saved through obedience to the laws and ordinances of the Gospel. *(Address from the First Presidency of the Church to the world, delivered to and accepted by vote of the Church in general conference, April 1907)* CR1907Apr(Appendix)4

### Elder Joseph Fielding Smith

[Respecter of persons] does not mean that the Lord does not respect those who obey him in all things more than he does the ungodly. Without question the Lord does respect those who love him and keep his commandments more than he does those who rebel against him. The proper interpretation of this passage is that the Lord is not partial and grants to each man, if he will repent, the same privileges and opportunities of salvation and exaltation. He is just to every man, both the righteous and the wicked. He will receive any soul who will turn from iniquity to righteousness, and will love him with a just love and bless him with all that the Father has to give; but let it not be thought that he will grant the same blessings to those who will not obey him and keep his law. If the Lord did bless the rebellious as he does the righteous, without their repentance, then he would be a respecter of persons. CHMR1:255; DCSM:6

**Elder Joseph F. Smith**

God is not a respecter of persons. The rich man may enter into the kingdom of heaven as freely as the poor, if he will bring his heart and affections into subjection to the law of God and to the principle of truth; if he will place his affections upon God, his heart upon the truth, and his soul upon the accomplishment of God's purposes, and not fix his affections and his hopes upon the things of the world. (*General conference, Oct. 1875*) TLDP:714

**Joseph Smith,**
*receiving the Word of the Lord*

And again, verily I say unto you, O inhabitants of the earth: I the Lord am willing to make these things known unto all flesh; 35. For I am no respecter of persons. . . . (*Revelation received during conference of elders of the Church, Nov. 1, 1831*) D&C 1:34-35

**Joseph Smith,**
*receiving the Word of the Lord*

And for your salvation I give unto you a commandment, for I have heard your prayers, and the poor have complained before me, and the rich have I made, and all flesh is mine, and I am no respecter of persons. (*Commandments to Saints in conference, Jan. 2, 1831*) D&C 38:16

**Rudger Clawson**

Now let me impress upon your minds the fact that it takes just as much to save the dead as the living, and whatever ordinance is conferred upon the living for their salvation in the Kingdom of God must also be conferred upon the dead. Hence these glorious temples which have been erected in our midst, that ordinances may be performed therein for the living and the dead. In this we see again that God is no respecter of persons, and that He is feeling after the dead as well as after the living. We cannot be made perfect without our fathers and mothers and our ancestors, and they cannot be made perfect without us. CR1904Oct:37

**Related Witnesses:**

**Paul**

I charge thee before God, and the Lord Jesus Christ, and the elect angels, that thou observe these things without preferring one before another, doing nothing by partiality. (*Paul writes to his assistant Timothy, about A.D. 64*) 1Tim.5:21

**Joseph Smith,**
*receiving the Word of the Lord*

And again I say unto you, let every man esteem his brother as himself. 26. For what man among you having twelve sons, and is no respecter of them, and they serve him obediently, and he saith unto the one: Be thou clothed in robes and sit thou here; and to the other: Be thou clothed in rags and sit thou there—and looketh upon his sons and saith I am just? (*Commandments to Saints in conference, Jan. 2, 1831*) D&C 38:25-26

**Mormon**

But little children are alive in Christ, even from the foundation of the world; if not so, God is a partial God, and also a changeable God, and a respecter to persons; for how many little children have died without baptism! . . . 18. For I know that God is not a partial God, neither a changeable being; but he is unchangeable from all eternity to all eternity. (*Epistle of Mormon to his son Moroni, prior to A.D. 384*) Moro.8:12,18

**James E. Talmage**

Now when we say that the Lord is not pleased with those churches, we do not mean that he is not pleased with the members thereof. We hold that God is no respecter of persons, but, on the contrary, that he will acknowledge good in any soul, no matter whether that person belongs to a church or not. But the Lord is not pleased with those churches that have been constructed by men and then labeled with his name. . . . ¶ I do not understand that all members of those churches are to meet destruction, physically or otherwise. He is speaking there of the church collectively, and he is not pleased with it; but individually he may be well pleased with many of his sons and daughters who have been under an environment that has led them into those churches which are not of God. CR1928Oct:120

---

299. **The gospel is universally applicable to all people everywhere; it will bring to each person exactly what is necessary for salvation.**

**N. Eldon Tanner**

Regardless of country, clime, or condition, the gospel of Jesus Christ applies to every individual just the same. It is a way of life that each can accept, and if lived, will bring greater joy, success, and happiness than anything else in the world. In fact, it sets forth in all simplicity the principles of the gospel established by Jesus Christ while he was here upon the earth. ("Christ's Worldwide Church," EN1974Jul:6) TLDP:237-38

**Francis M. Lyman**

The Gospel is suited to all the conditions of mankind. It will meet every requirement of man, and it will satisfy every rational ambition and every righteous desire of the human heart. It is perfect in every respect. It is broad enough and deep enough for the rich and for the poor, for the intelligent and for the ignorant. It will bring to every person exactly what is necessary for his salvation. If men need to be humbled, it will school them. If they need to be exalted, it will lift them up. If they have need to be reformed, it will reform them. In fact, as I have said, it will meet all the requirements of human nature. CR1899Apr:37

**Elder John Taylor**

[The everlasting gospel] is adapted to the wants of the human family, to the world morally, socially, religiously and politically. It is not a sickly, sentimental, effeminate plaything; not a ghostly, spiritual, sing-song, ethereal dream, but a living, sober, matter-of-fact reality, adapted to body and spirit, to earth and heaven, to time and eternity. It enters into all the ramifications of life. It does not adopt itself to the philosophy, politics, creeds and opinions of men, but fashions them in its divine mould. It cannot be twisted into the multitudinous latitudinarian principles of a degenerate world; but lifts all that are in the world, who will be subject to its precepts, to its own ennobling, exalted, and dignified standard. It searches all truth, and grasps at all intelligence; it is the revealed living and abiding will of God to man; a connection between the heavens and the earth; it is nature, philosophy, heavens and earth, time and eternity united; it is the philosophy of the heavens and the earth, of God, and angels, and saints. ("What Is Mormonism?", The Mormon, July 28, 1855, p.1) TLDP:238

**Stephen L. Richards**

The organizations of the Church are established in such a manner that service may be rendered by everyone within its membership to the ultimate benefit of every other member. It is a mutual plan whereby each may help every other and the common good may be promoted. ¶ So that, in brief, the gospel fulfills every requirement of a human life. CR1920Apr:98-99

**Related Witnesses:**

**Joseph Smith**

We believe that through the Atonement of Christ, all mankind may be saved, by obedience to the laws and ordinances of the Gospel. (The third of the thirteen Articles of Faith; letter to John Wentworth, March 1, 1842) AofF:3

**Peter**

Then Peter opened his mouth, and said, Of a truth I perceive that God is no respecter of persons: 35. But in every nation he that feareth him, and worketh righteousness, is accepted with him. (Peter in a vision is commanded to take the gospel to the Gentiles) Acts 10:34-35

**Bruce R. McConkie**

Further, the gospel is in operation in all the worlds created by the Father and the Son. Their work and their glory, in all the infinite creations that their hands have made, is to bring to pass immortality and eternal life for the children of the Father. Through the atonement of Christ, the inhabitants of all these worlds have power to become his sons and daughters, to become joint-heirs with him of all the glory of his Father's kingdom. . . . (The Promised Messiah, p. 286) TLDP:238

**James E. Talmage**

More is included in the gospel than all Scripture thus far written. . . . The Gospel is broad enough, and deep enough, and of such towering heights as to surpass the powers of the greatest mind to comprehend and yet so simple in its fundamentals as to satisfy the honest inquiry of the child. CR1918Apr:160,163

**Rudger Clawson**

And let me say to you, brethren and sisters, that the heights and the depths of the Gospel are quite beyond our reach. The finite mind is not capable of wholly comprehending the great plan of redemption. We, occasionally, have a glimpse of its power and beauty; but we must learn line upon line, precept upon precept, here a little and there a little, until we come up to the full stature of a man in Christ Jesus. It cannot be comprehended in a day, or a month, or a year, it is the study of a life-time. CR1904Oct:35

---

**300. The gospel was preached from the beginning, starting with Adam.**

**Joseph Smith,**
*translating the Book of Moses*

And thus the Gospel began to be preached, from the beginning, being declared by holy angels sent forth from the presence of God, and by his own voice, and by the gift of the Holy Ghost. 59. And thus all things were confirmed unto Adam, by an holy ordinance, and the Gospel preached, and a decree sent forth, that it should be in the world, until the end thereof; and thus it was. Amen. (Revelation to Moses about the beginning of man on earth) Moses 5:58-59

**Bruce R. McConkie**

Anyone who, with Moroni, knows, "That God is the same yesterday, today, and forever, and in him there is no variableness neither shadow of changing" (Morm. 9:9), also knows, automatically and instinctively, that Adam had the gospel of Jesus Christ in the same literal sense that the same plan of salvation was enjoyed by Paul. Modern religionists, with the light before them, choose darkness rather than light if they elect to believe that an eternal and unchangeable God saves one soul on one set of standards and another soul in some other way. (The Promised Messiah, pp. 285-87) TLDP:235-36

**Joseph Smith,**
*translating the Book of Moses*
And he called upon our father Adam by his own voice, saying: I am God; I made the world, and men before they were in the flesh. 52. And he also said unto him: If thou wilt turn unto me, and hearken unto my voice, and believe, and repent of all thy transgressions, and be baptized, even in water, in the name of mine Only Begotten Son, who is full of grace and truth, which is Jesus Christ, the only name which shall be given under heaven, whereby salvation shall come unto the children of men, ye shall receive the gift of the Holy Ghost, asking all things in his name, and whatsoever ye shall ask, it shall be given you. (*The record of Moses: Enoch recounts God speaking to Adam*) Moses 6:51-52

**President Joseph Fielding Smith**
We announce that this plan of salvation, this gospel plan, has been revealed to men in successive dispensations beginning with our father Adam, the first man; that it was known to Enoch and Noah, to Abraham and Moses; that it was proclaimed in plainness to the ancient inhabitants of the American continent; and that it is the same plan which was taught by Jesus and Peter and Paul, and the former Latter-day Saints who lived in the meridian of time. ¶ And further—and this is exceedingly important where all men now living are concerned—we believe that following a long night of darkness, unbelief, and departure from the truths of pure and perfect Christianity, the Lord in his infinite wisdom has again restored to earth the fullness of the everlasting gospel. CR1971Apr:5

**Elder Joseph F. Smith**
Undoubtedly the knowledge of this law [of sacrifice] and of other rites and ceremonies was carried by the posterity of Adam into all lands, and continued with them, more or less pure, to the flood, and through Noah, who was a "preacher of righteousness" to those who succeeded him, spreading out into all nations and countries, Adam and Noah being the first of their dispensations to receive them from God. What wonder, then, that we should find relics of Christianity, so to speak, among the heathens

and nations who know not Christ, and whose histories date back beyond the days of Moses, and even beyond the flood, independent of and apart from the records of the Bible. The ground taken by infidels, that "Christianity" sprang from the heathen, it being found that they have many rites similar to those recorded in the Bible, &c, is only a vain and foolish attempt to blind the eyes of men and dissuade them from their faith in the Redeemer of the world, and from their belief in the Scriptures of divine truth, for if the heathen have doctrines and ceremonies resembling to some extent those which are recorded in the Scriptures, it only proves, what is plain to the Saints, that these are the traditions of the fathers handed down from generation to generation, from Adam, through Noah, and that they will cleave to the children to the latest generation, though they may wander into darkness and perversion, until but a slight resemblance to their origin, which was divine, can be seen. *(In 13th Ward, Feb. 9, 1873, JD15:325)* TLDP:29

**Related Witnesses:**
(Author's Note: The following witnesses show that the Gospel was Preached to Abraham, to Enoch and Noah, and to ancient Israel):

**Paul**
And the scripture, foreseeing that God would justify the heathen through faith, preached before the gospel unto Abraham, saying, In thee shall all nations be blessed. (*Letter to the churches of Galatia in Asia Minor, about A.D. 55*) Gal.3:8

**Paul**
For unto us was the gospel preached, as well as unto them: but the word preached did not profit them, not being mixed with faith in them that heard it. (*Letter to the Jewish members of the Church, about A.D. 60*) Heb.4:2 [See Heb.3:15-19 for context.]

**Joseph Smith,**
*translating the Book of Moses*
And the Lord said unto me: Go to this people, and say unto them—Repent, lest I come out and smite them with a curse, and they die. 11. And he gave unto me a commandment that I should baptize in the name of the Father, and of the Son, which is full of grace and truth, and of the Holy Ghost, which beareth record of the Father and the Son. 12. And it came to pass that Enoch continued to call upon all the people, save it were the people of Canaan, to repent; (*Enoch talks to the Lord face to face*) Moses 7:10-12

**Joseph Smith,**
*translating the Book of Moses*
And it came to pass that Noah continued his preaching unto the people, saying: Hearken,

and give heed unto my words; 24. Believe and repent of your sins and be baptized in the name of Jesus Christ, the Son of God, even as our fathers, and ye shall receive the Holy Ghost, that ye may have all things made manifest; and if ye do not this, the floods will come in upon you; nevertheless they hearkened not. *(The record of Moses: The Lord has told Noah, "My spirit shall not always strive with man . . . and if men do not repent I will send in the floods. . . ." Moses 8:17)* Moses 8:23-24

### Joseph Smith

[T]he Book of Mormon; 9. . . . contains . . . the fullness of the gospel of Jesus Christ to the Gentiles and to the Jews also; *(Revelation on Church Organization and Government, April 1830; the Book of Mormon proves the divinity of the latter-day work)* D&C 20:8-9

---

301. **Every person will at some time have opportunity to hear the gospel, whether on earth or in the spirit world.**

### Elder Joseph Fielding Smith

The Lord has made it known that his mercy extends to the uttermost bounds and that every soul is entitled to hear the gospel plan, either in this life or in the spirit world. All who hear and believe, repenting and receiving the gospel in its fulness, whether living or dead, are heirs of salvation in the celestial kingdom of God. (Doctrines of Salvation, 2:133) DGSM:85

### President John Taylor

And this provision [the Atonement] applies not only to the living, but also to the dead, so that all men who have existed in all ages, who do exist now, or who will exist while the earth shall stand, may be placed upon the same footing, and that all men may have the privilege, living or dead, of accepting the conditions of the great plan of redemption provided by the Father, through the Son, before the world was; and that the justice and mercy of God may be applied to every being, living or dead, that ever has existed, that does now exist, or that ever will exist. (The Mediation and Atonement, p. 181) TLDP:38

### John A. Widtsoe

Man's earth-career is designed to enable him to acquire more power, more development, and therefore more joy. In the nature of existence, it is impossible for an intelligent being to attain the highest degree of joy unless other like beings move along with him. The Great Plan will succeed only if all, or at least a majority of

those who accepted it are saved. The Church, a part of the Great Plan, must have as its main purpose the saving of all human beings. All must be saved! The work of the Church cannot be completed until all have at least heard the truth and have been given the chance to accept it. There can be no talk of a few souls before the throne of God, with the many in hell. The great mission of the Church must always be to bring all men into a knowledge and acceptance of the truth. This is the cementing purpose of the Church. (A Rational Theology, p. 122) TLDP:411

### George F. Richards

The Gospel of Jesus Christ is the prescribed law by which all men are to be judged and by it to be condemned or justified according to merit. Justice demands, therefore, that all men shall have the privilege of learning and of receiving or rejecting the Gospel and its ordinances. God has graciously made provision through the Gospel that such shall be the case. ("All May Be Saved," IE1936Apr:201) TLDP:246

### Joseph Smith,
#### *receiving the Word of the Lord*

For verily the voice of the Lord is unto all men, and there is none to escape; and there is no eye that shall not see, neither ear that shall not hear, neither heart that shall not be penetrated. . . . 4. And the voice of warning shall be unto all people, by the mouths of my disciples, whom I have chosen in these last days. *(Revelation received during conference of elders of the Church, Nov. 1, 1831; preface to the doctrines given to the Church)* D&C 1:2,4

### Joseph Smith

For it shall come to pass in that day, that every man shall hear the fulness of the gospel in his own tongue, and in his own language, through those who are ordained unto this power, by the administration of the Comforter, shed forth upon them for the revelation of Jesus Christ. *(Revelation received March 8, 1833; the gospel to be preached to the nations of Israel, to the Gentiles, and to the Jews)* D&C 90:11

**Related Witnesses:**
### President Joseph F. Smith

But behold, from among the righteous, he organized his forces and appointed messengers, clothed with power and authority, and commissioned them to go forth and carry the light of the gospel to them that were in darkness, even to all the spirits of men; and thus was the gospel preached to the dead. 31. And the chosen messengers went forth to declare the acceptable day of the Lord and proclaim liberty to the captives who were bound, even unto all who would repent of their sins and receive the gospel. 32. Thus was the gospel preached to those who had died in their sins, without a knowledge of the truth, or in transgression, having rejected the prophets. (*Vision regarding the Savior's visit to the spirits of the dead, Oct. 3, 1918*) D&C 138:30-32

### John

And I saw another angel fly in the midst of heaven, having the everlasting gospel to preach unto them that dwell on the earth, and to every nation, and kindred, and tongue, and people, 7. Saying with a loud voice, Fear God, and give glory to him; for the hour of his judgment is come: and worship him that made heaven, and earth, and the sea, and the fountains of waters. (*The Apostle John sees the gospel restored in the last days by angelic ministry*) Rev.14:6-7

### President Joseph F. Smith

The dead who repent will be redeemed, through obedience to the ordinances of the house of God. (*Vision regarding the Savior's visit to the spirits of the dead, Oct. 3, 1918*) D&C 138:58

---

### 302. A physical body is essential to obtaining a fulness of joy in the celestial kingdom of God.

### Joseph Smith

We came to this earth that we might have a body and present it pure before God in the celestial kingdom. The great principle of happiness consists in having a body. The devil has no body, and herein is his punishment. He is pleased when he can obtain the tabernacle of man, and when cast out by the Savior he asked to go into the herd of swine, showing that he would prefer a swine's body to having none. ¶ All beings who have bodies have power over those who have not. (*At organization of school of instruction*) DGSM:28

### Joseph Smith

For man is spirit. The elements are eternal, and spirit and element, inseparably connected, receive a fulness of joy; 34. And when separated, man cannot receive a fulness of joy. (*Revelation at Kirtland, Ohio, May 6, 1833*) D&C 93:33,34

### President Joseph F. Smith

I beheld that they were filled with joy and gladness, and were rejoicing together because the day of their deliverance was at hand. 16. They were assembled awaiting the advent of the Son of God into the spirit world, to declare their redemption from the bands of death. 17. Their

sleeping dust was to be restored unto its perfect frame, bone to his bone, and the sinews and the flesh upon them, the spirit and the body to be united never again to be divided, that they might receive a fulness of joy. . . . 50. For the dead had looked upon the long absence of their spirits from their bodies as a bondage. 51. These the Lord taught, and gave them power to come forth, after his resurrection from the dead, to enter into his Father's kingdom and there to be crowned with immortality and eternal life. . . . 56. Even before they were born, they, with many others, received their first lessons in the world of spirits and were prepared to come forth in the due time of the Lord to labor in his vineyard for the salvation of the souls of men. (*Vision regarding the Savior's visit to the spirits of the dead, Oct. 3, 1918*) D&C 138:15-17,50-51,56

### Elder Joseph Fielding Smith

At one time we were in the presence of our Eternal Father. . . . We knew what kind of a being he is. . . . And we wanted to be like him. And because we wanted to be like him, we are here. We could not be like him and stay in his presence, because we did not have glorious bodies of flesh and bones. We were just spirits, and the spirit does not have flesh and bones. But we saw him in his glory and it was made known to us that by keeping his commandments and observing every covenant that would be given to us on earth, we could come back again into his presence, receiving our bodies in the resurrection from the dead—our spirits and bodies being united again, inseparably, never again to be divided. ¶ If we will just be true and faithful to every covenant, to every principle of truth that he has given us, then after the resurrection we would come back into his presence and we would be just like he is. We would have the same kind of bodies—bodies that would shine like the sun. (Take Heed to Yourselves, p. 345) DGSM:28

### Joseph Smith, *translating the Book of Moses*

And in that day Adam blessed God and was filled, and began to prophesy concerning all the families of the earth, saying: Blessed be the name of God, for because of my transgression my eyes are opened, and in this life I shall have joy, and again in the flesh I shall see God. (*The record of Moses: Adam realizes that through Adam and Eve's transgression they may receive joy and eternal life, and he therefore blesses the name of God*) Moses 5:10

### Marion G. Romney

[A]s the offspring of God, we inherit the capability of reaching, in full maturity, the status of our heavenly parents just as we inherit from our mortal parents the capability to attain to their mortal status; and . . . since God has a body of flesh and bones, it was necessary and perfectly natural for us, his spirit offspring, to obtain such bodies in order that we might be like him; . . . coming to earth was the means provided for us to obtain these bodies. CR1976Apr:118

### James E. Talmage

Man in his mortal state is the union of a preexistent spirit with a body composed of earthly elements. This union of spirit and body marks progress from the unembodied to the embodied condition, and is an inestimable advancement in the soul's onward course. The penalty incurred by proud Lucifer and his rebel hordes for their attempt to thwart the divine purpose in the matter of man's agency was the doom of being denied bodies of flesh. Mortal birth is a boon to which only those spirits who kept their first estate are eligible (see Jude 6). Expressive of the awful state of the utterly unregenerate among men, of those who have sunk to such depths in sin as to become "sons of perdition" the Lord has applied the extreme malediction that for such it were better never to have been born (see Matt. 26:24; D&C 76:32). AF:428

**Related Witnesses:**

### Joseph Smith

And the spirit and the body are the soul of man. 16. And the resurrection from the dead is the redemption of the soul. (*Revelation received Dec. 27/28, 1832; the "olive leaf message of peace"*) D&C 88:15-16

---

**HYMNS Written by Prophets Applicable to this Topic**

### Parley P. Pratt
*Behold Thy Sons and Daughters, Lord*
HYMNS:238

Behold thy sons and daughters, Lord,
On whom we lay our hands.
Thy have fulfilled the gospel word
And bowed at thy commands.

Oh, now send down the heav'nly dove
And overwhelm their souls
With peace and joy and perfect love,
As lambs within thy fold.

Seal them by thine own Spirit's pow'r,
Which purifies from sin,
And may they find, from this good hour,
They are adopted in.

Increase their faith, confirm their hope,
And guide them in the way.
With comfort bear their spirits up
Until the perfect day.

# List of Doctrines

## GOVERNMENTS: Civil Government

*Doctrines Located in This Topic*

303. Civil governments should exist for the benefit of the governed.

304. Civil governments should secure to all individuals freedom to worship how, where, or what they may.

305. Civil governments should function by the voice of the people.

306. Church and state should remain separate from each other, neither one interfering with the rights and functions of the other.

307. Promoting righteous civil government and sharing the burden of government is the responsibility of every citizen.

308. Each individual contributes to good civil government by living a righteous life and by influencing others to do the same.

309. We are to sustain and uphold the government under which we reside.

*Doctrines on GOVERNMENTS: Civil Government Located in Other Topics*

80. Church discipline is ecclesiastical only and can only affect a member's standing in the Church.

540. We are to pray for those who have civil authority over us.

# GOVERNMENTS: Civil Government

**303. Civil governments should exist for the benefit of the governed.**

### Joseph Smith

We believe that governments were instituted of God for the benefit of man; and that he holds men accountable for their acts in relation to them, both in making laws and administering them, for the good and safety of society. 2. We believe that no government can exist in peace, except such laws are framed and held inviolate as will secure to each individual the free exercise of conscience, the right and control of property, and the protection of life. *(Declaration of belief regarding governments and laws, Aug. 17, 1835)* D&C 134:1-2

### Elder Ezra Taft Benson

The function of government is to protect life, liberty, and property, and anything more or less than this is usurpation and oppression. CR1968Apr:49

### President David O. McKay

I believe with others that government, institutions, and organizations exist primarily for the purpose of securing to the individual his rights, his happiness, and proper development of his character. When organizations fail to accomplish this purpose, their usefulness ends. "So act," says Kant, "as to treat humanity, whether in your own person or that of another, in every case as an end, never as a means only." ¶ In all ages of the world men have been prone to ignore the personality of others, to disregard men's rights by closing against them the opportunity to develop. The worth of man is a good measuring rod by which we may judge the rightfulness or the wrongfulness of a policy or principle, whether in government, in business or in social activities. CR1962Oct:5-6

**Related Witnesses:**

### Mosiah, son of Benjamin, *quoted by Mormon*

And now I desire that this inequality should be no more in this land, especially among this my people; but I desire that this land be a land of liberty, and every man may enjoy his rights and privileges alike, so long as the Lord sees fit that we may live and inherit the land, yea, even as long as any of our posterity remains upon the face of the land. *(Mosiah tells the people unrighteous kings lead the people to sin, about 92 B.C.)* Mosiah 29:32

**304. Civil governments should secure to all individuals freedom to worship how, where, or what they may.**

### Joseph Smith

We believe that religion is instituted of God; and that men are amenable to him, and to him only, for the exercise of it, unless their religious opinions prompt them to infringe upon the rights and liberties of others; but we do not believe that human law has a right to interfere in prescribing rules of worship to bind the consciences of men, nor dictate forms for public or private devotion; that the civil magistrate should restrain crime, but never control conscience; should punish guilt, but never suppress the freedom of the soul. . . . 7. We believe that rulers, states, and governments have a right, and are bound to enact laws for the protection of all citizens in the free exercise of their religious belief; but we do not believe that they have a right in justice to deprive citizens of this privilege, or proscribe them in their opinions, so long as a regard and reverence are shown to the laws and such religious opinions do not justify sedition nor conspiracy. *(Declaration of belief regarding governments and laws, Aug. 17, 1835)* D&C 134:4,7

### President Brigham Young, *quoted by John A. Widtsoe*

We believe that the Lord has been preparing that when he should bring forth his work that, when the set time should fully come, there might be a place upon his footstool where sufficient liberty of conscience should exist, that his Saints might dwell in peace under the broad panoply of constitutional law and equal rights. In this view we consider that the men in the Revolution were inspired by the Almighty, to throw off the shackles of the mother government, with her established religion. For this cause were Adams, Jefferson, Franklin, Washington, and a host of others inspired to deeds of resistance to the acts of the King of Great Britain, who might also have been led to those aggressive acts, for aught we know, to bring to pass the purposes of God, in thus establishing a new government upon a principle of greater freedom, a basis of self-government allowing the free exercise of religious worship. *(In Tabernacle, Feb. 18, 1855, JD2:170)* DBY:359-60

### Mormon

But it came to pass in the latter end of the seventeenth year, there came a man into the land of Zarahemla, and he was Anti-Christ, for he began to preach unto the people against the prophecies which had been spoken by the prophets, concerning the coming of Christ. 7. Now there was no law against a man's belief; for it was strictly contrary to the commands of God that there should be a law which should bring men on to unequal grounds. 8. For thus saith the scripture: Choose ye this day, whom ye will serve. 9. Now if a man desired to serve God, it was his privilege; or rather, if he believed in God it was his privilege to serve him; but if he did not believe in him there was no law to punish him. 10. But if he murdered he was punished unto death; and if he robbed he was also punished; and if he stole he was also punished; and if he committed adultery he was also punished; yea, for all this wickedness they were punished. 11. For there was a law that men should be judged according to their crimes. Nevertheless, there was no law against a man's belief; therefore, a man was punished only for the crimes which he had done; therefore all men were on equal grounds. (*Korihor, Anti-Christ comes to Zarahemla, 74 B.C.*) Alma 30:6-11

**Joseph Smith**

We claim the privilege of worshiping Almighty God according to the dictates of our own conscience, and allow all men the same privilege, let them worship how, where, or what they may. (*The eleventh of the thirteen Articles of Faith; letter to John Wentworth, March 1, 1842*) AofF:11

**President Heber J. Grant,
J. Reuben Clark, Jr., David O. McKay,**
(First Presidency)

We condemn the outcome which wicked and designing men are now planning, namely: the worldwide establishment and perpetuation of some form of Communism on the one side, or of some form of Nazism or Fascism on the other. Each of these systems destroys liberty, wipes out free institutions, blots out free agency, stifles free press and free speech, crushes out freedom of religion and conscience. Free peoples cannot and do not survive under these systems. Free peoples the world over will view with horror the establishment of either Communism or Nazism as a worldwide system. Each system is fostered by those who deny the right and the ability of the common people who govern themselves. We proclaim that the common people have both this right and this ability. ¶ We review our declaration that international disputes can and should be settled by peaceful means. This is the way of the Lord. CR1942Oct:15

**Related Witnesses:**

**Joshua**

Now therefore fear the LORD, and serve him in sincerity and in truth: and put away the gods which your fathers served on the other side of the flood, and in Egypt; and serve ye the LORD. 15. And if it seem evil unto you to serve the LORD, choose you this day whom ye will serve; whether the gods which your fathers served that were on the other side of the flood, or the gods of the Amorites, in whose land ye dwell: but as for me and my house, we will serve the LORD. (*Joshua counsels the people of Israel*) Josh.24:14-15

---

## 305. Civil governments should function by the voice of the people.

**Joseph Smith**

In the United States the people are the government, and their united voice is the only sovereign that should rule, the only power that should be obeyed, and the only gentlemen that should be honored at home and abroad, on the land and on the sea. Wherefore, were I the president of the United States, by the voice of a virtuous people, I would honor the old paths of the venerated fathers of freedom; I would walk in the tracks of the illustrious patriots who carried the ark of the Government upon their shoulders with an eye single to the glory of the people, and when that people petitioned to abolish slavery in the slave states, I would use all honorable means to have their prayers granted, and, give liberty to the captive by paying the Southern gentlemen a reasonable equivalent for his property, that the whole nation might be free indeed! (*From Joseph's "Views of the Powers and Policy of the Government of the United States," Feb. 7, 1844*) HC6:208

**Mosiah, son of Benjamin,
quoted by Mormon**

Now it is not common that the voice of the people desireth anything contrary to that which is right; but it is common for the lesser part of the people to desire that which is not right; therefore this shall ye observe and make it your law—to do your business by the voice of the people. 27. And if the time comes that the voice of the people doth choose iniquity, then is the time that the judgments of God will come upon you; yea, then is the time he will visit you with great destruction even as he has hitherto visited this land. (*Mosiah tells the people unrighteous kings lead the people to sin, about 92 B.C.*) Mosiah 29:26-27

**Mosiah, son of Benjamin,
quoted by Mormon**

And I command you to do these things in the fear of the Lord; and I command you to do these things, and that ye have no king; that if these people commit sins and iniquities they shall be answered upon their own heads. 31. For behold I say unto you, the sins of many people have been caused by the iniquities of their kings; therefore their iniquities are answered upon the heads of their kings. 32. And now I desire that this inequality should be no more in this land, especially among this my people; but I desire that this land be a land of liberty, and every man may enjoy his rights and privileges alike, so long as the Lord sees fit that we may live and inherit the land, yea, even as long as any of our posterity remains upon the face of the land. (*Mosiah tells the people unrighteous kings lead the people to sin, about 92 B.C.*) Mosiah 29:30-32

**President Brigham Young,**
*quoted by John A. Widtsoe*

A republican government consists in letting the people rule by their united voice, without a dissension, —in learning what is for the best, and unitedly doing it. That is true republicanism. (*In Bowery, Sept. 13, 1857, JD5:228*) DBY:365

**President Brigham Young,**
*quoted by John A. Widtsoe*

[I]nstead of seeking to destroy the very best Government in the world, as seems to be the fears of some, we, like all other good citizens, should seek to place those men in power, who will feel the obligations and responsibilities they are under to a mighty people; who would feel and realize the important trusts reposed in them by the voice of the people who call them to administer law under the solemn sanction of an oath of fidelity to that heaven inspired instrument, to the inviolate preservation of which we look for the perpetuity of our free institutions. (*In Tabernacle, Feb. 18, 1855, JD2:175*) DBY:362

**Related Witnesses:**

**Parley P. Pratt**

God is the origin of power, the Sovereign. He made the people and the earth, and He has the right to reign. There will be good times and good government, when the world will acknowledge the God of heaven as the Lawgiver, and not till then; and if I could live under His government, I should be thankful, although I am a real Republican in principle, and would rather live under the voice of the people than the voice of one man. But it will be for the good and happiness of man when that government is established, which we pray for when we say, "Thy kingdom come, Thy will be done on earth as it is in heaven;" and until that time arrives we must pray for it. (*Conference of the Twelve, Boylston Hall, Boston, Mass., Sept. 9, 1843*) HC6:15

**Elder Ezra Taft Benson**

Keep in mind that the people who have created

their government can give to that government only such powers as they themselves have. They cannot give that which they do not possess. . . . ¶ The proper function of government is limited only to those spheres of activity within which the individual citizen has the right to act. By deriving its just powers from the governed, government becomes primarily a mechanism for defense against bodily harm, theft, involuntary servitude. It cannot claim the power to redistribute the wealth or force reluctant citizens to perform acts of charity against their will. Government is created by man. No man can delegate a power that he does not possess. The creature cannot exceed the creator. . . .CR1968Oct:18-19

**Mosiah, son of Benjamin,**
*quoted by Mormon*

Therefore, if it were possible that you could have just men to be your kings, who would establish the laws of God, and judge this people according to his commandments, yea, if ye could have men for your kings who would do even as my father Benjamin did for this people—I say unto you, if this could always be the case then it would be expedient that ye should always have kings to rule over you. . . .16. Now I say unto you, that because all men are not just it is not expedient that ye should have a king or kings to rule over you. 17. For behold, how much iniquity doth one wicked king cause to be committed, yea, and what great destruction! (*Mosiah tells the people unrighteous kings lead the people to sin, about 92 B.C.*) Mosiah 29:13,16-17

**Author's Note:** Civil governments should function by the voice of the people (D-305)—until Christ shall reign, until the millennial government when a theocracy will replace civil governments as we know them.

---

**306. Church and state should remain separate from each other, neither one interfering with the rights and functions of the other.**

**President Joseph F. Smith**

The Church of Jesus Christ of Latter-day Saints holds to the doctrine of the separation of church and state; the non-interference of church authority in political matters; and the absolute freedom and independence of the individual in the performance of his political duties. If, at any time, there has been conduct at variance with this doctrine, it has been in violation of the well settled principles and policy of the Church.

¶ We declare that from principle and policy, we favor: ¶ The absolute separation of church and state; ¶ No domination of the state by the church; ¶ No church interference with the functions of the state; ¶ No state interference with the functions of the church, or with the free exercise of religion. ¶ The absolute freedom of the individual from the domination of ecclesiastical authority in political affairs; ¶ The equality of all churches before the law. . . . ¶ . . . [I]t is sometimes pointed out that the members of the Church are looking for the actual coming of a Kingdom of God on earth, that shall gather all kingdoms of the world into one visible, divine empire, over which the risen Messiah shall reign. . . . ¶ [Neither] our belief in divine revelation, or our anticipation of the coming kingdom of God, weakens in any degree the genuineness of our allegiance to our country. When the divine empire will be established, we may not know any more than other Christians who pray, "Thy kingdom come, Thy will be done, in earth as it is in heaven;" but we do know that our allegiance and loyalty to country are strengthened by the fact that while awaiting the advent of the Messiah's kingdom, we are under a commandment from God to be subject to the powers that be, until He comes "whose right it is to reign." (*Joseph F. Smith, An Address from the First Presidency of the Church to the world, delivered to and accepted by vote of the Church in general conference, April 1907*) CR1907Apr(Appendix)14

### Elder Ezra Taft Benson

Let us first consider the origin of those freedoms we have come to know as human rights. Rights are either God-given as part of the divine plan or they are granted by government as part of the political plan. Reason, necessity, tradition, and religious convictions all lead me to accept the divine origin of these rights. If we accept the premise that human rights are granted by government, then we must be willing to accept the corollary that they can be denied by government. ¶ I support the doctrine of separation of church and state as traditionally interpreted to prohibit the establishment of an official national religion. But this does not mean that we should divorce government from any formal recognition of God. To do so strikes a potentially fatal blow at the concept of the divine origin of our rights and unlocks the door for an easy entry of future tyranny. If Americans should ever come to believe that their rights and freedoms are instituted among men by politicians and bureaucrats, then they will no longer carry the proud inheritance of their forefathers, but will grovel before their masters seeking favors and dispensations, a throwback to the feudal system of the Dark Ages. ¶ Since God created man with certain inalienable rights, and man, in turn, created government to help secure and safeguard those rights, it follows that man is superior to the creature which he created. Man is superior to government and should remain master over it, not the other way around. Even the nonbeliever can appreciate the logic of this relationship. ¶ A government is nothing more or less than a relatively small group of citizens who have been hired, in a sense, by the rest of us to perform certain functions and discharge certain responsibilities which have been authorized. The government itself has no innate power or privilege to do anything. Its only source of authority and power is from the people who created it. CR1968Oct:18

### President Heber J. Grant

The Church stands for the separation of church and state. The Church has no civil political functions. As the Church may not assume the functions of the state, so the state may not assume the functions of the church. The Church is responsible for and must carry on the work of the Lord, directing the conduct of its members, one towards the other, as followers of the lowly Christ, not forgetting the humble, the poor and needy, and those in distress, leading them all to righteous living and a spiritual life that shall bring them to salvation, exaltation, and eternal progression in wisdom, knowledge, understanding and power. . . . ¶ The state is responsible for the civil control of its citizens or subjects, for their political welfare, and for the carrying forward of political policies, domestic, and foreign, of body politic. For these policies, their success or failure, the state is alone responsible and it must carry its burdens. All these matters involve and directly affect Church members because they are part of the body politic, and members must give allegiance to their sovereign and render it loyal service when called thereto. But the Church, itself, as such, has no responsibility for these policies, as to which it has no means of doing more than urging its members fully to render that loyalty to their country and to free institutions which the loftiest patriotism calls for. ¶ Nevertheless, as a correlative of the principle of separation of the church and the State, themselves, there is an obligation running from every citizen or subject to the state. This obligation is voiced in that Article of Faith which declares: ¶ "We believe in being subject to kings, presidents, rulers, and magistrates, in obeying, honoring, and sustaining the law." CR1942Apr:92-93

**Author's Note:** Church and state should remain separate from each other, neither one interfering with the rights and functioning of the other—until Christ shall reign, until the millennial government when a theocracy will replace civil governments as we know them.

---

307. **Promoting righteous civil government and sharing the burden of government is the responsibility of every citizen.**

**Mormon**

And he told them that these things ought not to be; but that the burden should come upon all the people, that every man might bear his part. (*King Benjamin tells the people that even a righteous king ought not bear all the burdens of government*) Mosiah 29:34

**Elder John Taylor**

As we have progressed the mist has been removed, and in relation to these matters, the Elders of Israel begin to understand that they have something to do with the world politically as well as religiously, that it is as much their duty to study correct political principles as well as religious, and to seek to know and comprehend the social and political interests of man, and to learn and be able to teach that which would be best calculated to promote the interests of the world. (*In Tabernacle, April 13, 1862, JD9:340*) TLDP:261

**Joseph Smith**

We believe that governments were instituted of God for the benefit of man; and that he holds men accountable for their acts in relation to them, both in making laws and administering them, for the good and safety of society. . . . 3. We believe that all governments necessarily require civil officers and magistrates to enforce the laws of the same; and that such as will administer the law in equity and justice should be sought for and upheld by the voice of the people if a republic. . . . 5. We believe that all men are bound to sustain and uphold the respective governments in which they reside, while protected in their inherent and inalienable rights by the laws of such governments; . . . 8. . . . [F]or the public peace and tranquility all men should step forward and use their ability in bringing offenders against good laws to punishment. (*Declaration of belief regarding governments and laws, Aug. 17, 1835*) D&C 134:1,3,5,8

**Joseph Smith,**
*receiving the Word of the Lord*

I, the Lord God, make you free, therefore ye are free indeed; and the law also maketh you free. 9. Nevertheless, when the wicked rule the people mourn. 10. Wherefore, honest men and wise men should be sought for diligently, and good men and wise men ye should observe to uphold; otherwise whatsoever is less than these cometh of evil. (*Revelation received Aug. 6, 1833 in consequence of the persecution of the saints, the Lord justifies the Saints in befriending the constitutional law of the land*) D&C 98:8-10

**Richard L. Evans,**
*also quoting Joseph Smith*

Of course the world has troubles, uncertainties, problems. Of course we are impatient and puzzled at times, but the means and the reason for improving and repenting and for solving the problems are given us in our Father's plan and purposes. ¶ May I cite two oft-quoted scriptures, and put some added emphasis on them: ¶ "Verily I say, men should be anxiously engaged in a *good* cause, and do many things of their own free will, and bring to pass much *righteousness* (D&C 58:27, italics added)." ¶ The emphasis could well be on *good* and *righteousness.* ¶ Another: "Wherefore, honest men and wise men should be sought for diligently, and good men and wise men ye should observe to uphold. . . ." (D&C 98:10) ¶ I infer from this that we have an *obligation* to be active in public issues, in civic problems, and to provide honest and good men and wise men to serve and give leadership on public affairs. ¶ We shouldn't be sideline sitters. CR1968Oct:44

**President Spencer W. Kimball**

The only way we can keep our freedom is to work at it. Not some of us. All of us. Not some of the time, but all of the time. ¶ So if you value your citizenship and want to keep it for yourself and your children and their children, give it your faith, your belief, and give it your active support in civic affairs. (The Teachings of Spencer W. Kimball, p. 405) TLDP:261

**Henry D. Moyle**

If we are to be a God-fearing nation and enjoy the blessings of peace, then each one of us who has faith in God must do our duty, take our part to accomplish our purpose in government. We should become intimately familiar with those who are active politically; we ought to be part and parcel of them. They should not be strangers to us. We should see to it that those men who have true qualities of leadership are placed in positions of trust and responsibility in the government; these fundamental principles of truth apply to every political party alike. There is no hope and can be no hope for our government, or any government, to which this principle does not apply. . . . ¶ I hope and pray, my brethren and sisters, that we will not feel that politics has become so degraded that we are too good to participate. If any of us believe politics to be in that kind of state, we need only to enter into politics, go into it with our honesty and our integrity and our devotion to truth and to righteousness, and the standards will be raised. We cannot expect in this country a better government than the leaders are good, and so if we want a good government we must have good leaders. Let us participate in our mass meetings, in our party organization meetings, in our conventions; then when we go to the polls, we may have somebody worthy of our vote on our tickets. CR1952Apr:36-37

**Anthony W. Ivins**

My idea of loyal citizenship is just to abide loyally by the laws of our state and country, to sustain loyally the men who enact those laws, and the men who execute them. You ask me the question, Does our citizenship require us to sustain and uphold men who are not righteous in the administration of the law; does it require us to acknowledge and sustain and uphold laws which are not just? No, it does not; but it requires that those laws be changed or abrogated or amended if experience proves that they are not good, wholesome laws; and the same with men who administer them. There may be times when men go wrong; there may be times when they sell the authority which they have for money; there may be times when they are not honest; there may be times when it becomes necessary to remove them; but that, too, must be done lawfully; it must be done patiently; it must be done in the order that is provided by the law of the country, and not arbitrarily. (IE1921Jul:840) TLDP:261

**Related Witnesses:**

**Elder Ezra Taft Benson**

Could many of our ills today have resulted from our failure to train a strong citizenry from the only source we have—the boys and girls of each community? Have they grown up to believe in politics without principle, pleasure without conscience, knowledge without effort, wealth without work, business without morality, science without humanity, worship without sacrifice? ¶ I do not believe the greatest threat to our future is from bombs or guided missiles. I do not think our civilization will die that way. I think it will die when we no longer care, when the spiritual forces that make us wish to be right and noble die in the hearts of men, when we disregard the importance of law and order. CR1968Apr:50

**308. Each individual contributes to good civil government by living a righteous life and by influencing others to do the same.**

**Anthony W. Ivins**

My idea of citizenship is, to be true to every principle of right, as our conscience prompts us to do the right. God has planted in the hearts of all men knowledge of good and evil, and I believe that no man or woman does wrong without knowing it. That is what makes us responsible before God and before the law for our acts. We know it. . . .Whenever we violate that, either as it applies to our loyalty to the Church or to the Government, we cease to be good citizens as we might and ought to be, and we cease to be devoted members of the Church to which we profess allegiance, as we might be. (IE1921-Jul:840) TLDP:261

**N. Eldon Tanner**

When I was in East Germany meeting with the district presidents in that area, I was most encouraged to see how these men were prepared to honor and sustain the law of the country. . . . They all adopted the attitude that it was their responsibility to teach the Gospel wherever possible, to live its teachings strictly, and to encourage the members of the Church to live, as far as possible, all the commandments of God and the teachings of the Church under the existing laws of the country. They realized that living and teaching the Gospel and getting the people to accept it would do more for the cause of peace than anything else they could do. They expressed their belief and bore their testimonies that, if they kept the commandments of God and magnified their callings in the Church, all would be well and they would have nothing to fear. ("Submission to Secular Authority," Instructor, Oct. 1963, p. 353) MPSG1989:240

**L. Tom Perry**

We have been blessed with the light of the gospel to lead us and to guide and direct our lives. Through our understanding and study of the scriptures, we have a knowledge of the laws of the Lord by which we should govern our earthly conduct. With this great blessing comes an obligation to be a part of the communities in which we live. Our influence should be felt to safeguard the moral standards in the villages, in the towns, and in the cities where our homes are located in all parts of the world. I challenge you to become involved in lifting the moral standards of the communities where your homes are. CR1977Apr:89

### Neal A. Maxwell

Individual decency and constitutional viability are thus irrevocably intertwined. For instance, the loss of inner controls in individual citizens inevitably merely brings more outer controls with the resultant diminution of individual liberty. (*Grant Stake Bicentennial of the Constitution, May 1987*) MPSG1989:237

### President Ezra Taft Benson

We have no right to expect a higher degree of morality from those who represent us than what we ourselves are. In the final analysis, people generally get the kind of government they deserve. ("The Constitution: A Heavenly Banner," p. 28) MPSG1989:237

### Peter

Submit yourselves to every ordinance of man for the Lord's sake: whether it be to the king, as supreme; 14. Or unto governors, as unto them that are sent by him for the punishment of evildoers, and for the praise of them that do well. 15. For so is the will of God, that with well doing ye may put to silence the ignorance of foolish men: 16. As free, and not using your liberty for a cloke of maliciousness, but as the servants of God. (*Letter to the churches in modern Asia Minor, about A.D. 60*) 1Pet.2:13-16

### Related Witnesses:

### Mosiah, son of Benjamin, quoted by Mormon

Now it is not common that the voice of the people desireth anything contrary to that which is right. . . . 27. And if the time comes that the voice of the people doth choose iniquity, then is the time that the judgments of God will come upon you. . . .(*Mosiah tells the people unrighteous kings lead the people to sin, about 92 B.C.*) Mosiah 29:26-27

### Moroni, son of Mormon

Behold, this is a choice land, and whatsoever nation shall possess it shall be free from bondage, and from captivity, and from all other nations under heaven, if they will but serve the God of the land, who is Jesus Christ. . . . (*Moroni's comments, as he pauses in making the abridged record of the Jaredites covering the period of time of the Tower of Babel*) Ether 2:12

---

### 309. We are to sustain and uphold the government under which we reside.

### Howard W. Hunter

In some countries [the] supreme power is vested in one person, the sovereign. Other countries have republican forms of government in which sovereignty resides in the people, and the supreme power is usually expressed by the legislative body. Regardless of whether sovereignty is administered by an individual or by the people, citizens become subject to that supreme power. They have rights and privileges afforded them under the law, and they have the duty to comply with the provisions of the law. . . . ¶ Citizens do not have the right to take the law into their own hands or exercise physical force. The sovereign laws of the state must be sustained, and persons living under those laws must obey them for the good of the whole. In this regard The Church of Jesus Christ of Latter-day Saints takes a strong position. CR1968Apr:63; MPSG1989:239-40

### Joseph Smith

We believe that all men are bound to sustain and uphold the respective governments in which they reside, while protected in their inherent and inalienable rights by the laws of such governments; and that sedition and rebellion are unbecoming every citizen thus protected, and should be punished accordingly; and that all governments have a right to enact such laws as in their own judgments are best calculated to secure the public interest; at the same time, however, holding sacred the freedom of conscience. (*Declaration of belief regarding governments and laws, Aug. 17, 1835*) D&C 134:5

### Joseph Smith

Let no man break the laws of the land, for he that keepeth the laws of God hath no need to break the laws of the land. 22. Wherefore, be subject to the powers that be, until he reigns whose right it is to reign, and subdues all enemies under his feet. (*Revelation for the elders of the Church, Aug. 1, 1831*) D&C 58:21-22

### Joseph Smith

And thus all things shall be made sure, according to the laws of the land. (*Revelation May 1831*) D&C 51:6

### Joseph Smith, receiving the Word of the Lord

And now, verily I say unto you concerning the laws of the land, it is my will that my people should observe to do all things whatsoever I command them. 5. And that law of the land which is constitutional, supporting that principle of freedom in maintaining rights and privileges, belongs to all mankind, and is justifiable before me. 6. Therefore, I, the Lord, justify you, and your brethren of my church, in befriending that law which is the constitutional law of the land; 7. And as pertaining to law of man, whatsoever is more or less than this, cometh of evil. 8. I, the Lord God, make you free, therefore ye are free indeed; and the law also maketh you free. 9. Nevertheless, when the wicked rule the people mourn. 10. Wherefore, honest men and wise men should be sought for diligently, and good men and wise men ye should observe to uphold; otherwise whatsoever is less than these cometh of evil. (*Revelation received Aug. 6, 1833 in consequence of the persecution of the Saints in the United States*) D&C 98:4-10

### Joseph Smith

We believe in being subject to kings, presidents, rulers, and magistrates, in obeying, honoring, and sustaining the law. (*The twelfth of the thirteen Articles of Faith; letter to John Wentworth, March 1, 1842*) AofF:12

### President Joseph F. Smith

Neither in mental attitude nor in conduct have we [the Church] been disloyal to the government under whose guarantee of religious freedom our church was founded. . . . [W]e have no place in our hearts for disloyal sentiments, nor is there likelihood of treason in our conduct. . . . ¶ . . . [W]e declare to all men that there is nothing treasonable or disloyal in any ordinance, ceremony, or ritual of the Church. ¶ The overthrow of earthly governments; the union of church and state; domination of the state by the church; ecclesiastical interference with the political freedom and rights of the citizen,—all such things are contrary to the principles and policy of the Church, and directly at variance with the oft repeated declarations of its chief presiding authorities and of the Church itself, speaking through its general conferences. (*Address from the First Presidency of the Church to the world, delivered to and accepted by vote of the Church in general conference, April 1907*) CR1907Apr(Appendix)10,13

### Jesus,
### *recorded in Matthew*

Tell us therefore, What thinkest thou? Is it lawful to give tribute unto Caesar, or not? 18. But Jesus perceived their wickedness, and said, Why tempt ye me, ye hypocrites? 19. Shew me the tribute money. And they brought unto him a penny. 20. And he saith unto them, Whose is this image and superscription? 21. They say unto him, Caesar's. Then saith he unto them, Render therefore unto Caesar the things which are Caesar's; and unto God the things that are God's. Matt.22:17-21

### Paul

Render therefore to all their dues: tribute to whom tribute is due; custom to whom custom; fear to whom fear; honour to whom honour. (*Letter to the Church in Rome, about A.D. 55*) Rom.13:7

### Peter

Submit yourselves to every ordinance of man for the Lord's sake: whether it be to the king, as supreme; 14. Or unto governors, as unto them that are sent by him for the punishment of evildoers, and for the praise of them that do well. 15. For so is the will of God, that with well doing ye may put to silence the ignorance of foolish men: 16. As free, and not using your liberty for a cloke of maliciousness, but as the servants of God. (*Letter to the churches in modern Asia Minor, about A.D. 60*) 1Pet.2:13-16

### Related Witnesses:
### Joseph Smith

And it shall come to pass, that if any persons among you shall kill they shall be delivered up and dealt with according to the laws of the land; for remember that he hath no forgiveness; and it shall be proved according to the laws of the land. . . . 84. And if a man or woman shall rob, he or she shall be delivered up unto the law of the land. 85. And if he or she shall steal, he or she shall be delivered up unto the law of the land. 86. And if he or she shall lie, he or she shall be delivered up unto the law of the land. (*Revelation "embracing the law of the Church," Feb. 9, 1831*) D&C 42:79,84-86

**Author's Note:** With regard to the citation, "*A declaration of belief regarding governments and laws in general, adopted by unanimous vote at a general assembly of the Church held at Kirtland, Ohio, Aug. 17, 1835*": The occasion was a meeting of Church leaders, brought together to consider the proposed contents of the first edition of the Doctrine and Covenants. At that time this declaration was given the following preamble: "That our belief with regard to earthly governments and laws in general may not be misinterpreted nor misunderstood, we have thought proper to present at the close of this volume our opinion concerning the same." (Headnote to D&C Section 134) (HC2:247-249)

# List of Doctrines

## GRACE

# GRACE

**310. By faith we are saved by the grace of God, not by works alone without true faith.**

### Elder Joseph Fielding Smith

Paul taught these people—who thought that they could be saved by some power that was within them, or by observing the law of Moses—he pointed out to them the fact that if it were not for the mission of Jesus Christ, if it were not for this great atoning sacrifice, they could not be redeemed. And therefore it was by the grace of God that they are saved, not by any work on their part, for they were absolutely helpless. Paul was absolutely right. ¶ And on the other hand, James taught just as the Lord taught, just as Paul had taught in other scripture, that it is our duty, of necessity, to labor, to strive in diligence and faith, keeping the commandments of the Lord, if we would obtain that inheritance which is promised to the faithful, and which shall be given unto them through their faithfulness to the end. There is no conflict in the doctrines of these two men. There is no need for the world to be in conflict in regard to this question. It is merely due to the fact that they cannot or do not comprehend the mission of Jesus Christ. They do not understand what salvation means. They do not know upon what it is based. (Doctrines of Salvation, 2:310-11) TLDP:181

### Joseph Smith

Who cannot see, then, that salvation is the effect of faith? for, as we have previously observed, all the heavenly beings work by this principle; and it is because they are able so to do that they are saved, for nothing but this could save them. And this is the lesson which the God of heaven, by the mouth of his holy prophets, has been endeavoring to teach to the world. Hence we are told, that "Without faith it is impossible to please God"; and that salvation "is of faith, that it might be by grace, to the end the promise might be sure to all the seed." (Rom.4:16) And that Israel, who followed after the law of righteousness, has not attained to the law of righteousness. Wherefore? Because they sought it not by faith, but as it were by the works of the law; for they stumbled at that stumblingstone. (Rom.9:32) And Jesus said unto the man who brought his son to him, to get the devil who tormented him cast out: "If thou canst believe, all things are possible to him that believeth." (Mark 9:23) These with a multitude of other scriptures which might be quoted plainly set forth the light in which the Savior, as

well as the Former-day Saints, viewed the plan of salvation. That it was a system of faith—it begins with faith, and continues by faith; and every blessing which is obtained in relation to it is the effect of faith, whether it pertains to this life or that which is to come. To this all the revelations of God bear witness. . . . And through the whole history of the scheme of life and salvation, it is a matter of faith: every man received according to his faith— according as his faith was, so were his blessings and privileges; and nothing was withheld from him when his faith was sufficient to receive it. He could stop the mouths of lions, quench the violence of fire, escape the edge of the sword, wax valiant in fight, and put to flight the armies of the aliens; women could, by their faith, receive their dead children to life again; in a word, there was nothing impossible with them who had faith. All things were in subjection to the Former-day Saints, according as their faith was. ¶ 20. From this we may extend as far as any circumstances may require, whether on earth or in heaven, and we will find it the testimony of all inspired men, or heavenly messengers, that all things that pertain to life and godliness are the effects of faith and nothing else; all learning, wisdom and prudence fail, and every thing else as a means of salvation but faith. . . . For where faith is, there will the knowledge of God be also, with all things which pertain thereto— revelations, visions, and dreams, as well as every necessary thing, in order that the possessors of faith may be perfected, and obtain salvation. . . . And he who possesses it will, through it, obtain all necessary knowledge and wisdom, until he shall know God, and the Lord Jesus Christ, whom he has sent—whom to know is eternal life. Amen. (*Lectures on Faith delivered to the School of the Prophets, 1834-35*) LOF7:17,20

### Paul

But Israel, which followed after the law of righteousness, hath not attained to the law of righteousness. 32. Wherefore? Because they sought it not by faith, but as it were by the works of the law. For they stumbled at that stumblingstone; (*Letter to the Church in Rome, about A.D. 55*) Rom.9:31-32

### Paul

Knowing that a man is not justified by the works of the law, but by the faith of Jesus Christ, even we have believed in Jesus Christ, that we might be justified by the faith of Christ, and not by the works of the law: for by the works of the law shall no flesh be justified.

(*Letter to the churches of Galatia in Asia Minor, about* A.D. *55*) Gal.2:16

**Related Witnesses:**

**John A. Widtsoe**

The problem of faith as of every gift of the Lord, is twofold: to secure it, and to use it. We speak easily of faith, but altogether too often fail to use it. We recall that it is knowledge, high knowledge, but forget that it is also power, mighty power, and therefore fail to use the greatest force placed within our reach in every issue of life. It has been said: "Without faith it is impossible to please God;" and it may have been added that without the use of faith it is impossible to win the full happiness in life that the Lord has destined for his children. ¶ Latter-day Saints, trained in these truths, possessing a religion resting upon faith, should eagerly use their knowledge for their own and others' good. They should remember that faith may deliver us from evil and secure for us the good that we need. (Man and the Dragon, p. 142) TLDP:181

**Joseph Smith**

Yea, signs come by faith, unto mighty works, for without faith no man pleaseth God; and with whom God is angry he is not well pleased; wherefore, unto such he showeth no signs, only in wrath unto their condemnation. (*Revelation Aug. 1831*) D&C 63:11

**James**

Even so faith, if it hath not works, is dead, being alone. 18. Yea, a man may say, Thou hast faith, and I have works: shew me thy faith without thy works, and I will shew thee my faith by my works. 19. Thou believest that there is one God; thou doest well: the devils also believe, and tremble. 20. But wilt thou know, O vain man, that faith without works is dead? 21. Was not Abraham our father justified by works, when he had offered Isaac his son upon the altar? 22. Seest thou how faith wrought with his works, and by works was faith made perfect? 23. And the scripture was fulfilled which saith, Abraham believed God, and it was imputed unto him for righteousness: and he was called the Friend of God. 24. Ye see then how that by works a man is justified, and not by faith only. 25. Likewise also was not Rahab the harlot justified by works, when she had received the messengers, and had sent them out another way? 26. For as the body without the spirit is dead, so faith without works is dead also. (*Letter to his brethren in the church*) James 2:17-26

**Paul**

But God, who is rich in mercy, for his great love wherewith he loved us, 5. Even when we were dead in sins, hath quickened us together with Christ, (by grace ye are saved;) (*Letter to the Saints at Ephesus in Asia Minor, about* A.D. *62*) Eph.2:4-5

**Jacob, brother of Nephi,**
*quoted by Nephi*

Therefore, cheer up your hearts, and remember that ye are free to act for yourselves—to choose the way of everlasting death or the way of eternal life. 24. Wherefore, my beloved brethren, reconcile yourselves to the will of God, and not to the will of the devil and the flesh; and remember, after ye are reconciled unto God, that it is only in and through the grace of God that ye are saved. 25. Wherefore, may God raise you from death by the power of the resurrection, and also from everlasting death by the power of the atonement, that ye may be received into the eternal kingdom of God, that ye may praise him through grace divine. Amen. (*To the people of Nephi, 559-545 B.C.*) 2Ne.10:23-25

---

**311. Eternal life is a gift of God, and even though the obtaining of eternal life requires good works, it cannot be wholly earned by us.**

**Nephi, son of Lehi**

For we labor diligently to write, to persuade our children, and also our brethren, to believe in Christ, and to be reconciled to God; for we know that it is by grace that we are saved, after all we can do. (*The writings of Nephi, 559-545 B.C.*) 2Ne.25:23

**Bruce R. McConkie**

Jesus . . . makes a pronouncement of wondrous import: ¶ If thou wilt enter into life, keep the commandments. ¶ This is the sum and substance of the whole matter. Salvation, eternal life, rewards in all their degrees and varieties—all come by obedience to the laws and ordinances of the gospel. Salvation must be won; it is not a free gift. "Let us hear the conclusion of the whole matter: Fear God, and keep his commandments: for this is the whole duty of man." (Eccl. 12:13) But what of grace? Grace is the love, mercy, and condescension of God in making salvation available to men. "It is by grace that we are saved, after all we can do." (2Ne.25:23) Eternal life is freely available; salvation is free in that all may drink of the waters of life; all may come and partake; but none gains so high a reward as eternal life until he is tried and tested and found worthy, as were the ancients. . . . ¶ Eternal life can come to those only who put first in their lives the things of God's kingdom; who love the riches of eternity more than a handful of mortal pelf; who are willing to forsake all and follow Christ. Where a man's treasure is, there will his heart be also. (The Mortal Messiah, 3:302-04) TLDP:161

### Elder Joseph Fielding Smith

[W]e are all transgressors of the law to some extent, no matter how good we have tried to be—we are therefore unable in and of ourselves to receive redemption from our sins by any act of our own. ¶ . . .[I]t is by the grace of Jesus Christ that we are saved. (Doctrines of Salvation, 2:309) DCSM:34

### Joseph Smith,
### receiving the Word of the Lord

And, if you keep my commandments and endure to the end you shall have eternal life, which gift is the greatest of all the gifts of God. (Revelation for David Whitmer, June 1829) D&C 14:7

### Elder Heber J. Grant

God tells us in the Doctrine and Covenants there is no gift greater than the gift of salvation. We as Latter-day Saints have all started out for the gift of salvation, and we should so order our lives that when we have finished our work we shall be worthy to go back into the presence of our Father, and be worthy not only to receive an exaltation ourselves, but also to receive our wives and our children that have been sealed unto us that we shall possess them. No amount of testimony, no amount of knowledge, even knowledge that this is God's work will ever save a man . . . but the keeping of the commandments of God will entitle him to that blessing. CR1900Oct:59

### Orson F. Whitney

God's greatest gift is eternal life, but that pertains to Eternity. The greatest blessing that our Heavenly Father can bestow upon us in time, or while we are here, is the power to lay hold upon eternal life. The everlasting Gospel, through obedience to its every requirement, and the gift of the Holy Ghost, gives this power. It not only saves—it exalts men to where God and Christ dwell in the fulness of celestial glory. CR1929Oct:30

### Joseph Smith

If thou wilt do good, yea, and hold out faithful to the end, thou shalt be saved in the kingdom of God, which is the greatest of all the gifts of God; for there is no gift greater than the gift of salvation. (Revelation for Oliver Cowdery, April 1829) D&C 6:13

### Joseph Smith,
### receiving the Word of the Lord

And if you do these last commandments of mine, which I have given you, the gates of hell shall not prevail against you; for my grace is sufficient for you, and you shall be lifted up at the last day. (Revelation for Oliver Cowdery, David Whitmer and Martin Harris, the three special witnesses, June 1829) D&C 17:8

### Related Witnesses:
### Paul

For the wages of sin is death; but the gift of God is eternal life through Jesus Christ our Lord. (Letter to the Churchin Rome, about A.D. 55) Rom.6:23

### Jacob, brother of Nephi,
### quoted by Nephi

Wherefore, my beloved brethren, reconcile yourselves to the will of God, and not to the will of the devil and the flesh; and remember, after ye are reconciled unto God, that it is only in and through the grace of God that ye are saved. 25. Wherefore, may God raise you from death by the power of the resurrection, and also from everlasting death by the power of the atonement, that ye may be received into the eternal kingdom of God, that ye may praise him through grace divine. Amen. (To the people of Nephi, 559-545 B.C.) 2Ne.10:24-25

### Paul

For by grace are ye saved through faith; and that not of yourselves: it is the gift of God: 9. Not of works, lest any man should boast. (Letter to the Saints at Ephesus in Asia Minor, about A.D. 62) Eph.2:8-9

### Paul

Who hath saved us, and called us with an holy calling, not according to our works, but according to his own purpose and grace, which was given us in Christ Jesus before the world began, (Letter to his assistant Timothy, about A.D. 64) 2Tim.1:9

# List of Doctrines

## GRATITUDE

*Doctrines Located in This Topic*

312. God requires us to render thanks to Him.

*Doctrines on GRATITUDE Located in Other Topics*

522. Prayers are to contain expressions of gratitude.

# GRATITUDE

**312. God requires us to render thanks to Him.**

### Joseph Smith
And ye must give thanks unto God in the Spirit for whatsoever blessing ye are blessed with. *(Revelation relative to the gifts of the Spirit, March 8, 1831)* D&C 46:32

### Marion G. Romney
The Lord puts the commandment to be thankful along with other strong commandments. He said, "Thou shalt love the Lord thy God with all thy heart, with all thy might, mind, and strength; and in the name of Jesus Christ thou shalt serve him. Thou shalt love thy neighbor as thyself. Thou shalt not steal; neither commit adultery, nor kill, nor do anything like unto it. Thou shalt thank the Lord thy God in all things" (D&C 59:5-7). It is perfectly evident from this scripture that to thank the Lord in all things is not merely a courtesy. It is a commandment as binding upon us as any other commandment. ACR(San Jose)1977:12

### James E. Talmage
Gratitude is an ennobling quality in man; and he in whose soul it has no place is [defective]. . . . ¶ Gratitude is twin sister to humility; pride is a foe to both. The man who has come into close communion with God cannot fail to be thankful; for he feels, he knows, that for all he has and all he is, he is indebted to the Supreme Giver; and one would think that there is no need of commandment in the matter of thanksgiving. Yet we find that because of man's propensities toward forgetfulness and selfishness the Scriptures abound in admonitions to render thanks unto the Lord. . . . ¶ God requires thanksgiving, praise and worship, not for His gratification as the recipient of adulation, but for the good of His children who thus recognize and acknowledge Him, and so develop that abiding faith, such as shall lead to repentance, without which none can attain salvation in His kingdom. SNT:483,486

### Jacob, brother of Nephi,
*quoted by Nephi*
Behold, my beloved brethren, remember the words of your God; pray unto him continually by day, and give thanks unto his holy name by night. Let your hearts rejoice. *(Jacob teaches the people of Nephi, 559-545 B.C.)* 2Ne.9:52

### President David O. McKay
The young man who closes the door behind him, who draws the curtains, and there in silence pleads with God for help, should first pour out his soul in gratitude for health, for friends, for loved ones, for the gospel, for the manifestations of God's existence. He should first count his many blessings and name them one by one. CR1961Apr:8

### President Joseph F. Smith
Testimony bearing is chiefly for the benefit of those who bear the testimony, in that their gratitude and appreciation are deepened. Testimony bearing is not the accumulation of arguments or evidences solely for the satisfaction and testimony of others. Let the testimonies, then, of the young people include the training of their feelings by way of making them more appreciative and more thankful for the blessings they enjoy, and the children should be made to understand what these blessings are and how they come to them. It is an excellent way to make people helpful and thankful to others, by first making them thankful to God. (Gospel Doctrine, p. 208) TLDP:688

### Paul
In every thing give thanks: for this is the will of God in Christ Jesus concerning you. *(Letter to the Church at Thessalonica, comprising Jews and many pagan converts, A.D. 50)* 1Thess.5:18

### Hugh B. Brown
How rich and radiant is the soul of a man who has a thankful heart. His gratitude increases with his unfolding awareness of himself, the universe and his Creator. Appreciation, like love, enriches both giver and receiver, and, when spontaneously expressed in word or deed, reveals a depth and delicacy of fine-grain character. True gratitude is motivated by a recognition of favors received. Its counterfeit is fawning anticipation of favors to come. ¶ Serious consideration of the mystery of life, its vastness and incalculability, gives depth to appreciation for blessings gratuitously bestowed. They who have eyes to see, ears to hear, understanding hearts, will see the bounteous love of God everywhere manifest and will be inclined to reverently remove their shoes and exclaim: ¶ "For the rock and for the river, The valley's fertile sod, For the strength of the hills we bless thee, Our God, our fathers' God." ["For the Strength of the Hills," HYMNS:35] ("Gratitude Is a Spiritual Attribute," Instructor, Nov. 1957, p. 332) TLDP:269-70

### Recorded in 1 Chronicles
Give thanks unto the LORD, call upon his name, make known his deeds among the people. *(David delivers a Psalm of Thanksgiving)* 1Chr.16:8

### Elder Joseph Fielding Smith
One of the greatest sins, both in magnitude and

extent—for it enters into the lives of every one of us without exception to some degree—is the sin of ingratitude. When we violate a commandment, no matter how small and insignificant we may think it to be, we show our ingratitude to our Redeemer. It is impossible for us to comprehend the extent of his suffering when he carried the burden of the sins of the whole world, a punishment so severe that we are informed that blood came from the pores of his body, and this was before he was taken to the cross. The punishment of physical pain coming from the nails driven in his hands and feet, was not the greatest of his suffering, excruciating as that surely was. The greater suffering was the spiritual and mental anguish coming from the load of our transgressions which he carried. If we understood the extent of that suffering and his suffering on the cross, surely none of us would wilfully be guilty of sin. We would not give way to the temptations, the gratification of unholy appetites and desires and Satan could find no place in our hearts. As it is, whenever we sin, we show our ingratitude and disregard of the suffering of the Son of God by and through which we shall rise from the dead and live forever. If we really understood and could feel even to a small degree, the love and gracious willingness on the part of Jesus Christ to suffer for our sins we would be willing to repent of all our transgressions and serve him. (The Restoration of All Things, p. 199) TLDP:270

### Mormon

And he commanded them that they should observe the sabbath day, and keep it holy, and also every day they should give thanks to the Lord their God. (*Alma organizes the Church of Christ and ordains priests, about 148 B.C.*) Mosiah 18:23

### Elder Spencer W. Kimball

Ingratitude is a distressing sin which kindles the Lord's anger. (See D&C 59:21.) It is often manifest in "disobedience to parents," which Paul condemns. Many young people demand and receive much from parents and then show little or no gratitude, as though the parents owed it to them without any consideration or appreciation on their part. There must have been children in Paul's day who thanklessly took for granted their many blessings and opportunities, for he continued to warn the saints at Rome and others against this weakness. ¶ When the Savior healed the ten lepers and only one thanked him, he pointed out the nine ingrates as a lesson to all when he said, "Were there not ten cleansed?" (Luke 17:17)

Adults as well as the youth are often guilty, being disobedient and unthankful to their Heavenly Father who gives them all. Many fail to show their gratitude through service, through family prayers, through the payment of their tithes, and in numerous other ways God has a right to expect. (The Miracle of Forgiveness, pp. 58-59) TLDP:270

**Related Witnesses:**

### Jesus,
#### recorded in Luke

And it came to pass, as he went to Jerusalem, that he passed through the midst of Samaria and Galilee. 12. And as he entered into a certain village, there met him ten men that were lepers, which stood afar off: 13. And they lifted up their voices, and said, Jesus, Master, have mercy on us. 14. And when he saw them, he said unto them, Go shew yourselves unto the priests. And it came to pass, that, as they went, they were cleansed. 15. And one of them, when he saw that he was healed, turned back, and with a loud voice glorified God, 16. And fell down on his face at his feet, giving him thanks: and he was a Samaritan. 17. And Jesus answering said, Were there not ten cleansed? but where are the nine? 18. There are not found that returned to give glory to God, save this stranger. 19. And he said unto him, Arise, go thy way: thy faith hath made thee whole. (*Jesus heals the ten lepers, one returns to give thanks*) Luke 17:11-19

### N. Eldon Tanner

If children pray for their parents, it makes them more appreciative of their parents, and as they pray for one another, they feel closer to one another and part of each other, especially as they realize that they are talking to their Father in heaven while on their knees. (Prayer, p. 129) MPSG1983:130

**Author's Note:** Gratitude expressed with the spirit of the Lord will have its best opportunity to reach those who hear the words spoken. "[F]or when a man speaketh by the power of the Holy Ghost the power of the Holy Ghost carrieth it unto the hearts of the children of men." (*Nephi's writings, between 559-545 B.C.*) (2Ne.33:1)

# List of Doctrines

## HELL

# HELL

313. In the postmortal spirit world, the spirits of the wicked live in a state of unhappiness or misery, called hell, until the day of redemption and final judgment.

### George Q. Cannon
I have thought sometimes that some of our people are inclined to think there is no hell and that nobody is going to hell. I tell you there will be a large number of people go to hell; they will suffer torment and will go where there is weeping and wailing and gnashing of teeth; they will be in outer darkness and suffer far beyond anything we can conceive of. Latter-day Saints especially who commit sin, if they die in their sin, will go to hell, and they will suffer torment there until the day of redemption. But think of the length of time during which they will be in this torment! (Gospel Truth, 1:85) TLDP:639

### Elder Joseph Fielding Smith
All liars, and sorcerers, and adulterers and all who love and make a lie, shall not receive the resurrection at this time, but for a thousand years shall be thrust down into hell where they shall suffer the wrath of God until they pay the price of their sinning, if it is possible, by the things which they shall suffer. [See Church News, April 23, 1932, p. 6.] ¶ These are the "Spirits of men who are to be judged and are found under condemnation; And these are the rest of the dead; and they live not again until the thousand years are ended, neither again, until the end of the earth." [D&C 88: 100-01]. . . . ¶ These are the hosts of the telestial world who are commanded to "suffer the wrath of God on earth;" and who are "cast down to hell and suffer the wrath of Almighty God, until the fulness of times, when Christ shall have subdued all enemies under his feet, and shall have perfected his work" [Era, vol 45, p. 781; D&C 76:104-06]. . . . ¶ This suffering will be a means of cleansing, or purifying, and through it the wicked shall be brought to a condition whereby they may, through the redemption of Jesus Christ, obtain immortality. Their spirits and bodies shall be again united, and they shall dwell in the telestial kingdom. But this resurrection will not come until the end of the world. (Doctrines of Salvation, 2:295-98) TLDP:564-65

### Parley P. Pratt
[T]o those who deserve it [The spirit world after mortality] . . . is a place of punishment, a purgatory or hell, where spirits are buffeted till the day of redemption. (Key to the Science of Theology, pp. 132-33) TLDP:637

### Peter
For if God spared not the angels that sinned, but cast them down to hell, and delivered them into chains of darkness, to be reserved unto judgment; . . . (*Peter says the Lord knows how to reserve the unjust unto the day of judgement; letter to members of the Church, about A.D. 60-64*) 2Pet.2:4

### Alma, the younger,
*quoted by Mormon*
And then shall it come to pass, that the spirits of the wicked, yea, who are evil—for behold, they have no part nor portion of the Spirit of the Lord; for behold, they chose evil works rather than good; therefore the spirit of the devil did enter into them, and take possession of their house—and these shall be cast out into outer darkness; there shall be weeping, and wailing, and gnashing of teeth, and this because of their own iniquity, being led captive by the will of the devil. 14. Now this is the state of the souls of the wicked, yea, in darkness, and a state of awful, fearful looking for the fiery indignation of the wrath of God upon them; thus they remain in this state, as well as the righteous in paradise, until the time of their resurrection. (*Alma speaks to his son Corianton, concerning the resurrection of the dead, about 73 B.C.*) Alma 40:13-14

### James E. Talmage
That righteous and unrighteous dwell apart during the interval between death and resurrection is clear. Paradise, or as the Jews like to designate that blessed abode, "Abraham's bosom," [See parable of Lazarus and the Rich man in Luke 16:19-31.] is not the place of final glory, any more than the hell to which the rich man's spirit was consigned is the final habitation of the condemned. To that preliminary or intermediate state, however, men's works do follow them; and the dead shall surely find that their abode is that for which they have qualified themselves while in the flesh. JTC:468

### Joseph Smith
These are they who are liars, and sorcerers, and adulterers, and whoremongers, and whosoever loves and makes a lie. 104. These are they who suffer the wrath of God on earth. 105. These are they who suffer the vengeance of eternal fire. 106. These are they who are cast down to hell and suffer the wrath of Almighty God, until the fulness of times, when Christ shall have subdued all enemies under his feet, and shall have perfected his work; (*Vision to Joseph and Sidney Rigdon, Feb. 16, 1832*) D&C 76:103-106

### Jacob, brother of Nephi,
*quoted by Nephi*

O how great the goodness of our God, who prepareth a way for our escape from the grasp of this awful monster; yea, that monster, death and hell, which I call the death of the body, and also the death of the spirit. 11. And because of the way of deliverance of our God, the Holy One of Israel, this death, of which I have spoken, which is the temporal, shall deliver up its dead; which death is the grave. 12. And this death of which I have spoken, which is the spiritual death, shall deliver up its dead; which spiritual death is hell; wherefore, death and hell must deliver up their dead, and hell must deliver up its captive spirits, and the grave must deliver up its captive bodies, and the bodies and the spirits of men will be restored one to the other; and it is by the power of the resurrection of the Holy One of Israel. (*Jacob teaches the doctrine of the atonement to the people of Nephi, 559-545 B.C.*) 2Ne.9:10-12

### Elder Joseph Fielding Smith

Those who enter into the telestial kingdom . . . are the ungodly, the filthy who suffer the wrath of God on earth, who are thrust down to hell where they will be required to pay the uttermost farthing before their redemption comes. These are they who receive not the gospel of Christ and consequently could not deny the Holy Spirit while living on the earth. ¶ They have no part in the first resurrection and are not redeemed from the devil and his angels until the last resurrection, because of their wicked lives and their evil deeds. Nevertheless, even these are heirs of salvation, but before they are redeemed and enter the kingdom, they must repent of their sins, and receive the gospel, and bow the knee, and acknowledge that Jesus is the Christ, the Redeemer of the world. (Doctrines of Salvation, 2:22) DGSM:93

**Related Witnesses:**

### James E. Talmage

Upon all who reject the word of God in this life will fall the penalties provided; but after the debt has been paid the prison doors shall be opened, and the spirits once confined in suffering, then chastened and clean, shall come forth to partake of the glory provided for their class. AF:134

### Joseph Smith

There is no pain so awful as that of suspense. This is the punishment of the wicked; their doubt, anxiety and suspense cause weeping, wailing and gnashing of teeth. (*General conference, Nauvoo, April 1843*) HC5:340

### Joseph Smith

The great misery of departed spirits in the world

of spirits, where they go after death, is to know that they come short of the glory that others enjoy and that they might have enjoyed themselves, and they are their own accusers. (*At the Stand in Nauvoo, Ill., June 11, 1843*) HC5:425

### James E. Talmage

The false assumption, based upon sectarian dogma, that in the hereafter there shall be but two places, states or conditions for the souls of mankind—heaven or hell, with the same glory in all parts of the one and the same terrors throughout the other—is untenable in the light of divine revelation. AF:82-83

### John

And I saw the dead, small and great, stand before God; and the books were opened: and another book was opened, which is the book of life: and the dead were judged out of those things which were written in the books, according to their works. 13. And the sea gave up the dead which were in it; and death and hell delivered up the dead which were in them: and they were judged every man according to their works. (*John sees the judgment of man at the end of the Millennium*) Rev.20:12-13

**Author's Note:** Bruce R. McConkie explains why the word "hell" is used by prophets: "Messianic prophecies . . . describe in a most graphic way how the Lord saves men from the direful fate that would be theirs if he had not atoned for their sins. It is known as freeing the hosts of men from prison—from the prison of death, of hell, of the devil, and of endless torment. And how apt and pointed the illustration is, for the prisons of ancient times were hell holes of death, disease, and despair. They were dungeons of filth, corruption, and creeping denizens. Sheol itself was known as the pit, the dungeon of despair, the nether realms of torment, the Hades of hell. To be in prison was worse than a living hell, and to be freed therefrom was to arise from death to life. It is no wonder that the prophetic mind seized upon this illustration to teach what the Redeemer would do to ransom men from the fate that would be theirs if there were no atonement." (The Promised Messiah, pp. 238-39)

---

314. **Hell is not endless; there is an exit to hell as well as an entrance—there is an end to the torment of the damned.**

### James E. Talmage

Even to hell there is an exit as well as an

entrance; and when sentence has been served, commuted perhaps by repentance and its attendant works, the prison doors shall open and the penitent captive be afforded opportunity to comply with the law, which he aforetime violated. . . . ¶ The inhabitants of the telestial world—the lowest of the kingdoms of glory prepared for resurrected souls, shall include those "who are thrust down to hell" and "who shall not be redeemed from the devil until the last resurrection." (D&C 76:82-85) And though these may be delivered from hell and attain to a measure of glory with possibilities of progression, yet their lot shall be that of "servants of the Most High, but where God and Christ dwell they cannot come, worlds without end." (v.112) ¶ Deliverance from hell is not admittance to heaven. (The Vitality of Mormonism, pp. 255-56) DGSM:93

### Joseph Smith,
### receiving the Word of the Lord

And surely every man must repent or suffer, for I, God, am endless. 5. Wherefore, I revoke not the judgments which I shall pass, but woes shall go forth, weeping, wailing and gnashing of teeth, yea, to those who are found on my left hand. 6. Nevertheless, it is not written that there shall be no end to this torment, but it is written endless torment. 7. Again, it is written eternal damnation; wherefore it is more express than other scriptures, that it might work upon the hearts of the children of men, altogether for my name's glory. 8. Wherefore, I will explain unto you this mystery, for it is meet unto you to know even as mine apostles. 9. I speak unto you that are chosen in this thing, even as one, that you may enter into my rest. 10. For, behold, the mystery of godliness, how great is it! For, behold, I am endless, and the punishment which is given from my hand is endless punishment, for Endless is my name. Wherefore— 11. Eternal punishment is God's punishment. 12. Endless punishment is God's punishment. *(A commandment of God for Martin Harris, March 1830)* D&C 19:4-12

### Elder Joseph Fielding Smith

Those who enter into the telestial kingdom . . . are the ungodly, the filthy who suffer the wrath of God on earth, who are thrust down to hell where they will be required to pay the uttermost farthing before their redemption comes. These are they who receive not the gospel of Christ and consequently could not deny the Holy Spirit while living on the earth. ¶ They have no part in the first resurrection and are not redeemed from the devil and his angels until the last resurrection, because of their wicked lives and their evil deeds. Nevertheless, even these are heirs of salvation, but before they are redeemed and enter the kingdom, they must repent of their sins, and receive the gospel, and bow the knee, and acknowledge that Jesus is the Christ, the Redeemer of the world. (Doctrines of Salvation, 2:22) DGSM:93

### James E. Talmage

What is it to be damned? Does it mean that all who come under that sentence shall be cast into hell, there to dwell forever and forever? The light of the century, given by the Lord, declares the falsity of that construction. ¶ Salvation is graded ever upward until it culminates in the glorious condition of exaltation. . . . [S]o [also] damnation is graded; else what did the Lord mean as recorded in the twelfth chapter of Mark . . . . "These shall receive greater damnation?" Well, if there be a greater damnation there are lesser degrees of damnation and the term is used in the sense of deprivation and forfeiture. That man enters into a degree of damnation who has forfeited his opportunities and therefore has rendered himself incapable of the advancement that would otherwise be possible. . . . ¶ [E]xcept for those few . . . who have betrayed their trust and who have forfeited the very ability to repent—and they are few—every soul that has ever been tabernacled in flesh upon the earth shall be redeemed and shall be saved in his degree of worthiness and desert. ¶ During this hundred years [since 1830 when the gospel was restored to earth] many other great truths not known before, have been declared to the people, and one of the greatest is that to hell there is an exit as well as an entrance. Hell is no place to which a vindictive judge sends prisoners to suffer and to be punished principally for his glory; but it is a place prepared for the teaching, the disciplining of those who failed to learn here upon the earth what they should have learned. True, we read of everlasting punishment, unending suffering, eternal damnation. That is a direful expression; but in his mercy the Lord has made plain what those words mean. "Eternal punishment," he says, is God's punishment, for he is eternal; and that condition or state or possibility will ever exist for the sinner who deserves and really needs such condemnation; but this does not mean that the individual sufferer or sinner is to be eternally and everlastingly made to endure and suffer. No man will be kept in hell longer than is necessary to bring him to a fitness for something better. When he reaches that stage the prison doors will open and there will be rejoicing among the hosts who welcome him into a better state. CR1930Apr:95-97

**James E. Talmage,**
*also quoting Joseph Smith*

So general were the ill effects of the commonly accepted doctrine, unscriptural and untrue though it was, regarding the endless torment awaiting every sinner, that even before the Church had been formally organized in the present dispensation, the Lord gave a revelation through the Prophet Joseph Smith touching this matter, in which we read: "And surely every man must repent or suffer; for I, God, am endless. Wherefore, I revoke not the judgments which I shall pass, but woes shall go forth, weeping, wailing and gnashing of teeth, yea, to those who are found on my left hand. Nevertheless, it is not written that there shall be no end to this torment, but it is written endless torment. Again, it is written eternal damnation. . . . For behold, I am endless, and the punishment which is given from my hand is endless punishment, for Endless is my name. Wherefore, Eternal punishment is God's punishment. Endless punishment is God's punishment." (D&C 19:4-10) AF:56

**Author's Note:** "There is an exit to hell as well as an entrance—there is an end to the torment of the damned," except for the sons of perdition. In the words of Bruce R. McConkie, "for those who are heirs of some salvation, which includes all except the sons of perdition (D&C 76:44), hell has an end, but for those who have wholly given themselves over for satanic purposes there is no redemption from the consuming fires and torment of conscience. They go on forever in the hell that is prepared for them." (Doctrinal New Testament Commentary, 3:578-79)

---

**315. Perdition is a permanent place of hell where there is no forgiveness and no redemption.**

**Elder Joseph Fielding Smith**

[A place has been prepared for the punishment of the wicked, it is a] place where those who cannot be redeemed and who are called sons of Perdition will go into outer darkness. This is the real hell where those who once knew the truth and had the testimony of it and then turned away and blasphemed the name of Jesus Christ, will go. These are they who have sinned against the Holy Ghost. For them there is no forgiveness, and the Lord said he had prepared a place for them. (Answers to Gospel Questions, 2:208-10) TLDP:127

**Joseph Smith,**
*quoted by Elder Joseph Fielding Smith*

[T]here have been remarks made concerning all men being redeemed from hell; but I say that those who sin against the Holy Ghost cannot be forgiven in this world or in the world to come; they shall die the second death. Those who commit the unpardonable sin are doomed to Gnolom—to dwell in hell, worlds without end. As they concoct scenes of bloodshed in this world, so they shall rise to that resurrection which is as the lake of fire and brimstone. Some shall rise to the everlasting burnings of God; for God dwells in everlasting burnings, and some shall rise to the damnation of their own filthiness, which is as exquisite a torment as the lake of fire and brimstone. (*To the Church in general conference—to a congregation of 20,000—, "King Follett Sermon" April 7, 1844*) (See HC6:302-317, also see The Words of Joseph Smith, pp. 340-62.) TPJS:361

**President Joseph F. Smith**

God will not condemn any man to utter destruction, neither shall any man be thrust down to hell irredeemably, until he has been brought to the possession of the greater light that comes through repentance and obedience to the laws and commandments of God; but if, after he has received light and knowledge, he shall sin against the light and will not repent, then, indeed, he becomes a lost soul, a son of perdition. ("I Know That My Redeemer Lives," IE1908Mar:381) TLDP:634

**Joseph Smith,**
*receiving the Word of the Lord*

Thus saith the Lord concerning all those who know my power, and have been made partakers thereof, and suffered themselves through the power of the devil to be overcome, and to deny the truth and defy my power— 32. They are they who are the sons of perdition, of whom I say that it had been better for them never to have been born; 33. For they are vessels of wrath, doomed to suffer the wrath of God, with the devil and his angels in eternity; 34. Concerning whom I have said there is no forgiveness in this world nor in the world to come— 35. Having denied the Holy Spirit after having received it, and having denied the Only Begotten Son of the Father, having crucified him unto themselves and put him to an open shame. 36. These are they who shall go away into the lake of fire and brimstone, with the devil and his angels— 37. And the only ones on whom the second death shall have any power. . . . 44. Wherefore, he saves all except them— they shall go away into everlasting punishment, which is endless punishment, which is eternal punishment, to reign with the devil and his angels in eternity, where their worm dieth not, and the fire is not quenched, which is their torment— 45. And the end thereof, neither the place thereof, nor their torment, no man knows; 46. Neither was it revealed, neither is, neither will be revealed unto man, except to them who are made partakers thereof; 47. Nevertheless, I, the Lord, show it by vision unto many, but straightway shut it up again; 48. Wherefore, the end, the width, the height, the depth, and the misery thereof, they understand not, neither any man except those who are ordained unto this condemnation. (*Vision to Joseph Smith and Sidney Rigdon, Feb. 16, 1832*) D&C 76:31-37,44-48

## Joseph Smith,
### receiving the Word of the Lord

[F]or, behold, the devil was before Adam, for he rebelled against me, saying, Give me thine honor, which is my power; and also a third part of the hosts of heaven turned he away from me because of their agency; 37. And they were thrust down, and thus came the devil and his angels; 38. And, behold, there is a place prepared for them from the beginning, which place is hell. (*Revelation received Sept. 1830*) D&C 29:36-38

# List of Doctrines

## HOLY GHOST

*Doctrines Located in This Topic*

### (1) Gift of the Holy Ghost

316. The gift of the Holy Ghost is bestowed on those who have repented of their sins and have been properly baptized.

317. The gift of the Holy Ghost differs from the temporary witness of the Spirit, for the gift conveys the right to the constant companionship of the Holy Ghost.

318. The gift of the Holy Ghost is bestowed by the laying on of hands by elders of the Church holding the authority of the Melchizedek Priesthood.

319. Although we may receive the gift of the Holy Ghost, we may benefit from that gift only to the extent that we make ourselves worthy to receive its manifestations.

320. The gift of the Holy Ghost is the right to the companionship of the Holy Ghost.

321. Receiving the Holy Ghost is a "baptism of fire" (it has a sanctifying, purifying effect on the person who has been baptized by water).

322. Only those who are baptized of the water *and* of the Spirit, namely, the Holy Ghost, will enter the kingdom of God.

323. The truth of all things may be made known to those who have received the gift of the Holy Ghost.

324. Members of the Church are entitled to revelation and guidance from the Holy Ghost.

### (2) Witness of Truth
### (Including The Spirit of Christ)

325. The Holy Ghost is one of three members of the Godhead.

326. The Holy Ghost is a (male) personage of spirit, having a spirit body only, which is in the form of a man.

327. The Holy Ghost bears witness of the Father and the Son.

328. The Holy Ghost acts as a comforter.

329. The Holy Ghost acts as a teacher and a revelator.

330. The manifestation of the Holy Ghost is more powerful and longer lasting than the visitation of an angel.

331. The Holy Ghost must finally seal (ratify, approve, justify) every ordinance, blessing, and performance of the gospel, before those acts become binding on earth and in heaven.

332. The Holy Ghost brings to a person's remembrance those truths that have been learned earlier.

333. The Holy Ghost enables a person to discern between good and evil spirits.

334. When a person speaks by the power of the Holy Ghost, the Holy Ghost will carry the message to the hearts of those who hear by that same Spirit.

335. Through faith and by the power of the Holy Ghost, we may know the truth of all things.

336. Those who blaspheme against the Holy Ghost will not be forgiven.

337. The Spirit of Christ gives light to every person who comes into the world.

338. The Spirit of God is the spirit of love and peace.

**Doctrines on HOLY GHOST
Located in Other Topics**

16. We can discern between good and evil when we have the Spirit of God.

59. Baptism in connection with the gift of the Holy Ghost is a cleanser and a purifier.

68. A person may learn that the Book of Mormon is true by reading it and by asking of God, who will manifest the truth of it by the power of the Holy Ghost.

91. Where two or three disciples of the Lord are gathered together in His name, His Spirit will be with them.

97. A person who *accepts* divine truth must obtain it by the Spirit of God from someone who *teaches* by that same Spirit.

99. To be converted is to have a change of heart—a heart that has been penetrated by the Spirit of the Lord.

183. Those who believe the testimony of the prophets will receive the manifestations of the Holy Ghost.

236. Spiritual gifts are distributed among the members of the Church.

288. There is a Godhead consisting of God the Eternal Father, His son Jesus Christ, and the Holy Ghost.

290. The three members of the Godhead (God the Father, His son Jesus Christ, and the Holy Ghost) are united in purpose.

296. The first principles and ordinances of the gospel are faith in the Lord Jesus Christ, repentance, baptism by immersion, and the laying on of hands for the gift of the Holy Ghost.

325. The Holy Ghost is one of three members of the Godhead.

461. Missionaries are to proclaim the gospel by the Spirit of God; they are to teach only as moved upon by the Holy Ghost.

526. The Spirit of God is received through the prayer of faith.

538. The Holy Ghost enables a person who prays to ask according to the will of God.

660. The Holy Ghost confirms the truth of the declarations of the Lord's witnesses.

681. We are to heed the promptings of the Holy Ghost.

698. The Lord promises that those who partake of the sacrament worthily, will have His Spirit to be with them.

804. Church members are to teach only under direction of the Spirit, without which they are commanded not to teach.

813. Testimonies of divine truths come through personal revelation.

842. God uses the Holy Ghost to impart truth to His children.

# HOLY GHOST

(1) **Gift of the Holy Ghost**
(2) **Witness of Truth**

## (1) Gift of the Holy Ghost

316. The gift of the Holy Ghost is bestowed on those who have repented of their sins and have been properly baptized.

### Elder Spencer W. Kimball
Every person who has reached or passed the age of accountability of eight years, and who with a totally repentant heart is baptized properly, positively will receive the Holy Ghost. If heeded, this member of the Godhead will guide, inspire, and warn, and will neutralize the promptings of the evil one. (Miracle of Forgiveness, pp. 14-15) TLDP:282

### James E. Talmage
[T]he actual companionship of the Holy Ghost, the divinely-bestowed right to His ministrations, the sanctifying baptism with fire, are given as a permanent and personal possession only to the faithful, repentant, baptized candidate for salvation; and with all such this gift shall abide unless it be forfeited through transgression. AF:149

### Joseph Smith
We believe that the first principles and ordinances of the Gospel are: first, Faith in the Lord Jesus Christ; second, Repentance; third, Baptism by immersion for the remission of sins; fourth, Laying on of hands for the gift of the Holy Ghost. (*The fourth of the thirteen Articles of Faith; letter to John Wentworth, March 1, 1842*) AofF:4

### Joseph Smith
Baptism is a sign to God, to angels, and to heaven that we do the will of God, and there is no other way beneath the heavens whereby God hath ordained for man to come to Him to be saved, and enter into the kingdom of God, except faith in Jesus Christ, repentance, and baptism for the remission of sins, and any other course is in vain; then you have the promise of the gift of the Holy Ghost. (*In the Grove near the temple at Nauvoo, Ill., March 20, 1842.*) HC4:555

### Joseph Smith,
#### translating the Book of Moses
And he also said unto him: If thou wilt turn unto me, and hearken unto my voice, and believe, and repent of all thy transgressions, and be baptized, even in water, in the name of mine Only Begotten Son, who is full of grace and truth, which is Jesus Christ, the only name which shall be given under heaven, whereby salvation shall come unto the children of men, ye shall receive the gift of the Holy Ghost, asking all things in his name, and whatsoever ye shall ask, it shall be given you. (*The record of Moses: Enoch testifies to the people*) Moses 6:52

**Related Witnesses:**
### Elder Harold B. Lee
Baptism by immersion symbolizes the death and burial of the man of sin; and the coming forth out of the water, the resurrection to a newness of spiritual life. After baptism, hands are laid upon the head of the baptized believer, and he is blessed to receive the Holy Ghost. Thus does the one baptized receive the promise or gift of the Holy Ghost or the privilege of being brought back into the presence of one of the Godhead, by obedience to whom and through his faithfulness one so blessed might receive the guidance and direction of the Holy Ghost in his daily walks and talks, even as Adam walked and talked in the Garden of Eden with God, his Heavenly Father. To receive such guidance and such direction from the Holy Ghost is to be spiritually reborn. CR1947Oct:64; DCSM:42

---

317. The gift of the Holy Ghost differs from the temporary witness of the Spirit, for the gift conveys the right to the constant companionship of the Holy Ghost.

### Joseph Smith
There is a difference between the Holy Ghost, and the gift of the Holy Ghost. Cornelius received the Holy Ghost before he was baptized; which was the convincing power of God unto him of the truth of the gospel; but he could not receive the gift of the Holy Ghost until after he was baptized. Had he not taken this sign, or ordinance upon him, the Holy Ghost which convinced him of the truth of God, would have left him. (Times and Seasons, April 15, 1842, p. 752) TLDP:276

### Elder Joseph Fielding Smith
The Lord will grant to any honest person who earnestly seeks to know the truth *one* manifestation by the Holy Ghost; but he is not entitled to repeated manifestations. After such a revelation is given, he is to act, for the Holy Ghost cannot be appealed to for continued manifestations until after baptism and the gift has been bestowed. (Answer to Gospel Questions, 4:89) TLDP:279

### Bruce R. McConkie

True it is that honest truth seekers come to know of the truth and divinity of the Lord's work by the power of the Holy Ghost: they receive a flash of revelation telling them that Jesus is the Lord, that Joseph Smith is his prophet, that the Book of Mormon is the mind and will and voice of the Lord, that the Church of Jesus Christ of Latter-day Saints is the only true and living Church upon the whole earth. They gain a testimony before baptism. But it is only after they pledge their all in the cause of Christ that they receive the gift of the Holy Ghost. . . . (The Millennial Messiah, pp. 98-99) DGSM:45

### James E. Talmage

In another sense the Holy Ghost has frequently operated for good through persons that were unbaptized; indeed, some measure of His power is given to all mankind; for, as seen already, the Holy Spirit is the medium of intelligence, of wise direction, of development, of life. Manifestations of the power of God, as made plain through the operations of the Spirit, are seen in the triumphs of ennobling art, the discoveries of science, and the events of history; with all of which the carnal mind may believe that God takes no direct concern. Not a truth has ever been made the property of humankind except through the power of that great Spirit who exists to do the bidding of the Father and the Son. And yet the actual companionship of the Holy Ghost, the divinely-bestowed right to His ministrations, the sanctifying baptism with fire, are given as a permanent and personal possession only to the faithful, repentant, baptized candidate for salvation; and with all such this gift shall abide unless it be forfeited through transgression. AF:149

### Elder Joseph Fielding Smith

Every man can receive manifestation of the Holy Ghost, even when he is out of the Church, if he is earnestly seeking for the light and for the truth. The Holy Ghost will come and give the man the testimony he is seeking, and then withdraw; and the man does not have a claim upon another visit or constant visits and manifestations from him. He may have the constant guidance of that other Spirit, the Spirit of Christ. Every man may receive such a manifestation from the Holy Ghost when he is seeking for the truth, but not the power to call upon the Holy Ghost whenever he feels he needs the help, as a man does who is a member of the Church. (Doctrines of Salvation, 1:42) TLDP:279

318. **The gift of the Holy Ghost is bestowed by the laying on of hands by elders of the Church holding the authority of the Melchizedek Priesthood.**

### Elder Wilford Woodruff

This holy gift [the Holy Ghost] is bestowed today as it was anciently, by the laying on of hands by men possessing the authority to administer in the ordinances of the Gospel. (*In Tabernacle, May 14, 1882, JD23:127*) TLDP:277

### Joseph Smith

Repent and be baptized in the name of Jesus Christ, according to the holy commandment, for the remission of sins; 14. And whoso doeth this shall receive the gift of the Holy Ghost, by the laying on of the hands of the elders of the church. (*Revelation received March 1831*) D&C 49:13-14

### Joseph Smith

An apostle is an elder, and it is his calling to baptize; . . . 41. And to confirm those who are baptized into the church, by the laying on of hands for the baptism of fire and the Holy Ghost, according to the scriptures; (*Revelation on Church Organization and Government, April 1830*) D&C 20:38,41

### Joseph Smith

He said this Aaronic Priesthood had not the power of laying on hands for the gift of the Holy Ghost, but that this should be conferred on us hereafter; and he commanded us to go and be baptized, and gave us directions that I should baptize Oliver Cowdery, and that afterwards he should baptize me. (*John the Baptist appears to Joseph Smith and Oliver Cowdery, May 15, 1829*) JS-H 1:70

### President Joseph F. Smith

The gift of the Holy Ghost . . . is not given unto all men until they repent of their sins and come to a state of worthiness before the Lord. Then they receive it by the laying on of the hands of those who are authorized of God to bestow his blessings upon the heads of the children of men. ("Editor's Table," IE1908Mar:380-81) TLDP:277

### Recorded in Luke

But when they believed Philip preaching the things concerning the kingdom of God, and the name of Jesus Christ, they were baptized, both men and women. 13. Then Simon himself believed also: and when he was baptized, he continued with Philip, and wondered, beholding the miracles and signs which were done. 14. Now when the apostles which were at Jerusalem heard that Samaria had received the word of God, they sent unto them Peter and John: 15. Who, when they were come down, prayed for them, that they might receive the Holy Ghost: 16. (For as yet he was fallen upon none of them: only they were baptized in the name of the Lord Jesus.) 17. Then laid they their hands on them, and they received the Holy Ghost. 18. And when Simon saw that through laying on of the apostles' hands the Holy Ghost was given, he offered them money, 19. Saying, Give me also this power, that on whomsoever I lay hands, he may receive the Holy Ghost. 20. But Peter said unto him, Thy money perish with thee, because thou hast thought that the gift of God may be purchased with money. (*Peter and John come to Samaria and confer the gift of the Holy Ghost*) Acts 8:12-20

### Paul
Wherefore I put thee in remembrance that thou stir up the gift of God, which is in thee by the putting on of my hands. (*Letter to his assistant Timothy, about A.D.64*) 2Tim.1:6

**Related Witnesses:**
### Moroni, son of Mormon
The words of Christ, which he spake unto his disciples, the twelve whom he had chosen, as he laid his hands upon them— 2. And he called them by name, saying: Ye shall call on the Father in my name, in mighty prayer; and after ye have done this ye shall have power that to him upon whom ye shall lay your hands, ye shall give the Holy Ghost; and in my name shall ye give it, for thus do mine apostles. 3. Now Christ spake these words unto them at the time of his first appearing; and the multitude heard it not, but the disciples heard it; and on as many as they laid their hands, fell the Holy Ghost. (*Moroni writes for the benefit of the Lamanites, A.D. 400-421*) Moro.2:1-3

---

319. **Although we may receive the gift of the Holy Ghost, we may benefit from that gift only to the extent we make ourselves worthy to receive its manifestations.**

### Elder Joseph Fielding Smith
[I]t is my judgment that there are many members of this Church who have been baptized for the remission of their sins, who have had hands laid upon their heads for the gift of the Holy Ghost, who have never received that gift, that is, the manifestations of it. Why? Because they have never put themselves in order to receive these manifestations. They have never humbled

themselves. They have never taken the steps that would prepare them for the companionship of the Holy Ghost. CR1958Oct:21
### Anthony W. Ivins
While the Holy Ghost may be conferred upon us, and is designed to be our guide and support, it is only restrained and manifested in its fulness in our guidance and defence in proportion to the degree to which we cultivate it and listen to its promptings. We may lose it entirely through indifference or transgression and once deprived of its presence we are left in darkness more dense than before its reception. Cultivate it, my brethren and sisters, and it will become in reality the iron rod, which is the word of God, and will lead us back to him. CR1934Apr:101-02
### President Spencer W. Kimball
The Holy Ghost is a personage of spirit and comes into our lives to lead us in the paths of righteousness. Each person on whom authoritative hands have been placed will receive the Holy Ghost. He will lead us unto all truth. And so we are a blessed people with all these special blessings. If one does not receive the great gift of the Holy Ghost, then it is his fault, that he hasn't been spiritual enough or close enough to Heavenly Father. (*Seoul Korea Area conference, Aug. 1975*) DGSM:45
### President Brigham Young, quoted by John A. Widtsoe
We want to live so as to have the Spirit every day, every hour of the day, every minute of the day, and every Latter-day Saint is entitled to the Spirit of God, to the power of the Holy Ghost, to lead him in his individual duties. (*In Tabernacle, May 15, 1864, JD10:296*) DBY:82
### John A. Widtsoe
The gift of the Holy Ghost confers upon a person the right to receive, as he may desire and need, the presence, light and intelligence of the Holy Ghost. It gives, as it were, an official claim upon the mighty assistance and comforting assurance of the Holy Ghost. When the servants of the Lord display a spiritual power beyond the command of man; when the grief-laden heart beats with joy; when failure is converted into victory, it is by the visitation of the Holy Ghost. It is the Spirit of God under the direction of the Holy Ghost that quickeneth all things. ¶ The gift of the Holy Ghost remains inoperative unless a person leads a blameless life. Worthiness determines whether a person shall enjoy the privileges promised when the "gift" is conferred. It is useless to expect this high official assistance unless there is daily conformity to the laws of the gospel. Faith and

prayer, out of the heart and unceasing, will fit a person for the presence of the Holy Ghost, and to such a life he will respond in power. ¶ Latter-day Saints have received, under the hands of those divinely empowered, this inexpressibly glorious "gift," which will lead them if they are fitted, into the companionship of the Holy Ghost, and win for them intelligence and power to win joy in life and exaltation in the world to come. Those who have been so blessed have not always understood the greatness of that which has been given them, or have not earnestly sought its help. So powerful a gift, with such boundless promise, justifies every attempt to cleanse body and soul. Certain it is, that only with the aid of the Holy Ghost shall we be able to rise to the heights of salvation of which we dream and for which we pray. (Man and the Dragon, pp. 150-51) TLDP:276-77

**Related Witnesses:**

**Moroni, son of Mormon**

O God, the Eternal Father, we ask thee in the name of thy Son, Jesus Christ, to bless and sanctify this bread to the souls of all those who partake of it; that they may eat in remembrance of the body of thy Son, and witness unto thee, O God, the Eternal Father, that they are willing to take upon them the name of thy Son, and always remember him, and keep his commandments which he hath given them, that they may always have his Spirit to be with them. Amen. (*Moroni, records the prayer for the sacramental bread, A.D. 400-421*) Moro.4:3

**George Q. Cannon**

The only way to maintain our position in the Kingdom of God is to so conduct ourselves that we may have a living testimony of the truth continually dwelling in our bosoms, to live so that the Spirit of the Lord may be a constant and abiding quest with us, whether in the privacy of our chamber, in the domestic circle or in the midst of the crowded thoroughfares, the busy scenes and anxious cares of life. He who will pursue this course will never lack for knowledge; he will never be in doubt or in darkness, nor will his mind ever be clouded by the gloomy pall of unbelief; on the contrary his hopes will be bright; his faith will be strong; his joy will be full; he will be able each succeeding day to comprehend the unfolding purposes of Jehovah and to rejoice in the glorious liberty and happiness which all the faithful children of God enjoy. ¶ .... We can only retain the testimony of the truth in our heart by living near unto God. If we call upon Him in faith to bless us and seek to enjoy the companionship of the Holy Spirit, so ordering our lives that God can,

consistently, bless us and the Spirit of the Lord can abide with us, we receive strength to overcome every evil and our minds instinctively recoil from the commission of any act which might grieve that Spirit or bring a stain upon our own character or upon the divine cause in which we are engaged. (Gospel Truth, 1:343-33) TLDP:284

**President Joseph F. Smith**

[We] should live so near to the Lord, be so humble in our spirits, so tractable and pliable, under the influence of the Holy Spirit, that we will be able to know the mind and will of the Father concerning us as individuals and as officers in the Church of Christ under all circumstances. And when we live so that we can hear and understand the whisperings of the still small voice of the Spirit of God, let us do whatsoever that Spirit directs, without fear of the consequences. It does not make any difference whether it meet the minds of carpers or critics, or of the enemies of the kingdom of God, or not. Is it agreeable to the will of the Lord? Is it compatible with the spirit of the great latter-day work in which we are engaged? Is the end aimed at likely to advance the Church and to strengthen it in the earth? If its trend is in that direction, let us do it, no matter what men may say or think. CR1903Oct:86

**Joseph Smith**

Let thy bowels also be full of charity towards all men, and to the household of faith, and let virtue garnish thy thoughts unceasingly; then shall thy confidence wax strong in the presence of God; and the doctrine of the priesthood shall distil upon thy soul as the dews from heaven. 46. The Holy Ghost shall be thy constant companion, and thy scepter an unchanging scepter of righteousness and truth; and thy dominion shall be an everlasting dominion, and without compulsory means it shall flow unto thee forever and ever. (*Revelation received while in Liberty Jail, March 20, 1839; the priesthood should be used only in righteousness*) D&C 121:45-46

**Mormon**

And the remission of sins bringeth meekness, and lowliness of heart; and because of meekness and lowliness of heart cometh the visitation of the Holy Ghost, which Comforter filleth with hope and perfect love, which love endureth by diligence unto prayer, until the end shall come, when all the saints shall dwell with God. (*Epistle to his son Moroni, prior to A.D. 384*) Moro.8:26

**Elder Joseph Fielding Smith**

The Holy Ghost will not dwell in unclean tabernacles or disobedient tabernacles. The

Holy Ghost will not dwell with that person who is unwilling to obey and keep the commandments of God or who violates those commandments willingly. In such a soul the spirit of the Holy Ghost cannot enter. ¶ That great gift comes to us only through humility and faith and obedience. Therefore, a great many members of the Church do not have that guidance. Then some cunning, crafty individual will come along teaching that which is not true, and without the guidance which is promised to us through our faithfulness, people are unable to discern and are led astray. It depends on our faithfulness and our obedience to the commandments of the Lord if we have the teachings, the enlightening instruction, that comes from the Holy Ghost. (Take Heed to Yourselves, p. 364) TLDP:279

**Elder Joseph F. Smith**

Of what use is it that we know the truth, if we lack its spirit? Our knowledge, in this event, becomes a condemnation to us, failing to bear fruit. It is not sufficient that we know the truth, but we must be humble and with this knowledge possess the spirit to actuate us to good deeds. Baptism, as well as all other outward ordinances, without the spirit accompanying, is useless. We remain but baptized sinners. ¶ It is the duty of the young men of Israel to seek first the Kingdom of God and his righteousness, and leave other things to follow; to seek the spirit of truth so as to possess the knowledge of God, which giveth them a desire for purity, light, truth; and a spirit to despise evil and to turn away from all that is not of God. ("Editor's Table," IE1899Jul:699-700) TLDP:284-85

---

320. **The gift of the Holy Ghost is the right to the companionship of the Holy Ghost.**

**Elder Joseph Fielding Smith**

What is the gift of the Holy Ghost? Nothing more nor less than the right to the companionship of the Holy Ghost. (Doctrines of Salvation, 1:40) TLDP:276

**Marion G. Romney**

The gift of the Holy Ghost is an endowment that gives one the right to enjoy the enlightenment, companionship, and guidance of the Spirit and the influence of the Holy Spirit as long as one complies with the commandments of God. (Learning for the Eternities, p. 22) TLDP:277

**Elder Harold B. Lee**

What do we mean when we say the *gift* of the

Holy Ghost? I think that perhaps one of the most lucid explanations is made by President Joseph F. Smith. He said: ¶ "Therefore, the presentation of 'gift' of the Holy Ghost simply confers upon a man the right to receive at any time, when he is worthy of it and desires it, the power and light of truth of the Holy Ghost, although he may often be left to his own spirit and judgment." [Gospel Doctrine, eleventh edition, 1959, pp. 60-61] ¶ The bestowal of the gift is actually, then, a command to so live that when we need and desire it, we may have the accomplishment of the power of the Holy Ghost. (*To seminary and institute teachers, June 1962*) (Stand Ye in Holy Places, pp. 56-57) TLDP:277

**James E. Talmage**

And yet the actual companionship of the Holy Ghost, the divinely-bestowed right to His ministrations, the sanctifying baptism with fire, are given as a permanent and personal possession only to the faithful, repentant, baptized candidate for salvation; and with all such this gift shall abide unless it be forfeited through transgression. AF:149

**Elder Joseph Fielding Smith**

This Comforter is, by his influence, to be a constant companion to every baptized person, and to administer unto the members of the church by revelation and guidance, knowledge of truth that they may walk in its light. It is the Holy Ghost who enlightens the mind of the truly baptized member. (Answers to Gospel Questions, 2:149-50) DGSM:12

---

321. **Receiving the Holy Ghost is a "baptism of fire" (it has a sanctifying, purifying effect on the person who has been baptized by water).**

**Marion G. Romney**

This "mighty change" wrought by the baptism of fire and the Holy Ghost should and does, if the proselyte is prepared to receive it, occur when he is baptized by immersion for the remission of sins and receives the laying on of hands for the gift of the Holy Ghost— the two required ordinances for being "born of water and of the spirit." (Look to God and Live, pp. 269-70) DGSM:49

**Bruce R. McConkie**

As starving men crave a crust of bread, as choking men thirst for water, so do the righteous yearn for the Holy Ghost. The Holy Ghost is a Revelator; he is a Sanctifier; he reveals truth, and he cleanses human souls. He is the Spirit of

Truth, and his baptism is one of fire; he burns dross and evil out of repentant souls as though by fire. The gift of the Holy Ghost is the greatest of all the gifts of God, as pertaining to this life; and those who enjoy that gift here and now, will inherit eternal life hereafter, which is the greatest of all the gifts of God in eternity. (The Mortal Messiah, 2:122) TLDP:276

### Nephi, son of Lehi

Wherefore, do the things which I have told you I have seen that your Lord and your Redeemer should do; for, for this cause have they been shown unto me, that ye might know the gate by which ye should enter. For the gate by which ye should enter is repentance and baptism by water; and then cometh a remission of your sins by fire and by the Holy Ghost. (*Nephi writes, between 559-545 B.C.*) 2Ne.31:17

### James E. Talmage

And yet the actual companionship of the Holy Ghost, the divinely-bestowed right to His ministrations, the sanctifying baptism with fire, are given as a permanent and personal possession only to the faithful, repentant, baptized candidate for salvation; and with all such this gift shall abide unless it be forfeited through transgression. AF:149

### John the Baptist,
### *recorded in Matthew*

I indeed baptize you with water unto repentance: but he that cometh after me is mightier than I, whose shoes I am not worthy to bear: he shall baptize you with the Holy Ghost, and with fire: (*John the Baptist baptizes the repentant*) Matt.3:11

### Joseph Smith

And of tenets thou shalt not talk, but thou shalt declare repentance and faith on the Savior, and remission of sins by baptism, and by fire, yea, even the Holy Ghost. (*A commandment of God for Martin Harris, March 1830*) D&C 19:31

### Joseph Smith,
### *receiving the Word of the Lord*

And this is my gospel—repentance and baptism by water, and then cometh the baptism of fire and the Holy Ghost, even the Comforter, which showeth all things, and teacheth the peaceable things of the kingdom. (*Revelation received Jan. 5, 1831*) D&C 39:6

### Joseph Smith,
### *translating Matthew,*
### *quoting, in part, John the Baptist*

I indeed baptize you with water, upon your repentance; and when he of whom I bear record cometh, who is mightier than I, whose shoes I am not worthy to bear, (or whose place I am not able to fill,) as I said, I indeed baptize

you before he cometh, that when he cometh he may baptize you with the Holy Ghost and fire. . . . 40. Thus came John, preaching and baptizing in the river of Jordan; bearing record, that he who was coming after him had power to baptize with the Holy Ghost and fire. (*John the Baptist baptizes the repentant*) JST(Matt.3:- 38,40 in Appendix)

**Related Witnesses:**

### Parley P. Pratt

The gift of the Holy Ghost . . . quickens all the intellectual faculties, increases, enlarges, expands, and purifies all the natural passions and affections, and adapts them, by the gift of wisdom, to their lawful use. It inspires, develops, cultivates, and matures all the fine-toned sympathies, joys, tastes, kindred feelings, and affections of our nature. It inspires virtue, kindness, goodness, tenderness, gentleness, and charity. It develops beauty of person, form, and features. It tends to health, vigor, animation, and social feeling. It invigorates all the faculties of the physical and intellectual man. It strengthens and gives tone to the nerves. In short, it is, as it were, marrow to the bone, joy to the heart, light to the eyes, music to the ears, and life to the whole being. (Key to the Science of Theology, p. 61) DGSM:45

### Jesus,
### *quoted by Mormon*

Now this is the commandment: Repent, all ye ends of the earth, and come unto me and be baptized in my name, that ye may be sanctified by the reception of the Holy Ghost, that ye may stand spotless before me at the last day. (*The resurrected Jesus instructs his twelve Nephite disciples, A.D. 34*) 3Ne.27:20

### Mormon

And it came to pass when they were all baptized and had come up out of the water, the Holy Ghost did fall upon them, and they were filled with the Holy Ghost and with fire. 14. And behold, they were encircled about as if it were by fire; and it came down from heaven, and the multitude did witness it, and did bear record; and angels did come down out of heaven and did minister unto them. (*The twelve disciples are baptized, A.D. 34*) 3Ne.19:13-14

---

322. Only those who are baptized of the water *and* of the Spirit, namely, the Holy Ghost, will enter the kingdom of God.

### Elder Joseph Fielding Smith

Now, baptism into the Church is not enough to

save us. It is for the remission of sins, that is true, but there is another baptism which is just as essential, and that is the baptism of the spirit, or the bestowal of the gift of the Holy Ghost. CR1958Oct:21

**Jesus,**
*quoted by Mormon*

Now this is the commandment: Repent, all ye ends of the earth, and come unto me and be baptized in my name, that ye may be sanctified by the reception of the Holy Ghost, that ye may stand spotless before me at the last day. (*The resurrected Jesus instructs his twelve Nephite disciples, A.D. 34*) 3Ne.27:20

**Jesus,**
*quoted by John*

There was a man of the Pharisees, named Nicodemus, a ruler of the Jews: 2. The same came to Jesus by night, and said unto him, Rabbi, we know that thou art a teacher come from God: for no man can do these miracles that thou doest, except God be with him. 3. Jesus answered and said unto him, Verily, verily, I say unto thee, Except a man be born again, he cannot see the kingdom of God. 4. Nicodemus saith unto him, How can a man be born when he is old? can he enter the second time into his mother's womb, and be born? 5. Jesus answered, Verily, verily, I say unto thee, Except a man be born of water and of the Spirit, he cannot enter into the kingdom of God. 6. That which is born of the flesh is flesh; and that which is born of the Spirit is spirit. 7. Marvel not that I said unto thee, Ye must be born again. 8. The wind bloweth where it listeth, and thou hearest the sound thereof, but canst not tell whence it cometh, and whither it goeth: so is every one that is born of the Spirit. (*Jesus tells Nicodemus men must be born again*) John 3:1-8

**Joseph Smith,**
*translating the Book of Moses*

That by reason of transgression cometh the fall, which fall bringeth death, and inasmuch as ye were born into the world by water, and blood, and the spirit, which I have made, and so became of dust a living soul, even so ye must be born again into the kingdom of heaven, of water, and of the Spirit, and be cleansed by blood, even the blood of mine Only Begotten; that ye might be sanctified from all sin, and enjoy the words of eternal life in this world, and eternal life in the world to come, even immortal glory; 60. For by the water ye keep the commandment; by the Spirit ye are justified, and by the blood ye are sanctified; . . . 64. And it came to pass, when the Lord had spoken with Adam, our father, that Adam cried unto

the Lord, and he was caught away by the Spirit of the Lord, and was carried down into the water, and was laid under the water, and was brought forth out of the water. 65. And thus he was baptized, and the Spirit of God descended upon him, and thus he was born of the Spirit, and became quickened in the inner man. 66. And he heard a voice out of heaven, saying: Thou art baptized with fire, and with the Holy Ghost. This is the record of the Father, and the Son, from henceforth and forever; (*The record of Moses: Enoch recounts God speaking to Adam*) Moses 6:59-60,64-66

**Related Witnesses:**

**Joseph Smith,**
*receiving the Word of the Lord*

And behold, whosoever believeth on my words, them will I visit with the manifestation of my Spirit; and they shall be born of me, even of water and of the Spirit— (*Revelation received at the request of Martin Harris, March 1829; the Lord promises to supply three witnesses to the Book of Mormon*) D&C 5:16

**John the Baptist,**
*recorded in Matthew*

I indeed baptize you with water unto repentance: but he that cometh after me is mightier than I, whose shoes I am not worthy to bear: he shall baptize you with the Holy Ghost, and with fire: (*John the Baptist baptizes the repentant*) Matt.3:11

**Joseph Smith,**
*translating Matthew,*
*quoting, in part, John the Baptist*

I indeed baptize you with water, upon your repentance; and when he of whom I bear record cometh, who is mightier than I, whose shoes I am not worthy to bear, (or whose place I am not able to fill,) as I said, I indeed baptize you before he cometh, that when he cometh he may baptize you with the Holy Ghost and fire. . . . 40. Thus came John, preaching and baptizing in the river of Jordan; bearing record, that he who was coming after him had power to baptize with the Holy Ghost and fire. (*John the Baptist baptizes the repentant*) JST(Matt.3:38,40 in Appendix)

**Recorded in Mark**

And it came to pass in those days, that Jesus came from Nazareth of Galilee, and was baptized of John in Jordan. 10. And straightway coming up out of the water, he saw the heavens opened, and the Spirit like a dove descending upon him: (*Mark writes of John the Baptist*) Mark 1:9-10

323. The truth of all things may be made known to those who have received the gift of the Holy Ghost.

### Moroni, son of Mormon

And by the power of the Holy Ghost ye may know the truth of all things. (*The final writings of Moroni, about A.D. 421*) Moro.10:5

### President John Taylor

Now, what did Jesus tell His disciples the Holy Ghost should do when it came? He promised—"It shall lead you into all truth!" What shall it do? Lead you into all truth—not into a diversity of sentiments, not into differences of doctrine, not into a variety of ordinances, but you shall see alike, comprehend alike and understand alike. "It shall lead you into all truth." *(In Assembly Hall, Feb. 11, 1883, JD23:374)* TLDP:272

### Delbert L. Stapley

The Holy Ghost is a revelator of truth. . . . CR1966Oct:112

### Jesus,
*quoted by John*

Howbeit when he, the Spirit of truth, is come, he will guide you into all truth: for he shall not speak of himself; but whatsoever he shall hear, that shall he speak: and he will shew you things to come. (*Jesus discourses on the mission of the Holy Ghost*) John 16:13

### Jesus,
*quoted by John*

And I will pray the Father, and he shall give you another Comforter, that he may abide with you for ever; 17. Even the Spirit of truth; whom the world cannot receive, because it seeth him not, neither knoweth him: but ye know him; for he dwelleth with you, and shall be in you. . . . 26. But the Comforter, which is the Holy Ghost, whom the Father will send in my name, he shall teach you all things, and bring all things to your remembrance, whatsoever I have said unto you. (*Jesus promises his disciples to send the Holy Ghost*) John 14:16-17,26

### Joseph Smith,
*quoted by Elder Joseph Fielding Smith*

[W]e believe that it [the gift of the Holy Ghost] . . . brings things past to our remembrance, leads us into all truth, and shows us of things to come; we believe that "no man can know that Jesus is the Christ, but by the Holy Ghost." (Editorial in "Times and Seasons," June 1842) HC5:27; TPJS:243; TLDP:274

### Joseph Smith,
*translating the Book of Moses*

Therefore it is given to abide in you; the record of heaven; the Comforter; the peaceable things of immortal glory; the truth of all things; that which quickeneth all things, which maketh alive all things; that which knoweth all things, and hath all power according to wisdom, mercy, truth, justice, and judgment. (*The record of Moses: Enoch recounts God speaking to Adam*) Moses 6:61

### President Spencer W. Kimball

Each person on whom authoritative hands have been placed will receive the Holy Ghost. He will lead us unto all truth. (*Seoul Korea Area conference, Aug. 1975)* DGSM:45

### Bruce R. McConkie

[I]t is only after [honest truth seekers] pledge their all in the cause of Christ that they receive the gift of the Holy Ghost, which is the heavenly endowment of which Jesus spoke. Then they receive a fulfillment of the promise: "by the power of the Holy Ghost ye may know the truth of all things." (Moro.10:5) Then they receive the "spirit of revelation," and the Lord tells them in their heart and in their mind whatsoever he will. (D&C 8:1-3) (The Millennial Messiah, pp. 98-99) DGSM:45

### Related Witnesses:

### Noah,
*quoted by Joseph Smith,*
*translating the Book of Moses*

Believe and repent of your sins and be baptized in the name of Jesus Christ, the Son of God, even as our fathers, and ye shall receive the Holy Ghost, that ye may have all things made manifest; and if ye do not this, the floods will come in upon you; nevertheless they hearkened not. (*The record of Moses: Noah preaches to the people*) Moses 8:24

---

324. Members of the Church are entitled to revelation and guidance from the Holy Ghost.

### Elder Joseph Fielding Smith

This Comforter is, by his influence, to be a constant companion to every baptized person, and to administer unto the members of the church by revelation and guidance, knowledge of the truth that they may walk in its light. It is the Holy Ghost who enlightens the mind of the truly baptized member. (Answers to Gospel Questions, 2:149-50) DGSM:12

### Elder Spencer W. Kimball

Every person who has reached or passed the age of accountability of eight years, and who with a totally repentant heart is baptized properly, positively will receive the Holy Ghost. If heeded, this member of the Godhead will guide, inspire, and warn, and will neutralize the promptings of the evil one. (Miracle of Forgiveness, pp. 14-15) TLDP:282

**Nephi, son of Lehi**

For behold, again I say unto you that if ye will enter in by the way, and receive the Holy Ghost, it will show unto you all things what ye should do. (*Nephi's writings, between 559-545 B.C.*) 2Ne.32:5

**Joseph Smith,**
*receiving the Word of the Lord*

Go your way whithersoever I will, and it shall be given you by the Comforter what you shall do and whither you shall go. (*Revelation for Thomas B. Marsh who had been baptized earlier in the month, received Sept. 30, 1830*) D&C 31:11

**Charles A. Callis**

The Holy Ghost is the genius of the Holy Priesthood. Remove from this body of men, clothed with this power, dispossess them, if that were possible of the guiding influence of the spirit of revelation and they would be as unproductive in the ministry as the dry sand on the seashore. ¶ The spirit of revelation directs the leaders of the Church in the appointment of officers. They pray to the Lord. "Thou, Lord, which knowest the hearts of all men, shew whether of these two thou hast chosen." The Lord is the searcher of the heart. He knows the qualifications, the most secret purposes and intentions and dispositions of all men. Every man whom we have sustained by our vote this afternoon, in the position to which he has been appointed, that man, I testify, has been chosen by the spirit of revelation, by the Holy Ghost, which, as I have stated, is the genius of the Priesthood. While this spirit remains in the Church—and it will remain forever—we need not be afraid that we will be led astray, for God loves us. He loves the men whom he has appointed and he will move upon them, by the Holy Spirit, to select men whom he has chosen to be overseers of the flock, "to feed the Church of God." CR1938Apr:100

**Related Witnesses:**

**Elder Spencer W. Kimball**

The Holy Ghost is a revelator. Every worthy soul is entitled to a revelation, and it comes through the Holy Ghost. ("The Fourth Article of Faith," Instructor, April 1955, p. 108) TLDP:274

**Joseph Smith,**
*quoted by Elder Joseph Fielding Smith*

[W]e believe that [the gift of the Holy Ghost] is necessary to make and to organize the Priesthood, that no man can be called to fill any office in the ministry without it; we also believe in prophecy, in tongues, in visions, and in revelations, in gifts, and in healings; and that these things cannot be enjoyed without the gift of the Holy Ghost. We believe that the Holy Ghost, and that holy men in these days speak by the same principle; we believe in its being a comforter and a witness bearer, that it brings things past to our remembrance, leads us into all truth, and shows us of things to come; we believe that "no man can know that Jesus is the Christ, but by the Holy Ghost." (Editorial in "Times and Seasons," June 1842) HC5:27; TPJS:243; TLDP:274

**President Brigham Young,**
*quoted by John A. Widtsoe*

The Holy Ghost reveals unto you things past, present, and to come; it makes your minds quick and vivid to understand the handiwork of the Lord. Your joy is made full in beholding the footsteps of our Father going forth among the inhabitants of the earth; this is invisible to the world, but it is made visible to the Saints, and they behold the Lord in his providences, bringing forth the work of the last days. (*In Bowery, Aug. 17, 1856, JD4:22*) DBY:161

**Charles W. Penrose**

Now this gift of the Holy Ghost, as I before remarked, is the greatest boon that can be conferred upon mortal men, because by it they can discern and comprehend the things of God, and without it they cannot. They may reflect upon them, ponder upon them, speculate about them; they may come to certain conclusions in their own minds by reason and logic, but they cannot obtain a knowledge of these things unless it is by the power and gift of the Holy Ghost, which is the spirit of revelation. (*In Tabernacle, May 1, 1880, JD22:89*) TLDP:282

---

## (2) Witness of Truth

### (Including The Spirit of Christ)

**325. The Holy Ghost is one of three members of the Godhead.**

**Elder Joseph Fielding Smith**

The Holy Ghost is the third member of the Godhead. He is a Spirit, in the form of a man. . . . The Holy Ghost is a personage of Spirit, and has a spirit body only. His mission is to bear witness of the Father and the Son and of all truth. . . . ¶ . . . . He is also called the Holy Spirit, the Spirit of God, the Spirit of the Lord, the Spirit of Truth, and the Comforter. (Doctrines of Salvation, 1:38) DGSM:11

**Elder Joseph Fielding Smith**

We know what has been revealed and that the Holy Ghost, sometimes spoken of as the Holy Spirit, and Comforter, is the third member of the Godhead, and that he, being in perfect harmony with the Father and the Son, reveals to man by the spirit of revelation and prophecy the truths of the gospel of Jesus Christ. Our great duty is so to live that we may be led constantly in light and truth by this Comforter so that we may not be deceived by the many false spirits that are in the world. (Doctrines of Salvation, 1:39) TLDP:271

**George F. Richards**

This is the office of the Holy Ghost, who is a personage of spirit, one of the trinity of the Godhead. It is his mission and office to bear witness of the Father and of the Son and of the truth of all things. "No man may know that Jesus is the Lord except by the Holy Ghost." CR1931Oct:101

**Charles W. Penrose**

The Holy Ghost as "a personage of spirit" . . . represents both the Father and the Son and is one of the Godhead. CR1916Apr:22

**Bruce R. McConkie**

We learn these truths relative to the Gods we worship: ¶ 1. They are three in number, three separate persons: the first is the Father, the second, the Son; and the third, the Holy Ghost. They are three individuals who meet together, counsel in concert, and as occasion requires, travel separately through all immensity. They are three holy men, two having bodies of flesh and bones, the third being a personage of spirit. (The Promised Messiah, p. 120) TLDP:228-29

**President Brigham Young,**
*quoted by John A. Widtsoe*

The Holy Ghost, we believe, is one of the characters that form the Trinity, or the Godhead. Not one person in three, nor three persons in one; but the Father, Son, and Holy Ghost are one in essence, as the hearts of three men who are united in all things. He is one of the three characters we believe in, whose office it is to administer to those of the human family who love the truth. I have stated that they are one, as the hearts of three men might be one. Lest you should mistake me, I will say that I do not wish you to understand that the Holy Ghost is a personage having a tabernacle, like the Father and the Son; but he is God's messenger that diffuses his influence through all the works of the Almighty. (*In Tabernacle, Nov. 29, 1857, JD6:95)* DBY:30

**Marion G. Romney**

As a member of the Godhead, and being one

with the Father and the Son, the Holy Ghost is, as are the Father and the Son, omniscient. He comprehends all truth having a knowledge of [all] things. (D&C 93:24) ("The Holy Ghost," EN1974May:90) MGSP:7

**Mormon**

And he hath brought to pass the redemption of the world, whereby he that is found guiltless before him at the judgment day hath it given unto him to dwell in the presence of God in his kingdom, to sing ceaseless praises with the choirs above, unto the Father, and unto the Son, and unto the Holy Ghost, which are one God, in a state of happiness which hath no end. (*Mormon invites the Lamanites of the latter days to believe in Christ, about A.D. 385*) Morm.7:7

**Related Witnesses:**

**Joseph Smith**

Which Father, Son, and Holy Ghost are one God, infinite and eternal, without end. Amen. (*Revelation on Church Organization and Government, April 1830*) D&C 20:28

**Nephi, son of Lehi**

And now, behold, this is my beloved brethren, this is the way; and there is none other way nor name given under heaven whereby man can be saved in the kingdom of God. And now, behold, this is the doctrine of Christ, and the only and true doctrine of the Father, and of the Son, and of the Holy Ghost, which is one God, without end. Amen. (*Nephi writes, between 559-545 B.C.*) 2Ne.31:21

**James E. Talmage**

The Holy Ghost, called also Spirit, and Spirit of the Lord, Spirit of God, Comforter, and Spirit of Truth, is not tabernacled in a body of flesh and bones, but is a personage of spirit; yet we know that the Spirit has manifested Himself in the form of a man. (See 1Ne.11:11) ¶ . . . . That the Spirit of the Lord is capable of manifesting Himself in the form and figure of man, is indicated by the wonderful interview between the Spirit and Nephi, in which He revealed Himself to the prophet, questioned him concerning his desires and belief, instructed him in the things of God, speaking face to face with the man. "I spake unto him," says Nephi, "as a man speaketh; for I beheld that he was in the form of a man; yet nevertheless, I knew that it was the Spirit of the Lord; and he spake unto me as a man speaketh with another." (See 1Ne.11:11.) AF:38,144-45

**Joseph Smith**

Which Father, Son, and Holy Ghost are one God, infinite and eternal, without end. Amen. (*Revelation on Church Organization and Government, April 1830*) D&C 20:28

### John

For there are three that bear record in heaven, the Father, the Word, and the Holy Ghost: and these three are one. (*John writes to the churches in Asia*) 1Jn.5:7

---

**326. The Holy Ghost is a (male) personage of spirit, having a spirit body only, which is in the form of a man.**

#### Charles W. Penrose

The Holy Ghost is a personage of spirit, as Jesus was when he was Jehovah. . . . He [Jesus] was a personage of spirit, and he came here to the earth that he might be exactly like his brethren and like his Father, and have a body made of the lower elements of the universe. . . . ¶ . . . . But about the Holy Ghost, what about that? Why, he is a personage of spirit, an individual, a being, and he bears witness of the Father and of the Son and makes them plain to man. He is called by the Savior, the "Comforter." CR1921Apr:12-13

#### Charles W. Penrose

The Holy Ghost as "a personage of spirit," whom Jesus Christ said he would send from the Father, and who would not come unless Jesus went away (John 16:7) was not and is not a "being of tabernacle," but, without a body of flesh and bones, he represents both the Father and the Son and is one of the Godhead. (1Jn.5:7) CR1916Apr:22

#### Elder Joseph Fielding Smith

The Holy Ghost is the third member of the Godhead. He is a Spirit, in the form of a man. . . . The Holy Ghost is a personage of Spirit, and has a spirit body only. His mission is to bear witness of the Father and the Son and of all truth. ¶ As a spirit personage the Holy Ghost has size and dimensions. He does not fill the immensity of space, and cannot be everywhere present in person at the same time. He is also called the Holy Spirit, the Spirit of God, the Spirit of the Lord, the Spirit of Truth, and the Comforter. (Doctrines of Salvation, 1:38) DGSM:11

#### Joseph Smith

The Father has a body of flesh and bones as tangible as man's; the Son also; but the Holy Ghost has not a body of flesh and bones, but is a personage of Spirit. Were it not so, the Holy Ghost could not dwell in us. (*Revelation April 2, 1830*) D&C 130:22

#### Joseph Smith

The sign of the dove was instituted before the creation of the world, a witness for the Holy Ghost, and the devil cannot come in the sign of a dove. The Holy Ghost is a personage, and is in the form of a personage. It does not confine itself to the form of the dove, but in sign of the dove. The Holy Ghost cannot be transformed into a dove; but the sign of a dove was given to John to signify the truth of the deed, as the dove is an emblem or token of truth and innocence. (*Sunday meeting at Nauvoo Temple, Jan. 29, 1843*) DGSM:11; TPJS:276

---

**327. The Holy Ghost bears witness of the Father and the Son.**

#### George F. Richards

This is the office of the Holy Ghost, who is a personage of spirit, one of the trinity of the Godhead. It is his mission and office to bear witness of the Father and of the Son and of the truth of all things. "No man may know that Jesus is the Lord except by the Holy Ghost." CR1931Oct:100-01

#### Joseph Smith

As well as those who should come after, who should believe in the gifts and callings of God by the Holy Ghost, which beareth record of the Father and of the Son; (*Revelation April 1830; the Holy Ghost bears record of the Father and the Son*) D&C 20:27

#### Jesus, quoted by Mormon

And the Holy Ghost beareth record of the Father and me; and the Father giveth the Holy Ghost unto the children of men, because of me. (*The resurrected Jesus instructs his twelve Nephite disciples, A.D. 34*) 3Ne.28:11

#### Joseph Smith

"And then the angel spake, saying 'This thing is a similitude of the sacrifice of the Only Begotten of the Father, who is full of grace and truth. And thou shalt do all that thou doest in the name of the Son, and thou shalt repent and call upon God in the name of the Son for evermore.' And in that day the Holy Ghost fell upon Adam, which beareth record of the Father and the Son." ¶ 25. This last quotation, or summary, shows this important fact, that though our first parents were driven out of the garden of Eden, and were even separated from the presence of God by a vail, they still retained a knowledge of his existence, and that sufficiently to move them to call upon him. And further, that no sooner was the plan of redemption revealed to man, and he began to call upon God, than the Holy Spirit was given, bearing record of the Father and Son. (*Lectures on Faith delivered to the School of the Prophets, 1834-35*) LOF2:24-25

**Joseph Smith,**
*translating the Book of Moses*
And in that day the Holy Ghost fell upon Adam, which beareth record of the Father and the Son, saying: I am the Only Begotten of the Father from the beginning, henceforth and forever, that as thou hast fallen thou mayest be redeemed, and all mankind, even as many as will. (*The record of Moses: Adam receives the testimony of the Holy Ghost*) Moses 5:9

**Marion G. Romney**
One who receives the witness of the Holy Ghost has a sure knowledge that God lives; that he is our Father in heaven; that Jesus Christ is our Elder Brother in the spirit and the Only Begotten Son of the father in the flesh, our Savior and Redeemer. Such a one knows that the universal order in the heavens above, in the earth beneath, and in the waters under the earth, all give evidence that God lives; he knows that the testimonies of the prophets concerning the Father, Son and Holy Ghost are accurate and true. Secure in this knowledge, his life has purpose. ¶ The gospel of Jesus Christ becomes for him what Paul said it is, "The power of God unto salvation." (Rom.1:16) CR1967Oct:137

**Elder Joseph Fielding Smith**
The Holy Ghost is a personage of Spirit, and has a spirit body only. His mission is to bear witness of the Father and the Son and of all truth. (Doctrines of Salvation, 1:38) DGSM:11

**Related Witnesses:**
**James E. Talmage**
The Office of the Holy Ghost in His ministrations among men is described in scripture. He is a teacher sent from the Father; and unto those who are entitled to His tuition He will reveal all things necessary for the soul's advancement. Through the influences of the Holy Spirit the powers of the human mind may be quickened and increased, so that things past may be brought to remembrance. He will serve as a guide in things divine unto all who will obey Him, enlightening every man, in the measure of his humility and obedience; unfolding the mysteries of God, as the knowledge thus revealed may effect greater spiritual growth; conveying knowledge from God to man; sanctifying those who have been cleansed through obedience to the requirements of the Gospel; manifesting all things; and bearing witness unto men concerning the existence and infallibility of the Father and the Son. ¶ . . . . The power of the Holy Ghost then, is the spirit of prophecy and revela-

tion; His office is that of enlightenment of the mind, quickening of the intellect, and sanctification of the soul. AF:147

**Joseph Smith,**
*quoted by Elder Joseph Fielding Smith*
We believe that the Holy Ghost, and that holy men in these days speak by the same principle; we believe in its being a comforter and a witness bearer, that it brings things past to our remembrance, leads us into all truth, and shows us of things to come; we believe that "no man can know that Jesus is the Christ, but by the Holy Ghost." (Editorial in "Times and Seasons," June 1842) HC5:27; TPJS:243; TLDP:274

**Jesus,**
*quoted by John*
But when the Comforter is come, whom I will send unto you from the Father, even the Spirit of truth, which proceedeth from the Father, he shall testify of me: (*Jesus promises his disciples to send the Holy Ghost*) John 15:26

---

**328. The Holy Ghost acts as a comforter.**

**John A. Widtsoe**
The gift of the Holy Ghost confers upon a person the right to receive, as he may desire and need, the presence, light and intelligence of the Holy Ghost. It gives, as it were, an official claim upon the mighty assistance and comforting assurance of the Holy Ghost. When the servants of the Lord display a spiritual power beyond the command of man; when the grief-laden heart beats with joy; when failure is converted into victory, it is by the visitation of the Holy Ghost. (Man and the Dragon, pp. 150-51) TLDP:276-77

**Jesus,**
*quoted by John*
And I will pray the Father, and he shall give you another Comforter, that he may abide with you for ever; 17. Even the Spirit of truth; whom the world cannot receive, because it seeth him not, neither knoweth him: but ye know him; for he dwelleth with you, and shall be in you. . . . 26. But the Comforter, which is the Holy Ghost, whom the Father will send in my name, he shall teach you all things, and bring all things to your remembrance, whatsoever I have said unto you. (*Jesus comforts the Twelve in anticipation of his crucifixion*) John 14:16-17,26

**Jesus,**
*quoted by John*
But when the Comforter is come, whom I will send unto you from the Father, even the Spirit of truth, which proceedeth from the Father, he

shall testify of me: . . . (*Jesus promises his disciples to send the Holy Ghost*) John 15:26

**Recorded in Luke**

Then had the churches rest throughout all Judaea and Galilee and Samaria, and were edified; and walking in the fear of the Lord, and in the comfort of the Holy Ghost, were multiplied. Acts 9:31

**Joseph Smith**

[W]e believe that it [the gift of the Holy Ghost] is necessary to make and to organize the Priesthood, that no man can be called to fill any office in the ministry without it; we also believe in prophecy, in tongues, in visions, and in revelations, in gifts, and in healings; and that these things cannot be enjoyed without the gift of the Holy Ghost. We believe that the Holy Ghost, and that holy men in these days speak by the same principle; we believe in its being a comforter and a witness bearer, that it brings things past to our remembrance, leads us into all truth, and shows us of things to come; we believe that "no man can know that Jesus is the Christ, but by the Holy Ghost." (Editorial in "Times and Seasons," June 1842) HC5:27

**Joseph Smith,**
*receiving the Word of the Lord*

And this is my gospel—repentance and baptism by water, and then cometh the baptism of fire and the Holy Ghost, even the Comforter, which showeth all things, and teacheth the peaceable things of the kingdom. (*Revelation Jan. 5, 1831*) D&C 39:6

**Francis M. Lyman**

It is not possible for us to perform the labors that are required of us as Latter-day Saints—to preach the Gospel among the nations, to gather together the people, to build temples, and to perform in those temples the labors that are necessary for the salvation of the living and the dead—except we are aided by the Holy Ghost, the Comforter. It is not possible for men who stand at the head of this Church to direct, or to give counsel . . . to preside with dignity and in a manner pleasing to God, unless we enjoy the Holy Ghost. It is not possible for us as parents, to preside in our families, to set good examples before them, to set and keep our houses in order—as it is necessary they should be kept, that we may have salvation—unless we enjoy the Holy Ghost. It is not possible for us as individuals to be Saints, unless we enjoy the Holy Ghost. (*In Assembly Hall, Feb. 24, 1884, JD25:61*) TLDP:275

**Related Witnesses:**

**Joseph Smith,**
*receiving the Word of the Lord*

Go your way whithersoever I will, and it shall be given you by the Comforter what you shall do and whither you shall go. (*Revelation for Thomas B. Marsh who had been baptized earlier in the month, received Sept. 30, 1830*) D&C 31:11

**Mormon**

And the remission of sins bringeth meekness, and lowliness of heart; and because of meekness and lowliness of heart cometh the visitation of the Holy Ghost, which Comforter filleth with hope and perfect love. . . . (*Epistle of Mormon to his son Moroni, prior to A.D. 384*) Moro.8:26

**Elder Joseph Fielding Smith**

This Comforter is, by his influence, to be a constant companion to every baptized person, and to administer unto the members of the church by revelation and guidance, knowledge of the truth that they may walk in its light. (Answers to Gospel Questions, pp. 149-50) DGSM:12

---

**329. The Holy Ghost acts as a teacher and a revelator.**

**Joseph Smith,**
*receiving the Word of the Lord*

Yea, behold, I will tell you in your mind and in your heart, by the Holy Ghost, which shall come upon you and which shall dwell in your heart. 3. Now, behold, this is the spirit of revelation; behold, this is the spirit by which Moses brought the children of Israel through the Red Sea on dry ground. (*Revelation for Oliver Cowdery, April 1829*) D&C 8:2-3

**Moroni, son of Mormon**

And by the power of the Holy Ghost ye may know the truth of all things. (*Moroni's final writings, about A.D. 421*) Moro.10:5

**Jesus,**
*quoted by John*

But the Comforter, which is the Holy Ghost, whom the Father will send in my name, he shall teach you all things, and bring all things to your remembrance, whatsoever I have said unto you. (*Jesus promises his disciples to send the Holy Ghost*) John 14:26

**Jesus,**
*recorded in Luke*

And when they bring you unto the synagogues, and unto magistrates, and powers, take ye no thought how or what thing ye shall answer, or what ye shall say: 12. For the Holy Ghost shall teach you in the same hour what ye ought to say. (*Jesus teaches the multitude*) Luke 12:11-12

**Nephi, son of Lehi**

For behold, again I say unto you that if ye will enter in by the way, and receive the Holy Ghost, it will show unto you all things what ye should do. (*Nephi's writings, between 559-545 B.C.*) 2Ne.32:5

### Alma, the younger,
### quoted by Mormon

Behold, I say unto you they are made known unto me by the Holy Spirit of God. Behold, I have fasted and prayed many days that I might know these things of myself. And now I do know of myself that they are true; for the Lord God hath made them manifest unto me by his Holy Spirit; and this is the spirit of revelation which is in me. 47. And moreover, I say unto you that it has thus been revealed unto me, that the words which have been spoken by our fathers are true, even so according to the spirit of prophecy which is in me, which is also by the manifestation of the Spirit of God. (*Alma testifies to the people of the truth of the doctrine, about 83 B.C.*) Alma 5:46-47

### President Lorenzo Snow

There is a way by which persons can keep their consciences clear before God and man, and that is to preserve within them the spirit of God, which is the spirit of revelation to every man and woman. It will reveal to them, even in the simplest of matters, what they shall do, by making suggestions to them. We should try to learn the nature of this spirit, that we may understand its suggestions, and then we will always be able to do right. This is the grand privilege of every Latter-day Saint. We know that it is our right to have the manifestations of the spirit every day of our lives. . . . From the time we receive the Gospel, go down into the waters of baptism and have hands laid upon us afterwards for the gift of the Holy Ghost, we have a friend, if we do not drive it from us by doing wrong. That friend is the Holy Spirit, the Holy Ghost, which partakes of the things of God and shows them unto us. This is a grand means that the Lord has provided for us, that we may know the light, and not be groveling continually in the dark. CR1899Apr:52; DCSM:25

### President John Taylor

This same Comforter has been given, in connection with the Gospel in these days, for our enlightenment, for our instruction, for our guidance, that we may have a knowledge of things that are past, of the dealings of God with the human family, of the principles of truth that have been developed in the different ages, of the position of the world and its relationship to God in those different ages, of its position in years that are past and gone, and of its present status. It is also given for our enlightenment, that we may be enabled to conduct all things according to the mind and will of God, and in accordance with His eternal laws and those principles which exist in the heavens, and which have been provided by God for the salvation and exaltation of a fallen world; also for the manifestation of principles which have been and will be developed in the interest of man, not only pertaining to this world, but also to that which is to come; through which medium the Lord will make known His plans and designs to His Priesthood and His people in His own due time. (*In Logan Tabernacle in connection with dedication of Logan Temple, May 18, 1884, JD25:178-79*) TLDP:281

### Parley P. Pratt

The gift of the Holy Ghost . . . quickens all the intellectual faculties, increases, enlarges, expands, and purifies all the natural passions and affections, and adapts them, by the gift of wisdom, to their lawful use. It inspires, develops, cultivates, and matures all the fine-toned sympathies, joys, tastes, kindred feelings, and affections of our nature. It inspires virtue, kindness, goodness, tenderness, gentleness, and charity. . . . ¶ Such is the gift of the Holy Ghost, and such are its operations when received through the lawful channel—the divine, eternal priesthood. (Key to the Science of Theology, pp. 61-62) DGSM:45

**Related Witnesses:**

### John A. Widtsoe

The gift of the Holy Ghost confers upon a person the right to receive, as he may desire and need, the presence, light and intelligence of the Holy Ghost. It gives, as it were, an official claim upon the mighty assistance and comforting assurance of the Holy Ghost. When the servants of the Lord display a spiritual power beyond the command of man; when the grief-laden heart beats with joy; when failure is converted into victory, it is by the visitation of the Holy Ghost. It is the Spirit of God under the direction of the Holy Ghost that quickeneth all things. . . . ¶ Latter-day Saints have received, under the hands of those divinely empowered, this inexpressibly glorious "gift," which will lead them if they are fitted, into the companionship of the Holy Ghost, and win for them intelligence and power to win joy in life and exaltation in the world to come. Those who have been so blessed have not always understood the greatness of that which has been given them, or have not earnestly sought its help. So powerful a gift, with such boundless promise, justifies every attempt to cleanse body and soul. Certain it is, that only with the aid of the Holy Ghost shall we be able to rise to the heights of salvation of which we dream and for which we pray. (Man and the Dragon, pp. 150-51) TLDP:276-77

---

330. The manifestation of the Holy Ghost is more powerful and longer lasting than the visitation of an angel.

### Elder Joseph Fielding Smith

Christ is the second person in the Godhead. But Christ has himself declared that the manifestations we might have of the Spirit of Christ, or from a visitation of an angel, a tangible resurrected being, would not leave the impression and would not convince us and place within us that something which we cannot get away from which we receive through a manifestation of the Holy Ghost. [Luke 16:27-31; D&C 5:7] Personal visitations might become dim as time goes on, but this guidance of the Holy Ghost is renewed and continued, day after day, year after year, if we live to be worthy of it. (Doctrines of Salvation, 1:44) DCSM:33

### John A. Widtsoe

Without the help that we receive from the constant presence of the Holy Spirit, and from possible holy angels, the difficulties of life would be greatly multiplied. . . . In fact, the constant presence of the Holy Spirit would seem to make such a constant, angelic companionship unnecessary. (Gospel Interpretations, pp. 28-29) TLDP:26

### Elder Joseph Fielding Smith

The Spirit of God speaking to the spirit of man has power to impart truth with greater effect and understanding than the truth can be imparted by personal contact even with heavenly beings. Through the Holy Ghost the truth is woven into the very fibre and sinews of the body so that it cannot be forgotten. So positive and powerful are the teachings of the Spirit that when a man receives this knowledge and partakes of this power of God, which can only come after receiving the covenants and obligations belonging to the new and everlasting covenant, and he then turns away from this knowledge and these covenants, he sins knowingly. (Doctrines of Salvation, 1:47-48) TLDP:270

### Elder Wilford Woodruff

Now, if you have the Holy Ghost with you—and everyone ought to have—I can say unto you that there is no greater gift, there is no greater blessing, there is no greater testimony given to any man on earth. You may have the administration of angels; you may see many

miracles; you may see many wonders in the earth; but I claim that the gift of the Holy Ghost is the greatest gift that can be bestowed upon man. (Deseret Weekly, April 6, 1889, p. 451) TLDP:275

**Related Witnesses:**

### Joseph Smith,
*quoted by Elder Joseph Fielding Smith*

This first Comforter or Holy Ghost has no other effect than pure intelligence. It is more powerful in expanding the mind, enlightening the understanding, and sorting the intellect with present knowledge, of a man who is of the literal seed of Abraham, than one that is a Gentile, though it may not have half as much visible effect upon the body; for as the Holy Ghost falls upon one of the literal seed of Abraham, it is calm and serene; and his whole soul and body are only exercised by the pure spirit of intelligence; while the effect of the Holy Ghost upon a Gentile, is to purge out the old blood, and make him actually of the seed of Abraham. That man that has none of the blood of Abraham (naturally) must have a new creation by the Holy Ghost. In such a case, there may be more of a powerful effect upon the body, and visible to the eye, than upon an Israelite, while the Israelite at first might be far before the Gentile in pure intelligence. (*The Prophet gives instruction on various doctrines, June 27, 1839*) TPJS:149-50

### Jesus,
*recorded in Luke*

Then he said, I pray thee therefore, father, that thou wouldest send him to my father's house: 28. For I have five brethren; that he may testify unto them, lest they also come into this place of torment. 29. Abraham saith unto him, They have Moses and the prophets; let them hear them. 30. And he said, Nay, father Abraham: but if one went unto them from the dead, they will repent. 31. And he said unto him, If they hear not Moses and the prophets, neither will they be persuaded, though one rose from the dead. (*Jesus gives the parable of the rich man and Lazarus*) Luke 16:27-31

### Joseph Smith,
*receiving the Word of the Lord*

Behold, if they will not believe my words, they would not believe you, my servant Joseph, if it were possible that you should show them all these things which I have committed unto you. (*Revelation received at the request of Martin Harris, March 1829*) D&C 5:7

**Author's Note:** Angels visit but they do not stay. The Holy Ghost stays. In the 29th chapter of Alma, the prophet Alma desired that he might be an angel to preach to the world with angelic power and authority. ("O that I were an angel, and could have the wish of mine heart, that I might go forth and speak with the trump of God, with a voice to shake the earth, and cry repentance unto every people!") Alma then promptly repented of that wish, knowing that angelic preaching is not the Lord's pattern for teaching his children. The Lord's pattern is to reveal his truths to prophets; the prophets (not angels) testify to men. Following the testimony of the prophets the Holy Ghost confirms the truth to the hearts of the listeners. ¶ Angels visit but they do not stay. The Holy Ghost stays. It is a gift. Joseph Smith was taught by angelic visitation. Moroni came to him three times in one night—and a fourth time the next morning, but he did not stay. This principle is consistent throughout the history of the world. Even Adam and Eve received only brief visits from the Lord. None of the prophets after Adam— Enoch, Noah, Abraham, Isaac, Jacob, Joseph, Moses, Elijah, Jeremiah, Isaiah, Lehi, Nephi, Peter, Paul, Joseph Smith—enjoyed "in-house" heavenly guests who stayed a fortnight or more. These heavenly visitors come to prophets, deliver their messages and leave. Why? Why are they not available for long periods of time to give seemingly needed counsel and accurate advice? The role of an angel is to deliver his message and leave, leave to allow each person to work out his own salvation. Each man must do many things of his own free will. Strength comes from pondering, from working it out in your mind, even as Oliver Cowdery was instructed "But, behold, I say unto you, that you must study it out in your mind; then you must ask me if it be right, and if it is right I will cause that your bosom shall burn within you; therefore, you shall feel that it is right." (D&C 9:8) ¶ Our Heavenly Father wants us to become like him. To do so we must get the experience of arriving at decisions. All of us in our church callings should seek divine guidance. We should listen to the always available prompting of the Spirit, as we employ our God given minds and talents to magnify our callings. The divine principle of growth is the seemingly slow method of thinking and praying, of purifying ourselves to make of us the kind of person the Holy Ghost can inspire. Performing the duties of parenthood, of church callings, being faithful stewards while sanctifying our own spirits is the road to achievement and completeness. It is how we become God-like and perfect. Thus each of us must suffer a little, ago-

nize a little. We must listen to the Spirit as we fast and pray, as we ponder and seek guidance. We thereby develop personal characteristics that give us growth. We learn how to accept responsibility, how to magnify our callings—to make our calling and election sure.

---

331. **The Holy Ghost must finally seal (ratify, approve, justify) every ordinance, blessing, and performance of the gospel, before those acts become binding on earth and in heaven.**

**Elder Joseph Fielding Smith**
The Holy Spirit of Promise is the Holy Ghost who places the stamp of approval upon every ordinance: baptism, confirmation, ordination, marriage. The promise is that the blessings will be received through faithfulness. ¶ If a person violates a covenant, whether it be of baptism, ordination, marriage or anything else, the Spirit withdraws the stamp of approval, and the blessings will not be received. ¶ Every ordinance is sealed with a promise of a reward based upon faithfulness. The Holy Spirit withdraws the stamp of approval where covenants are broken. (Doctrines of Salvation, 1:45) DGSM:12

**Elder Joseph Fielding Smith**
I will make an explanation of the expression, "Sealed by the Holy Spirit of Promise." This does not have reference to marriage for time and all eternity only, but to every ordinance and blessing of the gospel. Baptism into the Church is sealed by this Spirit, likewise confirmation, ordination, and all ordinances as well as marriage for time and all eternity. ¶ The meaning of this expression is this: Every covenant, contract, bond, obligation, oath, vow, and performance, that man receives through the covenants and blessings of the gospel, is sealed by the Holy Spirit with a promise. The promise is that the blessing will be obtained, if those who seek it are true and faithful to the end. If they are not faithful, then the Holy Spirit will withdraw the blessing and the promise comes to an end. (Doctrines of Salvation, 2:94-95) TLDP:286-87

**Melvin J. Ballard**
A man and woman may by fraud and deception obtain admittance to the house of the Lord and may receive the pronouncement of the Holy Priesthood, giving to them, so far as lies in their power, these blessings. We may deceive men, but we cannot deceive the Holy Ghost, and our blessings will not be eternal unless they are also sealed by the Holy Spirit of Promise, the Holy

Ghost, one who reads the thoughts and hearts of men and gives his sealing approval to the blessings pronounced upon their heads. Then it is binding, efficacious, and of full force. (Sermons and Missionary Services of Melvin J. Ballard, pp. 236-37) TLDP:286

### Bruce R. McConkie

Men are justified in what they do when their deeds conform to divine standards. Righteous acts are approved of the Lord; they are ratified by the Holy Ghost; they are sealed by the Holy Spirit of Promise; or, in other words, they are justified by the Spirit. Such divine approval must be given to "all covenants, contracts, bonds, obligation, oaths, vows, performances, connections, associations, or expectations"—that is, to all things—if they are to have "efficacy, virtue, or force in and after the resurrection from the dead." (D&C 132:7) Such a requirement is part of the terms and conditions of the gospel covenant. (The Promised Messiah, p. 344) TLDP:284

### Joseph Smith,
*receiving the Word of the Lord*

And verily I say unto you, that the conditions of this law are these: All covenants, contracts, bonds, obligations, oaths, vows, performances, connections, associations, or expectations, that are not made and entered into and sealed by the Holy Spirit of promise, of him who is anointed, both as well for time and for all eternity, and that too most holy, by revelation and commandment through the medium of mine anointed, whom I have appointed on the earth to hold this power (and I have appointed unto my servant Joseph to hold this power in the last days, and there is never but one on the earth at a time on whom this power and the keys of this priesthood are conferred), are of no efficacy, virtue, or force in and after the resurrection from the dead; for all contracts that are not made unto this end have an end when men are dead. . . . 19. And again, verily I say unto you, if a man marry a wife by my word, which is my law, and by the new and everlasting covenant, and it is sealed unto them by the Holy Spirit of promise, by him who is anointed, unto whom I have appointed this power and the keys of this priesthood; and it shall be said unto them—Ye shall come forth in the first resurrection; and if it be after the first resurrection, in the next resurrection; and shall inherit thrones, kingdoms, principalities, and powers, dominions, all heights and depths—then shall it be written in the Lamb's Book of Life, that he shall commit no murder whereby to shed innocent blood, and if ye abide in my covenant, and commit no mur-

der whereby to shed innocent blood, it shall be done unto them in all things whatsoever my servant hath put upon them, in time, and through all eternity; and shall be of full force when they are out of the world; and they shall pass by the angels, and the gods, which are set there, to their exaltation and glory in all things, as hath been sealed upon their heads, which glory shall be a fulness and a continuation of the seeds forever and ever. (*Revelation relating to the new and everlasting covenant, including the eternal nature of the marriage covenant, July 12, 1843, [1831]*) D&C 132:7,19

### Elder Harold B. Lee,
*also quoting Joseph Smith*

I want to comment about this one statement: "by the Spirit ye are justified." Now I've struggled with that statement, and I have found a definition that seems to indicate to me what I'm sure the Lord intended to convey. The definition that I think is significant says: "Justify means to pronounce free from guilt or blame, or to absolve." Now if the Spirit, the Holy Ghost, is to pronounce one free from guilt or blame, or to absolve, then we begin to see something of the office of the Holy Ghost that relates to the subject about which we are talking: what it means to be born of the Spirit. ¶ I shall inject here another phrase that is oft discussed (and I think is misunderstood) and to which we try to attach some mysteries. This phrase, where the Lord directs that all of these things are to be eternal, is: "must be sealed by the Holy Spirit of promise." Let me refer first to the 76th section of the Doctrine and Covenants. Speaking of those who are candidates for celestial glory, the Lord says: ¶ "They are they who received the testimony of Jesus, and believed on his name and were baptized after the manner of his burial . . . That by keeping the commandments they might be washed and cleansed from all their sins, and receive the Holy Spirit by the laying on of the hands . . . And who overcome by faith, and are sealed by the Holy Spirit of Promise, which the Father sheds forth upon all those who are just and true." (D&C 76:51-53) ¶ In other words, baptism is only efficacious, and the initiatory ordinance is applicable, when it is sealed by the Holy Spirit of Promise. We have that same phrase repeated in section 132, verse 19, for the Lord is speaking now of celestial marriage. ¶ ". . . [I]f a man marry a wife by my word . . . and it is sealed unto them by the Holy Spirit of Promise . . . they shall pass by the angels, and the gods, which are set there, to their exaltation and glory in all things. . . ." ¶ And with reference to the priesthood, when the

Lord discusses in the 84th section the oath and covenant, exactly the same principle is implied. By the laying on of hands we get the promise of power and authority, but it will not be ours—worlds without end—unless we keep our part of the covenant. (*To seminary and institute teachers, June 1962*) (Stand Ye in Holy Places, pp. 51-52) TLDP:332-33

**Related Witnesses:**

**Joseph Smith**

And who overcome by faith, and are sealed by the Holy Spirit of promise, which the Father sheds forth upon all those who are just and true. (*Vision to Joseph Smith and Sidney Rigdon, Feb. 16, 1832*) D&C 76:53

**Paul**

In whom ye also trusted, after that ye heard the word of truth, the gospel of your salvation: in whom also after that ye believed, ye were sealed with that holy Spirit of promise, 14. Which is the earnest of our inheritance until the redemption of the purchased possession, unto the praise of his glory. (*Letter to the Saints at Ephesus in Asia Minor, about A.D. 62*) Eph.1:13-14

---

**332.** The Holy Ghost brings to a person's remembrance those truths that have been learned earlier.

**Jesus,**
*quoted by John*

But the Comforter, which is the Holy Ghost, whom the Father will send in my name, he shall teach you all things, and bring all things to your remembrance, whatsoever I have said unto you. (*Jesus, anticipating his crucifixion, promises his disciples the Holy Ghost in his stead*) John 14:26

**Elder Spencer W. Kimball**

The Holy Ghost is a revelator. . . . ¶ He is a reminder and will bring to our remembrance the things which we have learned and which we need in the time thereof. He is an inspirer and will put words in our mouths, enlighten our understandings and direct our thoughts. (The Teachings of Spencer W. Kimball, p. 23) DGSM:12

**President Brigham Young,**
*quoted by John A. Widtsoe*

The Holy Ghost reveals unto you things past, present, and to come; it makes your minds quick and vivid to understand the handiwork of the Lord. Your joy is made full in beholding the footsteps of our Father going forth among the inhabitants of the earth; this is invisible to the world, but it is made visible to the Saints, and they behold the Lord in his providences, bringing forth the work of the last days. (*In Bowery, Aug. 17, 1856, JD4:22*) DBY:161

**James E. Talmage**

Through the influences of the Holy Spirit the powers of the human mind may be quickened and increased, so that things past may be brought to remembrance. ¶ . . . . The power of the Holy Ghost then, is the spirit of prophecy and revelation; His office is that of enlightenment of the mind, quickening of the intellect, and sanctification of the soul. AF:147

**President Joseph F. Smith**

The office of the Holy Ghost is to bear record of Christ, or to testify of him, and confirm the believer in the truth, by bringing to his recollection things that have passed, and showing or revealing to the mind things present and to come. "But the Comforter, which is the Holy Ghost, whom the Father will send in my name, he shall teach you all things, and bring all things to your remembrance, whatsoever I have said unto you." "He will guide you into all truth." Thus, without the aid of the Holy Ghost no man can know the will of God, or that Jesus is the Christ—the Redeemer of the world, or that the course he pursues, the work he performs, or his faith, are acceptable to God, and such as will secure to him the gift of eternal life, the greatest of all gifts. (John 14:26; 16:13) (Gospel Doctrine, p. 101) TLDP:273

---

**333.** The Holy Ghost enables a person to discern between good and evil spirits.

**President Brigham Young**

People are liable in many ways to be led astray by the power of the adversary, for they do not fully understand that it is a hard matter for them to always distinguish the things of God from the things of the devil. There is but one way by which they can know the difference, and that is by the light of the spirit of revelation, even the spirit of our Lord Jesus Christ. . . . ¶ Consequently, it becomes us, as Saints, to cleave to the Lord with all our hearts and seek unto Him until we do enjoy the light of His Spirit, that we may discern between the righteous and the wicked, and understand the difference between false spirits and true. (*In Bowery, Oct. 6, 1855, JD3:43-44*) TLDP:232

**Joseph Smith**

"[N]o man knows the things of God, but by the Spirit of God," so no man knows the spirit of the devil, and his power and influence, but by possessing intelligence which is more than human, and having unfolded through the medium of the Priesthood the mysterious operations of his devices; without knowing the angelic form, the sanctified look and gesture, and the zeal that is frequently manifested by him for the glory of God, together with the prophetic spirit, the gracious influence, the godly appearance, and the holy garb, which are so characteristic of his proceedings and his mysterious windings. ¶ A man must have the discerning of spirits before he can drag into daylight this hellish influence and unfold it unto the world in all its soul-destroying, diabolical, and horrid colors; for nothing is a greater injury to the children of men than to be under the influence of a false spirit when they think they have the Spirit of God. . . . ¶ As we have noticed before, the great difficulty lies in the ignorance of the nature of spirits, of the laws by which they are governed, and the signs by which they may be known; if it requires the Spirit of God to know the things of God; and the spirit of the devil can only be unmasked through that medium, then it follows as a natural consequence that unless some person or persons have a communication, or revelation from God, unfolding to them the operation of the spirit, they must eternally remain ignorant of these principles; for I contend that if one man cannot understand these things but by the Spirit of God, ten thousand men cannot; it is alike out of the reach of the wisdom of the learned, the tongue of the eloquent, the power of the mighty. And we shall at last have to come to this conclusion, whatever we may think of revelation, that without it we can neither know nor understand anything of God, or the devil; (Editorial in the Times & Seasons, April 1, 1842) HC4:573-74

### George Q. Cannon

It requires the utmost care upon the part of the people who have received the Spirit of the Lord by the laying on of hands to distinguish between the voice of that Spirit and the voice of their own hearts or other spirits which may take possession of them. Experience and watchfulness will enable the Saint to recognize the voice of the Holy Spirit. ¶ It is a still, small voice in the hearts of the children of men. It is not boisterous, loud or aggressive, and if those who receive it carefully watch its suggestions, it will develop more and more within them, and it will become an unfailing source of revelation. But the necessity always remains of exercising care in distinguishing its voice from the voice of other influences in the heart. (Gospel Truth, 1:182) TLDP:285

### Joseph Smith

And again, to some it is given by the Holy Ghost to know the differences of administration, as it will be pleasing unto the same Lord, according as the Lord will, suiting his mercies according to the conditions of the children of men. 16. And again, it is given by the Holy Ghost to some to know the diversities of operations, whether they be of God, that the manifestations of the Spirit may be given to every man to profit withal. 23. And to others the discerning of spirits. (Revelation relative to governing and conducting meetings, March 8, 1831) D&C 46:15-16,23

### Joseph Smith

A man must have the discerning of spirits . . . and how is he to obtain this gift if there are no gifts of the Spirit? And how can these gifts be obtained without revelation? (Editorial in the Times & Seasons, April 1, 1842) HC4:574

**Related Witnesses:**

#### President Brigham Young, quoted by John A. Widtsoe

An individual who holds a share in the Priesthood, and continues faithful to his calling, who delights himself continually in doing the things God requires at his hands, and continues through life in the performance of every duty will secure to himself not only the privilege of receiving, but the knowledge how to receive the things of God, that he may know the mind of God continually; and he will be enabled to discern between right and wrong, between the things of God and the things that are not of God. And the Priesthood—the Spirit that is within him, will continue to increase until it becomes like a fountain of living water; until it is like the tree of life; until it is one continued source of intelligence and instruction to that individual. (In Tabernacle, Jan. 27, 1856, JD3:192) DBY:132

#### Alma, the younger, quoted by Mormon

Now Zeezrom, seeing that thou hast been taken in thy lying and craftiness, for thou hast not lied unto men only but thou hast lied unto God; for behold, he knows all thy thoughts, and thou seest that thy thoughts are made known unto us by his Spirit; (Alma contends with Zeezrom, about 82 B.C.) Alma 12:3

#### Ammon, son of Mosiah, quoted by Mormon

And it came to pass that Ammon, being filled with the Spirit of God, therefore he perceived the thoughts of the king. And he said unto him: Is it because thou hast heard that I defended thy servants and thy flocks, and slew seven of their brethren with the sling and with the sword, and smote off the arms of others, in order to defend thy flocks and thy servants; behold, is it this that causeth thy marvelings? 17. I say unto you, what is it, that thy marvelings are so great? Behold, I am a man, and am thy servant; therefore, whatsoever thou desirest which is right, that will I do. 18. Now when the king had heard these words, he marveled again, for he beheld that Ammon could discern his thoughts; but notwithstanding this, king Lamoni did open his mouth, and said unto him: Who art thou? Art thou that Great Spirit, who knows all things? (*King Lamoni is speechless in Ammon's presence, about 90 B.C.*) Alma 18:16-18

### Jacob, brother of Nephi

But behold, hearken ye unto me, and know that by the help of the all-powerful Creator of heaven and earth I can tell you concerning your thoughts, how that ye are beginning to labor in sin, which sin appeareth very abominable unto me, yea, and abominable unto God. (*Jacob teaches the Nephites in the temple, 544-421 B.C.*) Jacob 2:5

### Amulek,
#### quoted by Mormon

Now they knew not that Amulek could know of their designs. But it came to pass as they began to question him, he perceived their thoughts, and he said unto them: O ye wicked and perverse generation, ye lawyers and hypocrites, for ye are laying the foundation of the devil; for ye are laying traps and snares to catch the holy ones of God. (*Amulek answers the lawyers and the people in Ammonihah, about 82 B.C.*) Alma 10:17

### Stephen L. Richards,
#### also quoting Paul and Joseph Smith

. . . I believe [the gifts of the Gospel] have spiritual foundation. This conclusion seems to be borne out by the scriptures. The Apostle Paul tells his brethren: ¶ "Now there are diversities of gifts, but the same Spirit. . . ." ¶ Modern revelation emphasizes this diversity: ¶ "To some it is given by the Holy Ghost to know that Jesus Christ is the Son of God. . . . " ¶ "To others it is given to believe on their words." (D&C 46:13-14) ¶ The gift of discernment is essential to the leadership of the Church. I never ordain a bishop or set apart a president of a stake without invoking upon him this divine blessing, that he may read the lives and hearts of his people and call forth the best within them. The gift and power of discernment in this world of contention between the forces of good and the power of evil is essential equipment for every son and daughter of God. There could be no such mass dissensions as endanger the security of the world, if its

populations possessed this great gift in larger degree. . . . ¶ Every member in the restored Church of Christ could have this gift if he willed to do so. He could not be deceived with the sophistries of the world. He could not be led astray by pseudo-prophets and subversive cults. Even the inexperienced would recognize false teachings, in a measure at least. With this gift they would be able to detect something of the disloyal, rebellious, and sinister influences which not infrequently prompt those who seemingly take pride in the destruction of youthful faith and loyalties. Discerning parents will do well to guard their children against such influences and such personalities and teachings before irreparable damage is done. The true gift of discernment is often premonitory. A sense of danger should be heeded to be of value. We give thanks for a set of providential circumstances which avert an accident. We ought to be grateful every day of our lives for this sense which keeps alive a conscience which constantly alerts us to the dangers inherent in wrongdoers and sin. CR1950Apr:163

### Abraham O. Woodruff

The Bishop has a right to the gift of discernment, whereby he may tell whether these spirits are of God or not, and if they are not they should not have place in the congregations of the Saints. CR1901Apr:12

### Paul

To another the working of miracles; to another prophecy; to another discerning of spirits; to another divers kinds of tongues; to another the interpretation of tongues: (*Paul writes to the Church at Corinth, Greece, about A.D. 55*) 1Cor.12:10

---

334. **When a person speaks by the power of the Holy Ghost, the Holy Ghost will carry the message to the hearts of those who hear by that same Spirit.**

### Joseph Smith,
#### receiving the Word of the Lord

Therefore, why is it that ye cannot understand and know, that he that receiveth the word by the Spirit of truth receiveth it as it is preached by the Spirit of truth? 22. Wherefore, he that preacheth and he that receiveth, understand one another, and both are edified and rejoice together. (*Revelation for the elders of the Church, May 1831*) D&C 50:21-22

### J. Reuben Clark, Jr.

How shall we know when the things they have

spoken were said as they were "moved upon by the Holy Ghost?" I have given some thought to the question, and the answer thereto so far as I can determine, is: We can tell when the speakers are "moved upon by the Holy Ghost" only when we, ourselves, are "moved upon by the Holy Ghost." In a way, this completely shifts the responsibility from them to us to determine when they so speak. (*"When Are the Writings or Sermons of Church Leaders Entitled to the Claim of Scripture?" An address delivered to seminary and institute of religion personnel, July 7, 1954*) DCSM:144

### President Brigham Young, quoted by John A. Widtsoe

The preacher needs the power of the Holy Ghost to deal out to each heart a word in due season, and the hearers need the Holy Ghost to bring forth the fruits of the preached word of God to his glory. (*In Bowery, Sept. 16, 1860, JD8:167*) DBY:333

### Moroni, son of Mormon

And when ye shall receive these things, I would exhort you that ye would ask God, the Eternal Father, in the name of Christ, if these things are not true; and if ye shall ask with a sincere heart, with real intent, having faith in Christ, he will manifest the truth of it unto you, by the power of the Holy Ghost. 5. And by the power of the Holy Ghost ye may know the truth of all things. (*The final writings of Moroni, about A.D. 421*) Moro.10:4-5

### Nephi, son of Lehi

[F]or when a man speaketh by the power of the Holy Ghost the power of the Holy Ghost carrieth it unto the hearts of the children of men. (*Nephi's writings, between 559-545 B.C.*) 2Ne.33:1

### Elder Ezra Taft Benson

It takes revelation to perceive revelation. CR1985Oct:47

### Related Witnesses:
### Recorded in Luke

While Peter yet spake these words, the Holy Ghost fell on all them which heard the word. 45. And they of the circumcision which believed were astonished, as many as came with Peter, because that on the Gentiles also was poured out the gift of the Holy Ghost. 46. For they heard them speak with tongues, and magnify God. Then answered Peter, 47. Can any man forbid water, that these should not be baptized, which have received the Holy Ghost as well as we? (*After Peter received a vision teaching him to take the gospel to the Gentiles, he preached to Jew and Gentile about Christ*) Acts 10:44-47

### President Brigham Young

What is it that convinces man? It is the influence of the Almighty, enlightening his mind, giving instruction to the understanding. When that inhabits the body, that which comes from the regions of glory is enlightened by the influence, power, and Spirit of the Father of light, it swallows up the organization which pertains to this world. Those who are governed by this influence lose sight of all things pertaining to mortality; they are wholly influenced by the power of eternity, and lose sight of time. All the honor, wisdom, strength, and whatsoever is considered desirable among men, yea, all that pertains to this organization, which is in any way independent of that which came from the Father of our spirits, is obliterated to them and they hear and understand by the same power and spirit that clothe the Deity, and the holy beings in His presence. Anything besides that influence will fail to convince any person of the truth of the gospel of salvation. This is the reason why I love to hear men testify to the various operations of the Holy Spirit upon them—it is at once interesting and instructive. When a subject is treated upon with all the calculation, method, tact, and cunning of men, with the effusions of worldly eloquence, before a congregation endowed with the power of the Holy Ghost, and filled with the light of eternity, they can understand the subject, trace its bearings, place all its parts where they belong, and dispose of it according to the unalterable laws of truth. ("Statement from Brigham Young concerning the Holy Ghost," IE1947Jan:5, see JD1:90) TLDP:279-80

### Joseph Smith, quoted by Elder Joseph Fielding Smith

This is good doctrine. It tastes good. I can taste the principles of eternal life, and so can you. They are given to me by the revelations of Jesus Christ; and I know that when I tell you these words of eternal life as they are given to me, you taste them, and I know that you believe them. You say honey is sweet, and so do I. I can also taste the spirit of eternal life. I know that it is good; and when I tell you of these things which were given me by inspiration of the Holy Spirit, you are bound to receive them as sweet, and rejoice more and more. (*To the Church in general conference—to a congregation of 20,000—, "King Follett Sermon" April 7, 1844*) (See HC6:302-317, also see The Words of Joseph Smith, pp. 340-62.) HC6:312; TPJS:354

### Orson F. Whitney

It is all-important that we should possess that Spirit, whether we preach or sing or pray.

Prayers unprompted by it do not ascend to Heaven; sermons uninspired by it fail to touch the heart of the hearer; and the songs that are sung in our worshiping assemblies, if not in tune with it, are but discords in the ear of Deity. CR1931Apr:61

---

335. Through faith and by the power of the Holy Ghost, we may know the truth of all things.

### Moroni, son of Mormon

Behold, I would exhort you that when ye shall read these things, if it be wisdom in God that ye should read them, that ye would remember how merciful the Lord hath been unto the children of men, from the creation of Adam even down unto the time that ye shall receive these things, and ponder it in your hearts. 4. And when ye shall receive these things, I would exhort you that ye would ask God, the Eternal Father, in the name of Christ, if these things are not true; and if ye shall ask with a sincere heart, with real intent, having faith in Christ, he will manifest the truth of it unto you, by the power of the Holy Ghost. 5. And by the power of the Holy Ghost ye may know the truth of all things. (*Moroni's final writings, about A.D. 421*) Moro.10:3-5

### President Brigham Young, quoted by John A. Widtsoe

Our faith is concentrated in the Son of God, and through him in the Father; and the Holy Ghost is their minister to bring truths to our remembrance, to reveal new truths to us, and teach, guide, and direct the course of every mind, until we become perfected and prepared to go home, where we can see and converse with our Father in Heaven. (*In Tabernacle, Nov. 29, 1857, JD6:98*) DBY:26

### Joseph Smith, receiving the Word of the Lord

Oliver Cowdery, verily, verily, I say unto you, that assuredly as the Lord liveth, who is your God and your Redeemer, even so surely shall you receive a knowledge of whatsoever things you shall ask in faith, with an honest heart, believing that you shall receive a knowledge concerning the engravings of old records, which are ancient, which contain those parts of my scripture of which has been spoken by the manifestation of my Spirit. 2. Yea, behold, I will tell you in your mind and in your heart, by the Holy Ghost, which shall come upon you and which shall dwell in your heart. 3. Now, behold, this is the spirit of revelation; behold,

this is the spirit by which Moses brought the children of Israel through the Red Sea on dry ground. (*Revelation for Oliver Cowdery, April 1829*) D&C 8:1-3

### Joseph Smith, receiving the Word of the Lord

And now, verily, verily, I say unto thee, put your trust in that Spirit which leadeth to do good—yea, to do justly, to walk humbly, to judge righteously; and this is my Spirit. 13. Verily, verily, I say unto you, I will impart unto you of my Spirit, which shall enlighten your mind, which shall fill your soul with joy; 14. And then shall ye know, or by this shall you know, all things whatsoever you desire of me, which are pertaining unto things of righteousness, in faith believing in me that you shall receive. (*Revelation for Hyrum Smith, May 1829*) D&C 11:12-14

### Bruce R. McConkie

True it is that honest truth seekers come to know the truth and divinity of the Lord's work by the power of the Holy Ghost: they receive a flash of revelation telling them that Jesus is the Lord, that Joseph Smith is his prophet, that the Book of Mormon is the mind and will and voice of the Lord, that the Church of Jesus Christ of Latter-day Saints is the only true and living Church upon the whole earth. They gain a testimony before baptism. But it is only after they pledge their all in the cause of Christ that they receive the gift of the Holy Ghost, which is the heavenly endowment of which Jesus spoke. Then they receive a fulfillment of the promise: "by the power of the Holy Ghost ye may know the truth of all things." (Moro.10:5) Then they receive the "spirit of revelation," and the Lord tells them in their heart and in their mind whatsoever he will. (D&C 8:1-3) (The Millennial Messiah, pp. 98-99) DGSM:45

### Nephi, son of Lehi

And it came to pass after I, Nephi, having heard all the words of my father, concerning the things which he saw in a vision, and also the things which he spake by the power of the Holy Ghost, which power he received by faith on the Son of God—and the Son of God was the Messiah who should come—I, Nephi, was desirous also that I might see, and hear, and know of these things, by the power of the Holy Ghost, which is the gift of God unto all those who diligently seek him, as well in times of old as in the time that he should manifest himself unto the children of men. 18. For he is the same yesterday, to-day, and forever; and the way is prepared for all men from the foundation of the world, if it so be that they repent and come unto him. 19. For he that diligently seeketh shall find; and the mysteries of God shall be unfolded unto them, by the power of the Holy Ghost, as well in these times as in times of old, and as well in times of old as in times to come; wherefore, the course of the Lord is one eternal round. (*Nephi's writings, 600-592 B.C.*) 1Ne.10:17-19

### Elder Joseph Fielding Smith

Every man can receive manifestation of the Holy Ghost, even when he is out of the Church, if he is earnestly seeking for the light and for the truth. The Holy Ghost will come and give the man the testimony he is seeking, and then withdraw; and the man does not have claim upon another visit or constant visits and manifestations from him. He may have the constant guidance of that other Spirit, the Spirit of Christ. Every man may receive such a manifestation from the Holy Ghost when he is seeking for the truth, but not the power to call upon the Holy Ghost whenever he feels he needs the help, as a man does who is a member of the Church. (Doctrines of Salvation, 1:42) TLDP:279

### Elder Joseph Fielding Smith

The Lord will grant to any honest person who earnestly seeks to know the truth *one* manifestation by the Holy Ghost; but he is not entitled to repeated manifestations. After such a revelation is given, he is to act, for the Holy Ghost cannot be appealed to for continued manifestations until after baptism and the gift has been bestowed. (Answers to Gospel Questions, 4:89) TLDP:279

### Related Witnesses:
#### Joseph Smith,
*translating the Book of Moses*
And he also said unto him: If thou wilt turn unto me, and hearken unto my voice, and believe, and repent of all thy transgressions, and be baptized, even in water, in the name of mine Only Begotten Son, who is full of grace and truth, which is Jesus Christ, the only name which shall be given under heaven, whereby salvation shall come unto the children of men, ye shall receive the gift of the Holy Ghost, asking all things in his name, and whatsoever ye shall ask, it shall be given you. (*The record of Moses: Enoch recounts God speaking to Adam*) Moses 6:52

---

**336. Those who blaspheme against the Holy Ghost will not be forgiven.**

#### Joseph Smith

[O]ur Savior says, that all manner of sin and blasphemy shall be forgiven men wherewith they shall blaspheme; but the blasphemy against the Holy Ghost shall not be forgiven, neither in this world, nor in the world to come, evidently showing that there are sins which may be forgiven in the world to come, although the sin of blasphemy [against the Holy Ghost] cannot be forgiven. (*Editorial in Times and Seasons, April 15, 1842*) HC4:596

#### Jesus,
*recorded in Matthew*
Wherefore I say unto you, All manner of sin and blasphemy shall be forgiven unto men: but the blasphemy against the Holy Ghost shall not be forgiven unto men. 32. And whosoever speaketh a word against the Son of man, it shall be forgiven him: but whosoever speaketh against the Holy Ghost, it shall not be forgiven him, neither in this world, neither in the world to come. (*Jesus speaks to the people about blasphemy against the Holy Ghost*) Matt.12:31-32

#### Jesus,
*recorded in Mark*
Verily I say unto you, All sins shall be forgiven unto the sons of men, and blasphemies wherewith soever they shall blaspheme: 29. But he that shall blaspheme against the Holy Ghost hath never forgiveness, but is in danger of eternal damnation: 30. Because they said, He hath an unclean spirit. (*Jesus teaches about blasphemy against the Holy Ghost*) Mark 3:28-30

#### Jesus,
*recorded in Luke*
And whosoever shall speak a word against the Son of man, it shall be forgiven him: but unto him that blasphemeth against the Holy Ghost it shall not be forgiven. (*Jesus teaches the multitude*) Luke 12:10

#### Elder Joseph Fielding Smith
This is the real hell [a place where those who cannot be redeemed and who are called sons of perdition will go into outer darkness] where those who once knew the truth and had the testimony of it and then turned away and blasphemed the name of Jesus Christ, will go. These are they who have sinned against the Holy Ghost. For them there is no forgiveness, and the Lord said he had prepared a place for them. (Answers to Gospel Questions, 2:208-10) TLDP:127

#### Related Witnesses:
##### Recorded in Leviticus
And he that blasphemeth the name of the LORD, he shall surely be put to death, and all the congregation shall certainly stone him: as

well the stranger, as he that is born in the land, when he blasphemeth the name of the LORD, shall be put to death. (*Revelation to Moses for the children of Israel*) Lev.24:16

**Author's Note:** The Bible dictionary defines *blasphemy* as follows: "Generally denotes contemptuous speech concerning God, or concerning something that stands in a sacred relation toward God, such as his temple, his law, or his prophet." (Bible Dictionary, p. 625)

---

**337. The Spirit of Christ gives light to every person who comes into the world.**

**Joseph Smith**
For the word of the Lord is truth, and whatsoever is truth is light, and whatsoever is light is Spirit, even the Spirit of Jesus Christ. 46. And the Spirit giveth light to every man that cometh into the world; and the Spirit enlighteneth every man through the world, that hearkeneth to the voice of the Spirit. (*Revelation on priesthood received with six elders, Sept. 22/23, 1832*) D&C 84:45-46

**Bruce R. McConkie**
Our understanding of the Light of Christ is limited. Finite powers and capacities cannot comprehend that which is infinite. But we do know certain basic principles. . . . ¶ . . . . That it enlightens the mind and quickens the understanding of every person born into the world (all have a conscience!). . . . ¶ . . . . That it strives with all men (the Holy Ghost testifies but does not strive) unless and until they rebel against light and truth, at which time the striving ceases, and in that sense the Spirit is withdrawn; ¶ . . . . That those who hearken to its voice come unto Christ, receive his gospel, are baptized, and gain the gift of the Holy Ghost. (The Promised Messiah, pp. 208-09) DGSM:44

**President Harold B. Lee**
In determining that which is right in the sight of God let us consider this question of your conscience that we talk so much about. The scriptures speak of an influence to be found throughout the universe that gives life and light to all things, which is called variously the Light of Truth, the Light of Christ, or the Spirit of God. "That (is) the true Light that lighteth every man that cometh into the world." (John 19) It is that which "enlighteneth your eyes. . . . and quickeneth your understandings." (D&C 88:11) Every one of you born into this world enjoys the blessing of this Light that shall never cease to strive

with you until you are led to that further light from the gift of the Holy Ghost that may be received only upon condition of repentance and baptism into the Kingdom of God. (Decisions for Successful Living, p. 144) DGSM:44

**John**
That was the true Light, which lighteth every man that cometh into the world. (*The record of the Apostle John, testifying of the Savior*) John 1:9

**Joseph Smith,**
*receiving the Word of the Lord*
And that I am the true light that lighteth every man that cometh into the world; (*Revelation received at Kirtland, Ohio, May 6, 1833*) D&C 93:2

**Joseph Smith**
He that ascended up on high, as also he descended below all things, in that he comprehended all things, that he might be in all and through all things, the light of truth; 7. Which truth shineth. This is the light of Christ. As also he is in the sun, and the light of the sun, and the power thereof by which it was made. 8. As also he is in the moon, and is the light of the moon, and the power thereof by which it was made; 9. As also the light of the stars, and the power thereof by which they were made; 10. And the earth also, and the power thereof, even the earth upon which you stand. 11. And the light which shineth, which giveth you light, is through him who enlighteneth your eyes, which is the same light that quickeneth your understandings; 12. Which light proceedeth forth from the presence of God to fill the immensity of space— 13. The light which is in all things, which giveth life to all things, which is the law by which all things are governed, even the power of God who sitteth upon his throne, who is in the bosom of eternity, who is in the midst of all things. (*Revelation, Feb. 27, 1833*) D&C 88:6-13

**Elder Joseph Fielding Smith**
We very frequently quote from one of the revelations the words of the Lord to this effect, that "The glory of God is intelligence," and I wonder if we ourselves really comprehend what it means. We stop in the middle of sentence. That is not the end of the sentence, for the Lord says, "The glory of God is intelligence, or in other words light and truth." And then he adds that "light and truth forsaketh that evil one." ¶ When we have the Spirit of the Lord we have intelligence—light and truth. . . . It is pure intelligence, if you please, and he who has it has the power to discern between right and wrong, truth and error, and he will follow righteousness. CR1933Oct:60

**Mormon**

For behold, the Spirit of Christ is given to every man, that he may know good from evil; wherefore, I show unto you the way to judge; for every thing which inviteth to do good, and to persuade to believe in Christ, is sent forth by the power and gift of Christ; wherefore ye may know with a perfect knowledge it is of God. . . . 18. And now, my brethren, seeing that ye know the light by which ye may judge, which light is the light of Christ, see that ye do not judge wrongfully; for with that same judgment which ye judge ye shall also be judged. 19. Wherefore, I beseech of you, brethren, that ye should search diligently in the light of Christ that ye may know good from evil. . . . Moro.7:16,18-19

---

338. The Spirit of God is the spirit of love and peace.

**Paul**

For God hath not given us the spirit of fear; but of power, and of love, and of a sound mind. (*Paul writes to his assistant Timothy, about A.D. 64*) 2Tim.1:7

**John**

There is no fear in love; but perfect love casteth out fear: because fear hath torment. He that feareth is not made perfect in love. (*John writes to the churches in Asia*) 1Jn.4:18

**Mormon**

Wo be unto them that shall pervert the ways of the Lord after this manner, for they shall perish except they repent. Behold, I speak with boldness, having authority from God; and I fear not what man can do; for perfect love casteth out all fear. . . . 26. And the remission of sins bringeth meekness, and lowliness of heart; and because of meekness and lowliness of heart cometh the visitation of the Holy Ghost, which Comforter filleth with hope and perfect love. . . . (*Mormon writes to his son Moroni, prior to A.D. 384*) Moro.8:16,26

**Paul**

But the fruit of the Spirit is love, joy, peace, longsuffering, gentleness, goodness, faith, 23. Meekness, temperance: against such there is no law. 24. And they that are Christ's have crucified the flesh with the affections and lusts. 25. If we live in the Spirit, let us also walk in the Spirit. (*Paul writes to the churches of Galatia in Asia Minor, about A.D. 55; he instructs them to walk not after the flesh but after the Spirit*) Gal.5:22-25

**Related Witnesses:**
**Jesus,**
*quoted by John*

Peace I leave with you, my peace I give unto you: not as the world giveth, give I unto you. Let not your heart be troubled, neither let it be afraid. (*Jesus comforts the Twelve in anticipation of his crucifixion*) John 14:27

**Joseph Smith,**
*receiving the Word of the Lord*

Learn of me, and listen to my words; walk in the meekness of my Spirit, and you shall have peace in me. (*A commandment of God for Martin Harris, March 1830*) D&C 19:23

---

**HYMNS Written by Prophets Applicable to this Topic**

**Parley P. Pratt**
*Father in Heaven, We Do Believe*
HYMNS:180

Father in Heav'n, we do believe
The promise thou hast made;
Thy word with meekness we receive,
Just as thy Saints have said.

We now repent of all our sin
And come with broken heart,
And to thy covenant enter in
And choose the better part.

O Lord, accept us while we pray,
And all our sins forgive;
New life impart to us this day,
And bid the sinners live.

Humbly we take the sacrament
In Jesus' blessed name;
Let us receive thru covenant
The Spirit's heav'nly flame.

We will be buried in the stream
In Jesus' blessed name,
And rise, while light shall on us beam
The Spirit's heav'nly flame.

Baptize us with the Holy Ghost
And seal us as thine own,
That we may join the ransomed host
And with the Saints be one.

### Parley P. Pratt
*Behold Thy Sons and Daughters, Lord*
HYMNS:238

Behold thy sons and daughters, Lord,
On whom we lay our hands.
They have fulfilled the gospel word
And bowed at thy commands.

Oh, now send down the heav'nly dove
And overwhelm their souls
With peace and joy and perfect love,
As lambs within thy fold.

Seal them by thine own Spirit's pow'r,
Which purifies from sin,
And may they find, from this good hour,
They are adopted in.

Increase their faith, confirm their hope,
And guide them in the way.
With comfort bear their spirits up
Until the perfect day.

### Gordon B. Hinckley
*My Redeemer Lives*
HYMNS:135

I know that my Redeemer lives,
Triumphant Savior, Son of God,
Victorious over pain and death,
My King, my Leader, and my Lord.

He lives, my one sure rock of faith,
The one bright hope of men on earth,
The beacon to a better way,
The light beyond the veil of death.

Oh, give me thy sweet Spirit still,
The peace that comes alone from thee,
The faith to walk the lonely road
That leads to thine eternity.

# List of Doctrines

## HOME TEACHING

# HOME TEACHING

339. Home teachers are priesthood home visitors whose duty is to inquire into the well-being of the family, and to see if parents and children are doing their family duties and assuming their church responsibilities.

### Elder Harold B. Lee

The Priesthood visitors are to be thinking of a new name instead of *teacher* attached to these priesthood visitors. The word *teaching* suggests that they are to go there to teach a gospel message, and that primarily isn't what we expect the home teachers of today to do. They are home visitors; they are priesthood home visitors to inquire into the health of the family and to see if they are doing their family duties, and if they are assuming their Church responsibilities. (*Seminar of Regional Representatives, April 1969, pp. 20-21*) TLDP:517

### Elder Spencer W. Kimball

When the home teachers go into every home and motivate parents, especially fathers, to teach their children by example and verbal teaching, can it be conceived that there will need to be penal institutions, divorce courts, special counseling service? Will there be need for reformatories, courts, and jails? . . . ¶ When home teachers serve their few families as faithfully and as continuously as their bishops do their many families; when home teachers live the commandments near perfection; when they enter into every phase of the life of their charges; then will Satan be bound. . . . ¶ Blessed will be the day when all home teachers, those working on the missionary, genealogical, and the welfare and all programs, become home teachers in every sense of the word, looking after every facet of the lives of their families—spiritual, temporal, financial, moral, marital. That will be the happy day! The great umbrella is available. It will protect no one from the storm, the tempest, the danger unless it is spread. (*Seminar of Regional Representatives, April 1967*) (*The Teachings of Spencer W. Kimball, p. 524*) TLDP:517

### Marion G. Romney

It is the responsibility of the Priesthood of the Church to see that every program of the Church is carried forward for the perfection of the Saints, and that it succeeds. That is the duty of the Home Teacher to see that the members of the families participate in every organization and that they should participate, from their age and their circumstances, and to help perfect their lives. (*Seminar of Regional Representatives, Oct. 1969, p. 15*) TLDP:517

### Marion G. Romney

Home teaching is not limited to a specific gospel principle or church activity. By divine injunction home teaching supports and sustains all home and church programs and activities for teaching the gospel. ¶ What, then, is home teaching? ¶ Home teaching, properly functioning, brings to the home of each member two priesthood bearers divinely commissioned and authoritatively called into the service by their priesthood leader and bishop. . . . ¶ Not only is home teaching a divine call; it is also universal, so far as Melchizedek Priesthood bearers and priests and teachers are concerned. ("The Responsibilities of Home Teachers," EN1973Mar:12,14) TLDP:517-18

### Bruce R. McConkie

There is no substitute for home teaching. We do not need to appoint special fellowshipping committees to help reactivate elders or prospective elders. We do not need to issue a special call or make special arrangements for fellowshipping work. Instead, we use home teachers to do the things that by revelation they are commanded to do. Home teaching is one of the best resources in the Church. Home teachers visit in the homes of the members, watch over and strengthen the Saints, see that there is no iniquity in their lives, and see that all do their duties. . . . ("Only an Elder," EN1975Jun:68) TLDP:518

### Bruce R. McConkie

Home teachers are priesthood representatives, and home teaching is the priesthood way of watching over the Church. Through it, priesthood quorums guide and strengthen their members so they in turn can perfect their families. Through it, fathers, families, and individuals are so guided that they do their duty, keep the commandments, and gain salvation. Properly performed, home teaching is the Lord's way of making all of the blessings of the gospel available to all the members of his kingdom. (Let Every Man Learn His Duty, p. 23) TLDP:518

### President David O. McKay

To perform fully our duty as a home teacher, we should be continually aware of the attitudes, the activities and interests, the problems, the employment, the health, the happiness, the plans and purposes, the physical, temporal, and spiritual needs and circumstances of everyone—of every child, every youth, and every adult in the homes and families that have been placed in our trust and care. ("For the Perfecting of the Saints," IE1968Jan:2) TLDP:517

**Related Witnesses:**
### Joseph Smith
The teacher's duty is to watch over the church always, and be with and strengthen them; 54. And see that there is no iniquity in the church, neither hardness with each other, neither lying, backbiting, nor evil speaking; 55. And see that the church meet together often, and also see that all the members do their duty. (*Revelation on Church Organization and Government, April 1830*) D&C 20:53-55

**Author's Note:** When the home teachers find something amiss, their responsibility is not one of authority but of priesthood love. They are to "guide and strengthen their members so they in turn can perfect their families."

340. Home teachers are (two) priest-
      hood bearers divinely commis-
      sioned and authoritatively called
      by their priesthood leader and
      bishop to visit the homes of the
      members.

### Marion G. Romney
Home teaching, properly functioning, brings to the home of each member two priesthood bearers divinely commissioned and authoritatively called into the service by their priesthood leader and bishop. . . . ¶ Not only is home teaching a divine call; it is also universal, so far as Melchizedek Priesthood bearers and priests and teachers are concerned. ("The Responsibilities of Home Teachers," EN1973Mar:12,14) TLDP:517-18

### Bruce R. McConkie
Home teachers have status. Their calls are official. They have been sent by their quorum president, by the bishop, and by the Lord. They should visit frequently in their assigned homes. They are there to do the things listed in section 20 of the Doctrine and Covenants. ("Only an Elder," EN1975Jun:68) TLDP:518

### Elder Harold B. Lee
Home teaching, in essence, means that we consider separately each individual member of the family. . . . Home teaching . . . is to help the parents with home problems in their efforts to teach their families the fundamentals of parental responsibility. . . . Quorum leaders were given the responsibility of selecting, training, and supervising quorum members in visiting with and teaching assigned families of their own quorum members. CR1967Oct:100

# List of Doctrines

## HONESTY AND INTEGRITY

*Doctrines Located in This Topic*

341. We must live honestly.

342. We must not steal.

343. We must not defraud.

344. Employers must not exploit their employees.

345. Employees must not cheat their employers.

346. We are to return that which we borrow.

347. We shall not lie but always speak the truth.

348. Righteous ends cannot justify unrighteous means (to achieve any righteous objective, lofty as it may be, no person should perform any unrighteous act, insignificant as it may seem).

349. We are to keep the promises we make.

350. A hypocrite cannot be saved (in the celestial kingdom).

*Doctrines on HONESTY AND INTEGRITY Located in Other Topics*

165. The devil is the father of all lies.

767. We are not to bear false witness or accuse others falsely.

824. The Lord judges us by what we are in our minds and hearts, not by how we may appear to others.

857. We are not to gamble or take money without giving fair value in return.

# HONESTY AND INTEGRITY

**Author's Note:** Dictionary definition of *Honest*: [Derived from the word HONOR] "Fair in dealing with others; free from trickishness, fraud, or theft; upright; just; equitable; sincere; candid; or unreserved; honorable; reputable. . . ." (The New Webster Encyclopedic Dictionary of the English Language, p. 408) ¶ Dictionary definition of the word *Integrity*: "Behavior in accordance with a strict code of values, moral, artistic, etc.; honesty; entirety; the quality of wholeness; something without mark or stain; soundness." (The New Webster Encyclopedic Dictionary of the English Language, p. 448)

## 341. We must live honestly.

### Joseph Smith
We believe in being honest, true, chaste, benevolent, virtuous, and in doing good to all men; indeed, we may say that we follow the admonition of Paul—We believe all things, we hope all things, we have endured many things, and hope to be able to endure all things. If there is anything virtuous, lovely, or of good report or praiseworthy, we seek after these things. (*The thirteenth of the thirteen Articles of Faith; letter to John Wentworth, March 1, 1842*) AofF:13

### Mark E. Petersen
But we do not believe in honesty merely as a matter of policy. It is far more important than that. Honesty is a principle of salvation in the kingdom of God. Without it there can be no salvation. Just as no man or woman can be saved without baptism, so no one can be saved without honesty. As we cannot advance in the kingdom of heaven without a resurrection, so we cannot move into celestial realms without honesty. CR1971Oct:63

### Joseph Smith
And let every man deal honestly, and be alike among this people, and receive alike, that ye may be one, even as I have commanded you. (*Revelation to Joseph Smith, May 1831*) D&C 51:9

### Elder George Albert Smith
I want to say to you that the punishment that is meted out to those who are dishonest in our day, when they are apprehended and haled before the courts of the land and punished for their crimes, is insignificant when compared with the spiritual punishment that befalls us when we transgress the law of honesty and violate that commandment of God. ("Law of Honesty," Deseret News, Jan. 7, 1933, Church Section, p. 6) TLDP:288

### Paul
Recompense to no man evil for evil. Provide things honest in the sight of all men. (*Paul's letter to the Church in Rome, about A.D. 55*) Rom.12:17

### Paul
Let us walk honestly, as in the day; not in rioting and drunkenness, not in chambering and wantonness, not in strife and envying. (*Paul's letter to* the Church in Rome, about A.D. 55) Rom.13:13

### Elder Spencer W. Kimball
Integrity may be defined as a quality of being complete, unbroken, whole, and unimpaired purity and moral soundness; it is unadulterated genuineness and deep sincerity. It is honesty and righteousness. ¶ Some people keep scrupulously clean their bodies, teeth, hair, and clothes, but permit their morals to degenerate. . . . Practically all dishonesty owes its existence and growth to this inward distortion we call self-justification. It is the first, the worst, and most insidious and damaging form of cheating—to cheat oneself. ACR(Mexico City)1972:27

### Elder Spencer W. Kimball
Another area in which numerous people show a lack of total honestly and integrity is on the highway. Is it dishonest to break speed limits? What are we doing to our children and others when we not only exceed limits but boast about it? Perhaps there are few of us who do not exhibit this fault, but is it right because many break the law? (*At Brigham Young University, June 1957*) (The Teachings of Spencer W. Kimball, p. 197) TLDP:289

### Joseph Smith,
*receiving the Word of the Lord*
Wherefore, let every man beware lest he do that which is not in truth and righteousness before me. (*Revelation for the elders of the Church, May 1831*) D&C 50:9

### Delbert L. Stapley
Honesty and integrity as perfected virtues in parents are more likely to become the heritage and rich endowments of their children. Parents cannot give to their children that which they do not possess. All these fine ideals and principles that are a part of the gospel teachings, together with all the virtues that make for good character and good life, should be perfected in each of us. In that perfection they become a part of our nature, and when parenthood comes, these virtues are more apt to be transmitted to our children. CR1971Apr:153

### Ezekiel
But if a man be just, and do that which is lawful and right. . . . 7. And hath not oppressed any, but hath restored to the debtor his pledge,

hath spoiled none by violence, hath given his bread to the hungry, and hath covered the naked with a garment; 8. He that hath not given forth upon usury, neither hath taken any increase, that hath withdrawn his hand from iniquity, hath executed true judgment between man and man, 9. Hath walked in my statutes, and hath kept my judgments, to deal truly; he is just, he shall surely live, saith the Lord GOD. (*Ezekiel preaches the word of the Lord*) Ezek.18:5,7-9

### Related Witnesses:

#### President Brigham Young,
#### *quoted by John A. Widtsoe*

Simple truth, simplicity, honesty, uprightness, justice, mercy, love, kindness, do good to all and evil to none, how easy it is to live by such principles! A thousand times easier than to practice deception! (*In Tabernacle, Aug. 7, 1870, JD14:76*) DBY:232

#### Paul

Finally, brethren, whatsoever things are true, whatsoever things are honest, whatsoever things are just, whatsoever things are pure, whatsoever things are lovely, whatsoever things are of good report; if there be any virtue, and if there be any praise, think on these things. (*Letter from Rome to the Church at Philippi in Macedonia*) Philip.4:8

#### Mormon

And they [the people of Ammon] were among the people of Nephi, and also numbered among the people who were of the church of God. And they were also distinguished for their zeal towards God, and also towards men; for they were perfectly honest and upright in all things; and they were firm in the faith of Christ, even unto the end. (*Honest, upright, zealous members of the Church choose death at the hands of their enemies rather than taking up the sword against them*) Alma 27:27

#### Paul

And herein do I exercise myself, to have always a conscience void of offence toward God, and toward men. (*Paul answers before Felix*) Acts 24:16

---

## 342. We must not steal.

#### Recorded in Exodus

Thou shalt not steal. (*The Lord reveals the eighth of the Ten Commandments to Moses*) Ex.20:15

#### Jesus,
#### *recorded in Matthew*

He saith unto him, Which? Jesus said, Thou shalt do no murder, Thou shalt not commit adultery, Thou shalt not steal, Thou shalt not bear false witness, . . . (*Jesus instructs the young man who had great possessions*) Matt.19:18

#### Elder Spencer W. Kimball

The theft of pennies or dollars or commodities may impoverish little the one from whom the goods are taken, but it is a shrivelling, dwarfing process to the one who steals. (*At Brigham Young University, June 1957*) (The Teachings of Spencer W. Kimball, p. 198) TLDP:289

#### President Spencer W. Kimball

We are appalled at the reported dishonesty in many communities in our land; that the loss through shoplifting and allied dishonest tricks runs into billions of dollars in this country alone. ¶ The Lord told Adam's posterity and carved it into the stone plates, "Thou shalt not steal." (Ex.20:15) All parents should train their children against this deadly thing which can destroy their characters. Honesty is socially and culturally right. Liars and cheaters are both dishonest and alien to our culture. Dishonesty of all kinds is most reprehensible. "Thou shalt not steal." ¶ We call upon the . . . members of this church to be honest, full of integrity, pay for what they get, and take only that which they have properly paid for. We must teach our children honor and integrity. CR1975Apr:6

#### Joseph Smith,
#### *receiving the Word of the Lord*

Thou shalt not steal; and he that stealeth and will not repent shall be cast out. (*Revelation "embracing the law of the Church," Feb. 9, 1831*) D&C 42:20

#### Joseph Smith,
#### *receiving the Word of the Lord*

And if he or she shall steal, he or she shall be delivered up unto the law of the land. (*Revelation "embracing the law of the Church," Feb. 9, 1831*) D&C 42:85

#### Recorded in Exodus

And he that stealeth a man, and selleth him, or if he be found in his hand, he shall surely be put to death. (*The Lord reveals his laws to ancient Israel*) Ex.21:16

#### Mormon

And thus they might go forth and preach the word according to their desires, for the king had been converted unto the Lord, and all his household; therefore he sent his proclamation throughout the land unto his people, that the word of God might have no obstruction, but that it might go forth throughout all the land, that his people might be convinced concerning the wicked traditions of their fathers, and that they might be convinced that they were all brethren, and that they ought not to murder, nor to plunder, nor to steal, nor to commit adultery, nor to commit any manner of wickedness. *(Religious freedom is proclaimed by the king of the Lamanites)* Alma 23:3

**Paul**

Know ye not that the unrighteous shall not inherit the kingdom of God? Be not deceived: neither fornicators, nor idolaters, nor adulterers, nor effeminate, nor abusers of themselves with mankind, 10. Nor thieves, nor covetous, nor drunkards, nor revilers, nor extortioners, shall inherit the kingdom of God. *(Paul writes to the Church at Corinth, Greece, about A.D. 55)* 1Cor.6:9-10

**Related Witnesses:**

**Dallin H. Oaks**

[N]ot all stealing is at gunpoint or by dark of night. Some theft is by deception, where the thief manipulates the confidence of his victim. ¶ The white collar cousin of stealing is fraud, which gets its gain by lying about an essential fact in a transaction. ¶ Scheming promoters with glib tongues and ingratiating manners deceive their neighbors into investments the promoters know to be more speculative than they dare to reveal. CR1986Oct:25

---

### 343. We must not defraud.

**Recorded in Leviticus**

Thou shalt not defraud thy neighbour, neither rob him: the wages of him that is hired shall not abide with thee all night until the morning. *(Revelation to Moses)* Lev.19:13

**Paul**

That no man go beyond and defraud his brother in any matter: because that the Lord is the avenger of all such, as we also have forewarned you, and testified. *(Paul's letter to the Church at Thessalonica, comprising Jews and many pagan converts, A.D. 50)* 1Thess.4:6

**Albert E. Bowen**

Incurring obligations beyond a reasonable expectancy of the ability to meet them is a fruitful source of ultimate dishonesty. Men who would scorn to steal and who would be highly incensed at the suggestion of thievery, nevertheless do not hesitate to make engagements which they have no chance of meeting. When the day of reckoning comes they will covertly put their property out of reach and otherwise preserve what they have to the deprivation of those to whom they have given their word. It puts a heavy strain upon character to see the accumulations of years of toil appropriated to

the payment of debts incurred. One sees character crack under the strain. ¶ Buying on credit with no reasonable prospect of payment resembles taking outright what belongs to another in that both come about through uncontrolled desire to possess. The same kind of resistance is necessary in each case if desire is to be denied. The time to avoid the unpleasant consequence is before incurring the obligation. There is character-building strength in resisting. CR1938Oct:67

**Jesus,**
*recorded in Mark*

Thou knowest the commandments, Do not commit adultery, Do not kill, Do not steal, Do not bear false witness, Defraud not, Honour thy father and mother. *(Jesus instructs the young man who had great possessions)* Mark 10:19

**Paul**

Now therefore there is utterly a fault among you, because ye go to law one with another. Why do ye not rather take wrong? why do ye not rather suffer yourselves to be defrauded? 8. Nay, ye do wrong, and defraud, and that your brethren. *(Letter to the Church at Corinth, Greece, about A.D. 55)* 1Cor.6:7-8

**Recorded in Leviticus**

Ye shall do no unrighteousness in judgment, in meteyard, in weight, or in measure. 36. Just balances, just weights, a just ephah, and a just hin, shall ye have: I am the LORD your God, which brought you out of the land of Egypt. 37. Therefore shall ye observe all my statutes, and all my judgments, and do them: I am the LORD. *(Revelation to Moses)* Lev.19:35-37

**Related Witnesses:**

**Ezekiel**

But if a man be just, and do that which is lawful and right, . . . 8. He that hath not given forth upon usury, neither hath taken any increase, . . . *(Ezekiel preaches the word of the Lord)* Ezek.18:5,8

**Recorded in Deuteronomy**

Thou shalt not lend upon usury to thy brother; usury of money, usury of victuals, usury of any thing that is lent upon usury: *(Commandments to Israel through Moses)* Deut.23:19

**Elder Spencer W. Kimball**

Bankruptcies are common and numerous today. I hope bankruptcy proceedings are not intended to free men of their honest obligations. They may serve well to give the debtor a breathing period and an opportunity to make back the money but he should pay his honest obligations even though the law might have protected him against them. (The Teachings of Spencer W. Kimball, p. 196) TLDP:289

**Author's Note:**
Dictionary definition of *Usury* [A]n excessive or inordinate premium for the use of money borrowed. . . . (The New Webster Encyclopedic Dictionary of the English Language, p. 924)

---

**344. Employers must not exploit their employees.**

### Recorded in Deuteronomy

Thou shalt not oppress an hired servant that is poor and needy, whether he be of thy brethren, or of thy strangers that are in thy land within thy gates: 15. At his day thou shalt give him his hire, neither shall the sun go down upon it; for he is poor, and setteth his heart upon it: lest he cry against thee unto the LORD, and it be sin unto thee. (*Commandments to Israel through Moses: law given concerning making merchandise of men*) Deut.24:14-15

### George Q. Cannon

[W]hen employers agree to pay a certain price, or a certain kind of pay they should abide by their agreement. . . . These are practical duties. I would give more for a Latter-day Saint who, if I employed him to do me a job and he did it right, than I would for a man who would offer a long prayer and tell the Lord a great many things that might be very good, and did not do the work honestly. (*In Tabernacle, Oct. 9, 1881, JD22:325*) TLDP:288

### Paul

Masters, give unto your servants that which is just and equal; knowing that ye also have a Master in heaven. (*Paul writes from prison to the Church in Colossae, Asia Minor, about A.D. 60*) Col.4:1

### Dallin H. Oaks

An employee who receives the compensation agreed upon but does not perform the service agreed upon earns part of his living by injuring others. ¶ So does an employer who is unfair to his employees. . . . ¶ . . . . Of course, we understand that what an employer can pay his employees is limited by what his business can obtain for its products or services in a competitive marketplace. Contracts also impose limits on legitimate economic expectations. CR1986Oct:26

### James

Behold, the hire of the labourers who have reaped down your fields, which is of you kept back by fraud, crieth: and the cries of them which have reaped are entered into the ears of the Lord of sabaoth. (*Letter to his brethren in the Church*) James 5:4

### President Heber J. Grant

I have been impressed with the fact that there is a spirit growing in the world today to avoid giving service, an unwillingness to give value received, to try to see how little we can do and how much we can get for doing it. This is all wrong. Our spirit and aim should be to do all we possibly can, in a given length of time, for the benefit of those who employ us and for the benefit of those with whom we are associated. ¶ The other spirit—to get all we can, and give as little as possible in return—is contrary to the gospel of the Lord Jesus Christ. It is not right to desire something for which we do not give service or value received. That idea is all wrong, and it is only a question of time when the sheep and the goats will be separated. (*Gospel Standards, pp. 183-84*) TLDP:288

### Ezekiel

But if a man be just, and do that which is lawful and right, . . . 7. And hath not oppressed any, . . . 9. Hath walked in my statutes, and hath kept my judgments, to deal truly; he is just, he shall surely live, saith the Lord GOD. (*Ezekiel preaches the word of the Lord*) Ezek.18:5,7,9

### Jeremiah

Woe unto him that buildeth his house by unrighteousness, and his chambers by wrong; that useth his neighbour's service without wages, and giveth him not for his work; (*Revelation to Jeremiah, about 628 B.C.*) Jer.22:13

### Joseph Smith

[W]hen we undertake to cover our sins, or to gratify our pride, our vain ambition, or to exercise control or dominion or compulsion upon the souls of the children of men, in any degree of unrighteousness, behold, the heavens withdraw themselves; the Spirit of the Lord is grieved; and when it is withdrawn, Amen to the priesthood or the authority of that man. (*Revelation received in Liberty Jail, March 20, 1839; why many are called and few chosen*) D&C 121:37

**Related Witnesses:**

### Marvin J. Ashton

In recent days all of us have witnessed many who have weakened themselves even to the point of falling completely as they have sacrificed the leading principles of honesty and integrity in order to climb an artificial ladder of accomplishment. No lasting great personal heights are ever reached by those who step on others to try to push themselves upward. ¶ It is not surprising to learn that people who tell white lies soon become color-blind. ¶ Despite the endless examples of scandals in business, religion, and government, honesty and integrity are still the ingredients to strengthen [feeble] knees. CR1991Oct:99

## 345. Employees must not cheat their employers.

### President Heber J. Grant

I have been impressed with the fact that there is a spirit growing in the world today to avoid giving service, an unwillingness to give value received, to try to see how little we can do and how much we can get for doing it. This is all wrong. Our spirit and aim should be to do all we possibly can, in a given length of time, for the benefit of those who employ us and for the benefit of those with whom we are associated. ¶ The other spirit—to get all we can, and give as little as possible in return—is contrary to the gospel of the Lord Jesus Christ. It is not right to desire something for which we do not give service or value received. That idea is all wrong, and it is only a question of time when the sheep and the goats will be separated. (Gospel Standards, pp. 183-84) TLDP:288

### George Q. Cannon

Again, if a man employs you to do a piece of work, that work should be well done, whether he is there to see it done or not. And when employers agree to pay a certain price, or a certain kind of pay they should abide by their agreement. . . . These are practical duties. I would give more for a Latter-day Saint who, if I employed him to do me a job and he did it right, than I would for a man who would offer a long prayer and tell the Lord a great many things that might be very good, and did not do the work honestly. (In Tabernacle, Oct. 9, 1881, JD22:325) TLDP:288

### Dallin H. Oaks

An employee who receives the compensation agreed upon but does not perform the service agreed upon earns part of his living by injuring others. ¶ So does an employer who is unfair to his employees. . . . ¶ . . . . Of course, we understand that what an employer can pay his employees is limited by what his business can obtain for its products or services in a competitive marketplace. Contracts also impose limits on legitimate economic expectations. CR1986Oct:26

### Related Witnesses:

#### Marvin J. Ashton

In recent days all of us have witnessed many who have weakened themselves even to the point of falling completely as they have sacrificed the leading principles of honesty and integrity in order to climb an artificial ladder of accomplishment. No lasting great personal heights are ever reached by those who step on others to try to push themselves upward. ¶ It is not surprising to learn that people who tell white lies soon become color-blind. ¶ Despite the endless examples of scandals in business, religion, and government, honesty and integrity are still the ingredients to strengthen [feeble] knees. CR1991Oct:99

---

## 346. We are to return that which we borrow.

### President Brigham Young

If thou borrowest of thy neighbor, thou shalt restore that which thou hast borrowed; and if thou canst not repay then go straightway and tell thy neighbor, lest he condemn thee. (Revelation received Jan. 14, 1847) D&C 136:25

### George Q. Cannon

When a man says a thing to his neighbor, he should so live that his neighbor can have confidence in him. When he makes a promise that promise should be sacred, and if he cannot fulfil it, let him explain the reason so that confidence may be preserved. When we borrow we should repay; when we deal we should be upright in our dealing. (In Tabernacle, Oct. 9, 1881, JD22:325) TLDP:288

### King Benjamin,
#### quoted by Mormon

And I would that ye should remember, that whosoever among you borroweth of his neighbor should return the thing that he borroweth, according as he doth agree, or else thou shalt commit sin; and perhaps thou shalt cause thy neighbor to commit sin also. (King Benjamin addresses his people, about 124 B.C.) Mosiah 4:28

### Recorded in Exodus

And if a man borrow ought of his neighbour, and it be hurt, or die, the owner thereof being not with it, he shall surely make it good. (The Lord reveals his laws to ancient Israel) Ex.22:14

### Recorded in Psalms

The wicked borroweth, and payeth not again: but the righteous sheweth mercy, and giveth. Ps.37:21

### George Q. Cannon

When we borrow we should repay. . . . (In Tabernacle, Oct. 9, 1881, JD22:325) TLDP:288

### Related Witnesses:

#### President Brigham Young

If thou shalt find that which thy neighbor has lost, thou shalt make diligent search till thou shalt deliver it to him again. (Revelation, Jan. 14, 1847) D&C 136:26

### Recorded in Leviticus

And the LORD spake unto Moses, saying, 2. If a soul sin, and commit a trespass against the

LORD, and lie unto his neighbour in that which was delivered him to keep, or in fellowship, or in a thing taken away by violence, or hath deceived his neighbour; 3. Or have found that which was lost, and lieth concerning it, and sweareth falsely; in any of all these that a man doeth, sinning therein: 4. Then it shall be, because he hath sinned, and is guilty, that he shall restore that which he took violently away, or the thing which he hath deceitfully gotten, or that which was delivered him to keep, or the lost thing which he found, *(To Moses, the Lord reveals his laws for ancient Israel)* Lev.6:1-4

---

**347. We shall not lie but always speak the truth.**

**Zechariah**

These are the things that ye shall do; Speak ye every man the truth to his neighbour; execute the judgment of truth and peace in your gates: 17. And let none of you imagine evil in your hearts against his neighbour; and love no false oath: for all these are things that I hate, saith the LORD. *(The word of the Lord through the prophet Zechariah, about 518 B.C.)* Zech.8:16-17

**Marvin J. Ashton,**
*also quoting Joseph Smith*

How serious is lying? We have a clue when we read all through the scriptures that Satan is the father of lies. His method of teaching this evil practice is illustrated in the tenth section of the Doctrine and Covenants: "Yea, he [Satan] saith unto them: Deceive and lie. . . ; behold, this is no harm. And thus he . . . telleth them that it is no sin to lie. . . . And thus he . . . causeth them to catch themselves in their own snare." (D&C 10:25-26) ¶ Yet we can't hide behind the father of lies and say, "Satan made me do it." All he does is tell us, "This is no harm," and then he lets us catch ourselves in our own snare. ¶ It is a sin to lie. It is a tragedy to be the victim of lies. Being trapped in the snares of dishonesty and misrepresentation does not happen instantaneously. One little lie or dishonest act leads to another until the perpetrator is caught in the web of deceit. CR1982Apr:11

**Paul**

Wherefore putting away lying, speak every man truth with his neighbour: for we are members one of another. *(Letter to the Saints at Ephesus in Asia Minor, about A.D. 62)* Eph.4:25

**George Q. Cannon**

We should be honest, we should be truthful, our word should be like the words of the Lord, that

is, in our sphere. When a man says a thing to his neighbor, he should so live that his neighbor can have confidence in him. When he makes a promise that promise should be sacred, and if he cannot fulfil it, let him explain the reason so that confidence may be preserved. When we borrow we should repay; when we deal we should be upright in our dealing. I would like it to be the case among us that when a man has a horse to sell that he will tell all he knows about it and not endeavor to take advantage in any shape or form. The same with a wagon, a cow, a piece of land, or a house, or anything else, that a man will tell what he knows about these things, so that confidence may be maintained. *(In Tabernacle, Oct. 9, 1881, JD22:325)* TLDP:288

**Recorded in Proverbs**

The lip of truth shall be established for ever: but a lying tongue is but for a moment. 20. Deceit is in the heart of them that imagine evil: but to the counsellers of peace is joy. . . . 22. Lying lips are abomination to the LORD: but they that deal truly are his delight. Prov.12:19-20,22

**Mark E. Petersen**

We Latter-day Saints believe in God, and because we believe in him, we also believe there is a devil. But the devil himself is a liar—the father of lies—and those who choose to cheat and lie and deceive and misrepresent become his slaves. CR1971Oct:64-65

**Related Witnesses:**

**John**

And in their mouth was found no guile: for they are without fault before the throne of God. *(John sees the redeemed one hundred and forty-four thousand)* Rev.14:5

**Joseph Smith**

Take upon you the name of Christ, and speak the truth in soberness. *(Revelation received June 1829)* D&C 18:21

**Joseph Smith,**
*receiving the Word of the Lord*

Verily, verily, I say unto you, wo be unto him that lieth to deceive because he supposeth that another lieth to deceive, for such are not exempt from the justice of God. *(Revelation in respect to the lost 116 manuscript pages, summer of 1828)* D&C 10:28

---

**348. Righteous ends cannot justify unrighteous means (to achieve any righteous objective, lofty as it may be, no person should perform any unrighteous act, insignificant as it may seem).**

**Joseph Smith,**
*receiving the Word of the Lord*

Verily, verily, I say unto you, wo be unto him that lieth to deceive because he supposeth that another lieth to deceive, for such are not exempt from the justice of God. (*Revelation in respect to the lost 116 manuscript pages, summer of 1828*) D&C 10:28

**Marvin J. Ashton**

In recent days all of us have witnessed many who have weakened themselves even to the point of falling completely as they have sacrificed the leading principles of honesty and integrity in order to climb an artificial ladder of accomplishment. No lasting great personal heights are ever reached by those who step on others to try to push themselves upward. ¶ It is not surprising to learn that people who tell white lies soon become color-blind. ¶ Despite the endless examples of scandals in business, religion, and government, honesty and integrity are still the ingredients to strengthen [feeble] knees. CR1991Oct:99

**Stephen L. Richards**

[I]t will never profit you anything by deception to win your way into the temple. It is true that we may deceive our bishops, our presidents of stakes. Some may get recommends without revealing what they ought to reveal. It is useless. All the blessings of the temples are predicated upon faithfulness, upon obedience to the commandments. No blessing is effective unless it is based upon the good life of him who receives it. It is a mistake for anyone to think that by concealing or suppressing something that ought to be known he can secure a recommend to go to the temple. That is futile, and even worse than futile, because the suppressing of the fact is itself an additional offense. CR1959Apr:47

**Melvin J. Ballard**

A man and woman may by fraud and deception obtain admittance to the house of the Lord and may receive the pronouncement of the Holy Priesthood, giving to them, so far as lies in their power, these blessings. We may deceive men, but we cannot deceive the Holy Ghost, and our blessings will not be eternal unless they are also sealed by the Holy Spirit of Promise, the Holy Ghost, one who reads the thoughts and hearts of men and gives his sealing approval to the blessings pronounced upon their heads. Then it is binding, efficacious, and of full force. (*Sermons and Missionary Services of Melvin J. Ballard,* pp. 236-37) TLDP:286

**Related Witnesses:**

**Jeremiah**

Woe unto him that buildeth his house by unrighteousness, and his chambers by wrong; that useth his neighbour's service without wages, and giveth him not for his work; (*Revelation to Jeremiah, about 628 B.C.*) Jer.22:13

**Joseph Smith,**
*receiving the Word of the Lord*

Wherefore, let every man beware lest he do that which is not in truth and righteousness before me. (*Revelation for the elders of the Church, May, 1831*) D&C 50:9

---

**349. We are to keep the promises we make.**

**President Heber J. Grant**

The fundamental thing for a Latter-day Saint is to be honest. The fundamental thing for a Latter-day Saint is to value his word as faithfully as his bond; to make up his mind that under no circumstances, no matter how hard it may be, by and with the help of the Lord, he will dedicate his life and his best energies to making good his promises. ("As Other Men Judge Us," IE1938Jun:327) TLDP:288

**President Brigham Young**

Seek ye; and keep all your pledges one with another; and covet not that which is thy brother's. (*Revelation received Jan. 14, 1847*) D&C 136:20

**Joseph Smith**

Search diligently, pray always, and be believing, and all things shall work together for your good, if ye walk uprightly and remember the covenant wherewith ye have covenanted one with another. (*Revelation, March 8, 1833, wherein various individuals are counseled by the Lord to walk uprightly*) D&C 90:24

**George Q. Cannon**

When a man says a thing to his neighbor, he should so live that his neighbor can have confidence in him. When he makes a promise that promise should be sacred, and if he cannot fulfil it, let him explain the reason so that confidence may be preserved. (*In Tabernacle, Oct. 9, 1881, JD22:325*) TLDP:288

**Related Witnesses:**

**Mormon**

But after Alma had shown them the way that led to the land of Nephi the Lamanites would not keep their promise; but they set guards round about the land of Helam, over Alma and his brethren. (*The Lamanites promise freedom to Alma and his brethren in Helam, if they will show them the way to the land of Nephi*) Mosiah 23:37

**Moses**

I will be surety for him; of my hand shalt thou

require him: if I bring him not unto thee, and set him before thee, then let me bear the blame for ever: (*Judah promises to be surety for Benjamin, to persuade Jacob to send Benjamin to Egypt*) Gen.43:9

### Recorded in Numbers

If a man vow a vow unto the LORD, or swear an oath to bind his soul with a bond; he shall not break his word, he shall do according to all that proceedeth out of his mouth. (*Revelation to Moses for the children of Israel*) Num.30:2

---

### 350. A hypocrite cannot be saved (in the celestial kingdom).

#### Mark E. Petersen

Christians must learn that there is nothing Christlike in deception. There is no righteousness in hypocrisy. There is nothing good about a lie. ¶ We must recognize that if we are not honest we are not clean in the eyes of God, and that no unclean thing may enter his presence. CR1971Oct:65

### Recorded in Job

He also shall be my salvation: for an hypocrite shall not come before him. (*Job testifies of his confidence in the Lord*) Job 13:16

### Recorded in Job

For what is the hope of the hypocrite, though he hath gained, when God taketh away his soul? (*Job asserts his own righteousness*) Job 27:8

#### Joseph Smith,
##### receiving the Word of the Lord

But the hypocrites shall be detected and shall be cut off, either in life or in death, even as I will; and wo unto them who are cut off from my church, for the same are overcome of the world. 9. Wherefore, let every man beware lest he do that which is not in truth and righteousness before me. (*Revelation for the elders of the Church, May 1831*) D&C 50:8-9

#### President John Taylor

We may succeed in hiding our affairs from men; but it is written that for every word and every secret thought we shall have to give an account in the day when accounts have to be rendered before God, when hypocrisy and fraud of any kind will not avail us; for by our words and by our works we shall be justified, or by them we shall be condemned. (*On trip to Bear Lake, JD24:232*) TLDP:321

**Related Witnesses:**

#### Jesus,
##### recorded in Matthew

Woe unto you, scribes and Pharisees, hypocrites! for ye are like unto whited sepulchres, which indeed appear beautiful outward, but are within full of dead men's bones, and of all uncleanness. 28. Even so ye also outwardly appear righteous unto men, but within ye are full of hypocrisy and iniquity. (*Jesus warns the scribes and Pharisees*) Matt.23:27-28

### Recorded in Job

That the triumphing of the wicked is short, and the joy of the hypocrite but for a moment? (*Zophar the Naamanite shows the state and portion of the wicked*) Job 20:5

#### Joseph Smith

[A]nd those who are not pure, and have said they were pure, shall be destroyed, saith the Lord God. (*Revelation relating to the new and everlasting covenant, including the eternal nature of the marriage covenant, July 12, 1843, [1831]*) D&C 132:52

# List of Doctrines

## HUMILITY

### (Meekness; Submissiveness; Not proud)

*Doctrines Located in This Topic*

351. God wants us to be a humble people.

352. Humility is strength; it is not timidity, weakness, or self-abasement.

353. To be humble is to be teachable.

354. Humility precedes repentance.

355. The Lord chooses the humble to do His work.

356. The path to exaltation is through the valley of humility (to reach the mountain height we must traverse the valley below).

357. The humble person will be blessed with knowledge and strength.

358. By cultivating humility we can avoid the pitfalls of worldly pride and philosophies.

*Doctrines on HUMILITY Located in Other Topics*

515. The Lord responds to the prayer of the humble and penitent person.

629. Sorrow for sin is essential to the spirit of repentance.

875. The worldly wise, who will not humble themselves before God, will never enjoy eternal happiness.

# HUMILITY

## (Meekness; Submissiveness; Not proud)

**351. God wants us to be a humble people.**

### Joseph Smith

Be thou humble; and the Lord thy God shall lead thee by the hand, and give thee answer to thy prayers. (*Revelation for Thomas B. Marsh concerning the Twelve Apostles; received on the day on which the gospel was first preached in England, July 23, 1837*) D&C 112:10

### President Ezra Taft Benson

God will have a humble people. Either we can choose to be humble or we can be compelled to be humble. Alma said, "Blessed are they who humble themselves without being compelled to be humble." (Alma 32:16). . . . ¶ We must yield "to the enticings of the Holy Spirit," put off the prideful "natural man," become "a saint through the atonement of Christ the Lord," and become "as a child, submissive, meek, humble." (Mosiah 3:19) CR1989Apr:6-7

### King Benjamin,
#### *quoted by Mormon*

For the natural man is an enemy to God, and has been from the fall of Adam, and will be, forever and ever, unless he yields to the enticings of the Holy Spirit, and putteth off the natural man and becometh a saint through the atonement of Christ the Lord, and becometh as a child, submissive, meek, humble, patient, full of love, willing to submit to all things which the Lord seeth fit to inflict upon him, even as a child doth submit to his father. (*King Benjamin addresses his people, about 124 B.C.*) Mosiah 3:19

### King Benjamin,
#### *quoted by Mormon*

And again, believe that ye must repent of your sins and forsake them, and humble yourselves before God; and ask in sincerity of heart that he would forgive you; and now, if you believe all these things see that ye do them. 11. And again I say unto you as I have said before, that as ye have come to the knowledge of the glory of God, or if ye have known of his goodness and have tasted of his love, and have received a remission of your sins, which causeth such exceedingly great joy in your souls, even so I would that ye should remember, and always retain in remembrance, the greatness of God, and your own nothingness, and his goodness and long-suffering towards you, unworthy creatures, and humble yourselves even in the depths of humility, calling on the name of the Lord daily, and standing steadfastly in the faith of that which is to come, which was spoken by the mouth of the angel. 12. And behold, I say unto you that if ye do this ye shall always rejoice, and be filled with the love of God, and always retain a remission of your sins; and ye shall grow in the knowledge of the glory of him that created you, or in the knowledge of that which is just and true. (*King Benjamin addresses his people, about 124 B.C.*) Mosiah 4:10-12

### James

Humble yourselves in the sight of the Lord, and he shall lift you up. (*Letter of James to his brethren in the Church*) James 4:10

### Jesus,
#### *recorded in Luke*

And he spake this parable unto certain which trusted in themselves that they were righteous, and despised others: 10. Two men went up into the temple to pray; the one a Pharisee, and the other a publican. 11. The Pharisee stood and prayed thus with himself, God, I thank thee, that I am not as other men are, extortioners, unjust, adulterers, or even as this publican. 12. I fast twice in the week, I give tithes of all that I possess. 13. And the publican, standing afar off, would not lift up so much as his eyes unto heaven, but smote upon his breast, saying, God be merciful to me a sinner. 14. I tell you, this man went down to his house justified rather than the other: for every one that exalteth himself shall be abased; and he that humbleth himself shall be exalted. (*Jesus gives the parable of the Pharisee and publican*) Luke 18:9-14

### Jesus,
#### *recorded in Matthew*

At the same time came the disciples unto Jesus, saying, Who is the greatest in the kingdom of heaven? 2. And Jesus called a little child unto him, and set him in the midst of them, 3. And said, Verily I say unto you, Except ye be converted, and become as little children, ye shall not enter into the kingdom of heaven. 4. Whosoever therefore shall humble himself as this little child, the same is greatest in the kingdom of heaven. (*Jesus using a child as an example*) Matt.18:1-4

### Micah

He hath shewed thee, O man, what is good; and what doth the LORD require of thee, but to do justly, and to love mercy, and to walk humbly with thy God? (*The words of the prophet Micah*) Micah 6:8

### Alma, the younger,
#### *quoted by Mormon*

And now, because ye are compelled to be humble

blessed are ye; for a man sometimes, if he is compelled to be humble, seeketh repentance; and now surely, whosoever repenteth shall find mercy; and he that findeth mercy and endureth to the end the same shall be saved. 14. And now, as I said unto you, that because ye were compelled to be humble ye were blessed, do ye not suppose that they are more blessed who truly humble themselves because of the word? 15. Yea, he that truly humbleth himself, and repenteth of his sins, and endureth to the end, the same shall be blessed— yea, much more blessed than they who are compelled to be humble because of their exceeding poverty. 16. Therefore, blessed are they who humble themselves without being compelled to be humble; or rather, in other words, blessed is he that believeth in the word of God, and is baptized without stubbornness of heart, yea, without being brought to know the word, or even compelled to know, before they will believe. (*Alma preaches to the poor whose afflictions had humbled them, about 74 B.C.*) Alma 32:13-16

**Related Witnesses:**

**President Harold B. Lee**
The righteous man, although far superior to his fellows who are not, is humble and does not parade his righteousness to be seen of men but conceals his virtues. . . . He is not so much concerned about what he can get, but more about how much he can give to others. (Stand in Holy Places, pp. 332-33) MPSG1989:22

**Howard W. Hunter**
Humility is an attribute of godliness possessed by true Saints. . . . Our genuine concern should be for the success of others. CR1984Apr:89; MPSG1989:19

**Joseph Smith,**
*receiving the Word of the Lord*
Behold, thus saith the Lord unto my people— you have many things to do and to repent of; for behold, your sins have come up unto me, and are not pardoned, because you seek to counsel in your own ways. 15. And your hearts are not satisfied. And ye obey not the truth, but have pleasure in unrighteousness. 16. Wo unto you rich men, that will not give your substance to the poor, for your riches will canker your souls; and this shall be your lamentation in the day of visitation, and of judgment, and of indignation: The harvest is past, the summer is ended, and my soul is not saved! 17. Wo unto you poor men, whose hearts are not broken, whose spirits are not contrite, and whose bellies are not satisfied, and whose hands are not stayed from laying hold upon other men's goods, whose eyes are full of greediness, and who will not labor

with your own hands! (*Revelation at Kirtland, Ohio, June 1831*) D&C 56:14-17

**Jesus,**
*quoted by Mormon*
Therefore, whoso repenteth and cometh unto me as a little child, him will I receive, for of such is the kingdom of God. Behold, for such I have laid down my life, and have taken it up again; therefore repent, and come unto me ye ends of the earth, and be saved. (*The voice of the resurrected Jesus Christ to the Nephites immediately before he visited them, A.D. 34*) 3Ne.9:22

**Author's Note:** A dictionary definition of the word *Humble*: "Modest or meek in spirit, manner, or appearance: not proud or haughty. ¶ 'A spot where a man feels his own insignificance and may well learn to be humble,' Samuel Butler. ¶ Free from pride or vanity; modest; meek; unassuming. Respectful." (Webster's Third International Dictionary, p. 1101)

---

**352. Humility is strength; it is not timidity, weakness, or self-abasement.**

**Elder Spencer W. Kimball**
If the Lord was meek and lowly and humble, then to become humble one must do what He did in boldly denouncing evil, bravely advancing righteous works, courageously meeting every problem, becoming the master of himself and the situations about him and being near oblivious to personal credit. ¶ Humility is not . . . weak, vacillating, nor servile. . . . ¶ Humble and meek properly suggest virtues, not weaknesses. They suggest a consistent mildness of temper and an absence of wrath and passion. Humility suggests no affectation, no bombastic actions. It is not turbid nor grandiloquent. It is not servile submissiveness. It is not cowed nor frightened. No shadow or the shaking of a leaf terrorizes it. . . . ¶ . . . . Humility makes no bid for popularity and notoriety; demands no honors. . . . ¶ It is not self-abasement—the hiding in the corner, the devaluation of everything one does or thinks or says; but it is the doing of one's best in every case and leaving of one's acts, expressions, and accomplishments to largely speak for themselves. ("Humility," Brigham Young University Speeches of the Year, Provo, Utah, 16 Jan. 1963, pp. 2-4) TLDP:292

**Elder Spencer W. Kimball**
One can be bold and meek at the same time. One can be courageous and humble. (IE1963Aug: 656) MPSG1989:18

### Charles A. Callis

Among the cardinal virtues of the gospel is the praiseworthy virtue of humility. . . . I interpret humility as being strength. Humility expresses itself in lowly service, in volunteering for any service which will ameliorate the conditions, particularly the spiritual conditions of mankind. Humility does not mean to grovel, to be a sycophant. Humility is inward strength outwardly expressed in good works. Great souls attain to humility. CR1942Apr:42

### Elder Ezra Taft Benson

Humility does not mean weakness. It does not mean timidity. It does not mean fear. A man can be humble and fearless. A man can be humble and courageous. (*At seminar for new mission presidents, June 1979*) MPSG1989:18

### Elder Harold B. Lee

A meek man is defined as one who is not easily provoked or irritated and is forbearing under injury or annoyance. The meek man is the strong, the mighty, the man of complete self-mastery. He is the one who has the courage of his moral convictions, despite the pressure of the gang or the club. In controversy his judgment is the court of last resort and his sobered counsel quells the rashness of the mob. He is humble-minded; he does not bluster. "He that is slow to anger is better than the mighty. . . ." (Prov.16:32) He is a natural leader and is the chosen of army and navy, business and church, to lead where other men follow. He is the "salt" of the earth and shall inherit it. (Lesson in M Man and Gleaner Manual, 1950, Stand Ye in Holy Places, p. 346) TLDP:292

### Related Witnesses:

### Joseph Smith

And inasmuch as they were humble they might be made strong, and blessed from on high, and receive knowledge from time to time. (*Revelation during conference of elders of the Church, Nov. 1, 1831*) D&C 1:28

---

### 353. To be humble is to be teachable.

### Elder Spencer W. Kimball

Humility is teachableness—an ability to realize that all virtues and abilities are not concentrated in one's self. . . . ¶ Humility is never accusing nor contentious. . . . ¶ Humility is repentant and seeks not to justify its follies. It is forgiving others in the realization that there may be errors of the same kind or worse chalked up against itself. . . . ¶ Humility makes no bid for popularity and notoriety; demands no honors. . . . ¶ It is not self-abasement—the hiding in the corner,

the devaluation of everything one does or thinks or says; but it is the doing of one's best in every case and leaving of one's acts, expressions, and accomplishments to largely speak for themselves. ("Humility," Brigham Young University Speeches of the Year, Provo, Utah, 16 Jan. 1963) TLDP:292; DCSM:27

### Stephen L. Richards

[When men are humble] they acknowledge an intelligence far superior to their own and they seek guidance and wisdom from that source. CR1935Apr:30; MPSG1989:20

### President Ezra Taft Benson

We can choose to humble ourselves by receiving counsel and chastisement. CR1989Apr:7

### Joseph Smith,
### *receiving the Word of the Lord*

And now behold, verily I say unto you, I, the Lord, am not pleased with my servant Sidney Rigdon; he exalted himself in his heart, and received not counsel, but grieved the Spirit; (*Revelation, Aug. 1831*) D&C 63:55

### Joseph Smith,
### *receiving the Word of the Lord*

Verily thus saith the Lord unto you, my servant Lyman: Your sins are forgiven you, because you have obeyed my voice in coming up hither this morning to receive counsel of him whom I have appointed. (*Revelation for Lyman Sherman, Dec. 26, 1835 at Kirtland, Ohio*) D&C 108:1

### Related Witnesses:

### President Ezra Taft Benson

Humility responds to God's will—to the fear of His judgments and to the needs of those around us. CR1986Apr:6; MPSG1989:18

### Joseph Smith,
### *receiving the Word of the Lord*

Therefore, they must needs be chastened and tried, even as Abraham, who was commanded to offer up his only son. 5. For all those who will not endure chastening, but deny me, cannot be sanctified. (*Revelation, Dec. 16, 1833; the Saints are chastened and afflicted because of transgressions*) D&C 101:4-5

### Joseph Smith,
### *receiving the Word of the Lord*

My people must be tried in all things, that they may be prepared to receive the glory that I have for them, even the glory of Zion; and he that will not bear chastisement is not worthy of my kingdom. (*Revelation, Jan. 14, 1847*) D&C 136:31

### John A. Widtsoe

Joseph Smith was an obedient man. Humility always breeds obedience. (Joseph Smith: Seeker after Truth, Prophet of God, p. 333) MPSG1989:21

**Nephi, son of Lehi**

Know ye not that he was holy? But notwithstanding he being holy, he showeth unto the children of men that, according to the flesh he humbleth himself before the Father, and witnesseth unto the Father that he would be obedient unto him in keeping his commandments. (*Nephi tells why Christ was baptized, between 559-545 B.C.*) 2Ne.31:7

**Elder Spencer W. Kimball**

How does one get humble? To me, one must constantly be reminded of his dependence. On whom dependent? On the Lord. How remind one's self? By real, constant, worshipful, grateful prayer. (Humility, p. 657) MPSG1989:20

---

**354. Humility precedes repentance.**

**President Ezra Taft Benson**

My beloved brethren and sisters, as we cleanse the inner vessel, there will have to be changes made in our own personal lives, in our families, and in the Church. The proud do not change to improve, but defend their position by rationalizing. Repentance means change, and it takes a humble person to change. But we can do it. CR1986Apr:6; MPSG1989:22

**Alma, the younger,**
*quoted by Mormon*

And now, because ye are compelled to be humble blessed are ye; for a man sometimes, if he is compelled to be humble, seeketh repentance; and now surely, whosoever repenteth shall find mercy; and he that findeth mercy and endureth to the end the same shall be saved. 14. And now, as I said unto you, that because ye were compelled to be humble ye were blessed, do ye not suppose that they are more blessed who truly humble themselves because of the word? 15. Yea, he that truly humbleth himself, and repenteth of his sins, and endureth to the end, the same shall be blessed— yea, much more blessed than they who are compelled to be humble because of their exceeding poverty. (*Alma preaches to the poor whose afflictions had humbled them, about 74 B.C.*) Alma 32:13-16

**Elder Joseph Fielding Smith**

Mark you, the Lord says before a man comes into the Church he must have a desire, he must come with a broken heart and contrite spirit. What is a broken heart? One that is humble, one that is touched by the Spirit of the Lord, and which is willing to abide in all the covenants and the obligations which the Gospel entails. . . . Every baptized person who has fully repented, who comes into the Church with a broken heart and a contrite spirit, has made a covenant to continue with that broken heart, with that contrite spirit, which means a repentant spirit. CR1941Oct:93

**King Benjamin,**
*quoted by Mormon*

And again, believe that ye must repent of your sins and forsake them, and humble yourselves before God; and ask in sincerity of heart that he would forgive you; and now, if you believe all these things see that ye do them. 11. And again I say unto you as I have said before, that as ye have come to the knowledge of the glory of God, or if ye have known of his goodness and have tasted of his love, and have received a remission of your sins, which causeth such exceedingly great joy in your souls, even so I would that ye should remember, and always retain in remembrance, the greatness of God, and your own nothingness, and his goodness and long-suffering towards you, unworthy creatures, and humble yourselves even in the depths of humility, calling on the name of the Lord daily, and standing steadfastly in the faith of that which is to come, which was spoken by the mouth of the angel. 12. And behold, I say unto you that if ye do this ye shall always rejoice, and be filled with the love of God, and always retain a remission of your sins; and ye shall grow in the knowledge of the glory of him that created you, or in the knowledge of that which is just and true. (*King Benjamin addresses his people, about 124 B.C.*) Mosiah 4:10-12

**Joseph Smith**

And again, by way of commandment to the church concerning the manner of baptism—All those who humble themselves before God, and desire to be baptized, and come forth with broken hearts and contrite spirits, and witness before the church that they have truly repented of all their sins, and are willing to take upon them the name of Jesus Christ, having a determination to serve him to the end, and truly manifest by their works that they have received of the Spirit of Christ unto the remission of their sins, shall be received by baptism into his church. (*Revelation on Church Organization and Government, April 1830; laws governing repentance, justification, sanctification, and baptism are set forth*) D&C 20:37

---

**355. The Lord chooses the humble to do His work.**

**Elder Joseph Fielding Smith**

The Lord called Joseph Smith and others from

among the weak things of the world, because he and his associates were contrite and humble. The great and mighty ones in the nations the Lord could not use because of their pride and self-righteousness. . . . ¶ The Lord's ways are not man's ways, and he cannot choose those who in their own judgment are too wise to be taught. Therefore he chooses those who are willing to be taught and he makes them mighty even to the breaking down of the great and mighty. . . . When we think of our missionary system, we can see how the weak have gone forth among the strong ones and have prevailed. The mighty and strong ones have been broken down by the humble elders of the Church. CHMR1:255; DCSM:5

**Joseph Smith,**
*receiving the Word of the Lord*
And also gave commandments to others, that they should proclaim these things unto the world; and all this that it might be fulfilled, which was written by the prophets— 19. The weak things of the world shall come forth and break down the mighty and strong ones, that man should not counsel his fellow man, neither trust in the arm of flesh. . . . 23. That the fulness of my gospel might be proclaimed by the weak and the simple unto the ends of the world, and before kings and rulers. (*Revelation received during conference of elders of the Church, Nov. 1, 1831; preface to the doctrines given to the Church*) D&C 1:18-19,23

**Joseph Smith,**
*receiving the Word of the Lord*
Wherefore, I call upon the weak things of the world, those who are unlearned and despised, to thrash the nations by the power of my Spirit; (*Revelation to Joseph Smith and Sidney Rigdon, Dec. 1830*) D&C 35:13

**Joseph Smith**
And for this cause, that men might be made partakers of the glories which were to be revealed, the Lord sent forth the fulness of his gospel, his everlasting covenant, reasoning in plainness and simplicity— 58. To prepare the weak for those things which are coming on the earth, and for the Lord's errand in the day when the weak shall confound the wise, and the little one become a strong nation, and two shall put their tens of thousands to flight. 59. And by the weak things of the earth the Lord shall thrash the nations by the power of his Spirit. (*Revelation received Nov. 3, 1831*) D&C 133:57-59

**Moroni, son of Mormon,**
*receiving the Word of the Lord*
And if men come unto me I will show unto them their weakness. I give unto men weakness that they may be humble; and my grace is sufficient for all men that humble themselves before me; for if they humble themselves before me, and have faith in me, then will I make weak things become strong unto them. (*The Lord speaks to Moroni*) Ether 12:27

**Paul**
But God hath chosen the foolish things of the world to confound the wise; and God hath chosen the weak things of the world to confound the things which are mighty; (*Letter to the Church at Corinth, Greece, about A.D. 55*) 1Cor.1:27

**President Wilford Woodruff**
The Lord has chosen the weak things of the world to lead this people. Joseph Smith was but a young man when he died—not forty years of age. He lived nearly fourteen years after the organization of this Church. President Brigham Young followed him. Who was Brigham Young? He was a painter and glazier. He was a humble man. But the Lord called him to lead this people. You know what he has done, and the spirit that was with him. The Lord was with him, and he continued to lead this people by the power of God and by the revelation of Jesus Christ. He laid the foundation of a great work in these mountains of Israel. Many strangers who have recently visited us have marveled and wondered at Salt Lake City being laid out in the manner it was. . . . What was John Taylor? He was a wood turner, and he led the Church for quite a time. Wilford Woodruff was a miller and a farmer; that was about the highest ambition he ever arrived at as far as this world was concerned. That is about the way the Lord has chosen these men. Why did he not choose these learned and great men? As I have often said, he could not handle them. God has always chosen the weak things of the earth. (The Discourses of Wilford Woodruff, pp. 86-87) TLDP:294

**Related Witnesses:**
**Joseph Smith,**
*receiving the Word of the Lord*
Verily, thus saith the Lord unto you, my servant Joseph Smith, I am well pleased with your offering and acknowledgments, which you have made; for unto this end have I raised you up, that I might show forth my wisdom through the weak things of the earth. (*Revelation received Jan. 19, 1841*) D&C 124:1

**Recorded in 1 Samuel**
But the LORD said unto Samuel, Look not on his countenance, or on the height of his stature; because I have refused him: for the LORD seeth not as man seeth; for man looketh on the outward appearance, but the LORD looketh on the heart. (*The Lord through Samuel chooses*

*David to be king; Samuel examines Eliab, son of Jesse*) 1Sam.16:7

**Joseph Smith,**
*quoted by Elder Joseph Fielding Smith*

There are a great many wise men and women too in our midst who are too wise to be taught; therefore they must die in their ignorance, and in the resurrection they will find their mistake. Many seal up the door of heaven by saying, So far God may reveal and I will believe. (*At the Stand in Nauvoo, Ill., June 11, 1843*) TPJS:309; HC5:424

---

**356. The path to exaltation is through the valley of humility (to reach the mountain height we must traverse the valley below).**

**Anthon H. Lund**

If we want to attain greatness, we must not forget this virtue of humility. Perhaps many of those who feel so self-righteous will find that to cultivate humility is a hard task; still it is necessary. We look forward to exaltation, but to obtain this we must go through the valley of humility. We must go down into it, and then ascend, and before us is a destiny so bright that we cannot conceive it. CR1901Apr:22

**Alma, the younger,**
*quoted by Mormon*

And now, as I said unto you, that because ye were compelled to be humble ye were blessed, do ye not suppose that they are more blessed who truly humble themselves because of the word? 15. Yea, he that truly humbleth himself, and repenteth of his sins, and endureth to the end, the same shall be blessed—yea, much more blessed than they who are compelled to be humble because of their exceeding poverty. (*Alma preaches to the poor, about 74 B.C.*) Alma 32:14-15

**Recorded in Job**

When men are cast down, then thou shalt say, There is lifting up; and he shall save the humble person. (*Eliphaz accuses Job of sins and exhorts him to repent*) Job 22:29

**Jesus,**
*recorded in Matthew*

Blessed are the poor in spirit: for theirs is the kingdom of heaven. . . . 5. Blessed are the meek: for they shall inherit the earth. . . . 8. Blessed are the pure in heart: for they shall see God. 9. Blessed are the peacemakers: for they shall be called the children of God. (*Jesus teaches the multitude, about A.D. 30*) Matt.5:3,5,8-9

**Jesus,**
*quoted by Mormon*

Yea, blessed are the poor in spirit who come unto me, for theirs is the kingdom of heaven. . . . 5. And blessed are the meek, for they shall inherit the earth. . . . 8. And blessed are all the pure in heart, for they shall see God. 9. And blessed are all the peacemakers, for they shall be called the children of God. (*The resurrected Jesus Christ teaches the Nephite people, A.D. 34*) 3Ne.12:3,5,8-9

**Jesus,**
*recorded in Matthew*

But he that is greatest among you shall be your servant. 12. And whosoever shall exalt himself shall be abased; and he that shall humble himself shall be exalted. (*Jesus preaches to the multitude and his disciples about scribes and Pharisees*) Matt.23:11-12

**Jesus,**
*recorded in Luke*

I tell you, this man went down to his house justified rather than the other: for every one that exalteth himself shall be abased; and he that humbleth himself shall be exalted. (*Jesus gives the parable of the Pharisee and publican*) Luke 18:14

**Jesus,**
*quoted by Mormon*

Therefore, whoso repenteth and cometh unto me as a little child, him will I receive, for of such is the kingdom of God. Behold, for such I have laid down my life, and have taken it up again; therefore repent, and come unto me ye ends of the earth, and be saved. (*The voice of the resurrected Jesus Christ to the Nephites immediately before he visited them, A.D. 34*) 3Ne.9:22

**King Benjamin,**
*quoted by Mormon*

And again I say unto you as I have said before, that as ye have come to the knowledge of the glory of God, or if ye have known of his goodness and have tasted of his love, and have received a remission of your sins, which causeth such exceedingly great joy in your souls, even so I would that ye should remember, and always retain in remembrance, the greatness of God, and your own nothingness, and his goodness and long-suffering towards you, unworthy creatures, and humble yourselves even in the depths of humility, calling on the name of the Lord daily, and standing steadfastly in the faith of that which is to come, which was spoken by the mouth of the angel. 12. And behold, I say unto you that if ye do this ye shall always rejoice, and be filled with the love of God, and always retain a remission of your sins; and ye shall grow in the knowledge of the glory of him that created you, or in the knowledge of that which is just and true. (*King Benjamin addresses his people, about 124 B.C.*) Mosiah 4:11-12

**Related Witnesses:**

**Elder Joseph Fielding Smith**

Mark you, the Lord says before a man comes into the Church he must have a desire; he must come with a broken heart and a contrite spirit. ¶ What is a broken heart? One that is humble, one that is touched by the Spirit of the Lord, and which is willing to abide in all the covenants and the obligations which the Gospel entails. . . . ¶ Every baptized person who has fully repented, who comes into the Church with a broken heart and a contrite spirit, has made a covenant to continue with that broken heart, with that contrite spirit, which means a repentant spirit. He makes a covenant that he will do that. CR1941Oct:93

---

### 357. The humble person will be blessed with knowledge and strength.

**Joseph Smith**

And inasmuch as they were humble they might be made strong, and blessed from on high, and receive knowledge from time to time. (*Revelation during conference of elders of the Church, Nov. 1, 1831*) D&C 1:28

**Elder Joseph F. Smith**

You can obtain this knowledge [of the gospel truths] through repentance, humility, and seeking the Lord with full purpose of heart until you find Him. He is not afar off. It is not difficult to approach Him, if we will only do it with a broken heart and a contrite spirit, as did Nephi of old [see 2 Ne.4:32]. This was the way in which Joseph Smith, in his boyhood, approached Him. He went into the woods, knelt down, and in humility he sought earnestly to know which church was acceptable to God. He received an answer to his prayer, which he offered from the depths of his heart, and he received it in a way that he did not expect. CR1899Oct:71

**Moroni, son of Mormon**

And when I had said this, the Lord spake unto me, saying: Fools mock, but they shall mourn; and my grace is sufficient for the meek, that they shall take no advantage of your weakness; 27. And if men come unto me I will show unto them their weakness. I give unto men weakness that they may be humble; and my grace is sufficient for all men that humble themselves before me; for if they humble themselves before me,

and have faith in me, then will I make weak things become strong unto them. (*The Lord speaks to Moroni*) Ether 12:26-27

**Thomas S. Monson**

For those who humbly seek, there is no need to stumble or falter along the pathway leading to truth. It is well marked by our Heavenly Father. We must first have a desire to know for ourselves. We must study. We must pray. We must do the will of the Father. And then we will know the truth, and the truth will make us free. Divine favor will attend those who humbly seek it. CR1964Oct:19

**King Benjamin,**
*quoted by Mormon*

And again I say unto you as I have said before, that as ye have come to the knowledge of the glory of God, or if ye have known of his goodness and have tasted of his love, and have received a remission of your sins, which causeth such exceedingly great joy in your souls, even so I would that ye should remember, and always retain in remembrance, the greatness of God, and your own nothingness, and his goodness and long-suffering towards you, unworthy creatures, and humble yourselves even in the depths of humility, calling on the name of the Lord daily, and standing steadfastly in the faith of that which is to come, which was spoken by the mouth of the angel. 12. And behold, I say unto you that if ye do this ye shall always rejoice, and be filled with the love of God, and always retain a remission of your sins; and ye shall grow in the knowledge of the glory of him that created you, or in the knowledge of that which is just and true. (*King Benjamin addresses his people, about 124 B.C.*) Mosiah 4:11-12

**Jacob, brother of Nephi,**
*quoted by Nephi*

And whoso knocketh, to him will he open; and the wise, and the learned, and they that are rich, who are puffed up because of their learning, and their wisdom, and their riches—yea, they are they whom he despiseth; and save they shall cast these things away, and consider themselves fools before God, and come down in the depths of humility, he will not open unto them. (*Jacob teaches the doctrine of the atonement to the people of Nephi, 559-545 B.C.*) 2Ne.9:42

**Joseph Smith**

We are called to hold the keys of the mysteries of those things that have been kept hid from the foundation of the world until now. Some have tasted a little of these things, many of which are to be poured down from heaven upon the heads of babes; yea, upon the weak, obscure and despised ones of the earth. Therefore we beseech of you, brethren, that you bear with those who do not feel themselves more worthy than yourselves, while we exhort one another to a reformation with one and all, both old and young, teachers and taught, both high and low, rich and poor, bond and free, male and female; let honesty, and sobriety, and candor, and solemnity, and virtue, and pureness, and meekness, and simplicity crown our heads in every place; and in fine, become as little children, without malice, guile or hypocrisy. (*Epistle to the Church from Liberty Jail, Mar. 25, 1839*) HC3:296

**Related Witnesses:**

### Alma, the younger,
#### quoted by Mormon

And now Alma began to expound these things unto him, saying: It is given unto many to know the mysteries of God; nevertheless they are laid under a strict command that they shall not impart only according to the portion of his word which he doth grant unto the children of men, according to the heed and diligence which they give unto him. 10. And therefore, he that will harden his heart, the same receiveth the lesser portion of the word; and he that will not harden his heart, to him is given the greater portion of the word, until it is given unto him to know the mysteries of God until he know them in full. 11. And they that will harden their hearts, to them is given the lesser portion of the word until they know nothing concerning his mysteries; and then they are taken captive by the devil, and led by his will down to destruction. Now this is what is meant by the chains of hell. (*Alma contends with the lawyer Zeezrom, about 82 B.C.*) Alma 12:9-11

---

## 358. By cultivating humility we can avoid the pitfalls of worldly pride and philosophies.

### Oliver Cowdery

Should you in the least degree come short of your duty, great will be your condemnation; for the greater the calling the greater the transgression. I therefore warn you to cultivate great humility; for I know the pride of the human head. Beware, lest the flatterers of the world lift you up; beware, lest your affections be captivated by worldly objects. (*Oliver Cowdery addresses the Twelve, 1835*) HC2:195; MPSG1989:17

### Stephen L. Richards

Why is it so difficult to accept things on faith? I think I can suggest an answer. It is because we are so conceited. Men of the world are in the world only because they adopt the philosophy of the world, which is the philosophy of self-sufficiency. It is not a humble philosophy—it is highly egotistical. It makes men themselves the arbiters of all things. They look to no higher source than themselves for the solution of all questions. ¶ Such a philosophy is diametrically opposed to the philosophy of Christ, which is that of faith. When men adopt his philosophy they are humble—they acknowledge an intelligence far superior to their own and they seek guidance and wisdom from that source. When they adopt the philosophy of faith, they come out of the world, for the world, as a term in theology, is not a place but a condition or state of mind and feeling. It requires courage to come out of the world and adopt the philosophy of faith. Sometimes it subjects one to ridicule and to contempt of friends which are harder for most men to endure than physical pain; but because a thing is hard to do or hard to believe is no assurance that it is not right. CR1935Apr:30-31

### King Benjamin,
#### quoted by Mormon

For the natural man is an enemy to God, and has been from the fall of Adam, and will be, forever and ever, unless he yields to the enticings of the Holy Spirit, and putteth off the natural man and becometh a saint through the atonement of Christ the Lord, and becometh as a child, submissive, meek, humble, patient, full of love, willing to submit to all things which the Lord seeth fit to inflict upon him, even as a child doth submit to his father. (*King Benjamin addresses his people, about 124 B.C.*) Mosiah 3:19

### Richard L. Evans

May I suggest humility and never the pride of learning. Be patient. There may be some seeming discrepancies. Do not worry about them. Eternity is a long time. I have great respect for learning, for academic endeavor and the university atmosphere. I have spent many years of my life in one way or another going to or in being associated with some great institutions of learning. I have a great respect for science and scientists and for the search for truth. But remember this: science, after all (even when it is true and final and factual), is simply a man's discovering of a few things that God already knows and controls in his ordering of the universe. We are, after all, a bit like Newton who said of himself that he was like a child handling a few pebbles on the shore while the great, limitless, eternal sea was before him. God has not told us all he knows. We believe in continuous revelation. Be patient. Keep humble and balanced in all things. CR1961Apr:76

**Jesus,**
*recorded in Luke*

And he spake this parable unto certain which trusted in themselves that they were righteous, and despised others: 10. Two men went up into the temple to pray; the one a Pharisee, and the other a publican. 11. The Pharisee stood and prayed thus with himself, God, I thank thee, that I am not as other men are, extortioners, unjust, adulterers, or even as this publican. 12. I fast twice in the week, I give tithes of all that I possess. 13. And the publican, standing afar off, would not lift up so much as his eyes unto heaven, but smote upon his breast, saying, God be merciful to me a sinner. 14. I tell you, this man went down to his house justified rather than the other: for every one that exalteth himself shall be abased; and he that humbleth himself shall be exalted. (*Jesus gives the parable of the Pharisee and publican*) Luke 18:9-14

**President Ezra Taft Benson**

Humility responds to God's will—to the fear of His judgments and to the needs of those around us. To the proud, the applause of the world rings in their ears; to the humble, the applause of heaven warms their hearts. CR1986Apr:6; MPSG1989:18

**President Ezra Taft Benson**

Pride is the universal sin, the great vice. Yes, pride *is* the universal sin, the great vice. ¶ The antidote for pride is humility—meekness, submissiveness. It is the broken heart and contrite spirit. As Rudyard Kipling put it so well: ¶ The tumult and the shouting dies; ¶ The captains and the kings depart. ¶ Still stands thine ancient sacrifice, ¶ An humble and a contrite heart. ¶ Lord God of Hosts, be with us yet, ¶ Lest we forget, lest we forget. [HYMNS:80.] CR1989Apr:6

# List of Doctrines

## JESUS CHRIST:

### Appearances After His Crucifixion

*Doctrines Located in This Topic*

*Doctrines on JESUS CHRIST Located in Other Topics*

359. Jesus Christ rose from the dead after being crucified on a cross and buried in a tomb.

(See topic GOD)

360. The resurrected Christ appeared to many mortals in the Eastern Hemisphere following His crucifixion.

361. Christ appeared to the Nephite people in the Western Hemisphere soon after He was crucified.

362. Christ lives today—modern prophets have seen Him face to face and have talked with Him.

# JESUS CHRIST:

## Appearances After His Crucifixion

**359. Jesus Christ rose from the dead after being crucified on a cross and buried in a tomb.**

### President Heber J. Grant

We believe that Christ, divinely begotten, was born of woman, that He lived a mortal life, that He was crucified on the cross, that He died, His spirit leaving His body, and was buried, and was on the third day resurrected, His spirit and body re-uniting. We believe this is the exact pattern we shall all follow. We believe that all men will be resurrected, that "men will be punished for their own sins, and not for Adam's transgression." (*At memorial services, Zion Canyon, Utah, May 30, 1937)* MOFP6:33

### Mark E. Petersen

Next we affirm the Jesus Christ of Nazareth is indeed the Christ—he who was born in Bethlehem on the first Christmas . . . he who was persecuted by the religious cults of the day, was condemned to the cross, but who conquered death and the grave in a glorious resurrection on the third day afterward. CR1980Apr:93-94

### John

And he bearing his cross went forth into a place called the place of a skull. . . . 18. Where they crucified him, and two other with him, on either side one, and Jesus in the midst. . . . 30. When Jesus therefore had received the vinegar, he said, It is finished: and he bowed his head, and gave up the ghost. . . . 40. Then took they the body of Jesus, and wound it in linen clothes with the spices, as the manner of the Jews is to bury. 41. Now in the place where he was crucified there was a garden; and in the garden a new sepulchre, wherein was never man yet laid. 42. There laid they Jesus. . . . 20:17. Jesus saith unto her, Touch me not; for I am not yet ascended to my Father: but go to my brethren, and say unto them, I ascend unto my Father, and your Father; and to my God, and your God. (*Jesus is crucified and arises from dead; Mary Magdalene finds the tomb empty, sees Jesus whom she supposes to be a gardener; he speaks to her and she recognizes the risen Christ)* John 19:17-18,30,40-42; 20:17

### Jesus,
#### quoted by Mormon

Behold, I am Jesus Christ, whom the prophets testified shall come into the world. 11. And behold, I am the light and the life of the world; and I have drunk out of that bitter cup which the Father hath given me, and have glorified the

Father in taking upon me the sins of the world, in the which I have suffered the will of the Father in all things from the beginning. (*The risen Jesus Christ appears to the Nephite people on the American continent soon after his ascension into heaven following the crucifixion, A.D. 34)* 3Ne.11:10-11

### Bruce R. McConkie

Who, then, is the God of our Fathers, the god of Abraham, of Isaac, and of Jacob? He is the one who "yieldeth himself . . . as a man, into the hands of wicked men, to be lifted up . . . to be crucified . . . and to be buried in a sepulchre" (1 Ne.19:10), and to rise again in glory and triumph. He is Christ. It was Christ who appeared to Abraham. It was Christ who covenanted with him and then with Isaac and with Jacob. It was Christ of whom Nephi spoke when he said: "The fulness of mine intent is that I may persuade men to come unto the God of Abraham, and the God of Isaac, and the God of Jacob, and be saved." (1 Ne.6:4) ¶ . . . . Whatever the world may imagine, whatever any of the cultist sects of Christendom may attempt to expound relative to Jehovah, whatever the wisdom of men may suppose, the plain, unalterable fact is that the Lord Jehovah was the promised Savior, Redeemer, Deliverer, and Messiah, and that he is Christ. (The Promised Messiah, pp. 164-65) TLDP:305-06

### Related Witnesses:
#### Recorded in Luke

Now upon the first day of the week, very early in the morning, they came unto the sepulchre, bringing the spices which they had prepared, and certain others with them. 2. And they found the stone rolled away from the sepulchre. 3. And they entered in, and found not the body of the Lord Jesus. 4. And it came to pass, as they were much perplexed thereabout, behold, two men stood by them in shining garments: 5. And as they were afraid, and bowed down their faces to the earth, they said unto them, Why seek ye the living among the dead? 6. He is not here, but is risen: remember how he spake unto you when he was yet in Galilee, 7. Saying, The Son of man must be delivered into the hands of sinful men, and be crucified, and the third day rise again. (*Mary Magdalene and other women visit the tomb and receive the announcement by angels that Christ is resurrected)* Luke 24:1-7

### Jesus,
#### recorded in Luke

And as they thus spake, Jesus himself stood in

the midst of them, and saith unto them, Peace be unto you. 37. But they were terrified and affrighted, and supposed that they had seen a spirit. 38. And he said unto them, Why are ye troubled? and why do thoughts arise in your hearts? 39. Behold my hands and my feet, that it is I myself: handle me, and see; for a spirit hath not flesh and bones, as ye see me have. (*The risen Christ appears to the eleven Apostles*) Luke 24:36-39

**Mormon**

[S]oon after the ascension of Christ into heaven he did truly manifest himself unto them— 19. Showing his body unto them, . . . (*The risen Jesus Christ appears to the Nephite people on the American continent soon after his ascension into heaven following the crucifixion, A.D. 34*) 3Ne.10:18-19

---

**360. The resurrected Christ appeared to many mortals in the Eastern Hemisphere following His crucifixion.**

**James E. Talmage**

When Cleopas and his companion reached Jerusalem that night, they found the apostles and other devoted believers assembled in solemn and worshipful discourse within closed doors. Precautions of secrecy had been taken "for fear of the Jews." Even the apostles had been scattered by the arrest, arraignment, and judicial murder of their Master; but they and the disciples in general rallied anew at the word of His resurrection, as the nucleus of an army soon to sweep the world. The two returning disciples were received with the joyous announcement, "The Lord is risen indeed, and hath appeared to Simon." This is the sole mention made by the Gospel-writers of Christ's personal appearance to Simon Peter on that day. The interview between the Lord and His once recreant but now repentant apostle must have been affecting in the extreme. Peter's remorseful penitence over his denial of Christ in the palace of the high priest was deep and pitiful; he may have doubted that ever again would the Master call him His servant; but hope must have been engendered through the message from the tomb brought by the women, in which the Lord sent greetings to the apostles, whom for the first time He designated as His brethren, and from this honorable and affectionate characterization Peter had not been excluded; moreover, the angel's commission to the women had given prominence to Peter by particular mention. To

the repentant Peter came the Lord, doubtless with forgiveness and loving assurance. The apostle himself maintains a reverent silence respecting the visitation, but the fact thereof is attested by Paul as one of the definite proofs of the Lord's resurrection. JTC:687-88

**Recorded in Mark**

Now when Jesus was risen early the first day of the week, he appeared first to Mary Magdalene, out of whom he had cast seven devils. 10. And she went and told them that had been with him, as they mourned and wept. 11. And they, when they had heard that he was alive, and had been seen of her, believed not. 12. After that he appeared in another form unto two of them, as they walked, and went into the country. 13. And they went and told it unto the residue: neither believed they them. 14. Afterward he appeared unto the eleven as they sat at meat, and upbraided them with their unbelief and hardness of heart, because they believed not them which had seen him after he was risen. (*The risen Jesus Christ appears*) Mark 16:9-14

**Jesus,**
*recorded in Luke*

And as they thus spake, Jesus himself stood in the midst of them, and saith unto them, Peace be unto you. 37. But they were terrified and affrighted, and supposed that they had seen a spirit. 38. And he said unto them, Why are ye troubled? and why do thoughts arise in your hearts? 39. Behold my hands and my feet, that it is I myself: handle me, and see; for a spirit hath not flesh and bones, as ye see me have. (*The risen Christ appears to the eleven Apostles*) Luke 24:36-39

**Recorded in Acts**

The former treatise have I made, O Theophilus, of all that Jesus began both to do and teach, 2. Until the day in which he was taken up, after that he through the Holy Ghost had given commandments unto the apostles whom he had chosen: 3. To whom also he shewed himself alive after his passion by many infallible proofs, being seen of them forty days, and speaking of the things pertaining to the kingdom of God: (*Thus begins the second of a two-part work written to Theophilus, the first part known as the book of Luke*) Acts 1:1-3

**James E. Talmage**

Then Jesus said, "Come and dine"; and as the Host at the meal, He divided and distributed the bread and fish. We are not told that He ate with His guests. Everyone knew that it was the Lord who so hospitably served; yet on this, as on all other occasions of His appearing in the resurrected state, there was about Him an awe-inspiring and restraining demeanor. They would have liked to question Him, but durst not. John tells us that this was the "third time that Jesus shewed himself to his disciples, after that he was risen from the dead"; by which we understand the occasion to have been the third on which Christ had manifested Himself to the apostles, in complete or partial assembly; for, including also the appearing to Mary Magdalene, to the other women, to Peter, and to the two disciples on the country road, this was the seventh recorded appearance of the risen Lord. JTC:692

### Recorded in Matthew

And the angel answered and said unto the women, Fear not ye: for I know that ye seek Jesus, which was crucified. 6. He is not here: for he is risen, as he said. Come, see the place where the Lord lay. 7. And go quickly, and tell his disciples that he is risen from the dead; and, behold, he goeth before you into Galilee; there shall ye see him: lo, I have told you. 8. And they departed quickly from the sepulchre with fear and great joy; and did run to bring his disciples word. 9. And as they went to tell his disciples, behold, Jesus met them, saying, All hail. And they came and held him by the feet, and worshipped him. 10. Then said Jesus unto them, Be not afraid: go tell my brethren that they go into Galilee, and there shall they see me. . . . 16. Then the eleven disciples went away into Galilee, into a mountain where Jesus had appointed them. 17. And when they saw him, they worshipped him: but some doubted. (*The risen Jesus appears to the eleven Apostles*) Matt.28:5-10,16-17

**Related Witnesses:**

### Jesus,
### *quoted by John*

Jesus saith unto her, Touch me not; for I am not yet ascended to my Father: but go to my brethren, and say unto them, I ascend unto my Father, and your Father; and to my God, and your God. (*Mary Magdalene finds the tomb empty, sees Jesus whom she supposes to be a gardener; he speaks to her and she recognizes the risen Christ*) John 20:17

### Stephen

But he, being full of the Holy Ghost, looked up stedfastly into heaven, and saw the glory of God, and Jesus standing on the right hand of God, 56. And said, Behold, I see the heavens opened, and the Son of man standing on the right hand of God. (*Stephen receives and declares the vision of the Father and the Son, after which he is stoned to death*) Acts 7:55-56

### Paul

Whereupon as I went to Damascus with author-

ity and commission from the chief priests, 13. At midday, O king, I saw in the way a light from heaven, above the brightness of the sun, shining round about me and them which journeyed with me. 14. And when we were all fallen to the earth, I heard a voice speaking unto me, and saying in the Hebrew tongue, Saul, Saul, why persecutest thou me? it is hard for thee to kick against the pricks. 15. And I said, Who art thou, Lord? And he said, I am Jesus whom thou persecutest. 16. But rise, and stand upon thy feet: for I have appeared unto thee for this purpose, to make thee a minister and a witness both of these things which thou hast seen, and of those things in the which I will appear unto thee; (*Paul testifies before King Agrippa of the appearance of Jesus on the road to Damascus*) Acts 26:12-16

---

## 361. Christ appeared to the Nephite people in the Western Hemisphere soon after He was crucified.

### Howard W. Hunter,
### *also quoting Jesus,*
### *quoted by Mormon*

An account in the Book of Mormon, a second witness for Christ, gives us additional knowledge of the teachings of the Master. This record tells of his appearance to the people of this Western Hemisphere after his death and resurrection, adding much to our understanding of the great atoning sacrifice. ¶ . . . . A multitude assembled at the temple in the land Bountiful. . . . . They cast their eyes toward heaven and beheld a man clothed in a white robe who descended and stood in the midst of them. ¶ "And it came to pass that he stretched forth his hand and spake unto the people, saying: ¶ "Behold, I am Jesus Christ. . . . ¶ "Arise and come forth unto me, that ye may thrust your hands into my side, and also that ye may feel the prints of the nails in my hands and in my feet. . . ." [See 3Ne.11:14.] CR1973Apr:172-74

### James E. Talmage

The identity of Jesus Christ with the Jehovah of the Israelites was well understood by the Nephite prophets, and the truth of their teachings was confirmed by the risen Lord who manifested Himself unto them shortly after His ascension from the midst of the apostles at Jerusalem. JTC:38

### David B. Haight
### *also quoting Jesus,*
### *quoted by Mormon*

It may be beyond our own comprehension to realize what Jesus meant to Nephi when the resurrected Christ appeared on the western continent, saying, "Behold, I am Jesus Christ, whom the prophets testified shall come into the world. . . ." CR1974Apr:98

### Mormon

And now it came to pass that there were a great multitude gathered together, of the people of Nephi, round about the temple which was in the land Bountiful; and they were marveling and wondering one with another, and were showing one to another the great and marvelous change which had taken place. 2. And they were also conversing about this Jesus Christ, of whom the sign had been given concerning his death. 3. And it came to pass that while they were thus conversing one with another, they heard a voice as if it came out of heaven; and they cast their eyes round about, for they understood not the voice which they heard; and it was not a harsh voice, neither was it a loud voice; nevertheless, and notwithstanding it being a small voice it did pierce them that did hear to the center, insomuch that there was no part of their frame that it did not cause to quake; yea, it did pierce them to the very soul, and did cause their hearts to burn. 4. And it came to pass that again they heard the voice, and they understood it not. 5. And again the third time they did hear the voice, and did open their ears to hear it; and their eyes were towards the sound thereof; and they did look steadfastly towards heaven, from whence the sound came. 6. And behold, the third time they did understand the voice which they heard; and it said unto them: 7. Behold my Beloved Son, in whom I am well pleased, in whom I have glorified my name—hear ye him. 8. And it came to pass, as they understood they cast their eyes up again towards heaven; and behold, they saw a Man descending out of heaven; and he was clothed in a white robe; and he came down and stood in the midst of them; and the eyes of the whole multitude were turned upon him, and they durst not open their mouths, even one to another, and wist not what it meant, for they thought it was an angel that had appeared unto them. 9. And it came to pass that he stretched forth his hand and spake unto the people, saying: 10. Behold, I am Jesus Christ, whom the prophets testified shall come into the world. (*The risen Jesus Christ appears to the Nephite people on the American continent soon after his ascension into heaven following the crucifixion, A.D. 34*) 3Ne.11:1-10

### Mormon

[S]oon after the ascension of Christ into heaven he did truly manifest himself unto them— 19. Showing his body unto them, . . . 3Ne.10:18-19

### Related Witnesses:
#### President Brigham Young,
##### *quoted by John A. Widtsoe*

Jesus has been upon the earth a great many more times than you are aware of. When Jesus makes his next appearance upon the earth, but few of this Church will be prepared to receive him and see him face to face and converse with him; but he will come to his temple. Will he remain and dwell upon the earth a thousand years, without returning? He will come here, and return to his mansions where he dwells with his Father, and come again to the earth, and again return to his Father, according to my understanding. (*In Tabernacle, May 22, 1859, JD7:142*) DBY:114

## 362. Christ lives today—modern prophets have seen Him face to face and have talked with Him.

### Mark E. Petersen

He *is* the Savior of mankind! He *is* the Redeemer of all flesh! He *did* arise from the grave. . . . He *is* risen, as the angel said, in physical, corporeal reality. And he lives today! Our modern prophets have seen him face to face and have talked with him. We know that he lives and by his resurrection he will also give to each of us a victory over death, for we too shall be resurrected—physically and literally. We too shall live again. That is our testimony on this Easter day. ¶ We testify also that Christ has spoken again in our day, that he has raised up new prophets and through them has reestablished his Church on earth as it was originally when he called Peter, James, and John, Thomas, Judas, and others into the ministry. CR1980Apr:94

### Bruce R. McConkie

The fact of the resurrection is the most certain surety in all history; a cloud of witnesses testify thereto, including those in our day who also have seen and felt and handled; and all who will, may receive the same sure witness from the Holy Spirit of God. The resurrection from the dead—above all else—proves he is the Son of God. This is our witness; there is no doubt whatever; Jesus Christ is the Son of the living God who was crucified for the sins of the world. (The Mortal Messiah, 4:414-15) TLDP:317

### Joseph Smith

And now, after the many testimonies which have been given of him, this is the testimony, last of all, which we give of him: That he lives! 23. For we saw him, even on the right hand of

God; and we heard the voice bearing record that he is the Only Begotten of the Father—24. That by him, and through him, and of him, the worlds are and were created, and the inhabitants thereof are begotten sons and daughters unto God. (*Vision to Joseph Smith and Sidney Rigdon, Feb. 16, 1832*) D&C 76:22-24

**Related Witnesses:**

### Joseph Smith

After I had retired to the place where I had previously designed to go, having looked around me, and finding myself alone, I kneeled down and began to offer up the desires of my heart to God. I had scarcely done so, when immediately I was seized upon by some power which entirely overcame me, and had such an astonishing influence over me as to bind my tongue so that I could not speak. Thick darkness gathered around me, and it seemed to me for a time as if I were doomed to sudden destruction. 16. But, exerting all my powers to call upon God to deliver me out of the power of this enemy which had seized upon me, and at the very moment when I was ready to sink into despair and abandon myself to destruction—not to an imaginary ruin, but to the power of some actual being from the unseen world, who had such marvelous power as I had never before felt in any being—just at this moment of great alarm, I saw a pillar of light exactly over my head, above the brightness of the sun, which descended gradually until it fell upon me. 17. It no sooner appeared than I found myself delivered from the enemy which held me bound. When the light rested upon me I saw two Personages, whose brightness and glory defy all description, standing above me in the air. One of them spake unto me, calling me by name and said, pointing to the other—This is My Beloved Son. Hear Him! (*Joseph receives a visitation of the Father and the Son, spring of 1820*) JS-H 1:15-17

# List of Doctrines

## JOY AND HAPPINESS

*Doctrines Located in This Topic*

363. Happiness is the object and design of our existence.

364. True happiness and joy are not found in the frivolous or carnal pleasures of the world.

365. When we are actively engaged in a virtuous cause we can experience true happiness.

366. Keeping the commandments of God fosters happiness.

367. Only by entering the kingdom of god (the celestial kingdom) can we realize a fulness of joy.

*Doctrines on JOY AND HAPPINESS Located in Other Topics*

35. We cannot receive a fulness of joy in the celestial kingdom without the resurrection, in which our spirits and our bodies are inseparably reunited.

126. In the spirit world, after death, there is a separation of spirits that lasts until the resurrection and final judgment; the wicked go into a state of outer darkness, and the righteous go into a state of happiness.

188. In the Garden of Eden, Adam and Eve were in a state of innocence, not understanding good and evil, and having neither joy nor misery.

293. Before God sent us to the earth He prepared a plan of salvation for us.

302. A physical body is essential to obtaining a fulness of joy in the celestial kingdom of God.

740. Happiness comes from serving others.

750. It is more blessed to give than to receive (there is more joy in serving than in being served).

760. We experience joy when we choose the good and reject the evil.

762. The person who persists in sin cannot have joy, for wickedness never was happiness.

875. The worldly wise, who will not humble themselves before God, will never enjoy eternal happiness.

# JOY AND HAPPINESS

**363. Happiness is the object and design of our existence.**

**Joseph Smith,**
*quoted by Elder Joseph Fielding Smith*
Happiness is the object and design of our existence; and will be the end thereof, if we pursue the path that leads to it; and this path is virtue, uprightness, faithfulness, holiness, and keeping all the commandments of God. . . . ¶ . . . . [A]s God has designed our happiness—and the happiness of all His creatures, he never has—He never will institute an ordinance or give a commandment to His people that is not calculated in its nature to promote that happiness which He has designed, and which will not end in the greatest amount of good and glory to those who become the recipients of his law and ordinances. (*An essay recorded in the Journal History [HC5:134-35] Aug. 27, 1842*) TPJS:255-56; DGSM:27

**Lehi,**
*quoted by his son Nephi*
Adam fell that men might be; and men are, that they might have joy. (*Lehi teaches his sons, between 588-570 B.C.*) 2Ne.2:25

**Elder Lorenzo Snow**
There is nothing the Latter-day Saints can imagine that would afford them happiness that God has not unfolded to us. He has prepared everything for the Latter-day Saints that they could possibly wish or imagine in order to effect their complete happiness throughout the vast eternities. (*Teachings of Lorenzo Snow, p. 63*) DGSM:28

**President David O. McKay**
Pleasure is not the purpose of man's existence. Joy is. (*In Church News, Aug. 1951, Gospel Ideals, p. 492*) TLDP:318

**Joseph Smith,**
*translating the Book of Moses*
And in that day Adam blessed God and was filled, and began to prophesy concerning all the families of the earth, saying: Blessed be the name of God, for because of my transgression my eyes are opened, and in this life I shall have joy, and again in the flesh I shall see God. 11. And Eve, his wife, heard all these things and was glad, saying: Were it not for our transgression we never should have had seed, and never should have known good and evil, and the joy of our redemption, and the eternal life which God giveth unto all the obedient. (*The record of Moses: Adam realizes that through Adam and Eve's transgression they may receive joy and eternal life, and he therefore blesses the name of God*) Moses 5:10-11

---

**364. True happiness and joy are not found in the frivolous or carnal pleasures of the world.**

**James E. Talmage**
Happiness includes all that is really desirable of a true worth in pleasure, and much beside. Happiness is genuine gold, pleasure but gilded brass, which corrodes in the hand, and is soon converted into poisonous verdigris. Happiness is as the genuine diamond, which, rough and polished, shines with its own inimitable luster; pleasure is as the paste imitation that glows only when artificially embellished. Happiness is as the ruby, red as the heart's blood, hard and enduring; pleasure as stained glass, soft, brittle, and of but transitory beauty. ¶ Happiness is true food, wholesome, nutritious and sweet; it builds up the body and generates energy for action, physical, mental and spiritual; pleasure is but a deceiving stimulant which, like spirituous drink, makes one think he is strong when in reality enfeebled; makes him fancy he is well when in fact stricken with deadly malady. ¶ Happiness leaves no bad after-taste, it is followed by no depressing reaction; it calls for no repentance, brings no regret, entails no remorse; pleasure too often makes necessary repentance, contrition, and suffering; and, if indulged to the extreme, it brings degradation and destruction. ¶ True happiness is lived over and over again in memory, always with a renewal of the original good; a moment of unholy pleasure may leave a barbed sting, which, like a thorn in the flesh, is an ever-present source of anguish. ¶ Happiness is not akin with levity, nor is it one with light-minded mirth. It springs from the deeper fountains of the soul, and is not infrequently accompanied by tears. Have you never been so happy that you have had to weep? I have. ("A Greeting to the Missionaries," IE1913Dec:17) TLDP:318-19

**Alma, the younger**
*quoted by Mormon*
Behold, I say unto you, wickedness never was happiness. (*Alma speaks to his son Corianton, concerning the resurrection of the dead, about 73 B.C.*) Alma 41:10

**Rudger Clawson**
The man who expects to find a fulness of joy

in the light and frivolous pleasures of the world, or in matters pertaining strictly to the world, will be sadly disappointed, because it is said that a man whose heart is wedded to the things of the world is carnally minded, and we are told in the scriptures that to be carnally minded, or altogether worldly minded, is death, but to be spiritually minded is life eternal. There it is, and we should remember that as Latter-day Saints we must not give ourselves wholly and completely to worldly things, loving them above everything else. We have to deal with them, and we need them, too, but we must be spiritually minded if we will attain to a fulness of joy. CR1932Oct:10

**George Q. Cannon**
It is not given to men and women on the earth to be entirely satisfied, if they seek for satisfaction and happiness in worldly things. There is only one way in which perfect happiness can be obtained, and that is by having the Spirit of God. (Gospel Truth, 2:317-18) TLDP:319

**Related Witnesses:**
**President David O. McKay**
Pleasure is not the purpose of man's existence. Joy is. (Church News; Gospel Ideals, p. 492) TLDP:318

---

365. When we are actively engaged in a virtuous cause we can experience true happiness.

**Joseph Smith,**
*quoted by Elder Joseph Fielding Smith*
Happiness is the object and design of our existence; and will be the end thereof, if we pursue the path that leads to it; and this path is virtue, uprightness, faithfulness, holiness, and keeping all the commandments of God. *(An essay recorded in the Journal History, Aug. 27, 1842)* HC5:134-35; TPJS:255-56; DGSM:27

**Joseph Smith,**
*receiving the Word of the Lord*
Verily I say, men should be anxiously engaged in a good cause, and do many things of their own free will, and bring to pass much righteousness; 28. For the power is in them, wherein they are agents unto themselves. And inasmuch as men do good they shall in nowise lose their reward. *(Revelation for the elders of the Church, Aug. 1, 1831; the Lord instructs the Saints to counsel with each other and with the Lord)* D&C 58:27-28

**President Spencer W. Kimball**
The way for each person and each family to guard against the slings and arrows of the

Adversary and to prepare for the great day of the Lord, is to hold fast to the iron rod, to exercise greater faith, to repent of our sins and shortcomings, and to be anxiously engaged in the work of His kingdom on earth, which is The Church of Jesus Christ of Latter-day Saints. Herein lies the only true happiness for all our Father's children. CR1982Oct:4

**Rudger Clawson**
[Man] may get great happiness from what he does do in righteousness.... CR1932Oct:9

**President David O. McKay**
Man's greatest happiness comes from losing himself for the good of others. CR1963Oct:8

**Elder David O. McKay**
Actions in harmony with divine law and the laws of nature will bring happiness and those in opposition to divine truth, misery. Man is responsible not only for every deed, but also for every idle word and thought. CR1950Apr:33

**Related Witnesses:**
**President David O. McKay**
The first condition of happiness is a clear conscience. No man who does wrong or who is unvirtuous will be happy. . . . (Church News; Gospel Ideals, p. 498) TLDP:320

**Elder Heber J. Grant**
Make a motto in life; always try to assist someone else to carry his burden. The true key to happiness in life is to labor for the happiness of others. *(To students at University of Utah, 1901)* (Gospel Standards, p. 161) TLDP:320

**George Q. Cannon**
Whence comes your enjoyment? Whence come the glorious feelings that you have when you feel the best? Do they come from the outside? Do external circumstances produce real happiness of the kind that I describe? Doubtless, they contribute to happiness; but the purest joy, the greatest happiness, that which is most heavenly proceeds from within. A man must carry the principles of happiness and the love of God in his own breast, or he will not be happy. ¶ It is not true enjoyment when it comes from any other source. Not from without, therefore, must we expect happiness and exaltation, but from within. Deity is within us, and its development brings happiness and joy inexpressible. (Gospel Truth, 1:99) TLDP:319

**Nephi, son of Lehi**
And it came to pass that we lived after the manner of happiness. *(Nephi writes on plates shortly after the death of his father Lehi, 569-559 B.C.)* 2Ne.5:27

**Marion G. Romney**
The key to happiness is to get the Spirit and keep it. CR1961Oct:61

### Alma, the younger,
*quoted by Mormon*

41:10 Behold, I say unto you, wickedness never was happiness. . . . 42:8. Now behold, it was not expedient that man should be reclaimed from this temporal death, for that would destroy the great plan of happiness. (*Alma speaks to his son Corianton, concerning the resurrection of the dead, about 73 B.C.*) Alma 41:10; 42:8

**Author's Note:** Dennis F. Rasmussen writes this about happiness: "In the words of Aristotle, written over 2,300 years ago, happiness is 'an activity of soul in accordance with virtue' (I:vii). This idea will sound familiar to Latter-day Saints, who believe in being virtuous. . . . The final aim of all [man's] action is happiness. But as Aristotle saw, happiness is not an object, not a thing to be acted upon, not something to be kept, hoarded, or defended against thieves. Happiness is activity. . . . But happiness is not just any activity. It is '*an activity of soul in accordance with virtue.*' . . . The real test of our faith is how we act. There is deep wisdom, then, in a familiar idiom of Latter-day Saints. When we want to speak of someone's religious commitment, we do not usually say he is pious or observant or devout. Instead we say he is faithful, or, more commonly, we say he is *active*. A faithful member of the Church *is an active member*, because faith is the principle of action. . . . ¶ Now since happiness is 'an activity of soul in accordance with virtue,' not just acting, but acting in a certain way is required for happiness. We perform the actions that will finally yield happiness only by choosing first to follow virtue. . . . Only the virtuous, only those who seek the good, only those who keep God's commandments are worthy of happiness. And only those who are worthy of happiness can achieve it. This is not because God or anyone else would seek to withhold it, but because happiness is 'an activity of soul in accordance with virtue.'. . . Happiness requires, happiness *is* a virtuous or moral way of acting." (See Lectures on Faith in Historical Perspective, pp. 167-74.)

---

### 366. Keeping the commandments fosters happiness.

### King Benjamin,
*quoted by Mormon*

And moreover, I would desire that ye should consider on the blessed and happy state of those that keep the commandments of God. For behold, they are blessed in all things, both temporal and spiritual; and if they hold out faithful to the end they are received into heaven, that thereby they may dwell with God in a state of never-ending happiness. O remember, remember that these things are true; for the Lord God hath spoken it. (*King Benjamin addresses his people, about 124 B.C.*) Mosiah 2:41

### Elder George Albert Smith

The finest recipe that I could give, to obtain happiness, would be: Keep the commandments of the Lord. CR1934Oct:47-48

### Recorded in Proverbs

Where there is no vision, the people perish: but he that keepeth the law, happy is he. (*Proverb of Solomon, king of Israel*) Prov.29:18

### John A. Widtsoe

The more completely law is obeyed, the greater the consciousness of perfect joy. Throughout eternal life, increasing intelligence is attained, leading to greater adaptation to law, resulting in increasingly greater joy. Therefore it is that eternal life is the greatest gift of God, and that the plan of salvation is priceless. (A Rational Theology, p. 34) TLDP:320

### Joseph Smith,
*quoted by Elder Joseph Fielding Smith*

Happiness is the object and design of our existence; and will be the end thereof, if we pursue the path that leads to it; and this path is virtue, uprightness, faithfulness, holiness, and keeping all the commandments of God. . . . ¶ . . . . [A]s God has designed our happiness—and the happiness of all His creatures, he never has—He never will institute an ordinance or give a commandment to His people that is not calculated in its nature to promote that happiness which He has designed, and which will not end in the greatest amount of good and glory to those who become the recipients of his law and ordinances. (*An essay recorded in the Journal History Aug. 27, 1842*) HC5:134-35; TPJS:255-56; DGSM:27

**Related Witnesses:**

### Mormon

And it came to pass that there was no contention in the land, because of the love of God which did dwell in the hearts of the people. 16. And there were no envyings, nor strifes, nor tumults, nor whoredoms, nor lyings, nor murders, nor any manner of lasciviousness; and surely there could not be a happier people among all the people who had been created by the hand of God. (*Mormon abridges the account of the people of Nephi written by Nephi, one of the disciples of Christ, A.D. 36-60*) 4Ne.1:15-16

---

367. Only by entering the kingdom of God (the celestial kingdom) can we realize a fulness of joy.

### Elder George Albert Smith
What is this gospel to which we refer? It is the only power of God unto salvation, it is the only plan that will enable man to go back into the presence of his Maker and enjoy the celestial kingdom. It is the only plan that will bring peace and happiness to all the children of men, of every race and creed. CR1928Oct:93

### George F. Richards
Immortality is a means to an end, the end being the accomplishment of man's eternal salvation and glory. In support of this statement I call attention to the word of the Lord to the Prophet Joseph, as recorded in the Doctrine and Covenants, Sec. 93, verses 33 and 34, as follows: "For man is spirit. The elements are eternal, and spirit and element, inseparably connected, receive a fulness of joy; And when separated, man cannot receive a fulness of joy." Hence the importance of bringing about the immortality of man. ¶ . . . .The revelations of the Lord indicate to us the height, depth and grandeur of the glory of God to which the righteous may attain. Eternal life, as here used, being the greatest gift of God, must include a fulness of glory of God, in his celestial kingdom. [See D&C .76:54-60;132:20-24.] CR1916Apr:52

### John A. Widtsoe
The more completely law is obeyed, the greater the consciousness of perfect joy. Throughout eternal life, increasing intelligence is attained, leading to greater adaptation to law, resulting in increasingly greater joy. Therefore it is that eternal life is the greatest gift of God, and that the plan of salvation is priceless. (A Rational Theology, p. 34) TLDP:320

### Charles W. Penrose
The Lord has shown to us that the elements are eternal and that it requires the eternal union of spirit and element to obtain a fulness of joy. For the spirit part of man and the earthly, or temporal part just now, shall be united together perpetually, eternally, the body and the spirit being made one again, only joined together after the power of an endless life, that without that union a fulness of joy cannot be obtained. CR1914Oct:35

### Joseph Smith
For man is spirit. The elements are eternal, and spirit and element, inseparably connected, receive a fulness of joy; 34. And when separated, man cannot receive a fulness of joy. (Revelation at Kirtland, Ohio, May 6, 1833) D&C 93:33-34

### President Joseph F. Smith
I beheld that they were filled with joy and gladness, and were rejoicing together because the day of their deliverance was at hand. 16. They were assembled awaiting the advent of the Son of God into the spirit world, to declare their redemption from the bands of death. 17. Their sleeping dust was to be restored unto its perfect frame bone to his bone, and the sinews and the flesh upon them, the spirit and the body to be united never again to be divided, that they might receive a fulness of joy. . . . 50. For the dead had looked upon the long absence of their spirits from their bodies as a bondage. 51. These the Lord taught, and gave them power to come forth, after his resurrection from the dead, to enter into his Father's kingdom and there to be crowned with immortality and eternal life. (Vision regarding the Savior's visit to the spirits of the dead, Oct. 3, 1918) D&C 138:15-17,50-51

**Related Witnesses:**
### Rudger Clawson
"Men are, that they might have joy." We might say, God is that he might have joy, a fulness of joy, and so his Son Jesus Christ is that he might have a fulness of joy, and that would mean that God has a fulness of salvation, and that Jesus Christ has a fulness of salvation. They have attained to it. They have conquered. Jesus Christ has risen above his enemies. ¶ . . . . If a man cannot enter the kingdom of God he cannot rise to a fulness of joy, never, worlds without end. ¶ He may get some joy, he may get great happiness from what he does do in righteousness, but to get a fulness he must be born again. . . . CR1932Oct:9-10

### Lehi,
*quoted by his son Nephi*
Adam fell that men might be; and men are, that they might have joy. (Lehi explains the fall of Adam to his sons, 588-570 B.C.) 2Ne.2:25

# List of Doctrines

## JUDGMENT

386. Our final state after this life is determined by the choices we make (during this life and in the spirit world hereafter).

387. We receive our reward from him whom we choose to follow, whether we choose the Lord and the reward of exaltation, or the devil and the reward of damnation.

388. At the final judgment the wicked will be separated out from the righteous and consigned to the place prepared for the devil and his angels.

*Doctrines on JUDGMENT*
*Located in Other Topics*

14. We are each responsible for the choices we make through the exercise of our agency—and we must accept the immediate and eternal consequences of those decisions.

21. The Lord permits the righteous to be slain by the wicked that the wicked might exercise their agency and receive a just judgment at the last day.

126. In the spirit world, after death, there is a separation of spirits that lasts until the resurrection and final judgment; the wicked go into a state of outer darkness, and the righteous go into a state of happiness.

278. Jesus Christ is the judge of all.

313. In the postmortal spirit world, the spirits of the wicked live in a state of unhappiness or misery, called hell, until the day of redemption and final judgment.

617. We will be judged out of the records that are kept (on earth and in heaven).

715. Scripture is given from God to His prophets for (the blessing and judgment of) all people—not for members of His church alone.

824. The Lord judges us by what we are in our minds and hearts, not by how we may appear to others.

# JUDGMENT

**(1) Individual Accountability**
**(2) Judgment After Death**


**(1) Individual Accountability**

368. We are individually accountable to God for our actions.

**Paul**
So then every one of us shall give account of himself to God. (*Letter to the Church in Rome, about A.D. 55*) Rom.14:12

**President Joseph F. Smith**
I tell you the Lord is taking account of us. We are individually in His presence; we are individually a unit of the Kingdom of God, of the household of faith; and the Lord has cognizance of us, and will take note of us, and will record our works and our deeds. Thank God for that noble, that just, that godlike principle of the gospel of Jesus Christ, that every one of us will have to give an account for the deeds we do in the flesh, and that every man will be rewarded according to his works, whether they be good or evil. Thank God for that principle; for it is a just principle; it is Godlike. (*To Parowan Stake, Sept. 13, 1917, in answer to questions relating to the "Principle of Government in the Church"*) (See IE1917Nov:3-11.) MOFP5:86; TLDP:1

**James E. Talmage**
The doctrines of the Church are explicit in defining the relationship between the mortal probation and the future state, and in teaching individual accountability and the free agency of man. The Church affirms that in view of the responsibility under which every man rests, as the director of his own course, he must be and is free to choose in all things, from the life that leads to the celestial home to the career that is but the introduction to the miseries of perdition. Freedom to worship, or to refuse to worship, is a God-given right, and every soul must abide the result of his choice. AF:372

**Heber C. Kimball**
If I were to commit an impropriety, another person would not be justified in doing the same thing. If I violate the law of God I shall be condemned and will not escape upon the plea that somebody else did the same. Every man must answer for his own sin. (*In Bowery, Oct. 6, 1865, JD11:144*) TLDP:1

**Bruce R. McConkie**
No man, before the judgment bar, will be excused for believing false doctrines or doing evil acts on the excuse that he followed a minister, who he supposed taught true principles and gave good counsel, but who in fact declared false doctrine and wrought evil works. No matter that, in showy piety, we bear grievous burdens in the name of religion (as all the Jews did), or win great theological conflicts (as the Rabbis and scribes were wont to do), or display a superabundance of supposed good works (as some modern religionists suppose they do); no matter what else we may do in a false hope of gaining salvation—all that will matter in the day of judgment will be whether we have kept, truly and faithfully, the commandments of God. Let false ministers be damned, if such is the judgment they deserve; the members of their congregations must nonetheless work out their salvation by conforming to true principles of religion. (*The Mortal Messiah, 3:391*) TLDP:322

**Related Witnesses:**
**Peter**
Wherein they think it strange that ye run not with them to the same excess of riot, speaking evil of you: 5. Who shall give account to him that is ready to judge the quick and the dead. 6. For this cause was the gospel preached also to them that are dead, that they might be judged according to men in the flesh, but live according to God in the spirit. (*Letter to the churches in modern Asia Minor, about A.D. 60*) 1Pet.4:4-6

**John A. Widtsoe**
Membership in this Church involves personal responsibility. The Gospel of the Lord Jesus Christ presents the doctrine of individual salvation. There is no mass salvation in the Kingdom of God. One by one we enter into the glory of the Lord. I make my covenants alone. I go into the waters of baptism. No one can do that for me if I live on earth. Faith, repentance, baptism, the gift of the Holy Ghost, and all the things that pertain to the Gospel, I must accept myself. I cannot place the burden upon any one else. One of the simplest, as I have said, of all the principles of the Gospel, and one of the most important, is that we accept personal responsibility for the work of God's kingdom. CR1941Oct:76

**James E. Talmage**
But as to accountability for Adam's transgression, in all justice, Adam alone must answer. . . . [D]ivine justice forbids that we be accounted sinners solely because our parents transgressed. AF:428

369. God will judge us according to our words as well as our actions done in the body, whether open or secret.

### James E. Talmage

There is a plan of judgment divinely foreordained, by which every man will be called to answer for his deeds; and not for deeds alone but for his words also and even for the thoughts of his heart. "But I say unto you, That every idle word that men shall speak, they shall give account thereof in the day of judgment." These are the words of the Savior Himself. "And let none of you imagine evil in your hearts against his neighbor, and love no false oath: for all these are things that I hate, saith the Lord." AF:50

### Alma, the younger,
*quoted by Mormon*

For our words will condemn us, yea, all our works will condemn us; we shall not be found spotless; and our thoughts will also condemn us; and in this awful state we shall not dare to look up to our God; and we would fain be glad if we could command the rocks and the mountains to fall upon us to hide us from his presence. 15. But this cannot be; we must come forth and stand before him in his glory, and in his power, and in his might, majesty, and dominion, and acknowledge to our everlasting shame that all his judgments are just; that he is just in all his works, and that he is merciful unto the children of men, and that he has all power to save every man that believeth on his name and bringeth forth fruit meet for repentance. (*Alma contends with the lawyer Zeezrom, about 82 B.C.*) Alma 12:14-15

### Jesus,
*recorded in Matthew*

But I say unto you, That every idle word that men shall speak, they shall give account thereof in the day of judgment. 37. For by thy words thou shalt be justified, and by thy words thou shalt be condemned. (*Jesus speaks to the people about blasphemy against the Holy Ghost*) Matt.12:36-37

### King Benjamin,
*quoted by Mormon*

But this much I can tell you, that if ye do not watch yourselves, and your thoughts, and your words, and your deeds, and observe the commandments of God, and continue in the faith of what ye have heard concerning the coming of our Lord, even unto the end of your lives, ye must perish. And now, O man, remember, and perish not. (*King Benjamin addresses his people, about 124 B.C.*) Mosiah 4:30

### President John Taylor

We may succeed in hiding our affairs from men; but it is written that for every word and every secret thought we shall have to give an account in the day when accounts have to be rendered before God, when hypocrisy and fraud of any kind will not avail us; for by our words and by our works we shall be justified, or by them we shall be condemned. (*On trip to Bear Lake, JD24:232*) TLDP:321

### Elder David O. McKay

No man can disobey the word of God and not suffer for so doing. No sin, however secret, can escape retribution. True, you may lie and not be detected; you may violate virtue without its being known by any who would scandalize you; yet you cannot escape the judgment that follows such transgression. The lie is lodged in the recesses of your mind, an impairment of your character that will be reflected sometime, somehow in your countenance or bearing. Your moral turpitude, though only you, your accomplice, and God may ever know it, will canker your soul. ("The Constant Operation of Divine Law," IE1941Jul:395) TLDP:440

### Related Witnesses:
### John A. Widtsoe

The first expression of universal order is that a given cause always has the same effect. Under the same conditions, gasoline will always burst into flame when a lighted match is touched to it, or the finger burned if brought too near the fire. Yesterday, to-day and forever, like causes produce like effects. . . . ¶ The universal reign of law under which man lives not only offers the happy certainty of an orderly universe, but also the stern warning, that in a world where cause and effect are invariable, man cannot escape the effects of his actions. That is more terrible than the threat of a sulphurous hell. (Man and the Dragon, pp. 124, 129) TLDP:356

---

370. In His just judgment, God will take into account the thoughts and desires of our hearts.

### President Brigham Young,
*quoted by John A. Widtsoe*

This is a subject I have reflected upon a great deal, and I have come to the conclusion that we shall be judged according to the deeds done in the body and according to these thoughts and intents of the heart. (*In Tabernacle, Aug. 8, 1869, JD14:99*) DBY:382

**Joseph Smith,**
*receiving the Word of the Lord*
For I, the Lord, will judge all men according to
their works, according to the desire of their
hearts. (*Vision in Kirtland Temple, Jan. 21,
1836*) D&C 137:9

**Elder John Taylor**
We may deceive one another, and, in some circumstances, as counterfeit coin passes for that
which is considered true and valuable among
men. But God searches the hearts and tries the
reins of the children of men. He knows our
thoughts and comprehends our desires and feelings; he knows our acts and the motives which
prompt us to perform them. He is acquainted
with all the doings and operations of the human
family, and all the secret thoughts and acts of
the children of men are open and naked before
him, and for them he will bring them to judgment. (*In 14th Ward, Nov. 1873, JD16:301-02*)
DGSM:89

**Alma, the younger,**
*quoted by Mormon*
[A]nd our thoughts will also condemn us; and
in this awful state we shall not dare to look up
to our God; and we would fain be glad if we
could command the rocks and the mountains to
fall upon us to hide us from his presence. (*Alma
contends with the lawyer Zeezrom, about 82
B.C.*) Alma 12:14

**President John Taylor**
We may succeed in hiding our affairs from
men; but it is written that for every word and
every secret thought we shall have to give an
account in the day when accounts have to be
rendered before God, when hypocrisy and fraud
of any kind will not avail us; for by our words
and by our works we shall be justified, or by
them we shall be condemned. (*On trip to Bear
Lake, JD24:232*) TLDP:321

**Alma, the younger,**
*quoted by Mormon*
And it is requisite with the justice of God that
men should be judged according to their works;
and if their works were good in this life, and the
desires of their hearts were good, that they
should also, at the last day, be restored unto that
which is good. . . . 5. The one raised to happiness according to his desires of happiness, or
good according to his desires of good; and the
other to evil according to his desires of evil; for
as he has desired to do evil all the day long
even so shall he have his reward of evil when
the night cometh. 6. And so it is on the other
hand. If he hath repented of his sins, and
desired righteousness until the end of his days,
even so he shall be rewarded unto righteous-

ness. (*Alma speaks to his son Corianton, concerning the resurrection of the dead, about 73
B.C.*) Alma 41:3,5-6

**George Q. Cannon**
There are some laws that we are prevented
from obeying that have been declared to be
necessary to exaltation in the Celestial
Kingdom of our God. What will be the condition of those who do not obey these laws? God,
knowing all our desires, if He should see a spirit of willingness and obedience in our hearts,
will judge us accordingly. That which we cannot do we are not expected to do. God does not
ask impossible things from His children. But
He asks us to be obedient to Him and to carry
out His laws in our lives; and if for any reason
we cannot do this but are willing to do it, He
will accept the offering and the good desires
that we entertain in our hearts. (*Gospel Truth,
1:97-98*) TLDP:323

**Joseph Smith,**
*receiving the Word of the Lord*
Verily, verily, I say unto you, that when I give a
commandment to any of the sons of men to do
a work unto my name, and those sons of men
go with all their might and with all they have to
perform that work, and cease not their diligence, and their enemies come upon them and
hinder them from performing that work,
behold, it behooveth me to require that work no
more at the hands of those sons of men, but to
accept of their offerings. 50. And the iniquity
and transgression of my holy laws and commandments I will visit upon the heads of those
who hindered my work, unto the third and
fourth generation, so long as they repent not,
and hate me, saith the Lord God. 51. Therefore,
for this cause have I accepted the offerings of
those whom I commanded to build up a city
and a house unto my name, in Jackson county,
Missouri, and were hindered by their enemies,
saith the Lord your God. (*Revelation received
Jan. 19, 1841*) D&C 124:49-51

**Charles W. Penrose**
The Lord says that whenever he gives a commandment, no matter what it is about, to the
children of man, and they go to with their might
and endeavor to fulfil his commandment, and
do that which is required of them, and they are
prevented by their enemies, or by any other
means, from accomplishing it, he does not
require it any more at their hands. He accepts of
their offering. That has applied in the past, and
will apply in the future, and we should remember it. If God gives a commandment, and we do
not obey it, why he revokes it, and he revokes
the blessings. If he gives us a commandment to

do certain things, and we find ourselves unable to do them, either by restricted laws or any other obstacles in the way of physical force, the Lord requires them no more but accepts our offering, and he will visit his wrath and indignation upon those who prevent his people from accomplishing that which he required of their hands. CR1924Apr:13-14

**Related Witnesses:**

**King Benjamin,**

*quoted by Mormon*

But this much I can tell you, that if ye do not watch yourselves, and your thoughts, and your words, and your deeds, and observe the commandments of God, and continue in the faith of what ye have heard concerning the coming of our Lord, even unto the end of your lives, ye must perish. And now, O man, remember, and perish not. (*King Benjamin addresses his people, about 124 B.C.*) Mosiah 4:30

---

**371. There is no place we can go where God cannot find us.**

**Joseph Smith**

You cannot go anywhere but where God can find you out. All men are born to die, and all men must rise; all must enter eternity. (*Address at the Stand, Nauvoo, Ill., May 1844*) HC6:366

**Joseph Smith**

Hearken, O ye people of my church, saith the voice of him who dwells on high, and whose eyes are upon all men; yea, verily I say: Hearken ye people from afar; and ye that are upon the islands of the sea, listen together. 2. For verily the voice of the Lord is unto all men, and there is none to escape; and there is no eye that shall not see, neither ear that shall not hear, neither heart that shall not be penetrated. . . . 11. Wherefore the voice of the Lord is unto the ends of the earth, that all that will hear may hear: (*Revelation received during conference of elders of the Church Nov. 1, 1831; preface to the doctrines given to the Church*) D&C 1:1-2,11

**John A. Widtsoe**

By the intelligent operation and infinite extent of the holy spirit, the whole universe is held together and made as one unit. By its means there is no remoteness into which intelligent beings may escape the dominating will of God. By the holy spirit, the Lord is always with us, and "is nearer than breathing, and nearer than hands and feet.". . . ¶ So thoroughly permeated with the holy spirit is the immensity of space that every act and word and thought are recorded and transmitted everywhere, so that all who know how to read may

read. Thus we make an imperishable record of our lives. To those whose lives are ordered well this is a blessed conception; but to those of wicked lives, it is most terrible. . . . ¶ We cannot hide from the Master. (A Rational Theology, pp. 72-74) TLDP:363

**Delbert L. Stapley,**

*also quoting Joseph Smith*

"For verily the voice of the Lord is unto all men, and there is none to escape; and there is no eye that shall not see, neither ear that shall not hear, neither heart that shall not be penetrated. ¶ "And the rebellious shall be pierced with much sorrow. . . . (D&C 1:1-3) ¶ Thus we see that the voice of the Lord is to all men everywhere, and none can escape the judgment for violating his laws and commandments. CR1968Apr:26

---

**372. No individual will be held accountable for the commandments and doctrines of the gospel of Jesus Christ until that person has had opportunity to accept or reject the gospel.**

**James E. Talmage**

According to the technical definition of sin it consists in the violation of law, and in this strict sense sin may be committed inadvertently or in ignorance. It is plain, however, from the scriptural doctrine of human responsibility and the unerring justice of God, that in his transgressions as in his righteous deeds man will be judged according to his ability to comprehend and obey law. To him who has never been made acquainted with a higher law the requirements of that law do not apply in their fulness. For sins committed without knowledge—that is, for laws violated in ignorance—a propitiation has been provided in the atonement wrought through the sacrifice of the Savior; and sinners of this class do not stand condemned, but shall be given opportunity yet to learn and to accept or reject the principles of the Gospel. AF:52-53

**Jacob, brother of Nephi**

Wherefore, he has given a law; and where there is no law given there is no punishment; and where there is no punishment there is no condemnation; and where there is no condemnation the mercies of the Holy One of Israel have claim upon them, because of the atonement; for they are delivered by the power of him. 26. For the atonement satisfieth the demands of his justice upon all those who have not the law given to them, that they are delivered from that awful monster, death and hell, and the devil, and the lake of fire and brimstone, which is endless torment; and they are restored to that God who gave them breath, which is the Holy One of Israel. (*Jacob to the people of Nephi, 559-545 B.C.*) 2Ne.9:25-26

**Elder Joseph F. Smith**

We shall not be cast off . . . for those sins, which we ignorantly commit, which are the results of misunderstanding in all honesty before the Lord. The difficulty does not lie here; the danger lies in our failing to live up to that which we do know to be right and proper. For this we will be held responsible before the Lord; for this we will be judged and condemned unless we repent. (*In Tabernacle, July 7, 1878, JD20:26*) TLDP:323

**Paul**

For as many as have sinned without law shall also perish without law: and as many as have sinned in the law shall be judged by the law; (*Letter to the Church in Rome, about A.D. 55*) Rom.2:12

**Joseph Smith,**
*quoted by Elder Joseph Fielding Smith*

But while one portion of the human race is judging and condemning the other without mercy, the Great Parent of the universe looks upon the whole human family with a fatherly care and paternal regard; He views them as His offspring, and without any of those contracted feelings that influence the children of men, causes "His sun to rise on the evil and on the good, and sendeth rain on the just and on the unjust." He holds the reins of judgment in His hands; He is a wise Lawgiver, and will judge all men, not according to the narrow, contracted notions of men, but, "according to the deeds done in the body whether they be good or evil," or whether these deeds were done in England, America, Spain, Turkey, or India. He will judge them, "not according to what they have not, but according to what they have," those who have lived without law, will be judged without law, and those who have a law, will be judged by that law. We need not doubt the wisdom and intelligence of the Great Jehovah; He will award judgment or mercy to all nations according to their several deserts [sic], their means of obtaining intelligence, the laws by which they are governed, the facilities afforded them of obtaining correct information, and His inscrutable designs in relation to the human family; and when the designs of God shall be made manifest, and the curtain of futurity be withdrawn, we shall all of us eventually have to confess that the Judge of all the earth has done

right. (*In editorial from the Times and Seasons, recorded in the Prophet's journal, April 15, 1842*) TPJS:218

**Elder John Taylor**

There are heathen nations enveloped in idolatry; and if millions of people came into the world in those places surrounded with idolatry and superstition, it would be unjust for them to be punished for what they did not know. Hence, if they have no law, they will be judged without law; and God in his own wisdom will regulate their affairs, for it is their misfortune, not their individual offence, that has placed them in their present position. (The Government of God, p. 52) TLDP:323

**Mormon**

For behold that all little children are alive in Christ, and also all they that are without the law. For the power of redemption cometh on all them that have no law; wherefore, he that is not condemned, or he that is under no condemnation, cannot repent; and unto such baptism availeth nothing— (*Mormon writes to his son Moroni, prior to A.D. 384*) Moro.8:22

**Elder Spencer W. Kimball**

Knowledge of the gospel has come to many men and women in this life together with adequate opportunity to live it. Such will be judged by the gospel law. Should one not have had opportunities to hear and understand the gospel in this mortal life, that privilege will be given him hereafter. Judgment is according to knowledge and compliance. ¶ Latter-day Saints are in the first category. Having been blessed with the gospel privileges they are and will be judged on gospel criteria. (The Miracle of Forgiveness, pp. 12-13) TLDP:324

**Related Witnesses:**

**Alma, the younger,**
*quoted by Mormon*

Now I would that ye should remember, that inasmuch as the Lamanites have not kept the commandments of God, they have been cut off from the presence of the Lord. Now we see that the word of the Lord has been verified in this thing, and the Lamanites have been cut off from his presence, from the beginning of their transgressions in the land. 15. Nevertheless I say unto you, that it shall be more tolerable for them in the day of judgment than for you, if ye remain in your sins, yea, and even more tolerable for them in this life than for you, except ye repent. 16. For there are many promises which are extended to the Lamanites; for it is because of the traditions of their fathers that caused them to remain in their state of ignorance; therefore the Lord will be merciful unto them and prolong their existence in the land. 17. And at some period of time they will be brought to believe in his word, and to know of the incorrectness of the traditions of their fathers; and many of them will be saved, for the Lord will be merciful unto all who call on his name. (*Alma preaches repentance to the people of Ammonihah, about 82 B.C.*) Alma 9:14-17

### Paul

And I thank Christ Jesus our Lord, who hath enabled me, for that he counted me faithful, putting me into the ministry; 13. Who was before a blasphemer, and a persecutor, and injurious: but I obtained mercy, because I did it ignorantly in unbelief. 14. And the grace of our Lord was exceeding abundant with faith and love which is in Christ Jesus. 15. This is a faithful saying, and worthy of all acceptation, that Christ Jesus came into the world to save sinners; of whom I am chief. 16. Howbeit for this cause I obtained mercy, that in me first Jesus Christ might shew forth all longsuffering, for a pattern to them which should hereafter believe on him to life everlasting. (*Paul's letter to his assistant Timothy, about A.D. 64*) 1Tim.1:12-16

### King Benjamin,
#### quoted by Mormon

For behold, and also his blood atoneth for the sins of those who have fallen by the transgression of Adam, who have died not knowing the will of God concerning them, or who have ignorantly sinned. 12. But wo, wo unto him who knoweth that he rebelleth against God! For salvation cometh to none such except it be through repentance and faith on the Lord Jesus Christ. (*King Benjamin addresses his people, about 124 B.C.*) Mosiah 3:11-12

### Abinadi,
#### quoted by Mormon

And these are those who have part in the first resurrection; and these are they that have died before Christ came, in their ignorance, not having salvation declared unto them. And thus the Lord bringeth about the restoration of these; and they have a part in the first resurrection, or have eternal life, being redeemed by the Lord. (*Abinadi preaches to King Noah and his people that the prophets and those who have kept the commandments shall come forth in the first resurrection, about 148 B.C.*) Mosiah 15:24

---

**373.** Members of the Church will be held to a stricter accountability than those who have not heard the gospel.

### George Q. Cannon

The Latter-day Saints, I hold, will be held to stricter accountability than any other people on the face of the earth. . . . We must be a pure people or we will be scourged; we must be a holy people or God's anger will be kindled against us. . . . In proportion to the light which men have will they be judged, and God will reward them according to the deeds done in the body. (Gospel Truth, 1:93) TLDP:1

### Elder Wilford Woodruff

We will be held responsible before the Lord for the light we possess. We should be diligent and faithful in our labors, for if we turn our backs upon the truth, once having known it, we will be under a far greater condemnation than those who rejected the truth. What we may be called upon to suffer for the Gospel's sake is neither here nor there. (*In Tabernacle, June 12, 1881, JD22:176*) TLDP:1

### Elder Spencer W. Kimball

Knowledge of the gospel has come to many men and women in this life together with adequate opportunity to live it. Such will be judged by the gospel law. Should one not have had opportunities to hear and understand the gospel in this mortal life, that privilege will be given him hereafter. Judgment is according to knowledge and compliance. ¶ Latter-day Saints are in the first category. Having been blessed with the gospel privileges they are and will be judged on gospel criteria. (The Miracle of Forgiveness, pp. 12-13) TLDP:324

### Elder George Albert Smith

We will not be judged as our brothers and sisters of the world are judged; but according to the greater opportunities placed in our keeping. We will be among those who have received the word of the Lord, who have heard His sayings, and if we do them it will be to us eternal life, but if we fail condemnation will result. CR1906Oct:47

### Related Witnesses:
#### Peter

And if the righteous scarcely be saved, where shall the ungodly and the sinner appear? (*Peter writes to the churches in modern Asia Minor, about A.D. 60; the righteous will be tried and tested in all things*) 1Pet.4:18

### Elder Joseph F. Smith

We shall not be cast off . . . for those sins, which we ignorantly commit, which are the results of misunderstanding in all honesty before the Lord. The difficulty does not lie here; the danger lies in our failing to live up to that which we do know to be right and proper. For this we will be held responsible before the

Lord; for this we will be judged and condemned unless we repent. (*In Tabernacle, July 7, 1878, JD20:26*) TLDP:323

**Jesus,**
*recorded in Matthew*

For the kingdom of heaven is as a man travelling into a far country, who called his own servants, and delivered unto them his goods. 15. And unto one he gave five talents, to another two, and to another one; to every man according to his several ability; and straightway took his journey. 16. Then he that had received the five talents went and traded with the same, and made them other five talents. 17. And likewise he that had received two, he also gained other two. 18. But he that had received one went and digged in the earth, and hid his lord's money. 19. After a long time the lord of those servants cometh, and reckoneth with them. 20. And so he that had received five talents came and brought other five talents, saying, Lord, thou deliveredst unto me five talents: behold, I have gained beside them five talents more. 21. His lord said unto him, Well done, thou good and faithful servant: thou hast been faithful over a few things, I will make thee ruler over many things: enter thou into the joy of thy lord. (*Jesus speaks in parables about the kingdom of heaven*) Matt.25:14-21

**James**

Therefore to him that knoweth to do good, and doeth it not, to him it is sin. (*Letter to his brethren in the Church*) James 4:17

---

374. **Judgment on earth, to some extent, is given into the hands of certain priesthood leaders.**

**Charles W. Penrose**

But judgment, to a great extent, is given into the hands of certain quorums and councils in this Church. One body to exercise judgment is the bishopric, the bishopric of a ward are appointed and ordained to be judges. A bishop is a common judge in Israel to sit with his counselors in judgment upon transgressors and upon those whose difficulties cannot be settled by the teachers who visit them in their homes. . . . ¶ So when we are called upon to sit in judgment, either in a bishop's court or in a high council (to which the bishop's court may be appealed), if we are members of the high council, just remember what the Lord has said concerning such quorum or council. Every decision of these quorums that are organized must be given in justice, in righteousness, in equity, in fear of

the Lord, and with the desire to do what is right, not out of personal feeling. [See D&C 102:16.] Personal feelings ought to be banished from our souls when we sit in judgment having the right to sit in judgment. CR1916Oct:21-22

**President Joseph F. Smith**

Out of the things which have been written in the books, this people shall be judged, according to their works. The Lord shall make a record also, and out of that shall the whole world be judged. And you men of the holy Priesthood—you Apostles, Presidents, Bishops and High Priests in Zion—will be called upon to be the judge of the people. Therefore, it is expected that you shall set the standard for them to attain to, and see that they shall live according to the spirit of the Gospel, do their duty, and keep the commandments of the Lord. You shall make a record of their acts. You shall record when they are baptized, when they are confirmed, and when they receive the Holy Ghost by the laying on of hands. . . . You shall write their works . . . but we shall judge the people, first requiring them to do their duty. CR1901Apr:72

**Joseph Smith**

And verily in this thing ye have done wisely, for it is required of the Lord, at the hand of every steward, to render an account of his stewardship, both in time and in eternity. 4. For he who is faithful and wise in time is accounted worthy to inherit the mansions prepared for him of my Father. . . . 16. And now, verily I say unto you, that as every elder in this part of the vineyard must give an account of his stewardship unto the bishop in this part of the vineyard— (*Revelation received at an assemblage of elders and members, Dec. 4, 1831*) D&C 72:3-4,16

**Elder Harold B. Lee**

Acts that may affect your standing in the Church, or your right to privileges or advancement in the Church, are to be promptly confessed to the bishop whom the Lord has appointed as a shepherd over every flock and commissioned to be a common judge in Israel. He may hear such confession in secret and deal justly and mercifully, as each case warrants. (Decisions for Successful Living, p. 99) TLDP:551

**Elder Harold B. Lee**

I was in a stake conference recently where one of the bishops frankly stated that he had determined that he would never excommunicate any person no matter what the sin. I told him that if this was his true feeling, then he was in the wrong position—as a common judge in Israel. . . . When we let members lead a double and destructive life, instead of doing them a favor as we suppose, we damage them, sometimes, irreparably. We must let the light of gospel standards shine fully, and not try to deflect the penetrating rays of its standards. The gospel is to save men, not to condemn them, but to save it is sometimes necessary to confront and to discipline as the Lord has directed us. When individuals are on the wrong path, our task is to redirect them lovingly, and not to watch idly from our vantage point on the straight and narrow path. (*Address given at Regional Representatives' seminar, Oct. 1/2, 1969, pp. 11-12*) TLDP:81

## (2) Judgment After Death

375. Every person who belongs to the human family must eventually stand before the judgment seat of Christ to be judged.

### Mormon

And for this cause I write unto you, that ye may know that ye must all stand before the judgment seat of Christ, yea, every soul who belongs to the whole human family of Adam; and ye must stand to be judged of your works, whether they be good or evil; (*Mormon writes for the benefit of the Gentiles, the twelve tribes of Israel and the remnant of the descendants of Lehi, A.D. 363*) Morm.3:20

### President George Albert Smith

We are living eternal life, and our position hereafter will be the result of our lives here. Every man will be judged according to his works, and he will receive only that degree of glory that he has earned. CR1945Apr:139

### Amulek,
#### quoted by Mormon

[F]or behold, the day cometh that all shall rise from the dead and stand before God, and be judged according to their works. . . . 43. The spirit and the body shall be reunited again in its perfect form; both limb and joint shall be restored to its proper frame, even as we now are at this time; and we shall be brought to stand before God, knowing even as we know now, and have a bright recollection of all our guilt. (*Amulek answers the lawyer Zeezrom foretelling Christ's redemption of man, the resurrection and the final judgment, about 82 B.C.*) Alma 11:41,43

### Moroni, son of Mormon

[T]he trump shall sound; and they shall come forth, both small and great, and all shall stand before his bar, being redeemed and loosed from this eternal band of death, which death is a temporal death. 14. And then cometh the judgment of the Holy One upon them; and then cometh the time that he that is filthy shall be filthy still; and he that is righteous shall be righteous still; he that is happy shall be happy still; and he that is unhappy shall be unhappy still. (*Moroni addresses those who deny the revelations of God, A.D. 400-421*) Morm.9:13-14

### John

And I saw the dead, small and great, stand before God; and the books were opened: and another book was opened, which is the book of life: and the dead were judged out of those things which were written in the books, according to their works. 13. And the sea gave up the dead which were in it; and death and hell delivered up the dead which were in them: and they were judged every man according to their works. (*The Apostle John sees the judgment of man at the end of the Millennium*) Rev.20:12-13

### Nephi, son of Lehi

And it came to pass that I said unto them that it was a representation of things both temporal and spiritual; for the day should come that they must be judged of their works, yea, even the works which were done by the temporal body in their days of probation. 33. Wherefore, if they should die in their wickedness they must be cast off also, as to the things which are spiritual, which are pertaining to righteousness; wherefore, they must be brought to stand before God, to be judged of their works; and if their works have been filthiness they must needs be filthy; and if they be filthy it must needs be that they cannot dwell in the kingdom of God; if so, the kingdom of God must be filthy also. (*Nephi sees in vision the things his father Lehi had seen; he sees the dividing of the wicked from the righteous; he interprets the vision to his brothers, about 600-592 B.C.*) 1Ne.15:32-33

### Joseph Smith

No consideration whatever ought to deter us from showing ourselves approved in the sight of God, according to His divine requirement. Men not unfrequently forget that they are dependent upon heaven for every blessing which they are permitted to enjoy, and that for every opportunity granted them they are to give an account. You know, brethren, that when the Master in the Savior's parable of the stewards called his servants before him he gave them several talents to improve on while he should tarry abroad for a little season, and when he returned he called for an accounting. So it is now. Our Master is absent only for a little season, and at the end of it He will call each to render an account; and where the five talents were bestowed, ten will be required; and he that has made no improvement will be cast out as an unprofitable servant, while the faithful will enjoy everlasting honors. (*Written message from Kirtland, Ohio, to the brethren scattered abroad, Jan. 22, 1834)* HC2:23-24

**Related Witnesses:**

### Jacob, brother of Nephi,
### *quoted by Nephi*

The keeper of the gate is the Holy One of Israel; and he employeth no servant there; and there is none other way save it be by the gate; for he cannot be deceived, for the Lord God is his name. (*Jacob teaches the people of Nephi, 559-545 B.C.*) 2Ne.9:41

---

### 376. At the final judgment we will stand before God in our resurrected bodies.

#### James E. Talmage

The scriptures prove, that at the time of man's final judgment he will stand before the bar of God, clothed in his resurrected body, and this, irrespective of his condition of purity or guilt. AF:466

#### Amulek,
#### *quoted by Mormon*

Now, there is a death which is called a temporal death; and the death of Christ shall loose the bands of this temporal death, that all shall be raised from this temporal death. 43. The spirit and the body shall be reunited again in its perfect form; both limb and joint shall be restored to its proper frame, even as we now are at this time; and we shall be brought to stand before God, knowing even as we know now, and have a bright recollection of all our guilt. (*Amulek answers the lawyer Zeezrom, foretelling Christ's redemption and resurrection of man and the final judgment, about 82 B.C.*) Alma 11:42-43

#### President Joseph F. Smith

And in this space between death and the resurrection of the body, the two classes of souls remain, in happiness or in misery, until the time which is appointed of God that the dead shall come forth and be reunited both spirit and body, and be brought to stand before God and be judged according to their works. This is the final judgment. (Gospel Doctrine, p. 448) DGSM:84

#### Moroni, son of Mormon

And because of the redemption of man, which came by Jesus Christ, they are brought back

into the presence of the Lord; yea, this is wherein all men are redeemed, because the death of Christ bringeth to pass the resurrection, which bringeth to pass a redemption from an endless sleep, from which sleep all men shall be awakened by the power of God when the trump shall sound; and they shall come forth, both small and great, and all shall stand before his bar, being redeemed and loosed from this eternal band of death, which death is a temporal death. 14. And then cometh the judgment of the Holy One upon them; and then cometh the time that he that is filthy shall be filthy still; and he that is righteous shall be righteous still; he that is happy shall be happy still; and he that is unhappy shall be unhappy still. (*Moroni calls upon those who do not believe in Christ to repent, A.D. 400-421*) Morm.9:13-14

#### Jacob, brother of Nephi,
#### *quoted by Nephi*

And he suffereth this that the resurrection might pass upon all men, that all might stand before him at the great and judgment day. (*Jacob to the people of Nephi, 559-545 B.C.*) 2Ne.9:22

---

### 377. The dead will be judged from the books that are written on earth and in heaven.

#### President Joseph F. Smith

Out of the things which have been written in the books, this people shall be judged, according to their works. The Lord shall make a record also, and out of that shall the whole world be judged. And you men of the holy Priesthood—you Apostles, Presidents, Bishops and High Priests in Zion—will be called upon to be the judge of the people. Therefore, it is expected that you shall set the standard for them to attain to, and see that they shall live according to the spirit of the Gospel, do their duty, and keep the commandments of the Lord. You shall make a record of their acts. You shall record when they are baptized, when they are confirmed, and when they receive the Holy Ghost by the laying on of hands. . . . You shall write their works . . . but we shall judge the people, first requiring them to do their duty. CR1901Apr:72

#### Elder Spencer W. Kimball

Accordingly, men's deeds and thoughts must be recorded in heaven, and recording angels will not fail to make complete recordings of our thoughts and actions. We pay our tithing and the bishop records it in his book and gives us a receipt. But even if the entry fails to get in the ward record, we shall have full credit for the tithes we paid. There will be no omissions in the heavenly records, and they will all be available at the day of judgment. President John Taylor emphasized this: ¶ "Man sleeps the sleep of death, but the spirit lives where the record of his deeds is kept. ¶ "Man sleeps for a time in the grave, and by and by he rises again from the dead and goes to judgment; and then the secret thoughts of all men are revealed before him with whom we have to do; we cannot hide them: it would be in vain for a man to say, 'I did not do so and so,' the command would be, unravel and read the record which he has made of himself and let it testify in relation to these things, and all could gaze upon it." [In Journal of Discourses, 11:78-79] ¶ At that day we may be sure that we shall receive fair judgment. The judges will have the facts as they may be played back from our own records, and our voices and the pictures of our own acts and the recordings of our thoughts will testify against and for us. (The Miracle of Forgiveness, p. 109) TLDP:324-25

**Jesus,**
*quoted by Mormon*
For behold, out of the books which have been written, and which shall be written, shall this people be judged, for by them shall their works be known unto men. 26. And behold, all things are written by the Father; therefore out of the books which shall be written shall the world be judged. 27. And know ye that ye shall be judges of this people, according to the judgment which I shall give unto you, which shall be just. Therefore, what manner of men ought ye to be? Verily I say unto you, even as I am. (*The resurrected Jesus calls on the Nephites to repent in contemplation of the final judgment, A.D. 34*) 3Ne.27:25-27

**Related Witnesses:**
**John**
And I saw the dead, small and great, stand before God; and the books were opened: and another book was opened, which is the book of life: and the dead were judged out of those things which were written in the books, according to their works. 13. And the sea gave up the dead which were in it; and death and hell delivered up the dead which were in them: and they were judged every man according to their works. (*The Apostle John sees the final judgment of man*) Rev.20:12-13

**Nephi, son of Lehi**
Wherefore, because that ye have a Bible ye need not suppose that it contains all my words; neither need ye suppose that I have not caused more to be written. 11. For I command all men,

both in the east and in the west, and in the north, and in the south, and in the islands of the sea, that they shall write the words which I speak unto them; for out of the books which shall be written I will judge the world, every man according to their works, according to that which is written. 12. For behold, I shall speak unto the Jews and they shall write it; and I shall also speak unto the Nephites and they shall write it; and I shall also speak unto the other tribes of the house of Israel, which I have led away, and they shall write it; and I shall also speak unto all nations of the earth and they shall write it. (*Nephi writes the word of the Lord regarding the witnesses of the Bible and Book of Mormon*) 2Ne.29:10-12

**John A. Widtsoe**
So thoroughly permeated with the holy spirit is the immensity of space that every act and word and thought are recorded and transmitted everywhere, so that all who know how to read may read. Thus we make an imperishable record of our lives. To those whose lives are ordered well this is a blessed conception; but to those of wicked lives, it is most terrible. He who has the receiving apparatus, in whose hands the key is held, may read from the record of the holy spirit, an imperishable history of all that has occurred during the ages that have passed in the world's history. This solemn thought, that in the bosom of the holy spirit is recorded the whole history of the universe—our most secret thought and our faintest hope—helps man to walk steadily in the midst of the contending appeals of life. We cannot hide from the Master. (A Rational Theology, pp. 72-74) TLDP:363

---

**378. Christ will judge all people.**

**Jesus,**
*quoted by John*
For the Father judgeth no man, but hath committed all judgment unto the Son: . . . 27. And hath given him authority to execute judgment also, because he is the Son of man. (*Jesus addresses the Jews*) John 5:22,27

**James E. Talmage**
It is the prerogative of Jesus Christ to judge mankind, and He will do it as His own purposes, which are the purposes of His Father, may be best served. John records the words of Christ: "For the Father judgeth no man, but hath committed all judgment unto the Son: That all men should honor the Son even as they honor the Father." And Peter, while expounding

the Gospel to the devout Gentile, Cornelius, declared concerning Jesus Christ, that "it is he which was ordained of God to be the Judge of quick and dead." AF:51

**Bruce R. McConkie**

In his exalted state Christ has attained all power both in heaven and on earth so that the fulness of the godhead dwells in him; he has been exalted to the right hand of the Father, from whence, in due course, he shall come to judge all men. . . . ¶ The Son, not the Father, is the Judge of the whole earth, but his judgment is made in accordance with the will of the Father and therefore is just. . . . ¶ Because Jesus is the Son of Man of Holiness he has been given the power to execute judgment, to sit in judgment at the great and last day, to call all men forth in immortality to stand before his bar. (Doctrinal New Testament Commentary, 1:190) DGSM:89

**Jesus,**
*recorded in Matthew*

When the Son of man shall come in his glory, and all the holy angels with him, then shall he sit upon the throne of his glory: 32. And before him shall be gathered all nations: and he shall separate them one from another, as a shepherd divideth his sheep from the goats: 33. And he shall set the sheep on his right hand, but the goats on the left. (*Jesus gives the parable of the sheep and the goats; the sheep are placed on his right hand at the Lord's second coming*) Matt.25:31-33

**Elder John Taylor**

It is written that Jesus will judge not after the sight of the eye, or after the hearing of the ear, but with righteousness shall he judge the poor, and reprove with equity the meek of the earth. It is not because somebody has seen things, or heard anything by which a man will be judged and condemned, but it is because that record that is written by the man himself in the tablets of his own mind—that record that cannot lie—will in that day be unfolded before God and angels, and those who shall sit as judges. *(In Tabernacle, Feb. 5, 1865, JD11:79)* TLDP:324

**Joseph Smith,**
*quoted by Elder Joseph Fielding Smith*

He holds the reins of judgment in His hands; He is a wise Lawgiver, and will judge all men, not according to the narrow, contracted notions of men, but, "according to the deeds done in the body whether they be good or evil," or whether these deeds were done in England, America, Spain, Turkey, or India. He will judge them, "not according to what they have not, but according to what they have," those who have lived without law, will be judged without law,

and those who have a law, will be judged by that law. We need not doubt the wisdom and intelligence of the Great Jehovah; He will award judgment or mercy to all nations according to their several deserts. . . . (*In editorial from the Times and Seasons, recorded in the Prophet's journal, April 15, 1842*) TPJS:218

**Mormon**

And for this cause I write unto you, that ye may know that ye must all stand before the judgment-seat of Christ, yea, every soul who belongs to the whole human family of Adam; and ye must stand to be judged of your works, whether they be good or evil; (*Mormon writes for the benefit of the Gentiles, the twelve tribes of Israel and the remnant of the descendants of Lehi, A.D. 363*) Morm.3:20

**Related Witnesses:**

**Paul**

Because he hath appointed a day, in the which he will judge the world in righteousness by that man whom he hath ordained; whereof he hath given assurance unto all men, in that he hath raised him from the dead. (*Paul preaches on Mars' Hill about the unknown god*) Acts 17:31

---

379. **When the great day of judgment comes, Christ will use appointed priesthood agents to help Him judge the world.**

**Charles W. Penrose**

There is another thing connected with this that we ought to understand fully in our minds, and that is that the time will come, according to the revelations of God, concerning the resurrection, that judgment will be given into the hands of men who hold that priesthood, so that what they do in the judgment will be as though done by the Father or by the Son. . . . ¶ The great judgment that is to come will not be altogether performed by one individual sitting upon a great white throne and passing judgment upon the millions upon millions of the earth's inhabitants. God's house is a house of order, and the Lord will have agents appointed as he has now behind the veil as well as in the flesh, and when the great judgment comes, all will be judged according to their works, and the books will be opened, and the Book of Life will be scanned and the man's acts and the woman's acts upon the earth will be disclosed, and we will all confess in our souls that the judgment is just and righteous, because it will be uttered and delivered by one having authority and the seal of God will be upon it. [D&C 128:7-8] CR1916Oct:21-24

### President John Taylor

When we reflect upon the statement of creatures being judged without the law, the question arises as to who are to be their judges. We may here state that Christ is called the judge of the quick and the dead, the judge of all the earth. . . . ¶ It is also further stated that the Saints shall judge the world. Thus Christ is at the head, His apostles and disciples seem to take the next prominent part; then comes the action of the Saints, or other branches of the Priesthood, who it is stated shall judge the world. This combined Priesthood, it would appear, will hold the destiny of the human family in their hands and adjudicate in all matters pertaining to their affairs; and it would seem to be quite reasonable, if the Twelve Apostles in Jerusalem are to be the judges of the Twelve Tribes, and the Twelve Disciples on this continent are to be the judges of the descendants of Nephi, then the brother of Jared and Jared should be the judges of the Jaredites, their descendants; and further, that the First Presidency and Twelve who have officiated in our age, should operate in regard to mankind in this dispensation. (The Mediation and Atonement, pp. 155-56) TLDP:124

**Related Witnesses:**

### Paul

Do ye not know that the saints shall judge the world? and if the world shall be judged by you, are ye unworthy to judge the smallest matters? (*Letter to the Church at Corinth, Greece, about A.D. 55*) 1Cor.6:2

### Joseph Smith

And in whatsoever house ye enter, and they receive you not, ye shall depart speedily from that house, and shake off the dust of your feet as a testimony against them. 21. And you shall be filled with joy and gladness; and know this, that in the day of judgment you shall be judges of that house, and condemn them; (*Revelation at a Church conference, Jan. 25, 1832*) D&C 75:20-21

---

**380. The Twelve Apostles chosen by Jesus from among the Jews will judge the twelve tribes of Israel.**

### Jesus,
*recorded in Matthew*

And Jesus said unto them, Verily I say unto you, That ye which have followed me, in the regeneration when the Son of man shall sit in the throne of his glory, ye also shall sit upon twelve thrones, judging the twelve tribes of Israel. (*Jesus tells the Twelve that when they sit*

upon twelve thrones in judgment, those who have sacrificed much will receive eternal life) Matt.19:28

### Joseph Smith,
*receiving the Word of the Lord*

And again, verily, verily, I say unto you, and it hath gone forth in a firm decree, by the will of the Father, that mine apostles, the Twelve which were with me in my ministry at Jerusalem, shall stand at my right hand at the day of my coming in a pillar of fire, being clothed with robes of righteousness, with crowns upon their heads, in glory even as I am, to judge the whole house of Israel, even as many as have loved me and kept my commandments, and none else. (*Revelation received Sept. 1830*) D&C 29:12

### Nephi, son of Lehi

And the angel spake unto me, saying: Behold the twelve disciples of the Lamb, who are chosen to minister unto thy seed. 9. And he said unto me: Thou rememberest the twelve apostles of the Lamb? Behold they are they who shall judge the twelve tribes of Israel; wherefore, the twelve ministers of thy seed shall be judged of them; for ye are of the house of Israel. 10. And these twelve ministers whom thou beholdest shall judge thy seed. And, behold, they are righteous forever; for because of their faith in the Lamb of God their garments are made white in his blood. (*An angel shows Nephi a vision of the twelve disciples of Christ who were to be selected from the Nephites, between 600 and 592 B.C.*) 1Ne.12:8-10

### Mormon

Yea, behold, I write unto all the ends of the earth; yea, unto you, twelve tribes of Israel, who shall be judged according to your works by the twelve whom Jesus chose to be his disciples in the land of Jerusalem. 19. And I write also unto the remnant of this people, who shall also be judged by the twelve whom Jesus chose in this land; and they shall be judged by the other twelve whom Jesus chose in the land of Jerusalem. 20. And these things doth the Spirit manifest unto me; therefore I write unto you all. And for this cause I write unto you, that ye may know that ye must all stand before the judgment-seat of Christ, yea, every soul who belongs to the whole human family of Adam; and ye must stand to be judged of your works, whether they be good or evil; (*Mormon writes for the benefit of the Gentiles and the twelve tribes of Israel, A.D. 363*) Morm.3:18-20

### President John Taylor

It is also further stated that the Saints shall judge the world. Thus Christ is at the head, His

Apostles and disciples seem to take the next prominent part; then comes the action of the Saints, or other branches of the Priesthood, who it is stated shall judge the world. This combined Priesthood, it would appear, will hold the destiny of the human family in their hands and adjudicate in all matters pertaining to their affairs; and it would seem to be quite reasonable. If the Twelve Apostles in Jerusalem are to be the judges of the Twelve tribes, and the Twelve Disciples on this continent are to be the judges of the descendants of Nephi, then the brother of Jared and Jared should be the judges of the Jaredites, their descendants; and further, that the First Presidency and Twelve who have officiated in our age, should operate in regard to mankind in this dispensation. (The Mediation and Atonement, pp. 155-57) TLDP:324

---

### 381. The twelve disciples chosen by Jesus from among the Nephites will judge the Nephites.

#### Nephi, son of Lehi
And the angel spake unto me, saying: Behold the twelve disciples of the Lamb, who are chosen to minister unto thy seed. 9. And he said unto me: Thou rememberest the twelve apostles of the Lamb? Behold they are they who shall judge the twelve tribes of Israel; wherefore, the twelve ministers of thy seed shall be judged of them; for ye are of the house of Israel. 10. And these twelve ministers whom thou beholdest shall judge thy seed. And, behold, they are righteous forever; for because of their faith in the Lamb of God their garments are made white in his blood. (*An angel shows Nephi a vision of the twelve disciples of Christ who were to be selected from the Nephites, between 600 and 592 B.C.*) 1Ne.12:8-10

#### Mormon
Yea, behold, I write unto all the ends of the earth; yea, unto you, twelve tribes of Israel, who shall be judged according to your works by the twelve whom Jesus chose to be his disciples in the land of Jerusalem. 19. And I write also unto the remnant of this people, who shall also be judged by the twelve whom Jesus chose in this land; and they shall be judged by the other twelve whom Jesus chose in the land of Jerusalem. 20. And these things doth the Spirit manifest unto me; therefore I write unto you all. And for this cause I write unto you, that ye may know that ye must all stand before the judgment-seat of Christ, yea, every soul who belongs to the whole human family of Adam;

and ye must stand to be judged of your works, whether they be good or evil; (*Mormon writes for the benefit of the Gentiles and the twelve tribes of Israel, A.D. 363*) Morm.3:18-20

#### Jesus, quoted by Mormon
And know ye that ye shall be judges of this people, according to the judgment which I shall give unto you, which shall be just. Therefore, what manner of men ought ye to be? Verily I say unto you, even as I am. (*The resurrected Jesus instructs his twelve Nephite disciples, A.D. 34*) 3Ne.27:27

---

### 382. God's judgment is just: the final judgment will be just for everyone.

#### Mosiah, son of King Benjamin, quoted by Mormon
Now it is better that a man should be judged of God than of man, for the judgments of God are always just, but the judgments of man are not always just. (*King Mosiah proposes the appointment of righteous judges, about 92 B.C.*) Mosiah 29:12

#### George Q. Cannon
The Lord says that He is coming "to recompense unto every man according to his work, and measure to every man according to the measure to his fellow man." This is in keeping with the words of Jesus: [Luke 6:37-38 is quoted]. ¶ This is perfect justice. No one can complain with any good cause if he is recompensed according to his works or if he receives the same measure that he measures to his fellow man. But do we always think of this in all our transactions? If we all do, then we are in happy condition and will not be afraid to meet the consequences of all our acts when the Lord judges us. (Gospel Truth, 1:92) TLDP:320

#### Elder Spencer W. Kimball
On the earth there are many apparent injustices, when man must judge man and when uncontrollable situations seem to bring undeserved disaster, but in the judgment of God there will be no injustice and no soul will receive any blessing, reward, and glory which he has not earned, and no soul will be punished through deprivation or otherwise for anything of which he was not guilty. (*At Utah State University, Nov. 25, 1958*) (The Teachings of Spencer W. Kimball, p. 47) TLDP:321

#### Elder John Taylor
It is written that Jesus will judge not after the sight of the eye, or after the hearing of the ear,

but with righteousness shall he judge the poor, and reprove with equity the meek of the earth. It is not because somebody has seen things, or heard anything by which a man will be judged and condemned, but it is because that record that is written by the man himself in the tablets of his own mind—that record that cannot lie—will in that day be unfolded before God and angels, and those who shall sit as judges. *(In Tabernacle, Feb. 5, 1865, JD11:79)* TLDP:324

**Related Witnesses:**

**Jacob, brother of Nephi,**
*quoted by Nephi*

Prepare your souls for that glorious day when justice shall be administered unto the righteous, even the day of judgment, that ye may not shrink with awful fear; that ye may not remember your awful guilt in perfectness, and be constrained to exclaim: Holy, holy are thy judgments, O Lord God Almighty—but I know my guilt; I transgressed thy law, and my transgressions are mine; and the devil hath obtained me, that I am a prey to his awful misery. *(Jacob to the people of Nephi, 559-545 B.C.)* 2Ne.9:46

**Isaiah**

[A]nd he shall not judge after the sight of his eyes, neither reprove after the hearing of his ears: 4. But with righteousness shall he judge the poor, and reprove with equity for the meek of the earth: and he shall smite the earth with the rod of his mouth, and with the breath of his lips shall he slay the wicked. *(Isaiah prophesies, 740-659 B.C.)* Isa.11:3-4

---

383. Every person in the final judgment will be saved in a kingdom of glory (except the sons of perdition, who are cast into outer darkness).

**President Brigham Young,**
*quoted by John A. Widtsoe*

How many kingdoms there are has not been told to us; they are innumerable. The disciples of Jesus were to dwell with him. Where will the rest go? Into kingdoms prepared for them, where they will live and endure. Jesus will bring forth, by his own redemption, every son and daughter of Adam, except the sons of perdition, who will be cast into hell. Others will suffer the wrath of god—will suffer all the Lord can demand at their hands, or justice can require of them; and when they have suffered the wrath of God till the utmost farthing is paid, they will be brought out of prison. Is this dangerous doctrine to preach? Some consider it dangerous; but it is true that every person who

does not sin away the day of grace, and become an angel to the Devil, will be brought forth to inherit a kingdom of glory. *("The Three Glories", in Bowery, Aug. 26, 1860, JD8:154)* DBY:382

**Elder Joseph Fielding Smith**

Outer darkness is something which cannot be described, except that we know that it is to be placed beyond the benign and comforting influence of the Spirit of God—banished entirely from his presence. ¶ This extreme punishment will not be given to any but the sons of perdition. Even the wicked of the earth who never knew the power of God, after they have paid the price of their sinning—for they must suffer the excruciating torment which sin will bring—shall at last come forth from the prison house, repentant and willing to bow the knee and acknowledge Christ, to receive some influence of the Spirit of God in the telestial kingdom. . . . (Doctrines of Salvation, 2:220-21) TLDP:636

**President George Albert Smith**

We are living eternal life, and our position hereafter will be the result of our lives here. Every man will be judged according to his works, and he will receive only that degree of glory that he has earned. CR1945Apr:139

**Related Witnesses:**

**Paul**

There are also celestial bodies, and bodies terrestrial: but the glory of the celestial is one, and the glory of the terrestrial is another. 41. There is one glory of the sun, and another glory of the moon, and another glory of the stars: for one star differeth from another star in glory. *(Paul writes to the Church at Corinth, Greece, about A.D. 55)* 1Cor.15:40-42

**Joseph Smith**

And the glory of the celestial is one, even as the glory of the sun is one. 97. And the glory of the terrestrial is one, even as the glory of the moon is one. 98. And the glory of the telestial is one, even as the glory of the stars is one; for as one star differs from another star in glory, even so differs one from another in glory in the telestial world; *(Vision to Joseph Smith and Sidney Rigdon, Feb. 16, 1832)* D&C 76:96-98

---

384. There are three principal kingdoms, or degrees of glory, to which we are assigned after mortality.

**James E. Talmage**

The revelations of God have defined the following principal kingdoms or degrees of glory, as prepared through Christ for the children of men. ¶ 1. The Celestial Glory—There are some who have striven to obey all the divine commandments, who have accepted the testimony of Christ, obeyed "the laws and ordinances of the Gospel," and received the Holy Spirit; these are they who have overcome evil by godly works and who are therefore entitled to the highest glory; these belong to the Church of the Firstborn, unto whom the Father has given all things; they are made kings and priests of the Most High, after the order of Melchizedek; they possess celestial bodies, "whose glory is that of the sun, even the glory of God, the highest of all, whose glory the sun of the firmament is written of as being typical"; they are admitted to the glorified company, crowned with exaltation in the celestial kingdom. ¶ 2. The Terrestrial Glory—We read of others who receive glory of a secondary order, differing from the highest as "the moon differs from the sun in the firmament." These are they who, though honorable, failed to comply with the requirements for exaltation, were blinded by the craftiness of men and unable to receive and obey the higher laws of God. They proved "not valiant in the testimony of Jesus," and therefore are not entitled to the fulness of glory. ¶ 3. The Telestial Glory— There is another grade, differing from the higher orders as the stars differ from the brighter orbs of the firmament; this is for those who received not the testimony of Christ, but who nevertheless, did not deny the Holy Spirit; who have led lives exempting them from the heaviest punishment, yet whose redemption will be delayed until the last resurrection. In the telestial world there are innumerable degrees comparable to the varying light of the stars. Yet all who receive of any one of these orders of glory are at last saved, and upon them Satan will finally have no claim. AF:83-84

### Paul

There are also celestial bodies, and bodies terrestrial: but the glory of the celestial is one, and the glory of the terrestrial is another. 41. There is one glory of the sun, and another glory of the moon, and another glory of the stars: for one star differeth from another star in glory. 42. So also is the resurrection of the dead. It is sown in corruption; it is raised in incorruption: (*Paul writes to the Church at Corinth, Greece, about A.D. 55*) 1Cor.15:40-42

### Elder John Taylor

As eternal beings we all have to stand before him to be judged; and he has provided different degrees of glory—the celestial, the terrestrial, and the telestial glories—which are provided according to certain unchangeable laws which cannot be controverted. What will he do with them? For those who are ready to listen to him and be brought under the influence of the Spirit of God and be led by the principles of revelation and the light of heaven, and who are willing to yield to obedience to his commands at all times and carry out his purposes upon the earth, and who are willing to abide a celestial law, he has prepared for them a celestial glory, that they may be with him for ever and ever. And what about the others? They are not prepared to go there any more than lead is prepared to stand the same test as gold or silver; and there they cannot go. And there is a great gulf between them. But he [God] will do with them just as well as he can. A great many of these people in the world, thousands and hundreds of millions of them, will be a great deal better off through the interposition of the Almighty that they have any idea of. But they cannot enter into the celestial kingdom of God, where God and Christ are they cannot come. (*Quarterly conference, Salt Lake Stake, in Salt Lake Theatre, Jan. 6, 1879, JD20:116*) TLDP:325

### Joseph Smith

And again we bear record—for we saw and heard, and this is the testimony of the gospel of Christ concerning them who shall come forth in the resurrection of the just—. . . . 67. These are they who have come to an innumerable company of angels, to the general assembly and church of Enoch, and of the Firstborn. . . . 70. These are they whose bodies are celestial, whose glory is that of the sun, even the glory of God, the highest of all, whose glory the sun of the firmament is written of as being typical. 71. And again, we saw the terrestrial world, and behold and lo, these are they who are of the terrestrial, whose glory differs from that of the church of the Firstborn who have received the fulness of the Father, even as that of the moon differs from the sun in the firmament. . . . 80. And now this is the end of the vision which we saw of the terrestrial, that the Lord commanded us to write while we were yet in the Spirit. 81. And again, we saw the glory of the telestial, which glory is that of the lesser, even as the glory of the stars differs from that of the glory of the moon in the firmament. . . . 96. And the glory of the celestial is one, even as the glory of the sun is one. 97. And the glory of the terrestrial is one, even as the glory of the moon is one. 98. And the glory of the telestial is one, even as the glory of the stars is one; for as one star differs from another star in glory, even so differs one from another in glory in the telestial world; (*Vision to Joseph*

*Smith and Sidney Rigdon, February 16, 1832)*
D&C 76:50,67,70-71,80-81,96-98
**Related Witnesses:**
### James E. Talmage
The three kingdoms of widely differing glories are organized on an orderly plan of gradation. We have seen that the telestial kingdom comprises several subdivisions; this also is the case, we are told, with the celestial; and, by analogy, we conclude that a similar condition prevails in the terrestrial. Thus the innumerable degrees of merit amongst mankind are provided for in an infinity of graded glories. The celestial kingdom is supremely honored by the personal ministrations of the Father and the Son. The terrestrial kingdom will be administered through the higher, without a fulness of glory. The telestial is governed through the ministrations of the terrestrial, by "angels who are appointed to minister for them." HL:83

---

385. **At the final judgment we will be assigned to that degree of glory that we are willing to receive and able to abide.**

### President George Albert Smith
We are living eternal life, and our position hereafter will be the result of our lives here. Every man will be judged according to his works, and he will receive only that degree of glory that he has earned. CR1945Apr:139

### Elder Wilford Woodruff
If a man cannot abide a celestial law, he cannot receive a celestial glory, if a man cannot abide a terrestrial law he cannot receive a terrestrial glory; and if he cannot abide a telestial law he cannot receive a telestial glory, but will have to dwell in a kingdom which is not a kingdom of glory. This is according to the revelations of God to us. (*In Tabernacle, July 19, 1868, JD12:278*) TLDP:126-27

### Joseph Smith
And they who are not sanctified through the law which I have given unto you, even the law of Christ, must inherit another kingdom, even that of a terrestrial kingdom, or that of a telestial kingdom. 22. For he who is not able to abide the law of a celestial kingdom cannot abide a celestial glory. 23. And he who cannot abide the law of a terrestrial kingdom cannot abide a terrestrial glory. 24. And he who cannot abide the law of a telestial kingdom cannot abide a telestial glory; therefore he is not meet for a kingdom of glory. Therefore he must abide a kingdom which is not a kingdom of

glory. . . . 28. They who are of a celestial spirit shall receive the same body which was a natural body; even ye shall receive your bodies, and your glory shall be that glory by which your bodies are quickened. 29. Ye who are quickened by a portion of the celestial glory shall then receive of the same, even a fulness. 30. And they who are quickened by a portion of the terrestrial glory shall then receive of the same, even a fulness. 31. And also they who are quickened by a portion of the telestial glory shall then receive of the same, even a fulness. 32. And they who remain shall also be quickened; nevertheless, they shall return again to their own place, to enjoy that which they are willing to receive, because they were not willing to enjoy that which they might have received. 33. For what doth it profit a man if a gift is bestowed upon him, and he receive not the gift? Behold, he rejoices not in that which is given unto him, neither rejoices in him who is the giver of the gift. . . . 35. That which breaketh a law, and abideth not by law, but seeketh to become a law unto itself, and willeth to abide in sin, and altogether abideth in sin, cannot be sanctified by law, neither by mercy, justice, nor judgment. Therefore, they must remain filthy still. (*Revelation Dec. 27/28, 1832; obedience to celestial, terrestrial, or telestial law prepares men for those respective kingdoms and glories*) D&C 88:21-24,28-33,35

### James E. Talmage
Again, the Lord has said that according to the laws we obey here shall we receive from Him. We speak of rewards just as we speak of punishments. But rewards and punishments will come through truth by reference to what He had already revealed respecting the kingdoms or orders of glory, to this effect—If a man cannot or will not obey celestial laws, that is, live in accordance with the celestial requirements, he must not think that he is discriminated against when he is excluded from the celestial kingdom, because he could not abide it, he could not live there. If a man cannot or will not obey the terrestrial law he cannot rationally hope for a place in the terrestrial kingdom. If he cannot live the yet lower law—the telestial law—he cannot abide the glory of the telestial kingdom, and he will have to be assigned therefore to a kingdom without glory. I rejoice in the consistency and order of the Lord's plan and in His revelations to us. CR1929Oct:69

### Bruce R. McConkie
To gain the celestial kingdom, the Lord says: Ye must be "sanctified through the law which I have given unto you, even the law of Christ," which

law is the fulness of the gospel. The revealed word specifies that those who "abide the law of a terrestrial kingdom" shall obtain a terrestrial glory, and that those who "abide the law of a telestial kingdom" shall obtain a telestial glory. No such requirement is set forth for gaining a celestial glory. Instead, the revelation says that those who so obtain must be "*able* to abide the law of a celestial kingdom." (D&C 88:21-24) In other words, salvation in the celestial kingdom will come to all who are *able* to live the full law of Christ, even though they did not have opportunity so to do in the course of a mortal probation. (The Mortal Messiah, 1:74) TLDP:129

### President Brigham Young,
#### *quoted by John A. Widtsoe*

Some might suppose that it would be a great blessing to be taken and carried directly into heaven and there set down, but in reality that would be no blessing to such persons; they could not reap a full reward, could not enjoy the glory of the kingdom, and could not comprehend and abide the light thereof, but it would be to them a hell intolerable and I suppose would consume them much quicker than would hell fire. It would be no blessing to you to be carried into the celestial kingdom, and obliged to stay therein, unless you were prepared to dwell there. (*In Tabernacle, March 1856; JD3:221*) DBY:95; DGSM:92

### John

He that is unjust, let him be unjust still: and he which is filthy, let him be filthy still: and he that is righteous, let him be righteous still: and he that is holy, let him be holy still. 12. And, behold, I come quickly; and my reward is with me, to give every man according as his work shall be. (*The Apostle John sees the condition of the unjust on judgment day*) Rev.22:11-12

### Nephi, son of Lehi

And it came to pass that I said unto them that it was a representation of things both temporal and spiritual; for the day should come that they must be judged of their works, yea, even the works which were done by the temporal body in their days of probation. 33. Wherefore, if they should die in their wickedness they must be cast off also, as to the things which are spiritual, which are pertaining to righteousness; wherefore, they must be brought to stand before God, to be judged of their works; and if their works have been filthiness they must needs be filthy; and if they be filthy it must needs be that they cannot dwell in the kingdom of God; if so, the kingdom of God must be filthy also. 34. But behold, I say unto you, the kingdom of God is not filthy, and there cannot any unclean thing enter into the

kingdom of God; wherefore there must needs be a place of filthiness prepared for that which is filthy. 35. And there is a place prepared, yea, even that awful hell of which I have spoken, and the devil is the preparator of it; wherefore the final state of the souls of men is to dwell in the kingdom of God, or to be cast out because of that justice of which I have spoken. (*Nephi interprets his father Lehi's dream to his brothers, between 600-592 B.C.*) 1Ne.15:32-35

**Related Witnesses:**

### Amulek,
#### *quoted by Mormon*

Ye cannot say, when ye are brought to that awful crisis, that I will repent, that I will return to my God. Nay, ye cannot say this; for that same spirit which doth possess your bodies at the time that ye go out of this life, that same spirit will have power to possess your body in that eternal world. (*Amulek teaches the people this life is the time for men to prepare to meet God, 74 B.C.*) Alma 34:34

### Alma, the younger,
#### *quoted by Mormon*

For I perceive that ye are in the paths of righteousness; I perceive that ye are in the path which leads to the kingdom of God; yea, I perceive that ye are making his paths straight. 20. I perceive that it has been made known unto you, by the testimony of his word, that he cannot walk in crooked paths; neither doth he vary from that which he hath said; neither hath he a shadow of turning from the right to the left, or from that which is right to that which is wrong; therefore, his course is one eternal round. 21. And he doth not dwell in unholy temples; neither can filthiness or anything which is unclean be received into the kingdom of God; therefore I say unto you the time shall come, yea, and it shall be at the last day, that he who is filthy shall remain in his filthiness. (*Alma preaches to the people in Gideon, about 83 B.C.*) Alma 7:19-21

**Related Witnesses:**

### Moroni, son of Mormon

And then cometh the judgment of the Holy One upon them; and then cometh the time that he that is filthy shall be filthy still; and he that is righteous shall be righteous still; he that is happy shall be happy still; and he that is unhappy shall be unhappy still. (*Moroni addresses those who deny the revelations of God, A.D. 400-421*) Morm.9:14

### Jacob, brother of Nephi,
#### *quoted by Nephi*

And it shall come to pass that when all men shall have passed from this first death unto life, insomuch as they have become immortal, they must appear before the judgment-seat of the Holy One of Israel; and then cometh the judgment, and then must they be judged according to the holy judgment of God. 16. And assuredly, as the Lord liveth, for the Lord God hath spoken it, and it is his eternal word, which cannot pass away, that they who are righteous shall be righteous still, and they who are filthy shall be filthy still; wherefore, they who are filthy are the devil and his angels; and they shall go away into everlasting fire; prepared for them; and their torment is as a lake of fire and brimstone, whose flame ascendeth up forever and ever and has no end. (*Jacob to the people of Nephi, 559-545 B.C.*) 2Ne.9:15-16

### Paul
For this ye know, that no whoremonger, nor unclean person, nor covetous man, who is an idolater, hath any inheritance in the kingdom of Christ and of God. (*Letter to the Saints at Ephesus in Asia Minor, about A.D. 62*) Eph.5:5

### Paul
Know ye not that the unrighteous shall not inherit the kingdom of God? Be not deceived: neither fornicators, nor idolaters, nor adulterers, nor effeminate, nor abusers of themselves with mankind, 10. Nor thieves, nor covetous, nor drunkards, nor revilers, nor extortioners, shall inherit the kingdom of God. (*Paul's letter to the Church at Corinth, Greece, about A.D. 55*) 1Cor.6:9-10

**Author's Note:** If a wicked person comes to the judgment seat unrepentant, he remains wicked and cannot dwell in the kingdom of God; hence a person who is filthy because his works in mortality were filthy must remain filthy and cannot enter into the kingdom of God. The grace of God will not save such a one; hence the need for good works consistent with accepting Jesus Christ as the Savior. Also, it is likely deathbed repentance is not sufficient, a person must undergo a process of change from filthiness to purity.

---

### 386. Our final state after this life is determined by the choices we make (during this life and in the spirit world hereafter).

#### Elder John Taylor
Are we not the framers of our own destiny? Are we not the arbitrators of our fate? This is another part of my text, and I argue from it that it is our privilege to determine our own exaltation or degradation. It is our privilege to determine our

own happiness or misery in the world to come. (Gospel Kingdom, p. 341) DGSM:31

#### Joseph Smith
And they who remain shall also be quickened; nevertheless, they shall return again to their own place, to enjoy that which they are willing to receive, because they were not willing to enjoy that which they might have received. 33. For what doth it profit a man if a gift is bestowed upon him, and he receive not the gift? Behold, he rejoices not in that which is given unto him, neither rejoices in him who is the giver of the gift. (*Revelation Dec. 27/28, 1832*) D&C 88:32-33

#### Joseph Smith,
*receiving the Word of the Lord*
For behold, it is not meet that I should command in all things; for he that is compelled in all things, the same is a slothful and not a wise servant; wherefore he receiveth no reward. 27. Verily I say, men should be anxiously engaged in a good cause, and do many things of their own free will, and bring to pass much righteousness; 28. For the power is in them, wherein they are agents unto themselves. And inasmuch as men do good they shall in nowise lose their reward. 29. But he that doeth not anything until he is commanded, and receiveth a commandment with doubtful heart, and keepeth it with slothfulness, the same is damned. (*Revelation to the elders of the Church, Aug. 1, 1831*) D&C 58:26-29

#### Alma, the younger,
*quoted by Mormon*
And it is requisite with the justice of God that men should be judged according to their works; and if their works were good in this life, and the desires of their hearts were good, that they should also, at the last day, be restored unto that which is good. 4. And if their works are evil they shall be restored unto them for evil. Therefore, all things shall be restored to their proper order, every thing to its natural frame—mortality raised to immortality, corruption to incorruption—raised to endless happiness to inherit the kingdom of God, or to endless misery to inherit the kingdom of the devil, the one on one hand, the other on the other— 5. The one raised to happiness according to his desires of happiness, or good according to his desires of good; and the other to evil according to his desires of evil; for as he has desired to do evil all the day long even so shall he have his reward of evil when the night cometh. 6. And so it is on the other hand. If he hath repented of his sins, and desired righteousness until the end of his days, even so he shall be rewarded unto righteousness. 7. These are they that are

redeemed of the Lord; yea, these are they that are taken out, that are delivered from that endless night of darkness; and thus they stand or fall; for behold, they are their own judges, whether to do good or do evil. 8. Now, the decrees of God are unalterable; therefore, the way is prepared that whosoever will may walk therein and be saved. (*Alma speaks to his son Corianton, concerning the resurrection of the dead, about 73 B.C.*) Alma 41:3-8

### Alma, the younger, *quoted by Mormon*

Therefore, O my son, whosoever will come may come and partake of the waters of life freely; and whosoever will not come the same is not compelled to come; but in the last day it shall be restored unto him according to his deeds. 28. If he has desired to do evil, and has not repented in his days, behold, evil shall be done unto him, according to the restoration of God. (*Alma speaks to his son Corianton, about 73 B.C.; mortality is a probationary time to enable man to repent and serve God*) Alma 42:27-28

### President Brigham Young, *quoted by John A. Widtsoe*

The volition of the creature is free; this is a law of their existence and the Lord cannot violate his own law; were he to do that, he would cease to be God. He has placed life and death before his children, and it is for them to choose. If they choose life, they receive the blessing of life; if they choose death, they must abide the penalty. (*In Bowery, Aug. 19, 1866, JD11:272*) DBY:62; DGSM:31

### Paul

Be not deceived; God is not mocked: for whatsoever a man soweth, that shall he also reap. 8. For he that soweth to his flesh shall of the flesh reap corruption; but he that soweth to the Spirit shall of the Spirit reap life everlasting. 9. And let us not be weary in well doing: for in due season we shall reap, if we faint not. (*Paul writes to the churches of Galatia in Asia Minor, about A.D. 55*) Gal.6:7-9

### Samuel, the Lamanite, *quoted by Mormon*

And now remember, remember, my brethren, that whosoever perisheth, perisheth unto himself; and whosoever doeth iniquity, doeth it unto himself; for behold, ye are free; ye are permitted to act for yourselves; for behold, God hath given unto you a knowledge and he hath made you free. 31. He hath given unto you that ye might know good from evil, and he hath given unto you that ye might choose life or death; and ye can do good and be restored unto that which is good, or have that which is good restored unto

you; or ye can do evil, and have that which is evil restored unto you. (*Samuel preaches to the Nephites, about 6 B.C.*) Hel.14:30-31

387. **We receive our reward from him whom we choose to follow, whether we choose the Lord and the reward of exaltation, or the devil and the reward of damnation.**

### Mormon

For every man receiveth wages of him whom he listeth to obey, and this according to the words of the spirit of prophecy; therefore let it be according to the truth. And thus endeth the fifth year of the reign of the judges. (*In one year tens of thousands met death in war and were thus sent to the eternal world to reap their rewards according to their works, 87 B.C.*) Alma 3:27

### Alma, the younger, *quoted by Mormon*

Therefore, if a man bringeth forth good works he hearkeneth unto the voice of the good shepherd, and he doth follow him; but whosoever bringeth forth evil works, the same becometh a child of the devil, for he hearkeneth unto his voice, and doth follow him. 42. And whosoever doeth this must receive his wages of him; therefore, for his wages he receiveth death, as to things pertaining unto righteousness, being dead unto all good works. (*Alma teaches the people, about 83 B.C.*) Alma 5:41-42

### Elder John Taylor

For those who are ready to listen to [the Lord] and be brought under the influence of the Spirit of God and be led by the principles of revelation and the light of heaven, and who are willing to yield to obedience to his commands at all times and carry out his purposes upon the earth, and who are willing to abide a celestial law, he has prepared for them a celestial glory, that they may be with him for ever and ever. And what about the others? They are not prepared to go there any more than lead is prepared to stand the same test as gold or silver; and there they cannot go. And there is a great gulf between them. But he [God] will do with them just as well as he can. A great many of these people in the world, thousands and hundreds of million of them, will be a great deal better off through the interposition of the Almighty than they have any idea of. But they cannot enter into the celestial kingdom of God, where God and Christ are they cannot come. (*Quarterly conference, Salt Lake Stake, in Salt Lake Theatre, Jan. 6, 1879, JD20:116*) TLDP:325

### President Brigham Young,
*quoted by John A. Widtsoe*

[God] has placed life and death before his children, and it is for them to choose. If they choose life, they receive the blessing of life; if they choose death, they must abide the penalty. This is a law which has always existed from all eternity, and will continue to exist throughout all the eternities to come. Every intelligent being must have the power of choice, and God brings forth the results of the acts of his creatures to promote his Kingdom and subserve his purposes in the salvation and exaltation of his children. (*In Bowery, Aug. 19, 1866, JD11:272*) DBY:62; DGSM:31

**Related Witnesses:**

### King Benjamin,
*quoted by Mormon*

But, O my people, beware lest there shall arise contentions among you, and ye list to obey the evil spirit, which was spoken of by my father Mosiah. 33. For behold, there is a wo pronounced upon him who listeth to obey that spirit; for if he listeth to obey him, and remaineth and dieth in his sins, the same drinketh damnation to his own soul; for he receiveth for his wages an everlasting punishment, having transgressed the law of God contrary to his own knowledge. (*King Benjamin addresses his people, about 124 B.C.*) Mosiah 2:32-33

---

388. At the final judgment the wicked will be separated out from the righteous and consigned to the place prepared for the devil and his angels.

### Joseph Smith,
*receiving the Word of the Lord*

And again, verily, verily, I say unto you that when the thousand years are ended, and men again begin to deny their God, then will I spare the earth but for a little season; 23. And the end shall come, and the heaven and the earth shall be consumed and pass away, and there shall be a new heaven and a new earth. . . . 26. But, behold, verily I say unto you, before the earth shall pass away, Michael, mine archangel, shall sound his trump, and then shall all the dead awake, for their graves shall be opened, and they shall come forth—yea, even all. 27. And the righteous shall be gathered on my right hand unto eternal life; and the wicked on my left hand will I be ashamed to own before the Father; 28. Wherefore I will say unto them—Depart from me, ye cursed, into everlasting fire, prepared for

the devil and his angels. (*Revelation received Sept. 1830*) D&C 29:22-23,26-28

### John

And I saw a great white throne, and him that sat on it, from whose face the earth and the heaven fled away; and there was found no place for them. 12. And I saw the dead, small and great, stand before God; and the books were opened: and another book was opened, which is the book of life: and the dead were judged out of those things which were written in the books, according to their works. 13. And the sea gave up the dead which were in it; and death and hell delivered up the dead which were in them: and they were judged every man according to their works. 14. And death and hell were cast into the lake of fire. This is the second death. 15. And whosoever was not found written in the book of life was cast into the lake of fire. (*John sees the judgment of man at the end of the Millennium*) Rev.20:11-15

### Joseph Smith,
*receiving the Word of the Lord*

For in mine own due time will I come upon the earth in judgment, and my people shall be redeemed and shall reign with me on earth. 30. For the great Millennium, of which I have spoken by the mouth of my servants, shall come. 31. For Satan shall be bound, and when he is loosed again he shall only reign for a little season, and then cometh the end of the earth. 32. And he that liveth in righteousness shall be changed in the twinkling of an eye, and the earth shall pass away so as by fire. 33. And the wicked shall go away into unquenchable fire, and their end no man knoweth on earth, nor ever shall know, until they come before me in judgment. (*Revelation: message for the nations of the earth, Feb. 1831*) D&C 43:29-33

### Jesus,
*recorded in Matthew*

When the Son of man shall come in his glory, and all the holy angels with him, then shall he sit upon the throne of his glory: 32. And before him shall be gathered all nations: and he shall separate them one from another, as a shepherd divideth his sheep from the goats: 33. And he shall set the sheep on his right hand, but the goats on the left. . . . 41. Then shall he say also unto them on the left hand, Depart from me, ye cursed, into everlasting fire, prepared for the devil and his angels: . . . 46. And these shall go away into everlasting punishment: but the righteous into life eternal. (*Jesus gives the parable of the sheep and the goats; the sheep are placed on his right hand at the Lord's Second Coming*) Matt.25:31-33,41,46

### Elder Joseph Fielding Smith

Will the earth go back to the telestial order after the millennium? No, but the people on the face of the earth, many of them, will be like the Nephites who lived 200 years after the coming of Christ. They will rebel against the Lord knowingly, and the great last struggle will come, and the devil and his forces will be defeated: then the earth will die and receive its resurrection and become a celestial body. The resurrection of the wicked will take place as one of the last events before the earth dies. ¶ After the thousand years Satan will be loosed again and will go forth again to deceive the nations. Because men are still mortal, Satan will go out to deceive them. Men will again deny the Lord, but in doing so they will act with their eyes open and because they love darkness rather than light, and so they become sons of perdition. Satan will gather his hosts, both those on the earth and the wicked dead who will eventually also be brought forth in the resurrection. Michael, the Prince, will gather his forces and the last great battle will be fought. Satan will be defeated with his hosts. Then will come the end. Satan and those who follow him will be banished into outer darkness. (Doctrines of Salvation, 1:87-88) TLDP:407-08

### Elder Joseph Fielding Smith

All those who love wickedness, "who are liars, and sorcerers, and adulterers, and whoremongers, and whosoever loves and makes a lie," shall be sent to the telestial kingdom. There is still another group composed of those who have had a testimony of divine truth, who have had the guidance of the Spirit of the Lord, or Holy Ghost, and afterwards deny the truth and put Jesus Christ to open shame. These shall be cast out into "outer darkness." They are called sons of perdition. (Man: His Origin and Destiny, pp. 50-53) TLDP:(244)243-245

**Related Witnesses:**

### Melvin J. Ballard

[A]nd he has other sons and daughters who do not even attain unto the telestial kingdom. They are sons of perdition out with the devil and his angels, and though the Father has grieved over them, he still has not the power to rescue and save them because he gave them free agency, and they used that in such a manner that they have shut themselves out from his presence. But he is justified. He has performed his full duty by them. . . . (Sermons and Missionary Services of Melvin J. Ballard, pp. 255-57) TLDP:132

**HYMNS Written by Prophets**
**Applicable to this Topic**

### Bruce R. McConkie
*Come, Listen to a Prophet's Voice,* verse 4
HYMNS:21

Then heed the words of truth and light
That flow from fountains pure.
Yea, keep His law with all thy might
Till thine election's sure,
Till thou shalt hear the holy voice
Assure eternal reign,
While joy and cheer attend thy choice,
As one who shall obtain.

# List of Doctrines

## JUSTICE AND MERCY

*Doctrines Located in This Topic*

389. Divine justice requires that a penalty be paid for every sin.

390. Through the Atonement of Christ, mercy is available to all.

391. Justice is satisfied and mercy is extended to those who repent.

*Doctrines on JUSTICE AND MERCY Located in Other Topics*

45. Were it not for the Atonement, mercy could not be extended to sinners who, though they might repent, would nevertheless be compelled to suffer the rigorous demands of justice.

251. God is merciful.

784. Those who persist in sexual sin shall not inherit the kingdom of God (yet there is mercy for the sinner who repents).

# JUSTICE AND MERCY

**389. Divine justice requires that a penalty be paid for every sin.**

### Alma, the younger,
*quoted by Mormon*

Now, repentance could not come unto men except there were a punishment, which also was eternal as the life of the soul should be, affixed opposite to the plan of happiness, which was as eternal also as the life of the soul. 17. Now, how could a man repent except he should sin? How could he sin if there was no law? How could there be a law save there was a punishment? 18. Now, there was a punishment affixed, and a just law given, which brought remorse of conscience unto man. . . . 22. But there is a law given, and a punishment affixed, and a repentance granted; which repentance mercy claimeth; otherwise, justice claimeth the creature and executeth the law, and the law inflicteth the punishment; if not so, the works of justice would be destroyed, and God would cease to be God. 23. But God ceaseth not to be God, and mercy claimeth the penitent, and mercy cometh because of the atonement; and the atonement bringeth to pass the resurrection of the dead; and the resurrection of the dead bringeth back men into the presence of God; and thus they are restored into his presence, to be judged according to their works, according to the law and justice. 24. For behold, justice exerciseth all his demands, and also mercy claimeth all which is her own; and thus, none but the truly penitent are saved. 25. What, do ye suppose that mercy can rob justice? I say unto you, Nay; not one whit. If so, God would cease to be God. 26. And thus God bringeth about his great and eternal purposes, which were prepared from the foundation of the world. And thus cometh about the salvation and the redemption of men, and also their destruction and misery. (*Alma speaks to his son Corianton, concerning the resurrection of the dead, about 73 B.C.*) Alma 42:16-18,22-26

### Boyd K. Packer,
*also quoting Alma, the younger*

Each of us, without exception, one day will settle that spiritual account. We will, that day, face a judgment for our doings in mortal life and face a foreclosure of sorts. ¶ One thing I know; we will be justly dealt with. Justice, the eternal law of justice, will be the measure against which we settle this account. ¶ Justice is usually pictured holding a set of scales and blindfolded against the possibility that she may be partial or become sympathetic. There is no sympathy in justice alone—only justice! Our lives will be weighed on the scales of justice. ¶ The Prophet Alma declared: ¶ "Justice claimeth the creature and executeth the law, and the law inflicteth the punishment; if not so, the works of justice would be destroyed, and God would cease to be God." (Alma 42:22) ¶ I commend to you the reading of the 42nd chapter of Alma. It reveals the place of justice and should confirm that the poet spoke the truth when he said, "In the course of justice [only] none of us should see salvation." (Shakespeare, The Merchant of Venice, IV. i. 199-200) CR1977Apr:78-79

### Bruce R. McConkie

Adam fell. We know that this fall came because of transgression, and that Adam broke the law of God, became mortal and was thus subject to sin and disease and all the ills of mortality. We know that the effects of his fall passed upon all his posterity; all inherited a fallen state, a state of mortality, a state of temporal and spiritual death prevail. In this state all men sin. All are lost. All are fallen. All are cut off from the presence of God. All have become carnal, sensual, and devilish by nature. Such a way of life is inherent in this mortal existence. Thus all are in the grasp of justice, and because God is just, all must pay the penalty for their sins. ¶ This, Alma tells us, is the rationale "concerning the justice of God in the punishment of the sinner." Lost and fallen and sinful and carnal man has been in this state of opposition to God since the fall of Adam; such is his present state, and he will so remain forever, unless provision is made whereby he can escape from the grasp of justice. The provisions of the law of justice are so basic and so unvarying that if they ceased to operate, "God would cease to be God." (The Promised Messiah, pp. 244-45) TLDP:330

**Related Witnesses:**

### Jesus,
*recorded in Matthew*

Verily I say unto thee, Thou shalt by no means come out thence, till thou hast paid the uttermost farthing. (*Jesus teaches to "agree with thine adversary" lest he take thee to the judge and "thou be cast into prison," for even mankind's justice requires that a penalty be paid for every offense*) Matt.5:26

---

**390. Through the Atonement of Christ, mercy is available to all.**

### Elder Joseph Fielding Smith

In his infinite mercy, the Father heard the cries of

his children and sent His Only Begotten Son, who was not subject to death nor to sin, to provide the means of escape. This he did through his infinite atonement and the everlasting gospel. (Doctrines of Salvation, 1:127) TLDP:331

**Alma, the younger,**
*quoted by Mormon*
And now remember, my son, if it were not for the plan of redemption, (laying it aside) as soon as they were dead their souls were miserable, being cut off from the presence of the Lord. 12. And now, there was no means to reclaim men from this fallen state, which man had brought upon himself because of his own disobedience; 13. Therefore, according to justice, the plan of redemption could not be brought about, only on conditions of repentance of men in this probationary state, yea, this preparatory state; for except it were for these conditions, mercy could not take effect except it should destroy the work of justice. Now the work of justice could not be destroyed; if so, God would cease to be God. 14. And thus we see that all mankind were fallen, and they were in the grasp of justice; yea, the justice of God, which consigned them forever to be cut off from his presence. 15. And now, the plan of mercy could not be brought about except an atonement should be made; therefore God himself atoneth for the sins of the world, to bring about the plan of mercy, to appease the demands of justice, that God might be a perfect, just God, and a merciful God also. (*Alma speaks to his son Corianton, concerning the resurrection of the dead, about 73 B.C.*) Alma 42:11-15

**Boyd K. Packer,**
*also quoting Paul*
By eternal law, mercy cannot be extended save there be one who is both willing and able to assume our debt and pay the price and arrange the terms for our redemption. ¶ Unless there is a mediator, unless we have a friend, the full weight of justice untempered, unsympathetic, must, positively must fall on us. The full recompense for every transgression, however minor or however deep, will be exacted from us to the uttermost farthing. ¶ But know this: Truth, glorious truth, proclaims there is such a Mediator. ¶ "For there is one God, and one mediator between God and men, the man Christ Jesus." (1Tim.2:5) ¶ Through Him mercy can be fully extended to each of us without offending the eternal law of justice. . . . ¶ The extension of mercy will not be automatic. It will be through covenant with Him. It will be on His terms, His generous terms, which include, as an absolute essential, baptism by immersion for the remission of sins. ¶ All mankind can be pro-

tected by the law of justice, and at once each of us individually may be extended the redeeming and healing blessing of mercy. CR1977Apr:80

**Bruce R. McConkie**
As justice is the child of the fall, so mercy is the offspring of the atonement. "Mercy cometh because of the atonement," Alma says, "and mercy claimeth the penitent." If there were no atoning sacrifice there would be no mercy—only justice. (The Promised Messiah, pp. 244-45) TLDP:330

**Lehi,**
*quoted by his son Nephi*
Wherefore, redemption cometh in and through the Holy Messiah; for he is full of grace and truth. 7. Behold, he offereth himself a sacrifice for sin, to answer the ends of the law, unto all those who have a broken heart and a contrite spirit; and unto none else can the ends of the law be answered. 8. Wherefore, how great the importance to make these things known unto the inhabitants of the earth, that they may know that there is no flesh that can dwell in the presence of God, save it be through the merits, and mercy, and grace of the Holy Messiah, who layeth down his life according to the flesh, and taketh it again by the power of the Spirit, that he may bring to pass the resurrection of the dead, being the first that should rise. (*Lehi teaches his son Jacob, about the redemption of man from the fall of Adam, between 588-570 B.C.*) 2Ne.2:6-8

**Joseph Smith,**
*quoted by Elder Joseph Fielding Smith*
All are within the reach of pardoning mercy, who have not committed the unpardonable sin, which hath no forgiveness. . . . (*Items of instruction given by the Prophet at a conference in Nauvoo, Ill., Oct. 3, 1894*) HC4:425; TPJS:191

---

**391. Justice is satisfied and mercy is extended to those who repent.**

**Elder Joseph Fielding Smith**
Justice made certain demands, and Adam could not pay the price, so mercy steps in. The Son of God says: "I will go down and pay the price. I will be the Redeemer and redeem men from Adam's transgression. I will take upon me the sins of the world and redeem or save every soul from his own sins who will repent." That is the only condition. The Savior does not save anybody from his individual sins, only on condition of his repentance. So the effect of Adam's transgression was to place all of us in the pit with him. Then the Savior comes along, not

subject to that pit, and lowers the ladder. He comes down into the pit and makes it possible for us to use the ladder to escape. (Doctrines of Salvation, 1:123) TLDP:331

**Joseph Smith,**
*receiving the Word of the Lord*

[F]or I, the Lord forgive sins, and am merciful unto those who confess their sins with humble hearts; (*Revelation to the elders of the Church through Joseph Smith, Aug. 12, 1831*) D&C 61:2

**J. Reuben Clark, Jr.**

There is forgiveness for the sinner who truly repents. God's mercy is just as boundless as his justice. (The Latter-day Prophets and the Doctrine and Covenants, *2:320*) TLDP:331

**Bruce R. McConkie**

Truly, it is with the dead as with the living. The spirit offspring of Deity, whether encased in clay or roaming free in the realms of the departed dead, are all subject to the same eternal laws. Our Lord's infinite and eternal atonement reaches out to all in every sphere of creation. Freedom from the bondage of sin, from the chains of hell, from the darkness of doubt and despair come to both the quick and the dead on the same terms and conditions, and these are made operative through His atoning sacrifice. All must repent to be free. All must obey to gain gospel blessings. All must keep the commandments to merit mercy. (The Promised Messiah, p. 242) TLDP:232

**Elder Spencer W. Kimball**

There are many people who seem to rely solely on the Lord's mercy rather than on accomplishing their own repentance. One woman rather flippantly said, "The Lord knows my intents and that I'd like to give up my bad habits. He will understand and forgive me." But the scriptures will not bear this out. The Lord may temper justice with mercy, but he will never supplant it. Mercy can never replace justice. God is *merciful*, but he is also *just*. The Savior's atonement represents the mercy extended. Because of this atonement, all men can be saved. Most men can be exalted. ¶ Many have greatly misunderstood the place of mercy in the forgiveness program. Its role is not to give great blessings without effort. Were it not for the atonement of Christ, the shedding of his blood, the assumption by proxy of our sins, man could never be forgiven and cleansed. Justice and mercy work hand in hand. Having offered mercy to us in the overall redemption, the Lord must now let justice rule, for he cannot save us in our sins. . . . (The Miracle of Forgiveness, pp. 358-59) TLDP:331-32

**Related Witnesses:**
**Joseph Smith,**
*receiving the Word of the Lord*

But remember, God is merciful; therefore, repent of that which thou hast done which is contrary to the commandment which I gave you, and thou art still chosen, and art again called to the work; (*Revelation regarding the lost manuscript pages, July 1828*) D&C 3:10

# List of Doctrines

## JUSTIFICATION

*Doctrines Located in This Topic*

392. When a person *righteously* performs the ordinances and duties necessary for exaltation, those acts may be accepted (justified) by God.

393. Being born again (being quickened by the Spirit and receiving a change of heart after baptism by water and receiving the gift of the Holy Ghost) justifies a person before the Lord and starts that person toward sanctification.

*Doctrines on JUSTIFICATION Located in Other Topics*

438. A couple whose marriage is sealed by the power of the priesthood must yet live righteously throughout life for that marriage to survive death.

# JUSTIFICATION

**Author's Note:** "Justify means to pronounce free from guilt or blame, or to absolve." Elder Harold B. Lee (TLDP:332) ¶ To *justify,* as defined by Marvin R. Vincent, D.D., is "[T]he act or process by which a man is brought into a right state as related to God." He also defines *justification*: "Justification aims directly at *character.* It contemplates making the man himself right; . . ." (Word Studies in the New Testament, 3:39)

392. **When a person *righteously* performs the ordinances and duties necessary for exaltation, those acts may be accepted (justified) by God.**

**Bruce R. McConkie**

What, then, is the doctrine of justification. . . . To be justified is to be made righteous and therefore to be saved. Men are justified in what they do when their deeds conform to divine standards. Righteous acts are approved of the Lord; they are ratified by the Holy Ghost; they are sealed by the Holy Spirit of Promise; or, in other words, they are justified by the Spirit. Such divine approval must be given to "all covenants, contracts, bonds, obligations, oaths, vows, performances, connections, associations, or expectations"—that is, to all things—if they are to have "efficacy, virtue, or force in and after the resurrection from the dead." (D&C 132:7) Such a requirement is part of the terms and conditions of the gospel covenant. ¶ . . . . In the eternal sense, Israel consists of the members of the Church who keep the commandments and are thereby justified in this life and saved in the life to come. The wicked, of course, are not justified. (Alma 41:13-15) (The Promised Messiah, pp. 344-45) TLDP:333

**Elder Harold B. Lee**

I want to comment about this one statement: "by the Spirit ye are justified." Now I've struggled with that statement, and I have found a definition that seems to indicate to me what I'm sure the Lord intended to convey. The definition that I think is significant says: "Justify means to pronounce free from guilt or blame, or to absolve." Now if the Spirit, the Holy Ghost, is to pronounce one free from guilt or blame, or to absolve, then we begin to see something of the office of the Holy Ghost that relates to the subject about which we are talking: what it means to be born of the Spirit. ¶ I shall inject here another phrase that is oft discussed (and I think is misunderstood) and to which we try to attach some mysteries. This phrase, where the Lord directs that all of these things are to be eternal, is: "must be sealed by the Holy Spirit of promise." Let me refer first to the 76th section of the Doctrine and Covenants. Speaking of those who are candidates for celestial glory, the Lord says: ¶ "They are they who received the testimony of Jesus, and believed on his name and were baptized after the manner of his burial. . . . That by keeping the commandments they might be washed and cleansed from all their sins, and receive the Holy Spirit by the laying on of the hands. . . . And who overcome by faith, and are sealed by the Holy Spirit of Promise, which the Father sheds forth upon all those who are just and true." (D&C 76:51-53) ¶ In other words, baptism is only efficacious, and the initiatory ordinance is applicable, when it is sealed by the Holy Spirit of Promise. We have that same phrase repeated in section 132, verse 19, for the Lord is speaking now of celestial marriage. ¶ ". . . if a man marry a wife by my word . . . and it is sealed unto them by the Holy Spirit of Promise . . . they shall pass by the angels, and the gods, which are set there, to their exaltation and glory in all things. . . ." ¶ And with reference to the priesthood, when the Lord discusses in the 84th section the oath and covenant, exactly the same principle is implied. By the laying on of hands we get the promise of power and authority, but it will not be ours—worlds without end—unless we keep our part of the covenant. (Stand Ye in Holy Places, pp. 51-52) TLDP:332-333

**Joseph Smith,**
*receiving the Word of the Lord*

For all who will have a blessing at my hands shall abide the law which was appointed for that blessing, and the conditions thereof, as were instituted from before the foundation of the world. 6. And as pertaining to the new and everlasting covenant, it was instituted for the fulness of my glory; and he that receiveth a fulness thereof must and shall abide the law, or he shall be damned, saith the Lord God. 7. And verily I say unto you, that the conditions of this law are these: all covenants, contracts, bonds, obligations, oaths, vows, performances, connections, associations, or expectations, that are not made and entered into and sealed by the holy spirit of promise, of him who is anointed, both as well for time and for all eternity, and that too most holy, by revelation and commandment through the medium of mine anointed, whom I have appointed on the earth to hold this power (and I have appointed unto my servant Joseph to hold this power in the last days, and there is never but one on the earth at a time on whom this power and the keys of this priesthood are conferred), are of no efficacy, virtue, or force in and after the resurrection from the dead; for all contracts that are not made unto this end have an end when men are dead. 8. Behold, mine house is a house of order, saith the Lord God, and not a house of confusion. 9. Will I accept of an offering, saith the Lord, that is not made in my name? 10. Or will I receive at your hands that which I have not appointed? 11. And will I appoint unto you, saith the Lord, except it be by law, even as I and my father ordained unto you, before the world was? 12. I am the Lord thy God; and I give unto you this commandment—that no man shall come unto the Father but by me or by my word, which is my law, saith the Lord. 13. And everything that is in the world, whether it be ordained of men, by thrones, or principalities, or powers, or things of name, whatsoever they may be, that are not by me or by my word, saith the Lord, shall be thrown down, and shall not remain after men are dead, neither in nor after the resurrection, saith the Lord your God. (*Revelation relating to the terms of the new and everlasting covenant, July 12, 1843*) D&C 132:5-13

**Elder Joseph Fielding Smith**

Baptism is not merely a door into the kingdom, which entitles us to enter, bringing with us a trail of sins unrepented of. It is not that at all. We must not enter that door until our hearts are humble, our spirits contrite, and we give the assurance that we will serve the Lord in faithfulness and righteousness to the end. ¶ Again: "And we know that justification through the grace of our Lord and Savior Jesus Christ is just and true;" [D&C 20:30] ¶ That is, if we come into this Church with a broken heart and a contrite spirit, with a determination to forsake all our sins and live faithfully to the end, then we are justified, and the sanctification of the blood of Jesus Christ is efficacious, and we receive the blessings. ¶ "We know also, that sanctification through the grace of our Lord and Savior Jesus Christ is just and true, to all those who love and serve God with all their mights, minds, and strength." [D&C 20:31] CR1941Oct:93-94

**Related Witnesses:**

**Paul**

Know ye not that the unrighteous shall not inherit the kingdom of God? Be not deceived: neither fornicators, nor idolaters, nor adulterers, nor effeminate, nor abusers of themselves with mankind, 10. Nor thieves, nor covetous, nor drunkards, nor revilers, nor extortioners, shall inherit the kingdom of God. 11. And such were some of you: but ye are washed, but ye are sanctified, but ye are justified in the name of the Lord Jesus, and by the spirit of our God. (*Paul writes to the Church at Corinth, Greece, about A.D. 55*) 1Cor.6:9-11

**Joseph Smith**

And we know that all men must repent and believe on the name of Jesus Christ, and worship the Father in his name, and endure in faith on his name to the end, or they cannot be saved in the kingdom of God. 30. And we know that justification through the grace of our Lord and Savior Jesus Christ is just and true; 31. And we know also, that sanctification through the grace of our Lord and Savior Jesus Christ is just and true, to all those who love and serve God with all their mights, minds, and strength. 32. But there is a possibility that man may fall from grace and depart from the living God; 33. Therefore let the church take heed and pray always, lest they fall into temptation; 34. Yea, and even let those who are sanctified take heed also. (*Revelation on Church Organization and Government, April 1830; laws governing repentance, justification, sanctification are set forth*) D&C 20:29-34

**Nephi, son of Lehi**

And it came to pass that I said unto them that I knew that I had spoken hard things against the wicked, according to the truth; and the righteous have I justified, and testified that they should be lifted up at the last day; wherefore, the guilty taketh the truth to be hard, for it cutteth them to the very center. (*Nephi answers his brothers, 600-592 B.C.*) 1Ne.16:2

**Joseph Smith,**
*quoted by Elder Joseph Fielding Smith*

To be justified before God we must love one another: we must overcome evil; we must visit the fatherless and the widow in their affliction, and we must keep ourselves unspotted from the world: for such virtues flow from the great fountain of pure religion, strengthening our faith by adding every good quality that adorns the children of the blessed Jesus. We can pray in the season of prayer; we can love our neighbor as ourselves, and be faithful in tribulation, knowing that the reward of such is greater in the kingdom of heaven. What a consolation! What a joy! Let me live the life of the righteous, and let my reward be like his! (*Epistle to the Saints scattered abroad.*) (Messenger and Advocate, June 1835) TPJS:76; DGSM:50

**Joseph Smith,**
*translating the Book of Moses*

For by the water ye keep the commandment; by

the spirit ye are justified, and by the blood ye are sanctified; (*The record of Moses: Enoch recounts God speaking to Adam*) Moses 6:60

### Paul,
#### quoted by Joseph Smith,
#### translating Romans

Therefore ye are justified of faith and works, through grace, to the end the promise might be sure to all the seed; not to them only who are of the law, but to them also who are of the faith of Abraham; who is the father of us all. (*Letter to the Church in Rome, about* A.D. *55*) JST(Rom.4:16 fn. a)

### Paul

Therefore being justified by faith, we have peace with God through our Lord Jesus Christ. . . . 9. Much more then, being now justified by his blood, we shall be saved from wrath through him. (*Letter to the Church in Rome, about* A.D. *55*) Rom.5:1,9

### Jacob, brother of Nephi

And the hand of providence hath smiled upon you most pleasingly, that you have obtained many riches; and because some of you have obtained more abundantly than that of your brethren ye are lifted up in the pride of your hearts, and wear stiff necks and high heads because of the costliness of your apparel, and persecute your brethren because ye suppose that ye are better than they. 14. And now, my brethren, do ye suppose that God justifieth you in this thing? Behold, I say unto you, nay. But he condemneth you, and if ye persist in these things his judgments must speedily come unto you. (*Jacob denounces the love of riches among the Nephites, 544-421* B.C.) Jacob 2:13-14

**Author's Note:** A short-hand way of stating justification might be, as paraphrased from Bruce R. McConkie: Whatever the Holy Ghost endorses is justified.

---

393. **Being born again (being quickened by the Spirit and receiving a change of heart after baptism by water and receiving the gift of the Holy Ghost) justifies a person before the Lord and starts that person toward sanctification.**

### Elder Joseph Fielding Smith

Baptism is not merely a door into the kingdom, which entitles us to enter, bringing with us a trail of sins unrepented of. It is not that at all. We must not enter that door until our hearts are humble, our spirits contrite, and we give the

assurance that we will serve the Lord in faithfulness and righteousness to the end. ¶ Again: "And we know that justification through the grace of our Lord and Savior Jesus Christ is just and true;" [D&C 20:30] ¶ That is, if we come into this Church with a broken heart and a contrite spirit, with a determination to forsake all our sins and live faithfully to the end, then we are justified, and the sanctification of the blood of Jesus Christ is efficacious, and we receive the blessings. ¶ "We know also, that sanctification through the grace of our Lord and Savior Jesus Christ is just and true, to all those who love and serve God with all their mights, minds, and strength." [D&C 20:31] CR1941Oct:93-94

### Orson Pratt

The first effect of true faith is a sincere, true, and thorough repentance of all sins. . . . ¶ . . . . What does Paul mean when he says, "Therefore being justified by faith, we have peace with God, through our Lord Jesus Christ?" He means that faith is the starting point—the foundation and cause of our repentance and baptism which bring remission or justification; and being the cause which leads to those results, it is not improper to impute justification to faith. . . . All will admit that to believe with the heart leads to and includes repentance. ("True Faith," in Lectures on Faith, pp. 76-77) TLDP:178

### John A. Widtsoe

The gift of the Holy Ghost confers upon a person the right to receive, as he may desire and need, the presence, light and intelligence of the Holy Ghost. . . . ¶ The gift of the Holy Ghost remains inoperative unless a person leads a blameless life. Worthiness determines whether a person shall enjoy the privileges promised when the "gift" is conferred. It is useless to expect this high official assistance unless there is daily conformity to the laws of the gospel. Faith and prayer, out of the heart and unceasing, will fit a person for the presence of the Holy Ghost, and to such a life he will respond in power. ¶ Latter-day Saints have received, under the hands of those divinely empowered, this inexpressibly glorious "gift," which will lead them if they are fitted, into the companionship of the Holy Ghost, and win for them intelligence and power to win joy in life and exaltation in the world to come. Those who have been so blessed have not always understood the greatness of that which has been given them, or have not earnestly sought its help. So powerful a gift, with such boundless promise, justifies every attempt to cleanse body and soul. Certain it is, that only with the aid of the Holy Ghost shall we be able to rise to the heights of salvation of which we dream and for which we pray. (*Man and the Dragon,* pp. 150-51) TLDP:276-77

### Joseph Smith,
#### *translating the Book of Moses*

For by the water ye keep the commandment; by the spirit ye are justified, and by the blood ye are sanctified; (*The record of Moses: Enoch recounts God speaking to Adam*) Moses 6:60

**Related Witnesses:**

#### Paul

And such were some of you: but ye are washed, but ye are sanctified, but ye are justified in the name of the Lord Jesus, and by the spirit of our God. (*Letter to the Church at Corinth, Greece, about A.D. 55*) 1Cor.6:11

#### Elder Harold B. Lee

"Justify means to pronounce free from guilt or blame, or to absolve." Now if the Spirit, the Holy Ghost, is to pronounce one free from guilt or blame, or to absolve, then we begin to see something of the office of the Holy Ghost that relates to the subject about which we are talking: what it means to be born of the Spirit. *(To seminary and institute teachers, June 1962)* (Stand Ye in Holy Places, pp. 51-52) TLDP:332-33

#### Joseph Smith

And we know that all men must repent and believe on the name of Jesus Christ, and worship the Father in his name, and endure in faith on his name to the end, or they cannot be saved in the kingdom of God. 30. And we know that justification through the grace of our Lord and Savior Jesus Christ is just and true; 31. And we know also, that sanctification through the grace of our Lord and Savior Jesus Christ is just and true, to all those who love and serve God with all their mights, minds, and strength. (*Revelation on Church Organization and Government, April 1830; laws governing repentance, justification, sanctification, and baptism are set forth*) D&C 20:29-31

#### John A. Widtsoe

This understanding of the promise to Abraham places a heavy responsibility upon all who accept the gospel. As children of Abraham, they are under obligation to do the works of Abraham. The waters of baptism carry with them the promise on the part of the candidate that he will conform his life to the gospel of Jesus Christ, which of course was the gospel given, accepted, and practiced by Father Abraham. (Evidences and Reconciliations, p. 400) DGSM:58

#### James E. Talmage

The special purpose of baptism is to afford admission to the Church of Christ with remission of sins. What need of more words to prove the worth of this divinely appointed ordinance? What gift could be offered the human race greater than a sure means of obtaining forgiveness for transgression? Justice forbids the granting of universal and unconditional pardon for sins committed except through obedience to ordained law; but means simple and effective are provided whereby the penitent sinner may enter into a covenant with God, sealing that covenant with the sign that commands recognition in heaven, that he will submit himself to the laws of God; thus he places himself within the reach of Mercy, under whose protecting influence he may win eternal life. AF:111

#### Bruce R. McConkie

If you will read in the eighteenth chapter of Mosiah the account that took place at the waters of Mormon, you'll read what members of the Church do when they come in by baptism. They covenant to do certain things; for instance, one of the list of covenants there listed, recited is this: I covenant to stand as a witness of Christ, at all times, and in all places, and under all circumstances that I may be in even until death. That's one of the covenants we make. Now the overall covenant that we make is to keep the commandments. And the Lord, on his part, covenants with us that if we do what we there and then agree, he will pour out his Spirit upon us more abundantly, and he will give us eternal life in his kingdom. In other words, we in effect sign the everlasting covenant by the ordinance of baptism, and we make its terms and conditions binding upon us, and this is what makes us different from the generality of mankind. We receive the gift of the Holy Ghost, which is the right to the constant companionship of that member of the Godhead. And if we are guided thereby, then the sanctifying, cleansing, purifying, perfecting processes begin to operate in our lives, and in literal reality we become the saints of God, a peculiar and distinct people. That's what happens to us, at least if we keep our covenants— the covenants made in the waters of baptism. ACR(Brisbane)1976:15

#### George Q. Cannon

We need to be born again, and have new hearts put in us. There is too much of the old leaven about us. We are not born again as we should be. Do you not believe that we ought to be born again? Do you not believe that we should become new creatures in Christ Jesus, under the influence of the Gospel? All will say yes, who understand the Gospel. You must be born again. You must have new desires, new hearts, so to speak, in you. But what do we see? We see men following the ways of the world just as much as though they made no pretensions to being Latter-day Saints. Hundreds of people who are called Latter-day Saints you could not distinguish from the world. They have the same desires, the same feelings, the same aspirations, the same passions as the rest of the world. Is this how God wants us to be? No; He wants us to have new hearts, new desires. He wants us to be a changed people when we embrace His Gospel, and to be animated by entirely new motives, and have a faith that will lay hold of the promises of God. CR1899Oct:50

# List of Doctrines

## LAST DAYS

### The Signs of the Times
Events Preceding the Second Coming

*Doctrines Located in This Topic*

394. We are to look for the signs preceding the Second Coming of the Lord.

395. After the testimony of the elders of the Church in the last days shall come the testimony of the elements in commotion.

396. The calamities and judgments predicted for the last days shall come because of sin—the wickedness and disobedience of mankind.

397. The Church is charged with the responsibility to warn the people of God's impending judgments upon the wicked.

398. In the last days there shall be wars and rumors of wars.

399. Desolating plagues and sicknesses shall cover the land in the last days.

400. Before the Second Coming of the Lord, the sun shall be turned into darkness and the moon will appear as blood.

401. In the last days great physical calamities will occur and the whole earth shall be in commotion.

402. The righteous will be preserved from the calamities and judgments of the Lord in the last days.

403. The judgments and calamities prophesied to come in the last days will first come upon the disobedient and sinful within the Church.

404. In the last days the fulness of the gospel is to be given first to the Gentiles (non-Jews) and thereafter to the Jews.

405. The gospel shall be preached to all nations before the Second Coming of Christ.

406. In the last days false Christs and false prophets shall emerge showing great signs and wonders.

407. In the last days iniquity will abound.

408. Before the Lord comes in judgment the Lamanites will blossom as the rose.

409. The time will come when the wicked will be cleansed from the earth by fire.

# LAST DAYS continued

(See topic
SECOND COMING OF CHRIST.)

# LAST DAYS

## The Signs of the Times
### Events Preceding the Second Coming

**Author's Note:** *The Signs of The Times* defined by Bruce R. McConkie: *"Signs* are the recognizable events or occurrences which identify present and which portend future events. They are omens, prodigies, wonders, and marvels of abnormal occurrence. *Time* means the age, era, period, or dispensation involved. Thus the *signs of the times* for our age or dispensation are the marvelous events—differing in kind, extent, or magnitude from events of past *times*—which identify the dispensation of the fulness of times and presage the Second Advent of our Lord." [Italics added.] (DGSM:94)

394. We are to look for the signs preceding the Second Coming of the Lord.

**Nephi, son of Lehi**
But behold, the righteous that hearken unto the words of the prophets, and destroy them not, but look forward unto Christ with steadfastness for the signs which are given, notwithstanding all persecution—behold, they are they which shall not perish. (*Nephi foresees the destruction of his people, about 559-545 B.C.*) 2Ne.26:8
**Joseph Smith,**
*receiving the Word of the Lord*
And it shall come to pass that he that feareth me shall be looking forth for the great day of the Lord to come, even for the signs of the coming of the Son of Man. (*Revelation March 7, 1831; signs, wonders, and the resurrection are to attend the Second Coming*) D&C 45:39
**Bruce R. McConkie**
Ours is the dispensation of desolation and war that will be climaxed by a worldwide Armageddon of butchery and blood at the very hour of the coming of the Son of Man. Jesus speaks thus for the elect's sake: none others can read the signs of the times. Carnal men will consider war as a way of life and a norm of society, not as a scourge sent of God to cleanse the earth preparatory to the return of his Son. (The Mortal Messiah, 3:440-41) TLDP:345
**James E. Talmage**
Only through watchfulness and prayer may the signs of the times be correctly interpreted and the imminence of the Lord's appearing be apprehended. To the unwatchful and the wicked the event will be as sudden and unexpected as the coming of a thief in the night. But we are not left without definite information as to precedent signs. JTC:785-86
**Joseph Smith,**
*quoted by Elder Joseph Fielding Smith*
I will prophesy that the signs of the coming of the Son of man are already commenced. One pestilence will desolate after another. We shall

soon have war and bloodshed. The moon will be turned to blood. I testify of these things, and that the coming of the Son of Man is nigh, even at your doors. If our souls and our bodies are not looking forth for the coming of the Son of Man; and after we are dead, if we are not looking forth, we shall be among those who are calling for the rocks to fall upon them. (*The Prophet instructs the Twelve on priesthood, in the vicinity of Commerce, Ill., July 2, 1839*) HC3:390; TPJS:160; DGSM:95; TLDP:351
**Related Witnesses:**
**James E. Talmage**
It is the proud and they who do wickedly who close their eyes and their ears and their hearts to the signs of the times, to the word of the Gospel and to the testimony of the Christ. It has long been a favorite excuse of men who were not ready for the advent of the Lord, to say, "The Lord delayeth his coming." CR1916Apr:130
**LeGrand Richards**
While I was president of the Southern States Mission, one of our missionaries wrote in from Florida and said, "President Richards, I have been reading about the signs of the coming of the Lord." He said, "When the sun darkens and the moon ceases to give its light and the stars fall from heaven, everybody will know that he is coming." ¶ And I wrote back and said, "Probably they will know. The newspapers might announce some great phenomenon in the heavens, misplacement of planets, that have caused this consternation, and scientists will have their explanation to make of it, and unless they have faith in the Living God, unless as Jesus said, they can read the signs of the times, they may not know anything about what is going on in the world. ¶ " 'Why,' I said, 'if the inhabitants of this earth had the ability and the power to read the signs of the times, they would know that already the Lord has given far more than the darkening of the sun or obscuring the light of the moon or causing the stars to fall from heaven, for what he has accomplished in the establishment of his kingdom in the earth in

these latter days, and the unseen power operating in the world for the accomplishment of his purposes, are greater signs than any of these phenomena that we read about—the signs of his coming'." CR1951:Apr:40-41

### Paul

But ye, brethren, are not in darkness, that that day should overtake you as a thief. 5. Ye are all the children of light, and the children of the day: we are not of the night, nor of darkness. (*Letter to the Church at Thessalonica, comprising Jews and many pagan converts, A.D. 50*) 1Thess.5:4-5

### Bruce R. McConkie

Our souls cry out: "God hasten the day of the coming of thy Son," and yet we know that such cannot be. The day is fixed and the hour is set. The signs have been, are now, and will hereafter be shown forth. Our obligation is to discern the signs of the times lest we, with the world, be taken unawares. (The Millennial Messiah, p. 405) DGSM:96

---

395. After the testimony of the elders of the Church in the last days shall come the testimony of the elements in commotion.

### Melvin J. Ballard

You will find it recorded in one of the revelations to the Prophet Joseph Smith and the elders of this Church, that after the testimony of the elders should come the testimony of lightnings, of thunder, of earthquakes, of the sea heaving itself beyond its bounds, and of destruction, the elements being engaged in bearing testimony—the thunder would cry repentance. CR1923Oct:31-32

### Joseph Smith,
*receiving the Word of the Lord*

And after your testimony cometh wrath and indignation upon the people. 89. For after your testimony cometh the testimony of earthquakes, that shall cause groanings in the midst of her, and men shall fall upon the ground and shall not be able to stand. 90. And also cometh the testimony of the voice of thunderings, and the voice of lightnings, and the voice of tempests, and the voice of the waves of the sea heaving themselves beyond their bounds. (*Revelation Dec. 27/28, 1832; the "olive leaf message of peace"*) D&C 88:88-90

### President George Albert Smith,
### J. Reuben Clark, Jr., David O. McKay
(First Presidency)

At present the message of peace is being heralded to the world by more than 5000 duly commissioned servants of the Lord, representing The Church of Jesus Christ of Latter-day Saints. The mission of these ambassadors is to cry repentance unto this generation as well as to teach the Gospel of Jesus Christ in its fulness. Should this message be rejected, the Lord has warned the people as follows: ¶ "For after your testimony cometh the testimony of earthquakes, that shall cause groanings in the midst of her, and men shall fall upon the ground and shall not be able to stand. ¶ "And also cometh the testimony of the voice of thunderings, and the voice of lightnings, and the voice of tempests, and the voice of the waves of the sea heaving themselves beyond their bounds. ¶ "And all things shall be in commotion; and surely, men's hearts shall fail them; for fear shall come upon all people." (D&C 88:89-91) ¶ As the representatives of our Heavenly Father, we admonish people everywhere to turn unto the Lord and forsake evil, lest His judgments overtake them. Only through a return to the teachings of the Master can peace come to the world and the kingdom of God be made ready for the return of the Prince of Peace to reign as King of Kings and Lord of Lords. (*Christmas message in Church News*) MOFP6:283

### President Brigham Young,
*quoted by John A. Widtsoe*

All we have heard and we have experienced is scarcely a preface to the sermon that is going to be preached. When the testimony of the Elders ceases to be given, and the Lord says to them, "Come home: I will now preach my own sermons to the nations of the earth," all you now know can scarcely be called a preface to the sermon that will be preached with fire and sword, tempests, earthquakes, hail, rain, thunders and lightnings, and fearful destruction. What matters the destruction of a few railway cars? You will hear of magnificent cities, now idolized by the people, sinking in the earth, entombing the inhabitants. The sea will heave itself beyond its bounds, engulfing mighty cities. Famine will spread over the nations and nation will rise up against nation, kingdom against kingdom and states against states, in our own country and in foreign lands; and they will destroy each other, caring not for blood and lives of their neighbors, of their families, or for their own lives. (*In Bowery, July 1860; JD8:123*) DBY:111-12; DGSM:95

### Elder John Taylor

Before the Lord destroyed the old world, he directed Noah to prepare an ark; before the cities of Sodom and Gomorrah were destroyed, he told Lot to "flee to the mountains;" before Jerusalem was destroyed Jesus gave his disciples warning, and told them to "flee out of it;" and before the destruction of the world, a message is sent; after this, the nations will be judged, for God is now preparing his own kingdom for his own reign, and will not be thwarted by any conflicting influence, or opposing power. The testimony of God is first to be made known, the standard is to be raised; the gospel of the kingdom is to be preached to all nations, the world is to be warned, and then come the troubles. (The Government of God, p. 101) TLDP:328-29

**Related Witnesses:**

**Joseph Smith,**
*receiving the Word of the Lord*
Call ye, therefore, upon them with loud proclamation, and with your testimony, fearing them not, for they are as grass, and all their glory as the flower thereof which soon falleth, that they may be left also without excuse— 8. And that I may visit them in the day of visitation, when I shall unveil the face of my covering, to appoint the portion of the oppressor among hypocrites, where there is gnashing of teeth, if they reject my servants and my testimony which I have revealed unto them. 9. And again, I will visit and soften their hearts, many of them for your good, that ye may find grace in their eyes, that they may come to the light of truth, and the Gentiles to the exaltation or lifting up of Zion. 10. For the day of my visitation cometh speedily, in an hour when ye think not of; and where shall be the safety of my people, and refuge for those who shall be left of them? (*Revelation received Jan. 19, 1841*) D&C 124:7-10

---

396. The calamities and judgments predicted for the last days shall come because of sin—the wickedness and disobedience of mankind.

**Marion G. Romney,**
*also quoting James E. Talmage*
These forecasts are discomfiting. They come as no surprise, however, to Latter-day Saints, because we know that nearly a hundred and fifty years ago the Lord said that the conduct of the inhabitants of the earth, unless reformed, would bring disaster. [D&C 1:8-17]. . . . ¶ Calamities will come as a matter of cause and effect. They follow naturally "and inevitably the sins of mankind and the unregenerate state of the race." (Talmage, Improvement Era, June, 1921, p. 739) CR1977Apr:74,76

**Malachi**
For, behold, the day cometh, that shall burn as an oven; and all the proud, yea, and all that do wickedly, shall be stubble: and the day that cometh shall burn them up, saith the LORD of hosts, that it shall leave them neither root nor branch. (*The prophet Malachi to the people, about 430 B.C.*) Mal.4:1

**Charles A. Callis**
The people themselves are responsible for the calamities that befall them, but when they repent and turn unto the Lord, he hears their prayers. CR1938Oct:23

**Joseph Smith,**
*receiving the Word of the Lord*
For a desolating scourge shall go forth among the inhabitants of the earth, and shall continue to be poured out from time to time, if they repent not, until the earth is empty, and the inhabitants thereof are consumed away and utterly destroyed by the brightness of my coming. (*Revelation received at the request of Martin Harris, March 1829*) D&C 5:19

**President George Albert Smith**
I fear the time is coming . . . unless we can call the people of this world to repent of their sins and turn from the error of their ways, that the great war that has just passed will be an insignificant thing, as far as calamity is concerned, compared to that which is before us. CR1946Oct:149

**Elder George Albert Smith**
We are living in a period of time when upheavals in the world are daily, almost momentary. Marvelous things are occurring. The map of the world is changing. The order of government is being modified. In our own nation we are almost helpless before the problems that confront us, notwithstanding we are probably the wealthiest and most powerful nation in all the world. What is our difficulty, brethren and sisters? It is that men refuse to hear what the Lord has said. They refuse to pay attention to His wise counsel. They absolutely neglect to give credence to the things that He teaches us, and He will not be mocked. He gives us the advice and the counsel that we need, but He will not compel us. But if we refuse we lose our opportunity and it passes away from us, in many cases to return again no more forever. CR1933Apr:71

**Joseph Smith,**
*receiving the Word of the Lord*
And verily I say unto you, that they who go forth, bearing these tidings unto the inhabitants of the earth, to them is power given to seal both on earth and in heaven, the unbelieving and

rebellious; 9. Yea, verily, to seal them up unto the day when the wrath of God shall be poured out upon the wicked without measure—10. Unto the day when the Lord shall come to recompense unto every man according to his work, and measure to every man according to the measure which he has measured to his fellow man. 11. Wherefore the voice of the Lord is unto the ends of the earth, that all that will hear may hear: 12. Prepare ye, prepare ye for that which is to come, for the Lord is nigh; 13. And the anger of the Lord is kindled, and his sword is bathed in heaven, and it shall fall upon the inhabitants of the earth. 14. And the arm of the Lord shall be revealed; and the day cometh that they who will not hear the voice of the Lord, neither the voice of his servants, neither give heed to the words of the prophets and apostles, shall be cut off from among the people; 15. For they have strayed from mine ordinances, and have broken mine everlasting covenant; 16. They seek not the Lord to establish his righteousness, but every man walketh in his own way, and after the image of his own God, whose image is in the likeness of the world, and whose substance is that of an idol, which waxeth old and shall perish in Babylon, even Babylon the great, which shall fall. 17. Wherefore, I the Lord, knowing the calamity which should come upon the inhabitants of the earth, called upon my servant Joseph Smith, Jun., and spake unto him from heaven, and gave him commandments; (*Revelation received during conference of elders of the Church, Nov. 1, 1831; preface to the doctrines given to the Church*) D&C 1:8-17

### Mosiah, son of King Benjamin, quoted by Mormon

And if the time comes that the voice of the people doth choose iniquity, then is the time that the judgments of God will come upon you; yea, then is the time he will visit you with great destruction even as he has hitherto visited this land. (*Mosiah tells the people unrighteous kings lead the people to sin, about 92 B.C.*) Mosiah 29:27

### Nephi, son of Lehi

For behold, saith the prophet, the time cometh speedily that Satan shall have no more power over the hearts of the children of men; for the day soon cometh that all the proud and they who do wickedly shall be as stubble; and the day cometh that they must be burned. 16. For the time soon cometh that the fulness of the wrath of God shall be poured out upon all the children of men; for he will not suffer that the wicked shall destroy the righteous. 17. Wherefore, he will preserve the righteous by his power, even if it so be that the fulness of his wrath must come, and the righteous be preserved, even unto the destruction of their enemies by fire. Wherefore, the righteous need not fear; for thus saith the prophet, they shall be saved, even if it so be as by fire. . . . 22. And the righteous need not fear, for they are those who shall not be confounded. But it is the kingdom of the devil, which shall be built up among the children of men, which kingdom is established among them which are in the flesh— 23. For the time speedily shall come that all churches which are built up to get gain, and all those who are built up to get power over the flesh, and those who are built up to become popular in the eyes of the world, and those who seek the lusts of the flesh and the things of the world, and to do all manner of iniquity; yea, in fine, all those who belong to the kingdom of the devil are they who need fear, and tremble, and quake; they are those who must be brought low in the dust; they are those who must be consumed as stubble; and this is according to the words of the prophet. (*Nephi explains the prophecies written on the plates of brass, 588-570 B.C.*) 1Ne.22:15-17,22-23

### James E. Talmage

The great trouble with the world today, as I understand it, is that it has become idolatrous . . . defying the commandment written by the finger of God—'Thou shalt have no other Gods before me." . . . . Men are praising the gods of silver and of gold and of all the other valuable commodities that make up wealth, and the God in whose hand their breath is . . . they will not recognize. Do you wonder that wickedness and crime have increased to terrifying proportions under those conditions? The prophets of old foresaw it. They spoke of the days of wickedness and vengeance immediately precedent to the second coming of the Lord. . . . CR1930Oct:71

### Related Witnesses:

#### Joseph Smith, translating Matthew

Tell us when shall these things be which thou hast said concerning the destruction of the temple, and the Jews; and what is the sign of thy coming, and of the end of the world, or the destruction of the wicked, which is the end of the world? (*The disciples of Jesus come to Jesus privately to ask regarding the sign of his second coming*) JS-M 1:4

#### Joseph Smith, translating the Book of Moses

And it came to pass that Enoch saw the day of the coming of the Son of Man, in the last days, to dwell on the earth in righteousness for the space of a thousand years; 66. But before that day he saw great tribulations among the wicked; and he also saw the sea, that it was troubled, and men's hearts failing them, looking forth with fear for the judgments of the Almighty God, which should come upon the wicked. (*The record of Moses: the word of the Lord to Enoch*) Moses 7:65-66

**Joseph Smith,**
*receiving the Word of the Lord*

O, ye nations of the earth, how often would I have gathered you together as a hen gathereth her chickens under her wings, but ye would not! 25. How oft have I called upon you by the mouth of my servants, and by the ministering of angels, and by mine own voice, and by the voice of thunderings, and by the voice of lightnings, and by the voice of tempests, and by the voice of earthquakes, and great hailstorms, and by the voice of famines and pestilences of every kind, and by the great sound of a trump, and by the voice of judgment, and by the voice of mercy all the day long, and by the voice of glory and honor and the riches of eternal life, and would have saved you with an everlasting salvation, but ye would not! (*Revelation: message for the nations of the earth, Feb. 1831*) D&C 43:24-25

**Joseph Smith,**
*receiving the Word of the Lord*

And my people must needs be chastened until they learn obedience, if it must needs be, by the things which they suffer. (*Revelation for Zion's Camp, June 22, 1834*) D&C 105:6

**Samuel, the Lamanite,**
*quoted by Mormon*

And ye shall hear my words, for, for this intent have I come up upon the walls of this city, that ye might hear and know of the judgments of God which do await you because of your iniquities, and also that ye might know the conditions of repentance. (*Samuel prophesies the destruction of the Nephites unless they repent, 6 B.C.*) Hel.14:11

---

397. **The Church is charged with the responsibility to warn the people of God's impending judgments upon the wicked.**

**Joseph Smith,**
*receiving the Word of the Lord*

Behold, I sent you out to testify and warn the people, and it becometh every man who hath been warned to warn his neighbor. 82. There-fore, they are left without excuse, and their sins are upon their own heads. . . . 85. That their souls may escape the wrath of God, the desolation of abomination which awaits the wicked, both in this world and in the world to come. Verily, I say unto you, let those who are not the first elders continue in the vineyard until the mouth of the Lord shall call them, for their time is not yet come; their garments are not clean from the blood of this generation. (*Revelation Dec. 27/28, 1832; the "olive leaf message of peace."*) D&C 88:81-82,85

**Elder Wilford Woodruff**

The Lord has never sent judgments upon any generation which we have any knowledge of until he has raised up prophets and inspired men to warn the inhabitants of the earth. This is the course the Lord has dealt with all men from the days of Father Adam to the present time. (*Salt Lake Stake Conference, Jan. 9, 1881, JD22:206*) TLDP:329

**Joseph Smith,**
*receiving the Word of the Lord*

I will that my saints should be assembled upon the land of Zion; 37. And that every man should take righteousness in his hands and faithfulness upon his loins, and lift a warning voice unto the inhabitants of the earth; and declare both by word and by flight that desolation shall come upon the wicked. (*Revelation Aug. 1831*) D&C 63:36-37

**Orson Pratt**

In regard to the future, it has been a duty devolving upon me, in connection with hundreds of others, to declare not only the Gospel, but to portray before the people future events. There are great things in the future, and we are sometimes apt to forget them. We have been looking, for some time past, for the Lord to accomplish and fulfill the times of the Gentiles; or the times allotted to them, during which the testimonies of his servants should go forth among them, or in other words, the times of the warning of the Gentile nations. . . . These things have been sounded so long in the ears of the Latter-day Saints that I have sometimes thought they have become like a pleasing song, or like a dream, and that they scarcely realize that these great events are at hand, even at the doors. But if we can depend upon the word of the Lord, if we can depend upon modern revelation which God has given—there is a time of tribulations, of sorrow, of great judgment, of great wrath and indignation, to come upon the nations of the earth, such as has not been since the foundation of the world. And these things are not far off, but are near at hand. . . . CR1880Apr:86

**Related Witnesses:**

**Delbert L. Stapley**

God will hasten his work by opening the heavens and sending heavenly messengers to his prophets to warn his children to prepare themselves to receive their Lord at his second coming. CR1975Oct:71

**Elder Joseph Fielding Smith**

The Lord has placed upon us the responsibility to preach the gospel, but there is another great responsibility. I think some of our missionaries have had an idea that all we had to do was to make friends, and if they wanted to come in the church, well and good, and the missionaries have not realized that they were under the obligation to leave a warning, and it is just as necessary that we warn the world as it is to declare the way of eternal life. . . . ¶ Every missionary who goes out should see to it that he leaves his testimony, so that he will be free as the Lord has declared he should be in section four of the Doctrine and Covenants; and so that every man with whom he comes in contact should be warned and left without excuse, and thus the blood of every man be upon his own head. CR1946Apr:158

**Elder Wilford Woodruff**

The Lord has raised up prophets and apostles who have cried aloud to this generation, with the proclamation of the Gospel for half a century, and warned them of the judgments which were to come, and the inhabitants of the earth have rejected this testimony, and shed the blood of the Lord's anointed, and persecuted the Saints of God, and the consequence of this, "Darkness covers the earth, and gross darkness the people," and the Lord is withholding his spirit from the inhabitants of the earth, and the devil is ruling over his own kingdom, and wickedness and abominations of every kind have increased a hundred fold within the last few years, until the whole earth is filled with murders, whoredoms, blasphemies, and every crime in the black catalogue that was manifest in the antediluvian world, or Sodom and Gomorrah, until the whole earth groans under its abominations, and the heavens weep, and all eternity is pained, and the angels are waiting the great command to go forth and reap down the earth. This testimony I bear to all nations under heaven, and I know it is true by the inspiration of Almighty God. ("Epistle of Wilford Woodruff," Millennial Star, April 21, 1879, pp. 241, 245-46) TLDP:346

---

**398. In the last days there shall be wars and rumors of wars.**

**Joseph Smith,**
*receiving the Word of the Lord*

And in that day shall be heard of wars and rumors of wars, and the whole earth shall be in commotion, and men's hearts shall fail them, and they shall say that Christ delayeth his coming until the end of the earth. . . . 33. . . . [Y]et men will harden their hearts against me, and they will take up the sword, one against another, and they will kill one another. (*Revelation March 7, 1831 regarding the day of Christ's second coming*) D&C 45:26,33

**Jesus,**
*quoted by Joseph Smith,*
*translating Matthew*

And they shall hear of wars, and rumors of wars. 29. Behold I speak for mine elect's sake; for nation shall rise against nation, and kingdom against kingdom; there shall be famines, and pestilences, and earthquakes, in divers places. (*Jesus discourses on his second coming*) JS-M 1:28-29

**Joseph Smith,**
*quoted by Elder Joseph Fielding Smith*

There will be wars and rumors of wars. . . . (*General conference talk regarding the judgments to come before the Second Coming of Christ, April 1843*) HC5:337; TPJS:286; DGSM:95

**Bruce R. McConkie**

In the latter-day age of restoration, when once again the glorious wonders of the gospel are available to men, and when Israel is gathering again round the ancient standard, the powers of evil will be unleashed as never before in all history. Satan will then fight the truth and stir up the hearts of man to do evil and work wickedness to an extent and with an intensity never before known. . . . ¶ . . . . But when those of us who live in the day of restoration hear of wars; when voices of contention and conspiracy among us threaten to use the sword in this eventuality or that; when we hear reports and rumors about the use of atomic bombs, poisonous gases, and other weapons of unbelievable power and cruelty; when these things happen in our day, it is quite another thing. Such things are among the signs of the times, and the wars and desolations of our day will make the hostilities of the past seem like feeble skirmishes among childish combatants. ¶ Ours is the dispensation of desolation and war that will be climaxed by a worldwide Armageddon of butchery and blood at the very hour of the coming of the Son of Man. Jesus speaks thus for the elect's sake: none others can read the signs of the times. Carnal men will consider war as a way of life and a norm of society, not as a scourge sent of God to cleanse the earth preparatory to the return of his Son. (The Mortal Messiah, 3:440-41) TLDP:345

**George F. Richards**
The coming event of great importance, toward which the attention of the world is directed by the preaching of the gospel, is the second and glorious coming of our Lord and Savior, for whose coming all good Christians are anxiously awaiting. . . . ¶ Signs of the Lord's coming are seen in the wars and rumors of wars, famine, pestilence, the seas heaving themselves beyond their bounds, infidelity, apostasy, and wickedness of every conceivable character. ¶ They have transgressed the laws, changed the ordinances and broken the everlasting covenant, and sin and wickedness prevail throughout the earth. CR1947Oct:58

**Elder George Albert Smith**
The world will soon be devastated with war and carnage, with plague and all the distresses that the Lord has promised unless they repent; but he has indicated that they will not repent, and distress must come. CR1937Apr:36

**Related Witnesses:**
**President George Albert Smith**
I fear the time is coming . . . unless we can call the people of this world to repent of their sins and turn from the error of their ways, that the great war that has just passed will be an insignificant thing, as far as calamity is concerned, compared to that which is before us. CR1946Oct:149

**Bruce R. McConkie**
Before this earth becomes a fit habitat for the Holy One, it must be cleansed and purified. The wicked must be destroyed; peace must replace war, and the evil imaginations in the hearts of men must give way to desires for righteousness. How shall this be brought to pass? There are two ways: [one of which is] by plagues and pestilence and wars and desolation. The wicked shall slay the wicked, as did the Nephites and the Lamanites in the day of the extinction of the Nephites as a nation. . . . (The Millennial Messiah, p. 378) DGSM:95

---

**399. Desolating plagues and sick-nesses shall cover the land in the last days.**

**Joseph Smith**
[F]or a desolating sickness shall cover the land. (*Revelation March 7, 1831; signs and wonders to attend the Second Coming*) D&C 45:31

**President Brigham Young,**
**Heber C. Kimball, Willard Richards**
(First Presidency)
[T]he overflowing scourges of God's wrath shall destroy the nations, and depopulate the earth on account of the multiplied infidelity and abominations of the inhabitants thereof. . . . ¶ . . . [T]he increasing plagues and sickness in new and diversified forms, baffling the skill of the ablest physicians, and causing the wisdom of their wisest to perish . . . all these signs, and . . . many more like things [are the fulfillment of prophecies which] should come to pass in this generation, as signs of the second coming of the Son of Man, which is near at hand. . . . (*"Fifth General Epistle" to the Saints, April 7, 1851*) MOFP2:63-64

**Joseph Smith,**
*quoted by Elder Joseph Fielding Smith*
I will prophesy that the signs of the coming of the Son of Man are already commenced. One pestilence will desolate after another. (*Address to the Twelve, July 1839*) HC3:390; TPJS:160 DGSM:95

**Jesus,**
*quoted by Joseph Smith,*
*translating Matthew*
Behold I speak for mine elect's sake; for nation shall rise against nation, and kingdom against kingdom; there shall be famines, and pestilences, and earthquakes, in divers places. (*Jesus discourses on his second coming*) JS-M 1:29

**Bruce R. McConkie**
Before this earth becomes a fit habitat for the Holy One, it must be cleansed and purified. The wicked must be destroyed; peace must replace war, and the evil imaginations in the hearts of men must give way to desires for righteousness. How shall this be brought to pass? There are two ways: (1) By plagues and pestilence and wars and desolation. . . . Plagues will sweep the earth, as the Black Death ravaged Asia and Europe in the fourteenth century. . . . (2) Then, at his coming, the vineyard will be burned. The residue of the wicked will be consumed. (The Millennial Messiah, p. 378) DGSM:95

**Marion G. Romney**
Speaking to His apostles concerning our day, Jesus said: "They shall see an overflowing scourge; for a desolating sickness shall cover the land. ¶ "But my disciples shall stand in holy places, and shall not be moved; but among the wicked, men shall lift up their voices and curse God and die." [D&C 45:31-32] CR1977Apr:76-77

**400. Before the Second Coming of the Lord, the sun shall be turned into darkness and the moon will appear as blood.**

**President Joseph Fielding Smith**

Thus, the work of the Lord is advancing and all these things are signs of the near approach of our Lord. The words of the prophets are rapidly being fulfilled, but it is done on such natural principles that most of us fail to see it. Wonders in heaven and in the earth should be seen, and there should be fire, blood and pillars of smoke. Eventually the sun is to be turned into darkness and the moon as blood, and then shall come the great and dreadful day of the Lord. Some of these signs have been given; some are yet to come. The sun has not yet been darkened. We are informed that this will be one of the last acts just preceding the coming of the Lord. One wonders if we are not now seeing some of the signs in heaven. (Quoted by Albert L. Zobell, Jr.,"A Modern Prophet at Ninety-Five," EN1971Jul:33) TLDP:352-53

**Joseph Smith**

And before the day of the Lord shall come, the sun shall be darkened, and the moon be turned into blood, and the stars fall from heaven. (*Revelation March 7, 1831; signs, wonders, and the resurrection are to attend the Second Coming*) D&C 45:42

**Joseph Smith,**
*receiving the Word of the Lord*

[L]ift up your voice as with the sound of a trump, both long and loud, and cry repentance unto a crooked and perverse generation; preparing the way of the Lord for his second coming. 7. For behold, verily, verily, I say unto you, the time is soon at hand that I shall come in a cloud with power and great glory. 8. And it shall be a great day at the time of my coming, for all nations shall tremble. 9. But before that great day shall come, the sun shall be darkened, and the moon be turned into blood; and the stars shall refuse their shining, and some shall fall, and great destructions await the wicked. (*Jesus Christ in a revelation for Orson Pratt [age 19] Nov. 4, 1830, at Peter Whitmer, Sr., home*) D&C 34:6-9

**Joseph Smith,**
*quoted by Elder Joseph Fielding Smith*

Judah must return, Jerusalem must be rebuilt, and the temple, and water come out from under the temple, and the waters of the Dead Sea be healed. It will take some time to rebuild the walls of the city and the temple,

etc.; and all this must be done before the Son of Man will make his appearance. There will be wars and rumors of wars, signs in the heavens above and on the earth beneath, the sun turned into darkness and the moon to blood, earthquakes in divers places, the seas heaving beyond their bounds; then will appear one grand sign of the Son of Man in heaven. But what will the world do? They will say it is a planet, a comet, etc. But the Son of Man will come as the sign of the coming of the Son of Man, which will be as the light of the morning cometh out of the east. (*In General conference, convened on the floor of the Nauvoo Temple, April 6, 1843*) HC5:337; TPJS:286-87

**Joel**

And I will shew wonders in the heavens and in the earth, blood, and fire, and pillars of smoke. 31. The sun shall be turned into darkness, and the moon into blood, before the great and the terrible day of the Lord come. (*Joel, a prophet of Judah, prophesies*) Joel 2:30-31

**Author's Note:** The prophecy of Joel (Joel 2:28-32) was quoted by Peter on the day of Pentecost (Acts 2:17) and by the angel Moroni to Joseph Smith (JS-H 1:41).

**Related Witnesses:**

**Joseph Smith,**
*quoted by Elder Joseph Fielding Smith*

I will prophesy that the signs of the coming of the Son of Man are already commenced. One pestilence will desolate after another. We shall soon have war and bloodshed. The moon will be turned to blood. I testify of these things, and that the coming of the Son of Man is nigh, even at your doors. If our souls and our bodies are not looking forth for the coming of the Son of Man; and after we are dead, if we are not looking forth, we shall be among those who are calling for the rocks to fall upon them. (*Address to the Twelve, July 1839*) HC3:390; TPJS:160; DGSM:95; TLDP:351

---

**401. In the last days great physical calamities will occur and the whole earth shall be in commotion.**

**Bruce R. McConkie**

Nor is war all we face; as the crusades of carnage increase, so will the plagues and pestilence. Famine and disease will stalk the earth. And for some reason, as yet undiscovered by modern geologists, earthquakes will increase in number and intensity. These are the last days, and the judgments of God are at hand. ¶ All this shall be because iniquity abounds. Sin is the father of all the ills poured out upon mankind. (*The Mortal Messiah,* 3:440-41) TLDP:345

**Joseph Smith**

For not many days hence and the earth shall tremble and reel to and fro as a drunken man; and the sun shall hide his face, and shall refuse to give light; and the moon shall be bathed in blood; and the stars shall become exceedingly angry, and shall cast themselves down as a fig that falleth from off a fig-tree. (*Revelation Dec. 27/28, 1832*) D&C 88:87

**Joseph Smith,**
*receiving the Word of the Lord*

And there shall be earthquakes also in divers places, and many desolations; yet men will harden their hearts against me, and they will take up the sword, one against another, and they will kill one another. . . . 40. And they shall see signs and wonders, for they shall be shown forth in the heavens above, and in the earth beneath. 41. And they shall behold blood, and fire, and vapors of smoke. 42. And before the day of the Lord shall come, the sun shall be darkened, and the moon be turned into blood, and the stars fall from heaven. (*Revelation March 7, 1831; signs and wonders to attend the Second Coming*) D&C 45:33,40-42

**Melvin J. Ballard**

I believe that the Lord Jesus Christ was just geologist enough to know the time when this earth would quake, when the processes of nature should go forth to cause great upheavals, and knew the hour, just as an astronomer can predict the time of eclipse. The Lord Jesus knew when that would happen, and he knew it was coincident and immediately preceding the wonderful events that would happen in preparation of his coming. ¶ These are the last days spoken of by the prophets of old. These are the signs. CR1923Oct:32

**John**

The first angel sounded, and there followed hail and fire mingled with blood, and they were cast upon the earth: and the third part of trees was burnt up, and all green grass was burnt up. 8. And the second angel sounded, and as it were a great mountain burning with fire was cast into the sea: and the third part of the sea became blood; 9. And the third part of the creatures which were in the sea, and had life, died; and the third part of the ships were destroyed. (*John sees desolation poured out preceding the Second Coming*) Rev.8:7-9

**John**

And I beheld when he had opened the sixth seal, and, lo, there was a great earthquake; and the sun became black as sackcloth of hair, and the moon became as blood; 13. And the stars of heaven fell unto the earth, even as a fig tree casteth her untimely figs, when she is shaken of a mighty wind. (*John sees the signs of the times*) Rev.6:12-13

**President Brigham Young,**
*quoted by John A. Widtsoe*

All we have heard and we have experienced is scarcely a preface to the sermon that is going to be preached. When the testimony of the Elders ceases to be given, and the Lord says to them, "Come home: I will now preach my own sermons to the nations of the earth," all you now know can scarcely be called a preface to the sermon that will be preached with fire and sword, tempests, earthquakes, hail, rain, thunders and lightnings, and fearful destruction. What matters the destruction of a few railway cars? You will hear of magnificent cities, now idolized by the people, sinking in the earth, entombing the inhabitants. The sea will heave itself beyond its bounds, engulfing mighty cities. Famine will spread over the nations and nation will rise up against nation, kingdom against kingdom and states against states, in our own country and in foreign lands; and they will destroy each other, caring not for blood and lives of their neighbors, of their families, or for their own lives. (*In Bowery, July 1860, JD8:123*) DBY:111-12; DGSM:95

**Joseph Smith,**
*quoted by Elder Joseph Fielding Smith*

The coming of the Son of Man never will be—never can be till the judgments spoken of for this hour are poured out: which judgments are commenced. Paul says, "Ye are the children of the light, and not of the darkness, that that day should overtake you as a thief in the night." It is not the design of the Almighty to come upon the earth and crush it and grind it to powder, but he will reveal it to His servants the prophets. ¶ Judah must return, Jerusalem must be rebuilt, and the temple, and water come out from under the temple, and the waters of the Dead Sea be healed. It will take some time to rebuild the walls of the city and the temple, and etc.; and all this must be done before the Son of Man will make His appearance. There will be wars and rumors of wars, signs in the heavens above and on the earth beneath, the sun turned into darkness and the moon to blood, earthquakes in divers places, the seas heaving beyond their bounds; then will appear one grand sign of the Son of Man in heaven. But what will the world do? They will say it is a planet, a comet, etc. But the Son of man will come as the sign of the coming of the Son of Man, which will be as the light of the morning cometh out of the east. *(General conference talk regarding the judgments to come before the second coming of Christ, April 1843)* HC5:336-37; TPJS:286; DGSM:95

---

## 402. The righteous will be preserved from the calamities and judgments of the Lord in the last days.

### Nephi, son of Lehi

For the time soon cometh that the fulness of the wrath of God shall be poured out upon all the children of men; for he will not suffer that the wicked shall destroy the righteous. 17. Wherefore, he will preserve the righteous by his power, even if it so be that the fulness of his wrath must come, and the righteous be preserved, even unto the destruction of their enemies by fire. Wherefore, the righteous need not fear; for thus saith the prophet, they shall be saved, even if it so be as by fire. . . . 22. And the righteous need not fear, for they are those who shall not be confounded. *(Nephi explains the prophecies written on the plates of brass, 588-570 B.C.)* 1Ne.22:16-17,22

### Marion G. Romney,
### *also quoting James E. Talmage*

Through Malachi the Lord promised "Israel that by faithfulness the seasons should be made propitious, that nurturing rains should come, bringing such harvests that the people would lack room to store their products." (Talmage, Improvement Era, June 1921, p. 738; see Mal.3:8-12.) Like assurances have been given in these latter days. ¶ Nephi, envisioning and speaking of our day, said that God "will preserve the righteous by his power, . . . even unto the destruction of their enemies by fire. Wherefore, the righteous need not fear." (1Ne.22:17) ¶ Speaking to His apostles concerning our day, Jesus said: "They shall see an overflowing scourge; for a desolating sickness shall cover the land. ¶ "But my disciples shall stand in holy places, and shall not be moved; but among the wicked, men shall lift up their voices and curse God and die." [D&C 45:31-32] CR1977Apr:76-77

### Charles A. Callis

To men and likewise to nations the promises and threatenings of God are always conditional.

In the wisdom and goodness of God good behavior, sorrowful repentance and conversion can stay the approach of judgment, or at least secure a respite. People are given time by the Almighty to return to him through repentance. There is forgiveness with Him. Thus the Lord turns aside his judgments for a while at least. Nineveh's people were rescued. They were granted an extension of time. Judgments are conditional. The people themselves are responsible for the calamities that befall them, but when they repent and turn unto the Lord, he hears their prayers. CR1938Oct:23

### Melvin J. Ballard

Do you not know . . . that God knew what was coming; that he brought this people into these mountain valleys as a place of refuge when the storm shall come. We only hear the beginning of that storm. Dismal and distressful as has been its approach, while its thunders and its flashings have filled our hearts with terror, it is but the beginning of the storm. Oh, that it were passed, and that it were gone; but it is not, it is not! . . . . The storm in its fury shall rage; and all the powers of man cannot avert it. Only one thing can save them: their humiliation, their repentance will save them and nothing else can. CR1922Oct:59

### Joseph Smith,
### *receiving the Word of the Lord*

For I am no respecter of persons, and will that all men shall know that the day speedily cometh; the hour is not yet, but is nigh at hand, when peace shall be taken from the earth, and the devil shall have power over his own dominion. 36. And also the Lord shall have power over his saints, and shall reign in their midst, and shall come down in judgment upon Idumea, or the world. *(Revelation received during conference of elders of the Church, Nov. 1, 1831; preface to the doctrines given to the Church)* D&C 1:35-36

### President Lorenzo Snow

And then we should understand that the Lord has provided, when the days of trouble come upon the nations, a place for you and me, and we will be preserved as Noah was preserved, not in an ark, but we will be preserved by going into these principles of union by which we can accomplish the work of the Lord and surround ourselves with those things that will preserve us from the difficulties that are now coming upon the world, the judgments of the Lord. We can see, as we read in the newspapers, that they are coming upon the nations of the ungodly; and they would have been upon us if we had stayed among the nations, if the Lord had not inclined our ears and brought salvation to us, we would have been as they are. CR1900Oct:4

**Related Witnesses:**

**Joseph Smith,**
*receiving the Word of the Lord*

Wherefore, I command you again to repent, lest I humble you with my almighty power; and that you confess your sins, lest you suffer these punishments of which I have spoken, of which in the smallest, yea, even in the least degree you have tasted at the time I withdrew my Spirit. (*A commandment of God for Martin Harris, March 1830*) D&C 19:20

**President Wilford Woodruff**

So far as our temporal matters are concerned, we have got to go to work and provide for ourselves. The day will come when, as we have been told, we shall all see the necessity of making our own shoes and clothing and raising our own food, and uniting together to carry out the purposes of the Lord. We will be preserved in the mountains of Israel in the day of God's judgment. I therefore say to you, my brethren and sisters, prepare for that which is to come. ("Address given to Weber Stake," Millennial Star, Oct. 8, 1894, p. 644) TLDP:354

**Author's Note:** That the righteous will be preserved seems to be a *general* statement, for according to the prophet Joseph Smith, the righteous shall hardly escape all the judgments for all flesh is subject to suffer: ¶ "Sunday, 29.—Held meeting at my own house. After others had spoken I spoke and explained concerning the uselessness of preaching to the world about great judgments, but rather to preach the simple Gospel. Explained concerning the coming of the Son of Man; also that it is a false idea that the Saints will escape all the judgments, whilst the wicked suffer; for all flesh is subject to suffer, and 'the righteous shall hardly escape;' still many of the Saints will escape, for the just shall live by faith; yet many of the righteous shall fall a prey to disease, to pestilence, etc., by reason of the weakness of the flesh, and yet be saved in the Kingdom of God. So that it is an unhallowed principle to say that such and such have transgressed because they have been preyed upon by disease or death, for all flesh is subject to death; and the Savior has said, 'judge not, lest ye be judged'." (HC4:11)

---

403. **The judgments and calamities prophesied to come in the last days will first come upon the disobedient and sinful within the Church.**

**Peter**

For the time is come that judgment must begin at the house of God: and if it first begin at us, what shall the end be of them that obey not the gospel of God? (*Letter to the churches in modern Asia Minor, about A.D. 60*) 1Pet.4:17

**Elder John Taylor**

The judgments will begin at the house of God. We have to pass through some of these things, but it will only be a very little compared with the terrible destruction, the misery and suffering that will overtake the world who are doomed to suffer the wrath of God. It behooves us, as the Saints of God, to stand firm and faithful in the observance of his laws, that we may be worthy of his preserving care and blessing. (*At Ephraim, Utah, April 13, 1879, JD21:100*) TLDP:353

**Joseph Smith,**
*receiving the Word of the Lord*

Behold, vengeance cometh speedily upon the inhabitants of the earth, a day of wrath, a day of burning, a day of desolation, of weeping, of mourning, and of lamentation; and as a whirlwind it shall come upon all the face of the earth, saith the Lord. 25. And upon my house shall it begin, and from my house shall it go forth, saith the Lord; 26. First among those among you, saith the Lord, who have professed to know my name and have not known me, and have blasphemed against me in the midst of my house, saith the Lord. (*Revelation for Thomas B. Marsh concerning the Twelve Apostles; received on the day on which the gospel was first preached in England, July 23, 1837*) D&C 112:24-26

**Related Witnesses:**

**Elder Wilford Woodruff**

The parable of the ten virgins is intended to represent the second coming of the Son of man, the coming of the Bridegroom to meet the bride, the Church, the Lamb's wife, in the last days; and I expect that the Savior was about right when he said, in reference to the members of the Church, that five of them were wise and five were foolish; for when the Lord of heaven comes in power and great glory to reward every man according to the deeds done in the body, if he finds one-half of those professing to be members of his Church prepared for salvation, it will be as many as can be expected, judging by the course that many are pursuing. (*In new Tabernacle, Sept. 12, 1875, JD18:110*) TLDP:623

**Melvin J. Ballard**

Do you not know . . . that God knew what was coming; that he brought this people into these mountain valleys as a place of refuge when the storm shall come. We only hear the beginning of that storm. Dismal and distressful as has been its approach, while its thunders and its flashings have filled our hearts with terror, it is but the beginning of the storm. Oh, that it were passed, and that it were gone; but it is not, it is not! . . . The storm in its fury shall rage; and all the powers of man cannot avert it. Only one thing can save them: their humiliation, their repentance will save them and nothing else can. Therefore we stand in peril, many of us! For do you think that the Lord who has given us greater light and greater knowledge than the world, will pass us by in our sins and our transgressions? I say to you that if we do not live better than the world, if our standard of morality is not in excess of theirs, if we do not observe the law and maintain it better than any other people we ought to be ashamed of ourselves, and we shall stand under great condemnation before the Lord, because we know more than anybody else. The light and knowledge that the Lord has given to us place us in a very peculiar position, and if we are not careful the judgment of the Lord shall begin at the house of the Lord. CR1922Oct:59

---

404. In the last days the fulness of the gospel is to be given first to the Gentiles (non-Jews) and thereafter to the Jews.

### Elder Wilford Woodruff

No man knows the day or the hour when Christ will come, yet the generation has been pointed out by Jesus himself. He told his disciples when they passed by the temple as they walked out of Jerusalem that that generation should not pass away before not one stone of that magnificent temple should be left standing upon another and the Jews should be scattered among the nations; and history tells how remarkably that prediction was fulfilled. Moses and the prophets also prophesied of this as well as Jesus. The Savior, when speaking to his disciples of his second coming and the establishment of his kingdom on the earth, said the Jews should be scattered and trodden under foot until the times of the Gentiles were fulfilled. But, said he, when you see light breaking forth among the Gentiles, referring to the preaching of his gospel amongst them; when you see salvation offered to the Gentiles, and the Jews— the seed of Israel—passed by, the last first and the first last; when you see this you may know that the time of my second coming is at hand as surely as you know that summer is nigh when the fig tree puts forth its leaves; and when these

things commence that generation shall not pass away until all are fulfilled. (In Tabernacle, Jan. 1, 1871, JD14:5) TLDP:620

### Joseph Smith

They are the Twelve Apostles, who are called to the office of the Traveling High Council, who are to preside over the churches of the Saints, among the Gentiles, where there is a presidency established; and they are to travel and preach among the Gentiles, until the Lord shall command them to go to the Jews. They are to hold the keys of this ministry, to unlock the door of the Kingdom of heaven unto all nations, and to preach the Gospel to every creature. This is the power, authority, and virtue of their apostleship. ("Items of Instruction to the Twelve," Feb. 27, 1835; reported by Oliver Cowdery, clerk; "President Smith proposed the following question: 'What importance is there attached to the calling of these Twelve Apostles, different from the other callings or officers of the Church?' After the question was discussed by Councilors Patten, Young, Smith, and M'Lellin, President Joseph Smith, Jun., gave the foregoing decision.") HC2:2

### Elder Wilford Woodruff

Sometimes our neighbors and friends think hard of us because we call them Gentiles; but, bless your souls, we are all Gentiles. The Latter-day Saints are all Gentiles in a national capacity. The Gospel came to us among the Gentiles. We are not Jews, and the Gentile nations have got to hear the Gospel first. The whole Christian world have got to hear the Gospel, and when they reject it, the law will be bound and the testimony sealed, and it will turn to the house of Israel. Up to the present day we have been called to preach the Gospel to the Gentiles, and we have had to do it. For the last time we have been warning the world. . . . (In new Tabernacle, Sept. 12, 1875, JD18:112) DCSM:30

### Nephi, son of Lehi

[A]nd many generations after the Messiah shall be manifested in body unto the children of men, then shall the fulness of the gospel of the Messiah come unto the Gentiles, and from the Gentiles unto the remnant of our seed. (Nephi interprets his father Lehi's dream to his brothers, between 600-592 B.C.) 1Ne.15:13

### Related Witnesses:
#### Elder Joseph Fielding Smith

The Lord has caused Israel to mix with the nations and bring the Gentiles within the blessings of the seed of Abraham. We are preaching the gospel now in all parts of the world, and for what purpose? To gather out from the Gentile nations the lost sheep of the house of Israel. It is by this scattering that the Gentile nations have been blessed, and if they will truly repent they are entitled to all the blessings promised to Israel, "which are the blessings of salvation, even of life eternal." (Answers to Gospel Questions, 2:57) TLDP:210

**Joseph Smith,**
*receiving the Word of the Lord*
Wherefore it behooveth me that he should be ordained by you, Oliver Cowdery mine apostle; 11. This being an ordinance unto you, that you are an elder under his hand, he being the first unto you, that you might be an elder unto this church of Christ, bearing my name— 12. And the first preacher of this church unto the church, and before the world, yea, before the Gentiles; yea, and thus saith the Lord God, lo, lo! to the Jews also. Amen. (*Revelation to Joseph Smith given at the organization of the church, April 6, 1830*) D&C 21:10-12

**Joseph Smith**
And he further stated that the fulness of the Gentiles was soon to come in. (*Joseph Smith relates the angel Moroni's visit to him, Sept. 21, 1823*) JS-H 1:41

---

**405. The gospel shall be preached to all nations before the Second Coming of Christ.**

**President Brigham Young**
The Gospel of Jesus Christ must be preached to all nations for witness and a testimony; for a sign that the day has come, the set time for the Lord to redeem Zion, and gather Israel, preparatory to the coming of the Son of Man. (*In Tabernacle, Aug. 8, 1853, JD3:91*) TLDP:352

**President Joseph Fielding Smith**
We have attained the stature and strength that are enabling us to fulfill the commission given us by the Lord through the Prophet Joseph Smith that we should carry the glad tidings of the restoration to every nation and to all people. ¶ And not only shall we preach the gospel in every nation before the second coming of the Son of Man, but we shall make converts and establish congregations of Saints among them. ACR(Manchester)1971:5

**Jesus,**
*recorded in Matthew*
And this gospel of the kingdom shall be preached in all the world for a witness unto all nations; and then shall the end come. (*Jesus discourses on his second coming*) Matt.24:14

**LeGrand Richards**
For if this gospel that Jesus referred to was to be preached in all the world, it had to be done by his children. And hundreds of thousands of Latter-day Saint missionaries since that time have been all over the world—some 25,000 of them at the present time—to declare the restoration of the gospel as one of the steps in the preparation for the return of the Savior, for he so indicated that it must be preached in all the world. CR1978Apr:113

**President Brigham Young,**
**Heber C. Kimball, Willard Richards**
(First Presidency)
The unparalleled spread of the Gospel, in so short a space of time [twenty-one years at this writing], and the rapid gathering of the saints, is another token of Messiah's near approach. (*"Fifth General Epistle" to the Saints, April 7, 1851*) MOFP2:63-64

**Related Witnesses:**
**Joseph Smith,**
*receiving the Word of the Lord*
And the poor and the meek shall have the gospel preached unto them, and they shall be looking forth for the time of my coming, for it is nigh at hand— (*Revelation to Joseph Smith and Sidney Rigdon, Dec. 1830*) D&C 35:15

**Elder John Taylor**
Before the Lord destroyed the old world, he directed Noah to prepare an ark; before the cities of Sodom and Gomorrah were destroyed, he told Lot to "flee to the mountains;" before Jerusalem was destroyed Jesus gave his disciples warning, and told them to "flee out of it;" and before the destruction of the world, a message is sent; after this, the nations will be judged, for God is now preparing his own kingdom for his own reign, and will not be thwarted by any conflicting influence, or opposing power. The testimony of God is first to be made known, the standard is to be raised; the gospel of the kingdom is to be preached to all nations, the world is to be warned, and then come the troubles. (The Government of God, p. 101) TLDP:328-29

**James E. Talmage**
He will come with the body of flesh and bones in which His Spirit was tabernacled when he ascended from Mount Olivet. One of the characteristic features of the Church concerning that great, and in the language of the scripture, both glorious and terrible event, is its nearness. It is close at hand. The mission of the Church is to prepare the earth for the coming of the Lord. CR1916Apr:126

**Charles A. Callis**
The Church of Jesus Christ of Latter-day Saints

has been brought forth and established by the power of God and dedicated to the mission of preparing the way for the glorious coming of the Son of God to reign in the earth in truth and righteousness and peace. ¶ Would to God this glorious second coming of the Messiah might be in our day, but let it be sooner or later, in it we will rejoice. ¶ Truly, God will descend from the heavens in incomparable power and glory with all His holy angels, and He will stand upon the earth at the latter day. Then heaven and earth will meet. (Fundamentals of Religion: A Series of Radio Addresses [Independence, Missouri: Zion's Printing and Publishing Co., 1945], p. 40) TLDP:623

**Author's Note:** Reference is made to "the end of the world," which is the end of, or destruction of, the wicked. This, however, does not mean the end of the *earth*. *End of the "world" is not end of the "earth:"* ¶ 4. . . . Tell us when shall these things be which thou hast said concerning the destruction of the temple, and the Jews; and what is the sign of thy coming, and of the end of the world, or the destruction of the wicked, which is the end of the world? (*The disciples of Jesus come to Jesus privately to ask regarding the sign of his second coming*) (JS-M 1:4)

---

406. In the last days false Christs and false prophets shall emerge showing great signs and wonders.

### Jesus,
#### *recorded in Matthew*
For there shall arise false Christs, and false prophets, and shall shew great signs and wonders; insomuch that, if it were possible, they shall deceive the very elect. (*Jesus answers his disciples regarding his second coming and the last days*) Matt.24:24

#### President Brigham Young,
#### Heber C. Kimball, Willard Richards
(First Presidency)
[T]he increase of seers, and wizards, and diviners, and familiar spirits, and soothsayers, and astrologers, who are charming the nations with their magic arts, lulling the foolish to sleep with their magnetic influence, deceiving priests and people by their necromancy, calling rain, snow, and fire from heaven, and scattering abroad hoar frost like a winter's night . . . all these signs, and . . . many more like things [are the fulfillment of prophecies which] should come to pass in this generation, as signs of the second coming of the Son of Man, which is near at

hand. . . . (*"Fifth General Epistle" to the Saints, April 7,1851*) MOFP2:63-64

#### Bruce R. McConkie
In the day preceding our Lord's return, false religions will cover the earth. Each will be, as it were, a false Christ, inviting men to this or that system of salvation; each will have its own ministers and evangelists who, as false prophets, will propound its doctrines and extol its wonder. (The Mortal Messiah, 3:436-37) TLDP:30

#### Elder Harold B. Lee
False prophets and Christs, as foretold by the Savior, may come to deceive us not alone in the name of religion, but if we can believe the history of Italy and Germany and Russia, they may come under the label of politicians or of social planners or so-called economists, deceitful in their offerings of a kind of salvation which may come under such guise. CR1950Oct:131

#### Bruce R. McConkie
True, there may be those deranged persons who suppose they are God, or Christ, or the Holy Ghost, or almost anything. None but the lunatic fringe among men, however, will give them a second serious thought. The promise of false Christs who will deceive, if it were possible, even the very elect, who will lead astray those who have made eternal covenant with the Lord, is a far more subtle and insidious evil. ¶ A false Christ is not a person. It is a false system of worship, a false church, a false cult that says: "Lo, here is salvation; here is the doctrine of Christ. Come and believe thus and so, and ye shall be saved." It is any concept or philosophy that says that redemption, salvation, sanctification, justification, and all of the promised rewards can be gained in any way except that set forth by the apostles and prophets. . . . ¶ We hear the voice of a false Christ when we hear the divines of the day preach that salvation comes by the grace of God, not of works lest any man should boast, but simply by believing in and confessing the Lord Jesus with one's lips; or that signs and gifts and miracles are done away; or that ministers have power to represent the Lord and preach his gospel because they have a feeling in their heart that such is the course they should pursue. ¶ We hear the voice of one false Christ, echoing from the camps of communism, expounding the devil-devised declaration that religion is the opiate of the people. We hear another such voice when races alien to Israel acclaim that the one God has no need for a Son to mediate between himself and fallen man. ¶ We see the works of false Christs when women and homosexuals are ordained to the priest-

hood, as it is supposed; or when elaborate rituals pervert and twist and add to the sacrament of the Lord's supper; or when sins are forgiven through the doing of penance and the paying of money, as it is supposed. ¶ Indeed, false Christs are everywhere. (The Millennial Messiah, pp. 48-50) TLDP:30-31

**Related Witnesses:**

### James E. Talmage

We are not justified in regarding miracles as infallible testimony of Divine power and authority, for powers of the baser sort work wonders, to the deceiving of many. The magicians of Egypt were able to imitate in small measure the miracles of Moses. [See Exodus 7: 8-25, 8:1-7] John the Revelator told of evil powers deceiving men by what seemed to be supernatural achievements, and he saw unclean spirits, whom he knew to be "the spirits of devils working miracles." (See Rev.13:13-14, and 16:13-14) And the Savior Himself by this solemn warning armed the disciples against deception: "For there shall arise false Christs, and false prophets, and shall shew great signs and wonders; insomuch that, if it were possible, they shall deceive the very elect." (Matt. 24:24) ¶ The distinguishing feature of a miraculous manifestation of the Holy Spirit, as contrasted with a wonder wrought through other agencies, lies in the fact that the former is always done in the name of Jesus Christ, and had for its object the fostering of faith and the furthering of Divine purposes. (The Vitality of Mormonism, pp. 123-24) TLDP:650

### George Q. Cannon

Now, the only safe course for you and all mankind to pursue is to obey the Priesthood, to listen to the teachings of the servants of God and never murmur against them. Then God's power will increase with you, and you will add knowledge to knowledge, light to light, and be brought back into the presence of God. Then, when false prophets arise and wonderful works are performed by them through the power of the evil one, you will not be deceived; for you will know that they are not of God. Though they may call fire down from Heaven, you will still cling to the Priesthood of God. (Gospel Truth, 2:297-98) TLDP:667

---

### 407. In the last days iniquity will abound.

### Bruce R. McConkie

In the latter-day age of restoration, when once again the glorious wonders of the gospel are available to men, and when Israel is gathering again round the ancient standard, the powers of evil will be unleashed as never before in all history. Satan will then fight the truth and stir up the hearts of man to do evil and work wickedness to an extent and with an intensity never before known. . . . ¶ . . . . Such things are among the signs of the times, and the wars and desolations of our day will make the hostilities of the past seem like feeble skirmishes among childish combatants. ¶ Ours is the dispensation of desolation and war that will be climaxed by a worldwide Armageddon of butchery and blood at the very hour of the coming of the Son of Man. Jesus speaks thus for the elect's sake: none others can read the signs of the times. Carnal men will consider war as a way of life and a norm of society, not as a scourge sent of God to cleanse the earth preparatory to the return of his Son. ¶ Nor is war all we face; as the crusades of carnage increase, so will the plagues and pestilence. Famine and disease will stalk the earth. And for some reason, as yet undiscovered by modern geologists, earthquakes will increase in number and intensity. These are the last days, and the judgments of God are at hand. ¶ All this shall be because iniquity abounds. Sin is the father of all the ills poured out upon mankind. (The Mortal Messiah, 3:440-41) TLDP:345

### Paul

This know also, that in the last days perilous times shall come. 2. For men shall be lovers of their own selves, covetous, boasters, proud, blasphemers, disobedient to parents, unthankful, unholy, 3. Without natural affection, trucebreakers, false accusers, incontinent, fierce, despisers of those that are good, 4. Traitors, heady, highminded, lovers of pleasures more than lovers of God; 5. Having a form of godliness, but denying the power thereof: from such turn away. 6. For of this sort are they which creep into houses, and lead captive silly women laden with sins, led away with divers lusts, 7. Ever learning, and never able to come to the knowledge of the truth. (*Paul writes to his assistant Timothy, about* A.D. *64*) 2Tim.3:1-7

### Jesus, quoted by Joseph Smith, translating Matthew

And now I show unto you a parable. Behold, wheresoever the carcass is, there will the eagles be gathered together; so likewise shall mine elect be gathered from the four quarters of the earth. 28. And they shall hear of wars, and rumors of wars. 29. Behold I speak for mine elect's sake;

for nation shall rise against nation, and kingdom against kingdom; there shall be famines, and pestilences, and earthquakes, in divers places. 30. And again, because iniquity shall abound, the love of men shall wax cold; but he that shall not be overcome, the same shall be saved. 31. And again, this Gospel of the Kingdom shall be preached in all the world, for a witness unto all nations, and then shall the end come, or the destruction of the wicked; 32. And again shall the abomination of desolation, spoken of by Daniel the prophet, be fulfilled. (*An extract from the translation of the Bible as revealed to Joseph Smith, about Sept. 1831; Christ speaks of his second coming*) JS-M 1:27-32

**Joseph Smith**

And the love of men shall wax cold, and iniquity shall abound. 28. And when the times of the Gentiles is come in, a light shall break forth among them that sit in darkness, and it shall be the fulness of my gospel; 29. But they receive it not; for they perceive not the light, and they turn their hearts from me because of the precepts of men. . . . 33. And there shall be earthquakes also in divers places, and many desolations; yet men will harden their hearts against me, and they will take up the sword, one against another, and they will kill one another. (*Revelation, March 7, 1831; signs and wonders to attend the Second Coming*) D&C 45:27-29,33

**Elder Wilford Woodruff**

The question may be asked why these judgments are coming upon the world in the last days? I answer because of the wickedness of the inhabitants thereof. . . . The Lord has raised up prophets and apostles who have cried aloud to this generation, with the proclamation of the Gospel for half a century, and warned them of the judgments which were to come, and the inhabitants of the earth have rejected this testimony, and shed the blood of the Lord's anointed, and persecuted the Saints of God, and the consequence of this, "Darkness covers the earth, and gross darkness the people," and the Lord is withholding his spirit from the inhabitants of the earth, and the devil is ruling over his own kingdom, and wickedness and abominations of every kind have increased a hundred fold within the last few years, until the whole earth is filled with murders, whoredoms, blasphemies, and every crime in the black catalogue that was manifest in the antediluvian world, or Sodom and Gomorrah, until the whole earth groans under its abominations, and the heavens weep, and all eternity is pained, and the angels are waiting the great command to go forth and reap

down the earth. This testimony I bear to all nations under heaven, and I know it is true by the inspiration of Almighty God. ("Epistle of Wilford Woodruff," Millennial Star, April 21, 1879, pp. 241, 245-46) TLDP:345-46

**Related Witnesses:**

**Jesus,**
*recorded in Matthew*

But as the days of Noe were, so shall also the coming of the Son of man be. 38. For as in the days that were before the flood they were eating and drinking, marrying and giving in marriage, until the day that Noe entered into the ark, 39. And knew not until the flood came, and took them all away; so shall also the coming of the Son of man be. (*Signs of the Second Coming are spoken of by the Savior*) Matt.24:37-39

**Joseph Smith**

I prophesy, in the name of the Lord God of Israel, anguish and wrath and tribulation and the withdrawing of the Spirit of God from the earth await this generation, until they are visited with utter desolation. This generation is as corrupt as the generation of the Jews that crucified Christ; and if He were here today, and should preach the same doctrine He did then, they would put Him to death. (*At the Stand east of the Nauvoo Temple, Oct. 15, 1843*) HC6:58

---

**408. Before the Lord comes in judgment the Lamanites will blossom as the rose.**

**Joseph Smith**

But before the great day of the Lord shall come, Jacob shall flourish in the wilderness, and the Lamanites shall blossom as the rose. (*Revelation, March 1831, refuting Shaker doctrines and elaborating on the Second Coming*) D&C 49:24

**Elder Wilford Woodruff**

I am looking for the fulfillment of all things that the Lord has spoken, and they will come to pass as the Lord God lives. Zion is bound to rise and flourish. The Lamanites will blossom as the rose on the mountains. I am willing to say here that, though I believe this, when I see the power of the nation destroying them from the face of the earth, the fulfilment of that prophecy is perhaps harder for me to believe than any revelation of God that I ever read. It looks as though there would not be enough left to receive the gospel; but notwithstanding this dark picture, every word that God has ever said of them will have its fulfilment, and they, by and by, will receive the gospel. It will be a day of God's power among them, and a nation will be born in a day. Their chiefs will be filled with the power of God and receive the gospel, and they will go forth and build the new Jerusalem, and we shall help them. (*In 13th Ward, Jan. 12, 1873, JD15:282*) TLDP:115

### Elder Spencer W. Kimball

The Lamanites must rise in majesty and power. We must look forward to the day when they will be "white and delightsome" ["pure and delightsome," 2Ne.30:6], sharing the freedoms and blessings which we enjoy; when they shall have economic security, culture, refinement, and education; when they shall be operating farms and businesses and industries and shall be occupied in the professions and in teaching; when they shall be organized into wards and stakes of Zion, furnishing much of their own leadership; when they shall build and occupy and fill the temples, and serve in them as the natives are now serving in the Hawaiian Temple where I found last year the entire service conducted by them and done perfectly. And in the day when their prophet shall come, one shall rise . . . "mighty among them . . . being an instrument in the hands of God, with exceeding faith, to work mighty wonders. . . ." (2Ne.3:24) ¶ Brothers and sisters, the florescence of the Lamanites is in our hands. CR1947Oct:22

### George Q. Cannon

[The Lamanites] are our brethren, being of the house of Israel and containing a purer strain of Israelitish blood than many members of the Church. It has been predicted, and the word of the Lord will no more fail in this respect than in any other, that they will yet become a white and delightsome people ["pure and delightsome" 2Ne.30:6], possessed of a very high degree of cultivation. ¶ They are to build the New Jerusalem, and we, who are of the Gentile nations, are to assist them in the work. The prospect of such a condition of things may humble our pride, but we may as well look squarely at the destiny which is before [them] . . . in the due time of the Lord they will be redeemed. (Gospel Truth, 2:98) TLDP:115

### Anthony W. Ivins

These Lamanites, are heirs to the promises, and God has said, without qualification, that He will give this land to them for an everlasting inheritance [3 Ne.20:13-14], that they shall be, with us, the builders of the New Jerusalem [3Ne.21:20-25]; the powers of heaven shall be among them, and they shall know the record of their fathers which has been brought to us

through the instrumentality of the Prophet Joseph Smith. CR1915Apr:112

### President Heber J. Grant

God gave us the Book of Mormon and the chief reason, as set forth in one of the revelations, is that it shall be the means of bringing to the descendants of Father Lehi the knowledge of the Redeemer of the world, and to establish them in the faith of their fathers. I bear witness to you that nothing on earth shall ever bring them out of their thraldom save the gospel of the Lord Jesus Christ. I rejoice, therefore, that the day dawn is breaking, the night is dispelling, and the day of their redemption cometh. CR1926Oct:40

### Related Witnesses:

#### Mormon

And it came to pass that those Lamanites who had united with the Nephites were numbered among the Nephites; 15. And their curse was taken from them, and their skin became white like unto the Nephites; 16. And their young men and their daughters became exceedingly fair, and they were numbered among the Nephites, and were called Nephites. And thus ended the thirteenth year. (*Converted Lamanites become white and are called Nephites, about A.D. 3-9)* 3Ne.2:14-16

**Author's Note:** Whether or not the Lamanites eventually become white skinned, it is clear from scripture that one of the signs of the last days will be that the Lamanites will blossom in the gospel sense. It will make no difference as to the color of their skin because the Lord " . . . inviteth them all to come unto him and partake of his goodness; and he denieth none that come unto him, black and white, bond and free, male and female; and he remembereth the heathen; and all are alike unto God, both Jew and Gentile." (See 2Ne.26:33.) Those who accept Christ and are valiant can become spotless, pure, fair, and white because of being cleansed by the Redeemer. "O then ye unbelieving, turn ye unto the Lord; cry mightily unto the Father in the name of Jesus, that perhaps ye may be found spotless, pure, fair, and white, having been cleansed by the blood of the Lamb, at that great and last day." (See Morm.9:6.) ¶ The Lamanites first received their dark skin "that they might not be enticing" to the Nephites who were living the gospel: "And he had caused the cursing to come upon them, yea, even a sore cursing, because of their iniquity. For behold, they had hardened their hearts against him, that they had become like unto a flint; wherefore, as they were white, and exceedingly fair and delightsome, that they might not be enticing unto my people the Lord God did cause a skin of blackness to come upon them." (See 2Ne.5:21.)

---

**409. The time will come when the wicked will be cleansed from the earth by fire.**

### Elder Joseph Fielding Smith
The cleansing of the earth of much of its iniquity, by blood, fire, earthquake, pestilence, and the display of angry elements, was to assist in preparing the way for the return of the lost tribes of Israel. . . . The great day of the coming of the lost tribes would be after the preparatory work had been accomplished in the destruction of wickedness in very great measure, and the way prepared in part for the coming of the Lord also and the building of his Holy City and Temple. CHMR1:378

### Malachi
For, behold, the day cometh, that shall burn as an oven; and all the proud, yea, and all that do wickedly, shall be stubble: and the day that cometh shall burn them up, saith the LORD of hosts, that it shall leave them neither root nor branch. (*The prophet Malachi to the people, about 430 B.C.*) Mal.4:1

### President Joseph F. Smith
Then [in the days of Noah] the world was destroyed by flood, now it is to be destroyed by war, pestilence, famine, earthquake, storms and tempest, the sea rolling beyond its bounds, malarious vapors, vermin, disease and by fire and the lightnings of God's wrath poured out for destruction upon Babylon. The cry of the angel unto the righteous of this dispensation is, "Come out of her, my people, that ye be not partakers of her sins, and that ye receive not of her plagues" (Rev.18:4). (Improvement Era, Vol. 14, p. 266; Gospel Doctrine, p. 104.) TLDP:327-28

### Joseph Smith,
*receiving the Word of the Lord*
And the great and abominable church, which is the whore of all the earth, shall be cast down by devouring fire, according as it is spoken by the mouth of Ezekiel the prophet, who spoke of these things, which have not come to pass but surely must, as I live, for abominations shall not reign. (*Revelation received Sept. 1830*) D&C 29:21

**Related Witnesses:**
### John
Therefore shall her plagues come in one day, death, and mourning, and famine; and she shall be utterly burned with fire: for strong is the Lord God who judgeth her. (*Babylon falls, lamented by her supporters*) Rev.18:8

### Joseph Smith
It is also the concurrent testimony of all the Prophets, that this gathering together of all the Saints, must take place before the Lord comes to "take vengeance upon the ungodly," and "to be glorified and admired by all those who obey the Gospel." The fiftieth Psalm, from the first to the fifth verse inclusive, describes the glory and majesty of that event. ¶ "The mighty God, and even the Lord hath spoken, and called the earth from the rising of the sun unto the going down thereof. Out of Zion, the perfection of beauty, God hath shined. Our God shall come, and shall not keep silence; a fire shall devour before Him, and it shall be very tempestuous round about Him. He shall call to the heavens from above, and to the earth (that He may judge the people). Gather my Saints together unto me; those that have made covenant with me by sacrifice." (*From "A Proclamation of the Presidency of the Church to the Saints," Jan. 8, 1841*) HC4:272

### Recorded in Psalms
The mighty God, even the LORD, hath spoken, and called the earth from the rising of the sun unto the going down thereof. 2. Out of Zion, the perfection of beauty, God hath shined. 3. Our God shall come, and shall not keep silence: a fire shall devour before him, and it shall be very tempestuous round about him. Ps.50:1-3

# List of Doctrines

## LAW: Divine Law

*Doctrines Located in This Topic*

410. All things throughout the universe are governed by divine law.

*Doctrines on LAW: Divine Law Located in Other Topics*

92. Members of the Church are to live the law of consecration when called upon to do so: they are to be ready at all times to consecrate their time, talents, money, and property to the building up of the kingdom of god on earth.

96. Members of the Church are to live the law of sacrifice: to be willing to make whatever sacrifices the Lord requires for the sake of the gospel.

392. When a person righteously performs the ordinances and duties necessary for exaltation, those acts may then be accepted (justified) by God.

393. Being born again (being quickened by the Spirit and receiving a change of heart after baptism by water and receiving the gift of the Holy Ghost) justifies a person before the Lord and starts that person toward sanctification.

487. All blessings flow from obedience to laws of God (to obtain a blessing we must obey the law appointed for that blessing).

751. Sin is the willful breaking of divine law.

828. The law of tithing was instituted because the people could not abide the greater law of consecration.

840. Divine truth is eternal—it abides and endures forever and has no end.

841. Divine truth is absolute, ultimate, and pure; it never varies.

# LAW: Divine Law

**410. All things throughout the universe are governed by divine law.**

### Anthon H. Lund

We believe that everything is ruled by law. We are thankful that it is so, for otherwise we would live in a world of chance, in a fearful uncertainty of what would happen next. I believe that the material laws that can be traced in the creation had an intelligent will behind them, that the laws themselves were never superior to the will of God. He made those laws, and by His power they became effective to accomplish His purposes. It is to Him that we pray, and we know he is almighty and does hear prayers, and though He uses material laws to carry out His plans, His will was never subjected to the laws, but the laws have ever been subservient to Him. Let no one think that God is impotent, that the laws He has made stand in the way of His hearing His children and answering their prayers. CR1916Apr:12

### Elder Joseph Fielding Smith

The entire universe teaches us that there is divine law governing all things; that a supreme intelligence controls to the remotest parts of space, as far as man is able to discern the universe. Because of this obedience to law, there is perfect order and harmony. CHMR2:298

### Elder Wilford Woodruff

The God of heaven, who created this earth and placed his children upon it, gave unto them a law whereby they might be exalted and saved in a kingdom of glory. For there is a law given unto all kingdoms, and all things are governed by law throughout the whole universe. Whatever law anyone keeps, he is preserved by that law, and he receives whatever reward that law guarantees unto him. It is the will of God that all his children should obey the highest law, that they may receive the highest glory that is ordained for all immortal beings. But God has given all his children an agency, to choose what law they will keep. (*"Epistle to the Saints Abroad," Oct. 26, 1886)* (Discourses of Wilford Woodruff, p. 10) TLDP:357

### Joseph Smith,
*quoted by Elder Joseph Fielding Smith*

God has made certain decrees which are fixed and immovable: for instance,—God set the sun, the moon, and the stars in the heavens, and gave them their laws, conditions and bounds, which they cannot pass, except by His commandment; they all move in perfect harmony in their sphere and order, and are as lights, wonders and signs unto us. The sea also has its bounds which it cannot pass. God has set many signs on the earth, as well as in the heavens; for instance, the oak of the forest, the fruit of the tree, the herb of the field—all bear a sign that seed hath been planted there; for it is a decree of the Lord that every tree, plant, and herb bearing seed should bring forth of its kind, and cannot come forth after any other law or principle. (*To a large congregation in the Grove, west of the Nauvoo Temple—a child had recently died, March 20, 1842)* HC4:554; TPJS:197

### L. Tom Perry,
*also quoting Joseph Smith*

"There is a law, irrevocably decreed in heaven before the foundations of this world, upon which all blessings are predicated— ¶ "And when we obtain any blessing from God, it is by obedience to that law upon which it is predicated." (D&C 130:20-21) ¶ The Lord has clearly chartered a course for us to obtain his blessings. He is bound by his divine law to bless us for our righteousness. The overwhelming question in each age is why each generation must test his law, when the Lord's performance from generation to generation has been absolutely consistent. CR1976Apr:98

### Related Witnesses:
### Joseph Smith

There is a law, irrevocably decreed in heaven before the foundations of this world, upon which all blessings are predicated— 21. And when we obtain any blessing from God, it is by obedience to that law upon which it is predicated. (*Revelation, April 2, 1843)* D&C 130:20-21

### Joseph Smith,
*receiving the Word of the Lord*

For all who will have a blessing at my hands shall abide the law which was appointed for that blessing, and the conditions thereof, as were instituted from before the foundation of the world. . . . 11. And will I appoint unto you, saith the Lord, except it be by law, even as I and my Father ordained unto you, before the world was? 12. I am the Lord thy God; and I give unto you this commandment—that no man shall come unto the Father but by me or by my word, which is my law, saith the Lord. (*Revelation relating to the new and everlasting covenant, including the eternal nature of the marriage covenant, July 12, 1843, [1831])* D&C 132:5,11-12

### George F. Richards

The laws of the gospel are the laws of God and are as perfect in their sphere as are the laws governing the universe and all nature. They originated from the same source, and when obeyed by man, they produce order and beauty. . . . ¶ The gospel law is that by which our Savior lived, and which made him what he was in life, and what he now is, enthroned in glory at the right hand of

God, the Father, in his celestial kingdom. ¶ The same gospel laws are intended to make us like the Savior and to save us with him in our Father's kingdom. He has given us our agency and power to overcome and live the law. CR1947Oct:56

### Lehi,
#### *quoted by his son Nephi*

And if ye shall say there is no law, ye shall also say there is no sin. If ye shall say there is no sin, ye shall also say there is no righteousness. And if there be no righteousness there be no happiness. And if there be no righteousness nor happiness there be no punishment nor misery. And if these things are not there is no God. And if there is no God we are not, neither the earth; for there could have been no creation of things, neither to act nor to be acted upon; wherefore, all things must have vanished away. (*Lehi teaches his son, Jacob, about the redemption of man from the fall of Adam, between 588-570 B.C.*) 2Ne.2:13

### John A. Widtsoe

The first expression of universal order is that a given cause always has the same effect. Under the same conditions, gasoline will always burst into flame when a lighted match is touched to it, or the finger burned if brought too near the fire. Yesterday, to-day and forever, like causes produce like effects. . . . ¶ The universal reign of law under which man lives not only offers the happy certainty of an orderly universe, but also the stern warning, that in a world where cause and effect are invariable, man cannot escape the effects of his actions. That is more terrible than the threat of a sulphurous hell. Law, therefore, is both a protector and a rewarder. . . . ¶ . . . . We live under a reign of law. On every hand the orderliness of the universe confronts us. The sun rises and sets; summer follows winter; seed time determines harvest; "as the twig is inclined, so the tree is bent." We are utterly unable to change the laws of nature. (Man and the Dragon, pp. 124, 129) TLDP:356

### John A. Widtsoe

Countless forces, surrounding man, are interacting in the universe. By no means can he withdraw himself from them. He has learned by experience that control of natural forces is obtained only when their laws are understood. When a certain thing is done in a certain manner, there is a definite, invariable result. No doubt it had often occurred to an intelligent being that he might wish it otherwise; but that is impossible. The only remedy is to comply with existing conditions, acknowledge the restraint of nature, gain further knowledge, array law against law, until the purpose of man has been accomplished. That is the process by which intelligent beings have acquired dominion over nature. Such acknowledgment of the existence of the law of cause and effect does not weaken man; strength lies in an intelligent subjection to rightful restraint. It has been the condition of progress from the beginning. The recognition of law and the obedience to law are sure signs that intelligent beings are progressing. (A Rational Theology, p. 118) TLDP:356

### Orson Pratt

The Lord wanted this intelligent being called man, to prove himself; inasmuch as he was an agent, He desired that he should show himself approved before his Creator. ¶ How could this be done without a commandment? Can you devise any possible means? Is there any person in this congregation having wisdom sufficient to devise any means by which an intelligent being can show himself approved before a superior intelligence, unless it be by administering to that man certain laws to be kept? No. Without law, without commandment or rule, there would be no possible way of showing his integrity: it could not be said that he would keep all the laws that govern superior orders of beings, unless he had been placed in a position to be tried, and thus proven whether he would keep them or not. . . . ¶ . . . . But could He not give a commandment, without affixing a penalty? He could not: it would be folly, even worse than folly, for God to give a law to an intelligent being, without affixing a penalty to it if it were broken. Why? Because all intelligent beings would discard the very idea of a law being given, which might be broken at pleasure, without the individuals breaking it being punished for their transgression. (*In Tabernacle, July 25, 1852, JD1:283*) TLDP:356-57

### Joseph Smith,
#### *receiving the Word of the Lord*

Fear not to do good, my sons, for whatsoever ye sow, that shall ye also reap; therefore, if ye sow good ye shall also reap good for your reward. (*Revelation to Joseph Smith and Oliver Cowdery, April 1829*) D&C 6:33

### Joseph Smith

It would seem also, that wicked spirits have their bounds, limits, and laws by which they are governed or controlled, and know their future destiny; (*Editorial in Times and Seasons, about April 1, 1842*) HC4:576

### Joseph Smith,
#### *quoted by Elder Joseph Fielding Smith*

[The Melchizedek Priesthood] is a perfect law of theocracy, and stands as God to give laws to the people, administering endless lives to the sons and daughters of Adam. (*From an address at the Stand in Nauvoo, Ill., Aug. 27, 1843,*) HC5:555; TPJS:322

# List of Doctrines

## LEADERSHIP:
### Duties of Priesthood Holders and Church Officers

*Doctrines Located in This Topic*

411. We are to be diligent in every calling, office and responsibility in the Church (we are to magnify our callings).

412. To be efficacious, all exercise of priesthood authority is to be done with unfeigned love, patience, gentleness, and meekness.

413. A calling to a position of leadership is a call to serve others; it is not for worldly honor.

414. A man receives the oath and covenant of the priesthood with a *covenant* of obedience.

415. A man receives the oath and covenant of the priesthood with a *covenant* of service to do the work assigned.

416. In the oath and covenant of the priesthood, God covenants with an *oath* that the man who faithfully keeps this covenant shall receive all the Father has (he shall receive exaltation).

417. Those upon whom the authority of the priesthood has been conferred can lose the power to exercise that priesthood authority when they are corrupted by sin.

418. A man called to administer in the Church is to also faithfully administer and set in order his own house.

419. The powers of heaven can only be controlled in righteousness.

420. The Lord authorizes priesthood holders to act as His agents (to do what He would do if He were personally present).

*Doctrines on LEADERSHIP: Duties of Priesthood Holders and Church officers Located in Other Topics*

105. Many of the valiant and noble spirits in the premortal world were chosen and foreordained to be born into the family of Jacob (Israel).

425. We are to strive to lift others—to strengthen the weak.

743. We are to perform active service for others, to show charity by action (by giving of personal time and substance).

874. The Lord selects teachable persons to do His work; He chooses those whom the world calls weak and foolish more frequently than those whom the world calls wise.

# LEADERSHIP:

## Duties of Priesthood Holders and Church Officers

### (Including the Oath And Covenant of the Priesthood)

411. We are to be diligent in every calling, office, and responsibility in the Church (we are to magnify our callings).

**Joseph Smith**

Let every man be diligent in all things. And the idler shall not have place in the church, except he repent and mend his ways. (*Revelation at a Church conference, Jan. 25, 1832*) D&C 75:29

**Joseph Smith**

Wherefore, now let every man learn his duty, and to act in the office in which he is appointed, in all diligence. 100. He that is slothful shall not be counted worthy to stand, and he that learns not his duty and shows himself not approved shall not be counted worthy to stand. Even so. Amen. (*Revelation on priesthood to Joseph in council with the Twelve, March 28, 1835*) D&C 107:99-100

**President Heber J. Grant**

I am thoroughly convinced that all the Lord wants of you and me or of any other man or woman in the Church is for us to perform our full duty and keep the commandments of God. CR1944Apr:10

**President Joseph F. Smith**

There is never a time, there never will come a time to those who hold the priesthood in the Church of Jesus Christ of Latter-day Saints, when men can say of themselves that they have done enough. So long as life lasts, and so long as we possess ability to do good, to labor for the upbuilding of Zion and for the benefit of the human family, we ought, with willingness, to yield with alacrity to the requirements made of us to do our duty, little or great. CR1914Apr:7

**Elder Joseph Fielding Smith**

"Wherefore, now let every man learn his duty, and to act in the office in which he is appointed, in all diligence. ¶ "He that is slothful shall not be counted worthy to stand, and he that learns not his duty and shows himself not approved shall not be counted worthy to stand. Even so. Amen." (D&C 107:99-100) ¶ This means that the man who accepts the priesthood also accepts the responsibilities that go with it. He promises that he will give service and make himself approved. If he breaks this covenant—for it is a covenant—then he will have to stand among those who do not exercise priesthood; he cannot stand among those who are approved. CR1966Apr:102

**Related Witnesses:**

**President Joseph F. Smith**

The great object and duty that devolves upon the Latter-day Saints is to learn, each man and each woman for himself and for herself, their individual duty as members of the Church. CR1915Apr:4

**President David O. McKay**

The successful leader knows his duties and responsibilities and also the members under his direction. The teacher knows his children, as well as the lessons. CR1968Oct:144

**President Brigham Young**

An individual who holds a share in the Priesthood, and continues faithful to his calling, who delights himself continually in doing the things God requires at his hands, and continues through life in the performance of every duty, will secure to himself not only the privilege of receiving, but the knowledge how to receive the things of God, that he may know the mind of God continually; and he will be enabled to discern between right and wrong, between the things of God and the things that are not of God. And the Priesthood—the Spirit that is within him, will continue to increase until it becomes like a fountain of living water; until it is like the tree of life; until it is one continued source of intelligence and instruction to that individual. (*In Tabernacle, Jan. 27, 1856, JD3:192*) TLDP:519

**Jacob, brother of Nephi**

Now, my beloved brethren, I, Jacob, according to the responsibility which I am under to God, to magnify mine office with soberness, and that I might rid my garments of your sins, I come up into the temple this day that I might declare unto you the word of God. (*Jacob teaches the Nephites in the temple, 544-421 B.C.*) Jacob 2:2

**Joseph Smith**

For whoso is faithful unto the obtaining these two priesthoods of which I have spoken, and the magnifying their calling, are sanctified by the Spirit unto the renewing of their bodies. (*Revelation on priesthood received with six elders, Sept. 22/23, 1832*) D&C 84:33

**Jacob, brother of Nephi**

For I, Jacob, and my brother Joseph had been consecrated priests and teachers of this people, by the hand of Nephi. 19. And we did magnify our office unto the Lord, taking upon us the responsibility, answering the sins of the people upon our own heads if we did not teach them the word of God with all diligence; wherefore, by laboring with our might their blood might not come upon our garments; otherwise their blood would come upon our garments, and we would not be found spotless at the last day. (*Jacob teaches the Nephites in the temple, 544-421 B.C.*) Jacob 1:18-19

### Enos,
#### quoted by Mormon

And while I was thus struggling in the spirit, behold, the voice of the Lord came into my mind again, saying: I will visit thy brethren according to their diligence in keeping my commandments. I have given unto them this land, and it is a holy land; and I curse it not save it be for the cause of iniquity; wherefore, I will visit thy brethren according as I have said; and their transgressions will I bring down with sorrow upon their own heads. (*Enos gives the word of the Lord to the Nephites, 544-421 B.C.*) Enos 1:10

### President Heber J. Grant,
### Anthony W. Ivins, Charles W. Nibley
(First Presidency)

Refrain from evil; do that which is good. Visit the sick, comfort those who are in sorrow, clothe the naked, feed the hungry, care for the widow and the fatherless. Observe the laws of health which the Lord has revealed, and keep yourselves unspotted from the sins of the world. Pay your tithes and offerings, and the Lord will open the windows of heaven and pour out blessings until there shall not be room to contain them. Be obedient to the laws of God and the civil laws of the country in which you reside, and uphold and honor those who are chosen to administer them. (*Centennial Message of the First Presidency to the Saints throughout the world and to the world*) CR1930Apr:13

**Author's Note:** The dictionary defines *diligent*: "Characterized by steady, earnest, attentive, and energetic application and effort in a pursuit, vocation, or study: not lackadaisical." Webster's Third International Dictionary, p. 633.

---

412. To be efficacious, all exercise of priesthood authority is to be done with unfeigned love, patience, gentleness, and meekness.

### Joseph Smith

No power or influence can or ought to be maintained by virtue of the priesthood, only by persuasion, by long-suffering, by gentleness and meekness, and by love unfeigned; 42. By kind-

ness, and pure knowledge, which shall greatly enlarge the soul without hypocrisy, and without guile— 43. Reproving betimes with sharpness, when moved upon by the Holy Ghost; and then showing forth afterwards an increase of love toward him whom thou hast reproved, lest he esteem thee to be his enemy; (*Revelation during conference of Church elders, Nov. 1, 1831*) D&C 121:41-43

### Joseph Smith

The decisions of these quorums, or either of them, are to be made in all righteousness, in holiness, and lowliness of heart, meekness and long suffering, and in faith, and virtue, and knowledge, temperance, patience, godliness, brotherly kindness and charity; 31. Because the promise is, if these things abound in them they shall not be unfruitful in the knowledge of the Lord. (*Revelation on priesthood received in council with the Twelve, March 28, 1835*) D&C 107:30-31

### President Harold B. Lee

The qualities of acceptable priesthood leadership are also carefully defined in this revelation [D&C 121]. One is to preside over the Church with patience and long-suffering, with gentleness and meekness and with love unfeigned. If one must discipline or reprove with sharpness, he must do it when moved upon by the Holy Ghost, but afterwards he should show forth love, lest the one he has reproved thinks him to be an enemy. In all of our priesthood callings, therefore, we must never forget that it is the business of the Church to save souls, and those over whom we preside are our Father's children, and he will aid us in our endeavors to save every one of them. ACR(Mexico City)1972:76

**Related Witnesses:**
### Joseph Smith

And faith, hope, charity and love, with an eye single to the glory of God, qualify him for the work. (*Revelation for Joseph Smith, Sr., Feb. 1829*) D&C 4:5

### Joseph Smith

And no one can assist in this work except he shall be humble and full of love, having faith, hope, and charity, being temperate in all things, whatsoever shall be entrusted to his care. (*Revelation for Joseph Knight, May 1829*) D&C 12:8

### Joseph Smith

And if you have not faith, hope, and charity, you can do nothing. (*Revelation received June 1829*) D&C 18:19

### President Joseph F. Smith

The great object and duty that devolves upon

the Latter-day Saints is to learn, each man and each woman for himself and for herself, their individual duty as members of the Church. Just as soon as a man or woman learns his and her duty to God and to those who are members with them in the household of faith, peace is established, love and good will are assured, no backbiting, no fault-finding, no bearing false witness against neighbors, no strife, no contention. For the moment that a Latter-day Saint learns his duty, he will learn that it is his business to make peace, to establish good will, to work righteousness, to be filled with the spirit of kindness, love, charity, and forgiveness; and, so far as he is concerned, there can be no war, no strife, no contention, no quarreling, no disunion; no factions can arise among the people who know their duty as Latter-day Saints. CR1915Apr:4

**President Brigham Young,**
*quoted by John A. Widtsoe*
Until a selfish, individual interest is banished from our minds, and we become interested in the general welfare, we shall never be able to magnify our holy Priesthood as we should. (*On visit to Utah, Juab, and Sanpete counties, June and July, 1865, JD11:115*) DBY:133

**Paul**
I therefore, the prisoner of the Lord, beseech you that ye walk worthy of the vocation wherewith ye are called, 2. With all lowliness and meekness, with longsuffering, forbearing one another in love; 3. Endeavouring to keep the unity of the Spirit in the bond of peace. (*Paul's letter to the Saints at Ephesus in Asia Minor, about A.D. 62*) Eph.4:1-3

**Paul**
And the servant of the Lord must not strive; but be gentle unto all men, apt to teach, patient, 25. In meekness instructing those that oppose themselves; if God peradventure will give them repentance to the acknowledging of the truth; (*Paul's letter to his assistant Timothy, about A.D. 64*) 2Tim.2:24-25

**Paul**
Giving no offence in any thing, that the ministry be not blamed: 4. But in all things approving ourselves as the ministers of God, in much patience, in afflictions, in necessities, in distresses, 5. In stripes, in imprisonments, in tumults, in labours, in watchings, in fastings; 6. By pureness, by knowledge, by longsuffering, by kindness, by the Holy Ghost, by love unfeigned, (*Paul's letter to the Church at Corinth, Greece, about A.D. 55*) 2Cor.6:3-6

**President John Taylor**
There is no authority associated with the Holy Priesthood except on the principle of persuasion, and no man has a right to plume himself upon any position he occupies in this Church, for he is simply a servant of God, and a servant of the people, and if any man attempts to use any kind of arbitrary authority, and act with any degree of unrighteousness, God will hold that man to an account for it, and we all of us have to be judged according to the deeds done in the body. We are here as saviours of men, and not as tyrants and oppressors. (*At Parowan, Utah, June 24, 1883, JD24:268*) TLDP:516

**President David O. McKay**
Now a word to you officers and leaders in the stakes and wards, in missions, and in temples. . . . ¶ Fellow workers, you and I cannot hope to exert even to a small degree the personality of our great teacher, Jesus Christ. Each one's personality may be compared to the Savior's personality only as one little sunbeam to the mighty sun itself; and yet, though infinitely less in degree, each leader's, each teacher's personality should be the same in kind. In the realm of character, each leader and teacher may be superior, and such a magnet as to draw around him or her, in an indescribable way, those whom he or she would lead or teach. It is the radiation of the light that attracts. . . . ¶ It is the leader's duty, or the teacher's duty, to teach the member to love—not the leader or teacher, but the truth of the gospel. Always, everywhere, we find Christ losing himself for his Father's will; and so also should our leaders and teachers, so far as their personalities are concerned, lose themselves for the truth he desires to have them teach. ¶ When the people came to Jesus and asked for bread, or the truth, he never turned them away with a stone. He always had truth to give. He understood it. It radiated from his being. He understood how to use illustrations, the natural things around him, to impress that truth upon his hearers. In other words, he was filled with his subject and then was enabled to give that subject to his hearers. It is not always what you say, but what you *are* that influences children, the young, or that influences your associates. . . . ¶ Let me give you briefly five things, among many others, that may characterize the successful leader or teacher in the Church: ¶ First: Implicit faith in the gospel of Jesus Christ as the light of the world, and a sincere desire to serve him. This condition of the soul will make for the companionship and guidance of the Holy Ghost. ¶ Second: Unfeigned love for the child, or member. Unfeigned—remember how the word is used by the Prophet Joseph Smith in that great

revelation in the Doctrine and Covenants: "by love unfeigned." Unfeigned love for the children or members, guided by determination to deal justly and impartially with every member of the Church. Honor the child or member, and the child or member will honor you. ¶ Third: Thorough preparation. The successful leader knows his duties and responsibilities and also the members under his direction. The teacher knows his children, as well as the lessons. ¶ Fourth: Cheerfulness—not forced but natural cheerfulness, springing spontaneously from a hopeful soul. ¶ Fifth: Power to act nobly. ¶ "If you want to be a teacher or leader just watch your acts and walk; If you want to be a teacher or leader, just be careful how you talk." ¶ If you want to radiate the light of the gospel, that radiation must first come from the leader himself. CR1968Oct:143-44

---

**413. A calling to a position of leadership is a call to serve others; it is not for worldly honor.**

**Joseph F. Smith,
Anthon H. Lund, Charles W. Penrose**
*(First Presidency)*
Priesthood is not given for the honor or aggrandizement of man, but for the ministry of service among those for whom the bearers of that sacred commission are called to labor. Be it remembered that even our Lord and Master, after long fasting, when faint in body and physically weakened by exhausting vigils and continued abstinence, resisted the arch tempter's suggestion that he use the authority and power of his Messiahship to provide for his own immediate needs. ¶ The God-given titles of honor and of more than human distinction associated with the several offices in and orders of the Holy Priesthood, are not to be used nor considered as are the titles originated by man; they are not for adornment nor are they expressive of mastership, but rather of appointment to humble service in the work of the one Master whom we profess to serve. ("On Titles," IE1914Mar:479) TLDP:516

**Joseph Smith**
Behold, there are many called, but few are chosen. And why are they not chosen? 35. Because their hearts are set so much upon the things of this world, and aspire to the honors of men, that they do not learn this one lesson— 36. That the rights of the priesthood are inseparably connected with the powers of heaven, and that the powers of heaven cannot be controlled

nor handled only upon the principles of righteousness. (*Revelation while in Liberty Jail, March 20, 1839; why many are called and few chosen*) D&C 121:34-36
**Related Witnesses:**
**Elder Joseph Fielding Smith**
We are under obligation as men holding the Priesthood to put to service the authority which we have received. If we do this then we shall have other responsibilities and glory added, and we shall receive an abundance, that is, the fulness of the Father's kingdom; but if we bury our Priesthood, then we are not entitled to receive any reward, we cannot be exalted. (The Way to Perfection, p. 221) TLDP:515
**President Brigham Young,
quoted by John A. Widtsoe**
Until a selfish, individual interest is banished from our minds, and we become interested in the general welfare, we shall never be able to magnify our holy Priesthood as we should. (*On visit to Utah, Juab, and Sanpete counties, June and July, 1865, JD11:115*) DBY:133
**President John Taylor**
There is no authority associated with the Holy Priesthood except on the principle of persuasion, and no man has a right to plume himself upon any position he occupies in this Church, for he is simply a servant of God, and a servant of the people, and if any man attempts to use any kind of arbitrary authority, and act with any degree of unrighteousness, God will hold that man to an account for it, and we all of us have to be judged according to the deeds done in the body. We are here as saviours of men, and not as tyrants and oppressors. (*At Parowan, Utah, June 24, 1883, JD24:268*) TLDP:516

---

**414. A man receives the oath and covenant of the priesthood with a *covenant* of obedience.**

**President Spencer W. Kimball**
The faithful in the priesthood are those who fulfill the covenant by "magnifying their calling" and living "by every word that proceedeth forth from the mouth of God." (D&C 84:33,44) Far more seems to be implied in these requirements than token obedience—far more is needed than mere attendance at a few meetings and token fulfillment of assignments. The perfection of body and spirit are implied, and that includes the kind of service that goes far beyond the normal definition of duty. (EN1975Jun:3, The Teachings of Spencer W. Kimball, pp. 496-97) TLDP:515

## Bruce R. McConkie

The covenant which a man makes when he receives an office in the Melchizedek Priesthood is threefold: ¶ 1. That he will receive and make a part of his life and being the Holy Priesthood and that he will honor it as the holy power and authority which it is; ¶ 2. That he will magnify his calling in the priesthood; that is, that he will minister in the duties of the office, that he will do the work assigned; and ¶ 3. That he will live by every word that proceedeth forth from the mouth of God; that is to say, he will keep the commandments and work righteousness. ACR(Lima)1977:18

## Elder Joseph Fielding Smith

"Wherefore, now let every man learn his duty, and to act in the office in which he is appointed, in all diligence. ¶ "He that is slothful shall not be counted worthy to stand, and he that learns not his duty and shows himself not approved shall not be counted worthy to stand. Even so. Amen." (D&C 107:99-100) ¶ This means that the man who accepts the priesthood also accepts the responsibilities that go with it. He promises that he will give service and make himself approved. If he breaks this covenant—for it is a covenant—then he will have to stand among those who do not exercise priesthood; he cannot stand among those who are approved. CR1966Apr:102

## Elder Joseph Fielding Smith

The Lord most emphatically declared that it is impossible for man to become like God without the Priesthood and obedience to his commandments. Man has the power to know all things, to become perfect and be bathed in light, knowledge and wisdom, if he will only humble himself and walk in the light and truth. The man who refuses and lives bound within his own wisdom can never attain to these great blessings of exaltation and progression. A man must have, and be obedient to, the power of the Priesthood; he must be in full harmony and fellowship with God from whom all knowledge, wisdom and power come. No matter how much knowledge a man may gain, in this life or in the life to come, he cannot obtain the fulness unless he holds and magnifies the Priesthood and continueth in God! The power, knowledge and wisdom in their fulness, will never be exercised by those who reject the counsels and covenants of the Gospel of Jesus Christ. These are the possessions to be given to the just and true, who become members of the Church of the Firstborn. (Man: His Origin and Destiny, p. 534) TLDP:519

## Delbert L. Stapley

[T]here are two main requirements of this oath and covenant. First is faithfulness, which denotes obedience to the laws of God and connotes true observance of all gospel standards. For better understanding of the oath and covenant of the priesthood, may I propound these questions: ¶ 1. Can a man be faithful who does not abide by the first two great commandments, to love the Lord God with all his heart, soul, strength, and mind, and his neighbor as himself? ¶ 2. Can a man be faithful who is not honest and truthful in all dealings and relationships with his fellow men? ¶ 3. Can a man be faithful who does not honor the Sabbath day and keep it holy, attend the Sacrament and priesthood meetings; also worthily fulfil all other duties in keeping with his callings and obligations that day? ¶ 4. Can a man be faithful who does not plan and arrange for daily family prayer in the home? ¶ 5. Can a man be faithful who does not teach his children the true principles of the gospel of Christ and then set them a worthy example by living according to those truths? ¶ 6. Can a man be faithful who does not observe and keep the Word of Wisdom? ¶ 7. Can a man be faithful who does not pay an honest tithing and fast offering? ¶ 8. Can a man be faithful who does not obey the law of chastity and is not morally clean in his life and habits? ¶ 9. Can a man be faithful who does not, through obedience and sacrifice, prepare himself worthily for the holy temples of God where he can receive his endowments and sealings in the higher ordinances of the gospel and thus bind his family happily and eternally together in love and understanding? ¶ 10. Can a man be faithful who does not honor and obey the laws of the land? ¶ Perhaps we could summarize by asking, "Can a man be faithful if he does not keep all the commandments of God? . . . CR1957Apr:76-77

## Joseph Smith,
### receiving the Word of the Lord

For whoso is faithful unto the obtaining these two priesthoods of which I have spoken, and the magnifying their calling, are sanctified by the Spirit unto the renewing of their bodies. . . . 35. And also all they who receive this priesthood receive me, saith the Lord; 36. For he that receiveth my servants receiveth me; 37. And he that receiveth me receiveth my Father; 38. And he that receiveth my Father receiveth my Father's kingdom; therefore all that my Father hath shall be given unto him. 39. And this is according to the oath and covenant which belongeth to the priesthood. 40. Therefore, all those who receive the priesthood, receive this oath and covenant of my Father, which he cannot break, neither can it be moved. . . . 43. And I now give unto you a commandment to beware concerning yourselves, to give diligent heed to the words of eternal life. 44. For you shall live by every word that proceedeth forth from the mouth of God. (*Revelation on priesthood with six elders, Sept. 22/23, 1832*) D&C 84:33,35-40,43-44

### Marion G. Romney

It is of utmost importance that we keep clearly in mind what the magnifying of our callings in the priesthood requires of us. I am persuaded that it requires at least the following three things: ¶ 1. That we obtain a knowledge of the gospel. ¶ 2. That we comply in our personal living with the standards of the gospel. ¶ 3. That we give dedicated service. CR1980Oct:64; DGSM:70

**Related Witnesses:**

### Joseph Smith

And no man receiveth a fulness unless he keepeth his commandments. 28. He that keepeth his commandments receiveth truth and light, until he is glorified in truth and knoweth all things. (*Revelation at Kirtland, Ohio, May 6, 1833*) D&C 93:27-28

### Elder Wilford Woodruff

If we have the holy priesthood upon our heads and do not live our religion, of all men we are under the greatest condemnation. (*In Tabernacle, June 6, 1880, JD21:125*) TLDP:514

### Elder Spencer W. Kimball

There is no limit to the power of the priesthood which you hold. The limit comes in you if you do not live in harmony with the Spirit of the Lord and you limit yourselves in the power you exert. (*Lamanite conference priesthood meeting, Nov. 1947*) DGSM:70

### Joseph Smith

Wherefore, now let every man learn his duty, and to act in the office in which he is appointed, in all diligence. 100. He that is slothful shall not be counted worthy to stand, and he that learns not his duty and shows himself not approved shall not be counted worthy to stand. Even so. Amen. (*Revelation on priesthood in council with the Twelve, March 28, 1835*) D&C 107:99-100

---

**415. A man receives the oath and covenant of the priesthood with a *covenant* of service to do the work assigned.**

### Joseph Smith

Wherefore, now let every man learn his duty, and to act in the office in which he is appointed, in all diligence. 100. He that is slothful shall not be counted worthy to stand, and he that learns

not his duty and shows himself not approved shall not be counted worthy to stand. Even so. Amen. (*Revelation on priesthood in council with the Twelve, March 28, 1835*) D&C 107:99-100

### President Spencer W. Kimball

Now you made an oath, when you received the priesthood. You made an oath, and you cannot with impunity ignore that oath. You promised. When the stake president or mission president interviews, or the bishop or branch president, he asks promises: "Will you? Do you? Have you done? Will you continue to do?" And with that oath and the promise, you move forward into your service in the Melchizedek Priesthood. ACR(Stockholm)1974:99

### Marion G. Romney

[I]t is of utmost importance that we keep clearly in mind what the magnifying of our callings in the priesthood requires of us. I am persuaded that it requires at least the following three things: ¶ 1. That we obtain a knowledge of the gospel. ¶ 2. That we comply in our personal living with the standards of the gospel. ¶ 3. That we give dedicated service. CR1980Oct:64; DGSM:70

### Delbert L. Stapley

Can a man magnify his calling who does not use his priesthood in righteousness for the blessing and benefit of his fellow men? CR1957Apr:77

### Elder John Taylor

We have been ordaining men in the various quorums for the last forty years; and what for? Merely to give them a place and position and the priesthood? No, I tell you nay; but that holding the holy priesthood you may magnify it and become the saviors of men. . . . ¶ It is time we were waking up to a sense of the position we occupy before God; for the day is not far distant when we will hear of wars and rumors of wars; not only rumors of wars, but wars themselves . . . and general carnage will spread through the lands, and if you do not magnify your callings, God will hold you responsible for those whom you might have saved had you done your duty. (*In Tabernacle, July 7, 1878, JD20:22-23*) TLDP:514

### President Joseph F. Smith

There is never a time, there never will come a time to those who hold the priesthood in the Church of Jesus Christ of Latter-day Saints, when men can say of themselves that they have done enough. So long as life lasts, and so long as we possess ability to do good, to labor for the upbuilding of Zion and for the benefit of the human family, we ought, with willingness, to yield with alacrity to the requirements made of us to do our duty, little or great. CR1914Apr:7

## Elder Joseph Fielding Smith

Because the responsibility of holding the priesthood is so great, all who receive it do so by an oath and a covenant. Honoring the covenant means that "the man who accepts the priesthood also accepts the responsibilities that go with it. He promises that he will give service and make himself approved." CR1966Apr:102; DGSM:69

## Bruce R. McConkie

The covenant which a man makes when he receives an office in the Melchizedek Priesthood is threefold: ¶ 1. That he will receive and make a part of his life and being the Holy Priesthood and that he will honor it as the holy power and authority which it is; ¶ 2. That he will magnify his calling in the priesthood; that is, that he will minister in the duties of the office, that he will do the work assigned; and ¶ 3. That he will live by every word that proceedeth forth from the mouth of God; that is to say, he will keep the commandments and work righteousness. ACR(Lima)1977:18

**Related Witnesses:**

### Jacob, brother of Nephi

And we did magnify our office unto the Lord, taking upon us the responsibility, answering the sins of the people upon our own heads if we did not teach them the word of God with all diligence; wherefore, by laboring with our might their blood might not come upon our garments; otherwise their blood would come upon our garments, and we would not be found spotless at the last day. (*Jacob teaches the Nephites in the temple, 544-421 B.C.*) Jacob 1:19

### Marion G. Romney

These transcendent blessings the Father promises the receiver of the Melchizedek Priesthood by an oath and covenant which he says ". . . he cannot break, neither can it be moved.". . . But these blessings . . . do not come by ordination alone. Ordination to the priesthood is a prerequisite to receiving them, but it does not guarantee them. For a man actually to obtain them, he must faithfully discharge the obligation which is placed upon him when he receives the priesthood; that is, he must magnify his calling. CR1962Apr:17

### Stephen L. Richards

That [service] is the mission of the Priesthood of God. The Priesthood of God means to me only the right to serve, in the name of God, God's children, and he who serves God's children in God's name is doing the greatest service for the Master that can be done. CR1917Oct:147

**416.** In the oath and covenant of the priesthood, God covenants with an *oath* that the man who faithfully keeps this covenant shall receive all the Father has (he shall receive exaltation).

## Bruce R. McConkie

The covenant which God makes [in connection with the Oath and Covenant of the Priesthood] is that he on his part will give the faithful all that his Father hath. In other words, he will give eternal life to those who keep their priesthood covenants. ¶ Now we have mentioned both an oath and a covenant where the Melchizedek Priesthood is concerned. The oath is the solemn promise of the Lord that all those who keep the priesthood covenant shall gain exaltation. That is to say, the Lord swears with an oath that his adopted and obedient sons shall be high priests forever after the order of Melchizedek (see D&C 76:57); they shall be joint heirs with his natural Son, who is Christ our Lord. ACR(Lima)1977:18

### Joseph Smith,
*receiving the Word of the Lord*

And he that receiveth my Father receiveth my Father's kingdom; therefore all that my Father hath shall be given unto him. 39. And this is according to the oath and covenant which belongeth to the priesthood. 40. Therefore, all those who receive the priesthood, receive this oath and covenant of my Father, which he cannot break, neither can it be moved. (*Revelation on priesthood with six elders, Sept. 22/23, 1832*) D&C 84:38-40

### President Joseph Fielding Smith

[W]hen we receive the Melchizedek Priesthood we do so by covenant. We solemnly promise to receive the priesthood, to magnify our callings in it, and to live by every word that proceedeth forth from the mouth of God. The Lord on his part promises us that if we keep the covenant, we shall receive all that the Father hath, which is life eternal. Can any of us conceive of a greater or more glorious agreement than this? CR1970Oct:91

### President Joseph Fielding Smith

To swear with an oath is the most solemn and binding form of speech known to the human tongue. . . . And so Christ is the great prototype where priesthood is concerned, as he is with reference to baptism and all other things. And so, even as the Father swears with an oath that his Son shall inherit all things through the priesthood, so he swears with an oath that all of us who magnify our callings in that same priesthood shall receive all that the Father hath. CR1970Oct:92

### Marion G. Romney

The Father, by oath and covenant, promises the receiver that if he does so magnify his priesthood he will be sanctified by the Spirit unto the renewing of his body . . . and receive the ". . . Father's kingdom; therefore," said the Savior, "all that my Father hath shall be given unto him." [D&C 84:38] ¶ These transcendent blessings the Father promises the receiver of the Melchizedek Priesthood by an oath and covenant which he says ". . . he cannot break, neither can it be moved."[D&C 84:40] But these blessings . . . do not come by ordination alone. Ordination to the priesthood is a prerequisite to receiving them, but it does not guarantee them. For a man actually to obtain them, he must faithfully discharge the obligation which is placed upon him when he receives the priesthood. . . . CR1962Apr:17

### Elder Joseph Fielding Smith

Every man who is ordained to an office in the Melchizedek Priesthood should realize fully just what that ordination means. He receives the Priesthood with an oath and covenant that he will magnify his calling and be faithful therein. This oath and covenant when received in the fullness will entitle a man to become a member of the Church of the Firstborn, and the elect of God. He receives the fullness of the Father's kingdom and is entitled, if faithful to the end, "to all that the Father hath." This oath and covenant cannot be treated lightly, and if broken and altogether turned from, the man thus guilty has no forgiveness, that is to say, he will not again have these privileges granted to him which bring exaltation, or "all that the Father hath." He will stand aside without these blessings, but does not become a son of perdition because of this serious offense. CHMR1:339

**Related Witnesses:**

### Joseph Smith

They are they into whose hands the Father has given all things— 56. They are they who are priests and kings, who have received of his fulness, and of his glory; 57. And are priests of the Most High, after the order of Melchizedek, which was after the order of Enoch, which was after the order of the Only Begotten Son. 58. Wherefore, as it is written, they are gods, even the sons of God— 59. Wherefore, all things are theirs, whether life or death, or things present, or things to come, all are theirs and they are Christ's, and Christ is God's. 60. And they shall overcome all things. (*Vision to Joseph Smith and Sidney Rigdon, Feb. 16, 1832*) D&C 76:55-60

### Joseph Smith, receiving the Word of the Lord

What I the Lord have spoken, I have spoken, and I excuse not myself; and though the heavens and the earth pass away, my word shall not pass away, but shall all be fulfilled, whether by mine own voice or by the voice of my servants, it is the same. (*Revelation received during conference of elders of the Church, Nov. 1, 1831; preface to the doctrines given to the Church*) D&C 1:38

---

**417. Those upon whom the authority of the priesthood has been conferred can lose the power to exercise that priesthood authority when they are corrupted by sin.**

### Elder Spencer W. Kimball

There is no limit to the power of the priesthood which you hold. The limit comes in you if you do not live in harmony with the Spirit of the Lord and you limit yourselves in the power you exert.(*Lamanite conference priesthood meeting, Nov. 1947*) DGSM:70

### Joseph Smith

That the rights of the priesthood are inseparably connected with the powers of heaven, and that the powers of heaven cannot be controlled nor handled only upon the principles of righteousness. 37. That they may be conferred upon us, it is true; but when we undertake to cover our sins, or to gratify our pride, our vain ambition, or to exercise control or dominion or compulsion upon the souls of the children of men, in any degree of unrighteousness, behold, the heavens withdraw themselves; the Spirit of the Lord is grieved; and when it is withdrawn, Amen to the priesthood or the authority of that man. (*Revelation received in Liberty Jail, March 20, 1839; why many are called and few chosen*) D&C 121:36-37

### Marion G. Romney

Every bearer of the Melchizedek Priesthood should give diligent and solemn heed to the implications of this oath and covenant which he has received. Failure to observe the obligations imposed by it is sure to bring disappointment, sorrow, and suffering. Total disregard of it will place one beyond the reach of the blessings of forgiveness. ACR(Mexico City)1972:73

**Related Witnesses:**

### Boyd K. Packer

The priesthood cannot be conferred like a diploma. It cannot be handed to you as a certificate. It cannot be delivered to you as a message or sent to you in a letter. It comes only by proper ordination. An authorized holder of the priesthood has to be there. He must place his hands upon your head and ordain you. . . . ¶ I have told you how the authority is given to you. The *power* you receive will depend on what you do with this sacred, unseen gift. ¶ Your authority comes through your ordination; your power comes through obedience and worthiness. (That All May Be Edified, pp. 28-29) DGSM:70

### Delbert L. Stapley

Can a man magnify his calling who does not banish all iniquity from his soul, that he may gain favor with God and thus enjoy power in the use of the priesthood to bless people? CR1957Apr:77

**Author's Note:** A priesthood ordinance properly performed, such as a baptism or the conferring of the priesthood, is not invalidated because the person performing the ordinance was unworthy. An unworthy priesthood holder will be limited in the ability to call upon the powers of heaven, or to be led by the Spirit, but if he is directed to perform an ordinance by someone in authority, that ordinance does not become invalid because of his sins. If grievous sins are known it is highly unlikely that the priesthood holder will be invited to participate in holy ordinances.

---

418. A man called to administer in the Church is to also faithfully administer and set in order his own house.

### James E. Faust

Those who would lead in this Church must set the example of personal righteousness. They should seek for the constant guidance of the Holy Spirit. They should have their lives and homes in order. They should be honest and prompt in the paying of their bills. They must be exemplary in all their conduct. They should be men of honor and integrity. CR1980Oct:53

### Hugh B. Brown

I should like to say to you fathers tonight that our conduct in our homes determines in large measure our worthiness to hold and exercise the priesthood, which is the power of God delegated to man. Almost any man can make a good showing when on parade before the public, but one's integrity is tested when "off duty." The real man is seen and known in the comparative solitude of the home. An office or title will not erase a fault nor guarantee a virtue. CR1962Apr:88

### Paul

One that ruleth well his own house, having his children in subjection with all gravity; 5. (For if a man know not how to rule his own house, how shall he take care of the church of God?) (*Paul writes to his assistant Timothy, setting forth the attributes of a bishop, about* A.D. *64*) 1Tim.3:4-5

### President David O. McKay

[A]s men of the priesthood, as women of the Church, [we have the responsibility] to make our homes such as will radiate to our neighbors harmony, love, community duties, loyalty. Let our neighbors see it and hear it. Never must there be expressed in a Latter-day Saint home an oath, a condemnatory term, an expression of anger or jealousy or hatred. Control it! Do not express it! You do what you can to produce peace and harmony, no matter what you may suffer. CR1963Apr:130

### Joseph Smith

Govern your house in meekness, and be steadfast. (*Revelation calling Thomas B. Marsh to preach the gospel, Sept. 30, 1830*) D&C 31:9

### Joseph Smith,
*receiving the Word of the Lord*

But I have commanded you to bring up your children in light and truth. 41. But verily I say unto you, my servant Frederick G. Williams, you have continued under this condemnation; 42. You have not taught your children light and truth, according to the commandments; and that wicked one hath power, as yet, over you, and this is the cause of your affliction. 43. And now a commandment I give unto you—if you will be delivered you shall set in order your own house, for there are many things that are not right in your house. 44. Verily, I say unto my servant Sidney Rigdon, that in some things he hath not kept the commandments concerning his children; therefore, first set in order thy house. 45. Verily, I say unto my servant Joseph Smith, Jun., or in other words, I will call you friends, for you are my friends, and ye shall have an inheritance with me— 46. I called you servants for the world's sake, and ye are their servants for my sake— 47. And now, verily I say unto Joseph Smith, Jun.—You have not kept the commandments, and must needs stand rebuked before the Lord; 48. Your family must needs repent and forsake some things, and give more earnest heed unto your sayings, or be removed out of their place. 49. What I say unto one I say unto all; pray always lest that wicked one have power in you, and remove you out of your place. 50. My servant Newel K. Whitney also, a bishop of my church, hath need to be chastened, and set in order his family, and see that they are more diligent and concerned at home, and pray always, or they shall be removed out of their place. (*The leading brethren are commanded to set their houses in order, Kirtland, Ohio, May 6, 1833*) D&C 93:40-50

### President Spencer W. Kimball

Our success, individually and as a Church, will largely be determined by how faithfully we focus on living the gospel in the home. Only as we see clearly the responsibilities of each individual and the role of families and homes can we properly understand that priesthood quorums and auxiliary organizations, even wards and stakes, exist primarily to help members live the gospel in the home. Then we can understand that people are more important than programs, and that Church programs should always support and never detract from gospel-centered family activities. . . . ¶ You will observe that all of these functions can best be accomplished through a strong home environment. ("Living the Gospel in the Home," EN1978May:101) TLDP:91

**Related Witnesses:**

### Delbert L. Stapley

Can a man be faithful who does not plan and arrange for daily family prayer in the home? CR1957Apr:76

### L. Tom Perry

Remember, he [the bishop] has the same obligations as other heads of households: to, first, be a good husband; second, be a good father; and third, discharge his responsibility to provide for his family. We should not interrupt his family time or prevent him from growing, accomplishing, and achieving in his professional pursuits. CR1982Oct:43

**Author's Note:** From the witnesses quoted, it is clear that this doctrine applies not only to priesthood leaders in the Church but to all other priesthood bearers, and to parents as well.

---

### 419. The powers of heaven can only be controlled in righteousness.

### Joseph Smith

[T]he rights of the priesthood are inseparably connected with the powers of heaven, and . . . the powers of heaven cannot be controlled nor handled only upon the principles of righteousness. 37. That they may be conferred upon us, it is true; but when we undertake to cover our sins, or to gratify our pride, our vain ambition, or

to exercise control or dominion or compulsion upon the souls of the children of men, in any degree of unrighteousness, behold, the heavens withdraw themselves; the Spirit of the Lord is grieved; and when it is withdrawn, Amen to the priesthood or the authority of that man. 38. Behold, ere he is aware, he is left unto himself, to kick against the pricks, to persecute the saints, and to fight against God. (*Revelation received in Liberty Jail, March 20, 1839; why many are called and few chosen*) D&C 121:36-38

### President Wilford Woodruff

Let all Israel remember that the eternal and everlasting Priesthood is bestowed upon us for the purpose alone of administering in the ordinances of life and salvation, both for the living and the dead, and no man on earth can use that Priesthood for any other purpose than for the work of the ministry, the perfecting of the Saints, edifying the body of Christ, establishing the Kingdom of Heaven, and redeeming Zion. If we attempt to use it for unrighteous purposes, like lightning from heaven, our power, sooner or later, falls, and we fail to accomplish the designs of God. ("A Communication from President Woodruff," Millennial Star, Aug. 1887, p. 546) TLDP:523

### President Harold B. Lee

The penalty if we do use our priesthood unrighteously is that the heavens withdraw themselves and the Spirit of the Lord is grieved. When we lose the Spirit, our priesthood authority is taken from us and we are left to ourselves "to kick against the pricks," when we are being irritated by the admonitions and instructions of our leaders. Then we begin to persecute the saints, which means criticize, and finally to fight against God, and the powers of darkness overtake us if we do not repent and turn from that evil course. (*At Mexico City Area conference, Melchizedek Priesthood session, Aug. 26, 1972*) (Stand Ye in Holy Places, pp. 253-54) TLDP:524

### President John Taylor

There is no authority associated with the Holy Priesthood except on the principle of persuasion, and no man has a right to plume himself upon any position he occupies in this Church, for he is simply a servant of God, and a servant of the people, and if any man attempts to use any kind of arbitrary authority, and act with any degree of unrighteousness, God will hold that man to an account for it, and we all of us have to be judged according to the deeds done in the body. We are here as saviours of men, and not as tyrants and oppressors. (*At Parowan, Utah, June 24, 1883, JD24:268*) TLDP:516

**Joseph F. Smith,**
**Anthon H. Lund, Charles W. Penrose**
(First Presidency)

Priesthood is not given for the honor or aggrandizement of man, but for the ministry of service among those for whom the bearers of that sacred commission are called to labor. Be it remembered that even our Lord and Master, after long fasting, when faint in body and physically weakened by exhausting vigils and continued abstinence, resisted the arch tempter's suggestion that he use the authority and power of his Messiahship to provide for his own immediate needs. ("On Titles," IE1914Mar:479) TLDP:516

**Related Witnesses:**

**Elder Joseph Fielding Smith**

Most men are inclined to abuse authority, especially those who wield it who are the least prepared to hold positions of trust. It has been the characteristic of men in power to use that power to gratify their own pride and vain ambitions. More misery has come to the inhabitants of this world through the exercise of authority by those who least deserved it, than from almost any other cause. Rulers of kingdoms in the past have oppressed their subjects, and where they had the power they have sought to increase their dominions. We have had some horrible examples of misplaced ambition which, in recent years, placed the very existence of humanity in peril. These conditions still prevail in high places bringing fear and consternation to the troubled world. ¶ There should not, however, be any of this unrighteous ambition within the Church, but everything should be done in the spirit of love and humility. CHMR2:178; DGSM:70

**Elder Spencer W. Kimball**

The Savior who was the head of the Church never ruled by force, but by kindness and long-suffering and love. So you branch presidents and you counselors go back and with greater love than ever before seek to give leadership to your branch as Christ does to the Church. (*Lamanite conference, priesthood meeting, Mesa, Arizona, Nov. 3, 1947*) (The Teachings of Spencer W. Kimball, p. 485) TLDP:359

**Elder Spencer W. Kimball**

One breaks the priesthood covenant by transgressing commandments—but also by leaving undone his duties. Accordingly, to break this covenant one needs only to do nothing. (The Teachings of Spencer W. Kimball, p. 497) TLDP:501

**Joseph Smith**

We have learned by sad experience that it is the nature and disposition of almost all men, as soon as they get a little authority, as they suppose, they will immediately begin to exercise unrighteous dominion. 40. Hence many are called, but few are chosen. (*Revelation received while in Liberty Jail, March 20, 1839; why many are called and few chosen*) D&C 121:39-40

---

**420. The Lord authorizes priesthood holders to act as His agents (to do what He would do if He were personally present).**

**President Joseph Fielding Smith**

We are the Lord's agents; we represent him; he has given us authority which empowers us to do all that is necessary to save and exalt ourselves as well as his other children in the world. ¶ We are ambassadors of the Lord Jesus Christ. Our commission is to represent him. We are directed to preach his gospel, to perform the ordinances of salvation, to bless mankind, to heal the sick and perhaps perform miracles, to do what he would do if he were personally present—and all this because we hold the holy priesthood. ¶ As the Lord's agents we are bound by his law to do what he wants us to do regardless of personal feelings or worldly enticements. Of ourselves we have no message of salvation, no doctrine that must be accepted, no power to baptize or ordain or marry for eternity. All these things come from the Lord, and anything we do with reference to them is the result of delegated authority. ¶ When we join the Church and receive the priesthood, we are expected to forsake many of the ways of the world and live as becometh saints. We are no longer to dress or speak or act or even think as others too often do. Many in the world use tea, coffee, tobacco, and liquor, and are involved in the use of drugs. Many profane and are vulgar and indecent, immoral and unclean in their lives, but all these things should be foreign to us. We are the saints of the Most High. We hold the holy priesthood. CR1971Apr:47

**Joseph Smith**

Wherefore, as ye are agents, ye are on the Lord's errand; and whatsoever ye do according to the will of the Lord is the Lord's business. 30. And he hath set you to provide for his saints in these last days, that they may obtain an inheritance in the land of Zion. (*Revelation to the elders of the Church at Kirtland, Ohio, Sept. 11, 1831*) D&C 64:29-30

**President Harold B. Lee**

You see, when one becomes a holder of the priesthood, he becomes an agent of the Lord.

He should think of his calling as though he were on the Lord's errand. That is what it means to magnify the priesthood. ACR(Mexico City)1972:77

**Elder John Taylor**

What is priesthood? . . . [I]t is the government of God, whether on the earth or in the heavens, for it is by that power, agency, or principle that all things are governed on the earth and in the heavens, and by that power that all things are upheld and sustained. . . . It is the power of God delegated to intelligences in the heavens and to men on the earth; and when we arrive in the celestial kingdom of God, we shall find the most perfect order and harmony existing, because there is the perfect pattern, the most perfect order of government carried out. . . . ("On Priesthood," Millennial Star, Nov. 1847, p. 321) TLDP:498

**John A. Widtsoe**

The Church, the community of persons with the intelligent faith and desire and practice, is the organized agency through which God deals with His children and presents His will. Moreover, the authority to act for God must be vested on earth in some one organization and not independently in every man. The Church through the Priesthood holds the authority for the use of man. Besides, it is the common law of the universe, that when intelligent beings are organized, as of one body, they progress faster, individually and collectively. The Church as the product of Priesthood therefore represents God on earth and is the official means of communication between man and God. PCG:180-81

**Related Witnesses:**

**Elder John Taylor**

There are different callings, and offices, and stations, and authorities in the holy priesthood, but it is all the same priesthood; and there are different keys, and powers, and responsibilities, but it is the same government; and all the priesthood are agents in that government, and all are requisite for the organization of the body, the upbuilding of Zion, and the government of his kingdom. ("On Priesthood," Millennial Star, Nov. 1847, p. 322) TLDP:498

**President Joseph F. Smith**

And as I wondered, my eyes were opened, and my understanding quickened, and I perceived that the Lord went not in person among the wicked and the disobedient who had rejected the truth, to teach them; 30. But behold, from among the righteous, he organized his forces and appointed messengers, clothed with power and authority, and commissioned them to go forth and carry the light of the gospel to them

that were in darkness, even to all the spirits of men; and thus was the gospel preached to the dead. (*Vision regarding the Savior's visit to the spirits of the dead, received Oct. 3, 1918*) D&C 138:29-30

**Author's Note:** This principle of agency—that priesthood holders act as agents of the Lord—extends further into the duties of priesthood bearers, that they organize and delegate the work to sub-agents, so to speak. Hence Jethro, priest of Midian, counseled Moses: "And it came to pass on the morrow, that Moses sat to judge the people: and the people stood by Moses from the morning unto the evening. 14. And when Moses' father in law saw all that he did to the people, he said, What is this thing that thou doest to the people? why sittest thou thyself alone, and all the people stand by thee from morning unto even? 15. And Moses said unto his father in law, Because the people come unto me to inquire of God: 16. When they have a matter, they come unto me; and I judge between one and another, and I do make them know the statutes of God, and his laws. 17. And Moses' father in law said unto him, The thing that thou doest is not good. 18. Thou wilt surely wear away, both thou, and this people that is with thee: for this thing is too heavy for thee; thou art not able to perform it thyself alone. 19. Hearken now unto my voice, I will give thee counsel, and God shall be with thee: Be thou for the people to Godward, that thou mayest bring the causes unto God: 20. And thou shalt teach them ordinances and laws, and shalt shew them the way wherein they must walk, and the work that they must do. 21. Moreover thou shalt provide out of all the people able men, such as fear God, men of truth, hating covetousness; and place such over them, to be rulers of thousands, and rulers of hundreds, rulers of fifties, and rulers of tens." (Ex.18:13-21)

# List of Doctrines

## LOVE OF NEIGHBOR

*Doctrines Located in This Topic*

421. We are to love one another.

422. We are to love our enemies.

423. We are to return good for evil, not evil for evil.

424. We are to judge righteously.

425. We are to strive to lift others —to strengthen the weak.

426. We are to love our neighbors as ourselves.

427. Without charity (the pure love of Christ), we cannot enter into the celestial kingdom.

*Doctrines on LOVE OF NEIGHBOR Located in Other Topics*

223. We are to forgive each other without condition, limitation, or exception.

224. When offended, we are to forgive the offending person and seek reconciliation.

498. We are to live peaceably and not contend one with another.

499. We are not to be angry with others.

530. We are to pray for the sinful person.

531. We are to pray for our enemies.

855. We are to impart of our substance for the benefit of those less fortunate.

(See topic SERVICE.)

# LOVE OF NEIGHBOR

**421. We are to love one another.**

### Jesus,
#### recorded in Matthew

Master, which is the great commandment in the law? 37. Jesus said unto him, Thou shalt love the Lord thy God with all thy heart, and with all thy soul, and with all thy mind. 38. This is the first and great commandment. 39. And the second is like unto it, Thou shalt love thy neighbour as thyself. 40. On these two commandments hang all the law and the prophets. (*Jesus gives the two great commandments*) Matt.22:36-40

### Jesus,
#### quoted by John

A new commandment I give unto you, That ye love one another; as I have loved you, that ye also love one another. 35. By this shall all men know that ye are my disciples, if ye have love one to another. (*Jesus washes the feet of his the Twelve after the Last Supper and commands them to love one another*) John 13:34-35

### Joseph Smith

It is a duty which every saint ought to render to his brethren freely—to always love them, and ever succor them. To be justified before God we must love one another: we must overcome evil; we must visit the fatherless and the widow in their affliction, and we must keep ourselves unspotted from the world: for such virtues flow from the great fountain of pure religion, strengthening our faith by adding every good quality that adorns the children of the blessed Jesus, we can pray in the season of prayer; we can love our neighbor as ourselves, and be faithful in tribulation. . . . (*Joseph instructs elders and Saints in Missouri*) (Messenger and Advocate, June 1835) HC2:229; TLDP:367

### Joseph Smith

It is a time-honored adage that love begets love. Let us pour forth love—show forth our kindness unto all mankind, and the Lord will reward us with everlasting increase; cast our bread upon the waters and we shall receive it after many days, increased to a hundredfold. Friendship is like Brother Turley in his blacksmith shop welding iron to iron; it unites the human family with its happy influence. ¶ I do not dwell upon your faults, and you shall not upon mine. Charity, which is love, covereth a multitude of sins, and I have often covered up all the faults among you; but the prettiest thing is to have no faults at all. We should cultivate a meek, quiet and peaceable spirit. (*At the Stand in Nauvoo, Ill., Sunday July 23, 1843*) HC5:517

### John

We love him, because he first loved us. 20. If a man say, I love God, and hateth his brother, he is a liar: for he that loveth not his brother whom he hath seen, how can he love God whom he hath not seen? 21. And this commandment have we from him, That he who loveth God love his brother also. (*John writes to the churches in Asia*) 1Jn.4:19-21

### Jesus,
#### quoted by John

This is my commandment, That ye love one another, as I have loved you. 13. Greater love hath no man than this, that a man lay down his life for his friends. (*Jesus teaches his disciples the perfect law of love*) John 15:12-13

### Recorded in Leviticus

Thou shalt not avenge, nor bear any grudge against the children of thy people, but thou shalt love thy neighbour as thyself: I am the LORD. (*Revelation to Moses for the children of Israel*) Lev.19:18

### Paul

[I]f there be any other commandment, it is briefly comprehended in this saying, namely, Thou shalt love thy neighbour as thyself. 10. Love worketh no ill to his neighbour: therefore love is the fulfilling of the law. (*Paul writes to the Church in Rome, about A.D. 55*) Rom.13:9-10

### Nephi, son of Lehi

[W]herefore, the Lord God hath given a commandment that all men should have charity, which charity is love, and except they should have charity they were nothing. (*Nephi gives commandments of God to Nephites, 559-545 B.C.*) 2Ne.26:30

### Mormon

[F]or if he have not charity he is nothing; wherefore he must needs have charity. 45. And charity suffereth long, and is kind, and envieth not, and is not puffed up, seeketh not her own, is not easily provoked, thinketh no evil, and rejoiceth not in iniquity but rejoiceth in the truth, beareth all things, believeth all things, hopeth all things, endureth all things. 46. Wherefore, my beloved brethren, if ye have not charity, ye are nothing, for charity never faileth. Wherefore, cleave unto charity, which is the greatest of all, for all things must fail— 47. But charity is the pure love of Christ, and it endureth forever; and whoso is found possessed of it at the last day, it shall be well with him. 48. Wherefore, my beloved brethren, pray unto the Father with all the energy of heart, that ye may be filled with this love, which he hath bestowed upon all who are true followers of his Son,

Jesus Christ; that ye may become the sons of God; that when he shall appear we shall be like him, for we shall see him as he is; that we may have this hope; that we may be purified even as he is pure. Amen. (*Mormon preaches in the synagogue, prior to* A.D. *384*) Moro.7:44-48

### Dallin H. Oaks,
### *also quoting Jesus,*
### *as recorded in Matthew*

We know . . . that even the most extreme acts of service—such as giving all of our goods to feed the poor—profit us nothing unless our service is motivated by the pure love of Christ. ¶ If our service is to be most efficacious, it must be accomplished for the love of God and the love of his children. . . . ¶ This principle—that our service should be for the love of God and the love of fellowmen rather than for personal advantage or any other lesser motive—is admittedly a high standard. The Savior must have seen it so, since he joined his commandment for selfless and complete love directly with the ideal of perfection . . . "Be ye therefore perfect, even as your Father which is in heaven is perfect." (Matt.5:48). . . . ¶ Service with all of our heart and mind is a high challenge for all of us. Such service must be free of selfish ambition. It must be motivated only by the pure love of Christ. . . . ¶ I know that God expects us to work to purify our hearts and our thoughts so that we may serve one another for the highest and best reason, the pure love of Christ. CR1984Oct:16

### N. Eldon Tanner

The most important thing that Jesus Christ taught when he was on earth is that we must love one another. ("Message from the First Presidency," EN1971Jan:3) TLDP:366

### Joseph Smith,
### *quoted by Elder Joseph Fielding Smith*

Love is one of the chief characteristics of Deity, and ought to be manifested by those who aspire to be the sons of God. A man filled with the love of God, is not content with blessing his family alone, but ranges through the whole world, anxious to bless the whole human race. (*Epistle to the Twelve, Oct. 19, 1840*) HC4:227; TPJS:174

**Related Witnesses:**

### Joseph Smith

And let every man esteem his brother as himself, and practise virtue and holiness before me. 25. And again I say unto you, let every man esteem his brother as himself. (*Commandments to Saints in conference, Jan. 2, 1831*) D&C 38:24-25

### Paul

Put on therefore, as the elect of God, holy and beloved, bowels of mercies, kindness, humble-ness of mind, meekness, longsuffering; 13. Forbearing one another, and forgiving one another, if any man have a quarrel against any: even as Christ forgave you, so also do ye. 14. And above all these things put on charity, which is the bond of perfectness. (*Paul writes from prison to the Church in Colossae, Asia Minor, about* A.D. *60*) Col.3:12-14

**Author's Note:** C.S. Lewis wrote profoundly about this business of loving one another: ¶ "It may be possible for each to think too much of his own potential glory hereafter; it is hardly possible for him to think too often or too deeply about that of his neighbour. The load, or weight, or burden of my neighbour's glory should be laid on my back, a load so heavy that only humility can carry it, and the backs of the proud will be broken. It is a serious thing to live in a society of possible gods and goddesses, to remember that the dullest and most uninteresting person you can talk to may one day be a creature which, if you saw it now, you would be strongly tempted to worship. . . . There are no ordinary people. You have never talked to a mere mortal. . . . [I]t is immortals whom we joke with, work with, marry, snub, and exploit. . . . This does not mean that we are to be perpetually solemn. We must play. But our merriment must be of that kind (and it is, in fact, the merriest kind) which exists between people who have, from the outset, taken each other seriously—no flippancy, no superiority, no presumption. And our charity must be a real and costly love, with deep feeling for the sins in spite of which we love the sinner—no mere tolerance, or indulgence which parodies love as flippancy parodies merriment. Next to the Blessed Sacrament itself, your neighbour is the holiest object presented to your senses." (The Weight of Glory, pp. 18-19)

---

### 422. We are to love our enemies.

### Jesus,
### *recorded in Matthew*

But I say unto you, Love your enemies, bless them that curse you, do good to them that hate you, and pray for them which despitefully use you, and persecute you; 45. That ye may be the children of your Father which is in heaven: for he maketh his sun to rise on the evil and on the good, and sendeth rain on the just and on the unjust. 46. For if ye love them which love you, what reward have ye? do not even the publicans the same? 47. And if ye salute your brethren only, what do ye more than others? do not even the publicans so? 48. Be ye therefore perfect, even as your Father which is in heaven is perfect. (*Jesus teaches the multitude to love their enemies*) Matt.5:44-48

### Bruce R. McConkie

All men will be judged by what is in their own hearts. If their souls are full of hatred and cursings, such characteristics shall be restored to them in the resurrection. Loving one's enemies and blessing one's cursers perfects the soul. (The Mortal Messiah, 2:142) TLDP:370

### Jesus,
### *recorded in Matthew*

But I say unto you which hear, Love your enemies, do good to them which hate you, 28. Bless them that curse you, and pray for them which despitefully use you. (*Jesus teaches his disciples about love*) Luke 6:27-28

### President Brigham Young,
### *quoted by John A. Widtsoe*

Do I say, Love your enemies? Yes, upon certain principles. But you are not required to love their wickedness; you are only required to love them so far as concerns a desire and effort to turn them from their evil ways, that they may be saved through obedience to the Gospel. (*In Tabernacle, April 22, 1860, JD8:71*) DBY:272

### Jesus,
### *quoted by Mormon*

But behold I say unto you, love your enemies, bless them that curse you, do good to them that hate you, and pray for them who despitefully use you and persecute you; 45. That ye may be the children of your Father who is in heaven; for he maketh his sun to rise on the evil and on the good. 46. Therefore those things which were of old time, which were under the law, in me are all fulfilled. 47. Old things are done away, and all things have become new. 48. Therefore I would that ye should be perfect even as I, or your Father who is in heaven is perfect. (*The resurrected Jesus Christ teaches the Nephite people, A.D. 34*) 3Ne.12:44-48

### Related Witnesses:
### John

He that saith he is in the light, and hateth his brother, is in darkness even until now. 10. He that loveth his brother abideth in the light, and there is none occasion of stumbling in him. 11. But he that hateth his brother is in darkness, and walketh in darkness, and knoweth not whither he goeth, because that darkness hath blinded his eyes. (*John to the churches in Asia*) 1Jn.2:9-11

### Elder Harold B. Lee

A brotherhood that seeks to establish the common good is as "sounding brass or a tinkling cymbal," except it be founded upon the divine principle of love of God and our neighbor as ourselves. One who says he loves God and is a follower of Jesus and yet hates his brother is false to himself and before the world, for no one can love God whom he has not seen and yet love not his brother whom he has seen. (See John 4:20.) The truest evidence that one loves God is that he keeps the commandments. (See John 2:3-4.) RSM1943Feb:84-87

## 423. We are to return good for evil, not evil for evil.

### Jesus,
### *recorded in Matthew*

Ye have heard that it hath been said, An eye for an eye, and a tooth for a tooth: 39. But I say unto you, That ye resist not evil: but whosoever shall smite thee on thy right cheek, turn to him the other also. 40. And if any man will sue thee at the law, and take away thy coat, let him have thy cloke also. 41. And whosoever shall compel thee to go a mile, go with him twain. 42. Give to him that asketh thee, and from him that would borrow of thee turn not thou away. . . . 44. But I say unto you, Love your enemies, bless them that curse you, do good to them that hate you, and pray for them which despitefully use you, and persecute you; . . . 46. For if ye love them which love you, what reward have ye? do not even the publicans the same? . . . 48. Be ye therefore perfect, even as your Father which is in heaven is perfect. (*Jesus Christ to the multitude, about A.D. 30*) Matt.5:38-42,44,46,48

### President John Taylor

Have I any ill feelings towards these people that persecute and proscribe us? No. I would do them good for evil, give blessings for curses; I would treat them well, treat them honorably. Let us be men of truth, honor and integrity; men that will swear to our own hurt and change not; men whose word will be our everlasting bond. If you see men hungry, feed them, no matter who they are; white, black, or red, Jew, Gentile or Mormon, or anybody else—feed them. If you see naked, clothe them. If you see sick, administer to them, and learn to be kind to all men; but partake not of their evil practices. (*General conference, Oct. 1884, JD25:312*) TLDP:368

### Jesus,
### *recorded in Luke*

And unto him that smiteth thee on the one cheek offer also the other; and him that taketh

away thy cloke forbid not to take thy coat also.
30. Give to every man that asketh of thee; and
of him that taketh away thy goods ask them not
again. 31. And as ye would that men should do
to you, do ye also to them likewise. 32. For if
ye love them which love you, what thank have
ye? for sinners also love those that love them.
33. And if ye do good to them which do good
to you, what thank have ye? for sinners also do
even the same. (*Jesus addresses his disciples*)
Luke 6:29-33

**Elder Spencer W. Kimball,**
*also quoting*
**President George Albert Smith**

Sometimes the spirit of forgiveness is carried to
the loftiest height—to rendering assistance to
the offender. Not to be revengeful, not to seek
what outraged justice might demand, to leave
the offender in God's hands—this is admirable.
But to return good for evil, this is the sublime
expression of Christian love. ¶ In this regard we
have the stimulating example of President
George Albert Smith. It was reported to him
that someone had stolen from his buggy the
buggy robe. Instead of being angry, he
responded: "I wish we knew who it was, so that
we could give him the blanket also, for he must
have been cold; and some food also, for he
must have been hungry." (The Miracle of
Forgiveness, pp. 282-84) TLDP:206-07

**Jesus,**
*quoted by Mormon*

But behold I say unto you, love your enemies,
bless them that curse you, do good to them that
hate you, and pray for them who despitefully
use you and persecute you; 45. That ye may be
the children of your Father who is in heaven;
for he maketh his sun to rise on the evil and on
the good. (*The resurrected Jesus Christ teaches
the Nephite people, A.D. 34*) 3Ne.12:44-45

**Related Witnesses:**

**Mormon**

Some were lifted up in pride, and others were
exceedingly humble; some did return railing for
railing, while others would receive railing and
persecution and all manner of afflictions, and
would not turn and revile again, but were humble and penitent before God. (*Much iniquity
abounds among the Nephites, A.D. 29-30*)
3Ne.6:13

**Mormon**

Nevertheless, the people did harden their
hearts, for they were led by many priests and
false prophets to build up many churches, and
to do all manner of iniquity. And they did
smite upon the people of Jesus; but the people
of Jesus did not smite again. And thus they did

dwindle in unbelief and wickedness, from year
to year, even until two hundred and thirty years
had passed away. (*Mormon abridges the
account of Nephi, son of Nephi, one of the disciples of Christ, A.D. 36-60*) 4Ne.1:34

**Joseph Smith**

Now, I speak unto you concerning your families
—if men will smite you, or your families, once,
and ye bear it patiently and revile not against
them, neither seek revenge, ye shall be rewarded; 24. But if ye bear it not patiently, it
shall be accounted unto you as being meted out
as a just measure unto you. (*Revelation
received Aug. 6, 1833 in consequence of the
persecution of the Saints*) D&C 98:23-24

---

### 424. We are to judge righteously.

**Jesus,**
*quoted by Joseph Smith,*
*translating Matthew*

Now these are the words which Jesus taught his
disciples that they should say unto the people.
Judge not unrighteously, that ye be not judged:
but judge righteous judgment. (*Jesus concludes
the Sermon on the Mount*) JST(Matt.7:1, fn. a)

**Charles W. Penrose**

Now, brothers and sisters, what the Savior
meant [Matt.7:1-2] was that you and I, in our
capacity as individuals, as members, outside of
any official duty imposed upon us, should not
sit in judgment upon one another. And yet we
do it, and sometimes we say things about one
another that we are not justified in saying. . . .
It is not our province as members of the
Church, to sit in judgment upon one another
and call bad names when we reflect upon the
acts of people. We have no right, even if we
are in official capacity, to form a one-sided
judgment. There are two sides to every such
question, if not more, always; and we should
hear both. . . . Hear the other side before you
begin to find fault, and pass judgment. Do not
let us pass judgment upon our fellow creatures,
our brothers and sisters, or even people in the
world. CR1916Oct:22

**Jesus,**
*quoted by John*

Judge not according to the appearance, but
judge righteous judgment. (*Jesus teaches in the
temple*) John 7:24

**Alma, the younger,**
*quoted by Mormon*

Therefore, my son, see that you are merciful
unto your brethren; deal justly, judge righteously, and do good continually; and if ye do all

these things then shall ye receive your reward; yea, ye shall have mercy restored unto you again; ye shall have justice restored unto you again; ye shall have a righteous judgment restored unto you again; and ye shall have good rewarded unto you again. 15. For that which ye do send out shall return unto you again, and be restored; therefore, the word restoration more fully condemneth the sinner, and justifieth him not at all. (*Alma instructs his son Corianton that every person receives again in the resurrection those characteristics and attributes acquired in mortality, about 73 B.C.*) Alma 41:14-15

### Joseph Smith,
### *receiving the Word of the Lord*
And now, verily, verily, I say unto thee, put your trust in that Spirit which leadeth to do good—yea, to do justly, to walk humbly, to judge righteously; and this is my Spirit. (*Revelation for Hyrum Smith, May 1829*) D&C 11:12

**Related Witnesses:**

### Recorded in 1 Samuel
But the LORD said unto Samuel, Look not on his countenance, or on the height of his stature; because I have refused him: for the LORD seeth not as man seeth; for man looketh on the outward appearance, but the LORD looketh on the heart. (*The Lord through Samuel chooses David to be king; Samuel examines Eliab, son of Jesse*) 1Sam.16:7

### Jesus,
### *recorded in Matthew*
Judge not, that ye be not judged. 2. For with what judgment ye judge, ye shall be judged: and with what measure ye mete, it shall be measured to you again. 3. And why beholdest thou the mote that is in thy brother's eye, but considerest not the beam that is in thine own eye? 4. Or how wilt thou say to thy brother, Let me pull out the mote out of thine eye; and, behold, a beam is in thine own eye? 5. Thou hypocrite, first cast out the beam out of thine own eye; and then shalt thou see clearly to cast out the mote out of thy brother's eye. (*Jesus concludes the Sermon on the Mount*) Matt.7:1-5

### Jesus,
### *recorded in Luke*
Judge not, and ye shall not be judged: condemn not, and ye shall not be condemned: forgive, and ye shall be forgiven: (*Jesus teaches his disciples some principles of love and service*) Luke 6:37

---

**425. We are to strive to lift others—to strengthen the weak.**

### President Ezra Taft Benson
We can choose to humble ourselves by conquering enmity toward our brothers and sisters, esteeming them as ourselves, and lifting them as high or higher than we are. (See D&C 38:24; 81:5; 84:106.) CR1989Apr:6

### Jacob, brother of Nephi
Think of your brethren like unto yourselves, and be familiar with all and free with your substance, that they may be rich like unto you. (*Jacob denounces the love of riches among the Nephites, 544-421 B.C.*) Jacob 2:17

### President Harold B. Lee
You cannot lift another soul until you are standing on higher ground than he is. . . . You cannot light a fire in another soul unless it is burning in your own soul. CR1973Apr:178

### Joseph Smith
And if any man among you be strong in the Spirit, let him take with him him that is weak, that he may be edified in all meekness, that he may become strong also. (*Revelation on priesthood received with six elders, Sept. 22/23, 1832*) D&C 84:106

### Thomas S. Monson,
### *also quoting Jeremiah*
Time passes. Circumstances change. Conditions vary. Unaltered is the divine command to succor the weak and lift up the hands which hang down and strengthen the feeble knees. Each of us has the charge to be not a doubter, but a doer; not a leaner, but a lifter. But our complacency tree has many branches, and each spring more buds come into bloom. Often we live side by side but do not communicate heart to heart. There are those within the sphere of our own influence who, with outstretched hands, cry out: "Is there no balm in Gilead . . . ?" (Jer. 8:22) Each of us must answer. CR1971Oct:171

### Joseph Smith
And if any man among you be strong in the Spirit, let him take with him him that is weak, that he may be edified in all meekness, that he may become strong also. (*Revelation on priesthood received with six elders, Sept. 22/23, 1832*) D&C 84:106

### Joseph Smith
Therefore, strengthen your brethren in all your conversation, in all your prayers, in all your exhortations, and in all your doings. (*Revelation for Lyman Sherman, Dec. 26, 1835*) D&C 108:7

### Joseph Smith,
### *receiving the Word of the Lord*
Wherefore, be faithful; stand in the office which I have appointed unto you; succor the weak, lift up the hands which hang down, and strengthen the feeble knees. (*Revelation for the*

*newly called counselor in First Presidency, Frederick G. Williams, March 1832)* D&C 81:5

**Paul**

Wherefore lift up the hands which hang down, and the feeble knees; (*Paul's letter to the Jewish members of the Church, about A.D. 60*) Heb.12:12

**Isaiah**

Strengthen ye the weak hands, and confirm the feeble knees. 4. Say to them that are of a fearful heart, Be strong, fear not: behold, your God will come with vengeance, even God with a recompence; he will come and save you. (*Israel shall be gathered and Zion built up*) Isa.35:3-4

**Related Witnesses:**

**Jesus,**
*recorded in Luke*

But I have prayed for thee, that thy faith fail not: and when thou art converted, strengthen thy brethren. (*Jesus talks to Peter, prior to departing for Gethsemane*) Luke 22:32

**Marvin J. Ashton**

No one ever lifted someone else without stepping toward higher ground. CR1973Oct:131

---

426. We are to love our neighbors as ourselves.

**Jesus,**
*recorded in Matthew*

Jesus said unto him, Thou shalt love the Lord thy God with all thy heart, and with all thy soul, and with all thy mind. 38. This is the first and great commandment. 39. And the second is like unto it, Thou shalt love thy neighbour as thyself. 40. On these two commandments hang all the law and the prophets. (*Jesus gives the two great commandments*) Matt.22:37-40

**John A. Widtsoe**

To love oneself—that is easy. Instinctively, from the first day, we have reached out for our own greater good. Every personal philosophy makes the man the center. To love our neighbor equally well—"that's the rub." His will is not our will; his ways, not our ways. Yet, only by the progress of all, can each gain the greatest advancement. The fundamental conceptions of a universe filled with eternal matter and forces, and a host of individual intelligent beings, make it clear that only by complete harmony of all intelligent beings can the interests of each be served, in the work of subjugating, by intelligent conquest, the forces of universal nature. ¶ To love one's neighbor, then, a man must first fully know his own origin and destiny and possible pow-

ers; then he may soon learn the need of loving his fellowman, if his love for himself shall grow great. This commandment is not inferior to the first. (*A Rational Theology, p. 188*) TLDP:367

**Mormon**

Thus did Alma teach his people, that every man should love his neighbor as himself, that there should be no contention among them. (*Alma teaches the people, 145-121 B.C.*) Mosiah 23:15

**Paul**

[I]f there be any other commandment, it is briefly comprehended in this saying, namely, Thou shalt love thy neighbour as thyself. 10. Love worketh no ill to his neighbour: therefore love is the fulfilling of the law. (*Letter to the Church in Rome, about A.D. 55*) Rom.13:9-10

**Joseph Smith**

Thou shalt love thy neighbor as thyself. (*Revelation, Aug. 7, 1831*) D&C 59:6

**James**

If ye fulfil the royal law according to the scripture, Thou shalt love thy neighbour as thyself, ye do well: 9. But if ye have respect to persons, ye commit sin, and are convinced of the law as transgressors. (*Letter to his brethren in the Church*) James 2:8-9

**Related Witnesses:**

**President Spencer W. Kimball**

We must remember that those mortals we meet in parking lots, offices, elevators, and elsewhere are that portion of mankind God has given us to love and to serve. It will do us little good to speak of the general brotherhood of mankind if we cannot regard those who are all around us as our brothers and sisters. (*At Sun Valley, Idaho, to Young Presidents Organization, Jan. 1977*) (The Teachings of Spencer W. Kimball, p. 483) TLDP:368

---

427. Without charity (the pure love of Christ), we cannot enter into the celestial kingdom.

**Marion G. Romney**

In this modern world plagued with counterfeits for the Lord's plan, we must not be misled into supposing that we can discharge our obligations to the poor and the needy by shifting the responsibility to some governmental or other public agency. Only by voluntarily giving out of an abundant love for our neighbors can we develop that charity characterized by Mormon as "the pure love of Christ." (Moro.7:47) This we must develop if we would obtain eternal life. CR1972Oct:115

### Mormon

[F]or if he have not charity he is nothing; wherefore he must needs have charity. . . . 46. Wherefore, my beloved brethren, if ye have not charity, ye are nothing, for charity never faileth. Wherefore, cleave unto charity, which is the greatest of all, for all things must fail— 47. But charity is the pure love of Christ, and it endureth forever; and whoso is found possessed of it at the last day, it shall be well with him. 48. Wherefore, my beloved brethren, pray unto the Father with all the energy of heart, that ye may be filled with this love, which he hath bestowed upon all who are true followers of his Son, Jesus Christ; that ye may become the sons of God; that when he shall appear we shall be like him, for we shall see him as he is; that we may have this hope; that we may be purified even as he is pure. Amen. (*Mormon preaches in the synagogue, prior to A.D. 384*) Moro.7:44,46-48

### Moroni, son of Mormon

And I know that this love which thou hast had for the children of men is charity; wherefore, except men shall have charity they cannot inherit that place which thou hast prepared in the mansions of thy Father. (*Moroni, having heard the Lord speak to him, addresses the Lord*) Ether 12:34

### Nephi, son of Lehi

[W]herefore, the Lord God hath given a commandment that all men should have charity, which charity is love, and except they should have charity they were nothing. (*Nephi gives commandments of God to Nephites, 559-545 B.C.*) 2Ne.26:30

### James E. Talmage

If man would win eternal life, he cannot afford to neglect the duty of love to his fellow, for "Love is the fulfilling of the law." AF:392

**Related Witnesses:**

### Marion G. Romney

Service is not something we endure on this earth so we can earn the right to live in the celestial kingdom. Service is the very fiber of which an exalted life in the celestial kingdom is made. CR1982Oct:135

### George F. Richards

The Lord expects us when he blesses us with the good things of this earth to remember those who are not so fortunate. We are to feed the hungry, clothe the naked, visit the sick, comfort those who mourn, and minister unto those who are poor and needy, and thus become of that class to whom the Lord, when he shall come, shall say: "Come, ye blessed of the Father, inherit the kingdom prepared for you from the foundation of the world." CR1939Oct:108-09

### George F. Richards

Activity in the cause inspires love for, and interest in it. I have proven to my satisfaction that when we work for the Lord we love him more, and as we love him more, we have more desire to work for, and serve him. It works both ways. . . . If we do not love him we will not give to him much valuable service. Love and service to God and man are necessary qualifications in order to obtain eternal life, the greatest gift of God to man. CR1919Oct:61

### Elder Joseph Fielding Smith

The man who does only those things in the Church which concern himself alone will never reach exaltation. For instance, the man who is willing to pray, to pay his tithes and offerings, and to attend to the ordinary duties which concern his own personal life, and nothing more, will never reach the goal of perfection. ¶ Service must be given in behalf of others. We must extend the helping hand to the unfortunate, to those who have not heard the truth and are in spiritual darkness, to the needy, the oppressed. Are you failing? CR1968Apr:12

### Jesus,
### *recorded in Matthew*

Then shall the King say unto them on his right hand, Come, ye blessed of my Father, inherit the kingdom prepared for you from the foundation of the world: 35. For I was an hungred, and ye gave me meat: I was thirsty, and ye gave me drink: I was a stranger, and ye took me in: 36. Naked, and ye clothed me: I was sick, and ye visited me: I was in prison, and ye came unto me. 37. Then shall the righteous answer him, saying, Lord, when saw we thee an hungred, and fed thee? or thirsty, and gave thee drink? 38. When saw we thee a stranger, and took thee in? or naked, and clothed thee? 39. Or when saw we thee sick, or in prison, and came unto thee? 40. And the King shall answer and say unto them, Verily I say unto you, Inasmuch as ye have done it unto one of the least of these my brethren, ye have done it unto me. (*Jesus gives the parable of the sheep and the goats; the sheep are placed on his right hand at the Lord's second coming*) Matt.25:34-40

### Spencer W. Kimball

If one really loves another, one would rather die for that person than to injure him. (*Copenhagen Denmark area conference, Aug. 5, 1976*) (The Teachings of Spencer W. Kimball, p. 279) TLDP:369

# List of Doctrines

## MAN: Mankind

*Doctrines Located in This Topic*

428. We have an immortal identity: there never will be a time when we will cease to exist as individuals.

429. We are in the physical image of God.

430. The spirit and body combined constitute our souls.

431. We will continue to exist forever with our own individual identity; a soul can never be annihilated.

432. As a child of God, each of us is of infinite worth.

433. Men and women may, at sometime in the future, become gods.

*Doctrines on MAN: Mankind Located in Other Topics*

106. Each individual's placement among the tribes, families, and nations of this world was determined by the kind of life he or she lived in the premortal state.

144. Those who inherit exaltation in the celestial kingdom will thereafter become gods.

454. The worth of souls is great in the sight of God (each individual is precious in His sight).

# MAN: Mankind

**Author's Note:** Use of male gender terms in modern day writing tends to exclude or diminish the female role. For this reason the doctrines and principles in this book have been stated to avoid, where possible, the use of the word "man" and the pronoun "he." I have also tried to replace the word "mankind" in many instances with "all people." However, for the purposes of this topic, the words "man" and "mankind" best fit the scriptures and are hence retained in the topic title.

428. We have an immortal identity: there never will be a time when we will cease to exist as individuals.

**President Lorenzo Snow**

In considering ourselves and how we have been organized and what we are doing, we discover that there is immortality connected with us. We are immortal beings. That which dwells in this body of ours is immortal, and will always exist. Our individuality will always continue. Eternities may begin, eternities may end, and still we shall have our individuality. Our identity is insured. We will be ourselves, and nobody else. Whatever changes may arise, whatever worlds may be made or pass away, our identity will always remain the same; and we will continue on improving, advancing and increasing in wisdom, intelligence, power and dominion, worlds without end. Our present advancement is simply a starting out, as it were, on this path of immortality. Whatever may have been our past, how long we may have existed before this, or whether there ever was a time when we did not exist, there is one thing sure—our being in the future will never be annihilated, never destroyed. . . . But there is no such thing as our passing out of existence. CR1901Apr:2

**President Spencer W. Kimball**

We are eternal beings. We have no way of comprehending how long we dwelt in the presence of God as his spirit children. We are here in mortality for a moment of testing and trial. Then we will come forth in the resurrection, receive an inheritance in whatever kingdom we deserve, and go on living the commandments to all eternity. . . . [T]he life that is to be is forever. It will have no end. Men will rise from the grave and not die after. Life is eternal, unending; never after the resurrection will the children of our Father taste death. CR1978Oct:71

**President Joseph F. Smith**

I refer to our identity, our indestructible, immortal identity. . . . ¶ We will meet the same identical being that we associated with here in the flesh—not some other soul, some other being, or the same being in some other form—but the same identity and the same form and likeness, the same person we knew and were

associated with in our mortal existence, even to the wounds in the flesh. Not that a person will always be marred by scars, wounds, deformities, defects or infirmities, for these will be removed in their course. . . . (*At funeral of Rachel Grant, mother of President Heber J. Grant, IE1909Jun:591*) MPSG1970-71:41-42

**Joseph Smith,**
*quoted by Elder Joseph Fielding Smith*

Intelligence is eternal and exists upon a self-existent principle. It is a spirit from age to age and there is no creation about it. All the minds and spirits that God ever sent into the world are susceptible of enlargement. The first principles of man are self-existent with God. God himself, finding he was in the midst of spirits and glory, because he was more intelligent, saw proper to institute laws whereby the rest could have a privilege to advance like himself. The relationship we have with God places us in a situation to advance in knowledge. He has power to institute laws to instruct the weaker intelligences, that they may be exalted with Himself, so that they might have one glory upon another, and all that knowledge, power, glory, and intelligence, which is requisite in order to save them in the world of spirits. ¶ This is good doctrine. It tastes good. I can taste the principles of eternal life, and so can you. They are given to me by the revelations of Jesus Christ; and I know that when I tell you these words of eternal life as they are given to me, you taste them, and I know that you believe them. You say honey is sweet, and so do I. I can also taste the spirit of eternal life. I know that it is good; and when I tell you of these things which were given me by inspiration of the Holy Spirit, you are bound to receive them as sweet, and rejoice more and more. (*To the Church in general conference—to a congregation of 20,000—, "King Follett Sermon," April 7, 1844*) (See HC6:302-17, also see The Words of Joseph Smith, pp. 340-62) HC6:311-12; TPJS:354

**Related Witnesses:**

**President Joseph F. Smith**

We believe in the pre-existence of man as a spirit, and in the future state of individual existence, in which every soul shall find its place, as determined by justice and mercy, with opportunities of endless progression, in varied conditions of eternity. (*Address from the First Presidency of the Church to the world, delivered to and accepted by vote of the Church in general conference, April 1907*) CR1907Apr(Appendix)4

### Parley P. Pratt

Gods, angels and men are all of one species, one race, one great family, widely diffused among the planetary systems, as colonies, kingdoms, nations, etc. ¶ The great distinguishing difference between one portion of this race and another consists in the varied grades of intelligence and purity, and also in the variety of spheres occupied by each, in the series of progressive being. ¶ An immortal man, possessing a perfect organization of spirit, flesh, and bones, and perfected in his attributes in all the fulness of celestial glory is called *a god.* (Key to the Science of Theology, pp. 40-41) TLDP:374

---

### 429. We are in the physical image of God.

### Moses

And God said, Let us make man in our image, after our likeness: and let them have dominion over the fish of the sea, and over the fowl of the air, and over the cattle, and over all the earth, and over every creeping thing that creepeth upon the earth. 27. So God created man in his own image, in the image of God created he him; male and female created he them. (*Revelation to Moses regarding the creation of man*) Gen.1:26-27

### President Joseph F. Smith

We hold that man is verily the child of God, formed in His image, endowed with divine attributes, and possessing power to rise from the gross desires of earth to the ennobling aspirations of heaven. (*Address from the First Presidency of the Church to the world, delivered to and accepted by vote of the Church in general conference, April 1907*) CR1907Apr(Appendix)4

### Joseph Smith,
#### translating the Book of Moses

And I, God, said unto mine Only Begotten, which was with me from the beginning: Let us make man in our image, after our likeness; and it was so. And I, God, said: Let them have dominion over the fishes of the sea, and over the fowl of the air, and over the cattle, and over all the earth, and over every creeping thing that creepeth upon the earth. 27. And I, God, created man in mine own image, in the image of mine

Only Begotten created I him; male and female created I them. (*The record of Moses: God makes man and gives him dominion over all*) Moses 2:26-27

### President Brigham Young

Man is made in the image of his Maker, and ... he is His exact image, having eye for eye, forehead for forehead, eyebrows for eyebrows, nose for nose, cheekbones for cheekbones, mouth for mouth, chin for chin, ears for ears, precisely like our Father in heaven. (*In new Tabernacle, July 11, 1869, JD13:146*) TLDP:171

### President Brigham Young,
#### quoted by John A. Widtsoe

I now see before me beings who are in the image of those heavenly personages who are enthroned in glory and crowned with eternal lives in the very image of those beings who organized the earth and its fulness, and who constitute the Godhead. (*In Tabernacle, March 23, 1862, JD9:246*) DBY:25

### President Brigham Young,
#### quoted by John A. Widtsoe

When we look upon the human face we look upon the image of our Father and God; there is a divinity in each person, male and female; there is the heavenly, there is the divine and with this is amalgamated the human, the earthly, the weaker portions of our nature, and it is the human that shrinks in the presence of the divine, and this accounts for our man-fearing spirit, and it is all there is of it. (*In Tabernacle, April 27, 1862, JD9:291*) DBY:51;

### Ammon, son of Mosiah,
#### quoted by Mormon

Ammon said unto him: I am a man; and man in the beginning was created after the image of God, and I am called by his Holy Spirit to teach these things unto this people, that they may be brought to a knowledge of that which is just and true; (*Ammon responds to King Lamoni, about 90 B.C.*) Alma 18:34

### President Heber J. Grant,
### Anthony W. Ivins, Charles W. Nibley
#### (First Presidency)

Man is the child of God, formed in the divine image and endowed with divine attributes, and even as the infant son of an earthly father and mother is capable in due time of becoming a man, so that undeveloped offspring of celestial parentage is capable, by experience through ages and aeons, of evolving into a God. ("'Mormon' View of Evolution," IE1925Sep:1090-91) MOFP5:244

### Mormon

And a prophet of the Lord have they slain; yea, a chosen man of God, who told them of their wickedness and abominations, and prophesied of many things which are to come, yea, even the coming of Christ. 27. And because he said unto them that Christ was the God, the Father of all things, and said that he should take upon him the image of man, and it should be the image after which man was created in the beginning; or in other words, he said that man was created after the image of God, and that God should come down among the children of men, and take upon him flesh and blood, and go forth upon the face of the earth— 28. And now, because he said this, they did put him to death; (*King Limhi recounts the history of his people to Ammon and the throng assembled; he says a prophet [Abinadi] was slain because he testified that Christ was the God and Father of all things*) Mosiah 7:26-28

### Thomas S. Monson

When we realize that we have actually been made in the image of God, all things are possible. John Mott, a recipient of the Nobel Prize, indicated that this particular knowledge, a knowledge that we have been created in the image of God, is the single greatest segment of knowledge that can come to man in mortality. Mr. Mott, who is not a member of our church, indicated that that knowledge would give man a profound new sense of power and strength. ¶ We know that such is the case. We know that in and of ourselves we can do but little, but motivated with the spirit and knowledge that we have been created in the image of God, we can accomplish great things. ACR(Helsinki)1976:7

---

### 430. The spirit and body combined constitute our souls.

#### Joseph Smith

And the spirit and the body are the soul of man. (*Revelation received Dec. 27/28, 1832*) D&C 88:15

#### Joseph Smith,
*quoted by Elder Joseph Fielding Smith*

God made a tabernacle and put a spirit into it, and it became a living soul. . . . How does [the Bible] read in the Hebrew? It does not say in the Hebrew that God created the spirit of man. It says, "God made man out of the earth and put into him Adam's spirit, and so became a living body." (*To the Church in general conference— to a congregation of 20,000—, "King Follett Sermon," April 7, 1844*) (See HC6:302-17, also see The Words of Joseph Smith, pp. 340-62.) HC6:310; TPJS:354

### James E. Talmage

It is peculiar to the theology of the Latter-day Saints that we regard the body as an essential part of the soul. Read your dictionaries, the lexicons, and encyclopedias, and you will find that nowhere, outside of the Church of Jesus Christ, is the solemn and eternal truth taught that the soul of man is the body and the spirit combined. It is quite the rule to regard the soul as that incorporeal part of men, that immortal part which existed before the body was framed and which shall continue to exist after that body has gone to decay; nevertheless, that is not the soul; that is only a part of the soul; that is the spirit-man, the form in which every individual of us, and every individual human being, existed before called to take a tabernacle in the flesh. It has been declared in the solemn word of revelation, that the spirit and the body constitute the soul of man; and therefore, we should look upon this body as something that shall endure in the resurrected state, beyond the grave, something to be kept pure and holy. CR1913Oct:117

### Moses

And the LORD God formed man of the dust of the ground, and breathed into his nostrils the breath of life; and man became a living soul. (*Revelation to Moses with respect to the Creation*) Gen.2:7

### J. Reuben Clark, Jr.

[Christ's] real mission was to redeem man from the Fall of Adam by the atonement He made. We declare this is the greatest gift that ever came to man, for without it there would be no immortality of the soul, which is "the spirit and the body of man." ("I Am the Resurrection and the Life," IE1943Jan:63) TLDP:38

### Jacob, brother of Nephi,
*quoted by Nephi*

O how great the plan of our God! For on the other hand, the paradise of God must deliver up the spirits of the righteous, and the grave deliver up the body of the righteous; and the spirit and the body is restored to itself again, and all men become incorruptible, and immortal, and they are living souls, having a perfect knowledge like unto us in the flesh, save it be that our knowledge shall be perfect. (*Jacob recounts to the people of Nephi the covenants of the Lord made to the house of Israel, 559-545 B.C.*) 2Ne.9:13

### George F. Richards

The word immortal means not mortal; that is, not subject to the power of death. I would define immortality as being that state to which we attain in the progress of life when we have passed through death and the resurrection, the spirit and body being reunited and inseparably connected, constituting the soul of man prepared to receive a fulness of the glory of God. CR1916Apr:52

**President Brigham Young**

All spirits came from God, and they came pure from his presence, and were put into earthly tabernacles, which were organized for that express purpose; and so the spirit and the body became a living soul. If these souls should live, according to the law of heaven, God ordained that they should become temples prepared to inherit all things. (*In Tabernacle, Aug. 15, 1852, JD6:291*) TLDP:426

**Related Witnesses:**

**President Brigham Young, quoted by John A. Widtsoe**

After the body and spirit are separated by death, what, pertaining to this earth, shall we receive first? The body; that is the first object of a divine affection beyond the grave. We first come in possession of the body. The spirit has overcome the body, and the body is made subject in every respect to that divine principle God has planted in the person. The spirit within is pure and holy, and goes back pure and holy to God, dwells in the spirit world pure and holy, and, by and by, will have the privilege of coming and taking the body again. Some person holding the keys of the resurrection, having previously passed through that ordeal, will be delegated to resurrect our bodies, and our spirits will be there and prepared to enter into their bodies. Then, when we are prepared to receive our bodies, they are the first earthly objects that bear divinity personified in the capacity of the man. Only the body dies; the spirit is looking forth. (*In Bowery, July 28, 1861, JD9:139*) DBY:373

**President John Taylor**

Man is a dual being, possessed of body and spirit, made in the image of God, and connected with him and with eternity. He is a God in embryo and will live and progress throughout the eternal ages, if obedient to the laws of the Godhead, as the Gods progress throughout the eternal ages. (*General conference, April 1882, JD23:65*) TLDP:374

**John A. Widtsoe**

Man is immortal. The physical elements of earth cannot be destroyed, but only changed in their combinations; neither can the element of elements, the dominating element, the personality of man, be destroyed; but only changed as from an earthly to a spiritual condition. Man came on earth to win a body; only in association with the body, resurrected and purified, can

he approach the heights of salvation. The power to secure again the body buried in the grave comes from the vicarious sacrifice of our elder brother, the Lord Jesus Christ. He died that our journey on earth might not be in vain. (Man and the Dragon, p. 174) TLDP:375

**431. We will continue to exist forever with our own individual identity; a soul can never be annihilated.**

**President Lorenzo Snow**

That which dwells in this body of ours is immortal, and will always exist. Our individuality will always continue. Eternities may begin, eternities may end, and still we shall have our individuality. Our identity is insured. We will be ourselves, and nobody else. Whatever changes may arise, whatever worlds may be made or pass away, our identity will always remain the same; and we will continue on improving, advancing and increasing in wisdom, intelligence, power and dominion, worlds without end. Our present advancement is simply a starting out, as it were, on this path of immortality. Whatever may have been our past, how long we may have existed before this, or whether there ever was a time when we did not exist, there is one thing sure—our being in the future will never be annihilated, never destroyed. CR1901Apr:2

**Elder Joseph Fielding Smith**

A soul cannot be destroyed. ¶ Every soul born into this world shall receive the resurrection and immortality and shall endure forever. Destruction does not mean, then, annihilation. When the Lord says they shall be destroyed, he means that they shall be banished from his presence, that they shall be cut off from the presence of light and truth, and shall not have the privilege of gaining this exaltation; and that is destruction. (Doctrines of Salvation, 2:227-28) DCSM:19

**President Joseph F. Smith**

I refer to our identity, our indestructible, immortal identity. . . . (*Funeral of Rachel Grant, mother of President Heber J. Grant, IE1909Jun:591*) MPSG1970-71:41

**John A. Widtsoe**

Man is immortal. The physical elements of earth cannot be destroyed, but only changed in their combinations; neither can the element of elements, the dominating element, the personality of man, be destroyed; but only changed as from an earthly to a spiritual condition. (Man and the Dragon, p. 174) TLDP:375

### Alma, the younger,
*quoted by Mormon*

And now behold, I say unto you then cometh a death, even a second death, which is a spiritual death; then is a time that whosoever dieth in his sins, as to a temporal death, shall also die a spiritual death; yea, he shall die as to things pertaining unto righteousness. (*Alma contends with the lawyer Zeezrom, about 82 B.C.*) Alma 12:16

**Related Witnesses:**

### Samuel, the Lamanite,
*quoted by Mormon*

Yea, and it bringeth to pass the condition of repentance, that whosoever repenteth the same is not hewn down and cast into the fire; but whosoever repenteth not is hewn down and cast into the fire; and there cometh upon them again a spiritual death, yea, a second death, for they are cut off again as to things pertaining to righteousness. (*Samuel preaches to the Nephites, about 6 B.C.*) Hel.14:18

### President Joseph F. Smith

Their sleeping dust was to be restored unto its perfect frame bone to his bone, and the sinews and the flesh upon them, the spirit and the body to be united never again to be divided, that they might receive a fulness of joy. (*Vision regarding the Savior's visit to the spirits of the dead, Oct. 3, 1918*) D&C 138:17

---

### 432. As a child of God, each of us is of infinite worth.

### Joseph Smith

Remember the worth of souls is great in the sight of God; . . . (*Revelation received June 1829*) D&C 18:10

### George Q. Cannon

God in His infinite mercy has revealed to us a great truth. It is a truth that, when understood by us, gives a new light to our existence, and inspires us with the most exalted hopes. That truth is that God is our Father, and we are His children. What a tender relationship! What a feeling of nearness it creates within us! What? God my Father? Am I indeed His son? Am I indeed His daughter? Do I belong to the family of God? Is this literally true? The answer is, Yes. God has revealed it, that we are literally His children, His offspring; that we are just as much His children as our offspring are our children; that He begot us; and that we existed with Him in the family relationship as His children. What an immensity of vision is given to us in this truth! What a field for reflection! And how our hearts should be inspired with great

hopes and anticipations to think that the Being under whose direction this earth was organized, who governs the planets and controls the universe, who causes the rotation of the seasons and makes this earth so beautiful and such a delightful place of habitation, is our Father, and that we are His children, descended from Him! What illimitable hopes the knowledge of this inspires us with! ¶ Now, this is the truth. We humble people; we who feel ourselves sometimes so worthless, so good-for-nothing; we are not so worthless as we think. There is not one of us but what God's love has been expended upon. There is not one of us that He has not cared for and caressed. There is not one of us that He has not desired to save, and that He has not devised means to save. There is not one of us that He has not given His angels charge concerning. We may be insignificant and contemptible in our own eyes, and in the eyes of others, but the truth remains that we are the children of God, and that He has actually given His angels—invisible beings of power and might—charge concerning us, and they watch over us and have us in their keeping. ("Our Pre-existence and Present Probation," *Contributor*, Oct. 1890, p. 476) TLDP:376

### Richard L. Evans

We know of no one in life who isn't an Important Person. We know of no man on the street (or in the gutter, for that matter) who isn't a child of God with the same rights and with the same relationship to his Father in heaven as all the rest of us have. ¶ We know of no one, young or old, from infants to elderly individuals, whose past or whose potential we would want to appraise as being unimportant. We know of no one we might see in any public place—on subways or busses, or walking in shabby shoes—or any boy selling papers, or any abandoned urchin, who doesn't have an inestimable, unknown potential here and hereafter. (Richard L. Evans: The Man and the Message, p. 304) TLDP:375-76

### Marvin J. Ashton

I am certain our Heavenly Father is displeased when we refer to ourselves as "nobody". How fair are we when we classify ourselves a "nobody"? How fair are we to our families? How fair are we to our God? ¶ We do ourselves a great injustice when we allow ourselves, through tragedy, misfortune, challenge, discouragement, or whatever the earthly situation, to so identify ourselves. No matter how or where we find ourselves, we cannot with any justification, label ourselves "nobody". ¶ As children of God we are somebody. He will build us, mold us, and magnify us if we will but hold our heads up, our arms out, and walk with him. What a great blessing to be created in his image and know of our true potential in and through him! What a great blessing to know that in his strength we can do all things! CR1973Apr:21

**John A. Widtsoe**

Many sorrows of man are due to a false conception of man's relationship to the Lord and his fellowman. There can be little respect for human welfare of life, if man is but a higher animal, an accidental intruder on earth, or a creature of God, made at his pleasure, as children make mud pies. Man is a very son of God, begotten of God; he was the Father in the beginning. Since he is of a divine pedigree, with a spark of divinity within him, he rises immeasurably in the world of things. ¶ Then, the brotherhood of man, spoken of so lightly, often with a sneer, acquires a profound meaning. All men are children of God; brothers in fact; of the same divine pedigree; with the same high destiny; under the same loving guidance of the Father of the spirits of men. Then, every man must assume some of God's own responsibility in caring for the children of men. A person cannot let his very brothers go hungry, unclothed, shelterless or bowed down in sorrow. He cannot be cruel to them, and be true to his royal descent. CR1939Oct:98-99

**Marion G. Romney**

The truth I desire to emphasize today is that we mortals are in very deed the literal offspring of God. If men understood, believed, and accepted this truth and lived by it, our sick and dying society would be reformed and redeemed, and men would have peace here and now and eternal joy in the hereafter. ¶ Members of The Church of Jesus Christ of Latter-day Saints accept this concept as a basic doctrine of their theology. The lives of those who have given it thought enough to realize its implications are controlled by it; it gives meaning and direction to all their thoughts and deeds. This is so because they know that it is the universal law of nature in the plant, animal, and human worlds for reproducing offspring to reach in final maturity the likeness of their parents. ¶ They reason that the same law is in force with respect to the offspring of God. Their objective is, therefore, to someday be like their heavenly parents. ¶ They not only so reason; they know they may so become because God has revealed the fact that it is his work and glory to bring to pass their eternal life (Moses 1:39), which is the life God lives. CR1973Apr:133

## 433. Men and women may, at some time in the future, become gods.

**Joseph Smith,**
*receiving the Word of the Lord*

And again, verily I say unto you, if a man marry a wife by my word, which is my law, and by the new and everlasting covenant, and it is sealed unto them by the Holy Spirit of promise, by him who is anointed, unto whom I have appointed this power and the keys of this priesthood; and it shall be said unto them—Ye shall come forth in the first resurrection; and if it be after the first resurrection, in the next resurrection; and shall inherit thrones, kingdoms, principalities, and powers, dominions, all heights and depths— then shall it be written in the Lamb's Book of Life, that he shall commit no murder whereby to shed innocent blood, and if ye abide in my covenant, and commit no murder whereby to shed innocent blood, it shall be done unto them in all things whatsoever my servant hath put upon them, in time, and through all eternity; and shall be of full force when they are out of the world; and they shall pass by the angels, and the gods, which are set there, to their exaltation and glory in all things, as hath been sealed upon their heads, which glory shall be a fulness and a continuation of the seeds forever and ever. 20. Then shall they be gods, because they have no end; therefore shall they be from everlasting to everlasting, because they continue; then shall they be above all, because all things are subject unto them. Then shall they be gods, because they have all power, and the angels are subject unto them. (*Revelation relating to the new and everlasting covenant, including the eternal nature of the marriage covenant, July 12, 1843, [1831]*) D&C 132:19-20

**John A. Widtsoe**

To enter the highest of these degrees in the celestial kingdom is to be exalted in the kingdom of God. Such exaltation comes to those who receive the higher ordinances of the Church, such as the temple endowment, and afterwards are sealed in marriage for time and eternity, whether on earth or in the hereafter. Those who are so sealed continue the family relationship eternally. Spiritual children are begotten by them. They carry on the work of salvation for the hosts of waiting spirits. They who are so exalted become even as the gods. They will be "from everlasting to everlasting, because they continue." [D&C 132:20] (Evidences and Reconciliations, pp. 200-01) TLDP:163-64

**Wilford Woodruff**

There are a few individuals in this dispensation

who will inherit celestial glory, and a few in other dispensations; but before they receive their exaltation they will have to pass through and submit to whatever dispensation God may decree. But for all this they will receive their reward—they will become Gods, they will inherit thrones, kingdoms, principalities and powers through the endless ages of eternity, and to their increase there will be no end, and the heart of man has never conceived of the glory that is in store for the sons and daughters of God who keep the celestial law. (*At funeral services of two small children who had been burned to death, June 24, 1875, JD18:39*) TLDP:130

### James E. Talmage

[T]he Church proclaims the eternal truth: '*As man is, God once was; as God is, man may be.*' With such a future, well may man open his heart to the stream of revelation, past, present, and to come; . . . AF:390

### President Spencer W. Kimball

Each one of you has it within the realm of his possibility to develop a kingdom over which you will preside as its king and God. You will need to develop yourself and grow in ability and power and worthiness, to govern such a world with all of its people. You are sent to this earth not merely to have a good time or to satisfy urges or passions or desires. You are sent to this earth, not to ride merry-go-rounds, airplanes, automobiles, and have what the world calls "fun." ¶ You are sent to this world with a very serious purpose. You are sent to school, for that matter, to begin as a human infant and grow to unbelievable proportions in wisdom, judgment, knowledge, and power. That is why you and I cannot be satisfied with saying merely "I like that or want that." That is why in our childhood and our youth and our young adulthood we must stretch and grow and remember and prepare for the later life when limitations will terminate so that we can go on and on and on. (*To young men and young women at University of Utah institute, Oct. 1976*) DGSM:29

### Elder Lorenzo Snow

Through a continual course of progression, our heavenly Father has received exaltation and glory, and he points us out the same path; and inasmuch as he is clothed with power, authority, and glory, he says, 'Walk ye up and come in possession of the same glory and happiness that I possess.' (*Sermon to a male and female audience in Tabernacle, Oct. 1857, JD5:313*) DGSM:92

### Joseph Smith

Here, then, is eternal life—to know the only wise and true God; and you have got to learn how to be gods yourselves, and to be kings and priests to God, the same as all gods have done before you, namely, by going from one small degree to another, and from a small capacity to a great one; from grace to grace, from exaltation to exaltation, until you attain to the resurrection of the dead, and are able to dwell in everlasting burnings, and to sit in glory, as do those who sit enthroned in everlasting power. (*To the Church in general conference—to a congregation of 20,000—, "King Follett Sermon," April 7, 1844*) (See HC6:302-17, also see The Words of Joseph Smith, pp. 340-62.) HC6:306

### Related Witnesses:

### Bruce R. McConkie

Now, this plan [plan of salvation] was to enable his spirit children to grow from their primeval spirit state to a state of glory and dignity and exaltation so that they would be like him—like the Father. The name of the kind of life that God the Father lives is eternal life. This name describes wholly and completely the nature and kind of life he possesses; his life includes having power and dominion, might and glory and omnipotence, and also it includes living in the family relationship. In God's instance, we were among his spirit offspring. (*Making Our Calling and Election Sure, pp. 5-6, in Brigham Young University Speeches of the Year, 1969*) MPSG1974/75:8-9

### Bruce R. McConkie

But we do know that our Eternal Father . . . lives in the family unit. We do know that we are his children, created in his image, endowed with power and ability to become like him. CR1974Apr:103

### Joseph Smith

[S]alvation consists in the glory, authority, majesty, power and dominion which Jehovah possesses and in nothing else; and no being can possess it but himself or one like him. (*Lectures on Faith delivered to the School of the Prophets, 1834-35*) LOF7:9

### Joseph Smith

This fills up the measure of information on this subject, and shows most clearly that the Savior wished his disciples to understand that they were to be partakers with him in all things, not even his glory excepted. (*Lectures on Faith delivered to the School of the Prophets, 1834-35*) LOF7:14

### Joseph Smith,
### *receiving the Word of the Lord*

I am Jesus Christ, the Son of God, who was crucified for the sins of the world, even as many as will believe on my name, that they may become the sons of God, even one in me as I am one in the Father, as the Father is one in me, that we may be one. (*Revelation to Joseph Smith and Sidney Rigdon, Dec. 1830*) D&C 35:2

**Joseph Smith**

That by keeping the commandments they might be washed and cleansed from all their sins, and receive the Holy Spirit by the laying on of the hands of him who is ordained and sealed unto this power; . . . 54. They are they who are the church of the Firstborn. 55. They are they into whose hands the Father has given all things— 56. They are they who are priests and kings, who have received of his fulness, and of his glory; 57. And are priests of the Most High, after the order of Melchizedek, which was after the order of Enoch, which was after the order of the Only Begotten Son. 58. Wherefore, as it is written, they are gods, even the sons of God. . . . 62. These shall dwell in the presence of God and his Christ forever and ever. . . . 70. These are they whose bodies are celestial, whose glory is that of the sun, even the glory of God, the highest of all, whose glory the sun of the firmament is written of as being typical. (*Vision to Joseph Smith and Sidney Rigdon, Feb. 16, 1832*) D&C 76:52,54-58,62,70

**President Spencer W. Kimball**

Now, the sealing for eternity gives to you eternal leadership. The man will have the authority of the priesthood, and if he keeps his life in order he will become a god. . . . The Lord created this earth for us and made it a beautiful place to live. He promised us that if we would live the right way we could come back to him and be like him. ACR(Sao Paulo)1975:43; DGSM:71

# List of Doctrines

## MARRIAGE: Husband and Wife

*Doctrines Located in This Topic*

434. When a man and woman marry, they are to be united as one.

435. Marriage is ordained of God and is designed to be an eternal union of man and woman.

436. The temple marriage sealing ordinance is essential for exaltation in the celestial kingdom (it is a prerequisite to exaltation in the highest degree of the celestial kingdom).

437. A marriage not performed with the sealing power of the priesthood is not valid after this life.

438. A couple whose marriage is sealed by the power of the priesthood must yet live righteously throughout life for that marriage to survive death.

439. Husbands are to love and be considerate of their wives.

440. Husbands are not to abuse their wives.

441. Wives are to follow the righteous counsel of their husbands.

442. Divorce contravenes the law of God.

*Doctrines on MARRIAGE: Husband and Wife Located in Other Topics*

112. The sealing ordinance of marriage is an everlasting covenant between God and those who are sealed.

142. To receive exaltation (the highest degree in the celestial kingdom) a person must be married in the new and everlasting covenant.

(See topic
FAMILY AND PARENTHOOD.)

# MARRIAGE: Husband and Wife

**434. When a man and woman marry, they are to be united as one.**

### Jesus,
### *recorded in Mark*

But from the beginning of the creation God made them male and female. 7. For this cause shall a man leave his father and mother, and cleave to his wife; 8. And they twain shall be one flesh: so then they are no more twain, but one flesh. 9. What therefore God hath joined together, let not man put asunder. (*Jesus answers the Pharisees, teaching the higher law of marriage*) Mark 10:6-9

### President Spencer W. Kimball

[O]ur partnerships with our eternal companions, our wives, must be full partnerships. . . . ¶ Our sisters do not wish to be indulged or to be treated condescendingly; they desire to be respected and revered as our sisters and our equals. . . . We will be judged, as the Savior said on several occasions, by whether or not we love one another and treat one another accordingly and by whether or not we are of one heart and one mind. We cannot be the Lord's if we are not one! CR1979Oct:71-72

### Bruce R. McConkie

This is the very heart and core of the whole matter. God made man, male and female created he them, so they could marry; so they could provide bodies for his spirit children; so they could create for themselves eternal family units. God brought the woman unto the man and gave her to him to be his wife. He did it in Eden, before the fall; all things were then immortal; death had not entered the world. The first marriage—performed by the Lord God himself—was a celestial marriage, an eternal marriage, a union of Adam and Eve that was destined to last forever. There was no death; there was to be no divorce; the man and his wife were to be one flesh forever. Such was the pattern. All men thereafter should be as their first parents. Men and women should marry as did Adam and Eve—in celestial marriage—and should cleave unto each other as the divine pattern required. What God does is forever. And what he hath joined in eternal union, let not man put asunder. Divorce is no part of the eternal plan. (The Mortal Messiah, 3:294-95) TLDP:383

### Paul

For this cause shall a man leave his father and mother, and shall be joined unto his wife, and they two shall be one flesh. (*Paul writes to the Saints at Ephesus in Asia Minor, about A.D. 62*) Eph.5:31

### Moses

And the LORD God said, It is not good that the man should be alone; I will make him an help meet for him. . . . 24. Therefore shall a man leave his father and his mother, and shall cleave unto his wife: and they shall be one flesh. (*Revelation to Moses with respect to the Creation; woman is created*) Gen.2:18,24

### Joseph Smith

Wherefore, it is lawful that he should have one wife, and they twain shall be one flesh, and all this that the earth might answer the end of its creation; (*Revelation refuting the Shaker doctrine of celibacy, March 1831*) D&C 49:16-17

**Related Witnesses:**

### Paul

And unto the married I command, yet not I, but the Lord, Let not the wife depart from her husband: (*Letter to the Church at Corinth, Greece, about A.D. 55*) 1Cor.7:10

### Elder Ezra Taft Benson

Adam and Eve provide us with an ideal example of a covenant marriage relationship. They labored together; they had children together; they prayed together; and they taught their children the gospel—together. This is the pattern God would have all righteous men and women imitate. (Woman, p. 70) TLDP:388

### Joseph Smith,
### *receiving the Word of the Lord*

Thou shalt love thy wife with all thy heart, and shalt cleave unto her and none else. (*Revelation "embracing the law of the Church," Feb. 9, 1831*) D&C 42:22

### Elder Spencer W. Kimball

In a properly charted Latter-day Saint marriage, one must be conscious of the need to forget self and love one's companion more than self. There will not be postponement of parenthood, but a desire for children as the Lord intended, and without limiting the family as the world does. The children will be wanted and loved. There will be fidelity and confidence; eyes will never wander and thoughts will never stray toward extra-marital romance. In a very literal sense, husband and wife will keep themselves for each other only, in mind and body and spirit. . . . ¶ There are those married people who permit their eyes to wander and their hearts to become vagrant, who think it is not improper to flirt a little, to share their hearts and have desire for someone other than the wife or the husband. The Lord says in definite terms: "Thou shalt love thy wife with all thy heart, and shalt cleave unto her and none else." (D&C 42:22) [Italics added.] ¶ The words *none else* eliminate everyone and everything. The spouse then becomes pre-eminent in the life of the husband or wife and neither social life nor occupational life nor political life nor any other interest nor person nor thing shall ever take precedence over the companion spouse. We sometimes find women who absorb and hover over the children at the expense of the husband, sometimes even estranging them from him. This is in direct violation of the command: *None else.* (The Miracle of Forgiveness, p. 250) TLDP:387

**Author's Note:** Definition of *to cleave*: To adhere closely. To remain faithful. (The Random House Dictionary of the English Language, p. 384)

**435. Marriage is ordained of God and is designed to be an eternal union of man and woman.**

**Elder Harold B. Lee**

Now let us consider the first marriage that was performed after the earth was organized [Adam and Eve]. . . . Here was a marriage performed by the Lord between two immortal beings, for until sin entered the world their bodies were not subject to death. He made them one, not merely for time, for any definite period; they were to be one throughout the eternal ages. (Decisions for Successful Living, p. 125) DGSM:75-76

**President Joseph F. Smith**

Why did He teach us the principle of eternal union of man and wife? Because God knew that we were His children here, to remain His children forever and ever, and that we were just as truly individuals, and that our individuality was as identical as that of the Son of God, and would therefore continue . . . worlds without end, so that the man receiving his wife by the power of God, for time and for all eternity, would have the right to claim her and she to claim her husband, in the world to come. Neither would be changed, except from mortality to immortality, neither would be other than himself or herself, but they will have their identity in the world to come, precisely as they exercise their individuality and enjoy their identity here. God has revealed this principle, and it has its bearing upon the evidence that we possess of the actual, literal resurrection of the body, just as it is and as the prophets have declared it in the Book of Mormon. CR1912Apr:136-37

**President Joseph F. Smith**

To the Latter-day Saints, marriage is not designed by our heavenly Father to be merely an

earthly union, but one that shall survive the vicissitudes of time, and endure for eternity, bestowing honor and joy in this world, glory and eternal lives in the worlds to come. (*Address from the First Presidency of the Church to the world, delivered to and accepted by vote of the Church in general conference, April 1907*) CR1907Apr(Appendix)7

**Joseph Smith,**
*receiving the Word of the Lord*

And again, verily I say unto you, if a man marry a wife by my word, which is my law, and by the new and everlasting covenant, and it is sealed unto them by the Holy Spirit of promise, by him who is anointed, unto whom I have appointed this power and the keys of this priesthood; and it shall be said unto them—Ye shall come forth in the first resurrection; and if it be after the first resurrection, in the next resurrection; and shall inherit thrones, kingdoms, principalities, and powers, dominions, all heights and depths— then shall it be written in the Lamb's Book of Life, that he shall commit no murder whereby to shed innocent blood, and if ye abide in my covenant, and commit no murder whereby to shed innocent blood, it shall be done unto them in all things whatsoever my servant hath put upon them, in time, and through all eternity; and shall be of full force when they are out of the world; and they shall pass by the angels, and the gods, which are set there, to their exaltation and glory in all things, as hath been sealed upon their heads, which glory shall be a fulness and a continuation of the seeds forever and ever. 20. Then shall they be gods, because they have no end; therefore shall they be from everlasting to everlasting, because they continue; then shall they be above all, because all things are subject unto them. Then shall they be gods, because they have all power, and the angels are subject unto them. (*Revelation relating to the new and everlasting covenant, including the eternal nature of the marriage covenant, July 12, 1843, [1831]*) D&C 132:19-20

**Charles W. Penrose**

Under the law of God a man and woman should be joined together for all eternity, she to be bone of his bone, and flesh of his flesh, spirit answering to spirit, soul to soul, joined together with an eternal bond, to exist in life, in death, in the resurrection, and throughout the countless ages of eternity; this was the union at "the beginning;" that is the right kind of marriage, and the marriage that we Latter-day Saints should support and sustain and teach to our children, that they may enter into it prepared to gain the benefits thereof. CR1911Apr:37

**President Spencer W. Kimball**

The greatest joys of true married life can be continued. The most beautiful relationships of parents and children can be made permanent. The holy association of families can be never-ending if husband and wife have been sealed in the holy bond of eternal matrimony. Their joys and progress will never end, but this will never fall into place of its own accord. . . . ¶ God has restored the knowledge of temples and their purposes. On the earth this day are holy structures built to this special work of the Lord, and each is the house of the Lord. In these temples, by duly constituted authority, are men who can seal husbands and wives and their children for all eternity. This is a fact even though it is unknown to many. (Teachings of Spencer W. Kimball, p. 297; sermon, 1974) DGSM:75

**James E. Talmage**

Marriage, as regarded by the Latter-day Saints, is ordained of God and designed to be an eternal relationship of the sexes. With this people it is not merely a temporal contract to be of effect on earth during the mortal existence of the parties, but a solemn agreement which is to extend beyond the grave. In the complete ordinance of marriage, the man and the woman are placed under covenant of mutual fidelity, not "until death doth you part," but "for time and for all eternity." A contract as far reaching as this, extending not only throughout time but into the domain of the hereafter, requires for its validation an authority superior to that of earth; and such an authority is found in the Holy Priesthood, which, given of God, is eternal. Any power less than this, while of effect in this life, is void as to the state of the human soul beyond the grave. AF:403

**Related Witnesses:**

**Paul**

Nevertheless neither is the man without the woman, neither the woman without the man, in the Lord. 12. For as the woman is of the man, even so is the man also by the woman; but all things of God. (*Letter to the Church at Corinth, Greece, about* A.D. 55) 1Cor.11:11-12

**President Spencer W. Kimball**

Marriage is ordained of God. It is not merely a social custom. Without proper and successful marriage, one will never be exalted. (Teachings of Spencer W. Kimball, p. 291; sermon, 1971) DGSM:75

**President Heber J. Grant**

There is no doubt in the mind of any true Latter-day Saint, man or woman, as to the fact of individual existence beyond the grave, as to the fact that we shall know each other, and as to

the endless duration of the covenant of marriage that has been performed in the house of the Lord for time and eternity. ("A Promise of Possibilities," IE1941Jun:329) TLDP:382

**Jesus,**
*recorded in Matthew*

And said, For this cause shall a man leave father and mother, and shall cleave to his wife: and they twain shall be one flesh? 6. Wherefore they are no more twain, but one flesh. What therefore God hath joined together, let not man put asunder. (*Jesus answers the Pharisees and teaches about marriage and divorce*) Matt.19:5-6

**Joseph Smith**

And again, verily I say unto you, that whoso forbiddeth to marry is not ordained of God, for marriage is ordained of God unto man. 16. Wherefore, it is lawful that he should have one wife, and they twain shall be one flesh, and all this that the earth might answer the end of its creation; 17. And that it might be filled with the measure of man, according to his creation before the world was made. (*Revelation refuting the Shaker doctrine of celibacy, March 1831*) D&C 49:15-17

**President Spencer W. Kimball**

It is the normal thing to marry. It was arranged by God in the beginning, long before this world's mountains were ever formed. Remember: "Neither is the man without the woman, neither the woman without the man." (1Cor.11:11) . . . Every person should want to be married because that is what God in heaven planned for us. (Teachings of Spencer W. Kimball, p. 291; sermon, 1976) DGSM:75

**Recorded in Ecclesiastes**

Two are better than one; because they have a good reward for their labour. 10. For if they fall, the one will lift up his fellow: but woe to him that is alone when he falleth; for he hath not another to help him up. (*Reflections of a son of David the king*) Eccl.4:9-10

---

436. The temple marriage sealing ordinance is essential for exaltation in the celestial kingdom (it is a prerequisite to exaltation in the highest degree of the celestial kingdom).

**President Harold B. Lee**

For remember, brethren, that only those who enter into the new and everlasting covenant of marriage in the temple for time and eternity, only those will have the exaltation in the celestial kingdom. That is what the Lord tells us. CR1973Oct:120

### Elder Spencer W. Kimball

Clearly, attaining eternal life is not a matter of goodness only. This is one of the two important elements, but one must practice righteousness *and* receive the ordinances. People who do not bring their lives into harmony with God's laws and who do not receive the necessary ordinances either in this life or (if that is impossible) in the next, have thus deprived themselves, and will remain separate and single in the eternities. There they will have no spouses, no children. If one is going to be in God's kingdom of exaltation, where God dwells in all his glory, one will be there as a husband or a wife and not otherwise. Regardless of his virtues, the single person, or the one married for this life only, cannot be exalted. All normal people should marry and rear families. To quote Brigham Young: "No man can be perfect without the woman, so no woman can be perfect without a man to lead her. I tell you the truth as it is in the bosom of eternity. If he wishes to be saved, he cannot be saved without a woman by his side." ¶ Celestial marriage is that important. (The Miracle of Forgiveness, p. 245) TLDP:380

### Joseph Smith

In the celestial glory there are three heavens or degrees; 2. And in order to obtain the highest, a man must enter into this order of the priesthood, meaning the new and everlasting covenant of marriage; 3. And if he does not, he cannot obtain it. 4. He may enter into the other, but that is the end of his kingdom; he cannot have an increase. (*Instructions, May 16/17, 1843*) D&C 131:1-4

### Hugh B. Brown

Without the sealing ordinances of temple marriage, man cannot achieve a godlike stature or receive a fullness of joy because the unmarried person is not a whole person, is not complete. ("The LDS Concept of Marriage," IE1962Aug:572) TLDP:380

### President Spencer W. Kimball

I remember we had in our community in Arizona a good man who passed away. He and his lovely wife had resisted the teachings of the Church. And the wife, when he died, said, "I know that we will be associated as husband and wife through eternity." But she could say that a thousand times and it would still not come true because they were not humble enough to accept the law of marriage. They may receive other blessings, but not exaltation. That is reserved for those who are faithful and who obey the

commandments. (*Tokyo Japan area conference, Aug. 1975*) DGSM:77

### Joseph Smith

Except a man and his wife enter into an everlasting covenant and be married for eternity, while in this probation, by the power and authority of the Holy Priesthood, they will cease to increase when they die; that is, they will not have any children after the resurrection. But those who are married by the power and authority of the priesthood in this life, and continue without committing the sin against the Holy Ghost, will continue to increase and have children in the celestial glory. (*Instructions on the priesthood given Brother and Sister Benjamin F. Johnson at Ramus, Ill., May 16, 1843*) HC5:391

### Elder Joseph Fielding Smith

Since marriage is ordained of God, and the man is not without the woman, neither the woman without the man in the Lord, there can be no exaltation to the fullness of the blessings of the celestial kingdom outside of the marriage relation. A man cannot be exalted singly and alone; neither can a woman. Each must have a companion to share the honors and blessings of this great exaltation. Marriage for time and all eternity brings to pass the crowning glory of our Father's kingdom by which his children become his heirs, into whose hands he gives all things. ¶ If a man and his wife are saved in separate kingdoms, for instance, the celestial and terrestrial, automatically the sealing is broken; it is broken because of the sins of one of the parties. No one can be deprived of exaltation who remains faithful. In other words, an undeserving husband cannot prevent a faithful wife from an exaltation and vice versa. In this case the faithful servant would be given to someone who is faithful. (Doctrines of Salvation, 2:65) TLDP:379

### Joseph Smith,
### *receiving the Word of the Lord*

And again, verily I say unto you, if a man marry a wife by my word, which is my law, and by the new and everlasting covenant, and it is sealed unto them by the Holy Spirit of promise, by him who is anointed, unto whom I have appointed this power and the keys of this priesthood; and it shall be said unto them—Ye shall come forth in the first resurrection; and if it be after the first resurrection, in the next resurrection; and shall inherit thrones, kingdoms, principalities, and powers, dominions, all heights and depths—then shall it be written in the Lamb's Book of Life, that he shall commit no murder whereby to shed innocent blood, and if ye abide in my covenant, and commit no murder whereby to shed innocent blood, it shall be done unto them in all things whatsoever my servant hath put upon them, in time, and through all eternity; and shall be of full force when they are out of the world; and they shall pass by the angels, and the gods, which are set there, to their exaltation and glory in all things, as hath been sealed upon their heads, which glory shall be a fulness and a continuation of the seeds forever and ever. 20. Then shall they be gods, because they have no end; therefore shall they be from everlasting to everlasting, because they continue; then shall they be above all, because all things are subject unto them. Then shall they be gods, because they have all power, and the angels are subject unto them. (*Revelation relating to the new and everlasting covenant, including the eternal nature of the marriage covenant, July 12, 1843, [1831]*) D&C 132:19-20

### James E. Talmage

This system of holy matrimony, involving covenants for both time and eternity, is known distinctively as *Celestial Marriage*, and is understood to be the order of marriage that exists in the celestial worlds. This sacred ordinance is administered by the Church to those only who are adjudged to be of worthy life, fit to be admitted to the House of the Lord; for this holy rite, together with others of eternal validity, may be solemnized only within the temples reared and dedicated for such exalted service. . . . ¶ . . . . The ordinance of celestial marriage, whereby the contracting parties, whether living or dead, are united under the authority of the Holy Priesthood for time and eternity, is known distinctively as the ceremony of *Sealing in Marriage*. Husband and wife so united are said to be sealed, whereas if united under the lesser law for time only, either by secular or ecclesiastical authority, they are only married. HL:88-89

**Related Witnesses:**

### Parley P. Pratt

All persons who attain to the resurrection, and to salvation, without these eternal ordinances, or sealing covenants, will remain in a *single state*, in their saved condition, without the joys of eternal union with the other sex, and consequently without a crown, without a kingdom, without the power to increase. ¶ Hence, they are angels, and are not gods; and are ministering spirits, or servants, in the employ and under the direction of the Royal Family of heaven—the princes, kings and priests of eternity. (Key to the Science of Theology, pp. 169-70) TLDP:379

### President Spencer W. Kimball

Marriage is ordained of God. It is not merely a social custom. Without proper and successful marriage, one will never be exalted. (Teachings of Spencer W. Kimball, p. 291; sermon, 1976) DGSM:75

### President Spencer W. Kimball

No one who voluntarily rejects marriage here in mortality has any assurance of eternal life. ("Marriage is Honorable," Brigham Young University Speeches of the Year, 1973, p. 268) TLDP:380

### Bruce R. McConkie

Men are not saved alone and women do not gain an eternal fulness except in and through the continuation of the family unit in eternity. Salvation is a family affair. ¶ . . . . That is, the man and his wife together, and not either one of them alone, shall be exalted. They shall have eternal life; they shall fill the full measure of their creation; they shall inherit, receive, and possess all things. ACR(Nuku'alofa)1976:34

### Marion G. Romney

The new and everlasting covenant of celestial marriage is the gate to exaltation in the celestial kingdom. CR1962Apr:17

### Paul

Nevertheless neither is the man without the woman, neither the woman without the man, in the Lord. 12. For as the woman is of the man, even so is the man also by the woman; but all things of God. (*Letter to the Church at Corinth, Greece, about A.D. 55*) 1Cor.11:11-12

---

### 437. A marriage not performed with the sealing power of the priesthood is not valid after this life.

### President Joseph F. Smith

Unless man and wife are married by the power of God and by his authority, they become single again, they have no claim upon each other, after death; their contract is filled by that time, and is therefore of no force in and after the resurrection from the dead, nor after they are dead; . . . therefore, when they are out of the world, they neither marry nor are given in marriage, but become as angels in heaven. ("Marriage God-Ordained and Sanctioned," IE1902Jul:716) TLDP:381

### Joseph Smith,
*receiving the Word of the Lord*

Therefore, if a man marry him a wife in the world, and he marry her not by me nor by my word, and he covenant with her so long as he is in the world and she with him, their covenant and marriage are not of force when they are dead, and when they are out of the world;

therefore, they are not bound by any law when they are out of the world. 16. Therefore, when they are out of the world they neither marry nor are given in marriage; but are appointed angels in heaven, which angels are ministering servants, to minister for those who are worthy of a far more, and an exceeding, and an eternal weight of glory. 17. For these angels did not abide my law; therefore, they cannot be enlarged, but remain separately and singly, without exaltation, in their saved condition, to all eternity; and from henceforth are not gods, but are angels of God forever and ever. (*Revelation relating to the new and everlasting covenant, including the eternal nature of the marriage covenant, July 12, 1843, [1831]*) D&C 132:15-17

### President Heber J. Grant,
### J. Reuben Clark, Jr., David O. McKay
### (First Presidency)

Amongst His earliest commands to Adam and Eve, the Lord said: "Multiply and replenish the earth." He has repeated that commandment in our day. He has again revealed in this, the last dispensation, the principle of the eternity of the marriage covenant. He has restored to the earth the authority for entering into that covenant, and has declared that it is the only due and proper way of joining husband and wife, and the only means by which the sacred family relationship may be carried beyond the grave and through eternity. He has declared that this eternal relationship may be created only by the ordinances which are administered in the holy temples of the Lord, and therefore that His people should marry only in His temple in accordance with such ordinances. CR1942Oct:12

### Elder Joseph Fielding Smith

Naturally, if men and women, when they marry become members of the family of God, and are entitled to the blessings of eternal increase after the resurrection, the ordinance and covenant of marriage must be by divine authority. The privilege to perform such marriages cannot be promiscuously assumed by any individual or minister. There is but one at a time who holds these divine keys. He has the authority to delegate authority to others to perform marriages for time and for all eternity, and unless this authority is granted, marriages for time and eternity would not be binding beyond this mortal life. Naturally those who wish to marry must subscribe to the laws of the state. No minister or even elder of the Church has the authority to perform marriages and seal for time and all eternity except those who have been duly delegated the authority from the one who holds these divine keys—the President of the Church. (Answers to Gospel Questions, 4:146) TLDP:381

### Related Witnesses:
### Joseph Smith,
### *receiving the Word of the Lord*

And verily I say unto you, that the conditions of this law are these: All covenants, contracts, bonds, obligations, oaths, vows, performances, connections, associations, or expectations, that are not made and entered into and sealed by the Holy Spirit of promise, of him who is anointed, both as well for time and for all eternity, and that too most holy, by revelation and commandment through the medium of mine anointed, whom I have appointed on the earth to hold this power (and I have appointed unto my servant Joseph to hold this power in the last days, and there is never but one on the earth at a time on whom this power and the keys of this priesthood are conferred), are of no efficacy, virtue, or force in and after the resurrection from the dead; for all contracts that are not made unto this end have an end when men are dead. (*Revelation relating to the new and everlasting covenant, including the eternal nature of the marriage covenant, July 12, 1843, [1831]*) D&C 132:7

### Elder John Taylor

Why is a woman sealed to man for time and all eternity? Because there is legitimate power on earth to do it. This power will bind on earth and in heaven; it can loose on earth, and it is loosed in heaven; it can seal on earth, and it is sealed in heaven. There is a legitimate, authorized agent of God upon earth; this sealing power is regulated by him; hence what is done by that, is done right, and is recorded. When the books are opened, every one will find his proper mate and have those that belong to him, and every one will be deprived of that which is surreptitiously obtained. (*General conference, April 1853, JD1:232*) TLDP:381

### James E. Talmage

Marriage covenants authorized and sealed by that God-given power, endure, if the parties thereto are true to their troth, not through mortal life alone, but through time and all eternity. Thus the worthy husband and wife who have been sealed under the everlasting covenant shall come forth in the day of the resurrection to receive their heritage of glory, immortality, and eternal lives. (Young Womens' Journal, Oct. 1914, p. 604) DGSM:77

### Boyd K. Packer

Seal is the right word, therefore, to be used to represent spiritual authority. In this case it is not represented by an imprint, by a wax impression, by an embossment, or by a ribbon; nor by an engravement on a signet, or by a stamp, or by a gold design pressed onto a document. The seal of official authority relating to spiritual matters, like other things spiritual, can be identified by the influence that is felt when the sealing power is exercised. ¶ The sealing power represents the transcendent delegation of spiritual authority from God to man. The keeper of that sealing power is the Lord's chief representative here upon earth. That is the position of consummate trust and authority. We speak often of holding the key to that sealing power in the Church. ¶ Much of the teaching relating to the deeper spiritual things in the Church, particularly in the temple, is symbolic. We use the word *keys* in a symbolic way. Here the keys of priesthood authority represent the limits of the power extended from beyond the veil to mortal man to act in the name of God upon the earth. The words *seal* and *keys* and *priesthood* are closely linked together. (The Holy Temple, p. 82) DGSM:76

### Jesus,
### *recorded in Matthew*

And I will give unto thee the keys of the kingdom of heaven: and whatsoever thou shalt bind on earth shall be bound in heaven: . . . (*Jesus instructs his disciples, he addresses Peter*) Matt.16:19

---

**438. A couple whose marriage is sealed by the power of the priesthood must yet live righteously throughout life for that marriage to survive death.**

### Elder Spencer W. Kimball

Now, all Latter-day Saints are not going to be exalted. All people who have been through the holy temple are not going to be exalted. The Lord says, "Few there be that find it." For there are the two elements: (1) the sealing of a marriage in the holy temple, and (2) righteous living through one's life thereafter to make that sealing permanent. Only through proper marriage—and I repeat that—only through proper marriage . . . can one find that strait way, the narrow path. No one can ever have life, real life, in any other way under any other program. ("Marriage is Honorable," Brigham Young University Speeches of the Year, 1973, pp. 265-66) TLDP:183

### Elder Joseph Fielding Smith

We can say most positively that all those who are married in the temple for time and all eternity receive their blessings and enter their covenants with these promises based upon their faithfulness. If it so happens that they do sin and break their covenants, but have not sinned unto death, they will have to repent completely and faithfully of all their sins or they will never enter the celestial glory. No unrepentant person who remains in his sins will ever enter into the glories of the celestial kingdom. (Answers to Gospel Questions, 1:73) TLDP:183

### Joseph Smith

But those who are married by the power and authority of the priesthood in this life, and continue without committing the sin against the Holy Ghost, will continue to increase and have children in the celestial glory. (*Instructions on the priesthood to Brother and Sister Benjamin F. Johnson at Ramus, Ill., May 16, 1843*) TPJS:300-01; HC5:391; DGSM:77

### Bruce R. McConkie

Righteous acts are approved of the Lord; they are ratified by the Holy Ghost; they are sealed by the Holy Spirit of Promise; or, in other words, they are justified by the Spirit. Such divine approval must be given to "all covenants, contracts, bonds, obligations, oaths, vows, performances, connections, associations, or expectations"—that is, to all things—if they are to have "efficacy, virtue, or force in and after the resurrection from the dead." (D&C 132:7) Such a requirement is part of the terms and conditions of the gospel covenant. ¶ . . . . In the eternal sense, Israel consists of the members of the Church who keep the commandments and are thereby justified in this life and saved in the life to come. The wicked, of course, are not justified. (Alma 41:13-15) (The Promised Messiah, pp. 344-45) TLDP:333

### Joseph Smith,
### *receiving the Word of the Lord*

And again, verily I say unto you, if a man marry a wife by my word, which is my law, and by the new and everlasting covenant, and it is sealed unto them by the Holy Spirit of promise, by him who is anointed, unto whom I have appointed this power and the keys of this priesthood; and it shall be said unto them—Ye shall come forth in the first resurrection; and if it be after the first resurrection, in the next resurrection; and shall inherit thrones, kingdoms, principalities, and powers, dominions, all heights and depths—then shall it be written in the Lamb's Book of Life, that he shall commit no murder whereby to shed innocent blood, and if ye abide in my covenant, and commit no murder whereby to shed innocent blood, it shall be done unto them in all things whatsoever my servant hath put upon them, in time, and through all eternity; and shall be of full force when they are out of the world; and they shall pass by the angels, and the gods, which are set there, to their exaltation and glory in all things, as hath been sealed upon their heads, which glory shall be a fulness and a continuation of the seeds forever and ever. (*Revelation relating to the new and everlasting covenant, including the eternal nature of the marriage covenant, July 12, 1843, [1831]*) D&C 132:19

**Related Witnesses:**

**President Brigham Young**

Those who are faithful will continue to increase, and this is the great blessing the Lord has given to, or placed within the reach of, the children of man, even to be capable of receiving eternal lives. ¶ To have such a promise so sealed upon our heads, which no power on earth, in heaven, or beneath the earth can take from us, to be sealed up to the day of redemption and have the promise of eternal lives, is the greatest gift of all. (*In Tabernacle, June 3, 1855, JD2:301*) TLDP:384-85

**Author's Note:** Elder Bruce R. McConkie, prior to his calling to be a latter-day prophet/apostle, wrote the following, which has since been quoted in the Church published *Doctrines of the Gospel Student Manual*: "The Holy Spirit of Promise is the Holy Spirit *promised* the saints, or in other words the Holy Ghost. This name-title is used in connection with the sealing and ratifying power of the Holy Ghost, that is, the power given him to ratify and approve the righteous acts of men so that those acts will be binding on earth and in heaven. . . . ¶ To seal is to *ratify*, to *justify*, or to *approve.* Thus an act which is sealed by the Holy Spirit of Promise is one which is ratified by the Holy Ghost; it is one which is approved by the Lord; and the person who has taken the obligation upon himself is justified by the Spirit in the thing he has done. ¶ The ratifying seal of approval is put upon an act only if those entering the contract are worthy as a result of personal righteousness to receive the divine approbation. They "are sealed by the Holy Spirit of promise, which the Father sheds forth upon all those who are *just* and *true.*" (D&C 76:53) If they are not just and true and worthy the ratifying seal is withheld. (Mormon Doctrine, pp. 361-62; DGSM:77)

**439. Husbands are to love and be considerate of their wives.**

**President Spencer W. Kimball**

As the Lord loves his church and serves it, so

men should love their wives and serve them and their families. . . . ¶ Husbands are commanded: "Love your wives, even as Christ also loved the church, and gave himself for it." (Eph.5:25) And that is a high ambition. ¶ And here is the answer: Christ loved the Church and its people so much that he voluntarily endured persecution for them, suffered humiliating indignities for them, stoically withstood pain and physical abuse for them, and finally gave his precious life for them. ¶ When the husband is ready to treat his household in that manner, not only the wife, but all the family will respond to his leadership. Certainly if fathers are to be respected, they must merit respect. If they are to be loved, they must be consistent, lovable, understanding, and kind and must honor their priesthood. ACR(Stockholm)1974:46-47

**Gordon B. Hinckley**

As a husband [a man], would live with respect for his wife, standing side by side with her, never belittling her nor demeaning her but rather encouraging her in the continued development of her talents and in the church activities which are available to her. He would regard her as the greatest treasure of his life, one with whom he can share his concerns, his innermost thoughts, his ambitions and hopes. There would never be in that home any "unrighteous dominion" of husband over wife (see D&C 121:37,39), no assertion of superiority, but rather an expression in living which says that these two are equally yoked. ¶ No man can please his Heavenly Father who fails to respect the daughters of God. No man can please his Heavenly Father who fails to magnify his wife and companion, and nurture and build and strengthen and share with her. CR1985Apr:65

**President David O. McKay**

Let us instruct young people who come to us, to know that a woman should be queen of her own body. The marriage covenant does not give the man the right to enslave her or to abuse her or to use her merely for the gratification of his passion. Your marriage ceremony does not give you that right. ¶ Second, let them remember that gentleness and consideration after the ceremony [are] just as appropriate and necessary and beautiful as gentleness and consideration before the wedding. ¶ Third, let us realize that manhood is not undermined by the practicing of continence, notwithstanding what some psychiatrists claim. Chastity is the crown of beautiful womanhood, and self-control is the source of true manhood, if you will know it, not indulgence. . . . ¶ Let us teach our young men to enter into matrimony with the idea that each will be just as courteous and considerate of a wife after the ceremony as during courtship. CR1952Apr:86-87; TLDP:389

**President Spencer W. Kimball**

Brethren, love your wives. Be kind to your wives. They are not your chattels. They do not belong to you for your service. They are your partners. Love them; really love them, and stay close to them, and consider with them the family problems. And the Lord will bring down upon you blessings you have been unable to even imagine at this time. ACR(Stockholm)1974:104

**Paul**

Husbands, love your wives, even as Christ also loved the church, and gave himself for it; 26. That he might sanctify and cleanse it with the washing of water by the word, 27. That he might present it to himself a glorious church, not having spot, or wrinkle, or any such thing; but that it should be holy and without blemish. 28. So ought men to love their wives as their own bodies. He that loveth his wife loveth himself. 29. For no man ever yet hated his own flesh; but nourisheth and cherisheth it, even as the Lord the church: 30. For we are members of his body, of his flesh, and of his bones. 31. For this cause shall a man leave his father and mother, and shall be joined unto his wife, and they two shall be one flesh. 32. This is a great mystery: but I speak concerning Christ and the church. 33. Nevertheless let every one of you in particular so love his wife even as himself; and the wife see that she reverence her husband. (*Paul writes to the Saints at Ephesus in Asia Minor, about* A.D. *62*) Eph.5:25-33

**Related Witnesses:**

**Joseph Smith,**
*receiving the Word of the Lord*

Thou shalt love thy wife with all thy heart, and shalt cleave unto her and none else. (*Revelation "embracing the law of the Church," Feb. 9, 1831*) D&C 42:22

**Paul**

Husbands, love your wives, and be not bitter against them. (*Letter from prison to the Church in Colossae, Asia Minor, about* A.D. *60*) Col.3:19

**James E. Faust**

There are a few simple, relevant questions which each person, whether married or contemplating marriage, should honestly ask in an effort to become "one flesh." They are: ¶ First, am I able to think of the interest of my marriage and partner first before I think of my own desires? ¶ Second, how deep is my commitment to my companion, aside from any

other interests? ¶ Third, is he or she my best friend? ¶ Fourth, do I have respect for the dignity of my partner as a person of worth and value? ¶ Fifth, do we quarrel over money? Money itself seems neither to make a couple happy, nor the lack of it, necessarily, to make them unhappy, but money is often a symbol of selfishness. ¶ Sixth, is there a spiritually sanctifying bond between us? CR1977Oct:13

**Joseph Smith**

Women have claim on their husbands for their maintenance, until their husbands are taken. . . . (*Revelation, April 30, 1832*) D&C 83:2

**Recorded in Ecclesiastes**

Live joyfully with the wife whom thou lovest all the days of the life of thy vanity, which he hath given thee under the sun. . . . (*Reflections of a son of David the king*) Eccl.9:9

---

**440. Husbands are not to abuse their wives.**

**President David O. McKay**

Let us instruct young people who come to us, to know that a woman should be queen of her own body. The marriage covenant does not give the man the right to enslave her or to abuse her or to use her merely for the gratification of his passion. Your marriage ceremony does not give you that right. ¶ Second, let them remember that gentleness and consideration after the ceremony [are] just as appropriate and necessary and beautiful as gentleness and consideration before the wedding. ¶ Third, let us realize that manhood is not undermined by the practicing of continence, notwithstanding what some psychiatrists claim. CR1952Apr:86-87; TLDP:389

**Mark E. Petersen**

Recognizing her as a co-creator with God, will any of us attempt to seduce her, or defile her, or abuse her? Identifying her as a daughter of God, and a co-creator of life with him, do we not see why the Almighty places sex sin next to murder in his category of crime? Is there anything Christlike in any act that would degrade womanhood or cheapen the true concept of motherhood? ¶ Or is it Christlike to be cruel or unkind to any woman, or even discourteous, whether in public or in private? Which of us has the right to belittle his wife in or out of the home, as some habitually do? CR1968Oct:101

**President David O. McKay**

[C]onditions that cause divorce are violations of [Christ's] divine teachings. Some of these are: ¶ Unfaithfulness on the part of either the husband or wife, or both, habitual drunkenness, physical violence, long imprisonment that disgraces the wife and family, the union of an innocent girl to a reprobate—in these and perhaps other cases there may be circumstances which make the continuance of the marriage state a greater evil than divorce. But these are extreme cases—they are the mistakes, the calamities in the realm of marriage. If we could remove them I would say there never should be a divorce. It is Christ's ideal that home and marriage should be perpetual—eternal. (Treasures of Life, pp. 66-67) TLDP:396

### President George Albert Smith

Now it does not make any difference to me what a man's politics is; as long as he observes the advice of our Heavenly Father, he will be a safe companion and associate. We should not lose our tempers and abuse one another. I want to say that nobody ever abused anybody else when he had the spirit of the Lord. It is always when we have some other spirit. CR1950Oct:7-8

**Related Witnesses:**

### Jacob, brother of Nephi

For behold, I, the Lord, have seen the sorrow, and heard the mourning of the daughters of my people in the land of Jerusalem, yea, and in all the lands of my people, because of the wickedness and abominations of their husbands. 32. And I will not suffer, saith the Lord of Hosts, that the cries of the fair daughters of this people, which I have led out of the land of Jerusalem, shall come up unto me against the men of my people, saith the Lord of Hosts. 33. For they shall not lead away captive the daughters of my people because of their tenderness, save I shall visit them with a sore curse, even unto destruction; for they shall not commit whoredoms, like unto them of old, saith the Lord of Hosts. . . . 35. Behold, ye have done greater iniquities than the Lamanites, our brethren. Ye have broken the hearts of your tender wives. . . . (*Jacob speaks to the people of Nephi denouncing unchastity*) Jacob 2:31-33,35

### President Spencer W. Kimball

We are greatly concerned with the fact that the press continues to report many cases of child abuse. We are much concerned that there would be a single parent that would inflict damages on a child. . . . ¶ Let no Latter-day Saint parent ever be guilty of the heinous crime of abusing one of Christ's little ones! CR1978Apr:5

### President Spencer W. Kimball

Total chastity before marriage and total fidelity after are still the standard from which there can be no deviation without sin, misery, and unhap-

piness. The breaking of the seventh commandment usually means the breaking of one or more homes. ¶ Delinquent adults still tend to produce delinquent children. . . . CR1980Oct:4

### Jacob, brother of Nephi

Behold, the Lamanites your brethren, whom ye hate because of their filthiness and the cursing which hath come upon their skins, are more righteous than you; for they have not forgotten the commandment of the Lord, which was given unto our father—that they should have save it were one wife, and concubines they should have none, and there should not be whoredoms committed among them. 6. And now, this commandment they observe to keep; wherefore, because of this observance, in keeping this commandment, the Lord God will not destroy them, but will be merciful unto them; and one day they shall become a blessed people. 7. Behold, their husbands love their wives, and their wives love their husbands; and their husbands and their wives love their children; and their unbelief and their hatred towards you is because of the iniquity of their fathers; wherefore, how much better are you than they, in the sight of your great Creator? (*Jacob addresses the Nephites and directs his words to those who are not pure in heart, 544-421 B.C.*) Jacob 3:5-7

---

## 441. Wives are to follow the righteous counsel of their husbands.

### President Spencer W. Kimball

One of the most provocative and profound statements in holy writ is that of Paul wherein he directs husbands and wives in their duty to each other and to the family. First, he commands the women: "Wives, submit yourselves unto your own husbands, as unto the Lord. For the husband is head of the wife, even as Christ is the head of the church: And he is the Saviour of the body. Therefore as the church is subject unto Christ, so let the wives be to their own husbands in every thing." (Eph.5:22-24) ¶ If you analyze that very carefully, you can see that the Lord is not requiring women to be subject to their husbands if their husbands are bad and wicked and demanding. This is no idle jest, no facetious matter. Much is said in those few words "as unto the Lord." As the Lord loves his church and serves it, so men should love their wives and serve them and their families. ¶ A woman would have no fears of being imposed upon, nor of any dictorial measure, nor of improper demands if the husband were self-sacrificing and worthy. Certainly no sane woman would hesitate to give submission to her own really righteous husband in everything. We are sometimes shocked to see the wife taking over the leadership of the family, naming the one to pray, the place to be, the things to do. ACR(Stockholm)1974:46-47

**Paul**

Wives, submit yourselves unto your own husbands, as unto the Lord. 23. For the husband is the head of the wife, even as Christ is the head of the church: and he is the saviour of the body. 24. Therefore as the church is subject unto Christ, so let the wives be to their own husbands in every thing. (*Letter to the Saints at Ephesus in Asia Minor, about* A.D. *62*) Eph.5:22-24

**President Joseph F. Smith**

There is no higher authority in matters relating to the family organization, and especially when that organization is presided over by one holding the higher Priesthood, than that of the father. The authority is time honored, and among the people of God in all dispensations it has been highly respected and often emphasized by the teachings of the prophets who were inspired of God. The patriarchal order is of divine origin and will continue throughout time and eternity. . . . This patriarchal order has its divine spirit and purpose, and those who disregard it under one pretext or another are out of harmony with the spirit of God's laws as they are ordained for recognition in the home. It is not merely a question of who is perhaps the best qualified. Neither is it wholly a question of who is living the most worthy life. It is a question largely of law and order. (1902; Juvenile Instructor, Gospel Doctrine, pp. 286-87) MPSG1988:226

**Paul**

Wives, submit yourselves unto your own husbands, as it is fit in the Lord. (*Letter from prison to the Church in Colossae, Asia Minor, about* A.D. *60*) Col.3:18

**Related Witnesses:**

**President Brigham Young,**
**quoted by John A. Widtsoe**

It is not my general practice to counsel the sisters to disobey their husbands. . . . But I never counselled a woman to follow her husband to the Devil. (*In Tabernacle, Sept. 11, 1853, JD1:77*) DBY:200-01

**Paul**

Nevertheless let every one of you in particular so love his wife even as himself; and the wife see that she reverence her husband. (*Paul writes to the Saints at Ephesus in Asia Minor, about* A.D. *62*) Eph.5:33

**Elder Ezra Taft Benson**

We hear much talk—even among some of our own sisters—about so-called "alternative lifestyles" for women. It is maintained that some women are better suited for careers than for marriage and motherhood, or that a combination of both family and career is not inimical to either. Some have even been so bold as to suggest that the Church move away from the "Mormon woman stereotype" of homemaking and rearing children. God grant that dangerous philosophy will never take root among our Latter-day Saint women! ¶ I repeat: You are elect because you were elected to a certain work. How glorious is the knowledge that you are dignified by the God of heaven to be wives and mothers in Zion! (Woman, p. 70) TLDP:390

## 442. Divorce contravenes the law of God.

**Stephen L. Richards**

The remedy for domestic problems and irritations is not divorce, but repentance. I am thoroughly convinced in my heart that this is true, and I hope you will approve of that interpretation. I am sure that there is much that can be done to lessen this great evil. ¶ A long time ago I was a practicing attorney. I have investigated domestic problems. I have seen and tried divorce suits, and heard the evidence of the parties. As I look back over my experiences and observations, I can recall few instances where repentance of bad conduct on the part of the man or woman or both would not have been the answer. We are commanded to repent of all sin, and while I hesitate to say it for fear of hurting the feelings of some, I am constrained to believe that divorce is sin. If sin is an infraction of God's law, then surely this separation is in that category. There has been repeated before in our presence that great commandment: ¶ "For this cause shall a man leave his father and mother, and cleave to his wife; ¶ "And they twain shall be one flesh. . . . ¶ "What therefore God hath joined together, let no man put asunder." [Mark 10:7-9] ¶ So divorce contravenes the law of God. There may be exceptions to be treated with some tolerance, but for my own part I am fearful of any interpretation which does not put divorce in the category of evil and sin. CR1954Oct:80

**Elder Joseph Fielding Smith**

The word of the Lord is definite that when a man and a woman marry they become "one flesh," and therefore, they should never separate except where the most serious offenses in violation of the covenant warrant its being broken. Divorce is not a part of the gospel plan and there never would be any occasion for it if the man and his wife were sincerely, humbly, living in accordance with the gospel of Jesus Christ. It never could happen if the man and wife had in their hearts the pure love which they should hold for each other. No divorce ever comes where there is in the hearts of husband and wife, the pure love of Christ, for that love is based in righteousness, and righteousness is an enemy of sin. (The Restoration of All Things, p. 239) TLDP:396-97

### Bruce R. McConkie

Under the law of Moses, divorce came easily; but recently freed from Egyptian slavery, the chosen race had yet to attain the social, cultural, and spiritual stability that exalts marriage to its proper place in the eternal scheme of things. Men were empowered to divorce their wives for any unseemly thing. "It hath been said, Whosoever shall put away his wife, let him give her a writing of divorcement." ¶ No such low and base standard is acceptable under gospel law. Thus Jesus summarized his perfect marriage order by saying: "But I say unto you, That whosoever shall put away his wife, saving for the cause of fornication, causeth her to commit adultery: and whosoever shall marry her that is divorced committeth adultery." Divorce is totally foreign to celestial standards, a verity that Jesus will one day expound in more detail to the people of Jewry. For now, as far as the record reveals, he merely specifies the high law that his people should live, but that is beyond our capability even today. If husbands and wives lived the law as the Lord would have them live it, they would neither do nor say the things that would even permit the fleeting thought of divorce to enter the mind of their eternal companions. Though we today have the gospel, we have yet to grow into that high state of marital association where marrying a divorced person constitutes adultery. The Lord has not yet given us the high standard he here named as that which ultimately will replace the Mosaic practice of writing a bill of divorcement. (The Mortal Messiah, 2:138-39) TLDP:397-98

### President David O. McKay

In the light of scripture, ancient and modern, we are justified in concluding that Christ's ideal pertaining to marriage is the unbroken home, and conditions that cause divorce are violations of his divine teachings. Some of these are: ¶ Unfaithfulness on the part of either the husband or wife, or both, habitual drunkenness, physical violence, long imprisonment that disgraces the wife and family, the union of an innocent girl to a reprobate—in these and perhaps other cases there may be circumstances which make the continuance of the marriage state a greater evil than divorce. But these are extreme cases—they are the mistakes, the calamities in the realm of marriage. If we could remove them I would say there never should be a divorce. It is Christ's ideal that home and marriage should be perpetual—eternal. ¶ To look upon marriage as a mere contract that may be entered into at pleasure in response to a romantic whim, or for selfish purposes, and severed at the first difficulty or misunderstanding that may arise, is an evil meriting severe condemnation, especially in cases wherein children are made to suffer because of such separation. . . . ¶ A child has the right to feel that in his home he has a place of refuge, a place of protection from the dangers and evils of the outside world. Family unity and integrity are necessary to supply this need. (Treasures of Life, pp. 66-67) TLDP:396

### President Spencer W. Kimball

The ugly dragon of divorce has entered into our social life. Little known to our grandparents and not even common among our parents, this cancer has come to be so common in our own day that nearly every family has been cursed by its destructive machinations. This is one of the principal tools of Satan to destroy faith, through breaking up happy homes and bringing frustration of life and distortion of thought. ("Marriage and Divorce," Brigham Young University Speeches of the Year, 1976, p. 143) TLDP:397

### Related Witnesses:

### Stephen L. Richards

There never could be a divorce in this Church if the husband and wife were keeping the commandments of God. CR1949Apr:136

# List of Doctrines

## MILLENNIUM

# MILLENNIUM

**443. The ushering in of the Millennium will occur with the Second Coming of Christ.**

**Joseph Smith,**
*receiving the Word of the Lord*
For I will reveal myself from heaven with power and great glory, with all the hosts thereof, and dwell in righteousness with men on earth a thousand years, and the wicked shall not stand. (*Revelation received Sept. 1830; Christ's second coming ushers in the Millennium*) D&C 29:11

**Bruce R. McConkie**
The time for the Second Coming of Christ is as fixed and certain as was the hour of his birth. It will not vary as much as a single second from the divine decree. He will come at the appointed time. The Millennium will not be ushered in prematurely. . . . (The Millennial Messiah, p. 26) DGSM:104

**Joseph Smith,**
*translating the Book of Moses*
And it came to pass that Enoch saw the day of the coming of the Son of Man, in the last days, to dwell on the earth in righteousness for the space of a thousand years; (*Revelation to Moses recording the word of the Lord to Enoch*) Moses 7:65

**Elder Joseph Fielding Smith**
We speak of the time when the earth shall be cleansed from sin as the millennium. We look forward to it; the prophets have spoken of it. ¶ In our own day messengers have come from the presence of the Lord declaring that it is even now at our doors, and yet many, even among the Latter-day Saints, go about their affairs as though this coming of the Lord Jesus Christ and the ushering in of this reign of peace had been indefinitely postponed for many generations. I say to you that it is at our doors. I say this with all confidence because the Lord has said it. His messengers have said it as they have come from his presence bearing witness of him. (Doctrines of Salvation, 3:55) TLDP:399

**Bruce R. McConkie**
The millennial day is one in which the Lord himself will dwell with men. This is a boon of inestimable worth. We can scarcely conceive of the glory and wonder of it all. The Lord Jesus Christ, the King of heaven, our Savior and Redeemer, the Lord God Omnipotent dwelling among men! (The Millennial Messiah, p. 652) TLDP:403

**Related Witnesses:**
**Elder Joseph Fielding Smith**
This new heaven and new earth are our own earth and its heavens renewed to the primitive beauty and condition. This is not the great last change which shall come at the end of the earth, but the change to take place at the coming of Jesus Christ. Moreover, when this change comes all things will be set in order. Enmity between man and man and beast and beast will cease. . . . ¶ In this restitution the sea will be driven back to the north and the land will again be in one place. The mountains shall be thrown down and the valleys exalted. This scripture has been looked upon as being merely a figure of speech, but it is a literal change which will take place when Christ comes. . . . (The Restoration of All Things, pp. 23-24) TLDP:399-400

**Paul**
And to you who are troubled rest with us, when the Lord Jesus shall be revealed from heaven with his mighty angels, 8. In flaming fire taking vengeance on them that know not God, and that obey not the gospel of our Lord Jesus Christ: 2Thess.1:7-8

---

**444. Christ will reign on earth for the space of a thousand years.**

**Bruce R. McConkie**
[W]hen we speak of the Lord returning to reign personally upon the earth, we are talking about a literal return. We have in mind a King ruling on a throne. We mean that laws will come forth from a Lawgiver; that judges will be restored as of old; that there will be a full end of all nations as these now exist: that earth's new King will have dominion and power over all the earth; and that Israel, the chosen people, will possess the kingdom and have everlasting dominion. . . . ¶ . . . Christ shall provide the government. He shall reign on the throne of David forever. Peace shall prevail, and justice and judgment shall be the order of the day. And it is Israel, the chosen ones, over whom he shall reign in a kingdom that shall never cease. There is nothing figurative about this; it is not something that can be spiritualized away. It is the coming reality; it shall surely come to pass. . . . (The Millennial Messiah, pp. 596-97, 600) TLDP:401

**Joseph Smith**
[C]hrist and the resurrected Saints will reign over the earth during the thousand years. They will not probably dwell upon the earth, but will visit it when they please or when it is necessary to govern it. There will be wicked men on the earth during the thousand years. The heathen

nations who will not come up to worship will be visited with the judgments of God, and must eventually be destroyed from the earth. (*In a conversation with Judge Adams, Springfield, Ill., Dec. 30, 1842*) HC5:212

**Joseph Smith,**
*translating the Book of Moses*

And there shall be mine abode, and it shall be Zion, which shall come forth out of all the creations which I have made; and for the space of a thousand years the earth shall rest. 65. And it came to pass that Enoch saw the day of the coming of the Son of Man, in the last days, to dwell on the earth in righteousness for the space of a thousand years; (*Revelation to Moses recording the word of the Lord to Enoch*) Moses 7:64-65

**Elder Joseph Fielding Smith**

Through the revelations given to the prophets we learn that during the reign of Jesus Christ for a thousand years, eventually all people will embrace the truth. (Answers to Gospel Questions, 1:108-11) TLDP:406

**Joseph Smith,**
*receiving the Word of the Lord*

For in mine own due time will I come upon the earth in judgment, and my people shall be redeemed and shall reign with me on earth. 30. For the great Millennium, of which I have spoken by the mouth of my servants, shall come. 31. For Satan shall be bound, and when he is loosed again he shall only reign for a little season, and then cometh the end of the earth. 32. And he that liveth in righteousness shall be changed in the twinkling of an eye, and the earth shall pass away so as by fire. 33. And the wicked shall go away into unquenchable fire, and their end no man knoweth on earth, nor ever shall know, until they come before me in judgment. (*Message for the nations of the earth, Feb. 1831*) D&C 43:29-33

**Related Witnesses:**

**President Brigham Young**

When all nations are so subdued to Jesus that every knee shall bow and every tongue shall confess, there will still be millions on the earth who will not believe in him; but they will be obliged to acknowledge his kingly government. (*In Tabernacle, May 22, 1859, JD7:142*) TLDP:400

---

**445. In the Millennium, Satan will be bound and unable to tempt any person.**

**Joseph Smith,**
*receiving the Word of the Lord*

For the great Millennium, of which I have spo-

ken by the mouth of my servants, shall come. 31. For Satan shall be bound, and when he is loosed again he shall only reign for a little season, and then cometh the end of the earth. (*Message for the nations of the earth, Feb. 1831*) D&C 43:30-31

**Joseph Smith**

[A]nd Satan shall be bound, that old serpent, who is called the devil, and shall not be loosed for the space of a thousand years. (*Revelation received Dec. 27/28, 1832*) D&C 88:110

**Daniel H. Wells**

We read that Satan shall be bound a thousand years. How is this to be accomplished? By our becoming so impregnated with the principles of the Gospel—with the Holy Ghost—that the enemy will have no place in us or in our families, and shedding forth that influence in our neighborhoods. . . . Then will he not be bound? Yes, so far as this earth is concerned; and that is the way in which it is to be done, in my humble opinion. He will be chained to all intents and purposes when he can have no influence—no power—no tabernacles into which he can enter; he will then have no place of entertainment. When he finds that he is cornered that close, will he not consider himself bound? I think he will, whether he thinks so or not. (*In Tabernacle, March 22, 1857, JD5:43*) TLDP:401

**John**

And I saw an angel come down from heaven, having the key of the bottomless pit and a great chain in his hand. 2. And he laid hold on the dragon, that old serpent, which is the Devil, and Satan, and bound him a thousand years, 3. And cast him into the bottomless pit, and shut him up, and set a seal upon him, that he should deceive the nations no more, till the thousand years should be fulfilled: and after that he must be loosed a little season. . . . (*John sees Satan bound during the Millennium*) Rev.20:1-3

**President Brigham Young,**
*quoted by John A. Widtsoe*

The Millennium consists in this—every heart in the Church and kingdom of God being united in one: the Kingdom increasing to the overcoming of everything opposed to the economy of heaven, and Satan being bound, and having a seal set upon him. All things else will be as they are now, we shall eat, drink, and wear clothing. (*At opening of the new Tabernacle, April 6, 1852, JD1:203*) DBY:115

**Bruce R. McConkie**

What does it mean to bind Satan? How is he Bound? Our revelation says: "And in that day Satan shall not have power to tempt any man." (D&C 101:28) Does this mean that power is withdrawn from Satan so that he can no longer entice men to do evil? Or does it mean that men no longer succumb to his enticements because their hearts are so set on righteousness that they refuse to forsake that which is good to follow him who is evil? Clearly it means the latter. Satan was not bound in heaven, in the very presence of God, in the sense that he was denied the right and power to preach false doctrine and to invite men to walk away from that God whose children they were: nay, in this sense, he could not have been bound in heaven, for even he must have his agency. ¶ How, then, will Satan be bound during the Millennium? It will be by the righteousness of the people. . . . ¶ . . . . Thus Satan is bound because he "shall have power over the hearts of the children of men no more, for a long time." (2Ne.30:18) Thus the probationary nature of man's second estate is preserved even during the Millennium. It is not that men cannot sin, for the power is in them to do so—they have their agency—but it is that they do not sin because Satan is subject to them, and they are not enticed by his evil whisperings. (The Millennial Messiah, pp. 668-69) TLDP:401

**George Q. Cannon**

We talk about Satan being bound. Satan will be bound by the power of God; but he will be bound also by the determination of the people of God not to listen to him, not to be governed by him. The Lord will not bind him and take his power from the earth while there are men and women willing to be governed by him. That is contrary to the plan of salvation. To deprive men of their agency is contrary to the purposes of God. . . . ¶ Satan only gains power over man through man's exercise of his own agency; and when Satan shall be bound, as the Lord says he will be for a thousand years, one of the great powers that will help bring this to pass will be man's agency. The Lord has never forced men against their will to obey Him. He never will do so. If Satan, therefore, has power with man, it is because man yields to his influence. . . . ¶ The time is not far distant when great judgments will be poured out upon the wicked inhabitants of the earth. Every Prophet who has looked forward to our day has seen and predicted that the wicked would be destroyed. Their destruction means the destruction of Satan's power. The righteous will be left, and because of their righteousness the Lord will have mercy upon them; they, exercising their agency in the right direction, will bring down His blessings upon them to such an extent that Satan will be bound. CR1897Oct:64

**Related Witnesses:**
**Joseph Smith**
And in that day Satan shall not have power to tempt any man. *(The nature of life during the Millennium is set forth)* D&C 101:28
**Joseph Smith**
And Satan shall be bound, that he shall have no place in the hearts of the children of men. *(Revelation March 7, 1831; signs and wonders to attend the Second Coming)* D&C 45:55
**Nephi, son of Lehi**
For behold, saith the prophet, the time cometh speedily that Satan shall have no more power over the hearts of the children of men; for the day soon cometh that all the proud and they who do wickedly shall be as stubble; and the day cometh that they must be burned. . . . 26. And because of the righteousness of his people, Satan has no power; wherefore, he cannot be loosed for the space of many years; for he hath no power over the hearts of the people, for they dwell in righteousness, and the Holy One of Israel reigneth. *(Nephi explains to his brethren the meaning of the things which he read from the plates of brass, about 588-570 B.C.)* 1Ne.22:15,26
**Nephi, son of Lehi**
Wherefore, all things which have been revealed unto the children of men shall at that day be revealed; and Satan shall have power over the hearts of the children of men no more, for a long time. And now, my beloved brethren, I make an end of my sayings. *(Nephi foretells of the last days, 559-545 B.C.)* 2Ne.30:18
**Delbert L. Stapley**
The only way Satan can be bound is for people to forsake his temptations and enticements to do evil, and to walk uprightly and circumspectly before the Lord. (See 1Tim.6:5-7) CR1971Oct:101

---

**446. The devil will be loosed for a short time after the Millennium and wickedness will again abound upon the earth.**

**Joseph Smith,**
*receiving the Word of the Lord*
For the great Millennium, of which I have spoken by the mouth of my servants, shall come. 31. For Satan shall be bound, and when he is loosed again he shall only reign for a little season, and then cometh the end of the earth. *(Message to the nations of the earth, Feb. 1831)* D&C 43:30-31
**Joseph Smith**
[A]nd Satan shall be bound, that old serpent,

who is called the devil, and shall not be loosed for the space of a thousand years. 111. And then he shall be loosed for a little season, that he may gather together his armies. 112. And Michael, the seventh angel, even the archangel, shall gather together his armies, even the hosts of heaven. 113. And the devil shall gather together his armies; even the hosts of hell, and shall come up to battle against Michael and his armies. 114. And then cometh the battle of the great God; and the devil and his armies shall be cast away into their own place, that they shall not have power over the saints any more at all. (*Revelation, Dec. 27/28, 1832*) D&C 88:110-14

**Elder Joseph Fielding Smith**

After the thousand years Satan will be loosed again and will go forth again to deceive the nations. Because men are still mortal, Satan will go out to deceive them. Men will again deny the Lord, but in doing so they will act with their eyes open and because they love darkness rather than light, and so they become sons of perdition. Satan will gather his hosts, both those on the earth and the wicked dead who will eventually also be brought forth in the resurrection. Michael, the Prince, will gather his forces and the last great battle will be fought. Satan will be defeated with his hosts. Then will come the end. Satan and those who follow him will be banished into outer darkness. (Doctrines of Salvation, 1:87-88) TLDP:407:08

**John**

And when the thousand years are expired, Satan shall be loosed out of his prison, 8. And shall go out to deceive the nations which are in the four quarters of the earth, Gog and Magog, to gather them together to battle: the number of whom is as the sand of the sea. (*John sees the judgment of man at the end of the Millennium*) Rev.20:7-8

**Bruce R. McConkie**

John tells us, "Satan shall be loosed out of his prison." (Rev.20:7) This means that once again men will begin to give heed to his enticements. Satan was bound among the Nephites during their golden era. None of the people were then subject to his wiles; all lived in righteousness, and all were saved. But in A.D. 201, "there began to be among them those who were lifted up in pride, such as the wearing of costly apparel, and all manner of fine pearls, and of the fine things of the world. And from that time forth they did have their goods and their substance no more common among them. And they began to be divided into classes; and they began to build up churches unto themselves to get gain, and began to deny the true church of Christ."

(4Ne.1:24-26). . . . ¶ Satan will be loosed because he is no longer bound by the righteousness of the people. ¶ "And when he [Satan] is loosed again he shall only reign for a little season, and then cometh the end of the earth." (D&C 43:31) (The Millennial Messiah, pp. 694-95) TLDP:408-09

---

**447. After the Millennium, a final war between the devil with his hosts and the hosts of heaven will result in the expulsion of the devil from the earth forever.**

**Joseph Smith**

. . . Satan shall be bound, that old serpent, who is called the devil, and shall not be loosed for the space of a thousand years. 111. And then he shall be loosed for a little season, that he may gather together his armies. 112. And Michael, the seventh angel, even the archangel, shall gather together his armies, even the hosts of heaven. 113. And the devil shall gather together his armies; even the hosts of hell, and shall come up to battle against Michael and his armies. 114. And then cometh the battle of the great God; and the devil and his armies shall be cast away into their own place, that they shall not have power over the saints any more at all. (*Revelation, Dec. 27/28, 1832*) D&C 88:110-14

**Elder Joseph Fielding Smith**

After the thousand years Satan will be loosed again and will go forth again to deceive the nations. Because men are still mortal, Satan will go out to deceive them. Men will again deny the Lord, but in doing so they will act with their eyes open and because they love darkness rather than light, and so they become sons of perdition. Satan will gather his hosts, both those on the earth and the wicked dead who will eventually also be brought forth in the resurrection. Michael, the Prince, will gather his forces and the last great battle will be fought. Satan will be defeated with his hosts. Then will come the end. Satan and those who follow him will be banished into outer darkness. (Doctrines of Salvation, 1:87-88) TLDP:407-08

**John**

And when the thousand years are expired, Satan shall be loosed out of his prison, 8. And shall go out to deceive the nations which are in the four quarters of the earth, Gog and Magog, to gather them together to battle: the number of whom is as the sand of the sea. 9. And they went up on the breadth of the earth, and compassed the camp of the saints about, and the beloved city: and fire came down from God out of heaven, and devoured them. 10. And the devil that deceived them was cast into the lake of fire and brimstone, where the beast and the false prophet are, and shall be tormented day and night for ever and ever. (*John sees the judgment of man at the end of the Millennium*) Rev.20:7-10

**Related Witnesses:**

### Joseph Smith

The battle of Gog and Magog will be after the millennium. (*In his office in Nauvoo, Ill., the Prophet spoke about a number of things to his scribe, March 4, 1843*) HC5:298

---

**448. The earth will undergo a purifying process to make it a fit residence for its millennial inhabitants; it will be cleansed from sin and shall rest a thousand years from the wickedness that has been upon it.**

### Elder Joseph Fielding Smith

We speak of the time when the earth shall be cleansed from sin as the millennium. We look forward to it; the prophets have spoken of it. (Doctrines of Salvation, 3:55) TLDP:399

### Elder Joseph Fielding Smith, *also quoting Franklin D. Richards*

As Isaiah has predicted, we will, when Christ comes, have "new heavens and a new earth:" for, "behold, I create new heavens and a new earth: and the former shall not be remembered, nor come into mind." (Isa.65:17-25) This great change will be when the earth is cleansed of its iniquity and becomes a terrestrial body. Speaking of this, the authors in the "Compendium," have said: "The earth will go through a purifying process to fit it for the residence of its millennial inhabitants" [Franklin D. Richards and James A. Little, A Compendium of the Doctrines of the Gospel, rev. ed. (Salt Lake City: Deseret Book Co., 1925), pp. 185-86]. CHMR1:294

### Joseph Smith, *translating the Book of Moses*

And behold, Enoch saw the day of the coming of the Son of Man, even in the flesh; and his soul rejoiced, saying: The Righteous is lifted up, and the Lamb is slain from the foundation of the world; and through faith I am in the bosom of the Father, and behold, Zion is with me. 48. And it came to pass that Enoch looked upon the earth; and he heard a voice from the bowels thereof, saying: Wo, wo is me, the mother of men; I am pained, I am weary,

because of the wickedness of my children. When shall I rest, and be cleansed from the filthiness which is gone forth out of me? When will my Creator sanctify me, that I may rest, and righteousness for a season abide upon my face? . . . 64. And there shall be mine abode, and it shall be Zion, which shall come forth out of all the creations which I have made; and for the space of a thousand years the earth shall rest. 65. And it came to pass that Enoch saw the day of the coming of the Son of Man, in the last days, to dwell on the earth in righteousness for the space of a thousand years; (*Revelation to Moses recording the word of the Lord to Enoch*) Moses 7:47-48,64-65

### Mark E. Petersen

The Savior will come in judgment with rewards for the righteous and destruction for the wicked. When he begins his millennial reign, there must be a cleansed earth to receive him. He will not reign over a sinful world. Hence wickedness will be overthrown, wars will end, and peace will come. ¶ For such a vast and world-shaking appearance, a worldwide preparation is required. The people—those who will survive the great events of that day—will have to be taught, as the people in the Meridian of Time were taught by John the Baptist. A modern people must be prepared to receive the Lord. ¶ This preparation will come only through a worldwide preaching of the restored gospel "in the hour of God's judgment." The scriptures say it would be brought to earth by angelic ministry (see Rev.14:6-7) and then be preached in all the world as a warning to all nations (Matt.24:14). ¶ This preaching will convert the righteous who earnestly look forward to Christ's coming, and they will join his Church. It is to be by the same means used by John the Baptist. . . . ¶ Millions of people now converted to the restored gospel are preparing to meet him. When the time comes, they will be ready. (Malachi and the Great and Dreadful Day, p. 21) TLDP:624

**Related Witnesses:**

### Isaiah

The whole earth is at rest, and is quiet: they break forth into singing. (*Israel shall be gathered and enjoy millennial rest*) Isa.14:7

### Parley P. Pratt

In the resurrection which now approaches, and in connection with the glorious coming of Jesus Christ, the earth will undergo a change in its physical features, climate, soil, productions; and in its political, moral, and spiritual government. ¶ Its mountains will be levelled, its valleys exalted, its swamps and sickly places will be drained and become healthy, while its burning deserts, and its frigid polar regions, will be redeemed and become temperate and fruitful. (Key to the Science of Theology, pp. 139-40) TLDP:621

---

**449. In the Millennium not everyone will belong to the Lord's church.**

**Elder Joseph Fielding Smith**
Some members of the Church have an erroneous idea that when the millennium comes all of the people are going to be swept off the earth except righteous members of the Church. That is not so. There will be millions of people, Catholics, Protestants, agnostics, Mohammedans, people of all classes, and of all beliefs, still permitted to remain upon the face of the earth, but they will be those who have lived clean lives, those who have been free from wickedness and corruption. All who belong, by virtue of their good lives, to the terrestrial order, as well as those who have kept the celestial laws, will remain upon the face of the earth during the millennium. ¶ Eventually, however, the knowledge of the Lord will cover the earth as the waters do the sea. But there will be need for the preaching of the gospel, after the millennium is brought in, until all men are either converted or pass away. (Church News, Nov. 3, 1934; Doctrines of Salvation, 1:86) DGSM:105

**Elder Joseph Fielding Smith**
When the reign of Jesus Christ comes during the millennium, only those who have lived the telestial law will be removed. It is recorded in the Bible and other standard works of the Church that the earth will be cleansed of all its corruption and wickedness. Those who have lived virtuous lives, who have been honest in their dealings with their fellow man and have endeavored to do good to the best of their understanding shall remain. . . . ¶ So we learn that all corruptible things, whether men or beasts or element, shall be consumed; but all that does not come under this awful edict shall remain. Therefore, the honest and upright of all nations, kindreds, and beliefs who have kept the terrestrial as well as the celestial law, will remain. Under these conditions people will enter the great reign of Jesus Christ, carrying with them their beliefs and religious doctrines. Their agency will not be taken from them. . . . ¶ The saying that there will be wicked men on the earth during the millennium has been misunderstood by many, because the Lord declared that the wicked shall not stand, but shall be consumed. In using this term "wicked" it should be interpreted in the language of the Lord as

recorded in the Doctrine and Covenants, Section 84, verses 49-53. Here the Lord speaks of those who have not received the gospel as being "wicked" as they are still under the bondage of sin, having not been baptized. "The inhabitants of the terrestrial order will remain on the earth during the Millennium, and this class is without the gospel ordinances.". . . (Answers to Gospel Questions, 1:108-11) TLDP:406

**President Brigham Young**
In the millennium men will have the privilege of being Presbyterians, Methodists or Infidels, but they will not have the privilege of treating the name and character of Deity as they have done heretofore. No, but every knee shall bow and every tongue confess to the glory of God the Father that Jesus is the Christ. (*In new Tabernacle, Aug. 16, 1868, JD12:274*) TLDP:406

**President Brigham Young**
If the Latter-day Saints think, when the kingdom of God is established on the earth, that all the inhabitants of the earth will join the Church called Latter-day Saints, they are egregiously mistaken. I presume there will be as many sects and parties then as now. Still, when the kingdom of God triumphs, every knee shall bow and every tongue confess that Jesus is the Christ, to the glory of the Father. Even the Jews will do it then, but will the Jews and Gentiles be obliged to belong to the Church of Jesus Christ of Latter-day Saints? No; not by any means. . . . They will cease their persecutions against the Church of Jesus Christ, and they will be willing to acknowledge that the Lord is God and that Jesus is the Savior of the world. (*In Tabernacle, [On the murder of Dr. Robinson, Dec. 23, 1866, JD11:275*) TLDP:405-06

**President Brigham Young**
When all nations are so subdued to Jesus that every knee shall bow and every tongue shall confess, there will still be millions on the earth who will not believe in him; but they will be obliged to acknowledge his kingly government. (*In Tabernacle, May 22, 1859, JD7:142*) TLDP:400

**Bruce R. McConkie**
The prophetic word that sets forth what is to be during the Millennium speaks of "new heavens and a new earth, wherein dwelleth righteousness." (2Pet.3:13) It says that every corruptible thing shall be consumed when the vineyard is burned. And yet the Prophet Joseph Smith said: "There will be wicked men on the earth during the thousand years. The heathen nations who will not come up to worship will be visited with the judgments of God, and must eventually be destroyed from the earth."

(TPJS:268-69) Taken together, these concepts mean that wickedness that is telestial in nature, wickedness that consists of living after the manner of the world, that wickedness which is carnal, sensual, and devilish by nature—all such shall cease. Those who so live will be destroyed. They are the tares of the earth. ¶ But wickedness is a matter of degree, and even those who are upright and decent by worldly standards but who reject the gospel and do not worship the true God are considered to be wicked by gospel standards. They are "under the bondage of sin." They do not accept the message of the restoration and gain a remission of their sins in the waters of baptism. "And by this you may know the righteous from the wicked, and that the whole world groaneth under sin and darkness even now." (D&C 84:49-53). . . . There will be many churches on earth when the Millennium begins. False worship will continue among those whose desires are good, "who are honorable men of the earth," but who have been "blinded by the rest upon them until they repent and believe the gospel or are destroyed," as the Prophet said. It follows that missionary work will continue into the Millennium until all who remain are converted. Then "the earth shall be full of the knowledge of the Lord, as the waters cover the sea." (Isa.11:9) Then every living soul on earth will belong to The Church of Jesus Christ of Latter-day Saints. (The Millennial Messiah, pp. 651-52) TLDP:407

**Joseph Smith**

[C]hrist and the resurrected Saints will reign over the earth during the thousand years. They will not probably dwell upon the earth, but will visit it when they please or when it is necessary to govern it. There will be wicked men on the earth during the thousand years. The heathen nations who will not come up to worship will be visited with the judgments of God, and must eventually be destroyed from the earth. (*In a conversation with Judge Adams, Springfield, Ill., Dec. 30, 1842*) HC5:212

---

450. There shall be harmony, love, and peace in the Millennium; the violence of both people and beasts will cease.

**Joseph Smith,**
*receiving the Word of the Lord*

And in that day the enmity of man, and the enmity of beasts, yea, the enmity of all flesh, shall cease from before my face. (*Revelation Dec. 16, 1833; the nature of life during the Millennium is set forth*) D&C 101:26

**Elder Joseph Fielding Smith**

This new heaven and new earth are our own earth and its heavens renewed to the primitive beauty and condition. This is not the great last change which shall come at the end of the earth, but the change to take place at the coming of Jesus Christ. Moreover, when this change comes all things will be set in order. Enmity between man and man and beast and beast will cease. . . . (The Restoration of All Things, pp. 23-24) TLDP:399-400

**Elder Joseph Fielding Smith**

It shall be in that day that the lion shall lie down with the lamb and eat straw as the ox, and all fear, hatred, and enmity shall depart from the earth because all things having hate in their hearts shall pass away; and there shall come a change, a change over men, a change over the beasts of the field, and upon all things living upon the face of the earth. ¶ According to this word I have read there shall be harmony, and love, and peace, and righteousness because Satan is bound that he cannot tempt any man, and that will be the condition that shall be upon the earth for 1,000 years. (Doctrines of Salvation, 3:58) DGSM:104

**Orson Pratt**

It is then that the enmity of the beasts of the field as well as that of all flesh will cease; no more one beast of prey devouring and feasting upon another that is more harmless in its nature; no more will this enmity be found in the fish of the sea, or in the birds of the air. This change will be wrought upon all flesh when Jesus comes; not a change to immortality, but a change sufficient to alter the ferocious nature of beasts, birds and fishes. In those days the lion will eat straw like the ox; he will no more be the terror of the forest, but will be perfectly harmless, and gentleness will characterize all the wild and ferocious animals, as well as the venomous serpents, so much so that the little child might lead them and play with them, and nothing shall hurt or destroy in all the holy mountain of the Lord, all things becoming, in some measure, as when they were first created. (*In Tabernacle, June 23, 1878, JD20:18*) TLDP:402

**Isaiah**

And he shall judge among the nations, and shall rebuke many people: and they shall beat their swords into plowshares, and their spears into pruninghooks: nation shall not lift up sword against nation, neither shall they learn war any more. (*Isaiah sees the latter-day temple, the gathering of Israel, and millennial judgment and peace*) Isa.2:4

**Related Witnesses:**

### Isaiah

And righteousness shall be the girdle of his loins, and faithfulness the girdle of his reins. 6. The wolf also shall dwell with the lamb, and the leopard shall lie down with the kid; and the calf and the young lion and the fatling together; and a little child shall lead them. 7. And the cow and the bear shall feed; their young ones shall lie down together: and the lion shall eat straw like the ox. 8. And the sucking child shall play on the hole of the asp, and the weaned child shall put his hand on the cockatrice' den. 9. They shall not hurt nor destroy in all my holy mountain: for the earth shall be full of the knowledge of the LORD, as the waters cover the sea. (*Isaiah's prophecies, near 700 B.C.*) Isa.11:5-9 (See JS-H 1:40)

### Bruce R. McConkie

Thus, when we speak of the Lord returning to reign personally upon the earth, we are talking about a literal return. . . . ¶ He shall reign on the throne of David forever. Peace shall prevail, and justice and judgment shall be the order of the day. And it is Israel, the chosen ones, over whom he shall reign in a kingdom that shall never cease. There is nothing figurative about this; it is not something that can be spiritualized away. It is the coming reality; it shall surely come to pass. . . . ¶ The eventual triumph of the Lord's people is assured; there is to be a millennial day of glory and honor and peace; (The Millennial Messiah, pp. 596-97, 600) TLDP:401

### Isaiah

The wolf and the lamb shall feed together, and the lion shall eat straw like the bullock: and dust shall be the serpent's meat. They shall not hurt nor destroy in all my holy mountain, saith the LORD. (*Isaiah speaks of the Millennium*) Isa.65:25

---

**451. In the Millennium there will be no more weeping, no sorrow or pain, and no fear of death.**

### John

And God shall wipe away all tears from their eyes; and there shall be no more death, neither sorrow, nor crying, neither shall there be any more pain: for the former things are passed away. (*The Apostle John sees the earth in its millennial state*) Rev.21:4

### Isaiah

And I will rejoice in Jerusalem, and joy in my people: and the voice of weeping shall be no more heard in her, nor the voice of crying. (*Isaiah's words prophesying of the rejoicing and triumph of the Lord's people during the Millennium*) Isa.65:19

### Joseph Smith

And in that day Satan shall not have power to tempt any man. 29. And there shall be no sorrow because there is no death. 30. In that day an infant shall not die until he is old; and his life shall be as the age of a tree; 31. And when he dies he shall not sleep, that is to say in the earth, but shall be changed in the twinkling of an eye, and shall be caught up, and his rest shall be glorious. (*Revelation, Dec. 16, 1833; the nature of life during the Millennium is set forth*) D&C 101:28-31

**Related Witnesses:**

### Elder Joseph Fielding Smith

[M]en shall live free from sin and free from the ravages of disease and death until they reach the age of 100 years. Infants shall not die, they shall live until they have filled the measure of their mortal creation. In fact, mortality shall be reduced to a minimum. (Doctrines of Salvation, 3:58) TLDP:402

### Elder Joseph Fielding Smith

In the course of the thousand years all men will either come into the Church, or kingdom of God, or they will die and pass away. In that day there will be no death until men are old. Children will not die but will live to the age of a tree. Isaiah says this is 100 years. When the time comes for men to die, they will be changed in the twinkling of an eye, and there will be no graves. (Doctrines of Salvation, 1:86-87) TLDP:406

### James E. Talmage

It is evident from citations given and from all Scripture bearing upon the subject, that the Millennium is to precede the consummation spoken of as "the end of the world." In the era of peace both mortal and immortalized beings will tenant the earth; and though sin will not be wholly abolished nor death banished, the powers of righteousness shall be dominant. (The Vitality of Mormonism, p. 178) TLDP:405

---

**452. In the millennial era of peace, there will be a mingling of mortal and immortal beings.**

### James E. Talmage

It is evident from citations given and from all Scripture bearing upon the subject, that the Millennium is to precede the consummation spoken of as "the end of the world." In the era of peace both mortal and immortalized beings will tenant the earth; and though sin will not be wholly abolished nor death banished, the powers of righteousness shall be dominant. (The Vitality of Mormonism, p. 178) TLDP:405

### Bruce R. McConkie

During the Millennium there will, of course, be two kinds of people on earth. There will be those who are mortal, and those who are immortal. There will be those who have been changed or quickened or transfigured or translated (words fail us to describe their state), and those who have gone through a second change, in the twinkling of an eye, so as to become eternal in nature. There will be those who are on probation, for whom earth life is a probationary estate, and who are thus working out their own salvation, and those who have already overcome the world and have entered into a fulness of eternal joy. There will be those who will yet die in the sense of being changed from their quickened state to a state of immortality, and those who, having previously died, are then living in a resurrected state. There will be those who are subject to the kings and priests who rule forever in the house of Israel, and those who, as kings and priests, exercise power and dominion in the everlasting kingdom of Him whose we are. There will be those who, as mortals, provide bodies for the spirit children of the Father, for the spirits whose right it is to come to earth and gain houses for their eternal spirits, and those who, as immortals (Abraham is one), are already begetting spirit children of their own. There will be those for whom the fulness of eternal glory is ahead, and those who, again like Abraham, have already entered into their exaltation and sit upon their thrones and are not angels but are gods forever and ever. (The Millennial Messiah, pp. 644-45) TLDP:405

### Elder Joseph Fielding Smith

During this time of peace, when the righteous shall come forth from their graves, they shall mingle with mortal men on the earth and instruct them. The veil which separates the living from the dead will be withdrawn and mortal men and the ancient saints shall converse together. Moreover, in perfect harmony shall they labor for the salvation and exaltation of the worthy who have died without the privileges of the gospel. (Doctrines of Salvation, 2:251-52) TLDP:405

### Related Witnesses:

### James E. Talmage

With Christ shall come those who have already been resurrected; and His approach shall be the means of inaugurating a general resurrection of the righteous dead, while the pure and just who are still in the flesh shall be instantaneously changed from the mortal to the immortal state and shall be caught up with the newly resurrected to meet the Lord and His celestial company, and shall descend with Him. JTC:787

---

### 453. The great work of the Millennium shall be temple work for the redemption of the dead.

### President Joseph F. Smith

That this work [the deliverance of spirits from prison] may be hastened so that all who believe, in the spirit world, may receive the benefit of deliverance, it is revealed that the great work of the Millennium shall be the work in the temples for the redemption of the dead; and then we hope to enjoy the benefits of revelation through the Urim and Thummim, or by such means as the Lord may reveal concerning those for whom the work shall be done, so that we may not work by chance, or by faith alone, without knowledge, but with the actual knowledge revealed unto us. (IE1901Dec:145-47, Gospel Doctrine, p. 438) DGSM:104

### President Brigham Young

Do you know what the Millennium is for, and what work will have to be done during that period? Suppose the Christian world were now one in heart, faith, sentiment and works, so that the Lord could commence the Millennium in power and glory, do you know what would be done? Would you sit and sing yourselves away to everlasting bliss? No, I reckon not. I think there is a work to be done then which the whole world seems determined we shall not do. What is it? To build temples. . . . What are we going to do in these temples? . . . In these temples we will officiate in the ordinances of the Gospel of Jesus Christ for our friends, for no man can enter the kingdom of God without being born of the water and of the Spirit. We will officiate for them who are in the spirit world, where Jesus went to preach to the spirits, as Peter has written in the third chapter, verses 18, 19, and 20, of his first epistle. . . . ¶ We will also have hands laid on us for the reception of the Holy Ghost; and then we will receive the washing and anointings for and in their behalf, preparatory to their becoming heirs of God and joint-heirs with Christ. (In Tabernacle, April 24, 1870, JD13:329-30) TLDP:404

### President Brigham Young

To accomplish this work there will have to be not only one temple but thousands of them, and thousands and tens of thousands of men and women will go into those temples and officiate for people who have lived as far back as the Lord shall reveal. (*In Bowery, June 22, 1856, JD3:372*) TLDP:404

### Elder Wilford Woodruff

When the Savior comes, a thousand years will be devoted to this work of redemption; and Temples will appear all over this land of Joseph—North and South America—and also in Europe and elsewhere; and all the descendants of Shem, Ham, and Japheth, who received not the Gospel in the flesh, must be officiated for in the Temples of God, before the Savior can present the kingdom to the Father, saying, "It is finished." (*In new Tabernacle, Sept. 16, 1877, JD19:230*) TLDP:404

### Elder Joseph Fielding Smith

The great work of the millennium shall be performed in the temples which shall cover all parts of the land and into which the children shall go to complete the work for their fathers, which they could not do when in this mortal life for themselves. ¶ In this manner those who have passed through the resurrection, and who know all about people and conditions on the other side, will place in the hands of those who are in mortality, the necessary information by and through which the great work of salvation for every worthy soul shall be performed, and thus the purposes of the Lord, as determined before the foundation of the world, will be fully consummated. (Doctrines of Salvation, 2:251-52) TLDP:405

**Related Witnesses:**

### Bruce R. McConkie

Before he comes, many of the lost sheep of Israel must be gathered out of Babylon into the stakes of Zion, stakes now organized and yet to be organized in all nations. Before he comes, Zion must be built up, temples must rise wherever there are stakes, and the promises made to the fathers must be planted in the hearts of the children. (The Millennial Messiah, pp. 572-73) TLDP:625-26

---

**HYMNS Written by Prophets Applicable to this Topic**

### Parley P. Pratt
*Come, O Thou King of Kings*
HYMNS:59

Come, O thou King of Kings!
We've waited long for thee,
With healing in thy wings
To set thy people free.
Come, thou desire of nations, come;
Let Israel now be gathered home.

Come, make an end to sin
And cleanse the earth by fire,
And righteousness bring in,
That Saints may tune the lyre
With songs of joy, a happier strain,
To welcome in thy peaceful reign.

Hosannas now shall sound
From all the ransomed throng,
And glory echo round
A new triumphal song;
The wide expanse of heaven fill
With anthems sweet from Zion's hill.

Hail! Prince of life and peace!
Thrice welcome to thy throne!
While all the chosen race
Their Lord and Savior own,
The heathen nations bow the knee,
And ev'ry tongue sounds praise to thee.

### John Taylor
*Go, Ye Messengers of Glory*
HYMNS:262

Go, ye messengers of glory;
Run, ye legates of the skies.
Go and tell the pleasing story
That a glorious angel flies,
Great and mighty, Great and mighty,
With a message from the skies.

Go to ev'ry tribe and nation;
Visit ev'ry land and clime.
Sound to all the proclamation;
Tell to all the truth sublime:
That the gospel, That the gospel
Does in ancient glory shine.

Go, to all the gospel carry;
Let the joyful news abound.
Go till ev'ry nation hear you,
Jew and Gentile greet the sound.
Let the gospel, Let the gospel
Echo all the earth around.

Bearing seed of heav'nly virtue,
Scatter it o'er all the earth.
Go! Jehovah will support you;
Gather all the sheaves of worth.
Then, with Jesus, Then, with Jesus
Reign in glory on the earth.

# List of Doctrines

## MISSIONARY WORK

*Doctrines Located in This Topic*

454. The worth of souls is great in the sight of God (each individual is precious in His sight).

455. The gospel shall be preached in all the world to every nation, kindred, tongue, and people.

456. The day will come when all people will hear the fulness of the gospel in their own language.

457. The gospel is to be preached to every person on earth.

458. Missionaries are to serve the Lord with all their heart, might, mind, and strength.

459. The gospel is to be proclaimed by the weak and simple.

460. Those who preach the gospel to the world shall say nothing but repentance (they shall preach only with the desire to bring people to repentance and faith in God).

461. Missionaries are to proclaim the gospel by the Spirit of God; they are to teach only as moved upon by the Holy Ghost.

462. The preaching of the gospel has a more powerful effect on the minds of people who hear it, to lead them to do right, than anything else.

463. The Lord will support and strengthen the efforts of those who are called to proclaim the gospel.

464. There is joy in missionary service—the Lord greatly blesses the lives of those who serve as missionaries to the world.

465. People are not to function as missionaries unless they are set apart and authorized to preach the gospel by one who has authority.

466. Every person who has received the gospel is under obligation to take the gospel to his or her neighbor.

467. The Saints of God are to be a light to the world by setting an example of righteous living.

*Doctrines on MISSIONARY WORK Located in Other Topics*

87. One of the (threefold) missions of the Church is to proclaim the gospel to the world.

# MISSIONARY WORK continued

97. A person who *accepts* divine truth must obtain it by the Spirit of God from someone who *teaches* by that same Spirit.

237. Some are given the gift of speaking in tongues; others are given the interpretation of tongues.

334. When a person speaks by the power of the Holy Ghost, the Holy Ghost will carry the message to the hearts of those who hear by that same Spirit.

372. No individual will be held accountable for the commandments and doctrines of the gospel of Jesus Christ until that person has had opportunity to accept or reject the gospel.

508. The work of the Lord thrives under opposition and persecution.

815. When teachers (missionaries and speakers) bear testimony of a gospel truth they have taught, the Spirit of God witnesses the truth thereof to the heart of the honest seeker.

874. The Lord selects teachable persons to do His work; He chooses those whom the world calls weak and foolish more frequently than those whom the world calls wise.

**454.** The worth of souls is great in the sight of God (each individual is precious in His sight).

### Joseph Smith
Remember the worth of souls is great in the sight of God; 11. For, behold, the Lord your Redeemer suffered death in the flesh; wherefore he suffered the pain of all men, that all men might repent and come unto him. 12. And he hath risen again from the dead, that he might bring all men unto him, on conditions of repentance. (*Revelation, June 1829*) D&C 18:10-12

### Rudger Clawson
And how are we to determine the value of souls? This matter has been determined for us also by revelation. The souls of men are so precious in the sight of God that He gave to the world His Only Begotten Son, that by the shedding of His blood He might draw all men unto Him. That is why the great Prophet of this dispensation, Joseph Smith, and these others, John Whitmer, Oliver Cowdery, David Whitmer, and the rest, were called to bring souls unto Christ. And if one of these men should labor all his days, and bring save it be one soul unto Christ, and that one should be his wife, what great joy he would have with his wife in heaven. Then if he should labor all his days and bring unto Christ the souls of his wife and his children, and none else perchance, how great would be his joy in heaven with his wife and children. CR1901Apr:7-8; DCSM:35

### President David O. McKay
The Prophet Joseph Smith was given the divine message: "Remember the worth of souls is great in the sight of God. . . ." (D&C 18:10) Such is the philosophy expressed by the Redeemer in the seemingly paradoxical statement ". . . he that loseth his life for my sake shall find it." (Matt.10:39) The meaning of this becomes clear in the light of another passage which says, "Inasmuch as ye have done it unto one of the least of these my brethren, ye have done it unto me." (Matt.25:40) Just to be associated with men striving toward such an aim is a joy, and to assist them in their quest, an inspiration. If you are true followers of the Savior, you are striving to serve your fellowmen in love. CR1966Apr:108

### Elder Ezra Taft Benson
You remember, the Lord said to the Prophet Joseph: "Remember the worth of souls is great in the sight of God; For, behold, the Lord your Redeemer suffered death in the flesh; wherefore he suffered the pain of all men, that all men might repent and come unto him." (D&C 18:10-11) ¶

The Lord said to Moses: "For behold, this is my work and my glory—to bring to pass the immortality and eternal life of man." (Moses 1:39) ¶ This is our first interest as a Church—to build character, to save and exalt the souls of the children of men. CR1953Apr:39

**Related Witnesses:**

### Elder Ezra Taft Benson
I know, my brethren and sisters, that the sweetest work in all the world is the work in which we are engaged in helping to save and exalt the souls of the children of men. There isn't anything so important, so precious, so enjoyable, so soul-satisfying. CR1953Apr:39

### George F. Richards
That there are living among us many people who need what we have to offer—the gospel message—there can be no question from the fact that they are being converted in great numbers within the stakes and wards of the Church. The souls of these inactive members and non-members among us are as precious as the souls of people in foreign countries and in the islands of the seas where our missionaries are laboring. CR1950Apr:25

### President Heber J. Grant
The missionary work of the Latter-day Saints is the greatest of all the great works in all the world. CR1921Oct:5

### Elder George Albert Smith
My understanding is that the most important mission that I have in this life is: first to keep the commandments of God, as they have been taught to me; and next, to teach them to my Father's children who do not understand them. CR1916Oct:50

### Elder Spencer W. Kimball
There isn't anything else more important than taking the gospel to the world. ACR (Manchester)1971:22

---

**455.** The gospel shall be preached in all the world to every nation, kindred, tongue, and people.

### Joseph Smith
And this gospel shall be preached unto every nation, and kindred, and tongue, and people. (*Revelation, Nov. 3, 1831; the gospel restored through Joseph Smith to be preached to all nations*) D&C 133:37

### David B. Haight,
*also quoting Jesus,*
*as recorded in Matthew*
"Go ye therefore, and teach all nations"

(Matt.28:19). The prophet emphasizes that the Savior knew the bounds of the earth when he said that. He did not say to go only to Egypt or Greece or the Arab world or Rome; he knew of all the nations that existed then, and the nations that would emerge. He, the Creator, knew what growth would take place then, today, and in the future. ("Your Purpose and Responsibility," Brigham Young University Speeches of the Year, 1977, p. 130) TLDP:411

### Jesus,
#### recorded in Matthew

And this gospel of the kingdom shall be preached in all the world for a witness unto all nations; and then shall the end come. *(Jesus discourses on his second coming)* Matt.24:14

### Joseph Smith

[T]he Standard of Truth has been erected; no unhallowed hand can stop the work from progressing; persecutions may rage, mobs may combine, armies may assemble, calumny may defame, but the truth of God will go forth boldly, nobly, and independent till it has penetrated every continent, visited every clime, swept every country, and sounded in every ear, till the purposes of God shall be accomplished and the great Jehovah shall say the work is done. *(In Wentworth letter, March 1, 1842: "At the request of Mr. John Wentworth, Editor . . . Chicago Democrat, I have written [this] sketch of the rise, progress, persecution, and faith of the Latter-day Saints. . . .")* (Full account recorded in HC4:535-41) HC4:540

### President Joseph Fielding Smith

We have attained the stature and strength that are enabling us to fulfill the commission given us by the Lord through the Prophet Joseph Smith that we should carry the glad tidings of the restoration to every nation and to all people. ¶ And not only shall we preach the gospel in every nation before the second coming of the Son of Man, but we shall make converts and establish congregations of Saints among them. ACR(Manchester)1971:5

### Boyd K. Packer

Since baptism is essential there must be an urgent concern to carry the message of the gospel of Jesus Christ to every nation, kindred, tongue, and people. That came as a commandment from Him. ¶ His true servants will be out to convert all who will hear to the principles of the gospel and they will offer them that one baptism which He proclaimed as essential. . . . ¶ The powerful missionary spirit and the vigorous missionary activity in The Church of Jesus Christ of Latter-day Saints becomes a very significant witness that the true gospel and that the

authority are possessed here in the Church. We accept the responsibility to preach the gospel to every person on earth. And if the question is asked, "You mean you are out to convert the entire world?" the answer is, "Yes, we will try to reach every living soul." ¶ Some who measure that challenge quickly say, "Why, that's impossible! It cannot be done!" ¶ To that we simply say, "Perhaps, but we shall do it anyway." CR1975Oct:145

### Joseph Smith

And then cometh the day when the arm of the Lord shall be revealed in power in convincing the nations, the heathen nations, the house of Joseph, of the gospel of their salvation. 11. For it shall come to pass in that day, that every man shall hear the fulness of the gospel in his own tongue, and in his own language, through those who are ordained unto this power, by the administration of the Comforter, shed forth upon them for the revelation of Jesus Christ. *(Revelation, March 8, 1833; depicting the day when the arm of the Lord shall be revealed in power)* D&C 90:10-11

### Jesus,
#### recorded in Matthew

Go ye therefore, and teach all nations, baptizing them in the name of the Father, and of the Son, and of the Holy Ghost: *(The risen Jesus commands the eleven Apostles to teach all nations)* Matt.28:19

### Jesus,
#### recorded in Mark

And he said unto them, Go ye into all the world, and preach the gospel to every creature. *(The risen Jesus Christ to the eleven Apostles)* Mark 16:15

**Related Witnesses:**
### Joseph Smith,
#### receiving the Word of the Lord

Go ye into all the world, preach the gospel to every creature, acting in the authority which I have given you, baptizing in the name of the Father, and of the Son, and of the Holy Ghost. *(Revelation, Nov. 1831)* D&C 68:8

**Related Witnesses:**
### Ammon, son of Mosiah
#### quoted by Mormon

Now my brethren, we see that God is mindful of every people, whatsoever land they may be in; yea, he numbereth his people, and his bowels of mercy are over all the earth. Now this is my joy, and my great thanksgiving; yea, and I will give thanks unto my God forever. Amen. *(Ammon extols the mercy of God who has not forgotten this branch of the tree of Israel, 90-77 B.C.)* Alma 26:37

**456. The day will come when all people will hear the fulness of the gospel in their own language.**

**Joseph Smith**

For it shall come to pass in that day, that every man shall hear the fulness of the gospel in his own tongue, and in his own language, through those who are ordained unto this power, by the administration of the Comforter, shed forth upon them for the revelation of Jesus Christ. (*Revelation, March 8, 1833; depicting the day when the arm of the Lord shall be revealed in power*) D&C 90:11

**Elder Joseph Fielding Smith**

The promise is made that the day shall come when "every man shall hear the fulness of the Gospel in his own tongue, and in his own language through those who are ordained to this power, by the administration of the comforter, shed forth upon them for the revelation of Jesus Christ." It is the plan from the foundation of the earth that every soul shall have the opportunity of hearing the Gospel. . . . In order that the Gospel might be declared among the nations and kindreds and tongues, the Lord commanded that the elders should study languages and with all good books be prepared to carry the message so that people could hear it in their own tongue. This was one great opportunity presented in the school of the prophets. It is a remarkable fact that the elders of the Church going forth to foreign lands have had the gift of tongues by which they have learned to speak these foreign tongues within very brief periods of time. . . . ¶ It is the requirement of the Lord that his servants prepare themselves by study and by faith and become acquainted with peoples, languages and world conditions so that they may be more fully prepared to preach and teach the Gospel. CHMR1:390

**Related Witnesses:**

**Alma, the younger,**
*quoted by Mormon*

For behold, the Lord doth grant unto all nations, of their own nation and tongue, to teach his word, yea, in wisdom, all that he seeth fit that they should have; therefore we see that the Lord doth counsel in wisdom, according to that which is just and true. (*Alma having had an earnest desire to cry repentance to every people—even that he might be an angel to speak with a voice to shake the earth—now discerns the Lord's way of teaching each nation and tongue, about 76 B.C.*) Alma 29:8

**President Brigham Young,**
*quoted by John A. Widtsoe*

Some may receive the gift of tongues, that they will get up and speak in tongues, and speak in many other languages beside their mother tongue, the language that they were brought up in, that they were first taught, and be able to proclaim the Gospel of life and salvation that all men could understand it. (*At Paris, Idaho, Aug. 31, 1873, JD16:164*) DBY:161

**Joseph Smith**

Also, I saw Elder Brigham Young standing in a strange land, in the far south and west, in a desert place, upon a rock in the midst of about a dozen men of color, who appeared hostile. He was preaching to them in their own tongue. . . . (*The Prophet sees many things in a vision, Jan. 21, 1836*) HC2:381

**Joseph Smith**

[T]he gift of tongues by the power of the Holy Ghost in the Church, is for the benefit of the servants of God to preach to unbelievers, as on the day of Pentecost. When devout men from every nation shall assemble to hear the things of God, let the Elders preach to them in their own mother tongue, whether it is German, French, Spanish or "Irish," or any other. . . . (*Remarks at a public meeting of the Saints at the Prophet's house, Dec. 26, 1841*) HC4:485

**457. The gospel is to be preached to every person on earth.**

**Boyd K. Packer**

We accept the responsibility to preach the gospel to every person on earth. And if the question is asked, "You mean you are out to convert the entire world?" the answer is, "Yes. We will try to reach every living soul." CR1975Oct:145

**Jesus,**
*recorded in Mark*

And he said unto them, Go ye into all the world, and preach the gospel to every creature. (*The risen Jesus Christ to the eleven Apostles*) Mark 16:15

**Elder George Albert Smith**

Upon us, as elders of this Church, has been laid the obligation to go into all the world and preach the gospel unto every creature. We have received a wonderful gift, but with that gift comes a great responsibility. We have been blessed of the Lord with a knowledge beyond our fellows, and with that knowledge comes the requirement that we divide it with His children wherever they may be. CR1922Apr:53

**John A. Widtsoe**

In the Church of Christ [our desire is] to bring about the highest joy for all mankind. ¶ . . . . In the nature of existence, it is impossible for an intelligent being to attain the highest degree of joy unless other like beings move along with him. The Great Plan will succeed only if all, or at least a majority of those who accepted it, are saved. The Church, a part of the Great Plan, must have as its main purpose the saving of all human beings. All must be saved! The work of the Church cannot be completed until all have at least heard the truth and have been given the chance to accept it. There can be no talk of a few souls before the throne of God, with the many in hell. The great mission of the Church must always be to bring all men into a knowledge and acceptance of the truth. This is the cementing purpose of the Church. (A Rational Theology, p. 122) TLDP:411

**President Brigham Young**

It is necessary that all have the privilege of receiving or rejecting eternal truth, that they may be prepared to be saved, or be prepared to be damned. (*In Tabernacle, Dec. 18, 1859, JD7:139*) TLDP:410

**Related Witnesses:**
**Joseph Smith**

Let them preach by the way, and bear testimony of the truth in all places, and call upon the rich, the high and the low, and the poor to repent. (*Revelation for the elders of the Church, Aug. 1, 1831*) D&C 58:47

**Joseph Smith,**
*receiving the Word of the Lord*

[F]or I, the Lord, have a great work for thee to do, in publishing my name among the children of men. . . . 8. And by thy word many high ones shall be brought low, and by thy word many low ones shall be exalted. (*Revelation for Thomas B. Marsh, July 23, 1837*) D&C 112:6,8

**Alma, the younger,**
*quoted by Mormon*

O that I were an angel, and could have the wish of mine heart, that I might go forth and speak with the trump of God, with a voice to shake the earth, and cry repentance unto every people! 2. Yea, I would declare unto every soul, as with the voice of thunder, repentance and the plan of redemption, that they should repent and come unto our God, that there might not be more sorrow upon all the face of the earth. 3. But behold, I am a man, and do sin in my wish; for I ought to be content with the things which the Lord hath allotted unto me. . . . 6. Now, seeing that I know these things, why should I desire more than to perform the work to which I have been called? 7. Why should I desire that I were an angel, that I could speak unto all the ends of the earth? . . . 9. I know that which the Lord hath

commanded me, and I glory in it. I do not glory of myself, but I glory in that which the Lord hath commanded me; yea, and this is my glory, that perhaps I may be an instrument in the hands of God to bring some soul to repentance; and this is my joy. (*Alma discourses on the principle of repentance, about 76 B.C.*) Alma 29:1-3,6-7,9

**Ammon, son of Mosiah**
*quoted by Mormon*

Now my brethren, we see that God is mindful of every people, whatsoever land they may be in; yea, he numbereth his people, and his bowels of mercy are over all the earth. Now this is my joy, and my great thanksgiving; yea, and I will give thanks unto my God forever. Amen. (*Ammon extols the mercy of God who has not forgotten this branch of the tree of Israel, 90-77 B.C.*) Alma 26:37

---

458. **Missionaries are to serve the Lord with all their heart, might, mind, and strength.**

**Elder Joseph Fielding Smith**

It is true that not every man is a natural missionary, and there are those who shrink from the responsibility of raising their voices in proclamation of the Gospel, and yet this is an obligation that we owe to this fallen world. The elders in the very beginning had been commanded to serve the Lord with all their "heart, might, mind and strength," for the field is white and ready for the harvest. A penalty was to be inflicted upon those who failed and they were not to stand blameless at the last day. The preaching of the Gospel was to be a means to them by which they were not to perish, but bring salvation to their souls. There are many who have been sent forth who have had a fear of man, yet the Lord has promised to support them in their labors if they will trust in him. CHMR1:220-21

**Joseph Smith**

Therefore, O ye that embark in the service of God, see that ye serve him with all your heart, might, mind and strength, that ye may stand blameless before God at the last day. . . . 4. For behold the field is white already to harvest; and lo, he that thrusteth in his sickle with his might, the same layeth up in store that he perisheth not, but bringeth salvation to his soul; (*Revelation through Joseph Smith to his father, Feb. 1829*) D&C 4:2,4

**Joseph Smith,**
*receiving the Word of the Lord*

And even so will I gather mine elect from the

four quarters of the earth, even as many as will believe in me, and hearken unto my voice. 7. Yea, verily, verily, I say unto you, that the field is white already to harvest; wherefore, thrust in your sickles, and reap with all your might, mind, and strength. 8. Open your mouths and they shall be filled, and you shall become even as Nephi of old, who journeyed from Jerusalem in the wilderness. 9. Yea, open your mouths and spare not, and you shall be laden with sheaves upon your backs, for lo, I am with you. 10. Yea, open your mouths and they shall be filled, saying: Repent, repent, and prepare ye the way of the Lord, and make his paths straight; for the kingdom of heaven is at hand; (*Revelation for Ezra Thayre and Northrop Sweet, Oct. 1830*) D&C 33:6-10

### Elder George Albert Smith

One of the very first revelations that was given by our heavenly Father, as contained in the Doctrine and Covenants, reads as follows: "Now behold, a marvelous work is about to come forth among the children of men. Therefore, O ye that embark in the service of God, see that ye serve him with all your heart, might, mind and strength, that ye may stand blameless before God at the last day." [D&C 4:1-2] ¶ Now, I do not understand that we are serving God with all our might if we forsake his children, or if we spend so much of our time selfishly building up ourselves, accumulating things of this life, and leave his children in darkness, when we could bring them into the light. My understanding is that the most important mission that I have in this life is: first, to keep the commandments of God, as they have been taught to me; and next, to teach them to my Father's children who do not understand them. It makes little difference, when I go to the other side, whether I have been a man of wealth in this world or not, unless I have used that wealth to bless my fellow men. Though I be a wanderer in this world, and suffer for the necessities of life, if by reason of the knowledge that my Father has given me, I devote myself to the instruction of his children, to planting faith in their hearts, to dissipating the errors that have come to them by tradition, I believe when I go to the other side that I will find there a bank account that will be beyond compare with what I would have, if I lived for the things of this earth alone. CR1916Oct:50-51

---

### 459. The gospel is to be proclaimed by the weak and simple.

### Joseph Smith,
*receiving the Word of the Lord*

That the fulness of my gospel might be proclaimed by the weak and the simple unto the ends of the world, and before kings and rulers. (*Revelation during conference of elders of the Church, Nov. 1, 1831*) D&C 1:23

### President Joseph Fielding Smith

In the early days of this dispensation, the Lord said to those called in his ministry, "that every man might speak in the name of God the Lord, even the Savior of the world; . . . That the fulness of my gospel might be proclaimed by the weak and the simple unto the ends of the world, and before kings and rulers." (D&C 1:20,23) ¶ To those called "to go forth to preach" his gospel and to all "the elders, priests and teachers" of his church, he said: They "shall teach the principles of my gospel, which are in the Bible and the Book of Mormon," and the other scriptures, "as they shall be directed by the Spirit." (See D&C 42:11-13) ¶ As agents of the Lord we are not called or authorized to teach the philosophies of the world or the speculative theories of our scientific age. Our mission is to preach the doctrines of salvation in plainness and simplicity as they are revealed and recorded in the scriptures. CR1970Oct:5

### Paul

For ye see your calling, brethren, how that not many wise men after the flesh, not many mighty, not many noble, are called: 27. But God hath chosen the foolish things of the world to confound the wise; and God hath chosen the weak things of the world to confound the things which are mighty; (*Letter to the Church at Corinth, Greece, about A.D. 55*) 1Cor.1:26-27

### President David O. McKay

Again was given the divine injunction for authorized servants to be sent forth to the East and to the West, to the North and to the South that "every man might speak in the name of God the Lord, even the Savior of the world; That faith also might increase in the earth; That mine everlasting covenant might be established; That the fulness of my gospel might be proclaimed by the weak and the simple unto the ends of the world, and before kings and rulers." (D&C 1:20-23) ¶ In Section 4 of the Doctrine and Covenants, the Prophet Joseph Smith received a revelation that "behold, a marvelous work is about to come forth among the children of men. ¶ "Therefore, O ye that embark in the service of God see that ye serve him with all your heart, might, mind and strength, that ye may stand blameless before God at the last day." (D&C 4:1-2) ¶ When this revelation was given to the Prophet Joseph, he was only 23 years of age. The Book of Mormon was not yet published, no man had been ordained to the priesthood. The Church was not organized; yet the statement was made and written without qualification that "a marvelous work [was] about to come forth among the children of men." ¶ Another significant feature of this revelation, and of others given about the same period, is the naming of essential qualifications of those who were to participate in the bringing about of this marvelous work. These qualifications were not the possession of wealth, not social distinction, not political preferment, not military achievement, not nobility of birth; but a desire to serve God with all your "heart, might, mind and strength"—spiritual qualities that contribute to nobility of soul. I repeat: No popularity, no wealth, no theological training in church government—yet "a marvelous work [was] about to come forth among the children of men." CR1966Oct:86

**Related Witnesses:**

### George Q. Cannon

I do hope that, as soon as you get into your fields of labor, you will not apologize to the people for your weaknesses, and tell them how incapable and unfitted you are for such positions as you may hold. . . . Go into your fields of labor as men of God, appointed by Him to minister unto them the things pertaining to their salvation, and they will find that you have power which no other men, devoid of the authority you have, possess. (Gospel Truth, 2:78) TLDP:422

### Stephen L. Richards

I wish to bring forward a few items which justify this conclusion that our young men missionaries are ministers of religion. I grant you that they do not always look as other ministers look. They may be disappointing to some in formality and grace of expression. Many of them may not have attained the scholastic standing reached by most of the profession. What is the missionary's training for the ministry? ¶ First, he is usually reared in a home presided over by a man of the priesthood, who, in certain aspects at least, may be looked on as a man of the ministry. The functions of the ministry are carried forward in large measure in the future missionary's home. Prayer, blessings, scriptural and religious learning are features of his early environment. He is accorded the opportunity of participation. He prays, he sings, he reads, he studies, and in adolescent years, joins in sacred religious ordinances. ¶ Second, in the religious educational program of the Church, he becomes identified with the organizations of the Church. His mother may bring him to Sunday School as a baby; he toddles into the infant classes; and from then on he is taught, and he learns the literature of the Church and the ways of the Lord. ¶ Third, he is integrated into a spiritual society. His recreation, which not infrequently brings the contacts which enable him to choose his life's partner, is supervised and directed under religious auspices, whose constant endeavor it is to clarify and define the ultimate goals of life. In the atmosphere of such spirituality, his spirit nature is nurtured and developed. His liberal participation in all such institutions and exercises is calculated for the development of that spirituality. What I may ask, is more essential to a ministerial calling? ¶ Fourth, there then comes to the adolescent youth training and experience without counterpart in any other institutions of which I am aware. He enters the quorums of the priesthood. At the age of twelve he is first ordained and inducted into a group of approximately his own age. ¶ He is taught the history of the priesthood and he is made to understand that the power conferred upon him, even though a mere youth, derives from the authentic power given by the Lord Jesus Christ through his servants to those selected to receive the priesthood in this dispensation of time, and from whom it has come in direct and authentic succession to this boy. He has respect for this calling, and he seeks to discharge his duties as a youthful holder of the priesthood of the Lord. Is that training for a minister in the gospel of Christ? Is there anything taught in the seminaries of ecclesiastical learning more important as a groundwork for ministerial service than actual participation in the functions and offices of the priesthood? ¶ Well, this young man continues through the various gradations of the priesthood, always being given and assuming larger participation in the functions of the Church and the blessing of the people. ¶ Fifth, much of the education of the young man, not only in the Sunday School, the other auxiliary organizations, and the priesthood quorum, but also in his academic training, is directed toward acquisition of theological learning and capacity to live and expound the principles of the gospel. Church schools, institutes, and seminaries are available to him in this preparation. ¶ If he avails himself of all these privileges, I say he is prepared for missionary service and for ordination and setting apart to go forth as an ambassador and minister of the Lord Jesus Christ in teaching the gospel to the people and performing ministerial services among them. I hope that never again in our own country or in other countries will the ministerial status of our missionaries be seriously questioned. CR1955Oct:97-98

**Joseph Smith**

From a retrospect of the requirements of the servants of God to preach the Gospel . . . if a Priest understands his duty, his calling, and ministry, and preaches by the Holy Ghost, his enjoyment is as great as if he were one of the Presidency; and his services are necessary in the body, as are also those of Teachers and Deacons. *(Joseph instructs the priesthood in Kirtland Temple, April 1837)* HC2:478

**President Heber J. Grant**

There is nothing that qualifies a man so much for preaching the gospel of the Lord Jesus Christ as to study the revelations that the Lord has seen fit to give us in our day. CR1925Oct:6

---

460. Those who preach the gospel to the world shall say nothing but repentance (they shall preach only with the desire to bring people to repentance and faith in God).

**Elder Joseph Fielding Smith**

In the revelation to Oliver Cowdery, and to several others who came to ask what the Lord would have them do, the Lord said: "Say nothing but repentance unto this generation; keep my commandments, and assist to bring forth my work." We must not infer from this expression that those who went forth to preach were limited in their teachings so that all they could say was "repent from your sins," but in teaching the principles of the Gospel they should do so with the desire to teach repentance to the people and bring them in humility to a realization of the need for remission of sins. Even today, in all of our preaching it should be with the desire to bring people to repentance and faith in God. CHMR1:42

**Elder Brigham Young,**
**Heber C. Kimball, John E. Page,**
**Elder Wilford Woodruff,**
**Elder John Taylor,**
**George Albert Smith (1817-1875)**

Be careful that you teach not for the word of God, the commandments of men, nor the doctrines of men nor the ordinances of men, inasmuch as you are God's messengers; study the word of God and preach it, and not your opinions, for no man's opinion is worth a straw: advance no principle but what you can prove, for

one scriptural proof is worth ten thousand opinions: we would moreover say, abide by that revelation which says, "preach nothing but repentance to this generation," and leave the further mysteries of the kingdom, till God shall tell you to preach them, which is not now. ("To the Elders of the Church of Jesus Christ of Latter Day Saints, to the Churches Scattered Abroad, and to All the Saints," Times and Seasons, Nov. 1839, p. 13) TLDP:418-19

**Joseph Smith,**
*receiving the Word of the Lord*

Wherefore, you are called to cry repentance unto this people. 15. And if it so be that you should labor all your days in crying repentance unto this people, and bring, save it be one soul unto me, how great shall be your joy with him in the kingdom of my Father! . . . 20. Contend against no church, save it be the church of the devil. *(Revelation, June 1829)* D&C 18:14-15,20

**Joseph Smith,**
*quoted by Elder Joseph Fielding Smith*

Oh, ye elders of Israel, hearken to my voice; and when you are sent into the world to preach, tell those things you are sent to tell; preach and cry aloud, "Repent ye, for the kingdom of heaven is at hand; repent and believe the Gospel." Declare the first principles, and let mysteries alone, lest ye be overthrown. *(General conference in Nauvoo, Ill., April 8, 1843, on the floor of the temple, HC5:344)* TPJS:292

**Joseph Smith,**
*receiving the Word of the Lord*

And now, behold, I say unto you, that the thing which will be of the most worth unto you will be to declare repentance unto this people, that you may bring souls unto me, that you may rest with them in the kingdom of my Father. Amen. *(Revelation for John Whitmer, June 1829)* D&C 15:6

**Joseph Smith,**
*receiving the Word of the Lord*

Behold, the field is white already to harvest; therefore, whoso desireth to reap, let him thrust in his sickle with his might, and reap while the day lasts, that he may treasure up for his soul everlasting salvation in the kingdom of God. . . . 6. Now, as you have asked, behold, I say unto you, keep my commandments, and seek to bring forth and establish the cause of Zion; . . . 9. Say nothing but repentance unto this generation; keep my commandments, and assist to bring forth my work, according to my commandments, and you shall be blessed. *(Revelation for Oliver Cowdery, April 1829)* D&C 6:3,6,9

**Related Witnesses:**
**Mormon**

And thus, notwithstanding there being many

churches they were all one church, yea, even the church of God; for there was nothing preached in all the churches except it were repentance and faith in God. (*Alma establishes churches throughout Zarahemla, about 120 B.C.*) Mosiah 25:22

**Mormon**

And it came to pass that Alma, having authority from God, ordained priests; even one priest to every fifty of their number did he ordain to preach unto them, and to teach them concerning the things pertaining to the kingdom of God. 19. And he commanded them that they should teach nothing save it were the things which he had taught, and which had been spoken by the mouth of the holy prophets. 20. Yea, even he commanded them that they should preach nothing save it were repentance and faith on the Lord, who redeemed his people. (*Alma organizes the Church of Christ, about 148 B.C.*) Mosiah 18:18-20

**Alma, the younger,**
*quoted by Mormon*

Preach unto them repentance, and faith on the Lord Jesus Christ. . . . (*Alma instructs his son Helaman, about 73 B.C.*) Alma 37:33

**Jesus,**
*recorded in Matthew*

How think ye? if a man have an hundred sheep, and one of them be gone astray, doth he not leave the ninety and nine, and goeth into the mountains, and seeketh that which is gone astray? 13. And if so be that he find it, verily I say unto you, he rejoiceth more of that sheep, than of the ninety and nine which went not astray. (*Jesus teaches his disciples the parable of the lost sheep*) Matt.18:12-13

**Samuel, the Lamanite,**
*quoted by Mormon*

And he said unto them: Behold, I, Samuel a Lamanite, do speak the words of the Lord which he doth put into my heart; and behold he hath put it into my heart to say unto this people that the sword of justice hangeth over this people; and four hundred years pass not away save the sword of justice falleth upon this people. 6. Yea, heavy destruction awaiteth this people, and it surely cometh unto this people, and nothing can save this people save it be repentance and faith on the Lord Jesus Christ, who surely shall come into the world, and/shall suffer many things and shall be slain for his people. (*Samuel prophesies the destruction of the Nephites unless they repent, 6 B.C.*) Hel.13:5-6

**Jesus,**
*recorded in Matthew*

For the Son of man is come to save that which was lost. [JST(Matt.18:11 fn. c) . . . and to call sinners to repentance. . . .] (*Jesus teaches his disciples the parable of the lost sheep*) Matt.18:11

---

**461.** **Missionaries are to proclaim the gospel by the Spirit of God; they are to teach only as moved upon by the Holy Ghost.**

**Joseph Smith,**
*receiving the Word of the Lord*

Verily I say unto you, he that is ordained of me and sent forth to preach the word of truth by the Comforter, in the Spirit of truth, doth he preach it by the Spirit of truth or some other way? 18. And if it be by some other way it is not of God. 19. And again, he that receiveth the word of truth, doth he receive it by the Spirit of truth or some other way? 20. If it be some other way it is not of God. 21. Therefore, why is it that ye cannot understand and know, that he that receiveth the word by the Spirit of truth receiveth it as it is preached by the Spirit of truth? 22. Wherefore, he that preacheth and he that receiveth, understand one another, and both are edified and rejoice together. (*Revelation for the elders of the Church, May 1831*) D&C 50:17-22

**Joseph Smith,**
*receiving the Word of the Lord*

My servant, Orson Hyde, was called by his ordination to proclaim the everlasting gospel, by the Spirit of the living God, from people to people, and from land to land, in the congregations of the wicked, in their synagogues, reasoning with and expounding all scriptures unto them. 2. And, behold, and lo, this is an ensample unto all those who were ordained unto this priesthood, whose mission is appointed unto them to go forth— 3. And this is the ensample unto them, that they shall speak as they are moved upon by the Holy Ghost. (*Revelation, Nov. 1831*) D&C 68:1-3

**Henry D. Moyle**

Some may ask the question as to how we convert others to the truth. The answer is, we do not. Conversion comes from above. Our part in this work is to plant the seeds of truth. These seeds are born of our conviction when we testify of the divine mission of Jesus Christ, the Son of the Living God, who offered himself as a sacrifice for the sins of the world. We rely upon the gift and power of the Holy Ghost to carry our message into the hearts of our listeners and witness unto them the truthfulness of our stated conviction. CR1961Apr:101-02

**President Brigham Young**

Let one go forth who is careful to logically

prove all he says by numerous quotations from the revelations, and let another travel with him who can say, by the power of the Holy Ghost, Thus saith the Lord, and tell what the people should believe—what they should do—how they should live, and teach them to yield to the principles of salvation—though he may not be capable of producing a single logical argument—though he may tremble under a sense of his weakness, cleaving to the Lord for strength, as such men generally do, you will invariably find that the man who testifies by the power of the Holy Ghost will convince and gather many more of the honest and upright than will the merely logical reasoner. (*Instructions to missionaries in historian's office, April 25, 1860, JD8:53*) TLDP:419-20

**Related Witnesses:**

**President Brigham Young**

Nothing short of a testimony by the power of the Holy Ghost would bring light and knowledge to them—bring them in their hearts to repentance. Nothing short of that would ever do. (*In Bowery, Oct. 7, 1857, JD5:327*) TLDP:420

**President Spencer W. Kimball**

Actually, the missionary does not convert anyone: the Holy Ghost does the converting. The power of conversion is directly associated with the Holy Ghost, for no person can be truly converted and know that Jesus is the Christ save by the power of the Holy Ghost. ("It Becometh Every Man," EN1977Oct:3, The Teachings of Spencer W. Kimball, p. 570) TLDP:420

**Henry D. Moyle**

There is no power on earth by which we can penetrate the souls of men, the equal of that radiation of love and affection which will naturally pass from us to those to whom we bring truth and light and knowledge and understanding. CR1953Apr:127

---

462. **The preaching of the gospel has a more powerful effect on the minds of people who hear it, to lead them to do right, than anything else.**

**Mormon**

And now, as the preaching of the word had a great tendency to lead the people to do that which was just—yea, it had had more powerful effect upon the minds of the people than the sword, or anything else, which had happened unto them—therefore Alma thought it was expedient that they should try the virtue of the word

of God. (*Alma heads a mission to reclaim the apostate Zoramites, about 74 B.C.*) Alma 31:5

**President Spencer W. Kimball**

As a vital link in the conversion process, we should bear our testimonies that the gospel is true; our testimonies may well be the spark that ignites the conversion process. Consequently, we have a double responsibility; we must testify of the things we know, feel, and have felt, and we must live so the Holy Ghost can be with us and convey our words in power to the heart of the investigator. ("It Becometh Every Man," EN1977Oct:3, The Teachings of Spencer W. Kimball, p. 138) TLDP:420

**Joseph Smith**

And again, he that receiveth the word of truth, doth he receive it by the Spirit of truth or some other way? 20. If it be some other way it is not of God. 21. Therefore, why is it that ye cannot understand and know, that he that receiveth the word by the Spirit of truth receiveth it as it is preached by the Spirit of truth? 22. Wherefore, he that preacheth and he that receiveth, understand one another, and both are edified and rejoice together. (*Revelation for the elders of the Church, May 1831*) D&C 50:19-22

**Elder Joseph Fielding Smith**

This revelation [D&C 5:7-10] declared that this generation shall have the word of the Lord through Joseph Smith. There may be some who think that this is unreasonable, and the Lord should use some miraculous means to convert the world. Frequently when strangers . . . hear the story of the coming forth of the Book of Mormon, they ask if the plates are in some museum where they may be seen. Some of them with some scientific training, express themselves to the effect that if the scholars could see and examine the plates and learn to read them, they would then bear witness to the truth of the Book of Mormon and the veracity of Joseph Smith, and the whole world would then be converted. When they are informed that the angel took the plates back again, they turn away in their skepticism, shaking their heads. But the Lord has said: "For my thoughts are not your thoughts, neither are your ways my ways, saith the Lord. For as the heavens are higher than the earth, so are my ways higher than your ways, and my thoughts than your thoughts." (Isa.55:8-9) We have learned that people are not converted by miracles or by examining records. If the Lord had placed the [Book of Mormon] plates where the scholars could examine them, they would have scoffed at them just as much as they do today. People are converted by their hearts being penetrated by the

Spirit of the Lord when they humbly hearken to the testimonies of the Lord's servants. The Jews witnessed the miracles of our Lord, but this did not prevent them from crying out against him and having him crucified. CHMR1:39-40; DCSM:13

### Elder Wilford Woodruff

The whole secret of our success as far as making converts is concerned is, that we preach the same Gospel in all its simplicity and plainness that Jesus preached, and that the Holy Ghost rests upon those who receive it, filling their hearts with joy and gladness unspeakable, and making them as one; and they then know of the doctrine for themselves whether it be of God or man. (*In Tabernacle, May 14, 1882, JD23:129*) TLDP:419

---

463. The Lord will support and strengthen the efforts of those who are called to proclaim the gospel.

### President Brigham Young

I would like to impress upon the minds of the brethren, that he who goes forth in the name of the Lord, trusting in Him with all his heart, will never want for wisdom to answer any question that is asked him, or to give any counsel that may be required to lead the people in the way of life and salvation, and he will never be confounded worlds without end. . . . Go in the name of the Lord, trust in the name of the Lord, lean upon the Lord, and call upon the Lord fervently and without ceasing, and pay no attention to the world. (*In Tabernacle, April 14, 1867, JD12:34*) TLDP:421-22

### Jesus,
*recorded in Matthew*

Go ye therefore, and teach all nations, baptizing them in the name of the Father, and of the Son, and of the Holy Ghost: 20. Teaching them to observe all things whatsoever I have commanded you: and, lo, I am with you alway, even unto the end of the world. Amen. (*The risen Jesus commands the eleven disciples to teach all nations*) Matt.28:19-20

### Stephen L. Richards

I am not discouraged because I recognize that our numbers are still relatively small. Some one has said that there is but one Latter-day Saint to every ten thousand in the population of the world. It would seem an almost impossible task to disseminate the principles of truth with such a minority. But I remember that old saying that "God and one man are a majority" and

I have confidence to state that if we keep ourselves in line with our duties; if we fully live these principles of the truth that we are charged to teach, God will give us power, He will magnify our work, He will make our messages reach into the far corners of the earth. He will sustain His own. CR1940Oct:34

### Joseph Smith,
*receiving the Word of the Lord*

Yea, verily, verily, I say unto you, that the field is white already to harvest; wherefore, thrust in your sickles, and reap with all your might, mind, and strength. 8. Open your mouths and they shall be filled, and you shall become even as Nephi of old, who journeyed from Jerusalem in the wilderness. 9. Yea, open your mouths and spare not, and you shall be laden with sheaves upon your backs, for lo, I am with you. 10. Yea, open your mouths and they shall be filled, saying: Repent, repent, and prepare ye the way of the Lord, and make his paths straight; for the kingdom of heaven is at hand; (*Revelation for Ezra Thayre and Northrop Sweet, Oct. 1830*) D&C 33:7-10

### Elder John Taylor

These missionaries are now going to school to teach others, and in teaching others they themselves will be instructed, and when they rise to speak in the name of Israel's God, if they live in purity and holiness and before him, He will give them words and ideas of which they never dreamed before. I have travelled hundreds and thousands of miles to preach this gospel among all grades and conditions of men, and there is one thing that always gave me satisfaction—I never yet found a man in any part of the world who could overturn one principle that has been communicated to us; they will attempt it, but error is a very singular weapon with which to combat truth; it never can vanquish it. ¶ When men go forth in the name of Israel's God there is no power on earth that can overturn the truths they advocate. Men may misrepresent and calumniate them; they may circulate false reports, for as a general thing men love lies better than truth; but when men go forth possessing the truths of the everlasting gospel which God has revealed, they have a treasure within them that the world knows nothing about; they have the light of revelation, the fire of the Holy Ghost, and the power of the priesthood within them—a power that they know very little about even themselves, which, like a well-spring of life, is rising, bursting, bubbling, and spreading its exhilarating streams around. Why, says the Lord, with you I will confound the nations of the earth, with you I will overturn their kingdoms.

(*In Tabernacle, April 14, 1867, JD12:396-97*)
TLDP:422

### Elder John Taylor

I will tell you the first thing I used to do when I went preaching, particularly when I went to a fresh place—and that was to go aside to some place, anywhere I could get, into a field, a barn, into the woods, or my closet, and ask God to bless me and give me wisdom to meet all the circumstances with which I might have to contend; and the Lord gave me the wisdom I needed and sustained me. If you pursue a course of this kind, he will bless you also. Do not trust in yourselves, but study the best books—the Bible and Book of Mormon—and get all the information you can, and then cleave to God and keep yourselves free from corruption and pollution of every kind, and the blessings of the Most High will be with you. (*In Tabernacle, April 14, 1867, JD12:398*) (The Gospel Kingdom, p. 240) TLDP:422

### Orson Pratt

Brethren, I will prophesy that the power of the Lord God of Israel will be with you . . . and the way will be open before you, and the Lord will visit the hearts of the people before you arrive among them, and make manifest to them by visions and dreams that you are the servants of God, before they shall see your faces. And you will receive heavenly visions to comfort you, and dreams to give you knowledge of the things of God, if you prove faithful before him. I will prophesy this in the name of the Lord God of Israel. . . . (Masterful Discourses and Writings of Orson Pratt, p. 35) TLDP:422

**Related Witnesses:**

### Joseph Smith,
*receiving the Word of the Lord*

Behold, this is the promise of the Lord unto you, O ye my servants. 6. Wherefore, be of good cheer, and do not fear, for I the Lord am with you, and will stand by you: and ye shall bear record of me, even Jesus Christ, that I am the Son of the living God, that I was, that I am, and that I am to come. (*Revelation, Nov. 1831*) D&C 68:5-6

### Recorded in Exodus

And Moses said unto the LORD, O my Lord, I am not eloquent, neither heretofore, nor since thou hast spoken unto thy servant: but I am slow of speech, and of a slow tongue. 11. And the LORD said unto him, Who hath made man's mouth? or who maketh the dumb, or deaf, or the seeing, or the blind? have not I the LORD? 12. Now therefore go, and I will be with thy mouth, and teach thee what thou shalt say. (*Moses is called by the Lord to deliver Israel from bondage*) Ex.4:10-12

**464.** There is joy in missionary service—the Lord greatly blesses the lives of those who serve as missionaries to the world.

### Thomas S. Monson

We [the Church] care because the Lord, who knows the source of all happiness, has asked us to do it [share the gospel with others] and has assured us blessings and happiness and joy if we will do it. We care because when we share the gospel with others, we unavoidably get outside of ourselves; we think and pray and work for the blessing of others, and this only further enriches and quickens us by the Holy Spirit. The list of by-products to ourselves is endless—growth in our testimonies, growth in our knowledge of the gospel, growth in our faith, more answered prayers. The eternal truth is: that which we willingly share, we keep; and that which we selfishly keep to ourselves, we lose. We care because we want all of our members everywhere to be happy. Is there any better reason? ("Status Report on Missionary Work," EN1977Oct:11) TLDP:424

### Elder George Albert Smith

It is not an easy task; it is not a pleasant thing, perhaps, to be called out into the world, to leave our dear ones, but I say to you that it will purchase for those who are faithful, for those who discharge that obligation as they may be required, peace and happiness beyond all understanding, and will prepare them that, in due time, when life's labor is complete, they will stand in the presence of their Maker, accepted of Him because of what they have done. CR1922Apr:53

### Elder George Albert Smith

A hundred years ago yesterday the Lord commenced this work. . . . ¶ At that time he gave certain information. . . . The Lord said: "For, behold, I will bless all those who labor in my vineyard with a mighty blessing, and they shall believe on his words, which are given him through me by the Comforter, which manifesteth that Jesus was crucified by sinful men for the sins of the world, yea, for the remission of sins unto the contrite heart." [D&C 21:9] ¶ I call attention to the fact that he made a promise that he would bless all those who labored in his vineyard, and since that time thousands of men and women have gone into the world to advocate the truth. I have met and visited with hundreds, yes and with thousands of them myself, and I have never heard one bear any other testimony than that the Lord had blessed him and given him great joy when he labored in his service. CR1930Apr:66

**Joseph Smith,**
*receiving the Word of the Lord*

Remember the worth of souls is great in the sight of God; . . . 13. And how great is his joy in the soul that repenteth! . . . 15. And if it so be that you should labor all your days in crying repentance unto this people, and bring, save it be one soul unto me, how great shall be your joy with him in the kingdom of my Father! 16. And now, if your joy will be great with one soul that you have brought unto me into the kingdom of my Father, how great will be your joy if you should bring many souls unto me! (*Revelation, June 1829*) D&C 18:10,13,15-16

**Joseph Smith,**
*receiving the Word of the Lord*

And now, behold, I say unto you, that the thing which will be of the most worth unto you will be to declare repentance unto this people, that you may bring souls unto me, that you may rest with them in the kingdom of my Father. Amen. (*Revelation for Peter Whitmer, Fayette, N.Y., June 1829*) D&C 16:6

**President Heber J. Grant**

In all my labors I got nearer to the Lord, and accomplished more, and had more joy while in the mission field than ever before or since. Man is that he may have joy, and the joy that I had in the mission field was superior to any I have ever experienced elsewhere. Get it into your hearts, young people, to prepare yourselves to go out into the world where you can get on your knees and draw nearer to the Lord than in any other labor. ("The President Speaks: Excerpts from the Utterances of Heber J. Grant," IE1936Nov:659) TLDP:423

**Related Witnesses:**

**Stephen L. Richards**

The knowledge, the tolerance, the adventure, the polish, and the experience which worldwide travel brings have been, during the whole history of the Church, the product of our missionary system. I feel sure that in no other communities on the earth is the percentage of those who have "seen the world" so large as in the villages, towns, and cities of the Latter-day Saints. ¶ Such benefits, however, while important, are but incidental. The more vital results are deeper then enlarged information and polish. The fundamental character of our manhood and womanhood has been improved. Sacrifice has taught self-control. Giving has made for generosity as it always does. Teaching the virtues has brought them into application, and high spirituality has ingrained testimony and soul development. The general uplift in all standards of living which the Church has brought to its adherents is in no small measure directly attributable to its missionary system. CR1945Oct:55

**Joseph Smith,**
*receiving the Word of the Lord*

For, behold, I will bless all those who labor in my vineyard with a mighty blessing. . . . (*Revelation received April 6, 1830*) D&C 21:9

**Joseph Smith,**
*receiving the Word of the Lord*

Behold, the field is white already to harvest; therefore, whoso desireth to reap, let him thrust in his sickle with his might, and reap while the day lasts, that he may treasure up for his soul everlasting salvation in the kingdom of God. . . . 9. Say nothing but repentance unto this generation; keep my commandments, and assist to bring forth my work, according to my commandments, and you shall be blessed. (*Revelation for Oliver Cowdery, April 1829*) D&C 6:3,9

**President Brigham Young,**
*quoted by John A. Widtsoe*

Those faithful Elders who have testified of this work to thousands of people on the continents and islands of the seas will see the fruits of their labors, whether they have said five words or thousands. They may not see these fruits immediately, and perhaps, in many cases, not until the Millennium, but the savor of their testimony will pass down from father to son. (*In Bowery, Aug. 12, 1860, JD8:142*) DBY:329

---

**465. People are not to function as missionaries unless they are set apart and authorized to preach the gospel by one who has authority.**

**Joseph Smith**

We believe that a man must be called of God, by prophecy, and by the laying on of hands by those who are in authority, to preach the Gospel and administer in the ordinances thereof. (*The fifth of the thirteen Articles of Faith; letter to John Wentworth, March 1, 1842*) AofF:5

**Elder Wilford Woodruff**

Men cannot legally and authoritatively go forth to preach the Gospel until they are sent: and men cannot hear the word and be converted by the same unless they hear it through the mouth of a preacher who is sent, and who has power to administer in the ordinances of the Gospel. (*In Assembly Hall, March 26, 1882, JD23:78*) TLDP:417

**Joseph Smith,**
*receiving the Word of the Lord*

Again I say unto you, that it shall not be given

to any one to go forth to preach my gospel, or to build up my church, except he be ordained by some one who has authority, and it is known to the church that he has authority and has been regularly ordained by the heads of the church. (*Revelation "embracing the law of the Church," Feb. 9, 1831*) D&C 42:11

**Elder Lorenzo Snow**

We send our elders to preach the Gospel. Who sends them? President Woodruff? In one sense, no. The God of Israel sends them. It is His work. There is no mortal man that is so much interested in the success of an elder when he is preaching the Gospel as the Lord that sent him to preach to the people who are the Lord's children. (Millennial Star, July 16, 1894, p. 451) TLDP:417

**Joseph Smith**

And again, verily I say unto you, those who desire in their hearts, in meekness, to warn sinners to repentance, let them be ordained unto this power. (*Revelation, Aug. 1831*) D&C 63:57

**Elder Spencer W. Kimball**

"We believe that a man must be called of God, by prophecy, and by the laying on of hands, by those who are in authority to preach the Gospel and administer in the ordinances thereof." ¶ In accordance with this policy each missionary is called of God through the president of the Church. This is the way that Aaron received his call. Moses, the Lord's prophet, gave to him the call from the Lord. ¶ In the assigning of missionaries there are numerous factors, the chief one being the inspiration received by the Missionary Executive Committee, who review carefully and prayerfully all of the recommendations sent to them by the stakes and missions. As this committee makes recommendations, it considers numerous factors: worthiness, age, experience, military status, home, finances, health, language ability, desires, quotas, limitations of countries, requests, nationality, general attitudes, and the needs of the various missions. When all these factors have been duly weighed, a sincere effort is made to ascertain where the person can make the greatest contribution; the inspiration of the Lord is sought earnestly. The tentative assignment is made subject to approval by the president of the Church, who then signs the call and has it mailed to the prospective missionary. ("How Is the Missionary's Place of Assignment Determined?" NE1972Feb:37) TLDP:417

---

466. **Every person who has received the gospel is under obligation to take the gospel to his or her neighbor.**

**George F. Richards**

Every man and every woman that comes into the Church, every convert, is expected of the Lord to be a missionary for him, whether he be called to labor at home or abroad, or having no calling whatever specially given unto him. CR1933Oct:115

**President Brigham Young,**
*quoted by John A. Widtsoe*

We wish the brethren to understand the facts just as they are; that is, there is neither man or woman in this Church who is not on a mission. That mission will last as long as they live, and it is to do good, to promote righteousness, to teach the principles of truth, and to prevail upon themselves and everybody around them to live those principles that they may obtain eternal life. (*Words to departing missionaries, April 1867, JD12:19*) DBY:322

**Elder George Albert Smith**

It is my firm conviction . . . that unless we stir ourselves more than we are doing, that when we go to the other side of the veil, we will meet there men and women who have been our neighbors, and associates, and lived among us, that will condemn us because we have been so inconsiderate of them in not telling them of the truth of the gospel of our Lord. CR1916Oct:49-50

**Joseph Smith,**
*receiving the Word of the Lord*

Behold, I sent you out to testify and warn the people, and it becometh every man who hath been warned to warn his neighbor. 82. Therefore, they are left without excuse, and their sins are upon their own heads. (*Revelation, Dec. 27/28, 1832; the "olive leaf message of peace"*) D&C 88:81-82

**John A. Widtsoe**

In our pre-existent state, in the day of the great council, we made a certain agreement with the Almighty. The Lord proposed a plan, conceived by him. We accepted it. Since the plan is intended for all men, we become parties to the salvation of every person under the plan. We agreed, right then and there, to be not only saviors for ourselves, but measurably saviors for the whole human family. We went into partnership with the Lord. The working out of the plan became then not merely the Father's work, and the Savior's work, but also our work. The least of us, the humblest, is in partnership with the Almighty in achieving the purpose of the eternal plan of salvation. . . . (Utah Genealogical and Historical Magazine, Oct. 1934) MPSG1967:87

**Joseph Smith,**
*receiving the Word of the Lord*

And now, behold, I say unto you, that the thing

which will be of the most worth unto you will be to declare repentance unto this people, that you may bring souls unto me, that you may rest with them in the kingdom of my Father. Amen. *(Revelation for Peter Whitmer, Fayette, N.Y., June 1829)* D&C 16:6

### Joseph Smith

After all that has been said, the greatest and most important duty is to preach the Gospel. *(Joseph addresses the quorums of the priesthood in Kirtland Temple, April 1837)* HC2:478; DCSM:39

### Orson F. Whitney

The obligation of saving souls rests upon every man and woman in this Church—if not with equal weight, at least proportionately, according to their strength, their time, their opportunities, their abilities; and they cannot get out from under this responsibility on the plea that it belongs only to such and such persons. Did not the Lord say, through Joseph the Seer, at the beginning of this work, "Behold, it is a day of warning, and not of many words: Therefore, let every soul that is warned, warn its neighbor"? [See D&C 63:58, 88:81] CR1913Oct:99

### Related Witnesses:
#### President Heber J. Grant

I want to emphasize that we as a people have one supreme thing to do, and that is to call upon the world to repent of sin, to come to God. And it is our duty above all others to go forth and proclaim the gospel of the Lord Jesus Christ, the restoration again to the earth of the plan of life and salvation. . . . We have so much to look after, so many business interests, so many important things, so far as dollars and cents are concerned, that we are neglecting the one great thing of all; namely, the proclaiming of the gospel, and making what people call sacrifices but what actually are the exact opposite. We have in very deed the pearl of great price. We have that which is of more value than all the wealth and the scientific information which the world possesses. We have the plan of life and salvation. The first great commandment was to love the Lord our God with all our hearts, might, mind and strength; and the second was like unto it, to love our neighbor as ourselves. And the best way in the world to show our love for our neighbor is to go forth and proclaim the gospel of the Lord Jesus Christ, of which he has given us an absolute knowledge concerning its divinity. CR1927Apr:175-76

---

467. The Saints of God are to be a light to the world by setting an example of righteous living.

### Francis M. Lyman

If you be converted and are true Latter-day Saints, we want you to convert your neighbors—and convert them by your living. No stronger testimony can be borne in regard to the principles of honesty, temperance, justice, mercy, truth and morality, than for a man to live those principles and doctrines. No testimony is stronger. People may question what we say and what testimony we bear, but they cannot question our lives. If a man lives an honest life, meets his obligations, if he is a true man and lives a godly and upright life, dealing with his fellow men as he would that men should deal with him, if he is true and faithful in every line, no man can say nay to what that man does, for it is unquestionable, it is the facts as they exist and are eternal. CR1908Apr:18-19

### Elder George Albert Smith

My understanding is that the most important mission that I have in this life is: first, to keep the commandments of God, as they have been taught to me; and next, to teach them to my Father's children who do not understand them. . . . ¶ It is not necessary for you to be called to go into the mission field in order to proclaim the truth. Begin on the man who lives next door by inspiring confidence in him, by inspiring love in him for you because of your righteousness, and your missionary work has already begun. CR1916Oct:50-51; DCSM:12

### Jesus,
#### *recorded in Matthew*

Ye are the light of the world. A city that is set on an hill cannot be hid. 15. Neither do men light a candle, and put it under a bushel, but on a candlestick; and it giveth light unto all that are in the house. 16. Let your light so shine before men, that they may see your good works, and glorify your Father which is in heaven. *(Jesus Christ teaches the multitude, about A.D. 30)* Matt.5:14-16

### Jesus,
#### *recorded in Matthew*

Ye shall know them by their fruits. Do men gather grapes of thorns, or figs of thistles? 17. Even so every good tree bringeth forth good fruit; but a corrupt tree bringeth forth evil fruit. 18. A good tree cannot bring forth evil fruit, neither can a corrupt tree bring forth good fruit. 19. Every tree that bringeth not forth good fruit is hewn down, and cast into the fire. 20. Wherefore by their fruits ye shall know them. *(Jesus concludes his sermon on the mount)* Matt.7:16-20

### John A. Widtsoe

So we need, in this Church and Kingdom, for

our own and the world's welfare, a group of men and women in their individual lives who shall be as a light to the nations, and rally standards for the world to follow. Such a people must be different from the world as it now is. There is no opportunity for Latter-day Saints to say we shall be as the world is, unless the world has the same aim that we have. We are here to build Zion to Almighty God, for the blessing of all the world. In that aim we are unique and different from all other peoples. We must respect that obligation, and not be afraid of it. We cannot walk as other men, or talk as other men, or do as other men, for we have a different destiny, obligation, and responsibility placed upon us, and we must fit ourselves for that great destiny and obligation. CR1940Apr:36

### Joseph Smith,
*receiving the Word of the Lord*

Therefore, blessed are ye if ye continue in my goodness, a light unto the Gentiles, and through this priesthood, a savior unto my people Israel. The Lord hath said it. Amen. (*Revelation, Nov. 27, 1832*) D&C 86:11

### Joseph Smith

For they were set to be a light unto the world, and to be the saviors of men; 10. And inasmuch as they are not the saviors of men, they are as salt that has lost its savor, and is thenceforth good for nothing but to be cast out and trodden under foot of men. (*Revelation at Kirtland, Ohio, Feb. 24, 1834; why the Lord permitted persecution; those who prevail are those who are obedient*) D&C 103:9-10

### Joseph Smith

It is a time-honored adage that love begets love. Let us pour forth love—show forth our kindness unto all mankind, and the Lord will reward us with everlasting increase; cast our bread upon the waters and we shall receive it after many days, increased to a hundredfold. Friendship is like Brother Turley in his blacksmith shop welding iron to iron; it unites the human family with its happy influence. (*In meeting at the Stand in Nauvoo, Ill., July 23, 1843*) HC5:517

### Paul

Let no man despise thy youth; but be thou an example of the believers, in word, in conversation, in charity, in spirit, in faith, in purity. (*Paul writes to his assistant Timothy, about A.D. 64*) 1Tim.4:12

### Elder Joseph Fielding Smith

It is the duty of every member of the Church to preach the gospel by precept and by example. (Take Heed to Yourselves, p. 72) TLDP:415

### Peter

Having your conversation honest among the Gentiles: that, whereas they speak against you as evildoers, they may by your good works, which they shall behold, glorify God in the day of visitation. (*Peter to the churches in Asia Minor, about A.D. 60*) 1Pet.2:12

**Author's Note:** Results of a *bad* example: "And thus ended the eighth year of the reign of the judges; and the wickedness of the church was a great stumbling-block to those who did not belong to the church; and thus the church began to fail in its progress." (Alma 4:10)

---

### HYMNS Written by Prophets
### Applicable to this Topic

#### John Taylor
*Go, Ye Messengers of Glory*
HYMNS:262

Go, ye messengers of glory;
Run, ye legates of the skies.
Go and tell the pleasing story
That a glorious angel flies,
Great and mighty, Great and mighty,
With a message from the skies.

Go to ev'ry tribe and nation;
Visit ev'ry land and clime.
Sound to all the proclamation;
Tell to all the truth sublime:
That the gospel, That the gospel
Does in ancient glory shine.

Go, to all the gospel carry;
Let the joyful news abound.
Go till ev'ry nation hear you,
Jew and Gentile greet the sound.
Let the gospel, Let the gospel
Echo all the earth around.

Bearing seed of heav'nly virtue,
Scatter it o'er all the earth.
Go! Jehovah will support you;
Gather all the sheaves of worth.
Then, with Jesus, Then, with Jesus
Reign in glory on the earth.

#### John Taylor
*Go, Ye Messengers of Heaven*
HYMNS:327

Go, ye messengers of heaven,
Chosen by divine command;
Go and publish free salvation
To a dark, benighted land.

Go to island, vale, and mountain;
There fulfill the great command;
Gather out the sons of Jacob
To possess the promised land.

When your thousands all are gathered,
And their prayers for you ascend,
And the Lord has crowned with blessings
All the labors of your hand,

Then the song of joy and transport
Will from ev'ry land resound;
Then the nations long in darkness
By the Savior will be crowned.

# List of Doctrines

## MORTAL LIFE: Second Estate

*Doctrines Located in This Topic*

468. Those who come to earth are those who were faithful in the premortal life (they kept their First Estate).

469. Those who successfully meet the trials of life on earth will inherit eternal life in the celestial kingdom of glory.

470. One reason we came to earth was to obtain physical bodies of flesh and bone.

471. Mortality is a time for testing and trial, to prove whether we will keep the commandments of God.

472. Our life on earth is a probationary period, a time to prepare for eternal life.

473. The body is a temple in which the Spirit of God may dwell.

474. On earth those who accept the gospel are given the opportunity to receive the necessary eternal ordinances of salvation.

*Doctrines on MORTAL LIFE Located in Other Topics*

1. Life on earth is a probationary state in which every individual who attains the age of accountability is tested.

106. Each individual's placement among the tribes, families, and nations of this world was determined by the kind of life he or she lived in the premortal state.

189. Before the Fall, Adam was not subject to death.

195. After the Fall, Adam and Eve were granted a probationary time to repent and serve God.

196. As a result of the Fall, Adam and Eve experienced pain and sorrow, which are part of mortality.

# MORTAL LIFE: Second Estate

468. Those who come to earth are those who were faithful in the premortal life (they kept their First Estate).

### President Heber J. Grant

We have been placed upon this earth because of our faithfulness in having kept our first estate. The labors that we performed in the sphere that we left before we came here have had a certain effect upon our lives here, and to a certain extent they govern and control the lives that we lead here, just the same as the labors that we do here will control and govern our lives when we pass from this stage of existence. ("Reward of Conscience," Improvement Era, Feb. 1943, p. 75) TLDP:496

### Abraham,
### *quoted by Joseph Smith*

And they who keep their first estate shall be added upon; and they who keep not their first estate shall not have glory in the same kingdom with those who keep their first estate; and they who keep their second estate shall have glory added upon their heads for ever and ever. (*Abraham learns about the creation of the earth, of pre-earth existence, foreordination and the second estate of man*) Abr.3:26

### Elder Joseph Fielding Smith

The people who inhabit this earth were all living in the spirit life before they came to this earth. The Lord informs us that this earth was designed, before its foundations were formed, for the abode of the spirits who kept their first estate, and all such must come here and receive their tabernacles of flesh and bones, and this is according to the number, or measure, of man according to his creation before the world was made. CHMR1:209

### James E. Talmage

Man in his mortal state is the union of a preexistent spirit with a body composed of earthly elements. This union of spirit and body marks progress from the unembodied to the embodied condition, and is an inestimable advancement in the soul's onward course. The penalty incurred by proud Lucifer and his rebel hordes for their attempt to thwart the divine purpose in the matter of man's agency was the doom of being denied bodies of flesh. Mortal birth is a boon to which only those spirits who kept their first estate are eligible (see Jude 6). Expressive of the awful state of the utterly unregenerate among men, of those who have sunk to such depths in sin as to become "sons of perdition" the Lord has applied the extreme malediction

that for such it were better never to have been born (see Matt.26:24; D&C 76:32). The blessedness of advancement to the mortal state lies in the possibilities of achievement therein. Mortality is the preparatory school for eternity. Its curriculum is comprehensive and exacting. In its laboratories we pupils meet the experiences that test and try to conclusive demonstration the individual effect of precept and profession. For the founding and maintenance of this school the earth was created. AF:428

### Elder Harold B. Lee

There is no truth more plainly taught in the Gospel than that our condition in the next world will depend upon the kind of lives we live here. "All that are in the graves shall hear his voice, and shall come forth; they that have done evil, unto the resurrection of damnation." (John 5:28-29) Is it not just as reasonable to suppose that the conditions in which we now live have been determined by the kind of lives we lived in the preexistent world of spirits? That the apostles understood this principle is indicated by their question to the Master when the man who was blind from his birth was healed of his blindness. "Master, who did sin, this man or his parents that he was born blind?" (John 9:2) Now perhaps you will have a partial answer to some of your questions as to why, if God is a just Father, that some of his children are born of an enlightened race and in a time when the Gospel is upon the earth, while others are born of a heathen parentage in a benighted, backward country. . . . ¶ The privilege of obtaining a mortal body on this earth is seemingly so priceless that those in the spirit world, even though unfaithful or not valiant, were undoubtedly permitted to take mortal bodies although under penalty of racial or physical or nationalistic limitations. Between the extremes of the "noble and the great" spirits, whom God would make his rulers, and the disobedient and the rebellious who were cast out with Satan, there were obviously many spirits with varying degrees of faithfulness. May we not assume from these teachings that the progress and development we made as spirits have brought privileges and blessings here according to our faithfulness in the spirit world? (Decisions for Successful Living, pp. 164-65) TLDP:497

### Related Witnesses:
### Elder Joseph Fielding Smith

The punishment of Satan and the third of the host of heaven who followed him, was that they were denied the privilege of being born into this world and receiving mortal bodies. They did not keep their first estate and were denied the opportunity of eternal progression. The Lord cast them out into the earth, where they became the tempters of mankind—the devil and his angels. (Doctrines of Salvation, 1:65) DGSM:15

**Paul**

Blessed be the God and Father of our Lord Jesus Christ, who hath blessed us with all spiritual blessings in heavenly places in Christ: 4. According as he hath chosen us in him before the foundation of the world, that we should be holy and without blame before him in love: (*Letter to the Saints at Ephesus in Asia Minor, about A.D. 62*) Eph.1:3-4

**Paul**

But we are bound to give thanks alway to God for you, brethren beloved of the Lord, because God hath from the beginning chosen you to salvation through sanctification of the Spirit and belief of the truth: 14. Whereunto he called you by our gospel, to the obtaining of the glory of our Lord Jesus Christ. (*Letter to the Church at Thessalonica, comprising Jews and many pagan converts, A.D. 50*) 2Thess.2:13-14

---

**469. Those who successfully meet the trials of life on earth will inherit eternal life in the celestial kingdom of glory.**

**Marion G. Romney**

The spirits who kept their first estate—that was their spirit estate—are added upon, as promised, by receiving mortal bodies as they are born here upon this earth as human souls. ¶ The promise is that if they keep this, their second (that is, our mortal) estate, they "shall have glory added upon their heads for ever and ever." ¶ . . . [W]e came to earth for two purposes: one, to obtain physical bodies of flesh and bone in the likeness of our Heavenly Father; and two, to be proved—to see if we "will do all things whatsoever the Lord" our God commands us. CR1976Apr:118-19

**Abraham,**
*quoted by Joseph Smith*

And we will prove them herewith, to see if they will do all things whatsoever the Lord their God shall command them; 26. And they who keep their first estate shall be added upon; and they who keep not their first estate shall not have glory in the same kingdom with those who keep their first estate; and they who keep their second estate shall have glory added upon their heads for ever and ever. (*Abraham learns about the creation of the earth and the second estate of man*) Abr.3:25-26

**President Brigham Young**

All intelligent beings who are crowned with crowns of glory, immortality, and eternal lives must pass through every ordeal appointed for intelligent beings to pass through, to gain their glory and exaltation. Every calamity that can come upon mortal beings will be suffered to come upon the few, to prepare them to enjoy the presence of the Lord. If we obtain the glory that Abraham obtained, we must do so by the same means that he did. . . . We must pass through the same experience, and gain the knowledge, intelligence, and endowments that will prepare us to enter into the celestial kingdom of our Father and God. . . . Every trial and experience you have passed through is necessary for your salvation. (*At Provo, Utah, Aug. 26, 1860, JD8:150*) TLDP:426-27

**Alma, the younger,**
*quoted by Mormon*

And we see that death comes upon mankind, yea, the death which has been spoken of by Amulek, which is the temporal death; nevertheless there was a space granted unto man in which he might repent; therefore this life became a probationary state; a time to prepare to meet God; a time to prepare for that endless state which has been spoken of by us, which is after the resurrection of the dead. (*Alma responds to the chief ruler, Antionah, regarding Adam and Eve's expulsion from the Garden of Eden, about 82 B.C.*) Alma 12:24

**Elder Harold B. Lee**

There is no truth more plainly taught in the Gospel than that our condition in the next world will depend upon the kind of lives we live here. "All that are in the graves shall hear his voice, and shall come forth; they that have done evil, unto the resurrection of damnation." (John 5:28-29) (Decisions for Successful Living, pp. 164-65) TLDP:497

**Joseph Smith,**
*receiving the Word of the Lord*

And thus did I, the Lord God, appoint unto man the days of his probation—that by his natural death he might be raised in immortality unto eternal life, even as many as would believe; (*Revelation received Sept. 1830; the Fall and the Atonement bring salvation*) D&C 29:43

**President Heber J. Grant**

The object of our being placed upon the earth is that we may work out an exaltation, that we may prepare ourselves to go back and dwell with our Heavenly Father; and our Father, knowing the faults and failings of men, has given us certain commandments to obey, and if we will examine those requirements and the things that devolve upon us we will find that they are all for our individual benefit and advancement. The school of life in which we are placed and the lessons that are given to us by our Father will make of us exactly what he desires, so that we may be prepared to dwell with him. ("How to Be 'Saved,'" IE1945Mar:123) TLDP:427

---

**470. One reason we came to earth was to obtain physical bodies of flesh and bone.**

**Marion G. Romney**

[W]e came to earth for two purposes: one, to obtain physical bodies of flesh and bone in the likeness of our Heavenly Father; and two, to be proved—to see if we "will do all things whatsoever the Lord" our God commands us. CR1976Apr:119

**Marion G. Romney**

[A]s the offspring of God, we inherit the capability of reaching, in full maturity, the status of our heavenly parents just as we inherit from our mortal parents the capability to attain to their mortal status; and . . . since God has a body of flesh and bones, it was necessary and perfectly natural for us, his spirit offspring, to obtain such bodies in order that we might be like him; . . . coming to earth was the means provided for us to obtain these bodies. CR1976Apr:118

**Joseph Smith,**
*quoted by Elder Joseph Fielding Smith*

We came to this earth that we might have a body and present it pure before God in the celestial kingdom. The great principle of happiness consists in having a body. The devil has no body, and herein is his punishment. He is pleased when he can obtain the tabernacle of man, and when cast out by the Savior he asked to go into the herd of swine, showing that he would prefer a swine's body to having none. ¶ All beings who have bodies have power over those who have not. The devil has no power over us only as we permit him. (*At organization of school of instruction, Jan. 1841*) DGSM:28; TLDP:62; TPJS:181

**Elder Joseph F. Smith**

It is absolutely necessary that we should come to the earth and take upon us tabernacles; because if we did not have tabernacles we could not be like God, or like Jesus Christ. God has a tabernacle of flesh and bone. He is an organized being just as we are, who are now in the flesh. Jesus Christ . . . had a fleshly tabernacle; He was crucified on the cross; and his body was raised from the dead. . . . We are

precisely in the same condition and under the same circumstances that God our Heavenly Father was when He was passing through this or a similar ordeal. We are destined to come forth out of the grave as Jesus did, and to obtain immortal bodies as He did. . . . This is the object of our existence in the world. (*In Assembly Hall, Feb. 17, 1884, JD25:58-59*) TLDP:426

**President Brigham Young,**
*quoted by John A. Widtsoe*

Our mortal bodies are all important to us: without them we never can be glorified in the eternities that will be. We are in this state of being for the express purpose of obtaining habitations for our spirits to dwell in, that they may become personages of tabernacle. (*In Tabernacle, Feb. 23, 1862, JD9:286*) DBY:56

**James E. Talmage**

Man in his mortal state is the union of a preexistent spirit with a body composed of earthly elements. This union of spirit and body marks progress from the unembodied to the embodied condition, and is an inestimable advancement in the soul's onward course. The penalty incurred by proud Lucifer and his rebel hordes for their attempt to thwart the divine purpose in the matter of man's agency was the doom of being denied bodies of flesh. AF:428

**Related Witnesses:**

**President Brigham Young,**
*quoted by John A. Widtsoe*

Our bodies are all important to us, though they may be old and withered, emaciated with toil, pain, and sickness, and our limbs bent with rheumatism, all uniting to hasten dissolution, for death is sown in our mortal bodies. The food and drink we partake of are contaminated with the seeds of death, yet we partake of them to extend our lives until our allotted work is finished, when our tabernacles, in a state of ripeness, are sown in the earth to produce immortal fruit. Yet, if we live our holy religion and let the spirit reign, it will not become dull and stupid, but as the body approaches dissolution the spirit takes a firmer hold on that enduring substance behind the veil, drawing from the depths of that eternal Fountain of Light sparkling gems of intelligence which surround the frail and sinking tabernacle with a halo of immortal wisdom. (*In Tabernacle, Feb. 23, 1862) JD9:288*) DBY:56-57

---

**471. Mortality is a time for testing and trial, to prove whether we will keep the commandments of God.**

## Abraham,
### quoted by Joseph Smith

And we will prove them herewith, to see if they will do all things whatsoever the Lord their God shall command them; 26. And they who keep their first estate shall be added upon; and they who keep not their first estate shall not have glory in the same kingdom with those who keep their first estate; and they who keep their second estate shall have glory added upon their heads for ever and ever. (*Abraham learns about the creation of the earth and the second estate of man*) Abr.3:25-26

### James E. Talmage

The purpose of our mortal probation is that of education, training, trial, and test, whereby we demonstrate whether we will obey the commandments of the Lord our God and so lay hold on the boundless opportunities of advancement in the eternal worlds, or elect to do evil and forfeit the boon of citizenship in the Kingdom of Heaven. (The Vitality of Mormonism, p. 238) TLDP:427

### Joseph Smith,
### receiving the Word of the Lord

For if you will that I give unto you a place in the celestial world, you must prepare yourselves by doing the things which I have commanded you and required of you. (*Revelation, March 1832*) D&C 78:7

### Joseph Smith,
### receiving the Word of the Lord

Therefore, be not afraid of your enemies, for I have decreed in my heart, saith the Lord, that I will prove you in all things, whether you will abide in my covenant, even unto death, that you may be found worthy. 15. For if ye will not abide in my covenant ye are not worthy of me. (*Revelation received Aug. 6, 1833 in consequence of the persecution of the Saints in the United States*) D&C 98:14-15

### Joseph Smith,
### receiving the Word of the Lord

And again, verily I say unto you, I command you again to build a house to my name, even in this place, that you may prove yourselves unto me that ye are faithful in all things whatsoever I command you, that I may bless you, and crown you with honor, immortality, and eternal life. (*Revelation, Jan. 19, 1841*) D&C 124:55

### Bruce R. McConkie

In this mortal probation it is the design and purpose of the Lord to test us: to see if we will believe in him and obey his laws now that we no longer dwell in his presence, hear his voice, and see his face. He already knows how we respond—what we believe and how we act—

when we walk by sight. Now he is testing our devotion to him when we walk by faith: when his presence is veiled, his voice is afar off, and his face is seen by few men only. (The Promised Messiah, p. 84) TLDP:429

### President Brigham Young

We are placed on this earth to prove whether we are worthy to go into the celestial world, the terrestrial, or the telestial, or to hell, or to any other kingdom or place, and we have enough of life given us to do this. (*At Great Salt Lake City, March 8, 1857, JD4:269*) TLDP:426

**Related Witnesses:**

### President Joseph F. Smith

It is only by obedience to the laws of God that men can rise above the petty weaknesses of mortality. CR1903Oct:1-2; DGSM:28

---

**472. Our life on earth is a probationary period, a time to prepare for eternal life.**

### James E. Talmage

Mortality is the preparatory school for eternity. Its curriculum is comprehensive and exacting. In its laboratories we pupils meet the experiences that test and try to conclusive demonstration the individual effect of precept and profession. For the founding and maintenance of this school the earth was created. AF:428

### Alma, the younger,
### quoted by Mormon

And we see that death comes upon mankind, yea, the death which has been spoken of by Amulek, which is the temporal death; nevertheless there was a space granted unto man in which he might repent; therefore this life became a probationary state; a time to prepare to meet God; a time to prepare for that endless state which has been spoken of by us, which is after the resurrection of the dead. (*Alma responds to the chief ruler, Antionah, regarding Adam and Eve's expulsion from the Garden of Eden, about 82 B.C.*) Alma 12:24

### President Brigham Young

My people must be tried in all things, that they may be prepared to receive the glory that I have for them, even the glory of Zion; and he that will not bear chastisement is not worthy of my kingdom. (*Revelation received at Winter Quarters, Jan. 14, 1847*) D&C 136:31

### President Spencer W. Kimball

Each one of you has it within the realm of his possibility to develop a kingdom over which you will preside as its king and god. You will need to develop yourself and grow in ability and power and worthiness, to govern such a world with all of its people. You are sent to this earth not merely to have a good time or to satisfy urges or passions or desires. You are sent to this earth, not to ride merry-go-rounds, airplanes, automobiles, and have what the world calls "fun." ¶ You are sent to this world with a very serious purpose. You are sent to school, for that matter, to begin as a human infant and grow to unbelievable proportions in wisdom, judgment, knowledge, and power. That is why you and I cannot be satisfied with saying merely "I like that or want that." That is why in our childhood and our youth and our young adulthood we must stretch and grow and remember and prepare for the later life when limitations will terminate so that we can go on and on and on. (*University of Utah institute, Oct. 1976*) DGSM:29

**President Brigham Young**
All intelligent beings who are crowned with crowns of glory, immortality, and eternal lives must pass through every ordeal appointed for intelligent beings to pass through, to gain their glory and exaltation. Every calamity that can come upon mortal beings will be suffered to come upon the few, to prepare them to enjoy the presence of the Lord. If we obtain the glory that Abraham obtained, we must do so by the same means that he did. . . . We must pass through the same experience, and gain the knowledge, intelligence, and endowments that will prepare us to enter into the celestial kingdom of our Father and God. . . . Every trial and experience you have passed through is necessary for your salvation. (*At Provo, Utah, Aug. 26, 1860, JD8:150*) TLDP:426

**Amulek,**
*quoted by Mormon*
For behold, this life is the time for men to prepare to meet God; yea, behold the day of this life is the day for men to perform their labors. 33. And now, as I said unto you before, as ye have had so many witnesses, therefore, I beseech of you that ye do not procrastinate the day of your repentance until the end; for after this day of life, which is given us to prepare for eternity, behold, if we do not improve our time while in this life, then cometh the night of darkness wherein there can be no labor performed. (*Amulek teaches the people that this life is the time for men to prepare to meet God, 74 B.C.*) Alma 34:32-33

**Elder George Albert Smith**
We are not here to while away the hours of this life and then pass to a sphere of exaltation; but we are here to qualify ourselves day by day for the positions that our Father expects us to fill hereafter. CR1905Apr:61-62

**Elder Spencer W. Kimball**
Is there not wisdom in his [God's] giving us trials that we might rise above them, responsibilities that we might achieve, work to harden our muscles, sorrows to try our souls? Are we not exposed to temptations to test our strength, sickness that we might learn patience, death that we might be immortalized and glorified? (Faith Precedes the Miracle, p. 97) DGSM:28

**Related Witnesses:**
**John**
To him that overcometh will I grant to sit with me in my throne, even as I also overcame, and am set down with my Father in his throne. (*The Apostle John writes the invitation of Jesus to overcome the world*) Rev.3:21

**Richard L. Evans**
Keep courage. Do not feel sorry for yourselves. Whatever you do, do not feel sorry for yourselves. You live in a great age of opportunity. I remember the words of one very sharp and shrewd observer who said, "Whenever I hear someone sigh and say that life is hard, I am tempted to ask 'compared to what?'" What are the alternatives? No one ever promised us it would be easy. It is a schooling; it is an opportunity; it is a learning period, and a wonderful one. Despite all the disappointments and difficulties, the great and ultimate rewards are beyond price. CR1961Apr:76

---

**473.** The body is a temple in which the Spirit of God may dwell.

**Paul**
Know ye not that ye are the temple of God, and that the Spirit of God dwelleth in you? 17. If any man defile the temple of God, him shall God destroy; for the temple of God is holy, which temple ye are. (*Paul writes to the Church at Corinth, Greece, about A.D. 55*) 1Cor.3:16-17

**Paul**
What? know ye not that your body is the temple of the Holy Ghost which is in you, which ye have of God, and ye are not your own? 20. For ye are bought with a price: therefore glorify God in your body, and in your spirit, which are God's. (*Paul writes to the Church at Corinth, Greece, about A.D. 55*) 1Cor.6:19-20

**Mark E. Petersen**
That which is sacred has long been protected from the eyes of the curious public. It has been true from the earliest times. Did the masses of the people obtain admission to the sacred tabernacle of ancient Israel? Could they view or handle the ark of the covenant? Were they

admitted into the sacred precincts of the Holy Temple built anciently to the name of the Lord? Are they permitted into the Holy of Holies of any age? ¶ The human body is as sacred as any building ever erected, whether temple or tabernacle itself. It provides a mortal home for our own spirits, which are divine, the very offspring of God, and it may be a resting place for the Holy Spirit to which all followers of God are entitled. ¶ Should it be desecrated? Is it not as much an act of desecration to expose the sacred human temple to the public gaze, as it would have been for ancient Israel to expose the Ark of Covenant to the eyes of the jeering mobs? ¶ Can temples made with stone and brick be any more sacred than the human temple? (A Faith to Live By, pp. 311-12) TLDP:63

### Joseph Smith
The elements are the tabernacle of God; yea, man is the tabernacle of God, even temples; and whatsoever temple is defiled, God shall destroy that temple. (*Revelation received at Kirtland, Ohio, May 6, 1833*) D&C 93:35

**Related Witnesses:**
#### President Brigham Young
All spirits came from God, and they came pure from his presence, and were put into earthly tabernacles, which were organized for that express purpose; and so the spirit and the body became a living soul. If these souls should live, according to the law of heaven, God ordained that they should become temples prepared to inherit all things. (*In Tabernacle, Aug. 15, 1852, JD6:291*) TLDP:426

#### John A. Widtsoe
The spirit within must speak through a mortal body, subject to disease and death. The eternal spirit is restricted by the conditions of the body, which is of the earth, a result of all physical good and evil to which man has given himself since the days of Adam. During the long history of the race, both strength and weakness have no doubt been added to the body. It possesses inborn, inherent qualities, which man finds it difficult to ignore. Under the best conditions, the body is weaker than the spirit within. It is likely that the spirit inhabiting the finest earthly body is infinitely greater than its expression through that body. The spirit speaks only as our bodies allow; and, since our bodies differ greatly, there is in them another source of man's inequality. In fact, the inequality of man comes largely from the inequality of body, through which the eternal spirit often tries in vain to speak. (A Rational Theology, p. 138) TLDP:62-63

## 474. On earth those who accept the gospel are given the opportunity to receive the necessary eternal ordinances of salvation.

### Elder Joseph Fielding Smith
There is no exaltation in the kingdom of God without the fulness of priesthood. How could a man be an heir in that kingdom without priesthood? While the sisters do not hold the priesthood, they share in the fulness of its blessings in the celestial kingdom with their husbands. These blessings are obtained through obedience to the ordinances and covenants of the House of the Lord. The Prophet Joseph Smith once said: "If a man gets a fulness of the priesthood of God, he has to get it . . . by keeping all the commandments and obeying all the ordinances of the house of the Lord." To obtain the fulness of the priesthood does not mean that a man must become president of the Church. . . . The Lord has made it possible for every man in this Church, through his obedience, to receive the fulness of the priesthood through the ordinances of the temple of the Lord. This cannot be received anywhere else. ¶ So being ordained an elder, or a high priest, or an apostle, or even president of the Church, is not the thing that brings the exaltation, but obedience to the laws and the ordinances and the covenants required of those who desire to become members of the Church of the Firstborn as these are administered in the House of the Lord. To become a member of the Church of the Firstborn, as I understand it, is to become one of the inner circle. We are all members of The Church of Jesus Christ of Latter-day Saints by being baptized and confirmed, and there are many who seem to be content to remain such without obtaining the privileges of exaltation. The Lord has made it possible for us to become members of the Church of the Firstborn by receiving the blessings of the House of the Lord, and "overcoming all things." Thus we become heirs, "priests and kings, who have received of his fulness, and of his glory," who shall "dwell in the presence of God and his Christ forever and ever," with full exaltation. (Take Heed to Yourselves, pp. 112-14) TLDP:166

### Elder Wilford Woodruff
They will not baptize anybody in the spirit world; there is no baptism there; there is no marrying or giving in marriage there; all these ordinances have to be performed on the earth. Paul says, in referring to this subject—"Why are ye baptized for the dead? If the dead rise not why then are ye baptized for the dead?" The Lord holds us responsible for going to and

building Temples, that we may attend therein to the ordinances necessary for the salvation of the dead. *(In new Tabernacle, Sept. 12, 1875, JD18:114)* TLDP:61

**Elder Joseph Fielding Smith**

This mortal probation was to be a brief period, just a short span linking the eternity past with the eternity future. Yet it was to be a period of tremendous importance. It would either give to those who received it the blessing of eternal life, which is the greatest gift of God, and thus qualify them for godhood as sons and daughters of our Eternal Father, or, if they rebelled and refused to comply with the laws and ordinances which were provided for their salvation, it would deny them the great gift and they would be assigned, after the resurrection, to some inferior sphere according to their works. This life is the most vital period in our eternal existence. It is filled with awful responsibilities and dangers. Here we are face to face with innumerable temptations. Lucifer, formerly a son of the morning, now Satan, the deceiver, is here with his rebellious hosts to tempt us and lead us astray. (Doctrines of Salvation, 1:69) TLDP:429

**Joseph Smith,**
*quoted by Elder Joseph Fielding Smith*

One of the ordinances of the house of the Lord is baptism for the dead. God decreed before the foundation of the world that the ordinances should be administered in a font prepared for that purpose in the house of the Lord. *(Sunday sermon at the Stand, Nauvoo, Ill., June 11, 1843)* TPJS:308

**Joseph Smith,**
*receiving the Word of the Lord*

For, for this cause I commanded Moses that he should build a tabernacle, that they should bear it with them in the wilderness, and to build a house in the land of promise, that those ordinances might be revealed which had been hid from before the world was. 39. Therefore, verily I say unto you, that your anointings, and your washings, and your baptisms for the dead, and your solemn assemblies, and your memorials for your sacrifices by the sons of Levi, and for your oracles in your most holy places wherein you receive conversations, and your statutes and judgments, for the beginning of the revelations and foundation of Zion, and for the glory, honor, and endowment of all her municipals, are ordained by the ordinance of my holy house, which my people are always commanded to build unto my holy name. 40. And verily I say unto you, let this house be built unto my name, that I may reveal mine ordinances there-

in unto my people; *(Revelation to Joseph Smith, Jan. 19, 1841)* D&C 124:38-40

**John A. Widtsoe**

Now the concern of the Church is to bring all men into the celestial kingdom. It has no interest in the other, lower kingdoms. Every doctrine, principle, and item of organization within the Church pertains to the celestial glory. The manner of entrance into this the highest kingdom is therefore made clear. Any person who wishes to enter it must have faith and repent from his sins. Then he must be baptized, and receive the gift of the Holy Ghost by one who has divine authority to perform such ordinances. There are principles and ordinances which in their entirety belong peculiarly to the higher kingdom. ¶ After having laid the foundation for his claim to celestial membership and association, he must, to receive all available blessings of this kingdom, comply with the many requirements of life within the Church. He belongs to "those who are valiant and inspired with the true independence of heaven, who will go forth boldly in the service of their God leaving others to do as they please, determined to do right, though all mankind should take the opposite course." All this having been done, he is qualified to enter the celestial kingdom. Indeed, he is then, even on earth, in the celestial kingdom of God. ¶ Naturally, those who enter the celestial kingdom are of various attainments. There is not absolute uniformity anywhere among the children of God. Their innate capacities and their use of the law of free agency make them different, often widely so. Therefore, the members of the highest kingdom are also grouped, according to the Prophet Joseph Smith into three "degrees." [See D&C 131:1.] ¶ To enter the highest of these degrees in the celestial kingdom is to be exalted in the kingdom of God. Such exaltation comes to those who receive the higher ordinances of the Church, such as the temple endowment, and afterwards are sealed in marriage for time and eternity, whether on earth or in the hereafter. Those who are so sealed continue the family relationship eternally. Spiritual children are begotten by them. They carry on the work of salvation for the hosts of waiting spirits. They who are so exalted become even as the gods. They will be "from everlasting to everlasting, because they continue." [D&C 132:20] (Evidences and Reconciliations, pp. 200-01) TLDP:163-64

**Related Witnesses:**

**Joseph Smith**

Ordinances instituted in the heavens before the foundation of the world, in the priesthood, for the salvation of men, are not to be altered or changed. All must be saved on the same principles. . . . ¶ All men who become heirs of God and joint heirs with Jesus Christ will have to receive the fulness of the ordinances of his kingdom; and those who will not receive all the ordinances will come short of the fullness of that glory, if they do not lose the whole. (*Sunday sermon at the Stand, Nauvoo, Ill., June 11, 1843*) DGSM:52; TPJS:308

**Joseph Smith**

We believe that through the Atonement of Christ, all mankind may be saved, by obedience to the laws and ordinances of the Gospel. (*The third of the thirteen Articles of Faith; letter to John Wentworth, March 1, 1842*) AofF:3

**Alma, the younger,**
*quoted by Mormon*

Now these ordinances were given after this manner, that thereby the people might look forward on the Son of God, it being a type of his order, or it being his order, and this that they might look forward to him for a remission of their sins, that they might enter into the rest of the Lord. (*Alma instructs the people that high priests were ordained because of righteousness, about 82 B.C.*) Alma 13:16

# List of Doctrines

## MUSIC

# MUSIC

**475. We are to worship God by singing hymns.**

**Joseph Smith,**
*receiving the Word of the Lord*
And it shall be given thee, also, to make a selection of sacred hymns, as it shall be given thee, which is pleasing unto me, to be had in my church. 12. For my soul delighteth in the song of the heart; yea, the song of the righteous is a prayer unto me, and it shall be answered with a blessing upon their heads. (*Revelation for Emma Smith, July 1830*) D&C 25:11-12

**Elder Joseph F. Smith**
When we listen to this choir . . . we listen to music, and music is truth. Good music is gracious praise of God. It is delightsome to the ear, and it is one of our most acceptable methods of worshipping God. And those who sing in this choir and in all the choirs of the Saints, should sing with the Spirit and with understanding. They should not sing merely because it is a profession, or because they have a good voice; but they should sing also because they have the spirit of it and can enter into the spirit of prayer and praise to God who gave them their sweet voices. My soul is always lifted up and my spirit cheered and comforted when I hear good music. I rejoice in it very much indeed. CR1899Oct:69

**Paul**
Let the word of Christ dwell in you richly in all wisdom; teaching and admonishing one another in psalms and hymns and spiritual songs, singing with grace in your hearts to the Lord. (*Paul writes from prison to the Church in Colossae, Asia Minor, about A.D. 60*) Col.3:16

**Bruce R. McConkie**
Music is part of the language of the Gods. It has been given to man so he can sing praises to the Lord. It is a means of expressing, with poetic words and in melodious tunes, the deep feelings of rejoicing and thanksgiving found in the hearts of those who have testimonies of the divine Sonship and who know of the wonders and glories wrought for them by the Father, Son, and Holy Spirit. Music is both in the voice and in the heart. Every true saint finds his heart full of songs of praise to his Maker. Those whose voices can sing forth the praises found in their hearts are twice blest. "Be filled with the Spirit," Paul counseled, "Speaking to yourselves in psalms and hymns and spiritual songs, singing and making melody in your heart to the Lord." (Eph.5:18-19) Also: "Let the word of Christ dwell in you richly in all

wisdom; teaching and admonishing one another in psalms and hymns and spiritual songs, singing with grace in your hearts to the Lord." (Col.3:16) (The Promised Messiah, pp. 553-54) TLDP:431

**Related Witnesses:**
**Isaiah,**
*quoted by Nephi, son of Lehi,*
Behold, God is my salvation; I will trust, and not be afraid; for the Lord JEHOVAH is my strength and my song; he also has become my salvation. . . . 5. Sing unto the Lord; for he hath done excellent things; this is known in all the earth. (*Nephi records the words of Isaiah from the brass plates, 559-545 B.C.*) 2Ne.22:2,5

**Isaiah**
And in that day shall ye say, Praise the LORD, call upon his name, declare his doings among the people, make mention that his name is exalted. 5. Sing unto the LORD; for he hath done excellent things: this is known in all the earth. (*Isaiah prophesies, 740-659 B.C.*) Isa.12:4-5

**King Benjamin,**
*quoted by Mormon*
I say unto you that I have caused that ye should assemble yourselves together that I might rid my garments of your blood, at this period of time when I am about to go down to my grave, that I might go down in peace, and my immortal spirit may join the choirs above in singing the praises of a just God. (*King Benjamin addresses his people, about 124 B.C.*) Mosiah 2:28

**Paul**
What is it then? I will pray with the spirit, and I will pray with the understanding also: I will sing with the spirit, and I will sing with the understanding also. (*Letter to the Church at Corinth, Greece, about A.D. 55*) 1Cor.14:15

**Joseph Smith**
And it shall come to pass that the righteous shall be gathered out from among all nations, and shall come to Zion, singing with songs of everlasting joy. (*Revelation, March 7, 1831; signs, wonders, and the resurrection are to attend the Second Coming*) D&C 45:71

**Recorded in Job**
Where wast thou when I laid the foundations of the earth? declare, if thou hast understanding. . . . 7. When the morning stars sang together, and all the sons of God shouted for joy? (*The Lord teaches Job; he asks him questions*) Job 38:4,7

**Author's Note:** The hymn sung by Jesus and his Apostles at the Last Supper may have been the Jewish Hallel, according to Marvin R.

Vincent: "Very probably the second part of the Jewish Hallel or Hallelujah, embracing Ps. cxv., cxvi., cxvii., cxviii." (Words Studies in the New Testament, 1:139) ¶ "And when they had sung an hymn, they went out into the mount of Olives." (Matt.26:30)

---

**476. Appropriate music can increase our spiritual sensitivity.**

**Elder David O. McKay**

Music is truly the universal language, and when it is excellently expressed, how deeply it moves our souls! (Gospel Ideals, p. 256) TLDP:430

**Boyd K. Packer**

There are many references in the scriptures, both ancient and modern, that attest to the influence of righteous music. The Lord, Himself, was prepared for His greatest test through its influence, for the scripture records: "And when they had sung an hymn, they went out into the mount of Olives." (Mark 14:26) CR1973Oct:25

**President Heber J. Grant**

The singing of our sacred hymns, written by the servants of God, has a powerful effect in converting people to the principles of the Gospel, and in promoting peace and spiritual growth. Singing is a prayer to the Lord, as He has said: "For my soul delighteth in the song of the heart; yea, the song of the righteous is a prayer unto me, and it shall be answered with a blessing upon their heads." [D&C 25:12] ("Songs of the Heart," IE1940Sep:522) TLDP:431

**Elder Heber J. Grant**

I am confident that the hymns of Zion, when sung with the proper spirit, bring a peaceful and heavenly influence into our homes, and also aid in preaching the gospel of Jesus Christ. (Gospel Standards, p. 170) TLDP:432

**Mark E. Petersen**

Families would profit by having hymn books in their homes, and using them. In our "family hour" we may use our hymns to good advantage. ¶ A hymn in the home will go far toward bringing into it a spirit of love and worship, just as it does in a meeting in the ward. (A Faith to Live By, p. 170) TLDP:432

**Elder Spencer W. Kimball**

The responsibility for producing, selecting, and performing music for the Church requires discrimination, taste, knowledge, and the proper spirit: in short, it requires the best efforts that our best musicians can give inasmuch as we are using gifts which the Lord has given us for the purpose of building up his kingdom and as a

demonstration of our faith and love for him. We are in a position, as musicians, to touch the souls of those who listen. (The Teachings of Spencer W. Kimball, pp. 519-20) TLDP:431

**President Heber J. Grant**

The Lord has given a revelation wherein he has said that his soul delighteth in the song of the heart, that it is a prayer unto him, and that it shall be answered with a blessing upon our heads. Let us remember the kind of songs the Lord likes, songs with the Gospel in them. I have gone to conferences where I have heard three or four anthems, with the words of which I could not agree. They were sung to good music but they were not good doctrine. CR1931Apr:132

**Related Witnesses:**

**President George Albert Smith,**
**J. Reuben Clark, Jr., David O. McKay**
(First Presidency)

Recently, this question came before the First Presidency and the Twelve who unanimously approved the recommendation that the ideal condition is to have absolute quiet during the passing of the sacrament, and that we look with disfavor upon vocal solos, duets, group singing, or instrumental music during the administration of this sacred ordinance. ¶ There is no objection to having appropriate music during the preparation of the emblems, but after the prayer is offered, perfect silence should prevail until the bread and the water have been partaken of by the full congregation. *(Letter to presidents of stakes and bishops of wards, May 2, 1946)* MOFP6:252-53

---

**477. Some music can be used for wicked purposes; such music is to be shunned.**

**Boyd K. Packer**

In our day music itself has been corrupted. Music can, by its tempo, by its beat, by its intensity, dull the spiritual sensitivity of men. . . . ¶ Young people, you cannot afford to fill your mind with the unworthy hard music of our day. It is *not* harmless. It can welcome onto the stage of your mind unworthy thoughts and set the tempo to which they dance and to which you may act. ¶ You degrade yourself when you identify with all of those things which seem now to surround such extremes in music: the shabbiness, the irreverence, the immorality, and the addictions. Such music as that is not worthy of you. You should have self-respect. ¶ You are a son or a daughter of

Almighty God. He has inspired a world full of wonderful things to learn and to do, uplifting music of many kinds that you may enjoy. CR1973Oct:21,25

**Bruce R. McConkie**
Unfortunately not all music is good and edifying. Lucifer uses much that goes by the name of music to lead people to that which does not edify and is not of God. Just as language can be used to bless or curse, so music is a means of singing praises to the Lord or of planting evil thoughts and desires in the minds of men. Of that music which meets the divine standard and has the Lord's approval, he says: "My soul delighteth in the song of the heart; yea, the song of the righteous is a prayer unto me, and it shall be answered with a blessing upon their heads." (D&C 25:12) (The Promised Messiah, pp. 553-54) TLDP:431

**Elder John Taylor**
Our object is to get and to cleave to everything that is good, and to reject everything that is bad. One reason why religious people in the world are opposed to music and theaters is because of the corruption that is mixed up with them. Wicked and corrupt men associate themselves with these things, and degrade them; but is this any reason that the saints should not enjoy the gifts of God? Is that a correct principle? Certainly not. It is for them to grasp at everything that is good, and calculated to promote the happiness of the human family. (*In 13th Ward, Jan. 5, 1873, JD15:271*) (The Gospel Kingdom, p. 62) TLDP:431-32

**President Harold B. Lee,**
**N. Eldon Tanner, Marion G. Romney**
(First Presidency)
Through music, man's ability to express himself extends beyond the limits of the spoken language in both subtlety and power. Music can be used to exalt and inspire or to carry messages of degradation and destruction. It is therefore important that as Latter-day Saints we at all times apply the principles of the gospel and seek the guidance of the Spirit in selecting the music with which we surround ourselves. (Priesthood Bulletin, Aug. 1973, p. 3) TLDP:432

**Related Witnesses:**
**President Heber J. Grant**
The Lord has given a revelation wherein he has said that his soul delighteth in the song of the heart, that it is a prayer unto him, and that it shall be answered with a blessing upon our heads. Let us remember the kind of songs the Lord likes, songs with the Gospel in them. I have gone to conferences where I have heard

three or four anthems, with the words of which I could not agree. They were sung to good music but they were not good doctrine. CR1931Apr:132

---

**478. It is appropriate to enjoy good music for purposes besides worship.**

**President Brigham Young,**
*quoted by John A. Widtsoe*
There is no music in hell, for all good music belongs to heaven. Sweet harmonious sounds give exquisite joy to human beings capable of appreciating music. I delight in hearing harmonious tones made by the human voice, by musical instruments, and by both combined. Every sweet musical sound that can be made belongs to the Saints and is for the Saints. Every flower, shrub and tree to beautify, and to gratify the taste and smell, and every sensation that gives to man joy and felicity are for the Saints who receive them from the Most High. (*At the dedication of the new theater in Great Salt Lake, March 6, 1862, JD9:244*) DBY:242-43

**Elder John Taylor**
Why, there are some people who think that the fiddle, for instance, is an instrument of the devil and it is quite wrong to use it. I do not think so, I think it is a splendid thing to dance by. But some folks think that we should not dance. Yes, we should enjoy life in any way we can. Some people object to music. Why, music prevails in the heavens, and among the birds! God has filled them with it. There is nothing more pleasing and delightful then it is to go into the woods or among the bushes early in the morning and listen to the warbling and rich melody of the birds, and it is strictly in accordance with the sympathies of our nature. We have no idea of the excellence of the music we shall have in heaven. It may be said of that, as the apostle Paul has said in relation to something else— "Eye hath not seen, nor ear heard, neither have entered into the heart of man, the things which God hath prepared for them that love him." (1Cor.2:9) We have no idea of the excellency, beauty, harmony and symphony of the music in the heavens. ¶ Our object is to get and to cleave to everything that is good, and to reject everything that is bad. One reason why religious people in the world are opposed to music and theaters is because of the corruption that is mixed up with them. Wicked and corrupt men associate themselves with these things, and degrade them; but is this any reason that the

saints should not enjoy the gifts of God? Is that a correct principle? Certainly not. It is for them to grasp at everything that is good, and calculated to promote the happiness of the human family. (*In 13th Ward, Jan. 5, 1873, JD15:271*) (The Gospel Kingdom, p. 62) TLDP:431-32

**President Brigham Young**

Some wise being organized my system, and gave me my capacity, [and] put into my heart and brain something that delights, charms, and fills me with rapture at the sound of sweet music. . . . It was the Lord, our heavenly Father, who gave the capacity to enjoy these sounds, and which we ought to do in His name, and to His glory. (*In Tabernacle, April 9, 1852, JD1:48*) TLDP:430

**President Brigham Young**

If thou art merry, praise the Lord with singing, with music, with dancing, and with a prayer of praise and thanksgiving. (*Revelation, Jan. 14, 1847*) D&C 136:28

**Related Witnesses:**
**President Brigham Young**

If the people were all righteous, it would do to dance, and to have music, feasting and merriment. But what fellowship has Christ with Belial? Or what fellowship has light with darkness? or what union have the sons and daughters of God with the children of this world, who fear not God nor regard man. All amusement in which saints and sinners are mingled tends to corruption, and has a baneful influence in religious society. (*An epistle of the Twelve Apostles to the Church, Oct. 1, 1844*) HC7:282

**Joseph Smith**

A large party took a new year's supper at my house, and had music and dancing till morning. I was in my private room with my family, Elder John Taylor and other friends. (*Entry by the Prophet in his journal, Jan. 1, 1844*) HC6:155

**Joseph Smith**

A large party supped at my house, and spent the evening in music, dancing, &c., in a most cheerful and friendly manner. (*At this party Orrin Porter Rockwell made a surprise appearance after nearly a year's false imprisonment in Missouri*) HC6:134-35

**President Wilford Woodruff,**
**George Q. Cannon, Joseph F. Smith**
(First Presidency)

We desire to see this [Tabernacle] choir not only maintain the high reputation it has earned at home and abroad, but become the highest exponent of the "Divine Art" in all the land; and the worthy head, example and leader of all other choirs and musical bodies in the Church, inspiring musicians and poets with purest

sentiment and song and harmony, until its light shall shine forth to the world undimmed, and nations shall be charmed with its music. (*Letter to Tabernacle Choir, Salt Lake City, Utah, Feb. 11, 1895. The First Presidency had accompanied the Tabernacle Choir to the World's Fair in Chicago, Ill., Sept. 1893, when the choir had won second prize in a national contest. The choir's concert at the World's Fair was the beginning of a great missionary work to be accomplished by this musical organization. This letter contains the commendation for their work and a set of rules or regulations governing membership and participation in the choir*) MOFP3:267

**President Joseph F. Smith,**
**Anthon H. Lund, Charles W. Penrose**
(First Presidency)

The progress in music, both vocal and instrumental, in Utah has been general and gratifying. So with different branches of art. (*Christmas Greeting*) (Deseret News, Dec. 20, 1913) MOFP4:297

---

**HYMNS Written by Prophets**
**Applicable to this Topic**

**Bruce R. McConkie**
*I Believe in Christ*, First verse
HYMNS:134

I believe in Christ; he is my King!
With all my heart to him I'll sing;
I'll raise my voice in praise and joy,
In grand amens my tongue employ.
I believe in Christ; he is God's Son.
On earth to dwell his soul did come.
He healed the sick; the dead he raised.
Good works were his; his name be praised.

# List of Doctrines

## OBEDIENCE TO GOD

*Doctrines Located in This Topic*

479. We are to live the law of obedience (which is that the Saints of God shall do all things the Lord commands).

480. We are to heed the words of the Lord as they come from His servants, the living and ancient prophets.

481. The Lord gives us commandments that we may know how to act to obtain eternal salvation.

482. When God commands, He prepares a way for us to carry out His commandments.

483. The Lord requires active obedience, not just passive acceptance.

484. A way to test a doctrine is to live it.

485. If we keep the Lord's commandments, He is bound by His promises to bless us.

486. Those who keep the Lord's commandments may be blessed with temporal (as well as spiritual) blessings.

487. All blessings flow from obedience to laws of God (to obtain a blessing we must obey the law appointed for that blessing).

488. We can find peace by obeying the commandments of God.

489. When we obey the word of the Lord our souls are enlarged.

490. We are never to disobey God because of our fear of what mortals can do to us.

491. Members of the Lord's church who refuse to keep His commandments will not be saved (in the celestial kingdom).

*Doctrines on OBEDIENCE TO GOD Located in Other Topics*

77. We are to learn in our youth to keep the commandments of God.

101. We must endure to the end keeping all the commandments, in order to receive the gift of eternal life in the celestial kingdom of God.

137. To merit the gift of eternal life in the celestial kingdom, we must be baptized and receive the gift of the Holy Ghost, we must render obedience to the laws and ordinances of the gospel, and we must endure to the end.

174. To obtain eternal life in the celestial kingdom, a person must have faith in Christ, keep the commandments, and endure to the end.

177. To obtain eternal exaltation a person must have knowledge that the course of life which he or she is pursuing is according to the will of God.

186. Faith in Christ is increased by obedience to the word of God.

414. A man receives the oath and covenant of the priesthood with a covenant of obedience.

513. Keeping the commandments of God assists us in obtaining answers to our prayers.

634. Obedience---living the commandments of the Lord---is one of the requisites for repentance.

697. In partaking of the sacrament, we make solemn covenants with the Lord.

# OBEDIENCE TO GOD

479. We are to live the law of obedience (which is that the Saints of God shall do all things the Lord commands).

### Bruce R. McConkie

We have made . . . solemn, sacred, holy covenants, pledging ourselves before gods and angels. ¶ We are under covenant to live the law of obedience. ¶ We are under covenant to live the law of sacrifice. ¶ We are under covenant to live the law of consecration. . . . ¶ It is our privilege to consecrate our time, talents, and means to build up his kingdom. We are called upon to sacrifice, in one degree or another, for the furtherance of his work. Obedience is essential to salvation; so, also, is service; and so, also, are consecration and sacrifice. CR1975Apr:76

### Joseph Smith,
*receiving the Word of the Lord*

[F]or this cause I have sent you—that you might be obedient, and that your hearts might be prepared to bear testimony of the things which are to come; (*Revelation for the elders of the Church, Aug. 1, 1831*) D&C 58:6

### Joseph Smith,
*receiving the Word of the Lord*

Therefore, be not afraid of your enemies, for I have decreed in my heart, saith the Lord, that I will prove you in all things, whether you will abide in my covenant, even unto death, that you may be found worthy. 15. For if ye will not abide in my covenant ye are not worthy of me. (*Revelation received Aug. 6, 1833 in consequence of the persecution of the Saints in the United States*) D&C 98:14-15

### Joseph Smith,
*receiving the Word of the Lord*

He that receiveth my law and doeth it, the same is my disciple; and he that saith he receiveth it and doeth it not, the same is not my disciple, and shall be cast out from among you; (*Revelation, Feb. 4, 1831*) D&C 41:5

### Joseph Smith,
*receiving the Word of the Lord*

And, if you keep my commandments and endure to the end you shall have eternal life, which gift is the greatest of all the gifts of God. (*Revelation for David Whitmer, June 1829*) D&C 14:7

### Jesus,
*recorded in Matthew*

Not every one that saith unto me, Lord, Lord, shall enter into the kingdom of heaven; but he that doeth the will of my Father which is in heaven. (*Jesus Christ teaches the multitude, about A.D. 30*) Matt.7:21

### Abraham,
*quoted by Joseph Smith*

And we will prove them herewith, to see if they will do all things whatsoever the Lord their God shall command them; 26. And they who keep their first estate shall be added upon; and they who keep not their first estate shall not have glory in the same kingdom with those who keep their first estate; and they who keep their second estate shall have glory added upon their heads for ever and ever. (*Abraham learns about the creation of the earth and the second estate of man*) Abr.3:25-26

### President Joseph Fielding Smith

If we love him [the Lord] we will keep his commandments. ¶ Should there be any who offend or fail to keep the commandments of the Lord, then it is evidence that they do not love him. We must obey them. We show by our works that we love the Lord our God with all our hearts, with all our might, mind, and strength; and in the name of Jesus Christ we serve him and love our neighbor as ourself. This is the word of the Lord as it has been revealed in these modern times for the guidance of Israel. ("Keep the Commandments," IE1970Aug:2) DGSM:47

### Joseph Smith

That which is wrong under one circumstance, may be, and often is, right under another. ¶ God said, "Thou shalt not kill;" at another time He said "Thou shalt utterly destroy." This is the principle on which the government of heaven is conducted—by revelation adapted to the circumstances in which the children of the kingdom are placed. Whatever God requires is right, no matter what it is, although we may not see the reason thereof till long after the events transpire. (*Essay on Happiness, Aug. 1842*) HC5:135

### Boyd K. Packer

Obedience to God can be the very highest expression of independence. Just think of giving to him the one thing, the one gift, that he would never take. Think of giving him that one thing that he would never wrest from you. . . . ¶ Obedience—that which God will never take by force—he will accept when freely given. And he will then return to you freedom that you can hardly dream of—the freedom to feel and to know, the freedom to do, and the freedom to be, at least a thousandfold more than we offer him. Strangely enough, the key to freedom is obedience. . . . ¶ We should put ourselves in a position before our Father in heaven and say, individually, "I do not want to do what I want to do. I want to do what thou wouldst have me do." Suddenly, like any father, the Lord could say, "Well, there is one more of my children almost free from the need of constant supervision." *(Brigham Young University, 1971)* DGSM:47-48

### King Benjamin,
*quoted by Mormon*

And under this head ye are made free, and there is no other head whereby ye can be made free. There is no other name given whereby salvation cometh; therefore, I would that ye should take upon you the name of Christ, all you that have entered into the covenant with God that ye should be obedient unto the end of your lives. Mosiah 5:8

---

**480. We are to heed the words of the Lord as they come from His servants, the living and ancient prophets.**

### Mark E. Petersen

So if you really desire to avoid deceptions, if you really desire to do that which is right and proper, then you take advantage of the safeguard that the Lord has given you in the organization of this Church. And you remember that if you will follow the teachings of your inspired prophets, seers, and revelators, of your apostles, of your pastors and teachers, your bishops and your stake presidents, you won't need to wonder whether or not such and such a doctrine is a deception, whether it is false or whether it is true, because those authorized servants of the Lord will lead you into paths of righteousness, and they will keep you on the right track. ¶ Salvation comes not by being tossed about by every wind of doctrine but by learning the truth as it is taught by the inspired, authorized leaders of the Church, and then having learned that truth, by living up to it and enduring in faithfulness unto the very end. . . . ¶ If you would know the will of the Lord, so that you may obtain your salvation, then obtain your knowledge of the will of the Lord from his authorized servants whom he has set in this Church. CR1945Oct:92

### Joseph Smith

And the arm of the Lord shall be revealed; and the day cometh that they who will not hear the voice of the Lord, neither the voice of his servants, neither give heed to the words of the prophets and apostles, shall be cut off from among the people; 15. For they have strayed from mine ordinances, and have broken mine everlasting covenant; 16. They seek not the Lord to establish his righteousness, but every man

walketh in his own way, and after the image of his own God, whose image is in the likeness of the world, and whose substance is that of an idol, which waxeth old and shall perish in Babylon, even Babylon the great, which shall fall. *(Revelation during conference of elders of the Church, Nov. 1, 1831)* D&C 1:14-16

### Elder Harold B. Lee

Now the only safety we have as members of this church is to do exactly what the Lord said to the Church in that day when the Church was organized. We must learn to give heed to the words and commandments that the Lord shall give through his prophet, "as he receiveth them, walking in all holiness before me; . . . as if from mine own mouth in all patience and faith." (D&C 21:4-5) There will be some things that take patience and faith. You may not like what comes from the authority of the Church. It may contradict your political views. It may contradict your social views. It may interfere with your social life. . . . ¶ . . . . Your safety and ours depends upon whether or not we follow the ones whom the Lord has placed to preside over his church. He knows whom he wants to preside over this church, and he will make no mistake. The Lord doesn't do things by accident. . . . Let us keep our eye on the President of the Church. . . . CR1970Oct:152-53; DCSM:45

### Anthon H. Lund

The Lord in comforting the Saints told them that if they would listen to his counsel, the gates of hell should not have power over them, and this promise is the same to you and to me inasmuch as we listen to the counsels of inspired men. As I understand the expression "the gates of hell," it means those things which lead to hell in fact are the entrances to it. How many things there are that lead to those gates. How many things we have to be warned against and which we have to watch out for, because if we yield to them, they will lead us to the gates of hell! Let us each and every one examine ourselves and know well the path in which we are walking and avoid everything that we know is wrong and forbidden by the Lord, well knowing that if we yield to such we have not the promise that the gates of hell shall not have power over us; on the other hand if we perform our duty, live according to the testimony which God has given us, we need not fear, for He will lead us in the paths of righteousness that lead to eternal life. CR1913Apr:10-11

### Marvin J. Ashton

To obey the gospel law is to yield obedience to those divinely called to preside over us. ACR(Munich)1973:23

**Related Witnesses:**

### Joseph Smith,
*receiving the Word of the Lord*

Behold, there shall be a record kept among you; and in it thou shalt be called a seer, a translator, a prophet, an apostle of Jesus Christ, an elder of the church through the will of God the Father, and the grace of your Lord Jesus Christ, . . . 4. Wherefore, meaning the church, thou shalt give heed unto all his words and commandments which he shall give unto you as he receiveth them, walking in all holiness before me; 5. For his word ye shall receive, as if from mine own mouth, in all patience and faith. 6. For by doing these things the gates of hell shall not prevail against you; yea, and the Lord God will disperse the powers of darkness from before you, and cause the heavens to shake for your good, and his name's glory. (*Revelation received at the organization of the Church, April 6, 1830*) D&C 21:1,4-6

### Marvin J. Ashton

Another worthy personal commitment I challenge you with this day is this. "Help me, Oh Lord, to obey thee through thine appointed leaders." Any Church member not obedient to the leaders of this Church will not have the opportunity to be obedient to the prompting of the Lord. ¶ From the Doctrine and Covenants I quote: "For all who will have a blessing at my hands shall abide the law which was appointed for that blessing, and the conditions thereof, as were instituted from before the foundation of the world." (D&C 132:5) ACR(Munich)1973:23

### Erastus Snow

From my earliest association with the people of God, my mind has been to let my will and my feelings be subject to the guidance of the Spirit of the Lord, and also to the counsel of the living oracles; and so far as my private feelings are concerned, if I have any, let them be thrown under the table, or kicked out of the window, or any where else to get them out of my way. ¶ If I can learn what is the mind and will and feeling of my brethren that are placed over me, and learn what is for the interest and welfare of the kingdom of God on the earth, I am ready to endeavor to walk in that way continually that will enable me to accomplish what they desire of me. My experience has taught me from the beginning that this is the only frame of mind that can ensure us happiness, and it is the only course that can give us success; and whenever I have deviated from it I have invariably paid dearly for it. Have I learned this from my own experience, or from the experience of others? From both sources; and all my observation has taught me this principle. Naturally speaking, we all of us have our likes and dislikes, and our peculiar notions. We have a certain line of policy marked out that we think would please ourselves, and our minds are bent in that direction. But my experience has taught me that we ought not to try to please ourselves, any farther than we have the mind of Christ, and are enlightened and inspired by the Holy Ghost. Then we shall have no stakes set but those that can be easily pulled up; and as Latter-day Saints, it is in accordance with our covenants which we have entered into that we will serve God and not ourselves; that is to say, if we serve ourselves we will do it in serving our Master, and if we build ourselves up we will do it in building up the kingdom of God upon the earth. (Quoted by J.V. Long, "Remarks by Elder Erastus Snow," Deseret News Weekly, April 23, 1862, p. 338) TLDP:435

---

### 481. The Lord gives us commandments that we may know how to act to obtain eternal salvation.

### Joseph Smith,
*receiving the Word of the Lord*

And again, I say unto you, I give unto you a new commandment, that you may understand my will concerning you; 9. Or, in other words, I give unto you directions how you may act before me, that it may turn to you for your salvation. (*Revelation, April 26, 1832*) D&C 82:8-9

### Joseph Smith

We cannot keep all the commandments without first knowing them, and we cannot expect to know all, or more than we now know unless we comply with or keep those we have already received. (*Essay on Happiness, Aug. 1842*) HC5:135

### Joseph Smith

There is a law, irrevocably decreed in heaven before the foundations of this world, upon which all blessings are predicated— 21. And when we obtain any blessing from God, it is by obedience to that law upon which it is predicated. (*Revelation, April 2, 1830*) D&C 130:20-21

### Joseph Smith,
*receiving the Word of the Lord*

For all who will have a blessing at my hands shall abide the law which was appointed for that blessing, and the conditions thereof, as were instituted from before the foundation of the world. . . . 11. And will I appoint unto you, saith the Lord, except it be by law, even as I and my Father ordained unto you, before the world was?

12. I am the Lord thy God; and I give unto you this commandment—that no man shall come unto the Father but by me or by my word, which is my law, saith the Lord. (*Revelation relating to the new and everlasting covenant, including the eternal nature of the marriage covenant, July 12, 1843, [1831]*) D&C 132:5,11-12

**Joseph Smith,**
*receiving the Word of the Lord*

For if you will that I give unto you a place in the celestial world, you must prepare yourselves by doing the things which I have commanded you and required of you. (*Revelation, March 1832*) D&C 78:7

**President Joseph F. Smith**

There is no liberty that men enjoy or pretend to enjoy in the world that is not founded in the will and in the law of God and that does not have the truth for its underlying principle and foundation. It is error that makes bondsmen. It is untruth that degrades mankind. It is error and the lack of knowledge of God's laws and God's will that leaves men in the world on a par with the brute creation. CR1904Apr:4

**Samuel, the Lamanite,**
*quoted by Mormon*

And now remember, remember, my brethren, that whosoever perisheth, perisheth unto himself; and whosoever doeth iniquity, doeth it unto himself; for behold, ye are free; ye are permitted to act for yourselves; for behold, God hath given unto you a knowledge and he hath made you free. 31. He hath given unto you that ye might know good from evil, and he hath given unto you that ye might choose life or death; and ye can do good and be restored unto that which is good, or have that which is good restored unto you; or ye can do evil, and have that which is evil restored unto you. (*Samuel preaches to the Nephites, about 6 B.C.*) Hel.14:30-31

**Mark E. Petersen**

One of the great things about the gospel is that the Lord determined that in order for us to become like him we must be held strictly in a certain line of living. We must make it clear to ourselves as we study the gospel that there is a definite way that we must travel and that we must not vary from it. The gospel is very specific. We cannot vary from the way the Lord gives us because we must consider the commandments as a formula whereby we may build into ourselves the Christlike traits of character that were required, and in doing so then we become Christlike. ACR(Manchester)1976:11

**Related Witnesses:**

**Joseph Smith**

An actual knowledge to any person, that the course of life which he pursues is according to the will of God, is essentially necessary to enable him to have that confidence in God, without which no person can obtain eternal life. It was this that enabled the ancient saints to endure all their afflictions and persecutions, and to take joyfully the spoiling of their goods, knowing (not believing merely) that they had a more enduring substance. (Heb.10:34). . . . ¶ 4. Such was, and always will be, the situation of the saints of God, that unless they have an actual knowledge that the course they are pursuing is according to the will of God they will grow weary in their minds, and faint; . . . (*Lectures on Faith delivered to the School of the Prophets, 1834-35*) LOF6:2,4

**J. Reuben Clark, Jr.**

[O]bedience must often precede knowledge. CR1950Apr:181

**Boyd K. Packer**

Latter-day Saints are not obedient because they are compelled to be obedient. They are obedient because they know certain spiritual truths and have decided, as an expression of their own individual agency, to obey the commandments of God. . . . ¶ . . . . Those who talk of blind obedience may appear to know many things, but they do not understand the doctrines of the gospel. There is an obedience that comes from a knowledge of the truth that transcends any external form of control. We are not obedient because we are blind, we are obedient because we can see. CR1983Apr:89-90

**Elder Spencer W. Kimball**

When men obey commands of a creator, it is not blind obedience. How different is the cowering of a subject to his totalitarian monarch and the dignified, willing obedience one gives to his God. The dictator is ambitious, selfish, and has ulterior motives. God's every command is righteous, every directive purposeful, and all for the good of the governed. The first may be blind obedience, but the latter is certainly faith obedience. CR1954Oct:52

**N. Eldon Tanner**

We do not suggest blind obedience, but obedience by faith in those things which may not be fully understood by man's limited comprehension, but which in the infinite wisdom of God are for man's benefit and blessing. CR1977Oct:67

---

482. When God commands, He prepares a way for us to carry out His commandments.

### Nephi, son of Lehi

And it came to pass that I, Nephi, said unto my father: I will go and do the things which the Lord hath commanded, for I know that the Lord giveth no commandments unto the children of men, save he shall prepare a way for them that they may accomplish the thing which he commandeth them. *(Nephi responds to his father Lehi, who has given him a commandment of the Lord, 600-592 B.C.)* 1Ne.3:7

### Nephi, son of Lehi

And thus we see that the commandments of God must be fulfilled. And if it so be that the children of men keep the commandments of God he doth nourish them, and strengthen them, and provide means whereby they can accomplish the thing which he has commanded them; wherefore, he did provide means for us while we did sojourn in the wilderness. *(Nephi writes about how the Lord sustained his family as they approached the seashore, prior to building the ship, 592 B.C.)* 1Ne.17:3

### Elder Heber J. Grant

No obstacles are insurmountable when God commands and we obey. CR1899Oct:18

### Elder Joseph F. Smith

[S]o long as the Latter-day Saints are content to obey the commandments of God . . . so long our heavenly Father is bound by his oath and covenant to protect them from every opposing foe, and to help them to overcome every obstacle that can possible be arrayed against them, or thrown in their pathway. *(General conference, April 8, 1883, JD24:176)* (Gospel Doctrine, pp. 50-51) TLDP:436

**Related Witnesses:**

### John A. Widtsoe

Strict obedience to the laws of the Lord makes a person sensitive to spiritual impressions and messages. The clean life, earnest desire and sincere prayer of Joseph Smith placed him within the range of true spiritual experience. Spiritual power always follows complete devotion to the cause of the Lord. (Man and the Dragon, p. 171) TLDP:437

**Author's Note:** Although the Lord will provide a way to carry out his commandments, it is possible that our enemies may come upon us and hinder our most diligent efforts to be obedient to a command of the Lord. In such cases, the Lord may require us no more to perform that work. See D&C 124:49-53.

---

**483. The Lord requires active obedience, not just passive acceptance.**

### Jesus, *recorded in Matthew*

Not every one that saith unto me, Lord, Lord, shall enter into the kingdom of heaven; but he that doeth the will of my Father which is in heaven. *(Jesus Christ teaches the multitude, about A.D. 30)* Matt.7:21

### Joseph Smith, *receiving the Word of the Lord*

He that receiveth my law and doeth it, the same is my disciple; and he that saith he receiveth it and doeth it not, the same is not my disciple, and shall be cast out from among you; *(Revelation, Feb. 4, 1831)* D&C 41:5

### Mark E. Petersen

There is no reward for half-hearted obedience. We must become vigorous and enthusiastic about living our religion, for God commands that we serve him with *all* our heart, with *all* our might, with *all* our strength, and with the very best of our intelligence. ¶ With him there can be no halfway measures. We must be fully *for* him or we may be classed with those who are *against* him. CR1980Apr:96

### James

But be ye doers of the word, and not hearers only, deceiving your own selves. *(James writes to his brethren in the Church)* James 1:22

### President Brigham Young, Heber C. Kimball, Jedediah M. Grant
#### (First Presidency)

To the Elders abroad, we say, "be diligent in all your labours, be faithful in your testimony to the people, and when they receive the truth, learn them to live and practice their holy religion." It is easy to bear persecution, to contend for the faith, and even to die for it; the hardest of all is to live it, to be always actuated by its holy influences and practice it in all the walks of life. It is not a plaything or mere toy to believe, amuse ourselves with at our convenience, and then lay aside, but a tangible, every day experience and solid fact, entering into every avenue of business, of pastime and repose, as well as into the spiritually religious exercises of the mind. ¶ In fact we have no requirement or duty upon this earth only to serve God, keep His commandments, gather the Saints, and build up His kingdom thereon; for this we live, for this we expect to die. But the main difficulty with the Saints is to live their holy religion, and pursue that course which will ensure unto them its blessings and privileges, and that increase of faith, intelligence, and improvement which they may enjoy. ¶ It is a small matter to devote and dedicate ourselves and all we have to the cause of truth, and the building up of the kingdom of God upon the earth, but it is of importance to rightly apply ourselves and our means where we may do the most good. It is important that we be obedient and passive in the hands of the servants of God, and when we have embraced the truth, and placed ourselves with all we have upon the altar, to so remain, regardless alike of friend or foe, sunshine or shade, peace or plenty, of war, famine, and pestilence. It is our duty not only to profess and be believers, but to work out our salvation, continuing faithful in all things, even unto the end. MOFP2:184-85

### Mark E. Petersen

Half obedience will be rejected as readily as full violation, and maybe quicker, for half rejection and half acceptance is but a sham, an admission of lack of character, a lack of love for Him. It is actually an effort to live on both sides of the line. CR1982Apr:21

### President Heber J. Grant

Of what good is our faith, our repentance, our baptism, and all the sacred ordinances of the gospel by which we have been made ready to receive the blessings of the Lord, if we fail, on our part, to keep the commandments? All that we expect, or all that we are promised, is predicated on our own actions, and if we fail to act, or to do the work which God has required of us, we are little better than those who have not received the principles and ordinances of the gospel. We have only started, and when we rest there, we are not following our faith by our works, and are under condemnation, our salvation is not attained. ("Commandments and Promises: A New Year's Message," IE1921Jan:259) TLDP:436

### Related Witnesses:

#### Jesus,
##### quoted by Joseph Smith,
##### translating Matthew

For the day soon cometh, that men shall come before me to judgment, to be judged according to their works. JST(Matt.7:21 fn. e)

---

### 484. A way to test a doctrine is to live it.

#### Jesus,
##### quoted by John

Jesus answered them, and said, My doctrine is not mine, but his that sent me. 17. If any man will do his will, he shall know of the doctrine, whether it be of God, or whether I speak of myself. (*Jesus teaches in the temple*) John 7:16-17

#### John A. Widtsoe

I was brought up in scientific laboratories, where I was taught to test things, never to be satisfied unless a thing was tested. We have the right to test the Gospel of the Lord Jesus Christ. By testing it I mean living it, trying it out. Do you question the Word of Wisdom? Try it. Do you question the law of tithing? Practice it. Do you doubt the virtue of attending meetings? Attend them. Only then shall we be able to speak of these things intelligently and in such a way as to be respected by those who listen to us. Those who live the Gospel of Jesus Christ gain this higher knowledge, this greater testimony, this ultimate assurance that this is the truth. It is the way to truth. CR1938Oct:129

### Elder Harold B. Lee

All the principles and ordinances of the gospel are in a sense but invitations to learning the gospel by the practice of its teachings. No person knows the principle of tithing until he pays tithing. No one knows the principle of the Word of Wisdom until he keeps the Word of Wisdom. Children, or grownups for that matter, are not converted to tithing, the Word of Wisdom, keeping the Sabbath day holy, or prayer by hearing someone talk about these principles. We learn the gospel by living it. (Instructor, June 1963, pp. 220-24; Stand Ye in Holy Places, p. 215) TLDP:439

### Elder George Albert Smith

[P]raying is one thing and prayers are important, but living is the thing that will bring us power with our Heavenly Father. Living the gospel of Jesus Christ will give us influence with our fellows among the children of men. Keeping the commandments of God will give us strength and assurance that not anything else can give us. CR1943Apr:90

---

### 485. If we keep the Lord's commandments, He is bound by His promises to bless us.

#### Joseph Smith,
##### receiving the Word of the Lord

I, the Lord, am bound when ye do what I say; but when ye do not what I say, ye have no promise. (*Revelation, April 26, 1832*) D&C 82:10

#### Joseph Smith

There is a law, irrevocably decreed in heaven before the foundations of this world, upon which all blessings are predicated— 21. And when we obtain any blessing from God, it is by obedience to that law upon which it is predicated. (*Revelation, April 2, 1830*) D&C 130:20-21

#### President Joseph F. Smith

To please [God] we must not only worship him

with thanksgiving and praise but render willing obedience to his commandments. By so doing he is bound to bestow his blessings; for it is upon this principle (obedience to law) that all blessings are predicated. (Quoted by F. W. Otterstrom in "A Journey to the South: Gems from President Smith's Talks to the People on the Way," IE1917Dec:104) TLDP:436-37

### Elder Joseph F. Smith

So long as the Latter-day Saints are content to obey the commandments of God, to appreciate the privileges and blessings which they enjoy in the Church, and will use their time, their substance, in honor to the name of God, to build up Zion, and to establish truth and righteousness in the earth, so long our heavenly Father is bound by his oath and covenant to protect them from every opposing foe, and to help them to overcome every obstacle that can possibly be arrayed against them, or thrown in their pathway. (*General conference, April 8, 1883, JD24:176*) (Gospel Doctrine, pp. 50-51) TLDP:436

### Bruce R. McConkie

We must remind ourselves of how the law of forgiveness operates, for the Lord, who himself ordained the laws, is also himself bound to uphold and sustain and conform to them. The Lord forgives sins, but he does it in harmony with the laws he ordained before the world was. (The Mortal Messiah, 2:50-51) TLDP:205

**Related Witnesses:**

### Joseph Smith,
*receiving the Word of the Lord*

Therefore, be ye as wise as serpents and yet without sin; and I will order all things for your good, as fast as ye are able to receive them. Amen. (*Revelation, Aug. 6, 1836*) D&C 111:11

### James E. Talmage

Faith is a Gift of God. . . . No compulsion is used in bringing men to a knowledge of God; yet, as fast as we open our hearts to the influences of righteousness, the faith that leads to life eternal will be given us of our Father. AF:97

### Bruce R. McConkie

If we, as a people, keep the commandments of God; if we take the side of the Church on all issues, both religious and political; if we take the Holy Spirit for our guide; if we give heed to the words of the apostles and prophets who minister among us—then, from an eternal standpoint, all things will work together for our good. CR1980Apr:100

### Joseph Smith

How long can rolling waters remain impure? What power shall stay the heavens? As well might man stretch forth his puny arm to stop the Missouri river in its decreed course, or to turn it up stream, as to hinder the Almighty from pouring down knowledge from heaven upon the heads of the Latter-day Saints. D&C 121:33

### Jarom,
*quoted by Mormon*

Inasmuch as ye will keep my commandments ye shall prosper in the land. (*Jarom records how the word of the Lord was verified as the righteous Nephites successfully withstood the onslaughts of the Lamanites, 399 B.C.*) Jarom 1:9

### Mormon,
*quoting Amaron*

Inasmuch as ye will not keep my commandments ye shall not prosper in the land. (*Amaron writes the words of the Lord spoken to his ancestors*) Omni 1:6

---

**486. Those who keep the Lord's commandments may be blessed with temporal (as well as spiritual) blessings.**

### King Benjamin,
*quoted by Mormon*

And moreover, I would desire that ye should consider on the blessed and happy state of those that keep the commandments of God. For behold, they are blessed in all things, both temporal and spiritual; and if they hold out faithful to the end they are received into heaven, that thereby they may dwell with God in a state of never-ending happiness. O remember, remember that these things are true; for the Lord God hath spoken it. (*King Benjamin addresses his people, about 124 B.C.*) Mosiah 2:41

### Recorded in Leviticus

If ye walk in my statutes, and keep my commandments, and do them; 4. Then I will give you rain in due season, and the land shall yield her increase, and the trees of the field shall yield their fruit. 5. And your threshing shall reach unto the vintage, and the vintage shall reach unto the sowing time: and ye shall eat your bread to the full, and dwell in your land safely. 6. And I will give peace in the land, and ye shall lie down, and none shall make you afraid: and I will rid evil beasts out of the land, neither shall the sword go through your land. 7. And ye shall chase your enemies, and they shall fall before you by the sword. 8. And five of you shall chase an hundred, and an hundred of you shall put ten thousand to flight: and your enemies shall fall before you by the sword. 9. For I will have respect unto you, and make you fruitful, and multiply you, and establish my covenant with you. 10. And ye shall eat old store, and bring forth the old because of the new. 11. And I will set my tabernacle among you: and my soul shall not abhor you. 12. And I will walk among you, and will be your God, and ye shall be my people. (*Revelation to Moses for the children of Israel*) Lev.26:3-12

**Elder Spencer W. Kimball**

The Lord delights to give us all. He created the earth for us and gave to us as stewards all that it affords. "The fulness of the earth is yours," he said, but this fabulous gift came upon condition that we unreservedly obey his commands. ("When Is One Rich?", Salt Lake Tribune-Telegram, May 28, 1949; The Teachings of Spencer W. Kimball, p. 358) TLDP:714-15

**President Heber J. Grant,**
*also quoting Samuel, the Israelite*

Faith is a gift of God, and when people have faith to live the Gospel, and to listen to the counsel of those who preside in the wards and stakes, and of the General Authorities of the Church, it has been my experience that they have been abundantly blessed of the Lord, and that many of them have come out of great financial and other difficulties in a most miraculous and wonderful way. "Obedience [to obey] is better than sacrifice, and to hearken than the fat of rams." [1Sam.15:22] ("Further Facts on Following Counsel," IE1936Jun:332) TLDP:437

**Joseph Smith**

Behold, the Lord requireth the heart and a willing mind; and the willing and obedient shall eat the good of the land of Zion in these last days. (*Revelation for the elders of the Church at Kirtland, Ohio, Sept. 11, 1831*) D&C 64:34

**Elder Harold B. Lee**

I wish we could take a lesson from the testimony of a man in this city who conducts a business here, who wrote and told me about a little experience he had when during the so-called depression of the past years, he thought he was going to lose everything that he had, and so he fasted and prayed that the Lord would show him how to save his business, and he said: "One morning just as it was breaking daylight I felt the still small voice which said to me: 'If you will only but keep God's commandments, you will be given all the wisdom necessary to save your business.'" ¶ Simple, but a great powerful truth—if we will only keep God's commandments, the wisdom sufficient to our needs will be given us! CR1949Apr:51

**Mormon**

Blessed art thou and thy children; and they shall be blessed, inasmuch as they shall keep my commandments they shall prosper in the land. But remember, inasmuch as they will not keep my commandments they shall be cut off from the presence of the Lord. (*Mormon records how the word of the Lord given to Lehi about 588 B.C. is verified in 71 B.C.*) Alma 50:20

**Mormon,**
*quoting Amaron*

Inasmuch as ye will not keep my commandments ye shall not prosper in the land. (*Amaron writes the words of the Lord spoken to his ancestors*) Omni 1:6

**Related Witnesses:**

**Jarom,**
*quoted by Mormon*

Inasmuch as ye will keep my commandments ye shall prosper in the land. (*Jarom records how the word of the Lord was verified as the righteous Nephites successfully withstood the onslaughts of the Lamanites, 399 B.C.*) Jarom 1:9

**Elder David O. McKay**

The development of our spiritual nature should concern us most. Spirituality is the highest acquisition of the soul, the divine in man; "the supreme, crowning gift that makes him king of all created things." It is the consciousness of victory over self and of communion with the infinite. It is spirituality alone which really gives one the best in life. ¶ It is something to supply clothing to the scantily clad, to furnish ample food to those whose table is thinly spread, to give activity to those who are fighting desperately the despair that comes from enforced idleness, but after all is said and done, the greatest blessings that will accrue from the Church Security Plan [welfare program] are spiritual. Outwardly, every act seems to be directed toward the physical: remaking of dresses and suits of clothes, canning fruits and vegetables, storing foodstuffs, choosing of fertile fields for settlement—all seem strictly temporal, but permeating all these acts, inspiring and sanctifying them, is the element of spirituality. CR1936Oct:103

---

**487. All blessings flow from obedience to laws of God (to obtain a blessing we must obey the law appointed for that blessing).**

**Elder Ezra Taft Benson**

God, our Heavenly Father, governs His children by law. He has instituted laws for our perfection. If we obey His laws, we receive the blessings pertaining to those laws. If we do not obey, we receive the consequences. CR1983Apr:70

**Joseph Smith**

There is a law, irrevocably decreed in heaven before the foundations of this world, upon which all blessings are predicated— 21. And when we obtain any blessing from God, it is by obedience to that law upon which it is predicated. *(Revelation, April 2, 1830)* D&C 130:20-21

**Joseph Smith,**
*receiving the Word of the Lord*

For all who will have a blessing at my hands shall abide the law which was appointed for that blessing, and the conditions thereof, as were instituted from before the foundation of the world. *(Revelation relating to the new and everlasting covenant, including the eternal nature of the marriage covenant, July 12, 1843, [1831])* D&C 132:5

**Joseph Smith,**
*receiving the Word of the Lord*

I, the Lord, am bound when ye do what I say; but when ye do not what I say, ye have no promise. *(Revelation, April 26, 1832)* D&C 82:10

**President Joseph F. Smith**

To please [God] we must not only worship him with thanksgiving and praise but render willing obedience to his commandments. By so doing he is bound to bestow his blessings; for it is upon this principle (obedience to law) that all blessings are predicated. (Quoted by F. W. Otterstrom in "A Journey to the South: Gems from President Smith's Talks to the People on the Way," IE1917Dec:104) TLDP:436-37

**Francis M. Lyman**

Since President Snow has been talking so plainly upon this subject [of tithe paying], there have been a class of people who have undertaken to take advantage of his promise to the Latter-day Saints in regard to this law [of tithing], that if for the future they would observe this law faithfully the past should be forgiven. There have been men guilty of breaches of the laws of morality and honesty who have claimed that if they now pay their tithing all their sins will be forgiven them. President Snow never announced any such doctrine as that. He could not announce such a doctrine as that. But the Lord is perfectly able to say to us that if we will observe this law of finance . . . for the future and keep this commandment, our past negligence of the law of tithing will be forgiven. He is competent to say that if we will repent of [any of our] sins and serve God with all our hearts for the future, our sins will be forgiven us; but not otherwise. The forgiveness of sins is predicated upon faith in God, repentance and reformation and baptism. Sins are not forgiven through the payment of tithing, nor through the partaking of the sacra-ment, nor observing the Word of Wisdom, or prayer. *There are blessings attached to each of these important requirements of the Gospel* [italics added]; but if a man would have his sins forgiven . . . he must repent of all his sins, turn unto the Lord with full purpose of heart and sin no more. Then God will forgive him and redeem him from his sins; but not by paying tithing. . . . ¶ [page 36] Do you not remember when the Salt Lake Temple was dedicated in 1893, how everybody was allowed to go in there, transgressors and all? . . . The prophet Wilford Woodruff announced then that the sins of the Latter-day Saints were forgiven; but who are Latter-day Saints? Who are the men and women to whom President Woodruff referred? Any man who had not repented? No. . . . He was only announcing that the work you and I are engaged in is genuine, and that we were forgiven so far as we had complied with these laws. He never meant that a man who was an adulterer, or horse thief, was to be forgiven because he went into that Temple, without having . . . repented. President Woodruff could not say that; no Prophet could say it. The Father could not say it, only upon the principles of repentance, reformation and righteousness. CR1899Oct:34,36

**Marion G. Romney**

I plead with you young Aaronic Priesthood bearers—and all of us—to determine now, in your youth, to put your trust in the Lord, and by obeying his commandments earn the right to receive specific blessings he has promised for specific types of living—those given in the Word of Wisdom, for example, when he said that "all saints who remember to keep and do these sayings, walking in obedience to the commandments, shall receive health in their navel and marrow to their bones;" CR1979Apr:57

**Related Witnesses:**
**President Spencer W. Kimball**

All blessings, then, are conditional upon faithfulness. One is ordained to the priesthood with a conditional promise; one is married and sealed in the temple on condition of his faithfulness. And so far as I know there is nothing—no blessing in the world—that anyone can receive except through faithfulness. ("The Example of Abraham," EN1975Jun:3-4) TLDP:436

**Joseph Smith**

If a man gets a fullness of the priesthood of God, he has to get it in the same way that Jesus Christ obtained it, and that was by keeping all the commandments and obeying all the ordinances of the house of the Lord. *(At the Stand in Nauvoo, Ill., June 11, 1843)* HC5:424

**488. We can find peace by obeying the commandments of God.**

**Joseph Smith,**
*receiving the Word of the Lord*

Learn of me, and listen to my words; walk in the meekness of my Spirit, and you shall have peace in me. (*A commandment of God for Martin Harris, March 1830*) D&C 19:23

**Elder Spencer W. Kimball**

Peace, joy, satisfaction, happiness, growth, contentment, all come with the righteous living of the commandments of God. The one who delights in all of the worldly luxuries of today, at the expense of spirituality, is living but for the moment. His day is coming; retribution is sure. CR1952Apr:23-24

**Richard L. Evans**

I have a great respect for all men and their beliefs, but think it not a strange thing that in a kingdom, the kingdom of God, there should be specific requirements and commandments, and a way that God has given for our realizing the highest happiness and peace and progress. CR1961Apr:77

**Related Witnesses:**

**Joseph Smith,**
*receiving the Word of the Lord*

Be faithful and diligent in keeping the commandments of God, and I will encircle thee in the arms of my love. (*Revelation to Joseph Smith and Oliver Cowdery, April 1829*) D&C 6:20

---

**489. When we obey the word of the Lord our souls are enlarged.**

**Frances M. Lyman**

For there is an advantage, there is a blessing and an enlargement of the soul that comes to the man who obeys the word and will of the Lord. It is better that we have done God's will than that we should have need to be forgiven for neglecting it. It is better not to have been a sinner . . . God has designed that we should not be sinners, but that we should live lives of purity and righteousness and walk in obedience to His will, as the Savior did. CR1899Oct:35

**Joseph Smith**

He that keepeth his commandments receiveth truth and light, until he is glorified in truth and knoweth all things. (*Revelation May 6, 1833; Christ received a fulness of all truth and man, by obedience, may do likewise*) D&C 93:28

**Joseph Smith**

And all saints who remember to keep and do these sayings, walking in obedience to the commandments. . . . 19. . . . shall find wisdom and great treasures of knowledge, even hidden treasures; . . . (*Revelation, Feb. 27, 1833*) D&C 89:18-19

**Elder Ezra Taft Benson**

The Lord will increase our knowledge, wisdom, and capacity to obey when we obey His fundamental laws. This is what the Prophet Joseph Smith meant when he said we could have "sudden strokes of ideas" which come into our minds as "pure intelligence." (See Teachings of the Prophet Joseph Smith, p.151). This is revelation. We must learn to rely on the Holy Ghost so we can use it to guide our lives and the lives of those for whom we have responsibility. CR1983Apr:71-72

**Elder Ezra Taft Benson**

Listen to the spiritual promise; "All saints who remember to keep and do these sayings, walking in obedience to the commandments . . . shall find wisdom and great treasures of knowledge, even hidden treasures." (D&C 89:18-19) ¶ Some have thought this promise was contingent on just keeping the provisions of the Word of Wisdom. But you will notice we will walk in obedience to all the commandments. Then we shall receive specific spiritual promises. This means we must obey the law of tithing, keep the Sabbath day holy, keep morally clean and chaste, and obey all other commandments. . . . ¶ I do not believe that a member of the Church can have an active, vibrant testimony of the gospel without keeping the commandments. A testimony is to have current inspiration to know the work is true, not something we receive only once. The Holy Ghost abides with those who honor, respect, and obey God's laws. And it is that Spirit which gives inspiration to the individual. CR1983Apr:71-72

**John A. Widtsoe**

There is only one way . . . to obtain and possess this mighty spirit . . . which guides the Church today and enlightens every soul, and that is by obeying strictly, with all our might, as far as we poor mortal beings are able, the laws of the Gospel. If we obey, if we practice in our lives the truths given us, then as certainly as we do that, the enlivening spirit of light, of revelation, of understanding will come to us, comprehension will enter our minds and hearts and we shall know the true joy of being Latter-day Saints. CR1934Oct:11

**Related Witnesses:**

**Joseph Smith**

The Spirit of Revelation is in connection with these blessings. A person may profit by noticing the first intimation of the spirit of revelation;

for instance, when you feel pure intelligence flowing into you, it may give you sudden strokes of ideas, so that by noticing it, you may find it fulfilled the same day or soon; (i.e.) those things that were presented unto your minds by the Spirit of God, will come to pass; and thus by learning the Spirit of God and understanding it, you may grow into the principle of revelation, until you become perfect in Christ Jesus. (*Joseph instructs the Twelve in conference, June 27, 1839*) TPJS:151; DGSM:5

### Elder Joseph F. Smith

There is not a man born into the world, but has a portion of the Spirit of God, and it is that Spirit of God which gives to his spirit understanding. . . . [I]nasmuch as he puts forth his efforts in the proper direction, then he is entitled to an increased portion of the Spirit of the Almighty to inspire him to increased intelligence, to increased prosperity and happiness in the world; but in proportion as he prostitutes his energies for evil, the inspiration of the Almighty is withdrawn from him, until he becomes so dark and so benighted, that so far as his knowledge of God is concerned, he is quite as ignorant as a dumb brute. (Gospel Doctrine, p. 63) TLDP:365

### Jesus,
#### *quoted by John*

He that hath my commandments, and keepeth them, he it is that loveth me: and he that loveth me shall be loved of my Father, and I will love him, and will manifest myself to him. . . . 23. . . . If a man love me, he will keep my words: and my Father will love him, and we will come unto him, and make our abode with him. John 14:21,23

---

### 490. We are never to disobey God because of our fear of what mortals can do to us.

### Joseph Smith

For, behold, you should not have feared man more than God. Although men set a naught the counsels of God, and despise his words— 8. Yet you should have been faithful; and he would have extended his arm and supported you against all the fiery darts of the adversary; and he would have been with you in every time of trouble. (*Revelation regarding the lost manuscript pages, July 1828*) D&C 3:7-8

### Marvin J. Ashton

Much of the unrest and confusion in the world today is caused by man's fear to obey God because of the pressures of man. Certainly if we want peace, progress, and prosperity, it will come through adherence to God's principles. We have no need to fear if we keep God's commandments. ACR(Munich)1973:23

### Jesus,
#### *recorded in Matthew*

And fear not them which kill the body, but are not able to kill the soul: but rather fear him which is able to destroy both soul and body in hell. (*Christ instructs, empowers, and sends the Twelve Apostles forth to preach, minister, and heal the sick*) Matt.10:28

### Recorded in Psalms

The LORD is on my side; I will not fear: what can man do unto me? 7. The LORD taketh my part with them that help me: therefore shall I see my desire upon them that hate me. 8. It is better to trust in the LORD than to put confidence in man. Ps.118:6-8

### Joseph Smith,
#### *receiving the Word of the Lord*

But with some I am not well pleased, for they will not open their mouths, but they hide the talent which I have given unto them, because of the fear of man. Wo unto such, for mine anger is kindled against them. 3. And it shall come to pass, if they are not more faithful unto me, it shall be taken away, even that which they have. (*Revelation for certain elders of the Church, Aug. 8, 1831*) D&C 60:2-3

### Recorded in Proverbs

The fear of man bringeth a snare: but whoso putteth his trust in the LORD shall be safe. Prov.29:25

### Joseph Smith,
#### *receiving the Word of the Lord*

The Son of Man hath descended below them all. Art thou greater than he? 9. Therefore, hold on thy way, and the priesthood shall remain with thee; for their bounds are set, they cannot pass. Thy days are known, and thy years shall not be numbered less; therefore, fear not what man can do, for God shall be with you forever and ever. (*The word of the Lord to Joseph Smith while in Liberty Jail, March 1839*) D&C 122:8-9

### Paul

So that we may boldly say, The Lord is my helper, and I will not fear what man shall do unto me. (*Letter to the Jewish members of the Church, about A.D. 60*) Heb.13:6

### Mormon

. . . I fear not what man can do; for perfect love casteth out all fear. (*Mormon writes to his son Moroni, prior to A.D. 384*) Moro.8:16

### Related Witnesses:
#### Helaman, son of Alma, the younger,
#### *quoted by Mormon*

Now they never had fought, yet they did not

fear death; and they did think more upon the liberty of their fathers than they did upon their lives; yea, they had been taught by their mothers, that if they did not doubt, God would deliver them. (*Helaman's two thousand stripling sons fight with miraculous power and none of them are slain, 62 B.C.*) Alma 56:47

**Recorded in Psalms**

Yea, though I walk through the valley of the shadow of death, I will fear no evil: for thou art with me; thy rod and thy staff they comfort me. (*A psalm of David*) Ps.23:4

**Elder David O. McKay**

No man can disobey the word of God and not suffer for so doing. No sin, however secret, can escape retribution. True, you may lie and not be detected; you may violate virtue without its being known by any who would scandalize you; yet you cannot escape the judgment that follows such transgression. The lie is lodged in the recesses of your mind, an impairment of your character that will be reflected sometime, somehow in your countenance or bearing. Your moral turpitude, though only you, your accomplice, and God may ever know it, will canker your soul. ("The Constant Operation of Divine Law," IE1941Jul:395) TLDP:440

---

491. Members of the Lord's church who refuse to keep His commandments will not be saved (in the celestial kingdom).

**Joseph Smith**

[T]o get salvation we must not only do some things, but everything which God has commanded. Men may preach and practice everything except those things which God commands us to do, and will be damned at last. We may tithe mint and rue, and all manner of herbs, and still not obey the commandments of God. The object with me is to obey and teach others to obey God in just what He tells us to do. It mattereth not whether the principle is popular or unpopular, I will always maintain a true principle, even if I stand alone in it. (*The Prophet speaks following a lecture by an Episcopalian minister in the assembly room in Nauvoo, Ill.*) HC6:223

**Marvin J. Ashton**

Any Church member not obedient to the leaders of this Church will not have the opportunity to be obedient to the prompting of the Lord. ¶ From the Doctrine and Covenants I quote: "For all who will have a blessing at my hands shall abide the law which was appointed for that blessing, and the conditions thereof, as were

instituted from before the foundation of the world." (D&C 132:5) ACR(Munich)1973:23

**Joseph Smith,**
*receiving the Word of the Lord*

Hearken, O ye people who profess my name, saith the Lord your God; for behold mine anger is kindled against the rebellious, and they shall know mine arm and mine indignation, in the day of visitation and of wrath upon the nations. 2. And he that will not take up his cross and follow me, and keep my commandments, the same shall not be saved. [See Author's Note, below.] 3. Behold, I, the Lord, command; and he that will not obey shall be cut off in mine own due time, after I have commanded and the commandment is broken. (*Revelation received at Kirtland, Ohio, June 1831*) D&C 56:1-3

**King Benjamin,**
*quoted by Mormon*

But wo, wo unto him who knoweth that he rebelleth against God! For salvation cometh to none such except it be through repentance and faith on the Lord Jesus Christ. (*King Benjamin addresses his people, about 124 B.C.*) Mosiah 3:12

**Delbert L. Stapley**

[O]ne goal that most of us share in this life is the desire to achieve true joy and lasting happiness. There is only one way to do this, and that is by being obedient to all the commandments of God. As members of The Church of Jesus Christ of Latter-day Saints, we have voluntarily entered into holy covenants, promising to obey the Lord's commandments. Willing, righteous obedience leads to celestial life: indeed, there is no eternal progress without it. CR1977Oct:26

**Joseph Smith,**
*receiving the Word of the Lord*

Behold, I, the Lord, have looked upon you, and have seen abominations in the church that profess my name. . . . 8. But the hypocrites shall be detected and shall be cut off, either in life or in death, even as I will; and wo unto them who are cut off from my church, for the same are overcome of the world. (*Revelation for the elders of the Church, May 1831*) D&C 50:4,8

**Paul**

Being filled with all unrighteousness, fornication, wickedness, covetousness, maliciousness; full of envy, murder, debate, deceit, malignity; whisperers, 30. Backbiters, haters of God, despiteful, proud, boasters, inventors of evil things, disobedient to parents, 31. Without understanding, covenantbreakers, without natural affection, implacable, unmerciful: 32. Who knowing the judgment of God, that they which commit such things are worthy of death, not only do the same, but have pleasure in them that do them. (*Paul's letter to the Church in Rome regarding the unrighteous, about A.D. 55*) Rom.1:29-32

**Related Witnesses:**

**Elder John Taylor**

If the Lord can have a people to listen to his law, there may be a chance to establish his kingdom upon the earth: if not, the only way he can establish his kingdom is to remove them from the earth, or give up his kingdom until another time; for it is impossible to establish his kingdom without having a people obedient to him. . . . ¶ . . . [W]here there is not a feeling of obedience, the Spirit of God will be withdrawn; people cannot retain it and be in rebellion against the authorities and counsels of the church and kingdom of God. (*In Bowery, Sept. 20, 1857, JD5:265*) TLDP:433

**Joseph Smith**

For although a man may have many revelations, and have power to do many mighty works, yet if he boasts in his own strength, and sets at naught the counsels of God, and follows after the dictates of his own will and carnal desires, he must fall and incur the vengeance of a just God upon him. (*Revelation regarding the lost manuscript pages, July 1828*) D&C 3:4

**Joseph Smith,**
*receiving the Word of the Lord*

Therefore, whosoever belongeth to my church need not fear, for such shall inherit the kingdom of heaven. (*Revelation received 1828*) D&C 10:55

**Recorded in Deuteronomy**

Behold, I set before you this day a blessing and a curse; 27. A blessing, if ye obey the commandments of the LORD your God, which I command you this day: 28. And a curse, if ye will not obey the commandments of the LORD your God, but turn aside out of the way which I command you this day, to go after other gods, which ye have not known. (*Commandments to Israel through Moses*) Deut.11:26-28

**Joseph Smith,**
*receiving the Word of the Lord*

For I the Lord cannot look upon sin with the least degree of allowance; . . . (*Revelation through Joseph Smith during conference of elders of the Church, Nov. 1, 1831*) D&C 1:31

**Author's Note:** All men will be saved in a kingdom of glory (except those few "sons of Perdition") but the salvation as spoken of here (D&C 56:2) appears to refer to eternal life, to the celestial kingdom.

**HYMNS Written by Prophets Applicable to this Topic**

**Bruce R. McConkie**
*Come, Listen to a Prophet's Voice*
HYMNS:21

Then heed the words of truth and light
That flow from fountains pure.
Yea, keep His law with all thy might
Till thine election's sure,
Till thou shalt hear the holy voice
Assure eternal reign,
While joy and cheer attend thy choice,
As one who shall obtain.

**Orson F. Whitney**
*Savior, Redeemer of My Soul*
HYMNS:112

Savior, Redeemer of my soul,
Whose mighty hand hath made me whole,
Whose wondrous pow'r hath raised me up
And filled with sweet my bitter cup!
What tongue my gratitude can tell,
O gracious God of Israel.

Never can I repay thee, Lord,
But I can love thee.
Thy pure word, Hath it not been my one delight,
My joy by day, my dream by night?
Then let my lips proclaim it still,
And all my life reflect thy will.

O'errule mine acts to serve thine ends.
Change frowning foes to smiling friends.
Chasten my soul till I shall be
In perfect harmony with thee.
Make me more worthy of thy love,
And fit me for the life above.

# List of Doctrines

## ORDINANCES

*Doctrines Located in This Topic*

492. We must receive all the essential ordinances of the gospel if we are to gain exaltation in the celestial kingdom of God.

493. Although a man by his ordination holds authority of the priesthood, before he can lawfully perform any ordinance, he must receive authorization from one who holds the keys in the Church for the administration of that ordinance.

*Doctrines on ORDINANCES Located in Other Topics*

55. The specific form and words of the baptismal ordinance have been prescribed by revelation from the Lord.

75. Little children (babies) are to be blessed before the Church.

108. God's people are a covenant making people.

133. The Saints in the latter days cannot be made perfect without doing the ordinance work for their dead, nor can the dead be made perfect without this work being done for them.

179. The elder who has sufficient faith in Christ may heal the sick.

296. The first principles and ordinances of the gospel are faith in the Lord Jesus Christ, repentance, baptism by immersion, and the laying on of hands for the gift of the Holy Ghost.

474. On earth those who accept the gospel are given the opportunity to receive the necessary eternal ordinances of salvation.

570. To administer in the ordinances of the gospel, a man must hold priesthood authority.

574. Power of the priesthood extends beyond the grave, hence that which is bound on earth is also bound in heaven—ordinances performed on earth are valid in heaven.

697. In partaking of the sacrament, we make solemn covenants with the Lord.

809. Certain ordinances are to be administered only in a holy temple (including: baptisms for the dead; washings and annointings; endowments and sealings for the living and for the dead).

810. The temple endowment comprises the receiving of certain sacred ordinances necessary to enable us to gain salvation (in the celestial kingdom).

# ORDINANCES

**Author's Note:** Ordinances are rites or ceremonies essential to salvation and exaltation in the celestial kingdom of God, such as baptism, celestial marriage, temple endowments and sealings, and the sacrament. Other rites or ceremonies are *helpful* but not necessary for spiritual salvation, such as blessing of children, blessings of comfort or consolation, healing of sick, and dedication of graves. (See Mormon Doctrine, pp. 548-49.)

**492. We must receive all the essential ordinances of the gospel if we are to gain exaltation in the celestial kingdom of God.**

**Joseph Smith,**
*quoted by Elder Joseph Fielding Smith*
There are a great many wise men and women too in our midst who are too wise to be taught; therefore they must die in their ignorance, and in the resurrection they will find their mistake. Many seal up the door of heaven by saying, So far God may reveal and I will believe. ¶ All men who become heirs of God and joint heirs with Jesus Christ will have to receive the fulness of the ordinances of his kingdom; and those who will not receive all the ordinances will come short of the fullness of that glory, if they do not lose the whole. (*At the Stand in Nauvoo, Ill., June 11, 1843*) HC5:424; TPJS:309

**Elder Spencer W. Kimball**
Clearly, attaining eternal life is not a matter of goodness only. This is one of the two important elements, but one must practice righteousness *and* receive the ordinances. People who do not bring their lives into harmony with God's laws and who do not receive the necessary ordinances either in this life or (if that is impossible) in the next, have thus deprived themselves, and will remain separate and single in the eternities. There they will have no spouses, no children. If one is going to be in God's kingdom of exaltation, where God dwells in all his glory, one will be there as a husband or a wife and not otherwise. Regardless of his virtues, the single person, or the one married for this life only, cannot be exalted. All normal people should marry and rear families. To quote Brigham Young: "No man can be perfect without the woman, so no woman can be perfect without a man to lead her. I tell you the truth as it is in the bosom of eternity. If he wishes to be saved, he cannot be saved without a woman by his side." ¶ Celestial marriage is that important. (The Miracle of Forgiveness, p. 245) TLDP:380

**Elder Wilford Woodruff**
No man ever did or ever will obtain salvation, only through the ordinances of the gospel and

through the name of Jesus. There can be no change in the Gospel; all men that are saved from Adam to infinitum are saved by the one system of salvation. The Lord may give many laws and many commandments to suit the varied circumstances and conditions of his children throughout the world, such as giving a law of carnal commandment to Israel, but the laws and principles of the Gospel do not change. (*In Bowery, June 12, 1863, JD10:217*) TLDP:441

**President Brigham Young,**
*quoted by John A. Widtsoe*
There is no ordinance that God has delivered by his own voice, through his Son Jesus Christ, or by the mouths of any of his Prophets, Apostles or Evangelists, that is useless. Every ordinance, every commandment and requirement is necessary for the salvation of the human family. (*In Tabernacle, July 17, 1870, JD13:215*) DBY:152

**Related Witnesses:**
**Elder Joseph Fielding Smith**
Will those who enter the terrestrial and telestial kingdoms have to have the ordinance of baptism? No! Baptism is the door into the celestial kingdom. The Lord made this clear to Nicodemus. We are not preaching a salvation for the inhabitants of the terrestrial or the telestial kingdoms. All of the ordinances of the gospel pertain to the celestial kingdom, and what the Lord will require by way of ordinances, if any, in the other kingdoms he has not revealed. (Doctrines of Salvation, 2:329) TLDP:441

**Elder Joseph F. Smith**
So far as I know there is not an ordinance of the Church now enjoyed or practiced that was not revealed to the Church by the Prophet Joseph Smith. I know of no new doctrine that has been revealed. Principles that were revealed to the Prophet Joseph Smith have grown and developed more fully and clearly to the understanding; but we have received nothing new that I know of. Yet, if we should receive something new, through the proper channels of the Church, we should be as ready and willing to receive it as we were, or would be, to receive the same at the hands of the Prophet Joseph himself. CR1900Oct:47

**Author's Note:** What is an ordinance? John A. Widtsoe says: ¶ "An ordinance is an earthly symbol of a spiritual reality. It is usually also an act of symbolizing a covenant or agreement with the Lord. Finally, it is nearly always an act in anticipation of a blessing from heaven. An ordinance, then, is distinctly an act that connects heaven and earth, the spiritual and the temporal." PCG:366 ¶ *Ordinance* defined by Boyd K. Packer: "The word *ordinance* means, 'a religious or ceremonial observance'; 'an established rite'." ¶ The Oxford English Dictionary (Oxford, England, 1970) gives as the first definition of the word *order*, 'arrangement in ranks or rows,' and as the second definition, 'arrangement in sequence or proper relative position.' At first glance that may not strike a person as having much religious significance, but indeed it has." (See The Holy Temple, pp. 144-45.)

493. Although a man by his ordination holds authority of the priesthood, before he can lawfully perform any ordinance, he must receive authorization from one who holds the keys in the Church for the administration of that ordinance.

**John A. Widtsoe**
Every man holding the Priesthood of God, may exercise its power in behalf of himself and family. He may seek revelations for his own guidance; he may administer to his own family; teach, rebuke and bless them, he may bear witness everywhere of the truth of the Gospel and seek to help his fellowmen. In all this, his Priesthood will sustain him. ¶ But no man may exercise the power of his Priesthood for the Church except by appointment of those who hold the keys of the Priesthood—that is, those called to presiding positions. A Priest has authority to baptize, but may not exercise that power, unless called to do so by the authority presiding over the division of the Church in which he lives. Thus, confusion is avoided, and order is preserved, without in any degree violating the rights of the Priesthood. Every holder of the Priesthood may and should use it, always, for his personal welfare; but officially for the Church only when authorized to do so. PCG:73
**President Joseph F. Smith,**
**John R. Winder, Anthon H. Lund**
(First Presidency)
The leading fact to be remembered is that the Priesthood is greater than any of its offices; and that any man holding the Melchizedek Priesthood may, by virtue of its possession, per-

form any ordinance pertaining thereto, or connected therewith, when called upon to do so by one holding the proper authority, which proper authority is vested in the President of the Church, or in any whom he may designate. *("The Priesthood and its Offices," article published by the First Presidency in May 1902)* MOFP4:42-43
**Elder Joseph F. Smith,**
**quoted by John A. Widtsoe**
[THERE IS A] DISTINCTION BETWEEN KEYS OF THE PRIESTHOOD AND PRIESTHOOD. The Priesthood in general is the authority given to man to act for God. Every man ordained to any degree of the Priesthood, has this authority delegated to him. ¶ But it is necessary that every act performed under this authority shall be done at the proper time and place, in the proper way, and after the proper order. The power of directing these labors constitutes the keys of the Priesthood. In their fulness, the keys are held by only one person at a time, the prophet and president of the Church. He may delegate any portion of this power to another, in which case that person holds the keys of that particular labor. Thus, the president of a temple, the president of a stake, the bishop of a ward, the president of a mission, the president of a quorum, each holds the keys of the labors performed in that particular body or locality. His Priesthood is not increased by this special appointment, for a seventy who presides over a mission has no more Priesthood than a seventy who labors under his direction; and the president of an elders' quorum, for example, has no more Priesthood than any member of that quorum. But he holds the power of directing the official labors performed in the mission or the quorum, or in other words, the keys of that division of that work. So it is throughout all the ramifications of the Priesthood—a distinction must be carefully made between the general authority, and the directing of the labors performed by that authority. (IE1901Jan:230) PCG:200-01
**Elder Joseph Fielding Smith**
I have no right, notwithstanding I belong to the Council of the Twelve, to baptize one of my own children without first going to the bishop in the ward where I live and getting his consent, because he holds the keys for that ward to which I belong as member. I have never baptized any of my children except—and I have baptized nearly all of them as far as I could do and on their birthdays, too, when they were eight years old—except I have gone to the bishop and gained his sanction to perform that ordi-

nance and to confirm them members of the Church. ¶ I have no right to go into a stake of Zion and ordain a man an elder without the appointment coming to me from the presidency of the stake, after the man to be ordained has been voted upon by those who have the right to vote to sustain him in that stake. If a man goes into a stake to perform an ordinance and he is not sent, if he is not called, he is violating authority, he is doing that which he has no right to do, and it is not valid. ¶ All this authority radiates from the President of the Church. The President of this Church could say, if the Lord gave him that inspiration, that we shall not preach the gospel any more in the New England states, or in the United States, or in Europe, and there would not be an elder in this Church that would have any authority, notwithstanding his priesthood, to go into any place where he had been forbidden to go and preach the gospel, if the President of the Church withdrew the authority. (Doctrines of Salvation, 3:136-37) TLDP:442

**Related Witnesses:**

### John A. Widtsoe

The one baptizing must be properly appointed by the presiding officer. If the candidate desires a particular individual, or if a father desires to baptize a child, this may be granted provided the man is worthy and willing. PCG:368

### Joseph Smith

The power, glory and blessings of the Priesthood could not continue with those who received ordination only as their righteousness continued; for Cain also being authorized to offer sacrifice, but not offering it in righteousness, was cursed. It signifies, then, that the ordinances must be kept in the very way God has appointed; otherwise their Priesthood will prove a cursing instead of a blessing. ¶ If Cain had fulfilled the law of righteousness as did Enoch, he could have walked with God all the days of his life, and never failed of a blessing. . . . ¶ Elijah was the last Prophet that held the keys of the Priesthood, and who will, before the last dispensation, restore the authority and deliver the keys of the Priesthood, in order that all the ordinances may be attended to in righteousness. . . . Why send Elijah? Because he holds the keys of the authority to administer in all the ordinances of the Priesthood; and without the authority is given, the ordinances could not be administered in righteousness. (*From an article on priesthood, read at a general conference held in Nauvoo, Ill., Oct. 5, 1840*) HC4:209,11

### Boyd K. Packer

The word *ordinance* means, "a religious or cer-

emonial observance"; "an established rite." ¶ The *Oxford English Dictionary* (Oxford, England, 1970) gives as the first definition of the word *order*, "arrangement in ranks or rows," and as the second definition, "arrangement in sequence or proper relative position." At first glance that may not strike a person as having much religious significance, but indeed it has. ¶ Among the ordinances we perform in the Church are these: baptism, sacrament, naming and blessing of infants, administering to the sick, setting apart to callings in the Church, ordaining to offices. In addition there are higher ordinances, performed in the temples. These include washings, anointings, the endowment, and the sealing ordinance, spoken of generally as temple marriage. ¶ The word *ordinance* comes from the word order, which means, "a rank, a row, a series." The word *order* appears frequently in the scriptures. Some examples are: " . . . established the *order* of the Church" (Alma 8:1); ". . . all things should be restored to their proper *order* " (D&C 20:68), "mine house is a house of *order*" (D&C 132:8). Mormon even defined *depravity* as being "without *order*" (Moro.9:18). ¶ The word *ordain*, a close relative to the other two words, has, as its first definition, "to put in order, arrange, make ready, prepare"; also, "to appoint or admit to the ministry of the Christian church . . . by the laying on of hands or other symbolic action." ¶ From all this dictionary work there comes the impression that an ordinance, to be valid, must be done in proper order. (The Holy Temple, pp. 144-45) TLDP:442-43

### Joseph Smith,
#### receiving the Word of the Lord

Behold, mine house is a house of order, saith the Lord God, and not a house of confusion. (*Revelation relating to the new and everlasting covenant, including the eternal nature of the marriage covenant, July 12, 1843, [1831]*) D&C 132:8

### Joseph Smith

. . . that all things may be done in order. (*Revelation on Church Organization and Government, April 1830*) D&C 20:68

### Joseph Smith

For all things must be done in order, and by common consent in the church, by the prayer of faith. (*Revelation for Oliver Cowdery, Sept. 1830*) D&C 28:13

### Joseph Smith

Let all these things be done in order; . . . (*Revelation for the elders of the Church, Aug. 1, 1831*) D&C 58:55

**Joseph Smith**

. . . that all things may be done in order and in solemnity before him, according to truth and righteousness. (*Revelation on priesthood, received as the Twelve met in council, March 28, 1835*) D&C 107:84

**Paul**

Let all things be done decently and in order. (*Letter to the Church at Corinth, Greece, about A.D. 55*) 1Cor.14:40

**Bruce R. McConkie**

The death of these priests for performing an unauthorized ordinance [Lev.10:1-2] gives us insight into how the Lord deals with those of his people, at least, who do that which he has not authorized them to do. Certainly in principle, and to some degree the same condemnation, in a spiritual sense, rests upon all ministers who perform unauthorized ordinances. (The Mortal Messiah, 1:82) TLDP:443

**Joseph Smith,**
*receiving the Word of the Lord*

Again I say unto you, that it shall not be given to any one to go forth to preach my gospel, or to build up my church, except he be ordained by some one who has authority, and it is known to the church that he has authority and has been regularly ordained by the heads of the church. (*Revelation "embracing the law of the Church," Feb. 9, 1831*) D&C 42:11

**Joseph Smith**

We believe that a man must be called of God, by prophecy, and by the laying on of hands by those who are in authority, to preach the Gospel and administer in the ordinances thereof. (*The fifth of the thirteen Articles of Faith; letter to John Wentworth, March 1, 1842*) AofF:5

**President Joseph F. Smith**

Several examples have occurred in the history of the Church where men through transgression, duly proved and decided upon by the constituted authorities, have been stopped from acting in the Priesthood, which is just as effectual as taking away their Priesthood would be, if it were possible; but this has taken no ordination from them, and if in such cases the transgressors should repent and make complete and satisfactory restitution, they would still hold the same Priesthood which they held before they were silenced, or stopped from acting. A person once ordained a bishop, an elder, or high priest, continues to hold those offices. A bishop is still a bishop though he may remove to another ward, or for other reason temporarily lose his calling. But in case he is wanted to act in a new office, or place, and the proper authorities call him to act, it is not necessary to re-ordain him a bishop;

he would only need to be set apart for his new calling. So with other officers in the Priesthood, once having received the Priesthood, it cannot be taken from them, except by transgression so serious that they must forfeit their standing in the Church. But, as stated, their right to officiate, may be suspended or stopped. The Lord can take away the power and efficacy of their ordinations, and will do so if they transgress. No endowments or blessings in the House of the Lord, no patriarchal blessings, no ordination to the Priesthood, can be taken away, once given. To prevent a person for cause from exercising the rights and privileges of acting in the offices of the Priesthood, may be and has been done, and the person so silenced still remain a member of the Church, but this does not take away from him any Priesthood that he held. (*In a Church published statement, "Order of the Priesthood," April 1908*) MOFP4:174-175

**King Benjamin,**
*quoted by Mormon*

And see that all these things are done in wisdom and order; for it is not requisite that a man should run faster than he has strength. And again, it is expedient that he should be diligent, that thereby he might win the prize; therefore, all things must be done in order. (*King Benjamin concludes his discourse, about 124 B.C.*) Mosiah 4:27

**President Joseph F. Smith,**
*quoted by John A. Widtsoe*

We have found occasionally that men blessed with some peculiar gift of the spirit have exercised it in an unwise—shall we say, improper—manner. For instance: brethren strongly gifted with the power of healing have visited far and near amongst the Saints (to the neglect sometimes of other duties), until it has almost become a business with them, and their visits to the homes of the Saints have assumed somewhat the character of those of a physician, and the people have come to regard the power so manifested as if coming from man, and he himself has sometimes grown to so feel, and not that he was simply an instrument in the hands of God of bringing blessings to their house. This view is exceedingly unfortunate when indulged in, and is apt to result in the displeasure of the Lord. It has sometimes ended in the brother possessing this gift, if he encouraged such a feeling, losing his power to bless and heal. Departures from the recognized order and discipline of the Church should therefore be discountenanced and discouraged. (Juvenile Instructor, vol. 37, pp. 50-51, Jan. 15, 1902) PCG:75

# List of Doctrines

## PATRIARCHAL BLESSINGS

### Also: Blessings by Fathers of Family Members

*Doctrines Located in This Topic*

494. Patriarchs are called and ordained to bestow patriarchal blessings upon the people.

495. Patriarchal blessings are inspired priesthood blessings that declare the lineage of the recipient; they include other blessings and may entail a prophetic statement of the life mission of the recipient.

496. Patriarchal blessings are a valuable aid to help us on our life's journey, to point the path we should take to serve God.

497. Every father who holds the Melchizedek Priesthood has the right to give blessings to his own family in his capacity as patriarch to the family.

# PATRIARCHAL BLESSINGS

## Also: Blessings by Fathers of Family Members

494. Patriarchs are called and ordained to bestow patriarchal blessings upon the people.

### President Joseph F. Smith

We have a number of patriarchs in the Church, whose duty it is to bestow blessings upon the heads of those who seek blessings at their hands. They are fathers. They hold the evangelical office in the Church. It is their business and right to bestow blessings upon the people, to make promises unto them in the name of the Lord, as it may be given them by the inspiration of the Holy Spirit, to comfort them in the hours of sorrow and trouble, to strengthen their faith by the promises that shall be made to them through the Spirit of God, and to be fathers indeed of the people, leading them into all truth. CR1904Oct:4

### President Heber J. Grant,
### J. Reuben Clark, Jr., David O. McKay
(First Presidency)

The patriarchal office is one of blessing, not of administration. Patriarchal blessings are the only blessings that patriarchs are specifically ordained and sustained to give. (*From letter of instruction defining the role of Church patriarchs, May 15, 1943*) MOFP6:194

### President Spencer W. Kimball

The patriarch is a prophet entitled to the revelations of the Lord to each individual on whose head he places his hands. He may indicate the lineage of the individual, but he may also pour out blessings that are prophetic to the individual for his life. ACR(Seoul)1975:39

### Patriarch Eldred G. Smith

Every holder of the priesthood who is head of a family, has the right to bless members of his own family. However, it is not priesthood order for him to declare the blessings of the lineage of Israel. This is the specific responsibility of an ordained patriarch. For that reason, among others, we go to ordained patriarchs to receive those blessings. CR1960Apr:65

### Related Witnesses:
### John A. Widtsoe

To look upon a patriarch as a fortune-teller is an offense to the Priesthood; the patriarch only indicates the gifts the Lord would give us, if we labor for them. He helps us by pointing out the divine goal which we may enjoy if we pay the price. (Evidences and Reconciliations, p. 323) TLDP:458

495. Patriarchal blessings are inspired priesthood blessings that declare the lineage of the recipient; they include other blessings and may entail a prophetic statement of the life mission of the recipient.

### Patriarch Eldred G. Smith

Then the question comes, what is a patriarchal blessing? It is different from any other blessing one might receive. The first requirement and that which makes it primarily different from other blessings, is that the ordained patriarch has the right to declare the blessings of Israel, or the line of Israel through which the blessings shall come. The blessings of Israel are leadership blessings, and leadership blessings are the blessings of the priesthood. This is the main difference between patriarchal blessings and blessings given by others. CR1960Apr:65

### President Heber J. Grant,
### J. Reuben Clark, Jr., David O. McKay
(First Presidency)

Patriarchal blessings contemplate inspired declaration of the lineage of the recipient, and also, where so moved upon by the Spirit, an inspired and prophetic statement of the life mission of the recipient, together with such blessings, cautions, and admonitions as the patriarch may be prompted to give for the accomplishment of such life's mission, it always being made clear that the realization of all promised blessings is conditioned upon faithfulness to the Gospel of our Lord, whose servant the patriarch is. ¶ All such blessings are recorded and generally only one such blessing should be adequate for each person's life. The sacred nature of the patriarchal blessing must of necessity urge all patriarchs to most earnest solicitation of divine guidance for their prophetic utterances and superior wisdom for cautions and admonitions. (*From letter of instruction defining the role of Church patriarchs, May 15, 1943*) MOFP6:194

### Related Witnesses:
### President Spencer W. Kimball

There is no guarantee that the blessings will be fulfilled unless the individual subscribes to the program, but I bear my testimony to you that none of the blessings he pronounces will fail if the participant of the blessing fully subscribes. ACR(Seoul)1975:39

### John A. Widtsoe

These blessings are possibilities predicated upon

faithful devotion to the cause of truth. They must be earned. Otherwise they are but empty words. Indeed, they rise to their highest value when used as ideals, specific possibilities, toward which we may strive throughout life. (Evidences and Reconciliations, p. 323) TLDP:459

**Author's Note:** The First Presidency under President Heber J. Grant in 1943, and again, the First Presidency under President George Albert Smith in 1947, instructed that generally only one patriarchal blessing should be necessary: ¶ "All such blessings are recorded and generally only one such blessing should be adequate for each person's life. The sacred nature of the patriarchal blessing must of necessity urge all patriarchs to most earnest solicitation of divine guidance for their prophetic utterances and superior wisdom for cautions and admonitions." (MOFP6:194,261)

---

496. Patriarchal blessings are a valuable aid to help us on our life's journey, to point the path we should take to serve God.

### Elder Joseph Fielding Smith

The main purpose of the blessing is to be a guide to the individual who receives it, to encourage him, to direct him, to help him as he journeys through life. ¶ My uncle, John Smith, who gave as many blessings I suppose as anybody, said one day to me in the presence of others, "When I give a patriarchal blessing, the dividing line between time and eternity disappears." If that be the case, I guess I ought to be willing to accept it. Then there may be things in these blessings that pertain to our future existence. There might be promises made to us that are not fulfilled here that will be fulfilled. For instance, suppose a patriarch says in giving a blessing to a young woman that she shall be married and that she will have posterity, and yet she dies without posterity. Married for time and all eternity in the temple of the Lord, she receives there the blessings of eternal lives, which is a continuation of the seeds forever. Perhaps the patriarch, in giving her a blessing of posterity, sees beyond the veil; so I don't think we should be too hasty in condemning a patriarch when he promises posterity, and then in this life that blessing is not fulfilled. We may ourselves be at fault in judging in matters of that kind. (*Address delivered to Brigham Young University Church history and philosophy instructors, June 15, 1956*) TLDP:460

### John A. Widtsoe

The patriarchal blessing should be read and reread. It should be made useful in life. This should be done with faith in spiritual blessings. ¶ It is a gift of the Lord. The purpose of asking for the blessing must be remembered. It must be read with intelligent consideration of its meaning. Attention should be fixed upon the one great meaning of the blessing rather than upon particular statements. There must be no quibbling about the time or place when the promises should be fulfilled or about the man who gave it. As the blessing was given through the inspiration of the Lord, so its meaning will be made clear by the same power; and its fulfillment will be in His hands. Above all, it must ever be remembered that every blessing is conditioned upon our faithfulness. (Evidences and Reconciliations, p. 324) TLDP:460

### Patriarch Eldred G. Smith

If you can discover the keynote in your blessing, it will be an index to point the way of life for you, or the path that you should go to serve God. These blessings are an eternal anchor for our soul with the Lord. They are just as eternal and binding upon us, through our faithfulness, as were the blessings given by Adam, Abraham, Jacob, or any other patriarch of past times. Because of their eternal nature the Lord has required that they be recorded so that we have a record of them in the archives of the Church, and each individual is given a copy of his blessing so that he might have it available for himself. CR1960Apr:66

### Patriarch Eldred G. Smith

Now, if we are going to receive only one blessing, then it is important that we get that blessing at a proper time in our life. The question often comes to me, at what age should my children receive their patriarchal blessings? I discourage anyone under twelve years of age. If I were a stake patriarch and giving blessings to people in my community, I think I would raise that age. I think the best age is between fifteen and twenty-five. However, every baptized member of the Church is entitled to receive a patriarchal blessing. He should be old enough to understand the meaning and purpose and value of a patriarchal blessing to the extent that he has a personal desire to receive such a blessing, and not because a group is getting blessings, or because friends or neighbors are getting blessings, or because an adult or parent has the desire that the child should receive a blessing. CR1960Apr:66

**497.** Every father who holds the Melchizedek Priesthood has the right to give blessings to his own family in his capacity as patriarch to the family.

### John A. Widtsoe

Every father, having children born to him under the covenant, is to them as a patriarch, and he has the right to bless his posterity in the authority of the Priesthood which he holds. The patriarchs of old commonly blessed their children, as, for example, Isaac (Genesis, chapter 27), Jacob (Genesis, chapter 49), Lehi (Book of Mormon, 2 Nephi, chapters 2, 3, 4). (Evidences and Reconciliations, p. 321) TLDP:459

### Elder Joseph Fielding Smith

In the writings of President John Taylor the statement is made. "Every father, after he has received his patriarchal blessing, is a patriarch to his own family: which blessings will be just as legal as those conferred by any patriarch of the Church; in fact it is his right: and a patriarch in blessing his children, can only bless as his mouthpiece." (The Gospel Kingdom, page 146) . . . ¶ The statement of President John Taylor is true with this qualification: The father must hold the Melchizedek Priesthood, that is, have the office of an elder, seventy, or high priest. ¶ The privilege of giving these blessings, of course, is limited to the immediate members of the family. ¶ The difference between such blessings and those given by the regularly appointed patriarch is that the blessings of the father are not recorded in a book and filed eventually in the archives of the Church. The father may record such blessings for family use. ¶ In my opinion, a father will be better qualified to give such blessings if he has been to the temple and had his wife and children sealed to him. There would be no need for a father to get a recommend from the mission president or stake president in order to bless his own child. However, the father should use discretion in giving such blessings, and they should be confined to members of his family who are members of the Church. (Answers to Gospel Questions, p. 321) TLDP:469

### Patriarch Eldred G. Smith

Every holder of the priesthood who is head of a family, has the right to bless members of his own family. However, it is not priesthood order for him to declare the blessings of the lineage of Israel. This is the specific responsibility of an ordained patriarch. For that reason, among others, we go to ordained patriarchs to receive those blessings. CR1960Apr:65

# List of Doctrines

## PEACE

### (Peace versus Contention and War)

*Doctrines Located in This Topic*

498. We are to live peaceably and not contend one with another.

499. We are not to be angry with others.

500. Contention begets contention, revenge begets revenge, and war begets more war.

501. We are to avoid litigation in the courts.

502. Those who are not the cause of war or contention are justified in defending themselves against the enemy who comes against them.

503. The righteous shall receive a reward of inner peace and contentment—the kind of peace only the Lord can give.

504. Christ is the bringer of peace.

505. The Holy Ghost can give peace to the soul of the righteous.

*Doctrines on PEACE Located in Other Topics*

328. The Holy Ghost is a comforter.

450. There shall be harmony, love, and peace in the Millennium; the violence of both people and beasts will cease.

488. We can find peace by obeying the commandments of God.

636. Repentance brings peace of conscience.

742. We reap the good that we sow.

774. Pride leads to contention.

# PEACE

## (Peace versus Contention and War)

**498. We are to live peaceably and not contend one with another.**

### Nephi, son of Lehi

And again, the Lord God hath commanded that men should not murder; that they should not lie; that they should not steal; that they should not take the name of the Lord their God in vain; that they should not envy; that they should not have malice; that they should not contend one with another; that they should not commit whoredoms; and that they should do none of these things; for whoso doeth them shall perish. (*Nephi gives commandments of God to Nephites, 559-545 B.C.*) 2Ne.26:32

### President Ezra Taft Benson

Arguments, fights, unrighteous dominion, generation gaps, divorces, spouse abuse, riots, and disturbances all fall into this category of pride. ¶ Contention in our families drives the Spirit of the Lord away. It also drives many of our family members away. Contention ranges from a hostile spoken word to worldwide conflicts. CR1989Apr:5

### George Q. Cannon

[I]t is the duty of every man and woman in this Church to live at peace with him and herself, and then to live at peace with everybody else, husbands with wives, wives with husbands, parents with children, children with parents, brothers with sisters and sisters with brothers; this is the duty that God requires at our hands. I am speaking now of something which is not an abstract theory, that cannot be carried out; I am speaking of that which can be carried out, which every one of us can carry out, and of results which can be accomplished in the midst of this people. (*In 14th Ward, July 25, 1880, JD22:103*) TLDP:471

### King Benjamin,
#### *quoted by Mormon*

And ye will not have a mind to injure one another, but to live peaceably, and to render to every man according to that which is his due. 14. And ye will not suffer your children that they go hungry, or naked; neither will ye suffer that they transgress the laws of God, and fight and quarrel one with another, and serve the devil, who is the master of sin, or who is the evil spirit which hath been spoken of by our fathers, he being an enemy to all righteousness. 15. But ye will teach them to walk in the ways of truth and soberness; ye will teach them to love one another, and to serve one another.

(*King Benjamin to his people, about 124 B.C.*) Mosiah 4:13-15

### President Heber J. Grant,
### J. Reuben Clark, Jr., David O. McKay
#### (First Presidency)

The mission of the Church of Jesus Christ of Latter-day Saints is to establish peace. The living Christ is its head. Under Him over one hundred thousand men in the Church are divinely authorized to represent Him in variously assigned positions. It is the duty of these representatives to manifest brotherly love, first toward one another, then toward all mankind; to seek unity, harmony and peace in organizations within the Church, and then, by precept and example, extend these virtues throughout the world. ("Greetings from the First Presidency," Liahona, the Elder's Journal, Dec. 22, 1936, p. 315) TLDP:471-72

### Jesus,
#### *quoted by Mormon*

For verily, verily I say unto you, he that hath the spirit of contention is not of me, but is of the devil, who is the father of contention, and he stirreth up the hearts of men to contend with anger, one with another. 30. Behold, this is not my doctrine, to stir up the hearts of men with anger, one against another; but this is my doctrine, that such things should be done away. (*The resurrected Jesus Christ addresses his Nephite disciples, A.D. 34*) 3Ne.11:29-30

### Paul

Recompense to no man evil for evil. Provide things honest in the sight of all men. 18. If it be possible, as much as lieth in you, live peaceably with all men. 19. Dearly beloved, avenge not yourselves, but rather give place unto wrath: for it is written, Vengeance is mine; I will repay, saith the Lord. 20. Therefore if thine enemy hunger, feed him; if he thirst, give him drink: for in so doing thou shalt heap coals of fire on his head. 21. Be not overcome of evil, but overcome evil with good. (*Paul's letter to the Church in Rome, about A.D. 55*) Rom.12:17-21

### Mormon,
#### *receiving the Word of the Lord*

Turn, all ye Gentiles, from your wicked ways; and repent of your evil doings, of your lyings and deceivings, and of your whoredoms, and of your secret abominations, and your idolatries, and of your murders, and your priestcrafts, and your envyings, and your strifes, and from all your wickedness and abominations, and come unto me, and be baptized in my name, that ye may receive a remission of your sins, and be filled with the Holy Ghost, that ye may be numbered with my people who are of the house of Israel. (*Jesus Christ commands Mormon to write these words, between A.D. 326-385*) 3Ne.30:2

### President Joseph F. Smith

The great object and duty that devolves upon the Latter-day Saints is to learn, each man and each woman for himself and for herself, their individual duty as members of the Church. Just as soon as a man or woman learns his and her duty to God and to those who are members with them in the household of faith, peace is established, love and good will are assured, no backbiting, no fault-finding, no bearing false witness against neighbors, no strife, no contention. For the moment that a Latter-day Saint learns his duty, he will learn that it is his business to make peace, to establish good will, to work righteousness, to be filled with the spirit of kindness, love, charity, and forgiveness; and, so far as he is concerned, there can be no war, no strife, no contention, no quarreling, no disunion; no factions can arise among the people who know their duty as Latter-day Saints. CR1915Apr:4

---

## 499. We are not to be angry with others.

### Recorded in Psalms

Cease from anger, and forsake wrath: fret not thyself in any wise to do evil. (*A psalm of David*) Ps.37:8

### Jesus,
### *quoted by Mormon*

But I say unto you, that whosoever is angry with his brother shall be in danger of his judgment. And whosoever shall say to his brother, Raca, shall be in danger of the council; and whosoever shall say, Thou fool, shall be in danger of hell fire. (*The resurrected Jesus Christ to the Nephite people, A.D. 34*) 3Ne.12:22

### Jesus,
### *quoted by Mormon*

For verily, verily I say unto you, he that hath the spirit of contention is not of me, but is of the devil, who is the father of contention, and he stirreth up the hearts of men to contend with anger, one with another. 30. Behold, this is not my doctrine, to stir up the hearts of men with anger, one against another; but this is my doctrine, that such things should be done away. (*The resurrected Jesus Christ addresses his Nephite disciples, A.D. 34*) 3Ne.11:29-30

### Elder David O. McKay

The soul is the fountain from which the peace of the world will spring. Centered in the heart also are the enemies to peace—"avarice, ambition,

envy, anger, and pride." These and other vices which bring misery into the world must be eradicated before men will "beat their swords into ploughshares and their spears into pruning hooks." Before permanent peace is assured there shall have to be felt in the hearts of men more consideration for others—there shall have to be manifested around the coming peace table at least a little of the Christ spirit—"Do unto others as you would have others do unto you." ("Faith in Christ—The World's Greatest Need," IE1944Jan:62) TLDP:463-64

### President David O. McKay

[W]e leave this conference today with greater responsibility than ever before, as men of the priesthood, as women of the Church, to make our homes such as will radiate to our neighbors harmony, love, community duties, loyalty. Let our neighbors see it and hear it. Never must there be expressed in a Latter-day Saint home an oath, a condemnatory term, an expression of anger or jealousy or hatred. Control it! Do not express it! You do what you can to produce peace and harmony, no matter what you may suffer. CR1963Apr:130

### Mormon

And now behold, my son, I fear lest the Lamanites shall destroy this people; for they do not repent, and Satan stirreth them up continually to anger one with another. (*Mormon to his son Moroni, prior to A.D. 385*) Moro.9:3

### Joseph Smith

For Satan putteth it into their hearts to anger against you, and to the shedding of blood. (*Revelation, Aug. 1831*) D&C 63:28

### Paul

But now ye also put off all these; anger, wrath, malice, blasphemy, filthy communication out of your mouth. (*Paul's letter from prison to the Church in Colossae, Asia Minor, about A.D. 60*) Col.3:8

### Recorded in Proverbs

He that is slow to anger is better than the mighty; and he that ruleth his spirit than he that taketh a city. (*Proverb of Solomon, king of Israel*) Prov.16:32

### Jonah

Then said the LORD, Doest thou well to be angry? (*Jonah expresses his displeasure with the Lord's mercy upon the people, about 780-755 B.C.*) Jonah 4:4

**Related Witnesses:**
### President Spencer W. Kimball

In quiet, restrained, divine dignity he stood when they cast their spittle in his face. He remained composed. They pushed him around. Not an angry word escaped his lips. They slapped his face and beat his body. Yet he stood resolute, unintimidated. ¶ Literally did he follow his own admonition when he turned his other cheek to be also slapped and smitten. And yet, he showed no cringing, gave no denials, offered no rebuttals. When false mercenary witnesses were paid to lie about him, he seemed to condemn them not. They twisted his words and misinterpreted his meanings, yet he was calm and unflustered. Had he not taught, "Pray for them which despitefully use you"? (Matt.5:44), . . . . ¶ Neither did he say anything to the people who called for Barrabas, crying "Release unto us Barrabas" (Luke 23:18). Even when they cried for his blood, saying, "Crucify him, crucify him" (Luke 23:21)—yet he showed no bitterness nor venom nor condemnation. Only tranquility. This is divine dignity, power, control, restraint. Barrabas for Christ! Barrabas released, Christ crucified. The worst and the best; the just and the unjust; the Holy one crucified, the degenerate malefactor released. Yet no revenge, no name-calling, no condemnation. No lightning struck them, though it could have done. No earthquake, though a severe one could have come. No angels with protective weapons, though legions were ready. No escape, though he could have been translated and moved from their power. He stood and suffered in mind and body. "Bless them that curse you," he had taught (Matt.5:44). . . . ¶ . . . . He had said, "Love your enemies." Now he showed how much one can love his enemies. He was dying on the cross for those who had nailed him there. As he died, he experienced such agonies that no man had ever before or has since experienced. Yet he cried out, "Father, forgive them; for they know not what they do" (Luke 23:34). Was this not the last word—the supreme act? How divine to forgive those who were killing him—those who were clamoring for his blood! He had said, "Pray for them which despitefully use you," and here he was praying for them. His life met perfectly his teachings. "Be ye therefore perfect" was his command to us. With his life, his death, and his resurrection, Jesus truly has shown us the way. ("Jesus of Nazareth," EN1980Dec:6-8) TLDP:307

**Author's Note:** *Anger*: "A feeling of sudden and strong displeasure and antagonism directed against the cause of an assumed wrong or injury." (Funk & Wagnalls Standard College Dictionary, p. 56) ¶ Matthew and Third Nephi quoted above are identical except Matthew contains the qualifying phrase "without a cause." (See Matt.5:22 and compare with 3Ne.12:12.)

**500. Contention begets contention, revenge begets revenge, and war begets more war.**

**Jesus,**
*recorded in Matthew*
[T]hey that take the sword shall perish with the sword. (*Jesus speaks to Peter whose sword, in defense of Jesus, has cut off the ear of the Jewish high priest's servant*) Matt.26:52

**President Heber J. Grant,**
**J. Reuben Clark, Jr., David O. McKay**
(First Presidency)
But there is an eternal law that rules war and those who engage in it. It was given when, Peter having struck off the ear of Malchus, the servant of the High Priest, Jesus reproved him, saying: ¶ "Put up again thy sword into his place: for all they that take the sword shall perish with the sword." (Matt.26:52) ¶ The Savior thus laid down a general principle upon which He placed no limitations as to time, place, cause, or people involved. He repeated it in this dispensation when he told the people if they tried to secure the land of Zion by blood, then "Lo, your enemies are upon you." This is a universal law, for force always begets force; it is the law of "an eye for an eye, a tooth for a tooth" (Ex.21:24; Lev.24:20); it is the law of the unrighteous and wicked but it operates against the righteous who may be involved. CR1942Apr:95

**President Heber J. Grant,**
**J. Reuben Clark, Jr., David O. McKay**
(First Presidency)
[W]ar will be ended only by superior armed forces, by increased number of swifter and stronger planes, by more shattering bombs and other weapons of destruction; but Peace will be maintained only by nobler men and by more Christ-like nations. (*Annual Christmas message of First Presidency, Dec. 19, 1942, IE1943Jan:10-11*) MOFP6:189

**President Heber J. Grant,**
**J. Reuben Clark, Jr., David O. McKay**
(First Presidency)
Not until Freedom triumphs, and a just peace comes may we hope for "good will among men." When a soldier sees his "buddy's" body torn and mangled beside him, he madly, desperately seeks revenge. Multiply that soldier by millions, and you readily see how hate, not good will, governs the hearts and actions of mankind. Thus war makes men vicious and arouses in them brutal instincts. It prompts the abrogation of all moral obligations. (*Annual Christmas message of First Presidency, Dec. 19, 1942 IE1943Jan:10-11*) MOFP6:189

### Elder Joseph Fielding Smith

Sin begets sin; the darkness grows until the love of truth turns to hatred, and the love of God is overcome by the wicked desire to destroy all that is just and true. (Doctrines of Salvation, 1:49) TLDP:634-35

**Related Witnesses:**

### Mormon

But, behold, the judgments of God will overtake the wicked; and it is by the wicked that the wicked are punished; for it is the wicked that stir up the hearts of the children of men unto bloodshed. (*Mormon continues to record his account of war and carnage, about 363 B.C.*) Morm.4:5

### Joseph Smith

It is a time-honored adage that love begets love. Let us pour forth love—show forth our kindness unto all mankind, and the Lord will reward us with everlasting increase; cast our bread upon the waters and we shall receive it after many days, increased to a hundredfold. Friendship is like Brother Turley in his blacksmith shop welding iron to iron; it unites the human family with its happy influence. (*In meeting at the Stand in Nauvoo, Ill., July 23, 1843*) HC5:517

### Jesus,
*recorded in Matthew*

Ye have heard that it hath been said, An eye for an eye, and a tooth for a tooth: 39. But I say unto you, That ye resist not evil: but whosoever shall smite thee on thy right cheek, turn to him the other also. 40. And if any man will sue thee at the law, and take away thy coat, let him have thy cloke also. 41. And whosoever shall compel thee to go a mile, go with him twain. (*Jesus Christ to the multitude, about A.D. 30*) Matt.5:38-41

### Joseph Smith,
*receiving the Word of the Lord*

Now, I speak unto you concerning your families—if men will smite you, or your families, once, and ye bear it patiently and revile not against them, neither seek revenge, ye shall be rewarded; 24. But if ye bear it not patiently, it shall be accounted unto you as being meted out as a just measure unto you. (*Revelation received Aug. 6, 1833 in consequence of the persecution of the Saints*) D&C 98:23-24

### Mormon

And again, he saith: If my people shall sow filthiness they shall reap the chaff thereof in the whirlwind; and the effect thereof is poison. 31. And again he saith: If my people shall sow filthiness they shall reap the east wind, which bringeth immediate destruction. 32. And now,

behold, the promise of the Lord is fulfilled, and ye are smitten and afflicted. 33. But if ye will turn to the Lord with full purpose of heart, and put your trust in him, and serve him with all diligence of mind, if ye do this, he will, according to his own will and pleasure, deliver you out of bondage. (*King Limhi has just recounted the history of his people to Ammon and the throng assembled; he says a prophet [Abinadi] was slain by the wicked—because he testified that Christ was the God and Father of all things*) Mosiah 7:30-33

---

### 501. We are to avoid litigation in the courts.

### President Joseph F. Smith

Be reconciled with each other. Do not go to the courts of the Church nor to the courts of the land for litigation. Settle your own troubles, and difficulties; . . . there is only one way in which a difficulty existing between man and man can be truly settled, and that is when they get together and settle it between them. The courts cannot settle troubles between me and my brother. If they decide against him, and in my favor, of course I receive it with gladness, and praise the judge because he has favored me, but my brother is not satisfied at all, and condemns the decision, and is embittered against me. So the only way to settle a trouble between brethren is for them to get together and settle it between themselves and let it be settled fully and forever. CR1916Oct:7-8

### Paul

But brother goeth to law with brother, and that before the unbelievers. 7. Now therefore there is utterly a fault among you, because ye go to law one with another. Why do ye not rather take wrong? why do ye not rather suffer yourselves to be defrauded? 8. Nay, ye do wrong, and defraud, and that your brethren. (*Letter to the Church at Corinth in Greece, about A.D. 55*) 1Cor.6:6-8

### President Brigham Young,
*quoted by John A. Widtsoe*

My spiritual enjoyment must be obtained by my own life, but it would add much to the comfort of the community, and to my happiness, as one with them, if every man and woman would live their religion, and enjoy the light and glory of the Gospel for themselves, be passive, humble and faithful; rejoice continually before the Lord, attend to the business they are called to do, and be sure never to do anything wrong. ¶ All would then be peace, joy, and tranquility, in our streets and in our houses. Litigation would cease, there would be no difficulties before the High Council and Bishops' Courts, and courts, turmoil, and strife would not be known. ¶ Then we would have Zion, for all would be pure in heart. (*In Tabernacle, March 16, 1856, JD3:255*) DBY:119

### Dallin H. Oaks

Persons who prosecute frivolous lawsuits do not measure up to this high standard [that of being involved only in activities upon which they can ask the blessings of the Lord]. Groundless litigation rewards some plaintiffs handsomely, but it injures everyone else by raising the price of products and services. CR1986Oct:26

**Related Witnesses:**

### Paul

Dare any of you, having a matter against another, go to law before the unjust, and not before the saints? 2. Do ye not know that the saints shall judge the world? and if the world shall be judged by you, are ye unworthy to judge the smallest matters? 3. Know ye not that we shall judge angels? how much more things that pertain to this life? (*Letter to the Church at Corinth, Greece, about A.D. 55*) 1Cor.6:1-3

### John A. Widtsoe

It should always be remembered that the Church exists to save, not to condemn men. Every effort should be made to have contending parties settle their own difficulties, with the aid of ward teachers if necessary; and to induce those who have erred to tread the way of forgiveness and thus make unnecessary the calling together of a Church tribunal of justice. ¶ Should it be necessary to call a person to a Church trial, those composing the council must use every endeavor to bring about reconciliation or confession in humility. Excommunication should be the last resort. ¶ All should be eager to keep those who are in the Church in full fellowship with the community of Saints. PCG:215

### Joseph Smith,
*quoted by Elder Joseph Fielding Smith*

Brethren, bear and forbear one with another, for so the Lord does with us. Pray for your enemies in the Church and curse not your foes without: for vengeance is mine, saith the Lord, and I will repay. To every ordained member, and to all, we say, be merciful and you shall find mercy. Seek to help save souls, not to destroy them: (Messenger and Advocate, 1:137-38) TPJS:77

### Recorded in Leviticus

Thou shalt not hate thy brother in thine heart: thou shalt in any wise rebuke thy neighbour,

and not suffer sin upon him. 18. Thou shalt not avenge, nor bear any grudge against the children of thy people, but thou shalt love thy neighbour as thyself: I am the LORD. (*Revelation to Moses for the children of Israel*) Lev.19:17-18

### President John Taylor
### George Q. Cannon
(First Presidency)

Fifty-two years have passed since this [D&C 98:4-15] was given to the Church, and we are now witnessing its fulfillment. The Saints are required to do whatsoever the Lord commands them, to live by every word which proceedeth forth out of the mouth of God. They are also instructed to befriend every constitutional law of the land; for such laws support the principle of freedom; they maintain rights and privileges. This, as a people, we have striven to do from the beginning of our organization. We have ever been a law-abiding people. Times without number we have suffered the most grievous wrongs without resenting them. We have ever thought it better to suffer wrong than to do wrong. (*Epistle from the First Presidency to the Church, Oct. 6, 1885*) MOFP3:28-29

**Author's Note:** In the Prophet's Journal History of the Church appears the following from a report of the high council committee, accepted by the high council in Nauvoo, January 28, 1842: "Who, observing these things [set forth in 1Cor.6:1-10], would go to law distressing his brother, thereby giving rise to hardness, evil speaking, strifes and animosities among those who have covenanted to keep the commandments of God—who have taken upon them the name of Saints, and if Saints are to judge angels, and also to judge the world—why then are they not competent to judge in temporal matters, especially in trivial cases, taking the law of the Lord for their guide, brotherly kindness, charity, &c., as well as the law of the land? Brethren, these are evils which ought not to exist among us. We hope the time will speedily arrive when these things will be done away, and everyone stand in the office of his calling, as a faithful servant of God, building each other up, bearing each other's infirmities, and so fulfill the law of Christ." (HC4:505)

---

502. Those who are not the cause of war or contention are justified in defending themselves against the enemy who comes against them.

## Mormon

Nevertheless, the Nephites were inspired by a better cause, for they were not fighting for monarchy nor power but they were fighting for their homes and their liberties, their wives and their children, and their all, yea, for their rites of worship and their church. 46. And they were doing that which they felt was the duty which they owed to their God; for the Lord had said unto them, and also unto their fathers, that: Inasmuch as ye are not guilty of the first offense, neither the second, ye shall not suffer yourselves to be slain by the hands of your enemies. 47. And again, the Lord has said that: Ye shall defend your families even unto bloodshed. Therefore for this cause were the Nephites contending with the Lamanites, to defend themselves, and their families, and their lands, their country, and their rights, and their religion. (*Moroni arms the Nephites against the Lamanites who have come against them to war, about 73 B.C.*) Alma 43:45-47

### President David O. McKay

There are . . . two conditions which may justify a truly Christian man to enter—mind you, I say *enter, not begin*—a war: (1) an attempt to dominate and to deprive another of his free agency, and (2) loyalty to his country. Possibly there is a third, viz., defense of a weak nation that is being unjustly crushed by a strong, ruthless one. ¶ Paramount among these reasons, of course, is the defense of man's freedom. An attempt to rob man of his free agency caused dissension even in heaven. (Gospel Ideals, p. 287) TLDP:713

### Joseph Smith,
*quoted by Elder Joseph Fielding Smith*

The prediction is that army will be against army: it may be that the Saints will have to beat their ploughs into swords, for it will not do for men to sit down patiently and see their children destroyed. (*From an address at the Stand, Nauvoo, Ill., May 12, 1844*) TPJS:366

### Joseph Smith

It has been our study to avoid contention, and we have never interfered with others until they have thrown down the gauntlet; and as we have not been up to the present the aggressors so we are determined for the future not to be the aggressors. (*From an editorial in the first issue of Nauvoo Neighbor, May 1843*) HC5:381

### Elder Joseph Fielding Smith

Is there ever a time when war, or the taking up of arms is justified? ¶ Yes, there are such times. There have been many instances when the Lord has justified the taking up of arms and has approved his people in their obedience to such cause. When it becomes necessary for a righteous people to take arms against their enemies who are the aggressors, in protection of their lives and in the defense of their possessions, the Lord has approved. (Answers to Gospel Questions, 3:50-51) TLDP:713

### Joseph Smith,
*receiving the Word of the Lord*

And again, this is the law that I gave unto mine ancients, that they should not go out unto battle against any nation, kindred, tongue, or people, save I, the Lord, commanded them. 34. And if any nation, tongue, or people should proclaim war against them, they should first lift a standard of peace unto that people, nation, or tongue; 35. And if that people did not accept the offering of peace, neither the second nor the third time, they should bring these testimonies before the Lord; 36. Then I, the Lord, would give unto them a commandment, and justify them in going out to battle against that nation, tongue, or people. 37. And I, the Lord, would fight their battles, and their children's battles, and their children's children's, until they had avenged themselves on all their enemies, to the third and fourth generation. (*Revelation received Aug. 6, 1833 in consequence of the persecution of the Saints in Missouri*) D&C 98:33-37

### Related Witnesses:
### President Heber J. Grant,
### J. Reuben Clark, Jr.,David O. McKay
(First Presidency)

Thus the Church is and must be against war. The Church itself cannot wage war, unless and until the Lord shall issue new commands. It cannot regard the war as a righteous means of settling international disputes; these should and could be settled—the nations agreeing—by peaceful negotiation and adjustment. ¶ But the Church membership are citizens or subjects of sovereignties over which the Church has no control. The Lord Himself has told us to "Befriend that law which is the constitutional law of the land." CR1942Apr:94

### President Brigham Young,
*quoted by John A. Widtsoe*

Of one thing I am sure; God never institutes war; God is not the author of confusion or of war; they are the results of the acts of the children of men. Confusion and war necessarily come as the results of the foolish acts and policy of men; but they do not come because God desires they should come. If the people, generally, would turn to the Lord, there would never be any war. Let men turn from their iniquities and sins and, instead of being covetous and wicked, turn to God and seek to promote peace and happiness throughout the land, and wars would cease. We expect to see the day when swords shall be turned into ploughshares, spears into pruning hooks, and when men shall learn war no more. This is what we want. We are for peace, plenty and happiness to all the human family. (*In new Tabernacle, July 11, 1869, JD13:149*) DBY:366-67

## 503. The righteous shall receive a reward of inner peace and contentment—the kind of peace only the Lord can give.

**Jesus,**
*quoted by John*

Peace I leave with you, my peace I give unto you: not as the world giveth, give I unto you. Let not your heart be troubled, neither let it be afraid. (*Jesus comforts the Twelve in anticipation of his crucifixion*) John 14:27

**President Brigham Young,**
*quoted by John A. Widtsoe*

Thrust a man into prison and bind him with chains, and then let him be filled with the comfort and with the glory of eternity, and that prison is a palace to him. Again, let a man be seated upon a throne with power and dominion in this world, ruling his millions and millions and without that peace which flows from the Lord of Hosts—without that contentment and joy that come from heaven, his palace is a prison; his life is a burden to him; he lives in fear, in dread, and in sorrow. But when a person is filled with the peace and power of God, all is right with him. (*In Bowery, July 5, 1857, JD5:1-2*) DBY:33

**Joseph Smith**

But learn that he who doeth the works of righteousness shall receive his reward, even peace in this world and eternal life in the world to come. (*Revelation, Aug. 7, 1831*) D&C 59:23

**Marion G. Romney**

The fruits of the gospel are the only objectives worthy of life's full efforts. Their possessor obtains true wealth—wealth in the Lord's view of values. We need to constantly deepen our understandings and sharpen our realization of what the fruits of the gospel are. ¶ The Lord has defined them as "peace in this world, and eternal life in the world to come." (D&C 59:23) It is a bit difficult to define the "peace in this world" referred to in the revelation, but we may be assured that it is not the ease, luxury, and freedom from struggle envisioned by the

world's utopian dreamers. Jesus told his apostles that it would be found by them even in their days of tribulation. "Peace I leave with you," he said, "my peace I give unto you." And then, by way of caution, it seems to me, he added, "not as the world giveth, give I unto you." (John 14:27) ¶ A little later he reemphasized this statement in these words: "These things I have spoken unto you, that in me ye might have peace. In the world ye shall have tribulation." (John 16:33) ¶ Convincing evidence of the truth of this saying of the Master has come out of the most severe experiences. I suppose that the last few days of the Prophet Joseph Smith's life were crowded with about as much tribulation as any human being could endure. He was hounded by traitors, impeached by misguided and falsely accusing associates, called to account, promised protection, and then abandoned by his government. That all the while he knew he was approaching martyrdom is clear from the record. . . . ¶ . . . . In this setting, knowing that his own life would be taken from him by force and violence, and viewing the trials and suffering that would be visited upon his believing followers, he said to the company who were with him, "I am going like a lamb to the slaughter, but I am as calm as a summer's morning." (HC6:555) ¶ This is a classic of a person having at the same time tribulation in this world and peace in Christ. (Learning for Eternities, pp. 93-94) TLDP:462

**Joseph Smith**

I am going like a lamb to the slaughter, but I am calm as a summer's morning. I have a conscience void of offense toward God and toward all men. If they take my life I shall die an innocent man. . . . (*The words of the Prophet, en route to Carthage, Ill., where he was killed, June 24, 1844*) HC6:555

**Elder John Taylor**

Peace is the gift of God. Do you want peace? Go to God. Do you want peace in your families? Go to God. Do you want peace to brood over your families? If you do, live your religion, and the very peace of God will dwell and abide with you, for that is where peace comes from, and it doesn't dwell anywhere else. . . . ¶ Some in speaking of war and troubles, will say are you not afraid? No, I am a servant of God, and this is enough, for Father is at the helm. It is for me to be as clay in the hands of the potter, to be pliable and walk in the light of the countenance of the Spirit of the Lord, and then no matter what comes. Let the lightnings flash and the earthquakes bellow, God is at the helm, and I feel like saying but little, for the Lord God

Omnipotent reigneth and will continue his work until he has put all enemies under his feet, and his kingdom extends from the rivers to the ends of the earth. (*In Tabernacle, May 18, 1862, JD10:56,58*) TLDP:460

**Related Witnesses:**

### Elder Harold B. Lee

You who are engaged in deadly combat where all the forces of earth and hell seem to be combined to destroy life, if you have the assurance of the existence of things divine, you will be at peace even in the face of impending doom and though you walk through the valley of the shadow of death, you will fear no evil, but will feel the nearness of God's presence. (Youth and the Church, p. 52) TLDP:461-62

### Jesus,
#### quoted by John

These things I have spoken unto you, that in me ye might have peace. In the world ye shall have tribulation: but be of good cheer; I have overcome the world. (*Jesus tells his disciples of his death, resurrection, and divine Sonship*) John 16:33

---

### 504. Christ is the bringer of peace.

#### Bruce R. McConkie

Jesus' words bring peace; the preaching of the word to believing souls brings peace; the gospel is a message of peace, of peace on earth and good will to men. Peace is one of the gifts of the Spirit. No matter that there is persecution and sorrow and evil; the war cry of the saints is, "Be of good cheer," for Jesus has overcome the world. (The Mortal Messiah, 4:104) TLDP:468

#### Bruce R. McConkie

What, then, say the scriptures as to peace—whose it is, whence it comes, and how struggling, feeble, wayward man may gain it? ¶ 1. They say: *Peace comes from Jehovah.* "Jehovah," or, as it has been Anglicized in the translation process, "the Lord" says the Psalmist, "will bless his people with peace." (Ps.29:11) "He will speak peace unto his people, and to his saints." (Ps.85:8) The great blessing, revealed through Moses and pronounced upon all Israel, contained the promise: "The Lord lift up his countenance upon thee, and give thee peace." (Num.6:26) And it was Jehovah himself who said, "If ye walk in my statutes, and keep my commandments, and do them, . . . I will give peace in the land." (Lev.26:3-6) He it is who promises to make, with the righteous of all ages, his "covenant of peace," which is the gospel covenant. (Ezek.37:26; Isa.54:10) ¶ . . . . It is

clear that the Lord Jehovah is the source of peace for his people. It is also clear that the promised Messiah would bring peace to those same people. Fully aware of these verities, the Lord Jesus—whose very birth had been heralded by angelic choirs singing "Glory to God in the highest, and on earth peace, good will toward men" (Luke 2:14)—this same Jesus near the climax of his ministry said: "Peace I leave with you, my peace I give unto you" (John 14:27) and "in me ye might have peace." (John 16:33) (The Promised Messiah, pp. 211-13) TLDP:469-71

### Isaiah

How beautiful upon the mountains are the feet of him that bringeth good tidings, that publisheth peace. . . . (*Isaiah predicts the birth of the Messiah*) Isa.52:7

### Jesus,
#### quoted by John

Peace I leave with you, my peace I give unto you: not as the world giveth, give I unto you. Let not your heart be troubled, neither let it be afraid. (*Jesus comforts the Twelve in anticipation of his crucifixion*) John 14:27

### Jesus,
#### quoted by John

These things I have spoken unto you, that in me ye might have peace. In the world ye shall have tribulation: but be of good cheer; I have overcome the world. (*Jesus tells his disciples of his death, resurrection, and divine Sonship*) John 16:33

### Jesus,
#### quoted by John

Then said Jesus to them again, Peace be unto you: as my Father hath sent me, even so send I you. (*The risen Jesus appears to his assembled disciples*) John 20:21

### Paul

For God is not the author of confusion, but of peace, as in all churches of the saints. (*Paul writes to the Church at Corinth, Greece, about A.D. 55*) 1Cor.14:33

### Recorded in Luke

Glory to God in the highest, and on earth peace, good will toward men. (*An angel from God appears to shepherds announcing the birth of Jesus Christ*) Luke 2:14

---

### 505. The Holy Ghost can give peace to the soul of the righteous.

#### Marion G. Romney

The function of the Holy Ghost is to guide men in the way of truth and peace. Jesus referred to him as "the Spirit of truth" when he said to his disciples: "Howbeit when he, the Spirit of truth, is come, he will guide you into all truth: . . . and he will shew you things to come." (John 16:13) CR1968Apr:115

### Delbert L. Stapley

The Holy Ghost is also a comforter; it has the power to give peace to the soul of the righteous. . . . ¶ It is the Holy Ghost, or the Comforter, that fills us with hope and perfect love. (Moro.8:26) Men find peace, contentment, and comfort when by the Holy Ghost they gain a testimony of the Christ. Without this spirit, one cannot teach correct doctrine. CR1966Oct:113-14

### Joseph Smith,
*receiving the Word of the Lord*

And this is my gospel—repentance and baptism by water, and then cometh the baptism of fire and the Holy Ghost, even the Comforter, which showeth all things, and teacheth the peaceable things of the kingdom. (*Revelation, Jan. 5, 1831*) D&C 39:6

### Joseph Smith,
*translating the Book of Moses*

Therefore it is given to abide in you; the record of heaven; the Comforter; the peaceable things of immortal glory; the truth of all things; that which quickeneth all things, which maketh alive all things; that which knoweth all things, and hath all power according to wisdom, mercy, truth, justice, and judgment. (*The record of Moses: Enoch recounts God speaking to Adam*) Moses 6:61

### Paul

But the fruit of the Spirit is love, joy, peace, longsuffering, gentleness, goodness, faith, 23. Meekness, temperance: against such there is no law. 24. And they that are Christ's have crucified the flesh with the affections and lusts. 25. If we live in the Spirit, let us also walk in the Spirit. (*Paul writes to the churches of Galatia in Asia Minor, about A.D. 55; he instructs them to walk not after the flesh but after the Spirit*) Gal.5:22-25

# List of Doctrines

## PERSECUTION

*Doctrines Located in This Topic*

506. Apostates are prone to persecute the Church.

507. Satan influences people to persecute the Saints.

508. The work of the Lord thrives under opposition and persecution.

509. We are to bear persecution with patience.

*Doctrines on PERSECUTION
Located in Other Topics*

7. Those who live godly lives can expect criticism for their well doing.

29. A person who falls away, after having been enlightened by the Spirit of God, becomes more hardened—worse than if that person had never known the things of God.

# PERSECUTION

**506. Apostates are prone to persecute the Church.**

**Joseph Smith**

Strange as it may appear at first thought, yet it is no less strange than true, that notwithstanding all the professed determination to live godly, apostates after turning from the faith of Christ, unless they have speedily repented, have sooner or later fallen into the snares of the wicked one, and have been left destitute of the Spirit of God, to manifest their wickedness in the eyes of multitudes. From apostates the faithful have received the severest persecutions. Judas was rebuked and immediately betrayed his Lord into the hands of His enemies, because Satan entered into him. There is a superior intelligence bestowed upon such as obeyed the Gospel with full purpose of heart, which, if sinned against, the apostate is left naked and destitute of the Spirit of God, and he is, in truth, nigh unto cursing, and his end is to be burned. When once that light which was in them is taken from them they become as much darkened as they were previously enlightened, and then, no marvel, if all their power should be enlisted against the truth, and they, Judas like, seek the destruction of those who were their greatest benefactors. What nearer friend on earth, or in heaven, had Judas than the Savior? And his first object was to destroy Him. . . . From what source emanated the principle which has ever been manifested by apostates from the true Church to persecute with double diligence, and seek with double perseverance, to destroy those whom they once professed to love, with whom they once communed, and with whom they once covenanted to strive with every power in righteousness to obtain the rest of God? Perhaps our brethren will say the same that caused Satan to seek to overthrow the kingdom of God, because he himself was evil, and God's kingdom is holy. (*Written message to the elders of the Church in Kirtland, Ohio, and elsewhere, Jan. 1834*) HC2:22-23

**President David O. McKay**

The Church is little, if at all, injured by persecution and calumnies from ignorant, misinformed, or malicious enemies. A greater hindrance to its progress comes from faultfinders, shirkers, commandment-breakers, and apostate cliques within its own ecclesiastical and quorum groups. ¶ So it is with any government. It is the enemy from within that is most menacing, especially when it threatens to disintegrate established forms of good government. CR1967Oct:9

**President Harold B. Lee**

When we lose the Spirit, our priesthood authority is taken from us and we are left to ourselves "to kick against the pricks," when we are being irritated by the admonitions and instructions of our leaders. Then we begin to persecute the saints, which means criticize, and finally to fight against God, and the powers of darkness overtake us if we do not repent and turn from that evil course. (*Mexico City Area Conference, Melchizedek Priesthood session, Aug. 26, 1972*) (Stand Ye in Holy Places, pp. 253-54) TLDP:524

**George F. Richards**

Men and women have gone about the country, in this and in other lands, lecturing against the Church and its leaders. Magazine articles and books by the score, of a venomous and libelous character, have been written, published, and circulated against us. Apostates from the Church have opposed it in various ways, while the work of the Lord against which their fiery darts have been directed, goes steadily forward. CR1946Apr:95-96

**Elder Ezra Taft Benson,**
*also quoting J. Reuben Clark, Jr.*

Yes, within the Church today there are tares among the wheat and wolves within the flock. As President Clark stated, "The ravening wolves are amongst us, from our own membership, and they, more than any others, are clothed in sheep's clothing because they wear the habiliments of the priesthood. . . . We should be careful of them. . . ." (Era, May 1949, p. 268. See also Conference Report, April 1949, p. 163.) ¶ The wolves amongst our flock are more numerous and devious today than when President Clark made this statement. . . . ¶ Not only are there apostates within our midst, but there are also apostate doctrines that are sometimes taught in our classes and from our pulpits and that appear in our publications. And these apostate precepts of men cause our people to stumble. CR1969Apr:11

**Related Witnesses:**
**Joseph Smith**

[T]he rights of the priesthood are inseparably connected with the powers of heaven, and that the powers of heaven cannot be controlled nor handled only upon the principles of righteousness. 37. That they may be conferred upon us, it is true; but when we undertake to cover our sins, or to gratify our pride, our vain ambition, or to exercise control or dominion or compulsion upon the souls of the children of men, in any degree of unrighteousness, behold, the heavens withdraw themselves; the Spirit of the Lord is grieved; and when it is withdrawn, Amen to the priesthood or the authority of that man. 38. Behold, ere he is aware, he is left unto himself, to kick against the pricks, to persecute the saints, and to fight against God. (*Revelation received while in Liberty Jail, March 20, 1839; Why many are called and few chosen*) D&C 121:36-38

**Mormon**

For they saw and beheld with great sorrow that the people of the church began to be lifted up in the pride of their eyes, and to set their hearts upon riches and upon the vain things of the world, that they began to be scornful, one towards another, and they began to persecute those that did not believe according to their own will and pleasure. (*Iniquity enters the Church in Zarahemla, 84 B.C.*) Alma 4:8

---

**507. Satan influences people to persecute the Saints.**

**Bruce R. McConkie**

Persecution—the heritage of the faithful—whence does it come? Who wields the sword that slays the saints, and who hurls the spear that pierces the side of Him who hangs on the cross? ¶ Answers: It is a joint undertaking; a confederacy of evil powers unite to do the deeds; all participants play their parts as actors on an evil stage. Satan is the ultimate author; priests and ministers of false religions stir up the basest of men, who in turn wield the sword, and the legal processes of both church and state combine to justify, approve, and authorize the insane madness that fights the truth. ¶ Persecution is an essential part of the creeds of all false religions. There is an eternal law—a law as eternal as heaven and earth and the universe—that truth will prevail. Left to itself true religion—though it may be delayed or hindered in its progress—must and will prevail. The only effective weapon of false religions—and it yields only momentary success—is to persecute true believers. (The Mortal Messiah, 2:317) TLDP:479

**Elder Joseph F. Smith**

The hatred of the wicked always has and always will follow the Priesthood and the Saints. The devil will not lose sight of the power of God vested in man—the Holy Priesthood. He fears it, he hates it, and will never cease to stir up the hearts of the debased and corrupt in anger and malice towards those who hold this power, and to persecute the

Saints, until he is bound. (*In Tabernacle, April 2, 1877, JD19:24*) TLDP:139

**Mark E. Petersen**

Next we affirm that Jesus Christ of Nazareth is indeed the Christ—he who was born in Bethlehem on the first Christmas . . . he who was persecuted by the religious cults of the day, was condemned to the cross, but who conquered death and the grave in a glorious resurrection on the third day afterward. CR1980Apr:93-94

**Related Witnesses:**

**Paul**

And I thank Christ Jesus our Lord, who hath enabled me, for that he counted me faithful, putting me into the ministry; 13. Who was before a blasphemer, and a persecutor, and injurious: but I obtained mercy, because I did it ignorantly in unbelief. (*Paul's letter to his assistant Timothy, about A.D. 64*) 1Tim.1:12-13

**Bruce R. McConkie**

Persecution is one of the chief weapons in the hands of false priests; they use it to preserve their false religions. Truth stands on its own; error must be defended by the sword. False ministers fear the truth because by it their crafts are in danger. They practice priestcrafts to get gain and the praise of the world, neither of which will be theirs if true religion sweeps them into a deserved oblivion. (The Mortal Messiah, 2:393) TLDP:479

**Mormon**

For they saw and beheld with great sorrow that the people of the church began to be lifted up in the pride of their eyes, and to set their hearts upon riches and upon the vain things of the world, that they began to be scornful, one towards another, and they began to persecute those that did not believe according to their own will and pleasure. (*Iniquity enters the Church in Zarahemla, 84 B.C.*) Alma 4:8

---

**508. The work of the Lord thrives under opposition and persecution.**

**President Brigham Young,**
*quoted by John A. Widtsoe*

Every time they persecute and try to overcome this people, they elevate us, weaken their own hands, and strengthen the hands and arms of this people. And every time they undertake to lessen our number, they increase it. And when they try to destroy the faith and virtue of this people, the Lord strengthens the feeble knees, and confirms the wavering in faith and power in God, in light, and intelligence.

Righteousness and power with God increase in this people in proportion as the Devil struggles to destroy it. (*In Bowery, Oct. 21, 1860, JD8:225-26*) DBY:351

### George F. Richards

Persecution is, and always has been, a heritage of the Saints of God. Men and women have gone about the country, in this and in other lands, lecturing against the Church and its leaders. Magazine articles and books by the score, of a venomous and libelous character, have been written, published, and circulated against us. Apostates from the Church have opposed it in various ways, while the work of the Lord against which their fiery darts have been directed, goes steadily forward. ¶ Mormonism has for more than a century, been thus pelted with vituperation, deceit, and falsehood, but by every attack it has become more widely known. The work of the Lord thrives under opposition and persecution. "Truth is mighty and will prevail." ¶ We do not court opposition and persecution, but when it comes, we are not so greatly disturbed, for we know our ground, that this is the work of the Lord, and that God is at the helm, guiding the good ship into a safe harbor. CR1946Apr:95-96

### George Q. Cannon

[T]hat which we term persecution is only the discipline necessary for our development. There is a great destiny in store for this people, and they never can attain unto it unless they pass through just such scenes as they have passed through in the past, and such scenes as they doubtless will have to pass through of a more trying character in the future. This is the discipline that is necessary to purify us, to prepare us in every respect for the fulfilling of that high destiny that awaits us. . . . ¶ Every measure that has been taken against us since then, designed for our overthrow, has only taught us our strength. It has compelled us to go to the fountain of all strength, to God our Eternal Father. (*In Tabernacle, June 22, 1884, JD25:240-41*) TLDP:480

### Abraham O. Woodruff

No weapon that has ever been formed against Zion has prospered. The efforts of the evil one to destroy the work of the Lord have only tended to spread it abroad. The persecutions which have been heaped upon this people have been the means of cementing us together, drawing us more closely to God, and making us more united and powerful. It is the heritage of the saints of God to be misrepresented and persecuted by the insincere and the wicked; but their efforts have never blocked the progress of the

work of our Eternal Father. On the contrary, the labors of our most bitter enemies have been among the main factors in spreading the work abroad. The Lord has turned the wrath of the wicked to his own glory. Had it not been for the persecution of the Latter-day Saints, the mustard seed would not have been cast abroad; but in the attempt to destroy the mustard stalk, to which the Savior compared the Gospel, they have scattered the seed, and it has taken root wherever it has fallen. . . . I thank God that it is not his purposes which have failed, but the purposes of man. This should be an encouragement to every Latter-day Saint and a strong testimony that this is the work of God. It ought to be a testimony also to those who have sought to bring to naught the purposes of God. CR1901Oct:11

### George Q. Cannon

Hostile legislation and opposition have but one tendency as a rule, that is, to drive us closer together, to make the cause a common one, to cause us to feel united. (*Gospel Truth, 2:36*) TLDP:479

**Related Witnesses:**

### President Joseph F. Smith

This Church stands in no danger from opposition and persecution from without. There is more to fear in carelessness, sin and indifference, from within; more danger that the individual will fail in doing right and in conforming his life to the revealed doctrines of our Lord and Savior Jesus Christ. If we do the right, all will be well, the God of our fathers will sustain us, and every opposition will tend only to the further spread of the knowledge of truth. ("The Probable Cause," IE1903Jun:629) TLDP:480

### Joseph Smith

Our missionaries are going forth to different nations, and in Germany, Palestine, New Holland, Australia, the East Indies, and other places, the Standard of Truth has been erected; no unhallowed hand can stop the work from progressing; persecutions may rage, mobs may combine, armies may assemble, calumny may defame, but the truth of God will go forth boldly, nobly, and independent, till it has penetrated every continent, visited every clime, swept every country, and sounded in every ear, till the purposes of God shall be accomplished, and the Great Jehovah shall say the work is done. (*In Wentworth letter, March 1, 1842: "At the request of Mr. John Wentworth, Editor . . . Chicago Democrat, I have written [this] sketch of the rise, progress, persecution, and faith of the Latter-day Saints. . . ."* Full account recorded in HC4:535-41) HC4:540

### President Brigham Young,
#### quoted by John A. Widtsoe

When we look at the Latter-day Saints, we ask, is there any necessity of their being persecuted? Yes, if they are disobedient. Is there any necessity of chastening a son or a daughter? Yes, if they are disobedient. But suppose they are perfectly obedient to every requirement of their parents, is there any necessity of chastening them then? If there is, I do not understand the principle of it. I have not yet been able to see the necessity of chastening an obedient child, neither have I been able to see the necessity of chastisement from the Lord upon a people who are perfectly obedient. (*In old Tabernacle, Nov. 29, 1868, JD12:308)* DBY:350

---

### 509. We are to bear persecution with patience.

### President Joseph F. Smith,
### John R. Winder, Anthon H. Lund
#### (First Presidency)

Slander, false witness and the shafts of malice are arrayed against the Church and its authorities, as may be expected until Satan is bound and falsehood is conquered by divine truth. It is our duty to bear such things with patience, and not permit ourselves to be aroused to anger or retaliation. We should stand up for the right, and as far as possible ignore the wrong-doers. The knowledge that God is with us, and that his work will prevail, should buoy us up under every difficulty and every trial, having the conviction that the Lord will cause even "the wrath of man to praise him." ("Greetings from the First Presidency," IE1906Jan:247) TLDP:478

### President John Taylor

Have I any ill feelings towards these people that persecute and proscribe us? No. I would do them good for evil, give blessings for curses; I would treat them well, treat them honorably. . . . If you see men hungry, feed them, no matter who they are; white, black, or red, Jew, Gentile or Mormon, or anybody else—feed them. If you see naked clothe them. If you see sick, administer to them, and learn to be kind to all men; but partake not of their evil practices. (*General conference, Oct. 1884, JD25:312)* TLDP:368

### Joseph Smith,
#### receiving the Word of the Lord

And all they who suffer persecution for my name, and endure in faith, though they are called to lay down their lives for my sake yet shall they partake of all this glory. 36. Where-fore, fear not even unto death; for in this world your joy is not full, but in me your joy is full. 37. Therefore, care not for the body, neither the life of the body; but care for the soul, and for the life of the soul. 38. And seek the face of the Lord always, that in patience ye may possess your souls, and ye shall have eternal life. (*Revelation at the time of great persecution in Missouri, Dec. 16, 1833*) D&C 101:35-38

### Joseph Smith

An actual knowledge to any person, that the course of life which he pursues is according to the will of God, is essentially necessary to enable him to have that confidence in God, without which no person can obtain eternal life. It was this that enabled the ancient saints to endure all their afflictions and persecutions, and to take joyfully the spoiling of their goods, knowing (not believing merely) that they had a more enduring substance (Heb.10:34). 3. Having the assurance that they were pursuing a course which was agreeable to the will of God, they were enabled to take, not only the spoiling of their goods, and the wasting of their substance, joyfully, but also to suffer death in its most horrid forms; knowing (not merely believing) that when this earthly house of their tabernacle was dissolved, they had a building of God, a house not made with hands, eternal in the heavens (2Cor.5:1). 4. Such was, and always will be, the situation of the saints of God, that unless they have an actual knowledge that the course they are pursuing is according to the will of God they will grow weary in their minds, and faint; for such has been, and always will be, the opposition in the hearts of unbelievers and those that know not God against the pure and unadulterated religion of heaven (the only thing which insures eternal life), that they will persecute to the uttermost all that worship God according to his revelations, receive the truth in the love of it, and submit themselves to be guided and directed by his will; and drive them to such extremities that nothing short of an actual knowledge of their being the favorites of heaven, and of their having embraced the order of things which God has established for the redemption of man, will enable them to exercise that confidence in him, necessary for them to overcome the world, and obtain that crown of glory which is laid up for them that fear God. (*Lectures on Faith delivered to the School of the Prophets, 1834-35*) LOF6:2-4

#### Related Witnesses:
### Paul

So that we ourselves glory in you in the churches of God for your patience and faith in all your persecutions and tribulations that ye endure: 5. Which is a manifest token of the righteous judgment of God, that ye may be counted worthy of the kingdom of God, for which ye also suffer: (*Letter to the Church at Thessalonica, comprising Jews and many pagan converts, A.D. 50*) 2Thess.1:4-5

### Jesus,
#### *quoted by Mormon*
But behold I say unto you, love your enemies, bless them that curse you, do good to them that hate you, and pray for them who despitefully use you and persecute you; 45. That ye may be the children of your Father who is in heaven; for he maketh his sun to rise on the evil and on the good. 46. Therefore those things which were of old time, which were under the law, in me are all fulfilled. 47. Old things are done away, and all things have become new. 48. Therefore I would that ye should be perfect even as I, or your Father who is in heaven is perfect. (*The resurrected Jesus Christ teaches the Nephite people, A.D. 34*) 3Ne.12:44-48

### Jesus,
#### *recorded in Matthew*
But I say unto you, Love your enemies, bless them that curse you, do good to them that hate you, and pray for them which despitefully use you, and persecute you; 45. That ye may be the children of your Father which is in heaven: for he maketh his sun to rise on the evil and on the good, and sendeth rain on the just and on the unjust. 46. For if ye love them which love you, what reward have ye? do not even the publicans the same? 47. And if ye salute your brethren only, what do ye more than others? do not even the publicans so? 48. Be ye therefore perfect, even as your Father which is in heaven is perfect. (*Jesus teaches the multitude to love their enemies*) Matt.5:44-48

### Mormon
Some were lifted up in pride, and others were exceedingly humble; some did return railing for railing, while others would receive railing and persecution and all manner of afflictions, and would not turn and revile again, but were humble and penitent before God. (*Much iniquity abounds among the Nephites, A.D. 29-30*) 3Ne.6:13

### Joseph Smith,
#### *quoted by Elder Joseph Fielding Smith*
He that will war the true Christian warfare against the corruptions of these last days will have wicked men and angels of devils, and all the infernal powers of darkness continually arrayed against him. When wicked and corrupt men oppose, it is a criterion to judge if a man is warring the Christian warfare. When all men speak evil of you falsely, blessed are ye. Shall a man be considered bad, when men speak evil of him? No. If a man stands and opposes the world of sin, he may expect to have all wicked and corrupt spirits arrayed against him. But it will be but a little season, and all these afflictions will be turned away from us, inasmuch as we are faithful, and are not overcome by these evils. By seeing the blessings of the endowment rolling on, and the kingdom increasing and spreading from sea to sea, we shall rejoice that we were not overcome by these foolish things. (*At Relief Society meeting, Nauvoo, Ill., minutes by Eliza R. Snow*) HC5:139-41; TPJS:259

### George Q. Cannon
The Lord does not permit his enemies, nor the enemies of His people, to prevail over them for any length of time when they are living near unto Him and complying strictly with His will. (*Gospel Truth, 2:37*) TLDP:479-80

# List of Doctrines

## PRAYER

*Doctrines Located in This Topic*

### (1) Answers to Prayers

510. God answers prayers.

511. Desire and effort are both necessary to obtain divine assistance through prayer.

512. When the Lord answers our prayers, it may not always be with the answer we expect or desire.

513. Keeping the commandments of God assists us in obtaining answers to our prayers.

514. Purity and cleanliness from sin assist us in obtaining answers to our prayers.

515. The Lord responds to the prayer of the humble and penitent person.

516. The Lord answers the prayers of His servants according to the degree of their faith (and His holy purposes).

### (2) How to Pray

517. We are to address our prayers to God the Father in the name of Jesus Christ the Son.

518. In our prayers we are to address the Father with respect by using the pronouns "Thee," "Thou," "Thine," and "Thy."

519. We are not to offer vain, repetitious prayers.

520. There are times when we are to pray on our knees.

521. We are to pray vocally as well as silently in the heart.

### (3) What to Pray for— Content of Prayer

522. Prayers are to contain expressions of gratitude.

523. We are to pray for forgiveness of our sins.

524. It is appropriate to pray for our temporal needs: asking for the blessing of God upon all we possess and upon all our labors.

525. Through prayer we can receive divine direction concerning whatever we seek to undertake.

526. The Spirit of God is received through the prayer of faith.

527. We are to pray for our family members.

528. We are to pray for our neighbors, for the welfare of those around us.

529. We are to pray for the sick.

530. We are to pray for the sinful person.

531. We are to pray for our enemies.

## PRAYER continued

532. We are to pray for a testimony of the gospel.

533. We are to pray for our own spiritual welfare.

534. We are to pray that we can conquer Satan.

535. We are to pray for help to resist temptation.

536. In times of sorrow and affliction we are to pray for help from the Lord.

537. We are to pray for what is right—for what is in accord with the will of God.

538. The Holy Ghost enables a person who prays to ask according to the will of God.

539. We are to pray for those who have religious authority over us.

540. We are to pray for those who have civil authority over us.

541. In our prayers we are to dedicate ourselves and all that we have to God.

542. Through prayer we can obtain protection from peril.

543. Through prayer we can receive knowledge of divine truth (the mysteries of God).

### (4) When to Pray

544. We are to pray in the morning and evening of every day.

545. We are to live with the spirit of prayer always in our hearts.

546. We are to call upon the Lord while He is near.

### (5) Where to Pray

547. We are to pray in all places wherein we find ourselves.

548. We are to have secret prayer.

549. We are to pray in public as well as in secret.

550. We are to hold family prayer morning and night.

### (6) Prayer Is Essential

551. We are commanded to pray.

*Doctrines on PRAYER*
*Located in Other Topics*

215. Parents are to teach their children to pray.

222. Fasting is to be coupled with prayer and meditation.

817. Gospel study and prayer are necessary means for obtaining a testimony of the gospel.

# PRAYER

(1) **Answers to Prayers**
(2) **How to Pray**
(3) **What to Pray for—**
     **Content of Prayer**
(4) **When to Pray**
(5) **Where to Pray**
(6) **Prayer Is Essential**

## 1) Answers to Prayers

510. God answers prayers.

### Mormon
And as surely as Christ liveth he spake these words unto our fathers, saying: Whatsoever thing ye shall ask the Father in my name, which is good, in faith believing that ye shall receive, behold, it shall be done unto you. (*Mormon preaches in the synagogue, prior to A.D. 384*) Moro.7:26

### James
If any of you lack wisdom, let him ask of God, that giveth to all men liberally, and upbraideth not; and it shall be given him. 6. But let him ask in faith, nothing wavering. For he that wavereth is like a wave of the sea driven with the wind and tossed. (*Letter from James to his brethren in the Church*) James 1:5-6

### Joseph Smith
But ye are commanded in all things to ask of God, who giveth liberally; and that which the Spirit testifies unto you even so I would that ye should do in all holiness of heart, walking uprightly before me, considering the end of your salvation, doing all things with prayer and thanksgiving, that ye may not be seduced by evil spirits, or doctrines of devils, or the commandments of men; for some are of men, and others of devils. (*Revelation relative to governing and conducting meetings, March 8, 1831*) D&C 46:7

### Elder Joseph Fielding Smith
There is no reason in the world why any soul should not know where to find the truth. If he will only humble himself and seek in the spirit of humility and faith, going to the Lord just as the Prophet Joseph Smith went to the Lord to find the truth, he will find it. There's no doubt about it. There is no reason in the world, if men would only hearken to the whisperings of the Spirit of the Lord and seek as he would have them seek for the knowledge and understanding of the gospel of Jesus Christ, for them not to find it—no reason, except the hardness of their hearts and their love of the world. "Knock, and

it shall be opened unto you." This is my testimony, I know it is true. CR1951Apr:59

### Joseph Smith,
*receiving the Word of the Lord*
Therefore, if you will ask of me you shall receive; if you will knock it shall be opened unto you. . . . 14. Verily, verily, I say unto thee, blessed art thou for what thou hast done; for thou hast inquired of me, and behold, as often as thou hast inquired thou hast received instruction of my Spirit. If it had not been so, thou wouldst not have come to the place where thou art at this time. 15. Behold, thou knowest that thou hast inquired of me and I did enlighten thy mind; and now I tell thee these things that thou mayest know that thou hast been enlightened by the Spirit of truth; . . . (*Revelation to Joseph Smith and Oliver Cowdery, April 1829*) D&C 6:5,14-15

### Boyd K. Packer
Put difficult questions in the back of your mind and go about your lives. Ponder and pray quietly and persistently about them. ¶ The answer may not come as a lightning bolt. It may come as a little inspiration here and a little there, "line upon line, precept upon precept" (D&C 98:12). ¶ Some answers will come from reading the scriptures, some from hearing speakers. And, occasionally, when it is important, some will come by very direct and powerful inspiration. The promptings will be clear and unmistakable. CR1979Oct:30; DGSM:33

### Marion G. Romney
Just as there are many forms of prayers, so there are many types of revelation. Sometimes the Lord has answered prayers with the spoken word. . . . Sometimes the Lord puts thoughts in our minds in answer to prayers. . . . Sometimes the Lord, and perhaps more frequently in this way than in most other ways, gives us peace in our minds. ACR(Taipei)1975:7

### President Brigham Young,
*quoted by John A. Widtsoe*
When you have labored faithfully for years, you will learn this simple fact—that if your hearts are aright, and you still continue to be obedient, continue to serve God, continue to pray, the Spirit of revelation will be in you like a well of water springing up to everlasting life. Let no person give up prayer because he has not the spirit of prayer, neither let any earthly circumstance hurry you while in the performance of this important duty. By bowing down before the Lord to ask him to bless you, you will simply find this result—God will multiply blessings on you temporally and spiritually. Let a merchant, a farmer, a mechanic, any person

in business, live his religion faithfully, and he need never lose one minute's sleep by thinking about his business; he need not worry in the least, but trust in God, go to sleep and rest. I say to this people—pray, and if you cannot do anything else, read a prayer aloud that your family may hear it, until you get a worshiping spirit, and are full of the riches of eternity, then you will be prepared at any time to lay hands on the sick, or to officiate in any of the ordinances of this religion. (*In old Tabernacle, Nov. 17, 1867, JD12:103*) DBY:46

### Recorded in Psalms

I will instruct thee and teach thee in the way which thou shalt go: I will guide thee with mine eye. Ps.32:8

### Elder John Taylor

And do not forget to call upon the Lord in your family circles, dedicating yourselves and all you have to God every day of your lives; and seek to do right, and cultivate the spirit of union and love, and the peace and blessing of the Living God will be with us, and He will lead us in the paths of life; and we shall be sustained and upheld by all the holy angels and the ancient patriarchs and men of God, and the veil will become thinner between us and our God, and we will approach nearer to him, and our souls will magnify the Lord of hosts. (*At Provo, Utah, Nov. 30, 1879, JD20:361*) TLDP:488

### Isaiah

Then shalt thou call, and the LORD shall answer; thou shalt cry, and he shall say, Here I am. If thou take away from the midst of thee the yoke, the putting forth of the finger, and speaking vanity; 10. And if thou draw out thy soul to the hungry, and satisfy the afflicted soul; then shall thy light rise in obscurity, and thy darkness be as the noonday: 11. And the LORD shall guide thee continually, and satisfy thy soul in drought, and make fat thy bones: and thou shalt be like a watered garden, and like a spring of water, whose waters fail not. (*The Lord commands Isaiah to teach the people in fasting to serve the needy, thereby to be able to pray to the Lord and receive answers*) Isa.58:9-11

### Jesus, *recorded in Matthew*

Ask, and it shall be given you; seek, and ye shall find; knock, and it shall be opened unto you: 8. For every one that asketh receiveth; and he that seeketh findeth; and to him that knocketh it shall be opened. (*Jesus concludes the Sermon on the Mount*) Matt.7:7-8

### Jesus, *quoted by Mormon*

And now I go unto the Father, And verily I say unto you, whatsoever things ye shall ask the Father in my name shall be given unto you. 29. Therefore, ask, and ye shall receive; knock, and it shall be opened unto you; for he that asketh, receiveth; and unto him that knocketh, it shall be opened. (*The resurrected Jesus teaches the Nephites to pray*) 3Ne.27:28-29

### Joseph Smith, *receiving the Word of the Lord*

Draw near unto me and I will draw near unto you; seek me diligently and ye shall find me; ask, and ye shall receive; knock, and it shall be opened unto you. 64. Whatsoever ye ask the Father in my name it shall be given unto you, that is expedient for you; 65. And if ye ask anything that is not expedient for you, it shall turn unto your condemnation. (*Revelation, Dec. 27/28, 1832*) D&C 88:63-65

### John

Behold, I stand at the door, and knock: if any man hear my voice, and open the door, I will come in to him, and will sup with him, and he with me. . . . . 22. He that hath an ear, let him hear what the Spirit saith unto the churches. (*The Apostle John writes the invitation of Jesus to overcome the world*) Rev.3:20,22

### Joseph Smith, *receiving the Word of the Lord*

Let them ask and they shall receive, knock and it shall be opened unto them, and be made known from on high, even by the Comforter, whither they shall go. (*Revelation received at a Church conference, Jan. 25, 1832*) D&C 75:27

### John A. Widtsoe

Whoever in absolute desire to know the truth places himself in harmony with divine forces and approaches God in humble prayer, with full surrender of inherited or acquired prejudices, will learn to his complete satisfaction that there is a God in Heaven, whose loving will is operative on earth. Just as the turning of the dial of the radio enables us to hear the messages of distant broadcasting stations, so we may tune ourselves in prayer for truth to hear the messages that come from heavenly places. Man is more than a machine; he can so purify himself, establish earnest desire, and forget his selfish needs, as to receive through prayer the final assurance of the existence of the Lord of Heaven and Earth. This method or test is within the reach of all, humble or great, rich or poor. Happy is the man who thus enters into the abundant knowledge of divine things. ("The Articles of Faith," IE1935May:288) TLDP:490

### Jeremiah

Call unto me, and I will answer thee, and shew thee great and mighty things, which thou knowest not. *(The word of the Lord came to Jeremiah, about 628 B.C.)* Jer.33:3

### President David O. McKay

I would have them [the youth of Israel] have the trust in him which the little blind girl had in her father. One day she was sitting on his lap in the train, and a friend sitting by said, "Let me rest you," and he reached over and took the little child on his lap. The father said to her "Do you know who is holding you?" "No," she replied, "but you do." ¶ Just so real should be the trust which our boys and girls have in their Father in heaven. If our young people will have this faith, and so approach the Lord, . . . great blessings will come to them here and now. CR1961Apr:7

### Jesus,
#### recorded in Matthew

Jesus answered and said unto them, Verily I say unto you, If ye have faith, and doubt not, ye shall not only do this which is done to the fig tree, but also if ye shall say unto this mountain, Be thou removed, and be thou cast into the sea; it shall be done. 22. And all things, whatsoever ye shall ask in prayer, believing, ye shall receive. *(Jesus' disciples marvel at the cursing of the fig tree)* Matt.21:21-22

**Related Witnesses:**

### Joseph Smith,
#### receiving the Word of the Lord

For he will give unto the faithful line upon line, precept upon precept; and I will try you and prove you herewith. *(Revelation received Aug. 6, 1833, in consequence of the persecution of the Saints)* D&C 98:12

### Moroni, son of Mormon

And it came to pass that the Lord commanded them that they should go forth into the wilderness, yea, into that quarter where there never had man been. And it came to pass that the Lord did go before them, and did talk with them as he stood in a cloud, and gave directions whither they should travel. 6. And it came to pass that they did travel in the wilderness, and did build barges, in which they did cross many waters, being directed continually by the hand of the Lord. *(Moroni's abridgement of the record of the Jaredites covering the period of time of the Tower of Babel)* Ether 2:5-6

### Joseph Smith,
#### receiving the Word of the Lord

Hearken unto me, saith the Lord your God, and I will speak unto my servant Edward Partridge, and give unto him directions; for it must needs be that he receive directions how to organize this people. *(Revelation, May 1831)* D&C 51:1

### Joseph Smith,
#### receiving the Word of the Lord

And again, I say unto you, I give unto you a new commandment, that you may understand my will concerning you; 9. Or, in other words, I give unto you directions how you may act before me, that it may turn to you for your salvation. 10. I, the Lord, am bound when ye do what I say; but when ye do not what I say, ye have no promise. *(Revelation, April 26, 1832)* D&C 82:8-10

### Joseph Smith,
#### receiving the Word of the Lord

And now, again, I speak unto you, my servant Joseph, concerning the man that desires the witness— 24. Behold, I say unto him, he exalts himself and does not humble himself sufficiently before me; but if he will bow down before me, and humble himself in mighty prayer and faith, in the sincerity of his heart, then will I grant unto him a view of the things which he desires to see. *(Revelation received at the request of Martin Harris, March 1829)* D&C 5:23-24

---

511. Desire and effort are both necessary to obtain divine assistance through prayer.

### N. Eldon Tanner

If we pray that his will be done, we must be prepared to do our part. My father said to me when I was a boy, "If you want your prayers to be answered, you'd better get on your feet and go to work." There is no use praying for the kingdom to come and his will to be done unless we are prepared to do something about it. CR1974Apr:75-76

### Joseph Smith,
#### receiving the Word of the Lord

Behold, you have not understood; you have supposed that I would give it unto you, when you took no thought save it was to ask me. 8. But, behold, I say unto you, that you must study it out in your mind; then you must ask me if it be right, and if it is right I will cause that your bosom shall burn within you; therefore, you shall feel that it is right. 9. But if it be not right you shall have no such feelings, but you shall have a stupor of thought that shall cause you to forget the thing which is wrong; . . . *(Revelation for Oliver Cowdery, April 1829; the Book of Mormon is translated by study and by spiritual confirmation)* D&C 9:7-9

### Bruce R. McConkie

It is not, never has been, and never will be the design and purpose of the Lord—however much we seek him in prayer—to answer all our problems and concerns without struggle and effort on our part. This mortality is a probationary estate. In it we have our agency. We are being tested to see how we will respond in various situations; how we will decide issues; what course we will pursue while we are here walking, not by sight, but by faith. Hence, we are to solve our own problems and then to counsel with the Lord in prayer and receive a spiritual confirmation that our decisions are correct. ("Why the Lord Ordained Prayer," EN1976Jan:11) TLDP:488

### President Joseph F. Smith

Again, while prayer is essential and is one of the fundamental principles of the gospel of Jesus Christ, it is nonsense for a person to pray only, and not work. A well-balanced person would naturally do everything he could do and at the same time petition the Lord to help him in his efforts, thus aiding to bring about his desires. By work, patience and integrity, such a person would support his prayers by so living that the Lord could be justified in granting his petitions. The commandments which the Lord has given us, in ages past, and those now being revealed, teach us that human desire and effort are necessary to obtain divine assistance. ("Strive to Be as Broad as the Gospel," IE1912Jul:843) TLDP:487

### Ammon, son of Mosiah
#### *quoted by Mormon*

Yea, he that repenteth and exerciseth faith, and bringeth forth good works, and prayeth continually without ceasing—unto such it is given to know the mysteries of God; yea, unto such it shall be given to reveal things which never have been revealed; yea, and it shall be given unto such to bring thousands of souls to repentance, even as it has been given unto us to bring these our brethren to repentance. (*Ammon addresses his brethren, 90-77 B.C.*) Alma 26:22

### Elder Spencer W. Kimball

We pray for enlightenment, then go to with all our might and our books and our thoughts and righteousness to get the inspiration. We ask for judgment, then use all our powers to act wisely and develop wisdom. We pray for success in our work and then study hard and strive with all our might to help answer our prayers. When we pray for health we must live the laws of health and do all in our power to keep our bodies well and vigorous. We pray for protection and then take reasonable precaution to avoid danger. There must be works with faith. How foolish it would be to ask the Lord to *give* us knowledge, but how wise to ask the Lord's help to acquire knowledge, to study constructively, to think clearly, and to retain things that we have learned. How stupid to ask the Lord to protect us if we unnecessarily drive at excessive speeds, or if we eat or drink destructive elements or try foolhardy stunts. (Faith Precedes the Miracle, p. 205) TLDP:485-86

### Elder Spencer W. Kimball

When we pray, do we just speak, or do we also listen? Our Savior said: ¶ Behold, I stand at the door, and knock: if any man hear my voice, and open the door, I will come in to him, and will sup with him, and he with me. (Rev.3:20) ¶ The promise is made to everyone. There is no discrimination, no favored few, but the Lord has not promised to crash the door. He stands and knocks. If we do not listen, he will not sup with us nor give answer to our prayers. We must learn how to listen, grasp, interpret, understand. The Lord stands knocking. He never retreats. But he will never force himself upon us. If our distance from him increases, it is we who have moved and not the Lord. (Faith Precedes the Miracle, p. 208) TLDP:481

### Related Witnesses:
#### Alma, the younger,
#### *quoted by Mormon*

And they began from that time forth to call on his name; therefore God conversed with men, and made known unto them the plan of redemption, which had been prepared from the foundation of the world; and this he made known unto them according to their faith and repentance and their holy works. (*Alma responds to the chief ruler, Antionah, regarding Adam and Eve's expulsion from the Garden of Eden, about 82 B.C.*) Alma 12:30

---

### 512. When the Lord answers our prayers, it may not always be with the answer we expect or desire.

### Hyrum Mack Smith

The time has come when our prayers in behalf of many of our loved ones have not been answered, but those for whom we have prayed have been taken away. But, my brethren and sisters, because they are taken away, is that any sign that our prayers were not heard by our Father in heaven? Not in the least. It is but an evidence that God knows best, that His will is not our will, and that the time had come when He saw it wiser not to answer that prayer. How often do parents have to deny the prayers and petitions of their own children? Notwithstanding the child desires a thing greatly, and can see no reason why he should not have it, yet in the greater wisdom of the parent his request is denied and the supposed blessing is withheld. But that is no evidence that the prayer was not considered by the parent; it is simply an evidence that the parent knows best when to give and when to withhold. CR1902Apr:20-21

### Elder Spencer W. Kimball
How should we pray? We should pray in faith, but with awareness that when the Lord answers it may not be with the answer we expect or desire. Our faith must be that God's choice for us is right. (Faith Precedes the Miracle, p. 207) TLDP:487

### Elder Spencer W. Kimball
Prayers are not always answered as we wish them to be. Even the Redeemer's prayer in Gethsemane was answered in the negative. (*Jordan seminary graduation, May 14, 1954*) (The Teachings of Spencer W. Kimball, p. 124) TLDP:487-88

### John A. Widtsoe
The Being of higher intelligence, to whom the request is directed, may or may not grant the prayer, but some answer will be given. Prayer has been said to be "the soul's sincere desire." Only when it is such will the fullest answer be obtained, and it is doubtful if such a prayer is ever refused. No prayer is unheard. . . . A man should pray always; his heart should be full of prayer; he should walk in prayer. Answers will then be heard as God pleases. Seldom is a man greater than his private prayers. ¶ To become properly tuned with the guiding intelligent Being, one must give himself to the matter devotedly desired in the form of prayer, and then support it with all his works. Prayer is active and not passive. If a thing is wanted a man must try to secure it. Then, as a man devotes all of himself to the subject of the prayer, his attitude becomes such as to make him susceptible to the answer when it shall be sent. Prayer may be said to be the soul's whole desire. (A Rational Theology, pp. 76-77) TLDP:480-81

### J. Reuben Clark, Jr.
And I urge on you, brothers and sisters, that when you pray, let that central thought always be with you, and do not always expect that the answer to your prayer will come in the way in which you desire it. CR1958Oct:46

**Related Witnesses:**
### Joseph Smith,
*receiving the Word of the Lord*
Behold, and lo, I am the Lord thy God, and,

will answer thee as touching this matter. 3. Therefore, prepare thy heart to receive and obey the instructions which I am about to give unto you; for all those who have this law revealed unto them must obey the same. (*Revelation relating to the new and everlasting covenant, including the eternal nature of the marriage covenant, July 12, 1843 [1831]*) D&C 132:2-3

### Jeremiah
Then all the captains of the forces, and Johanan the son of Kareah, and Jezaniah the son of Hoshaiah, and all the people from the least even unto the greatest, came near, 2. And said unto Jeremiah the prophet, Let, we beseech thee, our supplication be accepted before thee, and pray for us unto the LORD thy God, even for all this remnant; (for we are left but a few of many, as thine eyes do behold us:) 3. That the LORD thy God may shew us the way wherein we may walk, and the thing that we may do. 4. Then Jeremiah the prophet said unto them, I have heard you; behold, I will pray unto the LORD your God according to your words; and it shall come to pass, that whatsoever thing the LORD shall answer you, I will declare it unto you; I will keep nothing back from you. 5. Then they said to Jeremiah, The LORD be a true and faithful witness between us, if we do not even according to all things for the which the LORD thy God shall send thee to us. 6. Whether it be good, or whether it be evil, we will obey the voice of the LORD our God, to whom we send thee; that it may be well with us, when we obey the voice of the LORD our God. (*Johanan, a military leader, asks Jeremiah to obtain instructions from the Lord for him and his people, about 628 B.C.*) Jer.42:1-6

---

**513. Keeping the commandments of God assists us in obtaining answers to our prayers.**

### John
And whatsoever we ask, we receive of him, because we keep his commandments, and do those things that are pleasing in his sight. (*John writes to the churches in Asia*) 1Jn.3:22

### Mark E. Petersen
Prayer is powerful indeed when accompanied by works of righteousness, but prayer alone is but lip service. The Almighty spurns lip service. Empty words are but symptoms of hypocrisy to him. He is a God of action—a God of works as well as of faith. He demands obedience to him if we are to receive help from him.

Are we ready to thus obey him? We cannot deal in half-way measures—not with God—and neither can we serve two masters. CR1968Apr:62

**Amulek,**
*quoted by Mormon*

And now behold, my beloved brethren, I say unto you, do not suppose that this is all; for after ye have done all these things, if ye turn away the needy, and the naked, and visit not the sick and afflicted, and impart of your substance, if ye have, to those who stand in need—I say unto you, if ye do not any of these things, behold, your prayer is vain, and availeth you nothing, and ye are as hypocrites who do deny the faith. (*Amulek teaches the people to pray earnestly for the welfare of themselves and their fellowmen, about 74 B.C.*) Alma 34:28

**Bruce R. McConkie**

No one can pray with perfect faith unless he keeps the commandments. ("The Ten Commandments of a Peculiar People," Brigham Young University Speeches of the Year, 1975, p. 38) TLDP:487

**Peter**

For the eyes of the Lord are over the righteous, and his ears are open unto their prayers: but the face of the Lord is against them that do evil. (*Peter writes to the churches in modern Asia Minor, about A.D. 60*) 1Pet.3:12

**Elder Joseph F. Smith**

If faithful, we have a right to claim the blessings of the Lord upon the labor of our hands, our temporal labors. CR1898Apr:9-10

**Related Witnesses:**

**King Benjamin,**
*quoted by Mormon*

For the Lord hath heard thy prayers, and hath judged of thy righteousness, and hath sent me to declare unto thee that thou mayest rejoice; and that thou mayest declare unto thy people, that they may also be filled with joy. (*King Benjamin addresses his people, about 124 B.C.*) Mosiah 3:4

**Alma, the younger,**
*quoted by Mormon*

[A]nd I myself was caught in a snare, and did many things which were abominable in the sight of the Lord, which caused me sore repentance; 10. Nevertheless, after much tribulation, the Lord did hear my cries, and did answer my prayers, and has made me an instrument in his hands in bringing so many of you to a knowledge of his truth. (*Alma enjoins the people to trust no man to be their teacher who is not a man of God, reminding them of his own sins as a priest of King Noah, before his conversion, 145-121 B.C.*) Mosiah 23:9-10

**514. Purity and cleanliness from sin assist us in obtaining answers to our prayers.**

**Joseph Smith**

And if ye are purified and cleansed from all sin, ye shall ask whatsoever you will in the name of Jesus and it shall be done. (*Revelation for the elders of the Church, May 1831*) D&C 50:29

**James E. Talmage**

If you would have your personal prayers reach the Divine destination to which they are addressed, see to it that they are transmitted by a current of pure sincerity, free from the resistance of unrepented sin. Let those who assemble in the sacred circle of united prayer have a care that each is individually clean, lest the supplication be nullified through the obstruction of an offending member. ("The Parable of the Defective Battery," IE1914Feb:285) TLDP:487

**Marion G. Romney**

[A]s a result of righteous living, we shall so enjoy the companionship of the Spirit that he will dictate to us what we should ask. On this point the Lord said: "He that asketh in the Spirit asketh according to the will of God; wherefore it is done even as he asketh." (D&C 46:30) ¶ I didn't understand this scripture until I had had a lot of experiences. When you live so that the Lord can dictate what you pray for, then you will receive whatever you ask for, because you will ask according to his will; "wherefore, it is done even as he asketh." And again: " . . . if ye are purified and cleansed from all sin, ye shall ask whatsoever you will in the name of Jesus and it shall be done. But know this, it shall be given you what you shall ask. . . ." (D&C 50:29-30) (Learning for the Eternities, pp. 117-18) TLDP:487

**Elder George Albert Smith**

Reference has been made in this conference to the importance of seeking the Lord in prayer. And we should know that our prayers will not avail us much unless we repent of our sins. Faith, repentance, baptism by immersion for the remission of sins, laying on of hands for the gift of the Holy Ghost, are the fundamental teachings of our Heavenly Father to us, and have been the groundwork of the Church since it was organized. CR1944Oct:95

**Related Witnesses:**

**Moroni, son of Mormon**

Now when the people saw that they must perish they began to repent of their iniquities and cry unto the Lord. 35. And it came to pass that when they had humbled themselves sufficiently before the Lord he did send rain upon the face of the earth. (*Moroni's abridgement of the writings of Ether, who wrote about 550 B.C.*) Ether 9:34-35

**Abinadi,**
*quoted by Mormon*

And it shall come to pass that except this people repent and turn unto the Lord their God, they shall be brought into bondage; and none shall deliver them, except it be the Lord the Almighty God. 24. Yea, and it shall come to pass that when they shall cry unto me I will be slow to hear [respond to] their cries; yea, and I will suffer them that they be smitten by their enemies. 25. And except they repent in sackcloth and ashes, and cry mightily to the Lord their God, I will not hear [respond to] their prayers, neither will I deliver them out of their afflictions; and thus saith the Lord, and thus hath he commanded me. (*Abinadi speaks the word of the Lord to the people of the wicked king Noah, about 150 B.C.*) Mosiah 11:23-25

**515. The Lord responds to the prayer of the humble and penitent person.**

**Recorded in Chronicles**

If my people, which are called by my name, shall humble themselves, and pray, and seek my face, and turn from their wicked ways; then will I hear from heaven, and will forgive their sin, and will heal their land. (*The Lord accepts the completed temple and instructs Solomon*) 2Chr.7:14

**Elder Spencer W. Kimball**

A humble prayer on bended knees, followed by the other works, is the invisible switch to tune us with the infinite and bring to us programs of knowledge, inspiration, and faith. (*At Brigham Young University, March 19, 1946*) (The Teachings of Spencer W. Kimball, p. 62) TLDP:490

**Joseph Smith**

Be thou humble; and the Lord thy God shall lead thee by the hand, and give thee answer to thy prayers. (*Revelation for Thomas B. Marsh, who has prayed in behalf of the Twelve, July 23, 1837*) D&C 112:10

**Joseph Smith**

And inasmuch as they were humble they might be made strong, and blessed from on high, and receive knowledge from time to time. (*Revelation received at a conference of Church elders; the true gospel to be preached, Nov. 1, 1831*) D&C 1:28

**Joseph Smith,**
*receiving the Word of the Lord*

Let him that is ignorant learn wisdom by humbling himself and calling upon the Lord his God,

that his eyes may be opened that he may see, and his ears opened that he may hear; 33. For my Spirit is sent forth into the world to enlighten the humble and contrite, and to the condemnation of the ungodly. (*Revelation relating to the new and everlasting covenant, July 12, 1843*) D&C 136:32-33

**Joseph Smith,**
*receiving the Word of the Lord*

And now, again, I speak unto you, my servant Joseph, concerning the man that desires the witness— 24. Behold, I say unto him, he exalts himself and does not humble himself sufficiently before me; but if he will bow down before me, and humble himself in mighty prayer and faith, in the sincerity of his heart, then will I grant unto him a view of the things which he desires to see. (*Revelation through Joseph Smith at the request of Martin Harris, March 1829*) D&C 5:23-24

**President Heber J. Grant**

No individual who is humble and prayerful before God and supplicates Him every day for the light and inspiration of His Holy Spirit, will ever become lifted up in the pride of his heart, or feel that the intelligence and the wisdom that he possesses are all-sufficient for him. ¶ The prayerful and humble man will always realize and feel that he is dependent upon the Lord for every blessing that he enjoys, and in praying to God he will not only pray for the light and the inspiration of His Holy Spirit to guide him, but he will feel to thank Him for the blessings that he receives, realizing that life, that health, that strength, and that all the intelligence which he possesses come from God, who is the Author of his existence. ¶ If we do not keep this channel of communication open between us and our Heavenly Father, then are we robbed of the light and inspiration of His Spirit, and of that feeling of gratitude and thanksgiving that fills our hearts and that desire to praise God for His goodness and mercy to us. ("Personal and Family Prayer," IE1942Dec:779) TLDP:489

**Elder Harold B. Lee**

If all our selfish motives, then, and all our personal desires, and expediency, would be subordinated to a desire to know the will of the Lord, one could have the companionship of heavenly vision. CR1946Oct:146

**King Benjamin,**
*quoted by Mormon*

And again I say unto you as I have said before, that as ye have come to the knowledge of the glory of God, or if ye have known of his goodness and have tasted of his love, and have received a remission of your sins, which causeth such exceedingly great joy in your souls, even so I would that ye should remember, and always retain in remembrance, the greatness of God, and your own nothingness, and his goodness and long-suffering towards you, unworthy creatures, and humble yourselves even in the depths of humility, calling on the name of the Lord daily, and standing steadfastly in the faith of that which is to come, which was spoken by the mouth of the angel. 12. And behold, I say unto you that if ye do this ye shall always rejoice, and be filled with the love of God, and always retain a remission of your sins; and ye shall grow in the knowledge of the glory of him that created you, or in the knowledge of that which is just and true. (*King Benjamin addresses his people, about 124 B.C.*) Mosiah 4:11-12

**Related Witnesses:**

**Isaiah**

. . . Thus saith the LORD, the God of David thy father, I have heard thy prayer, I have seen thy tears: behold, I will heal thee. . . . (*Isaiah brings the word of the Lord to Hezekiah, who has pleaded with the Lord to let him live*) 2Kgs.20:5

---

**516. The Lord answers the prayers of His servants according to the degree of their faith (and His holy purposes).**

**John A. Widtsoe**

If we want something for this Church and Kingdom, or if we want something for our individual lives, we must have a great, earnest, overpowering desire for that thing. We must reach out for it, with full faith in our Heavenly Father that the gift may be given us. Then it would seem as if the Lord himself cannot resist our petition. If our desire is strong enough, if our whole will is tempered and attuned to that which we desire, if our lives make us worthy of the desired gift, the Lord, by his own words, is bound to give us that which we desire, in his own time and in his own manner. CR1935Apr:82

**President David O. McKay**

I have cherished from childhood the truth that God is a personal being, and is, indeed, our Father whom we can approach in prayer and receive answers thereto. I cherish as one of the dearest experiences of life the knowledge that God hears the prayer of faith. It is true that the answers to our prayers may not always come as direct and at the time, nor in the manner, we anticipate; but they do come, and at a time and in a manner best for the interests of him who offers the supplication. CR1969Apr:152-53

**Mormon**

And again, the angel said: Behold, the Lord hath heard the prayers of his people, and also the prayers of his servant, Alma, who is thy father; for he has prayed with much faith concerning thee that thou mightest be brought to the knowledge of the truth; therefore, for this purpose have I come to convince thee of the power and authority of God, that the prayers of his servants might be answered according to their faith. (*Alma, the younger, and the four sons of Mosiah, have been seeking to destroy the Church when an angel appears to them commanding them to cease their evil course, 100-92 B.C.*) Mosiah 27:14

**Elder Joseph F. Smith**

It is not such a difficult thing to learn how to pray. It is not the words we use particularly that constitute prayer. Prayer does not consist of words altogether. True, faithful, earnest prayer consists more in the feeling that rises from the heart and from the inward desire of our spirits to supplicate the Lord in humility and in faith, that we may receive his blessings. It matters not how simple the words may be, if our desires are genuine and we come before the Lord with a broken heart and a contrite spirit to ask Him for that which we need. . . . ¶ My brethren and sisters, do not learn to pray with your lips only. Do not learn a prayer by heart, and say it every morning and evening. That is something I dislike very much. It is true that a great many people fall into the rut of saying over a ceremonious prayer. They begin at a certain point, and they touch at all the points along the road until they get to the winding-up scene; and when they have done, I do not know whether the prayer has ascended beyond the ceiling of the room or not. CR1899Oct:69,71-72

**Joseph Smith,**
*receiving the Word of the Lord*

And, behold, all the remainder of this work does contain all those parts of my gospel which my holy prophets, yea, and also my disciples, desired in their prayers should come forth unto this people. 47. And I said unto them, that it should be granted unto them according to their faith in their prayers; . . . (*Revelation in respect to the lost 116 manuscript pages, 1828*) D&C 10:46-47

**Elder Spencer W. Kimball**

How should we pray? We should pray in faith, but with awareness that when the Lord answers it may not be with the answer we expect or desire. Our faith must be that God's choice for us is right. (Faith Precedes the Miracle, p. 207) TLDP:487

### Nephi, son of Lehi

[Y]et the words of the righteous shall be written, and the prayers of the faithful shall be heard. . . . [ed. note: be responded to.] (*Nephi foretells of the last days and the coming forth of the Book of Mormon, 559-545 B.C.*) 2Ne.26:15

**Related Witnesses:**

### J. Reuben Clark, Jr.

Brethren and sisters, let us continue to be a praying people. Let us pray, keeping in mind some of the great principles involved therein. Let us go to our Heavenly Father for his advice, his counsel, his help. He will always answer if we are righteous in our asking, and if we are asking for righteous things that would be for our good and benefit. CR1958Oct:47

### Moroni, son of Mormon

And he knoweth their prayers, that they were in behalf of their brethren. And he knoweth their faith, for in his name could they remove mountains; and in his name could they cause the earth to shake; and by the power of his word did they cause prisons to tumble to the earth; yea, even the fiery furnace could not harm them, neither wild beasts nor poisonous serpents, because of the power of his word. 25. And behold, their prayers were also in behalf of him that the Lord should suffer to bring these things forth. (*Moroni writes of the Saints who preceded him, about A.D. 419-420*) Morm.8:24-25

### Boyd K. Packer,
### *also quoting Paul*

Answers to prayers come in a quiet way. The scriptures describe that voice of inspiration as a still, small voice. ¶ If you really try, you can learn to respond to that voice. ¶ In the early days of our marriage, our children came at close intervals. As parents of little children will know, in those years it is quite a novelty for them to get an uninterrupted night of sleep. . . . ¶ We finally divided our children into "his" and "hers" for night tending. She would get up for the new baby, and I would get up for the one cutting teeth. ¶ One day we came to realize that each would hear only the one to which we were assigned, and would sleep very soundly through the cries of the other. ¶ We have commented on this over the years, convinced that you can train yourself to hear what you want to hear, to see and feel what you desire, but it takes some conditioning. ¶ There are so many of us who go through life and seldom, if ever, hear that voice of inspiration, because "the natural man receiveth not the things of the Spirit of God: for they are foolishness unto him: neither can he know them, because they are spiritually discerned."(1Cor.2:14) CR1979Oct:28; DGSM:33

### President Spencer W. Kimball

Sometimes ideas flood our mind as we listen after our prayers. Sometimes feelings press upon us. A spirit of calmness assures us that all will be well. But always, if we have been honest and earnest [in our prayers] we will experience a good feeling—a feeling of warmth for our Father in Heaven and a sense of his love for us. (EN1981Oct:5) DGSM:34

### Joseph Smith,
### *receiving the Word of the Lord*

Verily, verily, I say unto you, even as you desire of me so it shall be unto you; and if you desire, you shall be the means of doing much good in this generation. (*Revelation to Joseph Smith and Oliver Cowdery, April 1829*) D&C 6:8

---

## (2) How to Pray

517. We are to address our prayers to God the Father in the name of Jesus Christ the Son.

### President Joseph F. Smith

We . . . accept without any question the doctrines we have been taught by the Prophet Joseph Smith and by the Son of God himself, that we pray to God, the Eternal Father, in the name of his only begotten Son, to whom also our father Adam and his posterity have prayed from the beginning. CR1916Oct:6

### Nephi, son of Lehi

But behold, I say unto you that ye must pray always, and not faint; that ye must not perform any thing unto the Lord save in the first place ye shall pray unto the Father in the name of Christ, that he will consecrate thy performance unto thee, that thy performance may be for the welfare of thy soul. (*Nephi writes, between 559-545 B.C.*) 2Ne.32:9

### Jesus,
### *quoted by John*

[T]hat whatsoever ye shall ask of the Father in my name, he may give it you. (*Jesus addresses his disciples who have been chosen to serve him*) John 15:16

### Mormon

. . . And as surely as Christ liveth he spake these words unto our fathers, saying: Whatsoever thing ye shall ask the Father in my name, which is good, in faith believing that ye shall receive, behold, it shall be done unto you. (*Mormon preaches in the synagogue, prior to A.D. 384*) Moro.7:26

### Mormon

And the twelve did teach the multitude; and

behold, they did cause that the multitude should kneel down upon the face of the earth, and should pray unto the Father in the name of Jesus. (*The twelve disciples of the resurrected Jesus minister to the Nephites, A.D. 34*) 3Ne.19:6

**Jesus,**
*quoted by Mormon*

And now I go unto the Father, And verily I say unto you, whatsoever things ye shall ask the Father in my name shall be given unto you. (*The resurrected Jesus instructs his twelve Nephite disciples, A.D. 34*) 3Ne.27:28

**Joseph Smith,**
*receiving the Word of the Lord*

Whatsoever ye ask the Father in my name it shall be given unto you, that is expedient for you; . . . (*Revelation, Dec. 27/28, 1832*) D&C 88:64

**Joseph Smith,**
*receiving the Word of the Lord*

I give unto you these sayings that you may understand and know how to worship, and know what you worship, that you may come unto the Father in my name, and in due time receive of his fulness. (*The Lord speaks by revelation at Kirtland, Ohio, May 6, 1833*) D&C 93:19

**President Brigham Young,**
*quoted by John A. Widtsoe*

When you approach the throne of grace and petition the Father, in the name of the Savior who has redeemed the world, do you use the name as the name of a stranger? If you understand your own religion, you petition that Personage as you would one of your brethren in the flesh. Is this strange to you? It should bring near to you things that pertain to eternity, give your reflections and views a more exalted cast, stamp your daily actions with truth and honesty, and cause you to be, filled with the Spirit and power of God. (*In Tabernacle, Oct. 6, 1859, JD7:274-75*) DBY:43

**Joseph Smith,**
*translating the Book of Moses*

Wherefore, thou shalt do all that thou doest in the name of the Son, and thou shalt repent and call upon God in the name of the Son forevermore. (*The record of Moses: an angel of the Lord appears to Adam and instructs him to pray to God*) Moses 5:8

**Related Witnesses:**

**Moroni, son of Mormon**

And they did kneel down with the church, and pray to the Father in the name of Christ, saying: 3. O God, the Eternal Father, we ask thee in the name of thy Son, Jesus Christ, to bless and sanctify this bread to the souls of all those who partake of it; that they may eat in remembrance of the body of thy Son, and witness unto thee, O God, the Eternal Father, that they are willing to take upon them the name of thy Son, and always remember him, and keep his commandments which he hath given them, that they may always have his Spirit to be with them. Amen. (*Moroni writes for the benefit of the Lamanites, A.D. 400-421*) Moro.4:2-3

**Elder Joseph Fielding Smith**

Everything that we do should be done in the name of Jesus Christ. CR1940Apr:95; DGSM:43

**Marion G. Romney**

[N]o divine commandment has been more frequently repeated than the commandment to pray in the name of the Lord Jesus Christ. CR1979Oct:20; DGSM:32

---

**518. In our prayers we are to address the Father with respect by using the pronouns "Thee," "Thou," "Thine" and "Thy."**

**Elder Spencer W. Kimball**

In all our prayers, it is well to use the pronouns thee, thou, thy, and thine instead of you, your, and yours inasmuch as they have come to indicate respect. (Faith Precedes the Miracle, p. 201) TLDP:483

**Dallin H. Oaks**

When we go to worship in a temple or a church, we put aside our working clothes and dress ourselves in something better. This change of clothing is a mark of respect. Similarly, when we address our Heavenly Father, we should put aside our working words and clothe our prayers in special language of reverence and respect. In offering prayers in the English language, members of our church do not address our Heavenly Father with the same words we use in speaking to a fellow worker, to an employee or employer, or to a merchant in the marketplace. We use special words that have been sanctified by use in inspired communications, words that have been recommended to us and modeled for us by those we sustain as prophets and inspired teachers. . . . ¶ Modern English has no special verbs or pronouns that are intimate, familiar, or honorific. When we address prayers to our Heavenly Father in English, our only available alternatives are the common words of speech like *you* and *your* or the dignified but uncommon words like *thee, thou,* and *thy* that were used in the King James version of the Bible almost five hundred years ago. Latter-day Saints, of course, prefer the latter. In our prayers we use language that is dignified and different, even archaic. . . . ¶ [p. 19]. . . . In our day the English words *thee, thou, thy,* and *thine* are suitable for the language of prayer. CR1993Apr:17,19

### Elder Spencer W. Kimball

I have noticed . . . the youth . . . who address the Father with the words "you" and "yours." The Presidency of the Church are quite anxious that everybody address the Lord with the pronouns "thee" and "thou" and "thine" and "thy". . . . Youth may feel that "you" and "yours" are a little more affectionate. But would you do what you can to change this pattern? (*Addressing seminary and institute faculty, June 18, 1962*) MPSG1983:132

### Stephen L. Richards

I think, my brethren, that in the quorums and in the classes, you would do well, as in the homes also, to teach the language of prayer "Thee and Thou," rather than "you." It always seems disappointing to me to have our Father in Heaven, our Lord, addressed as "you." It is surprising how much we see of this in the mission field among the young men who come to serve there. I think you might make note of it, and avail yourselves of any opportunities that may come in order to teach the sacred and reverential language of prayer. CR1951Oct:175

### L. Tom Perry,
### *also quoting Stephen L. Richards*

[U]se the sacred language of prayer. We should always address Deity by using the sacred pronouns *thou, thee, thy,* and *thine.* The late President Stephen L. Richards gave us this wise counsel: ¶ ". . . . teach the language of prayer—'Thee and Thou,' rather than 'you'." CR1983Oct:14

### L. Tom Perry

[I]t is good to use the sacred pronouns of the scriptures—*thee, thou, thy,* and *thine*—when addressing Deity in prayer, instead of the more common pronouns *you, your,* and *yours.* By doing so, we show greater respect to our Heavenly Father. CR1993Apr:112

---

### 519. We are not to offer vain, repetitious prayers.

### Bruce R. McConkie

We do not give memorized, ritualistic, or repetitious prayers. We seek the guidance of the Spirit and suit every prayer to the needs of the moment, with no thought of using the same words on successive occasions. CR1984Apr:44

### Jesus,
### *recorded in Matthew*

But when ye pray, use not vain repetitions, as the heathen do. (*Jesus teaches his disciples the Lord's Prayer*) Matt.6:7

### James E. Talmage

In the same spirit the Preacher denounce hypocritical prayers—the saying of prayers in place of praying. . . . He who would really pray—pray as nearly as possible as Christ prayed, pray in actual communion with God to whom the prayer is addressed—will seek privacy, seclusion, isolation; if opportunity permits he will retire to his chamber, and will shut the door, that none may intrude; there he may pray indeed, if the spirit of prayer be in his heart; and this course was commended by the Lord. Wordy supplications, made up largely of reiterations and repetitions such as the heathen use, thinking that their idol deities will be pleased with their much speaking, were forbidden. ¶ It is well to know that prayer is not compounded of words, words that may fail to express what one desires to say, words that so often cloak inconsistencies, words that may have no deeper source than the physical organs of speech, words that may be spoken to impress mortal ears. The dumb may pray, and that too with the eloquence that prevails in heaven. Prayer is made up of heart throbs and the righteous yearnings of the soul, of supplication based on the realization of need, of contrition and pure desire. JTC:237-38

### Jesus,
### *quoted by Mormon*

But when ye pray, use not vain repetitions, as the heathen, for they think that they shall be heard for their much speaking. 8. Be not ye therefore like unto them, for your Father knoweth what things ye have need of before ye ask him. (*The resurrected Jesus teaches the Nephites the Lord's Prayer, A.D. 34*) 3Ne.13:7-8

### President Joseph F. Smith

We do not have to cry unto him with many words. We do not have to weary him with long prayers. What we do need, and what we should do as Latter-day Saints, for our own good, is to go before him often, to witness unto him that we remember him and that we are willing to take upon us his name, keep his commandments, work righteousness; and that we desire his Spirit to help us. Then, if we are in trouble, let us go to the Lord and ask him directly and specifically to help us out of the trouble that we are in; and let the prayer come from the heart, let it not be in words that are worn into ruts in the beaten tracks of common use, without thought or feeling in the use of those words. Let us speak the simple words, expressing our need, that will appeal most truly to the Giver of every good and perfect gift. (Gospel Doctrine, p. 221) TLDP:482

**Author's Note:** *Vain repetitions*: Idle, hollow, or useless repetitions.

---

### 520. There are times when we are to pray on our knees.

**Marion G. Romney**
I think every Latter-day Saint ought to go to his knees night and morning in secret prayer. CR1961Oct:61

**Joseph Smith**
Let him offer himself in prayer upon his knees before God, in token or remembrance of the everlasting covenant. (*Revelation, Dec. 27/28, 1832*) D&C 88:131

**Joseph Smith**
It is expedient that the church meet together often to partake of bread and wine in the remembrance of the Lord Jesus; 76. And the elder or priest shall administer it; and after this manner shall he administer it—he shall kneel with the church and call upon the Father in solemn prayer, . . . (*Revelation on Church Organization and Government, April 1830*) D&C 20:75-76

**President Spencer W. Kimball**
The Church urges that there be family prayer every night and every morning. It is a kneeling prayer with all or as many members of the family present as possible. ("Prayer," NE1978Mar:15) MPSG1983:129

**Mormon**
And the twelve did teach the multitude; and behold, they did cause that the multitude should kneel down upon the face of the earth, and should pray unto the Father in the name of Jesus. (*The twelve disciples of the resurrected Jesus minister to the Nephites, A.D. 34*) 3Ne.19:6

**Recorded in Psalms**
O come, let us worship and bow down: let us kneel before the Lord our maker. (*A psalm of David*) Ps.95:6

**Gordon B. Hinckley**
I know of no single practice that will have a more salutary effect upon your lives than the practice of kneeling together as you begin and close each day. Somehow the little storms that seem to afflict every marriage are dissipated when, kneeling before the Lord, you thank him for one another, in the presence of one another,

and then together invoke his blessings upon your lives, your home, your loved ones, and your dreams. CR1971Apr:83

**Joseph F. Merrill**
In the spirit of helpfulness let me give you a key. When in doubt go on your knees in humility with an open mind and a pure heart with a real desire to do the Lord's will, and pray earnestly and sincerely for divine guidance. Persist in praying in this way until you get an answer that fills your bosom with joy and satisfaction. It will be God's answer. CR1941Apr:50-51

**N. Eldon Tanner**
If children pray for their parents, it makes them more appreciative of their parents, and as they pray for one another, they feel closer to one another and part of each other, especially as they realize that they are talking to their Father in heaven while on their knees. . . . CR1967Oct:55

**Related Witnesses:**

**L. Tom Perry**
When you are on your knees in prayer, there is an overwhelming feeling of gratitude to the Lord for the many blessings that he bestows on his children. CR1983Oct:15

**Recorded in Luke**
And he came out, and went, as he was wont, to the mount of Olives; and his disciples also followed him. . . . 41. And he was withdrawn from them about a stone's cast, and kneeled down, and prayed, . . . 45. And when he rose up from prayer, and was come to his disciples, he found them sleeping for sorrow, . . . (*Jesus suffers in Gethsemane*) Luke 22:39,41,45

**Enos,**
*quoted by Mormon*
And my soul hungered; and I kneeled down before my Maker, and I cried unto him in mighty prayer and supplication for mine own soul; and all the day long did I cry unto him; yea, and when the night came I did still raise my voice high that it reached the heavens. (*Enos prays mightily and gains a remission of sins, 544-421 B.C.*) Enos 1:4

**Recorded in Daniel**
Now when Daniel knew that the writing was signed, he went into his house; and his windows being open in his chamber toward Jerusalem, he kneeled upon his knees three times a day, and prayed, and gave thanks before his God, as he did aforetime. (*Daniel worships the Lord in defiance of a decree of Darius the king*) Dan.6:10

---

### 521. We are to pray vocally as well as silently in the heart.

**Joseph Smith,**
*receiving the Word of the Lord*

And again, I command thee that thou shalt pray vocally as well as in thy heart; yea, before the world as well as in secret, in public as well as in private. (*A commandment of God for Martin Harris, March 1830*) D&C 19:28

**Joseph Smith,**
*receiving the Word of the Lord*

Behold, I manifest unto you, Joseph Knight, by these words, that you must take up your cross, in the which you must pray vocally before the world as well as in secret, and in your family, and among your friends, and in all places. (*Revelation given in response to the earnest desire of Joseph Knight, Sr. and four other brethren to know of their respective duties, April 1930*) D&C 23:6

**President Spencer W. Kimball**

It was a prayer, a very special prayer, which opened this whole dispensation! It began with a young man's first vocal prayer. I hope that not too many of our prayers are silent, even though when we cannot pray vocally, it is good to offer a silent prayer in our hearts and in our minds. CR1979Oct:4; DGSM:33

**Related Witnesses:**

**Amulek,**
*quoted by Mormon*

But this is not all; ye must pour out your souls in your closets, and your secret places, and in your wilderness. 27. Yea, and when you do not cry unto the Lord, let your hearts be full, drawn out in prayer unto him continually for your welfare, and also for the welfare of those who are around you. (*Amulek teaches the people to pray, about 74 B.C.*) Alma 34:26-27

**Joseph Smith**

So, in accordance with this, my determination to ask of God, I retired to the woods to make the attempt. It was on the morning of a beautiful, clear day, early in the spring of eighteen hundred and twenty. It was the first time in my life that I had made such an attempt, for amidst all my anxieties I had never as yet made the attempt to pray vocally. . . . 18. My object in going to inquire of the Lord was to know which of all the sects was right, that I might know which to join. No sooner, therefore, did I get possession of myself, so as to be able to speak, than I asked the Personages who stood above me in the light, which of all the sects was right (for at this time it had never entered into my heart that all were wrong)—and which I should join. (*Joseph receives a visitation of the Father and the Son, spring of 1820*) JS-H 1:14,18

**Elder Joseph F. Smith**

It is not the words we use particularly that constitute prayer. Prayer does not consist of words, altogether. True, faithful, earnest prayer consists more in the feeling that rises from the heart and from the inward desire of our spirits to supplicate the Lord in humility and in faith, that we may receive his blessings. CR1899Oct:69; DCSM:22

## (3) What to Pray for—
## Content of Prayer

**522. Prayers are to contain expressions of gratitude.**

**John A. Widtsoe**

A prayer is not complete unless gratitude for blessings is expressed. It is by the power of the Lord that we live and move and have our being. This should be frankly stated gratefully as we pray to our Father in Heaven. (Evidences and Reconciliations, 1:313) MGSP:8

**Joseph Smith**

And ye must give thanks unto God in the Spirit for whatsoever blessing ye are blessed with. (*Revelation, March 8, 1831*) D&C 46:32

**Joseph Smith**

Thou shalt thank the Lord thy God in all things. (*Revelation, Aug. 7, 1831*) D&C 59:7

**President David O. McKay**

The young man who closes the door behind him, who draws the curtains, and there in silence pleads with God for help, should first pour out his soul in gratitude for health, for friends, for loved ones, for the gospel, for the manifestations of God's existence. He should first count his many blessings and name them one by one. CR1961Apr:7-8

**Alma, the younger,**
*quoted by Mormon*

Counsel with the Lord in all thy doings, and he will direct thee for good; yea, when thou liest down at night lie down unto the Lord, that he may watch over you in your sleep; and when thou risest in the morning let thy heart be full of thanks unto God; and if ye do these things, ye shall be lifted up at the last day. (*Alma instructs his son Helaman, about 73 B.C.*) Alma 37:37

**Alma, the younger,**
*quoted by Mormon*

And now I would that ye should be humble, and be submissive and gentle; easy to be entreated; full of patience and long-suffering; being temperate in all things; being diligent in keeping the commandments of God at all times; asking for whatsoever things ye stand in need, both spiritual and temporal; always returning thanks unto God for whatsoever things ye do receive. (*Alma to the people in Gideon, about 83 B.C.*) Alma 7:23

### Elder Spencer W. Kimball

For whom and what should we pray? We should express gratitude for past blessings. . . . (Faith Precedes the Miracle, p. 202) TLDP:485-86

### Paul

In every thing give thanks: for this is the will of God in Christ Jesus concerning you. (*Paul's letter to the Church at Thessalonica, comprising Jews and many pagan converts, A.D. 50*) 1Thess.5:18

### President Heber J. Grant

The prayerful and humble man will always realize and feel that he is dependent upon the Lord for every blessing that he enjoys, and in praying to God he will not only pray for the light and the inspiration of His Holy Spirit to guide him, but he will feel to thank Him for the blessings that he receives, realizing that life, that health, that strength, and that all the intelligence which he possesses come from God, who is the Author of his existence. ("Personal and Family Prayer," IE1942Dec:779) TLDP:489

### King Benjamin, quoted by Mormon

And behold also, if I, whom ye call your king, who has spent his days in your service, and yet has been in the service of God, do merit any thanks from you, O how you ought to thank your heavenly King! 20. I say unto you, my brethren, that if you should render all the thanks and praise which your whole soul has power to possess, to that God who has created you, and has kept and preserved you, and has caused that ye should rejoice, and has granted that ye should live in peace one with another— 21. I say unto you that if ye should serve him who has created you from the beginning, and is preserving you from day to day, by lending you breath, that ye may live and move and do according to your own will, and even supporting you from one moment to another—I say, if ye should serve him with all your whole souls yet ye would be unprofitable servants. (*King Benjamin addresses his people, about 124 B.C.*) Mosiah 2:19-21

### Marion G. Romney

Frequently, prayers are requests for specific blessings. They may, however, and should, include expressions of thanksgiving, praise, worship, and adoration. CR1978Apr:73

### Recorded in Psalms

O give thanks unto the LORD; call upon his name: make known his deeds among the people. 2. Sing unto him, sing psalms unto him: talk ye of all his wondrous works. 3. Glory ye in his holy name: let the heart of them rejoice that seek the LORD. 4. Seek the LORD, and his strength: seek his face evermore. 5. Remember his marvellous works that he hath done; his wonders, and the judgments of his mouth; Ps.105:1-5

### Related Witnesses:

### Bruce R. McConkie

[Thanks for Life and Hope of Eternal Life:] Then, in thanking the Lord for the blessings of mortal life, and the hope of immortality and eternal life, we might properly say such things as: ¶ Father, we thank thee for life itself, for this mortal probation in which we as pilgrims, far from our heavenly home, are gaining experiences that could be gained in no other way. We thank thee that thou didst ordain and establish the great and eternal plan of salvation whereby we, as thy spirit children, are given power, if faithful and true in all things, to advance and progress and become like thee. CR1984Apr:45

### Bruce R. McConkie

[Thanks for Restoration of the Gospel:] With reference to the restoration of the glorious gospel in our day, prayers might include expressions along these lines: ¶ And now, O thou God of our Fathers, we are grateful and rejoice in what thou hast done for us in our day. ¶ With all our hearts we thank thee for the restoration of the gospel; that the voice of God is heard again; that the heavens, long sealed, have been rent; that holy angels, bringing priesthoods and keys and light and truth, now minster among us. ¶ We stand in reverent awe at the realization that thou and thy Beloved Son came to Joseph Smith in the spring of 1820 to usher in the dispensation of the fulness of times. ¶ We marvel that thou didst send Moroni to reveal the Book of Mormon; Moses to empower us to gather Israel from the Egypt of the world into the Zion of God; and Elijah to confer upon us the power to bind on earth and have our acts sealed everlastingly in the heavens. ¶ How grateful we are that Elias brought back the gospel of Abraham, so that we, as children of the covenant, might have a continuation of the family unit in eternity. CR1984Apr:45

### Bruce R. McConkie

[Thanks for the Atonement of Christ:] We thank thee for sending thy Holy Son Jesus to be the Savior and Redeemer; to put into full operation all of the terms and conditions of thy great and eternal plan of salvation; to save us from death, hell, the devil, and endless torment. ¶ O how we glory in him and in his blessed name, rejoicing everlastingly that he has ransomed us from temporal and spiritual death; that he is the one Mediator between us and thee; that he has reconciled us unto thee, not imputing unto us our sins, but healing us with his stripes. ¶ We thank thee, O our Father, that thou gavest thine Only Begotten Son so that we, believing in him, shall not perish, but have everlasting life; that he, amid the blood and agonies of Gethsemane, and the blood and cruelties of Calvary, bore our sins on condition of repentance. CR1984Apr:45

---

### 523. We are to pray for forgiveness of our sins.

#### Mark E. Petersen
The formula of forgiveness is plainly set forth in the scriptures. First, men must forsake their sins. Then they must confess to the Lord and also to those against whom they have sinned, asking for forgiveness. Grievous sins which affect the standing in the Church should be made known to the bishop of the ward. One of the important factors in our escape from sin is the matter of making restitution to those against whom we have sinned. This we should do so far as it is within our power—the Lord expects we must also be willing to forgive other people who have offended us and finally we must press forward in doing the works of righteousness for the rest of our lives. (Your Faith and You, pp. 92-93) TLDP:205

#### Jesus,
*recorded in Luke*
And he said unto them, When ye pray, say, Our Father which art in heaven, Hallowed be thy name. Thy kingdom come. Thy will be done, as in heaven, so in earth. 3. Give us day by day our daily bread. 4. And forgive us our sins; for we also forgive every one that is indebted to us. (*Jesus teaches his disciples the Lord's Prayer and teaches the efficacy of prayer*) Luke 11:2-4

#### Jesus,
*quoted by Mormon*
After this manner therefore pray ye: Our Father who art in heaven, hallowed be thy name. 10. Thy will be done on earth as it is in heaven. 11. And forgive us our debts, as we forgive our debtors. (*The resurrected Jesus teaches the Nephites the Lord's Prayer, A.D. 34*) 3Ne.13:9-11

#### President Brigham Young,
*quoted by John A. Widtsoe*
When you get up in the morning, before you suffer yourselves to eat one mouthful of food, call your wife and children together, bow down before the Lord, ask him to forgive your sins,

and protect you through the day, to preserve you from temptation and all evil, to guide your steps aright, that you may do something that day that shall be beneficial to the Kingdom of God on the earth. Have you time to do this? Elders, sisters, have you time to pray? (*In Tabernacle, Ogden, Utah, May 26, 1872, JD15:36*) DBY:44

**Related Witnesses:**

#### John
If we say that we have no sin, we deceive ourselves, and the truth is not in us. 9. If we confess our sins, he is faithful and just to forgive us our sins, and to cleanse us from all unrighteousness. 10. If we say that we have not sinned, we make him a liar, and his word is not in us. (*Letter to the churches in Asia*) 1Jn.1:8-10

#### Bruce R. McConkie
We confess our sins before thee and seek remission thereof, lest anything stand between us and thee in receiving a free flow of thy Spirit. CR1984Apr:46

#### Elder Spencer W. Kimball
[Enos] writes: ¶ "and all the day long did I cry unto him;" ¶ Here is no casual prayer; no worn phrases; no momentary appeal by silent lips. All the day long, with seconds turning into minutes, and minutes into hours and hours. But when the sun had set, relief had still not come, for repentance is not a single act nor forgiveness an unearned gift. So precious to him was communication with and approval of his Redeemer that his determined soul pressed on without ceasing. ¶ "yea, and when the night came I did still raise my voice high that it reached the heavens." (Enos 4) ¶ Could the Redeemer resist such determined imploring? How many have thus persisted? How many, with or without serious transgressions, have ever prayed all day and into the night? Have many ever wept and prayed for ten hours? for five hours? for one? for thirty minutes? for ten? Our praying is usually measured in seconds and yet with a heavy debt to pay we still expect forgiveness of our sins. We offer pennies to pay the debt of thousands of dollars. (Faith Precedes the Miracle, p. 211) TLDP:481

#### Enos,
*quoted by Mormon*
And my soul hungered; and I kneeled down before my Maker, and I cried unto him in mighty prayer and supplication for mine own soul; and all the day long did I cry unto him; yea, and when the night came I did still raise my voice high that it reached the heavens. 5. And there came a voice unto me, saying: Enos, thy sins are forgiven thee, and thou shalt be

blessed. (*Enos prays mightily and gains a remission of sins, 544-421 B.C.*) Enos 1:4-5

**Nephi, son of Lehi**

And it came to pass that I did frankly forgive them all that they had done, and I did exhort them that they would pray unto the Lord their God for forgiveness. And it came to pass that they did so. And after they had done praying unto the Lord we did again travel on our journey towards the tent of our father. (*Nephi forgives his brethren who had bound him with cords, about 600-592 B.C.*) 1Ne.7:21

**Joseph Smith**

In consequence of these things, I often felt condemned for my weakness and imperfections; when, on the evening of the above-mentioned twenty-first of September, after I had retired to my bed for the night, I betook myself to prayer and supplication to Almighty God for forgiveness of all my sins and follies, and also for a manifestation to me, that I might know of my state and standing before him; for I had full confidence in obtaining a divine manifestation, as I previously had one. (*Joseph relates the angel Moroni's visit to him, Sept. 21, 1823*) JS-H 1:29

**Author's Note:** Sins are not forgiven *solely* through prayer but following appropriate repentance. As stated by Francis M. Lyman: ¶ "The forgiveness of sins is predicated upon faith in God, repentance and reformation and baptism. Sins are not forgiven through the payment of tithing, nor through the partaking of the sacrament, nor observing the Word of Wisdom, or prayer. There are blessings attached to each of these important requirements of the Gospel; but if a man would have his sins forgiven, and be allowed to enter into the Church, he must have faith in God, and in his Son Jesus Christ, and in the Holy Ghost, he must repent of all his sins, turn unto the Lord with full purpose of heart and sin no more. Then God will forgive him and redeem him from his sins; but not by paying tithing. . . . But we want our names recorded in the Lamb's Book of Life, and it is not done by the observance of any one principle alone, but to every principle there are special blessings promised." (CR1899Oct:34)

---

524. **It is appropriate to pray for our temporal needs: asking for the blessing of God upon all we possess and upon all our labors.**

**Elder Spencer W. Kimball**

We pray for everything that is needed and dig-

nified and proper. I heard a boy about fourteen years of age in family prayer imploring the Lord to protect the family sheep upon the hill. It was snowing and bitterly cold. I heard a family pray for rain when a severe drought was on and conditions were desperate. (Faith Precedes the Miracle, p. 206) TLDP:485-86

**Amulek,**
*quoted by Mormon*

Yea, humble yourselves, and continue in prayer unto him. 20. Cry unto him when ye are in your fields, yea, over all your flocks. 21. Cry unto him in your houses, yea, over all your household, both morning, mid-day, and evening. 22. Yea, cry unto him against the power of your enemies. 23. Yea, cry unto him against the devil, who is an enemy to all righteousness. 24. Cry unto him over the crops of your fields, that ye may prosper in them. 25. Cry over the flocks of your fields, that they may increase. (*Amulek teaches the people to pray, about 74 B.C.*) Alma 34:19-25

**Bruce R. McConkie**

As for our temporal needs, I would feel no hesitancy in saying such things as: . . . ¶ We need food, clothing, and shelter; we need schooling and proper employment; we need wisdom in our business and professional enterprises. ¶ Grant us according to our needs, giving us neither poverty nor riches, but feeding us with food convenient for us. CR1984Apr:46

**Joseph Smith,**
*quoted by Elder Joseph Fielding Smith*

We would say to the brethren, seek to know God in your closets, call upon him in the fields. Follow the directions of the Book of Mormon, and pray over, and for your families, your cattle, your flocks, your herds, your corn, and all things that you possess; ask the blessing of God upon all your labors, and everything that you engage in. (Times and Seasons, June 1842) HC5:31; TPJS:247; DGSM:33

**Elder Joseph F. Smith**

If faithful, we have a right to claim the blessings of the Lord upon the labor of our hands, our temporal labors. The farmer has a right to ask the Lord for blessings upon his farm, upon the labor that he bestows upon it. He has a right to claim the blessings of the Lord upon the animals that are necessary to the cultivation of his farm. He has a right to ask God to bless the grain that he sows and the seeds of the fruit that he plants in the soil. It is his privilege, not only to ask and claim these blessings at the hand of the Lord, but it is his right and privilege to receive blessings from God upon his labor, upon his farm, and upon all that he puts his hand unto in righteousness. It is our privilege to ask God to remove the curse from the earth, and to make it fruitful. If we will live so that we shall be entitled to his favor, and so that we may justly and righteously claim the blessings and gifts that he has promised unto his Saints, then that which we ask will be given, and we shall receive and enjoy them more abundantly. It is our privilege to ask God to bless the elements that surround us and to temper them for our good, and we know he will hear and answer the prayers of his people, according to their faith. CR1898Apr:9-10

**Related Witnesses:**

### Mormon

And there had been murders, and contentions, and dissensions, and all manner of iniquity among the people of Nephi; nevertheless for the righteous' sake, yea, because of the prayers of the righteous, they were spared. (*Writing about the condition of the Nephites, 60 B.C.*) Alma 62:40

### James

Elias was a man subject to like passions as we are, and he prayed earnestly that it might not rain: and it rained not on the earth by the space of three years and six months. 18. And he prayed again, and the heaven gave rain, and the earth brought forth her fruit. (*James writes to his brethren in the Church*) James 5:17-18

### Mormon

And it came to pass that so great were their afflictions that they began to cry mightily to God. 11. And Amulon commanded them that they should stop their cries; and he put guards over them to watch them, that whosoever should be found calling upon God should be put to death. 12. And Alma and his people did not raise their voices to the Lord their God, but did pour out their hearts to him; and he did know the thoughts of their hearts. 13. And it came to pass that the voice of the Lord came to them in their afflictions, saying: Lift up your heads and be of good comfort, for I know of the covenant which ye have made unto me; and I will covenant with my people and deliver them out of bondage. 14. And I will also ease the burdens which are put upon your shoulders, that even you cannot feel them upon your backs, even while you are in bondage; and this will I do that ye may stand as witnesses for me hereafter, and that ye may know of a surety that I, the Lord God, do visit my people in their afflictions. .... 21. Yea, and in the valley of Alma they poured out their thanks to God because he had been merciful unto them, and eased their burdens, and had delivered them out of bondage; for they were in bondage, and none could deliver them except it were the Lord their God. 22. And they gave thanks to God, yea, all their men and all their women and all their children that could speak lifted their voices in the praises of their God. (*Amulon puts taskmasters over Alma—the converted priest of King Noah—and his people; the Lord delivers them from bondage, 145-121 B.C.*) Mosiah 24:10-14,21-22

---

525. Through prayer we can receive divine direction concerning whatever we seek to undertake.

### Alma, the younger, *quoted by Mormon*

Counsel with the Lord in all thy doings, and he will direct thee for good; yea, when thou liest down at night lie down unto the Lord, that he may watch over you in your sleep; and when thou risest in the morning let thy heart be full of thanks unto God; and if ye do these things, ye shall be lifted up at the last day. (*Alma instructs his son Helaman, about 73 B.C.*) Alma 37:37

### Elder Harold B. Lee

If there should come a problem as to what kind of business a man should be engaged in, whether he should invest in this matter or that, whether he should marry this girl or marry that girl, where he should marry, and how he should marry, when it comes to the prosecuting of the work to which we are assigned, how much more certainly would those decisions be made, if always we recalled that all we do, and the decisions we make, should be made with that eternal goal in mind, with an eye single to the ultimate glory of man in the celestial world. ¶ If all our selfish motives, then, and all our personal desires, and expediency, would be subordinated to a desire to know the will of the Lord, one could have the companionship of heavenly vision. If your problems be too great for human intelligence or too much for human strength, you too, if you are faithful and appeal rightly unto the source of divine power, might have standing by you in your hour of peril or great need an angel of God, whose you are and whom you serve. One who lives thus worthy of a testimony that God lives and that Jesus is the Christ, and who is willing to reach out to him in constant inquiry to know if his course is approved is the one who is living life to its full abundance here, and is preparing for the celestial world, which is to live eternally with his Heavenly Father. CR1946Oct:146

### Joseph Smith, *quoted by Elder Joseph Fielding Smith*

We would say to the brethren . . . ask the blessing

of God upon all your labors, and everything that you engage in. (Times and Seasons, June 1842) HC5:31; TPJS:247; DGSM:33

**Elder Spencer W. Kimball**

We pray for help in carrying out our church callings. (Faith Precedes the Miracle, p. 207) TLDP:485-86

**President David O. McKay**

All over this land there are thousands and tens of thousands of students who are struggling to get an education. In the Church, let us teach these students that if they want to succeed in their lessons, they should seek their God; that the greatest Teacher known to the world stands near to guide them. Once the student feels that he can approach the Lord through prayer, he will receive confidence that he can get his lessons, that he can write his speech, that he can stand up before his fellow students and deliver his message without fear of failure. Confidence comes through sincere prayer. ¶ . . . . It is not imagination, if we approach God sincerely seeking light and guidance from him, our minds will be enlightened and our souls thrilled by his Spirit. Washington sought it; Lincoln received it; Joseph Smith knew it; and the testimony, the evidence of the Prophet Joseph's inspiration is manifest to all who will but open their eyes to see and their hearts to understand. CR1961Apr:8

**Related Witnesses:**

**President Spencer W. Kimball**

[W]e have pleaded long and earnestly in behalf of these, our faithful brethren, spending many hours in the Upper Room of the Temple supplicating the Lord for divine guidance. 10. He has heard our prayers, and by revelation has confirmed that the long-promised day has come when every faithful, worthy man in the Church may receive the holy priesthood, with power to exercise its divine authority, and enjoy with his loved ones every blessing that flows therefrom, including the blessings of the temple. (*On Sept. 30, 1978, at a general conference of the Church, President N. Eldon Tanner presented— and it was accepted by the Saints assembled as revelation—what is now known as "Official Declaration 2," from which this excerpt is taken)* D&C OD 2:9-10

**Bruce R. McConkie**

As to personal blessings that prepare us for salvation, our thoughts might be couched in expressions along this line: ¶ Bless us in our families that husbands and wives may love each other and cleave unto each other; that parents may bring up their children in light and truth; that children, thus brought up in the nurture and admonition of the Lord, may honor their fathers

and their mothers by living as their righteous ancestors lived. ¶ O Father, there are those among us, not a few in number, who desire and are worthy to have eternal companions. Wilt thou prepare the way before them that they may have the desires of their hearts in righteousness. . . . ¶ O Father we rejoice in the gifts of the Spirit and seek them in greater abundance. Let testimony and revelation and visions and miracles multiply among us. ¶ Let us know the wonders of eternity, even those things which eye has not seen, nor ear heard, nor have yet entered into the heart of man. CR1984Apr:46-47

---

**526. The Spirit of God is received through the prayer of faith.**

**Marion G. Romney**

Prayer is the key that opens the door to the Spirit of the Lord. The Lord told us in this dispensation, when the Church was very young, that we were to pray always that we would be conquerors. He told the Prophet Joseph to "pray always, . . . that you may conquer Satan, and that you may escape the hands of the servants of Satan that do uphold his work." (D&C 10:5) ACR(Taipei)1975:7

**Joseph Smith,**
*receiving the Word of the Lord*

Pray always, and I will pour out my Spirit upon you, and great shall be your blessing—yea, even more than if you should obtain treasures of earth and corruptibleness to the extent thereof. (*A commandment of God for Martin Harris, March 1830*) D&C 19:38

**Joseph Smith**

And the Spirit shall be given unto you by the prayer of faith; and if ye receive not the Spirit ye shall not teach. (*Revelation, Feb. 9, 1831*) D&C 42:14

**Joseph Smith,**
*receiving the Word of the Lord*

Draw near unto me and I will draw near unto you; seek me diligently and ye shall find me; ask, and ye shall receive; knock, and it shall be opened unto you. 64. Whatsoever ye ask the Father in my name it shall be given unto you, that is expedient for you; . . . (*Revelation, Dec. 27/28, 1832*) D&C 88:63-64

**Elder John Taylor**

Do not forget to call upon the Lord in your family circles, dedicating yourselves and all you have to God every day of your lives; and seek to do right, and cultivate the spirit of union and love, and the peace and blessing of the Living God will be with us, and He will lead us in the paths of life; and we shall be sustained and upheld by all the holy angels and the ancient patriarchs and men of God, and the veil will become thinner between us and our God, and we will approach nearer to him, and our souls will magnify the Lord of hosts. (*In Tabernacle, Provo, Utah, Nov. 30, 1879, JD20:361*) MPSG1983:128

### President David O. McKay

It is not imagination, if we approach God sincerely seeking light and guidance from him, our minds will be enlightened and our souls thrilled by his Spirit. Washington sought it; Lincoln received it; Joseph Smith knew it; and the testimony, the evidence of the Prophet Joseph's inspiration is manifest to all who will but open their eyes to see and their hearts to understand. CR1961Apr:8

**Related Witnesses:**

### President Brigham Young

Let him that is ignorant learn wisdom by humbling himself and calling upon the Lord his God, that his eyes may be opened that he may see, and his ears opened that he may hear; 33. For my Spirit is sent forth into the world to enlighten the humble and contrite, and to the condemnation of the ungodly. (*Revelation received Jan. 14, 1847*) D&C 136:32-33

### Jesus,
#### quoted by Mormon

I perceive that ye are weak, that ye cannot understand all my words which I am commanded of the Father to speak unto you at this time. 3. Therefore, go ye unto your homes, and ponder upon the things which I have said, and ask of the Father, in my name, that ye may understand, and prepare your minds for the morrow, and I come unto you again. (*The resurrected Jesus directs the people to pray for understanding, A.D. 34*) 3Ne.17:2-3

---

### 527. We are to pray for our family members.

### Elder Spencer W. Kimball

We pray for our own family members, their incomings and outgoings, their travels, their work, and all pertaining to them. When children pray audibly for their brothers and sisters, it is likely that quarreling and conflicts and jarrings will be lessened. (Faith Precedes the Miracle, p. 204) TLDP:485-86

### Amulek,
#### quoted by Mormon

Cry unto him in your houses, yea, over all your household, both morning, mid-day, and even-

ing. . . . 27. Yea, and when you do not cry unto the Lord, let your hearts be full, drawn out in prayer unto him continually for your welfare, and also for the welfare of those who are around you. (*Amulek teaches the people to pray, about 74 B.C.*) Alma 34:21,27

### President Spencer W. Kimball

We pray for loved ones, the sick, and those in need. We pray for the frustrated, the disturbed, the sinful. ("Prayer," New Era, March 1978, p. 15) MPSG1983:130

### Jesus,
#### quoted by Mormon

Pray in your families unto the Father, always in my name, that your wives and your children may be blessed. (*The resurrected Jesus commands the Nephite people to pray, A.D. 34*) 3Ne.18:21

### N. Eldon Tanner

If children pray for their parents, it makes them more appreciative of their parents, and as they pray for one another, they feel closer to one another and part of each other, especially as they realize that they are talking to their Father in heaven while on their knees in family or secret prayer. Then is when we forget our differences and think of the best in others, and pray for their well-being and for strength to overcome our own weaknesses. There is no doubt that we are better people when we try to tune in to the Spirit of our Father in heaven so that we might communicate with him and express our desire to do his will as we pray for his blessings. CR1967Oct:55-56

### Joseph Smith,
#### quoted by Elder Joseph Fielding Smith

Follow the directions of the Book of Mormon, and pray over, and for, your families, your cattle, your flocks, your herds, your corn, and all things that you possess; ask the blessing of God upon all your labors, and everything that you engage in. (Times and Seasons, June 1842) TPJS:247; DGSM:33

---

### 528. We are to pray for our neighbors, for the welfare of those around us.

### Amulek,
#### quoted by Mormon

[L]et your hearts be full, drawn out in prayer unto him continually for your welfare, and also for the welfare of those who are around you. 28. And now behold, my beloved brethren, I say unto you, do not suppose that this is all; for after ye have done all these things, if ye turn away the needy, and the naked, and visit not the sick and afflicted, and impart of your substance, if ye have, to those who stand in need—I say unto you, if ye do not any of these things, behold, your prayer is vain, and availeth you nothing, and ye are as hypocrites who do deny the faith. 29. Therefore, if ye do not remember to be charitable, ye are as dross, which the refiners do cast out, (it being of no worth) and is trodden under foot of men. (*Amulek teaches the people to pray and to be charitable, about 74 B.C.*) Alma 34:27-29

### James
Confess your faults one to another, and pray one for another, that ye may be healed. The effectual fervent prayer of a righteous man availeth much. (*James writes to his brethren in the Church*) James 5:16

### President Spencer W. Kimball
We pray for loved ones, the sick, and those in need. We pray for the frustrated, the disturbed, the sinful. ("Prayer," New Era, March 1978, p. 15) MPSG1983:130

### Related Witnesses:
### Joseph Smith
The nearer we get to our heavenly Father, the more we are disposed to look with compassion on perishing souls; we feel that we want to take them upon our shoulders, and cast their sins behind our backs. . . . If you would have God have mercy on you, have mercy on one another. (*In Relief Society meeting, at the Grove, Nauvoo, Ill., June 9, 1842*) HC5:24

---

### 529. We are to pray for the sick.

### James
And the prayer of faith shall save the sick, and the Lord shall raise him up; and if he have committed sins, they shall be forgiven him. 16. Confess your faults one to another, and pray one for another, that ye may be healed. The effectual fervent prayer of a righteous man availeth much. (*James writes to his brethren in the Church*) James 5:15-16

### President Spencer W. Kimball
We pray for loved ones, the sick, and those in need. We pray for the frustrated, the disturbed, the sinful. ("Prayer," New Era, March 1978, p. 15) MPSG1983:130

### Elder Spencer W. Kimball
Our petitions are also for the sick and afflicted. The Lord will hear our sincere prayers. He may not always heal them, but he may give them peace or courage or strength to bear up.

We do not forget in our prayers the folks who need blessings almost more than the physically imperfect—the frustrated and confused people, the tempted, the sinful, the disturbed. . . . (Faith Precedes the Miracle, p. 206) TLDP:485-86

### President Brigham Young,
### quoted by John A. Widtsoe
Parents, have you ever noticed that your children have exercised faith for you when you have been sick? The little daughter, seeing you sick, will lift her heart with a pure, angelic-like prayer to heaven; and disease is rebuked when that kind of faith is exercised. God bless the children! I pray that they may live and be reared up in righteousness, that God may have a people that will spread and establish one universal reign of peace, and possess the powers of the world to come. (*In Bowery, July 8, 1860, JD8:117*) DBY:206

### Related Witnesses:
### Jesus,
### recorded in Matthew
Howbeit this kind goeth not out but by prayer and fasting. (*Jesus heals a lunatic boy and teaches his disciples the principle of faith*) Matt.17:21

### Bruce R. McConkie
O Father, there are those among us who are sick and afflicted, who suffer from disease, and who are not appointed unto death. O thou Great Physician, pour out thy healing power upon thy Saints. ¶ O Lord, increase our faith, and let the sick be healed and the dead raised even in greater numbers than at present. ¶ But above this, O thou God of healing, wilt thou cause him who came with healing in his wings also to heal us spiritually. CR1984Apr:46

**Author's Note:** Examples of prayer for the sick in early latter-day Church history recorded by Joseph Smith: ¶ "Six, p.m., I met with my Brother Hyrum, William Law, Newel K. Whitney, and Willard Richards in my private room, where we had a season of prayer for Brother Law's little daughter, who was sick, and Emma, who was somewhat better." (HC6:31) ¶ "Thursday, 12.—Prayer-meeting in my room. We prayed for William Marks, who was sick." (HC6:54) ¶ "Sunday, 3.—I arrived at the assembly room and found all present: except Hyrum and his wife. He had slipped and turned his knee joint backward, and sprained the large muscle of his leg, and I had been ministering unto him. Emma had been unwell during the night. . . . We also prayed for Nathan Pratt, who was very sick, Hyrum, and others. I afterwards instructed them in the things of the Priesthood." (HC6:98) ¶ "A prayer-meeting held this evening in the assembly room. I was not present. Brigham Young presided. Several sick persons were prayed for." (HC6:108) ¶ "Prayer-meeting in the assembly room. Prayed for Sister Richards and others, who were sick." (HC6:211) ¶ "President Rigdon offered an affectionate appeal for the prayers of the Saints on behalf of the sick, and then prayer by Elder George J. Adams." (HC6:297) ¶ "Prayer meeting in the evening; the brethren prayed for the sick...." (HC6:346)

---

**530. We are to pray for the sinful person.**

### President Spencer W. Kimball

We pray for loved ones, the sick, and those in need. We pray for the frustrated, the disturbed, the sinful. ("Prayer," New Era, March 1978, p. 15) MPSG1983:130

### Joseph Smith

One of the most pleasing scenes that can transpire on earth, is, when a sin has been committed by one person against another, to forgive that sin: and then, according to the sublime and perfect pattern of the Savior, pray to our Father in heaven, to forgive also. ("A Friendly Hint to Missouri," Times and Seasons, March 15, 1844, p. 473) TLDP:206

### Elder Spencer W. Kimball

We do not forget in our prayers the folks who need blessings almost more than the physically imperfect—the frustrated and confused people, the tempted, the sinful, the disturbed. . . . (Faith Precedes the Miracle, p. 206) TLDP:485-86

### Jesus,
*recorded in Matthew*

But I say unto you, Love your enemies, bless them that curse you, do good to them that hate you, and pray for them which despitefully use you, and persecute you; . . . (*Jesus teaches the multitude to love their enemies*) Matt.5:44

**Related Witnesses:**

### Recorded in Numbers

Therefore the people came to Moses, and said, We have sinned, for we have spoken against the LORD, and against thee; pray unto the LORD, that he take away the serpents from us. And Moses prayed for the people. (*Israel in the wilderness is plagued with fiery serpents*) Num.21:7

---

**531. We are to pray for our enemies.**

### Jesus,
*recorded in Matthew*

But I say unto you, Love your enemies, bless

them that curse you, do good to them that hate you, and pray for them which despitefully use you, and persecute you; . . . (*Jesus teaches the multitude to love their enemies*) Matt.5:44

### Elder Spencer W. Kimball

We pray for our enemies. This will soften our hearts, and perhaps theirs, and we may better seek good in them. And this prayer should not be confined to national enemies but should extend to neighbors, members of the family, and all with whom we have differences. . . . (Faith Precedes the Miracle, p. 203) TLDP:485-86

### Jesus,
*quoted by Mormon*

But behold I say unto you, love your enemies, bless them that curse you, do good to them that hate you, and pray for them who despitefully use you and persecute you; 45. That ye may be the children of your Father who is in heaven; for he maketh his sun to rise on the evil and on the good. (*The resurrected Jesus Christ teaches the Nephite people, A.D. 34*) 3Ne.12:44-45

**Related Witnesses:**

### Enos,
*quoted by Mormon*

And after I, Enos, had heard these words, my faith began to be unshaken in the Lord; and I prayed unto him with many long strugglings for my brethren, the Lamanites. (*The voice of the Lord comes into Enos' mind in response to an earnest prayer for his enemies, the Lamanites, 544-421 B.C.*) Enos 1:11

---

**532. We are to pray for a testimony of the gospel.**

### Thomas S. Monson

But even with all this, the prime element of any conversion is personal prayer. When a person gets down on his or her knees and prays to Heavenly Father about the message that he or she has heard, that's when conversion really starts to take place. There cannot be conversion without prayer, without recognition of a power higher than our own. Until a person comes to the point where he or she desires to really communicate with our eternal Heavenly Father, conversion will always be elusive. But it can be conclusive once powerful, personal prayer takes place. In a sense, our role through all of our exposures and introductions of the Church to others through member missionaries, books, magazines, films, lessons, meetings, etc., is simply to stimulate individuals to receive personal revelation from our Heavenly Father. Once that happens, all the rest falls into place.

("Status Report on Missionary Work," EN1977Oct:14) TLDP:486

**Reed Smoot**

I thought this morning that I would refer to the question of prayer, for it is so vital to a man and woman, no matter what position they hold, in order that they may maintain a testimony, if they have one, of the Gospel of Jesus Christ; and if they haven't yet that testimony, I know of no better way in all the world to receive it than to plead with our Heavenly Father that it may be granted unto them. I know whereof I speak, because it was only through the humiliation of my soul and the prayers ascending to my God, at the request of the mother who gave me birth, that I received a testimony that this is God's work; and every prediction made by the servants of God in any age since it was established upon this earth, shall be fulfilled. CR1932Oct:85

**George O. Cannon**

Prayer is to the soul like the irrigating stream to our dry and parched fields and orchards. Prayer nourishes, strengthens and imparts vitality to the seed. The seed grows under the influence of prayer. But where prayer is neglected, the results are just as we see them when we neglect to irrigate our fields and orchards. That which is planted there begins to wither and dry up. ¶ So it is with the word of God in the human soul; it must be watered by the Spirit of God. Prayer must be exercised in order to invoke the power and blessing of God to rest upon it. Then the seed grows; the tree grows and florishes; its branches spread abroad and fill the whole man, and he knows that it is the word of God that he has received. He has a living and abiding testimony in his heart concerning it, and doubt has no room within him. But let him neglect his prayers, let him neglect to cultivate the seed and to watch over it, then it begins to wither, and he begins to doubt and to ask himself whether this is indeed the work of God. (Gospel Truth, 1:345) TLDP:484-85

**John A. Widtsoe**

Whoever in absolute desire to know the truth places himself in harmony with divine forces and approaches God in humble prayer, with full surrender of inherited or acquired prejudices, will learn to his complete satisfaction that there is a God in Heaven, whose loving will is operative on earth. ("The Articles of Faith," IE1935May:288) TLDP:490

**Related Witnesses:**

**John A. Widtsoe**

Those who live the Gospel of Jesus Christ gain this higher knowledge, this greater testimony, this ultimate assurance that this is the truth. It is the way to truth. All the while, brethren and sisters, we must seek help from the great unseen world about us, from God and his messengers. We call that prayer. A man never finds perfect peace, never reaches afar unless he penetrates to some degree the unseen world, and reaches out to touch the hands, as it were, of those who live in that unseen world, the world out of which we came, the world into which we shall go. CR1938Oct:129

---

533. We are to pray for our own spiritual welfare.

**President Joseph F. Smith**

What do you pray for? You pray that God may recognize you, that he may hear your prayers, and that he may bless you with his Spirit, and that he may lead you into all truth and show you the right way; that he will warn you against wrong and guide you into the right path; that you may not fall astray, that you may not veer into the wrong way unto death, but that you may keep in the narrow way.... So we pray for what we need. (Gospel Doctrine, p. 215) TLDP:484

**Amulek,**
*quoted by Mormon*

Yea, and when you do not cry unto the Lord, let your hearts be full, drawn out in prayer unto him continually for your welfare, and also for the welfare of those who are around you. (*Amulek teaches the people to pray, about 74 B.C.*) Alma 34:27

**Elder Spencer W. Kimball**

For whom and what should we pray? We should express gratitude for past blessings.... ¶ We pray for the poor and needy, and at the same time remember our obligation to do something for them.... ¶ We pray for the missionaries.... ¶ We pray for our enemies. This will soften our hearts, and perhaps theirs, and we may better seek good in them. And this prayer should not be confined to national enemies but should extend to neighbors, members of the family, and all with whom we have differences.... ¶ We pray for righteousness but do not expect the Lord to *make* us good. He will help us to perfect ourselves, and as we pray for controls and exercise those controls, we grow toward perfection. ¶ We pray for ourselves and our children and all that pertains to us, as Mormon suggests: ¶ . . . hearken unto the words of the Lord, and ask the Father in the name of Jesus for what things soever ye shall stand in need. . . .

(Morm.9:27) ¶ We pray for our fellow believers. . . . ¶ We pray for enlightenment, then go to with all our might and our books and our thoughts and righteousness to get the inspiration. We ask for judgment, then use all our powers to act wisely and develop wisdom. We pray for success in our work and then study hard and strive with all our might to help answer our prayers. When we pray for health we must live the laws of health and do all in our power to keep our bodies well and vigorous. We pray for protection and then take reasonable precaution to avoid danger. There must be works with faith. How foolish it would be to ask the Lord to *give* us knowledge, but how wise to ask the Lord's help to acquire knowledge, to study constructively, to think clearly, and to retain things that we have learned. How stupid to ask the Lord to protect us if we unnecessarily drive at excessive speeds, or if we eat or drink destructive elements or try foolhardy stunts. ¶ We pray for forgiveness. . . . ¶ We pray for everything that is needed and dignified and proper. I heard a boy about fourteen years of age in family prayer imploring the Lord to protect the family sheep upon the hill. It was snowing and bitterly cold. I heard a family pray for rain when a severe drought was on and conditions were desperate. I heard a young girl praying for help in her examinations that were coming up that day. . . . ¶ We pray for help in carrying out our church callings. (Faith Precedes the Miracle, pp. 202-07) TLDP:485-86

### Moroni, son of Mormon

[A]sk the Father in the name of Jesus for what things soever ye shall stand in need. Doubt not, but be believing, and begin as in times of old, and come unto the Lord with all your heart, and work out your own salvation with fear and trembling before him. 28. Be wise in the days of your probation; strip yourselves of all uncleanness; ask not, that ye may consume it on your lusts, but ask with a firmness unshaken, that ye will yield to no temptation, but that ye will serve the true and living God. (*Moroni addresses those who deny the revelations of God, A.D. 400-421*) Morm.9:27-28

### Amulek,
*quoted by Mormon*

Yea, cry unto him against the power of your enemies. 23. Yea, cry unto him against the devil, who is an enemy to all righteousness. (*Amulek teaches the people to pray, about 74 B.C.*) Alma 34:22-23

### Elder Wilford Woodruff

Whenever you are in doubt about any duty or work which you have to perform, never proceed to do anything until you go and labour in prayer and get the Holy Spirit. Wherever the Spirit dictates you to go or to do, that will be right; and, by following its dictates, you will come out right. (*In Bowery, April 9, 1857, JD5:85*) TLDP:484

### Richard L. Evans

Most of us might be disposed to pray for unbroken good fortune, for uninterrupted happiness, for perpetual prosperity, for victory, for assured success, for affluence and ease. But life isn't an uninterrupted holiday; nor, obviously, was it intended to be. Rather it is a time of training, and often of trial, of education, and of self-effort, as evidenced by the Lord God when he expelled Adam and Eve from Eden and said that they should eat bread by the sweat of their brow. ¶ It is not the usual purpose of prayer to serve us like Aladdin's lamp, to bring us ease without effort. Prayer is not a matter of asking only. It should not be always as the beggar's upturned hand. Often the purpose of prayer is to give us strength to do what needs to be done, wisdom to see the way to solve our own problems, and ability to do our best in our tasks. ¶ We need to pray not only for freedom from difficulty but for strength to endure, for faith and fortitude to face what sometimes must be faced. (Richard L. Evans: The Man and the Message, p. 289) TLDP:486

**Related Witnesses:**

### President Spencer W. Kimball

We pray for understanding, wisdom, judgment. ("Prayer," New Era, March 1978, p. 15) MPSG1983:130

---

### 534. We are to pray that we can conquer Satan.

### Joseph Smith

Pray always that you may come off conqueror; yea, that you may conquer Satan, and that you may escape the hands of the servants of Satan that do uphold his work. (*Revelation in respect to the lost 116 manuscript pages, 1828*) D&C 10:5

### Joseph Smith,
*receiving the Word of the Lord*

What I say unto one I say unto all; pray always lest that wicked one have power in you, and remove you out of your place. (*Revelation received at Kirtland, Ohio, May 6, 1833*) D&C 93:49

### Amulek,
*quoted by Mormon*

Yea, cry unto him against the power of your enemies. 23. Yea, cry unto him against the devil, who is an enemy to all righteousness.

*(Amulek teaches the people to pray, about 74 B.C.)* Alma 34:22-23

**Elder Joseph Fielding Smith**

We may be definitely sure that the Lord will not permit Satan to deceive the earnest seeker after truth when he sincerely prays. (Answers to Gospel Questions, 3:85) TLDP:136

**Jesus,**
*quoted by Mormon*

Verily, verily, I say unto you, ye must watch and pray always, lest ye be tempted by the devil, and ye be led away captive by him. . . . 18. Behold, verily, verily, I say unto you, ye must watch and pray always lest ye enter into temptation; for Satan desireth to have you, that he may sift you as wheat. 19. Therefore ye must always pray unto the Father in my name; . . . *(The resurrected Jesus commands the Nephite people to pray, A.D. 34)* 3Ne.18:15,18-19

**Related Witnesses:**

**Joseph F. Merrill**

Brethren and sisters, let us not be deceived. There are many agents of Satan abroad in the land and some of them may be self-deceived, not knowing that they are in the power of the evil one. However, the spirit of the devil among this people may be detected by all honest, sincere members who keep the commandments of the Lord. The spirit of the Lord is comforting, joy-producing, love-inspiring, help-giving. The spirit of the devil is manifested in fault-finding, envy, selfishness, hatred, deceit, dishonesty, and produces misery, sin and crime. . . . ¶ In the spirit of helpfulness let me give you a key. When in doubt go on your knees in humility with an open mind and a pure heart with a real desire to do the Lord's will, and pray earnestly and sincerely for divine guidance. Persist in praying in this way until you get an answer that fills your bosom with joy and satisfaction. It will be God's answer. If obedient to this answer you will always act as the President indicates. You will then be safe. CR1941Apr:50-51

---

### 535. We are to pray for help to resist temptation.

**Jesus,**
*recorded in Mark*

Watch ye and pray, lest ye enter into temptation. The spirit truly is ready, but the flesh is weak. *(Jesus at Gethsemane finds Peter, James and John asleep and addresses Peter)* Mark 14:38

**George O. Cannon**

Prayer is the bulwark of the Saints. It shields and protects those who offer it in sincerity and faith. Without prayer man is exposed to wicked temptations and to every evil. When he goes unto the Lord in humility, he shows Him his weaknesses and the dangers by which he is surrounded. This prompts him who prays to seek unto God for strength to overcome his weaknesses and to resist every temptation. His faith is strengthened by having his prayers answered. He has communion with his Heavenly Father through the Holy Ghost, and that Spirit becomes his constant companion and guide. (Gospel Truth, 2:169) TLDP:489

**Joseph Smith**

Pray always, lest you enter into temptation and lose your reward. *(Revelation for Thomas B. Marsh, Sept. 30, 1830)* D&C 31:12

**Jesus,**
*recorded in Matthew*

After this manner therefore pray ye: Our Father which art in heaven, Hallowed be thy name. 10. Thy kingdom come. Thy will be done in earth, as it is in heaven. 11. Give us this day our daily bread. 12. And forgive us our debts, as we forgive our debtors. 13. And lead us not into temptation, but deliver us from evil: For thine is the kingdom, and the power, and the glory, for ever. Amen. *(Jesus teaches the disciples the Lord's Prayer)* Matt.6:9-13

**Jesus,**
*recorded in Luke*

And when he was at the place, he said unto them, Pray that ye enter not into temptation. *(Jesus suffers in Gethsemane)* Luke 22:40

**Jesus,**
*recorded in Matthew*

Watch and pray, that ye enter not into temptation: the spirit indeed is willing, but the flesh is weak. *(Jesus addresses Peter before he continues his prayer in Gethsemane)* Matt.26:41

**Related Witnesses:**

**George Q. Cannon**

It is by prayer that the most correct conceptions can be obtained of the majesty of our God and of His purity and holiness. No man or woman can be in a proper condition to withstand temptation or be properly on his or her guard who does not pray. It is a direct command from the Lord, often repeated in His word, constantly declared by His servants, that it is the duty of His children to pray to Him without ceasing. When they do not bow the knee, it is still their duty to pray in their hearts. (Gospel Truth, 2:166-67) TLDP:489

**536. In times of sorrow and affliction we are to pray for help from the Lord.**

### Neal A. Maxwell

It is both proper and important for us in our afflictions and trials to ask for relief through fasting, prayer, and priesthood blessings. But after all we can do, we then submit to God's will as did Jesus in Gethsemane and on the cross, when, in anguish, He posed aloud the possibility that the cup might pass from Him. On that occasion, the key word that expressed Jesus' attribute of submissiveness was "nevertheless." (Even As I Am, p. 47) TLDP:9

### President Brigham Young

If thou art sorrowful, call on the Lord thy God with supplication, that your souls may be joyful. (*Revelation, Jan. 14, 1847*) D&C 136:29

### President Joseph F. Smith

We do not have to cry unto him with many words. We do not have to weary him with long prayers. What we do need, and what we should do as Latter-day Saints, for our own good, is to go before him often, to witness unto him that we remember him and that we are willing to take upon us his name, keep his commandments, work righteousness; and that we desire his Spirit to help us. Then, if we are in trouble, let us go to the Lord and ask him directly and specifically to help us out of the trouble that we are in; and let the prayer come from the heart, let it not be in words that are worn into ruts in the beaten tracks of common use, without thought or feeling in the use of those words. Let us speak the simple words, expressing our need, that will appeal most truly to the Giver of every good and perfect gift. (Gospel Doctrine, p. 221) TLDP:482

**Related Witnesses:**

### President Brigham Young,
#### quoted by John A. Widtsoe

I know it is hard to receive chastisement, for no chastisement is joyous, but grievous at the time it is given; but if a person will receive chastisement and pray for the Holy Spirit to rest upon him, that he may have the Spirit of truth in his heart, and cleave to that which is pleasing to the Lord, the Lord will give him grace to bear the chastisement, and he will submit to and receive it, knowing that it is for his good. (*In Bowery, Oct. 6, 1855, JD3:47*) DBY:227

### Elder John Taylor

I rejoice in afflictions, for they are necessary to humble and prove us, that we may comprehend ourselves, become acquainted with our weakness and infirmities; and I rejoice when I triumph over them, because God answers my prayers, therefore I feel to rejoice all the day long. (*In Tabernacle, report on mission to Europe, Aug. 22, 1852, JD1:17*) TLDP:5

### Gordon B. Hinckley

I know of no single practice that will have a more salutary effect upon your lives than the practice of kneeling together as you begin and close each day. Somehow the little storms that seem to afflict every marriage are dissipated when, kneeling before the Lord, you thank him for one another, in the presence of one another, and then together invoke his blessings upon your lives, your home, your loved ones, and your dreams. ¶ God then will be your partner, and your daily conversations with him will bring peace into your hearts and a joy into your lives that can come from no other source. Your companionship will sweeten through the years; your love will strengthen. Your appreciation for one another will grow. CR1971Apr:83

---

**537. We are to pray for what is right—for what is in accord with the will of God.**

### Jesus,
#### quoted by Mormon

And whatsoever ye shall ask the Father in my name, which is right, believing that ye shall receive, behold it shall be given unto you. (*The resurrected Jesus commands the Nephite people to pray, A.D. 34*) 3Ne.18:20

### Marion G. Romney

The time will come when we shall know the will of God before we ask. Then everything for which we pray will be right. That will be when, as a result of righteous living, we shall so enjoy the companionship of the Spirit that he will dictate to us what we should ask. On this point the Lord said: "He that asketh in the Spirit asketh according to the will of God; wherefore it is done even as he asketh." (D&C 46:30) ¶ I didn't understand this scripture until I had had a lot of experiences. When you live so that the Lord can dictate what you pray for, then you will receive whatever you ask for, because you will ask according to his will; "wherefore, it is done even as he asketh." And again: ". . . if ye are purified and cleansed from all sin, ye shall ask whatsoever you will in the name of Jesus and it shall be done. But know this, it shall be given you what you shall ask. . . ." (D&C 50:29-30) (Learning for the Eternities, pp. 117-18) TLDP:487

**Joseph Smith,**
*receiving the Word of the Lord*
Whatsoever ye ask the Father in my name it shall
be given unto you, that is expedient for you; . . .
(*Revelation, Dec. 27/28, 1832*) D&C 88:64

**Joseph Smith**
He that asketh in the Spirit asketh according to
the will of God; wherefore it is done even as he
asketh. (*Revelation relative to governing and
conducting meetings, March 8, 1831*) D&C 46:30

**Neal A. Maxwell**
Petitioning in prayer has taught me, again and
again, that the vault of heaven with all its blessings is to be opened only by a combination lock.
One tumbler falls when there is faith; a second
when there is personal righteousness; the third
and final tumbler falls only when what is sought
is, in God's judgment—not ours—right for us.
Sometimes we pound on the vault door for
something we want very much and wonder why
the door does not open. We would be very
spoiled children if that vault door opened any
more easily than it does. I can tell, looking back,
that God truly loves me by inventorying the petitions He has refused to grant me. Our rejected
petitions tell us much about ourselves but also
much about our flawless Father. ("Insights,"
New Era, April 1978, p.6) DGSM:34

**Related Witnesses:**

**President Brigham Young,**
*quoted by John A. Widtsoe*
If we draw near to him, he will draw near to us;
if we seek him early, we shall find him; if we
apply our minds faithfully and diligently day by
day, to know and understand the mind and will
of God, it is as easy as, yes, I will say easier
than it is to know the minds of each other, for to
know and understand ourselves and our own
being is to know and understand God and his
being. (*In Tabernacle, April 17, 1870,
JD13:312*) DBY:42

**President Heber J. Grant**
The minute a man stops supplicating God for
his spirit and direction, just so soon he starts
out to become a stranger to him and his works.
When men stop praying for God's spirit, they
place confidence in their own unaided reason,
and they gradually lose the spirit of God, just
the same as near and dear friends, by never
writing to or visiting with each other, will
become strangers. ("Some Sentence Sermons,"
IE1944Aug:481) TLDP:481

---

**538. The Holy Ghost enables a person
who prays to ask according to the
will of God.**

**Elder Spencer W. Kimball**
The Holy Ghost is a revelator. . . . ¶ He is an
inspirer and will put words in our mouths,
enlighten our understandings and direct our
thoughts. (The Teachings of Spencer W.
Kimball, p. 23) DGSM:12

**Joseph Smith**
He that asketh in the Spirit asketh according to
the will of God; wherefore it is done even as he
asketh. (*Revelation relative to the gifts of the
spirit, March 8, 1831*) D&C 46:30

**Joseph Smith**
Remember that that which cometh from above
is sacred, and must be spoken with care, and by
constraint of the Spirit; and in this there is no
condemnation; and ye receive the Spirit through
prayer; wherefore, without this there remaineth
condemnation. (*Revelation at Kirtland, Ohio,
August 1831*) D&C 63:64

**Bruce R. McConkie**
Pray by the power of the Holy Ghost. This is
the supreme and ultimate achievement in
prayer. The promise is: "The Spirit shall be
given unto you by the power of faith" (D&C
42:14), "and if ye are purified and cleansed
from all sin, ye shall ask whatsoever you will
in the name of Jesus and it shall be done
(D&C 50:29). Of the coming millennial era,
when prayers shall be perfected, the scripture
says: "And in that day whatsoever any man
shall ask, it shall be given unto him" (D&C
101:27). ("Why the Lord Ordained Prayer,"
EN1976Jan:11) TLDP:483-84

**Marion G. Romney**
The time will come when we shall know the
will of God before we ask. Then everything
for which we pray will be right. That will be
when, as a result of righteous living, we shall
so enjoy the companionship of the Spirit that
he will dictate to us what we should ask. On
this point the Lord said: "He that asketh in the
Spirit asketh according to the will of God;
wherefore it is done even as he asketh." (D&C
46:30) ¶ I didn't understand this scripture until
I had had a lot of experiences. When you live
so that the Lord can dictate what you pray for,
then you will receive whatever you ask for,
because you will ask according to his will;
"wherefore, it is done even as he asketh." And
again: " . . . if ye are purified and cleansed
from all sin, ye shall ask whatsoever you will
in the name of Jesus and it shall be done. But
know this, it shall be given you what you shall
ask. . . ." (D&C 50:29-30) (Learning for the
Eternities, pp. 117-18) TLDP:487

**Orson F. Whitney**
It is all-important that we should possess that

Spirit, whether we preach or sing or pray. Prayers unprompted by it do not ascend to Heaven; sermons uninspired by it fail to touch the heart of the hearer; and the songs that are sung in our worshiping assemblies, if not in tune with it, are but discords in the ear of Deity. CR1931Apr:61

**Related Witnesses:**

**Paul**

Likewise the Spirit also helpeth our infirmities: for we know not what we should pray for as we ought: but the Spirit itself maketh intercession for us with groanings which cannot be uttered. (*Paul writes to the Church in Rome, about A.D. 55*) Rom.8:26

**John**

And this is the confidence that we have in him, that, if we ask any thing according to his will, he heareth us: 15. And if we know that he hear us, whatsoever we ask, we know that we have the petitions that we desired of him. (*Letter to the churches in Asia*) 1Jn.5:14-15

**Mormon**

And now, I do not know all things; but the Lord knoweth all things which are to come; wherefore, he worketh in me to do according to his will. (*Mormon describes his selection of records that he abridges and that he includes in the plates which eventually comprise the Book of Mormon, A.D. 385*) WofM1:7

**President Brigham Young,**
***quoted by John A. Widtsoe***

The Lord has said, go into the waters of baptism and be baptized for the remission of your sins, and you shall receive a witness that I am telling you the truth. How? . . . by the Spirit that shall come unto you through obedience, which will make you feel like little children, and cause you to delight in doing good, to love your Father in Heaven and the society of the righteous. . . . [Y]ou will feel a glow, as of fire, burning within you; and if you open your mouths to talk you will declare ideas which you did not formerly think of; they will flow into your mind, even such as you have not thought of for years. (*In Tabernacle, Feb. 17, 1856, JD3:211*) DBY:331

**Joseph Smith,**
***receiving the Word of the Lord***

Draw near unto me and I will draw near unto you; . . . (*Revelation, Dec. 27/28, 1832*) D&C 88:63

**Joseph Smith**

And if ye are purified and cleansed from all sin, ye shall ask whatsoever you will in the name of Jesus and it shall be done. 30. But know this, it shall be given you what you shall ask; and as ye are appointed to the head, the spirits shall be subject unto you. (*Revelation for the elders of the Church, May 1831*) D&C 50:29-30

---

**539. We are to pray for those who have religious authority over us.**

**Elder Ezra Taft Benson**

Pray in your homes morning and evening. Pray for civil magistrates and leaders even when you do not agree with them. Pray for the leaders of the Church. Pray, as you have been counseled, that the doors of nations of the world will be opened to the preaching of the gospel. CR1978Apr:48

**Elder Spencer W. Kimball**

We pray for the Church leaders. If children all their days in their turn at family prayers and in their secret prayers remember before the Lord the leaders of the Church, they are quite unlikely to ever fall into apostasy. . . . The children who pray for the brethren will grow up loving them, speaking well of them, honoring and emulating them. Those who daily hear the leaders of the Church spoken of in prayer in deep affection will more likely believe the sermons and admonitions they will hear. . . . (Faith Precedes the Miracle, p. 203) TLDP:485-86

**Elder Joseph F. Smith**

There never should be a day pass but all the people composing the Church should lift up their voices in prayer to the Lord to sustain his servants who are placed to preside over them. Not only should they do this in behalf of the president of the stake and his counselors, but they should do it in behalf of the high council, before whom, in connection with the presidency of the stake, matters of vast importance to the members of the Church are brought from time to time for their judgment and counsel. These men should have the faith of their people to sustain them in discharge of their duties in order that they may be strong in the Lord. (Gospel Doctrine, p. 223) TLDP:665

**Reed Smoot**

Prayer is practiced in the Kingdom of God. Part of our prayers should be devoted to our leaders: they have great responsibilities. Oh, so many of the people do not realize the responsibilities that fall upon the President and his Counselors these days. It has been so from the beginning and as long as there is life it will continue to be so. Let us pray for our leaders at all times instead of criticizing them, pray that they may be given courage to continue with unflagging zeal from year to year; pray for the power of God to be upon them. CR1940Oct:21

**540. We are to pray for those who have civil authority over us.**

### Elder Ezra Taft Benson

Pray in your homes morning and evening. Pray for civil magistrates and leaders even when you do not agree with them. Pray for the leaders of the Church. Pray, as you have been counseled, that the doors of nations of the world will be opened to the preaching of the gospel. CR1978Apr:48

### Paul

I exhort therefore, that, first of all, supplications, prayers, intercessions, and giving of thanks, be made for all men; 2. For kings, and for all that are in authority; that we may lead a quiet and peaceable life in all godliness and honesty. 3. For this is good and acceptable in the sight of God our Saviour; 4. Who will have all men to be saved, and to come unto the knowledge of the truth. (*Paul writes to his assistant Timothy, about* A.D. *64*) 1Tim.2:1-4

### Elder John Taylor

[I]t is proper for well disposed persons to wait the Lord's time, to be peaceable and quiet, and to pray for kings, governors, and authorities. This was what Jeremiah taught the children of Israel to do, "and seek the peace of the city wherein I have caused you to be carried away captives, and pray, unto the Lord for it, for in the peace thereof shall you have peace." xxix. 7. It is very evident, from what has been shown, that there is no proper government nor rule upon the face of the earth; that there are no kings who are anointed, or legally appointed of God; and that, however much disposed any of them may feel to benefit the world, it is out of their jurisdiction, it requires a power, spirit, and intelligence, which they do not possess. We see, moreover, that tumults, commotions, rebellions, and resistance are not the way to do it. It requires more wisdom than that which emperors, kings, princes, or the wisest of men possess, to bring out of the wild chaos, the misery, and desolation that have overspread the world, the beautiful order, peace, and happiness portrayed by the prophets as the reign of the kingdom of God. (The Government of God, pp. 58, 67-78) TLDP:260

### Elder John Taylor

We ought to pray for these people, for those that are in authority, that they may be led in the right way, that they may be preserved from evil, that they may administer the government in righteousness, and that they may pursue a course that will receive the approbation of heaven. Well, what else? Then we ought to pray for

ourselves that when any plans or contrivances or opposition to the law of God, to the church and kingdom of God, or to his people, are introduced, and whenever we are sought to be made the victims of tyranny and oppression, that the hand of God may be over us and over them to paralyze their acts and protect us. (*In Assembly Hall, Jan. 4, 1880, JD21:68*) TLDP:260-61

---

**541. In our prayers we are to dedicate ourselves and all that we have to God.**

### Elder John Taylor

Do not forget to call upon the Lord in your family circles, dedicating yourselves and all you have to God every day of your lives; and seek to do right, and cultivate the spirit of union and love, and the peace and blessing of the Living God will be with us, and He will lead us in the paths of life; and we shall be sustained and upheld by all the holy angels and the ancient patriarchs and men of God, and the veil will become thinner between us and our God, and we will approach nearer to him, and our souls will magnify the Lord of hosts. (*In Provo Tabernacle, Nov. 1879, JD20:361*) MPSG1983:128

### Elder John Taylor

[D]o you bow in meekness and with sincere desire to seek the blessing of God upon you and your household? That is the way we ought to do, and cultivate a spirit of devotion and trust in God, dedicating ourselves to him, and seeking his blessings. (*At American Fork, Utah, Nov. 1879, JD21:118*) DGSM:33

### President Brigham Young,
*quoted by John A. Widtsoe*

Say your prayers always before going to work. Never forget that. A father—the head of the family—should never miss calling his family together and dedicating himself and them to the Lord of Hosts, asking the guidance and direction of his Holy Spirit to lead them through the day—that very day. Lead us this day, guide us this day, preserve us this day, save us from sinning against thee or any being in heaven or on earth this day! If we do this every day, the last day we live we will be prepared to enjoy a higher glory. (*In new Tabernacle, Aug. 9, 1868, JD12:261*) DBY:44

**Related Witnesses:**

### President Brigham Young,
### Heber C. Kimball, Jedediah M. Grant
(First Presidency)

It is a small matter to devote and dedicate ourselves and all we have to the cause of truth, and the building up of the kingdom of God upon the earth, but it is of importance to rightly apply ourselves and our means where we may do the most good. It is important that we be obedient and passive in the hands of the servants of God, and when we have embraced the truth, and placed ourselves with all we have upon the altar, to so remain, regardless alike of friend or foe, sunshine or shade, peace or plenty, of war, famine, and pestilence. (*Thirteenth General Epistle of the First Presidency*) (Deseret News, Oct. 29, 1855) (MOFP2:185) TLDP:433-44

**Bruce R. McConkie**

It is our privilege to consecrate our time, talents, and means to build up his kingdom. We are called upon to sacrifice, in one degree or another, for the furtherance of his work. Obedience is essential to salvation: so, also, is service; and so, also, are consecration and sacrifice. CR1975Apr:76

**Joseph Smith**

Now for a man to consecrate his property, wife and children, to the Lord, is nothing more nor less than to feed the hungry, clothe the naked, visit the widow and fatherless, the sick and afflicted, and do all he can to administer to their relief in their afflictions, and for him and his house to serve the Lord. (*Letter to the Church from Liberty Jail, Mo., Dec. 16, 1838*) HC3:231

**Boyd K. Packer**

Each year a number of men are called to preside over missions. In each case this requires the man's wife and family to accompany him to some distant place and live there for three years. This is a matter of great importance to the family. If the husband accepts the call he must leave his occupation, making such arrangements as he can obtain a leave of absence from his employer or to find someone to carry on his business. Sometimes the later reentry into his employment is left unsettled. He gives up political preference, his other interests, his hobbies. He turns away from every worldly ambition in accepting the call. ¶ His wife is equally affected. Her home, the garden, her social position, perhaps some of her family will be left behind for the years of the call. Frequently the call comes at a time when there is the promise of marriage for one of the children, or the coming of grandchildren. The probability is that the parents will not be present during these very important occasions in the lives of their children. Children who accompany the parents are affected too, sometimes more deeply and personally than are the parents. After several years of struggle a young man may have just made

the athletic team. Or a young woman perhaps has achieved some position in the school or community that is very desirable to her. ¶ What does a person do when he is asked to set aside every personal interest and go away for three years on call of the servants of the Lord? That depends on how he regards his covenants. ¶ I have met mission presidents and their wives in the training session prior to their departure and have met them in the distant parts of the world in the mission field. I never fail to be impressed with one thought. We are here to receive a mortal body. We are here to be tested. Who will pass the test? Are there men and are there women and are there children in the world who will turn aside from all that they hold dear to respond to a call from the Lord? Is there such dedication in the world? Insofar as these mission presidents and their families are concerned, the question has to that time been answered. ¶ We covenant with the Lord to devote our time, talents and means to His kingdom. (The Holy Temple, pp. 163-64) TLDP:103

**Bruce R. McConkie**

[Pattern for prayer:] And now, O God, thou Everlasting Elohim, knowing thy mind and will with reference to all these expressions of thanksgiving and all these petitions for blessings, we covenant before thee that we will keep thy commandments and love and serve thee all our days. ¶ Let this, then, be our covenant, that from this hour we will walk in all thy ways, blameless, obedient, faithful, true to every trust, having love one for another, testifying in word and in deed that we are thy people, the sheep of thy pasture, thine elect and chosen children. CR1984Apr:44,47

---

**542. Through prayer we can obtain protection from peril.**

**Elder Harold B. Lee**

If all our selfish motives, then and all our personal desires, and expediency, would be subordinated to a desire to know the will of the Lord, one could have the companionship of heavenly vision. If your problems be too great for human intelligence or too much for human strength, you too, if you are faithful and appeal rightly unto the source of divine power, might have standing by you in your hour of peril or great need an angel of God, whose you are and whom you serve. One who lives thus worthy of a testimony that God lives and that Jesus is the Christ, and who is willing to reach out to him in constant inquiry to know if his course is approved, is the one who is living life to its full abundance here, and is preparing for the celestial world, which is to live eternally with his Heavenly Father. CR1946Oct:146

**Elder Spencer W. Kimball**

We pray for protection and then take reasonable precaution to avoid danger. (Faith Precedes the Miracle, p. 205) TLDP:485-86

**John A. Widtsoe**

Prayer is a request for further light, protection or whatever else is desired. (A Rational Theology, pp. 76-77) TLDP:480-81

**Related Witnesses:**

**Mormon**

And it came to pass that so great were their afflictions that they began to cry mightily to God. 11. And Amulon commanded them that they should stop their cries; and he put guards over them to watch them, that whosoever should be found calling upon God should be put to death. 12. And Alma and his people did not raise their voices to the Lord their God, but did pour out their hearts to him; and he did know the thoughts of their hearts. 13. And it came to pass that the voice of the Lord came to them in their afflictions, saying: Lift up your heads and be of good comfort, for I know of the covenant which ye have made unto me; and I will covenant with my people and deliver them out of bondage. 14. And I will also ease the burdens which are put upon your shoulders, that even you cannot feel them upon your backs, even while you are in bondage; and this will I do that ye may stand as witnesses for me hereafter, and that ye may know of a surety that I, the Lord God, do visit my people in their afflictions. . . . 21. Yea, and in the valley of Alma they poured out their thanks to God because he had been merciful unto them, and eased their burdens, and had delivered them out of bondage; for they were in bondage, and none could deliver them except it were the Lord their God. 22. And they gave thanks to God, yea, all their men and all their women and all their children that could speak lifted their voices in the praises of their God. (*Amulon puts taskmasters over Alma—the converted priest of King Noah—and his people; the Lord delivers them from bondage, 145-121 B.C.*) Mosiah 24:10-14,21-22

---

543. Through prayer we can receive knowledge of divine truth (the mysteries of God).

**Joseph Smith**

If thou shalt ask, thou shalt receive revelation upon revelation, knowledge upon knowledge, that thou mayest know the mysteries and peaceable things—that which bringeth joy, that which bringeth life eternal. (*Revelation "embracing the law of the Church," Feb. 9, 1831*) D&C 42:61

**Ammon, son of Mosiah**
*quoted by Mormon*

Yea, he that repenteth and exerciseth faith, and bringeth forth good works, and prayeth continually without ceasing—unto such it is given to know the mysteries of God; yea, unto such it shall be given to reveal things which never have been revealed; yea, and it shall be given unto such to bring thousands of souls to repentance, even as it has been given unto us to bring these our brethren to repentance. (*Ammon addresses his brethren, 90-77 B.C.*) Alma 26:22

**President Joseph F. Smith**

What do you pray for? You pray that God may recognize you, that he may hear your prayers, and that he may bless you with his Spirit, and that he may lead you into all truth. (Gospel Doctrine, p. 215) TLDP:484

**President David O. McKay**

[Inspiration] is not imagination. If we approach God sincerely seeking light and guidance from him, our minds will be enlightened and our souls thrilled by his Spirit. Washington sought it; Lincoln received it; Joseph Smith knew it; and the testimony, the evidence of the Prophet Joseph's inspiration is manifest to all who will but open their eyes to see and their hearts to understand. CR1961Apr:8

**President Brigham Young,**
*quoted by John A. Widtsoe*

When you approach the throne of grace and petition the Father, in the name of the Savior who has redeemed the world. . . . [I]t should bring near to you things that pertain to eternity, give your reflections and views a more exalted cast, stamp your daily actions with truth and honesty, and cause you to be filled with the Spirit and power of God. (*In Tabernacle, Oct. 6, 1859, JD7:274-75*) DBY:43

**Related Witnesses:**

**Boyd K. Packer**

Put difficult questions in the back of your mind and go about your lives. Ponder and pray quietly and persistently about them. ¶ The answer may not come as a lightning bolt. It may come as a little inspiration here and a little there, "line upon line, precept upon precept" (D&C 98:12). ¶ Some answers will come from reading the scriptures, some from hearing speakers.

And, occasionally, when it is important, some will come by very direct and powerful inspiration. The promptings will be clear and unmistakable. CR1979Oct:30; DGSM:33

### Joseph Smith
He that keepeth his commandments receiveth truth and light, until he is glorified in truth and knoweth all things. (*Revelation received at Kirtland, Ohio, May 6, 1833*) D&C 93:28

### Isaiah
Whom shall he teach knowledge? and whom shall he make to understand doctrine? . . . 10. For precept must be upon precept, precept upon precept; line upon line, line upon line; here a little, and there a little: . . . (*The words of Isaiah, 740-659 B.C.; revelation comes line upon line*) Isa.28:9-10

**Author's Note:** According to Smith and Sjodahl Commentary on page 141, *mystery* is defined as follows: "A mystery is a truth that cannot be known except through divine revelation—a sacred secret."

### (4) When to Pray

**544. We are to pray in the morning and evening of every day.**

### President Joseph F. Smith
[O]bserve that great commandment given of the Master, always to remember the Lord, to pray in the morning, and in the evening, and always remember to thank him for blessings that you receive day by day. . . . It is the commandment of the Lord that we shall remember God morning and evening, and as the Book of Mormon tells us, "at all times." We should carry with us the spirit of prayer throughout every duty that we have to perform in life. Why should we? One of the simple reasons that appeals to my mind with great force is that man is so utterly dependent upon God! CR1914Oct:6; DGSM:33

### Alma, the younger,
*quoted by Mormon*
Counsel with the Lord in all thy doings, and he will direct thee for good; yea, when thou liest down at night lie down unto the Lord, that he may watch over you in your sleep; and when thou risest in the morning let thy heart be full of thanks unto God; and if ye do these things, ye shall be lifted up at the last day. (*Alma instructs his son Helaman, about 73 B.C.*) Alma 37:37

### Marion G. Romney
I think every Latter-day Saint ought to go to his knees night and morning in secret prayer. . . . I

grew up in a home where we had family prayers every night and morning. A good time to have morning family prayer is just before the morning meal. And a good time for the evening prayer is just before the evening meal. CR1961Oct:61

### Amulek,
*quoted by Mormon*
Yea, humble yourselves, and continue in prayer unto him. 20. Cry unto him when ye are in your fields, yea, over all your flocks. 21. Cry unto him in your houses, yea, over all your household, both morning, mid-day, and evening. (*Amulek teaches the people to pray, about 74 B.C.*) Alma 34:19-21

### President Spencer W. Kimball
The Church urges that there be family prayer every night and every morning. It is a kneeling prayer with all or as many members of the family present as possible. ("Prayer," New Era, March 1978, p.15) MPSG1983:129

### John A. Widtsoe
No prayer is unheard. The place and time of prayer are of less importance. Morning, noon and night, prayer is always fitting. However, it is well to be orderly, and to beget habits of prayer, and certain hours of the day should therefore be set aside for prayer, both in private and in the family. (A Rational Theology, pp. 76-77) TLDP:480-81

**Related Witnesses:**
### Mormon
And he commanded them that they should observe the sabbath day, and keep it holy, and also every day they should give thanks to the Lord their God. (*Alma organizes the Church of Christ and ordains priests, about 148 B.C.*) Mosiah 18:23

### King Benjamin,
*quoted by Mormon*
And again I say unto you as I have said before, that as ye have come to the knowledge of the glory of God, or if ye have known of his goodness and have tasted of his love, and have received a remission of your sins, which causeth such exceedingly great joy in your souls, even so I would that ye should remember, and always retain in remembrance, the greatness of God, and your own nothingness, and his goodness and long-suffering towards you, unworthy creatures, and humble yourselves even in the depths of humility, calling on the name of the Lord daily, and standing steadfastly in the faith of that which is to come, which was spoken by the mouth of the angel. (*King Benjamin addresses his people, about 124 B.C.*) Mosiah 4:11

**Author's Note:** Marion G. Romney spoke in the 52nd Primary conference, April 1958, saying: "To this day, my conscience won't let me go to bed at night or leave my room in the morning without saying my prayers on my knees, if I am where I can get on my knees. If I am where I can't get on my knees, I say them as I lie in my bed."

---

**545. We are to live with the spirit of prayer always in our hearts.**

**Bruce R. McConkie**

"Pray always." (See 2Ne.32:9.) So it is written—meaning: Pray regularly, consistently, day in and day out; and also, live with the spirit of prayer always in your heart, so that your thoughts, words, and acts are always such as will please Him who is Eternal. Amulek speaks of praying "both morning, mid-day, and evening," and says we should pour out our souls to the Lord in our closets, in our secret places, and in the wilderness. (See Alma 34:17-29.) Jesus commanded both personal and family prayer: "Watch and pray always," he said: and also, "Pray in your families unto the Father, always in my name, that your wives and your children may be blessed." (3Ne.18:15,21) ("Why the Lord Ordained Prayer," EN1976Jan:11) TLDP:491

**Rudger Clawson**

How impressive are those few simple words in regard to prayer! [D&C 19:28,38] They enter into a man's life and comprehend his whole existence, at least from the years of his accountability until he passes into the grave. He must pray under all circumstances. Prayer is not reserved for the Sabbath day or for any particular occasion. It is not only to be used at the general conferences of the Church, but the spirit of prayer must be in our hearts unceasingly. We must pray in our families; we must pray in secret; we must pray in our hearts. The spirit of prayer must be with us when we retire at night and when we arise in the morning. It must be upon us when we leave our homes for our daily employment; in the office; in the shop; in the field; in the mountains or in the valleys; or wherever we are. We are told . . . that if that spirit is upon us the Lord will bless us, and the blessings which will come in answer to prayer will be of more importance to us than treasures of the earth. CR1904Apr:42-43

**President Brigham Young,**
*quoted by John A. Widtsoe*

I do not know any other way for the Latter-day Saints than for every breath to be virtually a prayer for God to guide and direct his people, and that he will never suffer us to possess anything that will be an injury to us. I am satisfied that this should be the feeling of every Latter-day Saint in the world. If you are making a bargain, if you are talking in the house, visiting in the social party, going forth in the dance, every breath should virtually be a prayer that God will preserve us from sin and from the effects of sin. (*In Tabernacle, Ogden, Utah, June 11, 1864, JD10:313)* DBY:43-44

**President Joseph F. Smith**

It is the commandment of the Lord that we shall remember God morning and evening, and as the Book of Mormon tells us, "at all times." We should carry with us the spirit of prayer throughout every duty that we have to perform in life. Why should we? One of the simple reasons that appeals to my mind with great force is that man is so utterly dependent upon God! CR1914Oct:6

**Related Witnesses:**

**Paul**

Pray without ceasing. (*Paul writes to the Church at Thessalonica, comprised of Jews and many pagan converts, A.D. 50)* 1Thess.5:17

**Elder Wilford Woodruff**

We should call upon the Lord in mighty prayer, and make all our wants known unto Him. For if He does not protect and deliver us and save us, no other power will. Therefore our trust is entirely in Him. Therefore our prayers should ascend into the ears of our Heavenly Father day and night. ("An Epistle from the President of the Twelve Apostles," Millennial Star, Dec. 1886, p. 806) TLDP:481

**Amulek,**
*quoted by Mormon*

Yea, humble yourselves, and continue in prayer unto him. 20. Cry unto him when ye are in your fields, yea, over all your flocks. 21. Cry unto him in your houses, yea, over all your household, both morning, mid-day, and evening. (*Amulek teaches the people to pray, about 74 B.C.)* Alma 34:19-21

**Joseph Smith,**
*receiving the Word of the Lord*

And again, I command thee that thou shalt pray vocally as well as in thy heart; yea, before the world as well as in secret, in public as well as in private. . . . 38. Pray always, and I will pour out my Spirit upon you, and great shall be your blessing—yea, even more than if you should obtain treasures of earth and corruptibleness to the extent thereof. (*A commandment of God for Martin Harris, March 1830)* D&C 19:28,38

**Joseph Smith**

Pray always, lest you enter into temptation and lose your reward. *(Revelation for Thomas B. Marsh, Sept. 30, 1830)* D&C 31:12

**Joseph Smith**

Pray always that you may come off conqueror; yea, that you may conquer Satan, and that you may escape the hands of the servants of Satan that do uphold his work. *(Revelation in respect to the lost 116 manuscript pages, 1828)* D&C 10:5

**Joseph Smith,**
*receiving the Word of the Lord*

What I say unto one I say unto all; pray always lest that wicked one have power in you, and remove you out of your place. *(The Lord speaks by revelation to Joseph at Kirtland, Ohio, May 6, 1833)* D&C 93:49

**Jesus,**
*recorded in Luke*

Watch ye therefore, and pray always, that ye may be accounted worthy to escape all these things that shall come to pass, and to stand before the Son of man. *(Jesus tells of the signs that shall precede his second coming)* Luke 21:36

---

**546. We are to call upon the Lord while He is near.**

**Joseph Smith,**
*receiving the Word of the Lord*

And again, verily I say unto you, my friends, I leave these sayings with you to ponder in your hearts, with this commandment which I give unto you, that ye shall call upon me while I am near— 63. Draw near unto me and I will draw near unto you; seek me diligently and ye shall find me; ask, and ye shall receive; knock, and it shall be opened unto you. 64. Whatsoever ye ask the Father in my name it shall be given unto you, that is expedient for you; 65. And if ye ask anything that is not expedient for you, it shall turn unto your condemnation. *(Revelation, Dec. 27/28, 1832)* D&C 88:62-65

**Isaiah**

Seek ye the LORD while he may be found, call ye upon him while he is near: . . . *(Isaiah says come and drink, salvation is free; seek the Lord while he is near, 740-659 B.C.)* Isa.55:6

**Joseph Smith,**
*quoted by Elder Joseph Fielding Smith*

Repent ye, repent ye, and embrace the everlasting covenant, and flee to Zion, before the overflowing scourge overtake you, for there are those now living upon the earth whose eyes shall not be closed in death until they see all these things, which I have spoken, fulfilled.

Remember these things; call upon the Lord while He is near, and seek Him while He may be found, is the exhortation of your unworthy servant. *(Letter to the editor of a newspaper published in Rochester, New York, Jan. 4, 1833)* HC1:315-16; TPJS:18

**Related Witnesses:**

**President Joseph F. Smith**

We should live so near to the Lord, be so humble in our spirits, so tractable and pliable, under the influence of the Holy Spirit, that we will be able to know the mind and will of the Father concerning us as individuals and as officers in the Church of Christ under all circumstances. And when we live so that we can hear and understand the whisperings of the still small voice of the Spirit of God, let us do whatsoever that Spirit directs, without fear of the consequences. It does not make any difference whether it meet the minds of carpers or critics, or of the enemies of the kingdom of God, or not. Is it agreeable to the will of the Lord? Is it compatible with the spirit of the great latter-day work in which we are engaged? Is the end aimed at likely to advance the Church and to strengthen it in the earth? If its trend is in that direction, let us do it, no matter what men may say or think. CR1903Oct:86

**John A. Widtsoe**

God is a personal being of body—a body limited in extent. He cannot, therefore, at a given moment be personally everywhere. Time and space surround him as they surround us. Nevertheless, it is known that God, by his power, will and word, is everywhere present. The Lord must, therefore, be in possession of other agencies whereby his will may be transmitted at his pleasure to the uttermost confines of space. The chief agent employed by God to communicate his will to the universe is the holy spirit, which must not be confused with the Holy Ghost, the personage who is the third member of the Godhead. The holy spirit permeates all the things of the universe, material and spiritual. By the holy spirit the will of God is radio-transmitted, broadcasted as it were. It forms what may be called the great system of communication among the intelligent beings of the universe. The holy spirit vibrates with intelligence; it takes up the word and will of God as given by him or by his personal agents, and transmits the message to the remotest parts of space. By the intelligent operation and infinite extent of the holy spirit, the whole universe is held together and made as one unit. By its means there is no remoteness into which intelligent beings may escape the dominating will of

God. By the holy spirit, the Lord is always with us, and "is nearer than breathing, and nearer than hands and feet." . . . ¶ By the holy spirit, which fills every person, man may obtain information from the Lord. By its means comes the messages which transcend the ordinary methods of acquiring knowledge. By it man may readily communicate with God, or God with him. When a person utters his prayer in faith, it is impressed upon the holy spirit, and transmitted, so that God may read the man's desire. (A Rational Theology, pp. 72-74) TLDP:363

**Related Witnesses:**

**President Brigham Young,**
*quoted by John A. Widtsoe*

If we draw near to him, he will draw near to us; if we seek him early, we shall find him; if we apply our minds faithfully and diligently day by day, to know and understand the mind and will of God, it is as easy as, yes, I will say easier than it is to know the minds of each other, for to know and understand ourselves and our own being is to know and understand God and his being. (*In Tabernacle, April 17, 1870, JD13:312*) DBY:42

---

## (5) Where to Pray

**547.** We are to pray in all places wherein we find ourselves.

**Amulek,**
*quoted by Mormon*

Yea, humble yourselves, and continue in prayer unto him. 20. Cry unto him when ye are in your fields, yea, over all your flocks. 21. Cry unto him in your houses, yea, over all your household, both morning, mid-day, and evening. 22. Yea, cry unto him against the power of your enemies. 23. Yea, cry unto him against the devil, who is an enemy to all righteousness. 24. Cry unto him over the crops of your fields, that ye may prosper in them. 25. Cry over the flocks of your fields, that they may increase. 26. But this is not all; ye must pour out your souls in your closets, and your secret places, and in your wilderness. 27. Yea, and when you do not cry unto the Lord, let your hearts be full, drawn out in prayer unto him continually for your welfare, and also for the welfare of those who are around you. (*Amulek teaches the people to pray, about 74 B.C.*) Alma 34:19-27

**Bruce R. McConkie**

Amulek speaks of praying "both morning, mid-day, and evening," and says we should pour out our souls to the Lord in our closets, in our secret places, and in the wilderness. (See Alma 34:17-29.) Jesus commanded both personal and family prayer: "Watch and pray always," he said: and also, "Pray in your families unto the Father, always in my name, that your wives and your children may be blessed." (3Ne.18:15,21) ("Why the Lord Ordained Prayer," EN1976Jan:11) TLDP:491

**Joseph Smith,**
*quoted by Elder Joseph Fielding Smith*

We would say to the brethren, seek to know God in your closets, call upon him in the fields. Follow the directions of the Book of Mormon, and pray over, and for, your families, your cattle, your flocks, your herds, your corn, and all things that you possess; ask the blessing of God upon all your labors, and everything that you engage in. (Times and Seasons, June 1842) TPJS:247; DGSM:33

**Rudger Clawson**

[Man] must pray under all circumstances. Prayer is not reserved for the Sabbath day or for any particular occasion. It is not only to be used at the general conferences of the Church, but the spirit of prayer must be in our hearts unceasingly. We must pray in our families; we must pray in secret; we must pray in our hearts. The spirit of prayer must be with us when we retire at night and when we arise in the morning. It must be upon us when we leave our homes for our daily employment; in the office; in the shop; in the field; in the mountains or in the valleys; or wherever we are. We are told . . . that if that spirit is upon us the Lord will bless us, and the blessings which will come in answer to prayer will be of more importance to us than treasures of the earth. CR1904Apr:42-43; DCSM:38-39

---

**548.** We are to have secret prayer.

**Elder Wilford Woodruff**

You should enter your secret closets, and call upon the name of the Lord. Many of you have learned how to pray; then fail not to let your prayers ascend up into the ears of the God of Sabaoth; and He will hear you. I think sometimes that we do not fully comprehend the power that we have with God in knowing how to approach Him acceptably. All that these men holding the Priesthood, and all that our sisters need do, is to live near to God, and call upon Him, pouring out their soul's desires in behalf of Israel, and their power will be felt, and their confidence in God will be strengthened. (*At Nephi, Utah, Jan. 27, 1883, JD24:55*) TLDP:488

### Jesus,
*recorded in Matthew*

But thou, when thou prayest, enter into thy closet, and when thou hast shut thy door, pray to thy Father which is in secret; and thy Father which seeth in secret shall reward thee openly. (*Jesus' Sermon on the Mount; he teaches how to pray*) Matt.6:6

### Jesus,
*quoted by Mormon*

And when thou prayest thou shalt not do as the hypocrites, for they love to pray, standing in the synagogues and in the corners of the streets, that they may be seen of men. Verily I say unto you, they have their reward. 6. But thou, when thou prayest, enter into thy closet, and when thou hast shut thy door, pray to thy Father who is in secret; and thy Father, who seeth in secret, shall reward thee openly. (*The resurrected Jesus teaches the Nephites how to pray*, A.D. 34) 3Ne.13:5-6

### Reed Smoot

I say also to all members of the Church of Jesus Christ of Latter-day Saints, that if they will attend to their prayers, make the hearthstone of the home an altar for prayer, where the words from sincere hearts appeal to our father in Heaven, pray honestly, morning and evening, with the family and in secret; I promise them that they will never apostatize from this Church. . . . ¶ Let us pray early and late, and let the prayer not only be by the lips but from the heart. Let us pray in secret and in public. CR1908Oct:78

### Joseph Smith,
*receiving the Word of the Lord*

And again, I command thee that thou shalt pray vocally as well as in thy heart; yea, before the world as well as in secret, in public as well as in private. . . . (*A commandment of God for Martin Harris, March 1830*) D&C 19:28

### President Heber J. Grant

One of the requirements made of the Latter-day Saints is that they shall be faithful in attending to their prayers, both their secret and family prayers. The object that our Heavenly Father has in requiring this is that we may be in communication with Him, and that we may have a channel open between us and the heavens whereby we can bring down upon ourselves blessings from above. CR1944Apr:11

### Rudger Clawson

We must pray in our families; we must pray in secret; we must pray in our hearts. The spirit of prayer must be with us when we retire at night and when we arise in the morning. It must be upon us when we leave our homes for our daily employment; in the office; in the shop; in the field; in the mountains or in the valleys; or wherever we are. We are told . . . that if that spirit is upon us the Lord will bless us, and the blessings which will come in answer to prayer will be of more importance to us than treasures of the earth. CR1904Apr:42-43; DCSM:38-39

### Joseph Smith,
*receiving the Word of the Lord*

Behold, I manifest unto you, Joseph Knight, by these words, that you must take up your cross, in the which you must pray vocally before the world as well as in secret, and in your family, and among your friends, and in all places. (*Revelation given in response to the earnest desire of Joseph Knight, Sr. and four other brethren to know of their respective duties, April 1930*) D&C 23:6

### Joseph Smith

And visit the house of each member, and exhort them to pray vocally and in secret and attend to all family duties. (*Revelation on Church Organization and Government, explains the duties of priests, April 1830*) D&C 20:47

### Amulek,
*quoted by Mormon*

But this is not all; ye must pour out your souls in your closets, and your secret places, and in your wilderness. (*Amulek teaches the people to pray, about 74 B.C.*) Alma 34:26

### President David O. McKay

I cannot think that a Latter-day Saint will hold enmity in his heart if he will sincerely, in secret, pray God to remove from his heart all feelings of envy and malice toward any of his fellow men. Guidance? Yes, God will be there to guide and direct him who will seek him in faith with all his might and with all his soul. . . . ¶ . . . . Inspiration. It is not imagination, if we approach God sincerely seeking light and guidance from him, our minds will be enlightened and our souls thrilled by his Spirit. Washington sought it; Lincoln received it; Joseph Smith knew it; and the testimony, the evidence of the Prophet Joseph's inspiration is manifest to all who will but open their eyes to see and their hearts to understand. CR1961Apr:8

---

**549. We are to pray in public as well as in secret.**

### Joseph Smith,
*receiving the Word of the Lord*

And again, I command thee that thou shalt pray vocally as well as in thy heart; yea, before the world as well as in secret, in public as well as in private. (*A commandment of God for Martin Harris, March 1830*) D&C 19:28

**Joseph Smith,**
*receiving the Word of the Lord*
Behold, I manifest unto you, Joseph Knight, by these words, that you must take up your cross, in the which you must pray vocally before the world as well as in secret, and in your family, and among your friends, and in all places. (*Revelation given in response to the earnest desire of Joseph Knight, Sr. and four other brethren to know of their respective duties, April 1930*) D&C 23:6

**President Spencer W. Kimball**
Difficult as it seems, I have found when praying, other than in private and secret, that it is better to be concerned with communicating tenderly and honestly with God, rather than worrying over what the listeners may be thinking. The echoing of "amen" by the listeners is evidence of their accord and approval. Of course, the setting of prayers needs to be taken into account. This is one reason why public prayers, or even family prayers, cannot be the whole of our praying. CR1979Oct:4-5

**Reed Smoot**
Let us pray early and late, and let the prayer not only be by the lips but from the heart. Let us pray in secret and in public. CR1908Oct:78

---

**550. We are to hold family prayer morning and night.**

**President Spencer W. Kimball**
The Church urges that there be family prayer every night and every morning. It is a kneeling prayer with all or as many members of the family present as possible. Many have found the most effective time is at the breakfast and at the dinner table. Then it is least difficult to get the family members together. These prayers need not be long, especially if little children are on their knees. All of the members of the family, including the little ones, should have opportunity to be mouth in the prayer, in turn. ("Prayer," New Era, March 1978, p.15) MPSG1983:129

**President Spencer W. Kimball**
Our Father in Heaven has given us the blessing of prayer to help us succeed in our all-important activities of home and life. I know that if we pray fervently and righteously, individually and as a family, when we arise in the morning and when we retire at night, and around our tables at mealtime, we will not only knit together as loved ones but we will grow spiritually. We have so much need for our Heavenly

Father's help as we seek to learn gospel truths and then live them, and as we seek his help in the decisions of our lives. It is especially in our family circles where our children can learn how to talk to Heavenly Father by listening to their parents. They can learn about heartfelt and honest prayer from such experiences. (The Teachings of Spencer W. Kimball, p. 116) TLDP:491

**Marion G. Romney**
I think every Latter-day Saint ought to go to his knees night and morning in secret prayer. . . . I grew up in a home where we had family prayers every night and morning. A good time to have morning family prayer is just before the morning meal. And a good time for the evening prayer is just before the evening meal. CR1961Oct:61

**George O. Cannon**
No family that fails to attend to family prayers in the proper season can keep up with the progress of the Kingdom of God. Such families fall behind in everything. They become dark in their minds, dull in their spirits and lose what little faith they may possess. They are guilty of gross ingratitude, and this is a great sin. The Spirit of God is grieved and will withdraw itself from every person who does not appreciate the goodness of God to him and who fails to render Him that worship and thanksgiving which are due to Him as our Creator and Protector. (Gospel Truth, 2:168-69) TLDP:491

**Reed Smoot**
I say also to all members of the Church of Jesus Christ of Latter-day Saints, that if they will attend to their prayers, make the hearthstone of the home an altar for prayer, where the words from sincere hearts appeal to our father in Heaven, pray honestly, morning and evening, with the family and in secret; I promise them that they will never apostatize from this Church. . . . CR1908Oct:78

**Related Witnesses:**
**Gordon B. Hinckley**
I know of no single practice that will have a more salutary effect upon your lives than the practice of kneeling together as you begin and close each day. Somehow the little storms that seem to afflict every marriage are dissipated when, kneeling before the Lord, you thank him for one another, in the presence of one another, and then together invoke his blessings upon your lives, your home, your loved ones, and your dreams. ¶ God then will be your partner, and your daily conversations with him will bring peace into your hearts and a joy into your lives that can come from no other source. Your

companionship will sweeten through the years; your love will strengthen. Your appreciation for one another will grow. CR1971Apr:83

**Jesus,**
*quoted by Mormon*
Pray in your families unto the Father, always in my name, that your wives and your children may be blessed. (*The resurrected Jesus commands the Nephite people to pray, A.D. 34*) 3Ne.18:21

**Elder John Taylor**
[D]o not forget to call upon the Lord in your family circles, dedicating yourselves and all you have to God every day of your lives; and seek to do right, and cultivate the spirit of union and love, and the peace and blessing of the Living God will be with us, and He will lead us in the paths of life; and we shall be sustained and upheld by all the holy angels and the ancient patriarchs and men of God, and the veil will become thinner between us and our God, and we will approach nearer to him, and our souls will magnify the Lord of hosts. (*In Provo Tabernacle, Nov. 1879; JD20:361*) MPSG1983:128

**Elder John Taylor**
Do you have prayers in your family? . . . And when you do, do you go through the operation like the grinding of a piece of machinery, or do you bow in meekness and with a sincere desire to seek the blessing of God upon you and your household? That is the way that we ought to do, and cultivate a spirit of devotion and trust in God, dedicating ourselves to him, and seeking his blessings. (*At American Fork, Utah, Nov. 1879; JD21:118*) DGSM:33

**President Heber J. Grant**
One of the requirements made of the Latter-day Saints is that they shall be faithful in attending to their prayers, both their secret and family prayers. The object that our Heavenly Father has in requiring this is that we may be in communication with Him, and that we may have a channel open between us and the heavens whereby we can bring down upon ourselves blessings from above. CR1944Apr:11

**N. Eldon Tanner**
Family prayer in any home will draw the family closer together and result in better feeling between father and mother, between parents and children, and between one child and another. If children pray for their parents, it makes them more appreciative of their parents, and as they pray for one another, they feel closer to one another and part of each other, especially as they realize that they are talking to their Father in heaven while on their knees in family or

secret prayer. Then is when we forget our differences and think of the best in others, and pray for their well-being and for strength to overcome our own weaknesses. There is no doubt that we are better people when we try to tune in to the spirit of our Father in heaven so that we might communicate with him and express our desire to do his will as we pray for his blessings. CR1967Oct:55-56

---

## (6) Prayer Is Essential

### 551. We are commanded to pray.

**Marion G. Romney**
There isn't any commandment from the Lord that is repeated more often than the commandment to pray to the Lord. . . . ¶ Prayer is the key that opens the door to the Spirit of the Lord. The Lord told us in this dispensation, when the Church was very young, that we were to pray always that we would be conquerors. He told the Prophet Joseph to "pray always, . . . that you may conquer Satan, and that you may escape the hands of the servants of Satan that do uphold his work." (D&C 10:5) ACR(Taipei)1975:7

**Joseph Smith,**
*receiving the Word of the Lord*
Pray always, and I will pour out my Spirit upon you, and great shall be your blessing—yea, even more than if you should obtain treasures of earth and corruptibleness to the extent thereof. (*A commandment of God for Martin Harris, March 1830*) D&C 19:38

**Reed Smoot**
The Prophet Joseph Smith told President John Taylor that if he would pray earnestly every day of his life, he would never apostatize from the Church. I say also to all members of the Church of Jesus Christ of Latter-day Saints, that if they will attend to their prayers, make the hearthstone of the home an altar for prayer, where the words from sincere hearts appeal to our father in Heaven, pray honestly, morning and evening, with the family and in secret; I promise them that they will never apostatize from this Church. . . . ¶ I know that God will bless His people if they will attend to their prayers honestly and sincerely. Prayer is a duty. Why? Because God says that He desires His people to pray. And far greater than a duty, prayer is a privilege to every Latter-day Saint, and that privilege should be exercised by every member of the Church. No matter whether it be child, man, or woman, we should

value our souls; and, as we value our soul's eternal happiness, as we value the salvation of mankind, the fulfillment of the decrees of God, the extension of the Church of Jesus Christ of Latter-day Saints, the eradication of all vices in our midst, as we value the great principles of temperance, virtue, truth, and charity, so let us pray. Let us pray early and late, and let the prayer not only be by the lips but from the heart. Let us pray in secret and in public. CR1908Oct:78

### President Brigham Young,
### *quoted by John A. Widtsoe*
It matters not whether you or I feel like praying, when the time comes to pray, pray. If we do not feel like it, we should pray till we do. And if there is a heavy storm coming on and our hay is likely to be wet, let it come. You will find that those who wait till the Spirit bids them pray, will never pray much on this earth. (*In Tabernacle, Nov. 1869, JD13:155*) DBY:44

### President Brigham Young,
### *quoted by John A. Widtsoe*
The Lord says, I will be sought unto by my people for the blessings that they need. And instead of our classing prayer among the duties devolving upon us as Latter-day Saints, we should live so as to deem it one of the greatest privileges accorded to us; for were it not for the efficacy of prayer what would have become of us both as a people and as individuals? (*In Richfield, Utah, April 22, 1877, JD19:222*) DBY:43

### Jesus,
### *recorded in Matthew*
Ask, and it shall be given you; seek, and ye shall find; knock, and it shall be opened unto you: . . . (*Jesus concludes the Sermon on the Mount*) Matt.7:7

### Jesus,
### *quoted by Mormon*
And whatsoever ye shall ask the Father in my name, which is right, believing that ye shall receive, behold it shall be given unto you. 21. Pray in your families unto the Father, always in my name, that your wives and your children may be blessed. (*The resurrected Jesus commands the Nephite people to pray, A.D. 34*) 3Ne.18:20-21

### George Q. Cannon
It is by prayer that the most correct conceptions can be obtained of the majesty of our God and of His purity and holiness. No man or woman can be in a proper condition to withstand temptation or be properly on his or her guard who does not pray. It is a direct command from the Lord, often repeated in His word, constantly declared by His servants, that it is the duty of his children to pray to Him without ceasing. When they do not bow the knee, it is still their duty to pray in their hearts. (Gospel Truth, 2:166-67) TLDP:489

### President Heber J. Grant
One of the requirements made of the Latter-day Saints is that they shall be faithful in attending to their prayers, both their secret and family prayers. The object that our Heavenly Father has in requiring this is that we may be in communication with Him, and that we may have a channel open between us and the heavens whereby we can bring down upon ourselves blessings from above. CR1944Apr:11

### Elder John Taylor
[D]o you bow in meekness and with sincere desire to seek the blessing of God upon you and your household? That is the way we ought to do, and cultivate a spirit of devotion and trust in God, dedicating ourselves to him, and seeking his blessings. (The Gospel Kingdom, p. 284) DGSM:33

### Nephi, son of Lehi
But behold, I say unto you that ye must pray always, and not faint; that ye must not perform any thing unto the Lord save in the first place ye shall pray unto the Father in the name of Christ, that he will consecrate thy performance unto thee, that thy performance may be for the welfare of thy soul. (*Nephi writes, between 559-545 B.C.*) 2Ne.32:9

### Nephi, son of Lehi
[I]f ye would hearken unto the Spirit which teacheth a man to pray ye would know that ye must pray; for the evil spirit teacheth not a man to pray, but teacheth him that he must not pray. (*Nephi's writings, between 559-545 B.C.*) 2Ne.32:8

### Jesus,
### *recorded in Matthew*
But when ye pray, use not vain repetitions, as the heathen do: for they think that they shall be heard for their much speaking. 8. Be not ye therefore like unto them: for your Father knoweth what things ye have need of, before ye ask him. 9. After this manner therefore pray ye: Our Father which art in heaven, Hallowed be thy name. 10. Thy kingdom come. Thy will be done in earth, as it is in heaven. 11. Give us this day our daily bread. 12. And forgive us our debts, as we forgive our debtors. 13. And lead us not into temptation, but deliver us from evil: For thine is the kingdom, and the power, and the glory, for ever. Amen. (*Jesus' Sermon on the Mount; he teaches how to pray*) Matt.6:7-13

**Related Witnesses:**
**President Brigham Young,**
*quoted by John A. Widtsoe*
If the Devil says you cannot pray when you are angry, tell him it is none of his business, and pray until that species of insanity is dispelled and serenity is restored to the mind. (*In Tabernacle, May 24, 1863, JD10:175*) DBY:45

**President Brigham Young,**
*quoted by John A. Widtsoe*
When we neglect any one of these duties, the enemy says, "I have made so much ground." If the Devil can induce an Elder to drink a little, he is not satisfied with this triumph, but says to him, "Your wife and children know it, don't pray tonight." The Elder says to his family, "I feel tired tonight, we won't have prayers." The enemy says, "I have gained another point." You indulge still further, and you will find other excuses. Your head is not right, your heart is not right, your conscience is not right, and you retire again without praying. By and by, you begin to doubt something the Lord has revealed to us, and it is not long before such a one is led away captive of the Devil. (*At Logan, Utah, Aug. 15, 1876, JD18:216*) DBY:81

**President Joseph F. Smith**
Again, while prayer is essential and is one of the fundamental principles of the gospel of Jesus Christ, it is nonsense for a person to pray only, and not work.  A well-balanced person would naturally do everything that he could do and at the same time petition the Lord to help him in his efforts, thus aiding to bring about his desires.  By work, patience and integrity, such a person would support his prayers by so living that the Lord could be justified in granting his petitions.  The commandments which the Lord has given us, in ages past, and those now being revealed, teach us that human desire and effort are necessary to obtain divine assistance. ("Strive to Be as Broad as the Gospel," IE1912Jul:843) TLDP:487

---

**HYMNS Written by Prophets**
**Applicable to this Topic**

**John A. Widtsoe**
*Lead Me into Life Eternal*
HYMNS:45

Lead me into life eternal
By the gospel's holy call.
Let thy promise rest upon me;
Grant me ready strength for all.

Father, all my heart I give thee;
All my service shall be thine.
Guide me as I search in weakness;
Let thy loving light be mine.

Hear me as I pray in meekness;
Let my strength be as thy day.
Give me faith, the greater knowledge;
Father, bless me as I pray.

**Parley P. Pratt**
*Father In Heaven, We Do believe*
HYMNS:180

Father in Heav'n, we do believe
The promise thou hast made;
Thy word with meekness we receive,
Just as thy Saints have said.

We now repent of all our sin
And come with broken heart,
And to thy covenant enter in
And choose the better part.

O Lord, accept us while we pray,
And all our sins forgive;
New life impart to us this day,
And bid the sinners live.

**Gordon B. Hinckley**
*My Redeemer Lives*
HYMNS:135

[*Ed. note: See particularly the last verse*]
I know that my Redeemer lives,
Triumphant Savior, Son of God,
Victorious over pain and death,
My King, my Leader, and my Lord.

He lives, my one sure rock of faith,
The one bright hope of men on earth,
The beacon to a better way,
The light beyond the veil of death.

Oh, give me thy sweet Spirit still,
The peace that comes alone from thee,
The faith to walk the lonely road
That leads to thine eternity.

# List of Doctrines

## PREMORTAL LIFE

*Doctrines Located in This Topic*

552. Prior to life on earth we lived as spirits in a premortal world.

553. Our spirit bodies are in the same form as the spirit body of Jesus Christ.

554. The spirits of people and the spirits of animals and plants in the premortal world were in the same form as their mortal bodies.

555. We were instructed and prepared for earth life in the premortal world.

556. When the plan of salvation was presented in the premortal world, each person had the opportunity of accepting or rejecting it.

557. Memory of our premortal existence was taken from us when we were sent to earth.

558. We are spirit children of God—His literal offspring.

559. As spirit children of God in the premortal world we were not all alike; each of us had different talents and dispositions.

560. In the premortal world the Lord called (foreordained) certain persons to fulfill special assignments and missions on earth.

561. In the premortal world the Lord chose those who were to be rulers in the church of God on earth.

562. Demonstrated worthiness was the basis upon which those in the premortal world were called and chosen (foreordained) to minister in the Lord's vineyard on earth.

563. In the premortal world God knew each of us individually before we were born into mortality.

564. Physical deformities upon birth into mortal life are not punishment for misbehavior of the spirit in premortal life.

565. Every spirit born on earth is innocent.

566. The devil rebelled against God in the premortal world, sought to take control of the kingdom of God, and there was war in heaven.

567. As a result of the war in the premortal world, the devil and a third part of the hosts of heaven were thrust out.

*Doctrines on PREMORTAL LIFE Located in Other Topics*

13. Before the earth was created, the spirits of all people were free to act for themselves.

104. In the premortal existence, because of their faithfulness, the people of Israel were foreordained to become a chosen nation on earth.

105. Many of the valiant and noble spirits in the premortal world were chosen and foreordained to be born into the family of Jacob (Israel).

156. In the premortal existence the devil was an angel of God in a position of authority with God.

157. In the premortal existence the devil was ambitious and sought to exalt himself to the glory and honor of God.

158. In the premortal existence the devil's plan was to destroy the agency of the spirit sons and daughters of God.

159. The devil and his followers failed to keep their First Estate (in the premortal life); hence, they were denied the privilege of being born into the world and receiving mortal bodies.

262. Before the earth was created Jesus Christ was with God the Father in a premortal life.

468. Those who come to earth are those who were faithful in the premortal life (they kept their First Estate).

# PREMORTAL LIFE

**552. Prior to life on earth we lived as spirits in a premortal world.**

### Elder Joseph Fielding Smith

In the pre-existence we dwelt in the presence of God our Father. When the time arrived for us to be advanced in the scale of our existence and pass through this mundane probation, councils were held and the spirit children were instructed in matters pertaining to conditions in mortal life, and the reason for such an existence. In the former life we were spirits. In order that we should advance and eventually gain the goal of perfection, it was made known that we would receive tabernacles of flesh and bones and have to pass through mortality where we would be tried and proved to see if we, by trial, would prepare ourselves for exaltation. We were made to realize, in the presence of our glorious Father, who had a tangible body of flesh and bones which shone like the sun, that we were, as spirits, far inferior in our station to him. (Doctrines of Salvation, 1:57) DGSM:14

### Abraham,
#### quoted by Joseph Smith

Now the Lord had shown unto me, Abraham, the intelligences that were organized before the world was; and among all these there were many of the noble and great ones; 23. And God saw these souls that they were good, and he stood in the midst of them, and he said: These I will make my rulers; for he stood among those that were spirits, and he saw that they were good; and he said unto me: Abraham, thou art one of them; thou wast chosen before thou wast born. 24. And there stood one among them that was like unto God, and he said unto those who were with him: We will go down, for there is space there, and we will take of these materials, and we will make an earth whereon these may dwell; 25. And we will prove them herewith, to see if they will do all things whatsoever the Lord their God shall command them; (*Abraham learns of pre-earth life and foreordination*) Abr.3:22-25

### J. Reuben Clark, Jr.

[T]he Sacred Records make it clear that the Father and the Son were not alone in their eternal abode; that they dwelt amongst untold Heavenly Hosts; that a great schism arose amongst these hosts; that part of them rebelled against the Father, led by Lucifer, a son of the Morning, who sought to make himself above God; that a war ensued; that Lucifer and his followers, a third of the hosts of heaven were cast out and down into the bottomless pit, becoming the devil and his angels. Modern revelation makes all this very clear. . . . ¶ There is no place in this great plan, framed in the Council of Heaven, for that arch-heresy first preached, if not invented by Tertullian, and still proclaimed by a large part of the sectarian world, that our spirits had no premortal existence, but are propagated, like our mortal bodies, by our mortal parents. ¶ Our spirits were created by our Heavenly Father. We existed before we came to earth. (On the Way to Immortality and Eternal Life, pp. 21-31) MPSG1968-69:14-15

### James E. Talmage

[T]he spirits of mankind passed through a stage of existence prior to their earthly probation. This antemortal period is oftentimes spoken of as the stage of primeval childhood or first estate. That these spirits existed as organized intelligences and exercised their free agency during that primeval stage is clear from the declaration of the Lord to Abraham: "And they who keep their first estate shall be added upon; and they who keep not their first estate shall not have glory in the same kingdom with those who keep their first estate; and they who keep their second estate shall have glory added upon their heads forever and ever." ¶ No one who accepts Jesus Christ as the Son of God can consistently deny His antemortal existence, or question His position as one of the Godhead before He came to earth as Mary's Son. . . . Yet Christ was born a child among mortals; and it is consistent to infer that if His earthly birth was the union of a preexistent or antemortal spirit with a mortal body such also is the birth of every member of the human family. ¶ But we are not left to mere inference on a basis of analogy; the scriptures plainly teach that the spirits of mankind are known and numbered unto God before their earthly advent. In his farewell administration to Israel Moses sang: "Remember the days of old . . . When the Most High divided to the nations their inheritance, when he separated the sons of Adam, he set the bounds of the people according to the number of the children of Israel." From this we learn that the earth was allotted to the nations, according to the number of the children of Israel; it is evident therefore that the number was known prior to the existence of the Israelitish nation in the flesh; this is most easily explained on the basis of previous existence in which the spirits of the future nation were known. ¶ No chance is possible, therefore, in the number or extent of the temporal creations of God. The population of the earth is fixed according to the number of spirits appointed to take tabernacles of flesh upon this planet; when these have all come forth in the order and time appointed, then, and not till then, shall the end come. AF:174-76

**Jeremiah**

Before I formed thee in the belly I knew thee; and before thou camest forth out of the womb I sanctified thee, and I ordained thee a prophet unto the nations. *(The Lord to Jeremiah, about 628 B.C.)* Jer.1:5

**Elder George Albert Smith**

When God created the earth and placed our first parents upon it, He did not leave them without knowledge concerning Himself. It is true that there had been taken from them the remembrance of their pre-existent life, but in His tender mercy He talked with them and later He sent His choice servants to instruct them in the things pertaining to eternal life. CR1928Oct:90-91

**Paul**

According as he hath chosen us in him before the foundation of the world, that we should be holy and without blame before him in love: *(Letter to the Saints at Ephesus in Asia Minor, about A.D. 62)* Eph.1:4

**Recorded in Job**

Where wast thou when I laid the foundations of the earth? declare, if thou hast understanding. 5. Who hath laid the measures thereof, if thou knowest? or who hath stretched the line upon it? 6. Whereupon are the foundations thereof fastened? or who laid the corner stone thereof; 7. When the morning stars sang together, and all the sons of God shouted for joy? Job 38:4-7

**Recorded in Proverbs**

The LORD possessed me in the beginning of his way, before his works of old. 23. I was set up from everlasting, from the beginning, or ever the earth was. 24. When there were no depths, I was brought forth; when there were no fountains abounding with water. 25. Before the mountains were settled, before the hills was I brought forth: 26. While as yet he had not made the earth, nor the fields, nor the highest part of the dust of the world. 27. When he prepared the heavens, I was there: when he set a compass upon the face of the depth: 28. When he established the clouds above: when he strengthened the fountains of the deep: 29. When he gave to the sea his decree, that the waters should not pass his commandment: when he appointed the foundations of the earth: 30. Then I was by him, as one brought up with him: and I was daily his delight, rejoicing always before him; 31. Rejoicing in the habitable part of his earth; and my delights were with the sons of men. *(Proverb of Solomon, king of Israel)* Prov.8:22-31

**Related Witnesses:**

**President Joseph F. Smith**

Even before they were born, they, with many others, received their first lessons in the world of spirits and were prepared to come forth in the due time of the Lord to labor in his vineyard for the salvation of the souls of men. *(Vision of the Savior's visit to the spirits of the dead, Oct. 3, 1918)* D&C 138:56

**Joseph Smith,**
*receiving the Word of the Lord*

[F]or, behold, the devil was before Adam, for he rebelled against me, saying, Give me thine honor, which is my power; and also a third part of the hosts of heaven turned he away from me because of their agency; *(Revelation received Sept. 1830)* D&C 29:36

**Joseph Smith,**
*receiving the Word of the Lord*

And now, verily I say unto you, I was in the beginning with the Father, and am the Firstborn; . . . 23. Ye were also in the beginning with the Father; that which is Spirit, even the Spirit of truth; *(The Lord speaks by revelation at Kirtland, Ohio, May 6, 1833)* D&C 93:21,23

**Boyd K. Packer**

There is no way to make sense out of life without a knowledge of the doctrine of premortal life. ¶ The idea that mortal birth is the beginning is preposterous. There is no way to explain life if you believe that. ¶ The notion that life ends with mortal death is ridiculous. There is no way to face life if you believe that. ¶ When we understand the doctrine of premortal life, then things fit together and make sense. We then know that little boys and little girls are not monkeys, nor are their parents, nor were theirs, to the very beginning generation. ¶ We are the children of God, created in his image. ¶ Our child-parent relationship to God is clear. ¶ The purpose for the creation of this earth is clear. ¶ The testing that comes in mortality is clear. ¶ The need for a redeemer is clear. ¶ When we do understand that principle of the gospel, we see a Heavenly Father and a Son; we see an atonement and a redemption. ¶ We understand why ordinances and covenants are necessary. ¶ We understand the necessity for baptism by immersion for the remission of sins. We understand why we renew that covenant by partaking of the sacrament. CR1983Oct:22

---

553. **Our spirit bodies are in the same form as the spirit body of Jesus Christ.**

### President Joseph F. Smith, John R. Winder, Anthon H. Lund
(First Presidency)

All men and women are in the similitude of the universal Father and Mother, and are literally the sons and daughters of Deity. ¶ "God created man in His own image." This is just as true of the spirit as it is of the body, which is only the clothing of the spirit, its complement; the two together constituting the soul. The spirit of man is in the form of man, and the spirits of all creatures are in the likeness of their bodies. This was plainly taught by the Prophet Joseph Smith (D&C 77:2). MOFP4:203

### Marion G. Romney
The nature of the spirit is plainly revealed in the scriptures. A clear word picture of a spirit is recorded in the third chapter of Ether in the Book of Mormon, which gives an account of the appearance of Jesus Christ, as a spirit, some 2200 years before he was born to Mary in the flesh. The record says that Jesus stood before the brother of Jared in the form and likeness of man and said: ¶ ". . . Behold, I am Jesus Christ. . . . ¶ ". . . Seest thou that ye are created after mine own image? Yea, even all men were created in the beginning after mine own image. ¶ "Behold, this body, which ye now behold, is the body of my spirit; and man have I created after the body of my spirit; and even as I appear unto thee to be in the spirit will I appear unto my people in the flesh." ¶ Corroborating this truth, Jesus declared to Joseph Smith, as late as 1833: ¶ ". . . I was in the beginning with the Father, and am the First-born [meaning, of course, the firstborn spirit]; ¶ "Ye were also in the beginning with the Father; that which is Spirit. . . ." (D&C 93:21,23) CR1973Apr:134

### Joseph Smith
Q. What are we to understand by the four beasts, spoken of in the same verse? ¶ A. They are figurative expressions, used by the Revelator, John, in describing heaven, the paradise of God, the happiness of man, and of beasts, and of creeping things, and of the fowls of the air; that which is spiritual being in the likeness of that which is temporal; and that which is temporal in the likeness of that which is spiritual; the spirit of man in the likeness of his person, as also the spirit of the beast, and every other creature which God has created. (*Revelation in connection with his translating of the scriptures—Rev.4:6, March 1832*) D&C 77:2

### Bruce R. McConkie
But we do know that our Eternal Father . . . lives in the family unit. We do know that we are

his children, created in his image, endowed with power and ability to become like him. CR1974Apr:103

### Moroni, son of Mormon, *also quoting Jesus*
And it came to pass that when the brother of Jared had said these words, behold, the Lord stretched forth his hand and touched the stones one by one with his finger. And the veil was taken from off the eyes of the brother of Jared, and he saw the finger of the Lord; and it was as the finger of a man, like unto flesh and blood; and the brother of Jared fell down before the Lord, for he was struck with fear. 7. And the Lord saw that the brother of Jared had fallen to the earth; and the Lord said unto him: Arise, why hast thou fallen? 8. And he saith unto the Lord: I saw the finger of the Lord, and I feared lest he should smite me; for I knew not that the Lord had flesh and blood. 9. And the Lord said unto him: Because of thy faith thou hast seen that I shall take upon me flesh and blood; and never has man come before me with such exceeding faith as thou hast; for were it not so ye could not have seen my finger. Sawest thou more than this? 10. And he answered: Nay; Lord, show thyself unto me. 11. And the Lord said unto him: Believest thou the words which I shall speak? 12. And he answered: Yea, Lord, I know that thou speakest the truth, for thou art a God of truth, and canst not lie. 13. And when he had said these words, behold, the Lord showed himself unto him, and said: Because thou knowest these things ye are redeemed from the fall; therefore ye are brought back into my presence; therefore I show myself unto you. 14. Behold, I am he who was prepared from the foundation of the world to redeem my people. Behold, I am Jesus Christ. I am the Father and the Son. In me shall all mankind have life, and that eternally, even they who shall believe on my name; and they shall become my sons and my daughters. 15. And never have I showed myself unto man whom I have created, for never has man believed in me as thou hast. Seest thou that ye are created after mine own image? Yea, even all men were created in the beginning after mine own image. 16. Behold, this body, which ye now behold, is the body of my spirit; and man have I created after the body of my spirit; and even as I appear unto thee to be in the spirit will I appear unto my people in the flesh. (*Christ, before he is born into the world, shows himself to be in the image of man*) Ether 3:6-16

554. The spirits of people and the spirits of animals and plants in the premortal world were in the same form as their mortal bodies.

### President Joseph F. Smith, John R. Winder, Anthon H. Lund
(First Presidency)

The spirit of man is in the form of man, and the spirits of all creatures are in the likeness of their bodies. This was plainly taught by the Prophet Joseph Smith (D&C 77:2). (*From an Official Statement of the First Presidency, IE1909Nov:75-81*) MOFP4:203

### Bruce R. McConkie

Man and all forms of life existed as spirit beings and entities before the foundations of this earth were laid. There were spirit men and spirit beasts, spirit fowls and spirit fishes, spirit plants and spirit trees. Every creeping thing, every herb and shrub, every amoeba and tadpole, every elephant and dinosaur—all things—existed as spirits, as spirit beings before they were placed naturally upon the earth. (The Millennial Messiah, pp. 642-43) DGSM:16

### Joseph Smith

Q. What are we to understand by the four beasts, spoken of in the same verse? ¶ A. They are figurative expressions, used by the Revelator, John, in describing heaven, the paradise of God, the happiness of man, and of beasts, and of creeping things, and of the fowls of the air; that which is spiritual being in the likeness of that which is temporal; and that which is temporal in the likeness of that which is spiritual; the spirit of man in the likeness of his person, as also the spirit of the beast, and every other creature which God has created. (*Revelation in connection with his translating of the scriptures—Rev.4:6, March 1832*) D&C 77:2

### Joseph Smith, translating the Book of Moses

And every plant of the field before it was in the earth, and every herb of the field before it grew. For I, the Lord God, created all things, of which I have spoken, spiritually, before they were naturally upon the face of the earth. For I, the Lord God, had not caused it to rain upon the face of the earth. And I, the Lord God, had created all the children of men; and not yet a man to till the ground; for in heaven created I them; and there was not yet flesh upon the earth, neither in the water, neither in the air; . . . 7. And I, the Lord God, formed man from the dust of the ground, and breathed into his nostrils the breath of life; and man became a living soul, the first flesh upon the earth, the first man also; nevertheless, all things were before created; but spiritually were they created and made according to my word. (*The Lord reveals to Moses the creation of the earth and of man*) Moses 3:5,7

### Moses

These are the generations of the heavens and of the earth when they were created, in the day that the LORD God made the earth and the heavens, 5. And every plant of the field before it was in the earth, and every herb of the field before it grew: for the LORD God had not caused it to rain upon the earth, and there was not a man to till the ground. (*Revelation to Moses with respect to the Creation*) Gen.2:4-5

### Related Witnesses:
### Parley P. Pratt

The spirit of man consists of an organization of the elements of spiritual matter in the likeness and after the pattern of the fleshly tabernacle. It possesses, in fact, all the organs and parts exactly corresponding to the outward tabernacle. (Key to the Science of Theology, p. 79) DGSM:14

---

555. We were instructed and prepared for earth life in the premortal world.

### Elder Joseph Fielding Smith

In the pre-existence we dwelt in the presence of God our Father. When the time arrived for us to be advanced in the scale of our existence and pass through this mundane probation, councils were held and the spirit children were instructed in matters pertaining to conditions in mortal life, and the reason for such an existence. (Doctrines of Salvation, 1:57) DGSM:14

### Elder Joseph F. Smith

Our spirits existed before they came to this world. They were in the councils of the heavens before the foundations of the earth were laid. We were there. We sang together with the heavenly hosts for joy when the foundations of the earth were laid, and when the plan of our existence upon this earth and redemption were mapped out. We were there; we were interested, and we took a part in this great preparation. We were unquestionably present in those councils when that wonderful circumstance occurred when Satan offered himself as a savior of the world if he could but receive the honor and glory of the Father for doing it. But Jesus said, "Father, thy will be done, and the glory be thine forever." Wherefore, because Satan rebelled against God, and sought to destroy the agency of man, the Father rejected him and he was cast out, but Jesus was accepted. We were, no doubt, there, and took part in all those scenes, we were vitally concerned in the carrying out of these great plans and purposes, we understood them, and it was for our sakes they were decreed, and are to be consummated. (Gospel Doctrine, pp. 93-94) TLDP:494-95

### Bruce R. McConkie

We are his offspring. We were spirit children: he was glorified and exalted in the life that went before. We could tell the difference between our spirit bodies and the glorified and exalted body which he possessed. He taught us eternal truths: there came into our hearts the great desire to progress and advance and become like him so that we could have glorified and exalted bodies and so that we could live in the family unit as he lived in the family unit. And as a consequence, he ordained and established what is called a plan of salvation. The Prophet Joseph Smith said, "God, himself, finding he was in the midst of spirits and glory," ordained laws whereby they progress and become like him. ACR(Brisbane)1976:14

### President Lorenzo Snow

When we lived in the other life we had no doubt some understanding with reference to our duties in this life when we were permitted to come to this our second estate. And very likely we put ourselves under certain obligations that we would discharge certain duties devolving upon us when we came here into our second estate. And we had rendered ourselves worthy to come upon this earth for the purpose of securing those blessings that could only be obtained by observing the laws pertaining to our present estate. CR1898Apr:12

### President Joseph F. Smith

Even before they were born, they, with many others, received their first lessons in the world of spirits and were prepared to come forth in the due time of the Lord to labor in his vineyard for the salvation of the souls of men. (*Vision regarding the Savior's visit to the spirits of the dead, Oct. 3, 1918*) D&C 138:56

### Related Witnesses:

#### Elder Joseph F. Smith

Our spirits . . . were in the councils of the heavens before the foundations of the earth were laid. We were there. We sang together with the heavenly hosts for joy when the foundations of the earth were laid, and when the plan of our existence upon this earth and redemption were mapped out. We were there; we were interested, and we took a part in this great preparation. . . . We were vitally con-

cerned in the carrying out of these great plans and purposes, we understood them, and it was for our sakes they were decreed, and are to be consummated. (Gospel Doctrine, pp. 93-94) MPSG1985:78-79

### President Lorenzo Snow

We are in the world for a purpose. We are not here accidentally. We came here because we were willing to come, and because it was the wish of our Father in heaven that we should come. ¶ We undoubtedly saw very clearly that there was no other way for us to secure what the Father had in store for us. CR1901Apr:2

### Joseph Smith,
### *quoted by Elder Joseph Fielding Smith*

At the first organization in heaven we were all present, and saw the Savior chosen and appointed and the plan of salvation made, and we sanctioned it. (*At the organization of a school of instruction, Jan. 1841*) TPJS:181; MPSG1987:39; DGSM:21

### Abraham,
### *quoted by Joseph Smith*

And there stood one among them that was like unto God, and he said unto those who were with him: We will go down, for there is space there, and we will take of these materials, and we will make an earth whereon these may dwell; 25. And we will prove them herewith, to see if they will do all things whatsoever the Lord their God shall command them; 26. And they who keep their first estate shall be added upon; and they who keep not their first estate shall not have glory in the same kingdom with those who keep their first estate; and they who keep their second estate shall have glory added upon their heads for ever and ever. 27. And the Lord said: Whom shall I send? And one answered like unto the Son of Man: Here am I, send me. And another answered and said: Here am I, send me. And the Lord said: I will send the first. (*Abraham learns of pre-earth life and foreordination*) Abr.3:24-27

### Marion G. Romney

Abraham's account of the great pre-earth heavenly council identifies both God and Satan as participators in that council. (Read Abr.3.) ¶ Marvelous and important is the knowledge revealed in that account—knowledge of things as they were in the distant past, concerning God the Father and his spirit children, and concerning his plans for the creation of this earth. It refers to the gospel plan and identifies Christ and Satan. CR1971Apr:22-23

### Paul

Paul, a servant of God, and an apostle of Jesus Christ, according to the faith of God's elect, and the acknowledging of the truth which is after godliness; 2. In hope of eternal life, which God, that cannot lie, promised before the world began; (*Letter to his companion Titus, about A.D. 64*) Titus 1:1-2

### Bruce R. McConkie

One of the saddest examples of a misconceived and twisted knowledge of an otherwise glorious concept is the all-too-common heresy that there were two plans of salvation; that the Father (presumptively at a loss to know what to do) asked others for proposals; that Christ offered a plan involving agency and Lucifer proposed a plan denying agency; that the Father chose between them; and that Lucifer, his plan being rejected, rebelled, and then there was war in heaven. ¶ Even a cursory knowledge of the overall scheme of things reassures spiritually discerning persons that all things center in the Father; that the plan of salvation which he designed was to save his children, Christ included; and that neither Christ nor Lucifer could of themselves save anyone. As Jesus said: 'The Son can do nothing of himself. . . . I can of mine own self do nothing.' (John 5:19,30) ¶ There is, of course, a sense in which we may refer to Lucifer's proposed modifications of the Father's plan as Lucifer's plan, and Christ made the Father's plan his own by adoption. But what is basically important in this respect is to know that the power to save is vested in the Father, and that he originated, ordained, created, and established his own plan; that he announced it to his children; and that he then asked for a volunteer to be the Redeemer, the Deliverer, the Messiah, who would put the eternal plan of the Eternal Father into eternal operation. (The Mortal Messiah, pp. 48-49 n.3) DGSM:15

### Joseph Smith

The first principles of man are self-existent with God. God himself, finding he was in the midst of spirits and glory, because he was more intelligent, saw proper to institute laws where by the rest could have a privilege to advance like himself. The relationship we have with God places us in a situation to advance in knowledge. He has power to institute laws to instruct the weaker intelligences, that they may be exalted with Himself, so that they might have one glory upon another, and all that knowledge, power, glory, and intelligence, which is requisite in order to save them in the world of spirits. (*To the Church in general conference—to a congregation of 20,000—"King Follett Sermon," April 7, 1844*) (See HC6:302-17, also see The Words of Joseph Smith, pp. 340-62) HC6:312

**556. When the plan of salvation was presented in the premortal world, each person had the opportunity of accepting or rejecting it.**

### Joseph Smith,
*quoted by Elder Joseph Fielding Smith*

At the first organization in heaven we were all present, and saw the Savior chosen and appointed and the plan of salvation made, and we sanctioned it. (*Jan. 1841, at organization of a school of instruction*) TPJS:181; MPSG1987:39

### Elder Joseph Fielding Smith

When the plan of redemption was presented and Jesus was chosen to be the Redeemer of the world, some rebelled. They were not willing to accept him as "the Lamb slain from the foundation of the world." . . . In this great rebellion in heaven, Lucifer, or Satan, a son of the morning, and one-third of the hosts thereof were cast out into the earth because Lucifer sought to destroy the free agency of man and the one-third of the spirits sided with him. He sought the throne of God, and put forth his plan in boldness in that great council, declaring that he would save all, that not one soul should be lost, provided God would give him the glory and the honor. When his plan was rejected for a better one, he rebelled and said, as Isaiah states the case: "I will ascend into heaven, I will exalt my throne above the stars of God. . . . I will be like the Most High.". . . ¶ There were no neutrals in the war in heaven. All took sides either with Christ or with Satan. (Doctrines of Salvation, 1:64,64-66) TLDP:495

### John A. Widtsoe

In our pre-existent state, in the day of the great council, we made a certain agreement with the Almighty. The Lord proposed a plan, conceived by him. [ed. note: conceived by the Almighty God; see Bruce R. McConkie, above, in D-555] We accepted it. Since the plan is intended for all men, we become parties to the salvation of every person under the plan. We agreed, right then and there, to be not only saviors for ourselves, but measurably saviors for the whole human family. We went into partnership with the Lord. The working out of the plan became then not merely the Father's work, and the Savior's work, but also our work. The least of us, the humblest, is in partnership with the Almighty in achieving the purpose of the eternal plan of salvation. . . . (Utah Genealogical and Historical Magazine, Oct. 1934) MPSG1967:87

Related Witnesses:
**Alma, the younger,**
*quoted by Mormon*
And this is the manner after which they were ordained—being called and prepared from the foundation of the world according to the fore-knowledge of God, on account of their exceed-ing faith and good works; in the first place being left to choose good or evil; therefore they having chosen good, and exercising exceeding-ly great faith, are called with a holy calling, yea, with that holy calling which was prepared with, and according to, a preparatory redemp-tion for such. 4. And thus they have been called to this holy calling on account of their faith, while others would reject the Spirit of God on account of the hardness of their hearts and blindness of their minds, while, if it had not been for this they might have had as great privi-lege as their brethren. 5. Or in fine, in the first place they were on the same standing with their brethren; thus this holy calling being prepared from the foundation of the world for such as would not harden their hearts, being in and through the atonement of the Only Begotten Son, who was prepared—(*Alma instructs the people how God calls and ordains men to teach, about 82 B.C.*) Alma 13:3-5

---

**557. Memory of our premortal exi-stence was taken from us when we were sent to earth.**

**Elder George Albert Smith**
When God created the earth and placed our first parents upon it, He did not leave them without knowledge concerning Himself. It is true that there had been taken from them the remem-brance of their pre-existent life, but in His ten-der mercy He talked with them and later He sent His choice servants to instruct them in the things pertaining to eternal life. CR1928Oct:90-91

**Bruce R. McConkie**
Back there [in the premortal life] we were tested as spirit beings, down here we were to be tested as mortal beings, as individuals having mortal bodies which would be subject to the lusts and appetites of mortality—of the flesh. Whereas, back there we underwent a test to determine how we would keep the commandments when we walked by sight and when we were in the presence of the Eternal Father, down here we were to undergo a test to determine how we would respond to his laws when we walked by faith and no longer remembered the life that we had in his presence. ACR(Brisbane)1976:14

**Neal A. Maxwell,**
*also quoting Orson Hyde*
*and Elder Joseph F. Smith*
Agreeing to enter this second estate . . . was like agreeing in advance to anesthetic—the anesthetic of forgetfulness. Doctors do not de-anesthetize a patient, in the midst of what was previously authorized, to ask him, again, if it should be continued. We agreed to come here and to undergo certain experiences under cer-tain conditions. ¶ Elder Orson Hyde said, "We have forgotten! . . . But our forgetfulness can-not alter the facts." (JD7:315) Yet, on occa-sions, there are inklings. President Joseph F. Smith observed how "we often catch spark from the awakened memories of the immortal soul, which lights up our whole being as with the glory of our former home." (Gospel Doctrine, p. 14) CR1985Oct:21

**President Brigham Young,**
*quoted by John A. Widtsoe*
I want to tell you, each and every one of you, that you are well acquainted with God our Heavenly Father, or the great Elohim. You are all well acquainted with him, for there is not a soul of you but what has lived in his house and dwelt with him year after year; and yet you are seeking to become acquainted with him, when the fact is, you have merely forgotten what you did know. (*In Tabernacle, Feb. 1857, JD4:216*) DBY:50

**Elder Joseph Fielding Smith**
Notwithstanding this fact that our recollection of former things was taken away, the character of our lives in the spirit world has much to do with our disposition, desires and mentality here in mortal life. The spirit influences the body to a great extent, just as the body in its desires and cravings has an influence on the spirit. The Lord has caused it to be so, therefore those who were "noble and great ones" in that former world, the Lord fore-ordained to be his prophets and rulers here; for he knew them before they were born, and through the action of the spirit on the body, he knows they will be likely to serve him here. Environment and many other causes, however, have great influence on the progress and destiny of man, but we must not lose sight of the fact that the characteristics of the spirit which were developed through many ages of a former existence play a very important part in our progression through mortal life. ("Is Man Immortal?" IE1916Mar:426) TLDP:496

**Related Witnesses:**
**President Joseph F. Smith**
Our knowledge of persons and things before we came here, combined with the divinity awak-ened within our souls through obedience to the

gospel, powerfully affects, in my opinion, all our likes and dislikes, and guides our preferences in the course of this life, provided we give careful heed to the admonitions of the Spirit. ¶ All those salient truths which come home so forcibly to the head and heart seem but the awakening of the memories of the spirit. Can we know anything here that we did not know before we came? Are not the means of knowledge in the first estate equal to those of this? I think that the spirit, before and after this probation, possess greater facilities, aye, manifold greater, for the acquisition of knowledge, than while manacled and shut up in the prisonhouse of mortality. (*Letter to O. F. Whitney, about 1883*) TLDP:496; MPSG1970-71:27-28

---

### 558. We are spirit children of God—His literal offspring.

**President Joseph F. Smith,
John R. Winder, Anthon H. Lund**
(First Presidency)
All men and women are in the similitude of the universal Father and Mother, and are literally the sons and daughters of Deity. "God created man in His own image." This is just as true of the spirit as it is of the body, which is only the clothing of the spirit, its complement; the two together constituting the soul. The spirit of man is in the form of man, and the spirits of all creatures are in the likeness of their bodies. This was plainly taught by the Prophet Joseph Smith (D&C 77:2). (*From an official statement of First Presidency, IE1909Nov:75-81*) MOFP4:203

**Elder George Albert Smith**
It does seem strange that so many people doubt our divine ancestry, and that God is the Father of our spirits; yet from the very beginning, from the very earliest period of which we have any record in this world, He has been teaching men and women this fact. . . . CR1928Oct:90-91

**President Brigham Young,
quoted by John A. Widtsoe**
Things were first created spiritually: the Father actually begat the spirits, and they were brought forth and lived with him. . . ." (*In Tabernacle, Feb. 8, 1857, JD4:218*) DBY:50

**President Brigham Young,
quoted by John A. Widtsoe**
We are all his children. We are his sons and daughters naturally, and by the principles of eternal life. We are brethren and sisters. (*In new Tabernacle, May 1970, JD13:178*) DBY:53

**Marion G. Romney**
That man is a child of God is the most impor-

tant knowledge available to mortals. Such knowledge is beyond the ken of the uninspired mind. Neither logic, science, philosophy, nor any other field of worldly learning has ever been, or ever will be, able to find it out. Those who limit their search to such learning techniques will continue to be as they always have been, "Ever learning, and never able to come to the knowledge of the truth." (2Tim.3:7) ¶ The only means by which such knowledge can be had is divine revelation. Fortunately for us . . . it has been so revealed repeatedly from Adam until today. CR1973Apr:136

**Bruce R. McConkie**
But we do know that our Eternal Father . . . lives in the family unit. We do know that we are his children, created in his image, endowed with power and ability to become like him. CR1974Apr:103

**Joseph Smith**
That by him, and through him, and of him, the worlds are and were created, and the inhabitants thereof are begotten sons and daughters unto God. (*Vision to Joseph Smith and Sidney Rigdon, Feb. 16, 1832*) D&C 76:24

**Paul**
The Spirit itself beareth witness with our spirit, that we are the children of God: (*Paul writes to the Church in Rome, about A.D. 55*) Rom.8:16

**Paul**
Furthermore we have had fathers of our flesh which corrected us, and we gave them reverence: shall we not much rather be in subjection unto the Father of spirits, and live? (*Paul writes to the Jewish members of the Church, about A.D. 60*) Heb.12:9

**Marion G. Romney**
The theory that man is other than the offspring of God has been, and so long as it is accepted and acted upon, will be, a major factor in blocking man's spiritual growth and in corrupting his morals. . . . ¶ The concept that man is a beast relieves him of a sense of accountability and encourages him to adopt the fatalistic attitude of "eat, drink, and be merry, for tomorrow we die.". . . ¶ The aspirations, desires, and motivations of one who accepts, believes, and by the power of the Holy Spirit obtains a witness to the truth that he is a begotten son or daughter unto God differs from the aspirations of him who believes otherwise, as the growing vine differs from the severed branch. ¶ Knowing that he is a child of God, one does not doubt whether to "deem himself a God or Beast." He is not of "chaos . . . thought," driven by "passion" and "all confused." He is not "fix'd like a plant on his

peculiar spot, to draw nutrition, propagate, and rot." He thinks of himself, as the scriptures teach, possessed of the innate ability, as are all other reproducing offspring, to reach in final maturity the status of his heavenly parents and have "glory added upon [his] head for ever and ever." (Abr.3:26) This is his goal. [Quotations are from Alexander Pope] CR1973Apr:135-36

**Related Witnesses:**

### Paul
Forasmuch then as we are the offspring of God, we ought not to think that the Godhead is like unto gold, or silver, or stone, graven by art and man's device. (*Paul preaches on Mars' Hill about the Unknown God*) Acts 17:29

### Bruce R. McConkie
To begin with, there is a God in heaven who is infinite and eternal, an everlasting, glorified, exalted Being. He has a tabernacle of flesh and bones. He is a resurrected and holy and perfected man, and we are his offspring. We are his spirit children. He lives in the family unit. We are members of his family. We lived in this premortal life with him for an infinite period of time. We were on probation; we were being schooled and tested and examined; we were given the laws and the circumstances so that we could progress and advance. What he did for us was to ordain a plan of salvation. ("Making Our Calling and Election Sure," Brigham Young University Speeches of the Year, pp. 5-6) MPSG1974-75:8

### Joseph Smith,
### *translating the Book of Moses*
And I, the Lord God, had created all the children of men; and not yet a man to till the ground; for in heaven created I them; and there was not yet flesh upon the earth, neither in the water, neither in the air; (*The Lord reveals to Moses the creation of the earth and of man*) Moses 3:5

---

**559. As spirit children of God in the premortal world we were not all alike; each of us had different talents and dispositions.**

### Elder Joseph Fielding Smith
The spirits of men were not equal. They may have had an equal start, and we know they were all innocent in the beginning; but the right of free agency which was given to them enabled some to outstrip others, and thus, through the eons of immortal existence, to become more intelligent, more faithful for they were free to act for themselves, to receive the truth or rebel against it. (Doctrines of Salvation, 1:59) MPSG1985:78

### Bruce R. McConkie
Being subject to law, and having their agency, all the spirits of men, while yet in the Eternal Presence, developed aptitudes, talents, capacities, and abilities of every sort, kind, and degree. During the long expanse of life which then was, an infinite variety of talents and abilities came into being. As the ages rolled, no two spirits remained alike. Mozart became a musician; Einstein centered his interest in mathematics; Michelangelo turned his attention to painting. Cain was a liar, a schemer, a rebel who maintained a close affinity to Lucifer. Abraham and Moses and all of the prophets sought and obtained the talent for spirituality. Mary and Eve were two of the greatest of all the spirit daughters of the Father. The whole house of Israel, known and segregated out from their fellows, was inclined toward spiritual things. And so it went through all the hosts of heaven, each individual developing such talents and abilities as his soul desired. (The Mortal Messiah, 1:23) TLDP:497

### James E. Talmage
Thus the natures, dispositions, and tendencies of men are known to the Father of their spirits, even before they are born into mortality. The word of the Lord came unto Jeremiah, telling him that before he was conceived in the flesh he had been ordained to be a prophet unto the nations. . . . ¶ Doubtless He knows of some spirits that they await only the opportunity of choice between good and evil to choose the latter and to accomplish their own destruction. . . . There are others whose integrity and faithfulness have been demonstrated in their pristine state; the Father knows how unreservedly they may be trusted, and many of them are called even in their mortal youth to special and exalted labors as commissioned servants of the Most High. AF:172-74

### Abraham,
### *quoted by Joseph Smith*
Now the Lord had shown unto me, Abraham, the intelligences that were organized before the world was; and among all these there were many of the noble and great ones; 23. And God saw these souls that they were good, and he stood in the midst of them, and he said: These I will make my rulers; for he stood among those that were spirits, and he saw that they were good; and he said unto me: Abraham, thou art one of them; thou wast chosen before thou wast born. 24. And there stood one among them that was like unto God, and he said unto those who were with him: We will go down, for there is

space there, and we will take of these materials, and we will make an earth whereon these may dwell; 25. And we will prove them herewith, to see if they will do all things whatsoever the Lord their God shall command them; (*Abraham learns of pre-earth life and foreordination*) Abr.3:22-25

### Elder David O. McKay
From this revelation [Abr. 3:23], we may infer two things: first, that there were among those spirits [in pre-mortal life] different degrees of intelligence, varying grades of achievement, retarded and advanced spiritual attainment; second, that there were no national distinctions among those spirits such as Americans, Europeans, Asiatics, Australians, etc. Such "bounds of habitation" would have to be "determined" when the spirits entered their earthly existence or second estate. . . . ¶ . . . . Our place in this world would then be determined by our own advancement or condition in the pre-mortal state, just as our place in our future existence will be determined by what we do here in mortality. ¶ When, therefore, the Creator said to Abraham, and to others of his attainment, "You I will make my rulers," there could exist no feeling of envy or jealousy among the million other spirits, for those who were "good and great" were but receiving their just reward. (*Home Memories of President David O. McKay*, pp. 228-30) DGSM:14

### Elder Joseph Fielding Smith
The spirits of men were created with different dispositions and likes and talents. Some evidently were mechanically inclined, from them have come our inventors. Some loved music and hence they have become great musicians. We evidently brought to this world some if not all of the inclinations and talents that we had there. The fact that one person finds one bent, like mathematics easy and another finds it difficult, may, in my judgment, be traced to the spirit existence. So with other talents and skills. It was these characteristics that enabled our Eternal Father to choose certain individuals for certain work on the earth, such as Adam, Abraham, Moses and Joseph Smith. The Lord chose Cyrus and named him one hundred years before he was born to perform the work assigned to him on the earth. It is my judgment that thousands of others were chosen for their special fields because they showed talents and dispositions in that spirit world. (*Answers to Gospel Questions*, 5:138-39) TLDP:202

### Bruce R. McConkie
In this prior life, this premortal existence, this preexistence, we developed various capacities

and talents. Some developed them in one field and some in another. The most important of all fields was the field of spirituality, the ability, the talent, the capacity to recognize truth. ("Making Our Calling and Election Sure," Brigham Young University Speeches of the Year, 1969, pp. 5-6) MPSG1974-75:9

### Bruce R. McConkie
When we come into mortality, we bring the talents, capacities, and abilities acquired by obedience to law in our prior existence. Mozart composed and published sonatas when but eight years of age because he was born with musical talent. Melchizedek came into this world with such faith and spiritual capacity that "when a child he feared God, and stopped the mouths of lions, and quenched the violence of fire." (Gen.14:26, Inspired Version) CR1974Apr:103; MPSG1976-77:221-22

---

**560. In the premortal world the Lord called (foreordained) certain persons to fulfill special assignments and missions on earth.**

### Bruce R. McConkie
The work to be done by John the Baptist, by the ancient Twelve, by Columbus, by the signers of the Declaration of Independence, and by the framers of the Constitution of the United States were all known and arranged for in advance. And all these are but illustrations and patterns, for all of the Lord's work is planned and prepared in advance, and those who are called and chosen to do the work receive their commission and ordination from him, first in the preexistence and then, if they remain true and faithful, again here in mortality. CR1974Apr:102-03; MPSG1987:42

### President John Taylor
There are thousands of men upon the earth today, among the Saints of God, of whom it was decreed before they came that they should occupy the positions they have occupied and do occupy, and many of them have performed their part and gone home; others are left to still fulfill the duties and responsibilities devolving upon them. (*At funeral service of Bishop Miller, July 24, 1882, JD23:177*) TLDP:202

### Elder Wilford Woodruff
Here we are a handful of people chosen out of some twelve or fourteen hundred millions of people; and my faith in regard to this matter is that before we were born . . . we were chosen to come forth in this day and generation and do the work which God has designed should be

done. (*In Assembly Hall, July 3, 1880, JD21:193*) TLDP:202

### Elder Joseph Fielding Smith

The spirits of men were created with different dispositions and likes and talents. Some evidently were mechanically inclined, from them have come our inventors. Some loved music and hence they have become great musicians. We evidently brought to this world some if not all of the inclinations and talents that we had there. The fact that one person finds one bent, like mathematics easy and another finds it difficult, may, in my judgment, be traced to the spirit existence. So with other talents and skills. It was these characteristics that enabled our Eternal Father to choose certain individuals for certain work on the earth, such as Adam, Abraham, Moses and Joseph Smith. The Lord chose Cyrus and named him one hundred years before he was born to perform the work assigned to him on the earth. It is my judgment that thousands of others were chosen for their special fields because they showed talents and dispositions in that spirit world. (Answers to Gospel Questions, 5:138-39) TLDP:202

### Elder Joseph Fielding Smith

During the ages in which we dwelt in the premortal state we not only developed our various characteristics and showed our worthiness and ability, or the lack of it, but we were also where such progress could be observed. It is reasonable to believe that there was a Church organization there. The heavenly beings were living in a perfectly arranged society. Every person knew his place. Priesthood, without any question, had been conferred and the leaders were chosen to officiate. Ordinances pertaining to that pre-existence were required and the love of God prevailed. Under such conditions it was natural for our Father to discern and choose those who were most worthy and evaluate the talents of each individual. He knew not only what each of us could do, but what each of us *would* do when put to the test and when responsibility was given us. Then, when the time came for our habitation on mortal earth, all things were prepared and the servants of the Lord chosen and ordained to their respective missions. (The Way to Perfection, pp. 50-51) DGSM:14

### Related Witnesses:

### Bruce R. McConkie

There was only one Christ, and there is only one Mary. Each was noble and great in the preexistence, and each was foreordained to the ministry he or she performed. We cannot but think that the Father would choose the greatest female spirit to be the mother of his Son, even as

he chose the male spirit like unto him to be the Savior. (The Millennial Messiah, pp. 326-27, n.4) MPSG1987:41

### Nephi, son of Lehi

And I said unto him: A virgin, most beautiful and fair above all other virgins. 16. And he said unto me: Knowest thou the condescension of God? 17. And I said unto him: I know that he loveth his children; nevertheless, I do not know the meaning of all things. 18. And he said unto me: Behold, the virgin whom thou seest is the mother of the Son of God, after the manner of the flesh. 19. And it came to pass that I beheld that she was carried away in the Spirit; and after she had been carried away in the Spirit for the space of a time the angel spake unto me, saying: Look! 20. And I looked and beheld the virgin again, bearing a child in her arms. (*Nephi in a vision sees Mary, the mother of the Son of God, hundreds of years before her coming to earth, 600-592 B.C.*) 1Ne.11:15-20

### Nephi, son of Lehi

And I looked and beheld a man among the Gentiles, who was separated from the seed of my brethren by the many waters; and I beheld the Spirit of God, that it came down and wrought upon the man; and he went forth upon the many waters, even unto the seed of my brethren, who were in the promised land. 13. And it came to pass that I beheld the Spirit of God, that it wrought upon other Gentiles; and they went forth out of captivity, upon the many waters. (*An angel shows Nephi the discovery and colonizing of America, 600-592 B.C.*) 1Ne.13:12-13

### Joseph Smith,
*receiving the Word of the Lord*

And for this purpose have I established the Constitution of this land, by the hands of wise men whom I raised up unto this very purpose, and redeemed the land by the shedding of blood. (*Revelation at the time of great persecution in Missouri, Dec. 16, 1833, affirming the purpose of the Constitution was to protect the rights and agency of individuals—see verses 77-79*) D&C 101:80

---

**561. In the premortal world the Lord chose those who were to be rulers in the church of God on earth.**

### Joseph Smith,
*quoted by Elder Joseph Fielding Smith*

Every man who has a calling to minister to the inhabitants of the world was ordained to that very purpose in the Grand Council of heaven before this world was. I suppose I was ordained to this very office in that Grand Council. (*Sunday sermon at the Stand in Nauvoo, Ill., May 1844*) TPJS:365; DGSM:57; MPSG1987:40

**President Joseph F. Smith**

I observed that they [The Prophet Joseph Smith, and my father, Hyrum Smith, Brigham Young, John Taylor, Wilford Woodruff, and other choice spirits who were reserved to come forth in the fulness of times to take part in laying the foundations of the great latter-day work] were also among the noble and great ones who were chosen in the beginning to be rulers in the Church of God. 56. Even before they were born, they, with many others, received their first lessons in the world of spirits and were prepared to come forth in the due time of the Lord to labor in his vineyard for the salvation of the souls of men. (*Vision regarding the Savior's visit to the spirits of the dead, Oct. 3, 1918*) D&C 138:55-56

**Elder Joseph F. Smith**

No doubt all the prominent men who have figured in any dispensation of the Gospel since the days of our father, Adam, until the present, were inspired of the Almighty from their childhood, and were chosen and selected even from or before their birth. (*In Assembly Hall, Feb. 17, 1884, JD25:52*) TLDP:201

**Bruce R. McConkie**

I believe that Spencer W. Kimball was foreordained to be the president of The Church of Jesus Christ of Latter-day Saints; to be the prophet, seer, and revelator to the Lord's people; and to be the mouthpiece of God on earth for the time and season that lies ahead. . . . ¶ But more than mortal birth, more than mortal preparation are involved. He was born in the household of faith for a reason, and it was not this life alone that prepared him to stand as a minister of light and truth and salvation to his fellow mortals. The fact is, he is a spirit son of God who was called and chosen and foreordained before the foundations of the earth were laid, and he is now fulfilling the destiny designed for him from the preexistence, and promised him, in our presence, as we sat with him in the grand council when God himself was there. . . . President Kimball now wears the mantle of Joseph Smith and was a participant in the operation of the same law of foreordination. CR1974Apr:100-01; MPSG1975-76:53

**Bruce R. McConkie**

May I say there is no chance involved in the call of these brethren to direct the Lord's work on earth. . . . He selects and foreordains his

ministers; he sends them to earth at the times before appointed; he guides and directs their continuing mortal preparations; and he then calls them to those positions they were foreordained to receive from before the foundations of the earth. CR1974Apr:101

**Abraham,**
**quoted by Joseph Smith**

Now the Lord had shown unto me, Abraham, the intelligences that were organized before the world was; and among all these there were many of the noble and great ones; 23. And God saw these souls that they were good, and he stood in the midst of them, and he said: These I will make my rulers; for he stood among those that were spirits, and he saw that they were good; and he said unto me: Abraham, thou art one of them; thou wast chosen before thou wast born. 24. And there stood one among them that was like unto God, and he said unto those who were with him: We will go down, for there is space there, and we will take of these materials, and we will make an earth whereon these may dwell; 25. And we will prove them herewith, to see if they will do all things whatsoever the Lord their God shall command them; (*Abraham learns of pre-earth life and foreordination*) Abr.3:22-25

**Alma, the younger,**
**quoted by Mormon**

And this is the manner after which they were ordained—being called and prepared from the foundation of the world according to the foreknowledge of God, on account of their exceeding faith and good works; in the first place being left to choose good or evil; therefore they having chosen good, and exercising exceedingly great faith, are called with a holy calling, yea, with that holy calling which was prepared with, and according to, a preparatory redemption for such. 4. And thus they have been called to this holy calling on account of their faith, while others would reject the Spirit of God on account of the hardness of their hearts and blindness of their minds, while, if it had not been for this they might have had as great privilege as their brethren. 5. Or in fine, in the first place they were on the same standing with their brethren; thus this holy calling being prepared from the foundation of the world for such as would not harden their hearts, being in and through the atonement of the Only Begotten Son, who was prepared—(*Alma instructs the people how God calls and ordains men to teach, about 82 B.C.*) Alma 13:3-5

**Elder Wilford Woodruff**

Joseph Smith was ordained before he came here, the same as Jeremiah was. Said the Lord unto him, "Before you were begotten I knew you," etc. ¶ So do I believe with regard to this people, so do I believe with regard to the apostles, the high priests, seventies and the elders of Israel bearing the holy priesthood. I believe they were ordained before they came here; and I believe the God of Israel has raised them up, and has watched over them from their youth, and has carried them through all the scenes of life both seen and unseen, and has prepared them as instruments in his hands to take this kingdom and bear it off. If this be so, what manner of men ought we to be? If anything under the heavens should humble men before the Lord and before one another, it should be the fact that we have been called of God. (*General conference, Oct. 10, 1880, JD21:317*) TLDP:202

**Related Witnesses:**

### President Brigham Young,
### *quoted by John A. Widtsoe*

It was decreed in the counsels of eternity, long before the foundations of the earth were laid, that he, Joseph Smith, should be the man, in the last dispensation of this world, to bring forth the word of God to the people, and receive the fulness of the keys and power of the Priesthood of the Son of God. The Lord had his eyes upon him, and upon his father, and upon his father's father, and upon their progenitors clear back to Abraham, and from Abraham to the flood, from the flood to Enoch, and from Enoch to Adam. He has watched that family and that blood as it has circulated from its fountain to the birth of that man. He was fore-ordained in eternity to preside over this last dispensation. (*In Tabernacle, Oct. 1859, JD7:289*) DBY:108 DGSM:63

### Jeremiah

Before I formed thee in the belly I knew thee; and before thou camest forth out of the womb I sanctified thee, and I ordained thee a prophet unto the nations. (*Revelation, the word of the Lord to Jeremiah, about 628 B.C.*) Jer.1:5

### Paul

According as he hath chosen us in him before the foundation of the world, that we should be holy and without blame before him in love: (*Letter to the Saints at Ephesus in Asia Minor, about A.D. 62*) Eph.1:4

---

562. **Demonstrated worthiness was the basis upon which those in the premortal world were called and chosen (foreordained) to minister in the Lord's vineyard on earth.**

### Elder Joseph Fielding Smith

During the ages in which we dwelt in the premortal state we not only developed our various characteristics and showed our worthiness and ability, or the lack of it, but we were also where such progress could be observed. It is reasonable to believe that there was a Church organization there. The heavenly beings were living in a perfectly arranged society. Every person knew his place. Priesthood, without any question, had been conferred and the leaders were chosen to officiate. Ordinances pertaining to that pre-existence were required and the love of God prevailed. Under such conditions it was natural for our Father to discern and choose those who were most worthy and evaluate the talents of each individual. He knew not only what each of us could do, but what each of us *would* do when put to the test and when responsibility was given us. Then, when the time came for our habitation on mortal earth, all things were prepared and the servants of the Lord chosen and ordained to their respective missions. (The Way to Perfection, pp. 50-51) DGSM:14

### Alma, the younger,
### *quoted by Mormon*

And this is the manner after which they were ordained—being called and prepared from the foundation of the world according to the foreknowledge of God, on account of their exceeding faith and good works; in the first place being left to choose good or evil; therefore they having chosen good, and exercising exceedingly great faith, are called with a holy calling, yea, with that holy calling which was prepared with, and according to, a preparatory redemption for such. 4. And thus they have been called to this holy calling on account of their faith, while others would reject the Spirit of God on account of the hardness of their hearts and blindness of their minds, while, if it had not been for this they might have had as great privilege as their brethren. 5. Or in fine, in the first place they were on the same standing with their brethren; thus this holy calling being prepared from the foundation of the world for such as would not harden their hearts, being in and through the atonement of the Only Begotten Son, who was prepared—(*Alma instructs the people how God calls and ordains men to teach, about 82 B.C.*) Alma 13:3-5

### Bruce R. McConkie

This election to a chosen lineage is based on pre-existent worthiness and is thus made "according to the foreknowledge of God." (1Pet.1:2) Those so grouped together during their mortal probation have more abundant opportunities to make and keep the covenants of salvation, a right which they earned by pre-existent devotion to the cause of righteousness. As part of this election, Abraham and others of the noble and great spirits were chosen before they were born for the particular missions assigned to them in this life. (Doctrinal New Testament Commentary, 2:274) MPSG1987:41

**Bruce R. McConkie**

Back there [in the premortal life] we were tested as spirit beings, down here we were to be tested as mortal beings, as individuals having mortal bodies which would be subject to the lusts and appetites of mortality—of the flesh. Whereas, back there we underwent a test to determine how we would keep the commandments when we walked by sight and when we were in the presence of the Eternal Father, down here we were to undergo a test to determine how we would respond to his laws when we walked by faith and no longer remembered the life that we had in his presence. ACR(Brisbane)1976:14

**Elder David O. McKay**

From this revelation [Abraham 3:23], we may infer two things: first, that there were among those spirits [in premortal life] different degrees of intelligence, varying grades of achievement, retarded and advanced spiritual attainment; second, that there were no national distinctions among those spirits such as Americans, Europeans, Asiatics, Australians, etc. Such "bounds of habitation" would have to be "determined" when the spirits entered their earthly existence or second estate. . . . ¶ . . . . Our place in this world would then be determined by our own advancement or condition in the pre-mortal state, just as our place in our future existence will be determined by what we do here in mortality. ¶ When, therefore, the Creator said to Abraham, and to others of his attainment, "You I will make my rulers," there could exist no feeling of envy or jealousy among the million other spirits, for those who were "good and great" were but receiving their just reward. (Home Memories of President David O. McKay, pp. 228-30) DGSM:14

---

**563. In the premortal world God knew each of us individually before we were born into mortality.**

**James E. Talmage**

Thus the natures, dispositions, and tendencies of men are known to the Father of their spirits, even before they are born into mortality. The word of the Lord came unto Jeremiah, telling him that before he was conceived in the flesh he had been ordained to be a prophet unto the nations. . . . ¶ Doubtless He knows of some spirits that they await only the opportunity of choice between good and evil to choose the latter and to accomplish their own destruction. . . . There are others whose integrity and faithfulness have been demonstrated in their pristine state; the Father knows how unreservedly they may be trusted, and many of them are called even in their mortal youth to special and exalted labors as commissioned servants of the Most High. . . . ¶ But we are not left to mere inference on a basis of analogy; the scriptures plainly teach that the spirits of mankind are known and numbered unto God before their earthly advent. In his farewell administration to Israel Moses sang: "Remember the days of old . . . When the Most High divided to the nations their inheritance, when he separated the sons of Adam, he set the bounds of the people according to the number of the children of Israel." From this we learn that the earth was allotted to the nations, according to the number of the children of Israel; it is evident therefore that the number was known prior to the existence of the Israelitish nation in the flesh; this is most easily explained on the basis of previous existence in which the spirits of the future nation were known. ¶ No chance is possible, therefore, in the number or extent of the temporal creations of God. The population of the earth is fixed according to the number of spirits appointed to take tabernacles of flesh upon this planet; when these have all come forth in the order and time appointed, then, and not till then, shall the end come. AF:172-76

**Elder Joseph Fielding Smith**

Under such conditions it was natural for our Father to discern and choose those who were most worthy and evaluate the talents of each individual. He knew not only what each of us could do, but what each of us *would* do when put to the test and when responsibility was given us. Then, when the time came for our habitation on mortal earth, all things were prepared and the servants of the Lord chosen and ordained to their respective missions. (The Way to Perfection, pp. 50-51) DGSM:14

**Elder Joseph Fielding Smith**

The numbers of the children of Israel were known and the bounds of their habitation fixed, in the days of old when the Lord divided to the nations their inheritance. We conclude, therefore, that there must have been a division of the spirits of men in the spiritual world, and those who were appointed to be the children of Israel were separated and prepared for a special inheritance. (Doctrines of Salvation, 1:59) TLDP:202-03

### Bruce R. McConkie

This election to a chosen lineage is based on pre-existent worthiness and is thus made "according to the foreknowledge of God." (1Pet. 1:2) Those so grouped together during their mortal probation have more abundant opportunities to make and keep the covenants of salvation, a right which they earned by pre-existent devotion to the cause of righteousness. As part of this election, Abraham and others of the noble and great spirits were chosen before they were born for the particular missions assigned to them in this life. (Doctrinal New Testament Commentary, 2:274) MPSG1987:41

**Related Witnesses:**

### President Brigham Young, quoted by John A. Widtsoe

I want to tell you, each and every one of you, that you are well acquainted with God our Heavenly Father, or the great Elohim. You are all well acquainted with him, for there is not a soul of you but what has lived in his house and dwelt with him year after year; and yet you are seeking to become acquainted with him, when the fact is, you have merely forgotten what you did know. ¶ There is not a person here to-day but what is a son or a daughter of that Being. In the spirit world their spirits were first begotten and brought forth, and they lived there with their parents for ages before they came here. This, perhaps, is hard for many to believe, but it is the greatest nonsense in the world not to believe it. If you do not believe it, cease to call him Father; and when you pray, pray to some other character. (*In Tabernacle, Feb. 8, 1857, JD4:216*) DBY:50

### Recorded in Deuteronomy

Remember the days of old, consider the years of many generations: ask thy father, and he will shew thee; thy elders, and they will tell thee. 8. When the most High divided to the nations their inheritance, when he separated the sons of Adam, he set the bounds of the people according to the number of the children of Israel. (*Moses' farewell administration to Israel*) Deut.32:7-8

### Peter

Elect according to the foreknowledge of God the Father, through sanctification of the Spirit, unto obedience and sprinkling of the blood of Jesus Christ: Grace unto you, and peace, be multiplied. (*Letter to the churches in modern Asia Minor, about A.D. 60*) 1Pet.1:2

---

**564. Physical deformities upon birth into mortal life are not punishment for misbehavior of the spirit in premortal life.**

### Elder Joseph Fielding Smith

We must in all reason conclude that some physical defect at birth is due to some accident or other cause that can be laid at the door of mortal conditions and not to some premortal defect or punishment in the spirit world. When the disciples came to the Savior and asked the question concerning the man who was born blind, the question whether this defect came upon him because of a condition existing in the spirit world, he gave them the assurance that such was not the case. We have reason to believe that every spirit that comes into this world was whole and free from such defects in the pre-existence. ¶ We are subject to all the vicissitudes that go with a temporal existence, sickness and physical defects as well as health, but such things will not exist in the world of spirits nor in the kingdom of God after the resurrection. The Lord has made this perfectly clear. (Answers to Gospel Questions) MPSG1972-73:55-56

### John, also quoting Jesus

And as Jesus passed by, he saw a man which was blind from his birth. 2. And his disciples asked him, saying, Master, who did sin, this man, or his parents, that he was born blind? 3. Jesus answered, Neither hath this man sinned, nor his parents: but that the works of God should be made manifest in him. (*Jesus heals a man born blind, on the Sabbath*) John 9:1-3

### James E. Faust

The Savior's teaching that handicaps are not punishment for sin, either in the parents or the handicapped, can also be understood and applied in today's circumstances. How can it possibly be said that an innocent child born with a special problem is being punished? Why should parents who have kept themselves free from social disease, addicting chemicals, and other debilitating substances which might affect their offspring imagine that the birth of a disabled child is some form of divine disapproval? Usually, both the parents and the children are blameless. CR1984Oct:72-73

### James E. Talmage

We are not warranted, however, in assuming that all bodily ills are the result of culpable sin; and against such a conception stands the Lord's combined instruction and rebuke to those who, in the case of a man born blind, asked who had sinned, the man or his parents to bring so grievous an affliction upon him, to which inquiry our Lord replied that the man's blindness was due neither to his own sin nor to that of his parents. JTC:192

**James E. Talmage**

Jesus and His disciples saw the sightless one upon the street. The poor man lived by begging. The disciples, eager to learn, asked: "Master, who did sin, this man, or his parents, that he was born blind?" The Lord's reply was: "Neither hath this man sinned, nor his parents: but that the works of God should be made manifest in him." The disciples' question implied their belief in a state of moral agency and choice antedating mortality; else, how could they have thought of the man having sinned so as to bring upon himself congenital blindness? We are expressly told that he was born blind. That he might have been a sufferer from the sins of his parents was conceivable. The disciples evidently had been taught the great truth of an antemortal existence. It is further to be seen that they looked upon bodily affliction as the result of personal sin. Their generalization was too broad; for, while as shown by instances heretofore cited, individual wickedness may and does bring physical ills in its train, man is liable to err in his judgment as to the ultimate cause of affliction. The Lord's reply was sufficing; the man's blindness would be turned to account in bringing about a manifestation of divine power. JTC:412-13

---

565. Every spirit born on earth is innocent.

**Joseph Smith**

Every spirit of man was innocent in the beginning; and God having redeemed man from the fall, men became again, in their infant state, innocent before God. (*Revelation, May 6, 1833*) D&C 93:38

**Delbert L. Stapley**

We learn from this revelation [D&C 93:38] that in the beginning of mortal life all mankind is innocent before God and, therefore, is like the beginning river of water, pure and undefiled. As the polluted tributaries of water enter the main stream, our lives too become polluted when we allow tributaries of evil and wickedness to enter. It is these tributaries of evil we must be concerned about and fortify ourselves against. Wickedness never was happiness, but to the contrary, it is depressing; it destroys conscience and ultimately the spiritual life of the constant, erring individual. CR1971Oct:104

**Elder Joseph Fielding Smith**

[T]he spirits of men were not equal. They may have had an equal start, and we know they were all innocent in the beginning; but the right of free agency which was given to them enabled some to outstrip others, and thus, through the eons of immortal existence, to become more intelligent, more faithful for they were free to act for themselves, to receive the truth or rebel against it. (Doctrines of Salvation, 1:59) MPSG1985:78

---

566. The devil rebelled against God in the premortal world, sought to take control of the kingdom of God, and there was war in heaven.

**Elder Joseph Fielding Smith**

When the plan of redemption was presented and Jesus was chosen to be the Redeemer of the world, some rebelled. They were not willing to accept him as "the Lamb slain from the foundation of the world." . . . In this great rebellion in heaven, Lucifer, or Satan, a son of the morning, and one-third of the hosts thereof were cast out into the earth because Lucifer sought to destroy the free agency of man and the one-third of the spirits sided with him. He sought the throne of God, and put forth his plan in boldness in that great council, declaring that he would save all, that not one soul should be lost, provided God would give him the glory and the honor. When his plan was rejected for a better one, he rebelled and said, as Isaiah states the case: "I will ascend into heaven, I will exalt my throne above the stars of God. . . . I will be like the Most High.". . . ¶ There were no neutrals in the war in heaven. All took sides either with Christ or with Satan. (Doctrines of Salvation, 1:64-66) TLDP:495

**Joseph Smith**

And this we saw also, and bear record, that an angel of God who was in authority in the presence of God, who rebelled against the Only Begotten Son whom the Father loved and who was in the bosom of the Father, was thrust down from the presence of God and the Son, 26. And was called Perdition, for the heavens wept over him—he was Lucifer, a son of the morning. 27. And we beheld, and lo, he is fallen! is fallen, even a son of the morning! 28. And while we were yet in the Spirit, the Lord commanded us that we should write the vision; for we beheld Satan, that old serpent, even the devil, who rebelled against God, and sought to take the kingdom of our God and his Christ— (*Vision to Joseph Smith and Sidney Rigdon, Feb. 16, 1832*) D&C 76:25-28

**Joseph Smith,**
*translating the Book of Moses*

And I, the Lord God, spake unto Moses, saying: That Satan, whom thou hast commanded in the name of mine Only Begotten, is the same which was from the beginning, and he came before me, saying—Behold, here am I, send me, I will be thy son, and I will redeem all mankind, that one soul shall not be lost, and surely I will do it; wherefore give me thine honor. 2. But, behold, my Beloved Son, which was my Beloved and Chosen from the beginning, said unto me—Father, thy will be done, and the glory be thine forever. 3. Wherefore, because that Satan rebelled against me, and sought to destroy the agency of man, which I, the Lord God, had given him, and also, that I should give unto him mine own power; by the power of mine Only Begotten, I caused that he should be cast down; 4. And he became Satan, yea, even the devil, the father of all lies, to deceive and to blind men, and to lead them captive at his will, even as many as would not hearken unto my voice. (*Revelation, 1830; Moses describes the fall of Satan*) Moses 4:1-4

**Joseph Smith,**
*receiving the Word of the Lord*

And it came to pass that Adam, being tempted of the devil—for, behold, the devil was before Adam, for he rebelled against me, saying, Give me thine honor, which is my power; and also a third part of the hosts of heaven turned he away from me because of their agency; 37. And they were thrust down, and thus came the devil and his angels; 38. And, behold, there is a place prepared for them from the beginning, which place is hell. (*Revelation received Sept. 1830; the fall of Adam and the atonement of Christ bring salvation*) D&C 29:36-38

**George F. Richards**

I call attention to the war that took place in heaven of which we read in the Bible, the 12th chapter of Revelation, and the Pearl of Great Price [Moses 4:1-4], where one of our Father's sons who was regarded as a noble and great one, presented a plan for our salvation that would oblige us to comply with the law without the exercise of our agency, and he would take away from our Father in heaven his honor and his glory. In that council in heaven the Firstborn of the Father in the spirit came forward with a simple but forceful declaration: "Father, thy will be done, and the glory be thine forever." ¶ The battle was fought, whatever its nature, upon this platform of principles, and we have reason to believe that we were among those who stood with the Savior, our Elder Brother,

true and faithful, and those who rebelled were cast out and down. . . . CR1941Oct:20-21

**President John Taylor**

The question then arose [in the pre-mortal heaven], how, and upon what principle, should the salvation, exaltation and eternal glory of God's sons be brought about? It is evident that at that Council certain plans had been proposed and discussed, and that after a full discussion of those principles, and the declaration to the Father's will pertaining to His design, Lucifer came before the Father, with a plan of his own, saying, "Behold I, send me, I will be thy Son, and I will redeem all mankind, that one soul shall not be lost, and surely I will do it; wherefore, give me thine honor." But Jesus, on hearing this statement made by Lucifer, said, "Father, thy will be done, and the glory be thine forever." . . . He also wished the glory to be given to his Father, who, as God the Father, and the originator and designer of the plan, had a right to all the honor and glory. But Lucifer wanted to introduce a plan contrary to the will of his Father, and then wanted His honor, and said; "I will save every soul of man, wherefore give me thine honor." He wanted to go contrary to the will of his Father, and presumptuously sought to deprive man of his free agency . . . and again, Lucifer wanted the honor and power of his Father, to enable him to carry out principles which were contrary to the Father's wish. (The Mediation and Atonement, pp. 93-94) TLDP:494

**John**

And there was war in heaven: Michael and his angels fought against the dragon; and the dragon fought and his angels, 8. And prevailed not; neither was their place found any more in heaven. 9. And the great dragon was cast out, that old serpent, called the Devil, and Satan, which deceiveth the whole world: he was cast out into the earth, and his angels were cast out with him. (*John sees the War in Heaven*) Rev.12:7-9

---

**567.** As a result of the war in the premortal world, the devil and a third part of the hosts of heaven were thrust out.

**Joseph Smith,**
*receiving the Word of the Lord*

And it came to pass that Adam, being tempted of the devil—for, behold, the devil was before Adam, for he rebelled against me, saying, Give me thine honor, which is my power; and also a third part of the hosts of heaven turned he away from me because of their agency; 37. And they were thrust down, and thus came the devil and his angels; 38. And, behold, there is a place prepared for them from the beginning, which place is hell. (*Revelation in presence of six elders, Sept. 1830*) D&C 29:36-38

### Elder Joseph Fielding Smith

We learn that our Father called a council, and the plan of salvation was presented to all. Lucifer rebelled and led away one-third of the spirits, and they were cast out with him. . . . ¶ It was necessary that all should have the plan of salvation placed before them in that spirit existence, otherwise there could have been no rebellion against the plan and if all had not had the privilege of receiving or rejecting it, there could have been no punishment for rebellion. (*Answers to Gospel Questions*) MPSG1972-73:49-50

### Elder Joseph Fielding Smith

The punishment of Satan and the third of the host of heaven who followed him, was that they were denied the privilege of being born into this world and receiving mortal bodies. They did not keep their first estate and were denied the opportunity of eternal progression. The Lord cast them out into the earth, where they became the tempters of mankind—the devil and his angels. (Doctrines of Salvation, 1:65) DGSM:15

### President Brigham Young, *quoted by John A. Widtsoe*

In regard to the battle in heaven . . . how much of a battle it was I have forgotten. I cannot relate the principal circumstances, it is so long since it happened; but I do not think it lasted very long; for when Lucifer, the Son of the Morning, claimed the privilege of having the control of this earth, and redeeming it, a contention arose; but I do not think it took long to cast down one-third of the hosts of heaven, as it is written in the Bible. But let me tell you that it was one-third part of the spirits who were prepared to take tabernacles upon this earth, and who rebelled against the other two-thirds of the heavenly host; and they were cast down to this world. It is written that they were cast down to the earth. They were cast down to this globe—to this terra firma that you and I walk upon, and whose atmosphere we breathe. One-third part of the spirits that were prepared for this earth rebelled against Jesus Christ, and were cast down to the earth, and they have been opposed to him from that day to this, with Lucifer at their head. He is their general—Lucifer, the Son of the Morning. He was once a brilliant and influential character in heaven, and we will know more about him hereafter. (*In Bowery, July 19, 1857, JD5:54-55*) DBY:54-55

### Related Witnesses:
#### John

And there was war in heaven: Michael and his angels fought against the dragon; and the dragon fought and his angels, 8. And prevailed not; neither was their place found any more in heaven. 9. And the great dragon was cast out, that old serpent, called the Devil, and Satan, which deceiveth the whole world: he was cast out into the earth, and his angels were cast out with him. (*The Apostle John sees the War in Heaven*) Rev.12:7-9

#### Peter

For if God spared not the angels that sinned, but cast them down to hell, and delivered them into chains of darkness, to be reserved unto judgment; (*Peter writes to members of the Church, about A.D. 60 to 64*) 2Pet.2:4

#### Jesus, *recorded in Luke*

And he said unto them, I beheld Satan as lightning fall from heaven. (*Jesus speaks to the Seventy*) Luke 10:18

#### Jacob, brother of Nephi, *quoted by Nephi*

O the wisdom of God, his mercy and grace! For behold, if the flesh should rise no more our spirits must become subject to that angel who fell from before the presence of the Eternal God, and became the devil, to rise no more. (*Jacob teaches the Atonement to the people of Nephi, 559-545 B.C.*) 2Ne.9:8

#### John

Therefore rejoice, ye heavens, and ye that dwell in them. Woe to the inhabiters of the earth and of the sea! for the devil is come down unto you, having great wrath, because he knoweth that he hath but a short time. 13. And when the dragon saw that he was cast unto the earth, he persecuted the woman which brought forth the man child. (*John sees the War in Heaven*) Rev.12:12-13

#### Joseph Smith, *translating the Book of Moses*

Wherefore, because that Satan rebelled against me, and sought to destroy the agency of man, which I, the Lord God, had given him, and also, that I should give unto him mine own power; by the power of mine Only Begotten, I caused that he should be cast down; 4. And he became Satan, yea, even the devil, the father of all lies, to deceive and to blind men, and to lead them captive at his will, even as many as would not hearken unto my voice. (*The record of Moses: the Lord describes Satan's rebellion in the premortal world*) Moses 4:3-4

### Isaiah

How art thou fallen from heaven, O Lucifer, son of the morning! how art thou cut down to the ground, which didst weaken the nations! 13. For thou hast said in thine heart, I will ascend into heaven, I will exalt my throne above the stars of God: I will sit also upon the mount of the congregation, in the sides of the north: 14. I will ascend above the heights of the clouds; I will be like the most High. 15. Yet thou shalt be brought down to hell, to the sides of the pit. 16. They that see thee shall narrowly look upon thee, and consider thee, saying, Is this the man that made the earth to tremble, that did shake kingdoms; (*Lucifer is cast out of heaven for rebellion*) Isa.14:12-16

### Joseph Smith

And this we saw also, and bear record, that an angel of God who was in authority in the presence of God, who rebelled against the Only Begotten Son whom the Father loved and who was in the bosom of the Father, was thrust down from the presence of God and the Son, 26. And was called Perdition, for the heavens wept over him—he was Lucifer, a son of the morning. 27. And we beheld, and lo, he is fallen! is fallen, even a son of the morning! 28. And while we were yet in the Spirit, the Lord commanded us that we should write the vision; for we beheld Satan, that old serpent, even the devil, who rebelled against God, and sought to take the kingdom of our God and his Christ— 29. Wherefore, he maketh war with the saints of God, and encompasseth them round about. (*Vision to Joseph Smith and Sidney Rigdon, Feb. 16, 1832*) D&C 76:25-29

# List of Doctrines

## PRIESTHOOD: Authority and Power

### The Priesthood after the Order of the Son of God

*Doctrines Located in This Topic*

568. Priesthood is divine authority and divine power.

569. Divine authority is received only by ordination to the priesthood through the laying on of hands by commissioned servants of the Lord who themselves have likewise received such authority.

570. To administer in the ordinances of the gospel a man must hold priesthood authority.

571. No person may hold any office in the Church unless called and publicly given assignment by someone who has priesthood authority to issue the call.

572. All worthy male members of the Church may be ordained to the priesthood without regard to race or color.

573. The authority of the Melchizedek Priesthood was given to Joseph Smith by the ancient Apostles Peter, James, and John.

574. Power of the priesthood extends beyond the grave, hence that which is bound on earth is also bound in heaven—ordinances performed on earth are valid in heaven.

575. Elijah, the ancient prophet, personally restored the sealing powers of the priesthood to earth in these latter days.

576. The powers of heaven are controlled and handled by priesthood bearers.

577. Only upon principles of righteousness can a priesthood bearer manage the powers of heaven.

578. Authority of the priesthood is to be exercised in a pure spirit of love and kindness.

579. The Lord gives His authorized servants power over devils.

*Doctrines on PRIESTHOOD: AUTHORITY AND POWER Located in Other Topics*

168. The priesthood of God has power over the devil.

465. People are not to function as missionaries unless they are set apart and authorized to preach the gospel by one who has authority.

493. Although a man by his ordination holds authority of the priesthood, before he can lawfully perform any ordinance, he must receive authorization from one who holds the keys in the Church for the administration of that ordinance.

# PRIESTHOOD: Authority and Power
## The Priesthood after the Order of the Son of God

**568. Priesthood is divine authority and divine power.**

### President Joseph F. Smith

What is the Priesthood? It is nothing more nor less than the power of God delegated to man by which man can act in the earth for the salvation of the human family, in the name of the Father and the Son and the Holy Ghost, and act legitimately; not assuming that authority, nor borrowing it from generations that are dead and gone, but authority that has been given in this day in which we live by ministering angels and spirits from above, direct from the presence of God. . . . It is the same power and Priesthood that was committed to the disciples of Christ while he was upon the earth, that whatsoever they should bind on earth should be bound in heaven and whatsoever they should loose on earth should be loosed in heaven. CR1904Oct:5; DGSM:67

### Joseph Smith

The Melchizedek Priesthood holds the right of presidency, and has power and authority over all the offices in the church in all ages of the world, to administer in spiritual things. (*Revelation on priesthood, received as the Twelve met in council, March 28, 1835*) D&C 107:8

### Elder Harold B. Lee

Priesthood defined is the power of God given to man to act for Him in all things pertaining to the salvation of man—and I should add, within the limitations of each endowment of authority by the laying on of hands. *(Mission presidents' seminar, July 2, 1961)* (Stand Ye in Holy Places, p. 266) TLDP:519

### Elder John Taylor

What is priesthood? . . . [I]t is the government of God, whether on the earth or in the heavens, for it is by that power, agency, or principle that all things are governed on the earth and in the heavens, and by that power that all things are upheld and sustained. It governs all things—it directs all things—it sustains all things—and has to do with all things that God and truth are associated with. It is the power of God delegated to intelligences in the heavens and to men on the earth. (Millennial Star, Nov. 1847, 1:321) DGSM:67

### President John Taylor

The power manifested by the Priesthood is simply the power of God, for He is the head of the Priesthood, with Jesus as our President and great High Priest; and it is upon this principle that all the works of God have been accomplished, whether on the earth or in the heavens; and any manifestation of power through the Priesthood on the earth is simply a delegated power from the Priesthood in the heavens, and the more the Priesthood on the earth becomes assimilated with and subject to the Priesthood in the heavens the more of this power shall we possess. (The Mediation and Atonement, p. 88) TLDP:499

### Elder Wilford Woodruff

Our Heavenly Father performs all His works— the creation of worlds, the redemption of worlds—by the power of the Eternal Priesthood. And no man on the earth, from the days of Father Adam to the present time, has ever had power to administer in any of the ordinances of life and salvation only by the power of the Holy Priesthood. You will find this to be the case in the whole history of the Prophets of God. *(In Tabernacle, July 20, 1883, JD24:242)* TLDP:500

### President Wilford Woodruff

All the organizations of the priesthood have power. The Deacon has power, through the priesthood which he holds. So has the Teacher. They have power to go before the Lord and have their prayers heard and answered, as well as the prophet, the seer, or the revelator has. It is by this priesthood that the work of God has been accomplished. It is by this priesthood that men have ordinances conferred upon them, that their sins are forgiven, and that they are redeemed. For this purpose has it been revealed and sealed upon our heads. (Millennial Star, Sept. 1890, pp. 595-96) TLDP:499-500

### President Brigham Young, quoted by John A. Widtsoe

The Priesthood of God, that was given to the ancients and is given to men in the latter days, is co-equal in duration with eternity—is without beginning of days or end of life. It is unchangeable in its system of government and its Gospel of salvation. It gives to Gods and angels their supremacy and power, and offers wealth, influence, posterity, exaltations, power, glory, kingdoms and thrones, ceaseless in their duration, to all who will accept them on the terms upon which they are offered. *(In Bowery, Sept. 28, 1862, JD10:5)* DBY:49

### Delbert L. Stapley

There is a difference between the authority of the priesthood and the power of the priesthood. . . .

A man may have the priesthood conferred upon him, but through inactivity, disobedience, and violating the commandments of God he will not gain power in the priesthood. The priesthood may lie dormant in an individual, the power of it never realized whereby miracles can be performed. Such an inactive person denies himself personal benefits, as well as denying others who could be uplifted and blessed had he been faithful. (Quoted by Larry Hiller in "The South American Area Conferences," EN1975Jun:74) TLDP:500

**Related Witnesses:**

**Boyd K. Packer**

Your authority comes through your ordination; your power comes through obedience and worthiness. . . . ¶ Power in the priesthood comes from doing your duty in ordinary things: attending meetings, accepting assignments, reading the scriptures, keeping the Word of Wisdom. (That All May Be Edified, pp. 29-30) TLDP:500

**Elder David O. McKay**

If at this moment each one of you were asked to state in one sentence or phrase the most distinguishing feature of the Church of Jesus Christ of Latter-day Saints, what would be your answer? It occurs to me now that my answer would be this: ¶ Divine authority by direct revelation. ¶ There are those who claim authority through historical descent, others from the scriptures, but this Church stands out as making the distinctive claim that the authority of the priesthood has come directly from God the Father and the Son, by revelation to Joseph Smith. . . . ¶ Correlated with that revelation [the vision of the Father to Joseph Smith introducing the Son] is another fundamental fact, that the Lord is interested in his people, that the whole human family is related as his children, and he loves them, and that he has authorized men to officiate among the children of the world, to bring them back into his presence. CR1937Apr:121-22

**Joseph Smith**

That the rights of the priesthood are inseparably connected with the powers of heaven, and that the powers of heaven cannot be controlled nor handled only upon the principles of righteousness. (*Revelation received in Liberty Jail, March 20, 1839; why many are called and few chosen*) D&C 121:36

**Joseph Smith**

For unto you, the Twelve, and those, the First Presidency, who are appointed with you to be your counselors and your leaders, is the power of this priesthood given, for the last days and for the last time, in the which is the dispensation of the fulness of times. (*Revelation for Thomas B. Marsh concerning the Twelve Apostles, July 23, 1837*) D&C 112:30

**Elder Spencer W. Kimball**

There is no limit to the power of the priesthood which you hold. The limit comes in you if you do not live in harmony with the Spirit of the Lord and you limit yourselves in the power you exert. *(Lamanite conference, priesthood meeting)* (The Teachings of Spencer W. Kimball, p. 498) TLDP:500

**President Spencer W. Kimball**

It would be unfortunate if you received the total power of God all at once if you were not wholly ready for it, because you might make many mistakes. You might make people well when they ought to pass away. You might make many, many errors if you had no limitations to your priesthood. So the Lord has very wisely given to you priesthood commensurate with your need and your ability to handle it. . . . ¶ But as fast as a man is worthy and able to handle it, the Lord will give him these powers. *(Sao Paulo area conference, priesthood session)* (The Teachings of Spencer W. Kimball, p. 501) TLDP:500

---

**569.** Divine authority is received only by ordination to the priesthood through the laying on of hands by commissioned servants of the Lord who themselves have likewise received such authority.

**Joseph Smith**

We believe that a man must be called of God, by prophecy, and by the laying on of hands by those who are in authority, to preach the Gospel and administer in the ordinances thereof. (*The fifth of the thirteen Articles of Faith; letter to John Wentworth, March 1, 1842*) AofF:5

**James E. Talmage**

Ordination of Men to the Ministry, as sanctioned by scriptural precedent and established by direct revelation of God's will, is to be effected through the gift of prophecy and by the imposition of hands by those who are in authority. By prophecy is meant the right to receive and the power to interpret manifestations of the divine will. That the laying on of hands is usual as a part of the ordinance is seen in several of the instances already cited; nevertheless the scriptures record numerous ordinations to the offices of the Priesthood without specific statement concerning the imposition of hands or any other details. Such instances do not warrant the conclusion that the laying on of hands was omitted; and in the light of modern revelation it is clear that the imposition of hands was a usual accompaniment of ordination as also of confirming blessings and of bestowing the Holy Ghost. AF:164-65

### Joseph Smith

Accordingly we went and were baptized. I baptized him first, and afterwards he baptized me—after which I laid my hands upon his head and ordained him to the Aaronic Priesthood, and afterwards he laid his hands on me and ordained me to the same Priesthood—for so we were commanded. 72. The messenger who visited us on this occasion and conferred this Priesthood upon us, said that his name was John, the same that is called John the Baptist in the New Testament, and that he acted under the direction of Peter, James and John, who held the keys of the Priesthood of Melchizedek, which Priesthood, he said, would in due time be conferred on us, and that I should be called the first Elder of the Church, and he (Oliver Cowdery) the second. It was on the fifteenth day of May, 1829, that we were ordained under the hand of this messenger, and baptized. (*John the Baptist appears to Joseph Smith and Oliver Cowdery, May 15, 1829*) JS-H 1:71-72

### N. Eldon Tanner

We often hear the Church referred to as a democracy when, in reality, instead of being a church where the body is governed by people elected as representatives, the Church is a theocracy where God directs his Church through representatives chosen by Him. As one of our Articles of Faith says: "We believe that a man must be called of God, by prophecy, and by the laying on of hands, by those who are in authority to preach the Gospel and administer in the ordinances thereof" (Article of Faith 5). That is the way in which Joseph Smith was chosen by the Lord as president of his Church and set apart by those authorized by the Lord to do so. ("Administration of the Restored Church," *Devotional Speeches of the Year*, 1977, p. 202) TLDP:83

**Related Witnesses:**

### Elder Harold B. Lee

Priesthood defined is the power of God given to man to act for Him in all things pertaining to the salvation of man—and I should add, within the limitations of each endowment of authority by the laying on of hands. (*Mission presidents' seminar, July 2, 1961*) (Stand Ye in Holy Places, p. 266) TLDP:519

### Elder Wilford Woodruff

He [Joseph Smith] lived until he received every key, ordinance and law ever given to any man on the earth, from Father Adam down, touching this dispensation. He received powers and keys from under the hands of Moses for gathering the house of Israel in the last days; he received under the hands of Elias the keys of sealing the hearts of the fathers to the children, and the hearts of the children to the fathers; he received under the hands of Peter, James and John, the Apostleship, and everything belonging thereto; he received under the hands of Moroni all the keys and powers required of the stick of Joseph in the hands of Ephraim; he received under the hand of John the Baptist the Aaronic Priesthood, with all its keys and powers, and every other key and power belonging to this dispensation, and I am not ashamed to say that he was a Prophet of God, and he laid the foundation of the greatest work and dispensation that has ever been established on the earth. (*In new Tabernacle, Oct. 1873, JD16:267*) DGSM:68

### Mormon

And now it came to pass that after Alma had made an end of speaking unto the people of the church, which was established in the city of Zarahemla, he ordained priests and elders, by laying on his hands according to the order of God, to preside and watch over the church. (*Alma sets the Church in order in Zarahemla, about 83 B.C.*) Alma 6:1

### Elder Ezra Taft Benson

Our boys twelve years of age, if worthy, receive the Holy Priesthood by the laying on of hands, and our young men are hardly more than boys when at nineteen they receive the Holy Melchizedek Priesthood, the authority to officiate in the most sacred ordinances known to man. CR1948Oct:99

---

## 570. To administer in the ordinances of the gospel a man must hold priesthood authority.

### President Joseph F. Smith

We affirm that to administer in the ordinances of the Gospel, authority must be given of God; and that this authority is the power of the Holy Priesthood. (*Address to the world, adopted by vote of Saints assembled in general conference*) CR1907Apr(appendix)4

### Joseph Smith

We believe that a man must be called of God, by prophecy, and by the laying on of hands by those who are in authority, to preach the Gospel and administer in the ordinances thereof. (*The fifth of the thirteen Articles of Faith; letter to John Wentworth, March 1, 1842)* AofF:5

**Bruce R. McConkie**

God's ministers are ordained. They have the holy priesthood conferred upon them and are ordained by the laying on of hands to officiate in specific offices and callings. (Doctrinal New Testament Commentary, 1:748) DGSM:67-68

**Joseph Smith,**
*receiving the Word of the Lord*

Again I say unto you, that it shall not be given to any one to go forth to preach my gospel, or to build up my church, except he be ordained by some one who has authority, and it is known to the church that he has authority and has been regularly ordained by the heads of the church. (*Revelation "embracing the law of the Church," Feb. 9, 1831*) D&C 42:11

**Elder Wilford Woodruff**

[The priesthood] is the authority of God in heaven to the sons of men to administer in any of the ordinances of his house. There never was a man and never will be a man, in this or any other age of the world, who has power and authority to administer in one of the ordinances of the house of God, unless he is called of God as was Aaron, unless he has the holy Priesthood and is administered to by those holding that authority. (*In new Tabernacle, Oct. 8, 1873, JD16:266*) TLDP:514

**Elder Wilford Woodruff**

What is the priesthood for? It is to administer the ordinances of the gospel, even the gospel of our Father in heaven, the eternal God, the Eloheim of the Jews and the God of the Gentiles, and all he has ever done from the beginning has been performed by and through the power of the priesthood. (*In Tabernacle, June 1878, JD19:360*) DGSM:68

**James E. Talmage**

When the Lord established his Church amongst the Nephites upon this continent, he told those who were chosen and ordained unto whom authority was given, just how to administer the ordinance of baptism. They were to say: "Having authority given me of Jesus Christ, I baptize you in the name of the Father and of the Son, and of the Holy Ghost." That does not give us in this age any such authority. The words that Christ spoke unto his apostles of old would be no authority unto the apostles today, nor unto any of the elders of the Church. I repeat, the words that he, the Lord, spoke unto the disciples who were chosen from among the Nephites would be no authority unto us; but in this day and age he has spoken again, and has given that same power and authority to speak in

his name, and to administer the ordinances of the gospel, after the pattern that he has set; and therefore the elders and priests who take candidates into the waters of baptism today, declare that they have authority given them; and, being commissioned of Jesus Christ, they baptize in the name of the Father and of the Son and of the Holy Ghost. CR1924Apr:68; DCSM:46

**Related Witnesses:**
**Joseph Smith**

The power and authority of the higher, or Melchizedek Priesthood, is to hold the keys of all the spiritual blessings of the church— 19. To have the privilege of receiving the mysteries of the kingdom of heaven, to have the heavens opened unto them, to commune with the general assembly and church of the Firstborn, and to enjoy the communion and presence of God the Father, and Jesus the mediator of the new covenant. 20. The power and authority of the lesser, or Aaronic Priesthood, is to hold the keys of the ministering of angels, and to administer in outward ordinances, the letter of the gospel, the baptism of repentance for the remission of sins, agreeable to the covenants and commandments. (*Revelation on priesthood, received as the Twelve met in council, March 28, 1835*) D&C 107:18-20

**James E. Talmage**

Ordination of Men to the Ministry, as sanctioned by scriptural precedent and established by direct revelation of God's will, is to be effected through the gift of prophecy and by the imposition of hands by those who are in authority.... AF:164-65

**President Brigham Young,**
*quoted by John A. Widtsoe*

There is no act of a Latter-day Saint—no duty required—no time given, exclusive and independent of the Priesthood. Everything is subject to it, whether preaching, business, or any other act pertaining to the proper conduct of this life. (*In Provo, Utah, June 6, 1858, JD7:66*) DBY:133

**Recorded in Acts**

Now there were in the church that was at Antioch certain prophets and teachers; as Barnabas, and Simeon that was called Niger, and Lucius of Cyrene, and Manaen, which had been brought up with Herod the tetrarch, and Saul. 2. As they ministered to the Lord, and fasted, the Holy Ghost said, Separate me Barnabas and Saul for the work whereunto I have called them. 3. And when they had fasted and prayed, and laid their hands on them, they sent them away. (*Saul and Barnabas called to missionary service*) Acts 13:1-3

### Mormon

And now it came to pass that after Alma had made an end of speaking unto the people of the church, which was established in the city of Zarahemla, he ordained priests and elders, by laying on his hands according to the order of God, to preside and watch over the church. (*Alma sets the Church in Zarahemla in order, about 83 B.C.*) Alma 6:1

### Jesus,
#### quoted by Mormon

And the Lord said unto him: I give unto you power that ye shall baptize this people when I am again ascended into heaven. (*The resurrected Jesus Christ gives priesthood authority to Nephi son of Helaman, A.D. 34*) 3Ne.11:21

### Jesus,
#### quoted by Mormon

And when the multitude had eaten and were filled, he said unto the disciples: Behold there shall one be ordained among you, and to him will I give power that he shall break bread and bless it and give it unto the people of my church, unto all those who shall believe and be baptized in my name. (*The resurrected Jesus Christ teaches the Nephite people, A.D. 34*) 3Ne.18:5

### Jesus,
#### quoted by John

Ye have not chosen me, but I have chosen you, and ordained you, that ye should go and bring forth fruit, and that your fruit should remain: that whatsoever ye shall ask of the Father in my name, he may give it you. (*Jesus addresses his disciples who have been chosen to serve him*) John 15:16

### Jacob, brother of Nephi,
#### quoted by Nephi

Behold, my beloved brethren, I, Jacob, having been called of God, and ordained after the manner of his holy order, and having been consecrated by my brother Nephi, unto whom ye look as a king or a protector, and on whom ye depend for safety, behold ye know that I have spoken unto you exceedingly many things. (*Jacob teaches the people of Nephi, 559-545 B.C.*) 2Ne.6:2

### Joseph Smith

It is the duty of the Twelve, also, to ordain and set in order all the other officers of the church, agreeable to the revelation which says: 59. To the church of Christ in the land of Zion, in addition to the church laws respecting church business— 60. Verily, I say unto you, saith the Lord of Hosts, there must needs be presiding elders to preside over those who are of the office of an elder; 61. And also priests to preside over those who are of the office of a priest; 62. And also

teachers to preside over those who are of the office of a teacher, in like manner, and also the deacons— 63. Wherefore, from deacon to teacher, and from teacher to priest, and from priest to elder, severally as they are appointed, according to the covenants and commandments of the church. 64. Then comes the High Priesthood, which is the greatest of all. 65. Wherefore, it must needs be that one be appointed of the High Priesthood to preside over the priesthood, and he shall be called President of the High Priesthood of the Church; (*Revelation on priesthood received as he met in council with the Twelve, March 28, 1835*) D&C 107:58-65

### President Joseph F. Smith

But behold, from among the righteous, he organized his forces and appointed messengers, clothed with power and authority, and commissioned them to go forth and carry the light of the gospel to them that were in darkness, even to all the spirits of men; and thus was the gospel preached to the dead. (*Vision of the Savior's visit to the spirits of the dead, Oct. 3, 1918*) D&C 138:30

### Joseph Smith

The person who is called of God and has authority from Jesus Christ to baptize, shall go down into the water with the person who has presented himself or herself for baptism, and shall say, calling him or her by name: Having been commissioned of Jesus Christ, I baptize you in the name of the Father, and of the Son, and of the Holy Ghost. Amen. (*Revelation on Church Organization and Government, April 1830; laws governing repentance, justification, sanctification, and baptism are set forth*) D&C 20:73

---

**571.** No person may hold any office in the Church unless called and publicly given assignment by someone who has priesthood authority to issue the call.

### Bruce R. McConkie

All of the organizational things which the Church does—that is, the procedures which it follows and the officers which it appoints—must be done by common consent, by much faith and prayer. . . . ¶ General Church business cannot be transacted in secret. No man, for instance, could be appointed in secret to head the Church or to carry on some supposed great program for the salvation of men. Conferences are to transact the business of the Church. ¶ . . . . No man can so much as be ordained to any office in the Church without a vote of the Church. There is no such thing as a secret ordination to office, either high or low, in the Church of Christ. The Lord does not work in dark corners. His great works are trumpeted in the ears of all living so that every soul who is willing to do so may learn of them. (Common Consent pamphlet, 1955, pp. 12-13) TLDP:96

### Joseph Smith,
*receiving the Word of the Lord*

Again I say unto you, that it shall not be given to any one to go forth to preach my gospel, or to build up my church, except he be ordained by some one who has authority, and it is known to the church that he has authority and has been regularly ordained by the heads of the church. *(Revelation "embracing the law of the Church," Feb. 9, 1831)* D&C 42:11

### Mark E. Petersen

Neither does the Lord allow for any secret ordinations in his work. To be valid, everything is done publicly and by the vote of the people. Said the Savior, ". . . It shall not be given to anyone to go forth to preach my gospel, or to build up my church, except he be ordained by some one who has authority, and it is known to the church that he has authority and has been regularly ordained by the heads of the church." (D&C 42:11) ¶ And then the Lord said, ". . . All things shall be done by common consent in the church . . ." which means by public knowledge and public vote. (D&C 26:2) CR1974pr:82

### Boyd K. Packer,
*also quoting Joseph Smith*

One more thing: You can receive the priesthood only from one who has the authority and "it is known to the church that he has authority." (D&C 42:11) ¶ . . . . The priesthood is very, very precious to the Lord. He is very careful about how it is conferred, and by whom. It is never done in secret. CR1981Oct:46-47

### Related Witnesses:
### Joseph Smith

We believe that a man must be called of God, by prophecy, and by the laying on of hands by those who are in authority, to preach the Gospel and administer in the ordinances thereof. *(The fifth of the thirteen Articles of Faith; letter to John Wentworth, March 1, 1842)* AofF:5

### Stephen L. Richards

This Church is not democratic. This Church is a kingdom. We don't make the laws. God makes the laws. We ourselves do not appoint authorities and the administrators, they are appointed by the inspiration that emanates from him. ¶ We have a democratic method in that we sustain those who are appointed. Without that sustaining vote they cannot legally function. All the people

in the whole ward cannot unanimously nominate a bishop. The President of the Church cannot install himself unless the majority of the people sustain him. Never forget that this is a kingdom and never forget the laws of the Church are not man-made. *(To Las Vegas , Nev. priesthood meeting, four combined wards)* (Church News, Nov. 22, 1951, p. 2) TLDP:98

### Paul

And no man taketh this honour unto himself, but he that is called of God, as was Aaron. *(Letter to the Jewish members of the Church, about A.D. 60)* Heb.5:4

### Joseph Smith,
*receiving the Word of the Lord*

And again, verily I say unto you, those who desire in their hearts, in meekness, to warn sinners to repentance, let them be ordained unto this power. *(Revelation, Aug. 1831)* D&C 63:57

### Joseph Smith,
*receiving the Word of the Lord*

Behold, I command you that you need not suppose that you are called to preach until you are called. *(Revelation for Hyrum Smith, May 1829)* D&C 11:15

### Jesus,
*quoted by John*

Ye have not chosen me, but I have chosen you, and ordained you, that ye should go and bring forth fruit, and that your fruit should remain: that whatsoever ye shall ask of the Father in my name, he may give it you. *(Jesus addresses his disciples)* John 15:16

### Joseph Smith,
*receiving the Word of the Lord*

That as many as shall come before my servants Sidney Rigdon and Joseph Smith, Jun., embracing this calling and commandment, shall be ordained and sent forth to preach the everlasting gospel among the nations— . . . 7. And this commandment shall be given unto the elders of my church, that every man which will embrace it with singleness of heart may be ordained and sent forth, even as I have spoken. *(Revelation for Edward Partridge, Dec. 1830)* D&C 36:5,7

---

572. All worthy male members of the Church may be ordained to the priesthood without regard to race or color.

### President Spencer W. Kimball,
### N. Eldon Tanner, Marion G. Romney
(First Presidency)

To Whom it may Concern: ¶ On September 30, 1978, at the 148th Semiannual General

Conference of The Church of Jesus Christ of Latter-day Saints, the following was presented by President N. Eldon Tanner, First Counselor in the First Presidency of the Church: ¶ In early June of this year, the First Presidency announced that a revelation had been received by President Spencer W. Kimball extending priesthood and temple blessings to all worthy male members of the Church. President Kimball has asked that I advise the conference that after he had received this revelation, which came to him after extended meditation and prayer in the sacred rooms of the holy temple, he presented it to his counselors, who accepted it and approved it. It was then presented to the Quorum of the Twelve Apostles, who unanimously approved it, and was subsequently presented to all other General Authorities, who likewise approved it unanimously. ¶ President Kimball has asked that I [N. Eldon Tanner] now read this letter: ¶ June 8, 1978. ¶ To all general and local priesthood officers of The Church of Jesus Christ of Latter-day Saints throughout the world: ¶ Dear Brethren, ¶ As we have witnessed the expansion of the work of the Lord over the earth, we have been grateful that people of many nations have responded to the message of the restored gospel, and have joined the Church in ever-increasing numbers. This, in turn, has inspired us with a desire to extend to every worthy member of the Church all of the privileges and blessings which the gospel affords. ¶ Aware of the promises made by the prophets and presidents of the Church who have preceded us that at some time, in God's eternal plan, all of our brethren who are worthy may receive the priesthood, and witnessing the faithfulness of those from whom the priesthood has been withheld, we have pleaded long and earnestly in behalf of these, our faithful brethren, spending many hours in the Upper Room of the Temple supplicating the Lord for divine guidance. ¶ He has heard our prayers, and by revelation has confirmed that the long-promised day has come when every faithful, worthy man in the Church may receive the holy priesthood, with power to exercise its divine authority, and enjoy with his loved ones every blessing that flows therefrom, including the blessings of the temple. ¶ Accordingly, all worthy male members of the Church may be ordained to the priesthood without regard for race or color. Priesthood leaders are instructed to follow the policy of carefully interviewing all candidates for ordination to either the Aaronic or the Melchizedek Priesthood to

insure that they meet the established standards for worthiness. ¶ We declare with soberness that the Lord has now made known his will for the blessing of all his children throughout the earth who will hearken to the voice of his authorized servants, and prepare themselves to receive every blessing of the gospel. (*Published message of the First Presidency of the Church, June 8, 1978; presented to and accepted by the Church in general conference, Sept. 1978*) D&C OD 2:1-12

### N. Eldon Tanner

Recognizing Spencer W. Kimball as the prophet, seer, and revelator, and president of The Church of Jesus Christ of Latter-day Saints, it is proposed that we as a constituent assembly accept this revelation [all worthy male members of the Church may be ordained to the priesthood without regard for race or color] as the word and will of the Lord. All in favor please signify by raising your right hand. Any opposed by the same sign. ¶ The vote to sustain the foregoing motion was unanimous in the affirmative. ¶ Salt Lake City, Utah, September 30, 1978. (*Published message of the First Presidency of the Church, June 8, 1978; presented to and accepted by the Church in general conference, Sept. 1978*) D&C OD 2:14-16

### James E. Faust

God, through his prophets, has given the priesthood in recent times the great challenge to advance worldwide the holy work in which we are engaged. All worthy men may now be given the priesthood. With the coming of these inspired changes, I wonder if there has been an enlarging of altitude based upon the exalted principles the Savior taught. Has the extended responsibility of the priesthood caused us to have a better understanding of our work? CR1983Apr:60

**Author's Note:** In 1974, four years before the revelation effectively extending the priesthood to blacks, President Kimball at a press conference stated: "Blacks and the priesthood: I am not sure that there will be a change, although there could be. We are under the dictates of our Heavenly Father, and this is not my policy or the Church's policy. It is the policy of the Lord who established it, and I know of no change, although we are subject to revelations of the Lord in case he should ever wish to make a change." (*Press conference upon being ordained 12th president of The Church of Jesus Christ of Latter-day Saints, Dec. 1973*) (EN1974Jan:2)

573. The authority of the Melchizedek Priesthood was given to Joseph Smith by the ancient Apostles, Peter, James, and John.

### Elder Joseph Fielding Smith

The Melchizedek Priesthood was restored to Joseph Smith and Oliver Cowdery by Peter, James and John. This authority commissioned them to officiate in the ordinances of baptism and confirmation and ordination to the priesthood and the preaching of the gospel in all the world. The power which Elijah restored is the power to seal and bind for eternity. It has to do more particularly with the ordinances of the temple and reaches out and embraces the dead as well as the living in its scope. And this is the real significance of the turning of the hearts of the fathers to the children and the hearts of the children to their fathers. This authority provides the means by which the fathers who are dead, and who died without the privilege of the gospel, may receive the ordinances of the gospel vicariously by their children performing them in the temples. (The Restoration of All Things, pp. 172-73) TLDP:616

### Elder Joseph Fielding Smith

In the restoration of authority it was necessary that John the Baptist—the messenger who was formerly sent to prepare the way—should first come. Then Peter, James, and John, who held the keys of the greater priesthood had to come and give their power that the Church could be organized on the earth. (Doctrines of Salvation, 1:174) TLDP:559

### Joseph Smith,
*receiving the Word of the Lord*

And also with Peter, and James, and John, whom I have sent unto you, by whom I have ordained you and confirmed you to be apostles, and especial witnesses of my name, and bear the keys of your ministry and of the same things which I revealed unto them; 13. Unto whom I have committed the keys of my kingdom, and a dispensation of the gospel for the last times; and for the fulness of times, in the which I will gather together in one all things, both which are in heaven, and which are on earth; (*Revelation, Aug. 1830*) D&C 27:12-13

### James E. Talmage

A short time after this event, Peter, James, and John appeared to Joseph Smith and Oliver Cowdery, and ordained the two to the higher or Melchizedek Priesthood, bestowing upon them the keys of the apostleship, which these heavenly messengers had held and exercised in

the former Gospel dispensation. This order of Priesthood holds authority over all the offices in the Church, and includes power to administer in spiritual things; consequently all the authorities and powers necessary to the establishment and development of the Church were by this visitation restored to earth. AF:171

### President Brigham Young,
*quoted by John A. Widtsoe*

How came these Apostles, these Seventies, these High Priests, and all this organization we now enjoy? It came by revelation. . . . Joseph . . . received a revelation, and ordained High Priests. You read in the book of Doctrine and Covenants how he received the Priesthood in the first place. It is there stated how Joseph received the Aaronic Priesthood. John the Baptist came to Joseph Smith and Oliver Cowdery. . . . You read in the revelation that Joseph was ordained, as it is written. When he received the Melchizedek Priesthood, he had another revelation. Peter, James, and John came to him. You can read the revelation at your leisure. When he received this revelation in Kirtland, the Lord revealed to him that he should begin and ordain High Priests; and he then ordained quite a number. . . . These were the first that were ordained to this office in the Church. I relate this to show you how Joseph proceeded step by step in organizing the Church. At that time there were no Seventies nor Twelve Apostles. (*In Mill Creek Ward, May 7, 1861, JD9:88-89*) DBY:142

### Related Witnesses:
#### Joseph Smith

The messenger who visited us on this occasion, and conferred this Priesthood upon us, said that his name was John, the same that is called John the Baptist in the New Testament, and that he acted under the direction of Peter, James and John who held the keys of the Priesthood of Melchizedek, which Priesthood he said would in due time be conferred on us, and that I should be called the first Elder of the Church, and he (Oliver Cowdery) the second. It was on the 15th day of May, 1829, that we were ordained under the hand of this messenger and baptized. (*Entry in the Prophet's journal, 1829*) HC1:40-41

#### Joseph Smith

How have we come at the Priesthood in the last days? It came down, down, in regular succession. Peter, James, and John had it given to them and they gave it to others. (*The Prophet instructs the Twelve on priesthood, in the vicinity of Commerce, Ill., July 2, 1839*) HC3:387

### Elder Wilford Woodruff

He [Joseph Smith] lived until he received every key, ordinance and law ever given to any man on the earth, from Father Adam down, touching this dispensation. He received powers and keys from under the hands of Moses for gathering the house of Israel in the last days; he received under the hands of Elias the keys of sealing the hearts of the fathers to the children, and the hearts of the children to the fathers; he received under the hands of Peter, James and John, the Apostleship, and everything belonging thereto; he received under the hands of Moroni all the keys and powers required of the stick of Joseph in the hands of Ephraim; he received under the hand of John the Baptist the Aaronic Priesthood, with all its keys and powers; and every other key and power belonging to this dispensation, and I am not ashamed to say that he was a Prophet of God, and he laid the foundation of the greatest work and dispensation that has ever been established on the earth. (*In new Tabernacle, Oct. 1873, JD16:267*) DGSM:68

### Joseph Smith

And again, what do we hear? Glad tidings from Cumorah! Moroni, an angel from heaven, declaring the fulfilment of the prophets—the book to be revealed. A voice of the Lord in the wilderness of Fayette, Seneca county, declaring the three witnesses to bear record of the book! The voice of Michael on the banks of the Susquehanna, detecting the devil when he appeared as an angel of light! The voice of Peter, James, and John in the wilderness between Harmony, Susquehanna county, and Colesville, Broome county, on the Susquehanna river, declaring themselves as possessing the keys of the kingdom, and of the dispensation of the fulness of times! 21. And again, the voice of God in the chamber of old Father Whitmer, in Fayette, Seneca county, and at sundry times, and in divers places through all the travels and tribulations of this Church of Jesus Christ of Latter-day Saints! And the voice of Michael, the archangel; the voice of Gabriel, and of Raphael, and of divers angels, from Michael or Adam down to the present time, all declaring their dispensation, their rights, their keys, their honors, their majesty and glory, and the power of their priesthood; giving line upon line, precept upon precept; here a little, and there a little; giving us consolation by holding forth that which is to come, confirming our hope! (*Epistle to the Church, Sept. 6, 1842, at Nauvoo, Ill; all of the keys, powers, and authorities have been restored*) D&C 128:20-21

574. **Power of the priesthood extends beyond the grave, hence that which is bound on earth is also bound in heaven—ordinances performed on earth are valid in heaven.**

### John A. Widtsoe

Marriages may be consummated within the Church for all time—not merely until death doth them part. Family relationships may be continued throughout the eternities. The power of the Priesthood extends beyond the grave. Temple work, including baptism, the endowment, sealing, etc., is a function of the Priesthood. It is by this power that work for the dead may be done. It is by the power of the Priesthood. It is by the power of the Priesthood that a person may attain celestial glory. Without [the power of the] Priesthood one cannot enter the presence of God. (Program of the Church, p. 129) TLDP:500

### Joseph Smith

Now, the nature of this ordinance consists in the power of the priesthood, by the revelation of Jesus Christ, wherein it is granted that whatsoever you bind on earth shall be bound in heaven, and whatsoever you loose on earth shall be loosed in heaven. Or, in other words, taking a different view of the translation, whatsoever you record on earth shall be recorded in heaven, and whatsoever you do not record on earth shall not be recorded in heaven; for out of the books shall your dead be judged, according to their own works, whether they themselves have attended to the ordinances in their own propria persona, or by the means of their own agents, according to the ordinance which God has prepared for their salvation from before the foundation of the world, according to the records which they have kept concerning their dead. 9. It may seem to some to be a very bold doctrine that we talk of—a power which records or binds on earth and binds in heaven. Nevertheless, in all ages of the world, whenever the Lord has given a dispensation of the priesthood to any man by actual revelation, or any set of men, this power has always been given. Hence, whatsoever those men did in authority, in the name of the Lord, and did it truly and faithfully, and kept a proper and faithful record of the same, it became a law on earth and in heaven, and could not be annulled, according to the decrees of the great Jehovah. This is a faithful saying. Who can hear it? 10. And again, for the precedent, Matthew 16:18, 19: *And I say also unto thee, That thou art Peter, and upon this rock I will build my church; and the gates of hell shall not prevail against it. And I will give unto thee the keys of the kingdom of heaven: and whatsoever thou shalt bind on earth shall be bound in heaven; and whatsoever thou shalt loose on earth shall be loosed in heaven. (Epistle to the Church, Sept. 6, 1842, at Nauvoo, Ill., regarding the ordinance of baptism)* D&C 128:8-10

### Joseph Smith,
### *receiving the Word of the Lord*

And verily, verily, I say unto you, that whatsoever you seal on earth shall be sealed in heaven; and whatsoever you bind on earth, in my name and by my word, saith the Lord, it shall be eternally bound in the heavens; and whosesoever sins you remit on earth shall be remitted eternally in the heavens; and whosesoever sins you retain on earth shall be retained in heaven. *(Revelation relating to the new and everlasting covenant, including the eternal nature of the marriage covenant, July 12, 1843 [1831])* D&C 132:46

### Elder Joseph Fielding Smith

Elijah came to *restore* to the earth, by conferring on mortal prophets duly commissioned of the Lord, *the fulness of the power of priesthood. This priesthood holds the keys of binding and sealing on earth and in heaven of all the ordinances and principles pertaining to the salvation of man,* that they may thus become valid in the celestial kingdom of God. . . . ¶ It is by virtue of this authority that ordinances are performed in the temples for *both* the living and the dead. It is the power which unites for eternity husbands and wives, when they enter into marriage according to the eternal plan. *It is the authority by which parents obtain the claim of parenthood,* concerning their children, through all eternity and not only for time, which makes eternal the family in the kingdom of God. (Doctrines of Salvation, 2:117) MPSG1984:9

### President Joseph F. Smith

What is the Priesthood? It is nothing more nor less than the power of God delegated to man by which man can act in the earth for the salvation of the human family, in the name of the Father and the Son and the Holy Ghost, and act legitimately; not assuming that authority, nor borrowing it from generations that are dead and gone, but authority that has been given in this day in which we live by ministering angels and spirits from above, direct from the presence of God. . . . It is the same power and Priesthood that was committed to the disciples of Christ while he was upon the earth, that whatsoever they should bind on earth should be bound in

heaven and whatsoever they should loose on earth should be loosed heaven. CR1904Oct:5; DGSM:67

### Boyd K. Packer

Nevertheless, in the Church we hold sufficient authority to perform all of the ordinances necessary to redeem and to exalt the whole human family. And, because we have the keys to the sealing power, what we bind in proper order here will be bound in heaven. Those keys—the keys to seal and bind on earth, and have it bound in heaven—represent the consummate gift from our God. With that authority we can baptize and bless, we can endow and seal, and the Lord will honor our commitments. (The Holy Temple, p. 150-51) TLDP:509

### President John Taylor

We have now finished this Temple, and some people inquire, what is it for? For many things: that our sealings and ordinances may be performed in a manner that will be acceptable before God and the holy angels; that whatsoever is bound on the earth according to the laws of the eternal Priesthood shall be bound in the heavens; that there may be a connecting link between the living and the dead. *(At Logan, Utah, May 18, 1884, JD25:185)* TLDP:674

### Related Witnesses:
### Bruce R. McConkie

Since the earthly church, which is a kingdom, prepares men for the heavenly kingdom, which is in the celestial world, it follows that what is bound on earth is bound in heaven, and what is loosed on earth is loosed in heaven. If the Lord's legal administrators baptize repentant and worthy souls on earth, that baptism is binding in heaven and admits the faithful to celestial rest. If those legal administrators seal a worthy and faithful man to a worthy and faithful woman in the everlasting covenant of marriage, that marriage is binding in heaven and the blessed recipients of so great a bounty come forth in the resurrection as husband and wife and enter into eternal glory. And if the Lord's lawfully empowered servants, acting in his name and with his authorization, sever sinners from among the saints and turn them over to the buffetings of Satan on earth, all that might have been theirs is loosed in heaven, and they shall fail to gain what might have been theirs. It matters not whether the binding or loosing is done by the mouth of the Lord himself or by his servants who do and say what he directs. "Whether by mine own voice or by the voice of my servants, it is the same," he says. (D&C 1:38) (The Mortal Messiah, 3:39-40) TLDP:616

### Elder Joseph Fielding Smith

What is bound or sealed in the temples of the Lord, is also sealed in heaven. This is the great authority which Elijah restored. It also covers ordinances performed for the living as well as for the dead. The Prophet said that all of the ordinances for the living are required in behalf of all the dead who are entitled to the fulness of the exaltation. (See D&C 6:183-184.) CHMR2:329

### Elder Joseph Fielding Smith

This sealing power bestowed upon Elijah, is the power which binds husbands and wives, and children to parents for time and eternity. It is the binding power existing in every Gospel ordinance. . . . It is by this power that all the ordinances pertaining to salvation are bound, or sealed, and it was the mission of Elijah to come, and restore it so that the curse of confusion and disorder would not exist in the kingdom of God. (Elijah the Prophet and His Mission and Salvation Universal, p. 5) TLDP:617

### Jesus,
*recorded in Matthew*

And I will give unto thee the keys of the kingdom of heaven: and whatsoever thou shalt bind on earth shall be bound in heaven: and whatsoever thou shalt loose on earth shall be loosed in heaven. (*Jesus instructs his disciples, he addresses Peter*) Matt.16:19

### Joseph Smith,
*receiving the Word of the Lord*

For I have conferred upon you the keys and power of the priesthood, wherein I restore all things, and make known unto you all things in due time. 46. And verily, verily, I say unto you, that whatsoever you seal on earth shall be sealed in heaven; and whatsoever you bind on earth, in my name and by my word, saith the Lord, it shall be eternally bound in the heavens; and whosoever sins you remit on earth shall be remitted eternally in the heavens; and whosoever sins you retain on earth shall be retained in heaven. (*Revelation relating to the new and everlasting covenant, including the eternal nature of the marriage covenant, July 12, 1843, [1831]*) D&C 132:45-46

### Mormon

Behold, I give unto you power, that whatsoever ye shall seal on earth shall be sealed in heaven; and whatsoever ye shall loose on earth shall be loosed in heaven; and thus shall ye have power among this people. (*The Lord gives Nephi son of Helaman the sealing power, about 23-20 B.C.*) Hel.10:7

**575.** Elijah, the ancient prophet, personally restored the sealing powers of the priesthood to earth in these latter days.

### Elder Joseph Fielding Smith

Elijah came to restore to the earth, by conferring on mortal prophets duly commissioned of the Lord, the fulness of the power of priesthood. This priesthood holds the keys of binding and sealing on earth and in heaven of all the ordinances and principles pertaining to the salvation of man, that they may thus become valid in the celestial kingdom of God. . . . (Doctrines of Salvation, 2:117) MPSG84:9

### Elder Joseph Fielding Smith

In the fourth chapter Malachi speaks again of the coming of the Son of God, in these words: ¶ For, behold, the day cometh, that shall burn as an oven; and all the proud, yea, and all that do wickedly, shall be stubble: and the day that cometh shall burn them up, saith the LORD of hosts, that it shall leave them neither root nor branch. (Mal.4:1) ¶ This will happen when our savior comes in his glory to take vengeance upon the ungodly and take his place as King of kings and Lord of lords. Then this prophet Malachi goes on to say that before that day can come, which will be terrible, Elijah the prophet was to come. . . . ¶ The whole world ought to take notice of this prediction [Mal.4:5-6], but the world does not understand it. Surely the signs of the times point to the fact that the great and dreadful day is near, even at our doors. The fig tree, figuratively, is putting forth her leaves. The turmoil, trouble, the war and bloodshed that we have seen, and which we still see, all point to the fact that this day for the coming of the Son of God is near. Therefore, Elijah the prophet is due to appear. I am sure you agree with me that he has already appeared, for we have it so recorded by the testimony of witnesses. It was on the third day of April, 1836, when he came to the Kirtland Temple, to Joseph Smith and Oliver Cowdery, and conferred upon them the keys of his priesthood and told them he came in fulfilment of the prophecy of Malachi, to turn the hearts of the fathers to the children, and the children to their fathers, lest the whole earth be smitten with a curse. CR1948Apr:132

### Joseph Smith

After this vision had closed, another great and glorious vision burst upon us; for Elijah the prophet, who was taken to heaven without tasting death, stood before us, and said: 14. Behold, the time has fully come, which was spoken of by the mouth of Malachi—testifying that he Elijah, should be sent, before the great and dreadful day of the Lord come— 15. To turn the hearts of the fathers to the children, and the children to the fathers, lest the whole earth be smitten with a curse— 16. Therefore, the keys of this dispensation are committed into your hands; and by this ye may know that the great and dreadful day of the Lord is near, even at the doors. (*Vision manifested to Joseph Smith and Oliver Cowdery in the Kirtland Temple, April 3, 1836*) D&C 110:13-16

**Joseph Smith**

Elijah was the last Prophet that held the keys of the Priesthood, and who will, before the last dispensation, restore the authority and deliver the keys of the Priesthood, in order that all the ordinances may be attended to in righteousness. It is true that the Savior had authority and power to bestow this blessing; but the sons of Levi were too prejudiced. "And I will send Elijah the Prophet before the great and terrible day of the Lord," etc., etc. Why send Elijah? Because he holds the keys of the authority to administer in all the ordinances of the Priesthood; and without the authority is given, the ordinances could not be administered in righteousness. (*Article on priesthood, read to the Church in general conference, Oct. 1840*) HC4:211

**James E. Talmage**

Malachi predicted the coming of Elijah especially commissioned with power to inaugurate the work of cooperation between the fathers and the children, and announced this mission as a necessary preliminary to "the great and dreadful day of the Lord." The angel Moroni confirmed the truth and significance of this prediction in an emphatic reiteration as already set forth. Joseph Smith and his associate in the ministry, Oliver Cowdery, solemnly testify that they were visited by Elijah the prophet, in the Temple at Kirtland, Ohio, on the third day of April, 1836; on which occasion the ancient prophet declared to the prophet of the latter days that the day spoken of by Malachi had come: "Therefore," continued he, "the keys of this dispensation are committed into your hands; and by this ye may know that the great and dreadful day of the Lord is near, even at the doors." The particular nature of the union of the fathers and the children, upon which Malachi, Moroni, and Elijah laid great stress, has been explained as comprising vicarious ordinances, including baptism for the dead who have passed from earth without a knowledge of the Gospel or opportunity of complying with its laws and

ordinances. In the teaching and practice of this doctrine, The Church of Jesus Christ of Latter-day Saints stands alone amongst all the churches professing Christianity. AF:16

**President Brigham Young,**
*quoted by John A. Widtsoe*

Suppose we are ready to go into the temples of God to officiate for our fathers and our grandfathers—for our ancestors back for hundreds of years, who are all looking to see what their children are doing upon the earth. The Lord says, I have sent the keys of Elijah the Prophet —I have imparted that doctrine to turn the hearts of the fathers to the children, and the hearts of the children to the fathers. (*In Tabernacle, Aug. 15, 1852, JD6:296*) DBY:408

**Related Witnesses:**

**James E. Talmage**

The Church today cites as authority for its administration of ordinances in behalf of the dead, the special bestowal of this power and office through the ministry of Elijah, and furthermore, the Church holds that the giving of that power marked the fulfilment of Malachi's portentous prediction. There appears an element of particular fitness in the fact that the minister through whom this great work has been inaugurated in the present dispensation, is none other than Elijah—who, not having passed the portals of death, held a peculiar and special relation to both the dead and the living. As to the fidelity with which the Church has served under this special commission, the temples it has reared with such sacrifice and self-denial on the part of its devoted adherents, and the ordinance work already performed therein, are sufficient proof. HL:71-72

**(The angel) Moroni, son of Mormon,**
*quoted by Joseph Smith*

Behold, I will reveal unto you the Priesthood, by the hand of Elijah the prophet, before the coming of the great and dreadful day of the Lord. (*Extract from words of the angel Moroni to Joseph Smith, Sept. 21, 1823*) D&C 2:1

---

**576. The powers of heaven are controlled and handled by priesthood bearers.**

**Joseph Smith**

[T]he rights of the priesthood are inseparably connected with the powers of heaven, and that the powers of heaven cannot be controlled nor handled only upon the principles of righteousness. 37. That they may be conferred upon us, it is true; but when we undertake to cover our sins, or to gratify our pride, our vain ambition, or to exercise control or dominion or compulsion upon the souls of the children of men, in any degree of unrighteousness, behold, the heavens withdraw themselves; the Spirit of the Lord is grieved; and when it is withdrawn, Amen to the priesthood or the authority of that man. (*Revelation received while in Liberty Jail, March 20, 1839; why many are called and few chosen*) D&C 121:36-37

### Elder Spencer W. Kimball

There is no limit to the power of the priesthood which you hold. The limit comes in you if you do not live in harmony with the Spirit of the Lord and you limit yourselves in the power you exert. (*Lamanite conference, priesthood meeting, Nov. 1947*) (The Teachings of Spencer W. Kimball, p. 498) TLDP:500

### John A. Widtsoe

Marriages may be consummated within the Church for all time—not merely until death doth them part. Family relationships may be continued throughout the eternities. The power of the Priesthood extends beyond the grave. Temple work, including baptism, the endowment, sealing, etc., is a function of the Priesthood. It is by this power that work for the dead may be done. It is by the power of the Priesthood. (Program of the Church, p. 129) TLDP:500

### Joseph Smith

The power and authority of the higher, or Melchizedek Priesthood, is to hold the keys of all the spiritual blessings of the church— 19. To have the privilege of receiving the mysteries of the kingdom of heaven, to have the heavens opened unto them, to commune with the general assembly and church of the Firstborn, and to enjoy the communion and presence of God the Father, and Jesus the mediator of the new covenant. (*Revelation on priesthood, received as the Twelve met in council, March 28, 1835*) D&C 107:18-19

### President Joseph F. Smith

What is the Priesthood? It is nothing more nor less than the power of God delegated to man by which man can act in the earth for the salvation of the human family. . . . It is the same power and Priesthood that was committed to the disciples of Christ while he was upon the earth, that whatsoever they should bind on earth should be bound in heaven and whatsoever they should loose on earth should be loosed in heaven. CR1904Oct:5; DGSM:67

### Elder John Taylor

What is priesthood? . . . it is the government of God, whether on the earth or in the heavens, for it is by that power, agency, or principle that all things are governed on the earth and in the heavens, and by that power that all things are upheld and sustained. It governs all things—it directs all things—it sustains all things—and has to do with all things that God and truth are associated with. It is the power of God delegated to intelligences in the heavens and to men on the earth. (Millennial Star, Nov. 1847, p. 321) DGSM:67

### Elder Joseph Fielding Smith

The Melchizedek Priesthood was restored to Joseph Smith and Oliver Cowdery by Peter, James and John. This authority commissioned them to officiate in the ordinances of baptism and confirmation and ordination to the priesthood and the preaching of the gospel in all the world. The power which Elijah restored is the power to seal and bind for eternity. It has to do more particularly with the ordinances of the temple and reaches out and embraces the dead as well as the living in its scope. (The Restoration of All Things, pp. 172-73) TLDP:616

### Elder Joseph Fielding Smith

This priesthood holds the keys of binding and sealing on earth and in heaven of all the ordinances and principles pertaining to the salvation of man, that they may thus become valid in the celestial kingdom of God. . . . It is by virtue of this authority that ordinances are performed in the temples for *both* the living and the dead. It is the power which unites for eternity husbands and wives, when they enter into marriage according to the eternal plan. It is the authority by which parents obtain the claim of parenthood, concerning their children, through all eternity and not only for time, which makes eternal the family in the kingdom of God. (Doctrines of Salvation, 2:117) MPSG84:9

### Joseph Smith

Now, the nature of this ordinance consists in the power of the priesthood, by the revelation of Jesus Christ, wherein it is granted that whatsoever you bind on earth shall be bound in heaven, and whatsoever you loose on earth shall be loosed in heaven. . . . 9. It may seem to some to be a very bold doctrine that we talk of—a power which records or binds on earth and binds in heaven. Nevertheless, in all ages of the world, whenever the Lord has given a dispensation of the priesthood to any man by actual revelation, or any set of men, this power has always been given. Hence, whatsoever those men did in authority, in the name of the Lord, and did it truly and faithfully, and kept a proper and faithful record of the same, it became a law on earth and in heaven, and could not be annulled, according to the decrees of the great Jehovah. . . . *(Epistle to the Church, Sept. 6, 1842, at Nauvoo, Ill., regarding the ordinance of baptism)* D&C 128:8-9

**Related Witnesses:**

### Joseph Smith,
*receiving the Word of the Lord*

I came unto mine own, and mine own received me not; but unto as many as received me gave I power to do many miracles, and to become the sons of God; and even unto them that believed on my name gave I power to obtain eternal life. *(Revelation received March 7, 1831)* D&C 45:8

### President Joseph Fielding Smith

We are the Lord's agents; we represent him; he has given us authority which empowers us to do all that is necessary to save and exalt ourselves as well as his other children in the world. ¶ We are ambassadors of the Lord Jesus Christ. Our commission is to represent him. We are directed to preach his gospel, to perform the ordinances of salvation, to bless mankind, to heal the sick and perhaps perform miracles, to do what he would do if he were personally present—and all this because we hold the holy priesthood. CR1971Apr:47

### President Spencer W. Kimball

It would be unfortunate if you received the total power of God all at once if you were not wholly ready for it, because you might make many mistakes. You might make people well when they ought to pass away. You might make many, many errors if you had no limitations to your priesthood. So the Lord has very wisely given to you priesthood commensurate with your need and your ability to handle it. . . . ¶ But as fast as a man is worthy and able to handle it, the Lord will give him these powers. *(Sao Paulo area conference, priesthood session)* (The Teachings of Spencer W. Kimball, p. 501) TLDP:500

### Paul

And God hath set some in the church, first apostles, secondarily prophets, thirdly teachers, after that miracles, then gifts of healings, helps, governments, diversities of tongues. *(Paul writes to the Church at Corinth, Greece, about A.D. 55)* 1Cor.12:28

### Boyd K. Packer

President Kimball mentioned also the authority to command the elements, to walk on the water. The Lord has this power, but He has not given it to mortals, although there are times when righteous men have been inspired to command the forces of nature and have been obeyed. ¶ Nevertheless, in the Church we hold sufficient authority to perform all of the ordinances nec-essary to redeem and to exalt the whole human family. And, because we have the keys to the sealing power, what we bind in proper order here will be bound in heaven. Those keys—the keys to seal and bind on earth, and have it bound in heaven—represent the consummate gift from our God. With that authority we can baptize and bless, we can endow and seal, and the Lord will honor our commitments. (The Holy Temple, pp. 150-51) TLDP:509

---

### 577. Only upon principles of right-eousness can a priesthood bearer manage the powers of heaven.

### Joseph Smith

Behold, there are many called, but few are chosen. And why are they not chosen? 35. Because their hearts are set so much upon the things of this world, and aspire to the honors of men, that they do not learn this one les-son— 36. That the rights of the priesthood are inseparably connected with the powers of heaven, and that the powers of heaven cannot be controlled nor handled only upon the prin-ciples of righteousness. 37. That they may be conferred upon us, it is true; but when we undertake to cover our sins, or to gratify our pride, our vain ambition, or to exercise control or dominion or compulsion upon the souls of the children of men, in any degree of unrighteousness, behold, the heavens with-draw themselves; and the Spirit of the Lord is grieved; and when it is withdrawn, Amen to the priesthood or the authority of that man. *(Revelation received while in Liberty Jail, March 20, 1839: why many are called and few chosen)* D&C 121:34-37

### Joseph Smith

The power, glory and blessings of the Priest-hood could not continue with those who re-ceived ordination only as their righteousness continued; for Cain also being authorized to offer sacrifice, but not offering it in righteous-ness, was cursed. It signifies, then, that the ordinances must be kept in the very way God has appointed; otherwise their Priesthood will prove a cursing instead of a blessing. ¶ If Cain had fulfilled the law of righteousness as did Enoch, he could have walked with God all the days of his life, and never failed of a blessing. . . . *(From an article on priesthood, read at a general conference of the Church by Robert B. Thompson, and included as part of minutes of the conference held in Nauvoo, Ill., Oct. 5, 1840)* HC4:209

### President Harold B. Lee

The penalty if we do use our priesthood unrighteously is that the heavens withdraw themselves and the Spirit of the Lord is grieved. When we lose the Spirit, our priesthood authority is taken from us and we are left to ourselves "to kick against the pricks," when we are being irritated by the admonitions and instructions of our leaders. Then we begin to persecute the saints, which means criticize, and finally to fight against God, and the powers of darkness overtake us if we do not repent and turn from that evil course. (*Mexico City area conference, Melchizedek Priesthood session, Aug. 26, 1972*) (Stand Ye in Holy Places, pp. 253-54) TLDP:524

### Elder Wilford Woodruff

You cannot use the priesthood for any other purpose under heaven but to build up the kingdom and do the will of God; and when you attempt to do otherwise your power will be taken from you. CR1880Apr:83

### President Wilford Woodruff

Let all Israel remember that the eternal and everlasting Priesthood is bestowed upon us for the purpose alone of administering in the ordinances of life and salvation, both for the living and the dead, and no man on earth can use that Priesthood for any other purpose than for the work of the ministry, the perfecting of the Saints, edifying the body of Christ, establishing the Kingdom of Heaven, and redeeming Zion. If we attempt to use it for unrighteous purposes, like lightning from heaven, our power, sooner or later, falls, and we fail to accomplish the designs of God. ("A Communication from President Woodruff," Millennial Star, Aug. 1887, p. 546) TLDP:523

### Elder Joseph F. Smith

This [D&C 84:33-41] makes a very serious matter of receiving this covenant and this Priesthood; for those who receive it must, like God himself, abide in it, and must not fail, and must not be moved out of the way; for those who receive this oath and covenant and turn away from it, and cease to do righteously and to honor this covenant, and will to abide in sin, and repent not, there is no forgiveness for them either in this life or in the world to come. CR1898Apr:65

### Boyd K. Packer

Your authority comes through your ordination; your power comes through obedience and worthiness. . . . ¶ Power in the priesthood comes from doing your duty in ordinary things: attending meetings, accepting assignments, reading the scriptures, keeping the Word of Wisdom. (That All May Be Edified, pp. 29-30) TLDP:500

### Marion G. Romney

These transcendent blessings the Father promises the receiver of the Melchizedek Priesthood by an oath and covenant which he says " . . . he cannot break, neither can it be moved." . . . But these blessings . . . do not come by ordination alone. Ordination to the priesthood is a prerequisite to receiving them, but it does not guarantee them. For a man actually to obtain them, he must faithfully discharge the obligation which is placed upon him when he receives the priesthood. CR1962Apr:17

### Hugh B. Brown

I should like to say to you fathers tonight that our conduct in our homes determines in large measure our worthiness to hold and exercise the priesthood, which is the power of God delegated to man. Almost any man can make a good showing when on parade before the public, but one's integrity is tested when "off duty." The real man is seen and known in the comparative solitude of the home. An office or title will not erase a fault nor guarantee a virtue. CR1962Apr:88

---

## 578. Authority of the priesthood is to be exercised in a pure spirit of love and kindness.

### President Harold B. Lee

The qualities of acceptable priesthood leadership are also carefully defined in this revelation [see D&C 121]. One is to preside over the Church with patience and long-suffering, with gentleness and meekness and with love unfeigned. If one must discipline or reprove with sharpness, he must do it when moved upon by the Holy Ghost, but afterwards he should show forth love, lest the one he has reproved thinks him to be an enemy. In all of our priesthood callings, therefore, we must never forget that it is the business of the Church to save souls, and those over whom we preside are our Father's children, and he will aid us in our endeavors to save every one of them. ACR(Mexico City)1972:76

### Joseph Smith

We have learned by sad experience that it is the nature and disposition of almost all men, as soon as they get a little authority, as they suppose, they will immediately begin to exercise unrighteous dominion. 40. Hence many are called, but few are chosen. 41. No power or influence can or ought to be maintained by virtue of the priesthood, only by persuasion, by long-suffering, by gentleness and meekness, and by love unfeigned; 42. By kindness, and

pure knowledge, which shall greatly enlarge the soul without hypocrisy, and without guile— 43. Reproving betimes with sharpness, when moved upon by the Holy Ghost; and then showing forth afterwards an increase of love toward him whom thou hast reproved, lest he esteem thee to be his enemy; (*Revelation received while in Liberty Jail, March 20, 1839; the priesthood should be used only in righteousness*) D&C 121:39-43
**Joseph Smith**
Behold, there are many called, but few are chosen. And why are they not chosen? 35. Because their hearts are set so much upon the things of this world, and aspire to the honors of men, that they do not learn this one lesson— 36. That the rights of the priesthood are inseparably connected with the powers of heaven, and that the powers of heaven cannot be controlled nor handled only upon the principles of righteousness. 37. That they may be conferred upon us, it is true; but when we undertake to cover our sins, or to gratify our pride, our vain ambition, or to exercise control or dominion or compulsion upon the souls of the children of men, in any degree of unrighteousness, behold, the heavens withdraw themselves; the Spirit of the Lord is grieved; and when it is withdrawn, Amen to the priesthood or the authority of that man. (*Revelation through Joseph Smith while in Liberty Jail, March 20, 1839; why many are called and few chosen*) D&C 121:34-37
**Joseph Smith**
The decisions of these quorums, or either of them, are to be made in all righteousness, in holiness, and lowliness of heart, meekness and long suffering, and in faith, and virtue, and knowledge, temperance, patience, godliness, brotherly kindness and charity; (*Revelation on priesthood, received as the Twelve met in council, March 28, 1835*) D&C 107:30
**President John Taylor**
There is no authority associated with the Holy Priesthood except on the principle of persuasion, and no man has a right to plume himself upon any position he occupies in this Church, for he is simply a servant of God, and a servant of the people, and if any man attempts to use any kind of arbitrary authority, and act with any degree of unrighteousness, God will hold that man to an account for it, and we all of us have to be judged according to the deeds done in the body. We are here as saviours of men, and not as tyrants and oppressors. (*At Parowan, Utah, June 24, 1883, JD24:268*) TLDP:516
**Elder Joseph Fielding Smith**
Most men are inclined to abuse authority, espe-

cially those who wield it who are the least prepared to hold positions of trust. It has been the characteristic of men in power to use that power to gratify their own pride and vain ambitions. More misery has come to the inhabitants of this world through the exercise of authority by those who least deserved it, than from almost any other cause. Rulers of kingdoms in the past have oppressed their subjects, and where they had the power they have sought to increase their dominions. We have had some horrible examples of misplaced ambition which, in recent years, placed the very existence of humanity in peril. These conditions still prevail in high places bringing fear and consternation to the troubled world. ¶ There should not, however, be any of this unrighteous ambition within the Church, but everything should be done in the spirit of love and humility. CHMR2:178; DGSM:70
**President Joseph F. Smith**
For the moment that a Latter-day Saint learns his duty, he will learn that it is his business to make peace, to establish good will, to work righteousness, to be filled with the spirit of kindness, love, charity, and forgiveness; and, so far as he is concerned, there can be no war, no strife, no contention, no quarreling, no disunion; no factions can arise among the people who know their duty as Latter-day Saints. CR1915Apr:4
**Related Witnesses:**
**Hugh B. Brown**
While the Church, which was organized under divine direction, is the kingdom of God on earth, its membership consists of men and women who are not yet made perfect. It is a mixed society with an international complexion, subject in varying degrees to the weaknesses of humanity. It does not claim to be a picture gallery where every portrait is a masterpiece; therefore, Church membership requires continued tolerance, charity, and love of fellow men. CR1958Apr:109-10

---

**579. The Lord gives His authorized servants power over devils.**

**Heber C. Kimball**
I have no fears of anything myself; I do not fear all the devils in hell nor on the earth. I have seen the time, whether in the body or out of it I do not know, but I saw legions of devils; they came by thousands and tens of thousands, and thousands of men will, no doubt, give way before they yield the field; but when they come against me and my brethren, we, having

the priesthood, had power to withstand them all, for we were of God. You have heard President Young preach that a man, with the power of God upon him, all the devils in hell could not do anything with him; but if a man enters into the spirit world in his sins, the devil will have power over him to lead him captive at his will. (Deseret News Weekly, Aug. 20, 1862, p. 58) TLDP:499

**Jesus,**
*recorded in Luke*

And the seventy returned again with joy, saying, Lord, even the devils are subject unto us through thy name. 18. And he said unto them, I beheld Satan as lightning fall from heaven. 19. Behold, I give unto you power to tread on serpents and scorpions, and over all the power of the enemy: and nothing shall by any means hurt you. 20. Notwithstanding in this rejoice not, that the spirits are subject unto you; but rather rejoice, because your names are written in heaven. (*Jesus speaks to the Seventy*) Luke 10:17-20

**Joseph Smith,**
*translating the Book of Moses*

And it came to pass that Moses began to fear exceedingly; and as he began to fear, he saw the bitterness of hell. Nevertheless, calling upon God, he received strength, and he commanded, saying: Depart from me, Satan, for this one God only will I worship, which is the God of glory. 21. And now Satan began to tremble, and the earth shook; and Moses received strength, and called upon God, saying: In the name of the Only Begotten, depart hence, Satan. 22. And it came to pass that Satan cried with a loud voice, with weeping, and wailing, and gnashing of teeth; and he departed hence, even from the presence of Moses, that he beheld him not. 23. And now of this thing Moses bore record; but because of wickedness it is not had among the children of men. (*Revelation to Joseph Smith, 1830; Satan appears to Moses*) Moses 1:20-23

**Elder Spencer W. Kimball**

Not even Lucifer, the Star of the Morning, the arch-enemy of mankind, can withstand the power of the priesthood of God. CR1964Apr:96

**Jesus,**
*recorded in Mark*

And these signs shall follow them that believe; In my name shall they cast out devils; they shall speak with new tongues; (*The risen Jesus Christ to the eleven Apostles*) Mark 16:17

**President Brigham Young,**
*quoted by John A. Widtsoe*

Do you think that we are always going to remain the same size? I am not a stereotyped Latter-day Saint, and do not believe in the doctrine. Every year the Elders of Israel are improv-

ing and learning, and have more power, more influence with the Heavens, more power over the elements, and over diseases, and over the power of Satan, who has ruled this earth from the days of the fall until now. We have to gain power until we break the chain of the enemy. (*In Bowery, Sept. 23, 1860, JD8:185*) DBY:92

**James E. Talmage**

The scriptures declare that certain signs shall attend the Church of Christ, among them the gifts of tongues, healing, immunity from threatening death and the power to control evil spirits. AF:25

**Related Witnesses:**

**Elder Joseph F. Smith**

The hatred of the wicked always has and always will follow the Priesthood and the Saints. The devil will not lose sight of the power of God vested in man—the Holy Priesthood. He fears it, he hates it, and will never cease to stir up the hearts of the debased and corrupt in anger and malice towards those who hold this power, and to persecute the Saints, until he is bound. (*In Tabernacle, April 2, 1877, JD19:24*) TLDP:139

**Elder John Taylor**

Who is Satan? A being powerful, energetic, deceptive, insinuating; and yet necessary to develop the evil, as there are bitters, to make us appreciate the sweet; darkness, to make us appreciate the light; evil and sorrows, that we may appreciate the good; error that we may be enabled to appreciate truth; misery, in order that we may appreciate happiness. . . . ¶ But again, who is Satan? He is a being of God's own make, under his control, subject to his will, cast out of heaven for rebellion; and when his services can be dispensed with, an angel will cast him into the bottomless pit. Can he fight against and overcome God? verily, No! Can he alter the designs of God? verily, No! Satan may rage, but the Lord can confine him within proper limits. He may instigate rebellion against God, but the Lord can bind him in chains. (The Government of God, pp. 80-81) TLDP:141

**President Brigham Young,**
*quoted by John A. Widtsoe*

When men overcome as our faithful brethren have, and go where they see Joseph, who will dictate them and be their head and Prophet all the time, they have power over all disembodied evil spirits, for they have overcome them. Those evil spirits are under the command and control of every man that has had the Priesthood on him, and has honored it in the flesh, just as much as my hand is under my control. (*Funeral sermon for Jedediah M. Grant, in Tabernacle, Dec. 4, 1856, JD4:132*) DBY:378

# List of Doctrines

## PRIESTHOOD: Church Government

*Doctrines Located in This Topic*

### (1) Church Government

580. There are two orders of the priesthood in the Church, the Melchizedek and Aaronic.

581. All authorities or offices in the Church are appendages to the Melchizedek Priesthood.

582. Officers in the Church are chosen by the Lord, not by the people.

583. No one should seek or aspire to be appointed to any specific office or calling in the Church.

584. Priesthood leaders have the right to counsel Church members in temporal as well as spiritual matters.

585. Leaders in the Church are chosen by the Lord then accepted by the people—God appoints, the people sustain: government of the Church is by consent of the governed.

### (2) Common Consent

586. No person may function in the Church in *any* official capacity without the consent of the people, after the call to serve has been made.

587. All organizational things that the Church does—the procedures that it follows and the officers that it appoints—must be done by common consent.

### (3) Aaronic Priesthood

588. The Aaronic Priesthood administers in matters pertaining to the temporal welfare of the people.

589. The Aaronic Priesthood was restored to earth by John the Baptist, who personally bestowed the keys thereof upon Joseph Smith and Oliver Cowdery.

590. The Aaronic Priesthood is called the lesser priesthood because it is an appendage to the greater Melchizedek Priesthood.

591. The bishop holds the keys and authority of presidency of the Aaronic Priesthood.

### (4) Melchizedek Priesthood

592. The "Holy Priesthood after the order of the Son of God" is also called the Melchizedek Priesthood.

593. Priesthood is the ruling, presiding, governing authority in the Church.

# PRIESTHOOD: Church Government continued

594. The Church of Jesus Christ of Latter-day Saints is directed and governed by revelation from God through priesthood authorities.

595. The Melchizedek Priesthood administers primarily in the spiritual matters of the Church.

596. The Melchizedek Priesthood always presides over the Aaronic Priesthood.

597. The President of the Church alone holds the fulness of the keys of the priesthood, the power of directing the labors of the priesthood.

598. Three high priests form the First Presidency, the presiding council in the Church.

599. The Quorum of the Twelve Apostles stands next in authority to the First Presidency in the Church.

600. Each office in the priesthood (elder, seventy, high priest, bishop, Apostle, etc.) is a calling that derives all of its authority from the priesthood; officers hold different callings, but the same priesthood.

601. Except for the President of the Church, all priesthood holders have designated limits to their authority.

*Doctrines on PRIESTHOOD: Church Government Located in Other Topics*

90. The latter-day church of Christ has the same organization that Jesus Himself established while He was on the earth.

111. The oath and covenant of the priesthood is an everlasting covenant between God and each man who receives the Melchizedek Priesthood ordination.

246. Those appointed by the Lord to watch over the Church are entitled to the discernment of all the gifts of the Spirit.

493. Although a man by his ordination holds authority of the priesthood, before he can lawfully perform any ordinance, he must receive authorization from one who holds the keys in the Church for the administration of that ordinance.

539. We are to pray for those who have religious authority over us.

571. No person may hold any office in the Church unless called and publicly given assignment by someone who has priesthood authority to issue the call.

## PRIESTHOOD: Church Government

(1) Church Government
(2) Common Consent
(3) Aaronic Priesthood
(4) Melchizedek Priesthood

### (1) Church Government

580. There are two orders of the priest-hood in the Church, the Melchizedek and Aaronic.

**Joseph Smith**

There are, in the church, two priesthoods, namely, the Melchizedek and Aaronic, including the Levitical Priesthood. . . . 6. But there are two divisions or grand heads—one is the Melchizedek Priesthood, and the other is the Aaronic or Levitical Priesthood. . . . 13. The second priesthood is called the Priesthood of Aaron, because it was conferred upon Aaron and his seed, throughout all their generations. 14. Why it is called the lesser priesthood is because it is an appendage to the greater, or the Melchizedek Priesthood, and has power in administering outward ordinances. (*Revelation on priesthood, received as the Twelve met in council, March 28, 1835*) D&C 107:1,6,13-14

**Joseph Smith,**
*quoted by Elder Joseph Fielding Smith*

There are two Priesthoods spoken of in the Scriptures, viz., the Melchizedek and the Aaronic or Levitical. Although there are two Priesthoods, yet the Melchizedek Priesthood comprehends the Aaronic or Levitical Priesthood, and is the grand head, and holds the highest authority which pertains to the priest-hood, and the keys of the Kingdom of God in all ages of the world to the latest posterity on the earth; and is the channel through which all knowledge, doctrine, the plan of salvation and every important matter is revealed from heaven. ¶ Its institution was prior to the "foundation of this earth, or the morning stars sang together, or the Sons of God shouted for joy," and is the highest and holiest Priesthood, and is after the order of the Son of God, and all other Priest-hoods are only parts, ramifications, powers and blessings belonging to the same, and are held, controlled, and directed by it. (*From an article on priesthood read at a general conference of the Church by Robert B. Thompson, and included as part of minutes of the conference held in Nauvoo, Ill., Oct. 5, 1840, see HC4:207-12*) TPJS:166-67

**President Joseph F. Smith**

The Church has two characteristics—the temporal and the spiritual, and one is not without the other. We maintain that both are essential and that one without the other is incomplete and ineffectual. Hence, the Lord instituted in the government of the Church two Priesthoods—the lesser or Aaronic, having special charge of the temporal, and the higher or Melchizedek, looking to the spiritual welfare of the people. (Gospel Doctrine, p. 150) DGSM:68

**James A. Talmage**

The Church of Jesus Christ of Latter-day Saints recognizes two orders of Priesthood, the lesser called the Aaronic, the greater known as the Melchizedek order. AF:186

---

581. All authorities or offices in the Church are appendages to the Melchizedek Priesthood.

**President Joseph F. Smith**

There is no office growing out of this Priesthood that is or can be greater than the Priesthood itself. It is from the Priesthood that the office derives its authority and power. No office gives authority to the Priesthood. No office adds to the power of the Priesthood. But all offices in the Church derive their power, their virtue, their authority, from the Priesthood. If our brethren would get this principle thoroughly established in their minds, there would be less misunderstanding in relation to the functions of government in the Church than there is. Today the question is, which is the greater—the high priest or the seventy—the seventy or the high priest? I tell you that neither of them is the greater, and neither of them is the lesser. Their callings lie in different directions, but they are from the same Priesthood. If it were necessary, the Seventy, holding the Melchizedek Priesthood, as he does, I say *if it were necessary,* he could ordain a high priest; and if it were necessary for a high priest to ordain a seventy, he could do that. Why? Because both of them hold the Melchizedek Priesthood. Then again, if it were necessary, though I do not expect the necessity will ever arise, and there was no man left on earth holding the Melchizedek Priesthood, except an elder—that elder, by the inspiration of the Spirit of God and by the direction of the Almighty, could proceed, and should proceed, to organize the Church of Jesus Christ in all its perfection, because he holds the Melchizedek Priesthood. But the house of God is a house of order, and while the other officers remain in the Church, we must observe the order of the priesthood, and we must perform ordinances and ordinations strictly in accordance with that order, as it has been established in the Church through the instrumentality of the Prophet Joseph Smith and his successors. CR1903Oct:87

**Joseph Smith**

There are, in the church, two priesthoods, namely, the Melchizedek and Aaronic, including the Levitical Priesthood. . . . 5. All other authorities or offices in the church are appendages to this Melchizedek Priesthood. 6. But there are two divisions or grand heads—one is the Melchizedek Priesthood, and the other is the Aaronic or Levitical Priesthood. . . . 8. The Melchizedek Priesthood holds the right of presidency, and has power and authority over all the offices in the church in all ages of the world, to administer in spiritual things. 9. The Presidency of the High Priesthood, after the order of Melchizedek, have a right to officiate in all the offices in the church. 10. High priests after the order of the Melchizedek Priesthood have a right to officiate in their own standing, under the direction of the presidency, in administering spiritual things, and also in the office of an elder, priest (of the Levitical order), teacher, deacon, and member. 11. An elder has a right to officiate in his stead when the high priest is not present. 12. The high priest and elder are to administer in spiritual things, agreeable to the covenants and commandments of the church; and they have a right to officiate in all these offices of the church when there are no higher authorities present. . . . 17. But as a high priest of the Melchizedek Priesthood has authority to officiate in all the lesser offices, he may officiate in the office of bishop when no literal descendant of Aaron can be found, provided he is called and set apart and ordained unto this power by the hands of the Presidency of the Melchizedek Priesthood. (*Revelation on priesthood, received as the Twelve met in council, March 28, 1835*) D&C 107:1,5-6,8-12,17

**Boyd K. Packer**

The higher priesthood, the Melchizedek Priesthood, always presides over the Aaronic, or the lesser, Priesthood. Aaron was the high priest, or the presiding priest, of the Aaronic Priesthood. But Moses presided over Aaron because Moses held the Melchizedek Priesthood. ¶ The fact that it is called the lesser priesthood does not diminish at all the importance of the Aaronic Priesthood. The Lord said it is necessary to the Melchizedek Priesthood. (See D&C 84:29.)

Any holder of the higher priesthood should feel greatly honored to perform the ordinances of the Aaronic Priesthood, for they have great spiritual importance. (That All May Be Edified, p. 25) TLDP:507

**President Joseph F. Smith**

I have the right to bless. I hold the keys of the Melchizedek Priesthood and of the office and power of patriarch. It is my right to bless; for all the keys and authority and power pertaining to the government of the Church and to the Melchizedek and Aaronic Priesthood are centered in the presiding officer of the Church. There is no business nor office within the Church, that the President of the Church may not fill, and may not do, if it is necessary, or if it is required of him to do it. He holds the office of patriarch; he holds the office of high priest and of apostle, of seventy, of elder, of bishop and of priest, teacher and deacon in the Church; all these belong to the Presidency of the Church of Jesus Christ of Latter-day Saints, and they can officiate in any and in all of these callings when occasion requires. CR1915Oct:7

**Related Witnesses:**

**Elder John Taylor**

While the power of the higher, or Melchizedek is to hold the keys of all the spiritual blessings of the Church; . . . and to preside over all the spiritual officers of the Church, yet the Presidency of the High Priesthood, after the order of Melchizedek, have a right to officiate in all the offices in the Church, both spiritual and temporal. (Items on Priesthood, p. 31) TLDP:507

---

**582. Officers in the Church are chosen by the Lord, not by the people.**

**Stephen L. Richards**

This Church is not democratic. This Church is a kingdom. We don't make the laws. God makes the laws. We ourselves do not appoint authorities and the administrators, they are appointed by the inspiration that emanates from him. ¶ We have a democratic method in that we sustain those who are appointed. Without that sustaining vote they cannot legally function. All the people in the whole ward cannot unanimously nominate a bishop. The President of the Church cannot install himself unless the majority of the people sustain him. Never forget that this is a kingdom and never forget the laws of the Church are not manmade. (*In Las Vegas, Nev., priesthood meeting, four combined wards*) (Church News, Nov. 22, 1951, p. 2) TLDP:98

### President Joseph F. Smith

There is no officer in the Church of Jesus Christ of Latter-day Saints chosen by the body. The Lord has given us His way to do these things. He has revealed to us that it is the duty of the presiding authorities to appoint and call; and then those whom they choose for any official position in the Church shall be presented to the body. If the body reject them, they are responsible for that rejection. They have the right to reject, if they will, or to receive them and sustain them by their faith and prayers. CR1907Apr:4

### Elder Harold B. Lee,
#### *also quoting Parley P. Pratt*

We sometimes hear people who talk about the Church as a democracy. Well, it isn't any such thing. Democracy means a government where the sole authority is vested in the people—the right to nominate, the right to release, to change. The Church is not a democracy. It is more like a kingdom than a democracy—and yet it is not wholly like a kingdom, except that we accept the Lord as the king, who has under His direction an earthly head who operates and becomes His mouthpiece. It is an organization that is defined more accurately as a theocracy, which means that it is something like a kingdom as the world would define it, and yet something like a democracy. . . . ¶ Let me read you something by Parley P. Pratt that appeared in the Millennial Star in 1845. It was called a "Proclamation." ¶ "The legislative, judicial, and executive power is vested in Him (the Lord). He reveals the laws, and he elects, chooses, or appoints the officers; and holds the right to reprove, to correct, or even to remove them at pleasure. Hence the necessity of a constant intercourse by direct revelation between Him and His Church. As a precedent for the foregoing facts, we refer to the examples of all ages as recorded in the Scriptures. ¶ "This order of government began in Eden—God appointed Adam to govern the earth and gave him laws. ¶ "It was perpetuated in a regular succession from Adam to Noah to Melchizedek, Abraham, Isaac, Jacob, Joseph, Moses, Samuel, the prophets, John, Jesus and his apostles. All, and each of which were chosen by the Lord, and not by the people." (Millennial Star, March 1843, 5:150, Stand Ye in Holy Places, pp. 150-51) TLDP:83

### George Q. Cannon

God gave revelations unto this Church in exceeding great plainness, and there was one principle that was emphatically dwelt upon and enforced, namely, that there was but one channel, one channel alone, through which the word of God and the commandments of God should come to this people. The word of God was not to come from the people up. It was not vox populi, vox dei, but it was to be vox dei, vox populi—that is, the voice of God and then the voice of the people—from God downward through the channel that He should appoint; by the means that He should institute, that word should come to the people, and when obeyed by the people would bring the union and the love and the strength consequent upon union and love. And this has been the peculiarity and the excellence of this work of God thus far in the earth. Its excellence has consisted in this. Its power, its glory, the glory that we have as a people, the glory that belongs to the Church of God in this peculiar feature, that the word of God to us comes from God and not from the people. It is received by the people, accepted by the people, submitted to by the people, and this has produced the union and the love, as I have said, that have characterized the work thus far in its progress in the earth. (*In Assembly Hall, Dec. 2, 1883, JD24:362-63*) TLDP:247-48

**Related Witnesses:**

### President Joseph F. Smith

Nominations to Church office may be made by revelation; and the right of nomination is usually exercised by those holding high authority. . . . (*Address from the First Presidency of the Church to the world, delivered to and accepted by vote of the Church in general conference, April 1907*) CR1907Apr(Appendix)9

### Marion G. Romney

The Lord has set up a perfectly safe procedure in placing the power of nomination in the presiding officers, because in back of the government of the Church in the earth is the Lord Jesus Christ himself. I believe that when the Presidency of this Church nominates a person for an office, it is not a personal nomination. I have the confidence in the Presidency and that testimony of the divinity of this Church. I believe that the Lord Jesus Christ reveals to them through the Spirit of the Holy Ghost the men they should name to office, and I believe that same Spirit will inspire and direct the presidents of stakes and bishops of wards and the heads of other organizations in this Church, if they will live for such inspiration, so that when they name people for office, they will name them under the inspiration of the Holy Spirit. CR1947Oct:40

### Paul

For every high priest taken from among men is ordained for men in things pertaining to God. . . . 4. And no man taketh this honour unto himself, but he that is called of God, as was Aaron. (*Letter to the Jewish members of the Church, about A.D. 60*) Heb.5:1,4

### Joseph Smith,
*receiving the Word of the Lord*

For I have given him the keys of the mysteries, and the revelations which are sealed, until I shall appoint unto them another in his stead. (*Revelation for Oliver Cowdery, Sept. 1830*) D&C 28:7

### Marion G. Romney

No one should seek to be appointed to any particular office in the Church. Such an aspiration is not a righteous desire; it is a self-serving ambition. We should have a motivating desire to magnify our callings in the priesthood, whatever they may be. We should demonstrate that desire by living the gospel and diligently performing whatever service we are called upon to render. Holding a particular office in the Church will never save a person. One's salvation depends upon how well he discharges the duties of the service to which he is called. CR1973Apr:116-17

---

**583. No one should seek or aspire to be appointed to any specific office or calling in the Church.**

### Marion G. Romney

No one should seek to be appointed to any particular office in the Church. Such an aspiration is not a righteous desire; it is a self-serving ambition. We should have a motivating desire to magnify our callings in the priesthood, whatever they may be. We should demonstrate that desire by living the gospel and diligently performing whatever service we are called upon to render. Holding a particular office in the Church will never save a person. One's salvation depends upon how well he discharges the duties of the service to which he is called. CR1973Apr:116-17

### J. Reuben Clark, Jr.

In the service of the Lord, it is not where you serve but how. In The Church of Jesus Christ of Latter-day Saints, one takes the place to which one is duly called, which place one neither seeks nor declines. CR1951Apr:154

### J. Reuben Clark, Jr.

Furthermore, the actual procedure for voting is normally by the uplifted hand of those present. No electioneering, no speech-making, no stating of objections, no proposing of candidates, no vocal demonstration of any kind is in order. . . . ¶ The result of this system is that there has never been any politics in the Church. Churchmen do not seek Church office. The best evidence that a man is unfit for Church office is the fact that he wants it. CR1940Apr:72

### President Joseph F. Smith,
### Anthon H. Lund, Charles W. Penrose
(First Presidency)

Priesthood is not given for the honor or aggrandizement of man, but for the ministry of service among those for whom the bearers of that sacred commission are called to labor. Be it remembered that even our Lord and Master, after long fasting, when faint in body and physically weakened by exhausting vigils and continued abstinence, resisted the arch tempter's suggestion that he use the authority and power of his Messiahship to provide for his own immediate needs. ¶ The God-given titles of honor and of more than human distinction associated with the several offices in and orders of the Holy Priesthood, are not to be used nor considered as are the titles originated by man; they are not for adornment nor are they expressive of mastership, but rather of appointment to humble service in the work of the one Master whom we profess to serve. ("On Titles," IE1914Mar:479) TLDP:516

### Dallin H. Oaks

Some may serve for hope of earthly reward. Such a man or woman might serve in Church positions or in private acts of mercy in an effort to achieve prominence or cultivate contacts that would increase income or aid in acquiring wealth. Others might serve in order to obtain worldly honors, prominence, or power. ¶ The scriptures have a word for gospel service "for the sake of riches and honor;" it is "priestcraft" (Alma 1:16). . . . ¶ Service that is ostensibly unselfish but is really for the sake of riches or honor surely comes within the Savior's condemnation of those who "outwardly appear righteous unto men, but within . . . are full of hypocrisy and iniquity" (Matt.23:28). Such service earns no gospel reward. CR1984Oct:14

### Howard W. Hunter

It is easy to understand why a proud man fails. He is content to rely upon himself only. This is evident in those who seek social position or who push others aside to gain position in fields of business, government, education, sports, or other endeavors. . . . History bears record that those who have exalted themselves have been abased, but the humble have been exalted. On every busy street there are Pharisees and publicans. It may be that one of them bears our name. CR1984Apr:89; MPSG1989:19

### Stephen L. Richards

This Church is not democratic. This Church is a kingdom. We don't make the laws. God makes the laws. We ourselves do not appoint authorities and the administrators, they are appointed by the inspiration that emanates from him. ¶ We have a democratic method in that we sustain those who are appointed. Without that sustaining vote they cannot legally function. All the people in the whole ward cannot unanimously nominate a bishop. The President of the Church cannot install himself unless the majority of the people sustain him. Never forget that this is a kingdom and never forget the laws of the Church are not man-made. (*In Las Vegas, Nev., priesthood meeting, four combined wards*) (Church News, Nov. 22, 1951, p. 2) TLDP:98

### Jesus,
#### recorded in Luke
For whosoever exalteth himself shall be abased; and he that humbleth himself shall be exalted. (*Jesus teaches humility as he eats bread at the house of one of the chief Pharisees, observing how many of those that were invited chose the chief rooms*) Luke 14:11

### Joseph Smith,
#### receiving the Word of the Lord
And also let my servant William W. Phelps stand in the office to which I have appointed him, and receive his inheritance in the land; 41. And also he hath need to repent, for I, the Lord, am not well pleased with him, for he seeketh to excel, and he is not sufficiently meek before me. (*Revelation for the elders of the Church, Aug. 1, 1831*) D&C 58:40-41

### Nephi, son of Lehi
He commandeth that there shall be no priestcrafts; for, behold priestcrafts are that men preach and set themselves up for a light unto the world, that they may get gain and praise of the world; but they seek not the welfare of Zion. (*Nephi gives commandments of God to Nephites, 559-545 B.C.*) 2Ne.26:29

### Related Witnesses:
#### President Joseph F. Smith
Nominations to Church office may be made by revelation; and the right of nomination is usually exercised by those holding high authority. . . . (*Address from the First Presidency of the Church to the world, delivered to and accepted by vote of the Church in general conference, April 1907*) CR1907Apr(Appendix)9

#### Joseph Smith
We believe that a man must be called of God, by prophecy, and by the laying on of hands by those who are in authority, to preach the Gospel and administer in the ordinances thereof. (*The fifth of the thirteen Articles of Faith; letter to John Wentworth, March 1, 1842*) AofF:5

#### President Ezra Taft Benson
We are tempted daily to elevate ourselves above others and diminish them. ¶ The proud make every man their adversary by pitting their intellects, opinions, works, wealth, talents, or any other worldly measuring device against others. In the words of C. S. Lewis: "Pride gets no pleasure out of having something, only out of having more of it than the next man. . . . It is the comparison that makes you proud: the pleasure of being above the rest. Once the element of competition has gone, pride has gone." (Mere Christianity, New York: Macmillan 1952, pp. 109-10) CR1989Apr:4

### Alma, the younger,
#### quoted by Mormon
And now, O my son, ye are called of God to preach the word unto this people. (*Alma speaks to his son, Corianton, concerning the resurrection of the dead, about 73 B.C.*) Alma 42:31

### Joseph Smith
Which commandments were given to Joseph Smith, Jun., who was called of God, and ordained an apostle of Jesus Christ, to be the first elder of this church; 3. And to Oliver Cowdery, who was also called of God, an apostle of Jesus Christ, to be the second elder of this church, and ordained under his hand; (*Revelation on Church Organization and Government, April 1830*) D&C 20:2-3

### Mormon
Now the cause of this iniquity of the people was this—Satan had great power, unto the stirring up of the people to do all manner of iniquity, and to the puffing them up with pride, tempting them to seek for power, and authority, and riches, and the vain things of the world. (*Much iniquity abounds among the Nephites, A.D. 29-30*) 3Ne.6:15

### Isaiah
How art thou fallen from heaven, O Lucifer, son of the morning! how art thou cut down to the ground, which didst weaken the nations! 13. For thou hast said in thine heart, I will ascend into heaven, I will exalt my throne above the stars of God: I will sit also upon the mount of the congregation, in the sides of the north: 14. I will ascend above the heights of the clouds; I will be like the most High. (*Lucifer is cast out of heaven for rebellion*) Isa.14:12-14

### John
Nevertheless among the chief rulers also many believed on him; but because of the Pharisees they did not confess him, lest they should be put out of the synagogue: 43. For they loved the praise of men more than the praise of God. (*Although Jesus had done many miracles before the people, yet they feared man more than God*) John 12:42-43

584. Priesthood leaders have the right to counsel Church members in temporal as well as spiritual matters.

### President Joseph F. Smith

That the Church claims the right to counsel and advise her members in temporal as will as spiritual affairs is admitted. Leading Church officials, men of practical experience in pioneer life, have aided the people in establishing settlements throughout the inter-mountain west, and have given them, gratuitously, the benefit of their broader knowledge of things, through counsel and direction, which the people have followed to their advantage; and both the wisdom of the leaders and the good sense of the people are vindicated in the results achieved. All this has been done without the exercise of arbitrary power. It has resulted from wise counsels, persuasively given and willingly followed. (*Address from the First Presidency of the Church to the world, delivered to and accepted by vote ι the Church in general conference, April 1907*) CR1907Apr(Appendix)8

### Gordon B. Hinckley

The Lord intended that a priesthood quorum should be far more than a class in theology on Sunday mornings. Of course, the building of spirituality and the strengthening of testimony through effective gospel teaching is an important priesthood responsibility. But this is only a segment of the quorum function. Each quorum must be a working brotherhood for every member if its purpose is to be realized. There must be instruction in principles of personal and family preparedness. If effectively taught, such instruction will become preventative welfare, because the quorum member and his family, equipped with such knowledge, will be the better prepared to handle many difficulties that might arise. The teaching of financial and resource management, home production and storage, the fostering of such activities as will promote physical, emotional, and spiritual health might all be the proper and legitimate concerns of the presidency of the quorum in behalf of its members. ¶ Furthermore, the quorum becomes a resource of organized and disciplined manpower available to the bishop and stake president in carrying forward the production and processing of welfare commodities. It is in the quorum that the strong hands of willing men are found to thin the beets, to haul the hay, to build the fences, and to carry forward the myriad requirements of our welfare projects. ("Welfare Responsibilities of the Priesthood Quorums," EN1977Nov:86) TLDP:513

### Elder Lorenzo Snow

This priesthood or authority in which we stand is the medium or channel through which our Heavenly Father has purposed to communicate light, intelligence, gifts, powers, and spiritual and temporal salvation, unto the present generation. ("A Hint to the Wise," Millennial Star, July 1841, p. 38) TLDP:498

### Elder John Taylor

While the power of the higher, or Melchizedek is to hold the keys of all the spiritual blessings of the Church; . . . and to preside over all the spiritual officers of the Church, yet the Presidency of the High Priesthood, after the order of Melchizedek, have a right to officiate in all the offices in the Church, both spiritual and temporal. (Items on Priesthood, p. 31) TLDP:507

### J. Reuben Clark, Jr., quoted by Gordon B. Hinckley

In his temporal administrations, the bishop looks at every needy person as a temporary problem, caring for them until they can help themselves; the priesthood must look at their needy brethren as a continuing problem until not only his temporal needs are met, but his spiritual ones also. As a concrete example—a bishop extends help while the artisan or craftsman is out of work and in want; a priesthood quorum sets him up in work and tries to see that he goes along until fully self-supporting and active in his priesthood duties. ("Welfare Responsibilities of the Priesthood Quorums," EN1977Nov:86) TLDP:513

## (2) Common Consent

585. Leaders in the Church are chosen by the Lord then accepted by the people—God appoints, the people sustain: government of the Church is by consent of the governed.

### President Harold B. Lee

The leaders are chosen by the Lord and not by the people. The Church is not a democracy. We must not speak of the Church as a democracy. It is true that the people have a voice in the kingdom of God. No officer is to preside over a branch or a stake until he is sustained by a vote of that body over which he is to preside. They may reject, but they do not nominate and they do not release. That is done by a higher authority. ("The Place of the Prophet, Seer, and Revelator," The Charge to Religious Educators, p. 136) TLDP:98

**Stephen L. Richards**

This Church is not democratic. This Church is a kingdom. We don't make the laws. God makes the laws. We ourselves do not appoint authorities and the administrators, they are appointed by the inspiration that emanates from him. ¶ We have a democratic method in that we sustain those who are appointed. Without that sustaining vote they cannot legally function. All the people in the whole ward cannot unanimously nominate a bishop. The President of the Church cannot install himself unless the majority of the people sustain him. Never forget that this is a kingdom and never forget the laws of the Church are not man-made. (*In Las Vegas, Nev. priesthood meeting, four combined wards*) (Church News, Nov. 22, 1951, p. 2) TLDP:98

**J. Reuben Clark, Jr.**

Again speaking in terms of political science, in the Church the nominating power rests in a group, the General Authorities, but the sustaining or electing power rests in the body of the Church, which under no circumstances nominates officers, the function of the Church body being solely to sustain or to elect. In fact, as will be seen, the General Authority or other officer is proposed to the body of the Church for their sustaining vote. . . . ¶ Furthermore, the actual procedure for voting is normally by the uplifted hand of those present. No electioneering, no speech-making, no stating of objections, no proposing of candidates, no vocal demonstration of any kind is in order. Anyone seeking to do any of these things would not only be out of order as a matter of procedure, but would be likewise breaking the peace of the State by interrupting and disturbing a public assembly, would be subject to arrest as a disturber of the peace, and if necessary, would have to be so dealt with as a matter of public order. This assembly might be called the "voting booth" of the Church. . . . ¶ It is obvious that only members of the Church are entitled to vote, and an excommunicant is not a member. ¶ Anyone not desiring to sustain anyone proposed may not only indicate his dissent here but he may, if he wishes, present his objections to the proper authority of the Church, and will be given an appropriate hearing. This is the rule and order of the Church. . . . ¶ With this view of the rights, powers, and duties of the President of the High Priesthood of the Church, and also of the First Presidency, it is clear that the sustaining vote by the people is not, and is not to be regarded as, a mere matter of form, but on the contrary a matter of the last gravity. Every per-

son is entitled to indicate whether or not he or she can sustain the officer proposed. While all the Church members vote and sustain the officer, yet the sustaining Priesthood power comes from the Priesthood itself. Your voting will result in the Church body's acknowledging the administration of the man appointed by revelation as the Presiding High Priest over the High Priesthood of the Church. CR1940Apr:71-72

**Elder John Taylor**

Who have we for our ruling power? Where and how did he obtain his authority? . . .[It] is by the voice of God and the voice of the people, that our present President obtained his authority. . . . He obtains his authority first from God, and secondly from the people. . . . Is there a monarch, potentate, or power under the heavens that undergoes a scrutiny as fine as this? No, there is not; and yet this is done twice a year, before all the Saints in the world. Here are legitimacy and rule. You place the power in their hands to govern, dictate, regulate, and put in order the affairs of the kingdom of God. This is, Vox Dei vox populi. God appoints, the people sustain. (*In Tabernacle, April 8, 1853, JD1:229-30*) TLDP:95

**President Joseph F. Smith**

We deny the existence of arbitrary power in the Church; and this because its government is moral government purely, and its forces are applied through kindness, reason, and persuasion. Government by consent of the governed is the rule of the Church. . . . ¶ Nominations to Church office may be made by revelation; and the right of nomination is usually exercised by those holding high authority, but it is a law that no person is to be ordained to any office in the Church, where there is a regularly organized branch of the same, without the vote of its members. This law is operative as to all the officers of the Church, from the president down to the deacon. The ecclesiastical government itself exists by the will of the people; elections are frequent, and the members are at liberty to vote as they choose. True, the elective principle here operates by popular acceptance, rather than through popular selection, but it is none the less real. . . . The Church officers in the exercise of their functions, are answerable to the Church. No officer, however exalted his position, is exempt from this law. All decisions, rulings and conduct of officials are subject to investigation, correction, revision and final rejection by the general assembly of the priesthood of the Church, its final court of appeal. Even the President, its highest officer, is subject to these laws and special provision is made for his trial, and, if necessary, his deposition. (*Address from the First Presidency of the Church to the world, delivered to and accepted by vote of the Church in general conference, April 1907*) CR1907Apr(Appendix)8

**President Joseph F. Smith**

There is no officer in the Church of Jesus Christ of Latter-day Saints chosen by the body. The Lord has given us His way to do these things. He has revealed to us that it is the duty of the presiding authorities to appoint and call; and then those whom they choose for any official position in the Church shall be presented to the body. If the body reject them, they are responsible for that rejection. They have the right to reject, if they will, or to receive them and sustain them by their faith and prayers. CR1907Apr:4

**Orson F. Whitney**

Obedient to the divine mandate spoken to them in Father Whitmer's humble home [HC1:61], Joseph and Oliver took steps to ascertain whether or not their brethren would sanction their ordination as Elders of the Church and were willing to come under their spiritual tutelage. ¶ What!—exclaims one. After these men had communed with heavenly beings and received from them commandments for their guidance; after receiving divine authority to preach the Gospel, administer its ordinances, and establish once more on earth the long absent Church of Christ! After all this must they go before the people and ask their consent to organize them and preside over them as a religious body? Yes, that was precisely the situation. Notwithstanding all those glorious manifestations, they were not yet fully qualified to hold the high positions unto which they had been divinely called. One element was lacking—the consent of the people. Until that consent was given, there could be no church with these people as its members and those men as its presiding authorities. The Great Ruler of all never did and never will foist upon any of his people, in branch, ward, stake or Church capacity, a presiding officer whom they are not willing to accept and uphold. ¶ Happily for all concerned, the brethren associated with Joseph and Oliver on that memorable sixth of April of the year 1830, did sanction their ordination, did "decide by vote" to accept them as their "spiritual teachers." ¶ But suppose it had been otherwise. Suppose the brethren in question had not been willing to accept the men whom the Lord had chosen, but had lifted their hands against instead of for them. What would have been the result? Would such action have taken from Joseph and Oliver their Priesthood or their gifts

and powers as seers, prophets and revelators of the Most High? No. Any more than it would have blotted out the fact that Joseph had seen God, and that he and Oliver had communed with angels sent from Heaven to ordain them. Their brethren had not given them the Priesthood, had not made them prophets and seers, and they would have remained such regardless of any adverse action on the part of their associates. The Gospel, the Priesthood, the keys of the Kingdom of Heaven are not within the gift of the membership of the Church. They are bestowed by the Head of the Church, Jesus Christ, in person or by proxy, and without his consent no power on earth or under the earth could take them away. ¶ But if the vote had been unfavorable, this would have resulted: The brethren and sisters who were waiting to be admitted into the Church would have closed the door in their own faces, would have cut themselves off from a most precious privilege, would have deprived themselves of the inestimable benefits flowing from the exercise of the gifts and powers possessed by the men divinely commissioned to inaugurate this great Latter-day Work; and they could have gone elsewhere, and under divine direction, have organized the Church of Christ among any people worthy to constitute its membership and willing that these men should be their leaders. But the vote was in their favor, thank the Lord! and we who are here today are among the beneficiaries of that act of faith and humility. CR1930Oct:44-46

**Orson Pratt**

What! the people have a right to reject those whom the Lord names? Yes, they have this right, he gave it to them. "Let them be approved of or not approved of;" showing that he had respect to the people themselves, that they should vote and give their general voice to either sustain or not to sustain. (*In new Tabernacle, Oct. 5, 1877, JD19:119*) TLDP:95

**John A. Widtsoe**

Every officer of the Priesthood or auxiliary organizations, though properly nominated, holds his position in the Church only with the consent of the people. Officers may be nominated by the Presidency of the Church, but unless the people accept them as officials, they cannot exercise the authority of the offices to which they have been called. All things in the Church must be done by common consent. This makes the people, men and women, under God, the rulers of the Church. Even the President of the Church, before he can fully enter upon his duties, or continue in the office, must be sustained by the people. It is the common custom in the Church to vote on Church officers in the general stake and ward conferences. This gives every member an opportunity to vote for or against the officers. Meanwhile, the judiciary system of the Church is such that there is ample provision whereby any officer of the Church, if found in error, may be brought to justice and if found guilty be removed from his position. ¶ The doctrine of common consent is fundamental in the Church, and is coincident with the fact that the Church belongs to all the people. Since the authority of the Priesthood is vested in all the people, it follows that the officials of the Priesthood must be responsible to the people. The responsibility and work of the Church are not only for but by the people as a whole. (A Rational Theology, p. 109) TLDP:96

**Bruce R. McConkie**
All of the organizational things which the Church does—that is, the procedures which it follows and the officers which it appoints—must be done by common consent, by much faith and prayer. . . . ¶ General Church business cannot be transacted in secret. No man, for instance, could be appointed in secret to head the Church or to carry on some supposed great program for the salvation of men. Conferences are to transact the business of the Church. ¶ . . . . No man can so much as be ordained to any office in the Church without a vote of the Church. There is no such thing as a secret ordination to office, either high or low, in the Church of Christ. The Lord does not work in dark corners. His great works are trumpeted in the ears of all living so that every soul who is willing to do so may learn of them. (Common Consent pamphlet, 1955, pp. 12-13) TLDP:96

**Related Witnesses:**

**Elder Harold B. Lee,**
*also quoting Parley P. Pratt*
Let me read you something by Parley P. Pratt that appeared in the Millennial Star in 1845. It was called a "Proclamation." ¶ "The legislative, judicial, and executive power is vested in Him (the Lord). He reveals the laws, and he elects, chooses, or appoints the officers; and holds the right to reprove, to correct, or even to remove them at pleasure. Hence the necessity of a constant intercourse by direct revelation between Him and His Church." (Stand Ye in Holy Places, pp. 150-51) TLDP:83

**Joseph Smith**
We were, however, commanded to defer this our ordination until such time as it should be practicable to have our brethren, who had been and who should be baptized, assembled together, when we must have their sanction to our

thus proceeding to ordain each other, and have them decide by vote whether they were willing to accept us as spiritual teachers or not. . . . *(Joseph, speaking of the word of the Lord that came to him and his co-laborer in the farmhouse of Peter Whitmer, directing them to ordain each other to the office of elder)* HC1:61

**Joseph Smith**
The rise of the Church of Christ in these last days, being one thousand eight hundred and thirty years since the coming of our Lord and Savior Jesus Christ in the flesh, it being regularly organized and established agreeable to the laws of our country, by the will and commandments of God, in the fourth month, and on the sixth day of the month which is called April— *(Revelation on Church Organization and Government, April 1830)* D&C 20:1

---

**586. No person may function in the Church in *any* official capacity without the consent of the people, after the call to serve has been made.**

**Elder Joseph Fielding Smith**
No man can preside in this Church in any capacity without the consent of the people. [D&C 26:2] The Lord has placed upon us the responsibility of sustaining by vote those who are called, to various positions of responsibility. No man, should the people decide to the contrary, could preside over any body of Latter-day Saints . . . as they are assembled in conference, or other capacity, by the uplifted hand, to sustain or to reject; and I take it that no man has the right to raise his hand in opposition, or with contrary vote, unless he has a reason for doing so that would be valid if presented before those who stand at the head. In other words, I have no right to raise my hand in opposition to a man who is appointed to any position in this Church simply because I may not like him, or because of some personal disagreement or feeling I may have, but only on the grounds that he is guilty of wrongdoing, of transgression of the laws of the Church which would disqualify him for the position which he is called to hold. That is my understanding of it. CR1919Jun:92

**Bruce R. McConkie**
Church officers are empowered to act within the scope of their appointments, only if they are first, called by revelation, and second, sustained by vote of the Church. The appointment comes by revelation. Conferences are empowered to approve or disapprove when the names of

church officers are read. (Common Consent pamphlet, 1955, pp. 12-13) TLDP:96

### John A. Widtsoe

Every officer of the Priesthood or auxiliary organizations, though properly nominated, holds his position in the Church only with the consent of the people. Officers may be nominated by the Presidency of the Church, but unless the people accept them as officials, they cannot exercise the authority of the offices to which they have been called. All things in the Church must be done by common consent. This makes the people, men and women, under God, the rulers of the Church. Even the President of the Church, before he can fully enter upon his duties, or continue in the office, must be sustained by the people. It is the common custom in the Church to vote on Church officers in the general stake and ward conferences. This gives every member an opportunity to vote for or against the officers. Meanwhile, the judiciary system of the Church is such that there is ample provision whereby any officer of the Church, if found in error, may be brought to justice and if found guilty be removed from his position. ¶ The doctrine of common consent is fundamental in the Church, and is coincident with the fact that the Church belongs to all the people. Since the authority of the Priesthood is vested in all the people, it follows that the officials of the Priesthood must be responsible to the people. The responsibility and work of the Church are not only for but by the people as a whole. (A Rational Theology, p. 109) TLDP:96

### President Joseph F. Smith

They are faithful men chosen by inspiration. The Lord has given us the way to do these things. He has revealed to us that it is the duty of the presiding authorities to appoint and call and then those whom they choose for any official position in the Church shall be presented to the body. If the body reject them, they are responsible for that rejection. They have the right to reject, if they will, or to receive them and sustain them by their faith and prayers. That is strictly in accordance with the rule laid down of the Lord. CR1907Apr:4

---

587. All organizational things that the Church does—the procedures that it follows, and the officers that it appoints—must be done by common consent.

### Bruce R. McConkie

All of the organizational things which the Church does—that is, the procedures which it follows and the officers which it appoints—must be done by common consent, by much faith and prayer. . . . ¶ General Church business cannot be transacted in secret. No man, for instance, could be appointed in secret to head the Church or to carry on some supposed great program for the salvation of men. Conferences are to transact the business of the Church. ¶ . . . . No man can so much as be ordained to any office in the Church without a vote of the Church. There is no such thing as a secret ordination to office, either high or low, in the Church of Christ. The Lord does not work in dark corners. His great works are trumpeted in the ears of all living so that every soul who is willing to do so may learn of them. ¶ . . . . Even after a proper ordination, the elders of the Church have not power to act independently of the direction of the Church. They cannot presume to have any right or prerogative that has not been specifically given to them. Those holding priestly offices just have certificates of ordination. Elders must be properly recommended for special labors and must carry certificates so certifying. And no elder can receive a license to act in his calling without a vote of the Church, or by direction of a conference. ¶ . . . . Church officers are empowered to act within the scope of their appointments, only if they are first, called by revelation, and second, sustained by vote of the Church. The appointment comes by revelation. Conferences are empowered to approve or disapprove when the names of church officers are read. (Common Consent pamphlet, 1955, pp. 12-13) TLDP:96

### President John Taylor

We convene in conference in the various stakes that everything pertaining to the interests of the stakes may be considered in those conferences, and that all matters may be properly represented, and all the saints have the privilege of voting for or against those officers who are presented to the conference for their acceptance. It is also usual to vote for the officers of wards in the wards over which they preside, such as bishops and their counselors, with all the lesser priesthood, so that there may be perfect unanimity in all our acts. Because the church of God is based upon the principle of perfect freedom of action. . . . It is proper that all of these authorities should be presented from time to time before the people, that all the people everywhere, not only in a stake, but in all the stakes, as well as at the general conference, may have the opportunity if they know of anything wrong, anything immoral or unrighteous associated with the acts of any of the leading authorities of the church, of speaking of it, that everything and everybody may be properly presented and that the conduct of all men may be intelligently scrutinized; for, if we cannot bear the scrutiny of our brethren upon earth, how shall we be able to meet the scrutiny and investigations of our Heavenly Father when we shall stand before him. And if there is anything immoral or unrighteous, of any kind, it is proper and expedient that it be righted; and this applies quite as much to the presidency, the twelve, and the leading authorities as to any other individual in the church, in order that everything may be presented in its proper form, and everybody have a full opportunity of offering his ideas and views in regard to these matters. (*At Ogden, Utah, Jan. 21, 1883, JD24:32-33*) TLDP:97

### Mark E. Petersen
But there is more than voting to the system the Lord has instituted by which we "sustain" the officers of the Church. There is an expression of determination or purpose in it likewise. There is the token of a covenant. ¶ As we vote to sustain our Church officers we permit them to act and officiate in their callings: but we also pledge our support of them, which means that we will follow their inspired direction, we will cooperate in carrying forward the program of the Church, and willingly accept assignments of responsibilities from them. ¶ The work of the Church is not confined to a few men only. Every person in it must take a part. Every one must "work out his soul's salvation," by participating in the program of the Church. Each assignment accepted and fulfilled means further soul development, added skill in activity, deeper faith and testimony. ¶ It is the inactive who "rust" and fail in development. Without "works" faith is dead. ¶ Sustaining the authorities of the Church is as much a principle of the Gospel as baptism or the resurrection. Without the co-operative effort which is permitted by it, there would be chaos. (A Faith to Live By, p. 310) TLDP:97-98

### Related Witnesses:
#### Mark E. Petersen
At times, particularly in the smaller units of the Church, opposition votes are cast. Occasionally it is suggested that a branch be discontinued, or that it be merged with another ward or branch. Never is action taken to effect such a proposal without first submitting the matter to the vote of the people concerned. ¶ This voting is no rubber stamp procedure. There have been times when the proposals have been turned down by the people, and the

change has never been made. And this has been done without any prejudice on the part of the presiding officials. ¶ It is inherent in the organization of the Church that its work shall be done "by the voice of the people." No appointment is ever thrust upon the people. (A Faith to Live By, p. 309) TLDP:96

## (3) Aaronic Priesthood

**588. The Aaronic Priesthood administers in matters pertaining to the temporal welfare of the people.**

### President Joseph F. Smith
The Church has two characteristics—the temporal and the spiritual, and one is not without the other. We maintain that both are essential and that one without the other is incomplete and ineffectual. Hence, the Lord instituted in the government of the Church two Priesthoods—the lesser or Aaronic, having special charge of the temporal, and the higher or Melchizedek, looking to the spiritual welfare of the people. (Gospel Doctrine, p. 150) DGSM:68

### Elder John Taylor
The lesser priesthood is a part of, or an appendage to the greater, or the Melchizedek priesthood, and has power in administering outward ordinances. The lesser or Aaronic priesthood can make appointments for the greater in preaching; can baptize, administer the sacrament, attend to the tithing, buy lands, settle people in possessions, divide inheritances, look after the poor, take care of the properties of the church, attend generally to temporal affairs. (Gospel Kingdom, p. 155) DGSM:68

### Elder Joseph Fielding Smith
We may be sure that the Aaronic Priesthood will never be taken from the earth while mortality endures, for there will always be need for temporal direction and the performance of ordinances pertaining to "the preparatory Gospel." CHMR1:62; DCSM:28

### Related Witnesses:
#### Boyd K. Packer
Those who hold the Aaronic Priesthood, or the preparatory priesthood, hold the authority, when specifically directed, to perform those ordinances that belong to that priesthood. They can baptize. They can bless the sacrament and perform every service relating to the lesser priesthood. They cannot confirm someone a member of the Church, however, for that takes a higher authority. (The Holy Temple, p. 150-51) TLDP:509

**Elder Joseph F. Smith**

The Melchizedek Priesthood holds the keys of all the spiritual blessings of the Church, of the mysteries of the kingdom of heaven, of communion with the general assembly and Church of the first born, and the presence of God, the Father, and Jesus, the Mediator. ¶ The Aaronic Priesthood is an appendage to the first, and holds the keys of the ministering of angels, and the outward ordinances and letter of the gospel, the baptism of repentance for the remission of sins, agreeable to the covenants and commandments. (Gospel Doctrine, p. 191) TLDP:508

**Joseph Smith**

The power and authority of the lesser, or Aaronic Priesthood, is to hold the keys of the ministering of angels, and to administer in outward ordinances, the letter of the gospel, the baptism of repentance for the remission of sins, agreeable to the covenants and commandments. (*Revelation on priesthood, received as the Twelve met in council, March 28, 1835*) D&C 107:20

**Joseph Smith**

Why it is called the lesser priesthood is because it is an appendage to the greater, or the Melchizedek Priesthood, and has power in administering outward ordinances. (*Revelation on priesthood, received as the Twelve met in council, March 28, 1835*) D&C 107:14

**Joseph Smith**

And the lesser priesthood continued, which priesthood holdeth the key of the ministering of angels and the preparatory gospel; 27. Which gospel is the gospel of repentance and of baptism, and the remission of sins, and the law of carnal commandments, which the Lord in his wrath caused to continue with the house of Aaron among the children of Israel until John, whom God raised up, being filled with the Holy Ghost from his mother's womb. (*Revelation on priesthood received in the presence of six elders, Sept. 22/23, 1832*) D&C 84:26-27

**John the Baptist,**
*quoted by Joseph Smith*

Upon you my fellow servants, in the name of Messiah I confer the Priesthood of Aaron, which holds the keys of the ministering of angels, and of the gospel of repentance, and of baptism by immersion for the remission of sins; and this shall never be taken again from the earth, until the sons of Levi do offer again an offering unto the Lord in righteousness. (*John the Baptist ordains Joseph Smith and Oliver Cowdery to the Aaronic Priesthood, May 15, 1829*) D&C 13:1

**President Wilford Woodruff**

I had the administration of angels while holding the office of a priest. I had visions and revelations. I traveled thousands of miles. I baptized men, though I could not confirm them because I had not the authority to do it. ¶ I speak of these things to show that a man should not be ashamed of any portion of the priesthood. (Millennial Star, 1891, 53:641-42) DCSM:28

---

**589. The Aaronic Priesthood was restored to earth by John the Baptist, who personally bestowed the keys thereof upon Joseph Smith and Oliver Cowdery.**

**President David O. McKay**

Throughout this conference you have heard testimony from men who, with tears in their eyes, if you were close enough to see, their lips quivering with emotion, testified that they know that God lives, that Jesus is the Christ, and that the Father and the Son appeared to the Prophet Joseph Smith and gave instructions about organizing Christ's Church; and that Peter, James, and John, who held the authority from the Christ himself, gave that authority in this dispensation; that the Melchizedek Priesthood was bestowed upon the Prophet Joseph and Oliver Cowdery; that John the Baptist, who baptized Jesus Christ, bestowed the Aaronic Priesthood. CR1967Oct:151

**President Heber J. Grant**

We claim . . . authority and declare to all the world that John the Baptist, who held the keys of authority to baptize, restored the Aaronic priesthood, and bestowed it upon Joseph Smith and Oliver Cowdery. CR1935Apr:8

**Elder Joseph Fielding Smith**

Peter, James, and John conferred upon Joseph Smith and Oliver Cowdery the Melchizedek Priesthood. Before that time John the Baptist came and conferred upon them the Aaronic Priesthood. CR1967Apr:98

**Marion G. Romney**

John the Baptist, who held the keys of the Aaronic Priesthood in the days of Jesus, now a resurrected person, came to earth and laid his hands upon the heads of Joseph Smith and Oliver Cowdery and conferred upon them "the Priesthood of Aaron, which holds the keys of the ministering of angels, and of the gospel of repentance, and of baptism by immersion for the remission of sins." (D&C 13) CR1958Oct:96

**Delbert L. Stapley**

It seems fitting that the man who testified of the Savior, John the Baptist, has come and conferred upon Joseph Smith and Oliver Cowdery, the Aaronic Priesthood, and that later the three men, Peter, James, and John, who were with the Savior on the Mount when he was transfigured before them, and God again testified of his Son, should come and confer upon the Prophet Joseph and Oliver Cowdery the Melchizedek Priesthood, the priesthood after the order of the Son of God that has to do with the spiritual endowments, authorities, and blessings of God's church. CR1954Oct:48

### Joseph Smith

We still continued the work of translation, when, in the ensuing month (May 1829), we on a certain day went into the woods to pray and inquire of the Lord respecting baptism for the remission of sins, that we found mentioned in the translation of the plates. While we were thus employed, praying and calling upon the Lord, a messenger from heaven descended in a cloud of light, and having laid his hands upon us, he ordained us, saying: 69. Upon you my fellow servants, in the name of Messiah, I confer the Priesthood of Aaron, which holds the keys of the ministering of angels, and of the gospel of repentance, and of baptism by immersion for the remission of sins; and this shall never be taken again from the earth until the sons of Levi do offer again an offering unto the Lord in righteousness. 70. He said this Aaronic Priesthood had not the power of laying on hands for the gift of the Holy Ghost, but that this should be conferred on us hereafter; and he commanded us to go and be baptized, and gave us directions that I should baptize Oliver Cowdery, and that afterwards he should baptize me. 71. Accordingly we went and were baptized. I baptized him first, and afterwards he baptized me—after which I laid my hands upon his head and ordained him to the Aaronic Priesthood, and afterwards he laid his hands on me and ordained me to the same Priesthood— for so we were commanded. 72. The messenger who visited us on this occasion and conferred this Priesthood upon us, said that his name was John, the same that is called John the Baptist in the New Testament, and that he acted under the direction of Peter, James and John, who held the keys of the Priesthood of Melchizedek, which Priesthood, he said, would in due time be conferred on us, and that I should be called the first Elder of the Church, and he (Oliver Cowdery) the second. It was on the fifteenth day of May, 1829, that we were ordained under the hand of this messenger, and baptized. (*John the Baptist appears to Joseph Smith and Oliver Cowdery, May 15, 1829*) JS-H 1:68-72

### Related Witnesses:

#### Joseph Smith,
##### *receiving the Word of the Lord*

Behold, this is wisdom in me; wherefore, marvel not, for the hour cometh that I will drink of the fruit of the vine with you on the earth, and with Moroni, whom I have sent unto you to reveal the Book of Mormon, containing the fulness of my everlasting gospel, to whom I have committed the keys of the record of the stick of Ephraim; . . . 7. And also John the son of Zacharias, which Zacharias he (Elias) visited and gave promise that he should have a son, and his name should be John, and he should be filled with the spirit of Elias; 8. Which John I have sent unto you, my servants, Joseph Smith, Jun., and Oliver Cowdery, to ordain you unto the first priesthood which you have received, that you might be called and ordained even as Aaron; (*Revelation to Joseph Smith through a heavenly messenger, Aug. 1830*) D&C 27:5,7-8

#### Elder Wilford Woodruff

He [Joseph Smith] lived until he received every key, ordinance and law ever given to any man on the earth, from Father Adam down, touching this dispensation. . . . [H]e received under the hand of John the Baptist the Aaronic Priesthood, with all its keys and powers, and every other key and power belonging to this dispensation, and I am not ashamed to say that he was a Prophet of God, and he laid the foundation of the greatest work and dispensation that has ever been established on the earth. (*In new Tabernacle, Oct. 1873, JD16:267*) DGSM:68

#### John the Baptist,
##### *quoted by Joseph Smith*

Upon you my fellow servants, in the name of Messiah I confer the Priesthood of Aaron, which holds the keys of the ministering of angels, and of the gospel of repentance, and of baptism by immersion for the remission of sins; and this shall never be taken again from the earth, until the sons of Levi do offer again an offering unto the Lord in righteousness. (*Ordination of Joseph Smith and Oliver Cowdery to the Aaronic Priesthood, May 15, 1829, by the hands of an angel who announced himself as John the Baptist and who explained that he was acting under the direction of Peter, James, and John, the ancient Apostles, who held the keys of the higher, Melchizedek Priesthood*) D&C 13:1

---

590. The Aaronic Priesthood is called the lesser priesthood because it is an appendage to the greater Melchizedek Priesthood.

**Joseph Smith**

The second priesthood is called the Priesthood of Aaron, because it was conferred upon Aaron and his seed, throughout all their generations. 14. Why it is called the lesser priesthood is because it is an appendage to the greater, or the Melchizedek Priesthood, and has power in administering outward ordinances. (*Revelation on priesthood, received as the Twelve met in council, March 28, 1835*) D&C 107:13-14

**Elder John Taylor**

The lesser priesthood is a part of, or an appendage to the greater, or the Melchizedek priesthood, and has power in administering outward ordinances. The lesser or Aaronic priesthood can make appointments for the greater in preaching; can baptize, administer the sacrament, attend to the tithing, buy lands, settle people in possessions, divide inheritances, look after the poor, take care of the properties of the church, attend generally to temporal affairs. . . . They hold the keys of the ministering of angels and administer in outward ordinances, the letter of the gospel, and the baptism of repentance for the remission of sins. (Gospel Kingdom, p. 155) DGSM:68

**Boyd K. Packer**

The higher priesthood, the Melchizedek Priesthood, always presides over the Aaronic, or the lesser, Priesthood. Aaron was the high priest, or the presiding priest, of the Aaronic Priesthood. But Moses presided over Aaron because Moses held the Melchizedek Priesthood. ¶ The fact that it is called the lesser priesthood does not diminish at all the importance of the Aaronic Priesthood. The Lord said it is necessary to the Melchizedek Priesthood. (See D&C 84:29.) Any holder of the higher priesthood should feel greatly honored to perform the ordinances of the Aaronic Priesthood, for they have great spiritual importance. (That All May Be Edified, p. 25) TLDP:507

**President Brigham Young,**
*quoted by John A. Widtsoe*

The office of a Bishop belongs to the lesser Priesthood. He is the highest officer in the Aaronic Priesthood, and has the privilege of using the Urim and Thummim—has the administration of angels, if he has faith, and lives so that he can receive and enjoy the blessings Aaron enjoyed. At the same time, could Aaron rise up and say, "I have as much power and authority as you, Moses?" No; for Moses held the keys and authority above all the rest upon the earth. He holds the keys of the Priesthood of Melchizedek, which is the Priesthood of the Son of God, which holds the keys of all these Priesthoods, dispensing the blessings and privileges of both Priesthoods to the people, as he did in the days of the Children of Israel when he led them out of Egypt. (*At Mill Creek Ward, May 7, 1861, JD9:87*) DBY:143

**James A. Talmage**

The Church of Jesus Christ of Latter-day Saints recognizes two orders of Priesthood, the lesser called the Aaronic, the greater known as the Melchizedek order. AF:186

**Related Witnesses:**

**Joseph Smith**

And again, the offices of elder and bishop are necessary appendages belonging unto the high priesthood. 30. And again, the offices of teacher and deacon are necessary appendages belonging to the lesser priesthood, which priesthood was confirmed upon Aaron and his sons. (*Revelation on priesthood, received in the presence of six elders, Sept. 22/23, 1832*) D&C 84:29-30

**Joseph Smith**

He said this Aaronic Priesthood had not the power of laying on hands for the gift of the Holy Ghost, but that this should be conferred on us hereafter; and he commanded us to go and be baptized, and gave us directions that I should baptize Oliver Cowdery, and that afterwards he should baptize me. (*John the Baptist appears to Joseph Smith and Oliver Cowdery, May 15, 1829*) JS-H 1:70

**Joseph Smith**

The second priesthood is called the Priesthood of Aaron, because it was conferred upon Aaron and his seed, throughout all their generations. (*Revelation on priesthood, received as the Twelve met in council, March 28, 1835*) D&C 107:13

**James E. Talmage**

The Aaronic Priesthood is named after Aaron, who was given to Moses as his mouthpiece, to act under his direction in the carrying out of God's purposes respecting Israel. For this reason it is sometimes called the Lesser Priesthood; but though lesser, it is neither small nor insignificant. AF:186

---

**591. The bishop holds the keys and authority of presidency of the Aaronic Priesthood.**

**Joseph Smith**

The second priesthood is called the Priesthood of Aaron, because it was conferred upon Aaron and his seed, throughout all their generations. 14. Why it is called the lesser priesthood is because it is an appendage to the greater, or the Melchizedek Priesthood, and has power in administering outward ordinances. 15. The bishopric is the presidency of this priesthood, and holds the keys or authority of the same. (*Revelation on priesthood, received as the Twelve met in council, March 28, 1835*) D&C 107:13-15

**Joseph Smith**

Also the duty of the president over the Priesthood of Aaron is to preside over forty-eight priests, and sit in council with them, to teach them the duties of their office, as is given in the covenants— 88. This president is to be a bishop; for this is one of the duties of this priesthood. (*Revelation on priesthood, received as the Twelve met in council, March 28, 1835*) D&C 107:87-88

**Elder Joseph Fielding Smith**

The bishop is the presiding officer in the Aaronic Priesthood. The bishop of a ward presides over the Aaronic Priesthood of the ward, and as he also holds the office of high priest, he also, by virtue of that fact, is the president of the ward and has jurisdiction over all the people. CHMR:1:259

**President Brigham Young,**
*quoted by John A. Widtsoe*

The office of a Bishop belongs to the lesser Priesthood. He is the highest officer in the Aaronic Priesthood, and has the privilege of using the Urim and Thummim—has the administration of angels, if he has faith, and lives so that he can receive and enjoy the blessings Aaron enjoyed. At the same time, could Aaron rise up and say, "I have as much power and authority as you, Moses?" No; for Moses held the keys and authority above all the rest upon the earth. He holds the keys of the Priesthood of Melchizedek, which is the Priesthood of the Son of God, which holds the keys of all these Priesthoods, dispensing the blessings and privileges of both Priesthoods to the people, as he did in the days of the Children of Israel when he led them out of Egypt. (*At Mill Creek Ward, May 7, 1861, JD9:87*) DBY:143

**Related Witnesses:**

**Joseph Smith**

But, as a high priest of the Melchizedek Priesthood has authority to officiate in all the lesser offices he may officiate in the office of bishop when no literal descendant of Aaron can be found, provided he is called and set apart and ordained unto this power, under the hands of the First Presidency of the Melchizedek Priesthood. (*Revelation, Nov. 1831*) D&C 68:19

**Joseph Smith**

Wherefore, the office of a bishop is not equal unto it [to the High Priesthood]; for the office of a bishop is in administering all temporal things; 69. Nevertheless a bishop must be chosen from the High Priesthood, unless he is a lit-

eral descendant of Aaron; . . . (*Revelation on priesthood, received as the Twelve met in council, March 28, 1835*) D&C 107:68-69

## (4) Melchizedek Priesthood

592. The "Holy Priesthood after the order of the Son of God" is also called the Melchizedek Priesthood.

**Joseph Smith**

Why the first is called the Melchizedek Priesthood is because Melchizedek was such a great high priest. 3. Before his day it was called the Holy Priesthood, after the Order of the Son of God. 4. But out of respect or reverence to the name of the Supreme Being, to avoid the too frequent repetition of his name, they, the church, in ancient days, called that priesthood after Melchizedek, or the Melchizedek Priesthood. (*Revelation on priesthood, received as the Twelve met in council, March 28, 1835*) D&C 107:2-4

**Joseph Smith,**
*receiving the Word of the Lord*

Verily I say unto you, I now give unto you the officers belonging to my Priesthood, that ye may hold the keys thereof, even the Priesthood which is after the order of Melchizedek, which is after the order of my Only Begotten Son. (*Revelation received Jan. 19, 1841, Nauvoo, Ill.*) D&C 124:123

**Elder John Taylor**

We find that after the days of Noah an order was introduced called the patriarchal order, in which every man managed his own family affairs. And prominent men among them were kings and priests unto God, and officiated in what is known among us as the priesthood of the Son of God, or the priesthood after the order of Melchizedek. Man began again to multiply on the face of the earth, and the heads of families became their kings and priests, that is, the fathers of their own people. (*General conference, Oct. 1874, JD17:207*) TLDP:504

**James E. Talmage,**
*also quoting Joseph Smith*

The Melchizedek Priesthood is named after the king of Salem, a great High Priest before whose day it was known as "the Holy Priesthood, after the Order of the Son of God. But out of respect or reverence to the name of the Supreme Being, to avoid the too frequent repetition of his name, they, the Church, in ancient days, called that priesthood after Melchizedek." [See D&C 107:3-4] AF:186-87

### President Brigham Young,
*quoted by John A. Widtsoe*

Abraham was faithful to the true God; he overthrew the idols of his father and obtained the Priesthood after the order of Melchizedek, which is after the order of the Son of God, and a promise that of the increase of his seed there should be no end; when you obtain the holy Priesthood, which is after the order of Melchizedek, sealed upon you, and the promise that your seed shall be numerous as the stars in the firmament, or as the sands upon the seashore, and of your increase there shall be no end, you have then got the promise of Abraham, Isaac, and Jacob, and all the blessings that were conferred upon them. (*On a visit to Utah, Juab, and Sanpete counties, Utah, June and July, 1865, JD11:118*) DBY:106

### President Brigham Young,
*quoted by John A. Widtsoe*

Moses held the keys and authority above all the rest upon the earth. He holds the keys of the Priesthood of Melchizedek, which is the Priesthood of the Son of God, which holds the keys of all these Priesthoods, dispensing the blessings and privileges of both Priesthoods to the people, as he did in the days of the Children of Israel when he led them out of Egypt. (*At Mill Creek Ward, May 7, 1861, JD9:87*) DBY:143

**Related Witnesses:**

### President John Taylor

When the gospel was given to the Jews, all the gifts and graces and powers thereof, accompanied it. It was accompanied by the Eternal Priesthood—which is after the order of the Son of God, without which no man can administer in the ordinances of life and salvation. (*In Tabernacle, July 20, 1883, JD24:240*) TLDP:86

---

### 593. Priesthood is the ruling, presiding, governing authority in the Church.

### President Joseph F. Smith

The Priesthood after the order of the Son of God is the ruling, presiding authority in the Church. It is divided into its various parts— the Melchizedek and the Aaronic—and all the quorums or councils are organized in the Church, each with special duties and special callings; not clashing with one another, but all harmonious and united. In other words, there is no government in the Church of Jesus Christ separate and apart, above, or outside of the holy Priesthood or its authority. We have our Relief Societies, Mutual Improvement Associations, Primary Associations and Sunday Schools, and we may organize, if we choose, associations for self-help among ourselves, not subject to our enemies, but for our good and the good of our people, but these organizations are not quorums or councils of the Priesthood, but are auxiliary to, and under it; organized by virtue of the holy Priesthood. They are not outside of, nor above it, nor beyond its reach. They acknowledge the principle of the Priesthood. (Gospel Doctrine, p. 144) TLDP:510 [quoted in part in DGSM:68]

### Joseph Smith

The Melchizedek Priesthood holds the right of presidency, and has power and authority over all the offices in the church in all ages of the world, to administer in spiritual things. 9. The Presidency of the High Priesthood, after the order of Melchizedek, have a right to officiate in all the offices in the church. (*Revelation on priesthood, received as the Twelve met in council, March 28, 1835*) D&C 107:8-9

### Elder John Taylor

While the power of the higher, or Melchizedek is to hold the keys of all the spiritual blessings of the Church; . . . and to preside over all the spiritual officers of the Church, yet the Presidency of the High Priesthood, after the order of Melchizedek, have a right to officiate in all the offices in the Church, both spiritual and temporal. (Items on Priesthood, p. 31) TLDP:507

**Related Witnesses:**

### Joseph Smith

Again, the duty of the president over the office of elders is to preside over ninety-six elders, and to sit in council with them, and to teach them according to the covenants. 90. This presidency is a distinct one from that of the seventy, and is designed for those who do not travel into all the world. 91. And again, the duty of the President of the office of the High Priesthood is to preside over the whole church, and to be like unto Moses— 92. Behold, here is wisdom; yea, to be a seer, a revelator, a translator, and a prophet, having all the gifts of God which he bestows upon the head of the church. 93. And it is according to the vision showing the order of the Seventy, that they should have seven presidents to preside over them, chosen out of the number of the seventy; 94. And the seventh president of these presidents is to preside over the six; 95. And these seven presidents are to choose other seventy besides the first seventy to whom they belong, and are to preside over them; (*Revelation on priesthood, received as the Twelve met in council, March 28, 1835*) D&C 107:89-95

### Joseph Smith,
*receiving the Word of the Lord*

Verily, I say unto you, saith the Lord of Hosts, there must needs be presiding elders to preside over those who are of the office of an elder; 61. And also priests to preside over those who are of the office of a priest; 62. And also teachers to preside over those who are of the office of a teacher, in like manner, and also the deacons— 63. Wherefore, from deacon to teacher, and from teacher to priest, and from priest to elder, severally as they are appointed, according to the covenants and commandments of the church. 64. Then comes the High Priesthood, which is the greatest of all. 65. Wherefore, it must needs be that one be appointed of the High Priesthood to preside over the priesthood, and he shall be called President of the High Priesthood of the Church, 66. Or, in other words, the Presiding High Priest over the High Priesthood of the Church. (*Revelation on priesthood, March 28, 1835*) D&C 107:60-66

### Elder Harold B. Lee
*also quoting Parley P. Pratt*

We sometimes hear people who talk about the Church as a democracy. Well, it isn't any such thing. Democracy means a government where the sole authority is vested in the people—the right to nominate, the right to release, to change. The Church is not a democracy. It is more like a kingdom than a democracy—and yet it is not wholly like a kingdom, except that we accept the Lord as the king, who has under His direction an earthly head who operates and becomes His mouthpiece. It is an organization that is defined more accurately as a theocracy, which means that it is something like a kingdom as the world would define it, and yet something like a democracy. . . . ¶ Let me read you something by Parley P. Pratt that appeared in the Millennial Star in 1845. It was called a "Proclamation." ¶ "The legislative, judicial, and executive power is vested in Him (the Lord). He reveals the laws, and he elects, chooses, or appoints the officers; and holds the right to reprove, to correct, or even to remove them at pleasure. Hence the necessity of a constant intercourse by direct revelation between Him and His Church. As a precedent for the foregoing facts, we refer to the examples of all ages as recorded in the Scriptures. ¶ "This order of government began in Eden—God appointed Adam to govern the earth and gave him laws. ¶ "It was perpetuated in a regular succession from Adam to Noah to Melchizedek, Abraham, Isaac, Jacob, Joseph, Moses, Samuel, the prophets, John, Jesus and his apostles. All, and

each of which were chosen by the Lord, and not by the people." (Millennial Star, March 1843, p. 150; Stand Ye in Holy Places, pp. 150-51) TLDP:83

### Joseph Smith,
*quoted by Elder Joseph Fielding Smith*

I will inform you that it is contrary to the economy of God for any member of the Church, or any one, to receive instruction for those in authority, higher than themselves; therefore you will see the impropriety of giving heed to them; but if any person have a vision or a visitation from a heavenly messenger, it must be for his own benefit and instruction; for the fundamental principles, government, and doctrine of the Church are vested in the keys of the kingdom. *(Letter to Jared Carter, from Kirtland, Ohio, April 13, 1833)* HC1:338-39; TPJS:21

---

## 594. The Church of Jesus Christ of Latter-day Saints is directed and governed by revelation from God through priesthood authorities.

### Hugh B. Brown

Divine revelation has always been a characteristic of the living Church—it is absolutely essential to its continued existence in an organized state on the earth. . . . ¶ The Church of Jesus Christ was established and is now directed by revelation, and that fact is largely responsible for the appeal which this new Church makes, and when I say "new," I wish to emphasize that to us it is not new but a restoration of that which was . . . .That the Church is progressive and responsive to revealed truth is evidenced by our further declaration that we believe that God will yet reveal many great and important things. ¶ This church . . . is not committed to any formal or inflexible creed, but its members are taught to believe in and live by the revelations of the past and present and thus prepare themselves for the revelations yet to come. Our concepts and even our faith must be held subject to new light. . . . ¶ So we may trace the line of revelators, men who have stood, each in his time, as the medium through whom God speaks to his people, from Moses to Joshua, through the Judges, on to David and Solomon and down to Zachariah and Malachi. Christ himself, came to this world to reveal God to men, and he himself was led and directed by revelation from his Father while he dwelt on this earth. . . . ¶ All the prophets and leaders of ancient times were led, directed, chosen, inspired by God himself through revelation. ¶ We think we are justified in anticipating future revelation, and we believe that it will be surpassing in importance and glorious fulness anything that has yet been revealed. We believe that he will continue to reveal himself as long as man continues his probation here on earth. CR1961Oct:94-97

**Parley P. Pratt,**
*quoted by Elder Harold B. Lee*

Let me read you something by Parley P. Pratt that appeared in the Millennial Star in 1845. It was called a "Proclamation." ¶ "The legislative, judicial, and executive power is vested in Him (the Lord). He reveals the laws, and he elects, chooses, or appoints the officers; and holds the right to reprove, to correct, or even to remove them at pleasure. Hence the necessity of a constant intercourse by direct revelation between Him and His Church." (Millennial Star, March 1843, p. 150; Stand Ye in Holy Places, pp. 150-51) TLDP:83

**George Q. Cannon**

The same spirit of revelation that Moses had . . . rests upon him who holds the presidency as senior apostle in the midst of the people of God. The apostles of this Church have all the authority, they have all the keys, . . . all the spirit of revelation necessary to lead this people into the presence of the Lamb in the celestial kingdom of our God. . . . ¶ But it is the truth, that the same spirit of revelation that rested upon Moses, and which enabled him to lead the children of Israel through the Red Sea, rests upon the servants of God in the midst of this people, and you will find it so to your entire satisfaction if you will listen to their counsels and be guided by them. (*At Hyde Park, Nov. 2, 1879, JD21:270-71*) DCSM:19

**President John Taylor**

The Lord never had—and never will have to the end of time—a Church on earth without Prophets, Apostles, and inspired men. Whenever the Lord had a people on the earth that He acknowledged as such, that people were led by revelation. No man can find anything contrary to this. When the gospel was given to the Jews, all the gifts and graces and powers thereof, accompanied it. It was accompanied by the Eternal Priesthood—which is after the order of the Son of God, without which no man can administer in the ordinances of life and salvation. (*In Tabernacle, July 20, 1883, JD24:240*) TLDP:86

**Bruce R. McConkie**

Now there isn't any language that can possibly overstate, that can overemphasize, the dignity and glory of the office of an elder. Elders are ministers of Christ. They are called to administer in spiritual things. They do everything that an Aaronic Priesthood holder does. In addition, they lay on hands for the gift of the Holy Ghost. They conduct meetings as they are guided by the Holy Spirit. ACR(Lima)1977:18

**Related Witnesses:**

**President Joseph F. Smith**

Take away the organization of the Church, and its power would cease. Every part of its organization is necessary and essential to its perfect existence. Disregard, ignore, or omit any part and you start imperfection in the Church; and if we should continue in that way we would find ourselves like those of old, being led by error, superstition, ignorance and by the cunning and craftiness of men. We would soon leave out here a little and there a little, here a line and there a precept, until we would become like the rest of the world: divided, disorganized, confused, and without knowledge, without revelation or inspiration, and without Divine authority or power. CR1915Apr:5

**Elder John Taylor**

The Melchizedek priesthood holds the mysteries of the revelations of God. Wherever that priesthood exists, there also exists a knowledge of the laws of God; and wherever the gospel has existed, there has always been revelation; and where there has been no revelation, there never has been the true gospel. (*In new Tabernacle, May 1870, JD13:231*) DGSM:68

**Joseph Smith**

The power and authority of the higher, or Melchizedek Priesthood, is to hold the keys of all the spiritual blessings of the church— 19. To have the privilege of receiving the mysteries of the kingdom of heaven, to have the heavens opened unto them, to commune with the general assembly and church of the Firstborn, and to enjoy the communion and presence of God the Father, and Jesus the mediator of the new covenant. (*Revelation on priesthood, received as the Twelve met in council, March 28, 1835*) D&C 107:18-19

**Joseph Smith**

And this greater priesthood administereth the gospel and holdeth the key of the mysteries of the kingdom, even the key of the knowledge of God. 20. Therefore, in the ordinances thereof, the power of godliness is manifest. 21. And without the ordinances thereof, and the authority of the priesthood, the power of godliness is not manifest unto men in the flesh; (*Revelation on priesthood, received in the presence of six elders, Sept. 22/23, 1832*) D&C 84:19-21

**Joseph Smith,**
*receiving the Word of the Lord*
For I have given him the keys of the mysteries, and the revelations which are sealed, until I shall appoint unto them another in his stead. (*Revelation for Oliver Cowdery, Sept. 1830*) D&C 28:7

**Elder Lorenzo Snow**
The priesthood or authority in which we stand is the medium or channel through which our Heavenly Father has purposed to communicate light, intelligence, gifts, powers, and spiritual and temporal salvation unto the present generation. (Millennial Star, 1841, 2:39) DGSM:68

---

**595. The Melchizedek Priesthood administers primarily in the spiritual matters of the Church.**

**Joseph Smith**
The Melchizedek Priesthood holds the right of presidency, and has power and authority over all the offices in the church in all ages of the world, to administer in spiritual things. . . . 10. High priests after the order of the Melchizedek Priesthood have a right to officiate in their own standing, under the direction of the presidency, in administering spiritual things, and also in the office of an elder, priest (of the Levitical order), teacher, deacon, and member. . . . 18. The power and authority of the higher, or Melchizedek Priesthood, is to hold the keys of all the spiritual blessings of the church— 19. To have the privilege of receiving the mysteries of the kingdom of heaven, to have the heavens opened unto them, to commune with the general assembly and church of the Firstborn, and to enjoy the communion and presence of God the Father, and Jesus the mediator of the new covenant. (*Revelation on priesthood, received as the Twelve met in council, March 28, 1835*) D&C 107:8,10,18-19

**Elder John Taylor**
While the power of the higher, or Melchizedek is to hold the keys of all the spiritual blessings of the Church; . . . and to preside over all the spiritual officers of the Church, yet the Presidency of the High Priesthood, after the order of Melchizedek, have a right to officiate in all the offices in the Church, both spiritual and temporal. (Items on Priesthood, p. 31) TLDP:507

**Elder Joseph F. Smith**
The Melchizedek Priesthood holds the keys of all the spiritual blessings of the Church, of the mysteries of the kingdom of heaven, of communion with the general assembly and Church of

the First Born, and the presence of God, the Father, and Jesus, the Mediator. ¶ The Aaronic Priesthood is an appendage to the first, and holds the keys of the ministering of angels, and the outward ordinances and letter of the gospel, the baptism of repentance for the remission of sins, agreeable to the covenants and commandments. (Gospel Doctrine, p. 191) TLDP:508

**President Joseph F. Smith**
The Church has two characteristics—the temporal and the spiritual, and one is not without the other. We maintain that both are essential and that one without the other is incomplete and ineffectual. Hence, the Lord instituted in the government of the Church two Priesthoods—the lesser or Aaronic, having special charge of the temporal, and the higher or Melchizedek, looking to the spiritual welfare of the people. (Gospel Doctrine, p. 150) DGSM:68

**Bruce R. McConkie**
Now let us speak of the offices in the Melchizedek Priesthood. "*Elders* are ministers of Christ; they are called to administer in spiritual things (D&C 107:12). . . ." ACR(Lima)1977:18

**Elder Lorenzo Snow**
The priesthood or authority in which we stand is the medium or channel through which our Heavenly Father has purposed to communicate light, intelligence, gifts, powers, and spiritual and temporal salvation unto the present generation. (Millennial Star, 1841, 2:39) DGSM:68

---

**596. The Melchizedek Priesthood always presides over the Aaronic Priesthood.**

**Boyd K. Packer**
The higher priesthood, the Melchizedek Priesthood, always presides over the Aaronic, or the lesser, Priesthood. Aaron was the high priest, or the presiding priest, of the Aaronic Priesthood. But Moses presided over Aaron because Moses held the Melchizedek Priesthood. ¶ The fact that it is called the lesser priesthood does not diminish at all the importance of the Aaronic Priesthood. The Lord said it is necessary to the Melchizedek Priesthood. (See D&C 84:29.) Any holder of the higher priesthood should feel greatly honored to perform the ordinances of the Aaronic Priesthood, for they have great spiritual importance. (That All May Be Edified, p. 25) TLDP:507

**Boyd K. Packer**
You always hold one of these [Aaronic priesthood] offices. When you receive the next higher office, you still retain the authority of the

first. For instance, when you become a priest, you still have authority to do all that you did as a deacon and teacher. Even when you receive the higher priesthood, you keep all of the authority of, and, with proper authorization, can act in the offices of, the lesser priesthood. (That All May Be Edified, p. 25) TLDP:507

**President Joseph F. Smith**

[A]ll the keys and authority and power pertaining to the government of the Church and to the Melchizedek and Aaronic Priesthood are centered in the presiding officer of the Church. There is no business nor office within the Church, that the President of the Church may not fill, and may not do, if it is necessary, or if it is required of him to do it. He holds the office of patriarch; he holds the office of high priest and of apostle, of seventy, of elder, of bishop and of priest, teacher and deacon in the Church; all these belong to the Presidency of the Church of Jesus Christ of Latter-day Saints, and they can officiate in any and in all of these callings when occasion requires. CR1915Oct:7

**Bruce R. McConkie**

Elders are ministers of Christ. They are called to administer in spiritual things. They do everything that an Aaronic Priesthood holder does. In addition, they lay on hands for the gift of the Holy Ghost. They conduct meetings as they are guided by the Holy Spirit. ACR(Lima)1977:18

**Joseph Smith,**
*quoted by Elder Joseph Fielding Smith*

Although there are two Priesthoods, yet the Melchizedek Priesthood comprehends the Aaronic or Levitical Priesthood, and is the grand head, and holds the highest authority which pertains to the priesthood, and the keys of the Kingdom of God in all ages of the world to the latest posterity on the earth; and is the channel through which all knowledge, doctrine, the plan of salvation and every important matter is revealed from heaven. ¶ Its institution was prior to the "foundation of this earth, or the morning stars sang together, or the Sons of God shouted for joy," and is the highest and holiest Priesthood, and is after the order of the Son of God, and all other Priesthoods are only parts, ramifications, powers and blessings belonging to the same, and are held, controlled, and directed by it. (*From an article on priesthood, read at a general conference of the Church by Robert B. Thompson, and included as part of minutes of the conference held in Nauvoo, Ill., Oct. 5, 1840*) TPJS:166-67

**597.** The President of the Church alone holds the fulness of the keys of the priesthood, the power of directing the labors of the priesthood.

**President Joseph F. Smith**

The Priesthood in general is the authority given to man to act for God. Every man ordained to any degree of the Priesthood, has this authority delegated to him. ¶ But it is necessary that every act performed under this authority shall be done at the proper time and place, in the proper way, and after the proper order. The power of directing these labors constitutes the keys of the Priesthood. In their fulness, the keys are held by only one person at a time, the prophet and president of the Church. He may delegate any portion of this power to another, in which case that person holds the keys of that particular labor. Thus, the president of a temple, the president of a stake, the bishop of a ward, the president of a mission, the president of a quorum, each holds the keys of the labors performed in that particular body or locality. His Priesthood is not increased by this special appointment, for a seventy who presides over a mission has no more Priesthood than a seventy who labors under his direction; and the president of an elder's quorum, for example, has no more Priesthood than any member of that quorum. But he holds the power of directing the official labors performed in the mission or the quorum, or in other words, the keys of that division of that work. So it is throughout all the ramifications of the Priesthood—a distinction must be carefully made between the general authority, and the directing of the labors performed by that authority. (Gospel Doctrine, p. 136) TLDP:508; DGSM:68 (in part)

**President Joseph F. Smith**

[A]ll the keys and authority and power pertaining to the government of the Church and to the Melchizedek and Aaronic Priesthood are centered in the presiding officer of the Church. There is no business nor office within the Church, that the President of the Church may not fill, and may not do, if it is necessary, or if it is required of him to do it. He holds the office of patriarch; he holds the office of high priest and of apostle, of seventy, of elder, of bishop and of priest, teacher and deacon in the Church; all these belong to the Presidency of the Church of Jesus Christ of Latter-day Saints, and they can officiate in any and in all of these callings when occasion requires. CR1915Oct:7

**Joseph Smith,**
*receiving the Word of the Lord*

Unto whom I have given the keys of the kingdom, which belong always unto the Presidency of the High Priesthood: (*Revelation for the Prophet's newly called counselor in the First Presidency, Frederick G.Williams, March 1832*) D&C 81:2

**Joseph Smith,**
*receiving the Word of the Lord*

For I have given him the keys of the mysteries, and the revelations which are sealed, until I shall appoint unto them another in his stead. (*Revelation for Oliver Cowdery, Sept. 1830*) D&C 28:7

**Boyd K. Packer**

[T]hose who hold the Melchizedek Priesthood can perform the ordinances relating to the higher priesthood. But unless they are given special authorization they cannot endow, nor seal, nor perform those ordinances that pertain to the temple. ¶ There are limits. ¶ I heard President Kimball say on one occasion, as other Presidents of the Church have said, that while he holds all of the keys that are held upon the earth, there are keys that he does not hold. There are keys that have not been given to him as President of the Church, because they are reserved to higher power and authority. For instance, he said that he does not hold the keys of the resurrection. The Lord holds them, but He has not delegated them—neither anciently, nor to modern prophets. . . . ¶ Nevertheless, in the Church we hold sufficient authority to perform all of the ordinances necessary to redeem and to exalt the whole human family. And, because we have the keys to the sealing power, what we bind in proper order here will be bound in heaven. Those keys—the keys to seal and bind on earth, and have it bound in heaven—represent the consummate gift from our God. With that authority we can baptize and bless, we can endow and seal, and the Lord will honor our commitments. (The Holy Temple, pp. 150-51) TLDP:509

**Elder Joseph Fielding Smith**

Only one man at a time on the earth holds the keys of the priesthood; only one man at a time has the power to receive revelations for the Church; but the Lord has made it possible for every man in this Church, through his obedience, to receive the fulness of the priesthood through the ordinances of the temple of the Lord. This cannot be received anywhere else. (Doctrines of Salvation, 3:131-33) TLDP:503-04

**Elder Joseph Fielding Smith**

The new and everlasting covenant is the fulness of the gospel. It is composed of "All covenants,

contracts, bonds, obligations, oaths, vows, performances, connections, associations, or expectations" that are sealed upon members of the Church by the Holy Spirit of promise, or the Holy Ghost, by the authority of the President of the Church who holds the keys. The President of the Church holds the keys of the Melchizedek Priesthood. He delegates authority to others and authorizes them to perform the sacred ordinances of the priesthood. (Answers to Gospel Questions, 1:65) DCSM:46

**President Joseph F. Smith,**
**John R. Winder, Anthon H. Lund**
(First Presidency)

The leading fact to be remembered is that the Priesthood is greater than any of its offices; and that any man holding the Melchizedek Priesthood may, by virtue of its possession, perform any ordinance pertaining thereto, or connected therewith, when called upon to do so by one holding the proper authority, which proper authority is vested in the President of the Church, or in any whom he may designate. Every officer in the Church is under his direction, and he is directed of God. He is also selected of the Lord to be the head of the Church, and so becomes, when the Priesthood of the Church (which includes its officers), and its members, shall have so accepted and upheld him. (D&C 197:22) No man can justly presume to have authority to preside, merely by virtue of his Priesthood. . . . ¶ Every man holding the Holy Melchizedek Priesthood may act in any capacity and do all things that such Priesthood authorizes, it makes no difference what office in that Priesthood he holds, providing he is called upon by proper authority to so officiate; but he would have no right to depart from the limitations of his office, unless he is specially called upon by one whose calling, from those over him up to the head, would clearly authorize him to give such instructions. It is always to be presumed, also, that order will be observed, and that the servants of the Lord will not depart from that order, and call upon men to do things which the law of the Priesthood and the nature of their office, does not authorize, unless there is special occasion for it. The Lord says that all things are governed by law. (See D&C 88:42.) It is not consistent, for instance, to imagine that the Lord would call upon a deacon to baptize. (Officially published: IE1902May:549-51) MOFP4:43-44

**Jesus,**
*recorded in Matthew*

And I will give unto thee the keys of the kingdom of heaven: and whatsoever thou shalt bind on earth shall be bound in heaven: and whatsoever thou shalt loose on earth shall be loosed in heaven. (*Jesus instructs his disciples; he addresses Peter*) Matt.16:19

**Related Witnesses:**

**Elder Wilford Woodruff**

He [Joseph Smith] lived until he received every key, ordinance and law ever given to any man on the earth, from Father Adam down, touching this dispensation. He received powers and keys from under the hands of Moses for gathering the house of Israel in the last days; he received under the hands of Elias the keys of sealing the hearts of the fathers to the children, and the hearts of the children to the fathers; he received under the hands of Peter, James and John, the Apostleship, and everything belonging thereto; he received under the hands of Moroni all the keys and powers required of the stick of Joseph in the hands of Ephraim; he received under the hand of John the Baptist the Aaronic Priesthood, with all its keys and powers, and every other key and power belonging to this dispensation, and I am not ashamed to say that he was a Prophet of God, and he laid the foundation of the greatest work and dispensation that has ever been established on the earth. (*In new Tabernacle, Oct. 1873, JD16:267*) DGSM:68

**Author's Note:** The Apostles of the Church have all the authority, they have all the keys, but only the President has the power to exercise those keys. ¶ President Brigham Young said: ¶ "All the Priesthood, all the keys, all the gifts, all the endowments, and everything preparatory to entering back into the presence of the Father and of the Son is in, composed of, circumscribed by, or I might say incorporated within the circumference of the Apostleship." (TLDP:522) Brigham Young also said: "I say unto you that the Quorum of the Twelve have the keys of the kingdom of God in all the world." (HC7:233)

---

598. **Three high priests form the First Presidency, the presiding council in the Church.**

### Joseph Smith

The Presidency of the High Priesthood, after the order of Melchizedek, have a right to officiate in all the offices in the church. . . . 22. Of the Melchizedek Priesthood, three Presiding High Priests, chosen by the body, appointed and ordained to that office, and upheld by the confidence, faith, and prayer of the church, form a quorum of the Presidency of the Church. 23. The twelve traveling councilors are called to be the

Twelve Apostles, or special witnesses of the name of Christ in all the world—thus differing from other officers in the church in the duties of their calling. 24. And they form a quorum, equal in authority and power to the three presidents previously mentioned. (*Revelation on priesthood, received as the Twelve met in council, March 28, 1835*) D&C 107:9,22-24

### President Joseph F. Smith

We have the council of the first presidency consisting of three presiding high priests who are called of God and appointed to preside over the Church and over the Priesthood of God, and I want to say here that it does not follow and never has followed that the members of the first presidency of the Church are necessarily to be ordained apostles. They hold by virtue of their rights as presidents of the Church all the keys and all the authority that pertains to the Melchizedek Priesthood, which comprehends and comprises all of the appendages to that priesthood, the lesser priesthood and all the offices in the priesthood from first to last, and from least to greatest. CR1913Apr:4

### Elder Joseph Fielding Smith

Three high priests form the First Presidency, the presiding quorum in the Church. The power of presidency is vested in these three and they have authority to receive the mysteries of the kingdom. The President of the Church has vested in him the fulness of the Priesthood, and all the keys of authority over the Priesthood. He alone holds the sealing power in its fulness, and he delegates the authority to others. (See D&C 132:7.) ¶ The twelve apostles form the second quorum in authority in the Church. They have delegated to them the duty and responsibility to preach the Gospel, and to see that it is taught in all the world. The apostles constitute the traveling council of the Church. It is their duty, under the First Presidency, to ordain patriarchs and to set in order all the other officers of the Church. (D&C 132:39,58) They constitute the quorum of special witnesses for Jesus Christ, and it is their duty to testify of him by the power of the Holy Ghost in all the world. CHMR2:20

### President Brigham Young, *quoted by John A. Widtsoe*

In trying all matters of doctrine, to make a decision valid, it is necessary to obtain a unanimous voice, faith and decision. In the capacity of a Quorum, the three First Presidents must be one in their voice; the Twelve Apostles must be unanimous in their voice; to obtain a righteous decision upon any matter that may come before them, as you may read in the Doctrine and Covenants. Whenever you see these Quorums unanimous in their declaration, you may set it down as true. (*At Mill Creek Ward, May 7, 1861, JD9:91-92*) DBY:133

**Related Witnesses:**

**Elder John Taylor**

[The kingdom of God] has its First Presidency, its Prophets and Apostles, its Seventies and High Priests, its Bishops, Teachers, and Deacons, and every appendage that is necessary to completeness, and to promote the happiness and welfare of the human family, and for all purposes of government on this earth and in the heavens. Or, in other words, this organization is a pattern of things in the heavens and is the medium or channel through which the blessings of God flow to his people on the earth, and through which intelligence is communicated concerning all subjects with which the Saints are concerned, whether they relate to this world or to the world which is to come. (*In Tabernacle, Oct. 7, 1859, JD7:323*) TLDP:85-86

**Elder John Taylor**

The First Presidency has authority over all matters pertaining to the Church. ("The Organization of the Church," Millennial Star, Nov. 1851, pp. 337-38) TLDP:521

**President Joseph F. Smith**

If the Presidency were to be killed off, then the Council of the Twelve Apostles would stand in their place and preside until the Presidency should be restored; and if they and the First Presidency were all killed off, then the Seventies would come forward and they would establish the order of Zion and renew the order of the Priesthood upon the earth; and if all the Seventies were killed off, and yet there was one Elder, possessing the Melchizedek Priesthood, he would have authority to organize the Church, under the command of God and the guidance of His Holy Spirit, as Joseph did in the beginning; that it should be re-established in its perfect form. So you can see that this organization is well-nigh indestructible. (Elders' Journal, Nov. 1, 1906, p. 46) TLDP:94

---

**599. The Quorum of the Twelve Apostles stands next in authority to the First Presidency in the Church.**

**Elder John Taylor**

The First Presidency has authority over all matters pertaining to the Church. ¶ The next in order are the Twelve Apostles, whose calling is to preach the gospel, or see it preached, to all the world. They hold the same authority in all parts of the world that the First Presidency do at home, and act under their direction. They are called by revelation and sanctioned by the people. The Twelve have a president. . . . This presidency is obtained by seniority of age and ordination. ("The Organization of the Church," Millennial Star, Nov. 1851, pp. 337-38) TLDP:521

**Joseph Smith**

The twelve traveling councilors are called to be the Twelve Apostles, or special witnesses of the name of Christ in all the world—thus differing from other officers in the church in the duties of their calling. 24. And they form a quorum, equal in authority and power to the three presidents previously mentioned. (*Revelation on priesthood, received as the Twelve met in council, March 28, 1835*) D&C 107:23-24

**President Joseph F. Smith**

I want here to correct an impression that has grown up to some extent among the people, and that is, that the Twelve Apostles possess equal authority with the First Presidency in the Church. This is correct when there is no other Presidency but the Twelve Apostles; but so long as there are three presiding Elders who possess the presiding authority in the Church, the authority of the Twelve Apostles is not equal to theirs. If it were so, there would be two equal authorities and two equal quorums in the Priesthood, running parallel, and that could not be, because there must be a head. Therefore, so long as there is a First Presidency in the Church they hold supreme authority in the Church, and the Twelve Apostles are subject unto them and do not possess the same authority as they do as a presiding quorum. When the Presidency are not here, or when the Lord takes away the man who is called to be the President of the Church and the quorum of three Presidents is thereby dissolved, then the authority of the Twelve rises to the dignity of Presidents of the Church and not until then. Some people have thought also that the quorum of Seventies possess equal authority with the First Presidency and with the Twelve. So they would if there was no Presidency and no Twelve, and only seventy Elders called Seventies in the Church, but their authority is not equal to that of the First Presidency while the First Presidency lives, nor to that of the Twelve Apostles. (Elders' Journal, Nov. 1906, p. 43) TLDP:250-51

**President Joseph F. Smith**

If the Presidency were to be killed off, then the Council of the Twelve Apostles would stand in their place and preside until the Presidency should be restored; and if they and the First Presidency were all killed off, then the Seventies would come forward and they would establish the order of Zion and renew the order of the Priesthood upon the earth; and if all the Seventies were killed off, and yet there was one Elder, possessing the Melchizedek Priesthood, he would have authority to organize the Church, under the command of God and the guidance of His Holy Spirit, as Joseph did in the beginning; that it should be re-established in its perfect form. So you can see that this organization is well-nigh indestructible. (Elders' Journal, Nov. 1, 1906, p. 46) TLDP:94

**President Brigham Young,**
*quoted by John A. Widtsoe*

Suppose that Sidney Rigdon and Frederick G. Williams had been taken away or had apostatized, as one of them did soon after the revelation I have referred to was given, and there had been only Joseph Smith left of the First Presidency, would he alone have had authority to set in order the Kingdom of God on the earth? Yes. Again: Suppose that eleven of the Twelve had been taken away by the power of the Adversary, that one Apostle has the same power that Joseph had, and could preach, baptize, and set in order the whole Kingdom of God upon the earth, as much so as the Twelve were they all together. Again: If in the providence of God he should permit the enemy to destroy these two first Quorums, and then destroy the Quorum of the Seventy, all but one man, what is his power? It would be to go and preach, baptize, confirm, lay on hands, ordain, set in order, build up, and establish the whole Kingdom of God as it is now. Suppose the enemy had power to destroy all but one of the High Priests from the face of the earth, what would that one possess in the power of his Priesthood? He would have power and authority to go and preach, baptize, confirm, ordain, and set in order the Kingdom of God in all its perfection on the earth. Could he do this without revelation? No. Could the Seventies? No. Could the Twelve? No. And we ask, could Joseph Smith or the First Presidency do this without revelation? No. Not one of them could do such a work without revelation direct from God. I can go still further. Whoever is ordained to the office of an Elder to a certain degree possesses the keys of the Melchizedek Priesthood; and suppose only one Elder should be left on the earth, could he go and set in order the Kingdom of God? Yes, by revelation. *(At Mill Creek Ward, May 7, 1861, JD9:88)* DBY:138-39

**Elder Joseph Fielding Smith**

While the Prophet Joseph Smith stands at the head of this dispensation for all eternity, yet it became necessary in the government of the Church for others to be invested with divine power to stand to direct and preside over the affairs of the kingdom of God on the earth to succeed him after he was taken from mortality. Therefore the Lord made provision for this emergency and in this revelation said: "Nevertheless, through you shall the oracles be given to another, yea, even unto the church." The interpretation of the term "oracles" as used in this revelation is given in the dictionary to be "an infallible authority." For the perpetuity of the Church that provision must be made for a successor to the president who holds the keys, when he shall pass away. The word of the Lord was fulfilled wherein he said that through Joseph Smith the oracles should be given to the Church, and by command of the Lord the Prophet, in Nauvoo a few months before his death, called the apostles together and said to them that the Lord has commanded him to confer upon them all the keys and authorities which he had had conferred upon him, so that the work could be "rolled off" of his shoulders onto theirs. He thereupon conferred upon them this divine governing power, but this governing could not be exercised by any one of the twelve while the Prophet was living. Upon his death the right to preside and set in order and to hold the keys of authority in the Priesthood and in the Church, rightfully belonged to President Brigham Young and by authority of the ordination he had received under the hands of Joseph Smith and by being sustained by his brethren and the Church, he was vested with the supreme power. So likewise each of his successors, President John Taylor, Wilford Woodruff and all the Presidents of the Church down to the present have exercised this authority by divine right when the position of presidency in the presiding council has come to them. Each of the apostles when he is ordained has conferred upon him all the keys and authorities which were given by Joseph Smith to the apostles before his death. These brethren, however, cannot exercise these authorities except when the occasion arises that they come to the presidency. Before that time the powers lie dormant. This is one reason why they are sustained as prophets, seers and revelators in the Church, but there can be but one revelator for the Church at a time. CHMR1:388-89

**Elder Harold B. Lee**

To those who ask the question: How is the President of the Church chosen or elected? the correct and simple answer should be a quotation of the fifth Article of Faith: "We believe that a man must be called of God, by prophecy, and by the laying on of hands, by those who are in authority to preach the Gospel and administer in the ordinances thereof." ¶ The beginning of the call of one to be President of the Church actually begins when he is called, ordained, and set apart to become a member of the Quorum of the Twelve Apostles. Such a call by prophecy, or in other words, by the inspiration of the Lord to the one holding the keys of presidency, and the subsequent ordination and setting apart by the laying on of hands by that same authority, places each apostle in a priesthood quorum of twelve men holding the apostleship. ¶ Each apostle so ordained under the hands of the President of the Church, who holds the keys of the kingdom of God in concert with all other ordained apostles, has given to him the priesthood authority necessary to hold every position in the Church, even to a position of presidency over the Church if he were called by the presiding authority and sustained by a vote of a constituent assembly of the membership of the Church. ¶ The Prophet Joseph Smith declared that "where the president is not, there is no First Presidency." Immediately following the death of a president, the next ranking body, the Quorum of the Twelve Apostles, become the presiding authority, with the President of the Twelve automatically becoming the acting President of the Church until a President of the Church is officially ordained and sustained in his office. CR1970Apr:123

### George Q. Cannon

Every man who is ordained to the fulness of Apostleship, has the power and the authority to lead and guide the people of God whenever he is called upon to it, and the responsibility rests upon him. . . . And while it is the right of all the Twelve Apostles to receive revelation, for each one to be a Prophet, to be a Seer, to be a Revelator, and to hold the keys in the fulness, it is only the right of one man at a time to exercise that power in relation to the whole people, and to give revelation and counsel, and direct the affairs of the Church—of course, always acting in conjunction with his fellow-servants. And while we say that the Twelve Apostles have the right to govern, that the Twelve have the authority, that the Twelve Apostles are the men who preside—when we say this, we do not mean that every one of the Twelve is going to give revelation to this great people, that every one of the Twelve has the right to counsel and dictate and regulate the affairs of the Church as emergencies may arise, independent of the rest. The Church is not governed like Zion's Co-operative Institution, by a Board of Directors; this is not God's design. It is

governed by men who hold the keys of the Apostleship, who have the right and authority. Any one of them, should an emergency arise, can act as President of the Church, with all the powers, with all the authority, with all the keys, and with every endowment necessary to obtain revelation from God, and to lead and guide this people in the path that leads to the celestial glory; but there is only one man at a time who can hold the keys, who can dictate, who can guide, who can give revelation to the Church. The rest must acquiesce in his action, the rest must be governed by his counsels, the rest must receive his doctrines. (*In new Tabernacle, Oct. 8, 1877, JD19:233-34*) TLDP:250

**Related Witnesses:**

#### Joseph Smith,
*receiving the Word of the Lord*

For unto you, the Twelve, and those, the First Presidency, who are appointed with you to be your counselors and your leaders, is the power of this priesthood given, for the last days and for the last time, in the which is the dispensation of the fulness of times. 31. Which power you hold, in connection with all those who have received a dispensation at any time from the beginning of the creation; 32. For verily I say unto you, the keys of the dispensation, which ye have received, have come down from the fathers, and last of all, being sent down from heaven unto you. (*Revelation for Thomas B. Marsh concerning the Twelve Apostles, July 23, 1837*) D&C 112:30-32

#### Joseph Smith

They are the Twelve Apostles, who are called to the office of the Traveling High Council, who are to preside over the churches of the Saints, among the Gentiles, where there is a presidency established; and they are to travel and preach among the Gentiles, until the Lord shall command them to go to the Jews. They are to hold the keys of this ministry, to unlock the door of the Kingdom of heaven unto all nations, and to preach the Gospel to every creature. This is the power, authority, and virtue of their apostleship. (*"Items of Instruction to the Twelve," Feb. 27, 1835, reported by Oliver Cowdery, clerk; "President Smith proposed the following question: 'What importance is there attached to the calling of these Twelve Apostles, different from the other callings or officers of the Church?' After the question was discussed by Councilors Patten, Young, Smith, and M'Lellin, President Joseph Smith, Jun., gave the [foregoing] decision"*) HC2:200

**600. Each office in the priesthood (elder, seventy, high priest, bishop, Apostle, etc.) is a calling that derives all of its authority from the priesthood; officers hold different callings, but the same priesthood.**

### President Joseph F. Smith, John R. Winder, Anthon H. Lund
(First Presidency)

The leading fact to be remembered is that the Priesthood is greater than any of its offices; and that any man holding the Melchizedek Priesthood may, by virtue of its possession, perform any ordinance pertaining thereto, or connected therewith, when called upon to do so by one holding the proper authority, which proper authority is vested in the President of the Church, or in any whom he may designate. . . . An office in the Priesthood is a calling, like apostles, high priest, seventy, elder, and derives all its authority from the Priesthood; these officers hold different callings, but the same Priesthood. (Officially published: IE1902May:549-51) MOFP4:42-43; TLDP:520

### President Joseph F. Smith

There is no office growing out of this Priesthood that is or can be greater than the Priesthood itself. It is from the Priesthood that the office derives its authority and power. No office gives authority to the Priesthood. No office adds to the power of the Priesthood. But all offices in the Church derive their power, their virtue, their authority, from the Priesthood. If our brethren would get this principle thoroughly established in their minds, there would be less misunderstanding in relation to the functions of government in the Church than there is. Today the question is, which is the greater—the High Priest or the Seventy—the Seventy or the High Priest? I tell you that neither of them is the greater, and neither of them is the lesser. Their callings lie in different directions, but they are from the same Priesthood. If it were necessary, the Seventy, holding the Melchizedek Priesthood, as he does, I say *if it were necessary*, he could ordain a High Priest; and if it were necessary for a High Priest to ordain a seventy, he could do that. Why? Because both of them hold the Melchizedek Priesthood. Then again, if it were necessary, though I do not expect the necessity will ever arise, and there was no man left on earth holding the Melchizedek Priesthood, except an Elder—that Elder, by the inspiration of the Spirit of God and by the direction of the Almighty, could pro-

ceed, and should proceed, to organize the Church of Jesus Christ in all its perfection, because he holds the Melchizedek Priesthood. But the house of God is a house of order, and while the other officers remain in the Church, we must observe the order of the priesthood, and we must perform ordinances and ordinations strictly in accordance with that order, as it has been established in the Church through the instrumentality of the Prophet Joseph Smith and his successors. CR1903Oct:87

### President Brigham Young, quoted by John A. Widtsoe

[A] person who is ordained to the office of an Elder in this Kingdom has the same Priesthood that the High Priests, that the Twelve Apostles, that the Seventies, and that the First Presidency hold; but all are not called to be one of the Twelve Apostles nor are all called to be one of the First Presidency, nor to be one of the First Presidents of all the Seventies, nor to be one of the Presidents of a Quorum of Seventies, nor to preside over the High Priests' Quorum; but every man in his order and place, possessing a portion of the same Priesthood, according to the gifts and callings to each. *(At Mill Creek Ward, May 7, 1861, JD9:89)* DBY:134

### Elder John Taylor

There are different callings, and offices, and stations, and authorities in the holy priesthood, but it is all the same priesthood; and there are different keys, and powers, and responsibilities, but it is the same government; and all the priesthood are agents in that government, and all are requisite for the organization of the body, the upbuilding of Zion, and the government of his kingdom. ("On Priesthood," Millennial Star, Nov. 1847, p. 322) TLDP:498

### Related Witnesses:

### Elder Joseph Fielding Smith

Do not think because somebody has a higher office in this Church than you have that you are barred from blessings, because you can go into the temple of the Lord and get *all* the blessings there are that have been revealed, if you are faithful; you can have them sealed upon you as an *elder* in this Church, and then you have *all* that any man can get. There have to be offices in the Church, and we are not all called to the same calling, but you can get the fulness of the priesthood in the temple of the Lord by obeying this which I have read to you. I want to make this emphatic. . . . ¶ To obtain the fulness of the priesthood does not mean that a man must become President of the Church. Every man who is faithful and will receive these ordinances and blessings obtains a fulness of the priesthood, and the Lord has said that "he makes them equal in power, and in might, and in dominion." Only one man at a time on the earth holds the *keys* of the priesthood; only one man at a time has the power to receive revelations for the Church; but the Lord has made it possible for every man in this Church, through his obedience, to receive the fulness of the priesthood through the ordinances of the temple of the Lord. This cannot be received anywhere else. (Doctrines of Salvation, 3:131-33) TLDP:503-04

**Bruce R. McConkie**

Now let us speak of the offices in the Melchizedek Priesthood. "*Elders* are ministers of Christ; they are called to administer in spiritual things (D&C 107:12), 'To teach, expound, exhort, baptize, and watch over the church; And to confirm the church by the laying on of the hands, and the giving of the Holy Ghost. . . . The elders are to conduct the meetings as they are led by the Holy Ghost, according to the commandments and revelations of God.' (D&C 20:42-45; D&C 46:2) They are to preach the gospel (D&C 53:3), teach from the scriptures (D&C 42:12), administer to the sick (D&C 42:43-52; James 5:14-15), function in the church court system (D&C 42:80), and perform any duty that can be done by a holder of the lesser priesthood." (D&C 20:38-67) (*Mormon Doctrine, 2nd ed., p. 215; italics added*) ¶ *Elders* are to perfect the Saints, to feed the flock of God, to work in the organizations of the Church, to lead people to eternal life in our Father's kingdom. All holders of the Melchizedek Priesthood serve as elders. The President of the Church is the presiding elder in the Church. Apostles are elders; so also are seventies, high priests, and patriarchs. There is no way of overstating the importance of the office of an elder. ¶ Now there isn't any language that can possibly overstate, that can overemphasize, the dignity and glory of the office of an elder. Elders are ministers of Christ. They are called to administer in spiritual things. They do everything that an Aaronic Priesthood holder does. In addition, they lay on hands for the gift of the Holy Ghost. They conduct meetings as they are guided by the Holy Spirit. They preach the gospel. They teach from the scriptures. They administer to the sick. They are called upon to perfect the Saints, to feed the flock of God, to work in the organizations of the Church, to lead people to eternal life in our Father's kingdom. Now every holder of the Melchizedek Priesthood is an elder. There is with us tonight the presiding elder in the Church. I am an Apostle, and an Apostle is

an elder. We rejoice in that calling. All of the work that we do in the temples to make salvation and exaltation available to our ancestors is predicated upon the fact that our dead ancestors are ordained elders. We perform the ordinance for and on their behalf. Every elder makes the covenant of exaltation, and the Lord says to him, "If you magnify your calling [which means if you do the work of an elder], then I, the Lord, will give you all that my Father hath." (See D&C 84:34-39.) Which is to say, you shall have exaltation. And so elders save themselves, and they have power to save others. . . . ¶ *High priests* are elders with a special call and ordination to perfect the Saints, to preside over Church organizations, to guide the destinies of the Lord's people in any area. They serve as standing presidents. Members of stake presidencies, high councils, and bishoprics are all ordained high priests. ACR(Lima)1977:18

601. **Except for the President of the Church, all priesthood holders have designated limits to their authority.**

**Boyd K. Packer**

Now I make another comparison as I explain something that is understood by relatively few. It is common in the world for institutions to declare authority and at once strictly limit the extent of what is being delegated. For instance, in a branch bank the manager may have authorization to make loans up to a certain amount. If someone requests a loan larger than that amount, then a supervisor must approve it. For even larger amounts the regulations of the bank may require that only the president and chief executive officer himself may approve the loan. ¶ If a commitment for a loan is made by a branch manager within the policy, the bank will honor it, even though that manager may later quit and go to work for a competing bank. . . . ¶ The practice of delegating authority, and at once limiting it, is so commonly demonstrated in business and education, in government, in cultural organizations, that we should not have difficulty in understanding that principle in the Church. ¶ A missionary is given authority to teach and to baptize. Given certain approval, he can ordain someone to a priesthood office. If he is an elder, however, he cannot ordain someone to be a seventy or a high priest, for his authority is limited. Similarly, a bishop can call and release within the limits of his jurisdiction. But he could not,

for instance, set apart a stake high councilor. . . .
¶ Those who hold the Aaronic Priesthood, or
the preparatory priesthood, hold the authority,
when specifically directed, to perform those
ordinances that belong to that priesthood.
They can baptize. They can bless the sacrament and perform every service relating to the
lesser priesthood. They cannot confirm someone a member of the Church, however, for that
takes a higher authority. ¶ On the same principle, those who hold the Melchizedek
Priesthood can perform the ordinances relating
to the higher priesthood. But unless they are
given special authorization they cannot endow,
nor seal, nor perform those ordinances that pertain to the temple. ¶ There are limits. (The
Holy Temple, pp. 150-51) TLDP:509

**President Joseph F. Smith,**
**John R. Winder, Anthon H. Lund**
(First Presidency)

The leading fact to be remembered is that the
Priesthood is greater than any of its offices;
and that any man holding the Melchizedek
Priesthood may, by virtue of its possession, perform any ordinance pertaining thereto, or connected therewith, when called upon to do so by
one holding the proper authority, which proper
authority is vested in the President of the
Church, or in any whom he may designate. . . .
(Officially published: IE1902May:549-51)
MOFP4:43; TLDP:520

**Related Witnesses:**
**President Joseph F. Smith**

There is no office growing out of this
Priesthood that is or can be greater than the
Priesthood itself. It is from the Priesthood that
the office derives its authority and power. No
office gives authority to the Priesthood. No
office adds to the power of the Priesthood. But
all offices in the Church derive their power,
their virtue, their authority, from the Priesthood.
CR1903Oct:87

**President Brigham Young,**
*quoted by John A. Widtsoe*

[A] person who is ordained to the office of an
Elder in this Kingdom has the same Priesthood
that the High Priests, that the Twelve Apostles,
that the Seventies, and that the First Presidency
hold; but all are not called to be one of the
Twelve Apostles nor are all called to be one of
the First Presidency, nor to be one of the First
Presidents of all the Seventies, nor to be one of
the Presidents of a Quorum of Seventies, nor to
preside over the High Priests' Quorum; but
every man in his order and place, possessing a
portion of the same Priesthood, according to the
gifts and callings to each. *(At Mill Creek Ward,*

*May 7, 1861, JD9:89)* DBY:134

**Elder Harold B. Lee**

Priesthood defined is the power of God given to
man to act for Him in all things pertaining to
the salvation of man—and I should add, within
the limitations of each endowment of authority
by the laying on of hands. *(Mission presidents'
seminar, July 2, 1961)* (Stand Ye in Holy
Places, p. 266) TLDP:519

# List of Doctrines

## PROPHETS, SEERS AND REVELATORS

*Doctrines Located in This Topic*

602. The Lord's way of teaching us is through prophet witnesses.

603. Beginning with Adam, the Lord has continually sent prophets to the people to instruct them in the principles of the gospel.

604. The Lord chooses righteous men as His prophet witnesses.

605. Prophets are not perfect men (the Lord chooses His prophets from the ranks of ordinary men).

606. A prophet is a revelator who declares the will of God to the people.

607. The role of prophets is to teach the gospel to the world.

608. A prophet may foretell future events, both temporal and spiritual.

609. Joseph Smith was a prophet in these latter days.

610. We are to receive the words of the President of the Church as if they came from the mouth the Lord.

611. The President of the Church will never lead the Saints astray or send forth counsel to the world that is contrary to the mind and will of the Lord.

612. Apostles are prophets.

*Doctrines on PROPHETS, SEERS AND REVELATORS Located in Other Topics*

255. Prophets bear witness of God's existence.

561. In the premortal world the Lord chose those who were to be rulers in the church of God on earth.

645. Joseph Smith was chosen and called by the Lord to be a latter-day prophet.

712. Written scripture is the recorded testimony of prophets who receive gospel truths by revelation from the Lord.

718. In addition to written scripture we need continuous revelation from living prophets to guide us.

874. The Lord selects teachable persons to do His work; He chooses those whom the world calls weak and foolish more frequently than those whom the world calls wise.

# PROPHETS, SEERS AND REVELATORS

**602. The Lord's way of teaching us is through prophet witnesses.**

### Elder Joseph Fielding Smith

If the Lord wished he could preach this gospel to the world by declaring it from the heavens. He could have his angels blow their trumpets and declare the message of salvation in the ears of all the world. Would not that be a much easier way to get the message of truth before the world than the expensive way of sending messengers clothed with authority at great expense and toil to try to teach the world? ¶ But the ways of the Lord are not man's ways. He works through his witnesses, and in establishing his work in every age, he uses the few, not the many. Never since the beginning has the Lord declared himself to the unbelieving world, but he has sent out his messengers to preach the gospel to the world. (Church News, 1939; Doctrines of Salvation, 1:208-09) TLDP:733

### Mark E. Petersen

Always when the Lord has had a people on the earth whom he has recognized as his own, he has led them by living prophets to whom he has given guidance from heaven. ¶ While the people remained faithful anciently, one prophet after another was raised up by the Almighty in a long series of divine appointments. Thus we had many men of God mentioned in both Old and New Testaments. ¶ A similar line of inspired men now has been established in modern times. This was accomplished as a result of the restoration of the gospel of the Lord Jesus Christ through his latter-day seer, Joseph Smith. . . . ¶ Although he is a God of communication, he follows a particular method of transmitting knowledge to man. It is an unchanging pattern, which is, that he always speaks to the people through living prophets. CR1972Oct:150

### LeGrand Richards

We read in the scriptures the word of Amos the Prophet that: "Surely the Lord God will do nothing, but he revealeth his secret unto his servants the prophets." (Amos 3:7) ¶ So that if the Lord should ever undertake to fulfil the promises made to the Prophet Joseph Smith and to Isaiah and to Daniel, then we would have to look to find that work headed by a prophet, because God could not do, according to his plan and purposes, the work he decreed he would do without a prophet. Thank God for the prophets of this dispensation. CR1962Apr:41

### Francis M. Lyman

It has been the living oracles of God that produced the written word, and that always must produce the written word—not the written word that produces the living oracles. But the living oracles are those men whom God has chosen and has inspired and given responsibility to. Those are the living oracles of God, and they are the men that the Lord sustains and strengthens and preserves, and to whom He reveals His mind and will. CR1897Oct:18

### Elder Ezra Taft Benson

The most important prophet, so far as we are concerned, is the one who is living in our day and age. This is the prophet who has today's instructions from God to us today. God's revelation to Adam did not instruct Noah how to build the ark. Every generation has need of the ancient scripture plus the current scripture from the living prophet. Therefore, the most crucial reading and pondering which you should do is of the latest inspired words from the Lord's mouthpiece. ACR(Seoul)1975:52

### Elder Joseph Fielding Smith

We are called upon in this life to walk by faith, not by sight, not by the proclamation of heavenly messengers with the voice of thunder, but by the proclamation of accredited witnesses whom the Lord sends and by whom every word shall be established CHMR1:40; DCSM:13

**Related Witnesses:**

### Joseph Smith,
*receiving the Word of the Lord*

And the testimony of three witnesses will I send forth of my word. 16. And behold, whosoever believeth on my words, them will I visit with the manifestation of my Spirit; and they shall be born of me, even of water and of the Spirit. *(Revelation at the request of Martin Harris, March 1829; the Lord promises to supply three witnesses to the Book of Mormon)* D&C 5:15-16

### Elder Joseph Fielding Smith

In giving the world the testimony of three witnesses in addition to Joseph Smith, the Lord fulfilled the law. We are called upon in this life to walk by faith, not by sight, not by the proclamation of heavenly messengers with the voice of thunder, but by the proclamation of accredited witnesses whom the Lord sends and by whom every word shall be established. CHMR1:40; DCSM:13

### Nephi, son of Lehi

Wherefore, the Lord God will proceed to bring forth the words of the book; and in the mouth of as many witnesses as seemeth him good will he establish his word; and wo be unto him that rejecteth the word of God! *(Nephi foretells of the last days and the coming forth of the Book of Mormon, 559-545 B.C.)* 2Ne.27:14

### President Harold B. Lee

If you want to know what the Lord would have the Saints know and to have his guidance and direction for the next six months, get a copy of the proceedings of this conference, and you will have the latest word of the Lord as far as the Saints are concerned. CR1973Oct:168

### Nephi, son of Lehi

For I command all men, both in the east and in the west, and in the north, and in the south, and in the islands of the sea, that they shall write the words which I speak unto them; for out of the books which shall be written I will judge the world, every man according to their works, according to that which is written. 12. For behold, I shall speak unto the Jews and they shall write it; and I shall also speak unto the Nephites and they shall write it; and I shall also speak unto the other tribes of the house of Israel, which I have led away, and they shall write it; and I shall also speak unto all nations of the earth and they shall write it. 13. And it shall come to pass that the Jews shall have the words of the Nephites, and the Nephites shall have the words of the Jews; and the Nephites and the Jews shall have the words of the lost tribes of Israel; and the lost tribes of Israel shall have the words of the Nephites and the Jews. (*The Lord speaks to Nephi about the latter-day gentiles, many of whom shall reject the Book of Mormon, 559-545 B.C.*) 2Ne.29:11-13

---

**603. Beginning with Adam, the Lord has continually sent prophets to the people to instruct them in the principles of the gospel.**

### Elder George Albert Smith

It does seem strange that so many people doubt our divine ancestry, and that God is the Father of our spirits; yet from the very beginning, from the very earliest period of which we have any record in this world, He has been teaching men and women this fact. . . . ¶ When God created the earth and placed our first parents upon it, He did not leave them without knowledge concerning Himself. It is true that there had been taken from them the remembrance of their pre-existent life, but in His tender mercy He talked with them and later He sent His choice servants to instruct them in the things pertaining to eternal life. CR1928Oct:90-91

### Joseph Smith

Some say the kingdom of God was not set up on the earth until the day of Pentecost, and that John did not preach the baptism of repentance for the remission of sins; but I say, in the name of the Lord, that the kingdom of God was set up on the earth from the days of Adam to the present time. Whenever there has been a righteous man on earth unto whom God revealed His word and gave power and authority to administer in His name, and where there is a priest of God—a minister who has power and authority from God to administer in the ordinances of the gospel and officiate in the priesthood of God, there is the kingdom of God; and, in consequence of rejecting the Gospel of Jesus Christ and the Prophets whom God hath sent, the judgments of God have rested upon people, cities, and nations, in various ages of the world, which was the case with the cities of Sodom and Gomorrah, that were destroyed for rejecting the Prophets. ¶ Now I will give my testimony. I care not for man. I speak boldly and faithfully and with authority. How is it with the kingdom of God? Where did the kingdom of God begin? Where there is no kingdom of God there is no salvation. What constitutes the kingdom of God? Where there is a prophet, a priest, a righteous man unto whom God gives His oracles, there is the kingdom of God; and where the oracles of God are not, there the kingdom of God is not. (*Speech at Nauvoo Temple, Jan. 22, 1843: setting up the Kingdom of God* ) HC5:256-57; TLDP:333

### Bruce R. McConkie

Every prophet from the beginning on down was a witness of the Lord Jesus. They all bore testimony that salvation was in him. They all worshiped the Father in the name of Christ. They all taught that men received a remission of sins by faith and repentance and baptism, because of the atoning sacrifice which he would work out. Now that's the plan of salvation, and there has never been an age and there has never been a people and there has never been a time when the voice and mind and purposes of the Lord have been known in which prophets have not borne that witness. From the day of Adam to John the Baptist, all of the proclamations the prophets made could be termed Messianic prophecies. That is, they foretold the coming of the Messiah. They were climaxed by what John the Baptist said: "Behold the Lamb of God, which taketh away the sin of the world." (John 1:29) And all of the witness and all of the assurance that any of the inspired apostles and prophets have made since the day of Christ are termed testimony. We bear testimony of that which has been. The testimony which we bear is that Jesus is the Lord. ACR(Sydney)1976:20

### Bruce R. McConkie

Dispensations are those periods of time when

the plan of salvation, the Word—the Eternal Word—is dispensed to men on earth. How many there have been we do not know. I suppose there have been ten; maybe there have been twenty; there could have been more. I am speaking now not of what sometimes are called dispensations in the sense that John the Baptist and Paul and some of the other prophets had special appointments. I am speaking of those great eras or periods, of those designated portions of the earth's history, when the Lord, through one man, gives his word to the whole world and makes all the prophets, and all the seers, and all the administrators, and all the apostles of that period subject to, and exponents of, what came through that individual. What this means is that the head of a gospel dispensation stands as one of the ten or twenty greatest spirits who have so far been born on earth. ¶ We know very little about the caliber of men who will be born during the Millennium. Many great spirits will come then. It seems reasonable to suppose, however, that the Lord has singled out certain ones who had special spiritual talents and capabilities to come to earth in periods of turmoil and wickedness and rebellion and evil, to be lights and guides to the world. This gives us a little perspective of what is involved in the life and in the status and position of Joseph Smith. ¶ You start out with the Lord Jesus, and then you have Adam and Noah. Thereafter come the dispensation heads. Then you come to the prophets, to apostles, to the elders of Israel, and to wise and good and sagacious men who have the spirit of light and understanding. Every dispensation head is a revealer of Christ for his day; every prophet is a witness of Christ; and every other prophet or apostle who comes is a reflection and an echo and an exponent of the dispensation head. All such come to echo to the world and to expound and unfold what God has revealed through the man who was appointed to give his eternal word to the world for that era. Such is the dispensation concept. ("This Generation Shall Have My Word through You," EN1980Jun:54) TLDP:536

**Mark E. Petersen**

Always when the Lord has had a people on the earth whom he has recognized as his own, he has led them by living prophets to whom he has given guidance from heaven. ¶ While the people remained faithful anciently, one prophet after another was raised up by the Almighty in a long series of divine appointments. Thus we had many men of God mentioned in both Old and New Testaments. ¶ A similar line of inspired men now has been established in modern times.

This was accomplished as a result of the restoration of the gospel of the Lord Jesus Christ through his latter-day seer, Joseph Smith. . . . ¶ Although he is a God of communication, he follows a particular method of transmitting knowledge to man. It is an unchanging pattern, which is, that he always speaks to the people through living prophets. CR1972Oct:150

**Related Witnesses:**

**Elder Ezra Taft Benson**

The most important prophet, so far as we are concerned, is the one who is living in our day and age. This is the prophet who has today's instructions from God to us today. God's revelation to Adam did not instruct Noah how to build the ark. Every generation has need of the ancient scripture plus the current scripture from the living prophet. Therefore, the most crucial reading and pondering which you should do is of the latest inspired words from the Lord's mouthpiece. ACR(Seoul)1975:52

**James E. Talmage**

We believe that God is as willing today as He ever has been to reveal His mind and will to man, and that He does so through His appointed servants—prophets, seers, and revelators—invested through ordination with the authority of the Holy Priesthood. We rely therefore on the teachings of the living oracles of God as of equal validity with the doctrines of the written word. AF:6

---

**604. The Lord chooses righteous men as His prophet witnesses.**

**Joseph Smith**

Whenever there has been a righteous man on earth unto whom God revealed His word and gave power and authority to administer in His name, and where there is a priest of God—a minister who has power and authority from God to administer in the ordinances of the gospel and officiate in the priesthood of God, there is the kingdom of God. . . . What constitutes the kingdom of God? Where there is a prophet, a priest, a righteous man unto whom God gives His oracles, there is the kingdom of God; and where the oracles of God are not, there the kingdom of God is not. (*Speech at Nauvoo Temple, Jan. 22, 1843: setting up the Kingdom of God* ) HC5:256-57; TLDP:333

**James E. Talmage**

In specific terms the promise was made in olden times that the Lord would recognize the medium of prophecy through which to make His will and purposes known to man: "Surely the Lord God will do nothing, but he revealeth his secret unto his servants the prophets." Not all men may attain the position of special revelators: "The secret of the Lord is with them that fear him; and he will show them his covenant." Such men are oracles of truth, privileged counselors, friends of God. AF:270-71

### Nephi, son of Lehi

And these twelve ministers whom thou beholdest shall judge thy seed. And, behold, they are righteous forever; for because of their faith in the Lamb of God their garments are made white in his blood. (*In a vision, an angel shows Nephi how the twelve disciples and the Twelve Apostles shall judge Israel*) 1Ne.12:10

### Joseph Smith,
*receiving the Word of the Lord*

And again, verily, verily, I say unto you, and it hath gone forth in a firm decree, by the will of the Father, that mine apostles, the Twelve which were with me in my ministry at Jerusalem, shall stand at my right hand at the day of my coming in a pillar of fire, being clothed with robes of righteousness, with crowns upon their heads, in glory even as I am, to judge the whole house of Israel, even as many as have loved me and kept my commandments, and none else. (*Revelation received Sept. 1830; Christ's second coming ushers in the Millennium*) D&C 29:12

### Joseph Smith

And if they persecute you, so persecuted they the prophets and righteous men that were before you. . . . (*Joseph Smith writes to the Church: the Saints are to proceed with the construction of the temple notwithstanding persecution, Sept. 1, 1842*) D&C 127:4

### John Taylor and Willard Richards

[T]he murder of Abel, the assassination of hundreds, the righteous blood of all the holy Prophets, from Abel to Joseph, sprinkled with the best blood of the Son of God, as the crimson sign of remission, only carries conviction to the bosoms of all intelligent beings, that the cause is just and will continue. . . . (*To the Church by way of consolation at the loss of the Prophet Joseph, and his brother Hyrum, July 1, 1844, signed by John Taylor, Willard Richards, and W. W. Phelps*) HC7:152

### Mormon

And because he hath done this, my beloved brethren, have miracles ceased? Behold I say unto you, Nay; neither have angels ceased to minister unto the children of men. 30. For behold, they are subject unto him, to minister according to the word of his command, showing themselves unto them of strong faith and a firm mind in every form of godliness. (*Mormon preaches about Christ in the synagogue, prior to A.D. 384*) Moro.7:29-30

**Related Witnesses:**

### Joseph Smith

A majority may form a quorum when circumstances render it impossible to be otherwise— 29. Unless this is the case, their decisions are not entitled to the same blessings which the decisions of a quorum of three presidents were anciently, who were ordained after the order of Melchizedek, and were righteous and holy men. 30. The decisions of these quorums, or either of them, are to be made in all righteousness, in holiness, and lowliness of heart, meekness and long suffering, and in faith, and virtue, and knowledge, temperance, patience, godliness, brotherly kindness and charity; 31. Because the promise is, if these things abound in them they shall not be unfruitful in the knowledge of the Lord. (*Revelation on priesthood, received as the Twelve met in council, March 28, 1835*) D&C 107:28-31

### Jesus,
*quoted by John*

Ye have not chosen me, but I have chosen you, and ordained you, that ye should go and bring forth fruit, and that your fruit should remain: that whatsoever ye shall ask of the Father in my name, he may give it you. (*Jesus addresses his disciples who have been chosen to serve him*) John 15:16

### Paul

And no man taketh this honour unto himself, but he that is called of God, as was Aaron. (*Letter to the Jewish members of the Church, about A.D. 60*) Heb.5:4

### Peter

And we are witnesses of all things which he did both in the land of the Jews, and in Jerusalem; whom they slew and hanged on a tree: 40. Him God raised up the third day, and shewed him openly; 41. Not to all the people, but unto witnesses chosen before of God, even to us, who did eat and drink with him after he rose from the dead. (*Peter preaches about Christ*) Acts 10:39-41

### President Joseph F. Smith

Among the great and mighty ones who were assembled in this vast congregation of the righteous were Father Adam, the Ancient of Days and father of all, (*Vision of the Savior's visit to the spirits of the dead, Oct. 3, 1918*) D&C 138:38

### Paul

By faith Noah, being warned of God of things not seen as yet, moved with fear, prepared an ark to the saving of his house; by the which he condemned the world, and became heir of the righteousness which is by faith. (*Paul writes to the Jewish members of the Church on faith, about A.D. 60*) Heb.11:7

### James

And the scripture was fulfilled which saith, Abraham believed God, and it was imputed unto him for righteousness: and he was called the Friend of God. (*Letter to his brethren in the church*) James 2:23

### Paul

Even as Abraham believed God, and it was accounted to him for righteousness. (*Letter to the churches of Galatia in Asia Minor, about A.D. 55*) Gal.3:6

### Joseph Smith

That the rights of the priesthood are inseparably connected with the powers of heaven, and that the powers of heaven cannot be controlled nor handled only upon the principles of righteousness. (*Revelation received while in Liberty Jail, March 20, 1839; why many are called and few chosen*) D&C 121:36

### Joseph Smith,
#### receiving the Word of the Lord

For thus saith the Lord—I, the Lord, am merciful and gracious unto those who fear me, and delight to honor those who serve me in righteousness and in truth unto the end. 6. Great shall be their reward and eternal shall be their glory. 7. And to them will I reveal all mysteries, yea, all the hidden mysteries of my kingdom from days of old, and for ages to come, will I make known unto them the good pleasure of my will concerning all things pertaining to my kingdom. 8. Yea, even the wonders of eternity shall they know, and things to come will I show them, even the things of many generations. (*Vision to Joseph Smith and Sidney Rigdon, Feb. 16, 1832*) D&C 76:5-8

---

605. **Prophets are not perfect men (the Lord chooses His prophets from the ranks of ordinary men).**

### Boyd K. Packer

The prophets, as they walk and live among men, are common, ordinary men. Men called to apostolic positions are given a people to redeem. Theirs is the responsibility to lead those people in such a way that they win the battles of life and conquer the ordinary temptations and passions and challenges. And then, speaking figuratively, it is as though these prophets are tapped on the shoulder and

reminded: "While you carry such responsibility to help others with their battles, you are not excused from your own challenges of life. You too will be subject to passions, temptations, challenges. Win those battles as best you can."
¶ Some people are somehow dissatisfied to find in the leading servants of the Lord such ordinary mortals. They are disappointed that there is not some obvious mystery about those men; it is almost as if they are looking for the strange and the occult. To me, however, it is a great testimony that the prophets anciently and the prophets today are called out from the ranks of the ordinary men. It should not lessen our faith, for example, to learn that Elijah was discouraged at times, even despondent. (See 1Kgs.19:4.)
¶ This calling forth of ordinary men for extraordinary purposes is as evident during the Savior's earthly mission as in former and later eras. (The Holy Temple, p. 102) TLDP:537-38

### Joseph F. Merrill

Do the people of the Church want a safe guide to what is well for them to do? It is this: Keep in harmony with the Presidency of this Church. Accept and follow the teachings and advice of the President. At every Conference we raise our hands to sustain the President as prophet, seer and revelator. Is it consistent to do this and then go contrary to his advice? Is anyone so simple as to believe he is serving the Lord when he opposes the President? Of course, the President is not infallible. He makes no claims to infallibility. But when in his official capacity he teaches and advises the members of the Church relative to their duties, let no man who wants to please the Lord say aught against the counsels of the President. CR1941Apr:51

### Charles W. Penrose

We do not believe in the infallibility of man. When God reveals anything it is truth, and truth is infallible. No President of the Church has claimed infallibility. (IE1912Sep:1045) TLDP:537

### George Q. Cannon

The First Presidency cannot claim, individually or collectively, infallibility. The infallibility is not given to men. They are fallible. (Gospel Truth, 1:206) TLDP:537

### George Q. Cannon

The Presidency of the Church have to walk just as you walk. They have to take steps just as you take steps. They have to depend upon the revelations of God as they come to them. They cannot see the end from the beginning as the Lord does. They have their faith tested as you have your faith tested. . . . ¶ It is just as necessary that the Presidency and the Apostles should be tried as it is that you should be tried. It is as necessary that our faith should be called into exercise as that your faith should be called into exercise. We can see a certain distance in the light of the Spirit of God as it reveals to us His mind and His will, and we can take these steps with perfect security, knowing that they are the right steps to be taken. But as to what the result will be, that is for the God of Israel to control. That is the way in which the Church of God has always been led, and it will always be led in that way until He comes who is our King, our Lawgiver and our President, even Jesus Christ. (Gospel Truth, 1:346) TLDP:537

**Related Witnesses:**

### Joseph Smith

I told them that a prophet was a prophet only when he was acting as such. (*On Feb. 8, 1843, the Prophet was visiting with "a brother and sister from Michigan, who thought that 'a prophet is always a prophet.'"*) HC5:265

### Joseph Smith

I never told you I were perfect; but there is no error in the revelations which I have taught. (*At the Stand, May 12, 1844, Nauvoo, Ill.*) HC6:366

---

## 606. A prophet is a revelator who declares the will of God to the people.

### John A. Widtsoe

In the course of time the word "prophet" has come to mean, perhaps chiefly, a man who receives revelations and directions from the Lord. The principal business of a prophet has mistakenly been thought to foretell coming events, to utter prophecies, which is only one of the several prophetic functions. ¶ In the sense that a prophet is a man who receives revelations from the Lord, the titles "seer and revelator" merely amplify the larger and inclusive meaning of the title "prophet." (Evidences and Reconciliations, 1:204-05) DCSM:44

### J. Reuben Clark, Jr.

Only the President of the Church, the Presiding High Priest, is sustained as Prophet, Seer and Revelator for the Church, and he alone has the right to receive revelations for the church, either new or amendatory, or to give authoritative interpretations of scriptures that shall be binding on the Church, or change in any way the existing doctrines of the Church. He is God's sole mouthpiece on earth for the Church of Jesus Christ of Latter-day Saints, the only true Church. He alone may declare the mind and will of God to his people. No officer of any other Church in the world has this high right and lofty prerogative. . . . (Church News, July 13, 1954) MPSG1989:66

### James E. Talmage

To become an authorized minister of the Gospel, "a man must be called of God, by prophecy, and by the laying on of hands, by those who are in authority," and those in authority must have been similarly called. When thus commissioned, he speaks by a power greater than his own in preaching the Gospel and in administering the ordinances thereof; he may verily become a prophet unto the people. The Lord has consistently recognized and honored his servants so appointed. He has magnified their office in proportion to their worthiness, making them living oracles of the divine will. . . . ¶ It is a privilege of the Holy Priesthood to commune with the heavens, and to learn the immediate will of the Lord; this communion may be effected through the medium of dreams and visions, by Urim and thummim, through the visitation of angels, or by the higher endowment of face to face communication with the Lord. The inspired utterances of men who speak by the power of the Holy Ghost are scripture unto the people. In specific terms the promise was made in olden times that the Lord would recognize the medium of prophecy through which to make His will and purposes known to man: "Surely the Lord God will do nothing, but he revealeth his secret unto his servants the prophets." Not all men may attain the position of special revelators: "The secret of the Lord is with them that fear him; and he will show them his covenant." Such men are oracles of truth, privileged counselors, friends of God. AF:270-71

### James E. Talmage

We believe that God is as willing today as He ever has been to reveal His mind and will to man, and that He does so through His appointed servants—prophets, seers, and revelators— invested through ordination with the authority of the Holy Priesthood. We rely therefore on the teachings of the living oracles of God as of equal validity with the doctrines of the written word. AF:6

### Mark E. Petersen

The Church of Jesus Christ, then, should always be led by living apostles and prophets who would receive the constant guidance of heaven. They would continue always in the Church as seers and revelators for the people. ¶ But as they so ministered they would be providing also new and additional scripture appropriate to the times in which they lived, according to the Lord's pattern. ¶ The prophets of the early Christian church ministered in their day just as the Old Testament prophets did during the preceding centuries. And why? Because they followed this same divine pattern, for as Amos explained, the Lord works only through prophets. (Amos 3:7) ¶ When there are no prophets, there is no divine direction, and without such guidance the people walk in darkness. . . . CR1978Apr:95

**Jeremiah**

The prophet that hath a dream, let him tell a dream; and he that hath my word, let him speak my word faithfully. . . . *(Revelation to Jeremiah, about 628 B.C.)* Jer.23:28

**Patriarch Joseph F. Smith**

When Heber J. Grant, whom you have sustained, and I expect will again sustain [as President of the Church] before this conference is over, issues instruction as prophet, seer, and revelator, that word should be scripture to us. It is the word of the Lord Himself through His prophet, and it may be that sometimes that advice is not exactly in accordance with our personal desires. It has never been the business of a prophet of God, to tell people what they wanted to hear; it is the business of a prophet, and I imagine it is a very unpleasant business sometimes, to tell the people what the Lord wants them to know and to do, and we who hold the Priesthood should take the Church seriously enough to be obedient to the scriptures. CR1943Apr:76

**Elder Joseph Fielding Smith**

There has been much speculation in relation to the statement of the Lord to the Prophet Joseph Smith, "For his word ye shall receive, as if from mine own mouth, in all patience and faith." This is the word which the Lord gave to Israel in relation to Moses. It is just as true in the case of any other person who is sustained as the mouthpiece of the Almighty. Later, in speaking of his inspired servants, the Lord said: "And whatsoever they shall speak when moved upon by the Holy Ghost shall be scripture, shall be the will of the Lord, shall be the mind of the Lord, shall be the word of the Lord, shall be the voice of the Lord, and the power of God unto salvation." (D&C 68:4) In this dispensation the same characteristics are shown by the people as were in ancient times. We are more inclined to accept as the word of the Lord something which was uttered in some former dispensation, but look with critical eye and unbelief upon that which the Lord delivers today through his chosen servant—and this is true whether it is Joseph Smith or some other President of the

Church—"the gates of hell shall not prevail against us." CHMR1:107-08; DCSM:44-45

**Related Witnesses:**

**Jeremiah**

Then came the word of the LORD unto the prophet Jeremiah. . . . *(Revelation to Jeremiah, about 628 B.C.)* Jer.37:6

**Joseph Smith,**
*receiving the Word of the Lord*

[W]hether by mine own voice or by the voice of my servants, it is the same. *(Revelation during a conference of elders of the Church, Nov. 1, 1831)* D&C 1:38

**Joseph Smith,**
*receiving the Word of the Lord*

For his word ye shall receive, as if from mine own mouth, in all patience and faith. *(Revelation given at the organization of the Church, April 6, 1830)* D&C 21:5

**Elijah**

And there came a writing to him from Elijah the prophet, saying, Thus saith the LORD. . . . *(Elijah admonishes Jehoram, king of Israel)* 2Chr.21:12

**Isaiah**

And Isaiah the prophet the son of Amoz came unto him, and said unto him, Thus saith the LORD. . . . *(Isaiah visits the dying king Hezekiah)* Isa.38:1

**Amos**

Surely the Lord GOD will do nothing, but he revealeth his secret unto his servants the prophets. *(Amos the prophet reveals the way of the Lord)* Amos 3:7

**Recorded in Numbers**

And he said, Hear now my words: If there be a prophet among you, I the LORD will make myself known unto him in a vision, and will speak unto him in a dream. *(Revelation to Moses for the children of Israel)* Num.12:6

**Elijah**

And it came to pass at the time of the offering of the evening sacrifice, that Elijah the prophet came near, and said, LORD God of Abraham, Isaac, and of Israel, let it be known this day that thou art God in Israel, and that I am thy servant, and that I have done all these things at thy word. *(Elijah challenges the priests of Baal and calls down fire from heaven)* 1Kgs.18:36

**Recorded in 1 Kings**

And, behold, there came a prophet unto Ahab king of Israel, saying, Thus saith the LORD, . . . *(The king of Israel consults with the prophet before battle)* 1Kgs.20:13

**Peter**

For the prophecy came not in old time by the will of man: but holy men of God spake as they were moved by the Holy Ghost. (*Peter writes to members of the Church, about* A.D. *60-64*) 2Pet.1:21

**Recorded in Deuteronomy**

When a prophet speaketh in the name of the LORD, if the thing follow not, nor come to pass, that is the thing which the LORD hath not spoken, but the prophet hath spoken it presumptuously: thou shalt not be afraid of him. (*Commandments to Israel through Moses*) Deut.18:22

---

**607. The role of prophets is to teach the gospel to the world.**

**John A. Widtsoe**

A prophet is a teacher. That is the essential meaning of the word. He teaches the body of truth, the gospel, revealed by the Lord to man; and under inspiration explains it to the understanding of the people. He is an expounder of truth. Moreover, he shows that the way to human happiness is through obedience to God's law. He calls to repentance those who wander away from the truth. He becomes a warrior for the consummation of the Lord's purposes with respect to the human family. The purpose of his life is to uphold the Lord's plan of salvation. All this he does by close communion with the Lord, until he is "full of power by the spirit of the Lord." (Evidences and Reconciliations, 1:204-05) DCSM:44

**Hugh B. Brown**

A prophet should be primarily a teacher of men, an expounder of the things of God. The inspiration of the Almighty must give him understanding, and when given he must declare it fearlessly to the people of his time who can help others to see, a teacher sent of God to instruct a people, to enlighten an age. This is the primary office of a prophet. CR1969Apr:52

**Bruce R. McConkie**

A true prophet is a teacher of righteousness to whom the truths of the gospel have been revealed and who presents them to his fellowmen so they can become heirs of salvation in the highest heaven. A true prophet is a witness, a living witness, one who knows, and one who testifies. Such a one, if need be, foretells the future and reveals to men what the Lord reveals to him. (The Mortal Messiah, pp. 2:169) TLDP:538

**Anthony W. Ivins**

The word, prophet, defined in the Hebrew language, means one who has been called to denounce sin and foretell the consequences and

punishment of it. He is to be above all else a preacher of righteousness, to call the people back from idolatry, to faith in the living God and when moved upon by the Spirit of the Lord to foretell coming events. But more particularly a prophet is to be an expounder of present duties and an interpreter of the meaning and application of the written word. CR1933Oct:84

**N. Eldon Tanner**

This is the mission of the prophets of God: to preach repentance. And though it does not make for popularity, it must be done. We are told that the people were angry with Nephi but that he ministered with power and with great authority. CR1975Apr:53

**Joseph Smith**

They are the Twelve Apostles, who are called to the office of the Traveling High Council, who are to preside over the churches of the Saints, among the Gentiles, where there is a presidency established; and they are to travel and preach among the Gentiles, until the Lord shall command them to go to the Jews. They are to hold the keys of this ministry, to unlock the door of the Kingdom of heaven unto all nations, and to preach the Gospel to every creature. This is the power, authority, and virtue of their apostleship. (*"Items of Instruction to the Twelve," Feb. 27, 1835, reported by Oliver Cowdery, clerk; "President Smith proposed the following question: 'What importance is there attached to the calling of these Twelve Apostles, different from the other callings or officers of the Church?' After the question was discussed by Councilors Patten, Young, Smith, and M'Lellin, Joseph Smith gave the [foregoing] decision*) HC2:200

**Elder Wilford Woodruff**

The full set time is come for the Lord to set His hand to accomplish these mighty events; and as He has done in other ages, so has He done now—He has raised up a Prophet, and is revealing unto him His secrets. Through that Prophet He has brought to light the fullness of the everlasting Gospel to the present generation, and is again once more for the last time establishing His Church upon the foundation of the ancient Apostles and Prophets, which is revelation, Jesus Christ being the chief corner stone. (*At a conference of the Twelve, Boylston Hall, Boston, Mass., Sept. 10, 1843*) HC6:24

**Related Witnesses:**

**Jesus,**
*recorded in Mark*

And he said unto them, Go ye into all the world, and preach the gospel to every creature. 16. He that believeth and is baptized shall be saved; but he that believeth not shall be damned. . . . 20. And they went forth, and preached everywhere, the Lord working with them, and confirming the word with signs following. Amen. (*The risen Jesus Christ to the eleven Apostles*) Mark 16:15-16,20

**Peter**

And he commanded us to preach unto the people, and to testify that it is he which was ordained of God to be the Judge of quick and dead. 43. To him give all the prophets witness, that through his name whosoever believeth in him shall receive remission of sins. (*Peter preaches about Christ*) Acts 10:42-43

**Paul**

God, who at sundry times and in divers manners spake in time past unto the fathers by the prophets, 2. Hath in these last days spoken unto us by his Son, whom he hath appointed heir of all things, by whom also he made the worlds; (*Paul writes to the Jewish members of the Church, about A.D. 60*) Heb.1:1-2

---

**608. A prophet may foretell future events, both temporal and spiritual.**

**Anthony W. Ivins**

A prophet is not only one who foretells events that are to come, but one who, inspired of the Lord, instructs people in that which they ought to do in the day of their own probation, that they may be brought back into the presence of the Lord. CR1914Oct:92

**John A. Widtsoe**

The principle business of a prophet has mistakenly been thought to foretell coming events, to utter prophecies, which is only one of the several prophetic functions. (Evidences and Reconciliations, 1:205) DCSM:44

**Joseph Smith,**
*quoted by Elder Joseph Fielding Smith*

Study the prophecies, and rejoice that God grants unto the world Seers and Prophets. They are they who saw the mysteries of godliness; they saw the flood before it came; they saw angels ascending and descending upon a ladder that reached from earth to heaven; they saw the stone cut out of the mountain, which filled the whole earth; they saw the Son of God come from the regions of bliss and dwell with men on earth; they saw the deliverer come out of Zion, and turn away ungodliness from Jacob; they saw the glory of the Lord when he showed the transfiguration of the earth on the mount; they saw every mountain laid low and every valley exalted when the Lord was taking vengeance upon the wicked;

they saw truth spring out of the earth, and righteousness look down from heaven in the last days, before the Lord came the second time to gather his elect; they saw the end of wickedness on earth, and the Sabbath of creation crowned with peace; they saw the end of the glorious thousand years, when Satan was loosed for a little season; they saw the day of judgment when all men received according to their works, and they saw the heaven and the earth flee away to make room for the city of God, when the righteous receive an inheritance in eternity. (Evening and Morning Star, Aug. 1832) TPJS:12-13

**Bruce R. McConkie**

A true prophet is a witness, a living witness, one who knows, and one who testifies. Such a one, if need be, foretells the future and reveals to men what the Lord reveals to him. (The Mortal Messiah, 2:169) TLDP:538

**Related Witnesses:**

**Recorded in Deuteronomy**

When a prophet speaketh in the name of the LORD, if the thing follow not, nor come to pass, that is the thing which the LORD hath not spoken, but the prophet hath spoken it presumptuously: thou shalt not be afraid of him. (*Commandments to Israel through Moses*) Deut.18:22

**Anthony W. Ivins**

He is to be above all else a preacher of righteousness, to call the people back from idolatry, to faith in the living God and when moved upon by the Spirit of the Lord to foretell coming events. . . . ¶ We at the present day have an entirely different relationship to prophecy than had those who lived at the time that many of the most important of the prophecies made were uttered. People of Bible days looked hopefully and in faith forward to the fulfillment of the words of the prophets. ¶ We look backward and see that many, very many of those important predictions have been fulfilled. (*To the Church in general conference; he talks about a prophet's calling*) CR1933Oct:84

**Nephi, son of Lehi**

And I, Nephi, said unto them: Behold they were manifest unto the prophet by the voice of the Spirit; for by the Spirit are all things made known unto the prophets, which shall come upon the children of men according to the flesh. 3. Wherefore, the things of which I have read are things pertaining to things both temporal and spiritual; . . . (*Nephi explains the prophecies written on the plates of brass, 588-570 B.C.*) 1Ne.22:2-3

**Jeremiah**

The prophet which prophesieth of peace, when

the word of the prophet shall come to pass, then shall the prophet be known, that the LORD hath truly sent him. (*Revelation to Jeremiah, about 628 B.C.*) Jer.28:9

### Ezekiel

And when this cometh to pass, (lo, it will come,) then shall they know that a prophet hath been among them. (*Ezekiel the prophet receives a vision from God*) Ezek.33:33

### Recorded in Matthew

Now all this was done, that it might be fulfilled which was spoken of the Lord by the prophet. . . . (*Matthew anticipates the coming birth of Jesus*) Matt.1:22

---

### 609. Joseph Smith was a prophet in these latter days.

**President Heber J. Grant,**
**J. Reuben Clark, Jr., David O. McKay**
(First Presidency)

We solemnly declare that in these the latter-days, God has again spoken from the heavens through His chosen Prophet, Joseph Smith; that the Lord has, through that same Prophet, again revealed in its fulness His gospel—the plan of life and salvation; that through that Prophet and his associates He has restored His holy Priesthood to the earth, from which it had been taken because of the wickedness of men; and that all the rights, powers, keys, and functions appertaining to the Priesthood as so restored are now vested in and exercised by the chosen and inspired leadership of His Church—The Church of Jesus Christ of Latter-day Saints, even as the Priesthood has been exercised on the earth from the Beginning until this day, whenever His Church was here or His work had place among the children of men. CR1942Apr:88

**Joseph Smith,**
*receiving the Word of the Lord*

I give unto you my servant Joseph to be a presiding elder over all my church, to be a translator, a revelator, a seer, and prophet. (*Revelation received Jan. 19, 1841*) D&C 124:125

**Stephen L. Richards**

I know that Joseph Smith was a prophet of the living God, and the work he was instrumental in setting upon the earth is the veritable kingdom of our Father in heaven. CR1951Oct:118

**Anthon H. Lund**

Joseph Smith was a prophet of God. His teachings prove that what he taught was divinely inspired. Some of his prophecies have been fulfilled, and others remain to be fulfilled. His predictions have not been guesswork. . . . Now it is

reasonable to suppose that if the Lord raised up a Prophet, that Prophet would say something in regard to these two important things—the nation and the Church, and he did. . . . He prophesied that the Church should go to the Rocky Mountains. . . . In regard to the nation he plainly foretold where the Rebellion should begin and what its results should be. CR1899Oct:13

**President Brigham Young,**
*quoted by John A. Widtsoe*

It was decreed in the counsels of eternity, long before the foundations of the earth were laid, that he, Joseph Smith, should be the man, in the last dispensation of this world, to bring forth the word of God to the people, and receive the fulness of the keys and power of the Priesthood of the Son of God. The Lord had his eyes upon him, and upon his father, and upon his father's father, and upon their progenitors clear back to Abraham, and from Abraham to the flood, from the flood to Enoch, and from Enoch to Adam. He has watched that family and that blood as it has circulated from its fountain to the birth of that man. He was fore-ordained in eternity to preside over this last dispensation. (*In Tabernacle, Oct. 1859, JD7:289*) DBY:108; DGSM:63

**Related Witnesses:**

**Joseph Smith,**
*receiving the Word of the Lord*

Behold, there shall be a record kept among you; and in it thou shalt be called a seer, a translator, a prophet, an apostle of Jesus Christ, an elder of the church through the will of God the Father, and the grace of your Lord Jesus Christ, (*Revelation given at the organization of the Church, April 6, 1830; Joseph Smith is called by the Lord to be a seer, translator, prophet, Apostle and elder of the Church*) D&C 21:1

**Joseph Smith,**
*receiving the Word of the Lord*

Which commandments were given to Joseph Smith, Jun., who was called of God, and ordained an apostle of Jesus Christ, to be the first elder of this church; (*Revelation on Church Organization and Government, April 1830*) D&C 20:2

**President Brigham Young**

[T]o Joseph Smith, whom I did call upon by mine angels, my ministering servants, and by mine own voice out of the heavens, to bring forth my work; 38. Which foundation he did lay, and was faithful; and I took him to myself. 39. Many have marveled because of his death; but it was needful that he should seal his testimony with his blood, that he might be honored and the wicked might be condemned.

*(Revelation received at Winter Quarters, Jan. 14, 1847) D&C 136:37-39*

**Lehi,**
*quoted by his son Nephi*

Wherefore, Joseph truly saw our day. And he obtained a promise of the Lord, that out of the fruit of his loins the Lord God would raise up a righteous branch unto the house of Israel; not the Messiah, but a branch which was to be broken off, nevertheless, to be remembered in the covenants of the Lord that the Messiah should be made manifest unto them in the latter days, in the spirit of power, unto the bringing of them out of darkness unto light—yea, out of hidden darkness and out of captivity unto freedom. 6. For Joseph truly testified, saying: A seer shall the Lord my God raise up, who shall be a choice seer unto the fruit of my loins. 7. Yea, Joseph truly said: Thus saith the Lord unto me: A choice seer will I raise up out of the fruit of thy loins; and he shall be esteemed highly among the fruit of thy loins. And unto him will I give commandment that he shall do a work for the fruit of thy loins, his brethren, which shall be of great worth unto them, even to the bringing of them to the knowledge of the covenants which I have made with thy fathers. 8. And I will give unto him a commandment that he shall do none other work, save the work which I shall command him. And I will make him great in mine eyes; for he shall do my work. 9. And he shall be great like unto Moses, whom I have said I would raise up unto you, to deliver my people, O house of Israel. 10. And Moses will I raise up, to deliver thy people out of the land of Egypt. 11. But a seer will I raise up out of the fruit of thy loins; and unto him will I give power to bring forth my word unto the seed of thy loins—and not to the bringing forth my word only, saith the Lord, but to the convincing them of my word, which shall have already gone forth among them. 12. Wherefore, the fruit of thy loins shall write; and the fruit of the loins of Judah shall write; and that which shall be written by the fruit of thy loins, and also that which shall be written by the fruit of the loins of Judah, shall grow together, unto the confounding of false doctrines and laying down of contentions, and establishing peace among the fruit of thy loins, and bringing them to the knowledge of their fathers in the latter days, and also to the knowledge of my covenants, saith the Lord. *(Lehi speaks to his son Joseph, saying that the Joseph who was carried captive into Egypt received revelation from the Lord foretelling that a seer would be raised up by the Lord whose name would be Joseph, and his*

*father's name would also be Joseph, and this seer [Joseph Smith] would be like unto Joseph in Egypt and like Moses)* 2Ne.3:5-12

**Mark E. Petersen**

Adam brought the keys of the First Presidency. Joseph Smith received the keys of the First Presidency from Adam, who came back and visited him. Joseph Smith received the power of the gathering of Israel through Moses, who came back to see him. Elijah brought back the powers that we use in connection with our temple work. ACR(Mexico City)1972:61

**Joseph Smith**

I certify you, brethren, that the gospel which was preached of me is not after man; for I neither received it of man, neither was I taught it, but by the revelation of Jesus Christ. (Times and Seasons, Feb. 1840, p. 55) TLDP:558

---

**610.  We are to receive the words of the President of the Church as if they came from the mouth the Lord.**

**Elder Joseph Fielding Smith**

There has been much speculation in relation to the statement of the Lord to the Prophet Joseph Smith, "For his word ye shall receive, as if from mine own mouth, in all patience and faith." This is the word which the Lord gave to Israel in relation to Moses. It is just as true in the case of any other person who is sustained as the mouthpiece of the Almighty. Later, in speaking of his inspired servants, the Lord said: "And whatsoever they shall speak when moved upon by the Holy Ghost shall be scripture, shall be the will of the Lord, shall be the mind of the Lord, shall be the word of the Lord, shall be the voice of the Lord, and the power of God unto salvation." (D&C 68:4) In this dispensation the same characteristics are shown by the people as were in ancient times. We are more inclined to accept as the word of the Lord something which was uttered in some former dispensation, but look with critical eye and unbelief upon that which the Lord delivers today through his chosen servant—and this is true whether it is Joseph Smith or some other President of the Church—"the gates of hell shall not prevail against us." CHMR1:107-08; DCSM:44-45

**Joseph Smith,**
*receiving the Word of the Lord*

Behold, there shall be a record kept among you; and in it thou shalt be called a seer, a translator, a prophet, an apostle of Jesus Christ, an elder of the church through the will of God the Father, and the grace of your Lord Jesus Christ, . . . 4.

Wherefore, meaning the church, thou shalt give heed unto all his words and commandments which he shall give unto you as he receiveth them, walking in all holiness before me; 5. For his word ye shall receive, as if from mine own mouth, in all patience and faith. (*Revelation given at the organization of the Church, April 6, 1830*) D&C 21:1,4-5

### Elder Harold B. Lee

Now the only safety we have as members of this church is to do exactly what the Lord said to the Church in that day when the Church was organized. We must learn to give heed to the words and commandments that the Lord shall give through his prophet, "as he receiveth them, walking in all holiness before me; . . . as if from mine own mouth in all patience and faith." (D&C 21:4-5) There will be some things that take patience and faith. You may not like what comes from the authority of the Church. It may contradict your political views. It may contradict your social views. It may interfere with your social life. But if you listen to these things, as if from the mouth of the Lord himself, with patience and faith, the promise is that "the gates of hell shall not prevail against you; yea, and the Lord God will disperse the powers of darkness from before you, and cause the heavens to shake for your good, and his name's glory." ¶ . . . . Your safety and ours depends upon whether or not we follow the ones whom the Lord has placed to preside over his church. He knows whom he wants to preside over this church, and he will make no mistake. The Lord doesn't do things by accident. . . . ¶ Let us keep our eye on the President of the Church. CR1970Oct:152-53; DCSM:45

### Marion G. Romney

I would like now to suggest some tests which can safely be used to distinguish the genuine from the counterfeit. . . . ¶ . . . . Now the fourth and last test I shall mention is: Does it come through the proper Church channel? . . .The Lord could not have made it any plainer that one's authority must come through the established order of the Church, and the President of the Church stands at the head of that order. The Lord has placed him there. . . . ¶ . . . . Now one of Moses' greatest callings was to be a lawgiver, to declare the Word of God. Only the President can declare the doctrines of the Church. . . . ¶ "For his word ye shall receive, as if from mine own mouth, in all patience and faith." (D&C 21:5) ¶ Such is the obligation of this Priesthood with respect to our present Prophet, Seer, and Revelator, President David O. McKay. . . . ¶ Now, brethren, if we will keep

these things in mind, we shall not be deceived by false teachings. I remember years ago when I was a bishop I had President Grant talk to our ward. After the meeting, I drove him home. . . . Standing by me, he put his arm over my shoulder and said: "My boy, you always keep your eye on the President of the Church, and if he ever tells you to do anything, and it is wrong, and you do it, the Lord will bless you for it." Then with a twinkle in his eye, he said, "But you don't need to worry. The Lord will never let his mouthpiece lead the people astray." CR1960Oct:76-78

### Elder Ezra Taft Benson

Let me give you a crucial key to help you avoid being deceived. It is this—learn to keep your eye on the Prophet. He is the Lord's mouthpiece and the only man who can speak for the Lord today. Let his inspired counsel take precedence. Let his inspired words be a basis for evaluating the counsel of all lesser authorities. Then live close to the spirit so you may know the truth of all things. ("Our Immediate Responsibility," Brigham Young University Speeches of the Year, 1966, p. 13) TLDP:534

### Joseph F. Merrill

Do the people of the Church want a safe guide to what is well for them to do? It is this: Keep in harmony with the Presidency of this Church. Accept and follow the teachings and advice of the President. At every Conference we raise our hands to sustain the President as prophet, seer and revelator. Is it consistent to do this and then go contrary to his advice? Is anyone so simple as to believe he is serving the Lord when he opposes the President? Of course, the President is not infallible. He makes no claims to infallibility. But when in his official capacity he teaches and advises the members of the Church relative to their duties, let no man who wants to please the Lord say aught against the counsels of the President. CR1941Apr:51

**Related Witnesses:**

### Joseph Smith,
### *receiving the Word of the Lord*

[W]hether by mine own voice or by the voice of my servants, it is the same. (*Revelation during a conference of elders of the Church, Nov. 1, 1831*) D&C 1:38

### Joseph Smith

And the arm of the Lord shall be revealed; and the day cometh that they who will not hear the voice of the Lord, neither the voice of his servants, neither give heed to the words of the prophets and apostles, shall be cut off from among the people. . . . (*Revelation during a conference of elders of the Church, Nov. 1, 1831)* D&C 1:14

**Charles W. Penrose**

We don't want to prevent men from thinking. I have heard some of my brethren say, "Well, do you want to stop men from thinking?" Not at all. Liberty to think and liberty to act upon the thought if you don't infringe the rights others. . . . [B]ut my brethren, it isn't your province nor mine to introduce theories into the Church that are not in accordance with the revelations that have been given. Don't forget that. And if any change in policy is to be introduced, it is to come through the proper channel. The Lord said only his servant Joseph should do that while he lived, and then after he died others were to be called to occupy the place, and the key is in the hands of the man who stands at the head, if any change is to be introduced in our Church. CR1918Apr:21-22

---

611. **The President of the Church will never lead the Saints astray or send forth counsel to the world that is contrary to the mind and will of the Lord.**

**President Joseph Fielding Smith**

Now, brethren, I think there is one thing which we should have exceedingly clear in our minds. Neither the President of the Church, nor the First Presidency, nor the united voice of the First Presidency and the Twelve will ever lead the Saints astray or send forth counsel to the world that is contrary to the mind and will of the Lord. ¶ An individual may fall by the wayside, or have views, or give counsel which falls short of what the Lord intends. But the voice of the First Presidency and the united voice of those others who hold with them the keys of the kingdom shall always guide the Saints and the world in those paths where the Lord wants them to be. CR1972Apr:99; MPSG1989:58

**Elder Harold B. Lee**

We are not dependent only upon the revelations given in the past as contained in our standard works—as wonderful as they are. . . . We have a mouthpiece to whom God does and is revealing his mind and will. God will never permit him to lead us astray. As has been said, God would remove us out of our place if we should attempt to do it. You have no concern. Let the management and government of God, then, be with the Lord. Do not try to find fault with the management and affairs that pertain to him

alone and by revelation through his prophet—his living prophet, his seer, and his revelator. *(To seminary and institute of religion personnel, July 1964, p. 16)* DCSM:45

**Marion G. Romney**

Now one of Moses' greatest callings was to be a law-giver, to declare the Word of God. Only the President can declare the doctrines of the Church. . . . ¶ "For his word ye shall receive, as if from mine own mouth, in all patience and faith." (D&C 21:5) ¶ Such is the obligation of this Priesthood with respect to our present Prophet, Seer, and Revelator, President David O. McKay. . . . ¶ Now, brethren, if we will keep these things in mind, we shall not be deceived by false teachings. I remember years ago when I was a bishop I had President Grant talk to our ward. After the meeting, I drove him home. . . . Standing by me, he put his arm over my shoulder and said: "My boy, you always keep your eye on the President of the Church, and if he ever tells you to do anything, and it is wrong, and you do it, the Lord will bless you for it." Then with a twinkle in his eye, he said, "But you don't need to worry. The Lord will never let his mouthpiece lead the people astray." CR1960Oct:77-78

**President Joseph F. Smith**

I testify in the name of Israel's God that He will not suffer the head of the Church, him whom He has chosen to stand at the head, to transgress His laws and apostatize; the moment he should take a course that would in time lead to it, God would take him away. Why? Because to suffer a wicked man to occupy that position, would be to allow, as it were, the fountain to become corrupted, which is something He will never permit. *(At Ogden, Utah, June 21, 1883, JD24:192)* TLDP:248

**Related Witnesses:**

**President Joseph F. Smith, Anthon H. Lund, Charles W. Penrose**
*(First Presidency)*

The counsels of the Lord through the channel he has appointed will be followed with safety. Therefore, O! ye Latter-day Saints, profit by these words of warning. *(Published message of the First Presidency of the Church, IE1913Sept:1149)* MOFP4:286

**Joseph Smith,**
*receiving the Word of the Lord*

Exalt not yourselves; rebel not against my servant Joseph; for verily I say unto you, I am with him, and my hand shall be over him; and the keys which I have given unto him, and also to youward, shall not be taken from him till I come. *(Revelation for Thomas B. Marsh*

*concerning the Twelve Apostles, July 23, 1837)*
D&C 112:15

**Recorded in Deuteronomy**

But the prophet, which shall presume to speak a
word in my name, which I have not commanded him to speak, or that shall speak in the name
of other gods, even that prophet shall die.
(*Commandments to Israel through Moses*)
Deut.18:20-22

**Author's Note:** In October 6, 1890, President
Wilford Woodruff made the following statement in general conference: "I say to Israel, the
Lord will never permit me nor any other man
who stands as President of this Church, to lead
you astray. It is not in the program. It is not the
mind of God. If I were to attempt that, the Lord
would remove me out of my place, and so He
will any other man who attempts to lead the
children of men astray from the oracles of God
and from their duty." (Discourses of Wilford
Woodruff, p. 212-13)

---

612. Apostles are prophets.

**Joseph Smith**

I then called upon the quorums and congregation of Saints to acknowledge the Twelve
Apostles, who were present, as Prophets, Seers,
Revelators, and special witnesses to all the
nations of the earth, holding the keys of the
kingdom, to unlock it, or cause it to be done,
among them, and uphold them by their prayers,
which they assented to by rising. (*At the dedication of the Kirtland Temple, March 27, 1836*)
HC2:417

**Elder Harold B. Lee**

All members of the First Presidency and the
Twelve are regularly sustained as "prophets,
seers, and revelators," as you have done today.
This means that any one of the apostles, so chosen and ordained, could preside over the
Church if he were "chosen by the body [which
has been interpreted to mean, the entire Quorum of the Twelve, appointed and ordained to
that office, and upheld by the confidence, faith,
and prayer of the church," to quote from a revelation on this subject, on one condition, and that
being that he was the senior member, or the
president, of that body. (See D&C 107:22.)
CR1970Apr:123

**President Brigham Young**

The Bible says God hath set in the church, first
Apostles, then comes Prophets, afterwards,
because the keys and power of the Apostleship
are greater than that of the Prophets. (*Important*

*conference at Nauvoo, Ill., "...thousands having
arrived on the ground by ten o'clock a.m.,..."*
*Oct. 6, 1844)* HC7:288

**Author's Note:** Once a year, in addition to the
president of the Church, the counselors in the
First Presidency and the Twelve Apostles are sustained as Prophets, Seers and Revelators in a
General Conference of the Church. (For examples, see CR1901Nov:80; CR1944Apr:12-13;
CR1945Oct:5,13; CR1951Apr:138,147;
CR1970Apr:103,109; CR1972Oct:6,12;
CR1974Apr:55,61; CR1986Apr:93.) In addition to the president of the Church and
Apostles, the Patriarchs to the Church have also
been sustained by the Church as prophets. No
patriarch to the Church, however, has been sustained since Oct. 6, 1979.

# List of Doctrines

## PURITY AND RIGHTEOUSNESS

*Doctrines Located in This Topic*

613. We are to purify and cleanse ourselves from all sin.

614. No unclean thing can enter the kingdom of God.

615. The pure in heart shall see God.

616. Righteousness binds the devil; we are to take upon us the armor of righteousness as a protection against the evil one.

*Doctrines on PURITY AND RIGHT-EOUSNESS Located in Other Topics*

12. God will not force any person to do good, nor can a person be forced by Satan to do evil.

59. Baptism in connection with the gift of the Holy Ghost is a cleanser and a purifier.

127. In the postmortal spirit world the spirits of the righteous enter a condition of peace and rest, called paradise, until their resurrection.

250. God is no respecter of persons (He has no favorites except upon grounds of their degree of righteousness).

392. When a person *righteously* performs the ordinances and duties necessary for exaltation, those acts may be accepted (justified) by God.

402. The righteous will be preserved from the calamities and judgments of the Lord in the last days.

419. The powers of heaven can only be controlled in righteousness.

503. The righteous shall receive a reward of inner peace and contentment—the kind of peace that only the Lord can give.

514. Purity and cleanliness from sin assists us in obtaining answers to our prayers.

577. Only upon principles of righteousness can a priesthood bearer manage the powers of heaven.

754. Sin makes a person spiritually unclean.

761. Because no unclean thing can inherit the celestial kingdom, we cannot enter that kingdom unless we have repented of our sins.

820. Our minds should be occupied with virtuous and righteous thoughts.

## PURITY AND RIGHTEOUSNESS continued

821. We are to abstain from impure thoughts.

847. The Saints can accomplish any purpose of the Lord when fully united in righteousness.

877. Our bodies should be kept clean and pure; hence, we are to be concerned with the nature of the food and drink taken into our bodies.

893. Zion is the pure in heart.

894. Zion is wherever the organization of the Church of God is—where the pure in heart are gathered.

*(See topic SANCTIFICATION.)*

# PURITY AND RIGHTEOUSNESS

**613. We are to purify and cleanse ourselves from all sin.**

### Jesus,
*quoted by John*

Beloved, now are we the sons of God, and it doth not yet appear what we shall be: but we know that, when he shall appear, we shall be like him; for we shall see him as he is. 3. And every man that hath this hope in him purifieth himself, even as he is pure. (*An epistle of the Apostle John*) 1Jn.3:2-3

### Mormon

Wherefore, my beloved brethren, pray unto the Father with all the energy of heart, that ye may be filled with this love, which he hath bestowed upon all who are true followers of his Son, Jesus Christ; that ye may become the sons of God; that when he shall appear we shall be like him, for we shall see him as he is; that we may have this hope; that we may be purified even as he is pure. Amen. (*Mormon preaches in the synagogue, prior to A.D. 384*) Moro.7:48

### Joseph Smith

He that is ordained of God and sent forth, the same is appointed to be the greatest, notwithstanding he is the least and the servant of all. 27. Wherefore, he is possessor of all things; for all things are subject unto him, both in heaven and on the earth, the life and the light, the Spirit and the power, sent forth by the will of the Father through Jesus Christ, his Son. 28. But no man is possessor of all things except he be purified and cleansed from all sin. 29. And if ye are purified and cleansed from all sin, ye shall ask whatsoever you will in the name of Jesus and it shall be done. (*Revelation for the elders of the Church, May 1831*) D&C 50:26-29

### Joseph Smith,
*receiving the Word of the Lord*

And a commandment I give unto thee—that thou shalt write for him; and the scriptures shall be given, even as they are in mine own bosom, to the salvation of mine own elect; 21. For they will hear my voice, and shall see me, and shall not be asleep, and shall abide the day of my coming; for they shall be purified, even as I am pure. (*Revelation to Joseph Smith and Sidney Rigdon, Dec. 1830*) D&C 35:20-21

### Paul

Lay hands suddenly on no man, neither be partaker of other men's sins: keep thyself pure. (*Paul's letter to his assistant Timothy, about A.D. 64*) 1Tim.5:22

### Paul

But in a great house there are not only vessels of gold and of silver, but also of wood and of earth; and some to honour, and some to dishonour. 21. If a man therefore purge himself from these, he shall be a vessel unto honour, sanctified, and meet for the master's use, and prepared unto every good work. 22. Flee also youthful lusts: but follow righteousness, faith, charity, peace, with them that call on the Lord out of a pure heart. (*Paul's letter to his assistant Timothy, about A.D. 64*) 2Tim.2:20-22

### Paul

Having therefore these promises, dearly beloved, let us cleanse ourselves from all filthiness of the flesh and spirit, perfecting holiness in the fear of God. (*Paul's letter to the Church at Corinth, Greece, about A.D. 55*) 2Cor.7:1

### Isaiah,
*quoted by Jesus,*
*quoted by Mormon*

And then shall a cry go forth: Depart ye, depart ye, go ye out from thence, touch not that which is unclean; go ye out of the midst of her; be ye clean that bear the vessels of the Lord. (*The resurrected Jesus Christ teaches that when the fulness of the gospel is preached to the Israelites, "they shall believe in me, that I am Jesus Christ," A.D. 34*) 3Ne.20:41

### James

Wherefore lay apart all filthiness and superfluity of naughtiness, and receive with meekness the engrafted word, which is able to save your souls. (*Letter of James to his brethren in the Church*) James 1:21

**Related Witnesses:**

### President Spencer W. Kimball

A clean conscience with a chaste body and a virtuous mind brings power, happiness, and peace which no unvirtuous person can or ever will enjoy to the same extent. ACR(Sydney)1976:54

### Boyd K. Packer

There is a great cleansing power. Know that you can be clean. If you are outside of the Church, the covenant of baptism itself represents, among other things, a washing and a cleansing. ¶ For those of you who are in the Church there is a way, not entirely painless, but certainly possible. You can stand clean and spotless before him. Guilt will be gone, and you can be at peace. Go to your bishop or your branch president. He holds the key to this cleansing power. Go and have an interview with him, and then you do what he says, and you can become clean again. ACR(Stockholm)1974:84

### Recorded in Numbers

And a man that is clean shall gather up the ashes of the heifer, and lay them up without the camp in a clean place, and it shall be kept for the congregation of the children of Israel for a water of separation: it is a purification for sin. (*Revelation to Moses for the children of Israel*) Num.19:9

**Isaiah**

And he laid it upon my mouth, and said, Lo, this hath touched thy lips; and thine iniquity is taken away, and thy sin purged. (*Isaiah sees the Lord, his sins are forgiven*) Isa.6:7

---

### 614. No unclean thing can enter the kingdom of God.

**Mark E. Petersen**

As no unclean thing can enter the presence of the Lord, so no liar nor cheat nor hypocrite can abide in his kingdom. . . . ¶ . . . . We Latter-day Saints believe in God, and because we believe in him, we also believe there is a devil. But the devil himself is a liar—the father of lies—and those who choose to cheat and lie and deceive and misrepresent become his slaves. CR1971Oct:64-65

**Nephi, son of Lehi**

But behold, I say unto you, the kingdom of God is not filthy, and there cannot any unclean thing enter into the kingdom of God; wherefore there must needs be a place of filthiness prepared for that which is filthy. 35. And there is a place prepared, yea, even that awful hell of which I have spoken, and the devil is the preparator of it; wherefore the final state of the souls of men is to dwell in the kingdom of God, or to be cast out because of that justice of which I have spoken. (*Nephi interprets his father Lehi's dream to his brothers, between 600-592 B.C.*) 1Ne.15:34-35

**Elder Spencer W. Kimball**

The road of life is plainly marked according to the divine purpose, the map of the gospel of Jesus Christ is made available to the travelers, the destination of eternal life is clearly established. At that destination our Father waits hopefully, anxious to greet his returning children. Unfortunately, many will not arrive. ¶ The reason is forthrightly stated by Nephi—" . . . There cannot any unclean thing enter into the kingdom of God. . . ." (1Ne.15:34) And again, " . . . no unclean thing can dwell with God. . . ." (1Ne.10:21) To the prophets the term unclean in this context means what it means to God. To man the word may be relative in meaning—one minute speck of dirt does not make a white shirt or dress unclean, for example. But to God who is perfection, cleanliness means moral and personal cleanliness. Less than that is, in one degree or another, uncleanliness and hence cannot dwell

with God. (The Miracle of Forgiveness, p. 19) DGSM:39

**Paul**

Now the works of the flesh are manifest, which are these; Adultery, fornication, uncleanness, lasciviousness, 20. Idolatry, witchcraft, hatred, variance, emulations, wrath, strife, seditions, heresies, 21. Envyings, murders, drunkenness, revellings, and such like: of the which I tell you before, as I have also told you in time past, that they which do such things shall not inherit the kingdom of God. (*Paul's letter to the churches of Galatia in Asia Minor, about A.D. 55*) Gal.5:19-21

**Paul**

For this ye know, that no whoremonger, nor unclean person, nor covetous man, who is an idolater, hath any inheritance in the kingdom of Christ and of God. (*Paul's letter to the Saints at Ephesus in Asia Minor, about A.D. 62*) Eph.5:5

**Amulek,**
*quoted by Mormon*

And I say unto you again that he cannot save them in their sins; for I cannot deny his word, and he hath said that no unclean thing can inherit the kingdom of heaven; therefore, how can ye be saved, except ye inherit the kingdom of heaven? Therefore, ye cannot be saved in your sins. (*Amulek contends with the wicked Zeezrom, about 82 B.C.*) Alma 11:37

**Jesus,**
*quoted by Mormon*

And no unclean thing can enter into his kingdom; therefore nothing entereth into his rest save it be those who have washed their garments in my blood, because of their faith, and the repentance of all their sins, and their faithfulness unto the end. (*The resurrected Jesus Christ instructs his disciples, A.D. 34-35*) 3Ne.27:19

**Related Witnesses:**
**Nephi, son of Lehi**

Wherefore, if ye have sought to do wickedly in the days of your probation, then ye are found unclean before the judgment-seat of God; and no unclean thing can dwell with God; wherefore, ye must be cast off forever. (*Nephi's writings, 600-592 B.C.*) 1Ne.10:21

**Joseph Smith,**
*translating the Book of Moses*

Wherefore teach it unto your children, that all men, everywhere, must repent, or they can in nowise inherit the kingdom of God, for no unclean thing can dwell there, or dwell in his presence; for, in the language of Adam, Man of Holiness is his name, and the name of his Only Begotten is the Son of Man, even Jesus Christ, a righteous Judge, who shall come in the meridian of time. (*The record of Moses: Enoch recounts God speaking to Adam*) Moses 6:57

### John

And he carried me away in the spirit to a great and high mountain, and shewed me that great city, the holy Jerusalem, descending out of heaven from God, . . . 27. And there shall in no wise enter into it any thing that defileth, neither whatsoever worketh abomination, or maketh a lie: but they which are written in the Lamb's book of life. (*John sees the earth in its millennial state*) Rev.21:10,27

---

### 615. The pure in heart shall see God.

### Jesus,
#### *recorded in Matthew*

Blessed are the pure in heart: for they shall see God. (*Jesus Christ to the multitude, about A.D. 30*) Matt.5:8

### Jesus,
#### *quoted by Mormon*

And blessed are all the pure in heart, for they shall see God. (*The resurrected Jesus Christ teaches the Nephite people, A.D. 34*) 3Ne.12:8

### Joseph Smith,
#### *receiving the Word of the Lord*

And inasmuch as my people build a house unto me in the name of the Lord, and do not suffer any unclean thing to come into it, that it be not defiled, my glory shall rest upon it; 16. Yea, and my presence shall be there, for I will come into it, and all the pure in heart that shall come into it shall see God. 17. But if it be defiled I will not come into it, and my glory shall not be there; for I will not come into unholy temples. (*Revelation dealing with the affairs of the persecuted Saints in Missouri, Aug. 2, 1833*) D&C 97:15-17

**Related Witnesses:**
### Jacob, brother of Nephi

But behold, I, Jacob, would speak unto you that are pure in heart. Look unto God with firmness of mind, and pray unto him with exceeding faith, and he will console you in your afflictions, and he will plead your cause, and send down justice upon those who seek your destruction. 2. O all ye that are pure in heart, lift up your heads and receive the pleasing word of God, and feast upon his love; for ye may, if your minds are firm, forever. 3. But, wo, wo, unto you that are not pure in heart, that are filthy this day before God; for except ye repent the land is cursed for your sakes; and the Lamanites, which are not filthy like unto you, nevertheless they are cursed with a sore cursing, shall scourge you even unto destruction.

(*Jacob addresses the Nephites, those who are pure in heart, 544-421 B.C.*) Jacob 3:1-3

### President Brigham Young

Therefore, marvel not at these things, for ye are not yet pure; ye can not yet bear my glory; but ye shall behold it if ye are faithful in keeping all my words that I have given you, from the days of Adam to Abraham, from Abraham to Moses, from Moses to Jesus and his apostles, and from Jesus and his apostles to Joseph Smith, whom I did call upon by mine angels, my ministering servants, and by mine own voice out of the heavens, to bring forth my work; (*Revelation received at Winter Quarters, Jan. 14, 1847*) D&C 136:37

---

### 616. Righteousness binds the devil; we are to take upon us the armor of righteousness as a protection against the evil one.

### President Joseph F. Smith

The more righteous and upright, pure and undefiled, the Latter-day Saints become, the less power will Satan have over them, for in proportion to your unity and uprightness, honesty, and fidelity to the cause in which you are engaged, in such proportion will the power of the adversary be weakened, and those who are seeking to entice your sons and daughters into haunts of shame, and dens of wickedness, that they might be defiled, corrupted, wicked and like the rest of them will have less power over you, if you will watch your children better, and live better lives yourselves. CR1911Oct:11

### Joseph Smith,
#### *receiving the Word of the Lord*

Wherefore, lift up your hearts and rejoice, and gird up your loins, and take upon you my whole armor, that ye may be able to withstand the evil day, having done all, that ye may be able to stand. 16. Stand, therefore, having your loins girt about with truth, having on the breastplate of righteousness, and your feet shod with the preparation of the gospel of peace, which I have sent mine angels to commit unto you; 17. Taking the shield of faith wherewith ye shall be able to quench all the fiery darts of the wicked; 18. And take the helmet of salvation, and the sword of my Spirit, which I will pour out upon you, and my word which I reveal unto you, and be agreed as touching all things whatsoever ye ask of me, and be faithful until I come, and ye shall be caught up, that where I am ye shall be also. Amen. (*Revelation received through a heavenly messenger, Aug. 1830*) D&C 27:15-18

### Paul

Put on the whole armour of God, that ye may be able to stand against the wiles of the devil. 12. For we wrestle not against flesh and blood, but against principalities, against powers, against the rulers of the darkness of this world, against spiritual wickedness in high places. 13. Wherefore take unto you the whole armour of God, that ye may be able to withstand in the evil day, and having done all, to stand. 14. Stand therefore, having your loins girt about with truth, and having on the breastplate of righteousness; 15. And your feet shod with the preparation of the gospel of peace; 16. Above all, taking the shield of faith, wherewith ye shall be able to quench all the fiery darts of the wicked. 17. And take the helmet of salvation, and the sword of the Spirit, which is the word of God: (*Paul writes to the Saints at Ephesus in Asia Minor, about* A.D. 62) Eph.6:11-17

### Nephi, son of Lehi

And because of the righteousness of his people, Satan has no power; wherefore, he cannot be loosed for the space of many years; for he hath no power over the hearts of the people, for they dwell in righteousness, and the Holy One of Israel reigneth. (*Nephi explains the prophecies written on the plates of brass, 588-570 B.C.*) 1Ne.22:26

### Nephi, son of Lehi

And I said unto them that it [the rod of iron] was the word of God; and whoso would hearken unto the word of God, and would hold fast unto it, they would never perish; neither could the temptations and the fiery darts of the adversary overpower them unto blindness, to lead them away to destruction. (*Nephi interprets his father Lehi's dream to his brothers, between 600-592 B.C.*) 1Ne.15:24

### Related Witnesses:

#### Joseph Smith,
*receiving the Word of the Lord*

Yet you should have been faithful; and he would have extended his arm and supported you against all the fiery darts of the adversary; and he would have been with you in every time of trouble. (*Revelation regarding lost manuscript pages, July 1828.*) D&C 3:8

#### Lehi,
*quoted by his son Nephi*

Awake, my sons; put on the armor of righteousness. Shake off the chains with which ye are bound, and come forth out of obscurity, and arise from the dust. (*Lehi exhorts his sons to put on the armor of God, 588-570 B.C.*) 2Ne.1:23

### James

Submit yourselves therefore to God. Resist the devil, and he will flee from you. (*James writes his brethren in the Church*) James 4:7

---

# List of Doctrines

## RECORDS AND RECORD KEEPING

*Doctrines Located in This Topic*

617. We will be judged out of the records that are kept (on earth and in heaven).

618. The "book of life" is the record kept in heaven.

619. The Lord commands the Church to keep records.

620. Keeping personal journals can bless us and our posterity.

*Doctrines on RECORDS AND RECORD KEEPING Located in Other Topics*

377. The dead will be judged from the books that are written on earth and in heaven.

## RECORDS AND RECORD KEEPING

**617. We will be judged out of the records that are kept (on earth and in heaven).**

**Jesus,**
*quoted by Mormon*
For behold, out of the books which have been written, and which shall be written, shall this people be judged, for by them shall their works be known unto men. 26. And behold, all things are written by the Father; therefore out of the books which shall be written shall the world be judged. (*The resurrected Jesus calls on the Nephites to repent in contemplation of the final judgment,* A.D. *34*) 3Ne.27:25-26

**Elder Spencer W. Kimball**
Accordingly, men's deeds and thoughts must be recorded in heaven, and recording angels will not fail to make complete recordings of our thoughts and actions. We pay our tithing and the bishop records it in his book and gives us a receipt. But even if the entry fails to get in the ward record, we shall have full credit for the tithes we paid. There will be no omissions in the heavenly records, and they will all be available at the day of judgment. President John Taylor emphasized this: Man sleeps the sleep of death, but the spirit lives where the record of his deeds is kept. ¶ Man sleeps for a time in the grave, and by and by he rises again from the dead and goes to judgment; and then the secret thoughts of all men are revealed before him with whom we have to do; we cannot hide them: it would be in vain for a man to say, "I did not do so and so," the command would be, unravel and read the record which he has made of himself and let it testify in relation to these things, and all could gaze upon it. [JD11:78-79] ¶ At that day we may be sure that we shall receive fair judgment. The judges will have the facts as they may be played back from our own records, and our voices and the pictures of our own acts and the recordings of our thoughts will testify against and for us. (The Miracle of Forgiveness, p.109) TLDP:324-25

**Elder Spencer W. Kimball**
It is well for all of us to realize that our thought sins as well as all other sins are recorded in heaven. (The Miracle of Forgiveness, p.108) TLDP:691

**John**
And I saw the dead, small and great, stand before God; and the books were opened: and another book was opened, which is the book of life: and the dead were judged out of those things which were written in the books, according to their works. (*The Apostle John sees the judgment of man at the end of the Millennium*) Rev.20:12

**Joseph Smith**
You will discover in this quotation that the books were opened; and another book was opened, which was the book of life; but the dead were judged out of those things which were written in the books, according to their works; consequently, the books spoken of must be the books which contained the record of their works, and refer to the records which are kept on the earth. And the book which was the book of life is the record which is kept in heaven; . . . 8. Now, the nature of this ordinance consists in the power of the priesthood, by the revelation of Jesus Christ, wherein it is granted that whatsoever you bind on earth shall be bound in heaven, and whatsoever you loose on earth shall be loosed in heaven. Or, in other words, taking a different view of the translation, whatsoever you record on earth shall be recorded in heaven, and whatsoever you do not record on earth shall not be recorded in heaven; for out of the books shall your dead be judged, according to their own works, whether they themselves have attended to the ordinances in their own propria persona, or by the means of their own agents, according to the ordinance which God has prepared for their salvation from before the foundation of the world, according to the records which they have kept concerning their dead. (*Joseph writes to the Church giving further directions on baptism for the dead, Sept. 6, 1842*) D&C 128:7-8

**Related Witnesses:**
**Jesus,**
*also quoting Malachi,*
*quoted by Mormon*
Then they that feared the Lord spake often one to another, and the Lord hearkened and heard; and a book of remembrance was written before him for them that feared the Lord, and that thought upon his name. 17. And they shall be mine, saith the Lord of Hosts, in that day when I make up my jewels; and I will spare them as a man spareth his own son that serveth him. (*The resurrected Jesus Christ teaches the Nephite people, expounding and quoting the words of the prophet Malachi,* A.D. *34, see Malachi 3*) 3Ne.24:16-17

**Elder John Taylor**
It is written that Jesus will judge not after the sight of the eye, or after the hearing of the ear, but with righteousness shall he judge the poor, and reprove with equity the meek of the earth.

It is not because somebody has seen things, or heard anything by which a man will be judged and condemned, but it is because that record that is written by the man himself in the tablets of his own mind—that record that cannot lie—will in that day be unfolded before God and angels, and those who shall sit as judges. (*In Tabernacle, Feb. 5, 1865, JD11:79*) TLDP:324

### 618. The "book of life" is the record kept in heaven.

**Joseph Smith,**
*also quoting John*
You will discover in this quotation [Rev.20:12] that the books were opened; and another book was opened, which was the book of life; but the dead were judged out of those things which were written in the books, according to their works; consequently, the books spoken of must be the books which contained the record of their works, and refer to the records which are kept on the earth. And the book which was the book of life is the record which is kept in heaven; . . . that in all your recordings it may be recorded in heaven. 8. Now, the nature of this ordinance consists in the power of the priesthood, by the revelation of Jesus Christ, wherein it is granted that whatsoever you bind on earth shall be bound in heaven, and whatsoever you loose on earth shall be loosed in heaven. Or, in other words, taking a different view of the translation, whatsoever you record on earth shall be recorded in heaven, and whatsoever you do not record on earth shall not be recorded in heaven; for out of the books shall your dead be judged, according to their own works, whether they themselves have attended to the ordinances in their own propria persona, or by the means of their own agents, according to the ordinance which God has prepared for their salvation from before the foundation of the world, according to the records which they have kept concerning their dead. 9. It may seem to some to be a very bold doctrine that we talk of—a power which records or binds on earth and binds in heaven. Nevertheless, in all ages of the world, whenever the Lord has given a dispensation of the priesthood to any man by actual revelation, or any set of men, this power has always been given. Hence, whatsoever those men did in authority, in the name of the Lord, and did it truly and faithfully, and kept a proper and faithful record of the same, it became a law on earth and in heaven, and could not be annulled, according to the decrees of the great Jehovah. This is a faith-

ful saying. Who can hear it? (*Joseph writes to the Church giving further directions on baptism for the dead, after quoting Rev.20:12, Sept. 6, 1842*) D&C 128:7-9

**Alma, the younger,**
*quoted by Mormon*
The names of the wicked shall not be mingled with the names of my people; 58. For the names of the righteous shall be written in the book of life, and unto them will I grant an inheritance at my right hand. . . . (*Alma teaches the people, about 83 B.C.*) Alma 5:57-58

**President Brigham Young,**
*quoted by John A. Widtsoe*
The names of every son and daughter of Adam are already written in the Lamb's Book of Life. Is there ever a time when they will be taken out of it? Yes, when they become sons of perdition, and not till then. Every person has the privilege of retaining it there for ever and ever. If they neglect that privilege, then their names will be erased, and not till then. All the names of the human family are written there, and the Lord will hold them there until they come to the knowledge of the truth, that they can rebel against him, and can sin against the Holy Ghost; then they will be thrust down to hell, and their names be blotted out from the Lamb's Book of Life. (*In Tabernacle, Aug. 15, 1852, JD6:297*) DBY:387-88

**John**
And there shall in no wise enter into it any thing that defileth, neither whatsoever worketh abomination, or maketh a lie: but they which are written in the Lamb's book of life. (*The Apostle John sees the celestial kingdom*) Rev.21:27

**Related Witnesses:**
**Paul**
And I intreat thee also, true yokefellow, help those women which laboured with me in the gospel, with Clement also, and with other my fellowlabourers, whose names are in the book of life. (*Paul writes from Rome to the Church at Philippi in Macedonia*) Philip.4:3

**John**
He that overcometh, the same shall be clothed in white raiment; and I will not blot out his name out of the book of life, but I will confess his name before my Father, and before his angels. (*Jesus invites all to overcome, as he overcame*) Rev.3:5

**Joseph Smith,**
*receiving the Word of the Lord*
Behold, this is pleasing unto your Lord, and the angels rejoice over you; the alms of your prayers have come up into the ears of the Lord

of Sabaoth, and are recorded in the book of the names of the sanctified, even them of the celestial world. (*The Lord speaks to Joseph by revelation, Dec. 27/28, 1832*) D&C 88:2

### Francis M. Lyman

The forgiveness of sins is predicated upon faith in God, repentance and reformation and baptism. Sins are not forgiven through the payment of tithing, nor through the partaking of the sacrament, not observing the Word of Wisdom, or prayer. There are blessings attached to each of these important requirements of the Gospel; but if a man would have his sins forgiven, and be allowed to enter into the Church, he must have faith in God, and in his Son Jesus Christ, and in the Holy Ghost, he must repent of all his sins, turn unto the Lord with full purpose of heart and sin no more. Then God will forgive him and redeem him from his sins; but not by paying tithing. . . . But we want our names recorded in the Lamb's Book of Life, and it is not done by the observance of any one principle alone, but to every principle there are special blessings promised. CR1899Oct:34

### Bruce R. McConkie

All who bear testimony by the power of the Holy Ghost are blessed; their inspired utterances are recorded in heaven for the angels—their fellowservants—to look upon. (The Mortal Messiah, 3:38) TLDP:689

### Jesus,
#### *recorded in Luke*

Notwithstanding in this rejoice not, that the spirits are subject unto you; but rather rejoice, because your names are written in heaven. (*Jesus speaks to the Seventy who have reported their experiences*) Luke 10:20

### John

And if any man shall take away from the words of the book of this prophecy, God shall take away his part out of the book of life, and out of the holy city, and from the things which are written in this book. (*John addresses those who hear the words of his book of prophecy, the book of Revelation*) Rev.22:19

### Daniel

And at that time shall Michael stand up, the great prince which standeth for the children of thy people: and there shall be a time of trouble, such as never was since there was a nation even to that same time: and at that time thy people shall be delivered, every one that shall be found written in the book. (*In the last days Michael shall deliver Israel from their troubles*) Dan.12:1

### Joseph Smith,
#### *quoted by Elder Joseph Fielding Smith*

Until we have perfect love we are liable to fall

and when we have a testimony that our names are sealed in the Lamb's book of life we have perfect love and then it is impossible for false Christs to deceive us; . . . (*General conference held Oct. 25, 1831 at home of Sirenes Burnet, Orange, Ohio*) (Far West Record, p. 23) TPJS:9

**Author's Note:** The *Book of Life* is defined in the Bible Dictionary as follows: "Book of Life Spoken of in Philip. 4:3; Rev. 3:5; 13:8; 17:8; 20:12; 21:27; 22:19; cf. Dan. 12:1-4; Luke 10:20. In one sense the book of life is the sum total of one's thoughts and actions—the record of his life. However, the scriptures indicate that a heavenly record is kept of the faithful, whose names are recorded, as well as an account of their righteous deeds (D&C 88:2; 128:7)."

---

## 619. The Lord commands the Church to keep records.

### Anthon H. Lund

At the beginning of this revelation [D&C 21:1] we were told that there should be a recorder in the Church, that records should be kept among the people. This important work in the Church, of keeping records, was commanded; and if we read farther on we will find that John Whitmer was appointed to be Church Recorder, to write the events of the Church. I mention this to show you how important this part of our Church government is, to keep a history, to keep a record of what takes place. CR1913Apr:11

### Elder Joseph Fielding Smith

The matter of record keeping is one of the most important duties devolving on the Church. In the early days of the Church, because of lack of experience, this duty was neglected, therefore many important historical events were not recorded. Even today it is difficult to impress upon clerks in stakes, wards and missions the importance of proper record keeping. CHMR1:103

### Joseph Smith,
#### *receiving the Word of the Lord*

Behold, there shall be a record kept among you; . . . (*Revelation to Joseph Smith given at the organization of the Church, April 6, 1830*) D&C 21:1

### Jesus,
#### *quoted by Mormon*

And it came to pass that Nephi remembered that this thing had not been written. 13. And it came to pass that Jesus commanded that it should be written; therefore it was written according as he commanded. (*The resurrected*

*Jesus Christ instructs his disciples among Nephite people, A.D. 34)* 3Ne.23:12-13

**Joseph Smith**

I wrote a few words of revelation to you concerning a recorder. I have had a few additional views in relation to this matter, which I now certify. That is, it was declared in my former letter that there should be a recorder, who should be eye-witness, and also to hear with his ears, that he might make a record of a truth before the Lord. *(Joseph writes to the Church giving further directions on baptism for the dead, Sept. 6, 1842)* D&C 128:2

**Related Witnesses:**

**Joseph Smith**

After prayer by President Joseph Smith, Jun., he said, if we heard patiently, he could lay before the council an item which would be of importance. He had for himself, learned a fact by experience, which, on recollection, always gave him deep sorrow. It is a fact, if I now had in my possession, every decision which had been had upon important items of doctrine and duties since the commencement of this work, I should not part with them for any sum of money; but we have neglected to take minutes of such things, thinking, perhaps, that they would never benefit us afterwards; which, if we had them now, would decide almost every point of doctrine which might be agitated. But this has been neglected, and now we cannot bear record to the Church and to the world, of the great and glorious manifestations which have been made to us with that degree of power and authority we otherwise could, if we now had these things to publish abroad. *(Oliver Cowdery, clerk of the meeting, takes minutes of Joseph Smith's instructions to the Twelve, in Joseph's home at Kirtland, Ohio, Feb. 27, 1835)* HC2:198-99

**President George Albert Smith**

Each of them [the temples] has been built to one great eternal purpose: to serve as a House of the Lord, to provide a place sacred and suitable for the performing of holy ordinances that bind on earth as in heaven—ordinances for the dead and for the living that assure those who receive them and who are faithful to their covenants, the possession and association of their families, worlds without end, and exaltation with them in the celestial kingdom of our Father. ("The Tenth Temple," IE1945Oct:561) TLDP:675

---

**620. Keeping personal journals can bless us and our posterity.**

**President Spencer W. Kimball**

We renew our appeal for the keeping of individual journals and records and compiling family histories. . . . [S]ome families possess some spiritual treasures because ancestors have recorded the events surrounding their conversion to the gospel and other happenings of interest, including many miraculous blessings and spiritual experiences. . . . I promise you that if you will keep your journals and records they will indeed be a source of great inspiration to your families, to your children, your grandchildren, and others, on through generations. CR1978Oct:4-5

**Gordon B. Hinckley**

To you young women of today, who are old or young, may I suggest that you write, that you keep journals, that you express your thoughts on paper. Writing is a great discipline. It is a tremendous educational effort. It will assist you in various ways, and you will bless the lives of many—your families and others—now and in the years to come, as you put on paper some of your experiences and some of your musings. CR1984Oct:111

**Related Witnesses:**

**Elder Ezra Taft Benson**

[S]ome things which have not changed: ¶ . . . . Our responsibility to keep a journal and to write our own personal histories and those of our ancestors, particularly those who belong to the first four generations of our pedigree, has not changed. CR1978Oct:40-41

**Adam S. Bennion**

To you parents, as you dream dreams for the children you cherish, may I offer these suggestions: ¶ 1. Make sure that your children know our pioneer story. Let it not be said in any Latter-day Saint home that the children grow up in ignorance of the achievements of their forebears. Both you and they will stir to the materials in the books already quoted in this address and in such other publications as: ¶ Family Journals and Diaries. . . . CR1954Apr:101

**Joseph Smith**

Since I have been engaged in laying the foundation of the Church of Jesus Christ of Latter-day Saints, I have been prevented in various ways from continuing my journal and history in a manner satisfactory to myself or in justice to the cause. Long imprisonments, vexatious and long-continued law suits, the treachery of some of my clerks, the death of others, and the poverty of myself and brethren from continued plunder and driving, have prevented my handing down to posterity a connected memorandum of events desirable to all lovers of truth; yet I have

continued to keep up a journal in the best manner my circumstances would allow, and dictate
for my history from time to time, as I have had
opportunity so that the labors and suffering of
the first Elders and Saints of this last kingdom
might not wholly be lost to the world. (*Journal
entry, Dec. 11, 1841, explaining the Prophet's
difficulties in writing the annals of the Church*)
HC4:470

### President Brigham Young,
### quoted by John A. Widtsoe

You may remember it and lay it to heart, and if
you wish, write it in your journals that some of
the best spirits that have ever been sent to earth
are coming at the present time. (*Given on visits
to Utah, Juab, and Sanpete counties, Utah,
June and July, 1865, JD11:117*) DBY:109

**Author's Note:** Joseph Smith inserted in his
own journal the following excerpt from a letter
to the Editor written by a George Mitchelson
and printed in the *Millennial Star*. Joseph headed it, "Importance of Elders Keeping Journals,
Case of Healing Recorded:" ¶ "MR. EDI-
TOR:—The idea has frequently crossed my
mind, that were the Elders of the Church of
Jesus Christ in this age to keep a journal of
their travels and ministry, and record all the
healings and miracles they had witnessed from
time to time,—that should their separate journals be afterwards collected together and published in a volume, I am inclined to believe that
a far greater number of manifest displays of the
power of God would be therein recorded than is
found in the journals of the Elders of the
Church of Jesus Christ in the early ages, at least
so far as they are faithfully handed down to us
in the New Testament Scriptures." (HC6:186)

# List of Doctrines

## REPENTANCE

*Doctrines Located in This Topic*

### (1) The Role of Repentance

621. All people are commanded to repent.

622. Repentance is essential to salvation: we cannot be saved while we carry our sins with us.

623. Repentance is an ongoing process: whenever we sin—at any time in life—we are to repent.

624. We must suffer divine punishment for our sins unless we repent.

### (2) True Repentance

625. We are to repent in our hearts.

626. Temporary suffering is an integral part of the process of true repentance.

627. Repentance must not be procrastinated.

628. Repeated repentance following the same repeated transgressions is not complete repentance.

### (3) Steps of Repentance

629. Sorrow for sin is essential to the spirit of repentance.

630. Abandonment of sin is a necessary part of repentance.

631. Confession of sin is a necessary part of repentance.

632. Confession of sins is to be made to the appropriate persons—not all sins are to be confessed publicly but are to be confessed where the confession belongs.

633. Making restitution, as much as is possible, is part of complete repentance.

634. Obedience—living the commandments of the Lord—is one of the requisites for repentance.

### (4) Obtaining Forgiveness

635. There can be complete divine forgiveness of sin.

636. Repentance brings peace of conscience.

*Doctrines on REPENTANCE*
*Located in Other Topics*

37. The Atonement of Christ makes it possible for us to return to presence of the Lord.

# REPENTANCE continued

45. Were it not for the Atonement, mercy could not be extended to sinners who, though they might repent, would nevertheless be compelled to suffer the rigorous demands of justice.

48. Unrepentant persons cannot receive the full benefit of the Atonement; they will be resurrected but they must suffer for their sins.

51. Baptism is required of children only when they arrive at the age of accountability—when they are capable of repentance.

52. Only those who have truly repented may be baptized.

73. Little children have no need of repentance or baptism.

296. The first principles and ordinances of the gospel are faith in the Lord Jesus Christ, repentance, baptism by immersion, and the laying on of hands for the gift of the Holy Ghost.

354. Humility precedes repentance.

391. Justice is satisfied and mercy is extended to those who repent.

460. Those who preach the gospel to the world shall say nothing but repentance (they shall preach only with the desire to bring people to repentance and faith in God).

# REPENTANCE

## (1) The Role of Repentance

621. All people are commanded to repent.

**Joseph Smith,**
*receiving the Word of the Lord*

Hearken and hear, O ye inhabitants of the earth. Listen, ye elders of my church together, and hear the voice of the Lord; for he calleth upon all men, and he commandeth all men everywhere to repent. (*Revelation given for the elders of The Church of Jesus Christ of Latter-day Saints, Nov. 3, 1831*) D&C 133:16

**President Brigham Young**
**Heber C. Kimball, Jedediah M. Grant**
(First Presidency)

To all the honest in heart throughout the world, both of high and low degree, we say "repent, and be baptized for the remission of your sins," obey the ordinances of the Gospel through the administrations of the servants of the living God, for the judgments of the Almighty are upon you, flee therefore from the sinks of iniquity and corruption, lest the fiery indignation of the Lord also consume you with the wicked, of whom He has decreed that He will empty the earth. (*Twelfth General Epistle of the Presidency, Aug. 11, 1855*) (Deseret News, April 25, 1855) TLDP:544-45; MOFP2:171

**Alma, the younger,**
*quoted by Mormon*

O that I were an angel, and could have the wish of mine heart, that I might go forth and speak with the trump of God, with a voice to shake the earth, and cry repentance unto every people! 2. Yea, I would declare unto every soul, as with the voice of thunder, repentance and the plan of redemption, that they should repent and come unto our God, that there might not be more sorrow upon all the face of the earth. (*Alma has an earnest desire to cry repentance to every people—even that he might be an angel to speak with a voice to shake the earth, about 76 B.C.*) Alma 29:1-2

**Jesus,**
*quoted by Mormon*

And this is my doctrine, and it is the doctrine which the Father hath given unto me; and I bear record of the Father, and the Father beareth record of me, and the Holy Ghost beareth record of the Father and me; and I bear record that the Father commandeth all men, everywhere, to repent and believe in me. (*The resurrected Jesus Christ addresses his Nephite disciples, A.D. 34*) 3Ne.11:32

**Jacob, brother of Nephi,**
*quoted by Nephi*

And he commandeth all men that they must repent, and be baptized in his name, having perfect faith in the Holy One of Israel, or they cannot be saved in the kingdom of God. 24. And if they will not repent and believe in his name, and be baptized in his name, and endure to the end, they must be damned; for the Lord God, the Holy One of Israel, has spoken it. (*Jacob teaches the people of Nephi, 559-545 B.C.*) 2Ne.9:23-24

**Joseph Smith,**
*translating the Book of Moses*

Wherefore, thou shalt do all that thou doest in the name of the Son, and thou shalt repent and call upon God in the name of the Son forevermore. . . . 14. And the Lord God called upon men by the Holy Ghost everywhere and commanded them that they should repent; 15. And as many as believed in the Son, and repented of their sins, should be saved; and as many as believed not and repented not, should be damned; and the words went forth out of the mouth of God in a firm decree; wherefore they must be fulfilled. (*Revelation to Moses given to Joseph Smith, concerning Adam and Eve after they were driven out of the Garden of Eden*) Moses 5:8,14-15

**Jacob, brother of Nephi,**
*quoted by Nephi*

O how great the holiness of our God! For he knoweth all things, and there is not anything save he knows it. 21. And he cometh into the world that he may save all men if they will hearken unto his voice; for behold, he suffereth the pains of all men, yea, the pains of every living creature, both men, women, and children, who belong to the family of Adam. 22. And he suffereth this that the resurrection might pass upon all men, that all might stand before him at the great and judgment day. 23. And he commandeth all men that they must repent, and be baptized in his name, having perfect faith in the Holy One of Israel, or they cannot be saved in the kingdom of God. 24. And if they will not repent and believe in his name, and be baptized in his name, and endure to the end, they must be damned; for the Lord God, the Holy One of Israel, has spoken it. (*Jacob teaches the people of Nephi, 559-545 B.C.*) 2Ne.9:20-24

**Related Witnesses:**

### Peter

Repent ye therefore, and be converted, that your sins may be blotted out, when the times of refreshing shall come from the presence of the Lord; (*Peter preaches repentance*) Acts 3:19

### Moroni, son of Mormon

O then ye unbelieving, turn ye unto the Lord; cry mightily unto the Father in the name of Jesus, that perhaps ye may be found spotless, pure, fair, and white, having been cleansed by the blood of the Lamb, at that great and last day. (*Moroni calls upon those who do not believe in Christ to repent, A.D. 400-421*) Morm.9:6

### King Benjamin,
*quoted by Mormon*

And again, believe that ye must repent of your sins and forsake them, and humble yourselves before God; and ask in sincerity of heart that he would forgive you; and now, if you believe all these things see that ye do them. (*King Benjamin addresses his people, about 124 B.C.*) Mosiah 4:10

### Jesus,
*recorded in Matthew*

But when Jesus heard that, he said unto them, They that be whole need not a physician, but they that are sick. 13. But go ye and learn what that meaneth, I will have mercy, and not sacrifice: for I am not come to call the righteous, but sinners to repentance. (*Jesus eats with sinners to the consternation of the Pharisees*) Matt.9:12-13

### Joseph Smith,
*receiving the Word of the Lord*

Wherefore, I, the Lord, have said that the fearful, and the unbelieving, and all liars, and whosoever loveth and maketh a lie, and the whoremonger, and the sorcerer, shall have their part in that lake which burneth with fire and brimstone, which is the second death. 18. Verily I say, that they shall not have part in the first resurrection. (*Revelation received at Kirtland, Ohio, Aug. 1831*) D&C 63:17-18

---

622. **Repentance is essential to salvation: we cannot be saved while we carry our sins with us.**

### President Joseph F. Smith

No man can be saved in the kingdom of God in sin. No man will ever be forgiven of his sins by the just Judge, except he repent of his sins. No man will ever be freed from the power of death unless he is born again as the Lord Almighty has decreed, and declared to the world by the mouth of his Son in the meridian of time, and as he has declared it again in this dispensation through the Prophet Joseph Smith. Men can only be saved and exalted in the kingdom of God in righteousness, therefore we must repent of our sins, and walk in the light as Christ is in the light, that his blood may cleanse us from all sins, and that we may have fellowship with God and receive of his glory and exaltation. CR1907Oct:4

### President Joseph F. Smith

You cannot take a murderer, a suicide, an adulterer, a liar, or one who was or is thoroughly abominable in his life here, and simply by the performance of an ordinance of the gospel, cleanse him from sin and usher him into the presence of God. God has not instituted a plan of that kind, and it cannot be done. He has said you shall repent of your sins. The wicked will have to repent of their wickedness. Those who die without the knowledge of the gospel will have to come to the knowledge of it, and those who sin against light will have to pay the uttermost farthing for their transgression and their departure from the gospel, before they can ever get back to it. Do not forget that. Do not forget it, you elders in Israel, nor you, mothers in Israel, either; and, when you seek to save either the living or the dead, bear it in mind that you can only do it on the principle of their repentance and acceptation of the plan of life. That is the only way in which you can succeed. CR1907Oct:6-7

### Helaman,
*quoted by Mormon*

And remember also the words which Amulek spake unto Zeezrom, in the city of Ammonihah; for he said unto him that the Lord surely should come to redeem his people, but that he should not come to redeem them in their sins, but to redeem them from their sins. 11. And he hath power given unto him from the Father to redeem them from their sins because of repentance; therefore he hath sent his angels to declare the tidings of the conditions of repentance, which bringeth unto the power of the Redeemer, unto the salvation of their souls. (*Helaman preaches to his sons, 30 B.C.*) Hel.5:10-11

### Elder Joseph Fielding Smith

There can be no salvation without repentance. A man cannot enter into the kingdom of God in his sins. It would be a very inconsistent thing for a man to come into the presence of the Father and to dwell in God's presence in his sins. . . . ¶ I think there are a great many people upon the earth, many of them perhaps in the Church—at least some in the Church—who have an idea they can go through this life doing as they please, violating the commandments of the Lord and yet eventually they are going to come into his presence. They think they are going to repent, perhaps in the spirit world. ¶ They ought to read these words of Moroni: [Morm.9:3-5 is quoted.] ¶ Do you think that a man whose life has been filled with corruption, who has been rebellious against God, who has not had the spirit of repentance, would be happy or comfortable should he be permitted to come into the presence of God? (Doctrines of Salvation, 1:195-96) TLDP:544

### Moroni, son of Mormon

Then will ye longer deny the Christ, or can ye behold the Lamb of God? Do ye suppose that ye shall dwell with him under a consciousness of your guilt? Do ye suppose that ye could be happy to dwell with that holy Being, when your souls are racked with a consciousness of guilt that ye have ever abused his laws? 4. Behold, I say unto you that ye would be more miserable to dwell with a holy and just God, under a consciousness of your filthiness before him, than ye would to dwell with the damned souls in hell. (*Moroni calls upon those who do not believe in Christ to repent, A.D. 400-421*) Morm.9:3-4

### President Brigham Young

Now, my brethren, you who have sinned, repent of your sins. I can say to you in regard to Jesus and the atonement (it is so written, and I firmly believe it), that Christ has died for all. He has paid the full debt, whether you receive the gift or not. But if we continue to sin, to lie, steal, bear false witness, we must repent of and forsake that sin to have the full efficacy of the blood of Christ. Without this it will be of no effect; repentance must come, in order that the atonement may prove a benefit to us. (*In Bowery, April 8, 1867, JD11:375*) TLDP:544

### Amulek,
### quoted by Mormon

And I say unto you again that he cannot save them in their sins; for I cannot deny his word, and he hath said that no unclean thing can inherit the kingdom of heaven; therefore, how can ye be saved, except ye inherit the kingdom of heaven? Therefore, ye cannot be saved in your sins. (*Amulek contends with the wicked Zeezrom, about 82 B.C.*) Alma 11:37

### Related Witnesses:
### President David O. McKay

Every principle and ordinance of the gospel of Jesus Christ is significant and important in con-

tributing to the progress, happiness, and eternal life of man; but there is none more essential to the salvation of the human family than the divine and eternally operative principle, repentance. Without it, no one can be saved. Without it, no one can even progress. (Man May Know for Himself: Teachings of President David O. McKay, p. 43) DGSM:38

### Alma, the younger,
### quoted by Mormon

For I perceive that ye are in the paths of righteousness; I perceive that ye are in the path which leads to the kingdom of God; yea, I perceive that ye are making his paths straight. 20. I perceive that it has been made known unto you, by the testimony of his word, that he cannot walk in crooked paths; neither doth he vary from that which he hath said; neither hath he a shadow of turning from the right to the left, or from that which is right to that which is wrong; therefore, his course is one eternal round. 21. And he doth not dwell in unholy temples; neither can filthiness or anything which is unclean be received into the kingdom of God; therefore I say unto you the time shall come, yea, and it shall be at the last day, that he who is filthy shall remain in his filthiness. (*Alma preaches to the people in Gideon, about 83 B.C.*) Alma 7:19-21

### Elder Spencer W. Kimball

You will arise about the way you die. You will not change very much. You cannot repent on the Word of Wisdom violation in the spirit world because you have no body which you must change. You can hardly change its urges and desires and its pleadings and pullings in the spirit world. This is the time to put your lives in order. (*Brigham Young University stake conference*) (The Teachings of Spencer W. Kimball, p. 41) TLDP:546

### James E. Talmage

The Latter-day Saints believe and teach that repentance will be possible, and indeed required of the yet unrepentant, even after death; and they affirm that this doctrine is supported by scripture both ancient and modern. HL:67-68

### Marion G. Romney

All have sinned. Each person is therefore unclean to the extent to which he has sinned, and because of that uncleanness is banished from the presence of the Lord so long as the effect of his own wrongdoing is upon him. CR1982Apr:9

### President Spencer W. Kimball

Man can transform himself and he must. Man has in himself the seeds of godhood, which can germinate and grow and develop. As the acorn becomes the oak, the mortal man becomes a god. It is within his power to lift himself by his very bootstraps from the plane on which he finds himself to the plane on which he should be. It may be a long, hard lift with many obstacles, but it is a real possibility. *(At Brigham Young University, Sept. 1974)* (The Teachings of Spencer W. Kimball, p. 28) DGSM:52

---

623. Repentance is an ongoing process: whenever we sin—at any time in life—we are to repent.

### Richard L. Evans
Repentance is part of the process of progress, of learning, of maturing, of recognizing law, of recognizing results; it is a process of facing facts. Every correcting of a mistake is a kind of repentance; every sincere apology is a kind of repentance; every improvement is a kind of repentance; every conquering of an unhealthful habit. ("Repentance—a Foremost Principle," IE1965Jan:43) DGSM:38

### Mormon
Therefore I say unto you, Go; and whosoever transgresseth against me, him shall ye judge according to the sins which he has committed; and if he confess his sins before thee and me, and repenteth in the sincerity of his heart, him shall ye forgive, and I will forgive him also. 30. Yea, and as often as my people repent will I forgive them their trespasses against me. *(The voice of the Lord to Alma, about 120-100 B.C.)* Mosiah 26:29-30

### James E. Talmage
Wilful persistency in sin may lead to the loss and forfeiture of the ability to repent; and for man to procrastinate the day of repentance is to invite and eventually to insure such forfeiture. HL:67

### Moroni, son of Mormon
But as oft as they repented and sought forgiveness, with real intent, they were forgiven. *(Moroni writes for the benefit of the Lamanites, A.D. 400-421)* Moro.6:8

### Hugh B. Brown
When we speak of the continual need of repentance, let it not be understood that we refer to a cycle of sinning and repenting and sinning again. That is not complete repentance. We must see the right and follow it, recognize the wrong and forsake it with a "Godly sorrow" if we would obtain the blessing of complete repentance. A growing conception of the good life must be accompanied by constant adjustment thereto if one would achieve harmony with the will of God. (Eternal Quest, pp. 99-102) DGSM:39

### Elder Spencer W. Kimball
It is true that the great principle of repentance is always available, but for the wicked and rebellious there are serious reservations to this statement. For instance, sin is intensely habit-forming and sometimes moves men to the tragic point of no return. Without repentance there can be no forgiveness, and without forgiveness all the blessings of eternity hang in jeopardy. As the transgressor moves deeper and deeper in his sin, the error is entrenched more deeply and the will to change is weakened, it becomes increasingly near-hopeless, and he skids down and down until either he does not want to climb back or he has lost the power to do so. (The Miracle of Forgiveness, p.117) DGSM:39

**Author's Note:** But repeated repentance following the same repeated transgressions is not complete repentance. The prophet Joseph Smith said: "Repentance is a thing that cannot be trifled with every day. Daily transgression and daily repentance is not that which is pleasing in the sight of God. " (HC3:379)

---

624. We must suffer divine punishment for our sins unless we repent.

### Elder Joseph Fielding Smith
All sin, no matter what nature it is, is a violation of a constituted law or commandment and hence is worthy of punishment unless the price is paid. That price could be in physical or mental suffering or by otherwise paying the debt. The scriptures inform us that for every sin there must be compensation, either by repentance or punishment. (Seek Ye Earnestly, p. 151) TLDP:633

### Joseph Smith,
*receiving the Word of the Lord*
And surely every man must repent or suffer, for I, God, am endless. . . . 15. Therefore I command you to repent—repent, lest I smite you by the rod of my mouth, and by my wrath, and by my anger, and your sufferings be sore—how sore you know not, how exquisite you know not, yea, how hard to bear you know not. 16. For behold, I, God, have suffered these things for all, that they might not suffer if they would repent; 17. But if they would not repent they must suffer even as I; 18. Which suffering caused myself, even God, the greatest of all, to tremble because of pain, and to bleed at every pore, and to suffer both body and spirit—and would that I might not drink the bitter cup, and shrink— 19. Nevertheless, glory be to the Father, and I partook and finished my preparations unto the children of

men. 20. Wherefore, I command you again to repent, lest I humble you with my almighty power; and that you confess your sins, lest you suffer these punishments of which I have spoken, of which in the smallest, yea, even in the least degree you have tasted at the time I withdrew my Spirit. (*Christ announces himself and gives a commandment of God for Martin Harris, March 1830*) D&C 19:4,15-20

### Orson Hyde and Hyrum Smith

We now close our epistle by saying unto you the Lord has commanded us to purify ourselves, to wash our hands and our feet, that He may testify to His Father and our Father, to His God and our God, that we are clean from the blood of this generation; and before we could wash our hands and our feet we were constrained to write this letter. Therefore, with the feelings of inexpressible anxiety for your welfare, we say again, Repent, repent, or Zion must suffer, for the scourge and judgment must come upon her. (*Epistle from a conference of twelve high priests, Kirtland, Ohio, Jan. 14, 1833*) HC1:320

### Alma, the younger, quoted by Mormon

Yea, I would declare unto every soul, as with the voice of thunder, repentance and the plan of redemption, that they should repent and come unto our God, that there might not be more sorrow upon all the face of the earth. (*Alma has an earnest desire to cry repentance to every people— even that he might be an angel to speak with a voice to shake the earth, about 76 B.C.*) Alma 29:2

### Alma, the younger, quoted by Mormon

But there is a law given, and a punishment affixed, and a repentance granted; which repentance mercy claimeth; otherwise, justice claimeth the creature and executeth the law, and the law inflicteth the punishment; if not so, the works of justice would be destroyed, and God would cease to be God. 23. But God ceaseth not to be God, and mercy claimeth the penitent, and mercy cometh because of the atonement; and the atonement bringeth to pass the resurrection of the dead; and the resurrection of the dead bringeth back men into the presence of God; and thus they are restored into his presence, to be judged according to their works, according to the law and justice. 24. For behold, justice exerciseth all his demands, and also mercy claimeth all which is her own; and thus, none but the truly penitent are saved. (*Alma speaks to his son Corianton concerning the resurrection of the dead, about 73 B.C.*) Alma 42:22-24

### Nephi, son of Lehi

But behold, if the inhabitants of the earth shall repent of their wickedness and abominations they shall not be destroyed, saith the Lord of Hosts. (*Nephi foretells of the last days, 559-545 B.C.*) 2Ne.28:17

### Related Witnesses:

#### Joseph Smith

For the indignation of the Lord is kindled against their abominations and all their wicked works. (*Revelation dealing with the affairs of the persecuted Saints in Missouri, Aug. 2, 1833*) D&C 97:24

#### Moroni, son of Mormon

And thus we see that the Lord did visit them in the fulness of his wrath, and their wickedness and abominations had prepared a way for their everlasting destruction. (*Moroni's abridgement of the writings of Ether, who wrote about 550 B.C.*) Ether 14:25

#### Nephi, son of Lehi

And that great pit, which hath been digged for them by that great and abominable church, which was founded by the devil and his children, that he might lead away the souls of men down to hell—yea, that great pit which hath been digged for the destruction of men shall be filled by those who digged it, unto their utter destruction, saith the Lamb of God; not the destruction of the soul, save it be the casting of it into that hell which hath no end. 4. For behold, this is according to the captivity of the devil, and also according to the justice of God, upon all those who will work wickedness and abomination before him. (*An angel instructs Nephi, about 600-592 B.C.*) 1Ne.14:3-4

#### James E. Talmage

So general were the ill effects of the commonly accepted doctrine, unscriptural and untrue though it was, regarding the endless torment awaiting every sinner, that even before the Church had been formally organized in the present dispensation, the Lord gave a revelation through the Prophet Joseph Smith touching this matter, in which we read: "And surely every man must repent or suffer; for I, God, am endless. Wherefore, I revoke not the judgments which I shall pass, but woes shall go forth, weeping, wailing and gnashing of teeth, yea, to those who are found on my left hand. Nevertheless, it is not written that there shall be no end to this torment, but it is written endless torment. Again, it is written eternal damnation. . . . For behold, I am endless, and the punishment which is given from my hand is endless punishment, for Endless is my name. Wherefore, Eternal punishment is God's punishment. Endless punishment is God's punishment." (D&C 19:4-10) AF:56

## (2) True Repentance

### 625. We are to repent in our hearts.

#### Moroni, the Prophet General
##### *quoted by Mormon*
Do ye suppose that God will look upon you as guiltless while ye sit still and behold these things? Behold I say unto you, Nay. Now I would that ye should remember that God has said that the inward vessel shall be cleansed first, and then shall the outer vessel be cleansed also. (*Moroni complains to Pahoran of the government's neglect of the armies, about 62 B.C.*) Alma 60:23

#### Elder Spencer W. Kimball
In connection with repentance, the scriptures use the phrase, "with all his heart" (See D&C 42:25). Obviously this rules out any reservations. Repentance must involve an all-out, total surrender to the program of the Lord. (The Miracle of Forgiveness, p. 203) TLDP:548

#### President Lorenzo Snow
Do not be discouraged, brethren. If you cannot become perfect at once; if you see that you have weaknesses which have brought you into some trouble, do not be discouraged; but repent of that which you have done wrong, by which you have lost more or less of the Spirit of God, tell the Lord what you have done, and resolve in your hearts that you will do it no more. Then the Spirit of the Lord will be upon you. CR1898Oct:56

#### Moroni, son of Mormon
But as oft as they repented and sought forgiveness, with real intent, they were forgiven. (*Moroni writes for the benefit of the Lamanites, A.D. 400-421*) Moro.6:8

#### Charles A. Callis
The reward of repentance is a new man, a new birth. Think of the sweet influence that repentance brings. It changes the heart. It makes us feel that we have no more disposition to do evil, but to do good continually. Our Heavenly Father entreats us to be correct in manner, proper in our conduct, and an example and a light unto all mankind. Oh, the strength, the beauty there is in purity of heart! CR1941Oct:83

#### King Benjamin,
##### *quoted by Mormon*
And they had viewed themselves in their own carnal state, even less than the dust of the earth. And they all cried aloud with one voice, saying: O have mercy, and apply the atoning blood of Christ that we may receive forgiveness of our sins, and our hearts may be purified; for we believe in Jesus Christ, the Son of God, who created heaven and earth, and all things; who

shall come down among the children of men. . . . 10. And again, believe that ye must repent of your sins and forsake them, and humble yourselves before God; and ask in sincerity of heart that he would forgive you; and now, if you believe all these things see that ye do them. (*King Benjamin addresses his people, about 124 B.C.*) Mosiah 4:2,10

#### Mormon
Therefore I say unto you, Go; and whosoever transgresseth against me, him shall ye judge according to the sins which he has committed; and if he confess his sins before thee and me, and repenteth in the sincerity of his heart, him shall ye forgive, and I will forgive him also. (*The voice of the Lord to Alma, about 120-100 B.C.*) Mosiah 26:29

#### President Harold B. Lee
When you have done all you can within your power to overcome your mistakes, and you have determined in your heart that you will never repeat them again, then you can have that peace of conscience by which you will know that your sins have been forgiven. ACR(Mexico City)1972:103

#### Ezekiel
Cast away from you all your transgressions, whereby ye have transgressed; and make you a new heart and a new spirit: for why will ye die, O house of Israel? (*Ezekiel preaches the word of the Lord*) Ezek.18:31

#### Related Witnesses:
#### Jesus,
##### *recorded in Matthew*
Woe unto you, scribes and Pharisees, hypocrites! for ye make clean the outside of the cup and of the platter, but within they are full of extortion and excess. 26. Thou blind Pharisee, cleanse first that which is within the cup and platter, that the outside of them may be clean also. (*Jesus warns the scribes and Pharisees*) Matt.23:25-26

#### Recorded in 1 Samuel
But the LORD said unto Samuel, Look not on his countenance, or on the height of his stature; because I have refused him: for the LORD seeth not as man seeth; for man looketh on the outward appearance, but the LORD looketh on the heart. (*The Lord through Samuel chooses David to be king; Samuel examines Eliab, son of Jesse*) 1Sam.16:7

#### Jesus,
##### *recorded in Mark*
There is nothing from without a man, that entering into him can defile him: but the things which come out of him, those are they that defile the man. . . . 18. . . . Do ye not perceive,

that whatsoever thing from without entereth into the man, it cannot defile him; 19. Because it entereth not into his heart, but into the belly, and goeth out into the draught, purging all meats? 20. And he said, That which cometh out of the man, that defileth the man. 21. For from within, out of the heart of men, proceed evil thoughts, adulteries, fornications, murders, 22. Thefts, covetousness, wickedness, deceit, lasciviousness, an evil eye, blasphemy, pride, foolishness: 23. All these evil things come from within, and defile the man. (*Jesus instructs the people*) Mark 7:15,18-23

---

626. Temporary suffering is an integral part of the process of true repentance.

### President Spencer W. Kimball

If a person hasn't suffered, he hasn't repented. I don't care how many times he says he has. If he hasn't suffered, he hasn't repented. He has got to go through a change in his system whereby he suffers and then forgiveness is a possibility. (*Priesthood leadership meeting, Oct. 1974*) (The Teachings of Spencer W. Kimball, p. 99) TLDP:548

### President Spencer W. Kimball

Many people cannot repent until they have suffered much. They cannot direct their thoughts into new, clean channels. They cannot control their acts. They cannot plan their future properly until they have lost values that they did not seem to fully appreciate. Therefore, the Lord has prescribed excommunication, disfellowshipment, or probation. ("What Is True Repentance?" EN1974May:4; The Teachings of Spencer W. Kimball, pp. 97-98) TLDP:546-47

### President Spencer W. Kimball

Suffering is a very important part of repentance. One has not begun to repent until he has suffered intensely for his sins. (*Copenhagen area conference, Aug. 5, 1976*) (The Teachings of Spencer W. Kimball, p. 88) TLDP:548

### Abraham H. Cannon

Then we want them [men] to be filled with the spirit of repentance, which follows faith, and which is the natural result of faith in God; for if men are filled with faith in the Father and in the Son, they will naturally desire to place themselves in a condition to be fit associates for such holy beings, and *they will look back upon their past lives with sorrow* [Italics supplied]—with a sorrow which will prompt them to be more righteous, more God-fearing, more upright, in the future. Then repentance of sin will come upon

them; . . . a repentance that prompts men to make restitution, as far as it is possible for them to do so, for the sins which they have committed, and to restore four-fold, if necessary, in order to obtain pardon for the wrong done. (Millennial Star, July 18, 1895, p. 453) TLDP:546

**Related Witnesses:**

### Elder Harold B. Lee

And so it is when one has sinned so seriously that to hold further membership or to hold the holy priesthood would be as a stumbling block and burden rather than a blessing. In the wisdom of the Lord, these privileges are taken from him that he might be ground as "clay in the hands of the potter," again tried and tested, until he is again worthy to receive these holy blessings. (*To Brigham Young University student body, Oct. 2, 1956*) (Stand Ye in Holy Places, p. 119) TLDP:79

### Elder Joseph Fielding Smith

All sin, no matter what nature it is, is a violation of a constituted law or commandment and hence is worthy of punishment unless the price is paid. That price could be in physical or mental suffering or by otherwise paying the debt. The scriptures inform us that for every sin there must be compensation, either by repentance or punishment. (Seek Ye Earnestly, p. 151) TLDP:633

### Marion G. Romney

[T]here are many among us whose distress and suffering are unnecessarily prolonged because they do not complete their repentance by confessing their sins. . . . ¶ Repeatedly he [the Savior] says that he forgives the sins of those who confess their sins with humbleness of heart, " . . . who have not sinned unto death." CR1955Oct:124

### Elder Joseph F. Smith

True repentance is not only sorrow for sins, and humble penitence and contrition before God, but it involves the necessity of turning away from them, a discontinuance of all evil practices and deeds, a thorough reformation of life, a vital change from evil to good, from vice to virtue, from darkness to light. Not only so, but to make restitution, so far as it is possible, for all the wrongs we have done, to pay our debts, and restore to God and man their rights—that which is due them from us. This is true repentance, and *the exercise of the will and all the powers of body and mind is demanded* [Italics supplied], to complete this glorious work of repentance. (Gospel Doctrine, pp. 100-01) TLDP:549

**Author's Note:** It appears that by our accepting temporary suffering in *this* life as part of the process of repentance, by accepting punishment now for our sins—such as the temporary loss of the blessings of the gospel through disfellowshipment or excommunication, the pain and sorrow of facing our sins and those we have sinned against, the sometimes agonizing endeavor of making restitution, the pain of abandoning sin (changing bad habits)—by going through the painful process of repentance *now* we can avoid ultimate divine punishment and exquisite and unbearable suffering in the afterlife for our wrongdoing.

---

### 627. Repentance must not be procrastinated.

#### Amulek,
#### *quoted by Mormon*

And now, my brethren, I would that, after ye have received so many witnesses, seeing that the holy scriptures testify of these things, ye come forth and bring fruit unto repentance. 31. Yea, I would that ye would come forth and harden not your hearts any longer; for behold, now is the time and the day of your salvation; and therefore, if ye will repent and harden not your hearts, immediately shall the great plan of redemption be brought about unto you. 32. For behold, this life is the time for men to prepare to meet God; yea, behold the day of this life is the day for men to perform their labors. 33. And now, as I said unto you before, as ye have had so many witnesses, therefore, I beseech of you that ye do not procrastinate the day of your repentance until the end; for after this day of life, which is given us to prepare for eternity, behold, if we do not improve our time while in this life, then cometh the night of darkness wherein there can be no labor performed. 34. Ye cannot say, when ye are brought to that awful crisis, that I will repent, that I will return to my God. Nay, ye cannot say this; for that same spirit which doth possess your bodies at the time that ye go out of this life, that same spirit will have power to possess your body in that eternal world. 35. For behold, if ye have procrastinated the day of your repentance even until death, behold, ye have become subjected to the spirit of the devil, and he doth seal you his; therefore, the Spirit of the Lord hath withdrawn from you, and hath no place in you, and the devil hath all power over you; and this is the final state of the wicked. 36. And this I know, because the Lord hath said he dwelleth not in unholy temples, but in the hearts of the righteous doth he dwell; yea, and he has also said that the righteous shall sit down in his kingdom, to go no more out; but their garments should be made white through the blood of the Lamb. (*Amulek teaches the people that this life is the time for men to prepare to meet God, 74 B.C.*) Alma 34:30-36

#### Joseph Smith,
#### *quoted by Elder Joseph Fielding Smith*

We should take warning and not wait for the deathbed to repent, as we see the infant taken away by death, so may the youth and middle aged, as well as the infant, be suddenly called into eternity. Let this, then, prove as a warning to all not to procrastinate repentance, or wait till a deathbed for it is the will of God that man should repent and serve Him in health, and in the strength and power of his mind, in order to secure His blessing, and not wait until he is called to die. (*To a large assembly in the Grove near the Nauvoo Temple; the body of a deceased child of Mr. Windsor P. Lyon being before the assembly, March 1842*) TPJS:197; DGSM:39

#### Melvin J. Ballard

It is my judgment that any man or woman can do more to conform to the laws of God in one year in this life than they could in ten years when they are dead. The spirit only can repent and change, and then the battle has to go forward with the flesh afterwards. It is much easier to overcome and serve the Lord when both the flesh and spirit are combined as one. This is the time when men are more pliable and susceptible. When clay is pliable, it is much easier to change than when it gets hard and sets. (Sermons and Missionary Services of Melvin J. Ballard, p. 241) DGSM:39

#### James E. Talmage

As the time of repentance is procrastinated, the ability to repent grows weaker; neglect of opportunity in holy things develops inability. AF:104

#### James E. Talmage

Wilful persistency in sin may lead to the loss and forfeiture of the ability to repent; and for man to procrastinate the day of repentance is to invite and eventually to insure such forfeiture. HL:67

#### James E. Talmage

But, because there is hope of repentance beyond the veil, procrastinate not the day of your repentance; for, as the Prophet Alma has pointed out, you may find that the gift of repentance will be withheld from you a long, long time on account of your unworthiness. For repentance is a gift from God, and when man forfeits it he loses the power to repent; he can't turn away from his sins with a contrite heart and with a desire to forsake them, once and for ever. O, Latter-day Saints, ye men and women of Israel, listen unto the voices of those who speak to you under the inspiration of the power of God, and heed them; for by hearing we are condemned, if we follow not in the path that is pointed out to us as the path of our duty. CR1913Oct:121

**Elder Spencer W. Kimball**

It is true that the great principle of repentance is always available, but for the wicked and rebellious there are serious reservations to this statement. For instance, sin is intensely habit-forming and sometimes moves men to the tragic point of no return. Without repentance there can be no forgiveness, and without forgiveness all the blessings of eternity hang in jeopardy. As the transgressor moves deeper and deeper in his sin, the error is entrenched more deeply and the will to change is weakened, it becomes increasingly near-hopeless, and he skids down and down until either he does not want to climb back or he has lost the power to do so. (The Miracle of Forgiveness, p. 117) DGSM:39

**Elder George Albert Smith**

What is our difficulty, brethren and sisters? It is that men refuse to hear what the Lord has said. They refuse to pay attention to His wise counsel. They absolutely neglect to give credence to the things that He teaches us, and He will not be mocked. He gives us the advice and the counsel that we need, but He will not compel us. But if we refuse, we lose our opportunity and it passes away from us, in many cases to return again no more forever. CR1933Apr:71

**Alma, the younger,**
*quoted by Mormon*

And now, my brethren, I wish from the inmost part of my heart, yea, with great anxiety even unto pain, that ye would hearken unto my words, and cast off your sins, and not procrastinate the day of your repentance; (*Alma preaches repentance to his brethren in the gospel, about 82 B.C.*) Alma 13:27

**Related Witnesses:**

**Recorded in Psalms**

I made haste, and delayed not to keep thy commandments. Ps.119:60

**Joseph Smith,**
*receiving the Word of the Lord*

And he that repents not, from him shall be taken even the light which he has received; for my Spirit shall not always strive with man, saith the Lord of Hosts. (*Revelation received during conference of elders of the Church, Nov. 1, 1831*) D&C 1:33

**628. Repeated repentance following the same repeated transgressions is not complete repentance.**

**Joseph Smith,**
*quoted by Elder Joseph Fielding Smith*

Repentance is a thing that cannot be trifled with every day. Daily transgression and daily repentance is not that which is pleasing in the sight of God. (*Joseph instructs the brethren at a conference of the Twelve, June 1839*) HC3:379; TPJS:148; DGSM:39

**Elder Spencer W. Kimball**

Those who feel that they can sin and be forgiven and then return to sin and be forgiven again and again must straighten out their thinking. Each previously forgiven sin is added to the new one and the whole gets to be a heavy load. ¶ Thus when a man has made up his mind to change his life, there must be no turning back. Any reversal, even in a small degree, is greatly to his detriment. (The Miracle of Forgiveness, p. 170) TLDP:548

**Elder Joseph Fielding Smith**

Now, when people come into this Church they should, by all means, subscribe to the regulations which the Lord himself has laid down by commandment. But does that mean that after we are in the Church, after we have confessed our sins and have forsaken them, that we can return to them after membership has been secured? That would not be consistent. Woe unto all those who are disobedient after they have made the preparation which is expressed in this commandment [See 2Ne.9:27.] which I have read to you—woe unto them. CR1941Oct:93

**Hugh B. Brown**

When we speak of the continual need of repentance, let it not be understood that we refer to a cycle of sinning and repenting and sinning again. That is not complete repentance. We must see the right and follow it, recognize the wrong and forsake it with a "Godly sorrow" if we would obtain the blessing of complete repentance. A growing conception of the good life must be accompanied by constant adjustment thereto if one would achieve harmony with the will of God. (Eternal Quest, pp. 99-102) DGSM:39

**President Harold B. Lee**

The miracle of forgiveness is available to all of those who turn from their evil doings and return no more, because the Lord has said in a revelation to us in our day: " . . . go your ways and sin no more; but unto that soul who sinneth [meaning again] shall the former sins return, saith the

Lord your God." (D&C 82:7) Have that in mind, all of you who may be troubled with a burden of sin. CR1973Apr:178

**President Brigham Young**

You cannot constantly be sinning a little and repenting, and retain the Spirit of the Lord as your constant companion. (*In Tabernacle, Feb. 16, 1862, JD9:220*) TLDP:546

**Related Witnesses:**

**Joseph Smith**

[G]o your ways and sin no more; but unto that soul who sinneth [meaning again] shall the former sins return, saith the Lord your God. (*Revelation, April 30, 1832*) D&C 82:7

**President Harold B. Lee**

When you have done all you can within your power to overcome your mistakes, and you have determined in your heart that you will never repeat them again, then you can have that peace of conscience by which you will know that your sins have been forgiven. ACR(Mexico City)1972:103

---

## (3) Steps of Repentance

**Author's Note:** Elder Spencer W. Kimball is quoted hereafter stating repentance seems to fall into five steps. The Doctrinal Restatements that follow cover each of these five steps. They are:

1. Sorrow for sin.
2. Abandonment of sin.
3. Confession of sin.
4. Restitution for sin.
5. Doing the will of the Lord.

**629. Sorrow for sin is essential to the spirit of repentance.**

**Elder Spencer W. Kimball**

Repentance seems to fall into five steps: ¶ 1. Sorrow for sin. ¶ 2. Abandonment of sin. ¶ 3. Confession of sin. ¶ 4. Restitution for sin. ¶ 5. Doing the will of the Lord. ("Be Ye Clean," Brigham Young University Speeches of the Year, Provo, 1954, pp. 8-9) TLDP:550

**Abraham H. Cannon**

Then we want them [men] to be filled with the spirit of repentance, which follows faith, and which is the natural result of faith in God; for if men are filled with faith in the Father and in the Son, they will naturally desire to place themselves in a condition to be fit associates for such holy beings, and they will look back upon their past lives with sorrow—with a sorrow

which will prompt them to be more righteous, more God-fearing, more upright, in the future. Then repentance of sin will come upon them; . . . a repentance that prompts men to make restitution, as far as it is possible for them to do so, for the sins which they have committed, and to restore four-fold, if necessary, in order to obtain pardon for the wrong done. (Millennial Star, July 18, 1895, p. 453) TLDP:546

**Elder Joseph F. Smith**

True repentance is not only sorrow for sins, and humble penitence and contrition before God, but it involves the necessity of turning away from them, a discontinuance of all evil practices and deeds, a thorough reformation of life, a vital change from evil to good, from vice to virtue, from darkness to light. Not only so, but to make restitution, so far as it is possible, for all the wrongs we have done, to pay our debts, and restore to God and man their rights—that which is due them from us. This is true repentance, and the exercise of the will and all the powers of body and mind is demanded, to complete this glorious work of repentance. (Gospel Doctrine, pp. 100-01) TLDP:549; DGSM:40, in part.

**George Q. Cannon**

If you and I and all who profess to be the followers of the Lord Jesus will bow down before him with humble hearts, each of us with a broken heart and contrite spirit, what will be the effect? Why, we will confess our faults to him, because they will be plain in our sight, we will see ourselves in the light of the Spirit of God, and the spirit of repentance will rest down upon us. (*In Tabernacle, July 27, 1879, JD20:289*) TLDP:546

**Orson Pratt,**
*quoted by James E. Talmage*

Repentance, then, is not only a confession of sins, with a sorrowful, contrite heart, but a fixed, settled purpose to refrain from every evil way. AF:102

**Related Witnesses:**

**King Benjamin,**
*quoted by Mormon*

And again, believe that ye must repent of your sins and forsake them, and humble yourselves before God; and ask in sincerity of heart that he would forgive you; and now, if you believe all these things see that ye do them. 11. And again I say unto you as I have said before, that as ye have come to the knowledge of the glory of God, or if ye have known of his goodness and have tasted of his love, and have received a remission of your sins, which causeth such exceedingly great joy in your souls, even so I would that ye should remember, and always retain in remembrance, the greatness of God, and your own nothingness, and his goodness and long-suffering towards you, unworthy creatures, and humble yourselves even in the depths of humility, calling on the name of the Lord daily, and standing steadfastly in the faith of that which is to come, which was spoken by the mouth of the angel. 12. And behold, I say unto you that if ye do this ye shall always rejoice, and be filled with the love of God, and always retain a remission of your sins; and ye shall grow in the knowledge of the glory of him that created you, or in the knowledge of that which is just and true. (*King Benjamin addresses his people, about 124 B.C.*) Mosiah 4:10-12

### James E. Talmage

As soon as one has come to recognize the existence and authority of God, he feels a respect for divine laws, and a conviction of his own unworthiness. His wish to please the Father, whom he has so long ignored, will impel him to forsake sin; and this impulse will acquire added strength from the sinner's natural and commendable desire to make reparation, if possible, and so avert the dire results of his own waywardness. With the zeal inspired by fresh conviction, he will crave an opportunity of showing by good works the sincerity of his newly developed faith; and he will regard the remission of his sins as the most desirable of blessings. AF:99

### King Benjamin, *quoted by Mormon*

And now I ask, can ye say aught of yourselves? I answer you, Nay. Ye cannot say that ye are even as much as the dust of the earth; yet ye were created of the dust of the earth; but behold, it belongeth to him who created you. (*King Benjamin addresses his people, about 124 B.C.*) Mosiah 2:25

### Elder Spencer W. Kimball

Repentance is the key to forgiveness. It opens the door to happiness and peace and points the way to salvation in the kingdom of God. It unlocks the spirit of humility in the soul of man and makes him contrite of heart and submissive to the will of God. (The Miracle of Forgiveness, p. 133) TLDP:553

**Author's Note:** In the process of repentance we remind ourselves of the greatness of God, his goodness and longsuffering toward us, and in comparison we recognize we are nothing, thus humbling ourselves before God in the depths of humility and sorrow for sins.

## 630. Abandonment of sin is a necessary part of repentance.

### Elder Spencer W. Kimball

There is one crucial test of repentance. This is abandonment of the sin. Providing that a person discontinues his sin with the right motives—because of a growing consciousness of the gravity of the sin and a willingness to comply with the laws of the Lord—he is genuinely repenting. This criterion has been set by the Lord: "By this ye may know if a man repenteth of his sins—behold, he will confess them and forsake them." (D&C 58:43) (The Miracle of Forgiveness, p. 163) TLDP:548

### Joseph Smith

By this ye may know if a man repenteth of his sins—behold, he will confess them and forsake them. (*Revelation for the elders of the Church, Aug. 1, 1831*) D&C 58:43

### President Joseph F. Smith

True repentance is not only sorrow for sins, and humble penitence and contrition before God, but it involves the necessity of turning away from them, a discontinuance of all evil practices and deeds, a thorough reformation of life, a vital change from evil to good, from vice to virtue, from darkness to light. Not only so, but to make restitution, so far as it is possible, for all the wrongs we have done, to pay our debts, and restore to God and man their rights—that which is due to them from us. (Gospel Doctrine, p. 100) DGSM:40

### President Brigham Young

Now, my brethren, you who have sinned, repent of your sins. I can say to you in regard to Jesus and the atonement (it is so written, and I firmly believe it), that Christ has died for all. He has paid the full debt, whether you receive the gift or not. But if we continue to sin, to lie, steal, bear false witness, we must repent of and forsake that sin to have the full efficacy of the blood of Christ. Without this it will be of no effect; repentance must come, in order that the atonement may prove a benefit to us. (*In Bowery, April 8, 1867, JD11:375*) TLDP:544

### Elder Joseph Fielding Smith

Now, when people come into this Church they should, by all means, subscribe to the regulations which the Lord himself has laid down by commandment. But does that mean that after we are in the Church, after we have confessed our sins and have forsaken them, that we can return to them after membership has been secured? That would not be consistent. Woe unto all those who are disobedient after they have made the preparation which is expressed in this commandment [2Ne.9:27] which I have read to you—woe unto them. CR1941Oct:93

**Hugh B. Brown**

When we speak of the continual need of repentance, let it not be understood that we refer to a cycle of sinning and repenting and sinning again. That is not complete repentance. We must see the right and follow it, recognize the wrong and forsake it with a "Godly sorrow" if we would obtain the blessing of complete repentance. A growing conception of the good life must be accompanied by constant adjustment thereto if one would achieve harmony with the will of God. (Eternal Quest, pp. 99-102) DGSM:39

**King Benjamin,**
*quoted by Mormon*

And again, believe that ye must repent of your sins and forsake them, and humble yourselves before God; and ask in sincerity of heart that he would forgive you; and now, if you believe all these things see that ye do them. (*King Benjamin addresses his people, about 124 B.C.*) Mosiah 4:10

**President Brigham Young**

You cannot constantly be sinning a little and repenting, and retain the Spirit of the Lord as your constant companion. (*In Tabernacle, Feb. 16, 1862, JD9:220*) TLDP:546

**Related Witnesses:**
**Joseph Smith**

Go ye out from Babylon. Be ye clean that bear the vessels of the Lord. (*Revelation received Nov. 3, 1831; the Saints are to prepare for the Second Coming*) D&C 133:5

**Joseph Smith,**
*receiving the Word of the Lord*

Verily, thus saith the Lord: It shall come to pass that every soul who forsaketh his sins and cometh unto me, and calleth on my name, and obeyeth my voice, and keepeth my commandments, shall see my face and know that I am; (*Revelation received at Kirtland, Ohio, May 6, 1833*) D&C 93:1

**Joseph Smith**

Repentance is a thing that cannot be trifled with every day. Daily transgression and daily repentance is not that which is pleasing in the sight of God. (*Joseph instructs the brethren at a conference of the Twelve, June 1839*) HC3:379; DGSM:39; TPJS:148

---

**631. Confession of sin is a necessary part of repentance.**

**Joseph Smith**

By this ye may know if a man repenteth of his sins—behold, he will confess them and forsake them. (*Revelation for the elders of the Church, Aug. 1, 1831*) D&C 58:43

**Joseph Smith,**
*receiving the Word of the Lord*

Wherefore, I command you again to repent, lest I humble you with my almighty power; and that you confess your sins, lest you suffer these punishments of which I have spoken, . . . (*A commandment of God for Martin Harris, March 1830*) D&C 19:20

**Elder Spencer W. Kimball**

It follows that the ideal confession is voluntary, not forced. It is induced from within the offender's soul, not sparked by being found out in the sin. Such confession, like the voluntary humility of which Alma spoke (Alma 32:13-16), is a sign of growing repentance. It indicates the sinner's conviction of sin and his desire to abandon the evil practices. The voluntary confession is infinitely more acceptable in the sight of the Lord than is forced admission, lacking humility, wrung from an individual by questioning when guilt is evident. Such forced admission is not evidence of the humble heart which calls forth the Lord's mercy: " . . . For I, the Lord, forgive sins, and am merciful unto those *who confess* their sins with humble hearts." (D&C 61:2, italics added) (The Miracle of Forgiveness, p. 181) TLDP:551

**Joseph Smith,**
*receiving the Word of the Lord*

Nevertheless, he has sinned; but verily I say unto you, I, the Lord, forgive sins unto those who confess their sins before me and ask forgiveness, who have not sinned unto death. (*Revelation for the elders of the Church at Kirtland, Ohio, Sept. 11, 1831*) D&C 64:7

**Marion G. Romney**

[T]here are many among us whose distress and suffering are unnecessarily prolonged because they do not complete their repentance by confessing their sins. . . . ¶ Repeatedly he [the Savior] says that he forgives the sins of those who confess their sins with humbleness of heart, " . . . who have not sinned unto death." CR1955Oct:124

**Mormon**

Therefore I say unto you, Go; and whosoever transgresseth against me, him shall ye judge according to the sins which he has committed; and if he confess his sins before thee and me, and repenteth in the sincerity of his heart, him shall ye forgive, and I will forgive him also. 30. Yea, and as often as my people repent will I forgive them their trespasses against me. (*The voice of the Lord to Alma, about 120-100 B.C.*) Mosiah 26:29-30

### Recorded in Proverbs

He that covereth his sins shall not prosper: but whoso confesseth and forsaketh them shall have mercy. Prov.28:13

### John

If we confess our sins, he is faithful and just to forgive us our sins, and to cleanse us from all unrighteousness. (*Letter to the churches in Asia*) 1Jn.1:9

**Related Witnesses:**

### Mormon

And it came to pass that they did preach with great power, insomuch that they did confound many of those dissenters who had gone over from the Nephites, insomuch that they came forth and did confess their sins and were baptized unto repentance, and immediately returned to the Nephites to endeavor to repair unto them the wrongs which they had done. (*Nephi and Lehi, sons of Helaman, preach to the Lamanites and convert Nephite dissenters in Zarahemla, about 30 B.C.*) Hel.5:17

---

632. Confession of sins is to be made to the appropriate persons—not all sins are to be confessed publicly but are to be confessed where the confession belongs.

### Elder Harold B. Lee

That confession must be made first to him or her who has been most wronged by your acts. A sincere confession is not merely admitting guilt after the proof is already in evidence. If you have "offended many persons openly," your acknowledgment is to be made openly and before those whom you have offended that you might show your shame and humility and willingness to receive a merited rebuke. If your act is secret and has resulted in injury to no one but yourself, your confession should be in secret, that your Heavenly Father who hears in secret may reward you openly. Acts that may affect your standing in the Church, or your right to privileges or advancement in the Church, are to be promptly confessed to the bishop whom the Lord has appointed as a shepherd over every flock and commissioned to be a common judge in Israel. He may hear such confession in secret and deal justly and mercifully, as each case warrants. The unbaptized who is in sin may by following a similar course receive at the hands of an authorized elder of the Church, if otherwise prepared by an understanding of the gospel, baptism for the remission of his sins. (Decisions for Successful Living, p. 99) TLDP:551

### Marion G. Romney

We are to confess all our sins to the Lord. For transgressions which are wholly personal, affecting none but ourselves and the Lord, confession to ourselves and him would seem to be sufficient. . . . ¶ For misconduct which affects another, confession should also be made to the offended one and his forgiveness sought. ¶ Finally, where one's transgressions are of such a nature as would, unrepented of, put in jeopardy his right to membership or fellowship in the Church of Christ, full and effective confession requires confession by the repentant sinner to his bishop or other proper presiding Church officer—not that the Church officer could forgive him the sin (for this power rests in the Lord himself and those only to whom he specifically delegates the power), but rather that the Church, acting through its duly appointed officers (the power is not in the officer but in the Church), might with full knowledge of the facts take such action with respect to Church discipline as the circumstances require and merit. CR1980Oct:71; DGSM:40

### Elder Spencer W. Kimball

Knowing the hearts of men, and their intents, and their abilities to repent and regenerate themselves, the Lord waits to forgive until the repentance has matured. The transgressor must have a "broken heart and a contrite spirit" and be willing to humble himself and do all that is required. The confession of his major sins to a proper Church authority is one of those requirements made by the Lord. These sins include adultery, fornication, other sexual transgressions, and other sins of comparable seriousness. This procedure of confession assures proper controls and protection for the Church and its people and sets the feet of the transgressor on the path of true repentance. ¶ Many offenders in their shame and pride have satisfied their consciences, temporarily at least, with a few silent prayers to the Lord and rationalized that this was sufficient confession of their sins. "But I have confessed my sin to my Heavenly Father," they will insist, "and that is all that is necessary." This is not true where a major sin is involved. Then two sets of forgiveness are required to bring peace to the transgressor— one from the proper authorities of the Lord's Church, and one from the Lord himself. This is brought out in the Lord's clarification of Church administration as he gave it to Alma: "Therefore I say unto you, Go; and whosoever transgresseth against me, him shall ye judge according to the sins which he has committed; and if he confess his sins before thee and me, and repenteth in the sincerity of his heart, him shall ye forgive, and I will forgive him also." (See Mosiah 26:29.) ¶ From this, and from the Lord's word to modern Israel— " . . . confessing thy sins unto thy brethren, and before the Lord" (See D&C 59:12.)—it is plain that there are two confessions to make: one to the Lord and the other to "the brethren," meaning the proper ecclesiastical officers. (The Miracle of Forgiveness, pp. 179-80) TLDP:552-53

### President Brigham Young,
#### quoted by John A. Widtsoe
. . . I believe in coming out and being plain and honest with that which should be made public, and in keeping to yourselves that which should be kept. If you have your weaknesses, keep them hid from your brethren as much as you can. You never hear me ask the people to tell their follies. But when we ask the brethren, as we frequently do, to speak in sacrament meetings, we wish them, if they have injured their neighbors, to confess their wrongs; but do not tell about your nonsensical conduct that nobody knows of but yourselves. Tell to the public that which belongs to the public. If you have sinned against the people, confess to them. If you have sinned against a family or a neighborhood, go to them and confess. If you have sinned against your Ward, confess to your Ward. If you have sinned against one individual, take that person by yourselves and make your confession to him. And if you have sinned against your God, or against yourselves, confess to God, and keep the matter to yourselves, for I do not want to know anything about it. (*In Tabernacle, March 10, 1860, JD8:362*) DBY:158

### President Brigham Young,
#### quoted by John A. Widtsoe
If children have sinned against their parents, or husbands against their wives, or wives against their husbands, let them confess their faults one to another and forgive each other, and there let the confession stop; and then let them ask pardon from their God. Confess your sins to whoever you have sinned against, and let it stop there. If you have committed a sin against the community, confess to them. If you have sinned in your family, confess there. Confess your sins, iniquities, and follies, where that confession belongs, and, learn to classify your actions. (*In Tabernacle, Nov. 9, 1856, JD4:79*) DBY:204

### Elder Spencer W. Kimball
While the major sins such as those listed earlier in this chapter call for confession to the proper Church authorities, clearly such confession is neither necessary nor desirable for all sins.

Those of lesser gravity but which have offended others, marital differences, minor fits of anger, disagreements and such—should instead be confessed to the person or persons hurt and the matter should be cleared between the persons involved, normally without a reference to a Church authority. And if one confesses his sins, there is an obligation on the part of Church membership to accept and forgive, to eradicate from their hearts the memory of the transgression or ill feelings. (The Miracle of Forgiveness, p. 185) TLDP:551-52

**Related Witnesses:**
### Elder Spencer W. Kimball
Generally it is unwise and quite unnecessary to confess the same sin over and over again. If a major transgression has been fully confessed to and cleared by the proper authority, the person may usually clear himself in any future interview by explaining that this is so and giving the authority's name. Providing there has been no repetition of the offense, nor a commission of any other serious transgression, usually the matter may be considered settled. (The Miracle of Forgiveness, pp. 187-88) TLDP:552

---

### 633. Making restitution, as much as is possible, is part of complete repentance.

### Elder Joseph F. Smith
When we commit sin, it is necessary that we repent of it and make restitution as far as lies in our power. When we cannot make restitution for the wrong we have done, then we must apply for the grace and mercy of God to cleanse us from that iniquity. ¶ Men cannot forgive their own sins; they cannot cleanse themselves from the consequences of their sins. Men can stop sinning and can do right in the future, and so far their acts are acceptable before the Lord and worthy of consideration. But who shall repair the wrongs they have done to themselves and to others, which it seems impossible for them to repair themselves? By the atonement of Jesus Christ the sins of the repentant shall be washed away; though they be crimson they shall be made white as wool. This is the promise given to you. We who have not paid our tithing in the past, and are therefore under obligations to the Lord, which we are not in position to discharge, the Lord requires that no longer at our hands, but will forgive us for the past if we will observe this law honestly in the future. That is generous and kind, and I feel grateful for it. CR1899Oct:41-42

## Recorded in Leviticus

Then it shall be, because he hath sinned, and is guilty, that he shall restore that which he took violently away, or the thing which he hath deceitfully gotten, or that which was delivered him to keep, or the lost thing which he found, 5. Or all that about which he hath sworn falsely; he shall even restore it in the principal, and shall add the fifth part more thereto, and give it unto him to whom it appertaineth, in the day of his trespass offering. (*To Moses, the Lord reveals his laws for ancient Israel*) Lev.6:4-5

## Elder Spencer W. Kimball

One may trespass in ignorance. Should anyone be in sin yet be unaware of the evil nature of his actions, he should be required to make restitution so far as possible when brought to a realization of his sin. . . . ¶ A thief or burglar may make partial restitution by returning that which was stolen. A liar may make the truth known and correct to some degree the damage done by the lie. A gossip who has slandered the character of another may make partial restitution through strenuous effort to restore the good name of the person he harmed. If by sin or carelessness the wrongdoer has destroyed property, he may restore or pay for it in full or in part. ¶ If a man's actions have brought sorrow and disgrace to his wife and children, in his restitution he must make every effort to restore their confidence and love by an overabundance of filial devotion and fidelity. This is true also of wives and mothers. Likewise if children have wronged their parents, a part of their program of repentance must be to right those wrongs and to honor their parents. ¶ As a rule there are many things which a repentant soul can do to make amends. "A broken heart and a contrite spirit" will usually find ways to restore to some extent. The true spirit of repentance demands that he who injures shall do everything in his power to right the wrong. (The Miracle of Forgiveness, pp. 194-95) TLDP:550

## Ezekiel

If the wicked restore the pledge, give again that he had robbed, walk in the statutes of life, without committing iniquity; he shall surely live, he shall not die. (*Ezekiel preaches the word of the Lord*) Ezek.33:15

## President Harold B. Lee

If the time comes when you have done all that you can to repent of your sins, whoever you are, wherever you are, and have made amends and restitution to the best of your ability; if it be something that will affect your standing in the Church and you have gone to the proper authorities, then you will want that confirming answer as to whether or not the Lord has accepted of you. In your soul-searching, if you seek for and you find that peace of conscience, by that token you may know that the Lord has accepted of your repentance. CR1973Apr:177; DGSM:41

## Abraham H. Cannon

Then repentance of sin will come upon them; . . . a repentance that prompts men to make restitution, as far as it is possible for them to do so, for the sins which they have committed, and to restore four-fold, if necessary, in order to obtain pardon for the wrong done. (Millennial Star, July 18, 1895, p. 453) TLDP:546

## Recorded in Numbers

Then they shall confess their sin which they have done: and he shall recompense his trespass with the principal thereof, and add unto it the fifth part thereof, and give it unto him against whom he hath trespassed. (*Revelation to Moses for the children of Israel*) Num.5:7

**Related Witnesses:**

### Mormon

And it came to pass that they did preach with great power, insomuch that they did confound many of those dissenters who had gone over from the Nephites, insomuch that they came forth and did confess their sins, and were baptized unto repentance, and immediately returned to the Nephites to endeavor to repair unto them the wrongs which they had done. (*Nephi and Lehi, sons of Helaman, preach to the Lamanites and convert Nephite dissenters in Zarahemla, about 30 B.C.*) Hel.5:17

---

634. Obedience—living the commandments of the Lord—is one of the requisites for repentance.

### President Spencer W. Kimball

One of the requisites for repentance is the living of the commandments of the Lord. Perhaps few people realize that as an important element; though one may have abandoned a particular sin and even confessed it to his bishop, yet he is not repentant if he has not developed a life of action and service and righteousness, which the Lord has indicated to be very necessary: "He that repents and does the commandments of the Lord shall be forgiven." (D&C 1:32) ("What Is True Repentance?" EN1974May:4; The Teachings of Spencer W. Kimball, p. 105) TLDP:548

### John A. Widtsoe

To repent is first to turn from old practices. Thus, he who violates any of God's laws renders himself liable to certain punishment, but, if he repents, and sins no more, the punishments are averted. Naturally, such a change of heart and action can come only after faith has been established. No man will change a habit without a satisfactory reason. In fact, all the actions of men should be guided by reason. Repentance then is a kind of obedience or active faith; and is great in proportion to the degree of faith possessed by the individual. Certainly, the repentance of no man can transcend his faith, which includes his knowledge. . . . ¶ To repent is more than to turn from incorrect practices. It implies also the adoption of new habits. The man who has turned from his sins, may learn of a law, which he has never violated, yet which if obeyed, means progress for him. If he does not follow such a law, but remains neutral in its presence, he certainly is a sinner. To repent from such sin, is to obey each higher law as it appears. In the spiritual life, it is impossible for the person who desires the greatest joy to remain passive in the presence of new principles. He must embrace them; live them; make them his own. . . . ¶ The obedience yielded to the new knowledge is a kind of repentance. When a person, in religion or science, ceases to break law, he ceases from active evil; when he accepts a new law, he ceases from passive evil. No repentance can be complete which does not cease from both active and passive evil. ¶ Viewed in this manner, then, repentance is obedience to law and is active faith. The law, before it is obeyed, must be understood—that is, faith must precede repentance. Therefore, the obedience yielded can increase only with the knowledge or faith of the individual. As the Prophet Joseph Smith stated it, "No man can be saved in ignorance" and "a person is saved no faster than he gains intelligence." ¶ Repentance is as truly the second principle of action for individuals, in the domain of science as of theology. (Joseph Smith as Scientist, pp. 80-82) TLDP:547-48

**Joseph Smith,**
*receiving the Word of the Lord*
Verily, thus saith the Lord: It shall come to pass that every soul who forsaketh his sins and cometh unto me, and calleth on my name, and obeyeth my voice, and keepeth my commandments, shall see my face and know that I am; (*Revelation received at Kirtland, Ohio, May 6, 1833*) D&C 93:1

**George Teasdale**
Our message to the sinner is that if he will repent, cease to do evil and learn to do well, he shall receive a remission of his sins, through obedience to the Gospel and dedicating the rest of his life to the service of God. What a bright

and glorious outlook, to be redeemed from sin and to have the privilege of walking in the light, receiving salvation, and obtaining a glorious resurrection! CR1903Oct:50

**President Brigham Young,**
**Heber C. Kimball, Jedediah M. Grant**
(First Presidency)
To all the honest in heart throughout the world, both of high and low degree, we say "repent, and be baptized for the remission of your sins," obey the ordinances of the Gospel through the administrations of the servants of the living God, for the judgments of the Almighty are upon you, flee therefore from the sinks of iniquity and corruption, lest the fiery indignation of the Lord also consume you with the wicked, of whom He has decreed that He will empty the earth. (*Twelfth General Epistle of the Presidency, Aug. 11, 1855*) (Deseret News, April 25, 1855) MOFP2:171; TLDP:544-45
**Related Witnesses:**
**Elder Joseph Fielding Smith**
Now, when people come into this Church they should, by all means, subscribe to the regulations which the Lord himself has laid down by commandment. But does that mean that after we are in the Church, after we have confessed our sins and have forsaken them, that we can return to them after membership has been secured? That would not be consistent. Woe unto all those who are disobedient after they have made the preparation which is expressed in this commandment [2Ne.9:27] which I have read to you—woe unto them. CR1941Oct:93

**Joseph Smith**
For unless a person does know that he is walking according to the will of God, it would be offering an insult to the dignity of the Creator were he to say that he would be a partaker of his glory when he should be done with the things of this life. But when he has this knowledge, and most assuredly knows that he is doing the will of God, his confidence can be equally strong that he will be a partaker of the glory of God. (*Lectures on Faith delivered to the School of the Prophets, 1834-35*) LOF6:6

## (4) Obtaining Forgiveness

635. There can be complete divine forgiveness of sin.

### George F. Richards
The burden of sin and remorse is something to be dreaded and to be avoided. The Savior has provided, however, a means by which the sins

of deepest dye may be forgiven, and that, by repentance and obedience unto the laws and ordinances of the gospel, made effective through the atonement of our Lord and Savior, Jesus Christ. CR1946Apr:98

**Joseph Smith,**
*receiving the Word of the Lord*

Nevertheless, he that repents and does the commandments of the Lord shall be forgiven; 33. And he that repents not, from him shall be taken even the light which he has received; for my Spirit shall not always strive with man, saith the Lord of Hosts. (*Revelation through Joseph Smith during conference of elders of the Church, Nov. 1, 1831*) D&C 1:32-33

**Ezekiel**

But if the wicked will turn from all his sins that he hath committed, and keep all my statutes, and do that which is lawful and right, he shall surely live, he shall not die. 22. All his transgressions that he hath committed, they shall not be mentioned unto him: in his righteousness that he hath done he shall live. . . . 27. Again, when the wicked man turneth away from his wickedness that he hath committed, and doeth that which is lawful and right, he shall save his soul alive. (*Ezekiel preaches the word of the Lord*) Ezek.18:21-22,27

**George Teasdale**

He hath said to the sinner, "When the wicked man turneth away from his wickedness that he hath committed, and doeth that which is lawful and right, he shall save his soul alive" [Ezek.18:27]. This is a precious promise to the erring children of the Father. Our message to the sinner is that if he will repent, cease to do evil and learn to do well, he shall receive a remission of his sins, through obedience to the Gospel and dedicating the rest of his life to the service of God. What a bright and glorious outlook, to be redeemed from sin and to have the privilege of walking in the light, receiving salvation, and obtaining a glorious resurrection! CR1903Oct:50

**President Harold B. Lee**

If the time comes when you have done all that you can to repent of your sins, whoever you are, wherever you are, and have made amends and restitution to the best of your ability; if it be something that will affect your standing in the Church and you have gone to the proper authorities, then you will want that confirming answer as to whether or not the Lord has accepted of you. In your soul-searching, if you seek for and you find that peace of conscience, by that token you may know that the Lord has accepted of your repentance. Satan would have you think

otherwise and sometimes persuade you that now having made one mistake, you might go on and on without turning back. That is one of the great falsehoods. The miracle of forgiveness is available to all of those who turn from their evil doings and return no more, because the Lord has said in a revelation to us in our day: " . . . go your ways and sin no more; but unto that soul who sinneth [meaning again] shall the former sins return, saith the Lord your God." (D&C 82:7) Have that in mind, all of you who may be troubled with a burden of sin. (*Revelation received at Kirtland, Ohio, May 6, 1833*) CR1973Apr:177-78

**Joseph Smith,**
*receiving the Word of the Lord*

Verily, thus saith the Lord: It shall come to pass that every soul who forsaketh his sins and cometh unto me, and calleth on my name, and obeyeth my voice, and keepeth my commandments, shall see my face and know that I am; (*Revelation received at Kirtland, Ohio, May 6, 1833*) D&C 93:1

**Joseph Smith,**
*receiving the Word of the Lord*

Behold, he who has repented of his sins, the same is forgiven, and I, the Lord, remember them no more. (*Revelation for the elders of the Church, Aug. 1, 1831*) D&C 58:42

**Joseph Smith,**
*receiving the Word of the Lord*

Nevertheless, he has sinned; but verily I say unto you, I, the Lord, forgive sins unto those who confess their sins before me and ask forgiveness, who have not sinned unto death. (*Revelation for the elders of the Church at Kirtland, Ohio, Sept. 11, 1831*) D&C 64:7

**Joseph Smith,**
*receiving the Word of the Lord*

Behold, verily thus saith the Lord unto you, O ye elders of my church, who are assembled upon this spot, whose sins are now forgiven you, for I, the Lord, forgive sins, and am merciful unto those who confess their sins with humble hearts; (*Revelation to the elders of the Church, Aug. 12, 1831*) D&C 61:2

**Marion G. Romney**

Forgiveness is as wide as repentance. Every person will be forgiven for all the transgression of which he truly repents. If he repents of all his sins, he shall stand spotless before God because of the atonement of our Master and Savior Jesus Christ. . . . Such is the gift of God's merciful plan of redemption. CR1955Oct:124

**Isaiah**

Wash you, make you clean; put away the evil of your doings from before mine eyes; cease to do evil; . . . 18. Come now, and let us reason together, saith the LORD: though your sins be as scarlet, they shall be as white as snow; though they be red like crimson, they shall be as wool. (*Isaiah preaches the word of the Lord*) Isa.1:16,18

### Moroni, son of Mormon

But as oft as they repented and sought forgiveness, with real intent, they were forgiven. (*Moroni writes for the benefit of the Lamanites, A.D. 400-421*) Moro.6:8

### Moroni, son of Mormon

O then ye unbelieving, turn ye unto the Lord; cry mightily unto the Father in the name of Jesus, that perhaps ye may be found spotless, pure, fair, and white, having been cleansed by the blood of the Lamb, at that great and last day. (*Moroni calls upon those who do not believe in Christ to repent, A.D. 400-421*) Morm.9:6

### Peter,
### *recorded in Acts*

Repent ye therefore, and be converted, that your sins may be blotted out, when the times of refreshing shall come from the presence of the Lord; (*Peter preaches repentance*) Acts 3:19

**Related Witnesses:**

### Elder Joseph Fielding Smith

It appears to me the most extreme folly to believe, much less to teach, that the atonement of Jesus Christ merely paved the way for the remission and forgiveness of the sins of those who truly repent; and after one has truly repented and been baptized, he still must pay the price to some extent for his transgressions. This means that the man has not been truly forgiven, but is placed on probation with a penalty attached. This idea, which has so often been taught by saying that the holes remain after the nails are withdrawn, is a false doctrine when applied to the atonement for the truly repentant sinner. (Doctrines of Salvation, 2:332) TLDP:555

### Jeremiah

[T]hey shall all know me, from the least of them unto the greatest of them, saith the LORD; for I will forgive their iniquity, and I will remember their sin no more. (*Jeremiah speaks of the last days*) Jer.31:34

**Author's Note:** To be forgiven of sins means to receive a complete release from the penalty for sins. This is a remission of sins.

---

636. Repentance brings peace of conscience.

### Marion G. Romney

To these witnesses I add my testimony that repentance brings to the soul who has faith in the Lord Jesus Christ and his gospel forgiveness, with the attendant blessings of "peace" and "rest". CR1980Oct:73

### King Benjamin,
### *quoted by Mormon*

And it came to pass that after they had spoken these words the Spirit of the Lord came upon them, and they were filled with joy, having received a remission of their sins, and having peace of conscience, because of the exceeding faith which they had in Jesus Christ who should come, according to the words which king Benjamin had spoken unto them. (*King Benjamin concludes his discourse, about 124 B.C.*) Mosiah 4:3

### President Harold B. Lee

In your soul-searching, if you seek for and you find that peace of conscience, by that token you may know that the Lord has accepted of your repentance. Satan would have you think otherwise and sometimes persuade you that now having made one mistake, you might go on and on without turning back. That is one of the great falsehoods. The miracle of forgiveness is available to all of those who turn from their evil doings and return no more, because the Lord has said in a revelation to us in our day: " . . . go your ways and sin no more; but unto that soul who sinneth [meaning again] shall the former sins return, saith the Lord your God." (D&C 82:7) Have that in mind, all of you who may be troubled with a burden of sin. CR1973-Apr:177-78

### Boyd K. Packer

I repeat, as Bishop Featherstone said, my young friends, that there is a great cleansing power. Know that you can be clean. If you are outside of the Church, the covenant of baptism itself represents, among other things, a washing and a cleansing. ¶ For those of you who are in the Church there is a way, not entirely painless, but certainly possible. You can stand clean and spotless before him. Guilt will be gone, and you can be at peace. Go to your bishop or your branch president. He holds the key to this cleansing power. Go and have an interview with him, and then you do what he says, and you can become clean again. ACR(Stockholm) 1974:84

### Richard L. Evans

And you who are tried and tempted by appetites, by evil in its subtle shapes; you who have been careless in your conduct, who have lived the kind of lives that fall short of what you know you should have lived—and are contending with conscience and are torn inside your-selves: You also are not alone in life, for the Lord God who gave you life has also given the glorious principle of repentance, which, upon sincere turning away from false ways, can restore again the blessed peace that comes with quiet conscience. (Richard L. Evans: The Man and the Message, p. 139) TLDP:553-54

**Elder Spencer W. Kimball**
Confession brings peace. How often have peo-ple departed from my office relieved and lighter of heart than for a long time! Their burdens were lighter, having been shared. They were free. The truth had made them free. ¶ Having warned of excruciating pain and punishments, the Lord said: ". . . confess your sins, lest you suffer these punishments of which I have spo-ken, . . . " (D&C 19:20) There is substantial psychological strength in confession. Confession is not only the revealing of errors to proper authorities, but the sharing of burdens to lighten them. One lifts at least part of his bur-den and places it on other shoulders which are able and willing to help carry the load. Then there comes satisfaction in having taken anoth-er step in doing all that is possible to rid oneself of the burden of transgression. (The Miracle of Forgiveness, pp. 187-88) TLDP:552

**Related Witnesses:**
**Joseph Smith**
For unless a person does know that he is walk-ing according to the will of God, it would be offering an insult to the dignity of the Creator were he to say that he would be a partaker of his glory when he should be done with the things of this life. But when he has this knowl-edge, and most assuredly knows that he is doing the will of God, his confidence can be equally strong that he will be a partaker of the glory of God. (Lectures on Faith delivered to the School of the Prophets, 1834-35) LOF6:6

**Alma, the younger**
*quoted by Mormon*
Now, how could a man repent except he should sin? How could he sin if there was no law? How could there be a law save there was a pun-ishment? 18. Now, there was a punishment affixed, and a just law given, which brought remorse of conscience unto man. 19. Now, if there was no law given—if a man murdered he should die—would he be afraid he would die if he should murder? 20. And also, if there was no law given against sin men would not be afraid to sin. 21. And if there was no law given, if men sinned what could justice do, or mercy either, for they would have no claim upon the creature? 22. But there is a law given, and a

punishment affixed, and a repentance granted; which repentance mercy claimeth; otherwise, justice claimeth the creature and executeth the law, and the law inflicteth the punishment; if not so, the works of justice would be destroyed, and God would cease to be God. (Alma speaks to his son Corianton concerning the resurrec-tion of the dead, about 73 B.C.) Alma 42:17-22

**John**
And they which heard it, being convicted by their own conscience, went out one by one, beginning at the eldest, even unto the last: and Jesus was left alone, and the woman standing in the midst. (Jesus says he that is without sin, let him cast the first stone, when the scribes and Pharisees bring before him a woman taken in adultery) John 8:9

**Paul**
Now the Spirit speaketh expressly, that in the lat-ter times some shall depart from the faith, giving heed to seducing spirits, and doctrines of devils; 2. Speaking lies in hypocrisy; having their con-science seared with a hot iron; (Letter to his assistant Timothy, about A.D. 64) 1Tim.4:1-2

**Alma, the younger**
*quoted by Mormon*
Yea, and I know that good and evil have come before all men; he that knoweth not good from evil is blameless; but he that knoweth good and evil, to him it is given according to his desires, whether he desireth good or evil, life or death, joy or remorse of conscience. (Alma discourses on the principle of repentance, about 76 B.C.) Alma 29:5

**Paul**
And herein do I exercise myself, to have always a conscience void of offence toward God, and toward men. (Paul defends himself and his doc-trine before Felix) Acts 24:16

**HYMNS Written by Prophets**
**Applicable to this Topic**

**Parley P. Pratt**
*Father in Heaven, We Do Believe*
HYMNS:180

Father in Heav'n, we do believe
The promise thou hast made;
Thy word with meekness we receive,
Just as thy Saints have said.

We now repent of all our sin
And come with broken heart,
And to thy covenant enter in
And choose the better part.

O Lord, accept us while we pray,
And all our sins forgive;
New life impart to us this day,
And bid the sinners live.

Humbly we take the sacrament
In Jesus' blessed name;
Let us receive thru covenant
The Spirit's heav'nly flame.

We will be buried in the stream
In Jesus' blessed name,
And rise, while light shall on us beam
The Spirit's heav'nly flame.

Baptize us with the Holy Ghost
And seal us as thine own,
That we may join the ransomed host
And with the Saints be one.

# List of Doctrines

## RESTORATION

### Restoration of the Gospel—and the Church—in the Dispensation of the Fulness of Time

*Doctrines Located in This Topic*

637. The restoration of all things in the last days was foretold by prophets of God.

638. The land of America was prepared for the restoration of all things in the latter days.

639. All the keys, power and authority of the priesthood have now been restored.

640. The gospel was restored to earth in these latter days by many ancient prophets, who visited the earth for that purpose.

641. The restored gospel will remain on earth until the end of time, never to be taken away again.

642. The restoration of the gospel in the latter days is the "marvelous work and a wonder" of the Lord.

643. The Church of Jesus Christ of Latter-day Saints was organized in these latter days by divine authority.

644. The Lord gave Joseph Smith the gift to translate the Book of Mormon plates, that this generation would have the word of the Lord.

645. Joseph Smith was chosen and called by the Lord to be a latter-day prophet.

*Doctrines on RESTORATION Located in Other Topics*

27. Present-day Christian churches have departed from the principles of the original Christian faith.

82. The restored church of Jesus Christ was organized on April 6, 1830, by divine revelation that specified this precise date.

131. The prophet Elijah restored to Joseph Smith the sealing power—power to seal together those who dwell on earth, and to seal those on earth to those who dwell in heaven.

230. Moses delivered the keys of the gathering of Israel to Joseph Smith.

575. Elijah, the ancient prophet, personally restored the sealing powers of the priesthood to earth in these latter days.

589. The Aaronic priesthood was restored to earth by John the Baptist, who personally bestowed the keys thereof upon Joseph Smith and Oliver Cowdery.

# RESTORATION

## Restoration of the Gospel—and the Church in the Dispensation of the Fulness of Time

**637.** The restoration of all things in the last days was foretold by prophets of God.

### Joseph Smith

All the ordinances and duties that ever have been required by the Priesthood under the directions and commandments of the Almighty in any of the dispensations, shall all be had in the last dispensation, therefore all things had under the authority of the Priesthood at any former period, shall be had again, bringing to pass the restoration spoken of by the mouth of all the Holy Prophets. ("History of Joseph Smith," Deseret News Weekly, Oct. 5, 1854, p. 107) TLDP:556

### James E. Talmage

It is further evident from the scriptures that the dispensation of the Gospel in the latter days is to be one of restoration and restitution, truly a "dispensation of the fulness of times." Paul declares it to be the good pleasure of the Lord, "That in the dispensation of the fulness of times he might gather together in one all things in Christ, both which are in heaven, and which are on earth; even in him." This prediction finds a parallel in an utterance of the prophet Nephi: "Wherefore, all things which have been revealed unto the children of men shall at that day be revealed." And in accord with this is the teaching of Peter: "Repent ye therefore, and be converted, that your sins may be blotted out, when the times of refreshing shall come from the presence of the Lord; And he shall send Jesus Christ, which before was preached unto you: Whom the heaven must receive until the times of restitution of all things, which God hath spoken by the mouth of all his holy prophets since the world began." AF:19

### Peter,
### recorded in Acts

Repent ye therefore, and be converted, that your sins may be blotted out, when the times of refreshing shall come from the presence of the Lord; 20. And he shall send Jesus Christ, which before was preached unto you: 21. Whom the heaven must receive until the times of restitution of all things, which God hath spoken by the mouth of all his holy prophets since the world began. (Peter preaches repentance) Acts 3:19-21

### Paul

Having made known unto us the mystery of his will, according to his good pleasure which he hath purposed in himself: 10. That in the dis-

pensation of the fulness of times he might gather together in one all things in Christ, both which are in heaven, and which are on earth; even in him. (Letter to the Saints at Ephesus in Asia Minor, about A.D. 62) Eph.1:9-10

### Nephi, son of Lehi

Wherefore, all things which have been revealed unto the children of men shall at that day be revealed. . . . (Nephi foretells of the last days, 559-545 B.C.) 2Ne.30:18

### Related Witnesses:
### John

And I saw another angel fly in the midst of heaven, having the everlasting gospel to preach unto them that dwell on the earth, and to every nation, and kindred, and tongue, and people, 7. Saying with a loud voice, Fear God, and give glory to him; for the hour of his judgment is come: and worship him that made heaven, and earth, and the sea, and the fountains of waters. (John sees the gospel restored in the last days by angelic ministry) Rev.14:6-7

### Malachi

Behold, I will send my messenger, and he shall prepare the way before me: and the Lord, whom ye seek, shall suddenly come to his temple, even the messenger of the covenant, whom ye delight in: behold, he shall come, saith the Lord of hosts. (To the people of Israel, about 430 B.C.) Mal.3:1

### President Spencer W. Kimball

Now, with the doctrines perverted, the priesthood gone, the organization corrupted, and the knowledge lost, there must come another awakening. And, as the prophet Daniel prophesied millennia ago, there finally came a day when another restoration of truth should come, this time never to be lost. We have that promise now, that even though individuals may fall the Church and the gospel are here to stay, and all the powers of the earth and hell cannot effect total apostasy again. ("Absolute Truth," Brigham Young University Speeches of the Year, 1977, p. 141) TLDP:559

### Daniel

Daniel answered in the presence of the king, and said, The secret which the king hath demanded cannot the wise men, the astrologers, the magicians, the soothsayers, shew unto the king; 28. But there is a God in heaven that revealeth secrets, and maketh known to the king Nebuchadnezzar what shall be in the latter days. Thy dream, and the visions of thy head upon thy bed, are these; . . . 34. Thou sawest till that a stone was cut out without hands, which smote the image upon his feet that were of iron and clay, and brake them to pieces. 35. . . . and the stone that smote the image became a great mountain, and filled the whole earth. *(Daniel interprets Nebuchadnezzar's dream of a stone cut from the mountain without hands)* Dan.2:27-28,34-35

### James E. Talmage

The visiting angel, Moroni, then repeated several prophecies which are recorded in the ancient scriptures. . . . Among other scriptures, Moroni cited the prophecies of Isaiah relating to the restoration of scattered Israel, and the promised reign of righteousness on earth, saying that the predictions were about to be fulfilled; also the words of Peter to the Jews, concerning the prophet who Moses said would be raised up, explaining that the prophet referred to was Jesus Christ, and that the day was near at hand when all who rejected the words of the Savior would be cut off from among the people. AF:11-12

### James E. Talmage

Ancient prophecy has been fulfilled in the restoration of the Gospel and the reestablishment of the Church upon the earth through his instrumentality. AF:14

### Joseph Smith,
*receiving the Word of the Lord*

And, behold, all the remainder of this work does contain all those parts of my gospel which my holy prophets, yea, and also my disciples, desired in their prayers should come forth unto this people. 47. And I said unto them that it should be granted unto them according to their faith in their prayers; *(Revelation in respect to the lost 116 manuscript pages, 1828)* D&C 10:46-47

---

### 638. The land of America was prepared for the restoration of all things in the latter days.

### Elder Joseph F. Smith

The Lord Almighty has prepared the way for the coming forth of the kingdom of God in this dispensation by establishing the republican government of the United States; a government affording the widest liberty and the greatest freedom to man that has ever been known to exist among men, outside of those governed by the direct communication of heaven. It was part of the design of the Almighty when He influenced our fathers to leave the old world

and come to this continent; He had a hand in the establishment of this government; He inspired the framers of the Constitution and the fathers of this nation to contend for their liberties; and He did this upon natural principles, that the way might be prepared, and that it might be possible for Him to establish His kingdom upon the earth, no more to be thrown down. *(At Logan, Utah, Feb. 6, 1881, JD22:44-45)* TLDP:557

### President Spencer W. Kimball

This restoration was preceded by a long period of preparation. The Pilgrims and other Europeans were inspired to find this American haven of refuge and thus people this land with honest and God-fearing citizens. Washington and his fellows were inspired to revolt from England and bring political liberty to this land, along with the more valuable treasure of religious liberty so that the soil might be prepared for the seed of the truth when it should again be sown. ("Absolute Truth," Brigham Young University Speeches of the Year, 1977, p. 141) TLDP:557

### Mark E. Petersen

The restoration of the gospel should be viewed through a perspective of two thousand years. ¶ It was not a sudden thing. Neither was it "done in a corner," . . . ¶ In its preparation it was a world movement requiring centuries of time. It involved the discovery of a new continent and its colonization by selected peoples. ¶ It encompassed wars between world powers of two centuries ago. Even the renaissance of medieval Europe was a part of this mighty drama, for an awakening of mankind was stimulated in the Dark Ages. ¶ The fundamental element of freedom in the world—the fight for both religious and political liberty—the firm establishment of human rights beginning with the Magna Charta—were all involved. (The Great Prologue, p. 1) TLDP:557-58

### Mark E. Petersen

Do you understand the steps that were taken? There was the great apostasy, then the preservation of the Western Hemisphere, next Columbus and the colonization movement, the Revolutionary War to set the colonists free, and then a constitutional form of government which guaranteed free speech and free religion, free assembly and free press. ¶ All of these events were acts of God leading up to one thing—the restoration of the gospel. It was only half a dozen years or so after America was established as a free constitutional nation that one of the great spirits in the preexistence was sent to earth to be born on December 23, 1805, in a little farmhouse; and he was named Joseph Smith. ("The Great Prologue," Brigham Young University Speeches of the Year, 1974, p. 468) TLDP:558

---

**639. All the keys, power, and authority of the priesthood have now been restored.**

**Elder Joseph Fielding Smith**

In this restoration it is necessary that the Church of Jesus Christ in its simplicity and truth be restored. All the keys and powers of priesthood held by the prophets of former dispensations must be conferred upon God's chosen representatives on the earth. In this manner all the authority and keys of priesthood of the past are to flow into the most glorious and greatest of dispensations, like clear streams flowing into a mighty river. The everlasting covenant once given to the ancients, and which Isaiah says was broken, must be restored. (Doctrines of Salvation, 1:167-68) DGSM:63

**President Heber J. Grant,
J. Reuben Clark, Jr., David O. McKay**
(First Presidency)

We solemnly declare that in these the latter-days, God has again spoken from the heavens through His chosen Prophet, Joseph Smith; that the Lord has, through that same Prophet, again revealed in its fulness His gospel,—the plan of life and salvation; that through that Prophet and his associates He has restored His holy Priesthood to the earth, from which it had been taken because of the wickedness of men; and that all the rights, powers, keys, and functions appertaining to the Priesthood as so restored are now vested in and exercised by the chosen and inspired leadership of His Church,—The Church of Jesus Christ of Latter-day Saints, even as the Priesthood has been exercised on the earth from the Beginning until this day, whenever His Church was here or His work had place among the children of men. CR1942Apr:88

**Joseph Smith**

For unto you, the Twelve, and those, the First Presidency, who are appointed with you to be your counselors and your leaders, is the power of this priesthood given, for the last days and for the last time, in the which is the dispensation of the fulness of times. 31. Which power you hold, in connection with all those who have received a dispensation at any time from the

beginning of the creation; 32. For verily I say unto you, the keys of the dispensation, which ye have received, have come down from the fathers, and last of all, being sent down from heaven unto you. (*Revelation for Thomas B. Marsh concerning the Twelve Apostles, July 23, 1837*) D&C 112:30-32

**President Brigham Young,
quoted by John A. Widtsoe**

It was decreed in the counsels of eternity, long before the foundations of the earth were laid, that he, Joseph Smith, should be the man, in the last dispensation of this world, to bring forth the word of God to the people, and receive the fulness of the keys and power of the Priesthood of the Son of God. (*In Tabernacle, Oct. 1859, JD7:289*) DBY:108; DGSM:63

**James E. Talmage**

However, [the restoration of the Book of Mormon scripture which is] a record of the Gospel is not the Gospel itself. Authority to administer in the saving ordinances of the Gospel is essential to the effective preaching and administration thereof; this was restored through John the Baptist, who brought the Aaronic Priesthood, and through Peter, James, and John, who brought again to earth the Melchizedek Priesthood. AF:415

**Orson F. Whitney**

Joseph Smith's next great service to the race was in opening this gospel dispensation—the Dispensation of the Fulness of times. What does that mean? To dispense is to distribute or deal out in portions, as when the sacrament of the Lord's Supper is dispensed to a religious congregation. In a larger sense, it signifies the opening of the heavens and the sending forth of the gospel and the powers of the Priesthood, as a boon and blessing to mankind. The term "dispensation" also defines the period during which these saving and exalting principles, thus sent forth, continue operative in pristine power and purity. There have been many dispensations of the gospel, though men know little concerning them. The gospel of Christ is more than "the power of God unto salvation;" it is the power of God unto exaltation, and was instituted as such before this earth rolled into existence, before Adam fell, and consequently before man had need of redemption and salvation. It is the way of eternal progress, the path to perfection, and has been upon earth in a series of dispensations reaching like a mighty chain from the days of Adam down to the present time. The great difference between this dispensation and all others is, that this is the last and the greatest, virtually all dispensations rolled into one. CR1920Apr:122

### Joseph Smith,
*receiving the Word of the Lord*

Behold, this is wisdom in me; wherefore, marvel not, for the hour cometh that I will drink of the fruit of the vine with you on the earth, and with Moroni, whom I have sent unto you to reveal the Book of Mormon, containing the fulness of my everlasting gospel, to whom I have committed the keys of the record of the stick of Ephraim; 6. And also with Elias, to whom I have committed the keys of bringing to pass the restoration of all things spoken by the mouth of all the holy prophets since the world began, concerning the last days; 7. And also John the son of Zacharias, which Zacharias he (Elias) visited and gave promise that he should have a son, and his name should be John, and he should be filled with the spirit of Elias; 8. Which John I have sent unto you, my servants, Joseph Smith, Jun., and Oliver Cowdery, to ordain you unto the first priesthood which you have received, that you might be called and ordained even as Aaron; 9. And also Elijah, unto whom I have committed the keys of the power of turning the hearts of the fathers to the children, and the hearts of the children to the fathers, that the whole earth may not be smitten with a curse; 10. And also with Joseph and Jacob, and Isaac, and Abraham, your fathers, by whom the promises remain; 11. And also with Michael, or Adam, the father of all, the prince of all, the ancient of days; 12. And also with Peter, and James, and John, whom I have sent unto you, by whom I have ordained you and confirmed you to be apostles, and especial witnesses of my name, and bear the keys of your ministry and of the same things which I revealed unto them; 13. Unto whom I have committed the keys of my kingdom, and a dispensation of the gospel for the last times; and for the fulness of times, in the which I will gather together in one all things, both which are in heaven, and which are on earth; (*Revelation to Joseph Smith through a heavenly messenger, Aug. 1830*) D&C 27:5-13

**Author's Note:** As to "Dispensations," President John Taylor spoke the following: ¶ "We have had in the different ages various dispensations; for instance what may be called the Adamic dispensation, the dispensation of Noah, the dispensation of Abraham, the dispensation of Moses and of the Prophets who associated with that dispensation; the dispensation of Jesus Christ, when he came to

take away the sins of the world by the sacrifice of himself, and in and through those various dispensations, certain principles, powers, privileges and Priesthoods have been developed. But in the dispensation of the fullness of times a combination or a fullness, a completeness of all those dispensations was to be introduced among the human family. If there was anything pertaining to the Adamic, (or what we may term more particularly the patriarchal) dispensation, it would be made manifest in the last days. If there was anything associated with Enoch and his city, and the gathering together of his people, or of the translation of his city, it would be manifested in the last days. If there was anything associated with the Melchizedek Priesthood in all its forms, powers, privileges and blessings at any time or in any part of the earth, it would be restored in the last days. If there was anything connected with the Aaronic Priesthood, that also would be developed in the last times. If there was anything associated with the Apostleship and Presidency that existed in the days of Jesus, or that existed in this continent, it would be developed in the last times; for this is the dispensation of the fullness of times, embracing all other times, all principles, all powers, all manifestations, all Priesthoods and the powers thereof that have existed in any age, in any part of the world, but have been kept hid from the wise and prudent, shall be revealed unto babes and sucklings in this the dispensation of the fullness of times." (JD22:298-99; TLDP:143)

---

640. The gospel was restored to earth in these latter days by many ancient prophets, who visited the earth for that purpose.

#### Elder Joseph Fielding Smith
The Elias who was to restore all things is a composite Elias. In other words, the restoration was not made by one personage, but many, and in speaking of Elias coming to restore all things, the Lord was using that title in a plural meaning, having in mind all the prophets who came to restore the fulness of the gospel. This would include John the Baptist, Peter, James and John, and every ancient prophet who restored keys from the days of Adam down. (Doctrines of Salvation, 1:174) TLDP:559

#### James E. Talmage
Restoration of the Church—From the facts

already stated it is evident that the Church was literally driven from the earth; in the first ten centuries immediately following the ministry of Christ the authority of the Holy Priesthood was lost from among men, and no human power could restore it. But the Lord in His mercy provided for the reestablishment of His Church in the last days, and for the last time; and prophets of olden time foresaw this era of renewed enlightenment, and sang in joyous tones of its coming. This restoration was effected by the Lord through the Prophet Joseph Smith, who, together with Oliver Cowdery, in 1829, received the Aaronic Priesthood under the hands of John the Baptist; and later the Melchizedek Priesthood under the hands of the former-day apostles, Peter, James, and John. By the authority thus bestowed the Church has been again organized with all its former completeness, and mankind once more rejoices in the priceless privileges of the counsels of God. The Latter-day Saints declare their high claim to the true Church organization, similar in all essentials to the organization effected by Christ among the Jews. This people of the last days profess to have the Priesthood of the Almighty, the power to act in the name of God, which power commands respect both on earth and in heaven. AF:185

### Parley P. Pratt, John Taylor, and Willard Richards

Remember, REMEMBER that the priesthood and the keys of power are held in eternity as well as in time, and, therefore, the servants of God who pass the veil of death are prepared to enter upon a greater and more effectual work, in the speedy accomplishment of the restoration of all things spoken of by his holy prophets. ¶ Remember that all the prophets and saints who have existed since the world began, are engaged in this holy work, and are yet in the vineyard, as well as the laborers of the eleventh hour, and are all pledged to establish the kingdom of God on the earth, and to give judgment unto the saints: therefore, none can hinder the rolling on of the eternal purposes of the great Jehovah. (*Excerpt from a letter—also signed by W. W. Phelps—from Nauvoo, Ill., shortly after the martyrdom of Joseph Smith, July 15, 1844*) HC7:189

### Mark E. Petersen

Adam brought the keys of the First Presidency. Joseph Smith received the keys of the First Presidency from Adam, who came back and visited him. Joseph Smith received the power of the gathering of Israel through Moses, who came back to see him. Elijah brought back the

powers that we use in connection with our temple work. ACR(Mexico City)1972:61

### LeGrand Richards

The Lord has raised up the Prophet Joseph Smith, as has been testified in this conference, and we have more revealed truth through him than any prophet that has ever lived upon the face of this earth as far as our records show. He has brought us things from those dead prophets who were to come to restore all things before the Savior could come again. CR1975Oct:76

### Joseph Smith

[I]t is necessary in the ushering in of the dispensation of the fulness of times, which dispensation is now beginning to usher in, that a whole and complete and perfect union, and welding together of dispensations, and keys, and powers, and glories should take place, and be revealed from the days of Adam even to the present time. And not only this, but those things which never have been revealed from the foundation of the world, but have been kept hid from the wise and prudent, shall be revealed unto babes and sucklings in this, the dispensation of the fulness of times. 19. Now, what do we hear in the gospel which we have received? A voice of gladness! A voice of mercy from heaven; and a voice of truth out of the earth; glad tidings for the dead; a voice of gladness for the living and the dead; glad tidings of great joy. How beautiful upon the mountains are the feet of those that bring glad tidings of good things, and that say unto Zion: Behold, thy God reigneth! As the dews of Carmel, so shall the knowledge of God descend upon them! 20. And again, what do we hear? Glad tidings from Cumorah! Moroni, an angel from heaven, declaring the fulfilment of the prophets—the book to be revealed. A voice of the Lord in the wilderness of Fayette, Seneca county, declaring the three witnesses to bear record of the book! The voice of Michael on the banks of the Susquehanna, detecting the devil when he appeared as an angel of light! The voice of Peter, James, and John in the wilderness between Harmony, Susquehanna county, and Colesville, Broome county, on the Susquehanna river, declaring themselves as possessing the keys of the kingdom, and of the dispensation of the fulness of times! 21. And again, the voice of God in the chamber of old Father Whitmer, in Fayette, Seneca county, and at sundry times, and in divers places through all the travels and tribulations of this Church of Jesus Christ of Latter-day Saints! And the voice of Michael, the archangel; the voice of Gabriel, and of Raphael, and of divers angels, from Michael or Adam down to the present time, all declaring their dispensation, their rights, their keys, their honors, their majesty and glory, and the power of their priesthood; giving line upon line, precept upon precept; here a little, and there a little; giving us consolation by holding forth that which is to come, confirming our hope! (*Written directions to the Church on baptism for the dead, Sept. 6, 1842*) D&C 128:18-21

**Joseph Smith,**
*receiving the Word of the Lord*
Behold, this is wisdom in me; wherefore, marvel not, for the hour cometh that I will drink of the fruit of the vine with you on the earth, and with Moroni, whom I have sent unto you to reveal the Book of Mormon, containing the fulness of my everlasting gospel, to whom I have committed the keys of the record of the stick of Ephraim; 6. And also with Elias, to whom I have committed the keys of bringing to pass the restoration of all things spoken by the mouth of all the holy prophets since the world began, concerning the last days; 7. And also John the son of Zacharias, which Zacharias he (Elias) visited and gave promise that he should have a son, and his name should be John, and he should be filled with the spirit of Elias; 8. Which John I have sent unto you, my servants, Joseph Smith, Jun., and Oliver Cowdery, to ordain you unto the first priesthood which you have received, that you might be called and ordained even as Aaron; 9. And also Elijah, unto whom I have committed the keys of the power of turning the hearts of the fathers to the children, and the hearts of the children to the fathers, that the whole earth may not be smitten with a curse; 10. And also with Joseph and Jacob, and Isaac, and Abraham, your fathers, by whom the promises remain; 11. And also with Michael, or Adam, the father of all, the prince of all, the ancient of days; 12. And also with Peter, and James, and John, whom I have sent unto you, by whom I have ordained you and confirmed you to be apostles, and especial witnesses of my name, and bear the keys of your ministry and of the same things which I revealed unto them; 13. Unto whom I have committed the keys of my kingdom, and a dispensation of the gospel for the last times; and for the fulness of times, in the which I will gather together in one all things, both which are in heaven, and which are on earth; (*Revelation to Joseph Smith through a heavenly messenger, Aug. 1830*) D&C 27:5-13

**Related Witnesses:**
**Joseph Smith**
After this vision closed, the heavens were again opened unto us; and Moses appeared before us, and committed unto us the keys of the gathering of Israel from the four parts of the earth, and the leading of the ten tribes from the land of the north. 12. After this, Elias appeared, and committed the dispensation of the gospel of Abraham, saying that in us and our seed all generations after us should be blessed. 13. After this vision had closed, another great and glorious vision burst upon us; for Elijah the prophet, who was taken to heaven without tasting death, stood before us, and said: 14. Behold, the time has fully come, which was spoken of by the mouth of Malachi—testifying that he [Elijah] should be sent, before the great and dreadful day of the Lord come— 15. To turn the hearts of the fathers to the children, and the children to the fathers, lest the whole earth be smitten with a curse— 16. Therefore, the keys of this dispensation are committed into your hands; and by this ye may know that the great and dreadful day of the Lord is near, even at the doors. (*Vision manifested to Joseph Smith and Oliver Cowdery in the Kirtland Temple, April 3, 1836*) D&C 110:11-16

**641. The restored gospel will remain on earth until the end of time, never to be taken away again.**

**President Spencer W. Kimball**
Now, with the doctrines perverted, the priesthood gone, the organization corrupted, and the knowledge lost, there must come another awakening. And, as the prophet Daniel prophesied millennia ago, there finally came a day when another restoration of truth should come, this time never to be lost. We have that promise now, that even though individuals may fall the Church and the gospel are here to stay, and all the powers of the earth and hell cannot effect total apostasy again. ("Absolute Truth," Brigham Young University Speeches of the Year, 1977, p. 141) TLDP:559

**Daniel**
And in the days of these kings shall the God of heaven set up a kingdom, which shall never be destroyed: and the kingdom shall not be left to other people, but it shall break in pieces and consume all these kingdoms, and it shall stand for ever. (*Daniel interprets Nebuchadnezzar's dream of a stone cut from the mountain without hands*) Dan.2:44

**LeGrand Richards,**
*also quoting Daniel*

Then he [Daniel] told him [king Nebuchadnezzar] about the rise and fall of the kingdoms of this world until the latter days (and we live in the latter days), when the God of heaven would "set up a kingdom, which shall never be destroyed: and the kingdom shall not be left to other people." (Dan.2:44) How could God set up such a kingdom as that which would endure forever without a prophet through whom he could work to establish his kingdom? ¶ Then he said it would be as a stone, cut without hands—in other words, it would have a small beginning, and this kingdom started with six men and has grown, as Daniel said it would, to become a great mountain and fill the whole earth. (See Dan.2:35.) No other group of religious worshipers is growing by leaps and bounds as is this church today, because the God of heaven has established it according to his promise. CR1975Oct:76

**Elder Ezra Taft Benson,**
*also paraphrasing Daniel*

The prophet Daniel described the beginning and remarkable growth of the Church as a small stone which would become a great mountain and fill the entire earth! (see Dan.2:34-35,44). ¶ .... The growth of the Church, like the growth of grass or trees, has been almost imperceptible to the eye, but little by little, line by line, precept by precept, the Church has matured. . . . ¶ There were those who thought the Church would fail with the deaths of the martyrs Joseph and Hyrum, but they did not perceive, as Daniel foretold, that this latter-day kingdom should "never be destroyed." (Dan.2:44). CR1980Apr:44-45

**Gordon B. Hinckley,**
*also quoting Daniel*

Under President Benson's leadership, the work of the Lord will continue to move forward. No power under the heavens can deflect it from its course. We may expect that there will be some who will try. Their efforts will be like chipping away at a granite block with a chisel of wood. The stone will not be damaged, but the chisel will be broken. ¶ As Daniel declared in prophecy: "The God of heaven set up [this] kingdom, which shall never be destroyed: and the kingdom shall not be left to other people, . . . and it shall stand for ever." (*Ezra Taft Benson was sustained as President of the Church at this conference*) CR1986Apr:62

**L. Tom Perry**

The Lord was preparing for the establishment of the gospel again on the earth for the last time, and starting preparation for the return of his Son. This time the Restoration was to be permanent. ("He Hath Given a Law unto All Things," Brigham Young University Speeches of the Year, 1977, p. 185) TLDP:559

**Parley P. Pratt**

This court of inquisition inquired diligently into our belief of the seventh chapter of Daniel concerning the kingdom of God, which should subdue all other kingdoms and stand forever. And when told that we believed in that prophecy, the court turned to the clerk and said: "Write that down; it is a strong point for treason." Our lawyer observed as follows: "Judge, you had better make the Bible treason." The court made no reply. (*A civil court trial in which the judge asked "much concerning our views of the prophecy of Daniel . . . as if it were treason to believe the Bible," [Joseph Smith], Nov. 1838.*) Autobiography of Parley P. Pratt, p. 230) HC3:212 f.n.

**Related Witnesses:**

**President Brigham Young,**
*quoted by John A. Widtsoe*

All is right. God can carry on his own work. This Kingdom will stand forever. (*In Tabernacle, June 3, 1860, JD8:69*) DBY:442

**Bruce R. McConkie**

Truly the world is and will be in commotion, but the Zion of God will be unmoved. The wicked and ungodly shall be swept from the Church, and the little stone will continue to grow until it fills the whole earth. CR1980Apr:99

---

**642. The restoration of the gospel in the latter days is the "marvelous work and a wonder" of the Lord.**

**John A. Widtsoe**

Unknown, untaught, with no reputation, [Joseph Smith] should have been forgotten in the small hamlet, almost nameless, in the backwoods of a great state; but he dared to say that the work that he was doing, under God's instruction, was to become a marvel and a wonder in the world. We know, my brethren and sisters, that whether it be friend or enemy who speaks of us, if he is a sober-thinking, honest man, he will declare that whatever in his opinion the foundations of this work may be—we know the foundations—it is a marvelous work and a wonder, none like it in the long history of the world. The truths set loose by the Prophet Joseph Smith have touched every man of faith throughout the whole civilized world, and measurable changed their beliefs for good. CR1946Apr:21-22

### President Heber J. Grant

This "marvelous work and a wonder" has come to pass and has spread all over the world where there has been religious liberty; and from every land and from every clime honest, faithful, God-fearing men and women have heard the sound of the true voice of the shepherd through his servants who have gone forth to proclaim the Gospel. And men of great influence have been gathered into this Church. Men like John Taylor, who presided over the Church, heard the sound of this Gospel and embraced it and gathered to Zion, and labored with all the power and ability that they possessed for the advancement of God's kingdom. Year by year this great and wonderful work has rolled on and we are becoming known as God-fearing people, as a people with a destiny that is sure to be fulfilled. CR1929Oct:9

### Nephi, son of Lehi

And the Lord will set his hand again the second time to restore his people from their lost and fallen state. Wherefore, he will proceed to do a marvelous work and a wonder among the children of men. (*Nephi prophesies, about 559-554 B.C.*) 2Ne.25:17

### Orson F. Whitney

Seven hundred years before the birth of our Savior, a prophet of God upon the eastern hemisphere predicted the coming forth of "a marvelous work and a wonder." "Mormonism," so called, according to the faith of its adherents, is the fulfilment of that ancient prediction. And indeed it would be difficult to conceive of anything more marvelous, more wonderful, than the foundation facts upon which rests the Church of Jesus Christ of Latter-day Saints. What could be more strange, more unexpected, than the re-opening of the heavens in an age when it was believed and asserted that the heavens were permanently sealed, that God no longer spoke to man, that revelation had ceased, and that angels would never again commune with earth's inhabitants? But lo! the heavens are opened; angels come to earth; and not only this, but God himself descends from his glorious throne and appears unto man, opening the last and greatest of the gospel dispensations. An angel reveals the hidden past of the American continent—the Book of Mormon, containing the fulness of the gospel, a history of the Americans in pre-historic times, and a prophecy of their wondrous future. An angel restores the Aaronic priesthood, which holds the keys of repentance and baptism; and other angels bring back the higher or Melchizedek priesthood, holding the keys of heavenly mysteries; and

under this delegated divine authority, without which no man can lawfully represent God, or administer the sacred ordinances of the gospel, the Church of Christ is organized once more upon the earth. Truly, a marvelous work and a wonder—so marvelous, so wonderful, that most men reject it, deeming it a fable. And yet it is nothing more nor less than the plain fulfilment of prophecy. CR1916Oct:51

### John A. Widtsoe

Not only in numbers have we become a "marvelous work and a wonder" in a little less than one hundred years; but in a greater and a larger sense have we become a marvelous people, for we have impressed our thought upon the whole world. The world does not believe today as it did ninety years ago. A few days ago I picked up a recent number of a great magazine, and my feelings were roused within me and my testimony increased, when I found one of the writers declaring to the readers of the magazine that "God cannot look upon sin with the least degree of tolerance," borrowed almost word for word, from section one of the Doctrine and Covenants. In such a way have the doctrines taught by the despised Latter-day Saints been appropriated by the nations of the earth; and whether the people of the earth accept the inspiration of Joseph Smith, nevertheless, in fact, the whole current of human thought has been changed by the doctrines of this people. That is perhaps the greatest achievement of "Mormonism." . . . CR1921Oct:108-09

**Related Witnesses:**

### Joseph Smith,
#### *receiving the Word of the Lord*

And by your hands I will work a marvelous work among the children of men, unto the convincing of many of their sins, that they may come unto repentance, and that they may come unto the kingdom of my Father. (*Revelation, June 1829*) D&C 18:44

### Isaiah,
#### *quoted by Nephi, son of Lehi,*

Therefore, I will proceed to do a marvelous work among this people, yea, a marvelous work and a wonder, for the wisdom of their wise and learned shall perish, and the understanding of their prudent shall be hid. (*Nephi records on the plates, about 559-545 B.C.*) 2Ne.27:26

### Isaiah

Therefore, behold, I will proceed to do a marvellous work among this people, even a marvellous work and a wonder: for the wisdom of their wise men shall perish, and the understanding of their prudent men shall be hid. (*The Apostasy, the Restoration, and the coming forth* of the Book of Mormon are foretold by Isaiah, 740-659 B.C.) Isa.29:14

**Joseph Smith**

Now behold, a marvelous work is about to come forth among the children of men. (*Revelation for his father, Feb. 1829*) D&C 4:1

**Joseph Smith**

A great and marvelous work is about to come forth unto the children of men. (*Revelation to Joseph and to Oliver Cowdery, April 1829*) D&C 6:1

**Joseph Smith,**
**quoted by Elder Joseph Fielding Smith**

[I]t is left for us to see, participate in and help to roll forward the Latter-day glory, "the dispensation of the fulness of times, when God will gather together all things that are in heaven, and all things that are upon the earth," "even in one," . . . a work that God and angels have contemplated with delight for generations past; that fired the souls of the ancient patriarchs and prophets; a work that is destined to bring about the destruction of the powers of darkness, the renovation of the earth, the glory of God, and the salvation of the human family. (*Editorial in Times and Seasons, April 1842*) TPJS:231-32; DGSM:63

**Anthony W. Ivins**

This is a dispensation, the greatest that was ever ushered in in the history of the world, because it comprehends all that has been before it and all that shall come after it. CR1932Oct:5

---

643. The Church of Jesus Christ of Latter-day Saints was organized in these latter days by divine authority.

**President Joseph F. Smith**

We affirm that through the ministration of immortal personages, the Holy Priesthood has been conferred upon men in the present age, and that under this divine authority the Church of Christ has been organized. (*Address from the First Presidency of the Church to the world, delivered to and accepted by vote of the Church in general conference, April 1907*) CR1907Apr(Appendix)4

**Joseph Smith**

The rise of the Church of Christ in these last days, being one thousand eight hundred and thirty years since the coming of our Lord and Savior Jesus Christ in the flesh, it being regularly organized and established agreeable to the laws of our country, by the will and commandments of God, in the fourth month, and on the sixth day of the month which is called April—

2. Which commandments were given to Joseph Smith, Jun., who was called of God, and ordained an apostle of Jesus Christ, to be the first elder of this church; 3. And to Oliver Cowdery, who was also called of God, an apostle of Jesus Christ, to be the second elder of this church, and ordained under his hand; 4. And this according to the grace of our Lord and Savior Jesus Christ, to whom be all glory, both now and forever. Amen. (*Revelation on Church Organization and Government, April 1830*) D&C 20:1-4

**Hugh B. Brown**

The Church of Jesus Christ was established and is now directed by revelation, and that fact is largely responsible for the appeal which this new Church makes, and when I say "new," I wish to emphasize that to us it is not new but a restoration of that which was. CR1961Oct:95

**President Wilford Woodruff**

Joseph Smith was an illiterate man; but afterwards his teachers and instructors were angels—Apostles who had dwelt in the flesh in the days of Jesus. He was in a condition where he received testimonies and teachings from men that the world did not receive; and he had power to organize the Church in a manner that all the Christian world combined could not do. Why? Because a man, no matter how wealthy or how learned, cannot give a thing that he does not possess. They had not power to organize this Church, because they did not possess the Priesthood. But Joseph Smith held that Priesthood and had power to organize the Church. (*At stake conference in Logan, Utah, Nov. 1, 1891*) MOFP3:223; TLDP:558

**President David O. McKay**

This organization [the Church] is established by divine revelation, and there is nothing else in all the world that can so effectively take care of its members. (*President David O. McKay quoted by Henry D. Taylor in "The Church Welfare Plan"*) MPSG1989:105

**Related Witnesses:**
**Joseph Smith**

I certify you, brethren, that the gospel which was preached of me is not after man; for I neither received it of man, neither was I taught it, but by the revelation of Jesus Christ. (Times and Seasons, Feb. 1840, p. 55) TLDP:558

**Hugh B. Brown**

The restored gospel of Jesus Christ does not base its claim to authority on apostolic succession, nor did it begin with a protest against or attempt to reform other churches. Furthermore, this Church did not have its beginning in scholarly analysis of the gospel as taught in the

Bible. Its founder, at the time of his first vision, did not claim to be a profound student of theology, and he knew little of the writings of the early church fathers. His message came as a direct revelation from heaven. CR1958Apr:109

**Joseph Smith,**
*receiving the Word of the Lord*
Hearken, O ye people of my church, to whom the kingdom has been given. . . . *(Revelation, March 7, 1831)* D&C 45:1

---

644. The Lord gave Joseph Smith the gift to translate the Book of Mormon plates, that this generation would have the word of the Lord.

**Joseph Smith,**
*receiving the Word of the Lord*
And you have a gift to translate the plates; and this is the first gift that I bestowed upon you; and I have commanded that you should pretend to no other gift until my purpose is fulfilled in this; for I will grant unto you no other gift until it is finished. . . . 6. For hereafter you shall be ordained and go forth and deliver my words unto the children of men. . . . 10. But this generation shall have my word through you; *(Revelation, March 1829)* D&C 5:4,6,10

**Elder John Taylor**
In the short space of twenty years, he [Joseph Smith] has brought forth the Book of Mormon, which he translated by the gift and power of God, and has been the means of publishing it on two continents; has sent the fulness of the everlasting gospel, which it contained, to the four quarters of the earth; has brought forth the revelations and commandments which compose this book of Doctrine and Covenants, and many other wise documents and instructions for the benefit of the children of men; gathered many thousands of the Latter-day Saints, founded a great city, and left a fame and name that cannot be slain. *(John Taylor records the martyrdom of Joseph and Hyrum Smith, June 27, 1844)* D&C 135:3

**Joseph Smith,**
*receiving the Word of the Lord*
Behold, this is wisdom in me; wherefore, marvel not, for the hour cometh that I will drink of the fruit of the vine with you on the earth, and with Moroni, whom I have sent unto you to reveal the Book of Mormon, containing the fulness of my everlasting gospel, to whom I have committed the keys of the record of the stick of Ephraim; *(Revelation to Joseph Smith through a heavenly messenger, Aug. 1830)* D&C 27:5

**President Brigham Young,**
*quoted by John A. Widtsoe*
When Joseph first received the knowledge of the plates that were in the hill Cumorah, he did not then receive the keys of the Aaronic Priesthood, he merely received the knowledge that the plates were there, and that the Lord would bring them forth, and that they contained the history of the aborigines of this country. He received the knowledge that they were once in possession of the Gospel, and from that time he went on, step by step, until he obtained the plates, and the Urim and Thummim and had power to translate them. *(In Third Ward Meeting House, June 23, 1874, JD18:239-40)* DBY:461

**Joseph Smith,**
*receiving the Word of the Lord*
And after having received the record of the Nephites, yea, even my servant Joseph Smith, Jun., might have power to translate through the mercy of God, by the power of God, the Book of Mormon. *(Revelation during conference of elders of the Church, Nov. 1, 1831)* D&C 1:29

**Joseph Smith,**
*receiving the Word of the Lord*
And gave him power from on high, by the means which were before prepared, to translate the Book of Mormon; 9. Which contains a record of a fallen people, and the fulness of the gospel of Jesus Christ to the Gentiles and to the Jews also; 10. Which was given by inspiration, and is confirmed to others by the ministering of angels, and is declared unto the world by them— 11. Proving to the world that the holy scriptures are true, and that God does inspire men and call them to his holy work in this age and generation, as well as in generations of old; 12. Thereby showing that he is the same God yesterday, today, and forever. Amen. *(Revelation on Church Organization and Government, April 1830; the Book of Mormon proves the divinity of the latter-day work)* D&C 20:8-12

**Related Witnesses:**
**President Spencer W. Kimball**
By the power of God other books of scripture [in addition to the Bible] have come into being. Vital and priceless records of ancient America, with teachings of Christ, another testimony of his divinity, form the Book of Mormon, which we declare to be divine scripture, contemporary with and sustaining the Bible. CR1977Apr:115

---

645. Joseph Smith was chosen and called by the Lord to be a latter-day prophet.

### President Heber J. Grant,
### J. Reuben Clark, Jr., David O. McKay
(First Presidency)

We solemnly declare that in these the latter-days, God has again spoken from the heavens through His chosen Prophet, Joseph Smith; that the Lord has, through that same Prophet, again revealed in its fulness His gospel,—the plan of life and salvation; that through that Prophet and his associates He has restored His holy Priesthood to the earth, from which it had been taken because of the wickedness of men; and that all the rights, powers, keys, and functions appertaining to the Priesthood as so restored are now vested in and exercised by the chosen and inspired leadership of His Church,—The Church of Jesus Christ of Latter-day Saints, even as the Priesthood has been exercised on the earth from the Beginning until this day, whenever His Church was here or His work had place among the children of men. CR1942Apr:88; MOFP:6:149

### Gordon B. Hinckley,
### *also quoting Parley P. Pratt*

Is it any wonder that this work moves on from nation to nation, from people to people? Is it any wonder that it grows in strength and numbers, in influence and interest, notwithstanding its critics and naysayers? It is the work of God restored to the earth through a prophet [Joseph Smith] of whom Parley P. Pratt his contemporary, said: ¶ "His works will live to endless ages, and unnumbered millions yet unborn will mention his name with honor, as a noble instrument in the hands of God, who, during his short and youthful career, laid the foundation of that kingdom spoken of by Daniel, the prophet, which should break in pieces all other kingdoms and stand forever." (Autobiography of Parley Parker Pratt, p.46) ("The Lengthened Shadow of the Hand of God," EN1987May:59) MPSG1989:230-31

### Stephen L. Richards

I know that Joseph Smith was a prophet of the living God, and the work he was instrumental in setting upon the earth is the veritable kingdom of our Father in heaven. CR1951Oct:118

### Joseph Smith,
### *receiving the Word of the Lord*

Which commandments were given to Joseph Smith, Jun., who was called of God, and ordained an apostle of Jesus Christ, the first elder of this church; (*Revelation on Church Organization and Government, April 1830*) D&C 20:2

### Joseph Smith,
### *receiving the Word of the Lord*

Behold, there shall be a record kept among you;

and in it thou shalt be called a seer, a translator, a prophet, an apostle of Jesus Christ, an elder of the church through the will of God the Father, and the grace of your Lord Jesus Christ, (*Revelation received at the organization of the Church, April 6, 1830; Joseph Smith is called by the Lord to be a seer, translator, prophet, Apostle and elder of the Church*) D&C 21:1

### President Brigham Young,
### *quoted by John A. Widtsoe*

When Joseph first received the knowledge of the plates that were in the hill Cumorah, he did not then receive the keys of the Aaronic Priesthood, he merely received the knowledge that the plates were there, and that the Lord would bring them forth, and that they contained the history of the aborigines of this country. He received the knowledge that they were once in possession of the Gospel, and from that time he went on, step by step, until he obtained the plates, and the Urim and Thummim and had power to translate them. ¶ This did not make him an Apostle, it did not give to him the keys of the Kingdom, nor make him an Elder in Israel. He was a Prophet, and had the spirit of prophecy, and had received all this before the Lord ordained him. And when the Lord, by revelation, told him to go to Pennsylvania, he did so, and finished the translation of the Book of Mormon; and when the Lord, in another revelation, told him to come back into New York State, and to go to old Father Whitmer's . . . he did so, and had meetings, and gathered up a few who believed in his testimony. He received the Aaronic Priesthood, and then he received the keys of the Melchizedek Priesthood, and organized the Church. He first received the power to baptize, and still did not know that he was to receive any more until the Lord told him there was more for him. Then he received the keys of the Melchizedek Priesthood and had power to confirm after he had baptized, which he had not before. He would have stood precisely as John the Baptist stood had not the Lord sent his other messengers, Peter, James and John, to ordain Joseph to the Melchizedek Priesthood. (*In Third Ward Meeting House, June 23, 1874, JD18:239-40*) DBY:461

### President Brigham Young,
### *quoted by John A. Widtsoe*

It was decreed in the counsels of eternity, long before the foundations of the earth were laid, that he, Joseph Smith, should be the man, in the last dispensation of this world, to bring forth the word of God to the people, and receive the fulness of the keys and power of the Priesthood of the Son of God. The Lord had his eyes upon him, and upon his father, and upon his father's father, and upon their progenitors clear back to Abraham, and from Abraham to the flood, from the flood to Enoch, and from Enoch to Adam. He has watched that family and that blood as it has circulated from its fountain to the birth of that man. He was foreordained in eternity to preside over this last dispensation. (*In Tabernacle, Oct. 9, 1859, JD7:289*) DBY:108

**Related Witnesses:**

**Joseph Smith,**
*receiving the Word of the Lord*
Behold thou art Joseph, and thou wast chosen to do the work of the Lord. . . . (*Revelation, July 1828*) D&C 3:9

**Joseph Smith**
He . . . said . . . he was a messenger sent from the presence of God to me . . . that God had a work for me to do. (*Joseph relates the angel Moroni's visit to him Sept. 21, 1823*) JS-H 1:33

**Joseph Smith,**
*receiving the Word of the Lord*
Wherefore, I the Lord, knowing the calamity which should come upon the inhabitants of the earth, called upon my servant Joseph Smith, Jun., and spake unto him from heaven, and gave him commandments; (*Revelation received during conference of elders of the Church, Nov. 1, 1831*) D&C 1:17

**Elder John Taylor**
Joseph Smith, the Prophet and Seer of the Lord, has done more, save Jesus only, for the salvation of men in this world, than any other man that ever lived in it. In the short space of twenty years, he has brought forth the Book of Mormon, which he translated by the gift and power of God, and has been the means of publishing it on two continents; has sent the fulness of the everlasting gospel, which it contained, to the four quarters of the earth; has brought forth the revelations and commandments which compose this book of Doctrine and Covenants, and many other wise documents and instructions for the benefit of the children of men; gathered many thousands of the Latter-day Saints, founded a great city, and left a fame and name that cannot be slain. He lived great, and he died great in the eyes of God and his people; and like most of the Lord's anointed in ancient times, has sealed his mission and his works with his own blood; and so has his brother Hyrum. In life they were not divided, and in death they were not separated! (*John Taylor records the martyrdom of Joseph and Hyrum Smith, June 27, 1844*) D&C 135:3

**Joseph Smith**
I give unto you my servant Joseph to be a pre-siding elder over all my church, to be a translator, a revelator, a seer, and prophet. (*Revelation, Jan. 19, 1841*) D&C 124:125

**Joseph Smith,**
*receiving the Word of the Lord*
Verily, I say unto you, that woe shall come unto the inhabitants of the earth if they will not hearken unto my words; 6. For hereafter you shall be ordained and go forth and deliver my words unto the children of men. 7. Behold, if they will not believe my words, they would not believe you, my servant Joseph, if it were possible that you should show them all these things which I have committed unto you. 8. Oh, this unbelieving and stiffnecked generation—mine anger is kindled against them. 9. Behold, verily I say unto you, I have reserved those things which I have entrusted unto you, my servant Joseph, for a wise purpose in me, and it shall be made known unto future generations; 10. But this generation shall have my word through you; (*Revelation received at the request of Martin Harris, March 1829*) D&C 5:5-10

**Marion G. Romney**
Some people have said that Joseph Smith was an unlearned man. He was an unlearned man in the things of the world, but the day he came out of the grove, following the first vision, he was the most learned person in the world in the things that count. When he came out of that grove, he knew more than all the world put together about the great question of the resurrection, which had been argued from the time man began to think seriously, because he had seen standing before him, the resurrected Christ. When he came out of that grove, he knew more about the nature of God than all the world. There had been many books written; philosophers had spent their lives trying to find out the nature of God, but when God took Joseph in hand to reach him, he cut through all material things and taught Joseph the truth about these and many other important things. CR1946Apr:37

**Lehi,**
*quoted by his son Nephi*
Wherefore, Joseph truly saw our day. And he obtained a promise of the Lord, that out of the fruit of his loins the Lord God would raise up a righteous branch unto the house of Israel; not the Messiah, but a branch which was to be broken off, nevertheless, to be remembered in the covenants of the Lord that the Messiah should be made manifest unto them in the latter days, in the spirit of power, unto the bringing of them out of darkness unto light—yea, out of hidden darkness and out of captivity unto freedom. 6.

For Joseph truly testified, saying: A seer shall the Lord my God raise up, who shall be a choice seer unto the fruit of my loins. 7. Yea, Joseph truly said: Thus saith the Lord unto me: A choice seer will I raise up out of the fruit of thy loins; and he shall be esteemed highly among the fruit of thy loins. And unto him will I give commandment that he shall do a work for the fruit of thy loins, his brethren, which shall be of great worth unto them, even to the bringing of them to the knowledge of the covenants which I have made with thy fathers. 8. And I will give unto him a commandment that he shall do none other work, save the work which I shall command him. And I will make him great in mine eyes; for he shall do my work. 9. And he shall be great like unto Moses, whom I have said I would raise up unto you, to deliver my people, O house of Israel. 10. And Moses will I raise up, to deliver thy people out of the land of Egypt. 11. But a seer will I raise up out of the fruit of thy loins; and unto him will I give power to bring forth my word unto the seed of thy loins—and not to the bringing forth my word only, saith the Lord, but to the convincing them of my word, which shall have already gone forth among them. (*Lehi speaks to his son—named Joseph—saying that the Joseph who was carried captive into Egypt received revelation from the Lord foretelling that a seer would be raised up by the Lord whose name would be Joseph, and his father's name would also be Joseph, and this seer [Joseph Smith] would be like unto Joseph in Egypt and like Moses*) 2Ne.3:5-11

**Joseph Smith,**
*receiving the Word of the Lord*
And I have sent forth the fulness of my gospel by the hand of my servant Joseph; and in weakness have I blessed him; (*Revelation to Joseph Smith and Sidney Rigdon, Dec. 1830*) D&C 35:17

**President Wilford Woodruff**
Joseph Smith was an illiterate man; but afterwards his teachers and instructors were angels—Apostles who had dwelt in the flesh in the days of Jesus. He was in a condition where he received testimonies and teachings from men that the world did not receive; and he had power to organize the Church in a manner that all the Christian world combined could not do. Why? Because a man, no matter how wealthy or how learned, cannot give a thing that he does not possess. They had not power to organize this Church, because they did not possess the Priesthood. But Joseph Smith held that Priesthood and had power to organize the Church. (*At stake conference in Logan, Utah, Nov. 1, 1891*) MOFP3:223; TLDP:558

**Melvin J. Ballard**
I understand from this that the Lord plainly knew the condition of the world, what it was in 1830, and what it would be today. . . . Knowing the calamities that were coming to his children, unless they changed their course, knowing their disposition that there would be no repentance in their hearts, and yet with a great desire to save them, he called upon his servant, Joseph Smith, to warn men, to call repentance, and others to join in this great proclamation to all men: "Repent, for the Kingdom of God is at hand." CR1923Oct:30-31

**Mark E. Petersen**
It was only half a dozen years or so after America was established as a free constitutional nation that one of the great spirits in the preexistence was sent to earth to be born on December 23, 1805, in a little farmhouse; and he was named Joseph Smith. ("The Great Prologue," Brigham Young University Speeches of the Year, 1974, p. 468) TLDP:558

**Elder Joseph Fielding Smith**
If Joseph Smith was verily a prophet, and if he told the truth when he said that he stood in the presence of angels sent from the Lord, and obtained keys of authority, and the commandment to organize the Church of Jesus Christ once again on the earth, then this knowledge is of the most vital importance to the entire world. No man can reject that testimony without incurring the most dreadful consequences, for he cannot enter the kingdom of God. It is, therefore, the duty of every man to investigate that he may weigh this matter carefully and know the truth. (Doctrines of Salvation, 1:189-90) TLDP:559

---

**HYMNS Written by Prophets**
**Applicable to this Topic**

**Parley P. Pratt**
*The Morning Breaks,* Verses 3,4,5
HYMNS:1

The Gentile fulness now comes in,
And Israel's blessings are at hand.
Lo, Judah's remnant, cleansed from sin,
Lo, Judah's remnant, cleansed from sin,
Shall in their promised Canaan stand.

Jehovah speaks! Let earth give ear,
And Gentile nations turn and live.
His mighty arm is making bare,
His mighty arm is making bare
His cov'nant people to receive.

Angels from heav'n and truth from earth
Have met, and both have record borne;
Thus Zion's light is bursting forth,
Thus Zion's light is bursting forth
To bring her ransomed children home.

**Parley P. Pratt**
*An Angel from on High*
HYMNS:13

An angel from on high
The long, long silence broke;
Descending from the sky,
These gracious words he spoke:
Lo! in Cumorah's lonely hill
A sacred record lies concealed.
Lo! in Cumorah's lonely hill
A sacred record lies concealed.

Sealed by Moroni's hand,
It has for ages lain
To wait the Lord's command,
From dust to speak again.
It shall again to light come forth
To usher in Christ's reign on earth.
It shall again to light come forth
To usher in Christ's reign on earth.

It speaks of Joseph's seed
And makes the remnant known
Of nations long since dead,
Who once had dwelt alone.
The fulness of the gospel, too,
Its pages will reveal to view.
The fulness of the gospel, too,
Its pages will reveal to view.

The time is now fulfilled,
The long-expected day;
Let earth obedience yield
And darkness flee away.
Remove the seals; be wide unfurled
Its light and glory to the world.
Remove the seals; be wide unfurled
Its light and glory to the world.

Lo! Israel filled with joy
Shall now be gathered home,
Their wealth and means employ
To build Jerusalem,
While Zion shall arise and shine
And fill the earth with truth divine,
While Zion shall arise and shine
And fill the earth with truth divine.

**Parley P. Pratt**
*Truth Eternal*
HYMNS:4

Truth eternal, truth divine,
In thine ancient fulness shine!
Burst the fetters of the mind
From the millions of mankind!

Truth again restored to earth,
Opened with a prophet's birth.
Priests of heaven's royal line
Bear the keys of truth divine!

Truth shall triumph as the light
Chases far the misty night.
Endless ages own its sway,
Clad in everlasting day.

# List of Doctrines

## RESURRECTION

*Doctrines Located in This Topic*

646. Resurrection is the raising from death to life the mortal body to an immortal body and the spirit uniting with the body.

647. The resurrection is universal: every person will be saved from *physical* death regardless of whether he or she has done good or evil in this life.

648. The spirit and the body shall be reunited again in a perfect form.

649. In the resurrection we will maintain our personal identity (our talents, attributes, and skills will rise with us).

650. A resurrected being is no longer subject to death.

651. The resurrected body will have flesh and bones.

652. There are two major resurrections: the first resurrection for the just, the second for the unjust.

653. Many of the righteous dead were resurrected immediately after Christ was resurrected.

654. Animals will be resurrected.

*Doctrines on RESURRECTION Located in Other Topics*

33. The Atonement of Christ secures the universal and unconditional resurrection of the body for both the wicked and the righteous.

34. Without the atoning sacrifice of Jesus Christ there would be no resurrection of our bodies.

35. We cannot receive a fulness of joy in the celestial kingdom without the resurrection, in which the spirit and the body are inseparably reunited.

152. Those who are to inhabit the telestial kingdom are first cast down to hell in the spirit world before they are redeemed from the devil in the last RESURRECTION.

268. Through the process of death and resurrection, Jesus Christ's spirit was reunited with his body.

302. A physical body is essential to obtaining a fulness of joy in the celestial kingdom of God.

# RESURRECTION

**646. Resurrection is the raising from death to life the mortal body to an immortal body, and the spirit uniting with the body.**

### Hyrum Mack Smith
Death is the dissolution of the body, and the resurrection is the reanimation of the body; yea the actual and literal reuniting of the Spirit with the body. . . . ¶ It is the mortal body that dies, not the immortal spirit. The spirit which is alive and does not die cannot be resurrected. The body dies when the spirit departs from it. Resurrection means to come from death unto life, and as it is the body that dies, it is the body that must be raised up and brought to life again. The term resurrection is never used save in connection with the body. CR1917Apr:31-32

### Amulek,
### *quoted by Mormon*
Now, there is a death which is called a temporal death; and the death of Christ shall loose the bands of this temporal death, that all shall be raised from this temporal death. 43. The spirit and the body shall be reunited again in its perfect form; both limb and joint shall be restored to its proper frame, even as we now are at this time; and we shall be brought to stand before God, knowing even as we know now, and have a bright recollection of all our guilt. 44. Now, this restoration shall come to all, both old and young, both bond and free, both male and female, both the wicked and the righteous; and even there shall not so much as a hair of their heads be lost; but every thing shall be restored to its perfect frame, as it is now, or in the body, and shall be brought and be arraigned before the bar of Christ the Son, and God the Father, and the Holy Spirit, which is one Eternal God, to be judged according to their works, whether they be good or whether they be evil. 45. Now, behold, I have spoken unto you concerning the death of the mortal body, and also concerning the resurrection of the mortal body. I say unto you that this mortal body is raised to an immortal body, that is from death, even from the first death unto life, that they can die no more; their spirits uniting with their bodies, never to be divided; thus the whole becoming spiritual and immortal, that they can no more see corruption. (*Amulek answers the wicked Zeezrom, foretelling Christ's redemption of man, about 82 B.C.*) Alma 11:42-45

### James E. Talmage
The Church of Jesus Christ of Latter-day Saints teaches the doctrine of a literal resurrection; an actual reunion of the spirits of the dead and the tabernacles with which they were clothed during mortal probation; and transition from mortality to immortality in the case of some who will be in the flesh at the time of the Lord's advent, and who, because of individual righteousness, are to be spared the sleep of the grave. The Bible is replete with testimony regarding the quickening of the dead. Human knowledge of the resurrection rests wholly upon revelation. Pagan peoples have little or no conception of an actual coming forth of the dead unto life. AF:344-45

### Alma, the younger,
### *quoted by Mormon*
I say unto thee, my son, that the plan of restoration is requisite with the justice of God; for it is requisite that all things should be restored to their proper order. Behold, it is requisite and just, according to the power and resurrection of Christ, that the soul of man should be restored to its body, and that every part of the body should be restored to itself. 3. And it is requisite with the justice of God that men should be judged according to their works; and if their works were good in this life, and the desires of their hearts were good, that they should also, at the last day, be restored unto that which is good. 4. And if their works are evil they shall be restored unto them for evil. Therefore, all things shall be restored to their proper order, every thing to its natural frame—mortality raised to immortality, corruption to incorruption—raised to endless happiness to inherit the kingdom of God, or to endless misery to inherit the kingdom of the devil, the one on one hand, the other on the other— (*Alma speaks to his son Corianton concerning the resurrection of the dead, about 73 B.C.*) Alma 41:2-4

### Jacob, brother of Nephi,
### *quoted by Nephi*
And because of the way of deliverance of our God, the Holy One of Israel, this death, of which I have spoken, which is the temporal, shall deliver up its dead; which death is the grave. 12. And this death of which I have spoken, which is the spiritual death, shall deliver up its dead; which spiritual death is hell; wherefore, death and hell must deliver up their dead, and hell must deliver up its captive spirits, and the grave must deliver up its captive bodies, and the bodies and the spirits of men will be restored one to the other; and it is by the power of the resurrection of the Holy One of Israel. 13. O how great the plan of our God! For on the other hand, the paradise of God must deliver up the spirits of the righteous, and the grave

deliver up the body of the righteous; and the spirit and the body is restored to itself again, and all men become incorruptible, and immortal, and they are living souls, having a perfect knowledge like unto us in the flesh, save it be that our knowledge shall be perfect. (*Jacob teaches the doctrine of the Atonement to the people of Nephi, 559-545 B.C.*) 2Ne.9:11-13

### Elder John Taylor

Man is an eternal being, composed of body and spirit: his spirit existed before he came here; his body exists with the spirit in time, and after death the spirit exists without the body. In the resurrection, both body and spirit will finally be reunited; and it requires both body and spirit to make a perfect man, whether in time, or eternity. (The Government of God, p. 27) DGSM:87

### Joseph Smith

And the spirit and the body are the soul of man. 16. And the resurrection from the dead is the redemption of the soul. (*Revelation, Dec. 27/28, 1832; the "olive leaf message of peace"*) D&C 88:15-16

### Related Witnesses:

### Alma, the younger,
*quoted by Mormon*

Behold, I say unto you, that there is no resurrection—or, I would say, in other words, that this mortal does not put on immortality, this corruption does not put on incorruption—until after the coming of Christ. 3. Behold, he bringeth to pass the resurrection of the dead. But behold, my son, the resurrection is not yet. Now, I unfold unto you a mystery; nevertheless, there are many mysteries which are kept, that no one knoweth them save God himself. But I show unto you one thing which I have inquired diligently of God that I might know—that is concerning the resurrection. 4. Behold, there is a time appointed that all shall come forth from the dead. Now when this time cometh no one knows; but God knoweth the time which is appointed. (*Alma to his son Corianton, about 73 B.C.*) Alma 40:2-4

### Alma, the younger,
*quoted by Mormon*

The soul shall be restored to the body, and the body to the soul; yea, and every limb and joint shall be restored to its body; yea, even a hair of the head shall not be lost; but all things shall be restored to their proper and perfect frame. 24. And now, my son, this is the restoration of which has been spoken by the mouths of the prophets— (*Alma speaks to his son Corianton concerning the resurrection of the dead, about 73 B.C.*) Alma 40:23-24

### President Joseph F. Smith

Their sleeping dust was to be restored unto its perfect frame, bone to his bone, and the sinews and the flesh upon them, the spirit and the body to be united never again to be divided, that they might receive a fulness of joy. (*Vision received regarding the Savior's visit to the spirits of the dead, Oct. 3, 1918*) D&C 138:17

---

**647. The resurrection is universal: every person will be saved from *physical* death regardless of whether he or she has done good or evil in this life.**

### Elder Joseph F. Smith

Every creature that is born in the image of God will be resurrected from the dead. . . . But just as sure as we go down into the grave, through the transgression of our first parents, by whom death came into the world, so sure will we be resurrected from the dead by the power of Jesus Christ. It matters not whether we have done well or ill, whether we have been intelligent or ignorant, or whether we have been bondsmen or slaves or freemen, all men will be raised from the dead. (Millennial Star, March 12, 1896, p. 162) DGSM:88

### President Joseph F. Smith

The spirits of all men, as soon as they depart from this mortal body, whether they are good or evil, we are told in the Book of Mormon, are taken home to that God who gave them life, where there is a separation, a partial judgment, and the spirits of those who are righteous are received into a state of happiness which is called paradise, a state of rest, a state of peace, where they expand in wisdom, where they have respite from all their troubles, and where care and sorrow do not annoy. The wicked, on the contrary, have no part nor portion in the Spirit of the Lord, and they are cast into outer darkness, being led captive, because of their own iniquity, by the evil one. And in this space between death and the resurrection of the body, the two classes of souls remain, in happiness or in misery, until the time which is appointed of God that the dead shall come forth and be reunited both spirit and body, and be brought to stand before God and be judged according to their works. This is the final judgment. (Gospel Doctrine, p. 448) DGSM:84

### Alma, the younger,
*quoted by Mormon*

And behold, again it hath been spoken, that there is a first resurrection, a resurrection of all those who have been, or who are, or who shall be, down to the resurrection of Christ from the dead. 17. Now, we do not suppose that this first resurrection, which is spoken of in this manner, can be the resurrection of the souls and their consignation to happiness or misery. Ye cannot suppose that this is what it meaneth. 18. Behold, I say unto you, Nay; but it meaneth the reuniting of the soul with the body, of those from the days of Adam down to the resurrection of Christ. 19. Now, whether the souls and the bodies of those of whom has been spoken shall all be reunited at once, the wicked as well as the righteous, I do not say; let it suffice; that I say that they all come forth; or in other words, their resurrection cometh to pass before the resurrection of those who die after the resurrection of Christ. . . . 23. The soul shall be restored to the body, and the body to the soul; yea, and every limb and joint shall be restored to its body; yea, even a hair of the head shall not be lost; but all things shall be restored to their proper and perfect frame. 24. And now, my son, this is the restoration of which has been spoken by the mouths of the prophets— (*Alma speaks to his son Corianton concerning the resurrection of the dead, about 73 B.C.*) Alma 40:16-19,23-24

### Alma, the younger,
#### *quoted by Mormon*

I say unto thee, my son, that the plan of restoration is requisite with the justice of God; for it is requisite that all things should be restored to their proper order. Behold, it is requisite and just, according to the power and resurrection of Christ, that the soul of man should be restored to its body, and that every part of the body should be restored to itself. 3. And it is requisite with the justice of God that men should be judged according to their works; and if their works were good in this life, and the desires of their hearts were good, that they should also, at the last day, be restored unto that which is good. 4. And if their works are evil they shall be restored unto them for evil. Therefore, all things shall be restored to their proper order, every thing to its natural frame—mortality raised to immortality, corruption to incorruption—raised to endless happiness to inherit the kingdom of God, or to endless misery to inherit the kingdom of the devil, the one on one hand, the other on the other— (*Alma speaks to his son Corianton concerning the resurrection of the dead, about 73 B.C.*) Alma 41:2-4

### James E. Talmage

The Extent of the Atonement is universal, applying alike to all descendants of Adam. Even the unbeliever, the heathen, and the child who dies before reaching the years of discretion, all are redeemed by the Savior's self-sacrifice from the individual consequences of the fall. AF:77

### Jesus,
#### *quoted by John*

Marvel not at this: for the hour is coming, in the which all that are in the graves shall hear his voice, 29. And shall come forth; they that have done good, unto the resurrection of life; and they that have done evil, unto the resurrection of damnation. (*Jesus addresses the Jews*) John 5:28-29

### Related Witnesses:
#### President Joseph F. Smith

As Jesus was born of woman, lived and grew to manhood, was put to death and raised from the dead to immortality and eternal life, so it was decreed in the beginning that man should be, and will be, through the atonement of Jesus, in spite of himself, resurrected from the dead. Death came upon us without the exercise of our agency; we had no hand in bringing it originally upon ourselves; it came because of the transgression of our first parents. Therefore, man, who had no hand in bringing death upon himself, shall have no hand in bringing again life unto himself; for as he dies in consequence of the sin of Adam, so shall he live again, whether he will or not, by the righteousness of Jesus Christ, and the power of his resurrection. ("I Know That My Redeemer Lives," IE1908Mar:385) TLDP:561

#### Paul

For since by man came death, by man came also the resurrection of the dead. 22. For as in Adam all die, even so in Christ shall all be made alive. (*Paul writes to the Church at Corinth, Greece, about A.D. 55*) 1Cor.15:21-22

#### President Heber J. Grant

We believe that Christ . . . was crucified upon the cross, that He died, His spirit leaving His body, and was buried, and was on the third day resurrected, His spirit and body re-uniting, . . that He is a resurrected being, and that in His pattern, every man, woman, and child that ever lived, shall come forth from the grave a resurrected being, even as Christ is a resurrected being. ("Mortality—A Moment in Eternity," Millennial Star, June 24, 1937, pp. 395-96) TLDP:561

### Amulek,
#### *quoted by Mormon*

Therefore the wicked remain as though there had been no redemption made, except it be the loosing of the bands of death; for behold, the day cometh that all shall rise from the dead and stand before God, and be judged according to their works. 42. Now, there is a death which is called a temporal death; and the death of Christ shall loose the bands of this temporal death, that all shall be raised from this temporal death. 43. The spirit and the body shall be reunited again in its perfect form; both limb and joint shall be restored to its proper frame, even as we now are at this time; and we shall be brought to stand before God, knowing even as we know now, and have a bright recollection of all our guilt. (*Amulek contends with the wicked Zeezrom, about 82 B.C.*) Alma 11:41-43

### Elder Joseph Fielding Smith
So Jesus did for us something that we could not do for ourselves, through his infinite atonement. On the third day after the crucifixion he took up his body and gained the keys of the resurrection, and thus has power to open the graves for all men, but this he could not do until he had first passed through death himself and conquered. (Doctrines of Salvation, 1:128) DGSM:88

### Joseph Smith,
*receiving the Word of the Lord*
But, behold, verily I say unto you, before the earth shall pass away, Michael, mine archangel, shall sound his trump, and then shall all the dead awake, for their graves shall be opened, and they shall come forth—yea, even all. (*Revelation in presence of six elders, Sept. 1830*) D&C 29:26

### Jacob, brother of Nephi,
*quoted by Nephi*
And he suffereth this that the resurrection might pass upon all men, that all might stand before him at the great and judgment day. (*To the people of Nephi, 559-545 B.C.*) 2Ne.9:22

### Enoch,
*quoted by Moses,*
*quoted by Joseph Smith,*
*translating the Book of Moses*
And righteousness will I send down out of heaven; and truth will I send forth out of the earth, to bear testimony of mine Only Begotten; his resurrection from the dead; yea, and also the resurrection of all men. (*Revelation to Moses recording the word of the Lord to Enoch*) Moses 7:62

---

## 648. The spirit and the body shall be reunited again in a perfect form.

### President Joseph F. Smith
Their sleeping dust was to be restored unto its perfect frame, bone to his bone, and the sinews and the flesh upon them, the spirit and the body to be united never again to be divided, that they might receive a fulness of joy. (*Vision regarding the Savior's visit to the spirits of the dead, Oct. 3, 1918*) D&C 138:17

### Amulek,
*quoted by Mormon*
Now, there is a death which is called a temporal death; and the death of Christ shall loose the bands of this temporal death, that all shall be raised from this temporal death. 43. The spirit and the body shall be reunited again in its perfect form; both limb and joint shall be restored to its proper frame, even as we now are at this time; and we shall be brought to stand before God, knowing even as we know now, and have a bright recollection of all our guilt. 44. Now, this restoration shall come to all, both old and young, both bond and free, both male and female, both the wicked and the righteous; and even there shall not so much as a hair of their heads be lost; but every thing shall be restored to its perfect frame, as it is now, or in the body, and shall be brought and be arraigned before the bar of Christ the Son, and God the Father, and the Holy Spirit, which is one Eternal God, to be judged according to their works, whether they be good or whether they be evil. (*Amulek answers the wicked Zeezrom, foretelling Christ's redemption of man and the final judgment, about 82 B.C.*) Alma 11:42-44

### John Taylor
Man is an eternal being, composed of body and spirit: his spirit existed before he came here; his body exists with the spirit in time, and after death the spirit exists without the body. In the resurrection, both body and spirit will finally be reunited; and it requires both body and spirit to make a perfect man, whether in time, or eternity. (The Government of God, p. 27) DGSM:87

### Related Witnesses:
### President Joseph F. Smith
What a glorious thought it is, to me at least, and it must be to all who have conceived of the truth or received it in their hearts, that those from whom we have to part here, we will meet again and see as they are. We will meet the same identical being that we associated with here in the flesh—not some other soul, some other being, or the same being in some other form, but the same identity and the same form and likeness, the same person we knew and were associated with in our mortal existence, even to the wounds in the flesh. Not that a person will always be marred by scars, wounds, deformities, defects or infirmities, for these will be removed in their course, in their proper time, according to the merciful providence of God. Deformity will be removed; defects will be eliminated, and men and women shall attain to the perfection of their spirits, to the perfection that God designed in the beginning. (*At funeral*

*services of Rachel Grant, mother of President Heber J. Grant)* (Gospel Doctrine, p. 23) DGSM:88

## Alma, the younger, quoted by Mormon

The soul shall be restored to the body, and the body to the soul; yea, and every limb and joint shall be restored to its body; yea, even a hair of the head shall not be lost; but all things shall be restored to their proper and perfect frame. 24. And now, my son, this is the restoration of which has been spoken by the mouths of the prophets— *(Alma speaks to his son Corianton concerning the resurrection of the dead, about 73 B.C.)* Alma 40:23-24

### Elder Spencer W. Kimball

I am confident that when we come back with our bodies again, there will be no aches or pains. There will be no wrinkles or deformities. I am sure that if we can imagine ourselves at our very best, physically, mentally, spiritually, that is the way we will come back—perhaps not as a child or youth, perhaps in sweet and glorious maturity, but not in age or infirmity or distress or pain or aches. *(At a funeral service)* (The Teachings of Spencer W. Kimball, p. 45) TLDP:563

### Elder Joseph Fielding Smith

The question is frequently discussed in our classes in Sunday School, Mutual and Priesthood quorums, whether or not a body will come forth deformed, if deformed in this mortal life; or with some part missing, such as if a limb, or other part was lost while in mortal life. The answer has been given in the most emphatic and positive manner in the scriptures. The mortal body will not grow in the grave, for that is contrary to nature. So each body will come forth the same stature as when laid in the earth. Children will rise as they were laid away, but after the resurrection their bodies will grow to the full stature of their spirits. Deformities will be erased and in the resurrection will be made whole. CHMR2:301

### President Joseph F. Smith

Would we be satisfied to be imperfect? Would we be satisfied to be decrepit? Would we be satisfied to remain for ever and ever in the form of infirmity incident to age? No! Would we be satisfied to see the children we bury in their infancy remain as children only, throughout the countless ages of eternity? No! Neither would the spirit that did possess the tabernacles of our children be satisfied to remain in that condition. But we know our child will not be compelled to remain a child in stature always, for it was revealed from God, the fountain of truth, through Joseph Smith the prophet, in this dispensation, that in the resurrection of the dead the child that was buried in its infancy will come up in the form of the child that it was when it was laid down, then it will begin to develop. From the day of the resurrection, the body will develop until it reaches the full measure of the stature of its spirit, whether it be male or female. If the spirit possessed the intelligence of God and the aspirations of mortal souls, it could not be satisfied with anything less than this. You will remember we are told that the spirit of Jesus Christ visited one of the ancient prophets and revealed himself to him, and he declared his identity, that he was the same Son of God that was to come in the meridian of time. He said he would appear in the flesh just as he appeared to that prophet. He was not an infant; He was a grown, developed spirit, possessing the form of man and the form of God, the same form as when he came and took upon him a tabernacle and developed it to the full stature of his spirit. These are truths that have been revealed to us. What for? To give us intelligent hope; to give us intelligent aspiration; to lead us to think, to hope, to labor and accomplish what God has aimed and does aim and design that we should accomplish, not only in this life but in the life to come. ("Our Indestructible, Immortal Identity," IE1909Jun:593-94) TLDP:562

### President Brigham Young

At the sound of the trumpet of God every particle of our physical structures necessary to make our tabernacles perfect will be assembled, to be rejoined with the spirit, every man in his order. No one particle will be lost. *(Sermon delivered in 1875)* ("The Resurrection," Elder's Journal, July 1904, p. 153) TLDP:562-63

---

649. In the resurrection we will maintain our personal identity (our talents, attributes, and skills will rise with us).

### President Joseph F. Smith

[Christ] rose, and He preserved His identity. . . . So it will be with you and with every son and daughter of Adam, born into the world. You will not lose your identity any more than Christ did. You will be brought forth from death to life again, just as sure as Christ was brought forth from death to life again. . . . ¶ Neither [husband or wife] would be changed, except from mortality to immortality, neither would be other than himself or herself; but they will have their identity in the world to come, precisely as they exercise their individuality and enjoy their identity here. God has revealed this principle. CR1912Apr:135-36

### Neal A. Maxwell

If we ponder just what it is that will rise with us in the resurrection, it seems clear that our intelligence will rise with us, meaning not simply our IQ, but also our capacity to receive and apply truth. Our talents, attributes, and skills will rise with us; certainly also our capacity to learn, our degree of self-discipline, and our capacity to work. (We Will Prove Them Herewith, p. 12) TLDP:563-64

### Jacob, brother of Nephi,
### quoted by Nephi

And assuredly, as the Lord liveth, for the Lord God hath spoken it, and it is his eternal word, which cannot pass away, that they who are righteous shall be righteous still, and they who are filthy shall be filthy still; wherefore, they who are filthy are the devil and his angels; and they shall go away into everlasting fire, prepared for them; . . . (To the people of Nephi, 559-545 B.C.) 2Ne.9:16

### Elder Spencer W. Kimball

I am sure that if we can imagine ourselves at our very best, physically, mentally, spiritually, that is the way we will come back—perhaps not as a child or youth, perhaps in sweet and glorious maturity, but not in age or infirmity or distress or pain or aches. (At a funeral service) (The Teachings of Spencer W. Kimball, p. 45) TLDP:563

### Joseph Smith

Whatever principle of intelligence we attain unto in this life, it will rise with us in the resurrection. 19. And if a person gains more knowledge and intelligence in this life through his diligence and obedience than another, he will have so much the advantage in the world to come. (Revelation, April 2, 1830) D&C 130:18-19

### Alma, the younger,
### quoted by Mormon

O, my son, this is not the case; but the meaning of the word restoration is to bring back again evil for evil, or carnal for carnal, or devilish for devilish—good for that which is good; righteous for that which is righteous; just for that which is just; merciful for that which is merciful. 14. Therefore, my son, see that you are merciful unto your brethren; deal justly, judge righteously, and do good continually; and if ye do all these things then shall ye receive your reward; yea, ye shall have mercy restored unto you again; ye shall have justice restored unto you again; ye shall have a righteous judgment restored unto you again; and ye shall have good

rewarded unto you again. 15. For that which ye do send out shall return unto you again, and be restored; therefore, the word restoration more fully condemneth the sinner, and justifieth him not at all. (Alma speaks to his son Corianton concerning the resurrection of the dead, about 73 B.C.) Alma 41:13-15

### President Joseph F. Smith

What a glorious thought it is, to me at least, and it must be to all who have conceived of the truth or received it in their hearts, that those from whom we have to part here, we will meet again and see as they are. We will meet the same identical being that we associated with here in the flesh—not some other soul, some other being, or the same being in some other form, but the same identity and the same form and likeness, the same person we knew and were associated with in our mortal existence, even to the wounds in the flesh. Not that a person will always be marred by scars, wounds, deformities, defects or infirmities, for these will be removed in their course, in their proper time, according to the merciful providence of God. Deformity will be removed; defects will be eliminated, and men and women shall attain to the perfection of their spirits, to the perfection that God designed in the beginning. (At funeral services of Rachel Grant, mother of President Heber J. Grant) (Gospel Doctrine, p. 23) DGSM:88

---

### 650. A resurrected being is no longer subject to death.

### Elder Joseph Fielding Smith

A soul cannot be destroyed. ¶ Every soul born into this world shall receive the resurrection and immortality and shall endure forever. Destruction does not mean, then, annihilation. When the Lord says they shall be destroyed, he means that they shall be banished from his presence, that they shall be cut off from the presence of light and truth, and shall not have the privilege of gaining this exaltation; and that is destruction. (Doctrines of Salvation, 2:227-28) DCSM:19

### Elder Joseph Fielding Smith

After the resurrection from the dead our bodies will be spiritual bodies, but they will be bodies that are tangible, bodies that have been purified, but they will nevertheless be bodies of flesh and bones, but they will not be blood bodies, they will no longer be quickened by blood but quickened by the spirit which is eternal and they shall become immortal and shall never die. CR1917Apr:63

**President Joseph F. Smith**

Their sleeping dust was to be restored unto its perfect frame, bone to his bone, and the sinews and the flesh upon them, the spirit and the body to be united never again to be divided, that they might receive a fulness of joy. (*Vision regarding the Savior's visit to the spirits of the dead, Oct. 3, 1918*) D&C 138:17

**Amulek,**
*quoted by Mormon*

Now, there is a death which is called a temporal death; and the death of Christ shall loose the bands of this temporal death, that all shall be raised from this temporal death. 43. The spirit and the body shall be reunited again in its perfect form. . . . 45. Now, behold, I have spoken unto you concerning the death of the mortal body, and also concerning the resurrection of the mortal body. I say unto you that this mortal body is raised to an immortal body, that is from death, even from the first death unto life, that they can die no more; their spirits uniting with their bodies, never to be divided; thus the whole becoming spiritual and immortal, that they can no more see corruption. (*Amulek answers the wicked Zeezrom, foretelling Christ's redemption of man and the final judgment, about 82 B.C.*) Alma 11:42-43,45

**Related Witnesses:**

**Paul**

Knowing that Christ being raised from the dead dieth no more; death hath no more dominion over him. 10. For in that he died, he died unto sin once: but in that he liveth, he liveth unto God. (*Paul writes to the Church in Rome, about A.D. 55*) Rom.6:9-10

**Jacob, brother of Nephi,**
*quoted by Nephi*

And because of the way of deliverance of our God, the Holy One of Israel, this death, of which I have spoken, which is the temporal, shall deliver up its dead; which death is the grave. 12. And this death of which I have spoken, which is the spiritual death, shall deliver up its dead; which spiritual death is hell; wherefore, death and hell must deliver up their dead, and hell must deliver up its captive spirits, and the grave must deliver up its captive bodies, and the bodies and the spirits of men will be restored one to the other; and it is by the power of the resurrection of the Holy One of Israel. 13. O how great the plan of our God! For on the other hand, the paradise of God must deliver up the spirits of the righteous, and the grave deliver up the body of the righteous; and the spirit and the body is restored to itself again, and all men become incorruptible, and immortal, and they are living souls, having a perfect knowledge like unto us in the flesh, save it

be that our knowledge shall be perfect. (*Jacob teaches the doctrine of the Atonement to the people of Nephi, 559-545 B.C.*) 2Ne.9:11-13

**Elder John Taylor**

Man is an eternal being, composed of body and spirit: his spirit existed before he came here; his body exists with the spirit in time, and after death the spirit exists without the body. In the resurrection, both body and spirit will finally be reunited; and it requires both body and spirit to make a perfect man, whether in time, or eternity. (The Government of God, p. 27) TLDP:560

**Paul**

But now is Christ risen from the dead, and become the firstfruits of them that slept. 21. For since by man came death, by man came also the resurrection of the dead. 22. For as in Adam all die, even so in Christ shall all be made alive. (*Letter to the Church at Corinth, Greece, about A.D. 55*) 1Cor.15:20-22

---

**651. The resurrected body will have flesh and bones.**

**Elder Joseph Fielding Smith**

After the resurrection from the dead our bodies will be spiritual bodies, but they will be bodies that are tangible, bodies that have been purified, but they will nevertheless be bodies of flesh and bones, but they will not be blood bodies, they will no longer be quickened by blood but quickened by the spirit which is eternal and they shall become immortal and shall never die. CR1917Apr:63

**Alma, the younger,**
*quoted by Mormon*

I say unto thee, my son, that the plan of restoration is requisite with the justice of God; for it is requisite that all things should be restored to their proper order. Behold, it is requisite and just, according to the power and resurrection of Christ, that the soul of man should be restored to its body, and that every part of the body should be restored to itself. (*Alma speaks to his son Corianton concerning the resurrection of the dead, about 73 B.C.*) Alma 41:2

**James E. Talmage**

This enunciation of the resurrection, so plainly made that the most unlettered could understand, must have offended any Sadducees present, for they emphatically denied the actuality of the resurrection. The universality of a resurrection is here unquestionably affirmed; not only the righteous but even those who merit condemnation are to come forth from their graves in their bodies of flesh and bones. JTC:210

**Joseph Smith**

There are two kinds of beings in heaven, namely: Angels, who are resurrected personages, having bodies of flesh and bones— 2. For instance, Jesus said: Handle me and see, for a spirit hath not flesh and bones, as ye see me have. 3. Secondly: the spirits of just men made perfect, they who are not resurrected, but inherit the same glory. (*Instructions given at Nauvoo, Ill., Feb. 9, 1843; keys given whereby messengers from beyond the veil may be identified*) D&C 129:1-3

**Alma, the younger,**
*quoted by Mormon*

The soul shall be restored to the body, and the body to the soul; yea, and every limb and joint shall be restored to its body; yea, even a hair of the head shall not be lost; but all things shall be restored to their proper and perfect frame. 24. And now, my son, this is the restoration of which has been spoken by the mouths of the prophets— (*Alma speaks to his son Corianton concerning the resurrection of the dead, about 73 B.C.*) Alma 40:23-24

**Amulek,**
*quoted by Mormon*

Now, there is a death which is called a temporal death; and the death of Christ shall loose the bands of this temporal death, that all shall be raised from this temporal death. 43. The spirit and the body shall be reunited again in its perfect form; both limb and joint shall be restored to its proper frame, even as we now are at this time; and we shall be brought to stand before God, knowing even as we know now, and have a bright recollection of all our guilt. 44. Now, this restoration shall come to all, both old and young, both bond and free, both male and female, both the wicked and the righteous; and even there shall not so much as a hair of their heads be lost; but every thing shall be restored to its perfect frame, as it is now, or in the body, and shall be brought and be arraigned before the bar of Christ the Son, and God the Father, and the Holy Spirit, which is one Eternal God, to be judged according to their works, whether they be good or whether they be evil. 45. Now, behold, I have spoken unto you concerning the death of the mortal body, and also concerning the resurrection of the mortal body. I say unto you that this mortal body is raised to an immortal body, that is from death, even from the first death unto life, that they can die no more; their spirits uniting with their bodies, never to be divided; thus the whole becoming spiritual and immortal, that they can no more see corruption. (*Amulek answers the wicked Zeezrom fore-*

telling Christ's redemption of man and the final judgment, about 82 B.C.*) Alma 11:42-45

**Related Witnesses:**
**President Joseph F. Smith**

What a glorious thought it is, to me at least, and it must be to all who have conceived of the truth or received it in their hearts, that those from whom we have to part here, we will meet again and see as they are. We will meet the same identical being that we associated with here in the flesh—not some other soul, some other being, or the same being in some other form, but the same identity and the same form and likeness, the same person we knew and were associated with in our mortal existence, even to the wounds in the flesh. Not that a person will always be marred by scars, wounds, deformities, defects or infirmities, for these will be removed in their course, in their proper time, according to the merciful providence of God. Deformity will be removed; defects will be eliminated, and men and women shall attain to the perfection of their spirits, to the perfection that God designed in the beginning. (*At funeral services of Rachel Grant, mother of President Heber J. Grant*) (Gospel Doctrine, p. 23) DGSM:88

**Joseph Smith**

As concerning the resurrection I will merely say that all men will come from the grave as they lie down, whether old or young, there will not be "added unto their stature one cubit;" neither taken from it; all will be raised by the power of God, having spirit in their bodies, and not blood. (Times and Seasons, April 15, 1842, p. 752) TLDP:562

**President Spencer W. Kimball**

When the body is resurrected, we will have our limbs and all our facilities. We will not have blood in our veins, but we will have the Spirit of the Lord in our veins so that we can move forward into an everlasting life. ACR(Manilla)1975:51

**James E. Talmage**

A resurrected body, though of tangible substance, and possessing all the organs of the mortal tabernacle, is not bound to earth by gravitation, nor can it be hindered in its movements by material barriers. To us who conceive of motion only in the directions incident to the three dimensions of space, the passing of a solid, such as a living body of flesh and bones, through stone walls, is necessarily incomprehensible. But that resurrected beings move in accordance with laws making such passage possible and to them natural, is evidenced not only by the instance of the risen Christ, but by the movements of other resurrected personages.

Thus, in September, 1823, Moroni, the Nephite prophet who had died about A.D. 400, appeared to Joseph Smith in his chamber, three times during one night, coming and going without hindrance incident to walls of roof (see JS-H 2:43; also The Articles of Faith, pp. 11-13). That Moroni was a resurrected man is shown by his corporeity manifested in his handling of the metallic plates on which was inscribed the record known to us as the Book of Mormon. So also resurrected beings possess the power of rendering themselves visible or invisible to the physical vision of mortals. JTC:698

### James E. Talmage

It would appear unnecessary to cite at greater length in substantiating our affirmation that Jesus Christ was God even before He assumed a body of flesh. During that antemortal period there was essential difference between the Father and the Son, in that the former had already passed through the experiences of mortal life, including death and resurrection, and was therefore a Being possessed of a perfect, immortalized body of flesh and bones, while the Son was yet unembodied. Through His death and subsequent resurrection Jesus the Christ is today a Being like unto the Father in all essential characteristics. JTC:38-39

### Joseph Smith

Some will say that they have seen a spirit; that he offered them his hand, but they did not touch it. This is a lie. First, it is contrary to the plan of God: a spirit cannot come but in glory; an angel has flesh and bones; we see not their glory. (*The Prophet instructs the Twelve on priesthood, in the vicinity of Commerce, Ill., July 2, 1839*) HC3:392

### Joseph Smith

The Father has a body of flesh and bones as tangible as man's; the Son also; but the Holy Ghost has not a body of flesh and bones, but is a personage of Spirit. Were it not so, the Holy Ghost could not dwell in us. (*Revelation, April 2, 1830*) D&C 130:22

### Jesus,
#### recorded in Luke

And as they thus spake, Jesus himself stood in the midst of them, and saith unto them, Peace be unto you. 37. But they were terrified and affrighted, and supposed that they had seen a spirit. 38. And he said unto them, Why are ye troubled? and why do thoughts arise in your hearts? 39. Behold my hands and my feet, that it is I myself: handle me, and see; for a spirit hath not flesh and bones, as ye see me have. (*The risen Christ appears to the Apostles and others*) Luke 24:36-39

**652. There are two major resurrections: the first resurrection for the just, the second for the unjust.**

### Joseph Smith

And the saints that are upon the earth, who are alive, shall be quickened and be caught up to meet him. 97. And they who have slept in their graves shall come forth, for their graves shall be opened; and they also shall be caught up to meet him in the midst of the pillar of heaven— 98. They are Christ's, the first fruits, they who shall descend with him first, and they who are on the earth and in their graves, who are first caught up to meet him; and all this by the voice of the sounding of the trump of the angel of God. 99. And after this another angel shall sound, which is the second trump; and then cometh the redemption of those who are Christ's at his coming; who have received their part in that prison which is prepared for them, that they might receive the gospel, and be judged according to men in the flesh. 100. And again, another trump shall sound, which is the third trump; and then come the spirits of men who are to be judged, and are found under condemnation; 101. And these are the rest of the dead; and they live not again until the thousand years are ended, neither again, until the end of the earth. 102. And another trump shall sound, which is the fourth trump, saying: There are found among those who are to remain until that great and last day, even the end, who shall remain filthy still. (*Revelation, Dec. 27/28, 1832; the "olive leaf message of peace"*) D&C 88:96-102

### Elder Joseph Fielding Smith

While there was a general resurrection of the righteous at the time Christ arose from the dead, it is customary for us to speak of the resurrection of the righteous at the Second Coming of Christ as the first resurrection. It is first to us, for we have little thought or concern over that which is past. The Lord has promised that at the time of his Second Advent the graves will be opened, and the just shall come forth to reign with him on the earth for a thousand years. . . . ¶ In modern revelation given to the Church, the Lord has made known more in relation to this glorious event. There shall be at least two classes which shall have the privilege of the resurrection at this time: First, those who "shall dwell in the presence of God and his Christ forever and ever" [D&C 76:62]; and second, honorable men, those who belong to the terrestrial kingdom as well as those of the celestial kingdom. . . . ¶ After the Lord and the righteous who are caught up to meet him have descended upon the earth, there will come to pass another resurrection. This may be considered as a part of the first, although it comes later. In this resurrection will come forth those of the terrestrial order, who were not worthy to be caught up to meet him, but who are worthy to come forth to enjoy the millennial reign. . . . ¶ Also in this class will be numbered those who died without law and hence are not under condemnation for a violation of the commandments of the Lord. The promise is made to them of redemption from death in the following words: "and then shall the heathen nations be redeemed, and they that knew no law shall have part in the first resurrection; and it shall be tolerable for them" [D&C 45:54]. These, too, shall partake of the mercies of the Lord and shall receive the reuniting of spirit and body inseparably, thus becoming immortal, but not with the fulness of the glory of God. . . . ¶ All liars, and sorcerers, and adulterers and all who love and make a lie, shall not receive the resurrection at this time, but for a thousand years shall be thrust down into hell where they shall suffer the wrath of God until they pay the price of their sinning, if it is possible, by the things which they shall suffer. [See Church News, Apr 23, 1932, p. 6.] ¶ These are the "spirits of men who are to be judged and are found under condemnation; And these are the rest of the dead; and they live not again until the thousand years are ended, neither again, until the end of the earth" [D&C 88:100-01]. ¶ These are the hosts of the telestial world who are commanded to "suffer the wrath of God on earth;" and who are "cast down to hell and suffer the wrath of Almighty God, until the fulness of times, when Christ shall have subdued all enemies under his feet, and shall have perfected his work;" [Era, vol. 45, p. 781; D&C 76:104-06]. . . . ¶ This suffering will be a means of cleansing, or purifying, and through it the wicked shall be brought to a condition whereby they may, through the redemption of Jesus Christ, obtain immortality. Their spirits and bodies shall be again united, and they shall dwell in the telestial kingdom. But this resurrection will not come until the end of the world. (Doctrines of Salvation, 2:295-98) TLDP:564-65

**Joseph Smith**

And [the dead] shall come forth; they who have done good in the resurrection of the just, and they who have done evil in the resurrection of the unjust. (*Vision to Joseph Smith and Sidney Rigdon, Feb. 16, 1832*) D&C 76:17

**Joseph Smith**

For the day cometh that the Lord shall utter his voice out of heaven; the heavens shall shake and the earth shall tremble, and the trump of God shall sound both long and loud, and shall say to the sleeping nations: Ye saints arise and live; ye sinners stay and sleep until I shall call again. (*Revelation, Feb. 1831*) D&C 43:18

**Paul**

And have hope toward God, which they themselves also allow, that there shall be a resurrection of the dead, both of the just and unjust. (*Paul testifies before the procurator, Felix*) Acts 24:15

**Joseph Smith**

And again we bear record—for we saw and heard, and this is the testimony of the gospel of Christ concerning them who shall come forth in the resurrection of the just— 51. They are they who received the testimony of Jesus, and believed on his name and were baptized after the manner of his burial, being buried in the water in his name, and this according to the commandment which he has given— 52. That by keeping the commandments they might be washed and cleansed from all their sins, and receive the Holy Spirit by the laying on of the hands of him who is ordained and sealed unto this power; 53. And who overcome by faith, and are sealed by the Holy Spirit of promise, which the Father sheds forth upon all those who are just and true. 54. They are they who are the church of the Firstborn. 55. They are they into whose hands the Father has given all things— 56. They are they who are priests and kings, who have received of his fulness, and of his glory; 57. And are priests of the Most High, after the order of Melchizedek, which was after the order of Enoch, which was after the order of the Only Begotten Son. 58. Wherefore, as it is written, they are gods, even the sons of God— 59. Wherefore, all things are theirs, whether life or death, or things present, or things to come, all are theirs and they are Christ's, and Christ is God's. 60. And they shall overcome all things. 61. Wherefore, let no man glory in man, but rather let him glory in God, who shall subdue all enemies under his feet. 62. These shall dwell in the presence of God and his Christ forever and ever. 63. These are they whom he shall bring with him, when he shall come in the clouds of heaven to reign on the earth over his people. 64. These are they who shall have part in the first resurrection. 65. These are they who shall come forth in the resurrection of the just. . . . 102. Last of all, these all are they who will not be gathered with the saints, to be caught up unto the church of the Firstborn, and received into the cloud. 103. These are they who are liars, and sorcerers, and adulterers, and whoremongers, and whosoever loves and makes a lie. 104. These are they who suffer the wrath of God on earth. 105. These are they who suffer the vengeance of eternal fire. 106. These are they who are cast down to hell and suffer the wrath of Almighty God, until the fulness of times, when Christ shall have subdued all enemies under his feet, and shall have perfected his work; (*Vision to Joseph Smith and Sidney Rigdon, Feb. 16, 1832*) D&C 76:50-65,102-06

**John**

[A]nd they lived and reigned with Christ a thousand years. 5. But the rest of the dead lived not again until the thousand years were finished. This is the first resurrection. 6. Blessed and holy is he that hath part in the first resurrection: on such the second death hath no power, but they shall be priests of God and of Christ, and shall reign with him a thousand years. (*The Apostle John sees the judgment of man at the end of the Millennium*) Rev.20:4-6

**Jesus,**
*quoted by John*

Marvel not at this: for the hour is coming, in the which all that are in the graves shall hear his voice, 29. And shall come forth; they that have done good, unto the resurrection of life; and they that have done evil, unto the resurrection of damnation. (*Jesus addresses the Jews*) John 5:28-29

**Daniel**

And many of them that sleep in the dust of the earth shall awake, some to everlasting life, and some to shame and everlasting contempt. (*Daniel tells of the two resurrections*) Dan.12:2

**James E. Talmage**

Two General Resurrections are mentioned in the scriptures, and these may be specified as first and final, or as the resurrection of the just and the resurrection of the unjust. The first was inaugurated by the resurrection of Jesus Christ, immediately following which many of the saints came forth from their graves. A continuation of this, the resurrection of the just, has been in operation since, and will be greatly extended, or brought to pass in a general way, in connection with the coming of Christ in His glory. The final resurrection will be deferred until the end of the thousand years of peace, and will be in connection with the last judgment. AF:348

**Related Witnesses:**

**Paul**

For the Lord himself shall descend from heaven with a shout, with the voice of the archangel, and with the trump of God: and the dead in Christ shall rise first: . . . (*Paul writes to the Church at Thessalonica, comprising Jews and many pagan converts, A.D. 50*) 1Thess.4:16

**Elder Wilford Woodruff**

While I was upon my knees praying, my room was filled with light. I looked up and a messenger stood by my side. I arose, and this personage told me he had come to instruct me. . . . ¶ Then he showed me the resurrection of the dead—what is termed the first and second resurrection. In the first resurrection I saw no graves, nor anyone raised from the grave. I saw legions of celestial beings, men and women who had received the Gospel, all clothed in white robes. In the form they were presented to me, they had already been raised from the grave. After this, he showed me what is termed the second resurrection. Vast fields of graves were before me, and the Spirit of God rested upon the earth like a shower of gentle rain, and when that fell upon the graves they were opened, and a immense host of human beings came forth. They were just as diversified in their dress as we are here, or as they were laid down. ("Obtain the Spirit of God," Millennial Star, Sept. 28, 1905, p. 612) TLDP:564

**Melvin J. Ballard**

When you see men and women in the resurrection, we shall see them in very bloom of their glorious manhood and womanhood, and he has promised all who would keep his commandments and obey the gospel of the Lord Jesus Christ, the restoration of their houses, glorified, immortalized, celestialized, fitted to dwell in the presence of God. ¶ To those who cannot subscribe to those terms, and yet obey others, the lesser law, Jesus has promised a terrestrial body, not so glorious, and yet immortal and eternal, and still to those who cannot do so much, but only obey in part, a telestial body suited to the kingdom in which they dwell. Thus we fix our status in that resurrection, though the resurrection is a fact without our action. Our action makes it either glorious—the resurrection of the just; or the resurrection of the unjust. (Sermons and Missionary Services of Melvin J. Ballard, p. 186) TLDP:565-66

**Abinadi,**
*quoted by Mormon*

And there cometh a resurrection, even a first resurrection; yea, even a resurrection of those that have been, and who are, and who shall be, even until the resurrection of Christ—for so shall he be called. 22. And now, the resurrection of all the prophets, and all those that have believed in their words, or all those that have kept the commandments of God, shall come forth in the first resurrection; therefore, they are the first resurrection. 23. They are raised to dwell with God who has redeemed them; thus they have eternal life through Christ, who has broken the bands of death. 24. And these are those who have part in the first resurrection; and these are they that have died before Christ came, in their ignorance, not having salvation declared unto them. And thus the Lord bringeth about the restoration of these; and they have a part in the first resurrection, or have eternal life, being redeemed by the Lord. 25. And little children also have eternal life. (*Abinadi preaches to King Noah and his people, about 148 B.C.*) Mosiah 15:21-25

---

**653. Many of the righteous dead were resurrected immediately after Christ was resurrected.**

**James E. Talmage**
Two General Resurrections are mentioned in the scriptures, and these may be specified as first and final, or as the resurrection of the just and the resurrection of the unjust. The first was inaugurated by the resurrection of Jesus Christ, immediately following which many of the saints came forth from their graves. A continuation of this, the resurrection of the just, has been in operation since, and will be greatly extended, or brought to pass in a general way, in connection with the coming of Christ in His glory. The final resurrection will be deferred until the end of the thousand years of peace, and will be in connection with the last judgment. AF:348

**Recorded in Matthew**
Jesus, when he had cried again with a loud voice, yielded up the ghost. 51. And, behold, the veil of the temple was rent in twain from the top to the bottom; and the earth did quake, and the rocks rent; 52. And the graves were opened; and many bodies of the saints which slept arose, 53. And came out of the graves after his resurrection, and went into the holy city, and appeared unto many. (*Jesus is crucified*) Matt.27:50-53

**James E. Faust**
Mary was not to be the only witness of the miracle of the Resurrection. Although the Savior was the "first-fruits" of them that slept (1Cor.15:23), the scriptures testify that "many bodies of the saints which slept arose, and came out of the grave after his resurrection, and went into the holy city, and appeared unto many." (Matt.27:52-53) CR1985Apr:39

**Elder Ezra Taft Benson**
The resurrection is a reality. The scriptures are replete with evidence. Almost immediately

after the glorious resurrection of the Lord, Matthew records: "And the graves were opened; and many bodies of the saints which slept arose, ¶ "And came out of the graves after his resurrection, and went into the holy city, and appeared unto many." CR1971Apr:17-18

**Elder Joseph Fielding Smith**
While there was a general resurrection of the righteous at the time Christ arose from the dead, it is customary for us to speak of the resurrection of the righteous at the Second Coming of Christ as the first resurrection. It is the first to us, for we have little thought or concern over that which is past. (Doctrines of Salvation, 2:295-98) TLDP:564-65

**James E. Talmage**
Christ had risen; and following Him many of the righteous dead on the western continent rose from their graves, and appeared as resurrected, immortalized beings among the survivors of the land-wide destruction; even as in Judea many of the saints had been raised immediately after the resurrection of Christ. JTC:724

**James E. Talmage**
The victory over death was made manifest in the resurrection of the crucified Christ; He was the first to pass from death to immortality and so is justly known as "the first fruits of them that slept." That the resurrection of the dead so inaugurated is to be extended to every one who has or shall have lived is proved by an abundance of scriptural evidence. Following our Lord's resurrection, others who had slept in the tomb arose and were seen of many, not as spirit-apparitions but as resurrected beings possessing immortalized bodies: "And the graves were opened; and many bodies of the saints which slept arose, and came out of the graves after his resurrection, and went into the holy city, and appeared unto many." JTC:23

**Related Witnesses:**
**Elder Joseph Fielding Smith**
It is the opinion of some that the resurrection is going on all the time now, but this is purely speculation without warrant in the scriptures. It is true that the Lord has power to call forth any person or persons from the dead, as he may desire, especially if they have a mission to perform which would require their resurrection. For example, we have the cases of Peter, James, and Moroni. ¶ We are given to understand that the first resurrection yet future, which means the coming forth of the righteous, will take place at one particular time, which is when our Savior shall appear in the clouds of heaven, when he shall return to reign. For us to speculate whether or not the Prophet Joseph Smith,

Hyrum Smith, Brigham Young, and others have been called forth, without any revelation from the Lord, is merely supposition. When the Lord wants any of these men, he has the power to call them, but the first resurrection, with which we have any future concern, will commence when Christ comes. (Doctrines of Salvation, 2:299-300) DGSM:89

### Paul

For as in Adam all die, even so in Christ shall all be made alive. 23. But every man in his own order: Christ the firstfruits; afterward they that are Christ's at his coming. (*Paul writes to the Church at Corinth, Greece, about* A.D. 55) 1Cor.15:22-23

### 654. Animals will be resurrected.

#### Elder Joseph Fielding Smith

The Lord created all things for a purpose. Nothing has he created to be destroyed, but that all things might endure forever. . . . ¶ So we see that the Lord intends to save, not only the earth and the heavens, not only man who dwells upon the earth, but all things which he has created. The animals, the fishes of the sea, the fowls of the air, as well as man, are to be re-created, or renewed, through the resurrection, for they too are living souls. CR1928Oct:99-100

#### Joseph Smith,
*receiving the Word of the Lord*

And again, verily, verily, I say unto you that when the thousand years are ended, and men again begin to deny their God, then will I spare the earth but for a little season; 23. And the end shall come, and the heaven and the earth shall be consumed and pass away, and there shall be a new heaven and a new earth. 24. For all old things shall pass away, and all things shall become new, even the heaven and the earth, and all the fulness thereof, both men and beasts, the fowls of the air, and the fishes of the sea; 25. And not one hair, neither mote, shall be lost, for it is the workmanship of mine hand. (*Revelation in presence of six elders, Sept. 1830*) D&C 29:22-25

#### Joseph Smith

John saw curious looking beasts in heaven; he saw every creature that was in heaven,—all the beasts, fowls and fish in heaven,—actually there, giving glory to God. How do you prove it? (See Rev.5:13.) "And every creature which is in heaven, and on the earth, and under the earth, and such as are in the sea, and all that are in them, heard I saying, Blessing, and honour, and glory, and power, be unto him that sitteth

upon the throne, and unto the Lamb for ever and ever." ¶ I suppose John saw beings there of a thousand forms, that had been saved from ten thousand times ten thousand earths like this,—strange beasts of which we have no conception: all might be seen in heaven. The grand secret was to show John what there was in heaven. John learned that God glorified himself by saving all that his hands had made, whether beasts, fowls, fishes or men; and he will glorify himself with them. ¶ Says one, "I cannot believe in the salvation of beasts." Any man who would tell you that this could not be, would tell you that the revelations are not true. John heard the words of the beasts giving glory to God, and understood them. God who made the beasts could understand every language spoken by them. The four beasts were four of the most noble animals that had filled the measure of their creation, and had been saved from other worlds, because they were perfect: they were like angels in their sphere. We are not told where they came from, and I do not know; but they were seen and heard by John praising and glorifying God. [See Rev.4:6] (*General conference of the Church held on the floor of the Nauvoo Temple, April 8, 1843*) HC5:343-44

#### President Joseph F. Smith,
#### John R. Winder, Anthon H. Lund
(First Presidency)

He made the tadpole and the ape, the lion and the elephant but He did not make them in His own image, nor endow them with Godlike reason and intelligence. Nevertheless, the whole animal creation will be perfected and perpetuated in the Hereafter, each class in its 'distinct order or sphere,' and will enjoy 'eternal felicity.' That fact has been made plain in this dispensation (D&C 77:3). (*Christmas greetings, Dec. 18, 1909*) MOFP4:207

**Related Witnesses:**

#### Joseph Smith

Q. Are the four beasts limited to individual beasts, or do they represent classes or orders? ¶ A. They are limited to four individual beasts, which were shown to John, to represent the glory of the classes of beings in their destined order or sphere of creation, in the enjoyment of their eternal felicity. (*Revelation in connection with Joseph's translation of the scriptures, Rev.4:6, March 1832*) D&C 77:3

# List of Doctrines

## REVELATION

*Doctrines Located in This Topic*

### (1) Law of Witnesses

655. When the Lord wants the people to learn any essential truth, He will teach it to them over and over again through the repeated witnesses of prophets.

656. The Lord continually reveals His word to prophets for the contemporary guidance of His people, while He also preserves ancient and contemporary records as continual testimony and witness of His doctrines.

657. All revelations from heaven are harmonious with each other.

658. True doctrine is in harmony with the recorded revealed word of God in all scriptures (i.e., the standard works).

659. Unless a doctrine is in harmony with the teachings of contemporary prophets it cannot be considered true doctrine.

660. The Holy Ghost confirms the truth of the declarations of the Lord's witnesses.

### (2) Revelation to the Church

661. Revelation to the Church is continuous.

662. Only the President of the Church—the prophet, seer, and revelator—has the right to receive new revelation for the Church (or amendatory revelations, or to give authoritative interpretations of scriptures, or to change in any way the existing doctrines of the Church).

663. For new revelation to be binding on the Church (when the President of the Church receives revelation for the Church), it must be proclaimed universally to the Church.

### (3) Revelation to Individuals

664. Only by revelation from God can we gain knowledge about God; we cannot learn about the existence and character of God by reasoning alone.

665. "Mysteries of God" (those divine truths that bring about salvation and eternal life) are available to us only by revelation from God.

# REVELATION continued

666. Revelation from God to each of us as individuals is necessary for our salvation.

667. Revelation to individuals and to the Church comes line upon line, precept upon precept.

668. If we are obedient to the light He has given us, God will reveal more truth and knowledge to us.

669. Personal righteousness is a prerequisite for receiving revelation.

670. Individual men and women can receive revelation to guide them within their own spheres of authority (they will not receive divine instructions for those higher in authority than they).

671. Every Church member is entitled to revelation in the performance of his or her calling in the Church.

## (4) Recognizing Revelation

672. One way God communicates to us is by giving us peace to our minds and souls.

673. The spirit of revelation is perceived when a person senses an inward flowing of pure intelligence, giving sudden strokes of ideas.

674. The spirit of revelation is perceived when a person senses an enlarging of the soul and an enlightening of the understanding.

675. God at times speaks to us with a still, small voice of revelation.

676. Revelation comes at times through dreams.

677. Revelation comes at times as an audible voice from heaven.

678. Revelation comes at times through angels sent with messages.

679. Revelation comes at times by visions.

680. Revelation of the truth of a matter comes by the process of first studying it out, then asking the Lord if the conclusion is right; the Lord then induces a burning in the bosom if it is right, or else He causes a stupor of thought if the decision is wrong—causing a forgetting of that which is wrong.

681. We are to heed the promptings of the Holy Ghost.

*Doctrines on REVELATION*
*Located in Other Topics*

324. Members of the Church are entitled to revelation and guidance from the Holy Ghost.

# REVELATION continued

362. Christ lives today—modern prophets have seen Him face to face and have talked with Him.

602. The Lord's way of teaching us is through prophet witnesses.

604. The Lord chooses righteous men as His prophet witnesses.

606. A prophet is a revelator who declares the will of God to the people.

610. We are to receive the words of the President of the Church as if they came from the mouth the Lord.

611. The President of the Church will never lead the Saints astray or send forth counsel to the world that is contrary to the mind and will of the Lord.

712. Written scripture is the recorded testimony of prophets who receive gospel truths by revelation from the Lord.

813. Testimonies of divine truths come through personal revelation.

819. Only by revelation can a person know and testify that Jesus Christ is the Son of God.

# REVELATION

**(1) Law of Witnesses**
**(2) Revelation to the Church**
**(3) Revelation to Individuals**
**(4) Recognizing Revelation**

**Author's Note:** Every truth of the gospel intended as a testimony to the world is revealed from God to men through the recorded witness of *many* prophets in written scriptures. Every asserted doctrine and every interpretation of scripture must be tested against those recorded testimonies and be in harmony with them.

## (1) Law of Witnesses

655. When the Lord wants the people to learn any essential truth, He will teach it to them over and over again through the repeated witnesses of prophets.

**Boyd K. Packer**
I wish to share a few thoughts about a basic doctrine of the Church. . . . ¶ . . . . [I]nstruction vital to our salvation is not hidden in an obscure verse or phrase in the scriptures. To the contrary, essential truths are repeated over and over again. CR1984Oct:81

**Elder Joseph Fielding Smith**
There is a law definitely stated in the scriptures governing testimony and the appointment of witnesses. This law the Lord has always followed in granting new revelation to the people. ¶ All down through the ages this law has been a fixed and definite one. If we had perfect records of all ages, we would find that whenever the Lord has established a dispensation, there has been more than one witness to testify for him. Paul in writing to the Corinthians said: "In the mouth of two or three witnesses shall every word be established." [2Cor.13:1, the divine law of witnesses given to Israel.] (Church News, 1939; Doctrines of Salvation 1:203) TLDP:733

**Bruce R. McConkie**
This law . . . is that the Lord always sends his word by witnesses who testify of its truth and divinity; that one witness alone, though he speaks the truth, is not enough to bind his hearers; that two or more witnesses always unite their voices to make the divinely borne testimony binding on earth and sealed everlastingly in the heavens; and that thus, in the mouth of two or three witnesses every word shall be established. (The Mortal Messiah, 2:76) TLDP:733

**Elder Joseph Fielding Smith**
In giving the world the testimony of three witnesses in addition to Joseph Smith, the Lord fulfilled the law. We are called upon in this life

to walk by faith, not by sight, not by the proclamation of heavenly messengers with the voice of thunder, but by the proclamation of accredited witnesses whom the Lord sends and by whom every word shall be established. CHMR1:40; DCSM:13

**Nephi, son of Lehi**
Wherefore, the Lord God will proceed to bring forth the words of the book; and in the mouth of as many witnesses as seemeth him good will he establish his word; and wo be unto him that rejecteth the word of God! (*Nephi foretells of the last days and the coming forth of the Book of Mormon, 559-545 B.C.*) 2Ne.27:14

**Joseph Smith**
One thing more in order to prove the work as we proceed. It is necessary to have witnesses, two or three of whose testimonies, according to the laws or rules of God and man, are sufficient to establish any one point. (*Letter to James A. Bennett, Nov. 13, 1843*) HC6:76

**Joseph Smith,**
*receiving the Word of the Lord*
And now, behold, I give unto you, and also unto my servant Joseph, the keys of this gift, which shall bring to light this ministry; and in the mouth of two or three witnesses shall every word be established. (*Revelation for Oliver Cowdery, April 1829*) D&C 6:28

**Nephi, son of Lehi**
And my brother, Jacob, also has seen him as I have seen him; wherefore, I will send their words forth unto my children to prove unto them that my words are true. Wherefore, by the words of three, God hath said, I will establish my word. Nevertheless, God sendeth more witnesses, and he proveth all his words. (*Nephi testifies that he and his brother, Jacob, have each seen the Redeemer, 559-545 B.C.*) 2Ne.11:3

**Moroni, son of Mormon**
And in the mouth of three witnesses shall these things be established; and the testimony of three, and this work, in the which shall be shown forth the power of God and also his word, of which the Father, and the Son, and the

Holy Ghost bear record—and all this shall stand as a testimony against the world at the last day. (*The record of Moroni*) Ether 5:4

**Joseph Smith**

[T]hat in the mouth of two or three witnesses every word may be established. (*Joseph writes to the Church giving further directions on baptism for the dead, Sept. 6, 1842*) D&C 128:3

**Joseph Smith,**
*receiving the Word of the Lord*

And the testimony of three witnesses will I send forth of my word. 16. And behold, whosoever believeth on my words, them will I visit with the manifestation of my Spirit; and they shall be born of me, even of water and of the Spirit— (*Revelation at the request of Martin Harris, March 1829; the Lord promises to supply three witnesses to the Book of Mormon*) D&C 5:15-16

**Mark E. Petersen**

The chief reason we have the Book of Mormon is that in the mouth of two or three witnesses shall all things be established. (See 2Cor.13:1.) We have the Bible; we also have the Book of Mormon. They constitute two voices—two volumes of scripture—from two widely separated ancient peoples, both bearing testimony to the divinity of the Lord Jesus Christ. ¶ But we also have two other scriptural witnesses also, making four altogether. They are the modern scriptures given as revelations through the Prophet Joseph Smith, and they, too, declare that Jesus is the Christ, the Savior, the Creator, the long-promised Messiah. CR1978Apr:98

**Paul**

This is the third time I am coming to you. In the mouth of two or three witnesses shall every word be established. (*Paul writes to the Church at Corinth, Greece, reminding the Saints that he has already given them two witnesses—two visits, two preachings—and that this epistle is the third, about A.D. 55*) 2Cor.13:1

**Elder Joseph Fielding Smith**

It was necessary . . . that there should be other witnesses and that Joseph Smith should not stand alone. . . . This is according to the law of witnesses which the Lord established in the very beginning. (See Deut.19:15; John 5:30-32; John 8:12-14; 2Cor.13:1.) ¶ The consequences following the rejection of such strong, divine, and attested witness, is exceedingly great. CHMR1:73

**Related Witnesses:**

**Bruce R. McConkie**

All the prophets of all the ages bear the same testimony; all preach the same saving truths; all bear witness of the same Atoning One. (The Mortal Messiah, 3:401) TLDP:535

**Bruce R. McConkie**

Jesus himself, *repeatedly*, bluntly, plainly, *over and over again* testified of his own divine Sonship. [italics added] (Doctrinal New Testament Commentary, 1:198-99) TLDP:317

**J. Reuben Clark, Jr.**

I have said to you brethren, *over and over again*, and I *repeat* it tonight. . . . [italics added] CR1949Apr:184

**President Joseph F. Smith,**
**Anthon H. Lund, Charles W. Penrose**
**(First Presidency)**
**Council of the Twelve**

The scriptures plainly and *repeatedly* affirm that God is the Creator of the earth and the heavens and all things that in them are. [italics added] (*Pamphlet, "The Father and The Son; A Doctrinal Exposition by The First Presidency and The Twelve," published by the Church, June 30, 1916. Reprinted in AF:420-26. For details, see MOFP5:23-34*) AF:421; MOFP5:26

**Elder Spencer W. Kimball**

Sexual sin receives *repeated* condemnation in the scriptures. [italics added] (The Miracle of Forgiveness, p. 24) TLDP:71

**President Spencer W. Kimball**

We have *repeatedly* affirmed the position of the Church in unalterably opposing all abortions, except in two rare instances. . . . [italics added] CR1976Oct:6

**President Heber J. Grant,**
**J. Reuben Clark, Jr., David O. McKay**
**(First Presidency)**

[T]he Lord said: "Multiply and replenish the earth." He has *repeated* that commandment in our day. He has again revealed in this, the last dispensation, the principle of the eternity of the marriage covenant. [italics added] CR1942Oct:12; MOFP6:177

**George Q. Cannon**

It is a direct command from the Lord, often *repeated* in His word, constantly declared by His servants, that it is the duty of his children to pray to Him without ceasing. [italics added] (Gospel Truth, 2:166-67) TLDP:489

**Marion G. Romney**

There isn't any commandment from the Lord that is *repeated* more often than the commandment to pray to the Lord. . . . [italics added] ACR(Taipei)1975:7

**Nephi, son of Lehi**

For I command all men, both in the east and in the west, and in the north, and in the south, and in the islands of the sea, that they shall write the words which I speak unto them; for out of the books which shall be written I will judge the world, every man according to their works, according to that which is written. 12. For behold, I shall speak unto the Jews and they shall write it; and I shall also speak unto the Nephites and they shall write it; and I shall also speak unto the other tribes of the house of Israel, which I have led away, and they shall write it; and I shall also speak unto all nations of the earth and they shall write it. 13. And it shall come to pass that the Jews shall have the words of the Nephites, and the Nephites shall have the words of the Jews; and the Nephites and the Jews shall have the words of the lost tribes of Israel; and the lost tribes of Israel shall have the words of the Nephites and the Jews. (*The Lord speaks to Nephi about the latter-day gentiles, many of whom shall reject the Book of Mormon, 559-545 B.C.*) 2Ne.29:11-13

### Bruce R. McConkie
Every prophet from the beginning on down was a witness of the Lord Jesus. They all bore testimony that salvation was in him. They all worshipped the Father in the name of Christ. They all taught that men received a remission of sins by faith and repentance and baptism, because of the atoning sacrifice which he would work out. . . . And all of the witness and all of the assurance that any of the inspired apostles and prophets have made since the day of Christ are termed testimony. ACR(Sydney)1976:20

### Jacob, brother of Nephi
Behold, my brethren, he that prophesieth, let him prophesy to the understanding of men; for the Spirit speaketh the truth and lieth not. Wherefore, it speaketh of things as they really are, and of things as they really will be; wherefore, these things are manifested unto us plainly, for the salvation of our souls. But behold, we are not witnesses alone in these things; for God also spake them unto prophets of old. (*Jacob's writings, 544-521 B.C.*) Jacob 4:13

### Elder Joseph Fielding Smith
It is wrong to take one passage of scripture and isolate it from all other teachings dwelling on the same subject. We should bring together all that has been said by authority on the question. . . . Therefore we must find out what else has been said about salvation. (Doctrines of Salvation, 2:95) TLDP:615

### President Joseph F. Smith
We have nothing that is not in common with the Latter-day Saints. We know nothing, and we will preach nothing to the people except that which the Lord God has revealed, and we advise and counsel those who are in authority, and whose duty and business it is to teach and preach the principles of the gospel to the world and to the Latter-day Saints, to confine their teachings and their instructions to the word of God that has been revealed. CR1917Oct:5

### Jesus,
### *recorded in Matthew*
But if he will not hear thee, then take with thee one or two more, that in the mouth of two or three witnesses every word may be established. (*Jesus teaches his disciples the principle of forgiveness*) Matt.18:16

### President Joseph F. Smith,
### Anthon H. Lund, Charles W. Penrose
(First Presidency)
The First Presidency have nothing to advance concerning pre-existing states, but that which is contained in the revelations to the Church. The written standards of scripture show. . . . (*Published message of the First Presidency of the Church, Jan. 1912; IE1912Mar:417*) MOFP4:264

### Thomas B. Marsh, Orson Hyde,
### William Smith, David W. Patten,
### Wm. E. M'Lellin, Orson Pratt,
### Brigham Young, Parley P. Pratt,
### John F. Boynton, Heber C. Kimball,
### Luke S. Johnson, Lyman E. Johnson
TESTIMONY OF THE TWELVE APOSTLES TO THE TRUTH OF THE BOOK OF DOCTRINE AND COVENANTS. ¶ The Testimony of the Witnesses to the Book of the Lord's Commandments, which He gave to His Church through Joseph Smith, Jun., who was appointed by the voice of the Church for this purpose: ¶ We, therefore, feel willing to bear testimony to all the world of mankind, to every creature upon the face of all the earth and upon the islands of the sea, that the Lord has borne record to our souls, through the Holy Ghost shed forth upon us, that these commandments were given by inspiration of God, and are profitable for all men, and are verily true. ¶ We give this testimony unto the world, the Lord being our helper; and it is through the grace of God the Father, and His Son, Jesus Christ, that we are permitted to have this privilege of bearing this testimony unto the world, that the children of men may be profited thereby. (*This written testimony of the Twelve Apostles was included in the introduction to the publication of the Doctrine and Covenants [Book of Commandments] in 1835*) D&C Intro

### Recorded in Deuteronomy
One witness shall not rise up against a man for any iniquity, or for any sin, in any sin that he sinneth: at the mouth of two witnesses, or at the mouth of three witnesses, shall the matter be established. (*Commandments to Israel through Moses*) Deut.19:15

**Jesus,**
*quoted by John*

Then spake Jesus again unto them, saying, I am the light of the world: he that followeth me shall not walk in darkness, but shall have the light of life. 13. The Pharisees therefore said unto him, Thou bearest record of thyself; thy record is not true. 14. Jesus answered and said unto them. . . . 17. It is also written in your law, that the testimony of two men is true. 18. I am one that bear witness of myself, and the Father that sent me beareth witness of me. (*Jesus responds to the Pharisees who accuse him of bearing record of himself without witnesses, as he teaches the people in the temple*) John 8:12-14,17-18

**Elder Joseph Fielding Smith**

The law given to Israel in the beginning was that in the mouth of two or three witnesses all things should be established. (Answers to Gospel Questions, 1:204) TLDP:733

**Author's Note:** The question arises, where can we go to find these "repeated witnesses of prophets," referred to in this doctrine (D-655)? ¶ In the Gospel Principles Manual appears the following important statement: "The Church of Jesus Christ of Latter-day Saints accepts four books as scripture: the Bible, the Book of Mormon, the Doctrine and Covenants, and the Pearl of Great Price. These books are called the standard works of the Church. . . . ¶ In addition to these four books of scripture, the inspired words of our living prophets become scripture to us. Their words come to us through conferences, Church publications, and instructions to local priesthood leaders." (GP:49,51-52) ¶ Those *words of prophets* that are binding scripture on the saints and the world *because they are officially published by the Church*, are located in the following five types of official Church publications: ¶ (1) The Standard Works. ¶ (2) Conference Reports: Church published speeches and writings of the Latter-day prophets of the Church of Jesus Christ of Latter-day Saints. ¶ (3) Church published books or writings of Apostles (i.e. published by authority of the prophets: the First Presidency of the Church and/or the Council of the Twelve). ¶ (4) Church published priesthood and Relief Society manuals, institute and other lesson manuals. These are writings promulgated under authority of the President of the Church, the living prophet, whose right it is to speak for the Lord. (But we have not included in this definition of Church publications Church *sponsored* writings, such as the Church News and Church magazines—Ensign, New Era, Friend,

or Improvement Era—because the living prophet and President of the Church does not control the contents or officially promulgate these publications. ¶ (5) New revelations, or amendatory revelations, presented by the President, prophet, seer and revelator of the Church to the Church as a whole, and accepted by the Church as a whole at a general conference, and which are then sent (i.e. published) to the stakes and wards of the Church over the signatures of the First Presidency, or sent/published to the Church in the regular papers or magazines which are under the control of the Church, as revelation to the Church by the Lord through his prophet in the spirit of "Thus saith the Lord!" ¶ Since by the mouth of two or three witnesses every word is to be established, when a concept appears only once and is NOT repeated by prophetic witness it is not doctrine of the Church. ¶ When the Lord wants his children to learn and understand any doctrine, he will teach it to them through the spirit of prophecy by the *repeated* influence of the Holy Ghost. That same spirit will prompt more than one prophet to reiterate the doctrine. Two or more witnesses (prophets) must affirm the doctrine. Their testimonies or witnesses may all be found within the standard works; there may be but one in the standard works yet other witnesses expounding the doctrine in Church writings published under direction of the President, prophet, seer, and revelator of the Church, the First Presidency or Council of the Twelve; there may be a doctrine given to the Church and authoritatively sent (i.e. published) to the Church through a latter-day prophet/president and subsequently renewed in other writings published under the direction of the President/prophet; there may be several repetitions of the doctrine by prophets in conference talks and other Church published writings; but always, by the testimony of two or more witnesses shall every word of the Lord be established. ¶ Such is the pattern the Lord has given us from the beginning as verified by scripture: ". . . [I]n the mouth of two or three witnesses shall every word be established." (D&C 6:28)

656. The Lord continually reveals His word to prophets for the contemporary guidance of His people, while He also preserves ancient and contemporary records as continual testimony and witness of His doctrines.

### Hugh B. Brown

[W]e cannot believe that [God's] Church in one dispensation would be blessed and led by . . . "live" revelation and in another dispensation leave a distraught and imperiled world with only the recorded messages of ancient prophets, some of which messages were for specific purposes and under special circumstances. We believe that revelation both "live" and recorded is now, and will continue to be, available to men. Whenever the Lord has recognized his Church, he has given through his prophets messages of warning, instruction, and hope. . . . CR1961Oct:94-95

### President Joseph F. Smith

The theology of our Church is the theology taught by Jesus Christ and His apostles, the theology of scripture and reason. It not only acknowledges the sacredness of ancient scripture, and the binding force of divinely-inspired acts and utterances in ages past; but also declares that God now speaks to man in this final Gospel dispensation. (*Address from the First Presidency of the Church to the world, delivered to and accepted by vote of the Church in general conference, April 1907*) CR1907Apr(Appendix)4

### Marion G. Romney

Even though these testimonies of Jesus and the ancient prophets concerning the person and nature of God are clear and convincing, the Lord does not require us to rely upon them alone. He has never required the people of one age to rely upon the records of the past alone. At the beginning of every dispensation he has revealed himself anew. . . . ¶ God has, from the beginning, seen fit to place a knowledge of himself within the reach of all men. We who are his present witnesses are but discharging our responsibility when we bring these testimonies of the prophets and our own testimonies as to the form and nature of God to your attention. ¶ To the extent we do bring them to your attention, the responsibility passes from us to you to determine the credibility of the witnesses and their testimonies. Let no man underestimate the importance of his decision concerning this matter. To know God and his Son Jesus Christ is life eternal. Without such knowledge no man can be saved. And the only way to get it is to obtain a personal witness to the truth of the revelations which God the Father and Jesus Christ, his Son, have given of themselves. CR1967Oct:135-36

### Orson Pratt,
#### quoted by the First Presidency:
#### President Brigham Young,
#### Heber C. Kimball, Daniel H. Wells

Upon what principle are we to be one? It is by hearkening in all things to that eternal and ever-lasting Priesthood which has been conferred upon mortal man upon the earth. When I say that Priesthood, I mean the individual who holds the keys thereof. He is the standard—the living oracle to the Church. ¶ "But," says one, "suppose that we hearken to the word of God in the Old and New Testament—suppose that we hearken to the word of God in the Book of Doctrine and Covenants—suppose we hearken to the word of God in the Book of Mormon, and at the same time we feel disposed in our hearts to lay aside the living oracles, what then?" I would answer, in the first place, that the premises are false. Why? The very moment that we set aside the living oracles we set aside the revelations of God. Why? Because the revelations of God command us plainly that we shall hearken to the living oracles. Hence, if we undertake to follow the written word, and at the same time do not give heed to the living oracles of God, the written word will condemn us: it shows that we do not follow it according to our profession. (*As introduction to the address of Orson Pratt, from which this quotation is taken, the following appeared: "On the 29th of January, in the Tabernacle, Elder Orson Pratt, senior, addressed the Saints; and, through an oversight, a portion of his remarks was printed in . . . the Deseret News, previous to being carefully revised. Since then, those remarks have been examined by brother Pratt and the Council, and are now printed as agreed upon by them." Published message of the First Presidency of the Church, Deseret News, Sept. 22, 1860*) MOFP2:217

### James E. Talmage

We believe that God is as willing today as He ever has been to reveal His mind and will to man, and that He does so through His appointed servants—prophets, seers, and revelators—invested through ordination with the authority of the Holy Priesthood. We rely therefore on the teachings of the living oracles of God as of equal validity with the doctrines of the written word. AF:6

### President Spencer W. Kimball

Since that momentous day in 1820, additional scripture has continued to come, including the numerous and vital revelations flowing in a never-ending stream from God to his prophets on earth. . . . ¶ I say, in the deepest of humility, but also by the power and force of a burning testimony in my soul, that from the prophet of our own year, the communication line is unbroken, the authority is continuous, a light brilliant and penetrating, continues to shine. The sound of the voice of the Lord is a continuous melody and a thunderous appeal. For nearly a century and a half there has been no interruption. CR1977Apr:115

**Orson F. Whitney**

My Greek Catholic friend, whether he knew it or not, had hit upon the great distinguishing feature that differentiates God's Church from all other churches under the sun—in this, that while they are founded upon books and traditions and the precepts of men, this Church is built upon the rock of Christ, upon the principle of immediate and continuous revelation. The Latter-day Saints do not do things because they happen to be printed in a book. They do not do things because God told the Jews to do them; nor do they do or leave undone anything because of instructions that Christ gave to the Nephites. Whatever is done by this Church is because God, speaking from heaven in our day, has commanded this Church to do it. No book presides over this Church, and no book lies at its foundation. You cannot pile up books enough to take the place of God's priesthood, inspired by the power of the Holy Ghost. . . . Divine revelation adapts itself to the circumstances and conditions of men, and change ensues as God's progressive work goes on to its destiny. There is no book big enough or good enough to preside over this Church. ¶ In saying this, I speak with all due reverence of the written word of God. . . . (*Elder Whitney's "Greek Catholic friend" had said that it "made him shudder when he saw people sipping the water" instead of wine for sacrament—his church does not recognize the principle of continuous revelation*) CR1916Oct:55

---

**657.** All revelations from heaven are harmonious with each other.

**President Joseph F. Smith, John R. Winder, Anthon H. Lund**
(First Presidency)

Truth has but one source, and all revelations from heaven are harmonious with each other. (*Published message of the First Presidency of the Church, Nov. 1909*) MOFP4:199

**President Joseph F. Smith, Anthon H. Lund, Charles W. Penrose**
(First Presidency)
*quoted by*
**President George Albert Smith, J. Reuben Clark, Jr., David O. McKay**
*(First Presidency)*

When visions, dreams, tongues, prophecy, impressions, or an extraordinary gift of inspiration conveys something out of harmony with the accepted revelations of the Church or contrary to the decisions of its constituted authorities, Latter-day Saints may know that it is not of God, no matter how plausible it may appear. Also, they should understand that directions for the guidance of the Church will come by revelation, through the head. . . . ¶ Be not led by any spirit or influence that discredits established authority . . . or leads away from the direct revelations of God for the government of the Church. The Holy Ghost does not contradict its own revealings. Truth is always harmonious with itself. (*Published message of the First Presidency of the Church, Dec. 29, 1945, republishing a message of the previous First Presidency in 1913*) MOFP6:244-45

**Marion G. Romney**

I would like now to suggest some tests which can safely be used to distinguish the genuine from the counterfeit. . . . ¶ . . . . *The teaching must not only come under the proper label [that of Jesus Christ], but it must also conform to the other teaching[s] of the Gospel of Jesus Christ.* [Italics by Marion G. Romney] CR1960Oct:76-77

**Elder Joseph Fielding Smith**

If I should say something which is contrary to that which is written in the standard works of the Church, and accepted by the Authorities of the Church and approved by the Church generally, no one is under any obligation to accept it. Everything I say and everything that any other person says must square itself with that which the Lord has revealed, or it should be rejected. CR1943Oct:97

**Bruce R. McConkie**

The issue then was—and now is—how to identify the true prophets; how to know who among the professing prophets represent the Lord and who have no such divine commission; how to tell the true from the false. ¶ . . . . Is their doctrine true and sound and in harmony with all that is found in Holy Writ? . . . And does the Lord God give his Holy Spirit to attest the truth of their words and to approve the acts that they do? Without true prophets there is no salvation; false prophets lead people astray; men choose, at the peril of their salvation, the prophets whom they follow. (The Mortal Messiah, 2:170-71) TLDP:538

**Related Witnesses:**

**President Heber J. Grant**

The Book of Mormon is in absolute harmony from start to finish with other sacred scriptures. There is not a doctrine taught in it that does not harmonize with the teachings of Jesus Christ. . . . It is in every way a true witness for God, and it sustains the Bible and is in harmony with the Bible. No group of men can write a book of six or seven hundred pages that is a fraud and have it in harmony in every particular with the scriptures that were given to us by the prophets of God and by Jesus Christ and his Apostles. CR1929Apr:128-29

**President Joseph F. Smith,**
**Anthon H. Lund, Charles W. Penrose**
(First Presidency)

But anything at discord with that which comes from God through the head of the Church is not to be received as authoritative or reliable. *(Published message of the First Presidency of the Church)* IE1913Sept:1148-49; MOFP4:285

**President Heber J. Grant**

The Book of Mormon does not in any degree conflict with or take the place of the Holy Bible, but is the strongest corroborative evidence in existence of the divine origin of that sacred record. CR1930Apr:10

**James E. Talmage**

The Church of Jesus Christ of Latter-day Saints accepts the Holy Bible as the foremost of her standard works, first among the books which have been proclaimed as her written guides in faith and doctrine. In the respect and sanctity with which the Latter-day Saints regard the Bible they are of like profession with Christian denominations in general, but differ from them in the additional acknowledgment of certain other scriptures as authentic and holy, which others are in harmony with the Bible, and serve to support and emphasize its facts and doctrines. AF:214

---

**658. True doctrine is in harmony with the recorded revealed word of God in all scriptures (i.e., the Standard Works).**

**Elder Joseph Fielding Smith**

[W]e should prove every doctrine by the revelations of the Lord; by those principles of eternal truth which have been revealed for our guidance. We have certain standards which have been accepted and by which we are to be governed. ¶ If I should say something which is contrary to that which is written in the standard works of the church, and accepted by the authorities of the church and approved by the church generally, no one is under any obligation to accept it. Everything I say and everything that any other person says must square itself with that which the Lord has revealed, or it should be rejected. CR1943Oct:97

**Albert E. Bowen**

In my view there is only one safety; there is only one cure; and that is to take the pure and unadulterated word of God and set that up as our standard of measurement and measure every creed and doctrine and dogma by that yardstick. That which will not square with the declarations of Almighty God we can lay aside as unsuited for the need of man, and orient ourselves again in that declaration of Peter, re-echoed by Paul, by all the disciples of the Christ, so long as his teachings remained undefiled and uncorrupted and set that up as the guide to our course of life. CR1952Apr:66

**Elder Harold B. Lee**

It is not to be thought that every word spoken by the General Authorities is inspired, or that they are moved upon by the Holy Ghost in everything they read and write. Now you keep that in mind. I don't care what his position is, if he writes something or speaks something that goes beyond anything that you can find in the standard church works, unless that one be the prophet, seer, and revelator—please note that one exception—you may immediately say, "Well, that is his own idea." And if he says something that contradicts what is found in the standard church works (I think that is why we call them "standard"—it is the standard measure of all that men teach), you may know by that same token that it is false, regardless of the position of the man who says it. *(To seminary and institute of religion faculty, July 1964)* DCSM:144

**Charles W. Penrose**

We don't want to prevent men from thinking. I have heard some of my brethren say, "Well, do you want to stop men from thinking?" Not at all. Liberty to think and liberty to act upon the thought if you don't infringe the rights others. . . . [B]ut my brethren, it isn't your province nor mine to introduce theories into the Church that are not in accordance with the revelations that have been given. Don't forget that. And if any change in policy is to be introduced, it is to come through the proper channel. The Lord said only his servant Joseph should do that while he lived, and then after he died others were to be called to occupy the place, and the key is in the hands of the man who stands at the head, if any change is to be introduced in our Church. CR1918Apr:21-22

**Marion G. Romney**

I would like now to suggest some tests which can safely be used to distinguish the genuine from the counterfeit. . . . ¶ . . . . *The teaching must not only come under the proper label [that of Jesus Christ], but it must also conform to the other teaching[s] of the Gospel of Jesus Christ.* [italics by Marion G. Romney] CR1960Oct:76-77

### Elder Joseph Fielding Smith

The world today is full of vain philosophy, full of doctrine that is not of the Lord, full of false conclusions, ideas and theories that were not a part of the gospel in the days of the Son of God and hence are not a part of it now, but on the contrary are in absolute contradiction of the truth. . . . The worship of reason, of false philosophy, is greater now than it was then. Men are depending upon their own reason to find out God. . . . They are not seeking for the Spirit of the Lord, they are not striving to know God in the manner he has marked out by which he may be known, but they are walking in their own way, believing in their own man-made philosophies, and teaching the doctrines of devils and not the doctrines of the Son of God. . . . ¶ I want to say to the Latter-day Saints that it is our duty to put our faith in the revealed word of God, to accept that which has come through inspiration, through revelation unto his servants, the prophets, both ancient and modern, and whenever you find any doctrine, any idea, any expression from any source whatsoever that is in conflict with that which the Lord has revealed and which is found in the holy scriptures, you may be assured that it is false and you should put it aside and stand firmly grounded in the truth in prayer and in faith, relying upon the Spirit of the Lord, for knowledge, for wisdom, concerning these principles of truth. CR1917Apr:59-60,64

### President Joseph F. Smith, Anthon H. Lund, Charles W. Penrose
#### (First Presidency)

When visions, dreams, tongues, prophecy, impressions or any extraordinary gift of inspiration, convey something out of harmony with accepted revelations of the Church or contrary to the decisions of its constituted authorities, Latter-day Saints may know that it is not of God, no matter how plausible it may appear. Also, they should understand that directions for the guidance of the Church will come, by revelation, through the head. All faithful members are entitled to the inspiration of the Holy Spirit for themselves, their families, and for those over whom they are appointed and ordained to preside. But anything at discord with that which comes from God through the head of the Church is not to be received as authoritative or reliable. In secular as well as spiritual affairs, saints may receive divine guidance and revelation affecting themselves, but this does not convey authority to direct others, and is not to be accepted when contrary to Church covenants, doctrine or discipline, or to known facts, demonstrated truths, or good common sense. No person has the right to induce his fellow members of the Church to engage in speculations or take stock in ventures of any kind on the specious claim of divine revelation, or vision, or dream, especially when it is in opposition to the voice of recognized authority, local or general. The Lord's Church "is a house of order." It is not governed by individual gifts or manifestations, but by the order and power of the Holy Priesthood as sustained by the voice and vote of the Church in its appointed conferences. . . . ¶ . . . . The Holy Ghost does not contradict its own revealings. Truth is always harmonious with itself. Piety is often the cloak of error. The counsels of the Lord through the channel he has appointed will be followed with safety, therefore, Oh! ye Latter-day Saints, profit by these words of warning. (Published message of the First Presidency of the Church) IE1913Sept:1148-49; MOFP4:285

### Related Witnesses:
#### Peter

Knowing this first, that no prophecy of the scripture is of any private interpretation. 21. For the prophecy came not in old time by the will of man: but holy men of God spake as they were moved by the Holy Ghost. (Letter to members of the Church, about A.D. 60-64) 2Pet.1:20-21

#### Gordon B. Hinckley

The remarkable organization of the Church . . . was framed by him [Joseph Smith] as he was directed by revelation, and no modification or adaptation of that organization is ever considered without searching the revelations set forth by the Prophet. CR1977Apr:95

#### John A. Widtsoe

For a number of years I was engaged in reading the sermons of Brigham Young, having in mind a compilation of his wise sayings for the benefit of the saints. I was amazed to note how closely, how carefully, he followed the doctrine laid down by the Prophet Joseph Smith, who himself only taught the pure, unchanged Gospel of the Lord Jesus Christ. As I read on, studying the teachings of those who came after Brigham Young, I found the same thing to be true. I have listened in this tabernacle, for many years, to the words of President Heber J. Grant, and I have found him likewise a teacher of the same doctrine that was taught by Joseph Smith, by Brigham Young, and by the others who have preceded President Grant in his high office. There has been no deviation in his teachings from fundamental truth; not by a hair's breadth. ¶ In this changelessness of fundamental teaching lies not only a testimony of the truth of this great work, but also a principle of comfort to all who belong to the Church. . . . I can cling safely to the Church, to the Gospel of Jesus Christ; it has steadying power, it does not change nor vary. It is the same today, yesterday and forever. . . . ¶ Do not misunderstand me as I speak on this theme. Every man clothes his ideas in his own words. Joseph Smith did not speak as Heber J. Grant speaks. The principles, the ideas were the same, but the words used, the forms of expression, belong to the speaker; and every man has a right to express as best he can in the words God gives him, the eternal truths that he may obtain from a divine source. ¶ Again, do not misunderstand me. I do not mean that this Church and kingdom is static, that we stand still. I believe in a living, growing Church, which is in need of and does receive revelation from day to day. Nothing is more certain to me than that we are founded on revelation from God, and that we are guided daily by such revelation. We shall have revelation for our guidance to the end of time; but such new revelations as may come will never supersede, destroy or abrogate the fundamental principles upon which this Church rests its body of doctrine. A new revelation merely adds and develops and more nearly completes that which has formerly been given. CR1934Oct:9-10

---

659. **Unless a doctrine is in harmony with the teachings of contemporary prophets it cannot be considered true doctrine.**

### Charles W. Penrose

[B]ut my brethren, it isn't your province nor mine to introduce theories into the Church that are not in accordance with the revelations that have been given. Don't forget that. And if any change in policy is to be introduced, it is to come through the proper channel. The Lord said only his servant Joseph should do that while he lived, and then after he died others were to be called to occupy the place, and the key is in the hands of the man who stands at the head, if any change is to be introduced in our Church. CR1918Apr:21-22

### President Joseph F. Smith,
### Anthon H. Lund, Charles W. Penrose
(First Presidency)

But anything at discord with that which comes from God through the head of the Church is not to be received as authoritative or reliable. (*Published message of the First Presidency of the Church*) IE1913Sept:1148-49; MOFP4:285

### Orson Pratt,
*quoted by the First Presidency:*
*President Brigham Young,*
*Heber C. Kimball, Daniel H. Wells*

Upon what principle are we to be one? It is by hearkening in all things to that eternal and everlasting Priesthood which has been conferred upon mortal man upon the earth. When I say that Priesthood, I mean the individual who holds the keys thereof. He is the standard—the living oracle to the Church. ¶ "But," says one, "suppose that we hearken to the word of God in the Old and New Testament—suppose that we hearken to the word of God in the Book of Doctrine and Covenants—suppose we hearken to the word of God in the Book of Mormon, and at the same time we feel disposed in our hearts to lay aside the living oracles, what then?" I would answer, in the first place, that the premises are false. Why? The very moment that we set aside the living oracles we set aside the revelations of God. Why? Because the revelations of God command us plainly that we shall hearken to the living oracles. Hence, if we undertake to follow the written word, and at the same time do not give heed to the living oracles of God, the written word will condemn us: it shows that we do not follow it according to our profession. (*As introduction to the address of Orson Pratt, from which this quotation is taken, the following appeared: "On the 29th of January, in the Tabernacle, Elder Orson Pratt, senior, addressed the Saints; and, through an oversight, a portion of his remarks was printed in . . . the Deseret News, previous to being carefully revised. Since then, those remarks have been examined by brother Pratt and the Council, and are now printed as agreed upon by them." Published message of the First Presidency of the Church, Deseret News, Sept. 22, 1860*) MOFP2:217

### Elder Joseph Fielding Smith

I want to say to the Latter-day Saints that it is our duty to put our faith in the revealed word of God, to accept that which has come through inspiration, through revelation unto his servants, the prophets, both ancient and modern, and whenever you find any doctrine, any idea, any expression from any source whatsoever that is in conflict with that which the Lord has revealed and which is found in the holy scriptures, you may be assured that it is false and you should put it aside and stand firmly grounded in the truth in prayer and in faith, relying upon the Spirit of the Lord, . . . CR1917Apr:59-60,64

**President Joseph F. Smith,
Anthon H. Lund, Charles W. Penrose**
(First Presidency)
Be not led by any spirit or influence that discredits established authority and contradicts true scientific principles and discoveries, or leads away from the direct revelations of God for the government of the Church. The Holy Ghost does not contradict its own revealings. Truth is always harmonious with itself. Piety is often the cloak of error. The counsels of the Lord through the channel he has appointed will be followed with safety, therefore, Oh! ye Latter-day Saints, profit by these words of warning. (*Published message of the First Presidency of the Church*) IE1913Sept:1148-49; MOFP4:285

**John A. Widtsoe**
Again, do not misunderstand me. I do not mean that this Church and kingdom is static, that we stand still. I believe in a living, growing Church, which is in need of and does receive revelation from day to day. Nothing is more certain to me than that we are founded on revelation from God, and that we are guided daily by such revelation. We shall have revelation for our guidance to the end of time; but such new revelations as may come will never supersede, destroy or abrogate the fundamental principles upon which this Church rests its body of doctrine. A new revelation merely adds and develops and more nearly completes that which has formerly been given. CR1934Oct:9-10

**J. Reuben Clark,
on behalf of the First Presidency**
You are not, whether high or low, to change the doctrines of the Church or to modify them, as they are declared by and in the Standard Works of the Church and by those whose authority it is to declare the mind and will of the Lord to the Church. The Lord had declared he is "the same yesterday, today, and forever." (*Speaking on behalf of the First Presidency [see letter of First Presidency, MOFP6:208-09] to seminary, institute, and Church school teachers at Aspen Grove. Entire speech published in Deseret News, Church Section, Aug. 13, 1938, and in IE1938Sep:520ff; reprinted in MOFP6:44-58. The speech was extracted for use as Lesson 18 of the Melchizedek Priesthood course of study, 1969-70, p. 129ff*) MOFP6:55

**President George Albert Smith,
J. Reuben Clark, Jr., David O. McKay**
(First Presidency)
When visions, dreams, tongues, prophecy, impressions, or an extraordinary gift of inspiration conveys something out of harmony with the accepted revelations of the Church or contrary to the decisions of its constituted authorities, Latter-day Saints may know that it is not of God, no matter how plausible it may appear. Also, they should understand that directions for the guidance of the Church will come by revelation, through the head. . . . ¶ Be not led by any spirit or influence that discredits established authority . . . or leads away from the direct revelations of God for the government of the Church. The Holy Ghost does not contradict its own revealings. Truth is always harmonious with itself. (*Published message of the First Presidency of the Church, Dec. 29, 1945, republishing a message of the previous First Presidency in 1913, comprised of Joseph F. Smith, Anthon H. Lund, and Charles W. Penrose*) MOFP6:244-45

**660. The Holy Ghost confirms the truth of the declarations of the Lord's witnesses.**

**J. Reuben Clark, Jr.**
The question is how shall we know when the things they have spoken were said as they were 'moved upon by the Holy Ghost?' I have given some thought to the question, and the answer thereto so far as I can determine, is: We can tell when the speakers are 'moved upon by the Holy Ghost,' only when we, ourselves, are 'moved upon by the Holy Ghost.' In a way, this completely shifts the responsibility from them to us to determine when they so speak. (*To seminary and institute faculties, Brigham Young University, July 7, 1954*) DCSM:144

**Recorded in Acts**
While Peter yet spake these words, the Holy Ghost fell on all them which heard the word. (*After Peter received a vision teaching him to take the gospel to the gentiles, he preached to Jew and gentile about Christ*) Acts 10:44

**Elder Ezra Taft Benson**
It takes revelation to perceive revelation. CR1985Oct:47

**Joseph Smith**
Therefore, why is it that ye cannot understand and know, that he that receiveth the word by the Spirit of truth receiveth it as it is preached by the Spirit of truth? 22. Wherefore, he that preacheth and he that receiveth, understand one another, and both are edified and rejoice together. (*Revelation for the elders of the Church, May 1831*) D&C 50:21-22

**Jesus,
quoted by John**
But the Comforter, which is the Holy Ghost,

whom the Father will send in my name, he shall teach you all things, and bring all things to your remembrance, whatsoever I have said unto you. *(Jesus, anticipating his crucifixion, promises his disciples the Holy Ghost in his stead)* John 14:26

### George F. Richards

The things contained in the Book of Mormon are the things of God given to the children of men by the inspiration and power of the Holy Ghost, and so are the things contained in the Doctrine and Covenants, in the Pearl of Great Price, and in the Holy Bible, which books constitute the standard works of the Church of Jesus Christ of Latter-day Saints. If we can enjoy that measure of the Holy Ghost which is felt by and which actuated those prophets of God who spoke the things contained in these books, and wrote them, we will understand as they understood, and they will not be mysteries unto us. Every Latter-day Saint who is faithful, having accepted the first principles and ordinances of the Gospel, having had the Holy Ghost conferred upon him, if he is true to these things, will know the truth when he reads it or when he hears it spoken. . . . ¶ By the power of the Holy Ghost, which we through righteousness have a right to enjoy, we know that all of those who have spoken in this conference in our hearing have spoken by the power of the Lord. They have spoken words of truth, and words which will make for salvation if we will receive them in good and honest hearts and live with them. This is the office of the Holy Ghost, who is a personage of spirit, one of the trinity of the godhead. It is his mission and office to bear witness of the Father and of the Son and of the truth of all things. "No man may know that Jesus is the Lord except by the Holy Ghost." CR1931Oct:100-01

### Nephi, son of Lehi

[F]or when a man speaketh by the power of the Holy Ghost the power of the Holy Ghost carrieth it unto the hearts of the children of men. *(Nephi's writings, 559-545 B.C.)* 2Ne.33:1

**Related Witnesses:**

### President George Albert Smith, J. Reuben Clark, Jr., David O. McKay
(First Presidency)

Be not led by any spirit or influence that discredits established authority . . . or leads away from the direct revelations of God for the government of the Church. The Holy Ghost does not contradict its own revealings. Truth is always harmonious with itself. *(Published message of the First Presidency of the Church, Dec. 29, 1945, republishing a message of the previous First Presidency in 1913, comprised of*

*Joseph F. Smith, Anthon H. Lund, and Charles W. Penrose)* MOFP6:245

### Moroni, son of Mormon

And when ye shall receive these things, I would exhort you that ye would ask God, the Eternal Father, in the name of Christ, if these things are not true; and if ye shall ask with a sincere heart, with real intent, having faith in Christ, he will manifest the truth of it unto you, by the power of the Holy Ghost. 5. And by the power of the Holy Ghost ye may know the truth of all things. *(Moroni's final writings, about A.D. 421)* Moro.10:4-5

---

## (2) Revelation to the Church

### 661. Revelation to the Church is continuous.

#### Elder Wilford Woodruff

The Lord never had—and never will have to the end of time—a Church on the earth without Prophets, Apostles, and inspired men. Whenever the Lord had a people on the earth that He acknowledged as such, that people were led by revelation. *(In Tabernacle, July 20, 1883, JD24:240)* TLDP:568

#### Boyd K. Packer

Revelation is a continuous principle in the Church. In one sense the Church is still being organized. As light and knowledge are given, as prophecies are fulfilled and more intelligence is received, another step forward can be taken. (The Holy Temple, p. 137) TLDP:569

#### Hugh B. Brown

Divine revelation has always been a characteristic of the living Church—it is absolutely essential to its continued existence in an organized state on the earth. . . . ¶ Without continued revelation there can be no authorized ministry on the earth, and without authorized officers there can be no Church of Christ. . . . ¶ . . . [W]e cannot believe that [God's] Church in one dispensation would be blessed and led by . . . "live" revelation and in another dispensation leave a distraught and imperiled world with only the recorded messages of ancient prophets, some of which messages were for specific purposes and under special circumstances. We believe that revelation both "live" and recorded is now, and will continue to be, available to men. Whenever the Lord has recognized his Church, he has given through his prophets messages of warning, instruction, and hope. . . . ¶ So we may trace the line of revelators, men who have stood, each in his time, as the medium through whom God speaks to his people, from Moses to Joshua, through the Judges, on to David and Solomon and down to Zachariah and Malachi. Christ himself, came to this world to reveal God to men, and he himself was led and directed by revelation from his Father while he dwelt on this earth. . . . ¶ The scriptures, then, are not only replete with evidence, but conclusive in proving that God does and always has, whenever there has been a dispensation of the gospel upon the earth, been in touch with his people. . . . ¶ From the scriptures cited [John 7:3; Gen.5:24; Luke 1:28,31; John 12:49-50; 1Cor.2:10-11; Eph.1:10] and many others, it seems evident that revelation from God to man has been a vital characteristic and standard procedure in all dispensations of the gospel. All the prophets and leaders of ancient times were led, directed, chosen, inspired by God himself through revelation. CR1961Oct:94-96

### John A. Widtsoe

Again, do not misunderstand me. I do not mean that this church and kingdom is static, that we stand still. I believe in a living, growing church, which is in need of and does receive revelation from day to day. Nothing is more certain to me than that we were founded in revelation from God, and that we are guided daily by such revelation. We shall have revelation for our guidance to the end of time: but such new revelations as may come will never supersede, destroy or abrogate the fundamental principles upon which this Church rests its body of doctrine. A new revelation merely adds and develops and more nearly completes that which has formerly been given. CR1934Oct:10

### George Q. Cannon

As Latter-day Saints, we need constantly the guidance of Jehovah. We have the Bible, the Book of Mormon and the Book of Doctrine and Covenants; but all these books, without the living oracles and a constant stream of revelation from the Lord, would not lead any people into the Celestial Kingdom of God. This may seem a strange declaration to make, but strange as it may sound, it is nevertheless true. ¶ Of course, these records are all of infinite value. They cannot be too highly prized, nor can they be too closely studied. But in and of themselves, with all the light that they give, they are insufficient to guide the children of men and to lead them into the presence of God. To be thus led requires a living priesthood and constant revelation from God to the people according to the circumstances in which they may be placed. (Gospel Truth, 1:323) TLDP:568

### President Spencer W. Kimball

Since that momentous day in 1820, additional scripture has continued to come, including the numerous and vital revelations flowing in a never-ending stream from God to his prophets on earth. Many of these revelations are recorded in another scripture called the Doctrine and Covenants. Completing our Latter-day Saint scriptures is the Pearl of Great Price, another record of revelation and translated writings of both ancient and modern prophets. ¶ There are those who would assume that with the printing and binding of these sacred records, that would be the "end of the prophets." But again we testify to the world that revelation continues and that the vaults and files of the Church contain these revelations which come month to month and day to day. We testify also that there is, since 1830 when The Church of Jesus Christ of Latter-day Saints was organized, and will continue to be, so long as time shall last, a prophet, recognized of God and his people, who will continue to interpret the mind and will of the Lord. . . . ¶ I say, in the deepest of humility, but also by the power and force of a burning testimony in my soul, that from the prophet of the Restoration to the prophet of our own year, the communication line is unbroken, the authority is continuous, a light brilliant and penetrating continues to shine. The sound of the voice of the Lord is a continuous melody and a thunderous appeal. For nearly a century and a half there has been no interruption. CR1977Apr:115

### Related Witnesses:
### President Spencer W. Kimball

Never again will God be hidden from his children on the earth. Revelation is here to remain. ¶ In the early years of his newly established dispensation, the Lord set his divine law of succession, and prophets have followed each other and will continue to follow each other in never-ending divine appointed succession, and the secrets of the Lord will be revealed without measure. ¶ Man never needs to stand alone. Every faithful person may have the inspiration for his own limited kingdom. But the Lord definitely calls prophets today and reveals his secrets unto them as he did yesterday, he does today, and will do tomorrow: that is the way it is. CR1977Apr:115

### Joseph Smith

We believe all that God has revealed, all that He does now reveal, and we believe that He will yet reveal many great and important things pertaining to the Kingdom of God. (*The ninth of the thirteen Articles of Faith; letter to John Wentworth, March 1, 1842*) AofF:9

### Moroni, son of Mormon

And again I speak unto you who deny the revelations of God, and say that they are done away, that there are no revelations, nor prophecies, nor gifts, nor healing, nor speaking with tongues, and the interpretation of tongues; 8. Behold I say unto you, he that denieth these things knoweth not the gospel of Christ; yea, he has not read the scriptures; if so, he does not understand them. 9. For do we not read that God is the same yesterday, today, and forever, and in him there is no variableness neither shadow of changing? (*Moroni addresses those who deny the revelations of God, A.D. 400-421*) Morm.9:7-9

**President Joseph F. Smith**
The theology of our Church is the theology taught by Jesus Christ and His apostles, the theology of scripture and reason. It not only acknowledges the sacredness of ancient scripture, and the binding force of divinely-inspired acts and utterances in ages past; but also declares that God now speaks to man in this final Gospel dispensation. (*Address from the First Presidency of the Church to the world, delivered to and accepted by vote of the Church in general conference, April 1907*) CR1907Apr(Appendix)4

**Gordon B. Hinckley**
To the world we give our witness that there is revelation of the word of God as certainly in the atomic age as there was in the age of Jeremiah. It is just that simple and just that true. CR1964Apr:39

**Joseph Smith**
Abraham received all things, whatsoever he received, by revelation and commandment, by my word, saith the Lord, and hath entered into his exaltation and sitteth upon his throne. (*Revelation relating to the new and everlasting covenant, July 12, 1843*) D&C 132:29

**Amos**
Surely the Lord GOD will do nothing, but he revealeth his secret unto his servants the prophets. (*Amos prophesies the downfall of Israel, about 770-750 B.C.*) Amos 3:7

**Author's Note:** From the very beginning when revelation to man began with Adam, revelation to prophets and to the Church has been continuous. Elder Joseph F. Smith spoke about this in 1873. He said that the Lord's laws, rites and ceremonies existed from the beginning: ¶ "Undoubtedly the knowledge of [the law of sacrifice] and of other rites and ceremonies was carried by the posterity of Adam into all lands, and continued with them, more or less pure, to the flood, and through Noah . . . to those who succeeded him, spreading out into all nations and countries, Adam and Noah being the first

of their dispensations to receive them from God. What wonder, then, that we should find relics of Christianity, so to speak, among the heathens and nations who know not Christ, and whose histories date back beyond the days of Moses, and even beyond the flood, independent of and apart from the records of the Bible. The ground taken by infidels, that 'Christianity' sprang from the heathen, it being found that they have many rites similar to those recorded in the Bible, &c, is only a vain and foolish attempt to blind the eyes of men and dissuade them from their faith in the Redeemer of the world, and from their belief in the Scriptures of divine truth, for if the heathen have doctrines and ceremonies resembling to some extent those which are recorded in the Scriptures, it only proves what is plain to the Saints, that these are the traditions of the fathers handed down from generation to generation, from Adam, through Noah, and that they will cleave to the children to the latest generation, though they may wander into darkness and perversion, until but a slight resemblance to their origin, which was divine, can be seen." (JD15:325)

---

662. Only the President of the Church—the prophet, seer, and revelator—has the right to receive new revelation for the Church (or amendatory revelations, or to give authoritative interpretations of scriptures, or to change in any way the existing doctrines of the Church).

**J. Reuben Clark, Jr.**
Only the President of the Church, the Presiding High Priest, is sustained as Prophet, Seer and Revelator for the Church, and he alone has the right to receive revelations for the church, either new or amendatory, or to give authoritative interpretations of scriptures that shall be binding on the Church, or change in any way the existing doctrines of the Church. He is God's sole mouthpiece on earth for the Church of Jesus Christ of Latter-day Saints, the only true Church. He alone may declare the mind and will of God to his people. No officer of any other Church in the world has this high right and lofty prerogative. . . . ¶ When any one except the President of the Church undertakes to proclaim a revelation from God for the guidance of the Church, we may know he is not "moved upon by the Holy Ghost." ¶ When any one except the President of the Church undertakes to

proclaim one unsettled doctrine of the Church, we may know that he is not "moved upon by the Holy Ghost," unless he is acting under the direction and by the authority of the President. ¶ Of these things we may have a confident assurance without chance for doubt or quibbling. (Church News, July 13, 1954) MPSG1989:66

### Delbert L. Stapley

I bear witness to you, my brothers and sisters, that God sustains him [the living prophet] and no one else in the world today but him, because he has the holy calling of prophet, seer, and revelator, representing the Lord upon the earth in our time. He only has the right to revelation for the people of the Church, and if all people would understand that, they would not be tossed about by those who would seek to divert their minds from the Church and its glorious principles. . . . ¶ [I]f the people of the Church understand the calling and position of the chosen and anointed prophet of God, they will be fortified against false teachers and anti-Christs, and we do have them among us. CR1953Oct:70; DCSM:45

### James E. Talmage

The Lord observes the principle of order and fitness in giving revelation to His servants. Though it is the privilege of any person to live so as to merit this gift in the affairs of his special calling, only those appointed and ordained to the offices of presidency are to be revelators to the people at large. Concerning the President of the Church, who at the time of the revelation here referred to was the Prophet Joseph Smith, the Lord has said to the elders of the Church: "And this ye shall know assuredly, that there is none other appointed unto you to receive commandments and revelations until he be taken, if he abide in me. . . . And this shall be a law unto you, that ye receive not the teachings of any that shall come before you as revelations or commandments; And this I give unto you that you may not be deceived, that you may know they are not of me." [D&C 43:3,5-6] AF:209

### Joseph Smith,
*receiving the Word of the Lord*

For behold, verily, verily, I say unto you, that ye have received a commandment for a law unto my church, through him whom I have appointed unto you to receive commandments and revelations from my hand. 3. And this ye shall know assuredly—that there is none other appointed unto you to receive commandments and revelations until he be taken, if he abide in me. 4. But verily, verily, I say unto you, that none else shall be appointed unto this gift except it be through him; for if it be taken from him he shall not have power except to appoint another in his stead. 5. And this shall be a law unto you, that ye receive not the teachings of any that shall come before you as revelations or commandments; 6. And this I give unto you that you may not be deceived, that you may know they are not of me. 7. For verily I say unto you, that he that is ordained of me shall come in at the gate and be ordained as I have told you before, to teach those revelations which you have received and shall receive through him whom I have appointed. (*Revelation: message for the nations of the earth, Feb. 1831*) D&C 43:2-7

### Elder Ezra Taft Benson

Let me give you a crucial key to help you avoid being deceived. It is this—learn to keep your eye on the Prophet. He is the Lord's mouthpiece and the only man who can speak for the Lord today. Let his inspired words be a basis for evaluating the counsel of all lesser authorities. Then live close to the Spirit so you may know the truth of all things. (*At Brigham Young University, Oct. 1966*) MPSG1989:58

### Charles W. Penrose

We don't want to prevent men from thinking. I have heard some of my brethren say, "Well, do you want to stop men from thinking?" Not at all. Liberty to think and liberty to act upon the thought if you don't infringe the rights others. . . . [B]ut my brethren, it isn't your province nor mine to introduce theories into the Church that are not in accordance with the revelations that have been given. Don't forget that. And if any change in policy is to be introduced, it is to come through the proper channel. The Lord said only his servant Joseph should do that while he lived, and then after he died others were to be called to occupy the place, and the key is in the hands of the man who stands at the head, if any change is to be introduced in our Church. CR1918Apr:21-22

### President George Albert Smith,
### J. Reuben Clark, Jr., David O. McKay,
(First Presidency)

When visions, dreams, tongues, prophecy, impressions, or an extraordinary gift of inspiration conveys something out of harmony with the accepted revelations of the Church or contrary to the decisions of its constituted authorities, Latter-day Saints may know that it is not of God, no matter how plausible it may appear. Also, they should understand that directions for the guidance of the Church will come by revelation, through the head. (*Published message of the First Presidency of the Church, Dec.29,*

*1945, republishing a message of the previous First Presidency in 1913, comprised of Joseph F. Smith, Anthon H. Lund, and Charles W. Penrose)* MOFP6:244

### Boyd K. Packer

Revelation continues in the Church: the prophet receiving it for the Church; the president for his stake, his mission, or his quorum; the bishop for his ward; the father for his family; the individual for himself. CR1974Apr:139

### Elder Ezra Taft Benson

The most important prophet, so far as we are concerned, is the one who is living in our day and age. This is the prophet who has today's instructions from God to us today. God's revelation to Adam did not instruct Noah how to build the ark. Every generation has need of the ancient scripture plus the current scripture from the living prophet. Therefore, the most crucial reading and pondering which you should do is of the latest inspired words from the Lord's mouthpiece. ACR(Seoul)1975:52; MPSG1989:58-59

### Mark E. Petersen

The Church of Jesus Christ, then, should always be led by living apostles and prophets who would receive the constant guidance of heaven. They would continue always in the Church as seers and revelators for the people. ¶ But as they so ministered they would be providing also new and additional scripture appropriate to the times in which they lived, according to the Lord's pattern. ¶ The prophets of the early Christian church ministered in their day just as the Old Testament prophets did during the preceding centuries. And why? Because they followed this same divine pattern, for as Amos explained, the Lord works only through prophets. (Amos.3:7) ¶ When there are no prophets, there is no divine direction, and without such guidance the people walk in darkness. . . . ¶ The world has been so confused by the conflicting creeds of men that the truth had to be given to mankind once again to disabuse their minds and correct their thinking. There was only one way in which this could be done and that was by new revelation. But to have new revelation requires the presence of a prophet to receive it, for as Amos said, the Lord will not act except through prophets. (See Amos 3:7.) CR1978Apr:95,98

**Related Witnesses:**

### Joseph Smith,
*receiving the Word of the Lord*

But, behold, verily, verily, I say unto thee, no one shall be appointed to receive commandments and revelations in this church excepting my servant Joseph Smith, Jun., for he receiveth them even as Moses. 3. And thou shalt be obedient unto the things which I shall give unto him, even as Aaron, to declare faithfully the commandments and the revelations, with power and authority unto the Church. 4. And if thou art led at any time by the Comforter to speak or teach, or at all times by the way of commandment unto the church, thou mayest do it. 5. But thou shalt not write by way of commandment, but by wisdom; 6. And thou shalt not command him who is at thy head, and at the head of the church; 7. For I have given him the keys of the mysteries, and the revelations which are sealed, until I shall appoint unto them another in his stead. *(Revelation for Oliver Cowdery, Sept. 1830)* D&C 28:2-7

### J. Reuben Clark, Jr.

You are not, whether high or low, to change the doctrines of the Church or to modify them, as they are declared by and in the Standard Works of the Church and by those whose authority it is to declare the mind and will of the Lord to the Church. The Lord had declared he is "the same yesterday, today, and forever." *(Speaking in behalf of the First Presidency [see letter of First Presidency, MOFP6:208-09] to seminary, institute, and Church school teachers at Aspen Grove. Entire speech published in Deseret News, Church Section, Aug. 13, 1938 and in IE1938Sep:520ff; reprinted in MOFP6:44-58. The speech was extracted for use as Lesson 18 of the Melchizedek Priesthood course of study 1969-70, p. 129ff)* MPSG1969-70:137

### Amos

Surely the Lord GOD will do nothing, but he revealeth his secret unto his servants the prophets. *(Amos prophesies the downfall of Israel, about 770-750 B.C.)* Amos 3:7

### Elder Joseph Fielding Smith

Let me add that when a revelation comes for the guidance of this people, you may be sure that it will not be presented in some mysterious manner contrary to the order of the Church. It will go forth in such form that the people will understand that it comes from those who are in authority, for it will be sent either to the presidents of stakes and the bishops of the wards over the signatures of the presiding authorities, or it will be published in some of the regular papers or magazines under the control and direction of the church, or it will be presented before such a gathering as this at a general conference. It will not spring up in some distant part of the Church and be in the hands of some obscure individual without authority, and thus be circulated among the Latter-day Saints. Now, you may remember this. . . . ¶ Now, the Lord is not going to give unto any woman in this Church a revelation for the Church. He is not going to give unto any man in this Church, other than the one who is properly appointed, a revelation for the guidance of the Church, for everything will be done in order. CR1918Oct:55

**President Joseph Fielding Smith**
Now, brethren, I think there is one thing which we should have exceedingly clear in our minds. Neither the President of the Church, nor the First Presidency, nor the united voice of the First Presidency and the Twelve will ever lead the Saints astray or send forth counsel to the world that is contrary to the mind and will of the Lord. ¶ An individual may fall by the wayside, or have views, or give counsel which falls short of what the Lord intends. But the voice of the First Presidency and the united voice of those others who hold with them the keys of the kingdom shall always guide the Saints and the world in those paths where the Lord wants them to be. CR1972Apr:99; MPSG1989:58

**President Joseph F. Smith**
. . . I know this, that God has organized his Church in the earth, and I know that when he designs or purposes to make any change in the matter of governing or controlling or presiding over the affairs of his Church, that he will make the change, and that he will make it in such a way that the whole people of the Church, who are doing right, will understand and accept it. I know that the Lord will not raise up "Tom, Dick, or Harry," here, there and everywhere, claiming to be Christ, or "one mighty and strong," claiming to be inspired and called to do some wonderful thing. The Lord will not deal with men in that way; that while the organization of the Church exists, while quorums and councils of the Priesthood are intact in the Church, the Lord will reveal his purposes through them and not through "Tom, Dick, or Harry." Put that in your little notebooks now, and remember it; it is true. CR1912Apr:10

**Patriarch Joseph F. Smith**
When Heber J. Grant, whom you have sustained [as President of the Church], and I expect will again sustain before this conference is over, issues instruction as prophet, seer, and revelator, that word should be scripture to us. It is the word of the Lord Himself through His prophet, and it may be that sometimes that advice is not exactly in accordance with our personal desires. It has never been the business of a prophet of God to tell people what they wanted to hear; it is the business of a prophet, and I imagine it is a very unpleasant business

sometimes, to tell the people what the Lord wants them to know and to do, and we who hold the Priesthood should take the Church seriously enough to be obedient to the scriptures. CR1943Apr:76

**Joseph Smith**
And again, the duty of the President of the office of the High Priesthood is to preside over the whole church, and to be like unto Moses— 92. Behold, here is wisdom; yea, to be a seer, a revelator, a translator, and a prophet, having all the gifts of God which he bestows upon the head of the church. (*Revelation on priesthood, received as the Twelve met in council, March 28, 1835*) D&C 107:91-92

**Joseph Smith,**
*quoted by Elder Joseph Fielding Smith*
I will inform you that it is contrary to the economy of God for any member of the Church, or any one, to receive instructions for those in authority higher than themselves; therefore you will see the impropriety of giving heed to them; but if any person have a vision or a visitation from a heavenly messenger, it must be for his own benefit and instruction; for the fundamental principles, government, and doctrine of the Church are vested in the keys of the kingdom. (*Letter to Jared Carter, April 13, 1833*) HC1:338; TPJS:21; DGSM:5

**Author's Note:** When the Lord wants his children to learn and understand any doctrine, He will teach it to them by the repeated influence of the Holy Ghost through His witnesses the prophets: that same Spirit will prompt more than one prophet to reiterate the doctrine, hence two or more witnesses will always affirm the doctrine. Observe how any new doctrine first comes to men by revelation through the President of the Church, be it new, amendatory or an authoritative interpretation changing in any way the existing doctrines of the Church. Thereafter the Apostles of the Lord, who are ordained prophets, teach that new or amended doctrine by the repeated influence of the Holy Ghost, thus verifying in a sense the revelation given to the President of the Church. But the reverse is not the pattern of the Lord. Apostles do not come forth with new or modified revelation to the Church, for that is the calling of its President. By heeding the teachings of the Apostles we can obtain a greater understanding, a keener insight into revealed doctrines as the Holy Ghost verifies to us those truths spoken by the Apostles. We come thereby to that "unity of the faith" spoken of by Paul: "Till we all come in the unity of the faith, and of the knowledge of the Son of God, unto a perfect man, unto the measure of the stature of the fulness of Christ:" (Eph.4:13) ¶ We lose much on those occasions when we prefer to use our intellectual talent and judgment in matters pertaining to the Spirit instead of our spiritual discernment. When the Holy Ghost speaks through a prophet, we ought to let the Holy Ghost in us give full credence to those inspired words of the prophet. The Spirit should override the talent of our meager intellects. We ought to humbly and gratefully honor and respect those scriptural expressions of prophetic witnesses so they become part of our own spiritual fiber. Then the spirit in us will also find room for deep gratitude toward those worthy prophets through whom the Lord has spoken.

663. For new revelation to be binding on the Church (when the President of the Church receives revelation for the Church), it must be proclaimed universally to the Church.

### Elder Joseph Fielding Smith

Let me add that when a revelation comes for the guidance of this people, you may be sure that it will not be presented in some mysterious manner contrary to the order of the Church. It will go forth in such form that the people will understand that it comes from those who are in authority, for it will be sent either to the presidents of stakes and the bishops of the wards over the signatures of the presiding authorities, or it will be published in some of the regular papers or magazines under the control and direction of the church, or it will be presented before such a gathering as this at a general conference. It will not spring up in some distant part of the Church and be in the hands of some obscure individual without authority, and thus be circulated among the Latter-day Saints. Now, you may remember this. . . . ¶ Now I maintain that there is no occasion for any member of this Church to have a doubt in his mind regarding matters of revelation as coming for the guidance of the Church, because when such things come they will come in the proper channels and be presented by those who are ordained to this calling and who are known to the Church. CR1918Oct:55-56

### President Joseph F. Smith

. . . I know this, that God has organized his Church in the earth, and I know that when he designs or purposes to make any change in the matter of governing or controlling or presiding over the affairs of his Church, that he will make the change, and that he will make it in such a way that the whole people of the Church, who are doing right, will understand and accept it. I know that the Lord will not raise up "Tom, Dick, or Harry," here, there and everywhere, claiming to be Christ, or "one mighty and strong," claiming to be inspired and called to do some wonderful thing. The Lord will not deal with men in that way; that while the organization of the Church exists, while quorums and councils of the Priesthood are intact in the Church, the Lord will reveal his purposes through them and not through "Tom, Dick, or Harry." Put that in your little notebooks now, and remember it; it is true. CR1912Apr:10

### President Heber J. Grant,
### Anthony W. Ivins, J. Reuben Clark, Jr.
(First Presidency)

It is alleged [by an apostate group] that on September 26-27, 1886, President John Taylor received a revelation from the Lord [pertaining to continued polygamous marriages]. . . . ¶ [S]o far as the authorities of the Church are concerned and so far as the members of the Church are concerned, since this pretended revelation, if ever given, was never presented to and adopted by the Church or by any council of the Church . . . the said pretended revelation could have no validity and no binding effect and force upon Church members, and action under it would be unauthorized, illegal, and void. (*Official statement from the First Presidency, June 17, 1933*) MOFP5:327

**Related Witnesses:**

### Patriarch Joseph F. Smith

When Heber J. Grant, whom you have sustained [as President of the Church], and I expect will again sustain before this conference is over, issues instruction as prophet, seer, and revelator, that word should be scripture to us. It is the word of the Lord Himself through His prophet, and it may be that sometimes that advice is not exactly in accordance with our personal desires. It has never been the business of a prophet of God to tell people what they wanted to hear; it is the business of a prophet, and I imagine it is a very unpleasant business sometimes, to tell the people what the Lord wants them to know and to do, and we who hold the Priesthood should take the Church seriously enough to be obedient to the scriptures. CR1943Apr:76

### President Joseph F. Smith

The theology of our Church is the theology taught by Jesus Christ and His apostles, the theology of scripture and reason. It not only acknowledges the sacredness of ancient scripture, and the binding force of divinely inspired acts and utterances in ages past; but also declares that God now speaks to man in this final Gospel dispensation. (*Address from the First Presidency of the Church to the world, delivered to and accepted by vote of the Church in general conference, April 1907*) CR1907Apr(Appendix)4

## (3) Revelation to Individuals

664. Only by revelation from God can we gain knowledge about God; we cannot learn about the existence and character of God by reasoning alone.

### Charles W. Penrose

No man by his own researches can find out God. He may, by reason and reflection, by observing and pondering upon the wonders of creation, by studying his own internal and external nature, come to the sure conclusion that there is a God, and to a very small extent make an estimate of His character. But unless the Almighty manifests Himself in some manner, finite man can never obtain a knowledge of infinite Deity. The speculations of human beings concerning God are many and various, and a vast number of their conclusions inconsistent and vain. Human learning, no matter how extensive, and human research, no matter how profound, are of necessity inadequate alone to the acquisition of a knowledge of divine things. Hence an unlettered person enlightened direct from God, will know more of Deity than the most erudite collegian who has not received this divine illumination. (*Mission pamphlet, 1929*) MDPS:9

### Joseph Smith

As we have been indebted to a revelation which God made of himself to his creatures, in the first instance, for the idea of his existence, so in like manner we are indebted to the revelations which he has given to us for a correct understanding of his character, perfections, and attributes; because without the revelations which he has given to us, no man by searching could find out God. (*Lectures on Faith delivered to the School of the Prophets, 1834-35*) LOF3:7

### Joseph Smith,
*receiving the Word of the Lord*

And now I speak unto you, the Twelve—Behold, my grace is sufficient for you; you must walk uprightly before me and sin not. . . . 33. And I, Jesus Christ, your Lord and your God, have spo-

ken it. 34. These words are not of men nor of man, but of me; wherefore, you shall testify they are of me and not of man; 35. For it is my voice which speaketh them unto you; for they are given by my Spirit unto you, and by my power you can read them one to another; and save it were by my power you could not have them; (*Revelation received June 1829*) D&C 18:31,33-35

**Related Witnesses:**

### Nephi, son of Lehi

For he that diligently seeketh shall find; and the mysteries of God shall be unfolded unto them, by the power of the Holy Ghost, as well in these times as in times of old, and as well in times of old as in times to come; wherefore, the course of the Lord is one eternal round. (*Nephi's writings, 600-592 B.C.*) 1Ne.10:19

### Joseph Smith

The object . . . is to show to this class the way by which mankind were first made acquainted with the existence of a God; that it was by a manifestation of God to man, and that God continued, after man's transgression, to manifest himself to him and to his posterity; and, notwithstanding they were separated from his immediate presence that they could not see his face, they continued to hear his voice, ¶ 31. Adam, thus being made acquainted with God, communicated the knowledge which he had unto his posterity; and it was through this means that the thought was first suggested to their minds that there was a God, which laid the foundation for the exercise of their faith, through which they could obtain a knowledge of his character and also of his glory. . . . ¶ 54. We have now shown how it was that the first thought ever existed in the mind of any individual that there was such a Being as a God, who had created and did uphold all things: that it was by reason of the manifestation which he first made to our father Adam, when he stood in his presence, and conversed with him face to face, at the time of his creation. (*Lectures on Faith delivered to the School of the Prophets, 1834-35*) LOF2:30-31,54

### Recorded in Job

Canst thou by searching find out God? canst thou find out the Almighty unto perfection? 8. It is as high as heaven; what canst thou do? deeper than hell; what canst thou know? 9. The measure thereof is longer than the earth, and broader than the sea. (*Zophar the Naamathite asks, can man by searching find out God?*) Job 11:7-9

### Jacob, brother of Nephi

Behold, great and marvelous are the works of the Lord. How unsearchable are the depths of the mysteries of him; and it is impossible that man should find out all his ways. And no man knoweth of his ways save it be revealed unto him; wherefore, brethren, despise not the revelations of God. (*Jacob makes his record on plates of metal, 544-421 B.C.*) Jacob 4:8

**Marion G. Romney**

That man is a child of God is the most important knowledge available to mortals. Such knowledge is beyond the ken of the uninspired mind. Neither logic, science, philosophy, nor any other field of worldly learning has ever been, or ever will be, able to find it out. Those who limit their search to such learning techniques will continue to be as they always have been, "Ever learning, and never able to come to the knowledge of the truth." (2Tim.3:7) ¶ The only means by which such knowledge can be had is divine revelation. Fortunately for us . . . it has been so revealed repeatedly from Adam until today. CR1973Apr:136

---

665. **"Mysteries of God" (those divine truths that bring about salvation and eternal life) are available to us only by revelation from God.**

**Elder Joseph Fielding Smith**

The Lord has promised to reveal his mysteries to those who serve him in faithfulness. . . . There are no mysteries pertaining to the Gospel, only as we, in our weakness fail to comprehend Gospel truth. . . . The "simple" principles of the Gospel, such as baptism, the atonement, are mysteries to those who do not have the guidance of the Spirit of the Lord. CHMR1:43; DCSM:15

**Joseph Smith**

For thus saith the Lord—I, the Lord, am merciful and gracious unto those who fear me, and delight to honor those who serve me in righteousness and in truth unto the end. 6. Great shall be their reward and eternal shall be their glory. 7. And to them will I reveal all mysteries, yea, all the hidden mysteries of my kingdom from days of old, and for ages to come, will I make known unto them the good pleasure of my will concerning all things pertaining to my kingdom. 8. Yea, even the wonders of eternity shall they know, and things to come will I show them, even the things of many generations. 9. And their wisdom shall be great, and their understanding reach to heaven; and before them the wisdom of the wise shall perish, and the understanding of the prudent shall come to naught. 10. For by my Spirit will I enlighten them, and by my power will I make known

unto them the secrets of my will—yea, even those things which eye has not seen, nor ear heard, nor yet entered into the heart of man. (*Vision to Joseph Smith and Sidney Rigdon, Feb. 16, 1832*) D&C 76:5-10

**Joseph Smith,**
*quoted by Elder Joseph Fielding Smith*

[I]f it requires the Spirit of God to know the things of God; and the spirit of the devil can only be unmasked through that medium, then it follows as a natural consequence that unless some person or persons have a communication, or revelation from God, unfolding to them the operation of the spirit, they must eternally remain ignorant of these principles; for I contend that if one man cannot understand these things but by the Spirit of God, ten thousand men cannot; it is alike out of the reach of the wisdom of the learned, the tongue of the eloquent, the power of the mighty. And we shall at last have to come to this conclusion, whatever we may think of revelation, that without it we can neither know nor understand anything of God, or the devil; . . . (Editorial in Times and Seasons, April 1842) HC4:573-74; TPJS:203-04

**Joseph Smith**

If thou shalt ask, thou shalt receive revelation upon revelation, knowledge upon knowledge, that thou mayest know the mysteries and peaceable things—that which bringeth joy, that which bringeth life eternal. . . . 65. Behold, thou shalt observe all these things, and great shall be thy reward; for unto you it is given to know the mysteries of the kingdom, but unto the world it is not given to know them. . . . 68. Therefore, he that lacketh wisdom, let him ask of me, and I will give him liberally and upbraid him not. (*Revelation "embracing the law of the Church," Feb. 9, 1831*) D&C 42:61,65,68

**Paul**

But as it is written, Eye hath not seen, nor ear heard, neither have entered into the heart of man, the things which God hath prepared for them that love him. 10. But God hath revealed them unto us by his Spirit: for the Spirit searcheth all things, yea, the deep things of God. 11. For what man knoweth the things of a man, save the spirit of man which is in him? even so the things of God knoweth no man, but the Spirit of God. 12. Now we have received, not the spirit of the world, but the spirit which is of God; that we might know the things that are freely given to us of God. 13. Which things also we speak, not in the words which man's wisdom teacheth, but which the Holy Ghost teacheth; comparing spiritual things with spiritual. 14. But the natural man receiveth not the things of the Spirit of God: for they are foolishness unto him: neither can he know them, because they are spiritually discerned. 15. But he that is spiritual judgeth all things, yet he himself is judged of no man. 16. For who hath known the mind of the Lord, that he may instruct him? But we have the mind of Christ. *(Paul writes to the Church at Corinth, Greece, about A.D. 55)* 1Cor.2:9-16

### Ammon, son of Mosiah,
### *quoted by Mormon*

Yea, he that repenteth and exerciseth faith, and bringeth forth good works, and prayeth continually without ceasing—unto such it is given to know the mysteries of God; yea, unto such it shall be given to reveal things which never have been revealed; yea, and it shall be given unto such to bring thousands of souls to repentance, even as it has been given unto us to bring these our brethren to repentance. *(Ammon addresses his brethren, 90-77 B.C.)* Alma 26:22

### Elder Joseph F. Smith

If I have learned something through prayer, supplication, and perseverance in seeking to know the truth, and I tell it to you, it will not be knowledge unto you. I can tell you how you can obtain it, but I cannot give it to you. If we receive this knowledge, it must come from the Lord. He can touch your understandings and your spirits, so that you shall comprehend perfectly and not be mistaken. But I cannot do that. You can obtain this knowledge through repentance, humility, and seeking the Lord with full purpose of heart until you find Him. He is not afar off. It is not difficult to approach Him, if we will only do it with a broken heart and a contrite spirit, as did Nephi of old. [2Ne.4:32] This was the way in which Joseph Smith, in his boyhood, approached Him. He went into the woods, knelt down, and in humility he sought earnestly to know which church was acceptable to God. He received an answer to his prayer, which he offered down in the depths of his heart, and he received it in a way that he did not expect. CR1899Oct:71

### Joseph Smith

The best way to obtain truth and wisdom is not to ask it from books, but to go to God in prayer, and obtain divine teaching. *(Conference in Nauvoo, Ill., Oct. 1841)* HC4:425

### Mormon,
### *also quoting King Benjamin*

And he also taught them concerning the records which were engraven on the plates of brass, saying: My sons, I would that ye should remember that were it not for these plates, which contain these records and these com-

mandments, we must have suffered in ignorance, even at this present time, not knowing the mysteries of God. *(King Benjamin teaches his sons the language and prophecies of their fathers, about 130 B.C.)* Mosiah 1:3

### Related Witnesses:
### Paul

For after that in the wisdom of God the world by wisdom knew not God, it pleased God by the foolishness of preaching to save them that believe. 22. For the Jews require a sign, and the Greeks seek after wisdom: 23. But we preach Christ crucified, unto the Jews a stumblingblock, and unto the Greeks foolishness; 24. But unto them which are called, both Jews and Greeks, Christ the power of God, and the wisdom of God. *(Letter to the Church at Corinth, Greece, about A.D. 55)* 1Cor.1:21-24

### Joseph Smith

The God of heaven, understanding most perfectly the constitution of human nature, and the weakness of men, knew what was necessary to be revealed, and what ideas must be planted in their minds in order that they might be enabled to exercise faith in him unto eternal life. *(Lectures on Faith delivered to the School of the Prophets, 1834-35)* LOF4:2

### President John Taylor

As we are all made in the image of God, and as God is the God and Father of the spirits of all flesh, it is His right, it is His prerogative to communicate with the human family. We are told that there is a spirit in man and the inspiration of the Almighty giveth it understanding. God having made the earth, made the people to inhabit it, and made all things that exist therein, has a right to dictate, has a right to make known His will, has a right to communicate with whom He will and control matters as He sees proper: it belongs to Him by right. *(In Tabernacle, Oct. 8, 1882, JD23:260)* TLDP:566

### Joseph Smith

And again, he that receiveth the word of truth, doth he receive it by the Spirit of truth or some other way? 20. If it be some other way it is not of God. 21. Therefore, why is it that ye cannot understand and know, that he that receiveth the word by the Spirit of truth receiveth it as it is preached by the Spirit of truth? 22. Wherefore, he that preacheth and he that receiveth, understand one another, and both are edified and rejoice together. *(Revelation for the elders of the Church, May 1831)* D&C 50:19-22

### Joseph Smith,
### *translating the Book of Moses*

And thus the Gospel began to be preached, from the beginning, being declared by holy angels sent forth from the presence of God, and by his own voice, and by the gift of the Holy Ghost. (*The record of Moses concerning Adam and Eve after they were driven out of the Garden of Eden*) Moses 5:58

### Amos

Surely the Lord GOD will do nothing, but he revealeth his secret unto his servants the prophets. (*Amos prophesies the downfall of Israel, about 770-750 B.C.*) Amos 3:7

**Related Witnesses:**

#### Joseph Smith

And this greater priesthood administereth the gospel and holdeth the key of the mysteries of the kingdom, even the key of the knowledge of God. (*Revelation on priesthood received with six elders, Sept. 22/23, 1832*) D&C 84:19

**Author's Note:** According to Smith and Sjodahl in their commentary on page 141: "A mystery is a truth that cannot be known except through divine revelation—a sacred secret." (DCSM:15)

---

666. Revelation from God to each of us as individuals is necessary for our salvation.

#### President Brigham Young

Without revelation direct from heaven it is impossible for any person to fully understand the plan of salvation. We often hear it said that the living oracles must be in the Church, in order that the kingdom of God may be established and prosper on the earth. I will give another version of this sentiment. I say that the living oracles of God, or the Spirit of revelation must be in each and every individual, to know the plan of salvation and keep in the path that leads them to the presence of God. (*In Tabernacle, April 7, 1862, JD9:279*) TLDP:572

#### President Brigham Young, quoted by John A. Widtsoe

No person [no being] possesses intelligence, in any degree, that he has not received from the God of heaven, or, in other words, from the Fountain of all intelligence, whether he acknowledges his God in it or not. No man, independent of the Great Ruler of the universe, is capable of devising that which we see and are well acquainted with. All mechanism, good government, wholesome principle, and true philosophy of whatever name or nature, flows from God to finite man. What for? To determine what he will do with it. It is for his improvement and advancement in the arts of

civilized life, mortality, and true religion. This has been taught you from the beginning as the unmistakable features of our holy religion. (*In Tabernacle, May 22, 1859, JD7:141*) DBY:148

#### President Brigham Young, quoted by John A. Widtsoe

There is only one way to obtain power and influence in the Kingdom of God, and only one way to obtain foreknowledge, and that is to live so that that influence will come from our Creator, enlightening the mind and revealing things that are past, present and future pertaining to the earth and its inhabitants, and to the dealings of God with the children of men; in short, there is no source of true information outside of the Spirit of Revelation; it maketh manifest all things, and revealeth the dispositions of communities and of individuals. By possessing this Spirit, mankind can obtain power that is durable, beneficial, and that will result in a higher state of knowledge, of honor, and of glory. This can be obtained only by strictly marking the path of truth, and walking faithfully therein. (*In Tabernacle, March 8, 1863, JD10:104-05*) DBY:147

#### Bruce R. McConkie

If we build our house of salvation on the rock of personal revelation, if we build it on the revealed reality that Jesus is the Lord, if we build it on him who is the Eternal Rock—it will stand forever. CR1981Apr:103

#### Elder Joseph F. Smith

Now if we are permitted to believe that the Lord revealed himself to the ancients of whose deeds we read in the Holy Scriptures, it seems to me that there is no good reason for believing that it is not necessary that he should reveal himself in this day to others who desire to be guided by his Spirit and inspiration. Every new truth which grows into living action in the lives of men is a revelation in itself from God, and without the revelation of additional truth, men would not progress in this world, but, left to themselves, would retrograde, being cut off from the light and life of the great fountain of all intelligence, the Father of all. (Gospel Doctrine, p. 37) TLDP:572

#### Elder Ezra Taft Benson

The Lord will increase our knowledge, wisdom, and capacity to obey when we obey His fundamental laws. This is what the Prophet Joseph Smith meant when he said we could have "sudden strokes of ideas" which come into our minds as "pure intelligence." (See Teachings of the Prophet Joseph Smith, p. 151.) This is revelation. We must learn to rely on the Holy Ghost so we can use it to guide our lives and the lives of those for whom we have responsibility. CR1983Apr:71-72

---

667. Revelation to individuals and to the Church comes line upon line, precept upon precept.

**Nephi, son of Lehi**
For behold, thus saith the Lord God: I will give unto the children of men line upon line, precept upon precept, here a little and there a little; and blessed are those who hearken unto my precepts, and lend an ear unto my counsel, for they shall learn wisdom; for unto him that receiveth I will give more; and from them that shall say, We have enough, from them shall be taken away even that which they have. (*Nephi foretells the last days, 559-545 B.C.*) 2Ne.28:30

**Elder Joseph Fielding Smith**
The Lord could not reveal to the Church in the beginning all the knowledge and organization which would be essential to the full and complete organization of the Church. Had this been done, it would have been like an overwhelming flood that would have brought destruction. The truth had to come piecemeal—line upon line, precept upon precept, just like knowledge comes to all of us. CHMR1:95; DCSM:42

**Elder Joseph Fielding Smith**
Revelation is promised us through our faithfulness. . . . The Lord withholds much that he would otherwise reveal if the members of the Church were prepared to receive it. . . . ¶ We have little occasion to clamor for more revelation when we refuse to heed what the Lord has revealed for our salvation. (Doctrines of Salvation, 1:283) DGSM:5

**Joseph Smith**
And again, the voice of God in the chamber of old Father Whitmer, in Fayette, Seneca county, and at sundry times, and in divers places through all the travels and tribulations of this Church of Jesus Christ of Latter-day Saints! And the voice of Michael, the archangel; the voice of Gabriel, and of Raphael, and of divers angels, from Michael or Adam down to the present time, all declaring their dispensation, their rights, their keys, their honors, their majesty and glory, and the power of their priesthood; giving line upon line, precept upon precept; here a little, and there a little; giving us consolation by holding forth that which is to come, confirming our hope! (*Epistle to the Church, Sept. 6, 1842, at Nauvoo, Ill.; all of the keys, powers, and authorities have been restored*) D&C 128:21

**Joseph Smith,**
*quoted by Elder Joseph Fielding Smith*
We consider that God has created man with a mind capable of instruction, and a faculty which may be enlarged in proportion to the heed and diligence given to the light communicated from heaven to the intellect; and that the nearer man approaches perfection, the clearer are his views, and the greater his enjoyments, till he has overcome the evils of his life and lost every desire for sin; and like the ancients, arrives at that point of faith where he is wrapped in the power and glory of his Maker and is caught up to dwell with Him. But we consider that this is a station to which no man ever arrived in a moment: he must have been instructed in the government and laws of that kingdom by proper degrees, until his mind is capable in some measure of comprehending the propriety, justice, equality, and consistency of the same. (*From an epistle to the elders of the Church in Kirtland, Ohio, and to their brethren "abroad," Jan. 22, 1834*) HC2:4-24; TPJS:51

**Rudger Clawson**
And let me say to you, brethren and sisters, that the heights and the depths of the Gospel are quite beyond our reach. The finite mind is not capable of wholly comprehending the great plan of redemption. We, occasionally, have a glimpse of its power and beauty; but we must learn line upon line, precept upon precept, here a little and there a little, until we come up to the full stature of a man in Christ Jesus. It cannot be comprehended in a day, or a month, or a year, it is the study of a lifetime. CR1904Oct:35

**President Joseph F. Smith**
Even Christ himself was not perfect at first; he received not a fulness at first, but he received grace for grace, and he continued to receive more and more until he received a fulness. Is not this to be so with the children of men? Is any man perfect? Has any man received a fulness at once? Have we reached a point wherein we may receive the fulness of God, of his glory, and his intelligence? No; and yet, if Jesus, the Son of God, and the Father of the heavens and the earth in which we dwell, received not a fulness at the first, but increased in faith, knowledge, understanding and grace until he received a fulness, is it not possible for all men who are born of women to receive little by little, line upon line, precept upon precept, until they shall receive a fulness, as he has received a fulness, and be exalted with him in the presence of the father? (*In Tabernacle, March 16, 1902*) (Gospel Doctrine, p. 68) TLDP:474

### Alma, the younger,
*quoted by Mormon*

It is given unto many to know the mysteries of God; nevertheless they are laid under a strict command that they shall not impart only according to the portion of his word which he doth grant unto the children of men, according to the heed and diligence which they give unto him. 10. And therefore, he that will harden his heart, the same receiveth the lesser portion of the word; and he that will not harden his heart, to him is given the greater portion of the word, until it is given unto him to know the mysteries of God until he know them in full. 11. And they that will harden their hearts, to them is given the lesser portion of the word until they know nothing concerning his mysteries; and then they are taken captive by the devil, and led by his will down to destruction. (*Alma contends with the wicked Zeezrom, about 82 B.C.*) Alma 12:9-11

### Bruce R. McConkie

But not all people in all ages and under all circumstances are prepared to receive the fulness of all gospel truths. The Lord gives his word to men line upon line, precept upon precept, here a little and there a little, confirming their hope, building each new revelation upon the foundations of the past, giving his children only that portion of his word which they are able to bear. ¶ When the elders of Israel go forth to proclaim the gospel to the world, they are subject to two commandments that the spiritually untutored might assume are contradictory. In one of them the Lord says: "Teach the principles of my gospel, which are in the Bible and the Book of Mormon." (D&C 42:12) Does this mean they are free to teach all they know about all of the doctrines found in the standard works? In another revelation, the Lord says, "Declare glad tidings. . . . And of tenets thou shalt not talk, but thou shalt declare repentance and faith on the Savior, and remission of sins by baptism and by fire, yea, even the Holy Ghost."(D&C 19:29-31) The clear meaning, of course, is that the servants of the Lord go forth to teach what people are prepared to receive, nothing more. They are to declare glad tidings, to proclaim the message of the restoration, to teach the simple and easy doctrines, and to leave the mysteries alone. They are not to present lessons in calculus to students who must first learn arithmetic; they are not to reveal the mysteries of the kingdom until people believe the first principles: they are to give milk before meat. ¶ Alma summarized the restrictions under which preachers of righteousness serve by saying: "It is given unto many to know the mysteries of God; nevertheless they are laid under a strict command that they shall not impart only according to the portion of his word which he doth grant unto the children of men, according to the heed and diligence which they give unto him." (See Alma 12:9.) Such is the universal principle; it is not how much the teacher knows, but how much the student is prepared to receive. Strong and deep doctrine, spoken to rebellious people, drives them further away and widens the gulf between them and the saints of God. . . . ¶ . . . . Even the true saints—the believing disciples, those who have accepted the gospel and received the gift of the Holy Ghost—are not prepared to receive all things. We have the fulness of the everlasting gospel, meaning we have every truth, power, priesthood, and key needed to enable us to gain the fulness of salvation in our Father's kingdom. But we do not have, and are not yet prepared to receive, the fulness of gospel truth. (The Mortal Messiah, 2:235-37) TLDP:672-73

---

**668. If we are obedient to the light He has given us, God will reveal more truth and knowledge to us.**

### John A. Widtsoe

There is only one way . . . to obtain and possess this mighty spirit . . . which guides the Church today and enlightens every soul, and that is by obeying strictly, with all our might, as far as we poor mortal beings are able, the laws of the Gospel. If we obey, if we practice in our lives the truths given us, then as certainly as we do that, the enlivening spirit of light, of revelation, of understanding will come to us, comprehension will enter our minds and hearts and we shall know the true joy of being Latter-day Saints. CR1934Oct:11

### Nephi, son of Lehi

For behold, thus saith the Lord God: I will give unto the children of men line upon line, precept upon precept, here a little and there a little; and blessed are those who hearken unto my precepts, and lend an ear unto my counsel, for they shall learn wisdom; for unto him that receiveth I will give more; and from them that shall say, We have enough, from them shall be taken away even that which they have. (*Nephi foretells the last days, 559-545 B.C.*) 2Ne.28:30

### Elder Ezra Taft Benson

The Lord will increase our knowledge, wisdom, and capacity to obey when we obey His fundamental laws. This is what the Prophet Joseph Smith meant when he said we could have "sudden strokes of ideas" which come into our minds as "pure intelligence." (See Teachings of the Prophet Joseph Smith, p. 151.) This is revelation. CR1983Apr:71-72

### Joseph Smith

He that keepeth his commandments receiveth truth and light, until he is glorified in truth and knoweth all things. (*Revelation received May 6, 1833; Christ received a fulness of all truth and man by obedience may do likewise*) D&C 93:28

### President Brigham Young,
### *quoted by John A. Widtsoe*

An individual who holds a share in the Priesthood, and continues faithful to his calling, who delights himself continually in doing the things God requires at his hands, and continues through life in the performance of every duty will secure to himself not only the privilege of receiving, but the knowledge how to receive the things of God, that he may know the mind of God continually; and he will be enabled to discern between right and wrong, between the things of God and the things that are not of God. And the Priesthood—the Spirit that is within him, will continue to increase until it becomes like a fountain of living water; until it is like the tree of life; until it is one continued source of intelligence and instruction to that individual. (*In Tabernacle, Jan. 27, 1856, JD3:192*) DBY:132

### Alma, the younger,
### *quoted by Mormon*

It is given unto many to know the mysteries of God; nevertheless they are laid under a strict command that they shall not impart only according to the portion of his word which he doth grant unto the children of men, according to the heed and diligence which they give unto him. 10. And therefore, he that will harden his heart, the same receiveth the lesser portion of the word; and he that will not harden his heart, to him is given the greater portion of the word, until it is given unto him to know the mysteries of God until he know them in full. 11. And they that will harden their hearts, to them is given the lesser portion of the word until they know nothing concerning his mysteries; and then they are taken captive by the devil, and led by his will down to destruction. (*Alma contends with the wicked Zeezrom, about 82 B.C.*) Alma 12:9-11

### Jedediah M. Grant

If this people wish any more law, doctrine, and policy, let them live to the doctrines and revelations which they have already received. ¶ Whoever reflects for a moment will perceive that there is plenty of truth on hand for them to observe, and that more is coming continually and that too faster than we obey. The light is shining upon us direct from heaven, from the throne of light. Can good come from hell? Will light come from darkness? If light can only come from heaven, then the priesthood is the channel for it to flow through. That channel is here, and that God from whom the light comes is the being to govern the world. Then love God, the doctrines and revelations that he gives, and do the best you know how, and you shall have all that you can eat, drink, wear, understand, and make wise use of: Amen. (Deseret News Weekly, April 2, 1856, p. 28) TLDP:575

---

## 669. Personal righteousness is a prerequisite for receiving revelation.

### Elder Joseph Fielding Smith

Revelation is promised us through our faithfulness. . . . The Lord withholds much that he would otherwise reveal if the members of the Church were prepared to receive it. . . . ¶ We have little occasion to clamor for more revelation when we refuse to heed what the Lord has revealed for our salvation. (Doctrines of Salvation, 1:283) DGSM:5

### President Brigham Young,
### *quoted by John A. Widtsoe*

There is only one way to obtain power and influence in the Kingdom of God, and only one way to obtain foreknowledge, and that is to live so that that influence will come from our Creator. . . . This can be obtained only by strictly marking the path of truth, and walking faithfully therein. (*In Tabernacle, March 8, 1863, JD10:104-05*) DBY:147

### Joseph Smith,
### *receiving the Word of the Lord*

For thus saith the Lord—I, the Lord, am merciful and gracious unto those who fear me, and delight to honor those who serve me in righteousness and in truth unto the end. 6. Great shall be their reward and eternal shall be their glory. 7. And to them will I reveal all mysteries, yea, all the hidden mysteries of my kingdom from days of old, and for ages to come, will I make known unto them the good pleasure of my will concerning all things pertaining to my kingdom. 8. Yea, even the wonders of eternity shall they know, and things to come will I show them, even the things of many generations. 9. And their wisdom shall be great, and their understanding reach to heaven; and before them the wisdom of the wise shall perish, and the understanding of the prudent shall come to naught. 10. For by my Spirit will I enlighten them, and by my power will I make known unto them the secrets of my will—yea, even those things which eye has not seen, nor ear heard, nor yet entered into the heart of man. (*Vision to Joseph Smith and Sidney Rigdon, Feb. 16, 1832*) D&C 76:5-10

### Joseph Smith,
### receiving the Word of the Lord

Let thy bowels also be full of charity towards all men, and to the household of faith, and let virtue garnish thy thoughts unceasingly; then shall thy confidence wax strong in the presence of God; and the doctrine of the priesthood shall distil upon thy soul as the dews from heaven. 46. The Holy Ghost shall be thy constant companion, and thy scepter an unchanging scepter of righteousness and truth; and thy dominion shall be an everlasting dominion, and without compulsory means it shall flow unto thee forever and ever. (*Revelation received in Liberty Jail, March 20, 1839; the priesthood should be used only in righteousness*) D&C 121:45-46

### Joseph Smith

And if ye are purified and cleansed from all sin, ye shall ask whatsoever you will in the name of Jesus and it shall be done. (*Revelation for the elders of the Church, May 1831*) D&C 50:29

### Joseph Smith

And all saints who remember to keep and do these sayings, walking in obedience to the commandments. . . . 19. . . . shall find wisdom and great treasures of knowledge, even hidden treasures; (*Revelation, Feb. 27, 1833*) D&C 89:18-19

### Elder Ezra Taft Benson

Listen to the spiritual promise; "All saints who remember to keep and do these sayings, walking in obedience to the commandments . . . shall find wisdom and great treasures of knowledge, even hidden treasures." (D&C 89:18-19) ¶ Some have thought this promise was contingent on just keeping the provisions of the Word of Wisdom. But you will notice we will walk in obedience to all the commandments. Then we shall receive specific spiritual promises. This means we must obey the law of tithing, keep the Sabbath day holy, keep morally clean and chaste, and obey all other commandments. . . . ¶ I do not believe that a member of the Church can have an active, vibrant testimony of the gospel without keeping the commandments. A testimony is to have current inspiration to know the work is true, not something we receive only once. The Holy Ghost abides with those who honor, respect, and obey God's laws. And it is that Spirit which gives inspiration to the individual. CR1983Apr:71-72

### Ammon, son of Mosiah,
### quoted by Mormon

Yea, he that repenteth and exerciseth faith, and bringeth forth good works, and prayeth continually without ceasing—unto such it is given to know the mysteries of God; yea, unto such it shall be given to reveal things which never have been revealed. . . . (*Ammon addresses his brethren, 90-77 B.C.*) Alma 26:22

### President Heber J. Grant

The Lord gives to many of us the still, small voice of revelation. It comes as vividly and strongly as though it were with a great sound. It comes to each man, according to his needs and faithfulness, for guidance in matters that pertain to his own life. CR1945Apr:9

### Abraham O. Woodruff

It is the right of every Latter-day Saint, who is living in accordance to the commandments of the Lord, to know of the truthfulness, correctness, and righteousness of every enactment that is made by the Church of Christ, for we believe in revelation. We believe that God will manifest these things unto us, not simply to those who stand at the head of the Church, but to all the members of the Church of Christ. It is our privilege to know and understand whether anything that is done by the Church is right or not, if we are living in accordance with the commandments of the Lord. CR1899Oct:62

### Elder Joseph F. Smith

If I have learned something through prayer, supplication, and perseverance in seeking to know the truth, and I tell it to you, it will not be knowledge unto you. I can tell you how you can obtain it, but I cannot give it to you. If we receive this knowledge, it must come from the Lord. He can touch your understandings and your spirits, so that you shall comprehend perfectly and not be mistaken. But I cannot do that. You can obtain this knowledge through repentance, humility, and seeking the Lord with full purpose of heart until you find Him. He is not afar off. It is not difficult to approach Him, if we will only do it with a broken heart and a contrite spirit, as did Nephi of old. [2Ne.4:32] This was the way in which Joseph Smith, in his boyhood, approached Him. He went into the woods, knelt down, and in humility he sought earnestly to know which church was acceptable to God. He received an answer to his prayer, which he offered down in the depths of his heart, and he received it in a way that he did not expect. CR1899Oct:71

### Nephi, son of Lehi

And it came to pass after I, Nephi, having heard all the words of my father, concerning the things which he saw in a vision, and also the things which he spake by the power of the Holy Ghost, which power he received by faith on the Son of God—and the Son of God was the Messiah who should come—I, Nephi, was desirous also that I might see, and hear, and know of these things, by the power of the Holy Ghost, which is the gift of God unto all those who diligently seek him, as well in times of old as in the time that he should manifest himself unto the children of men. 18. For he is the same yesterday, to-day, and forever; and the way is prepared for all men from the foundation of the world, if it so be that they repent and come unto him. 19. For he that diligently seeketh shall find; and the mysteries of God shall be unfolded unto them, by the power of the Holy Ghost, as well in these times as in times of old, and as well in times of old as in times to come; wherefore, the course of the Lord is one eternal round. (*Nephi's writings, 600-592 B.C.*) 1Ne.10:17-19

**Related Witnesses:**
### Elder Spencer W. Kimball
For many it seems hard to accept as revelation those numerous . . . revelations which come to prophets as deep, unassailable impressions settling down on the prophet's mind and heart as dew from heaven or as the dawn displaces the darkness of night. ¶ The burning bushes, the smoking mountains, the sheets of four-footed beasts, the Cumorahs, and the Kirtlands were realities; but they were the exceptions. The great volume of revelation came to Moses and to Joseph and comes to today's prophet in the less spectacular way—that of deep impressions, without spectacle or glamour or dramatic events. ¶ Always expecting the spectacular, many may miss entirely the constant flow of revealed communication. ¶ When in a Thursday temple meeting, after prayer and fasting, important decisions are made, new missions and new stakes are created, new patterns and policies initiated, the news is taken for granted and possibly thought of as mere human calculations. But to those who sit in the intimate circles and hear the prayers of the prophet and the testimony of the man of God; to those who see the astuteness of his deliberations and the sagacity of his decisions and pronouncements, to them he is verily a prophet. To hear him conclude important new developments with such solemn expressions as "the Lord is pleased;" "that move is right;" "our Heavenly Father has spoken," is to know positively. ACR(Munich)1973:76-77

**670. Individual men and women can receive revelation to guide them within their own spheres of authority (they will not receive divine instructions for those higher in authority than they).**

### Joseph Smith,
*quoted by Elder Joseph Fielding Smith*
I will inform you that it is contrary to the economy of God for any member of the Church, or any one, to receive instructions for those in authority higher than themselves; therefore you will see the impropriety of giving heed to them; but if any person have a vision or a visitation from a heavenly messenger, it must be for his own benefit and instruction; for the fundamental principles, government, and doctrine of the Church are vested in the keys of the kingdom. (*Letter to Jared Carter, April 13, 1833*) HC1:338; TPJS:21; DGSM:5

### Joseph Smith,
*receiving the Word of the Lord*
Behold, I say unto thee, Oliver, that it shall be given unto thee that thou shalt be heard by the church in all things whatsoever thou shalt teach them by the Comforter, concerning the revelations and commandments which I have given. 2. But, behold, verily, verily, I say unto thee, no one shall be appointed to receive commandments and revelations in this church excepting my servant Joseph Smith, Jun., for he receiveth them even as Moses. 3. And thou shalt be obedient unto the things which I shall give unto him, even as Aaron, to declare faithfully the commandments and the revelations, with power and authority unto the church. 4. And if thou art led at any time by the Comforter to speak or teach, or at all times by the way of commandment unto the church, thou mayest do it. 5. But thou shalt not write by way of commandment, but by wisdom; 6. And thou shalt not command him who is at thy head, and at the head of the church; 7. For I have given him the keys of the mysteries, and the revelations which are sealed, until I shall appoint unto them another in his stead. (*Revelation for Oliver Cowdery, Sept. 1830*) D&C 28:1-7

### James E. Talmage
The Lord observes the principle of order and fitness in giving revelation to His servants. Though it is the privilege of any person to live so as to merit this gift in the affairs of his special calling, only those appointed and ordained to the offices of presidency are to be revelators to the people at large. AF:209

## Boyd K. Packer

Revelation continues in the Church: the prophet receiving it for the Church; the president for his stake, his mission, or his quorum; the bishop for his ward; the father for his family; the individual for himself. CR1974Apr:139

## President Joseph F. Smith

I say to you that there is revelation in the Church. The Lord not only blesses the men who stand at the head and hold the keys of the kingdom, but He also blesses every faithful individual with the spirit of inspiration. He gives His people revelation for their own guidance, wherein they keep His commandments and serve Him. That is a blessing promised and within their power to receive. CR1910Oct:41

## President Joseph F. Smith

I believe that every individual in the Church has just as much right to enjoy the spirit of revelation and the understanding from God which that spirit of revelation gives him, for his own good, as the bishop has to enable him to preside over his ward. Every man has the privilege to exercise these gifts and these privileges in the conduct of his own affairs, in bringing up his children in the way they should go, and in the management of his farm, his flocks, his herds, and in the management of his business, if he has business of other kinds to do; it is his right to enjoy the spirit of revelation and of inspiration to do the right thing, to be wise and prudent, just and good in every thing that he does. I know that this is a true principle. CR1912Apr:9-10

## President Spencer W. Kimball

Never again will God be hidden from his children on the earth. Revelation is here to remain. . . . ¶ . . . . Man never needs to stand alone. Every faithful person may have the inspiration for his own limited kingdom. But the Lord definitely calls prophets today and reveals his secrets unto them as he did yesterday, he does today, and will do tomorrow: that is the way it is. CR1977Apr:115

## Russell M. Nelson

The father in the home next door will not receive revelation for his neighbor's family. CR1984Oct:40

## Related Witnesses:

### James

If any of you lack wisdom, let him ask of God, that giveth to all men liberally, and upbraideth not; and it shall be given him. (James writes to his brethren in the Church) James 1:5

### Jesus,
*quoted by Mormon*

And whatsoever ye shall ask the Father in my name, which is right, believing that ye shall receive, behold it shall be given unto you. (The

*resurrected Jesus commands the Nephite people to pray, A.D. 34)* 3Ne.18:20

---

671. Every Church member is entitled to revelation in the performance of his or her calling in the Church.

### Joseph Smith,
*quoted by Elder Joseph Fielding Smith*

It is also the privilege of any officer in this Church to obtain revelations, so far as relates to his particular calling and duty in the Church. *(In solemn assembly in Kirtland Temple, April 6, 1837)* TPJS:111; DGSM:5

### Elder Lorenzo Snow

[I]n every circumstance and condition surrounding the Latter-day Saints, while in the performance of their duties, they are entitled to supernatural aid from the Holy Spirit, to help in the various conditions surrounding them, and in the duties that they are required to perform. CR1898Apr:12

### President Joseph F. Smith

The gift of revelation does not belong to one man solely. It is not a gift that pertains to the Presidency of the Church and the Twelve Apostles alone. It is not confined to the presiding authorities of the Church. It belongs to every individual member of the Church; and it is the right and privilege of every man, every woman, and every child who has reached the years of accountability to enjoy the spirit of revelation, and to be possessed of the spirit of inspiration in the discharge of their duties as members of the Church. CR1912Apr:5

### James E. Talmage

The Lord observes the principle of order and fitness in giving revelation to His servants. Though it is the privilege of any person to live so as to merit this gift in the affairs of his special calling, only those appointed and ordained to the offices of presidency are to be revelators to the people at large. AF:209

### Joseph F. Merrill

Revelation is needed not only to guide the organization and teachings of the Church, but also to enable the members to function acceptably in their respective duties. One thing that is characteristic of the Latter-day Saints is their assurance that God lives, that this is His accepted Church and that He helps His children according to their worthiness and needs. Experience has taught them the validity of certain scriptural teachings relative to the individual receiving divine revelations. CR1941Apr:47-48

### Abraham O. Woodruff

We are told that we are agents unto ourselves, and that we ought to be engaged in bringing to pass much righteousness. When we are placed to preside over a Ward it is not necessary to go to the President of the Church to ask about every little matter, but we are entitled to the spirit of God and to the revelations of the Lord Jesus Christ in our calling. If we are energetic and are working in the calling whereunto the Lord has called us, he will reveal many great and important things unto us, and he will bring to our minds many suggestions and ideas with regard to the government of our Ward. So with presidents of Stakes and High Councils and other officers of the Church. CR1900Oct:15

**Related Witnesses:**

### Joseph Smith,
*quoted by Elder Joseph Fielding Smith*

I will inform you that it is contrary to the economy of God for any member of the Church, or any one, to receive instruction for those in authority higher than themselves; therefore you will see the impropriety of giving heed to them; but if any person have a vision or a visitation from a heavenly messenger, it must be for his own benefit and instruction; for the fundamental principles, government, and doctrine of the Church are vested in the keys of the kingdom. (*Letter, April 13, 1833*) TPJS:21; DGSM:5

---

## (4) Recognizing Revelation

672. **One way God communicates to us is by giving us peace to our minds and souls.**

### Thomas S. Monson

Rarely is the assurance communicated by a flashing sign or a loud voice. Rather, the language of the Spirit is gentle, quiet, uplifting to the heart and soothing to the soul. ¶ At times, the answers to our questions and the responses to our daily prayers come to us through silent promptings of the Spirit. ¶ We watch. We wait. We listen for that still, small voice. CR1985Apr:85-86

### Elder Spencer W. Kimball

[Revelations] . . . come to prophets as deep, unassailable impressions settling down on the prophet's mind and heart as dew from heaven or as the dawn displaces the darkness of night. ACR(Munich)1973:77

### Elder Spencer W. Kimball

The burning bushes, the smoking mountains, the sheets of four-footed beasts, the Cumorahs, and the Kirtlands were realities; but they were the exceptions. The great volume of revelation came to Moses and to Joseph and comes to today's prophet in the less spectacular way— that of deep impressions, without spectacle or glamour or dramatic events. ¶ Always expecting the spectacular, many will miss entirely the constant flow of revealed communication. ACR(Munich)1973:77

### George Q. Cannon

It should be the aim of every one professing to be a Latter-day Saint not to leave his chamber in the morning until he comes out feeling that spirit of peace, with his brow unruffled with care, with a consciousness of having communed with God and that he knows his standing with him. When he leaves his chamber having that spirit, he will diffuse joy and gladness throughout his entire household. Should anything occur to disturb the serenity of a Latter-day Saint he ought to step aside and ask God in the name of Jesus to remove it and to pour out the spirit of peace and consolation upon him to fill his heart. At night too, the same Spirit of peace should be sought for. (*In Tabernacle, July 27, 1879, JD20:292*) TLDP:471

### Joseph Smith,
*receiving the Word of the Lord*

And the place where it is my will that you should tarry, for the main, shall be signalized unto you by the peace and power of my Spirit, that shall flow unto you. (*Revelation received at Salem, Mass., Aug. 6, 1836*) D&C 111:8

### Joseph Smith,
*receiving the Word of the Lord*

Verily, verily, I say unto you, if you desire a further witness, cast your mind upon the night that you cried unto me in your heart, that you might know concerning the truth of these things. 23. Did I not speak peace to your mind concerning the matter? What greater witness can you have than from God? (*Revelation for Oliver Cowdery, April 1829*) D&C 6:22-23

**Related Witnesses:**

### Helaman, son of Alma, the younger,
*quoted by Mormon*

Therefore we did pour out our souls in prayer to God, that he would strengthen us and deliver us out of the hands of our enemies, yea, and also give us strength that we might retain our cities, and our lands, and our possessions, for the support of our people. 11. Yea, and it came to pass that the Lord our God did visit us with assurances that he would deliver us; yea, insomuch that he did speak peace to our souls, and did grant unto us great faith, and did cause us that we should hope for our deliverance in him. (*The Lord speaks peace to Helaman while in battle*) Alma 58:10-11

**Elder Harold B. Lee**
If we will live worthy, then the Lord will guide us—by a personal appearance, or by His actual voice, or by His voice coming into our mind, or by impressions upon our heart and our soul. And oh, how grateful we ought to be if the Lord sends us a dream in which are revealed to us the beauties of the eternity or a warning and direction for our special comfort. Yes, if we so live, the Lord will guide us for our salvation and for our benefit. *(To Brigham Young University student body)* (Stand Ye in Holy Places, p. 144) TLDP:575

**Recorded in Numbers**
The Lord lift up his countenance upon thee, and give thee peace. *(The words of the Lord to Moses for Aaron and his sons)* Num.6:26

---

673. **The spirit of revelation is perceived when a person senses an inward flowing of pure intelligence, giving sudden strokes of ideas.**

**Joseph Smith,**
*quoted by Elder Joseph Fielding Smith*
The Spirit of Revelation is in connection with these blessings. A person may profit by noticing the first intimation of the spirit of revelation; for instance, when you feel pure intelligence flowing into you, it may give you sudden strokes of ideas, so that by noticing it, you may find it fulfilled the same day or soon; (i.e.,) those things that were presented unto your minds by the Spirit of God, will come to pass; and thus by learning the Spirit of God and understanding it, you may grow into the principle of revelation, until you become perfect in Christ Jesus. *(Instructions to the Twelve, June 27, 1839)* TPJS:151; DGSM:5

**Elder Ezra Taft Benson**
The Lord will increase our knowledge, wisdom, and capacity to obey when we obey His fundamental laws. This is what the Prophet Joseph Smith meant when he said we could have "sudden strokes of ideas" which come into our minds as "pure intelligence." (See Teachings of the Prophet Joseph Smith, p. 151.) This is revelation. We must learn to rely on the Holy Ghost so we can use it to guide our lives and the lives of those for whom we have responsibility. CR1983Apr:71-72;

**President Harold B. Lee**
When there come to you things that your mind does not know, when you have a sudden thought that comes to your mind, if you will learn to give heed to these things that come from the Lord you will learn to walk by the spirit of revelation. ACR(Mexico City)1972:49

**President Brigham Young,**
*quoted by John A. Widtsoe*
The Lord has said, go into the waters of baptism and be baptized for the remission of your sins, and you shall receive a witness that I am telling you the truth. How? . . . You will feel kind to your children, to your brothers and sisters, to your parents and neighbors, and to all around you; you will feel a glow, as of fire, burning within you; and if you open your mouths to talk you will declare ideas which you did not formerly think of; they will flow into your mind, even such as you have not thought of for years. The Scriptures will be opened to you, and you will see how clear and reasonable everything is which this or that Elder teaches you. Your hearts will be comforted, you can lie down and sleep in peace, and wake up with feelings as pleasant as the breezes of summer. This is a witness to you. *(In Tabernacle, Feb. 17, 1856, JD3:211)* DBY:331

**Related Witnesses:**
**Joseph Smith,**
*receiving the Word of the Lord*
Yea, behold, I will tell you in your mind and in your heart, by the Holy Ghost, which shall come upon you and which shall dwell in your heart. 3. Now, behold, this is the spirit of revelation; behold, this is the spirit by which Moses brought the children of Israel through the Red Sea on dry ground. *(Revelation for Oliver Cowdery, April 1829)* D&C 8:2-3

**Enos,**
*quoted by Mormon*
Now, it came to pass that when I had heard these words I began to feel a desire for the welfare of my brethren, the Nephites; wherefore, I did pour out my whole soul unto God for them. 10. And while I was thus struggling in the spirit, behold, the voice of the Lord came into my mind again, . . . *(Enos gives the word of the Lord to the Nephites, 544-421 B.C.)* Enos 1:9-10

**Joseph Smith**
[A]fter man was created, he was not left without intelligence or understanding, to wander in darkness and spend an existence and doubt (on the great and important point which effected his happiness) as to the real fact by whom he was created, or unto whom he was amenable for his conduct. God conversed with him face to face. In his presence he was permitted to stand, and from his own mouth he was permitted to receive instruction. He heard his voice, walked before him and gazed upon his glory, while intelligence

burst upon his understanding, and enabled him to give names to the vast assemblage of his Maker's works. (*Lectures on Faith delivered to the School of the Prophets, 1834-35*) LOF2:18

**Joseph Smith,**
*quoted by Elder Joseph Fielding Smith*
One great evil is, that men are ignorant of the nature of spirits; their power, laws, government, intelligence, &c., and imagine that when there is anything like power, revelation, or vision manifested, that it must be of God. Hence the Methodists, Presbyterians, and others frequently possess a spirit that will cause them to lie down, and during its operation, animation is frequently entirely suspended; they consider it to be the power of God, and a glorious manifestation from God—a manifestation of what? Is there any intelligence communicated? Are the curtains of heaven withdrawn, or the purposes of God developed? Have they seen and conversed with an angel—or have the glories of futurity burst upon their view? No! but their body has been inanimate, the operation of their spirit suspended, and all the intelligence that can be obtained from them when they arise, is a shout of "glory," or "hallelujah," or some incoherent expression; but they have had "the power." (Editorial in Times and Seasons, April 1842) HC4:572; TPJS:203-04

---

674. **The spirit of revelation is perceived when a person senses an enlarging of the soul and an enlightening of the understanding.**

**Alma, the younger,**
*quoted by Mormon*
Now, we will compare the word unto a seed. Now, if ye give place, that a seed may be planted in your heart, behold, if it be a true seed, or a good seed, if ye do not cast it out by your unbelief, that ye will resist the Spirit of the Lord, behold, it will begin to swell within your breasts; and when you feel these swelling motions, ye will begin to say within yourselves—It must needs be that this is a good seed, or that the word is good, for it beginneth to enlarge my soul; yea, it beginneth to enlighten my understanding, yea, it beginneth to be delicious to me. (*Alma preaches to the poor whose afflictions had humbled them; he compares the word of God to a seed, about 74 B.C.*) Alma 32:28

**President Brigham Young,**
*quoted by John A. Widtsoe*
There is only one way to obtain power and influence in the Kingdom of God, and only one

way to obtain foreknowledge, and that is to live so that that influence will come from our Creator, enlightening the mind and revealing things that are past, present and future pertaining to the earth and its inhabitants, and to the dealings of God with the children of men; in short, there is no source of true information outside of the Spirit of Revelation; it maketh manifest all things, and revealeth the dispositions of communities and of individuals. By possessing this Spirit, mankind can obtain power that is durable, beneficial, and that will result in a higher state of knowledge, of honor, and of glory. This can be obtained only by strictly marking the path of truth, and walking faithfully therein. (*In Tabernacle, March 8, 1863, JD10:104-05*) DBY:147

**President Brigham Young**
What is it that convinces man? It is the influence of the Almighty, enlightening his mind, giving instruction to the understanding. When that inhabits the body, that which comes from the regions of glory is enlightened by the influence, power, and Spirit of the Father of light, it swallows up the organization which pertains to this world. Those who are governed by this influence lose sight of all things pertaining to mortality; they are wholly influenced by the power of eternity, and lose sight of time. All the honor, wisdom, strength, and whatsoever is considered desirable among men, yea, all that pertains to this organization, which is in any way independent of that which came from the Father of our spirits, is obliterated to them and they hear and understand by the same power and spirit that clothe the Deity, and the holy beings in His presence. ("Statement from Brigham Young concerning the Holy Ghost," IE1947Jan:5, JD1:90) TLDP:279

**President Joseph F. Smith**
I believe that the Lord has revealed to the children of men all that they know. I do not believe that any man has discovered any principle in science, or art, in mechanism, or mathematics, or anything else, that God did not know before he did. Man is indebted to the source of all intelligence and truth for the knowledge that he possesses; and all who will yield obedience to the promptings of the Spirit which leads to virtue, to honor, to the love of God and man, and to the love of truth and that which is enobling and enlarging to the soul, will get a clearer, a more expansive, and a more direct and conclusive knowledge of God's truths than anyone else can do. CR1902Apr:85-86

**Parley P. Pratt**
The gift of the Holy Ghost adapts itself to all these organs or attributes. It quickens all the

intellectual faculties, increases, enlarges, expands, and purifies all the natural passions and affections, and adapts them, by the gift of wisdom, to their lawful use. It inspires, develops, cultivates, and matures all the fine-toned sympathies, joys, tastes, kindred feelings, and affections of our nature. It inspires virtue, kindness, goodness, tenderness, gentleness, and charity. It develops beauty of person, form, and features. It tends to health, vigor, animation, and social feeling. It invigorates all the faculties of the physical and intellectual man. It strengthens and gives tone to the nerves. In short, it is, as it were, marrow to the bone, joy to the heart, light to the eyes, music to the ears, and life to the whole being. (Key to the Science of Theology, p. 61) TLDP:280; DGSM:45

### Marion G. Romney
The gift of the Holy Ghost is an endowment that gives one the right to enjoy the enlightenment, companionship, and guidance of the Spirit and the influence of the Holy Spirit as long as one complies with the commandments of God. (Learning for the Eternities, p. 22) TLDP:277

### Bruce R. McConkie
"Come unto me" and receive my Spirit, and then shall ye have power to learn of me. This is the great and grand secret. This is the course that is provided for us and for all men, and it is provided in the wisdom of him who knoweth all things. This is the sole and only way to learn of Christ within the full sense and meaning of his tender and solicitous invitation. "No man can know that Jesus is the Lord, but by the Holy Ghost." Little slivers of truth come to all who seek to know; occasional flashes of lightening give glimpses of the eternal realities that are hidden by the gloom and darkness of unbelief. But to learn and know those truths which reveal the Son of Man in his majesty and beauty and that prepare the truth seeker to be one with his Lord, such rays of the noonday sun shine forth only upon those who gain the enlightening companionship of the Holy Spirit. (The Mortal Messiah, 1:17) TLDP:283

### Related Witnesses:
### President Joseph F. Smith
[In the words of Job], "There is a spirit in man; and the inspiration of the Almighty giveth them understanding." It is this inspiration from God, proceeding throughout all his creations, that enlighteneth the children of men; and it is nothing more nor less than the Spirit of Christ, that enlighteneth the mind, that quickeneth the understanding, and that prompteth the children of men to do that which is good and to eschew that which is evil; which quickens the con-

science of man and gives him intelligence to judge between good and evil, light and darkness, right and wrong. We are indebted to God for this intelligence that we possess. It is by the spirit which lighteth every man that cometh into the world that our minds are quickened and our spirits enlightened with understanding and intelligence. And all men are entitled to this. It is not reserved for the obedient alone; but it is given unto all the children of men that are born into the world. ("I Know That My Redeemer Lives," IE1908Mar:380-81) TLDP:362

---

## 675. God at times speaks to us with a still, small voice of revelation.

### Mormon
And it came to pass that while they were thus conversing one with another, they heard a voice as if it came out of heaven; and they cast their eyes round about, for they understood not the voice which they heard; and it was not a harsh voice, neither was it a loud voice; nevertheless, and notwithstanding it being a small voice it did pierce them that did hear to the center, insomuch that there was no part of their frame that it did not cause to quake; yea, it did pierce them to the very soul, and did cause their hearts to burn. (*God the Father testifies of his Beloved Son, A.D. 34*) 3Ne.11:3

### Mormon
And it came to pass when they heard this voice, and beheld that it was not a voice of thunder, neither was it a voice of a great tumultuous noise, but behold, it was a still voice of perfect mildness, as if it had been a whisper, and it did pierce even to the very soul— (*The Lamanites, who have imprisoned Nephi and Lehi, see them protected by a circle of fire, and hear a voice commanding them to repent, about 30 B.C.*) Hel.5:30

### President Heber J. Grant
The Lord gives to many of us the still, small voice of revelation. It comes as vividly and strongly as though it were with a great sound. CR1945Apr:9

### Recorded in 1 Kings
[B]ut the LORD was not in the wind: and after the wind an earthquake; but the LORD was not in the earthquake: 12. And after the earthquake a fire; but the LORD was not in the fire: and after the fire a still small voice. (*Elijah challenges the priests of Baal and calls down fire from heaven*) 1Kgs.19:11-12

### George Q. Cannon
It requires the utmost care upon the part of the people who have received the Spirit of the Lord

by the laying on of hands to distinguish between the voice of that Spirit and the voice of their own hearts or other spirits which may take possession of them. Experience and watchfulness will enable the Saint to recognize the voice of the Holy Spirit. ¶ It is a still, small voice in the hearts of the children of men. It is not boisterous, loud or aggressive, and if those who receive it carefully watch its suggestions, it will develop more and more within them, and it will become an unfailing source of revelation. But the necessity always remains of exercising care in distinguishing its voice from the voice of other influences in the heart. (Gospel Truth, 1:182) TLDP:285

**Nephi, son of Lehi**
Ye are swift to do iniquity but slow to remember the Lord your God. Ye have seen an angel, and he spake unto you; yea, ye have heard his voice from time to time; and he hath spoken unto you in a still small voice, but ye were past feeling, that ye could not feel his words. . . . (*Nephi answers his rebellious brothers, about 591 B.C.*) 1Ne.17:45

**President Joseph F. Smith**
And when we live so that we can hear and understand the whisperings of the still small voice of the Spirit of God, let us do whatsoever that Spirit directs, without fear of the consequences. . . . [L]et us do it, no matter what men may say or think. CR1903Oct:86

**Joseph Smith**
Yea, thus saith the still small voice, which whispereth through and pierceth all things, and often times it maketh my bones to quake while it maketh manifest. . . . (*Revelation, Nov. 27, 1832*) D&C 85:6

**Bruce R. McConkie**
Sad though it be, few are the men who hear the audible voice, thundering from Sinai, revealing in prophetic ears the mind and will of Jehovah; few are they who hear the still small voice, whispering in prophetic ears, revealing the principles and ordinances of the gospel; but millions comprise the hosts of earth's inhabitants who have before them the recorded words of holy men who wrote as they were prompted from on high. And all those who read these words—words preserved in the holy scriptures—and who do so by the power of the Holy Ghost can testify that they have heard the Lord's voice and know his words. (D&C 18:33-36) (The Mortal Messiah, 3:403) TLDP:283

**Related Witnesses:**
**Bruce R. McConkie**
A true prophet is one who has the testimony of Jesus; one who knows by personal revelation that Jesus Christ is the Son of the living God,

and that he was to be—or has been—crucified for the sins of the world; one to whom God speaks and who recognizes the still small voice of the Spirit. (The Mortal Messiah, pp. 168-70) TLDP:538

---

**676. Revelation comes at times through dreams.**

**George F. Richards**
The Lord has revealed to me, by dreams, something more than I have ever understood or felt before about the love for God and the love for fellow men. I believe in dreams. The Lord has given me dreams, which to me, are just as real and as much from God as was the dream of King Nebuchadnezzar which was the means of saving a nation from starvation, or the dream of Lehi who through a dream led his colony out of the old country, across the mighty deep to this promised land, or any other dreams that we read of in the scripture. ¶ It is not out of place for us to have important dreams, for we read in the scriptures: "And it shall come to pass in the last days, saith God, I will pour out of my Spirit upon all flesh: and your sons and your daughters shall prophesy, and your young men shall see visions, and your old men shall dream dreams." (Acts 2:17) ¶ More than forty years ago I had a dream, which I am sure was from the Lord. In this dream I was in the presence of the Savior as he stood in mid-air. He spoke no word to me, but my love for him was such that I have not words to explain. I know that no mortal man can love the Lord as I experienced that love for the Savior unless God reveals it unto him. I would have remained in his presence, but there was a power drawing me away from him, and as a result of that dream I had this feeling, that no matter what might be required at my hands, what the gospel might entail unto me, I would do what I should be asked to do, even to the laying down of my life. CR1946Oct:139

**Joseph Smith**
We believe that we have a right to revelations, visions, and dreams from God, our heavenly Father; and light and intelligence, through the gift of the Holy Ghost, in the name of Jesus Christ, on all subjects pertaining to our spiritual welfare, if it so be that we keep his commandments, so as to render ourselves worthy in his sight. (Times and Seasons, Feb. 1840, p. 54) TLDP:570

**Elder Harold B. Lee**
If we will live worthy, then the Lord will guide us—by a personal appearance, or by His actual

voice, or by His voice coming into our mind, or by impressions upon our heart and our soul. And oh, how grateful we ought to be if the Lord sends us a dream in which are revealed to us the beauties of the eternity or a warning and direction for our special comfort. Yes, if we so live, the Lord will guide us for our salvation and for our benefit. *(To Brigham Young University student body)* (Stand Ye in Holy Places, p. 144) TLDP:575

**James E. Talmage**

Visions and Dreams have constituted a means of communication between God and men in every dispensation of the Priesthood. In general, visions are manifested to the waking senses whilst dreams are given during sleep. In the vision, however, the senses may be so affected as to render the person practically unconscious, at least oblivious to ordinary occurrences, while he is able to discern the heavenly manifestation. In the earlier dispensations, the Lord frequently communicated through dreams and visions, oftentimes revealing to prophets the events of the future even to the latest generations. Consider the case of Enoch, unto whom the Lord spoke face to face, showing him the course of the human family unto and beyond the second coming of the Savior. The brother of Jared because of his righteousness was so blessed of God as to be shown all the inhabitants of the earth, both those who had previously existed and those who were to follow. Unto Moses the will of God was made known with the visual manifestation of fire. Lehi received through dreams his instructions to leave Jerusalem; and on many subsequent occasions the Lord communicated with this patriarch of the western world by dreams and visions. AF:205-06

**Marion G. Romney**

Now I know, my brothers and sisters and friends, and bear witness to the fact that revelation from the Lord comes through the spoken word, by personal visitation, by messengers from the Lord, through dreams, and by way of visions, and by the voice of the Lord coming into one's mind. ¶ Most often, however, revelation comes to us by means of the still, small voice. . . . CR1978Apr:76

**James E. Talmage**

Revelation is the communication or disclosure of the will of God directly to man. Under circumstances best suiting the divine purposes, through the dreams of sleep or in waking visions of the mind, by voices without visional appearance or by actual manifestations of the Holy Presence before the eye, God makes known His designs, and instructs His revelators. AF:208

**Related Witnesses:**

**Moses**

And Joseph dreamed a dream, and he told it to his brethren: and they hated him yet the more. . . . 9. And he dreamed yet another dream, and told it to his brethren, and said, Behold, I have dreamed a dream more; and, behold, the sun and the moon and the eleven stars made obeisance to me. *(Joseph dreams that his parents and brothers make obeisance to him)* Gen.37:5,9

**Recorded in Matthew**

But while he thought on these things, behold, the angel of the Lord appeared unto him in a dream, saying, Joseph, thou son of David, fear not to take unto thee Mary thy wife: for that which is conceived in her is of the Holy Ghost. *(Joseph, espoused to Mary, learns she is with child)* Matt.1:20

**Nephi, son of Lehi**

And it came to pass that the Lord commanded my father, even in a dream, that he should take his family and depart into the wilderness. *(The Lord, in a dream, warns faithful Lehi to go into the wilderness, 600 B.C.)* 1Ne.2:2

**Moses**

And Jacob went out from Beer-sheba, and went toward Haran. 11. And he lighted upon a certain place, and tarried there all night, because the sun was set; and he took of the stones of that place, and put them for his pillows, and lay down in that place to sleep. 12. And he dreamed, and behold a ladder set up on the earth, and the top of it reached to heaven: and behold the angels of God ascending and descending on it. 13. And, behold, the LORD stood above it, and said, I am the LORD God of Abraham thy father, and the God of Isaac: the land whereon thou liest, to thee will I give it, and to thy seed; 14. And thy seed shall be as the dust of the earth, and thou shalt spread abroad to the west, and to the east, and to the north, and to the south: and in thee and in thy seed shall all the families of the earth be blessed. 15. And, behold, I am with thee, and will keep thee in all places whither thou goest, and will bring thee again into this land; for I will not leave thee, until I have done that which I have spoken to thee of. 16. And Jacob awaked out of his sleep, and he said, Surely the LORD is in this place; and I knew it not. *(Jacob receives the vision of a ladder reaching up into heaven)* Gen.28:10-16

**President Joseph F. Smith,
Anthon H. Lund, Charles W. Penrose**
(First Presidency)
*quoted by*
**President George Albert Smith,
J. Reuben Clark, Jr., David O. McKay**
*(First Presidency)*
When visions, dreams, tongues, prophecy,

impressions, or an extraordinary gift of inspiration conveys something out of harmony with the accepted revelations of the Church or contrary to the decisions of its constituted authorities, Latter-day Saints may know that it is not of God, no matter how plausible it may appear. Also, they should understand that directions for the guidance of the Church will come by revelation, through the head. (*Published message of the the First Presidency of the Church, Dec. 29, 1945, republishing a message of the previous First Presidency in 1913*) MOFP6:244

---

677. Revelation comes at times as an audible voice from heaven.

**Elder Harold B. Lee**

If we will live worthy, then the Lord will guide us—by a personal appearance, or by His actual voice, or by His voice coming into our mind, or by impressions upon our heart and our soul. . . . Yes, if we so live, the Lord will guide us for our salvation and for our benefit. *(To Brigham Young University student body)* (Stand Ye in Holy Places, p. 144) TLDP:575

**Marion G. Romney**

Now I know, my brothers and sisters and friends, and bear witness to the fact that revelation from the Lord comes through the spoken word, by personal visitation, by messengers from the Lord, through dreams, and by way of visions, and by the voice of the Lord coming into one's mind. ¶ Most often, however, revelation comes to us by means of the still, small voice. . . . CR1978Apr:76

**James E. Talmage**

Revelation is the communication or disclosure of the will of God directly to man. Under circumstances best suiting the divine purposes, through the dreams of sleep or in waking visions of the mind, by voices without visional appearance or by actual manifestations of the Holy Presence before the eye, God makes known His designs, and instructs His revelators. AF:208

**Joseph Smith**

[A]fter man was created, he was not left without intelligence or understanding, to wander in darkness and spend an existence and doubt (on the great and important point which effected his happiness) as to the real fact by whom he was created, or unto whom he was amenable for his conduct. God conversed with him face to face. In his presence he was permitted to stand, and from his own mouth he was permitted to receive instruction. He heard his voice, walked

before him and gazed upon his glory, while intelligence burst upon his understanding, and enabled him to give names to the vast assemblage of his Maker's works. ¶ 19. Though man [Adam] did transgress, his transgression did not deprive him of the previous knowledge with which he was endowed relative to the existence and glory of his Creator; for no sooner did he hear his voice than he sought to hide himself from his presence. (*Lectures on Faith delivered to the School of the Prophets, 1834-35*) LOF2:18-19

**Related Witnesses:**

**Joseph Smith**

After Adam had been driven out of the garden . . . he called upon the name of the Lord, and so did Eve, his wife, also. "And they heard the voice of the Lord, from the way toward the Garden of Eden, speaking unto them, and they saw him not, for they were shut out from his presence; and he gave unto them commandments that they should worship the Lord their God, and should offer the firstlings of their flocks for an offering unto the Lord. (*Lectures on Faith delivered to the School of the Prophets, 1834-35*) LOF2:22

**Peter**

For he received from God the Father honour and glory, when there came such a voice to him from the excellent glory, This is my beloved Son, in whom I am well pleased. 18. And this voice which came from heaven we heard, when we were with him in the holy mount. (*Peter writes to members of the Church, about A.D. 60-64*) 2Pet.1:17-18

**Joseph Smith**

I was once praying very earnestly to know the time of the coming of the Son of Man, when I heard a voice repeat the following: 15. Joseph, my son, if thou livest until thou art eighty-five years old, thou shalt see the face of the Son of Man; therefore let this suffice, and trouble me no more on this matter. (*Revelation, April 2, 1830*) D&C 130:14-15

**Mormon**

And it came to pass that there came a voice as if it were above the cloud of darkness, saying: Repent ye, repent ye, and seek no more to destroy my servants whom I have sent unto you to declare good tidings. 30. And it came to pass when they heard this voice, and beheld that it was not a voice of thunder, neither was it a voice of a great tumultuous noise, but behold, it was a still voice of perfect mildness, as if it had been a whisper, and it did pierce even to the very soul— 31. And notwithstanding the mildness of the voice, behold the earth shook exceedingly, and the walls of the prison trembled again, as if it were about to tumble to the earth; and behold the cloud of darkness, which had overshadowed them, did not disperse— 32. And behold the voice came again, saying: Repent ye, repent ye, for the kingdom of heaven is at hand; and seek no more to destroy my servants. And it came to pass that the earth shook again, and the walls trembled. 33. And also again the third time the voice came, and did speak unto them marvelous words which cannot be uttered by man; and the walls did tremble again, and the earth shook as if it were about to divide asunder. (*The Lamanites, who have imprisoned Nephi and Lehi, see them protected by a circle of fire, about 30 B.C.*) Hel.5:29-33

**Recorded in Matthew**

And Jesus, when he was baptized, went up straightway out of the water: and, lo, the heavens were opened unto him, and he saw the Spirit of God descending like a dove, and lighting upon him: 17. And lo a voice from heaven, saying, This is my beloved Son, in whom I am well pleased. (*Jesus is baptized by John to fulfill all righteousness*) Matt.3:16-17

**Jesus,**
*quoted by John*

Father, glorify thy name. Then came there a voice from heaven, saying, I have both glorified it, and will glorify it again. 29. The people therefore, that stood by, and heard it, said that it thundered: others said, An angel spake to him. 30. Jesus answered and said, This voice came not because of me, but for your sakes. (*Jesus in contemplation of his death addresses God the Father*) John 12:28-30

**Nephi, son of Lehi**

Ye are swift to do iniquity but slow to remember the Lord your God. Ye have seen an angel, and he spake unto you; yea, ye have heard his voice from time to time; and he hath spoken unto you in a still small voice, but ye were past feeling, that ye could not feel his words; wherefore, he has spoken unto you like unto the voice of thunder, which did cause the earth to shake as if it were to divide asunder. (*Nephi answers his rebellious brothers, about 591 B.C.*) 1Ne.17:45

---

678. **Revelation comes at times through angels sent with messages.**

**Elder Wilford Woodruff**

I have had the administration of angels in my day and time, though I never prayed for an angel. I have had, in several instances, the

administration of holy messengers. . . . ¶ [A]s a general thing, angels do not administer to anybody on the earth unless it is to preserve the lives of good men, or to bring the gospel, or to perform a work that men cannot do for themselves. (Discourses of Wilford Woodruff, pp. 286-87) DGSM:5

**Marion G. Romney**

Now I know, my brothers and sisters and friends, and bear witness to the fact that revelation from the Lord comes through the spoken word, by personal visitation, by messengers from the Lord, through dreams, and by way of visions, and by the voice of the Lord coming into one's mind. ¶ Most often, however, revelation comes to us by means of the still, small voice. . . . CR1978Apr:76

**Delbert L. Stapley,**
*also quoting Mormon*

King Lamoni addressed his Lamanite subjects and urged them not to take up arms against their brothers, saying: "And the great God has had mercy on us, . . . because he loveth our souls as well as he loveth our children; therefore, in his mercy he doth visit us by his angels, that the plan of salvation might be made known unto us as well as unto future generations." (Alma 24:14) ¶ Personally, I do not believe the angels of God could refuse to visit a person who fully keeps the first and great commandment. CR1968Oct:29

**Related Witnesses:**
**Recorded in Luke**

And in the sixth month the angel Gabriel was sent from God unto a city of Galilee, named Nazareth, 27. To a virgin espoused to a man whose name was Joseph, of the house of David; and the virgin's name was Mary. 28. And the angel came in unto her, and said, Hail, thou that art highly favoured, the Lord is with thee: blessed art thou among women. (*The angel Gabriel announces to Mary that she shall be the mother of the Son of God*) Luke 1:26-28

**Recorded in Luke**

And there appeared unto him an angel of the Lord standing on the right side of the altar of incense. 12. And when Zacharias saw him, he was troubled, and fear fell upon him. 13. But the angel said unto him, Fear not, Zacharias: for thy prayer is heard; and thy wife Elisabeth shall bear thee a son, and thou shalt call his name John. . . . 19. And the angel answering said unto him, I am Gabriel, that stand in the presence of God; and am sent to speak unto thee, and to shew thee these glad tidings. (*The angel Gabriel promises Zacharias that his wife will bear a son*) Luke 1:11-13,19

## Joseph Smith

While I was thus in the act of calling upon God, I discovered a light appearing in my room, which continued to increase until the room was lighter than at noonday, when immediately a personage appeared at my bedside, standing in the air, for his feet did not touch the floor. 31. He had on a loose robe of most exquisite whiteness. It was a whiteness beyond anything earthly I had ever seen; nor do I believe that any earthly thing could be made to appear so exceedingly white and brilliant. His hands were naked, and his arms also, a little above the wrist; so, also, were his feet naked, as were his legs, a little above the ankles. His head and neck were also bare. I could discover that he had no other clothing on but this robe, as it was open, so that I could see into his bosom. 32. Not only was his robe exceedingly white, but his whole person was glorious beyond description, and his countenance truly like lightning. The room was exceedingly light, but not so very bright as immediately around his person. When I first looked upon him, I was afraid; but the fear soon left me. 33. He called me by name, and said unto me that he was a messenger sent from the presence of God to me, and that his name was Moroni; that God had a work for me to do; and that my name should be had for good and evil among all nations, kindreds, and tongues, or that it should be both good and evil spoken of among all people. (*Joseph relates the angel Moroni's visit to him, Sept. 21, 1823*) JS-H 1:30-33

## Mormon

And as I said unto you, as they were going about rebelling against God, behold, the angel of the Lord appeared unto them; and he descended as it were in a cloud; and he spake as it were with a voice of thunder, which caused the earth to shake upon which they stood; . . . 14. And again, the angel said: Behold, the Lord hath heard the prayers of his people, and also the prayers of his servant, Alma, who is thy father; for he has prayed with much faith concerning thee that thou mightest be brought to the knowledge of the truth; therefore, for this purpose have I come to convince thee of the power and authority of God, that the prayers of his servants might be answered according to their faith. . . . 17. And now it came to pass that these were the last words which the angel spake unto Alma, and he departed. (*Alma, the younger, and the four sons of Mosiah were seeking to destroy the Church when an angel appeared to them commanding them to cease their evil course, 100-92 B.C.*) Mosiah 27:11,14,17

## Recorded in Acts

He saw in a vision evidently about the ninth hour of the day an angel of God coming in to him, and saying unto him, Cornelius. 4. And when he looked on him, he was afraid, and said, What is it, Lord? And he said unto him, Thy prayers and thine alms are come up for a memorial before God. (*Cornelius, a centurion and a devout man, receives a vision in answer to prayer*) Acts 10:3-4

## Bruce R. McConkie

And as it is with the elders on earth, so it is with their fellow servants beyond the veil. The words of the angels of God in heaven are scripture, for, "Angels speak by the power of the Holy Ghost; wherefore, they speak the words of Christ." (2Ne.32:3) (The Promised Messiah, pp. 23) TLDP:539

---

## 679. Revelation comes at times by visions.

### James E. Talmage

Visions and Dreams have constituted a means of communication between God and men in every dispensation of the Priesthood. In general, visions are manifested to the waking senses whilst dreams are given during sleep. In the vision, however, the senses may be so affected as to render the person practically unconscious, at least oblivious to ordinary occurrences, while he is able to discern the heavenly manifestation. In the earlier dispensations, the Lord frequently communicated through dreams and visions, oftentimes revealing to prophets the events of the future even to the latest generations. Consider the case of Enoch, unto whom the Lord spoke face to face, showing him the course of the human family unto and beyond the second coming of the Savior. The brother of Jared because of his righteousness was so blessed of God as to be shown all the inhabitants of the earth, both those who had previously existed and those who were to follow. Unto Moses the will of God was made known with the visual manifestation of fire. Lehi received through dreams his instructions to leave Jerusalem; and on many subsequent occasions the Lord communicated with this patriarch of the western world by dreams and visions. AF:205-06

### Joseph Smith

We believe that we have a right to revelations, visions, and dreams from God, our heavenly Father; and light and intelligence, through the gift of the Holy Ghost, in the name of Jesus Christ, on all subjects pertaining to our spiritual welfare;

if it so be that we keep his commandments, so as to render ourselves worthy in his sight. (*Times and Seasons, Feb. 1840, p. 54*) TLDP:570

**Marion G. Romney**

Now I know, my brothers and sisters and friends, and bear witness to the fact that revelation from the Lord comes through the spoken word, by personal visitation, by messengers from the Lord, through dreams, and by way of visions, and by the voice of the Lord coming into one's mind. ¶ Most often, however, revelation comes to us by means of the still, small voice. . . . CR1978Apr:76

**Peter**

And it shall come to pass in the last days, saith God, I will pour out of my Spirit upon all flesh: and your sons and your daughters shall prophesy, and your young men shall see visions, and your old men shall dream dreams. Acts 2:17

**James E. Talmage**

It is a privilege of the Holy Priesthood to commune with the heavens, and to learn the immediate will of the Lord; this communion may be effected through the medium of dreams and visions, by the Urim and Thummim, through the visitation of angels, or by the higher endowment of face to face communication with the Lord. AF:270

**President Brigham Young**

If you will follow the doctrines, and be guided by the precepts of that book [the Bible] it will direct you where you may see as you are seen, where you may converse with Jesus Christ, have the visitation of angels, have dreams, visions, and revelations, and understand and know God for yourselves. (*In Tabernacle, July 1853, JD1:243*) DBY:126; DGSM:5

**Related Witnesses:**

**Joseph Smith**

By the power of the Spirit our eyes were opened and our understandings were enlightened, so as to see and understand the things of God— 13. Even those things which were from the beginning before the world was, which were ordained of the Father, through his Only Begotten Son, who was in the bosom of the Father, even from the beginning; 14. Of whom we bear record; and the record which we bear is the fulness of the gospel of Jesus Christ, who is the Son, whom we saw and with whom we conversed in the heavenly vision. (*Vision to Joseph Smith and Sidney Rigdon, Feb. 16, 1832*) D&C 76:12-14

**Recorded in Acts**

He saw in a vision evidently about the ninth hour of the day an angel of God coming in to him, and saying unto him, Cornelius. 4. And when he looked on him, he was afraid, and said, What is it, Lord? And he said unto him, Thy prayers and thine alms are come up for a memorial before God. (*Cornelius, a centurion and a devout man, receives a vision in answer to prayer*) Acts 10:3-4

**Nephi, son of Lehi**

And it came to pass after I, Nephi, having heard all the words of my father, concerning the things which he saw in a vision, and also the things which he spake by the power of the Holy Ghost, which power he received by faith on the Son of God—and the Son of God was the Messiah who should come—I, Nephi, was desirous also that I might see, and hear, and know of these things, by the power of the Holy Ghost, which is the gift of God unto all those who diligently seek him, as well in times of old as in the time that he should manifest himself unto the children of men. (*Nephi's writings, 600-592 B.C.*) 1Ne.10:17

**Recorded in Acts**

And he became very hungry, and would have eaten: but while they made ready, he fell into a trance, 11. And saw heaven opened, and a certain vessel descending unto him, as it had been a great sheet knit at the four corners, and let down to the earth: 12. Wherein were all manner of fourfooted beasts of the earth, and wild beasts, and creeping things, and fowls of the air. 13. And there came a voice to him, Rise, Peter; kill, and eat. 14. But Peter said, Not so, Lord; for I have never eaten any thing that is common or unclean. 15. And the voice spake unto him again the second time, What God hath cleansed, that call not thou common. 16. This was done thrice: and the vessel was received up again into heaven. 17. Now while Peter doubted in himself what this vision which he had seen should mean, behold, the men which were sent from Cornelius had made inquiry for Simon's house, and stood before the gate, 18. And called, and asked whether Simon, which was surnamed Peter, were lodged there. 19. While Peter thought on the vision, the Spirit said unto him, Behold, three men seek thee. 20. Arise therefore, and get thee down, and go with them, doubting nothing: for I have sent them. (*Peter went up upon the housetop to pray*) Acts 10:10-20

**Paul**

At midday, O king, I saw in the way a light from heaven, above the brightness of the sun, shining round about me and them which journeyed with me. 14. And when we were all fallen to the earth, I heard a voice speaking unto me, and saying in the Hebrew tongue, Saul, Saul, why persecutest thou me? it is hard for thee to kick against the pricks. 15. And I said, Who art thou, Lord? And he said, I am Jesus whom thou persecutest. 16. But rise, and stand upon thy feet: for I have appeared unto thee for this purpose, to make thee a minister and a witness both of these things which thou hast seen, and of those things in the which I will appear unto thee; 17. Delivering thee from the people, and from the Gentiles, unto whom now I send thee, 18. To open their eyes, and to turn them from darkness to light, and from the power of Satan unto God, that they may receive forgiveness of sins, and inheritance among them which are sanctified by faith that is in me. 19. Whereupon, O king Agrippa, I was not disobedient unto the heavenly vision: (*Paul testifies before King Agrippa of the appearance of Jesus on the road to Damascus*) Acts 26:13-19

### Ezekiel

In the visions of God brought he me into the land of Israel, and set me upon a very high mountain, by which was as the frame of a city on the south. (*A heavenly ministrant shows Ezekiel, in a vision, a city wherein is the temple, and shows him the form and size of the temple*) Ezek.40:2

---

680. Revelation of the truth of a matter comes by the process of first studying it out, then asking the Lord if the conclusion is right; the Lord then induces a burning in the bosom if it is right, or else He causes a stupor of thought if the decision is wrong—causing a forgetting of that which is wrong.

### Joseph Smith,
*receiving the Word of the Lord*

Behold, you have not understood; you have supposed that I would give it unto you, when you took no thought save it was to ask me. 8. But, behold, I say unto you, that you must study it out in your mind; then you must ask me if it be right, and if it is right I will cause that your bosom shall burn within you; therefore, you shall feel that it is right. 9. But if it be not right you shall have no such feelings, but you shall have a stupor of thought that shall cause you to forget the thing which is wrong; therefore, you cannot write that which is sacred save it be given you from me. (*Revelation for Oliver Cowdery, April 1829; the Book of Mormon is translated by study and by spiritual confirmation*) D&C 9:7-9

### Melvin J. Ballard

There is a key given in the ninth section of the book of Doctrine and Covenants, which would be very profitable for the Latter-day Saints to follow even now. You remember the circumstance of Oliver Cowdery translating portions of the Book of Mormon, and then all became darkness to him and he could not proceed. He inquired of the Lord to know why it was, and the answer came that he had taken no thought save it was to ask the Lord, and left the burden of responsibility there. ¶ You do not know what to do today to solve your financial problems, what to plant, whether to buy or sell cattle, sheep or other things. It is your privilege to study it out: counsel together with the best wisdom and judgment the Lord shall give you, reach your conclusions, and then go to the Lord with it, tell him what you have planned to do. If the thing you have planned to do is for your good and your blessing, and you are determined to serve the Lord, pay your tithes and your offerings and keep his commandments, I promise you that he will fulfill that promise upon your head, and your bosom shall burn within you if the thing you have planned to do is right, and you shall know by the whisperings of the Spirit that it is right. But if it is not right you shall have no such feelings, but you shall have a stupor of thought, and your hearts will be turned away from that thing. CR1931Apr:37

### Elder Joseph Fielding Smith

[A] similar privilege is given to any member of the Church who seeks knowledge in the spirit of prayer and faith. The Lord will cause the feeling of security and truth to take hold of the individual and burn within the bosom, and there will be an overwhelming feeling that the thing is right. Missionaries have felt the manifestation of this gift while laboring in the field; when searching the scriptures; when speaking before congregations on the streets and in public gatherings. When you have been listening to some inspired speaker who has presented a new thought to you, have you not felt that burning within and the satisfaction in your heart that this new thought is true? On the other hand, have you experienced the feeling of stupor, gloom, or uneasiness when some thought has been presented which was in conflict with the revealed word of the Lord, and you have felt by this manifestation of the Spirit that what was said is not true? It is a great gift, which all may receive, to have this spirit of discernment, or revelation, for it is the spirit of revelation. CHMR1:51; DCSM:21

### Marion G. Romney

Now, I tell you that you can make every decision

in your life correctly if you can learn to follow the guidance of the Holy Spirit. This you can do if you will discipline yourself to yield your own feelings to the promptings of the Spirit. Study your problems and prayerfully make a decision. Then take that decision and say to him, in a simple, honest supplication, "Father, I want to make the right decision. I want to do the right thing. This is what I think I should do: let me know if it is the right course." Doing this, you can get the burning in your bosom, if your decision is right. If you do not get the burning, then change your decision and submit a new one. When you learn to walk by the Spirit, you never need to make a mistake. CR1961Oct:60-61

**Bruce R. McConkie**

"Oh, I prayed about it. I said, 'O God, if the Book of Mormon is true, strike me dead;' and here I am." ¶ My unspoken impulse was to give this rejoinder: "But Reverend, you have to pray in faith!" ¶ This account dramatizes another of our problems in teaching those who read the Book of Mormon how to read it in order to gain the promised witness by the power of the Holy Ghost. ¶ The pattern was set in the experience of Oliver Cowdery. . . . ¶ Oliver tried to translate and failed. Then came the divine word: "Behold, you have not understood; you have supposed that I would give it unto you, when you took no thought save it was to ask me." That is, he had not done all that in his power lay; he had expected the Lord to do it all merely because he asked. "But, behold, I say unto you," the divine word continued, "that you must study it out in your mind; then you must ask me if it be right, and if it is right I will cause that your bosom shall burn within you; therefore, you shall feel that it is right.". . . ¶ . . . . [This test] calls for us simply to read, ponder, and pray—all in the spirit of faith and with an open mind. To keep ourselves alert to the issues at hand—as we do read, ponder, and pray—we should ask ourselves a thousand times, "Could any man have written this book?" ¶ And it is absolutely guaranteed that sometime between the first and thousandth time this question is asked, every sincere and genuine truth seeker will come to know by the power of the Spirit that the Book of Mormon is true. . . . CR1983Oct:105-06

**Related Witnesses:**

**Joseph Smith**

This is good doctrine. It tastes good. I can taste the principles of eternal life, and so can you. They are given to me by the revelations of Jesus Christ; and I know that when I tell you these words of eternal life as they are given to me, you taste them, and I know that you believe them. You say honey is sweet, and so do I. I can also taste the spirit of eternal life. I know that it is good; and when I tell you of these things which were given me by inspiration of the Holy Spirit, you are bound to receive them as sweet, and rejoice more and more. (*To the Church in general conference—to a congregation of 20,000—"King Follett Sermon," April 7, 1844*) (See HC6:302-17, also see The Words of Joseph Smith, pp. 340-62.) HC6:312; TPJS:354

**Author's Note:** This gospel principle, set forth in D-680, was first introduced in a specific context, namely, when Oliver Cowdery was trying to translate portions of the Book of Mormon. All became darkness to him and he could not proceed. He inquired of the Lord to know why it was, and the answer came that he had taken no thought save it was to ask the Lord, and left the burden of responsibility there. Prophets since that time have quoted this scripture (D&C 9:7-9) in broader contexts to include many other situations in life, where we feel a need to call on the Lord for help.

---

**681. We are to heed the promptings of the Holy Ghost.**

**Joseph Smith,**
*receiving the Word of the Lord*

Yea, behold, I will tell you in your mind and in your heart, by the Holy Ghost, which shall come upon you and which shall dwell in your heart. 3. Now, behold, this is the spirit of revelation; behold, this is the spirit by which Moses brought the children of Israel through the Red Sea on dry ground. 4. Therefore this is thy gift; apply unto it, and blessed art thou, for it shall deliver you out of the hands of your enemies, when, if it were not so, they would slay you and bring your soul to destruction. D&C 8:2-4

**Anthony W. Ivins**

While the Holy Ghost may be conferred upon us, and is designed to be our guide and support, it is only restrained and manifested in its fulness in our guidance and defense in proportion to the degree to which we cultivate it and listen to its promptings. We may lose it entirely through indifference or transgression and once deprived of its presence we are left in darkness more dense than before its reception. Cultivate it, my brethren and sisters, and it will become in reality the iron rod, which is the word of God, and will lead us back to him. CR1934Apr:101-02

**Thomas S. Monson,**
*also quoting John*

We watch. We wait. We listen for that still, small voice. When it speaks, wise men and women obey. We do not postpone following promptings of the Spirit. . . . ¶ Never, never, never postpone following a prompting. ¶ As we pursue the journey of life, let us learn the language of the Spirit. May we remember and respond to the Master's gentle invitation: "Behold, I stand at the door, and knock: if any man hear my voice, and open the door, I will come in to him." (Rev.3:20) CR1985Apr:86-87

**Francis M. Lyman**

The Latter-day Saints are as sensitive to the movements and operations of the Spirit of the Lord as the thermometer is to the presence of heat and cold. CR1901Apr:48-49

**Marion G. Romney**

Now, I tell you that you can make every decision in your life correctly if you can learn to follow the guidance of the Holy Spirit. This you can do if you will discipline yourself to yield your own feelings to the promptings of the Spirit. Study your problems and prayerfully make a decision. Then take that decision and say to him, in a simple, honest supplication, "Father, I want to make the right decision. I want to do the right thing. This is what I think I should do: let me know if it is the right course." Doing this, you can get the burning in your bosom, if your decision is right. If you do not get the burning, then change your decision and submit a new one. When you learn to walk by the Spirit, you never need to make a mistake. CR1961Oct:60-61

**Joseph Smith,**
*receiving the Word of the Lord*

But ye are commanded in all things to ask of God, who giveth liberally; and that which the Spirit testifies unto you even so I would that ye should do in all holiness of heart, walking uprightly before me, considering the end of your salvation, doing all things with prayer and thanksgiving, that ye may not be seduced by evil spirits, or doctrines of devils, or the commandments of men; for some are of men, and others of devils. (*Revelation, March 8, 1831*) D&C 46:7

**Peter**

And this voice which came from heaven we heard, when we were with him in the holy mount. 19. We have also a more sure word of prophecy; whereunto ye do well that ye take heed, as unto a light that shineth in a dark place, until the day dawn, and the day star arise

in your hearts: 20. Knowing this first, that no prophecy of the scripture is of any private interpretation. 21. For the prophecy came not in old time by the will of man: but holy men of God spake as they were moved by the Holy Ghost. (*Letter to members of the Church*) 2Pet.1:18-21

**James E. Faust**

We acknowledge and testify that the same witness of Christ's divinity as received by Peter is also our sacred knowledge. ¶ Personal revelation comes as a testimony of truth and as guidance in spiritual and temporal matters. Members of the Church know that the promptings of the Spirit may be received upon all facets of life, including daily, ongoing decisions (see D&C 42:61). How could anyone think of making an important decision such as "Who is to be my companion?", and "How will I live?" without seeking the inspiration of the Almighty God. CR1980Apr:16

**Elder Joseph Fielding Smith**

We have to pass through pain and sorrow and are constantly in need of protection against sin and error. This is given us through the Spirit of God if we will but heed it. All of this was made known to us in the preexistence, and yet we were glad to take the risk. (Doctrines of Salvation, 1:69) TLDP:429

**George Q. Cannon**

Every man and woman who has received the truth should live in such a manner before the Lord as to have the light of the Holy Spirit constantly beaming upon their hands. They should be in close communion, through that Holy Spirit, with their God, so that if they had to stand alone in the midst of a gainsaying world they should be living witnesses to the truth of the Gospel and the power of God manifested in these days, and that if even the Priesthood from Zion were to be withdrawn from their midst, they could stand firm and unshaken, enjoying the light of revelation and having the consciousness that God was directing them in all their ways. ("Eternal Vigilance is the Price of Safety," Millennial Star, Jan. 3, 1863, p. 9) TLDP:284

**George Q. Cannon**

The only way to maintain our position in the Kingdom of God is to so conduct ourselves that we may have a living testimony of the truth continually dwelling in our bosoms, to live so that the Spirit of the Lord may be a constant and abiding quest with us, whether in the privacy of our chamber, in the domestic circle or in the midst of the crowded thoroughfares, the busy scenes and anxious cares of life. He who will pursue this course will never lack for knowledge; he will never be in doubt or in darkness, nor will his mind ever be clouded by the gloomy pall of unbelief; on the contrary his hopes will be bright; his faith will be strong; his joy will be full; he will be able each succeeding day to comprehend the unfolding purposes of Jehovah and to rejoice in the glorious liberty and happiness which all the faithful children of God enjoy. ¶ . . . . We can only retain the testimony of the truth in our heart by living near unto God. If we call upon Him in faith to bless us and seek to enjoy the companionship of the Holy Spirit, so ordering our lives that God can, consistently, bless us and the Spirit of the Lord can abide with us, we receive strength to overcome every evil and our minds instinctively recoil from the commission of any act which might grieve that Spirit or bring a stain upon our own character or upon the divine cause in which we are engaged. (Gospel Truth, 1:343-44) TLDP:284

**President Joseph F. Smith**
We should live so near to the Lord, be so humble in our spirits, so tractable and pliable under the influence of the Holy Spirit, that we will be able to know the mind and will of the Father concerning us as individuals and as officers in the Church of Christ under all circumstances. And when we live so that we can hear and understand the whisperings of the still small voice of the Spirit of God, let us do whatsoever that Spirit directs, without fear of the consequences. It does not make any difference whether it meet the minds of carpers or critics, or of the enemies of the kingdom of God, or not. Is it agreeable to the will of the Lord? Is it compatible with the spirit of the great latter-day work in which we are engaged? Is the end aimed at likely to advance the Church and to strengthen it in the earth? If its trend is in that direction, let us do it, no matter what men may say or think. CR1903Oct:86

**President David O. McKay**
That man is not at peace who is untrue to the whisperings of Christ, the promptings of his conscience. He cannot be at peace when he is untrue to his better self, when he transgresses the law of righteousness, either in dealing with himself, in indulging in passion or in appetites, yielding to the temptations of the flesh, or being untrue to trust, transgressing the law of righteousness in dealing with his fellow men. (Pathways to Happiness, pp. 136-37) TLDP:463

**Related Witnesses:**
**Stephen L. Richards**
The gift of discernment is essential to the leadership of the Church. I never ordain a bishop or set apart a president of a stake without invoking upon him this divine blessing, that he may read the lives and hearts of his people and call forth the best within them. The gift and power of discernment in this world of contention between the forces of good and the power of evil is essential equipment for every son and daughter of God. There could be no such mass dissensions as endanger the security of the world, if its populations possessed this great gift in larger degree. . . . ¶ . . . . Every member in the restored Church of Christ could have this gift if he willed to do so. He could not be deceived with the sophistries of the world. He could not be led astray by pseudo-prophets and subversive cults. Even the inexperienced would recognize false teachings, in a measure at least. With this gift they would be able to detect something of the disloyal, rebellious, and sinister influences which not infrequently prompt those who seemingly take pride in the destruction of youthful faith and loyalties. Discerning parents will do well to guard their children against such influences and such personalities and teachings before irreparable damage is done. The true gift of discernment is often premonitory. A sense of danger should be heeded to be of value. We give thanks for a set of providential circumstances which avert an accident. We ought to be grateful every day of our lives for this sense which keeps alive a conscience which constantly alerts us to the dangers inherent in wrongdoers and sin. CR1950Apr:163

**Joseph Smith,**
*receiving the Word of the Lord*
Again I say, hearken ye elders of my church, whom I have appointed: Ye are not sent forth to be taught, but to teach the children of men the things which I have put into your hands by the power of my Spirit; 16. And ye are to be taught from on high. Sanctify yourselves and ye shall be endowed with power, that ye may give even as I have spoken. (*Revelation: message for the nations of the earth, Feb. 1831*) D&C 43:15-16

**President Joseph F. Smith**
I believe that the Lord has revealed to the children of men all that they know. I do not believe that any man has discovered any principle in science, or art, in mechanism, or mathematics, or anything else, that God did not know before he did. Man is indebted to the source of all intelligence and truth, for the knowledge that he possesses; and all who will yield obedience to the promptings of the Spirit . . . will get a clearer, a more expansive, and a more direct and conclusive knowledge of God's truths than anyone else can do. CR1902Apr:85-86

**Joseph Smith,**
*quoted by Elder Joseph Fielding Smith*

We consider that God has created man with a mind capable of instruction, and a faculty which may be enlarged in proportion to the heed and diligence given to the light communicated from heaven to the intellect. . . . TPJS:51

**Elder Joseph Fielding Smith**

If we persist in the violation of the Sabbath day, the time comes when our conscience becomes seared, and we fail to heed its warnings or its call for spiritual food. Surely it is not unreasonable for us to be commanded to obey the Sabbath when the Lord has given us six-sevenths of our time for all temporal purposes. ("What Can We Do on the Sabbath?", IE1955-Jan:15) TLDP:583

**Alma, the younger,**
*quoted by Mormon*

And now, my son, I would that ye should understand that these things are not without a shadow; for as our fathers were slothful to give heed to this compass (now these things were temporal) they did not prosper; even so it is with things which are spiritual. 44. For behold, it is as easy to give heed to the word of Christ, which will point to you a straight course to eternal bliss, as it was for our fathers to give heed to this compass, which would point unto them a straight course to the promised land. 45. And now I say, is there not a type in this thing? For just as surely as this director did bring our fathers, by following its course, to the promised land, shall the words of Christ, if we follow their course, carry us beyond this vale of sorrow into a far better land of promise. (*Alma instructs his son Helaman, about 73 B.C.*) Alma 37:43-45

**Jesus,**
*recorded in Luke*

Take heed therefore that the light which is in thee be not darkness. 36. If thy whole body therefore be full of light, having no part dark, the whole shall be full of light, as when the bright shining of a candle doth give thee light. (*Jesus preaches to the people, who were "gathered thick together," about not placing a light under a bushel*) Luke 11:35-36

**Henry D. Moyle**

Throughout the history of the Church innumerable examples of spiritual guidance are found. One which I have cherished since childhood is an early experience of Wilford Woodruff. ¶ While traveling in New England, on assignment by Brigham Young, President Woodruff drove his carriage into the yard of Brother Williams. Brother Orson Hyde drove a wagon by the side of his carriage. He had only

been there few minutes when the Spirit said to him, "Get up and move that carriage." When he told his wife that he had to move the carriage, she asked, "What for?" He answered, "I don't know." ¶ That was all she asked on such occasions. When he told her that he did not know, that was enough. President Woodruff got up and moved his carriage four or five rods, and put the off fore wheel against the corner of the house. He then returned to bed. The same Spirit said, "Go and move your animals from the oak tree." They were two hundred yards from his carriage. He moved his horses and put them in a little hickory grove. Again he went to bed. In thirty minutes a whirlwind came up and broke that oak tree off within two feet of the ground. It swept over three or four fences and fell square in the dooryard, near Brother Orson Hyde's wagon, and right where the carriage had stood. What would have been the consequences if he had not listened to that Spirit? Why, President Woodruff, his wife, and children doubtless would have been killed. ¶ That was the still, small voice to him—no thunder, no lightning, but the still small voice of the Spirit of God. It saved his life. It was the Spirit of revelation. ¶ We all can afford to develop a sensitiveness to the promptings of the Spirit in all things pertaining to our physical as well as our spiritual well-being. ¶ In speaking on this, Joseph Fielding Smith said, "The testimony of the Holy Ghost is Spirit speaking to spirit, and is not confined solely to the natural or physical sense." CR1957Apr:33-34

**Joseph Smith,**
*receiving the Word of the Lord*

But, behold, I say unto you, that you must study it out in your mind; then you must ask me if it be right, and if it is right I will cause that your bosom shall burn within you; therefore, you shall feel that it is right. 9. But if it be not right you shall have no such feelings, but you shall have a stupor of thought that shall cause you to forget the thing which is wrong; therefore, you cannot write that which is sacred save it be given you from me. D&C 9:8-9

**Joseph Smith,**
*receiving the Word of the Lord*

Behold, I say unto you, David, that you have feared man and have not relied on me for strength as you ought. 2. But your mind has been on the things of the earth more than on the things of me, your Maker, and the ministry whereunto you have been called; and you have not given heed unto my Spirit, and to those who were set over you, but have been persuaded by those whom I have not commanded. 3.

Wherefore, you are left to inquire for yourself at my hand, and ponder upon the things which you have received. (*Revelation, Sept. 30, 1830; David Whitmer is chastened for failure to serve diligently*) D&C 30:1-3

---

## HYMNS Written by Prophets Applicable to this Topic

### Bruce R. McConkie
*I Believe in Christ*
HYMNS:134

I believe in Christ; he is my King!
With all my heart to him I'll sing;
I'll raise my voice in praise and joy,
In grand amens my tongue employ.
I believe in Christ; he is God's Son.
On earth to dwell his soul did come.
He healed the sick; the dead he raised.
Good works were his; his name be praised.

I believe in Christ; oh, blessed name!
As Mary's Son he came to reign
'Mid mortal men, his earthly kin,
To save them from the woes of sin.
I believe in Christ, who marked the path,
Who did gain all his Father hath,
Who said to men: "Come, follow me,
That ye, my friends, with God may be."

I believe in Christ—my Lord, my God!
My feet he plants on gospel sod.
I'll worship him with all my might;
He is the source of truth and light.
I believe in Christ; he ransoms me.
From Satan's grasp he sets me free,
And I shall live with joy and love
In his eternal courts above.

I believe in Christ; he stands supreme!
From him I'll gain my fondest dream;
And while I strive through grief and pain,
His voice is heard: "Ye shall obtain."
I believe in Christ; so come what may,
With him I'll stand in that great day
When on this earth he comes again
To rule among the sons of men.

### Parley P. Pratt
*As the Dew from Heaven Distilling*
HYMNS:149

As the dew from heav'n distilling
Gently on the grass descends
And revives it, thus fulfilling
What thy providence intends,

Let thy doctrine, Lord, so gracious,
Thus descending from above,
Blest by thee, prove efficacious
To fulfill thy work of love.

Lord, behold this congregation;
Precious promises fulfill.
From thy holy habitation
Let the dews of life distill.

Let our cry come up before thee.
Thy sweet Spirit shed around,
So the people shall adore thee
And confess the joyful sound.

# List of Doctrines

## SABBATH DAY

### The Law of the Sabbath

*Doctrines Located in This Topic*

682. We are to keep the Sabbath holy as a sacred day.

683. Sabbath day observance is a distinguishing characteristic of God's chosen people.

684. Observance of the weekly Sabbath (generally on *Sunday, the first day of the week*) is commanded by the Lord.

685. The Sabbath is a day for us to rest; we are not to work at our temporal labors.

686. We are not to permit our children, our guests, servants, or our animals to labor on the Sabbath.

687. On the Sabbath we are to worship God in church.

688. The Sabbath is set apart for partaking of the sacrament (for renewing sacred covenants).

689. Observing the Sabbath can help a person keep unspotted from worldly enticements.

690. We are to do good deeds on the Sabbath day.

691. On the Sabbath day food is to be prepared with "singleness of heart."

692. We are not to do business or work at our jobs on the Sabbath.

693. We should refrain from shopping on the Sabbath day, and from participating in commercial activities.

694. The Sabbath is not a day for seeking pleasure and recreation.

# SABBATH DAY

## The Law of the Sabbath

**682.** We are to keep the Sabbath holy as a sacred day.

### President David O. McKay

Keeping holy the Sabbath Day is a law of God, resounding through the ages from Mt. Sinai. You cannot transgress the law of God without circumscribing your spirit. . . . [O]ur Sabbath, the first day of the week, commemorates the greatest event in all history: Christ's resurrection and his visit as a resurrected being to his assembled Apostles. His birth, of course, was necessary, and just as great, so I say this is one of the greatest events in all history. CR1956Oct:90

### Moses

Remember the sabbath day, to keep it holy. 9. Six days shalt thou labour, and do all thy work: 10. But the seventh day is the sabbath of the LORD thy God: in it thou shalt not do any work, thou, nor thy son, nor thy daughter, thy manservant, nor thy maidservant, nor thy cattle, nor thy stranger that is within thy gates: 11. For in six days the LORD made heaven and earth, the sea, and all that in them is, and rested the seventh day: wherefore the LORD blessed the sabbath day, and hallowed it. (*The Lord reveals the fourth of the Ten Commandments to Moses*) Ex.20:8-11

### Elder Joseph Fielding Smith

The commandment to keep holy the Sabbath day is just as binding upon the people of the earth today as it ever was. While it is true that man was not made for the Sabbath, but the Sabbath for man, we should not misinterpret this saying and ignore this great commandment, for that would incur the displeasure of the Lord. The inhabitants of Zion were instructed that they were to be faithful in the observance of this day. They were to go to the house of prayer, with contrite spirits, and broken hearts, bearing testimony of the goodness of God to them. CHMR1:218

### Joseph Smith,
*receiving the Word of the Lord*

And that thou mayest more fully keep thyself unspotted from the world, thou shalt go to the house of prayer and offer up thy sacraments upon my holy day; 10. For verily this is a day appointed unto you to rest from your labors, and to pay thy devotions unto the Most High; 11. Nevertheless thy vows shall be offered up in righteousness on all days and at all times; 12.

But remember that on this, the Lord's day, thou shalt offer thine oblations and thy sacraments unto the Most High, confessing thy sins unto thy brethren, and before the Lord. 13. And on this day thou shalt do none other thing, only let thy food be prepared with singleness of heart that thy fasting may be perfect, or, in other words, that thy joy may be full. (*Revelation, Aug. 7, 1831*) D&C 59:9-13

### Joseph Smith

And the inhabitants of Zion shall also observe the Sabbath day to keep it holy. (*Revelation received at the request of several elders, Nov. 1831*) D&C 68:29

### Bruce R. McConkie

The law of the Sabbath is so basic, so fundamental, that the Lord Jehovah named it as number four in the Ten Commandments themselves. The first three commandments call upon men to worship the Lord and reverence his great and holy name. The fourth gives us the Sabbath day as the weekly occasion on which we perfect our worship and put ourselves in tune to the full with Him by whom all things are. It is in no sense an exaggeration nor does it overstate the fact one whit to say that any person who keeps the Sabbath, according to the revealed pattern, will be saved in the celestial kingdom. The Sabbath is a day of worship; the requirement to rest from our labors, to do no servile work therein, is simply an incident to the real purpose of the day. Vital as it is to refrain from toil and to turn away from temporalities, these requirements are for the purpose of putting men in a position to do what should be done on the Sabbath, that is, to worship the Father in the name of the Son, to worship him in Spirit and in truth. True worship includes keeping the commandments, and those who devote their Sabbaths to true and proper worship obtain the encouragement that leads to full obedience. (The Promised Messiah, pp. 390-91) TLDP:577-78

### Mormon

And he commanded them that they should observe the sabbath day, and keep it holy, and also every day they should give thanks to the Lord their God. (*Alma organizes the Church of Christ and ordains priests, about 148 B.C.*) Mosiah 18:23

### Recorded in Exodus

And the Lord spake unto Moses, saying, 13. Speak thou also unto the children of Israel, saying, Verily my sabbaths ye shall keep: for it is a sign between me and you throughout your generations; that ye may know that I am the Lord that doth sanctify you. 14. Ye shall keep the sabbath therefore; for it is holy unto you: every one that defileth it shall surely be put to death: for whosoever doeth any work therein, that soul shall be cut off from among his people. 15. Six days may work be done; but in the seventh is the sabbath of rest, holy to the LORD: whosoever doeth any work in the sabbath day, he shall surely be put to death. (*The Lord instructs Moses about keeping the Sabbath, for a blessing to present and future generations of Israel*) Ex.31:12-15

**Related Witnesses:**

**Elder Spencer W. Kimball**

To many, Sabbath breaking is a matter of little moment, but to our Heavenly Father it is one of the principal commandments. It is a test to "see if we will do all things" commanded. . . . (The Teachings of Spencer W. Kimball, p. 217) DGSM:73

**Mark E. Petersen**

No law in all scripture has been more clearly defined than that of the Sabbath. From the time of Genesis to our own day, there has been no subject spoken of more directly or repeatedly than the Sabbath. ¶ It is one of the laws most dear to the heart of God. Yet it is noted far more in its desecration than in its acceptance and proper observance. CR1975Apr:70

**Moses**

And God blessed the seventh day, and sanctified it: because that in it he had rested from all his work which God created and made. (*Revelation to Moses with respect to the Creation*) Gen.2:3

**Jarom,**
*quoted by Mormon*

And now, behold, two hundred years had passed away, and the people of Nephi had waxed strong in the land. They observed to keep the law of Moses and the sabbath day holy unto the Lord. And they profaned not; neither did they blaspheme. And the laws of the land were exceedingly strict. (*The Nephites keep the law of Moses and look forward to the coming of Christ, 420 B.C.*) Jarom 1:5

---

**683. Sabbath day observance is a distinguishing characteristic of God's chosen people.**

**Bruce R. McConkie**

Sabbath worship, that system which singles out one day in seven to be used exclusively for spiritual things, is a sign which identifies the Lord's people. Whatever the world may do, day in and day out, without cessation, in the way of toil and revelry, the saints of God rest from their labors and pay their devotions to the Most High on his holy Sabbath. True religion always has and always will call for a Sabbath on which men rest from their temporal labors and work exclusively on spiritual matters. True religion requires—it is not optional; it is mandatory—that one day in seven be devoted exclusively to worshipping the Father in Spirit and in truth. Without a Sabbath of rest and worship, men's hearts will never be centered on the things of the Spirit sufficiently to assure them of salvation. (The Promised Messiah, pp. 390-91) TLDP:577-78

**Moses**

Speak thou also unto the children of Israel, saying, Verily my sabbaths ye shall keep: for it is a sign between me and you throughout your generations; that ye may know that I am the LORD that doth sanctify you. . . . 16. Wherefore the children of Israel shall keep the sabbath, to observe the sabbath throughout their generations, for a perpetual covenant. 17. It is a sign between me and the children of Israel for ever: for in six days the LORD made heaven and earth, and on the seventh day he rested, and was refreshed. (*The Lord instructs Moses about keeping the Sabbath, for a blessing to present and future generations of Israel*) Ex.31:13,16-17

**President Brigham Young**

This people called Latter-day Saints are required by the revelations that the Lord has given, to assemble themselves together on this day. . . . In this commandment we are required to come together and repent of our sins and confess our sins and partake of the bread and of the wine, or water, in commemoration of the death and sufferings of our Lord and Savior. (*At Paris, Idaho, Aug. 31, 1873, JD16:168*) TLDP:582

**Ezekiel**

Moreover also I gave them my sabbaths, to be a sign between me and them, that they might know that I am the LORD that sanctify them. (*The Lord through Ezekiel points out that Israel has rebelled and failed to keep the commandments and has polluted the Sabbath*) Ezek.20:12

**Elder Spencer W. Kimball**

The Sabbath day is given throughout the generations of man for a perpetual covenant. It is a sign between the Lord and his children forever. ("The Fourth Commandment," M Man-Gleaner Manual for 1963-64, p. 265) DGSM:73-74

**Related Witnesses:**
**Elder George Albert Smith**
This very day upon which we meet here to worship, viz, the Sabbath, has become the play-day of this great nation—the day set apart by thousands to violate the commandment that God gave long, long ago, and I am persuaded that much of the sorrow and distress that is afflicting and will continue to afflict mankind is traceable to the fact that they have ignored his admonition to keep the Sabbath day holy. CR1935Oct:120

---

**684. Observance of the weekly Sabbath (generally on *Sunday, the first day of the week*) is commanded by the Lord.**

**James E. Talmage**
The Church accepts Sunday as the Christian Sabbath and proclaims the sanctity of the day. We admit without argument that under the Mosaic law the seventh day of the week, Saturday, was designated and observed as the holy day, and that the change from Saturday to Sunday was a feature of the apostolic administration following the personal ministry of Jesus Christ. Greater than the question of this day or that in the week is the actuality of the weekly Sabbath, to be observed as a day of special and particular devotion to the service of the Lord. AF:407

**James E. Talmage**
The Church of Jesus Christ teaches that Sunday is the acceptable day for Sabbath observance, on the authority of direct revelation specifying the Lord's Day as such. In this, a new dispensation, and verily the last—the Dispensation of the Fulness of Times—the law of the Sabbath has been reaffirmed unto the Church. It is to be noted that the revelation [D&C 59th Section] . . . was given to the Church on a Sunday—August 7, 1831. AF:409

**President David O. McKay**
There is a third reason. Keeping holy the Sabbath Day is a law of God, resounding through the ages from Mt. Sinai. You cannot transgress the law of God without circumscribing your spirit. Finally, our Sabbath, the first day of the week, commemorates the greatest event in all history: Christ's resurrection and his visit as a resurrected being to his assembled Apostles. CR1956Oct:90

**President Brigham Young,**
*quoted by John A. Widtsoe*
You take this book (the book of Doctrine and Covenants) and you will read here that the Saints are to meet together on the Sabbath day. It is what we call the first day of the week. No matter whether it is the Jewish Sabbath or not, I do not think there is anybody who can bring facts to prove which is the seventh day, or when Adam was put in the garden, or the day about which the Lord spoke to Moses. This matter is not very well known, so we call the day on which we rest and worship God the first day of the week. This people called Latter-day Saints, are required by the revelations that the Lord has given, to assemble themselves together on this day. In this commandment we are required to come together and repent of our sins and confess our sins and partake of the bread and of the wine, or water, in commemoration of the death and sufferings of our Lord and Savior. (*At Paris, Idaho, Aug. 31, 1873, JD16:168*) DBY:164

**Elder Joseph Fielding Smith**
My beloved brethren and sisters, I want to talk to you briefly on our responsibilities in regard to the Sabbath day. In the beginning the Lord chose the last day after the creation as the Sabbath, and that continued until the resurrection of Christ. After the resurrection of our Savior, the Sabbath day was transferred to the Lord's day or the first day of the week, contrary to the ideas of some professed Christians. CR1963Apr:21

**Related Witnesses:**
**John**
Then the same day at evening, being the first day of the week, when the doors were shut where the disciples were assembled for fear of the Jews, came Jesus and stood in the midst, and saith unto them, Peace be unto you. (*The risen Jesus appears to his assembled disciples*) John 20:19

**Joseph Smith,**
*receiving the Word of the Lord*
And that thou mayest more fully keep thyself unspotted from the world, thou shalt go to the house of prayer and offer up thy sacraments upon my holy day; 10. For verily this is a day appointed unto you to rest from your labors, and to pay thy devotions unto the Most High; 11. Nevertheless thy vows shall be offered up in righteousness on all days and at all times; 12. But remember that on this, the Lord's day, thou shalt offer thine oblations and thy sacraments unto the Most High, confessing thy sins unto thy brethren, and before the Lord. (*Revelation received Aug. 7, 1831*) D&C 59:9-12

**Howard W. Hunter**
"But the seventh day is the sabbath of the Lord thy God: in it thou shalt not do any work, thou, nor thy son, nor thy daughter, thy manservant,

nor thy maidservant, nor thy cattle, nor thy stranger that is within thy gates. . . ." [See Ex.20:8-11.] CR1965Apr:56-57

**Elder Joseph Fielding Smith**

Now, we have some people professing Christianity who are very intense upon the idea that the old Sabbath day should be maintained. The Lord himself changed the day. The Saints in olden times, that is, after the resurrection of Christ, accepted the date of the resurrection as their Sabbath, and they called it the Lord's day. It was on that day that John, in prayer before the Lord, received the great revelation known to us as the "apocalypse." CR1963Apr:21

**Recorded in Acts**

And upon the first day of the week, when the disciples came together to break bread, Paul preached unto them, ready to depart on the morrow; and continued his speech until midnight. (*Paul preaches at the seacoast town of Troas, a Roman colony*) Acts 20:7

**Author's Note:** In some areas of the world the Church endorses holding the Sabbath day on a day other than the first day of the week, such as the sixth day (as in Islamic countries) and the seventh day (in Israel).

---

685. **The Sabbath is a day for us to rest; we are not to work at our temporal labors.**

**Moses**

Six days may work be done; but in the seventh is the sabbath of rest, holy to the LORD: whosoever doeth any work in the sabbath day, he shall surely be put to death. (*The Lord instructs Moses about keeping the Sabbath, for a blessing to present and future generations of Israel*) Ex.31:15

**Elder Joseph Fielding Smith**

This is a day in which we should rest from all our manual labors, and from all secular duties that require our attention on the six other days of the week. By obedience to this law we are to have power over evil and more fully be able to keep the commandments of the Lord and be unspotted from the sins of the world. The purpose for this day of Sabbath rest many members of the Church, apparently, fail to see, and they make excuses for not observing it as the Lord has directed in this revelation. In his abundant wisdom, the Lord has granted to us six days out of seven in which we may perform any legitimate labor for our temporal needs, but he asks that we spend the seventh day in each week,

laying aside all other duties, to serve him, and spend time in reflection and study of the things which pertain to our eternal salvation. This is not an inconsistent demand. It was not made for the purpose of giving pleasure to the Lord, but for our own spiritual uplift and preparation for the things which are to come. The spiritual side of man needs attention, to be fed the things of spiritual life, to be mellowed by thought, humility and prayer, and instructed in the things of the Kingdom of God. Moreover, we need that fellowship which contact with our fellow members in the Church brings to us. This Sabbath day has been set apart that mankind may spend their time in worship and have their minds centered on the things of God, free from the influences and distractions of the business and work-a-day world. A little reflection will reveal to us the reasonableness of this demand made on us and our time by our Father in heaven, and that it is given for our own good. CHMR1:218

**Moses**

Six days shall work be done: but the seventh day is the sabbath of rest, an holy convocation; ye shall do no work therein: it is the sabbath of the LORD in all your dwellings. (*To Moses the Lord reveals his laws for ancient Israel*) Lev.23:3

**Joseph Smith,**
*receiving the Word of the Lord*

For verily this is a day appointed unto you to rest from your labors, and to pay thy devotions unto the Most High; . . . (*Revelation, Aug. 7, 1831, with respect to the keeping of the Sabbath holy*) D&C 59:10

**Bruce R. McConkie**

Whatever the world may do, day in and day out, without cessation, in the way of toil and revelry, the saints of God rest from their labors and pay their devotions to the Most High on his holy Sabbath. True religion always has and always will call for a Sabbath on which men rest from their temporal labors and work exclusively on spiritual matters. True religion requires—it is not optional; it is mandatory—that one day in seven be devoted exclusively to worshipping the Father in Spirit and in truth. Without a Sabbath of rest and worship, men's hearts will never be centered on the things of the Spirit sufficiently to assure them of salvation. (The Promised Messiah, pp. 390-91) TLDP:577-78

**President Heber J. Grant,**
**Anthony W. Ivins, Charles W. Nibley**
(First Presidency)

Let all unnecessary labor be suspended and let no encouragement be given by the attendance

of members of the Church at places of amusement and recreation on the Sabbath day. If Sunday is spent in our meetings and in our homes great blessings will come to our families and communities. (Liahona, the Elder's Journal, Oct. 8, 1940, pp. 195-96) MOFP5:260
**Related Witnesses:**
### Elder Spencer W. Kimball
In Hebrew the term *Sabbath* means "rest". It contemplates quiet tranquillity, peace of mind and spirit. It is a day to get rid of selfish interests and absorbing activities. ¶ The Sabbath day is given throughout the generations of man for a perpetual covenant. It is a sign between the Lord and his children forever. It is a day in which to worship and to express our gratitude and appreciation to the Lord. It is a day on which to surrender every worldly interest and to praise the Lord humbly, for humility is the beginning of exaltation. It is a day not for affliction and burden but for rest and righteous enjoyment. . . . ¶ The Sabbath is a day on which to take inventory—to analyze our weaknesses, to confess our sins to our associates and our Lord. It is a day on which to fast in "sackcloth and ashes." It is a day on which to read good books, a day to contemplate and ponder, a day to study lessons for priesthood and auxiliary organizations, a day to study the scriptures and to prepare sermons, a day to nap and rest and relax, a day to visit the sick, a day to preach the gospel, a day to proselyte, a day to visit quietly with the family and get acquainted with our children, a day for proper courting, a day to do good, a day to drink at the fountain of knowledge and of instruction, a day to seek forgiveness of our sins, a day for the enrichment of our spirit and our soul, a day to restore us to our spiritual stature, a day to partake of the emblems of his sacrifice and atonement, a day to contemplate the glories of the gospel and of the eternal realms, a day to climb high on the upward path toward our Heavenly Father. . . . ¶ . . . . It seems the Lord's idea of a full and abundant Sabbath is the worship and the learning of him and partaking of his sacrament. He would have us fill the day with useful and spiritual activities. He would have us do these things with thanksgiving and cheerful hearts and countenances. . . . When one shall have taken care of his religious duties in spirit as well as by the letter and shall have filled in the interims with these constructive activities, there will be little temptation to falter. ¶ People frequently wonder where to draw the line: what is worthy and what is unworthy to do upon the Sabbath. But if one loves the Lord with all his heart, might, mind, and strength; if one can put away selfishness and curb desire; if one can measure each Sabbath activity by the yardstick of worshipfulness; if one is honest with his Lord and with himself; if one offers a "broken heart and a contrite spirit," it is quite unlikely that there will be Sabbath breaking in that person's life. (The Teachings of Spencer W. Kimball, pp. 215-16, 218-19) DGSM:73-74; TLDP:580

### Elder Spencer W. Kimball
[The Sabbath day] is a day not for lavish banqueting, but a day of simple meals and spiritual feasting; not a day of abstinence from food, except fast day, but a day when maid and mistress might be relieved from the preparation. . . . It is a day when animals may be turned out to graze and rest; when the plow may be stored in the barn and other machinery cooled down; a day when employer and employee, master and servant may be free from plowing, digging, toiling. It is a day when the office may be locked and business postponed, and troubles forgotten; a day when man may be temporarily released from that first injunction, "In the sweat of thy face shalt thou eat bread, till thou return unto the ground." (Gen.3:19) It is a day when bodies may rest, minds relax and spirits grow. It is a day when songs may be sung, prayers offered, sermons preached, and testimonies borne, and when man may climb high, almost annihilating time, space, and distance between himself and his Creator. (The Teachings of Spencer W. Kimball, pp. 215-16) DGSM:73-74

---

**686. We are not to permit our children, our guests, servants, or our animals to labor on the Sabbath.**

### Moses
Six days thou shalt labour, and do all thy work: 14. But the seventh day is the sabbath of the LORD thy God: in it thou shalt not do any work, thou, nor thy son, nor thy daughter, nor thy manservant, nor thy maidservant, nor thine ox, nor thine ass, nor any of thy cattle, nor thy stranger that is within thy gates; that thy manservant and thy maidservant may rest as well as thou. (*Moses reviews the Ten Commandments before Israel*) Deut.5:13-14
### Moses
But the seventh day is the sabbath of the LORD thy God: in it thou shalt not do any work, thou, nor thy son, nor thy daughter, thy manservant, nor thy maidservant, nor thy cattle, nor thy stranger that is within thy gates: . . . (*The Lord reveals the fourth of the Ten Commandments to Moses*) Ex.20:10

### Abinadi,
*quoted by Mormon*

Six days shalt thou labor, and do all thy work;
18. But the seventh day, the sabbath of the Lord
thy God, thou shalt not do any work, thou, nor
thy son, nor thy daughter, thy man-servant, nor
thy maid-servant, nor thy cattle, nor thy
stranger that is within thy gates; (*Abinadi
teaches the Ten Commandments to the people
of the wicked King Noah, about 148 B.C.*)
Mosiah 13:17-18

---

687. On the Sabbath we are to worship
God in church.

### Joseph Smith,
*receiving the Word of the Lord*

And that thou mayest more fully keep thyself
unspotted from the world, thou shalt go to the
house of prayer and offer up thy sacraments
upon my holy day; 10. For verily this is a day
appointed unto you to rest from your labors,
and to pay thy devotions unto the Most High;
11. Nevertheless thy vows shall be offered up in
righteousness on all days and at all times; 12.
But remember that on this, the Lord's day, thou
shalt offer thine oblations and thy sacraments
unto the Most High, confessing thy sins unto
thy brethren, and before the Lord. 13. And on
this day thou shalt do none other thing, only let
thy food be prepared with singleness of heart
that thy fasting may be perfect, or, in other
words, that thy joy may be full. (*Revelation,
Aug. 7, 1831*) D&C 59:9-13

### Elder Spencer W. Kimball

A man of my acquaintance remained home each
Sabbath and justified himself by saying that he
could benefit more by reading a good book at
home than by attending the sacrament meeting
and listening to a poor sermon. But the home,
sacred as it should be, is not the house of prayer.
In it no sacrament is administered; in it is not
found the fellowship with members, nor the
confession of sins to the brethren. The mountains may be termed the temples of God and the
forests and streams his handiwork, but only in
the meeting house, or house of prayer, can be
fulfilled all the requirements of the Lord. And
so he has impressed upon us that: "It is expedient that the church meet together often to partake of bread and wine in the remembrance of
the Lord Jesus." (D&C 20:75) (The Teachings
of Spencer W. Kimball, p. 220) DGSM:73

### Elder Joseph Fielding Smith

The spiritual side of man needs attention, to be
fed the things of spiritual life, to be mellowed

by thought, humility and prayer, and instructed
in the things of the Kingdom of God.
Moreover, we need that fellowship which contact with our fellow members in the Church
brings to us. This Sabbath day has been set
apart that mankind may spend their time in
worship and have their minds centered on the
things of God free from the influences and distractions of the business and work-a-day world.
A little reflection will reveal to us the reasonableness of this demand made on us and our
time by our Father in heaven, and that it is
given for our own good. CHMR1:218

### President Joseph F. Smith

The Sabbath is a day when, with your brethren
and sisters, you should attend the meetings of
the Saints, prepared to partake of the sacrament
of the Lord's supper; having first confessed your
sins before the Lord and your brethren and sisters, and forgiven your fellows as you expect the
Lord to forgive you. (Gospel Doctrine, p. 245)
TLDP:578

### Elder John Taylor

In meeting together on Sabbath days we assemble generally for the purpose of renewing our
spiritual strength by partaking of the emblems
of the broken body and shed blood of our Lord
and Savior Jesus Christ, communing with our
own hearts and reflecting upon things pertaining to the kingdom of God, and of speaking and
listening to those things that have a tendency to
enlighten our minds and establish us in the
faith, to increase and confirm our hopes, and to
enable us to press onward with avidity, confidence, and renewed determination in the path
which the Lord has marked out for us to travel
in. (*In new Tabernacle, Nov. 5, 1876,
JD18:278*) TLDP:582

**Related Witnesses:**

### Elder Harold B. Lee

For Latter-day Saints, to offer up "sacraments"
in the house of prayer as the Lord commands
means for you to present your devotions before
the Lord in the form of songs of praise, prayers
and thanksgiving, testimonies, and the partaking of the sacrament and the study of the word
of God. In its most widely accepted usage it
means for you to stand for any sacred right or
ceremony whereby you affirm your allegiance
to your Heavenly Father and His Son. (*Radio
Address in 1960*) (Ye Are the Light of the
World, p. 72) DGSM:73

### Elder Ezra Taft Benson

Now, what about those activities that do not fit
the spirit or purpose of the Sabbath? It seems to
me that the following should be avoided on the
Sabbath: ¶ —Overworking and staying up late

Saturday so that you are exhausted the next day. ¶ —Filling the Sabbath so full of extra meetings that there is no time for prayer, meditation, family fellowship, and counseling. ("Keeping the Sabbath Day Holy," EN1971May:6-7) TLDP:581-82

---

**688. The Sabbath day is set apart for partaking of the sacrament (for renewing sacred covenants).**

**Elder Joseph Fielding Smith**

In the present dispensation, at the time of the organization of the Church, the Lord said: "It is expedient that the church meet together often to partake of bread and wine in the remembrance of the Lord Jesus." . . . ¶ To meet together often for this purpose is a requirement made of members of the Church, which is just as binding upon them in its observance as the requirement in relation to any other principle or ordinance of the gospel. No member of the Church who refuses to observe this sacred ordinance can retain the inspiration and guidance of the Holy Ghost. (Doctrines of Salvation, 2:338) DGSM:54; TLDP:588

**President Joseph F. Smith**

The Sabbath is a day when, with your brethren and sisters, you should attend the meetings of the Saints, prepared to partake of the sacrament of the Lord's supper; having first confessed your sins before the Lord and your brethren and sisters, and forgiven your fellows as you expect the Lord to forgive you. (Gospel Doctrine, p. 245) TLDP:578

**Elder David O. McKay**

My brethren and sisters, do we always stop to think, on that sacred Sabbath day when we meet together to partake of the sacrament, that we witness, promise, obligate ourselves, in the presence of one another, and in the presence of God, that we will do certain things? . . . ¶ . . . . It is good to meet together and especially to renew our covenants with God in that holy sacrament. CR1929Oct:14-15

**Elder David O. McKay**

I desire to say this morning that I feel impressed to emphasize what the Lord has designated as the most important meeting in the Church, and that is the sacrament meeting. In this very text which I have read [D&C 20:75], given to Joseph Smith by revelation, the Lord refers to that special meeting. "It is expedient that the church meet together often." Not for these general purposes to which I have made brief reference, but for the specific purpose of

partaking of the sacrament. He has designated a particular prayer to be offered on that occasion. He has prescribed for us only a few set prayers, one of which is the blessing on the bread and water. ¶ Let us first consider the importance of this sacrament. It is not the only sacrament in the Church. It is particularly designated "The Lord's Supper." But if you will recall the occasion on which that was given or instituted you will agree with me that the Lord himself, the Savior, attached great importance to it. He had met with his twelve disciples in the upper room in Jerusalem. . . . He had partaken of the passover with them in accordance with the Jewish practice, and then he took bread and brake it and said, "Take, eat; this is my body, which is broken for you." He took the cup and blessed it, and said, "Drink ye all of it in remembrance of the blood which is shed for you, and this do in remembrance of me till I come; till we eat and drink in the kingdom of the Father." That was given just a few hours before his crucifixion. That alone establishes its importance. . . . [W]e learn further that the Lord himself revealed the significance of the sacrament to Paul, and Paul gave specific instruction to the Church at Corinth, in regard to the partaking of these important and sacred emblems. Again in this dispensation the Lord revealed specifically how this part of the worship should be conducted. All God's ordinances and ceremonies are sacred but it seems to me that there is more importance attached to this than perhaps to any other sacrament or ceremony in the Church of Christ. CR1929Oct:11

**President Spencer W. Kimball**

But we do not go to Sabbath meetings to be entertained or even solely to be instructed. We go to worship the Lord. It is an individual responsibility, and regardless of what is said from the pulpit, if one wishes to worship the Lord in spirit and in truth, he may do so by attending his meetings, partaking of the sacrament, and contemplating the beauties of the gospel. If the service is a failure to you, you have failed. No one can worship for you; you must do your own waiting upon the Lord. ("The Sabbath—A Delight," EN1978Jan:4-5) TLDP:579-80

**Related Witnesses:**

**Joseph Smith**

It is expedient that the church meet together often to partake of bread and wine in the remembrance of the Lord Jesus; (*Revelation on Church Organization and Government, April 1830*) D&C 20:75

**Elder Harold B. Lee**

For Latter-day Saints, to offer up "sacraments"

in the house of prayer as the Lord commands means for you to present your devotions before the Lord in the form of songs of praise, prayers and thanksgiving, testimonies, and the partaking of the sacrament. . . . (*Radio Address, 1960*) (Ye Are the Light of the World, p. 72) DGSM:73

**Moroni, son of Mormon**

And the church did meet together oft, to fast and to pray, and to speak one with another concerning the welfare of their souls. 6. And they did meet together oft to partake of bread and wine, in remembrance of the Lord Jesus. (*Moroni writes for the benefit of the Lamanites, A.D. 400-421*) Moro.6:5-6

**Jesus,**
*quoted by Mormon*

And it came to pass that Jesus commanded his disciples that they should bring forth some bread and wine unto him. 2. And while they were gone for bread and wine, he commanded the multitude that they should sit themselves down upon the earth. 3. And when the disciples had come with bread and wine, he took of the bread and brake and blessed it; and he gave unto the disciples and commanded that they should eat. 4. And when they had eaten and were filled, he commanded that they should give unto the multitude. 5. And when the multitude had eaten and were filled, he said unto the disciples: Behold there shall one be ordained among you, and to him will I give power that he shall break bread and bless it and give it unto the people of my church, unto all those who shall believe and be baptized in my name. 6. And this shall ye always observe to do, even as I have done, even as I have broken bread and blessed it and given it unto you. 7. And this shall ye do in remembrance of my body, which I have shown unto you. And it shall be a testimony unto the Father that ye do always remember me. And if ye do always remember me ye shall have my Spirit to be with you. 8. And it came to pass that when he said these words, he commanded his disciples that they should take of the wine of the cup and drink of it, and that they should also give unto the multitude that they might drink of it. 9. And it came to pass that they did so, and did drink of it and were filled; and they gave unto the multitude, and they did drink, and they were filled. 10. And when the disciples had done this, Jesus said unto them: Blessed are ye for this thing which ye have done, for this is fulfilling my commandments, and this doth witness unto the Father that ye are willing to do that which I have command-

ed you. (*The resurrected Jesus institutes the sacrament among the Nephites, A.D. 34*) 3Ne.18:1-10

---

689. **Observing the Sabbath can help a person keep unspotted from worldly enticements.**

**Joseph Smith,**
*receiving the Word of the Lord*

And that thou mayest more fully keep thyself unspotted from the world, thou shalt go to the house of prayer and offer up thy sacraments upon my holy day; (*Revelation, Aug. 7, 1831, with respect to the keeping of the Sabbath holy*) D&C 59:9

**Mark E. Petersen**

We constantly talk about the worldliness of the present day and speak of the fact that our young people face more serious temptations than did those of a generation ago, and this is probably true. Also, more parents seem to be caught up in the worldliness of today than was the case a generation ago. ¶ What can we do to protect ourselves under these hazardous circumstances? How can we better help our young people to remain unspotted from the world? ¶ The Lord gives us the answer, and says that it can be done by sincerely observing the Sabbath day. Most people have never thought of it in this way, but note the words of the Lord in this regard: "That thou mayest more fully keep thyself unspotted from the world"—note these words—"that thou mayest more fully keep thyself unspotted from the world, thou shalt go to the house of prayer and offer up thy sacraments upon my holy day." (D&C 59:9) ¶ Think about that for a moment. Do we really believe in God—sincerely? Are we convinced that he knows what he is talking about? If we are, then will we take him and his word seriously? Or will we further trifle with divine revelation? ¶ The Lord knows what he is talking about. Sabbath observance will help us to more fully remain unspotted from the world. CR1975Apr:70

**President David O. McKay**

A second purpose for keeping holy the Sabbath Day is: "That thou mayest more fully keep thyself unspotted from the world." Contemplation during that sacred hour, self-communion, and higher than that, communion in thought and feeling with the Lord—the realization that He is near enough to be aware of what you are thinking. What you think about—is really what you are. . . . CR1956Oct:90

### Elder Joseph Fielding Smith

By obedience to this law we are to have power over evil and more fully be able to keep the commandments of the Lord and be unspotted from the sins of the world. The purpose for this day of Sabbath rest many members of the Church, apparently, fail to see, and they make excuses for not observing it as the Lord has directed in this revelation. . . . It was not made for the purpose of giving pleasure to the Lord, but for our own spiritual uplift and preparation for the things which are to come. The spiritual side of man needs attention, to be fed the things of spiritual life, to be mellowed by thought, humility and prayer, and instructed in the things of the Kingdom of God. Moreover, we need that fellowship which contact with our fellow members in the Church brings to us. This Sabbath day has been set apart that mankind may spend their time in worship and have their minds centered on the things of God free from the influences and distractions of the business and work-a-day world. A little reflection will reveal to us the reasonableness of this demand made on us and our time by our Father in heaven, and that it is given for our own good. CHMR1:218

### Elder Harold B. Lee

May we not hope that in addition to our worshipful activities on the Lord's Day we might also on that day reduce the drudgery of the home to a minimum, and that outside the home only essential chores will be performed. Make this a day of prayerful, thoughtful study of the scriptures and other good books. While filled with the joy of the Sabbath, write a letter to your sweetheart or an absent loved one or a friend who may need your spiritual strength. Make your homes the places for the singing and playing of beautiful music in harmony with the spirit of the day. At evening's close as you gather at your fireside with the family alone or with friends, discuss the precious truths of the gospel and close with the benediction of family prayer. My experience has taught me that the prompting of the conscience to a faithful Church member is the safest indicator as to that which is contrary to the spirit of worship on the Sabbath Day. (Decisions for Successful Living, p. 148) TLDP:579

**Related Witnesses:**

### James

Pure religion and undefiled before God and the Father is this, To visit the fatherless and widows in their affliction, and to keep himself unspotted from the world. (*Letter to his brethren in the Church*) James 1:27

**690. We are to do good deeds on the Sabbath day.**

### President Spencer W. Kimball

The Sabbath is a holy day in which to do worthy and holy things. Abstinence from work and recreation is important, but insufficient. The Sabbath calls for constructive thoughts and acts, and if one merely lounges about doing nothing on the Sabbath, he is breaking it. To observe it, one will be on his knees in prayer, preparing lessons, studying the gospel, meditating, visiting the ill and distressed, writing letters to missionaries, taking a nap, reading wholesome material, and attending all the meetings of that day at which he is expected. ("The Sabbath—A Delight," EN1978Jan:4-5) TLDP:579-80

### Elder Spencer W. Kimball

[The Sabbath is] a day to visit the sick, a day to preach the gospel, a day to proselyte, a day to visit quietly with the family and get acquainted with our children, a day for proper courting, a day to do good. . . . ("The Fourth Commandment," M Man-Gleaner Manual for 1963-64, p. 265; The Teachings of Spencer W. Kimball, p. 216) DGSM:74

### Jesus,
*recorded in Matthew*

Wherefore it is lawful to do well on the sabbath days. (*Jesus answers the Pharisees, who maintained a tradition against healing on the Sabbath, by healing a man's withered hand*) Matt.12:12

### Jesus,
*recorded in Luke*

And it came to pass on the second sabbath after the first, that he went through the corn fields; and his disciples plucked the ears of corn, and did eat, rubbing them in their hands. 2. And certain of the Pharisees said unto them, Why do ye that which is not lawful to do on the sabbath days? 3. And Jesus answering them said, Have ye not read so much as this, what David did, when himself was an hungred, and they which were with him; 4. How he went into the house of God, and did take and eat the shewbread, and gave also to them that were with him; which it is not lawful to eat but for the priests alone? 5. And he said unto them, That the Son of man is Lord also of the sabbath. 6. And it came to pass also on another sabbath, that he entered into the synagogue and taught: and there was a man whose right hand was withered. 7. And the scribes and Pharisees watched him, whether he would heal on the sabbath day; that they might find an accusation against him. 8. But he knew their thoughts, and said to the man which had the withered hand, Rise up, and stand forth in the midst. And he arose and stood forth. 9. Then said Jesus unto them, I will ask you one thing; Is it lawful on the sabbath days to do good, or to do evil? to save life, or to destroy it? 10. And looking round about upon them all, he said unto the man, Stretch forth thy hand. And he did so: and his hand was restored whole as the other. 11. And they were filled with madness; and communed one with another what they might do to Jesus. (*Jesus heals on the Sabbath*) Luke 6:1-11

### Jesus,
### *recorded in Luke*

And, behold, there was a woman which had a spirit of infirmity eighteen years, and was bowed together, and could in no wise lift up herself. 12. And when Jesus saw her, he called her to him, and said unto her, Woman, thou art loosed from thine infirmity. 13. And he laid his hands on her: and immediately she was made straight, and glorified God. 14. And the ruler of the synagogue answered with indignation, because that Jesus had healed on the sabbath day, and said unto the people, There are six days in which men ought to work: in them therefore come and be healed, and not on the sabbath day. 15. The Lord then answered him, and said, Thou hypocrite, doth not each one of you on the sabbath loose his ox or his ass from the stall, and lead him away to watering? 16. And ought not this woman, being a daughter of Abraham, whom Satan hath bound, lo, these eighteen years, be loosed from this bond on the sabbath day? 17. And when he had said these things, all his adversaries were ashamed: and all the people rejoiced for all the glorious things that were done by him. (*Jesus heals a woman on the Sabbath*) Luke 13:11-17

### President Joseph F. Smith

God made or designated the Sabbath day for a day of rest, a day of worship, a day for goodly deeds, and for humility and penitence, and the worship of the Almighty in spirit and in truth. CR1915Apr:10

---

**691.** On the Sabbath food is to be prepared with "singleness of heart."

### Joseph Smith,
### *receiving the Word of the Lord*

And on this day thou shalt do none other thing, only let thy food be prepared with singleness of

heart that thy fasting may be perfect, or, in other words, that thy joy may be full. (*Revelation, Aug. 7, 1831, with respect to the keeping of the Sabbath holy*) D&C 59:13

### Elder Spencer W. Kimball

[The Sabbath day] is a day not for lavish banqueting, but a day of simple meals and spiritual feasting; not a day of abstinence from food, except fast day, but a day when maid and mistress might be relieved from the preparation. (The Teachings of Spencer W. Kimball, p. 215) DGSM:73-74

### President Joseph F. Smith

On the Sabbath day you are to do no other thing than to prepare your food with singleness of heart, that your fasting may be perfect, and your joy may be full. This is what the Lord calls fasting and prayer. ¶ The reason for this required course upon the Sabbath day is also plainly stated in the revelations. It is that one may more fully keep himself unspotted from the world; and to this end, also, the Saints are required to go to the house of prayer and offer up their sacraments on the Sabbath day. (Gospel Doctrine, p. 245) TLDP:578

### Bruce R. McConkie

Except for the preparation of modest meals, or the pulling of the ox from the mire, as it were, on this the Lord's day, we do no other things except to worship the Lord in spirit and in truth. (The Mortal Messiah, 1:203) TLDP:580-81

**Related Witnesses:**
### Elder Harold B. Lee

May we not hope that in addition to our worshipful activities on the Lord's Day we might also on that day reduce the drudgery of the home to a minimum, and that outside the home only essential chores will be performed. Make this a day of prayerful, thoughtful study of the scriptures and other good books. While filled with the joy of the Sabbath, write a letter to your sweetheart or an absent loved one or a friend who may need your spiritual strength. Make your homes the places for the singing and playing of beautiful music in harmony with the spirit of the day. At evening's close as you gather at your fireside with the family alone or with friends, discuss the precious truths of the gospel and close with the benediction of family prayer. My experience has taught me that the prompting of the conscience to a faithful Church member is the safest indicator as to that which is contrary to the spirit of worship on the Sabbath Day. (Decisions for Successful Living, p. 148) TLDP:579

**692. We are not to do business or work at our jobs on the Sabbath.**

**Bruce R. McConkie**

In the very nature of things, true Sabbath worship precludes worldly activities. Hence on that day we rest from all servile work; we lay our temporal pursuits aside for the moment; we refrain from recreational activities; we let our crops and our herds fend for themselves and our shops and our factories remain closed and idle; we leave the fish in the streams and the golf clubs in the locker room. Except for the preparation of modest meals, or the pulling of the ox from the mire, as it were, on this the Lord's day, we do no other things except to worship the Lord in spirit and in truth. (The Mortal Messiah, 1:203) TLDP:580-81

**Elder Spencer W. Kimball**

The Savior repeatedly insists upon the hallowing of the Sabbath day. He recognized the fact that livestock must be loosed from the stall and taken to water and fed and that other chores must be done. He recognized also that the ox might get into the mire or the ass fall into the pit; but neither in the letter nor in the spirit did he ever approve the use of the Sabbath for ordinary and regular work or for amusements and play. . . . (M Man-Gleaner manual for 1963/64; The Teachings of Spencer W. Kimball, p. 216) TLDP:580

**Dallin H. Oaks**

[A]n owner who keeps his business open on Sunday prevents his employees from attending worship services and being with their families on the Sabbath. Modern-day prophets have encouraged us not to shop on Sunday. . . . Those of us who shop on the Sabbath cannot escape responsibility for encouraging business to remain open on that day. Essential services must be provided, but most Sabbath transactions could be avoided if merchants and customers were determined to avoid doing business on the Lord's day. CR1986Oct:26

**President Spencer W. Kimball**

It is true that some people must work on the Sabbath. And, in fact, some of the work that is truly necessary—caring for the sick, for example—may actually serve to hallow the Sabbath. However, in such activities our motives are a most important consideration. ¶ When men and women are willing to work on the Sabbath to increase their wealth, they are breaking the commandments; for money taken in on the Sabbath, if the work is unnecessary, is unclean money. Can you imagine a person laboring on the Sabbath in defiance of the Lord's command, and

then bringing a tithe or other portion of the ill-gained fruits of this labor to Him as an offering? Just as in Old Testament times, offerings presented to the Lord must be "without blemish," and unnecessary Sabbath-day earnings can never be such. ("The Sabbath—A Delight," EN1978Jan:5) TLDP:581

**Nehemiah**

In those days saw I in Judah some treading wine presses on the sabbath, and bringing in sheaves, and lading asses; as also wine, grapes, and figs, and all manner of burdens, which they brought into Jerusalem on the sabbath day: and I testified against them in the day wherein they sold victuals. 16. There dwelt men of Tyre also therein, which brought fish, and all manner of ware, and sold on the sabbath unto the children of Judah, and in Jerusalem. 17. Then I contended with the nobles of Judah, and said unto them, What evil thing is this that ye do, and profane the sabbath day? 18. Did not your fathers thus, and did not our God bring all this evil upon us, and upon this city? yet ye bring more wrath upon Israel by profaning the sabbath. (Nehemiah corrects abuses and re-institutes Sabbath observance) Neh.13:15-18

**President Joseph F. Smith**

Men are not resting from their labors when they plow, and plant and haul and dig. They are not resting when they linger around the home all day on Sunday, doing odd jobs that they have been too busy to do on other days. (Gospel Doctrine, p. 246) TLDP:581

**Related Witnesses:**

**Elder Ezra Taft Benson**

Now, what about those activities that do not fit the spirit or purpose of the Sabbath? It seems to me that the following should be avoided on the Sabbath: ¶ —Overworking and staying up late Saturday so that you are exhausted the next day. ¶ —Filling the Sabbath so full of extra meetings that there is no time for prayer, meditation, family fellowship, and counseling. ("Keeping the Sabbath Day Holy," EN1971May:6-7) TLDP:581-82

---

**693. We should refrain from shopping on the Sabbath day, and from participating in commercial activities.**

**President Ezra Taft Benson,**
**Gordon B. Hinckley, Thomas S. Monson**
(First Presidency)

We should refrain from shopping on the Sabbath and participating in other commercial and sporting activities that now commonly desecrate the Sabbath. *(Published letter, Sept. 28, 1992, from First Presidency to all priesthood leaders directed to be read in sacrament meetings throughout the Church)*

### Dallin H. Oaks

Modern-day prophets have encouraged us not to shop on Sunday. . . . Those of us who shop on the Sabbath cannot escape responsibility for encouraging business to remain open on that day. Essential services must be provided, but most Sabbath transactions could be avoided if merchants and customers were determined to avoid doing business on the Lord's day. CR1986Oct:26

### President Spencer W. Kimball

We call attention also to the habit in which many buy their commodities on the Sabbath. Many employed people would be released for rest and worship on the Sabbath if we did not shop on that day. Numerous excuses and rationalizations are presented to justify the Sunday buying. We call upon all of you to keep the Sabbath holy and make no Sunday purchases. CR1974Oct:6

### President Spencer W. Kimball

Sabbath-breakers too are those who buy commodities or entertainment on the Sabbath, thus encouraging pleasure palaces and business establishments to remain open—which they otherwise would not do. If we buy, sell, trade, or support such on the Lord's day we are as rebellious as the children of Israel, the dire consequences of whose transgressions against this and other commandments should be a permanent warning to us all. ("The Sabbath—A Delight," EN1978Jan:5) TLDP:581

### President Joseph F. Smith

Men are not showing zeal and ardor in their religious faith and duty when they hustle off early Sunday morning on the cars, in teams, in automobiles, to the canyons, the resorts, and to visit friends or places of amusement with their wives and children. (Gospel Doctrine, p. 246) TLDP:581

### Elder Ezra Taft Benson

Now, what about those activities that do not fit the spirit or purpose of the Sabbath? It seems to me that the following should be avoided on the Sabbath: . . . ¶ —Taking trips to canyons or resorts, visiting friends socially, joy riding, wasting time, and engaging in other amusements. (See DBY:165.) ¶ —Playing vigorously and going to movies. . . . ¶ —Shopping or supporting with your patronage businesses that operate on Sunday, such as grocery stores, supermarkets, restaurants, and service stations. ("Keeping the Sabbath Day Holy," EN1971May:6-7) TLDP:581-82

**Related Witnesses:**
### President Heber J. Grant, Anthony W. Ivins, Charles W. Nibley
(First Presidency)

Let all unnecessary labor be suspended and let no encouragement be given by the attendance of members of the Church at places of amusement and recreation on the Sabbath day. If Sunday is spent in our meetings and in our homes great blessings will come to our families and communities. (Liahona, the Elders' Journal, Oct. 8, 1940, pp. 195-96) MOFP5:260

---

### 694. The Sabbath is not a day for seeking pleasure and recreation.

### President Joseph F. Smith

Men are not showing zeal and ardor in their religious faith and duty when they hustle off early Sunday morning on the cars, in teams, in automobiles, to the canyons, the resorts, and to visit friends or places of amusement with their wives and children. They are not paying their devotions in this way to the Most High. ¶ Not in seeking pleasure and recreation do they offer their time and attention in the worship of the Lord; nor can they thus rejoice in the spirit of forgiveness and worship that comes with partaking of the holy sacrament. ¶ Boys and young men are not fasting with singleness of heart that their joy may be full when they spend the Sabbath day loafing around the village ice-cream stand or restaurant, playing games, or in buggy riding, fishing, shooting, or engaged in physical sports, excursions and outings. Such is not the course that will keep them unspotted from the world, but rather one that will deprive them of the rich promises of the Lord, giving them sorrow instead of joy, and unrest and anxiety instead of the peace that comes with works of righteousness. ¶ Let us play and take recreation to our hearts' content during other days, but on the Sabbath let us rest, worship, go to the house of prayer, partake of the sacrament, eat our food with singleness of heart, and pay our devotions to God, that the fulness of the earth may be ours, and that we may have peace in this world and eternal life in the world to come. (Gospel Doctrine, p. 246) TLDP:581

### Elder Spencer W. Kimball

The Savior repeatedly insists upon the hallowing of the Sabbath day. He recognized the fact that livestock must be loosed from the stall and taken to water and fed and that other chores must be done. He recognized also that the ox might get into the mire or the ass fall into the pit; but neither in the letter nor in the spirit did he ever approve the use of the Sabbath for ordinary and regular work or for amusements and play. . . . (M Man-Gleaner manual for 1963/64, The Teachings of Spencer W. Kimball, p. 216) TLDP:580

### President Heber J. Grant,
### Anthony W. Ivins, Charles W. Nibley
(First Presidency)

The Lord's day is a holy day—not a holiday. It has been set apart as a day of rest and worship. A sacred Sabbath begets reverence for God. It is not pleasing in His sight that the day be given over to pleasure seeking in places of amusement or elsewhere. ¶ Sunday Schools and meetings have been so arranged as to meet the convenience of the people and leave a considerable portion of the Sabbath day without Church appointments. We earnestly appeal to the people to keep their meeting appointments faithfully and to utilize that portion of Sunday not appointed for meetings in promoting family association in the home, with the purpose of stimulating and establishing greater home fealty, a closer companionship among parents and children, and more intimate relations among all kindred. ¶ We believe that it is unnecessary for families to go beyond their own homes or those of their kindred for the relaxation and association which are proper for the Sabbath day, and we therefore discourage more traveling than is necessary for this purpose and attendance upon appointed meetings. ¶ Let all unnecessary labor be suspended and let no encouragement be given by the attendance of members of the Church at places of amusement and recreation on the Sabbath day. If Sunday is spent in our meetings and in our homes great blessings will come to our families and communities. (Liahona, the Elders' Journal, Oct. 8, 1940, pp. 195-96) MOFP5:260

# List of Doctrines

## SACRAMENT OF THE LORD'S SUPPER

*Doctrines Located in This Topic*

695. Jesus instituted the sacrament as the symbol of His atoning sacrifice.

696. The sacrament of the Lord's Supper is an ordinance of the gospel.

697. In partaking of the sacrament we renew solemn covenants made with the Lord.

698. The Lord promises that those who partake of the sacrament worthily will have His spirit to be with them.

699. Liquids other than wine and food other than bread may be used as emblems in the observance of the sacrament.

700. The bread of the sacrament is a symbol of the Savior's broken flesh; the wine is a symbol of His spilled blood: the bread is not the actual flesh of Christ, the wine is not His actual blood.

701. The Lord has designated those who may officiate in the administration of the sacrament.

702. The Lord has established the words to be used for the blessing of the emblems of the sacrament.

703. The sacrament is for those who believe in Christ and have been baptized, namely, members of the Church of Jesus Christ of Latter-day Saints.

704. Before partaking of the sacrament we are to examine ourselves to determine that we are worthy.

705. Although unworthy persons should not take the sacrament, they are not to be removed from Church services, rather they are to be loved and cared for.

*Doctrines on SACRAMENT OF THE LORD'S SUPPER Located in Other Topics*

688. The Sabbath day is set apart for partaking of the sacrament (for renewing sacred covenants).

## SACRAMENT OF THE LORD'S SUPPER

695. Jesus instituted the sacrament as the symbol of His atoning sacrifice.

### James E. Talmage

While Jesus with the Twelve still sat at table, He took a loaf or cake of bread, and having reverently given thanks and by blessing sanctified it, He gave a portion to each of the apostles, saying: "Take, eat; this is my body"; or, according to the more extended account, "This is my body which is given for you: this do in remembrance of me." Then, taking a cup of wine, He gave thanks and blessed it, and gave it unto them with the command: "Drink ye all of it; for this is my blood of the new testament, which is shed for many for the remission of sins. But I say unto you, I will not drink henceforth of this fruit of the vine, until that day when I drink it new with you in my Father's kingdom." In this simple but impressive manner was instituted the ordinance, since known as the Sacrament of the Lord's Supper. The bread and wine, duly consecrated by prayer, become emblems of the Lord's body and blood, to be eaten and drunk reverently, and in remembrance of Him. JTC:596-97

### President John Taylor

Previous to the offering up of Himself, as the great expiatory sacrifice, having fulfilled the law and made it honorable, and having introduced the Gospel, He met with his disciples, as already noticed, to eat the Passover. He then told them, "With desire I have desired to eat this passover with you before I suffer." To eat what with you? The Sacrament of the Lord's Supper. Thus He [ate] both, for the two ceremonies centered in Him, He was the embodiment of both, He was the Being provided before the foundation of the earth, and prophesied of by men of God throughout all the preceding ages; and also on account of whom the sacrifices were offered up by all the servants of the Lord, from the fall of Adam to that time; and all the various atonements heretofore offered pointed to Him, for whom they were all made and in whom they all centered. (The Mediation and Atonement, p. 125) TLDP:584

### Elder Harold B. Lee

By the partaking of the sacrament you are participating in one of the most sacred ordinances of the Church. It has a similar significance to us today that the sacrifice of burnt offerings, given to Adam, had to the saints before the advent of the Savior upon the earth. When the sacrifice of burnt offerings was first given it was for the purpose of reminding Adam of the great atoning sacrifice of the Son of God that should transpire in the meridian of time, by which Adam and his posterity might be loosed from the bonds of death and if they were faithful to the gospel plan might partake of eternal life with our Heavenly Father in his kingdom. With the sacrifice of Jesus, by which he, "the just" suffered for "the unjust," the sacrifice of burnt offerings, as it had been observed up to that time, was fulfilled (3Ne.9:19-20). In its place he instituted at the time of the Last Supper, before his crucifixion, the holy sacrament, by which the meaning of his great atoning sacrifice would be had in everlasting remembrance. The purpose and meaning of the sacrament and the seriousness that should accompany your partaking of it is clearly set forth in the Master's words as understood by the Apostle Paul: "This do ye . . . in remembrance of me. For as often as ye eat this bread, and drink this cup, ye do show the Lord's death till he come. Wherefore whosoever shall eat this bread, and drink this cup of the Lord, unworthily, shall be guilty of the body and blood of the Lord. But let a man examine himself, and so let him eat of the bread, and drink of that cup. For he that eateth and drinketh unworthily, eateth and drinketh damnation to himself, not discerning the Lord's body. For this cause many are weak and sickly among you, and many sleep." (1Cor.11:25-30) All this is done for the one divine purpose, as declared by the Lord, "that thou mayest more fully keep thyself unspotted from the world." (D&C 59:9) (Decisions for Successful Living, pp. 146-47) TLDP:584

### Elder Joseph F. Smith

When Jesus came and suffered, "the just for the unjust," . . . the law of sacrifice was fulfilled, and in the stead thereof he gave another law, which we call the "Sacrament of the Lord's Supper," by which his life and mission, his death and resurrection, the great sacrifice he had offered for the redemption of man, should be kept in everlasting remembrance. . . . Therefore, this law is to us, what the law of sacrifice was to those who lived prior to the first coming of the Son of Man, until He shall come again. Therefore, we must honor and keep it sacredly. (*In 13th Ward, Feb. 9, 1873, JD15:324*) TLDP:584

**Related Witnesses:**

### Jesus,
### *quoted by Mormon*

And it came to pass that Jesus commanded his disciples that they should bring forth some bread and wine unto him. 2. And while they were gone for bread and wine, he commanded the multitude that they should sit themselves down upon the earth. 3. And when the disciples had come with bread and wine, he took of the bread and brake and blessed it; and he gave unto the disciples and commanded that they should eat. 4. And when they had eaten and were filled, he commanded that they should give unto the multitude. 5. And when the multitude had eaten and were filled, he said unto the disciples: Behold there shall one be ordained among you, and to him will I give power that he shall break bread and bless it and give it unto the people of my church, unto all those who shall believe and be baptized in my name. 6. And this shall ye always observe to do, even as I have done, even as I have broken bread and blessed it and given it unto you. 7. And this shall ye do in remembrance of my body, which I have shown unto you. And it shall be a testimony unto the Father that ye do always remember me. And if ye do always remember me ye shall have my Spirit to be with you. 8. And it came to pass that when he said these words, he commanded his disciples that they should take of the wine of the cup and drink of it, and that they should also give unto the multitude that they might drink of it. 9. And it came to pass that they did so, and did drink of it and were filled; and they gave unto the multitude, and they did drink, and they were filled. 10. And when the disciples had done this, Jesus said unto them: Blessed are ye for this thing which ye have done, for this is fulfilling my commandments, and this doth witness unto the Father that ye are willing to do that which I have commanded you. 11. And this shall ye always do to those who repent and are baptized in my name; and ye shall do it in remembrance of my blood, which I have shed for you, that ye may witness unto the Father that ye do always remember me. And if ye do always remember me ye shall have my Spirit to be with you. (*The resurrected Jesus institutes the sacrament among the Nephites, A.D. 34*) 3Ne.18:1-11

**Jesus,**
*recorded in Luke*
And he took bread, and gave thanks, and brake it, and gave unto them, saying, This is my body which is given for you: this do in remembrance of me. 20. Likewise also the cup after supper, saying, This cup is the new testament in my blood, which is shed for you. (*Jesus institutes the sacrament with the Twelve at the feast of the Passover*) Luke 22:19-20

**Jesus,**
*recorded in Matthew*
And as they were eating, Jesus took bread, and blessed it, and brake it, and gave it to the disciples, and said, Take, eat; this is my body. 27. And he took the cup, and gave thanks, and gave it to them, saying, Drink ye all of it; 28. For this is my blood of the new testament, which is shed for many for the remission of sins. (*Jesus keeps the Passover with the Twelve and institutes the sacrament at the Last Supper*) Matt.26:26-28

**Joseph Smith**
It is expedient that the church meet together often to partake of bread and wine in the remembrance of the Lord Jesus; (*Revelation on Church Organization and Government, April 1830*) D&C 20:75

---

696. The sacrament of the Lord's Supper is an ordinance of the gospel.

**Jesus,**
*quoted by Joseph Smith,*
*translating Mark*
And as oft as ye do this ordinance, ye will remember me in this hour that I was with you and drank with you of this cup, even the last time in my ministry. (*Jesus keeps the Passover with the Twelve and institutes the sacrament at the Last Supper*) JST Mark 14:24

**David B. Haight**
The weekly opportunity of partaking of the sacrament of the Lord's Supper is one of the most sacred ordinances of The Church of Jesus Christ of Latter-day Saints and is further indication of His love for all of us. Associated with the partaking of the sacrament are principles that are fundamental to man's advancement and exaltation in the kingdom of God and the shaping of one's spiritual character. CR1983Apr:16-17

**Bruce R. McConkie**
To keep his saints in constant remembrance of their obligation to accept and obey him—or in other words, to eat his flesh and drink his blood—the Lord has given them the sacramental ordinance. This ordinance, performed in remembrance of his broken flesh and spilled blood, is the means provided for men, formally and repeatedly, to assert their belief in the divinity of Christ, and to affirm their determination to serve him and keep his commandments; or, in other words, in this ordinance—in a spiritual, but not a literal sense—men eat his flesh and drink his blood. (Doctrinal New Testament Commentary, 1:358) DGSM:54

### President Wilford Woodruff

No man or woman should eat the bread and drink of the cup at the Sacrament who entertains hard feelings against any of his or her brethren and sisters. They should be taught the importance of settling all their difficulties and removing all causes of ill-feeling, so that no condemnation will rest upon them for partaking of this holy ordinance unworthily. (*Letter of the First Presidency to the president and counselors of the St. George Stake, Utah, April 1888*) MOFP3:164

### Elder Joseph Fielding Smith

To meet together often for this purpose [partaking of the sacrament] is a requirement made of members of the Church, which is just as binding upon them in its observance as the requirement in relation to any other principle or ordinance of the gospel. No member of the Church who refuses to observe this sacred ordinance can retain the inspiration and guidance of the Holy Ghost. (Doctrines of Salvation, 2:338) DGSM:54

---

**697. In partaking of the sacrament we renew solemn covenants made with the Lord.**

### N. Eldon Tanner

To pay a bill or a note is a pledge that is very important; to keep one's word in anything one says or agrees to do is a pledge. When one joins the Church, he pledges certain things as he goes into the waters of baptism. When accepting the priesthood, we make a very definite covenant with the Lord. When partaking of the sacrament, we renew our covenants. Notice that I am using covenants, promises, and pledges interchangeably. CR1966Oct:98

### Delbert L. Stapley

[About] covenants: (1) The gospel of our Lord Jesus Christ is a covenant between God and his people. (2) When baptized by an authorized servant of God, we covenant to do God's will and to obey his commandments. (3) By partaking of the Sacrament we renew all covenants entered into with the Lord and pledge ourselves to take upon us the name of his Son, to always remember him and keep his commandments. (4) There is an oath and covenant which belongs to the priesthood wherein men receiving this holy power pledge themselves faithfully to keep all the commandments of God and to magnify their callings in the priesthood, which is God's gift of his power and authority unto them. (5) In connection with all ordinances pertaining to the temples of our God, men and women accept covenants and obligations which relate to the endowment and to the eternity of the marriage and family relationship. All these doctrines and more are necessary and vital to the salvation, exaltation and eternal happiness of God's children. CR1965Oct:14

### Elder Joseph Fielding Smith

Each member of the Church should have in mind the three great covenants that are made by partaking of these tokens, which are: ¶ First: That they are willing to take upon them the name of the Son. ¶ Second: That they will always remember him. ¶ Third: That they will keep his commandments, which he has given them. ¶ How do we take upon us the name of the Son? The Church is called by his name, and we are to remember that by partaking of the sacrament, we acknowledge his hand in our redemption from death, which is the gift to all men, and in the remission of our individual sins which comes through our obedience in keeping his commandments. ¶ King Benjamin has given us an excellent understanding of what is meant by taking upon us the name of the Son. Because of the covenant we make, we are spiritually begotten sons and daughters of Jesus Christ. We become his sons and daughters, because he has redeemed us and given us life, thus defeating the power of the grave. [See Mosiah 5:8-12] ¶ To "always remember him" does not mean simply to remember that he was crucified; but to keep in mind constantly the reasons why, and what blessings have come to each of us through his death and resurrection. We are to remember the great suffering and what it cost him to make the great atonement. We are to remember that he did it because of his love, not only for those who believe on him, but also for the whole world. . . . ¶ The third thing to remember is that we covenant to keep his commandments. How can a member of the Church partake of the sacrament and renew these covenants, and then go forth from this sacred assembly, and deliberately break any of the divine commandments! In doing such a thing we bring condemnation to our souls. Far better for members of the Church never to partake of these emblems, thus renewing these three covenants, than to partake of them and then go forth to commit sin. It is, however, a solemn commandment from the Lord, that we do partake of the sacrament. Those who repeatedly and constantly disregard this commandment and remain away from this sacrament meeting, will lose the Spirit of the Lord, for his Spirit will not dwell in those who fail to renew these covenants in a consistent manner. (Answers to Gospel Questions, 3:3-5) TLDP:585

### President David O. McKay

My brethren and sisters, do we always stop to think, on that sacred Sabbath day when we meet together to partake of the sacrament, that we witness, promise, obligate ourselves, in the presence of one another, and in the presence of God, that we will do certain things? Note them. ¶ The first: We are willing to take upon ourselves the name of the Son. In doing so we choose him as our leader and our ideal; and he is the one perfect character in all the world. ¶ The second: That we will always remember him. Not just on Sunday, but on Monday, in our daily acts, in our self-control. When our brother hurts us, we are going to try to master our feelings and not retaliate in the same spirit of anger. When a brother treats us with contempt, we are going to try to return kindness. That's the spirit of the Christ, and that's what we have promised—that we will do our best to achieve these high standards of Christian principles. ¶ The third: We promised to " . . . keep his commandments which he has given . . ."—tithing, fast offerings, the Word of Wisdom, kindness, forgiveness, love. The obligation of a member of the Church of Jesus Christ is great, because obedience to these principles gives life, eternal life. CR1929Oct:14

### J. Reuben Clark, Jr.

Before the Meridian of Time and the birth of the Messiah, mankind looked forward thereto. Before that, all of the rituals pertaining to the gospel looked to the Messiah, to his birth. . . . Since that time, we honor him, and our ritual, the sacrament, relates back to that time. We make covenants when we partake of the sacrament. CR1953Oct:39

### Elder Joseph Fielding Smith

I have often wondered if we fully realize the significance and importance of the covenants we make in partaking of these emblems in remembrance of the body and blood of Jesus Christ. It is our duty carefully and thoughtfully to consider the nature of these prayers, when we hear them offered in our meetings. (Doctrines of Salvation, 2:344-45) DGSM:53

**Related Witnesses:**

### Joseph Smith

O God, the Eternal Father, we ask thee in the name of thy Son, Jesus Christ, to bless and sanctify this bread to the souls of all those who partake of it, that they may eat in remembrance of the body of thy Son, and witness unto thee, O God, the Eternal Father, that they are willing to take upon them the name of thy Son, and always remember him and keep his commandments which he has given them; that they may always have his Spirit to be with them. Amen. . . . 79.

O God, the Eternal Father, we ask thee in the name of thy Son, Jesus Christ, to bless and sanctify this wine to the souls of all those who drink of it, that they may do it in remembrance of the blood of thy Son, which was shed for them; that they may witness unto thee, O God, the Eternal Father, that they do always remember him, that they may have his Spirit to be with them. Amen. (*Revelation on Church Organization and Government; the sacramental prayers are given, April 1830*) D&C 20:77,79

### David B. Haight

The weekly opportunity of partaking of the sacrament of the Lord's Supper is one of the most sacred ordinances of the Church of Jesus Christ of Latter-day Saints and is further indication of His love for all of us. Associated with the partaking of the sacrament are principles that are fundamental to man's advancement and exaltation in the kingdom of God and the shaping of one's spiritual character. We should reflect in our own weekday conduct the spiritual renewal and commitments made on Sunday. . . . ¶ We all have regrets for words or deeds or thoughts from Sabbath to Sabbath that we should like to erase from our souls. Perhaps we have erred against someone or injured them; or, if there is ill feeling in our heart, we should repent, obtain forgiveness from those affected or transgressed against, then humbly, with a contrite spirit, prepare ourselves to be worthy to partake of the sacrament. . . . ¶ By partaking of the sacrament each Sunday we receive the encouragement and strength to keep the commandments of God, to live uprightly, virtuously, and honestly. . . . ¶ The sacrament is one ordinance that allows us to experience a personal relationship to God and enlarges our knowledge and understanding of Him and His Only Begotten Son. ¶ Our personal reward for compliance with the covenants and obligations in the ordinance of the sacrament becomes the companionship of God's Holy Spirit. This is the light that leads to eternal life. CR1993Apr:16-17

### Elder Spencer W. Kimball

The Savior emphasized that the tangible bread and water of the Sacrament were to remind us continually of the sacrifice he made for us and for renewal of our covenants of righteousness. (The Teachings of Spencer W. Kimball, p. 220) DGSM:53

### Bruce R. McConkie

When they [who have been baptized] thereafter partake worthily of the sacrament, they renew the covenant made in the waters of baptism. The two covenants are the same. (The Promised Messiah, p. 386) DGSM:54

### Alma, the elder,
### quoted by Mormon

Now I say unto you, if this be the desire of your hearts, what have you against being baptized in the name of the Lord, as a witness before him that ye have entered into a covenant with him, that ye will serve him and keep his commandments, that he may pour out his Spirit more abundantly upon you? (*Alma organizes the Church of Christ and performs baptisms, about 148 B.C.*) Mosiah 18:10

### Paul

And when he had given thanks, he brake it, and said, Take, eat: this is my body, which is broken for you: this do in remembrance of me. 25. After the same manner also he took the cup, when he had supped, saying, This cup is the new testament in my blood: this do ye, as oft as ye drink it, in remembrance of me. 26. For as often as ye eat this bread, and drink this cup, ye do shew the Lord's death till he come. (*Letter to the Church at Corinth, Greece, about A.D. 55*) 1Cor.11:24-26

### Anthon H. Lund

The institution of the Lord's supper is strong evidence of the divinity and foreknowledge of the Savior, and what could be more impressive and powerful to call to mind the sublime sacrifice he made than that of partaking of broken bread to remember his body; and drinking from the cup to remember his blood that was shed for all for the remission of sins? Jesus knew that abstract teaching might easily be forgotten, that men would remember the concrete better, and hence many of his excellent lessons were given in parables, and that this, the greatest event, might be vividly impressed on all, he gave this glorious ordinance in a tangible form, to look at and partake of. CR1916Oct:13

---

**698.** The Lord promises that those who partake of the sacrament worthily will have His spirit to be with them.

### Bruce R. McConkie

When we partake worthily of the sacrament ordinance we renew the covenant made in the waters of baptism. Once again we covenant to remember and rely upon the atoning sacrifice of Christ, to take his name upon us, and to keep his commandment. He in turn promises us that we shall always have his Spirit to be with us and that we shall have eternal life in his Father's kingdom. (The Promised Messiah, pp. 385-86) TLDP:585-86

### Elder George Albert Smith

Before partaking of this sacrament, our hearts should be pure; our hands should be clean; we should be divested of all enmity toward our associates; we should be at peace with our fellow men; and we should have in our hearts a desire to do the will of our Father and to keep all of His commandments. If we do this, partaking of the sacrament will be a blessing to us and will renew our spiritual strength. CR1908Apr:35

### Melvin J. Ballard,
### quoted by David B. Haight

Some years ago, Elder Melvin J. Ballard wrote: ¶ "I am a witness that there is a spirit attending the administration of the sacrament that warms the soul from head to foot; you feel the wounds of the spirit being healed, and the load is lifted. Comfort and happiness come to the soul that is worthy and truly desirous of partaking of this spiritual food." CR1983Apr:16

### Jesus,
### quoted by Mormon

And when the multitude had eaten and were filled, he said unto the disciples: Behold there shall one be ordained among you, and to him will I give power that he shall break bread and bless it and give it unto the people of my church, unto all those who shall believe and be baptized in my name. 6. And this shall ye always observe to do, even as I have done, even as I have broken bread and blessed it and given it unto you. 7. And this shall ye do in remembrance of my body, which I have shown unto you. And it shall be a testimony unto the Father that ye do always remember me. And if ye do always remember me ye shall have my Spirit to be with you. 8. And it came to pass that when he said these words, he commanded his disciples that they should take of the wine of the cup and drink of it, and that they should also give unto the multitude that they might drink of it. 9. And it came to pass that they did so, and did drink of it and were filled; and they gave unto the multitude, and they did drink, and they were filled. 10. And when the disciples had done this, Jesus said unto them: Blessed are ye for this thing which ye have done, for this is fulfilling my commandments, and this doth witness unto the Father that ye are willing to do that which I have commanded you. 11. And this shall ye always do to those who repent and are baptized in my name; and ye shall do it in remembrance of my blood, which I have shed for you, that ye may witness unto the Father that ye do always remember me. And if ye do always remember me ye shall have my Spirit to be with you. (*The resurrected Jesus institutes the sacrament among the Nephites, A.D. 34*) 3Ne.18:5-11

**Related Witnesses:**

**Joseph Smith**

O God, the Eternal Father, we ask thee in the name of thy Son, Jesus Christ, to bless and sanctify this bread to the souls of all those who partake of it, that they may eat in remembrance of the body of thy Son, and witness unto thee, O God, the Eternal Father, that they are willing to take upon them the name of thy Son, and always remember him and keep his commandments which he has given them; that they may always have his Spirit to be with them. Amen. . . . 79. O God, the Eternal Father, we ask thee in the name of thy Son, Jesus Christ, to bless and sanctify this wine to the souls of all those who drink of it, that they may do it in remembrance of the blood of thy Son, which was shed for them; that they may witness unto thee, O God, the Eternal Father, that they do always remember him, that they may have his Spirit to be with them. Amen. (*Revelation on Church Organization and Government; the sacramental prayers are given, April 1830*) D&C 20:77,79

**Jesus,**
*quoted by Mormon*

And he said unto them: He that eateth this bread eateth of my body to his soul; and he that drinketh of this wine drinketh of my blood to his soul; and his soul shall never hunger nor thirst, but shall be filled. 9. Now, when the multitude had all eaten and drunk, behold, they were filled with the Spirit; and they did cry out with one voice, and gave glory to Jesus, whom they both saw and heard. (*The resurrected Jesus provides bread and wine miraculously and again administers the sacrament*) 3Ne.20:8-9

**Joseph Smith,**
*receiving the Word of the Lord*

I, the Lord, am bound when ye do what I say; but when ye do not what I say, ye have no promise. (*Revelation, April 26, 1832*) D&C 82:10

---

699. **Liquids other than wine and food other than bread may be used as emblems in the observance of the sacrament.**

**Joseph Smith,**
*receiving the Word of the Lord*

For, behold, I say unto you, that it mattereth not what ye shall eat or what ye shall drink when ye partake of the sacrament, if it so be that ye do it with an eye single to my glory—remembering unto the Father my body which was laid down for you, and my blood which was shed for the remission of your sins. 3. Wherefore, a commandment I give unto you, that you shall not purchase wine neither strong drink of your enemies; (*Revelation to Joseph through a heavenly messenger, Aug. 1830*) D&C 27:2-3

**President Brigham Young**

The Lord has said to us it mattereth not what we partake of when we administer the sup to the people, inasmuch as we do it with an eye single to the glory of God; it is then acceptable to him. Consequently we use water as though it were wine; for we are commanded to drink not of wine for this sacred purpose except it be made by our own hands. (*At Brigham City, Utah, Aug. 19, 1877, JD19:92*) TLDP:587-88

**James E. Talmage**

In instituting the sacrament among both the Jews and the Nephites, Christ used bread and wine as the emblems of His body and blood; and in this, the dispensation of the fulness of times, He has revealed His will that the saints meet together often to partake of bread and wine in this commemorative ordinance. But He has also shown that other forms of food and drink may be used in place of bread and wine. Soon after the Church had been organized in the present dispensation, the Prophet Joseph Smith was about to purchase wine for sacramental purposes, when a messenger from God met him and delivered the following instructions: "For, behold, I say unto you, that it mattereth not what ye shall eat or what ye shall drink when ye partake of the sacrament, if it so be that ye do it with an eye single to my glory—remembering unto the Father my body which was laid down for you, and my blood which was shed for the remission of your sins. Wherefore, a commandment I give unto you, that you shall not purchase wine neither strong drink of your enemies; Wherefore, you shall partake of none except it is made new among you; yea, in this my Father's kingdom which shall be built up on the earth." Upon this authority, the Latter-day Saints administer water in their sacramental service, in preference to wine. AF:159

**Related Witnesses:**

**Elder Joseph Fielding Smith**

In the present dispensation, at the time of the organization of the Church, the Lord said: "It is expedient that the church meet together *often* to partake of bread and wine in the remembrance of the Lord Jesus." Then follow the exact words which are to be used in blessing the bread and the wine, or water, which by revelation has been substituted for wine. [D&C 20:75] (Doctrines of Salvation, 2:338) TLDP:588

---

700. **The bread of the sacrament is a symbol of the Savior's broken flesh; the wine is a symbol of His spilled blood: the bread is not the actual flesh of Christ, the wine is not His actual blood.**

**Elder George Albert Smith**

We believe that the sacrament is not the literal body and blood of our Lord; in other words, we do not believe in the doctrine of Transubstantiation. CR1908Apr:36

**Anthon H. Lund**

A great number of Christian sects and denominations claim that this [Matt.26:26,28] did not signify that the bread and wine were emblems, but that we partake really of his flesh and blood, in the administration of the sacrament. ¶ Transubstantiation means that the bread changes by the blessing into his flesh, and the wine into his blood. This is not our opinion. We believe that the bread and wine are simply emblems of his body and blood. If we could imagine ourselves in that sacred room where he and his disciples were having the last evening together, where they partook of the paschal meal, and where he instituted this holy ordinance, we should see him then standing before the disciples, saying to them of the bread, "This is my body," and of the contents of the cup, "This is my blood," and yet we should see him standing in the full vigor of health and the blood circulating in his veins. It was not his blood in the cup, for he calls it at the very same time, "this fruit of the vine." It was wine he gave unto them, but it represented his blood that was to be shed for the remission of sins. CR1916Oct:13

**Bruce R. McConkie**

To keep his saints in constant remembrance of their obligation to accept and obey him—or in other words, to eat his flesh and drink his blood—the Lord has given them the sacramental ordinance. This ordinance, performed in remembrance of his broken flesh and spilled blood, is the means provided for men, formally and repeatedly, to assert their belief in the divinity of Christ, and to affirm their determination to serve him and keep his commandments; or, in other words, in this ordinance—in a spiritual, but not a literal sense—men eat his flesh and drink his blood. (Doctrinal New Testament Commentary, 1:358) DGSM:54

**Jesus,**
*quoted by Joseph Smith,*
*translating Mark*

And as they did eat, Jesus took bread, and blessed, and brake it, and gave to them, and said, Take, and eat. 21. Behold, this is for you to do in remembrance of my body; for as oft as ye do this ye will remember this hour that I was with you. 22. And he took the cup, and when he had given thanks, he gave it to them: and they all drank of it. 23. And he said unto them, This is in remembrance of my blood which is shed for many, and the new testament which I give unto you; for of me ye shall bear record unto all the world. 24. And as oft as ye do this ordinance, ye will remember me in this hour that I was with you and drank with you of this cup, even the last time in my ministry. 25. Verily I say unto you, Of this ye shall bear record; for I will drink no more of the fruit of the vine with you, until that day that I drink it new in the kingdom of God. (*Jesus keeps the Passover with the Twelve and institutes the sacrament at the Last Supper*) JST Mark 14:20-25

**Related Witnesses:**

**Jesus,**
*quoted by Joseph Smith,*
*translating Matthew*

For this is in remembrance of my blood of the new testament, which is shed for as many as shall believe on my name, for the remission of their sins. (*Jesus keeps the Passover with the Twelve and institutes the sacrament at the Last Supper*) JST Matt.26:24

**Jesus,**
*recorded in Matthew*

And as they were eating, Jesus took bread, and blessed it, and brake it, and gave it to the disciples, and said, Take, eat; this is my body. 27. And he took the cup, and gave thanks, and gave it to them, saying, Drink ye all of it; 28. For this is my blood of the new testament, which is shed for many for the remission of sins. (*Jesus keeps the Passover with the Twelve and institutes the sacrament at the Last Supper*) Matt.26:26-28

**Jesus,**
*quoted by John*

And Jesus said unto them, I am the bread of life: he that cometh to me shall never hunger; and he that believeth on me shall never thirst. (*After Jesus fed the five thousand, the people came to Jesus and he taught them the difference between physical and spiritual food*) John 6:35

**Jesus,**
*quoted by John*

Jesus answered and said unto her, If thou knewest the gift of God, and who it is that saith to thee, Give me to drink; thou wouldest have asked of him, and he would have given thee living water. (*Jesus teaches the woman of Samaria at Jacob's well*) John 4:10

**Bruce R. McConkie**

Jesus, celebrating the Feast of the Passover, thus dignifying and fulfilling the law to the full, initiated the sacrament of the Lord's supper. Sacrifice stopped and sacrament started. It was the end of the old era, the beginning of the new. Sacrifice looked forward to the shed blood and bruised flesh of the Lamb of God. The sacrament was to be in remembrance of his spilt blood and broken flesh, the emblems, bread and wine, typifying such as completely as had the shedding of the blood of animals in their days. (Doctrinal New Testament Commentary, 1:719-20) DGSM:54-55

**Author's Note:** It is interesting to observe that in January, 1932, the First Presidency published the following as part of "Details About the Sacrament:" ¶ In the administration of this sacred ordinance, it is desirable that the bread provided should be in medium slices, and it should be broken in fair-sized pieces. It is, of course, desirable to avoid having a large surplus of broken bread on hand. (MOFP5:307.)

---

**701. The Lord has designated those who may officiate in the administration of the sacrament.**

**Elder George Albert Smith**

The Lord has indicated the importance of the sacrament in another way. There are certain of the Priesthood who are not permitted to officiate in this ordinance. The Deacon or Teacher may not administer the sacrament, and those who bear no Priesthood, cannot act in this capacity. The Lord has certainly emphasized its importance by designating those who may officiate. . . . We should partake of it in humility, with preparation of clean hands and pure hearts, and with a desire to be acceptable to our Father; then we will receive it worthily, and rejoice in the blessing that comes to us by reason of it. CR1908Apr:36

**Jesus,**
*quoted by Mormon*

And when the multitude had eaten and were filled, he said unto the disciples: Behold there shall one be ordained among you, and to him will I give power that he shall break bread and bless it and give it unto the people of my church, unto all those who shall believe and be baptized in my name. (*The resurrected Jesus*

institutes the sacrament among the Nephites, A.D. 34) 3Ne.18:5

**Joseph Smith**

And the elder or priest shall administer it; and after this manner shall he administer it. . . . (*Revelation on Church Organization and Government; instructions regarding the sacrament, April 1830*) D&C 20:76

**Joseph Smith**

The priest's duty is to preach, teach, expound, exhort, and baptize, and administer the sacrament, . . . (*Revelation on Church Organization and Government, April 1830*) D&C 20:46

---

**702. The Lord has established the words to be used for the blessing of the emblems of the sacrament.**

**Elder David O. McKay**

He has prescribed for us only a few set prayers, one of which is the blessing on the bread and water. CR1929Oct:11

**Elder George Albert Smith**

I admonish you, my brethren, that when we officiate in administering the sacrament, we repeat, if possible, the exact words given by revelation, and that we do so with the Spirit of the Lord. CR1908Apr:37

**Joseph Smith**

It is expedient that the church meet together often to partake of bread and wine in the remembrance of the Lord Jesus; 76. And the elder or priest shall administer it; and after this manner shall he administer it—he shall kneel with the church and call upon the Father in solemn prayer, saying: 77. O God, the Eternal Father, we ask thee in the name of thy Son, Jesus Christ, to bless and sanctify this bread to the souls of all those who partake of it, that they may eat in remembrance of the body of thy Son, and witness unto thee, O God, the Eternal Father, that they are willing to take upon them the name of thy Son, and always remember him and keep his commandments which he has given them; that they may always have his Spirit to be with them. Amen. 78. The manner of administering the wine—he shall take the cup also, and say: 79. O God, the Eternal Father, we ask thee in the name of thy Son, Jesus Christ, to bless and sanctify this wine to the souls of all those who drink of it, that they may do it in remembrance of the blood of thy Son, which was shed for them; that they may witness unto thee, O God, the Eternal Father, that they do always remember him, that they may have his Spirit to be with them. Amen. *(Revelation on Church Organization and Government, April 1830; sacramental prayers are given)* D&C 20:75-79

### Moroni, son of Mormon

The manner of their elders and priests administering the flesh and blood of Christ unto the church; and they administered it according to the commandments of Christ; wherefore we know the manner to be true; and the elder or priest did minister it— 2. And they did kneel down with the church, and pray to the Father in the name of Christ, saying: 3. O God, the Eternal Father, we ask thee in the name of thy Son, Jesus Christ, to bless and sanctify this bread to the souls of all those who partake of it; that they may eat in remembrance of the body of thy Son, and witness unto thee, O God, the Eternal Father, that they are willing to take upon them the name of thy Son, and always remember him, and keep his commandments which he hath given them, that they may always have his Spirit to be with them. Amen. *(Moroni records the prayer for the sacramental bread, A.D. 400-42)* Moro.4:1-3

### Moroni, son of Mormon

The manner of administering the wine— Behold, they took the cup, and said: 2. O God, the Eternal Father, we ask thee, in the name of thy Son, Jesus Christ, to bless and sanctify this wine to the souls of all those who drink of it, that they may do it in remembrance of the blood of thy Son, which was shed for them; that they may witness unto thee, O God, the Eternal Father, that they do always remember him, that they may have his Spirit to be with them. Amen. *(Moroni records the prayer for the sacramental wine, A.D. 400-42)* Moro.5:1-2

**Author's Note:** Aside from the temple ordinances, the Lord has designated only three set prayers which are to be repeated word for word: the sacrament prayer over the bread, the sacrament prayer over the water, and the baptismal prayer.

---

703. **The sacrament is for those who believe in Christ and have been baptized, namely, members of The Church of Jesus Christ of Latter-day Saints.**

### Elder Spencer W. Kimball

The sacrament is for the saints, for those who have actually made covenants at the waters of baptism. . . . ¶ If a person, not a member of the

Church, is in the congregation, we do not forbid him partaking of it, but would properly advise that the sacrament is for the renewing of covenants. And, since he has not made the true covenant of baptism or temple covenant, he is exempt. However, his partaking of the sacrament if he is clean and worthy and devout would not bring upon him any condemnation as it would for those who have made solemn covenants and then have ignored or defiled them. *(Letter, May 1963)* (The Teachings of Spencer W. Kimball, pp. 226-27) DGSM:55

### James E. Talmage

There is an absence of scriptural sanction for giving the sacrament to any who are not members in full fellowship in the Church of Jesus Christ. Christ administered the ordinance on the eastern continent to the apostles; and we have record of their giving it to those only who had assumed the name of Christ. Amongst His western fold, Christ established the law that only the actual members of His Church should partake. In promising to ordain one among them with power to officiate in the sacrament, the Savior specified that the one so chosen should give it unto the people of His Church, unto all those who believed and were baptized in His name. Only those who had been so baptized were called the Church of Christ. Continuing His instructions to the disciples concerning the sacrament, the Savior said: "This shall ye always do to those who repent and are baptized in my name." AF:158

### Jesus,
#### quoted by Mormon

And when they had eaten and were filled, he commanded that they should give unto the multitude. 5. And when the multitude had eaten and were filled, he said unto the disciples: Behold there shall one be ordained among you, and to him will I give power that he shall break bread and bless it and give it unto the people of my church, unto all those who shall believe and be baptized in my name. *(The resurrected Christ instructs the twelve disciples in observance of the sacrament, A.D. 34)* 3Ne.18:4-5

**Related Witnesses:**

### Elder Joseph Fielding Smith

Contrary to the expressed opinion of some who think that the partaking of the sacrament at such an early age "detracts from its meaning," we sincerely proclaim that the permitting of small children to partake when it is explained to them acts upon their minds exactly to the contrary. Perhaps some of us fail to comprehend the depth of a small child's mind. Surely little children in the Primary class can understand that the sacrament is a sacred ordinance when they are carefully taught. Then again we may say, even if they are too small to comprehend, the practice is teaching them that it is a sacred ordinance, and this will eventually bear fruit. It seems that a child in the kindergarten class is surely capable of realizing that the sacrament is a special privilege, having relationship to the sacrifice of our Redeemer on the cross. (Answers to Gospel Questions, 5:67) TLDP:588

---

704. Before partaking of the sacrament we are to examine ourselves to determine that we are worthy.

### Elder George Albert Smith

Before partaking of this sacrament, our hearts should be pure; our hands should be clean; we should be divested of all enmity toward our associates; we should be at peace with our fellow men; and we should have in our hearts a desire to do the will of our father and to keep all of His commandments. If we do this, partaking of the sacrament will be a blessing to us and will renew our spiritual strength. CR1908Apr:35

### Joseph Smith

How long do you suppose a man may partake of this ordinance unworthily, and the Lord not withdraw His Spirit from him? How long will he thus trifle with sacred things, and the Lord not give him over to the buffetings of Satan until the day of redemption! The Church should know if they are unworthy from time to time to partake, lest the servants of God be forbidden to administer it. Therefore our hearts ought to be humble, and we to repent of our sins, and put away evil from among us. (*Remarks to newly baptized members of the Church prior to their partaking of the sacrament*) HC2:204; DGSM:55

### Elder Spencer W. Kimball

And every time we take the bread and water, there should be a reconsecration, a rededication. When we are not living the commandments, when we are in transgression, when we have angers and hatreds and bitterness, we should consider seriously if we should take the sacrament. (*To seminary and institute teachers, 1962*) (The Teachings of Spencer W. Kimball, p. 225) TLDP:586

### Paul

Wherefore whosoever shall eat this bread, and drink this cup of the Lord, unworthily, shall be guilty of the body and blood of the Lord. 28. But let a man examine himself, and so let him eat of that bread, and drink of that cup. 29. For he that eateth and drinketh unworthily, eateth and drinketh damnation to himself, not discerning the Lord's body. 30. For this cause many are weak and sickly among you, and many sleep. (*Letter to the Church at Corinth, Greece, about A.D. 55*) 1Cor.11:27-30

### President Wilford Woodruff,
### *in behalf of the Council of the Apostles*

No man or woman should eat the bread and drink of the cup at the Sacrament who entertains hard feelings against any of his or her brethren and sisters. They should be taught the importance of settling all their difficulties and removing all causes of ill-feeling, so that no condemnation will rest upon them for partaking of this holy ordinance unworthily. By paying strict attention to this, the Wards will be kept in a healthy condition, the Spirit of the Lord will flow freely to the people, and the blessings of heaven will be upon them. (*Letter to the presidency of the St. George Utah Stake, April 1888*) MOFP3:164; TLDP:587

### Francis M. Lyman

It is not pleasing in the sight of the Lord, for us to partake of the sacrament if there be hard feelings in our hearts, if there be jealousness, if there be enmity or strife, if we are not in fellowship with the Church, if we are not keeping the commandments of the Lord, if we are not living in peace, if we are not obedient to the counsels of heaven; I say that it is not pleasing in the sight of the Lord to partake of the sacrament under such circumstances. (*In Assembly Hall, Feb. 24, 1884, JD25:61*) TLDP:587

**Related Witnesses:**

### Elder Spencer W. Kimball

However, his [a non-member's] partaking of the sacrament if he is clean and worthy and devout would not bring upon him any condemnation as it would for those who have made solemn covenants and then have ignored or defiled them. (*Letter, May 1963*) (The Teachings of Spencer W. Kimball, p. 227) DGSM:55

---

705. Although unworthy persons should not take the sacrament, they are not to be removed from Church services, rather they are to be loved and cared for.

### James E. Talmage

The direct word of the Lord unto the saints in this dispensation instructs them to permit no one in transgression to partake of the sacrament until reconciliation has been made; nevertheless the saints are commanded to exercise abundant charity toward their erring fellows, not casting them out from the assemblies yet withholding the sacrament from them. ¶ In our system of Church organization the local ecclesiastical officers are charged with the responsibility of administering the sacrament, and the people are required to keep themselves worthy to partake of the sacred emblems. AF:157-58

**Joseph Smith**

Ye are also commanded not to cast any one who belongeth to the church out of your sacrament meetings; nevertheless, if any have trespassed, let him not partake until he makes reconciliation. (*Revelation relative to governing and conducting meetings, March 8, 1831*) D&C 46:4

**Jesus,**
*quoted by Mormon*

And now behold, this is the commandment which I give unto you, that ye shall not suffer any one knowingly to partake of my flesh and blood unworthily, when ye shall minister it; 29. For whoso eateth and drinketh my flesh and blood unworthily eateth and drinketh damnation to his soul; therefore if ye know that a man is unworthy to eat and drink of my flesh and blood ye shall forbid him. 30. Nevertheless, ye shall not cast him out from among you, but ye shall minister unto him and shall pray for him unto the Father, in my name; and if it so be that he repenteth and is baptized in my name, then shall ye receive him, and shall minister unto him of my flesh and blood. (*The resurrected Christ instructs his twelve disciples in observance of the sacrament, A.D. 34*) 3Ne.18:28-30

**Related Witnesses:**

**Elder Spencer W. Kimball**

The sacrament is for the saints, for those who have actually made covenants at the waters of baptism. . . . ¶ If a person, not a member of the Church, is in the congregation, we do not forbid him partaking of it, but would properly advise that the sacrament is for the renewing of covenants. And, since he has not made the true covenant of baptism or temple covenant, he is exempt. However, his partaking of the sacrament if he is clean and worthy and devout would not bring upon him any condemnation as it would for those who have made solemn covenants and then have ignored or defiled them. (*Letter, May 1963*) (The Teachings of Spencer W. Kimball, pp. 226-27) DGSM:55

**HYMNS Written by Prophets Applicable to this Topic**

**Parley P. Pratt**
*Father in Heaven, We Do Believe*
HYMNS:180

Father in Heav'n, we do believe
The promise thou hast made;
Thy word with meekness we receive,
Just as thy Saints have said.

We now repent of all our sin
And come with broken heart,
And to thy covenant enter in
And choose the better part.

O Lord, accept us while we pray,
And all our sins forgive;
New life impart to us this day,
And bid the sinners live.

Humbly we take the sacrament
In Jesus' blessed name;
Let us receive thru covenant
The Spirit's heav'nly flame.

We will be buried in the stream
In Jesus' blessed name,
And rise, while light shall on us beam
The Spirit's heav'nly flame.

Baptize us with the Holy Ghost
And seal us as thine own,
That we may join the ransomed host
And with the Saints be one.

# List of Doctrines

## SANCTIFICATION
### Perfection

*Doctrines Located in This Topic*

706. Sanctification is a process whereby we eventually become pure and spotless before God.

707. Christ would have us be perfect, even as He is perfect.

708. If we sanctify ourselves so our minds become single to God and His glory, we may one day see the face of the Lord (for some, this may occur in mortal life).

709. He who faithfully magnifies his calling in the priesthood will be sanctified by the Spirit and receive the fulness of the Father's kingdom; he will receive all the Father has.

710. A sanctified person cannot look upon sin without abhorrence.

711. Even those who are sanctified may fall from grace, for all of us must endure in faith to the end or we cannot be saved in the kingdom of God.

*Doctrines on SANCTIFICATION Located in Other Topics*

5. Suffering can refine, purify, and perfect our nature.

86. One of the (three-fold) missions of the Church is to perfect the Saints.

133. The Saints in the latter days cannot be made perfect without doing the ordinance work for their dead, nor can the dead be made perfect without this work being done for them.

321. Receiving the Holy Ghost is a "baptism of fire" (it has a sanctifying, purifying effect on the person who has been baptized by water).

393. Being born again (being quickened by the Spirit and receiving a change of heart after baptism by water and receiving the gift of the Holy Ghost) justifies a person before the Lord and starts that person toward sanctification.

# SANCTIFICATION
## Perfection

**706. Sanctification is a process whereby we eventually become pure and spotless before God.**

### Bruce R. McConkie
Those who go to the celestial kingdom of heaven have to be sanctified, meaning that they become clean and pure and spotless. They've had evil and sin and iniquity burned out of their souls as though by fire, and the figurative expression there is "the baptism of fire." Here again it is a *process*. Nobody is sanctified in an instant, suddenly. But if we keep the commandments and press forward with steadfastness after baptism then degree by degree and step by step we sanctify our souls until that glorious day when we're qualified to go where God and angels are. ("Jesus Christ and Him Crucified," Brigham Young University Speeches of the Year, 1976, p. 399) TLDP:605

### President Brigham Young
I will put my own definition to the term sanctification, and say it consists in overcoming every sin and bringing all into subjection to the law of Christ. God has placed in us a pure spirit; when this reigns predominant, without let or hindrance, and triumphs over the flesh and rules and governs and controls as the Lord controls the heavens and the earth, this I call the blessing of sanctification. Will sin be perfectly destroyed? No, it will not, for it is not so designed in the economy of Heaven. . . . ¶ Do not suppose that we shall ever in the flesh be free from temptations to sin. Some suppose that they can in the flesh be sanctified body and spirit and become so pure that they will never again feel the effects of the power of the adversary of truth. Were it possible for a person to attain to this degree of perfection in the flesh, he could not die, neither remain in a world where sin predominates. Sin has entered into the world, and death by sin. (*In Tabernacle, May 1863*) TLDP:604; MPSG1985:205 (in part)

### Moroni, son of Mormon
Yea, come unto Christ, and be perfected in him, and deny yourselves of all ungodliness; and if ye shall deny yourselves of all ungodliness, and love God with all your might, mind and strength, then is his grace sufficient for you, that by his grace ye may be perfect in Christ; and if by the grace of God ye are perfect in Christ, ye can in nowise deny the power of God. 33. And again, if ye by the grace of God are perfect in Christ, and deny not his power, then are ye sanctified in Christ by the grace of God, through the shedding of the blood of Christ, which is in the covenant of the Father unto the remission of your sins, that ye become holy, without spot. (*Moroni's final writings, about A.D. 421*) Moro.10:32-33

**Related Witnesses:**
### Bruce R. McConkie
To be sanctified is to be cleansed from all sin; it is to stand pure and spotless before the Lord; it is to overcome the world and be a fit candidate for a celestial inheritance. The "sanctified" are "them of the celestial world." (D&C 88:2) The Holy Ghost is a sanctifier. His baptism of fire burns dross and evil out of repentant souls as though by fire. Sanctification comes only to the obedient; it is the truth of heaven—the very word of God, his everlasting gospel—which sanctifies the souls of men. (The Mortal Messiah, 4:114) TLDP:605

### Jesus,
*quoted by Mormon*
And no unclean thing can enter into his kingdom; therefore nothing entereth into his rest save it be those who have washed their garments in my blood, because of their faith, and the repentance of all their sins, and their faithfulness unto the end. 20. Now this is the commandment: Repent, all ye ends of the earth, and come unto me and be baptized in my name, that ye may be sanctified by the reception of the Holy Ghost, that ye may stand spotless before me at the last day. (*The resurrected Jesus Christ instructs his twelve Nephite disciples, A.D. 34*) 3Ne.27:19-20

### Delbert L. Stapley,
*also quoting Mormon*
"Nevertheless they did fast and pray oft, and did wax stronger and stronger in their humility, and firmer and firmer in the faith of Christ unto the filling their souls with joy and consolation, yea, even to the purifying and the sanctification of their hearts, which sanctification cometh because of their yielding their hearts unto God." (Hel.3:35) ¶ My brothers and sisters, if we fast and pray often I am sure that we, too, can wax stronger and stronger in our faith and in our humility, that our hearts will be filled with joy and consolation; that we will also purify and sanctify our hearts, which sanctification will come because we do yield our hearts unto God. CR1951Oct:126

### Hugh B. Brown
Nothing but the gospel of love, the restored gospel of Jesus Christ, which we gratefully proclaim, can save the world or the individual from

the dangers that threaten us. This is a gospel of character-building activity, of invincible faith and the courage that is born of faith; of repentance, the doorway to progress; of sanctification through baptism of water and of the Spirit, the doorway, to the celestial kingdom. CR1963Apr:8

### Paul

Know ye not that the unrighteous shall not inherit the kingdom of God? Be not deceived: neither fornicators, nor idolaters, nor adulterers, nor effeminate, nor abusers of themselves with mankind, 10. Nor thieves, nor covetous, nor drunkards, nor revilers, nor extortioners, shall inherit the kingdom of God. 11. And such were some of you: but ye are washed, but ye are sanctified, but ye are justified in the name of the Lord Jesus, and by the Spirit of our God. *(Letter to the Church at Corinth, Greece, about A.D. 55)* 1Cor.6:9-11

### Alma, the younger,
*quoted by Mormon*

Now they, after being sanctified by the Holy Ghost, having their garments made white; being pure and spotless before God, could not look upon sin save it were with abhorrence; and there were many, exceedingly great many, who were made pure and entered into the rest of the Lord their God. *(Alma instructs the people that high priests were ordained because of righteousness, about 82 B.C.)* Alma 13:12

### President Brigham Young

When the will, passions, and feelings of a person are perfectly submissive to God and His requirements, that person is sanctified. It is for my will to be swallowed up in the will of God, that will lead me into all good, and crown me ultimately with immortality and eternal lives. *(In Tabernacle, April 1853, JD2:123)* DGSM:50

### Enoch,
*quoted by Joseph Smith,*
*translating the Book of Moses*

That by reason of transgression cometh the fall, which fall bringeth death, and inasmuch as ye were born into the world by water, and blood, and the spirit, which I have made, and so became of dust a living soul, even so ye must be born again into the kingdom of heaven, of water, and of the Spirit, and be cleansed by blood, even the blood of mine Only Begotten; that ye might be sanctified from all sin, and enjoy the words of eternal life in this world, and eternal life in the world to come, even immortal glory; 60. For by the water ye keep the commandment; by the Spirit ye are justified, and by the blood ye are sanctified; *(The record of Moses: Enoch testifies to the people)* Moses 6:59-60

### Joseph Smith

And we know also, that sanctification through the grace of our Lord and Savior Jesus Christ is just and true, to all those who love and serve God with all their mights, minds, and strength. *(Revelation on Church Organization and Government, April 1830; laws governing repentance, justification, sanctification, and baptism are set forth)* D&C 20:31

### Mormon

Nevertheless they did fast and pray oft, and did wax stronger and stronger in their humility and firmer and firmer in the faith of Christ, unto the filling their souls with joy and consolation, yea, even to the purifying and the sanctification of their hearts, which sanctification cometh because of their yielding their hearts unto God. *(The more humble part of the Nephite Church members suffer persecutions, 41 B.C.)* Hel.3:35

**Author's Note:** Doctrine D-706 states "Sanctification is a *process* whereby we eventually become pure and spotless before God." The "elect" are chosen and called elect because they merit the appellation, and yet not quite because of merit, but because they have gone through a *process*, have *become* godlike, have *become* elect spirits. The elect are not "rewarded" for good works, but they have become elect because they have *developed* into godlike spirits. There is no selection on any other basis than *change of character.* There are no arbitrary placements, no selections because of rank or family or worldly nobility or talent. God is no respecter of persons, choosing one over the other without worthiness: "Because their hearts are set so much upon the things of this world, and aspire to the honors of men, that they do not learn this one lesson— ¶ "That the rights of the priesthood are inseparably connected with the powers of heaven, and that the powers of heaven cannot be controlled nor handled only upon the principles of righteousness. ¶ "That they may be conferred upon us, it is true; but when we undertake to cover our sins, or to gratify our pride, our vain ambition, or to exercise control or dominion or compulsion upon the souls of the children of men, in any degree of unrighteousness, behold, the heavens withdraw themselves; the Spirit of the Lord is grieved; and when it is withdrawn, Amen to the priesthood or the authority of that man." (D&C 121:35-37)

---

707. Christ would have us be perfect, even as He is perfect.

### Moroni, son of Mormon

Yea, come unto Christ, and be perfected in him, and deny yourselves of all ungodliness; and if ye shall deny yourselves of all ungodliness, and love God with all your might, mind and strength, then is his grace sufficient for you, that by his grace ye may be perfect in Christ; and if by the grace of God ye are perfect in Christ, ye can in nowise deny the power of God. 33. And again, if ye by the grace of God are perfect in Christ, and deny not his power, then are ye sanctified in Christ by the grace of God, through the shedding of the blood of Christ, which is in the covenant of the Father unto the remission of your sins, that ye become holy, without spot. (*Moroni's final writings, about A.D. 421*) Moro.10:32-33

### Jesus,
#### *quoted by Mormon*

Therefore, what manner of men ought ye to be? Verily I say unto you, even as I am. (*The resurrected Jesus Christ teaches the Nephites, A.D. 34*) 3Ne.27:27

### Jesus,
#### *quoted by Mormon*

Therefore I would that ye should be perfect even as I, or your Father who is in heaven is perfect. (*The resurrected Jesus Christ teaches the Nephite people, A.D. 34*) 3Ne.12:48

### Jesus,
#### *recorded in Matthew*

Be ye therefore perfect, even as your Father which is in heaven is perfect. (*Jesus Christ teaches the multitude near Jerusalem, about A.D. 30*) Matt.5:48

### Jesus,
#### *quoted by Joseph Smith, translating Matthew*

Ye are therefore commanded to be perfect. . . . (*Jesus teaches the multitude to love their enemies*) JST(Matt.5:48 fn. a)

**Related Witnesses:**

### President Spencer W. Kimball

Each one of you has it within the realm of his possibility to develop a kingdom over which you will preside as its king and God. You will need to develop yourself and grow in ability and power and worthiness, to govern such a world with all of its people. You are sent to this earth not merely to have a good time or to satisfy urges or passions or desires. You are sent to this earth, not to ride merry-go-rounds, airplanes, automobiles, and have what the world calls "fun." ¶ You are sent to this world with a very serious purpose. You are sent to school, for that matter, to begin as a human infant and grow to unbelievable proportions in wisdom,

judgment, knowledge, and power, that is why you and I cannot be satisfied with saying merely "I like that or want that." That is why in our childhood and our youth and our young adulthood we must stretch and grow and remember and prepare for the later life when limitations will terminate so that we can go on and on and on. (*To University of Utah Institute of Religion students, Oct. 1976*) DGSM:29

---

708. **If we sanctify ourselves so our minds become single to God and His glory, we may one day see the face of the Lord (for some, this may occur in mortal life).**

### Joseph Smith,
#### *receiving the Word of the Lord*

And if your eye be single to my glory, your whole bodies shall be filled with light, and there shall be no darkness in you; and that body which is filled with light comprehendeth all things. 68. Therefore, sanctify yourselves that your minds become single to God, and the days will come that you shall see him; for he will unveil his face unto you, and it shall be in his own time, and in his own way, and according to his own will. (*Revelation, Dec. 27/28, 1832*) D&C 88:67-68

### Mark E. Petersen

Through righteous living we invite the Holy Spirit in, and when it enters our bodies it sanctifies them with a holy influence and prepares us for the spiritual blessings which may be enjoyed by the faithful. ¶ The principle of sanctification is one with which many Latter-day Saints are unfamiliar, yet one which everyone should study, for the Lord commands us to sanctify ourselves "that your minds become single to God, and the days will come that you shall see him, for he will unveil his face unto you, and it shall be in his own time and according to his own will." (D&C 88:68) ¶ On the day the Church was organized the Lord told the Prophet Joseph Smith that "sanctification through the grace of our Lord and Savior Jesus Christ is just and true, to all those who love and serve God with all their mights, minds and strength." (D&C 20:31) ¶ But unless our bodies are clean and ready for the Holy Spirit to enter, it cannot sanctify them, and without sanctification, can we be admitted to His presence? (Why the Religious Life? pp. 252-53) TLDP:605

### Joseph Smith,
#### *receiving the Word of the Lord*

Verily thus saith the Lord: It shall come to pass that every soul who forsaketh his sins and cometh unto me, and calleth on my name, and obeyeth my voice, and keepeth my commandments, shall see my face and know that I am; (*Revelation at Kirtland, Ohio, May 6, 1833*) D&C 93:1

### Joseph Smith,
### *receiving the Word of the Lord*

And again, verily I say unto you that it is your privilege, and a promise I give unto you that have been ordained unto this ministry, that inasmuch as you strip yourselves from jealousies and fears, and humble yourselves before me, for ye are not sufficiently humble, the veil shall be rent and you shall see me and know that I am—not with the carnal neither natural mind, but with the spiritual. 11. For no man has seen God at any time in the flesh, except quickened by the Spirit of God. (*Revelation, Nov. 1831*) D&C 67:10-11

### Joseph Smith

Let us here observe, that after any portion of the human family are made acquainted with the important fact that there is a God, who has created and does uphold all things, the extent of their knowledge respecting his character and glory will depend upon their diligence and faithfulness in seeking after him, until, like Enoch, the brother of Jared, and Moses, they shall obtain faith in God, and power with him to behold him face to face. (*Lectures on Faith delivered to the School of the Prophets, 1834-35*) LOF2:55

### Recorded in Job

For I know that my redeemer liveth, and that he shall stand at the latter day upon the earth: 26. And though after my skin worms destroy this body, yet in my flesh shall I see God: 27. Whom I shall see for myself, and mine eyes shall behold, and not another; though my reins be consumed within me. (*Job prophecies of his own resurrection and exaltation*) Job 19:25-27

### Related Witnesses:
### George F. Richards

The Lord has revealed to me, by dreams, something more than I have ever understood or felt before about the love for God and the love for fellow men. I believe in dreams. The Lord has given me dreams, which to me, are just as real and as much from God as was the dream of King Nebuchadnezzar which was the means of saving a nation from starvation, or the dream of Lehi who through a dream led his colony out of the old country, across the mighty deep to this promised land, or any other dreams that we read of in the scripture. ¶ It is not out of place for us to have important dreams, for we read in the scriptures: "And it shall come to pass in the last days, saith God, I will pour out of my Spirit upon all flesh: and your sons and your daughters shall prophesy, and your young men shall see visions, and your old men shall dream dreams." (Acts 2:17) ¶ More than forty years ago I had a dream, which I am sure was from the Lord. In this dream I was in the presence of the Savior as he stood in mid-air. He spoke no word to me, but my love for him was such that I have not words to explain. I know that no mortal man can love the Lord as I experienced that love for the Savior unless God reveals it unto him. I would have remained in his presence, but there was a power drawing me away from him, and as a result of that dream I had this feeling, that no matter what might be required at my hands, what the gospel might entail unto me, I would do what I should be asked to do, even to the laying down of my life. CR1946Oct:139

### Melvin J. Ballard

I know, as well as I know that I live and look into your faces, that Jesus Christ lives, and he is the Redeemer of the world, that he arose from the dead with a tangible body, and still has that real body which Thomas touched when he thrust his hands into his side and felt that wound of the spear, and also the prints of the nails in his hands. I know by the witness and the revelations of God to me that Thomas told the truth. I know by witness that Joseph Smith told the truth, for mine eyes have seen. For in the visions of the Lord to my soul, I have seen Christ's face, I have heard his voice. I know that he lives, that he is the Redeemer of the World, and that as he arose from the dead, a tangible and real individual, so shall all men arise in the resurrection from the dead. CR1920Apr:40-41

### Nephi, son of Lehi

And now I, Nephi, write more of the words of Isaiah, for my soul delighteth in his words. For I will liken his words unto my people, and I will send them forth unto all my children, for he verily saw my Redeemer, even as I have seen him. 3. And my brother, Jacob, also has seen him as I have seen him; wherefore, I will send their words forth unto my children to prove unto them that my words are true. Wherefore, by the words of three, God hath said, I will establish my word. Nevertheless, God sendeth more witnesses, and he proveth all his words. (*Nephi testifies that he and his brother Jacob have each seen the Redeemer, 559-545 B.C.*) 2Ne.11:2-3

### Joseph Smith

Therefore, in the ordinances thereof, the power of godliness is manifest. 21. And without the ordinances thereof, and the authority of the priesthood, the power of godliness is not manifest unto men in the flesh; 22. For without this no man can see the face of God, even the Father, and live. 23. Now this Moses plainly taught to the children of Israel in the wilderness, and sought diligently to sanctify his people that they might behold the face of God; 24. But they hardened their hearts and could not endure his presence; therefore, the Lord in his wrath, for his anger was kindled against them, swore that they should not enter into his rest while in the wilderness, which rest is the fulness of his glory. (*Revelation on priesthood received with six elders, Sept. 22/23, 1832*) D&C 84:20-24

**Author's Note:** There are several well known reports of individuals who have seen the Lord in visions or dreams. (There is no doubt in my mind but what there are many, many more instances that have not been publicly disclosed, due to the sacred nature of the experience.) Here are some examples of known reports: ¶ In the course of a temple meeting of the First Presidency and the Council of the Twelve, January 7, 1919, Melvin J. Ballard related the following: "I remember one testimony, among the many testimonies which I have received. You will pardon me for referring to it. Two years ago about this time, I had been on the Fort Peck Reservation for several days with the brethren, solving the problems connected with our work among the Lamanites. There was no precedent for us to follow, and we just had to go to the Lord and tell Him our troubles, and get inspiration and help from Him. On this occasion I had sought the Lord, under such circumstances, and that night I received a wonderful manifestation and impression which has never left me. I was carried to this place—into this room. I saw myself here with you. I was told there was another privilege that was to be mine; and I was led into a room where I saw, seated on a raised platform, the most glorious being I have ever conceived of, and was taken forward to be introduced to Him. As I approached He smiled, called my name, and stretched out His hands toward me. If I live to be a million years old I shall never forget that smile. He put His arms around me and kissed me, as He took me into His bosom, and He blessed me until my whole being was thrilled. As He finished I fell at His feet, and there saw the marks of the nails; and as I kissed them, with deep joy swelling through my whole being, I felt that I was in heaven indeed. The

feeling that came to my heart then was: Oh! if I could live worthy, though it would require fourscore years, so that in the end when I have finished I could go into His presence and receive the feeling that I then had in His presence, I would give everything that I am and ever hope to be!" (*Melvin J. Ballard, Crusader for Righteousness, p. 66; also, Marion G. Romney: His Life and Faith, p. 64*) ¶ George Q. Cannon recorded the following: "I know that God lives, I know that Jesus lives; for I have seen Him." (*Deseret Weekly, Oct. 6, 1896*) ¶ George F. Richards reported in a General Conference: ". . . I had a dream, which I am sure was from the Lord. In this dream I was in the presence of the Savior as he stood in mid-air. He spoke no word to me, but my love for him was such that I have not words to explain. I know that no mortal man can love the Lord as I experienced that love for the Savior, unless God reveals it unto him. . . . [A]s a result of that dream I had this feeling, that no matter what the gospel might entail unto me, I would do what I should be asked to do, even to the laying down of my life." (CR1946Oct:139) ¶ According to the record of Nephi, he and his brother Jacob saw the Lord, and the prophet Isaiah as well: "for he [Isaiah] verily saw my Redeemer, even as I have seen him. And my brother, Jacob, also has seen him as I have seen him; . . ." (2Ne.11:2-3)

---

**709.** He who faithfully magnifies his calling in the priesthood will be sanctified by the Spirit and receive the fulness of the Father's kingdom; he will receive all the Father has.

### Elder Joseph Fielding Smith
Every man who is ordained to an office in the Melchizedek Priesthood should realize fully just what that ordination means. He receives the Priesthood with an oath and covenant that he will magnify his calling and be faithful therein. This oath and covenant when received in the fullness will entitle a man to become a member of the Church of the Firstborn, and the elect of God. He receives the fullness of the Father's kingdom and is entitled, if faithful to the end, "to all that the Father hath." This oath and covenant cannot be treated lightly, and if broken and altogether turned from, the man thus guilty has no forgiveness, that is to say, he will not again have these privileges granted to him which bring exaltation, or "all that the Father hath." He will stand aside without these

blessings, but does not become a son of perdition because of this serious offense. The oath and covenant belonging to the Priesthood, pertains to the Melchizedek Priesthood and not to the Aaronic, although it is also a serious matter to turn away or violate that blessing. CHMR1:339

### President Joseph Fielding Smith

And so Christ is the great prototype where priesthood is concerned, as he is with reference to baptism and all other things. And so, even as the Father swears with an oath that his Son shall inherit all things through the priesthood, so he swears with an oath that all of us who magnify our callings in that same priesthood shall receive all that the Father hath. CR1970Oct:92

### Joseph Smith,
### *receiving the Word of the Lord*

For whoso is faithful unto the obtaining these two priesthoods of which I have spoken, and the magnifying their calling, are sanctified by the Spirit unto the renewing of their bodies. 34. They become the sons of Moses and of Aaron and the seed of Abraham, and the church and kingdom, and the elect of God. 35. And also all they who receive this priesthood receive me, saith the Lord; 36. For he that receiveth my servants receiveth me; 37. And he that receiveth me receiveth my Father; 38. And he that receiveth my Father receiveth my Father's kingdom; therefore all that my Father hath shall be given unto him. (*Revelation on priesthood, Sept. 22/23, 1832*) D&C 84:33-38

### Joseph Smith

They are they into whose hands the Father has given all things— 56. They are they who are priests and kings, who have received of his fulness, and of his glory; 57. And are priests of the Most High, after the order of Melchizedek, which was after the order of Enoch, which was after the order of the Only Begotten Son. 58. Wherefore, as it is written, they are gods, even the sons of God— 59. Wherefore, all things are theirs, whether life or death, or things present, or things to come, all are theirs and they are Christ's, and Christ is God's. 60. And they shall overcome all things. (*Vision to Joseph and Sidney Rigdon, Feb. 16, 1832*) D&C 76:55-60

### Joseph Smith

He that is ordained of God and sent forth, the same is appointed to be the greatest, notwithstanding he is the least and the servant of all. 27. Wherefore, he is possessor of all things; for all things are subject unto him, both in heaven and on the earth, the life and the light, the Spirit and the power, sent forth by the will of the Father

through Jesus Christ, his Son. 28. But no man is possessor of all things except he be purified and cleansed from all sin. (*Revelation for the elders of the Church, May 1831*) D&C 50:26-28

### Bruce R. McConkie

The covenant which a man makes when he receives an office in the Melchizedek Priesthood is threefold: ¶ 1. That he will receive and make a part of his life and being the Holy Priesthood and that he will honor it as the holy power and authority which it is; ¶ 2. That he will magnify his calling in the priesthood; that is, that he will minister in the duties of the office, that he will do the work assigned; and ¶ 3. That he will live by every word that proceedeth forth from the mouth of God; that is to say, he will keep the commandments and work righteousness. ¶ The covenant which God makes is that he on his part will give the faithful all that his Father hath. In other words, he will give eternal life to those who keep their priesthood covenants. ¶ Now we have mentioned both an oath and a covenant where the Melchizedek Priesthood is concerned. The oath is the solemn promise of the Lord that all those who keep the priesthood covenant shall gain exaltation. That is to say, the Lord swears with an oath that his adopted and obedient sons shall be high priests forever after the order of Melchizedek (see D&C 76:57); they shall be joint heirs with his natural Son, who is Christ our Lord. ACR(Lima)1977:18

### Related Witnesses:
### President Spencer W. Kimball

[T]he highest achievement of spirituality comes as we conquer the flesh. We build character as we encourage people to care for their own needs. ¶ As givers gain control of their desires and properly see other needs in light of their own wants, then the powers of the gospel are released in their lives. They learn that by living the great law of consecration they insure not only temporal salvation, but also spiritual sanctification. CR1977Oct:123

### Joseph Smith

And we ask thee, Holy Father, that thy servants may go forth from this house armed with thy power, and that thy name may be upon them, and thy glory be round about them, and thine angels have charge over them; (*Prayer given to Joseph Smith by revelation to be offered at dedication of Kirtland Temple, March 27, 1836*) D&C 109:22

### Marion G. Romney

[A] priesthood bearer with serious intentions of so magnifying his calling as to merit the blessing of the "covenant which belongeth to the priesthood" should be conversant with all the instructions given to guide us in our personal conduct—both those recorded in the scriptures and those being received currently by the living prophets. One can scarcely hope to be fortified "against the wiles of the devil" by putting "on the whole armor of God" (see Eph.6:11) unless he knows what that armor is. CR1980Oct:65-66

### Marion G. Romney

Ordination to the priesthood is a prerequisite to receiving [blessings], but does not guarantee them. For a man actually to obtain them, he must faithfully discharge the obligation which is placed upon him when he receives the priesthood; that is, he must magnify his calling. CR1962Apr:17; MPSG1988:31

### Joseph Smith

And unto him that repenteth and sanctifieth himself before the Lord shall be given eternal life. (*Revelation received Nov. 3, 1831*) D&C 133:62

### Joseph Smith,
*receiving the Word of the Lord*

And they who are not sanctified through the law which I have given unto you, even the law of Christ, must inherit another kingdom, even that of a terrestrial kingdom, or that of a telestial kingdom. (*Revelation, Dec. 27/28, 1832; obedience to celestial, terrestrial, or telestial law prepares men for those respective kingdoms and glories*) D&C 88:21

**Author's Note:** Magnify refers to what we do with our calling. Delbert L. Stapley amplified on this: "Sometimes we hear brethren refer to 'magnifying the priesthood.' While many of us are guilty of making this erroneous statement, it isn't the priesthood we magnify; it is one's office and calling in the priesthood. It [the priesthood] cannot be enlarged upon because there is no authority or power greater in the universe." (*Conference report, Mexico and Central America area conference, 1972, p. 64*)

---

### 710. A sanctified person cannot look upon sin without abhorrence.

### Alma, the younger,
*quoted by Mormon*

Therefore they were called after this holy order, and were sanctified, and their garments were washed white through the blood of the Lamb. 12. Now they, after being sanctified by the Holy Ghost, having their garments made white, being pure and spotless before God, could not look upon sin save it were with abhorrence; and

there were many, exceedingly great many, who were made pure and entered into the rest of the Lord their God. 13. And now, my brethren, I would that ye should humble yourselves before God, and bring forth fruit meet for repentance, that ye may also enter into that rest. (*Alma instructs the people that high priests were called on account of righteousness, about 82 B.C.*) Alma 13:11-13

### Delbert L. Stapley

Man can only become spotless and sanctified by the reception of the Holy Ghost in his personal life. The Holy Ghost is a cleansing and purifying agent to all who receive it and are righteous. This means that sin and iniquity are spiritually burned out of the repentant person. He then receives a remission of sins, and his soul is sanctified and made clean for the Holy Ghost to abide in him. The cleansed person enjoys a newness of life and becomes a new creature in the spirit. CR1966Oct:112

**Related Witnesses:**

### President Brigham Young

When through the Gospel the Spirit in man has so subdued the flesh that he can live without wilful transgression, the Spirit of God unites with his spirit, they become congenial companions, and the mind and will of the Creator is thus transmitted to the creature. (*In Tabernacle, Feb. 1862, JD9:288*) MPSG1985:205

### Mormon

And they did look upon shedding the blood of their brethren with the greatest abhorrence; and they never could be prevailed upon to take up arms against their brethren; and they never did look upon death with any degree of terror, for their hope and views of Christ and the resurrection; therefore, death was swallowed up to them by the victory of Christ over it. 29. Therefore, they would suffer death in the most aggravating and distressing manner which could be inflicted by their brethren, before they would take the sword or cimeter to smite them. 30. And thus they were a zealous and beloved people, a highly favored people of the Lord. (*Honest, zealous members of the Church choose death at the hands of their enemies rather than taking the sword against them*) Alma 27:28-30

### Joseph Smith

We consider that God has created man with a mind capable of instruction, and a faculty which may be enlarged in proportion to the heed and diligence given to the light communicated from heaven to the intellect; and that the nearer man approaches perfection, the clearer are his views, and the greater his enjoyments, till he has overcome the evils of his life and lost every desire for sin; and like the ancients, arrives at that point of faith where he is wrapped in the power and glory of his Maker and is caught up to dwell with Him. (*Excerpt from a letter from the First Presidency in Kirtland, Ohio, to the brethren scattered abroad, Jan. 22, 1834*) TPJS:51

### Recorded in Psalms
I rejoice at thy word, as one that findeth great spoil. 163. I hate and abhor lying: but thy law do I love. 164. Seven times a day do I praise thee because of thy righteous judgments. 165. Great peace have they which love thy law: and nothing shall offend them. 166. LORD, I have hoped for thy salvation, and done thy commandments. 167. My soul hath kept thy testimonies; and I love them exceedingly. 168. I have kept thy precepts and thy testimonies: for all my ways are before thee. Ps.119:162-68

### Habakkuk
Thou art of purer eyes than to behold evil, and canst not look on iniquity. . . . (*The prophet Habakkuk addresses the Lord, about 600 B.C.*) Hab.1:13

### Joseph Smith,
### *receiving the Word of the Lord*
For I the Lord cannot look upon sin with the least degree of allowance; (*Revelation received during conference of elders of the Church, Nov. 1, 1831*) D&C 1:31

### Alma, the younger,
### *quoted by Mormon*
[F]or the Lord cannot look upon sin with the least degree of allowance. (*Alma blesses the earth for the sake of the righteous, 73 B.C.*) Alma 45:16

### Jacob, brother of Nephi,
### *quoted by Nephi*
Behold, my soul abhorreth sin, and my heart delighteth in righteousness; and I will praise the holy name of my God. (*Jacob teaches the people of Nephi, 559-545 B.C.*) 2Ne.9:49

### Jacob, brother of Nephi
But behold, hearken ye unto me, and know that by the help of the all-powerful Creator of heaven and earth I can tell you concerning your thoughts, how that ye are beginning to labor in sin, which sin appeareth very abominable unto me, yea, and abominable unto God. (*Jacob teaches the Nephites in the temple, 544-421 B.C.*) Jacob 2:5

---

711. **Even those who are sanctified may fall from grace, for all of us must endure in faith to the end or we cannot be saved in the kingdom of God.**

### Joseph Smith
The doctrine that the Presbyterians and Methodists have quarreled so much about— once in grace, always in grace, or falling away from grace, I will say a word about. They are both wrong. Truth takes a road between them both, for while the Presbyterian says "once in grace, you cannot fall;" the Methodist says: "You can have grace today, fall from it tomorrow, next day have grace again; and so follow on, changing continually." But the doctrine of the Scriptures and the spirit of Elijah would show them both false, and take a road between them both; for, according to the Scripture, if men have received the good word of God, and tasted of the powers of the world to come, if they shall fall away, it is impossible to renew them again, seeing they have crucified the Son of God afresh, and put Him to an open shame; so there is a possibility of falling away; you could not be renewed again, and the power of Elijah cannot seal against this sin, for this is a reserve made in the seals and power of the Priesthood. (*At the Stand in Nauvoo, Ill., Sunday, March 10, 1844*) HC6:252-53

### Joseph Smith
And we know that all men must repent and believe on the name of Jesus Christ, and worship the Father in his name, and endure in faith on his name to the end, or they cannot be saved in the kingdom of God. . . . 32. But there is a possibility that man may fall from grace and depart from the living God; 33. Therefore let the church take heed and pray always, lest they fall into temptation; 34. Yea, and even let those who are sanctified take heed also. (*Revelation on Church Organization and Government, April 1830*) D&C 20:29,32-34

### Elder Joseph Fielding Smith
If a person violates a covenant, whether it be of baptism, ordination, marriage or anything else, the Spirit withdraws the stamp of approval, and the blessings will not be received. Every ordinance is sealed with a promise of reward based upon faithfulness. The Holy Spirit withdraws the stamp of approval where covenants are broken. (Doctrines of Salvation, 1:45) MPSG1985:204

### Elder Joseph Fielding Smith
Sanctification is also true. Through the praise of the Father, we may be sanctified from all sin through acceptance of the Gospel and compliance with all the ordinances. We are told that those "who overcome by faith, and are sealed by the Holy Spirit of promise, which the father sheds forth upon all those who are just and true" will be entitled to become sons of God. (See D&C 76:53-54 and Moses 7:57-60) The

Lord has said: "But there is a possibility that even those who are cleansed may fall from grace and depart from the living God." What can bring greater sorrow than to see one who has enjoyed the spirit of the Gospel and the power of the Holy Ghost fall from grace and turn to evil practices? How careful we should be to walk the way of truth and constantly be seeking the companionship of the Holy Spirit that we be not led into temptation and fall. CHMR1:94

**Related Witnesses:**
### Elder Joseph Fielding Smith
Never in the history of the world, that is, in the history of the Church, have there been so many temptations, so many pitfalls, so many dangers, to lure away the members of the Church from the path of duty and from righteousness, as we find today. Every day of our lives we come in contact with these temptations, these dangers. We should continue in the spirit of prayer and faith, remembering that there is this possibility that we may turn from the grace of the living God, and fall unless we continue in that humility, in the exercise of faith and obedience to every principle of truth. CR1941Oct:94

### Joseph Smith,
*receiving the Word of the Lord*
The blasphemy against the Holy Ghost, which shall not be forgiven in the world nor out of the world, is in that ye commit murder wherein ye shed innocent blood, and assent unto my death, after ye have received my new and everlasting covenant, saith the Lord God; and he that abideth not this law can in nowise enter into my glory, but shall be damned, saith the Lord. (*Revelation relating to the new and everlasting covenant, July 12, 1843; law given relative to blasphemy against the Holy Ghost*) D&C 132:27

### Jesus,
*quoted by Mormon*
And no unclean thing can enter into his kingdom; therefore nothing entereth into his rest save it be those who have washed their garments in my blood, because of their faith, and the repentance of all their sins, and their faithfulness unto the end. (*The resurrected Jesus Christ instructs his twelve Nephite disciples, A.D. 34*) 3Ne.27:19

# List of Doctrines

## SCRIPTURE

*Doctrines Located in This Topic*

### (1) Scripture in General

712. Written scripture is the recorded testimony of prophets who receive gospel truths by revelation from the Lord.

713. Written scriptures are preserved and made available to us because they are vital to our salvation.

714. The Lord at times commands His prophets to hide up sacred records so they can be made available at a future time.

715. Scripture is given from God to His prophets for (the blessing and judgment of) all people—not for members of His church alone.

716. The Bible, the Book of Mormon, the Doctrine and Covenants, and the Pearl of Great Price (the Standard Works of the Church) are written scriptures.

717. The word of the Lord is not confined to the Bible.

718. In addition to written scripture we need continuous revelation from living prophets to guide us.

719. Revelations do not have to be published in written form to be scripture.

720. Inspired prophetic utterances, both oral and written, are scripture.

### (2) Scripture Study

721. We are to read and study the scriptures regularly.

722. Parents are to teach their children to study the scriptures.

723. Answers to personal problems can come through scripture study.

724. Members of the Church are to read the Book of Mormon particularly.

725. Reading the scriptures enlarges our spiritual endowments.

*Doctrines on SCRIPTURE*
*Located in Other Topics*

655. When the Lord wants the people to learn any essential truth, He will teach it to them over and over again through the witnesses of prophets.

666. Revelation from God to each of us as individuals is necessary for our salvation.

817. Gospel study and prayer are necessary means for obtaining a testimony of the gospel.

(See topics BIBLE;
BOOK OF MORMON; and TRUTH.)

# SCRIPTURE

## (1) Scripture in General
## (2) Scripture Study

### (1) Scripture in General

712. Written scripture is the recorded testimony of prophets who receive gospel truths by revelation from the Lord.

**Mark E. Petersen**

It is an infallible sign of the true church that it has in it divinely chosen, living prophets to guide it, men who receive current revelation from God and whose recorded works become new scripture. ¶ It is an infallible sign of the true church also that it will produce new and additional scripture arising out of the ministrations of those prophets. This unfailing pattern of God is clearly made manifest through his dealings with his people from the beginning. CR1978Apr:95-96

**Bruce R. McConkie**

Prophetic utterances, both oral and written, are scripture. "To some it is given by the Holy Ghost to know that Jesus Christ is the Son of God, and that he was crucified for the sins of the world." (D&C 46:13) Testimonies borne by such persons, when moved upon by the Spirit, are scripture. In fact, all the elders of the Church, by virtue of their ordination, are called "to proclaim the everlasting gospel, by the Spirit of the living God," with this promise: "Whatsoever they shall speak when moved upon by the Holy Ghost shall be scripture, shall be the will of the Lord, shall be the mind of the Lord, shall be the word of the Lord, shall be the voice of the Lord, and the power of God unto salvation." (D&C 68:1,4) And as it is with the elders on earth, so it is with their fellow servants beyond the veil. The words of the angels of God in heaven are scripture, for, "Angels speak by the power of the Holy Ghost; wherefore, they speak the words of Christ." (2Ne.32:3) ¶ . . . . Such scripture as is canonized—meaning, at the present moment, the Bible, the Book of Mormon, the Doctrine and Covenants, and the Pearl of Great Price—comes from prophets who held positions of leadership and trust in the Lord's earthly kingdom. It is binding upon the Church and the world and is the standard by which all men shall be judged when they shall stand before the pleasing bar of the great Jehovah to receive according to their works. (The Promised Messiah, pp. 24-25) TLDP:606

**Joseph Smith**

And gave him power from on high, by the means which were before prepared, to translate the Book of Mormon; 9. Which contains a record of a fallen people, and the fulness of the gospel of Jesus Christ to the Gentiles and to the Jews also; 10. Which was given by inspiration, and is confirmed to others by the ministering of angels, and is declared unto the world by them— 11. Proving to the world that the holy scriptures are true, and that God does inspire men and call them to his holy work in this age and generation, as well as in generations of old; 12. Thereby showing that he is the same God yesterday, today, and forever. Amen. (*Revelation on Church Organization and Government, April 1830; the Book of Mormon proves the divinity of the latter-day work*) D&C 20:8-12

**Elder Wilford Woodruff**

Here is the Bible, the record of the Jews, given by the inspiration of the Lord through Moses and the ancient Patriarchs and Prophets. Is it an imposture, and as the infidels say, the work of man? No, it is not in the power of any man who ever breathed the breath of life to make such a book without the inspiration of the Almighty. (*General conference, April 1873, JD16:35*) TLDP:610

**Lehi,**
*quoted by his son Nephi*

For behold, Laban hath the record of the Jews and also a genealogy of my forefathers, and they are engraven upon plates of brass. 4. Wherefore, the Lord hath commanded that thou and thy brothers should go unto the house of Laban, and seek the records, and bring them down hither into the wilderness. . . . 19. And behold, it is wisdom in God that we should obtain these records. . . . 20. And also that we may preserve unto them the words which have been spoken by the mouth of all the holy prophets, which have been delivered unto them by the Spirit and power of God, since the world began, even down unto this present time. (*Lehi instructs his son Nephi, 600-592 B.C.*) 1Ne.3:3-4,19-20

**President Spencer W. Kimball**

By the power of God other books of scripture [in addition to the Bible] have come into being. Vital and priceless records of ancient America, with teachings of Christ, another testimony of his divinity, form the Book of Mormon, which we declare to be divine scripture, contemporary with and sustaining the Bible. ¶ Since that momentous day in 1820, additional scripture has continued to come, including the numerous and vital revelations, flowing in a never-ending stream from God to his prophets on the earth.

Many of these revelations are recorded in another scripture called the Doctrine and Covenants. Completing our latter-day scriptures is the Pearl of Great Price, another record of revelation and translated writings of both ancient and modern prophets. ¶ There are those who would assume that with the printing and binding of these sacred records, that would be the "end of the prophets." But again we testify to the world that revelation continues and that the vaults and files of the Church contain these revelations which come month to month and day to day. CR1977Apr:115

**Elder George Albert Smith**

That he [Joseph Smith] might be a witness of the living God the Lord gave to him by revelation the contents of this record that I hold in my hand, (the Doctrine and Covenants) containing over four hundred pages of instruction to the children of men. . . . ¶ The Bible, Book of Mormon, Doctrine and Covenants, and Pearl of Great Price, do not contain the wisdom of men alone, but of God. . . . [T]hey contain the word of the Lord. What matter it though we understand Homer and Shakespeare and Milton, and I might enumerate all the great writers of the world; if we have failed to read the scriptures we have missed the better part of this world's literature. ¶ . . . . [God] called his sons one by one, and they gave their lives that we might have the Old Testament. He sent his only begotten Son into the world, and his life was sacrificed in order that we might have the teachings of the New Testament. The prophets of God recorded in the Book of Mormon laid down their lives and sealed their testimonies with their blood, in order that the children of men might know what the Father desired of them. He sent the Prophet Joseph Smith, and he gave his life together with his brother Hyrum, in order that we might have the truths contained in the sacred record known as the Doctrine and Covenants. CR1917Oct:41-44

**Author's Note:** In contrast to the recorded testimony of prophets, it is interesting to read of the "loose writings" of men as depicted by President Harold B. Lee, as follows: "There are among us many loose writings predicting the calamities which are about to overtake us. Some of these have been publicized as though they were necessary to wake up the world to the horrors about to overtake us. Many of these are from sources upon which there cannot be unquestioned reliance. ¶ Are you priesthood bearers aware of the fact that we need no such publications to be forewarned, if we were only

conversant with what the scriptures have already spoken to us in plainness? ¶ Let me give you the sure word of prophecy on which you should rely for your guide instead of these strange sources which may have great political implications. ¶ Read the 24th chapter of Matthew—particularly that inspired version as contained in the Pearl of Great Price. [JS-M] ¶ Then read the 45th section of the Doctrine and Covenants where the Lord, not man, has documented the signs of the times. ¶ Now turn to section 101 and section 133 of the Doctrine and Covenants and hear the step-by step recounting of events leading up to the coming of the Savior. ¶ Finally, turn to the promises the Lord makes to those who keep the commandments when these judgments descend upon the wicked, as set forth in the Doctrine and Covenants, section 38. ¶ Brethren, these are some of the writings with which you should concern yourselves, rather than commentaries that may come from those whose information may not be the most reliable and whose motives may be subject to question. And may I say, parenthetically, most of such writers are not handicapped by having any authentic information on their writings." (CR1972Oct:128)

**Related Witnesses:**

**Bruce R. McConkie**

We have in the Holy Scriptures—those inspired and canonized utterances of the holy prophets; those heaven-sent fragments from the records of eternity; those words and phrases spoken by the power of the Holy Ghost—we have in these sacred writings the plan and the pattern, the laws and the requirements, the gospel recitations, that will guide us to eternal life in our Father's kingdom. They chart the course we must pursue to gain peace in this life and glory and honor in the life to come. (The Mortal Messiah, 1:265) TLDP:606

**Jacob, brother of Nephi**

Behold, my brethren, he that prophesieth, let him prophesy to the understanding of men; for the Spirit speaketh the truth and lieth not. Wherefore, it speaketh of things as they really are, and of things as they really will be; wherefore, these things are manifested unto us plainly, for the salvation of our souls. But behold, we are not witnesses alone in these things; for God also spake them unto prophets of old. (Jacob's scriptural writings, 544-521 B.C.) Jacob 4:13

**Moroni, son of Mormon**

And in the mouth of three witnesses shall these things be established; and the testimony of three, and this work, in the which shall be shown forth the power of God and also his word, of which the Father, and the Son, and the Holy Ghost bear record—and all this shall stand as a testimony against the world at the last day. (*The record of Moroni*) Ether 5:4

**President Joseph F. Smith**

I say to my brethren that the book of Doctrine and Covenants contains some of the most glorious principles ever revealed to the world, some that have been revealed in greater fulness than they were ever revealed before to the world; and this, in fulfilment of the promises of the ancient prophets that in the latter times, the Lord would reveal things to the world that had been kept hid from the foundation thereof; and the Lord has revealed them through the Prophet Joseph Smith. CR1913Oct:9

**Nephi, son of Lehi**

And my brother, Jacob, also has seen him as I have seen him; wherefore, I will send their words forth unto my children to prove unto them that my words are true. Wherefore, by the words of three, God hath said, I will establish my word. Nevertheless, God sendeth more witnesses, and he proveth all his words. (*Nephi testifies that he and his brother Jacob have each seen the Redeemer, 559-545 B.C.*) 2Ne.11:3

**Jesus,**
*quoted by Mormon*

And now it came to pass that when Jesus had said these words he said unto them again, after he had expounded all the scriptures unto them which they had received, he said unto them: Behold, other scriptures I would that ye should write, that ye have not. 7. And it came to pass that he said unto Nephi: Bring forth the record which ye have kept. 8. And when Nephi had brought forth the records, and laid them before him, he cast his eyes upon them and said: 9. Verily I say unto you, I commanded my servant Samuel, the Lamanite, that he should testify unto this people, that at the day that the Father should glorify his name in me that there were many saints who should arise from the dead, and should appear unto many, and should minister unto them. And he said unto them: Was it not so? 10. And his disciples answered him and said: Yea, Lord, Samuel did prophesy according to thy words, and they were all fulfilled. 11. And Jesus said unto them: How be it that ye have not written this thing, that many saints did arise and appear unto many and did minister unto them? 12. And it came to pass that Nephi remembered that this thing had not been written. 13. And it came to pass that Jesus commanded that it should be written; therefore it was written according as he commanded. 14. And now it

came to pass that when Jesus had expounded all the scriptures in one, which they had written, he commanded them that they should teach the things which he had expounded unto them. (*The resurrected Jesus Christ instructs his disciples among the Nephite people, A.D. 34*) 3Ne.23:6-14

---

**713.** Written scriptures are preserved and made available to us because they are vital to our salvation.

**Bruce R. McConkie**

They [the holy scriptures] tell how all men—not the ancients only—may hear the voice of God, entertain angelic messengers, and enjoy the outpourings of the Holy Spirit. The Holy Scriptures are given to guide men to that state of spiritual enlightenment and perfection attained by those of old who worked out their salvation. ¶ "The holy scriptures," Paul told his beloved Timothy, "are able to make thee wise unto salvation through faith which is in Christ Jesus." The scriptures open the door; they mark the course we must pursue; they identify the strait and narrow path; they testify of Christ and his laws; they engender faith; their worth cannot be revealed, men must walk therein to gain the desired eternal reward. (The Mortal Messiah, 1:266) TLDP:608

**Lehi,**
*quoted by his son Nephi*

And it came to pass that he spake unto me, saying: Behold I have dreamed a dream, in the which the Lord hath commanded me that thou and thy brethren shall return to Jerusalem. 3. For behold, Laban hath the record of the Jews and also a genealogy of my forefathers, and they are engraven upon plates of brass. 4. Wherefore, the Lord hath commanded me that thou and thy brothers should go unto the house of Laban, and seek the records, and bring them down hither into the wilderness. . . . 19. And behold, it is wisdom in God that we should obtain these records, that we may preserve unto our children the language of our fathers; 20. And also that we may preserve unto them the words which have been spoken by the mouth of all the holy prophets, which have been delivered unto them by the Spirit and power of God, since the world began, even down unto this present time. (*Lehi instructs his son Nephi, 600-592 B.C.*) 1Ne.3:2-4,19-20

**Elder George Albert Smith**

Will our Father hold us guiltless when we go home, if we have failed to teach our children the importance of these sacred records? I think not. He called his sons one by one, and they gave their lives that we might have the Old Testament. He sent his only begotten Son into the world, and his life was sacrificed in order that we might have the teachings of the New Testament. The prophets of God recorded in the Book of Mormon laid down their lives and sealed their testimonies with their blood, in order that the children of men might know what the Father desired of them. He sent the Prophet Joseph Smith, and he gave His life, together with his brother Hyrum, in order that we might have the truths contained in the sacred record known as the Doctrine and Covenants. Do you suppose that after the Lord has done all this for us, has given to this world the choicest and sweetest of men and women, whose lives have been dedicated to the blessing of mankind, many of them sealing their testimony with their blood, has placed within our reach the excellent teachings contained in these holy records, that he will consider us appreciative if we fail to teach them to our families, and to impress them upon those with whom we come in contact? CR1917Oct:43-44

### George Q. Cannon

It is of infinite importance that we should value and preserve these records because in them is contained the revelations of God to His children in former times. (Gospel Truth, 1:324) TLDP:612-13

### Mormon

Now these things are written unto the remnant of the house of Jacob; and they are written after this manner, because it is known of God that wickedness will not bring them forth unto them; and they are to be hid up unto the Lord that they may come forth in his own due time. 13. And this is the commandment which I have received; and behold, they shall come forth according to the commandment of the Lord, when he shall see fit, in his wisdom. 14. And behold, they shall go unto the unbelieving of the Jews; and for this intent shall they go—that they may be persuaded that Jesus is the Christ, the Son of the living God; that the Father may bring about, through his most Beloved, his great and eternal purpose, in restoring the Jews, or all the house of Israel, to the land of their inheritance, which the Lord their God hath given them, unto the fulfilling of his covenant; 15. And also that the seed of this people may more fully believe his gospel, which shall go forth unto them from the Gentiles; . . . (*Mormon's writings, A.D. 375-380; the Book of Mormon shall come forth to convince all Israel that Jesus is the Christ*) Morm.5:12-15

### Elder Joseph Fielding Smith

The Lord has given so many revelations in our own day. We have this Doctrine and Covenants full of them, all pertaining unto the Latter-day Saints and to the world. For this is not our book alone. This Doctrine and Covenants is my book and your book; but more than that, it belongs to all the infidels; to the Catholics, to the Presbyterians, to the Methodists, to the infidel, to the non-believer. It is his book if he will accept it, if he will receive it. The Lord has given it unto the world for their salvation. If you do not believe it, you read the first section in this book, the preface, and you will find that the Lord has sent this book and the things which it contains unto the people afar off, on the islands of the sea, in foreign lands, and his voice is unto all people, that all may hear. CR1919Oct:146

### Nephi, son of Lehi

And upon these I write the things of my soul, and many of the scriptures which are engraven upon the plates of brass. For my soul delighteth in the scriptures, and my heart pondereth them, and writeth them for the learning and the profit of my children. (*Nephi writes on plates shortly after the death of his father Lehi, 588-570 B.C.*) 2Ne.4:15

**Related Witnesses:**

### L. Tom Perry

Oh, how I can bear witness to the value of the scriptures in my life. I am absolutely convinced that they have answers to every problem in life. When a problem develops, after praying for instruction from the Lord, you ought to turn to the scriptures to find your answer. ACR(San Jose)1977:15; TLDP:608

### Nephi, son of Lehi

Behold the Lord slayeth the wicked to bring forth his righteous purposes. It is better that one man should perish than that a nation should dwindle and perish in unbelief. 14. And now, when I, Nephi, had heard these words, I remembered the words of the Lord which he spake unto me in the wilderness, saying that: Inasmuch as thy seed shall keep my commandments, they shall prosper in the land of promise. 15. Yea, and I also thought that they could not keep the commandments of the Lord according to the law of Moses, save they should have the law. 16. And I also knew that the law was engraven upon the plates of brass. 17. And again, I knew that the Lord had delivered Laban into my hands for this cause—that I might obtain the records according to his commandments. 18. Therefore I did obey the voice of the Spirit, and took Laban by the hair of the head, and I smote off his head with his own sword. (*Writings of Nephi, 600-592 B.C.*) 1Ne.4:13-18

### George Q. Cannon

This book [the Bible] is of priceless worth; its

value cannot be established by anything that is known among men upon which value is fixed. . . . To the Latter-day Saints it should always be a precious treasure. Beyond any people now upon the face of the earth, they should value it, for the reason that from its pages, from the doctrines set forth by its writers, the epitome of the plan of salvation which is there given unto us, we derive the highest consolation, we obtain the greatest strength. It is, as it were, a constant fountain sending forth streams of living life to satisfy the souls of all who peruse its pages. (Gospel Truth, 2:248) TLDP:610

**Joseph Smith**

This he forbade me, saying that I must have no other object in view in getting the plates but to glorify God, and must not be influenced by any other motive than that of building his kingdom; otherwise I could not get them. (*Joseph's record of the obtaining of the Book of Mormon plates*) JS-H 1:46

**Mormon**

And they discovered a people, who were called the people of Zarahemla. Now, there was great rejoicing among the people of Zarahemla; and also Zarahemla did rejoice exceedingly, because the Lord had sent the people of Mosiah with the plates of brass which contained the record of the Jews. . . . 17. And at the time that Mosiah discovered them, they had become exceedingly numerous. Nevertheless, they had had many wars and serious contentions, and had fallen by the sword from time to time; and their language had become corrupted; and they had brought no records with them; and they denied the being of their Creator; and Mosiah, nor the people of Mosiah, could understand them. (*Mosiah and his followers discover the people of Zarahemla, the Mulekites, 279-130 B.C.*) Omni 1:14,17

**Joseph Smith**

Whatsoever they shall speak when moved upon by the Holy Ghost shall be scripture, shall be the will of the Lord, shall be the mind of the Lord, shall be the word of the Lord, shall be the voice of the Lord, and the power of God unto salvation. (*Revelation, Nov. 1831*) D&C 68:4

**Nephi, son of Lehi**

And it mattereth not to me that I am particular to give a full account of all the things of my father, for they cannot be written upon these plates, for I desire the room that I may write of the things of God. 4. For the fulness of mine intent is that I may persuade men to come unto the God of Abraham, and the God of Isaac, and the God of Jacob, and be saved. 5. Wherefore, the things which are pleasing unto the world I do not write, but the things which are pleasing

unto God and unto those who are not of the world. 6. Wherefore, I shall give commandment unto my seed, that they shall not occupy these plates with things which are not of worth unto the children of men. (*The writings of Nephi, 600-592 B.C.*) 1Ne.6:3-6

**Nephi, son of Lehi**

For we labor diligently to write, to persuade our children, and also our brethren, to believe in Christ, and to be reconciled to God; for we know that it is by grace that we are saved, after all we can do. (*The writings of Nephi, 559-545 B.C.*) 2Ne.25:23

**President Harold B. Lee**

We need to make sure, that so far as lies in our power, we don't leave the homes of our people without . . . copies of the Book of Mormon, the Bible, the Doctrine and Covenants, the Pearl of Great Price. We ought to see to it, somehow, that they have these precious scriptures, not just dissertations from the scriptures, but the scriptures themselves and read from what's in those precious books. (*At Sunday School session of general conference, Oct. 5, 1973*) MPSG84:2

---

**714. The Lord at times commands His prophets to hide up sacred records so they can be made available at a future time.**

**Mormon**

And it came to pass that when three hundred and twenty years had passed away, Ammaron, being constrained by the Holy Ghost, did hide up the records which were sacred—yea, even all the sacred records which had been handed down from generation to generation, which were sacred—even until the three hundred and twentieth year from the coming of Christ. 49. And he did hide them up unto the Lord that they might come again unto the remnant of the house of Jacob according to the prophecies and the promises of the Lord. And thus is the end of the record of Ammaron. (*Mormon abridges the account of Nephi, son of Nephi, one of the disciples of Christ, A.D. 36-60*) 4Ne.1:48-49

**Oliver Cowdery**

This Book was written on plates of gold and handed down from father to son for many ages and generations. ¶ It was then that the people prospered and were strong and mighty; they cultivated the earth, built buildings and cities, and abounded in all good things, as the palefaces now do. ¶ But they became wicked; they killed one another and shed much blood; they killed their prophets and wise men, and sought to destroy the

Book. The Great Spirit became angry and would speak to them no more; they had no more good and wise dreams; no more visions, no more angels sent among them by the Great Spirit; and the Lord commanded Mormon and Moroni, their last wise men and prophets to hide the Book in the earth that it might be preserved in safety and be found and made known in the latter-day to the palefaces who should possess the land that they might again make it known to the red men, in order to restore them to the knowledge of the will of the Great Spirit and to His favor. *(Speech to the Delaware Indians near Buffalo, N.Y., 1831)* HC1:183-84 (Footnote)

#### Nephi, son of Lehi
Wherefore, when thou hast read the words which I have commanded thee, and obtained the witnesses which I have promised unto thee, then shalt thou seal up the book again, and hide it up unto me, that I may preserve the words which thou hast not read, until I shall see fit in mine own wisdom to reveal all things unto the children of men. 23. For behold, I am God; and I am a God of miracles; and I will show unto the world that I am the same yesterday, today, and forever; and I work not among the children of men save it be according to their faith. *(Nephi prophesies of the coming forth of the Book of Mormon and records the words of the Lord foretelling the time when Joseph Smith would be instructed to hide up the plates from which he has translated the Book of Mormon, 599-545 B.C.)* 2Ne.27:22-23

#### Moroni, son of Mormon
And now, after that, they have all dwindled in unbelief; and there is none save it be the Lamanites, and they have rejected the gospel of Christ; therefore I am commanded that I should hide them up again in the earth. 4. Behold, I have written upon these plates the very things which the brother of Jared saw; and there never were greater things made manifest than those which were made manifest unto the brother of Jared. 5. Wherefore the Lord hath commanded me to write them; and I have written them. And he commanded me that I should seal them up; and he also hath commanded that I should seal up the interpretation thereof; wherefore I have sealed up the interpreters, according to the commandment of the Lord. 6. For the Lord said unto me: They shall not go forth unto the Gentiles until the day that they shall repent of their iniquity, and become clean before the Lord. 7. And in that day that they shall exercise faith in me, saith the Lord, even as the brother of Jared did, that they may become sanctified in

me, then will I manifest unto them the things which the brother of Jared saw, even to the unfolding unto them all my revelations, saith Jesus Christ, the Son of God, the Father of the heavens and of the earth, and all things that in them are. *(Moroni writes the word of the Lord, A.D. 384-421)* Ether 4:3-7

#### Moroni, son of Mormon
Therefore I will write and hide up the records in the earth; and whither I go it mattereth not. *(Mormon writes to his son Moroni, prior to A.D. 384)* Morm.8:4

**Related Witnesses:**
#### Moroni, son of Mormon
And it came to pass that the army of Coriantumr did pitch their tents by the hill Ramah; and it was that same hill where my father Mormon did hide up the records unto the Lord, which were sacred. *(Moroni's abridgement of the writings of Ether, who wrote about 550 B.C.)* Ether 15:11

**Author's Note:** John, the beloved disciple, wrote on parchment which he hid and which came into the hands of Joseph Smith, who translated it. ¶ Hugh Nibley writes the following about hiding up holy documents: "At any rate, we now have proof [referencing to the *"Assumption of Moses,"* apocryphal document and the *Dead Sea Scrolls*] both of the tradition and practice in Israel of hiding up holy documents as the only means of conveying them in their purity to the men of another and a distant age." ("The Prophetic Book of Mormon," p.75)

---

715. Scripture is given from God to His prophets for (the blessing and judgment of) all people—not for members of His church alone.

#### Bruce R. McConkie
Such scripture as is canonized—meaning, at the present moment, the Bible, the Book of Mormon, the Doctrine and Covenants, and the Pearl of Great Price—comes from prophets who held positions of leadership and trust in the Lord's earthly kingdom. It is binding upon the Church and the world and is the standard by which all men shall be judged when they shall stand before the pleasing bar of the great Jehovah to receive according to their works. (The Promised Messiah, pp. 24-25) TLDP:606

#### Elder Joseph Fielding Smith
The Lord has given so many revelations in our own day. We have this Doctrine and Covenants full of them, all pertaining unto the Latter-day Saints and to the world. For this is not our book

alone. This Doctrine and Covenants is my book and your book; but more than that, it belongs to all the world; to the Catholics, to the Presbyterians, to the Methodists, to the infidel, to the non-believer. It is his book if he will accept it, if he will receive it. The Lord has given it unto the world for their salvation. If you do not believe it, you read the first section in this book, the preface, and you will find that the Lord has sent this book and the things which it contains unto the people afar off, on the islands of the sea, in foreign lands, and his voice is unto all people, that all may hear. And so I say it belongs to all the world, not only to the Latter-day Saints, and they will be judged by it, and you will be judged by it. We will all be judged by it, by the things which this book contains and by the things which the other books contain which are holy scripture, which the Lord has given unto us; and if we fail to comprehend these things, if we will not search, if we will not study, if we will not take hold on the things which the Lord has revealed unto us, then his condemnation shall rest upon us, and we shall be removed from his presence and from his kingdom. And I say that in all soberness, because it is true. CR1919Oct:146

**Joseph Smith,**
*receiving the Word of the Lord*
Hearken, O ye people of my church, saith the voice of him who dwells on high, and whose eyes are upon all men; yea, verily I say: Hearken ye people from afar; and ye that are upon the islands of the sea, listen together. 2. For verily the voice of the Lord is unto all men, and there is none to escape; and there is no eye that shall not see, neither ear that shall not hear, neither heart that shall not be penetrated. . . . 4. And the voice of warning shall be unto all people, by the mouths of my disciples, whom I have chosen in these last days. (*Revelation received during conference of elders of the Church, Nov. 1, 1831; preface to the doctrines given to the Church*) D&C 1:1-2,4

**Elder Ezra Taft Benson**
A hundred and thirty years ago, when the elders were assembled in conference to determine whether the revelations should be published to the world, the Lord saw fit to give revelation to his Church, which was also directed to the world. He referred to it as his "Preface" or his "Introduction to his Book of Commandments," and it is the first section of the Doctrine and Covenants. . . . ¶ So our message is a world message. It is intended for all of our Father's children. When God the Father and his Son Jesus Christ saw fit to come here to earth and appear to

a boy prophet, surely such a visitation was intended to bless all of our Father's children. CR1961Apr:113-14

**President Brigham Young,**
*quoted by John A. Widtsoe*
The revelations of the Lord to his creatures are adapted to the lowest capacity, and they bring life and salvation to all who are willing to receive them. (*In Tabernacle, May 21, 1871, JD14:136*) DBY:124

**Related Witnesses:**
**Joseph Smith,**
*receiving the Word of the Lord*
Behold, this is mine authority, and the authority of my servants, and my preface unto the book of my commandments, which I have given them to publish unto you, O inhabitants of the earth. (*Revelation received during conference of elders of the Church, Nov. 1, 1831; preface to the doctrines given to the Church*) D&C 1:6

**Joseph Smith,**
*receiving the Word of the Lord*
Wherefore the voice of the Lord is unto the ends of the earth, that all that will hear may hear: (*Revelation received during conference of elders of the Church, Nov. 1, 1831; preface to the doctrines given to the Church*) D&C 1:11

---

**716.** The Bible, the Book of Mormon, the Doctrine and Covenants, and the Pearl of Great Price (the Standard Works of the Church) are written scriptures.

**Bruce R. McConkie**
Such scripture as is canonized—meaning, at the present moment, the Bible, the Book of Mormon, the Doctrine and Covenants, and the Pearl of Great Price—comes from prophets who held positions of leadership and trust in the Lord's earthly kingdom. It is binding upon the Church and the world and is the standard by which all men shall be judged when they shall stand before the pleasing bar of the great Jehovah to receive according to their works. (*The Promised Messiah, pp. 24-25*) TLDP:606

**Elder George Albert Smith**
My brethren and sisters, all the truth that is advocated in all the teachings of men, necessary for our salvation, is contained within the lids of the books that I have already mentioned (i.e. Bible, Book of Mormon, Doctrine and Covenants, and Pearl of Great Price). CR1917Oct:43

**Elder George Albert Smith**
That he [Joseph Smith] might be a witness of

the living God the Lord gave to him by revelation the contents of this record that I hold in my hand, (the Doctrine and Covenants) containing over four hundred pages of instruction to the children of men. . . . ¶ The Bible, Book of Mormon, Doctrine and Covenants, and Pearl of Great Price, do not contain the wisdom of men alone, but of God. . . . [T]hey contain the word of the Lord. CR1917Oct:41-44

**President Harold B. Lee**
We need to make sure, that so far as lies in our power, we don't leave the homes of our people without . . . copies of the Book of Mormon, the Bible, the Doctrine and Covenants, the Pearl of Great Price. We ought to see to it, somehow, that they have these precious scriptures, not just dissertations from the scriptures, but the scriptures themselves and read from what's in those precious books. (*At Sunday School session of general conference, Oct. 5, 1973*) MPSG84:2

**Related Witnesses:**

**Mark E. Petersen**
The chief reason we have the Book of Mormon is that in the mouth of two or three witnesses shall all things be established. (See 1Cor.13:1.) We have the Bible; we also have the Book of Mormon. They constitute two voices—two volumes of scripture—from two widely separated ancient peoples, both bearing testimony to the divinity of the Lord Jesus Christ. ¶ But we also have two other scriptural witnesses also, making four altogether. They are the modern scriptures given as revelations through the Prophet Joseph Smith, and they, too, declare that Jesus is the Christ, the Savior, the Creator, the long-promised Messiah. CR1978Apr:98

**Joseph Smith,**
*receiving the Word of the Lord*
And now, behold, I give unto you, and also unto my servant Joseph, the keys of this gift, which shall bring to light this ministry; and in the mouth of two or three witnesses shall every word be established. (*Revelation for Oliver Cowdery, April 1829*) D&C 6:28

**Author's Note:** In the Gospel Principles manual published by the Church and distributed broadly throughout the Church for generations (and hence published and re-published by the prophets of the Church) the following statement appears: "The Church of Jesus Christ of Latter-day Saints accepts four books as scripture: the Bible, the Book of Mormon, the Doctrine and Covenants, and the Pearl of Great Price. These books are called the standard works of the Church. . . ." (Gospel Principles, pp. 51-52.)

**717. The word of the Lord is not confined to the Bible.**

**James E. Talmage**
In the respect and sanctity with which the Latter-day Saints regard the Bible they are of like profession with Christian denominations in general, but differ from them in the additional acknowledgment of certain other scriptures as authentic and holy, which others are in harmony with the Bible, and serve to support and emphasize its facts and doctrines. AF:214

**Nephi, son of Lehi**
For I command all men, both in the east and in the west, and in the north, and in the south, and in the islands of the sea, that they shall write the words which I speak unto them; for out of the books which shall be written I will judge the world, every man according to their works, according to that which is written. 12. For behold, I shall speak unto the Jews and they shall write it; and I shall also speak unto the Nephites and they shall write it; and I shall also speak unto the other tribes of the house of Israel, which I have led away, and they shall write it; and I shall also speak unto all nations of the earth and they shall write it. 13. And it shall come to pass that the Jews shall have the words of the Nephites, and the Nephites shall have the words of the Jews; and the Nephites and the Jews shall have the words of the lost tribes of Israel; and the lost tribes of Israel shall have the words of the Nephites and the Jews. (*The Lord speaks to Nephi about the latter-day gentiles, many of whom shall reject the Book of Mormon, 559-545 B.C.*) 2Ne.29:11-13

**Elder Joseph Fielding Smith**
The canon of scripture is not full. There are many books of scripture mentioned in the Bible which we do not have. There are numerous prophecies in the scriptures where the Lord has promised to speak again, even in these latter days. (The Restoration of All Things, p. 72) TLDP:613

**President Brigham Young,**
*quoted by John A. Widtsoe*
The Bible is true. It may not all have been translated aright, and many precious things may have been rejected in the compilation and translation of the Bible; but we understand, from the writings of one of the Apostles, that if all the sayings and doings of the Savior had been written, the world could not contain them. I will say that the world could not understand them. They do not understand what we have on record, nor the character of the Savior, as delineated in the Scriptures; and yet it is one of the simplest

things in the world, and the Bible, when it is understood, is one of the simplest books in the world, for, as far as it is translated correctly, it is nothing but truth, and in truth there is no mystery save to the ignorant. The revelations of the Lord to his creatures are adapted to the lowest capacity, and they bring life and salvation to all who are willing to receive them. (*In Tabernacle, May 21, 1871, JD14:135*) DBY:124

### Lehi,
#### quoted by his son Nephi

And it came to pass that he spake unto me, saying: Behold I have dreamed a dream, in the which the Lord hath commanded me that thou and thy brethren shall return to Jerusalem. 3. For behold, Laban hath the record of the Jews and also a genealogy of my forefathers, and they are engraven upon plates of brass. 4. Wherefore, the Lord hath commanded me that thou and thy brothers should go unto the house of Laban, and seek the records, and bring them down hither into the wilderness. . . . 19. And behold, it is wisdom in God that we should obtain these records, that we may preserve unto our children the language of our fathers; 20. And also that we may preserve unto them the words which have been spoken by the mouth of all the holy prophets, which have been delivered unto them by the Spirit and power of God, since the world began, even down unto this present time. (*Lehi's instructions to his son Nephi, 600-592 B.C.*) 1Ne.3:2-4,19-20

### Mark E. Petersen

It is an infallible sign of the true church that it has in it divinely chosen, living prophets to guide it, men who receive current revelation from God and whose recorded works become new scripture. ¶ It is an infallible sign of the true church also that it will produce new and additional scripture arising out of the ministrations of those prophets. This unfailing pattern of God is clearly made manifest through his dealings with his people from the beginning. CR1978Apr:95-96

### President Spencer W. Kimball

By the power of God other books of scripture [in addition to the Bible] have come into being. Vital and priceless records of ancient America, with teachings of Christ, another testimony of his divinity, form the Book of Mormon, which we declare to be divine scripture, contemporary with and sustaining the Bible. ¶ Since that momentous day in 1820, additional scripture has continued to come, including the numerous and vital revelations flowing in a never-ending stream from God to his prophets on the earth. Many of these revelations are recorded in

another scripture called the Doctrine and Covenants. Completing our Latter-day scriptures is the Pearl of Great Price, another record of revelation and translated writings of both ancient and modern prophets. ¶ There are those who would assume that with the printing and binding of these sacred records, that would be the "end of the prophets." But again we testify to the world that revelation continues and that the vaults and files of the Church contain these revelations which come month to month and day to day. CR1977Apr:115

### Related Witnesses:
#### Nephi, son of Lehi

Yea, and I also thought that they could not keep the commandments of the Lord according to the law of Moses, save they should have the law. 16. And I also knew that the law was engraven upon the plates of brass. 17. And again, I knew that the Lord had delivered Laban into my hands for this cause—that I might obtain the records according to his commandments. (*Writings of Nephi in the Book of Mormon, 600-592 B.C.*) 1Ne.4:15-17

---

**718.** In addition to written scripture we need continuous revelation from living prophets to guide us.

### Elder John Taylor

Those books [the scriptures] are good for example, precedent, and investigation, and for developing certain laws and principles; but they do not, they cannot touch every case required to be adjudicated and set in order; we require a living tree—a living fountain—living intelligence, proceeding from the living priesthood in heaven, through the living priesthood on earth. ("On Priesthood," Millennial Star, Nov. 1, 1847, p. 323) TLDP:612

### George Q. Cannon

As Latter-day Saints, we need constantly the guidance of Jehovah. We have the Bible, the Book of Mormon and the Book of Doctrine and Covenants; but all these books, without the living oracles and a constant stream of revelation from the Lord, would not lead any people into the Celestial Kingdom of God. This may seem a strange declaration to make, but strange as it may sound, it is nevertheless true. ¶ Of course, these records are all of infinite value. They cannot be too highly prized, nor can they be too closely studied. But in and of themselves, with all the light that they give, they are insufficient to guide the children of men and to lead them into the presence of God. To be thus led requires a living Priesthood and constant revelation from

God to the people according to the circumstances in which they may be placed. ¶ A great many people fall into error very frequently by quoting and seeking to apply to present conditions revelation which were given to the Church in early days and which were especially adapted to the circumstances then existing. Of course, it is appropriate to quote from the revelations concerning principle; but in many instances the revelations that are contained in the Book of Doctrine and Covenants are not, I may say—and I say it with some degree of care—suited to the circumstances and conditions in which we are placed. They were given to the Church at a time when just such revelations were required. Nor must we fall into the idea that the world has adopted, that the Bible is all that is necessary for man's salvation. . . . ¶ It is of infinite importance that we should value and preserve these records because in them is contained the revelations of God to His children in former times. But with all these there is still something more needed for our salvation, and that is the living word of God. We need the revelations of Jesus adapted to our condition and circumstances day by day and for the guidance and control of the Church of Christ in the various circumstances in which it is from time to time placed. . . . ¶ There are revelations in that book concerning counsel and the management of affairs that are not binding upon us only so far as they are applicable to us. When, however, it comes to the revelations concerning principle, then those revelations are unalterable and they will stand as long as heaven and earth will endure, because they are true. (Gospel Truth, 1:323-24) TLDP:612-13

### Mark E. Petersen

It is an infallible sign of the true church that it has in it divinely chosen, living prophets to guide it, men who receive current revelation from God and whose recorded works become new scripture. ¶ It is an infallible sign of the true church also that it will produce new and additional scripture arising out of the ministrations of those prophets. This unfailing pattern of God is clearly made manifest through his dealings with his people from the beginning. CR1978Apr:95-96

### Bruce R. McConkie

Further, there is the practical matter of interpretation and of equating and of comparing the written word with the continuing stream of oral utterances that, because the speaking voice has been inspired from on high, are themselves also scripture. Principles revealed in one day must be applied to new situations in another time; the

ancient scriptures must tell what the word of God, given anciently, means today. ¶ It takes an inspired man to understand and interpret an inspired utterance. No one but a prophet can envision the true and full meaning of prophetic words. Any person of normal mentality can absorb some of the intended meaning from the scriptures, but no one can plumb the depths unless enlightened by the same power that gave the revealed truths in the first instance. Hence, "no prophecy of the scripture is of any private interpretation," as Peter said. Why? Because "the prophecy came not in old time by the will of man: but holy men of God spake as they were moved by the Holy Ghost." (2Pet.1:20-21) Similarly, holy men of God, as moved upon by the Holy Ghost, are the only ones who can make authoritative and complete statements as to the meaning and application of revealed truth. (The Mortal Messiah, 1:267-68) TLDP:613-14

### Orson F. Whitney

My Greek Catholic friend, whether he knew it or not, had hit upon the great distinguishing feature that differentiates God's Church from all other churches under the sun—in this, that while they are founded upon books and traditions and the precepts of men, this Church is built upon the rock of Christ, upon the principle of immediate and continuous revelation. The Latter-day Saints do not do things because they happen to be printed in a book. They do not do things because God told the Jews to do them; nor do they do or leave undone anything because of instructions that Christ gave to the Nephites. Whatever is done by this Church is because God, speaking from heaven in our day, has commanded this Church to do it. No book presides over this Church, and no book lies at its foundation. You cannot pile up books enough to take the place of God's priesthood, inspired by the power of the Holy Ghost. . . . Divine revelation adapts itself to the circumstances and conditions of men, and change ensues as God's progressive work goes on to its destiny. There is no book big enough or good enough to preside over this Church. ¶ In saying this, I speak with all due reverence of the written word of God. . . . (*Elder Whitney's "Greek Catholic friend" had said that it "made him shudder when he saw people sipping the water" instead of wine for sacrament— his church does not recognize the principle of continuous revelation*) CR1916Oct:55

### Related Witnesses:

### Joseph Smith

And gave him power from on high, by the means which were before prepared, to translate the Book of Mormon; 9. Which contains a record of a fallen people, and the fulness of the gospel of Jesus Christ to the Gentiles and to the Jews also; 10. Which was given by inspiration, and is confirmed to others by the ministering of angels, and is declared unto the world by them— 11. Proving to the world that the holy scriptures are true, and that God does inspire men and call them to his holy work in this age and generation, as well as in generations of old; 12. Thereby showing that he is the same God yesterday, today, and forever. Amen. (*Revelation on Church Organization and Government, April 1830; the Book of Mormon proves the divinity of the latter-day work*) D&C 20:8-12

---

### 719. Revelations do not have to be published in written form to be scripture.

#### President Joseph F. Smith
We are blest with revelation; the Church is built upon that foundation. All the revelations given do not have to be written. The inspiration may come as the Lord directs them. It does not have to be printed in a book. We have revelations that have been given that have been written; some of them have been published, some of them have not. CR1910Oct:41

#### Joseph Smith
And, behold, and lo, this is an ensample unto all those who were ordained unto this priesthood, whose mission is appointed unto them to go forth— 3. And this is the ensample unto them, that they shall speak as they are moved upon by the Holy Ghost. 4. And whatsoever they shall speak when moved upon by the Holy Ghost shall be scripture, shall be the will of the Lord, shall be the mind of the Lord, shall be the word of the Lord, shall be the voice of the Lord, and the power of God unto salvation. (*Revelation received at the request of several elders, Nov. 1831*) D&C 68:2-4

#### James E. Talmage
We believe that God is as willing today as He ever has been to reveal His mind and will to man, and that He does so through His appointed servants—prophets, seers, and revelators— invested through ordination with the authority of the Holy Priesthood. We rely therefore on the teachings of the living oracles of God as of equal validity with the doctrines of the written word. AF:6

#### President Wilford Woodruff
I will refer to a certain meeting I attended in the town of Kirtland in my early days. At that meeting some remarks were made . . . with regard to the living oracles and with regard to the written word of God. . . . [A] leading man in the church . . . talked upon the subject, and said: "You have got the word of God before you here in the Bible, Book of Mormon, and Doctrine and Covenants; you have the written word of God, and you who give revelations should give revelations according to those books, as what is written in those books is the word of God. We should confine ourselves to them." When he concluded, Brother Joseph turned to Brother Brigham Young and said, "Brother Brigham, I want you to take the stand, and tell us your views with regard to the written word of God." Brother Brigham took the stand, and he took the Bible, and laid it down; he took the Book of Mormon, and laid it down; and he took the Book of Doctrine and Covenants, and laid it down before him, and he said: "There is the written word of God to us, concerning the work of God from the beginning of the world, almost, to our day." "And now," said he, "when compared with the living oracles those books are nothing to me; those books do not convey the word of God direct to us now, as do the words of a Prophet or a man bearing the Holy Priesthood, in our day and generation. I would rather have the living oracles than all the writing in the books." That was the course he pursued. When he was through, Brother Joseph said to the congregation. "Brother Brigham has told you the word of the Lord, and he has told you the truth." ¶ . . . . The Bible is all right, the Book of Mormon is all right, the Doctrine and Covenants is all right, and they proclaim the work of God and the word of God in the earth in this day and generation until the coming of the Son of Man; but the Holy Priesthood is not confined particularly to those books, that is, it did not cease when those books were made. CR1897Oct:22-23

#### Related Witnesses:
##### George Q. Cannon
I want to teach you not to go to the book alone but beyond it—to the fountain whence it emanated—to Him who has filled us with noble and lofty aspirations, Who has brought us into intimate connection with Himself by revealing unto us His Gospel. We ought not to depend for our salvation and exaltation upon books but upon the Creator of the world, Who inspired the men who wrote this book [the Bible]. Possession of God's Spirit enables us to know whether this book is what it professes to be, and exalts us to the same level as the men whose narratives are here found. ¶ In making

these remarks it is not my wish to weaken your love for this book, but it is to give you to understand that it alone is not all that is necessary to build up the Kingdom of God. It is to induce you to look beyond it to the Being Who is the fountain of revelation and Who is the true source of all intelligence, so that if this book were burned and destroyed—if the millions of other books were all destroyed—there would still be a fountain of intelligence accessible to you from the life-giving stream, of which you might eternally drink. ¶ It was not books alone that directed the ancients; the law of God was written in their hearts. They drank at the fountain of knowledge which God had opened up unto them as it flowed forth pure from himself and thus were enabled to write the records which we now so much venerate. It is our privilege to receive and enjoy this same Spirit and knowledge. (Gospel Truth, 2:250-51) TLDP:613

---

720. Inspired prophetic utterances, both oral and written, are scripture.

### Bruce R. McConkie

Prophetic utterances, both oral and written, are scripture. "To some it is given by the Holy Ghost to know that Jesus Christ is the Son of God, and that he was crucified for the sins of the world." (D&C 46:13) Testimonies borne by such persons, when moved upon by the Spirit, are scripture. In fact, all the elders of the Church, by virtue of their ordination, are called "to proclaim the everlasting gospel, by the Spirit of the living God," with this promise: "Whatsoever they shall speak when moved upon by the Holy Ghost shall be scripture, shall be the will of the Lord, shall be the mind of the Lord, shall be the word of the Lord, shall be the voice of the Lord, and the power of God unto salvation." (D&C 68:1,4) And as it is with the elders on earth, so it is with their fellow servants beyond the veil. The words of the angels of God in heaven are scripture, for, "Angels speak by the power of the Holy Ghost; wherefore, they speak the words of Christ." (2Ne.32:3). . . . ¶ . . . . In our day the First Presidency and the Twelve are sustained as prophets, seers, and revelators to the whole Church, with the revealed provision that the President of the Church, who is the senior apostle of God on earth at any given time, shall "preside over the whole church" and "be like unto Moses," being "a seer, a revelator, a translator, and a prophet, having all the gifts of God which he bestows upon the head of the Church." (D&C 107:91-92) ¶ Such scripture as is canonized—meaning, at the present moment, the Bible, the Book of Mormon, the Doctrine and Covenants, and the Pearl of Great Price—comes from prophets who held positions of leadership and trust in the Lord's earthly kingdom. It is binding upon the Church and the world and is the standard by which all men shall be judged when they shall stand before the pleasing bar of the great Jehovah to receive according to their works. (The Promised Messiah, pp. 24-25) TLDP:606

### Elder Ezra Taft Benson

The most important prophet, so far as we are concerned, is the one who is living in our day and age. This is the prophet who has today's instructions from God to us today. God's revelation to Adam did not instruct Noah how to build the ark. Every generation has need of the ancient scripture plus the current scripture from the living prophet. Therefore, the most crucial reading and pondering which you should do is of the latest inspired words from the Lord's mouthpiece. ACR(Seoul)1975:52; MPSG1989:58-59

### Henry D. Moyle

The older I get and the closer the contact I have with the President of the Church, the more I realize that the greatest of all scriptures which we have in the world today is current scripture. What the mouthpiece of God says to his children is scripture. ("Beware of Temptation," Brigham Young University tri-stake fireside, Jan. 6, 1963, p. 7) TLDP:606

### George Q. Cannon

We have been blessed as a people with an abundance of revelation. Some have deceived themselves with the idea that because revelations have not been written and published, therefore there has been a lessening of power in the Church of Christ. This is a very great mistake, as we will find out sooner or later. This Church has been continually led by the spirit of revelation. The spirit of revelation has been here in our conference. The addresses that have been delivered have been made under the inspiration of the Holy Ghost, and they are the word of God unto this people, binding upon them, and they will be judged by these words that we have heard. CR1900Oct:64

### James E. Talmage

To become an authorized minister of the Gospel, "a man must be called of God, by prophecy, and by the laying on of hands, by those who are in authority," and those in authority must have been similarly called. When thus commissioned, he speaks by a power greater than his own in preaching the Gospel and in administering the ordinances thereof; he may verily become a prophet unto the people. The Lord has consistently recognized and honored his servants so appointed. He has magnified their office in proportion to their worthiness, making them living oracles of the divine will. . . . ¶ It is a privilege of the Holy Priesthood to commune with the heavens, and to learn the immediate will of the Lord; this communion may be effected through the medium of dreams and visions, by Urim and Thummim, through the visitation of angels, or by the higher endowment of face to face communication with the Lord. The inspired utterances of men who speak by the power of the Holy Ghost are scripture unto the people. In specific terms the promise was made in olden times that the Lord would recognize the medium of prophecy through which to make His will and purposes known to man: "Surely the Lord God will do nothing, but he revealeth his secret unto his servants the prophets." Not all men may attain the position of special revelators: "The secret of the Lord is with them that fear him; and he will show them his covenant." Such men are oracles of truth, privileged counselors, friends of God. AF:270-71

### Elder Joseph Fielding Smith

[W]hen the brethren, the authorities of the church, the elders of Israel, speak unto the people, and they have the Spirit of the Lord, they speak by inspiration, and, as we read in Section 1 of the Doctrine and Covenants, when they so speak, that which they say is scripture, and the Lord will recognize it as such, and it is binding upon the people when they so speak as if he himself spoke unto them; but when they speak unto the people by inspiration, as they do from time to time, it will be in order and according to the doctrines and the revelations which have been given to the Church, so that all who hear may understand. CR1918Oct:56

### Related Witnesses:
#### President Harold B. Lee

If you want to know what the Lord would have the Saints know and to have his guidance and direction for the next six months, get a copy of the proceedings of this conference, and you will have the latest word of the Lord as far as the Saints are concerned. CR1973Oct:168

#### Jacob, brother of Nephi

Behold, my brethren, he that prophesieth, let him prophesy to the understanding of men; for the Spirit speaketh the truth and lieth not. Wherefore, it speaketh of things as they really are, and of things as they really will be; where-fore, these things are manifested unto us plainly, for the salvation of our souls. But behold, we are not witnesses alone in these things; for God also spake them unto prophets of old. (*Jacob's scriptural writings, 544-521 B.C.*) Jacob 4:13

#### Mark E. Petersen

It is an infallible sign of the true church that it has in it divinely chosen, living prophets to guide it, men who receive current revelation from God and whose recorded works become new scripture. ¶ It is an infallible sign of the true church also that it will produce new and additional scripture arising out of the ministrations of those prophets. This unfailing pattern of God is clearly made manifest through his dealings with his people from the beginning. CR1978Apr:95-96

#### Joseph Smith

And, behold, and lo, this is an ensample unto all those who were ordained unto this priesthood, whose mission is appointed unto them to go forth— 3. And this is the ensample unto them, that they shall speak as they are moved upon by the Holy Ghost. 4. And whatsoever they shall speak when moved upon by the Holy Ghost shall be scripture, shall be the will of the Lord, shall be the mind of the Lord, shall be the word of the Lord, shall be the voice of the Lord, and the power of God unto salvation. 5. Behold, this is the promise of the Lord unto you, O ye my servants. 6. Wherefore, be of good cheer, and do not fear, for I the Lord am with you, and will stand by you: and ye shall bear record of me, even Jesus Christ, that I am the Son of the living God, that I was, that I am, and that I am to come. (*Revelation at the request of several elders, Nov. 1831*) D&C 68:2-6

#### Peter

Knowing this first, that no prophecy of the scripture is of any private interpretation. 21. For the prophecy came not in old time by the will of man: but holy men of God spake as they were moved by the Holy Ghost. (*Letter to members of the Church, about A.D. 60-64*) 2Pet.1:20-21

**Author's Note:** In the Gospel Principles manual published by the Church and distributed broadly throughout the Church (and hence published and re-published by the prophets of the Church) the following pertinent statement appears: "In addition to these four books of scripture, [the Standard Works] the inspired words of our living prophets become scripture to us. Their words come to us through conferences, Church publications, and instructions to local priesthood leaders." (Gospel Principles, pp. 51-52)

## (2) Scripture Study

**721. We are to read and study the scriptures regularly.**

### President Ezra Taft Benson,
### *also quoting*
### President Spencer W. Kimball

In a First Presidency message in 1976, President Kimball said: ¶ "I am convinced that each of us, at least some time in our lives, must discover the scriptures for ourselves—and not just discover them once, but rediscover them again and again. . . . ¶ "The Lord is not trifling with us when he gives us these things, for 'unto whomsoever much is given, of him shall be much required.' (Luke 12:48) Access to these things means responsibility for them. We must study the scriptures according to the Lord's commandment (see 3Ne.23:1-5); and we must let them govern our lives." (En1976Sept:4-5). . . . ¶ I add my voice to these wise and inspired brethren [referencing President Spencer W. Kimball, Bruce R. McConkie and Boyd K. Packer] and say to you that one of the most important things you can do as priesthood leaders is to immerse yourselves in the scriptures. Search them diligently. Feast upon the words of Christ. Learn the doctrine. Master the principles that are found therein. There are few other efforts that will bring greater dividends to your calling. There are few other ways to gain greater inspiration as you serve. . . . ¶ I urge you to recommit yourselves to a study of the scriptures. Immerse yourselves in them daily so you will have the power of the Spirit to attend you in your callings. Read them in your families and teach your children to love and treasure them. Then prayerfully and in counsel with others, seek every way possible to encourage the members of the Church to follow your example. (*To the Church in a priesthood leadership meeting, April 4, 1986; published in the Ensign by direction of President Benson*) EN1986May:81-82

### Jesus,
### *quoted by John*

Search the scriptures; for in them ye think ye have eternal life: and they are they which testify of me. (*Jesus addresses the Jews*) John 5:39

### President Spencer W. Kimball

Perhaps you have noticed that for many years the General Authorities have urged us all with increasing frequency and in a spirit of love to adopt a program of daily gospel study in our homes, both as individuals and as families . . . scarcely a meeting comes to a close without an inspired admonition from priesthood leaders to read and study the scriptures. . . . ¶ . . . I ask us all to honestly evaluate our performance in scripture study. It is a common thing to have a few passages of scripture at our disposal, floating in our minds, as it were, and thus to have the illusion that we know a great deal about the gospel. In this sense, having a little knowledge can be a problem indeed. I am convinced that each of us, at some time in our lives, must discover the scriptures for ourselves—and not just discover them once, but rediscover them again and again. (*Published message of the First Presidency of the Church*) EN1976Sep:2

### Joseph Smith,
### *receiving the Word of the Lord*

[S]tudy my word which hath gone forth among the children of men. . . . (*Revelation for Hyrum Smith, May 1829*) D&C 11:22

### Mark E. Petersen

It is through reading the scriptures that we learn what the Lord requires of us. If we do not know these requirements, how can we live them? There are two reasons why it is our responsibility to read the scriptures and know what the Lord's requirements are: that we may obey them and obtain our salvation, and that we may know by what rules we shall be judged at the last day. (*Malachi and the Great and Dreadful Day, p. 16*) TLDP:614

### President Spencer W. Kimball

Study the scriptures. Thus you may gain strength through the understanding of eternal things. You young women need this close relationship with the mind and will of our Eternal Father. We want our sisters to be scholars of the scriptures as well as our men. ¶ You need an acquaintanceship with his eternal truths for your own well-being, and for the purposes of teaching your own children and all others who come within your influence. (*Women's fireside, 1978*) (The Teachings of Spencer W. Kimball, p. 129) TLDP:607

### Bruce R. McConkie

Treasure up the Lord's word. Possess it, own it, make it yours by both believing it and living it. For instance: the voice of the Lord says that if men have faith, repent, and are baptized, they shall receive the Holy Ghost. It is not sufficient merely to know what the scripture says. One must treasure it up, meaning take it into his possession so affirmatively that it becomes a part of his very being; as a consequence, in the illustration given, one actually receives the companionship of the Spirit. Obviously such persons will not be deceived where the signs of the times and the Second Coming of the Messiah are concerned. (Doctrinal New Testament Commentary, 1:662) DGSM:96

### Elder Joseph Fielding Smith

It is the duty of the members of this Church to make themselves familiar with the revelations as they have been given and with the commandments as they have been taught in these revelations, or have been presented in them and given to the people, that they may know the truth which makes us free. CR1931Oct:17-18

**Related Witnesses:**

### Peter

We have also a more sure word of prophecy; whereunto ye do well that ye take heed, as unto a light that shineth in a dark place, until the day dawn, and the day star arise in your hearts: 20. Knowing this first, that no prophecy of the scripture is of any private interpretation. 21. For the prophecy came not in old time by the will of man: but holy men of God spake as they were moved by the Holy Ghost. (*Peter writes to members of the Church, about* A.D. *60-64*) 2Pet.1:19-21

### George Q. Cannon

The inspired books are superior to all others. No matter how good books may be nor how good the men may be who write them, they are not the standard works of the Church. The Bible, the Book of Mormon, the Book of Doctrine and Covenants and the Pearl of Great Price are the standard works. Others may be written under the influence of the Spirit of God, but they are not the word of God to the people. (Gospel Truth, 2:246) TLDP:608-09

### Paul

All scripture is given by inspiration of God, and is profitable for doctrine, for reproof, for correction, for instruction in righteousness: 17. That the man of God may be perfect, throughly furnished unto all good works. (*Paul writes to his assistant Timothy, about* A.D. *64*) 2Tim.3:16-17

### Alma, the younger,
#### quoted by Mormon

And Alma said unto them: Behold, ye have said that ye could not worship your God because ye are cast out of your synagogues. But behold, I say unto you, if ye suppose that ye cannot worship God, ye do greatly err, and ye ought to search the scriptures; if ye suppose that they have taught you this, ye do not understand them. (*Alma tells the people that the scriptures testify of the Son of God, about 74 B.C.*) Alma 33:2

### President Brigham Young,
#### quoted by John A. Widtsoe

Do you read the Scriptures, my brethren and sisters, as though you were writing them a thousand, two thousand, or five thousand years ago? Do you read them as though you stood in the place of the men who wrote them? If you do not

feel thus, it is your privilege to do so, that you may be as familiar with the spirit and meaning of the written word of God as you are with your daily walk and conversation, or as you are with your workmen or with your households. (*In Tabernacle, Oct. 8, 1859, JD7:333)* DBY:128

### Mormon

And it came to pass after he had made an end of speaking unto the people many of them did believe on his words, and began to repent, and to search the scriptures. (*Alma has been preaching repentance to his brethren in the gospel, about 82 B.C.*) Alma 14:1

---

## 722. Parents are to teach their children to study the scriptures.

### Elder George Albert Smith

In our homes . . . it is our privilege, nay, it is our duty, to call our families together to be taught the truths of the Holy scriptures. In every home, children should be encouraged to read the word of the Lord, as it has been revealed to us in all dispensations. We should read the Bible, the Book of Mormon, the Doctrine and Covenants, and the Pearl of Great Price; not only read it in our homes, but explain it to our children, that they may understand the . . . dealings of God with the peoples of the earth. CR1914Apr:12

### President Ezra Taft Benson

I urge you to recommit yourselves to a study of the scriptures. Immerse yourselves in them daily so you will have the power of the Spirit to attend you in your callings. Read them in your families and teach your children to love and treasure them. Then prayerfully and in counsel with others, seek every way possible to encourage the members of the Church to follow your example. (*To the Church in a priesthood leadership meeting, April 4, 1986; published in the Ensign by direction of President Benson*) EN1986May:81-82

### President Ezra Taft Benson

Children, support your parents in their efforts to have daily family scripture study. Pray for them as they pray for you. The Adversary does not want scripture study to take place in our homes, and so he will create problems if he can. But we must persist. Perhaps each family member can take a turn reading a verse at a time. Comments could follow. Maybe you can study by subject. Perhaps assignments might be made. CR1986Apr:99

## 723. Answers to personal problems can come through scripture study.

### President Spencer W. Kimball

The years have taught me that if we energetically pursue this worthy personal goal [of scripture study] in a determined and conscientious manner, we shall indeed find answers to our problems and peace in our hearts. We shall experience the Holy Ghost broadening our understanding, find new insights, witness an unfolding pattern of all scripture; and the doctrines of the Lord shall come to have more meaning to us than we ever thought possible. (*Area conference, Manila, Philippines, 1975*) (Teachings of Spencer W. Kimball, p. 135) TLDP:607

### Jacob, brother of Nephi

And it supposeth me that they have come up hither to hear the pleasing word of God, yea, the word which healeth the wounded soul. (*Jacob teaches the Nephites in the temple, 544-421 B.C.*) Jacob 2:8

### L. Tom Perry

Oh, how I can bear witness to the value of the scriptures in my life. I am absolutely convinced that they have answers to every problem in life. When a problem develops, after praying for instruction from the Lord, you ought to turn to the scriptures to find your answer. ACR(San Jose)1977:15; TLDP:608

### President Ezra Taft Benson,
### *also quoting Jacob, brother of Nephi*

Do you have members in your stakes whose lives are shattered by sin or tragedy, who are in despair and without hope? Have you longed for some way to reach out and heal their wounds, soothe their troubled souls? The prophet Jacob offers just that with this remarkable promise: "And it supposeth me that they have come up hither to hear the pleasing word of God, the word which healeth the wounded soul." (Jacob 2:8) (*To the Church in a priesthood leadership meeting, April 4, 1986; published in the Ensign by direction of President Benson*) EN1986May:81-82

### President Ezra Taft Benson

Often we spend great effort in trying to increase the activity levels in our stakes. . . . to raise the percentages of those attending sacrament meetings . . . to get a higher percentage of our young men on missions . . . to improve the numbers of those marrying in the temple. . . . But when individual members and families immerse themselves in the scriptures regularly and consistently, these other areas of activity will automatically come. Testimonies will increase. Commitment will be strengthened. Families

will be fortified. Personal revelation will flow. (*To the Church in a priesthood leadership meeting, April 4, 1986; published in the Ensign by direction of President Benson*) EN1986May:80

**Related Witnesses:**

### Richard L. Evans

The whole intent of scripture is one of establishing our relationship with God, our Father, and with his Son, our Savior, and with the eternal plans and purposes for each and all of us, and our relationships to life—and to one another also. CR1959Oct:127

### Paul

For whatsoever things were written aforetime were written for our learning, that we through patience and comfort of the scriptures might have hope. (*Letter to the Church in Rome, about A.D. 55*) Rom.15:4

### President Joseph F. Smith

The Scriptures . . . are intended to enlarge man's spiritual endowments and to reveal and intensify the bond of relationship between him and his God. (Gospel Doctrine, p. 46) TLDP:607

---

## 724. Members of the Church are to read the Book of Mormon particularly.

### Elder Joseph Fielding Smith

No member of this Church can stand approved in the presence of God who has not seriously and carefully read the Book of Mormon. . . . CR1961Oct:18

### Marion G. Romney

Nephi tells us that its [the Book of Mormon's] contents "shall go from generation to generation as long as the earth shall stand; . . . and the nations who shall possess them [the teachings of the Book of Mormon] shall be judged of them according to the words which are written." (2Ne.25:22) ¶ For me there could be no more impelling reason for reading the Book of Mormon than this statement that we who have the Book of Mormon shall be judged by what is written in it. ¶ Moroni says that the very reason the book has been given to us is that we may know the "decrees of God" (Ether 2:11) set forth therein and by obedience to them escape the calamities which are to follow disobedience. . . . ¶ There is another reason why we should read the Book of Mormon: By doing so we will fill and refresh our minds with a constant flow of the "water" which Jesus said would be in us "a well of water springing up into everlasting life" (John 4:14). We must obtain a continuing supply of this water if we are to resist evil and retain the blessings of being born again. . . . ¶ If we would avoid adopting the evils of the world, we must pursue a course which will daily feed our minds with, and call them back to, the things of the Spirit. I know of no better way to do this than by daily reading the Book of Mormon. CR1980Apr:87-88

**President Ezra Taft Benson**

Unless we read the Book of Mormon and give heed to its teachings, the Lord has stated in section 84 of the Doctrine and Covenants that the whole Church is under condemnation. CR1986Apr:4

**Elder Ezra Taft Benson**

Is the Book of Mormon true? Yes. ¶ Who is it for? Us. ¶ What is its purpose? To bring men to Christ. ¶ How does it do this? By testifying of Christ and revealing his enemies. ¶ How are we to use it? We are to get a testimony of it, we are to teach from it, we are to hold it up as a standard and "hiss it forth." ¶ Have we been doing this? Not as we should, nor as we must. ¶ Do eternal consequences rest upon our response to this book? Yes, either to our blessing or our condemnation. CR1975Apr:94-95

**Elder Heber J. Grant**

I rejoice in the wonderful spirit of the Book of Mormon. I believe that it is one of the greatest missionaries in the hands of the Elder that it is possible for him to have. I believe that no man can open that book and read it with a prayerful heart, and ask God, in the name of Jesus Christ, for a testimony regarding its divinity, but what the Lord will manifest unto him by His Spirit the truth of the book. Now that is the promise made in the book itself and God has performed it; He has done it in thousands of cases. There is a mark of divinity in this book; and I maintain that no man can read, for instance the 36th chapter, the commandments of Alma to his son Helaman, without receiving an impression of this kind. CR1908Apr:57

---

## 725. Reading the scriptures enlarges our spiritual endowments.

**President Joseph F. Smith**

The Scriptures . . . are intended to enlarge man's spiritual endowments and to reveal and intensify the bond of relationship between him and his God. (Gospel Doctrine, p. 46) TLDP:607

**Bruce R. McConkie**

The Holy Scriptures are given to guide men to that state of spiritual enlightenment and perfection attained by those of old who

worked out their salvation. ¶ "The holy scriptures," Paul told his beloved Timothy, "are able to make thee wise unto salvation through faith which is in Christ Jesus." The scriptures open the door; they mark the course we must pursue; they identify the strait and narrow path; they testify of Christ and his laws; they engender faith; their worth cannot be revealed, men must walk therein to gain the desired eternal reward. (The Mortal Messiah, 1:266) TLDP:608

### Mormon

And now, as the preaching of the word had a great tendency to lead the people to do that which was just—yea, it had had more powerful effect upon the minds of the people than the sword, or anything else, which had happened unto them—therefore Alma thought it was expedient that they should try the virtue of the word of God. (Alma heads a mission to reclaim the apostate Zoramites, about 74 B.C.) Alma 31:5

### Nephi, son of Lehi

Angels speak by the power of the Holy Ghost; wherefore, they speak the words of Christ. Wherefore, I said unto you, feast upon the words of Christ; for behold, the words of Christ will tell you all things what ye should do. (Nephi's writings, 559-545 B.C.) 2Ne.32:3

### Marion G. Romney

If we would avoid adopting the evils of the world, we must pursue a course which will daily feed our minds with, and call them back to, the things of the Spirit. I know of no better way to do this than by daily reading the Book of Mormon. CR1980Apr:88

### Paul

For the word of God is quick and powerful, and sharper than any two-edged sword, piercing even to the dividing asunder of soul and spirit, and of joints and marrow, and is a discerner of the thoughts and intents of the heart. (Paul's letter to the Jewish members of the Church, about A.D. 60) Heb.4:12

### President Spencer W. Kimball

The years have taught me that if we energetically pursue this worthy personal goal [of scripture study] in a determined and conscientious manner, we shall indeed find answers to our problems and peace in our hearts. We shall experience the Holy Ghost broadening our understanding, find new insights, witness an unfolding pattern of all scripture; and the doctrines of the Lord shall come to have more meaning to us than we ever thought possible. (Area conference, Manila, Philippines, 1975) (The Teachings of Spencer W. Kimball, p. 135) TLDP:607

**Related Witnesses:**
### Joseph Smith
Never did any passage of scripture come with
more power to the heart of man than this did at
this time to mine. It seemed to enter with great
force into every feeling of my heart. I reflected
on it again and again, knowing that if any person needed wisdom from God, I did; for how to
act I did not know, and unless I could get more
wisdom than I then had, I would never know;
for the teachers of religion of the different sects
understood the same passages of scripture so
differently as to destroy all confidence in settling the question by an appeal to the Bible.
*(Joseph relates the background of his experi-
ence of the vision of the Father and the Son that
occurred in the spring of 1820)* JS-H 1:12

# List of Doctrines

## SECOND COMING OF CHRIST

### Events at the Second Coming, and Doctrines Specifically Referring to the Second Coming

*Doctrines Located in This Topic*

726. Christ will come again, this time to reign personally upon the earth.

727. At His second coming, the Lord will come in power and great glory; He will not come in secret.

728. The day and the hour of the second coming of the Lord is not known by any person, and will not be known (even by angels) until He comes.

729. The Savior's second coming has been foretold by Old and New Testament prophets, by angels, and by the Savior Himself.

730. At His second coming, the Savior will appear first to those in the New Jerusalem in America, then to the Jews in Jerusalem, and finally to all the world.

731. The second coming of the Lord is near; it will come as "a thief in the night."

732. The earth will be in great upheaval at the Savior's second coming.

733. The Lord will be clothed in red apparel when He appears to all the world at His second coming.

734. At the second coming of the Lord, the wicked will weep and wail and try to hide themselves from the glory of His presence.

735. Faithful Saints, both living and dead, will be caught up to meet Christ at His second coming.

736. The Jews will acknowledge Jesus as the Christ at His second coming.

737. When the Lord comes in the last days He will set His foot upon the Mount of Olives and it shall cleave in twain.

738. The second coming of Christ will usher in the Millennium.

739. The Saints must prepare for the Second Coming.

*Doctrines on SECOND COMING OF CHRIST Located in Other Topics*

443. The ushering in of the Millennium will occur with the second coming of Christ.

(See topic LAST DAYS.)

# SECOND COMING OF CHRIST

## Events at the Second Coming, and Doctrines Specifically Referring to the Second Coming

**726. Christ will come again, this time to reign personally upon the earth.**

### President Brigham Young

We believe that Jesus Christ will descend from heaven to earth again even as He ascended into heaven. "Behold, He cometh with clouds, and every eye shall see Him, and they also which pierced Him: and all kindreds of the earth shall wail because of Him." He will come to receive His own, and rule and reign king of nations as He does king of saints; "For He must reign, till He hath put all enemies under His feet. The last enemy that shall be destroyed is death." He will banish sin from the earth and its dreadful consequences, tears shall be wiped from every eye and there shall be nothing to hurt or destroy in all God's holy mountain. (*In Bowery, June 18, 1865, JD11:123*) TLDP:620

### Joseph Smith,
### *receiving the Word of the Lord*

For in mine own due time will I come upon the earth in judgment, and my people shall be redeemed and shall reign with me on earth. 30. For the great Millennium, of which I have spoken by the mouth of my servants, shall come. (*Message for the nations of the earth, Feb. 1831*) D&C 43:29-30

### Joseph Smith

These are they whom he shall bring with him, when he shall come in the clouds of heaven to reign on the earth over his people. (*Vision to Joseph and to Sidney Rigdon, Feb. 16, 1832*) D&C 76:63 (See verses 58-63)

### Elder Wilford Woodruff

The Lord Jesus Christ is coming to reign on earth. The world may say that he delays his coming until the end of the earth. But they know neither the thoughts nor the ways of the Lord. The Lord will not delay his coming because of their unbelief, and the signs both in heaven and earth indicate that it is near. The fig trees are leafing in sight of all the nations of the earth, and if they had the Spirit of God they could see and understand them. (*General conference, April 1873, JD16:35*) TLDP:621

### Joseph Smith

We believe . . . that Christ will reign personally upon the earth. . . . (*The tenth of the thirteen Articles of Faith; letter to John Wentworth, March 1, 1842*) AofF:10

### Charles A. Callis

The Church of Jesus Christ of Latter-day Saints has been brought forth and established by the power of God and dedicated to the mission of preparing the way for the glorious coming of the Son of God to reign in the earth in truth and righteousness and peace. ¶ Would to God this glorious second coming of the Messiah might be in our day, but let it be sooner or later, in it we will rejoice. ¶ Truly, God will descend from the heavens in incomparable power and glory with all His holy angels, and He will stand upon the earth at the latter day. Then heaven and earth will meet. (*Fundamentals of Religion: A Series of Radio Addresses*) TLDP:623

### Nephi, son of Lehi

And the time cometh speedily that the righteous must be led up as calves of the stall, and the Holy One of Israel must reign in dominion, and might, and power, and great glory. 25. And he gathereth his children from the four quarters of the earth; and he numbereth his sheep, and they know him; and there shall be one fold and one shepherd; and he shall feed his sheep, and in him they shall find pasture. 26. And because of the righteousness of his people, Satan has no power; wherefore, he cannot be loosed for the space of many years; for he hath no power over the hearts of the people, for they dwell in righteousness, and the Holy One of Israel reigneth. (*Nephi explains the prophecies written on the plates of brass, 588-570 B.C.*) 1Ne.22:24-26

### Isaiah

Then the moon shall be confounded, and the sun ashamed, when the LORD of hosts shall reign in mount Zion, and in Jerusalem, and before his ancients gloriously. (*Isaiah prophesies, near 700 B.C.*) Isa.24:23

### Related Witnesses:
### Joseph Smith,
### *receiving the Word of the Lord*

And there shall be mine abode, and it shall be Zion, which shall come forth out of all the creations which I have made; and for the space of a thousand years the earth shall rest. 65. And it came to pass that Enoch saw the day of the coming of the Son of Man, in the last days, to dwell on the earth in righteousness for the space of a thousand years; (See Moses 7:62-65.) (*Revelation to Moses recording the word of the Lord to Enoch*) Moses 7:64-65

### Joseph Smith,
*receiving the Word of the Lord*

Thus saith the Lord; for I am God, and have sent mine Only Begotten Son into the world for the redemption of the world, and have decreed that he that receiveth him shall be saved, and he that receiveth him not shall be damned— 6. And they have done unto the Son of Man even as they listed; and he has taken his power on the right hand of his glory, and now reigneth in the heavens, and will reign till he descends on the earth to put all enemies under his feet, which time is nigh at hand— *(Revelation, March 1831)* D&C 49:5-6

### Micah

And I will make her that halted a remnant, and her that was cast far off a strong nation: and the LORD shall reign over them in mount Zion from henceforth, even for ever. *(Micah prophesies, about 740-700 B.C.)* Micah 4:7

### Recorded in Matthew

When the Son of man shall come in his glory, and all the holy angels with him, then shall he sit upon the throne of his glory: 32. And before him shall be gathered all nations: and he shall separate them one from another, as a shepherd divideth his sheep from the goats: 33. And he shall set the sheep on his right hand, but the goats on the left. 34. Then shall the King say unto them on his right hand, Come, ye blessed of my Father, inherit the kingdom prepared for you from the foundation of the world: . . . *(Jesus gives the parable of the sheep and the goats; the sheep are placed on his right hand at the Lord's second coming)* Matt.25:31-34

### Recorded in Mark

And then shall they see the Son of man coming in the clouds with great power and glory. 27. And then shall he send his angels, and shall gather together his elect from the four winds, from the uttermost part of the earth to the uttermost part of heaven. *(The Lord will come after the sun and moon are darkened)* Mark 13:26-27

---

## 727. At His second coming, the Lord will come in power and great glory; He will not come in secret.

### Orson Pratt

The second advent of the Son of God is to be something altogether of a different nature from anything that has hitherto transpired on the face of the earth, accompanied with great power and glory, something that will not be done in a small portion of the earth like Palestine, and seen only by a few; but it will be an event that will be seen by all—all flesh shall see the glory of the Lord; when he reveals himself the second time, every eye, not only those living at that time in the flesh, in mortality on the earth, but also the very dead themselves, they also who pierced him, those who lived eighteen hundred years ago, who were engaged in the cruel act of piercing his hands and his feet and his side, will also see him at that time. *(In 15th Ward, March 1876, JD18:170)* DGSM:102

### Joseph Smith,
*receiving the Word of the Lord*

And then they shall look for me, and, behold, I will come; and they shall see me in the clouds of heaven, clothed with power and great glory; with all the holy angels. . . . *(Revelation, March 7, 1831; signs and wonders to attend the Second Coming)* D&C 45:44

### Jesus,
*recorded in Matthew*

Wherefore if they shall say unto you, Behold, he is in the desert; go not forth: behold, he is in the secret chambers; believe it not. 27. For as the lightning cometh out of the east, and shineth even unto the west; so shall also the coming of the Son of man be. 28. For wheresoever the carcase is, there will the eagles be gathered together. 29. Immediately after the tribulation of those days shall the sun be darkened, and the moon shall not give her light, and the stars shall fall from heaven, and the powers of the heavens shall be shaken: 30. And then shall appear the sign of the Son of man in heaven: and then shall all the tribes of the earth mourn, and they shall see the Son of man coming in the clouds of heaven with power and great glory. *(Jesus foretells his second coming to his disciples)* Matt.24:26-30

### Elder John Taylor

There is something also to be looked to in the future. The Son of God has again to figure in the grand drama of the world. He has been here once and "In his humiliation his judgment was taken away.". . . Jesus accomplished what He was sent to do, and, feeling satisfied of this, when he was about to leave the earth he said he had finished the work his Father gave him to do. But there was another work, another event that was to transpire in the latter days, when he should not be led as a lamb to the slaughter or be like a sheep before the shearers: when he would not act in that state of humiliation and quiescence, but when he will go forth as a man of war and tread down the people in his anger and trample them in his fury, when blood should be on his garments and the day of vengeance in his heart, when he would rule the nations with an iron rod and break them to pieces like a potter's vessel. . . . When he comes again he comes to take vengeance on the ungodly and to bring deliverance unto his Saints; "For the day of vengeance," it is said, "is in my heart and the year of my redeemed is come." [Isaiah 63:4] It behooves us to be made well aware which class we belong to, that if we are not already among the redeemed we may immediately join that society, that when the Son of God shall come the second time with all the holy angels with him, arrayed in power and great glory to take vengeance on them that know not God and obey not the Gospel, or when he shall come in flaming fire, we shall be among that number who shall be ready to meet him with gladness in our hearts and hail him as our great deliverer and friend. (*In Tabernacle, Feb. 22, 1863, JD10:115*) TLDP:622

### Joseph Smith,
*receiving the Word of the Lord*

For I will reveal myself from heaven with power and great glory, with all the hosts there-of. . . . (*Revelation, Sept. 1830; Christ's second coming ushers in the Millennium*) D&C 29:11

### Charles A. Callis

Truly, God will descend from the heavens in incomparable power and glory with all His holy angels, and He will stand upon the earth at the latter day. Then heaven and earth will meet. (*Fundamentals of Religion: A Series of Radio Addresses, p. 40*) TLDP:623

### Elder Ezra Taft Benson,
*also quoting Joseph Smith*

His first appearance will be to the righteous Saints who have gathered to the New Jerusalem. In this place of refuge they will be safe from the wrath of the Lord, which will be poured out without measure on all nations. . . . ¶ The second appearance of the Lord will be to the Jews. To these beleaguered sons of Judah, surrounded by hostile Gentile armies, who again threaten to overrun Jerusalem, the Savior—their Messiah—will appear and set His feet on the Mount of Olives, "and it shall cleave in twain, and the earth shall tremble, and reel to and fro, and the heavens shall also shake." (D&C 45:48) ¶ The Lord Himself will then rout the Gentile armies, decimating their forces (see Ezek.38,39). Judah will be spared, no longer to be persecuted and scattered. . . . ¶ The third appearance of Christ will be to the rest of the world. . . . ¶ All nations will see Him "in the clouds of heaven, clothed with power and great glory; with all the holy angels. . . . ¶ "And the Lord shall utter his voice, and all the ends of the earth shall hear it; and the nations of the earth shall mourn, and they that have laughed shall see their folly. ¶ "And

calamity shall cover the mocker, and the scorner shall be consumed; and they that have watched for iniquity shall be hewn down and cast into the fire." ¶ Yes, come He will! (New Era, Dec. 1980, pp. 49-50) DGSM:101

### Charles W. Penrose

The great and crowning advent of the Lord will be subsequent to these two appearances [to the New Jerusalem and to the Jews]; but who can describe it in the language of mortals? The tongue of man falters, and the pen drops from the hand of the writer, as the mind is rapt in contemplation of the sublime and awful majesty of his coming to take vengeance on the ungodly and to reign as King of the whole earth. ¶ He comes! The earth shakes, and the tall mountains tremble; the mighty deep rolls back to the north as in fear, and the rent skies glow like molten brass. He comes! The dead Saints burst forth from their tombs, and "those who are alive and remain" are "caught up" with them to meet him. The ungodly rush to hide themselves from his presence, and call upon the quivering rocks to cover them. He comes! with all the hosts of the righteous glorified. The breath of his lip strikes death to the wicked. His glory is a consuming fire. The proud and rebellious are as stubble; they are burned and "left neither root nor branch." He sweeps the earth "as with the besom [broom] of destruction." He deluges the earth with the fiery floods of his wrath, and the filthiness and abominations of the world are consumed. Satan and his dark hosts are taken and bound—the prince of the power of the air has lost his dominion, for He whose right it is to reign has come, and "the kingdoms of this world have become the kingdoms of our Lord and of his Christ." (Millennial Star, Sept. 1859, p. 583) DGSM:101

**Related Witnesses:**

### Joseph Smith,
*receiving the Word of the Lord*

Behold, it is my will, that all they who call on my name, and worship me according to mine everlasting gospel, should gather together, and stand in holy places; 23. And prepare for the revelation which is to come, when the veil of the covering of my temple, in my tabernacle, which hideth the earth, shall be taken off, and all flesh shall see me together. (*Revelation, Dec. 16, 1833*) D&C 101:22-23

### Isaiah

And the glory of the LORD shall be revealed, and all flesh shall see it together: for the mouth of the LORD hath spoken it. (*Isaiah speaks, "Comfort ye, comfort ye my people, saith your God" 740-659 B.C.*) Isa.40:5

### Joseph Smith

The coming of the Son of Man never will be—never can be, till the judgments spoken of for this hour are poured out: which judgments are commenced. Paul says, "Ye are the children of the light, and not of the darkness, that that day should overtake you as a thief in the night." It is not the design of the Almighty to come upon the earth and crush it and grind it to powder, but he will reveal it to His servants the prophets. ¶ Judah must return, Jerusalem must be rebuilt, and the temple, and water come out from under the temple, and the waters of the Dead Sea be healed. It will take some time to rebuild the walls of the city and the temple, and etc; and all this must be done before the Son of Man will make His appearance. There will be wars and rumors of wars, signs in the heavens above and on the earth beneath, the sun turned into darkness and the moon to blood, earthquakes in divers places, the seas heaving beyond their bounds; then will appear one grand sign of the Son of Man in heaven. But what will the world do? They will say it is a planet, a comet, etc. But the Son of Man will come as the sign of the coming of the Son of Man, which will be as the light of the morning cometh out of the east. (*General conference, speaking on the judgments to come before the Second Coming of Christ, April 1843*) HC5:336-37

### John,
### *quoted by Joseph Smith,*
### *translating the Book of Revelation*

For behold, he cometh in the clouds with ten thousands of his saints in the kingdom, clothed with the glory of his Father. And every eye shall see him, and they who pierced him: and all kindreds of the earth shall wail because of him. Even so, Amen. JST(Rev.1:7 in appendix)

### Paul

For the Lord himself shall descend from heaven with a shout, with the voice of the archangel, and with the trump of God. . . . (*Paul writes to the Church at Thessalonica that the Lord shall come again and the dead shall rise, A.D. 50*) 1Thess.4:16

---

728. **The day and the hour of the second coming of the Lord is not known by any person, and will not be known (even by angels) until He comes.**

### James E. Talmage

The precise time of Christ's Coming has not been made known to man. By learning to com-

prehend the signs of the times, by watching the development of the work of God among the nations, and by noting the rapid fulfilment of significant prophecies, we may perceive the progressive evidence of the approaching event: "But the hour and the day no man knoweth, neither the angels in heaven, nor shall they know until he comes." His coming will be a surprise to those who have ignored His warnings, and who have failed to watch. "As a thief in the night" will be the coming of the day of the Lord unto the wicked. "Watch therefore, for ye know neither the day nor the hour wherein the Son of Man cometh." AF:328

### Joseph Smith,
### *receiving the Word of the Lord*

[Christ] now reigneth in the heavens, and will reign till he descends on the earth to put all enemies under his feet, which time is nigh at hand—7. I, the Lord God, have spoken it; but the hour and the day no man knoweth, neither the angels in heaven, nor shall they know until he comes. (*Revelation, March 1831*) D&C 49:6-7

### Joseph Smith

Yea, let the cry go forth among all people: Awake and arise and go forth to meet the Bridegroom; behold and lo, the Bridegroom cometh; go ye out to meet him. Prepare yourselves for the great day of the Lord. 11. Watch, therefore, for ye know neither the day nor the hour. (*All are commanded to flee from Babylon, come to Zion, and prepare for the great day of the Lord*) D&C 133:10-11

### Joseph Smith

Jesus Christ never did reveal to any man the precise time that He would come. Go and read the Scriptures, and you cannot find anything that specifies the exact hour He would come; and all that say so are false teachers. (*Sermon on Elias, Elijah and Messiah, Sunday, March 10, 1844*) HC6:254; TPJS:341; DGSM:101

### Jesus,
### *recorded in Matthew*

But of that day and hour knoweth no man, no, not the angels of heaven, but my Father only. (*Jesus foretells his second coming to his disciples*) Matt.24:36

### Jesus,
### *quoted by Joseph Smith,*
### *translating Matthew*

But of that day, and hour, no one knoweth; no, not the angels of God in heaven, but my Father only. (*An extract from the translation of the Bible as revealed to Joseph Smith, about Sept. 1831; Christ speaks of his second coming*) JS-M 1:40

### Elder Wilford Woodruff

No man knows the day or the hour when Christ

will come, yet the generation has been pointed out by Jesus himself. He told his disciples when they passed by the temple as they walked out of Jerusalem that that generation should not pass away before not one stone of that magnificent temple should be left standing upon another and the Jews should be scattered among the nations; and history tells how remarkably that prediction was fulfilled. Moses and the prophets also prophesied of this as well as Jesus. The Savior, when speaking to his disciples of his second coming and the establishment of his kingdom on the earth, said the Jews should be scattered and trodden under foot until the times of the Gentiles were fulfilled. But, said he, when you see light breaking forth among the Gentiles, referring to the preaching of his gospel amongst them; when you see salvation offered to the Gentiles, and the Jews—the seed of Israel—passed by, the last first and the first last; when you see this you may know that the time of my second coming is at hand as surely as you know that summer is nigh when the fig tree puts forth its leaves; and when these things commence that generation shall not pass away until all are fulfilled. (*In Tabernacle, Jan. 1, 1871, JD14:5*) TLDP:620

### Elder Joseph Fielding Smith

Do not think that he delayeth his coming. I want to say to you that many of the signs of the coming of the Son of God have been given and others will be given, so we may, if we will, know that the coming of the Son of God is even now, figuratively speaking, at our doors. The Lord isn't going to tell me when he is coming; he is not going to tell you; he is not going to tell anybody else—for he has made it definitely clear that he is going to come like the thief comes: when he is not expected. ("The Blessings of Eternal Glory," Brigham Young University Speeches of the Year, 1968, p. 10) TLDP:621

### Charles W. Penrose

There are quite a number of people who set the date to the time of the coming of the Savior. . . . That is all wrong; that should not be done. The Lord has not, at any time, so far as I am aware, in all my searchings in the revelations that have come to the earth, set a date for the coming of the Savior to reign on the earth. CR1924Apr:14

---

729. **The Savior's second coming has been foretold by Old and New Testament prophets, by angels, and by the Savior Himself.**

### Elder Wilford Woodruff

No man knows the day or the hour when Christ

will come, yet the generation has been pointed out by Jesus himself. He told his disciples when they passed by the temple as they walked out of Jerusalem that that generation should not pass away before not one stone of that magnificent temple should be left standing upon another and the Jews should be scattered among the nations; and history tells how remarkably that prediction was fulfilled. Moses and the prophets also prophesied of this as well as Jesus. The Savior, when speaking to his disciples of his second coming and the establishment of his kingdom on the earth, said the Jews should be scattered and trodden under foot until the times of the Gentiles were fulfilled. But, said he, when you see light breaking forth among the Gentiles, referring to the preaching of his gospel amongst them; when you see salvation offered to the Gentiles, and the Jews—the seed of Israel—passed by, the last first and the first last; when you see this you may know that the time of my second coming is at hand as surely as you know that summer is nigh when the fig tree puts forth its leaves; and when these things commence that generation shall not pass away until all are fulfilled. (*In Tabernacle, Jan. 1, 1871, JD14:5*) TLDP:620

### Joseph Smith,
### *translating the Book of Moses*

And it came to pass that Enoch saw the day of the coming of the Son of Man, in the last days, to dwell on the earth in righteousness for the space of a thousand years; (*Moses relates Enoch's vision*) Moses 7:65

### Related Witnesses:
### Malachi

Behold, I will send my messenger, and he shall prepare the way before me: and the Lord, whom ye seek, shall suddenly come to this temple, even the messenger of the covenant, whom ye delight in: behold, he shall come, saith the LORD of hosts. 2. But who may abide the day of his coming? and who shall stand when he appeareth? for he is like a refiner's fire, and like fullers' soap: (*The prophet Malachi to the people, about 430 B.C.*) Mal.3:1-2

### Malachi,
### *quoted by Jesus,*
### *quoted by Mormon*

But who may abide the day of his coming, and who shall stand when he appeareth? For he is like a refiner's fire, and like fuller's soap. (*The resurrected Christ instructs his Nephite disciples to write the words which the Father had given Malachi concerning the Second Coming, which words he then gives to them, A.D. 34*) 3Ne.24:2

**Jesus,**
*recorded in Matthew*

For the Son of man shall come in the glory of his Father with his angels; and then he shall reward every man according to his works. *(Jesus speaks to his disciples and foretells his death and resurrection)* Matt.16:27

**Recorded in Acts**

. . . Ye men of Galilee, why stand ye gazing up into heaven? this same Jesus, which is taken up from you into heaven, shall so come in like manner as ye have seen him go into heaven. *(The Apostles witness the ascent of Jesus to heaven and two angels speak to them)* Acts 1:11

**Joseph Smith,**
*receiving the Word of the Lord*

And the saints also shall hardly escape; nevertheless, I, the Lord, am with them, and will come down in heaven from the presence of my Father and consume the wicked with unquenchable fire. *(Revelation, Aug. 1831)* D&C 63:34

**President Brigham Young**

We believe that Jesus Christ will descend from heaven to earth again even as He ascended into heaven. "Behold, He cometh with clouds, and every eye shall see Him, and they also which pierced Him: and all kindreds of the earth shall wail because of Him." He will come to receive His own, and rule and reign king of nations as He does king of saints; "For He must reign, till He hath put all enemies under His feet. The last enemy that shall be destroyed is death." He will banish sin from the earth and its dreadful consequences, tears shall be wiped from every eye and there shall be nothing to hurt or destroy in all God's holy mountain. *(In Bowery, June 18, 1865, JD11:123)* TLDP:620

**Joseph Smith,**
*quoted by Elder Joseph Fielding Smith*

When I contemplate the rapidity with which the great and glorious day of the coming of the Son of Man advances, when He shall come to receive His Saints unto Himself, where they shall dwell in His presence, and be crowned with glory and immortality: when I consider that soon the heavens are to be shaken, and the earth tremble and reel to and fro; and that the heavens are to be unfolded as a scroll when it is rolled up; and that every mountain and island are to flee away, I cry out in my heart, What manner of persons ought we to be in all holy conversation and godliness! *(In letter to Moses C. Nickerson, Upper Canada, from the Prophet in Kirtland, Ohio, Nov. 19, 1833)* HC1:441-43; TPJS:29

**Author's Note:** The second coming of Christ is mentioned over 1,800 times in the Bible, according to Sterling W. Sill: ¶ "The most often mentioned event in the entire Bible is that wonderful, yet awful experience that we will have when Jesus Christ shall come to judge our world. There are many important gospel doctrines mentioned in the Bible only briefly, and some not at all. The new birth is mentioned in the Bible nine times; baptism is mentioned 52 times, repentance is mentioned 89, but the second coming of Christ is mentioned over 1,500 times in the Old Testament and 300 times in the New Testament. If God thought this subject that important, he must have wanted us to do something about it." *(CR1966Apr:19)*

---

730. **At His second coming, the Savior will appear first to those in the New Jerusalem in America, then to the Jews in Jerusalem, and finally to all the world.**

**Elder Ezra Taft Benson,**
*also quoting Joseph Smith*

His first appearance will be to the righteous Saints who have gathered to the New Jerusalem. In this place of refuge they will be safe from the wrath of the Lord, which will be poured out without measure on all nations. . . . ¶ The second appearance of the Lord will be to the Jews. To these beleaguered sons of Judah, surrounded by hostile Gentile armies, who again threaten to overrun Jerusalem, the Savior—their Messiah—will appear and set His feet on the Mount of Olives, "and it shall cleave in twain, and the earth shall tremble, and reel to and fro, and the heavens shall also shake." *(D&C 45:48)* ¶ The Lord Himself will then rout the Gentile armies, decimating their forces (see Ezek. 38,39). Judah will be spared, no longer to be persecuted and scattered. . . . ¶ The third appearance of Christ will be to the rest of the world. . . . ¶ All nations will see Him "in the clouds of heaven, clothed with power and great glory; with all the holy angels. . . ." *(New Era, Dec. 1980, p.49)* DGSM:101

**President Brigham Young,**
*quoted by John A. Widtsoe*

When he comes again, he will not come as he did when the Jews rejected him; neither will he appear first at Jerusalem when he makes his second appearance on the earth; but he will appear first on the land where he commenced his work in the beginning, and planted the Garden of Eden, and that was done in the land of America. ¶ When the Savior visits Jerusalem, and the Jews look upon him, and see the wounds in his hands and in his side and in his feet, they will then know that they have persecuted and put to death the true Messiah, and then they will acknowledge him, but not till then. They have confounded his first and second coming, expecting his first coming to be as a mighty prince instead of as a servant. They will go back by and by to Jerusalem and own their Lord and Master. We have no feelings against them. (*In Tabernacle, Dec. 23, 1866, JD11:279*) DBY:122

**Bruce R. McConkie**

Before the Lord Jesus descends openly and publicly in the clouds of glory, attended by all the hosts of heaven; before the great and dreadful day of the Lord sends terror and destruction from one end of the earth to the other; before he stands on Mount Zion, or sets his feet on Olivet, or utters his voice from an American Zion or a Jewish Jerusalem; before all flesh shall see him together; before any of his appearances, which taken together comprise the second coming of the Son of God—before all these, there is to be a secret appearance to selected members of his Church. He will come in private to his prophet and to the apostles then living. Those who have held keys and powers and authorities in all ages from Adam to the present will also be present. (The Millennial Messiah, pp. 578-79) DGSM:101

**Related Witnesses:**

**Charles W. Penrose**

His [Christ's] next appearance [after his appearance in the New Jerusalem] will be among the distressed and nearly vanquished sons of Judah. At the crisis of their fate, when the hostile troops of several nations are ravaging the city and all the horrors of war are overwhelming the people of Jerusalem, he will set his feet upon the Mount of Olives, which will cleave and part asunder at his touch. (Millennial Star, Sept. 1859, p. 583) DGSM:101

**Hugh B. Brown**

To the wicked, the second coming will be a great and dreadful day, a day of sorrow and desolation, of burning and vengeance and judgment. ¶ "For the presence of the Lord shall be as the melting fire that burneth, and as the fire which causeth the waters to boil." [D&C 133:41] ¶ But to the righteous who have waited faithfully and kept his laws, the second coming will be a day devoutly to be desired, when injustice will cease and wickedness be vanished. ¶ The Lord will undoubtedly make many successive appearances in various parts of the earth, and Malachi asks: ¶ "Who may abide the day of his coming? and who shall stand when he appeareth?" [Mal.3:2] ("We Rededicate Our Lives to Establish the Kingdom of God," Church News, 28 Nov. 1964, p. 15) TLDP:622

**Bruce R. McConkie**

[A]nd the New Jerusalem will become, in all her glory and magnificence, the spiritual capital of the world. Jehovah himself will come to the new temple, there to be constructed after the order of his new kingdom, and the saints shall worship in those sacred halls for a thousand years. . . . (The Mortal Messiah, 3:446-47) TLDP:349-50

**Joseph Smith**

And it shall be called the New Jerusalem, a land of peace, a city of refuge, a place of safety for the saints of the Most High God; 67. And the glory of the Lord shall be there, and the terror of the Lord also shall be there, insomuch that the wicked will not come unto it, and it shall be called Zion. (*Revelation, March 7, 1831; the Saints are commanded to gather and build the New Jerusalem*) D&C 45:66-67

**Jesus,**
**quoted by Mormon**

And they shall assist my people, the remnant of Jacob, and also as many of the house of Israel as shall come, that they may build a city, which shall be called the New Jerusalem. 24. And then shall they assist my people that they may be gathered in, who are scattered upon all the face of the land, in unto the New Jerusalem. 25. And then shall the power of heaven come down among them; and I also will be in the midst. (*The resurrected Jesus Christ to the Nephite people, A.D. 34*) 3Ne.21:23-25

**Joseph Smith,**
**receiving the Word of the Lord**

And then shall the Lord set his foot upon this mount, and it shall cleave in twain, and the earth shall tremble, and reel to and fro, and the heavens also shall shake. . . . 51. And then shall the Jews look upon me and say: What are these wounds in thine hands and in thy feet? 52. Then shall they know that I am the Lord; for I will say unto them: These wounds are the wounds with which I was wounded in the house of my friends. I am he who was lifted up. I am Jesus that was crucified. I am the Son of God. 53. And then shall they weep because of their iniquities; then shall they lament because they persecuted their king. (*Revelation, March 7, 1831; Christ shall stand on the Mount of Olives, and the Jews shall see the wounds in his hands and feet*) D&C 45:48,51-53

**Zechariah**

And I will pour upon the house of David, and upon the inhabitants of Jerusalem, the spirit of grace and of supplications: and they shall look upon me whom they have pierced, and they shall mourn for him, as one mourneth for his only son, and shall be in bitterness for him, as one that is in bitterness for his firstborn. (*The word of the Lord to Zechariah regarding the Second Coming, the final great war at Jerusalem—then the Jews shall look upon him they crucified*) Zech.12:10

**Zechariah**
For I will gather all nations against Jerusalem to battle; and the city shall be taken, and the houses rifled, and the women ravished; and half of the city shall go forth into captivity, and the residue of the people shall not be cut off from the city. 3. Then shall the LORD go forth, and fight against those nations, as when he fought in the day of battle. 4. And his feet shall stand in that day upon the mount of Olives, which is before Jerusalem on the east, and the mount of Olives shall cleave in the midst thereof toward the east and toward the west, and there shall be a very great valley; and half of the mountain shall remove toward the north, and half of it toward the south. 5. And ye shall flee to the valley of the mountains; for the valley of the mountains shall reach unto Azal: yea, ye shall flee, like as ye fled from before the earthquake in the days of Uzziah king of Judah: and the LORD my God shall come, and all the saints with thee. (*Zechariah prophesies that at his second coming the Lord shall fight for Israel*) Zech.14:2-5

---

731. The second coming of the Lord is near; it will come as "a thief in the night."

**James E. Talmage**
To the unwatchful and the wicked the event will be as sudden and unexpected as the coming of a thief in the night. But we are not left without definite information as to precedent signs. JTC:785-86

**James E. Talmage**
The precise time of Christ's coming has not been made known to man. By learning to comprehend the signs of the times, by watching the development of the work of God among the nations, and by noting the rapid fulfilment of significant prophecies, we may perceive the progressive evidence of the approaching event: "But the hour and the day no man knoweth, neither the angels in heaven, nor shall they know until he comes." His coming will be a surprise to those who have ignored His warnings, and who have failed to watch. "As a thief

in the night" will be the coming of the day of the Lord unto the wicked. "Watch therefore, for ye know neither the day nor the hour wherein the Son of Man cometh." AF:328

**Joseph Smith**
And again, verily I say unto you, the coming of the Lord draweth nigh, and it overtaketh the world as a thief in the night— 5. Therefore, gird up your loins, that you may be the children of light, and that day shall not overtake you as a thief. (*Revelation for Warren A. Cowdery, called to serve as a local presiding officer in the Church, Nov. 25, 1834*) D&C 106:4-5

**Paul**
For yourselves know perfectly that the day of the Lord so cometh as a thief in the night. 3. For when they shall say, Peace and safety; then sudden destruction cometh upon them, as travail upon a woman with child; and they shall not escape. 4. But ye, brethren, are not in darkness, that that day should overtake you as a thief. (*Letter to the Church at Thessalonica, comprising Jews and many pagan converts, A.D. 50*) 1Thess.5:2-4

**Elder Joseph Fielding Smith**
Do not think that he delayeth his coming. I want to say to you that many of the signs of the coming of the Son of God have been given and others will be given, so we may, if we will, know that the coming of the Son of God is even now, figuratively speaking, at our doors. The Lord isn't going to tell me when he is coming; he is not going to tell you; he is not going to tell anybody else—for he has made it definitely clear that he is going to come like the thief comes: when he is not expected. ("The Blessings of Eternal Glory," Brigham Young University Speeches of the Year, 1968, p. 10) TLDP:621

**Jesus,**
*recorded in Matthew*
Watch therefore: for ye know not what hour your Lord doth come. 43. But know this, that if the goodman of the house had known in what watch the thief would come, he would have watched, and would not have suffered his house to be broken up. 44. Therefore be ye also ready: for in such an hour as ye think not the Son of man cometh. (*Jesus foretells his second coming to his disciples*) Matt.24:42-44

---

732. The earth will be in great upheaval at the Savior's second coming.

**Parley P. Pratt**
In the resurrection which now approaches, and

in connection with the glorious coming of Jesus Christ, the earth will undergo a change in its physical features, climate, soil, productions; and in its political, moral, and spiritual government. ¶ Its mountains will be levelled, its valleys exalted, its swamps and sickly places will be drained and become healthy, while its burning deserts, and its frigid polar regions, will be redeemed and become temperate and fruitful. (Key to the Science of Theology, pp. 139-40) TLDP:621

**Elder Joseph Fielding Smith**

As Isaiah has predicted, we will, when Christ comes, have "new heavens and a new earth:" for, "behold, I create new heavens and a new earth: and the former shall not be remembered, nor come into mind." (Isa.65:17-25) This great change will be when the earth is cleansed of its iniquity and becomes a terrestrial body. Speaking of this, the authors in the "Compendium," have said: "The earth will go through a purifying process to fit it for the residence of its millennial inhabitants." [Franklin D. Richards and James A. Little, A Compendium of the Doctrines of the Gospel, rev. ed. (Salt Lake City: Deseret Book Co., 1925), pp. 185-86]. CHMR1:294

**President Brigham Young**

Do you think there is calamity abroad now among the people? Not much. All we have yet heard and all we have experienced is scarcely a preface to the sermon that is going to be preached. When the testimony of the Elders ceases to be given, and the Lord says to them, "Come home; I will now preach my own sermons to the nations of the earth," all you now know can scarcely be called a preface to the sermon that will be preached with fire and sword, tempests, earthquakes, hail, rain, thunders and lightnings, and fearful destruction. What matters the destruction of a few railway cars? You will hear of magnificent cities, now idolized by the people, sinking in the earth, entombing the inhabitants. The sea will heave itself beyond its bounds, engulfing mighty cities. Famine will spread over the nations, and nation will rise up against nation, kingdom against kingdom, and states against states, in our own country and in foreign lands; and they will destroy each another, caring not for the blood and lives of their neighbors, of their families, or for their own lives. (In Bowery, July 15, 1860, JD8:123) TLDP:344-45

**Orson F. Whitney**

Marvel not, my hearers, that all things are in commotion. The hour of God's judgment is at hand. War, famine, pestilence, earthquake,

tempest and tidal wave—these are among the predicted signs of the Savior's second coming. Tyranny and wickedness must be overthrown, and the way prepared for him who, though gracious and merciful to all, and forgiving to sinners who repent, "cannot look upon sin with the least degree of allowance." Earth must be freed from all oppression and cleansed from all iniquity. It is God's house; he is coming to live in it, and to make of it a glorified mansion. The world is in its Saturday night; house-cleaning is in progress; and the work of purification must be done and out of the way before the Lord of the Sabbath appears. ("The Everlasting Gospel," IE1925Feb:317) TLDP:345

**Joseph Smith,**
*quoted by Elder Joseph Fielding Smith*

When I contemplate the rapidity with which the great and glorious day of the coming of the Son of Man advances, when He shall come to receive His Saints unto Himself, where they shall dwell in His presence, and be crowned with glory and immortality: when I consider that soon the heavens are to be shaken, and the earth tremble and reel to and fro; and that the heavens are to be unfolded as a scroll when it is rolled up; and that every mountain and island are to flee away, I cry out in my heart, What manner of persons ought we to be in all holy conversation and godliness! (In letter to Moses C. Nickerson, Upper Canada, from the Prophet in Kirtland, Ohio, Nov. 19, 1833) HC1:441-43; TPJS:29

**Related Witnesses:**

**Joseph Smith**

For not many days hence and the earth shall tremble and reel to and fro as a drunken man; and the sun shall hide his face, and shall refuse to give light; and the moon shall be bathed in blood; and the stars shall become exceedingly angry, and shall cast themselves down as a fig that falleth from off a fig-tree. (Revelation, Dec. 27/28, 1832; the "olive leaf message of peace") D&C 88:87

**Joseph Smith**

And it shall be a voice as the voice of many waters, and as the voice of a great thunder, which shall break down the mountains, and the valleys shall not be found. 23. He shall command the great deep, and it shall be driven back into the north countries, and the islands shall become one land; 24. And the land of Jerusalem and the land of Zion shall be turned back into their own place, and the earth shall be like as it was in the days before it was divided. (At the Second Coming the lost tribes of Israel shall return) D&C 133:22-24

**Joseph Smith**

Wherefore, be not deceived, but continue in steadfastness, looking forth for the heavens to be shaken, and the earth to tremble and to reel to and fro as a drunken man, and for the valleys to be exalted, and for the mountains to be made low, and for the rough places to become smooth—and all this when the angel shall sound his trumpet. (*Revelation, March 1831, refuting Shaker doctrines and elaborating on the Second Coming*) D&C 49:23

**John**

And there were voices, and thunders, and lightnings; and there was a great earthquake, such as was not since men were upon the earth, so mighty an earthquake, and so great. 19. And the great city was divided into three parts, and the cities of the nations fell: and great Babylon came in remembrance before God, to give unto her the cup of the wine of the fierceness of his wrath. 20. And every island fled away, and the mountains were not found. (*John sees the time when the nations will assemble for Armageddon and the second coming of Christ, thereafter*) Rev.16:18-20

---

**733. The Lord will be clothed in red apparel when He appears to all the world at His second coming.**

**Joseph Smith**

And it shall be said: Who is this that cometh down from God in heaven with dyed garments; yea, from the regions which are not known, clothed in his glorious apparel, traveling in the greatness of his strength? 47. And he shall say: I am he who spake in righteousness, mighty to save. 48. And the Lord shall be red in his apparel, and his garments like him that treadeth in the wine-vat. (*Revelation received Nov. 3, 1831; the Saints are to prepare for the Second Coming*) D&C 133:46-48

**Isaiah**

Wherefore art thou red in thine apparel, and thy garments like him that treadeth in the winefat? 3. I have trodden the winepress alone; and of the people there was none with me: for I will tread them in mine anger, and trample them in my fury; and their blood shall be sprinkled upon my garments, and I will stain all my raiment. (*Isaiah sees the last days and the second coming of the Lord, 740-659 B.C.*) Isa.63:2-3

**John**

And I saw heaven opened, and behold a white horse; and he that sat upon him was called Faithful and True, and in righteousness he doth judge and make war. 12. His eyes were as a flame of fire, and on his head were many crowns; and he had a name written, that no man knew, but he himself. 13. And he was clothed with a vesture dipped in blood: and his name is called The Word of God. (*John sees the day when Christ shall rule the nations as King of kings and Lord of lords*) Rev.19:11-13

**Elder John Taylor**

But there was another work, another event that was to transpire in the latter days, when he should not be led as a lamb to the slaughter or be like a sheep before the shearers: when he would not act in that state of humiliation and quiescence, but when he will go forth as a man of war and tread down the people in his anger and trample them in his fury, when blood should be on his garments. . . . When he comes again he comes to take vengeance on the ungodly and to bring deliverance unto his Saints; "For the day of vengeance," it is said, "is in my heart and the year of my redeemed is come." [Isa.63:4] It behooves us to be made well aware which class we belong to, that if we are not already among the redeemed we may immediately join that society, that when the Son of God shall come the second time with all the holy angels with him, arrayed in power and great glory to take vengeance on them that know not God and obey not the Gospel, or when he shall come in flaming fire, we shall be among that number who shall be ready to meet him with gladness in our hearts and hail him as our great deliverer and friend. (*In Tabernacle, Feb. 22, 1863, JD10:115-16*) TLDP:622

---

**734. At the second coming of the Lord, the wicked will weep and wail and try to hide themselves from the glory of His presence.**

**Joseph Smith**

And there shall be weeping and wailing among the hosts of men; (*Revelation received Sept. 1830*) D&C 29:15

**Isaiah**

And they shall go into the holes of the rocks, and into the caves of the earth, for fear of the LORD, and for the glory of his majesty, when he ariseth to shake terribly the earth. . . . 21. To go into the clefts of the rocks, and into the tops of the ragged rocks, for fear of the LORD, and for the glory of his majesty, when he ariseth to shake terribly the earth. (*The proud and the wicked shall be brought low at the Second Coming*) Isa.2:19,21

**Alma, the younger,**
*quoted by Mormon*

For our words will condemn us, yea, all our works will condemn us; we shall not be found spotless; and our thoughts will also condemn us; and in this awful state we shall not dare to look up to our God; and we would fain be glad if we could command the rocks and the mountains to fall upon us to hide us from his presence. (*Alma contends with the wicked Zeezrom, about 82 B.C.*) Alma 12:14

**Joseph Smith**

And the Lord shall utter his voice, and all the ends of the earth shall hear it; and the nations of the earth shall mourn, and they that have laughed shall see their folly. (*Revelation, March 7, 1831; Christ shall stand on the Mount of Olives, and the Jews shall see the wounds in his hands and feet*) D&C 45:49-50

**Isaiah,**
*quoted by Nephi, son of Lehi,*
*quoted by Mormon*

O ye wicked ones, enter into the rock, and hide thee in the dust, for the fear of the Lord and the glory of his majesty shall smite thee. 11. And it shall come to pass that the lofty looks of man shall be humbled, and the haughtiness of men shall be bowed down, and the Lord alone shall be exalted in that day. 12. For the day of the Lord of Hosts soon cometh upon all nations, yea, upon every one; yea, upon the proud and lofty, and upon every one who is lifted up, and he shall be brought low. (*Nephi records the words of Isaiah from the brass plates, 559-545 B.C.*) 2Ne.12:10-12

---

735. **Faithful Saints, both living and dead, will be caught up to meet Christ at His second coming.**

**James E. Talmage**

With Christ shall come those who have already been resurrected; and His approach shall be the means of inaugurating a general resurrection of the righteous dead, while the pure and just who are still in the flesh shall be instantaneously changed from the mortal to the immortal state and shall be caught up with the newly resurrected to meet the Lord and His celestial company, and shall descend with Him. JTC:787

**Joseph Smith**

And the Saints that are upon the earth, who are alive, shall be quickened and be caught up to meet him. 97. And they who have slept in their graves shall come forth, for their graves shall be opened; and they also shall be caught up to

meet him in the midst of the pillar of heaven—98. They are Christ's, the first fruits, they who shall descend with him first, and they who are on the earth and in their graves, who are first caught up to meet him; and all this by the voice of the sounding of the trump of the angel of God. (*The Lord speaks to Joseph by revelation, Dec. 27/28, 1832*) D&C 88:96-98

**Joseph Smith**

But before the arm of the Lord shall fall, an angel shall sound his trump, and the saints that have slept shall come forth to meet me in the cloud. 46. Wherefore, if ye have slept in peace blessed are you; for as you now behold me and know that I am, even so shall ye come unto me and your souls shall live, and your redemption shall be perfected; and the saints shall come forth from the four quarters of the earth. (*Revelation, March 7, 1831; signs, wonders, and the resurrection are to attend the Second Coming*) D&C 45:45-46

**Paul**

For the Lord himself shall descend from heaven with a shout, with the voice of the archangel, and with the trump of God: and the dead in Christ shall rise first: 17. Then we which are alive and remain shall be caught up together with them in the clouds, to meet the Lord in the air: and so shall we ever be with the Lord. (*Paul writes to the Church at Thessalonica that the Lord shall come again and the dead shall rise, A.D. 50*) 1Thess.4:16-17

**Bruce R. McConkie**

Christ's, the first fruits—who are they? They are all those who were with him in his resurrection. They are all those of Enoch's city, a righteous people who were translated and who then gained full immortality when Christ rose from his tomb. They are all those of ages past who have burst the bands of death. They are the living saints who are quickened by the power of God and are caught up to meet their Lord in the air. . . . (The Millennial Messiah, p. 636) DGSM:102

**Related Witnesses:**

**Paul,**
*quoted by Joseph Smith,*
*translating 1 Thessalonians*

Then they who are alive, shall be caught up together into the clouds with them who remain, to meet the Lord in the air; and so shall we be ever with the Lord. (*Letter to the Church at Thessalonica, comprising Jews and many pagan converts, A.D. 50*) JST(1Thess.4:17 fn. a)

**Joseph Smith**

These are they whom he shall bring with him, when he shall come in the clouds of heaven to reign on the earth over his people. (*Vision to Joseph Smith and Sidney Rigdon, Feb. 16, 1832*) D&C 76:63

---

736. The Jews will acknowledge Jesus as the Christ at His second coming.

### Joseph Smith,
*receiving the Word of the Lord*
And then shall the Jews look upon me and say: What are these wounds in thine hands and in thy feet? 52. Then shall they know that I am the Lord; for I will say unto them: These wounds are the wounds with which I was wounded in the house of my friends. I am he who was lifted up. I am Jesus that was crucified. I am the Son of God. 53. And then shall they weep because of their iniquities; then shall they lament because they persecuted their king. (*Revelation, March 7, 1831, signs and wonders to attend the Second Coming of Christ*) D&C 45:51-53

### Elder Wilford Woodruff
The Jews have got to gather to their own land in unbelief. They will go and rebuild Jerusalem and their temple. They will take their gold and silver from the nations and will gather to the Holy Land, and when they have done this and rebuilt their city, the Gentiles . . . will go up against Jerusalem to battle and to take a spoil and a prey; and then when they have taken one-half of Jerusalem captive and distressed the Jews for the last time on the earth, their Great Deliverer, Shiloh, will come. They do not believe in Jesus of Nazareth now, nor ever will until he comes and sets his foot on Mount Olivet and it cleaves in twain, one part going towards the East and the other towards the West. Then, when they behold the wounds in his hands and in his feet, they will say, "Where did you get them?" and he will reply "I am Jesus of Nazareth, King of the Jews, your Shiloh, him whom you crucified." Then, for the first time will the eyes of Judah be opened. They will remain in unbelief until that day. This is one of the events that will transpire in the latter day. (*In 13th Ward, Jan. 12, 1873, JD15:277-78*) TLDP:349

### Zechariah
And I will pour upon the house of David, and upon the inhabitants of Jerusalem, the spirit of grace and of supplications: and they shall look upon me whom they have pierced, and they shall mourn for him, as one mourneth for his only son, and shall be in bitterness for him, as one that is in bitterness for his firstborn. (*Zechariah prophesies, about 518 B.C.*) Zech.12:10

### President Brigham Young
When he comes again, he will not come as he did when the Jews rejected him; neither will he appear first at Jerusalem when he makes his second appearance on the earth; but he will appear first on the land where he commenced his work in the beginning, and planted the Garden of Eden, and that was done in the land of America. ¶ When the Savior visits Jerusalem, and the Jews look upon him, and see the wounds in his hands and in his side and in his feet, they will then know that they have persecuted and put to death the true Messiah, and then they will acknowledge him, but not till then. They have confounded his first and second coming, expecting his first coming to be as a mighty prince instead of as a servant. They will go back by and by to Jerusalem and own their Lord and Master. We have no feelings against them. (*In Tabernacle, Dec. 23, 1866, JD11:279*) DBY:122

### Related Witnesses:
### Zechariah
And one shall say unto him, What are these wounds in thine hands? Then he shall answer, Those with which I was wounded in the house of my friends. (*Zechariah prophesies, about 518 B.C.*) Zech.13:6

---

737. When the Lord comes in the last days He will set His foot upon the Mount of Olives and it shall cleave in twain.

### Joseph Smith
And then shall the Lord set his foot upon this mount, and it shall cleave in twain, and the earth shall tremble, and reel to and fro, and the heavens also shall shake. (*Revelation, March 7, 1831; signs and wonders to attend the Second Coming*) D&C 45:48

### Zechariah
And his feet shall stand in that day upon the mount of Olives, which is before Jerusalem on the east, and the mount of Olives shall cleave in the midst thereof toward the east and toward the west, and there shall be a very great valley; and half of the mountain shall remove toward the north, and half of it toward the south. (*Zechariah prophesies that at his second coming the Lord shall fight for Israel, about 518 B.C.*) Zech.14:4

### Elder Wilford Woodruff
[The Jews] do not believe in Jesus of Nazareth now, nor ever will until he comes and sets his foot on Mount Olivet and it cleaves in twain,

one part going towards the East and the other towards the West. Then, when they behold the wounds in his hands and in his feet, they will say, "Where did you get them?" and he will reply "I am Jesus of Nazareth, King of the Jews, your Shiloh, him whom you crucified." Then, for the first time will the eyes of Judah be opened. They will remain in unbelief until that day. This is one of the events that will transpire in the latter day. (*In 13th Ward, Jan. 12, 1873, JD15:277-78*) TLDP:349

**Related Witnesses:**

### James E. Talmage

He will come with the body of flesh and bones in which His Spirit was tabernacled when he ascended from Mount Olivet. CR1916Apr:126

---

### 738. The second coming of Christ will usher in the Millennium.

#### Elder Wilford Woodruff

When the Savior comes, a thousand years will be devoted to this work of redemption; and Temples will appear all over this land of Joseph—North and South America—and also in Europe and elsewhere; and all the descendants of Shem, Ham, and Japheth, who received not the Gospel in the flesh, must be officiated for in the Temples of God, before the Savior can present the kingdom to the Father, saying, "It is finished." (*In new Tabernacle, Sept. 16, 1877, JD19:230*) TLDP:404

#### Joseph Smith,
*receiving the Word of the Lord*

For in mine own due time will I come upon the earth in judgment, and my people shall be redeemed and shall reign with me on earth. 30. For the great Millennium, of which I have spoken by the mouth of my servants, shall come. 31. For Satan shall be bound, and when he is loosed again he shall only reign for a little season, and then cometh the end of the earth. 32. And he that liveth in righteousness shall be changed in the twinkling of an eye, and the earth shall pass away so as by fire. 33. And the wicked shall go away into unquenchable fire, and their end no man knoweth on earth, nor ever shall know, until they come before me in judgment. (*Revelation: message for the nations of the earth, Feb. 1831*) D&C 43:29-33

#### Elder Joseph Fielding Smith

We speak of the time when the earth shall be cleansed from sin as the Millennium. We look forward to it; the prophets have spoken of it. ¶ In our own day messengers have come from the presence of the Lord declaring that it is even now at our doors, and yet many, even among the Latter-day Saints, go about their affairs as though this coming of the Lord Jesus Christ and the ushering in of this reign of peace had been indefinitely postponed for many generations. I say to you that it is at our doors. I say this with all confidence because the Lord has said it. His messengers have said it as they have come from his presence bearing witness of him. (Doctrines of Salvation, 3:55) TLDP:399

#### Bruce R. McConkie

Thus, when we speak of the Lord returning to reign personally upon the earth, we are talking about a literal return. We have in mind a King ruling on a throne. We mean that laws will come forth from a Lawgiver; that judges will be restored as of old; that there will be a full end of all nations as these now exist; that earth's new King will have dominion and power over all the earth; and that Israel, the chosen people, will possess the kingdom and have everlasting dominion. . . . ¶ . . . Christ shall provide the government. He shall reign on the throne of David forever. Peace shall prevail, and justice and judgment shall be the order of the day. And it is Israel, the chosen ones, over whom he shall reign in a kingdom that shall never cease. There is nothing figurative about this; it is not something that can be spiritualized away. It is the coming reality; it shall surely come to pass. . . . ¶ The eventual triumph of the Lord's people is assured; there is to be a millennial day of glory and honor and peace; the fulness of the earth shall be theirs in that day, and all nations and kingdoms shall serve and obey them. But all the promised rewards need not be deferred until that day. Even now the saints can begin the process of inheriting the kingdom. They have power to begin to reap some of the millennial rewards. (The Millennial Messiah, pp. 596-97,600) TLDP:401

---

### 739. The Saints must prepare for the Second Coming.

#### Elder Wilford Woodruff

The parable of the ten virgins is intended to represent the second coming of the Son of man, the coming of the Bridegroom to meet the bride, the Church, the Lamb's wife, in the last days; and I expect that the Savior was about right when he said, in reference to the members of the Church, that five of them were wise and five were foolish; for when the Lord of heaven comes in power and great glory to reward every man according to the deeds done in the body, if he finds one-half of those professing to be members of his Church prepared for salvation, it will be as many as can be expected, judging by the course that many are pursuing. (*In new Tabernacle, Sept. 12, 1875*) TLDP:623

**Jesus,**
*recorded in Matthew*

Then shall the kingdom of heaven be likened unto ten virgins, which took their lamps, and went forth to meet the bridegroom. 2. And five of them were wise, and five were foolish. 3. They that were foolish took their lamps, and took no oil with them: 4. But the wise took oil in their vessels with their lamps. 5. While the bridegroom tarried, they all slumbered and slept. 6. And at midnight there was a cry made, Behold, the bridegroom cometh; go ye out to meet him. 7. Then all those virgins arose, and trimmed their lamps. 8. And the foolish said unto the wise, Give us of your oil; for our lamps are gone out. 9. But the wise answered, saying, Not so; lest there be not enough for us and you: but go ye rather to them that sell, and buy for yourselves. 10. And while they went to buy, the bridegroom came; and they that were ready went in with him to the marriage: and the door was shut. 11. Afterward came also the other virgins, saying, Lord, Lord, open to us. 12. But he answered and said, Verily I say unto you, I know you not. 13. Watch therefore, for ye know neither the day nor the hour wherein the Son of man cometh. (*Jesus gives the parable of the ten virgins*) Matt.25:1-13

**Joseph Smith,**
*receiving the Word of the Lord*

And at that day, when I shall come in my glory, shall the parable be fulfilled which I spake concerning the ten virgins. 57. For they that are wise and have received the truth, and have taken the Holy Spirit for their guide, and have not been deceived—verily I say unto you, they shall not be hewn down and cast into the fire, but shall abide the day. 58. And the earth shall be given unto them for an inheritance; and they shall multiply and wax strong, and their children shall grow up without sin unto salvation. 59. For the Lord shall be in their midst, and his glory shall be upon them, and he will be their king and their lawgiver. (*Revelation, March 7, 1831; signs, wonders, and the resurrection are to attend the Second Coming*) D&C 45:56-59

**Charles A. Callis**

The Church of Jesus Christ of Latter-day Saints has been brought forth and established by the power of God and dedicated to the mission of preparing the way for the glorious coming of the Son of God to reign in the earth in truth and

righteousness and peace. ¶ Would to God this glorious second coming of the Messiah might be in our day, but let it be sooner or later, in it we will rejoice. ¶ Truly, God will descend from the heavens in incomparable power and glory with all His holy angels, and He will stand upon the earth at the latter day. Then heaven and earth will meet. (*Fundamentals of Religion: A Series of Radio Addresses*) TLDP:623

**Elder Harold B. Lee**

A people to receive the coming of the Lord, must be taught the personality and the nature of God and his Son, Jesus Christ. . . . ¶ How can one meet a person whose identity is unknown? How can one be prepared to meet a person about whom he has no knowledge? How can one be prepared to meet a being whose personality he cannot comprehend? . . . ¶ Another requisite of that preparation to receive the Lord at the beginning of his millennial reign demands that the people be taught to accept the divinity of the mission of Jesus as the Savior of the world. . . . ¶ That last declaration of the Prophet Alma [Alma 11:37] points to still another requirement, as I see it, for a people to be prepared to receive the Savior's coming. We must be cleansed and purified and sanctified to be made worthy to receive and abide that holy presence. . . . ¶ How can this cleansing take place? The answer is: through holy ordinances which the Lord has established for that purpose. . . . ¶ And now, finally, there is still one more thing that is necessary, to my thinking, before that preparation is made for the millennial reign. We must accept the divine mission of the Prophet Joseph Smith as the instrumentality through which the restoration of the gospel and the organization of The Church of Jesus Christ was accomplished. Each member of the Church, to be prepared for the millennial reign, must receive a testimony, each for himself, of the divinity of the work established by Joseph Smith. CR1956Oct:61-62

**Delbert L. Stapley**

Let us be sure we thoroughly understand the most important things we can do to prepare ourselves for our Lord's second coming to earth and, by our obedience and faithfulness, escape his punishment. ¶ The following are important considerations. We must set our lives and homes in order. This means a searching of our souls, an admittance of wrongdoing, and repentance where needed. It means keeping all of God's commandments. It means loving our neighbor. It means living an exemplary life. It means being good husbands and wives. It means teaching and training our children in the ways of righteousness. It means being honest in all our doings, in business and at home. It means spreading the gospel of Jesus Christ to all the peoples of the world. ¶ The Lord has said: "I will hasten my work in its time." (D&C 88:73) ¶ There is an urgency in his work. Time is getting short. This sense of urgency in promoting the Lord's kingdom in these last days does not arise out of panic, but out of a desire to move swiftly and surely to establish and strengthen his kingdom among all people who are seeking the light and truth of the gospel, which is God's plan of life for all his children. ¶ God will hasten his work by opening the heavens and sending heavenly messengers to his prophets to warn his children to prepare themselves to receive their Lord at his second coming. CR1975Oct:71

### James E. Talmage
The mission of the Church is to prepare the earth for the coming of the Lord. CR1916Apr:126

### LeGrand Richards
For if this gospel that Jesus referred to was to be preached in all the world, it had to be done by his children. And hundreds of thousands of Latter-day Saint missionaries since that time have been all over the world . . . to declare the restoration of the gospel as one of the steps in the preparation for the return of the Savior, for he so indicated that it must be preached in all the world. CR1978Apr:113

### Bruce R. McConkie
The Second Coming is a day of judgment, a day of rewards, a day of vengeance for the wicked, a day of glory and honor for the righteous. It is a day for which all man prepare by the lives that they live. Those who live as becometh saints shall be as their Lord; those who walk in carnal paths shall be cast out. (The Mortal Messiah, 3:51) TLDP:625

### Mark E. Petersen
The Savior will come in judgment with rewards for the righteous and destruction for the wicked. When he begins his millennial reign, there must be a cleansed earth to receive him. He will not reign over a sinful world. Hence wickedness will be overthrown, wars will end, and peace will come. ¶ For such a vast and world-shaking appearance, a worldwide preparation is required. The people—those who will survive the great events of that day—will have to be taught, as the people in the Meridian of Time were taught by John the Baptist. A modern people must be prepared to receive the Lord. ¶ This preparation will come only through a worldwide preaching of the restored gospel "in the hour of God's judgment." The scriptures say it would be brought to earth by angelic ministry (see Rev.14:6-7) and then be preached in all the world as a warning to all nations (Matt.24:14). ¶ This preaching will convert the righteous who earnestly look forward to Christ's coming, and they will join his Church. It is to be by the same means used by John the Baptist. To carry on the work in an orderly manner, the Lord fully restored his Church and priesthood in our day, and decreed that missionaries should go to every nation, kindred, tongue, and people, just as in ancient times. ¶ All of this was done under the immediate direction of the Savior himself, who sent holy angels to minister to the Prophet Joseph Smith. ¶ Joseph was the Lord's forerunner to begin the preparation for the Second Coming of the Lord. This work still goes on under the direction of living prophets who have succeeded Joseph, and it will continue worldwide until the Lord says "enough." Then he will come. ¶ Millions of people now converted to the restored gospel are preparing to meet him. When the time comes, they will be ready. (Malachi and the Great and Dreadful Day, p. 21) TLDP:624

# List of Doctrines

## SERVICE

*Doctrines Located in This Topic*

740. Happiness comes from serving others.

741. Christlike service is giving without thought of recompense.

742. We reap the good that we sow.

743. We are to perform active service for others, to show charity by action (by giving of personal time and substance).

744. We are to minister to the physical needs of others.

745. We are to minister to the spiritual needs of others.

746. We are to give genuinely from the heart when we give.

747. We need the experience of serving others that we might develop Christlike characters, to qualify us to return to the presence of the Lord.

748. A person who serves another serves God.

749. We are to be eagerly engaged in doing many things of our own free will (we are not to wait for specific commands or formal church callings to do good works).

750. It is more blessed to give than to receive (there is more joy in serving than in being served).

*Doctrines on SERVICE Located in Other Topics*

94. Persons who have acquired more possessions than they can manage and use properly are to freely impart the surplus to the needy.

95. Those who refuse to share what they have will not gain exaltation.

856. We are not to engage in acts of priestcraft: performing church service for material gain or rendering benevolent service to others for riches or honor.

861. We are to care for the poor, the needy, and the sick and afflicted.

(See topic LOVE OF NEIGHBOR.)

# SERVICE

## 740. Happiness comes from serving others.

### President David O. McKay

Man's greatest happiness comes from losing himself for the good of others. CR1963Oct:8

### Marion G. Romney

"[A]nd surely there could not be a happier people among all the people who had been created by the hand of God." (4Ne.1:16) ¶ Why were these people so happy? Because they were free of the shackles of selfishness and had learned what the Lord knows—that ultimate joy comes only through service. CR1981Oct:132

### Gordon B. Hinckley

It seems to me that he [the Savior] is saying to each of us that unless we lose ourselves in the service of others our lives are largely lived to no real purpose. . . . He who lives only unto himself withers and dies, while he who forgets himself in the service of others grows and blossoms in this life and in eternity. ("Forget Yourself," Brigham Young University Speeches of the Year, 1977, p. 43) TLDP:630

**Related Witnesses:**

### Jesus,
*recorded in Luke*

For whosoever will save his life shall lose it: but whosoever will lose his life for my sake, the same shall save it. (*Jesus teaches his disciples*) Luke 9:24

### Jesus,
*quoted by John*

He that loveth his life shall lose it; and he that hateth his life in this world shall keep it unto life eternal. (*Jesus foretells his death*) John 12:25

### Jesus,
*recorded in Matthew*

He that findeth his life shall lose it: and he that loseth his life for my sake shall find it. (*Jesus trains and instructs the Twelve*) Matt.10:39

### Elder Spencer W. Kimball

Only when you lift a burden, God will lift your burden. Divine paradox this! The man who staggers and falls because his burden is too great can lighten that burden by taking on the weight of another's burden. You get by giving, but your part of giving must be given first. (*To Rotary Club, 1935*) (The Teachings of Spencer W. Kimball, p. 251) TLDP:630

### President Heber J. Grant

Make a motto in life; always try to assist someone else to carry his burden, The true key to happiness in life is to labor for the happiness of others. (*To University of Utah students*) (Gospel Standards, p. 161) TLDP:320

## 741. Christlike service is giving without thought of recompense.

### Thomas S. Monson

The beloved apostles noted well his example. He lived not so to be ministered unto, but to minister; not to receive, but to give; not to save his life, but to pour it out for others. CR1971Oct:171

### President Spencer W. Kimball

Never did the Savior give in expectation. I know of no case in his life in which there was an exchange. He was always the giver, seldom the recipient. Never did he give shoes, hose, or a vehicle; never did he give perfume, a shirt, or a fur wrap. His gifts were of such a nature that the recipient could hardly exchange or return the value. His gifts were rare ones: eyes to the blind, ears to the deaf, and legs to the lame; cleanliness to the unclean, wholeness to the infirm, and breath to the lifeless. His gifts were opportunity to the downtrodden, freedom to the oppressed, light in the darkness, forgiveness to the repentant, hope to the despairing. His friends gave him shelter, food, and love. He gave them of himself, his love, his service, his life. The wise men brought him gold and frankincense. He gave them and all their fellow mortals resurrection, salvation, and eternal life. We should strive to give as he gave. To give of oneself is a holy gift. (Pamphlet, 1978; The Teachings of Spencer W. Kimball, pp. 246-47) TLDP:628

### Dallin H. Oaks,
*also quoting Jesus,*
*recorded in Matthew*

This principle—that our service should be for the love of God and the love of fellowmen rather than for personal advantage or any other lesser motive—is admittedly a high standard. The Savior must have seen it so, since he joined his commandment for selfless and complete love directly with the ideal of perfection. . . . "Be ye therefore perfect, even as your Father which is in heaven is perfect." (Matt.5:48) . . . ¶ Service with all of our heart and mind is a high challenge for all of us. Such service must be free of selfish ambition. It must be motivated only by the pure love of Christ. . . . ¶ I know that God expects us to work to purify our hearts and our thoughts so that we may serve one another for the highest and best reason, the pure love of Christ. CR1984Oct:16

### Marion G. Romney

The United Order exalts the poor and humbles the rich. In the process both are sanctified. The poor, released from the bondage and humiliating limitations of poverty, are enabled as free men to rise to their full potential, both temporally and spiritually. The rich, by consecration and by imparting of their surplus for the benefit of the poor, not by constraint but willingly as an act of free will, evidence that charity for their fellowmen characterized by Mormon as "the pure love of Christ." (Moro.7:47) CR1966Apr:97

### James E. Talmage

Charity, or almsgiving, even though it be associated with the sincerest of motives, devoid of all desire for praise or hope of return, is but a feeble manifestation of the love that is to make one's neighbor as dear to him as himself; the love that suffers long; that envies not others; that vaunts not itself; that knows no pride; that subdues selfishness; that rejoices in the truth. AF:392

**Related Witnesses:**

### Marion G. Romney

In this modern world plagued with counterfeits for the Lord's plan, we must not be misled into supposing that we can discharge our obligations to the poor and the needy by shifting the responsibility to some governmental or other public agency. Only by voluntarily giving out of an abundant love for our neighbors can we develop that charity characterized by Mormon as "the pure love of Christ." (Moro.7:47) This we must develop if we would obtain eternal life. CR1972Oct:115

### James E. Talmage

The Church of the present day can point to a stupendous labor of benevolence already accomplished and still in progress. One of the most glorious monuments of its work is seen in the missionary labor which has ever been a characteristic feature of its activities. Actuated by no other motives than pure love for humanity and a desire to fulfil the commands of God respecting mankind, the Church sends out every year hundreds of missionaries to proclaim the Gospel of eternal life to the world, and that too without money or price. Multitudes of these devoted servants have suffered contumely and insult at the hands of those whom they sought to benefit; and not a few have given their lives with the seal of the martyr upon their testimony and work. AF:392-93

### Joseph Smith,
*quoted by Elder Joseph Fielding Smith*

[I]f there are any among you who aspire after their own aggrandizement, and seek their own opulence, while their brethren are groaning in poverty, and are under sore trials and temptations, they cannot be benefited by the intercession of the Holy Spirit, which maketh intercession for us day and night with groanings that cannot be uttered. *(Epistle to the Church from Liberty Jail, Mo., March 25, 1839)* TPJS:141

## 742. We reap the good that we sow.

### Joseph Smith

It is a time-honored adage that love begets love. Let us pour forth love—show forth our kindness unto all mankind, and the Lord will reward us with everlasting increase; cast our bread upon the waters and we shall receive it after many days, increased to a hundredfold. Friendship is like Brother Turley in his blacksmith shop welding iron to iron; it unites the human family with its happy influence. *(In meeting at the Stand in Nauvoo, Ill., July 23, 1843)* HC5:517

### Paul

Be not deceived; God is not mocked: for whatsoever a man soweth, that shall he also reap. 8. For he that soweth to his flesh shall of the flesh reap corruption; but he that soweth to the Spirit shall of the Spirit reap life everlasting. *(Paul writes to the churches of Galatia in Asia Minor, about A.D. 55; he instructs them to walk not after the flesh but after the Spirit)* Gal.6:7-8

### Recorded in Proverbs

The liberal soul shall be made fat: and he that watereth shall be watered also himself. Prov.11:25

### Paul

He which soweth sparingly shall reap also sparingly; and he which soweth bountifully shall reap also bountifully. *(Paul writes to the Church at Corinth, Greece, about A.D. 55)* 2Cor.9:6

### Joseph Smith

[E]very man may improve upon his talent, that every man may gain other talents, yea, even an hundred fold. . . . *(Revelation, April 26, 1832)* D&C 82:18

### Joseph Smith

But learn that he who doeth the works of righteousness shall receive his reward, even peace in this world and eternal life in the world to come. *(Revelation, Aug. 7, 1831)* D&C 59:23

### Jesus,
*recorded in Luke*

Judge not, and ye shall not be judged: condemn not, and ye shall not be condemned: forgive, and ye shall be forgiven: 38. Give, and it shall be given you; good measure, pressed down, and shaken together, and running over, shall men give into your bosom. For with the same measure that ye mete withal it shall be measured to you again. (*Jesus teaches his disciples some principles of love and service*) Luke 6:37-38

**Recorded in Proverbs**

A man that hath friends must shew himself friendly: and there is a friend that sticketh closer than a brother. (*Proverbial literature*) Prov.18:24

**Related Witnesses:**

**Paul**

And let us not be weary in well doing: for in due season we shall reap, if we faint not. (*Letter to the churches of Galatia in Asia Minor, about A.D. 55*) Gal.6:9

**Recorded in Proverbs**

Iron sharpeneth iron; so a man sharpeneth the countenance of his friend. (*Proverb of Solomon, king of Israel*) Prov.27:17

---

**743.** We are to perform active service for others, to show charity by action (by giving of personal time and substance).

**Marvin J. Ashton**

True love is a process. True love requires personal action. Love must be continuing to be real. Love takes time. . . . How hollow, how empty if our love is no deeper than the arousal of momentary feeling or the expression in words of what is no more lasting than the time it takes to speak them. A group of college students recently indicated to me their least favorite expression to come from us as the older set is, "If there is ever anything I can do to help you, please let me know." They, as do others, much prefer actions over conversation. ¶ We must at regular and appropriate intervals speak and reassure others of our love and the long time it takes to prove it by our actions. Real love does take time. . . . ¶ Undoubtedly our Heavenly Father tires of expressions of love in words only. He has made it clear through his prophets and his words that his ways are ways of commitment, and not conversation. He prefers performance over lip service. CR1975Oct:160-61

**Amulek,**
*quoted by Mormon*

[L]et your hearts be full, drawn out in prayer unto him continually for your welfare, and also for the welfare of those who are around you. 28. And now behold, my beloved brethren, I say unto you, do not suppose that this is all; for after ye have done all these things, if ye turn away the needy, and the naked, and visit not the sick and afflicted, and impart of your substance, if ye have, to those who stand in need—I say

unto you, if ye do not any of these things, behold, your prayer is vain, and availeth you nothing, and ye are as hypocrites who do deny the faith. 29. Therefore, if ye do not remember to be charitable, ye are as dross, which the refiners do cast out, (it being of no worth) and is trodden under foot of men. (*Amulek teaches the people to pray and to be charitable, about 74 B.C.*) Alma 34:27-29

**John A. Widtsoe**

Love is a positive active force. It helps the loved one. If there is need, love tries to supply it. If there is weakness, love supplants it with strength. . . . Love that does not help is a faked or transient love. (An Understanding Religion, pp. 72-73) TLDP:368

**James**

What doth it profit, my brethren, though a man say he hath faith, and have not works? can faith save him? 15. If a brother or sister be naked, and destitute of daily food, 16. And one of you say unto them, Depart in peace, be ye warmed and filled; notwithstanding ye give them not those things which are needful to the body; what doth it profit? (*James writes to his brethren in the Church*) James 2:14-16

**Related Witnesses:**

**James**

Pure religion and undefiled before God and the Father is this, To visit the fatherless and widows in their affliction, and to keep himself unspotted from the world. (*James writes to his brethren in the Church*) James 1:27

**President Brigham Young,**
*quoted by John A. Widtsoe*

To explain how much confidence we should have in God, I were I using a term to suit myself, I should say implicit confidence. I have faith in my God, and that faith corresponds with the works I produce. I have no confidence in faith without works. (*In Bowery, Aug. 17, 1856, JD4:24*) DBY:155

**President Brigham Young,**
*quoted by John A. Widtsoe*

The most effectual way to establish the religion of Heaven is to live it, rather than to die for it: I think I am safe in saying that there are many of the Latter-day Saints who are more willing to die for their religion than to live it faithfully. There is no other proof can be adduced to God, angels, and men, than that a people faithfully live their religion, than that they repent truly of their sins, obey the law of baptism for the remission of sins, and then continue to do the works of righteousness day by day. (*In Bowery, Aug. 3, 1862, JD9:333*) DBY:221

## 744. We are to minister to the physical needs of others.

**George F. Richards**

The Lord expects us when he blesses us with the good things of this earth to remember those who are not so fortunate. We are to feed the hungry, clothe the naked, visit the sick, comfort those who mourn, and minister unto those who are poor and needy, and thus become of that class to whom the Lord, when he shall come, shall say: "Come, ye blessed of the Father, inherit the kingdom prepared for you from the foundation of the world." CR1939Oct:108-09

**Joseph Smith,**
*receiving the Word of the Lord*

For the earth is full, and there is enough and to spare; yea, I prepared all things, and have given unto the children of men to be agents unto themselves. 18. Therefore, if any man shall take of the abundance which I have made, and impart not his portion, according to the law of my gospel, unto the poor and the needy, he shall, with the wicked, lift up his eyes in hell, being in torment. (*Revelation concerning the United Order, April 23, 1834*) D&C 104:17-18

**President John Taylor**

If you see men hungry, feed them, no matter who they are; white, black, or red, Jew, Gentile or Mormon, or anybody else—feed them. If you see men naked, clothe them. If you see men sick, administer to them, and learn to be kind to all men; but partake not of their evil practices. (*General conference, Oct. 1884, JD25:313*) TLDP:368

**Joseph Smith,**
*receiving the Word of the Lord*

And remember in all things the poor and the needy, the sick and the afflicted, for he that doeth not these things, the same is not my disciple. (*Revelation to the elders of the Church, June 7, 1831; various elders sent to preach the gospel*) D&C 52:40

**King Benjamin,**
*quoted by Mormon*

And also, ye yourselves will succor those that stand in need of your succor; ye will administer of your substance unto him that standeth in need; and ye will not suffer that the beggar putteth up his petition to you in vain, and turn him out to perish. 17. Perhaps thou shalt say: The man has brought upon himself his misery; therefore I will stay my hand, and will not give unto him of my food, nor impart unto him of my substance that he may not suffer, for his punishments are just— 18. But I say unto you, O man, whosoever doeth this the same hath great cause to repent; and except he repenteth of that which he hath done he perisheth forever, and hath no interest in the kingdom of God. 19. For behold, are we not all beggars? Do we not all depend upon the same Being, even God, for all the substance which we have, for both food and raiment, and for gold, and for silver, and for all the riches which we have of every kind. 20. And behold, even at this time, ye have been calling on his name, and begging for a remission of your sins. And has he suffered that ye have begged in vain? Nay; he has poured out his Spirit upon you, and has caused that your hearts should be filled with joy, and has caused that your mouths should be stopped that ye could not find utterance, so exceedingly great was your joy. 21. And now, if God, who has created you, on whom you are dependent for your lives and for all that ye have and are, doth grant unto you whatsoever ye ask that is right, in faith, believing that ye shall receive, O then, how ye ought to impart of the substance that ye have one to another. . . . 26. And now, for the sake of these things which I have spoken unto you—that is, for the sake of retaining a remission of your sins from day to day, that ye may walk guiltless before God—I would that ye should impart of your substance to the poor, every man according to that which he hath, such as feeding the hungry, clothing the naked, visiting the sick and administering to their relief, both spiritually and temporally, according to their wants. (*King Benjamin addresses his people, about 124 B.C.*) Mosiah 4:16-21,26

**Jesus,**
*recorded in Matthew*

Then shall the King say unto them on his right hand, Come, ye blessed of my Father, inherit the kingdom prepared for you from the foundation of the world: 35. For I was an hungred, and ye gave me meat: I was thirsty, and ye gave me drink: I was a stranger, and ye took me in: 36. Naked, and ye clothed me: I was sick, and ye visited me: I was in prison, and ye came unto me. 37. Then shall the righteous answer him, saying, Lord, when saw we thee an hungred, and fed thee? or thirsty, and gave thee drink? 38. When saw we thee a stranger, and took thee in? or naked, and clothed thee? 39. Or when saw we thee sick, or in prison, and came unto thee? 40. And the King shall answer and say unto them, Verily I say unto you, Inasmuch as ye have done it unto one of the least of these my brethren, ye have done it unto me. (*Jesus gives the parable of the sheep and the goats; the sheep are placed on his right hand at the Lord's second coming*) Matt.25:34-40

**Related Witnesses:**

**Mormon**

And it came to pass in the thirty and sixth year, the people were all converted unto the Lord, upon all the face of the land, both Nephites and Lamanites, and there were no contentions and disputations among them, and every man did deal justly one with another. 3. And they had all things common among them; therefore there were not rich and poor, bond and free, but they were all made free, and partakers of the heavenly gift. (*Mormon abridges the account of Nephi son of Nephi, one of the disciples of Christ, A.D. 36-60*) 4Ne.1:2-3

---

**745. We are to minister to the spiritual needs of others.**

**Jesus,**
*recorded in Matthew*

But I have prayed for thee, that thy faith fail not: and when thou art converted, strengthen thy brethren. (*Jesus talks to Peter, prior to departing for Gethsemane*) Luke 22:32

**President Joseph Fielding Smith**

The man who does only those things in the Church which concern himself alone will never reach exaltation. For instance, the man who is willing to pray, to pay his tithes and offerings, and to attend to the ordinary duties which concern his own personal life, and nothing more, will never reach the goal of perfection. ¶ Service must be given in behalf of others, We must extend the helping hand to the unfortunate, to those who have not heard the truth and are in spiritual darkness, to the needy, the oppressed. Are you failing? CR1968Apr:12

**King Benjamin,**
*quoted by Mormon*

. . . I would that ye should impart of your substance to the poor, every man according to that which he hath, such as feeding the hungry, clothing the naked, visiting the sick and administering to their relief, both spiritually and temporally, according to their wants. (*King Benjamin addresses his people, about 124 B.C.*) Mosiah 4:26

**Marvin J. Ashton**

Love demands action if it is to be continuing. Love is a process. Love is not a declaration. Love is not an announcement. Love is not a passing fancy. Love is not an expediency. Love is not a convenience. "If ye love me, keep my commandments" and "If ye love me feed my sheep" are God-given proclamations that should remind us we can often best show our love through the processes of feeding and keeping. . . . ¶ . . . . Certainly the best way for us to show our love in keeping and feeding is by taking the time to prove it hour by hour and day by day. Our expressions of love and comfort are empty if our actions don't match. God loves us to continue. Our neighbors and families love us if we will but follow through with sustaining support and self-sharing. True love is as eternal as life itself. Who is to say the joys of eternity are not wrapped up in continuous feeding, keeping, and caring? CR1975Oct:160-61

**Gordon B. Hinckley**

We shall continue the great work that goes on in our temples, an unmatched work of love reaching out even to those who have gone beyond the veil of death. Can there be a greater labor of love than this? It comes more nearly of partaking of the Spirit of the Lord himself, who gave his life as a vicarious sacrifice for all of us, than any other work of which I know. It is done in the name of him whose salvation is universal. CR1982Oct:113

**Neal A. Maxwell**

We poorly serve the cause of the Lord, at times, with programmatic superficiality and by our lack of empathy for those who drift in despair. ¶ Truly, we live and walk on "a streetful of splendid strangers," whom we are to love and serve even if they are uninterested in us! CR1983Apr:11

**Peter**

Then Peter said, Silver and gold have I none; but such as I have give I thee: In the name of Jesus Christ of Nazareth rise up and walk. (*Peter and John heal a man lame from birth*) Acts 3:6

**Related Witnesses:**

**Charles A. Callis**

Among the cardinal virtues of the gospel is the praiseworthy virtue of humility. . . . I interpret humility as being strength. Humility expresses itself in lowly service, in volunteering for any service which will ameliorate the conditions, particularly the spiritual conditions of mankind. CR1942Apr:42

**Recorded in Deuteronomy**

And he humbled thee, and suffered thee to hunger, and fed thee with manna, which thou knewest not, neither did thy fathers know; that he might make thee know that man doth not live by bread only, but by every word that proceedeth out of the mouth of the LORD doth man live. (*Revelation to Moses for the children of Israel; the Lord tests Israel—eating manna*) Deut.8:3

**Joseph Smith,**
*receiving the Word of the Lord*

And remember in all things the poor and the

needy, the sick and the afflicted, for he that doeth not these things, the same is not my disciple. (*Revelation "embracing the law of the Church," Feb. 9, 1831*) D&C 52:40

## 746. We are to give genuinely from the heart when we give.

**Paul**

Every man according as he purposeth in his heart, so let him give; not grudgingly, or of necessity: for God loveth a cheerful giver. (*Paul writes to the Church at Corinth, Greece, about A.D. 55*) 2Cor.9:7

**Thomas S. Monson,**
*also quoting Jeremiah*

Often we live side by side but do not communicate heart to heart. There are those within the sphere of our own influence who, with outstretched hands, cry out: "Is there no balm in Gilead. . .?" (Jer.8:22) Each of us must answer. CR1971Oct:171

**Dallin H. Oaks,**
*also quoting Jesus,*
*recorded in Matthew*

We know . . . that even the most extreme acts of service—such as giving all of our goods to feed the poor—profit us nothing unless our service is motivated by the pure love of Christ. ¶ If our service is to be most efficacious, it must be accomplished for the love of God and the love of his children. . . . ¶ This principle—that our service should be for the love of God and the love of fellowmen rather than for personal advantage or any other lesser motive—is admittedly a high standard. The Savior must have seen it so, since he joined his commandment for selfless and complete love directly with the ideal of perfection. . . . "Be ye therefore perfect, even as your Father which is in heaven is perfect" (Matt.5:48). . . . ¶ Service with all of our heart and mind is a high challenge for all of us. Such service must be free of selfish ambition. It must be motivated only by the pure love of Christ. . . . ¶ I know that God expects us to work to purify our hearts and our thoughts so that we may serve one another for the highest and best reason, the pure love of Christ. CR1984Oct:16

**Dallin H. Oaks**

"It is obeying God willingly that is accepted," an anonymous writer has said. "The Lord hates that which is forced—it is rather a tax than an offering." ¶ Although those who serve out of a fear of punishment or out of a sense of duty undoubtedly qualify for the blessings of heaven, there are still higher reasons for service. CR1984Oct:15

**Joseph Smith**

It is a duty which every saint ought to render to his brethren freely—to always love them, and ever succor them. To be justified before God we must love one another: we must overcome evil; we must visit the fatherless and the widow in their affliction, and we must keep ourselves unspotted from the world: for such virtues flow from the great fountain of pure religion, strengthening our faith by adding every good quality that adorns the children of the blessed Jesus, we can pray in the season of prayer; we can love our neighbor as ourselves, and be faithful in tribulation, knowing that the reward of such is greater in the kingdom of heaven. What a consolation! What a joy! Let me live the life of the righteous, and let my reward be like this! ("To the Saints, Scattered Abroad," *Messenger and Advocate,* June 1835) HC2:229

**Mormon**

For behold, God hath said a man being evil cannot do that which is good; for if he offereth a gift, or prayeth unto God, except he shall do it with real intent it profiteth him nothing. 7. For behold, it is not counted unto him for righteousness. 8. For behold, if a man being evil giveth a gift, he doeth it grudgingly; wherefore it is counted unto him the same as if he had retained the gift; wherefore he is counted evil before God. (*Mormon preaches in the synagogue, prior to A.D. 384*) Moro.7:6-8

**Richard L. Evans**

There are some things we can't buy. There are some things in which we can't simply give money as a substitute for personal service. So I think perhaps we should repent of going through too many mechanics, and assuming that we have done the job when we have simply been through the motions—when we have paid the dues, attended the meetings, set up committees, and repeated the mottoes and the phrases. The gift without the giver is a very empty and hollow thing. Service must be an experience in the giving of oneself as well as of material things. It is a sharing experience, or it misses much of the result that is hoped for it. (Richard L. Evans: The Man and the Message, p. 239) TLDP:629

**Related Witnesses:**

**Amulek,**
*quoted by Mormon*

[L]et your hearts be full, drawn out in prayer unto him continually for your welfare, and also for the welfare of those who are around you. (*Amulek teaches the people to pray, about 74 B.C.*) Alma 34:27

747. We need the experience of serving others that we might develop Christlike characters, to qualify us to return to the presence of the Lord.

**Marion G. Romney**

The Lord doesn't really need us to take care of the poor. He could take care of them without our help if it were his purpose to do so. "I, the Lord," he said, "stretched out the heavens, and built the earth, my very handiwork; and all things therein are mine. ¶ "And it is my purpose to provide for my saints, for all things are mine." (D&C 104:14-15) ¶ . . . . No, the Lord doesn't really need us to care for the poor, but we need this experience; for it is only through our learning how to take care of each other that we develop within us the Christlike love and disposition necessary to qualify us to return to his presence. CR1981Oct:130-31

**J. Reuben Clark, Jr.,**
*quoted by Marion G. Romney*

"The real long-term objective of the welfare plan is the building of character in the members of the Church, givers and receivers, rescuing all that is finest down deep inside of them and bringing to flower and fruitage the latent richness of the spirit, which after all is the mission and purpose and reason for being of this church. (*In a special meeting of stake presidencies, Oct. 2, 1936*) CR1981Oct:130

**Orson Pratt**

As love decreases, wickedness, hatred, and misery increases; and the more wicked individuals or nations become, the less capable they are of loving others and making them happy; and vice versa, the more righteous a people become the more they are qualified for loving others and rendering them happy. ("Celestial Marriage: A Revelation on the Patriarchal Order of Matrimony, or Plurality of Wives," The Seer, Oct. 1853, p. 156) TLDP:370

**Bruce R. McConkie**

All men will be judged by what is in their own hearts. If their souls are full of hatred and cursings, such characteristics shall be restored to them in the resurrection. Loving one's enemies and blessing one's cursers perfects the soul. (The Mortal Messiah, 2:142) TLDP:370

**President Spencer W. Kimball**

Service to others deepens and sweetens this life while we are preparing to live in a better world. It is by serving that we learn to serve. When we are engaged in the service of our fellowmen, not only do our deeds assist them, but we also put our own problems in a fresher perspective.

When we concern ourselves more with others, there is less time to be concerned with ourselves. In the midst of serving, there is the promise of Jesus that by losing ourselves, we find ourselves. (President Kimball Speaks Out, p. 39) TLDP:630

**Elder Spencer W. Kimball**

A striking personality and good character is achieved by practice, not merely by thinking it. Just as a pianist masters the intricacies of music through hours and weeks of practice, so mastery of life is achieved by the ceaseless practice of mechanics which make up the art of living. Daily unselfish service to others is one of the rudimentary mechanics of the successful life. "For whosoever will save his life," the Galilean said, "shall lose it, and whosoever will lose his life for my sake shall find it." (Matt.16:25) What a strange paradox this! And yet one needs only to analyze it to be convinced of its truth. *(Commencement at Safford, Arizona, High School, 1939)* (The Teachings of Spencer W. Kimball, p. 250) TLDP:630

---

748. A person who serves another serves God.

**Thomas S. Monson**

We know that when we serve our fellowmen, we are only in the service of our God. (See Mosiah 2:17.) We have the responsibility to serve as though the entire future of the Church depended upon you or upon me. ACR(Copenhagen) 1976:31

**King Benjamin,**
*quoted by Mormon*

Behold, I say unto you that because I said unto you that I had spent my days in your service, I do not desire to boast, for I have only been in the service of God. 17. And behold, I tell you these things that ye may learn wisdom; that ye may learn that when ye are in the service of your fellow beings ye are only in the service of your God. (*King Benjamin addresses his people, about 124 B.C.*) Mosiah 2:16-17

**John A. Widtsoe**

Every man must assume some of God's own responsibility in caring for the children of men. A person cannot let his very brothers go hungry, unclothed, shelterless or bowed down in sorrow. He cannot be cruel to them, and be true to his royal descent. CR1939Oct:98-99

**Joseph Smith,**
*receiving the Word of the Lord*

And inasmuch as ye impart of your substance unto the poor, ye will do it unto me; and they shall be laid before the bishop of my church and his counselors, two of the elders, or high priests, such as he shall appoint or has appointed and set apart for that purpose. . . . 38. For inasmuch as ye do it unto the least of these, ye do it unto me. (*King Benjamin addresses his people, about 124 B.C.*) D&C 42:31,38

**Jesus,**
*recorded in Matthew*

Then shall the King say unto them on his right hand, Come, ye blessed of my Father, inherit the kingdom prepared for you from the foundation of the world: 35. For I was an hungred, and ye gave me meat: I was thirsty, and ye gave me drink: I was a stranger, and ye took me in: 36. Naked, and ye clothed me: I was sick, and ye visited me: I was in prison, and ye came unto me. 37. Then shall the righteous answer him, saying, Lord, when saw we thee an hungred, and fed thee? or thirsty, and gave thee drink? 38. When saw we thee a stranger, and took thee in? or naked, and clothed thee? 39. Or when saw we thee sick, or in prison, and came unto thee? 40. And the King shall answer and say unto them, Verily I say unto you, Inasmuch as ye have done it unto one of the least of these my brethren, ye have done it unto me. (*Jesus gives the parable of the sheep and the goats; the sheep are placed on his right hand at the Lord's second coming*) Matt.25:34-40

**Related Witnesses:**

**Joseph Smith,**
*receiving the Word of the Lord*

And remember in all things the poor and the needy, the sick and the afflicted, for he that doeth not these things, the same is not my disciple. (*Revelation "embracing the law of the Church,"* Feb. 9, 1831) D&C 52:40

---

**749.** We are to be eagerly engaged in doing many things of our own free will (we are not to wait for specific commands or formal church callings to do good works).

**Joseph Smith,**
*receiving the Word of the Lord*

For behold, it is not meet that I should command in all things; for he that is compelled in all things, the same is a slothful and not a wise servant; wherefore he receiveth no reward. 27. Verily I say, men should be anxiously engaged in a good cause, and do many things of their own free will, and bring to pass much righteousness; 28. For the power is in them, wherein they are agents unto themselves. And inasmuch as men do good they shall in nowise lose their

reward. 29. But he that doeth not anything until he is commanded, and receiveth a commandment with doubtful heart, and keepeth it with slothfulness, the same is damned. (*Revelation for the elders of the Church, Aug. 1, 1831; the Lord instructs the Saints to counsel with each other and with the Lord*) D&C 58:26-29

**President Brigham Young**

The children of men are made as independent in their sphere as the Lord is in His, to prove themselves, pursue which path they please, and choose the evil or the good. For those who love the Lord, and do His will, all is right, and they shall be crowned; but those who hate His ways shall be damned, for they choose to be damned. (*In Tabernacle, April 9, 1852, JD1:49*) TLDP:12

**Joseph Smith**

It is a duty which every saint ought to render to his brethren freely—to always love them, and ever succor them. To be justified before God we must love one another: we must overcome evil; we must visit the fatherless and the widow in their affliction, and we must keep ourselves unspotted from the world: for such virtues flow from the great fountain of pure religion, strengthening our faith by adding every good quality that adorns the children of the blessed Jesus, we can pray in the season of prayer; we can love our neighbor as ourselves, and be faithful in tribulation, knowing that the reward of such is greater in the kingdom of heaven. What a consolation! What a joy! Let me live the life of the righteous, and let my reward be like this! ("To the Saints, Scattered Abroad," Messenger and Advocate, June 1835) HC2:229

**John A. Widtsoe**

[E]very man must assume some of God's own responsibility in caring for the children of men. A person cannot let his very brothers go hungry, unclothed, shelterless or bowed down in sorrow. He cannot be cruel to them, and be true to his royal descent. CR1939Oct:98-99

**Thomas S. Monson,**
*also quoting Jeremiah*

Time passes. Circumstances change. Conditions vary. Unaltered is the divine command to succor the weak and lift up the hands which hang down and strengthen the feeble knees. Each of us has the charge to be not a doubter, but a doer; not a leaner, but a lifter. But our complacency tree has many branches, and each spring more buds come into bloom. Often we live side by side but do not communicate heart to heart. There are those within the sphere of our own influence who, with outstretched hands, cry out: "Is there no balm in Gilead. . . ?" (Jer.8:22) Each of us must answer. CR1971Oct:171

## Elder Joseph Fielding Smith

Of course salvation and exaltation must come through the free will without coercion and by individual merit in order that righteous rewards may be given and proper punishment be meted out to the transgressor. (Answers to Gospel Questions, 2:20) TLDP:10

## Marion G. Romney

"For behold, this is my work and my glory— to bring to pass the immortality and eternal life of man." (Moses 1:39) Hence, we see the complete unselfishness of our Father in Heaven. His whole work and glory is to bring eternal life and happiness to his children. Should not our whole purpose in this life, therefore, be made up of righteous service one to another? If not, how can we ever hope to be as he is? CR1981Oct:132

## George F. Richards

The Lord expects us when he blesses us with the good things of this earth to remember those who are not so fortunate. We are to feed the hungry, clothe the naked, visit the sick, comfort those who mourn, and minister unto those who are poor and needy, and thus become of that class to whom the Lord, when he shall come, shall say: "Come, ye blessed of the Father, inherit the kingdom prepared for you from the foundation of the world." CR1939Oct:108-09

## Thomas S. Monson

The beloved apostle [John] noted well his example. He lived not so to be ministered unto, but to minister; not to receive, but to give; not to save his life, but to pour it out for others. CR1971Oct:171

## Bruce R. McConkie

Now I think it is perfectly clear that the Lord expects far more of us than we sometimes render in response. We are not as other men. We are the saints of God and have the revelations of heaven. Where much is given much is expected. We are to put first in our lives the things of his kingdom. CR1975Apr:76

## Related Witnesses:

### President Wilford Woodruff

By virtue of this agency you and I and all mankind are made responsible beings, responsible for the course we pursue, the lives we live, the deeds we do in the body. ("Discourse," Millennial Star, Oct. 1889, p. 642) DGSM:30

### President David O. McKay

Free agency is the impelling source of the soul's progress. It is the purpose of the Lord that man become like him. In order for man to achieve this it was necessary for the Creator first to make him free. ("Free Agency . . . the Gift Divine," IE1962Feb:86) TLDP:11

## Albert E. Bowen

There is no soul-growth in any act done under compulsion. It is an immutable law of life that mental or spiritual growth comes only out of self-effort. CWP:14

## Joseph Smith

But ye are commanded in all things to ask of God, who giveth liberally; and that which the Spirit testifies unto you even so I would that ye should do in all holiness of heart, walking uprightly before me, considering the end of your salvation, doing all things with prayer and thanksgiving, that ye may not be seduced by evil spirits, or doctrines of devils, or the commandments of men; for some are of men, and others of devils. (Revelation relative to governing and conducting meetings, March 8, 1831) D&C 46:7

## Jacob, brother of Nephi, quoted by Nephi

Therefore, cheer up your hearts, and remember that ye are free to act for yourselves—to choose the way of everlasting death or the way of eternal life. (Jacob to the people of Nephi, 559-545 B.C.) 2Ne.10:23

## Joseph Smith, receiving the Word of the Lord

But, behold, I say unto you, that you must study it out in your mind; then you must ask me if it be right, and if it is right I will cause that your bosom shall burn within you; therefore, you shall feel that it is right. (Revelation for Oliver Cowdery, April 1829) D&C 9:8

**Author's Note:** We must do many things of our own free will. Strength comes from pondering, from working it out in our minds, even as Oliver Cowdery was instructed: "But, behold, I say unto you, that you must study it out in your mind; then you must ask me if it be right, and if it is right I will cause that your bosom shall burn within you; therefore, you shall feel that it is right." (See D&C 9:8.) ¶ Our Heavenly Father wants us to become like him. To do so we must get the experience of arriving at decisions. In our Church callings we seek for divine guidance, listen to the always available prompting of the Spirit as we employ our God given minds and talents to magnify our callings. The divine principle of growth is the seemingly slow method of thinking and praying, of purifying ourselves to make of ourselves the kind of persons the Holy Ghost can inspire. Serving our neighbors, performing the duties of parenthood, of Church callings, being faithful stewards while sanctifying our own spirits is the road to achievement and completeness. It is how we become God-like and perfect. Thus each of us must suffer a little, agonize a little. We must listen to the Spirit as we fast and pray, as we ponder and seek guidance. We thereby develop personal characteristics that give us growth. We learn how to accept responsibility, how to magnify our callings—to make our calling and election sure.

---

**750. It is more blessed to give than to receive (there is more joy in serving than in being served).**

**Paul**

I have shewed you all things, how that so labouring ye ought to support the weak, and to remember the words of the Lord Jesus, how he said, It is more blessed to give than to receive. (*Paul reveals a teaching of Jesus*) Acts 20:35

**Marion G. Romney**

[M]ay I remind you that you cannot give yourself poor in this work; you can only give yourself rich. I have satisfied myself regarding the truthfulness of the statement made to me by Elder Melvin J. Ballard as he set me apart for my mission in 1920: "A person cannot give a crust to the Lord without receiving a loaf in return." ¶ The Savior taught that it is more blessed to give than to receive (see Acts 20:35). Through church welfare, both the giver and the receiver are blessed in unique ways—each to the sanctification and salvation of his eternal soul. CR1980Oct:137

**J. Reuben Clark, Jr.**

But there was another element involved in [the Welfare program], and that was based upon the Savior's principle announced in the Sermon on the Mount, "It is more blessed to give than to receive." And the history of the Welfare movement shows that there has come into the church an ever-increasing spirituality because of the giving which has been incident to the carrying on of the Welfare work. That giving has been not alone a giving of money or provisions or clothing or fuel, but a giving of manual labor, and of all the contributions, the latter has perhaps brought the most of a feeling of common brotherhood as men of all training and occupation have worked side by side in a Welfare garden or other project. CR1943Oct:12-13

**J. Reuben Clark, Jr.**

There is something very remarkable about what we have to give under the gospel plan. No matter how much we give of truth, of good example, of righteous living, our stores, our blessings increase, not decrease, by that which we give away. CR1946Oct:85

**Related Witnesses:**

**Paul**

But this I say, He which soweth sparingly shall reap also sparingly; and he which soweth bountifully shall reap also bountifully. (*Paul writes to the Church at Corinth, Greece, about A.D. 55*) 2Cor.9:6

**Elder Harold B. Lee**

When you begin to make service to meet other's needs your constant practice, you are beginning a program that will make you successful in your chosen field and your own needs will begin automatically to take care of themselves. This great idea in action has made great inventors, great statesmen, great business leaders. . . . ¶ When you lose yourselves in the unselfish service to others, you will unconsciously forget your own wants and they will be supplied most likely because of the reciprocal service or patronage of those whom you have thus served. (Decisions for Successful Living, p. 200) TLDP:629

**Jesus,**
*recorded in Luke*

Give, and it shall be given unto you; good measure, pressed down, and shaken together, and running over, shall men give into your bosom. For with the same measure that ye mete withal it shall be measured to you again. (*Jesus teaches his disciples some principles of love and service*) Luke 6:38

**Henry D. Moyle**

We will become mightier and more powerful in our own right in direct proportion to the service and contribution we make to strengthen the Church. CR1962Apr:90

# List of Doctrines

## SIN

773. We are not to boast in our own wisdom, power, or possessions (rather, we should give honor to God).

774. Pride leads to contention.

775. The proud will not inherit eternal life.

776. At the end of this world the proud will be burned as stubble when God cleanses the earth by fire.

### (5) Sexual Immorality

777. Every person should be chaste, free of sexual sin.

778. Sexual sin stands in its enormity next to murder.

779. Men and women are not to commit adultery.

780. The adulterer who repents can be forgiven.

781. Men and women are not to have sexual relations outside of marriage.

782. Men are not to have sexual relations with other men, or women with other women.

783. We are not to have carnal relations with animals.

784. Those who persist in sexual sin shall not inherit the kingdom of God (yet there is mercy for the sinner who repents).

### (6) Sorcery

785. Sorcery (including divination, enchantments, necromancy, witchcraft, wizardry, and the like) is an abomination to the Lord.

### (7) Unrighteous Dominion

786. We are not to abuse the authority given us—to exercise unrighteous dominion or power.

### (8) Worshipping False Gods

787. We are not to worship any other being but God.

788. Whatever we set our hearts and our trust in most becomes, in a sense, our god; if our god is not the true and living God of Israel, we are laboring in idolatry.

789. We are not to worship idols.

*Doctrines on SIN*
*Located in Other Topics*

8. Physical handicaps or disease are not necessarily the result of sin.

11. We have the ability to discern between good and evil and the agency to choose between the two.

20. We have a dual nature: one, related to the earthly life; the other, akin to the divine; by following after the enticings of the Spirit we can overcome the inclinations of the flesh.

36. Because we sin, we would all be forever banned from the presence of God were it not for the Atonement of Christ.

39. The atoning Savior was Himself free from sin.

48. Unrepentant persons cannot receive the full benefit of the Atonement; they will be resurrected but they must suffer for their sins.

72. Children are innocent and are not under penalty of sin when born into mortality.

151. Those who will inherit the telestial kingdom will be the wicked people of the earth, such as adulterers and deliberate liars.

163. The devil is the author of all sin, the source of all evil on earth.

197. The Fall of Adam subjected all people to the enticings of Satan.

198. The body of flesh subjects us to enticements toward physical gratification.

207. Abortion is a sinful, evil practice and Church members are not to submit to or perform an abortion—except in specific rare instances.

247. A gift from God may be taken away when a person fails to heed the counsel of God; the light received shall be taken from the person who does not repent.

358. By cultivating humility we can avoid the pitfalls of worldly pride and philosophies.

364. True happiness and joy are not found in the frivolous or carnal pleasures of the world.

369. God will judge us according to our words as well as our actions done in the body, whether open or secret.

389. Divine justice requires that a penalty be paid for every sin.

396. The calamities and judgments predicted for the last days shall come because of sin—the wickedness and disobedience of mankind.

412. To be efficacious, all exercise of priesthood authority is to be done with unfeigned love, patience, gentleness, and meekness.

# SIN continued

417. Those upon whom the authority of the priesthood has been conferred can lose the power to exercise that priesthood authority when they are corrupted by sin.

440. Husbands are not to abuse their wives.

535. We are to pray for help to resist temptation.

578. Authority of the priesthood is to be exercised in a pure spirit of love and kindness.

613. We are to purify and cleanse ourselves from all sin.

622. Repentance is essential to salvation: we cannot be saved while we carry our sins with us.

710. A sanctified person cannot look upon sin without abhorrence.

848. Lust for money is the root of much evil.

852. They who possess great riches tend to succumb to the sin of pride.

(See topic REPENTANCE.)

# SIN

**(1) Sin in General**
**(2) Evil Speaking**
**(3) Murder**
**(4) Pride**
**(5) Sexual Immorality**
  1. Chastity
  2. Adultery
  3. Fornication
  4. Homosexuality
  5. Bestiality
  6. Repentance from Sexual Sin
**(6) Sorcery**
**(7) Unrighteous Dominion**
**(8) Worshipping False Gods**

## (1) Sin in General

751. Sin is the willful breaking of divine law.

**Orson F. Whitney**

Sin is the transgression of divine law. A man sins when he violates his conscience, going contrary to light and knowledge—not the light and knowledge that has come to his neighbor, but that which has come to himself. He sins when he does the opposite of what he knows to be right. Up to that point he only blunders. One may suffer painful consequences for only blundering, but he cannot commit sin unless he knows better than to do the thing in which the sin consists. One must have a conscience before he can violate it. (Cowley and Whitney on Doctrine, pp. 435-36) TLDP:631

**John**

Whosoever committeth sin transgresseth also the law: for sin is the transgression of the law. (*John writes to the churches in Asia*) 1Jn.3:4

**Elder Harold B. Lee**

Sin is something so universal that all of you know about it, and all preachers of righteousness and indeed all honest souls are opposed to it. Sin may be defined as any want of conformity to or transgression of a rule or law or right or duty, as made known by your conscience or the revealed word of God. Such non-conformity or transgression of divine law might be either by omission or commission, or in other words sin may be either the willful breaking of divine law or you may sin by your failure and neglect in thought, word or deed to keep the commandments of the Lord. One may sin by being hasty in judgment on vital issues or where the welfare of a human soul is at stake, and "he that

forgiveth not his brother his trespasses standeth condemned before the Lord; for there remaineth in him the greater sin." (D&C 64:9) (Decisions for Successful Living, p. 82) TLDP:631

**James**

Therefore to him that knoweth to do good, and doeth it not, to him it is sin. (*James writes to his brethren in the Church*) James 4:17

**President Brigham Young,**
*quoted by John A. Widtsoe*

Sin consists in doing wrong when we know and can do better, and it will be punished with a just retribution, in the due time of the Lord. (*In Tabernacle, Dec. 18, 1853*) DBY:28

752. There is no sin without knowledge of good and evil.

**Alma, the younger,**
*quoted by Mormon*

[H]e that knoweth not good from evil is blameless. . . . (*Alma discourses on the principle of repentance, about 76 B.C.*) Alma 29:5

**Orson F. Whitney**

Sin is the transgression of divine law. A man sins when he violates his conscience, going contrary to light and knowledge—not the light and knowledge that has come to his neighbor, but that which has come to himself. He sins when he does the opposite of what he knows to be right. Up to that point he only blunders. One may suffer painful consequences for only blundering, but he cannot commit sin unless he knows better than to do the thing in which the sin consists. One must have a conscience before he can violate it. (Cowley and Whitney on Doctrine, pp. 435-36) TLDP:631

**Jesus,**
*quoted by John*

Jesus said unto them, If ye were blind, ye should have no sin: but now ye say, We see; therefore your sin remaineth. (*Jesus responds to the Pharisees*) John 9:41

**Jacob, brother of Nephi,**
*quoted by Nephi*

Wherefore, he has given a law; and where there is no law given there is no punishment; and where there is no punishment there is no condemnation. . . . (*Jacob to the people of Nephi, 559-545 B.C.*) 2Ne.9:25

**James E. Talmage**

According to the technical definition of sin it consists in the violation of law, and in this strict sense sin may be committed inadvertently or in ignorance. It is plain, however, from the scriptural doctrine of human responsibility and the unerring justice of God, that in his transgressions as in his righteous deeds man will be judged according to his ability to comprehend and obey law. To him who has never been made acquainted with a higher law the requirements of that law do not apply in their fulness. For sins committed without knowledge—that is, for laws violated in ignorance—a propitiation has been provided in the atonement wrought through the sacrifice of the Savior; and sinners of this class do not stand condemned, but shall be given opportunity yet to learn and to accept or reject the principles of the Gospel. AF:52-53

### Elder Joseph F. Smith

We shall not be cast off . . . for those sins, which we ignorantly commit, which are the results of misunderstanding in all honesty before the Lord. The difficulty does not lie here; the danger lies in our failing to live up to that which we do know to be right and proper. For this we will be held responsible before the Lord; for this we will be judged and condemned unless we repent. (*In Tabernacle, July 7, 1878, JD20:26*) TLDP:323

**Related Witnesses:**

### James

Therefore to him that knoweth to do good, and doeth it not, to him it is sin. (*James writes to his brethren in the Church*) James 4:17

### Alma, the younger, quoted by Mormon

And now, how much more cursed is he that knoweth the will of God and doeth it not, than he that only believeth, or only hath cause to believe, and falleth into transgression? (*Alma preaches to the poor whose afflictions had humbled them, about 74 B.C.*) Alma 32:19

### Joseph Smith, quoted by Elder Joseph Fielding Smith

Again, if men sin wilfully after they have received the knowledge of the truth, there remaineth no more sacrifice for sin, but a certain fearful looking for of judgment and fiery indignation to come, which shall devour these adversaries. (*Letter to the Church from Liberty Jail, Dec. 16, 1838*) HC3:226-33; TPJS:128

### Joseph Smith

[I]t becometh every man who hath been warned to warn his neighbor. 82. Therefore, they are left without excuse, and their sins are upon their own heads. (*Revelation Dec. 27/28, 1832; the "olive leaf message of peace"*) D&C 88:81-82

### Lehi, quoted by his son Nephi

[T]hey would have remained in a state of innocence, having no joy, for they knew no misery; doing no good, for they knew no sin. (*Lehi teaches his sons, between 588-570 B.C.*) 2Ne.2:23

---

### 753. We are to shun all evil.

#### President Joseph F. Smith

It is not necessary that our young people should know of the wickedness carried on in any place. Such knowledge is not elevating, and it is quite likely that more than one young man can trace the first step of his downfall to a curiosity which led him into questionable places. Let the young men of Zion, whether they be on missions or whether they be at home, shun all dens of infamy. It is not necessary that they should know what is going on in such places. No man is better or stronger for such knowledge. Let them remember that "the knowledge of sin tempteth to its commission," and then avoid those temptations that in time to come may threaten their virtue and their standing in the Church of Christ. (Juvenile Instructor, vol. 37, May 1902, p. 304; Gospel Doctrine, p. 373) TLDP:631

#### Recorded in Proverbs

My son, if sinners entice thee, consent thou not. Prov.1:10

#### Elder Spencer W. Kimball

The importance of not accommodating temptation in the least degree is underlined by the Savior's example. Did not he recognize the danger when he was on the mountain with his fallen brother, Lucifer, being sorely tempted by that master tempter? He could have opened the door and flirted with danger by saying, "All right, Satan, I'll listen to your proposition. I need not succumb, I need not yield, I need not accept—but I'll listen." ¶ Christ did not so rationalize. He positively and promptly closed the discussion, and commanded: "Get thee hence, Satan," meaning, likely, "Get out of my sight—get out of my presence—I will not listen—I will have nothing to do with you." Then, we read, "the devil leaveth him." ¶ This is our proper pattern, if we would prevent sin rather than be faced with the much more difficult task of curing it. As I study the story of the Redeemer and his temptations, I am certain he spent his energies fortifying himself against temptation rather than battling with it to conquer it. (The Miracle of Forgiveness, p. 216) TLDP:681

#### John A. Widtsoe

Naturally the question arises: How could these men [Oliver Cowdery and David Whitmer], both of whom had seen the angelic guardian of the plates from which the Book of Mormon was translated and the plates themselves, and one of whom in addition had been privileged to have conversed with heavenly beings, John the Baptist, Peter, James and John—how could such men so conduct themselves as to endanger their Church membership or be content to remain outside the Church? They had knowledge, beyond that of other men, of the reality and divinity of the events which led to the organization of The Church of Jesus Christ of Latter-day Saints. ¶ The answer to the question is simple, well understood by all. These brethren did not use their knowledge in conformity with the order of the Church as set forth in the revelations of the Lord. That is, they entered forbidden paths; they did not obey the commandments of God. The practices of their lives did not correspond with their knowledge. CR1938Apr:49

**Related Witnesses:**

### Jesus,
*recorded in Matthew*

And fear not them which kill the body, but are not able to kill the soul: but rather fear him which is able to destroy both soul and body in hell. *(Jesus trains and instructs the Twelve)* Matt.10:28

### Nephi, son of Lehi

Awake, my soul! No longer droop in sin. Rejoice, O my heart, and give place no more for the enemy of my soul. *(Nephi writes on plates shortly after the death of his father Lehi, 588-570 B.C.)* 2Ne.4:28

### Nephi, son of Lehi

O Lord, wilt thou redeem my soul? Wilt thou deliver me out of the hands of mine enemies? Wilt thou make me that I may shake at the appearance of sin? *(Nephi writes on plates shortly after the death of his father Lehi, 588-570 B.C.)* 2Ne.4:31

---

## 754. Sin makes a person spiritually unclean.

### Marion G. Romney

All men have sinned. Each person is therefore unclean to the extent to which he has sinned, and because of that uncleanness is banished from the presence of the Lord so long as the effect of his own wrongdoing is upon him. CR1982Apr:9

### Paul

Unto the pure all things are pure: but unto them that are defiled and unbelieving is nothing pure;

but even their mind and conscience is defiled. 16. They profess that they know God; but in works they deny him, being abominable, and disobedient, and unto every good work reprobate. *(Paul's letter to his companion Titus, about A.D. 64)* Titus 1:15-16

### Elder Joseph Fielding Smith

The Spirit of the Lord will not dwell in unclean tabernacles, and when the spirit is withdrawn, darkness supersedes the light, and apostasy will follow. This is one of the greatest evidences of the divinity of this latter-day work. In other organizations men may commit all manner of sin and still retain their membership, because they have no companionship with the Holy Ghost to lose: but in the Church when a man sins and continues without repentance, the Spirit is withdrawn, and when he is left to himself the adversary takes possession of his mind and he denies the faith. (Doctrines of Salvation, 3:309) TLDP:632

### Recorded in Psalms

Who shall ascend into the hill of the LORD? or who shall stand in his holy place? 4. He that hath clean hands, and a pure heart; who hath not lifted up his soul unto vanity, nor sworn deceitfully. Ps.24:3-4

### King Benjamin,
*quoted by Mormon*

For the natural man is an enemy to God, and has been from the fall of Adam, and will be, forever and ever, unless he yields to the enticings of the Holy Spirit, and putteth off the natural man and becometh a saint through the atonement of Christ the Lord, and becometh as a child, submissive, meek, humble, patient, full of love, willing to submit to all things which the Lord seeth fit to inflict upon him, even as a child doth submit to his father. *(King Benjamin addresses his people, about 124 B.C.)* Mosiah 3:19

### Amulek,
*quoted by Mormon*

And I say unto you again that he cannot save them in their sins; for I cannot deny his word, and he hath said that no unclean thing can inherit the kingdom of heaven; therefore, how can ye be saved, except ye inherit the kingdom of heaven? Therefore, ye cannot be saved in your sins. *(Amulek contends with the lawyer Zeezrom, about 82 B.C.)* Alma 11:37

### Alma, the younger,
*quoted by Mormon*

And he doth not dwell in unholy temples; neither can filthiness or anything which is unclean be received into the kingdom of God; therefore I say unto you the time shall come, yea, and it shall be at the last day, that he who is filthy shall remain in his filthiness. (*Alma preaches to the people in Gideon, about 83 B.C.*) Alma 7:21

**Jacob, brother of Nephi**

But, wo, wo, unto you that are not pure in heart, that are filthy this day before God; for except ye repent the land is cursed for your sakes; and the Lamanites, which are not filthy like unto you, nevertheless they are cursed with a sore cursing, shall scourge you even unto destruction. (*Jacob addresses the Nephites, those who are pure in heart, 544-421 B.C.*) Jacob 3:3

---

**755. The Lord cannot look upon sin with the least degree of allowance.**

**Joseph Smith,**
*receiving the Word of the Lord*

For I the Lord cannot look upon sin with the least degree of allowance; 32. Nevertheless, he that repents and does the commandments of the Lord shall be forgiven; 33. And he that repents not, from him shall be taken even the light which he has received; for my Spirit shall not always strive with man, saith the Lord of Hosts. (*Revelation received at a conference of elders of the Church, Nov. 1, 1831*) D&C 1:31-33

**Orson F. Whitney**

Marvel not, my hearers, that all things are in commotion. The hour of God's judgment is at hand. War, famine, pestilence, earthquake, tempest and tidal wave—these are among the predicted signs of the Savior's second coming. Tyranny and wickedness must be overthrown, and the way prepared for him who, though gracious and merciful to all, and forgiving to sinners who repent, "cannot look upon sin with the least degree of allowance." Earth must be freed from all oppression and cleansed from all iniquity. It is God's house; he is coming to live in it, and to make of it a glorified mansion. The world is in its Saturday night; house cleaning is in progress; and the work of purification must be done and out of the way before the Lord of the Sabbath appears. ("The Everlasting Gospel," IE1925Feb:317) TLDP:345

**Jacob, brother of Nephi**

But behold, hearken ye unto me, and know that by the help of the all-powerful Creator of heaven and earth I can tell you concerning your thoughts, how that ye are beginning to labor in sin, which sin appeareth very abominable unto me, yea, and abominable unto God. (*Jacob teaches the Nephites in the temple, 544-421 B.C.*) Jacob 2:5

**Elder George Albert Smith**

Think of that—the suggestion that a little sin

will be justified, yet in the very first revelation contained in the Doctrine and Covenants, that which is known as the Preface, we find these words: "For I the Lord cannot look upon sin with the least degree of allowance." ¶ Yet there are those who would say that because it is a little sin our Heavenly Father does not care. ¶ . . . . Whether it be a lie intended to affect a religious organization, a business organization, a political organization, or an individual, the lie will brand the one who tells it, and sooner or later he will have to account for the wrong he has committed. CR1932Oct:28-29

**Alma, the younger,**
*quoted by Mormon*

And he said: Thus saith the Lord God—Cursed shall be the land, yea, this land, unto every nation, kindred, tongue, and people, unto destruction, which do wickedly, when they are fully ripe; and as I have said so shall it be; for this is the cursing and the blessing of God upon the land, for the Lord cannot look upon sin with the least degree of allowance. (*Alma blesses the earth for the sake of the righteous, 73 B.C.*) Alma 45:16

**Elder Spencer W. Kimball**

And through it all we must remember that the pleading sinner, desiring to make restitution for his acts, must also forgive others of all offenses committed against him. The Lord will not forgive us unless our hearts are fully purged of all hate, bitterness and accusation against our fellowmen. . . . ¶ The Lord says: ¶ . . . I the Lord cannot look upon sin with the least degree of allowance; ¶ Nevertheless, he that repents and does the commandments of the Lord shall be forgiven. (D&C 1:31-32) (The Miracle of Forgiveness, p. 200-01) TLDP:550

**Related Witnesses:**

**John A. Widtsoe**

Not only in numbers have we become a "marvelous work and a wonder" in a little less than one hundred years; but in a greater and a larger sense have we become a marvelous people, for we have impressed our thought upon the whole world. The world does not believe today as it did ninety years ago. A few days ago I picked up a recent number of a great magazine, and my feelings were roused within me and my testimony increased, when I found one of the writers declaring to the readers of the magazine that "God cannot look upon sin with the least degree of tolerance," borrowed almost word for word, from section one of the Doctrine and Covenants. In such a way have the doctrines taught by the despised Latter-day Saints been appropriated by the nations of the earth; and whether the people of the earth accept the inspiration of Joseph Smith, nevertheless, in fact, the whole current of human thought has been changed by the doctrines of this people. That is perhaps the greatest achievement of "Mormonism." CR1921Oct:108-09

---

**756. There is sin in omission: to know the will of God and fail to act is sin.**

### James

Therefore to him that knoweth to do good, and doeth it not, to him it is sin. (*James writes to his brethren in the Church*) James 4:17

### Elder Harold B. Lee

Sin may be defined as any want of conformity to or transgression of a rule or law or right or duty, as made known by your conscience or the revealed word of God. Such non-conformity or transgression of divine law might be either by omission or commission, or in other words sin may be either the willful breaking of divine law or you may sin by your failure and neglect in thought, word or deed to keep the commandments of the Lord. One may sin by being hasty in judgment on vital issues or where the welfare of a human soul is at stake, and "he that forgiveth not his brother his trespasses standeth condemned before the Lord; for there remaineth in him the greater sin." (D&C 64:9) (Decisions for Successful Living, p. 82) TLDP:631

### Alma, the younger,
### *quoted by Mormon*

And now, how much more cursed is he that knoweth the will of God and doeth it not, than he that only believeth, or only hath cause to believe, and falleth into transgression? (*Alma preaches to the poor whose afflictions had humbled them, about 74 B.C.*) Alma 32:19

### Elder Spencer W. Kimball

Yes, sins of omission have much in common with those of commission. As we have seen, one common feature is their potential for damning the sinner. (The Miracle of Forgiveness, p. 101) TLDP:631

---

**757. All people sin.**

### Paul

For all have sinned, and come short of the glory of God; (*Paul writes to the Church in Rome, about A.D. 55*) Rom.3:23

### Joseph Smith

[A]nd as all men sin[,] forgive the transgressions

of thy people, and let them be blotted out forever. (*Prayer given to Joseph Smith by revelation and offered at the dedication of the Kirtland Temple on March 27, 1836*) D&C 109:34

### Marion G. Romney

From the days of Adam until today, Satan has fought against Christ for the souls of men. Every person who has reached the age of accountability, except Jesus, has yielded in some degree to sin, some more and some less, but all save Jesus only have yielded sufficiently to be barred from the presence of God. This means that every person must be cleansed through the atonement of Jesus Christ in order to reenter the society of God. ("Jesus—Savior and Redeemer," Brigham Young University Speeches of the Year, 1978, p. 11) TLDP:633

### John

If we say that we have no sin, we deceive ourselves, and the truth is not in us. 9. If we confess our sins, he is faithful and just to forgive us our sins, and to cleanse us from all unrighteousness. 10. If we say that we have not sinned, we make him a liar, and his word is not in us. (*John writes to the churches in Asia*) 1Jn.1:8-10

### Elder Heber J. Grant

I do not believe that any man lives up to his ideals, but if we are striving, if we are working, if we are trying, to the best of our ability, to improve day by day, then we are in the line of our duty. If we are seeking to remedy our own defects, if we are so living that we can ask God for light, for knowledge, for intelligence, and above all, for His Spirit, that we may overcome our weaknesses, then, I can tell you, we are in the straight and narrow path that leads to life eternal. Then we need have no fear. CR1909Apr:111; DGSM:40

### Recorded in Ecclesiastes

For there is not a just man upon earth, that doeth good, and sinneth not. (*Reflections of a son of David the king*) Eccl.7:20

### Paul

As it is written, There is none righteous, no, not one: (*Letter to the Church in Rome, about A.D. 55*) Rom.3:10

**Related Witnesses:**

### Jesus,
### *quoted by John*

He that is without sin among you, let him first cast a stone at her. (*The scribes and Pharisees bring a woman taken in adultery before Jesus*) John 8:7

### Francis M. Lyman

For there is an advantage, there is a blessing and an enlargement of the soul that comes to the man who obeys the word and will of the

Lord. It is better that we have done God's will than that we should have need to be forgiven for neglecting it. It is better not to have been a sinner. It is better that our sins should be very light, and not of a serious nature, than that they should be deadly sins. It is better that we should live without sin, and be like the Son of God. It is not necessary that we should be sinners. God has designed that we should not be sinners, but that we should live lives of purity and righteousness and walk in obedience to His will, as the Savior did. CR1899Oct:35

---

### 758. When we commit sins we must suffer the penalties.

#### President Spencer W. Kimball

We are concerned that too many times the interviewing leader in his personal sympathies for the transgressor, and in his love perhaps for the family of the transgressor, is inclined to waive the discipline which that transgressor demands. ¶ Too often a transgressor is forgiven and all penalties waived when that person should have been disfellowshipped or excommunicated. Too often a sinner is disfellowshipped when he or she should have been excommunicated. ¶ . . . . There can be no forgiveness without real and total repentance, and there can be no repentance without punishment. This is as eternal as is the soul. ¶ . . . . [W]hen a man has committed sin, he must suffer. It is an absolute requirement—not by the bishop—but it is a requirement by nature and by the very part of a man. CR1975Apr:116

#### John A. Widtsoe

The eternal power of choice was respected by the Lord himself. That throws a flood of light on the "Fall." It really converts the command into a warning, as much as if to say, if you do this thing, you will bring upon yourself a certain punishment. . . . ¶ In the heavens above, as in the earth below, law prevails. No one can escape the consequences of the acceptance or rejection of law. Cause and effect are eternally related. (Evidences and Reconciliations, pp. 192-95) TLDP:187-88

#### Elder Wilford Woodruff

I have never committed a sin in this Church and kingdom, but what it has cost me a thousand times more than it was worth. We cannot sin with impunity; we cannot neglect any counsel with impunity, but what it will bring sorrow. (In Assembly Hall, July 4, 1880, JD21:284) TLDP:631

#### Elder Spencer W. Kimball

We might add that one's position makes no dif-

ference to the inescapability of the consequences of sin. In the Church, the bishop, the stake president, the apostle—all are subject to the same laws of right living, and penalties follow their sins just as for the other members of the Church. None are exempt from the results of sin, as regards either Church action against the offender or the effects of sin upon the soul. (The Miracle of Forgiveness, p. 145) TLDP:632

#### President Harold B. Lee

The heaviest burden that one has to bear in this life is the burden of sin. CR1973Apr:177

#### Joseph Smith,
*receiving the Word of the Lord*

Therefore I command you to repent—repent, lest I smite you by the rod of my mouth, and by my wrath, and by my anger, and your sufferings be sore—how sore you know not, how exquisite you know not, yea, how hard to bear you know not. 16. For behold, I, God, have suffered these things for all, that they might not suffer if they would repent; 17. But if they would not repent they must suffer even as I; 18. Which suffering caused myself, even God, the greatest of all, to tremble because of pain, and to bleed at every pore, and to suffer both body and spirit—and would that I might not drink the bitter cup, and shrink— 19. Nevertheless, glory be to the Father, and I partook and finished my preparations unto the children of men. 20. Wherefore, I command you again to repent, lest I humble you with my almighty power; and that you confess your sins, lest you suffer these punishments of which I have spoken, of which in the smallest, yea, even in the least degree you have tasted at the time I withdrew my Spirit. (*Christ announces himself and gives a commandment of God for Martin Harris, March 1830*) D&C 19:15-20

#### Jeremiah

[Y]our sins have witholden good things from you. (*The prophet Jeremiah foretells judgments to be poured out upon the Jews because of their sins*) Jer.5:25

#### N. Eldon Tanner

There is no happiness in sin, and when we depart from the path of righteousness we begin to do those things which will inevitably lead us to unhappiness and misery and loss of freedom. CR1977Apr:21

---

### 759. The final consequence of unrepented sin is spiritual death.

#### Paul

For the wages of sin is death; but the gift of

God is eternal life through Jesus Christ our Lord. (*Paul writes to the Church in Rome, about A.D. 55*) Rom.6:23

### Amulek,
#### quoted by Mormon

And I say unto you again that he cannot save them in their sins; for I cannot deny his word, and he hath said that no unclean thing can inherit the kingdom of heaven; therefore, how can ye be saved, except ye inherit the kingdom of heaven? Therefore, ye cannot be saved in your sins. (*Amulek contends with the lawyer Zeezrom, about 82 B.C.*) Alma 11:37

### President Spencer W. Kimball

One must come to a realization of the seriousness of his sin. Since the beginning there has been in the world a wide range of sins. Many of them involve harm to others, but every sin is against ourselves and God, for sins limit our progress, curtail our development, and estrange us from good people, good influences, and from our Lord. (President Kimball Speaks Out, p. 6) TLDP:633

### James

[S]in, when it is finished, bringeth forth death. (*James writes to his brethren in the Church*) James 1:15

### President Joseph F. Smith

Self-respect, deference for sacred things, and personal purity are the beginnings and the essence of wisdom. The doctrines of the gospel, the Church restraint, are like schoolmasters to keep us in the line of duty. If it were not for these schoolmasters, we would perish and be overcome by the evil about us. We see men who have freed themselves from Church restraint and from the precious doctrines of the gospel, who perish about us every day! They boast of freedom, but are the slaves of sin. ¶ Let me admonish you to permit the gospel schoolmaster to teach you self-respect and to keep you pure and free from secret sins that bring not only physical punishment, but sure spiritual death. You cannot hide the penalty which God has affixed to them—a penalty often worse than death. It is the loss of self-respect, it is physical debility, it is insanity, indifference to all powers that are good and noble—all these follow in the wake of the sinner in secret, and of the unchaste. Unchastity, furthermore, not only fixes its penalty on the one who transgresses, but reaches out unerring punishment to the third and fourth generation, making not only the transgressor a wreck, but mayhap involving scores of people in his direct line of relationship, disrupting family ties, breaking the hearts of parents, and causing a black stream of sor-

row to overwhelm their lives. (Gospel Doctrine, p. 335) TLDP:631-32

### Paul

The sting of death is sin; and the strength of sin is the law. (*Letter to the Church at Corinth, Greece, about A.D. 55*) 1Cor.15:56

### Nephi, son of Lehi

Therefore remember, O man, for all thy doings thou shalt be brought into judgment. 21. Wherefore, if ye have sought to do wickedly in the days of your probation, then ye are found unclean before the judgment-seat of God; and no unclean thing can dwell with God; wherefore, ye must be cast off forever. (*Nephi's writings, 600-592 B.C.*) 1Ne.10:20-21

### Jesus,
#### quoted by Mormon

And no unclean thing can enter into his kingdom; therefore nothing entereth into his rest save it be those who have washed their garments in my blood, because of their faith, and the repentance of all their sins, and their faithfulness unto the end. 20. Now this is the commandment: Repent, all ye ends of the earth, and come unto me and be baptized in my name, that ye may be sanctified by the reception of the Holy Ghost, that ye may stand spotless before me at the last day. (*The resurrected Jesus Christ calls on the Nephites to repent in contemplation of the final judgment, A.D. 34*) 3Ne.27:19-20

### Jesus,
#### recorded in Matthew

And fear not them which kill the body, but are not able to kill the soul: but rather fear him which is able to destroy both soul and body in hell. (*Christ instructs, empowers, and sends the Twelve Apostles forth to preach, minister, and heal the sick*) Matt.10:28

**Related Witnesses:**

### Jeremiah

[Y]our sins have withholden good things from you. (*The prophet Jeremiah foretells judgments to be poured out upon the Jews because of their sins*) Jer.5:25

---

### 760. We experience joy when we choose the good and reject the evil.

### Lehi,
#### quoted by his son Nephi

And now, behold, if Adam had not transgressed he would not have fallen, but he would have remained in the garden of Eden. And all things which were created must have remained in the same state in which they were after they were created; and they must have remained forever, and had no end. 23. And they would have had no children; wherefore they would have remained in a state of innocence, having no joy, for they knew no misery; doing no good, for they knew no sin. 24. But behold, all things have been done in the wisdom of him who knoweth all things. 25. Adam fell that men might be; and men are, that they might have joy. (*Lehi teaches his sons, between 588-570 B.C.*) 2Ne.2:22-25

### John A. Widtsoe

After their expulsion from Eden into the earth as it is, Adam exults: ". . . . Blessed be the name of God, for because of my transgression my eyes are opened, and in this life I shall have joy, and again in the flesh I shall see God." And Eve seemed almost jubilant: ". . . . Were it not for our transgression we never should have had seed, and never should have known good and evil, and the joy of our redemption, and the eternal life which God giveth unto all the obedient." (Moses 5:10-11) ¶ These were not the words of sinners or of repentant sinners. This was spoken by people who had met and accepted a great challenge, with which, as they imply, God was pleased. . . . ¶ In the joy of Adam and Eve after the "Fall" lies hidden, perhaps, a principle which disputants about this subject have not understood, and which may not as yet be fully comprehended. However, in modern revelation, a clue to understanding of the "Fall" is given, which may be the key to the apparent contradiction. ¶ After Adam had been supplied with a body made "from the dust of the ground," and placed in the garden of Eden, instructions were given him: ¶ "And I, the Lord God, commanded the man, saying: Of every tree of the garden thou mayest freely eat. But of the tree of the knowledge of good and evil, thou shalt not eat of it, *nevertheless, thou mayest choose for thyself, for it is given unto thee;* but, remember that I forbid it, for in the day thou eatest thereof thou shalt surely die." (Moses 3:16-17, italics added) ¶ Though a command had been given, Adam was permitted to exercise his free agency. "Thou mayest choose for thyself." The eternal power of choice was respected by the Lord himself. That throws a flood of light on the "Fall." It really converts the command into a warning, as much as if to say, if you do this thing, you will bring upon yourself a certain punishment; but do it if you choose. ¶ Such was the problem before our first parents: to remain forever at selfish ease in the Garden of Eden, or to face unselfishly tribulation and death, in bringing to pass the purposes of the Lord for a host of waiting spirit children. They chose the latter. ¶ *This they did with open eyes and minds as to consequences.* The memory of their former estates may have been dimmed, but the gospel had been taught them during their sojourn in the Garden of Eden. They could not have been left in complete ignorance of the purpose of their creation. Brigham Young frankly said: "Adam was as conversant with his Father who placed him upon this earth as we are conversant with our earthly parents." [DBY:104] The Prophet Joseph taught that "Adam received commandments and instructions from God; this was the order from the beginning." [TPJS:168] ¶ The choice that they made raises Adam and Eve to pre-eminence among all who have come on earth. The Lord's plan was given life by them. They are indeed, as far as this earth is concerned, our loving father and mother. The "Fall" and the consequent redeeming act of Jesus became the most glorious events in the history of mankind. ¶ In the heavens above, as in the earth below, law prevails. No one can escape the consequences of the acceptance or rejection of law. Cause and effect are eternally related. The Lord had warned Adam and Eve of the hard battle with earth conditions if they chose to eat of the tree of the knowledge of good and evil. He would not subject his son and daughter to hardship and the death of their bodies unless it be of their own choice. They must choose for themselves. They chose wisely, in accord with the heavenly law of love for others. ¶ In life all must choose at times. Sometimes, two possibilities are good; neither is evil. Usually, however, one is of greater import than the other. When in doubt, each must choose that which concerns the good of others—the greater law—rather than that which chiefly benefits ourselves—the lesser law. The greater must be chosen whether it be law or thing. That was the choice made in Eden. . . . ¶ . . . . It is a thrilling thought that Adam and Eve were not coerced to begin God's work on earth. They chose to do so, by the exercise of their free agency. It is the lesson for all their children: Seek the truth, choose wisely, and carry the responsibility for our acts. (Evidences and Reconciliations, pp. 192-95) TLDP:188

### President John Taylor

Thus we find: Firstly, that Adam and Eve both considered that they had gained, instead of suffered loss, through their disobedience to that law; for they made the statement, that if it had not been for their transgression they never would "have known good and evil." And again, they would have been incapable of increase; and without that increase the designs of God in relation to the formation of the earth and man could not have been accomplished; for one great object of the creation of the world was the propagation of the human species, that bodies might be prepared for those spirits who already existed, and who, when they saw the earth formed, shouted for joy. . . . ¶ . . . . God's plan in relation to man was that he should fall, and having fallen and obtained a knowledge of good and evil (which knowledge he could not have obtained without placing himself in that position), then it became necessary that he should know concerning the atonement and redemption which should be brought about through the mediation of Jesus Christ. (The Mediation and Atonement, pp. 130, 187) TLDP:182-83

**Related Witnesses:**

**Joseph Smith,**
*translating the Book of Moses*

Blessed be the name of God, for because of my transgression my eyes are opened, and in this life I shall have joy, and again in the flesh I shall see God. 11. And Eve, his wife, heard all these things and was glad, saying: Were it not for our transgression we never should have had seed, and never should have known good and evil, and the joy of our redemption, and the eternal life which God giveth unto all the obedient. (*The record of Moses: Adam prophesies concerning all the families of the earth*) Moses 5:10-11

**Joseph Smith,**
*translating the Book of Moses*

And I, the Lord God, commanded the man, saying: Of every tree of the garden thou mayest freely eat, 17. But of the tree of the knowledge of good and evil, thou shalt not eat of it, nevertheless, thou mayest choose for thyself, for it is given unto thee; but, remember that I forbid it, for in the day thou eatest thereof thou shalt surely die. (*The Lord reveals to Moses the placing of man in the Garden of Eden*) Moses 3:16-17

**Alma, the younger,**
*quoted by Mormon*

Now behold, my son, I will explain this thing unto thee. For behold, after the Lord God sent our first parents forth from the garden of Eden, to till the ground, from whence they were taken—yea, he drew out the man, and he placed at the east end of the garden of Eden, cherubim, and a flaming sword which turned every way, to keep the tree of life— 3. Now, we see that the man had become as God, knowing good and evil; and lest he should put forth his hand, and

take also of the tree of life, and eat and live forever, the Lord God placed cherubim and the flaming sword, that he should not partake of the fruit— 4. And thus we see, that there was a time granted unto man to repent, yea, a probationary time, a time to repent and serve God. (*Alma speaks to his son Corianton; mortality is a probationary time to enable man to repent and serve God, about 73 B.C.*) Alma 42:2-4

**Nephi, son of Lehi**

Awake, my soul! No longer droop in sin. Rejoice, O my heart, and give place no more for the enemy of my soul. (*Nephi writes on plates shortly after the death of his father Lehi, 588-570 B.C.*) 2Ne.4:28

**Alma, the younger,**
*quoted by Mormon*

Behold, I say unto you, wickedness never was happiness. (*Alma speaks to his son Corianton, concerning the resurrection of the dead, about 73 B.C.*) Alma 41:10

---

761. Because no unclean thing can inherit the celestial kingdom, we cannot enter that kingdom unless we have repented of our sins.

**Marion G. Romney**

All men have sinned. Each person is therefore unclean to the extent to which he has sinned, and because of that uncleanness is banished from the presence of the Lord so long as the effect of his own wrongdoing is upon him. CR1982Apr:9

**Amulek,**
*quoted by Mormon*

And I say unto you again that he cannot save them in their sins; for I cannot deny his word, and he hath said that no unclean thing can inherit the kingdom of heaven; therefore, how can ye be saved, except ye inherit the kingdom of heaven? Therefore, ye cannot be saved in your sins. (*Amulek contends with the lawyer Zeezrom, about 82 B.C.*) Alma 11:37

**Alma, the younger,**
*quoted by Mormon*

For I perceive that ye are in the paths of righteousness; I perceive that ye are in the path which leads to the kingdom of God; yea, I perceive that ye are making his paths straight. 20. I perceive that it has been made known unto you, by the testimony of his word, that he cannot walk in crooked paths; neither doth he vary from that which he hath said; neither hath he a shadow of turning from the right to the left, or from that which is right to that which is wrong; therefore, his course is one eternal round. 21. And he doth not dwell in unholy temples; neither can filthiness or anything which is unclean be received into the kingdom of God; therefore I say unto you the time shall come, yea, and it shall be at the last day, that he who is filthy shall remain in his filthiness. (*Alma preaches to the people in Gideon, about 83 B.C.*) Alma 7:19-21

### Joseph Smith

But no man is possessor of all things except he be purified and cleansed from all sin. (*Revelation received for the elders of the Church, May 1831*) D&C 50:28

**Related Witnesses:**

#### Elder Joseph Fielding Smith

Cleanliness of life will bring the reward of exaltation and an eternal existence in the kingdom of God. If we choose the evil, the reward will be in punishment. Eventually every sin will have to be righted. Our Savior paid the price of our transgressions if we do not sin a sin worthy of eternal death and humbly keep his commandments; otherwise he has said, we must suffer even as did he. CR1964Apr:108

#### Recorded in Psalms

Who shall ascend into the hill of the LORD? or who shall stand in his holy place? 4. He that hath clean hands, and a pure heart; who hath not lifted up his soul unto vanity, nor sworn deceitfully. Ps.24:3-4

---

762. **The person who persists in sin cannot have joy, for wickedness never was happiness.**

#### Alma, the younger,
#### *quoted by Mormon*

Behold, I say unto you, wickedness never was happiness. (*Alma speaks to his son Corianton, concerning the resurrection of the dead, about 73 B.C.*) Alma 41:10

#### Delbert L. Stapley

We learn from this revelation [D&C 93:38] that in the beginning of mortal life all mankind is innocent before God and, therefore, is like the beginning river of water, pure and undefiled. As the polluted tributaries of water enter the main stream, our lives too become polluted when we allow tributaries of evil and wickedness to enter. It is these tributaries of evil we must be concerned about and fortify ourselves against. Wickedness never was happiness, but to the contrary, it is depressing; it destroys conscience and ultimately the spiritual life of the constant, erring individual. CR1971Oct:105

#### James E. Talmage

Happiness leaves no bad after-taste, it is followed by no depressing reaction; it calls for no repentance, brings no regret, entails no remorse; pleasure too often makes necessary repentance, contrition, and suffering; and, if indulged to the extreme, it brings degradation and destruction. ¶ True happiness is lived over and over again in memory, always with a renewal of the original good; a moment of unholy pleasure may leave a barbed sting, which, like a thorn in the flesh, is an ever-present source of anguish. ("A Greeting to the Missionaries," IE1913Dec:173) TLDP:318-19

---

## (2) Evil Speaking

763. **We are not to speak evil of another—to slander or malign others.**

#### James

Speak not evil one of another, brethren. He that speaketh evil of his brother, and judgeth his brother, speaketh evil of the law, and judgeth the law: but if thou judge the law, thou art not a doer of the law, but a judge. (*James writes to his brethren in the Church*) James 4:11

#### Stephen L. Richards

[T]here are many who are thoughtless, who speak lightly and carelessly and disrespectfully of leaders and principles and sacred phases of this Church. I think it is a shame to jest about sacred things and sometimes it is as blasphemous as taking the name of God in vain. I rebuke those who do it and I call upon them to stop and think. If they will but think, I believe they will realize the incalculable harm they do, the faith they destroy and the unhappiness they bring. ¶ .... Certain it is that a large part of the unhappiness of the world results from inconsiderate judgment. Many a pillow is wet with the sobs of those who are its victims. We cannot read the hearts of man [of men]. We may not know their good intentions. We often judge them by their failures, and we are unkind enough to circulate our judgment in the form of rumors and gossip and thus do irreparable damage. CR1938Oct:117

#### Paul

Let all bitterness, and wrath, and anger, and clamour, and evil speaking, be put away from you, with all malice: 32. And be ye kind one to another, tenderhearted, forgiving one another, even as God for Christ's sake hath forgiven you. (*Letter to the Saints at Ephesus in Asia Minor, about A.D. 62*) Eph.4:31-32

### Joseph Smith

We ask thee, Holy Father, to confound, and astonish, and to bring to shame and confusion, all those who have spread lying reports abroad, over the world, against thy servant or servants, if they will not repent, when the everlasting gospel shall be proclaimed in their ears; 30. And that all their works may be brought to naught, and be swept away by the hail, and by the judgments which thou wilt send upon them in thine anger, that there may be an end to lyings and slanders against thy people. (*Prayer given to Joseph Smith by revelation and offered at the dedication of the Kirtland Temple on March 27, 1836*) D&C 109:29-30

### Joseph Smith

Thy voice shall be a rebuke unto the transgressor; and at thy rebuke let the tongue of the slanderer cease its perverseness. (*Revelation for Thomas B. Marsh concerning the Twelve Apostles; received on the day on which the gospel was first preached in England, July 23, 1837*) D&C 112:9

### Recorded in Psalms

Whoso privily slandereth his neighbour, him will I cut off: him that hath an high look and a proud heart will not I suffer. Ps.101:5

### Recorded in Psalms

Keep thy tongue from evil, and thy lips from speaking guile. Ps.34:13

### Related Witnesses:

#### Joseph Smith,
##### quoted by Elder Joseph Fielding Smith

When all men speak evil of you falsely, blessed are ye. Shall a man be considered bad, when men speak evil of him? No. If a man stands and opposes the world of sin, he may expect to have all wicked and corrupt spirits arrayed against him. But it will be but a little season, and all these afflictions will be turned away from us, inasmuch as we are faithful, and are not overcome by these evils. By seeing the blessings of the endowment rolling on, and the kingdom increasing and spreading from sea to sea, we shall rejoice that we were not overcome by these foolish things. (*At Relief Society meeting, Nauvoo, Ill., minutes by Eliza R. Snow*) HC5:139-41; TPJS:259

### Recorded in Proverbs

He that hideth hatred with lying lips, and he that uttereth a slander, is a fool. 21. The lips of the righteous feed many: but fools die for want of wisdom. Prov.10:18,21

---

**764. We should not gossip about others.**

### Recorded in Leviticus

Thou shalt not go up and down as a talebearer among thy people: neither shalt thou stand against the blood of thy neighbour: I am the LORD. (*Revelation to Moses for the children of Israel*) Lev.19:16

### Elder Spencer W. Kimball

Of course, no one sees himself in this category. It is always the other person who gossips, invents tales, slanders, and is double-tongued. But are not we all guilty to some degree and do not all of us need introspection, self-analysis and then repentance? (The Miracle of Forgiveness, p. 52) TLDP:289-90

### Stephen L. Richards

Certain it is that a large part of the unhappiness in the world results from inconsiderate judgment. Many a pillow is wet with the sobs of those who are its victims. We cannot read the hearts of man. We may not know their good intentions. We often judge them by their failures, and are unkind enough to circulate our judgment in the form of rumors and gossip and thus do irreparable damage. CR1938Oct:117

### President David O. McKay

Many of us . . . nurse our ill will until it grows to hatred; then this hatred expresses itself in faultfinding and even slander, "whose whisper over the world's diameter as level as a cannon to its mouth, transports its poison shot." Backbiting, faultfinding are weeds of discord and thrive best in superficial minds, as fungus grows best on weakened plants. ¶ "Bear ye one another's burdens," but do not add to those burdens by gossiping about your neighbors or by spreading slander. (Pathways to Happiness, p. 211) TLDP:467

### Paul

And let these also first be proved; then let them use the office of a deacon, being found blameless. 11. Even so must their wives be grave, not slanderers, sober, faithful in all things. (*Paul writes to his assistant Timothy, about A.D. 64*) 1Tim.3:10-11

### Paul

Being filled with all unrighteousness . . . wickedness, covetousness, maliciousness; full of envy, . . . debate, deceit, malignity; whisperers, 30. Backbiters, haters of God, despiteful, proud, boasters, inventors of evil things, . . . 32. Who knowing the judgment of God, that they which commit such things are worthy of death, not only do the same, but have pleasure in them. (*Paul writes to the Church in Rome regarding the unrighteous, about A.D. 55*) Rom.1:29-30,32

### Related Witnesses:

#### Jesus,
##### recorded in Matthew

But I say unto you, That every idle word that

men shall speak, they shall give account thereof in the day of judgment. 37. For by thy words thou shalt be justified, and by thy words thou shalt be condemned. (*Jesus teaches the people*) Matt.12:36-37

**Author's Note:** *Gossiper:* A person who perpetuates rumors, or slanders, or is double-tongued, or invents tales, etc., etc.

---

### 765. We are not to use vulgar or filthy language.

#### Paul
Let no corrupt communication proceed out of your mouth, but that which is good to the use of edifying, that it may minister grace unto the hearers. (*Paul writes to the Saints at Ephesus in Asia Minor, about A.D. 62*) Eph.4:29

#### Elder Spencer W. Kimball
Included in this group of sinners are those mentioned by Paul: flatterers, double-tongued, slanderers, filthy communicators, those who are envious, spiteful, jealous, bitter, biters and devourers of each other, defilers, revilers, evil speakers, provokers, haters, inventors of evil things, stumbling blocks. ¶ Of course, no one sees himself in this category. . . . But are not we all guilty to some degree and do not all of us need introspection, self-analysis and then repentance? (The Miracle of Forgiveness, p. 52) TLDP:289-90

#### James
But the tongue can no man tame; it is an unruly evil, full of deadly poison. 9. Therewith bless we God, even the Father; and therewith curse we men, which are made after the similitude of God. 10. Out of the same mouth proceedeth blessing and cursing. My brethren, these things ought not so to be. 11. Doth a fountain send forth at the same place sweet water and bitter? 12. Can the fig tree, my brethren, bear olive berries? either a vine, figs? so can no fountain both yield salt water and fresh. 13. Who is a wise man and endued with knowledge among you? let him shew out of a good conversation his works with meekness of wisdom. (*James writes to his brethren in the Church*) James 3:8-13

#### Stephen L. Richards
I cannot pass this point without importuning some of my brethren to stop swearing. No man can love God and damn him any more than he can love his wife and damn her. Think again, please. Think of the utter futility of this vulgar habit. Think of its effect on youth. Men teach boys profanity. It is not congenital with the

race. It is the nature of man to love God and not to damn him. CR1938Oct:117

#### Elder Brigham Young, Heber C. Kimball Orson Pratt, William Smith, Lyman Wight, Elder Wilford Woodruff, Elder John Taylor, George A. Smith, and Willard Richards
When you arrive on our shores, and while sailing up our rivers, you need not be surprised if your ears are saluted by the false and filthy language of wicked and designing men who are ever ready to speak evil of the things they understand not, and who would gladly blast the character of the Prophet of the Most High God, and all connected with him, with their foul anathemas, beyond anything you ever thought of. We would not dishearten you, neither would we have you ignorant of the worst that awaits the righteous. ¶ If the Saints are not prepared to rejoice and be glad when they hear the name of the Prophet and their own name cast out as evil, as gluttonous, winebibber, friend of publicans and sinners, Beelzebub, thief, robber and murderer, they are not prepared for the gathering. The wheat and tares must grow together till the harvest; at the harvest the wheat is gathered together into the threshing floor, so with the Saints—the stakes are the threshing floor. Here they will be threshed with all sorts of difficulties, trials, afflictions and everything to mar their peace, which they can imagine, and thousands which they cannot imagine, but he that endures the threshing till all the chaff, superstition, folly and unbelief are pounded out of him, and does not suffer himself to be blown away as chaff by the foul blast of slander, but endures faithfully to the end, shall be saved. (*Epistle of the Twelve to the Saints in England and elsewhere, Nov. 15, 1841*) HC4:451-52

#### President Joseph Fielding Smith
When we join the Church and receive the priesthood, we are expected to forsake many of the ways of the world and live as becometh saints. We are no longer to dress or speak or act or even think as others too often do. Many in the world use tea, coffee, tobacco, and liquor, and are involved in the use of drugs. Many profane and are vulgar and indecent, immoral and unclean in their lives, but all these things should be foreign to us. We are the saints of the Most High. We hold the holy priesthood. CR1971Apr:47

#### Paul
But now ye also put off all these; anger, wrath, malice, blasphemy, filthy communication out of your mouth. 9. Lie not one to another, seeing that ye have put off the old man with his deeds;

10. And have put on the new man, which is renewed in knowledge after the image of him that created him: (*Letter from prison to the Church in Colossae, Asia Minor, about* A.D. *60*) Col.3:8-10

#### Joseph Smith

How vain and trifling have been our spirits, our conferences, our councils, our meetings, our private as well as public conversations—too low, too mean, too vulgar, too condescending for the dignified characters of the called and chosen of God. . . . (*Epistle to the Church from Liberty Jail, March 25, 1839*) HC3:295-96

**Related Witnesses:**

#### Jesus,
#### *quoted by Mormon*

Even so every good tree bringeth forth good fruit; but a corrupt tree bringeth forth evil fruit. 18. A good tree cannot bring forth evil fruit, neither a corrupt tree bring forth good fruit. (*The resurrected Jesus teaches the Nephites,* A.D. *34*) 3Ne.14:17-18

#### Joseph Smith,
#### *receiving the Word of the Lord*

Verily I say unto you, ye are clean, but not all; and there is none else with whom I am well pleased; 11. For all flesh is corrupted before me; and the powers of darkness prevail upon the earth, among the children of men, in the presence of all the hosts of heaven— (*Revelation of commandments to Saints in conference, Jan. 2, 1831*) D&C 38:10-11

---

766. **We shall not profane the name of God; we are to use the name of the Lord reverently.**

#### Dallin H. Oaks

This scripture [D&C 63:61-62] shows that we take the name of the Lord in vain when we use his name without authority. This obviously occurs when the sacred names of God the Father and his Son, Jesus Christ, are used in what is called profanity: in hateful cursings, in angry denunciations, or as marks of punctuation in common discourse. . . . ¶ Profanity is profoundly offensive to those who worship the God whose name is desecrated. We all remember how a prophet reacted from a hospital bed when an operating room attendant stumbled and cursed in his presence. Even half-conscious, Elder [Spencer W.] Kimball "recoiled and implored: 'Please! Please! That is my Lord whose names you revile.'" CR1986Apr:66,68

**Recorded in Leviticus**

Neither shall ye profane my holy name; but I will be hallowed among the children of Israel: I am the LORD which hallow you, (*Revelation to Moses for the children of Israel*) Lev.22:32

**Recorded in Leviticus**

[N]either shalt thou profane the name of thy God: I am the LORD. (*Revelation to Moses for the children of Israel*) Lev.18:21

#### President Joseph F. Smith

I say to the fathers and mothers of Israel, and to the boys who have been born in the Church of Jesus Christ of Latter-day Saints: I say it to men and boys throughout the world, as far as my words may go—I plead with you, I implore you not to offend the Lord, nor to offend honorable men and women, by the use of profanity. ("A Sermon on Purity," IE1903May:504) TLDP:89

#### Ezekiel

And I will sanctify my great name, which was profaned among the heathen, which ye have profaned in the midst of them; and the heathen shall know that I am the LORD, saith the Lord GOD, when I shall be sanctified in you before their eyes. (*The word of the Lord to Israel, through the prophet Ezekiel*) Ezek.36:23

#### Stephen L. Richards

I cannot pass this point without importuning some of my brethren to stop swearing. No man can love God and damn him any more than he can love his wife and damn her. Think again, please. Think of the utter futility of this vulgar habit. Think of its effect on youth. Men teach boys profanity. It is not congenital with the race. It is the nature of man to love God and not to damn him. CR1938Oct:117

**Recorded in Exodus**

Thou shalt not take the name of the LORD thy God in vain; for the LORD will not hold him guiltless that taketh his name in vain. (*The Lord reveals the third of the Ten Commandments to Moses*) Ex.20:7

#### Abinadi,
#### *quoted by Mormon*

Thou shalt not take the name of the Lord thy God in vain; for the Lord will not hold him guiltless that taketh his name in vain. (*Abinadi teaches the Ten Commandments to the people of the wicked King Noah, about 148* B.C.) Mosiah 13:15

#### Joseph Smith,
#### *receiving the Word of the Lord*

Wherefore, let all men beware how they take my name in their lips— 62. For behold, verily I say, that many there be who are under this condemnation, who use the name of the Lord, and use it in vain, having not authority. (*Revelation, Aug. 1831*) D&C 63:61-62

### President Brigham Young

Keep yourselves from evil to take the name of the Lord in vain, for I am the Lord your God, even the God of your fathers, the God of Abraham and of Isaac and of Jacob. (*Revelation received at Winter Quarters, Jan. 14, 1847*) D&C 136:21

**Related Witnesses:**

### Joseph Smith

Remember that that which cometh from above is sacred, and must be spoken with care, and by constraint of the Spirit; and in this there is no condemnation, and ye receive the Spirit through prayer; wherefore, without this there remaineth condemnation. (*Revelation received at Kirtland, Ohio, Aug. 1831*) D&C 63:64

### Jesus,
### *quoted by Joseph Smith,*
### *translating Matthew*

And the mysteries of the kingdom ye shall keep within yourselves; for it is not meet to give that which is holy unto the dogs; neither cast ye your pearls unto swine, lest they trample them under their feet. 11. For the world cannot receive that which ye, yourselves, are not able to bear; wherefore ye shall not give your pearls unto them, lest they turn again and rend you. (*Jesus concludes the Sermon on the Mount*) JST Matt.7:10-11

### Joseph Smith

For it is not meet that the things which belong to the children of the kingdom should be given to them that are not worthy, or to dogs, or the pearls to be cast before swine. (*Revelation, Feb. 4, 1831*) D&C 41:6

### Recorded in Leviticus

Speak unto Aaron and to his sons, that they separate themselves from the holy things of the children of Israel, and that they profane not my holy name in those things which they hallow unto me: I am the LORD. (*Revelation to Moses for the children of Israel*) Lev.22:2

**Author's Note:** *Profane*: "Irreverent toward God or holy things; speaking or spoken, acting or acted in contempt of sacred things or implying it; blasphemous; polluted; [desecrated]." (The New Webster Encyclopedic Dictionary of the English Language, p. 663)

---

**767. We are not to bear false witness or accuse others falsely.**

### Recorded in Exodus

Thou shalt not bear false witness against thy neighbour. (*The Lord reveals the ninth of the Ten Commandments to Moses*) Ex.20:16

### Recorded in Exodus

Thou shalt not raise a false report: put not thine hand with the wicked to be an unrighteous witness. (*The Lord reveals his laws for ancient Israel pertaining to integrity and godly conduct*) Ex.23:1

### Elder Spencer W. Kimball

The sin of false witness is committed in many ways. Guilty ones are gossipers and bearers of tales, whisperers, those destitute of truth, liars, quarrelers, deceitful persons. Sometimes these weaknesses are thought of as minor, yet they break hearts, destroy reputations and wreck lives. . . . ¶ Included in this group of sinners are those mentioned by Paul: flatterers, double-tongued, slanderers, filthy communicators, those who are envious, spiteful, jealous, bitter, biters and devourers of each other, defilers, revilers, evil speakers, provokers, haters, inventors of evil things, stumbling blocks. ¶ Of course, no one sees himself in this category. It is always the other person who gossips, invents tales, slanders, and is double-tongued. But are not we all guilty to some degree and do not all of us need introspection, self-analysis and then repentance? (The Miracle of Forgiveness, p. 52) TLDP:289-90

### Joseph Smith,
### *receiving the Word of the Lord*

And those who swear falsely against my servants, that they might bring them into bondage and death— 19. Wo unto them; because they have offended my little ones they shall be severed from the ordinances of mine house. (*Revelation received while in Liberty Jail, March 20, 1839*) D&C 121:18-19

### Elder Brigham Young, Heber C. Kimball
### Orson Pratt, William Smith, Lyman Wight,
### Elder Wilford Woodruff,
### Elder John Taylor, George A. Smith,
### and Willard Richards

When you arrive on our shores, and while sailing up our rivers, you need not be surprised if your ears are saluted by the false and filthy language of wicked and designing men who are ever ready to speak evil of the things they understand not, and who would gladly blast the character of the Prophet of the Most High God, and all connected with him, with their foul anathemas, beyond anything you ever thought of. (*Epistle of the Twelve to the Saints in abroad, Nov. 15, 1841*) HC4:451

### George F. Richards

Why did the Lord give the commandment? ¶ "Thou shalt not bear false witness against thy neighbor." (Ex.20:16) ¶ He gave it because of the subtle methods of the adversary in his effort to divide and tear asunder the love and the unity of the Lord's people! To bear false witness may not appear to be a very serious offense, but its results are far-reaching and cruel, hence, the use made of it by the instigator of evil. The Lord warns us against this evil practice. Bearing false witness, talebearing, slander, gossip, scandal, fault-finding, backbiting, and evil speaking are in the same category of evil practice and are some of the means employed by Satan to disunite us as a people and destroy brotherly love, kindness, and helpfulness toward one another. ¶ . . . . By the spirit of Satan one bears false witness and broadcasts the weakness of his neighbor. He becomes a talebearer, a character assassin. He robs his neighbor of that which greatly impoverishes his neighbor without enriching himself. He makes others miserable and unhappy and has within himself the kingdom of Satan. ¶ . . . . We should be doubly careful not to do any injury we cannot repair. When we bear false witness, we injure at least four: ourselves, him about whom we speak, him to whom we speak, and the Lord. CR1947Apr:24-25

### Jesus,
*recorded in Matthew*

He saith unto him, Which? Jesus said, Thou shalt do no murder, Thou shalt not commit adultery, Thou shalt not steal, Thou shalt not bear false witness, (*Jesus instructs the young man who had great possessions*) Matt.19:18

### Paul

For this, Thou shalt not commit adultery, Thou shalt not kill, Thou shalt not steal, Thou shalt not bear false witness, Thou shalt not covet; and if there be any other commandment, it is briefly comprehended in this saying, namely, Thou shalt love thy neighbour as thyself. (*Letter to the Church in Rome, about A.D. 55*) Rom.13:9

---

## (3) Murder

768. We are not to commit murder.

### Jacob, brother of Nephi,
*quoted by Nephi*

Wo unto the murderer who deliberately killeth, for he shall die. (*Jacob to the people of Nephi, 559-545 B.C.*) 2Ne.9:35

### Recorded in Exodus

Thou shalt not kill. (*The Lord reveals the sixth of the Ten Commandments to Moses*) Ex.20:13

### Russell M. Nelson,
*also quoting Alma, the younger,*
*quoted by Mormon*

Of those who shed innocent blood, a prophet declared: "The judgments which [God] shall

exercise . . . in his wrath [shall] be just and the blood of the innocent shall stand as a witness against them, yea, and cry mightily against them at the last day." (Alma 14:11) CR1985Apr:15-16

### Alma, the younger,
*quoted by Mormon*

For behold, if ye deny the Holy Ghost when it once has had place in you, and ye know that ye deny it, behold, this is a sin which is unpardonable; yea, and whosoever murdereth against the light and knowledge of God, it is not easy for him to obtain forgiveness; yea, I say unto you, my son, that it is not easy for him to obtain a forgiveness. (*Alma to his son Corianton, about 73 B.C.*) Alma 39:6

### Joseph Smith,
*receiving the Word of the Lord*

And now, behold, I speak unto the church. Thou shalt not kill; and he that kills shall not have forgiveness in this world, nor in the world to come. 19. And again, I say, thou shalt not kill; but he that killeth shall die. (*Revelation "embracing the law of the Church," Feb. 9, 1831*) D&C 42:18-19

### President Spencer W. Kimball

The leaders of the Church continually cry out against that which is intolerable in the sight of the Lord; against pollution of mind and body and our surroundings; against vulgarity, stealing, lying, cheating, false pride, blasphemy, and drunkenness; against fornication, adultery, homosexuality, abortion, and all other abuses of the sacred power to create; against murder and all that is like unto it; against all manner of degradation and sin. CR1982Oct:4

### Jesus,
*recorded in Matthew*

And, behold, one came and said unto him, Good Master, what good thing shall I do, that I may have eternal life? 17. And he said unto him, Why callest thou me good? there is none good but one, that is, God: but if thou wilt enter into life, keep the commandments. 18. He saith unto him, Which? Jesus said, Thou shalt do no murder, Thou shalt not commit adultery, Thou shalt not steal, Thou shalt not bear false witness, (*Jesus instructs the young man who had great possessions*) Matt.19:16-18

### Dallin H. Oaks

The Savior's Golden Rule says we are [our brother's keeper]. Satan says we are not. ¶ . . . . The sin may be murder, robbery, or theft. It may be fraud or deception. . . . Always the excuse is the same: "Am I my brother's keeper?" CR1986Oct:25

### Nephi, son of Lehi

And again, the Lord God hath commanded that

men should not murder; that they should not lie; that they should not steal; that they should not take the name of the Lord their God in vain; that they should not envy; that they should not have malice; that they should not contend one with another; that they should not commit whoredoms; and that they should do none of these things; for whoso doeth them shall perish. (*Nephi gives commandments of God to the Nephites, 559-545 B.C.*) 2Ne.26:32

**Related Witnesses:**

### Amulek,
### quoted by Mormon

And when Amulek saw the pains of the women and children who were consuming in the fire, he also was pained; and he said unto Alma: How can we witness this awful scene? Therefore let us stretch forth our hands, and exercise the power of God which is in us, and save them from the flames. 11. But Alma said unto him: The Spirit constraineth me that I must not stretch forth mine hand; for behold the Lord receiveth them up unto himself, in glory; and he doth suffer that they may do this thing, or that the people may do this thing unto them, according to the hardness of their hearts, that the judgments which he shall exercise upon them in his wrath may be just; and the blood of the innocent shall stand as a witness against them, yea, and cry mightily against them at the last day. (*Believers in the word of God are burned, about 82 B.C.*) Alma 14:10-11

### Elder Spencer W. Kimball

The laws of both of the land and of God recognize a great difference between murder and wilful slaughter and manslaughter which is not premeditated. Likewise men unfortunately must take others' lives in war. Some of our conscientious young men have been disturbed and concerned as they have been compelled to kill. There are mitigating circumstances but certainly the blame and responsibility rest heavily upon the heads of those who brought about the war, making necessary the taking of life. It is conceivable that even in war there may be many times when there is legitimate choice and enemy combatants could be taken prisoner rather than be killed. (The Miracle of Forgiveness, p. 129) TLDP:714

### Elder Harold B. Lee

There are many who are troubled and their souls harrowed by the haunting question of the position of the soldier who in combat kills the enemy. Again, the First Presidency has commented: ¶ "When, therefore, constitutional law, obedient to those principles, calls the Manhood of the Church into the armed service of any

country to which they owe allegiance, their highest civic duty requires that they meet that call. If, hearkening to that call and obeying those in command over them, they shall take the lives of those who fight against them, that will not make of them murderers, nor subject them to the penalty that God has prescribed for those who kill, beyond the principles to be mentioned shortly; for it would be a cruel God that would punish his children as moral sinners for acts done by them as the innocent instrumentalities of a sovereign whom he has told them to obey and whose will they were powerless to resist." (Ye Are the Light of the World, pp. 252-53) TLDP:713-14

### Joseph Smith

Abraham was commanded to offer his son Isaac; nevertheless, it was written: Thou shalt not kill. Abraham, however, did not refuse, and it was accounted unto him for righteousness. (*Revelation recorded July 12, 1843*) D&C 132:36

### Russell M. Nelson

The Church of Jesus Christ of Latter-day Saints has consistently opposed the practice of abortion. . . . ¶ Now is there hope for those who have so sinned without full understanding, who now suffer heartbreak? Yes. So far as is known, the Lord does not regard this transgression as murder. And "as far as has been revealed, a person may repent and be forgiven for the sin of abortion." CR1985Apr:16

### Recorded in Deuteronomy

And this is the case of the slayer, which shall flee thither, that he may live: Whoso killeth his neighbour ignorantly, whom he hated not in time past; 5. As when a man goeth into the wood with his neighbour to hew wood, and his hand fetcheth a stroke with the axe to cut down the tree, and the head slippeth from the helve, and lighteth upon his neighbour, that he die; he shall flee unto one of those cities, and live: (*Commandments to Israel through Moses*) Deut.19:4-5

---

### 769. We are not to commit suicide.

### George Q. Cannon

[Suicide] seems to be one of the results of Satan's increased influence over the children of men. Having no tabernacle himself, he would like to prompt every child of God to destroy his body. When a human being becomes possessed of the devil, the tabernacle is soon wrecked; for neither he nor his companion spirits know to what use to put a fleshly tabernacle except to destroy it. ¶ Man did not create himself. He did not furnish his spirit with a human dwelling place. It is God who created man, both body and spirit. Man has no right, therefore, to destroy that which he had no agency in creating. They who do so are guilty of murder, self-murder it is true; but they are no more justified in killing themselves than they are in killing others. What difference of punishment there is for the two crimes, I do not know; but it is clear that no one can destroy so precious a gift as that of life without incurring a severe penalty. ("Topics of the Times," Juvenile Instructor, Sept. 1886, pp. 274-75) TLDP:126

**Elder Spencer W. Kimball**

It is not sufficient that we do not kill or commit murder, but we should protect others from such crimes. Not only is suicide a crime, but one is obligated to protect and save and prolong his own life. Not only shall we not take life, but it is obligatory upon us to give life, both by bearing children into mortality and by leading people toward eternal life by teaching, proselyting and influencing them strongly toward that end. (The Miracle of Forgiveness, pp. 98-99) TLDP:126

**President John Taylor and George Q. Cannon**

(First Presidency)

There is another evil that is growing amongst the peoples of the world that is not unfelt amidst the Latter-day Saints. It is the crime of self-murder. Suicide should be made odious among the people of God, it should be emphasized as a deadly sin, and no undue feelings of tenderness toward the unfortunate dead, or of sympathy towards the living bereaved, should prevent us denouncing it as a crime against God and humanity, against the Creator and the creature. It is true that the exact enormity of the act is not defined with minute detail in the Holy Scriptures, or the limits of its punishment given; but to believers in the God whom we worship it has always been regarded as a sin of great magnitude; and in many countries especial pains have been taken to discourage it, by refusal to bury in consecrated ground, by indignities offered to the lifeless remains, or by such lack of funereal observances as would produce a peculiar and horrifying effect upon the survivors. Now, while not advocating measures of this description, we do not think that the same laudations and panegyrics should be pronounced over the self-murderer as are so freely uttered over the faithful Saint who has gone to his eternal rest. There is a difference in their death, and that difference should be impressed upon the living, unless the deceased, at the time

of the rash act, was in such a mental condition as not to be wholly responsible for his actions; but again, if this condition be the result of sin, of departure from God's laws, then the unfortunate one, like the inebriate, is not altogether free from the responsibility of acts committed while in this state of mental derangement; if he is not censurable for the act itself, he is for the causes that induced it. In such cases the mantle of charity must not be stretched so widely, in our desire to protect our erring friends, as to reflect dishonor on the work of God, or contempt for the principles of the everlasting Gospel. There is an unfortunate tendency in the natures of many to palliate sins by which they are not personally injured, but we must not forget that such palliation frequently increases the original wrong, and brings discredit on the Church and dishonor to the name and work of our blessed Redeemer; in other words, to save the feelings of our friends we are willing to crucify afresh the Lord of life and glory. *(Epistle read at general conference, Coalville, Utah, Oct. 1886)* MOFP3:88-89

**Author's Note:** M. Russell Ballard wrote a helpful article on suicide, saying, in part: " 'Persons subject to great stress may lose control of themselves and become mentally clouded to the point that they are no longer accountable for their acts' (Bruce R. McConkie, Mormon Doctrine, p. 771). ¶ When [the Lord] does judge us, I feel he will take all things into consideration: our genetic and chemical make-up, our mental state, . . . our health, and so forth." (EN1987Oct:7-8)

## 770. The useless killing of animals is displeasing to the Lord.

**Joseph Smith**

And wo be unto man that sheddeth blood or that wasteth flesh and hath no need. *(Revelation, March 1831)* D&C 49:21

**Hyrum Mack Smith**

But although God has ordained animals for the use of man, He has not sanctioned the order of things under which some have an abundance of food and clothing, while others are destitute; for that very reason "the world lieth in sin" [D&C 49:20]. Nor must man waste animal life. To kill, when not necessary, is a sin akin to murder. "A righteous man regardeth the life of his beast" (Prov.12:10). Man has been entrusted with sovereignty over the animal kingdom (Gen.1:21), that he may learn to govern, as God rules, by the power of love and justice, and become fit for his eternal destiny as a ruler of worlds. A tyrant who has learned nothing but selfishness and cruelty can hope for no position of trust hereafter in the kingdom of the Father. (Doctrine and Covenants Commentary, Hyrum M. Smith and Janne M. Sjodahl, p. 286) TLDP:28

### President Joseph F. Smith

I do not believe any man should kill animals or birds unless he needs them for food, and then he should not kill innocent little birds that are not intended for food for man. I think it is wicked for men to thirst in their souls to kill almost everything which possesses animal life. It is wrong, and I have been surprised at prominent men whom I have seen whose very souls seemed to be athirst for the shedding of animal blood. (Gospel Doctrine, p. 266) TLDP:28

### President Spencer W. Kimball

Now, I also would like to add some of my feelings concerning the unnecessary shedding of blood and destruction of life. . . . ¶ And not less with reference to the killing of innocent birds is the wildlife of our country that live upon the vermin that are indeed enemies to the farmer and to mankind. It is not only wicked to destroy them, it is a shame, in my opinion. I think that this principle should extend not only to the bird life but to the life of all animals. . . . The Lord gave us all the animals. Seemingly, he thought it was important that all these animals be on the earth for our use and encouragement. CR1978Oct:64

### Elder Ezra Taft Benson,
*also quoting Joseph Smith*

In this revelation the Lord counsels us to use meat sparingly [see D&C 89]. I have often felt that the Lord is further counseling us in this revelation against indiscriminately killing animals, for He has said elsewhere in scripture, "Wo be unto man that sheddeth blood or that wasteth flesh and hath no need." [D&C 49:21] CR1983Apr:71

---

## (4) Pride

### 771. We are not to be proud.

### President Ezra Taft Benson,
*also quoting Alma, the younger*

In the scriptures there is no such thing as righteous pride. It is always considered as a sin. We are not speaking of a wholesome view of self-worth which is established by a close relationship with God. But we are speaking of pride as

the universal sin, as someone has described it. . . . ¶ Essentially, pride is a "my will" rather than "thy will" approach to life. The opposite of pride is humbleness, meekness, submissiveness (see Alma 13:28), or teachableness. . . . ¶ Pride does not look up to God and care about what is right. It looks sideways to man and argues who is right. . . . ¶ [Pride] is self-will as opposed to God's will. It is the fear of man over the fear of God. ¶ Humility responds to God's will—to fear of His judgments and the needs of those around us. To the proud, the applause of the world rings in their ears; to the humble, the applause of heaven warms their hearts. CR1986Apr:5-6; MPSG1989:18 (in part)

### Joseph Smith

And again, thou shalt not be proud in thy heart; let all thy garments be plain, and their beauty the beauty of the work of thine own hands; (*Revelation "embracing the law of the Church," Feb. 9, 1831*) D&C 42:40

### Joseph Smith,
*receiving the Word of the Lord*

[T]he riches of the earth are mine to give; but beware of pride, lest ye become as the Nephites of old. (*Revelation of commandments to Saints in conference, Jan. 2, 1831*) D&C 38:39

### Joseph Smith

But beware of pride, lest thou shouldst enter into temptation. (*Revelation given in response to the earnest desire of Joseph Knight, Sr. and four other brethren to know of their respective duties, April 1930*) D&C 23:1

### Joseph Smith

We would say, beware of pride also; for well and truly hath the wise man said, that pride goeth before destruction, and a haughty spirit before a fall. And again, outward appearance is not always a criterion by which to judge our fellow man; but the lips betray the haughty and overbearing imaginations of the heart; by his words and his deeds let him be judged. (*Epistle to the Church from Liberty Jail, March 25, 1839*) HC3:295

### Peter

Likewise, ye younger, submit yourselves unto the elder. Yea, all of you be subject one to another, and be clothed with humility: for God resisteth the proud, and giveth grace to the humble. 6. Humble yourselves therefore under the mighty hand of God, that he may exalt you in due time: (*Letter to the churches in modern Asia Minor, about A.D. 60*) 1Pet.5:5-6

### Jesus,
*recorded in Luke*

For whosoever exalteth himself shall be abased; and he that humbleth himself shall be exalted.

*(Jesus teaches humility and gives the parable of the great supper)* Luke 14:11

### Jeremiah

Hear ye, and give ear; be not proud: for the LORD hath spoken. *(Revelation to Jeremiah, about 628 B.C.)* Jer.13:15

**Related Witnesses:**

### Paul

Charge them that are rich in this world, that they be not highminded, nor trust in uncertain riches, but in the living God, who giveth us richly all things to enjoy; *(Paul's letter to his assistant Timothy, about A.D. 64)* 1Tim.6:17

### Joseph Smith,
*receiving the Word of the Lord*

And also he hath need to repent, for I, the Lord, am not well pleased with him, for he seeketh to excel, and he is not sufficiently meek before me. *(Revelation referring to Wm. W. Phelps, Aug. 1, 1831)* D&C 58:41

### Nephi, son of Lehi

[T]hey sell themselves for naught; for, for the reward of their pride and their foolishness they shall reap destruction. . . . *(The writings of Nephi, 559-545 B.C.)* 2Ne.26:10

---

**772. We are not to be concerned about status or position.**

### Mormon

But it came to pass in the twenty and ninth year there began to be some disputings among the people; and some were lifted up unto pride and boastings because of their exceedingly great riches, yea, even unto great persecutions; 11. For there were many merchants in the land, and also many lawyers, and many officers. 12. And the people began to be distinguished by ranks, according to their riches and their chances for learning, yea, some were ignorant because of their poverty, and others did receive great learning because of their riches. 13. Some were lifted up in pride, and others were exceedingly humble; some did return railing for railing, while others would receive railing and persecution and all manner of afflictions, and would not turn and revile again, but were humble and penitent before God. *(Much iniquity abounds among the Nephites, A.D. 29-30)* 3Ne.6:10-13

**Related Witnesses:**

### John

Nevertheless among the chief rulers also many believed on him; but because of the Pharisees they did not confess him, lest they should be put out of the synagogue: 43. For they loved the praise of men more than the praise of God.

*(Although Jesus had done many miracles before the people, yet they feared man more than God.)* John 12:42-43

### Mormon

For behold, the Lord had blessed them so long with the riches of the world that they had not been stirred up to anger, to wars, nor to bloodshed; therefore they began to set their hearts upon their riches; yea, they began to seek to get gain that they might be lifted up one above another; therefore they began to commit secret murders, and to rob and to plunder, that they might get gain. *(The Lamanites and the Nephites prosper and become exceedingly rich, 29 B.C.)* Hel.6:17

### Joseph Smith,
*receiving the Word of the Lord*

And also he hath need to repent, for I, the Lord, am not well pleased with him, for he seeketh to excel, and he is not sufficiently meek before me. *(Revelation referring to Wm. W. Phelps, Aug. 1, 1831)* D&C 58:41

### Joseph Smith,
*receiving the Word of the Lord*

And behold, how oft you have transgressed the commandments and the laws of God, and have gone on in the persuasions of men. 7. For, behold, you should not have feared man more than God. Although men set at naught the counsels of God, and despise his words— . . . *(The Lord reproves Martin Harris and Joseph Smith regarding the lost manuscript pages, July 1828)* D&C 3:6-7

### Joseph Smith,
*receiving the Word of the Lord*

Behold, I say unto you, David, that you have feared man and have not relied on me for strength as you ought. 2. But your mind has been on the things of the earth more than on the things of me, your Maker, and the ministry whereunto you have been called; and you have not given heed unto my Spirit, and to those who were set over you, but have been persuaded by those whom I have not commanded. *(Revelation, Sept. 30, 1830; David Whitmer is chastened for failure to serve diligently)* D&C 30:1-2

### Mormon

And there was a strict command throughout all the churches that there should be no persecutions among them, that there should be an equality among all men; 4. That they should let no pride nor haughtiness disturb their peace; that every man should esteem his neighbor as himself, laboring with their own hands for their support. *(Mosiah forbids persecution, 100-92 B.C.)* Mosiah 27:3-4

773. We are not to boast in our own wisdom, power, or possessions (rather, we should give honor to God).

### Alma, the younger,
*quoted by Mormon*

See that ye are not lifted up unto pride; yea, see that ye do not boast in your own wisdom, nor of your much strength. 12. Use boldness, but not overbearance; and also see that ye bridle all your passions, that ye may be filled with love; see that ye refrain from idleness. (*Alma to his son Shiblon, about 73 B.C.*) Alma 38:11-12

### President Ezra Taft Benson,
*also quoting Paul*

Most of us think of pride as self-centeredness, conceit, boastfulness, arrogance, or haughtiness. All of these are elements of the sin, but the heart, or core, is still missing. ¶ The central feature of pride is enmity—enmity toward God and enmity toward our fellowmen. Enmity means "hatred toward, hostility to, or a state of opposition." It is the power by which Satan wishes to reign over us. ¶ Pride is essentially competitive in nature. We pit our will against God's. When we direct our pride toward God, it is in the spirit of "my will and not thine be done." As Paul said, they "seek their own, not the things which are Jesus Christ's."(Philip.2:-21) ¶ Our will in competition to God's will allows desires, appetites, and passions to go unbridled. (See Alma 38:12; 3Ne.12:30.) ¶ The proud cannot accept the authority of God giving direction to their lives. (See Hel.12:6.) They pit their perceptions of truth against God's great knowledge, their abilities versus God's priesthood power, their accomplishments against His mighty works. ¶ . . . . The proud wish God would agree with them. They aren't interested in changing their opinions to agree with God's. CR1989Apr:3-4

### Mormon

Yea, how quick to be lifted up in pride; yea, how quick to boast, and do all manner of that which is iniquity; and how slow are they to remember the Lord their God, and to give ear unto his counsels, yea, how slow to walk in wisdom's paths! 6. Behold, they do not desire that the Lord their God, who hath created them, should rule and reign over them; notwithstanding his great goodness and his mercy towards them, they do set at naught his counsels, and they will not that he should be their guide. (*Mormon abridges the record of Helaman and observes how the Lord chastens his people, about 7 B.C.*) Hel.12:5-6

### Ammon, son of Mosiah,
*quoted by Mormon*

And it came to pass that when Ammon had said these words, his brother Aaron rebuked him, saying: Ammon, I fear that thy joy doth carry thee away unto boasting. 11. But Ammon said unto him: I do not boast in my own strength, nor in my own wisdom; but behold, my joy is full, yea, my heart is brim with joy, and I will rejoice in my God. 12. Yea, I know that I am nothing; as to my strength I am weak; therefore I will not boast of myself, but I will boast of my God, for in his strength I can do all things; yea, behold, many mighty miracles we have wrought in this land, for which we will praise his name forever. (*Ammon glories in the Lord because of the conversion of many Lamanites, 90-77 B.C.*) Alma 26:10-12

### Joseph Smith,
*receiving the Word of the Lord*

For although a man may have many revelations, and have power to do many mighty works, yet if he boasts in his own strength, and sets at naught the counsels of God, and follows after the dictates of his own will and carnal desires, he must fall and incur the vengeance of a just God upon him. (*The Lord reproves Martin Harris and Joseph Smith regarding the lost manuscript pages, July 1828*) D&C 3:4

### Paul

For by grace are ye saved through faith; and that not of yourselves: it is the gift of God: 9. Not of works, lest any man should boast. 10. For we are his workmanship, created in Christ Jesus unto good works, which God hath before ordained that we should walk in them. (*Letter to the Saints at Ephesus in Asia Minor, about A.D. 62*) Eph.2:8-10

### James

But now ye rejoice in your boastings: all such rejoicing is evil. (*Letter to his brethren in the Church*) James 4:16

### Related Witnesses:
### Mormon

And because of this their great wickedness, and their boastings in their own strength, they were left in their own strength; therefore they did not prosper, but were afflicted and smitten, and driven before the Lamanites, until they had lost possession of almost all their lands. (*Nephite dissenters and Lamanites join forces, there is great slaughter of the Nephites who had become wicked, including some who professed to belong to the Church, about 35-31 B.C.*) Hel.4:13

### President Ezra Taft Benson

In the pre-earthly council, Lucifer placed his

proposal in competition with the Father's plan as advocated by Jesus Christ. He wished to be honored above all others. In short, his prideful desire was to dethrone God. CR1989Apr:4

### Joseph Smith,
### *translating the Book of Moses*

And I, the Lord God, spake unto Moses, saying: That Satan, whom thou hast commanded in the name of mine Only Begotten, is the same which was from the beginning, and he came before me, saying—Behold, here am I, send me, I will be thy son, and I will redeem all mankind, that one soul shall not be lost, and surely I will do it; wherefore give me thine honor. 2. But, behold, my Beloved Son, which was my Beloved and Chosen from the beginning, said unto me—Father, thy will be done, and the glory be thine forever. 3. Wherefore, because that Satan rebelled against me, and sought to destroy the agency of man, which I, the Lord God, had given him, and also, that I should give unto him mine own power; by the power of mine Only Begotten, I caused that he should be cast down; (*The record of Moses: The Lord describes Satan's rebellion in the premortal world*) Moses 4:1-3

### Ammon, son of Mosiah,
### *quoted by Mormon*

Now have we not reason to rejoice? Yea, I say unto you, there never were men that had so great reason to rejoice as we, since the world began; yea, and my joy is carried away, even unto boasting in my God; for he has all power, all wisdom, and all understanding; he comprehendeth all things, and he is a merciful Being, even unto salvation, to those who will repent and believe on his name. 36. Now if this is boasting, even so will I boast; for this is my life and my light, my joy and my salvation, and my redemption from everlasting wo. Yea, blessed is the name of my God, who has been mindful of this people, who are a branch of the tree of Israel, and has been lost from its body in a strange land; yea, I say, blessed be the name of my God, who has been mindful of us, wanderers in a strange land. (*Ammon extols the mercy of God who has not forgotten this branch of the tree of Israel, 90-77 B.C.*) Alma 26:35-36

### Paul

Where is boasting then? It is excluded. By what law? of works? Nay: but by the law of faith. (*Letter to the Church in Rome, about A.D. 55*) Rom.3:27

**Author's Note:** "*Boast*": To speak or possess with pride. (Funk & Wagnalls Standard College Dictionary, p. 153)

## 774. Pride leads to contention.

### President Ezra Taft Benson

Another face of pride is contention. Arguments, fights, unrighteous dominion, generation gaps, divorces, spouse abuse, riots, and disturbances all fall into this category of pride. ¶ Contention in our families drives the Spirit of the Lord away. It also drives many of our family members away. Contention ranges from a hostile spoken word to worldwide conflicts. . . . CR1989Apr:5

### Recorded in Proverbs

Only by pride cometh contention. . . . Prov.13:10

### Recorded in Proverbs

He that is of a proud heart stirreth up strife. . . . Prov.28:25

### President David O. McKay

Centered in the heart also are the enemies to peace—"avarice, ambition, envy, anger, and pride." These and other vices which bring misery into the world must be eradicated before men will "beat their swords into ploughshares and their spears into pruning hooks." Before permanent peace is assured there shall have to be felt in the hearts of men more consideration for others— there shall have to be manifested around the coming peace table at least a little of the Christ spirit—"Do unto others as you would have others do unto you." ("Faith in Christ—The World's Greatest Need," IE1944Jan:62) TLDP:463-64

**Related Witnesses:**

### Mormon

Nevertheless, there were many among them who began to be proud, and began to contend warmly with their adversaries, even unto blows; yea, they would smite one another with their fists. (*There began to be contention by some Church members, notwithstanding there was a strict law in the Church against persecution among themselves and with those who did not belong to the Church, about A.D. 90*) Alma 1:22

### Mormon

For they saw and beheld with great sorrow that the people of the church began to be lifted up in the pride of their eyes, and to set their hearts upon riches and upon the vain things of the world, that they began to be scornful, one towards another, and they began to persecute those that did not believe according to their own will and pleasure. (*Iniquity enters the Church in Zarahemla, 84 B.C.*) Alma 4:8

### President Joseph F. Smith

Just as soon as a man or woman learns his and her duty to God and to those who are members with them in the household of faith, peace is established, love and good will are assured, no back-biting, no fault-finding, no bearing false witness against neighbors, no strife, no contention. For the moment that a Latter-day Saint learns his duty, he will learn that it is his business to make peace, to establish good will, to work righteousness, to be filled with the spirit of kindness, love, charity, and forgiveness; and, so far as he is concerned, there can be no war, no strife, no contention, no quarreling, no disunion; no factions can arise among the people who know their duty as Latter-day Saints. CR1915Apr:4

### Mormon

And now it came to pass in the forty and third year of the reign of the judges, there was no contention among the people of Nephi save it were a little pride which was in the church, which did cause some little dissensions among the people, which affairs were settled in the ending of the forty and third year. 2. And there was no contention among the people in the forty and fourth year; neither was there much contention in the forty and fifth year. (*Mormon records the history of the Nephites from the record of Helaman son of Alma, the younger, about 49-46 B.C.*) Hel.3:1-2

---

### 775. The proud will not inherit eternal life.

#### Alma, the younger,
*quoted by Mormon*

Behold, are ye stripped of pride? I say unto you, if ye are not ye are not prepared to meet God. Behold ye must prepare quickly; for the kingdom of heaven is soon at hand, and such an one hath not eternal life. (*Alma teaches the people, about 83 B.C.*) Alma 5:28

#### Jacob, brother of Nephi

O that ye would listen unto the word of his commands, and let not this pride of your hearts destroy your souls! (*Jacob denounces the love of riches among the Nephites, 544-421 B.C.*) Jacob 2:16

#### Malachi

For, behold, the day cometh, that shall burn as an oven; and all the proud, yea, and all that do wickedly, shall be stubble: and the day that cometh shall burn them up, saith the LORD of hosts, that it shall leave them neither root nor branch. (*The prophet Malachi to the people, about 430 B.C.*) Mal.4:1

#### Related Witnesses:

##### Joseph Smith,
*receiving the Word of the Lord*

Be not ashamed, neither confounded; but be admonished in all your high-mindedness and pride, for it bringeth a snare upon your souls. (*Revelation, March 8, 1833, wherein various individuals are counseled by the Lord to walk uprightly*) D&C 90:17

### Recorded in Psalms

[H]im that hath an high look and a proud heart will not I suffer. Ps.101:5

### Recorded in Proverbs

These six things doth the LORD hate: yea, seven are an abomination unto him: 17. A proud look, a lying tongue, and hands that shed innocent blood, 18. An heart that deviseth wicked imaginations, feet that be swift in running to mischief, 19. A false witness that speaketh lies, and he that soweth discord among brethren. Prov.6:16-19

---

### 776. At the end of this world the proud will be burned as stubble when God cleanses the earth by fire.

#### President Ezra Taft Benson

At the end of this world, when God cleanses the earth by fire, the proud will be burned as stubble and the meek shall inherit the earth. CR1989Apr:3

#### Malachi,
*quoted by Mormon*

For behold, the day cometh that shall burn as an oven; and all the proud, yea, and all that do wickedly, shall be stubble; and the day that cometh shall burn them up, saith the Lord of Hosts, that it shall leave them neither root nor branch. (*The resurrected Jesus Christ teaches the Nephite people, expounding and quoting the words of the prophet Malachi, A.D. 34; see Malachi 4*) 3Ne.25:1

#### Joseph Smith,
*receiving the Word of the Lord*

For the hour is nigh and the day soon at hand when the earth is ripe; and all the proud and they that do wickedly shall be as stubble; and I will burn them up, saith the Lord of Hosts, that wickedness shall not be upon the earth; (*Revelation received Sept. 1830; Christ's second coming ushers in the Millennium*) D&C 29:9

#### Joseph Smith

For behold, the day cometh that shall burn as an oven, and all the proud, yea, and all that do wickedly shall burn as stubble; for they that come shall burn them, saith the Lord of Hosts, that it shall leave them neither root nor branch. (*The angel Moroni instructs Joseph, Sept. 21, 1823*) JS-H 1:37

### Malachi

For, behold, the day cometh, that shall burn as an oven; and all the proud, yea, and all that do wickedly, shall be stubble: and the day that cometh shall burn them up, saith the LORD of hosts, that it shall leave them neither root nor branch. (*The prophet Malachi to the people, about 430 B.C.*) Mal.4:1

---

### (5) Sexual Immorality

1. Chastity
2. Adultery
3. Fornication
4. Homosexuality
5. Bestiality
6. Repentance from Sexual Sin

### 1. Chastity

777. Every person should be chaste, free of sexual sin.

### President Heber J. Grant, J. Reuben Clark, Jr., David O McKay
(First Presidency)

By virtue of the authority in us vested as the First Presidency of the Church, we warn our people who are offending, of the degradation, the wickedness, the punishment that attend upon unchastity; we urge you to remember the blessings which flow from the living of the clean life; we call upon you to keep, day in and day out, the way of strictest chastity, through which only can God's choice gifts come to you and His spirit abide with you. ¶ How glorious is he who lives the chaste life. He walks unfearful in the full glare of the noonday sun, for he is without moral infirmity. He can be reached by no shafts of base calumny, for his armor is without flaw. His virtue cannot be challenged by any just accuser, for he lives above reproach. His cheek is never blotched with shame, for he is without hidden sin. He is honored and respected by all mankind, for he is beyond their censure. He is loved by the Lord, for he stands without blemish. The exaltations of eternities await his coming. CR1942Oct:11-12

### Melvin J. Ballard

Certainly our teachers were right when they held up an ideal that virtue was as sacred as life itself, and that we had better lose our lives than lose our virtue . . . . [N]ext to the crime of murder itself is the crime of sexual impurity. CR1929Apr:69

### Joseph Smith

We believe in being honest, true, chaste, benevolent, virtuous, and in doing good to all men; indeed, we may say that we follow the admonition of Paul—We believe all things, we hope all things, we have endured many things, and hope to be able to endure all things. If there is anything virtuous, lovely, or of good report or praiseworthy, we seek after these things. (*The thirteenth of the thirteen Articles of Faith; letter to John Wentworth, March 1, 1842*) AofF:13

### President Spencer W. Kimball

May I talk to you just a moment or two about that which is most dear and precious above all things. Can you think what it would be? Would it be bonds, stocks, or diamonds? Would it be herds or flocks? Would it be automobiles and houses? Would it be medals in athletics? This is the greatest blessing, the most dear and precious above all things—above all things. It cannot be purchased with money, but may be enjoyed by all, even those of humble circumstances as well as the affluent, as much by the high school student as by those who have doctors degrees. Even mortal life when placed upon the balance scales weighs less. That of which I speak is chastity and virtue. The lack of it has caused rivers of tears to flow, broken numerous homes, and deprived large numbers of innocent children. ACR(Sydney)1976:54

### Mormon

[T]hat which was most dear and precious above all things, which is chastity and virtue— (*Mormon to his son Moroni, prior to A.D. 384*) Moro.9:9

### John A. Widtsoe

Virtue is youth's dearest possession; and chastity is the strongest bulwark against the many temptations of life. Of all earthly possessions virtue should be cherished most. If one values life's happiness, one must enter the married state with an unstained, unviolated body. (IE1940Oct:637) TLDP:67

### J. Reuben Clark, Jr.

[O]ne of the worst of the teachings that come [to the youth] is that teaching which is becoming too common, that the sex-urge is a natural urge to be gratified like the urge for drink or for food. Satan has not invented any more unrighteous, hideous doctrine than that, and he knows it. CR1957Apr:87

### Jesus, *recorded in Matthew*

Ye have heard that it was said by them of old time, Thou shalt not commit adultery: 28. But I say unto you, That whosoever looketh on a woman to lust after her hath committed adultery with her already in his heart. (*Jesus Christ to the multitude, about A.D. 30*) Matt.5:27-28

### Jacob, brother of Nephi

For I, the Lord God, delight in the chastity of women. And whoredoms are an abomination before me; thus saith the Lord of Hosts. (*Jacob teaches the Nephites in the temple, 544-421 B.C.*) Jacob 2:28

### Jacob, brother of Nephi

And now I, Jacob, spake many more things unto the people of Nephi, warning them against fornication and lasciviousness, and every kind of sin, telling them the awful consequences of them. (*Jacob speaks to the people of Nephi denouncing unchastity*) Jacob 3:12

**Related Witnesses:**

### President Heber C. Grant,
### J. Reuben Clark, Jr., David O. McKay
(First Presidency)

To the youth of the Church . . . above all we plead with you to live clean, for the unclean life leads only to suffering, misery, and woe physically, —and spiritually it is the path to destruction. How glorious and near to the angels is youth that is clean; this youth has joy unspeakable here and eternal happiness hereafter. Sexual purity is youth's most precious possession; it is the foundation of all righteousness. Better dead, clean, than alive, unclean. CR1942Apr:89

### Paul

Let not sin therefore reign in your mortal body, that ye should obey it in the lusts thereof. (*Paul's letter to the Church in Rome, about A.D. 55*) Rom.6:12

### Paul

This I say then, Walk in the Spirit, and ye shall not fulfil the lust of the flesh. 17. For the flesh lusteth against the Spirit, and the Spirit against the flesh: and these are contrary the one to the other: so that ye cannot do the things that ye would. (*Letter to the churches of Galatia in Asia Minor, about A.D. 55*) Gal.5:16-17

### Melvin J. Ballard

Men . . . have no true conception of the sacredness of the most marvelous power with which God has endowed mortal men—the power of creation. Even though that power may be abused and may become a mere harp of pleasure to the wicked, nevertheless it is the most sacred and holy and divine function with which God has endowed man. (Sermons and Missionary Services of Melvin J. Ballard, p. 167) TLDP:524

### Peter

Dearly beloved, I beseech you as strangers and pilgrims, abstain from fleshly lusts, which war against the soul; 12. Having your conversation honest among the Gentiles: that, whereas they speak against you as evildoers, they may by your good works, which they shall behold, glorify God in the day of visitation. (*Peter to the churches in modern Asia Minor, about A.D. 60*) 1Pet.2:11-12

### Joseph Smith,
### receiving the Word of the Lord

Therefore, cease from all your light speeches, from all laughter, from all your lustful desires, from all your pride and light-mindedness, and from all your wicked doings. (*Revelation received Dec. 27/28, 1832*) D&C 88:121

### John

Love not the world, neither the things that are in the world. If any man love the world, the love of the Father is not in him. 16. For all that is in the world, the lust of the flesh, and the lust of the eyes, and the pride of life, is not of the Father, but is of the world. 17. And the world passeth away, and the lust thereof: but he that doeth the will of God abideth for ever. (*Letter to the churches in Asia*) 1Jn.2:15-17

### President Spencer W. Kimball

To be specific, let us postulate clearly and unmistakably that all sexual life outside of the proper marriage association—I said the proper marriage association—are evil and forbidden by God, and the unrepentant and those who indulge in these will be disillusioned. ¶ Easy it is to create excuses and escapes to cover our own weaknesses. The fornicator minimizes his sins. The robber justifies his thievery. The pervert says that God made him that way. The petter rationalizes his act into insignificance. Let it be understood without equivocation that the common indulgences are transgressions, for sin is the breaking of the divine law. ACR(Sydney)1976:54

### Marion G. Romney,
### also quoting J. Reuben Clark, Jr.

[A]s President Clark used to say, the Lord has made no "fine distinctions . . . between fornication and adultery" (CR1949Oct:194). Nor may I add, between adultery and sex perversion. CR1974Apr:117-18

**Author's Note:** *Chaste*: "Pure in character or conduct; not indecent." "Not guilty of unlawful sexual intercourse; virtuous." (Funk & Wagnalls Standard College Dictionary, p. 231) ¶ *Lust*: Longing desire; eagerness to possess or enjoy; depraved affection or desire; more especially, sexual appetite; unlawful desire of sexual pleasure; concupiscence. (The New Webster Encyclopedic Dictionary of the English Language, p. 505)

**778. Sexual sin stands in its enormity next to murder.**

### President Heber J. Grant,
### J. Reuben Clark, Jr., David O. McKay
(First Presidency)

The doctrine of this Church is that sexual sin— the illicit sexual relations of men and women— stands, in its enormity, next to murder. ¶ The Lord has drawn no essential distinctions between fornication, adultery, and harlotry or prostitution. Each has fallen under His solemn and awful condemnation. ¶ You youths of Zion, you cannot associate in non-marital, illicit sex relationships, which is fornication, and escape the punishments and the judgments which the Lord has declared against this sin. The day of reckoning will come just as certainly as night follows day. They who would palliate this crime and say that such indulgence is but a sinless gratification of a normal desire, like appeasing hunger and thirst, speak filthiness with their lips. Their counsel leads to destruction; their wisdom comes from the Father of Lies. ¶ You husbands and wives who have taken on solemn obligations of chastity in the holy temples of the Lord and who violate those sacred vows by illicit sexual relations with others, you not only commit the vile and loathsome sin of adultery, but you break the oath you yourselves made with the Lord Himself before you went to the altar for your sealing. You become subject to the penalties which the Lord has prescribed for those who breach their covenants with Him. CR1942Oct:11

### Melvin J. Ballard

I call you, my brethren, to work, to pray and to guard the flocks over whom God hath made you overseers . . . that we shall live up to the standards under which I was raised, and you were raised, that we shall teach our sons and daughters that next to murder itself, is the crime of sexual impurity. We have that standard. We expect the boy to be just as clean and as pure as the girl whom he marries, to be his wife and the mother of his children. CR1921Oct:102

### Melvin J. Ballard

[N]ext to the crime of murder itself is the crime of sexual impurity. CR1929Apr:69

### Hyrum Mack Smith

"Thou shalt not commit adultery." Another soul destroying crime which is very rare among the Latter-day Saints. There is no other sin, save murder only, that will so soon destroy the spiritual and moral life of men—why, it is spiritual suicide to participate in any such deadly crime. CR1906Oct:44-45

### President Harold B. Lee

I want to warn this great body of priesthood against that great sin of Sodom and Gomorrah, which has been labeled as a sin second only in seriousness to the sin of murder. I speak of the sin of adultery . . . and besides this, the equally grievous sin of homosexuality, which seems to be gaining momentum with social acceptance in the Babylon of the world, of which Church members must not be part. CR1972Oct:127

**Related Witnesses:**

### Alma, the younger,
### *quoted by Mormon*

And this is not all, my son. Thou didst do that which was grievous unto me; for thou didst forsake the ministry, and did go over into the land of Siron, among the borders of the Lamanites, after the harlot Isabel. 4. Yea, she did steal away the hearts of many; but this was no excuse for thee, my son. Thou shouldst have tended to the ministry wherewith thou wast entrusted. 5. Know ye not, my son, that these things are an abomination in the sight of the Lord; yea, most abominable above all sins save it be the shedding of innocent blood or denying the Holy Ghost? (*Alma to his son Corianton, about 73 B.C.*) Alma 39:3-5

### President Joseph F. Smith

What has come to be known in present day literature as the social evil is a subject of perennial discussion, and the means proposed for dealing with it are topics of contention and debate. That the public conscience is aroused to the seriousness of the dire condition due to sexual immorality is a promising indication of prospective betterment. No more loathsome cancer disfigures the body and soul of society today than the frightful affliction of sexual sin. It vitiates the very fountains of life, and bequeaths its foul effects to the yet unborn as a legacy of death. It lurks in hamlet and city, in the mansion and in the hovel as a ravening beast in wait for prey; and it skulks through the land in blasphemous defiance of the laws of God and man. (*Published by the President in the Improvement Era, June 1917*) MOFP5:63-64

---

## 2. Adultery

**779. Men and women are not to commit adultery.**

### Recorded in Exodus

Thou shalt not commit adultery. (*The Lord reveals the seventh of the Ten Commandments to Moses*) Ex.20:14

### Hyrum Mack Smith

"Thou shalt not commit adultery." Another soul destroying crime which is very rare among the Latter-day Saints. There is no other sin, save murder only, that will so soon destroy the spiritual and moral life of men—why, it is spiritual suicide to participate in any such deadly crime. We do not sustain it; and we do not suffer it; we do not tolerate it; and we do not commit it, as a people. So far as I am concerned I will not support any man or any set of men who are seducers and who commit this deadly sin, be they whom they may, within or without the Church of God; neither will I sustain the men, or the publications, or the party that protect or sustain such corruption. CR1906Oct:44-45

### President Spencer W. Kimball

To be specific, let us postulate clearly and unmistakably that all sexual life outside of the proper marriage association—I said the proper marriage association—are evil and forbidden by God, and the unrepentant and those who indulge in these will be disillusioned. ¶ Easy it is to create excuses and escapes to cover our own weaknesses. The fornicator minimizes his sins. The robber justifies his thievery. The pervert says that God made him that way. The petter rationalizes his act into insignificance. Let it be understood without equivocation that the common indulgences are transgressions, for sin is the breaking of the divine law. ACR(Sydney)1976:54

### Jesus,
#### recorded in Matthew

He saith unto him, Which? Jesus said, Thou shalt do no murder, Thou shalt not commit adultery. . . . (*Jesus instructs the young man who had great possessions*) Matt.19:18

### Marion G. Romney,
#### also quoting J. Reuben Clark, Jr.

One of the most corrupting and debasing vices rampant in our society today is unchastity. Let us be ever mindful that from Sinai the Lord thundered, "Thou shalt not commit adultery." (Ex.20:14) ¶ The penalty for so doing under the Mosaic law was death. Notwithstanding the fact that in this generation's corrupt permissiveness its violation is tolerated with impunity, under God's divine law it is as it has always been, a soul-destroying sin. Its self-executing penalty is spiritual death. No unforgiven adulterer is magnifying his calling in the priesthood; and as President Clark used to say, the Lord has made no "fine distinctions . . . between fornication and adultery" (CR1949Oct:194). Nor may I add, between adultery and sex perversion. CR1974Apr:117-18

### President Heber J. Grant,
### J. Reuben Clark, Jr., David O. McKay
#### (First Presidency)

The doctrine of this Church is that sexual sin—the illicit sexual relations of men and women—stands, in its enormity, next to murder. ¶ The Lord has drawn no essential distinctions between fornication, adultery, and harlotry or prostitution. . . . ¶ . . . . You husbands and wives who have taken on solemn obligations of chastity in the holy temples of the Lord and who violate those sacred vows by illicit sexual relations with others, you not only commit the vile and loathsome sin of adultery, but you break the oath you yourselves made with the Lord himself before you went to the altar for your sealing. You become subject to the penalties which the Lord has prescribed for those who breach their covenants with Him. CR1942Oct:11

### Joseph Smith,
#### receiving the Word of the Lord

Thou shalt love thy wife with all thy heart, and shalt cleave unto her and none else. 23. And he that looketh upon a woman to lust after her shall deny the faith, and shall not have the Spirit; and if he repents not he shall be cast out. 24. Thou shalt not commit adultery; and he that committeth adultery, and repenteth not, shall be cast out. 25. But he that has committed adultery and repents with all his heart, and forsaketh it, and doeth it no more, thou shalt forgive; 26. But if he doeth it again, he shall not be forgiven, but shall be cast out. (*Revelation "embracing the law of the Church," Feb. 9, 1831*) D&C 42:22-26

### Joseph Smith,
#### receiving the Word of the Lord

And if any man or woman shall commit adultery, he or she shall be tried before two elders of the church, or more, and every word shall be established against him or her by two witnesses of the church, and not of the enemy; but if there are more than two witnesses it is better. 81. But he or she shall be condemned by the mouth of two witnesses; and the elders shall lay the case before the church, and the church shall lift up their hands against him or her, that they may be dealt with according to the law of God. (*Revelation "embracing the law of the Church," Feb. 9, 1831*) D&C 42:80-81

### Joseph Smith,
#### receiving the Word of the Lord

And as ye have asked concerning adultery, verily, verily, I say unto you, if a man receiveth a wife in the new and everlasting covenant, and if she be with another man, and I have not appointed unto her by the holy anointing, she hath committed adultery and shall be destroyed.

42. If she be not in the new and everlasting covenant, and she be with another man, she has committed adultery. 43. And if her husband be with another woman, and he was under a vow, he hath broken his vow and hath committed adultery. (*Revelation received Feb. 4, 1831*) D&C 132:41-43

**Abinadi,**
*quoted by Mormon*

Thou shalt not commit adultery. . . . (*Abinadi teaches the Ten Commandments to the people of the wicked King Noah, about 148 B.C.*) Mosiah 13:22

**Alma, the younger,**
*quoted by Mormon*

Know ye not, my son, that these things are an abomination in the sight of the Lord; yea, most abominable above all sins save it be the shedding of innocent blood or denying the Holy Ghost? (*Alma chastises his son for going after the harlot Isabel, about A.D. 73*) Alma 39:5

**Joseph Smith**

Thou shalt love thy neighbor as thyself. Thou shalt not steal; neither commit adultery, nor kill, nor do anything like unto it. (*Revelation, Aug. 7, 1831*) D&C 59:6

**Jesus,**
*recorded in Matthew*

Ye have heard that it was said by them of old time, Thou shalt not commit adultery: 28. But I say unto you, That whosoever looketh on a woman to lust after her hath committed adultery with her already in his heart. (*Jesus teaches the multitude, about A.D. 30*) Matt.5:27-28

**Related Witnesses:**

**Recorded in Proverbs**

But whoso committeth adultery with a woman lacketh understanding: he that doeth it destroyeth his own soul. Prov.6:32

**Paul**

So then if, while her husband liveth, she be married to another man, she shall be called an adulteress: but if her husband be dead, she is free from that law; so that she is no adulteress, though she be married to another man. (*Paul's letter to the Church in Rome, about A.D. 55*) Rom.7:3

---

**780.** The adulterer who repents can be forgiven.

**Joseph Smith,**
*receiving the Word of the Lord*

But he that has committed adultery and repents with all his heart, and forsaketh it, and doeth it no more, thou shalt forgive; 26. But if he doeth

it again, he shall not be forgiven, but shall be cast out. (*Revelation "embracing the law of the Church," Feb. 9, 1831*) D&C 42:25-26

**President Spencer W. Kimball**

When the unmarried yield to the lust which induces intimacies, it is called fornication, and when married people do so it is called adultery. The forgiveness, as stated, can come only through a total repentance. One has not repented of evil sins until he has suffered terribly. There must be an admission of sin to the proper Church authorities and a total change of the life—transformation. ACR(Santiago)1977:5

**Elder Spencer W. Kimball**

If adultery or fornication justified the death penalty in the old days, and still in Christ's day, is the sin any less today because the laws of the land do not assess the death penalty for it? Is the act less grievous? There must be a washing, a purging, a changing of attitudes, a correcting of appraisals, a strengthening toward self-mastery. And these cleansing processes cannot be accomplished as easily as taking a bath or shampooing the hair, or sending a suit of clothes to the cleaners. There must be many prayers, and volumes of tears. There must be more than a verbal acknowledgement. There must be an inner conviction giving to the sin its full diabolical weight. "My sins are disgusting—loathsome" one could come to think about his baser sins, like the Psalmist who used these words: "My wounds stink and are corrupt because of my foolishness." (Ps.38:5) ¶ There must be increased devotion and much thought and study. There must be a re-awakening, a fortification, a re-birth. And this takes energy and time and often is accompanied with sore embarrassment, heavy deprivations and deep trials, even if indeed one is not excommunicated from the Church, losing all spiritual blessings. (The Miracle of Forgiveness, p. 155) TLDP:74

**Related Witnesses:**

**Boyd K. Packer**

There is a great cleansing power. Know that you can be clean. If you are outside of the Church, the covenant of baptism itself represents, among other things, a washing and a cleansing. ¶ For those of you who are in the Church there is a way, not entirely painless, but certainly possible. You can stand clean and spotless before him. Guilt will be gone, and you can be at peace. Go to your bishop or your branch president. He holds the key to this cleansing power. Go and have an interview with him, and then you do what he says, and you can become clean again. ACR(Stockholm)1974:84

## 3. Fornication

**781. Men and women are not to have sexual relations outside of marriage.**

**President Heber J. Grant,
J. Reuben Clark, Jr., David O. McKay**
(First Presidency)

The doctrine of this Church is that sexual sin—the illicit sexual relations of men and women—stands, in its enormity, next to murder. ¶ The Lord has drawn no essential distinctions between fornication, adultery, and harlotry or prostitution. Each has fallen under His solemn and awful condemnation. ¶ You youths of Zion, you cannot associate in non-marital, illicit sexual relationships, which is fornication, and escape the punishments and the judgements which the Lord has declared against this sin. The day of reckoning will come just as certainly as night follows day. They who would palliate this crime and say that such indulgence is but a sinless gratification of a normal desire, like appeasing hunger and thirst, speak filthiness with their lips. Their counsel leads to destruction; their wisdom comes from the Father of Lies. ¶ You husbands and wives who have taken on solemn obligations of chastity in the holy temples of the Lord and who violate those sacred vows by illicit sexual relations with others, you not only commit the vile and loathsome sin of adultery, but you break the oath you yourselves made with the Lord himself before you went to the altar for your sealing. You become subject to the penalties which the Lord has prescribed for those who breach their covenants with Him. ¶ Of the harlots and those who visit them, God speaks in terms of divine contempt. They are they who have bargained away the eternity of bliss for the momentary pleasures of the flesh. ¶ The Lord will have only a clean people. CR1942Oct:11

**Elder Spencer W. Kimball**

Sexual sin receives repeated condemnation in the scriptures. To get our definitions clear, let us realize that heterosexual intercourse is the sin of fornication when committed by the unmarried and is adultery when indulged in by married people outside of their marriage covenants. Both are grievous sins in God's sight. (The Miracle of Forgiveness, p. 24 ) TLDP:71

**Alma, the younger,
quoted by Mormon**

And this is not all, my son. Thou didst do that which was grievous unto me; for thou didst for-

sake the ministry, and did go over into the land of Siron, among the borders of the Lamanites, after the harlot Isabel. 4. Yea, she did steal away the hearts of many; but this was no excuse for thee, my son. Thou shouldst have tended to the ministry wherewith thou wast entrusted. 5. Know ye not, my son, that these things are an abomination in the sight of the Lord; yea, most abominable above all sins save it be the shedding of innocent blood or denying the Holy Ghost? (Alma to his son Corianton, about 73 B.C.) Alma 39:3-5

**Boyd K. Packer**

There was provided in our bodies—and this is sacred—a power of creation, a light, so to speak, that has the power to kindle other lights. This gift was to be used only within the sacred bonds of marriage. Through the exercise of this power of creation, a mortal body may be conceived, a spirit enter into it, and a new soul born into this life. ¶ This power is good. It can create and sustain family life, and it is in family life that we find the foundations of happiness. It is given to virtually every individual who is born into mortality. It is a sacred and significant power, and I repeat, my young friends, that this power is good. ¶ You who are teenagers, like every other son and daughter of Adam and Eve, have this power within you. ¶ The power of creation—or may we say procreation—is not just an incidental part of the plan: it is essential to it. Without it the plan could not proceed. The misuse of it may disrupt the plan. CR1972Apr:136-37

**Elder Harold B. Lee**

The divine impulse within every true man and woman that impels companionship with the opposite sex is intended by our Maker as a holy impulse for a holy purpose—not to be satisfied as a mere biological urge or as a lust of the flesh in promiscuous associations, but to be reserved as an expression of true love in holy wedlock. (At Weber State College, 1972) (Ye Are the Light of the World, pp. 266-67) TLDP:68

**Joseph Smith,
receiving the Word of the Lord**

Thou shalt love thy wife with all thy heart, and shalt cleave unto her and none else. 23. And he that looketh upon a woman to lust after her shall deny the faith, and shall not have the Spirit; and if he repents not he shall be cast out. 24. Thou shalt not commit adultery; and he that committeth adultery, and repenteth not, shall be cast out. 25. But he that has committed adultery and repents with all his heart, and forsaketh it, and doeth it no more, thou shalt forgive; 26. But if he doeth it again, he shall not be forgiven, but shall be cast out. (*Revelation "embracing the law of the Church," Feb. 9, 1831*) D&C 42:22-26

**Related Witnesses:**

**Paul**

For this is the will of God, even your sanctification, that ye should abstain from fornication: 4. That every one of you should know how to possess his vessel in sanctification and honour; 5. Not in the lust of concupiscence, even as the Gentiles which know not God: (*Letter to the Church at Thessalonica, comprising Jews and many pagan converts, A.D. 50*) 1Thess.4:3-5

**Delbert L. Stapley**

[T]here are two main requirements of this oath and covenant. First is faithfulness, which denotes obedience to the laws of God and connotes true observance of all gospel standards. For better understanding of the oath and covenant of the priesthood, may I propound these questions: . . . ¶ Can a man be faithful who does not obey the law of chastity and is not morally clean in his life and habits? CR1957Apr:76

**President Heber J. Grant,**
**J. Reuben Clark, Jr., David O. McKay**
(First Presidency)

You who have observed the law of chastity have kept the temples of God undefiled. You can stand unabashed before the Lord. He loves you. He will bestow honor and reward upon you. Every overcoming of temptation brings strength and glory to the soul. CR1942Oct:10

**J. Reuben Clark, Jr.**

[T]o keep the Children of Israel from committing these sins, the Lord proceeds to name them and to prescribe penalties for their commission. I am going to name a few of them. ¶ First is incest. I am not enlarging on it. In the law incest included more than we now ascribe to it. It included marriage between people within prohibited relationships. The penalty for incest was death to both parties. ¶ Fornication— sometimes adultery and fornication are used interchangeably. But for certain kinds of fornication, the penalty was death. ¶ For adultery it was death for both parties. ¶ For homosexuality, it was death to the male and prescription or penalty for the female I do not know. ¶ . . . . Prostitution was called an abomination. ¶ After the Lord finished his listing of abominations recorded here, he continued: . . . "Ye shall therefore keep my statutes and my judgements, and shall not commit any of these abominations; neither any of your own nation, nor any stranger that sojourneth among you." CR1957Apr:87

**President David O. McKay,**
*quoted by Elder Spencer W. Kimball*

Your virtue is worth more than your life. Please, young folk, preserve your virtue even if you lose your lives. Do not tamper with sin . . . do not permit yourselves to be led into temptation. ¶ Conduct yourselves seemly and with due regard, particularly you young boys, to the sanctity of womanhood. Do not pollute it. (The Miracle of Forgiveness, p. 63) TLDP:67

## 4. Homosexuality

782. Men are not to have sexual relations with other men, or women with other women.

**Elder Spencer W. Kimball**

Because of the seriousness of this sin [of homosexuality] it carries a heavy penalty for the unrepentant. The offender may realize that disfellowshipment or excommunication is the penalty for heavy petting, adultery, fornication and comparable sins if there is not adequate repentance, yet he often supposes that because his acts have not been committed with the opposite sex he is not in sin. Let it therefore be clearly stated that the seriousness of the sin of homosexuality is equal to or greater than that of fornication or adultery; and that the Lord's Church will as readily take action to disfellowship or excommunicate the unrepentant practicing homosexual as it will the unrepentant fornicator or adulterer. (The Miracle of Forgiveness, pp. 81-82) TLDP:72

**President Harold B. Lee**

I want to warn this great body of priesthood against that great sin of Sodom and Gomorrah, which has been labeled as a sin second only in seriousness to the sin of murder. I speak of the sin of adultery . . . and besides this, the equally grievous sin of homosexuality, which seems to be gaining momentum with social acceptance in the Babylon of the world, of which Church members must not be part. CR1972Oct:127

**J. Reuben Clark, Jr.**

[T]o keep the Children of Israel from committing these sins, the Lord proceeds to name them and to prescribe penalties for their commission. I am going to name a few of them. ¶ First is incest. I am not enlarging on it. In the law incest included more than we now ascribe to it. It included marriage between people within prohibited relationships. The penalty for incest was death to both parties. ¶ Fornication—sometimes adultery and fornication are used interchangeably. But for certain kinds of fornication, the penalty was death. ¶ For adultery, it was death for both parties. ¶ For homosexuality, it was death to the male and the prescription or penalty for the female I do not know. ¶ . . . . Prostitution was called an abomination. ¶ After the Lord finished his listing of abominations recorded here, he continued: . . . "Ye shall therefore keep my statutes and my judgements, and shall not commit any of these abominations; neither any of your own nation, nor any stranger that sojourneth among you." CR1957Apr:87

**President Joseph Fielding Smith,**
**Harold B. Lee, N. Eldon Tanner**
(First Presidency)

[Church] leaders should generally approach these unhappy [homosexual] people in the true spirit of the gospel of love and understanding rather than of condemnation. They are sons and daughters of God and made in the image of God, and intended to become like God in righteousness and honor and integrity and virtue. ¶ They should be convinced through kind persuasion that a total continuing repentance could bring them forgiveness for the transgression. They can also be assured that in spite of all they may have heard from other sources, they can overcome and can return to total normal, happy living. ¶ Many of these people have reached their present depressed state on a long road of gradual deterioration and cannot be expected to perfect themselves instantly. Consequently, high ideals and positive programs should be suggested to them and frequent visits will help them gain self-mastery. ¶ The inspiration of the Lord will generally bring happy solutions to these problems. (His Servants Speak, pp. 157-58) TLDP:73

**Recorded in Leviticus**

If a man also lie with mankind, as he lieth with a woman, both of them have committed an abomination: they shall surely be put to death; their blood shall be upon them. (*Revelation to Moses for the children of Israel*) Lev.20:13

**Elder Spencer W. Kimball**

Prophets anciently and today condemn masturbation. It induces feelings of guilt and shame. It is detrimental to spirituality. It indicates slavery to the flesh, not that mastery of it and the growth toward godhood which is the object of our mortal life. Our modern prophet has indicated that no young man should be called on a mission who is not free from this practice. ¶ While we should not regard this weakness as the heinous sin which some other sexual practices are, it is of itself bad enough to require sincere repentance. What is more, it too

often leads to grievous sin, even to that sin against nature, homosexuality. For, done in private, it evolves often into mutual masturbation—practiced with another person of the same sex and thence into total homosexuality. . . . ¶ But let us emphasize that right and wrong, righteousness and sin, are not dependent upon man's interpretations, conventions and attitudes. Social acceptance does not change the status of an act, making wrong into right. If all the people in the world were to accept homosexuality, as it seems to have been accepted in Sodom and Gomorrah, the practice would still be deep, dark sin. . . . ¶ In this context, where stands the perversion of homosexuality? Clearly it is hostile to God's purpose in that it negates his first and great commandment to "multiply and replenish the earth." If the abominable practice became universal it would depopulate the earth in a single generation. It would nullify God's great program for his spirit children in that it would leave countless unembodied spirits in the heavenly world without the chance for the opportunities of mortality and would deny to all the participants in the practice the eternal life God makes available to us all. (The Miracle of Forgiveness, pp. 77-79, 81-82) TLDP:71-72

**Related Witnesses:**

**Paul**

Know ye not that the unrighteous shall not inherit the kingdom of God? Be not deceived: neither fornicators, nor idolaters, nor adulterers, nor effeminate, nor abusers of themselves with mankind, 10. Nor thieves, nor covetous, nor drunkards, nor revilers, nor extortioners, shall inherit the kingdom of God. 11. And such were some of you: but ye are washed, but ye are sanctified, but ye are justified in the name of the Lord Jesus, and by the Spirit of our God. (*Paul's letter to the Church at Corinth, Greece, about A.D. 55*) 1Cor.6:9-11

**Paul**

And likewise also the men, leaving the natural use of the woman, burned in their lust one toward another; men with men working that which is unseemly, and receiving in themselves that recompence of their error which was meet. (*Letter to the Church in Rome regarding the unrighteous, about A.D. 55*) Rom.1:27

**Recorded in Jude**

For there are certain men crept in unawares, who were before of old ordained to this condemnation, ungodly men, turning the grace of our God into lasciviousness, and denying the only Lord God, and our Lord Jesus Christ. . . . 7. Even as Sodom and Gomorrha, and the cities about them in like manner, giving themselves over to fornication, and going after strange flesh, are set forth for an example, suffering the vengeance of eternal fire. (*Letter of Jude, brother of James*) Jude 1:4,7

### President Spencer W. Kimball

To be specific, let us postulate clearly and unmistakably that all sexual life outside of the proper marriage association—I said the *proper* marriage association—are evil and forbidden by God, and the unrepentant and those who indulge in these will be disillusioned. ¶ The fornicator minimizes his sins. The robber justifies his thievery. The pervert says that God made him that way. The petter rationalizes his act into insignificance. Let it be understood without equivocation that the common indulgences are transgressions, for sin is the breaking of the divine law. [Italics by SWK] ACR(Sydney)1976:54

---

## 5. Bestiality

**783.** We are not to have carnal relations with animals.

### Recorded in Leviticus

Neither shalt thou lie with any beast to defile thyself therewith: neither shall any woman stand before a beast to lie down thereto: it is confusion. (*Revelation to Moses*) Lev.18:23

### J. Reuben Clark, Jr.

[T]o keep the Children of Israel from committing these sins, the Lord proceeds to name them and to prescribe penalties for their commission. . . . ¶ For Bestiality, it was death for both the man involved and for the woman. CR1957Apr:87

### Recorded in Leviticus

And if a man lie with a beast, he shall surely be put to death: and ye shall slay the beast. 16. And if a woman approach unto any beast, and lie down thereto, thou shalt kill the woman, and the beast: they shall surely be put to death; their blood shall be upon them. (*Revelation to Moses for the children of Israel*) Lev.20:15-16

---

## 6. Repentance from Sexual Sin

**784.** Those who persist in sexual sin shall not inherit the kingdom of God (yet there is mercy for the sinner who repents).

### Melvin J. Ballard

Certainly our teachers were right when they held up an ideal that virtue was as sacred as life itself, and that we had better lose our lives than lose our virtue. . . . [N]ext to the crime of murder itself is the crime of sexual impurity. . . . [T]he devil is apt to [make the sinner believe] that now he or she has committed this sin they are lost forever. Repentance is in order always, and mercy for the sinner. CR1929Apr:69

### Elder Spencer W. Kimball

If adultery or fornication justified the death penalty in the old days, and still in Christ's day, is the sin any less today because the laws of the land do not assess the death penalty for it? Is the act less grievous? There must be a washing, a purging, a changing of attitudes, a correcting of appraisals, a strengthening toward self-mastery. And these cleansing processes cannot be accomplished as easily as taking a bath or shampooing the hair, or sending a suit of clothes to the cleaners. There must be many prayers, and volumes of tears. There must be more than a verbal acknowledgement. There must be an inner conviction giving to the sin its full diabolical weight. "My sins are disgusting—loathsome" one could come to think about his baser sins, like the Psalmist who used these words: "My wounds stink and are corrupt because of my foolishness." (Ps.38:5) ¶ There must be increased devotion and much thought and study. There must be a re-awakening, a fortification, a re-birth. And this takes energy and time and often is accompanied with sore embarrassment, heavy deprivations and deep trials, even if indeed one is not excommunicated from the Church, losing all spiritual blessings. (The Miracle of Forgiveness, p. 155) TLDP:74

### President Spencer W. Kimball

To be specific, let us postulate clearly and unmistakably that all sexual life outside of the proper marriage association—I said the proper marriage association—are evil and forbidden by God, and the unrepentant and those who indulge in these will be disillusioned. ACR(Sydney)1976:54

### Paul

Know ye not that the unrighteous shall not inherit the kingdom of God? Be not deceived: neither fornicators, nor idolaters, nor adulterers, nor effeminate, nor abusers of themselves with mankind, 10. Nor thieves, nor covetous, nor drunkards, nor revilers, nor extortioners, shall inherit the kingdom of God. (*Letter to the Church at Corinth, Greece, 55 B.C.*) 1Cor.6:9-10

**Paul**

For this ye know, that no whoremonger, nor unclean person, nor covetous man, who is an idolater, hath any inheritance in the kingdom of Christ and of God. (*Letter to the Saints at Ephesus in Asia Minor, about A.D. 62*) Eph.5:5

**President Joseph Fielding Smith,**
**Harold B. Lee, N. Eldon Tanner**
(First Presidency)

[Church] leaders should generally approach these unhappy [homosexual] people in the true spirit of the gospel of love and understanding rather than of condemnation. They are sons and daughters of God and made in the image of God, and intended to become like God in righteousness and honor and integrity and virtue. ¶ They should be convinced through kind persuasion that a total continuing repentance could bring them forgiveness for the transgression. They can also be assured that in spite of all they may have heard from other sources, they can overcome and can return to total normal, happy living. ¶ Many of these people have reached their present depressed state on a long road of gradual deterioration and cannot be expected to perfect themselves instantly. Consequently, high ideals and positive programs should be suggested to them and frequent visits will help them gain self-mastery. ¶ The inspiration of the Lord will generally bring happy solutions to these problems. (His Servants Speak, pp. 157-58) TLDP:73

**Joseph Smith,**
*receiving the Word of the Lord*

And he that looketh upon a woman to lust after her shall deny the faith, and shall not have the Spirit; and if he repents not he shall be cast out. 24. Thou shalt not commit adultery; and he that committeth adultery, and repenteth not, shall be cast out. 25. But he that has committed adultery and repents with all his heart, and forsaketh it, and doeth it no more, thou shalt forgive; 26. But if he doeth it again, he shall not be forgiven, but shall be cast out. (*Revelation "embracing the law of the Church," Feb. 9, 1831*) D&C 42:23-26

**Related Witnesses:**

**President Spencer W. Kimball**

"Vice is a monster of such heinous mien," someone has said. But it is a monkey on your back. Its satisfactions are momentary, but the reaction is always disappointing and frustrating. Rationalization may sear the conscience, but the product of unchastity is remorse and sorrow. A clean conscience with a chaste body and a virtuous mind bring power, happiness, and peace which no unvirtuous person can or ever will enjoy to the same extent. [*See Alexander*

*Pope's An Essay on Man:*
  *"Vice is a monster of so frightful mein,*
  *As, to be hated, needs but to be seen;*
  *Yet seen too oft, familiar with her face,*
  *We first endure, then pity, then embrace."*]
                 ACR(Sydney)1976:54

## (6) Sorcery

**785. Sorcery (including divination, enchantments, necromancy, witchcraft, wizardry, and the like) is an abomination to the Lord.**

**Paul**

Now the works of the flesh are manifest, which are these; Adultery, fornication, uncleanness, lasciviousness, 20. Idolatry, witchcraft, hatred, variance, emulations, wrath, strife, seditions, heresies, 21. Envyings, murders, drunkenness, revellings, and such like: of the which I tell you before, as I have also told you in time past, that they which do such things shall not inherit the kingdom of God. (*Paul writes to the churches of Galatia in Asia Minor, about A.D. 55*) Gal.5:19-21

**Recorded in Deuteronomy**

When thou art come into the land which the LORD thy God giveth thee, thou shalt not learn to do after the abominations of those nations. 10. There shall not be found among you any one that maketh his son or his daughter to pass through the fire, or that useth divination, or an observer of times, or an enchanter, or a witch, 11. Or a charmer, or a consulter with familiar spirits, or a wizard, or a necromancer. 12. For all that do these things are an abomination unto the LORD: and because of these abominations the LORD thy God doth drive them out from before thee. 13. Thou shalt be perfect with the LORD thy God. 14. For these nations, which thou shalt possess, hearkened unto observers of times, and unto diviners: but as for thee, the LORD thy God hath not suffered thee so to do. (*Commandments to Israel through Moses*) Deut.18:9-14

**John**

But the fearful, and unbelieving, and the abominable, and murderers, and whoremongers, and sorcerers, and idolaters, and all liars, shall have their part in the lake which burneth with fire and brimstone: which is the second death. (*John sees the condition of mankind at judgment day*) Rev.21:8

**Micah**

And I will cut off witchcrafts out of thine hand; and

thou shalt have no more soothsayers: (*Micah prophesies, about 740-700 B.C.*) Micah 5:12

**Mormon**

And it came to pass that there were sorceries, and witchcrafts, and magics; and the power of the evil one was wrought upon all the face of the land, even unto the fulfilling of all the words of Abinadi, and also Samuel the Lamanite. (*Mormon writes about the people of his day, A.D. 327-328*) Morm.1:19

**Related Witnesses:**

**President Brigham Young,
Heber C. Kimball, Willard Richards**

(First Presidency)

[T]he increase of seers, and wizards, and diviners, and familiar spirits, and soothsayers, and astrologers, who are charming the nations with their magic arts, lulling the foolish to sleep with their magnetic influence, deceiving priests and people by their necromancy, calling rain, snow, and fire from heaven, and scattering abroad hoar frost like a winter's night . . . all these signs, and . . . many more like things [are the fulfillment of prophecies which] should come to pass in this generation, as signs of the second coming of the Son of Man, which is near at hand. . . . (*Fifth General Epistle to the Saints, April 7, 1851*) MOFP2:63-64

**Related Witnesses:**

**Recorded in 2 Chronicles**

And he caused his children to pass through the fire in the valley of the son of Hinnom: also he observed times, and used enchantments, and used witchcraft, and dealt with a familiar spirit, and with wizards: he wrought much evil in the sight of the LORD, to provoke him to anger. (*Manasseh reigns in wickedness and worships false gods; some acts of Manasseh recorded*) 2Chr.33:6

**Author's Note:** Following are dictionary definitions of some of the terms used in D-785: *Sorcery*: "Divination by the assistance or supposed assistance of evil spirits; magic; enchantment; witchcraft" (The New Webster Encyclopedic Dictionary of the English Language, p. 800). *Divination*: "The act of divining; a foretelling future events, or discovering things secret or obscure, by the aid of superior beings, or by certain rites, experiments, observations, etc." (The New Webster Encyclopedic Dictionary of the English Language p. 256). *Enchantment*: "The act of enchanting; the use of magic arts, spells, or charms; incantation" (The New Webster Encyclopedic Dictionary of the English Language, p. 286). *Necromancy*: "Divination by means of a pretended communication with the

dead; the black art; the art of magic or sorcery" (The New Webster Encyclopedic Dictionary of the English Language, p. 561). *Witchcraft*: "The practices of witches; sorcery; power more than natural; enchantment; fascination" (The New Webster Encyclopedic Dictionary of the English Language, p. 962). *Wizard*: "[A]n adept in the black art; a sorcerer; an enchanter; a magician; a conjurer" (The New Webster Encyclopedic Dictionary of the English Language, p. 962). ¶ I am including the following quotation from Joseph Smith on this subject of false spirits which is helpful in understanding why there is concern with the evil practices addressed in this doctrine: *¶ It is evident from the Apostles' writings, that many false spirits existed in their day, and had "gone forth into the world," and that it needed intelligence which God alone could impart to detect false spirits, and to prove what spirits were of God. The world in general has been grossly ignorant in regard to this one thing, . . . "for no man knows the things of God, but by the Spirit of God." ¶ The Egyptians were not able to discover the difference between the miracles of Moses and those of the magicians until they came to be tested together; and if Moses had not appeared in their midst, they would unquestionably have thought that the miracles of the magicians were performed through the mighty power of God, for they were great miracles that were performed by them—a supernatural agency was developed, and great power manifested. ¶ The witch of Endor is a no less singular personage; clothed with a powerful agency she raised the Prophet Samuel from his grave, and he appeared before the astonished king, and revealed unto him his future destiny. Who is to tell whether this woman is of God, and a righteous woman—or whether the power she possessed was of the devil, and she a witch as represented by the Bible? It is easy for us to say now, but if we had lived in her day, which of us could have unravelled the mystery? ¶ It would have been equally as difficult for us to tell by what spirit the Apostles prophesied, or by what power the Apostles spoke and worked miracles. Who could have told whether the power of Simon, the sorcerer, was of God or of the devil? ¶ There always did, in every age, seem to be a lack of intelligence pertaining to this subject. Spirits of all kinds have been manifested, in every age, and almost amongst all people. If we go among the pagans, they have their spirits; the Mohammedans, the Jews, the Christians, the Indians—all have their spirits, all have a supernatural agency, and all contend that their spirits are of God. Who shall solve the* *mystery? "Try the spirits," says John, but who is to do it? The learned, the eloquent, the philosopher, the sage, the divine—all are ignorant. The heathens will boast of their gods, and of the great things that have been unfolded by their oracles. The Mussulman will boast of his Koran, and of the divine communications that his progenitors have received. The Jews have had numerous instances, both ancient and modern, among them of men who have professed to be inspired, and sent to bring about great events, and the Christian world has not been slow in making up the number. ¶ "Try the spirits," but what by? Are we to try them by the creeds of men? What preposterous folly—what sheer ignorance—what madness! Try the motions and actions of an eternal being (for I contend that all spirits are such) by a thing that was conceived in ignorance, and brought forth in folly— a cobweb of yesterday! Angels would hide their faces, and devils would be ashamed and insulted, and would say, "Paul we know, and Jesus we know, but who are ye?" Let each man of society make a creed and try evil spirits by it, and the devil would shake his sides; it is all that he would ask—all that he would desire. Yet many of them do this, and hence "many spirits are abroad in the world." ¶ One great evil is, that men are ignorant of the nature of spirits; their power, laws, government, intelligence, &c., and imagine that when there is anything like power, revelation, or vision manifested, that it must be of God. Hence the Methodists, Presbyterians, and others frequently possess a spirit that will cause them to lie down, and during its operation, animation is frequently entirely suspended; they consider it to be the power of God, and a glorious manifestation from God—a manifestation of what? Is there any intelligence communicated? Are the curtains of heaven withdrawn, or the purposes of God developed? Have they seen and conversed with an angel—or have the glories of futurity burst upon their view? No! but their body has been inanimate, the operation of their spirit suspended, and all the intelligence that can be obtained from them when they arise, is a shout of "glory," or "hallelujah," or some incoherent expression; but they have had "the power." ¶ The Shaker will whirl around on his heel, impelled by a supernatural agency or spirit, and think that he is governed by the Spirit of God; and the Jumper will jump and enter into all kinds of extravagances. A Primitive Methodist will shout under the influence of that spirit, until he will rend the heavens with his cries; while the Quakers (or Friends) moved as they think, by*

*the Spirit of God, will sit still and say nothing. Is God the author of all this? If not of all of it, which does He recognize? Surely, such a heterogeneous mass of confusion never can enter into the kingdom of heaven.* (HC4:571-72)

## (7) Unrighteous Dominion

786. We are not to abuse the authority given us—to exercise unrighteous dominion or power.

### Elder Joseph Fielding Smith

Most men are inclined to abuse authority, especially those who wield it who are the least prepared to hold positions of trust. It has been the characteristic of men in power to use that power to gratify their own pride and vain ambitions. More misery has come to the inhabitants of this world through the exercise of authority by those who least deserved it, than from almost any other cause. Rulers of kingdoms in the past have oppressed their subjects, and where they had the power they have sought to increase their dominions. We have had some horrible examples of misplaced ambition which, in recent years, placed the very existence of humanity in peril. These conditions still prevail in high places bringing fear and consternation to the troubled world. ¶ There should not, however, be any of this unrighteous ambition within the Church, but everything should be done in the spirit of love and humility. CHMR2:178; DGSM:70

### Joseph Smith

Behold, there are many called, but few are chosen. And why are they not chosen? 35. Because their hearts are set so much upon the things of this world, and aspire to the honors of men, that they do not learn this one lesson— 36. That the rights of the priesthood are inseparably connected with the powers of heaven, and that the powers of heaven cannot be controlled nor handled only upon the principles of righteousness. 37. That they may be conferred upon us, it is true; but when we undertake to cover our sins, or to gratify our pride, our vain ambition, or to exercise control or dominion or compulsion upon the souls of the children of men, in any degree of unrighteousness, behold, the heavens withdraw themselves; the Spirit of the Lord is grieved; and when it is withdrawn, Amen to the priesthood or the authority of that man. 38. Behold, ere he is aware, he is left unto himself, to kick against the pricks, to persecute the saints, and to fight against God. 39. We have learned by sad experience that it is the nature and disposition of almost all men, as soon as they get a little authority, as they suppose, they will immediately begin to exercise unrighteous dominion. 40. Hence many are called, but few are chosen. (*Revelation received while in Liberty Jail, March 20, 1839; why many are called and few chosen*) D&C 121:34-40

### Orson F. Whitney

The great principle enunciated in the Declaration of Independence, that governments derive their just powers from the consent of the governed, permeates this Church and lies at the foundation of its government, determining the manner of the choice of men and women to hold office therein. This has always been the rule of the Church. There is no room in it for tyranny, for usurpation, for the exercise of unrighteous dominion. CR1907Apr:111

### Elder Wilford Woodruff

"Many are called, few are chosen." The Almighty has revealed in our day the reasons, but what a mighty host have wrecked their eternal hopes on those fatal reefs—love of the riches of this world, the honors and praises of men, and the exercises of unrighteous dominion. ¶ Let all Israel remember that the eternal and everlasting Priesthood is bestowed upon us for the purpose alone of administering in the ordinances of life and salvation, both for the living and the dead, and no man on earth can use that Priesthood for any other purpose than for the work of the ministry, the perfecting of the Saints, edifying the body of Christ, establishing the Kingdom of Heaven, and redeeming Zion. If we attempt to use it for unrighteous purposes, like lightning from heaven our power, sooner or later, falls, and we fail to accomplish the designs of God. (*In official announcement of the death of President John Taylor, Aug. 29, 1887*) MOFP3:131

### President Brigham Young, Heber C. Kimball, Willard Richards
(First Presidency)

The Church and Kingdom of God does not use any compulsion over the souls of men. Nor does it claim any right so to do. The Priesthood which it bears is Divine authority to administer in behalf of Deity in the truths and ordinances of salvation. Those who hold it are warned against seeking to exercise unrighteous dominion, and instructed that it can only be maintained "by persuasion, by longsuffering, by gentleness and meekness and by love unfeigned." The presiding authorities therein regulate the affairs of the Church by "common consent," and their jurisdiction is within, and not without, its ecclesiastical limits. Every member of the organization in every place is absolutely free as a citizen, and is not restrained of any liberty enjoyed by nonmembers. *(Sixth General Epistle of the First Presidency of the Church from Great Salt Lake Valley, Jan. 15, 1852)* MOFP4:82

### Bruce R. McConkie

Babylon is the communistic system that seeks to destroy freedom of people in all nations and kingdoms; it is the Mafia and crime syndicates that murder and rob and steal; it is the secret combinations that seek for power and unrighteous dominion over the souls of men. Babylon is the promoter of pornography; it is organized crime and prostitution; it is every evil and wicked and ungodly thing in our whole social structure." (The Millennial Messiah, p. 424) DGSM:98

### President Heber J. Grant, J. Reuben Clark, Jr., David O. McKay
(First Presidency)

The gospel of Christ is a gospel of love and peace, of patience and long suffering, of forbearance and forgiveness, of kindness and good deeds, of charity and brotherly love. Greed, avarice, base ambition, thirst for power, and unrighteous dominion over our fellow men, can have no place in the hearts of Latter-day Saints nor of God-fearing men everywhere. We of the Church must lead the life prescribed in the saying of the ancient prophet-warrior: ¶ "I seek not for power, but to pull it down. I seek not for honor of the world, but for the glory of my God, and the freedom and welfare of my country." (Alma 60:36) CR1942Apr:90

### Moroni, the Prophet General, quoted by Mormon

Behold, I am Moroni, your chief captain. I seek not for power, but to pull it down. I seek not for honor of the world, but for the glory of my God, and the freedom and welfare of my country. And thus I close mine epistle. (*Moroni complains to Pahoran of the government's neglect of the armies, about 62 B.C.*) Alma 60:36

### President Heber J. Grant, J. Reuben Clark, Jr., David O. McKay
(First Presidency)

That sin [of war], as Moroni of old said, is to the condemnation of those who "sit in their places of power in a state of thoughtless stupor," those rulers in the world who in a frenzy of hate and lust for unrighteous power and dominion over their fellow men, have put into motion eternal forces they do not comprehend and cannot control. God, in His own due time, will pass sentence upon them. ¶ "Vengeance is mine; I will repay, saith the Lord." (Rom.12:19) CR1942Apr:95-96

### Russell M. Nelson,
#### also quoting Joseph Smith

Like cutting the cord with clippers, it is possible to use spiritual power so carelessly as to destroy one's very connection to that power. I know a husband who dominates his wife as though she were his possession. . . . And I know a wife who dominates her husband to the point that he has lost all feelings of worth. ¶ Remember, "the rights of the priesthood are inseparably connected with the powers of heaven, and . . . the powers of heaven cannot be controlled nor handled *only* upon the principles of righteousness." (D&C 121:36; italics added by RMN) ¶ The unrighteous use of priesthood authority surely severs the connection to the Source of that authority. (See D&C 121:37.) CR1984Oct:40

### James E. Faust

As direction is given in the Church and in our homes, there should be no spirit of dictatorship and no *unrighteous dominion,* CR1983Apr:59

### Gordon B. Hinckley

There [should] never be in [the] home any "unrighteous dominion" of husband over wife (see D&C 121:37,39), no assertion of superiority, but rather an expression in living which says that these two are equally yoked. ¶ No man can please his Heavenly Father who fails to respect the daughters of God. No man can please his Heavenly Father who fails to magnify his wife and companion, and nurture and build and strengthen and share with her. CR1985Apr:65; DGSM:80

**Related Witnesses:**

#### President Ezra Taft Benson

Arguments, fights, unrighteous dominion, generation gaps, divorces, spouse abuse, riots, and disturbances all fall into this category of pride. CR1989Apr:5

### President Brigham Young,
#### quoted by John A. Widtsoe

Thrust a man into prison and bind him with chains, and then let him be filled with the comfort and with the glory of eternity, and that prison is a palace to him. Again, let a man be seated upon a throne with power and dominion in this world, ruling his millions and millions and without that peace which flows from the Lord of Hosts—without that contentment and joy that come from heaven, his palace is a prison; his life is a burden to him; he lives in fear, in dread, and in sorrow. But when a person is filled with the peace and power of God,

all is right with him. (*In Bowery, July 5, 1857, JD5:1-2*) DBY:33

#### Recorded in Luke

And the devil, taking him up into an high mountain, shewed unto him all the kingdoms of the world in a moment of time. 6. And the devil said unto him, All this power will I give thee, and the glory of them: for that is delivered unto me; and to whomsoever I will I give it. 7. If thou therefore wilt worship me, all shall be thine. 8. And Jesus answered and said unto him, Get thee behind me, Satan: for it is written, Thou shalt worship the Lord thy God, and him only shalt thou serve. (*The devil tempts Jesus*) Luke 4:5-8

---

## (8) Worshipping False Gods

**787.** We are not to worship any other being but God.

### Joseph Smith

And gave unto them commandments that they should love and serve him, the only living and true God, and that he should be the only being whom they should worship. (*Revelation on Church Organization and Government, April 1830*) D&C 20:19

#### Recorded in Exodus

I am the LORD thy God, which have brought thee out of the land of Egypt, out of the house of bondage. 3. Thou shalt have no other gods before me. (*The Lord reveals the first of the Ten Commandments to Moses*) Ex.20:2-3

#### Recorded in Exodus

For thou shalt worship no other god: for the LORD, whose name is Jealous, is a jealous God: (*The Lord commands Moses for Israel*) Ex.34:14

### Alma, the younger,
#### quoted by Mormon

But behold, I trust that ye are not in a state of so much unbelief as were your brethren; I trust that ye are not lifted up in the pride of your hearts; yea, I trust that ye have not set your hearts upon riches and the vain things of the world; yea, I trust that you do not worship idols, but that ye do worship the true and living God, and that ye look forward for the remission of your sins, with an everlasting faith, which is to come. (*Alma to the people in Gideon, about 83 B.C.*) Alma 7:6

#### Recorded in Deuteronomy

And it shall be, if thou do at all forget the LORD thy God, and walk after other gods, and serve them, and worship them, I testify against you this day that ye shall surely perish. 20. As the nations which the LORD destroyeth before your face, so shall ye perish; because ye would not be obedient unto the voice of the LORD your God. (*Revelation to Moses for the children of Israel*) Deut.8:19-20

**Related Witnesses:**

**Bruce R. McConkie**

True and saving worship is found only among those who know the truth about God and the Godhead and who understand the true relationship men should have with each member of that Eternal Presidency. ¶ It follows that the devil would rather spread false doctrine about God and the Godhead, and induce false feelings with reverence to any one of them, than almost any other thing he could do. The creeds of Christendom illustrate perfectly what Lucifer wants so-called Christian people to believe about Deity in order to be damned. ("Our Relationship with the Lord," Brigham Young University Speeches of the Year, 1981-82, p. 97) TLDP:751

**Jesus,**
*recorded in Matthew*

Again, the devil taketh him up into an exceeding high mountain, and sheweth him all the kingdoms of the world, and the glory of them; 9. And saith unto him, All these things will I give thee, if thou wilt fall down and worship me. 10. Then saith Jesus unto him, Get thee hence, Satan: for it is written, Thou shalt worship the Lord thy God, and him only shalt thou serve. (*The devil tempts Jesus*) Matt.4:8-10

---

788. Whatever we set our hearts and our trust in most becomes, in a sense, our god; if our god is not the true and living God of Israel, we are laboring in idolatry.

**President Spencer W. Kimball**

Few men have ever knowingly and deliberately chosen to reject God and his blessings. Rather, we learn from the scriptures that because the exercise of faith has always appeared to be more difficult than relying on things more immediately at hand, carnal man has tended to transfer his trust in God to material things. Therefore, in all ages when men have fallen under the power of Satan and lost the faith, they have put in its place a hope in the "arm of flesh" and in "gods of silver, and gold, of brass, iron, wood, and stone, which see not, nor hear, nor know" (Dan.5:23)—that is, in idols. . . . Whatever thing a man sets his heart and his trust in most is his god; and if his god doesn't

also happen to be the true and living God of Israel that man is laboring in idolatry. ("The False Gods We Worship;" EN1976Jun:4) DCCH:6

**Elder Spencer W. Kimball**

Modern idols or false gods can take such forms as clothes, homes, businesses, machines, automobiles, pleasure boats, and numerous other material deflectors from the path to godhood. What difference does it make that the item concerned is not shaped like an idol? Brigham Young said: "I would as soon see a man worshipping a little god made of brass or of wood as to see him worshipping his property." ¶ Intangible things make just as ready gods. Degrees and letters and titles can become idols. Many young men decide to attend college when they should be on missions first. The degree, and the wealth and the security which come through it, appear so desirable that the mission takes second place. Some neglect Church service through their college years, feeling to give preference to the secular training and ignoring the spiritual covenants they have made. ¶ Many people build and furnish a home and buy the automobile first—and then find they "cannot afford" to pay tithing. Whom do they worship? Certainly not the Lord of heaven and earth, for we serve whom we love and give first consideration to the object of our affection and desires. Young married couples who postpone parenthood until their degrees are attained might be shocked if their expressed preference were labeled idolatry. (Miracle of Forgiveness, pp. 40-41) DCSM:4-5

**James E. Talmage**

The great trouble with the world today, as I understand it, is that it has become idolatrous. We read of idolatry and think of it as a practice or series of practices in the past. This is an idolatrous generation, defying the commandment written by the finger of God—"Thou shalt have no other Gods before me." . . . Men are praising the gods of silver and of gold and of all the other valuable commodities that make up wealth, and the God in whose hand their breath is . . . they will not recognize. Do you wonder that wickedness and crime have increased to terrifying proportions under those conditions? The prophets of old foresaw it. They spoke of the days of wickedness and vengeance immediately precedent to the second coming of the Lord. . . . ¶ . . . . Are we worshipping the true and living God, or are we going idolatrously after the gods of gold and silver, of iron and wood, and brass, diamonds and other idols of wealth? Are we worshipping our farms, our cattle and sheep? Who is our God? To whom are we yielding homage, allegiance and worship? Not worship by means of words only, in ritualistic form, but worship in action, devotion, and sacrificial service? CR1930Oct:71,73

### Bruce R. McConkie

Fornication, adultery, and whoredoms, these are the terms the prophets use to describe the false worship, the devil's way of worship, the worship that is not of God. They are the most grievous of all sins save murder only, and they are used to denote the most degenerate of all states that can befall man save only his death and destruction, and that state is to worship false gods and thereby be cut off from any hope of salvation. . . . ¶ False worship brings damnation. (The Millennial Messiah, p. 435) TLDP:751

**Related Witnesses:**

### Joseph Smith

They seek not the Lord to establish his righteousness, but every man walketh in his own way, and after the image of his own God, whose image is in the likeness of the world, and whose substance is that of an idol, which waxeth old and shall perish in Babylon, even Babylon the great, which shall fall. (Revelation received during conference of elders of the Church, Nov. 1, 1831) D&C 1:16

### Daniel

But hast lifted up thyself against the LORD of heaven; and they have brought the vessels of his house before thee, and thou, and thy lords, thy wives, and thy concubines, have drunk wine in them; and thou hast praised the gods of silver, and gold, of brass, iron, wood, and stone, which see not, nor hear, nor know: and the God in whose hand thy breath is, and whose are all thy ways, hast thou not glorified: (Daniel reproves King Belshazzar for pride and idolatry) Dan.5:23

### Nephi, son of Lehi

O Lord, I have trusted in thee, and I will trust in thee forever. I will not put my trust in the arm of flesh; for I know that cursed is he that putteth his trust in the arm of flesh. Yea, cursed is he that putteth his trust in man or maketh flesh his arm. (Nephi writes on plates shortly after the death of his father Lehi, 588-570 B.C.) 2Ne.4:34

## 789. We are not to worship idols.

### Jacob, brother of Nephi,
#### quoted by Nephi

Yea, wo unto those that worship idols, for the devil of all devils delighteth in them. (Jacob to the people of Nephi, 559-545 B.C.) 2Ne.9:37

### Recorded in Exodus

Thou shalt not make unto thee any graven image, or any likeness of any thing that is in heaven above, or that is in the earth beneath, or that is in the water under the earth: 5. Thou shalt not bow down thyself to them, nor serve them: for I the LORD thy God am a jealous God, visiting the iniquity of the fathers upon the children unto the third and fourth generation of them that hate me; 6. And shewing mercy unto thousands of them that love me, and keep my commandments. (The Lord reveals the second of the Ten Commandments to Moses) Ex.20:4-6

### Recorded in Deuteronomy

When thou shalt beget children, and children's children, and ye shall have remained long in the land, and shall corrupt yourselves, and make a graven image, or the likeness of any thing, and shall do evil in the sight of the LORD thy God, to provoke him to anger: 26. I call heaven and earth to witness against you this day, that ye shall soon utterly perish from off the land whereunto ye go over Jordan to possess it; ye shall not prolong your days upon it, but shall utterly be destroyed. (Moses to the children of Israel) Deut.4:25-26

### Paul

Wherefore, my dearly beloved, flee from idolatry. (Letter to the Church at Corinth, Greece, about A.D. 55) 1Cor.10:14

### Recorded in Leviticus

Turn ye not unto idols, nor make to yourselves molten gods: I am the LORD your God. (Revelation to Moses) Lev.19:4

**Related Witnesses:**

### Recorded in Judges

And the children of Israel did evil in the sight of the LORD, and served Baalim: 12. And they forsook the LORD God of their fathers, which brought them out of the land of Egypt, and followed other gods, of the gods of the people that were round about them, and bowed themselves unto them, and provoked the LORD to anger. (The children of Israel after the death of Joshua) Judg.2:11-12

### Recorded in Deuteronomy

They provoked him to jealousy with strange gods, with abominations provoked they him to anger. 17. They sacrificed unto devils, not to God; to gods whom they knew not, to new gods that came newly up, whom your fathers feared not. (Moses to the children of Israel) Deut.32:16-17

### Recorded in 1 Chronicles

For great is the LORD, and greatly to be praised: he also is to be feared above all gods.

26. For all the gods of the people are idols: but the LORD made the heavens. (*David delivers a psalm of thanksgiving*) 1Chr.16:25-26

### Recorded in 2 Chronicles

And when he had broken down the altars and the groves, and had beaten the graven images into powder, and cut down all the idols throughout all the land of Israel, he returned to Jerusalem. (*Josiah, son of David, reigns in righteousness*) 2Chr.34:7

### Paul

As concerning therefore the eating of those things that are offered in sacrifice unto idols, we know that an idol is nothing in the world, and that there is none other God but one. 5. For though there be that are called gods, whether in heaven or in earth, (as there be gods many, and lords many,) 6. But to us there is but one God, the Father, of whom are all things, and we in him; and one Lord Jesus Christ, by whom are all things, and we by him. (*Letter to the Church at Corinth, Greece, about A.D. 55*) 1Cor.8:4-6

### John

And the rest of the men which were not killed by these plagues yet repented not of the works of their hands, that they should not worship devils, and idols of gold, and silver, and brass, and stone, and of wood: which neither can see, nor hear, nor walk: (*John sees the wars and plagues before the Lord comes*) Rev.9:20

# List of Doctrines

## SONS OF PERDITION

*Doctrines Located in This Topic*

790. Those who have received the Holy Ghost, had the heavens opened unto them and know God, who thereafter deny the Holy Ghost and sin against God, become sons of perdition and their sin shall have no forgiveness.

791. Satan is called Perdition.

792. Those in mortality who sink to the level of perdition (and the premortal hosts of heaven who followed Satan) are sons of perdition.

793. Sons of perdition will suffer the wrath of God and partake of the second death.

794. Those who become sons of perdition after having lived in mortality will be resurrected, but they will not be received into a kingdom of glory.

795. Only those who become sons of perdition will be able to comprehend the magnitude of their misery.

*Doctrines on SONS OF PERDITION Located in Other Topics*

315. Perdition is a permanent place of hell where there is no forgiveness and no redemption.

# SONS OF PERDITION

790. Those who have received the Holy Ghost, had the heavens opened unto them and know God, who thereafter deny the Holy Ghost and sin against God, become sons of perdition and their sin shall have no forgiveness.

## Joseph Smith

All sins shall be forgiven, except the sin against the Holy Ghost; for Jesus will save all except the sons of perdition. What must a man do to commit the unpardonable sin? He must receive the Holy Ghost, have the heavens opened unto him, and know God, and then sin against him. After a man has sinned against the Holy Ghost, there is no repentance for him. He has got to say that the sun does not shine while he sees it; he has got to deny Jesus Christ when the heavens have been opened unto him, and to deny the plan of salvation with his eyes open to the truth of it; and from that time he begins to be an enemy. This is the case with many apostates of the Church of Jesus Christ of Latter-day Saints. (*To the Church in general conference—to a congregation of 20,000—"King Follett Sermon," April 7, 1844*) (See HC6:302-17, also see The Words of Joseph Smith, pp. 340-62) HC6:314; DGSM:93

## Joseph Smith,
*receiving the Word of the Lord*

Thus saith the Lord concerning all those who know my power, and have been made partakers thereof, and suffered themselves through the power of the devil to be overcome, and to deny the truth and defy my power— 32. They are they who are the sons of perdition, of whom I say that it had been better for them never to have been born; 33. For they are vessels of wrath, doomed to suffer the wrath of God, with the devil and his angels in eternity; 34. Concerning whom I have said there is no forgiveness in this world nor in the world to come— 35. Having denied the Holy Spirit after having received it, and having denied the Only Begotten Son of the Father, having crucified him unto themselves and put him to an open shame. 36. These are they who shall go away into the lake of fire and brimstone, with the devil and his angels— (*Vision to Joseph Smith and Sidney Rigdon, Feb. 16, 1832*) D&C 76:31-36

## President Brigham Young

How much does it take to prepare a man, or woman, or any being, to become angels to the devil, to suffer with him to all eternity? Just as much as it does to prepare a man to go into the celestial kingdom, into the presence of the Father and the Son, and to be made an heir to His Kingdom, and all His glory, and be crowned with crowns of glory, immortality, and eternal lives. Now who will be damned to all eternity? Will any of the rest of mankind? No; not one of them. (*In Tabernacle, Aug. 8, 1852, JD3:93*) TLDP:634

## Jesus,
*recorded in Matthew*

Wherefore I say unto you, All manner of sin and blasphemy shall be forgiven unto men: but the blasphemy against the Holy Ghost shall not be forgiven unto men. 32. And whosoever speaketh a word against the Son of man, it shall be forgiven him: but whosoever speaketh against the Holy Ghost, it shall not be forgiven him, neither in this world, neither in the world to come. (*Jesus speaks to the people about blasphemy against the Holy Ghost*) Matt.12:31-32

## Charles W. Penrose

The "sons of perdition" are those who have received the Gospel, those to whom the Father has revealed the Son; those who know something concerning the plan of salvation; those who have had keys placed in their hands by which they could unlock the mysteries of eternity; those who received power to ascend to the highest pinnacle of the celestial glory; those who received power sufficient to overcome all things, and who, instead of using it for their own salvation, and in the interest of the salvation of others, prostituted that power and turned away from that which they knew to be true, denying the Son of God and putting Him to an open shame. All such live in the spirit of error, and they love it and roll it under the tongue as a sweet morsel; they are governed by Satan, becoming servants to him whom they list to obey, they become the sons of perdition, doomed to suffer the wrath of God reserved for the devil and his angels. (*In Assembly Hall, March 4, 1883, JD24:93*) TLDP:634

## James E. Talmage

Consider the word of the Lord regarding those whose sin is the unpardonable one, whose transgression has carried them beyond the present horizon of possible redemption; those who have sunk so low in their wickedness as to have lost the power and even the desire to attempt reformation. Sons of Perdition they are called. These are they who, having learned the power of God afterward renounce it; those who sin wilfully in the light of knowledge; those who open their hearts to the Holy Spirit and then put the Lord to a mockery and a shame by denying it; and those who commit murder wherein they shed innocent blood; these are they of whom the Savior has declared that it would be better for them had they never been born. These are to share the punishment of the devil and his angels—punishment so terrible that the knowledge is withheld from all except those who are consigned to this doom, though a temporary view of the picture is permitted to some. These sinners are the only ones over whom the second death hath power: "Yea, verily, the only ones who shall not be redeemed in the due time of the Lord." AF:54-55

### Elder Joseph Fielding Smith

[Hell is] a place where those who cannot be redeemed and who are called sons of Perdition will go into outer darkness. This is the real hell where those who once knew the truth and had the testimony of it and then turned away and blasphemed the name of Jesus Christ, will go. These are they who have sinned against the Holy Ghost. For them there is no forgiveness, and the Lord said he had prepared a place for them. (Answers to Gospel Questions, 2:210) TLDP:127

### Elder Joseph Fielding Smith

[I]t is only those who have the light through the priesthood and through the power of God and through their membership in the Church who will be banished forever from his influence into outer darkness to dwell with the devil and his angels. That is a punishment that will not come to those who have never known the truth. Bad as they may suffer, and awful as their punishment may be, they are not among that group which is to suffer the eternal death and banishment from all influence concerning the power of God. CR1958Oct:21

### Stephen L. Richards

It is a tremendous responsibility to bear the Holy Priesthood. I wish all of you—perhaps all did not—had heard what President Joseph Fielding Smith told us yesterday, something I have long believed, and I was glad to have sanction for my belief. He said in substance that there will be no Sons of Perdition who do not hold the Priesthood. I have believed that for years because I do not think that the Lord in his mercy would ever condemn a man to that indescribable penalty of being put out entirely from the Kingdom and from all grace unless that man knew that Jesus was the Christ, unless he knew the power of the Christ, and he could only know that, I think by holding the Priesthood. I believe that in the main that can be said to be true—that only men who hold the Priesthood of God stand in danger of that terrible penalty of being classed as outcasts. CR1958Oct:86

### Related Witnesses:
### Elder Spencer W. Kimball

The sin against the Holy Ghost requires such knowledge that it is manifestly impossible for the rank and file to commit such a sin. Comparatively few Church members will commit murder wherein they shed innocent blood, and we hope only few will deny the Holy Ghost. (The Teachings of Spencer W. Kimball, p. 23) TLDP:635

### Joseph Smith

[O]ur Savior says, that all manner of sin and blasphemy shall be forgiven men wherewith they shall blaspheme; but the blasphemy against the Holy Ghost shall not be forgiven, neither in this world, nor in the world to come, evidently showing that there are sins which may be forgiven in the world to come, although the sin of blasphemy [against the Holy Ghost] cannot be forgiven. (Editorial in "Times and Seasons," April 15, 1842) HC4:596

### Paul

For it is impossible for those who were once enlightened, and have tasted of the heavenly gift, and were made partakers of the Holy Ghost, 5. And have tasted the good word of God, and the powers of the world to come, 6. If they shall fall away, to renew them again unto repentance; seeing they crucify to themselves the Son of God afresh, and put him to an open shame. (*Paul writes to the Jewish members of the Church, about A.D. 60*) Heb.6:4-6

### Paul

For if we sin wilfully after that we have received the knowledge of the truth, there remaineth no more sacrifice for sins, 27. But a certain fearful looking for of judgment and fiery indignation, which shall devour the adversaries. (*Letter to the Jewish members of the Church, about A.D. 60*) Heb.10:26-27

### Joseph Smith

No man can commit the unpardonable sin after the dissolution of the body, not in this life, until he receives the Holy Ghost but they must do it in this world. (*To the Church in general conference—to a congregation of 20,000—"King Follett Sermon," April 7, 1844*) (See HC6:302-17, also see The Words of Joseph Smith, pp. 340-62) HC6:314; TPJS:357

---

### 791. Satan is called Perdition.

### Joseph Smith

And this we saw also, and bear record, that an angel of God who was in authority in the presence of God, who rebelled against the Only

Begotten Son whom the Father loved and who was in the bosom of the Father, was thrust down from the presence of God and the Son, 26. And was called Perdition, for the heavens wept over him—he was Lucifer, a son of the morning. 27. And we beheld, and lo, he is fallen! is fallen, even a son of the morning! 28. And while we were yet in the Spirit, the Lord commanded us that we should write the vision; for we beheld Satan, that old serpent, even the devil, who rebelled against God, and sought to take the kingdom of our God and his Christ— 29. Wherefore, he maketh war with the saints of God, and encompasseth them round about. 30. And we saw a vision of the sufferings of those with whom he made war and overcame, for thus came the voice of the Lord unto us: 31. Thus saith the Lord concerning all those who know my power, and have been made partakers thereof, and suffered themselves through the power of the devil to be overcome, and to deny the truth and defy my power— 32. They are they who are the sons of perdition, of whom I say that it had been better for them never to have been born; (*Vision to Joseph Smith and Sidney Rigdon, Feb. 16, 1832*) D&C 76:25-32

**James E. Talmage**

We learn of another class of souls whose sins are such as to place them beyond the present possibility of repentance and salvation. These are called sons of Perdition, children of the fallen angel who was once a Son of the Morning, Lucifer, now Satan, or Perdition. AF:371-72

---

792. **Those in mortality who sink to the level of perdition (and the premortal hosts of heaven who followed Satan) are sons of perdition.**

**James E. Talmage,**
*also quoting Joseph Smith*

The Sons of Perdition—We learn of another class of souls whose sins are such as to place them beyond the present possibility of repentance and salvation. These are called sons of Perdition, children of the fallen angel who was once a Son of the Morning, Lucifer, now Satan, or Perdition. These are they who have violated truth in the light of knowledge; who, having received the testimony of Christ, and having been endowed by the Holy Spirit, then deny the same and defy the power of God, crucifying the Lord afresh and putting Him to an open shame. This, the unpardonable sin, can be committed by those only who have received knowledge

and conviction of the truth, against which they then rebel. Their sin is comparable to the treason of Lucifer, by which he sought to usurp the power and glory of his God. Concerning them and their dreadful fate, the Lord has said: "They are they who are the sons of perdition, of whom I say that it had been better for them never to have been born; For they are vessels of wrath, doomed to suffer the wrath of God, with the devil and his angels in eternity; Concerning whom I have said there is no forgiveness in this world nor in the world to come. . . . And the only ones on whom the second death shall have any power; . . . they shall go away into everlasting punishment, which is endless punishment, which is eternal punishment, to reign with the devil and his angels in eternity, where their worm dieth not, and the fire is not quenched, which is their torment—And the end thereof, neither the place thereof, nor their torment, no man knows; Neither was it revealed, neither is, neither will be revealed unto man, except to them who are made partakers thereof; Nevertheless I, the Lord, show it by vision unto many, but straightway shut it up again; Wherefore, the end, the width, the height, the depth, and the misery thereof, they understand not, neither any man except those who are ordained unto this condemnation." [D&C 76:31-48] AF:371-72

**Joseph Smith**

Who glorifies the Father, and saves all the works of his hands, except those sons of perdition who deny the Son after the Father has revealed him. 44. Wherefore, he saves all except them—they shall go away into everlasting punishment, which is endless punishment, which is eternal punishment, to reign with the devil and his angels in eternity, where their worm dieth not, and the fire is not quenched, which is their torment— (*Vision to Joseph Smith and Sidney Rigdon, Feb. 16, 1832*) D&C 76:43-44

**Charles W. Penrose**

The "sons of perdition" are those who have received the Gospel, those to whom the Father has revealed the Son; those who know something concerning the plan of salvation; those who have had keys placed in their hands by which they could unlock the mysteries of eternity; those who received power to ascend to the highest pinnacle of the celestial glory; those who received power sufficient to overcome all things, and who, instead of using it for their own salvation, and in the interest of the salvation of others, prostituted that power and turned away from that which they knew to be true, denying the Son of God and putting Him to an open shame. All such live in the spirit of error, and they love it and roll it under the tongue as a sweet morsel; they are governed by Satan, becoming servants to him in whom they list to obey, they become the sons of perdition, doomed to suffer the wrath of God reserved for the devil and his angels. (*In Assembly Hall, March 4, 1883, JD24:93*) TLDP:634

### Joseph Smith,
*receiving the Word of the Lord*

Thus saith the Lord concerning all those who know my power, and have been made partakers thereof, and suffered themselves through the power of the devil to be overcome, and to deny the truth and defy my power— 32. They are they who are the sons of perdition, of whom I say that it had been better for them never to have been born; (*Vision to Joseph Smith and Sidney Rigdon, Feb. 16, 1832*) D&C 76:31-32

**Related Witnesses:**

### Elder Spencer W. Kimball

In the realms of perdition or the kingdom of darkness, where there is no light, Satan and the unembodied spirits of the pre-existence shall dwell together with those of mortality who retrogress to the level of perdition. These have sunk so low as to have lost the inclinations and ability to repent, consequently the gospel plan is useless to them as an agent of growth and development. (The Miracle of Forgiveness, p. 125) DGSM:93

### President Brigham Young,
*quoted by John A. Widtsoe*

Jesus will redeem the last and least of the sons of Adam, except the sons of perdition, who will be held in reserve for another time. They will become angels of the Devil. (*In Bowery, Aug. 26, 1860, JD8:154*) DBY:29

### Joseph Smith,
*receiving the Word of the Lord*

And it came to pass that Adam, being tempted of the devil—for, behold, the devil was before Adam, for he rebelled against me, saying, Give me thine honor, which is my power; and also a third part of the hosts of heaven turned he away from me because of their agency; 37. And they were thrust down, and thus came the devil and his angels; 38. And, behold, there is a place prepared for them from the beginning, which place is hell. (*Revelation, Sept. 1830*) D&C 29:36-38

### John

And there was war in heaven: Michael and his angels fought against the dragon; and the dragon fought and his angels, 8. And prevailed not; neither was their place found any more in heaven. 9. And the great dragon was cast out, that old serpent, called the Devil, and Satan, which deceiveth the whole world: he was cast out into the earth, and his angels were cast out with him. (*The Apostle John sees the War in Heaven*) Rev.12:7-9

### Peter

For if God spared not the angels that sinned, but cast them down to hell, and delivered them into chains of darkness, to be reserved unto judgment; (*Peter writes to members of the Church, about A.D. 60-64*) 2Pet.2:4

### Recorded in Jude

And the angels which kept not their first estate, but left their own habitation, he hath reserved in everlasting chains under darkness unto the judgment of the great day. (*Letter of Jude, brother of James*) Jude 1:6

---

**793.** Sons of perdition will suffer the wrath of God and partake of the Second Death.

### Joseph Smith,
*quoted by Elder Joseph Fielding Smith*

There have been remarks made concerning all men being redeemed from hell; but I say that those who sin against the Holy Ghost cannot be forgiven in this world or in the world to come; they shall die the second death. Those who commit the unpardonable sin are doomed to Gnolom—to dwell in hell, worlds without end. As they concoct scenes of bloodshed in this world, so they shall rise to that resurrection which is as the lake of fire and brimstone. Some shall rise to the everlasting burnings of God; for God dwells in everlasting burnings, and some shall rise to the damnation of their own filthiness, which is as exquisite a torment as the lake of fire and brimstone. (*To the Church in general conference—to a congregation of 20,000—"King Follett Sermon," April 7, 1844*) (See HC6:302-17, also see The Words of Joseph Smith, pp. 340-62.) TPJS:361

### George Q. Cannon

A careful reading of these verses [D&C 76:38-39], however, and especially of the preceding paragraphs, will show that the Lord does not, in this language, exclude even the sons of perdition from the resurrection. It is plain that the intention is to refer to them explicitly as the only ones on whom the second death shall have any power: "for *all the rest* shall be brought forth by the resurrection of the dead, through the triumph and the glory of the Lamb." This excluded class are the only ones on whom the second death shall have any power, and "the only ones who shall not be redeemed in the due time of the Lord after the sufferings of his wrath." ("The Resurrection As Affecting the Sons of Perdition," Juvenile Instructor, Feb. 15, 1900, p. 123) TLDP:635-36

**James E. Talmage**

Consider the word of the Lord regarding those whose sin is the unpardonable one. . . . These are to share the punishment of the devil and his angels—punishment so terrible that the knowledge is withheld from all except those who are consigned to this doom, though a temporary view of the picture is permitted to some. These sinners are the only ones over whom the second death hath power: "Yea, verily, the only ones who shall not be redeemed in the due time of the Lord." AF:54-55

**Joseph Smith**

For they [the sons of perdition] are vessels of wrath, doomed to suffer the wrath of God, with the devil and his angels in eternity. . . . 37. And the only ones on whom the second death shall have any power; 38. Yea, verily, the only ones who shall not be redeemed in the due time of the Lord, after the sufferings of his wrath. (*Vision to Joseph Smith and Sidney Rigdon, Feb. 16, 1832*) D&C 76:33,37-38

**Related Witnesses:**

**President Brigham Young**

What is that we call death, compared to the agonies of the second death? If people could see it, as Joseph and Sidney saw it, they would pray that the vision be closed up; for they could not endure the sight. (*At Logan, Utah, Aug. 15, 1876, JD18:217*) TLDP:647

**Elder Joseph Fielding Smith**

As all things have their opposites, there is a punishment which is the opposite to eternal life, which punishment is the "heaviest of all cursings." [See D&C 41:1.] This is the second or spiritual death, which is banishment from the presence of God and from his light and truth forever. (Doctrines of Salvation, 2:218) TLDP:647

**Marion G. Romney**

Spiritual death means banishment from God. It was the first death which passed upon Adam. It will be the last death to pass upon the still unrepentant at the days of final judgment. It is infinitely more far-reaching and terrible than physical death. . . . (Look to God and Live, p. 90) TLDP:646

**Joseph Smith,**
*receiving the Word of the Lord*

Hearken and hear, O ye my people, saith the Lord and your God, ye whom I delight to bless with the greatest of all blessings, ye that hear me; and ye that hear me not will I curse, that

have professed my name, with the heaviest of all cursings. (*Revelation received Feb. 4, 1831*) D&C 41:1

**Charles W. Penrose**

"Well, now," say some persons, "won't they [the sons of perdition] be redeemed some time? How do you know?" Why the Lord does not tell you and He says He will not do it. He says it is not revealed; the height and depth and the extent and the end thereof is not revealed, so do not try to find out for yourselves, without the Lord reveals something about it; and if He does He will not reveal it to you or me for the Church, but will reveal it to us, if at all, for our own enlightenment. CR1922Apr:31

---

**794. Those who become sons of perdition after having lived in mortality will be resurrected, but they will not be received into a kingdom of glory.**

**George Q. Cannon**

In many minds there has been a great misapprehension on the question of the resurrection. Some have had the idea, and have taught it, that the sons of perdition will not be resurrected at all. They base this idea, and draw this conclusion, from the 38th and 39th paragraphs of section 76 of the book of Doctrine and Covenants. . . . ¶ A careful reading of these verses [D&C 76:38-39], however, and especially of the preceding paragraphs, will show that the Lord does not, in this language, exclude even the sons of perdition from the resurrection. It is plain that the intention is to refer to them explicitly as the only ones on whom the second death shall have any power: "for *all the rest* shall be brought forth by the resurrection of the dead, through the triumph and the glory of the Lamb." This excluded class are the only ones on whom the second death shall have any power, and "the only ones who shall not be redeemed in the due time of the Lord after the sufferings of his wrath." ¶ This is by no means to say that they are to have no resurrection. Jesus our Lord and Savior died for all, and all will be resurrected. ("The Resurrection As Affecting the Sons of Perdition," Juvenile Instructor, Feb. 15, 1900, p. 123) TLDP:635-36

**Joseph Smith**

And he who cannot abide the law of a telestial kingdom cannot abide a telestial glory; therefore he is not meet for a kingdom of glory. Therefore he must abide a kingdom which is not a kingdom of glory. . . . 32. And they who remain shall also be quickened; nevertheless, they shall return again to their own place, to enjoy that which they are willing to receive, because they were not willing to enjoy that which they might have received. (*Revelation, Dec. 27/28, 1832; obedience to celestial, terrestrial, or telestial law prepares men for those respective kingdoms and glories*) D&C 88:24,32

**Joseph Smith**

Who glorifies the Father, and saves all the works of his hands, except those sons of perdition who deny the Son after the Father has revealed him. 44. Wherefore, he saves all except them—they shall go away into everlasting punishment, which is endless punishment, which is eternal punishment, to reign with the devil and his angels in eternity, where their worm dieth not, and the fire is not quenched, which is their torment— (*Vision to Joseph Smith and Sidney Rigdon, Feb. 16, 1832*) D&C 76:43-44

**Related Witnesses:**

**Recorded in Jude**

And the angels which kept not their first estate, but left their own habitation, he hath reserved in everlasting chains under darkness unto the judgment of the great day. (*Letter of Jude, brother of James*) Jude 1:6

**Elder Joseph F. Smith**

Every creature that is born in the image of God will be resurrected from the dead. . . . But just as sure as we go down into the grave, through the transgression of our first parents, by whom death came into the world, so sure will we be resurrected from the dead by the power of Jesus Christ. It matters not whether we have done well or ill, whether we have been intelligent or ignorant, or whether we have been bondsmen or slaves or freemen, all men will be raised from the dead. (Millennial Star, March 1896, p. 162) DGSM:88

**Author's Note:** However, the devil and his angels who rebelled in the premortal existence obtained no body, were not born on the earth and will never receive a resurrection. ¶ The phrase "save all except the sons of perdition," [DGSM:93] and "saves all the works of his hands, except those sons of perdition" (D&C 76:43) refers, I believe, to "saving from sin," as opposed to saving from the death of the body. Likewise, the phrase "the only ones who shall not be redeemed in the due time of the Lord," [D&C 76:38] must refer to redemption from sin, not redemption from death. James E. Talmage writes: "Yet all who receive of any one of these orders of glory [the telestial, terrestrial and celestial kingdoms] are at last saved,

and upon them Satan will finally have no claim." (See AF:84.) Hence the statement by Joseph F. Smith: "Every creature that is born in the image of God will be resurrected from the dead. . . . But just as sure as we go down into the grave, through the transgression of our first parents, by whom death came into the world, so sure will we be resurrected from the dead by the power of Jesus Christ. It matters not whether we have done well or ill, whether we have been intelligent or ignorant, or whether we have been bondsmen or slaves or freemen, all men will be raised from the dead." (Millennial Star, March 1896, p. 162) (DGSM:88)

**795. Only those who become sons of perdition will be able to comprehend the magnitude of their misery.**

**Elder Joseph Fielding Smith**

The extent of this punishment none will ever know except those who partake of it. That it is the most severe punishment that can be meted out to man is apparent. Outer darkness is something which cannot be described, except that we know that it is to be placed beyond the benign and comforting influence of the Spirit of God—banished entirely from his presence. ¶ This extreme punishment will not be given to any but the sons of perdition. Even the wicked of the earth who never knew the power of God, after they have paid the price of their sinning— for they must suffer the excruciating torment which sin will bring—shall at last come forth from the prison house, repentant and willing to bow the knee and acknowledge Christ, to receive some influence of the Spirit of God in the telestial kingdom. . . . ¶ With the sons of perdition, however, even this blessing is denied. They have wilfully made themselves servants of Satan and servants to him shall they remain forever. They place themselves beyond the power of repentance and beyond the mercies of God. (Doctrines of Salvation, 2:220-21) TLDP:636

**Joseph Smith**

Wherefore, he saves all except them—they shall go away into everlasting punishment, which is endless punishment, which is eternal punishment, to reign with the devil and his angels in eternity, where their worm dieth not, and the fire is not quenched, which is their torment— 45. And the end thereof, neither the place thereof, nor their torment, no man knows; 46. Neither was it revealed, neither is, neither

will be revealed unto man, except to them who
are made partakers thereof; 47. Nevertheless, I,
the Lord, show it by vision unto many, but
straightway shut it up again; 48. Wherefore, the
end, the width, the height, the depth, and the
misery thereof, they understand not, neither any
man except those who are ordained unto this
condemnation. (*Vision to Joseph Smith and
Sidney Rigdon, Feb. 16, 1832*) D&C 76:44-48
**James E. Talmage**
Consider the word of the Lord regarding those
whose sin is the unpardonable one. . . . These
are to share the punishment of the devil and his
angels—punishment so terrible that the knowledge is withheld from all except those who are
consigned to this doom, though a temporary
view of the picture is permitted to some. These
sinners are the only ones over whom the second
death hath power: "Yea, verily, the only ones
who shall not be redeemed in the due time of
the Lord." AF:54-55
**Related Witnesses:**
     **President Brigham Young**
What is that we call death, compared to the
agonies of the second death? If people could
see it, as Joseph and Sidney saw it, they would
pray that the vision be closed up; for they could
not endure the sight. (*At Logan, Utah, Aug. 15,
1876, JD18:217*) TLDP:647

# List of Doctrines

## SPIRITUAL DEATH

*Doctrines Located in This Topic*

796. Because of the Fall of Adam all people were cut off from the presence of the Lord and are considered spiritually dead.

797. There is a second spiritual death wherein the sons of perdition will be banished from the presence of God and from His light forever.

*Doctrines on SPIRITUAL DEATH Located in Other Topics*

47. Redemption from *spiritual death* through Christ's atonement is conditioned obedience to the laws and ordinances of the gospel.

125. Spiritual death is separation from the presence of God.

191. The Fall of Adam brought upon him spiritual death, the condition of being cut off from the presence of the Lord.

759. The final consequence of unrepented sin is spiritual death.

# SPIRITUAL DEATH

**796. Because of the Fall of Adam all people were cut off from the presence of the Lord and are considered spiritually dead.**

### Samuel, the Lamanite,
#### quoted by Mormon

Yea, behold, this death bringeth to pass the resurrection, and redeemeth all mankind from the first death—that spiritual death; for all mankind, by the fall of Adam being cut off from the presence of the Lord, are considered as dead, both as to things temporal and to things spiritual. (*Samuel preaches to the Nephites that Christ, through his death and resurrection, redeems men from temporal and spiritual death, about 6 B.C.*) Hel.14:16

### Bruce R. McConkie

The first death, in point of time, was spiritual. Spiritual death is to die as pertaining to the things of righteousness; it is to be cast out of the presence of the Lord, in which presence spirituality and righteousness abound. Adam died this death when he left Eden, and he remained dead until he was born again by the power of the Spirit following his baptism. ¶ Temporal death is the natural death. It consists of the separation of the body and the spirit, the one going to the grave, the other to a world of waiting spirits to await the day of resurrection. Adam died temporally within a thousand years, which is a day unto the Lord. ¶ Thus the *temporal fall* is to die and lose the house prepared as an habitation for the eternal spirit, and the *spiritual fall* is to be denied the presence of God and the righteousness which there abounds. ¶ "To atone is to ransom, reconcile, expiate, redeem, reclaim, absolve, propitiate, make amends, pay the penalty." (*Mormon Doctrine, 2nd ed., p. 62*) Our Lord's atoning sacrifice was one in which he conquered both temporal and spiritual death. (The Promised Messiah, p. 224) TLDP:647

### Alma, the younger,
#### quoted by Mormon

And now, ye see by this that our first parents were cut off both temporally and spiritually from the presence of the Lord; and thus we see they became subjects to follow after their own will. 8. Now behold, it was not expedient that man should be reclaimed from this temporal death, for that would destroy the great plan of happiness. 9. Therefore, as the soul could never die, and the fall had brought upon all mankind a spiritual death as well as a temporal, that is, they were cut off from the presence of the Lord, it was expedient that mankind should be reclaimed from this spiritual death. 10. Therefore, as they had become carnal, sensual, and devilish, by nature, this probationary state became a state for them to prepare; it became a preparatory state. 11. And now remember, my son, if it were not for the plan of redemption, (laying it aside) as soon as they were dead their souls were miserable, being cut off from the presence of the Lord. (*Alma speaks to his son Corianton, concerning the resurrection of the dead, about 73 B.C.*) Alma 42:7-11

### Marion G. Romney

Spiritual death means banishment from God. It was the first death which passed upon Adam. It will be the last death to pass upon the still unrepentant at the days of final judgment. It is infinitely more far-reaching and terrible than physical death. . . . ¶ Man, being within the grasp of the demands of justice, could not make the required atonement. So far as he was concerned, he was forever bound. By the exercise of his own will, he had incurred the penalty of the broken law, and he could not, by himself alone, remove the penalty. He had to be rescued by someone other than himself or remain forever spiritually dead. ¶ The required atonement had to be made by someone upon whom spiritual death had not passed, someone over whom the demands of justice had no claim. Such a one could be none other than a god—a god who, endowed with free agency, would in mortality submit himself to the temptations of Satan without once yielding thereto in any particular. . . . ¶ It is clear that our ability to repent, as well as the efficacy of our repentance, comes as a gift from the Redeemer. It is one of the fruits of his atonement. This gift men reject at their peril. Unless they exercise it, they remain spiritually dead. . . . For it takes repentance to bring one within reach of the atoning blood of Jesus Christ . . . while he that exercises no faith unto repentance is exposed to the whole law of the demands of justice. (Look to God and Live, pp. 90-92, 99-100) TLDP:646-47

### Elder Joseph F. Smith

. . . I want to speak a word or two in relation to another death, which is a more terrible death than that of the body. When Adam our first parent, partook of the forbidden fruit, transgressed the law of God, and became subject unto Satan, he was banished from the presence of God, and was thrust out into outer spiritual darkness. This was the first death. Yet living, he was dead—dead to God, dead to light and truth, dead spiritually; cast out from the presence of God; communication between the Father and the Son was cut off. He was as absolutely thrust out from the presence of God as was Satan and the hosts that followed him. That was spiritual death. But the Lord said that he would not suffer Adam nor his posterity to come to the temporal death until they should have the means by which they might be redeemed from the first death, which is spiritual. Therefore angels were sent unto Adam, who taught him the gospel, and revealed to him the principle by which he could be redeemed from the first death, and be brought back from banishment and outer darkness into the marvelous light of the gospel. He was taught faith, repentance and baptism for the remission of sins, in the name of Jesus Christ, who should come in the meridian of time and take away the sins of the world, and was thus given a chance to be redeemed from the spiritual death before he should die the temporal death. ¶ Now, all the world today, I am sorry to say, with the exception of a handful of people who have obeyed the new and everlasting covenant, are suffering this spiritual death. They are cast out from the presence of God. They are without God, without gospel truth, and without the power of redemption; for they know not God nor his gospel. In order that they may be redeemed and saved from the spiritual death which has spread over the world like a pall, they must repent of their sins, and be baptized by one having authority, for the remission of their sins, that they may be born of God. CR1899Oct:72

**Joseph Smith,**
*receiving the Word of the Lord*
Wherefore, it came to pass that the devil tempted Adam, and he partook of the forbidden fruit and transgressed the commandment, wherein he became subject to the will of the devil, because he yielded unto temptation. 41. Wherefore, I, the Lord God, caused that he should be cast out from the Garden of Eden, from my presence, because of his transgression, wherein he became spiritually dead, which is the first death, even that same death which is the last death, which is spiritual, which shall be pronounced upon the wicked when I shall say: Depart, ye cursed. 42. But, behold, I say unto you that I, the Lord God, gave unto Adam and unto his seed, that they should not die as to the temporal death, until I, the Lord God, should send forth angels to declare unto them repentance and redemption, through faith in the name of mine Only Begotten Son. 43. And thus did I, the Lord God, appoint unto man the days of his probation—that by his natural death he might be raised in immortality unto eternal life,

even as many as would believe; 44. And they that believe not unto eternal damnation; for they cannot be redeemed from their spiritual fall, because they repent not; 45. For they love darkness rather than light, and their deeds are evil, and they receive their wages of whom they list to obey. (*Revelation received in the presence of six elders, Sept. 1830*) D&C 29:40-45

---

**797. There is a second spiritual death wherein the sons of perdition will be banished from the presence of God and from His light forever.**

**Elder Joseph Fielding Smith**
As all things have their opposites, there is a punishment which is the opposite to eternal life, which punishment is the "heaviest of all cursings." [See D&C 41:1.] This is the second or spiritual death, which is banishment from the presence of God and from his light and truth forever. (Doctrines of Salvation, 2:218) TLDP:647

**Joseph Smith**
For they are vessels of wrath, doomed to suffer the wrath of God, with the devil and his angels in eternity. . . . 37. And the only ones on whom the second death shall have any power; 38. Yea, verily, the only ones who shall not be redeemed in the due time of the Lord, after the sufferings of his wrath. (*Vision to Joseph Smith and Sidney Rigdon, Feb. 16, 1832*) D&C 76:33,37-38

**Marion G. Romney**
Spiritual death means banishment from God. It was the first death which passed upon Adam. It will be the last death to pass upon the still unrepentant at the days of final judgment. It is infinitely more far-reaching and terrible than physical death. . . . (Look to God and Live, p. 90) TLDP:646

**Related Witnesses:**
**Joseph Smith,**
*quoted by Elder Joseph Fielding Smith*
There have been remarks made concerning all men being redeemed from hell; but I say that those who sin against the Holy Ghost cannot be forgiven in this world or in the world to come; they shall die the second death. Those who commit the unpardonable sin are doomed to Gnolom—to dwell in hell, worlds without end. As they concoct scenes of bloodshed in this world, so they shall rise to that resurrection which is as the lake of fire and brimstone. Some shall rise to the everlasting burnings of God; for God dwells in everlasting burnings, and some shall rise to the damnation of their

own filthiness, which is as exquisite a torment as the lake of fire and brimstone. *(To the Church in general conference—to a congregation of 20,000—"King Follett Sermon," April 7, 1844)* (See HC6:302-17, also see The Words of Joseph Smith, pp. 340-62.) TPJS:361

## Joseph Smith,
### *receiving the Word of the Lord*

Hearken and hear, O ye my people, saith the Lord and your God, ye whom I delight to bless with the greatest of all blessings, ye that hear me; and ye that hear me not will I curse, that have professed my name, with the heaviest of all cursings. *(Revelation received Feb. 4, 1831)* D&C 41:1

## George Q. Cannon

A careful reading of these verses [D&C 76:38-39], however, and especially of the preceding paragraphs, will show that the Lord does not, in this language, exclude even the sons of perdition from the resurrection. It is plain that the intention is to refer to them explicitly as the only ones on whom the second death shall have any power: "for *all the rest* shall be brought forth by the resurrection of the dead, through the triumph and the glory of the Lamb." This excluded class are the only ones on whom the second death shall have any power, and "the only ones who shall not be redeemed in the due time of the Lord after the sufferings of his wrath." ("The Resurrection As Affecting the Sons of Perdition," Juvenile Instructor, Feb. 15, 1900, p. 123) TLDP:635-36

## President Brigham Young

What is that we call death, compared to the agonies of the second death? If people could see it, as Joseph and Sidney saw it, they would pray that the vision be closed up; for they could not endure the sight. *(At Logan, Utah, Aug. 15, 1876, JD18:217)* TLDP:647

# List of Doctrines

## SUSTAINING CHURCH LEADERS

*Doctrines Located in This Topic*

798. Church members are to sustain priesthood authorities by following their counsel.

799. Church members are not to speak out against the Lord's anointed leaders.

800. Those who faithfully sustain the Church leaders will be blessed and supported by the Lord and will not be overcome by their enemies.

*Doctrines on SUSTAINING CHURCH LEADERS Located in Other Topics*

666. Revelation from God to each of us as individuals is necessary for our salvation.

670. Individual men and women can receive revelation to guide them within their own spheres of authority (they will not receive divine instructions for those higher in authority than they).

806. All members of the Church are to confine their public interpretations of doctrine to those that are in harmony with the President of the Church.

# SUSTAINING CHURCH LEADERS

**798. Church members are to sustain priesthood authorities by following their counsel.**

### Elder George Albert Smith

The obligation that we make when we raise our hands under such circumstances, is a most sacred one. It does not mean that we will go quietly on our way and be willing that the prophet of the Lord shall direct this work, but it means,—if I understand the obligation I assumed when I raised my hand—that we will stand behind him; we will pray for him; we will defend his good name, and we will strive to carry out his instructions as the Lord shall direct him to offer them to us while he remains in that position. CR1919Apr:40

### Mark E. Petersen

When we sustain our President, we agree to follow his direction. He is the mouthpiece of the Lord for today, and that has great and significant meaning. . . . ¶ As members of the Church, by voting to sustain our new President, we have placed ourselves under a solemn covenant to give diligent heed to the words of eternal life as he gives them to us. CR1974Apr:81

### Elder Harold B. Lee

President Grant used to say to us time and again: "Brethren, keep your eye on the President of this Church. If he tells you to do anything and it is wrong and you do it, the Lord will bless you for it. But you don't need to worry; the Lord will never let his mouthpiece lead this people astray." (*To Brigham Young University studentbody*) (Ye Are the Light of the World, p. 36) TLDP:666

### Marion G. Romney

I have never been very particular to determine when [Church leaders] were speaking as prophets of God and when they were speaking as men. It has never occurred to me that I had the ability to determine that. It has been the rule of my life to find out if I could, by listening closely to what they said and by asking the Lord to help me interpret it, what they had in mind for the Latter-day Saints to do and then do it. I am happy to say, not boastfully but gratefully, that I have never hesitated to follow the counsel of the Authorities of the Church, even though it crossed my social, professional, or political life. I am very grateful now that I may have some opportunity to associate more closely with them. CR1941Apr:123

**Related Witnesses:**

### Jesus,
#### *recorded in Matthew*

He that receiveth you receiveth me, and he that receiveth me receiveth him that sent me. 41. He that receiveth a prophet in the name of a prophet shall receive a prophet's reward; and he that receiveth a righteous man in the name of a righteous man shall receive a righteous man's reward. (*Jesus trains and instructs the Twelve*) Matt.10:40-41

### J. Reuben Clark, Jr.

In the service of the Lord, it is not where you serve but how. In The Church of Jesus Christ of Latter-day Saints, one takes the place to which one is duly called, which place one neither seeks nor declines. CR1951Apr:154

### Paul

Let every soul be subject unto the higher powers. For there is no power but of God: the powers that be are ordained of God. 2. Whosoever therefore resisteth the power, resisteth the ordinance of God: and they that resist shall receive to themselves damnation. (*Paul's letter to the Church in Rome, about A.D. 55*) Rom.13:1-2

### Joseph Smith

And the arm of the Lord shall be revealed; and the day cometh that they who will not hear the voice of the Lord, neither the voice of his servants, neither give heed to the words of the prophets and apostles, shall be cut off from among the people; (*Revelation received during a conference of elders of the Church, Nov. 1, 1831*) D&C 1:14

### Joseph Smith,
#### *receiving the Word of the Lord*

For he that receiveth my servants receiveth me; 37. And he that receiveth me receiveth my Father; 38. And he that receiveth my Father receiveth my Father's kingdom; therefore all that my Father hath shall be given unto him. 39. And this is according to the oath and covenant which belongeth to the priesthood. (*Revelation on priesthood received with six elders, Sept. 22/23, 1832*) D&C 84:36-39

### Russell M. Nelson

When you lift your arm to sustain the brethren as prophets, seers, and revelators you aren't lifting your arm simply to sustain Brother Nelson, Brother Oaks, Brother Maxwell, Brother Monson, and all those brethren with all their human frailties. You sustain them because the Lord has called them and the Lord works through them to accomplish his purposes. (*Unpublished address, March 31, 1985*) MPSG1989:61

### Recorded in Deuteronomy

And the man that will do presumptuously, and will not hearken unto the priest that standeth to minister there before the LORD thy God, or unto the judge, even that man shall die: and thou shalt put away the evil from Israel. 13. And all the people shall hear, and fear, and do no more presumptuously. (*Commandments to Israel through Moses*) Deut.17:12-13

**Elder Spencer W. Kimball**

We pray for the Church leaders. If children all their days in their turn at family prayers and in their secret prayers remember before the Lord the leaders of the Church, they are quite unlikely to ever fall into apostasy and into the class Peter mentioned: ". . . . Presumptuous are they, selfwilled, they are not afraid to speak evil of dignities." (2Pet.2:10) The children who pray for the brethren will grow up loving them, speaking well of them, honoring and emulating them. Those who daily hear the leaders of the Church spoken of in prayer in deep affection will more likely believe the sermons and admonitions they will hear. (Faith Precedes the Miracle, p. 203) MPSG1989:62

**Samuel, the Israelite**

And the men of David said unto him, Behold the day of which the LORD said unto thee, Behold, I will deliver thine enemy into thine hand, that thou mayest do to him as it shall seem good unto thee. Then David arose, and cut off the skirt of Saul's robe privily. 5. And it came to pass afterward, that David's heart smote him, because he had cut off Saul's skirt. 6. And he said unto his men, The LORD forbid that I should do this thing unto my master, the LORD's anointed, to stretch forth mine hand against him, seeing he is the anointed of the LORD. (*David finds Saul asleep in a cave and spares his life*) 1Sam.24:4-6

**Elder Brigham Young, Heber C. Kimball, John E. Page, Elder Wilford Woodruff, Elder John Taylor, George A. Smith**

Pray for the prosperity of Zion, for the Prophet and his counselors, for the Twelve, the High Council, the High Priests, the Seventies, the Elders, the Bishops, and all Saints—that God may bless them, and preserve His people in righteousness, and grant unto them wisdom and intelligence; that His kingdom may roll forth. (*Epistle of the Twelve to the elders of the Church and to all Saints, July 3, 1839*) HC3:395

**Joseph Smith,**
*receiving the Word of the Lord*

Cursed are all those that shall lift up the heel against mine anointed, saith the Lord, and cry they have sinned when they have not sinned before me, saith the Lord, but have done that which is meet in mine eyes, and which I commanded them. 17. But those who cry transgression do it because they are the servants of sin, and are the children of disobedience them-

selves. 18. And those who swear falsely against my servants, that they might bring them into bondage and death— 19. Wo unto them; because they have offended my little ones they shall be severed from the ordinances of mine house. 20. Their basket shall not be full, their houses and their barns shall perish, and they themselves shall be despised by those that flattered them. 21. They shall not have right to the priesthood, nor their posterity after them from generation to generation. 22. It had been better for them that a millstone had been hanged about their necks, and they drowned in the depth of the sea. (*Revelation received in Liberty Jail, March 20, 1839*) D&C 121:16-22

**Jacob, brother of Nephi,**
*quoted by Nephi*

O that cunning plan of the evil one! O the vainness, and the frailties, and the foolishness of men! When they are learned they think they are wise, and they hearken not unto the counsel of God, for they set it aside, supposing they know of themselves, wherefore, their wisdom is foolishness and it profiteth them not. And they shall perish. 29. But to be learned is good if they hearken unto the counsels of God. (*To the people of Nephi, 559-545 B.C.*) 2Ne.9:28-29

**Author's Note:** President Ezra Taft Benson once said that disobedience toward someone in authority usually involves pride: "Disobedience is essentially a prideful power struggle against someone in authority over us. It can be a parent, a priesthood leader, a teacher, or ultimately God. A proud person hates the fact that someone is above him. He thinks this lowers his position." (EN1989May:5)

---

**799. Church members are not to speak out against the Lord's anointed leaders.**

**George Q. Cannon**

God has chosen His servants. He claims it as His prerogative to condemn them, if they need condemnation. He has not given it to us individually to censure and condemn them. No man, however strong he may be in the faith, however high in the Priesthood, can speak evil of the Lord's anointed and find fault with God's authority on the earth without incurring His displeasure. The Holy Spirit will withdraw itself from such a man, and he will go into darkness. This being the case, do you not see how important it is that we should be careful? However difficult it may be for us to understand the reason for any action of the authorities of the Church, we should not too hastily call their acts in question and pronounce them wrong. (Gospel Truth 1:278) DCSM:4

**Elder Brigham Young, Heber C. Kimball, John E. Page, Elder Wilford Woodruff, Elder John Taylor, George A. Smith**

[B]ring no railing accusations against your brethren, especially take care that you do not against the authorities or Elders of the Church, for that principle is of the devil; he is called the accuser of the brethren; . . . (*Epistle of the Twelve to the elders of the Church and to all Saints, July 3, 1839)* HC3:394

**Elder Joseph Fielding Smith**

Again, we are granted the privilege by the will of the Lord, to vote to sustain, or reject, the officers in the Church. When we have sustained them we are duty bound to support them. Any person who raises his hand to sustain the President of the Church, or any other officer, and then goes straightway and criticizes or condemns, that man is a covenant breaker, for it is a covenant we take when we raise our hand and pledge our support. CHMR1:188

**Reed Smoot**

Prayer is practiced in the Kingdom of God. Part of our prayers should be devoted to our leaders: they have great responsibilities. Oh, so many of the people do not realize the responsibilities that fall upon the President and his Counselors these days. It has been so from the beginning and as long as there is life it will continue to be so. Let us pray for our leaders at all times instead of criticizing them, pray that they may be given courage to continue with unflagging zeal from year to year; pray for the power of God to be upon them. CR1940Oct:21

**George F. Richards**

We should be on the alert lest we be found rendering aid to Satan and hindering the work of the Lord. When we say anything bad about the leaders of the Church, whether true or false, we tend to impair their influence and their usefulness and are thus working against the Lord and his cause. When we speak well of our leaders, we tend to increase their influence and usefulness in the service of the Lord. In his absence our brother's character when assailed, should be defended, thus doing to others as we would be done by. The Lord needs the help of all of us. Are we helping or are we hindering? CR1947Apr:24

**Marion G. Romney**

Some members assume that one can be in full harmony with the spirit of the gospel, enjoy full fellowship in the Church, and at the same time be out of harmony with the leaders of the Church and the counsel and direction they give. Such a position is wholly inconsistent. . . . Those who profess to accept the gospel and who at the same time criticize and refuse to follow the counsel of the prophets are assuming an indefensible position. Such a spirit leads to apostasy. CR1983Apr:21

**Elder Harold B. Lee**

During the early days of the Church we passed through a period of slander and misrepresentation, and we came through. It drove us together because of enemies from the outside. And we survived it. We passed through a period of mobbing and driving, when lives were taken and blood was shed, and somehow the martyr gave us strength. We passed through an age of what we might call apostasy, or betrayal from the inside—one of the severest tests through which we have passed. We are now going through another test—a period of what we might call sophistication. This is a time when there are many clever people who are not willing to listen to the humble prophets of the Lord. And we have suffered a rather severe test. (Instructor, June 1965, p. 217) MPSG1989:59

**Elder David O. McKay**

Parents who speak at the table against the bishopric, against a teacher, stake president, or any other officer of the Church are, unwittingly, perhaps, but most assuredly lessening in their children's minds the respect and confidence in Church authorities. CR1944Apr:108

**Related Witnesses:**

**Elder Brigham Young, Heber C. Kimball, Orson Pratt, William Smith, Lyman Wight, Elder Wilford Woodruff, Elder John Taylor, George A. Smith Willard Richards**

[Y]ou need not be surprised if your ears are saluted by the false and filthy language of wicked and designing men who are ever ready to speak evil of the things they understand not, and who would gladly blast the character of the Prophet of the Most High God, and all connected with him, with their foul anathemas, beyond anything you ever thought of. We would not dishearten you, neither would we have you ignorant of the worst that awaits the righteous. (*In an epistle of the Twelve to the Saints in England and elsewhere, Nov. 15, 1841)* HC4:451

**Recorded in Jude**

Likewise also these filthy dreamers defile the flesh, despise dominion, and speak evil of dignities. (*Letter of Jude, brother of James)* Jude 1:8

**Peter**

The Lord knoweth how to deliver the godly out of temptations, and to reserve the unjust unto the day of judgment to be punished: 10. But chiefly them that walk after the flesh in the lust of uncleanness, and despise government. Presumptuous are they, selfwilled, they are not afraid to speak evil of dignities. (*Letter to members of the Church, about* A.D. *60-64*) 2Pet.2:9-10

**Recorded in Exodus**

And in the morning, then ye shall see the glory of the LORD; for that he heareth your murmurings against the LORD: and what are we, that ye murmur against us? 8. And Moses said, This shall be, when the LORD shall give you in the evening flesh to eat, and in the morning bread to the full; for that the LORD heareth your murmurings which ye murmur against him: and what are we? your murmurings are not against us, but against the LORD. (*The people of Israel in the wilderness murmur against their leaders for want of bread*) Ex.16:7-8

**Joseph Smith,**
*quoted by Elder Joseph Fielding Smith*

I shall triumph over my enemies: I have begun to triumph over them at home, and I shall do it abroad. All those that rise up against me will surely feel the weight of their iniquity upon their own heads. Those that speak evil of me and the Saints are ignorant or abominable characters, and full of iniquity. (*At Relief Society meeting, Nauvoo, Ill., minutes by Eliza R. Snow*) HC5:140; TPJS:258

**Joseph Smith,**
*quoted by Elder Joseph Fielding Smith*

The enemies of this people will never get weary of their persecution against the Church, until they are overcome. I expect they will array everything against me that is in their power to control, and that we shall have a long and tremendous warfare. He that will war the true Christian warfare against the corruptions of these last days will have wicked men and angels of devils, and all the infernal powers of darkness continually arrayed against him. When wicked and corrupt men oppose, it is a criterion to judge if a man is warring the Christian warfare. When all men speak evil of you falsely, blessed are ye. Shall a man be considered bad, when men speak evil of him? No. If a man stands and opposes the world of sin, he may expect to have all wicked and corrupt spirits arrayed against him. But it will be but a little season, and all these afflictions will be turned away from us, inasmuch as we are faithful, and are not overcome by these evils. By seeing the blessings of the endowment rolling on, and the kingdom increasing and spreading from sea to sea, we shall rejoice that we were not overcome by these foolish things.

(*At Relief Society meeting, Nauvoo, Ill., minutes by Eliza R. Snow*) HC5:139-141; TPJS:259

**800. Those who faithfully sustain the Church leaders will be blessed and supported by the Lord and will not be overcome by their enemies.**

**George Q. Cannon**

But as a servant of God I am willing to stake my reputation in making this statement, that if you will listen to the voice of God as manifested through His servant who stands at our head, you never will, from this time forward until eternity dawns upon you, you never will be overcome by your enemies, or by the enemies of God's kingdom. (*In Assembly Hall, Dec. 2, 1883, JD24:364-65*) TLDP:666-67

**Joseph F. Merrill**

Do the people of the Church want a safe guide to what is well for them to do? It is this: Keep in harmony with the Presidency of this Church. Accept and follow the teachings and advice of the President. At every Conference we raise our hands to sustain the President as prophet, seer and revelator. Is it consistent to do this and then go contrary to his advice? Is anyone so simple as to believe he is serving the Lord when he opposes the President? Of course, the President is not infallible. He makes no claims to infallibility. But when in his official capacity he teaches and advises the members of the Church relative to their duties, let no man who wants to please the Lord say aught against the counsels of the President. ¶ In the spirit of helpfulness let me give you a key. When in doubt go on your knees in humility with an open mind and a pure heart with a real desire to do the Lord's will, and pray earnestly and sincerely for divine guidance. Persist in praying in this way until you get an answer that fills your bosom with joy and satisfaction. It will be God's answer. If obedient to this answer you will always act as the President indicates. You will then be safe. CR1941Apr:51

**Elder Harold B. Lee**

Now the only safety we have as members of this Church is to do exactly what the Lord said to the Church in that day when the Church was organized. We must learn to give heed to the words and commandments that the Lord shall give through his prophet, "as he receiveth them, walking in all holiness before me; . . . as if from mine own mouth, in all patience and faith." (D&C 21:4-5) There will be some things that take patience and faith. You may not like what comes from the authority of the Church. It may contradict your political views. It may contradict your social views. It may interfere with some of your social life. But if you listen to these things, as if from the mouth of the Lord himself, with patience and faith, the promise is that "the gates of hell shall not prevail against you; yea, and the Lord God will disperse the powers of darkness from before you, and cause the heavens to shake for your good, and his name's glory." (D&C 21:6) CR1970Oct:152

### George F. Richards

My advice and counsel to the Latter-day Saints is that we keep near to the Authorities of this Church, and if we will follow their example and observe their teachings we will be on safe ground and cannot be undermined by the wiles and machinations of him who is the enemy of God and of man and who would destroy our faith and lead us from paths of virtue, truth, and honor, to degradation and to condemnation. CR1939Oct:108

### Related Witnesses:

#### Elder George Albert Smith

There is only one pathway of safety for me in this day and that is to follow those whom the Lord has appointed to lead. I may have my own ideas and opinions. I may set up my own judgment with reference to things, but I know that when my judgment conflicts with the teachings of those that the Lord has given to us to point the way, I should change my course. If I desire salvation I will follow the leaders that our Heavenly Father has given to us, as long as he sustains them. CR1937Apr:33

#### President Brigham Young
#### Heber C. Kimball, Willard Richards
(First Presidency)

Elders of Israel be faithful in your calling, feed the sheep, feed the lambs of the flock, and proclaim the gospel in all simplicity, meekness, and love, whenever you have the opportunity as it shall be given you by the power of the Holy Ghost, which you will always have for your counsellor if you are faithful; and let all the Saints give diligent heed unto the counsel of those who are over them in the Lord, upholding them by the prayer of faith, keeping themselves pure and humble, and they will never lack wisdom from above, and by faith and works search out your way to Zion. *(Third Epistle of the Presidency of the Church to the Saints scattered throughout the earth)* (Frontier Guardian, June 12, 1850, and Millennial Star, Aug. 15, 1850) MOFP2:48

# List of Doctrines

## TEACHING

*Doctrines Located in This Topic*

801. Teachers of the gospel are to teach the official views and doctrines of the Church set forth in the Church-published words of the prophets.

802. To convincingly teach the gospel we must live the gospel.

803. Before we can effectively teach the gospel we must first obtain an understanding of the gospel.

804. Church members are to teach only under direction of the spirit, without which they are commanded not to teach.

805. Church teachers are to avoid discussion of theories and "mysteries"—subjects not taught by the prophets.

806. All members of the Church are to confine their public interpretations of doctrine to those that are in harmony with the President of the Church.

*Doctrines on TEACHING Located in Other Topics*

28. Apostasy involves teaching or practicing false doctrine; having an apostate opinion, and either practicing or preaching it (after being corrected by one's bishop or higher authority) is apostasy.

86. One of the (threefold) missions of the Church is to perfect the Saints.

97. A person who *accepts* divine truth must obtain it by the Spirit of God from someone who *teaches* by that same Spirit.

167. The devil authors false doctrines.

212. Parents are to teach their children to honor and respect their parents.

213. Parents are commanded to teach their children by the time they are eight years old to understand the doctrines of faith, repentance, and baptism.

214. Parents are commanded to teach the gospel to their children.

215. Parents are to teach their children to pray.

815. When teachers (missionaries and speakers) bear testimony of a gospel truth they have taught, the Spirit of God witnesses the truth thereof to the heart of the honest seeker.

874. The Lord selects teachable persons to do His work; He chooses those whom the world calls weak and foolish more frequently than those whom the world calls wise.

**801.** Teachers of the gospel are to teach the official views and doctrines of the Church set forth in the Church-published words of the prophets.

### J. Reuben Clark, Jr.

You are to teach this Gospel using as your sources and authorities the Standard Works of the Church, and the words of those whom God has called to lead His people in these last days. You are not, whether high or low, to intrude into your work your own peculiar philosophy, no matter what its source or how pleasing or rational it seems to you to be. To do so would be to have as many different churches as we have seminaries—and that is chaos. ¶ You are not, whether high or low, to change the doctrines of the Church or to modify them, as they are declared by and in the Standard Works of the Church and by those whose authority it is to declare the mind and will of the Lord to the Church. The Lord has declared he is "the same yesterday, today, and forever." *(Speaking in behalf of the First Presidency [see letter of First Presidency, MOFP6:208-09] to seminary, institute, and Church school teachers at Aspen Grove. Entire speech published in Deseret News, Church Section, Aug. 13, 1938 and in IE1938Sep:520ff; copied in MOFP6:44-58. The speech was extracted for use as Lesson 18 of the Melchizedek Priesthood Course of Study, 1969-70, p. 129ff)* MOFP6:55; TLDP:671

### Elder Spencer W. Kimball

There are great numbers of unusually splendid and talented members of the Church all through the world who are intelligent and well-meaning, but I repeat again the statement I made in conference: That while they may think as they please, no one has the right to give his own private interpretations when he has been invited to teach in the organizations of the Church: he is a guest; he has been given an authoritative position and the stamp of approval is placed upon him, and those whom he teaches are justified in assuming that, having been chosen and sustained in the proper order, he represents the Church and the things which he teaches are *approved by the Church.* No matter how brilliant he may be and how many new truths he may think he has found, he has no right to go beyond the program of the Church. Certainly if any one or group of individuals have felt they have advanced inspiration or revelation, there is a way by which they can present it for approval. [Italics added] (The Teachings of Spencer W. Kimball, pp. 532-33) TLDP:672-73

### Mark E. Petersen

It is my full belief that whenever any of us accepts a position of any description in the Church, we accept along with it the responsibility of that office, whatsoever it may be. I believe that if a person accepts a position as a teacher in one of our organizations, or if he accepts the responsibility of preaching from the pulpit, such person accepts the responsibility which goes with that call. He becomes a representative of the Church in that position. Every teacher and every preacher therefore is duty bound, upon accepting such a call, to represent the official views and doctrines of the Church, and to teach those official doctrines in his class or from the pulpit with the one thought in mind that conversion is to come about in the hearts of those who listen to him. I do not believe that conversion to the truth comes through the teaching of half-truths or untruths. ¶ Our classrooms and our assembly rooms have been built at great expense with one thought in mind, and that is that in them we may teach the truth so that we may convert those who come there, so that they in turn will live the gospel and work out their salvation in the earth. CR1953Apr:83

### President Joseph F. Smith

We have nothing that is not in common with the Latter-day Saints. We know nothing, and we will preach nothing to the people except that which the Lord God has revealed, and we advise and counsel those who are in authority, and whose duty and business it is to teach and preach the principles of the gospel to the world and to the Latter-day Saints, to confine their teachings and their instructions to the word of God that has been revealed. CR1917Oct:5

### Mormon

And he commanded them that they should teach nothing save it were the things which he had taught, and which had been spoken by the mouth of the holy prophets. (*Alma organizes the Church of Christ and ordains priests, about 148 B.C.*) Mosiah 18:19

### Joseph Smith

And again, the elders, priests and teachers of this church shall teach the principles of my gospel, which are in the Bible and the Book of Mormon, in the which is the fulness of the gospel. 13. And they shall observe the covenants and church articles to do them, and these shall be their teachings, as they shall be directed by the Spirit. 14. And the Spirit shall be given unto you by the prayer of faith; and if ye receive not the Spirit ye shall not teach. 15. And all this ye shall observe to do as I have commanded concerning your teaching, until the fulness of my scriptures is given. (*Revelation "embracing the law of the Church" Feb. 9, 1831*) D&C 42:12-15

**President Ezra Taft Benson,**
*also quoting Mormon and Joseph Smith*
[W]hat should be the source for teaching the great plan of the Eternal God? The scriptures, of course—particularly the Book of Mormon. This should also include the other modern-day revelations. These should be coupled with the words of the Apostles and prophets and the promptings of the Spirit. Alma "commanded them that they should teach nothing save it were the things which he had taught, and which had been spoken by the mouth of the holy prophets" (Mosiah 18:19). The Doctrine and Covenants states: "Let them journey from thence preaching the word by the way, saying none other things than that which the prophets and apostles have written, and that which is taught them by the Comforter through the prayer of faith" (D&C 52:9). CR1987Apr:107

**Joseph Smith**
And let them journey from thence preaching the word by the way, saying none other things than that which the prophets and apostles have written, and that which is taught them by the Comforter through the prayer of faith. (*Revelation for the elders of the Church, June 7, 1831; various elders sent to preach the gospel*) D&C 52:9

**Orson Pratt**
Have we not a right to make up our minds in relation to the things recorded in the word of God, and speak about them, whether the living oracles believe our views or not? We have not the right. Why? Because the mind of man is weak: one man may make up his mind in this way, and another man may make up his mind in another way, and a third individual may have his views; and thus every man is left to be his own authority, and is governed by his own judgment, which he takes as his standard. ¶ Do you not perceive that this would, in a short time, cause a complete disunion and division of sentiment throughout the whole Church? (*Address printed in published message of the First Presidency of the Church, Sept. 22, 1860*) MOFP2:219

**Hyrum Smith**
And again I say unto you, an elder has no business to undertake to preach mysteries in any part of the world, for God has commanded us all to preach nothing but the first principles unto the world. Neither has any elder any authority to preach any mysterious thing to any branch of the church unless he has a direct commandment from God to do so. Let the matter of the grand

councils of heaven, and the making of Gods, worlds, and devils entirely alone: for you are not called to teach any such doctrine—for neither you nor the people are capacitated to understand any such principles—less so to teach them. For when God commands men to teach such principles the saints will receive them. Therefore beware what you teach! for the mysteries of God are not given to all men; and unto those to whom they are given they are placed under restrictions to impart only such as God will command them, and the residue is to be kept in a faithful breast, otherwise he will be brought under condemnation. By this God will prove his faithful servants, who will be called and numbered with the chosen. (Times and Seasons, March 15, 1844, p. 474) TLDP:671

**Elder Spencer W. Kimball**
There are those today who seem to take pride in disagreeing with the orthodox teachings of the Church and who present their own opinions which are at variance with the revealed truth. Some may be partially innocent in the matter; others are feeding their own egotism; and some seem to be deliberate. Men may think as they please, but they have no right to impose upon others their unorthodox views. Such persons should realize that their own souls are in jeopardy. The Lord said to us through the Prophet Joseph: ¶ "[T]each the principles of my gospel, which are in the Bible and the Book of Mormon, in the which is the fulness of the gospel. ¶ And they shall observe the covenants and church articles to do them, and these shall be their teachings, as they shall be directed by the Spirit. ¶ . . . . And if ye receive not the Spirit ye shall not teach." (D&C 42:12-14). . . . ¶ If one cannot accept and teach the program of the Church in an orthodox way without reservations, he should not teach. . . . ¶ And so we admonish the leaders in stakes, wards, and missions to be ever vigilant to see that no incorrect doctrines are promulgated in their classes or congregations. . . . And we warn again those who write or preach or otherwise teach subversive doctrines, that their punishment is sure for their "worm dieth not." CR1948Apr:109-10

**Related Witnesses:**
**Joseph Smith**
I was answered that I must join none of them, for they were all wrong; and the Personage who addressed me said that all their creeds were an abomination in his sight; that those professors were all corrupt; that: "They draw near to me with their lips, but their hearts are far from me, they teach for doctrines the commandments of men, having a form of godliness, but they deny

the power thereof." (*Vision of the Father and the Son, spring of 1820*) JS-H 1:19

**Jesus,**
*quoted by Mormon*

And now it came to pass that when Jesus had said these words he said unto them again, after he had expounded all the scriptures unto them which they had received. . . . 14. And now it came to pass that when Jesus had expounded all the scriptures in one, which they had written, he commanded them that they should teach the things which he had expounded unto them. (*The resurrected Jesus Christ instructs his disciples among the Nephite people, A.D. 34*) 3Ne.23:6,14

**Nephi, son of Lehi**

Now it came to pass that I, Nephi, did teach my brethren these things; and it came to pass that I did read many things to them, which were engraven upon the plates of brass, that they might know concerning the doings of the Lord in other lands, among people of old. 23. And I did read many things unto them which were written in the books of Moses; but that I might more fully persuade them to believe in the Lord their Redeemer I did read unto them that which was written by the prophet Isaiah; for I did liken all scriptures unto us, that it might be for our profit and learning. (*Nephi's writings, between 588-570 B.C.*) 1Ne.19:22-23

**President Harold B. Lee**

I say that we need to teach our people to find their answers in the scriptures. . . . But the unfortunate thing is that so many of us are not reading the scriptures. We do not know what is in them, and therefore we speculate about the things that we ought to have found in the scriptures themselves. I think that therein is one of our biggest dangers of today. ("Find the Answers in the Scriptures," EN1972Dec:3) MPSG1984:3

**Peter**

[T]here shall be false teachers among you, who privily shall bring in damnable heresies, even denying the Lord that bought them, and bring upon themselves swift destruction. (*Letter to members of the Church, about A.D. 60-64*) 2Pet.2:1

**Jesus,**
*recorded in Luke*

Woe unto you, lawyers! for ye have taken away the key of knowledge: [the fulness of the scriptures (see revised version)] ye entered not in yourselves, and them that were entering in ye hindered. (*Jesus reproaches the lawyers*) Luke 11:52

**President Heber J. Grant**

Teachers will do well to give up indoctrinating themselves in the Sectarianisms of the new

"Divinity School theology. . . ." ¶ In the teaching, the teachers will use verbiage and terminology which have become classic in the Church. . . . ¶ Furthermore, teachers will not advance their own theories about the Gospel or Gospel principles. (*Letter from First Presidency to Franklin L. West, Church commissioner of education, 1940*) MOFP6:209

**Author's Note:** See the topic in this book, REVELATION: (1) Law of Witness, which sets forth how we can always know what are the "official views" of the prophets. ¶ When a gospel teacher supplements a lesson with material outside the lesson manual, it would appear that this doctrine tells us that such material must harmonize with the official views of the Church! ¶ In a church or seminary classroom setting, a "spiritually prepared" teacher is often challenged by an intellectual argument from some gifted student who, not being at the moment in the same spirit, is able to intellectually conceive of alternate ideas, ideas that argue against the teacher's sound and correct interpretation of a doctrine—(sound and correct because the teacher is "spiritually prepared" and teaches doctrine derived from the witnesses of more than one prophet in written scripture). Church members lose much on those occasions when they prefer to use their intellectual talent and judgment in matters pertaining to the Spirit instead of their spiritual discernment. When the Holy Ghost speaks through several prophets who say the same thing, we ought to let the Holy Ghost in us give full credence to those inspired words of the prophets. The Spirit should override the talent of our meager intellects. We ought to humbly and gratefully honor and respect those scriptural expressions of prophetic witnesses so they become part of our own spiritual fiber. Then the Spirit in us will also find room for deep gratitude toward those worthy prophets through whom the Lord has spoken.

---

**802. To convincingly teach the gospel we must live the gospel.**

**President Heber J. Grant**

No man can teach the Gospel of Jesus Christ under the inspiration of the living God and with power from on high unless he is living it. He can go on as a member and we will pray for him, no matter how many years it may require, and we will never put a block in his way, because the Gospel is one of love and of forgiveness, but we want true men and women as our officers in the Priesthood and in the Relief Societies. And a man has no right to be in a high council who can not stand up and say that he knows the Gospel is true and that he is living it. CR1938Apr:15

**Marion G. Romney**
For those of us who desire to effectively share the gospel, there are some very important lessons taught in this message: We must put our lives in order so the Lord's Spirit can influence our thoughts and actions—so we can be taught from on high. ("Records of Great Worth," EN1980Sept:7) TLDP:670-71

**Paul**
Even so hath the Lord ordained that they which preach the gospel should live of the gospel. *(Paul writes to the Church at Corinth, Greece, about A.D. 55)* 1Cor.9:14

**Richard L. Evans**
Abstract qualities of character don't mean much in the abstract. It is how we live, how we serve, how we teach our children, what we do from day to day that both indicate what we are and determine what we are; and all the theory and all the speculation, all the quoting of scripture, all the searching of the mysteries, and all the splitting of hairs, and all the knowledge of the letter of the law don't in the final and saving sense amount to very much unless we live the gospel, unless we keep the commandments, unless we prove the principles, unless we live lives of effectiveness, sincerity, and service. CR1966Apr:89-90

**President Brigham Young,**
*quoted by John A. Widtsoe*
A few words now, with regard to preaching. The greatest and loudest sermon that can be preached, or that ever was preached on the face of the earth, is practice. No other is equal to it. *(In new Tabernacle, Aug. 16, 1868, JD12:271)* DBY:336

**Melvin J. Ballard**
The most powerful sermon any of us shall ever preach will be the sermon of our lives. CR1934Oct:115

**Hugh B. Brown**
What the teacher is counts for more than what he says. CR1963Apr:89

**Related Witnesses:**

**Jesus,**
*recorded in Matthew*
Whosoever therefore shall break one of these least commandments, and shall teach men so, he shall be called the least in the kingdom of heaven: but whosoever shall do and teach them, the same shall be called great in the kingdom of heaven. *(Jesus Christ teaches the multitude, about A.D. 30)* Matt.5:19

**Jesus,**
*quoted by Joseph Smith,*
*translating Matthew*
Whosoever, therefore, shall break one of these least commandments, and shall teach men so to do, he shall in no wise be saved in the kingdom of heaven; but whosoever shall do and teach these commandments of the law until it be fulfilled, the same shall be called great, and shall be saved in the kingdom of heaven. *(Jesus Christ teaches the multitude, about A.D. 30)* JST(Matt.5:21 in Appendix)

**Nephi, son of Lehi**
Yea, and there shall be many which shall teach after this manner, false and vain and foolish doctrines, and shall be puffed up in their hearts, and shall seek deep to hide their counsels from the Lord; and their works shall be in the dark. 10. And the blood of the saints shall cry from the ground against them. 11. Yea, they have all gone out of the way; they have become corrupted. 12. Because of pride, and because of false teachers, and false doctrine, their churches have become corrupted, and their churches are lifted up; because of pride they are puffed up. 13. They rob the poor because of their fine sanctuaries; they rob the poor because of their fine clothing; and they persecute the meek and the poor in heart, because in their pride they are puffed up. 14. They wear stiff necks and high heads; yea, and because of pride, and wickedness, and abominations, and whoredoms, they have all gone astray save it be a few, who are the humble followers of Christ; nevertheless, they are led, that in many instances they do err because they are taught by the precepts of men. 15. O the wise, and the learned, and the rich, that are puffed up in the pride of their hearts, and all those who preach false doctrines, and all those who commit whoredoms, and pervert the right way of the Lord, wo, wo, wo be unto them, saith the Lord God Almighty, for they shall be thrust down to hell! *(Nephi foretells of false teachers and false churches in the last days, and the coming forth of the Book of Mormon, 559-545 B.C.)* 2Ne.28:9-15

**Author's Note:** The Lord does not require perfection. We all sin, yet we are to strive to live the gospel principles. A teacher must not be a hypocrite, teaching what he or she does not even attempt to practice.

803. Before we can effectively teach the gospel we must first obtain an understanding of the gospel.

**Joseph Smith,**
*receiving the Word of the Lord*
Seek not to declare my word, but first seek to obtain my word, and then shall your tongue be loosed; then, if you desire, you shall have my Spirit and my word, yea, the power of God unto the convincing of men. (*Revelation for Hyrum Smith, May 1829*) D&C 11:21

**President Brigham Young,**
**Heber C. Kimball and Daniel H. Wells**
(First Presidency)
This should be a lasting lesson to the Elders of Israel not to undertake to teach doctrine they do not understand. If the Saints can preserve themselves in a present salvation day by day, which is easy to be taught and comprehended, it will be well with them hereafter. (*Published message of the First Presidency of the Church, Sept. 22, 1860*) MOFP2:223

**Marion G. Romney**
As Latter-day Saints, we are commissioned to deliver that which we receive from the Lord to those we teach. Sometimes, though, we attempt to teach without first obtaining the proper information and spirit. . . . ¶ For those of us who desire to effectively share the gospel, there are some very important lessons taught in this message: We must put our lives in order so the Lord's Spirit can influence our thoughts and actions—so we can be taught from on high. We must work and study his word with full desire until his teachings become our teachings. Then we will be able to speak with power and conviction. If we choose to follow some other path of preparation, we have no assurance of success. We will end up delivering our own ideas or some other man's ideas, and we will not be profitable servants of the Lord. The primary source of the Lord's word is in the standard works, augmented as needed by living prophets. ¶ I feel that it is important for us to become familiar with these spiritual fundamentals. When I pray for the Spirit of the Lord to help me in my life and to teach, I pray for the spirit of revelation, the help of the Holy Ghost. ("Records of Great Worth," EN1980Sept:7) TLDP:670-71

**Howard W. Hunter**
From the scriptures . . . several things are made abundantly clear: ¶ 1. Every bearer of the priesthood within his sphere of influence and responsibility is to teach the gospel through precept and example. That is, he should be teaching by the example of living the gospel; also through words, learning experiences, and instructional materials. ¶ 2. Every bearer of the priesthood is to prepare himself to be an effec-

tive teacher by study, prayer, and faith. ¶ 3. Every bearer of the priesthood should seek the direction of the Spirit to guide him in his own life and to inspire him in his teaching efforts. ¶ 4. Every bearer of the priesthood has a sacred stewardship in the kingdom of God. Our time, our talents, our property, our priesthood callings are part of this stewardship. CR1971Apr:49-50

**N. Eldon Tanner**
If teachers only knew it, they could find enlightenment in the scriptures on any subject they might be teaching. Through accepting and living the teachings of the gospel of Jesus Christ, they would be entitled to the additional light and knowledge that comes through the Holy Ghost and the Spirit of God by which a man may know the truth of all things. Their learning would be enhanced and their ability to impart and instruct would be greatly increased as the gifts of the Spirit worked upon them. ("Right Answers," EN1973Oct:3) TLDP:673

---

804. **Church members are to teach only under direction of the Spirit, without which they are commanded not to teach.**

**Elder Joseph Fielding Smith**
[N]o one should be called upon to teach and no one should attempt to teach the doctrines of the Church unless he is fully converted and has an abiding testimony of their truth. This testimony can only be received through prayerful study and obedience to all the commandments of the Lord. No man or woman can teach by the Spirit what he or she does not practice. Sincerity, integrity and loyalty are essential factors, and these will be accompanied by the spirit of prayer. The Comforter, "who knoweth all things," we should rely on, and then our teachings shall be approved of our Father in Heaven. CHMR1:184-85; DCSM:83

**Elder John Taylor**
There is no man living, and there never was a man living, who was capable of teaching the things of God only as he was taught, instructed and directed by the spirit of revelation proceeding from the Almighty. And then there are no people competent to receive true intelligence and to form a correct judgment in relation to the sacred principles of eternal life, unless they are under the influence of the same spirit, and hence speakers and hearers are all in the hands of the Almighty. (*General conference, April 1875, JD16:369*) TLDP:668

**Joseph Smith,**
*receiving the Word of the Lord*

Verily I say unto you, he that is ordained of me and sent forth to preach the word of truth by the Comforter, in the Spirit of truth, doth he preach it by the Spirit of truth or some other way? 18. And if it be by some other way it is not of God. 19. And again, he that receiveth the word of truth, doth he receive it by the Spirit of truth or some other way? 20. If it be some other way it is not of God. 21. Therefore, why is it that ye cannot understand and know, that he that receiveth the word by the Spirit of truth receiveth it as it is preached by the Spirit of truth? 22. Wherefore, he that preacheth and he that receiveth, understand one another, and both are edified and rejoice together. (*Revelation for the elders of the Church, May 1831*) D&C 50:17-22

**Joseph Smith,**
*receiving the Word of the Lord*

And again, the elders, priests and teachers of this church shall teach the principles of my gospel, which are in the Bible and the Book of Mormon, in the which is the fulness of the gospel. 13. And they shall observe the covenants and church articles to do them, and these shall be their teachings, as they shall be directed by the Spirit. 14. And the Spirit shall be given unto you by the prayer of faith; and if ye receive not the Spirit ye shall not teach. 15. And all this ye shall observe to do as I have commanded concerning your teaching, until the fulness of my scriptures is given. 16. And as ye shall lift up your voices by the Comforter, ye shall speak and prophesy as seemeth me good; . . . (*Revelation, Feb. 9, 1831*) D&C 42:12-16

**Joseph Smith**

A fanciful and flowery and heated imagination beware of; because the things of God are of deep import; and time, and experience, and careful and ponderous and solemn thoughts can only find them out. Thy mind, O man! if thou wilt lead a soul unto salvation, must stretch as high as the utmost heavens, and search into and contemplate the darkest abyss, and the broad expanse of eternity—thou must commune with God. How much more dignified and noble are the thoughts of God, than the vain imaginations of the human heart! None but fools will trifle with the souls of men. ¶ How vain and trifling have been our spirits, our conferences, our councils, our meetings, our private as well as public conversations—too low, too mean, too vulgar, too condescending for the dignified characters of the called and chosen of God, according to the purposes of His will, from before the foundation of the world! We are called to hold the keys of the mysteries of those things that have been kept hid from the founda-

tion of the world until now. (*Epistle to the Church from Liberty Jail, Mar. 25, 1839*) HC3:295-96

**Howard W. Hunter**

From the scriptures . . . several things are made abundantly clear: ¶ 1. Every bearer of the priesthood within his sphere of influence and responsibility is to teach the gospel through precept and example. That is, he should be teaching by the example of living the gospel; also through words, learning experiences, and instructional materials. ¶ 2. Every bearer of the priesthood is to prepare himself to be an effective teacher by study, prayer, and faith. ¶ 3. Every bearer of the priesthood should seek the direction of the Spirit to guide him in his own life and to inspire him in his teaching efforts. ¶ 4. Every bearer of the priesthood has a sacred stewardship in the kingdom of God. Our time, our talents, our property, our priesthood callings are part of this stewardship. CR1971Apr:49-50

**Related Witnesses:**
**Joseph Smith**

And let them journey from thence preaching the word by the way, saying none other things than that which the prophets and apostles have written, and that which is taught them by the Comforter through the prayer of faith. (*Revelation for the elders of the Church, June 7, 1831; various elders sent to preach the gospel*) D&C 52:9

---

**805. Church teachers are to avoid discussion of theories and "mysteries"—subjects not taught by the prophets.**

**Joseph Smith,**
*quoted by Elder Joseph Fielding Smith*

Oh ye elders of Israel, harken to my voice; and when you are sent into the world to preach, tell those things you are sent to tell; preach and cry aloud, "Repent ye, for the kingdom of heaven is at hand; repent and believe the Gospel." Declare the first principles, and let mysteries alone, lest ye be overthrown. Never meddle with the visions of beasts and subjects you do not understand. (*General conference in Nauvoo, Ill., April 8, 1843, on the floor of the temple*) HC5:344; TPJS:292; DCSM:15

**Elder Wilford Woodruff**

The books used [in the Sunday Schools and Improvement Associations] should be almost without exception, the revelations of God as contained in ancient and modern Scripture, together with the other works of the Church. . . . In the theological and other classes all discussions should be avoided as much as possible on subjects which God in His wisdom has not yet fully revealed. We know there are many persons who appear to take more delight in dwelling upon questions which are mysterious and cannot very well, in our present state of knowledge, be answered than they do upon those subjects which are plain and simple and essential to present progress. . . . In our theological classes, quorum meetings and other assemblies, therefore, these debatable questions need not be discussed or be dwelt upon. . . . (*An epistle to the Church from the President of the Twelve, Wilford Woodruff, upon the death of President John Taylor, Oct. 10, 1887*) MOFP3:139

**Elder Brigham Young, Heber C. Kimball, John E. Page, Elder Wilford Woodruff, Elder John Taylor, George Albert Smith**

Be careful that you teach not for the word of God the commandments of men, nor the doctrines of men, nor the ordinances of men, inasmuch as you are God's messengers. Study the word of God, and preach it and not your opinions, for no man's opinion is worth a straw. Advance no principle but what you can prove, for one scriptural proof is worth ten thousand opinions. We would moreover say, abide by that revelation which says "Preach nothing but repentance to this generation," and leave the further mysteries of the kingdom till God shall tell you to preach them, which is not now. (*Epistle from the Twelve Apostles, 1837*) HC3:395-96

**Bruce R. McConkie**

Every gospel teacher—from the Chief Elder, who is Christ, to the least and lowest of his servants—must determine, in all teaching situations, what portion of eternal truth he will offer to his hearers of the moment. The gospel and its eternal truths are always the same; what was true two thousand years ago is true today. . . . The Lord gives his word to men line upon line, precept upon precept, here a little and there a little, confirming their hope, building each new revelation upon the foundations of the past, giving his children only that portion of his word which they are able to bear. . . . [T]he servants of the Lord [are to] go forth to teach what people are prepared to receive, nothing more. They are to declare glad tidings, to proclaim the message of the restoration, to teach the simple and easy doctrines, and to leave the mysteries alone. They are not to present lessons in calculus to students who must first learn arithmetic; they are not to reveal the mysteries of the kingdom until people believe the first principles: they are to give milk before meat. ¶ Alma summarized the restrictions

under which preachers of righteousness serve by saying: "It is given unto many to know the mysteries of God; nevertheless they are laid under a strict command that they shall not impart only according to the portion of his word which he doth grant unto the children of men, according to the heed and diligence which they give unto him." Such is the universal principle; *it is not how much the teacher knows, but how much the student is prepared to receive.* [Italics added] Strong and deep doctrine, spoken to rebellious people, drives them further away and widens the gulf between them and the saints of God. [Alma 12:9] ¶ Even the true saints—the believing disciples, those who have accepted the gospel and received the gift of the Holy Ghost—are not prepared to receive all things. We have the fulness of the everlasting gospel, meaning we have every truth, power, priesthood, and key needed to enable us to gain the fulness of salvation in our Father's kingdom. But we do not have, and are not yet prepared to receive, the fulness of gospel truth. (The Mortal Messiah, 2:235-37) TLDP:672-73

**J. Reuben Clark, Jr.**

You are to teach this Gospel using as your sources and authorities the Standard Works of the Church, and the words of those whom God has called to lead His people in these last days. You are not, whether high or low, to intrude into your work your own peculiar philosophy, no matter what its source or how pleasing or rational it seems to you to be. To do so would be to have as many different churches as we have seminaries—and that is chaos. ¶ You are not, whether high or low, to change the doctrines of the Church or to modify them, as they are declared by and in the Standard Works of the Church and by those whose authority it is to declare the mind and will of the Lord to the Church. The Lord has declared he is "the same yesterday, today, and forever." (*Speaking in behalf of First Presidency [see letter of First Presidency, MOFP6:208-09] to seminary, institute, and Church school teachers at Aspen Grove. Entire speech published in Deseret News, Church Section, Aug. 13, 1938 and in IE1938Sep:520ff; copied in MOFP6:44-58. The speech was extracted for use as Lesson 18 of the Melchizedek Priesthood Course of Study 1969-70, p. 129ff*) MOFP6:55; TLDP:671

**Stephen L. Richards**

Another thing for which I am likewise grateful is that there is substantially no variance or uncertainty in our missionary teaching. It is not necessary that there be long debates or discussions as to interpretations of doctrine. What we teach is the revelations which, for the most part are direct, certain, and unequivocal in their import. If any mysteries seem to arise, we leave the solution of such mysteries for future revelation. The Lord has given us sufficient for this day and time, and for the people who live in the world. ¶ When I read of the discussions, debates, and sometimes controversies, arising among religious leaders and learned men as to the problems and programs for Christian churches, I assure you I am profoundly grateful to be identified with a lofty cause, whose course is so fully and accurately and permanently charted that all you have to do to know the way and perceive the light is to ask and discover what the revelations say and what the priesthood directs. It seems to me that all that should be necessary to guide the course of any Christian cause is a simple declaration of the divine nature of the Christ and his supremacy in the world as the author of divine law which governs in the affairs of men. CR1954Oct:96

**Related Witnesses:**
**President Joseph F. Smith,**
**Anthon H. Lund, Charles W. Penrose**
(First Presidency)
Dogmatic assertions do not take the place of revelation, and we should be satisfied with that which is accepted as doctrine, and not discuss matters that, after all disputes, are merely matters of theory. (*Published message of the First Presidency of the Church, Jan. 1912; IE1912Mar:418*) MOFP4:265

**President Heber J. Grant**
Teachers will do well to give up indoctrinating themselves in the Sectarianisms of the new "Divinity School theology. . . ." ¶ In the teaching, the teachers will use verbiage and terminology which have become classic in the Church. . . . ¶ Furthermore, teachers will not advance their own theories about the Gospel or Gospel principles. (*Letter from First Presidency to Franklin L. West, Church commissioner of education, 1940*) MOFP6:209

**J. Reuben Clark, Jr.,**
*quoting Matthew Cowley*
I am told that Brother Matt Cowley once voiced this idea: He said something of this sort, "You know, I am so busy trying to understand the first principles of the Gospel that I have no time for the mysteries." CR1960Apr:20

**Elder Joseph Fielding Smith**
We who are called and ordained to the ministry or to teach in The Church of Jesus Christ of Latter-day Saints carry a very grave responsibility. Every man that teaches holds a great responsibility. And he that teaches error and

leads men from the path of truth is committing one of the greatest crimes that it is possible for man to commit. If he, through his teachings, is presenting false doctrine, and leading men astray from that which is eternal truth, away from the kingdom of God, he is taking upon himself a grave responsibility for which he will have to answer at the judgment seat of God. ¶ The Lord said in one of the early revelations before the organization of the Church that the worth of souls is great in the sight of God. Then he said if a man should labor all his days and convert but one soul, he should have great joy in the kingdom of our Father, and if he should convert many souls, then much greater would be that joy. Reversing the picture, he who blinds one soul, he who spreads error, he who destroys, through his teachings, divine truth, truth that would lead a man to the kingdom of God and to its fulness, how great shall be his condemnation and his punishment in eternity. For the destruction of a soul is the destruction of the greatest thing that has ever been created. . . . ¶ No matter what you teach, if it is not of God, it is darkness. And eventually, no matter how well it may be received, it must come to an end. (Take Heed to Yourselves! pp. 190-91) TLDP:668

**Elder Joseph Fielding Smith**
The gospel is simple. There is nothing difficult about it. There are mysteries, no doubt. We do not need to bother about the mysteries, but the simple things pertaining to our salvation and exaltation we can understand. CR1958Oct:22

**Paul**
For if the trumpet give an uncertain sound, who shall prepare himself to the battle? 9. So likewise ye, except ye utter by the tongue words easy to be understood, how shall it be known what is spoken? for ye shall speak into the air. (*Paul writes to the Church at Corinth, Greece, about A.D. 55*) 1Cor.14:8-9

**Paul**
Yet in the church I had rather speak five words with my understanding, that by my voice I might teach others also, than ten thousand words in an unknown tongue. (*Paul writes to the Church at Corinth, Greece, about A.D. 55*) 1Cor.14:19

**Author's Note:** We are encouraged to *learn* the "mysteries of God," as Ammon states in Alma 26:22. But it appears we are not to *teach* the mysteries until they are confirmed by the law of witnesses, by the voice of many prophets. This way we can avoid teaching views which do not harmonize with the official views of the Church. Orson Pratt once publicly expressed his regret at having done this very thing. He said: "There are a few things which have been a source of sorrow to myself. . . . ¶ . . . . There are some points of doctrine which I have unfortunately thrown out before the people. ¶ At the time I expressed those views, I did most sincerely believe that they were in accordance with the word of God. I did most sincerely suppose that I was justifying the truth. But I have since learned from my brethren that some of the doctrines I had advanced . . . were incorrect." Elder Pratt then proceeded to say why it is important not to teach our own views, even though sincere. "Have we not a right to make up our minds in relation to the things recorded in the word of God, and speak about them, whether the living oracles believe our views or not? We have not the right. Why? Because the mind of man is weak: one man may make up his mind in this way, and another man may make up his mind in another way, and a third individual may have his views; and thus every man is left to be his own authority, and is governed by his own judgment, which he takes as his standard. ¶ Do you not perceive that this would, in a short time, cause a complete disunion and division of sentiment throughout the whole Church?" (MOFP2:219) ¶ (Orson Pratt was, at times, publicly criticized by Brigham Young for teaching incorrect doctrine. But it is of great interest to note Brigham Young's famous tribute to Orson Pratt: "If Elder Pratt was chopped up in inch pieces, each piece would cry out Mormonism is true!" (Brigham Young's secretary's journal, Oct. 1, 1860)

---

806. **All members of the Church are to confine their public interpretations of doctrine to those that are in harmony with the President of the Church.**

**President Brigham Young,**
**Elder Wilford Woodruff, George A. Smith,**
**Amasa M. Lyman, Ezra T. Benson,**
**Charles C. Rich, Elder Lorenzo Snow,**
**Erastus Snow, Franklin D. Richards,**
**George Q. Cannon**

It ought to have been known, years ago, by every person in the Church—for ample teachings have been given on the point—that no member of the Church has the right to publish any doctrines, as the doctrines of the Church of Jesus Christ of Latter-day Saints, without first submitting them for examination and approval to the First Presidency and the Twelve. There is but one man upon the earth, at one time, who holds the keys to receive commandments and revelations for

the Church, and who has the authority to write doctrines by way of commandment unto the Church. And any man who so far forgets the order instituted by the Lord as to write and publish what may be termed new doctrines, without consulting with the First Presidency of the Church respecting them, places himself in a false position, and exposes himself to the power of darkness by violating his Priesthood. ¶ While upon this subject, we wish to warn all the Elders of the Church, and to have it clearly understood by the members, that, in the future, whoever publishes any new doctrines without first taking this course, will be liable to lose his Priesthood. (*Published proclamation of the First Presidency of the Church and the Twelve, Oct. 21, 1865*) MOFP2:238-39

**Orson Pratt,**
*quoted by President Brigham Young*

There are a few things which have been a source of sorrow to myself, at different times, for many years. ¶ Perhaps you may be desirous to know what they are. I will tell you. There are some points of doctrine which I have unfortunately thrown out before the people. ¶ At the time I expressed those views, I did most sincerely believe that they were in accordance with the word of God. I did most sincerely suppose that I was justifying the truth. But I have since learned from my brethren that some of the doctrines I had advanced . . . were incorrect. Naturally being of a stubborn disposition, and having a kind of selfwill about me, and moreover supposing really and sincerely that I did understand what true doctrine was in relation to those points, I did not feel to yield to the judgment of my brethren, but believed they were in error. Now, was this right? No, it was not. Why? Because the Priesthood is the highest and only legitimate authority in the Church in these matters. ¶ How is it about this? Have we not a right to make up our minds in relation to the things recorded in the word of God, and speak about them, whether the living oracles believe our views or not? We have not the right. Why? Because the mind of man is weak: one man may make up his mind in this way, and another man may make up his mind in another way, and a third individual may have his views; and thus every man is left to be his own authority, and is governed by his own judgment, which he takes as his standard. ¶ Do you not perceive that this would, in a short time, cause a complete disunion and division of sentiment throughout the whole Church? . . . ¶ "You have made this confession," says one; "and now we want to ask you a question on the subject. What do you believe concerning those points now?" ¶

I will answer. . . . So far as revelation from the heavens is concerned, I have had none in relation to those points of doctrine. (*Published message of the First Presidency of the Church, including primarily an address of Orson Pratt, Sr., Sept. 22, 1860*) MOFP2:218-19

## Mark E. Petersen

I believe that if a person accepts a position as a teacher in one of our organizations, or if he accepts the responsibility of preaching from the pulpit, such person accepts the responsibility which goes with that call. He becomes a representative of the Church in that position. Every teacher and every preacher therefore is duty bound, upon accepting such a call, to represent the official views and doctrines of the Church, and to teach those official doctrines in his class or from the pulpit with the one thought in mind that conversion is to come about in the hearts of those who listen to him. I do not believe that conversion to the truth comes through the teaching of half-truths or untruths. ¶ Our classrooms and our assembly rooms have been built at great expense with one thought in mind, and that is that in them we may teach the truth so that we may convert those who come there, so that they in turn will live the gospel and work out their salvation in the earth. CR1953Apr:83

## J. Reuben Clark, Jr.

You are not, whether high or low, to change the doctrines of the Church or to modify them, as they are declared by and in the Standard Works of the Church and by those whose authority it is to declare the mind and will of the Lord to the Church. The Lord had declared he is "the same yesterday, today, and forever." (*Speaking in behalf of First Presidency [see letter of First Presidency, MOFP6:208-09] to seminary, institute, and Church school teachers at Aspen Grove. Entire speech published in Deseret News, Church Section, Aug. 13, 1938 and in IE1938Sep:520ff; copied in MOFP6:44-58. The speech was extracted for use as Lesson 18 of the Melchizedek Priesthood Course of Study 1969-70, p. 129ff*) MPSG1969-70:137

### Related Witnesses:

## Elder Spencer W. Kimball

There are those today who seem to take pride in disagreeing with the orthodox teachings of the Church and who present their own opinions which are at variance with the revealed truth. Some may be partially innocent in the matter; others are feeding their own egotism; and some seem to be deliberate. Men may think as they please, but they have no right to impose upon others their unorthodox views. Such persons should realize that their own souls are in jeopardy. The Lord said

to us through the Prophet Joseph: ¶ "[T]each the principles of my gospel, which are in the Bible and the Book of Mormon, in the which is the fulness of the gospel. ¶ And they shall observe the covenants and church articles to do them, and these shall be their teachings, as they shall be directed by the Spirit. ¶ . . . . And if ye receive not the Spirit ye shall not teach." (D&C 42:12-14). . . . ¶ If one cannot accept and teach the program of the Church in an orthodox way without reservations, he should not teach. . . . ¶ And so we admonish the leaders in stakes, wards, and missions to be ever vigilant to see that no incorrect doctrines are promulgated in their classes or congregations. . . . And we warn again those who write or preach or otherwise teach subversive doctrines, that their punishment is sure for their "worm dieth not." CR1948Apr:109

## Mormon

And he commanded them that they should teach nothing save it were the things which he had taught, and which had been spoken by the mouth of the holy prophets. (*Alma organizes the Church of Christ and ordains priests, about 148 B.C.*) Mosiah 18:19

## President Joseph F. Smith

We have nothing that is not in common with the Latter-day Saints. We know nothing, and we will preach nothing to the people except that which the Lord God has revealed, and we advise and counsel those who are in authority, and whose duty and business it is to teach and preach the principles of the gospel to the world and to the Latter-day Saints, to confine their teachings and their instructions to the word of God that has been revealed. CR1917Oct:5

## President Joseph Fielding Smith
## Anthon H. Lund, Charles W. Penrose
(First Presidency),
*quoted by*
## President George Albert Smith,
## J. Reuben Clark, Jr., David O. McKay
*(First Presidency)*

When visions, dreams, tongues, prophecy, impressions, or an extraordinary gift of inspiration conveys something out of harmony with the accepted revelations of the Church or contrary to the decisions of its constituted authorities, Latter-day Saints may know that it is not of God, no matter how plausible it may appear. Also, they should understand that directions for the guidance of the Church will come by revelation, through the head. (*Published message of the First Presidency of the Church, Dec. 29, 1945, republishing a message of the previous First Presidency in 1913*) MOFP6:244

# List of Doctrines

## TEMPLES

*Doctrines Located in This Topic*

807. The Lord commands the building of temples.

808. Temples are holy sanctuaries for sacred rites and ceremonies pertaining to the living and the dead.

809. Certain ordinances are to be administered only in a holy temple (including baptisms for the dead; washings and annointings; and endowments and sealings for the living and for the dead).

810. The temple endowment comprises the receiving of certain sacred ordinances necessary to enable us to gain salvation (in the celestial kingdom).

811. A temple is built that the Lord might have a place to manifest Himself to His people.

812. Church members must be clean and faithful to receive and benefit from the blessings of the temple.

*Doctrines on TEMPLES Located in Other Topics*

88. One of the (threefold) missions of the Church is to perform vicarious ordinances for the redemption of the dead.

235. The object of gathering the people of God in any age is for their salvation, that they might obtain the ordinances administered in holy temples.

436. The temple marriage sealing ordinance is essential for exaltation in the celestial kingdom (it is a prerequisite to exaltation in the highest degree of the celestial kingdom.)

453. The great work of the Millennium shall be temple work for the redemption of the dead.

(See topic
DEATH: (3) Work for the Dead.)

# TEMPLES

## 807. The Lord commands the building of temples.

### Bruce R. McConkie

[W]henever the Lord has had a people on earth, from the days of Adam to the present moment, he has always commanded them to build temples so that they could be taught how to gain eternal life, and so that all of the ordinances of salvation and exaltation could be performed for and on their behalf. (The Mortal Messiah, 1:100) TLDP:675-76

### President Spencer W. Kimball

We indicate that these revealed truths should come to the people in a house built to his name. The Lord said that all the anointings, baptisms for the dead, solemn assemblies, and memorials and oracles, and the revelations pertaining to the foundation of Zion should be done in these holy places, the temples. All such sacred matters should be attended to inside such a building as he commanded to be built. ACR(Auckland)1979:4

### Nathan,
### receiving the Word of the Lord

Go and tell my servant David, Thus saith the LORD, Shalt thou build me an house for me to dwell in? 6. Whereas I have not dwelt in any house since the time that I brought up the children of Israel out of Egypt, even to this day, but have walked in a tent and in a tabernacle. . . . 12. And when thy days be fulfilled, and thou shalt sleep with thy fathers, I will set up thy seed after thee. . . . 13. He shall build an house for my name. . . . (David offers to build a house for the Lord, and the prophet Nathan responds) 2Sam.7:5-6,12-13

### Joseph Smith,
### receiving the Word of the Lord

And again, verily I say unto you, how shall your washings be acceptable unto me, except ye perform them in a house which you have built to my name? 38. For, for this cause I commanded Moses that he should build a tabernacle, that they should bear it with them in the wilderness, and to build a house in the land of promise, that those ordinances might be revealed which had been hid from before the world was. (Revelation received Jan. 19, 1841, Nauvoo, Ill.) D&C 124:37-38

### Elder Joseph Fielding Smith

[T]he work of baptism and other saving ordinances for the dead; the endowments, and all the ordinances that have been revealed to be performed in the sacred edifices called temples, which we are under commandment from God always to build unto His holy name,—(D&C 124:39) these things have been revealed to us in this dispensation in greater fulness and in greater plainness than ever before in the history of the world so far as we know. CR1913Oct:9-10

## 808. Temples are holy sanctuaries for sacred rites and ceremonies pertaining to the living and the dead.

### Elder Brigham Young, Heber C. Kimball, Orson Pratt, Lyman Wight, Elder John Taylor, Elder Wilford Woodruff, George A. Smith, Willard Richards

The time has come when the great Jehovah would have a resting place on earth, a habitation for his chosen, where his law shall be revealed, and his servants be endowed from on high, to bring together the honest in heart from the four winds; where the saints may enter the Baptismal font for their dead relations, so that they may be judged according to men in the flesh, and live according to God in the spirit, and come forth in the celestial kingdom; . . . a place where all the ordinances shall be made manifest and the saints shall unite in the songs of Zion, even praise, thanksgiving and hallelujahs to God and the Lamb, that he has wrought out their deliverance, and bound Satan fast in chains. (Epistle of the Twelve to the brethren scattered abroad on the continent of America) (Times and Seasons, Oct. 15, 1841, p. 569) TLDP:674

### Joseph Smith,
### receiving the Word of the Lord

For, for this cause I commanded Moses that he should build a tabernacle, that they should bear it with them in the wilderness, and to build a house in the land of promise, that those ordinances might be revealed which had been hid from before the world was. 39. Therefore, verily I say unto you, that your anointings, and your washings, and your baptisms for the dead, and your solemn assemblies, and your memorials for your sacrifices by the sons of Levi, and for your oracles in your most holy places wherein you receive conversations, and your statutes and judgments, for the beginning of the revelations and foundation of Zion, and for the glory, honor, and endowment of all her municipals, are ordained by the ordinance of my holy house, which my people are always commanded to build unto my holy name. 40. And verily I say unto you, let this house be built unto my name, that I may reveal mine ordinances there-in unto my people; 41. For I deign to reveal unto my church things which have been kept hid from before the foundation of the world, things that pertain to the dispensation of the fulness of times. (*Revelation received Jan. 19, 1841; the Saints are commanded to build a temple*) D&C 124:38-41

### President George Albert Smith

Each of them [the temples] has been built to one great eternal purpose: to serve as a House of the Lord, to provide a place sacred and suitable for the performing of holy ordinances that bind on earth as in heaven—ordinances for the dead and for the living that assure those who receive them and who are faithful to their covenants, the possession and association of their families, worlds without end, and exaltation with them in the celestial kingdom of our Father. ("The Tenth Temple," IE1945Oct:561) TLDP:675

### Related Witnesses:

#### Joseph Smith,
#### *receiving the Word of the Lord*

Let the hearts of your brethren rejoice, and let the hearts of all my people rejoice, who have, with their might, built this house to my name. 7. For behold, I have accepted this house, and my name shall be here; and I will manifest myself to my people in mercy in this house. 8. Yea, I will appear unto my servants, and speak unto them with mine own voice, if my people will keep my commandments, and do not pollute this holy house. 9. Yea the hearts of thousands and tens of thousands shall greatly rejoice in consequence of the blessings which shall be poured out, and the endowment with which my servants have been endowed in this house. 10. And the fame of this house shall spread to foreign lands; and this is the beginning of the blessing which shall be poured out upon the heads of my people. Even so. Amen. (*Vision manifested to Joseph Smith and Oliver Cowdery in the Kirtland Temple, April 3, 1836*) D&C 110:6-10

---

809. Certain ordinances are to be administered only in a holy temple (including baptisms for the dead; washings and annointings; and endowments and sealings for the living and for the dead).

#### Joseph Smith,
#### *quoted by Elder Joseph Fielding Smith*

The declaration this morning is, that as soon as the Temple and baptismal font are prepared, we

calculate to give the Elders of Israel their washings and anointings, and attend to those last and more impressive ordinances, without which we cannot obtain celestial thrones. But there must be a holy place prepared for that purpose. There was a proclamation made during the time that the foundation of the Temple was laid to that effect, and there are provisions made until the work is completed, so that men may receive their endowments and be made kings and priests unto the Most High God, having nothing to do with temporal things, but their whole time will be taken up with things pertaining to the house of God. There must, however, be a place built expressly for that purpose, and for men to be baptized for their dead. (*General conference of the Church, April 8, 1844*) HC6:319; TPJS:362-63

#### Joseph Smith

What was the object of gathering the Jews, or the people of God in any age of the world? . . . ¶ The main object was to build unto the Lord a house whereby He could reveal unto His people the ordinances of His house and the glories of His kingdom, and teach the people the way of salvation; for there are certain ordinances and principles that, when they are taught and practiced, must be done in a place or house built for that purpose. ¶ It was the design of the councils of heaven before the world was, that the principles and laws of the priesthood should be predicated upon the gathering of the people in every age of the world. Jesus did everything to gather the people, and they would not be gathered, and He therefore poured out curses upon them. [See Matt.23:37-39.] Ordinances instituted in the heavens before the foundation of the world, in the priesthood, for the salvation of men, are not to be altered or changed. All must be saved on the same principles. ¶ It is for the same purpose that God gathers together His people in the last days, to build unto the Lord a house to prepare them for the ordinances and endowments, washings and anointings, etc. One of the ordinances of the house of the Lord is baptism for the dead. . . . ¶ If a man gets a fullness of the priesthood of God, he has to get it in the same way that Jesus Christ obtained it, and that was by keeping all the commandments and obeying all the ordinances of the house of the Lord. (*At the Stand in Nauvoo, Ill., June 11, 1843*) HC5:423-24

#### President Spencer W. Kimball

The Lord said, "I deign to reveal unto my church things which have been kept hid from before the foundation of the world, things that pertain to the dispensation of the fulness of times." (D&C 124:41) There are many people who say, "Well, all a church has to do is to go into a meeting and decide things." That of course, is not true, for the Lord is at the head of the church, and he guides his leaders aright. ¶ We indicate that these revealed truths should come to the people in a house built to his name. The Lord said that all the anointings, baptisms for the dead, solemn assemblies, and memorials and oracles, and the revelations pertaining to the foundation of Zion should be done in these holy places, the temples. All such sacred matters should be attended to inside such a building as he commanded to be built. ACR(Auckland)1979:4

### Bruce R. McConkie

Why have temples? They are built by the tithing and sacrifice of the Lord's people; they are dedicated and given to him; they become his earthly houses; in them the mysteries of the kingdom are revealed; in them the pure in heart see God; in them men are sealed up unto eternal life—all to the end that man may become as his Maker, and live and reign forever in the heavenly Jerusalem, as part of the general assembly and Church of the Firstborn, where God and Christ are the judge of all. Of temples the Lord says: "Therein are the keys of the holy priesthood ordained, that you may receive honor and glory." In them, he says, his saints shall receive washing, anointing, baptisms, revelation, oracles, conversations, statutes, judgment, endowments, and sealings. In them are held solemn assemblies. In them the fulness of the priesthood is received and the patriarchal order conferred upon men. In them the family unit is made eternal. Because of them life eternal is available. With temples men can be exalted; without them there is no exaltation (D&C 124:28-40; 131:1-4; 132:1-33). (The Mortal Messiah, 1:99) TLDP:675-76

### President Brigham Young

This Priesthood has been restored again, and by its authority we shall be connected with our fathers, by the ordinance of sealing. . . . This ordinance will not be performed anywhere but in a Temple; neither will children be sealed to their living parents in any other place than a Temple. . . . Children born unto parents before the latter enter into the fullness of the covenants, have to be sealed to them in a Temple to become legal heirs of the Priesthood. (At Franklin, Utah, Sept. 4, 1873, JD16:186) TLDP:676

### Joseph Smith,
*quoted by Elder Joseph Fielding Smith*

One of the ordinances of the house of the Lord is baptism for the dead. God decreed before the foundation of the world that the ordinances should be administered in a font prepared for the purpose in the house of the Lord. (*Sermon at the Stand, Nauvoo, Ill., June 11, 1843*) TPJS:308

### Joseph Smith,
*quoted by Elder Joseph Fielding Smith*

In regard to the law of the Priesthood, there should be a place where all nations shall come up from time to time to receive their endowments; and the Lord has said this shall be the place for the baptisms for the dead. (*From an address at the Stand, Nauvoo, Ill., May 12, 1844*) TPJS:367

### Joseph Smith,
*receiving the Word of the Lord*

For verily I say unto you, that after you have had sufficient time to build a house to me, wherein the ordinance of baptizing for the dead belongeth, and for which the same was instituted from before the foundation of the world, your baptisms for your dead cannot be acceptable unto me; 34. For therein are the keys of the holy priesthood ordained, that you may receive honor and glory. . . . 38. For, for this cause I commanded Moses that he should build a tabernacle, that they should bear it with them in the wilderness, and to build a house in the land of promise, that those ordinances might be revealed which had been hid from before the world was. 39. Therefore, verily I say unto you, that your anointings, and your washings, and your baptisms for the dead, and your solemn assemblies, and your memorials for your sacrifices by the sons of Levi, and for your oracles in your most holy places wherein you receive conversations, and your statutes and judgments, for the beginning of the revelations and foundation of Zion, and for the glory, honor, and endowment of all her municipals, are ordained by the ordinance of my holy house, which my people are always commanded to build unto my holy name. 40. And verily I say unto you, let this house be built unto my name, that I may reveal mine ordinances therein unto my people; 41. For I deign to reveal unto my church things which have been kept hid from before the foundation of the world, things that pertain to the dispensation of the fulness of times. (*Revelation received Jan. 19, 1841; the Saints are commanded to build a temple*) D&C 124:33-34,38-41

### Related Witnesses:
### Elder Joseph Fielding Smith

What is bound or sealed in the temples of the Lord, is also sealed in heaven. This is the great authority which Elijah restored. It also covers ordinances performed for the living as well as for the dead. The Prophet said that all of the ordinances for the living are required in behalf of all the dead who are entitled to the fulness of the exaltation. CHMR2:329

**Joseph Smith**

Yea the hearts of thousands and tens of thousands shall greatly rejoice in consequence of the blessings which shall be poured out, and the endowment with which my servants have been endowed in this house. (*Vision manifested to Joseph Smith and Oliver Cowdery in the Kirtland Temple, April 3, 1836*) D&C 110:9

**Author's Note:** There have been times when temple ordinances have been administered in places other than in temples. Before the Nauvoo Temple was built, baptisms for the dead were performed in the Mississippi River for a limited time. The Lord then told Joseph "after you have had sufficient time to build a house to me, wherein the ordinance of baptizing for the dead belongeth, and for which the same was instituted from before the foundation of the world, your baptisms for your dead cannot be acceptable unto me. . . ." (See D&C 124.) The temple endowment has also been administered outside the temple both in Nauvoo and in Great Salt Lake City while a temple was waiting to be built. (See HC6:319.) But since temples have been available, these ordinances are now performed only in temples.

---

810. **The temple endowment comprises the receiving of certain sacred ordinances necessary to enable us to gain salvation (in the celestial kingdom).**

### President Brigham Young, *quoted by John A. Widtsoe*

Your endowment is, to receive all those ordinances in the house of the Lord, which are necessary for you, after you have departed this life, to enable you to walk back to the presence of the Father, passing the angels who stand as sentinels, being enabled to give them the key words, the signs and tokens, pertaining to the holy Priesthood, and gain eternal exaltation in spite of earth and hell. (*Oration delivered on laying the South-East Cornerstone of the Salt Lake Temple, April 1853, JD2:31*) DBY:416; MPSG1988:157

### Joseph Smith, *quoted by Elder Joseph Fielding Smith*

The declaration this morning is, that as soon as

the Temple and baptismal font are prepared, we calculate to give the Elders of Israel their washings and anointings, and attend to those last and more impressive ordinances, without which we cannot obtain celestial thrones. But there must be a holy place prepared for that purpose. There was a proclamation made during the time that the foundation of the Temple was laid to that effect, and there are provisions made until the work is completed, so that men may receive their endowments and be made kings and priests unto the Most High God, having nothing to do with temporal things, but their whole time will be taken up with things pertaining to the house of God. There must, however, be a place built expressly for that purpose, and for men to be baptized for their dead. It must be built in this the central place; for every man who wishes to save his father, mother, brothers, sisters and friends, must go through all the ordinances for each one of them separately, the same as for himself, from baptism to ordination, washings and anointings, and receive all the keys and powers of the Priesthood, the same as for himself. . . . ¶ The Lord has an established law in relation to the matter: there must be a particular spot for the salvation of our dead. I verily believe there will be a place, and hence men who want to save their dead can come and bring their families, do their work by being baptized and attending to the other ordinances for their dead, and then may go back again to live and wait till they go to receive their reward. (*General conference of Church, April 8, 1844*) HC6:319; TPJS:362-63

**Related Witnesses:**

### Joseph Smith

You need an endowment, brethren, in order that you may be prepared and able to overcome all things; and those that reject your testimony will be damned. (*Remarks made in meeting with the Council of the Twelve, Nov. 12, 1835*) HC2:309

### Elder Joseph Fielding Smith

Temples, according to the revelations of the Lord, are sanctuaries specially dedicated for sacred rites and ceremonies pertaining to exaltation in the celestial kingdom of God. . . . Temples are sanctified for the purpose of performing rites for and making covenants with the pure in heart, who have proved themselves by faithful service worthy of the blessings of exaltation. (Doctrines of Salvation, 2:231) MPSG1988:156

### Joseph Smith

Yea the hearts of thousands and tens of thousands shall greatly rejoice in consequence of the blessings which shall be poured out, and the endowment with which my servants have been endowed in this house. (*Vision manifested to Joseph Smith and Oliver Cowdery in the Kirtland Temple, April 3, 1836*) D&C 110:9

### John A. Widtsoe

We live in a world of symbols. No man or woman can come out of the temple endowed as he should be, unless he has seen, beyond the symbol, the mighty realities for which the symbols stand. ¶ To the man or woman who goes through the temple, with open eyes, heeding the symbols and the covenants, and making a steady, continuous effort to understand the full meaning, God speaks his word, and revelations come. The endowment is so richly symbolic that only a fool would attempt to describe it; it is so packed full of revelations to those who exercise their strength to seek and see, that no human words can explain or make clear the possibilities that reside in the temple service. The endowment which was given by revelation can best be understood by revelation; and to those who seek most vigorously, with pure hearts, will the revelation be greatest. ("Temple Worship," *Utah Genealogical and Historical Magazine,* April 1921, pp. 62-63) MPSG1988:157-58

### James E. Talmage

The Temple Endowment, as administered in modern temples, comprises instruction relating to the significance and sequence of past dispensations, and the importance of the present as the greatest and grandest era in human history. This course of instruction includes a recital of the most prominent events of the creative period, the condition of our first parents in the Garden of Eden, their disobedience and consequent expulsion from that blissful abode, their condition in the lone and dreary world when doomed to live by labor and sweat, the plan of redemption by which the great transgression may be atoned, the period of the great apostasy, the restoration of the Gospel with all its ancient powers and privileges, the absolute and indispensable condition of personal purity and devotion to the right in present life, and a strict compliance with Gospel requirements. HL:99-100

---

### 811. A temple is built that the Lord might have a place to manifest Himself to His people.

### Bruce R. McConkie

What is a temple? It is a house of the Lord; a house of Deity that is built on earth; a house

prepared by the saints as a dwelling place for the Most High, in the most literal sense of the word; a house where a personal God personally comes. It is a holy sanctuary, set apart from the world, wherein the saints of God prepare to meet their Lord; where the pure in heart shall see God, according to the promises. . . . ¶ When the Lord comes from heaven to the earth, as he does more frequently than is supposed, where does he make his visitations? Those whom he visits know the answer; he comes to one of his houses. Whenever the Great Jehovah visits his people, he comes, suddenly as it were, to his temple. If he has occasion to come when he has no house on earth, his visit is made on a mountain, in a grove, in a wilderness area, or at some location apart from the tumults and contentions of carnal men; and in that event the place of his appearance becomes a temporary temple, a site used by him in place of the house his people would normally have prepared. (*The Mortal Messiah,* 1:98-99) TLDP:675-76

### Joseph Smith

For thou knowest that we have done this work through great tribulation; and out of our poverty we have given of our substance to build a house to thy name, that the Son of Man might have a place to manifest himself to his people. 6. And as thou hast said in a revelation, given to us, calling us thy friends, saying—Call your solemn assembly, as I have commanded you; 7. And as all have not faith, seek ye diligently and teach one another words of wisdom; yea, seek ye out of the best books words of wisdom, seek learning even by study and also by faith; 8. Organize yourselves; prepare every needful thing, and establish a house, even a house of prayer, a house of fasting, a house of faith, a house of learning, a house of glory, a house of order, a house of God; 9. That your incomings may be in the name of the Lord, that your outgoings may be in the name of the Lord, that all your salutations may be in the name of the Lord, with uplifted hands unto the Most High— 10. And now, Holy Father, we ask thee to assist us, thy people, with thy grace, in calling our solemn assembly, that it may be done to thine honor and to thy divine acceptance; 11. And in a manner that we may be found worthy, in thy sight, to secure a fulfilment of the promises which thou hast made unto us, thy people, in the revelations given unto us; 12. That thy glory may rest down upon thy people, and upon this thy house, which we now dedicate to thee, that it may be sanctified and consecrated to be holy, and that thy holy presence may be continually in this house; 13. And that all people who shall enter upon the threshold of the Lord's house may feel thy power, and feel constrained to acknowledge that thou hast sanctified it, and that it is thy house, a place of thy holiness. (*Prayer revealed to Joseph Smith, offered at dedication of Kirtland Temple on March 27, 1836*) D&C 109:5-13

### Joseph Smith,
### receiving the Word of the Lord

Let the hearts of your brethren rejoice, and let the hearts of all my people rejoice, who have, with their might, built this house to my name. 7. For behold, I have accepted this house, and my name shall be here; and I will manifest myself to my people in mercy in this house. 8. Yea, I will appear unto my servants, and speak unto them with mine own voice, if my people will keep my commandments, and do not pollute this holy house. (*Visions manifested to Joseph Smith and Oliver Cowdery in the Kirtland Temple, April 3, 1836*) D&C 110:6-8

**Related Witnesses:**

### President Spencer W. Kimball

The house of the Lord is functional. Every element in the design, decoration, atmosphere, and program of the temple contributes to its function, which is to teach. The temple teaches of Christ. It teaches of his ordinances. It is filled with his Spirit. There is an aura of deity. (*Dedication of remodeled Arizona Temple, April 15, 1975*) (The Teachings of Spencer W. Kimball, pp. 534-35) TLDP:675

---

**812. Church members must be clean and faithful to receive and benefit from the blessings of the temple.**

### Joseph Smith

And that no unclean thing shall be permitted to come into thy house to pollute it; 21. And when thy people transgress, any of them, they may speedily repent and return unto thee, and find favor in thy sight, and be restored to the blessings which thou hast ordained to be poured out upon those who shall reverence thee in thy house. (*Prayer revealed to Joseph Smith, offered at dedication of Kirtland Temple on March 27, 1836*) D&C 109:20-21

### Stephen L. Richards

[I]t will never profit you anything by deception to win your way into the temple. It is true that we may deceive our bishops, our presidents of stakes. Some may get recommends without revealing what they ought to reveal. It is useless. All the blessings of the temples are predicated

upon faithfulness, upon obedience to the commandments. No blessing is effective unless it is based upon the good life of him who receives it. It is a mistake for anyone to think that by concealing or suppressing something that ought to be known he can secure a recommend to go to the temple. That is futile, and even worse than futile, because the suppressing of the fact is itself an additional offense. CR1959Apr:47

### Elder Spencer W. Kimball

But all these ordinances are futile unless with them there is a great righteousness. . . . Sometimes people feel if they have complied with the more mechanical things that they are in line. And yet perhaps their hearts are not always pure. . . . With hearts that are absolutely purged and cleaned, and living the more mechanical things, we are prepared to come into the holy temple. (*Dedication of the Swiss Temple, Sept. 15, 1955*) (The Teachings of Spencer W. Kimball, pp. 536-37) TLDP:679

### President Spencer W. Kimball

This is the work of the Lord, and he has given it to us. It is our responsibility, our pleasure, and our privilege to carry this work forward. We should so organize ourselves and the work that it will go forward in leaps and bounds. In the book of Revelation, John saw that sometime in the future (and it is still in the future to us), those who were faithful and have cleansed their lives will work night and day in the holy temples. Evidently there will be then a constant succession of groups going through the temple somewhat like it was in the days of the Nauvoo Temple [just before the Saints crossed the plains]. ("The Things of Eternity—Stand We in Jeopardy?" EN1977Jan:7) TLDP:678

### Marion G. Romney

God grant that we may be worthy to stand in his presence when we come here. To come unworthily into this temple and receive our endowments will not prove to be a blessing to us. Every soul when he comes here should be at peace in his own heart; his feelings should be at peace toward every other person in the world; he should have no hard feelings toward anyone. There should be no feelings of competition, no feelings of jealousy, nothing but the Spirit of the Living God and love toward our fellow men and toward each other, for here in his house we literally stand in the presence of the Lord. God grant that we may do so worthily. ("The House of the Lord," IE1965Feb:120) MPSG1988:161

### Elder Joseph Fielding Smith

Temples, according to the revelations of the Lord, are sanctuaries specially dedicated for sacred rites and ceremonies pertaining to

exaltation in the celestial kingdom of God. . . .
Temples are sanctified for the purpose of performing rites for and making covenants with
the pure in heart, who have proved themselves
by faithful service worthy of the blessings of
exaltation. (Doctrines of Salvation, 2:231)
MPSG1988:156

### President David O. McKay

Therefore, may all who seek this holy temple
come with clean hands and pure hearts that thy
holy spirit may ever be present to comfort, to
inspire, and to bless. (*Dedicatory prayer for the
Los Angeles Temple; IE1956Apr:227*)
MPSG1988:158

**Related Witnesses:**

### Ezekiel

Moreover this they have done unto me: they
have defiled my sanctuary in the same day, and
have profaned my sabbaths. 39. For when they
had slain their children to their idols, then they
came the same day into my sanctuary to profane it; and, lo, thus have they done in the midst
of mine house. (*Ezekiel declares the abominations of Samaria and Jerusalem*) Ezek.23:38-39

### Ezekiel

And they shall teach my people the difference
between the holy and profane, and cause them
to discern between the unclean and the clean.
(*The Lord instructs Ezekiel to reverence the
house of the Lord*) Ezek.44:23

### Joseph Smith,
#### receiving the Word of the Lord

Yea, I will appear unto my servants, and speak
unto them with mine own voice, if my people
will keep my commandments, and do not pollute this holy house. (*Vision manifested to
Joseph Smith and Oliver Cowdery in the
Kirtland Temple, April 3, 1836*) D&C 110:8

### Joseph Smith

And go ye out from among the wicked. Save
yourselves. Be ye clean that bear the vessels of
the Lord. Even so. Amen. (*Revelation of commandments to Saints in conference, Jan. 2,
1831*) D&C 38:42

### Recorded in Leviticus

Only he shall not go in unto the vail, nor come
nigh unto the altar, because he hath a blemish;
that he profane not my sanctuaries: for I the
LORD do sanctify them. (*Revelation to Moses
for the children of Israel*) Lev.21:23

# List of Doctrines

## TESTIMONY

*Doctrines Located in This Topic*

813. Testimonies of divine truths come through personal revelation.

814. To be capable of entering into celestial glory, each person must eventually gain an independent, personal testimony (of the truth of the gospel and its doctrines).

815. When teachers (missionaries and speakers) bear testimony of a gospel truth they have taught, the Spirit of God witnesses the truth thereof to the heart of the honest seeker.

816. We can gain testimonies of the gospel and its divine truths for ourselves through obedience to God.

817. Gospel study and prayer are necessary means for obtaining a testimony of the gospel.

818. A desire to believe starts the process for developing faith and obtaining a testimony of the gospel.

819. Only by revelation can a person know and testify that Jesus Christ is the Son of God.

*Doctrines on TESTIMONY Located in Other Topics*

532. We are to pray for a testimony of the gospel.

803. Before we can effectively teach the gospel we must first obtain an understanding of the gospel.

(See topic
TRUTH: Knowledge of Truth.)

# TESTIMONY

## 813. Testimonies of divine truths come through personal revelation.

### Elder Joseph Fielding Smith

A testimony of the gospel is a convincing knowledge given by revelation to the individual who humbly seeks the truth. Its convincing power is so great that there can be no doubt left in the mind when the Spirit has spoken. It is the only way that a person can truly know that Jesus is the Christ and that his gospel is true. There are millions of people on the earth who believe that Jesus lived and died and that his work was for the salvation of souls; but unless they have complied with his commandments and have accepted his truth as it has been restored, they do not know and cannot know the full significance of his mission and its benefits to mankind. Only through humble repentance and submission to the plan of salvation can this be made known. The way is open to all if they will receive his truth and accept his ordinances and abide faithfully in them. (Answers to Gospel Questions, 3:31) TLDP:685

### Elder Harold B. Lee

[R]evelation by the power of the Holy Ghost is required for one to receive a testimony— . . . (Stand Ye in Holy Places, pp. 194-95) TLDP:686

### Elder Harold B. Lee

[T]he Lord has said it was not only important that there be revelation to his Church through his mouthpiece, the one who held the keys, but his Church must also be founded on personal revelation, that every member of the Church who has been baptized and has received the Holy Ghost must be admonished so to live that each might receive a personal testimony and a witness of the divine calling of him who was called to lead as the President of the Church, so that he will accept those words and that counsel as if from the mouth of the Lord himself. CR1953Apr:28

### Elder Joseph F. Smith

We know that the One in whom we trust is God, for it has been revealed to us. We are not in the dark, neither have we obtained our knowledge from any man, synod or collection of men, but through the revelation of Jesus. If there be any who doubt us, let them repent of their sins. Is there any harm in your forsaking your follies and evils, and in bowing in humility before God for his Spirit, and in obedience to the words of the Savior, being baptized for the remission of sins, and having hands laid upon you for the gift of the Holy Ghost, that you may have a witness for yourselves of the truth of the words we

speak to you? Do this humbly and honestly, and as sure as the Lord lives, I promise you that you will receive the testimony of this work for yourselves, and will know it as all the Latter-day Saints know it. This is the promise; it is sure and steadfast. It is something tangible; it is in the power of every man to prove for himself whether we speak the truth or whether we lie. We do not come as deceivers or impostors before the world; we do not come with the intention to deceive, but we come with plain simple truth, and leave it to the world to test it and get a knowledge for themselves. It is the right of every soul that lives—the high, low, rich, poor, great and small, to have this testimony for themselves inasmuch as they will obey the gospel. (In new Tabernacle, Nov. 15, 1868) (Gospel Doctrine, p. 83) TLDP:685

### Bruce R. McConkie

And having thus testified again of his divine Sonship, Jesus promises that upon the rock of revealed truth, the rock of revelation, the rock of personal testimony received by the power of the Holy Ghost—upon this rock he will build this Church. And thus it has ever been. (The Mortal Messiah, 3:38) TLDP:688

### Elder Ezra Taft Benson

A testimony is to have current inspiration to know the work is true, not something we receive only once. The Holy Ghost abides with those who honor, respect, and obey God's laws. And it is that Spirit which gives inspiration to the individual. CR1983Apr:72

### President Spencer W. Kimball

You may know. You need not be in doubt. Follow the prescribed procedures, and you may have an absolute knowledge that these things are absolute truths. The necessary procedure is: study, think, pray, and do. Revelation is the key. God will make it known to you once you have capitulated and have become humble and receptive. Having dropped all pride of your mental stature, having acknowledged before God your confusion, having subjected your egotism, and having surrendered yourself to the teaching of the Holy Spirit, you are ready to begin to learn. With preconceived religious notions stubbornly held, one is not teachable. The Lord has promised repeatedly that he will give you a knowledge of spiritual things when you have placed yourself in a proper frame of mind. He has counseled us to seek, ask, and search diligently. (The Teachings of Spencer W. Kimball, p. 63) TLDP:686

### Elder Joseph Fielding Smith

The impressions on the soul that come from the Holy Ghost are far more significant than a vision. It is where Spirit speaks to spirit, and the imprint upon the soul is far more difficult to erase. Every member of the Church should have the impressions on his soul made by the Holy Ghost that Jesus is the Son of God indelibly pictured so that they cannot be forgotten. We read that it is the Spirit that giveth life. (*"The Twelve Apostles," address to the seminary and institute faculty at Brigham Young University, 1958, p. 6*) TLDP:683

**Related Witnesses:**

**Moroni, son of Mormon**

And when ye shall receive these things, I would exhort you that ye would ask God, the Eternal Father, in the name of Christ, if these things are not true; and if ye shall ask with a sincere heart, with real intent, having faith in Christ, he will manifest the truth of it unto you, by the power of the Holy Ghost. 5. And by the power of the Holy Ghost ye may know the truth of all things. (*Moroni's final writings, about A.D. 421*) Moro.10:4-5

**Alma, the younger,**
*quoted by Mormon*

For I am called to speak after this manner, according to the holy order of God, which is in Christ Jesus; yea, I am commanded to stand and testify unto this people the things which have been spoken by our fathers concerning the things which are to come. 45. And this is not all. Do ye not suppose that I know of these things myself? Behold, I testify unto you that I do know that these things whereof I have spoken are true. And how do you suppose that I know of their surety? 46. Behold, I say unto you they are made known unto me by the Holy Spirit of God. Behold, I have fasted and prayed many days that I might know these things of myself. And now I do know of myself that they are true; for the Lord God hath made them manifest unto me by his Holy Spirit; and this is the spirit of revelation which is in me. 47. And moreover, I say unto you that it has thus been revealed unto me, that the words which have been spoken by our fathers are true, even so according to the spirit of prophecy which is in me, which is also by the manifestation of the Spirit of God. (*Alma testifies to the people of the truth of his teachings, about 83 B.C.*) Alma 5:44-47

---

814. **To be capable of entering into celestial glory, each person must eventually gain an independent, personal testimony (of the truth of the gospel and its doctrines).**

**President Brigham Young**

Those men, or those women, who know no more about the power of God, and the influences of the Holy Spirit, than to be led entirely by another person, suspending their own understanding, and pinning their faith upon another's sleeve, will never be capable of entering into the celestial glory, to be crowned as they anticipate; they will never be capable of becoming Gods. They cannot rule themselves, to say nothing of ruling others, but they must be dictated to every trifle, like a child. . . . They never can hold scepters of glory, majesty, and power in the celestial kingdom. Who will? Those who are valiant and inspired with the true independence of heaven, who will go forth boldly to do as they please, determined to do right, though all mankind besides should take the opposite course. (*In Tabernacle, Feb. 20, 1853, JD1:312*) TLDP:683-84

**Elder Harold B. Lee**

The time is here when each of you must stand on your own feet. Be converted, because no one can endure on borrowed light. You will have to be guided by the light within yourself. If you do not have it, you will not stand. (Stand Ye in Holy Places, p. 95) TLDP:684

**Elder Harold B. Lee,**
*quoting Heber C. Kimball*

President Heber C. Kimball, shortly after the Saints had arrived here in the mountains—and some, I suppose, were somewhat gloating over the fact that they had triumphed for a temporary period over their enemies—had this to say: . . . *we think we are secure here in the chambers of the everlasting hills where we can close those few doors of the canyons against mobs and persecutors, the wicked and the vile, who have always beset us with violence and robbery, but I want to say to you, my brethren, the time is coming when we will be mixed up in these now peaceful valleys to that extent that it will be difficult to tell the face of a Saint from the face of an enemy to the people of God. Then, brethren, look out for the great sieve, for there will be a great sifting time, and many will fall—for I say unto you there is a test, a TEST, a TEST coming, and who will be able to stand? . . . ¶ You imagine,* said he, *that you would have stood by [the Prophet Joseph Smith] when persecution raged and he was assailed by foes within and without. You would have defended him and been true to him in the midst of every trial. You think you would have been delighted to have shown your integrity in the days of mobs and traitors. ¶ Let me say to you, that many of you will see the time when you will have all the trouble, trial and persecution that you can stand, and plenty of opportunities to show that you are true to God and his work. This Church has before it many close places through which it will have to pass before the work of God is crowned with victory. To meet the difficulties that are coming, it will be necessary for you to have a knowledge of the truth of this work for yourselves. The difficulties will be of such a character that the man or woman who does not possess this personal knowledge or witness will fall. If you have not got the testimony, live right and call upon the Lord and cease not till you obtain it. If you do not you will not stand. ¶ Remember these sayings, for many of you will live to see them fulfilled. The time will come when no man nor woman will be able to endure on borrowed light. Each will have to be guided by the light within himself. If you do not have it, how can you stand?* (Life of Heber C. Kimball, pp. 446, 449-50) CR1965Oct:128

**President Brigham Young**

I am more afraid that this people have so much confidence in their leaders that they will not inquire for themselves of God whether they are led by Him. I am fearful they settle down in a state of blind self-security, trusting their eternal destiny in the hands of their leaders with a reckless confidence that in itself would thwart the purposes of God in their salvation, and weaken that influence they could give to their leaders, did they know for themselves, by the revelations of Jesus, that they are led in the right way. Let every man and woman know, by the whispering of the Spirit of God to themselves, whether their leaders are walking in the path the Lord dictates, or not. (*In Tabernacle, Jan. 12, 1862, JD9:150*) TLDP:684

**Heber C. Kimball,**
*quoted by Elder Ezra Taft Benson*

Elder Heber C. Kimball stated: "The time will come when no man or woman will be able to endure on borrowed light." (Orson F. Whitney, Life of Heber C. Kimball, 1888 edition, p. 461) CR1963Oct:18

**Elder Harold B. Lee**

And now, finally, there is still one more thing that is necessary, to my thinking, before that preparation is made for the millennial reign. We must accept the divine mission of the Prophet Joseph Smith as the instrumentality through which the restoration of the gospel and the organization of the Church of Jesus Christ was accomplished. Each member of the Church, to be prepared for the millennial reign, must receive a testimony, each for himself, of the divinity of the work established by Joseph

Smith. It was this that was taught plainly by the Saints after the advent of the Savior upon the earth, and one of the leaders in our day has said it again, when he declared, I suppose with reference to the parable of the five foolish and five wise virgins in the Master's parable, "The time will come when no man nor woman will be able to endure on borrowed light. Each will have to be guided by the light within himself." (Life of Heber C. Kimball, pp. 449-50) CR1956Oct:62

**Related Witnesses:**

**John A. Widtsoe**

The essential thought must ever be that a man does not, except in his spiritual infancy, accept a statement merely because the Church or someone in authority declares it correct, but because, under mature examination, it is found to be true and right and worthwhile. Conversion must come from within. (Program of the Church, p. 24) TLDP:686

**Henry D. Moyle**

And finally the missionaries go to bear witness to the world that God lives, that Jesus is the Christ, that through the gift and power of the Holy Ghost we may all receive this same testimony for ourselves, independent of all else in the world. When received, this testimony is all consuming, all embracing. We know who we are, where we came from, and where through strict obedience to the laws and ordinances of the gospel we may go. Life's purpose becomes absolute and fixed. Our testimony and knowledge of God cannot be lost except through transgression. With transgression we also lose the Spirit of God and the Holy Ghost as our comforter. CR1963Apr:46

**President David O. McKay**

Every individual stands independent in his sphere in that testimony, just as these thousands of incandescent lamps which make Salt Lake City so brilliant at night, each one of which stands and shines in its own sphere, yet the light in it is produced by the same power, the same energy from which all the other lights receive their energy. So each individual in the Church stands independently in his sphere, independently in the knowledge that God lives, that the Savior is the Redeemer of the world, and that the gospel of Jesus Christ has been restored through Joseph Smith the Prophet. CR1960Oct:6

**Stephen L. Richards**

I repeat what I have said in this pulpit before: My grandfather was the close friend and companion of this man [Joseph Smith]. He knew him as intimately as one man may know another. He had abundant opportunity to detect any flaws in his character and discover any deceit in his work. He found none, and he has left his testimony to his family and to all the world that this man was true, that he was divinely commissioned for the work he had to do, and that he gave his life to the fulfillment of his mission. I have complete assurance that Willard Richards did not lie about his friend, and on my own account, independent of my grandfather's testimony, borne out of the spirit within me, I know that Joseph Smith was a prophet of the Living God, and the work he was instrumental in setting up in the earth is the veritable kingdom of our Father in heaven. CR1951Oct:118

**Author's Note:** In regard to obtaining one's own testimony, Elder Bruce R. McConkie wrote, "In speaking of these wondrous things I shall use my own words, though you may think they are the words of scripture, words spoken by other apostles and prophets. ¶ True it is they were first proclaimed by others, but they are now mine, for the Holy Spirit of God has borne witness to me that they are true, *and it is now as though the Lord had revealed them to me in the first instance.* I have thereby heard his voice and know his word." [italics added] (New Witness for the Articles of Faith, p. xii) ¶ Albert Schweitzer expressed similar thoughts in a non-religious context, "Living truth is that alone which has it origin in thinking. Just as a tree bears year after year the same fruit and yet fruit which is each year new, so must all permanently valuable ideas be continually born again in thought. . . . It is only by confidence in our ability to reach truth by our own individual thinking, that we are capable of accepting truth from outside" (Out of My Life and Thought, p. 173). ¶ If we paraphrase Albert Schweitzer, we may say this about a personally obtained testimony: A testimony that Jesus is the Christ, that Joseph Smith is a prophet of God, or that the gospel is true—or that a particular gospel doctrine is true and is part of the divine plan of salvation revealed from God to man, must come from within us. It cannot successfully be forced upon us from without, no matter how willing a subject we may be. Just as a tree bears year after year the same fruit and yet fruit which is each year new, so for all gospel truths, to have real force and effect in us, to become part of us—to become our own truths—they must be born again quietly in the heart of each of us. Each of us must gain for ourselves, from the inside, our own assurance that the doctrine is true. The gospel truth, then, is not a truth for all

of us, but rather a truth for each of us. It is only by confidence in our ability to obtain such a testimony by our own individual effort that we are capable of accepting truth from the outside—from the scriptures or from the pulpit.

---

815. **When teachers (missionaries and speakers) bear testimony of a gospel truth they have taught, the Spirit of God witnesses the truth thereof to the heart of the honest seeker.**

### Bruce R. McConkie
We do two things; we teach and we testify. We have to teach first so that we will have a basis for a testimony. We don't just bear testimony promiscuously; we bear testimony to back up teaching. Missionaries teach and testify. ACR(Sydney)1976:19

### Nephi, son of Lehi
[F]or when a man speaketh by the power of the Holy Ghost the power of the Holy Ghost carrieth it unto the hearts of the children of men. (*Nephi's writings, between 559-545 B.C.*) 2Ne.33:1

### President Joseph F. Smith
The individual testimony is a personal possession. One cannot give his testimony to another, yet he is able to aid his earnest brother in gaining a true testimony for himself. The over-zealous missionary may be influenced by the misleading thought that the bearing of his testimony to those who have not before heard the Gospel message, is to convince or condemn, as the hearers accept or reject. The elder is sent into the field to preach the Gospel—the good news of its restoration to earth, showing by scriptural evidence the harmony of the new message with the predictions of earlier times; expounding the truths embodied in the first principles of the Gospel; then if he bear his testimony under divine inspiration, such a testimony is as a seal attesting the genuineness of the truths he has declared, and so appealing to the receptive soul whose ears have been saluted by the heaven-sent message. . . . ¶ But the voicing of one's testimony, however eloquently phrased or beautifully expressed, is no fit or acceptable substitute for the needed discourse of instruction and counsel expected in a general gathering of the people. ("Testimony Bearing," Juvenile Instructor, Aug. 1, 1906, p. 465) TLDP:688
**Related Witnesses:**
### Elder Joseph Fielding Smith
People are converted by their hearts being penetrated by the Spirit of the Lord when they

humbly hearken to the testimonies of the Lord's servants. CHMR1:39-40; DCSM:13

### Joseph Smith

Therefore, why is it that ye cannot understand and know, that he that receiveth the word by the Spirit of truth receiveth it as it is preached by the Spirit of truth? 22. Wherefore, he that preacheth and he that receiveth, understand one another, and both are edified and rejoice together. D&C 50:21-22

### President Brigham Young,
*quoted by John A. Widtsoe*

The preacher needs the power of the Holy Ghost to deal out to each heart a word in due season, and the hearers need the Holy Ghost to bring forth the fruits of the preached word of God to his glory. (*In Bowery, Sept. 16, 1860, JD8:167*) DBY:333

### Alma, the younger,
*quoted by Mormon*

And this is not all. Do ye not suppose that I know of these things myself? Behold, I testify unto you that I do know that these things whereof I have spoken are true. And how do ye suppose that I know of their surety? 46. Behold, I say unto you they are made known unto me by the Holy Spirit of God. Behold, I have fasted and prayed many days that I might know these things of myself. And now I do know of myself that they are true; for the Lord God hath made them manifest unto me by his Holy Spirit; and this is the spirit of revelation which is in me. 47. And moreover, I say unto you that it has thus been revealed unto me, that the words which have been spoken by our fathers are true, even so according to the spirit of prophecy which is in me, which is also by the manifestation of the Spirit of God. 48. I say unto you, that I know of myself that whatsoever I shall say unto you, concerning that which is to come, is true. . . . (*Alma testifies to the people of the truth of his teachings, about 83 B.C.*) Alma 5:45-48

### Paul

Then Agrippa said unto Paul, Almost thou persuadest me to be a Christian. 29. And Paul said, I would to God, that not only thou, but also all that hear me this day, were both almost, and altogether such as I am, except these bonds. (*Paul has asked King Agrippa "Believest thou the prophets? I know that thou believest"*) Acts 26:28-29

### John

It is also written in your law, that the testimony of two men is true. 18. I am one that bear witness of myself, and the Father that sent me beareth witness of me. (*The Pharisees accuse Jesus of bearing record of himself without witnesses; Jesus responds*) John 8:17-18

### Amulek,
*quoted by Mormon*

And now, behold, I will testify unto you of myself that these things are true. Behold, I say unto you, that I do know that Christ shall come among the children of men, to take upon him the transgressions of his people, and that he shall atone for the sins of the world; for the Lord God hath spoken it. (*Amulek teaches the people about the atonement of Christ, 74 B.C.*) Alma 34:8

### Nephi, son of Helaman,
*quoted by Mormon*

And now behold, Moses did not only testify of these things, but also all the holy prophets, from his days even to the days of Abraham. (*Nephi speaks to the wicked Nephites, about 23-20 B.C.*) Hel.8:16

### Nephi, son of Helaman,
*quoted by Mormon*

Behold now, I do not say that these things shall be, of myself, because it is not of myself that I know these things; but behold, I know that these things are true because the Lord God has made them known unto me, therefore I testify that they shall be. (*Nephi speaks to the wicked Nephites, about 23-20 B.C.*) Hel.7:29

**Author's Note:** For a marvelous scriptural example of the workings of the Spirit as a result of teaching and testifying, read Alma 22:3-18. Aaron's teachings to Lamoni's father result in the king's conversion, and in the king saying, "What shall I do that I may have this eternal life of which thou hast spoken? Yea, what shall I do that I may be born of God, having this wicked spirit rooted out of my breast, and receive his Spirit, that I may be filled with joy, that I may not be cast off at the last day? Behold, said he, I will give up all that I possess, yea, I will forsake my kingdom, that I may receive this great joy." Then in a prayer to God the king declares further that not only would he give up all his *possessions* to receive eternal life but he would, in his own words, "give away all my *sins* to know thee, and that I may be raised from the dead, and be saved at the last day." [Italics added.]

---

### 816. We can gain testimonies of the gospel and its divine truths for ourselves through obedience to God.

### Jesus,
*quoted by John*

If any man will do his will, he shall know of the

doctrine, whether it be of God, or whether I speak of myself. (*Jesus teaches in the temple*) John 7:17

### John A. Widtsoe

I was brought up in scientific laboratories, where I was taught to test things, never to be satisfied unless a thing was tested. We have the right to test the Gospel of the Lord Jesus Christ. By testing it I mean living it, trying it out. Do you question the Word of Wisdom? Try it. Do you question the law of tithing? Practice it. Do you doubt the virtue of attending meetings? Attend them. Only then shall we be able to speak of these things intelligently and in such a way as to be respected by those who listen to us. Those who live the Gospel of Jesus Christ gain this higher knowledge, this greater testimony, this ultimate assurance that this is the truth. It is the way to truth. All the while . . . we must seek help from the great unseen world about us, from God and his messengers. We call that prayer. A man never finds perfect peace, never reaches afar unless he penetrates to some degree the unseen world, and reaches out to touch the hands, as it were, of those who live in that unseen world, the world out of which we came, the world into which we shall go. CR1938Oct:129

### President Ezra Taft Benson

I do not believe that a member of the Church can have an active, vibrant testimony of the gospel without keeping the commandments. A testimony is to have current inspiration to know the work is true, not something we receive only once. The Holy Ghost abides with those who honor, respect, and obey God's laws. And it is that Spirit which gives inspiration to the individual. CR1983Apr:72

### Elder Joseph F. Smith

If there be any who doubt us, let them repent of their sins. Is there any harm in your forsaking your follies and evils, and in bowing in humility before God for his Spirit, and in obedience to the words of the Savior, being baptized for the remission of sins, and having hands laid upon you for the gift of the Holy Ghost, that you may have a witness for yourselves of the truth of the words we speak to you? Do this humbly and honestly, and as sure as the Lord lives, I promise you that you will receive the testimony of this work for yourselves, and will know it as all the Latter-day Saints know it. This is the promise; it is sure and steadfast. It is something tangible; it is in the power of every man to prove for himself whether we speak the truth or whether we lie. We do not come as deceivers or impostors before the world; we do not come with the intention to deceive, but we come with plain simple truth, and leave it to the world to test it and get a knowledge for themselves. It is the right of every soul that lives— the high, low, rich, poor, great and small, to have this testimony for themselves inasmuch as they will obey the gospel. (*In new Tabernacle, Nov. 15, 1868*) (Gospel Doctrine, p. 83) TLDP:685

### Elder Spencer W. Kimball

You may know. You need not be in doubt. Follow the prescribed procedures, and you may have an absolute knowledge that these things are absolute truths. The necessary procedure is: study, think, pray, and do. (The Teachings of Spencer W. Kimball, p. 63) TLDP:686

### Elder Joseph Fielding Smith

A testimony of the gospel is a convincing knowledge given by revelation to the individual who humbly seeks the truth. Its convincing power is so great that there can be no doubt left in the mind when the Spirit has spoken. It is the only way that a person can truly know that Jesus is the Christ and that his gospel is true. There are millions of people on the earth who believe that Jesus lived and died and that his work was for the salvation of souls; but unless they have complied with his commandments and have accepted his truth as it has been restored, they do not know and cannot know the full significance of his mission and its benefits to mankind. Only through humble repentance and submission to the plan of salvation can this be made known. The way is open to all if they will receive his truth and accept his ordinances and abide faithfully in them. (Answers to Gospel Questions, 3:31) TLDP:685

### Related Witnesses:

### President Spencer W. Kimball

Every time you bear your testimony it becomes strengthened. ("President Kimball Speaks Out on Testimony," NE1981Aug:7) TLDP:689

### John A. Widtsoe

First, to keep our testimony we must feed it, regularly and plentifully. The steps that lead to a testimony: desire, prayer, study, and practice, must be trodden continuously. . . . ¶ . . . . To keep his testimony, a person must increase in the use of gospel principles. There must be stricter conformity with the higher as well as the lesser laws of life—more activity in Church service; increasing charity and kindness; greater sacrifice for the common good; more readiness to help advance the plan of salvation; more truth in all we do. And as our knowledge of gospel law increases, our activity under gospel law must increase. . . . ¶ . . . . The dying testimony is easily recognized. The organizations and practices of the Church are ignored; the radio takes the place of the sacrament meeting; golf or motion pictures, the Sunday worship; the cup of coffee, instead of the Word of Wisdom; the cold, selfish hand instead of helpfulness, charity for the poor and the payment of tithing. ¶ Soon, the testimony is gone, and the former possessor walks about, somewhat sour and discontented, and always in his heart, unhappy. He has lost his most precious possession, and has found nothing to replace it. He has lost inward freedom, the gift of obedience to law. (Gospel Interpretations, pp. 37-39) TLDP:687

**Author's Note:** When we perform acts in obedience to the will of God, without yet full knowledge that it is of God, the act of doing seems to leave traces on the mind and on the physical system. Hence, "If any man will do his will, he shall know of the doctrine, whether it be of God. . . ." (John 7:17)

---

817. Gospel study and prayer are necessary means for obtaining a testimony of the gospel.

### President Spencer W. Kimball
You may *know*. You need not be in doubt. Follow the prescribed procedures, and you may have an absolute knowledge that these things are absolute truths. The necessary procedure is: study, think, pray, and do. Revelation is the key. God will make it known to you once you have capitulated and have become humble and receptive. Having dropped all pride of your mental stature, having acknowledged before God your confusion, having subjected your egotism, and having surrendered yourself to the teaching of the Holy Spirit, you are ready to begin to learn. With preconceived religious notions stubbornly held, one is not teachable. The Lord has promised repeatedly that he will give you a knowledge of spiritual things when you have placed yourself in a proper frame of mind. He has counseled us to seek, ask, and search diligently. (The Teachings of Spencer W. Kimball, p. 63) TLDP:686

### Joseph Smith,
*receiving the Word of the Lord*
Behold, you have not understood; you have supposed that I would give it unto you, when you took no thought save it was to ask me. 8. But, behold, I say unto you, that you must study it out in your mind; then you must ask me if it be right, and if it is right I will cause that your bosom shall burn within you; therefore, you shall feel that it is right. 9. But if it be not right you shall have no such feelings, but you shall have a stupor of thought that shall cause you to forget the thing which is wrong; . . . (*Revelation for Oliver Cowdery, April 1829; the Book of Mormon is translated by study and by spiritual confirmation*) D&C 9:7-9

### John A. Widtsoe
The steps that lead to a testimony: desire, prayer, study, and practice, must be trodden continuously. The desire for truth should stamp our every act; help from God in all things must be invoked; the study of the gospel, which has not been plumbed to its depth by any man, should be continued; and the practice of gospel principles, in all our labors, must never be forgotten. ¶ . . . . By a little such study every day, light will follow light, and understanding will increase. This is doubly important since we live in a changing world, which requires continuous applications of gospel truth to new conditions. (Gospel Interpretations, pp. 37-39) TLDP:687

### Elder Joseph F. Smith
If I have learned something through prayer, supplication, and perseverance in seeking to know the truth, and I tell it to you, it will not be knowledge unto you. I can tell you how you can obtain it, but I cannot give it to you. If we receive this knowledge, it must come from the Lord. He can touch your understandings and your spirits, so that you shall comprehend perfectly and not be mistaken. But I cannot do that. You can obtain this knowledge through repentance, humility, and seeking the Lord with full purpose of heart until you find Him. He is not afar off. It is not difficult to approach Him, if we will only do it with a broken heart and a contrite spirit, as did Nephi of old. [2 Ne. 4:32] This was the way in which Joseph Smith, in his boyhood, approached Him. He went into the woods, knelt down, and in humility he sought earnestly to know which church was acceptable to God. He received an answer to his prayer, which he offered down in the depths of his heart, and he received it in a way that he did not expect. CR1899Oct:71

### John A. Widtsoe
[E]vidences are not enough to gain a testimony of the truth. . . . I was brought up in scientific laboratories, where I was taught to test things, never to be satisfied unless a thing was tested. We have the right to test the Gospel of the Lord Jesus Christ. By testing it I mean living it, trying it out. Do you question the Word of Wisdom? Try it. Do you question the law of tithing? Practice it. Do you doubt the virtue of

attending meetings? Attend them. Only then shall we be able to speak of these things intelligently and in such a way as to be respected by those who listen to us. Those who live the Gospel of Jesus Christ gain this higher knowledge, this greater testimony, this ultimate assurance that this is the truth. It is the way to truth. All the while, brethren and sisters, we must seek help from the great unseen world about us, from God and his messengers. We call that prayer. A man never finds perfect peace, never reaches afar unless he penetrates to some degree the unseen world, and reaches out to touch the hands, as it were, of those who live in that unseen world, the world out of which we came, the world into which we shall go. CR1938Oct:129

**Related Witnesses:**

**George Q. Cannon**

Prayer is to the soul like the irrigating stream to our dry and parched fields and orchards. Prayer nourishes, strengthens and imparts vitality to the seed. The seed grows under the influence of prayer. But where prayer is neglected, the results are just as we see them when we neglect to irrigate our fields and orchards. That which is planted there begins to wither and dry up. ¶ So it is with the word of God in the human soul; it must be watered by the Spirit of God. Prayer must be exercised in order to invoke the power and blessing of God to rest upon it. Then the seed grows; the tree grows and flourishes; its branches spread abroad and fill the whole man, and he knows that it is the word of God that he has received. He has a living and abiding testimony in his heart concerning it, and doubt has no room within him. But let him neglect his prayers, let him neglect to cultivate the seed and to watch over it, then it begins to wither, and he begins to doubt and to ask himself whether this is indeed the work of God. (Gospel Truth, 1:345) TLDP:684-85

**Alma, the younger,**
*quoted by Mormon*

Behold, I say unto you they are made known unto me by the Holy Spirit of God. Behold, I have fasted and prayed many days that I might know these things of myself. And now I do know of myself that they are true; for the Lord God hath made them manifest unto me by his Holy Spirit; and this is the spirit of revelation which is in me. (*Alma testifies to the people of the truth of his teachings, about 83 B.C.*) Alma 5:46

**Reed Smoot**

I thought this morning that I would refer to the question of prayer, for it is so vital to a man and woman, no matter what position they hold, in order that they may maintain a testimony, if they have one, of the Gospel of Jesus Christ; and if they haven't yet that testimony, I know of no better way in all the world to receive it than to plead with our Heavenly Father that it may be granted unto them. I know whereof I speak, because it was only through the humiliation of my soul and the prayers ascending to my God, at the request of the mother who gave me birth, that I received a testimony that this is God's work; and every prediction made by the servants of God in any age since it was established upon this earth, shall be fulfilled. CR1932Oct:85

---

**818. A desire to believe starts the process for developing faith and obtaining a testimony of the gospel.**

**Alma, the younger,**
*quoted by Mormon*

But behold, if ye will awake and arouse your faculties, even to an experiment upon my words, and exercise a particle of faith, yea, even if ye can no more than desire to believe, let this desire work in you, even until ye believe in a manner that ye can give place for a portion of my words. 28. Now, we will compare the word unto a seed. Now, if ye give place, that a seed may be planted in your heart, behold, if it be a true seed, or a good seed, if ye do not cast it out by your unbelief, that ye will resist the Spirit of the Lord, behold, it will begin to swell within your breasts; and when you feel these swelling motions, ye will begin to say within yourselves—It must needs be that this is a good seed, or that the word is good, for it beginneth to enlarge my soul; yea, it beginneth to enlighten my understanding, yea, it beginneth to be delicious to me. (*Alma teaches the poor and compares the word of God to a seed, about 74 B.C.*) Alma 32:27-28

**Elder Harold B. Lee**

With these truths made clear, then—first, that a testimony follows the exercise of faith, and second, that revelation by the power of the Holy Ghost is required for one to receive a testimony—the next question of our truth-seeking friend would naturally be, "Just how does one prepare himself to receive that divine witness called testimony?" ¶ As one reads this whole text [Alma 32], he finds clearly prescribed the way by which all may receive a testimony or "knowledge by revelation" as defined above: first, desire; second, belief; third, faith; fourth, knowledge or testimony. . . . ¶ But now we must understand one thing more: Faith necessary to knowledge comes by "hearing the word of God," as Paul said. (Stand Ye in Holy Places, pp. 194-95) TLDP:686

**John A. Widtsoe**

The steps that lead to a testimony: desire, prayer, study, and practice, must be trodden continuously. The desire for truth should stamp our every act. . . . (Gospel Interpretations, p. 37) TLDP:687

**Related Witnesses:**

**Moroni, son of Mormon**

And when ye shall receive these things, I would exhort you that ye would ask God, the Eternal Father, in the name of Christ, if these things are not true; and if ye shall ask with a sincere heart, with real intent, having faith in Christ, he will manifest the truth of it unto you, by the power of the Holy Ghost. 5. And by the power of the Holy Ghost ye may know the truth of all things. (*Moroni's final writings, about A.D. 421*) Moro.10:4-5

---

819. Only by revelation can a person know and testify that Jesus Christ is the Son of God.

**President Lorenzo Snow**

But no person can know that Jesus is the Son of God, except by revelation. CR1900Apr:3

**Joseph Smith,**
*quoted by Elder Joseph Fielding Smith*

Salvation cannot come without revelation; it is in vain for anyone to minister without it. No man is a minister of Jesus Christ without being a Prophet. No man can be a minister of Jesus Christ except he has the testimony of Jesus; and this is the spirit of prophecy. Whenever salvation has been administered, it has been by testimony. Men of the present time testify of heaven and hell, and have never seen either; and I will say that no man knows these things without this. (*Explaining the priesthood, July 1839*) HC3:389-90; TPJS:160; MGSP:8 (in part)

**Elder Joseph Fielding Smith**

The impressions on the soul that come from the Holy Ghost are far more significant than a vision. It is where Spirit speaks to spirit, and the imprint upon the soul is far more difficult to erase. Every member of the Church should have the impressions on his soul made by the Holy Ghost that Jesus is the Son of God indelibly pictured so that they cannot be forgotten. We read that it is the Spirit that giveth life. (*"The Twelve Apostles," address to the semi-*nary and institute faculty at Brigham Young University, 1958) TLDP:683

**Elder Joseph Fielding Smith**

A testimony of the gospel is a convincing knowledge given by revelation to the individual who humbly seeks the truth. Its convincing power is so great that there can be no doubt left in the mind when the Spirit has spoken. It is the only way that a person can truly know that Jesus is the Christ and that his gospel is true. There are millions of people on the earth who believe that Jesus lived and died and that his work was for the salvation of souls; but unless they have complied with his commandments and have accepted his truth as it has been restored, they do not know and cannot know the full significance of his mission and its benefits to mankind. Only through humble repentance and submission to the plan of salvation can this be made known. The way is open to all if they will receive his truth and accept his ordinances and abide faithfully in them. (Answers to Gospel Questions, 3:31) TLDP:685

**Bruce R. McConkie**

"Come unto me" and receive my Spirit, and then shall ye have power to learn of me. This is the great and grand secret. This is the course that is provided for us and for all men, and it is provided in the wisdom of him who knoweth all things. This is the sole and only way to learn of Christ within the full sense and meaning of his tender and solicitous invitation. "No man can know that Jesus is the Lord, but by the Holy Ghost." Little slivers of truth come to all who seek to know; occasional flashes of lightning give glimpses of the eternal realities that are hidden by the gloom and darkness of unbelief. But to learn and know those truths which reveal the Son of Man in his majesty and beauty and that prepare the truth seeker to be one with his Lord, such rays of the noonday sun shine forth only upon those who gain the enlightening companionship of the Holy Spirit. (The Mortal Messiah, 1:1) TLDP:283

**Bruce R. McConkie**

A true prophet is one who has the testimony of Jesus; one who knows by personal revelation that Jesus Christ is the Son of the living God, and that he was to be—or has been—crucified for the sins of the world; one to whom God speaks and who recognized the still small voice of the Spirit. (See The Millennial Messiah, pp. 168-70) TLDP:538

**Bruce R. McConkie**

We have the testimony of the Lord Jesus. We are a testimony-bearing people. When we say we have a testimony of this work, we mean three things in particular: we mean, number

one; that we know by the revelations of the
Holy Spirit to our souls that Jesus is the Lord,
that he was born into the world as the literal
Son of God, that he came with the power of
immortality because God was his father and he
was thereby able to work out the infinite and
eternal atoning sacrifice. The atonement of the
Lord Jesus is the most important single thing in
all revealed religion. The second point in our
testimony is that God has in these last days,
through the instrumentality primarily of Joseph
Smith, restored anew the knowledge of Christ
and the knowledge of salvation and given again
every key and power and right and prerogative
that enables us men to do the things that will
save and exalt us in the highest heaven of the
celestial world. And the third great truth in a
testimony is to know that The Church of Jesus
Christ of Latter-day Saints as now constituted
with President Spencer W. Kimball as its presiding officer is, in the most literal and real and
full sense of the word, the kingdom of God on
earth, the only true and living church upon the
face of the whole earth, and the one place
where salvation is found. ¶ Now when we say
that we have a testimony of the divinity of the
work, we mean those three things. We mean
that the Holy Spirit of God has spoken to the
spirit within us so that we know by revelation—not simply by mental analysis or by
reason but by personal revelation born of the
Holy Spirit—that those three great verities are
precisely that. ACR(Sydney)1976:17
**Related Witnesses:**
### President Brigham Young,
*quoted by John A. Widtsoe*
If you will follow the doctrines, and be guided
by the precepts of that book [the Bible] it will
direct you where you may see as you are seen,
where you may converse with Jesus Christ,
have the visitation of angels, have dreams,
visions, and revelations, and understand and
know God for yourselves. (*In Tabernacle, July
1853, JD1:243*) DBY:126; DGSM:5

# List of Doctrines

## THOUGHTS AND INTENTIONS

*Doctrines Located in This Topic*

820. Our minds should be occupied with virtuous and righteous thoughts.

821. We are to abstain from impure thoughts.

822. Our thoughts are to be directed unto the Lord.

823. The Lord knows our thoughts and the intents of our hearts.

824. The Lord judges us by what we are in our minds and hearts, not by how we may appear to others.

825. We are what we think and what we feel in our hearts —and we generally act accordingly.

826. Our evil thoughts will condemn us.

*Doctrines on THOUGHTS AND INTENTIONS Located in Other Topics*

370. In His just judgment, God will take into account the thoughts and desires of our hearts.

625. We are to repent in our hearts.

# THOUGHTS AND INTENTIONS

**820.** Our minds should be occupied with virtuous and righteous thoughts.

### President Joseph F. Smith
I wish to say to all who read these lines that the key to purity is found in chaste thoughts, and the young man who obtains it will be able to unlock a rich storehouse of cleanliness enabling his life to be as the fresh morning. ("Three Threatening Dangers," IE1914Mar:478) TLDP:690

### Paul
Finally, brethren, whatsoever things are true, whatsoever things are honest, whatsoever things are just, whatsoever things are pure, whatsoever things are lovely, whatsoever things are of good report; if there be any virtue, and if there be any praise, think on these things. (*Paul writes from Rome to the Church at Philippi in Macedonia*) Philip.4:8

### Joseph Smith
[L]et virtue garnish thy thoughts unceasingly; then shall thy confidence wax strong in the presence of God; and the doctrine of the priesthood shall distil upon thy soul as the dews from heaven. (*Revelation received while in Liberty Jail, March 20, 1839; the priesthood should be used only in righteousness*) D&C 121:45

### Joseph Smith,
*receiving the Word of the Lord*
And if your eye be single to my glory, your whole bodies shall be filled with light, and there shall be no darkness in you; and that body which is filled with light comprehendeth all things. 68. Therefore, sanctify yourselves that your minds become single to God, and the days will come that you shall see him; for he will unveil his face unto you, and it shall be in his own time, and in his own way, and according to his own will. 69. Remember the great and last promise which I have made unto you; cast away your idle thoughts and your excess of laughter far from you. (*Revelation received Dec. 27/28, 1832; the "olive leaf message of peace"*) D&C 88:67-69

### Alma, the younger,
*quoted by Mormon*
[L]et all thy thoughts be directed unto the Lord. . . . (*Alma instructs his son Helaman, about 73 B.C.*) Alma 37:36

**Related Witnesses:**
### Recorded in Proverbs
The thoughts of the righteous are right: but the counsels of the wicked are deceit. Prov.12:5

**821.** We are to abstain from impure thoughts.

### Joseph Smith,
*receiving the Word of the Lord*
And he that looketh upon a woman to lust after her shall deny the faith, and shall not have the Spirit; and if he repents not he shall be cast out. (*Revelation "embracing the law of the Church," Feb. 9, 1831*) D&C 42:23

### Jesus,
*quoted by Mormon*
Behold, it is written by them of old time, that thou shalt not commit adultery; 28. But I say unto you, that whosoever looketh on a woman, to lust after her, hath committed adultery already in his heart. 29. Behold, I give unto you a commandment, that ye suffer none of these things to enter into your heart; 30. For it is better that ye should deny yourselves of these things, wherein ye will take up your cross, than that ye should be cast into hell. (*The resurrected Jesus Christ teaches the Nephite people, A.D. 34*) 3Ne.12:27-30

### Alma, the younger,
*quoted by Mormon*
For our words will condemn us, yea, all our works will condemn us; we shall not be found spotless; and our thoughts will also condemn us; and in this awful state we shall not dare to look up to our God; and we would fain be glad if we could command the rocks and the mountains to fall upon us to hide us from his presence. (*Alma contends with the wicked Zeezrom, about 82 B.C.*) Alma 12:14

### Jesus,
*recorded in Mark*
There is nothing from without a man, that entering into him can defile him: but the things which come out of him, those are they that defile the man. 16. If any man have ears to hear, let him hear. 17. And when he was entered into the house from the people, his disciples asked him concerning the parable. 18. And he saith unto them, Are ye so without understanding also? Do ye not perceive, that whatsoever thing from without entereth into the man, it cannot defile him; 19. Because it entereth not into his heart, but into the belly, and goeth out into the draught, purging all meats? 20. And he said, That which cometh out of the man, that defileth the man. 21. For from within, out of the heart of men, proceed evil thoughts, adulteries, fornications, murders, 22. Thefts, covetousness, wickedness, deceit, lasciviousness, an evil eye, blasphemy, pride, foolishness; 23. All these evil

things come from within, and defile the man. (*Jesus instructs the people*) Mark 7:15-23

**President David O. McKay**
"Tell me what you think about when you do not have to think, and I will tell you what you are." ¶ Temptation does not come to those who have not thought of it before. Keep your thoughts clean, and it will be easy to resist temptations as they come. (Gospel Ideals, p. 401) TLDP:690

**Isaiah**
Let the wicked forsake his way, and the unrighteous man his thoughts: and let him return unto the LORD, and he will have mercy upon him; and to our God, for he will abundantly pardon. (*740-659 B.C.*) Isa.55:7

**King Benjamin,**
*quoted by Mormon*
[I]f ye do not watch yourselves, and your thoughts . . . ye must perish. . . . (*King Benjamin addresses his people, about 124 B.C.*) Mosiah 4:30

**Paul**
Doth not behave itself unseemly, seeketh not her own, is not easily provoked, thinketh no evil; . . . (*Paul writes about charity to the Church at Corinth, Greece, about A.D. 55*) 1Cor.13:5

**Related Witnesses:**

**Boyd K. Packer**
Choose . . . a favorite hymn . . . one that makes you feel something akin to inspiration. Go over it in your mind carefully. Memorize it. . . . ¶ Now, use this hymn as the place for your thoughts to go. . . . Whenever you find these shady actors [shady thoughts] have slipped from the sidelines of your thinking onto the stage of your mind, put on this record, as it were. As the music begins and as the words form in your thoughts, the unworthy ones will slip shamefully away. It will change the whole mood on the stage of your mind. Because it is uplifting and clean, the baser thoughts will disappear. For, while virtue, by choice, will not associate with filth, evil cannot tolerate the presence of light. CR1986Oct:100

**Authors Note:** Elder Ezra Taft Benson said: "Sometimes we may have difficulty driving off the stage of our minds a certain evil thought. To drive it off, Elder Boyd K. Packer suggested that we sing an inspirational song of Zion, or think on its words." (Teachings of Ezra Taft Benson, p. 382)

**Moses**
And GOD saw that the wickedness of man was great in the earth, and that every imagination of the thoughts of his heart was only evil continually. 6. And it repented the LORD that

he had made man on the earth, and it grieved him at his heart. (*The people are ripe in iniquity; the Lord prepares the great flood*) Gen.6:5-6

**Recorded in Proverbs**
The thoughts of the wicked are an abomination to the LORD: but the words of the pure are pleasant words. Prov.15:26

---

**822. Our thoughts are to be directed unto the Lord.**

**Alma, the younger,**
*quoted by Mormon*
Yea, and cry unto God for all thy support; yea, let all thy doings be unto the Lord, and whithersoever thou goest let it be in the Lord; yea, let all thy thoughts be directed unto the Lord; yea, let the affections of thy heart be placed upon the Lord forever. 37. Counsel with the Lord in all thy doings, and he will direct thee for good; yea, when thou liest down at night lie down unto the Lord, that he may watch over you in your sleep; and when thou risest in the morning let thy heart be full of thanks unto God; and if ye do these things, ye shall be lifted up at the last day. (*Alma instructs his son Helaman, about 73 B.C.*) Alma 37:36-37

**Marion G. Romney**
If we would avoid adopting the evils of the world, we must pursue a course which will daily feed our minds with, and call them back to, the things of the spirit. I know of no better way to do this than by reading the Book of Mormon. . . . ¶ I am persuaded that it is irrational to hope to escape the lusts of the world without substituting for them as the subjects of our thoughts the things of the spirit. (Learning for the Eternities, pp. 83-84) TLDP:691

**Joseph Smith,**
*receiving the Word of the Lord*
Look unto me in every thought; doubt not, fear not. (*Revelation to Joseph Smith and Oliver Cowdery, April 1829*) D&C 6:36

**Recorded in Psalms**
The wicked, through the pride of his countenance, will not seek after God: God is not in all his thoughts. Ps.10:4

**Related Witnesses:**

**Recorded in Psalms**
In the multitude of my thoughts within me thy comforts delight my soul. Ps.94:19

**Mormon**
And again, when they thought of the immediate goodness of God, and his power in delivering Alma and his brethren out of the hands of the Lamanites and of bondage, they did raise their

voices and give thanks to God. (*King Mosiah reads to his people the account of Alma and his brethren and their afflictions; the people respond, about 120 B.C.*) Mosiah 25:10

---

## 823. The Lord knows our thoughts and the intents of our hearts.

**Joseph Smith,**
*receiving the Word of the Lord*
Yea, I tell thee, that thou mayest know that there is none else save God that knowest thy thoughts and the intents of thy heart. (*Revelation for Oliver Cowdery, April 1829*) D&C 6:16

**Joseph Smith,**
*receiving the Word of the Lord*
Behold, I say unto you, my servants Ezra and Northrop, open your ears and hearken to the voice of the Lord your God, whose word is quick and powerful, sharper than a two-edged sword, to the dividing asunder of the joints and marrow, soul and spirit; and is a discerner of the thoughts and intents of the heart. (*Revelation for Ezra Thayre and Northrop Sweet, Oct. 1830*) D&C 33:1

**Recorded in 1 Samuel**
But the LORD said unto Samuel, Look not on his countenance, or on the height of his stature; because I have refused him: for the LORD seeth not as man seeth; for man looketh on the outward appearance, but the LORD looketh on the heart. (*The Lord through Samuel chooses David to be king*) 1Sam.16:7

**Alma, the younger,**
*quoted by Mormon*
Now Zeezrom, seeing that thou hast been taken in thy lying and craftiness, for thou hast not lied unto men only but thou hast lied unto God; for behold, he knows all thy thoughts, and thou seest that thy thoughts are made known unto us by his spirit; . . . (*Alma contends with the wicked Zeezrom, about 82 B.C.*) Alma 12:3

**Recorded in Matthew**
And Jesus knew their thoughts. . . . (*The Pharisees said that Jesus cast out devils by the power of the devil*) Matt.12:25

**Recorded in 1 Chronicles**
And thou, Solomon my son, know thou the God of thy father, and serve him with a perfect heart and with a willing mind: for the Lord searchest all hearts, and understandeth all the imaginations of the thoughts: if thou seek him, he will be found of thee; but if thou forsake him, he will cast thee off for ever. (*Solomon has been told by King David that he has been chosen by*

the Lord to build a house unto the Lord) 1Chr.28:9

**Isaiah**
For I know their works and their thoughts. . . . (*The word of the Lord to Isaiah; the wicked shall be destroyed*) Isa.66:18

**Jesus,**
*recorded in Matthew*
And Jesus knowing their thoughts said, Wherefore think ye evil in your hearts? (*The scribes call it blasphemy when Jesus, healing a man with palsy, says, "thy sins be forgiven thee"*) Matt.9:4

**Paul**
For the word of God is quick and powerful, and sharper than any two-edged sword, piercing even to the dividing asunder of soul and spirit, and of joints and marrow, and is a discerner of the thoughts and intents of the heart. (*Paul writes to the Jewish members of the Church, about A.D. 60*) Heb.4:12

**Recorded in 1 Kings**
Then hear thou in heaven thy dwelling place, and forgive, and do, and give to every man according to his ways, whose heart thou knowest; (for thou, even thou only, knowest the hearts of all the children of men;) . . . (*King Solomon calls upon the Lord*) 1Kgs.8:39

**Related Witnesses:**
**Joseph Smith**
After we had received this revelation, Oliver Cowdery stated to me that after he had gone to my father's to board, and after the family had communicated to him concerning my having obtained the plates, that one night after he had retired to bed he called upon the Lord to know if these things were so, and the Lord manifested to him that they were true, but he had kept the circumstance entirely secret, and had mentioned it to no one; so that after this revelation was given, he knew that the work was true, because no being living knew of the thing alluded to in the revelation, but God and himself. (*Entry in Joseph's journal, April 1829*) HC1:35

**Joseph Smith,**
*translating the Book of Moses*
And Satan . . . knew not the mind of God, wherefore he sought to destroy the world. (*The Lord instructs Moses about the devil, the father of lies*) Moses 4:6

---

**Author's Note:** Only the Lord—and, at times and in part, his righteous servants—can know our thoughts and intents: "there is none else save God that knowest thy thoughts and the intents of thy heart." (D&C 6:16) Satan does not have this ability.

824. The Lord judges us by what we are in our minds and hearts, not by how we may appear to others.

**Recorded in 1 Samuel**
But the LORD said unto Samuel, Look not on his countenance, or on the height of his stature; because I have refused him: for the LORD seeth not as man seeth; for man looketh on the outward appearance, but the LORD looketh on the heart. (*The Lord through Samuel chooses David to be king; Samuel examines Eliab, son of Jesse*) 1Sam.16:7

**President George Albert Smith**
All at once there came to me this interpretation of what he [Karl Maeser] had said: Why of course you will be held accountable for your thoughts, because when your life is completed in mortality, it will be the sum of your thoughts. That one suggestion has been a great blessing to me all my life, and it has enabled me upon many occasions to avoid thinking improperly, because I realize that I will be when my life's labor is complete, the product of my thoughts. (Sharing the Gospel with Others, p. 63) TLDP:691

**Elder John Taylor**
We may deceive one another, and, in some circumstances, as counterfeit coin passes for that which is considered true and valuable among men. But God searches the hearts and tries the reins of the children of men. He knows our thoughts and comprehends our desires and feelings; he knows our acts and the motives which prompt us to perform them. He is acquainted with all the doings and operations of the human family, and all the secret thoughts and acts of the children of men are open and naked before him, and for them he will bring them to judgment. (*In Fourteenth Ward, Nov. 16, 1873, JD16:301-02*) TLDP:691

**President John Taylor**
We may succeed in hiding our affairs from men; but it is written that for every word and every secret thought we shall have to give an account in the day when accounts have to be rendered before God, when hypocrisy and fraud of any kind will not avail us; for by our words and by our works we shall be justified, or by them we shall be condemned. (*To some settlements on a trip to Bear Lake, JD24:232*) TLDP:691

**Related Witnesses:**

**Mormon**
Now when Alma saw this his heart was grieved; for he saw that they were a wicked and a perverse people; yea, he saw that their hearts

were set upon gold, and upon silver, and upon all manner of fine goods. . . . 28. Behold, O my God, their costly apparel, and their ringlets, and their bracelets, and their ornaments of gold, and all their precious things which they are ornamented with; and behold, their hearts are set upon them, and yet they cry unto thee and say— We thank thee, O God, for we are a chosen people unto thee, while others shall perish. (*Alma heads a mission to reclaim the apostate Zoramites and observes their customs, about 74 B.C.*) Alma 31:24,28

---

825. We are what we think and what we feel in our hearts—and we generally act accordingly.

**George Q. Cannon**
It is very true that "As he thinketh in his heart, so is he." (Prov.23:7) Words and actions are but the external fruits of the inward thoughts of the soul; they must be conceived there before they find their birth from the lips or the hands of the corporeal frame. Hence, we can see the necessity of properly governing our thoughts and of cultivating a habit of pure and correct thinking. (Gospel Truth, 2:200) TLDP:690

**Recorded in Proverbs**
For as he thinketh in his heart, so is he. . . . (*Proverbial literature*) Prov.23:7

**Marion G. Romney**
The great overall struggle in the world today is, as it has always been, for the souls of men. Every soul is personally engaged in the struggle, and he makes his fight with what is in his mind. In the final analysis the battleground is, for each individual, within himself. Inevitably he gravitates toward the subjects of his thoughts. Ages ago the wise man thus succinctly states this great truth: "As he thinketh in his heart, so is he" (Prov.23:7). CR1980Apr:88

**Elder Harold B. Lee**
Thought is the father of an act. No man ever committed murder who did not first become angry. No one ever committed adultery without a preceding immoral thought. The thief did not steal except he first coveted that which was his neighbor's. (Church News, Nov. 6, 1943; Stand Ye in Holy Places, p. 370) TLDP:690

**President David O. McKay**
Thoughts are the seeds of acts and precede them. Mere compliance with the word of the Lord, without a corresponding inward desire, will avail but little. Indeed, such outward actions and pretending phrases may be vehemently condemned. . . . ¶ . . . . What a man con-

tinually thinks about determines his actions in times of opportunity and stress. A man's reaction to his appetites and impulses when they are aroused gives the measure of that man's character. In these reactions are revealed the man's power to govern or his forced servility to yield. CR1951Oct:6,8

### Elder Spencer W. Kimball

Every thought that one permits through his mind leaves its trace. Thoughts are things. Our lives are governed a great deal by our thoughts. *(Brisbane, Australia Area Conference, March 1, 1976)* (The Teachings of Spencer W. Kimball, p. 154) TLDP:690

**Related Witnesses:**
### Jesus,
*recorded in Matthew*
Ye have heard that it was said by them of old time, Thou shalt not commit adultery: 28. But I say unto you, That whosoever looketh on a woman to lust after her hath committed adultery with her already in his heart. *(Jesus Christ to the multitude, about A.D. 30)* Matt.5:27-28

### Jesus,
*recorded in Matthew*
For where your treasure is, there will your heart be also. *(Jesus continues the Sermon on the Mount)* Matt.6:21

### Paul
Unto the pure all things are pure: but unto them that are defiled and unbelieving is nothing pure; but even their mind and conscience is defiled. *(Paul writes to his companion Titus, about A.D. 64)* Titus 1:15

---

## 826. Our evil thoughts will condemn us.

### Alma, the younger,
*quoted by Mormon*
For our words will condemn us, yea, all our works will condemn us; we shall not be found spotless; and our thoughts will also condemn us; and in this awful state we shall not dare to look up to our God; and we would fain be glad if we could command the rocks and the mountains to fall upon us to hide us from his presence. *(Alma contends with the wicked Zeezrom, about 82 B.C.)* Alma 12:14

### Elder David O. McKay
Actions in harmony with divine law and the laws of nature will bring happiness and those in opposition to divine truth, misery. Man is responsible not only for every deed, but also for every idle word and thought. ¶ "We are spinning our own fates good or evil, and never to be undone. Every smallest stroke of virtue or of

vice leaves its ever so little scar. The drunken Rip Van Winkle, in Jefferson's play, excuses himself for every fresh dereliction by saying, 'I won't count this time.' Well, he may not count it, and a kind Heaven may not count it; but it is being counted none the less. Down among the nerve-cells and fibers the molecules are counting it, registering and storing it up to be used against him when the next temptation comes." (William James) CR1950Apr:33-34

### King Benjamin,
*quoted by Mormon*
But this much I can tell you, that if ye do not watch yourselves, and your thoughts, and your words, and your deeds, and observe the commandments of God, and continue in the faith of what ye have heard concerning the coming of our Lord, even unto the end of your lives, ye must perish. And now, O man, remember, and perish not. *(King Benjamin addresses his people, about 124 B.C.)* Mosiah 4:30

### President Spencer W. Kimball
If we think that [poem] through, we will realize that it is very true, that the things we tolerate in our lives finally become a part of us. [See Alexander Pope's An Essay on Man, lines 217-20.] It means that all of the teachings that are given to us are fundamental and true and need to be followed. Ugly things, evil thoughts, and evil doings will take place in our lives if we think about them and tolerate them in our minds, and then we will suffer. Eventually we will pay for that which we have done.

[*"Vice is a monster of so frightful mein,
As, to be hated, needs but to be seen;
Yet seen too oft, familiar with her face,
We first endure, then pity, then embrace."*]
ACR(Manilla)1975:5

**Related Witnesses:**
### Moses
And GOD saw that the wickedness of man was great in the earth, and that every imagination of the thoughts of his heart was only evil continually. 6. And it repented the LORD that he had made man on the earth, and it grieved him at his heart. 7. And the LORD said, I will destroy man whom I have created from the face of the earth; both man, and beast, and the creeping thing, and the fowls of the air; for it repenteth me that I have made them. *(The people are ripe in iniquity; the Lord prepares the great flood)* Gen.6:5-7

# List of Doctrines

## TITHING

# TITHING

**827.** Members of the Lord's Church are to give as tithing one-tenth of all their increase annually.

### Howard W. Hunter
The law is simply stated as "one-tenth of all their interest." Interest means profit, compensation, increase. It is the wage of one employed, the profit from the operation of a business, the increase of one who grows or produces, or the income to a person from any other source. The Lord said it is a standing law "forever" as has been in the past. CR1964Apr:35

### President Joseph F. Smith
The law of tithing was instituted because the people could not abide the greater law. If we could live up to the law of consecration, then there would be no necessity for the law of tithing, because it would be swallowed up in the greater law. The law of consecration requires all; the law of tithing only requires one-tenth of your increase annually. (Millennial Star, June 1894, p. 386) TLDP:106

### Elder John Taylor
He [Elder Taylor] . . . said one of the clerks had asked whether any should be baptized who had not paid their tithing; it is our duty to pay our tithing, one-tenth of all we possess, and then one-tenth of our increase, and a man who has not paid his tithing is unfit to be baptized for his dead. It is as easy for a man who has ten thousand dollars to pay one thousand, as it is for a man who has but a little to pay one-tenth. It is our duty to pay our tithing. If a man has not faith enough to attend to these little things, he has not faith enough to save himself and his friends. It is a man's duty to attend to these things. The poor are not going to be deprived of these blessings because they are poor; no, God never reaps where he has not sown. This command is harder for the rich than the poor; a man who has one million dollars, if he should give one hundred thousand, he would think he was beggared forever. The Savior said, how hardly do they that have riches enter the kingdom of heaven. (*Conference in Nauvoo, Ill., Oct. 6, 1844; reported in the Times and Seasons*) HC7:292-93

### President Brigham Young
There have been so much inquiry it becomes irksome: the law is for a man to pay one-tenth of all he possesses for the erecting of the House of God, the spread of the gospel, and the support of the priesthood. When man comes into the church he wants to know if he must reckon his clothing, bad debts, lands, etc. It is the law to give one-tenth of what he has got, and then one-tenth of his increase or one-tenth of his time. (*Oct. 7, 1844, Brigham has been sustained as president of the Quorum of the Twelve, and as one of the First Presidency; he addresses the principle of tithing*) HC7:301

### Joseph Smith,
### *receiving the Word of the Lord*
And after that, those who have thus been tithed shall pay one-tenth of all their interest annually; and this shall be a standing law unto them forever, for my holy priesthood, saith the Lord. (*Revelation instituting the law of tithing in these latter days, July 8, 1839*) D&C 119:4

### President Joseph F. Smith
The tithing system of the Church . . . is in reality a system of free-will offerings. . . . [T]he members, by the law of the Church, are under moral obligation to pay one-tenth of their interest annually. . . . [T]here is no compulsory means of collecting this or any other Church revenue. Tithing is a voluntary offering for religious and charitable purposes. . . . (*Address from the First Presidency of the Church to the world, delivered to and accepted by vote of the Church in general conference, April 1907*) CR1907Apr(Appendix)9

**Related Witnesses:**

### Jacob (Israel),
### *quoted by Moses*
And this stone, which I have set for a pillar, shall be God's house: and of all that thou shalt give me I will surely give the tenth unto thee. (*Jacob covenants to pay tithes—after the vision of a ladder reaching up into heaven*) Gen.28:22

### Alma, the younger,
### *quoted by Mormon*
And it was this same Melchisedek to whom Abraham paid tithes; yea, even our father Abraham paid tithes of one-tenth part of all he possessed. (*Alma tells the people about the great high priest Melchizedek, about 82 B.C.*) Alma 13:15

### Paul
For this Melchisedec, king of Salem, priest of the most high God, who met Abraham returning from the slaughter of the kings, and blessed him; 2. To whom also Abraham gave a tenth part of all; first being by interpretation King of righteousness, and after that also King of Salem, which is, King of peace; . . . (*Letter to the Jewish members of the Church, about A.D. 60*) Heb.7:1-2

### Rudger Clawson
There are doubtless many of the people who only paid a partial tithing, or as Bishop Preston

says, "a little ten per cent," which he informs us is not ten per cent at all. Ten per cent is ten per cent, and a tithing is ten per cent, neither more nor less. When it is below that, the view has been held that it is simply an offering to the Lord. . . . ¶ . . . . We learned from President Cannon last night that the law of tithing is just as essential and as saving a principle as the principle of baptism or the laying on of hands. CR1900Apr:45

**Stephen L. Richards**

I have said in your presence before that tithing does not mean one-fiftieth, nor one-thirtieth, nor one-twentieth. Tithing means one-tenth. I have sometimes wondered what a part tithing means. I have never seen any definition of it, but I know what a tithing means. So far as I know, there is only one tithing, and that is one-tenth. So I believe that you brethren in authority could bring a lot of happiness to men and women throughout the Church if you yourselves would fully comply with this law that the Lord has given to us. CR1952Apr:84

**Malachi**

Will a man rob God? Yet ye have robbed me. But ye say, Wherein have we robbed thee? In tithes and offerings. 9. Ye are cursed with a curse: for ye have robbed me, even this whole nation. 10. Bring ye all the tithes into the storehouse, that there may be meat in mine house, and prove me now herewith, saith the LORD of hosts, if I will not open you the windows of heaven, and pour you out a blessing, that there shall not be room enough to receive it. (*The prophet Malachi to the people of Israel, about 430 B.C.*) Mal.3:8-10

**Jesus,**
*quoted by Mormon*

Will a man rob God? Yet ye have robbed me. But ye say: Wherein have we robbed thee? In tithes and offerings. . . . 10. Bring ye all the tithes into the storehouse. . . . (*The resurrected Christ commands the Nephites to write the words which the Father had given to Malachi, which he would now tell them, A.D. 34*) 3Ne.24:8,10

**President Lorenzo Snow**

The word of the Lord to you is not anything new; it is simply this: THE TIME HAS COME FOR EVERY LATTER-DAY SAINT WHO CALCULATES TO BE PREPARED FOR THE FUTURE AND TO HOLD HIS FEET STRONG UPON A PROPER FOUNDATION, TO DO THE WILL OF THE LORD AND PAY HIS TITHING IN FULL. That is the word of the Lord to you, and it will be the word of the Lord to every settlement throughout the land of Zion. . . . [T]he time has come when every man

should stand up and pay his tithing in full. (*At St. George, Utah, May 8, 1899*) MOFP3:313

**Author's Note:** The revelation through Joseph Smith instituting the law of tithing in the latter days, July 8, 1839, required the saints to pay their surplus property to the Church and thereafter to give as tithing one-tenth of their *interest* annually. (See D&C 119.) In 1844 Brigham Young said: "It is the law to give one-tenth of what he has got, and then one-tenth of his increase or one-tenth of his time." Since then the prophets have interpreted the word *interest* to mean *increase*, as can be observed from the witnesses quoted above. Howard W. Hunter makes it quite clear: "The law is simply stated as 'one-tenth of all their interest.' Interest means profit, compensation, increase. It is the wage of one employed, the profit from the operation of a business, the increase of one who grows or produces, or the income to a person from any other source." (CR1964Apr:35)

---

828. **The law of tithing was instituted because the people could not abide the greater law of consecration.**

**President Joseph F. Smith**

The law of tithing was instituted because the people could not abide the greater law. If we could live up to the law of consecration, then there would be no necessity for the law of tithing, because it would be swallowed up in the greater law. The law of consecration requires all; the law of tithing only requires one-tenth of your increase annually. (Millennial Star, June 1894, p. 386) TLDP:106

**Elder Joseph F. Smith**

Now, if we are not faithful to this law [of tithing], what evidence have we that we shall be faithful in other things? The Lord instituted it as a substitute, because of our lack of faith, for the higher law of consecration in which the Lord requires not only all that we have, but our hearts also; and by this substitute He designs to prove us, to see whether we will be obedient or not. I perceive in this principle something that is of greater worth to me than all the substance that I put into the storehouse of the Lord as tithing. CR1899Apr:68

**President Lorenzo Snow**

Joseph tried to develop [the Saints] so that they would conform to the law of consecration, which is in advance of the law of tithing, and is a principle which, as sure as I am speaking, you

and I will one day have to conform to.
CR1900Oct:61-62

### Francis M. Lyman

Before we enter upon the law of consecration, which is the celestial law of God in finance, it is necessary that we should take the training that we are now having under the law of tithing. ¶ You may be certain, my brethren and sisters, that any person who is not able to observe this law faithfully and well will never, worlds without end, be able to observe the law of consecration. The law of tithing is a stepping stone, and it is a law that will abide forever, because a great majority possibly of the children of God will not be able to reach the higher law. CR1899Oct:34

### Orson F. Whitney

Those who obey the Law of Tithing will be prepared to live the Law of Consecration. Those who do not obey it will not be prepared. That is the whole thing in a nut shell. We are tithed that the Church may have means to build and maintain temples and tabernacles, to found and sustain missions and schools, and otherwise carry on its great work throughout the world. But that is not all. The spiritual dividend that we draw from heaven as the reward of our obedience, is the principal purpose for which the Law of Tithing was instituted. All the rest is incidental or secondary. CR1931Apr:66

**Related Witnesses:**

### Melvin J. Ballard

No man can live the Order of Enoch who has not learned how to honestly live the law of tithing. CR1934Apr:70

# List of Doctrines

## TRANSLATED BEINGS

*Doctrines Located in This Topic*

829. Some mortals have been translated; in this state their bodies are changed so that they are not subject to disease, sorrow, or death.

830. Translated beings eventually undergo a change equivalent to death.

# TRANSLATED BEINGS

**829.** Some mortals have been trans- lated; in this state their bodies are changed so that they are not sub- ject to disease, sorrow, or death.

### Bruce R. McConkie

Some mortals have been translated. In this state they are not subject to sorrow or to disease or to death. No longer does blood (the life-giv- ing element of our present mortality) flow in their veins. Procreation ceases. If they then had children, their offspring would be denied a mortal probation, which all worthy spirits must receive in due course. They have power to move and live in both a mortal and an unseen sphere. All translated beings undergo another change in their bodies when they gain full immortality. This change is the equivalent of a resurrection. All mortals, after death, are also resurrected. In the resurrected state they are immortal and eternal in nature, and those among them who are privileged to live in the family unit have spirit children. Millennial man will live in a state akin to translation. His body will be changed so that it is no longer sub- ject to disease or death as we know it, although he will be changed in the twinkling of an eye to full immortality when he is a hundred years of age. He will, however, have children, and mor- tal life of a millennial kind will continue. (The Millennial Messiah, p. 644) TLDP:699-70

### Joseph Smith

Many have supposed that the doctrine of trans- lation was a doctrine whereby men were taken immediately into the presence of God, and into an eternal fullness, but this is a mistaken idea. Their place of habitation is that of the terrestrial order, and a place prepared for such characters He held in reserve to be ministering angels unto many planets, and who as yet have not entered into so great a fullness as those who are resur- rected from the dead. . . . ¶ Now it was evident that there was a better resurrection, or else God would not have revealed it unto Paul. Wherein then, can it be said a better resurrection? This distinction is made between the doctrine of the actual resurrection and translation: translation obtains deliverance from the tortures and suf- ferings of the body, but their existence will pro- long as to the labors and toils of the ministry, before they can enter into so great a rest and glory. (*From an article on priesthood, read at a general conference of the Church by Robert B. Thompson, and included as part of minutes of the conference held in Nauvoo, Ill., Oct. 5, 1840, HC4:207-12*) HC4:210

### George Q. Cannon

"Does translation imply an entire change in the body?" ¶ There is nothing written upon this sub- ject concerning Elijah, who was translated. But we have the words of the Lord in the Book of Mormon concerning the three Nephites unto whom the promise was made, in the words of Jesus, "For ye shall never taste of death." They were told that they should "never endure the pains of death," but when Jesus should come in His glory they were to "be changed in the twink- ling of an eye from mortality to immortality." They were not to have pain while they should "dwell in the flesh, neither sorrow save it be for the sins of the world." They were caught up into heaven, and it is recorded that they could not tell whether they were in the body or out of the body; "for it did seem unto them like a trans- figuration of them, that they were changed from this body of flesh into an immortal state." In speaking of them, the Prophet Mormon says, "Whether they were mortal or immortal from the day of their transfiguration" he knew not. ¶ This gives us a clear idea of the change that was wrought in these three Apostles. In the transla- tion of Elijah and others who may have been translated there doubtless were similar changes made such as the Prophet Mormon describes as having taken place in the case of the three Nephites. (Gospel Truth, 1:36-37) TLDP:699

### Jesus,
#### *quoted by Mormon*

And it came to pass when Jesus had said these words, he spake unto his disciples, one by one, saying: What is it that ye desire of me, after that I am gone to the Father? 2. And they all spake, save it were three, saying: We desire that after we have lived unto the age of man, that our ministry, wherein thou hast called us, may have an end, that we may speedily come unto thee in thy kingdom. 3. And he said unto them: Blessed are ye because ye desired this thing of me; therefore, after that ye are sev- enty and two years old ye shall come unto me in my kingdom; and with me ye shall find rest. 4. And when he had spoken unto them, he turned himself unto the three, and said unto them: What will ye that I should do unto you, when I am gone unto the Father? 5. And they sorrowed in their hearts, for they durst not speak unto him the thing which they desired. 6. And he said unto them: Behold, I know your thoughts, and ye have desired the thing which John, my beloved, who was with me in my ministry, before that I was lifted up by the Jews, desired of me. 7. Therefore, more blessed are ye, for ye shall never taste of death; but ye shall live to behold all the doings of the Father unto the children of men, even until all things shall be fulfilled according to the will of the Father, when I shall come in my glory with the powers of heaven. 8. And ye shall never endure the pains of death; but when I shall come in my glory ye shall be changed in the twinkling of an eye from mortality to immortality; and then shall ye be blessed in the kingdom of my Father. 9. And again, ye shall not have pain while ye shall dwell in the flesh, neither sorrow save it be for the sins of the world; and all this will I do because of the thing which ye have desired of me, for ye have desired that ye might bring the souls of men unto me, while the world shall stand. . . . 12. And it came to pass that when Jesus had spoken these words, he touched every one of them with his finger save it were the three who were to tarry, and then he departed. *(Nine of the twelve disciples desire and are promised an inheritance in Christ's kingdom when they die—the three Nephites desire and are given power over death so as to remain on the earth until Jesus comes again)* 3Ne.28:1-9,12

**Related Witnesses:**

### Paul

By faith Enoch was translated that he should not see death; and was not found, because God had translated him: for before his translation he had this testimony, that he pleased God. *(Letter to the Jewish members of the Church, about A.D. 60)* Heb.11:5

### President John Taylor

It would appear that the translated residents of Enoch's city are under the direction of Jesus, who is the Creator of worlds: and that He, holding the keys of the government of other worlds, could, in His administrations to them, select the translated people of Enoch's Zion, if He thought proper, to perform a mission to these various planets, and as death had not passed upon them, they could be prepared by Him and made use of through the medium of the Holy Priesthood to act as ambassadors, teachers, or messengers to those worlds over which Jesus holds the authority. . . . ¶ Each kingdom, or planet, and the inhabitants thereof, were blessed with the visits and presence of their Creator, in their several times and seasons. (The Mediation and Atonement, pp. 76-77) TLDP:699

### Joseph Smith, translating the Book of Moses

And it came to pass that the Lord showed unto Enoch all the inhabitants of the earth; and he beheld, and lo, Zion, in process of time, was taken up into heaven. And the Lord said unto

Enoch: Behold mine abode forever. . . . 27. And Enoch beheld angels descending out of heaven, bearing testimony of the Father and Son; and the Holy Ghost fell on many, and they were caught up by the powers of heaven into Zion. . . . 29. And Enoch said unto the Lord. . . . 31. And thou hast taken Zion to thine own bosom, from all thy creations. . . . *(The record of Moses: Enoch views the earth)* Moses 7:21,27,29,31

### Moses

And Enoch walked with God: and he was not; for God took him. *(The generations of Adam are set forth)* Gen.5:24

### Joseph Smith, receiving the Word of the Lord

I am the same which have taken the Zion of Enoch into mine own bosom. . . . *(Revelation of commandments to Saints in conference, Jan. 2, 1831)* D&C 38:4

### Joseph Smith, translating the Book of Moses

Wherefore, hearken ye together and let me show unto you even my wisdom—the wisdom of him whom ye say is the God of Enoch, and his brethren, 12. Who were separated from the earth, and were received unto myself—a city reserved until a day of righteousness shall come—a day which was sought for by all holy men, and they found it not because of wickedness and abominations; *(Revelation, March 7, 1831)* D&C 45:11-12

### Joseph Smith

Enoch was twenty-five years old when he was ordained under the hand of Adam; and he was sixty-five and Adam blessed him. 49. And he saw the Lord, and he walked with him, and was before his face continually; and he walked with God three hundred and sixty-five years, making him four hundred and thirty years old when he was translated. *(Revelation on priesthood received as the Twelve met in council, March 28, 1835)* D&C 107:48-49

### Bruce R. McConkie

Enoch and his whole city were translated, taken up bodily into heaven without tasting death. There they served and labored with bodies of flesh and bones, bodies quickened by the power of the Spirit, until that blessed day when they were with Christ in his resurrection. Then, in the twinkling of an eye, they were changed and became immortal in the full sense of the word. So it was also with Moses and Elijah, who were taken up bodily into heaven for reasons that will be manifest on the Mount of Transfiguration. They too were with the Lord Jesus in his resurrection. (See D&C 133:54-55.) (The Mortal Messiah, 3:52) TLDP:700

**Jesus,**
*quoted by John*

Peter seeing him saith to Jesus, Lord, and what shall this man do? 22. Jesus saith unto him, If I will that he tarry till I come, what is that to thee? follow thou me. *(Peter asks Jesus about John)* John 21:21-22

**John,**
*quoted by Joseph Smith,*
*translating a parchment record of John's*

And the Lord said unto me: John, my beloved, what desirest thou? For if you shall ask what you will, it shall be granted unto you. 2. And I said unto him: Lord, give unto me power over death, that I may live and bring souls unto thee. 3. And the Lord said unto me: Verily, verily, I say unto thee, because thou desirest this thou shalt tarry until I come in my glory, and shalt prophesy before nations, kindreds, tongues and people. *(Revelation given to Joseph Smith the Prophet and Oliver Cowdery, at Harmony, Pennsylvania, April 1829, when they inquired through the Urim and Thummim as to whether John, the beloved disciple, tarried in the flesh or had died. The revelation is a translated version of the record made on parchment by John and hidden up by himself.)* HC1:35-36; D&C 7:1-3

**Joseph Smith**

After this vision had closed, another great and glorious vision burst upon us; for Elijah the prophet, who was taken to heaven without tasting death, stood before us, . . . *(Vision manifested to Joseph Smith and Oliver Cowdery in the Kirtland Temple, April 3, 1836)* D&C 110:13

**Joseph Smith,**
*receiving the Word of the Lord*

Wherefore, I will that all men shall repent, for all are under sin, except those which I have reserved unto myself, holy men that ye know not of. *(Revelation, March 1831)* D&C 49:8

**Jesus,**
*recorded in Matthew*

Verily I say unto you, There be some standing here, which shall not taste of death, till they see the Son of man coming in his kingdom. *(Jesus speaks to his disciples and foretells his death and resurrection)* Matt.16:28

**Mormon**

And when Alma had done this he departed out of the land of Zarahemla, as if to go into the land of Melek. And it came to pass that he was never heard of more; as to his death or burial we know not of. 19. Behold, this we know, that he was a righteous man; and the saying went abroad in the church that he was taken up by the Spirit, or buried by the hand of the Lord, even as Moses. But behold, the scriptures saith

the Lord took Moses unto himself; and we suppose that he has also received Alma in the spirit, unto himself; therefore, for this cause we know nothing concerning his death and burial. *(Mormon records the disappearance of Alma, the younger, 73 B.C.)* Alma 45:18-19

---

**830. Translated beings eventually undergo a change equivalent to death.**

**Joseph Smith**

Translated bodies cannot enter into rest until they have undergone a change equivalent to death. Translated bodies are designed for future missions. *(Conference of the Church, Oct. 3, 1841, Nauvoo, Ill.)* HC4:425

**Elder Joseph Fielding Smith**

Translated beings are still mortal and will have to pass through the experience of death, or the separation of the spirit and the body, although this will be instantaneous. The people of the City of Enoch, Elijah, and others who received this great blessing of translation in ancient times, *before* the coming of our Lord, could not have received the resurrection, or the change from mortality to immortality at that time, because our Lord had not paid the debt which frees us from mortality and grants to us the resurrection and immortal life. ¶ Christ is the "resurrection and the life" and the first fruits of them that slept. Therefore, none could pass from mortality to immortality until our Savior completed his work for the redemption of man and had gained the keys of the resurrection, being the first to rise, having "life in himself" and the power to lay down his life and take it up again, thus freeing all men from the bondage which the fall had placed upon them. (Doctrines of Salvation, 2:300-01)   TLDP:700

**Elder Wilford Woodruff**

We acknowledge that through Adam all have died, that death through the fall must pass upon the whole human family, also upon the beasts of the field, the fishes of the sea and the fowls of the air and all the works of God, as far as this earth is concerned. It is a law that is unchangeable and irrevocable. It is true a few have been translated, and there will be living upon the earth thousands and millions of people when the Messiah comes in power and great glory to reward every man according to the deeds done in the body, who will be changed in the twinkling of an eye, from mortality to immortality. Nevertheless, they must pass through the ordeal of death involved in the change that will come from them. (May 14, 1882, Discourses of Wilford Woodruff, p. 244) TLDP:700

**Bruce R. McConkie**

Will translated beings ever die? Remember John's enigmatic words relative to his own translation: "Then went this saying abroad among the brethren, that that disciple should not die: yet Jesus said not unto him, He shall not die; but, If I will that he tarry till I come, what is that to thee?" (John 21:23) Note the distinction between avoiding death as such and living till the Lord comes. Then note that Jesus promises the Three Nephites, not that they shall not die, but that they "shall never taste of death" and shall not "endure the pains of death." Again it is an enigmatic declaration with a hidden meaning. There is a distinction between death as we know it and tasting of death or enduring the pains of death. As a matter of doctrine, death is universal; every mortal thing, whether plant or animal or man, shall surely die. Jacob said: "Death hath passed upon all men, to fulfil the merciful plan of the great Creator" (2Ne.9:6). There are no exceptions, not even among translated beings. Paul said: "As in Adam all die, even so in Christ shall all be made alive" (1Cor.15:22). Again the dominion of death over all is acclaimed. But the Lord says of all his saints, not that they will not die, but that: "those that die in me shall not taste of death, for it shall be sweet unto them; And they that die not in me, wo unto them, for their death is bitter" (D&C 42:46-47). The distinction is between dying as such and tasting of death itself. Again the Lord says: "He that liveth when the Lord shall come, and hath kept the faith, blessed is he; nevertheless, it is appointed to him to die at the age of man. Wherefore, children shall grow up until they become old; old men shall die; but they shall not sleep in the dust, but they shall be changed in the twinkling of an eye" (D&C 63:50-51). Thus, this change from mortality to immortality, though almost instantaneous, is both a death and a resurrection. Thus, translated beings do not suffer death as we normally define it, meaning the separation of body and spirit; nor do they receive a resurrection as we ordinarily describe it, meaning that the body rises from the dust and the spirit enters again into its fleshly home. But they do pass through death and are changed from mortality to immortality, in the eternal sense, and they thus both die and are resurrected in the eternal sense. This, we might add, is why Paul wrote: "Behold, I shew you a mystery; We shall not all sleep, but we shall all be changed. In a moment, in the twinkling of an eye, at the last trump; for the trumpet shall sound, and the dead shall be raised incorruptible, and we shall be changed" (1Cor.15:51-52). ¶ "And again, ye shall not have pain while ye shall dwell in the flesh, neither sorrow save it be for the sins of the world; and all this will I do because of the thing which ye have desired of me, for ye have desired that ye might bring the souls of men unto me, while the world shall stand." ¶ During the Millennium all men will be translated, as it were; in that day "there shall be no sorrow because there is no death. In that day an infant shall not die until he is old; and his life shall be as the age of a tree; And when he dies he shall not sleep, that is to say in the earth, but shall be changed in the twinkling of an eye, and shall be caught up, and his rest shall be glorious." (D&C 101:29-31) (The Mortal Messiah, 4:389-91) TLDP:700-01

# List of Doctrines

## TRUSTING IN GOD

*Doctrines Located in This Topic*

831. Love of God dispels fear.

832. There is nothing too hard for the Lord; for Him, all things are possible.

833. Those who serve the Lord need never fear, for He will be with them and succor them.

834. Courage emanates from righteous living and faith in God.

*Doctrines on TRUSTING IN GOD Located in Other Topics*

3. The Lord helps us bear tribulations.

10. God does not suffer us to be tried or tested beyond that which we are able to bear.

16. We can discern between good and evil when we have the Spirit of God.

18. Power to overcome Satan and his evil influence comes from God.

462. The preaching of the gospel has a more powerful effect on the minds of people who hear it, to lead them to do right, than anything else.

542. Through prayer we can obtain protection from peril.

# TRUSTING IN GOD

## 831. Love of God dispels fear.

**John**

There is no fear in love; but perfect love casteth out fear: because fear hath torment. He that feareth is not made perfect in love. We love him, because he first loved us. (*John writes to the churches in Asia about the love of God*) 1Jn.4:18-19.

**John**

And we have known and believed the love that God hath to us. God is love; and he that dwelleth in love dwelleth in God, and God in him. 17. Herein is our love made perfect, that we may have boldness in the day of judgment: because as he is, so are we in this world. 18. There is no fear in love; but perfect love casteth out fear: because fear hath torment. He that feareth is not made perfect in love. 19. We love him, because he first loved us. 20. If a man say, I love God, and hateth his brother, he is a liar: for he that loveth not his brother whom he hath seen, how can he love God whom he hath not seen? 21. And this commandment have we from him, That he who loveth God love his brother also. (*John writes about the love of God to the churches in Asia*) 1Jn.4:16-21

**Mormon**

Behold, I speak with boldness, having authority from God; and I fear not what man can do; for perfect love casteth out all fear. (*Mormon writes to his son Moroni expressing his own perfect love for little children, prior to A.D. 384*) Moro.8:16

**Related Witnesses:**

**Jesus,**
*quoted by John*

Peace I leave with you, my peace I give unto you: not as the world giveth, give I unto you. Let not your heart be troubled, neither let it be afraid. 28. Ye have heard how I said unto you, I go away, and come again unto you. If ye loved me, ye would rejoice, because I said, I go unto the Father: for my Father is greater than I. (*Jesus comforts the Twelve in anticipation of his crucifixion*) John 14:27-28

**Recorded in Psalms**

Yea, though I walk through the valley of the shadow of death, I will fear no evil: for thou art with me; thy rod and thy staff they comfort me. Ps.23:4

**Related Witnesses:**

**Paul**

That Christ may dwell in your hearts by faith; that ye, being rooted and grounded in love, 18. May be able to comprehend with all saints what is the breadth, and length, and depth, and height; 19. And to know the love of Christ, which passeth knowledge, that ye might be filled with all the fulness of God. (*Paul writes to the Saints at Ephesus in Asia Minor, about A.D. 62*) Eph.3:17-19

---

## 832. There is nothing too hard for the Lord; for Him, all things are possible.

**Moses**

Is any thing too hard for the LORD? At the time appointed I will return unto thee, according to the time of life, and Sarah shall have a son. (*The Lord promises Abraham and Sarah a son notwithstanding their old age*) Gen.18:14

**Jesus,**
*recorded in Matthew*

But Jesus beheld them, and said unto them, With men this is impossible; but with God all things are possible. (*Jesus teaches of the difficulty for a rich man to enter into the kingdom of God*) Matt.19:26

**Recorded in Luke**

And the angel said unto her, Fear not, Mary: for thou hast found favour with God. . . . 37. For with God nothing shall be impossible. (*The angel Gabriel tells Mary she shall be the mother of the Son of God*) Luke 1:30,37

**Jeremiah**

Ah Lord GOD! behold, thou hast made the heaven and the earth by thy great power and stretched out arm, and there is nothing too hard for thee: 18. Thou shewest lovingkindness unto thousands, and recompensest the iniquity of the fathers into the bosom of their children after them: the Great, the Mighty God, the LORD of hosts, is his name, 19. Great in counsel, and mighty in work: for thine eyes are open upon all the ways of the sons of men: to give every one according to his ways, and according to the fruit of his doings: 20. Which hast set signs and wonders in the land of Egypt, even unto this day, and in Israel, and among other men; and hast made thee a name, as at this day; 21. And hast brought forth thy people Israel out of the land of Egypt with signs, and with wonders, and with a strong hand, and with a stretched out arm, and with great terror; . . . (*Jeremiah prays, worshipping the Lord*) Jer.32:17-21

**Jeremiah**

Then came the word of the LORD unto Jeremiah, saying, 27. Behold, I am the LORD, the God of all flesh: is there any thing too hard for me? (*Revelation to Jeremiah, about 628 B.C.*) Jer.32:26-27

**833.** Those who serve the Lord need never fear, for He will be with them and succor them.

### Joseph Smith,
*receiving the Word of the Lord*

Wherefore, be of good cheer, and do not fear, for I the Lord am with you, and will stand by you. . . . (*The Lord promises to be with his servants who are called to preach the gospel, Nov. 1831*) D&C 68:6

### Isaiah,
*quoted by Jesus,*
*quoted by Mormon*

For ye shall not go out with haste nor go by flight; for the Lord will go before you, and the God of Israel shall be your rearward. (*The resurrected Jesus Christ teaches the Nephites using the words of Isaiah, A.D. 34*) 3Ne.20:42

### Ammon, son of Mosiah,
*quoted by Mormon*

Now when our hearts were depressed, and we were about to turn back, behold, the Lord comforted us, and said: Go amongst thy brethren, the Lamanites, and bear with patience thine afflictions, and I will give unto you success. (*Speaking to his brethren, Ammon recounts their successes and rejoices in the Lord, 90-77 B.C.*) Alma 26:27

### Alma, the younger,
*quoted by Mormon*

But if ye keep the commandments of God, and do with these things which are sacred according to that which the Lord doth command you, (for you must appeal unto the Lord for all things whatsoever ye must do with them) behold, no power of earth or hell can take them from you, for God is powerful to the fulfilling of all his words. 17. For he will fulfil all his promises which he shall make unto you, for he has fulfilled his promises which he has made unto our fathers. (*Alma instructs his son Helaman, about 73 B.C.*) Alma 37:16-17

### Amos

Seek good, and not evil, that ye may live: and so the LORD, the God of hosts, shall be with you, as ye have spoken. (*The word of the Lord to the house of Israel*) Amos 5:14

**Related Witnesses:**

### Moroni, the Prophet General,
*quoted by Mormon*

But now, ye behold that the Lord is with us; and ye behold that he has delivered you into our hands. And now I would that ye should understand that this is done unto us because of our religion and our faith in Christ. And now ye see that ye cannot destroy this our faith. (*General*

*Moroni commands the Lamanites to make a covenant of peace or be destroyed, about 74 B.C.*) Alma 44:3

### Recorded in 1 Samuel

David said moreover, The LORD that delivered me out of the paw of the lion, and out of the paw of the bear, he will deliver me out of the hand of this Philistine. And Saul said unto David, Go, and the LORD be with thee. (*The boy David goes against the giant Goliath*) 1Sam.17:37

### Jeremiah

Be not afraid of the king of Babylon, of whom ye are afraid; be not afraid of him, saith the LORD: for I am with you to save you, and to deliver you from his hand. (*The word of the Lord for Johanan and his captains, about 628 B.C.*) Jer.42:11

### Paul

Now the Lord of peace himself give you peace always by all means. The Lord be with you all. (*Letter to the Church at Thessalonica, comprising Jews and many pagan converts, A.D. 50*) 2Thess.3:16

### Daniel

If it be so, our God whom we serve is able to deliver us from the burning fiery furnace, and he will deliver us out of thine hand, O king. 18. But if not, be it known unto thee, O king, that we will not serve thy gods, nor worship the golden image which thou hast set up. . . . 23. And these three men, Shadrach, Meshach, and Abed-nego, fell down bound into the midst of the burning fiery furnace. 24. Then Nebuchadnezzar the king was astonied and rose up in haste, and spake, and said unto his counsellers, Did not we cast three men bound into the midst of the fire? They answered and said unto the king, True, O king. 25. He answered and said, Lo, I see four men loose, walking in the midst of the fire, and they have no hurt; and the form of the fourth is like the Son of God. 26. Then Nebuchadnezzar came near to the mouth of the burning fiery furnace, and spake, and said, Shadrach, Meshach, and Abed-nego, ye servants of the most high God, come forth, and come hither. Then Shadrach, Meshach, and Abed-nego, came forth of the midst of the fire. 27. And the princes, governors, and captains, and the king's counsellers, being gathered together, saw these men, upon whose bodies the fire had no power, nor was an hair of their head singed, neither were their coats changed, nor the smell of fire had passed on them. 28. Then Nebuchadnezzar spake, and said, Blessed be the God of Shadrach, Meshach, and Abed-nego, who hath sent his angel, and delivered his servants that trusted in him, and have changed the king's word, and yielded their bodies, that they might not serve nor worship any god, except their own God. (*King Nebuchadnezzar casts Shadrach, Meshach and Abed-nego into the fiery furnace because they refuse to worship his idol*) Dan.3:17-18,23-28

### Jesus,
#### recorded in Matthew

And he saith unto them, Why are ye fearful, O ye of little faith? Then he arose, and rebuked the winds and the sea; and there was a great calm. (*A tempest arises on the sea which causes Jesus' disciples to fear: "Master the tempest is raging, the billows are tossing high. . . ."*) Matt.8:26

**Author's Note:** *Fear* defined: "A painful emotion excited by an expectation of evil or the apprehension of impending danger." (The New Webster Encyclopedic Dictionary of the English Language, p. 321)

---

### 834. Courage emanates from righteous living and faith in God.

#### Mormon

And they were all young men, and they were exceedingly valiant for courage, and also for strength and activity; but behold, this was not all—they were men who were true at all times in whatsoever thing they were entrusted. 21. Yea, they were men of truth and soberness, for they had been taught to keep the commandments of God and to walk uprightly before him. (*Helaman takes command of the two thousand stripling sons of the people of Ammon, about 64 B.C.*) Alma 53:20-21

#### Helaman, son of Alma, the younger,
##### quoted by Mormon

And now I say unto you, my beloved brother Moroni, that never had I seen so great courage, nay, not amongst all the Nephites. 46. For as I had ever called them my sons (for they were all of them very young) even so they said unto me: Father, behold our God is with us, and he will not suffer that we should fall; then let us go forth; we would not slay our brethren if they would let us alone; therefore let us go, lest they should overpower the army of Antipus. 47. Now they never had fought, yet they did not fear death; and they did think more upon the liberty of their fathers than they did upon their lives; yea, they had been taught by their mothers, that if they did not doubt, God would deliver them. (*Helaman's two thousand stripling*

"*sons*" *fight with miraculous power and none of them are slain, 62 B.C.*) Alma 56:45-47

#### John A. Widtsoe

The gifts of faith are two: knowledge and power. These are to each other as the palm and fingers of a hand, or the charge and the gun to the speeding bullet. Where one is there is the other. These gifts were in the mind of the Apostle Paul when he defined faith as "the substance of things hoped for, the evidence of things not seen." From these chief gifts are derived many lesser ones, such as hope and courage, trust and contentment. Faith, once developed, contributes to the solution of every problem of life. (Man and the Dragon, p. 139) TLDP:178

#### Elder Ezra Taft Benson,
##### also quoting Paul

We all have our difficulties, our problems, our reversals. "Whom the Lord loveth He chasteneth." (Heb.12:6.) It is in the depths that men and women learn the lessons that help to build strong men and women, not at the pinnacle of success. In the hour of a man's success is his greatest danger. It sometimes takes a reversal to make us appreciate our blessings and to develop us into strong, courageous characters. We can meet every reversal that can possibly come with the help of the Lord. Every reversal can be turned to our benefit and blessing and can make us stronger, more courageous, more godlike. ACR(Manilla)1975:11

**Related Witnesses:**

#### Francis M. Lyman

Courage has its root in cheerfulness, and cheerfulness becomes rich and deep in a mind busy with earnest work. Doing good to others is a complete cure for the blues. Let the heart be warmed by love, and the mind, too much concerned in the failings and failures of self, begin to make plans for the happiness of others, and we will feel gladness coming into our own souls. It is a duty to be cheerful as well as courageous, for a happy man is of more value to the world than is a melancholy one. A buoyant spirit that fathers pleasant smiles and cheerful words helps the world forward, for joy is a tonic, it gives more energy than does hate, and directs its use in a wholesome way. But if a man would be cheerful, he must live at peace with his neighbors, and be ready to do more than his share of their common labors. He must be prepared to endure criticism, just and unjust, and invariably do good for evil. ("Manhood," IE1904Jan:176-77) TLDP:321

#### Richard L. Evans

Keep courage. Do not feel sorry for yourselves.

Whatever you do, do not feel sorry for yourselves. You live in a great age of opportunity. I
remember the words of one very sharp and
shrewd observer who said, "Whenever I hear
someone sigh and say that life is hard, I am
tempted to ask 'compared to what?'" What are
the alternatives? No one ever promised us it
would be easy. It is a schooling; it is an opportunity; it is a learning period, and a wonderful
one. Despite all the disappointments and difficulties, the great and ultimate rewards are
beyond price. CR1961Apr:76

**Author's Note:** *Courage* is "That quality of
mind which enables men to encounter danger
and difficulties with firmness, or without fear;"
(The New Webster Encyclopedic Dictionary of
the English Language, p.197)

# List of Doctrines

## TRUTH: Knowledge of Truth

*Doctrines Located in This Topic*

835. A person gains knowledge of truth through obedience to God.

836. God will give us knowledge of truth as fast as we are able to receive it.

837. The Lord teaches line upon line, precept upon precept, here a little, there a little.

838. To gain knowledge of truth requires our persistent effort.

839. All knowledge and intelligence we obtain in this life will rise with us in the resurrection.

840. Divine truth is eternal—it abides and endures forever and has no end.

841. Divine truth is absolute, ultimate, and pure; it never varies.

842. God uses the Holy Ghost to impart truth to His children.

843. Those who gain more knowledge of divine truth than others in this life have an advantage in the world to come.

844. It is impossible for a person to be saved in ignorance of the saving principles of the gospel.

*Doctrines on TRUTH Located in Other Topics*

187. By the exercise of faith in Christ, knowledge of divine truths can be received through the power of the Holy Ghost.

543. Through prayer we can receive knowledge of divine truth (the mysteries of God).

# TRUTH: Knowledge of Truth

**835. A person gains knowledge of truth through obedience to God.**

### President Joseph F. Smith

Man is indebted to the source of all intelligence and truth, for the knowledge that he possesses; and all who will yield obedience to the promptings of the Spirit, which lead to virtue, to honor, to the love of God and man, and to the love of truth and that which is ennobling and enlarging to the soul, will get a cleaner, a more expansive, and a more direct and conclusive knowledge of God's truths than anyone else can obtain. CR1902Apr:85-86

### Joseph Smith

He that keepeth his commandments receiveth truth and light, until he is glorified in truth and knoweth all things. (*Revelation received at Kirtland, Ohio, May 6, 1833*) D&C 93:28

### Joseph Smith

And all saints who remember to keep and do these sayings, walking in obedience to the commandments. . . . 19. . . . shall find wisdom and great treasures of knowledge, even hidden treasures; (*Revelation Feb. 27, 1833*) D&C 89:18-19

### Joseph Smith

That which is of God is light; and he that receiveth light, and continueth in God, receiveth more light; and that light groweth brighter and brighter until the perfect day. (*Revelation for the elders of the Church, May 1831*) D&C 50:24

### J. Reuben Clark, Jr.

[O]bedience must often precede knowledge. CR1950Apr:181

### John A. Widtsoe

To possess knowledge, and not to use it, or not to use it properly, is a sin. The failure of the human will to render obedience to God's law is not only unintelligent and unwise, it is sinful. On one occasion the Lord said to the Church, through the latter-day Prophet: "There are many who have been ordained among you, whom I have called but few of them are chosen. They who are not chosen have sinned a very grievous sin, in that they are walking in darkness at noon-day." Oliver Cowdery and David Whitmer were in the noon-day of knowledge, yet walked in darkness. Wisdom had departed from them. Therefore they were in sin. So may any man close his eyes in full sunlight and walk in darkness and commit a sin before God. The nations of earth, sated with knowledge, in the full light of a Gospel dispensation, walk in darkness. Therefore, the wages of sin are

theirs. Their wars and contentions are sinful before the Lord, and punishment will follow until they open their eyes to the light. ¶ The divine warning has been given: "If you keep not my commandments, the love of the Father shall not continue with you, therefore ye shall walk in darkness." Obedience to law leads to intelligence and wisdom and frees men from darkness and the charge of sin. CR1938Apr:51

### John A. Widtsoe

[I]t often happens that a person of limited knowledge but who earnestly and prayerfully obeys the law, rises to a higher intelligence or wisdom, than one of vast Gospel learning who does not comply in his daily life with the requirements of the Gospel. Obedience to law is a mark of intelligence. CR1938Apr:50

### John A. Widtsoe

Those who live the Gospel of Jesus Christ gain this higher knowledge, this greater testimony, this ultimate assurance that this is the truth. It is the way to truth. CR1938Oct:129

### Stephen L. Richards

From these statements (D&C 93:24-29) we learn important things about truth, first, that truth is knowledge; second, that it comprehends all things, past, present, and future; third, that it is opposed by an adversary; fourth, that it is of God; fifth, that it may only be received in fullness by keeping God's commandments. (Where is Wisdom? p. 143) TLDP:701

### Elder Ezra Taft Benson,
### *also quoting Joseph Smith*

The Lord will increase our knowledge, wisdom, and capacity to obey when we obey His fundamental laws. This is what the Prophet Joseph Smith meant when he said we could have "sudden strokes of ideas" which come into our minds as "pure intelligence." (See TPJS:151.) This is revelation. We must learn to rely on the Holy Ghost so we can use it to guide our lives and the lives of those for whom we have responsibility. CR1983Apr:71-72

**Related Witnesses:**

### Joseph Smith,
### *receiving the Word of the Lord*

And that wicked one cometh and taketh away light and truth, through disobedience, from the children of men, and because of the tradition of their fathers. 40. But I have commanded you to bring up your children in light and truth. (*The Lord speaks by revelation at Kirtland, Ohio, May 6, 1833*) D&C 93:39-40

### Joseph Smith

An actual knowledge to any person, that the course of life which he pursues is according to the will of God, is essentially necessary to enable him to have that confidence in God, without which no person can obtain eternal life. It was this that enabled the ancient saints to endure all their afflictions and persecutions, and to take joyfully the spoiling of their goods, knowing (not believing merely) that they had a more enduring substance. Heb.10:34. . . . ¶ 4. Such was, and always will be, the situation of the saints of God, that unless they have an actual knowledge that the course they are pursuing is according to the will of God they will grow weary in their minds, and faint; . . . *(Lectures on Faith delivered to the School of the Prophets, 1834-35)* LOF6:2,4

---

836. God will give us knowledge of truth as fast as we are able to receive it.

**Joseph Smith,**
*receiving the Word of the Lord*
Therefore, be ye as wise as serpents and yet without sin; and I will order all things for your good, as fast as ye are able to receive them. Amen. *(Revelation, Aug. 6, 1836)* D&C 111:11

**Joseph Smith,**
*receiving the Word of the Lord*
If thou shalt ask, thou shalt receive revelation upon revelation, knowledge upon knowledge, that thou mayest know the mysteries and peaceable things—that which bringeth joy, that which bringeth life eternal. . . . 65. Behold, thou shalt observe all these things, and great shall be thy reward; for unto you it is given to know the mysteries of the kingdom, but unto the world it is not given to know them. . . . 68. Therefore, he that lacketh wisdom, let him ask of me, and I will give him liberally and upbraid him not. *(Revelation "embracing the law of the Church," Feb. 9, 1831)* D&C 42:61,65,68

**Joseph Smith,**
*quoted by Elder Joseph Fielding Smith*
We consider that God has created man with a mind capable of instruction, and a faculty which may be enlarged in proportion to the heed and diligence given to the light communicated from heaven to the intellect; and that the nearer man approaches perfection, the clearer are his views, and the greater his enjoyments, till he has overcome the evils of his life and lost every desire for sin; and like the ancients, arrives at that point of faith where he is wrapped in the power and glory of his Maker and is caught up to dwell with Him. But we consider that this is a station to which no man

ever arrived in a moment: he must have been instructed in the government and laws of that kingdom by proper degrees, until his mind is capable in some measure of comprehending the propriety, justice, equality, and consistency of the same. *(Written message to the elders of the Church in Kirtland and elsewhere, Jan. 1834)* TPJS:51

**Joseph Smith,**
*quoted by Elder Joseph Fielding Smith*
The Lord deals with this people as a tender parent with a child, communicating light and intelligence and the knowledge of his ways as they can bear it. *(Discourse on 2nd Peter, first chapter, May 21, 1843)* HC5:401-03; TPJS:305

**James E. Talmage**
Faith a Gift of God . . . . No compulsion is used in bringing men to a knowledge of God; yet, as fast as we open our hearts to the influences of righteousness, the faith that leads to life eternal will be given us of our Father. AF:97

**Ammon, son of Mosiah**
*quoted by Mormon*
Yea, he that repenteth and exerciseth faith, and bringeth forth good works, and prayeth continually without ceasing—unto such it is given to know the mysteries of God; yea, unto such it shall be given to reveal things which never have been revealed; yea, and it shall be given unto such to bring thousands of souls to repentance, even as it has been given unto us to bring these our brethren to repentance. *(Ammon addresses his brethren, 90-77 B.C.)* Alma 26:22

**Related Witnesses:**
**Joseph Smith**
How long can rolling waters remain impure? What power shall stay the heavens? As well might man stretch forth his puny arm to stop the Missouri river in its decreed course, or to turn it up stream, as to hinder the Almighty from pouring down knowledge from heaven upon the heads of the Latter-day Saints. *(Revelation received in Liberty Jail, March 20, 1839)* D&C 121:33

**Jesus,**
*recorded in Matthew*
Ask, and it shall be given you; seek, and ye shall find; knock, and it shall be opened unto you: 8. For every one that asketh receiveth; and he that seeketh findeth; and to him that knocketh it shall be opened. *(Jesus concludes the Sermon on the Mount)* Matt.7:7-8

**Joseph Smith**
God shall give unto you knowledge by his Holy Spirit, yea, by the unspeakable gift of the Holy Ghost, that has not been revealed since the world was until now; 27. Which our forefathers

have awaited with anxious expectation to be revealed in the last times, which their minds were pointed to by the angels, as held in reserve for the fulness of their glory; 28. A time to come in the which nothing shall be withheld, whether there be one God or many gods, they shall be manifest. 29. All thrones and dominions, principalities and powers, shall be revealed and set forth upon all who have endured valiantly for the gospel of Jesus Christ. 30. And also, if there be bounds set to the heavens or to the seas, or to the dry land, or to the sun, moon, or stars— 31. All the times of their revolutions, all the appointed days, months, and years, and all the days of their days, months, and years, and all their glories, laws, and set times, shall be revealed in the days of the dispensation of the fulness of times— 32. According to that which was ordained in the midst of the Council of the Eternal God of all other gods before this world was, that should be reserved unto the finishing and the end thereof, when every man shall enter into his eternal presence and into his immortal rest. (*Revelation received in Liberty Jail, March 20, 1839*) D&C 121:26-32

---

837. The Lord teaches line upon line, precept upon precept, here a little, there a little.

### Isaiah

Whom shall he teach knowledge? and whom shall he make to understand doctrine? . . . 10. For precept must be upon precept, precept upon precept; line upon line, line upon line; here a little, and there a little: (*The words of Isaiah, 740-659 B.C.; revelation comes line upon line*) Isa.28:9-10

### Joseph Smith,
*receiving the Word of the Lord*

If thou shalt ask, thou shalt receive revelation upon revelation, knowledge upon knowledge, that thou mayest know the mysteries and peaceable things—that which bringeth joy, that which bringeth life eternal. (*Revelation "embracing the law of the Church," Feb. 9, 1831*) D&C 42:61

### George Q. Cannon

The possession and complete understanding of one truth or principle in the system is but the stepping-stone to the complete and perfect comprehension of its adjacent truth; and thus the investigator is gradually led on from one truth to another, until the mind is fully developed, and he beholds a grand and beautiful system, perfect in all its parts, and every truth hav-

ing such an intimate relationship with its fellow-truth, that to believe and fully grasp one with the mind is to believe and grasp the other. (Gospel Truth, 2:8) TLDP:704-05

### Nephi, son of Lehi

Wo be unto him that shall say: We have received the word of God, and we need no more of the word of God, for we have enough! 30. For behold, thus saith the Lord God: I will give unto the children of men line upon line, precept upon precept, here a little and there a little; and blessed are those who hearken unto my precepts, and lend an ear unto my counsel, for they shall learn wisdom; for unto him that receiveth I will give more; and from them that shall say, We have enough, from them shall be taken away even that which they have. (*Nephi foretells the last days, 559-545 B.C.*) 2Ne.28:29-30

### Boyd K. Packer

Revelation is a continuous principle in the Church. In one sense the Church is still being organized. As light and knowledge are given, as prophecies are fulfilled and more intelligence is received, another step forward can be taken. (The Holy Temple, p. 137) TLDP:569

### Bruce R. McConkie

The Lord gives his word to men line upon line, precept upon precept, here a little and there a little, confirming their hope, building each new revelation upon the foundations of the past, giving his children only that portion of his word which they are able to bear. . . . ¶ Alma summarized the restrictions under which preachers of righteousness serve by saying: "It is given unto many to know the mysteries of God; nevertheless they are laid under a strict command that they shall not impart only according to the portion of his word which he doth grant unto the children of men, according to the heed and diligence which they give unto him." Such is the universal principle; it is not how much the teacher knows, but how much the student is prepared to receive. Strong and deep doctrine, spoken to rebellious people, drives them further away and widens the gulf between them and the saints of God. . . . ¶ . . . . Even the true saints—the believing disciples, those who have accepted the gospel and received the gift of the Holy Ghost—are not prepared to receive all things. We have the fulness of the everlasting gospel, meaning we have every truth, power, priesthood, and key needed to enable us to gain the fulness of salvation in our Father's kingdom. But we do not have, and are not yet prepared to receive, the fulness of gospel truth. (The Mortal Messiah, 2:235-37) TLDP:672-73

### Joseph Smith

When you climb up a ladder, you must begin at

the bottom, and ascend step by step, until you arrive at the top; and so it is with the principles of the gospel—you must begin with the first, and go on until you learn all the principles of exaltation. But it will be a great while after you have passed through the veil before you will have learned them. It is not all to be comprehended in this world; it will be a great work to learn our salvation and exaltation even beyond the grave. (*To the Church in general conference—to a congregation of 20,000—"King Follett Sermon," April 7, 1844*) (See HC6:302-17, also see The Words of Joseph Smith, pp. 340-62.) TPJS:348; DGSM:29

**Elder Joseph Fielding Smith**
The truth had to come piecemeal—line upon line, precept upon precept, just like knowledge comes to all of us. CHMR1:95; DCSM:42

**Related Witnesses:**
**President Joseph F. Smith**
[A]s men grow in the knowledge of God, they shall become more and more like him unto the perfect day, when his knowledge shall cover the earth as the waters cover the deep. (Gospel Doctrine, p. 400) TLDP:339-40

**Boyd K. Packer**
Many elements of truth come only after a lifetime of preparation. CR1974Apr:138

---

**838. To gain knowledge of truth requires our persistent effort.**

**Howard W. Hunter**
As important as scientific research may be, the greatest quest is a search for God—to determine his reality, his personal attributes, and to secure a knowledge of the gospel of his Son Jesus Christ. It is not easy to find a perfect understanding of God. The search requires persistent effort, and there are some who never move themselves to pursue this knowledge. CR1974Oct:138

**Joseph Smith,**
**Hyrum Smith, Lyman Wight**
The things of God are of vast importance, and require time and experience as well as deep and solemn thought to find them out; and if we would bring souls to salvation it requires that our minds should rise to the highest heavens, search into and contemplate the lowest abyss, expand wide as eternity and hold communion with Deity. ("Copy of a Letter Written . . . While in Prison," Times and Seasons, May 1840, p. 102) TLDP:341-42

**Elder Joseph F. Smith**
If I have learned something through prayer,

supplication, and perseverance in seeking to know the truth, and I tell it to you, it will not be knowledge unto you. I can tell you how you can obtain it, but I cannot give it to you. If we receive this knowledge, it must come from the Lord. He can touch your understandings and your spirits, so that you shall comprehend perfectly and not be mistaken. But I cannot do that. You can obtain this knowledge through repentance, humility, and seeking the Lord with full purpose of heart until you find Him. He is not afar off. It is not difficult to approach Him, if we will only do it with a broken heart and a contrite spirit, as did Nephi of old. [2Ne.4:32] This was the way in which Joseph Smith, in his boyhood, approached Him. He went into the woods, knelt down, and in humility he sought earnestly to know which church was acceptable to God. He received an answer to his prayer, which he offered from the depths of his heart, and he received it in a way that he did not expect. CR1899Oct:71

**Ammon, son of Mosiah,**
***quoted by Mormon***
Yea, he that repenteth and exerciseth faith, and bringeth forth good works, and prayeth continually without ceasing—unto such it is given to know the mysteries of God; yea, unto such it shall be given to reveal things which never have been revealed; yea, and it shall be given unto such to bring thousands of souls to repentance, even as it has been given unto us to bring these our brethren to repentance. (*Ammon addresses his brethren, 90-77 B.C.*) Alma 26:22

**Elder Spencer W. Kimball**
God and his program will be found only in deep pondering, appropriate reading, much kneeling in devout, humble prayer, and in a sincerity born of need and dependence. ¶ These requirements having been fully met, there is no soul between the poles nor from ocean to ocean who may not positively obtain this knowledge, this hidden treasure of knowledge, this saving and exalting knowledge. . . . ¶ The ultimate and greatest of all knowledge, then, is to know God and his program for our exaltation. We may know him by sight, by sound, by feeling. While relatively few ever *do* really know him, everyone may know him. . . . CR1968Oct:130

**Alma, the younger,**
***quoted by Mormon***
It is given unto many to know the mysteries of God; nevertheless they are laid under a strict command that they shall not impart only according to the portion of his word which he doth grant unto the children of men, according to the heed and diligence which they give unto him.

10. And therefore, he that will harden his heart, the same receiveth the lesser portion of the word; and he that will not harden his heart, to him is given the greater portion of the word, until it is given unto him to know the mysteries of God until he know them in full. 11. And they that will harden their hearts, to them is given the lesser portion of the word until they know nothing concerning his mysteries; and then they are taken captive by the devil, and led by his will down to destruction. (*Alma contends with the wicked Zeezrom, about 82 B.C.*) Alma 12:9-11

### John A. Widtsoe

These . . . are the steps on the way to truth: Desire, prayer, study, and practice. They form the eternal price which must be paid for truth. ¶ This way must be found by each person for himself. Another cannot desire, pray, study, or practice in our stead and for us. Truth must be won individually. ¶ The way to truth is the way to a testimony of the truth of the restored gospel of Jesus Christ. Try it! It never fails those who travel it sincerely. Those who live most, live by truth. (Evidences and Reconciliations, 3:84-85) TLDP:705

**Related Witnesses:**

### Joseph Smith,
*receiving the Word of the Lord*

Behold, you have not understood; you have supposed that I would give it unto you, when you took no thought save it was to ask me. 8. But, behold, I say unto you, that you must study it out in your mind; then you must ask me if it be right, and if it is right I will cause that your bosom shall burn within you; therefore, you shall feel that it is right. 9. But if it be not right you shall have no such feelings, but you shall have a stupor of thought that shall cause you to forget the thing which is wrong; therefore, you cannot write that which is sacred save it be given you from me. (*Revelation for Oliver Cowdery, April 1829; the Book of Mormon is translated by study and by spiritual confirmation*) D&C 9:7-9

### J. Reuben Clark, Jr.

Thus God made clear that the gaining of knowledge is not to be like the commonplace work of earning a living. He who invades the domain of knowledge must approach it as Moses came to the burning bush; he stands on holy ground; he would acquire things sacred; he seeks to make his own the attributes of Deity, the truth which Christ declared he was (John 14:6), and which shall make us free (John 8:32), free of the shackles of time and space, which shall be no more. We must come to this quest of truth—in all regions of human knowledge whatsoever—not only in reverence, but with a spirit of wor-

ship. ¶ In all his promises and commandments about gaining knowledge, the Lord has never withheld from our quest any field of truth. Our knowledge is to be coterminous with the universe and is to reach out and to comprehend the laws and the workings of the deeps of the eternities. All domains of all knowledge belong to us. In no other way could the great law of eternal progression be satisfied. (*Charge to President Howard S. McDonald at his inauguration as president of Brigham Young University, Nov. 14, 1945, delivered by J. Reuben Clark, Jr., in behalf of the First Presidency, IE1946Jan:60-63*) MOFP6:231-32

### Elder Spencer W. Kimball

The Lord has promised repeatedly that he will give you a knowledge of spiritual things when you have placed yourself in a proper frame of mind. He has counseled us to seek, ask, and search diligently. (The Teachings of Spencer W. Kimball, p. 63) TLDP:686

---

839. **All knowledge and intelligence we obtain in this life will rise with us in the resurrection.**

### Joseph Smith

Whatever principle of intelligence we attain unto in this life, it will rise with us in the resurrection. 19. And if a person gains more knowledge and intelligence in this life through his diligence and obedience than another, he will have so much the advantage in the world to come. (*Revelation, April 2, 1830*) D&C 130:18-19

### Charles A. Callis,
*also quoting Joseph Smith*

The Prophet Joseph Smith said: "Whatever principle of intelligence we attain unto in this life, it will rise with us in the resurrection. And if a person gains more knowledge and intelligence in this life through his diligence and obedience than another he will have so much the advantage in the world to come." What knowledge? The pure knowledge that greatly enlarges the soul, that makes us more like God by giving more understanding of his glorious purposes. CR1939Oct:20

### President Spencer W. Kimball

Each one of you has it within the realm of his possibility to develop a kingdom over which you will preside as its king and God. You will need to develop yourself and grow in ability and power and worthiness, to govern such a world with all of its people. You are sent to this earth not merely to have a good time or to satisfy urges or passions or desires. You are sent to this earth, not to ride merry-go-rounds, air-planes, automobiles, and have what the world calls "fun." ¶ You are sent to this world with a very serious purpose. You are sent to school, for that matter, to begin as a human infant and grow to unbelievable proportions in wisdom, judgment, knowledge, and power, that is why you and I cannot be satisfied with saying mere-ly "I like that or want that." That is why in our childhood and our youth and our young adult-hood we must stretch and grow and remember and prepare for the later life when limitations will terminate so that we can go on and on and on. (*At University of Utah Institute of Religion, Oct. 1976*) DGSM:29

---

### 840. Divine truth is eternal—it abides and endures forever and has no end.

**Joseph Smith,**
*receiving the Word of the Lord*
[M]y Spirit is truth; truth abideth and hath no end; and if it be in you it shall abound. (*Revelation, Dec. 27/28, 1832; the "olive leaf message of peace"*) D&C 88:66

**Joseph Smith,**
*receiving the Word of the Lord*
Search these commandments, for they are true and faithful, and the prophecies and promises which are in them shall all be fulfilled. 38. What I the Lord have spoken, I have spoken, and I excuse not myself; and though the heavens and the earth pass away, my word shall not pass away, but shall all be fulfilled, whether by mine own voice or by the voice of my servants, it is the same. 39. For behold, and lo, the Lord is God, and the Spirit beareth record, and the record is true, and the truth abideth forever and ever. Amen. (*Revelation received during a con-ference of elders of the Church, Nov. 1, 1831*) D&C 1:37-39

**Charles W. Penrose**
The truth of God abideth forever. CR1911Oct:48

**Recorded in Psalms**
[A]nd the truth of the LORD endureth for ever. (*A psalm of David*) Ps.117:2

**Related Witnesses:**
**Joseph Smith,**
*receiving the Word of the Lord*
And truth is knowledge of things as they are, and as they were, and as they are to come; 25. And whatsoever is more or less than this is the spirit of that wicked one who was a liar from the beginning. 26. The Spirit of truth is of God. I am

the Spirit of truth, and John bore record of me, saying: He received a fulness of truth, yea, even of all truth; . . . (*The Lord speaks by revelation at Kirtland, Ohio, May 6, 1833*) D&C 93:24-26

---

### 841. Divine truth is absolute, ultimate, and pure; it never varies.

**Charles W. Penrose**
Truth does not change with the centuries. It will not change with the eternal ages. The truth of God abideth forever. That which is true, coming from Him in one age of the world, is true in another. [See D&C 93:24-25.] That which is true on one of His worlds that He has created, is true in all the worlds that He has caused to be organized and sent forth, each in its place, rolling in space, revolving upon its own axis, preserved in its own sphere, in its own orbit, and with the others contributing to the glory of God and bespeaking His handi-work. Truth never changes. Our conception of a truth may change as we grow in wisdom and understanding, and in clearness of spiritual vision. That which appeared to us to be true at one time we may find out later to be incorrect, and so it is we who change, and not the truth that changes. CR1911Oct:48

**J. Reuben Clark, Jr.**
These are some of the ultimate truths, which God has revealed to us. These truths endure; they are the same in all lands, and among all people, and at all times. They are changeless. They are the truths which must take precedence over all contrary theories, dogmas, hypotheses, or relative truths from whatever source or by whomsoever brought. These ultimate truths may not be questioned. All secular truths will, must, finally conform to these ultimate truths. ¶ He wounds, maims, and cripples a soul who raises doubts about or destroys faith in the ulti-mate truths. God will hold such a one strictly accountable; and who can measure the depths to which one shall fail who wilfully shatters in another the opportunity for celestial glory. These ultimate truths are royal truths to which all human wisdom and knowledge are subject. These truths point the way to celestial glory. (*Charge to President Howard S. McDonald at his inauguration as president of Brigham Young University, Nov. 14, 1945, delivered by J. Reuben Clark, Jr., in behalf of the First Presidency, IE1946Jan:60-63*) MOFP6:237

**President Spencer W. Kimball**
This true way of life is not a matter of opinion. There are absolute truths and relative truths.

The rules of dietetics have changed many times in my lifetime. Many scientific findings have changed from year to year. The scientists taught for decades that the world was once a nebulous, molten mass cast off from the sun, and later many scientists said it once was a whirl of dust which solidified. There are many ideas advanced to the world that have been changed to meet the needs of the truth as it has been discovered. There are relative truths, and there are also absolute truths which are the same yesterday, today, and forever—never changing. These absolute truths are not altered by the opinions of men. As science has expanded our understanding of the physical world, certain accepted ideas of science have had to be abandoned in the interest of truth. Some of these seeming truths were stoutly maintained for centuries. The sincere searching of science often rests only on the threshold of truth, whereas revealed facts give us certain absolute truths as a beginning point so we may come to understand the nature of man and the purpose of his life. ("Absolute Truth," Brigham Young University Speeches of the Year, 1977, p. 137-38) TLDP:706

### President Spencer W. Kimball

We learn about these absolute truths by being taught by the Spirit. These truths are 'independent' in their spiritual sphere and are to be discovered spiritually, though they may be confirmed by experience and intellect. (See D&C 93:30.) ("Absolute Truth," EN1978Sept:3-4) DGSM:3

### Elder Ezra Taft Benson

In the Church we have no fear that any discovery of new truths will ever be in conflict with these standards—with any fundamental basic principle which we advocate in the Gospel. Truth is always consistent. This fact gives to us as members of the Church a feeling of great security, a feeling of peace, a feeling of assurance. We know beyond any question that the truths which we advocate, the truths of the Gospel restored to the earth through the Prophet Joseph, are in very deed the truths of heaven. These truths will always be consistent with the discovery of any new truths, whether discovered in the laboratory, through research of the scientist, or whether revealed from heaven through prophets of God. Time is always on the side of truth. CR1958Apr:60

**Related Witnesses:**

### J. Reuben Clark, Jr.

Temporal truths relate to the materials, forces, compositions that are universe-wide, and to matters that generally are covered as matters of

science, economics, sociology, politics, and like matters—I am not listing, I am only indicating—they are essentially non-scriptural, except where the Lord has declared the truth. ¶ Spiritual truths include all matters relating to the principles and doctrines of religion, as generally termed, and all matters of scriptures dealing therewith, and all matters affecting the progress, development, and destiny of the soul of man. Again I am not listing, but indicating. ¶ The first matters, temporal truths, are not normally controlled by revelations of the Lord concerning them and are, so to say, in the public domain. They may be discussed, investigated, experimented upon, theorized about, and handled in any way we wish, with the exception noted. ¶ Spiritual truths, on the other hand, are to be found in and are governed and controlled by the revelations of our Heavenly Father as contained in the scriptures and in inspired utterances of his prophets. . . . As President Joseph F. Smith said, as already quoted: ¶ ". . . . There never was and never will be any conflict between truth revealed by the Lord to his servants, the prophets, and truth revealed by him to the scientist, who makes his discoveries through his research and study." ("The Genius of Our Church Organization," Brigham Young University Speeches of the Year, June 17, 1958, p. 16) TLDP:706

### Alma, the younger,
*quoted by Mormon*

I perceive that it has been made known unto you, by the testimony of his word, that he cannot walk in crooked paths; neither doth he vary from that which he hath said; neither hath he a shadow of turning from the right to the left, or from that which is right to that which is wrong; therefore, his course is one eternal round. (*Alma preaches to the people in Gideon, about 83 B.C.*) Alma 7:20

### Mormon

For I know that God is not a partial God, neither a changeable being; but he is unchangeable from all eternity to all eternity. (*Mormon writes to his son Moroni, prior to A.D. 384*) Moro.8:18

### Joseph Smith

For God doth not walk in crooked paths, neither doth he turn to the right hand nor to the left, neither doth he vary from that which he hath said, therefore his paths are straight, and his course is one eternal round. (*Revelation, July 1828*) D&C 3:2

### Joseph Smith,
*receiving the Word of the Lord*

Listen to the voice of the Lord your God, even Alpha and Omega, the beginning and the end, whose course is one eternal round, the same today as yesterday, and forever. (*Revelation to Joseph Smith and Sidney Rigdon, Dec. 1830*) D&C 35:1

---

842. God uses the Holy Ghost to impart truth to His children.

**Moroni, son of Mormon**
And by the power of the Holy Ghost ye may know the truth of all things. (*The final writings of Moroni, about A.D. 421*) Moro.10:5

**Nephi, son of Lehi**
For he that diligently seeketh shall find; and the mysteries of God shall be unfolded unto them, by the power of the Holy Ghost, as well in these times as in times of old, and as well in times of old as in times to come; wherefore, the course of the Lord is one eternal round. (*Nephi's writings, 600-592 B.C.*) 1Ne.10:19

**Delbert L. Stapley**
The Holy Ghost is a revelator of truth. . . . CR1966Oct:112

**Jesus,**
*recorded by John*
Howbeit when he, the Spirit of truth, is come, he will guide you into all truth: for he shall not speak of himself; but whatsoever he shall hear, that shall he speak: and he will shew you things to come. (*Jesus discourses on the mission of the Holy Ghost*) John 16:13

**Joseph Smith,**
*quoted by Elder Joseph Fielding Smith*
[W]e believe that it [the gift of the Holy Ghost] . . . brings things past to our remembrance, leads us into all truth, and shows us of things to come; we believe that "no man can know that Jesus is the Christ, but by the Holy Ghost." (Editorial in "Times and Seasons," June 1842) HC5:27; TPJS:243

**Joseph Smith,**
*receiving the Word of the Lord*
And again, he that receiveth the word of truth, doth he receive it by the Spirit of truth or some other way? 20. If it be some other way it is not of God. 21. Therefore, why is it that ye cannot understand and know, that he that receiveth the word by the Spirit of truth receiveth it as it is preached by the Spirit of truth? 22. Wherefore, he that preacheth and he that receiveth, understand one another, and both are edified and rejoice together. (*Revelation for the elders of the Church, May 1831*) D&C 50:19-22

**Joseph Smith**
Therefore, whoso readeth it, let him understand, for the Spirit manifesteth truth; . . . (*Revelation, March 9, 1833*) D&C 91:4

**Bruce R. McConkie**
True it is that honest truth seekers come to know of the truth and divinity of the Lord's work by the power of the Holy Ghost: they receive a flash of revelation telling them that Jesus is the Lord, that Joseph Smith is his prophet, that the Book of Mormon is the mind and will and voice of the Lord, that the Church of Jesus Christ of Latter-day Saints is the only true and living Church upon the whole earth. They gain a testimony before baptism. But it is only after they pledge their all in the cause of Christ that they receive the gift of the Holy Ghost, which is the heavenly endowment of which Jesus spoke. Then they receive a fulfillment of the promise: "by the power of the Holy Ghost ye may know the truth of all things." (Moro.10:5) Then they receive the "spirit of revelation," and the Lord tells them in their heart and in their mind whatsoever he will. (D&C 8:1-3) (The Millennial Messiah, pp. 98-99) DGSM:45

---

843. Those who gain more knowledge of divine truth than others in this life have an advantage in the world to come.

**Joseph Smith**
Whatever principle of intelligence we attain unto in this life, it will rise with us in the resurrection. 19. And if a person gains more knowledge and intelligence in this life through his diligence and obedience than another, he will have so much the advantage in the world to come. (*Revelation, April 2, 1830*) D&C 130:18-19

**Charles A. Callis**
The Prophet Joseph Smith said: "Whatever principle of intelligence we attain unto in this life, it will rise with us in the resurrection. And if a person gains more knowledge and intelligence in this life through his diligence and obedience than another he will have so much the advantage in the world to come." What knowledge? The pure knowledge that greatly enlarges the soul, that makes us more like God by giving more understanding of his glorious purposes. CR1939Oct:20

**Related Witnesses:**
**President Joseph F. Smith**
[A]s men grow in the knowledge of God, they shall become more and more like him unto the perfect day, when his knowledge shall cover the earth as the waters cover the deep. (Gospel Doctrine, p. 400) TLDP:339-40

**Elder Harold B. Lee**
Truth is the scepter of power, which if man

possesses, will give him "dominion" and the ability to "subdue all things." (Decisions for Successful Living, p. 188) TLDP:704

---

844. It is impossible for a person to be saved in ignorance of the saving principles of the gospel.

### Bruce R. McConkie

Man's hope of gaining salvation is in direct proportion to his knowledge of God and the laws of salvation. No man can be saved in ignorance of Jesus Christ and the laws of the gospel. Man is saved no faster then he gains knowledge of God and the saving truths recorded in the scriptures. A fountain cannot rise above its source; a people cannot live laws of which they are ignorant, nor believe in a Christ about whom they know little or nothing. The Lord expects his people to learn the doctrines of salvation. "Search these commandments" (D&C 1:37), is a decree which applies in principle to all revelations of all ages. (The Mortal Messiah, 2:81) TLDP:339

### Elder Joseph Fielding Smith

Now I say it boldly, all the knowledge that a man can gain in this world or beyond this world, independent of the spirit of God, the inspiration of the Almighty, will not lead him to a fulness. . . . ¶ . . . . It is, however, knowledge of the principles of the Gospel that will save men in the Kingdom of God. CR1939Apr:102-03

### Elder Ezra Taft Benson

The most vital knowledge you can learn is the saving truths of the gospel—the truths that will make the difference in your eternal welfare. The most vital words that you can read are those of the Presidents of the Church—particularly the living prophet—and those of the apostles and prophets. God encourages learning in many areas, and vocational skills will have increasing importance. There is much reading material that is available which is either time-wasting or corrupting. The best yardstick to use in discerning the worth of true knowledge and learning is to go first and foremost to the words of the Lord's prophets. ("In His Steps," Brigham Young University Speeches of the Year, 1979, p. 62) TLDP:706

### Joseph Smith,
*quoted by Elder Joseph Fielding Smith*

As far as we degenerate from God, we descend to the devil and lose knowledge, and without knowledge we cannot be saved, and while our hearts are filled with evil, we are studying evil, there is no room in our hearts for good, or

studying good. Is not God good? Then you be good; if He is faithful, then you be faithful. Add to your faith virtue, to virtue knowledge, and seek for every good thing. . . . ¶ A man is saved no faster than he gets knowledge, for if he does not get knowledge, he will be brought into captivity by some evil power in the other world, as evil spirits will have more knowledge, and consequently more power than many men who are on the earth. Hence it needs revelation to assist us, and give us *knowledge of the things of God.* [Italics supplied.] (*From a synopsis by Elder Wilford Woodruff of the Prophet's remarks in a talk in the Grove, Nauvoo, Ill., April 10, 1842*) HC4:588; TPJS:217; MPSG1972-73:7

### Joseph Smith,
*quoted by Elder Joseph Fielding Smith*

Add to your faith knowledge, etc. The principle of knowledge is the principle of salvation. This principle can be comprehended by the faithful and diligent; and every one that does not obtain knowledge sufficient to be saved will be condemned. The principle of salvation is given us through the knowledge of Jesus Christ. *(From a sermon at Yelrome, May 14, 1843, drawn from a synopsis by Elder Wilford Woodruff)* HC5:387-90; TPJS:297; MPSG1972-73:7

### Related Witnesses:
#### President Spencer W. Kimball

[W]e must recognize that secular knowledge alone can never save a soul nor open the celestial kingdom to anyone. . . . ¶ . . . . Yet secular knowledge can be most helpful to [those] who have found and are living those truths which lead one to eternal life, ("Seek Learning, Even by Study and Also by Faith," EN1983Sept:3) DGSM:3

#### Joseph Smith

It is impossible for a man to be saved in ignorance. *(Instructions, May 16/17, 1843)* D&C 131:6

#### Elder Spencer W. Kimball

God and his program will be found only in deep pondering, appropriate reading, much kneeling in devout, humble prayer, and in a sincerity born of need and dependence. ¶ These requirements having been fully met, there is no soul between the poles nor from ocean to ocean who may not positively obtain this knowledge, this hidden treasure of knowledge, this saving and exalting knowledge. . . . ¶ The ultimate and greatest of all knowledge, then, is to know God and his program for our exaltation. We may know him by sight, by sound, by feeling. While relatively few ever *do* really know him, everyone may know him. . . . CR1968Oct:130

### President Brigham Young,
### Heber C. Kimball, Willard Richards
(First Presidency)

If men would be great in goodness, they must be intelligent, for no man can do good unless he knows how; therefore seek after knowledge, all knowledge, and especially that which is from above, which is wisdom to direct in all things, and if you find any thing that God does not know, you need not learn that thing; but strive to know what God knows, and use that knowledge as God uses it, and then you will be like him; will see as you are seen, and know as you are known; and have charity, love one another, and do each other good continually, and for ever, even as for yourselves. ("Sixth General Epistle of the Presidency of The Church of Jesus Christ of Latter-day Saints," Millennial Star, Jan. 15, 1852, p. 22) TLDP:341

### Joseph Smith,
### *quoted by Elder Joseph Fielding Smith*

It is not to be wondered at that men should be ignorant, in a great measure, of the principles of salvation, and more especially of the nature, office, power, influence, gifts, and blessings of the gift of the Holy Ghost, when we consider that the human family have been enveloped in gross darkness and ignorance for many centuries past, without revelation, or any just criterion [by which] to arrive at a knowledge of the things of God, which can only be known by the Spirit of God. (Editorial in Times and Seasons, HC5:26-32, June 15, 1842) TPJS:242

**Author's Note:** Elder Joseph Fielding Smith wrote: "The Prophet did say that a man cannot be saved in ignorance, but in ignorance of what? He said that a man cannot be saved in ignorance of the saving principles of the gospel of Jesus Christ." (Doctrines of Salvation, 1:290)

# List of Doctrines

## UNITY

# UNITY

**845. The Saints of God are to be united with each other and with God.**

### Joseph Smith,
*receiving the Word of the Lord*
. . . I say unto you, be one; and if ye are not one ye are not mine. (*Revelation for the Saints in conference, Jan. 2, 1831*) D&C 38:27

### Joseph Smith,
*translating the Book of Moses*
And the Lord called his people ZION, because they were of one heart and one mind, and dwelt in righteousness; and there was no poor among them. (*The record of Moses: Enoch builds a city of holiness*) Moses 7:18

### Jesus,
*quoted by John*
That they all may be one; as thou, Father, art in me, and I in thee, that they also may be one in us: that the world may believe that thou hast sent me. 22. "And the glory which thou gavest me I have given them; that they may be one, even as we are one: 23. I in them, and thou in me, that they may be made perfect in one; and that the world may know that thou hast sent me, and hast loved them, as thou hast loved me. (*Jesus offers the great intercessory prayer for his Apostles*) John 17:21-23

### President John Taylor
Let the Presidency of my Church be one in all things; and let the twelve also be one in all things; and let them all be one with me as I am one with the Father. (*Revelation given through the President of the Church at Salt Lake City, Utah Territory, Oct. 13, 1882*) MOFP:2:348

### Elder Harold B. Lee
Then, besides those ordinances by which we are adopted into that oneness with the Father and the Son, he has given to us principles and ordinances all intended to the perfecting of his Saints, that this same unity might be realized. CR1950Apr:99

**Related Witnesses:**

### Jesus,
*recorded in Matthew*
. . . Every kingdom divided against itself is brought to desolation; and every city or house divided against itself shall not stand: (*Jesus lectures the Pharisees that devils are cast out by the power of God, not by the power of Satan*) Matt.12:25

**846. The gospel of Jesus Christ leads to unity among the Saints.**

### Elder Joseph F. Smith
The gospel has been restored to the earth, and the Priesthood again established, and both are enjoyed by this people; but those unacquainted with the working of the gospel and the Priesthood look upon us with wonder, and are astonished at the union that exists in our midst. We move as a man, almost; we hearken to the voice of our leader; we are united in our faith and in our work. The world can not understand this, and they behold it with wonder. ¶ Let me tell my brethren and friends that this is one of the effects of the gospel of Jesus Christ. We have become united in our faith by one baptism; we know that Jesus Christ lives, we know that he is our Savior and Redeemer; we have a testimony of this, independent of any written books, and we testify of these things to the world. This unison in the midst of the people called Latter-day Saints, and their prosperity, are hard for a great many to understand. (*Nov. 15, 1868*) (Gospel Doctrine, pp. 80-81) TLDP:708

### Francis M. Lyman
It is a great mystery to the people of the world how the Latter-day Saints hold so unitedly together as a people, why there is such a fraternal, binding feeling existing between them. Quite generally they look upon it as the result of compulsory power, exercised by the leaders of the Church. How incorrect this idea is! What holds this people together so solidly, and what makes them willing to labor for the salvation of the children of men, at the sacrifice of their own worldly affairs and interest, is answered in the text I have just to read to you. [See 3Ne.11:20-36.] . . . The Lord has spoken to us today by the inspiration of His Spirit. He has been present with us by His Spirit. Every Latter-day Saint has been moved upon by that same spirit, and record has been borne in our hearts that we have listened to the word and the will of the Lord. That is the power, the secret power, that binds our hearts together and makes them respond as one, no matter where we may be. We may be thousands of miles apart, yet we are in unison, because bound together and inspired by the one Spirit. It is the same Spirit which binds the Father and the Son and makes them one. As the Father and the Son are one, so are we one. This is accomplished through our faith, repenting of our sins, cleansing our hearts, and living lives of purity before Him. We may make a good start, but if we fail to continue in our good works and in our devotion to the Lord, that Spirit will diminish within us,

we are inclined to divide one against the other and receive the spirit of the world. Then it is that every man is for himself, following the imaginations of his own heart instead of being guided by the inspiration of the Holy Ghost. I would like us to understand and realize this. CR1904Apr:10-11

### Elder Harold B. Lee

Unity centers in heaven, even as the Master prayed, "Father, that we might be one." The Saints might become one with the Father and the Son, spiritually begotten by baptism and through the Holy Ghost even unto the renewing of their bodies as the Lord tells us, and thus, "become . . . the church and kingdom, and the elect of God" (D&C 84:34), and thus become adopted into the holy family, the Church and kingdom of God, the Church of the Firstborn. ¶ Then, besides those ordinances by which we are adopted into that oneness with the Father and the Son, he has given to us principles and ordinances all intended to the perfecting of his Saints, that this same unity might be realized. CR1950Apr:99

### Marion G. Romney

There is but one way that we can be united, and that way is to seek the Lord and his righteousness. (See 3Ne.13:33.) Unity comes by following the light from above. It does not come out of the confusions below. While men depend upon their own wisdom and walk in their own way, without the guidance of the Lord they cannot live in unity. Neither can they come to unity by following uninspired men. ¶ The way to unity is for us to learn the will of the Lord and then to do it. Until this basic principle is understood and observed, there will be no unity and peace on this earth. ¶ We of this Church can come to a unity and a oneness which will give us strength beyond anything we have yet enjoyed if we will obtain a sounder understanding of the principles of the gospel and come to a unity in our interpretations of present world conditions and trends. This we can do by prayerful study of the Lord's word, including that given to us through the living prophet. ¶ This is the way to come to a unity. If we will study the word of the Lord as it comes to us through the standard works and through the instructions of the living prophet and not harden our hearts, but humble ourselves and develop a real desire to understand its application to us in our own peculiar circumstances, and then ask the Lord in faith, believing that we shall receive (see D&C 18:18), all the while being diligent in keeping the commandments of the Lord, surely the path we should follow will be

made known unto us, and we will be able to face the world as a solid unit. ¶ Surely we need this unity and this strength in this day in which we live. We have a great opportunity, the opportunity to rise heavenward, to gain the spirit of the gospel as we have never enjoyed it before. This we can do by developing among us that unity required by the laws of the celestial kingdom. ¶ If, in the expediency of the moment, we set God aside to follow the teachings of men, we disown him. ¶ Only a united people, keeping God's commands, can expect the protection which he alone can give when the floods come, and the rains descend, and the winds blow, and beat upon our house. (See Matt.7:25.) ¶ It is my conviction that, since we are engaged in the Lord's work, we can accomplish everything he requires us to do if we will but be united. CR1983Apr:21-22

---

847. **The Saints can accomplish any purpose of the Lord when fully united in righteousness.**

### J. Reuben Clark, Jr.

I have said to you brethren, over and over again, and I repeat it tonight, that if we were really united, if we really saw eye to eye, and then would move in unison, there is nothing in the world, in righteousness, that we might not do in accordance with the will of the Lord and not to defeat his purposes. CR1949Apr:184

### Elder Harold B. Lee

If we would be united in paying our fast offerings and on serving the law of the fast as fully as the Lord has taught it, and if we were united in carrying out the principles of the welfare program as they have been given to us by our leaders today, we would be free from want and distress and would be able fully to care for our own. Our failure to be united would be to allow our needy to become the pawns of politicians in the public mart. ¶ If we were fully united as a people in our missionary work, we would rapidly hasten the day when the gospel would be preached to all people without and within the boundaries of the organized stakes of Zion. If we are not united, we will lose that which has been the lifeblood and which has fed and stimulated this Church for a generation. ¶ If we were fully united in keeping the law of sacrifice and paying our tithes as we have been schooled today, we would have sufficient to build our temples, our chapels, our schools of learning. If we fail to do that, we will be in the bondage of mortgage and debt. ¶ If we were united as a people in electing honorable men to high places in our civil government, regardless of the political party with which we have affiliation, we would be able to safeguard our communities and to preserve law and order among us. Our failure to be united means that we permit tyranny and oppression and taxation to the extent of virtual confiscation of our own property. ¶ If we are united in supporting our own official newspaper and magazines which are owned and operated by the Church and for Church members, there will always be in this Church a sure voice to the people, but if we fail to be united in giving this support, we permit ourselves to be subject to abuse, slander, and to misrepresentation without any adequate voice of defense. ¶ If we were united in safeguarding our youth from promiscuous associations that foster marriages out of the Church and out of the temples, by having socials and recreations as a united people, as has been the practice from our pioneer days, we would be building all our Latter-day Saint homes on a sure and happy foundation. Our failure to be united in these things will be our failure to receive eternal blessings that otherwise could be ours. ¶ If we were united in safeguarding the Church from false doctrines and error and in standing as watchmen upon the tower as teachers and leaders in watching over the Church, then we would be free from these things that cause many to stumble and fall and lose their faith. If we are not thus united, the wolves among us will be sowing the seeds of discord, disharmony, all tending to the destruction of the flock. ¶ If we were united in our temple work and in our genealogical research work, we would not be satisfied with the present temples only, but we would have sufficient work for temples yet to come, to the unlocking of the doors of opportunity to those beyond who are our own kin, and thus ourselves become saviors on Mount Zion. Our failure to be united will be our failure to perpetuate our family homes in the eternity. So we might multiply the blessings that could come to this people if they were fully united in the purposes of the Lord. CR1950Apr:96-97

**Elder Ezra Taft Benson**

There are some who would have us believe that the final test of the rightness of a course is whether everyone is united on it. But the Church does not seek unity, simply for unity's sake. The unity for which the Lord prayed and of which President McKay speaks is the only unity which God honors—that is, "Unity in righteousness," unity in principle. ¶ We cannot compromise good and evil in an attempt to have peace and unity in the Church, any more than the Lord could have compromised with Satan in order to avoid the War in Heaven. ("Our Immediate Responsibility," Brigham Young University Speeches of the Year, 1966, p. 8) TLDP:711

**Related Witnesses:**

**Jesus,**
*recorded in Luke*

He that is not with me is against me: and he that gathereth not with me scattereth. (*Jesus lectures the Pharisees that devils are cast out by the power of God, not by the power of Satan*) Luke 11:23

**Jesus,**
*recorded in Luke*

No servant can serve two masters: for either he will hate the one, and love the other; or else he will hold to the one, and despise the other. Ye cannot serve God and mammon. (*Jesus publicly teaches his disciples*) Luke 16:13

# List of Doctrines

## WEALTH

### Money and Carnal Riches

*Doctrines Located in This Topic*

848. Lust for money is the root of much evil.

849. The material things of the world are not true riches; only the riches of eternal life are lasting and permanent.

850. Wealth can be a blessing; riches are not inherently evil.

851. The Devil tempts us to covet riches and the material things of the earth.

852. They who possess great riches tend to succumb to the sin of pride.

853. We are to avoid financial debt.

854. The Lord favors neither the rich over the poor nor the poor over the rich.

855. We are to impart of our substance for the benefit of those less fortunate.

856. We are not to engage in acts of priestcraft: performing church service for material gain or rendering benevolent service to others for riches or honor.

857. We are not to gamble or take money without giving fair value in return.

*Doctrines on WEALTH Located in Other Topics*

92. Members of the Church are to live the law of consecration when called upon to do so: they are to be ready at all times to consecrate their time, talents, money, and property to the building up of the kingdom of God on earth.

93. Disciples of Christ should be more concerned with building up the kingdom of God than with acquiring the things of this world.

94. Persons who have acquired more possessions than they can manage and use properly are to freely impart the surplus to the needy.

96. Members of the Church are to live the law of sacrifice: to be willing to make whatever sacrifices the Lord requires for the sake of the gospel.

201. It was the design of the Lord that Adam and Eve (and all people born thereafter) should support themselves by their own labors.

211. Parents are to provide and care for their children.

788. Whatever we set our hearts and our trust in most becomes, in a sense, our god; if our god is not the true and living God of Israel, we are laboring in idolatry.

# WEALTH

## Money and Carnal Riches

**848. Lust for money is the root of much evil.**

### Elder Spencer W. Kimball

I am not against wealth, and I like to see people enjoy the blessings of this earth. Wealth ethically acquired and properly used is not evil—it is good. It is the love of it, the coveting of it, the lust for it, the compromises made for it which are evil. *(Beneficial Life convention, San Diego, 1966)* (The Teachings of Spencer W. Kimball, p. 358) TLDP:714-15

### Elder Wilford Woodruff

I do not find fault with riches. The gold and silver are the Lord's. We want houses building and we must cultivate the earth. This is all right. I do not find fault with a man getting rich, I find fault with our selling the kingdom of God, our birthright, selling the Gospel and depriving ourselves of eternal life, for the sake of gratifying the lusts of the flesh, the pride of life and the fashions of the world; and setting our hearts upon these things. *(In new Tabernacle, Sept. 12, 1875, JD18:121)* TLDP:714

### Paul

For the love of money is the root of all evil: which while some coveted after, they have erred from the faith, and pierced themselves through with many sorrows. *(Paul's letter to his assistant Timothy, about A.D. 64)* 1Tim.6:10

### Anthon H. Lund

The Lord, in one of His revelations given very early in the Church, says: "Seek not for riches but for wisdom, and behold the mysteries of God shall be unfolded unto you, and then shall you be made rich. Behold, he that hath eternal life is rich." ¶ The riches of eternal life we ought to seek, not the riches of the world. There is a raging thirst for riches in this land. The love of money is growing even in our midst. We do not look upon wealth in itself as a curse. We believe that those who can handle means rightly can do much to bless their fellows. But he who is ruled by the love of money is tempted to commit sin. The love of money is the root of all evil. . . . There is hardly a commandment but is violated through this seeking for riches. CR1903Apr:24

### Jesus,
*recorded in Matthew*

No man can serve two masters: for either he will hate the one, and love the other; or else he will hold to the one, and despise the other. Ye cannot serve God and mammon. *(Jesus teaches his disciples)* Matt.6:24

### George Q. Cannon

We must serve God with all our hearts, our love and affections reaching after Him, and the things of this world must be looked upon by us as secondary considerations. They are good enough in their place; right enough to be attended to; but subordinate always to the love of God. That should be the first love, greater than every other love. A man that loves a wife, a man that loves a child, a man that loves anything upon the earth more than God, is not a true Latter-day Saint. He may have a lovely wife, he may have a lovely child; he may have a rich farm, he may have stock, elegant residences, horses and carriages, together with an abundance of wealth to command all the comforts of the earth; but I tell you, as a servant of God, if he loves these things more than he loves God, he is not a true Latter-day Saint. *(At Hooperville, Utah, June 27, 1881, JD22:288-89)* TLDP:366

### Moroni, son of Mormon

For behold, ye do love money, and your substance, and your fine apparel, and the adorning of your churches, more than ye love the poor and the needy, the sick and the afflicted. 38. O ye pollutions, ye hypocrites, ye teachers, who sell yourselves for that which will canker, why have ye polluted the holy church of God? Why are ye ashamed to take upon you the name of Christ? Why do ye not think that greater is the value of an endless happiness than that misery which never dies—because of the praise of the world? 39. Why do ye adorn yourselves with that which hath no life, and yet suffer the hungry, and the needy, and the naked, and the sick and the afflicted to pass by you, and notice them not? 40. Yea, why do ye build up your secret abominations to get gain, and cause that widows should mourn before the Lord, and also orphans to mourn before the Lord, and also the blood of their fathers and their husbands to cry unto the Lord from the ground, for vengeance upon your heads? 41. Behold, the sword of vengeance hangeth over you; and the time soon cometh that he avengeth the blood of the saints upon you, for he will not suffer their cries any longer. *(Moroni's writings, about A.D. 400)* Morm.8:37-41

### Related Witnesses:

### Recorded in Proverbs

He that trusteth in his riches shall fall: but the righteous shall flourish as a branch. Prov.11:28

### Mormon

For behold, the Lord had blessed them so long with the riches of the world that they had not been stirred up to anger, to wars, nor to bloodshed; therefore they began to set their hearts upon their riches; yea, they began to seek to get gain that they might be lifted up one above another; therefore they began to commit secret murders, and to rob and to plunder, that they might get gain. . . . 31. And now behold, he had got great hold upon the hearts of the Nephites; yea, insomuch that they had become exceedingly wicked; yea, the more part of them had turned out of the way of righteousness, and did trample under their feet the commandments of God, and did turn unto their own ways, and did build up unto themselves idols of their gold and their silver. (*The Lamanites and the Nephites prosper and become exceedingly rich, 29 B.C.*) Hel.6:17,31

### Nephi, son of Helaman, quoted by Mormon

O repent ye, repent ye! Why will ye die? Turn ye, turn ye unto the Lord your God. Why has he forsaken you? . . . 21. But behold, it is to get gain, to be praised of men, yea, and that ye might get gold and silver. And ye have set your hearts upon the riches and the vain things of this world, for the which ye do murder, and plunder, and steal, and bear false witness against your neighbor, and do all manner of iniquity. 22. And for this cause wo shall come unto you except ye shall repent. . . . Hel.7:17,21-22

### Mormon

And it came to pass that Alma and Amulek came over to the land of Zarahemla, where Alma took Amulek to his own house, and did administer unto him in his tribulations, and strengthened him in the Lord, Amulek having forsaken all his gold, and silver, and his precious things, which were in the land of Ammonihah, for the word of God, he being rejected by those who were once his friends and also by his father and his kindred; . . . (*Amulek, who had great riches and influential friends, rebels against the Lord until he is taught the gospel by the prophet Alma; he thereafter forsakes his riches for the word of the Lord and is consequently blessed—albeit rejected by those so-called friends, about 81 B.C.*) Alma 15:16

---

849. The material things of the world are not true riches; only the riches of eternal life are lasting and permanent.

### Anthon H. Lund

The riches of eternal life we ought to seek, not the riches of the world. There is a raging thirst for riches in this land. The love of money is growing in our midst. We do not look upon wealth in itself as a curse. We believe that those who can handle means rightly can do much to bless their fellows. But he who is ruled by the love of money is tempted to commit sin. The love of money is the root of all evil. . . . There is hardly a commandment but is violated through this seeking for riches. CR1903Apr:24

### Joseph Smith

Seek not for riches but for wisdom, and behold, the mysteries of God shall be unfolded unto you, and then shall you be made rich. Behold, he that hath eternal life is rich. (*Revelation to Joseph and to Oliver Cowdery, April 1829*) D&C 6:7

### Francis M. Lyman

We will seek the riches of eternity here. We can take the riches of eternal life with us when we leave this sphere, but we cannot take the riches of this world. Yet the riches of this world are convenient and necessary and we cannot very well get along without them. But the riches of eternal life are lasting and permanent. They come from the good we accomplish, the righteousness we bring to pass, the purity to which we attain, the cleansing and purifying of our own hearts, that we may come as near being perfect in this life as our Father and his Son, Jesus Christ, are perfect. CR1899Apr:38

### President Joseph F. Smith

What are true riches? The love of your family, and the confidence of friends and neighbors; faith in God and obedience to his commandments,—not money, not wealth. (IE1902June:573) TLDP:716

### John

Because thou sayest, I am rich, and increased with goods, and have need of nothing; and knowest not that thou art wretched, and miserable, and poor, and blind, and naked: 18. I counsel thee to buy of me gold tried in the fire, that thou mayest be rich; and white raiment, that thou mayest be clothed, and that the shame of thy nakedness do not appear; and anoint thine eyes with eyesalve, that thou mayest see. (*The Apostle John writes the invitation of Jesus to overcome as he overcame*) Rev.3:17-18

### Related Witnesses:
### Recorded in Proverbs

He that trusteth in his riches shall fall: but the righteous shall flourish as a branch. Prov.11:28

### Paul

Charge them that are rich in this world, that

they be not highminded, nor trust in uncertain riches, but in the living God, who giveth us richly all things to enjoy; 18. That they do good, that they be rich in good works, ready to distribute, willing to communicate; 19. Laying up in store for themselves a good foundation against the time to come, that they may lay hold on eternal life. (*Paul's letter to his assistant Timothy, about* A.D. *64*) 1Tim.6:17-19

---

850. Wealth can be a blessing; riches are not inherently evil.

**Anthon H. Lund**

We do not look upon wealth in itself as a curse. We believe that those who can handle means rightly can do much to bless their fellows. But he who is ruled by the love of money is tempted to commit sin. The love of money is the root of all evil. . . . There is hardly a commandment but is violated through this seeking for riches. CR1903Apr:24

**Elder Spencer W. Kimball**

Wealth ethically acquired and properly used is not evil—it is good. It is the love of it, the coveting of it, the lust for it, the compromises made for it which are evil. (*Beneficial Life convention, San Diego, 1966*) (The Teachings of Spencer W. Kimball, p. 358) TLDP:714-15

**Elder Spencer W. Kimball**

But must one be poor to inherit eternal life? There is no such ultimatum. The Lord delights to give us all. He created the earth for us and gave to us as stewards all that it affords. "The fulness of the earth is yours." he said, but this fabulous gift came upon condition that we unreservedly obey his commands. The Lord indicts those who seek not earnestly the riches of eternity, but whose eyes are full of greediness. . . . ¶ Perhaps the sin is not in "things" but in our attitude toward and worship of "things." Unless an acquisitive person can positively accumulate and hold wealth while still giving full allegiance to God and his program—unless the rich man can keep the Sabbath, keep his mind and body and spirit uncontaminated, and give unstinted service to his fellowmen through God's appointed way—unless the affluent man has total control and can hold all his possessions in trust, subject to the call of the Lord through his authorized servants, then that man, for the good of his soul, should certainly "go and sell that thou hast and give to the poor, . . . and come and follow me." (Matt.19:21) ¶ "For where your treasure is, there will your heart be also." (Matt.6:21) (The Teachings of Spencer W. Kimball, p. 358) TLDP:714-15

**President Brigham Young, Heber C. Kimball, Willard Richards**
(First Presidency)

Gold is good in its place—it is good in the hands of a good man to do good with, but in the hands of a wicked man it often proves a curse instead of a blessing. Gold is a good servant, but a miserable, blind, and helpless god, and at last will have to be purified by fire, with all its followers. (*Third General Epistle of the Presidency of the Church, April 12, 1850, MOFP2:40-49*) MOFP2:46

**George Q. Cannon**

Wealth is a blessing when properly used. It adds to comfort; it contributes to happiness, and it enlarges usefulness. But when it is improperly used, it becomes an injury. When people set their affections upon it, are made vain and proud by it, think themselves a little better than their neighbor because of it, then it becomes a curse. (Gospel Truth, 2:319) TLDP:714

**Elder Joseph F. Smith**

Jesus said to his disciples, "A rich man shall hardly enter into the kingdom of heaven." (See Matt.19:16-23.) ¶ Is this because the rich man is rich? No. May not the rich man, who has the light of God in his heart, who possesses the principle and spirit of truth, and who understands the principle of God's government and law in the world, enter into the kingdom of heaven as easily, and be as acceptable there as the poor man may? Precisely. God is not a respecter of persons. The rich man may enter into the kingdom of heaven as freely as the poor, if he will bring his heart and affections into subjection to the law of God and to the principle of truth; if he will place his affections upon God, his heart upon the truth, and his soul upon the accomplishment of God's purposes, and not fix his affections and his hopes upon the things of the world. (*General conference, Oct. 1875*) (Gospel Doctrine, pp. 260-61) TLDP:714

---

851. The devil tempts us to covet riches and the material things of the earth.

**Joseph Smith,**
*translating the Book of Moses*

And Cain said unto the Lord: Satan tempted me because of my brother's flocks. And I was wroth also; for his offering thou didst accept and not mine; my punishment is greater than I can bear. (*The record of Moses: revelation to Moses concerning Cain and Able*) Moses 5:38

### President Wilford Woodruff,
*in behalf of the Council of the Twelve*

Those, however, who remember constantly the teachings of the Lord concerning the earth and its inhabitants, and who contribute of the means which the Lord gives them to assist the poor and help carry forward the work of God, exercise a check upon themselves and give Satan less power to lead them astray. Under the present system of affairs, those who supply themselves and their families with luxuries and advantages that are denied their neighbors, are in danger of becoming separated from the bulk of the people and forming a distinct class. (*General conference, Oct. 1887, epistle to Church; see MOFP3:133-55*) MOFP3:142-43; TLDP:716-17

### Joseph Smith

By this time, so deep were the impressions made on my mind, that sleep had fled from my eyes, and I lay overwhelmed in astonishment at what I had both seen and heard. But what was my surprise when again I beheld the same messenger at my bedside, and heard him rehearse or repeat over again to me the same things as before; and added a caution to me, telling me that Satan would try to tempt me (in consequence of the indigent circumstances of my father's family), to get the plates for the purpose of getting rich. This he forbade me, saying that I must have no other object in view in getting the plates but to glorify God, and must not be influenced by any other motive than that of building his kingdom; otherwise I could not get them. (*Joseph relates the angel Moroni's visit to him, Sept. 21, 1823*) JS-H 1:46

### Elder Joseph Fielding Smith

We should be on guard always to resist Satan's advances. He will appear to us in a person of a friend or a relative in whom we have confidence. He has power to place thoughts in our minds and to whisper to us in unspoken impressions to entice us to satisfy our appetites or desires and in various other ways he plays upon our weaknesses and desires. (Answers to Gospel Questions, 3:81) TLDP:137

**Related Witnesses:**

### President Heber J. Grant,
### J. Reuben Clark, Jr., David O. McKay
(First Presidency)

Satan is making war against all the wisdom that has come to men through their ages of experience. He is seeking to overturn and destroy the very foundations upon which society, government and religion rest. He aims to have man adopt theories and practices which he induced their forefathers, over the ages, to adopt and try,

only to be discarded by them when found unsound, impractical, and ruinous. He plans to destroy liberty and freedom—economic, political, and religious, and to set up in place thereof the greatest, most widespread, and the most complete tyranny that has ever oppressed men. He is working under such perfect disguise that many do not recognize either him or his methods. There is no crime he would not commit, no debauchery he would not set up, no plague he would not send, no heart he would not break, no life he would not take, no soul he would not destroy. He comes as a thief in the night, he is a wolf in sheep's clothing. Without their knowing it, the people are being urged down paths that lead only to destruction. Satan never before had so firm a grip on this generation as he has now. ("The Message of the First Presidency to the Church," IE1942Nov:761) TLDP:138

### Mormon

Now the cause of this iniquity of the people was this—Satan had great power, unto the stirring up of the people to do all manner of iniquity, and to the puffing them up with pride, tempting them to seek for power, and authority, and riches, and the vain things of the world. 16. And thus Satan did lead away the hearts of the people to do all manner of iniquity; therefore they had enjoyed peace but a few years. (*Much iniquity abounds among the Nephites, A.D. 29-30*) 3Ne.6:15-16

---

## 852. They who possess great riches tend to succumb to the sin of pride.

### Elder Wilford Woodruff

I do not find fault with riches. The gold and silver are the Lord's. We want houses building and we must cultivate the earth. This is all right. I do not find fault with a man getting rich, I find fault with our selling the kingdom of God, our birthright, selling the Gospel and depriving ourselves of eternal life, for the sake of gratifying the lusts of the flesh, the pride of life and the fashions of the world; and setting our hearts upon these things. (*In new Tabernacle, Sept. 12, 1875, JD18:121*) TLDP:714

### President Wilford Woodruff,
*in behalf of the Council of the Twelve*

This law of liberality appears to be one of the safeguards which the Lord has adopted to avert from his people the evil consequences which follow the possession of wealth. He has told us that the riches of the earth are His to give; but He has warned us to beware of pride, lest we become as the Nephites of old. We know the ruin it wrought for them, and we should spare no precaution to prevent wealth having a disastrous effect upon us. Many can endure poverty and be humble and live near the Lord who cannot bear riches. They become lifted up in pride and become covetous, and forget their God. . . . But the day will come when a more perfect order will be introduced. Then it will be said there are no poor and no rich in Zion—that is, we shall not be divided into classes, but shall all possess everything of this character necessary for our comfort and happiness. But until then, if we wish our families and ourselves to remain Latter-day Saints, we must be especially careful to guard against the deceitfulness of riches. (*General conference, Oct. 1887, epistle to Church; see MOFP3:133-55*) MOFP3:142-43; TLDP:716-17

**Mormon**

And it came to pass that the fifty and second year ended in peace also, save it were the exceedingly great pride which had gotten into the hearts of the people; and it was because of their exceedingly great riches and their prosperity in the land; and it did grow upon them from day to day. (*The more humble part of the Nephite Church members suffer persecutions, 41 B.C.*) Hel.3:36

**Mormon**

Now this great loss of the Nephites, and the great slaughter which was among them, would not have happened had it not been for their wickedness and their abomination which was among them; yea, and it was among those also who professed to belong to the church of God. 12. And it was because of the pride of their hearts, because of their exceeding riches, yea, it was because of their oppression to the poor, withholding their food from the hungry, withholding their clothing from the naked, and smiting their humble brethren upon the cheek, making a mock of that which was sacred, denying the spirit of prophecy and of revelation, murdering, plundering, lying, stealing, committing adultery, rising up in great contentions, and deserting away into the land of Nephi, among the Lamanites— (*Nephite dissenters join forces with the Lamanites; there is great slaughter of the Nephites who had become wicked, including some who professed to belong to the Church, about 35-31 B.C.*) Hel.4:11-12

**Mormon**

But it came to pass in the twenty and ninth year there began to be some disputings among the people; and some were lifted up unto pride and boastings because of their exceedingly great riches, yea, even unto great persecutions; 11. For there were many merchants in the land, and also many lawyers, and many officers. 12. And the people began to be distinguished by ranks, according to their riches and their chances for learning, yea, some were ignorant because of their poverty, and others did receive great learning because of their riches. 13. Some were lifted up in pride, and others were exceedingly humble; some did return railing for railing, while others would receive railing and persecution and all manner of afflictions, and would not turn and revile again, but were humble and penitent before God. 14. And thus there became a great inequality in all the land, insomuch that the church began to be broken up; . . . 15. Now the cause of this iniquity of the people was this—Satan had great power, unto the stirring up of the people to do all manner of iniquity, and to the puffing them up with pride, tempting them to seek for power, and authority, and riches, and the vain things of the world. (*Much iniquity abounds among the Nephites, A.D. 29-30*) 3Ne.6:10-15

**Jacob, brother of Nephi**

And the hand of providence hath smiled upon you most pleasingly, that you have obtained many riches; and because some of you have obtained more abundantly than that of your brethren ye are lifted up in the pride of your hearts, and wear stiff necks and high heads because of the costliness of your apparel, and persecute your brethren because ye suppose that ye are better than they. 14. And now, my brethren, do ye suppose that God justifieth you in this thing? Behold, I say unto you, Nay. But he condemneth you, and if ye persist in these things his judgments must speedily come unto you. 15. O that he would show you that he can pierce you, and with one glance of his eye he can smite you to the dust! 16. O that he would rid you from this iniquity and abomination. And, O that ye would listen unto the word of his commands, and let not this pride of your hearts destroy your souls! 17. Think of your brethren like unto yourselves, and be familiar with all and free with your substance, that they may be rich like unto you. 18. But before ye seek for riches, seek ye for the kingdom of God. 19. And after ye have obtained a hope in Christ ye shall obtain riches, if ye seek them; and ye will seek them for the intent to do good—to clothe the naked, and to feed the hungry, and to liberate the captive, and administer relief to the sick and the afflicted. 20. And now, my brethren, I have spoken unto you concerning pride; and those of you which have afflicted your neighbor, and persecuted him because ye were proud in your hearts, of the things which God hath given you, what say ye of it? 21. Do ye not suppose that such things are abominable unto him who created all flesh? And the one being is as precious in his sight as the other. And all flesh is of the dust; and for the selfsame end hath he created them, that they should keep his commandments and glorify him forever. 22. And now I make an end of speaking unto you concerning this pride. And were it not that I must speak unto you concerning a grosser crime, my heart would rejoice exceedingly because of you. (*Jacob denounces the love of riches to the Nephites, 544-421 B.C.*) Jacob 2:13-22

### Moroni, son of Mormon

And I know that ye do walk in the pride of your hearts; and there are none save a few only who do not lift themselves up in the pride of their hearts, unto the wearing of very fine apparel, unto envying, and strifes, and malice, and persecutions, and all manner of iniquities; and your churches, yea, even every one, have become polluted because of the pride of your hearts. 37. For behold, ye do love money, and your substance, and your fine apparel, and the adorning of your churches, more than ye love the poor and the needy, the sick and the afflicted. (*Moroni continues to write his last records on the plates that he hides up in the earth; he foresees the Nephite record shall come forth in a day of wickedness, degeneration and apostasy and says "I speak unto you as if ye were present, and yet ye are not . . . Jesus Christ has shown you unto me, and I know your doing," A.D. 401)* Morm.8:36-37

**Author's Note:** Not only the wealthy tend to succumb to the sin of pride. There are those who seek for status, or position, or power, who in that manner also tend to succumb to the sin of pride.

### 853. We are to avoid financial debt.

#### Reed Smoot

It is my hope and desire that the warning . . . to keep out of debt, and those who are in debt to get out as fast as possible, will be heeded. . . . I tell you that to an honest man there is no bondage controlled by human laws upon the face of the earth greater than the bondage of debt. . . . And when you are relieved, do not go in debt any more. CR1900Oct:6

#### J. Reuben Clark, Jr.

The First Presidency would like to urge every member of the Church to follow the example set by the Church and to live within his income. ¶ Anyone who lives beyond his income is invit-

ing disaster. Borrowed money is not income. Borrowing on capital account, within your reasonable capacity to pay, may be sound, depending upon circumstances. But borrowing to live on is unsound, whether it be an outright loan or installment buying. We urge the members to be frugal, thrifty, industrious, temperate, saving, and to live righteously. CR1940Apr:14-15

#### George Teasdale

I do not know how far we may be justified in going into debt; but we were admonished years ago by President John Taylor to keep out of debt. CR1898Apr:52

#### George Teasdale

The Lord has also commanded us to get out of debt, so that we may owe no man anything and be independent and keep the law of God. CR1900Apr:19

#### Elder Heber J. Grant

Now we desire that the Latter-day Saints shall be free from the bondage of debt. The Prophet of God has sounded the key-note to the people, "Pay your obligations, and do not grow in debt." CR1900Oct:35

#### Joseph Smith

Therefore, it is not right that any man should be in bondage one to another. (*Revelation, Dec. 16, 1833*) D&C 101:79 (See verses 69-79)

#### Paul

Render therefore to all their dues: tribute to whom tribute is due; custom to whom custom; fear to whom fear; honour to whom honour. 8. Owe no man any thing, but to love one another: for he that loveth another hath fulfilled the law. (*Paul's letter to the Church in Rome, about A.D. 55*) Rom.13:7-8

#### President Joseph F. Smith

Credit often involves persons in bankruptcy, and is most frequently at the root of all financial failure. It involves men in bondage which often works destruction to their characters as well as their whole course in life. Only the free are free, and no person in debt is free. Of all people on earth, the Saints should be the freest; and in order to fulfill the desires of their hearts as Latter-day Saints, they above all people should be free from debt. ¶ The Lord has taught his people to keep themselves free from all extravagance; and it is as much a duty we owe to our families, to live within our means, and protect them from debt, as it is to devote our lives in other ways to their temporal and spiritual progress and protection. In fact, keeping out of debt and holding ourselves financially free, are conditions upon which both temporal and spiritual progress depends. . . . ¶ The Saints should learn that it is not right, and leads to grave evil, to spend money on luxuries, for outings and other pleasure trips, that is not their own, or that has been obtained by going into debt for necessities. No luxuries for undue travel, dress, for eating or drinking, for amusement or entertainment, should be tolerated by the head of a family or demanded by its members, until the honest debts for necessities are cancelled. . . . To live within one's means, pay one's debts promptly, avoid credit as much as possible, both in giving and receiving, are old but worthy business maxims. Their observance should become a fixed habit with the man who desires to prosper in temporal affairs, and to lay the foundations of a character upon which a rich spiritual structure may be builded. ¶ Finally, while times are prosperous, get out of debt, and then keep out; pay as you go, and do your business on a cash basis. ("Avoid Debt and Credit," IE1905Sept:866-67) TLDP:731

**Related Witnesses:**

### Francis M. Lyman
A man cannot be comfortable spiritually who is in bondage financially. CR1904Oct:18

### Reed Smoot
I tell you that to an honest man there is no bondage controlled by human laws upon the face of the earth greater than the bondage of debt. CR1900Oct:6

### Francis M. Lyman,
### *also paraphrasing Marriner W. Merrill*
Repentance is necessary to salvation. Elder M. W. Merrill suggested that the first step to get out of debt was to quit going into debt; so I say that the very first step to repentance is to stop sinning. . . . CR1899Apr:38

### Recorded in Proverbs
The rich ruleth over the poor, and the borrower is servant to the lender. Prov.22:7

### J. Reuben Clark, Jr.
It is a rule of our financial and economic life in all the world that interest is to be paid on borrowed money. May I say something about interest? ¶ Interest never sleeps nor sickens nor dies; it never goes to the hospital; it works on Sundays and holidays; it never takes a vacation; it never visits nor travels; it takes no pleasure; it is never laid off work nor discharged from employment; it never works on reduced hours; it never has short crops nor droughts; it never pays taxes; it buys no food; it wears no clothes; it is unhoused and without home and so has no repairs, no replacements, no shingling, plumbing, painting, or white-washing; it has neither wife, children, father, mother, nor kinfolk to watch over and care for; it has no expense of living; it has neither weddings nor

births nor deaths; it has no love, no sympathy; it is as hard and soulless as a granite cliff. Once in debt, interest is your companion every minute of the day and night; you cannot shun it or slip away from it; you cannot dismiss it; it yields neither to entreaties, demands, nor orders; and whenever you get in its way or cross its course or fail to meet its demands, it crushes you. ("The Specter of Debt," IE1938Jun:328) TLDP:732

### Marriner W. Merrill
The easiest and shortest way to get out of debt is to first pay our tithing, promptly and honestly. CR1903Apr:66

### Marriner W. Merrill
I want to make you a promise . . . that if you will . . . begin now to pay your tithes and your offerings in full, if you will cease to sign notes, if you will cease to give mortgages on your homes, and retrench from this time forth, and turn to the Lord with full purpose of heart I will promise you that the way will be opened up and every faithful man and woman will be able to extricate himself and herself, and the time will be in your life time, when you will be a free people. There are some few people that are free now, and they do not owe any man anything. . . . Wait until we have the means and then make the purchase, and do not make the purchase until we have the means. . . . It is not a good thing, in my view, for individuals to do [to borrow]. It may be justifiable in the case of some large enterprise that would benefit the country and people, but as a rule for individuals to pattern after large corporations, they will fall if they do it. . . . As a rule . . . it has not been counsel of the Priesthood, so far as I have learned, for the people to obligate themselves beyond that which they were able to meet at any time. CR1898Apr:38-39

### Anthon H. Lund
I think . . . it is timely advice to our people to guard against the growing tendency to speculation and making investments when they have not the means wherewith to do it. It is not safe. We have prosperous times at present. We hope they may continue. But it would be very unwise to build upon the future, and not stand on a firm foundation in regard to financial matters. If any one wants to make investments, let him make them with his own means; not be too hopeful and borrow means beyond his ability to pay. CR1903Apr:24

### President Joseph F. Smith
My injunction, and the injunction of my brethren of the Presidency and of the Twelve, is, get out of debt; pay your honest obligations, free

yourselves so that you will be at liberty to perform any duty that you desire or that may be
asked of you for the upbuilding of Zion and the
spread of truth. CR1905Oct:3

---

**854. The Lord favors neither the rich
over the poor nor the poor over
the rich.**

### Elder Joseph F. Smith
God is not a respecter of persons. The rich man
may enter into the kingdom of heaven as freely
as the poor, if he will bring his heart and affections into subjection to the law of God and to
the principle of truth; if he will place his affections upon God, his heart upon the truth, and
his soul upon the accomplishment of God's purposes, and not fix his affections and his hopes
upon the things of the world. (*General conference, Oct. 1875*) TLDP:714

### Recorded in Proverbs
The rich and poor meet together: the LORD is
the maker of them all. Prov.22:2

### Joseph Smith,
*receiving the Word of the Lord*
And for your salvation I give unto you a commandment, for I have heard your prayers, and
the poor have complained before me, and the
rich have I made, and all flesh is mine, and I am
no respecter of persons. (*Revelation for Saints
in conference, Jan. 2, 1831*) D&C 38:16

### Rudger Clawson
We are led to understand from the scriptures that
God is no respecter of persons, and that these
social conditions that are in the world, and in
some degree perhaps in our midst, are not pleasing in His sight. . . . ¶ So, my brethren and sisters, if there are to be distinctions among us,
they must not be based on our financial condition, but rather upon the principle of righteousness. One man is better than another if he is
more righteous than the other. One man is more
acceptable to the Lord than another if he lives
nearer to the Lord than the other. CR1899Apr:4
**Related Witnesses:**

### Bruce R. McConkie
Either God treats all men the same or he is not
God. If he respects persons and shows partiality,
he does not possess those attributes of perfection
which make him the exalted being that he is.
(The Promised Messiah, p. 286) TLDP:221

---

**855. We are to impart of our substance
for the benefit of those less fortunate.**

### Dallin H. Oaks,
*also quoting Jesus,*
*recorded in Matthew*
We know . . . that even the most extreme acts of
service—such as giving all of our goods to feed
the poor—profit us nothing unless our service
is motivated by the pure love of Christ. ¶ If our
service is to be most efficacious, it must be accomplished for the love of God and the love of
his children. . . . ¶ This principle—that our service should be for the love of God and the love
of fellowmen rather than for personal advantage
or any other lesser motive—is admittedly a high
standard. The Savior must have seen it so, since
he joined his commandment for selfless and
complete love directly with the ideal of perfection. . . . "Be ye therefore perfect, even as your
Father which is in heaven is perfect."
(Matt.5:48). . . . ¶ Service with all of our heart
and mind is a high challenge for all of us. Such
service must be free of selfish ambition. It must
be motivated only by the pure love of Christ. . . .
¶ I know that God expects us to work to purify
our hearts and our thoughts so that we may
serve one another for the highest and best reason, the pure love of Christ. CR1984Oct:16-17

### King Benjamin,
*quoted by Mormon*
I would that ye should impart of your substance
to the poor, every man according to that which he
hath, such as feeding the hungry, clothing the
naked, visiting the sick and administering to their
relief, both spiritually and temporally, according
to their wants. (*King Benjamin addresses his people, about 124 B.C.*) Mosiah 4:26

### Jacob, brother of Nephi
Think of your brethren like unto yourselves,
and be familiar with all and free with your substance, that they may be rich like unto you. 18.
But before ye seek for riches, seek ye for the
kingdom of God. 19. And after ye have obtained a hope in Christ ye shall obtain riches, if
ye seek them; and ye will seek them for the
intent to do good—to clothe the naked, and to
feed the hungry, and to liberate the captive, and
administer relief to the sick and the afflicted.
(*Jacob denounces the love of riches among the
Nephites, 544-421 B.C.*) Jacob 2:17-19

### Joseph Smith,
*receiving the Word of the Lord*
For the earth is full, and there is enough and to
spare; yea, I prepared all things, and have given
unto the children of men to be agents unto
themselves. 18. Therefore, if any man shall take
of the abundance which I have made, and
impart not his portion, according to the law of
my gospel, unto the poor and the needy, he

shall, with the wicked, lift up his eyes in hell, being in torment. (*Revelation concerning the United Order, April 23, 1834*) D&C 104:17-18

**Joseph Smith,**
*quoted by Elder Joseph Fielding Smith*

[I]f there are any among you who aspire after their own aggrandizement, and seek their own opulence, while their brethren are groaning in poverty, and are under sore trials and temptations, they cannot be benefited by the intercession of the Holy Spirit, which maketh intercession for us day and night with groanings that cannot be uttered. (*In epistle to the Church from Liberty Jail, Missouri, March 25, 1839; see HC3:289-305*) TPJS:141

**Related Witnesses:**
**J. Reuben Clark, Jr.**

But there was another element involved in it [the Welfare Program], and that was based upon the Savior's principle announced in the Sermon on the Mount, "It is more blessed to give than to receive." And the history of the Welfare movement shows that there has come into the church an ever-increasing spirituality because of the giving which has been incident to the carrying on of the Welfare work. That giving has been not alone a giving of money or provisions or clothing or fuel, but a giving of manual labor, and of all the contributions the latter has perhaps brought the most of a feeling of common brotherhood as men of all training and occupation have worked side by side in a Welfare garden or other project. CR1943Oct:12-13

**Mormon**

And now, because of the steadiness of the church they began to be exceedingly rich, having abundance of all things whatsoever they stood in need—an abundance of flocks and herds, and fatlings of every kind, and also abundance of grain, and of gold, and of silver, and of precious things, and abundance of silk and fine-twined linen, and all manner of good homely cloth. 30. And thus, in their prosperous circumstances, they did not send away any who were naked, or that were hungry, or that were athirst, or that were sick, or that had not been nourished; and they did not set their hearts upon riches; therefore they were liberal to all, both old and young, both bond and free, both male and female, whether out of the church or in the church, having no respect to persons as to those who stood in need. 31. And thus they did prosper and become far more wealthy than those who did not belong to their church. 32. For those who did not belong to their church did indulge themselves in sorceries, and in idolatry

or idleness, and in babblings, and in envyings and strife; wearing costly apparel; being lifted up in the pride of their own eyes; persecuting, lying, thieving, robbing, committing whoredoms, and murdering, and all manner of wickedness; nevertheless, the law was put in force upon all those who did transgress it, inasmuch as it was possible. (*Those who were strong in the faith considered themselves equals, the priests supported themselves and the people cared for the poor, 91 B.C.*) Alma 1:29-32

856. **We are not to engage in acts of priestcraft: performing Church service for material gain or rendering benevolent service to others for riches or honor.**

**Dallin H. Oaks**

Some may serve for hope of earthly reward. Such a man or woman might serve in Church positions or in private acts of mercy in an effort to achieve prominence or cultivate contacts that would increase income or aid in acquiring wealth. Others might serve in order to obtain worldly honors, prominence, or power. ¶ The scriptures have a word for gospel service "for the sake of riches and honor;" it is "priestcraft" (Alma 1:16). . . . ¶ Service that is ostensibly unselfish but is really for the sake of riches or honor surely comes within the Savior's condemnation of those who "outwardly appear righteous unto men, but within . . . are full of hypocrisy and iniquity" (Matt.23:28). Such service earns no gospel reward. CR1984Oct:14

**Nephi, son of Helaman,**
*quoted by Mormon*

He commandeth that there shall be no priestcrafts; for, behold priestcrafts are that men preach and set themselves up for a light unto the world, that they may get gain and praise of the world; but they seek not the welfare of Zion. 30. Behold, the Lord hath forbidden this thing; wherefore, the Lord God hath given a commandment that all men should have charity, which charity is love, and except they should have charity they were nothing. Wherefore, if they should have charity they would not suffer the laborer in Zion to perish. 31. But the laborer in Zion shall labor for Zion; for if they labor for money they shall perish. (*Nephi gives commandments of God to Nephites, 559-545 B.C.*) 2Ne.26:29-31

**Peter**

The elders which are among you I exhort, who am also an elder, and a witness of the sufferings of Christ, and also a partaker of the glory that shall be revealed: 2. Feed the flock of God which is among you, taking the oversight thereof, not by constraint, but willingly; not for filthy lucre, but of a ready mind; (*Peter to the churches in modern Asia Minor, about* A.D. *60*) 1Pet.5:1-2

**Related Witnesses:**

### Micah

The heads thereof judge for reward, and the priests thereof teach for hire, and the prophets thereof divine for money: yet will they lean upon the LORD, and say, Is not the LORD among us? none evil can come upon us. (*The word of the Lord concerning Israel*) Micah 3:11

### Mormon,
#### *also quoting Alma, the younger*

And it came to pass that in the first year of the reign of Alma in the judgment-seat, there was a man brought before him to be judged, a man who was large, and was noted for his much strength. 3. And he had gone about among the people, preaching to them that which he termed to be the word of God, bearing down against the church; declaring unto the people that every priest and teacher ought to become popular; and they ought not to labor with their hands, but that they ought to be supported by the people. 4. And he also testified unto the people that all mankind should be saved at the last day, and that they need not fear nor tremble, but that they might lift up their heads and rejoice; for the Lord had created all men, and had also redeemed all men; and, in the end, all men should have eternal life. 5. And it came to pass that he did teach these things so much that many did believe on his words, even so many that they began to support him and give him money. 6. And he began to be lifted up in the pride of his heart, and to wear very costly apparel, yea, and even began to establish a church after the manner of his preaching. . . . 11. And it came to pass that he stood before Alma and pleaded for himself with much boldness. 12. But Alma said unto him: Behold, this is the first time that priestcraft has been introduced among this people. And behold, thou art not only guilty of priestcraft, but hast endeavored to enforce it by the sword; and were priestcraft to be enforced among this people it would prove their entire destruction. (*Priestcrafts and persecution spread among the people, 91* B.C.) Alma 1:2-6,11-12

### President Joseph F. Smith

Service in the interest of the Church is given, for the most part, without monetary compensation; where compensation is allowed it is mod-

erate; the high Church officials are not rich, but in the majority of cases are men of limited means, and where it is otherwise their wealth did not come from the tithes of the people; . . . (*Address from the First Presidency of the Church to the world, delivered to and accepted by vote of the Church in general conference, April 1907*) CR1907Apr(Appendix)10

### Paul

For there are many unruly and vain talkers and deceivers, specially they of the circumcision: 11. Whose mouths must be stopped, who subvert whole houses, teaching things which they ought not, for filthy lucre's sake. (*Paul's letter to his companion Titus, about* A.D. *64*) Titus 1:10-11

### Paul

This is a true saying, If a man desire the office of a bishop, he desireth a good work. 2. A bishop then must be blameless, the husband of one wife, vigilant, sober, of good behaviour, given to hospitality, apt to teach; 3. Not given to wine, no striker, not greedy of filthy lucre; but patient, not a brawler, not covetous; . . . 8. Likewise must the deacons be grave, not doubletongued, not given to much wine, not greedy of filthy lucre; (*Letter to his assistant Timothy, about* A.D. *64*) 1Tim.3:1-3,8

### Bruce R. McConkie

Persecution is one of the chief weapons in the hands of false priests; they use it to preserve their false religions. Truth stands on its own; error must be defended by the sword. False ministers fear the truth because by it their crafts are in danger. They practice priestcrafts to get gain and the praise of the world, neither of which will be theirs if true religion sweeps them into a deserved oblivion. (The Mortal Messiah, 2:393) TLDP:479

### President David O. McKay

A careful analysis of the organization of the Church of Jesus Christ of Latter-day Saints reveals the fact that it embodies all the strength of a strong central government and every virtue and necessary safeguard of a democracy. ¶ First, it has the authority of priesthood without the vice of priestcraft, every worthy man being entitled to a place in the governing quorums. (IE1961Jul:486-87) TLDP:247

### Mormon

And when the priests left their labor to impart the word of God unto the people, the people also left their labors to hear the word of God. And when the priest had imparted unto them the word of God they all returned again diligently unto their labors; and the priest, not esteeming himself above his hearers, for the preacher was no better than the hearer, neither was the teacher any better than the learner; and thus they were all equal, and they did all labor, every man according to his strength. (*Those who were strong in the faith considered themselves equals, the priests supported themselves and the people cared for the poor, 91 B.C.*) Alma 1:26

**Author's Note:** A dictionary definition of *priestcraft*: "Priestly policy or system of management based on temporal or material interest; policy of clergy to advance their own order." (The New Webster Encyclopedic Dictionary of the English Language, p. 659)

---

### 857. We are not to gamble or take money without giving fair value in return.

#### Stephen L. Richards

Now, there are a good many who will try to defend gambling. I have heard people say that all business is a gamble, that even life is a gamble. The latter statement is absolutely false to anyone who knows anything about life. There is no gamble about life, as everyone of you know. You know that it is all planned from the very beginning, and while we cannot foresee all the circumstances that will transpire, we know what life is. We know the course that life should take. We know its rewards and we know its penalties for infractions of the law. Life is not a gamble, and it is a mistake to say that business is a gamble. Anybody who understands the fundamentals of good business knows that it is not a gamble. Every legitimate business contemplates an exchange of values. One thing of value, services, for another thing of value, money or some other thing. All sound business is based solely on that principle—an exchange of values. ¶ That is not true of gambling—absolutely not. That is an effort to secure either something for nothing, or much more than what is invested in the gambling. . . . [I]t is the morality of it, my brethren, that I so much deplore because it puts men and women (and unfortunately there are many women who indulge) in a position where they are unable to appraise the sound values in life and in business, and it leads them on and on, like one who takes his first drink, until they may end up as alcoholics, or they may end up as gambling addicts, as this man calls them—compulsive gamblers. CR1958Oct:85

#### President Heber J. Grant, Anthony W. Ivins, Charles W. Nibley
(First Presidency)

The Church has been and now is unalterably opposed to gambling in any form whatever. It is opposed to any game of chance, occupation, or so-called business, which takes money from the person who may be possessed of it without giving value received in return. It is opposed to all practices the tendency of which is to encourage the spirit of reckless speculation, and particularly to that which tends to degrade or weaken the high moral standard which the members of the Church, and our community at large, have always maintained. MOFP5:245

#### Henry D. Moyle

No man ought to be very proud of his accomplishments if those accomplishments consist of capitalizing upon the human weaknesses and frailties of others. Generally speaking, it is the young people, the boys and girls, who are naturally inclined to be a little reckless. They get in the groove, as it were, in the habit of gambling, by learning that most vicious habit of trying to get something for nothing. It is prevalent today in the individual lives of our people and in all of our government units to give the people as much as possible for nothing and to see how little the people shall ultimately be required to work for what they get. I hope and pray that the day will come when every Latter-day Saint will stand for the enthroning of labor and industry and thrift. God bless us to be wise. . . . CR1950Oct:96

**Related Witnesses:**

#### President Joseph F. Smith

The Church does not approve of gambling but strongly condemns it as morally wrong, and classes also with this gambling, games of chance and lottery, of all kinds, and earnestly disapproves of any of its members engaging therein. ("Is Speculation a Legitimate Means of Earning a Livelihood?" IE1908Aug:807) TLDP:89

#### President Heber J. Grant

I have read nothing except condemnation of card-playing and the wasting of your time in doing something that brings no good, bodily, intellectually or in any way, and sometimes leads your children to become gamblers, because they become expert card-players. The Church as a Church requests its members not to play cards. I hope you understand me, and I want you to know that I am speaking for the Church when I ask the people to let cards alone. MOFP:5:250

### Delbert L. Stapley

The underworld of gambling and vice are constantly and unrelentingly exploiting the innocent and unsuspecting. ¶ Liquor interests and gambling operators partially justify their existence through the heavy taxes paid by them which they claim relieves tax burdens from the people. They fail to mention that by the use of their products and gambling devices, the customer pays the tax and receives no personal good from the product or activity. ¶ Some speculative business operators, also swindlers, with their schemes, stock promotions, and finance plans of an unsound and promotional nature. ¶ Promotions are not always truthful, also short of dependable facts and fail in fulfillment of promised income and rewards. CR1961Oct:22

### Mark E. Petersen

If you gamble . . . ask yourself if Christ is pleased. Ask yourself if such retrogression will bring you any nearer your purpose in life, that of becoming like our Savior. CR1968Oct:101

# List of Doctrines

## WELFARE PROGRAM OF THE CHURCH

*Doctrines Located in This Topic*

### (1) Prevention

858. Every adult has the responsibility to be self-reliant and independent in caring for his or her own economic needs.

859. Every adult has the responsibility to be self-reliant and independent in caring for his or her own emotional and spiritual needs.

860. Every adult has the responsibility for personal preparedness against emergency.

### (2) Temporary Assistance

861. We are to care for the poor, the needy, and the sick and afflicted.

862. Parents are to support their minor children.

863. Adult children have the responsibility to support their parents when they are in need.

864. If Church members are unable to sustain themselves, they are to call upon their own families, and then upon the Church, in that order.

865. Church members should not call upon the government for unearned welfare assistance.

866. The Lord's way for Church members to provide for the welfare of the needy is this: donations and offerings are to be given to the bishop, who in turn distributes them to the needy.

867. Fast offering donations are a Church-constituted means for providing for the poor.

868. Members of the Church are to contribute the value of two meals (at least) as a voluntary fast offering for the relief of those who are hungry or otherwise in distress.

869. We are to be very generous in the giving of fast offerings.

### (3) Rehabilitation

870. We are to be willing and eager to work for whatever welfare service we receive— to the extent of our abilities.

871. The Lord's way of providing welfare assistance prompts the individual to hasten his or her efforts to become independent again.

*Doctrines on WELFARE PROGRAM Located in Other Topics*

94. Persons who have acquired more possessions than they can manage and use properly are to freely impart the surplus to the needy.

201. It was the design of the Lord that Adam and Eve (and all people born thereafter) should support themselves by their own labors.

# WELFARE PROGRAM OF THE CHURCH

**(1) Prevention**
**(2) Temporary Assistance**
**(3) Rehabilitation**

## (1) Prevention

858. Every adult has the responsibility to be self-reliant and independent in caring for his or her own economic needs.

**John A. Widtsoe**
The activities of life center upon the business of making a living. Every man worthy of life desires to be able to sustain himself and a family of his own. This has always been an objective of the Latter-day Saints. In our welfare program the need of caring for the poor, necessary and beautiful as it is, is less important than the attempt to find ways and means to enable the poor to provide for themselves, and to raise the standard of living of all to meet their natural wants properly. Universal self-support will be a mighty defense against any enemy. A contented, self-supporting people will resist the cheap, enslaving offerings of evil. CR1940Oct:64

**Moses**
In the sweat of thy face shalt thou eat bread, till thou return unto the ground; for out of it wast thou taken: for dust thou art, and unto dust shalt thou return. (*Adam and Eve are cast out of the Garden of Eden to experience mortal life*) Gen.3:19

**Marion G. Romney**
It will require maximum effort for us to bring ourselves within the reach of the atoning blood of Jesus Christ so that we can be saved. There will be no government dole which can get us through the pearly gates. Nor will anyone go through those gates who wants to go through on the efforts of another. ¶ The first principle of action in Church Welfare is, therefore, for us to take care of ourselves as far as is possible. CR1979Apr:134

**Marion G. Romney**
We should strive to become self-reliant and not depend on others for our existence. ¶ Governments are not the only guilty parties. We fear many parents in the Church are making "gullible gulls" out of their children with their permissiveness and their doling out of family resources. Parents who place their children on the dole are just as guilty as a government which places its citizens on the dole. In fact, the actions of parents in this area can be more devastating than any government program. ¶ Bishops and other priesthood leaders can be guilty of making "gullible gulls" out of their ward members. Some members become financially or emotionally dependent on their bishops. A dole is a dole whatever its source. All of our Church and family actions should be directed toward making our children and members self-reliant. . . . ¶ Man cannot be an agent unto himself if he is not self-reliant. Herein we see that independence and self-reliance are critical keys to our spiritual growth. Whenever we get into a situation which threatens our self-reliance, we will find our freedom threatened as well. If we increase our dependence, we will find an immediate decrease in our freedom to act. . . . ¶ The key to making self-reliance spiritual is in using the freedom to comply with God's commandments. CR1982Oct:133-34

**President Harold B. Lee**
After giving his law to parents to teach and train their children to walk uprightly before the Lord, he indicated his displeasure relative to those among us who, in his language, "are idlers . . . and [our] children are also growing up in wickedness; they also seek not earnestly the riches of eternity, but their eyes are full of greediness." (D&C 68:31) ¶ If these words are clearly understood, we have been told where the roots of all evil are to be found. Our children have not been properly taught by parents in the home. Our communities have adopted policies which encourage idleness instead of work for those who want to work for what they need, and have failed to adopt measures to see that idleness and unemployment are reduced to the absolute minimum. CR1972Oct:61

**Marvin J. Ashton**
God help us to realize that money management is an important ingredient in proper personal welfare. Learning to live within our means should be a continuing process. We need to work constantly toward keeping ourselves free of financial difficulties. It is a happy day financially when time and interest are working for you and not against you. ¶ Money in the lives of Latter-day Saints should be used as a means of achieving eternal happiness. Careless and selfish uses cause us to live in financial bondage. We can't afford to neglect personal and family involvement in our money management. God will open the windows of heaven to us in these matters if we will but live close to him and keep his commandments. ("One for the Money," EN1975Jul:73) TLDP:731

**Related Witnesses:**
**Joseph Smith**
Let every man be diligent in all things. And the idler shall not have place in the church, except he repent and mend his ways. (*Revelation received at a Church conference, Jan. 25, 1832*) D&C 75:29

**Joseph Smith**
Cease to be idle; cease to be unclean; cease to find fault one with another; cease to sleep longer than is needful; retire to thy bed early, that ye may not be weary; arise early, that your bodies and your minds may be invigorated. (*Revelation Dec. 27/28, 1832; the "olive leaf message of peace"*) D&C 88:124

**Joseph Smith**
And the inhabitants of Zion also shall remember their labors, inasmuch as they are appointed to labor, in all faithfulness; for the idler shall be had in remembrance before the Lord. 31. Now, I, the Lord, am not well pleased with the inhabitants of Zion, for there are idlers among them. . . . (*Revelation received at the request of several elders, Nov. 1831*) D&C 68:30-31

**Joseph Smith,**
*receiving the Word of the Lord*
Thou shalt not be idle; for he that is idle shall not eat the bread nor wear the garments of the laborer. (*Revelation "embracing the law of the Church," received Feb. 9, 1831; "Although this revelation was given in connection with the law of consecration, the principles it teaches are consistent with the Church welfare plan,"* MPSG1988:102) D&C 42:42

**Joseph Smith**
Wo unto you poor men, whose hearts are not broken, whose spirits are not contrite . . . who will not labor with your own hands! (*Revelation at Kirtland, June 1831*) D&C 56:17

**Alma, the younger,**
*quoted by Mormon*
[S]ee that ye refrain from idleness. (*Alma to his son Shiblon*) Alma 38:12

**Marion G. Romney**
The first principle of action in Church Welfare is, therefore, for us to take care of ourselves as far as is possible. ¶ The second principle is that we should be so bound together as families that we shall sustain each other. Fathers and mothers are under a divine command to care for their children, and children have the responsibility to care for their parents. CR1979Apr:134

**Author's Note:** This principle of economic independence does not negate the appropriate partnership relationship in marriage where the breadwinner is usually the husband.

**859.** Every adult has the responsibility to be self-reliant and independent in caring for his or her own emotional and spiritual needs.

**Boyd K. Packer**
I have been concerned that we may be on the verge of doing to ourselves emotionally (and therefore spiritually) what we have been working so hard for generations to avoid materially. If we lose our emotional and spiritual self-reliance, we can be weakened quite as much, perhaps even more, than when we become dependent materially. On one hand, we counsel bishops to avoid abuses in the Church welfare program. On the other hand, we seem to dole out counsel and advice without the slightest thought that the member should solve the problem himself or turn to his family. Only when those resources are inadequate should he turn to the Church. ¶ We recognize at once that it would be folly to develop welfare production projects to totally sustain all of the members of the Church in every material need. We ought likewise to be very thoughtful before we develop a vast network of counseling programs with all of the bishops and branch presidents and everyone else doling out counsel in an effort to totally sustain our members in every emotional need. ¶ If we are not careful we can lose the power of individual revelation. . . . ¶ Has it occurred to you that many problems can be solved by reading the scriptures? We should all personally be familiar with the revelations. As part of your emotional self-reliance, read the scriptures. . . . ¶ I think an emotional dole system can be as dangerous as a material dole system, and we can become so dependent that we stand around waiting for the Church to do everything for us. ("Self-reliance," EN1975Aug:86) TLDP:724-25

**President Spencer W. Kimball**
Work brings happiness, self-esteem, and prosperity. It is the means of all accomplishment; it is the opposite of idleness. . . . ¶ . . . . The Church and its members are commanded by the Lord to be self-reliant and independent. ¶ The responsibility for each person's social, emotional, spiritual, physical, or economic well-being rests first upon himself, second upon his family, and third upon the Church if he is a faithful member thereof. ¶ No true Latter-day Saint, while physically or emotionally able, will voluntarily shift the burden of his own or his family's well-being to someone else. So long as he can, under the inspiration of the Lord and with his own labors, he will supply himself and

his family with the spiritual and temporal necessities of life. ¶ . . . . Because all things belong to the Lord, we are stewards over our bodies, minds, families, and properties. *(General conference, welfare session, Oct. 1977)* (The Teachings of Spencer W. Kimball, p. 366) TLDP:718-19

### Howard W. Hunter,
### *also quoting Joseph Smith*

There are some who ask why the Church is concerned with temporal affairs. The Church is interested in the welfare of each of its members. This interest therefore cannot be limited to man's spiritual needs alone but extends to every phase of his life. Social and economic needs are important to everyone. Man also has need for physical, mental, and moral guidance. Our lives cannot be one-sided, nor can we separate the spiritual from the temporal. The Lord has said: ¶ "Wherefore, verily I say unto you that all things unto me are spiritual, and not at any time have I given unto you a law which was temporal; neither any man, nor the children of men; neither Adam, your father, whom I created. ¶ "Behold, I gave unto him that he should be an agent unto himself; and I gave unto him commandment, but no temporal commandment gave I unto him, for my commandments are spiritual; they are not natural nor temporal neither carnal nor sensual." (D&C 29:34-35) ¶ The Lord makes no distinction between temporal and spiritual commandments, for he has said that all of his commandments are spiritual. When we understand the plan of life and salvation, this becomes evident to us. Mortality is just one part of our eternal life. ¶ We know where we came from. Holy writ tells us that we were born the spiritual children of our Heavenly Father, that we dwelt with him in a spiritual existence before our birth into mortality. The divine object of our coming to earth is to obtain a body of flesh and bones, to learn by the experiences which come to us in this mortal life the difference between good and evil, and to accomplish those things which the Lord commanded. Thus this life is the schoolroom of our journey through eternity. There is work to do and lessons to learn that we might prepare and qualify ourselves to go into the spiritual existence to follow. ¶ Man distinguishes between the temporal and the spiritual, probably because living in mortality between the spiritual pre-existence and the spiritual life hereafter, he fails to recognize the full significance of his activities during the years he spends on earth. To the Lord everything is both spiritual and temporal, and the laws he gives are consequently spiritual, because they concern spiritual beings. ¶ Every phase of our life, therefore becomes the concern of the Church. The great welfare program of the Church demonstrates this principle. The Church is interested in our social and our recreational needs, educational, family life, our business affairs, and all that we do. ¶ There is no way we can separate the activities of worship on the Sabbath day from the many pursuits of the weekday by calling one religious and the other temporal. Both are spiritual. God has ordained them thus, for they consist of our thoughts and actions as we wend our way through this part of eternity. Thus our business transactions, our daily labors, our trade or profession, or whatever we do become part of living the gospel. ¶ This imposes upon us a high duty and a high responsibility. If all men would live in obedience to these principles in their daily lives and in their dealings with each other, and if this same code would prevail among those who are in leadership among the peoples and nations of the world, righteousness would prevail, peace would return, and the blessings of the Lord would be showered down upon his children. ¶ Righteous living must start in the lives of individuals. *Each of us has the duty.* [Italics added] It must be incorporated into family living. Parents have the responsibility to live these principles and teach them to their children. Religion must be part of our living. The gospel of Jesus Christ must become the motivating influence in all that we do. There must be more striving within in order to follow the great example set by the Savior if we are to become more like him. This becomes our great challenge. CR1961Oct:108

### Related Witnesses:
#### Albert E. Bowen

We have a very practical religion. It pertains to our lives now. And the reward of observance of the law is not altogether postponed to a future on the other side of the grave. Building up the kingdom involves some very practical things. It is not altogether concerned with the non-material lying out in the ethereal realm. The building of meetinghouses, places of worship, schools, temples, for example, clearly is for spiritual purposes. But they involve a large element of the material. They are essential to the building up of the kingdom of God. And where would you classify the beautifying of your home; the making of refined surroundings? It is necessary to provide the things that sustain life, to master the arts and crafts and trades that meet the needs of progress and improvement. I do not think I can find the line that divides the spiritual from the temporal. CR1951Apr:124

**President Brigham Young,**
*quoted by John A. Widtsoe*

If we could only learn enough to be self-preserving and self-sustaining, we should then have learned what the Gods have learned before us, and what we must eventually learn before we can be exalted. (*In Tabernacle, Jan. 26, 1862, JD9:169)* DBY:255

**Marion G. Romney**

The first principle of action in Church Welfare is, therefore, for us to take care of ourselves as far as is possible. ¶ The second principle is that we should be so bound together as families that we shall sustain each other. Fathers and mothers are under a divine command to care for their children, and children have the responsibility to care for their parents. CR1979Apr:134

---

860. Every adult has the responsibility for personal preparedness against emergency.

**President Heber J. Grant,**
**J. Reuben Clark, Jr.,David O. McKay**
(First Presidency)

We renew the counsel given to the Saints from the days of Brigham Young until now—be honest, truthful, industrious, frugal, thrifty. In the day of plenty, prepare for the day of scarcity. The principle of the fat and lean kine is as applicable today as it was in the days when, on the banks of the Nile, Joseph interpreted Pharaoh's dream. Officials now warn us, and warn again, that scant days are coming. CR1942Apr:89

**President Spencer W. Kimball**

The principle of self-reliance stands behind the Church's emphasis on personal and family preparedness. Our progress in implementing the various facets of this personal and family preparedness is impressive, but there are still far too many families who have yet to heed the counsel to live providently. CR1978Apr:120

**President Spencer W. Kimball**

Some have become casual about keeping up their year's supply of commodities. . . . ¶ Should evil times come, many might wish they had filled all their fruit bottles and cultivated a garden in their backyards and planted a few trees and berry bushes and provided for their own commodity needs. ¶ The Lord planned that we would be independent of every creature. CR1974Oct:6

**Elder Ezra Taft Benson**

Our bishops storehouses are not intended to stock enough commodities to care for all the members of the Church. Storehouses are only established to care for the poor and the needy. For this reason, members of the Church have been instructed to personally store a year's supply of food, clothing, and, where possible, fuel. By following this counsel, most members will be prepared and able to care for themselves and their family members, and be able to share with others as may be needed. ("Ministering to Needs through the Lord's Storehouse System," EN1977May:82) TLDP:730

## (2) Temporary Assistance

861. We are to care for the poor, the needy, and the sick and afflicted.

**Russell M. Nelson**

Few, if any, of the Lord's instructions are stated more often, or given greater emphasis, than the commandment to care for the poor and the needy. CR1986Apr:32

**Joseph Smith,**
*receiving the Word of the Lord*

And behold, thou wilt remember the poor, and consecrate of thy properties for their support that which thou hast to impart unto them, with a covenant and a deed which cannot be broken. 31. And inasmuch as ye impart of your substance unto the poor, ye will do it unto me; . . . (*Revelation "embracing the law of the Church," Feb. 9, 1871; "Although this revelation was given in connection with the law of consecration, the principles it teaches are consistent with Church welfare plan,"MPSG-1988:102)* D&C 42:30-31

**Joseph Smith,**
*receiving the Word of the Lord*

Behold, I say unto you, that ye must visit the poor and the needy and administer to their relief, that they may be kept until all things may be done according to my law which ye have received. Amen. (*Revelation received in Kirtland, Ohio, Feb. 1831)* D&C 44:6

**George F. Richards**

The Lord expects us, when he blesses us with the good things of this earth, to remember those who are not so fortunate. We are to feed the hungry, clothe the naked, visit the sick, comfort those who mourn, and minister unto those who are poor and needy, and thus become of that class to whom the Lord, when he shall come, shall say: "Come, ye blessed of the Father, inherit the kingdom prepared for you from the foundation of the world." CR1939Oct:108-09

### Joseph Smith

Therefore, if any man shall take of the abundance which I have made, and impart not his portion, according to the law of my gospel, unto the poor and the needy, he shall, with the wicked, lift up his eyes in hell, being in torment. (*Revelation concerning the United Order, April 23, 1834*) D&C 104:18

### Jacob, brother of Nephi

Think of your brethren like unto yourselves, and be familiar with all and free with your substance, that they may be rich like unto you. 18. But before ye seek for riches, seek ye for the kingdom of God. 19. And after ye have obtained a hope in Christ ye shall obtain riches, if ye seek them; and ye will seek them for the intent to do good—to clothe the naked, and to feed the hungry, and to liberate the captive, and administer relief to the sick and the afflicted. (*Jacob denounces the love of riches among the Nephites, 544-421 B.C.*) Jacob 2:17-19

### King Benjamin, *quoted by Mormon*

I would that ye should impart of your substance to the poor, every man according to that which he hath, such as feeding the hungry, clothing the naked, visiting the sick and administering to their relief, both spiritually and temporally, according to their wants. (*King Benjamin addresses his people, about 124 B.C.*) Mosiah 4:26

---

## 862. Parents are to support their minor children.

### Joseph Smith

All children have claim upon their parents for their maintenance until they are of age. 5. And after that, they have claim upon the church . . . if their parents have not wherewith to give them inheritances. (*Revelation, April 30, 1832*) D&C 83:4-5

### Marion G. Romney

Fathers and mothers are under a divine command to care for their children. . . . CR1979Apr:134

### Boyd K. Packer

If a member is unable to sustain himself, then he is to call upon his own family, and then upon the Church, in that order, and not upon the government at all. ("Self-reliance," EN1975Aug:85) TLDP:728-29

### Paul

But if any provide not for his own, and specially for those of his own house, he hath denied the faith, and is worse than an infidel. (*Letter to his assistant Timothy, about A.D. 64*) 1Tim.5:8

### Russell M. Nelson

[T]he Lord's "own way" includes, first, reliance on self, then on the family. As parents care for their children, they in turn, may reciprocate when parents become less able. Family pride promotes solicitude for each member, taking priority over other assistance. (Handbook of the Relief Society, 1931, p. 22.) CR1986Apr:33

**Related Witnesses:**

### Elder Harold B. Lee

I have asked myself if the failure of children to take care of their aging parents, when they come to a day of want and are in need of sustenance, is due to the failure of parents, in the day gone by, to teach those same children to avoid the curse of idleness, and to be responsible in righteousness before our Heavenly Father. Unless we teach our children today correct principles, they, like some children today, will be thankless and without the natural affection necessary to cement this society upon a firm, determined foundation. Yes, it seems to me that in very deed, the welfare plan has been a kind of turning of the hearts of the children to the fathers and the fathers to the children, that we might be prolonged upon this land which the Lord our God has given us. CR1946Apr:71

---

## 863. Adult children have the responsibility to support their parents when they are in need.

### Marion G. Romney

The first principle of action in Church Welfare is, therefore, for us to take care of ourselves as far as is possible. ¶ The second principle is that we should be so bound together as families that we shall sustain each other. Fathers and mothers are under a divine command to care for their children, and children have the responsibility to care for their parents. CR1979Apr:134

### Jesus, *recorded in Matthew*

But he answered and said unto them, Why do ye also transgress the commandment of God by your tradition? 4. For God commanded, saying, Honour thy father and mother: and, He that curseth father or mother, let him die the death. 5. But ye say, Whosoever shall say to his father or his mother, It is a gift, by whatsoever thou mightest be profited by me; 6. And honour not his father or his mother, he shall be free. Thus have ye made the commandment of God of none effect by your tradition. 7. Ye hypocrites, well did Esaias prophesy of you, saying, 8. This people draweth nigh unto me with their mouth, and honoureth me with their lips; but their heart is far from me. 9. But in vain they do worship me, teaching for doctrines the commandments of men. (*Jesus answers the scribes and Pharisees who contend against him*) Matt.15:3-9

### Elder Harold B. Lee,
### also quoting Paul and Moses

To Timothy, the apostle Paul said: ¶ "But if any [man] provide not for his own, and specially for those of his own house, he hath denied the faith, and is worse than an infidel." (1Tim.5:8) ¶ And again the commandment from Mt. Sinai, and interpreted by the Master . . . to mean the taking care of aging parents by children: ¶ "Honour thy father and thy mother: that thy days may be long upon the land which the LORD thy God giveth thee. (Ex.20:12) ¶ From these two scriptures I make these two conclusions: In the first place those who refuse to care for their own are subject to a judgment more severe than that which would be meted out to one who lost his faith and had become as an infidel; and second, that those who refuse to honor father and mother in the way the Master explained, are jeopardizing their tenure upon this land which the Lord has given us. I have thought a great deal about that. I wonder whether that tenure shall be jeopardized because of the burdensome taxation that shall increase and grow until we are virtually displaced in our ownership, if we don't take care of our own, or I am wondering whether the Lord will withdraw his blessings, as Amulek declared in the thirty-fourth chapter of Alma, if we refuse to succor those who stand in need of help. ¶ And on the other hand, so far as children are concerned, I have remembered what the Apostle Paul said about that: He predicted a time would come in the last days, a perilous time when men should be lovers of their own selves, covetous, disobedient, unthankful, unholy, without natural affection. That sounds strangely familiar to the language of the Lord in this day, when he declared: ¶ "Now, I, the Lord, am not well pleased with the inhabitants of Zion, for there are idlers among them; and their children are also growing up in wickedness; they also seek not earnestly the riches of eternity, but their eyes are full of greediness. These things ought not to be, and must be done away from among them." (D&C 68:31,32) ¶ I have asked myself if the failure of children to take care of their aging parents, when they come to a day of want and are in need of sustenance, is due to the failure of parents, in the day gone by, to teach those same children to avoid the curse of idleness, and to be responsible in righteous-

ness before our Heavenly Father. Unless we teach our children today correct principles, they, like some children today, will be thankless and without the natural affection necessary to cement this society upon a firm, determined foundation. Yes, it seems to me that in very deed, the welfare plan has been a kind of turning of the hearts of the children to the fathers and the fathers to the children, that we might be prolonged upon this land which the Lord our God has given us. CR1946Apr:70-71

### Russell M. Nelson

The Lord's "own way" includes, first, reliance on self, then on the family. As parents care for their children, they in turn, may reciprocate when parents become less able. Family pride promotes solicitude for each member, taking priority over other assistance. (Handbook of the Relief Society, 1931, p. 22.) CR1986Apr:33

**Related Witnesses:**

### Recorded in Exodus

Honour thy father and thy mother: that thy days may be long upon the land which the LORD thy God giveth thee. (*The Lord reveals the fifth of the Ten Commandments to Moses*) Ex.20:12

### Paul

But if any provide not for his own, and specially for those of his own house, he hath denied the faith, and is worse than an infidel. (*Paul writes to his assistant Timothy, about A.D. 64*) 1Tim.5:8

**Author's Note:** Parents have claim upon their children for support to the extent that they cannot sustain themselves. ¶ No one should call for assistance until after his own resources and resourcefulness have run out: "It is important that you understand that, as a priesthood bearer, it is your responsibility to first care for your own temporal needs, next to care for the temporal needs of your family, and then for the temporal needs of others. This is a key welfare principle." (See MPSG1988:100.)

---

864. If Church members are unable to sustain themselves, they are to call upon their own families, and then upon the Church, in that order.

### Marion G. Romney

The first principle of action in Church Welfare is . . . for us to take care of ourselves as far as is possible. ¶ The second principle is that we should be so bound together as families that we shall sustain each other. Fathers and mothers are under a divine command to care for their children, and children have the responsibility to care for their parents. ¶ When Church members cannot provide for themselves and are not cared for by their families, they are to be cared for pursuant to the third principle of Church Welfare, which is, by divine command, that the membership of the Church shall care for them. ¶ The Lord has made these principles binding upon the Saints in every gospel dispensation. CR1979Apr:134

**Boyd K. Packer**

We have succeeded fairly well to establishing in the minds of Latter-day Saints that they should take care of their own material needs and then contribute to the welfare of those who cannot provide the necessities of life. If a member is unable to sustain himself, then he is to call upon his own family, and then upon the Church, in that order, and not upon the government at all. ("Self-reliance," EN1975Aug:85) TLDP:728-29

**Joseph Smith**

All children have claim upon their parents for their maintenance until they are of age. 5. And after that, they have claim upon the church, or in other words upon the Lord's storehouse, if their parents have not wherewith to give them inheritances. (*Revelation, April 30, 1832*) D&C 83:4-5

**Russell M. Nelson**

The Lord's "own way" includes, first, reliance on self, then on the family. As parents care for their children, they in turn, may reciprocate when parents become less able. Family pride promotes solicitude for each member, taking priority over other assistance. ¶ If one's family can't help, the Lord's "own way" includes the Church organization. The bishop is assisted by priesthood quorums and good sisters of the Relief Society, organized to look "to the wants of the poor, searching after objects of charity and . . . administering to their wants." (Handbook of the Relief Society, 1931, p. 22) CR1986Apr:33

**President Spencer W. Kimball**

The Church and its members are commanded by the Lord to be self-reliant and independent. ¶ The responsibility for each person's social, emotional, spiritual, physical, or economic well-being rests first upon himself, second upon his family, and third upon the Church if he is a faithful member thereof. ¶ No true Latter-day Saint, while physically or emotionally able, will voluntarily shift the burden of his own or his family's well-being to someone else. So long as he can, under the inspiration of the Lord and

with his own labors, he will supply himself and his family with the spiritual and temporal necessities of life. (*General conference, welfare session, Oct. 1977*) (The Teachings of Spencer W. Kimball, p. 366) TLDP:718-19

**Elder Ezra Taft Benson**

Occasionally, we receive questions as to the propriety of Church members receiving government assistance instead of Church assistance. Let me restate what is a fundamental principle. Individuals, to the extent possible, should provide for their own needs. Where the individual is unable to care for himself, his family should assist. Where the family is not able to provide, the Church should render assistance, not the government. We accept the basic principle that "though the people support the government, the government should not support the people." ¶ Latter-say Saints should not receive unearned welfare assistance from local or national agencies. This includes food stamps. Priesthood and Relief Society leaders should urge members to accept the Church welfare program and earn through the program that which they need, even though they may receive less food and money. By doing so, members will be spiritually strengthened, and they will maintain their dignity and self-respect. ("Ministering to Needs through the Lord's Storehouse System," EN1977May:84) TLDP:728

**Marion G. Romney**

We do not bless anybody when we do for them what they can do for themselves. The purpose of Welfare Services is to promote "independence, thrift, and self-respect," and every individual should value his or her independence and labor with all their might to maintain it by being self-sustaining. . . . ¶ Finally, the individual having done all he can to maintain himself, and members of his family having done what they can do to assist him, the Church, through Welfare Services, stands ready to see that such members, who will accept the program and work in it to the extent of their ability, are cared for, each "according to his family, according to his circumstances and his wants and needs." (D&C 51:3) CR1977Oct:115-16

**Marion G. Romney**

Obviously, no one should become a charge upon the public when his relatives are able to care for him. Every consideration of kindness, of justice, of fairness, of the common good, and of humanity requires this. CR1980Apr:114

**Related Witnesses:**

**Boyd K. Packer**

I have been concerned that we may be on the verge of doing to ourselves emotionally (and therefore spiritually) what we have been working so hard for generations to avoid materially. If we lose our emotional and spiritual self-reliance, we can be weakened quite as much, perhaps even more, than when we become dependent materially. On one hand, we counsel bishops to avoid abuses in the Church welfare program. On the other hand, we seem to dole out counsel and advice without the slightest thought that the member should solve the problem himself or turn to his family. Only when those resources are inadequate should he turn to the Church. ("Self-reliance," EN1975Aug:86) TLDP:724-25

---

### 865. Church members should not call upon the government for unearned welfare assistance.

**Boyd K. Packer**

We have succeeded fairly well to establishing in the minds of Latter-day Saints that they should take care of their own material needs and then contribute to the welfare of those who cannot provide the necessities of life. If a member is unable to sustain himself, then he is to call upon his own family, and then upon the Church, in that order, and not upon the government at all. ("Self-reliance," EN1975Aug:85) TLDP:728-29

**Elder Ezra Taft Benson**

Occasionally, we receive questions as to the propriety of Church members receiving government assistance instead of Church assistance. Let me restate what is a fundamental principle. Individuals, to the extent possible, should provide for their own needs. Where the individual is unable to care for himself, his family should assist. Where the family is not able to provide, the Church should render assistance, not the government. We accept the basic principle that "though the people support the government, the government should not support the people." ¶ Latter-say Saints should not receive unearned welfare assistance from local or national agencies. This includes food stamps. Priesthood and Relief Society leaders should urge members to accept the Church welfare program and earn through the program that which they need, even though they may receive less food and money. By doing so, members will be spiritually strengthened, and they will maintain their dignity and self-respect. ("Ministering to Needs through the Lord's Storehouse System," EN1977May:84) TLDP:728

**Marion G. Romney**

Obviously, no one should become a charge upon the public when his relatives are able to care for him. Every consideration of kindness, of justice, of fairness, of the common good, and of humanity requires this. CR1980Apr:114

**Marion G. Romney**

The first principle of action in Church Welfare is . . . for us to take care of ourselves as far as is possible. ¶ The second principle is that we should be so bound together as families that we shall sustain each other. Fathers and mothers are under a divine command to care for their children, and children have the responsibility to care for their parents. ¶ When Church members cannot provide for themselves and are not cared for by their families, they are to be cared for pursuant to the third principle of Church Welfare, which is, by divine command, that the membership of the Church shall care for them. ¶ The Lord has made these principles binding upon the Saints in every gospel dispensation. CR1979Apr:134

---

### 866. The Lord's way for Church members to provide for the welfare of the needy is this: donations and offerings are to be given to the bishop, who in turn distributes them to the needy.

**Russell M. Nelson**

As individual members of the Church, you and I participate in the Lord's "own way." At least once a month, we fast and pray and contribute generous offerings to funds that enable bishops to disperse aid. This is part of the law of the gospel. Each of us truly can help the poor and the needy, now, and wherever they are. And we, too, will be blessed and protected from apostasy by so doing. CR1986Apr:33

**J. Reuben Clark, Jr.**

In normal times, except for the few who are wholly incapacitated for work, and the few old folk without relatives to support them, the bishop's job is to afford temporary relief while the needy find re-employment. . . . ¶ Since the most pressing need was food, shelter, and clothing— the maintenance of life—the bishops were directed to adjust their organizations to intensify their work, to this end. Bishops' storehouses have been established for the collection of fuel, food, and clothing, these materials to come from the voluntary contributions of the people of the wards. Thus neighbors are to help neighbors, through the medium of the storehouse. This puts into the relief a personal sympathy that is wholesome for all, and tends to prevent imposition and over-reaching. There is an infinity of difference between the sack of flour that comes over the back fence from your next door neighbor and a sack that is sent to you from Washington. The one hallows the giver, and raises and enspirits, with the human love and sympathy behind it, him who thankfully eats it; the other debauches the hand which doles out that which is not his, and embitters and enslaves him who with malediction devours it. (*From an address at Estes Park, Colorado, pursuant to an invitation to speak on "Federal Relief—Emergency Measure or Permanent Program," June 20, 1939; entire address published in pamphlet distributed by the General Church Welfare Committee; MOFP6:63-88*) MOFP6:74

**Joseph Smith,**
*receiving the Word of the Lord*
And inasmuch as ye impart of your substance unto the poor, ye will do it unto me; and they shall be laid before the bishop of my church and his counselors, two of the elders, or high priests, such as he shall appoint or has appointed and set apart for that purpose. (*Revelation "embracing the law of the Church," Feb. 9, 1831; "Although this revelation was given in connection with the law of consecration, the principles it teaches are consistent with the Church welfare plan," MPSG1988:102*) D&C 42:31

**Related Witnesses:**
**Joseph Smith,**
*receiving the Word of the Lord*
I, the Lord, stretched out the heavens, and built the earth, my very handiwork; and all things therein are mine. 15. And it is my purpose to provide for my saints, for all things are mine. 16. But it must needs be done in mine own way; and behold this is the way that I, the Lord, have decreed to provide for my saints, that the poor shall be exalted, in that the rich are made low. 17. For the earth is full, and there is enough and to spare; yea, I prepared all things, and have given unto the children of men to be agents unto themselves. 18. Therefore, if any man shall take of the abundance which I have made, and impart not his portion, according to the law of my gospel, unto the poor and the needy, he shall, with the wicked, lift up his eyes in hell, being in torment. (*Revelation concerning the United Order, April 23, 1834*) D&C 104:14-18

**Joseph Smith**
And again, let the bishop appoint a storehouse unto this church; and let all things both in money and in meat, which are more than is needful for the wants of this people, be kept in

the hands of the bishop. (*Revelation, May 1831*) D&C 51:13

**Marion G. Romney**
Finally, the individual having done all he can to maintain himself, and members of his family having done what they can do to assist him, the Church, through Welfare Services, stands ready to see that such members, who will accept the program and work in it to the extent of their ability, are cared for, each "according to his family, according to his circumstances and his wants and needs." (D&C 51:3) CR1977Oct:115-16

**Marion G. Romney**
Thus, the bishop is to "visit the poor and the needy and administer to their relief," as a husband to the widow, as a parent to the orphan. And for temporal needs he is to draw from the storehouse. Spiritually he is to see that they are or become the pure in heart, that their spirits are contrite, that their "hearts are broken." CR1977Oct:118

**Marion G. Romney**
Everything we do in welfare services must be measured by its accomplishment in spiritual terms. Givers must give out of a righteous heart and with a willing spirit. Receivers must receive with thankfulness and gladness of heart. The Spirit must confirm a bishop's evaluation regarding assistance. It must lead a home teacher and a visiting teacher to know how to respond to needs of families to whom they are assigned. With righteous intent, participating in this great work sanctifies the soul and enlarges the mind. As we spiritually mature in fulfilling our welfare responsibilities, whatever they may be, we prepare ourselves to become "partakers of the divine nature." (See 2Pet.1:4.) CR1980Apr:115

**President Spencer W. Kimball**
Consecration is the giving of one's own time, talents, and means to care for those in need—whether spiritually or temporally—and in building the Lord's kingdom. In Welfare Services, members consecrate as they labor on production projects, donate materials to Deseret Industries, share their professional talents, give a generous fast offering, and respond to ward and quorum service projects. They consecrate their time in their home or visiting teaching. We consecrate when we give of ourselves. (*General conference, welfare session, Oct. 1977*) (The Teachings of Spencer W. Kimball, p. 36) TLDP:718-19

**J. Reuben Clark, Jr.**
[I]n lieu of residues and surpluses which were accumulated and built up under the United

Order, we, today, have our fast offerings, our Welfare donations, and our tithing, all of which may be devoted to the care of the poor, as well as for the carrying on of the activities and business of the Church. After all, the United Order was primarily designed to build up a system under which there should be no abjectly poor, and this is the purpose, also, of the Welfare Plan. . . . ¶ . . . . Furthermore, we had under the United Order a bishop's storehouse in which were collected the materials from which to supply the needs and the wants of the poor. We have a bishop's storehouse under the Welfare Plan, used for the same purpose. . . . ¶ . . . . Thus you will see, brethren, that in many of its great essentials, we have, as the Welfare Plan has now developed, the broad essentials of the United Order. CR1942Oct:57-58

---

### 867. Fast offering donations are a Church-constituted means for providing for the poor.

#### President Heber J. Grant
When fasting, members of the Church are advised to abstain from two meals each Fast Day and to contribute as a donation the amount saved thereby for the support of the worthy poor. . . . (*Published statement from the First Presidency of the Church, March 26, 1932*) MOFP5:307

#### President Heber J. Grant
Each member is asked to fast for two meals on the first Sunday in each month, and to give as a wholly voluntary contribution, the equivalent of these meals, which is used for the support of the poor. (*Published statement from the First Presidency of the Church, June 20, 1939*) MOFP6:72

#### Elder David O. McKay
Associated with this practice [of fasting] in the Church of Jesus Christ of Latter-day Saints is the giving of a fast offering, the underlying purpose and far-reaching benefits of which make the monthly observance of fast day one of the most significant features of this latter-day work. Besides the benefits already mentioned there are: First, all the spiritual uplift that comes from a Christ-like desire to serve one's fellowmen; and Second, an economic means which when carried out by a perfect and active organization will supply the needs of every worthy poor person within the confines of the organized branches of the Church. CR1932Apr:64-65

#### J. Reuben Clark, Jr.
[I]n lieu of residues and surpluses which were accumulated and built up under the United Order, we, today, have our fast offerings, our Welfare donations, and our tithing, all of which may be devoted to the care of the poor, as well as for the carrying on of the activities and business of the Church. After all, the United Order was primarily designed to build up a system under which there should be no abjectly poor, and this is the purpose, also, for the Welfare Plan. CR1942Oct:57-58

#### Related Witnesses:

##### Joseph Smith,
*receiving the Word of the Lord*
And remember in all things the poor and the needy, the sick and the afflicted, for he that doeth not these things, the same is not my disciple. (*Revelation for the elders of the Church, June 7, 1831; various elders sent to preach the gospel*) D&C 52:40

##### King Benjamin,
*quoted by Mormon*
And also, ye yourselves will succor those that stand in need of your succor; ye will administer of your substance unto him that standeth in need; and ye will not suffer that the beggar putteth up his petition to you in vain, and turn him out to perish. 17. Perhaps thou shalt say: The man has brought upon himself his misery; therefore I will stay my hand, and will not give unto him of my food, nor impart unto him of my substance that he may not suffer, for his punishments are just— 18. But I say unto you, O man, whosoever doeth this the same hath great cause to repent; and except he repenteth of that which he hath done he perisheth forever, and hath no interest in the kingdom of God. 19. For behold, are we not all beggars? Do we not all depend upon the same Being, even God, for all the substance which we have, for both food and raiment, and for gold, and for silver, and for all the riches which we have of every kind? 20. And behold, even at this time, ye have been calling on his name, and begging for a remission of your sins. And has he suffered that ye have begged in vain? Nay; he has poured out his Spirit upon you, and has caused that your hearts should be filled with joy, and has caused that your mouths should be stopped that ye could not find utterance, so exceedingly great was your joy. 21. And now, if God, who has created you, on whom you are dependent for your lives and for all that ye have and are, doth grant unto you whatsoever ye ask that is right, in faith, believing that ye shall receive, O then, how ye ought to impart of the substance that ye have one to another. . . . 26. And now, for the sake of these things which I have spoken unto you—that is, for the sake of retaining a

remission of your sins from day to day, that ye may walk guiltless before God—I would that ye should impart of your substance to the poor, every man according to that which he hath, such as feeding the hungry, clothing the naked, visiting the sick and administering to their relief, both spiritually and temporally, according to their wants. (*King Benjamin addresses his people, about 124 B.C.*) Mosiah 4:16-21,26

---

868. **Members of the Church are to contribute the value of two meals (at least) as a voluntary fast offering for the relief of those who are hungry or otherwise in distress.**

### President Heber J. Grant

Each member is asked to fast for two meals on the first Sunday in each month, and to give as a wholly voluntary contribution, the equivalent of these meals, which is used for the support of the poor. (*Published statement from the First Presidency of the Church, June 20, 1939*) MOFP6:72

### President David O. McKay

The regularly constituted fast consists of abstinence from food once each month, that is, it means missing two meals on the first Sunday of each month. The value of those two meals given as voluntary donation for the relief of those who are hungry or otherwise in distress constitutes the fast offering. Think what the sincere observance of this rule would mean spiritually if every man, woman, and child were to observe the fast and contribute the resultant offering, with the sincere desire of blessing the less fortunate brother or sister or sorrowing child! ¶ It is God's way. You say people don't like charity? Why, it should not be administered as charity; but as a co-operative plan of mutual service adopted for the benefit of all. ("On Fasting," IE1963Mar:156-57) TLDP:198

### Melvin J. Ballard

Our difficulty is that we have not all used the Lord's plan as we should. What ought that contribution, our fast offering, be, to be the equivalent of two meals? I would like to suggest that there isn't anything that this present generation needs so much as the power of self-control; appetite is stronger than will. Men's passions dominate their lives. If there is one thing that we need to recover, it is the power of self-control over the physical body; to deny it good food that would not be injurious, for two meals, has obtained a mastery over self; and the great-

est battle any of us shall ever fight is with self. ¶ I am charged to take possession of this house, this mortal tabernacle, and it is to be my servant. I am not to abuse it but keep it vigorous, clean, healthy, and strong. This exercise of controlling it once a month, that it must fast, is a healthy exercise of spiritual control over the material. If I can do this with regard to food, when this body craves something that is positively hurtful, then I have obtained power to say: "You cannot have it." Thus spiritual control over the body, in all its activities, may be secured, beginning with control over the appetite. (Sermons and Missionary Services of Melvin J. Ballard, p. 157) TLDP:199

### President Spencer W. Kimball

Each member should contribute a generous fast offering for the care of the poor and the needy. This offering should at least be the value of the two meals not eaten while fasting. ¶ "Sometimes we have been a bit penurious and figured that we had for breakfast one egg and that cost so many cents and then we give that to the Lord. I think that when we are affluent, as many of us are, that we ought to be very, very generous. . . . ¶ "I think we should . . . give, instead of the amount saved by our two meals of fasting, perhaps much, much more—ten times more when we are in a position to do it." ( See CR1974Apr:184.) CR1977Oct:126

### Delbert L. Stapley

Most Latter-day Saints, I think, understand the doing without two meals in connection with the monthly fast and giving the cash equivalent to the bishop as fast offerings, but I am wondering along with our fasting, do we gather our families together and pray with them that they may enjoy the blessings of the Lord? Do we also understand that the true fast presupposes self-restraint and purity of body by refraining from all bodily gratifications and indulgences? It seems to me that the soul cannot be humbled nor sanctified for the blessings of God unless this is true. CR1951Oct:123

### Mark E. Petersen

I believe that in many ways, here and now in mortality, we can begin to perfect ourselves. A certain degree of perfection is attainable in this life. . . . We can be one hundred percent perfect in paying a full and honest tithing. We can be one hundred percent perfect in abstaining from eating two meals on fast day and giving to the bishop as fast offering the value of those two meals from which we abstain. CR1950Apr:153

**Related Witnesses:**

### Marion G. Romney

If we will double our fast offerings, we shall

increase our own prosperity, both spiritually and temporally. This the Lord has promised, and this has been the record. ("Basics of Church Welfare," address to the Priesthood Board, March 6, 1974, p. 10) MPSG1986:117

**Delbert L. Stapley**

[T]here are two main requirements of this oath and covenant. First is faithfulness, which denotes obedience to the laws of God and connotes true observance of all gospel standards. For better understanding of the oath and covenant of the priesthood, may I propound. . . . ¶ . . . . Can a man be faithful who does not pay an honest tithing and fast offering? CR1957Apr:76

**Elder Harold B. Lee**

If we would be united in paying our fast offerings and observing the law of the fast as fully as the Lord has taught it, and if we were united in carrying out the principles of the welfare program as they have been given to us by our leaders today, we would be free from want and distress and would be able fully to care for our own. Our failure to be united would be to allow our needy to become the pawns of politicians in the public mart. CR1950Apr:96-97

---

**869. We are to be very generous in the giving of fast offerings.**

**Marion G. Romney**

Be liberal in your giving, that you yourselves may grow. Don't give just for the benefit of the poor, but give for your own welfare. Give enough so that you can give yourself into the kingdom of God through consecrating of your means and your time. Pay an honest tithing and a generous fast offering if you want the blessings of heaven. I promise every one of you who will do it that you will increase your own prosperity, both spiritually and temporally. The Lord will reward you according to your deeds. ("The Blessings of the Fast," EN1982Jul:4) TLDP:200

**Marion G. Romney**

While we await the redemption of Zion and the earth and the establishment of the United Order, we as bearers of the priesthood should live strictly by the principles of the United Order insofar as they are embodied in present church practices, such as fast offering, tithing, and the welfare activities. Through these practices we could as individuals, if we were of a mind to do so, implement in our own lives all the basic principles of the United Order. ¶ As you will recall, the principles underlying the United

Order are consecration and stewardships and then the contribution of surpluses into the bishop's storehouse. . . . ¶ What prohibits us from giving as much in fast offerings as we would have given in surpluses under the United Order? Nothing but our own limitations. CR1966Apr:100

**President Spencer W. Kimball**

Sometimes we have been a bit penurious and figured that we had for breakfast one egg and that cost so many cents and then we give that to the Lord. I think that when we are affluent, as many of us are, that we ought to be very, very generous. . . . ¶ I think we should . . . give, instead of the amount saved by our two meals of fasting, perhaps much, much more—ten times more when we are in a position to do it. CR1974Apr:184

**President Joseph F. Smith**

It is, therefore, incumbent upon every Latter-day Saint to give to his bishop, on fast day, the food that he or his family would consume for the day, that it may be given to the poor for their benefit and blessing; or, in lieu of the food that its equivalent amount, or if the person be wealthy a liberal donation, in money be so reserved and dedicated to the poor. . . . ("Observance of Fast Day," IE1902Dec:148-49) TLDP:198

**President Heber J. Grant**

Now, I believe that people are blessed in proportion to their liberality. I am not saying that they always make more dollars, perhaps. . . . I believe that to those who are liberal the Lord gives ideas, and they grow in capacity and ability more rapidly than those that are stingy. ("Settlement," IE1941Jan:9,56) TLDP:694

**Elder Heber J. Grant**

If the people will pay their tithes and offerings, they will not only be blessed in their material affairs, but they will be abundantly blessed with increased outpouring of the Spirit of the Lord. . . . ¶ I bear witness to you, as an Apostle of the Lord Jesus Christ, that material and spiritual prosperity is predicated upon the fulfillment of the duties and responsibilities that rest upon us a Latter-day Saints. CR1899Oct:19

**President Wilford Woodruff,**
*in behalf of the Council of the Twelve*

We have only to look around us to satisfy ourselves also, that those who are generous in contributing to God's work are favored of the Lord. This was the experience of ancient Israel, and it is our experience, Yet in regard to voluntary donations there is too much carelessness, notwithstanding all the precious promises connected therewith. The Saints should be reminded of the obligation which rests upon them. Our children, also, should be taught this duty, that it may become a fixed habit with them to punctually attend to these matters. Those who have strictly observed these requirements can testify to the great pleasure and many rewards they have received from their observance. ¶ This law of liberality appears to be one of the safeguards which the Lord has adopted to avert from his people the evil consequences which follow the possession of wealth. He has told us that the riches of the earth are His to give; but He has warned us to beware of pride, lest we become as the Nephites of old. We know the ruin it wrought for them, and we should spare no precaution to prevent wealth having a disastrous effect upon us. Many can endure poverty and be humble and live near the Lord who cannot bear riches. They become lifted up in pride and become covetous, and forget their God. Those, however, who remember constantly the teachings of the Lord concerning the earth and its inhabitants, and who contribute of the means which the Lord gives them to assist the poor and help carry forward the work of God, exercise a check upon themselves and give Satan less power to lead them astray. Under the present system of affairs, those who supply themselves and their families with luxuries and advantages that are denied their neighbors, are in danger of becoming separated from the bulk of the people and forming a distinct class. But the day will come when a more perfect order will be introduced. Then it will be said there are no poor and no rich in Zion—that is, we shall not be divided into classes, but shall all possess everything of this character necessary for our comfort and happiness. But until then, if we wish our families and ourselves to remain Latter-day Saints, we must be especially careful to guard against the deceitfulness of riches. (*General conference, Oct. 1887, epistle to the Church, see MOFP3:133-55*) MOFP3:142-43; TLDP:716-17

**Related Witnesses:**

**Paul**

Every man according as he purposeth in his heart, so let him give; not grudgingly, or of necessity: for God loveth a cheerful giver. (*Letter to the Church at Corinth, Greece, about A.D. 55*) 2Cor.9:7

---

## (3) Rehabilitation

870. We are to be willing and eager to work for whatever welfare service we receive—to the extent of our abilities.

**Marion G. Romney**

The obligation of the receiver to labor, to the extent of his ability, to sustain himself and dependents, is just as great, in God's economy, as is the obligation to contribute to the care of the needy. . . . ¶ As positive, however, as is this commandment against idleness, a disregard of it by the receiver does not justify Church members in failing to impart of their substance "according to the law of [the] gospel, unto the poor and the needy." (D&C 104:18) CR1972Oct:116

**J. Reuben Clark, Jr.**

At the time it [the welfare program] was put into operation, we called attention to the fact that while its immediate purpose was the caring for the poor, and only temporarily caring for them so far as the individuals were concerned, yet that back of and behind that service there were other considerations, among them being that we should rehabilitate temporally and spiritually those who received the assistance. It was also determined that the principle of help should be the actual need of the individual or family; there was not to be a fixed, uniform amount for each person. Also, in so far as it was practicable, everyone should work for what he received, if he were well. CR1943Oct:12

**Elder Ezra Taft Benson**

Priesthood and Relief Society leaders should urge members to accept the Church welfare program and earn through the program that which they need, even though they may receive less food and money. By doing so, members will be spiritually strengthened, and they will maintain their dignity and self-respect. ("Ministering to Needs through the Lord's Storehouse System," EN1977May:84) TLDP:728

**Related Witnesses:**

**Joseph Smith,**
*receiving the Word of the Lord*

Thou shalt not be idle; for he that is idle shall not eat the bread nor wear the garments of the laborer. (*Revelation "embracing the law of the Church," Feb. 9, 1831*) D&C 42:42

**Joseph Smith**

Wo unto you poor men, whose hearts are not broken, whose spirits are not contrite . . . who will not labor with your own hands! (*Revelation received at Kirtland, June 1831*) D&C 56:17

**Moses**

In the sweat of thy face shalt thou eat bread, till thou return unto the ground; for out of it wast thou taken: for dust thou art, and unto dust shalt thou return. (*Adam and Eve are cast out of the Garden of Eden to experience mortal life*) Gen.3:19

### J. Reuben Clark, Jr.

We must purge our hearts of the love of ease; we must put from our lives the curse of idleness. . . . CR1973Oct:97

**Author's Note:** "Every priesthood bearer should be willing and anxious to work for whatever he receives to the extent of his ability." (MPSG1988:101) ¶ Henry D. Taylor, quoting from *Christian Economics,* says "That which one man receives without working for it, another man must work for without receiving it." (MPSG1988:101)

---

871. The Lord's way of providing welfare assistance prompts the individual to hasten his or her efforts to become independent again.

#### President Spencer W. Kimball

The Lord's way builds individual self-esteem and develops and heals the dignity of the individual, whereas the world's way depresses the individual's view of himself and causes deep resentment. ¶ The Lord's way causes the individual to hasten his efforts to become economically independent again, even though he may have temporary need, because of special conditions, for help and assistance. The world's way deepens the individual's dependency on welfare programs and tends to make him demand more rather than encouraging him to return to economic independence. ¶ The Lord's way helps our members get a testimony for themselves about the gospel of work. For work is important to human happiness as well as productivity. The world's way, however, places greater and greater emphasis on leisure and upon the avoidance of work. . . . ¶ Do what you can to make our projects economically viable, so that we don't rationalize that the welfare project is good simply because it gets men together. Even though it is good for the priesthood to labor side by side, we can have the brotherhood of labor and the economic efficiency too. (*General conference, welfare session, April 1976*) (The Teachings of Spencer W. Kimball, p. 369) TLDP:722

#### J. Reuben Clark, Jr.

At the time it [the welfare program] was put into operation, we called attention to the fact that while its immediate purpose was the caring for the poor, and only temporarily caring for them so far as the individuals were concerned, yet that back of and behind that service there were other considerations, among them being that we should rehabilitate temporally and spiritually those who received the assistance. CR1943Oct:12

#### J. Reuben Clark, Jr., quoted by Gordon B. Hinckley

"The priesthood quorums in their extending of relief have not the obligation prescribed to the bishop. But the relationship of the priesthood, [and] the spirit of lofty unselfish brotherhood which it carries with it, do require that they individually and as quorums exert their utmost means of power to rehabilitate, spiritually and temporally, their erring and unfortunate brethren. In his temporal administrations, the bishop looks at every needy person as a temporary problem, caring for them until they can help themselves; the priesthood must look at their needy brethren as a continuing problem until not only his temporal needs are met, but his spiritual ones also. As a concrete example—a bishop extends help while the artisan or craftsman is out of work and in want; a priesthood quorum sets him up to work and tries to see that he goes along until fully self-supporting and active in his priesthood duties. (*J. Reuben Clark, Jr., "Bishops and Relief Society," July 9, 1941, pp. 17-18*). . . . ¶ "[Such] assistance may take the form of helping the needy brother in his actual need and problem, to build a home, or to start in a small business, or, if he be an artisan, to get him a kit of tools, or, if he be a farmer, to get him seeds, or to help him plant or harvest a crop, or to meet some urgent credit need he has, or to supply him with clothing, or shelter, or food, or medical assistance, or schooling for the children, or to give aid in any number of other ways." (*From Estes Park address, June 20, 1939; the address at Estes Park, Colorado, was given pursuant to an invitation to speak on "Federal Relief—Emergency Measure or Permanent Program;" published in pamphlet distributed by the General Church Welfare Committee; entire address MOFP6:63-88*) ("Welfare Responsibilities of the Priesthood Quorums," EN1977Nov:85) TLDP:727

#### Russell M. Nelson

Members of priesthood quorums and groups have a duty to rehabilitate, spiritually and temporally, their erring or unfortunate brethren. While a bishop extends aid to one temporarily out of work, the quorum arranges for his employment until fully self-supporting again. CR1986Apr:33

# List of Doctrines

## WISDOM

*Doctrines Located in This Topic*

872. We are to be diligent, yet we should not run faster or labor more than we have strength and means.

873. True wisdom comes from the inspiration of God (divine inspiration is greater than earthly experience, no matter how extensive that may be).

874. The Lord selects teachable persons to do His work; He chooses those whom the world calls weak and foolish more frequently than those whom the world calls wise.

875. The worldly wise, who will not humble themselves before God, will never enjoy eternal happiness.

872. We are to be diligent, yet we should not run faster or labor more than we have strength and means.

**Joseph Smith**
Do not run faster or labor more than you have strength and means to enable you to translate; but be diligent unto the end. (*Revelation received at Harmony, Pennsylvania, summer of 1828*) D&C 10:4

**Joseph Smith**
And no one can assist in this work except he shall be humble and full of love, having faith, hope, and charity, being temperate in all things, whatsoever shall be entrusted to his care. (*Revelation for Joseph Knight, Sen., May 1829*) D&C 12:8

**Alma, the younger,**
*quoted by Mormon*
And now, as ye have begun to teach the word even so I would that ye should continue to teach; and I would that ye would be diligent and temperate in all things. 11. See that ye are not lifted up unto pride; yea, see that ye do not boast in your own wisdom, nor of your much strength. 12. Use boldness, but not overbearance; and also see that ye bridle all your passions, that ye may be filled with love; see that ye refrain from idleness. (*Alma to his son Shiblon*) Alma 38:10-12

**King Benjamin,**
*quoted by Mormon*
And see that all these things are done in wisdom and order; for it is not requisite that a man should run faster than he has strength. And again, it is expedient that he should be diligent, that thereby he might win the prize; therefore, all things must be done in order. (*King Benjamin addresses his people, about 124 B.C.*) Mosiah 4:27

**Related Witnesses:**
**Alma, the younger,**
*quoted by Mormon*
And now I would that ye should be humble, and be submissive and gentle; easy to be entreated; full of patience and long-suffering; being temperate in all things; being diligent in keeping the commandments of God at all times; asking for whatsoever things ye stand in need, both spiritual and temporal; always returning thanks unto God for whatsoever things ye do receive. (*Alma preaches to the people in Gideon, about 83 B.C.*) Alma 7:23

**Author's Note:** Dictionary definition of *temperate*: "Marked by moderation: keeping or existing in the middle ground between extremes. Moderate in indulging appetite or desire." (Webster's Third International Dictionary, p. 232)

---

873. True wisdom comes from the inspiration of God (divine inspiration is greater than earthly experience, no matter how extensive that may be).

**Recorded in Job**
I said, Days should speak, and multitude of years should teach wisdom. 8. But there is a spirit in man: and the inspiration of the Almighty giveth them understanding. 9. Great men are not always wise: neither do the aged understand judgment. (*Elihu, admittedly a younger man than they, censures Job and his three friends*) Job 32:7-9

**President Joseph F. Smith**
I believe that the Lord has revealed to the children of men all that they know. I do not believe that any man has discovered any principle in science, or art, in mechanism, or mathematics, or anything else, that God did not know before he did. Man is indebted to the source of all intelligence and truth, for the knowledge that he possesses; and all who will yield obedience to the promptings of the Spirit . . . will get a clearer, a more expansive, and a more direct and conclusive knowledge of God's truths than anyone else can do. CR1902Apr:85-86

**Erastus Snow**
The foundation of all true education is the wisdom and knowledge of God. (*In Tabernacle, Oct. 8, 1867, JD12:178*) TLDP:149

**Recorded in Proverbs**
The fear of the LORD is the beginning of wisdom: and the knowledge of the holy is understanding. Prov.9:10

**J. Reuben Clark, Jr.**
Thus God made clear that the gaining of knowledge is not to be like the commonplace work of earning a living. He who invades the domain of knowledge must approach it as Moses came to the burning bush; he stands on holy ground; he would acquire things sacred; he seeks to make his own the attributes of Deity, the truth which Christ declared he was (John 14:6), and which shall make us free (John 8:32), free of the shackles of time and space, which shall be no more. We must come to this quest of truth—in all regions of human knowledge whatsoever—not only in reverence, but with a

spirit of worship. ¶ In all his promises and commandments about gaining knowledge, the Lord has never withheld from our quest any field of truth. Our knowledge is to be coterminous with the universe and is to reach out and to comprehend the laws and the workings of the deeps of the eternities. All domains of all knowledge belong to us. In no other way could the great law of eternal progression be satisfied. (*Charge to President Howard S. McDonald at his inauguration as president of Brigham Young University, Nov. 14, 1945, delivered by J. Reuben Clark, Jr., in behalf of the First Presidency, IE1946Jan:60-63)* MOFP6:231-32

**Related Witnesses:**

**Recorded in Proverbs**

Trust in the LORD with all thine heart; and lean not unto thine own understanding. 6. In all thy ways acknowledge him, and he shall direct thy paths. 7. Be not wise in thine own eyes: fear the LORD, and depart from evil. Prov.3:5-7

**James**

If any of you lack wisdom, let him ask of God, that giveth to all men liberally, and upbraideth not; and it shall be given him. (*Letter to his brethren in the Church*) James 1:5

**Recorded in Proverbs**

Wisdom is the principal thing; therefore get wisdom: and with all thy getting get understanding. Prov.4:7

**Jacob, brother of Nephi,**
**quoted by Nephi**

But to be learned is good if they hearken unto the counsels of God. (*Jacob teaches the people of Nephi, 559-545 B.C.*) 2Ne.9:29

**Paul**

Ever learning, and never able to come to the knowledge of the truth. (*Paul writes to his assistant Timothy describing apostasy in the last days, about A.D. 64*) 2Tim.3:7

---

**874. The Lord selects teachable persons to do His work; He chooses those whom the world calls weak and foolish more frequently than those whom the world calls wise.**

**Paul**

For ye see your calling, brethren, how that not many wise men after the flesh, not many mighty, not many noble, are called: 27. But God hath chosen the foolish things of the world to confound the wise; and God hath chosen the weak things of the world to confound the things which are mighty; (*Paul writes to the Church at Corinth, Greece, about A.D. 55*) 1Cor.1:26-27

**President Brigham Young,**
**quoted by John A. Widtsoe**

This people are mostly gathered from what are termed the laboring and middle classes. We have not gathered into this Church men that are by the world esteemed profound in their principles, ideas, and judgment. We have none in this Church that are called by them expert statesmen. How frequently it is cast at the Elders, when they are abroad preaching, that Joseph Smith, the founder of their Church and religion, was only a poor illiterate boy. That used to be advanced as one of the strongest arguments that could be produced against the doctrine of salvation, by the wise and learned of this world, though it is no argument at all. The Lord should have revealed himself to some of the learned priests or talented men of the age, say they, who could have done some good and borne off the Gospel by their influence and learning, and not to a poor, ignorant, unlettered youth. Not many wise, not many mighty, not many noble, speaking after the manner of men, are called; but God hath chosen the foolish things of the world to confound the wise, the weak things of the world to confound the things that are mighty; and base things of the world—things which are despised by the world, hath God in his wisdom chosen; yea, and things which are not, to bring to naught things that are, that no flesh should glory in his presence. (*In Tabernacle, Nov. 22, 1857, JD6:70*) DBY:321-22

**Jacob, brother of Nephi,**
**quoted by Nephi**

And whoso knocketh, to him will he open; and the wise, and the learned, and they that are rich, who are puffed up because of their learning, and their wisdom, and their riches—yea, they are they whom he despiseth; and save they shall cast these things away, and consider themselves fools before God, and come down in the depths of humility, he will not open unto them. 43. But the things of the wise and the prudent shall be hid from them forever—yea, that happiness which is prepared for the saints. (*Jacob to the people of Nephi, 559-545 B.C.*) 2Ne.9:42-43

**President Wilford Woodruff**

The Lord has chosen the weak things of the world to lead this people. Joseph Smith was but a young man when he died—not forty years of age. He lived nearly fourteen years after the organization of this Church. President Brigham Young followed him. Who was Brigham Young? He was a painter and glazier. He was a humble man. But the Lord called him to lead this people. You know what he has done, and the spirit that was with him. The Lord was with him, and he continued to lead this people by the power of God and by the revelation of Jesus Christ. He laid the foundation of a great work in these mountains of Israel. Many strangers who have recently visited us have marveled and wondered at Salt Lake City being laid out in the manner it was. . . . What was John Taylor? He was a wood turner, and he led the Church for quite a time. Wilford Woodruff was a miller and a farmer; that was about the highest ambition he ever arrived at as far as this world was concerned. That is about the way the Lord has chosen these men. Why did he not choose these learned and great men? As I have often said, he could not hadn't them. God has always chosen the weak things of the earth. (Millennial Star, 1891; The Discourses of Wilford Woodruff, pp. 86-87) TLDP:294

**Related Witnesses:**

### Paul

Ever learning, and never able to come to the knowledge of the truth. (*Letter to his assistant Timothy, about A.D. 64*) 2Tim.3:7

### Jacob, brother of Nephi,
*quoted by Nephi*

O that cunning plan of the evil one! O the vainness, and the frailties, and the foolishness of men! When they are learned they think they are wise, and they hearken not unto the counsel of God, for they set it aside, supposing they know of themselves, wherefore, their wisdom is foolishness and it profiteth them not. And they shall perish. 29. But to be learned is good if they hearken unto the counsels of God. (*Jacob teaches the people of Nephi, 559-545 B.C.*) 2Ne.9:28-29

---

875. The worldly wise, who will not humble themselves before God, will never enjoy eternal happiness.

### Joseph Smith,
*quoted by Elder Joseph Fielding Smith*

There are a great many wise men and women too in our midst who are too wise to be taught; therefore they must die in their ignorance, and in the resurrection they will find their mistake. (*At the Stand in Nauvoo, Ill., June 11,1843*) TPJS:309

### Jacob, brother of Nephi,
*quoted by Nephi*

And whoso knocketh, to him will he open; and the wise, and the learned, and they that are rich, who are puffed up because of their learning, and their wisdom, and their riches—yea, they are they whom he despiseth; and save they shall

cast these things away, and consider themselves fools before God, and come down in the depths of humility, he will not open unto them. 43. But the things of the wise and the prudent shall be hid from them forever—yea, that happiness which is prepared for the saints. (*Jacob to the people of Nephi, 559-545 B.C.*) 2Ne.9:42-43

### Elder Joseph Fielding Smith

Now I say it boldly, all the knowledge that a man can gain in this world or beyond this world, independent of the spirit of God, the inspiration of the Almighty, will not lead him to a fulness, and in defense of that I am going to read to you from section ninety-three of the Doctrine and Covenants: [verses 20-28 are quoted]. ¶ So with all our boasting, with all our understanding, with all the knowledge that we possess, let me say that this great knowledge that has been poured out upon man, and all that is truth has come from God, but with it all unless we humble ourselves and put ourselves in harmony with his truth and seek for the light which comes through the Spirit of truth, which is Jesus Christ, we will never gain a fulness of knowledge. ¶ I realize that it must eventually come to pass in the case of those who gain the exaltation and become sons of God, that they must in the eternities reach the time when they will know all things. They must know mathematics; they must know all the principles of science; they must be prepared in all things, by learning, by study, by faith, to comprehend these principles of eternal truth, even as our Father in heaven comprehends them, and unless men will put themselves in harmony with him and his Spirit and seek the light which comes through that Spirit they never will reach the goal of perfection in these things. It is, however, knowledge of the principles of the Gospel that will save men in the Kingdom of God. CR1939Apr:102-03

### President Brigham Young,
### Heber C. Kimball, Willard Richards
(First Presidency)

If men would be great in goodness, they must be intelligent, for no man can do good unless he knows how; therefore seek after knowledge, all knowledge, and especially that which is from above, which is wisdom to direct in all things, and if you find any thing that God does not know, you need not learn that thing; but strive to know what God knows, and use that knowledge as God uses it, and then you will be like him; will see as you are seen, and know as you are known; and have charity, love one another, and do each other good continually, and for ever, even as for yourselves. ¶ But if a man have all knowledge, and does not use it for good, it will prove a curse instead of a blessing as it did to Lucifer, the Son of the Morning. If a sinner is advised to repent, and be baptized for remission of his sins, and does it not, it will prove to his condemnation instead of a blessing, and he cannot receive the laying on of the hands of the Elders for the reception of the Holy Ghost. ("Sixth General Epistle of the Presidency of The Church of Jesus Christ of Latter-day Saints," Millennial Star, Jan. 15, 1852, p. 22) TLDP:341

**Related Witnesses:**
### Elder Spencer W. Kimball
God and his program will be found only in deep pondering, appropriate reading, much kneeling in devout, humble prayer, and in a sincerity born of need and dependence. ¶ These requirements having been fully met, there is no soul between the poles nor from ocean to ocean who may not positively obtain this knowledge, this hidden treasure of knowledge, this saving and exalting knowledge. . . . ¶ The ultimate and greatest of all knowledge, then, is to know God and his program for our exaltation. We may know him by sight, by sound, by feeling. While relatively few ever *do* really know him, everyone may know him. . . . CR1968Oct:130

### Howard W. Hunter
As important as scientific research may be, the greatest quest is a search for God—to determine his reality, his personal attributes, and to secure a knowledge of the gospel of his Son Jesus Christ. It is not easy to find a perfect understanding of God. The search requires persistent effort, and there are some who never move themselves to pursue this knowledge. CR1974Oct:138

### Recorded in Job
Great men are not always wise: neither do the aged understand judgment. Job 32:9

### Jacob, brother of Nephi, quoted by Nephi
But to be learned is good if they hearken unto the counsels of God. (*Jacob teaches the people of Nephi, 559-545 B.C.*) 2Ne.9:29

### Paul
Ever learning, and never able to come to the knowledge of the truth. (*Letter to his assistant Timothy, about A.D. 64*) 2Tim.3:7

### Recorded in Proverbs
Trust in the LORD with all thine heart; and lean not unto thine own understanding. 6. In all thy ways acknowledge him, and he shall direct thy paths. 7. Be not wise in thine own eyes: fear the LORD, and depart from evil. Prov.3:5-7

### Jacob, brother of Nephi
Wherefore, brethren, seek not to counsel the Lord, but to take counsel from his hand. For behold, ye yourselves know that he counseleth in wisdom, and in justice, and in great mercy, over all his works. (*Jacob makes his record on plates of metal, 544-421 B.C.*) Jacob 4:10

# List of Doctrines

## WORD OF WISDOM

*Doctrines Located in This Topic*

876. The Word of Wisdom is a commandment of the Lord.

877. Our bodies should be kept clean and pure; hence, we are to be concerned with the nature of the food and drink taken into our bodies.

878. Observance of the Word of Wisdom increases the health of both the body and the spirit.

879. We are not to drink alcoholic beverages.

880. We are not to use tobacco.

881. We are not to drink tea or coffee.

882. The use of a habit-forming drug of any kind violates the spirit of the Word of Wisdom and defiles both body and spirit.

883. The meat of animals is intended for our food, but we are to use it sparingly.

884. Wholesome herbs and fruits are intended for our food; we are to use them prudently.

885. A man who faithfully magnifies his priesthood calling may be sanctified by the Spirit to the renewal of his body, and the enjoyment of increased physical health.

886. By obedience to the Word of Wisdom we may gain great wisdom, understanding, and hidden treasures of knowledge.

*Doctrines on WORD OF WISDOM Located in Other Topics*

120. All plants and animals upon the earth were created for the benefit of human beings.

473. The body is a temple in which the Spirit of God may dwell.

# WORD OF WISDOM

**876. The Word of Wisdom is a commandment of the Lord.**

**Joseph Smith**

A Word of Wisdom, for the benefit of the council of high priests, assembled in Kirtland, and the church, and also the saints in Zion— 2. To be sent greeting; not by commandment or constraint, but by revelation and the word of wisdom, showing forth the order and will of God in the temporal salvation of all saints in the last days— 3. Given for a principle with promise, adapted to the capacity of the weak and the weakest of all saints, who are or can be called saints. 4. Behold, verily, thus saith the Lord unto you: In consequence of evils and designs which do and will exist in the hearts of conspiring men in the last days, I have warned you, and forewarn you, by giving unto you this word of wisdom by revelation— 5. That inasmuch as any man drinketh wine or strong drink among you, behold it is not good, neither meet in the sight of your Father, only in assembling yourselves together to offer up your sacraments before him. 6. And, behold, this should be wine, yea, pure wine of the grape of the vine, of your own make. 7. And, again, strong drinks are not for the belly, but for the washing of your bodies. 8. And again, tobacco is not for the body, neither for the belly, and is not good for man, but is an herb for bruises and all sick cattle, to be used with judgment and skill. 9. And again, hot drinks are not for the body or belly. (*Revelation, Feb. 27, 1833*) D&C 89:1-9

**Elder Spencer W. Kimball**

In 1851 President Brigham Young gave to this Church the Word of Wisdom as a final and definite commandment. From the time it was given to the Prophet Joseph until 1851 it was considered as a matter of preference or suggestion to the people, a word of advice and counsel. From 1851 until this day it is a commandment to all the members of the Church of Jesus Christ. (*Brigham Young University, stake conference*) (The Teachings of Spencer W. Kimball. p. 201) TLDP:739

**Elder Ezra Taft Benson**

In 1851, President Brigham Young proposed to the general conference of the Church that all Saints formally covenant to keep the Word of Wisdom. This proposal was unanimously upheld by the membership of the Church. Since that day, the revelation has been a binding commandment on all Church members. ¶ . . . . The Word of Wisdom is a law—a principle with a promise. If we obey the provisions of the law,

we receive the promises. If we do not, there will both temporal and spiritual consequences. CR1983Apr:70

**President Joseph F. Smith,**
*quoted by Elder Joseph Fielding Smith*

It [D&C 89] was not given, at that time, by way of commandment or restraint but by revelation, "a word of wisdom showing forth the order and will of God in the temporal salvation of all saints in the last days." Subsequently, years afterwards, from this stand, it was proclaimed from the mouth of the Prophet and President of the Church of Jesus Christ of Latter-day Saints, Brigham Young, that the time had come when this Word of Wisdom—then given not by commandment or constraint—was now a commandment of the Lord to the Church of Jesus Christ of Latter-day Saints, and the Lord required them to observe this Word of Wisdom and counsel, which is the will of God unto the people for their temporal salvation. CHMR1:384

**Marvin O. Ashton**

[The Word of Wisdom] is given as a commandment; the Word of Wisdom did proceed from the mouth of God to us as a people, and as the will of the Lord, and therefore we are under a command to observe it. CR1938Oct:57

**Elder Joseph Fielding Smith**

We sometimes hear it said that the Lord did not give the Word of Wisdom by commandment, and therefore some take advantage of a word and justify themselves in not observing this revelation. But let us remember that the Lord has also said that what he has here said is "adapted to the capacity of the weak and the weakest of all saints, who are or can be called saints." There were good reasons why it was not strictly commanded at the time the revelation was given, as already expressed. When men become sufficiently taught they were expected to observe what is here written. In fact the High Council of the Church over which the Prophet Joseph Smith presided declared in 1834 by unanimous vote after a full and free discussion on the subject, that, "No official member of this Church is worthy to hold an office after having the Word of Wisdom properly taught him; and he, the official member, neglecting to comply with or obey it." (*Essentials In Church History, p. 169*) CHMR1:383-84; TPJS:117

**Related Witnesses:**

**President Brigham Young,**
*quoted by John A. Widtsoe*

Now, Elders of Israel, if you have a right to chew tobacco, you have a privilege I have not; if you have a right to drink whiskey, you have a

right that I have not; if you have a right to transgress the Word of Wisdom, you have a right that I have not. (*Discourse on Word of Wisdom, April 7, 1867, JD12:30*) DBY:183
**President Brigham Young,
quoted by John A. Widtsoe**
I said to the saints at our last annual Conference, the Spirit whispers to me to call upon the Latter-day Saints to observe the Word of Wisdom, to let tea, coffee, and tobacco alone, and to abstain from drinking spirituous drinks. This is what the Spirit signifies through me. If the Spirit of God whispers this to his people through their leader, and they will not listen nor obey, what will be the consequences of their disobedience? Darkness and blindness of mind with regard to the things of God will be their lot; they will cease to have the spirit of prayer, and the spirit of the world will increase in them in proportion to their disobedience until they apostatize entirely from God and his ways. (*In Tooele, Utah, Aug. 17, 1867, JD12:117*) DBY:183

877. Our bodies should be kept clean and pure; hence, we are to be concerned with the nature of the food and drink taken into our bodies.

**James E. Talmage**
Sanctity of the Body—The Church teaches that everyone should regard his body as "the temple of God; and that he maintain its purity and sanctity as such. He is taught that the Spirit of the Lord dwells not in unclean tabernacles; and that therefore he is required to live according to the laws of health, which constitute part of the law of God. For the special guidance of His saints, the Lord has revealed the following: [Quoting the Word of Wisdom, D&C 89] AF:405
**Elder Joseph Fielding Smith**
From the organization of the Church until the Word of Wisdom was given the Lord had, by revelation, tried to impress upon the members of the Church the fact that their bodies should be kept clean and pure, for they were to be the eternal tabernacles of the spirits which dwell in them. One of the main purposes of this mortal life is to obtain these bodies and if they are not kept clean then they are not fit for exaltation. The doctrine of the Church in this respect transcend the teachings of any other people, and the purpose of this great revelation on the care and proper treatment of the body is that the body may be sanctified in truth and cleanliness, as well as the spirit. If we are to be immortal

beings and to dwell in the presence of the Father and the Son, then our bodies must be sanctified from all evil and become like theirs. John says, "Every man that hath this hope in him purifieth himself, even as he (Christ) is pure." (1Jn.3:3) CHMR1:383
**President Joseph F. Smith**
Everything has become degenerated from what it was in its primitive state. God made man pure, but he [man] has found out many inventions; his vices have become innumerable and his diseases multiplied. His taste has become vitiated and his judgment impaired. He has fallen—fallen—fallen from that dignified state that he once occupied on the earth, and it needs a restorative that man has not in his possession, wisdom which is beyond the reach of human intellect, the power which human philosophy, talent, and ingenuity cannot control. God only is acquainted with the fountain of action and the mainsprings of human events. He knows where disease is seated and what is the cause of it. He is also acquainted with the springs of health, the balm of Gilead—of life. He knows what course to pursue to restore mankind to the pristine excellency and primitive vigor and health. He has appointed the Word of Wisdom as one of the engines to bring about this thing, to remove the beastly appetites, the murderous disposition and the vitiated taste of man; to restore his body to health and vigor, and promote peace between him and the brute creation. ("Meaning of the Word of Wisdom," Improvement Era, Oct. 1901, pp. 945-46) TLDP:739
**John A. Widtsoe**
The Word of Wisdom is concerned largely with the nature of the food and drink taken into the body. That is in full accord with modern views. The positive teachings of the Word of Wisdom in the light of present-day science may be summarized as follows: ¶ 1. The Moderate Use of Meat. The flesh of animals should be used sparingly, chiefly in cold weather. ¶ 2. The Liberal Use of Fruits. Fruits of all kinds, especially fresh fruits, should be a regular part of the human dietary. ¶ 3. The Regular Use of Vegetables. All the recognized edible vegetables, leafy, root and tuber, should be eaten daily. The leafy vegetables and some of the others should be eaten in their fresh state. ¶ 4. The Basic Use of Grains. The daily dietary should include as its basis, properly prepared grains. The whole wheat kernel should preferably be ground for bread or porridge. All grains are good foods, but wheat is best for the use of man. Other seeds and nuts also form valuable foods. 5. Health-giving Beverages. Pure, fresh water should be drunk

freely, at arising and between meals throughout the day. Milk, fruit juices and grain extracts should supplement the intake of pure water in supplying the body with the necessary liquid. ¶ 6. Proper Period of Sleep. The body should be invigorated by regular, preferably early sleep, ending in early morning. ¶ 7. Habits of Regular Work and Play. Health requires regular and steady physical labor and intellectual effort. ¶ 8. A Correct Mental Attitude. Faith, hope, charity, and a constant seeking after the truth of life and the universe with a determination to accept it when found, form the foundation blocks for good health. A sound religious philosophy is a pre-requisite for good health. (Program of the Church, pp. 38-39) TLDP:741-42

**Related Witnesses:**

**Paul**

Know ye not that ye are the temple of God, and that the Spirit of God dwelleth in you? 17. If any man defile the temple of God, him shall God destroy; for the temple of God is holy, which temple ye are. (*Paul writes to the Church at Corinth, Greece, about* A.D. 55) 1Cor.3:16-17

**Joseph Smith**

The elements are the tabernacle of God; yea, man is the tabernacle of God, even temples; and whatsoever temple is defiled, God shall destroy that temple. (*Revelation received at Kirtland, Ohio, May 6, 1833*) D&C 93:35

**President Brigham Young,**
*quoted by John A. Widtsoe*

Mankind would not become attached to these unnecessary articles were it not for the poison they contain. The poisonous or narcotic properties in spirits, tobacco and tea are the cause of their being so much liked by those who use them. (*In new Tabernacle, Oct. 30, 1870, JD13:276*) DBY:184

**Paul**

What? know ye not that your body is the temple of the Holy Ghost which is in you, which ye have of God, and ye are not your own? 20. For ye are bought with a price: therefore glorify God in your body, and in your spirit, which are God's. (*Letter to the Church at Corinth, Greece, about* A.D. 55) 1Cor.6:19-20

**Recorded in Daniel**

But Daniel purposed in his heart that he would not defile himself with the portion of the king's meat, nor with the wine which he drank: therefore he requested of the prince of the eunuchs that he might not defile himself. (*Daniel and certain Hebrews are trained in the court of Nebuchadnezzar; they choose to eat plain food and drink no wine*) Dan.1:8

**878. Observance of the Word of Wisdom increases the health of both the body and the spirit.**

**Stephen L. Richards**

Every commandment of God is spiritual in nature. There are no carnal commandments. . . . The Word of Wisdom is spiritual. It is true that it enjoins the use of deleterious substances and makes provision for the health of the body. But the largest measure of good derived from its observance is in increased faith and the development of more spiritual power and wisdom. Likewise, the most regrettable and damaging effects of its infractions are spiritual, also, injury to the body may be comparatively trivial to the damage to the soul in the destruction of faith and the retardation of spiritual growth. So I say, every commandment involves a spiritual growth. So I say, every commandment involves a spiritual principle. CR1949Apr:141

**John A. Widtsoe**

Those who, because of their acceptance and use of the Word of Wisdom, possess a clean body, a clear mind and a spirit in tune with the infinite, are best able to assist in establishing the Kingdom of God on earth, and thereby to render greatest service to their fellow men. ¶ They also find the greatest happiness in life, for their capacity for joy is unhindered by a weak body, a dull mind, and dim spiritual vision. They find a new wealth of joy in every commonplace of life. They have eyes and they see; ears and they hear. Their understanding is reinforced with the spiritual light of truth. ¶ There are many laws of the Gospel that lead towards spirituality. Among them the Word of Wisdom stands unchallenged. (The Word of Wisdom; A Modern Interpretation, pp. 283-84) TLDP:743

**John A. Widtsoe**

A statement of the blessings that will follow the observance of the rules laid down in the Word of Wisdom: [D&C 89:18-21 is quoted] That is, the reward for keeping the Word of wisdom is four-fold. 1. Self-control is developed. That is implied in verse 3 of the revelation which states that the Word of Wisdom is "adapted to the capacity of the weak and the weakest of all Saints." 2. Strength of body, including resistance to contagion, is a result of wise living. 3. Clearness of mind is the gift of those whose bodies are in a healthy condition. 4. Spiritual power comes to all who conquer their appetites, live normally and look upward to God. (Program of the Church, pp. 37-38) TLDP:743

**Elder George Albert Smith**

I am fully convinced that the Lord in His mercy,

when He gave us the Word of Wisdom, gave it to us, not alone that we might have health while we live in the world, but that our faith might be strengthened, that our testimony of the divinity of the mission of our Lord and Master might be increased, that thereby we might be better prepared to return to His presence when our labor here is complete. CR1907Apr:19

**Joseph Smith**

A Word of Wisdom, for the benefit of the council of high priests, assembled in Kirtland, and the church, and also the saints in Zion—. . . . 18. And all saints who remember to keep and do these sayings, walking in obedience to the commandments, shall receive health in their navel and marrow to their bones; 19. And shall find wisdom and great treasures of knowledge, even hidden treasures; 20. And shall run and not be weary, and shall walk and not faint. 21. And I, the Lord, give unto them a promise, that the destroying angel shall pass by them, as the children of Israel, and not slay them. Amen. (*Revelation received Feb. 27, 1833*) D&C 89:1,18-21

**Elder Ezra Taft Benson,**
*also quoting Joseph Smith*

Scientific studies have confirmed that Latter-day Saints have less incidence of heart problems, all forms of cancer, and other diseases because of their adherence to the Word of Wisdom. ¶ These studies have demonstrated that not only will one live a longer life, but also that the quality of one's life will be better. . . . ¶ The Word of Wisdom allows us to know that the Lord is vitally concerned about the health of His Saints. He has graciously given us counsel for improving our health, endurance, and resistance to many diseases. ¶ The temporal promise for obedience is: They "shall receive health in their navel and marrow to their bones; . . . [they] shall run and not be weary and shall walk and not faint" (D&C 89:18,20). ¶ I have always felt, however, that the greater blessing of obedience to the Word of Wisdom and all other commandments is spiritual. ¶ Listen to the spiritual promise: "All saints who remember to keep and do these sayings, walking in obedience to the commandments, . . . shall find wisdom and great treasures of knowledge, even hidden treasures" (D&C 89:18,19). ¶ Some have thought this promise was contingent on just keeping the provisions of the Word of Wisdom. But you will notice we must walk in obedience to all the commandments. Then we shall receive specific spiritual promises. CR1983Apr:70-71

**Elder Spencer W. Kimball**

In the march to perfection through the conquering of sin, it is important to have the right perspective.

For example, some people get means and ends reversed. Many feel that the Word of Wisdom is for the principal purpose of increasing our health, increasing our mortal life, but a more careful study of the revelation (D&C 89) reveals that there is a deeper purpose. Of course, total observance will strengthen one's body, make it survive longer so that there will be a longer time in which to perfect the body and, especially, the spirit— looking toward eternal status and eternal joys. The Lord made solemn promises to ". . . all Saints who remember to keep and do these sayings, walking in obedience to the commandments . . ." (D&C 89:18) Here the commitments of the Lord were two-fold. First, he promised to such who obey that they shall ". . . receive health in their navel and marrow to their bones . . . ," that as a consequence of good health physically they "shall run and not be weary, and shall walk and not faint." This is a glorious promise. ¶ But the spiritual promises greatly exceed the physical. For those who observe these particular instructions and are obedient to all the Lord's commandments, the blessings really are increased and magnified. Such saints, he promises, shall be passed over by the angel of death and shall not be slain. This promise returns us to Exodus where we read that the Lord tested the faith of the children of Israel to see if they would follow the great Moses. ¶ Now the promise in the revelation above quoted is similar and dissimilar to ancient Israel's test, as comparisons generally are. In both circumstances there would be the element of passover, the element of obedience of faith without knowing all the reasons why. The "obedience of faith" is basic. Without it the miracle cannot happen. Had Israel not obeyed, their firstborn sons would not have been protected. ¶ For observing the Word of Wisdom the reward is life, not only prolonged mortal life but life eternal. No promise is made through the Word of Wisdom that the faithful observer will not die: "For as in Adam all die, even so in Christ shall all be made alive" (1Cor.15:22). With ancient Israel it was physical life or physical death. In our modern promise, it is spiritual life or spiritual death. If one ignores "these sayings" and fails in "obedience to the commandments" his death is certain, but if he obeys implicitly, his eternal life through perfection is assured. The angel of death cuts one short of mortal life for disobedience; the angel of light makes the way clear for the spiritual life eternal. (*The Miracle of Forgiveness*, pp. 210-11) TLDP:743

**Related Witnesses:**

**Elder David O. McKay**

Obedience to the Word of Wisdom develops

greater spiritual power, that spiritual power which comes from resistance. (Gospel Ideals, p. 398) TLDP:743

### 879. We are not to drink alcoholic beverages.

**Joseph Smith,**
*receiving the Word of the Lord*
That inasmuch as any man drinketh wine or strong drink among you, behold it is not good, neither meet in the sight of your Father, only in assembling yourselves together to offer up your sacraments before him. 6. And, behold, this should be wine, yea, pure wine of the grape of the vine, of your own make. 7. And, again, strong drinks are not for the belly, but for the washing of your bodies. (*Revelation, Feb. 27, 1833*) D&C 89:5-7

**President Joseph F. Smith**
Young men or middle-aged men who have had experience in the Church should not be ordained to the Priesthood nor recommended to the privileges of the House of the Lord, unless they will abstain from the use of tobacco and intoxicating drinks. This is the rule of the Church, and should be observed by all its members. (IE1916Feb:360) TLDP:740

**President Heber J. Grant,**
**J. Reuben Clark, Jr., David O. McKay**
(First Presidency)
Over the earth, and it seems particularly in America, the demon drink is in control. Drunken with strong drink, men have lost their reason; their counsel has been destroyed; their judgment and vision are fled; they reel forward to destruction. ¶ Drink brings cruelty into the home; it walks arm in arm with poverty; its companions are disease and plague; it puts chastity to flight; it knows neither honesty nor fair dealing; it is a total stranger to truth; it drowns conscience; it is the bodyguard of evil; it curses all who touch it. ¶ Drink has brought more woe and misery, broken more hearts, wrecked more homes, committed more crimes, filled more coffins, than all the wars the world has suffered. CR1942Oct:8

**Recorded in Judges**
And the angel of the LORD appeared unto the woman, and said unto her, Behold now, thou art barren, and bearest not: but thou shalt conceive, and bear a son. 4. Now therefore beware, I pray thee, and drink not wine nor strong drink, and eat not any unclean thing: (*An angel instructs the mother of Samson*) Judg.13:3-4

**Recorded in Proverbs**
Wine is a mocker, strong drink is raging: and

whosoever is deceived thereby is not wise. Prov.20:1

**Paul**
A bishop then must be blameless, the husband of one wife, vigilant, sober, of good behaviour, given to hospitality, apt to teach; 3. Not given to wine, no striker, not greedy of filthy lucre; but patient, not a brawler, not covetous; (*Letter to his assistant Timothy, about A.D. 64*) 1Tim. 3:2-3

**Related Witnesses:**
**Paul**
Know ye not that the unrighteous shall not inherit the kingdom of God? Be not deceived: neither fornicators, nor idolaters, nor adulterers, nor effeminate, nor abusers of themselves with mankind, 10. Nor thieves, nor covetous, nor drunkards, nor revilers, nor extortioners, shall inherit the kingdom of God. (*Paul writes to the Church at Corinth, Greece, about A.D. 55*) 1Cor.6:9-10

### 880. We are not to use tobacco.

**Joseph Smith,**
*receiving the Word of the Lord*
And again, tobacco is not for the body, neither for the belly, and is not good for man, but is an herb for bruises and all sick cattle, to be used with judgment and skill. (*Revelation, Feb. 27, 1833*) D&C 89:8

**Elder George Albert Smith**
I want to say to you, in my judgment, that the use of tobacco, a little thing as it seems to some men, has been the means of destroying their spiritual life, has been the means of driving from them the companionship of the Spirit of our Father, has alienated them from the society of good men and women, and has brought upon them the disregard and reproach of the children that have been born to them, and yet the devil will say to a man, Oh, it's only a little thing! CR1918Apr:40

**President Joseph F. Smith**
Young men or middle-aged men who have had experience in the Church should not be ordained to the Priesthood nor recommended to the privileges of the House of the Lord, unless they will abstain from the use of tobacco and intoxicating drinks. This is the rule of the Church, and should be observed by all its members. (IE1916Feb:360) TLDP:740

**President Brigham Young,**
*quoted by John A. Widtsoe*
I say to all the Elders of Israel, if it makes you sick and so sleepy that you cannot keep out of bed unless you have tobacco, go to bed and there lie. How long? Until you can get up and

go to your business like rational men, like men who have heads on their shoulders and who are not controlled by their foolish appetites. . . . Will it take a month? No matter if it does; if it takes three months, six months, or a year, it is better to lie there in bed until the influence of tea, coffee and liquor is out of the system, so that you may go about your business like rational persons, than to give way to these foolish habits. They are destructive to the human system; they filch money from our pockets, and they deprive the poor of the necessaries of life. *(In new Tabernacle, Oct. 30, 1870, JD13:278)* DBY:184

**Related Witnesses:**

**President Heber J. Grant**

I would like it known that if we as a people never used a particle of tea or coffee or of tobacco or of liquor, we would become one of the most wealthy people in the world. Why? Because we would have increased vigor of body, increased vigor of mind; we would grow spiritually; we would have a more direct line of communication with God, our Heavenly Father; we would be able to accomplish more—to say nothing about the fact that we do not produce these things that the Lord has told us to leave alone, and the money that is expended in breaking the Word of Wisdom goes away from our communities. ("Safeguard," IE1941Feb:73) TLDP:743

---

**881. We are not to drink tea or coffee.**

**Joseph Smith,**
*receiving the Word of the Lord*

And again, hot drinks are not for the body or belly. *(Revelation, Feb. 27, 1833)* D&C 89:9

**Joseph Smith,**
*quoted by John A. Widtsoe*

I understand that some of the people are excusing themselves in using tea and coffee, because the Lord only said "hot drinks" in the revelation of the Word of Wisdom. Tea and coffee are what the Lord meant when he said "hot drinks." (The Word of Wisdom; A Modern Interpretation, p. 75) TLDP:740

**President Brigham Young,**
*quoted by John A. Widtsoe*

This Word of Wisdom prohibits the use of hot drinks and tobacco. I have heard it argued that tea and coffee are not mentioned therein; that is very true; but what were the people in the habit of taking as hot drinks when that revelation was given? Tea and coffee. We were not in the habit of drinking water very hot, but tea and coffee — the beverages in common use. And the Lord said hot drinks are not good for the body nor

the belly, liquor is not good for the body nor the belly, but for the washing of the body, etc. Tobacco is not good, save for sick cattle, and for bruises and sores, its cleansing properties being then very useful. *(In new Tabernacle, Oct. 30, 1870, JD13:277)* DBY:182

**President Brigham Young,**
**Heber C. Kimball, Willard Richards**
(First Presidency)

The conference voted to observe the word of wisdom, and particularly to dispense with the use of tea, coffee, snuff, and tobacco, and in this thing as well as many others, what is good for the Saints in the mountains, is good for the Saints in other places, and if all who profess to be Saints would appropriate the funds lavished on luxuries, and articles unwise to use, to the benefit of the public works, we would soon see another "Temple of the Lord." *(Sixth General Epistle of the Presidency, Jan. 15, 1852; reference to "conference" is to the semi-annual conference of the Church, Sept. 7, 1851)* MOFP2:90

**Elder Joseph Fielding Smith**

So much stress has been placed upon the "don'ts" in this revelation that whenever we hear it mentioned the vision of prohibited liquors, tobaccos, teas, coffees, etc., comes before us. We seldom hear of the things mentioned which are "ordained for the constitution, nature, and use of man." The Lord has given us all good herbs, fruits, and grains. These are to be the main foods of men, beast, and fowls. But we should not overlook the fact that they are to be used with "prudence and thanksgiving." CHMR1:385

---

**882. The use of a habit-forming drug of any kind violates the spirit of the Word of Wisdom and defiles both body and spirit.**

**Marion G. Romney**

The use of a habit-forming drug of any kind violates the spirit of the Word of Wisdom and defiles both body and spirit. CR1974Apr:117

**Russell M. Nelson**

In 1833 the Prophet Joseph Smith received the Word of Wisdom by revelation. . . . Prophets in our generation and in this conference have told us also to avoid harmful drugs. Now medical science increasingly confirms the physical benefits of compliance with these teachings. CR1986Oct:87

**President Joseph Fielding Smith**

When we join the Church and receive the priesthood, we are expected to forsake many of the ways of the world and live as becometh saints. We are no longer to dress or speak or act or even think as others too often do. Many in the world use tea, coffee, tobacco, and liquor, and are involved in the use of drugs. Many profane and are vulgar and indecent, immoral and unclean in their lives, but all these things should be foreign to us. We are the saints of the Most High. We hold the holy priesthood. CR1971Apr:47

**Stephen L. Richards**

Every commandment of God is spiritual in nature. There are no carnal commandments. . . . The Word of Wisdom is spiritual. It is true that it enjoins the use of deleterious substances and makes provision for the health of the body. But the largest measure of good derived from its observance is in increased faith and the development of more spiritual power and wisdom. Likewise, the most regrettable and damaging effects of its infractions are spiritual, also, injury to the body may be comparatively trivial to the damage to the soul in the destruction of faith and the retardation of spiritual growth. So I say, every commandment involves a spiritual growth. So I say, every commandment involves a spiritual principle. CR1949Oct:141

**President David O. McKay**

A person's reaction to his appetites and impulses when they are aroused gives the measure of that person's character. In such reactions are revealed the man's power to govern or his forced servility to yield. That phase of the Word of Wisdom, therefore, which refers to intoxicants, drugs, and stimulants, goes deeper than the ill effects upon the body and strikes at the very root of character building itself. CR1964Apr:4

**Related Witnesses:**

**L. Tom Perry**

I stand before you today to accuse many of the husbands and fathers who are within the sound of my voice and throughout the world of failing in your two major God-given responsibilities. The reason for most of the problems we find in the world today must be laid at your door. Divorce, infidelity, dishonesty, the use of drugs, deterioration of family life, loss of identity, instability and unhappiness have resulted from the lack of your leadership in the home. CR1977Oct:95

---

883. **The meat of animals is intended for our food, but we are to use it sparingly.**

**Joseph Smith,**
*receiving the Word of the Lord*

Yea, flesh also of beasts and of the fowls of the air, I, the Lord, have ordained for the use of man with thanksgiving; nevertheless they are to be used sparingly; 13. And it is pleasing unto me that they should not be used, only in times of winter, or of cold, or famine. (*Revelation, Feb. 27, 1833*) D&C 89:12-13

**John A. Widtsoe**

The Word of Wisdom is concerned largely with the nature of the food and drink taken into the body. That is in full accord with modern views. . . . The flesh of animals should be used sparingly, chiefly in cold weather. (Program of the Church, pp. 38-39) TLDP:741

**John A. Widtsoe**

The Word of Wisdom does not contain a prohibition against meat eating, but urges its sparing use. Unfortunately, this advice is not generally observed, and man's health suffers in consequence. Many people eat too much meat; a few do not eat enough. (The Word of Wisdom; A Modern Interpretation, p. 260) TLDP:741

**John A. Widtsoe**

In the observance of the Word of Wisdom caution should be used. Personal opinions often color our practices. We have the right of free agency, but nevertheless we should not try to stretch the Word of Wisdom to conform with our own opinions. ¶ For example: The Word of Wisdom is not a system of vegetarianism. Clearly, meat is permitted. Naturally, that includes animal products, less subject than meat to putrefactive and other disturbances, such as eggs, milk, and cheese. These products cannot be excluded simply because they are not mentioned specifically. By that token most of our foodstuffs could not be eaten. ¶ That man can live without meat is well known, and he may live well if his knowledge is such as to enable him to choose adequate vegetable protein. And, all have the right if they so choose to live without meat. (Evidences and Reconciliations, 3:155-57) TLDP:741

**Ezra Taft Benson,**
*also quoting Joseph Smith*

In this revelation [D&C 89] the Lord counsels us to use meat sparingly. I have often felt that the Lord is further counseling us in this revelation against indiscriminately killing animals, for He has said elsewhere in scripture, "Wo be unto man that sheddeth blood or that wasteth flesh and hath no need." (D&C 49:21) CR1983Apr:71

**Joseph F. Merrill**

It is to flesh as an article in human diet that I wish to direct my attention. . . . [A]uthorities say that generally food has more to do with health than any other factor affecting health. . . . ¶ [T]he book continues ["How To Live," p. 251]: "Meat eating and a high-protein diet, instead of increasing one's endurance, have been shown like alcohol, actually to reduce it." ¶ . . . . Latter-day Saints, why should you complain of the scarcity or high price of flesh foods? Have you not known that in any case you should eat them sparingly? The Lord told you so. I have quoted from some of the highest authorities in the world to the effect that they are not essential to your physical well-being. But Americans did not know this until God revealed it to them through his Prophet, Joseph Smith. ¶ . . . . Americans eat too much meat, a non-essential in human diet, because all the proteins needed are available in . . . other foods. . . . CR1948Apr:72,73,75

---

884. Wholesome herbs and fruits are intended for our food; we are to use them prudently.

### Joseph Smith,
*receiving the Word of the Lord*
And again, verily I say unto you, all wholesome herbs God hath ordained for the constitution, nature, and use of man— 11. Every herb in the season thereof, and every fruit in the season thereof; all these to be used with prudence and thanksgiving. (*Revelation, Feb. 27, 1833*) D&C 89:10-11

### Elder Joseph Fielding Smith
So much stress has been placed upon the "don'ts" in this revelation that whenever we hear it mentioned the vision of prohibited liquors, tobaccos, teas, coffees, etc., comes before us. We seldom hear of the things mentioned which are "ordained for the constitution, nature, and use of man." The Lord has given us all good herbs, fruits, and grains. These are to be the main foods of men, beast, and fowls. But we should not overlook the fact that they are to be used with "prudence and thanksgiving." CHMR1:385

### John A. Widtsoe
The . . . positive part of the revelation is of first importance, since obedience to it lessens the appetite for injurious substances. . . . ¶ This part of the revelation further teaches, in addition to the sparing use of meat, that all wholesome vegetables, (herbs) fruits, and all grains, notably wheat, should be eaten for good health. . . . ¶ In the observance of the Word of Wisdom caution should be used. Personal opinions often color our practices. We have the right of

free agency, but nevertheless we should not try to stretch the Word of Wisdom to conform with our own opinions. ¶ For example: The Word of Wisdom is not a system of vegetarianism. Clearly, meat is permitted. Naturally, that includes animal products, less subject than meat to putrefactive and other disturbances, such as eggs, milk, and cheese. These products cannot be excluded simply because they are not mentioned specifically. By that token most of our foodstuffs could not be eaten. ¶ That man can live without meat is well known, and he may live well if his knowledge is such as to enable him to choose adequate vegetable protein. And, all have the right if they so choose to live without meat. ¶ The phrase "in the season thereof," referring to fruits and vegetables, has raised much speculation. It indicates simply the superior value of fresh foods as demonstrated by modern science, but does not necessarily prohibit the use of fruits or vegetables out of season if preserved by proper methods. (Evidences and Reconciliations, 3:155-57) TLDP:741

---

885. A man who faithfully magnifies his priesthood calling may be sanctified by the Spirit to the renewal of his body, and the enjoyment of increased physical health.

### Joseph Smith
For whoso is faithful unto the obtaining these two priesthoods of which I have spoken, and the magnifying their calling, are sanctified by the Spirit unto the renewing of their bodies. (*Revelation on priesthood with six elders, Sept. 22/23, 1832*) D&C 84:33

### Hugh B. Brown
The Lord said: ¶ ". . . whoso is faithful unto the obtaining these two priesthoods of which I have spoken, and the magnifying their calling, are sanctified by the Spirit unto the renewing of their bodies." (D&C 84:33) ¶ Brethren, I bear testimony to the fact that that promise has been realized in the lives of many of us. I know that it has been realized in the life of President David O. McKay, that he has been sanctified by the Spirit unto the renewing of his body, and some of the rest of us are better off today than were many years ago so far as physical health is concerned and we attribute that fact to his blessing. CR1963Apr:90; MPSG88:30

### Russell M. Nelson
Elder Anderson has followed what I label as the

Lord's prescription for a long and useful life. Those faithful in magnifying their calling are sanctified by the Spirit unto the renewing of their bodies. They become . . . the elect of God. (See D&C 84:33-34.) CR1985Oct:40

**President Spencer W. Kimball**
They shall be "sanctified by the Spirit unto the renewing of their bodies." I present to you the thought that President David O. McKay, who was in his nineties, President Joseph Fielding Smith, who was in his nineties, and all the Presidents of the Church since almost the beginning became men of advanced age, that their bodies were renewed, and their spirits were sanctified. ACR(Stockholm)1974:99; DGSM:70

**Abraham O. Woodruff**
I do not know that I have ever heard President Snow speak when his voice sounded clearer or more forceful than it did this morning, and this reminded me of the change that ofttimes comes over men when they are called of God to certain positions. In many instances their bodies and their minds seem to be renovated and renewed by the power of God within them. CR1900Oct:13

**Related Witnesses:**

**Paul**
But if the Spirit of him that raised up Jesus from the dead dwell in you, he that raised up Christ from the dead shall also quicken your mortal bodies by his Spirit that dwelleth in you. (*Letter to the Church in Rome, about* A.D. *55*) Rom.8:11

**Bruce R. McConkie**
We can be sanctified by the Spirit, have dross and evil burned out of us as though by fire, become clean and spotless, and be fit to dwell with gods and angels. ¶ The Holy Ghost is the Sanctifier. Those who magnify their callings in the priesthood "are sanctified by the Spirit unto the renewing of their bodies." (D&C 84:33) They are born again; they become new creatures of the Holy Ghost; they are alive in Christ. CR1977Oct:50

**Joseph Smith**
Behold he is a righteous man, may God Almighty lengthen out the old man's days; and may his trembling, tortured, and broken body be renewed, and in the vigor of health turn upon him, if it be Thy will, consistently, O God; and it shall be said of him, by the sons of Zion, while there is one of them remaining, that this man was a faithful man in Israel; therefore his name shall never be forgotten. (*Joseph blesses Joseph Knight, Sen., Aug. 22, 1842*) HC5:124-25

**Author's Note:** There is every reason why, correspondingly, the *sisters* in the Church may also enjoy the blessing of this doctrine.

---

886. **By obedience to the Word of Wisdom we may gain great wisdom, understanding, and hidden treasures of knowledge.**

**President Brigham Young**
It is a piece of good counsel which the Lord desires His people to observe, that they may live on the earth until the measure of their creation is full. This is the object the Lord had in view in giving the Word of Wisdom. To those who observe it He will give great wisdom and understanding, increasing their health, giving strength and endurance to the faculties of their bodies and minds until they shall be full of years upon the earth. This will be their blessing if they will observe His word with a good and willing heart and in faithfulness before the Lord. (*In old Tabernacle, Jan. 12, 1868, JD12:156*) TLDP:742

**President Heber J. Grant**
We are promised that if we obey the Word of Wisdom it will give us physical strength, whereby the destroying angel shall pass us by as he did the children of Israel. And we are promised that we shall have hidden treasures of knowledge if we live in accordance with the Word of Wisdom. CR1930Apr:188

**Elder Ezra Taft Benson,**
*also quoting Joseph Smith*
The temporal promise for obedience is: They "shall receive health in their navel and marrow to their bones; . . . [they] shall run and not be weary and shall walk and not faint" (D&C 89:18,20). ¶ I have always felt, however, that the greater blessing of obedience to the Word of Wisdom and all other commandments is spiritual. ¶ Listen to the spiritual promise: "All saints who remember to keep and do these sayings, walking in obedience *to the commandments,* . . . shall find wisdom and great treasures of knowledge, even hidden treasures." (D&C 89:18,19, italics added by ETB) ¶ Some have thought this promise was contingent on just keeping the provisions of the Word of Wisdom. But you will notice we must walk in obedience to *all* the commandments. Then we shall receive specific spiritual promises. CR1983Apr:70-71

# List of Doctrines

## WORSHIPPING GOD

### (Love of God and Reverence)

*Doctrines Located in This Topic*

887. We are to love the Lord our God with all our heart and soul.

888. We are commanded to worship God, the Father, in the name of the Son, Jesus Christ.

889. We are to manifest reverence in places of worship.

890. We are to revere God and His holy name.

891. To love Christ is to obey Him.

892. When we love God, the Spirit of God dwells in our hearts.

*Doctrines on WORSHIPPING GOD Located in Other Topics*

91. Where two or three disciples of the Lord are gathered together in His name, His Spirit will be with them.

286. God the Father is to be the object of our worship.

748. A person who serves another serves God.

(See topic SIN: (8) Worshipping False Gods.)

# WORSHIPPING GOD

## (Love of God and Reverence)

**887. We are to love the Lord our God with all our heart and soul.**

### Jesus,
#### *recorded in Matthew*

"Master, which is the great commandment in the law? 37. Jesus said unto him, Thou shalt love the Lord thy God with all thy heart, and with all thy soul, and with all thy mind. 38. This is the first and great commandment. 39. And the second is like unto it, Thou shalt love thy neighbour as thyself. 40. On these two commandments hang all the law and the prophets. (*Jesus gives the two great commandments*) Matt.22:36-40

### Joseph Smith,
#### *receiving the Word of the Lord*

Wherefore, I give unto them a commandment, saying thus: Thou shalt love the Lord thy God with all thy heart, with all thy might, mind, and strength; and in the name of Jesus Christ thou shalt serve him. 6. Thou shalt love thy neighbor as thyself. . . . (*Revelation, Aug. 7, 1831*) D&C 59:5-6

### Jesus,
#### *recorded in Mark*

Jesus answered him, The first of all the commandments is, Hear, O Israel; The Lord our God is one Lord: 30. And thou shalt love the Lord thy God with all thy heart, and with all thy soul, and with all thy mind, and with all thy strength: this is the first commandment. 31. And the second is like, namely this, Thou shalt love thy neighbour as thyself. There is none other commandment greater than these. (*A scribe asks Jesus, "Which is the first commandment of all?"*) Mark 12:29-31

### George Q. Cannon

We must serve God with all our hearts, our love and affections reaching after Him, and the things of this world must be looked upon by us as secondary considerations. They are good enough in their place; right enough to be attended to; but subordinate always to the love of God. That should be the first love, greater than every other love. A man that loves a wife, a man that loves a child, a man that loves anything upon the earth more than God, is not a true Latter-day Saint. He may have a lovely wife, he may have a lovely child; he may have a rich farm, he may have stock, elegant residences, horses and carriages, together with an abundance of wealth to command all the comforts of the earth; but I tell you, as a servant of God, if he

loves these things more than he loves God, he is not a true Latter-day Saint. (*At Hooperville, Utah, June 27, 1881, JD22:288-89*) TLDP:366

### Jesus,
#### *recorded in Luke*

And, behold, a certain lawyer stood up, and tempted him, saying, Master, what shall I do to inherit eternal life? 26. He said unto him, What is written in the law? how readest thou? 27. And he answering said, Thou shalt love the Lord thy God with all thy heart, and with all thy soul, and with all thy strength, and with all thy mind; and thy neighbour as thyself. 28. And he said unto him, Thou hast answered right: this do, and thou shalt live. (*Jesus answers the lawyer; he thereafter tells the story of the Good Samaritan—vs. 30-37*) Luke 10:25-28

### President Joseph F. Smith

We all need love in our souls, all the time: first, for God our heavenly Father, who is the giver of all good—love which encompasses our souls, our thoughts, our hearts, our minds, our strength, insomuch that we would willingly, if he required, give our lives as well as our time, talents, and substance in this world to the service of the living God who gives us all that we have. Then, if we can only have that love in our hearts, so much that we will love God more than business, more than money, more than earthly pleasures: that is, enjoy greater pleasure in the worship and love of God than we have in any other thing in the world, then we will be able to go to our neighbors or friends, when we think they have done something not just right, when we think they ought to be corrected, and we are the persons to correct them, we will go to them and help them to correct their errors and mistakes, and do it in the spirit of friendship and love. That is the duty of Latter-day Saints. (*At a temple fast meeting, Feb. 1918, published by the First Presidency in Improvement Era, May 1918*) MOFP5:91

### Moses

And now, Israel, what doth the LORD thy God require of thee, but to fear the LORD thy God, to walk in all his ways, and to love him, and to serve the LORD thy God with all thy heart and with all thy soul, (*Moses addresses Israel*) Deut.10:12

### Related Witnesses:
#### Elder Harold B. Lee

A brotherhood that seeks to establish the common good is as "sounding brass or a tinkling cymbal," except it be founded upon the divine principle of love of God and our neighbor as ourselves. One who says he loves God and is a follower of Jesus and yet hates his brother is false to himself and before the world, for no one can love God whom he has not seen and yet love not his brother whom he has seen. (See John 4:20.) The truest evidence that one loves God is that he keeps the commandments. (See John 2:3-4.) (Relief Society Magazine, Feb. 1943, pp. 84-87; Stand Ye in Holy Places, p. 225) TLDP:367

## 888. We are commanded to worship God, the Father, in the name of the Son, Jesus Christ.

### President Joseph F. Smith
We . . . accept without any question the doctrines we have been taught by the Prophet Joseph Smith and by the Son of God himself, that we pray to God, the Eternal Father, in the name of his only begotten Son, to whom also our father Adam and his posterity have prayed from the beginning. CR1916Oct:6

### Joseph Smith,
*translating the Book of Moses*
Wherefore, thou shalt do all that thou doest in the name of the Son, and thou shalt repent and call upon God in the name of the Son forevermore. (*Revelation to Moses; Adam and Eve receive commandments after being driven out of the Garden of Eden*) Moses 5:8

### Bruce R. McConkie
Christ worked out his own salvation by worshipping the Father. . . . ¶ . . . . All men must worship the Father in the same way Christ did in order to gain salvation. ¶ Thus spake the Lord: . . . ¶ I give unto you these sayings that you may understand and know how to worship, and know what you worship, that you may come unto the Father in my name, and in due time receive of his fulness. ("Our Relationship with the Lord," Brigham Young University Speeches of the Year, 1981-82, p. 99) TLDP:747

### Joseph Smith,
*receiving the Word of the Lord*
I give unto you these sayings that you may understand and know how to worship, and know what you worship, that you may come unto the Father in my name, and in due time receive of his fulness. (*The Lord speaks by revelation at Kirtland, Ohio, May 6, 1833*) D&C 93:19

### Joseph Smith
And again, I say unto you, all things must be done in the name of Christ, whatsoever you do in the Spirit; 32. And ye must give thanks unto

God in the Spirit for whatsoever blessing ye are blessed with. (*Revelation relative to governing and conducting meetings, March 8, 1831*) D&C 46:31-32

### President Brigham Young, quoted by John A. Widtsoe
Let every man and every woman call upon the name of the Lord, and that, too, from a pure heart, while they are at work as well as in their closet; while they are in public as well as while they are in private, asking the Father in the name of Jesus, to bless them, and to preserve and guide them, and to teach them, in the way of life and salvation and to enable them so to live that they will obtain this eternal salvation that we are after. (*In Bowery, June 9, 1872, JD15:63*) DBY:43

### President Brigham Young
When people assemble to worship they should leave their worldly cares where they belong, then their minds are in a proper condition to worship the Lord, to call upon him in the name of Jesus, and to get his Holy Spirit, that they may hear and understand things as they are in eternity, and know how to comprehend the providences of our God. This is the time for their minds to be open, to behold the invisible things of God, that he reveals by his Spirit. (*At Provo, Utah, July 13, 1855, JD3:53*) DBY:167

### Paul
And whatsoever ye do in word or deed, do all in the name of the Lord Jesus, giving thanks to God and the Father by him. (*Paul writes from prison to the Church in Colossae, Asia Minor, about A.D. 60*) Col.3:17

### Related Witnesses:
### Bruce R. McConkie
We do not worship the Son, and we do not worship the Holy Ghost. I know perfectly well what the scriptures say about worshiping Christ and Jehovah, but they are speaking in an entirely different sense—the sense of standing in awe and being reverentially grateful to him who has redeemed us. Worship in the true and saving sense is reserved for God the first, the Creator. ¶ Our revelations say that the Father "is infinite and eternal," that he created "man, male and female." ¶ And gave unto them commandments that they should love and serve him, the only living and true God, and that he should be the only being whom they should worship. [D&C 20:17-19] ¶ Jesus said: ¶ True worshippers shall [note that this is mandatory] worship the Father in spirit and in truth; for the Father seeketh such to worship him. ¶ For unto such hath God promised his Spirit. And they who worship him, must worship in spirit and in truth. [JST John 4:25-26] ¶ There is no other way, no other approved system of

worship. ("Our Relationship with the Lord," Brigham Young University Speeches of the Year, 1981-82, p. 98) TLDP:746-47

---

**889. We are to manifest reverence in places of worship.**

**Gordon B. Hinckley**

I invite you brethren of the priesthood, wherever you may be, and particularly you members of bishoprics, to begin an earnest effort to cultivate a more beautiful spirit of worship in our sacrament meetings and an attitude of increased reverence generally in our church buildings. . . . ¶ Socializing . . . should take place in the foyer, and when we enter the chapel we should understand that we are in sacred precincts. CR1987Apr:55

**Elder David O. McKay**

I believe there is one great need in the Church which you presidencies of stakes, bishoprics of wards, presidencies of quorums, and officers in auxiliaries, can supply. I have in mind the need of more reverence in our houses of worship, better order and discipline in our classrooms, in quorum meetings and in auxiliary groups. ¶ The more we try to cultivate the attributes of the Savior, the stronger we become in character and in spirituality, and those are the two great purposes of life, so to live that we may be susceptible to the inspiration of the Holy Ghost and to his guidance. CR1950Oct:162-63

**Recorded in Leviticus**

Ye shall keep my sabbaths, and reverence my sanctuary: I am the LORD. (*The Lord reveals his laws for ancient Israel to Moses*) Lev.19:30

**Howard W. Hunter**

Occasionally we visit too loudly, enter and leave meetings too disrespectfully in what should be an hour of prayer and purifying worship. Reverence is the atmosphere of heaven. CR1977Oct:81

**Howard W. Hunter**

Even the temple where Jesus taught and worshipped in Jerusalem was built in such a way as to establish respect for and devotion to the Father. . . . God must be approached carefully, respectfully, and with great preparation. . . . ¶ Never did Jesus show a greater tempest of emotion than in the cleansing of the temple. . . . The reason for the tempest [Christ's fury against the money exchangers in the temple] lies in just three words: "My Father's house." It was not an ordinary house; it was the house of God. It was erected for God's worship. It was a home for the reverent heart. It was intended to be a place of solace for men's woes and troubles, the very gate of heaven. CR1977Oct:80

**Joseph Smith**

And that all people who shall enter upon the threshold of the Lord's house may feel thy power, and feel constrained to acknowledge that thou hast sanctified it, and that it is thy house, a place of thy holiness. . . . 16. And that this house may be a house of prayer, a house of fasting, a house of faith, a house of glory and of God, even thy house; 17. That all the incomings of thy people, into this house, may be in the name of the Lord; 18. That all their outgoings from this house may be in the name of the Lord; 19. And that all their salutations may be in the name of the Lord, with holy hands, uplifted to the Most High; 20. And that no unclean thing shall be permitted to come into thy house to pollute it; 21. And when thy people transgress, any of them, they may speedily repent and return unto thee, and find favor in thy sight, and be restored to the blessings which thou hast ordained to be poured out upon those who shall reverence thee in thy house. (*Prayer given to Joseph Smith by revelation, offered at the dedication of the Kirtland Temple on March 27, 1836*) D&C 109:13,16-21

**President Spencer W. Kimball**

In a very real sense, what is said of the sacred temples of the Church is applicable to every "house of the Lord," whether it be a meetinghouse or any place where the Saints worship, or in fact, any Latter-day Saint home. ("We Should Be a Reverent People," pamphlet) MPSG1990:48

**Recorded in Exodus**

Now Moses kept the flock of Jethro his father in law, the priest of Midian: and he led the flock to the backside of the desert, and came to the mountain of God, even to Horeb. 2. And the angel of the LORD appeared unto him in a flame of fire out of the midst of a bush: and he looked, and, behold, the bush burned with fire, and the bush was not consumed. 3. And Moses said, I will now turn aside, and see this great sight, why the bush is not burnt. 4. And when the LORD saw that he turned aside to see, God called unto him out of the midst of the bush, and said, Moses, Moses. And he said, Here am I. 5. And he said, Draw not nigh hither: put off thy shoes from off thy feet, for the place whereon thou standest is holy ground. (*The Lord appears to Moses at the burning bush*) Ex.3:1-5

---

**890. We are to revere God and His holy name.**

**Joseph Smith**

Why the first is called the Melchizedek Priesthood is because Melchizedek was such a great high priest. 3. Before his day it was called the Holy Priesthood, after the Order of the Son of God. 4. But out of respect or reverence to the name of the Supreme Being, to avoid the too frequent repetition of his name, they, the church, in ancient days, called that priesthood after Melchizedek, or the Melchizedek Priesthood. *(Revelation on priesthood, received as the Twelve met in council, March 28, 1835)* D&C 107:2-4

**President David O. McKay**

Inseparable from the acceptance of the existence of God is an attitude of reverence. The greatest manifestation of spirituality is reverence; indeed, reverence is spirituality. Reverence is profound respect mingled with love. It is a "complex emotion made up of mingled feelings of the soul." Carlyle says it is "the highest of human feelings." If reverence is the highest, then irreverence is the lowest state in which a man can live in the world. Be that as it may, it is nevertheless true that an irreverent man has a crudeness about him that is repellant. He is cynical, often sneering, and always iconoclastic. ¶ Reverence embraces regard, deference, honor, and esteem. Without some degree of it, therefore, there would be no courtesy, no gentility, no consideration of others' feelings or of others' rights. Reverence is the fundamental virtue in religion. It is one of the signs of strength; irreverence, one of the surest indications of weakness. "No man will rise high," says one man, "who jeers at sacred things. The fine loyalties of life must be reverenced or they will be foresworn in the day of trial." . . . ¶ If there were more reverence in human hearts, there would be less room for sin and sorrow, and there would be increased capacity for joy and gladness. To make more cherished, more adaptable, more attractive this gem among brilliant virtues is a project worthy of the most united and prayerful efforts of every parent, every officer, and every member of the Church. CR1967Apr:86-87

**Recorded in Exodus**

Thou shalt not take the name of the LORD thy God in vain; for the LORD will not hold him guiltless that taketh his name in vain. *(The Lord reveals the third of the Ten Commandments to Moses)* Ex.20:7

**Howard W. Hunter**

The reverence of the Savior for our Father and the understanding of his love made the whole world hopeful and holy. . . . ¶ In the process of moral decline, reverence is one of the first virtues to disappear, and there should be serious concern about that loss in our times. . . . ¶ How careful Jesus was for even the name of his Father. . . . CR1977Oct:80

**Isaiah**

And in that day shall ye say, Praise the LORD, call upon his name, declare his doings among the people, make mention that his name is exalted. 5. Sing unto the LORD; for he hath done excellent things: this is known in all the earth. *(Isaiah prophesies, 740-659 B.C.)* Isa.12:4-5

---

**891. To love Christ is to obey Him.**

**Elder Joseph Fielding Smith**

If we love him [the Lord] we will keep his commandments. ¶ Should there be any who offend or fail to keep the commandments of the Lord, then it is evidence that they do not love him. We must obey them. We show by our works that we love the Lord our God with all our hearts, with all our might, mind, and strength; and in the name of Jesus Christ we serve him and love our neighbor as ourself. This is the word of the Lord as it has been revealed in these modern times for the guidance of Israel. ("Keep the Commandments," IE1970Aug:2) DGSM:47

**Jesus,**
*quoted by John*

If ye love me, keep my commandments. . . . 21. He that hath my commandments, and keepeth them, he it is that loveth me: and he that loveth me shall be loved of my Father, and I will love him, and will manifest myself to him. . . . 23. Jesus answered and said unto him, If a man love me, he will keep my words: and my Father will love him, and we will come unto him, and make our abode with him. *(Jesus instructs the Twelve in anticipation of his crucifixion)* John 14:15,21,23

**Mark E. Petersen**

Half obedience will be rejected as readily as full violation, and maybe quicker, for half rejection and half acceptance is but a sham, an admission of lack of character, a lack of love for Him. It is actually an effort to live on both sides of the line. CR1982Apr:21

**Joseph Smith,**
*receiving the Word of the Lord*

If thou lovest me thou shalt serve me and keep all my commandments. *(Revelation "embracing the law of the Church," Feb. 9, 1831)* D&C 42:29

**John**

For this is the love of God, that we keep his commandments: and his commandments are not grievous. *(Letter to the churches in Asia)* 1Jn.5:3

## 892. When we love God, the Spirit of God dwells in our hearts.

**Paul**

That Christ may dwell in your hearts by faith; that ye, being rooted and grounded in love, 18. May be able to comprehend with all saints what is the breadth, and length, and depth, and height; 19. And to know the love of Christ, which passeth knowledge, that ye might be filled with all the fulness of God. (*Paul writes to the Saints at Ephesus in Asia Minor, about A.D. 62*) Eph.3:17-19

**John**

And we have known and believed the love that God hath to us. God is love; and he that dwelleth in love dwelleth in God, and God in him. (*John writes to the churches in Asia*) 1Jn.4:16

**Jesus,**
*quoted by John*

Jesus answered and said unto him, If a man love me, he will keep my words: and my Father will love him, and we will come unto him, and make our abode with him. (*Jesus instructs the Twelve in anticipation of his crucifixion*) John 14:23

**Related Witnesses:**

**David B. Haight**

Love of God is the means of unlocking divine powers which help us to live worthily and to overcome the world. CR1982Oct:14

**John**

We love him, because he first loved us. (*John writes to the churches in Asia*) 1Jn.4:19

**Jesus,**
*recorded in Matthew*

Master, which is the great commandment in the law? 37. Jesus said unto him, Thou shalt love the Lord thy God with all thy heart, and with all thy soul, and with all thy mind. 38. This is the first and great commandment. 39. And the second is like unto it, Thou shalt love thy neighbour as thyself. 40. On these two commandments hang all the law and the prophets. (*Jesus gives the two great commandments*) Matt.22:36-40

**Paul**

But as it is written, Eye hath not seen, nor ear heard, neither have entered into the heart of man, the things which God hath prepared for them that love him. (*Paul writes to the Church at Corinth, Greece, about A.D. 55*) 1Cor.2:9

**Joseph Smith,**
*receiving the Word of the Lord*

For thus saith the Lord—I, the Lord, am merciful and gracious unto those who fear me, and delight to honor those who serve me in righteousness and in truth unto the end. 6. Great shall be their reward and eternal shall be their glory. 7. And to them will I reveal all mysteries, yea, all the hidden mysteries of my kingdom from days of old, and for ages to come, will I make known unto them the good pleasure of my will concerning all things pertaining to my kingdom. 8. Yea, even the wonders of eternity shall they know, and things to come will I show them, even the things of many generations. 9. And their wisdom shall be great, and their understanding reach to heaven; and before them the wisdom of the wise shall perish, and the understanding of the prudent shall come to naught. 10. For by my Spirit will I enlighten them, and by my power will I make known unto them the secrets of my will—yea, even those things which eye has not seen, nor ear heard, nor yet entered into the heart of man. (*Vision to Joseph Smith and Sidney Rigdon, Feb. 16, 1832*) D&C 76:5-10

**HYMNS Written by Prophets
Applicable to this Topic**

**Bruce R. McConkie**
*I Believe in Christ*
HYMNS:134

I believe in Christ; he is my King!
With all my heart to him I'll sing;
I'll raise my voice in praise and joy,
In grand amens my tongue employ.
I believe in Christ; he is God's Son.
On earth to dwell his soul did come.
He healed the sick; the dead he raised.
Good works were his; his name be praised.

I believe in Christ; oh, blessed name!
As Mary's Son he came to reign
'Mid mortal men, his earthly kin,
To save them from the woes of sin.
I believe in Christ, who marked the path,
Who did gain all his Father hath,
Who said to men: "Come, follow me,
That ye, my friends, with God may be."

I believe in Christ—my Lord, my God!
My feet he plants on gospel sod.
I'll worship him with all my might;
He is the source of truth and light.
I believe in Christ; he ransoms me.
From Satan's grasp he sets me free,
And I shall live with joy and love
In his eternal courts above.

I believe in Christ; he stands supreme!
From him I'll gain my fondest dream;
And while I strive through grief and pain,
His voice is heard: "Ye shall obtain."
I believe in Christ; so come what may,
With him I'll stand in that great day
When on this earth he comes again
To rule among the sons of men.

### Orson F. Whitney
*Savior, Redeemer of My Soul*
HYMNS:112

Savior, Redeemer of my soul,
Whose mighty hand hath made me whole,
Whose wondrous pow'r hath raised me up
And filled with sweet my bitter cup!
What tongue my gratitude can tell,
O gracious God of Israel.

Never can I repay thee, Lord,
But I can love thee.
Thy pure word, Hath it not been my one
delight,
My joy by day, my dream by night?
Then let my lips proclaim it still,
And all my life reflect thy will.

O'errule mine acts to serve thine ends.
Change frowning foes to smiling friends.
Chasten my soul till I shall be
In perfect harmony with thee.
Make me more worthy of thy love,
And fit me for the life above.

### Parley P. Pratt
*As the Dew from Heaven Distilling*
HYMNS:149

As the dew from heav'n distilling
Gently on the grass descends
And revives it, thus fulfilling
What thy providence intends.

Let thy doctrine, Lord, so gracious,
Thus descending from above,
Blest by thee, prove efficacious
To fulfill thy work of love.

Lord, behold this congregation;
Precious promises fulfill.
From thy holy habitation
Let the dews of life distill.

Let our cry come up before thee.
Thy sweet Spirit shed around,
So the people shall adore thee
And confess the joyful sound.

# List of Doctrines

## ZION

# ZION

**Author's Note:** About the fall of Babylon (the wicked) and the establishment of Zion (the pure in heart): Babylon is frequently contrasted with Zion, the wicked contrasted with the pure in heart. ¶ "Anciently Babylon was the chief capital city of the Babylonian empire," writes Bruce R. McConkie. "To the Lord's people anciently, Babylon was known as the center of iniquity, carnality, and worldliness. Everything connected with it was in opposition to all righteousness and had the effect of leading men downward to the destruction of their souls." (Mormon Doctrine, p. 68-69) ¶ Bruce R. McConkie defines *spiritual Babylon* thus: "In prophetic imagery, Babylon is the world with all its carnality and wickedness. Babylon is the degenerate social order created by lustful men who love darkness rather than light because their deeds are evil. . . . [I]t is the false churches that build false temples and worship false gods; it is every false philosophy . . . that leads men away from God and salvation. . . . [I]t is every evil and wicked and ungodly thing in our whole social structure." (The Millennial Messiah, p. 424; DGSM:98)

## 893. Zion is the pure in heart.

**Joseph Smith,**
*receiving the Word of the Lord*
Therefore, verily, thus saith the Lord, let Zion rejoice, for this is Zion—THE PURE IN HEART; therefore, let Zion rejoice, while all the wicked shall mourn. (*Revelation dealing with the affairs of the persecuted Saints in Missouri, Aug. 2, 1833*) D&C 97:21
**Elder George Albert Smith**
Will we make this Zion? Will we keep it to be Zion, because Zion means the pure in heart? CR1941Oct:99
**President John Taylor**
The Zion of God. What does it mean? The pure in heart in the first place. In the second place those who are governed by the law of God—the pure in heart who are governed by the law of God. (*At Malad, Idaho, Oct. 20, 1881, JD26:109*) TLDP:751
**President John Taylor**
The Zion of God must consist of men that are pure in heart and pure in life and spotless before God. At least that is what we have got to arrive at. We are not there yet, but we must get there before we shall be prepared to inherit glory and exaltation. Therefore a form of godliness will amount to but little with any of us, for he that knoweth the master's will and doeth it not shall be beaten with many stripes. It is "Not every one that saith unto me, Lord, Lord, shall enter into the kingdom of heaven; but he that doeth the will of My Father, which is in heaven." (Matt.7:21) These are doctrines of the gospel as I understand them. And it is not enough for us to embrace the gospel and to be gathered here to the land of Zion, and be associated with the people of God, attend our meetings and partake of the sacrament of the Lord's supper, and endeavor to move along without much blame of any kind attached to us.

For notwithstanding all this, if our hearts are not right, if we are not pure in heart before God, if we have not pure hearts and pure consciences, fearing God and keeping his commandments, we shall not unless we repent, participate in these blessings about which I have spoken and of which the prophets bear testimony. (*In Assembly Hall, Feb. 12, 1882*) (The Gospel Kingdom, pp. 89-90) TLDP:753
**Elder Harold B. Lee**
There are several meanings to the word Zion. ¶ It may have reference to the hill named Mt. Zion or by extension in the land of Jerusalem. [See Micah 4:2.] ¶ It has sometimes been used, as by the prophet Micah, to refer to the location of "the mountain of the house of the Lord"—as some place apart from Jerusalem. ¶ Zion was so called by Enoch in reference to the "City of Holiness," or the "City of Enoch." [See Moses 7:18-19.] The Land of Zion has been used to refer, in some connotations, to the Western Hemisphere. ¶ But there is another most significant use of the term by which the Church of God is called Zion, comprising, according to the Lord's own definition, "the pure in heart." (D&C 97:21) CR1968Oct:61-62
**Joseph Smith,**
*translating the Book of Moses*
And the Lord called his people ZION, because they were of one heart and one mind, and dwelt in righteousness; and there was no poor among them. 19. And Enoch continued his preaching in righteousness unto the people of God. And it came to pass in his days, that he built a city that was called the City of Holiness, even ZION. 20. And it came to pass that Enoch talked with the Lord; and he said unto the Lord: Surely Zion shall dwell in safety forever. But the Lord said unto Enoch: Zion have I blessed, but the residue of the people have I cursed. (*The record of Moses: Enoch builds a city of holiness*) Moses 7:18-20

### President Spencer W. Kimball

Zion can be built up only among those who are the pure in heart, not a people torn by covetousness or greed, but a pure and selfless people. Not a people who are pure in appearance, rather a people who are pure in heart. Zion is to be in the world and not of the world, not dulled by a sense of carnal security, nor paralyzed by materialism. No, Zion is not things of the lower, but of the higher order, things that exalt the mind and sanctify the heart. ¶ Zion is "every man seeking the interest of the neighbor, and doing all things with an eye single to the glory of God." (D&C 82:19) As I understand these matters, Zion can be established only by those who are pure in heart, and who labor for Zion; for if they labor for money they shall perish." (2Ne.26:31) ¶ May I suggest three fundamental things we must do if we are to "bring again Zion," three things for which we must labor for Zion must commit ourselves. ¶ First, we must eliminate the individual tendency to selfishness that snares the soul, shrinks the heart, and darkens the mind. . . . ¶ Second, we must cooperate completely and work in harmony one with the other. There must be unanimity in our decisions and unity in our actions. . . . ¶ If the Spirit of the Lord is to magnify our labors, then this spirit of oneness and cooperation must be the prevailing spirit in all that we do. . . . ¶ Third, we must lay on the altar and sacrifice whatever is required by the Lord. We begin by offering a "broken heart and a contrite spirit." We follow this by giving our best effort in our assigned fields of labor and callings. We learn our duty and execute it fully. Finally we consecrate our time, talents, and means as called upon by our file leaders and as prompted by the whisperings of the Spirit. CR1978Apr:122-24

**Related Witnesses:**

### Elder John Taylor

We can not build up a Zion unless we are in possession of the spirit of Zion, and of the light and intelligence that flow from God, and under the direction of the priesthood, the living oracles of God, to lead us in the paths of life. (*In old Tabernacle, Aug. 31, 1875, JD18:78-79*) TLDP:753

### Stephen L. Richards

There is no fence around Zion or the world, but to one of discernment, they are separated more completely than if each were surrounded with high unscalable walls. Their underlying concepts, philosophies, and purposes are at complete variance one with the other. The philosophy of the world is self-sufficient, egotistical, materialistic, and skeptical. The philosophy of

Zion is humility, not servility, but a willing recognition of the sovereignty of God and dependence on his providence. CR1951Oct:110

### President Spencer W. Kimball

[O]ne important end result of our labors, hopes, and aspirations in this work is the building of a Latter-day Zion, a Zion characterized by love, harmony, and peace—a Zion in which the Lord's children are as one. (*General conference, welfare session, April 1978*) (The Teachings of Spencer W. Kimball, p. 362) TLDP:754

### President John Taylor

We are here to build up the church of God, the Zion of God, and the kingdom of God, and to be on hand to do whatever God requires—first to purge ourselves from all iniquity, from covetousness and evil of every kind, to forsake sin of every sort, cultivate the Spirit of God, and help to build up his kingdom; to beatify Zion and have pleasant habitations, and pleasant gardens and orchards, until Zion shall be the most beautiful place there is on the earth. . . . Zion shall yet become the praise and the glory of the whole earth. (*In Bowery, June 1883, JD24:201*) DGSM:98

### President John Taylor

We will build up our Zion after the pattern that God will show us, and we will be governed by his law and submit to his authority and be governed by the holy priesthood and by the word and will of God. And then when the time comes that these calamities we read of, shall overtake the earth, those that are prepared will have the power of translation, as they had in former times, and the city will be translated. And Zion that is on the earth will rise, and the Zion above will descend, as we are told, and we will meet and fall on each other's necks and embrace and kiss each other. And thus the purposes of God to a certain extent will then be fulfilled. (*At Ogden, Utah, March 21, 1880, JD21:253*) TLDP:753

### Joseph Smith

In regard to the building up of Zion, it has to be done by the counsel of Jehovah, by the revelations of heaven; and we should feel to say, "if the Lord go not with us, carry us not up hence." (*Editorial in the Times and Seasons*) HC5:65

---

**894. Zion is wherever the organization of the Church of God is—where the pure in heart are gathered.**

### President Brigham Young

Where is Zion? Where the organization of the

Church of God is. And may it dwell spiritually in every heart; and may we so live as to always enjoy the Spirit of Zion! (*In Bowery, Oct. 14, 1860, JD8:205*) TLDP:752

### President Spencer W. Kimball

Now as we sing together "Come to Zion," we mean come to the ward—not to Salt Lake City—come to the ward, the branch, the mission, the stake, and give assistance to build up Zion. We used to think that one had to be in Salt Lake City to be in Zion, but it has been interpreted differently. Sometimes all of America is Zion, and we think of Zion as being where the pure in heart are located. So we hope you will stay here and build up a beautiful France Zion. Italy is the Zion for the Italians, Spain for the Spaniards, Portugal for the Portuguese, and Germany for the Germans. Scandinavia is Zion for the Scandinavians, and Japan for the Japanese. ACR(Paris)1976:3

**Related Witnesses:**

### Bruce R. McConkie

The place of gathering for the Mexican Saints is in Mexico; the place of gathering for the Guatemalan Saints is in Guatemala; the place of gathering for the Brazilian Saints is in Brazil; and so it goes throughout the length and breadth of the whole earth. Japan is for the Japanese; Korea is for the Koreans; Australia is for the Australians; every nation is the gathering place for its own people. ACR(Mexico City)1972:45

### President Spencer W. Kimball

The gathering of Israel is now in progress. Hundreds of thousands of people have been baptized into the Church. Millions more will join the Church. And this is the way that we will gather Israel. The English people will gather in England. The Japanese people will gather in the Orient. The Brazilian people will gather in Brazil. So that important element of the world history is already being accomplished. ¶ It is to be done by missionary work. It is your responsibility to attend to the missionary work. ACR(Sao Paulo)1975:73

### President Brigham Young

When Joseph first revealed the land where the Saints should gather, a woman in Canada asked if we thought that Jackson County would be large enough to gather all the people that would want to go to Zion. I will answer the question really as it is. Zion will extend, eventually, all over this earth. There will be no nook or corner upon the earth but what will be in Zion. It will all be Zion. I remember that the lady was answered by asking her whether she thought the ark was large enough to hold those that were to

go into it in the days of Noah? "Yes," was the reply. Then of course Zion will be just large enough to receive all that will be prepared to possess it, as the ark was. (*In Bowery, July 28, 1861, JD9:138*) TLDP:752

### President Lorenzo Snow

President Smith was talking yesterday about the land of Zion. Yes, surely, this entire continent is the land of Zion, and the time will come when there will be Temples established over every portion of the land, and we will go into these Temples and work for our kindred dead night and day, that the work of the Lord may be speedily accomplished, that Jesus may come and present the kingdom to His father. He is coming soon, too. But we will not hear His voice until we build up Jackson County. Now we should make preparation for this. We are not only going to have Zion throughout this continent, but we will have it over the whole earth. The whole earth is the Lord's. (*At St. George, Utah, May 8, 1899*) MOFP3:313-14

### President Joseph F. Smith,
### Anthon H. Lund, Charles W. Penrose
(First Presidency)

The steps taken toward the building of a Temple in Alberta, Canada, indicating the purpose of the Church to extend the blessing of holy ordinances for the living and the dead of *other lands than Utah and former dwelling places of Zion,* [italics added] have awakened new interest and confidence in the cause of salvation. More Church edifices have been erected and such property acquired than ever before in our history, and we congratulate all who sense the importance of these movements on that which has been accomplished. (*Christmas message published in Deseret News, Dec. 20, 1913, by the First Presidency*) MOFP4:295

### Joseph Smith

You know there has been great discussion in relation to Zion—where it is, and where the gathering of the dispensation is, and which I am now going to tell you. The prophets have spoken and written upon it; but I will make a proclamation that will cover a broader ground. The whole of America is Zion itself from north to south, and is described by the Prophets, who declare that it is the Zion where the mountain of the Lord should be, and that it should be in the center of the land. HC6:318-19

### Joseph Smith,
### *receiving the Word of the Lord*

Until the day cometh when there is found no more room for them; and then I have other places which I will appoint unto them, and they shall be called stakes, for the curtains or the strength of Zion. (*Revelation, Dec. 16, 1833*) D&C 101:21

### Matthew Cowley

In your homes where the priesthood of God exists, there is Zion. And to you whose lives are committed to righteousness, I say unto you, You are Zion. CR1952Apr:102

### President Joseph F. Smith, Anthon H. Lund, John Henry Smith
(First Presidency)

Seventy-eight years have passed since then, [since 1833 when the Saints were driven from Missouri] and though the dispossessed and driven people have never returned to Jackson county, yet that spot is still to them Zion, the place to which they or their children will eventually wend their way to rear upon its consecrated soil the city and temple of God. All other gathering places of the Saints, including their present homes in the region of the Rocky mountains, are merely "stakes" of Zion. (*Published in Deseret News by First Presidency, Nov. 4, 1911*) MOFP4:238

---

**895. Zion and her stakes are to be places of peace and safety for the Saints of God.**

### Elder George Albert Smith

He [the Lord] has told us in great plainness that the world will be in distress, that there will be warfare from one end of the world to the other, that the wicked shall slay the wicked and that peace shall be taken from the earth. And he has said, too, that the only place where there will be safety will be in Zion. Will we make this Zion? Will we keep it to be Zion, because Zion means the pure in heart? CR1941Oct:99

### Joseph Smith

And it shall be called the New Jerusalem, a land of peace, a city of refuge, a place of safety for the saints of the Most High God; 67. And the glory of the Lord shall be there, and the terror of the Lord also shall be there, insomuch that the wicked will not come unto it, and it shall be called Zion. 68. And it shall come to pass among the wicked, that every man that will not take his sword against his neighbor must needs flee unto Zion for safety. 69. And there shall be gathered unto it out of every nation under heaven; and it shall be the only people that shall not be at war one with another. 70. And it shall be said among the wicked: Let us not go up to battle against Zion, for the inhabitants of Zion are terrible; wherefore we

cannot stand. 71. And it shall come to pass that the righteous shall be gathered out from among all nations, and shall come to Zion, singing with songs of everlasting joy. (*The Lord calls upon the Saints to gather to Zion, March 7, 1831*) D&C 45:66-71

### Joseph Smith, receiving the Word of the Lord

Verily I say unto you all: Arise and shine forth, that thy light may be a standard for the nations; 6. And that the gathering together upon the land of Zion, and upon her stakes, may be for a defense, and for a refuge from the storm, and from wrath when it shall be poured out without mixture upon the whole earth. D&C 115:5-6

### Joseph Smith, translating the Book of Moses

And it came to pass that Enoch talked with the Lord; and he said unto the Lord: Surely Zion shall dwell in safety forever. But the Lord said unto Enoch: Zion have I blessed, but the residue of the people have I cursed. (*The record of Moses: Enoch talks to the Lord face to face*) Moses 7:20

**Related Witnesses:**

### Joseph Smith, receiving the Word of the Lord

For Zion must increase in beauty, and in holiness; her borders must be enlarged; her stakes must be strengthened; yea, verily I say unto you, Zion must arise and put on her beautiful garments. (*Revelation, April 26, 1832*) D&C 82:14

---

**896. Zion will prevail: no weapon that is formed against Zion shall prosper.**

### President John Taylor, and George Q. Cannon
(of the First Presidency)

God has said concerning Zion, that "no weapon that is formed against thee shall prosper; and every tongue that shall rise against thee in judgment thou shalt condemn. This is the heritage of the servants of the Lord, and their righteousness is of me, saith the Lord." ¶ Our history is one continued illustration of the fulfillment of this word of our God. We can truthfully ask, where is the weapon that has been formed against Zion which has prospered? The God of heaven is on our side. He has made promises to Zion which cannot fail. He is mightier than all of earth's hosts, and by His wonderful providence can bring to pass, in His own way, the fulfillment of all the words of His inspired servants. Upon this foundation we can rest secure. No weapon that is formed against Zion can prosper. . . . (*Epistle prepared for delivery in absentia at April general conference, 1886; published in pamphlet, May 1886)* MOFP3:70-71

### President John Taylor and George Q. Cannon
(of the First Presidency)

No weapon that is formed against Zion can prosper; and every tongue that shall rise against her in judgment shall be condemned. *(From an epistle read at general conference in Oct. 1886)* MOFP3:75

### Joseph Smith

Verily, thus saith the Lord unto you—there is no weapon that is formed against you shall prosper; 10. And if any man lift his voice against you he shall be confounded in mine own due time. *(Revelation given to Joseph Smith and Sydney Rigdon, Dec. 1, 1831)* D&C 71:9-10

### Joseph Smith

We ask thee, Holy Father, to establish the people that shall worship, and honorably hold a name and standing in this thy house, to all generations and for eternity; 25. That no weapon formed against them shall prosper; that he who diggeth a pit for them shall fall into the same himself; 26. That no combination of wickedness shall have power to rise up and prevail over thy people upon whom thy name shall be put in this house; *(Prayer given to Joseph Smith by revelation, offered at dedication of Kirtland Temple on March 27, 1836)* D&C 109:24-26

### President Wilford Woodruff, George Q. Cannon, Joseph F. Smith
(First Presidency)

There never was a time probably in our history when the Latter-day Saints needed more than they do at present the assistance which God has promised to render to us. He has made precious promises to His Church; among them He has said that no weapon that is formed against Zion shall prosper. This will be fulfilled to the very letter. The Lord's word cannot fail. But it is for us, as a people, to place ourselves in such a condition that we can ask the Lord in faith for these blessings, and receive them at His hand. We should so live that He will feel bound by His promises to come to our aid and to fulfil His word to us. We have never appealed to Him in vain. *(Letter to stake presidents, Dec. 2, 1889)* MOFP3:176

### Abraham O. Woodruff

No weapon that has ever been formed against Zion has prospered. The efforts of the evil one to destroy the work of the Lord have only tended to spread it abroad. The persecutions which have been heaped upon this people have been the means of cementing us together, drawing us more closely to God, and making us more united and powerful. It is the heritage of the saints of God to be misrepresented and persecuted by the insincere and the wicked; but their efforts have never blocked the progress of the work of our Eternal Father. On the contrary, the labors of our most bitter enemies have been among the main factors in spreading the work abroad. The Lord has turned the wrath of the wicked to his own glory. Had it not been for the persecution of the Latter-day Saints, the mustard seed would not have been cast abroad; but in the attempt to destroy the mustard stalk, to which the Savior compared the Gospel, they have scattered the seed, and it has taken root wherever it has fallen. . . . I thank God that it is not his purposes which have failed, but the purposes of man. This should be an encouragement to every Latter-day Saint and a strong testimony that this is the work of God. It ought to be a testimony also to those who have sought to bring to naught the purposes of God. CR1901Oct:11

### President Joseph F. Smith, Anthon H. Lund, Charles W. Penrose
(First Presidency)

After the excitement aroused by the outrageous and improbable stories against the elders and saints has subsided, investigation by rational persons ensues, the meetings held by our people are largely attended, conversions follow, or at least conviction that the people and principles so grossly maligned have been unjustly accused, and those who have figured in the falsehood stand condemned before their fellows. And thus the work goes on, in fulfillment of Divine promises and to the accomplishment of the warning of the world and the proclamation of the gospel of the Son of God, whose advent as the Babe of Bethlehem we delight to celebrate. Each Christmas day brings additional assurances that the word of the Lord to us in the beginning will certainly be fulfilled: "No weapon that is formed against you shall prosper, and the tongue that rises in judgment against you shall be condemned." *(Christmas message published by the First Presidency in Deseret News, Dec. 21, 1912)* MOFP4:278-79

### Related Witnesses:
### Daniel

And in the days of these kings shall the God of heaven set up a kingdom, which shall never be destroyed: and the kingdom shall not be left to other people, but it shall break in pieces and consume all these kingdoms, and it shall stand for ever. *(Daniel interprets Nebuchadnezzar's dream of a stone cut from the mountain without hands)* Dan.2:44

### Orson F. Whitney

The ancient Zion foreshadowed the Zion of the Last Days, with which it is destined to blend. In Enoch's day the Lord's people, consecrating to Him their all, became equal in earthly as in heavenly things; and the righteous unity resulting from that blest condition brought forth the peace and power of sanctity. So shall it be and more, when the Lord brings again Zion. (*Saturday Night Thoughts*, p. 117) TLDP:751

### Isaiah,
#### *quoted by Nephi, son of Lehi*

Hearken unto me, my people; and give ear unto me, O my nation; for a law shall proceed from me, and I will make my judgment to rest for a light for the people. 5. My righteousness is near; my salvation is gone forth, and mine arm shall judge the people. The isles shall wait upon me, and on mine arm shall they trust. 6. Lift up your eyes to the heavens, and look upon the earth beneath; for the heavens shall vanish away like smoke, and the earth shall wax old like a garment; and they that dwell therein shall die in like manner. But my salvation shall be forever, and my righteousness shall not be abolished. (*The prophecies of Isaiah as found in the Book of Mormon*) 2Ne.8:4-6

### President John Taylor

We are here to build up the church of God, the Zion of God, and the kingdom of God . . . to beautify Zion and have pleasant habitations, and pleasant gardens and orchards, until Zion shall be the most beautiful place there is on the earth. . . . Zion shall yet become the praise and the glory of the whole earth. (*In Bowery, June 1883, JD24:201*) DGSM:98

---

### 897. Zion (the New Jerusalem) will be established upon the American continent.

### President Brigham Young

This American continent will be Zion; for it is so spoken of by the prophets. Jerusalem will be rebuilt and will be the place of gathering, and the tribe of Judah will gather there; but this continent of America is the land of Zion. (*In Bowery, July 5, 1857, JD5:4*) TLDP:752

### Marion G. Romney

Zion, as used in this scripture [Isa.2:2-3], means America. In fact, America is Zion. At times the term is used to include both the North and South American continents. In some references the word Zion is used to designate the area in and about Jackson County, Missouri, where the New Jerusalem will be built, which

city is itself sometimes called Zion. From Zion the law of God shall eventually go forth into all the world. ("America's Fate and Ultimate Destiny," Brigham Young University Speeches of the Year, 1976, p. 326) TLDP:752

### Joseph Smith

We believe in the literal gathering of Israel and in the restoration of the Ten Tribes; that Zion (the New Jerusalem) will be built upon the American continent; that Christ will reign personally upon the earth; and, that the earth will be renewed and receive its paradisiacal glory. (*The tenth of the thirteen Articles of Faith; letter to John Wentworth, March 1, 1842*) AofF:10

### Elder Joseph Fielding Smith

In the day of regeneration, when all things are made new, there will be three great cities that will be holy. One will be the Jerusalem of old, which shall be rebuilt according to the prophecy of Ezekiel. [Ether 13:2-11] One will be the city of Zion, or of Enoch, which was taken from the earth when Enoch was translated and which will be restored; and the city Zion, or New Jerusalem, which is to be built by the seed of Joseph on this the American continent. [3Ne.20:21-22] DGSM:99; MPSG1972-73:135

### Elder Joseph Fielding Smith

When Joseph Smith translated the Book of Mormon, he learned that America is the land of Zion which was given to Joseph and his children and that on this land the City of Zion, or New Jerusalem, is to be built. He also learned that Jerusalem in Palestine is to be rebuilt and become a holy city. These two cities, one in the land of Zion and one in Palestine, are to become capitals for the kingdom of God during the millennium. (Church News, Nov. 21, 1931, Doctrines of Salvation, 3:71) DGSM:104

### Elder Wilford Woodruff

The Lord has said by the ancient prophets, that in the last days there should be deliverance in Jerusalem and in Mount Zion; and by the mouth of the modern prophet, seer, and revelator, pointed out the location of Zion [on the American Continent, AofF:10], and commanded the Saints among the Gentiles to gather thereunto and build it up, while the Jews gather to Jerusalem. The safety of the Saints depends as much upon their fulfilling his commandments, as the safety of Noah and Lot depended upon their obedience to the commands of God in their day and generation. ("A Word to the Wise Is Sufficient," Millennial Star, June 1845, p. 3) TLDP:207-08

### Jesus,
#### *quoted by Mormon*

And I will gather my people together as a man

gathereth his sheaves into the floor. . . . 22. And behold, this people will I establish in this land, unto the fulfilling of the covenant which I made with your father Jacob; and it shall be a New Jerusalem. And the powers of heaven shall be in the midst of this people; yea, even I will be in the midst of you. (*The resurrected Jesus Christ foretells the fulfilling of his covenant regarding the New Jerusalem, A.D. 34*) 3Ne.20:18,22

**Elder Joseph Fielding Smith**
While the Lord promised the children of Israel that they would be restored to their lands in Palestine, yet there are many predictions pointing to the gathering of scattered Israel first to this American Continent which the Lord has designated the land of Zion. It is here where all the descendants of the ten tribes are to come, while those of the house of Judah are to gather in Palestine. (The Restoration of All Things, p. 142) TLDP:209

**Joseph Smith,**
*receiving the Word of the Lord*
Wherefore I, the Lord, have said, gather ye out from the eastern lands, assemble ye yourselves together ye elders of my church; go ye forth into the western countries, call upon the inhabitants to repent, and inasmuch as they do repent, build up churches unto me. 65. And with one heart and with one mind, gather up your riches that ye may purchase an inheritance which shall hereafter be appointed unto you. 66. And it shall be called the New Jerusalem, a land of peace, a city of refuge, a place of safety for the saints of the Most High God; 67. And the glory of the Lord shall be there, and the terror of the Lord also shall be there, insomuch that the wicked will not come unto it, and it shall be called Zion. 68. And it shall come to pass among the wicked, that every man that will not take his sword against his neighbor must needs flee unto Zion for safety. 69. And there shall be gathered unto it out of every nation under heaven; and it shall be the only people that shall not be at war one with another. 70. And it shall be said among the wicked: Let us not go up to battle against Zion, for the inhabitants of Zion are terrible; wherefore we cannot stand. 71. And it shall come to pass that the righteous shall be gathered out from among all nations, and shall come to Zion, singing with songs of everlasting joy. (*Revelation, March 7, 1831*) D&C 45:64-71

**President David O. McKay**
Zion means, literally, a "sunny place" or "sunny mountain." It first designated an eminence in Palestine on which Jerusalem is built. In the Doctrine and Covenants, Zion has three designations: First, the land of America; sec-

ond, a specific place of gathering; and third, the pure in heart. ("Zion Shall Flourish," Instructor, Feb. 1959, p. 33) TLDP:751-52

**Joseph Smith**
You know there has been great discussion in relation to Zion—where it is, and where the gathering of the dispensation is, and which I am now going to tell you. The prophets have spoken and written upon it; but I will make a proclamation that will cover a broader ground. The whole of America is Zion itself from north to south, and is described by the Prophets, who declare that it is the Zion where the mountain of the Lord should be, and that it should be in the center of the land. HC6:318-19

**Moroni, son of Mormon**
Behold, Ether saw the days of Christ, and he spake concerning a New Jerusalem upon this land. 5. And he spake also concerning the house of Israel, and the Jerusalem from whence Lehi should come—after it should be destroyed it should be built up again, a holy city unto the Lord; wherefore, it could not be a new Jerusalem for it had been in a time of old; but it should be built up again, and become a holy city of the Lord; and it should be built unto the house of Israel. 6. And that a New Jerusalem should be built upon this land, unto the remnant of the seed of Joseph, for which things there has been a type. (*Moroni's abridgement of the writings of Ether, who wrote about 550 B.C.*) Ether 13:4-6

**President Joseph F. Smith,**
**Anthon H. Lund, John Henry Smith**
(First Presidency)
The Book of Mormon is replete with predictions of the glorious future of America. "The Land of Zion," where the New Jerusalem is to be built by a gathering of scattered Israel, preparatory to the second coming of the Messiah, and the beginning of the Millennial Reign. It shows how such men as Columbus, the Pilgrim fathers, the patriots of the revolution, and the "Gentiles" of today—meaning the people of the United States and of European nations—have been and are being used by the Almighty to bring about the great consummation. (*Published in Deseret News by the First Presidency, Nov. 4, 1911*) MOFP4:233

---

**898. In the last days, the law of God will go forth from Zion.**

**Isaiah,**
*quoted by Nephi, son of Lehi*
And it shall come to pass in the last days, when the mountain of the Lord's house shall be

established in the top of the mountains, and shall be exalted above the hills, and all nations shall flow unto it. 3. And many people shall go and say, Come ye, and let us go up to the mountain of the Lord, to the house of the God of Jacob; and he will teach us of his ways, and we will walk in his paths; for out of Zion shall go forth the law, and the word of the Lord from Jerusalem. (*Nephi records the words of Isaiah from the brass plates, 559-545*) 2Ne.12:2-3

### Marion G. Romney

Zion, as used in this scripture [Isa.2:2-3], means America. In fact, America is Zion. At times the term is used to include both the North and South American continents. In some references the word Zion is used to designate the area in and about Jackson County, Missouri, where the New Jerusalem will be built, which city is itself sometimes called Zion. From Zion the law of God shall eventually go forth into all the world. ("America's Fate and Ultimate Destiny," Brigham Young University Speeches of the Year, 1976, p. 326) TLDP:752

### Isaiah

And it shall come to pass in the last days, that the mountain of the LORD's house shall be established in the top of the mountains, and shall be exalted above the hills; and all nations shall flow unto it. 3. And many people shall go and say, Come ye, and let us go up to the mountain of the LORD, to the house of the God of Jacob; and he will teach us of his ways, and we will walk in his paths: for out of Zion shall go forth the law, and the word of the LORD from Jerusalem. (*Isaiah sees the latter-day temple and the gathering of Israel*) Isa.2:2-3

### Micah

And many nations shall come, and say, Come, and let us go up to the mountain of the LORD, and to the house of the God of Jacob; and he will teach us of his ways, and we will walk in his paths: for the law shall go forth of Zion, and the word of the LORD from Jerusalem. (*Micah prophesies, in the last days the temple shall built and Israel shall gather to it*) Micah 4:2

**Related Witnesses:**

### Isaiah
#### quoted by Nephi, son of Lehi

Hearken unto me, my people; and give ear unto me, O my nation; for a law shall proceed from me, and I will make my judgment to rest for a light for the people. 5. My righteousness is near; my salvation is gone forth, and mine arm shall judge the people. The isles shall wait upon me, and on mine arm shall they trust. 6. Lift up your eyes to the heavens, and look upon the earth beneath; for the heavens shall vanish

away like smoke, and the earth shall wax old like a garment; and they that dwell therein shall die in like manner. But my salvation shall be forever, and my righteousness shall not be abolished. (*The prophecies of Isaiah as found in the Book of Mormon*) 2Ne.8:4-6

### Hyrum Mack Smith

One great purpose of God in establishing Zion is to save the world, through its laws and institutions, from the curse of poverty and destitution. The object is to give to the world an entirely new social order, to establish a community in which even the poor would share the "fat things" with "the rich and the learned, the wise and the noble" (D&C 58:10). Zion is to be a place for the "supper of the house of the Lord"—a banquet hall—"unto which all nations shall be invited." There "the marriage feast of the Lamb" will be held when the time has come for God Omnipotent to reign upon this Earth (Rev. 19:7-9). It is the New Jerusalem, consisting of the City of Zion and the "Jerusalem which is above," that is, "the Bride of the Lamb" (Rev. 21:2; Gal. 4:26; Eph. 5:27). The two will be united when our Savior comes in His glory. "Blessed are they who are called unto the marriage supper of the Lamb." Yea, blessed are they who will be called to become citizens in the City of Zion. (The Doctrine and Covenants Commentary, Hyrum M. Smith and Janne M. Sjodahl, pp. 336-37) TLDP:751

---

### HYMNS Written by Prophets
### Applicable to this Topic

#### Parley P. Pratt
*The Morning Breaks,* Verses 3,4,5
HYMNS:1

The Gentile fulness now comes in,
And Israel's blessings are at hand.
Lo, Judah's remnant, cleansed from sin,
Lo, Judah's remnant, cleansed from sin
Shall in their promised Canaan stand.

Jehovah speaks! Let earth give ear,
And Gentile nations turn and live,
His mighty arm is making bare,
His mighty arm is making bare
His cov'nant people to receive.

Angels from heav'n and truth from earth
Have met, and both have record borne;
Thus Zion's light is bursting forth,
Thus Zion's light is bursting forth
To bring her ransomed children home.

**Parley P. Pratt**
*An Angel from on High,* 5th verse
HYMNS:13

Lo! Israel filled with joy
Shall now be gathered home,
Their wealth and means employ
To build Jerusalem,
While Zion shall arise and shine
And fill the earth with truth divine,
While Zion shall arise and shine
And fill the earth with truth divine.


**John Taylor**
*Go, Ye Messengers of Heaven*
HYMNS:327

Go, ye messengers of heaven,
Chosen by divine command;
Go and publish free salvation
To a dark, benighted land.

Go to island, vale, and mountain;
There fulfill the great command;
Gather out the sons of Jacob
To possess the promised land.

When your thousands all are gathered,
And their prayers for you ascend,
And the Lord has crowned with blessings
All the labors of your hand,

Then the song of joy and transport
Will from ev'ry land resound;
Then the nations long in darkness
By the Savior will be crowned.

# LIST OF LATTER-DAY PROPHETS

### Sustained as Prophets, Seers and Revelators

*(We Believe* quotes only Prophets, ancient and modern.
The modern, latter-day prophets are those listed below.)

| Prophet/Apostle | Born | Ordained Apostle | Sustained as President |
|---|---|---|---|
| Ashton, Marvin J. | 1915 | 1971 | |
| Ballard, Melvin J. | 1873 | 1919 | |
| Ballard, M. Russell | 1928 | 1985 | |
| Bennion, Adam S. | 1886 | 1953 | |
| Benson, Ezra Taft | 1811 | 1846 | |
| **Benson, Ezra Taft** | **1899** | **1943** | **1985 13th President** |
| Bowen, Albert E. | 1875 | 1937 | |
| Brown, Hugh B. | 1883 | 1958 | |
| Callis, Charles A. | 1865 | 1933 | |
| Cannon, Abraham H. | 1859 | 1889 | |
| Cannon, George Q. | 1827 | 1860 | |
| Cannon, Sylvester Q. | 1877 | 1938 | |
| Carrington, Albert | 1813 | 1870 | |
| Clark, J. Reuben, Jr. | 1871 | 1934 | |
| Clawson, Rudger | 1857 | 1898 | |
| Cowdery, Oliver | 1806 | 1829 | |
| Cowley, Matthew | 1897 | 1945 | |
| Cowley, Matthias F. | 1858 | 1897 | |
| Dyer, Alvin R. | 1903 | 1967 | |
| Evans, Richard L. | 1906 | 1953 | |
| Erying, Henry B. | 1933 | 1995 | |
| Faust, James E. | 1920 | 1978 | |
| **Grant, Heber J.** | **1856** | **1882** | **1918 Seventh President** |
| Grant, Jedediah M. | 1816 | 1854 | |
| Haight, David B. | 1906 | 1976 | |
| Hales, Robert D. | 1932 | 1994 | |
| Hinckley, Alonzo A. | 1870 | 1934 | |
| **Hinckley, Gordon B.** | **1910** | **1961** | **1995 Fifteenth President** |
| Holland, Jeffery R. | 1940 | 1994 | |
| **Hunter, Howard W.** | **1907** | **1959** | **1994 Fourteenth President** |
| Hyde, Orson | 1805 | 1835 | |
| Ivins, Anthony W. | 1852 | 1907 | |
| Johnson, Luke S. | 1807 | 1835 | |
| Johnson, Lyman E. | 1811 | 1835 | |
| Kimball, Heber C. | 1801 | 1835 | |
| **Kimball, Spencer W.** | **1895** | **1943** | **1973 Twelfth President** |
| **Lee, Harold B.** | **1899** | **1941** | **1972 Eleventh President** |
| Lund, Anthon H. | 1844 | 1889 | |
| Lyman, Amasa M. | 1813 | 1842 | |
| Lyman, Francis M. | 1840 | 1880 | |
| Lyman, Richard R. | 1870 | 1918 | |
| Marsh, Thomas B. | 1799 | 1835 | |
| Maxwell, Neal A. | 1926 | 1981 | |
| Merrill, Joseph F. | 1868 | 1931 | |
| Merrill, Marriner W. | 1835 | 1889 | |
| Monson, Thomas S. | 1927 | 1963 | |
| Morris, George Q. | 1874 | 1954 | |
| Moyle, Henry D. | 1889 | 1947 | |
| McConkie, Bruce R. | 1915 | 1972 | |
| **McKay, David O.** | **1873** | **1906** | **1951 Ninth President** |
| Morris, George Q. | 1874 | 1954 | |
| M'Lellin, William E. | 1806 | 1835 | |
| Nelson, Russell M. | 1924 | 1984 | |
| Oaks, Dallin H. | 1932 | 1984 | |
| Packer, Boyd K. | 1924 | 1970 | |
| Page, John E. | 1799 | 1838 | |

| Prophet/Apostle | Born | Ordained Apostle | Sustained as President |
|---|---|---|---|
| Patten, David W. | 1799 | 1835 | |
| Penrose, Charles W. | 1832 | 1904 | |
| Perry, L. Tom | 1922 | 1974 | |
| Petersen, Mark E. | 1900 | 1944 | |
| Pratt, Orson | 1811 | 1835 | |
| Pratt, Parley P. | 1807 | 1835 | |
| Rich, Charles C. | 1809 | 1849 | |
| Richards, Franklin D. | 1821 | 1849 | |
| Richards, George F. | 1861 | 1906 | |
| Richards, LeGrand | 1886 | 1952 | |
| Richards, Stephen L. | 1879 | 1917 | |
| Richards, Willard | 1804 | 1840 | |
| Romney, Marion G. | 1897 | 1951 | |
| Scott, Richard G. | 1928 | 1988 | |
| Smith, George A. | 1817 | 1839 | |
| **Smith, George Albert** | **1870** | **1903** | **1945 Eighth President** |
| Smith, John H. | 1848 | 1880 | |
| **Smith, Joseph** | **1805** | **1829** | **1832 First President** |
| **Smith, Joseph F.** | **1838** | **1866** | **1901 Sixth President** |
| **Smith, Joseph Fielding** | **1876** | **1910** | **1970 Tenth President** |
| Smith, Hyrum | 1800 | 1837 | |
| Smith, Hyrum Mack | 1872 | 1901 | |
| Smith, William | 1811 | 1835 | |
| Smoot, Reed | 1862 | 1900 | |
| Snow, Erastus | 1818 | 1849 | |
| **Snow, Lorenzo** | **1814** | **1849** | **1898 Fifth President** |
| Stapley, Delbert L. | 1896 | 1950 | |
| Talmage, James E. | 1862 | 1911 | |
| Tanner, N. Eldon | 1898 | 1961 | |
| **Taylor, John** | **1808** | **1838** | **1880 Third President** |
| Taylor, John W. | 1858 | 1884 | |
| Teasdale, George | 1831 | 1882 | |
| Thatcher, Moses | 1842 | 1879 | |
| Wells, Daniel H. | 1814 | 1857 | |
| Wight, Lyman | 1796 | 1841 | |
| Whitney, Orson F. | 1855 | 1906 | |
| Widtsoe, John A. | 1872 | 1921 | |
| Wirthlin, Joseph B. | 1917 | 1986 | |
| Woodruff, Abraham O. | 1872 | 1897 | |
| **Woodruff, Wilford** | **1807** | **1839** | **1889 Fourth President** |
| **Young, Brigham** | **1801** | **1835** | **1847 Second President** |
| Young, Brigham, Jr. | 1836 | 1864 | |
| Young, Joseph A. | 1834 | 1864 | |
| Young, John W. | 1844 | 1855 | (at age of 11) |

| *Patriarch | Born | Ordained Patriarch |
|---|---|---|
| Smith, Eldred G. | 1907 | 1947 |
| Smith, Hyrum | 1800 | 1841 |
| Smith, Hyrum G | 1879 | 1912 |
| Smith, John | 1781 | 1849 |
| Smith, John | 1832 | 1855 |
| Smith, Joseph, Sr. | 1771 | 1833 |
| Smith, Joseph Fielding | 1899 | 1942 |
| Smith, William | 1811 | 1845 |

* Until October 6, 1979, when Eldred G. Smith was the last ordained patriarch, patriarchs to the Church were sustained as "prophets, seers and revelators" along with the apostles and members of the First Presidency. After Eldred G. Smith no patriarch to the Church has been sustained.

# BIBLIOGRAPHY A

## Official Publications of
## The Church of Jesus Christ of Latter-day Saints
(See Endnote 1, *Official Publications of The Church of Jesus Christ of Latter-day Saints*)

*We Believe* deviates from the normal methods of citing sources. Instead of indicating the earliest available references, *We Believe* cites for its primary sources those works officially published by the Church. These publications appear here in BIBLIOGRAPHY A.

Since many quotations taken from these Church publications appeared in works that were originally published elsewhere, these earlier publications are listed in BIBLIOGRAPHY B.

All Church publications are cited in abbreviated form, as set forth in the List of Abbreviations that follows:

## LIST OF ABBREVIATIONS
(Abbreviations to the *Standard Works—Bible, Book of Mormon, Doctrine & Covenants, and Pearl of Great Price*—follow immediately *after* this first set.)

**ACR**     Area Conference Report. Cited: ACR(Amsterdam)1976:4 (conference report of Amsterdam Netherlands Area Conference 1976, p. 4). The following are the cities cited (in italics) followed by the country in which the city is located:

        *Amsterdam*, Netherlands
        *Auckland*, New Zealand
        *Brisbane*, Australia
        *Copenhagen*, Denmark
        *Helsinki*, Finland
        *Honolulu*, Hawaii
        *London*, England
        *Manchester*, England
        *Manila*, Philippines
        *Melbourne*, Australia
        *Mexico City*, Mexico
        *Munich*, Germany
        *Nuku'alofa*, Tonga
        *Lima*, Peru
        *Paris*, France
        *San Jose*, Costa Rica
        *Santiago*, Chile
        *Sao Paulo*, Brazil
        *Seoul*, Korea
        *Stockholm*, Sweden
        *Sydney*, Australia
        *Taipei*, Taiwan, Republic of China
        *Tokyo*, Japan

**AF**     *Articles of Faith*. James E. Talmage. Salt Lake City: Deseret Book Company, 1988. [Note: Original was published by The Church of Jesus Christ of Latter-day Saints, 1899. It was last revised by the author in 1924. In 1984 it was reprinted by Deseret Book Company without change, except for revised typography and pagination.]

**AofF**     See AofF in the abbreviations listings for the Standard Works.

**BD**     Bible Dictionary. Published and bound with the Standard Works. Salt Lake City: The Church of Jesus Christ of Latter-day Saints, 1979.

**CHMR**     *Church History and Modern Revelation*. Joseph Fielding Smith. 2 vols., Salt Lake City: The Church of Jesus Christ of Latter-day Saints, 1953.

**CR**     Conference Report of a general annual or semi-annual conference of the Church. Cited: CR1974Oct:127 (Conference Report, October 1974, p. 127). [See Endnote 2 Regarding Conference Reports.]

**CWP**     *The Church Welfare Plan* [Gospel Doctrine Department course of study]. Salt Lake City: The Church of Jesus Christ of Latter-day Saints, 1946.

**DBY**     *Discourses of Brigham Young*. Sel. John A. Widtsoe. Salt Lake City: Deseret Book Company, 1941. [Copyrighted by The Church of Jesus Christ of Latter-day Saints.]

**DCCH**     *Doctrine and Covenants and Church History* [teacher's supplement]. Salt Lake City: The Church of Jesus Christ of Latter-day Saints, 1984.

**DCSM**     *Doctrine and Covenants* [student manual]. Salt Lake City: The Church of Jesus Christ of Latter-day Saints, 1981.

**DGSM**     *Doctrines of the Gospel* [student manual, Church Educational System]. Salt Lake City: The Church of Jesus Christ of Latter-day Saints, 1986.

**EN**     *Ensign*. Cited EN1986Nov:27 (*Ensign*, Nov. 1986, p. 27). [Note: Only editorials by the First Presidency or by a member of the First Presidency, articles and speeches by the President of the Church, and some conference addresses have been quoted; other articles are *not* used.]

**GP**     *Gospel Principles*. Salt Lake City: The Church of Jesus Christ of Latter-day Saints, 1985.

**HC**     *The History of the Church of Latter Day Saints*. Salt Lake City: The Church of Jesus Christ of Latter-day Saints, 1902. [2nd edition includes Introduction and Notes by B. H. Roberts. 7 vols. Salt Lake City: Deseret Book Company, 1964.]

**HL**     *The House of the Lord*. James E. Talmage. Salt Lake City: The Church of Jesus Christ of Latter-day Saints, 1912.

**HYMNS**     *Hymns of The Church of Jesus Christ of Latter-day Saints*. Salt Lake City: The Church of Jesus Christ of Latter-day Saints, 1985.

**IE**     *Improvement Era*. Cited: IE1966Nov:27 (*Improvement Era*, Nov. 1966, p. 27). [Note: Only editorials by the First Presidency or by a member of the First Presidency, articles and speeches by the President of the Church, and some conference addresses have been quoted; other articles are *not* used.]

**JD**     *Journal of Discourses*. [See BIBLIOGRAPHY B. This is not an official Church publication.]

**JTC**     *Jesus the Christ*. James E. Talmage. Salt Lake City: Deseret Book Company, 1945. [Note: Published by The Church of Jesus Christ of Latter-day Saints, see Preface to the 1915 edition. The official announcement of being published by the Church is found in MOFP4:340; also see MOFP4:347.]

**JST**   Joseph Smith Translation. Cited: JST Heb.7:19–21. [JST footnotes in King James Translation published by The Church of Jesus Christ of Latter-day Saints cited: JST(Matt.7:1 fn. a.); Appendix cited: JST(John 1:4–9 in Appendix).]

**LOF**   *Lectures on Faith.* Salt Lake City: Deseret Book Company, 1985. Cited LOF5:3 (Lecture 5, paragraph 3.) [Note: Published by The Church of Jesus Christ of Latter-day Saints from 1835 to 1921 as part of the Doctrine and Covenants. The Lectures on Faith were first delivered at the School of the Prophets in Kirtland, Ohio, 1834–1835. For a text slightly modified for purposes of clarification, see *The Lectures on Faith in Historical Perspective.* Ed. by Larry E. Dahl and Charles D. Tate, Jr. Provo: Religious Studies Center, Brigham Young University, 1990.

**MDPS**   *"Mormon" Doctrine Plain and Simple.* 6th ed. Charles W. Penrose. Independence: the Missions of the Church of Jesus Christ of Latter-day Saints in America, Press of Zion's Printing and Publishing Company, 1929.

**MGSP**   *Missionary Gospel Study Program* [student manual]. Salt Lake City: The Church of Jesus Christ of Latter-day Saints, 1988.

**MOFP**   *Messages of the First Presidency.* Ed. by James R. Clark. 6 vols. Salt Lake City: Bookcraft, Inc., 1965. Cited: MOFP4:203 (*Messages of the First Presidency*, Volume 4, p. 203). [Note: These are statements from the First Presidency of the Church published at various times by various means, such as letters directed to the stakes of the Church. However, this six-volume set was not published by or under the direction of the Church. **Each referenced item has, therefore, been checked** to ensure it is an official, published message of the First Presidency that has been published under the guidance or control of the Church to preserve the integrity of the letter, article, or speech.

**MPSG**   *Melchizedek Priesthood Personal Study Guide* [also titled, *A Course of Study for the Melchizedek Priesthood Quorums*]. Salt Lake City: The Church of Jesus Christ of Latter-day Saints, published annually. Cited: MPSG1983:123 (Melchizedek Personal Study Guide, 1983, p. 123).

**PCG**   *Priesthood and Church Government.* John A. Widtsoe. Salt Lake City: Deseret Book Company, 1939. [Note: Compiled under the direction of the Council of Twelve and copyrighted by The Church of Jesus Christ of Latter-day Saints. Used as a course of study for Melchizedek Priesthood quorums.]

**RSM**   *Relief Society Magazine.* Salt Lake City: The Church of Jesus Christ of Latter-day Saints, published annually.

**STG**   *Sharing the Gospel* [Religion 130 course manual, Church Education System, Department of Seminaries and Institutes of Religion]. Salt Lake City: The Church of Jesus Christ of Latter-day Saints, 1976.

**SNT**   *Sunday Night Talks.* James E. Talmage. Salt Lake City: The Church of Jesus Christ of Latter-day Saints, 1930.

**TLDP**   *Teachings of the Latter-day Prophets* [a publication of limited circulation]. Salt Lake City: The Church of Jesus Christ of Latter-day Saints, 1986.

**TPJS**   *Teachings of the Prophet Joseph Smith.* Comp. Joseph Fielding Smith. Salt Lake City: Deseret Book Company, 1976. [Note: Original was published by The Church of Jesus Christ of Latter-day Saints, 1938.]

## ABBREVIATIONS FOR THE STANDARD WORKS
### (The Bible, Book of Mormon, Doctrine and Covenants, and Pearl of Great Price)
Published in 1979 by The Church of Jesus Christ of Latter-day Saints

*We Believe* deviates slightly from standard abbreviations for the Standard Works. These deviations are made to condense the text to accommodate the two-column format of this book. (For example 1 John 2:2, appears as 1Jn.2:2; 2 Thess. 1:2 appears as 2Thess.1:2.) Also, liberty has been taken to change source citations that are found *within* quoted passages to make such citations, where appropriate, conform to all other abbreviations in this book.

Abbreviations that follow are first in *numerical* order, then in *alphabetical* Order.

| | | |
|---|---|---|
| **1Chr.** | 1 Chronicles | Old Testament |
| **1Cor.** | 1 Corinthians | New Testament |
| **1Jn.** | 1 John | New Testament |
| **1Kgs.** | 1 Kings | Old Testament |
| **1Ne.** | 1 Nephi | Book of Mormon |
| **1Pet.** | 1 Peter | New Testament |
| **1Sam.** | 1 Samuel | Old Testament |
| **1Thess.** | 1 Thessalonians | New Testament |
| **1Tim.** | 1 Timothy | New Testament |
| **2Chr.** | 2 Chronicles | Old Testament |
| **2Cor.** | 2 Corinthians | New Testament |
| **2Jn.** | 2 John | New Testament |
| **2Kgs.** | 2 Kings | Old Testament |
| **2Ne.** | 2 Nephi | Book of Mormon |
| **2Pet.** | 2 Peter | New Testament |
| **2Sam.** | 2 Samuel | Old Testament |
| **2Thess.** | 2 Thessalonians | New Testament |
| **2Tim.** | 2 Timothy | New Testament |
| **3Jn.** | 3 John | New Testament |
| **3Ne.** | 3 Nephi | Book of Mormon |
| **4Ne.** | 4 Nephi | Book of Mormon |
| **Abr.** | Abraham | Pearl of Great Price |
| **Acts** | Acts | New Testament |
| **Alma** | Alma | Book of Mormon |
| **Amos** | Amos | Old Testament |
| **AofF** | Articles of Faith | Pearl of Great Price |
| **Col.** | Colossians | New Testament |
| **D&C** | Doctrine and Covenants | Doctrine and Covenants |
| **D&C OD** | Official Declaration | Doctrine and Covenants |
| **Dan.** | Daniel | Old Testament |
| **Deut.** | Deuteronomy | Old Testament |
| **Eccl.** | Ecclesiastes | Old Testament |
| **Enos** | Enos | Book of Mormon |
| **Eph.** | Ephesians | New Testament |
| **Esth.** | Esther | Old Testament |
| **Ether** | Ether | Book of Mormon |
| **Ex.** | Exodus | Old Testament |
| **Ezek.** | Ezekiel | Old Testament |
| **Ezra** | Ezra | Old Testament |

| Gal. | Galatians | New Testament |
|------|-----------|---------------|
| **Gen.** | Genesis | Old Testament |
| **Hab.** | Habakkuk | Old Testament |
| **Hag.** | Haggai | Old Testament |
| **Heb.** | Hebrews | New Testament |
| **Hel.** | Helaman | Book of Mormon |
| **Hosea** | Hosea | Old Testament |
| **Isa.** | Isaiah | Old Testament |
| **Jacob** | Jacob | Book of Mormon |
| **James** | James | New Testament |
| **Jarom** | Jarom | Book of Mormon |
| **Jer.** | Jeremiah | Old Testament |
| **Job** | Job | Old Testament |
| **Joel** | Joel | Old Testament |
| **John** | John | New Testament |
| **Jonah** | Jonah | Old Testament |
| **Josh.** | Joshua | Old Testament |
| **JS-H** | Joseph Smith—History | Pearl of Great Price |
| **JS-M** | Joseph Smith—Matthew | Pearl of Great Price |
| **Jude** | Jude | New Testament |
| **Judg.** | Judges | Old Testament |
| **Lam.** | Lamentations | Old Testament |
| **Lev.** | Leviticus | Old Testament |
| **Luke** | Luke | New Testament |
| **Mal.** | Malachi | Old Testament |
| **Mark** | Mark | New Testament |
| **Matt.** | Matthew | New Testament |
| **Micah** | Micah | Old Testament |
| **Morm.** | Mormon | Book of Mormon |
| **Moro.** | Moroni | Book of Mormon |
| **Moses** | Moses | Pearl of Great Price |
| **Mosiah** | Mosiah | Book of Mormon |
| **Nahum** | Nahum | Old Testament |
| **Neh.** | Nehemiah | Old Testament |
| **Num.** | Numbers | Old Testament |
| **Obad.** | Obadiah | Old Testament |
| **Omni** | Omni | Book of Mormon |
| **Philem.** | Philemon | New Testament |
| **Philip.** | Philippians | New Testament |
| **Prov.** | Proverbs | Old Testament |
| **Ps.** | Psalms | Old Testament |
| **Rev.** | Revelation | New Testament |
| **Rom.** | Romans | New Testament |
| **Ruth** | Ruth | Old Testament |
| **Song.** | Song of Solomon | Old Testament |
| **Titus** | Titus | New Testament |
| **WofM** | Words of Mormon | Book of Mormon |
| **Zech.** | Zechariah | Old Testament |
| **Zeph.** | Zephaniah | Old Testament |

## ENDNOTES TO BIBLIOGRAPHY A

### 1. Official Publications of The Church of Jesus Christ of Latter-day Saints:

An "Official Publication" of the Church is defined in this book as any printed matter officially promulgated or published by the Church, including:

(1) **The Standard Works**: Bible, Book of Mormon, Doctrine and Covenants, and Pearl of Great Price.

(2) **Official Conference Reports** of general annual or semiannual conferences of the Church and official conference reports of area conferences (see Endnote 2).

(3) **Melchizedek Priesthood Study Guides**, or manuals.

(4) **Church Lesson Manuals**: includes only those manuals actually published by The Church of Jesus Christ of Latter-day Saints.

(5) **Books or Pamphlets**, those published or copyrighted by The Church of Jesus Christ of Latter-day Saints, or by the President of the Church. [Note: The act of copyrighting in the United States consists in part of publishing the work to be copyrighted.]

(6) **Articles and Editorials** written by the President of the Church, the First Presidency, or President of the Quorum of the Twelve that have been published with the consent of the writer—actual or implied—in any Church-owned magazine and in the *Church News*. Not included are articles published in any other newspaper or magazine; this is because there is no assurance that the article has been printed exactly as was given.

(7) **Published Speeches** of the President of the Church published with his implied consent. This includes publication in any Church-owned magazine or in the *Church News*. Not included are articles published in any other newspaper or magazine; this is because there is no assurance that the article has been printed exactly as was given.

(8) **Letters** written by the First Presidency or President of the Church to a Church unit—as opposed to private letters not intended for publication. Most letters referred to are referenced in *Messages of the First Presidency* for ease of access, because official letters of the First Presidency are not otherwise generally available in libraries.

### 2. Conference Reports

Because the official reports of the general conference proceedings of the Church constitute a major resource for this book, the following information is provided:

"The institutionalization of the general conferences as we know them to be today dates back to the 1838–1841 period [of Church history] when the earliest consecutive precedents for the annual and semi-annual conferences and for their being held in the months of April and October were established." (See *A Study of the General Conferences of The Church of Jesus Christ of Latter-day Saints, 1830–1901*. Jay R. Lowe's master's thesis (Provo: Brigham Young University, 1972), p. 433.)

Printed reports of the proceedings of general conferences of the Church were first published in self-contained pamphlet form in April 1880 and again in October 1897. From that time to the present, conference reports have been published regularly. I have treated all conference reports that were printed in self-contained pamphlet or booklet form as official publications of the Church, even though the pamphlets prior to October 1921 indicate that they were published by the Deseret News

(Deseret Printing and Publishing Establishment, April 1880; Deseret News Publishing Co., 1898–1902; Deseret News, 1903–1919; and Deseret Book Company, 1920 and April 1921).

Although I have been unable to locate any official announcement regarding official or non-official publication of the conference reports prior to 1921, the Church seems to have sanctioned the printing of conference proceedings in pamphlet form since the first pamphlet was published in 1880. From the time of the publication of that Jubilee issue of April 1880 and continuing with the next issue in 1897, seventeen and a half years later, down to the present day, the Church has at the least permitted, and probably encouraged or directed the publication of annual and semiannual conference proceedings in pamphlet form. During all that time the conference reports have been faithfully printed and published with no disclaimer by the Church. (In October 1921 the conference report booklets contained for the first time the inscription, "Published by The Church of Jesus Christ of Latter-day Saints, Salt Lake City, Utah."

The fact that the Church controlled the companies that printed and published the conference report pamphlets adds further credence to the position that all the conference reports prior to October 1921 were "published" by the Church. The Deseret News (Deseret Printing and Publishing Establishment; Deseret News Publishing Co.) was either owned and controlled by the Church or was the "official organ of the Church" during the entire period in which the Deseret News printed and published those pamphlets containing the conference proceedings. (See *Voice in the West*, Wendell J. Ashton (New York: Duell, Sloan & Pearce, 1950), pp. 207–26.) On September 14, 1892, for example, the following announcement appeared in the *Deseret Evening News*: "On the first day of October next there will be an entire change in the management of the *Deseret News*. The paper, however, will . . . remain the *official organ* of the Church of Jesus Christ of Latter-day Saints."

The same may be said of the Deseret Book Company, which operated as an appendage to the Church. Deseret Book Company was formed in 1920, the year it published the 1920 issues of the conference reports. It published one more issue, the April 1921 issue, after which the conference booklets no longer displayed either the Deseret Book Company or the Deseret News inscriptions. (See *Voice in the West*, Ashton, p. 284; also see *Deseret Book Company 1866–1976*, (Salt Lake City: Deseret Book Company, 1976) p. 11.)

The Church has encouraged members to acquire and read the conference reports. In a preface to the first pamphlet published in April 1880, there appears the following explanation for publishing conference reports in pamphlet form:

> In compliance with widely expressed wish, we herewith publish the proceedings of the late Conference in pamphlet form. It is believed that in this shape the excellent and inspiring instructions imparted during the Conference will be made much more available for general reference and distribution, and will be appreciated by those who desire to preserve the services of the Jubilee Conference.

In the April 1929 general conference, Elder George F. Richards, a member of the Quorum of the Twelve, encouraged the Saints to obtain copies of the conference booklets:

> The proceedings of these meetings have been kept and will be printed verbatim and appear in a pamphlet or booklet known as the Conference Pamphlet, for distribution. I think that these pamphlets ought to be found more generally in the homes of the saints. I think we should publish a very great many more of them than we have had need for in the past. . . . ¶ . . . . The Lord has blessed the Church with some very efficient teachers of his word . . . and I appreciate them, and I would like the members of the Church to have the opportunity of receiving these gems of information and truth. If I can leave this word impressed upon the minds of Latter-day Saints in such a way that they will secure the Conference Pamphlet, and possibly in their home evenings consider it with their sons and daughters, then I shall feel that my remarks have not been made in vain. (Conference Report, April 1929, pp. 115, 116-17)

Prior to the publication of the 1880 conference proceedings in pamphlet form, select conference discourses were printed at random in various publications. Only in 1880 and thereafter were all of the conference talks printed and published together in a self-contained booklet. In contrast, the *Journal of Discourses* and other collections of discourses contain assembled talks by General Authorities and other leading brethren in the Church, all of which were *collected and printed privately*—not as conference reports, and not published by the Church. The institution of a regular annual and semiannual conference schedule does not seem to have become an established pattern in the Church until 1840. The reporting of the full proceedings of general conference sessions began forty years later with the Jubilee Conference in April 1880. (See *A Study of the General Conferences*, Lowe.)

# BIBLIOGRAPHY B

## Arranged by Title of Publication

See Bibliography A, List of Abbreviations, for descriptions of the official publications of The Church of Jesus Christ of Latter-day Saints that are frequently referenced in *We Believe.*

*Abundance of the Heart, The.* Arthur Henry King. Salt Lake City: Bookcraft, 1986.

*Abundant Life, The.* Hugh B. Brown. Salt Lake City: Bookcraft, 1965.

*Answers to Gospel Questions.* Comp. by Joseph Fielding Smith, Jr. 5 vols. Salt Lake City: Deseret Book Company, 1957–66.

*Approaching Zion.* Hugh Nibley. Salt Lake City: Deseret Book, 1989.

*Autobiography of Parley Parker Pratt.* Ed. by Parley P. Pratt. Salt Lake City: Deseret Book Company, 1938.

*Bible, A Bible, A.* Robert Matthews. Salt Lake City: Bookcraft, 1990.

*Brigham Young University Speeches of the Year.* Provo: Brigham Young University Press, published annually.

*Charge to Religious Educators, The.* Salt Lake City: The Church of Jesus Christ of Latter-day Saints, 1977.

*Church News.* Salt Lake City: Deseret News, published weekly.

*Cowley and Whitney on Doctrine.* Comp. Forace Green. Salt Lake City: Bookcraft, 1963.

*Decisions for Successful Living.* Harold B. Lee. Salt Lake City: Deseret Book Company, 1973.

*Discourses of Wilford Woodruff, The.* Sel. by G. Homer Durham. Salt Lake City: Bookcraft, 1946.

*Doctrinal New Testament Commentary.* Bruce R. McConkie. 3 vols. Salt Lake City: Bookcraft, 1965.

*Doctrine and Covenants Commentary.* Rev. ed. Hyrum M. Smith and Janne M. Sjodahl. Salt Lake City: Deseret Book Company, 1972.

*Doctrines of Salvation.* Joseph Fielding Smith. 3 vols. Salt Lake City: Bookcraft, 1954–56.

*Elijah the Prophet and His Mission, and Salvation Universal.* Joseph Fielding Smith. Salt Lake City: Deseret Book Company, 1957.

*Eternal Quest.* Sel. by Charles Manley Brown. Salt Lake City: Bookcraft, 1956.

*Even As I Am.* Neal A. Maxwell. Salt Lake City: Deseret Book Company, 1982.

*Evidences and Reconciliations.* Ed. by G. Homer Durham. 3 vols. in 1. Salt Lake City: Bookcraft, 1960.

*Faith Precedes the Miracle.* Spencer W. Kimball. Salt Lake City: Deseret Book Company, 1972.

*Faith to Live By, A.* Mark E. Petersen. Salt Lake City: Bookcraft, 1959.

*Far West Record.* Ed. by Donald Q. Cannon and Lyndon W. Cook. Salt Lake City: Deseret Book Company, 1983.

*Fundamentals of Religion: A Series of Radio Addresses.* Independence: Zion's Printing and Publishing Co., 1945.

*Funk & Wagnalls Standard College Dictionary.* Pleasantville: The Readers Digest Association, 1966.

*Gospel Doctrine.* 5th ed. Salt Lake City: Deseret Book Company, 1939.

*Gospel Ideals.* David O. McKay. Salt Lake City: Improvement Era, 1953.

*Gospel Interpretations.* John A. Widtsoe. Salt Lake City: Bookcraft, 1947.

*Gospel Kingdom, The.* John Taylor. Sel. by G. Homer Durham. Salt Lake City: Bookcraft, 1943.

*Gospel Standards.* Heber J. Grant. Comp. by G. Homer Durham. Salt Lake City: Improvement Era, 1941.

*Gospel Truth.* Sel. by Jerreld L. Newquist. 2 vols. Salt Lake City: Deseret Book Company, 1957.

*Gospel Themes.* Orson F. Whitney. Salt Lake City: The Church of Jesus Christ of Latter-day Saints, 1914.

*Government of God, The.* John Taylor. Liverpool: S. W. Richards, 1852.

*Great Prologue, The.* Mark E. Petersen. Salt Lake City: Deseret Book Company, 1975.

*Great Apostasy, The.* James E. Talmage. Salt Lake City: Deseret Book Company, 1968.

*His Servants Speak.* R. Clayton Brough. Bountiful: Horizon Publishers, 1975.

*Holy Temple, The.* Boyd K. Packer. Salt Lake City: Bookcraft, 1980.

*Home Memories of President David O. McKay.* Salt Lake City: Deseret Book Company, 1956.

*Isaiah for Today.* Mark E. Petersen. Salt Lake City: Deseret Book Company, 1981.

*Items on Priesthood.* John Taylor. Salt Lake City: George Q. Cannon and Sons, 1899.

*Joseph Smith as Scientist.* Salt Lake City: The General Board and Young Men's Mutual Improvement Association, 1908.

*Joseph Smith: Seeker after Truth, Prophet of God.* John A. Widtsoe. Salt Lake City: Bookcraft, 1957.

*Journal of Discourses.* 26 vols. Liverpool: R. D. and S. W. Richards, 1854–56. [Cited: JD1:232 (*Journal of Discourses*, Volume 1, p. 232).]

*Key to the Science of Theology.* Parley P. Pratt. 9th ed. Salt Lake City: Deseret Book Company, 1965.

*Kingdom of God, The.* Orson Pratt. Liverpool: R. James, Printer, 1848.

*Latter-day Prophets and the Doctrine and Covenants, The.* Roy W. Doxey. 4 vols. Salt Lake City: Deseret Book Company, 1978.

*Learning for the Eternities.* Marion G. Romney. Comp. by George J. Romney. Salt Lake City: Deseret Book Company, 1977.

*Lectures on Faith in Historical Perspective, The.* Dennis R. Rasmussen. Provo: Religious Study Center, Brigham Young University. [Dist. by Bookcraft, 1990.]

*Let Every Man Learn His Duty.* Marion G. Romney. Salt Lake City: Deseret Book Company, 1976.

*Look to God and Live.* Marion G. Romney. Comp. by George J. Romney. Salt Lake City: Deseret Book Company, 1971.

*Lord's Way, The.* Dallin H. Oaks. Salt Lake City: Deseret Book Company, 1991.

*Malachi and the Great and Dreadful Day.* Mark E. Petersen. Salt Lake City: Deseret Book Company, 1983.

*Man and the Dragon.* John A. Widtsoe. Salt Lake City: Bookcraft, 1945.

*Man: His Origin and Destiny.* Joseph Fielding Smith. Salt Lake City: Deseret Book Company, 1954.

*Man May Know for Himself: Teachings of President David O. McKay.* Comp. by Clare Midddlemiss. Salt Lake City: Deseret Book Company, 1967.

*Marion G. Romney: His Life and Faith.* F. Burton Howard. Salt Lake City: Bookcraft, 1988.

*Masterful Discourses and Writings of Orson Pratt.* Comp. by N. B. Lundwall Salt Lake City: Bookcraft, 1962.

*Matthew Cowley Speaks.* Salt Lake City: Deseret Book Company, 1954.

*Mediation and the Atonement, The.* John Taylor. Salt Lake City: Deseret News Co., 1882.

*Melvin J. Ballard, Crusader for Righteousness.* Salt Lake City: Melvin R. Ballard, 1966.

*Messages of the Doctrine and Covenants, The.* Ed. by G. Homer Durham. Salt Lake City: Bookcraft, 1969.

*Messages of the First Presidency.* James R. Clark. 6 vols. Salt Lake City: Bookcraft, 1965.

*Millennial Messiah, The.* Bruce R. McConkie. Salt Lake City: Deseret Book Company, 1982.

*Miracle of Forgiveness, The.* Spencer W. Kimball. Salt Lake City: Bookcraft, 1969.

*Mormon Doctrine.* Bruce R. McConkie. 2nd ed. Salt Lake City: Bookcraft, 1966.

*Mortal Messiah, The.* Bruce R. McConkie. 4 vols. Salt Lake City: Deseret Book Company, 1979–81.

*New Webster Encyclopedic Dictionary of the English Language, The.* Chicago: Consolidated Book Publishers, MCMLII.

*New Witness for the Articles of Faith, A.* Bruce R. McConkie. Salt Lake City: Deseret Book Company, 1985.

*On the Way to Immortality and Eternal Life.* J. Reuben Clark. Salt Lake City: Deseret Book Company, 1961.

*Out of My Life and Thoughts.* Albert Schweitzer. New York: Mentor Book. 1963.

*Pathways to Happiness.* Comp. by Llewelyn R. McKay. Salt Lake City: Bookcraft, 1957.

*Prayer.* Salt Lake City: Deseret Book Company, 1977.

*President Kimball Speaks Out.* Salt Lake City: Deseret Book Company, 1981.

*Program of the Church.* John A. Widtsoe. Salt Lake City: Deseret Book Company, 1937.

*Promised Messiah, The.* Bruce R. McConkie. Salt Lake City: Deseret Book Company, 1978.

*Prophetic Book of Mormon, The.* Hugh Nibley. Salt Lake City: Deseret Book Company, 1989.

*Random House Dictionary of the English Language, The.* 2nd ed. Unabridged. New York: Random House, Inc., 1987.

*Rational Theology, A.* John A. Widtsoe. Salt Lake City: Deseret Book Company, 1915.

*Restoration of All Things, The.* Joseph Fielding Smith. Salt Lake City: Deseret Book Company, 1945.

*Richard L. Evans: The Man and the Message.* Comp. by Richard L. Evans, Jr. Salt Lake City:

Bookcraft, 1973.

*Saturday Night Thoughts.* Orson F. Whitney. Salt Lake City: Deseret Book Company, 1921.

*Seek Ye Earnestly.* Joseph Fielding Smith. Salt Lake City: Deseret Book Company, 1970.

*Sermons and Missionary Services of Melvin J. Ballard.* Comp. by Bryant S. Hinckley. Salt Lake City: Deseret Book Company, 1949.

*Sharing the Gospel with Others.* Comp. by Preston Nibley. Salt Lake City: Deseret Book Company, 1948.

*Stand Ye in Holy Places.* Harold B. Lee. Salt Lake City: Deseret Book Company, 1974.

*Study of the General Conferences of The Church of Jesus Christ of Latter-day Saints, 1830–1901, A.* Jay R. Lowe. Master's thesis. Provo: Brigham Young University, 1972.

*Take Heed to Yourselves.* Joseph Fielding Smith. Salt Lake City: Deseret Book Company, 1971.

*Teachings of Ezra Taft Benson.* Ed. Salt Lake City: Bookcraft, 1988.

*Teachings of Lorenzo Snow, The.* Ed. by Clyde J. Williams. Salt Lake City: Bookcraft, 1984.

*Teachings of Spencer W. Kimball, The.* Ed. by Edward L. Kimball. Salt Lake City: Bookcraft, 1982.

*That All May Be Edified.* Boyd K. Packer. Salt Lake City: Publishers Press, 1982.

*Treasures of Life.* David O. McKay. Comp. by Clare Midddlemiss. Salt Lake City: Deseret Book Company, 1962.

*Understanding Religion, An.* John A. Widtsoe. Salt Lake City: Deseret Book Company, 1944.

*Vision, or the Degrees of Glory, The.* Comp. by N. B. Lundwall. Kaysville: Inland Printing Co., 1951.

*Visions of Zion.* Alexander B. Morrison. Salt Lake City: Deseret Book Company, 1993.

*Vitality of Mormonism, The.* James E. Talmage. Boston: Richard G. Badger, 1919.

*Way of the Master, The.* Hugh B. Brown. Salt Lake City: Bookcraft, 1974.

*Way to Perfection, The.* Joseph Fielding Smith. Salt Lake City: Genealogical Society of Utah, 1940.

*Weight of Glory, The.* C. S. Lewis. New York: Collier Books, Macmillan Publishing Company, 1980.

*We Will Prove Them Herewith.* Neal A. Maxwell. Salt Lake City: Deseret Book Company, 1982.

*Where is Wisdom?* Stephen L. Richards. Salt Lake City: Deseret Book Company, 1955.

*Why the Religious Life?* Mark E. Petersen. Salt Lake City: Deseret News Press, 1930.

*Woman.* Ezra Taft Benson. Salt Lake City: Deseret Book Company, 1979.

*Word of Wisdom; A Modern Interpretation, The.* Rev. ed. Salt Lake City: Deseret Book Company, 1950.

*Words of Joseph Smith, The.* Comp. by Andrew F. Ehat and Lyndon W. Cook. Salt Lake City: Bookcraft, 1980.

*Word Studies in the New Testament.* Marvin R. Vincent, D.D. 4 vols. McLean: Macdonald Publishing Company.

*Ye Are the Light of the World.* Harold B. Lee. Salt Lake City: Deseret Book Company, 1974.

*Your Faith and You.* Mark E. Petersen. Salt Lake City: Bookcraft, 1963.

# SCRIPTURE INDEX

The following scripture index cross-references all scripture quotations from the Standard Works of the Church to the Doctrinal Statement numbers—not to page numbers. Those who wish to mark the Doctrinal Statement numbers in their scriptures can do so from this Index.

**The Holy Bible** (King James Version—Published 1981 by The Church of Jesus Christ of Latter-day Saints)

**Old Testament**

**Genesis**

| | | | | | | | |
|---|---|---|---|---|---|---|---|
| 1:26 | D-118 D-429 | 22:2 | D-96 | 20:5 | D-789 | 22:2 | D-766 |
| 1:27 | D-118 D-204 | 22:10 | D-96 | 20:6 | D-789 | 22:32 | D-766 |
| | D-248 D-429 | 22:11 | D-96 | 20:7 | D-766 D-890 | 23:3 | D-685 |
| 1:28 | D-204 | 22:12 | D-96 | 20:8 | D-682 | 24:16 | D-336 |
| 1:29 | D-120 | 22:17 | D-102 | 20:9 | D-682 | 25:35 | D-94 |
| 2:1 | D-119 | 22:18 | D-102 | 20:10 | D-682 D-686 | 25:36 | D-94 |
| 2:2 | D-119 | 28:3 | D-103 | 20:11 | D-119 D-682 | 25:37 | D-94 |
| 2:4 | D-117 | 28:4 | D-103 | 20:12 | D-76 D-212 | 25:38 | D-94 |
| 2:3 | D-117 D-682 | 28:10 | D-676 | | D-863 | 26:3 | D-486 |
| 2:4 | D-117 D-554 | 28:11 | D-676 | 20:13 | D-768 | 26:4 | D-486 |
| 2:5 | D-117 D-554 | 28:12 | D-676 | 20:14 | D-779 | 26:5 | D-486 |
| 2:7 | D-430 | 28:13 | D-676 | 20:15 | D-342 | 26:6 | D-486 |
| 2:18 | D-205 D-434 | 28:14 | D-676 | 20:16 | D-767 | 26:7 | D-486 |
| 2:22 | D-205 | 28:15 | D-676 | 21:15 | D-76 | 26:8 | D-486 |
| 2:23 | D-205 | 28:16 | D-676 | 21:16 | D-342 | 26:9 | D-486 |
| 2:24 | D-205 D-434 | 28:22 | D-827 | 21:17 | D-76 | 26:10 | D-486 |
| 2:25 | D-205 | 35:9 | D-103 | 22:14 | D-346 | 26:11 | D-486 |
| 3:1 | D-192 | 35:10 | D-103 | 23:1 | D-767 | 26:12 | D-486 |
| 3:2 | D-192 | 35:11 | D-103 | 31:12 | D-682 | 26:33 | D-227 |
| 3:3 | D-192 | 37:5 | D-676 | 31:13 | D-682 D-683 | | |
| 3:4 | D-192 | 37:9 | D-676 | 31:14 | D-682 | **Numbers** | |
| 3:5 | D-192 | 43:9 | D-349 | 31:15 | D-682 D-685 | 5:7 | D-633 |
| 3:6 | D-192 D-193 | 46:2 | D-240 | 31:16 | D-683 | 6:26 | D-672 |
| 3:8 | D-190 | | | 31:17 | D-683 | 12:6 | D-606 |
| 3:16 | D-196 D-200 | **Exodus** | | 34:6 | D-251 | 16:22 | D-283 |
| 3:17 | D-201 | 3:1 | D-889 | 34:7 | D-251 | 19:9 | D-613 |
| 3:18 | D-201 | 3:2 | D-889 | 34:14 | D-787 | 21:7 | D-530 |
| 3:19 | D-201 D-858 | 3:3 | D-889 | | | 23:19 | D-252 |
| | D-870 | 3:4 | D-274 D-889 | **Leviticus** | | 30:2 | D-349 |
| 5:1 | D-118 | 3:5 | D-274 D-889 | 6:1 | D-346 | | |
| 5:2 | D-118 | 3:6 | D-274 | 6:2 | D-346 | **Deuteronomy** | |
| 5:24 | D-829 | 3:15 | D-274 | 6:3 | D-346 | 4:25 | D-789 |
| 6:5 | D-821 D-826 | 3:16 | D-274 | 6:4 | D-346 D-633 | 4:26 | D-789 |
| 6:6 | D-821 D-826 | 4:10 | D-463 | 6:5 | D-633 | 4:27 | D-229 |
| 6:7 | D-826 | 4:11 | D-463 | 18:21 | D-766 | 4:28 | D-229 |
| 9:1 | D-204 | 4:12 | D-463 | 18:23 | D-783 | 4:29 | D-229 |
| 12:2 | D-102 | 14:13 | D-178 D-184 | 19:4 | D-789 | 4:30 | D-229 |
| 12:3 | D-102 | 14:14 | D-178 D-184 | 19:13 | D-343 | 4:31 | D-229 |
| 17:1 | D-102 | 14:15 | D-178 D-184 | 19:16 | D-764 | 5:13 | D-686 |
| 17:2 | D-102 | 14:16 | D-178 D-184 | 19:17 | D-501 | 5:14 | D-686 |
| 17:3 | D-102 | 16:7 | D-799 | 19:18 | D-421 D-501 | 6:6 | D-214 |
| 17:4 | D-102 | 16:8 | D-799 | 19:30 | D-889 | 6:7 | D-214 |
| 17:5 | D-102 | 19:3 | D-103 | 19:35 | D-343 | 8:2 | D-1 D-4 |
| 17:6 | D-102 | 19:4 | D-103 | 19:36 | D-343 | 8:3 | D-745 |
| 17:7 | D-102 | 19:5 | D-103 | 19:37 | D-343 | 8:5 | D-216 |
| 18:14 | D-832 | 19:6 | D-103 | 20:13 | D-782 | 8:19 | D-787 |
| | | 20:2 | D-787 | 20:15 | D-783 | 8:20 | D-787 |
| | | 20:3 | D-787 | 20:16 | D-783 | 10:12 | D-887 |
| | | 20:4 | D-789 | 21:23 | D-812 | 11:18 | D-214 |

| | | | | | | | |
|---|---|---|---|---|---|---|---|
| 5:28 | D-777 D-779 | 8:33 | D-163 | 19:14 | D-73 | 25:12 | D-739 |
| | D-825 | 9:4 | D-821 D-823 | 19:16 | D-768 | 25:13 | D-739 |
| 5:38 | D-423 D-500 | 9:12 | D-621 | 19:17 | D-768 | 25:14 | D-373 |
| 5:39 | D-423 D-500 | 9:13 | D-621 | 19:18 | D-342 D-767 | 25:15 | D-373 |
| 5:40 | D-423 D-500 | 10:8 | D-241 D-243 | | D-768 D-779 | 25:16 | D-373 |
| 5:41 | D-423 D-500 | 10:28 | D-123 D-490 | 19:26 | D-832 | 25:17 | D-373 |
| 5:42 | D-423 | | D-753 D-759 | 19:28 | D-380 | 25:18 | D-373 |
| 5:44 | D-422 D-423 | 10:39 | D-740 | 19:29 | D-96 | 25:19 | D-373 |
| | D-509 D-530 | 10:40 | D-798 | 21:21 | D-510 | 25:20 | D-373 |
| | D-531 | 10:41 | D-798 | 21:22 | D-510 | 25:21 | D-373 |
| 5:45 | D-422 D-509 | 11:28 | D-3 | 22:17 | D-309 | 25:31 | D-378 D-388 |
| 5:46 | D-422 D-423 | 11:29 | D-3 | 22:18 | D-309 | | D-726 |
| | D-509 | 11:30 | D-3 | 22:19 | D-309 | 25:32 | D-378 D-388 |
| 5:47 | D-422 D-509 | 12:12 | D-690 | 22:20 | D-309 | | D-726 |
| 5:48 | D-422 D-423 | 12:25 | D-823 D-845 | 22:21 | D-309 | 25:33 | D-378 D-388 |
| | D-509 D-707 | 12:31 | D-336 D-790 | 22:36 | D-421 D-887 | | D-726 |
| 6:6 | D-548 | 12:32 | D-336 D-790 | | D-892 | 25:34 | D-427 D-726 |
| 6:7 | D-519 D-550 | 12:36 | D-369 D-764 | 22:37 | D-421 D-426 | | D-748 |
| 6:8 | D-550 | 12:37 | D-369 D-764 | | D-887 D-892 | 25:35 | D-427 D-744 |
| 6:9 | D-535 D-550 | 13:24 | D-25 | 22:38 | D-421 D-426 | | D-748 |
| 6:10 | D-535 D-550 | 13:25 | D-25 | | D-887 D-892 | 25:36 | D-427 D-744 |
| 6:11 | D-535 D-550 | 13:26 | D-25 | 22:39 | D-421 D-426 | | D-748 |
| 6:12 | D-535 D-550 | 13:27 | D-25 | | D-887 D-892 | 25:37 | D-427 D-744 |
| 6:13 | D-535 D-550 | 13:28 | D-25 | 22:40 | D-421 D-426 | | D-748 |
| 6:14 | D-225 | 13:29 | D-25 | | D-887 D-892 | 25:38 | D-427 D-744 |
| 6:15 | D-225 | 13:30 | D-25 | 23:11 | D-356 | | D-748 |
| 6:21 | D-825 | 14:30 | D-184 | 23:12 | D-356 | 25:39 | D-427 D-744 |
| 6:24 | D-848 | 14:31 | D-184 | 23:25 | D-625 | | D-748 |
| 6:25 | D-93 | 15:3 | D-863 | 23:26 | D-625 | 25:40 | D-427 D-744 |
| 6:26 | D-93 | 15:4 | D-76 D-863 | 23:27 | D-350 | | D-748 |
| 6:27 | D-93 | 15:5 | D-76 D-863 | 23:28 | D-350 | 25:41 | D-161 D-388 |
| 6:28 | D-93 | 15:6 | D-76 D-863 | 24:14 | D-405 D-455 | 25:46 | D-388 |
| 6:29 | D-93 | 15:7 | D-27 D-863 | 24:24 | D-25 D-406 | 26:26 | D-695 D-700 |
| 6:30 | D-93 | 15:8 | D-863 | 24:26 | D-727 | 26:27 | D-695 D-700 |
| 6:31 | D-93 | 15:9 | D-27 D-863 | 24:27 | D-727 | 26:28 | D-695 D-700 |
| 6:32 | D-93 | 15:28 | D-180 | 24:28 | D-727 | 26:36 | D-41 |
| 6:33 | D-93 | 16:19 | D-437 D-574 | 24:29 | D-727 | 26:37 | D-41 |
| 7:1 | D-424 | | D-597 D-597 | 24:30 | D-727 | 26:38 | D-41 |
| 7:2 | D-424 | 16:27 | D-729 | 24:35 | D-253 | 26:39 | D-41 D-279 |
| 7:3 | D-424 | 16:28 | D-829 | 24:36 | D-728 | 26:40 | D-41 |
| 7:4 | D-424 | 17:20 | D-178 | 24:37 | D-407 | 26:41 | D-41 D-535 |
| 7:5 | D-424 | 17:21 | D-529 | 24:38 | D-407 | 26:42 | D-41 D-279 |
| 7:7 | D-510 D-550 | 18:1 | D-351 | 24:39 | D-407 | 26:43 | D-41 |
| | D-836 | 18:2 | D-351 | 24:42 | D-731 | 26:44 | D-41 |
| 7:8 | D-510 D-836 | 18:3 | D-351 | 24:43 | D-731 | 26:45 | D-41 |
| 7:16 | D-467 | 18:4 | D-351 | 24:44 | D-731 | 26:46 | D-41 |
| 7:17 | D-467 | 18:11 | D-460 | 25:1 | D-739 | 26:52 | D-500 |
| 7:18 | D-467 | 18:12 | D-460 | 25:2 | D-739 | 27:46 | D-43 |
| 7:19 | D-467 | 18:13 | D-460 | 25:3 | D-739 | 27:50 | D-653 |
| 7:20 | D-467 | 18:16 | D-655 | 25:4 | D-739 | 27:51 | D-653 |
| 7:21 | D-479 D-483 | 18:19 | D-91 | 25:5 | D-739 | 27:52 | D-33 D-124 |
| 8:26 | D-833 | 18:20 | D-91 | 25:6 | D-739 | | D-653 |
| 8:28 | D-163 | 18:21 | D-223 | 25:7 | D-739 | 27:53 | D-33 D-124 |
| 8:29 | D-163 | 18:22 | D-223 | 25:8 | D-739 | | D-653 |
| 8:30 | D-163 | 19:5 | D-435 | 25:9 | D-739 | 28:5 | D-360 |
| 8:31 | D-163 | 19:6 | D-435 | 25:10 | D-739 | 28:6 | D-360 |
| 8:32 | D-163 | 19:13 | D-73 | 25:11 | D-739 | 28:7 | D-360 |

| | | | | | | | |
|---|---|---|---|---|---|---|---|
| 1:30 | D-491 D-764 | 2:10 | D-665 | 12:9 | D-236 D-241 | 5:19 | D-614 D-785 |
| 1:31 | D-491 | 2:11 | D-665 | | D-245 | 5:20 | D-614 D-785 |
| 1:32 | D-491 D-764 | 2:12 | D-665 | 12:10 | D-236 D-237 | 5:21 | D-614 D-785 |
| 2:12 | D-372 | 2:13 | D-665 | | D-238 D-244 | 5:22 | D-338 D-505 |
| 3:10 | D-757 | 2:14 | D-665 | | D-333 | 5:23 | D-338 D-505 |
| 3:23 | D-36 D-757 | 2:15 | D-665 | 12:11 | D-236 | 5:24 | D-338 D-505 |
| 3:27 | D-773 | 2:16 | D-665 | 12:28 | D-576 | 5:25 | D-338 D-505 |
| 5:1 | D-392 | 3:16 | D-473 D-821 | 13:5 | D-821 | 6:7 | D-386 D-742 |
| 5:3 | D-2 | | D-877 | 14:6 | D-238 | 6:8 | D-386 D-742 |
| 5:4 | D-2 | 3:17 | D-473 D-821 | 14:8 | D-805 | 6:9 | D-386 D-742 |
| 5:5 | D-2 | | D-877 | 14:9 | D-805 | | |
| 5:9 | D-392 | 6:1 | D-501 | 14:15 | D-475 | **Ephesians** | |
| 6:3 | D-56 D-58 | 6:2 | D-379 D-501 | 14:19 | D-805 | 1:3 | D-468 |
| 6:4 | D-56 D-58 | 6:3 | D-501 | 14:33 | D-504 | 1:4 | D-468 D-552 |
| 6:5 | D-56 D-58 | 6:6 | D-501 | 14:40 | D-493 | | D-561 |
| 6:9 | D-650 | 6:7 | D-343 D-501 | 15:20 | D-650 | 1:9 | D-637 |
| 6:10 | D-650 | 6:8 | D-343 D-501 | 15:21 | D-33 D-194 | 1:10 | D-637 |
| 6:12 | D-777 | 6:9 | D-342 D-385 | | D-647 D-650 | 1:13 | D-331 |
| 6:23 | D-136 D-311 | | D-392 D-706 | 15:22 | D-33 D-194 | 1:14 | D-331 |
| | D-759 | | D-782 D-784 | | D-647 D-650 | 2:4 | D-251 D-31( |
| 7:3 | D-779 | | D-879 | | D-653 | 2:5 | D-251 D-31( |
| 8:5 | D-198 | 6:10 | D-342 D-385 | 15:23 | D-33 D-653 | 2:8 | D-136 D-311 |
| 8:6 | D-198 | | D-392 D-706 | 15:29 | D-132 | | D-773 |
| 8:7 | D-198 | | D-782 D-784 | 15:40 | D-383 D-384 | 2:9 | D-136 D-311 |
| 8:8 | D-198 | | D-879 | 15:41 | D-383 D-384 | | D-773 |
| 8:11 | D-885 | 6:11 | D-392 D-393 | 15:42 | D-383 D-384 | 2:10 | D-773 |
| 8:16 | D-283 D-558 | | D-706 D-782 | 15:56 | D-759 | 2:19 | D-84 D-90 |
| 8:17 | D-283 | 6:19 | D-473 D-877 | | | 2:20 | D-84 D-90 |
| 8:26 | D-538 | 6:20 | D-378 D-473 | **2 Corinthians** | | 3:9 | D-114 |
| 9:31 | D-310 | | D-877 | 6:3 | D-412 | 3:17 | D-260 D-831 |
| 9:32 | D-310 | 7:10 | D-434 | 6:4 | D-412 | | D-892 |
| 10:14 | D-176 | 8:4 | D-789 | 6:5 | D-412 | 3:18 | D-260 D-831 |
| 12:17 | D-341 D-498 | 8:5 | D-291 D-789 | 6:6 | D-412 | | D-892 |
| 12:18 | D-498 | 8:6 | D-291 D-789 | 7:1 | D-613 | 3:19 | D-260 D-831 |
| 12:19 | D-21 D-498 | 9:14 | D-802 | 8:13 | D-94 | | D-892 |
| 12:20 | D-498 | 9:16 | D-87 | 8:14 | D-94 | 4:1 | D-412 |
| 12:21 | D-498 | 10:13 | D-10 D-18 | 8:15 | D-94 | 4:2 | D-412 |
| 13:1 | D-798 | 10:14 | D-789 | 9:6 | D-742 D-750 | 4:3 | D-412 |
| 13:2 | D-798 | 11:11 | D-435 D-436 | 9:7 | D-746 D-869 | 4:5 | D-297 |
| 13:7 | D-309 D-853 | 11:12 | D-435 D-436 | 11:13 | D-165 | 4:11 | D-86 D-90 |
| 13:8 | D-853 | 11:24 | D-697 | 11:14 | D-165 | 4:12 | D-86 D-90 |
| 13:9 | D-421 D-426 | 11:25 | D-697 | 11:15 | D-165 | 4:13 | D-86 D-90 |
| | D-767 | 11:26 | D-697 | 13:1 | D-655 | 4:14 | D-86 D-90 |
| 13:10 | D-421 D-426 | 11:27 | D-704 | | | 4:25 | D-347 |
| 13:13 | D-341 | 11:28 | D-704 | **Galatians** | | 4:29 | D-765 |
| 14:12 | D-368 | 11:29 | D-704 | 2:16 | D-310 | 4:31 | D-763 |
| 15:4 | D-723 | 11:30 | D-704 | 3:6 | D-107 D-604 | 4:32 | D-763 |
| | | 12:1 | D-236 | 3:7 | D-107 | 5:5 | D-385 D-614 |
| **1 Corinthians** | | 12:2 | D-236 | 3:8 | D-107 D-300 | | D-784 |
| 1:21 | D-665 | 12:3 | D-236 | 3:9 | D-107 | 5:22 | D-441 |
| 1:22 | D-665 | 12:4 | D-236 | 3:13 | D-107 | 5:23 | D-441 |
| 1:23 | D-665 | 12:5 | D-236 | 3:14 | D-107 | 5:24 | D-441 |
| 1:24 | D-665 | 12:6 | D-236 | 3:16 | D-107 | 5:25 | D-439 |
| 1:26 | D-459 D-874 | 12:7 | D-236 D-237 | 3:29 | D-107 | 5:26 | D-439 |
| 1:27 | D-355 D-459 | | D-238 | 5:13 | D-20 | 5:27 | D-439 |
| | D-874 | 12:8 | D-236 D-237 | 5:16 | D-777 | 5:28 | D-439 |
| 2:9 | D-892 D-665 | | D-238 | 5:17 | D-777 | 5:29 | D-439 |

## The Book of Mormon

| | | | | | | | |
|---|---|---|---|---|---|---|---|
| 29:2 | D-457 D-621 | 34:27 | D-521 D-527 | 41:4 | D-386 D-646 | 42:31 | D-251 D-583 |
| | D-624 | | D-528 D-548 | | D-647 | 43:45 | D-502 |
| 29:3 | D-457 | | D-743 D-746 | 41:5 | D-370 D-386 | 43:46 | D-502 |
| 29:5 | D-636 D-752 | | D-533 | 41:6 | D-370 D-386 | 43:47 | D-502 |
| 29:6 | D-457 | 34:28 | D-513 D-528 | 41:7 | D-386 | 44:3 | D-833 |
| 29:7 | D-457 | | D-743 | 41:8 | D-386 | 45:16 | D-710 D-755 |
| 29:9 | D-457 | 34:29 | D-528 D-743 | 41:10 | D-364 D-365 | 45:18 | D-829 |
| 29:8 | D-456 | 34:30 | D-627 | | D-760 D-761 | 45:19 | D-829 |
| 30:6 | D-304 | 34:31 | D-627 | | D-762 D-777 | 53:20 | D-834 |
| 30:7 | D-304 | 34:32 | D-472 D-627 | 41:11 | D-198 | 53:21 | D-834 |
| 30:8 | D-304 | 34:33 | D-472 D-627 | 41:13 | D-649 | 56:45 | D-834 |
| 30:9 | D-304 | 34:34 | D-385 D-627 | 41:14 | D-424 D-649 | 56:46 | D-834 |
| 30:10 | D-304 | 34:35 | D-627 | 41:15 | D-424 D-649 | 56:47 | D-184 D-490 |
| 30:11 | D-304 | 34:36 | D-627 | 42:2 | D-195 D-760 | | D-834 |
| 30:43 | D-182 | 36:3 | D-3 | | D-761 | 57:26 | D-184 |
| 30:44 | D-182 D-254 | 37:16 | D-833 | 42:3 | D-195 D-760 | 58:10 | D-672 |
| 30:52 | D-165 | 37:17 | D-833 | | D-761 | 58:11 | D-672 |
| 30:53 | D-165 | 37:33 | D-460 | 42:4 | D-195 D-760 | 60:13 | D-21 |
| 30:60 | D-162 | 37:35 | D-77 | | D-761 | 60:23 | D-625 |
| 31:5 | D-97 D-462 | 37:36 | D-77 D-820 | 42:5 | D-195 | 60:36 | D-786 |
| | D-725 | | D-822 | 42:6 | D-30 D-122 | 62:40 | D-524 |
| 31:24 | D-824 | 37:37 | D-77 D-522 | | D-191 | | |
| 31:28 | D-824 | | D-525 D-544 | 42:7 | D-30 D-122 | Helaman | |
| 32:13 | D-351 D-354 | | D-822 | | D-191 D-796 | 3:1 | D-774 |
| 32:14 | D-351 D-354 | 37:43 | D-681 | 42:8 | D-30 D-122 | 3:2 | D-774 |
| | D-356 | 37:44 | D-681 | | D-365 D-796 | 3:24 | D-83 |
| 32:15 | D-351 D-354 | 37:45 | D-681 | 42:9 | D-30 D-125 | 3:25 | D-83 |
| | D-356 | 38:5 | D-3 | | D-191 D-195 | 3:26 | D-83 |
| 32:16 | D-351 D-354 | 38:10 | D-872 | | D-198 D-796 | 3:27 | D-83 |
| 32:19 | D-752 D-756 | 38:11 | D-773 D-872 | 42:10 | D-30 D-195 | 3:28 | D-83 |
| 32:27 | D-185 D-818 | 38:12 | D-773 D-858 | | D-198 D-796 | 3:35 | D-706 |
| 32:28 | D-185 D-674 | | D-872 | 42:11 | D-30 D-390 | 3:36 | D-852 |
| | D-818 | 39:3 | D-778 D-781 | | D-796 | 4:11 | D-852 |
| 33:2 | D-721 | 39:4 | D-778 D-781 | 42:12 | D-30 D-390 | 4:12 | D-852 |
| 34:8 | D-815 | 39:5 | D-778 D-779 | 42:13 | D-30 D-45 | 4:13 | D-773 |
| 34:9 | D-36 | | D-781 | | D-390 | 5:10 | D-622 |
| 34:10 | D-36 | 39:6 | D-768 | 42:14 | D-30 D-45 | 5:11 | D-622 |
| 34:11 | D-36 | 40:2 | D-646 | | D-390 | 5:17 | D-631 D-633 |
| 34:12 | D-36 | 40:3 | D-646 | 42:15 | D-30 D-45 | 5:29 | D-677 |
| 34:15 | D-175 | 40:4 | D-646 | | D-390 | 5:30 | D-675 D-677 |
| 34:16 | D-175 | 40:11 | D-124 | 42:16 | D-389 | 5:31 | D-677 |
| 34:17 | D-175 | 40:12 | D-126 D-127 | 42:17 | D-389 D-636 | 5:32 | D-677 |
| 34:19 | D-524 D-544 | 40:13 | D-313 | 42:18 | D-389 D-636 | 5:33 | D-677 |
| | D-545 D-547 | 40:14 | D-126 D-127 | 42:19 | D-636 | 6:4 | D-2 175 |
| 34:20 | D-524 D-544 | | D-313 | 42:20 | D-636 | 6:17 | D-772 D-848 |
| | D-545 D-547 | 40:16 | D-647 | 42:21 | D-636 | 6:30 | D-164 |
| 34:21 | D-524 D-527 | 40:17 | D-647 | 42:22 | D-45 D-389 | 6:31 | D-848 |
| | D-544 D-545 | 40:18 | D-647 | | D-624 D-636 | 7:17 | D-848 |
| | D-547 | 40:19 | D-647 | 42:23 | D-45 D-389 | 7:21 | D-848 |
| 34:22 | D-524 D-533 | 40:23 | D-646 D-647 | | D-624 | 7:22 | D-848 |
| | D-534 D-547 | | D-648 D-651 | 42:24 | D-45 D-389 | 7:29 | D-815 |
| 34:23 | D-524 D-533 | 40:24 | D-646 D-647 | | D-624 | 8:16 | D-815 |
| | D-534 D-547 | | D-648 D-651 | 42:25 | D-45 D-389 | 8:24 | D-254 |
| 34:24 | D-524 D-547 | 41:2 | D-646 D-647 | 42:26 | D-389 | 10:3 | D-177 |
| 34:25 | D-524 D-547 | | D-651 | 42:27 | D-386 | 10:4 | D-177 |
| 34:26 | D-521 D-547 | 41:3 | D-370 D-386 | 42:28 | D-386 | 10:5 | D-177 |
| | D-548 | | D-646 D-647 | 42:30 | D-251 | 10:7 | D-574 |

## Doctrine and Covenants

| | | | | | | | | |
|---|---|---|---|---|---|---|---|
| 84:22 | D-708 | 88:17 | D-35 D-142 | 89:2 | D-876 | 93:39 | D-835 |
| 84:23 | D-708 | 88:18 | D-35 D-142 | 89:3 | D-876 | 93:40 | D-214 D-418 |
| 84:24 | D-708 | 88:19 | D-35 D-142 | 89:4 | D-876 | | D-835 |
| 84:25 | D-60 | 88:20 | D-35 D-142 | 89:5 | D-876 D-879 | 93:41 | D-214 D-418 |
| 84:26 | D-60 D-588 | 88:21 | D-142 D-385 | 89:6 | D-876 D-879 | 93:42 | D-214 D-418 |
| 84:27 | D-60 D-588 | | D-709 | 89:7 | D-876 D-879 | 93:43 | D-418 |
| 84:29 | D-90 D-590 | 88:22 | D-142 D-385 | 89:8 | D-876 D-880 | 93:44 | D-418 |
| 84:30 | D-90 D-590 | 88:23 | D-385 | 89:9 | D-876 D-881 | 93:45 | D-260 D-418 |
| 84:33 | D-71 D-107 | 88:24 | D-385 D-794 | 89:10 | D-884 | 93:46 | D-418 |
| | D-411 D-414 | 88:28 | D-385 | 89:11 | D-884 | 93:47 | D-418 |
| | D-709 D-885 | 88:29 | D-385 | 89:12 | D-883 | 93:48 | D-418 |
| 84:34 | D-71 D-107 | 88:30 | D-385 | 89:13 | D-883 | 93:49 | D-418 D-534 |
| | D-709 | 88:31 | D-385 | 89:18 | D-489 D-669 | | D-545 |
| 84:35 | D-71 D-414 | 88:32 | D-14 D-385 | | D-835 D-878 | 93:50 | D-418 |
| | D-709 | | D-386 D-794 | 89:19 | D-489 D-669 | 97:8 | D-96 |
| 84:36 | D-71 D-414 | 88:33 | D-14 D-295 | | D-835 D-878 | 97:15 | D-615 |
| | D-709 D-798 | | D-385 D-386 | 89:20 | D-878 | 97:16 | D-615 |
| 84:37 | D-71 D-414 | 88:34 | D-14 D-295 | 89:21 | D-878 | 97:17 | D-615 |
| | D-709 D-798 | 88:35 | D-14 D-385 | 90:10 | D-455 | 97:21 | D-893 |
| 84:38 | D-71 D-414 | 88:47 | D-254 | 90:11 | D-301 D-455 | 97:24 | D-624 |
| | D-416 D-709 | 88:62 | D-546 | | D-456 | 98:1 | D-3 D-6 |
| | D-798 | 88:63 | D-510 D-526 | 90:17 | D-775 | 98:2 | D-3 D-6 |
| 84:39 | D-414 D-416 | | D-546 | 90:24 | D-349 | 98:3 | D-2 D-3 D-6 |
| | D-798 | 88:64 | D-510 D-517 | 91:4 | D-842 | 98:4 | D-309 |
| 84:40 | D-111 D-414 | | D-526 D-537 | 93:1 | D-630 D-634 | 98:5 | D-309 |
| | D-416 | | D-546 | | D-635 D-708 | 98:6 | D-309 |
| 84:43 | D-414 | 88:65 | D-510 D-546 | 93:2 | D-276 D-337 | 98:7 | D-309 |
| 84:44 | D-414 | 88:66 | D-840 | 93:4 | D-271 | 98:8 | D-307 D-309 |
| 84:45 | D-276 D-337 | 88:67 | D-708 D-820 | 93:6 | D-262 | 98:9 | D-307 D-309 |
| 84:46 | D-276 D-337 | 88:68 | D-708 D-820 | 93:7 | D-262 | 98:10 | D-307 D-309 |
| 84:74 | D-49 | 88:69 | D-820 | 93:8 | D-262 | 98:12 | D-510 |
| 84:77 | D-260 | 88:81 | D-87 D-397 | 93:9 | D-262 D-276 | 98:13 | D-96 |
| 84:102 | D-251 | | D-466 D-752 | 93:10 | D-121 D-262 | 98:14 | D-96 D-471 |
| 84:106 | D-425 | 88:82 | D-397 D-466 | 93:11 | D-262 | | D-479 |
| 85:6 | D-675 | | D-752 | 93:12 | D-271 | 98:15 | D-96 D-113 |
| 86:1 | D-25 | 88:85 | D-397 | 93:13 | D-271 | | D-471 D-479 |
| 86:2 | D-25 | 88:87 | D-401 D-732 | 93:14 | D-271 | 98:23 | D-423 D-500 |
| 86:3 | D-25 D-70 | 88:88 | D-395 | 93:15 | D-271 D-285 | 98:24 | D-423 D-500 |
| 86:11 | D-467 | 88:89 | D-395 | 93:16 | D-271 | 98:33 | D-502 |
| 88:1 | D-71 | 88:90 | D-395 | 93:17 | D-271 | 98:34 | D-502 |
| 88:2 | D-71 D-618 | 88:96 | D-652 D-735 | 93:19 | D-517 D-888 | 98:35 | D-502 |
| 88:3 | D-71 | 88:97 | D-652 D-735 | 93:21 | D-262 D-263 | 98:36 | D-502 |
| 88:4 | D-70 D-71 | 88:98 | D-652 D-735 | | D-552 | 98:37 | D-502 |
| | D-135 | 88:99 | D-652 | 93:23 | D-552 | 101:1 | D-9 |
| 88:6 | D-42 D-276 | 88:100 | D-652 | 93:24 | D-840 | 101:2 | D-9 |
| | D-337 | 88:101 | D-652 | 93:25 | D-840 | 101:3 | D-9 |
| 88:7 | D-276 D-337 | 88:102 | D-652 | 93:26 | D-840 | 101:4 | D-9 D-353 |
| 88:8 | D-276 D-337 | 88:110 | D-445 D-446 | 93:27 | D-414 | 101:5 | D-9 D-353 |
| 88:9 | D-276 D-337 | | D-447 | 93:28 | D-414 D-489 | 101:6 | D-9 |
| 88:10 | D-276 D-337 | 88:111 | D-446 D-447 | | D-543 D-668 | 101:7 | D-9 |
| 88:11 | D-276 D-337 | 88:112 | D-446 D-447 | | D-835 | 101:8 | D-9 |
| 88:12 | D-276 D-337 | 88:113 | D-446 D-447 | 93:33 | D-35 D-116 | 101:9 | D-9 |
| 88:13 | D-276 D-337 | 88:114 | D-446 D-447 | | D-302 D-367 | 101:21 | D-894 |
| 88:15 | D-35 D-142 | 88:121 | D-777 | 93:34 | D-35 D-302 | 101:22 | D-727 |
| | D-302 D-430 | 88:124 | D-858 | | D-367 | 101:23 | D-727 |
| | D-646 | 88:131 | D-520 | 93:35 | D-473 D-877 | 101:26 | D-450 |
| 88:16 | D-35 D-142 | 89:1 | D-876 D-878 | 93:38 | D-72 D-565 | 101:28 | D-445 D-451 |
| | D-302 D-646 | | | | | | |

# Pearl of Great Price

# TOPIC INDEX

Because this book is encyclopedic in nature (because the topics are arranged in alphabetical order) this index is a supplementary, not a comprehensive index.

**Topic titles in this index are in bold type.**